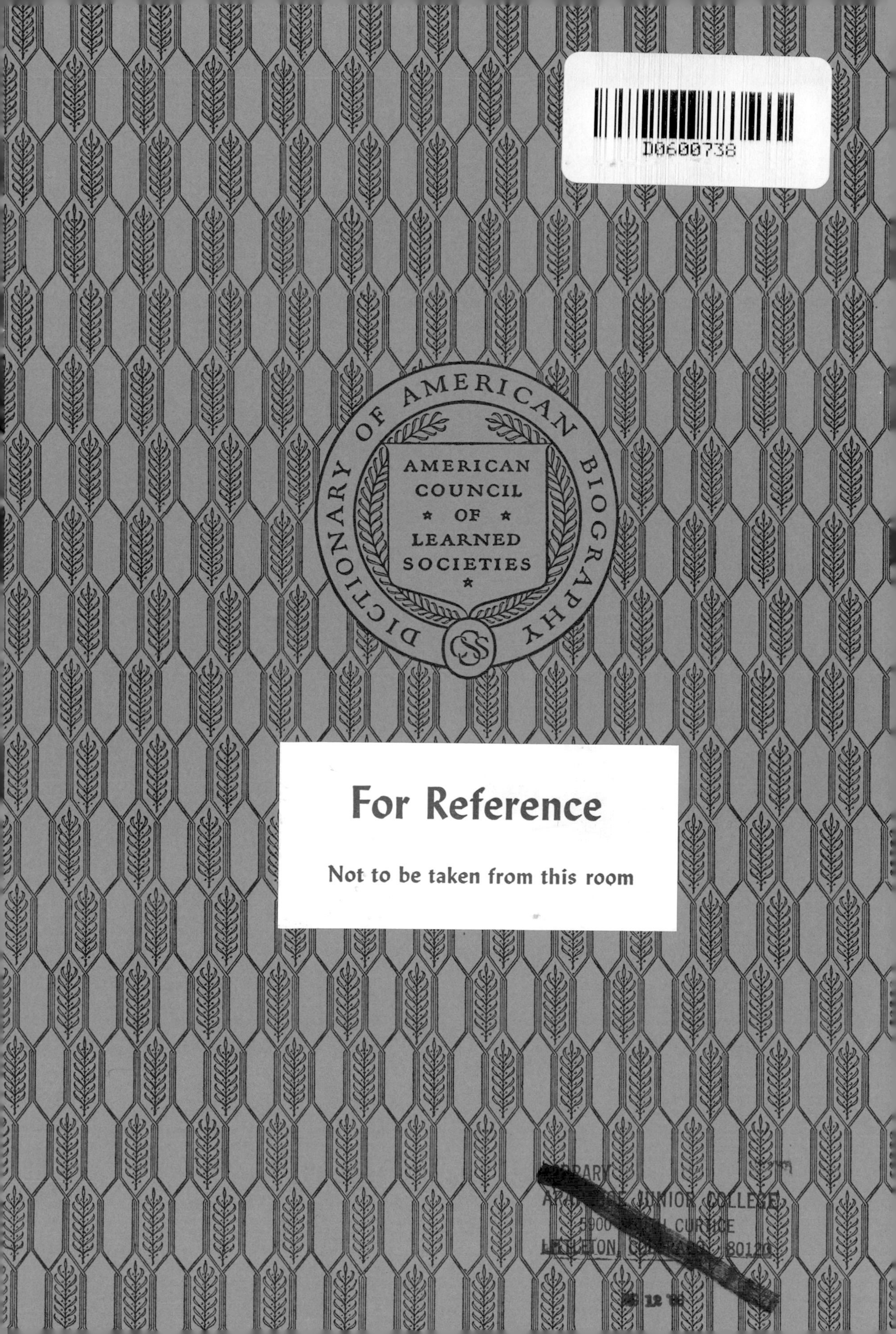
D0600738
DICTIONARY OF AMERICAN BIOGRAPHY
AMERICAN COUNCIL OF LEARNED SOCIETIES
For Reference
Not to be taken from this room

DICTIONARY
OF AMERICAN BIOGRAPHY

The *Dictionary of American Biography* was published originally in twenty volumes. Supplementary volumes were added in 1944 and 1958. This edition of the work combines all twenty-two volumes.

The present Volume I (Abbe–Brazer) contains Volumes I and II of the original edition, but these are now denominated "Part 1" and "Part 2" of the Volume. Volumes II through XI are arranged similarly, the Second Part in each instance representing a volume of the original series. For ease in reference, although the articles follow one another in strict alphabetical order, each Second Part is preceded by a half-title page which relates that Part to its place in the original numbering of the volumes.

The Errata list at the head of Volume I contains corrections of fact and additional data which have come to the attention of the Editors from the first publication of the work up to the present. Minor typographical corrections have been made in many instances directly on the plates.

PUBLISHED UNDER THE AUSPICES OF

THE AMERICAN COUNCIL OF LEARNED SOCIETIES

AMERICAN PHILOSOPHICAL SOCIETY

AMERICAN ACADEMY OF ARTS AND SCIENCES

AMERICAN ANTIQUARIAN SOCIETY

AMERICAN ORIENTAL SOCIETY

AMERICAN NUMISMATIC SOCIETY

AMERICAN PHILOLOGICAL ASSOCIATION

ARCHAEOLOGICAL INSTITUTE OF AMERICA

SOCIETY OF BIBLICAL LITERATURE AND EXEGESIS

MODERN LANGUAGE ASSOCIATION OF AMERICA

AMERICAN HISTORICAL ASSOCIATION

AMERICAN ECONOMIC ASSOCIATION

AMERICAN FOLKLORE SOCIETY

AMERICAN PHILOSOPHICAL ASSOCIATION

AMERICAN ANTHROPOLOGICAL ASSOCIATION

AMERICAN POLITICAL SCIENCE ASSOCIATION

BIBLIOGRAPHICAL SOCIETY OF AMERICA

ASSOCIATION OF AMERICAN GEOGRAPHERS

AMERICAN SOCIOLOGICAL SOCIETY

COLLEGE ART ASSOCIATION OF AMERICA

HISTORY OF SCIENCE SOCIETY

LINGUISTIC SOCIETY OF AMERICA

MEDIAEVAL ACADEMY OF AMERICA

AMERICAN MUSICOLOGICAL SOCIETY

ASSOCIATION FOR ASIAN STUDIES

AMERICAN SOCIETY FOR AESTHETICS

DICTIONARY
OF
American Biography

VOLUME IV

FRAUNCES - HIBBARD

Edited by

ALLEN JOHNSON

AND DUMAS MALONE

Charles Scribner's Sons *New York*

Prompted solely by a desire for public service the New York Times Company and its President, Mr. Adolph S. Ochs, have made possible the preparation of the manuscript of the Dictionary of American Biography through a subvention of more than $500,000 and with the understanding that the entire responsibility for the contents of the volumes rests with the American Council of Learned Societies.

Printed in the United States of America

C-4.64[V]

VOLUME IV, PART 1
FRAUNCES - GRIMKÉ

(VOLUME VII OF THE ORIGINAL EDITION)

CROSS REFERENCES FROM THIS VOLUME ARE MADE TO THE VOLUME NUMBERS OF THE ORIGINAL EDITION.

CONTRIBUTORS

VOLUME IV, PART I

Thomas P. Abernethy	T. P. A.
Adeline Adams	A. A.
James Truslow Adams	J. T. A.
Randolph G. Adams	R. G. A—s.
Robert Greenhalgh Albion	R. G. A—n.
Carroll S. Alden	C. S. A.
Edmund Kimball Alden	E. K. A.
L. P. Alford	L. P. A.
John Lincoln Alger	J. L. A.
Arthur A. Allen	A. A. A.
Francis G. Allinson	F. G. A.
William H. Allison	W. H. A.
Katharine H. Amend	K. H. A.
J. Douglas Anderson	J. D. A.
Katharine Anthony	K. A.
Percy M. Ashburn	P. M. A.
Frederick W. Ashley	F. W. A.
Kendric C. Babcock	K. C. B.
Christian A. Bach	C. A. B.
Christina H. Baker	C. H. B.
Frank Collins Baker	F. C. B.
Horace B. Baker	H. B. B.
Ray Palmer Baker	R. P. B—r.
Thomas S. Barclay	T. S. B.
Viola F. Barnes	V. F. B.
Claribel R. Barnett	C. R. B.
Harry M. Barrett	H. M. B.
George A. Barton	G. A. B—n.
Ernest Sutherland Bates	E. S. B—s.
Harold H. Bender	H. H. B.
Elbert J. Benton	E. J. B.
Edith R. Blanchard	E. R. B.
Arthur R. Blessing	A. R. B.
G. Alder Blumer	G. A. B—r.
Sarah G. Bowerman	S. G. B.
William K. Boyd	W. K. B.
Percy H. Boynton	P. H. B.
Robert Preston Brooks	R. P. B—s.
Everett S. Brown	E. S. B—n.
L. Parmly Brown	L. P. B.
Marshall S. Brown	M. S. B.
Philip M. Brown	P. M. B.
Robert M. Brown	R. M. B.
Solon J. Buck	S. J. B.
F. Lauriston Bullard	F. L. B.
William B. Cairns	W. B. C.
Isabel M. Calder	I. M. C.
Robert G. Caldwell	R. G. C.
Robert C. Canby	R. C. C.
Lester J. Cappon	L. J. C.
George I. Chadwick	G. I. C.
Joseph S. Chamberlain	J. S. C.
Arney R. Childs	A. R. C.
Hubert Lyman Clark	H. L. C.
Ernest W. Clement	E. W. C.
Frederick W. Coburn	F. W. C.
Fannie L. Gwinner Cole	F. L. G. C.
John R. Commons	J. R. C.
R. D. W. Connor	R. D. W. C
John Corbett	J. C.
Robert Spencer Cotterill	R. S. C.
E. Merton Coulter	E. M. C.
Avery O. Craven	A. O. C.
Nelson Antrim Crawford	N. A. C.
Merle E. Curti	M. E. C.
Chalmers G. Davidson	C. G. D.
Jerome Davis	J. D.
Davis R. Dewey	D. R. D.
Eleanor Robinette Dobson	E. R. D.
Elizabeth Donnan	E. D.
William Howe Downes	W. H. D.
Stella M. Drumm	S. M. D.
Raymond S. Dugan	R. S. D.
Lionel C. Durel	L. C. D.
Walter Prichard Eaton	W. P. E.
William G. Elliott	W. G. E.
Ephraim Emerton	E. E.
Charles R. Erdman, Jr.	C. R. E., Jr.
Hallie Farmer	H. F.
Harold U. Faulkner	H. U. F.
William W. Fenn	W. W. F.
H. H. Fisher	H. H. F.
John C. Fitzpatrick	J. C. F.
Percy Scott Flippin	P. S. F.
John E. Flitcroft	J. E. F.
Claude M. Fuess	C. M. F.
John F. Fulton	J. F. F.
Clifton Joseph Furness	C. J. F.
Ralph H. Gabriel	R. H. G.
Curtis W. Garrison	C. W. G.
George Harvey Genzmer	G. H. G.
Margaret Wadsworth Genzmer	M. W. G.
W. J. Ghent	W. J. G.
George W. Goble	G. W. G.
Armistead Churchill Gordon, Jr.	A. C. G., Jr.
H. P. Gould	H. P. G.
Lewis M. Gram	L. M. G.
Ruth Shepard Granniss	R. S. G.
Fletcher M. Green	F. M. G.
Charles Burton Gulick	C. B. G.

Contributors

J. Evetts Haley	J. E. H.
Laurence P. Hall	L. P. H.
Percival Hall	P. H.
Philip M. Hamer	P. M. H.
Edward P. Hamilton	E. P. H.
J. G. deR. Hamilton	J. G. deR. H.
Talbot Faulkner Hamlin	T. F. H.
Elizabeth Deering Hanscom	E. D. H.
Mary Bronson Hartt	M. B. H.
George C. Harvey	G. C. H.
Ellwood Hendrick	E. H.
Granville Hicks	G. H.
John Donald Hicks	J. D. H.
Edward M. Hinton	E. M. H.
John Haynes Holmes	J. H. H.
Lucius H. Holt	L. H. H.
Walter Hough	W. H.
Harvey J. Howard	H. J. H.
Leland Ossian Howard	L. O. H.
F. W. Howay	F. W. H.
Asher Isaacs	A. I.
Edith J. R. Isaacs	E. J. R. I.
Joseph Jackson	J. J.
James A. James	J. A. J.
M. C. James	M. C. J.
W. L. Jepson	W. L. J.
Guy B. Johnson	G. B. J.
Rufus M. Jones	R. M. J.
David Starr Jordan	D. S. J.
Whitman H. Jordan	W. H. J.
Louise Phelps Kellogg	L. P. K.
Fiske Kimball	F. K.
Edward C. Kirkland	E. C. K.
Allen Marshall Kline	A. M. K.
H. W. Howard Knott	H. W. H. K.
C. E. Krehbiel	C. E. K.
Gracie Brainerd Krum	G. B. K.
Kenneth S. Latourette	K. S. L.
James Melvin Lee	J. M. L.
Max Lerner	M. L.
William S. Lewis	W. S. L.
William E. Lingelbach	W. E. L.
Charles R. Lingley	C. R. L.
George W. Littlehales	G. W. L.
L. Leland Locke	L. L. L.
Ella Lonn	E. L.
Lincoln Lorenz	L. L.
Thomas Denton McCormick	T. D. M.
Thomas McCrae	T. M.
Philip B. McDonald	P. B. M.
Reginald C. McGrane	R. C. M.
S. S. McKay	S. S. M.
John H. T. McPherson	J. H. T. M.
W. C. Mallalieu	W. C. M.
Dumas Malone	D. M.
Helen Jo Scott Mann	H. J. S. M.
Isaac F. Marcosson	I. F. M.
Frederick H. Martens	F. H. M.
Albert P. Mathews	A. P. M.
David M. Matteson	D. M. M.
Lawrence S. Mayo	L. S. M.
Leila Mechlin	L. M.
Robert L. Meriwether	R. L. M—r.
George P. Merrill	G. P. M.
Douglass W. Miller	D. W. M.
William Snow Miller	W. S. M.
Edwin Mims, Jr.	E. M., Jr.
Broadus Mitchell	B. M.
Catherine Palmer Mitchell	C. P. M.
Samuel Chiles Mitchell	S. C. M.
Carl W. Mitman	C. W. M.
Frank Monaghan	F. M—n.
Fulmer Mood	F. M—d.
Robert E. Moody	R. E. M.
Albert B. Moore	A. B. M.
James G. Moore	J. G. M.
Samuel Eliot Morison	S. E. M.
Richard B. Morris	R. B. M.
Jarvis M. Morse	J. M. M.
Richard L. Morton	R. L. M—n.
Kenneth B. Murdock	K. B. M.
David S. Muzzey	D. S. M.
Frank Nash	F. N.
H. Edward Nettles	H. E. N.
Allan Nevins	A. N.
Lyman C. Newell	L. C. N.
Robert Hastings Nichols	R. H. N.
Roy F. Nichols	R. F. N.
Herman C. Nixon	H. C. N.
Harold J. Noble	H. J. N.
John Scholte Nollen	J. S. N.
Wallace Nutting	W. N.
Henry N. Ogden	H. N. O.
Rollo Ogden	R. O.
David Edward Owen	D. E. O.
Mildred B. Palmer	M. B. P.
Victor H. Paltsits	V. H. P.
Scott H. Paradise	S. H. P.
Fred Lewis Pattee	F. L. P—e.
Charles O. Paullin	C. O. P.
Frederic Logan Paxson	F. L. P—n.
Donald Culross Peattie	D. C. P.
James H. Peeling	J. H. P.
George J. Peirce	G. J. P.
Dexter Perkins	D. P.
Frederick T. Persons	F. T. P.
A. Everett Peterson	A. E. P.
James M. Phalen	J. M. P.
Isaac King Phelps	I. K. P.
Francis S. Philbrick	F. S. P.
David Philipson	D. P—n.
Paul Chrisler Phillips	P. C. P.
W. C. Plummer	W. C. P.
David deSola Pool	D. deS. P.
Edward Preble	E. P.
William K. Prentice	W. K. P.

Contributors

Richard J. Purcell	R. J. P.	Bertha Monica Stearns	B. M. S.
Arthur Hobson Quinn	A. H. Q.	Thomas Wood Stevens	T. W. S.
Charles W. Ramsdell	C. W. R.	John P. Sutherland	J. P. S—d.
Belle Rankin	B. R.	William W. Sweet	W. W. S.
William L. Raub	W. L. R.	Charles S. Sydnor	C. S. S.
P. O. Ray	P. O. R.	Frank A. Taylor	F. A. T.
Charles Dudley Rhodes	C. D. R.	William A. Taylor	W. A. T.
Irving B. Richman	I. B. R.	David Y. Thomas	D. Y. T.
Robert E. Riegel	R. E. R.	Charles C. Torrey	C. C. T.
Franklin L. Riley	F. L. R.	Frederick Tuckerman	F. T.
J. Fred Rippy	J. F. R.	Julius H. Tuttle	J. H. T.
David A. Robertson	D. A. R.	William T. Utter	W. T. U.
William A. Robinson	W. A. R.	John T. Vance	J. T. V.
James H. Ropes	J. H. R.	Eugene M. Violette	E. M. V.
Earle Dudley Ross	E. D. R.	Frank H. Vizetelly	F. H. V.
Frank Edward Ross	F. E. R.	John D. Wade	J. D. W.
Dunbar Rowland	D. R.	W. Randall Waterman	W. R. W.
George H. Ryden	G. H. R.	Raymond C. Werner	R. C. W.
Joseph Schafer	J. S.	Allan Westcott	A. W.
Charles Schuchert	C. S.	George F. Whicher	G. F. W.
Robert Francis Seybolt	R. F. S.	Arthur P. Whitaker	A. P. W.
Benjamin F. Shambaugh	B. F. S.	Allen Sinclair Will	A. S. W.
Muriel Shaver	M. S.	James F. Willard	J. F. W.
William Bristol Shaw	W. B. S.	Samuel Williston	S. W.
Fred W. Shipman	F. W. S.	Edwin B. Wilson	E. B. W.
Lester B. Shippee	L. B. S.	Louis R. Wilson	L. R. W.
Wilbur H. Siebert	W. H, S.	Albert T. Witbeck	A. T. W.
Joseph F. Siler	J. F. S.	Helen Sumner Woodbury	H. S. W.
Kenneth C. M. Sills	K. C. M. S.	Maude H. Woodfin	M. H. W.
Francis Butler Simkins	F. B. S.	Carter G. Woodson	C. G. W.
Edgar A. Singer, Jr.	E. A. S., Jr.	William Loring Worcester	W. L. W—r.
David Eugene Smith	D. E. S.	William H. Worrell	W. H. W.
Joe Patterson Smith	J. P. S—h.	Herbert F. Wright	H. F. W.
W. E. Smith	W. E. S.	Walter L. Wright, Jr.	W. L. W—t., Jr.
Thomas M. Spaulding	T. M. S.	John C. Wyllie	J. C. W.
Harris Elwood Starr	H. E. S.		

DICTIONARY OF
AMERICAN BIOGRAPHY

Fraunces — Grimké

FRAUNCES, SAMUEL (*c.* 1722–Oct. 10, 1795), tavern-keeper, household steward to President Washington, was a West Indian, probably of French extraction. His name is inseparably linked with Fraunces Tavern, the most noted hostelry of colonial New York. Fraunces appeared as the proprietor of the Masons' Arms on Broadway from 1759 to 1762, but in the latter year he bought the former De Lancey mansion at the corner of Broad and Pearl streets and in a few months it was carrying the "Sign of Queen Charlotte" (*New York Gazette or Weekly Post Boy,* July 26, 1762). A year later it bore the "Sign of the Queen's Head." In 1765 he left the tavern to establish a garden on the North River —"Vauxhall"—where for "Four shillings each Person" his guests might see "a Group of magnificent Wax Figures," but in 1770 he returned to his inn, which, as the Revolution approached, became known simply as Fraunces Tavern. Here "Black Sam," as Philip Freneau called him (*Poems,* ed. 1786, p. 321), achieved a reputation as a connoisseur of wines and a steward *par excellence,* and the place became a favorite rendezvous. It was there that the Sons of Liberty met in 1774 before they dumped East India tea into the river, and during the British occupancy of the island red-coated officers babbled over their cups as they "drunk deep" at Black Sam's table. In May 1783, when Washington and Sir Guy Carleton met at Tappan to confer on peace terms, the former secured Fraunces to provide the repast, and it was under the tavern roof late in the year that the evacuation of the city by the British was celebrated, and that Washington bade farewell to his officers. Both the American Congress and the New York state legislature voted moneys to Fraunces for kindnesses to American prisoners and other services to the patriot cause. When Washington moved to New York as the nation's first president, Fraunces accepted the stewardship of his household. He proved himself so indispensable that he was taken with the family to Philadelphia when that became the capital city, serving until June 9, 1794. He died the next year, survived by his wife, Elizabeth, two sons, and five daughters.

[H. R. Drowne, *A Sketch of Fraunces Tavern* (1919); M. F. Pierce, *The Landmark of Fraunces' Tavern* (1901); W. J. Davis, "Fraunces Tavern," in *Hist. Buildings of America* (1906), edited by Esther Singleton; Jared Sparks, *The Writings of Geo. Washington,* vol. XII (1837); *Gazette of the U. S.,* Oct. 13, 1795. Many original documents are preserved in the tavern. An abstract of Fraunces's will is to be found in the collection in the Pa. Hist. Soc.] A. E. P.

FRAZEE, JOHN (July 18, 1790–Feb. 24, 1852), pioneer sculptor, was born in poverty in the "upper village" of Rahway, N. J. His father, Reuben Frazee, was a carpenter, a descendant in the third generation from a godly Scottish family named Fraser or Frazer, who came to Amboy, N. J., among its earliest settlers. The change of the final *r* to *e* was a whim of the sculptor's grandfather. Soon after John's birth, his father abandoned his brood, and nothing was heard from him for nine years. The mother, whose maiden name was Brookfield, took the boy when he was five to the Brookfield farm, where he was reared under the kindly influence of his grandmother, and where of necessity he was soon set to work about the farm and home. He had little play, less schooling. Then the prodigal father returned, and sent young John to work for a brutal farmer named De Camp, in surroundings "most deplorable." At fourteen, however, the lad escaped unscathed to the Brookfield farm, where he labored cheerfully, with some brief snatches of longed-for schooling. At seventeen he was apprenticed to William Lawrence, a bricklayer and mason, who later became a licensed tavern-keeper. Between trowel, tankard, and hoe, John was busy. By day, he laid brick; on winter nights, says his friend Dunlap, he served "the reveler and the drunkard." Soon an unexpected opportunity came. Lawrence, having finished building a bridge over the Rahway River at Bridgeton, wished to have an inscription cut in the stone. Not one of the forty men working on the bridge would undertake it, but Frazee, with the inexperience of his eighteen years, rushed in and succeeded, his exploit being duly bruited abroad. His life in the Lawrence home was anything but dull. An elder brother was a fellow apprentice, and Lawrence himself, though untaught, was a man of keen mind. There was discussion, even thinking, and John spent his leisure in reading, drawing, and writing. Among his master's few books were two on "sacred harmony," from which he soon learned enough to become chorister for the Presbyterian Church in Rahway, and to teach psalmody in the season.

In 1810 Frazee was sent to work as a bricklayer for John Sanford, a contractor for the masonry on the New Brunswick bank, and there he met Ward Baldwin, a stone-cutter who had learned his trade while working on the famous City Hall in New York. Frazee was already spending eleven hours a day in bricklaying, but he was glad to spare four of the remaining hours in acquiring from Baldwin the art of hewing stone. Later, when Lawrence was building a stone house for Peter De Windt Smith, near Haverstraw, Frazee boldly offered to do all the so-called ornamental carving, asking for the work "in language as respectful as my illiterate abilities could summon" (*North American Quarterly Magazine,* July 1835, p. 4). Again his attempt was successful beyond hope. When the War of 1812 broke out, he turned to cutting tombstones to eke out a living. Years afterward, realizing his weakness even in this humble art, he wrote: "I knew nothing about the arts of antiquity. . . . The want of that knowledge . . . may easily be detected . . . in most of my works, prior to the year 1820" (*Ibid.,* p. 11). In 1813 he married Jane Probasco of Spotswood, N. J., bought a little house at Rahway, and added a workshop for stone-cutting, but the next year he moved to New Brunswick, N. J., where for two years he struggled heroically against both poverty and pestilence. At first his work was only in curbstones, milestones, and headstones; his earliest attempt to represent the human form was in 1815, when he made a figure of Grief for the tombstone of his infant son. His skill of hand increased with practise, and for several years he worked from thirteen to fifteen hours a day, spending his evenings carving in wood for cabinetmakers, or cutting steel letters for branding.

In 1818, with his brother William, Frazee opened a marble-shop in New York City, where he soon found ample employment in making mantels, tombstones, and church memorials. Dunlap relates that from 1819 to 1823 "his principal study was lettering, which he carried to high perfection" (*post,* II, 468). A figure of his three-year-old son, modeled in 1820, won him an interview with John Trumbull, who curtly told him that nothing in sculpture would be wanted "in this country, for yet a hundred years" (*North American Quarterly Magazine,* July 1835, p. 17). Frazee, chilled but not daunted, continued his efforts. His post-mortem memorial portrait of John Wells, dated 1824, and placed in St. Paul's Church, New York, was the first marble bust carved in this country by a native American, giving it a historic significance above that of Trumbull's mistaken prophecy. The memorial, for which the sculptor received $1,000, includes an inscribed tablet over-adorned with monumental items, but the portrait itself is soundly conceived and executed. Two years later, Frazee was one of the fifteen artists who, choosing fifteen others, founded the National Academy of Design. At its inception, he alone represented the art of sculpture.

Frazee's commissions increased as his work became known. At the instance of Hon. Gulian C. Verplanck, Congress appropriated a sum for a marble bust of John Jay, which was successfully carved by Frazee. Thomas W. Ward, of Boston, pleased with the sculptor's portrait of Nathaniel Prime, induced friends to order busts of Daniel Webster and of Nathaniel Bowditch. To help Frazee in producing a characteristic likeness, Webster, nothing loath, delivered an oration while posing. These two portraits were engaged for the Boston Athenæum with others including those of John Marshall, William Prescott, John Lovell, and Thomas H. Perkins. In addition to these Frazee chiseled busts of Andrew Jackson, Judge Story, Bishop Hobart, De Witt Clinton, and the Marquis de Lafayette. His self-portrait, of which the Pennsylvania Academy of the Fine Arts owns the original plaster cast (1828), is a straightforward rendering of a virile, ardent, shapely head, with clear-cut face. But Frazee's portraits represented only a part of his output; his activities in the marble-yard continued. Dissolving the connection with his brother, he formed in 1831 an advantageous partnership with Robert E. Launitz, and important work followed. A lithograph dated 1837 shows plan, elevation, and perspective of the New York Custom House and bears the inscription "John Frazee, architect and superintendent." This labor occupied him from 1834 to 1841. His first wife having died "of the pestilence" in 1832, leaving five of the ten children born to them, he married Lydia Place, daughter of Thomas Place of New York City. He died at Compton Mills, R. I., in the sixty-second year of his age.

[Frazee's autobiography was published in the *North Am. Quart. Mag.*, Apr., July 1835. His "Jersey neighbor," Wm. Dunlap, in his *Hist. of the Rise and Progress of the Arts of Design in the U. S.* (1834), presents a fairly complete memoir, from which practically all subsequent accounts are taken, including that found in Henry T. Tuckerman's *Book of the Artists* (1867). Lorado Taft's *History of American Sculpture* (1903) gives a critical estimate which is both sympathetic and logical, and contains an illustration of Frazee's self-portrait.]

A. A.

FRAZER, JOHN FRIES (July 8, 1812–Oct. 12, 1872), scientist, editor, teacher, was born in Philadelphia, Pa., the son of Robert and Elizabeth (Fries) Frazer, and the grandson of Col. Persifor Frazer [*q.v.*] of Revolutionary fame. The Frazer family was of Scotch origin, having come from the north of Ireland to settle in Pennsylvania early in the eighteenth century, while Elizabeth Fries, a daughter of John Fries, was German in descent. John Fries Frazer received his early education in the Philadelphia schools and in the private school of Capt. Partridge at Norwich, Conn. He graduated from the University of Pennsylvania in 1830. As a laboratory assistant to Prof. Alexander Dallas Bache [*q.v.*] he continued his studies and received the M.A. degree from the same institution in 1833. After making the preliminary preparations for the study of medicine, just as he was ready to enter the medical school he changed to the study of law. He completed his preparation for the bar under the direction of J. M. Scott, but after having been admitted, he found the profession scarcely suited to his taste. In 1836 he accepted a position as assistant to Henry D. Rogers, who was in charge of the first geological survey of Pennsylvania. The following year Frazer began to teach in the Philadelphia High School, where he served until 1844 when he succeeded Bache in the chair of chemistry and natural philosophy at the University of Pennsylvania. This position he held until 1872. He was one of the founders of the National Academy of Sciences (1863), a lecturer at Franklin Institute, and editor of its *Journal* from 1850 to 1866. As a scientist he was noteworthy for his able critical evaluation of the discoveries of others rather than for original contributions. He made no independent contributions to science, and the aid he gave Bache in the experiments that led to the first accurate determination of the daily variations of the magnetic needle in America and in the study of the interaction of the aurora borealis with magnetic forces were his only important collaborations. The pages of the *Journal of the Franklin Institute,* however, and the class-room lectures delivered over a period of more than twenty-five years were the mediums through which the work of experimental scientists was subjected to a keen critical analysis and passed on to the public. Although chemistry was Frazer's special branch of instruction his bent was always for mechanics. He was especially at home in the field of history of science, and hence viewed the sciences as the result of a long historical development. His interests were broad: his home was the Mid-Victorian salon for the *Intelligentsia* of Philadelphia, where he was found as happily conversant with the Greek and Latin classics or current French and English literature as with the subjects of his special field. On Sept. 1, 1838, he married Charlotte Jeffers Cave, a daughter of Thomas Cave. By her he had three children, one of whom, Persifor [*q.v.*], also attained distinction as a scientist.

[Persifor Frazer, *Gen. Persifor Frazer: a Memoir* (1907); J. L. LeConte, memoir in *Nat. Acad. Sci. Biog. Memoirs,* vol. I (1877), and in *Proc. Am. Phil. Soc.,* vol. XIII (1873); J. L. Chamberlain and others, *Univ. of Pa.* (1901), I, 335; *Penn Monthly,* Nov. and Dec. 1872; *Press* (Phila.) and *Phila. Inquirer,* Oct. 14, 1872.]

T. D. M.

FRAZER, OLIVER (Feb. 4, 1808–Feb. 9, 1864), portrait-painter, was born, probably in Jessamine County, Ky., the second son of Alexander Frazer, who had emigrated from Ireland after participating in Emmett's insurrection. His mother was Nancy Oliver of Lexington, Ky. When Frazer was a small child his father died, and he was indebted to his uncle, Robert Frazer, for his education. He attended the schools of Lexington until he was seventeen, when "the early development of his talent for drawing proved an interruption to the pursuit of his studies" (Price, *post,* p. 97), and he left school to go into the studio of Matthew H. Jouett [*q.v.*], from whom he had already gleaned what he knew of drawing. At Jouett's advice he was later sent to Philadelphia to study with Thomas Sully. In May 1834 he sailed for Europe. The first six months he spent in Paris, where he enjoyed the companionship of George P. A. Healy and Edwin Forrest. Later he pursued his studies in the schools of Berlin and Florence, but in 1835 he went to England, considering it the best place to study portraiture. After four years of European study he returned to Lexington, where in 1838 he married Martha Bell Mitchell, the daughter of Alexander Mitchell of Frankfort.

Frazer's success in Lexington was immediate. He demanded fifty dollars a portrait, the highest price in the city, and had no lack of patronage. His pictures of Henry Clay, Chief Justice George Robertson, M. T. Scott, president of the Bank of Kentucky, Joel T. Hart, and the group of his own wife and children were particularly felicitous. His work is marked by simplicity of line and firmness of texture, and generally preserves the virtues of eighteenth-century American painting. Personally, Frazer was eccentric and original, given to a proverbial irony and a not unbecoming hauteur. The uneven quality of his work was due in part to his temperamental inability to force himself to a standard, and in part to his sight, which in his later years was badly impaired. He died in Lexington.

[S. W. Price, *The Old Masters of the Bluegrass*, Filson Club Publications, no. 17, 1902; William Dunlap, *Hist. of the Rise and Progress of the Arts of Design in the U. S.* (3 vols., 1918); G. W. Ranck, *Hist. of Lexington, Ky.* (1872); Robt. Peter, *Hist. of Fayette County, Ky.* (1882), p. 374; G. N. Mackenzie, *Colonial Families of the U. S.*, II (1911), 86; information as to certain facts from Samuel M. Wilson of Lexington, Ky.] C. P. M.

FRAZER, PERSIFOR (Aug. 9, 1736–Apr. 24, 1792), Revolutionary soldier, was born in Newton township, then in Chester County, Pa., the son of John and Mary (Smith) Frazer. His ancestors came from Glasslough, County Monaghan, in the north of Ireland; his father emigrated to Pennsylvania in 1735. Persifor Frazer was both a merchant having commercial relations with the southern colonies and the West Indies, and an iron-master with an interest in the Deep Creek Iron Works which began operations in 1763. He was one of the merchants who signed the non-importation resolutions in 1765. After his marriage with Mary Worroll Taylor (Oct. 2, 1766), he took over the Sarum Iron Works, which had been founded in 1742 by her grandfather, Dr. John Taylor. In the opening days of the Revolution he was a delegate to the provincial council (Committee of Safety), and he served on various committees. In January 1776 he was appointed captain of Pennsylvania troops, and was made major Sept. 24, 1776, and lieutenant-colonel of the 5th Pennsylvania Oct. 4, 1776. During that year he was employed on Long Island in arresting Loyalists and suppressing their activities; he also took part in the later stage of the Canadian campaign, being engaged in the skirmish at Three Rivers. At different times he was occupied in recruiting, and was stationed in New York and New Jersey as well as in his own state. He was present at the battle of Brandywine, and almost immediately afterward he was captured while scouting, Sept. 16, 1777. Escaping from prison, Mar. 17, 1778, he fought at the battle of Monmouth, June 28, of which he gave a detailed account in a letter. On Oct. 9, 1778, his resignation was accepted by Washington. He declined the office of clothier-general of the Continental Army, to which he had been appointed, July 15, 1779. In the *Journals of the Military Expedition of Major-General John Sullivan* (1887), edited by Frederick Cook, there appears on the roster of officers the name: Lt. Col. Persifor Frazer, D.C.G. His descendant and biographer finds no confirmation of this record, nor family tradition of Frazer's presence with the expedition. He was treasurer of Chester County in 1781 and was elected that year to the Pennsylvania General Assembly, being reelected in 1782. On May 25, 1782, he was appointed brigadier-general of militia. In 1785 he was commissioner to the Wyoming Valley, where the claims of Connecticut conflicted with those of his state. He was appointed justice of the court of common pleas in 1786, and in that year register of wills, and he held this office until his death in 1792. Of his descendants several reached distinction, one of whom, his great-grandson Persifor [*q.v.*], collected the main data regarding the family.

[Persifor Frazer, *Notes and Papers of or Connected with Persifor Frazer in Glasslough, Ireland, and his Son, John Frazer of Phila.* (1906), and *General Persifor Frazer: a Memoir* (1907); *Pa. Mag. of Hist. and Biog.*, Oct. 1893, Apr. 1894, Apr., July, Oct. 1907; *Bull. Am. Iron and Steel Asso.*, vol. XXI (1887); obituary notice by Dr. Benj. Rush in Dunlap's *Am. Daily Advertiser* (Phila.), Apr. 30, 1792.] E. K. A.

FRAZER, PERSIFOR (July 24, 1844–Apr. 9, 1909), scientist, was born in Philadelphia, the son of John Fries Frazer [*q.v.*] and his wife, Charlotte Jeffers Cave. He was educated in private schools of Philadelphia and at the University of Pennsylvania, from which he received the B.A. and M.A. degrees in 1862 and 1865, respectively. He participated in the Civil War: in 1862–63 as a member of the United States Coast Survey attached to the South Atlantic Squadron; as a member of the first troop, Philadelphia city cavalry, during the Gettysburg campaign; and later as acting ensign attached to the Mississippi Squadron, where he served until the close of the war. On returning to Philadelphia he began the study of chemistry with the commercial firm of Booth & Garrett, but left after a few months to enter the Royal Saxon School of Mines at Freiberg, Germany. After spending three years at Freiberg he returned to America in 1869 to become mineralogist and metallurgist to the United States Geological Survey, then under the direction of Ferdinand V. Hayden [*q.v.*]. He wrote "Mines and Minerals of Colorado," which appeared in the *Third Annual Report* (1869) of the Survey. In 1870 he was appointed instructor of natural philosophy and chemistry at the University of Pennsylvania, succeeding his father as head of that department in 1872; and on the division of the department in 1873 he served one year as head of the department of chemistry.

Since by training and predilection he was more geologist than chemist, he resigned from the University to become assistant to J. P. Lesley [*q.v.*] in the Second Geological Survey of Pennsylvania. During the eight years that Frazer was connected with the survey his work was largely confined to the south-eastern counties, where the structure presented an intricate geological problem. His able study, published in five volumes of the *Reports* of the Second Geological Survey of Pennsylvania, has not been greatly modified by subsequent work. He served as general manager of the Central Virginia Iron Company, and a little later began to practise his profession as consulting and reporting geologist, metallurgist and mining engineer. This commercial work necessitated extensive travels in America and abroad, but the professional nature of his work did not detract from the purely scientific value of the reports published in that connection. Frazer was one of the founders of the *American Geologist,* and one of its editors from 1888 to 1905. In 1882 he was made professor of chemistry at Franklin Institute and was one of the editors of its *Journal* from 1881 to 1892. He was also noted for his researches in the characteristics of handwriting and the study of manuscript documents, making some original contributions, among which was the colorimeter, an instrument to determine the relative intensity and color value of ink-marks in handwriting. In this connection he published *A Manual of the Study of Documents to Establish the Individual Character of Handwriting and to Detect Fraud and Forgery* (1894). Later editions were published under the title: *Bibliotics; or The Study of Documents.* Later on he took up the study of the Bertillon system, and visited Bertillon in France to discuss his methods. In the capacity of handwriting and Bertillon expert, Frazer appeared at many trials, his most noted work in this connection being the Molineux murder case tried in the New York courts. He was one of the most prolific of the scientific writers of the period, his publications numbering about three hundred titles, most of which were articles in scientific magazines, particularly the *American Geologist* and *Journal of the Franklin Institute.* He was self-reliant and accurate in his search for scientific truths, but was often so vigorous in defense of that which he believed the truth that he gave offense to others. The Université de France bestowed upon him the degree of Docteur ès Sciences Naturelles in 1882, the first foreigner to receive this degree, and in 1890 the French government gave him the honorary title of Officier de l'Instruction Publique. In 1871 he married Isabella Nevins Whelen by whom he had four children.

[R. A. F. Penrose, in *Bull. Geol. Soc. of America,* Mar. 1910, has an excellent sketch of Frazer's life, with a bibliography of his most important published works. See also *University of Pennsylvania* (1901), ed. by J. L. Chamberlain and others, I, 358–59; *Bull. Am. Inst. Mining Engineers,* May 1909; *Military Order of the Loyal Legion of the U. S. Commandery of the State of Pa., Circular No. 16, Series of 1910*; *Jour. of the Franklin Inst.,* July 1909; *Public Ledger* (Phila.), Apr. 9, 1909; and Persifor Frazer, *Notes and Papers of or Connected with Persifor Frazer in Glasslough, Ireland, and his Son, John Frazer of Phila.* (1906).] T. D. M

FREAR, WILLIAM (Mar. 24, 1860–Jan. 7, 1922), agricultural chemist, educator, born in Reading, Pa., was descended from the French Huguenot, Hugo Freer, who was a patentee in the settlement of New Paltz, N. Y., in 1677. Abraham Frear, three generations removed from the pioneer, migrated to the Wyoming Valley in Pennsylvania in 1778. The Rev. George Frear of the fifth generation was a Baptist clergyman. His wife was Malvina Rowland, and of their children William was the eldest. During the father's pastorates at Reading and at Norristown, Pa., the son attended the public schools. Later the family moved to Lewisburg, Pa., where William attended Bucknell University, graduating in 1881. For the next two years he was assistant in science at Bucknell, at the same time taking summer courses at Harvard and studying under the guidance of Illinois Wesleyan University, from which he received the degree of Ph.D. in 1883. He then accepted an appointment in the United States Department of Agriculture, but left in 1885 to become assistant professor of agricultural chemistry at Pennsylvania State College. In 1886 he was made professor, and in the following year became vice-director and chief chemist of the experiment station. On July 18, 1900, he married Julia Reno of Greenville, Ky.

Frear's activities covered a wide range: he taught agricultural chemistry and meteorology; as an administrator he chose and organized research projects, and wrote bulletins and reports; and as chief chemist of the experiment station he conducted analytical work and applied the results in regulatory activities such as the Fertilizer and the Food and Drug acts. He was appointed and served for life on the federal and state committee on definitions and standards of foods and drugs. The results of this service are regarded as his greatest work, despite the fact that selfish and partisan politics after his death damaged its value for a time, if not permanently. In his own research he applied himself particularly to the study of lime as a fertilizer and to tobacco culture. As a leader in agricultural thought, in a pioneer day in agricultural education and scientific agriculture, he was remarkable for his breadth of vision.

[T. I. Mairs of the Pennsylvania State College has prepared an unpublished biographical sketch of Frear. Obituary notices appeared in the *Jour. of the Asso. of Official Agric. Chemists,* May 15, 1922, and the *Jour. of Industrial and Engineering Chemistry.* Information as to certain facts was supplied by Julia Reno Frear.]

I. K. P.

FREAS, THOMAS BRUCE (Nov. 2, 1868–Mar. 15, 1928), chemist, was born near Newark, Ohio, the son of Andrew and Mary (Bruce) Freas. His father was a farmer. Both parents died while he was a child, and he was brought up in the family of his uncle, Royal Bruce, who was also a farmer. He attended the local country school, then studied at odd times at Ohio Wesleyan University and at the state normal school at Ada. Following this training, he taught at various places in Kansas, continuing his education as he could afford to do so, first at the state normal school at Emporia and then for a semester at the state university at Lawrence. The financial depression of the nineties in the Middle West induced him to wander out to California. There he found work on a great fruit farm during vacations and studied at the Leland Stanford Junior University, from which he graduated in the class of 1896. On attaining his degree he accepted the post of principal of the high school at Hiawatha, Kan., where he gave instruction in the classics, although he had majored in physical science. In 1897 he joined the Western Electric Company as chemist in their Chicago establishment, and in the following year, on Dec. 28, he married Mary Kuhn of Leavenworth, Kan.

The wastefulness and inadequacy of chemical laboratory control and administration having already aroused his interest, Freas was prevailed upon to accept the post of curator of chemistry at Chicago University by Prof. Alexander Smith, who held the chair of inorganic chemistry. To improve his financial status and to get a closer insight into the production and costs of apparatus, he became manager of the scientific apparatus and supply house of Ernst Lietz at Chicago for two years. Then he returned to the university, where he developed the art of laboratory control. Meanwhile he studied, engaged in research, and achieved his doctorate by 1911. The special thermostats and the well-known Freas ovens for constant temperatures which he invented came into industrial and academic use wherever chemistry was practised. When Prof. Smith was called to New York to succeed Prof. Chandler at Columbia in 1911, he induced the trustees to offer an assistant professorship to Freas, which he accepted. Later he became associate professor, and finally full professor. Besides being purchasing agent and head of the physical administration of the chemical laboratories, on which subject he gave instruction to advanced students, he lectured on chemical thermodynamics, in which he was at once learned and profoundly informed.

Freas was a popular member of the faculty, and was singularly conscientious in the fulfilment of all his obligations. His concept of his duties to the university, to students, and also to his friends, at the expense of his own interests, impinged not only on his health but also caused him to leave unfinished a work which might have brought him a great reputation. This was an amazingly bold idea in the field of thermodynamics. Believing that it might be possible to retain as free energy the heat developed in the liquefaction of air and to resolve this into an available form, he conceived of an apparatus which would, in effect, be operated by the heat of the sun, previously contributed to the air, of which the waste products would be cold air and moisture. As far as he was able to carry out his computations, these were favorable rather than otherwise to the postulate that an engine, such as he had in mind, would develop and at the same time deliver several times the measure of its energy-cost as available energy. Two or three of the friends to whom he confided his ideas missed his concept of the apparatus as a sun-motor, and declared that he was merely chasing the will-o'-the-wisp of perpetual motion. Since he was of an extremely sensitive nature, this increased his reticence. For fear of being made the subject of ridicule he spoke of his research, which did not get beyond the mathematical stage, to but few persons. It is a matter of regret that he did not feel able to devote sufficient time and attention to this study to reach a definite conclusion.

[*Who's Who in America,* 1926–27; *Jour. of the Am. Chem. Soc.,* Apr. 1928; J. M. Cattell and Jacques Cattell, *Am. Men of Sci.* (4th ed., 1927); *Science,* Mar. 23, 1928; *N. Y. Times,* Mar. 17, 1928.]

E. H.

FREDERIC, HAROLD (Aug. 19, 1856–Oct. 19, 1898), journalist, novelist, was born in Utica, N. Y., of Dutch, French, and New England ancestry. His father, Henry De Motte Frederic, a descendant of early settlers in the Mohawk Valley, was by trade a decorator of furniture, but, obliged by ill health to seek out-door work, found employment on a railroad and was killed in an accident when Harold was eighteen months old. Mrs. Frederic, left in straitened circumstances, opened a dairy, in which the boy assisted as soon as he was able. Rising daily at 4:00 A. M., he would make deliveries before attending school, where his milk-stained clothes excited the ridicule of his fellow-pupils. At fourteen he became an office-boy on the *Utica Observer*. Developing considerable skill as a retoucher of photographic negatives, in 1873 he went to Boston to work for the firm of Allen & Rowell but soon found the eye-strain too severe and returned to Utica. During the period of enforced leisure that resulted, he wrote a few short stories which found their way into the Utica papers. After working for a time on a farm, he became, at the age of twenty, a reporter on the *Utica Observer*, at a salary of $9 a week, which enabled him to make an early and, ultimately, rather unhappy marriage. By 1880 he was one of the editors of his paper, and in 1882 became editor-in-chief of the *Albany Evening Journal*, one of the leading Republican organs of the state. He was never an ardent Republican, however—during his two years in Albany he was an intimate friend of Grover Cleveland—and on the bankruptcy of his paper in 1884 he was glad to take a more congenial position as London correspondent for the *New York Times*.

The rest of his life was spent in Europe. Almost immediately he showed his mettle by making in the summer of 1884 a hazardous tour of personal investigation through the cholera-stricken districts of Southern France and Italy. His minute reports, with elaborate tables showing the extent and spread of the disease, did much to reassure the people of the United States by demonstrating the dependence of cholera upon dirt and bad sewerage. In 1891 he went to Russia to investigate the persecution of the Jews, and his indictment of the government was so sweeping as virtually to close the Russian Empire to him thenceforward. His letters to the *New York Times* were published in book form in 1892 as *The New Exodus: A Study of Israel in Russia*. An analysis of the career and character of Emperor William II also was published, after its appearance in the *Times*, as *The Young Emperor* (1891). Always indifferent to culture, Frederic, despite his own inheritance, was profoundly skeptical of French civilization, while, on the other hand, his warm-heartedness made him an ardent supporter of the Irish in their struggle with England. Honest, fearless, and a keen observer, he was always a valued correspondent. Although his breezy Americanism made him deem it unnecessary to learn any foreign language, he was otherwise extremely conscientious in his work, continuing it even after a stroke of partial paralysis in August 1898, and sending his last weekly cable on the Saturday before his death. This occurred on Oct. 19, 1898, at Henley-on-the-Thames. An ardent Christian Scientist, he had refused medical aid, and his twenty-year-old daughter testified before the coroner's jury that he was insane. After weeks of deliberation their conclusion was merely that "the deceased was a strong-minded, obstinate and self-opinionated man."

That, in addition to his work as a journalist, Frederic should have been able, during his fourteen years abroad, to compose ten volumes of fiction, is evidence of his driving energy. He wrote rapidly, with little care for stylistic niceties—sometimes writing 4,000 words a day—and his first drafts were usually sent to the printer unrevised. His inspiration was initially derived from an extraordinarily vivid memory of the life of the Mohawk Valley, the scene of most of his works. These were at first—in *Seth's Brother's Wife* (1887), *The Lawton Girl* (1890), and *The Return of the O'Mahoney* (1892)—mere contributions to the local-color school of his day, but with *In the Valley* (1890), dealing with the American Revolution, and *The Copperhead* (1893) and *Marsena and Other Stories* (1894), dealing with the Civil War, Frederic became a worthy pioneer in the revival of the historical novel, while in his masterpiece, *The Damnation of Theron Ware* (published in England as *Illumination*, 1896), he transcended the limitations of his era and produced a work of enduring value. In his study of spiritual deterioration, which enjoyed a *succès de scandale* owing to the fact that its shallow hero is a Methodist minister, Frederic was the first to lay bare a fundamental weakness of American character in its tendency to rely upon a purely verbal moral idealism. The book, with its trenchant but not unsympathetic realism, pointed away from contemporary romanticism toward earlier and later work. Frederic was unable to surpass or even equal it. His last three novels, *March Hares* (1896), *Gloria Mundi* (posthumous, 1898), and *The Market Place* (posthumous, 1899), all dealing with English life, were written in failing health and during domestic trouble; they added little to his reputation.

[Good obituary in *N. Y. Times,* Oct. 20, 1898; introduction by Robt. Morss Lovett to 1924 ed. of *The Damnation of Theron Ware*; article by Louise Imogen Guiney in *Book Buyer,* Jan. 1899; *Saturday Rev.* (London), Oct. 22, Nov. 12, 1898; *Idler* (London), Nov. 1897; *Citizen* (Phila.), Sept. 1897; *Dial* (Chicago), Nov. 1, 1898.]

E. S. B—s.

FREEDMAN, ANDREW (Sept. 1, 1860–Dec. 4, 1915), capitalist, was born in New York City, the son of Joseph and Elizabeth (Davies) Freedman. After attending a public school on Thirteenth Street, he found employment in a wholesale dry-goods house, picked up a little law, and embarked in the real-estate business. By ways that are no longer traceable he achieved a conspicuous success. He had a hand in several large transactions, such as the sale of the Academy of Music in 1887, dealt extensively in Fifth Avenue properties, and exploited large tracts of land in the Bronx, which was then a sparsely settled outskirt of the city. Meanwhile he became a close friend of Richard Croker. When Croker married for the second time, Freedman acted as his best man. When Croker returned from his retirement abroad to reassume the leadership of Tammany Hall, Freedman came with him, was treasurer of the Democratic campaign in 1897, and was reputed to be a power in municipal politics. Mayor Van Wyck, it is said, stood ready to appoint him to any office that he might desire, but Freedman was busy with other projects. One of these was the Maryland Fidelity and Guarantee Company, which he organized in 1898. The company did a good deal of bonding for the city of Baltimore. Having sold out his holdings in it in 1903, Freedman next formed the Casualty Company of America, which grew so rapidly that in 1908 it had a premium income of $1,500,000. In 1909 he disposed of his interest in it to Lyman A. Spaulding and several other men. Another and more devious project of his was the building of the first New York subway. John B. McDonald, a contractor, came to him with the original idea, and together they secured the support of August Belmont. On Jan. 16, 1900, the contract was awarded to McDonald, whose bids for constructing the several sections totaled $35,000,000. Freedman's relations with the various building and operating companies concerned in the subway appear to have been highly complicated. At the time of his death a committee of the New York legislature was endeavoring to unravel some of the complications, but its efforts to get access to Freedman's papers were blocked by his executors, and the investigation was dropped. From 1894 to 1902 Freedman was the owner of the New York Baseball Club (the "Giants"), which he made the most remunerative enterprise of its kind. He was a director of thirteen corporations, most of them New York transit companies whose prosperity was somewhat dependent on local politics, and was a member of fourteen clubs. In New York he lived at Sherry's, on Fifth Avenue at Forty-fourth St.; he had a handsome estate, "Tower Hill," at Red Bank, N. J., where in the last year of his life he was laying out a model dairy farm and stocking it with pure-bred Holsteins. He never married. He collected pictures, particularly the work of French landscape-painters, bronzes, and silver, admired fast horses and fast yachts, and was generous to his friends. Himself a Jew, he left the bulk of his $7,000,000 estate to a non-sectarian home for the aged and made special provision that in it married couples might live out their lives in decent comfort and seclusion.

[*Who's Who in America,* 1914–15; *N. Y. Times,* Feb. 2, Dec. 4, 5, 8, 9, 10, 11, 1915, Feb. 10, Apr. 15, 1916; for other items about Freedman see *N. Y. Times Index.*]

G. H. G.

FREEMAN, BERNARDUS (d. 1741), Reformed Dutch clergyman, known also and more correctly as Freerman, is said to have been a native of Gilhuis in the Netherlands. Though a man of parts, he had little schooling and earned his living as a tailor, but the object of his ambition was the Reformed ministry. At the instigation of William Bancker, an Amsterdam merchant with correspondents in Albany, N. Y., he was ordained Mar. 16, 1700, by the Classis of Lingen as pastor of the Reformed church in Albany. The whole procedure was irregular, for the Dutch churches of New York were under the patronage of the Classis of Amsterdam, which, as Bancker well knew, had already chosen the Rev. John Lydius for the position. The rival dominies, sailing up the Hudson on the same boat, reached Albany in midsummer, handed their credentials to Elder Peter Schuyler, preached trial sermons, and awaited the decision of the congregation, which voted to receive Lydius. Freeman quickly found a charge at Schenectady and was appointed by Gov. Bellomont to work among the Indians and, incidentally, to discover what he could about the activities of the French to the north and west. In a short time he became unusually proficient in the Mohawk language and translated several religious texts for use among his converts. The Mohawks are said to have been deeply impressed by his way of intoning the Litany. Lawrence Claesse's *The Morning and Evening Prayer, the Litany, Church Catechism, Family Prayers, and Several*

Chapters of the Old and New-Testament, translated into the Mahaque Indian Language (New York, William Bradford, 1715) is based, in part at least, on Freeman's manuscript. In 1702 he received what purported to be a cali from the four churches—New Amersfort, Midwout (Flatbush), Breuckelen, and New Utrecht—in Kings County, L. I. This call turned out to be anything but unanimous, and the affair was further complicated by the fact that Freeman was in the employ of the government, that the people ot Schenectady were loath to part with him, and that he himself had conducted the negotiations with great awkwardness and perhaps with impropriety. Still worse was his action in securing a license as pastor of the Kings County churches from Gov. Cornbury. The result was an ecclesiastical quarrel that raged on Long Island for almost fourteen years and intruded into the council chamber of four provincial governors. In the midst of it the Rev. Vincentius Antonides was sent from Holland as a rival pastor. Ultimately the two men composed their differences and worked in harmony. Meanwhile Freeman had married, Aug. 25, 1705, Margareta Van Schaick of New York, through whom he acquired some property. With true missionary zeal he served scattered groups of German Reformed settlers in Queens County, on Staten Island, and in Monmouth County, N. J. He was one of the leading spirits in the Coetus party and a close friend of Theodorus Jacobus Frelinghuysen and John Henry Goetschius [*qq.v.*]. Such opportunities as he had for study he seems to have improved, and he published three books: *De Spiegel der Self-Kennes* (William Bradford, 1720); *De Weegshale de Gerade Gods* (William Bradford, 1721); and *Verdeediging van D. Bernardus Freeman* (J. Peter Zenger, 1726).

[*Ecclesiastical Records of the State of N. Y.*, see index volume (1916); E. B. O'Callaghan, ed., *Doc. Hist. State of N. Y.* (1849–51), and *Docs. Relative to the Col. Hist. State of N. Y.*, IV (1854); E. R. Purple, "Contributions to the Hist. of the Ancient Families of N. Y.," in *N. Y. Geneal. and Biog. Record*, Apr. 1876; H. R. Stiles, *Hist. of the City of Brooklyn*, vol. I (Brooklyn, 1867); T. M. Strong, *Hist of the Town of Flatbush in Kings County, L. I.* (type-facsimile of edition of 1842); *Tercentenary Studies 1928 Reformed Ch. in America* (1928). For his descendants, see W. W. Spooner, ed., *Hist. Families of America* (N. Y., n.d.), p. 280.]

G. H. G.

FREEMAN, FREDERICK KEMPER (June 15, 1841–Sept. 9, 1928), senior editor of "the press on wheels," son of Arthur Robertson and Mary Allison (Kemper) Freeman and nephew of James L. Kemper [*q.v.*], was born at the family home, "Greenfields," Culpeper County, Va. He attended an "old-field school" for several years and at the age of ten accompanied his uncle, Frederick Thomas Kemper, to Boonville, Mo., where he entered Kemper Family School, now Kemper Military School, of which his uncle was founder. He returned four years later to his parents' home then at Gordonsville, Va., where he attended Kemper College, conducted by a cousin. While a student at a college at Union, Monroe County (now West Virginia), he enlisted on May 9, 1861, in the Confederate army. After taking part in the battle of Manassas he was transferred to the Signal Corps, in which branch of the service he had attained the rank of lieutenant by the close of the war. In 1866, with his brother Legh (originally Leigh), he went West for the purpose of rebuilding the family fortune, and at old Kearney City, in Nebraska Territory, the two began the publication of the *Frontier Index*, a tri-weekly, from a hand-roller press abandoned by Gen. Joseph E. Johnston, who prior to 1861 was in command of United States troops in the West. The paper made its initial appearance in May 1866, but soon the "press on wheels" began to move. The brothers followed the temporary terminus points of the Union Pacific Railroad, doing what Freeman called a "land office" business in the printing of advertising circulars for miners, prospectors, adventurers, former soldiers, and railroad employees as they rushed into each new town. Their second place of publication was North Platte, to which they were moved by ox teams driven by Mexicans. In January 1867 they moved on to Julesburg, and a few months later the *Index* was one of the first enterprises to reach Cheyenne, where it was housed in a tent. Equipment was next shifted to Laramie, 105 miles farther west. Freeman was seriously injured on this move and for many months wrote editorials and news from a hospital bed at Ft. Sanders. Later he visited Brigham Young at Salt Lake City.

While Freeman was operating the *Index* at Laramie, Legh was publishing a branch paper at Bear River City, near coal-mines in northern Utah to which they had filed claim with the Federal government. They opened these veins and brought out coal to a country in which all fuel was costly and scarce. When the wealth of these mines became known, others who wanted the property incited a mob to burn the Freeman plant and to force the brothers out. In the resulting confusion of land titles, they lost all rights to the mines. This double loss prompted Freeman in 1869 to ship the equipment at Laramie to Corinne, near Ogden, Utah, where his brother resumed the publication of the *Index* under the title of *Freeman's Farmer*, and to return to Virginia. He had served on the Nebraska Territorial Council as adviser to Gov. David Butler in 1867, and was elected to the state Senate following Nebraska's admission to the Union. From 1869 to 1874 he lived in Virginia, removing then to Georgia where he became a pioneer pecan grower and where he engaged in the wholesale grocery business. His wife was Mary Julia Roper, whom he married in 1896.

[Freeman's own account of the *Frontier Index,* now in possession of his sister, Maria D. Freeman; private paper of Freeman family lent by Maria D. Freeman and Mrs. George Crane of Athens, Ga.; Jas. Melvin Lee, *Hist. of Am. Journalism* (1917); I. S. Bartlett, *Hist. of Wyoming* (1918), I, 454; *Editor and Publisher,* Apr. 20, 1929; *Banner Herald* (Athens, Ga.), Sept. 10, 1928.] H.J.S.M.

FREEMAN, JAMES (Apr. 22, 1759–Nov. 14, 1835), first Unitarian minister of King's Chapel, Boston, was born in Charlestown, Mass., a son of Constant and Lois (Cobb) Freeman, and a descendant of Samuel Freeman who emigrated to Watertown in 1630. He was a pupil of the celebrated master Lovell in the Boston Latin School where he excelled in the languages and mathematics. After graduation at Harvard in 1777 he spent the following year there in the study of theology. Although an ardent supporter of the colonial cause, he did not enlist for fear of injuring his father who, because of his business interests, was compelled to live in Quebec. After drilling troops on Cape Cod and spending two years in Quebec, he began to preach, and in September 1782 was chosen reader by the vestry of King's Chapel. This celebrated church, founded in 1686, was the first Episcopal church in New England, and during the eighteenth century was the place of worship of the royal governors and of prominent families of Boston. Many members of the congregation were Loyalists who with Dr. Henry Caner, the last Anglican rector, left Boston with the British troops at the evacuation. After sharing their building with the Old South, whose church had been dismantled by the British during the siege, the congregation were now preparing to resume their regular services. Theological liberalism was in the air in Boston, and on his proposal to revise the liturgy by the omission of its more distinctively Trinitarian portions, Freeman found himself supported by a majority of his congregation. The revision, which followed somewhat closely the draft of a reformed liturgy made by Dr. Samuel Clarke of London, was accepted by the proprietors of the Chapel on June 19, 1785, and before the end of the year the book was printed and in use. Application for ordination having been refused by Bishop Seabury of Connecticut and put off by the more sympathetic Bishop Provoost of New York, the congregation became impatient and decided to take the matter into their own hands. Accordingly Freeman was ordained by the senior warden, Dr. Thomas Bulfinch, on Sunday, Nov. 18, 1787, "to be the Rector, Minister, Priest, Pastor, Public Teacher and Teaching Elder of this Episcopal Church." Protests against the ordination by a minority of the congregation and by a number of the Episcopal clergy of Boston and vicinity were without avail, and thus *"The first Episcopal church in New England became the first Unitarian church in America"* (F. W. P. Greenwood, *A History of King's Chapel, in Boston,* 1833, p. 139). The congregation became strong and flourishing and Freeman's active and influential ministry continued till 1826 when failing health compelled him to retire to Newton where the remaining nine years of his life were spent.

Freeman was a member of the first school committee elected by the people of Boston and was for many years influential in shaping its educational policies. He was a founder of the Massachusetts Historical Society, its recording secretary from 1798 to 1812, and a valued contributor to its collections. He was also a member of the American Academy of Arts and Sciences and of the Massachusetts constitutional convention (1820–21). He had a genius for friendship, and his intimate circle embraced ministers of all shades of doctrinal belief, prominent among whom was Cheverus, the first Catholic bishop of Boston. His speech was simple and direct, and his sermons, in the purest English, were devoid of all oratorical embellishment. He recognized in Christ all the divine that could be made human, his view of the Redeemer being somewhere between that of the Arians, who made him neither God nor man, and that of the humanitarians, who made him merely a human being. Besides numerous sermons, addresses, and articles in the reviews, Freeman published *Sermons on Particular Occasions* in 1812, and in 1829 had printed *Eighteen Sermons and a Charge* as a gift to his parish. On July 17, 1783, he married Martha Curtis, widow of Samuel Clarke, adopting his wife's only son, who became the father of James Freeman Clarke [*q.v.*].

[F. W. P. Greenwood, *A Sermon Preached in King's Chapel the Sunday after the Funeral of the Rev. Jas. Freeman* (1835); and memoirs in *Mass. Hist. Soc. Colls.,* 3 ser. V (1836), and in Wm. Ware, *Am. Unit. Biog.,* I (1850); Jas. Freeman Clarke, memoirs in the *Western Messenger* (Cincinnati), Jan. 1836, in Wm. B. Sprague, *Annals of the Am. Pulpit,* VIII (1865), in *Memorial and Biog. Sketches* (1878), and *Remarks on the Life and Character of Jas. Freeman* (1886); F. Parkman, in *Christian Examiner* (Boston), Jan. 1836; H. W. Foote, "Jas. Freeman and King's Chapel, 1782–

87," the *Religious Mag. and Monthly Rev.* (Boston), June 1873, and *Annals of King's Chapel,* II (1896); Thos. Belsham, *Memoirs of the Late Rev. Theophilus Lindsey, M.A.* (London, 1812); S. A. Eliot, *Heralds of a Liberal Faith* (1910), vol. II.] F. T. P.

FREEMAN, JAMES EDWARDS (1808–Nov. 21, 1884), genre painter, writer, was the son of Joshua Edwards and Eliza (Morgan) Freeman, and a descendant of Samuel Freeman who emigrated to Watertown, Mass., with Gov. Winthrop in 1630. Freeman's family had removed to Indian Island, New Brunswick, shortly before his birth, but returned to the United States within a few years to settle in Otsego County, N. Y. The desire for artistic training led Freeman through many hardships to New York City, where in 1826 he applied to William Dunlap [*q.v.*] for instruction. On Dunlap's recommendation he was entered as a student in the National Academy of Design, where his application and precocity gained for him the affection and encouragement of the older artists. In 1833 he was elected to membership in the Academy. After a short residence in the ancestral home of James Fenimore Cooper, he left America in 1836 for Italy, where he remained, a voluntary expatriate, to the end of his life. In 1840 he was appointed consul to Ancona, a position which he held until July 1849. Most of the time he lived in Rome discharging his slight duties through an agent. Upon his own evidence it was an unimportant commission which he remembered chiefly for the expense it caused him.

As an artist, Freeman subscribed to the current taste for rich colors and human misery. Among his better-known pictures are "The Beggars," "The Flower Girl," "The Savoyard Boy in Italy," "Young Italy," and "The Bad Shoe," all of which were insipidly sentimental. He rarely exhibited his pictures in America. The last one to be shown before his death was "Mother and Child" which was hung in the National Academy Exhibit of 1868. His self-portrait was exhibited in the Centennial Exhibition of 1925, and later placed in the National Academy rooms on 33rd St. He published two volumes of memoirs, *Gatherings from an Artist's Portfolio* (1877), and *Gatherings from an Artist's Portfolio in Rome* (1883). They reveal an instinct for story telling and a genial disposition, but have no pretensions beyond presenting a slightly decorated picture of Bohemian life. In the advance of taste, Freeman's pictures lost their following. At the time of his death he was almost forgotten as an artist, and was remembered rather as a picturesque member of the old guard in the Roman art colony, and a charming example of a past age. He died in Rome. He had married Augusta Latilla, a sculptress, in 1845.

[Frederick Freeman, *Freeman Geneal.* (1875); C. E. Clement and Laurence Hutton, *Artists of the Nineteenth Century* (1885); William Dunlap, *Hist. of the Rise and Progress of the Arts of Design in the U. S.* (1918), III, 264; *Am. Art Annual,* IX, 44 (1911); W. M. Gillespie, *Rome: as Seen by a New Yorker* (1845), p. 181; H. T. Tuckerman, *Book of the Artists* (1867); *N. Y. Tribune,* Nov. 30, 1884; U. S. Dept. of State, *Reg. of all Officers and Agents in the Service of the U. S.,* 1843–47; state dept. records.] C. P. M.

FREEMAN, MARY ELEANOR WILKINS (Oct. 31, 1852–Mar. 13, 1930), writer, was born in Randolph, Mass., the daughter of Warren E. and Eleanor (Lothrop) Wilkins, both of old New England families. Her father was a carpenter, and for a time kept a small shop in Brattleboro, Vt., whither the family removed when she was a child. She was educated in the schools of Randolph and Brattleboro, and spent one year, 1870–71, at Mount Holyoke Female Seminary. After the death of her parents, about 1883, she returned to Massachusetts, which remained her home until her marriage some years later. It is noticeable that although many of her impressionable years were spent in Brattleboro, neither the exceeding beauty of southern Vermont nor the life of a small city is reflected in her most characteristic writings. The flat, inland scenery of eastern Massachusetts forms the background of her tales, and her people are essentially of the country. The setting of her best work is always that which she knew first and to which she returned. There are also no clearly discernible literary influences in her writings, although it is known that she was a lover of the great English novelists and was familiar with the work of some of the Russians. Her earliest stories and poems were published in a Sunday-school magazine for children, and later she wrote, mostly verse, for the juvenile monthly, *Wide Awake.* "A Shadow Family," her first adult story, was written for a Boston paper, and "Two Old Lovers," her second, appeared in *Harper's Bazaar* for Mar. 31, 1883. Her connection with the Harper publications thus begun was strengthened when Henry M. Alden accepted "A Humble Romance" for *Harper's Magazine* for June 1884. Public recognition of the quality of her work was almost immediate, and gradually her tales were gathered into volumes: *A Humble Romance* (1887); *A New England Nun* (1891); and many others. Her first stories were not the work of a girl, as was then generally supposed, but the work of a woman over thirty, who had the time as well as the natural ability for observation. Responding to the wide-spread interest in tales of local color, she caught the spirit of her rustic surroundings and soon came to be known as one of the chief exponents of New England rural life. On Jan. 1, 1902, Mary Wilkins was married to Dr. Charles M. Freeman and removed to his home in Metuchen, N. J. There she spent the remainder of her life, though the later years of her marriage were unhappy. The change of environment consequent on her marriage is reflected in several of her stories, especially in her novel *The Debtor* (1905); but her intellectual and esthetic home remained in the New England village.

Mrs. Freeman tried many kinds of writing. A play, *Giles Corey, Yeoman,* dealing with Salem witchcraft, was produced in the early nineties, and one or two of her stories were dramatized, but without success. She anticipated a popular vogue in mystery stories involving spiritism, but in this type she had not the qualities necessary for perfection. In short stories of country life she was master of herself and of her art. In that realm her work challenges comparison with the best of its kind, for it is there that she identified herself completely with her material. She seemed hardly to be an observer, certainly not an interpreter, yet she wrote with dispassionate objectivity, the more noteworthy because at the time sentimentality was appallingly popular. Such was the subtlety of her writing that some of its most artistic results may easily escape the unwary. The humor is characteristically elusive, and the style, at its best, has a rare note of inevitability. Fine writing Mrs. Freeman never attained; only seldom could she be fluent without prolixity. She was easily in the front rank of dialect writers. The speech of her characters is of New England, but it is old English and truly racial in that its distinctive quality lies not in separate words and idioms but in those cadences which denote the spirit of a people. Men and women share life's burdens, but it is through the women's somber eyes that the reader looks upon the incidents and characters of the tales; it is their problems and perplexities which she presents. She analyzed the strange manifestations of inbreeding and introspection and the inability of man to break the fetters of his own forging. Overworked, underfed, poorly clad, her people have no touch of squalor; life is to them always significant. It is the moral element in their natures, their adherence to the "painful right" that gives to them a dignity which at times approaches grandeur.

Despite her facility in handling the materials of a short story, Mrs. Freeman was unable to achieve a like facility with her novels. The best —*Jane Field* (1893), *Pembroke* (1894), *Jerome* (1897)—are good because of the qualities that give excellence to the tales, but even they lack organic unity. She could handle an incident, but not a plot; she could analyze dominating and perverting characteristics, but the final synthesis by which characters are created and placed in perspective was not within her power. In the field of her best work, however, she was given generous recognition not only in America, but in England and France as well, and final honors came to her in 1925 when she was awarded the William Dean Howells medal for fiction by the American Academy of Arts and Letters and was elected a member of the National Institute of Arts and Letters in 1926.

[At the time of Mrs. Freeman's greatest popularity many articles about her were published in literary journals. In many cases the biographical material was inaccurate and the criticism ephemeral. One penetrating essay, "Miss Wilkins: An Idealist in Masquerade," by Chas. Miner Thompson, appeared in the *Atlantic Monthly* for June 1899. There is also a brief but critical estimate of her work by F. L. Pattee in the chapter on the short story in *The Cambridge Hist. of Am. Literature,* II (1918), 390. The best French review appeared in the *Revue des Deux Mondes,* Aug. 1, 1896. See also the *N. Y. Times,* Mar. 9, 17, 24, 1923, Feb. 21, 1925, and Mar. 15, 1930. The date of her birth, which is usually incorrectly given, is taken from the town records of Randolph, Mass.; the same record gives her baptismal name as Mary Ella Wilkins.] E. D. H.

FREEMAN, NATHANIEL (Mar. 28, 1741–Sept. 20, 1827), patriot, physician, lawyer, magistrate, was born in Dennis near Yarmouth, Mass. His parents were Martha Otis and Edmund Freeman, through whom he was descended from Edmund, the original settler of Sandwich. After studying medicine under Dr. Cobb of Thompson, Conn., he returned to Sandwich about 1765 and began to practise. Then, at the suggestion of his great-uncle, James Otis, Sr., he read law. Thus doubly fitted for leadership he soon became prominent as an able young patriot devoted to the American cause. Frequently a moderator in Sandwich town meeting, he moulded patriot sentiment and checked the activities of spirited neighbors who favored the British connection. At the head of a large mob of determined men he dramatically prevented the courts from opening at Barnstable in September 1774. Soon after he was brutally attacked by a band of Loyalists who left him for dead, but he recovered. He became a member of the Sandwich committee of correspondence, and also represented the town at the Watertown Provincial Congress in 1775 by the authority of which he was successively appointed lieutenant-colonel, then colonel, of the first Barnstable county regiment. He negotiated with the Penobscot Indians and took part in the expedition against the British who held Rhode Island. At Cambridge he met Gen. Washington who employed him in 1779 on an important mission to West Point. With another officer he was able on this occasion to persuade Massachusetts soldiers whose terms were about to expire to continue longer in the public service. After the peace he served for many years in the state militia, resigning in 1793 with the rank of brigadier-general. From 1778 to 1780 he represented Sandwich in the legislature and in the latter year also reported on the state constitution to his fellow townsmen. The new Federal Constitution won his favor but he was an unsuccessful candidate for membership in the convention which ratified it. Although he was a supporter of strong government, the quality of his Federalism was tolerant enough to concede much merit to Thomas Jefferson.

With the war at an end, Freeman applied himself to law and to medicine. In the latter art he read much, and, despite the fact that he was instructed only by books, performed many difficult operations with notable success. He relinquished a flourishing practise in 1804. Meantime he had a seat on the bench as judge of the court of common pleas, and ultimately presided over the court as chief justice. From his legal duties he took time to prepare a *Charge to the Grand Jury . . . at Barnstable* (Boston, 1802), a work which furnishes an excellent statement of his opinions on law, religion, morals, and politics. He was a deeply religious man whose initial orthodoxy was covered in middle life by a sympathy for the liberal teachings of Joseph Priestley; but by 1814 he returned to the Trinitarian doctrines in which he had been bred. In addition to his other duties he prepared an augmented edition of Dr. William Enfield's *Prayers for the Use of Families* (Boston, 1794), and was one of the founders of Sandwich Academy. A chief delight was his library with its books on theology, medicine, and law. On May 5, 1763, he married Tryphosa Colton of Killingly, Conn. She died in 1796 and on Apr. 7, 1799, he married Elizabeth Gifford who survived him. Twenty children were born to him and of these eighteen arrived at maturity. His second son, Nathaniel, a member of Congress from 1795 till 1799, is sometimes confused with his father, but predeceased his parent by twenty-seven years.

[The best notice of Freeman is that by his friend James Thacher in *Am. Medic. Biog. . . .* (1828), II, 241–46. The same author's *Mil. Jour.* (1823) supplies additional information. See also Wm. Lincoln, *The Jours. of each Provincial Cong. of Mass. in 1774 and 1775* (1838); *Mass. Soldiers and Sailors of the Revolutionary War*, vol. VI (1899); Frederick Freeman, *The Hist. of Cape Cod* (2 vols., 1858–62), and *Freeman Geneal.* (1875).]

F. M—d.

FREEMAN, THOMAS (d. Nov. 8, 1821), civil engineer, astronomer, explorer, was born in Ireland, emigrating to America in 1784. He must at some time have received an excellent scientific education. Appointed one of the surveyors for the new capital of the United States, Mar. 25, 1794, he quickly demonstrated his ability by completing on June 25, 1795, the survey of the entire northern portion of the district. After planting the stones on the boundary he commenced the first topographic survey of the city, but resigned on July 7, 1796, to accept a commission as United States surveyor to chart the boundary line between the United States and Spain. Leaving Washington with Andrew Ellicott on Sept. 13, 1796, he arrived at Natchez, Feb. 24, 1797. On the boat trip down the Mississippi, he objected to the presence of a woman who was accompanying Ellicott. This objection, together with Ellicott's dilatory tactics in getting the survey started, finally resulted in an open break between the two men. Freeman was suspended from duty, and charges were preferred against him. Ellicott wrote his wife on Nov. 8, 1798, that the deposed engineer was "an idle, lying, troublesome, discontented, mischief-making man," and that he had expelled him from camp. The charges having been disproved, Freeman was appointed on Apr. 14, 1804, by President Jefferson to explore the Red and Arkansas Rivers. Word having been received that it would be dangerous to undertake this expedition on account of the hostility of the Spaniards, it was delayed until April 1806, when Freeman, accompanied by Peter Custis, a naturalist, Capt. Richard Sparks, and Lieut. Enoch Humphreys, with seventeen soldiers, left Fort Adams, Miss., and proceeded up the Red River in two flatboats. After traveling three months and reaching a point near the place where the present boundaries of Arkansas, Oklahoma, and Texas meet, the members of the party were stopped by a force of several hundred Spaniards and were obliged to return. Freeman's strategy and diplomacy on this occasion undoubtedly saved the party from destruction. As a result of his measurements and observations, the course of the lower Red River was for the first time accurately mapped. One of his astronomical observations was checked by engineers of the General Land Office in 1914 and found to be almost exactly correct (Arthur D. Kidder's report, Ferry Lake case, General Land Office). The next year he mapped out part of the boundary line between Tennessee and Alabama. In 1808 he was appointed to examine into the claims and trespass on public lands and on Jan. 10, 1811, he was commissioned surveyor of public lands of the United States south of Tennessee, with headquarters at Washington, Mississippi Territory.

He held the position until Nov. 8, 1821, when he died suddenly at Huntsville, Ala., having gone there on an inspection trip. Courteous, a maker and keeper of friends, of undoubted integrity and ability, he died poor, fighting the land speculators until the last.

[W. B. Bryan, *A Hist. of the Nat. Capital* (1914), vol. I; Thos. Freeman and Peter Custis, *An Account of the Red River, in La.* (1806); C. Van C. Mathews, *Andrew Ellicott: His Life and Letters* (1908); Dunbar Rowland, *Mississippi* (1907), I, 749–50, *Miss. Territorial Archives*, I (1905), 49, 73, 163, and *Official Letter Books of W. C. C. Claiborne, 1801–16* (1917), III, *passim*; Surveyor-General's Letter Books, nos. 53 and 54, General Land Office; *Ala. Republican* (Huntsville), Nov. 9, 1821; *Miss. State Gazette*, Nov. 24, 1821; manuscripts in the Lib. of Cong., and in the possession of the writer.] A. T. W.

FREER, CHARLES LANG (Feb. 25, 1856–Sept. 25, 1919), art collector and donor of the Freer Gallery of Art in Washington, was born at Kingston, N. Y., the son of Jacob R. and Phoebe Jane (Townsend) Freer. He was of French-Huguenot ancestry and was descended from one of the original patentees of New Paltz, N. Y. After attending a public school he entered the employ of a cement-manufacturing company near his home. At the age of sixteen he was a clerk in the general store of John C. Brodhead at Kingston, in a building which also housed the offices of the New York, Kingston & Syracuse Railroad, and in 1873 he was appointed to the office of paymaster of this railroad. In August 1876, when Frank G. Hecker became general superintendent of the Eel River Railroad with headquarters at Logansport, Ind., he selected Freer to accompany him and to serve as first accountant for the company, and later as its treasurer. Upon the absorption of the Eel River Railroad by the Wabash three years later, Freer and Hecker left the company and went to Detroit, Mich., where they lived for many years. There they organized the Peninsular Car Works, which later became the Peninsular Car Company and later still was merged with the Michigan Car Company. Of this corporation Senator James McMillan was chairman, and Freer was one of the managing directors. In 1899 Freer took an active part in consolidating thirteen of the car-building manufactories of the country in the organization known as the American Car & Foundry Company, but a year later he retired permanently from active business, and from that time to the end of his life devoted the greater part of his leisure to collecting works of art.

Freer had begun collecting in the early eighties, and among the first works he acquired were Whistler etchings. When a little later he bought Whistler pastels, he became eager to know the artist. The meeting was extremely unconventional and led to a remarkable friendship. From the nineties on Freer never went to Europe without seeing Whistler in London or Paris, and gradually he acquired his paintings, etchings, or drawings, either directly from him or from owners willing to sell. From this friendship also undoubtedly sprang Freer's increasing interest in Oriental art and his theories concerning art which not only colored but determined the direction of his collecting. By comparing the works of the great masters of the East with those of Whistler and a few other Western artists, he thought he discerned a definite relationship between them. In support of these theories, and as a sensitive art lover, he succeeded in bringing together, as the late Ernest L. Fenollosa has said, "first, by far the largest and most representative series of all the pictorial work of James McNeill Whistler that now exists in any one group, or that it is physically possible shall ever exist;—second, the most comprehensive and æsthetically valuable collection anywhere known of all the ancient glazed pottery of the world, Egyptian, Babylonian, Persian, Indian, Chinese, Korean, and Japanese;—and third, the finest and best unified group of masterpieces by the greatest Chinese and Japanese painters of all ages that exists outside of Japan, with the possible exception of that in the Boston Art Museum."

From 1900 to 1903 Freer spent much time in Europe; the following six years he spent chiefly in Asia and the Near East, adding through personal exploration and investigation to his collection of Oriental art, which by 1910 included over 8,000 rare and beautiful objects. Then his health failed and his travels ended, but to the last his interest in his collection and its development never ceased. His association with Senator McMillan, which undoubtedly increased his interest in the National Capital, and his promise to Whistler that his works should sometime be housed in a public gallery, preferably in Washington, doubtless led to his generous gifts to the nation. In 1906 he gave his entire collection, supplemented later by a sum of money to be expended for the erection of the Freer Gallery at Washington and for the establishment of a fund for additional acquisitions. At the time the deed was transferred it was understood that the collection should not pass out of Freer's possession during his lifetime, but he himself later withdrew this condition, and the building on the Mall designed under his direction was almost completed at the time of his death.

[E. R. and Joseph Pennell, *The Whistler Journal* (1921); E. L. Fenollosa, in the *Pacific Era*, Nov. 1907;

Leila Mechlin, in the *Century Mag.*, Jan. 1907; L. W. Havemeyer, in *Scribner's Mag.*, May 1923; Chas. Moore, *Washington Past and Present* (1929); *N. Y. Times*, Sept. 26, 1919. There are books of clippings at the Freer Gallery containing important contemporary notices about Freer and his collection.] L. M.

FRELINGHUYSEN, FREDERICK (Apr. 13, 1753–Apr. 13, 1804), lawyer, Revolutionary patriot, senator, was born near Somerville, Somerset County, N. J., the only son of the Rev. John and Dinah (Van Berg) Frelinghuysen, and the grandson of the Rev. Theodorus Jacobus Frelinghuysen [*q.v.*], who emigrated from Holland in 1720. His father died during the son's second year, and his mother, the daughter of a wealthy East India merchant, was about to return to her family in Amsterdam with her two small children when Jacob R. Hardenbergh [*q.v.*], a divinity student, who had been studying under her husband, persuaded her to become his wife. Brought up in a very religious household, Frederick yielded to his mother's desire that he enter the Christian ministry to the extent of studying theology for six months. Possibly the rigidity and strictness of his stepfather in regard to Sabbath observance and other matters may have discouraged young Frelinghuysen, who did not feel himself fitted for this profession. He then entered the College of New Jersey and was graduated in 1770. Taking up the study of the law he was admitted to the bar upon reaching his majority and began practise in Somerset County. Under the leadership of his college president, John Witherspoon, he was among the first in New Jersey to join the movement for independence from Great Britain. But twenty-two years of age, he was selected with John Witherspoon, Jonathan D. Sergeant, and William Paterson to represent his county in the Provincial Congress of 1775 and 1776. His votes in that body show him to have been one of the most uncompromising of those seeking complete separation from England. Throughout the war he varied his legislative duties with those of a very active military career. First a major of the Minute Men of his county, next a captain of artillery, major, and finally colonel and aide-de-camp to Gen. Philemon Dickinson, Frelinghuysen took part in the battles of Trenton, Princeton, and Monmouth. At Princeton his intimate knowledge of the local terrain was said to have been of great help to his superior officers (Mellick, *post*, p. 377). Elected Nov. 6, 1778, by his state legislature a member of the Continental Congress, he resigned his military command and position on the New Jersey Committee of Safety to serve in that body. Eight months of Congress was enough for an energetic young man whose heart was in the military struggle rather than the intrigues of politics. He resigned, giving as his reason his youth, but also his "situation [which was] peculiarly disagreeable" to him, and which he refused to explain for fear of causing more evil than good (letter to the speaker of the New Jersey Assembly in Lee, *post*, I, 9). He then served his state as clerk of court of Somerset County and as a member of the legislative council until 1782, when he consented to return to the Continental Congress for another year. Again in the state legislature, he served in the Assembly (1784, 1800, 1804), and in the Council (1790–92), and was a member of the New Jersey convention which ratified the Constitution. In 1790 he was appointed by President Washington a brigadier-general in the campaign against the western Indians, and in 1794, while a United States senator, he was commissioned a major-general of militia in the Whiskey Insurrection. His term in the Senate, extending from Dec. 5, 1793, until his resignation in May 1796, was uneventful. He was twice married. His first wife was Gertrude Schenck, who died in 1794. After her death he married Ann Yard.

[Theo. Frelinghuysen Chambers, *Early Germans of N. J.* (1895); F. B. Lee, *Geneal. and Memorial Hist. of the State of N. J.* (4 vols., 1910), I, 1–10; A. B. Mellick, Jr., *Story of an Old Farm* (1889); Talbot W. Chambers, *Memoir of the Life and Character of the Late Hon. Theo. Frelinghuysen* (1863), pp. 22–27; *Minutes of the Provincial Cong. and the Council of Safety of the State of N. J.* (Trenton, 1879); C. R. Erdman, Jr., *The N. J. Constitution of 1776* (1929).] C. R. E., Jr.

FRELINGHUYSEN, FREDERICK THEODORE (Aug. 4, 1817–May 20, 1885), statesman, direct descendant of Theodorus Jacobus Frelinghuysen [*q.v.*], and grandson of Frederick Frelinghuysen [*q.v.*], was the son of Frederick and Jane Dumont Frelinghuysen of Millstone, N. J., where he was born. On the death of his father, a lawyer of great promise, he was adopted at the age of three by his uncle, Theodore Frelinghuysen [*q.v.*]. After several years of study in the Somerville and Newark academies, young Frederick was admitted into the sophomore class in Rutgers College and graduated in 1836. His record there was not remarkable, though he impressed his classmates with his engaging personality and natural talents, notably in oratory. He studied law in the office of his uncle in Newark, was admitted to the bar in 1839, and succeeded to the latter's practise when he became chancellor of the University of the City of New York. Among his clients were the Central Railroad of New Jersey and the Morris Canal and Banking Company. He was appointed city attorney of Newark in 1849, and was later elected to the city council. With his friend Gov. Olden, he represented New Jersey at the Peace Congress held in Washington early in 1861 for the purpose of trying to avert secession. In the same year he was appointed attorney-general of New Jersey, and served until 1866 when he was chosen by Gov. Ward to represent New Jersey in the Senate. A Democratic legislature chose his successor in 1869. In July 1870 he was appointed by President Grant minister to Great Britain, an honor which he promptly declined, it is said, because he preferred an American atmosphere for the education of his children. The next year he returned to Washington as the choice of a Republican legislature to represent his state again in the Senate. There he achieved a position of commanding influence, particularly with his party associates who, like himself and Senator Conkling, affiliated themselves with the "Stalwarts." During his first term he fought hard for the impeachment of President Johnson, and was a member of the electoral commission which decided the election of President Hayes.

On leaving the Senate Frelinghuysen resumed the practise of law for a few years until requested by President Arthur to replace Secretary of State Blaine, whose political differences with the "Stalwarts" made his presence in the cabinet quite impossible. Temperamentally, Frelinghuysen was very different from the former secretary. There was nothing dramatic, experimental, or aggressive in his conduct of American foreign relations. He felt compelled, in fact, to reverse some of his predecessor's decisions, notably in the mediation of the United States in the dispute between Chile and Peru over the provinces of Tacna and Arica. This led Blaine and some of his friends to believe unjustly that there was a conspiracy to discredit him. There was no truculence in Frelinghuysen's diplomacy, though he insisted courteously and firmly on a due regard for American rights, as, for example, in the controversy with Great Britain concerning the plan for the construction of an interoceanic canal across Nicaragua. During his incumbency he favored closer commercial relations with the countries of Latin America upon the basis of reciprocity, vigorously supported American commercial interests in Germany and France, negotiated for a naval base at Pearl Harbor in Hawaii, and opened up treaty relations with Korea. He also authorized the participation of the United States in the Berlin Conference of 1884 which regulated the affairs of the Congo and mediated successfully a boundary dispute between Mexico and Guatemala which threatened the peace of that whole region. He always aimed with great patience and courtesy to show consideration for the rights of other nations and to create a feeling of generous good will in all his diplomatic negotiations. He was thus able to avoid critical situations and to leave no trying problems for his successors. Frelinghuysen served as secretary of state from Dec. 19, 1881, until his successor, Secretary Bayard, was appointed by President Cleveland on Mar. 4, 1885. Long public service had undermined his health, and he lived only a few weeks after returning to Newark. He was survived by his widow, Matilde E. Griswold, whom he had married on Jan. 25, 1842, and six children. A man of courtly personality, he had an inspiring sense of the dignity of life, and was actuated in all he did by sound judgment, delicate feeling, and conscientious devotion to principles and ideals.

[F. J. Hageman, "The Life, Character and Services of Frederick T. Frelinghuysen, LL.D.," in *Proc. N. J. Hist. Soc.*, 2 ser. IX (1887); F. B. Lee, *Geneal. and Memorial Hist. of the State of N. J.* (1910), vol. I; P. M. Brown, in *The Am. Secretaries of State and their Diplomacy* (1928), vol. VIII; W. E. Sackett, *Modern Battles of Trenton* (1895); *N. Y. Tribune*, May 21, 1885.]

P. M. B.

FRELINGHUYSEN, THEODORE (Mar. 28, 1787–Apr. 12, 1862), lawyer, senator, college president, was born in Franklin Township, Somerset County, N. J., the second son of Gen. Frederick Frelinghuysen [*q.v.*] and Gertrude (Schenck) Frelinghuysen. At thirteen, with his father's consent, he left the grammar school connected with Queen's College (later Rutgers), to pursue farming rather than a liberal education. Soon afterward, however, his stepmother, during his father's absence, packed him off to Dr. Finley's academy at Basking Ridge where he received an excellent primary education, and from there he went to Princeton, graduating second in his class in 1804. He then read law with Richard Stockton of Princeton, was admitted to the bar in 1808 as an attorney, in 1811 as a counselor, and in 1817 received the title of sergeant at law. He began his practise of the law in Newark where, in 1809, he married Charlotte, daughter of Archibald Mercer. Having no children of their own, they adopted a nephew, Frederick Theodore Frelinghuysen [*q.v.*]. The young lawyer's rise at the bar was rapid. Four years after his admittance he had an extensive and lucrative practise and in 1817 his abilities and personal character were so well recognized that he was made attorney-general of New Jersey. He received this appointment by the votes of a legislature, the majority of whose members were opposed to him in politics, a mark of the esteem in which he was held by his fellow citizens. Reëlected in 1822 and 1827, he served until his election to the United States Senate in 1829. In 1826 the legislature had appointed him justice of the state supreme court which he declined, preferring to continue his practise at the bar. The best evidence of his ability to plead a cause is found in his argument made in the case of *Hendrickson* vs. *Decow* (1 *N. J. Equity,* 577), in which he successfully defended the claims of the Orthodox Quakers.

Although serving but a single term as United States senator (1829–35), Frelinghuysen became a national figure. The influence which he exerted at Washington can be explained only by the universal respect in which he was held by members of both parties. His six-hour speech (Apr. 7, 8, and 9, 1830, *Register of Debates in Congress,* 21 Cong., 1 Sess., pp. 309–20) in opposition to the bill for the removal of the Cherokee and other southern Indians to territory west of the Mississippi, though unsuccessful in defeating the measure, brought him prominently before the nation. He became known as the "Christian statesman," probably as a result of a poem by William Lloyd Garrison praising Frelinghuysen for his stand on the Indian question, and designating him "Patriot and Christian." Daniel Webster, Henry Clay, and other well-known men paid tribute to the deep religious conviction of Frelinghuysen, and never did they resent in any way the solicitude with which he regarded their own personal religious lives (Chambers, *post,* pp. 178, 183). It was said of him that no American layman of his time was associated with so many great national organizations of religion and charity. For sixteen years he served as president of the American Board of Commissioners for Foreign Missions; from 1846 till his death he was president of the American Bible Society; president of the American Tract Society from 1842 to 1848; vice-president of the American Sunday School Union for fifty years; and for many years an officer of the American Colonization Society and of the American Temperance Union. Giving so much of his time and money, for he was a generous contributor to all these causes, it is not surprising that in 1835 Frelinghuysen seriously contemplated leaving the bar and entering the ministry (Chambers, *post,* p. 170). In 1839 he retired from his law practise and resigned as mayor of Newark, to which office he had been first elected in 1836 and reëlected in 1838, to accept the chancellorship of the University of the City of New York. In 1844 he made his last appearance in a political rôle, as the Whig candidate for vice-president. The defeat of the Whig ticket was a surprise and bitter disappointment to him, especially because of his great admiration and affection for his running mate, Henry Clay. Ironically the votes of the New York Abolitionists for Birney gave the state and the presidency to Polk.

Frelinghuysen's success as an academic administrator did not rival his success as a lawyer. It was in the legal forum that his peculiar gifts of quick insight, sharp discrimination, and impetuous eloquence were best displayed. His abandonment of the profession of the law in favor of an academic career was always regarded as a mistake by his friends of the New Jersey bar. After eleven years as chancellor of the University in New York he resigned to assume the presidency of Rutgers College. Since an acute illness had impaired his accustomed good health, he welcomed this change, believing that the work at Rutgers would not be so exacting as that in New York, where he was under the continual burden of raising funds. His connection with Rutgers was far from being nominal, however, and he engaged actively in the work of enlisting the aid of old friends of the college who renewed their support under the leadership of their distinguished president. The results were evidenced by the increase in the enrolment and endowment as well as in a greatly enlarged course of study. It was while serving at Rutgers that Frelinghuysen's active life came to a close. He contracted a severe cold while attending church on Washington's birthday, 1862, and died after a few weeks' illness. His first wife having died in 1854, on Oct. 14, 1857, he was married to Harriet Pumpelly of Owego, N. Y.

[Cortlandt Parker, *A Sketch of the Life and Pub. Services of Theo. Frelinghuysen* (1844), and *The Essex Bar* (1874); Talbot W. Chambers, *Memoir of the Life and Character of the Late Hon. Theo. Frelinghuysen* (1863); J. F. Folsom, *The Municipalities of Essex County, N. J.* (1925), III, 4–5; J. L. Chamberlain, *N. Y. University* (1901); W. H. S. Demarest, *A Hist. of Rutgers Coll., 1766–1924* (1924); W. L. Garrison, *Sonnets and Other Poems* (1843), pp. 69–71; *State Gazette and Republican* (Trenton, N. J.), Apr. 15, 1862; *N. Y. Tribune,* Apr. 14, 1862.]

C. R. E., Jr.

FRELINGHUYSEN, THEODORUS JACOBUS (1691–*c.* 1748), Reformed Dutch clergyman, was born in Germany at Lingen on the Ems near the Dutch border, the son of the local Reformed pastor, Johannes Hendricus Frielinghausen. He received most of his education from his father and from the Rev. Otto Verbrugge, later a professor at Gronigen, who persuaded him to learn Dutch so as to profit by the superior orthodoxy of Dutch theology. He was licensed in 1717 by the Classis of Emden, was a chaplain in 1718 at the Logumer Voorwerk in East Friesland, and in the same year was made subrector at Enkhuizen on the Zuiderzee in West Friesland. Soon thereafter, as the result of a chance meeting with the Rev. Sicco Tjadde, he accepted a call to the Dutch congregations of Raritan (founded 1699), New Brunswick, Six-Mile Run, Three-

Mile Run, and North Branch in the Raritan Valley in New Jersey. Frelinghuysen combined loyalty to the teachings of the Heidelberg Catechism with the methods and fanatical zeal of a master revivalist. On Jan. 17, 1720, shortly after his landing at New York, he preached for Dominie Henricus Boel and twice during the service omitted the Lord's Prayer where the rubric called for it. Boel, truculently orthodox and appetent of controversy, smelled heresy in the omissions and began to gird for battle. Frelinghuysen, meanwhile, threw himself into his work with tremendous zest. Many of his parishioners were quickly incensed by the directness of his preaching, the severity of his requirements for admission to the communion table, and the candor of his strictures on their manners, morals, and religious observances. Allying themselves with Boel and other New York clergymen, they carried on a long, stubborn, and unseemly warfare, which culminated in 1725 with the publication of a *Klagte* of 146 pages, drawn up it is believed by Boel's lawyer brother and signed by sixty-four heads of families. Frelinghuysen, however, was a match for them. With the help of Peter Henry Dorsius, Bernardus Freeman [*q.v.*], and other sympathizers, he vanquished his foes and lived his latter years in peace and honor. His congregations throve; revivals and "ingatherings" followed in his wake; his labors were commended by George Whitefield, Gilbert Tennent, and Jonathan Edwards. He did as much as any one to invoke the Great Awakening in the Middle Colonies, and the region where he wrought remains a stronghold of his denomination. He trained several men for the ministry, advocated the establishment of a college and theological seminary, urged the Dutch churches to govern themselves instead of deferring to the Classis of Amsterdam, and set an example by taking part in the unauthorized ordination of John Henry Goetschius [*q.v.*]. He published seven pamphlets of his sermons. His wife was Eva, daughter of Albert Terhune, a well-to-do farmer of Flatbush, L. I. Jacobus Schureman, a schoolmaster who accompanied him from Amsterdam, married her sister Autje. Frelinghuysen's two daughters married ministers; his five sons became ministers. The date of his death and the site of his grave are unknown.

[T. J. Frelinghuysen, *Sermons, Translated from the Dutch and Prefaced by a Sketch of the Author's Life by Rev. Wm. Demarest* (1856); E. T. Corwin, *Manual Reformed Ch. in America* (4th ed., 1902); J. P. De Bie and J. Loosjes, *Biographisch Woordenboek van Protestantsche Godgeleerden in Nederland* ('S-Gravenhage, n.d.); C. H. Maxson, *The Great Awakening in the Middle Colonies* (1920).]

G. H. G.

FRÉMONT, JESSIE BENTON (May 31, 1824–Dec. 27, 1902), writer, daughter of Senator Thomas Hart Benton [*q.v.*] and wife of John Charles Frémont, was the second of five children. Her mother was Elizabeth McDowell, and Jessie was born at her grandfather McDowell's estate near Lexington, Va. Here, in Washington, and in St. Louis, she passed her girlhood. She was tutored at home, much of the time by her father himself, in St. Louis went to an informal French school where she helped the master's wife with her preserving and acquired an easy familiarity with spoken French; studied Spanish—"the neighbor language," as her father called it—and in her early teens was sent to the fashionable boarding school kept by Miss English in Georgetown, D. C. At this time, as she later admitted, she was still something of a tomboy, given to climbing trees. At sixteen, a blooming, vigorous girl, full of fun, with an intellectual capacity beyond her years—the result in part of companionship with her father—she met young John Charles Frémont [*q.v.*], a lieutenant in the Topographical Corps, and in spite of the effort of her parents to postpone what seemed inevitable, she married him on Oct. 19, 1841.

For the first years after her marriage, during her explorer-husband's long absences, she lived in her father's house—continuing her studies under his supervision, translating confidential State Department papers from the Spanish, serving as his hostess, and becoming increasingly his companion during her mother's long invalidism. Frémont returned from his first important expedition in October 1842; their baby, Elizabeth, was born in November; and during the happy winter that followed, Jessie worked daily with her husband on the first of his vivid reports. When his second expedition (1843) was endangered by a letter recalling him to Washington, she suppressed the order, wrote to him to start at once without waiting for a reason, and when she had received word that he had acted immediately upon her message, wrote to the Department at Washington explaining what she had done. The expedition—a long one—was successful, and in the winter of 1844–45 Frémont and Jessie collaborated on the second report. Anxiety incident to Frémont's court martial in 1848 following his third expedition, told upon Jessie's health, and in the fall of that year her second baby died. In 1849, with her little girl, she went, by the Panama route, to meet Frémont in San Francisco, suffering a critical illness on the way. The hardships of the voyage and conditions in California on the eve of its admission as a state are described in her little volume, *A Year of American Travel*

(1878). The example of young Mrs. Frémont, reared in a very comfortable home, gallantly doing her own work in the frontier community and refusing to employ slaves, is said to have had an influence on the members of the convention which drafted California's Free-Soil constitution.

During the next five years she returned for a short time to Washington society as wife of the first senator from California; bore a son, and when he was but two months old saw her house burn to the ground in the San Francisco fire of 1851; visited Europe, 1852–53, being received cordially everywhere as the daughter of Senator Benton and the wife of the brilliant explorer and making lasting friendships in her own right; had another baby, who died; went back to her father's house to wait for Frémont's return from his fifth and most dangerous expedition (1853–54); and in May 1854 gave birth to another son. In her husband's unsuccessful campaign for the presidency (1856) her charm was exploited until " 'Frémont and Jessie' seemed to constitute the Republican ticket rather than Frémont and Dayton" (Nevins, *post*, II, 496–97). After another brief visit to Europe and three years on the California ranch and in San Francisco, where she encouraged and befriended the obscure young reporter, Bret Harte, there came the Civil War. Throughout Frémont's stormy military service she shared his intense anxiety, giving expression to the bitterness which he would not admit and even, on one occasion, attempting to argue with the President in his behalf. Her feeling is partially revealed in *The Story of the Guard: A Chronicle of the War* (1863).

After the war their home in New York City and their country place on the Hudson were centers of hospitality, but in the seventies they lost their entire fortune and for a time were in actual need. Faced by the problem of a young son whose health required a change of climate, and with no money to send him away, Mrs. Frémont offered Robert Bonner of the *New York Ledger* a series of articles at $100 each. He accepted her offer, and she began to contribute regularly to a number of periodicals, writing travel sketches, historical sketches, and stories for boys and girls. Selections from these papers were republished in book form: *Souvenirs of My Time* (1887); *Far West Sketches* (1890); *The Will and the Way Stories* (1891). She helped Frémont with the writing of the first and only published volume of his *Memoirs* (1887), and wrote for it a sketch of Senator Benton. (Another sketch of her father, which she wrote in 1879, was not published for many years; see New York *Independent*, Jan. 29, 1903.) In 1887 the Frémonts returned to California, and after her husband's death in 1890 Mrs. Frémont remained in Los Angeles with her daughter, living in a house given her by the ladies of Southern California. At her death in 1902 she was buried beside Frémont at Piermont on the Hudson.

[Mrs. Frémont's writings; Allan Nevins, *Frémont: the West's Greatest Adventurer* (2 vols., 1928); *Recollections of Elizabeth Benton Frémont* (1912), comp. by I. T. Martin; M. C. Kendall, "A Woman who has Lived History," *Overland Monthly*, Jan. 1, 1901; C. A. Moody, "Here was a Woman," *Out West* (Los Angeles), Feb. 1903, a good character sketch; Rebecca Harding Davis, "In Remembrance," *Independent* (N. Y.), Jan. 29, 1903; articles in *Los Angeles Times*, Dec. 28, 1902, and following issues.] E. R. D.

FRÉMONT, JOHN CHARLES (Jan. 21, 1813–July 13, 1890), explorer, politician, soldier, was the son of a French émigré school-teacher of Richmond, Va., Jean Charles Frémon, who eloped with Mrs. Anne Whiting Pryor of that city in 1811. They fled from Mrs. Pryor's aged husband to Savannah, Ga., where Frémont was born. While the father taught French and dancing in various parts of the South, the mother sometimes took boarders. The family spent some years in Norfolk, Va., and after the death of Frémon in 1818 his widow (if we may so call her in the absence of any marriage) removed to Charleston, S. C., where she supported several children on a meager inherited income. Frémont was precocious, handsome, and daring, and quickly showed an aptitude for obtaining protectors. A lawyer, John W. Mitchell, saw that he was given sufficient schooling to enter Charleston College in May 1829, and he remained there, with intervals of teaching in the country, till expelled for irregular attendance in 1831. Fortunately the college had grounded him in mathematics and the natural sciences. Fortunately also he had attracted the attention of Joel R. Poinsett, Jacksonian leader in the state, and shortly obtained through him an appointment as teacher of mathematics on the sloop of war *Natchez*. On this ship he cruised in South American waters in 1833.

Frémont's real career began when he resigned from the navy to become a second lieutenant in the United States Topographical Corps and to assist in surveying the route of a projected railway between Charleston and Cincinnati. In his work in the Carolina mountains he formed a strong taste for wilderness exploration. This was deepened when in 1837–38 he acted with another detachment of the Topographical Corps in a reconnaissance of the Cherokee country in Georgia, instituted by the government preparatory to the removal of the Indians. Ordered thence to Washington, Frémont obtained from Poinsett a place with the expedition of J. N. Nicollet [*q.v.*] for exploring the plateau between the upper Mississippi and Missouri Rivers. Nicollet, a scientist of high reputation in Paris and Washington, gave him an expert training in astronomical, topographical, and geological observation, for which Frémont's quick mind had a natural taste. He also received a thorough initiation into western frontier life, becoming intimate with such men as Henry Sibley of the American Fur Company, Joseph Renville, J. B. Faribault, and Étienne Provot, meeting large bodies of Sioux, and traversing much of the country between Fort Pierre on the Missouri and Fort Snelling on the Mississippi. Returning to Washington, he took bachelor quarters with Nicollet and collaborated with him upon a map and an elaborate scientific report.

The second turning-point in Frémont's life was his meeting with Senator Thomas Hart Benton, who was greatly interested in Nicollet's work, brought Frémont to his house, and gave him a new vision of the possibilities of western exploration and expansion to the Pacific. Frémont later wrote that his interviews with Benton were "pregnant with results and decisive of my life" (*Memoirs of My Life,* 1887, I, 65). He fell in love with the sixteen-year-old Jessie Benton. Alarmed by their obvious attachment, her father persuaded Poinsett, now secretary of war, to send the penniless lieutenant to explore the Des Moines River. Frémont, elated by his first independent commission, equipped an expedition in St. Louis, hired the botanist Charles Geyer, and during the spring and summer of 1841 creditably mapped much of Iowa Territory. Neither he nor the strong-willed Jessie Benton had swerved, however, from what was to prove a lifelong devotion, and when the Benton family remained obdurate, they were secretly married in Washington, on Oct. 19, 1841, by a Catholic priest. When Benton learned the fact in November he angrily ordered Frémont from his door, but relented when Jessie quoted the words of Ruth, "Whither thou goest, I will go." Thereafter Frémont found an invaluable adviser, patron, and protector in his father-in-law.

Frémont's first important exploration, a summer expedition in 1842 to the Wind River chain of the Rockies, was planned by Benton, Senator Lewis Linn, and other Westerners interested in the acquisition of Oregon, and marked him definitely as the successor of the now dying Nicollet. Its main object was to give a scientific examination to the Oregon Trail through South Pass and to report on the rivers, the fertility of the country, the best positions for forts, and the nature of the mountains beyond in Wyoming. Equipping a party of twenty-five in St. Louis with the aid of Cyprian Chouteau and obtaining by a lucky chance the services of Kit Carson as guide, Frémont left the Kansas River on June 15, 1842, followed the Platte toward the Rockies, crossed South Pass, and from the headwaters of the Green River explored the Wind River range, where he climbed what he mistakenly thought to be the highest peak of the Rockies, Frémont's Peak (13,730 feet). On his return he recklessly shot the rapids of the swollen Platte in a rubber boat and lost much of his equipment (F. S. Dellenbaugh, *Frémont and '49,* 1914, p. 65 ff.). He was back in Washington in October, and with Jessie Frémont's expert help, for she possessed high literary gifts, he composed a report which gave him a wide popular reputation (*Report of the Exploring Expedition to the Rocky Mountains,* 1843). Modeled on Irving's *Adventures of Captain Bonneville,* it showed a zest for adventure and a descriptive sparkle which appealed to the fast-growing interest in Oregon settlement. It furnished a scientific map of much of the Oregon Trail prepared by the topographer Charles Preuss, emphasized the fertility of the plains, and offered much practical advice to emigrants. Government publication was followed by numerous reprints. Congress, prompted by Benton, at once authorized a second expedition under Frémont which was to reach the South Pass by a different route, push to the Columbia, and examine the Oregon country, connecting on the Pacific with the coastal surveys by Commander Wilkes.

Frémont's second expedition of almost forty well-equipped men left the Missouri River in May 1843, with Thomas Fitzpatrick as guide, Preuss as topographer, and a twelve-pound howitzer cannon which he rashly obtained from Col. S. W. Kearny in St. Louis. Its departure was hastened by an urgent message from Jessie Frémont, who suppressed a War Department order requiring Frémont to return to Washington to explain his howitzer; the government objected to giving the expedition the appearance of a military reconnaissance. Benton later successfully defended his daughter's action. On the Arkansas River Frémont was joined by Kit Carson. After an unavailing effort to blaze a new trail through northern Colorado, he struck the regular Oregon Trail, on which he passed the main body of the great emigration of 1843; stopped to explore the Great Salt Lake; and pushed on by way of Fort Hall and Fort Boise to Marcus Whitman's mission on the Columbia. His endurance, energy, and resourcefulness were remarkable. Reaching the Dalles on Nov. 5, Frémont left the main body of his expedition while he went downstream to Fort Vancouver for supplies. He might then have retraced his steps to St. Louis. But under the spell of Benton's dream of acquiring the whole West, he resolved to turn south and explore the Great Basin between the Rockies and Sierras. Moving through Oregon to Pyramid Lake, which he named, and into Nevada, he reached the Carson River on Jan. 18, 1844. From a point near the site of Virginia City he resolved to cross the Sierra into California, a feat daring to the point of foolhardiness, yet despite the perils of cold and snow he accomplished it. Early in March he reached the Sacramento Valley and was hospitably received by Capt. August Sutter at his fort, where he refitted his party. While here he talked with the American settlers, now growing numerous, and formed a clear impression of the feeble Mexican hold upon California. Moving south till he struck the "Spanish Trail" from Los Angeles to Santa Fé, he followed this for some distance, crossed parts of the present states of Nevada and Utah, explored Utah Lake, and by way of Pueblo reached Bent's Fort on the Arkansas. Not until August 1844 did he arrive in St. Louis. His return was one of the sensations of the day. Accompanied by Jessie, he traveled to Washington and devoted the winter with her aid to his second report. It appeared at a fortunate moment, when Polk's victory had given impetus to policies of expansion. As detailed, vivid, and readable as the first report, with much careful scientific observation, it showed that the Oregon Trail was not difficult and that the Northwest was fertile and desirable. Senator Buchanan moved the printing of 10,000 copies.

With war with Mexico now clearly imminent and all eyes fixed on the West, it was easy for Benton to carry an appropriation for a third expedition under Frémont. Under the War Department, it was to execute a survey of the central Rockies, the Great Salt Lake region, and part of the Sierra Nevada. In St. Louis Frémont equipped sixty men, fully armed; Kit Carson was again called to be his guide, and two other distinguished frontiersmen, Joseph Walker and Alexander Godey, were enlisted. Frémont in his *Memoirs* (I, 422 ff.) states that it was secretly intended by Benton and George Bancroft, secretary of the navy, that if he reached California and found war had begun, he should transform his scientific force into a military body. Unquestionably he desired to play a rôle in conquering California, which had captivated him by its beauty and wealth, and this desire furnishes the key to his very controversial conduct there. Moving west by way of Bent's Fort, the Great Salt Lake, and the "Hastings Cut-Off," he reached the Ogden River, which he renamed the Humboldt, and divided his party in order to double his geographical information. On Dec. 9, 1845, after blazing a useful new trail across Nevada, he was again at Sutter's Fort. Under the pretext of obtaining fuller supplies, he took his men to Monterey and established contact there with the American consul, Thomas Larkin. In February 1846 he united with the other branch of his expedition near San Jose, thus giving the United States a formidable little force in the heart of California. The suspicious Mexican officials ordered him from the country but with headstrong audacity he promptly hoisted the American flag, defying them. Then, obviously playing for time, he moved north to Klamath Lake, where on May 8 he was overtaken by Lieut. A. H. Gillespie from Washington. Gillespie had brought dispatches to Larkin, of which he carried copies to Frémont, and according to the latter he also brought verbal instructions from Benton and Buchanan which justified aggressive action. There can be no question that he brought news that both Larkin and the commander of the American warship *Portsmouth* in San Francisco Bay expected war to begin in a few days (Larkin Manuscripts, State Department, letters of Apr. 17, 23, 1846). Frémont felt that his course was clear and turned back.

The result was that he played a prominent if at first hesitating rôle in the conquest of California. Hastening to Sutter's Fort, he made a display of force there which inspired the discontented American settlers in the Sacramento Valley to begin the Bear Flag revolt, and then (June 23) took up arms in their support. When news of actual war reached him on July 10 he actively cooperated with Sloat and Stockton in the conquest of California. His "California Battalion" of expedition-members and settlers marched to Monterey, took ship to San Diego, and with Stockton's force captured Los Angeles on Aug. 13. Frémont then went north to muster a larger force, was busy recruiting when a revolt wrested Los Angeles from the Americans, and returned only in time to assist Stockton and Gen. S. W. Kearny in the final capture of that town in January 1847. He accepted the Mexican surrender in the Capitulation of Couenga. Almost immediately he was involved in the bitter quarrel of Stockton and Kearny [*qq.v.*] over their respective authorities, caused by conflicting instructions from Washington. Taking Stockton's side, he was appointed by him civil governor of California, and exercised that authority for two months, until final orders from Washington established Kearny's supremacy. Kearny humiliated Frémont, detained him in defiance of Polk's orders that he be allowed to proceed to Mexico, and, taking him to Fort Leavenworth as a virtual prisoner, there arrested him upon charges of mutiny and insubordination. The quarrel was taken up with indiscreet energy by Benton. It resulted in a famous court martial in Washington (November 1847–January 1848) in which a panel of regular officers found Frémont guilty of mutiny, disobedience, and conduct prejudicial to order. Though President Polk remitted the penalty, Frémont, who found public sentiment on his side, indignantly resigned from the service.

This resignation was followed by a midwinter expedition (1848–49), at the expense of Benton and certain wealthy St. Louisans interested in a Pacific railroad, to find passes for such a line westward from the upper waters of the Rio Grande. It proved a disastrous venture. Eager to show that passage of the mountains was practicable in midwinter, Frémont ignored frontiersmen who warned him that the Sangre de Cristo and San Juan ranges were impassable. He was led astray by his guide "Old Bill" Williams, but he unwisely failed to turn back from the San Juan Mountains in time, and after intense suffering from cold, storms, and starvation, lost eleven men. Succored by Kit Carson and others in Taos, he proceeded to California, meeting on the Gila a troop of Sonora Mexicans who told him that gold had been discovered. Consul Larkin had recently purchased for him a tract of seventy square miles in the Sierra foothills, the Mariposa estate, and he hired the Mexicans to work there on shares. Within a few weeks his income from the diggings reached enormous sums—Jessie Frémont speaks of hundred-pound bags of gold dust—and he was able to acquire large realty interests in San Francisco, live on a generous scale in Monterey, and develop his Mariposa property. His election as United States senator in December 1850 gave him only the short term from Sept. 9, 1850, to Mar. 4, 1851.

Frémont remained essentially a Californian till the Civil War, but with restless energy spent much time outside the state. He served six weeks as senator in Washington, made a prolonged stay with his family in London and Paris (1852–53), gathering capital to work the quartz deposits at Mariposa, and conducted another winter exploration in search of a southern railway route to the Pacific (1853–54). In this expedition he reached central Utah with a small body of men after a journey of great hardship, demonstrating that practicable passes through the mountains existed between north latitude 37° and 38°. But the most important event of these years was his nomination for the presidency. His explorations and court martial had made him a national hero, while his aloofness from the slavery contest rendered him available. First approached by Democratic leaders, including Ex-Gov. John B. Floyd of Virginia and members of the influential Preston family, he pronounced himself vigorously for a free-soil Kansas and against enforcement of the Fugitive-Slave Law (Jessie Benton Frémont Manuscripts). Organizers of the new national Republican party, led by N. P. Banks, Henry Wilson, and John Bigelow, then took him up, and he was nominated at Philadelphia in June 1856. He had hoped that Simon Cameron would be named for vice-president, and always regarded the nomination of W. L. Dayton as one of the causes of his defeat. Possessing no taste or aptitude for politics, he played as passive a rôle as his opponent, Buchanan. In a campaign notable for abusiveness, much being made of his illegitimate birth and a mendacious report that he was a Catholic, he remained quietly at his Ninth St. home in New York. His defeat by Buchanan by an electoral vote of 174 to 114, and a popular vote of 1,838,169 to 1,341,264, was due partly to fear of Southern secession and partly to lack of campaign funds. Frémont shortly returned to California and devoted himself to his mining business, his title to Mariposa, then valued by some at ten million dollars, being confirmed by the federal Supreme Court in 1855.

The outbreak of the Civil War found Frémont in Europe raising more capital for Mariposa, and he attempted a bold service by hastening to England and on his own responsibility purchasing arms for the Federal cause (J. B. McMaster, *History of the People of the United States, During Lincoln's Administration,* 1927, p. 190). Lincoln wished to appoint him minister to France, but when Secretary Seward protested, appointed him major-general in charge of the department of the West, with headquarters at St. Louis, where he arrived July 25, 1861. The task before him was of tremendous difficulty; he had to organize an army in a slave state, largely disloyal, with few arms, few supplies, and limited numbers of raw volunteers for material, and with political and military enemies ready to make the most of every misstep. When he took charge guerrilla warfare was breaking out in Missouri, while his forces at Cairo, Ill., and Springfield, Mo., were menaced by superior armies. He accomplished much, reinforcing Cairo, fortifying St. Louis, organizing a squadron of river gunboats, arousing the enthusiasm of the German population, and training large bodies of men; but the defeats at Wilson's Creek, and Lexington were unfairly blamed upon him, he was justly accused of ostentation and reckless expenditures, and the attacks of Frank Blair cost him Lincoln's confidence. He blundered when on Aug. 30, 1861, he issued a rash proclamation declaring the property of Missourians in rebellion confiscated and their slaves emancipated; this act aroused the applause of radical Northerners, but Lincoln rightly regarded it as premature and when Frémont refused to retract issued an order modifying it. In response to growing complaints Lincoln sent first Montgomery Blair, and later Secretary Cameron and Lorenzo Thomas, to Missouri to investigate, and on the basis of their reports removed Frémont as he was leading an army in futile pursuit of Price's Confederate force (Nov. 2, 1861). The antagonisms aroused in the West by Frémont would alone have justified such action, but the removal was bitterly resented by radical anti-slavery men, and was indirectly censured by the congressional committee on the conduct of the war. Out of regard for this radical opinion, Lincoln in March 1862 appointed Frémont to command the mountain department in western Virginia. But he was given inadequate forces, his command was improperly divided by the government, Lincoln plainly distrusted him, and in May and June 1862 he was completely outgeneralled by "Stonewall" Jackson in the latter's brilliant Valley campaign. Lincoln then placed Frémont and his corps under the command of Pope, whom Frémont detested for his alleged insubordination in Missouri, and Frémont asked to be relieved.

Thereafter Frémont's history was one of adversity. Still popular with the radical Republicans who disliked Lincoln, he was nominated for the presidency on May 31, 1864, in Cleveland, by a convention of radicals, western Germans, and war Democrats. His candidacy disturbed the administration, and by a bargain between it and Frémont's radical supporters, Frémont ungracefully withdrew on Sept. 22, 1864, and Lincoln the next day dismissed the ultra-conservative Montgomery Blair from his cabinet. Frémont played no further part in public life. Turning to business, he proved unable to rescue his Mariposa estate from the embarrassments into which it had fallen during his preoccupation with the war, and by the end of 1864 had lost control of that property. For finance, as for war, he lacked essential qualities of judgment. He became interested in western railroads, and after purchasing the Kansas Pacific franchise and a part-interest in the Memphis & Little Rock, he became president and promoter of the Memphis & El Paso, which he dreamed of extending from Norfolk, Va., to San Diego, Cal. Though his methods were merely those characteristic of promoters in the flush years preceding 1873, the bankruptcy of the line in 1870 not only cost him the remnants of his fortune, but left his reputation under a cloud. Misleading advertisements in French papers, for which he was indirectly responsible, caused his indictment in that country. He never reëstablished himself, and was saved from poverty only by Jessie Benton Frémont's activities as an author, his appointment as territorial governor of Arizona (1878–83), and his restoration to the army as major-general, with pay on the retired list, early in 1890. In 1887 he made his home in California, but death came while he was temporarily staying in New York. He and his wife, who survived until 1902, are buried at Piermont on the Hudson. His whole later career had been a tragic anti-climax; but his fame as an explorer, in which his achievements were of very high rank, is commemorated by numerous place-names throughout the United States, and represents services which cannot be forgotten.

[The fullest work on Frémont's life is Allan Nevins, *Frémont, the West's Greatest Adventurer* (2 vols., 1928); it is based in part on family documents, and contains an extensive bibliography. It is supplemented by Frémont's *Memoirs of My Life* (1887), of which but one volume was ever published; by Mrs. Frémont's *Souvenirs of My Time* (1887), *Far West Sketches* (1890), and *A Year of American Travel* (1878), valuable in the order mentioned; and by F. S. Dellenbaugh's *Frémont and '49* (1914). Of less importance are S. N. Carvalho, *Incidents of Travel and Adventure in the Far West with Frémont's Last Expedition* (1857); John R. Howard, *Remembrance of Things Past* (1925), by a member of Frémont's staff in Missouri; the manuscript "Narrative of John C. Frémont's Expedition in Cal. 1845–46," by Thos. S. Martin, in the Bancroft Lib., Cal.; and John Fowler's manuscript paper on "The Bear Flag Revolt in Cal." (1846), in the same collection. *The Recollections of Elizabeth Benton Frémont* (1912), compiled by I. T. Martin, contains materials by his daughter. There is an obituary in the *N. Y. Tribune*, July 14, 1890. Cardinal Goodwin, *John Chas. Frémont: An Explanation of His Career* (1930), is an able but excessively hostile treatment which centers attention upon the Bear Flag Revolt, the events of 1861, and the subsequent railroad transactions. All of Frémont's papers which survive, many having been destroyed in a fire, are in the Bancroft Library.]

A. N.

FRENCH, AARON (Mar. 23, 1823–Mar. 24, 1902), inventor and pioneer manufacturer of railroad car springs, was born in Wadsworth, Medina County, Ohio, in 1823. The son of Philo and Mary (McIntyre) French, he was a descendant of early colonial stock. He attended school until he was twelve years old, after which he learned blacksmithing—a trade which then embraced working with metals and fashioning and repairing wheels, tools, springs, and other mechanical devices. By the time he was twenty he had held various jobs in different parts of the country. For two years he had worked for the Ohio Stage Company at Cleveland, Ohio, then, after a year in the employ of the Gayoso House in Memphis,

Tenn., he had become a western agent of the American Fur Company. At twenty, anxious to continue his education, he attended for a year the Archie McGregor Academy in Wadsworth, Ohio. In 1844 he went to St. Louis, but left in 1845 to work for Peter Young, a wagon-builder, at Carlyle, Clinton County, Ill. Becoming very ill, he was brought back to Ohio by his brother and was a semi-invalid during the four years which followed. After his return to active life he was employed in railroad blacksmith shops. In 1853 he was with the Cleveland & Pittsburgh Railroad in Cleveland and later was placed in charge of a similar shop of the same railroad at Wellsville, Ohio. Then, turning west again, he went to Racine, Wis., as superintendent of the blacksmithing of the Racine & Mississippi Railroad. Upon the outbreak of the Civil War he was among the first to volunteer but failed to pass the physical tests. He had made such a reputation for courage and fair-dealing during his short stay in Racine, however, that he was elected sheriff of the county. This position he resigned to move in 1862 to Pittsburgh, where he entered a partnership with Calvin Wells for the manufacture of the first steel springs for railroad cars. At first he employed eight or ten workmen and limited his output to elliptic springs under the Hazen patents, but the business grew rapidly, and within thirty years the force had increased to three hundred men. During these years he invented and put into use coiled and elliptic springs which effected a revolution in the railroad industry. He had reduced the weight of the car spring by two-thirds, and at the same time had increased its strength.

French died in 1902, on the day following his seventy-ninth birthday. Shortly before his death his business (the A. French Spring Company) had merged with the Railway Steel Spring Company of Pittsburgh. He was twice married. His first wife was Euphrasia Terrill of Liverpool, Medina County, Ohio, whom he married in 1848. After her death in 1871 he was married to Caroline B. Skeer. Personally he was modest and unassuming, and shunned publicity. He carried on his philanthropic work so quietly that the full extent of his benefactions cannot be ascertained, though he is known to have made generous gifts to the Georgia School of Technology.

[Notices at the time of French's death appeared in the *Pittsburgh Dispatch*, and the *Pittsburgh Post*. See also the *Biog. Rev. of Pittsburgh* (1897); *Encyc. of Pa.*, vol. I (1914); *Ann. Announcement of the Ga. School of Technology*, 1907–08.] A. I.

FRENCH, EDWIN DAVIS (Jan. 19, 1851–Dec. 8, 1906), engraver of silver and copper, was the son of Ebenezer French, a carpenter of North Attleboro, Mass., and his wife Ann Maria Norton. After preliminary schooling near his home and at the Connecticut Literary Institute of Suffield, French entered Brown University in 1866, but was forced by ill health to leave in his sophomore year. Two years later he entered the service of W. D. Whiting as a silver engraver in the Whiting Manufacturing Company of North Attleboro. He accompanied the firm to New York City in 1876, and was given charge of the engraving department, serving in that capacity until 1894, with the exception of the years from 1881 to 1883 when he was in North Attleboro as designer for F. M. Whiting.

Although almost twenty-five years of his life were devoted to silver engraving in the Whiting Company, French's interest in graphic art, which in his childhood had prompted elaborate woodshed exhibitions, persisted through his long industrial career, and at length induced him to desert silver for copper engraving. During his early years in New York he studied at home, compiling scrap-books of design and engraving. His formal training did not begin until 1883, when he entered the evening class of the Art Students' League as a student of William Sartain and later of George de Forest Brush and F. Edwin Elwell. He fell into book-plate engraving almost by accident. His initial attempt was inscribed "u sepe ars so ap" and was inserted in an authentic collection as a practical joke. It printed so well that he cut others, some of which were shown at the 1893–94 exhibition of the Architectural League of New York, with the result that he was soon obliged to resign from the Whiting Company to satisfy the demand for his plates. Of the approximately three hundred book-plates he engraved in the remaining twelve years of his life, many were designed for private libraries, but some of the most impressive were those cut for societies and institutions. These included *ex-libris* for the Colonial Dames, 1894, the Library of the Metropolitan Museum of Art, 1895, the Candidati and the Princeton Library, 1897, and the Hohenzollern Collection of the Harvard College Library, 1904. He carried out various other commissions for designs and engravings, of which the most notable were the title-page for *André's Journal*, published in 1903 by the Bibliophile Society, and twelve views of New York City, published severally by the Society of Iconophiles of the City of New York from February 1895 to March 1897.

French's engraving was notable for its dignity of design and its meticulous workmanship. His preoccupation with the decorative element of his plates, and his use of formal and simplified baroque, as well as his technical skill, were probably the result of his long apprenticeship as a silver engraver. Excepting his realistic cuts, which were accurate but uninteresting, his work was uniformly distinguished, and often striking. In his most successful plates he preserved the best traditions of line engraving, and was, at the time of his death, an acknowledged master of his craft. In 1885 he was elected to membership in the Art Students' League, and was for five years on the board of control, as treasurer in 1887 and as president from 1889 to 1891. He was interested in languages, particularly Volapük and Esperanto, in which he wrote for publication, corresponded actively, and made translations. He removed to Saranac Lake in 1897, where, with the exception of a trip to the South in 1899 and another to Europe in 1905–06, he remained until his death. He had married Mary Olivia Brainerd of Enfield, Conn., on Nov. 18, 1873.

[Ira H. Brainerd, *Edwin Davis French* (1908), contains a biographical sketch and a check-list of bookplates and other engravings. R. H. Lawrence, *Cat. of the Engravings Issued by the Soc. of Iconophiles* (1908), contains an autobiographical sketch. There are many published catalogues, particularly of his book-plates. Other material may be found in *Am. Art News*, Dec. 15, 1906; *Am. Art Annual*, 1907–08, p. 109; Frank Weitenkampf, *Am. Graphic Art* (1912); and *N. Y. Times*, Dec. 9, 10, 1906.] C. P. M.

FRENCH, LUCY VIRGINIA SMITH (Mar. 16, 1825–Mar. 31, 1881), author, the daughter of Mease W. and Elizabeth (Parker) Smith, was born in Accomac County, Va. Her parents came from families of wealth and culture. Her father, educator and lawyer, was chancellor of Virginia and successively professor of Greek and Latin and president of Washington College in Virginia. Her maternal grandfather, a merchant in the South American and East Indian trade, as an officer in the Revolution was known as "Fighting Tom Parker." Following the death of her mother, she and her younger sister were sent to Mrs. Hannah's School in Washington, Pa., where they were graduated. On their return to Virginia, as their father had remarried, the two girls were not happy, so they went to Memphis, Tenn., and became teachers. Virginia began also to write for the *Louisville Journal* under the name "L'Inconnue." In 1852 she became associate editor of the *Southern Ladies' Book*, New Orleans. She was married, on Jan. 12, 1853, to Col. Johns Hopkins French, a wealthy Tennessee stockman. One of her poems, called "One or Two," had made him resolve to ask the author to marry him. He went to Memphis for the purpose, met "L'Inconnue" by accident in a book-shop, and the wedding soon took place. During the twenty-eight years of their married life they lived at "Forest Home," in the mountains near McMinnville, Tenn. With abundant means and a husband who encouraged her, Mrs. French continued her literary work. From 1856 to 1879 she was literary editor of various newspapers and magazines, among them the *Southern Homestead*, Nashville; the *Rural Sun*, the *Sunny South*, the *Crusader*, and the *Ladies' Home*, all of Atlanta; and the *Southern Literary Messenger*, Richmond. She published several volumes: *Wind Whispers* (1856), a book of poems; *Istalilxo, the Lady of Tula* (1856), a five-act tragedy of Mexico before Cortez; *Legends of the South* (1867), a book of poems; *My Roses* (1872), a novel; and *Darlingtonia* (1879), a novel. Her work, both in prose and poetry, was thoroughly spontaneous. She wrote because she loved to, just as she painted, played upon the piano, embroidered, and worked in her garden. Some of her friendly critics deplored her lack of ambition and failure to devote herself more seriously to literature. Her home and her family were her first interest; writing shared second place with many other occupations. She was a woman of piquant beauty and charm, witty in conversation, liberal in her views. In the Civil War, which she had seen approaching, she remained a warm supporter of the Union and wrote in behalf of its restoration, yet she understood the South. Of her poems "Tecumseh's Foot" has been compared with Longfellow's "Hiawatha," and "The Great River" with Bryant's "The Prairies." The romantic and the heroic appealed to her and form the basis of both her prose and poetry. She handled blank verse well and had a sense of the dramatic which enabled her to produce good climax. Her verse is probably her best work. She died at McMinnville, after a long illness, and is buried in the little cemetery there.

[J. Virginia Benham, "L. Virginia French," in the *Am. Illustrated Meth. Mag.*, July 1900; J. W. Davidson, *The Living Writers of the South* (1869); Mary T. Tardy, ed., *The Living Female Writers of the South* (1872), and *Southland Writers* (1870); *Daily American* (Nashville), Apr. 3, 1881; information as to certain facts from Mrs. French's daughter, Mrs. P. D. Benham of Chattanooga, Tenn.] S. G. B.

FRENCH, WILLIAM HENRY (Jan. 13, 1815–May 20, 1881), soldier, was born in Baltimore, Md. He was appointed to West Point in 1833 from the District of Columbia, where his father, William French, was then living as an employee of the Post Office Department. Graduating in 1837, in the class of Sedgwick, Hooker, Bragg, Early, and Pemberton, he was commissioned in the 1st Artillery, and went at once to service in the Florida War. He was promoted to first lieutenant in 1838. In the Mexican War he was engaged in the siege of Vera Cruz, the battles of Cerro Gordo, Contreras, and Churubusco, and the capture of the city of Mexico; and was aide to Franklin Pierce, then a brigadier-general of volunteers, for some months after the city was taken. He reached his captaincy in 1848. In 1861, when Gen. Twiggs surrendered the government property in Texas to the secessionists, French moved the garrison of Fort Duncan, at Eagle Pass, to Fort Brown, at the mouth of the Rio Grande, marching over four hundred miles in sixteen days, and there embarked it for Key West. He remained in command there until November, meanwhile being promoted to major in the regular artillery and brigadier-general of volunteers. Assigned to the Army of the Potomac, he commanded a brigade in the Peninsular campaign, and a division at Antietam. He was appointed major-general of volunteers, Nov. 29, 1862, commanded a division at Fredericksburg and Chancellorsville, and the Harper's Ferry district during the Gettysburg campaign. He commanded the III Corps during the fall of 1863, at first with success, but Gen. Meade ascribed to the slowness of this corps the failure of the Mine Run campaign, and held French primarily to blame. In the reorganization of the army in 1864, and the consequent consolidation of corps, French was displaced, was mustered out of the volunteer service, and saw no further field service. He was promoted lieutenant-colonel in the regular army, Feb. 8, 1864, and colonel, July 2, 1877. He was retired from active service in 1880. His death occurred in Washington. French was a tall, bulky man; "a jovial companion, full of wit and sparkling humor," according to Gen. Cullum. He had a high reputation as an artillerist, assisted in the preparation of the system of light-artillery tactics used during the Civil War, and was employed frequently on technical board and inspection duties. Until the failure at Mine Run he was a more than ordinarily successful leader of troops, advancing step by step to the command of a brigade, a division, and finally a corps, but his conduct on that occasion destroyed Meade's previous confidence in him. French subsequently expressed the opinion that the difficulty was due to the personal enmity of one of his division commanders (unpublished letter).

[G. W. Cullum, *Biog. Reg.* (3rd ed., 1891), I, 676–79; obituary notice, by Gen. O. O. Howard, in *Twelfth Ann. Reunion Asso. Grads., U. S. Mil. Acad.* (1881), pp. 51–53; *Official Records (Army)*, 1 ser., vols. I, XI (pts. 1, 2), XIX (pt. 1), XXI, XXV (pt. 1), XXVII (pts. 1, 3), XXIX (pts. 1, 2); *Washington Post*, May 21, 1881; unpublished records in the War Dept.]

T. M. S.

FRENCH, WILLIAM MERCHANT RICHARDSON (Oct. 1, 1843–June 3, 1914), director of the Art Institute of Chicago, was born in Exeter, N. H. He was descended from a long line of distinguished New England ancestors. One grandfather, Daniel French, was for a time attorney-general of New Hampshire; the other, William Merchant Richardson [*q.v.*], was chief justice of that state. Henry Flagg French, his father, was a successful lawyer who indulged his taste for beauty in nature by practising, in a modest way, landscape gardening. Ann Richardson French, his mother, had a talent for drawing which both he and his brother, Daniel Chester French, the sculptor, inherited. After attending the public schools of Exeter and the Phillips Exeter Academy, French entered Harvard, from which he graduated in 1864. For about a year he served as a volunteer in the Northern army. Later he took a special course in civil engineering at the Massachusetts Institute of Technology, then in 1867 he settled in Chicago. From engineering work he went into landscape gardening, but gradually his interest in art and his desire that it be better understood led him to lecture and write on the subject, and in 1878 he became secretary of the Chicago Academy of Design. The following year a new society was organized under the name of the Chicago Academy of Fine Arts, which in December 1882 became the Art Institute of Chicago. He served this organization first as secretary and then, for thirty-five years, as director. Having conceived of an art museum as something more than a mere repository of works of art, he labored, in this position, to bring the enjoyment of such treasures within the reach of the common people. He was a charter member of the American Association of Museums and its president in 1907–08; a charter member and president, 1912–13, of the Chicago Literary Club; and for a number of years art editor of the *Chicago Tribune*. In 1907 he was made *Officier d'Académie* by the French government. When he died, after a brief illness, his funeral was held in Fullerton Memorial Hall at the Art Institute of Chicago. He was a man of rare administrative ability, culture, kindliness, and artistic gifts, and was especially remembered for his efforts in making the Art Institute a cultural influence in his community. French was married on Sept. 9, 1879, to Sarah M. Lovejoy, who died Aug. 8, 1881. On Mar. 27, 1890, he was married to Alice Helm, who with two sons survived him.

[*Who's Who in America*, 1912–13; *Bull. of the Art Inst. of Chicago*, July 1914; *Am. Art Annual*, 1914; *Am. Art News*, June 13, 1914; *Chicago News*, June 3, *Chicago Tribune*, June 4, 1914; information as to certain facts from French's brother, Daniel Chester French.] L. M.

FRENEAU, PHILIP MORIN (Jan. 2, 1752–Dec. 19, 1832), poet, editor, mariner, came of a Huguenot family whose earliest representative in America, André Fresneau, settled in New York in 1707, established himself as an importer of wines from France and the Canaries, and prospered. After the early death of the pioneer, his sons Andrew and Pierre Freneau, as the name became, continued with the business, the younger soon taking the lead. Married to Agnes, daughter of Richard Watson of Freehold, N. J., he established a home on Frankford St., which, furnished richly with books and works of art and much frequented by cultured visitors, became one of the centers of refinement in New York. Into this home was born Philip Freneau and five years later Peter, who afterward became a conspicuous figure in Charleston, S. C. With increasing prosperity, the family acquired for summer use "Mount Pleasant," near Middletown Point, N. J., a plantation destined to become in later years the home of the poet. The children were educated privately by tutors and with such care that Philip at the early age of fifteen was able to enter the sophomore class at the College of New Jersey (now Princeton), so thoroughly prepared that President Witherspoon wrote his mother a letter of congratulation. Here he was a classmate and perhaps a roommate of James Madison. Collaborating with his classmate, H. H. Brackenridge, he wrote a remarkable poem entitled "The Rising Glory of America" which was read by the latter at the graduating exercises of his class in 1771 and was issued as a pamphlet the next year in Philadelphia.

Even in college Freneau had visions of a poetic career. He had read widely in the English poets, and he had a scholarly acquaintance with the Latin and the Greek. He entered upon no profession; for a time he taught school; but constantly he wrote poetry. When the Revolution broke out he became fiercely active with his pen. Within a few months he published no fewer than eight pamphlet satires aimed at the British, among them *General Gage's Soliloquy* (1775) and *General Gage's Confession* (1775), all burning with invective. Poetry, however, was a poor profession for an ambitious man in the early days of the Revolution, and he turned to what seemed a promising and romantic opening, a secretaryship in the home of a prominent planter on the Island of Santa Cruz in the West Indies. The new environment, the romance of the Spanish Main, the tropic splendor of the islands, laid powerful hold upon his imagination, and during the three years that followed he wrote what must be regarded as his most significant poems, "Santa Cruz," "The Jamaica Funeral," and, especially, "The House of Night." Written before the opening of the romantic period in Europe, the latter poem has within it all the elements of the new romanticism. It places Freneau as one of the pioneers in the movement.

Returning to America after his long absence, having been captured by the British but released, he found the Revolution in full career. His mind, however, was upon the ocean. Always the sea called to the deeps within him, fascinated him, held him fast. He voyaged as supercargo of a brig plying between the Azores and New York, was chased more than once by British cruisers, and in the early spring set out again to visit the West Indies. He was scarcely clear of the American coast, however, when the ship was captured by a British man-of-war, and after a farcical trial he was remanded to the prison ship *Scorpion* in New York Harbor. From starvation and brutal treatment he fell into a decline, was removed to the hospital ship *Hunter,* where he found still more brutal treatment, but at last more dead than alive was exchanged and enabled to reach his home in New Jersey, where he soon regained his health. His experiences he later described realistically in *The British Prison-Ship: A Poem, in Four Cantoes* (1781).

During the next three years he was an employee in the Philadelphia Post-Office. He seems to have had much leisure time, for poetry now came in a steady stream from his pen, most of it being published in Francis Bailey's vigorous newspaper, the *Freeman's Journal,* which unquestionably Freneau helped to edit. Every movement of the "insolent foe," every new plight in which the Loyalists found themselves, he satirized with vigor, and he glorified the deeds of his fellow patriots in such lyrics as that commemorating the victory of Jones, and the lament over the dead at Eutaw Springs. It was during this period that he produced the most distinctive of the lyrics which won for him the sobriquet "the poet of the American Revolution." By temperament Freneau was restless and eager. After three years in the city his soul again was "tossing on the ocean." In 1784 he sailed as master of a brig bound for Jamaica and for several years led a stormy life on the Atlantic and Caribbean. He was shipwrecked, narrowly escaping destruction; he outrode a hurricane that destroyed the greater part of the shipping in West Indian waters; and he wrote a hurricane lyric at the height of the storm. No other American poet has known the ocean as he knew it or has pictured it more graphically.

This third marine period in his life was terminated in 1789 when he was married to Eleanor Forman of Middletown Point, and during the next seven or eight years he was engaged in newspaper work, editing first the New York *Daily Advertiser,* a sheet which he at once made important. Following the removal of the government to Philadelphia in 1791 and the resignation of John Pintard, an associate of Freneau's on the *Daily Advertiser,* as translating clerk of the Department of State, Jefferson offered Freneau the post at a salary of $250 a year. Freneau finally accepted the appointment, which was formally made Aug. 16, 1791, removed to Philadelphia, and there issued on Oct. 31 the first number of the *National Gazette.* As an antidote to the highly aristocratic *Gazette of the United States* of John Fenno [*q.v.*], a financial beneficiary of Hamilton, Freneau's sparkling paper more than fulfilled the hopes of Jefferson and Madison. Soon singling out Hamilton for attack as the chief monarchist, the democratic Freneau so discomfited that statesman that he himself entered the lists anonymously, charging his journalistic foe with being a subservient employee of Jefferson. That the Secretary of State had originally encouraged Freneau to publish his paper and used his influence to advance its interests seems indubitable. Freneau, however, was neither a hireling nor a truckler. He voiced his own convictions and in his continued support of Genet [*q.v.*] after Jefferson had repudiated that French minister, he showed his independence. A passionate democrat and consistent supporter of the principles of the French Revolution, Freneau more than any other journalist of the day quickened the democratic spirit of the new republic (Forman, *post,* p. 78). Jefferson said he "saved our Constitution, which was galloping fast into monarchy" (P. L. Ford, *The Writings of Thomas Jefferson,* I, 1892, p. 231). Washington, on the other hand, was incensed by the abuse of "that rascal Freneau" and complained of him bitterly to the Secretary of State, who, however, did not remove him. On Oct. 26, 1793, because of shortage of funds and the yellow-fever epidemic, the *National Gazette* was suspended, and, with the retirement of Jefferson from office soon thereafter, Freneau was compelled to resign his governmental position. He had taken a leading part in the French demonstrations of the period, dedicating to the new era of "the rights of man" a whole sheaf of lyrics, some of them of stirring eloquence.

After a short service as editor of a rural paper, the *Jersey Chronicle,* and then a longer period as editor of the distinctive New York journal, the *Time-Piece,* he retired from journalism and for the rest of his life alternated between the sea and his New Jersey farm. He lived until 1832, long enough to see the new school of Bryant and Irving and Cooper fully established. In December of that year, returning home from the country store through a blizzard, he lost his way and perished.

The first distinctive issue of his writings was *The Poems of Philip Freneau* (1786), from the press of his friend Bailey. This was followed by *The Miscellaneous Works of Mr. Philip Freneau Containing His Essays, and Additional Poems* (1788); *Poems Written between the Years 1768 and 1794, by Philip Freneau of New Jersey* (1795), printed by his own press; *Poems Written and Published during the American Revolutionary War* (2 vols., 1809); and *A Collection of Poems, on American Affairs . . . Written between the Year 1797 and the Present Time* (2 vols., 1815). Without adequate criticism, without an adequate reading public, and totally without literary atmosphere in a crude age, he nevertheless produced lyrics that still live. He wrote with romantic atmosphere and theme in "The House of Night"; he was the first in America to put the Indian distinctively into poetry, "The Indian Burying Ground" being his best effort; and his "The Wild Honeysuckle" has been called the "first stammer of nature poetry in America." Some of his songs of the sea put him even now among the leading American poets of the ocean. Unquestionably he was the most significant poetic figure in America before Bryant.

[V. H. Paltsits, *A Bibliog. of the Separate and Collected Works of Philip Freneau* (1903); F. L. Pattee, ed., *The Poems of Philip Freneau* (3 vols., 1902–07); H. H. Clark, ed., *Poems of Freneau* (1929); E. F. De Lancey, "Philip Freneau, The Huguenot Patriot Poet of the Revolution," *Proc. Huguenot Soc. of America,* vol. II, no. 2 (1891); Mary S. Austin, *Philip Freneau, The Poet of the Revolution* (1901); S. E. Forman, "The Pol. Activities of Philip Freneau," *Johns Hopkins Univ. Studies in Hist. and Pol. Science,* ser. XX, nos. 9–10 (1902); F. L. Pattee, "The Modernness of Philip Freneau," in *Sidelights on Am. Lit.* (1922).] F. L. P—e.

FREY, JOSEPH SAMUEL CHRISTIAN FREDERICK (Sept. 21, 1771–June 5, 1850), Presbyterian and Baptist clergyman, was born of Jewish parents at Mainstockheim in Lower Franconian Bavaria. His father, Samuel Levi, was a tutor; his mother kept a small shop. The boy was named Joseph Samuel and began early to study the Scriptures and the Talmud. At eighteen he became a tutor, at twenty-one a *chazan* (cantor), and not long after a *schochat* (butcher). After making a failure as helper to his mother, who had become a sutler in the train of the Prussian army, he set out on a walking tour. On the road he fell in with a Christian who set him to pondering the New Testament. Still ruminating over Christian doctrine, he worked for several years as a shoemaker's apprentice, and at Neubrandenburg in Mecklenburg-Strelitz on May 8, 1798, he finally discarded his phylactery and was baptized as Joseph Samuel Christian Frederick Frey. Subsequently, in Berlin, he exchanged Lutheranism for Moravianism, attended a missionary institute in Saxony, and went in 1801 to London, intending to proceed thence to Africa. Instead he studied and taught in a missionary seminary at Gosport under the Rev. David Bogue and in 1801 entered the service of the London Missionary Society. In 1806 he married Hannah Cohen, a converted Jewess. When the London Missionary Society broke up, Frey betook himself to another, but similar, organization, the London Society for Promoting Christianity among the Jews. As its agent Frey was very successful as a money raiser but failed completely as a converter of Jews. In May 1816, again out of employment, he decided to start over again in America. He arrived in New York with his family on Sept. 15, was welcomed by ministers and laymen to whom he brought letters of introduction, preached his first sermon in America the next Sunday evening, and was soon in charge of a small congregation in New York City. He was not ordained until Apr. 15, 1818. On Feb. 8, 1820, the American Society for Meliorating the Condition of the Jews was organized in New York and on Apr. 14 was regularly incorporated. The object of this society was not only to convert Jews to Christianity but to settle them as farmers in special communities. Frey was its agent from 1822 to 1826 and again from 1836 to 1839. He traveled up and down the country, preaching some three hundred sermons a year and telling the story of his life. Jews were still objects of curiosity in the United States, and wherever Frey went crowds flocked to gape at him and hear him preach. As in England he succeeded in creating much interest in the cause and in raising considerable sums of money, but he does not appear to have made a single convert. As in England, he was bitterly attacked by Jews and his character impugned. Finally he began to have doubts as to whether he had really been baptized a Christian. Concluding that a mere Lutheran sprinkling was no true baptism, he went to New York and was baptized by immersion Aug. 28, 1827, by the Rev. Archibald Maclay. His second term as agent for the Society was spent largely in England. In 1843–44 he traveled through the South and the Southwest and finally settled in Pontiac, Mich., where he died. His life had been laborious and unhappy. At heart he probably remained a Jew, his frequent changes of doctrine and abode being so many attempts to escape from his inner misery.

He was a prolific writer. Among his publications are: *The Converted Jew,* an autobiography (1809); *Narrative of the Rev. J. S. C. F. Frey* (1810); *A Hebrew Grammar in the English Language* (1813); *The Objects of the American Society for Meliorating the Condition of the Jews* (1827); *Essays on Christian Baptism* (1829); *Essays on the Passover* (1834); *Joseph and Benjamin: A Series of Letters on the Controversy between Jews and Christians . . .* (2 vols., 1835–36); *Judah and Israel, or the Restoration and Conversion of the Jews and Ten Tribes* (1837); *Course of Lectures on the Scripture Types* (1841); *Course of Lectures on the Messiahship of Christ* (1844). He edited *Van der Hooght's Hebrew Bible* (1811); *Biblia Hebraica* (1812); *A Hebrew, Latin, and English Dictionary* (2 vols., 1815); *A Hebrew and English Dictionary* (1839); *Theological Lectures of David Bogue* (1849).

[W. B. Sprague, *Annals of the Am. Pulpit,* vol. VI (1860); L. M. Friedman, *The Am. Soc. for Meliorating the Condition of the Jews and Joseph S. C. F. Frey its Missionary* (1925); Frey's own writings.] G. H. G.

FRICK, HENRY CLAY (Dec. 19, 1849–Dec. 2, 1919), coke and steel manufacturer, capitalist, came from typical American ancestry. His father, John W. Frick, of an old Swiss family, married Elizabeth Overholt, of wealthy Mennonite forebears who came originally from the Palatinate of the Rhine. Both the Fricks and the Overholts had come to America during the eighteenth century and settled in Pennsylvania. Henry Clay Frick was of the fourth generation in America on both sides of the family. He was born at West Overton in Westmoreland County, Pa., the second of six children, and was named for the leader of the Whig party. As a boy he was delicate, and all his life suffered intermittently from indigestion and rheumatism, although he grew from a slender youth into a stalwart man. At the age of eight he was able to help with the chores on his father's farm and to attend school during the winter. His education, which consisted of thirty months of actual tuition, ended when he was seventeen. Before this he had worked in his uncle's store to earn his board and the privilege of sleeping on the counter. Another uncle, who had a store at Mt. Pleasant, engaged him on a money basis when he was sixteen. While attending the Classical and Scientific Institute at Mt. Pleasant, and, for a few months, Otterbein University at Westerville, Ohio, he showed literary and artistic tastes as well as ambitious visions. Discharged by his uncle's partner, he worked for a short time in his grandfather Overholt's distillery at Bradford and then obtained a position in a store in Pittsburgh. Sickness intervened, and he became bookkeeper in the distillery at $1,000 a year shortly before his grandfather, the "squire of Westmoreland County," died.

While still retaining his bookkeeper's job, Frick at the age of twenty-one joined several associates in building and operating coke-ovens in the surrounding Connellsville coal district. To finance Frick & Company, he called on Judge Thomas Mellon in Pittsburgh and boldly borrowed money. Initial success and expansion were followed by the disastrous panic of 1873. Undespairing in the midst of financial stringency, Frick took advantage of the hard times to negotiate the sale of a local ten-mile railroad to the Baltimore & Ohio for a commission of $50,000, and increased his holdings of coal lands. Despite business difficulties and sickness, by the time he was thirty he had attained his ambition to be worth a million dollars; coke had risen in price from less than a dollar to five dollars a ton. With Andrew W. Mellon, son of his financial backer, and two other young men, he visited Europe for rest and relaxation. On Dec. 15, 1881, he married Adelaide Howard Childs, daughter of Asa P. Childs of Pittsburgh. On their wedding trip they dined in New York with Andrew Carnegie and his mother. The meeting led to Carnegie's acquiring stock in the H. C. Frick Coke Company. This came about through the help of Thomas Carnegie, younger brother of Andrew and a partner of Henry Phipps, Jr. Differences between Andrew Carnegie and Frick over labor problems developed in 1887, a year after Thomas Carnegie died. As Frick now owned less than a majority of the company's stock, he resigned as president but was reinstated in the following year and took a firm hand toward labor, in contrast to Carnegie's conciliatory attitude.

In 1889 the "coke king" was invited to acquire an interest in Carnegie Brothers & Company and to become chairman with the intention of reorganizing the steel business. So discouraging were the company's affairs that Carnegie and Phipps were considering selling out for a fraction of the amount they finally received from the Morgan syndicate twelve years later. The reorganization included the building of connecting railroads, the settling of staff jealousies, the improvement of operating methods, and the advancement of capable young men such as Charles M. Schwab and Thomas Morrison. For six years without a vacation, Frick rose at six, walked two miles to his office, was at his desk before eight, and did not leave until six. One of his first coups was to buy out the chief competitor of the Carnegie company, the Duquesne Steel Company, for a million dollars in bonds. At forty-one Frick was in control of the world's greatest steel and coke operations, employing 30,000 men.

One of the most notorious of all labor strikes was that at Homestead, Pa., in 1892. Beginning in a dispute over wages, it became a complicated case of the rights of private property against militant organized employees, a majority of whom were foreigners. Carnegie was in Scotland, and Frick was in full charge. He engaged with doubtful legality three hundred Pinkerton guards, who tried unsuccessfully to get to the plant on boats at night while a mob of strikers fired on them from the company's properties which they unlawfully held. The governor of the state and eight thousand of the national guard were required to recover the plant. Frick's firmness, much criticized though it was, finally won, but he himself was shot and stabbed by Alexander Berkman, a Russian anarchist. During these savage troubles, Frick showed personal courage and a reassuring trust in the principles of law and order.

During the 1890's Frick induced the Carnegie Steel Company to cooperate with Henry W. Oliver in buying iron-ore properties in the Lake Superior region, while Carnegie opposed or gave reluctant consent to such "pioneering." These ore mines proved exceedingly valuable. In 1899 negotiations by the Moore syndicate to take over the Carnegie and other companies were frustrated by the demoralization in the money market caused by the death of Roswell P. Flower. The conflicts between Carnegie and Frick had led the latter to encourage the formation of such a syndicate in order to buy out Carnegie. Differences over policy now caused the resignation of Frick as chairman, after eleven years of service, but he sued the company over a coke contract and won. In the important negotiations leading to the formation of the United States Steel Corporation in 1901, Frick played an essential part, acting as intermediary between Morgan and Rockefeller at a time when the tension was strained. Later as a director he gave valuable aid to the corporation. He also took part as director in railroad developments, particularly the Pennsylvania Railroad, and recommended the reorganization in 1905 of the Equitable Life Assurance Company.

After building a handsome residence on Fifth Avenue, Frick began collecting works of the old masters. The mansion, with its many treasures, and an endowment of $15,000,000, was willed to the public as a museum. He also made liberal donations to Princeton University, and left a park of 150 acres, with an endowment of $2,000,000, to the city of Pittsburgh. Besides his wife, a son and a daughter survived him. His reputation for determined views was due to his quick insight and perhaps also to a sensitiveness which dated back to his delicate health and artistic predilections as a boy. His birthplace is preserved as a historical museum.

[George Harvey's *Henry Clay Frick, the Man* (1928) is the best source. B. C. Forbes, in *Men Who are Making America* (1917) includes Frick among fifty leaders in industry. Obituary notices appeared in *Iron Age*, Dec. 11, 1919; *Iron Trade Rev.*, Dec. 4, 1919; *Engineering and Mining Jour.*, Dec. 13, 20, 1919; and the *N. Y. Times*, Dec. 3, 7, 1919. See also H. N. Casson, *The Romance of Steel* (1907); J. H. Bridge, *The Inside Hist. of the Carnegie Steel Company* (1903); Ida M. Tarbell, *Life of Elbert H. Gary* (1925).] P. B. M.

FRIDAY (*c.* 1822–May 13, 1881), an Arapaho sub-chief, was born probably in a migratory village somewhere on the Kansas-Colorado plains. At the age of nine, in the vicinity of the present Ulysses, in southwestern Kansas, he was lost by his parents and for seven days wandered about the desolate region alone. He was rescued by Thomas Fitzpatrick [*q.v.*], then head of the Rocky Mountain Fur Company. From the circumstance that he was found on a Friday (June 3, 1831), he received the name which clung to him ever afterward. Fitzpatrick sent him to St. Louis and had him put to school, where he proved an apt pupil. It seems likely that his benefactor intended to adopt him and to rear him according to the standards of the whites, but if so the plan was frustrated. His parents, hearing of the rescue, demanded that he be sent back to them, and though he at first refused to go he was later persuaded to make the journey. Ultimately he became reconciled to the savage life and remained with his people.

To Fitzpatrick, whom he occasionally encountered, he was devotedly attached; and his friendship for the whites is frequently mentioned in early chronicles. Rufus Sage, who rode a long journey with him in the summer of 1844, speaks of him as already a noted warrior, an expert buffalo hunter, and a leader among his people. In 1851 he attended the great Indian council near Fort Laramie and was chosen as one of the three delegates of the Arapahos to visit Washington with Fitzpatrick. By 1858 he was the leader of an independent band that roamed about the upper waters of the Cache la Poudre, in northern Colorado. During the Civil War, when most of the plains tribes took the war-path against the whites, he remained loyal in spite of persistent efforts to induce him to join the hostiles. Early in 1869 he gave up the Cache la Poudre country and with his followers joined the Northern Arapahos, under Medicine Man, in Wyoming. Many depredations were committed by these red-men but there is no evidence that Friday had any part in them, and it is certain that more than once he was able to save the lives of whites from the fury of his fellow tribesmen. In 1878 the Northern Arapahos were placed on the Shoshone reservation, on the Wind River. Friday continued to remain with them, and was employed by the government as an interpreter. He died, after a few days' illness, of heart disease.

Early accounts describe Friday as a handsome, highly intelligent and honest youth, whose manners were engaging and who spoke English fluently and well. Lieut. Lemly, who talked with him three years before his death, characterizes him as one who had wholly reverted to savagery; but the account is inconsistent with the subsequent report of Agent Charles Hatton, who comments on his death as a "severe blow to the tribe and to the agency." It seems probable that his undeviating friendship for the whites cost him the promotion to the head chieftainship of his people.

[Theodore Talbot, manuscript journal in the Lib. of Cong.; R. B. Sage, *Scenes in the Rocky Mountains, . . .* (1847 ed.), 294–96, 297–301; P. St. G. Cooke, *Scenes and Adventures in the Army* (1857), p. 401; F. A. Root and W. E. Connelley, *The Overland Stage to Cal.* (1901), pp. 347–48; F. V. Hayden, *Contributions to the Ethnography and Philol. of the Indian Tribes of the Miss. Valley* (1862), pp. 322–23; W. F. Raynolds, *Report on the Exploration of the Yellowstone River* (1868), p. 64; H. G. Nickerson, "Indian Depredations in Sweetwater County," *Wyoming Hist. Soc. Colls.*, I (1897), 181–82; H. R. Lemly, "Among the Arrapahoes," *Harper's New Monthly Mag.*, Mar. 1880; files of the Indian Office.] W. J. G.

FRIEDENWALD, AARON (Dec. 20, 1836–Aug. 26, 1902), physician, ophthalmologist, was born in Baltimore, Md., the son of Jonas and Merle (Bar) Stern Friedenwald. His father had come to the United States in 1832 from Hesse-Darmstadt, Germany, as a penniless immigrant, but had soon become a successful merchant and a prominent participant in all Jewish communal and charitable undertakings. After a common-school education Aaron entered an office but at the same time continued his studies and became proficient in Hebrew, German, and French. Having decided to study medicine he entered the office of Nathan R. Smith [*q.v.*] in the spring of 1858 and two years later received his degree in medicine from the University of Maryland. On Apr. 26, 1860, he left for Europe to begin a two-year post-graduate course of study, which he carried out in succession in Berlin, Paris, Prague, Vienna, and London, and which embraced both general medicine and ophthalmology. In his numerous letters he spoke with enthusiasm of von Graefe of Berlin and Arlt of Vienna, his masters in the latter branch. He also visited many places of interest, including the former homes of his parents. He returned to Baltimore in July 1862 with the intention of entering at once into ophthalmological as well as general practise, for since the retirement of George Frick there had not been a single eye specialist in the community. The city was at the time divided by the passions born of the Civil War, and although Friedenwald was a loyal yet conservative Unionist, some of his family and friends were sympathetic toward the South. During the latter part of 1863, not long after his marriage to Bertha Bamberger, he himself was imprisoned for a night as a suspected Confederate. His principal war service was as attending surgeon in a temporary hospital for the wounded from both armies.

Friedenwald's practise was not fairly under way until 1868 when he was able to move to 310 North Eutaw St. There he remained for the rest of his life. Although engaged in the roughest general practise, which at this early period included attendance at a smallpox infirmary, he had become well known as an ophthalmologist and his old teachers and friends supported him in this field. In 1873 he was appointed professor of diseases of the eye and ear in the College of Physicians and Surgeons and was a co-founder and the first president of the Maryland Ophthalmological Society. During the term 1889–90 he was president of the Medico-Chirurgical Faculty of Maryland and in 1890 took the initiative in the foundation of the Association of American Medical Colleges. He made a pleasure trip to Europe in 1895 and a pilgrimage to Palestine in 1898. In 1901 he began to suffer from an obscure gastro-enteric disorder and at Heidelberg in 1902 discovered that his ailment was a cancer of the stomach. Returning home for an operation he succumbed to post-operative complications. He published no major work. Of his two sons who became physicians, the elder compiled an elaborate biography of his father which in addition to many letters contains a list of fifty-four reprinted or manuscript addresses on professional, philanthropic, and miscellaneous subjects. Friedenwald was interested in many Jewish institutions among which were the Baltimore Hebrew Orphan Asylum, the Baron de Hirsch Commission, the Alliance Israelite Universelle, the Jewish Theological Seminary, Jewish Publication Society, and the Federation of American Zionists.

[Harry Friedenwald, *Life, Letters and Addresses of Aaron Friedenwald* (1906); "The Friedenwald Memorial Meeting," in the *Jour. of the Alumni of the Coll. of Physicians and Surgeons, Baltimore,* Jan. 1903; *Am. Encyc. and Dict. of Ophthalmol.,* vol. VII (1915); *Md. Medic. Jour.,* Sept. 1902; *Jour. Am. Medic. Asso.,* Sept. 6, 1902; *N. Y. Times,* Aug. 27, 1902.] E. P.

FRIEDLAENDER, ISRAEL (Sept. 8, 1876–July 5, 1920), Semitist, son of Pinkus and Gitel Ehrlich Friedlaender, was born at Kovel, Russian Poland. He laid the foundations of his scholarship in Warsaw. In Berlin at the University and the Rabbinerseminar, he gave it academic quality. After receiving his degree of doctor of philosophy from the University of Strassburg in 1901, he was there admitted as privatdocent in Semitic languages. Two years later he was called to New York to fill the Sabato Morais chair in Biblical literature and exegesis in the Jewish Theological Seminary of America. This position, as well as that of instructor of history at the Hebrew Teachers' Institute, he occupied until his death. As an Arabist interested especially in historical relations between Islam and Judaism he published many works of exact research, including, besides six on Maimonides, *Die Messiasidee in Islam* (1903), *The Heterodoxies of the Shiites* (1909), *Abdalah ben Saba* (1910), *Jewish Arabic Studies* (1910–13), *Muhammedanische Geschichtskonstruktionen* (1912), *Die Chadhirlegende und der Alexanderroman* (1913). In rapid succession he produced a number of technical historical papers and *The Political Ideal of the Prophets* (1910). His other literary and practical work reveals the many-sidedness and humanism of his scholarship. The World War threw Eastern European Jewry into the crucible of changing destiny. To illumine their problem in the light of history he wrote *The Jews of Russia and Poland* (1915), and translated from the Russian manuscript, S. M. Dubnow's *History of the Jews in Russia and Poland* (3 vols., 1916–20).

The problem of the survival of the Jew, and, still more, of Judaism, moved him deeply. As chairman of the Bureau of Jewish Education of New York City, he worked ardently for Jewish education, "mediating between the older generation and the new through the sincere piety of his life and his real modernity." Believing in the essential union of religion and nationalism in Judaism, he gave himself untiringly to the Zionist cause. He translated from Russian into German Dubnow's *Die Grundlagen des National Judentums* (1905), and from Hebrew into German Ahad Haam's *Am Scheideweg* (1905). He wrote profound and moving essays on various aspects of Jewish nationalism, collected in *Past and Present* (1919), and *Zionism and the World*

Peace (1919). He was motivated by the conviction that "Palestine is the Land of Promise, not only to the Jew but to the entire world—the promise of a higher and better social order." He cherished the purpose of settling in Palestine, and as an Arabist furthering an understanding between Arab and Jew.

Though the British conquest of Palestine in 1917 gave promise of realizing this dream, he found himself prevented from giving service in the land of his hopes. He could not rest, however, while he saw his people succumbing in myriads to typhus, famine, and massacre. With the consent of his wife, Lilian Ruth Bentwich, he left her and their six young children in the security of their American home, and in January 1920 set out for the Ukraine as commissioner of the Joint Distribution Committee of America. For five months he was held back in Poland by the virtual anarchy in the Ukraine, but, learning of the threat of new pogroms, though cognizant of all the personal dangers, he determined to push through and reach General Pilsudski in the hope of being able to avert fresh disaster from his people. He never reached his goal. On July 5, 1920, he and his companion, Rabbi Bernard Cantor (b. Buffalo, 1892), were shot down in cold blood by guerrilla soldiers of the Bolshevik army in the village of Kamenetz-Podolsk. Friedlaender, in his forty-fourth year, had achieved more than a life's measure of rich usefulness. By his charm, intellectual force, and the sterling sincerity of his character, he had exercised a potent, refining, and guiding influence on his generation, especially on the youth who knew him, and who have perpetuated his memory in a Jewish educational organization bearing his name. His significance for the Jewish cause which was his life's passion may best be summed up in his own eloquent words: "History is not made by philosophers, but by martyrs, by men whose lives are an object-lesson of their doctrines. The Jewish prophets were at once thinkers and martyrs. Not only did they think their ideals, they lived their ideals because they were not theirs but God's."

[*Memorial Meeting: Israel Friedlaender-Bernard Cantor* (1920); S. A. Poznanski, *Hatkufa*, VIII (1920), 483–88; Lilian Friedlaender and Alexander Marx, the *Menorah Jour.*, VI, 1920, pp. 337–50; Cyrus Adler, "Dr. Friedlaender of Blessed Memory," *The American Hebrew*, July 16, 1920; *N. Y. Times*, July 11, 13, 16, 1920.]

D. deS. P.

FRIES, FRANCIS (Oct. 17, 1812–Aug. 1, 1863), manufacturer, was descended from an old German family of gentle blood, which in the eighteenth century turned from war and court life to trade. His grandfather was Peter Konrad Fries, who, declining to be a merchant as his father desired, studied theology at Strasbourg and received the degree of Ph.D. in 1741. In 1757 he came under the influence of Nicholaus Ludwig, Count von Zinzendorf, the next year joined the Unitas Fratrum (Moravian church), later becoming a member of the Unity's Elders' Conference and holding important posts in this religious fellowship. The paternal grandmother of Francis Fries was Christiane Jäschke, daughter of a Moravian exile. His father, John Christian William Fries, after a Moravian education in Europe, crossed the ocean and settled in the Moravian colony of Wachovia (afterward Salem), in North Carolina. Here he married Elizabeth Nissen. His parents meant Francis to be a minister and sent him to the Moravian seminary, Nazareth Hall, in Pennsylvania. He decided against the ministry, however, returned to his home, and taught school for a time. He then read law with Emanuel Shober and entered practise, soon being appointed clerk of the court and master in equity.

His business career began when as agent of the new Salem [cotton] Manufacturing Company, he visited Paterson, N. J., and other northern points to purchase machinery, which in 1836 he installed in a factory building erected after his own plans. In 1838 he married Lizetta Vogler, by whom he had seven children. Two years later, with the assistance of his father-in-law, he commenced woolen manufacture. At first he operated only cards for making rolls of the wool brought in by farmers, and set up a little dyeing and fulling mill for finishing cloth woven in the homes of the countryside. Being successful in these enterprises, in 1842 he installed spinning machinery, and then looms. He was encouraged in his manufacturing by his friend Edwin M. Holt [*q.v.*] of Alamance, and they arranged to make alternate trips to the North to study developments in the older textile centers, afterward sharing their information. The South manufactured very little at this time, but the tradition of the Moravians in North Carolina was one of mechanical enterprise, and Fries did more than any one else to foster this spirit. His brother, Henry W. Fries, was admitted to partnership in 1846. Two years later they built a cotton factory which was conducted until 1880, when it was dismantled and became part of the woolen mill. Fries had other talents. As a member of the legislature in 1857 he gave special attention to revising the state system of taxation. He was an architect, designing the court-house for the new county of Forsyth and the main building for the Salem Female Academy, of which institution he was a principal supporter. He was once mayor of Salem. He was a promoter of the plank road from Fayetteville to western North Carolina and was associated with Gov. John M. Morehead in building the North Carolina Railroad, in which he was a director until his death. He built a tannery, and conducted a store. He was one in a small but important group which sought vainly to implant industry in the agricultural ante-bellum South.

[W. A. Blair in S. A. Ashe, ed., *Biog. Hist. of N. C.*, III (1905), 129–34; D. A. Tompkins, *Cotton Mill, Commercial Features* (1899), pp. 183–84.] B. M.

FRIES, JOHN (*c.* 1750–February 1818), insurgent, was born in Montgomery County, Pa., the son of Simon Fries, variously described as having been of Welsh, German, and Danish descent. He became a cooper's apprentice at an early age, but afterward abandoned the craft to become an itinerant auctioneer. In 1770 he was married to Margaret Brunner, and in 1775 moved to Bucks County, where he served as captain of a militia company in the Revolution and in the Whiskey Insurrection. Between times, accompanied by his dog, Whiskey, he presided at country-store vendues, where he was easily distinguishable by his shrewd but uncultured mind, ready wit, and fluency of speech in both English and German. He was a favorite wherever he went, for his practical philosophy appealed to the common sense of his listeners. He seems to have been largely responsible for the opposition to the direct federal property tax established by the acts of July 9 and 14, 1798, in anticipation of a war with France. He was present at a meeting held at John Kline's tavern in February 1799, assisted in drawing up a petition denouncing the tax, and later promised to raise a regiment of 700 men to prevent its collection. The Pennsylvania Germans, influenced by Fries and French brandy, erected liberty poles with cries of "Dämm de President, dämm de Congresz, dämm de Arischdokratz!" and spent enough money to have more than paid the tax. Assessors were ordered out of the country under threat of having their legs shot off; and Capt. Fries, with a feather in his hat, a sword and horse-pistol strapped to his side, led a band of fifty or sixty men—including a fifer and drummer—wearing red, white, and blue cockades, and proceeded to eject persistent collectors, and to liberate prisoners in custody of the federal marshal at Bethlehem. The area of belligerency was extended to include irate housewives who, by a liberal use of hot water, defended their homes from the measuring sticks of the assessors. By a proclamation, Mar. 12, 1799, President John Adams ordered the recalcitrant Pennsylvanians to submit to the laws, and sent Gen. MacPherson with a force of regular cavalry and militia to arrest a few rioters. Fries, busy at vendue when the troops appeared, did not complete the sale, but fled to a near-by swamp. At this point Whiskey brought the "Hot Water War" to an end by betraying his master's hiding-place. The insurgent leader was arrested, taken to Philadelphia for trial for treason, and twice sentenced to death, only to be pardoned by President Adams against the advice of his cabinet. Fries returned to Bucks County and followed his profession until his death. There is no evidence to support the story that he opened a tin shop in Philadelphia and became a rich and influential citizen.

[W. H. H. Davis, *The Fries Rebellion* (1899), and an article in the *Era Mag.* (Phila.), Aug. 1903; F. M. Eastman, *Courts and Lawyers of Pa.* (1922), ch. XXX, "The Fries Rebellion," reprinted in *Americana*, Jan. 1922; C. F. Adams, ed., *The Works of John Adams* (1850–56), *passim*; Horace Binney, *Leaders of the Old Bar of Phila.* (1859); Chas. H. Jones, *Memoir of William Rodman* (1867); *The Pennsylvania-German Soc.*, XXIX (1922), 162–63; *The Two Trials of John Fries* (1800), containing the stenographic notes of the trials taken by Thos. Carpenter.] T. D. M.

FRIEZE, HENRY SIMMONS (Sept. 15, 1817–Dec. 7, 1889), professor of Latin, thrice acting president, and patron of music, at the University of Michigan, was born in Boston, the son of Jacob and Betsey (Slade) Frieze. His father, a Universalist clergyman, teacher, and editor, was also an accomplished musician and a writer of political pamphlets. His mother is remembered for her refinement and gentleness. Frieze seems to have inherited a happy combination of intellectual power, awareness of beauty, and charm of personality. After preparatory schooling at Newport, he entered Brown University, supporting himself by teaching music and by playing the organ. Upon graduating, in 1841, he became a tutor at Brown, three years later founded the University Grammar School in Providence, and taught there until called to Michigan in 1854. In 1847 he was married in Providence to Anna Brownell Roffee.

Though a sound scholar Frieze was more the artist than the philologist. He loved literature, and, in spite of his contact with Germany shortly after his appointment at Michigan, was no more of an investigator than other American classical scholars of that day. His familiar school edition of Virgil's *Æneid* first appeared in 1860, *The Bucolics, Georgics and the First Six Books of the Æneid of Vergil,* and his *P. Vergili Maronis Opera* in 1883. His less-known work, *The Tenth and Twelfth Books of the Institutes of Quintilian,* was issued in 1865. Other publications include a number of addresses: *The Relations of the State University to Religion* (1888), *A Memorial Discourse on the Life and Services of Rev. Henry Philip Tappan* (1882), and *Art Museums and*

Their Connection with Public Libraries (1876); an article, "Vergilius and Virgilius" (*Latine et Graece*, October 1885); and *Giovanni Dupré, with Two Dialogues on Art from the Italian of Augusto Conti* (1886).

His visit to Germany did, however, convince him that American colleges were little better than gymnasia, and that higher education was the business of the State. He believed that the American high schools should relieve the universities of preparatory work, and that their pupils should be admitted to the universities by diploma. When President Haven [*q.v.*] resigned in 1869, and before James B. Angell [*q.v.*] was appointed, in 1871, Frieze had opportunity, as acting president, to effect the introduction of the diploma system. He could not foresee that in America this would often imperil the university by making it seem merely the last member of the public-school system. His admission of women (1870) was, of course, not German. Frieze was offered the presidency during the negotiations with Angell, but declined. He did, however, on two other occasions serve as acting president: during the absences of President Angell, from June 1880 to February 1882, and from October 1887 to January 1888. No president of Michigan is more honored in memory.

For twenty years Frieze continued to be heard as an organist. His piano was his sole temptation in hours pledged to work on his Virgil. He secured for Michigan a professorship of music, led in the establishment of the University School of Music, and otherwise promoted the musical life of the community. Under his successor in the chair of Latin, Francis W. Kelsey [*q.v.*], the University Musical Society, the Choral Union, and the May Festival continued to bear witness to the musical tastes of Frieze. His other project, the Art Museum, after a good start received less support. In June 1889, Kelsey was called to the department of Latin, and in the following December Frieze died. His grave, in Forest Hill Cemetery, Ann Arbor, is marked by an alumni memorial, copied from the tomb of Scipio and bearing the Horatian legend, *"Candidiorem animam terra non tulit."*

[The private papers of Frieze and his personal letters from Andrew D. White and others, preserved in the Univ. of Mich. library, reveal his rare personality. For the facts of his career, see E. M. Farrand, *Hist. of the Univ. of Mich.* (1885); B. A. Hinsdale, *Hist. of the Univ. of Mich.* (1906), ed. by I. N. Demmon; Wilfred Shaw, *The Univ. of Mich.* (1920); J. B. Angell, *A Memorial Discourse on the Life and Services of Henry Simmons Frieze* (1890), informing but eulogistic; *Detroit Free Press*, Dec. 8, 1889.] W. H. W.

FRISBIE, LEVI (Sept. 15, 1783–July 9, 1822), college professor, was born in Ipswich, Mass., the eldest child of Levi and Mehitable (Hale) Frisbie. His father (Apr. 11, 1748–Feb. 25, 1806) was one of the four students in the first graduating class (1771) of Dartmouth College. After studying divinity under President Eleazar Wheelock he was ordained and labored as a missionary among the Indians, first along the Muskingum in Ohio and later in Maine and Canada. On Feb. 7, 1776, he was installed as pastor of the First Congregational Church of Ipswich, where he continued until his death. The younger Frisbie received his preparatory education at Andover and helped to defray his expenses at Harvard College by copying papers for several hours a day while the college was in session and by teaching a school during the winter vacation. Upon his graduation in 1802 he went to Concord, where he taught for a year, and then began the study of the law. An affection of the eyes soon compelled him to relinquish his ambition, and thereafter he was unable to read for himself. Friends were at hand, however, who willingly read to him in Latin and English, and by laying a ruler or a thin octavo across the page as a guide to his hand he managed to write. In this way he acquired sufficient knowledge to discharge his duties as a teacher at Harvard and to be esteemed by his colleagues as an ornament to their society. He was tutor in Latin, 1805–11, professor of Latin, with no substantial change in his work, 1811–17, and Alford Professor of Natural Religion, Moral Philosophy, and Civil Polity from 1817 to the end of his life. He was also something, though not much, of a minor poet. On Sept. 10, 1815, he married Catherine Saltonstall Mellen of Cambridge. Of his literary remains the weightiest is the inaugural address delivered when he assumed the Alford professorship. In this he expounded the doctrine that the principles of ethics should be derived from the precepts and narratives of the Bible and pointed out the great service that literature might, but seldom does, do for morality. In dignified, academic language but much in the spirit of a New England Tertullian he denounced Chaucer, Swift, Pope, Fielding, Smollett, Goethe, Byron, and Moore for their licentious writings, but gave his approval to Cowper, Campbell, Scott, and, with reservations, to Maria Edgeworth. Andrews Norton reviewed the address at length and with enthusiasm in the *North American Review* (January 1818). Under the influence of his friend Norton he emancipated himself from some of the tenets of high Calvinism, but memories of his father's reasonings on providence, foreknowledge, will, and fate troubled him in hours of despondence. Sometime about 1821 he developed tuberculosis, and the disease ran its course quickly. "The last act of his life," wrote Norton, "was an expression of affection for his aged mother, who was adjusting his pillow."

[Andrews Norton, *A Collection of the Miscellaneous Writings of Prof. Frisbie with Some Notices of his Life and Character* (1823); *Harvard Quin. Cat. 1636–1915* (1915); *Vital Records of Ipswich, Mass., to 1850*, vols. I and II (1910); John Farrar, in *Boston Advertiser*, July 13, 1822. For the elder Frisbie see G. T. Chapman, *Sketches of the Alumni of Dartmouth Coll.* (1867), and F. Chase, *Hist. of Dartmouth Coll.*, vol. I (1891).] G. H. G.

FRISSELL, HOLLIS BURKE (July 14, 1851–Aug. 5, 1917), clergyman, educator, was born in the village of South Amenia, Dutchess County, N. Y., one of the four children of Rev. Amasa Cogswell and Lavinia (Barker) Frissell. His descent was from Joseph Frissell, a Scotchman, who was one of thirty-five men to receive grants in Woodstock, Conn., in the latter part of the seventeenth century. Ancestors on both sides were Revolutionary officers. His education began in a little red school-house and was continued in the old academy in Amenia where his mother had taught prior to her marriage, in a military school at College Hill, Poughkeepsie, in Dr. Dwight's School, New York City, in Phillips Andover, and at Yale. A schoolmate at Andover describes Frissell as already having "the scholar's stoop," a "quiet mirthfulness," a voice of "virile robustness and roundness," withal "soberminded, considerate, careful, in his movements leisurely, yet without any intimation of indolence" (manuscript letter of President C. F. Thwing, in office of the *Southern Workman*, Hampton Institute, Hampton, Va.). A good tenor voice was a bread-winning and friend-winning asset, "a better asset for college life than a high stand in mathematics" as a Yale classmate put it (J. C. Goddard, "Dr. Frissell at Yale," manuscript). This interest in music aided him to become president of the college glee club, the first Yale glee club to tour the country so far west as Chicago. His graduation in 1874 was followed by a teaching career of two years at De Garmo Institute, Rhinebeck, N. Y., after which he entered Union Theological Seminary. His course completed there in 1879, he served for a year as assistant pastor of the Madison Avenue Presbyterian Church in New York. An appeal to this church to assist the negroes of the South led him, in 1880, to pay a visit to Hampton Institute, Va., where he met Samuel Chapman Armstrong [*q.v.*], and was induced to become the school's chaplain (1880–93). He soon became much more than chaplain, assuming the responsibilities of principal on the many occasions when Armstrong was absent or ill. Therefore, Frissell, at forty-two, after an apprenticeship of thirteen years, was the logical successor to Armstrong when the latter died in 1893, and he continued to be principal of Hampton Institute until his death, almost a quarter century later.

Frissell's influence, however, went far beyond the limits of the Hampton campus. He held to the conviction that improved education for the Southern whites was a necessary preliminary to the education of negroes. Accordingly, as opportunity offered to interest people, both North and South, in this cause, that opportunity was seized. Never claiming credit as a leader, he was credited by those who knew him intimately with an exceptional quality of leadership and with wisdom as a counselor. Perhaps the most important series of conferences which he helped to organize, and in which he was always a leading spirit, was that begun at Capon Springs, W. Va., in 1898, out of which the Southern Education Board developed in 1901. To the wisely managed educational campaigns carried on by this Board, through the "Conferences for Education in the South" which were held annually in the several Southern states in rotation from 1901 to 1915, more than to any other single agency, the South owes a remarkable educational awakening.

As a member of the General Education Board, to which he was elected in 1906, Frissell was identified with the promotion of farm and health demonstrations. Traceable to suggestions offered by him are the Jeanes teachers' supervision of industrial education in the rural negro schools and the state agents' direction of negro education, the Cooperative Education Association of Virginia, and the Negro Organization Society. "No man in American public life," said a fellow Virginia educator, "has done more to heal the wounds of war, to bind the sections together, to unify the nation, to build up a finer and freer civilization on the ruins of an old order, than this unobtrusive missionary to a backward race" (President E. A. Alderman, *Southern Workman*, November 1917, p. 571). He married, Nov. 8, 1883, Julia F. Dodd, daughter of Judge Amzi Dodd of Bloomfield, N. J., who with one son survived him.

[A stenographic report of a chapel address, May 15, 1910, in which Frissell sketched his own life, in the office of the *Southern Workman*, Hampton Inst., Hampton, Va., is the best source of information about him. The same office has many letters from school and college mates, from trustees and friends of Hampton, and a sketch by Alice Carter. Printed material includes *Southern Workman*, Nov. 1917, memorial number; F. G. Peabody, *Education for Life* (1918); J. H. Oldham, "Hollis B. Frissell and Hampton," *Constructive Quart.*, Sept. 1918; R. R. Moton, *Finding a Way Out* (1920), and "Frissell the Builder," *Southern Workman*, June 1923; J. D. Eggleston, "Hollis Burke Frissell," *Ibid.*, Mar. 1924; *Biog. Record of the Class of 1874 in Yale*

College, pt. IV, 1874–1909 (1912), pt. V, 1909–19 (1919); *Who's Who in America*, 1914–15.] A. E. P.

FRITSCHEL, CONRAD SIGMUND (Dec. 2, 1833–Apr. 26, 1900), Lutheran theologian, was born in Nürnberg, Germany, the eldest of the three sons of Martin Heinrich and Katharina Esther (Kässler) Fritschel. His most abiding characteristic, a simple, whole-hearted piety, was manifest even in boyhood. In 1850, in accordance with his first ambition, he entered the Missionary Institute conducted by Friedrich Bauer; and when Bauer moved the school at Easter 1853 to Neuendettelsau, Johann Tobias Müller, the editor of the standard German-Latin edition of the Concordia, and Wilhelm Löhe, the famous pastor of Neuendettelsau, also became his teachers. All three, but especially Löhe, left a deep impress on Fritschel's mind. At this period the institute was engaged in training missionaries to work among the German Lutherans who were emigrating in large numbers to the United States and settling principally in the Middle West. Fritschel was ordained in Hamburg Apr. 23, 1854, as pastor of a congregation aboard ship and reached Dubuque, Iowa, July 28. There he joined Johannes Deindörfer and Georg Martin Grossmann [*qq.v.*], and on Aug. 24, 1854, at St. Sebald, Clayton County, Iowa, they, together with Michael Schüller, who had accompanied Fritschel from Germany, constituted themselves the Evangelical Lutheran Synod of Iowa. For the next two years Fritschel labored as a missionary in Platteville, Wis., and the surrounding territory, and then went to Detroit as pastor of a congregation belonging to the Buffalo Synod. On Aug. 22, 1858, he entered on what was to be his life-work as a professor in the Wartburg Seminary of the Iowa Synod. He filled this position until his death forty-two years later; for thirty-one years his shorter-lived brother, Gottfried Leonhard Wilhelm [*q.v.*], was his colleague. The two Fritschels were, in fact, the seminary. Together they trained the future ministers of the synod, formulated its theological position, and defended that position in a series of controversies with the theologians of the Missouri Synod. His eloquence and social gifts made Sigmund a favorite preacher or speaker for special occasions; whenever a corner-stone was laid throughout the length and breadth of the growing synod, a church dedicated, a school opened, an organ installed, a mortgage lifted, "Professor Senior" was invited to deliver the address. In 1860, when a debt of $7,000 threatened to close the seminary, he went in the steerage to Germany to collect funds. He met with extraordinary success not only in Germany but in Russia; the debt was paid, and new-made friends of the synod in Germany and Russia continued to give it support for almost a generation. He visited Germany again in 1866, 1871, and 1891. He was a standing delegate to the General Council of the Evangelical Lutheran Church in North America and exercised a considerable influence over its doctrinal and liturgical development. His contributions to theological journals were numerous, but he wrote no books. In 1899 his rugged health gave way; Bright's disease made its appearance; and Fritschel faced the one contingency that he dreaded—inactivity before his death. As the disease progressed he begged his family not to pray for the prolongation of his life. He died at Dubuque and was buried beside his brother at Mendota, Ill.

On Jan. 20, 1856, at Dubuque, Fritschel married Margarethe, daughter of Conrad Prottengeier. She with seven of their eleven children outlived him. Of the surviving children, John became director of Wartburg College and Max president of Wartburg Seminary; five of the six daughters married clergymen.

[*Reden und Ansprachen gehalten bei der Trauerfeier für Professor D. Sigmund Fritschel in Dubuque, Iowa, und Mendota, Ill.* (Chicago, n.d.); A. Spaeth, memoir with list of writings in *Luth. Ch. Rev.*, Jan. 1901; G. J. Fritschel, *Quellen und Dokumente zur Geschichte und Lehrstellung der ev.-luth. Synode von Iowa u. a. Staaten* (Chicago, n.d); W. Koller, *Die Missionsanstalt in Neuendettelsau* (Neuendettelsau, 1924); P. Bredow, *Erinnerungen aus dem Leben und Wirken eines amerikanisch-lutherischen Pastors* (privately printed, Waterloo, Iowa, 1904); *Dubuque Times*, Apr. 27, 1900; personal assistance from Fritschel's nephew, Prof. George J. Fritschel of Wartburg Seminary. See also bibliography to article on G. L. W. Fritschel.] G. H. G.

FRITSCHEL, GOTTFRIED LEONHARD WILHELM (Dec. 19, 1836–July 13, 1889), Lutheran theologian, was born in Nürnberg, Germany, the youngest of the three sons of Martin Heinrich and Katharina Esther (Kässler) Fritschel. In 1853 he followed his brother Conrad Sigmund [*q.v.*] into the Missionary Institute at Neuendettelsau, where he was profoundly influenced by Wilhelm Löhe. Completing his theological training with a year at the University of Erlangen under Franz Delitzsch, Theodosius Harnack, von Hofmann, and Thomasius, he came to the United States in the spring of 1857, was ordained at Dubuque on May 31 (Pentecost) by Georg Martin Grossmann [*q.v.*], and entered at once on his work as professor of theology in the Wartburg Seminary of the Iowa Synod. The seminary led for some years a precarious existence. To save expense it was moved in 1857 to St. Sebald, Clayton County, Iowa, where students, professors, and professors' families were housed in a single wooden building at the edge of the open prairie, five miles from the nearest settlement, almost a day's journey from a railroad. The next year his brother joined him as the second professor. Each professor, until 1864, received an annual salary of $100 together with an allowance for heat and light. Close to penury as their life must have been, in later years neither brother could remember that they had suffered by any real privation. Indeed, they reared and educated large families, collected a respectable library, and led an intense intellectual life. Gottfried studied the voluminous theologians of the sixteenth and seventeenth centuries and made himself a living concordance of Luther's writings. Such learning was necessary, for the synod was being attacked by the unceasing, rancorous, yet learned polemics of the Missouri Synod; and to Gottfried and Sigmund, almost alone, fell the task of defending the theological position of the Iowa Synod, which was substantially that of Wilhelm Löhe. Gottfried also rendered great service of an inconspicuous sort by mastering the English language and insisting that his pupils study English. To gain fluency and to improve his pronunciation, he overcame the shyness that he usually felt among strangers and taught for one summer semester in Upper Iowa University, where he was surrounded by English-speaking people. He learned Norwegian and Swedish and gave much encouragement to the Scandinavian Lutherans of the Northwest. His private studies were chiefly in Spanish literature and in geography; his brother noted that he excerpted some standard treatises on geography as carefully as he did the works of Luther. As a preacher he was less eloquent than Sigmund, but his quiet, sober reasoning drew thoughtful hearers to him. What most distinguished the man was a certain inner illumination: few have better illustrated the adage that the heart makes the theologian.

He was the author of *Passionsbetrachtungen* (1868; 2nd ed., 1876); *Geschichte der Christlichen Missionen unter den Indianern Nordamerikas in 17 und 18 Jahrhundert* (Nürnberg, 1870); *Theophilus,* a book for confirmands (1889), which he partly wrote and partly dictated during his last illness. He contributed numerous articles to Samuel Kistler Brobst's *Theologische Monatsheft,* and to the Iowa Synod's periodicals, the *Kirchenblatt* and the *Kirchliches Zeitschrift.* He was editor at various times of the *Kirchenblatt;* he and his brother edited the *Zeitschrift* from its founding in 1876. While on a missionary tour of the Dakotas in the summer of 1888 he became alarmingly ill and never recovered. The following Christmas he was compelled to give up his classes. He died at Mendota, Ill., where the seminary had been situated since 1874. On Aug. 29, 1858, at St. Sebald, Fritschel married Elise Eleanore, daughter of the Rev. Georg Köberle. She with seven of their ten children survived him. Five of the seven sons entered the service of the Iowa Synod.

[S. Fritschel, "Zur Erinnerung an G. L. W. Fritschel," in the *Kirchliche Zeitschrift,* vols. XIII–XIV (Waverly, Iowa, 1889–90); *In Memoriam: Zum Gedächtnis des selig entschlafenen G. L. W. Fritschel,* with list of writings (Waverly, Iowa, 1889); G. J. Fritschel, *Geschichte der Lutherischen Kirche in Amerika,* vol. II (Gütersloh, Germany, 1897); J. Deindörfer, *Geschichte der Evangel.-Luth. Synode von Iowa* (1897); G. J. Fritschel, *The Koeberle Family* (privately printed, 1927); personal assistance from Fritschel's son, Prof. George J. Fritschel of Wartburg Seminary. See also bibliography to article on C. S. Fritschel.] G. H. G.

FRITZ, JOHN (Aug. 21, 1822–Feb. 13, 1913), mechanical engineer, ironmaster, was born on a small farm in Londonderry township, Chester County, Pa., the oldest of seven children of George and Mary (Meharg) Fritz. His father, born in Germany, emigrated to the United States in 1802 with his parents. His mother was a native of Chester County and was of Scotch-Irish stock. Since the father was a millwright and machinist, as well as a farmer, the three sons went naturally into similar work. John attended school between intervals of helping on the farm. At sixteen he went to Parkesburg, in the same county, as an apprentice in blacksmithing and country machine work. At twenty-two he succeeded in obtaining a job as mechanic in the Norristown iron works of Moore & Hooven. Indefatigable, after the twelve-hour working day, he spent his evenings watching the rolls in the mill or learning iron-puddling. He was soon made night superintendent and a little later was practically in charge of the rolling-mill. So anxious was he to learn other phases of the iron business that in 1849 he left this hard-won position, paying $1,000 a year, to take one at $650 at Safe Harbor where Reeves, Abbott & Company were building a rail-mill and blast-furnace. In 1851 when a prolonged attack of fever and ague made work impossible, an opportunity arose for him to visit iron mines near Marquette, Mich. Upon his return he was unable to interest capitalists in mines so far from the eastern centers, although a half share in the Jackson mine could have been bought for $25,000. After further rest and a little uncertainty he superintended the rebuilding of the Kunzie blast-furnace on the Schuylkill near Philadelphia; this plant used the new anthracite fuel instead of charcoal or coke. In 1853 he and his brother George, with others, built a foundry and a machine-shop at Catasauqua to furnish supplies for the blast-furnaces and rolling-mills. A turning point in his career came in 1854 when he went to Johnstown, Pa., as general superintendent of the Cambria iron works. This company was in an unsatisfactory condition, both financially and mechanically, but Fritz determined to make it the "greatest rail-plant in the world." Against bankruptcy, hidebound opposition to his improvements, and the destruction of the mill by fire, he labored to build an efficient plant. He introduced three-high rolls in the face of a hostile attitude of the staff, and he avoided the use of gears whenever possible because of early exasperating difficulties with repairs. The machinery which he designed, although said to have been unduly heavy, was almost incapable of breakdown. Until 1860 he toiled without a vacation and then, tired of opposition, he resigned to become general superintendent and chief engineer for the Bethlehem Iron Company, which gave him cordial support. By 1863 the plant was turning out rails for use in the Civil War. In the blast-furnaces he startled conservative iron-masters by using a blast pressure as high as twelve pounds per square inch, for which he designed special blowers.

Fritz became one of a notable group, including his brother George, Robert W. Hunt, William R. Jones, and Alexander L. Holley, who applied the famous Bessemer process for making steel to American practise—the basis of a revolution in industry. Other outstanding improvements tried out in the Bethlehem plant were open-hearth furnaces, the Thomas basic process, the Whitworth forging-press, enormous steam-hammers, and automatic devices of many varieties. The plant attracted world-wide attention for its processes of turning out rails and armor-plate by quick, simplified methods; it was a pioneer in making armor-plate in America. In 1892, at the age of seventy, Fritz retired from active work. During the Civil War the government had shown its confidence by asking him to design a rolling-mill at Chattanooga, Tenn., in which rails damaged by the Confederates could be rerolled; his brother William was made superintendent of this plant. The government again honored him in 1897 when it selected him to make plans and estimates for a proposed government armor-plate works.

The John Fritz gold medal was established in 1902, on Fritz's eightieth birthday, by friends and associates in the engineering profession. At that time a dinner was given him at the Waldorf-Astoria hotel in New York, and he was made the first recipient of the medal. In 1893 he received the Bessemer gold medal of the Iron and Steel Institute of Great Britain, and in 1910 he received the Elliott Cresson medal of the Franklin Institute. Although a self-educated man, he was a member of the board of control of Lehigh University from its inception, and he gave and endowed an engineering laboratory for the university. In 1894 he was president of the American Institute of Mining Engineers, and in 1895–96 was president of the American Society of Mechanical Engineers. His autobiography, compiled at the request of friends, was written in direct, modest style from a point of view perhaps too close to the work which engrossed him, but it made available a remarkable record in American industry. In appearance Fritz showed his hard-working, unassuming nature in his strongly marked face. On Sept. 11, 1851, he was married to Ellen W. Maxwell, who died Jan. 29, 1908.

[*The Autobiog. of John Fritz* (1912); *Trans. Am. Inst. of Mining Engineers*, Aug., Oct., 1913; *Trans. Am. Soc. of Mech. Engineers, 1913* (1914); *Engineering and Mining Jour.*, Feb. 22, 1913; *Power*, Feb. 25, 1913; *Am. Machinist*, Feb. 20, 1913; *Machinery*, Mar. 1913; and obituaries in local newspapers.] P. B. M.

FRIZELL, JOSEPH PALMER (Mar. 13, 1832–May 4, 1910), hydraulic engineer, was born at Barford, Quebec, Canada. His parents, Oliver and Mary Beach Frizell, were natives of Vermont. He attended schools at Brownington, Vt., and Richmond, Canada, where he was especially apt in mathematics. His schooling was elementary, but he continued to instruct himself along the lines of mathematics and engineering, and is said even to have devised and put to practical use a certain form of calculus. In 1850 he went to work in one of the cotton-mills at Manchester, N. H. The hours of labor were long and little time was left for pleasure or study. Nevertheless, he continued his studies and in 1854 entered the office of the city engineer as an assistant. He remained there for two years and then moved down the river to Lowell, where he became an engineering assistant with the "Proprietors of the Locks and Canals on the Merrimack River," under James B. Francis [*q.v.*], the engineer of this company, and undoubtedly the foremost hydraulic engineer of his day in the United States. Nowhere could a young engineer have found a teacher so skilled both in the theory and practise of hydraulics. Francis, having just completed and published *The Lowell Hydraulic Experiments* (1855), was busily carrying out additional work, and under his tutelage Frizell worked and studied from 1857 to 1861 and from 1866 to 1867.

During the Civil War as an assistant civil engineer of the United States army, Frizell engaged largely upon work on fortifications along the Gulf Coast. After the war he returned to Lowell for a year and then with his wife, Julia

A. Bowes, whom he had married in 1864, he went to Davenport, Iowa. Returning to the East, from 1870 to 1878 he engaged in the practise of consulting engineering in Boston, and in the latter year patented an air compressor utilizing the direct action of falling water, which proved to be successful. He went West again in 1878 as an assistant civil engineer in the United States Engineers Department and was concerned with hydraulic investigations on the headwaters of the Mississippi. He was chief engineer of the board of public works of Austin, Tex., from 1890 to 1892, but in the next year he returned to Boston and reopened his engineering office. In 1900 he published the results of some of his researches in a thorough study entitled *Water Power, an Outline of the Development and Application of the Energy of Flowing Water.* It was the first practical book of its kind published in the United States and showed that its author was well abreast and in some ways in advance of his contemporaries. In later life he contributed many technical papers to various engineering societies. In 1903 he retired from active practise and from that time until his death he lived in Dorchester, Mass. He was a most able member of that class of engineers, largely self-taught, who established the basis upon which the modern science of hydraulics rests.

[A memoir of Frizell in the *Trans. Am. Soc. Civil Engineers,* Sept. 1911; *Boston Herald,* May 6, 1910; records of the Proprietors of the Locks and Canals, Lowell, Mass.] E. P. H.

FROHMAN, CHARLES (June 17, 1860–May 7, 1915), theatrical manager, was born at Sandusky, Ohio. His father, Henry Frohman, native of a suburb of Darmstadt, Germany, emigrated to the United States at the age of eighteen. After some experience as peddler in New York State, he established a cigar factory in Sandusky. Here he married Barbara Strauss, also a native of the Darmstadt vicinity. Charles was the youngest of three sons. The other two were Daniel and Gustave. Gustave was the first of the Frohmans to enter the theatrical business; he subsequently brought his two brothers into it, and all became conspicuously identified with dramatic production.

Early environment and a strong natural impulse helped to shape Charles Frohman's career. His father aspired to be an actor and directed many amateur performances of German classics in Sandusky. When Daniel was in his teens it was decided to educate the boys in New York, and the elder Frohman established a retail cigar business on lower Broadway, in the heart of what was then the Rialto. Into the shop came some of the most famous actors of the time, and their talk and work influenced Charles, who from boyhood had an indomitable ambition to be a factor in the theatre. His first contact with the theatre in a business way was made at the age of eight, selling souvenir copies of *The Black Crook,* which was then running at Niblo's Garden. When he was nine he made his only appearance on any stage as actor, taking the part of an extra page in the extravaganza, *The Field of the Cloth of Gold,* at the New York Theatre. His initial employment in the play-house was as ticket-seller at Hooley's Theatre in Brooklyn, which his brother Gustave had rented for a summer minstrel season. Charles was then fourteen, and during the daytime worked in the office of the *Daily Graphic.* He subsequently served his apprenticeship as advance agent to road companies, including Haverly's minstrels—The "Haverly Mastodons"—and the Madison Square Theatre troupes which toured the country after their New York runs. At the Madison Square the three Frohmans were associated under the same managerial roof for the first time.

In 1883 Charles Frohman first became an independent manager, taking the famous Wallack Theatre Company on tour. Subsequently he opened a booking office in New York and laid the foundation of what later became the powerful Theatrical Syndicate. His first great success as independent manager was the production of Bronson Howard's *Shenandoah* in 1889 at the Star Theatre in New York. When originally produced in Boston, the play was a failure. Frohman had faith in it and induced the author to make several changes. The result was a triumph which gave future stars like Henry Miller, Viola Allen, Wilton Lackaye, Effie Shannon, John E. Kellard, and Nannette Comstock a Broadway appearance. In 1892 Charles Frohman engaged John Drew [*q.v.*], who became the nucleus of the Empire Stock Company. This organization developed into the greatest of all American theatrical star factories. Out of it emerged such distinguished figures as Maude Adams, William Faversham, Arnold Daly, Ethel Barrymore, Margaret Anglin, Arthur Byron, Ida Conquest, Edna Wallace, W. J. Ferguson, Elsie De Wolfe, and many others. The Empire Stock Company marked an epoch in Frohman's life because it sponsored successes like *The Girl I Left Behind Me* (Jan. 25, 1893), which established a theatrical tradition. His career henceforth was on the expanding scale that was his boyhood dream. He became star-maker and play-arbiter, in the words of the press, "the Napoleon of the drama." He was the first to encourage Clyde Fitch and Augustus Thomas. Among the other playwrights whose works he produced were Sir James M. Barrie, David Belasco, Paul Potter, Bronson Howard, Henry Arthur Jones, Henry de Mille, Haddon Chambers, Charles Klein, Somerset Maugham, William Gillette, Alfred Sutro, Sir Arthur Wing Pinero, Louis N. Parker, Michael Morton, Anthony Hope, and Granville Barker.

Charles Frohman's relation with Sir James M. Barrie deserves a paragraph all its own. They represented two extremes. Barrie was silent, dour, and aloof, while Frohman was the bubbling impresario who lived in a blaze of action and publicity. Yet they got on famously. It was Frohman who first introduced the whimsical Scotch author to the general American public with *The Little Minister* (Sept. 27, 1897), in which Maude Adams had the principal part. Henceforth Miss Adams, Barrie, and Frohman formed an irresistible combination which scored success after success. The outstanding event was the production of *Peter Pan,* following *Quality Street.*

Charles Frohman gave the American theatre a buoyant, magnetic personality and the record of an astonishing achievement. He was influential not only in the development of the organized booking system which now exists but in that of the star system as well. Having strong individuality himself, he believed in capitalizing distinctive personal appeal in others. He was distinguished by two traits. One was his reckless disregard of the value of money. He produced unmindful of expense. The other was the sacredness of his pledged word. He never made a written contract with his stars or authors. What he promised to do became the proverbial bond. His exit from life was as dramatic as any production he ever staged. In April 1915, he put on a war play entitled *The Hyphen,* which marked his last personal direction. On the following May 1st, he sailed on the *Lusitania.* Six days later the vessel was torpedoed by a German submarine eight miles off the Head of Kinsale, within sight of the Irish coast. Frohman was one of a hundred Americans who went to their death. His last words were "Why fear death? It is the most beautiful adventure of life." Funeral services for him were held at Temple Emanu-El in New York City, and memorial services, at the instigation of various Frohman stars, in Los Angeles, San Francisco, Tacoma, Providence, and St. Martin-in-the-Fields, London. Frohman never married.

[I. F. Marcosson and Daniel Frohman, *Charles Frohman—Manager and Man* (1916); and J. D. Williams, "C. F.," in *Century Mag.,* Dec. 1915; *N. Y. Times,* May 8, 9, 1915.]

I. F. M.

FROST, ARTHUR BURDETT (Jan. 17, 1851–June 22, 1928), illustrator, humorist, was born in Philadelphia, the youngest son of John Frost and his wife Sarah Ann Burdett. His father, a Harvard graduate and a compiler of textbooks, died in 1859, leaving his family without adequate provision, and young Frost went to work at the age of fifteen, first in a wood-engraver's shop and later in the office of a lithographer. He sketched in the evenings, studying for a time under Thomas Eakins at the Philadelphia Academy of the Fine Arts, but was mainly, as he later insisted, "self-taught." His first opportunity to do illustrating came through William J. Clark, who perceived his comic talent and arranged for him to cut wood-engravings for a book by his brother, Charles H. Clark (Max Adeler), called *Out of the Hurly Burly* (1874). Although crude in comparison with his later work, these sketches marked the beginning of Frost's career as an illustrator. The following year he was on the staff of the New York *Graphic* and in 1876 entered the studio of Harper & Brothers. From that time his drawings appeared frequently, and by the end of the century he was probably the most popular illustrator in the country. In 1877 he went to London for work and study, but returned in 1878, finding England uncongenial to his entirely American genius.

Frost's early illustrations cover a wide range of subjects, from romantic pictures for an 1882 edition of *The Lady of the Lake* to humorous sketches for Lewis Carroll's *Rhyme? and Reason?* (1883) and utility drawings for *Harper's Magazine.* It appeared, however, that his true talent was for American folk pictures, to which he soon devoted himself. They fell mainly into two groups, comic line sketches in story sequence, and finished illustrations in pen and ink, oils, or water-color. Some of his humorous sketches appeared in book form as *Stuff and Nonsense* (1884), *The Bull Calf and Other Tales* (1892), and *Carlo* (1913), but most of them were published in periodicals. His more formal illustrations appeared in *Scribner's Magazine, Harper's Magazine* and *Collier's,* from which representative sketches were selected for the publication of his *Book of Drawings* in 1904. He was probably known best as the visual creator of Joel Chandler Harris's Uncle Remus, Brer Rabbit, Aunt Minervy Ann, and a whole gallery of animal characters. His first illustrations of this series appeared in *Uncle Remus and His Friends* (1892), followed by *Uncle Remus, His Songs and His Sayings* (1895), *The Chronicles of Aunt Minervy Ann* (1899), *The Tar-Baby and Other Rhymes of Uncle Remus* (1904), *Told by Uncle Remus* (1905), and finally *Uncle Remus Returns* (1918). Two of his pictures, "What Happened?" and "Somebody Blundered" were entered in the Paris Exposition of 1900.

Frost remained throughout his life an illustrator. Although he had an adequate knowledge of design, his talent was for dramatic incident rather than decorative compositions. His chin-whiskered farmers, his plantation negroes, his sportsmen and animals are picturesque in their own right, but are interesting mainly as specific characters confronted by specific situations. His hold on the affections of his public was certainly due to his sense of comedy. His humor never depended upon cheap wit or incongruity, but upon a knowledge and appreciation of character. He was acutely observant, and skilful in exaggerating and simplifying the facts he observed to suit his purposes. Moreover, he was so intensely interested in the people he created that he was able to engender in the spectator an attitude of actual participation. As a result, his drawings by their homely fidelity to nature and dramatic emphasis retained their freshness and flavor after the work of more pretentious contemporaries had become stale and uninteresting. With Mark Twain and Joel Chandler Harris, Frost definitely crystallized the tang and gusto of the American countryside. After his marriage to Emily Louise Phillips in 1883, he established himself on a small farm in Convent Station, N. J. In 1908 he removed to Paris where his two sons received artistic training, but returned to America in 1916, residing in New Jersey and Pennsylvania until 1924 when he went to Pasadena. He died there in the home of his son, John Frost, a California landscape-painter.

[N. S. Frost, *Frost Geneal. in Five Families* (1926), pp. 272, 275; H. C. Bunner, "A. B. Frost," in *Harper's Mag.*, Oct. 1892; *Art Digest*, July 1928; C. D. Gibson, "A. B. Frost," *Scribner's Mag.*, Nov. 1928; Perriton Maxwell, "A. B. Frost," *Pearson's Mag.*, Apr. 1908; *N. Y. Times*, June 24, 1928; N. Y. *World*, June 25, 1928.]
C. P. M.

FROTHINGHAM, ARTHUR LINCOLN (June 21, 1859–July 28, 1923), scholar, teacher, and author, was the only son of Arthur Lincoln and Jessie (Peabody) Frothingham. He was born in Boston, but soon after his birth his parents moved to Newton, Mass. He was a delicate child, and on this account, when he was about eight years old, his family went to live in Italy; first at Florence and soon afterwards at Rome, where they remained until 1883. Arthur was a pupil in a private school in Rome, pursued courses, especially in Oriental languages, at the Seminario di Sant' Apollinare and at the Università Reale at Rome, and in 1883 received the degree of Ph.D. from the University of Leipzig. Thus practically all of his formal education was European. In 1882 he was made fellow in Semitic languages at Johns Hopkins University, and he continued to hold this fellowship until 1885: in that year he became fellow by courtesy in Semitics, and for three years he delivered lectures at Johns Hopkins on Babylonian and Assyrian archeology and art. On June 12, 1886, he was appointed professor of archeology in the College of New Jersey at Princeton (now Princeton University), and continued a member of the faculty of this institution until he retired in June 1905. From 1886 until his death he made his home in Princeton. On Jan. 27, 1897, he married Helen Bulkley Post of Brooklyn, N. Y., who died in 1921.

In 1885 he founded the *American Journal of Archæology,* of which he was the managing editor until 1896, contributing much himself to its pages. He also joined in founding, in 1889, the *Princeton College Bulletin,* and was for a time one of its editors. He was secretary of the Archæological Institute of America in 1884, and associate director of the American School of Classical Studies in Rome in 1895–96. He was delegate from the United States to the International Congress on Art and Archæology at Rome in 1912, and read a paper before that congress on "The Origin of Rome and Running Water" (see also *American Journal of Archæology,* January–March 1912). Frothingham was a learned and brilliant scholar. Among his more important contributions are the following, published in the *American Journal of Archæology*: "Notes on Roman Artists of the Middle Ages" (1889–93); "Byzantine Artists in Italy from the Sixth to the Fifteenth Century" (1894); "Introduction of Gothic Architecture into Italy by the French Cistercian Monks" (1890–91); "Medusa, Apollo, and the Great Mother" (1911, 1915, 1922); "Diocletian and Mithra in the Roman Forum" (1914); "A New Mithraic Relief from Syria" (1918); "Babylonian Origin of Hermes, the Snake-God, and of the Caduceus" (1916). He also contributed notable articles on "The Architect in History" to the *Architectural Record* (February 1908; March, April, July 1909).

His keen observation enabled him to find what others overlooked, to discover new and significant facts or new explanations of known facts which shattered opinions and doctrines long regarded as incontestable. In a series of papers read at general meetings of the Archæological Institute of America, and in articles, chiefly in the *American Journal of Archæology* (1900, 1901, 1904), he developed his ideas of the origin, significance, and history of Roman memorial and triumphal arches, which at the time of his death he was intending to incorporate and extend in a large work of several volumes. "De la véritable Signification des Monuments Romans qu'on appelle 'Arcs de Triomphe' " appeared in the *Revue Archéologique* (September–October 1900); "A National Emblem of Liberty" in the *Architectural Record* (January 1908); and in articles entitled "Who Built the Arch of Constantine," in the *American Journal of Archæology* (1912, 1915), he sought to show that this arch was originally built under the Emperor Domitian, and afterward altered to serve as a monument of the Emperor Constantine. He discovered in the museum at Rouen the model in papier mâché from which, with some alterations, the Church of Saint Maclou at Rouen was built. Accounts of this discovery were published in *L'Académie des Inscriptions et Belles-Lettres, Monuments et Memoires* (*Fondation Eugène Piot,* XII, 1905), in the *Nation* (Mar. 9, 1905), and in the *Architectural Record* (August 1907). Perhaps his most far-reaching idea was one presented first in a paper before the Archæological Institute, Dec. 30, 1914, and afterward developed under the title "Ancient Orientation Unveiled" in the *American Journal of Archæology* (1917). He argued that many of the peoples of the ancient world may be assigned to one or other of two groups, according to their practise of orientation when consulting the signs of the gods in the heavens. This observation suggested the possibility that some primitive conceptions and ritualistic practises among the Etruscans and the Babylonians may have originated in the West, and may have been transmitted from the West to the East, instead of from the East to the West as commonly supposed.

His published books are: *Il Tesoro della Basilica di S. Pietro in Vaticano dal XIII al XV Secolo* (with Eugene Müntz, 1883); *Stephen Bar Sudaili, the Syrian Mystic, and the Book of Hierotheos* (1886); *A Text-Book of the History of Sculpture* (with Allan Marquand, 1896); *The Monuments of Christian Rome from Constantine to the Renaissance* (1908); *Roman Cities in Italy and Dalmatia* (1910); *A History of Architecture,* Volumes III and IV (1915), a sequel to Volumes I and II by Russell Sturgis; *Simplified Italian Manual* (1918); *Handbook of War Facts and Peace Problems* (4th ed., 1919); *Revolutionary Radicalism . . . Report of the Joint Legislative Committee Investigating Seditious Activities, filed Apr. 24, 1920 in the Senate of the State of New York* (with A. E. Stevenson, 4 vols., 1920).

[An outline of Frothingham's career is contained in *Who's Who in America,* 1922–23. Memorials were published by Harold N. Fowler in the *Am. Jour. Archæol.* (Oct.–Dec. 1923), and by Salomon Reinach in *Revue Archéologique* (Janvier–Juin 1924). There is an obituary in the *N. Y. Times,* July 29, 1923. The writer has also availed himself of the official records of Johns Hopkins and Princeton Universities, and of the personal recollections of Frothingham's sister, Miss Jessie Peabody Frothingham.]

W. K. P.

FROTHINGHAM, NATHANIEL LANGDON (July 23, 1793–Apr. 4, 1870), Unitarian clergyman, was born in Boston, the seventh of the nine children of Ebenezer and Joanna (Langdon) Frothingham, and the sixth in descent from William Frothingham, who was a selectman of Charlestown, Mass., in 1634 and founded a line of furniture-makers and carriage-builders. His father was a dealer in crockery and a tax assessor. Frothingham graduated from Harvard College in 1811, studied theology under the elder Henry Ware [*q.v.*] while acting as preceptor in rhetoric and oratory at Harvard, 1812–15, and was ordained in 1815 as pastor of the First Church of Boston. In 1818 he married Ann Gorham Brooks, daughter of Peter Chardon Brooks [*q.v.*] and sister of Mrs. Edward Everett and Mrs. Charles Francis Adams. He traveled in Europe in 1826–27, in 1849, and in 1859–60. In 1850, after thirty-five years of service, he resigned his charge and was made pastor emeritus. Besides many contributions to periodicals and numerous occasional sermons and pamphlets, he published *Sermons in the Order of a Twelve-Month* (1852); *Metrical Pieces, Translated and Original* (1855, 1856); and *Metrical Pieces, Part Two* (1870). His translations include the "Phenomena" of Aratus and poems by Propertius, Martial, Manzoni, Goethe, Schiller, Herder, Rückert, Uhland, Baron von Zedlitz, and Count von Auersperg—a list that suggests the extent of his reading in ancient and modern, especially German, literature. Three of his hymns—"O God, Whose presence glows in all"; "We meditate the day"; "O Lord of life and truth and grace"—have been deservedly praised. He was a dutiful pastor and a distinguished preacher and writer. His religion "was essentially the old one, softened by thought, knowledge, experience, feeling; a faith rather than a creed, a sentiment more than a dogma, not sharp in outline, but full of emotion and charged with conviction slightly illogical, perhaps, but firm" (*Boston Unitarianism,* p. 38). He was sufficiently conservative from both taste and principle to exclude Theodore Parker from the "Thursday Lecture" in his church, and sufficiently humane to develop a warm regard for Parker himself. Despite their wide differences of temper, he was greatly admired by Ralph Waldo Emerson: "I had a letter from Dr. Frothingham to-day. The sight of that man's handwriting is Parnassian. Nothing vulgar is connected with his name, but, on the contrary, every remembrance of wit and learning, and contempt of cant. In our Olympic games we love his fame. But that fame was bought by many years' steady rejection of all that is popular with our saints, and as persevering study of books which none else reads, and which he can convert to no temporary purpose. There is a scholar doing a scholar's office" (*Journals,* vol. IV, 1910, p. 272, Aug. 9, 1834). His happy life was finally broken by heavy afflictions: the death of his wife in 1863 and the complete loss, the next year, of his eyesight. Until his health gave way he continued at work, setting his affairs in order, dictating poems, and translating German hymns.

[O. B. Frothingham [*q.v.*], *Boston Unitarianism 1820–50* . . . (1890) and *Recollections and Impressions 1822–90* (1891); *Nation,* Aug. 21, 1890; *Proc. Mass. Hist. Soc. 1869–70* (1871); *Proc. Am. Acad. Arts and Sci.,* VIII (1873), 226–28; A. B. Ellis, *Hist. of the First Church in Boston 1630–1880* (1881); T. B. Wyman, *Frothingham Geneal.* (n.d.); J. McKean, *Sermon Delivered at the Ordination of the Rev. N. L. Frothingham* (1815); for list of published sermons see J. Sabin, *Dict. of Books Relating to America,* vol. VII (1875), and E. A. and G. L. Duyckinck, *Cyc. Am. Lit.* (rev. ed., 1875).] G. H. G.

FROTHINGHAM, OCTAVIUS BROOKS (Nov. 26, 1822–Nov. 27, 1895), Unitarian and independent clergyman, author, was born in Boston, the second of the five children of Nathaniel Langdon Frothingham [*q.v.*] and Ann Gorham Brooks. After his graduation from Harvard College in 1843 and from the Divinity School in 1846, he was ordained Mar. 10, 1847, as pastor of the North Church of Salem. Thirteen days later he married Caroline E. Curtis of Boston. In 1853 he sought relief from throat trouble by traveling in Europe. Until after his thirtieth year his inward life was as placid as the outward, but under the influence of his friend Theodore Parker his intellectual life was quickened and deepened and his energies unchained. By conviction a militant radical, temperamentally he remained to the end of his days a conservative and looked back with sympathy and almost with longing on the religion of his childhood. He soon broke with his Salem congregation over the question of slavery and removed to Jersey City in 1855 as pastor of a newly organized Unitarian society. His reputation as a man of extraordinary spiritual power grew rapidly, and in 1859 the Third Congregational Unitarian Society (later the Independent Liberal Church) was organized in New York by admirers who wished to see his influence extended.

This society, to which men and women of the most diverse faiths and aspirations were attracted, met first in Ebbit Hall, then in a church of its own, later in Lyric Hall, and finally in the Masonic Temple. During his twenty years as its pastor Frothingham was at the height of his powers and was looked upon as the intellectual heir of Theodore Parker. His beliefs, however, were even further removed than Parker's from traditional Christianity. To many people, even to his cousin Henry Adams (*Education of Henry Adams,* 1918, p. 35), his faith seemed "scepticism." His weekly sermons were broadcast in newspapers and pamphlets and aroused widespread attention and discussion. Finding himself outside the bounds of orthodox Unitarianism, Frothingham became one of the founders, in Boston, May 30, 1867, of the Free Religious Association and served until 1878 as its first president. In 1879 his health broke down, and he was compelled to give up active work. After a great public testimonial to its esteem and love for him, his congregation disbanded, and he went to Europe for a year of rest. On his return he took up his residence in Boston, where he lived in semi-retirement for the rest of his life. He never regained his health.

While a student he composed his one generally known hymn, "The Lord of Hosts, Whose guiding hand." Between 1863 and 1891 he wrote copiously, his most substantial books being *The Religion of Humanity* (1872); *The Safest Creed* (1874); *Theodore Parker: A Biography* (1874); *Transcendentalism in New England: A History* (1876); *Gerrit Smith: A Biography* (1877); *George Ripley* (1882); *Memoir of William Henry Channing* (1886); *Boston Unitarianism, 1820–1850: A Study of the Life and Work of Nathaniel Langdon Frothingham* (1890); and *Recollections and Impressions, 1822–1890* (1891). Unfortunately, his earlier works, written during the strenuous years in New York, are marred by serious errors and omissions; his later books, the products of his leisure, are far better. As a biographer he was honest, fair, candid, and sympathetic. He also wrote much for newspapers and periodicals, contributed several memoirs to the *Proceedings* of the Massachusetts Historical Society, and published some 150 sermons. He died in Boston; his body, at his earnest request, was cremated.

[The chief source of information is his *Recollections and Impressions, 1822–90* (1891). The fullest memoir is Josiah P. Quincy's in *Proc. Mass. Hist. Soc.,* 2 ser. X (1896), 507–39. For other writings by and about him see the sketch by his nephew, Paul R. Frothingham, in S. A. Eliot's *Heralds of a Liberal Faith,* III (1910), 120–27.] G. H. G.

FROTHINGHAM, PAUL REVERE (July 6, 1864–Nov. 27, 1926), clergyman and author, was born at Jamaica Plain, a suburb of Boston, Mass., the son of Thomas Bumstead and Annie Pearson (Lunt) Frothingham. He graduated from Harvard in 1886 and received there also the degrees of A.M. and S.T.B. in 1889. Three years later, on June 14, 1892, he married Anna C. Clapp. His only pastorates were with the First Congregational Society of New Bedford, Mass., 1889 to 1900, and the Arlington Street Church (Unitarian) in Boston, 1900 to his death. His father, a Boston merchant, was the son of the Rev. Nathaniel Langdon Frothingham [*q.v.*], minister of the First Church of Boston, 1815 to 1850, and his maternal grandfather, William Parsons Lunt, was for many years minister of the famous "Church of the Presidents" at Quincy, Mass. His father's brother, Octavius Brooks Frothingham [*q.v.*], was minister of the Third Unitarian Congregational Society in New York, 1860 to 1879. His grandmother Frothingham was a daughter of Peter C. Brooks [*q.v.*], a successful Boston merchant, and her sisters were the wives of Edward Everett and Charles Francis Adams. Through his ancestry Frothingham was thus connected with some of the most notable New England families and identified with all those currents of thought and social activities naturally associated with the name of Boston. Especially close were his ties with Harvard, to which he gave devoted service as one of the preachers to the University for sixteen years and as a member of the Board of Overseers for two terms of six years each.

His theological position was determined by the adjustments in religious thought which were taking place in the community about him. The fierce conflicts between the traditional forms of faith and the new scientific spirit had, so far as that community was concerned, ceased to trouble. The problem of his generation was to adapt the gains of the long controversy to the practical needs of society. Frothingham accepted the forms of the liberal church organization as he found them and strove to utilize them as best he could for the betterment of civic life. He was little concerned with names or formulas. He was a Unitarian by tradition and by conviction, but he was not led into the radical extremes which had limited the influence of his brilliant uncle. He was an individualist, but was able to see that the individual works best through organizations. As minister of a great city church he bore his part in its manifold activities. His preaching, both there and at the University, was effective because it was always the expression of his own personality tempered and controlled by understanding and respect for the opinions of others. On the twenty-fifth anniversary of his settlement at Arlington Street Church in 1925, which coincided with the centennial celebration of the American Unitarian Association, he gave expression to his matured thought in two memorable addresses: a sermon on the text, "Not perfect without us," published in *Twenty-Fifth Anniversary of the Installation of Rev. Paul Revere Frothingham, D.D., as Minister of the Arlington Street Church, Boston* (1926), and *Our Heritage of Faith* (1925), a summary of Unitarian accomplishment and a summons to new activity. In his later years he found his thoughts increasingly occupied with the great problems left open by the World War. An ardent patriot, he saw his country's greatness, not so much in her own prosperity based upon her conquest of the material world as in the part she might play in helping organized society toward the new consummation of a peace founded upon civic righteousness. In the League of Nations he beheld the concrete expression of this ideal and he threw himself heartily into its defense. He was a frequent attendant at its sessions and took every opportunity to urge the participation of the United States in its membership.

Frothingham was master of a direct and forceful literary style. His publications were largely of sermons and addresses. Only once did he attempt a work of greater dimensions, *Edward Everett, Orator and Statesman* (1925), a biography of his great-uncle by marriage. It was a task of peculiar difficulty to present to the readers of 1925 a public character whose qualities, extravagantly praised in his day, have ceased to appeal to the popular taste and judgment. The subject was one naturally adapted to a modern type of biographical method characterized by flippant depreciation and ridicule, but the author chose the wiser plan of emphasizing the greater qualities and explaining, while not concealing, the lesser ones. The result is a biography which is likely to stand as the final judgment of the second generation upon a notable historic figure.

In person Dr. Frothingham was tall, erect, alert in movement, with a quick flashing eye, a refined voice of unusual power and resonance, and a manner equally removed from familiarity and reserve. He was a natural leader in whatever form of associated life he chose to enter.

[Robt. Grant, "Memoir," *Proc. Mass. Hist. Soc.*, June 1927; S. M. Crothers, *Harv. Grads. Mag.*, Mar. 1927; *Twenty-fifth Anniversary of the Installation of Rev. Paul Revere Frothingham, D.D., as Minister of the Arlington Street Church, Boston* (1926); *Unitarian Year Book*, 1927–28; *Who's Who in America*, 1926–27; personal acquaintance.]

E. E.

FROTHINGHAM, RICHARD (Jan. 31, 1812–Jan. 29, 1880), historian, was born at

Charlestown, Mass., with which town he was prominently identified throughout his life. His father was Richard Frothingham, a descendant of William, who emigrated to Massachusetts from Yorkshire, England, in Winthrop's fleet. His mother was Mary Thompson. The boy attended two small private schools and a public school in Boston, entering business when eighteen years of age. After acting as a clerk for two concerns for short periods, he entered the employ of the Middlesex Canal Company, remaining with it from 1834 until its dissolution in 1860, having risen from subordinate positions to that of treasurer. He was one of the proprietors of the *Boston Post* and served as managing editor from 1852 to 1865, having been a prominent contributor both before and during his editorship. He was public-spirited and greatly interested in politics. Always a consistent Democrat, he was a delegate to the National Democratic Conventions in 1852 and 1876, and was several times a candidate for Congress from the 5th district. He was a member of the state legislature in 1840, 1842, 1844, 1850, and 1851; a delegate to the state constitutional convention in 1853; mayor of Charlestown for three successive terms, 1851–53; a member of the state board of health for a number of years; and from 1838 to 1843 one of the trustees of the Free Schools, much of the time serving as president of the board. He was also active in many organizations, such as the American Antiquarian Society; the New-England Historic Genealogical Society; and the Massachusetts Historical Society, of which last he was treasurer from 1847 to 1877. A Universalist in religion, he was one of the most prominent laymen of that denomination and a trustee and treasurer for eight years of Tufts College. Although he never held high office, he was essentially a public man and had a wide acquaintance among well-known men, beginning with Lafayette.

His most important work was as an historian, though with one exception he devoted his labor to the meticulous examination of local history. His most important books are: *The History of Charlestown, Mass.* (issued in seven numbers, 1845–49); *History of the Siege of Boston* (1849); *The Command in the Battle of Bunker Hill* (1850); *Life and Times of Joseph Warren* (1865, begun in 1849); and *The Rise of the Republic* (1872). He regarded the last as his greatest contribution; but while it has not by any means lost all its value as compared with later works, probably Frothingham's earlier and more limited studies and his one biography will be those for which scholars will longest be indebted to him. His indefatigable research and painstaking accuracy within his chosen field have left little for later students to accomplish. He was also a frequent contributor of important papers to the publications of the societies to which he belonged, notably to the Massachusetts Historical Society; and for several years he served on the board of editors for the *Collections* of that organization. The last eleven months of his life were clouded by some obscure brain trouble following an attack of pneumonia. He was survived by his wife, Vrylena Blanchard, whom he had married on Dec. 18, 1833. Six children were born to them.

[There is a brief account in *New-Eng. Hist. and Geneal. Reg.*, Oct. 1883; and a memoir by Chas. Deane in *Proc. Mass. Hist. Soc.*, 2 ser. I (1885), 381–93.]

J. T. A.

FRY, BIRKETT DAVENPORT (June 24, 1822–Jan. 21, 1891), lawyer, Confederate soldier, cotton manufacturer, was born in Kanawha County, Va. (now W. Va.), the son of Thornton and Eliza R. (Thompson) Fry and a great-grandson of Col. Joshua Fry [*q.v.*]. His maternal grandfather was Philip Rootes Thompson who had been a member of Congress from Virginia from 1801 to 1807. He received his education in Virginia Military Institute and in Washington College, Pennsylvania. In 1842 he was admitted to West Point, but withdrew after two years because of a deficiency in mathematics. He then studied law and was admitted to the bar in 1846. His military training secured him an appointment as first lieutenant of infantry in the regular army at the opening of the Mexican War. He was appointed Feb. 24, 1847, and two months later was transferred to Voltiguers. At the battle of Chapultepec he was mentioned in the report of the colonel for unusual courage. He received his discharge Aug. 31, 1848, and was presented with a sword by the state of Virginia "for gallant and meritorious service." The following year he made the journey across the plains to California and opened a law office in Sacramento. While there he took part in Walker's expedition to Nicaragua (1855) and rose to the rank of brigadier-general in the filibustering army. When the movement collapsed he was in California where he had been sent to secure recruits for Walker's army. He therefore escaped the fate which overtook most of the members of the expedition.

In 1853 Fry had married Martha (Micou) Baker, the daughter of William and Ann Micou of Augusta, Ga., and in 1859 he left the West and settled in Tallassee, Ala., where he became manager of a cotton-mill in which the family of his wife was interested. At the outbreak of the Civil War, he offered his services to the state of Alabama and was commissioned colonel of the 13th Regiment, Alabama Infantry. He accompanied this regiment to Virginia where it was assigned to the 5th Brigade in the Army of Virginia. Here he rendered heroic service. At Seven Pines he was wounded but refused to leave the field. At Sharpsburg, where he was officially commended by Gen. Hill, his arm was shattered and he was warned by the physicians that he could not hope to live unless he permitted it to be amputated. He refused, nevertheless, and did recover in time to participate in the battle of Chancellorsville where he was again wounded. At Gettysburg he led Archer's brigade in the attack upon Cemetery Ridge. In this attack he was wounded and taken prisoner. Nine months later he was exchanged and returned to the Army of Virginia. He received his commission as brigadier-general May 24, 1864, and was given command of Archer's and Walker's brigades which he led in the second battle of Cold Harbor. Shortly after this battle he was sent to Augusta, Ga., to command a military district, and remained there until the close of the war. The three years following the war he spent in Cuba, returning to Tallassee in 1868 to manage the cotton-mill once more. In 1881 he settled in Richmond, Va., and engaged in cotton-buying. In 1886 he became president of the Marshall Manufacturing Company and held this position until his death in 1891. Gen. Bragg described him as "a man of gunpowder reputation" and his career proves that he merited the tribute, though he was slight in build and quiet in manner. He was devoted to children and was very fond of flowers and animals.

[E. F. Barker, *Frye Geneal.* (1920), contains the best sketch. This has been supplemented by the *Official Records (Army)*; records in the War Department; papers in the possession of the Micou family; Wm. Walker, *The War in Nicaragua* (1860); R. A. Brock, in *Southern Hist. Soc. Papers,* vol. XVIII (1890); and the *Richmond Dispatch,* Jan. 22, 1891. The sketches in Thos. M. Owen's *Hist. of Ala. and Dict. of Ala. Biog.* (1921), vol. III, and the *Confed. Mil. Hist.* (1899), vol. VII, are brief and inaccurate in certain details.]

H. F.

FRY, JAMES BARNET (Feb. 22, 1827–July 11, 1894), soldier, writer, was born at Carrollton, Ill., the son of Gen. Jacob and Emily (Turney) Fry. He was graduated from the United States Military Academy in 1847, served as brevet second lieutenant of artillery during the Mexican War, was later instructor in artillery at West Point and Fortress Monroe, and for five years was adjutant at West Point. On Mar. 16, 1861, he was appointed an assistant adjutant-general of the army and brevetted captain, and after successive promotions was commissioned lieutenant-colonel as of Dec. 31, 1862. Meanwhile he had served for two months as aide-de-camp and adjutant-general on the staff of Gen. McDowell and a year as chief-of-staff of Gen. Buell [*q.v.*] in the Army of the Ohio. He was commended by McDowell for conduct at Manassas, and by Buell for gallantry at Shiloh and ability and zeal in the performance of his duties, and was recommended for appointment as brigadier-general of volunteers. His emphasis, throughout life, upon Buell's contribution to victory at Shiloh was unpalatable to Grant and Sherman (see *North American Review,* February 1886, p. 206). He was a leading witness before the military commission convened in November 1862 to investigate Buell's conduct after the battle of Perryville, and it was presumably feeling in the Senate against his commander which prevented confirmation of two nominations as brevet-colonel which Fry received in 1863.

When, however, the Bureau of the Provost-Marshal-General was created—to check desertions and physical exemptions, reorganize recruiting, and enforce conscription—Col. Fry (recommended by Gen. Grant as "the officer best fitted for that office by his experience") was detailed to the post on Mar. 17, 1863. He originated the basic organization of the Bureau and his final report showed that on the whole his administration of it was successful and economical. The Bureau did much to equalize the efforts of the states, systematize military organization, and bind together the people and the government, but it could not satisfy everybody in fixing state quotas or crediting past enlistments against them. Scandals arose, also, from the collusion of certain local provost-marshals with bounty-jumpers; national traditions were strong against conscription, and both these causes for discontent gave rise to the draft riots of Boston and New York in July 1863, and to Fry's later quarrel with Roscoe Conkling.

Fry received the rank of brigadier-general as of Apr. 21, 1864, but this rank expired with the Bureau on Aug. 28, 1866. Before that date the introduction by James G. Blaine in the House of Representatives of a bill for the reorganization of the army, making the Bureau permanent, led to a debate on that point between Blaine and Roscoe Conkling which was one of the most sensational in Congressional history (*Congressional Globe,* 39 Cong., 1 Sess., 2150–53, 2180–81, 2292–99). A House committee, appointed to consider the charges mutually made by Fry and Conkling, ignored the latter's because of the magnitude of the task involved in a study of the Bureau's operations, yet censured Fry for abuse of the privileges of the House in making his charges through

Representative Blaine (*House Report No. 93,* 39 Cong., 1 Sess.; this report, partisan and unjudicial, did Fry great injustice). The controversy was evidenced in obstinate struggles in the Senate over his successive nominations to higher rank, but by Feb. 14, 1868, he had been confirmed successively major-general by brevet "for faithful, meritorious and distinguished services" as provost-marshal-general; colonel by brevet "for gallant and meritorious services at the battle of Bull Run (1st)"; and brigadier-general by brevet "for gallant and meritorious services at the battles of Shiloh, Tennessee, and Perryville, Kentucky"—all as of Mar. 13, 1865.

He became a colonel, in the department of the Adjutant-General, as of Mar. 3, 1875, and served thereafter as adjutant-general of the military divisions of the Pacific, South, and Atlantic. In 1875 he published *A Sketch of the Adjutant General's Department, United States Army 1775–1875, with Some General Remarks on its Province,* which was followed by *The History and Legal Effects of Brevets in the Armies of Great Britain and the United States* (1877) and *Army Sacrifices; or, Briefs from Official Pigeon-holes: Sketches . . . illustrating the Services and Experiences of the Regular Army of the United States on the Indian Frontier* (1879). On July 1, 1881, he was retired at his own request, that he might devote himself to literary pursuits. In addition to aiding greatly in the preparation of *Battles and Leaders of the Civil War,* he published articles in periodicals, notably the *North American Review,* and several volumes: *McDowell and Tyler in the Campaign of Bull Run, 1861* (1884); *Operations of the Army under Buell from June 10th to October 30th, 1862, and the "Buell Commission"* (1884); *New York and the Conscription of 1863; a Chapter in the History of the Civil War* (1885); *Military Miscellanies* (1889), containing some material also issued separately as pamphlets; and *The Conkling and Blaine-Fry Controversy, in 1866* (1893). He died in 1894 at Newport, R. I., and was buried in the churchyard of St. James the Less, Philadelphia. A just characterization of him is that of Nicolay and Hay (*Abraham Lincoln,* 1890, VII, 6): "not only an accomplished soldier but an executive officer of extraordinary tact, ability, and industry."

[Biographical sketches of Fry are found in E. Miner, *Past and Present of Greene County, Ill.* (1905), and *Hist. of Greene and Jersey Counties, Ill.* (1885); an outline of his military career appears in G. W. Cullum, *Biog. Reg. Officers and Grads. U. S. Mil. Acad.* (3rd ed., 1891), II, 314. For his war record see *Official Records (Army), Battles and Leaders of the Civil War* (4 vols., 1887–89), and his own writings. His reports as provost-marshal-general appear in the *Official Records,* 3 ser. III, 125–46, 1046–73, IV, 925–34, V, 486–89, 599–932. The *N. Y. Herald,* July 12, and *N. Y. Tribune,* July 13, 1894, contain obituaries.] F. S. P.

FRY, JOSHUA (*c.* 1700–May 31, 1754), professor of mathematics at the College of William and Mary, surveyor, and pioneer, was born in Crewkerne, Somerset, England, the son of Joseph Fry. The records of Oxford University state that he matriculated at Wadham College, on Mar. 31, 1718, at the age of eighteen. He came to Virginia before 1720, and was vestryman and magistrate in Essex County. Here he married Mary (Micou) Hill, a widow, the daughter of Paul Micou, a physician. In 1729 he was made master of the grammar school connected with William and Mary, and in 1731 he became professor of natural philosophy and mathematics in the College. According to a contemporary, Fry later removed "to the back settlements in order to raise a fortune for his family." In 1744 he was living in Goochland County on Hardware River near Carter's Bridge, between the present Charlottesville and Scottsville. When Albemarle County was formed from Goochland in 1745, Joshua Fry, Gentleman, was made first presiding justice of the county, justice in the court of chancery, county surveyor, and one of the first two representatives from the county in the colonial House of Burgesses, in which body he remained an active member until his death. He was also appointed in 1745 county lieutenant, a position of great honor and responsibility. In 1746 he aided, as the King's representative, in establishing the boundaries of Lord Fairfax's grant in the Northern Neck. Three years later, Fry and Peter Jefferson were commissioned to run part of the Virginia-Carolina boundary line.

In 1752 Fry was commissioned with three others to treat with the Six Nations, together with the Shawnee, Mingo, and Delaware tribes. They secured the timely and important treaty of Logstown (near the forks of the Ohio) in which these tribes promised not to molest the English settlers southeast of the Ohio. Fry was appointed commander-in-chief of the militia in the spring of 1754 to put an end to French encroachments at the head of the Ohio, but he died in camp at Wills's Creek (at the site of Cumberland, Md.) on May 31, and was succeeded by the second in command, George Washington. One of the greatest services which Fry rendered the colony was the making, in connection with his friend Peter Jefferson, of a "Map of the Inhabited Parts of Virginia" (1751), one of the first and most interesting of the maps of Virginia. Fry accompanied it with an account of frontier settlements and of western lands, which he drew chiefly from his unusually large collection of source material relating to New France, and from conversations with his neighbor, Dr. Thomas Walker.

[P. Slaughter, *Memoirs of Col. Joshua Fry* (1880), usually accurate, but brief and requiring supplementation; Jos. Foster, *Alumni Oxonienses . . . 1715–1886,* vol. II (1888); W. G. Stanard, "Virginians at Oxford," *Wm. and Mary Coll. Quart.,* Oct. 1892; "Journal of the Meetings of the President and Masters of Wm. and Mary College," *Ibid.,* Jan. 1894; Manuscript Faculty Minutes at Wm. and Mary; Fairfax Harrison, "The Virginians on the Ohio and Mississippi in 1742," in *Va. Mag. Hist. and Biog.,* Apr. 1922, and "The Northern Neck Maps of 1737–1747," in *Wm. and Mary Coll. Quart. Hist. Mag.,* Jan. 1924; P. L. Phillips, "Some Early Maps of Va.," in *Va. Mag. Hist. and Biog.,* July 1907, stating that the revised copy of Fry and Jefferson's map, by John Dalrymple, is the one usually consulted, and that the date 1775 on some copies is doubtless an error; *The Official Records of Robt. Dinwiddie* (2 vols., 1883–84), ed. by R. A. Brock, containing sketch of Fry by the editor and papers relating to his part in the French and Indian War; Order Books and other county records in clerk's office, Charlottesville, Va.; Albemarle County Will Book, No. 2, p. 15.]

R. L. M—n.

FRY, RICHARD (fl. 1731–1741), paper-maker, bookseller, came from London to Boston in 1731, under agreement with Samuel Waldo, a wealthy New England merchant, to manufacture paper (*New-England Historical and Genealogical Register,* April 1875, p. 159). For three years he waited for the mill, which according to Waldo's contract was to have been ready within ten months. During this period he sold stationers' supplies and printed and distributed 1,200 copies of the poems of Stephen Duck (Isaiah Thomas, *History of Printing in America,* 1874, II, 224). He also formulated an ambitious project for reprinting the *Spectator,* provided orders for 300 sets could be obtained. "Stationer, bookseller, paper maker, and rag merchant," was his own description of himself at this time. In 1734 Waldo leased to him a mill on the Stroudwater, not far from Portland, and here he went with his family and began making paper. Within two years he was in financial difficulties which led to protracted litigation. The first case brought against him was for £70 arrears in rent. For this sum Waldo seized his paper-making machinery, which was already mortgaged. He was thus rendered unable to manufacture more paper, his sole means of support, and was plunged into trouble with the mortgagee. He was probably in Boston jail by the end of 1736 or the beginning of 1737, and from there he appealed one case after another for five years (court files of Suffolk County, Mass.).

Discussions of currency were engrossing the attention of Boston merchants at this time, and Fry, during his incarceration, wrote a treatise on currency for the consideration of the General Court (1739). His scheme was of greater interest than the usual land-bank project of the time, since it involved the creation of a chain of factories which should provide New England with a wide variety of products. Indeed, it probably had more value as a suggestion for the industrial development of the colonies than as a solution of the monetary difficulties of Massachusetts. While in prison Fry also signed, and in all likelihood formulated, two vigorous petitions to the General Court, asking for better treatment of prisoners, and sent to that body a communication charging one of the keepers with circulating bills of the land bank. His death occurred before August 1745, for in that month his widow, Martha Brook Fry, petitioned to be made administrator of his estate. It is possible to think of him as a "scheming adventurer" (A. McFarland Davis, *Colonial Currency Reprints,* 1911, III, 282), with a delusion of persecution, but the meager facts lend themselves equally well to a more favorable interpretation. He was a man of great energy and of active and ingenious mind, who, given a little more capital or creditors with greater patience, might have become a New England entrepreneur of wealth and position.

[The facts of Fry's life can be pieced together from the court files of Suffolk County, 1736–41, and advertisements in the Boston papers: *Weekly Rehearsal,* May 1, 1732, *Boston News Letter,* Oct. 17, 1734, *Boston Gazette,* May 28, 1739, and others. His *Scheme for a Paper Currency* was reprinted by the Club for Colonial Reprints (Providence, 1908), and by the Prince Society, *Colonial Currency Reprints* (1911), III, 255–77, both edited by Andrew McFarland Davis, who has, in his notes and introduction, brought together practically all that is known of Fry's career. Of the original of his treatise there is a unique copy in the John Carter Brown Library. See also *New Eng. Hist. and Geneal. Reg.,* July 1919.]

E. D.

FRY, WILLIAM HENRY (Aug. 10, 1815–Dec. 21, 1864), composer, music-critic, journalist, was the son of William and Ann (Fleeson) Fry, both Philadelphians. The father, a man of considerable prominence, was the publisher of the *National Gazette*; the mother was a grand-daughter of Judge Plunkett Fleeson. He was born in Philadelphia, and educated in his native city and at Mount St. Mary's College, Emmittsburg, Md. Though he showed an aptitude for music early in life, it attracted no especial attention until he taught himself to play the piano by listening to the lessons of an elder brother. He was then placed under the best teachers and began the study of harmony and counterpoint under the able musician, Leopold Meignen, a graduate of the Paris Conservatory. He composed his first overture when he was fourteen and when he was twenty the Philadelphia Philharmonic Society performed one of his later overtures and awarded him a gold medal. On June 4, 1845, he presented his first opera, *Leonora,* which is known as the first publicly performed grand opera written by a native American. The libretto, based on *The Lady of Lyons,* was written by his brother, Joseph R. Fry. It had several successful performances by the Seguin company, in Philadelphia at the Chestnut Street Theatre, and at the New York Academy of Music. In both places it ran for some time. Thirteen years later, in March 1858, it was revived in New York with an Italian translation and was produced under the direction of Carl Anschütz, with an excellent cast of Italian singers. The complete work was never published, but airs from it show traces of Irish melodies and are reminiscent of Donizetti and Balfe. A well-known drinking song is its most interesting number. He also wrote a few songs, piano pieces, and "chamber quartets," but his most important instrumental compositions were his four symphonies: *The Breaking Heart*; *A Day in the Country*; *Santa Claus, or the Christmas Symphony*; and *Childe Harold,* performed in New York and on tour by Jullien's Orchestra, brought to America in 1853.

Fry never followed music as a profession; in 1839 he entered the field of journalism in his father's office, and in 1844 he became editor of the Philadelphia *Public Ledger.* From 1846 to 1852 he was in Europe as Paris and London correspondent of the *New York Tribune,* the Philadelphia *Ledger,* and other newspapers. In 1852 he returned to New York as editorial writer and music-editor of the *Tribune.* He also made many political speeches, wrote on economic problems, and in 1861 received an appointment as secretary of legation at Turin. He retained his interest in music all his life, however, and continued to produce musical works and to give lectures on musical history. In 1855 he composed a *Stabat Mater,* and in 1863 completed his second opera, *Notre Dame de Paris.* The latter was successfully produced in Philadelphia, under Thomas, and later in New York, but the text, written by his brother Joseph, was unpoetic and rather uninteresting. With *Leonora,* it attained merely ephemeral success. Both operas contained ingratiating melodies, strongly imitative of French and Italian models, but Fry lacked dramatic force. While he can scarcely be considered a great composer, he was the first successful American opera composer, and his fluent pen and ready speech made him a power in furthering American music. He died in Santa Cruz, West Indies.

[Henry Simpson, *The Lives of Eminent Philadelphians* (1859); W. G. Armstrong, *A Record of the Opera in Philadelphia* (1884); L. C. Elson, *The Hist. of Am. Music* (rev. ed., 1925); F. L. Ritter, *Music in America* (1883); W. S. B. Mathews, *A Hundred Years of Music in America* (1889); Theo. Baker, *A Biog. Dict. of Musicians* (1900); *Dwight's Jour. of Music,* Apr. 6, 1861; *Musical Digest,* June 1930; *Pa. Mag. of Hist. and Biog.,* Apr. 1920; information as to certain facts from Thos. Ridgway, Philadelphia, Pa.]

F. L. G. C.

FRYE, JOSEPH (Mar. 8/19, 1711/12–July 25, 1794), soldier, was the ninth of the thirteen children of Sergeant John and Tabitha (Farnam) Frye of Andover, Mass., where the family had long been of local prominence. He began his military career, for which he is chiefly distinguished, in February 1744/5 as ensign in Hale's 5th Massachusetts Regiment which took part in the capture of Louisburg. From March 1747/48 until June 1749 he served with the rank of captain. During 1754 he was a lieutenant-colonel in Winslow's Kennebec expedition (*New-England Historical and Genealogical Register,* July 1873). Still with Winslow, he was a major in the expedition planned by Gov. Shirley which expelled a portion of the Acadians in 1755, performing the unpleasant duty of burning houses and forcing the rebellious settlers to submit to English rule (*Ibid.,* October 1879). In 1757, after Lord Loudoun had set his hand to military affairs in North America, Frye was commissioned to raise 1,800 troops to reinforce Gen. Webb for the proposed attack on Crown Point. When the English attempted to relieve the inadequate force within Fort William Henry in this campaign, the French and Indians under Montcalm surrounded both the fort and the relief forces, compelling Lieut.-Col. Munroe, Frye's superior in command, to surrender, Aug. 9, 1757. The French were unable to control their Indian allies, who, mad for blood and plunder, massacred many of the disarmed troops. Frye, himself, after hand-to-hand combat, reached Fort Edward naked, half-starved, and half-crazed. Prevented by the terms of the capitulation from serving for eighteen months, Frye did not reënlist until March 1759. From then to the close of 1760 he was the commanding officer at Fort Cumberland in Acadia. The chief problems of this routine service were feeding the destitute inhabitants who submitted to English control, disciplining his disorderly troops, and finally quelling an actual mutiny (Massachusetts Archives, LXXX, 395, 397).

On Mar. 3, 1762, in response to his petition, the Massachusetts General Court granted to Frye a township of land in the Maine district, and in 1770 he moved with his family from Andover to the new settlement, where he opened a store. The town was incorporated in January 1777 as Fryeburg, in honor of the grantee. He himself kept ten of the sixty rights and acted as proprietor's clerk from June 23, 1766, to Sept. 15, 1777. On

June 21, 1775, the Provincial Congress had appointed him major-general of Massachusetts militia. He served in this capacity at Falmouth from November to Jan. 10, 1776, when he was appointed (probably due to the influence of Gen. Artemas Ward) a brigadier-general in the Continental Army. He resigned on account of infirmities, Apr. 23, 1776. While a resident of Andover, Frye was representative to the General Court, 1751–55, 1762–63, 1764–65. He favored the separation of Maine from Massachusetts, and was a delegate from Fryeburg to the Portland convention of September 1786, which met to consider the measure. He married Mehitable Poor of Andover, Mar. 20/31, 1732/33.

[Mass. Archives; S. L. Bailey, *Hist. Sketches of Andover* (1880); *Maine Hist. Soc. Colls.*, vol. IV (1856), 2 ser. vol. II (1891); J. E. Baxter, *Doc. Hist. of Me.*, vols. XII–XVIII (1908–14); E. F. Barker, *Frye Geneal.* (1920); *The Centennial Celebration of the Settlement of Fryeburg, Me.* (1864); *Post* (Fryeburg, Me.), Nov. 9, 1915, June 6, 1916; *News* (Bethel, Me.), Dec. 24, 1898. See the *Port Folio*, May 1819, for Frye's experiences following the surrender of Fort William Henry.]
R. E. M.

FRYE, WILLIAM PIERCE (Sept. 2, 1831–Aug. 8, 1911), representative, and senator from Maine, was a prominent figure in the group of members of Congress from that state who almost dominated the federal government during the late years of the nineteenth century. The earliest ancestor of the family to reach America seems to have come from Hampshire, England, to Massachusetts in 1638. A great-great-grandfather of William Frye, Gen. Joseph Frye [*q.v.*], served as an officer in the French and Indian War and the Revolution. The father of William was Col. John M. Frye, one of the early settlers of Lewiston, and his mother was Alice M. Davis. It was in Lewiston that the future senator was born. He received his education in the public schools and in Bowdoin College. Frye seems to have been more fond of sport and of making friends than of serious application to study, so that he graduated (1850) in the third quarter of a class numbering thirty-two. Later, however, he became a member of the board of trustees of Bowdoin, and was honored with its LL.D. in 1889. On graduating from college, Frye entered upon the study of law in the office of William Pitt Fessenden, and engaged in practise in Rockland, Me., and later in Lewiston. While in Rockland he married, on Feb. 27, 1853, Caroline Frances Spear, who died on Dec. 21, 1900. Their family numbered three daughters. As a lawyer, Frye was described as possessing a capacity for grasping the essential elements of a case, an attractive manner and physique, and a well-modulated voice, together with imagination, earnestness, and courage. Such qualities in a Maine lawyer pointed almost inevitably to a political career, and in fact political offices soon followed in rapid succession.

He became a member of the state legislature in 1861, serving also in 1862 and 1867, and acting as a presidential elector in 1864. He was mayor of Lewiston in 1866–67, and attorney-general of Maine from 1867 to 1869. He was elected to the national House of Representatives in 1871. He was a delegate to the Republican National Conventions of 1876 and 1880, and served also on the Republican national executive committee during those campaigns, as he had in 1872. Of his ten years of service in the House, James G. Blaine wrote: "His rank as a debater was soon established, and he exhibited a degree of care and industry in committee work not often found among representatives who so readily command the attention of the House" (*Twenty Years of Congress,* II, 510). In the Forty-sixth Congress, serving with Garfield as a minority member of the committee on rules, he contributed to the notable simplification and codification of the rules of the House effected in 1880 (D. S. Alexander, *History and Procedure of the House of Representatives,* 1916, pp. 193–95). His capacity for debate, which Blaine noticed, was likewise observed by many others, and Frye became one of the most sought-for campaign speakers of his time.

On Mar. 15, 1881, he was chosen a senator from Maine to succeed Blaine, who had resigned to enter Garfield's cabinet. From that time until his death, Frye remained a member of the Senate. Accounts of his work in that body, written by members of both parties, scarcely differ in their general import. He was a strict Republican, holding firmly to the primary importance of a protective tariff. He was conservative in regard to government regulation of industry, and was commonly accounted one of the "Old Guard," as that term was used during the administrations of Roosevelt and Taft. He cared little for society, being, as Senator Nelson of Minnesota asserted, "emphatically a man of work." As a member of the committees on foreign relations and appropriations, and particularly as chairman for many years of the committee on commerce, Frye was one of the "wheel-horses" of the Senate. He was the author of several and the proponent of many other measures aimed at the revival of the American merchant marine. The rejection of the subsidy policy was the greatest disappointment of his public career.

He probably made his deepest impress on the history of his time during the McKinley administration. He had long been a thorough-going expansionist, anxious to acquire Caribbean territory, a transisthmian canal, and outposts in the Pacific. Some of his utterances in the period preceding the Spanish-American War were ill-advised for a member of the foreign relations committee and led Godkin, editor of the New York *Nation,* who hated Jingoes and Jingoism, to declare on one occasion that he had the same standards of international morality as William Walker or Captain Kidd (*Nation,* Feb. 11, 1897; see also Mar. 28, 1895). He was an important factor in securing the passage of the Hawaiian annexation resolution and an earnest supporter of McKinley's war policy. At the close of the war with Spain, Frye was placed by McKinley on the peace commission which met at Paris. During the resulting negotiations, he joined with Senator C. K. Davis and Whitelaw Reid in urging the acquisition of the entire Philippine archipelago, although the remaining members of the commission, W. R. Day and Judge George Gray, opposed such action. The advice of Frye and his associates was followed by the administration. Owing to the death of Vice-President Hobart during McKinley's first term, and the elevation of Vice-President Roosevelt to the executive chair in 1901, Frye as president *pro tempore* was the permanent presiding officer of the Senate for a period of about five years. During this time, he so commended himself to both parties that the Democrats initiated the movement which led to the presentation of a silver loving-cup to him at the close of the Fifty-sixth Congress. His death occurred in Lewiston on Aug. 8, 1911.

[See "William Pierce Frye. Memorial Addresses Delivered in the Senate and the House of Representatives," *Sen. Doc. 1145,* 62 Cong., 3 Sess. (1913); W. H. White, Jr., "Senator Wm. P. Frye," in *Just Maine Folks* (1924); J. G. Blaine, *Twenty Years of Cong.,* vol. II (1886); E. N. Dingley, *The Life and Times of Nelson Dingley, Jr.* (1902); *Independent,* Dec. 30, 1909; N. Y. *Sun,* Aug. 9, 1911; *Lewiston Evening Jour.,* Aug. 9, 10, 11, 1911; *Outlook,* Aug. 19, 1911; E. F. Barker, *Frye Geneal.* (1920). Date of birth is taken from *Who's Who in America,* 1899–1911; the year 1830 is given by many other authorities.] C. R. L.

FUERTES, ESTEVAN ANTONIO (May 10, 1838–Jan. 16, 1903), engineer, educator, was born in San Juan, Porto Rico, the son of Estevan and Demetria (Charbonnier) Fuertes. His father was a distinguished governmental official prominent in the social life of the island. The boy was given a good education for the times, first in the local schools, then at the University of Salamanca in Spain where he received a Ph.D. degree, and finally at the Rensselaer Polytechnic Institute in this country where he received an engineering degree in 1861, when he was twenty-three years old. Returning to Porto Rico in the same year, he was for two years an engineer in the public works department of the island, building roads, bridges, harbor improvements, and water-works. He then returned to this country and for six years was an engineer of the Croton Aqueduct Board under Alfred Craven, leaving because his sense of honesty and professional ethics would not allow him to acquiesce in the practises of the "Tweed ring." From 1869 to 1873 he engaged in private practise interrupted in 1870–71 when he went as engineer-in-chief with the exploratory expedition to Nicaragua. In 1873 he accepted the position as dean of the department of civil engineering at Cornell University. His acceptance was the result of a deliberate determination to devote himself to the upbuilding of a great technical school, and though the conditions at the University were disheartening enough to test the character of the bravest, he struggled valiantly through the long hard years that followed. Cornell was then at low ebb; the engineering department was housed in two rooms over the veterinary department, from which nauseating smells continually arose. Fuertes taught all the subjects in the department except mathematics and descriptive geometry. The time was ripe, however, for his leadership. With the recognition of the value of scholastic and scientific training in engineering, the drawbacks of the apprentice method were being realized, and Fuertes, awake to the situation, was resolved to put this vocation on an equal footing with the other learned professions. The course of training which he devised involved a great deal of laboratory work and perhaps it was his insistence on a judicious combination of practise and theory which was his greatest contribution to the educational methods of the time. He installed laboratories in all possible subjects, not only in chemistry and physics, surveying and astronomy, but also in hydraulics, bridge construction, and cement work. His own dexterity and precision were extraordinary, and for many years he personally made regular star observations by which the university tower clock was accurately controlled. His relations with the students were both severe and friendly. The poor and careless student was vigorously rated for his deficiencies, then cheered and encouraged. The influence of his personality, his idealism, and his enthusiasm was very widely felt. His early cultural training never left him. Always he was socially minded, affable, extremely courteous, and at the same time sensitive beyond the understanding of most of his associates. Due in part also to his nationality, he was most temperamental, quick-tempered as well as penitent and generous. He resigned from his active work on account of ill health in November 1902 and died in January 1903. He was married, on Dec. 21, 1860, to Mary Stone Perry of Troy, N. Y. He had two daughters and three sons, one of whom was Louis Agassiz Fuertes [*q.v.*].

[*Who's Who in America*, 1901–02; R. H. Thurston, in *Science*, Feb. 20, 1903; J. H. Selkreg, *Landmarks of Tompkins County, N. Y.* (1894); *Cornell Alumni News*, Nov. 12, 1902; Jan. 21, 1903; W. T. Hewett, *Cornell Univ.: A Hist.* (3 vols., 1905); *N. Y. Times*, Jan. 17, 1903.]

H. N. O.

FUERTES, LOUIS AGASSIZ (Feb. 7, 1874–Aug. 22, 1927), artist-naturalist, was born at Ithaca, N. Y. His father, Estevan Antonio Fuertes [*q.v.*], was a descendant of a prominent Spanish family. His mother, Mary Stone Perry Fuertes, of Dutch and English ancestry, was born in Troy, N. Y. His talent in drawing and his love of birds began to show at an early age and developed without particular encouragement from parents or friends. By the time he was eight or nine years old he had definitely focused his attention upon painting birds, and when he was fourteen, according to an autobiographical sketch, his career was definitely settled. He received his education in the public schools of Ithaca, N. Y., then in 1892 accompanied his parents to Europe and spent the year in a preparatory school in Zurich, Switzerland. On his return he entered Cornell University and was graduated with the class of 1897. In 1894, while on a glee club trip to Washington, D. C., he met Elliott Coues [*q.v.*] and showed him some of his paintings. The encouragement which he received from the ornithologist was apparently a deciding factor in his career. Following his graduation from Cornell he spent a year studying with Abbott H. Thayer, which improved his technique very materially, and with him and his son, Gerald Thayer, he went to Florida in the spring of 1898. This was the first of a series of expeditions which widened his knowledge of the birds of North America. In 1899 he went to Alaska with the famed Harriman expedition, and two years later he visited western Texas and New Mexico with a party from the United States Biological Survey. With Dr. F. M. Chapman, curator of birds at the American Museum in New York City, between 1902 and 1913 he visited the Bahamas, the Pacific Coast, the prairies of Saskatchewan and the Canadian Rockies, the Cuthbert Rookery in Florida, Yucatan and eastern Mexico, and Colombia, South America. In addition to these expeditions Fuertes visited Jamaica on his wedding journey in 1904; the Magdalen Islands and Bird Rock in 1909 with Leonard Cutler Sanford; and after a dozen years spent mostly in his studio at Ithaca, in 1926–27 he made an expedition to little-known parts of Abyssinia with Dr. Wilfred H. Osgood for the Field Museum of Natural History in Chicago. From 1923 to 1927 he was lecturer in ornithology at Cornell University.

Fuertes was a tireless worker in the field and never lost an opportunity to add to his collection of birds or sketches. At the time of his death he left a collection of some 3,500 beautifully prepared bird skins and over a thousand field and studio sketches of more than 400 different kinds of birds. His greatest collection, however, was the series of mental images of each bird which seemed to be indelibly impressed upon his mind with all the accuracy of a photographic plate. When examining a bird, his concentration was supreme; he was oblivious to everything about him; and during these moments, apparently, details of pose and expression were so fixed in his mind that years afterwards he could reproduce them with his pencil and brush without the slightest hesitation. His paintings, which illustrate most of the leading bird books published between 1896 and 1927, are characterized by a beauty of draftsmanship and a devotion to truth which are manifested not only in the accuracy of every detail of plumage and form, but in the perfection attained in reproducing the characteristic attitudes and expressions of each species. On June 2, 1904, Fuertes was married to Margaret F. Sumner of Ithaca, by whom he had two children. He was killed in a grade-crossing accident in 1927.

[F. M. Chapman, "Louis Agassiz Fuertes—Painter of Bird Portraits," the *Am. Museum Jour.*, May 1915 (reprinted in *Bird-Lore*, July–Aug. 1915), and "Louis Agassiz Fuertes," *Bird-Lore*, Sept.–Oct. 1927; A. A. Allen, "The Passing of a Great Teacher: Louis Agassiz Fuertes," *Bird-Lore*, Sept.–Oct. 1927; F. M. Chapman, "In Memoriam: Louis Agassiz Fuertes, 1874–1927," the *Auk*, Jan. 1928, containing a list of books illustrated by Fuertes; Harry Harris, "Examples of Recent Am. Bird Art," the *Condor*, Sept. 1926. There is a collection of letters, journals, and notes, as well as a representative collection of paintings by Louis Agassiz Fuertes, in the Fuertes Memorial Room, McGraw Hall, Cornell University.]

A. A. A.

FULLER, ANDREW S. (Aug. 3, 1828–May 4, 1896), horticulturist, editor, was born and brought up in a fruit-growing region. His parents lived at Utica, N. Y., when he was born, but soon moved to a small farm near Barre, N. Y. Andrew attended country school, but also did the usual chores which fell to a farmer's boy. In 1846 the family moved to Milwaukee, Wis., where he learned the carpenter's trade. With a natural interest in the growing of plants, he soon began to specialize in the construction of greenhouses. In 1851 he was married to Jennie Clippens. In 1855 he became manager of the greenhouses of William R. Prince of Flushing, Long Island. This position he held for two years; then, anxious to enter business for himself, he moved to Brooklyn and began the culture of small fruits, specializing in the improvement of the strawberry by cross-fertilization and selection. In this work he was a pioneer. Almost immediately he began writing on horticulture for *Life Illustrated*, the *New York Tribune*, and other publications. The *Tribune* distributed 300,000 of Fuller's strawberry plants as circulation premiums, helping to establish him financially as well as in reputation.

While living in Brooklyn he began to write his first book, *The Illustrated Strawberry Culturist* (1862). In 1860 he moved to Ridgewood, N. J., where he had purchased a tract of waste land. This he improved and used largely for experimental purposes, but he continued to write for various agricultural and horticultural papers. During 1866 and 1867 he was editor of *Woodward's Record of Horticulture*. He also continued his work on the *New York Tribune* until 1868, when he became agricultural editor of the newly established *Weekly Sun*, which position he held until 1894. On the *Sun* he was responsible for the distribution of seed potatoes with subscriptions. During his early years at Ridgewood he wrote *The Grape Culturist* (1864), *The Forest Tree Culturist* (1866), and *The Small Fruit Culturist* (1867). The last, the best of his works, was translated into German and published at Weimar in 1868. In 1871 Fuller became associate editor of *Moore's Rural New-Yorker*, later simply the *Rural New-Yorker*, and acted in this capacity for five years. In April 1876 he became part owner and editor-in-chief of the paper, but dropped these connections within a year. During his term of service on this publication his New Jersey farm was popularly referred to as "the *Rural New-Yorker's* trial grounds." Fuller was one of the founders of the New Jersey State Horticultural Society in 1875 (Carl R. Woodward, *The Development of Agriculture in New Jersey, 1640–1880*, 1926, p. 235), as well as a member of numerous other organizations. Meanwhile he continued his writing and his experimental work, particularly with fruits. His *Practical Forestry* appeared in 1884, *The Propagation of Plants* in 1887, and new editions of his other books at intervals. He constantly improved his own farm, adorning it with practically all the trees and shrubs native to the region and many others besides. He accumulated a large horticultural library and made extensive mineralogical and entomological collections. His collection of *Coleoptera* became eventually one of the best in the United States, and for them he built a special house. He was also a student of prehistoric American pottery. During the last ten years of his life he devoted much of his time to assembling data for *The Nut Culturist*, which he believed would be his best work and which was published (1896) shortly before his death. With characteristic energy he continued to write for various agricultural and horticultural periodicals through the latter years of his life. At the time of his death he was staff writer for the *Florists' Exchange*, the *American Agriculturist*, and the *American Gardener*. He died of neuralgia of the heart after a very brief illness. Fuller had keen powers of observation and a natural aptitude for systematic information. His writing was always vigorous, direct, and interesting.

[Obituaries appeared in the N. Y. *Sun*, and *N. Y. Tribune*, May 5, 1896, *Rural New-Yorker* and *Am. Agriculturist*, May 16, 1896. There is a sketch of Fuller by F. M. Hexamer in L. H. Bailey's *Cyc. of Am. Hort.*, III (1906), 616.] N. A. C.

FULLER, GEORGE (Jan. 17, 1822–Mar. 21, 1884), painter, was born in Deerfield, Mass., where his father, Aaron Fuller, a farmer of English descent, described as a serene, kindly man, diligent, and sufficiently prosperous, had taken for his second wife Fanny Negus of Petersham, Mass., who came of Welsh stock. George Fuller was the first of several children by this second marriage. Mrs. Fuller's grandfather was an officer in the Revolutionary army; her father, a lawyer, was an amateur painter; one of her brothers was a painter by profession; and her younger sister was a miniaturist. She herself, a sanguine, impulsive, emotional type, for a time stoutly opposed her eldest son's wish to become a painter; while her husband meant him to be a business man. Consequently when the boy was thirteen years old, he was taken to Boston, to work in a grocery. Finding this occupation irksome, he undertook the equally distasteful trade of selling shoes; but after a month or two he returned to the Deerfield farm, to which he continued to return after many wanderings throughout his life. About a year later, he joined a party of young men who were going to Illinois to make surveys for a new railroad. This time he was away from home about two years. His letters to his parents told of many adventures, hazards, and picturesque episodes, and abounded in comments upon men and events that showed unusual discernment for a lad in his teens. Returning to his home at the age of sixteen, he resumed his studies in the Deerfield Academy, but found time out of school hours to make many essays in painting, mainly in portraiture. In the words of his biographer, William Dean Howells, he was at that time "an ardent and susceptible youth, falling in love right and left, and full of a joyous life, at once buoyant and tranquil."

When it became evident that his artistic ambition was to be seriously reckoned with, he was permitted in 1841 to accompany his half-brother Augustus, a deaf-mute who painted miniatures, on a tour through northern New York for the purpose of painting portraits at fifteen to twenty dollars apiece. This expedition proved fairly successful. After it came a return to work on the farm. The following winter, 1841–42, the paternal opposition to his choice of a profession having been overcome by his persistency, he went to Albany, N. Y., to begin the serious study of painting in the studio of Henry Kirke Brown [*q.v.*], the sculptor, to whose instruction, counsel, and encouragement Fuller owed much. After nine months in Albany, he went to Boston to continue his studies during the two succeeding winters at the Boston Artists' Association. The summers he spent at home, helping on the farm. In 1843 he wrote to Brown: "I have concluded to see nature for myself, through the eyes of no one else, and put my trust in God, awaiting the result" (C. H. Caffin, *post,* p. 104). Fuller shared a studio in Boston with Thomas Ball [*q.v.*], the sculptor, on the top floor of 17½ Tremont Row. "We were then struggling after Allston's color," wrote Ball, years afterward; "I think the effect of his then admiration for that great artist can be traced in all Mr. Fuller's works." A great event in 1846 was the sale of his first imaginative picture, "A Nun at Confession," for the sum of six dollars. In 1847, at the solicitation of his friend and mentor, Brown, he went to New York and entered the life class in the school of the National Academy of Design. For the greater part of the next ten years he lived in New York, though three of the winters were passed in the South, at Charleston, Mobile, Augusta, and other places, where he painted a few portraits and made studies of negro life, some of which were utilized in his later work. He also lived for nearly a year in Philadelphia. His most intimate artist-friends in New York were Daniel Huntington, Sandford R. Gifford, Henry Peters Gray, J. Q. A. Ward, and the Cheney brothers. In 1857 he was elected an associate of the National Academy.

In 1859, the death of his father and the duty of supporting the surviving members of the family recalled him to the farm. Before settling down as a farmer at the old home, however, he was given his first opportunity to make a tour of Europe. In January 1860, with his friends William James Stillman and William H. Ames, he left New York in a sailing vessel bound for Liverpool. The voyage was tedious and stormy. In the five months that followed Fuller visited London, Paris, Florence, Rome, Venice, and other art capitals, making many sketches in the museums, and finding special pleasure in the works of the Venetians. In London he met Dante Gabriel Rossetti and Holman Hunt. His letters of this time do not throw any new light on the old masters, but they are interesting as the first impressions of a sensitive observer. He returned to the United States in the summer of 1860; and a year later married Agnes Higginson of Cambridge, Mass., and brought his bride to the Deerfield homestead. There he took seriously to farm work, and roamed no more for some fifteen years, almost forgotten save by a few old friends. They alone knew that he still painted in the intervals of farming, in an old carriage house converted into a studio. His subjects were portraits of his family and friends, landscapes, and, occasionally, ideal figures such as were later to be associated with his name. He was feeling his way in solitude; gradually evolving his own method of expression.

For a time his management of the farm promised to be successful. Many improvements were introduced. Tobacco culture was begun with excellent prospects of profit. A disastrous turn of the tide came in 1875, when the fall of prices forced him into insolvency. In this emergency there was nothing left to him but his art, and he resolved to capitalize it. He finished about a dozen pictures during the winter of 1875–76, sent them to Boston, where, in the spring, the first exhibition of his works was opened. His success was instantaneous and complete. A new chapter in his life was opened, and from this time forth he had no difficulty in finding buyers for whatever he painted. He now established himself in Boston once more, at the outset taking a studio at 12 West St., and moving a year or two later to 149-A Tremont St., in the Lawrence Building. In 1878 he made his reappearance at the National Academy exhibition with the "Turkey Pasture in Kentucky" and "By the Wayside"; in 1879 he sent to the Academy two pictures, "And She Was a Witch" and "The Romany Girl"; in 1880, "The Quadroon" and a portrait of a boy; and in 1881, "Winifred Dysart." To the exhibitions of the Society of American Artists he sent "Evening-Lorette," "Nydia," and "Priscilla Fauntleroy." Three of his paintings were seen at the exhibition of the Boston Art Club in 1882. He was now producing his best work, not only with the joy of creation, but with the satisfaction of knowing that he was understood. The tide of popular approval continued to rise; with the advent of "Winifred Dysart" and "The Romany Girl" it reached flood stage. The painter was hailed as a master of rare distinction; his pictures were called painted poetry. He had, in fact, made a special appeal to the latent idealism of the people, and the response was phenomenal.

His masterpiece, "Winifred Dysart," was bought by J. Montgomery Sears of Boston, and is now the property of the Worcester Art Museum. Finished in 1881, it was first seen in a Boston dealer's gallery, and then at the National Academy, where it created a sensation. "A dreamy picture, full of twilight haze, out of which looks a sweet-faced girl," was the simple description of it in Mr. Kurtz's *Academy Notes.* "No more fascinating, haunting, individual figure has come from a contemporary hand," wrote Mrs. Van Rensselaer (*post,* p. 207); "it had no prototype or inspiration in the work of any other brush." So welcome are the authentic marks of poetic feeling and imagination in a work of art, the chorus of praise became general; critics let themselves go and were lyrical in their enthusiasm. If all this was heartening for the artist, a rich recompense for so many years of patient striving, it was also one of the most significant manifestations of the sound acumen of his public, wholly unused as it was to such things in modern pictorial art as the elusive and mystical qualities of Fuller's work, but, as it proved, ready and eager for them. The prompt recognition of a personal note so rare and delicate was therefore not only Fuller's triumph, but a historic demonstration of zeal in the cause of moral and, as it were, spiritual beauty—those outward and visible signs of an inward and spiritual grace which relate Fuller to such remote predecessors as Botticelli and Memling. Such art as this connotes nobility and purity of character in the artist. Fuller was no ordinary man. "His heart was sound, his mind was clear, and his taste was sure," wrote Samuel Isham. That his was a singularly fine and sweet nature is the testimony of all who knew him. Extremely simple, modest, and unaffected, he was full of kindness and charity. He never uttered a word in disparagement of a colleague. If he could not praise, he held his peace. His influence was wholesome. When success and renown came to him, he was not in the least puffed up, but remained the same unassuming and gracious gentleman he had always been.

In the spring of 1884 another exhibition of his paintings was opened at the old Williams & Everett galleries in Boston. Twenty works were shown, the most important of the new canvases being "Arethusa," his last picture and the only nude subject he ever painted. It represented the Nereid celebrated in Shelley's poem, who changed herself into a fountain to escape the importunities of her lover Alpheus. This work now belongs to the Museum of Fine Arts, Boston. Another important painting was "Fidalma," a character in George Eliot's *Spanish Gypsy.* There were also "Nydia," the "Girl and Calf," and a number of portraits. While this exhibition was in progress, the artist was stricken suddenly with pneumonia, and died, Mar. 21, 1884, at his home in Brookline. He was buried at Deerfield. A few weeks later a memorial exhibition was held at the Museum of Fine Arts, Boston, containing no less than 175 paintings, an almost complete collection of his pictures. In 1886 a handsome memorial volume was published, containing a biography by William Dean Howells, an estimate by Francis D. Millet, reminiscences by William James Stillman and Thomas Ball, a sonnet by John G. Whittier, appreciations by John J. Enneking and William Baxter Closson, a list of the artist's works, and a number of illustrations, including a portrait of Fuller engraved by G. Kruell, "The Romany Girl" engraved by Timothy Cole, "Winifred Dysart" and three other subjects engraved by W. B. Closson, and etchings of Fuller's home and studio in Deerfield by Edmund H. Garrett, all the plates being printed by hand on Japanese paper.

[The memorial volume published in 1886, *George Fuller, His Life and Works,* edited by Josiah B. Millet, is the chief source of information, and is especially notable for Mr. Howells's intimate biographical sketch, with copious passages from the artist's correspondence. Next in value comes a chapter on Fuller in Mrs. Schuyler Van Rensselaer's *Six Portraits* (1889), pp. 190–236, one of the best examples of her critical appraisals. A well-considered appreciation is to be found in Charles H. Caffin's *Am. Masters of Painting* (1902), pp. 101–11. See also a brief chapter in Royal Cortissoz, *Am. Artists* (1923), pp. 57–66; Samuel Isham, *The Hist. of Am. Painting* (1927), pp. 390–94; Charles De Kay, "George Fuller, Painter," in *Mag. of Art,* Aug. 1889; F. D. Millet, "George Fuller" (published anonymously, but subsequently reprinted with the author's name in the memorial volume), in *Harper's Monthly,* Sept. 1884; Sidney Dickinson, "Geo. Fuller," in the *Bay State Monthly,* June 1884; W. H. Fuller, *Geneal. of Some Descendants of Thomas Fuller of Woburn* (1919).]
W. H. D.

FULLER, HENRY BLAKE (Jan. 9, 1857–July 28, 1929), novelist, was born in Chicago and educated in the city schools. His father, George Wood Fuller, cashier of the Home National Bank, was originally a New Yorker and his mother, Mary Josephine Sanford, came from Bridgeport, Conn. After a brief business experience he spent a full year in Europe, taking his place in the succession of Americans from

Irving onward whose enjoyment of European culture was heightened by the contrast between old Europe and new America. He made European sojourns, usually of six months each, in 1883, 1886, 1892, 1894, and 1896. In the eleven-year period beginning with 1890 Fuller published eight volumes: *The Chevalier of Pensieri-Vani* (1890, issued under the pseudonym of Stanton Page), *The Chatelaine of La Trinité* (1892), *The Cliff-Dwellers* (1893), *With the Procession* (1895), *The Puppet-Booth; Twelve Plays* (1896), *From the Other Side; Stories of Transatlantic Travel* (1898), *The Last Refuge; a Sicilian Romance* (1900), and *Under the Skylights* (1901). In these volumes there is a clear oscillation between cultured and courtly Europe and the raw Middle West. James G. Huneker (*Unicorns,* 1917, p. 84) speaks of him as the one "felicitous example of cosmopolitanism" to be classed with Henry James; but it was the Middle West to which he belonged and to which he was bound to return. There were first two narratives located in Italy, then two novels of Chicago, a sort of pivot in the little collection of plays, two more books with a European background and a somewhat dispirited return to the United States. Throughout his career he was a resident of Chicago, never, apparently, attempting to alienate himself from his native city; and he made no visits to Europe between 1896 and his final brief trip in 1924. The closeness of his connection with Chicago was shown in his cooperative literary activities. From the establishment of *Poetry: A Magazine of Verse* in 1912 to his death, he was a member of the advisory committee, reading copy, writing reviews, and frequently helping in the routine work of issuing the numbers. Before this, in 1901–02, he helped shape the book-review section of the *Chicago Evening Post,* and he maintained from 1911 to 1913 a somewhat looser connection with the *Chicago Record-Herald* as an editorial writer.

With the turn of the century the world seems to have been too much with this cosmopolite. The events of the Spanish-American War and the development of American imperialism horrified him. In 1899, unable to secure a publisher, he privately printed *The New Flag,* a violent attack on President McKinley and his policies. *Under the Skylights* (1901) turned from the promise of Chicago's vigor to the enervating influence of philistinism on potential art. After a long interval there appeared in 1908 *Waldo Trench, and Others; Stories of Americans in Italy,* a series of mocking satires on negligible people. His *Lines Long and Short* (1917), biographical sketches in various rhythms, was directed by name at various figures in American public life. Having none of his earlier suavity of tone, it was as mordant as Edgar Lee Masters's *Spoon River Anthology,* published two years earlier.

From the entrance of the United States into the World War until the end of his career, Fuller was content to lead the quiet life of a semi-recluse bachelor, seen here and there in the neighborhood of the University of Chicago, yet always shyly aloof. The last six months of his life were marked by an extraordinary return of creative energy. Stimulated by some of his friends, he undertook to resume the thread of his first book. In January 1929 he wrote and retranscribed a volume of over 50,000 words, with the title *Gardens of this World,* reviving some of the characters of his earliest work and introducing, in his own words, a lot of "new folks." In February, he swung to the Chicago type of story, and between then and April completed a somewhat longer work, *Not on the Screen,* a combined picture of social life and satire of screen scenario construction. In the following summer he was stricken with a fatal illness, only six weeks before the announced publication of *Gardens* and before he had even had the opportunity to see the first proofs of *Not on the Screen,* which was published in the winter (1930) following his death.

[Recollections of Fuller's friends have been gathered into a volume by Anna Morgan with the title, *Tributes to Henry B. from Friends* (1929). There is a check-list of his works in *Gardens of this World* (1929). See also "Fuller of Chicago," by R. M. Lovett, in the *New Republic,* Aug. 21, 1929; "Henry Blake Fuller: Civilized Chicagoan," by Victor Schultz, in the *Bookman,* Sept. 1929; Hamlin Garland, *Roadside Meetings* (1930); *Who's Who in America,* 1924–25; *Chicago Daily Tribune,* July 29, and *N. Y. Times,* July 29, Aug. 1, 1929.]

P. H. B.

FULLER, HIRAM (Sept. 6, 1814–Nov. 19, 1880), journalist, was born in Halifax, Plymouth County, Mass., the second of the eight children of Thomas and Sally (Sturtevant) Fuller, and the seventh in descent from Samuel Fuller, a physician, who emigrated from Norfolk to Holland in 1608, came to Plymouth in the *Mayflower* in 1620, and played a worthy part in the early history of the colony. Fuller received a good education in his native town, became a teacher at the age of sixteen, and in 1836 obtained the principalship of a small school in Providence, R. I. He proved so intelligent, amiable, and devoted that interested people built a school for him on Greene St., and at the dedication of the building, June 10, 1837, Ralph Waldo Emerson delivered the address. For a year and a half Margaret Fuller was one of his assistants.

This period of teaching is the most creditable in Fuller's career. He was proprietor of a bookstore in Providence for several years, and endeavored to assist local literary talent by bringing out *The Rhode Island Book* (1841), edited by Anne C. Lynch, who later became Mrs. Botta [*q.v.*]; but in 1843 he moved to New York and joined George Pope Morris and Nathaniel Parker Willis [*qq.v.*] in conducting the *New York Mirror.* Confiscatory postal rates soon forced them to make their weekly into a daily paper, the *Evening Mirror,* which Fuller continued to own and manage for fourteen years after the withdrawal of his partners. In October 1844 he improved his social and financial position by marrying Emilie Louise, daughter of John F. Delaplaine, an affluent New Yorker. In his editorial policy he was professedly non-partizan and unmistakably Protestant, white, and American. Embroiling himself with Edgar Allan Poe, he was so injudicious as to reprint the defamatory attack on him by Thomas Dunn English [*q.v.*]. Poe retorted with a libel suit and was awarded $225 damages. Fuller was among the first to discern presidential qualities in Gen. Zachary Taylor, who rewarded his insight with an appointment in the Navy Department. Under the pseudonym of "Belle Brittan" he wrote gossipy, diverting special correspondence of the Willisian variety, some of which was republished in *Belle Brittan on a Tour, at Newport, and Here and There* (1858) and *Sparks from a Locomotive, or Life and Liberty in Europe* (1859). As the Civil War approached he grew increasingly pro-Southern in his utterances, so that when hostilities opened he found it advisable to leave the country. In London he started a weekly paper, the *Cosmopolitan,* to represent the Confederate point of view, but he secured little encouragement and twice went bankrupt. He also wrote for *Fraser's Magazine* (September 1862–February 1863), signing himself "A White Republican," and published *Causes and Consequences of the Civil War in America* (1861); *The Flag of Truce: Dedicated to the Emperor of the French* (1862); *Curiosity Visits to Southern Plantations* (1863), "by a Northern Man"; *The Times! or The Flag of Truce* (Richmond, Va., 1863); and *North and South* (1863; 1864). By espousing the Southern cause he lost his friends and virtually ruined himself. In *Grand Transformation Scenes in the United States or Glimpses of Home after Thirteen Years Abroad* (1875) he tried eagerly to reinstate himself with Northern readers, but no one was any longer interested in him. He died obscurely in Paris, where for some years he had been living by newspaper work. His wife and an adopted daughter survived him.

[W. H. Fuller, *Geneal. of Some Descendants of Dr. Samuel Fuller of the Mayflower* (1910); H. L. Greene, "The Greene-St. School of Providence and its Teachers," *Pubs. R. I. Hist. Soc.,* new ser., VI (1898–99), 199–219; H. A. Beers, *Nathaniel Parker Willis* (1885); portrait and reading notice, *Ballou's Pictorial Drawing-Room Companion,* July 28, 1855; obituary, *New-Eng. Hist. & Geneal. Reg.,* Jan. 1881, p. 116.]

G. H. G.

FULLER, JOHN WALLACE (July 28, 1827–Mar. 12, 1891), Union soldier, was born at Harston, Cambridgeshire, England. His father, Benjamin Fuller, a Baptist clergyman and nephew of Rev. Andrew Fuller, one of the most famous English Baptists of his time, removed to the United States in 1833, and settled in Oneida County, N. Y. The boy attended the public schools for a time, but before he was fourteen years old went to work in a bookstore in Utica and his education was largely acquired there by reading in the intervals of work. He afterwards started in business for himself as a publisher and bookseller, and prospered until a considerable part of his plant was destroyed by fire in 1857. Meanwhile he was a hard-working officer of the militia, was city treasurer from 1852 to 1854, and occasionally wrote for local publications; one of his poems is said to have been commended by Charles Dickens. In 1851 he married Anna, daughter of Dr. Josiah Rathbun, a Utica physician. In 1858 he moved to Ohio and established a publishing and bookselling business in Toledo. At the outbreak of the Civil War he was asked to assist in drilling and disciplining new troops, and while so employed at Grafton, Va. (now W. Va.), he attracted the favorable notice of officers, who recommended him so strongly to the governor that he was appointed colonel of the new 27th Ohio Infantry, and was mustered in as such, Aug. 18, 1861. He served with his regiment in Pope's operations at New Madrid and Island No. 10, and having succeeded by seniority to the command of the brigade, led it at the battles of Iuka and Corinth. Originally the 1st Brigade, 2nd Division, Army of the Mississippi, its official designation was repeatedly changed as transfers and reorganizations took place, but throughout the war and afterwards it remained "Fuller's Brigade" in popular phrase, and for a considerable period, indeed, had no other official name. Through the greater part of 1863 it was in garrison in Tennessee, but it was in the field against Forrest near the end of that year, and in 1864, as a part of the XVI Corps, Army of the Tennessee (McPherson), it took part in the Atlanta campaign. Fuller was appointed brigadier-general of volunteers, Jan. 5, 1864. He was with the brigade in the two months of almost continuous fighting in northern Georgia. At the battle of Atlanta and for some time afterwards he was in command of the division. Again in charge of his brigade, he took part in the march to the sea and the campaign of the Carolinas. He resigned from the army Aug. 15, 1865, and resumed business in Toledo as senior member of the firm of Fuller, Childs & Company, wholesale boot and shoe merchants. He was collector of customs there from 1874 to 1881, and died in that city. Fuller's success as a soldier was largely due to his appreciation, at the outset, of the necessity of firm discipline and thorough training, an understanding which many of the volunteer officers acquired only through experience. Courteous and kindly in manner, always apparently cheerful, he was notably popular with those who served under him.

[Chas. H. Smith, *Hist. of Fuller's Ohio Brigade* (1909), contains a detailed account of the military operations of the brigade and a biographical sketch of its commander, by Oscar Sheppard. See also obituary notice published as *Mil. Order of the Loyal Legion of the U. S., Commandery of the State of Ohio, Circular No. 13* (1891); F. B. Heitman, *Hist. Reg. and Dict. U. S. Army* (1903), I, 440; *Official Records (Army)*, 1 ser., vols. XVII (pt. 1, for Iuka and Corinth), XXXVIII (pt. 3, for the Atlanta campaign), and XLVII (pt. 1, for the campaign of the Carolinas).] T. M. S.

FULLER, LEVI KNIGHT (Feb. 24, 1841–Oct. 10, 1896), inventor, manufacturer, governor of Vermont, was born at Westmoreland, N. H., the second son of Washington and Lucinda Constantine Fuller. His father was of old New England, his mother of German ancestry. In 1845 he moved with his parents to Bellows Falls, Vt., where he attended the public schools for several years. At the age of thirteen he felt obliged to leave school in order to make his own living. With only twenty-five cents in his pocket he left home, went to Brattleboro, Vt., and entered the employ of James A. Capen as a printer. For the next few years he worked at the trade and studied telegraphy in his leisure hours. He became deeply interested in the subject of electricity and showed a decided aptitude for mechanical pursuits. In 1856 he went to Boston and served an apprenticeship to a machinist, and also availed himself of the opportunity to pursue scientific studies in the evening schools. The following year he went to Burlington, Vt., as a telegraph operator, but returned to Brattleboro in 1860 to enter the employ of J. Estey & Company, later the Estey Organ Company, as mechanical engineer. He was actively identified with this concern in various capacities for the rest of his life, becoming in 1866 a member of the firm and its vice-president. In addition to these activities he maintained for a number of years a machine shop of his own for the manufacture of wood-working machinery and sewing-machines, and carried on scientific investigations of importance. He was awarded about fifty patents upon his inventions, most of which were appliances for organs. In the field of acoustics, a subject upon which he was a recognized authority, he was particularly interested in securing the adoption of "international pitch" for musical instruments.

After having achieved success in business, Fuller responded to the call of politics. He represented Windham County in the state Senate from 1880 to 1882 and served as chairman of the committee on finance. In 1886 he was elected lieutenant-governor on the ticket with E. J. Ormsbee. In 1892 he was nominated on the Republican ticket for governor and was elected despite the fact that it was an unfavorable year for the party through the country at large. His gubernatorial career is noteworthy for his enthusiastic advocacy of the cause of good roads. He was one of the pioneers in awakening public sentiment in this field at a time when little interest had been manifested in the subject. He was married on May 8, 1865, to Abby Emily Estey, daughter of Jacob and Desdemona Wood Estey. During his youth he became a member of the Baptist Church and throughout his life he was a liberal supporter of its activities and institutions, especially of the Vermont Academy at Saxtons River. He was also deeply interested in the advancement of the welfare of the negro and for several years was a member of the board of trustees of Shaw University. He was an active member of numerous scientific societies, the most important of which were the American Association for the Advancement of Science and the Society of American Engineers.

[See the *Vermonter,* Nov. 1896; Mary R. Cabot, *Annals of Brattleboro, 1681–1895,* vol. II (1922); W. H. Crockett, *Vermont: The Green Mountain State,* vol. IV (1921), *passim*; Hiram Carleton, *Geneal. and Family Hist. of the State of Vt.* (1903); J. B. Ullery, *Men of Vt.* (1894).] A. M. K.

FULLER, LOIE (Jan. 15, 1862–Jan. 1, 1928), dancer, the daughter of Reuben and Delilah Fuller, was born in the little settlement of Fullersburg, Ill., which was named after her forefathers. At the age of five she was beginning to play the piano and sing before groups of people and at thirteen she was a temperance lecturer, becoming popular chiefly because she used the "horrible example" as a method of appeal. While still in her teens she joined a group which was playing Shakespeare with little success. She studied for a time in Chicago, where she was finally engaged by James M. Hill to sing and act in Hooley's Opera House, and from there she went to New York. After a year spent in search of a position, she joined Nat Goodwin in the burlesque, *Little Jack Sheppard,* then appeared in Rider Haggard's *She* under the management of Charles Frohman. In both productions Miss Fuller achieved some success and immediately set out to capitalize it by heading a theatrical company of her own on a long South American tour which ended in disastrous bankruptcy. In 1889 she went to London and appeared in an ill-starred venture, *Caprice.* After several other failures she returned to New York.

The turning point of Miss Fuller's career came with a discovery made in an idle moment. As she was entertaining herself one day by twirling and twining a beautiful piece of material about her body before a mirror, the light from a window reflected in the mirror and onto the fabric, suggesting to her the possibilities latent in the combination of movement and color. A few days later, obtaining permission to dance before a producer, she exhibited the famous serpentine dance and explained to him the effects which changing lights would create. When she introduced her dance on the stage she won immediate success. From that time on she experimented with light and color and movement, producing and appearing in ballets in London, Paris, Berlin, and New York. Her début in Paris took place in 1892 in the Folies-Bergère in the *Fire Dance.*

During the World War Miss Fuller devoted herself to relief work in the Allied countries and won decorations from France, Belgium, and Rumania. After the war she developed a school of dancing in Paris, from which she sent out troupes to various cities. She considered her dancers as instruments of light rather than dancers, a conception which was her own, although her methods were imitated widely. In Europe, especially, she was very popular and numbered many notable people among her personal friends; foremost among them perhaps was Queen Marie of Rumania, with whom she traveled for a time in the United States in 1926. In 1908 Miss Fuller published *Quinze Ans de ma Vie,* which appeared in English in 1913 as *Fifteen Years of a Dancer's Life, with some account of her Distinguished Friends,* with an introduction by Anatole France. At some time during her career she entered into a common-law marriage with Col. William Hayes. Upon discovering that he already had a wife she instituted legal proceedings against him which resulted in his conviction (*N. Y. Times,* Jan. 2, 1928).

[In addition to the references cited, see Raymond Bouyer, "La Loie Fuller," *L'Artiste,* Dec. 1928; Isadora Duncan, *My Life* (1927); *Chicago Tribune,* Jan. 3, 1928. Information as to certain facts was given by Mrs. Nella Fuller Brookins, of Hinsdale, Ill.] M. S.

FULLER, MARGARET [See FULLER, SARAH MARGARET, 1810–1850].

FULLER, MELVILLE WESTON (Feb. 11, 1833–July 4, 1910), chief justice of the United States, was born at Augusta, Me., the son of Catherine Martin Weston and Frederick Augustus Fuller. Abundant in his ancestral lines were men eminent in the church, the law, or public life, college graduates, and educators. His father, paternal grandfather, father-in-law, and six uncles were lawyers or judges. After graduation from Bowdoin College (1853) he read law, attended for a year the Harvard Law School, was admitted to the bar of Maine in 1855, and entered practise in Augusta, becoming almost immediately a member and president of the common council, and also city counsel. He also worked on the *Age* of Augusta, a leading Democratic paper of the state.

In 1856 he removed to Chicago, and was admitted to the Illinois bar on June 15. Until 1878 he was most of the time associated with partners. His cases lay in almost all fields of the law, though real property and commercial law were the subjects of his greatest mastery. He had a quick intelligence, and worked with extraordinary ease and rapidity; but the primary cause of his great success was a patient thoroughness, which his other qualities might have led a man of less conscience to neglect. As years passed he did more and more work for fellow lawyers in difficult cases, yet was busy to the end of his practise with jury cases. He was facile of speech, earnest, thorough, and convincing in discussion, pertinacious and skilful in procedure; never dull, sometimes entertaining though hardly brilliant; and decidedly successful. Dignity, courtesy, moderation, learning, and a distinct personality marked him at the bar as later on the bench.

One of the most celebrated of his cases—one outcome of which was the establishment of the Reformed Protestant Episcopal Church—was his defense of Charles Edward Cheney [*q.v.*], the rector of Christ Church in Chicago, before an ecclesiastical tribunal, against charges of canonical disobedience; and later in derivative cases in the civil courts involving conflicting claims to the church property. In the ecclesiastical proceedings he displayed a mastery of canon law and patristic literature that vastly impressed the bar. Equally famous was the Lake Front litigation, involving the rights of Chicago in the shore of Lake Michigan. Notable, also, were cases involving monopolistic contracts between certain gas companies in Chicago; attacks upon long-term franchises granted by the state legislature to street railways in Chicago; and his services in building up the city's park system. He held a commanding position, and by a flawless personal and professional character had won the unbounded confidence of both bench and bar, when he was appointed to the Supreme Court.

His nomination to the Court met, nevertheless, with difficulties. He was a strong Democrat, and a predilection for politics had taken him into the Illinois constitutional convention of 1862, the legislature of 1863–64, and the national Democratic conventions of 1864, 1872, 1876, and 1880, in all of which bodies he was conspicuous. In the presidential election of 1884 he campaigned actively against his townsman and newspaper rival of youthful days, James G. Blaine. President Cleveland offered him a high diplomatic post and the solicitor-generalship, both of which he declined, and then nominated him as chief justice. He was confirmed on July 20, 1888, after prolonged delay, by a vote of 41 to 20 (*Journal of the Executive Proceedings of the Senate,* 50 Cong., 1 Sess., pp. 252, 254, 287, 313). The opposition was largely partisan, but in part due to the disappointment of friends of Edward J. Phelps [*q.v.*], whom the President had first favored, and in part to charges that Fuller was of lukewarm loyalty during the Civil War.

He performed the duties of the office with a versatile ability that demonstrated the adequacy of his training. It was a period of unparalleled industrial growth; of departures from national tradition in colonial expansion; of cases involving new problems of immigration and naturalization, the extension of the Constitution to the colonies, the interpretation of federal statutes against monopolies and of other legislation expressing national efforts at social control, novel and multitudinous applications of the state police power, and the application of constitutional restraints to the struggle between capital and labor. Fuller approached these questions as an old-time Democrat, friendly to the doctrine of state rights, and as a sincere believer in individualism. He inclined toward strict construction of all governmental powers as against the political liberty and economic initiative of the citizen, and of federal powers as against the rights of the states. He was resolute in insisting that the powers of Congress were limited, being derivable only from specific grants, reasonably construed, and not from any assumption of an underlying "national sovereignty." On the other hand, when he deemed the line rightly drawn he was unhesitant in giving to both the states and the federal government the logical and liberal development that constructive statesmanship required.

With little difficulty most of his decisions are adjustable to these simple principles. They need not here, however, be detailed. He was certainly not a reformer of legal procedure, even where reform seems to day to have been imperative. And though his human sympathies were frequently displayed in solicitude for the protection of women and family interests and for improved conditions for labor, his voice was consistently raised for the upholding of traditional rights of person and property against the regulating tendency of the time. He had too much human sympathy and scholarship to be a reactionary or obstructionist, tested by the views of his day; nevertheless, legislatures and courts (including his own) began within a few years after his death to move swiftly away from the principles of "property" and "freedom of contract" which he, with his colleagues, accepted as fundamental. His opinions (more than 850 in number) are marked by directness and clarity of reasoning, and by common sense. He was a good reasoner, at least, and his command of precedent frequently gave evidence of exhaustive research. As a presiding officer he was notable for dignity, and equally for tact, invariable good temper, simplicity, modesty, courtesy, and consideration for counsel. These qualities, indeed, marked him in all the relations of life. Probably no predecessor had equaled him as a business manager of the Court, nor enjoyed in like degree the affection of colleagues and the bar. After a long period of physical decline, he died of heart-failure at Sorrento, Me., where he had made his summer home for seventeen years.

He was a very active regent of the Smithsonian Institution throughout his judicial term; a trustee of the Peabody Education Fund, 1888–1910, and chairman of the Board, 1901–10; an overseer, 1875–79, and a trustee, 1894–1910, of Bowdoin College; a member of the American Venezuela–British Guiana Boundary Commission, and of the Venezuelan boundary arbitration tribunal, 1899; a member of the Permanent Court of Arbitration at The Hague, 1900–10; a representative of Great Britain on the arbitral tribunal which tried the matter of the Muscat dhows, 1905; a vice-president and an executive councillor of the American Society of International Law; and a fellow of the American Academy of Arts and Sciences of Boston.

Fuller was married twice: on June 28, 1858,

to Calista O. Reynolds of Chicago, who died Nov. 13, 1864; and on May 30, 1866, to Mary Ellen Coolbaugh of the same city, who died Aug. 17, 1904. He had two daughters by his first wife and five daughters and one son by his second. His home life was ideal. He was an omnivorous reader in all lines of literature, and his public addresses were studded with allusions and quotations drawn from modern, classical, and Biblical literature. A very human, kindly, honest, unpretentious man, he added to these qualities a keen humor and manners engaging and gracious, that made him a most agreeable companion. Formal society, however, did not attract him, though he was an inveterate first-nighter at the theatre. Rather short and light of body, he was physically vigorous and enduring. He had a flowing moustache and wore his heavy hair to the shoulder, even in middle life. Throughout life he was associated with many legal, political, social, and religious organizations. He was a devoted member of the Episcopal church. Chicago remained always the home of his heart, and his professional earnings, invested in real estate in that city, made him a wealthy man.

Fuller was frequently orator for the bar of Chicago. His eulogy of Sidney Breese is in *Proceedings of the Illinois State Bar Association*, 1879 (pp. 31–61); and his "Address in Commemoration of the Inauguration of George Washington as First President of the United States," delivered on Dec. 11, 1889, before Congress, is in 132 *United States Reports*, 705–34. His book-reviews (see the *Dial*, July 16, 1910) clearly reveal his political faith. Few of his other writings are in print.

[See biographies and appreciations of Fuller in *Chicago Legal News*, July 16, 1910; *Proc. of the Bar and Officers of the Supreme Court of the U. S. in Memory of Melville W. Fuller*, Dec. 10, 1910, including 219 *U. S. Reports* (1911), pp. vii–xxviii; S. M. Cullom, *Fifty Years of Pub. Service* (1911), pp. 236–42; *The Bench and Bar of Chicago* (1883), pp. 262–64; *Encyc. of Biog. of Ill.* (1894), II, 7–13; J. M. Palmer, ed., *The Bench and Bar of Ill.* (1899), I, 561–62, II, 647; *Chicago Daily Tribune, Chicago Record-Herald*, and N. Y. *Evening Post*, July 5, 1910. His family history is traced in W. H. Fuller, *Geneal. of Some Descendants of Edward Fuller of the Mayflower* (1908); his judicial opinions are analyzed in *Maine Law Rev.*, Jan. 1917; *Univ. of Pa. Law Rev.*, Oct. 1910; *Law Notes*, Aug. 1910.] F. S. P.

FULLER, RICHARD (Apr. 22, 1804–Oct. 20, 1876), Baptist clergyman, ninth of the ten children of Thomas and Elizabeth (Middleton) Fuller, was born in Beaufort, S. C., and died in Baltimore. About the time of his birth, his parents joined the Baptist church, but he was brought up more an Episcopalian, it seems, than anything else. He went to school in Beaufort, and in 1820, following the example of his brothers, he set out to attend college in the North. His career at Harvard was cut short in December 1822, in the midst of his junior year, when he developed symptoms of what was thought to be tuberculosis. A year or so of life in Northampton as prescribed by his doctors made him well again, and when his class was graduated in 1824, he was given his diploma, out of consideration for his past good record. Then he returned home and after a short period of private study, began to practise law. In August 1831, he was married to Charlotte Bull, daughter of James and Ann Stuart Bull. A few months after his marriage he was converted and in 1832 he entered the Baptist ministry and began in Beaufort a fifteen years' pastorate. He made a tour of Europe in 1836. In 1839 certain insinuations against the Catholic Church made in resolutions passed by the Prince William Temperance Society, petitioning the South Carolina legislature to enact a law of prohibition, gave rise to a controversy in the *Charleston Courier* (July 1839–Sept. 1839) between himself and his friend, John England [*q.v.*], the Catholic Bishop of Charleston, which, though protracted and stringent, was characterized by great personal courtesy on both sides (see *Letters Concerning the Roman Chancery*, 1840). Another public controversy of his was inaugurated in the latter part of 1844, when, at the request of the *Christian Reflector* of Philadelphia, he published in that paper an article explaining his belief that slavery was sanctioned by the Bible. The article was answered by his fellow Baptist divine, Francis Wayland [*q.v.*], who invited a reply. The ensuing argument, handled with great skill and decorum by both participants, was in 1845 put into a book, *Domestic Slavery Considered as a Scriptural Institution.* In 1847 he went to Baltimore where he was pastor of the Seventh Baptist Church, 1847–71, and of the Eutaw Place Church, 1871–76. His reason for going there was largely the position of the city between the North and the South, and its consequent preëminence as a place for observing the more and more turbulent aspect of sectional misunderstanding. In January 1851, before the American Colonization Society, meeting in Washington to consider some of the phases of this misunderstanding, he made an address, *Our Duty to the African Race* (1851), which was so wise, perspicacious, and temperate that it pleased nobody. During the Civil War he remained in Baltimore, doing what he could, then and afterward, to alleviate popular distress which he had long foreseen and loathed. He was a powerful and devout preacher, and though his adherence to Baptist doctrines at times verged upon complacency, he kept uppermost in his mind always the need of humility and tolerance. Among his published writings are: *Baptism and the Terms of Communion: an Argument* (1854); *Sermons* (1860); *A City or House Divided Against Itself. A Discourse Delivered . . . on the First Day of June, 1865, Being the Day of National Fasting and Humiliation* (1865), *Sermons Delivered . . . During His Ministry With the Seventh and Eutaw Churches, Baltimore, 1847–76* (1877).

[J. H. Cuthbert, *Life of Richard Fuller* (1879); Harvard Univ., *Quin. Cat.* (1915); Peter Guilday, *The Life and Times of John England*, II, 472–74.] J. D. W.

FULLER, ROBERT MASON (Oct. 27, 1845–Dec. 28, 1919), physician, pharmacist, inventor, was born in Schenectady, N. Y., the son of John Irwin and Louise (Gardner) Fuller. His father had been a merchant, manufacturer, and banker in New York City. He obtained his preliminary education at Union School in Schenectady. During 1861–63 he worked as a clerk in a drug store, at the same time studying pharmacy. Later he took a special chemistry course at Union College. His teacher in both of these branches was Prof. C. F. Chandler, from whom he received a certificate, and perhaps his special interest in toxicology. In a report to the United States government made in 1913 (quoted by Dr. Kebler, *post*), he stated that at the age of sixteen he had begun to experiment with the manufacture of tablet triturates. In 1863 he began the study of medicine at the Albany Medical School which gave him the degree of M.D. in 1865; and during this undergraduate period he was attached to the Ira Harris United States Hospital as assistant to Dr. Armsby, the professor of surgery at the Albany Medical School. For a short time he was at the front in the 6th Army Hospital Corps Hospital, at City Point, Va. In passing through Washington he chanced to be present at Ford's Theatre the night of Lincoln's assassination.

In connection with his early studies of toxicology he invented a method of using the photographic camera for demonstrating the presence of microcrystals of arsenic—a method which was to prove of value in forensic medicine. He also practised the photography of wounds with such success that some of his slides were inserted in the official *Medical and Surgical History of the War of the Rebellion.* After graduation he remained for a short time in Albany before removing permanently to New York City where he practised for forty years. He developed also an interest in the photography of skin diseases and used the camera with great success while serving as a lecturer on dermatology in the medical department of the University of the City of New York. After bacteria had been made visible by staining methods he became interested in this aspect of microphotography. Yet he seems never to have lost interest in tablet triturates, and in 1878, after a continuous study of seventeen years, he made his first report on this subject to the New York Academy of Medicine. The paper, entitled "Dose-Dispensing Simplified: An Easy, Economical and Accurate Method of Dispensing Medicine in a Compact and Palatable Form," appeared in full in the *Medical Record,* Mar. 9, 1878. He did not apply for a patent, and the manufacture and marketing of the triturates was taken over by Benjamin T. Fairchild, then chief of the dispensing department of Caswell, Hazard & Company. It was not until the formation of the firm of Fairchild & Brothers, however, that the triturates were brought directly to the attention of medical practitioners. At a later period (1881) this new firm joined forces with Horace Fraser under the firm name of Fraser & Company, which subsequently both manufactured and distributed the triturates. Full credit for originating and working out the principle of this innovation is unanimously assigned to Fuller, who has been long and justly known as the "father of the tablet triturate." After his retirement from practise about 1909 he returned to Schenectady and from that period until his death was chiefly interested in Union College and the Albany Medical School. For the former he assembled a library on chemistry, and to the latter he bequeathed $30,000. He never married. His only publication is a joint work with H. G. Piffard: *A Practical Treatise on Diseases of the Skin* (1891).

[*Albany Medic. Annals*, Feb. 1920; *N. Y. Times* and *Albany Evening Jour.*, Dec. 29, 1919; L. F. Kebler, "The Tablet Industry," in *Jour. Am. Pharmaceutical Asso.*, July 1914; A. V. V. Raymond, *Union Univ.* (3 vols., 1907); personal information from B. T. Fairchild.] E. P.

FULLER, SARAH MARGARET (May 23, 1810–July 19, 1850), Marchioness Ossoli, journalist, critic, social reformer, was born in Cambridgeport, near Boston, Mass., of typical Puritan ancestry. Her father, Timothy Fuller, was a lawyer and a graduate of Harvard. A member of the Massachusetts Senate and a representative in Congress, he played a considerable part in the politics of his day. Her mother, Margaret Crane, once a school-teacher, had no intellectual pretensions. Ten years younger than her husband, she left all authority to him. While she brought up the younger children, Mr. Fuller took full charge of the education of his daughter, who was a precocious child and a model pupil. Proud of her abilities, her father forced her progress. At the age of six she was introduced to Latin and two years later she was reading Ovid. Shakespeare, Cervantes, and Molière were also read before she had reached her teens. Two years at boarding-school, which were most unhappy, brought out the latent hysteria in the ambitious girl. Margaret afterward blamed her father for her broken health. She said that children should not read too early, as "they should not through books ante-date their actual experiences, but should take them gradually, as sympathy and interpretation are needed" (*Memoirs, post,* I, 31). When she was twenty-five, Emerson said of her that her reading was at the rate of Gibbon's.

Margaret's friendships with the intellectual leaders of her time began at an early age. She discussed philosophy while riding horse-back with James Freeman Clarke; read with Frederic Henry Hedge the German authors whom Carlyle had made the fashion; and confided in William Henry Channing "her secret hope of what Woman might be and do, as an author, in our Republic" (*Memoirs,* II, 7–8). Often satirized as a blue-stocking, she became along with Emerson the butt of many gibes aimed at Transcendentalism. She was accepted in this circle on a par with men like Alcott and Thoreau and developed in its atmosphere her talents as a talker.

From 1839 to 1844 her famous "conversations" were held in Boston. After several years of teaching and translating, Margaret hit upon this method of adding to her income while she exercised her talent. "Conversation is my natural element," she said. "I need to be called out, and never think alone, without imagining some companion" (*Memoirs,* I, 107). The purpose of the course, as her prospectus said, was to supply "a point of union to well-educated and thinking women, in a city which, with great pretensions to mental refinement, boasts, at present, nothing of the kind." The first class, composed of twenty-five ladies, came together in Elizabeth Peabody's room in West Street. The conversations were extremely popular and Margaret's reputation was soon made. Her pupils, whom Harriet Martineau once peevishly described as "gorgeous pedants," were drawn from the most intellectual and cultivated circles of Boston society. From her discussions with this group, she derived material and inspiration for her volume, *Woman in the Nineteenth Century* (1845). Though comparable with Mary Wollstonecraft's *Vindication of the Rights of Woman* (1792), the book did not attract the same degree of popular attention. It touched on all the issues of the future woman's movement, however, and quietly prepared the way in many isolated minds, although its view of woman's rights was too comprehensive and its tone too philosophical to gratify the militants of those early days. When the outcome of the Civil War made suffrage a burning issue, the ideas of Margaret Fuller were allowed to fall into the background. Her book was thus neglected and soon almost forgotten. Her life had more influence.

Margaret began her career as a journalist with the editorship of the *Dial,* the organ of the Transcendentalists. Ralph Waldo Emerson and George Ripley were joint editors with her. As editor-in-chief she was to have received two hundred dollars a year, but Emerson doubts whether even this modest salary was ever paid. She labored strenuously with her unpaid contributors but oftener than she liked she was obliged to fill her columns with her own contributions. The common criticism was that the *Dial* was too feminine. It ceased to exist when Margaret changed the scene of her activities from Boston to New York. While "far from being an original genius," as she once said of herself, she was one of the best of American critics. It was in this capacity that Horace Greeley invited her to join the staff of the *New York Tribune.* His wife, who had attended the conversations in Boston, was in favor of the plan, which offered among its terms a home in the Greeley household. Mr. Greeley, who was a great admirer of the *Dial,* had read the contributions of its hard-worked editor. He had been especially impressed by her *Summer on the Lakes, in 1843* (1844), the description of a journey to Chicago. Margaret's optimistic view of Western life accorded with the slogan of the *Tribune* editor: "Go west, young man, and grow up with the country." Mr. Greeley's enthusiasm for these papers, aided by the admiration of his wife for the talents of Miss Fuller, led him to offer her a position on his newspaper.

During the two years that she spent in New York—her business life as she called it—Margaret won her reputation as an American critic. The *Tribune* was famous for the excellence and freedom of its articles and reviews. Before the bar of Margaret's literary judgment came the work of Carlyle, Tennyson, and Browning. Like Mr. Greeley, she sometimes made enemies. Lowell, whom she derided as a poet, lampooned her as Miranda in his *Fable for Critics* (1864), yet she achieved a place as "one of the best-equipped, most sympathetic, and genuinely philosophical critics produced in America prior to 1850"

(*Cambridge History of American Literature,* I, 343). In the summer of 1846 she at last gratified her great desire to go to Europe. Her letters from abroad appeared from time to time on the front page of the *Tribune.* She visited Carlyle, Wordsworth, and Harriet Martineau, but one of her favorite poets had disappeared from London. "Browning has just married Miss Barrett, and gone to Italy," she wrote to her publisher. "I may meet them there" (*Memoirs,* II, 190). In Paris she visited George Sand and was profoundly impressed by her personality. In Rome she renewed her acquaintance with Mazzini, begun in London. By a romantic chain of circumstances she became deeply involved in the Roman Revolution.

In October 1847 she parted with her friends, the Springs, with whom she had been traveling in Europe, and returned to Rome for an indefinite sojourn. She took a furnished room in the Corso and prepared, like Goethe, to steep herself in Rome. A chance encounter with an Italian gentleman developed into friendship and still greater intimacy. Angelo Ossoli, ten years younger than Margaret, was handsome, penniless, and devoted. He had nothing to offer but himself and the title of Marquesa. In time the two were married; the exact date was never revealed. The marriage was first announced when their child was one year old. He had been born Sept. 5, 1848, in the ancient village of Rieti. Margaret left him with a nurse while she returned to play her part in the Roman Revolution. She and Ossoli were adherents of Mazzini. The husband, an officer in the republican service, fought courageously in the siege of 1849. Margaret assisted Princess Belgiojoso in the organization of the hospitals. Her occasional letters to the *Tribune* described the progress of the siege and strove to throw a favorable light on the tottering republic. On July 4, the French troops entered Rome. "In two days of French 'order,'" wrote Margaret, "more acts of violence have been committed than in two months under the Triumvirate." She sat with Ossoli in her chamber and refused to look out of the window. The Roman husband wept.

With Ossoli and her child, Margaret fled to Florence, where she took her husband's name and the title of Marquesa. She spent the winter writing a history of the Roman Revolution. Of this book, which was never to be published, Mrs. Browning said, "It would have been more equal to her faculties than anything she had ever yet produced." In the spring the manuscript was finished, and Margaret prepared to return to America to find a publisher. With her family she set sail from Leghorn May 17, 1850. On this ill-fated voyage, disasters followed close upon each other. The captain died of smallpox and Margaret's child almost succumbed to it. On the eve of their arrival in New York, the vessel ran into a storm and was shipwrecked off Fire Island. Margaret and Ossoli and little Angelino all perished in the waves. Of the three bodies only that of the child was recovered. The manuscript of Margaret's book on the Roman Revolution was lost without a trace. "For years afterwards," wrote Rebecca Spring, "if I went to the sea-shore, I would dream of Margaret, and always pleasantly. In my dream, she always seemed happy; it may be that the requiem of the winds and the waves was the best for her. She believed in the higher education of women and in equal rights for them as citizens. She would have rejoiced in the wonderful progress they have made in these things since her time. Let our sex never forget Margaret Fuller."

It was by her personality rather than her writings that Margaret Fuller impressed herself upon her generation. There were strange contradictions in her life which were a great puzzle to her contemporaries. Though always an invalid, she did the work of three women and sometimes "worked better when she was ill." Her eccentricities in early life made many enemies and were deprecated even by her friends, but those who knew her in Italy, as for instance Mrs. Story, testified that she had lost her arrogance and oddity and gained in tolerance and simplicity. A year after her death, a memorial volume was published by her New England friends. As scarcely any records of her foreign life survived, it gave no just account of her last eventful years. Mazzini and the Brownings were invited to contribute, but the papers which they wrote were lost and never came to light. The portrait which emerged from the two-volume memoirs was therefore chiefly drawn from Margaret's early years. Unfinished though it was, it reveals her as a noble and generous personality, a pathfinder whose brave hopes were realized by others. In 1869 her complete works were published under the direction of Horace Greeley. Besides *Summer on the Lakes* and *Woman in the Nineteenth Century,* they included her contributions to the *Tribune* in three volumes entitled *Literature and Art,* published in 1846 as *Papers on Literature and Art*; *Life Without and Life Within*; and *At Home and Abroad.*

[The *Memoirs of Margaret Fuller Ossoli* (2 vols., 1852) were edited by R. W. Emerson, W. H. Channing, and J. F. Clarke. *Margaret Fuller Ossoli* was written for the American Men of Letters Series by Thomas Wentworth Higginson (1884). Julia Ward Howe's *Margaret Fuller* (1883) emphasized her struggles as a pioneer. The short life by Andrew Macphail in *Essays in Puritanism* (1905) contained the first account of her Italian life which did not gloss over its unconventional aspects. See also Helen N. McMaster, *Margaret Fuller as a Literary Critic* (1928); Karl Knortz, *Brook Farm and Margaret Fuller* (1900); Katharine Anthony, *Margaret Fuller* (1920); W. H. Fuller, *Geneal. of Some Descendants of Thomas Fuller of Woburn* (1919).] K. A.

FULLER, THOMAS CHARLES (Feb. 27, 1832–Oct. 20, 1901), judge, the third child of Thomas and Catherine (Raboteau) Fuller, was born in Fayetteville, N. C. His father, a prosperous merchant, died young, and the mother took their three young children to Franklin County, the home of the Fuller family. After preparing for college in Louisburg where he spent most of his boyhood, Thomas Fuller entered in 1849 the University of North Carolina. Three years later he left college and entered the employ of a merchant in Fayetteville, but in 1855 he began the study of law under Judge Richmond M. Pearson and was admitted to the bar the following year. On Nov. 5, 1857, he married Caroline Douglas Whitehead of Fayetteville. He began practise in his native town and by 1860 had attained an excellent position at the bar. Unlike the majority of young lawyers of his day, he had no political ambitions, but he was deeply interested in politics. A Union Whig, he opposed secession as constitutionally unwarranted and as practically unwise, but when Lincoln called for troops he promptly took up arms, and joining the 1st North Carolina, was a participant in the battle of Bethel. At the close of his six months' enlistment he aided in raising a battery of light artillery of which he became first lieutenant. He remained in the service until 1863 when he was elected to the Confederate Congress. There, as its youngest member, he remained until the close of the war, voted generally with the peace party, and "labored for reconstruction." He was elected to the United States Congress in 1865 but was not seated. In 1868 he was once more nominated but was defeated. In 1872 he was candidate for elector on the Greeley ticket, but failing of election, was never again a candidate for public office. He resumed the practise of law in 1865 and quickly rose to a leading place in the bar of the state. In 1873 he moved to Raleigh. He was employed in many notable civil cases, but his chief reputation was made on the side of the defense in criminal practise which gave full scope to his superb talents before a jury. His legal learning, his careful preparation of a case for the jury, and his skill in the examination of witnesses excited the wonder and envy of his legal brethren, but the public knew him best as an advocate. Away from the bar he was known as an effective public speaker, and until he went on the bench he took part in every political campaign. In 1891 President Harrison made him a justice of the court of private land claims established to pass upon titles based on Mexican grants in the territory acquired from Mexico. He filled the place ably until his death in Raleigh ten years later. Personally, Fuller was a genial and sociable man, possessed of a ready wit and a gift for pleasant conversation.

[S. A. Ashe, ed., *Biog. Hist. of N. C.*, I (1905), 277; *Jour. of the Cong. of the Confed. States of America*, vol. VII (1905); Walter Clark, ed., *Histories of the Several Regiments and Battalions from N. C. in the Great War, 1861–65* (1901); *Official Records (Army)*; *News and Observer* (Raleigh, N. C.), Oct. 22, 1901.] J. G. deR. H.

FULLERTON, GEORGE STUART (Aug. 18, 1859–Mar. 23, 1925), philosopher, was one of seven children born to the Rev. Robert Stewart and Martha (White) Fullerton during their fifteen-year residence in India as missionaries. The American Fullertons are descended through Humphrey who about 1727 settled at Pequea, Pa., from a long line of Covenanters. From the marriage of Thomas, great-grandson of this Humphrey, with Elizabeth Stewart of Maryland, came that Robert Stewart who immediately after his wedding with Martha, daughter of the Rev. Robert White of Faggs Manor, Pa., set sail with his bride for India. A recent memoir, *Robert Stewart Fullerton, Letters and Narratives of Mutiny Days* (J. J. Lucas, Allahabad, 1928), recalls the horrors of the Indian Mutiny (1857), and the part played by this missionary family in the dangerous work of reconstruction. It was in no quiet times that their sixth child, George Stuart was born to them at the cantonment station, Fatehgarh. Six months later, the mother, newly widowed, returned with her four daughters and two surviving sons to America.

Fullerton's early career conformed closely to a family tradition which in his own generation returned two daughters (Dr. Anna M. and Mary) to India, and sent two sons (George S. and Edward G.) into the ministry. Not until his twenty-fifth year did the theologian yield to the philosopher in Fullerton, who having graduated from the University of Pennsylvania in 1879, pursued graduate studies at Princeton and Yale, was licensed to preach by a Presbyterian body, and was later ordained to the Protestant Episcopal ministry. In 1883, however, giving final expression to interests which had been forming throughout his student years, he accepted an instructorship in philosophy at the University of Pennsylvania. Here, in the course of the next twenty years, he developed that method of presenting philosophy which was less a lecture-form than a marvelously skilful adaptation of the classic "Socratic questioning."

The thought in which these years culminated did not appear in systematic form till the moment of their close, yet the minor works produced were neither few nor unimportant; their topics range through mathematics (*Conception of the Infinite,* 1887), theology (*Plain Argument for God,* 1889), philosophy (*On Sameness and Identity,* 1890), psychology (*On the Perception of Small Differences,* in collaboration with J. M. Cattell, 1892), historical interpretation (*On Spinozistic Immortality,* 1899). The ordering of such rich material into an organic whole demanded leisure for consecutive thought, but the more Fullerton became known in the academic world the more this leisure was denied him. Dean of the Graduate School and vice-provost from 1894 to 1896, he retained the latter office till 1898, when it became clear that only release from its heavy responsibilities would permit him to resume his philosophic work. The previous year, Mar. 8, 1897, had witnessed his marriage to Julia Winslow Dickerson, his first wife, Rebekah Daingerfield Smith, to whom he was married Jan. 26, 1884, having died in 1892; and now with adequate leisure, surrounded by every solicitude, his writing progressed rapidly toward the *System of Metaphysics* of 1904. Before this work reached completion, however, it had become increasingly plain that a health never robust, a strength always overtaxed, would be unequal to the continued strain of writing and lecturing in conjunction. In 1903, therefore, he resigned his Seybert professorship at Pennsylvania and accepted at Columbia a research professorship which conveyed the privilege of dividing his time between lecture-semesters at home and leisure-intervals abroad. Thus it happens that the *System,* published during the first year of his new professorship, presents the fruit of long labors in the old; but it happens, too, that its purport makes it no less a promise of things to come than a consummation of things gone before. It conveniently divides the philosopher's development into two periods. Taking these two periods together, his thought may be said to have found its beginnings in a Berkeleyan Idealism, its end in a New Realism. The earlier writings represent knowledge as setting out with "subjective data" (sensations), and acquiring with experience "beliefs" (expectations of sensation). From the skeptical implications of this philosophy Fullerton felt himself to have escaped when in the *System* he showed why the "elements of experience," with which all science must begin, are no more to be called "subjective" than "objective," since they become one or the other according as they are regarded as moments in the history of a mind, or aspects of an object observed. But if in 1904 this thought brought with it little more than a sense of escape from Idealism, by 1912, in *The World We Live In,* it had become an aggressive realism of the type its proponents of that day called "New": the "ideas," of which the earlier philosophy had supposed the world of experience to be composed, could only be called "ideas" by one already in possession of a physical world-order to which he might refer in locating mental states.

In arriving at this insight, Fullerton had no doubt put behind him certain historic errors; but no doubt, too, he looked upon this somewhat negative result as but a clearing of the ground for new constructions. World events defeated his private plans. Appointed to represent Columbia as first exchange professor to Austria in 1913–14, he chose as the subject of his Vienna lecture course "A Realistic Philosophy of Experience" the opening of which, given important place by the *Wiener Abendblatt* of the day, is reported to have found *ausserordentlichen Beifall*; and at its close Fullerton received at the hands of the Emperor the unusual distinction of nomination to an honorary professorship in the University of Vienna. At Munich he and Mrs. Fullerton were caught by the outbreak of the war, and here they were held till its close, with such consequences to the frail health of the philosopher as seem to have left him little strength for the more severe efforts of thought. On his return to America in 1918, his lectures at Vassar retained all their charm. His one volume of this period is unpretentious in scope, *A Handbook of Ethical Theory* (1922). Not long after this, his familiar letters begin to speak of "a tired mind in a tired body." Throughout his active life a masterful spirit had compelled to its service a machine little equal to the demands made on it. In his sixty-sixth year, at his home in Poughkeepsie, he took his own life.

In addition to the works already mentioned, he published *The Philosophy of Spinoza,* translated from the Latin and edited with notes (1894); *Introduction to Philosophy* (1906); *Die Amerikanischen Hochschulen* (1914); *Germany of Today* (1915).

[Dickinson S. Miller, "Fullerton and Philosophy," *New Republic,* May 13, 1925; John Marshall Gest, *Alumni Reg.,* Univ. of Pa., June 1925; Edgar A. Singer, Jr., *Fools Advice* (1925); *Yale Univ. Obit. Record* (1925); *Who's Who in America,* 1924–25; *N. Y. Times,* Mar. 24, 1925.]

E. A. S., Jr.

FULTON, JUSTIN DEWEY (Mar. 1, 1828–Apr. 16, 1901), Baptist clergyman, was born in Earlville, N. Y., the son of John J. and Clarissa (Dewey) Fulton. He spent his boyhood in Michigan attending school at Tecumseh, and later the state university (1848–51). He was graduated from the University of Rochester in 1852, from the Rochester Theological Seminary in 1854, and in May of that year was ordained. He was a minister in St. Louis (1854–55), in Sandusky, Ohio (1855–59), in Albany, N. Y. (1859–64), in Boston (1864–73), and then for many years in Brooklyn; from 1894 till his death he was in Somerville, Mass. He edited three religious papers, a publication of the Bible Union in St. Louis, and the *Christian in the World* and the *Watch Tower* in Brooklyn. In St. Louis, he made himself objectionable by his drastic pronouncements on slavery; in Brooklyn he withdrew from one church to establish another, and was temporarily suspended from the preachers' association; in Nova Scotia he harangued the country-side with such rancor as to get himself chained up to a lamp post; and in Somerville, as an old man of seventy, he disagreed with his parishioners and in a huff broke off relations with them. Whether as a preacher or as a lecturer he was a fervid orator, "admirably fitted," according to a contemporary account, for out-of-door speaking; his utterance was "like the flow of a mighty river, with force enough to turn all the mills for miles" (*Genealogy,* p. 212). One of his dearest themes was that honesty and hard work, coupled with the avoidance of whatever is not "useful," will inevitably lead to wealth and power; and he was always alert to denounce drinking, woman suffrage, and the drama. During the first part of his life the chief object of his condemnation was slavery, but after the Civil War, he finished off his concern with this matter by his adulatory sermon on the death of Lincoln (*Sermons Preached in Boston on the Death of Abraham Lincoln,* 1865), in which the sole error attributed to Lincoln is frequenting theatres, and by his *Memoir* (1866) of the business-man abolitionist, Timothy Gilbert. An antipathy of his more disturbing than all the others was Roman Catholicism, first the object of his attack in *The Outlook of Freedom: or The Roman Catholic Element in American History* (1856) and later in book and lecture and sermon until he died. *Why Priests Should Wed* (1888), delayed in publication because of alleged obscenity, *The Fight with Rome* (1889), *How to Win Romanists* (1898), and many other writings thunder his notions with a vigor which is notable for unction and sincerity but which seems in general too reckless of fact and effect. He was married three times, first to Sarah E. Norcross, and last, in 1897, to a school teacher forty years his junior, Jennie A. Chapman, by whom he had two children. Among his writings not already mentioned are *The True Woman* (1869) and *Rome in America* (1884), with a sketch of the author by R. S. MacArthur.

[*Who's Who in America,* 1899–1900; *Geneal. of the Fulton Family* (1900), comp. and ed. by H. R. Fulton; *Univ. of Mich., Gen. Cat. of Officers and Students 1837–1911* (1912); *Univ. of Rochester, Gen. Cat., 1850–1911* (1911); *Rochester Theol. Sem. Gen. Cat., 1850–1910* (1910); *N. Y. Times,* Apr. 17, 1901.]

J. D. W.

FULTON, ROBERT (Nov. 14, 1765–Feb. 24, 1815), artist, civil engineer, inventor, was born in Little Britain (later Fulton Township), Lancaster County, Pa. His ancestors had emigrated from Scotland to Ireland, and it was probably from Kilkenny in the latter country that the elder Robert Fulton came to America. By 1735 the latter had settled in the town of Lancaster, and in 1759 he married Mary Smith of Oxford Township, Chester County, Pa. In 1764 he purchased a farm near Lancaster and it was there that his son Robert was born a year later. After experimenting with farming for two years without success, the elder Fulton mortgaged his farm and returned with his family to Lancaster, where two years later he died, leaving practically no estate. The widow managed to keep her family of five children intact and gave them the rudiments of an education. When Robert was eight years old his mother sent him to a private school where his preliminary education was somewhat augmented.

From all accounts Fulton was not a brilliant scholar, but at the early age of ten he exhibited a genius for drawing. He showed, too, an unusual inventive trait, making his own pencils by hammering out the lead from the bits of sheet metal which he could secure. In 1778, when thirteen years old, he is said to have invented a sky-rocket when the town council because of the scarcity of candles forbade the use of them in honor of Independence Day. At the time of the Revolution, Lancaster was an important center for gun making and many prominent gunsmiths resided there. Young Fulton, because of his interest in mechanics, early made the acquaintance of such men and by observation learned much of their craft. He quickly became an expert gunsmith and supplied to the several established makers drawings for whole guns, and made computations of proportions and performances which were verified on the shooting-range. He also made many decorative designs for guns and these were always in great demand with the makers. As a boy, he enjoyed fishing but did not relish the physical labor of poling a boat, and as early as 1779 he devised a successful mechanism to propel a boat by paddle-wheels, manually operated, which he and his companions used on their fishing excursions on the Conestoga Creek at Lancaster. Meanwhile his talent for painting developed, and at the age of seventeen he went to Philadelphia to seek his fortune. Here he remained four years, supporting himself by making portraits and miniatures as well as by making mechanical drawings and painting landscapes. He was really successful in this work, and was able to save enough money to purchase a small farm in Washington County, Pa., for his mother and her family, giving her a deed to the property. Working so intensely, however, he seriously undermined his health and was advised to go abroad, preferably to London where an old family friend, Benjamin West, had settled and become famous. Accordingly, in 1786, Fulton left the United States and did not return to his native land for twenty years.

He spent his first years abroad in London, supporting himself by painting but following closely all scientific and engineering discussion and developments. Friendships formed with the Duke of Bridgewater and Lord Stanhope led to many schemes for the promotion of the useful arts which so engrossed Fulton's every thought that after 1793 he painted only for amusement or relaxation. Following his residence in London, he spent some time in Devonshire and was then for at least eighteen months a resident of Birmingham, whither he is thought to have gone because of his interest in the Duke of Bridgewater's canal projects then under way between Birmingham and the sea. His full time and thought were now given to engineering projects for internal improvements and the devising of mechanical equipment of various sorts. In 1794 he was in correspondence with Boulton & Watt concerning the purchase of a suitable steam-engine for boat propulsion. That year he secured a British patent for what he called a "double inclined plane" for raising and lowering canal boats; and soon thereafter patented a machine for sawing marble, for which he afterward received the medal of the Society for the Encouragement of Arts, Commerce, and Manufacturing; as well as a machine for spinning flax and one for twisting hemp rope.

Although reaching out in many directions in an endeavor to solve industrial problems, Fulton's energies were directed chiefly toward the development of canal systems, and one of his most widely used inventions of this period was a dredging-machine, or power shovel, for cutting canal channels. This was for a long time afterward a common machine in England. As his ideas on inland navigation matured, he wrote many essays, pamphlets, and letters upon all phases of the subject and sent them to persons who, he felt, could promote their advancement. In 1796 he published *A Treatise on the Improvement of Canal Navigation,* profusely illustrated by himself and containing drawings of many mechanical designs and even boats to show "the numerous advantages to be derived from small canals." He signed himself "Robert Fulton, Civil Engineer," which was the first formal announcement of his new occupation. Copies of this treatise were sent to Gen. Washington and the governor of Pennsylvania. It not only dealt with the practical contrivances for canals and the technicalities of his own inventions but also contained complete and accurate computations of all construction and operating costs. It contained, too, much argument and prophecy in regard to the economic and political advantages which would accrue to nations adopting great inland systems of canals.

That he was prepared to go further than the writing of treatises is well illustrated in his proposal for the construction of cast-iron aqueducts made in March 1796 to the Board of Agriculture of Great Britain. This contained complete plans and working drawings and involved the use of castings which could be "cast in the open sand" and erected with only the simplest and most inexpensive kind of staging. His plan required but few patterns, easily and cheaply made. One of these aqueducts was afterward erected over the Dee, twenty miles from Chester, consisting of eighteen spans of fifty-two feet, supported on pillars, the tallest of which in the middle of the valley was 126 feet high. The total length of the structure was about 300 yards, its width twenty feet, and its depth, six feet. Fulton also designed cast-iron bridge-structures for the carrying of roads across deep and wide valleys and inclined gradients. With all of his later proposals to the Board of Agriculture for these as well as for aqueducts he furnished complete detailed drawings and models and accurate computations of all costs. His double inclined plane invention of 1794, which is described in his canal treatise, was probably his most daring innovation. He proposed to take canal boats out of the canal and transport them overland by rail at certain parts of the route so as to avoid the high cost of construction in difficult country. Such inclined planes were actually built and found practicable in both England and the United States.

British interference with commerce during the European wars made of Fulton an avowed advocate of the freedom of the seas and led him to seek means of combating what he regarded as sea piracy, by whomever practised. He chose submarine warfare as the most effective weapon and for nine years, beginning in 1797, applied his energies and genius almost exclusively to the development of the submarine mine and torpedo. He was not in a financial position to undertake the necessary experiments alone, but believed that he might interest France sufficiently to gain her assistance. Accordingly, after preparing an essay on the general subject and forwarding it to the Directory, he repaired to Paris. Official France failed to recognize him immediately, but a fellow American, Joel Barlow [*q.v.*], residing in Paris, whom Fulton met on his arrival, became greatly interested and was his main financial support. His first experiments, made at Brest, were with a self-moving torpedo. The machine was intended to drive a cigar-shaped torpedo in a definite direction and to a predetermined place, there to fire a charge of gunpowder. The experiments were unsuccessful, however, and many months elapsed before Fulton could continue them, chiefly because of the lack of sufficient working capital.

Meanwhile, he obtained French patents for his several earlier inventions of canal equipment, and in order to support himself secured the adoption of his plans for the canal from Paris to Dieppe. He also painted in Paris what is thought to be the first panorama ever built. The subject was "l'Incendie de Moscow." A share in the admission fees yielded Fulton additional income. He also continued his submarine studies and finally, about 1799, obtained an audience with the French Directory only to have his plans summarily rejected. In 1800, however, Napoleon appointed a commission to examine thoroughly the schemes Fulton had in mind. Thus encouraged, he began experiments again, this time at Havre, and in the course of the winter of 1800–01 built a "diving boat," as he called it, which seems to have been remarkably successful. Accompanied by three mechanics he descended under water to depths of twenty-five feet. The depth was determined by the use of the barometer and the boat was directed by means of a compass. Fulton found that the boat steered as easily under water as above. Air was supplied to the occupants from a compressed air tank which enabled them to remain under water as long as four and a half hours. The performance of the *Nautilus,* as the boat was called, in its official trials before the French commission, was all that could be desired, and on Feb. 28, 1801, the Minister of the Marines and Colonies, under instructions from Napoleon, made a proposal to Fulton to proceed against British ships. His remuneration was to be proportional to the size of the vessel destroyed, a thirty-cannon frigate to yield the maximum, 400,000 francs. Fulton spent the summer reconnoitering the coast with the *Nautilus* but failed to overtake a British ship and accordingly received no reward for his efforts or for any of his experimental expenses. After this failure the French were no longer interested in his schemes. Had Napoleon been a naval man rather than an artillerist, Fulton's chances might have been better. The British meanwhile were by no means unaware of his experiments, for he still corresponded with his friends in England, and in 1803 the ministry, through a third party, made overtures to him, the result of which was that he agreed to discuss the character and applications of his invention and to demonstrate its practicability. The latter he tried to do in 1804 in an expedition against the French fleet in the harbor of Boulogne. Failure was again the result, caused by defective torpedoes. In spite of the fact that a year later, on Oct. 15, 1805, the value of his boat was proved by blowing up a heavy brig near Deal, England, British conservatism decided against the adoption of Fulton's invention and nothing came of his efforts. During the whole course of these experiments and negotiations Fulton had kept the United States officially informed of his activities, even though he did not believe that these inventions would be of immediate benefit to his native country.

He was greatly disappointed in his double failure with France and England, but was soothed somewhat by the revival of his interest in steamboats. This came about through a meeting with the newly appointed American minister to France, Robert R. Livingston [*q.v.*], who had been for a number of years deeply interested in steamboat developments in America and was still in possession of a monopoly granted by the New York legislature for the navigation of state waters by steamboats. The upshot of the meeting of these two men was that, while still experimenting with the *Nautilus,* Fulton entered into a legal agreement with Livingston, dated Oct. 10, 1802, to construct a steamboat for the purpose of navigating the Hudson River between New York and Albany. Livingston furnished the capital and Fulton applied his genius and energies to designing an experimental boat. By the early spring of 1803 the boat was completed and launched on the Seine, but the weight of the machinery placed in it was too great and it broke in two and sank. By Aug. 9, 1803, however, a new and stronger hull was built, the machinery installed, including Joel Barlow's patented steam boiler, and before a large crowd of spectators including a select committee of the National Academy, the new boat was successfully launched and was propelled slowly by the force of steam against the current at a speed of about four and a half miles an hour. This was so encouraging to Fulton that a day or two later he mailed an order to Boulton & Watt of England for a steam-engine for use in the boat proposed to be built in New York. Livingston also secured an extension of his New York monopoly for twenty years from 1803. Some years before this Fulton had about made up his mind to return to the United States, primarily to do what he could to bring about the adoption of his canal plans and the general improvement of inland conditions. This determination was materially strengthened by his friendship with Livingston, the success of his steamboat trial, and finally the failure of both France and England to take up his submarine schemes. Fully two years elapsed, however, after he placed his order for a steam-engine before he could return to America. He still had hopes that the British could be made to appreciate his submarine inventions; he had to secure permission for the export of his engine, and to keep after Boulton & Watt to hurry the building of it. He used the time also to gather all the information that he could relative to steamboat developments in England and France. Finally, in October 1806, Fulton sailed for New York, arriving two months later.

While the *Clermont,* as his new steamboat was named, was under construction, Fulton publicly demonstrated in the presence of naval experts the effectiveness of his torpedo invention by blowing up a brig in New York harbor, July 20, 1807. The *Clermont* was built by Charles Brown, a well-known New York ship-builder. It was 133 feet long, seven feet deep, and eighteen feet broad, and was decked over for a short distance at bow and stern. Under Fulton's immediate direction the Watt steam-engine was placed in the forward part of the boat and left open to view. Back of it was installed the twenty-foot boiler set in brick-work and housed over. Two side paddle-wheels, fifteen feet in diameter, propelled the boat. On Aug. 17, 1807, the *Clermont* began her memorable voyage up the Hudson to Albany and return. The elapsed time for the round trip was five days, but the *Clermont* was actually under way only sixty-two hours, the speed attained having been close to five miles an hour.

Until his death eight years later, Fulton was occupied with the establishment and management of steamboat lines, as well as with steamboat construction. The monopoly under which he operated caused many legal entanglements. Under his direction no fewer than seventeen steamboats, a torpedo-boat, and a ferryboat were constructed, after his designs and incorporating several patented details of both steam-engines and steam-vessels. At the time of his death a steamboat for the Russian government was in the process of building. While the War of 1812 was in progress, Fulton designed a steam war vessel in response to the demands of citizens of New York City for a means of harbor defense. The design was later submitted to Congress, which body after an investigation by naval experts authorized its construction in 1814. *Fulton the First,* as this vessel came to be known, was enormous for her period. The hull was double, like a catamaran, with a sixteen-foot paddle-wheel between the two parts, and was 156 feet long, fifty-six feet wide, and twenty feet deep. Her steam-engine cylinder was four feet in diameter and the engine stroke was five feet. Her armament consisted of thirty 32-pounders designed to discharge red-hot shot. Fulton did not live to see the boat in service. During these last years, too, he conducted many experiments on the firing of guns under water, which formed the foundation for subsequent developments.

"The grand achievement of Fulton was the direction of an enterprise which resulted in the production by Watt and his partners in Great Britain, and by Brown in New York, of a steamboat that could give commercial returns in its actual daily operation, and the institution of a 'line' of boats between New York and Albany, the success of which insured the introduction and continued operation of steam-vessels, with all the marvellous consequences of that great event. He was a prophet, inasmuch as he foresaw the outcome of this grand revolution, in which he was so active a participant and agent; and he was a statesman, in that he weighed justly and fully the enormous consequences of the introduction of steam navigation as an element of national greatness; but he has been recognized neither as prophet nor as statesman, both of which he was, but as the inventor of the steamboat—which he was not" (Thurston, *post,* pp. 48–49). Fulton married Harriet Livingston, the daughter of Walter Livingston, of "Teviotdale," Livingston Manor, N. Y., on Jan. 7, 1808, and died in New York at the age of fifty, survived by his widow and four children. He is buried in Old Trinity Churchyard, lower Broadway.

[C. D. Colden, *The Life of Fulton* (1817); Robt. H. Thurston, *Robt. Fulton* (1891); Alice C. Sutcliffe, *Robt. Fulton and the "Clermont"* (1909); H. W. Dickinson, *Robt. Fulton—Engineer and Artist—His Life and Works* (1913); W. B. Parsons, *Robt. Fulton and the Submarine* (1922); Geo. Iles, *Leading Am. Inventors* (1912); J. T. Lloyd, *Lloyd's Steamboat Directory* (1856); C. B. Todd, *Life and Letters of Joel Barlow* (1886); E. B. Livingston, *The Livingstons of Livingston Manor* (1910).] C. W. M.

FULTON, ROBERT BURWELL (Apr. 8, 1849–May 29, 1919), teacher, university executive, was born on a farm in Sumter County, Ala. His parents, William and Elizabeth K. (Frierson) Fulton, devoted their resources principally to the education of their children. In his seventeenth year he entered the sophomore class in the University of Mississippi, from which institution he graduated in 1869 with first honors in a class of twenty-one. After teaching a short time in Alabama and in New Orleans, he returned to his alma mater in March 1871 as assistant in the department of physics and astronomy. He continued his studies until he received the degree of M.A. in 1873, and maintained connection with the institution for thirty-three years thereafter, becoming professor in 1875 and chancellor in 1892.

During his first year as the executive head of the University, he abolished the preparatory department and in 1893 he introduced a summer session. Through his efforts the endowment was substantially increased by congressional grant of 23,040 acres of land in 1894. He was chiefly responsible for the development of a system of affiliated high schools which soon resulted in doubling the number of students and instructors in the University, for the enlargement of the physical equipment, the extension of the curriculum, and the addition of three professional schools. Owing to his initiative, the National Association of State Universities was organized in 1896, and in recognition of this service he was annually elected president of the association until 1903. He was president of the Southern Educational Association (1899), three times head of its department of higher education, and once head of the same department in the National Education Association. When the Mississippi Historical Society was organized (1890), he became a charter member, and served as archivist and member of the executive committee until the Society turned over its archives to the state in order to induce the legislature to establish a state department of archives and history. Elected to the first board of trustees of this newly created department in 1902, he served upon it until his removal from Mississippi four years later. At the same time, he was an active member of a commission in charge of the geological survey of the state. Forced from the chancellorship in 1906 by Gov. Vardaman, after the dismissal of a student with powerful political influence, he became superintendent of the Miller School in Albemarle County, Va., where he remained until his final retirement on a Carnegie pension twelve years later. In 1871 he had married Annie Rose, daughter of Landon C. Garland [*q.v.*], an educator of distinction. Before her death in 1893 she bore him four sons and a daughter. On Apr. 2, 1903, he married Florence Thompson, a member of a prominent family in New Orleans. Fulton was a man of striking personality. He had a keen sense of humor and his conversation abounded in choice epigrams and apt anecdotes. He made his home in New York City during the last months of his life and was buried in Rock Creek Cemetery, Washington, D. C.

[Sketches of Fulton will be found in *Univ. of Miss. Mag.*, Apr. 1902, pp. 20–21; *Bull. of the Univ. of Miss.*, "Hist. Cat., 1849–1909" (June 1910); *Who's Who in America*, 1918–19; *N. Y. Times*, May 31, 1919. For a list of his writings, see T. M. Owen, "A Bibliography of Miss.," in *Ann. Report of the Am. Hist. Asso. for 1899*, I, 710–11.] F. L. R.
D. M.

FUNK, ISAAC KAUFFMAN (Sept. 10, 1839–Apr. 4, 1912), clergyman, publisher, editor, was born at Clifton, Ohio, of Holland-Swiss stock. His father, John Funk, was a Universalist, and his mother, Martha Kauffman, a Lutheran. Isaac was educated for the Lutheran ministry, graduating from Wittenberg College, Springfield, Ohio, in 1860, and from the theological department there in 1861. Ordained that same year, he began his ministry in Indiana and later held pastorates in Carey, Ohio, and in Brooklyn, N. Y., where he was pastor of St. Matthew's English Lutheran Church from 1865 to 1872. Upon resigning this charge, he traveled in Europe, Egypt, and Palestine. After his return, he engaged in editorial work on the *Christian Radical*, then published in Pittsburgh, Pa.

In October 1876 Funk started in business, with desk room at 21 Barclay St., New York. He began by supplying books, pictures, and sundry necessities to ministers, of whose needs he was well aware. To meet one of these he founded the *Metropolitan Pulpit*, an aid in sermonic themes and Biblical exegesis. Two years later he changed the name to the *Complete Preacher*, changing it again in 1878 to the *Preacher and Homiletic Monthly*, and finally in 1885 to the

Homiletic Review. In 1877 he was joined by Adam Willis Wagnalls, a former classmate, and the two formed I. K. Funk & Company, known later as Funk & Wagnalls, and ultimately (1891) as the Funk & Wagnalls Company. The business was continued at 21 Barclay St., until it crowded all the other tenants out of the building, and then a store, occupying three floors, at 10-12 Dey St., was rented. Realizing that there was a demand for cheap books of the better kind, Funk announced a "Standard Series" of eleven works in large quarto, to which he added until it consisted of seventy-nine numbers. In 1884, by arrangement with Charles H. Spurgeon, his firm undertook the publication of Spurgeon's *The Treasury of David* (7 vols.), a standard work on the Psalms, which had a large sale. There followed in succeeding years other series of expository works, commentaries, and encyclopedias of various kinds, some of which are still standard books of reference.

A militant temperance advocate, in 1880 Funk started the *Voice,* as a temperance campaign paper, in the interests of the Prohibition party. A trial of eight weeks showed a demand for such a publication, and on Jan. 2, 1885, it began its career as a regular periodical, with a circulation which, during the political campaign of 1888, reached 700,000 copies. In the later eighties at Harriman, Tenn., he formed the East Tennessee Land Company, hoping to establish a prohibition center in that state, but the enterprise failed. Funk lost heavily, as did many of his followers, some of whom were very bitter over it. He was more successful, however, in establishing a residential center on Staten Island, which he called Prohibition Park.

In 1890 he launched the most successful of all his periodicals, the *Literary Digest,* of which he was the first editor. The crowning achievement of his literary career, *A Standard Dictionary of the English Language,* engaged his attention between the years 1890 and 1893. He originated the plans, selected the staff, superintended the editorial collaboration, and was editor-in-chief. He acted in the same capacity on a later edition of this book (1908–12), and was working on the manuscript for the letter "s" when he died. After the completion of the *Dictionary,* he began (1896) an active campaign for simplified spelling in the *Voice* and the *Literary Digest.* When, with the aid of the funds that Andrew Carnegie contributed to the movement, the Simplified Spelling Board was started, Funk gave it enthusiastic support. He also engaged in the production of *The Jewish Encyclopedia* (12 vols., 1901–06) projected by Dr. Isidore Singer, and throughout served as chairman of the editorial board under the direction of which the work was issued.

Funk's firm benefited through the lack of international copyright, and he was accused of reprinting authorized editions of books which other publishers had imported. For comments made in the *Evening Post* regarding the alleged piracy of an English work, he brought suit against E. L. Godkin for $250,000. The case was tried in February 1893, and although legal counsel deemed Godkin's attack legally indefensible, such was the skill of Joseph H. Choate in conducting the case for the defense that the verdict of the jury was in favor of Godkin and Funk had to pay the costs (Allan Nevins, *The Evening Post: a Century of Journalism,* 1922, p. 561).

As an editor, Funk contributed a number of trenchant and stirring articles to his publications. He was also the author of *The Next Step in Evolution* (1902), a religio-philosophical expression of his views; *The Widow's Mite and Other Psychic Phenomena* (1904), and *The Psychic Riddle* (1907). In 1901 he edited an edition of Croly's *Salathiel* which he issued under the title *Tarry Thou till I Come.* In 1863 he married at Carey, Ohio, Eliza Thompson, daughter of James and Janet Thompson. She died in 1868, and the following year he married her sister, Helen G. Thompson.

[*The New York Journalist* (1895); *Who's Who in America,* 1912–13; *Publisher's Weekly,* Apr. 13, 1912; *Literary Digest,* Apr. 13, 1912; F. H. Vizetelly, *The Development of the Dictionary* (1915); *N. Y. Times* and *N. Y. Tribune,* Aug. 5, 1912; *Homiletic Rev.,* May 1912; private information.]
F. H. V.

FUNSTON, FREDERICK (Nov. 9, 1865–Feb. 19, 1917), soldier, was the son of Edward Hogue and Ann Eliza (Mitchell) Funston, who moved about 1867 from New Carlisle, Ohio, where Frederick was born, to Iola, Kan., where he was brought up on a farm. The father served through the Civil War with Ohio troops, and, as "Fog Horn" Funston, had a long political career in the Kansas legislature and in Congress, where he was representative of the second Kansas district from 1884 until he was unseated in 1894. The boy was a rover. He worked at all the varied tasks about the farm, tried his hand at newspaper work, collected tickets on a railroad, and lasted two and a half years at the state university at Lawrence. While in college he was a "bantam," weighing about one hundred pounds, which were so well distributed over his short frame (five feet, five) that he was an unexpectedly handy man in any kind of fight. He was capable of real education and eventually acquired the training of a botanist, but he had no place in the formal discipline of the university. After 1888 he was on his own. He found a job as a special agent of the Department of Agriculture, and in the Death Valley expedition of 1891 made a creditable showing. Transferred to Alaska, he paddled a canoe in a hazardous trip of fifteen-hundred miles down the Yukon River from the Porcupine, and wrote a paper entitled "Botany of Yakutat Bay, Alaska" (*Contributions from the United States National Herbarium,* III, Jan. 15, 1896, p. 325).

The outbreak of the Cuban insurrection in 1895 found Funston footloose, and attracted to the Cuban cause by a speech of Gen. Daniel E. Sickles. His qualifications for the artillery service, for which he was accepted, were zeal and the fact that he had once "seen a salute fired to President Hayes at a county fair in Kansas" (*Memories of Two Wars,* p. 6). He was sent to Cuba from Charleston on the *Dauntless* in August 1896. Here, with Winchester Dana Osgood, who was killed in action, he served the artillery of Gomez; and after eighteen months of irregular warfare, having risen from captain to lieutenant-colonel, he came back to the United States on the eve of the war with Spain. Gov. John W. Leedy gave Funston command of the 20th Kansas Regiment on the strength of his Cuban experience. In May 1898 they were mustered in; and soon they were moved to the Pacific where they were to form part of a Philippine expeditionary force. They took no part in the operations against Spain, but in November 1898 they were sent to Manila, where they served in the brigade of Harrison Gray Otis in the division of Maj.-Gen. Arthur MacArthur. They distinguished themselves in the insurrection which began in the following winter. Funston was promoted to the rank of brigadier-general of volunteers and received the congressional medal of honor after the battle of Calumpit, in which he and a party of volunteers crossed the Rio Grande de Cagayán under fire and seized the skeleton of a broken railway bridge in the face of the enemy. The passage of the Army Act of Mar. 2, 1899, prepared the way for the withdrawal of the volunteer force, which was to be mustered out between Jan. 1 and June 30, 1901. Funston was ordered home for discharge, and an unwary general of regulars remarked when his retention for a permanent commission was broached: "I am making lieutenants of better stuff than Funston every day. Funston is a boss scout—that's all" (*Army and Navy Journal,* Apr. 13, 1901, p. 791).

Before the order for his return was complied with, Funston ascertained, from captured letters, the location of the headquarters of Aguinaldo, leader of the insurrection. On the night of Mar. 14, 1901, the *U. S. S. Vicksburg* set ashore on the northern end of the island of Luzon what purported to be a group of recruits hastening to Aguinaldo, with half a dozen American soldiers picked up as prisoners on the way. The recruits were Macabebe scouts, from a tribe that was loyal to the United States; the ostensible commander of the party was a former leader of the Filipinos who had surrendered to the United States but of whose capitulation Aguinaldo was unaware; the American prisoners were Funston and his assistants. The elaborate and hazardous ruse was a complete success. Once landed on the coast, the party worked its way through the jungle to Aguinaldo's camp, where it surprised and arrested the dictator. The party was picked up on Mar. 25 by the *Vicksburg,* at a prearranged spot, and three days later the news of the capture was sent out from Manila. Before the week was over the administration at Washington recognized this as "the most important single military event of the year in the Philippines" (Secretary of War, Annual Report, 1901, *House Document 2,* 57 Cong., 1 Sess., p. 32), and Funston was transferred to the regular army with his volunteer rank (*Milwaukee Sentinel,* Mar. 31, 1901).

Coming at the age of thirty-six to the grade of brigadier-general, he was many years younger than his ranking associates. He had the same type of opportunity that was about this time accorded to Leonard Wood and John J. Pershing, and like them he had to face and live with the disappointment of the junior officers in the regular army over whose heads he had been promoted. In 1906 he was on the spot when the earthquake shattered San Francisco. He was then in command of the military department of California, under Maj.-Gen. A. W. Greely, who commanded the division of the Pacific, but Greely was out of the division for the moment and Funston assumed charge in the emergency with a vigor that called forth a mild protest from his chief, who hurried back to his post of duty (*Annual Report of the War Department for the Fiscal Year Ended June 30, 1906,* III, 1906, "Report Pacific Mission," p. 165). After this Funston went to Cuba with the Taft mission, served in the Philippines and in Hawaii, and at the army service schools at Fort Leavenworth. In 1914 he was on the Texas border when the American intervention in Mexico occurred. He commanded the force that was sent to hold Vera Cruz, and was military governor of that city. He returned to Texas in November 1914, to command the troops on the border. He became a major-general Nov. 17, 1914, having previously acquiesced with good grace when other officers, senior in years though junior in rank, were promoted over him. He was still in command on the border when Pershing was sent into Mexico after Villa, but he died a few days after the orders had been issued for Pershing's withdrawal.

In 1898, while waiting in San Francisco for orders to proceed to the Philippines, he met, wooed, and married Eda Blankart of Oakland, Cal., an act which he described as "by all odds the smartest thing I ever did in my life" (*Memories of Two Wars*, p. 172).

[The obituary in the *Army and Navy Journal*, Feb. 24, 1917, p. 818, is excellent. Funston's own *Memories of Two Wars: Cuban and Philippine Experiences* (1911), is a vigorous and unconventional narrative. See also *Who's Who in America*, 1914–15; *Cong. Record*, 64 Cong., 2 Sess., p. 3702; *San Francisco Chronicle*, Feb. 20, 1917.] F. L. P—n.

FURLOW, FLOYD CHARLES (Apr. 9, 1877–Apr. 26, 1923), engineer, inventor, was born at Americus, Ga., the son of Charles T. and Carrie V. (Meriwether) Furlow. His father was a planter but while young Furlow was still a boy he became a Georgia state officer at the capital and moved with his family to Atlanta, Ga. Here Furlow prepared for college and entered the Georgia School of Technology in 1894, graduating with the degree of B.S. in mechanical engineering in 1897. After serving the school during the year 1897–98 as instructor of subfreshmen, Furlow devoted the next two years to postgraduate study in engineering, particularly metallurgy, at Worcester Polytechnic Institute, Worcester, Mass., and at several universities abroad. On his return to Atlanta in 1900, he was for a year adjunct professor in mathematics and head of the dormitories at the Georgia School of Technology. Continuing at the college the following year as junior professor in mechanical engineering in charge of mechanics and as lecturer in experimental engineering, he also established himself in business as a consulting engineer in Atlanta, undertaking especially construction engineering work. In 1902 he accepted the appointment as chief engineer of the Plunger Elevator Company of Worcester, Mass., and moved with his family there. Two years later he became vice-president of this company in New York, and after a year became chief engineer of the Otis Elevator Company, also in that city. In 1909 he was promoted to the position of general sales manager of the Otis Company, was made vice-president in 1911, and president in 1918, which position he held at the time of his death. In addition to his great business and administrative duties, Furlow maintained an especial interest in engineering research during his career, doing much work himself in electric, hydraulic, and steam engineering as well as in machine design. He specialized, however, in improvements in lifting machinery and elevators, and between 1906 and 1922 patents were issued to him on approximately twenty-five inventions, all of which were of great value in bringing the electric elevator to a high state of efficiency. These include elevator safety devices; a push-button-controlled electric plunger and elevator system; electrically controlled elevators; a speed regulator for plunger elevators; a variable landing device; a self-leveling elevator; and a micro-drive hydraulic elevator. Furlow was one of the first experimenters in X-ray photography in the United States and while a consulting engineer in Atlanta designed and built the first wireless apparatus in the South. In addition to his office as president of the Otis Elevator Company, he was the director of the Otis companies of Illinois, Missouri, Texas, Canada, and France, and was at one time reputed to be the highest salaried executive in the world. He was a member of many clubs and societies, including the American Association for the Advancement of Science, and the American Geographical Society. He married Nellie Johnson of Atlanta on Dec. 26, 1898, who with three children survived him at the time of his death in New York City.

[*Who's Who in America*, 1922–23; *N. Y. Times*, Apr. 27, 1923; correspondence with the National Alumni Association, Georgia School of Technology, Atlanta, Ga.; Patent Office records.] C. W. M.

FURMAN, JAMES CLEMENT (Dec. 5, 1809–Mar. 3, 1891), Baptist preacher, university president, son of Richard and Dorothea Maria (Burn) Furman, was born in Charleston and died near Greenville, S. C. His grandfather, Wood Furman, was in early life a merchant in New York City, but he removed to South Carolina and gave his time to teaching school, surveying, and farming. Richard Furman [*q.v.*] was for over thirty years pastor of the First Baptist Church in Charleston, a leader of his denomination in the state, and an author of considerable local reputation. Several of his sons became teachers and preachers. James Furman was sent to school in Charleston, and was a member of the class of 1826, College of Charleston. He was converted in the spring of 1828, and by that fall he was a licensed Baptist minister. He preached at a number of different places and for a while attended the Furman Theological Institution. He was ordained in 1832, and in 1833 he married Harriet E. Davis, daughter of the Rev. Jonathan Davis of Monticello, and entered upon a pastorate at Society Hill which he continued with only slight interruptions till 1844. After that he was "senior professor"—president, in actuality, it seems—of the Furman Theological Institution. It was here that he first displayed an ability to go out among the rank-and-file of citizens and procure funds for a cause that was dear to him. Once that ability was recognized, his progress was no longer a matter of question. In 1852 he was given the presidency of the newly organized Baptist institution, Furman University, in Greenville, a position which he retained till his resignation in 1879. His wife died in 1849, and about six years later he married her sister, Mary Glenn Davis. He was a delegate to the state secession convention. During the war his university was dormant, and he taught in the Greenville Female College. Hard times throughout the South in the late 1870's made many people unable to meet pledges which they had signed toward the maintenance of the university. There was rough sailing—dissension as to what to do about these pledges, restiveness among subordinates unsure of their next paycheck, murmurs to the effect that what the university really needed most was a younger president. After his resignation he continued to preach regularly, and he became an associate editor of the *Baptist Courier*. All his life he was a member and often an official of various Baptist boards, five times, for instance, vice-president of the Southern Association, and seven times president of the State Association. In his last years he took part, or was thought of as taking part through his paper, in several vigorous controversies. The most notable of these turned on whether or not the state could of right empower its university to charge no tuition fees when church schools were obliged to charge such fees to keep in operation. He was a strict disciplinarian in ecclesiastical matters, not hesitating when he thought proper to expel people from his communion. He would not tolerate divorce on any grounds whatever, and in general he distrusted women in public affairs. As for their *preaching,* he held that that was expressly forbidden in the Scriptures.

[McDonald Furman, "A Family of Educators," *Education,* Mar. 1897; H. T. Cook, *Life Work of J. C. Furman* (1926); Charleston *News and Courier,* Mar. 4, 1891.]

J. D. W.

FURMAN, RICHARD (Oct. 9, 1755–Aug. 25, 1825), Baptist clergyman, educator, was born in Esopus, N. Y. In the summer of 1755, his father, Wood Furman, a native of Long Island and a merchant in New York, had gone with his son to South Carolina, leaving temporarily in the North his wife, Rachel Brodhead, and their daughter. After Richard's birth, the mother went by sea with the two children to join her husband, and the family finally settled near Charleston. Wood Furman knew enough mathematics to do surveying, while his general intellectual ability led to his selection as local magistrate and judge of probate. He himself looked after the education of Richard, who had little if any conventional schooling. In May 1770 the family moved to the High Hills of Santee, where young Furman came under religious convictions and united with the Baptist Church. He began almost immediately to preach, and in May 1774, before he was nineteen, was ordained as pastor of the local church. The next November he married Elizabeth Haynesworth, whose brother had married Richard's only sister. Elizabeth died in June 1787, and on May 5, 1789, Furman married Dorothea Maria Burn.

As the Revolution approached, he took a positive stand on the side of the colonies. He even marched to Charleston with a company commanded by his brother, but Gov. Rutledge advised him to return home where his influence was strong. Later, Cornwallis placed a price upon his head, and Furman betook himself to North Carolina and Virginia till the war was over. Upon his return, although considerably under thirty, he was the outstanding leader of the Baptists of his state, and soon, of the South. In 1787 this position was made more strategic by his call to the pastorate of the Baptist Church at Charleston.

Furman was an influential member of the convention which in 1790 drew up a constitution for South Carolina; this abrogated the special privileges of the Episcopal Church and granted all religious denominations the right of incorporation. He became a Federalist in politics and was always a champion of strong, centralized authority. As a result, he favored an ecclesiastical polity which, in so democratic a group as the Baptists, called for a greater degree of centralization than that acceptable to most of his codenominationalists. He advocated no organization beyond what he considered necessary for efficient functioning in the varied enterprises dependent upon the churches, but he did not stress the safeguards to the independence of the local church which mark the slower evolutionary process of Baptist ecclesiasticism in recent times. As early as 1785, he brought forward a plan for the incorporation of the Charleston Baptist Association, and in 1819 he advocated the plan of the Charleston Association as a basis for uniting the Baptists of South Carolina in a General Association. This scheme was thwarted by conservatism and suspicion of centralization, but when, two years later, the Baptist State Convention was organized, he became inevitably its first president.

In no area was Furman's influence more important for the South and the Baptists than in that of education. As the Baptists had no school of theology until well along in the nineteenth century, he himself had often taken into his household young men who desired training for the ministry. In 1789, sensing the need of broader educational opportunities for prospective ministers, he devised a plan to secure funds for this purpose in the stronger churches, and this movement soon became more definitely organized with Furman as its official leader. When the proposal was made that the Baptists of South Carolina and Georgia unite in founding a collegiate institution, he was one of its leading proponents. He did not live to see the fruition of this effort, but within fifteen months of his death, his name was given to the academy and theological institution which soon became Furman University.

When the Baptists of the United States were awakened to their foreign missionary opportunity by the acquisition of Adoniram Judson and Luther Rice [*qq.v.*], Furman was alert to see the possibilities of "enlarged expressional activities," although the phrase arose at a later time. At the meeting called at Philadelphia in 1814 to organize the missionary and other general activities of the Baptists, he was from the first a recognized leader, and was chosen president of the new organization, the Baptist Triennial Convention of the United States. At its second meeting in 1817 he was reëlected to this office; his address at this time on ministerial education is considered to have been a factor in the establishment of Columbian College (George Washington University).

Although a number of Furman's discourses were printed, his writings do not bear much evidence of the tremendous personal influence which he exerted. For almost fifty years probably no one man in the South had a wider one. It was based upon sheer character and ability, and was always used for the higher interests of mankind. His chief biographer designates him as "the incarnation of the Anglo-Roman spirit of organization."

[H. T. Cook, *A Biog. of Richard Furman* (1923), though short, is the fullest account of Furman's career; his connection with educational movements is further traced by Cook in *Educ. in S. C. under Bapt. Control* (1912) and by W. J. McGlothlin, *Bapt. Beginnings in Educ., A Hist. of Furman Univ.* (1926). See also W. B. Sprague, *Annals Am. Pulpit*, vol. VI (1860); *Two Centuries of the First Bapt. Ch. of S. C., 1683–1883* (1889), ed. by H. A. Tupper; Colyer Meriwether, *Hist. of Higher Educ. in S. C.* (1889); McDonald Furman, "A Family of Educators," *Education*, Mar. 1897.]

W. H. A.

FURNAS, ROBERT WILKINSON (May 5, 1824–June 1, 1905), soldier, governor of Nebraska, agriculturist, was born near Troy, Miami County, Ohio, of English Quaker stock. His parents, William and Martha (Jenkins) Furnas, were natives of South Carolina, but their antipathy to slavery led them to remove to Ohio before Robert was born. The boy, left as an orphan in 1832, soon began to shift for himself. He learned several trades, including that of printer, and on reaching maturity tried out a number of different occupations without at first achieving notable success. In 1856 he emigrated to the tiny village of Brownville, Nebraska Territory, where he soon established the *Nebraska Advertiser,* a paper which came to exercise great influence in the South Platte region. After some hesitation the pioneer editor allied himself with the newly formed Republican party. He served four years, 1856–59, in the territorial legislature, but his otherwise excellent record as legislator was marred by the charge that his vote against the removal of the capital from Omaha had been secured by bribery, and in 1860 he retired temporarily from political life.

With the outbreak of the Civil War, Furnas, as an officer of the territorial militia, sought to awaken the people of the territory to their military responsibilities; later, as a colonel in the regular army, he organized three regiments of Indians in the Indian Territory, with whom he saw active service; and finally, he was largely instrumental in raising the 2nd Nebraska Cavalry, which he commanded in campaigns against the plains Indians. In 1864 he returned to civil life. After spending several years as an Indian agent, he resumed his editorial work, but soon relinquished it and reëntered politics. In 1872 he was elected governor of his state on the Republican ticket—a place which he held, however, with small satisfaction to himself, partly because the old charge of bribery rose again to plague him, and partly because the petty details of administrative work irked him. He made no effort to succeed himself.

Furnas's chief claim to fame lay in his lifelong devotion to agriculture. He was instrumental in establishing the territorial board of agriculture, and was for forty-four years an active member of it, usually as president or secretary.

He made the Nebraska State Fair his particular hobby and pride, found time to foster the work of numerous agricultural organizations, and represented Nebraska at fairs and expositions outside the state. He owned a farm in Nemaha County, and although he made little money as a farmer, he at one time was said to have operated the largest nursery in the state. He was as much interested as his friend J. Sterling Morton [*q.v.*] in the planting of trees, and according to a well-authenticated tradition the idea of Arbor Day originated with Furnas rather than with Morton. He was also interested in public education. As a member of the legislature he secured the passage of the first common-school law for Nebraska; he was twice regent of the state university; and in 1878 he took the lead in organizing the Nebraska State Historical Society. In his human dealings he was generally opinionated, but seldom dogmatic; decisive, but always courteous. He was twice married: on Oct. 29, 1845, to Mary E. McComas, who died in April 1897, and on Dec. 25, 1899, to Susannah (Emswiler) Jameson. By his first wife he was the father of eight children. He died in Lincoln, June 1, 1905, and was buried by the Masons, among whom he had long been prominent.

[Some Furnas correspondence and two volumes of Furnas scrap-books are in the possession of the Nebr. State Hist. Soc. A thesis by John L. McKinley, "The Political Career of Robt. W. Furnas," is in the library of the University of Nebraska. Other material is to be found in A. C. Edmunds, *Pen Sketches of Nebraskans* (1871), pp. 234–39; T. W. Tipton, *Forty Years of Nebr.* (1902), pp. 120–34; J. Sterling Morton and Albert Watkins, *Illustrated Hist. of Nebr.*, I (1905), 656–60; *Proc. and Colls. Nebr. State Hist. Soc.*, vol. XV (1907); *Morning World-Herald* (Omaha, Nebr.), June 2, 1905.]

J. D. H.

FURNESS, HORACE HOWARD (Nov. 2, 1833–Aug. 13, 1912), Shakespearian scholar, was born in Philadelphia, the third of the four children of the Rev. William Henry [*q.v.*] and Annis Pulling (Jenks) Furness. He graduated fifth in the class of 1854 at Harvard College and for the next two years traveled with his roommate, Atherton Blight, in Germany, Spain, the Crimea, and the Levant. Home in Philadelphia, he was admitted to the bar in November 1859 and in June 1860 married Helen Kate Rogers, daughter of Evans Rogers, a hardware merchant. They had four children. In 1874 Mrs. Furness published a *Concordance to Shakespeare's Poems.* After her death Oct. 30, 1883, the successive volumes of the New Variorum Shakespeare were dedicated to her memory. Like his father he was an active Abolitionist. As a student he had seen Anthony Burns [*q.v.*] returned to slavery; in December 1859 he helped to spirit the body of John Brown through Philadelphia; a year later he mailed Thomas Carlyle a photograph of a "scourged back" with the message: "Please observe an instance of *'hiring for life.'* God forgive you for your cruel jest and your blindness" (*Letters,* I, 156). Rejected for military service because of deafness, he served through the Civil War, in the field and on the lecture platform, as an agent of the Sanitary Commission. In 1866, having sufficient leisure and means, he entered upon what proved to be his life-work.

He was destined, it would seem, to edit Shakespeare. As an adolescent he had worshipped Fanny Kemble, a parishioner of his father's, and had attended her Shakespearian readings unfailingly. He was a second-year man at Harvard when Francis James Child [*q.v.*], his "alderliefest master," returned from his *Lehrjahre* under Jacob Grimm. His deafness, though it deprived him of music, the theatre, and such conversation as cannot be poured into an ear-trumpet, absolved him in large measure from the practise of his profession and left him free to work unhurried. Early in the sixties he made for himself "a mighty Variorum *Hamlet,* cutting out the notes of five or six editions besides the Variorum of 1821 and pasting them on a page with a little rivulet of text" (*Letters,* II, 54–55). It showed him that a New Variorum was needed. Encouraged by the Shakspere Society of Philadelphia, to which he had been elected in 1860, he planned such an edition, based on the Boswell-Malone Variorum of 1821, of *Romeo and Juliet.* While collating texts and assembling materials he discovered his genius. In 1870, through J. B. Lippincott & Company, he issued his prospectus; the play was published in 1871; and thereafter the stately terra-cotta and gold volumes, prized by students of Shakespeare the world over, appeared at remarkably regular intervals: *Macbeth* (1873); *Hamlet* (2 vols., 1877); *King Lear* (1880); *Othello* (1886); *The Merchant of Venice* (1888); *As You Like It* (1890); *The Tempest* (1892); *Midsummer Night's Dream* (1895); *The Winter's Tale* (1898); *Much Ado About Nothing* (1899); *Twelfth Night* (1901); *Love's Labour's Lost* (1904); *Antony and Cleopatra* (1907); and *Cymbeline,* published posthumously (1913). His treatment of the text was thoroughly conservative. For the first three plays he constructed his own, abandoning his original intention of using the Cambridge text; in *Macbeth* he seldom departed from the readings of the First Folio; for the succeeding plays he strove to reproduce as exactly as possible the text of his copy of the Folio; and in his notes he was almost invariably an advocate of the Folio readings. After *Romeo and Juliet* he did not depend on the Variorum of 1821 but traversed for himself the whole field of Shakespeare criticism. The chief merits of the New Variorum are its full record of variant readings and of the judgment of editors on disputed points, the monumental abstract of all previous criticism, and the wit, insight, and sense of its editor, who was "the most genial (in the German as in the English sense of the word), scholarly, and witty editor that ever shed light on the works of Shakespeare" (S. A. Tannenbaum in the *Dial*, July 16, 1913).

Furness was a devoted trustee of the University of Pennsylvania, was acting chairman of the University's Seybert Commission to investigate the phenomena of spiritualism, and was the author of the commission's *Preliminary Report* (1887). He translated Julius Wellhausen's German version of the *Psalms* (1898) for Paul Haupt's "Polychrome Bible." In *Records of a Lifelong Friendship* (1910) he published the correspondence between his father and Ralph Waldo Emerson. As deafness did not mar his perfect control of his voice, he continued until late in life to give public readings of Shakespeare and to deliver occasional addresses. Edwin Booth thought that in Furness the stage had lost a great actor. He was an expert gardener and a friend of Walt Whitman, cherished till the last his memories of a week with Richard Burton in Damascus, collected editions of Horace, cherished innumerable kittens, went annually to the Gulf of Mexico to fish for tarpon, and was universally beloved for his gentleness, kindness, and modesty. In his last years he bore manfully the frequent deaths of friends and relatives. His own death came suddenly and without pain at his home, "Lindenshade," in Wallingford, a suburb of Philadelphia.

[*Letters of Horace Howard Furness* (2 vols., 1922); *Old Penn: Weekly Rev. of the Univ. of Pa.*, Feb. 1, 1913 (Furness memorial number); F. A. Kemble, *Further Records* (1891); *Harvard Coll.: Report of the Class of 1854, 1854–94* (1894); *Letters of Chas. Eliot Norton* (2 vols., 1913); F. N. Thorpe, "Letters of H. H. Furness," *Lippincott's Mag.*, Apr. 1914; J. R. Hayes, "Gentlest and Kindliest," *Ibid.*, Dec. 1912; O. Wister, in *Harvard Grads.' Mag.*, Dec. 1912; Alois Brandl, in *Shakespeare-Jahrbuch*, vol. XLIX (1913); F. E. Schelling, in the *Nation*, Aug. 22, 1912; S. C. Chew, *Ibid.*, Aug. 29, 1912; Agnes Repplier, in the *Atlantic Monthly*, Nov. 1912; Taleott Williams, in the *Century Mag.*, Nov. 1912.]

G. H. G.

FURNESS, HORACE HOWARD (Jan. 24, 1865–Apr. 15, 1930), Shakespearian scholar, was born in Philadelphia, the second of the four children of Horace Howard [*q.v.*] and Helen Kate (Rogers) Furness. Like his father he spent almost his entire life in his birthplace. Upon his graduation from Harvard College in 1888, he returned home, attended courses in music and astronomy for three years at the University of Pennsylvania, and on May 3, 1890, married Louise Brooks Winsor, daughter of William Davis Winsor of Philadelphia, who died without issue May 1, 1929. In 1891 he became an instructor in physics in the Episcopal Academy and in 1900 published a laboratory manual that was used in several near-by schools. In 1901 he gave up teaching to join his father as co-editor of the New Variorum Shakespeare. After his apprentice work, a revised edition (1903) of *Macbeth*, in which, in conformity with the later plan of the series, he reprinted the Folio text *literatim*, he devoted himself to the historical plays, issuing *Richard III* (1908), *Julius Cæsar* (1913), *King John* (1919), and *Coriolanus* (1928). In 1920 he published a one-act play, *The Gloss of Youth*, dealing with a fancied episode in the lives of Shakespeare, Milton, and Cromwell. He was a trustee of the University of Pennsylvania, a member of several clubs and learned societies, and president of the Philadelphia Theatre Association. He was a man of great modesty and of many amiable qualities. He died of pneumonia in his sixty-sixth year. To the University of Pennsylvania he bequeathed the great Shakespearian library and collection of relics that had descended to him from his father, together with a $100,000 endowment for its maintenance.

When he began work on the New Variorum, Furness was unknown as a scholar, and the news of the arrangement was received with some misgiving. At his father's death the suggestion came simultaneously from various quarters that the completion of the edition be intrusted to a committee of scholars. Though the plan had advantages, it was hardly possible for Furness to assent to it, and he carried on the work, as an act of filial piety, with noble purpose and laborious industry. In general, the volumes that he edited were well received, but the most careful reviews of his work revealed numerous errors and shortcomings. (See especially S. A. Tannenbaum in the *Dial*, July 16, 1913, and Lawrence Mason in the *Journal of English and Germanic Philology*, July 1919, pp. 346–59.) How far they affect the total value of his work is a matter in dispute, but it is clear that in learning, critical judgment, originality, and mastery of detail he was not the equal of his father. It was his good fortune to be the son and pupil of the greatest of Shakespeare's editors, his misfortune that he must stand comparison with him.

[*Who's Who in America*, 1928–29; *N. Y. Times* and *Public Ledger* (Phila.), Apr. 16, 23, 1930; *Harvard*

Coll. Class of 1888, Secretary's Report No. V (1905) and *No. VII* (1913), with two portraits; editorial in the *Nation*, May 7, 1930.] G. H. G.

FURNESS, WILLIAM HENRY (Apr. 20, 1802–Jan. 30, 1896), Unitarian clergyman, was born in Boston, Mass., the son of William and Rebekah (Thwing) Furness. He attended a "dame's school" and the Latin School with his lifelong friend R. W. Emerson. He graduated in 1820 from Harvard and in 1823 from the Divinity School. After several months of preaching, he was called in the summer of 1824 to the Unitarian Church in Philadelphia, where he was ordained and installed Jan. 12, 1825. This church, founded by Dr. Priestley in 1796, had never previously had a pastor. The congregation grew rapidly under Furness's leadership and after three years a commodious house of worship was built which lasted through his ministry. In 1875 he became pastor emeritus, but continued to preach to his own people and elsewhere as long as he lived. It has been said that his life had two major interests. The first was the anti-slavery cause which he championed as early as 1824 until the close of the Civil War, in defiance of violence and social ostracism. His other interest was the study of the life of Jesus. As a student of the Jesus of history rather than the Christ of theology, he was a pioneer in pointing out the distinction between the two. He believed that Jesus represented humanity at its best, that the Gospels were historic documents, and that the New Testament miracles were wholly natural events. Out of this research developed several published works, of which the most important are the following: *Remarks on the Four Gospels* (1836); *Jesus and His Biographers* (1838); *A History of Jesus* (1850); *Thoughts on the Life and Character of Jesus of Nazareth* (1859); and *The Veil Partly Lifted* (1864).

Furness was one of the first American scholars to study and translate German literature, his most important translation being Daniel Schenkel's *Character of Jesus Portrayed* (1866), to which he added copious annotations. In his work of translation he was associated with his friend Rev. F. H. Hedge [*q.v.*], whom he assisted in the preparation of *Prose Writers of Germany* (1849). He also translated much German verse, of which his Schiller's *Song of the Bell* (1850) is probably the best. He was a hymn-writer of considerable merit, a collection of his best hymns being found in A. P. Putnam's *Singers and Songs of the Liberal Faith* (1875). He was a lover of art and a great promoter of artistic interests, and appreciated both the classic and the current in literature. Although a participant in the Unitarian and the slavery controversies, he never aroused antagonisms because he criticized ideas rather than persons. His circle of friends embraced those of all sects and creeds, prominent among whom was the Catholic Bishop of Philadelphia. He was a poor denominationalist and thought in terms of principles rather than of organization. He was married in 1825 to Annis Pulling Jenks of Salem, Mass., who died in 1884. Of their four children, two sons and a daughter survived them. One son, Horace Howard Furness, 1833–1912 [*q.v.*], attained distinction as a Shakespearian scholar.

[A comprehensive account of the life and work of Furness, with an extensive bibliography of his writings, is found in S. A. Eliot, ed., *Heralds of a Liberal Faith* (1910), vol. III. See also *Proc. Am. Philos. Soc. Memorial Vol.*, I (1900), 9–18; *Am. Ancestry*, IV (1889), 206; J. W. Jordan, ed., *A Hist. of Delaware County, Pa.* (1914); *Unit. Rev.*, Feb. 1875; *Athenæum*, Feb. 8, 1896; *Critic*, Feb. 8, 1896; *Christian Reg.*, Feb. 6, 1896; *Nation*, Feb. 6, 1896.] F. T. P.

FUSSELL, BARTHOLOMEW (Jan 9, 1794–Feb. 15, 1871), physician, reformer, was born in Chester County, Pa., the son of Bartholomew and Rebecca (Bond) Fussell. He was of mixed ancestry, with the English strain predominant. His father was a farmer and an approved Quaker minister. Fussell received his earliest instruction in a school erected by his father and taught by his sister Esther, who exercised a far-reaching influence over his intellectual development. While studying in the medical department of the University of Maryland, where he graduated M.D. in 1824, he supported himself by teaching and on Sundays conducted a free school for negro slaves, in which he had as many as sixty pupils at a time. Friendly contact with the negroes soon turned him into a militant Abolitionist, and Elisha Tyson of Baltimore initiated him into the duties of a station-master on the Underground Railroad. Shortly after his marriage to Lydia Morris, Fussell removed to Kennett Square, celebrated in Bayard Taylor's *Story of Kennett Square* (1866), in his native county, where he soon won renown as a physician of rare skill and devotion and as an Abolitionist who knew no fear. Into the business of sheltering escaped slaves and baffling their pursuers he seems to have entered with the zest of a sportsman, and his portly figure was conspicuous at the Philadelphia convention of 1833 that organized the American Anti-Slavery Society and issued its famous "Declaration of Sentiments." From the beginning he had been a friend of William Lloyd Garrison and had supported the *Genius of Universal Emancipation* and the *Liberator*. Though elsewhere in Chester County he had more than one encounter with hostile mobs, at

Kennett Square, thanks to his own prestige and to the persuasive eloquence of the peripatetic Charles Calistus Burleigh [*q.v.*], he was entrenched safely. When Gov. David R. Porter denounced the Abolitionists as traitors, John Greenleaf Whittier, in an unrepublished poem, defied him to

> Go hunt sedition! Search for that
> In every pedlar's cart of rags;
> Pry into every Quaker's hat
> And Dr. Fussell's saddle-bags,
> Lest treason wrap, with all its ills,
> Around his powders and his pills.

Largely through the influence of his sister, Esther Fussell Lewis, he also became an earnest advocate of temperance, of free elementary education, and of greater educational and professional opportunities for women. As early as 1840 he gave medical instruction to a class of women; he succeeded in interesting other doctors in his ideas; and as the result of his efforts the Female Medical College (renamed in 1867 the Woman's Medical College) of Pennsylvania was incorporated Mar. 11, 1850. Henry Gibbons, a son of William Gibbons [*q.v.*], was the chief incorporator; Fussell, though unable to take any direct part in the work, always remained deeply interested in it. After the death about 1838 of his first wife, he married Rebecca C. Hewes and moved to York, Pa., where he opened a school and continued to work for the emancipation of negroes. He died at Chester Springs at the home of one of his sons.

[Wm. Still, *The Underground Railroad* (1872); R. C. Smedley, *Hist. of the Underground Railroad* (Lancaster, Pa., 1883); J. G. Whittier, "The Antislavery Convention of 1833," *Atlantic Monthly*, Feb. 1874; S. T. Pickard, *Life and Letters of J. G. Whittier*, I (1894), 229; E. F. Cordell, *Medic. Annals of Md.* (1903); Clara Marshall, *Woman's Medic. Coll. of Pa.* (1897). The day of his death is taken from the *Public Ledger* (Phila.), Feb. 18, 1871.]

G. H. G.

GABB, WILLIAM MORE (Jan. 20, 1839–May 30, 1878), paleontologist, was born in Philadelphia. His father, Joseph H. Gabb, who kept a millinery shop, died about 1861, and his mother, Christiana Gabb, carried on the business. Graduating from the Jefferson Grammar School in 1852, he entered the Central High School, from which he received the B.A. degree in 1857. He followed the classical course, but he was especially interested in minerals and fossils, and whenever possible he visited the Academy of Natural Sciences, then the center of American natural history. He early determined on a career in geology and paleontology, and between 1857 and 1860 studied at Albany with James Hall, then the country's foremost paleontologist. Returning to Philadelphia in 1860, he became a member of the Academy, serving on its paleontological committees, and forming life friendships with many scientists. He also spent some time at the Smithsonian Institution in Washington, where he met the leaders in various fields of natural history.

His first official appointment came at the end of 1861, when he was chosen by Josiah D. Whitney to serve as paleontologist on the Geological Survey of California. He had been recommended as the best authority in America on Cretaceous marine paleontology—a considerable eminence for a youth of twenty-two to have reached, though a glance at his bibliography shows that he already had to his credit no fewer than twenty-two papers, fifteen of which were on Cretaceous fossils. He remained in California six years. In the field, he covered hundreds of miles on horseback, often in the territory of hostile Indians. His companion on one of these trips, William H. Brewer [*q.v.*], records that he was "curiously self-contained. He never seemed afraid, and never anxious in the presence of danger; he never lost his temper, and in various ways showed a peculiarly even disposition." The results of his early industry are apparent in the quarto paleontology volumes of the California Survey, of which Gabb was responsible for sections I and IV of the first volume and for all of the second (*Geological Survey of California, Paleontology*, vol. I, 1864; vol. II, 1869).

His attention was next directed to Lower California, whither he went in 1867, traversing the entire peninsula from north to south on muleback and crossing it ten times. These trips resulted in a report with a geologic map (A. H. Petermann, *Mittheilungen*, vol. XIV, 1868) that was the first to set forth the true structure of this Mexican peninsula. The following year he went to Santo Domingo to make a topographic and geologic survey of that country. Three years of work here led to a memoir of 200 pages, "On the Topography and Geology of Santo Domingo" (*Transactions of the American Philosophical Society*, new series, vol. XV, 1873), and a fine map which was combined with Schomburgk's work on Haiti (Petermann, *Mittheilungen*, vol. XX, 1874). In 1873, the government of Costa Rica entrusted to him the making of a survey of its province of Talamanca, then perhaps the least known of any part of Central or Isthmian America. Toward the end of his work in this tropical country, he suffered severely from coast fever, and finally contracted pneumonia, which left his lungs in a weakened state. Recovering, he returned to the United States in 1876, but shortly afterward started for Santo Domingo to develop a mining claim, only to be forced by illness to turn back to Philadelphia, where he died after a few weeks. The geographic phase of his work in Costa Rica appeared in 1875 in a government publication (*Anales de Instituto Fisico-Geografico Nacional de Costa Rica*), but the paleontologic monographs that he had planned to build upon the material collected were never to see the light of day, though in 1876 he published an ethnological study "On the Indian Tribes and Languages of Costa Rica" (*Proceedings of the American Philosophical Society,* XV, 1874–75). Gabb's work belongs to the pioneer period of paleontology and is chiefly exploratory and descriptive. His bibliography numbers eighty-eight titles. Of Cretaceous fossils alone he described at least 474, and such extensive description stamped his impress indelibly upon American Cretaceous and Tertiary paleontology.

[See memoir by W. H. Dall, with bibliography, in *Nat. Acad. Sci. Biog. Memoirs,* vol. VI (1909); J. S. Newberry in *Am. Jour. Sci.,* Aug. 1878, p. 164; *Nature,* July 11, 1878; *Public Ledger* (Phila.), June 1, 1878. Gabb's letters to the editors of the *Am. Jour. Sci.,* written during his stay in Central America and Santo Domingo, were published in abstract in that journal from 1871 to 1875.] C. S.

GADSDEN, CHRISTOPHER (Feb. 16, 1724–Aug. 28, 1805), merchant, Revolutionary leader, was born in Charleston, S. C., the son of Thomas and Elizabeth Gadsden. He was sent to a classical school in England, and thence to a counting-house in Philadelphia, was for a time purser on a British war vessel, but having married in 1746, returned to Charleston to enter business. By 1761 he had two stores in town, two in the country, and a plantation. In 1757 he entered the Assembly, in which he served for nearly thirty years. An attempt by Gov. Boone in 1762 to unseat him brought on a hot contest with the lower house. In the Stamp Act Congress of 1765 Gadsden distinguished himself by his arguments for colonial union and against recognition of the authority of Parliament (R. W. Gibbes, *Documentary History of the American Revolution,* 1855, pp. 7–9, and William Johnson, *Sketches of the Life and Correspondence of Nathanael Greene,* 1822, I, 265–66). He was now the acknowledged leader of the radicals of the province. In his political principles he was an excellent representative of the liberal portion of the South Carolina aristocracy—insistent on the rights of self-government, but with standards of public order and official responsibility practically precluding anything more democratic than popular rights with aristocratic leadership. Personal qualities rather than difference of principles put him far in advance of his fellows. Despite impetuosity to the point of rashness, and a temper that he controlled with the greatest difficulty, his integrity and religious zeal, his courage, optimism, and energy made him an invaluable champion. He found enthusiastic followers among the Charleston mechanics, skilled and responsible workmen who owned property and voted for members of the Assembly but did not sit in it. On the repeal of the Stamp Act he met with twenty-five of them and the party pledged themselves to the defense of American rights (Joseph Johnson, *post,* pp. 27–29, 35; Gibbes, *op. cit.,* pp. 10–11). For the next eight years, in the Assembly, in mass meetings which agreed upon and enforced non-importation, and in newspaper controversy, Gadsden was indefatigable. In 1774 he was elected one of the four delegates to the First Continental Congress. He left the Second Congress in January 1776 to take command as senior colonel in the newly organized South Carolina forces, but first served in the Provincial Congress, where in February he startled friend and foe alike by advocating complete independence. In June, he was in command of Fort Johnson when the British attacked Fort Moultrie, opposite his position. He became brigadier-general in the Continental Army in September following. The year 1778 saw the climax of his career. In the constitution adopted in March he and William Henry Drayton [*q.v.*] secured the disestablishment of the church, and popular election of senators, but the conservative revolutionists, led by John Rutledge [*q.v.*], succeeded in removing Gadsden from leadership in the Assembly by electing him vice-president. A riot against the administration of Rawlins Lowndes [*q.v.*] and Gadsden, because of its extension of time limit for taking an oath of allegiance, roused the latter's anger and probably occasioned the break which followed with his old friends, the mechanics. In the same year a dispute over the command of the Continental troops in the state led to his resignation, and to a bloodless duel with his rival, Gen. Robert Howe of North Carolina. After the fall of Charleston in 1780 he was paroled, but later taken to St. Augustine. On his refusal to give another parole he was put in close confinement for ten months until he was released by exchange. In 1782, alleging age and ill health, he refused the governorship tendered him by the Assembly. He sat in that body, however, for the next two years, and was one of the few who opposed confiscation and amercement of Loyalist property (Alexander Garden, *Anecdotes of the Revolutionary War,* 1822, p. 176). Popular feeling against the Loyalists, formation of political clubs which attempted to exert pressure on legislation, and threats of mob violence caused him intense uneasiness, and in 1784 he engaged in a bitter newspaper fight with such opponents, writing under his own name or that of "Steady and Open Republican" (see letters in the *Gazette of the State of South Carolina,* Apr. 22, 29, May 6, 13, July 15, 17, 26, 29, Aug. 2, 12, 19, Sept. 9). When the confusion subsided he withdrew from public life almost entirely. He sat in the state convention of 1788 and there voted for ratification of the United States Constitution, was one of the South Carolina presidential electors in 1789, and sat in the state constitutional convention of 1790. In the election of 1800 he bestirred himself for his old friend Adams, and grieved over his defeat (*The Works of John Adams,* ed. by C. F. Adams, vol. IX, 1854, p. 578). From the Revolution to his death in 1805 his chief business interest was his great thousand-foot wharf which he had completed about 1770. He was married three times: On Aug. 28, 1746, to Jane Godfrey; on Dec. 29, 1755, to Mary Hasell; and in 1776 to Anne Wragg.

[For sketches of Gadsden see David Ramsay, *The Hist. of S. C.* (1809), II, 457–66; F. A. Porcher in *S. C. Hist. Soc. Colls.,* vol. IV (1887); E. I. Renick, in *Pubs. Southern Hist. Asso.,* July 1898; Jos. Johnson, *Traditions and Reminiscences Chiefly of the Am. Revolution in the South* (1851). For his public career to 1783 see Edward McCrady, *Hist. of S. C. under the Royal Govt.* (1899) and *Hist. of S. C. in the Revolution* (2 vols., 1901–02); and E. C. Burnett, *Letters of Members of the Continental Cong.,* vol. I (1921). Additional bits of information are found in the compilations by A. S. Salley, Jr.: *Marriage Notices in the S. C. Gazette* (1902), pp. 11, 19, *Reg. of St. Philip's Parish* (1904), pp. 61, 183, *Marriage Notices in the S. C. and Am. General Gazette* (1914), p. 24; in *S. C. Hist. and Geneal. Mag.,* Jan. 1919; and in S. C. newspapers and the state archives.]

R. L. M—r.

GADSDEN, JAMES (May 15, 1788–Dec. 26, 1858), railroad president, promoter of Southern nationalism, minister to Mexico, was born in Charleston, S. C., the son of Philip and Catherine (Edwards) Gadsden and the grandson of Christopher Gadsden [*q.v.*] of Revolutionary note. He received his college education at Yale, where he graduated in 1806, and returned to his native city to enter business. Soon afterward he abandoned commercial life for the United States army, continuing in the service for more than a decade. During the War of 1812 he was a lieutenant of engineers and after its close he aided Andrew Jackson in the inspection of the military defenses of the Southwest and the Gulf Coast. Participating in the war against the Seminole Indians, he seized the correspondence which led to the military trial and execution of Robert C. Ambrister and Alexander Arbuthnot in 1818. He was soon given the rank of captain and charged with the construction of works of defense on the Gulf frontier. Late in 1820 he became a colonel with authority to inspect the southern division of the United States army. For eight months subsequent to August 1821 he was employed as adjutant-general, but when the Senate refused to ratify his appointment, he left the military service and went to Florida.

Here he remained for some sixteen years. In April 1823, President Monroe appointed him commissioner to effect the removal of the Seminoles to reservations in the southern portion of the territory. This he accomplished in the following September by the Treaty of Fort Moultrie. He then made a survey of the reservations and built the first roads of the United States government in Florida. In 1824 he became a member of its first territorial Legislative Council. Attracted by the fertile lands of this newly acquired region, he disposed of the property in Tennessee which he had purchased during his army days, and became a Florida planter. He was made restless, however, by his previous career. He felt that the joy of country life existed only in the imagination of the poets and longed for something more congenial than "ploughing the soil and subduing the forest" (Garber, *post,* p. 76). It may be seriously questioned whether he found what he sought in Florida politics, for his championship of nullification lost him the friendship of Jackson and he was uniformly defeated in his numerous campaigns for the privilege of representing the territory in Congress. After the devastations of the Seminole War, he returned in 1839 to his native city.

A year after he reached Charleston he became president of the Louisville, Cincinnati & Charleston Railroad, an enterprise in which he had been interested since 1835; and for ten years he continued in this position. The organization had been involved in difficulties by the panic of 1837 and disputes among the directors. In 1840 it owned only 136 miles of track and was burdened with a three-million-dollar debt. After Gadsden took charge the road was reincorporated (1842) as the South Carolina Railroad Company. He came into power with dreams of knitting the small isolated railways of the South into a great system and of connecting the whole with the Pacific Coast by means of a line along the southern frontier. He would make the West tributary to the South and, moreover, inaugurate a direct trade between the South and Europe. In this manner he would bring about an economic revival in the South and break the dependency of this region upon the Northeast.

These ambitions he sought to realize largely through Southern conventions. Already he had been present at the Augusta Convention of 1837, where he had been appointed a member of the committee of five instructed to draw up an address to the people of the South and Southwest urging the advantage of direct trade with Europe. He had also been chairman of another convention with similar purposes which had met in the same city in 1838; and he had been prominent in the Charleston Convention of 1839. He now became one of the prime promoters of the Memphis Commercial Convention of 1845, where he served on several committees and was chairman of the committee on railroads. Here he urged the construction of a railway to the Pacific, recommending the project to the South as a good investment. During the next five years he worked zealously but without success for the connection of sufficient southern roads to form a continuous line to the Mississippi. In 1850, stockholders demanding immediate dividends removed him from the presidency of the South Carolina Railroad Company, but his interest in the scheme of a southern transcontinental railroad persisted. By 1853 he had not only decided upon the route along the Gila River as the shortest and most practicable, but he had also become convinced that the purchase of territory from Mexico would be necessary to the realization of the project. For a brief period fortune turned in his direction. His friend Jefferson Davis became President Pierce's chief counselor and secretary of war, and through Davis's influence Gadsden was appointed minister to Mexico. He was first instructed to settle the Indian and the general-claims issues and to obtain only sufficient territory for the construction of a railway to the Gulf of California. Soon after his arrival in the city of Mexico, however, his ambitions expanded. He saw an opportunity to serve his beloved South by a large addition of territory. Santa Anna's needs appeared to be great and, believing that he might be forced by these and by intimidation to alienate a large portion of northern Mexico, including Lower California, Gadsden hastened to make known the situation at Washington. He soon received instructions to purchase as much territory as he could buy for $50,000,000. The event proved that he had been too optimistic. He succeeded, by taking advantage of the dire financial straits of the Dictator and by opportune use of threats, in obtaining only a small strip of territory, which, however, proved adequate for his original purpose, although he died long before the railway to the Pacific was constructed across the area.

This acquisition, known as the Gadsden Purchase, marked the culmination of Gadsden's career. He remained another three years in Mexico, as minister, but they were unhappy years, filled with no important achievement. Although he had been willing to prolong the rule of a dictator in order to serve his own section in the United States, he was really at heart a democrat and he desired to see the democratic-republican system prevail in Mexico. There were many monarchists in the country, however, and Gadsden thought that they were being encouraged by European Powers unfriendly to the United States. "He believed the European nations intended not only to dominate Mexico, but to form an offensive and defensive alliance with Guatemala [Central America?] and all the South American countries, restrict the maritime power of the United States, control Tehuantepec, preserve Cuba, return Santo Domingo to Spain, place Haiti under the protection of France, and check the progress of American expansion and ideas in general" (Rippy, *post,* p. 203). He maintained that, under the circumstances, it was the duty of the United States to withhold the final three-million-dollar payment on the Gadsden Purchase from a Mexican government which longed for a monarch from Europe, and to lend its support to the republican group with American sympathies. The secretary of state, William L. Marcy [*q.v.*], did not speedily respond to his advice, but Gadsden appears to have supported the democratic revolutionists fighting under the reform Plan of Ayutla with more eagerness than propriety. Numerous demands for his recall were the reward of his pains. Relieved from his post by Marcy, he returned to Charleston late in 1856, where two years later he died. His wife, Susanna Gibbes Hort, died shortly before her husband, and they left no children.

[P. N. Garber, *The Gadsden Treaty* (1923), and J. F. Rippy, *The U. S. and Mexico* (1925), both contain suggestive references to sources. Gadsden's activities in the Southern conventions may be gleaned from the contemporary newspapers of the cities where they assembled. Consult F. B. Dexter, *Biog. Sketches Grads. Yale Coll.,* vol. VI (1912); U. B. Phillips, *A Hist. of Transportation in the Eastern Cotton Belt* (1908); obituary in *Charleston Daily Courier,* Dec. 28, 1858.]

J. F. R.

GAFFNEY, MARGARET [See HAUGHERY, MARGARET GAFFNEY, *c.* 1814–1882].

GAGE, FRANCES DANA BARKER (Oct. 12, 1808–Nov. 10, 1884), reformer, author, was born in Marietta, Ohio, where her father, Col. Joseph Barker, a native of New Hampshire, was among the original settlers. Her mother, Elizabeth Dana, was connected with the Dana and Bancroft families of Massachusetts. Frances secured such an education as the little frontier community afforded. On Jan. 1, 1829, when not yet twenty-one, she married James L. Gage, a lawyer of McConnelsville, Ohio. In spite of the demands upon her made, ultimately, by a family of eight children, she found time for reading, writing, and even speaking on temperance, slavery, and woman's rights. She later wrote to Elizabeth Cady Stanton, "From 1849 to 1855 I lectured on this subject [woman's rights] in Ohio, Indiana, Illinois, Iowa, Missouri, Louisiana, Massachusetts, Pennsylvania, and New York, and wrote volumes for the press" (letter quoted in Parton, *post*, p. 386). In 1853 the family moved to St. Louis. Here Mrs. Gage's anti-slavery proclivities promptly branded her an Abolitionist, her articles were excluded from the press, and she herself was socially ostracized and threatened with violence. While in St. Louis the family suffered three disastrous fires, possibly the work of incendiaries, and James Gage failed in business and in health. Mrs. Gage thereupon took the post of assistant editor of an agricultural paper in Columbus, Ohio, which she held until the Civil War destroyed the circulation of the paper. On the outbreak of the war, four of her sons joined the Union armies, and in 1862 she went to Port Royal, Beaufort, and Paris Island, S. C., and Fernandina, Fla., where for thirteen months, with the aid of her daughter Mary, she ministered to the freedmen of the soldiers. She then returned North to lecture and arouse others to the needs of the freedmen and the armies. Later she served as an unsalaried agent of the Western Sanitary Commission in Memphis, Vicksburg, and Natchez. In September of 1864, however, her active war work was ended when she was thrown from her carriage in Galesburg, Ill., and crippled for a year. Following the war, she lectured widely on temperance. In August 1867, a stroke of paralysis brought her public life to an end, but she continued her writing, and, as "Aunt Fanny," became well known for her children's stories, sketches of social life, and poems. Her larger published works were *Elsie Magoon; or the Old Still-House in the Hollow* (1867), a temperance tale; *Poems* (1867); *Gertie's Sacrifice* (1869); and *Steps Upward* (1870). She was large and vigorous, with a kindly face, easy manners, and a rich fund of conversation. An excellent extemporaneous speaker who never failed to interest her audiences, she was much in demand, and rendered valuable aid to the various causes in which she became interested. She died in Greenwich, Conn.

[Elizabeth Cady Stanton, "Frances D. Gage," in Jas. Parton and others, *Eminent Women of the Age* (1868); E. F. Barker, *Barker Geneal.* (1927), p. 401; E. C. Stanton, S. B. Anthony, and M. J. Gage, *Hist. of Woman Suffrage* (3 vols., 1881–87), *passim*; L. P. Brockett and M. C. Vaughan, *Woman's Work in the Civil War* (1867), pp. 683–90; obituary in *N. Y. Tribune*, Nov. 13, 1884.]

W. R. W.

GAGE, LYMAN JUDSON (June 28, 1836–Jan. 26, 1927), banker, secretary of the treasury, was born at Deruyter, Madison County, N. Y. His ancestor, Thomas Gage, came from England before 1650 and settled in Yarmouth, Mass., but his parents, Eli A. and Mary (Judson) Gage, were natives of New York State. Lyman attended the common schools in Madison County and after his parents had moved in 1848 to Rome, N. Y., continued his education at the Rome Academy. When he was fourteen, his school days came to an end and he became a mail agent on the Rome & Watertown Railroad. When he was seventeen he entered the Oneida Central Bank of Rome as office boy and junior clerk. At this time his salary was one hundred dollars a year. In 1855 he left Rome for Chicago, where he secured employment as a clerk in a lumber-yard and planing-mill. Three years later he became a bookkeeper, at a salary of five hundred dollars a year, for the Merchants' Savings, Loan & Trust Company. In 1861 he was made cashier and in 1868 accepted a similar position with the First National Bank of Chicago. During the seventies he was one of the organizers, and treasurer, of "The Honest Money League of the North West," which inaugurated a vigorous campaign against irredeemable paper money. His writings at this time were widely circulated and he began to acquire a reputation as a sound, conservative business man. In May 1882 there was a reorganization of the First National Bank and he became vice-president and executive officer of the new corporation, whose cash capital amounted to three million dollars. The following year he was elected president of the American Bankers' Association, to which office he was twice reëlected. The Haymarket tragedy of 1886 brought home to him the necessity of reconciling the conflicting views of labor and capital. With other outstanding leaders in the industrial and labor world he organized a series of economic conferences which for three years conducted an open forum on current questions pertaining to labor and capital. While these meetings resulted in no tangible solution of the pressing economic problems, they helped to awaken public discussion, and, incidentally, Gage, by his tact and open-mindedness, gained that sympathy of the working classes which he held throughout his distinguished career. In 1891 he was elected president of the First National Bank, which office he held until he entered public life. His service (1890–91) as president of the Chicago board of directors of the World's Columbian Exposition first brought him into national prominence. It may truthfully be said that the success of the exposition was "largely due to his genius, tact, and wise counsel" (*Review of Reviews,* March 1897, p. 292).

Although originally a Republican and a member of the committee on arrangements for the National Republican Convention of 1880, he had supported Grover Cleveland for the presidency in 1884. Upon Cleveland's election in 1892, Gage was offered the post of secretary of the treasury but declined it. He was a vigorous opponent of "free silver" and cordially supported President Cleveland in his views on the currency question. During the panic of 1893 he proposed that the government issue $200,000,000 in bonds for subscription in treasury notes, which were then to be withdrawn from circulation, on the ground that "the government must be taken out of the note-issuing business" (D. R. Dewey, *Financial History of the United States,* 1903, p. 459). In the campaign of 1896 he was a stanch defender of the gold standard, and following the election, upon the refusal of Mark Hanna [*q.v.*] to accept appointment as secretary of the treasury, he was offered and accepted the office, to the great delight of President McKinley.

His management of the national finances during the Spanish-American War added greatly to his financial reputation. Congress, in June 1898, authorized the issue of $200,000,000 of government bonds bearing three per cent. interest. Great doubt was expressed at the time as to whether bonds carrying so low a rate of interest could be sold except at a discount. Secretary Gage popularized the loan, and within sixty days it was not only floated at par but oversubscribed. Gage was also influential in securing the passage of the Act of Mar. 14, 1900, which established the gold standard, but was unsuccessful in his efforts to obtain further legislation providing for a definite method of maintaining parity and an elastic currency (A. B. Hepburn, *History of Coinage and Currency in the United States,* 1903, pp. 396–408).

In 1902 he resigned his secretaryship, and from 1902 to 1906 he was president of the United States Trust Company of New York. In the latter year he retired from active business and moved to California, building a house at Point Loma where the Theosophical Society had a colony. Although he was always interested in psychical research, he was greatly annoyed by the report that he had become a Theosophist, maintaining that he was still "an old fashioned Methodist." He was married three times: in 1864 to Sarah Etheridge of Hastings, Minn., who died in 1874; on June 7, 1887, to Mrs. Cornelia (Washburne) Gage, his brother's widow, who died in 1901; and on Nov. 25, 1909, to Mrs. Frances Ada Ballou of San Diego, Cal. He died at San Diego in his ninety-first year.

[Moses P. Handy, "Lyman J. Gage," in *Rev. of Revs.* (N. Y.), Mar. 1897; *New-Eng. Hist. and Geneal. Reg.,* Apr. 1899; A. T. Andreas, *Hist. of Chicago* (3 vols., 1886); John Moses and Jos. Kirkland, *Hist. of Chicago* (2 vols., 1895); H. C. Morris, *The Hist. of the First National Bank of Chicago* (1902); F. M. Huston and A. Russel, *Financing an Empire: Hist. of Banking in Ill.* (1926), vol. I; H. H. Kohlsaat, *From McKinley to Harding* (1923); F. E. Leupp, *The Man Roosevelt* (1904); W. R. Thayer, *Life and Letters of John Hay* (1915), II, 154; *Who's Who in America,* 1926–27; obituaries in *Chicago Daily Tribune, N. Y. Times,* Jan. 27, 1927.] R. C. M.

GAGE, MATILDA JOSLYN (Mar. 24, 1826–Mar. 18, 1898), woman's suffrage advocate, and author, was born in Cicero, N. Y., the only daughter of Dr. Hezekiah and Helen (Leslie) Joslyn. Her mother was the daughter of Sir George Leslie of Scotland. Dr. Joslyn's home in Cicero appears to have been one of the intellectual centers of the community; he was keenly interested in reform movements of every kind and made his house the gathering place for such advanced thinkers as visited the town. The atmosphere in which Matilda spent her childhood and youth greatly influenced her character and life work. Her early education was received at home, where her father instructed her in physiology, Greek, and mathematics, and taught her to think for herself. Later she completed the liberal education afforded young women of the period at the Clinton Seminary. At eighteen she married Henry H. Gage, a merchant of Cicero, with whom she removed first to Syracuse, then to Manlius, and finally to Fayetteville, where she made her home in the same house for thirty-eight years. At the Syracuse National Woman's Rights Convention, Sept. 8–10, 1852, she made her first public appearance as an advocate of woman's rights. As the youngest woman taking part in the convention, she attracted not a little attention. Soon afterward she associated herself with Elizabeth Cady Stanton [*q.v.*], becoming one of the most effective of the woman's rights lecturers. She was also active in the organization of the suffrage movement. In 1869 she took part in the organization of both the New York State Woman's Suffrage Association and the National Woman's Suffrage Association, and served both of these organizations as president, or in some other official capacity, for many years. In 1878 she founded the Woman's National Liberal League, of which she remained the president until her death in 1898. She undertook also the literary advocacy of the cause, published *Woman as Inventor* (1870) and *Woman's Rights Catechism* (1871), joined with Elizabeth Cady Stanton and Susan B. Anthony [*q.v.*] in the authorship of *Woman's Declaration of Rights* (1876) and in 1880 issued *Who Planned the Tennessee Campaign of 1862? Or Anna Ella Carroll vs. Ulysses S. Grant.* On the historical status of woman, Mrs. Gage seems to have been better informed than any of her fellow crusaders, and *Woman, Church and State* (1893) she considered the most important of her works, although she is now remembered more commonly as joint author and editor with Mrs. Stanton and Miss Anthony of the first three volumes (1881–86) of their great *History of Woman Suffrage.* Besides these literary activities she published several of her speeches, contributed many articles on woman's rights to the public press, and edited and published *The National Citizen and Ballot Box* at Syracuse (1878–81). On several occasions she addressed congressional committees on the suffrage question. The closing years of her life were spent with a married daughter in Chicago, where the winter of 1897–98 found her busily engaged in the preparation of a paper to be read before the February meeting of the National American Woman's Suffrage Association—a meeting commemorating the fiftieth anniversary of the organized woman's suffrage movement. Ill health prevented her undertaking the journey to Washington, but she sent her paper, which was read to the convention. A few days later she suffered a paralytic stroke, and the end came quickly.

Matilda Joslyn Gage was one of the "strong minded" women of her age—a woman of rare courage, energy, and character. Her portrait seems to indicate no lack of sympathetic understanding, and the possession of a saving gift of humor. Intellectually she was without doubt among the ablest of the suffrage leaders of the nineteenth century. An excellent speaker and capable organizer, her greatest strength apparently lay in her thorough grasp of the historical status of woman through the ages. "She always had a knack of rummaging through old libraries," said Elizabeth Cady Stanton (*History of Woman Suffrage,* I, 466 n.), "bringing more startling facts to light than any woman I ever knew."

[In addition to the *Hist. of Woman Suffrage* see Ida H. Harper, *The Life and Work of Susan B. Anthony* (3 vols., 1899–1908); D. H. Bruce, *Onondaga's Centennial* (1896); *Woman's Jour.* (Boston), Mar. 26, 1898; *Woman's Tribune,* June 25, 1898; *Daily Inter Ocean* (Chicago), and *Boston Transcript,* Mar. 19, 1898.]

W. R. W.

GAGE, THOMAS (1721–Apr. 2, 1787), last royal governor of Massachusetts, was the second son of Thomas, first Viscount Gage, of the Irish peerage, and his first wife Benedicta (or Beata Maria Theresa) Hall of High Meadow, Gloucestershire. Young Thomas, born at Firle, Sussex, early entered the military profession, and on Jan. 30, 1741, was commissioned lieutenant in a new regiment, afterward known as the 48th Foot. Apparently he served as aide-de-camp to Lord Albemarle in Flanders, 1747–48, and after successive promotions became lieutenant-colonel of the 44th Foot on Mar. 2, 1751. In 1754 he went with his regiment to America under Gen. Braddock. He commanded an advance column on the march toward Fort Duquesne and on July 9 distinguished himself by gallant conduct and was wounded. He was also with the 44th at Oswego. In May 1758 he raised a provincial regiment, the 80th Foot, and in the same year commanded the light infantry in the Ticonderoga expedition under James Abercromby. After the fall of Niagara (July 1759), he was detached from Crown Point and, as brigadier-general, superseded Sir William Johnson. He commanded the rear-guard of Amherst's force which joined Murray's forces before Montreal on Sept. 6, 1760, and completed the conquest of Canada. For a time he was military governor of Montreal. In 1761 he was again promoted and became a major-general. Two years later, Amherst having returned to England, Gage was appointed commander-in-chief in North America with headquarters at New York. The next year the appointment was confirmed and he remained in charge of all American military affairs for nearly a decade, until he also returned to England in February 1773, leaving Gen. Haldimand in his place. While still in America he had been advanced in grade to lieutenant-general, and his services had received the approval of the home authorities.

After a short stay in England, he returned to the colonies to enter upon a better-known but more unfortunate phase of his career. In the spring of 1774 he was commissioned vice-admiral (Apr. 5) and "Captain-general and Governor-in-chief" (Apr. 7) of Massachusetts (*Colonial Society of Massachusetts Publications,* vol. II, 1913, pp. 279 ff., 174 ff.). He at once sailed for his new post, which proved to be that of the last governor of Massachusetts under royal authority; arrived at Boston May 13; and was sworn into office on the 17th (*Ibid.,* vol. XVII, 1915, p. 86).

As governor of Massachusetts, in succession to Thomas Hutchinson, he found a situation that might well have baffled a far wiser man than Gage ever was or claimed to be. The quarrel with the English government had reached a stage at which some of the leading radicals, such as Samuel Adams, not only made accommodation difficult but did all in their power to prevent it. Even if Gage had always acted wisely, which he did not, the more radical patriots would have done all they could to stultify his acts. The Massachusetts situation was not wholly unknown to the new governor. He had been sent to Boston in 1768 to assist in the adjustment of the difficulties caused in that year by the presence of British troops, and had expressed his own views in two publications which had been printed in 1769, *Letters to the Ministry from Governor Bernard, General Gage, and Commodore Hood,* and *Letters to the Right Honorable the Earl of Hillsborough from Governor Bernard, General Gage, and the Honorable His Majesty's Council for the Province of Massachusetts Bay.* The reflections which the patriots felt he had cast upon their party called forth Samuel Adams's reply, *An Appeal to the World.* Neither the patriots nor the Governor were therefore strangers to one another when they met in a new opposition in 1774. There was, however, a large loyal element, especially among the upper classes, and Gage was well received, so far as appearances went, when he entered upon his new duties.

Nevertheless, there were insuperable difficulties under the surface. The Governor reached Boston only three days after the news of the English retributive measures, including the Port Bill, and in addition to the usual instructions given to colonial governors he had received additional secret instructions from Lord Dartmouth, dated Apr. 9, 1774. According to these he was to use troops should "the Madness of the People" or the "Timidity, or want of Strength of the Peace Officers" appear to demand it (Adams, *post,* p. 299 n.). The patriots had formed committees of correspondence and a "Solemn League and Covenant," and on June 29 Gage issued a proclamation directed against this and other "illegal combinations" (*Proceedings of the Massachusetts Historical Society,* vol. XII, 1873, pp. 45 ff.). Under the Port Bill, Salem became the capital of the province and there the Governor remained during the summer, returning to Boston in the autumn. That town had taken the lead in refusing to acknowledge the validity of the appointment of councilors by writ of *mandamus.* The brewing trouble came to a head with the time for the assembling of the General Court in October. Under the lead of Boston a large number of towns instructed their delegates to join in forming a Provincial Congress, which met at Concord and at once undertook the administration of the province. There were thus two governments—the illegal revolutionary body sitting at Concord, supported by a majority of the people, and the royal government, or its shadow, sitting in Boston. On Nov. 5 Gage's effigy was publicly burned in the usual celebrations which marked Guy Fawkes's Day.

Early in 1775 Gage made several attempts to use the military to seize stores of supplies in near-by places, and on Apr. 18 came the celebrated expedition for the same purpose to Concord and Lexington which precipitated armed hostilities. On June 12, the Governor issued a proclamation establishing martial law but offering amnesty to all except Samuel Adams and John Hancock, and five days later, on June 17, was fought the battle of Bunker Hill. Gage was then shut up in Boston. His conduct of military affairs was severely criticized at home and it was evident that he was occupying a post beyond his abilities, but he was reappointed commander-in-chief in America in August. The position, however, was untenable. He soon after resigned and sailed from Boston on Oct. 10. His own brief account of his activities in America which he later gave to George Chalmers, may be found in the *Collections of the Massachusetts Historical Society* (4 ser., vol. IV, 1858, pp. 367 ff.). He remained in the army and was transferred from the colonelcy of the 22nd Foot, to which he had been assigned while in America, to that of the 17th, and afterward the 11th Dragoons. In November 1782 he was commissioned a full general. He died some five years later. On Dec. 8, 1758, he had married in New Jersey, Margaret, daughter of Peter Kemble, a member of the Council of that colony. By her he had five daughters and six sons, of whom the eldest surviving son, Henry, succeeded his uncle as third Viscount Gage.

[Sketch by H. M. Chichester in *Dict. Nat. Biog.,* with valuable references; Justin Winsor, *The Memorial Hist. of Boston* (1880–81), vols. II and III; Thos. Hutchinson, *The Hist. of the Province of Mass. Bay,* vol. III (1828); *A Report of the Record Commissioners of the City of Boston, Containing the Boston Town Records, 1758–69* (1886) and *1770–77* (1887); J. T. Adams, *Revolutionary New England, 1691–1776* (1923).]

J. T. A.

GAILLARD, DAVID DU BOSE (Sept. 4, 1859–Dec. 5, 1913), engineer, soldier, was the son of Samuel Isaac and Susan Richardson (Du Bose) Gaillard, and was descended from distinguished Huguenot ancestors, one of whom was broken on the wheel in 1616 for refusing to recant his Protestant faith. Born at Fulton, Sumter County, S. C., he lived at Clarendon with his grandparents until 1872, when he moved to Winnsboro, Fairfield County, in order to attend school at the Mount Zion Institute. Out of school hours he worked as a clerk in a general store. In 1880 he secured an appointment to West Point through competitive examination and on June 5, 1884, was graduated fifth in a brilliant class of thirty-one members. Immediately following his graduation he was commissioned second lieutenant of engineers. During the following three years he was a student and instructor at the Engineer School of Application, Willets Point, N. Y., and from 1887 to 1891 was on engineering duty in Florida. In the latter year, at the age of thirty-two, he was appointed a member of the important International Boundary Commission, reëstablishing the line between Mexico and the United States, on which work he was engaged for five years. Still a member of the commission, he served a brief period of duty at Fortress Monroe and on the Washington aqueduct in 1895, then from December 1895 to May 1898 he was in charge of the water-supply of the nation's capital. Meanwhile, on Oct. 25, 1895, he had reached a captaincy, and in the following year had spent some seven months in a survey of the Portland Channel in Alaska—a mission of some international importance.

War with Spain found Gaillard on duty as chief engineer with the staff of Gen. James F. Wade, but his genius for organization was soon recognized by appointment as colonel of the 3rd Regiment of Volunteer Engineers, which within a few months he had mustered in at Jefferson Barracks, Mo., and had taken to Cuba. Offensive operations having ceased, his regiment returned to the United States and was mustered out at Fort McPherson, Ga., May 17, 1899, commended by Gen. John C. Bates and Gen. James H. Wilson for soldierly performance of duty. He then served, from 1899 to 1901, as assistant to the engineer commissioner of the District of Columbia, and subsequently was placed in charge of river and harbor improvements on Lake Superior, with station at Duluth. Here he remained until 1903, when he was transferred to the Department of the Columbia. This gave him opportunity to publish in 1904 the valuable technical work entitled *Wave Action in Relation to Engineering Structures* (Professional Papers of the Corps of Engineers, No. 31)—a standard work on the subject. In the previous year he had been selected as a member of the initial General Staff Corps, and after short duty as such at Vancouver Barracks and St. Louis, was promoted major, Apr. 23, 1904, and spent the academic year 1904–05 as a student at the Army War College. Upon graduation he performed two years of general staff duty in Washington and in Cuba.

When President Roosevelt made Gen. Goethals chief engineer of the Panama Canal in 1907, the latter immediately placed Gaillard in charge of the department of dredging and excavation. With characteristic energy and ability, Gaillard organized the Chagres division comprising twenty-three miles of excavation from Gamboa to Gatun, and did much toward utilizing discarded French equipment and reducing costs. On July 1, 1908, under a general reorganization of canal work by Gen. Goethals, Gaillard was given charge of the central division, a distance of thirty-three miles between the Atlantic and the Pacific locks, and including excavation through the continental divide by the so-called Culebra Cut. His problem was colossal; many eminent engineers deemed the project impossible of fulfilment. As work progressed, difficulties increased, not the least of which were the great slides of earth in Culebra Cut which repeatedly threatened to bring operations to a standstill. By his indomitable will and resourcefulness, however, Gaillard made steady progress in the face of these discouragements, but on July 26, 1913, when about to witness the triumphal culmination of his arduous labors, he broke under the strain and never recovered. He was rushed for treatment to Johns Hopkins Hospital, Baltimore, where he passed away Dec. 5, 1913. The press of the entire country extolled his life, character, and services; both houses of Congress on Dec. 6, 1913, passed resolutions of regret and appreciation; by executive order, President Wilson changed the name of Culebra to Gaillard Cut; and by order of the secretary of war, the army post at Culebra was given the name of Camp Gaillard. Bronze memorial tablets in his honor were erected by his West Point class in Cullum Hall at the military academy, and by the American Huguenots in the Huguenot Church at Charleston, S. C. On Feb. 4, 1928, an additional tablet, given by the Gaillard family and Gaillard's old volunteer regiment, was unveiled on a prominent rock-face of Gaillard Cut, where passing ships of all countries and for all time, would be constantly reminded of his monumental achievement and self-sacrifice. He was survived by his wife, whom, as Katherine Ross Davis of Columbia, S. C., he had married in 1887; and by a son.

[*David Du Bose Gaillard: A Memorial Compiled and Published by the Third U. S. Volunteer Engineers* (1916); *Asso. Grads. of the U. S. Mil. Acad., Ann. Reunion*, June 12, 1914; *Who's Who in America*, 1912–13; *Evening Star* (Washington, D. C.), Dec. 5, 1913; *Sunday Star*, Feb. 5, 1928.]

C. D. R.

GAILLARD, EDWIN SAMUEL (Jan. 16, 1827–Feb. 2, 1885), surgeon, editor, and medical journalist, was born near Charleston, S. C. He attended South Carolina College (later the University of South Carolina), graduating in 1845, and then the Medical College of the State of South Carolina at Charleston, from which he graduated in March 1854. Establishing himself in Florida, he soon obtained a large practise. In 1857 he moved to New York and after a short interval went abroad for a year's study in Europe. In 1861 he settled in Baltimore and at the outbreak of the Civil War joined the Confederate army as assistant surgeon of the 1st Maryland Regiment, becoming brigade-surgeon in August of the same year. Four months later he was made a member of the medical examining board of the Army of Virginia. In May 1862 he lost his right arm in the battle of Seven Pines, but reported for duty three months later and was made medical director of military hospitals in Virginia and North Carolina. In December 1863 he became general inspector of Confederate hospitals and served in that capacity until the close of the war.

Settling in Richmond in 1865, Gaillard was made professor of the principles and practise of medicine and general pathology in the Medical College of Virginia and established the *Richmond Medical Journal.* In 1866 he received the prize of the Georgia Medical Association for an essay on diphtheria. In 1868 he took his journal with him to Louisville, Ky., and continued its publication until 1879 under the name of the *Richmond and Louisville Medical Journal.* He was at once made professor of medicine in the Kentucky School of Medicine, of which he later became dean, and in 1869 he became professor of general medicine and pathology in the Louisville Medical College of which he was one of the organizers and the first dean. In 1874 he established the *American Medical Weekly,* continuing as its editor until 1883. He was a vigorous writer in spite of the loss of his right arm. In 1879 he moved to New York City and from that date until 1883 he published, in addition to the *American Medical Weekly, Gaillard's Medical Journal.* He contributed numerous articles to his own and other medical papers, one of which, "Ozone: Its Relation to Health and Disease" (*Boston Medical and Surgical Journal,* Sept. 15–Nov. 10, 1864), was awarded the Fiske Fund Prize in 1861. Gaillard was married to Jane Marshall Thomas, daughter of Rev. Edward Thomas of Charleston, S. C., in 1856. She died in 1860, and in 1865 he was married to Mary Elizabeth Gibson, daughter of Prof. C. B. Gibson of Richmond, Va. By the latter marriage four children survived him.

[*Va. Medic. Monthly,* Feb. 1885; *Medic. Record* (N. Y.), Feb. 7, 1885; *N. Y. Medic. Jour.,* Feb. 14, 1885; *N. C. Medic. Jour.,* Feb. 1885; T. S. Bell, *Medic. and Surgic. Sci. as Expounded by E. S. Gaillard* (1869); editorial in the *Richmond and Louisville Medic. Jour.,* June 1871; *Am. Practitioner* (Louisville), supplement to issue of July 1871; *Georgia Medic. Companion,* Sept. 1872, pp. 564–72; R. F. Stone, *Biog. of Eminent Am. Physicians and Surgeons* (1894).] A. P. M.

GAILLARD, JOHN (Sept. 5, 1765–Feb. 26, 1826), United States senator, was born in St. Stephen's Parish, S. C., where his father had a large property in lands and slaves. His father, John Gaillard, was descended from one of the Huguenot immigrants to South Carolina of about 1685. His mother was Judith Peyre. With his brother Theodore he was admitted to the Middle Temple, London, July 15, 1782, but he never practised law. He married Mary Lord, daughter of Andrew Lord, Nov. 24, 1792, and established himself in St. Stephen's as a planter (*Miscellaneous Records,* 3M, p. 150, State Archives). His wife and an infant child were drowned in 1799, but a son Theodore survived by whom he had descendants. He never married again. From St. Stephen's he was elected in 1794 to the state House of Representatives, and in 1796 to the Senate, where he served until December 1804. He was faithful in attendance, and conservative in his votes. He was second on the ticket of Jefferson electors in 1804, and president of the Senate (*City Gazette,* Charleston, Dec. 3, 8, 1804). Elected to the United States Senate to fill the unexpired term of Pierce Butler, he took his seat on Jan. 31, 1805, having received 105 of the 134 votes cast. He was elected for the regular term in 1806, and served continuously until his death. In the Senate likewise he was a conservative Republican. He supported the administration in Jefferson's second term save in the impeachment of Judge Samuel Chase, for whom he voted on all articles. He opposed the bill to re-charter the first United States Bank as well as all moves to establish the second, and objected to federal aid for internal improvements. He voted for war in 1812 and supported the bills in the interest of slavery. He also voted for the tariff of 1816 although he considered the rates too high; the later tariffs with their increases of duties he consistently opposed. He developed almost as firm a hold upon the Senate as upon his state, for from 1814 until his death he was almost without exception the choice of the body for president *pro tempore.* He spent most of this time in the chair, due to the death in office of two vice-presidents, Clinton and Gerry, and the frequent absence of a third,

Tompkins (T. H. Benton, *Thirty Years' View,* 1854, I, 77). He was several times thanked by the Senate for this service. Senators Benton and Macon praised highly his skill, firmness, and tact in the performance of his duties, and paid tribute to the gentleness and polish of his manners. After several years of ill health, during which he continued at his post, he died in Washington, and was buried in the Congressional Cemetery.

[*S. C. Hist. and Geneal. Mag.,* July 1920; *Heads of Families, First Census, S. C.* (1908), p. 37; E. A. Jones, *Am. Members of the Inns of Court* (1924); *City Gazette and Commercial Daily Advertiser* (Charleston), and *Charleston Mercury,* Mar. 6, 1826. A manuscript "Chart of the Gaillard Family" is in the library of the S. C. Hist. Soc.] R. L. M—r.

GAILLARDET, THÉODORE FRÉDÉRIC (Apr. 7, 1808–Aug. 13, 1882), journalist, author, was born at Auxerre, department of the Yonne, France. He early studied law and was admitted to practise at Tonnerre (Yonne) where his family lived, but soon abandoned the law and went to Paris. There he became interested in the theatre and, under the influence of Victor Hugo and the romantic movement, wrote a play, *La Tour de Nesle,* brilliantly and successfully produced at the Théâtre de Porte-Saint-Martin in May 1832. The unwelcome collaboration of Alexander Dumas *père* in this play provoked a noted literary quarrel which culminated in six legal suits, in which Gaillardet was successful, and a duel in which both successfully escaped injury. Gaillardet wrote two more plays, *Georges, ou le criminel par Amour* and *Struensée, ou le Médecin de la Reine,* both produced the following year (1833) at the Théâtre de la Gaîté, before turning his attention to historical studies. His *Mémoires du Chevalier d'Éon,* an important study of one of the most enigmatical figures of the eighteenth century, was published in two volumes in 1836.

The following year Gaillardet accompanied his two brothers, one a physician and the other a merchant, to New Orleans. He planned a book on the United States in the fashion which De Tocqueville had established. From the time of his arrival in America he contributed to two Parisian newspapers: *La Presse* and *Le Journal des Débats.* As a preface to his American studies he traveled in Cuba and in Texas, and then went up the Mississippi Valley to Kentucky. A series of his articles on Louisiana, Mississippi, and Texas appeared in the *Journal des Débats* during 1839. After having visited the French populations of America he determined to found a newspaper for them and for the French language. This newspaper he built from the ruins of the *Courrier des États-Unis.* Founded in New York in 1828 by Joseph Bonaparte, it had been sold several years later to a German bookseller named Beer, who had just died when Gaillardet came to New York. This newspaper, with its few remaining subscribers, Gaillardet bought, and to it he gave new life. He assumed control in January 1840, and his generous and liberal program brought forth an immediate response. *"Nous ne serons ni Républicains, ni Carlistes, ni Philippistes; nous serons Français, ne pensant pas qu'il doive y avoir d'autres dénominations parmi nous à l'étranger"* (*Courrier des États-Unis,* Jan. 16, 1840). Of a party organ he made a national newspaper, the oldest French newspaper in America that has continued publication to the present time.

In 1848 Gaillardet, attracted by the newly founded republic in France, sold the newspaper to a Mr. Arpin of New Orleans and returned to Tonnerre, where his friends persuaded him to become a candidate for the National Assembly. There he found that his old enemy Dumas and Prince Louis-Napoleon were his opponents; Dumas and Gaillardet withdrew and Napoleon was elected. In this year he published *Profession de foi et considérations sur le système républicain des États-Unis présentées aux électeurs de l'Yonne* (1848). He had not entirely given up his journalistic career in New York, for he remained the Parisian political correspondent for the *Courrier* until his death in 1882. He numbered among his many friends in American public life James Buchanan, Charles G. Ingersoll, and Pierre Soulé, returned often to America, and in the presidential campaign of 1872 spoke for his friend Horace Greeley. After the publication of new material on the Chevalier d'Éon, he wrote another study, *Mémoires sur la Chevalière d'Éon,* which appeared in 1866. He died in 1882 at Plessis-Bouchard (near Franconville) where he had, in his retirement, become mayor of the village. His long-awaited book on America, *L'Aristocratie en Amérique,* brilliant though fragmentary, was published in 1883, the year after his death.

[Charles Glinel, *Alexandre Dumas et son œuvre* (Reims, 1884); *Courrier des États-Unis* (N. Y.), Jan. 14, 1840, Aug. 13, 15, 20, and 27, 1882; *N. Y. Times,* Aug. 15, 1882; *Le Siècle* and *Le Journal des Débats* (Paris), Aug. 14, 1882; information from H. P. Sampers of New York City; private information.] F. M—n.

GAINE, HUGH (1726/27–Apr. 25, 1807), printer and bookseller, was born of Scotch-Irish parentage at Belfast, Ireland, where he learned the printing art. Upon completion of his indenture he sailed for America, landing in New York City in 1745, "without basket or burden." He found work with James Parker and remained with him until 1752, the year in which for a few months he had a partnership with William Weyman, another printer, in the bookselling business. Gaine then established himself as printer and bookseller "on Hunter's Key," making several removals in 1753, 1754, and in 1757, when he went to "Hanover Square, near the Meal Market," to a three-story house which he purchased on Apr. 30, 1759. Here he conducted a printery, book-shop, and a general store, to which he added patent medicines in 1760. His place of business carried the sign of "Bible & Crown" and bore that of royalty until after the evacuation of New York by the British in 1783, after which it was known as "the Bible." Gaine promptly laid the foundations of a prosperous business in 1752, by beginning the series of Hutchin's almanacs and establishing (Aug. 3 or 8, no copy extant) his newspaper, the *New-York Mercury,* which lived through Nov. 10, 1783. He had difficulties with the Assembly of New York, because he printed some of its proceedings without authority, and was reprimanded, Nov. 14, 1753. Though Scotch-Irish, he chose the Anglican Church and party rather than the Presbyterian, and thus became involved in bitter controversy with William Livingston, John Morin Scott, and William Smith, after which, under a truce, he carried on his newspaper as a "free press," open to both parties. It was in this period that he printed in his paper the political essays known as the "Watch Tower" (1754–55). When in 1768–70 another ecclesiastical tilt occurred, Gaine printed only the effusions of the Episcopalians.

Twice he had contact with stamp acts: once when the New York Assembly levied a tax on vellum, parchment, and paper, which Gaine promptly charged against his subscribers (1757–59), and again in 1765, when he issued his newspaper without its title but with a substituted heading, "No Stamped Paper to be had," on Nov. 4, 11, and 18. In 1776, when the British were about to capture New York City, he removed some of his equipment to Newark, N. J., and printed there seven issues of his newspaper (Sept. 21–Nov. 2), as a Whig organ, while (Sept. 20–Nov. 4) his regular paper continued to appear in New York, but managed by Ambrose Serle, under Sir William Howe's direction, as a royalist sheet. Gaine regained control on Nov. 11 and retained it from that time until the end (1783). At the beginning of the Revolution he had leanings toward the Whigs, and perhaps expediency and property interest were chiefly responsible for his change of heart, though it seems certain that his later ardor for the British cause was sincere.

On Jan. 15, 1768, Gaine became public printer to the province. His public work embraced the printing of journals or votes, session laws, collected statutes, and speeches and proclamations of the governor, as well as paper currency. He also was official printer to the City of New York. In 1773 he, in partnership, set up a paper-mill at "Hempstead Harbor on Long-Island." In 1800 he gave up the printing business, but continued as a bookseller. Gaine married first, on Oct. 24, 1759, Sarah Robbins (died 1765), by whom he had a son and two daughters; and second, on Sept. 5, 1769, a widow, Mrs. Cornelia Wallace, by whom he had two daughters. He died in his eighty-first year and was buried in his family plot in the yard of Trinity Church. In his private relations Gaine was an active Mason, a member of the St. Patrick Society (then Protestant), and a vestryman of Trinity Church. He owned much real estate, including a fine large country seat on Manhattan Island, on Kings Bridge Road.

[The chief source is P. L. Ford, ed., *The Jours. of Hugh Gaine* (2 vols., 1902), of which vol. I has the biography and bibliography, while vol. II contains Gaine's journals of 1757–58, 1777–82, 1797–98, and seventeen letters, 1768–1806. Now largely superseded, and full of errors though of some use, is C. R. Hildebrun, *Sketches of Printers and Printing in Colonial N. Y.* (1895), pp. 72–88. An obituary appeared in the N. Y. *Evening Post,* Apr. 27, 1807. The history of Gaine's newspaper and extant files can also be traced in I. N. P. Stokes, *The Iconography of Manhattan Island,* II (1916), 422, 434–40, and index of vol. VI; and C. S. Brigham, "Bibliography of Am. Newspapers, 1690–1820," in *Proc. Am. Antiquarian Soc.,* Oct. 17, 1917, pp. 423, 456. The N. Y. Pub. Lib. has one of the best files of the *Mercury,* also Gaine's manuscript receipt book (1767–99) of private and business transactions, and other MSS. Ford's bibliography is well done, yet over fifty new titles have since been discovered.]

V. H. P.

GAINES, EDMUND PENDLETON (Mar. 20, 1777–June 6, 1849), soldier, was born in Culpeper County, Va. His father, James Gaines, was a Revolutionary soldier and the nephew of Edmund Pendleton, the famous lawyer. His mother was Elizabeth Strother. George Strother Gaines [*q.v.*] was his younger brother. At the close of the Revolution the family moved to North Carolina and a little later went west into Sullivan County, now a part of Tennessee. At the age of eighteen, Gaines saw service as a lieutenant in a company of riflemen organized for Indian warfare, and in 1797 entered the United States army as an ensign, being at once promoted to lieutenant. From 1801 to 1804 he was engaged in surveying a road from Nashville to Natchez and in 1804 was made military collector of Mobile and commandant at Fort

Stoddert, becoming captain in 1807. He made the arrest of Aaron Burr and was a witness at the latter's trial. With a view to resigning, he obtained a long leave and having studied law began practise in the Mississippi Territory, but the war with Great Britain brought him back into active service in 1812 with the rank of major. He was promoted at once to lieutenant-colonel, and in 1813 to colonel. At the battle of Chrysler's Field in 1813 his regiment covered the American retreat. He was made adjutant-general and put in command of Fort Erie, which he defended successfully against a long and heavy British attack. For this he was promoted to brigadier-general with a major-general's brevet, was thanked by Congress and given a gold medal, and received votes of thanks from five states and swords from Virginia, New York, and Tennessee. He was seriously wounded and took no further part in the war.

In 1817 he was sent south as commissioner to treat with the Creek Indians, and a little later was engaged with Jackson in the campaign against them and the Seminoles. He was in the Black Hawk War in 1832, and in 1835, when the Florida war began, he commanded an expedition against the Indians and was wounded in the mouth at Onithlacoochie. Bitter jealousy and enmity between him and Gen. Winfield Scott, which had developed long before, became open in this campaign. A court of inquiry held in 1837 to investigate their failure, while criticizing both, justified their military conduct. Gaines was violent in speech and in his formal defense compared Scott to Benedict Arnold. In 1838 Gaines submitted to the War Department a report on the defense of the western frontier in which he advocated floating batteries for harbor defense and a network of railroads in the interior. Disgruntled because of its unfavorable reception, he elaborated his defense plan in a memorial presented to Congress in 1840.

At the outbreak of the Mexican War, being then in command of the western department, he called upon Louisiana for volunteers to send to Zachary Taylor, and although the War Department at once reprimanded him, he called on Alabama, Mississippi, and Missouri for troops a few months later. A heated correspondence with Secretary Marcy followed, in which Gaines wrote of the official reprimands, "I carelessly submit to them, as they seem to be a source of pleasure to the War Department, and certainly inflict no injury on me" (*Senate Document 402*, 29 Cong., 1 Sess.). He was finally removed from the command of the department and ordered to Fortress Monroe for trial by court martial. He defended himself with much skill and with all his usual vehemence, maintaining that since Gen. Taylor, his subordinate in the department, had been given authority to call for volunteers, the authority necessarily belonged to him as well. The court, while declaring that he had no authority to call for troops, held that his undoubted patriotism and the real necessities of the case made him excusable, and accordingly recommended that all proceedings against him be stopped. Later he was placed in command of the eastern department. During his long service in the army Gaines was constantly at variance with the War Department. His official communications breathe anything but respect for authority or disposition to obedience. He was fiery, unrestrained, and often bitter. Full of suspicion of Gen. Scott, who barely outranked him, and of Gen. Macomb, who was promoted over them both, he was ever ready to believe himself the object of conspiracy and injustice. Scott hated him no less bitterly and during Gaines's later years made no secret of his belief that he was insane, stating it again and again in official communications.

Gaines was married three times: first, to Frances, daughter of Judge Harry Toulmin; second, to Barbara, daughter of Senator William and Mary (Granger) Blount of Tennessee, who died in 1836; and third, in 1839, to Mrs. Myra Whitney of New York, the daughter of Daniel Clark [*q.v.*]. Ten years later he died of cholera at New Orleans. His widow's name was conspicuous in the press for many years during the process of extensive litigation over her father's will.

[*Senate Doc. 224*, 24 Cong., 2 Sess.; *House Doc. 311*, 25 Cong., 2 Sess.; *House Doc. 150*, 28 Cong., 1 Sess.; *Senate Doc. 378*, 29 Cong., 1 Sess.; *Memorial of Edmund Pendleton Gaines to the Senate and House of Representatives* (1840); Samuel Perkins, *A Hist. of the Pol. and Mil. Events of the Late War between the U. S. and Gt. Britain* (1825); Jas. B. Longacre and Jas. Herring, *Nat. Portr. Gallery of Distinguished Americans*, vol. IV (1839); *Biog. of Edmund Pendleton Gaines, By a Friend* (1844); *U. S. Mag. and Democratic Rev.*, June 1848; L. P. Gaines, *Gaines Geneal.* (1918); T. M. Owen, "Wm. Strother of Virginia and his Descendants," *Pubs. Southern Hist. Asso.*, vol. II (1898); *Daily Picayune* (New Orleans), June 7, 1849.]

J. G. de R. H.

GAINES, GEORGE STROTHER (*c.* 1784–Jan. 21, 1873), Alabama pioneer, Indian agent, merchant, planter, was descended from Virginia aristocrats. Born in Stokes County, N. C., he was the son of James and Elizabeth (Strother) Gaines, the former a captain in the Revolutionary War and member of the North Carolina convention that ratified the Federal Constitution, and was a brother of Edmund Pendleton Gaines [*q.v.*]. At the age of ten, George Gaines removed with his parents to Sullivan County (now Tennessee), where he lived until he was appointed (1805) assistant factor of the government trading house at St. Stephens, in the Alabama part of the Mississippi Territory. He became factor the next year. The question of his education is obscure, and so is the reason for his appointment at twenty-one as Indian agent at a strategic place on the Spanish borderland. About 1812 he was married to his cousin, Ann Gaines of St. Stephens.

Pioneer life was raw in the Tombigbee Valley, and with the inflow of American settlers the Indians became restless and border troubles and trade rivalry with the Spanish grew apace. Friendly relations with the Choctaws and the success of American over Spanish trade (conducted through the powerful John Forbes Company) depended largely upon Gaines. By adroitness, fair dealing, and kindly ministrations to the Choctaws he commanded their esteem and won their trade; "his simple word became their law and his sympathy and kindness their abiding reliance" (*Mobile Daily Register,* June 19, 1872). Nor could the Philippics of the mighty Tecumseh detach the Choctaws from him. On the contrary, many of them helped to exterminate the Creek "Red Sticks" in the War of 1812. Gaines promoted among the Choctaws the idea of removing beyond the Mississippi, and when they were ready to go they insisted on his helping them to select their lands. His services to the pioneers of the Mississippi Territory were inestimable. The leadership of Gaines, John McKee [*q.v.*], and Judge Henry Toulmin in the Tombigbee Valley will compare favorably with that of the pioneer patriarchs on any sector of the American frontier. Gaines's "Reminiscences of Early Times in the Mississippi Territory" (*Mobile Daily Register,* June 19, 27, July 3, 10, 17, 1872) is a valuable contribution to pioneer history.

In 1819 he resigned the government factorage and in 1822 became a merchant at Demopolis, the site which he had helped the French colonists to select four years previously. He succeeded in business and represented Clarke and Marengo counties in the Alabama Senate from 1825 to 1827. From 1830 to 1856 he was a merchant in Mobile. He prospered in business, helped to promote the Mobile & Ohio Railroad, and for a time was president of the Mobile branch of the state bank. He did not succeed as bank director, nor did more hard-hearted men when there was a mad rush upon the state banks for loans. Gaines retired from business in 1856 and settled on his plantation at State Line, Miss. He was elected to the Mississippi legislature in 1861. In January 1873 this "patriarch of two states" lay down to rest amid the scenes of more than three-score years of pioneering and building. Gainesville, Ala., was named for him.

[H. S. Halbert, "Creek War Incidents," in *Trans. Ala. Hist. Soc.,* vol. II (1898); "Letters from G. S. Gaines relating to Events in South Ala., 1805–1814," *Ibid.,* vol. III (1899); G. S. Gaines, "Dancing Rabbit Creek Treaty," Ala. Dept. Archives and Hist., *Hist. and Patriotic Series,* No. 10 (1928); W. Brewer, *Ala.: Her Hist., Resources, War Record, and Pub. Men* (1872); A. B. Moore, *Hist. of Ala. and Her People,* vol. I (1927); T. M. Owen, *Hist. of Ala. and Dict. of Ala. Biog.* vol. III (1921); G. J. Leftwich in *Pubs. Miss. Hist. Soc., Centenary Ser.,* I (1916), 442–56; obituary in *Mobile Daily Register,* Jan. 25, 1873, repr. in the *Spectator* (North Port, Ala.), Feb. 4, 1873; newspaper clippings and manuscripts in Ala. Dept. Archives and Hist., Montgomery, Ala.; information from George J. Leftwich, Esq., Aberdeen, Miss., Dr. Toulmin Gaines, Mobile, Ala., and Dr. Erwin Craighead of the *Mobile Register and News-Item.*] A. B. M.

GAINES, JOHN POLLARD (Sept. 22, 1795–Dec. 9, 1857), lawyer, soldier, territorial governor, was born in Augusta County, Va., the son of Abner and Elizabeth (Mathews) Gaines, and reared, from early childhood, in Boone County, Ky. After receiving a thorough English education, he studied law, was admitted to the bar, and began practise in his home town of Walton. He served as a common soldier in the War of 1812, fighting in the battle of the Thames. On June 22, 1819, he married Elizabeth, daughter of Nicholas Kincaid of Versailles, Ky. When the Mexican War broke out he was commissioned major-general in Thomas Marshall's Kentucky cavalry brigade, and distinguished himself in the battle of Molino del Rey. In January 1847 he was captured by the Mexicans at Incarnacion and detained some months in a military prison, from which he escaped. He then served as aide-de-camp on the staff of Gen. Winfield Scott. Gaines had been a member for several terms of the Kentucky legislature. During his imprisonment in Mexico he was elected as a Whig from his district to the Thirtieth Congress (1847–49). His record in Congress is not significant. President Taylor appointed him governor of Oregon Territory after Abraham Lincoln declined that office. Gaines accepted, shipped with his family on the store ship *Supply* around the Horn, and arrived in San Francisco in July 1850. On the voyage two of his daughters, beautiful and accomplished young women, died of yellow fever. From San Francisco the Gaines family proceeded to Oregon on the ship-of-war *Falmouth,* arriving Aug. 15.

Gaines was received with much ceremony, but there was opposition to federal officers appointed from outside the Territory and there was also a tendency toward Democracy in politics which made his stiff Whiggism distinctly unpopular. He was a man of distinguished appearance, with great personal dignity, more than a touch of pompousness, and a rather marked deficiency of humor. He was under the influence of bad political advisers. While personally honorable, and devoted to the public welfare, he had the misfortune within a few months to see the people of the Territory factionalized, the legislature and the supreme court disrupted, and the interests of the community he had been sent to serve generally disturbed and jeopardized. The principal occasion of difficulty was the question of relocating the capital of the Territory, Oregon City and Salem being rivals for the honor. Those who urged the retention of Oregon City as the seat of government as well as the so-called "Salem Clique," were to some extent animated by speculative interest. The latter, through their organ the *Oregon Statesman,* edited by Asahel Bush, abused Gaines viciously. "Breakspeare" (W. L. Adams, *q.v.*) makes Bush say of him, keeping close to the language of his vitriolic sheet:

> "Have I not held him up to public scorn,
> As an old, pampered, shallow minded swine,
> Feeding and grunting round the public crib?"

By way of retaliation Gaines assaulted Bush on the street in Salem and so the unseemly quarrel raged month after month.

Technically, Gaines was at least half right. A majority of both houses of the legislature had voted to fix the permanent capital at Salem. Gaines favored Oregon City and, being in control of the funds appropriated by Congress for public buildings, he was able to checkmate the Salem party. He argued that the law locating the capital was unconstitutional because the enabling act had provided that no law could cover more than one subject, whereas the act in question not only fixed the capital at Salem and gave the penitentiary to Portland and the university to Marysville, but also provided for endowing the university. The opposition did not feel confident that their law would be held constitutional, and it was in fact pronounced null and void by the United States attorney-general, but, in any event, Congress would have to approve all territorial acts before they became operative. Congress eventually gave its approval to this and other laws passed by the majority of the legislature sitting at Salem, thus lowering Gaines's prestige. In 1853 his term of office expired. His wife was killed by accident in the fall of 1851, and a son Richard died soon afterward. About fifteen months after his wife's death, Gaines married Margaret B. Wands, one of the five women teachers sent to Oregon by Gov. Slade. He settled on a farm near Salem, where he spent the remainder of his life.

["Hist. of Ore.," vol. II, ch. v, in *The Works of H. H. Bancroft,* vol. XXX (1888), treats of Gaines's administration of the Territory. *Executive Doc. 96,* 32 Cong., 1 Sess., contains Attorney-General Crittenden's opinion on the capital location law submitted by Gaines; *Executive Doc. 104* contains the opinion of two Ore. supreme court judges on the validity of the same law; *House Misc. Doc. 9,* 32 Cong., 1 Sess., contains the memorial of the majority of the legislature, sitting at Salem, which condemned Gaines; *House Misc. Doc. 10* contains the journals of the pretended legislature sitting at Oregon City. See also *Cong. Globe,* 30 Cong., 1 Sess., App., p. 387; J. L. Peyton, *Hist. of Augusta County, Va.* (1882); Lyman Chalkley, *Chronicles of the Scotch-Irish Settlement in Va.,* II (1913), 295. An obituary notice is in *Weekly Oregonian,* Dec. 19, 1857.]

J. S.

GAINES, REUBEN REID (Oct. 30, 1836–Oct. 13, 1914), chief justice of the supreme court of Texas, was born in Sumter County, Ala., the son of Joab and Lucinda (McDavid) Gaines. His childhood was passed on a plantation cultivated by slave labor, his father being a planter of some means, and his early education was secured in country and private schools. After graduation from the University of Alabama in 1855, he entered the once-famous law school of Cumberland University, at Lebanon, Tenn., and in 1857 received from that institution the degree of LL.B. The next four years were devoted to the practise of law and to the management of his plantation at Selma, Ala. In March 1859 he married Louisa Shortridge, who was his constant companion through more than fifty years, and who survived him.

During the Civil War, Gaines served in the Confederate army until the final surrender at Salisbury, N. C., in 1865, at which time he had attained the rank of major. The experience must have been a high adventure, for his commanders were the celebrated cavalry leaders, John T. Morgan and Joseph Wheeler. But though he was severely wounded and served with distinction in most of the important western campaigns, in later life Gaines could seldom be persuaded to mention his career in the army. Few knew what rank he had borne; and in the South where colonel was the courtesy title of many citizens, his friends never heard him referred to by any military appellation.

The close of the war found the young lawyer ruined financially and face to face with the disastrous consequences of an economic and political revolution in his native state. Like many others, he turned his eyes toward Texas, young, full of possibilities, and comparatively untouched by war. He and his wife removed in 1868 to Clarksville, in Red River County, where he successfully engaged in the practise of law and established his reputation as a leading member of the Texas bar. As the result of a unique non-political convention of the lawyers of his district, Gaines was nominated and elected in 1876 judge for the sixth judicial district, a position in which he served until 1884. Two years later he became an associate justice of the supreme court. On the death of the celebrated Chief Justice Stayton in 1894, Gaines was appointed chief justice, and continued in this position by successive nominations and elections, always without opposition, until Jan. 5, 1911, when he resigned on account of the growing infirmities of age. His term of service lacked only a few months of completing a quarter of a century, the longest in the history of the court.

In the course of his work on the supreme court, Gaines delivered over a thousand written opinions. For twelve years his colleagues were Judge Frank A. Williams and Judge Thomas J. Brown. This period is known to Texas lawyers as that of the "strong court." Although the three judges were men of decided views, the twelve years during which they were associated were marked by only three instances of dissenting opinions, one by each of them, so careful were they to harmonize their views and reach conclusions in which they could all agree. The opinions of Gaines are clear and brief, marked by no elaborate display of legal learning. Their impersonal tone is in strange contrast to a vigorous and almost volcanic personality, about which many anecdotes have gathered.

[The best sketch of his career is A. E. Wilkinson, "Reuben Reid Gaines, Chief Justice of Texas," *Tex. Law Rev.*, Feb. 1924, pp. 183–94. See also the *Houston Post*, Jan. 6, 1911, Oct. 14, 1914; *Proc. Tex. Bar Asso.* (1915); and 107 *Tex. Reports*, 657. His decisions will be found in 65–103 *Tex. Reports*. His former colleague, Judge Williams, selects *Houston & Tex. Central Railway Co. et al.* vs. *State of Tex.*, 95 *Tex.*, 507, as probably the best single specimen of his judicial methods.]

R. G. C.

GAINES, WESLEY JOHN (Oct. 4, 1840–Jan. 12, 1912), clergyman, a leader in the establishment of the African Methodist Episcopal Church in the South, and for nearly twenty-four years bishop, was born a slave on the plantation of Gabriel Toombs, brother of Gen. Robert Toombs [*q.v.*], Wilkes County, Ga. He was the youngest of the fourteen children of William and Louisa Gaines. From childhood he showed an eagerness for knowledge, and as a youth, being too delicate physically for hard work, he had time to pursue it. Taught by a white boy, he learned the alphabet in a week and, by imitating copies in books he secured, he was soon able to write. The desire to be a preacher early took possession of him. In 1855 he went to a plantation in Stewart County and the following year, to one in Muscogee County. Here, in August 1863, he married Julia A. Camper. At the close of the war, he announced his intention of going into the ministry, and was encouraged by his former owner, Toombs, who himself was an official in a Methodist church. He was licensed to preach, June 1865, by Rev. J. L. Davies, a presiding elder of the Methodist Episcopal Church, South, but under the influence of an older brother, Rev. William Gaines, he soon joined the African Methodist Episcopal Church, and was commissioned to organize churches in Muscogee and Chattahoochee counties. In 1866 he was admitted to what was then the South Carolina Conference and ordained deacon at Savannah, Ga.; the following year he was ordained elder.

All his pastorates were in Georgia, where he served churches at Atlanta, Athens, Macon, and Columbus, displaying notable ability as an organizer and financial agent. Along with his duties he found time to improve his education, studying theology at Athens in 1870 under Matthew H. Henderson, rector of the Episcopal church there, and during the years 1875 to 1878, under Rev. Joseph S. Key, later a bishop of the Methodist Church, South. He did much to promote the education of his own people, being a founder, treasurer, and president of the board of trustees of Morris Brown College, Atlanta, a coeducational institution for colored students opened in 1885, and serving as trustee of Wilberforce University, Wilberforce, Ohio; vice-president of Payne Theological Seminary, Selma, Ala.; and president of the board of trustees of Edward Waters College, Jacksonville, Fla. He was long prominent in the administrative work of his church, and in 1888 the General Conference elected him bishop. As such for many years he supervised with marked success the work of the Second Episcopal District. In 1890 he published *African Methodism in the South*; and in 1897, *The Negro and the White Man*, in which he set forth in admirable spirit what he considered to be the possibilities and needs of the colored race in the United States. He died at Atlanta in his seventy-second year, having won the high regard of all classes.

[Gaines's *African Methodism in the South* contains a biographical sketch. See also Horace Talbert, *The Sons of Allen* (1906); *Centennial Encyc. of the A. M. E. Church* (1916), ed. by R. R. Wright; *Who's Who in America*, 1912–13; *Atlanta Jour.*, Jan. 13, 1912.]

H. E. S.

GALBERRY, THOMAS (1833–Oct. 10, 1878), Augustinian provincial and Catholic bishop of Hartford, was the son of Thomas and Margaret White Galberry of Naas, County Kildare, Ireland, who emigrated to Philadelphia in 1836. His religious character was so marked while he was attending the local schools, that his parents at a considerable sacrifice sent him to Villanova College from which he was graduated as class orator in 1851. Entering the Augustinian novitiate, Jan. 1, 1852, he made his solemn profession, Jan. 4, 1853, and on the completion of his theological course he was ordained by Bishop Neumann of Philadelphia in St. Augustine's Church, Dec. 20, 1856. For four years he acted successively as an instructor at Villanova, as a curate at St. Dennis's Church, Cobb's Creek, and as a pastor at Haverford, Pa.; then he was transferred to Lansingburg, N. Y. Here during a pastorate of ten years he established a cemetery, built a parochial school, and erected St. Augustine's Church. Because of his industry and business ability, he was appointed in 1866 superior of the Augustinian missions in the United States, which greatly widened his field of service. In 1870 he took charge of the Augustinian parish in Lawrence, Mass., where he remained until he was called to the rectorship of Villanova College in 1872. As president, he infused new life into the institution, improved scholarship and discipline, and constructed new buildings. In 1874, when the Commissariat of Our Lady of Good Counsel in the United States was instituted the Province of St. Thomas of Villanova, Galberry was named prior-provincial by the general of the order, and was continued in this position by the vote of his religious brethren when the first Augustinian chapter met on Dec. 18, 1874. This vote of commendation gave him true satisfaction.

Three months later, Galberry was dazed on reading in a newspaper that his appointment to the See of Hartford had been promulgated in a public consistory in Rome (Mar. 15, 1875). Feeling unequal to the task and not relishing this separation from his community, he forwarded a declination when the official notification reached him. The Holy See was not satisfied with his reasons, and a papal mandate of Feb. 17, 1876, enjoined his acceptance. Trained in obedience, the friar closed the affairs of his order and college and went to Hartford where he was consecrated by Archbishop Williams of Boston on Mar. 19, 1876. Almost immediately, he made his *ad limina* visit to Rome, incidentally visiting Augustinian priories in Italy, France, and Ireland. Returning to the diocese, he made the usual visitation, commenced the construction of St. Joseph's Cathedral, founded the *Connecticut Catholic* (later the *Catholic Transcript*) as a diocesan weekly paper, erected two churches, opened a boys' school, increased the number of female religious institutions in the diocese from six to seventeen, and encouraged the total abstinence movement. In two years of consistent work, Galberry accomplished much. Urged to go to Villanova for a rest, he was stricken with a hemorrhage on the way and died in a New York hotel. On Oct. 15 the archbishop of Boston performed the funeral services and Bishop De Goesbriant of Burlington pronounced the panegyric over his friend's remains which were buried under the high altar of his cathedral. Galberry's life was not picturesque; he was a humble religious who sought no fame, but loyally served his order and church as a preacher, an administrator, a kindly teacher, and a firm superior.

[R. H. Clarke, *Lives of the Deceased Bishops of the Cath. Ch. in the U. S.* (1888), III, 128–40; *Cath. Directory,* 1879, p. 39; J. A. Rooney, ed., *Conn. Cath. Year Book* (1877), pp. 35–44; J. H. O'Donnell, "Diocese of Hartford," in *Hist. of the Cath. Ch. in the New Eng. States* (1899), vol. II; T. S. Duggan, *The Cath. Ch. in Conn.* (1930); *Hartford Daily Courant,* Oct. 11, 14, 16, 1878.]

R. J. P.

GALE, BENJAMIN (Dec. 14, 1715–May 6, 1790), Connecticut physician and political writer, son of John and Mary Gale and grandson of Abel Gale, was born at Jamaica, Long Island, where his family had lived for three generations. Early in his childhood his parents removed to Goshen, Orange County, N. Y. After obtaining the degree of M.A. from Yale in 1733, he studied medicine and surgery with Dr. Jared Eliot [*q.v.*] of Killingworth, Conn., as his preceptor, and eventually (June 6, 1739) married Eliot's daughter, Hannah, by whom he had six daughters and two sons. Gale gradually took over his father-in-law's practise and settled permanently in Killingworth. As a physician he won a wide reputation in the colony, and is remembered for his *Historical Memoirs, relating to the Practice of Inoculation for the Small Pox, in the British American Provinces, particularly in New England*; read to the Royal Society of London May 23, 1765, by John Huxham (*Philosophical Transactions,* LV, 1766, 193–204). In it he advocated the use of mercury and antimony inunctions, prior to receiving the pustule. The paper was well written and is noteworthy for his use of the statistical method and for his record of the population and the mortality rates of Boston during epidemic years. He claimed that before the heavy metals were used, one in one hundred died after inoculation, afterward only one in eight hundred succumbed. His only other medical contribution was on dog bites (*Connecticut Journal,* Nov. 21, 1787). He carried on a large correspondence with English and Continental scientists, chiefly upon agricultural matters, and received a medal from the Society of Arts in London for devising an improved drill plough. He also wrote in 1783 *Observations on the culture of Smyrna Wheat* for the American Academy (*Memoirs of the American Academy of Arts and Sciences,* I, 1785, 381).

From 1747 until 1767 Gale served as representative in the General Assembly. "He was by nature intensely interested in politics, and when the rupture with England occurred was strongly in favor of the American cause, though too independent a thinker to give up the privilege of criticizing the measures adopted" (Dexter, *post,* p. 477). Thus in 1755 he published *The Present State of the Colony of Connecticut Considered,* which was an anonymous attack upon the claim of Yale to financial support from the Colonial Assembly. He violently opposed the Stamp Act, and in January 1765 remarked: "A more wicked scheme I think never was on foot, in this colony to destroy us" (*Historical Magazine,* May 1862, 138–39). On Feb. 27, 1775, he wrote to his friend, Silas Deane, "There is not public virtue enough in the Nation [England] to save them; they are doomed to remain a kingdom of Tyrants and Asses. But how much this Country must suffer in the conflict, God only knows" (*Collections of the Connecticut Historical Society,* II, 1870, 204). In November 1775 he became associated with David Bushnell [*q.v.*] in devising the "American Turtle," a kind of depth bomb with which they intended to blow up the fleet of the enemy (*Ibid.,* 315–18). During the Revolution and the period of the framing of the Constitution, he contributed anonymously to several of the colonial newspapers, to the detriment, so his contemporaries averred, of his professional activities. Finally he was an ardent Biblical critic, his chief theological work being *A brief Essay, or, An Attempt to Prove, from the Prophetick Writings of the Old and New Testament, what Period of Prophecy the Church of God is now Under* (1788). He is said to have stipulated that he be buried in such a position, that, when he rose from the dead (he predicted that his resurrection would occur in 1804), his eyes would look upon his own house.

[The best accounts of Gale are those of E. H. Jenkins, *Yale Jour. Biol. and Med.,* Mar. 1930, and F. B. Dexter, *Biog. Sketches of the Grads. of Yale Coll.,* I (1885), 477–80. See also Geo. Gale, *The Gale Family Records* (1866); *Geneal. of the Descendants of John Eliot* (1905); *Boston Medic. and Surgic. Jour.,* Apr. 1, 1840; James Thacher, *Am. Medic. Biog.* (1828), I, 267; *Conn. Hist. Soc. Colls.,* II (1870).]

J. F. F.

GALE, ELBRIDGE (Dec. 25, 1824–Nov. 7, 1907), Baptist clergyman, horticulturist, was born in Bennington, Vt., the son of Isaac and Lydia (Gardner) Gale. He grew up on a farm near North Bennington and as a boy was studious and thoughtful. His love of nature was doubtless stimulated by his close association with his grandfather, Solomon Gale, who was greatly interested in geology and for whom he collected much geological material. After graduating from the New Hampton Literary and Theological Institution, a Baptist school in New Hampshire, he attended Brown University, but serious illness terminated his course. He then began his ministerial career which lasted until 1870. He held Baptist pastorates successively at Johnson, Vt., where in 1853 he married Elizabeth Carpenter; at Pavilion, Ill.; and finally at Manhattan, Kan., whither he moved in 1864. From 1868 to 1871 he was superintendent of schools for Riley County. Throughout these years in the Middle West, he must have been profoundly interested in horticulture, for in 1870 he became "professor of horticulture and superintendent of the nursery" at the Kansas State Agricultural College at Manhattan. Later his title became "professor of botany and practical horticulture." This marked the end of his pastoral work and the beginning of his horticultural career, the first eight years of which he spent in the college. In 1875 he was elected to the presidency of the Kansas State Horticultural Society, continuing in that capacity until 1886, when he resigned, having in 1884 gone to southern Florida on account of his health.

In Florida Gale turned his attention to subtropical fruits and plants, and concerned himself particularly with less well developed varieties such as the mango, guava, avocado, and others. He considered the mango the most deserving of attention of the newer fruits, and it is with it, especially with the Mulgoba variety, that his name is the most intimately associated. In 1889 the United States Department of Agriculture imported from India a few trees each of several mango varieties, some of which were sent to Gale. Since he alone succeeded in saving a single tree of the Mulgoba variety, it was through him that the choicest of all mango varieties came to be known in southern Florida. His study of the cultural requirements and methods of propagation of the fruit advanced the efforts of the United States Department of Agriculture by many years. His devotion to horticultural interests and his faith in the possibilities of the West and South are exhibited in his presidential addresses before the state horticultural society of Kansas and in his extended correspondence with horticulturists of the federal government.

[George Gale, *The Gale Family Records* (1866); L. H. Bailey, *The Standard Cyc. of Horticulture,* vol. III (1915); *Country Life in America,* Feb. 1907; information as to certain facts from Gale's daughter, Mrs. W. H. Sanders, Manhattan, Kan., and from the librarian of the Am. Bapt. Hist. Soc.] H. P. G.

GALE, GEORGE WASHINGTON (Dec. 3, 1789–Sept. 13, 1861), Presbyterian clergyman, educator, was born at Stanford, Dutchess County, N. Y. His father was Josiah Gale, a son of emigrants who came from Yorkshire, according to family tradition; his mother, Rachel Mead, whose family came from Connecticut. After a varied experience of study and teaching, including a year in the Academy of Middlebury College, he was graduated from Union College in 1814. Five years later, after an interruption due to ill health, he completed the course at Princeton Theological Seminary and became pastor of a church in Adams, Jefferson County, N. Y. While here he was the theological instructor of Charles G. Finney [*q.v.*], the famous evangelist. Teacher and student did not agree in their theological views, but they remained good friends. In 1824, because of another break in health, Gale resigned his pastorate and a year later settled on a small farm in Western, Oneida County, N. Y. Here he developed a plan for making manual labor an essential feature in education. Impressed by the need of an educated ministry and by the lack of means of many who desired schooling, he took several young men into his family and gave them books and instruction in return for a few hours' work each day. This principle he also applied at the Oneida Institute in Whitesboro, N. Y., which was founded mainly by his efforts and of which he was the head from 1827 to 1834. During this time he formed the more ambitious purpose of establishing a college on the same principle, for both men and women, in what was then known as the West. His plan was to organize a company, purchase a tract of government land, sell part of it to individual members at an advanced price, and give the profits to the college. The result was the founding of Knox College and the town of Galesburg in Knox County, Ill. The college was chartered Feb. 15, 1837, as the Knox Manual Labor College. The manual labor feature, however, was apparently not a success, and after a few years the name of the institution was shortened to Knox College.

Gale was the first pastor of the local church, a trustee of the college until his death, president of the board for a few years, acting professor of languages until 1842, and from 1843 to 1857 professor of moral philosophy and belles-lettres. A man of intense religious convictions, he was chiefly concerned with the spiritual welfare of his fellow men and his greatest ambition was to bring about their salvation. His theological views were characterized by Finney as hyper-Calvinism. He was married three times: in 1820, at Troy, N. Y., to Harriet Selden; in 1841, at Galesburg, to Mrs. Esther (Williams) Coon; and in 1844, at New Haven, Conn., to Lucy Merriam.

[An unpublished autobiography in the possession of the Gale family; Geo. Gale, *The Gale Family Records* (1866); *Union Univ. Centennial Cat., 1795–1895* (1895); *Princeton Theol. Sem. Biog. Cat.* (1909); G. W. Gale, *A Brief Hist. of Knox Coll.* (1845); official records of Knox College; M. F. Webster, *The Story of Knox Coll.* (1912); *Memoirs of Rev. Charles G. Finney* (1876); date of death from probate records, Knox County Court.] W. L. R.

GALES, JOSEPH (Feb. 4, 1761–Aug. 24, 1841), journalist, reformer, was born at Eckington, near Sheffield, England, the eldest son of Thomas Gales, a village school-teacher who has been described as "an Israelite in whom there was no guile." He worked for his father and studied at night until he was thirteen years of age, at which time he was apprenticed to a printer in Manchester. The printer's shrewish wife threatened his life, and he fled with half a crown in his pocket to Eckington. He was then apprenticed to a kindly typographer in Newark-on-Trent, under whose guidance he became a master printer and binder. There he met Winifred Marshall, a cousin of Lord Melbourne, and married her on May 4, 1784. He established himself in the printing and publishing business in Sheffield, where he founded the weekly *Sheffield Register* in 1787. His wife, a novelist and student of the classics, helped him to make a home to which reformers were attracted. He was able, alert, mild-tempered, firm in his convictions, stalwart in physique, and a champion of liberalism and the cause of labor. He became popular with the radicals and laborers in North England. Joseph Priestley found in him a warm friend and helper in the cause of Unitarianism. He applauded the French Revolutionists; he sold Thomas Paine's *Rights of Man* and befriended the author; he advocated the abolition of slavery and imprisonment for debt, universal manhood suffrage, and the reform of the judicial system; and he very actively supported the Constitutional Society. His strictures on the Pitt government brought upon him the condemnation of that government, and after the suspension of the *habeas corpus,* he fled to Altona, Schleswig-Holstein, in 1794. Mrs. Gales sold the *Register* to his assistant editor, James Montgomery, the poet, and with her two children joined her husband. He improved his knowledge of shorthand, learned French and Spanish, and soon sailed with his family for America, landing at Philadelphia, July 30, 1795, after an eventful voyage. He obtained employment first as a compositor, then as bookkeeper and reporter for the *American Daily Advertiser,* in which capacity he startled the Americans by making the first verbatim report of proceedings in Congress.

He then bought and edited the *Independent Gazetteer.* Among his newly found friends were congressmen of North Carolina who persuaded him to establish a journal in their new state capital at Raleigh. He sold his paper to S. Harrison Smith and in the same year founded the weekly *Raleigh Register* (Oct. 22, 1799), a Jeffersonian journal. He served as mayor of Raleigh nineteen years and was elected state printer annually after 1800 until Jackson's party ousted him. In 1832 he transferred his journal, printing establishment, and bookstore to his son Weston Raleigh Gales and went to live with his son Joseph [*q.v.*] in Washington. He compiled the first two volumes (1834) of the *Annals of Congress* published by Gales & Seaton, served as secretary of the Peace Society, and was six years secretary and treasurer of the American Colonization Society. An ardent Unionist and emancipationist, he nevertheless believed only the states had the right to emancipate slaves. In 1839 careless expenditures and severe criticisms of the Colonization Society led to the employment of a financial secretary in his place. Gales, nearly fourscore, retired and returned to Raleigh, where he died.

[W. G. Briggs, "Joseph Gales, Editor of Raleigh's First Newspaper," in the *N. C. Booklet,* Oct. 1907; Mrs. J. R. Chamberlain, "Two Wake County Editors Whose Work Has Influenced the World," in *Proc. State Lit. and Hist. Commission of N. C.,* Dec. 1922; Josephine Seaton, *Wm. Winston Seaton: A Biog. Sketch* (1871); files of the *Raleigh Register* (1799–1833); obituary in *Raleigh Register and N. C. Gazette,* Aug. 27, 1841.]

W. E. S.

GALES, JOSEPH (Apr. 10, 1786–July 21, 1860), journalist, was born in Eckington, England, the eldest son of Joseph [*q.v.*] and Winifred (Marshall) Gales. In 1795 he was taken to America by his father who was a political refugee. Four years of his boyhood and youth were spent in Philadelphia, the remainder in Raleigh, N. C. His mother taught him to read Latin fluently and to appreciate the works of Shakespeare, Milton, and Adam Smith before he reached the age of fourteen years. He attended a private school in Raleigh, and later, for a time, the University of North Carolina, and learned the printer's trade from his father, who also taught him shorthand and sent him to Philadelphia and Washington to develop his skill as a reporter.

In 1807 he went to the Capital to report congressional proceedings for S. Harrison Smith, editor of the tri-weekly *National Intelligencer.* He sat next the vice-president and "shared his snuff-box" with him from 1807 to 1820 while he was the sole reporter of the proceedings of the Senate. In 1809 he was made a partner of Smith, and in 1810 he became sole proprietor of the *National Intelligencer,* the "recognized organ," or "Court Paper." In 1812 he took into partnership William W. Seaton [*q.v.*], who had been associated with the elder Gales on the *Raleigh Register* and had married the latter's daughter Sarah. The brothers-in-law equally divided their work and as long as Gales lived maintained a common bank-account. A warm supporter of Madison in the War of 1812, Gales volunteered as a private in a company of infantry which saw service about Washington, accepting hazardous missions to prove his loyalty to his adopted country. Meanwhile the paper, which was introduced to the public as a daily on Jan. 1, 1813, was published regularly until the invasion of Washington, the editors returning from camp on alternate days to supervise its preparation. When the British captured the Capital they destroyed Gales's library and equipment, but, at the earnest request of an old lady, spared his building. On Dec. 14, 1813, he married Sarah Juliana Maria Lee, daughter of Theodorick Lee of Virginia and niece of "Light-Horse Harry." They made their home on Ninth Street, just above "the Avenue," until business houses crowded them out. Gales had selected a likely spot for a country estate before he married, and later realized his dreams in "Eckington," about two miles from his office on New Jersey Avenue. Here he found recreation in walking or shooting, and indulged his taste for a rich cellar and a heavy table. His free giving and careless bookkeeping almost bankrupted him, but the guests entertained by the Galeses included the Adamses, Websters, and Calhouns, the British minister, and other celebrities.

Gales was responsible for most of the editorials in the *Intelligencer.* They were short and compact, unless the gibes of his enemies stirred him to retaliation. Contrary to the public opinion of his time, few statesmen wrote editorials for his paper. He was not a skilled "political" journalist. In turn a Republican, a Whig, and a Constitutional Democrat, he did not believe in government by the masses and considered the election of Andrew Jackson a national calamity. He warmly supported the United States Bank, national free education, and Clay's "American System"; encouraged liberalism in religion, being a member of the first Unitarian church organized in Washington; and materially aided the American Colonization Society. He had some share in local politics, being mayor of Washington from 1827 to 1830. His most permanent work, however, was the preservation of the proceedings of Congress throughout a considerable period. Condensed running reports of proceedings were printed in the *National Intelligencer,* the files of which are thus the most valuable sources of Congressional debates down to 1833, when the *Congressional Globe* began to report in more detail. Gales & Seaton also published, from 1825 to 1837, a *Register of Debates in Congress* (29 vols.), covering those years; the *Annals of Congress* (vols. I and II, 1834; vols. III–XLII, 1849–56), covering the period 1789–1824; and the *American State Papers* (38 vols., 1832–61). Although Gales was employing other reporters at the time of the Webster-Hayne debate, at Webster's request he reported that debate himself, and saved it in a volume of 100 pages.

[A. C. Clark, "Joseph Gales, Jr., Editor and Mayor," in *Columbia Hist. Soc. Records* (Washington, D. C.), vol. XXIII (1920); Frederic Hudson, *Journalism in the U. S.* (1873); Josephine Seaton, *Wm. Winston Seaton: A Biog. Sketch* (1871); files of the *Washington Globe* (1830–45); and the *National Intelligencer* (1810–60) and obituary in the latter, July 23, 1860; "The National Intelligencer and Its Editors," in *Atlantic Monthly,* Oct. 1860; H. W. Crew, *Centennial Hist. of the City of Washington* (1892); S. C. Busey, *Pictures of the City of Washington in the Past* (1898); W. B. Bryan, *A Hist. of the National Capital* (2 vols., 1916); A. K. McClure, *Recollections of Half a Century* (1902); letters in the Van Buren MSS. in the Lib. of Cong.]

W. E. S.

GALL (*c.* 1840–Dec. 5, 1894), a war chief of the Hunkpapa Sioux, was born on the Moreau River, S. Dak. An attempt in boyhood to eke out his scanty rations by eating the gall of an animal killed by a neighbor gave him his sobriquet, his Indian name being Pizi. Though of humble parentage and though at an early age he lost his father, he was "well brought up" according to Indian standards, receiving at the hands of his people the consideration usually given an orphan. As a young man he became a warrior of note. In the years immediately following the treaty of 1868 he allied himself with the hostile element that refused to remain on the reservation; and with the assumption by his fellow tribesman, Sitting Bull, of the rôle of medicine man and political leader, became that chieftain's military lieutenant. He was the principal war chief, though without supreme authority, in the battle of the Little Big Horn, June 25, 1876. He led the attack which routed Reno in the valley, immediately afterward cooperating with Crazy Horse in surrounding and annihilating Custer and then returning to the siege of Reno and Benteen on the bluffs. On the subsequent break-up of the Indian force he remained with Sitting Bull's band, which late in the year was forced across the line into Canada. In the fall of 1880 he quarreled with his leader, called him a coward and a fraud, and with a large number of followers returned to the United States. He was still belligerent, but after a half-hearted fight with the force of Maj. Guido Ilges, at Poplar River Agency, Mont., Jan. 3, 1881, surrendered with some 300 followers.

He settled as a farmer on the Standing Rock reservation, where he came under the influence of James McLaughlin, the Indian agent, and ultimately became a friend of the whites and a potent influence in inducing the Indians to accept the federal government's plan of educating their children. In 1886 he attended the reunion of survivors of the Little Big Horn battle on the field and gave to Capt. (afterward Gen.) Godfrey and others the first trustworthy account of the fight from an Indian standpoint. From 1889 he was a judge of the Court of Indian Offenses at the agency. In December of the same year he accompanied McLaughlin to Washington on a mission in behalf of the Sioux. He opposed the policies of Sitting Bull, and toward the end, fearing an attempt at assassination, asked to be armed. Though he seems to have taken no open part in combating the Messiah craze of 1890, he was known to look upon it with strong disfavor. He died at his home on Oak Creek, S. Dak.

McLaughlin describes him as a large man of noble presence and says that the finest typical picture of an Indian extant is a photograph of him taken about 1885. His military talents are conceded to have been of a high order, and his personal character won him the esteem of the whites with whom he came in contact. His influence with his tribesmen was shown in many instances, particularly in his bringing about the ratification of the Act of Mar. 2, 1889, the last agreement with the Sioux by which, for certain concessions, their great reservation was divided into separate reservations and certain portions ceded to the government. By McLaughlin, to whom he became closely attached and to whom he would often come "with personal affairs of staggering intimacy," he is regarded as one of the greatest men of his nation and the peer of Red Cloud and Spotted Tail.

[Jas. McLaughlin, *My Friend the Indian* (1910) and article in *Handbook of Am. Indians* (1907); Chas. A. Eastman (Ohiyesa), *Indian Heroes and Great Chieftains* (1918).] W. J. G.

GALLAGHER, HUGH PATRICK (Mar. 26, 1815–Mar. 10, 1882), Catholic priest, was born at Killygordon, Donegal, Ireland. Prior to his emigration to America in 1837 he had completed his philosophical course and was studying theology. He continued his study in the Seminary of St. Charles Borromeo in Overbrook, Pa., and was there ordained by Bishop F. P. Kenrick [*q.v.*] on Sept. 27, 1840. Assigned to St. Patrick's Church in Pottsville, he was so aroused by the ravages of intemperance that he formed a total abstinence society of about 5,000 members. He is said to have introduced in 1843 the Sisters of Mercy into the Pittsburgh diocese and to have founded in 1844 the *Pittsburgh Catholic.* As pastor of St. Peter's Church in Butler from 1841 to 1844, he ministered to 1,800 parishioners, largely German and Irish immigrants. Sent to Father Gallitzin's parish at Loretto in the latter year, he commenced a church which was completed by his brother and successor, Father Joseph A. Gallagher. He invited the Sisters of Mercy to establish schools; encouraged the Franciscan Brothers who founded their mother-house and St. Francis College for boys; and arranged a parochial budget based on pew rents. Appointed a theologian at the First Plenary Council of Baltimore, Gallagher attracted the attention of Bishop Alemany [*q.v.*] who induced him to go in 1852 to his California diocese.

The future career of "Father Hugh," as he came to be known in the frontier towns, mining camps, and in San Francisco, was colorful. He was of untold assistance to Archbishop Alemany as a leader of the Irish priests and congregations. An organizer and builder, he constructed St. Dominic's Church at Benicia, St. Peter's and St. Paul's at Yreka, and chapels or churches at Shasta, Weaverville, Carson City, Reno, Virginia City, and Stockton. He commenced the Church of the Immaculate Conception at Oakland and aided in building St. Mary's Cathedral, San Francisco. In 1853 he founded the *Catholic Standard,* the first Catholic paper on the Coast. The following year he brought from Rome the pallium for the newly named archbishop. At this time, while in Ireland, he enlisted a group of Presentation nuns from Cork and some Sisters of Mercy from Kinsale under Sister Mary Baptist Russell, a sister of Lord Chief Justice Russell of Killowen, who along with a few priests and seminarians accompanied him to California by way of the tedious New York–Panama route. As a patron of these communities, he aided in the establishment of schools, orphanages, a Magdalen home for wayward girls—for which he obtained a small legislative grant, and St. Mary's Hospital in San Francisco, which was presided over by Sister Mary Baptist for forty years. When the Adams Express Company closed their California offices in 1855, he was intrusted by miners and laborers with their savings, which in the aggregate amounted to millions. In 1861, with the aid of his brother, who had followed him westward, he created St. Joseph's parish and church with its model school and hall. Indeed, he is accredited with the introduction of the parochial school system into the diocese. In the hard years of 1869 and 1870 he successfully advocated the improvement of Golden Gate Park as a measure of unemployment relief. He made frequent pilgrimages to Europe and was in close correspondence with the Holy See. In time his robust constitution gave way. After a fruitless visit to Ireland in search of health, he retired to St. Mary's Hospital where he succumbed to pneumonia.

[A. A. Lambing, *A Hist. of the Cath. Ch. in the Dioceses of Pittsburgh and Allegheny* (1880); F. Kittell, *Souvenir of Loretto Centenary* (1899); M. E. Herron, *Sisters of Mercy in U. S.* (1928); W. Gleason, *Hist. of the Cath. Ch. in Cal.* (1872); *N. Y. Freeman's Jour.*, Oct. 10, 1854; *Ave Maria*, Apr. 1, 1882; *Daily Examiner* (San Francisco), Mar. 11, 14, 1882; *Morning Call* (San Francisco), Mar. 13, 14, 1882; *Monitor* (San Francisco), Mar. 15, 1882; the *Catholic* (Pittsburgh), Apr. 1, 1882.] R. J. P.

GALLAGHER, WILLIAM DAVIS (Aug. 21, 1808–June 27, 1894), editor, poet, public official, was born in Philadelphia, Pa., the son of Bernard Gallagher, an Irish refugee and compatriot of Robert Emmett, and Abigail Davis Gallagher, daughter of a Welsh farmer who died at Valley Forge while a soldier in Washington's army. He spent his youth with his widowed mother on a farm near Mount Pleasant, in Southern Ohio, and attended elementary school there. Later he attended a Lancasterian seminary. His first verse was published in 1824 in the *Literary Gazette.* In 1826 he began his journalistic career which for the next thirteen years was varied and financially precarious. He was connected successively with the *Western Tiller*; the *Cincinnati Emporium*; the *Cincinnati Register*; the *Western Minerva,* a literary magazine attempted in conjunction with his brother Francis; the *Backwoodsman,* a campaign paper at Xenia, Ohio, devoted to the presidential candidacy of Henry Clay; the *Cincinnati Mirror,* fourth literary periodical published west of the Alleghany Mountains; the *Western Literary Journal and Monthly Review*; the *Western Monthly Magazine and Literary Journal*; the *Ohio State Journal* at Columbus; and the *Hesperian,* his most important literary magazine. While he was at Xenia he was married to Emma Adamson, daughter of Captain Adamson of Boston.

Attracted by Gallagher's political correspondence for the paper, Charles Hammond, editor of the *Cincinnati Gazette,* invited him in 1839 to become his assistant at a liberal salary, and the days of his early struggle were ended. After Hammond's death in 1840, Gallagher did much political writing and took an active part in Whig politics. A brief editorship of the *Daily Message,* an Abolitionist newspaper, provided the only break in his connection with the *Gazette* until 1850 when he resigned to become private secretary to Thomas Corwin, secretary of the treasury. Two years later he bought an interest in the *Daily Courier* at Louisville, Ky., and assumed the editorship. He sold his interest in the *Courier* in 1854 and accepted the editorship of the *Western Farmer's Journal,* having found that his opposition to slavery made his paper unpopular.

Gallagher was a delegate to the Republican national convention of 1860, in which he supported Abraham Lincoln for the presidential nomination, and was one of those who carried the news to Springfield. When Salmon P. Chase was appointed secretary of the treasury he made Gallagher his secretary. President Lincoln later appointed him a special collector of customs and commercial agent in the upper Mississippi Valley. He intercepted provisions and stores valued at millions of dollars en route to the Confederates and turned them over to the Union armies. Later he was surveyor of customs for Louisville and pension agent. He suffered financial reverses after the war and for a time did clerical work as secretary of the Kentucky Land Company. He published his first volume of poetry, *Erato No. I,* in the spring of 1835 and followed it with *Erato No. II* in August 1835 and *Erato No. III* in 1837. He edited *Selections from the Poetical Literature of the West,* containing a number of his own poems, in 1841. His *Miami Woods, A Golden Wedding and Other Poems* was published in 1881 at Cincinnati. Much of his poetry appeared in newspapers and magazines. Many of his lyrics were set to music and were popularized in the theater. Preëminent among early Ohio poets, he exerted a formative influence in the Middle West comparable to that which his more distinguished New England contemporaries made felt in their wider field. In his blank verse of *Miami Woods,* which was Wordsworthian both in its style and in its sympathetic portrayal of nature, he immortalized the charm of the forests of Ohio as Bryant had the eastern woodlands and Longfellow the groves of Louisiana.

[W. H. Venable, "Wm. Davis Gallagher," *Ohio Archeol. and Hist. Quart.,* Mar., Sept. 1888, reprinted as a separate biography in 1889 and later in *Beginnings of Literary Culture in the Ohio Valley* (1891). See also Emerson Venable, *Poets of Ohio* (1909), pp. 15–33; the *Courier Jour.* (Louisville, Ky.), the *Louisville Commercial,* and the *Louisville Times,* June 28, 1894.]

D. W. M.

GALLATIN, ABRAHAM ALFONSE ALBERT (Jan. 29, 1761–Aug. 12, 1849), secretary of the treasury, diplomat, the son of Jean and Sophie Albertine (Rolaz) Gallatin, dropped the first two alliterative forenames, retaining only the Albert from his mother. As early as the fourteenth century his aristocratic family was prominent in the history of the Duchy of Savoy, and after the city of Geneva established its independence in 1536 the house furnished an almost unbroken succession of councilors and great lords of the syndic. Albert was the eleventh in direct descent from the Jean Gallatin who signed the decree which freed Geneva from the episcopal-papal control of Savoy. Left an orphan at the age of nine, he was taken into the care of a distant relative, Mlle. Catherine Pictet, whose wise and affectionate guidance won the lasting gratitude, if only the intermittent acknowledgment, of her ward. A rich heritage of culture, exposure to the exceptionally enlightened society of pre-revolutionary Geneva, and an excellent education at the Academy, from which he graduated in 1779, all combined to give the youth of eighteen a refinement of manners and an alertness of mind which he retained throughout the remaining three score and ten years of his life. But no amount of persuasion or pressure could keep the young Gallatin faithful to the aristocratic traditions of his family. He gravitated toward the more radical group of students in the Academy, applauded the summons of Rousseau to seek freedom from the conventions of civilization in a romantic return to nature, and felt something stifling in the political atmosphere of the oligarchy of Geneva. He indignantly refused his grandmother's offer to procure for him a lieutenant-colonelcy in the mercenary troops which her friend the Landgrave of Hesse was sending to George III to help put down the rebellion in the American colonies. Chafing under what he believed to be a disposition on the part of his guardian and family to force him into a distasteful career, Gallatin left Geneva a few weeks before his nineteenth birthday, without warning to family or friends, and in company with an impecunious but optimistic chum, Henri Serre, took passage at Bordeaux for America, "the land of freedom."

If Gallatin had refused to fight against the Americans as an officer of the Hessian troops, no more did he come, like the young Lafayette, to fight for the Americans. When he landed on the Massachusetts coast in the midsummer of 1780, the fortunes of Washington's army were at a low ebb. But Gallatin took no notice of this state of affairs. He had come to America for his own freedom, not hers. He had bought with his few thousand francs, not bullets to shoot at the British, but tea, a notorious commodity, to sell to the Americans. The statement that he "fought in our Revolution" (E. Channing, *A History of the United States,* IV, 1917, 266) is based on the slender fact that the young adventurer, not being able to sell to the impecunious farmers of Machias, Me., the stock of West Indian goods for which he had exchanged his tea, had sought relief from the monotony of a winter in that frontier village by joining a small group of volunteers who marched to Passamaquoddy Bay on the rumor of a British attack, and was for a few days "left accidentally in command of some militia, volunteers and Indians" there. "As I never met the enemy," he wrote sixty-five years later, "I have not the slightest claim to military services" (*Writings,* II, 621). He returned from the Maine frontier to the unwelcome atmosphere of puritanical Boston in the very month (October 1781) of Cornwallis's surrender at Yorktown; and during the year of the peace negotiations he was allowed by the president and fellows of Harvard College to give a sort of "extension course" in French to such students as secured the permission of parents or guardians to take it.

At Boston Gallatin met M. Savary, representative of a firm in Lyons which had a claim against the state of Virginia, and willingly joined him as companion and interpreter. Savary soon bought warrants at Philadelphia for 120,000 acres of land adjoining the "Washington bottom lands" on the south side of the Ohio, making over one-fourth (later one-half) of the purchase to Gallatin, on condition that the latter should give his personal attention to the development of the lands until the receipt of his patrimony on his twenty-fifth birthday (Jan. 29, 1786) should provide him with the funds for the purchase of his share of them. In the spring of 1784 Gallatin crossed the Alleghanies with a small exploring party and established headquarters and a store at Clare's Farm on the Monongahela River, in Fayette County, Pa., about four miles north of the Virginia line. A little later he located his permanent western home, "Friendship Hill," a few miles up the river. Henry Adams deplored the fact that a man of Gallatin's gifts was led by his youthful enthusiasm for Rousseau to bury his talents and sink his modest fortune in the wilderness of western Pennsylvania. It is true that Gallatin was neither a good farmer nor a successful land speculator; that neither his own need for cultural contacts nor his family's social ambitions found satisfaction in the bucolic atmosphere of "Friendship Hill." In his old age he wrote of his western land, "It is a troublesome and unproductive property, which has plagued me all my life. I could not have invested my patrimony in a more unprofitable manner" (Adams, *post,* p. 67). Yet the western residence was no political detriment. The obvious superiority of Gallatin's talents marked him from the first as a leader of the homespun democracy of western Pennsylvania, and caused him, before he had reached his thirty-ninth year, to be launched upon a public career which was to continue unbroken for almost four decades.

Gallatin made his début in politics as a member of a conference held at Harrisburg, in September 1788, to consider ways and means for revising the new Constitution of the United States, which had been ratified by the Pennsylvania convention the previous December by a vote of 46 to 23. The very presence of Gallatin at this conference classed him with the men who objected to the centralizing features of the Constitution. The radical resolutions which he prepared called for a single chamber of Congress, a strictly limited executive, elected for a brief term by popular vote, and a Supreme Court with no appellate jurisdiction except by writ of error from the state courts. Disappointed in his projects of colonization and dejected by the death of his bride of a few months, Sophia Allegre, whom he had brought from Richmond to the banks of the Monongahela, Gallatin thought seriously of returning to Geneva in 1789. But the impossibility of retrieving the money which he had sunk in real estate, together with the upheaval caused in his native city by the outbreak of the French Revolution, kept him in America. In the winter of 1789–90 he sat in the convention which revised the constitution of Pennsylvania, contributing notably to the discussions of the suffrage, representation, taxation, and the judiciary. In October 1790, he was elected to the state legislature as a representative of Fayette County, and was reëlected in 1791 and 1792 without a contest.

In a memorandum of his career in the legislature Gallatin wrote: "I enjoyed an extraordinary influence in that body, the more remarkable as I was always in a *party* minority. . . . The laboring oar was left almost exclusively to me. In the session of 1791–2 I was put on thirty-five committees, prepared all their reports, and drew all their bills" (Adams, p. 84). Reading of Gallatin's work for the reform of the penal code, the establishment of a state-wide system of public education, the removal of antiquated survivals from the statute law, and the abolition of slavery, one is strongly reminded of the vigorous program of Jefferson in the Virginia legislature in the years from 1776 to 1779. The parallelism extends even to the simile of "the laboring oar." But Gallatin's greatest service was in a field in which Jefferson was never more than a novice—public finance. Gallatin laid the foundation of his reputation by preparing the report of the committee of ways and means in his very first term, and thereafter was recognized as the leader of the House in financial legislation. His measures included proposals for the rehabilitation of the currency by the extinction of the state paper money, the full payment of the public debt in specie, the wise management of the funds from the sale of the public lands, the establishment of the Bank of Pennsylvania, and the creation of a revenue adequate to meet "all the expenses of government without any direct tax during the forty ensuing years" (Adams, p. 86). In many respects this program was similar to that which was being carried into effect at the same time by Alexander Hamilton as secretary of the treasury.

A democrat by conviction and a representative of the agricultural West, Gallatin naturally espoused the Republican cause in the sharp party struggle of the day. It was therefore a testimony to his personal prestige and accomplishments that the Federalist legislature of the state elected him on joint ballot (45 to 37) to the Senate of the United States, on Feb. 28, 1793. He took his seat at the opening of the Third Congress in December, but his eligibility was immediately challenged on the ground that he had not been nine years a citizen of the United States. On a fair interpretation of the Constitution Gallatin was entitled to his seat, but the Federalist Senate, for political reasons, deprived him of it by a vote of 14 to 12, on Feb. 28, 1794. Brief as his stay in the Senate had been, he had aroused the ire of the Federalists by a motion calling upon the secretary of the treasury for a detailed statement of the government's finances down to Jan. 1, 1794, a motion which drew from Hamilton a testy letter of complaint that he should be hectored by "unexpected, desultory, and distressing calls for lengthy and complicated statements" (Adams, pp. 117–18). It was not till the year 1800 that a law was passed requiring the secretary of the treasury to submit an annual report to Congress.

Gallatin was not greatly distressed by his removal from the Senate. On Nov. 1, 1793, he had married Hannah, the daughter of Commodore James Nicholson of New York, and was even more concerned to get his private affairs straightened out than to probe the administration of the public finances. His second wife, unlike the landlady's pretty daughter with whom he had eloped from Richmond four years before, was a woman of high family standing and wide social connections, with uncles and brothers in the navy, and sisters married to members of Congress. In April 1794, Gallatin sold his western lands to Robert Morris for $4,000 Pennsylvania currency, payable (but not paid) in three yearly instalments. The next month he took his bride to the rustic mansion on the Monongahela. The whole of their little fortune, as he confided to her, consisted in the notes of Morris, together with their farm and five or six hundred pounds in cash.

When, after an absence of a year and a half, he returned to his home in Fayette County, the whole of western Pennsylvania was seething with the Whiskey Rebellion, provoked by Hamilton's excise bill of 1791. A group of radicals, headed by a blatant demagogue named David Bradford, staged incendiary meetings, to which they summoned the militia in arms, terrorized Pittsburgh, forced revenue officers to flee for their lives, and urged the western counties to resist the law to the death. In this crisis Gallatin played a dominant rôle. With superb courage and persuasive oratory he faced the excited and armed crowd, enheartened the moderates, won over the wavering, and at last secured a vote of 34 to 23 in the revolutionary committee of sixty for peaceable submission to the law of the country. It is hardly an exaggeration to say that Gallatin saved western Pennsylvania from a civil war. When the militia which Washington had sent out under the command of Gov. Henry Lee of Virginia reached the scene of disturbance, it found, instead of "embattled farmers" to subdue, only a few lawbreakers to arrest and carry to Philadelphia for trial. Hamilton, who accompanied the troops to Pittsburgh, is said to have tried hard to show that Gallatin was implicated in disloyal propaganda, but no proof of the latter's disloyalty in the crisis of 1794 could be found. He had amply atoned for what he called his "only political sin" in acting as clerk of a meeting of the protesting farmers in Pittsburgh two years before. Nevertheless, such is the virulence of partisan rancor that to the end of his life he was maligned by his political opponents as the arch-instigator of the Whiskey Rebellion.

The inhabitants of the western counties pronounced a more just verdict on Gallatin's services when they elected him to the federal House of Representatives in the autumn of 1794. He took his seat at the opening of the Fourth Congress and served for three terms. These six years (1795–1801) constituted perhaps the stormiest period in American political history. In all the turmoil of debate over the Jay Treaty, the insults of the French Directory, the Alien and Sedition Acts, naval and commercial policies, the war with France, and the election of 1800, Gallatin showed an unrivaled grasp of constitutional and international law, great power of argument, and a calmness of temper unruffled by the personal attacks of the New England Federalists, who sneered at his foreign birth and French accent and grossly misrepresented the part he had taken in the Whiskey Rebellion. When Madison and William Branch Giles retired from the House in 1797, Gallatin became the recognized leader of the Republican minority. His signal service was in the field of finance. Insisting on the strict accountability of the Treasury to Congress, he caused the creation of a standing committee on finance (the famous committee of ways and means) to receive and advise on the reports of the secretary on revenues, debts, loans, expenditures, and estimates; and he urged that no moneys should be spent except for the specific purposes for which they had been appropriated. Secretary Wolcott wrote to Hamilton in desperation: "Gallatin . . . is evidently intending to break down this department, by charging it with an impracticable detail" (G. Gibbs, *Memoirs of the Administrations of Washington and John Adams,* 1846, II, 45). Against the combined opposition of the Federalist majority in the House and the Federalist officials in the cabinet Gallatin was unable to carry through his plan of financial reform, but he clearly announced the more orderly procedure which he himself was soon to follow as secretary of the treasury. In the last days of his final session in the House, during the Jefferson-Burr deadlock, as party leader he directed the fight for the election of Jefferson, displaying tact and firmness, refusing to be frightened or cajoled by the Federalists into schemes for a new election or a "regency," and remaining confident that the Burrite obstructionists would give way to the manifest will of the people.

That Gallatin should head the Treasury Department in the new administration was as inevitable as that Jefferson should head the administration itself. There was no other man in the Republican party to dispute his eminence in the field of finance. Appointed secretary of the treasury in May 1801, he held the position until February 1814, although ceasing to perform its actual duties in May 1813. No other secretary of the treasury has yet equaled Gallatin in length of service. The labor which he devoted to the details of the office in the first two years was the most arduous of his life, and, as he told his son long years afterward, it nearly undermined his constitution. Only the reading of his voluminous reports to Congress and his correspondence with his chief will enable one to gain an adequate idea of his large conception of the rôle of the guardian of the public treasure in an administration aiming at the establishment of pure Republican principles. For Gallatin was not content, as he wrote to Jefferson on Nov. 8, 1809, "to act the part of a mere financier, to become a contriver of taxes, a dealer of loans . . . fattening contractors, pursers and agents" (Adams, p. 410). He was a statesman first, shaping his policy to further the political and social ends which he envisaged as the destiny of the United States, a new and powerful nation, free from the burden of military and naval preëmptions, free from political entanglements with the Old World, free from the curse of party faction and the canker of social privilege. He felt that, by following the peaceful paths of industry and commerce, the country, favored by its geographical position and its abundant natural resources, would grow prosperous; and the government, without recourse to oppressive taxation, would not only have ample means to perform its restricted functions, but an increasing surplus to devote to national projects for education and internal improvements.

Gallatin's administration of the Treasury was made difficult by circumstances over which he had no control, such as the war with the Barbary pirates, the vexation of American commerce by British Orders in Council and Napoleonic decrees, the inefficient management of the Navy Department by Robert Smith, and the bitter, factious opposition in the Senate, against which he had but indifferent support from Jefferson and hardly any from the more temporizing Madison. The public debt on Jan. 1, 1801, was slightly over $80,000,000. By setting aside $7,-

300,000 (about three-fourths of the estimated revenue for 1802) each year for the payment of interest and principal, Gallatin calculated that, if peace continued, the debt would be wiped out by 1817. And so, undoubtedly, it would have been. After ten years of Gallatin's administration the debt had been reduced to $45,000,000, in spite of the Barbary wars, the purchase of Louisiana, and the commercial losses from embargoes and non-intercourse. But the War of 1812 sent the debt up to $123,000,000 and postponed its extinction twenty years beyond the date set by Gallatin. The internal revenue duties, which he was loath to sacrifice, in spite of his condemnation of them at the time of the Whiskey Rebellion, were swept away, on motion of John Randolph, in 1802. But a special Mediterranean fund of two and a half per cent increase in *ad valorem* duties was imposed in March 1804, to defray the expense of the Barbary wars. At the close of Jefferson's highly prosperous first administration all the expenses of the government, including the interest on the $11,250,000 stock for the Louisiana purchase, had been easily met, and the treasury showed a surplus of $1,000,000, which increased the next year (1806) to over $4,000,000.

Then came the evil days. In April 1807, a Tory majority of 200 was returned to Parliament, and George Canning became foreign secretary. "From the moment Mr. Canning and his party assumed power, the fate of Mr. Jefferson's Administration was sealed; . . . England was determined to recover her commerce and to take back her seamen, and America could not retain either by any means whatever; she had no alternative but submission or war, and either submission or war was equally fatal to Mr. Jefferson's Administration" (Adams, p. 356). The developments of the next six years, especially the American efforts to exert peaceful coercion by means of commercial restriction and the ultimate recourse to war, wrecked Gallatin's policies. Not only was he forced to become "a contriver of taxes, a dealer of loans," but he had to abandon the project which he had worked out with Jefferson for the expenditure of $20,000,000 in the construction of a vast system of canals and highways running from Maine to Georgia and connecting the eastern rivers with the Mississippi basin. With characteristic imperturbability and diligence he set himself to the unwelcome tasks which filled the last years of his secretaryship. To enforce the Embargo he had to issue orders as drastic as those which he had condemned in the Federalist régime. As the revenue from exports sank, the hated internal taxes had to be revived and extended. Congress refused to re-charter the Bank of the United States (1811), in spite of Gallatin's plea that it was a necessity, with the result that the paper of the prolific state banks compelled the suspension of specie payments outside the New England states. The latter maintained a constant opposition to "Mr. Madison's war." Of the $16,000,000 which Gallatin was authorized to raise in December 1812, Boston subscribed $75,000 as against $5,720,000 from New York and $6,858,000 from Philadelphia. Finally, the faction opposed to Gallatin in the Senate, led by Samuel Smith [*q.v.*], grew so bitter—after Gallatin had forced the latter's incompetent brother Robert Smith [*q.v.*] to resign from the State Department in 1811—that Gallatin became convinced of the futility of remaining longer in the cabinet. He took advantage of the Russian offer of mediation to request the President to send him to St. Petersburg.

When Gallatin dropped down Delaware Bay on May 9, 1813, on his voyage to Russia, he was leaving behind him forever the turmoil of American domestic politics. For the next ten years he was to be engaged almost uninterruptedly in diplomatic service abroad. The six months which he spent in St. Petersburg with James A. Bayard and John Quincy Adams were fruitless, owing to Great Britain's refusal to accept Russian mediation. Gallatin learned in October 1813 that the Senate had rejected his nomination as peace commissioner. When the British offered to treat with the United States directly, Madison omitted Gallatin's name from the new list of commissioners, supposing that he was coming back to his post at the Treasury. But Gallatin preferred to stay, and the President added his name as a fifth member of the commission, with Adams, Bayard, Henry Clay, and Jonathan Russell, appointing a new secretary of the treasury. This chapter of confusion resulted in Gallatin's name being at the foot instead of the head of the new commission, but it did not prevent him from again wielding "the laboring oar" when the British and the American negotiators finally set to work at Ghent in the midsummer of 1814. He not only prepared or revised the drafts on the most important points in dispute, with great patience and skill wearing down the exorbitant demands of the British, but with even greater patience and skill he kept a degree of harmony in the American commission itself between Adams and Clay, whose pugnacious tempers and sectional interests clashed over the relative value of the Newfoundland fisheries and the navigation of the Mississippi. There were moments in the autumn of 1814 when Gallatin despaired of the success of the negotiations and apprehended that the full force of the British army and navy, released by the triumph of the Allies over Napoleon, might be turned against the United States. But agricultural distress, a rapidly mounting debt, Macdonough's victory on Lake Champlain, the sound advice of Wellington, and the fluttering of European danger signals at Vienna, combined to persuade the British to follow the wiser course. The treaty of peace was signed at Ghent on Christmas eve, 1814. Henry Adams calls it "the special and peculiar triumph of Mr. Gallatin" (*post,* p. 546).

On completing his work at Ghent, Gallatin visited Geneva after an absence of thirty-five years, and arrived at Paris in March 1815, to be received in audience, cordially by the departing Bourbon King and rather brusquely by the returning Emperor. In April he crossed the Channel to England, where he labored, with Adams and Clay, to conclude a favorable commercial treaty with the British. On his return to America in September he was confronted with an embarrassment of choices. Friends in Philadelphia begged him to accept nomination for Congress; John Jacob Astor offered him a share of one-fifth of his lucrative business; Secretary of State Monroe urged him to accept the post of minister to France, which Madison had proffered to him before his return to America. Yielding to the wishes of his family, and perhaps to his own unacknowledged preference for a residence in Paris over one on the banks of the Monongahela, Gallatin accepted the French mission early in 1816, only to be faced in a few days with still another offer. Alexander J. Dallas resigned from the Treasury and Madison asked Gallatin to return to his place in the cabinet. He was only fifty-five years old, at the height of his powers. His continued service at the head of the Treasury would have been of far more value to his country than anything he could accomplish in France under the Bourbon Restoration. But he declined the Treasury post with the lame explanation that "an active young man" was needed, and sailed with his delighted family for France. The seven years in Paris (1816–23) were a diplomatic deadlock. Indeed, one gathers from the diary kept by Gallatin's son and secretary, James, that official business was completely stifled by social amenities at Paris. Gallatin performed his duties with conscientious diligence; like Martin Luther, he "could not do otherwise." But in the main business of his mission, the claims for injury done to American commerce by the Napoleonic decrees, he made no progress with the successive ministries of Louis XVIII; while the tangle of red tape caused by the interpretation of the Louisiana treaty could have been as well unraveled by a second-rate minister. The only service rendered by Gallatin on this mission at all comparable to that rendered at Ghent was the aid which he gave in 1818 to the American minister in London, Richard Rush, in negotiating a treaty renewing the commercial clauses of 1815, gaining some concessions in colonial trade and the Newfoundland fisheries, drawing the boundary line between the United States and Canada from the Lake of the Woods to the Rockies, and providing for the joint occupation of the Oregon Territory for a period of ten years.

Gallatin returned to America in the summer of 1823 to find the country already seething with the factional politics which brought to a speedy close the "era of good feeling." He reluctantly allowed his name to be used with Crawford's on the "regular" Republican ticket, only to be asked to withdraw it later, when Van Buren conceived the preposterous hope of inducing Clay to be content with vice-presidential ambitions. Gallatin acceded more readily to the second solicitation than to the first, for he had no personal desire for office. But the whole transaction was rather scabrous, and it confirmed the impression which Gallatin had formed on his return from Paris, that American politics had declined from the high level of principles by which he believed it was guided in the Jeffersonian era.

Gallatin anticipated retiring to the new stone mansion which he had built at "Friendship Hill" and living as a gentleman-farmer on his modest income of $2,000 a year. He actually spent only a single year at New Geneva, where his family, except for the second son Albert, chafed under a feeling of social rustication. In 1826 he was for a third time drafted for a foreign mission. When failing health obliged Rufus King to resign, President Adams persuaded Gallatin to accept the appointment to St. James's for such a period at least as would be necessary for the settlement of new difficulties over old questions, which had been accentuated by the accession of the implacable Canning to power in 1822 and the retaliatory navigation acts of Congress at the instigation of the no less implacable Adams. After laboring for more than a year in London, Gallatin came home in November 1827 with enough concessions to earn from the President, who was never over-generous in praise of a colleague or appreciation of a rival, congratulations on the "reason and good temper" with which he had accomplished the "salutary effect" of his mission. The commercial treaties of 1815 and 1818 were renewed, the joint occupation of Oregon was to be continued indefinitely, subject to a twelve-months notice of change by either party, and the settlement of the northeast boundary was left to the arbitration of a friendly sovereign, the King of the Netherlands. For two years after his return Gallatin was hard at work on the preparation of the historical data for the royal arbiter. The arbitration proved a failure, however, and the northeast boundary was not settled until Gallatin's old friend, Alexander Baring, now Lord Ashburton, came to America a decade later (1842).

Though Gallatin's public career ended with his mission of 1826–27 to England, the score and more years of life that remained to him were not spent in that bucolic retirement which had been his persistent illusion. He settled in New York City, and at the urgent solicitation of his friend John Jacob Astor accepted the presidency (1831–39) of the newly established National (later Gallatin) Bank, using his great influence in banking circles to hasten the return to specie payments after the disastrous panic of 1837. His *Considerations on the Currency and Banking System of the United States* (1831) was circulated as a campaign document in 1832 by the United States Bank. It is characteristic of the scrupulous honor of Gallatin that he refused to accept any pay from Nicholas Biddle for the use of his pamphlet. His *Memorial of the Committee Appointed by the "Free Trade Convention" held in Philadelphia in . . . 1831* (1832), a trenchant pamphlet condemning the high protective tariff, drew from Henry Clay a vituperative speech in which he charged Gallatin with being "still at heart an alien." In his eighty-fourth year he stood with superb courage before a hostile and turbulent crowd in New York to protest against the annexation of Texas as the prelude to a war of imperialistic aggression.

He was one of the founders and the first president of the council of the University of the City of New York in 1831, but withdrew his support from the institution when it fell under the influence of theological zealots. In 1843 he was made president of the New York Historical Society, in the gallery of whose building hangs the Powell portrait of him, with the penetrating, kindly, hazel eyes and the long aristocratic nose above the mobile mouth. But his most absorbing interest in these years was the study of Indian tribes. He has been called "the father of American ethnology." Founder of the American Ethnological Society in 1842, Gallatin defrayed most of the cost of its two volumes of *Transactions,* and wrote for them "Notes on the Semicivilized Nations of Mexico, Yucatan and Central America" and an introduction to "Hale's Indians of North-West America and Vocabularies of North America" (*Transactions American Ethnological Society,* vol. I, 1845; vol. II, 1848). He wrote to a friend in 1842 that except for his papers on the Indians all his writings were of only "a local and ephemeral importance." Posterity has not so judged them. His annual and special reports as secretary of the treasury, his diplomatic notes, his voluminous correspondence, his pamphlets on finance, the public lands, the tariff, the Oregon question, the French debt, and the Mexican War are still mines of information for the student of American history and economics. With his eighty-seventh year his powers began to wane. He had outlived his generation. During the winter of 1848–49 he was confined for the most part to his room, and in the spring he suffered the cruellest blow of all in the death of his wife, the companion of more than half a century. He was taken to the country home of his daughter Frances at Astoria, L. I., in the summer and there he died in her arms on Aug. 12, 1849, at the age of eighty-eight years and six months.

The services of this great financier, diplomat, and statesman have never been adequately recognized by his adopted country, partly, perhaps, because it was his adopted country. He never made parade of his patriotism, which was sincere and abiding. He never sought to ingratiate himself with the multitude by the specious art of aggressive or defensive oratory. His appeal was always addressed to men's reason and judgment, not to their emotions and prejudices. No prospect of political preferment or threat of personal loss could tempt or frighten him from what he felt to be the path of duty, honor, and truth. The false gods of wealth, power, and vulgar fame were as impotent to deflect his devotions as African idols are to attract the worship of a philosopher. In intellect he was the peer of any of his contemporaries—as constructive as Hamilton, as astute as Jefferson, as logical as Adams, as comprehensive as Webster. And in that innate nobility of character which meets malice with charity and "fears a stain as a wound" he was without a superior.

[The standard biography is Henry Adams, *The Life of Albert Gallatin* (1879), of which John A. Stevens, *Albert Gallatin* (1885), is hardly more than a condensation. *A Great Peacemaker, The Diary of James Gallatin* (1914) covers the years of his father's diplomatic career. Henry Adams also published *The Writings of Albert Gallatin* (3 vols., 1879), containing his letters from 1801 on, his speech of Jan. 1795 in the Pennsylvania legislature on the Whiskey Rebellion, six of his major pamphlets on political and financial questions, and a list of his publications. See also *Am. State Papers, Finance,* vols. I, II (1832), *Foreign Relations,* vols. III (1832), IV (1834), VI (1859); W. P. Bacon,

Ancestry of Albert Gallatin (1916); *N. Y. Tribune*, Aug. 13, 14, 1849. The unsorted Gallatin papers, now stored in the attic of the building of the N. Y. Hist. Soc., have not yet been made available.] D. S. M.

GALLAUDET, EDWARD MINER (Feb. 5, 1837–Sept. 26, 1917), educator of the deaf, was the youngest son of Thomas Hopkins [*q.v.*] and Sophia (Fowler) Gallaudet. He was born in Hartford, Conn., and spent his boyhood in an atmosphere which particularly fitted him for work with deaf children. He attended Trinity College, but was employed at the same time as a teacher of deaf pupils in the Hartford school. Through the influence of his father he was imbued with the idea of establishing an institution for the higher education of the deaf; thus the call which he received at twenty seemed to him providential. Amos Kendall [*q.v.*] and some of his friends in Washington were establishing a new school for deaf children in the District of Columbia, and young Gallaudet was invited to become its principal. In 1864, in response to the petitions of Kendall and Gallaudet, Congress granted to the Columbia Institution, over which Gallaudet presided as educational head, the right to confer collegiate degrees, and gave funds for the establishment of a faculty and buildings necessary to conduct higher education. A considerable number of free scholarships, also, were established by the government. Gradually the institution developed and in 1894 the advanced department became Gallaudet College.

Although Gallaudet was convinced of the value of the language of gestures in the training of the deaf, he was one of the first in the United States to advocate giving all deaf children instruction in speech and lip reading. He produced many valuable articles on methods of instruction of deaf pupils, over one hundred of which appeared in the *American Annals of the Deaf*. He also wrote *A Manual of International Law* (1879) and the *Life of Thomas Hopkins Gallaudet* (1888). The Convention of American Instructors of the Deaf, when it was incorporated in 1895, elected him to the presidency, in which office he remained continuously until his death. In 1912 he was made chevalier of the Legion of Honor by the French government. Gallaudet was married to Jane M. Fessenden of Hartford in July 1858. On Dec. 22, 1868, he was married to Susan Denison of Royalton, Vt. Six children survived him.

[E. A. Fay, "Edward Miner Gallaudet," *Am. Annals of the Deaf*, Nov. 1917; memorial edition of *Buff and Blue*, published by the undergraduates of Gallaudet College, Oct. 1917; E. M. Gallaudet, "A Hist. of the Columbia Inst. for the Deaf and Dumb," *Records of the Columbia Hist. Soc.*, vol. XV (1912); *Who's Who in America*, 1916–17; *Evening Star* (Washington, D. C.), Sept. 28, 1917.] P. H.

GALLAUDET, THOMAS (June 3, 1822–Aug. 27, 1902), missionary to the deaf, was the oldest child of Thomas Hopkins Gallaudet [*q.v.*] and Sophia Fowler. From his mother he inherited a fine physical constitution and a well-formed body, and from his father a deep and kindly interest in people. He was born and brought up near the school for the deaf at Hartford which his father had founded. Since his mother was deaf and many of his playmates were pupils of the school, he was soon familiar with the language of gestures, and became interested as a child in all things pertaining to the education and life of deaf people. He prepared to enter Yale University, but because of reduced family means he was sent to Washington (now Trinity) College, where he was graduated in 1842. Though he intended to begin at once to study for the Episcopal ministry, his father persuaded him first to teach in the public schools and then to accept a position in the New York Institution for the Deaf. In spite of family objection he became a communicant of the Episcopal Church, and continued to study for the ministry as he had time. On July 15, 1845, he was married to Elizabeth R. Budd, a charming young deaf woman whom he had met in the New York school. They resided with the Budd family in New York for a number of years.

In 1850 Gallaudet established a Bible class for deaf people in St. Stephen's Church. In the same year he was ordained a deacon in the Episcopal Church, and was made assistant rector of St. Stephen's in New York. In 1851 he was ordained to the priesthood and was then made assistant rector of St. Ann's, Morrisania. While ministering to a deaf girl who was slowly dying of tuberculosis he conceived the idea of founding in New York a church which should be the spiritual home of deaf people. When the plan developed, St. Ann's Church for Deaf-Mutes was established and regular services were begun in 1852 in a chapel of the University of the City of New York. Money was gradually collected, funds for a minister pledged, and on Oct. 1, 1858, Gallaudet gave up his teaching and devoted his time thereafter particularly to church and missionary work among the deaf. In 1859 a church building was purchased on West Eighteenth Street, near Fifth Avenue, which became headquarters for missionary work elsewhere, and permanent missions were soon established in other cities. On Nov. 30, 1862, Gallaudet became rector of St. Ann's Church, where he continued services for both hearing and deaf people until in

1898 a new church and parish house, for the exclusive use of deaf people, was erected on 148th Street. He was at the same time widely interested in various charitable institutions, and founded the home for aged and infirm deaf-mutes, later established near Poughkeepsie, which came to be known as the Gallaudet Home. He was also a member of the board of directors of the New York Institution for the Deaf where he had formerly taught, and always took the deepest interest in its welfare. He attended many national and international conferences on the education of the deaf, and constantly gave his testimony as to the value of the sign language. His home in New York became a haven for deaf people, and there, as servant and friend, he ministered to those who came to him for financial aid, for work, or for spiritual comfort.

[Thos. Gallaudet, "A Sketch of My Life," manuscript autobiography in the possession of John H. Kent; A. G. Draper, "Thos. Gallaudet," *Annals of the Deaf*, Nov. 1902; John H. Kent, "Rev. Thos. Gallaudet," *Ibid.*, Dec. 1922; *Churchman*, Sept. 6, 1902; *N. Y. Tribune*, Apr. 11, 1897; *N. Y. Times*, Aug. 28, 1902; and personal recollections of the writer.] P. H.

GALLAUDET, THOMAS HOPKINS (Dec. 10, 1787–Sept. 10, 1851), educator of the deaf, was born in Philadelphia, Pa., where his father, Peter Wallace Gallaudet, had established himself as a merchant. His paternal ancestors were French Huguenots who had settled in New York. His mother, Jane Hopkins, was of distinguished English descent, among whose ancestors were Thomas Hooker and John Hopkins. The family moved to Hartford when Thomas was thirteen, and two years later the boy entered the sophomore class at Yale, where he graduated in 1805. After a year in the law office of Chauncey Goodrich and another two years as a student of English literature and composition and as a tutor at Yale, Gallaudet was forced by the delicacy of his health to adopt a more active life. Accepting a position with a commercial house in New York he traveled for the company in Kentucky and Ohio and regained his health. In January 1812 he entered the Andover Theological Seminary, graduating in 1814, but with the return of ill health he declined to accept a ministerial position.

About this time Gallaudet became acquainted with a deaf child, Alice Cogswell, to whom he tried to teach the names of certain objects. Having read various treatises on the education of deaf children, he urged her father, Dr. Mason Cogswell, to obtain a regular teacher for the child. Cogswell and a number of friends finally raised a sum of money and proposed to send Gallaudet abroad to study methods of education employed in schools for the deaf there. Gallaudet accepted this mission, sailed for England in 1815, but was greatly disappointed by his reception there. The Institut Royal des Sourds-Muets in Paris, however, under the Abbé Sicard, threw open its doors to Gallaudet, and there he studied for several months. In 1816 he returned to the United States with Laurent Clerc, a brilliant deaf teacher of the Paris institution, and with his aid raised money for the first free American school for the deaf, which was established in Hartford in 1817. Gallaudet was made the principal of this school and remained in charge until 1830. During these thirteen years, despite his ill health and other discouraging circumstances, he was able to train for his profession a number of men who later became the heads of similar schools, and to establish the school on a firm basis.

Gallaudet's work was by no means confined to the education of the deaf. After leaving the Hartford school he was invited to take chairs at Dartmouth, the University of the City of New York, and other institutions, but declined all such offers to devote himself to more general educational and philanthropic work. He helped establish public normal schools in Connecticut, interested himself in the education of negroes, and fostered the advancement of manual training in the schools. He also advocated the higher education of women and stressed the need of well-trained women in the teaching profession. Despite the active demands upon his time he was able to publish a number of studies. His articles on the education of the deaf appeared in the early numbers of the *American Annals of the Deaf*. Other works include: *Discourses on Various Points of Christian Faith and Practise* (1818), a volume of his sermons; *The Child's Book on the Soul* (1830); and *Scripture Biography for the Young* (1838, 1839).

One of Gallaudet's first pupils at the Hartford school was Sophia Fowler, who soon after her graduation became his wife. Their oldest son, Thomas [*q.v.*], became a well-known minister to the deaf. Their youngest son, Edward Miner [*q.v.*], with the aid of Amos Kendall, established a school for the deaf in Washington. Later its advanced department became Gallaudet College, named in honor of Thomas Hopkins Gallaudet, to whose grateful memory deaf people of the country erected a monument by Daniel French, now on the grounds of the college.

[E. M. Gallaudet, *Life of Thos. Hopkins Gallaudet* (1888); Herman Humphrey, *The Life and Letters of the Rev. T. H. Gallaudet* (1857); Henry Barnard, *Tribute to Gallaudet* (1852); I. L. Peet, in *Am. Annals of the Deaf*, Jan. 1888; Edwin Booth, "Reminiscences of Gallaudet," *Ibid.*, July 1881; F. B. Dexter, *Biog. Sketches of the Grads. of Yale Coll.*, V (1911), 749–57; *Hartford Courant*, Sept. 11, 1851.] P. H.

GALLINGER, JACOB HAROLD (Mar. 28, 1837–Aug. 17, 1918), physician and politician, was the son of Jacob and Catharine (Cook) Gallinger. He was descended from Michael Gallinger, a German who settled in New York in 1754 and later removed to Canada. Born on a farm near Cornwall, Ont., the fourth in a large family of small means, he was apprenticed at the age of twelve to a printer and spent four years at Cornwall learning the trade. After a year in Ogdensburg, N. Y., and about the same period in a newspaper office in his native town, having saved a little money, he resolved to study medicine. In 1855 he entered the Medical Institute of Cincinnati, Ohio, receiving his degree three years later. In 1868 he also received the degree of M.D. from the New York Homœopathic Medical College. During his course in Cincinnati he supported himself by working at his old trade. After graduation he spent two years in further study and European travel, and in 1860 began practise at Keene, N. H. On Aug. 3 of the same year he married Mary Anna Bailey of Salisbury, N. H. Two years later he moved to Concord where he soon built up a large general practise. For the remainder of his life he was identified with a variety of interests in that city.

In spite of absorption in professional work he soon took an active part in municipal politics, displaying from the start an aptitude for party management which was destined to make him one of the most powerful political leaders in the history of the state. He was a member of the New Hampshire House in 1872–73 and in 1891, and of the Senate from 1878 to 1881, being president of the latter body during his last two terms. He took a prominent part in the constitutional convention of 1876. In 1882 he became chairman of the Republican state committee, a position which he held at varying intervals for a total of eighteen years and in which he displayed ability which made him a match even for the redoubtable William E. Chandler, with whom he repeatedly clashed.

In 1884 he was elected to Congress and as a member of the House (1885–89) became known as an indefatigable worker, his attention to claims and pensions earning the gratitude of many. He gained favorable notice by speeches against free silver and the Democratic tariff policy, but the principle of rotation, then strong in New Hampshire, forced his retirement at the expiration of his second term. In the same year he engaged in an unsuccessful contest with Chandler for the United States senatorship. After two years, apparently finding his professional work less attractive than politics, he again entered the senatorial contest, this time successfully, in spite of determined opposition from Senator Chandler and other leaders. From 1891 until his death he remained a dominant power in the state, his repeated reëlections to the Senate, the last one by popular vote, demonstrating both his political ability and his personal popularity. In the upper chamber he maintained his reputation as a tireless worker on committees and to the last took an active part in proceedings on the floor. He was a competent parliamentarian and an able, though hardly an outstanding, debater.

He was a strong partisan, and as an orthodox Republican supported high tariff, sound money, and in general those policies which appealed to the financial and industrial interests of the Eastern states. Intensely conservative, he had scant interest in most reforms or humanitarian projects. Notable exceptions, however, were prohibition and woman's suffrage; at the memorial services of Jan. 19, 1919, his junior colleague, Senator Hollis, declared that Gallinger's support had expedited by several years the adoption of the Eighteenth and Nineteenth Amendments, which by that time seemed assured. He expressed profound contempt for civil service reform and similar types of "Sunday school politics" (for interesting comment, see an open letter addressed to him by Carl Schurz, *Speeches, Correspondence and Political Papers of Carl Schurz,* 1913, V, 403–11). He was a stickler for senatorial prerogatives, his bitter quarrel with President Harrison over patronage, and, late in life, his successful fight against President Wilson's nomination of George Rublee for the Federal Trade Commission, being typical of the man. When the break between the "Old Guard" and "Insurgent" wings of the party developed, Gallinger, truculent and unabashed, took his place with the former group. Burly, pugnacious, self-confident, he was caricatured as the very embodiment of "stand-pattism."

He struggled, in season and out, for the establishment of a merchant marine, and in his last years gave ungrudging support to the war policy of the Wilson administration. Probably his greatest services, however, were rendered as chairman of the committee on the District of Columbia, services which offered no direct political reward but which are gratefully remembered by the inhabitants of the District and were commemorated by Congress in the establishment of the Gallinger Hospital. Announcing that he would not be satisfied until Washington became the most beautiful city in the world, he took an active and constructive part in legislation effecting its physical renovation and beautification. He was the author of the District medical practise act which brought about the suppression of the cruder forms of quackery that had flourished in the national capital, and handled, efficiently and intelligently, the enormous amount of routine legislation on District affairs.

[Published material includes: Jas. O. Lyford, "Senator Jacob H. Gallinger," *Granite Monthly,* Dec. 1908; John N. McClintock, "Hon. Jacob H. Gallinger, M.D.," *Ibid.,* Sept.–Oct. 1890; "Senator Gallinger's Rise to Prominence," *Washington Post,* Dec. 21, 1902; obituary material in *Boston Evening Transcript,* Aug. 17, 1918; *Manchester Union,* Aug. 19, 1918; *Washington Post,* Aug. 18, 1918; *Granite Monthly,* July–Sept. 1918; memorial addresses in Congress, printed as *Senate Doc. 454,* 65 Cong., 3 Sess. The N. H. Hist. Soc. has a considerable collection of Gallinger's political papers and correspondence.] W. A. R.

GALLITZIN, DEMETRIUS AUGUSTINE (Dec. 22, 1770–May 6, 1840), Catholic missionary, was born at The Hague, where his father, Prince Dmitriĭ Alekseievich Gallitzin (Golitsyn), a distinguished scientist and former privy counselor of Catharine II, was Russian ambassador after a service of fourteen years at the court of Louis XV, where he associated with Voltaire and the Encyclopedists. The Gallitzins boasted a medieval Lithuanian origin from a prince whose descendants furnished rulers for Poland, Hungary, and Bohemia. A Russian Gallitzin defeated Charles XII at Poltava. As became the heir of so exalted a family, Prince Dmitriĭ married Countess Amalia, daughter of the Prussian Field Marshal Von Schmettau and his Catholic wife, Baroness von Ruffert. Amalia was raised a Catholic in a Breslau convent; but as a result of later training in Berlin and her marriage to a deistic adherent of the Orthodox Greek Church, she lost interest in revealed religion.

Demetrius was reared in his father's faith and tutored by the ablest masters, as befitted a Russian aristocrat and companion of Frederick William, future King of The Netherlands and duke of Luxemburg. In his early childhood he had little association with his mother, whose salon was thronged by intellectuals, or with his father, who was collecting treasures for the Czar's palaces. Growing tired of society, however, Amalia, through the intervention of Diderot, lived apart from her husband, though their relations continued friendly, and gave her full attention to the education of her two children, first at The Hague, and later at Münster where her intimate circle included Goethe, Hamar, Jacobi, and the learned priest, Baron de Furstenberg. Such were the advantages of the young prince. In 1786, after a severe illness, Princess Amalia became a zealous Catholic, and the year following, her son entered the Catholic Church, taking the baptismal name of Augustine. On completion of his formal education, he was appointed aide-de-camp to the Austrian General Von Lilien, who was campaigning in Brabant against the French Revolutionists. Suddenly Gallitzin was retired by an imperial order barring foreigners from the service. Since the grand tour was impossible in disordered Europe, he obtained permission to spend two years traveling in the West Indies and the United States. Accompanied by Father Felix Brosius (later an American missionary), Augustine Smith or Schmet, as he called himself for convenience in traveling, sailed from Rotterdam to Baltimore where he arrived on Oct. 28, 1792, with letters of introduction including one to Bishop Carroll. Attracted by the bishop and the scholarly Parisian exiles of St. Sulpice who under Francis Nagot, S. S., had just established St. Mary's Seminary in Baltimore, the brilliant young traveler, who in addition to his native Russian tongue spoke Dutch, German, French, Polish, Italian, and some English, decided to renounce the dazzling life of the Czar's court and to devote himself to the struggling Church in America. On completion of the regular seminary course, Smith was ordained by Bishop Carroll (Mar. 18, 1795), being the first priest to receive his full theological training in the United States. Again he made a sacrifice when he rejected the scholarly seclusion of a seminary teacher for the rigorous life of a missionary.

Assigned to the stations of Port Tobacco and Conewago and to the German community of Baltimore, he covered on horse and foot an extensive territory, even venturing into unfriendly Virginia. In 1796, journeying 150 miles from Conewago on a sick call to Capt. Michael McGuire's settlement at the summit of the Alleghanies in modern Cambria County where a number of Maryland, German, and Irish Catholics had settled, he conceived the idea of a Catholic colony on this Pennsylvania frontier. Since McGuire had bequeathed 400 acres for the support of a resident priest, Bishop Carroll gave Smith the assignment (1799). With the aid of sturdy parishioners, he cleared the land, built a log-cabin, and erected a log chapel which was ready for Christmas services. From Loretto, the name he gave to the settlement, Father Smith attended the whole countryside, frequently going by sled or cart into the Indian country. Neither the solicitations of his mother and reconciled father nor the entreaties of friends could induce him to forsake his charge even for a visit. He decided to cast his lot in America and was naturalized at Huntington in 1802.

Buying land outright and as an agent of Henry Drinker of Philadelphia, he sold farms on easy terms to his Swiss, German, and Irish colonists, and erected a grist-mill and a tannery. Lax in collecting installments from shiftless settlers, he found himself in financial difficulties when the death of his father (1803) ended his remittances. Never accepting a salary, he supported himself from his model farm and cared for a number of orphans. Indeed his cabin was a Mecca for pioneers pushing westward, some of whom were little better than beggars. Despite his charities, he faced vicious attacks from ungrateful, self-willed colonists. Some resented his strict ecclesiastical rule; others were suspicious of his past; the Irish, stirred up by an occasional wandering Irish priest, resented a foreign pastor; Republicans were aroused by his Federalist sympathies, though in 1812 he exhorted his people to volunteer, and assisted Capt. Richard McGuire in training a company of soldiers. Smith in turn was dictatorial, condemning drunkenness, opposing unworthy candidates for local offices, and urging the idle to labor. Supported by the bishop and the better element in his fold, he prevailed over his defamers, who made public reparations. His identity was settled when, in 1809, the Pennsylvania legislature legalized the use of his family name and validated all papers which he had signed. Writing his injuries in sand, he marveled at the change when his neighbors were assured of his princely origin.

Gallitzin's colony was not a wild scheme, but under the circumstances it proved a costly venture. Granted permission by the Russian government to look after his father's estate, he refused to leave his colony. His agents, Baron de Furstenberg and two imperial counts, despite a Russian decree robbing him of his patrimony because of his departure from the empire, abandonment of his regiment, and ordination, arranged that his mother and sister would be recognized as heirs with the right to sell the estates and dispose of the proceeds (1807). Gallitzin had visions of settling his debts. His mother sent a few thousand dollars, but the lands were unproductive because of the Napoleonic wars, and the burning of Moscow brought heavy losses. On the death of his mother, his sister Maria Anna forwarded his diminished rentals, until her unfortunate marriage with the dissolute Prince de Salm whose debts and riotous extravagance absorbed the estate. Gallitzin was supposed to have expended about $150,000 on the colony, and was badly in debt. His mother's library brought some money, and the friendly King of the Netherlands bought the Gallitzin art collection for $20,000, though hardly half of the sum passed through Salm's hands to Prince Gallitzin. Baron de Maltitz, Russian ambassador, is said to have lighted a cigar with Gallitzin's note for $5,000 at a Washington dinner which he attended with his friend Henry Clay. Vouched for by the ambassador, in 1827 Gallitzin made a public appeal which brought aid from such noteworthy donors as Gregory XVI and Charles Carroll, for the missionary of Loretto had become widely known. By the close of his life his kind creditors, largely Protestants and Quakers of Baltimore and Philadelphia, were paid. To this end he had endured every privation, denying himself all luxuries.

Aroused by a local minister's sermon against "popery," he wrote a series of letters to the *Huntington Gazette,* which were published under the title, *Defence of Catholic Principles* (1816). Enlarged, this brochure went through repeated editions in the United States and Ireland and was translated for European circulation. In 1817 the minister's rejoinder brought *An Appeal to the Protestant Public,* which was followed by *A Letter to a Protestant Friend on the Holy Scriptures* (1820). Gallitzin was skilled in argument; and he was refreshingly tolerant, as befitted a tractarian of his cosmopolitan outlook. In 1834 he issued a pamphlet, *Six Letters of Advice to the Gentlemen Presbyterian Parsons Who Lately Met at Columbia for the Purpose of Declaring War Against the Catholic Church.* Friendly critics have seen the touch of Bossuet in his polemics and modern students find in them models of controversial literature.

Prince Gallitzin sought no ecclesiastical preferment, though his relations with Carroll and Bishop Egan of Philadelphia were most friendly. Bishop Flaget recommended him for the See of Cincinnati (1821), but Archbishop Maréchal is said to have blocked an appointment as he did later when Bishop Fenwick suggested his name for the See of Detroit (1833). Bishop Conwell of Philadelphia favored Gallitzin as his successor and named him vicar-general for Western Pennsylvania. For forty-one years he had labored alone in the heights of the Alleghanies, when, overtaxed by Lenten ministrations, he was overtaken by death. As he lay in state in his frame church, crowds paid their respects to the prince-priest who gave up a Moscow villa for a backwoodsman's cabin.

[Thomas Hayden, *Life and Character of Rev. Prince*

Demetrius A. de Gallitzin (1869); S. M. Brownson, *Life of Demetrius Augustine Gallitzin, Prince and Priest* (1873); Heinrich Lemcke, *Leben und Wirken* (1861); Ferdinand Kittell, *Souvenir of Loretto Centenary* (1899); Joseph Galland, *Die Fürstin Amalie von Gallitzin und ihre Freunde* (1880); J. M. Finotti, *Bibliographia Catholica Americana* (1872); F. E. Tourscher, *Diary and Visitation Record of Francis P. Kenrick* (1916); *Cath. Hist. Rev.*, Oct. 1927; *Cath. World*, June, Nov. 1865, Apr. 1895; *Biog. Ann.* (1841); *U. S. Cath. Hist. Mag.*, Apr. 1890; *Metropolitan*, May 1856; *Am. Cath. Hist. Researches*, see Index; *Pa. Mag. of Hist. and Biog.*, II, 378 (1878); *Littell's Living Age*, Dec. 1871; *North Am. Rev.*, Apr. 1859; *Lippincott's Mag.*, Feb. 1892; *Records Am. Cath. Hist. Soc.*, see Index, and especially vol. IV (1893), pp. 1–36; *Cath. Encyc.*, vol. VI.] R. J. P.

GALLOWAY, CHARLES BETTS (Sept. 1, 1849–May 12, 1909), bishop of the Methodist Episcopal Church, South, one of the eight children of Charles Betts and Adelaide (Dinkins) Galloway, was born in Kosciusko and died in Jackson, Miss. His ancestry was English, Scotch, Irish, and Welsh. His father, a physician of North Carolina origin, in 1863 moved the family residence from Kosciusko to Canton, in order to be near numerous relatives of his who were also living in Mississippi. Young Charles Galloway grew up in a hospitable, religious home, attended local schools and churches, and, entering the University of Mississippi as a sophomore, graduated fifth in his class in 1868, being not yet nineteen. The atmosphere of the University was favorable to religion, and Galloway's demonstrated ability as a public speaker made it natural that he should enter the ministry. He was licensed to preach in the summer following his graduation, and the following autumn was admitted on trial into the Mississippi Conference. On his twentieth birthday (1869) he was married to Harriet E. Willis of Vicksburg. His charm of personality and pronounced ability as a preacher caused his rapid advancement in the ministry. In 1873 he was sent to a church in Jackson, which, with the possible exception of one in Vicksburg, was the most important position his denomination could offer in Mississippi. He was here from 1873 to 1877 and again from 1881 to 1883, after which he was no longer an active pastor. From 1877 to 1881 he was in Vicksburg. There, in 1878, both he and his wife had yellow fever. His life was despaired of, and an obituary of him even appeared in a paper in Jackson. From 1882 to 1886 he was editor of the *New Orleans Christian Advocate*, and in 1886 he was made a bishop, the youngest Methodist to be raised to that position in America until that time. Though, according to the custom of his church, he presided over conferences in various states and mission fields throughout the connection, soon after his elevation to the episcopacy he made his home in Jackson.

Often referred to as the "missionary bishop of Methodism," he made extensive episcopal tours in the Orient and South America. Though in no sense fanatical, he was a leader in the prohibition movement in his state and section and in 1887 had a sharp but on the whole dignified newspaper controversy on this question with Jefferson Davis (Candler, *post*, pp. 211–54). Probably his greatest services were in the fields of education and race-relations. He was a trustee of the University of Mississippi from 1882 to 1894; he was a prime mover in the establishment of the Methodist institution, Millsaps College, Jackson, Miss., making a state-wide canvass for funds at the outset and serving as president of its board of trustees from 1889 until his death; he was long president of the board of education of his church and was for fifteen years a trustee of Vanderbilt University, being president of the board from 1905 to 1909. An active trustee of the John F. Slater Fund for the Advancement of Freedmen, he courageously withstood prejudice and passion and urged his fellow citizens to practise forbearance toward and do justice to the negroes.

Though impatient of narrow sectionalism, he was an enthusiastic student of the history of his state and a frequent contributor to the *Publications of the Mississippi Historical Society*. He wrote many essays, lectures, and public letters, some of which have been gathered into books. Among the most notable of these are: *A Circuit of the Globe* (1894); *Susanna Wesley* (1896); *Christianity and the American Commonwealth* (1898); *The South and the Negro* (1904); *Jefferson Davis, A Judicial Estimate* (1908); and *Great Men and Great Movements* (1914). In all of these he shows courage, practical good sense, and fair-mindedness. He was chiefly famed, however, as an orator, both in the pulpit and on the platform, and was not inaptly described as "golden-mouthed." His sermon at the opening of the ecumenical conference in London in 1901, and his address on L. Q. C. Lamar, delivered many times and regarded in the South as an oratorical classic, were particularly notable. Among the bishops of his church he was affectionately known as "Prince Charley," and it was said after his death that his was a type of greatness which made him preëminently useful and lovable (Mayes, *post*, p. 30). It would be hard to prove the claim advanced by his eulogists that he was the greatest of all Mississippians (Candler, p. 293), but he seems to have swayed the imagination of his state as not more than two or three others of its citizens have swayed it.

[Edward Mayes, "Chas. Betts Galloway," in *Miss. Hist. Soc. Pubs.*, vol XI (1910); W. A. Candler, *Bishop Charles Betts Galloway* (1927); T. J. Bailey, *Prohibition in Miss.* (1917); *Vanderbilt Univ. Quart.*, July 1909; *Vicksburg Herald*, May 13, 14, 1909; Nashville *Christian Advocate*, May 14, 21, 1909.] J. D. W.

GALLOWAY, JOSEPH (*c.* 1731–Aug. 29, 1803), colonial statesman, Loyalist, was born at West River, Anne Arundel County, Md., the son of Peter Bines Galloway and his wife, Elizabeth Rigbie (or Rigby). The family was prominent in trade and possessed large estates in Maryland and Pennsylvania. During Joseph's boyhood his father died, and shortly thereafter he removed to Philadelphia where he studied law. He early rose to eminence at the bar and became one of the most popular pleaders of the time. On Oct. 18, 1753, he married Grace Growden, daughter of Lawrence Growden, one of the richest and most influential men of the province. Galloway's writings show that he had a good knowledge of the classics, history, and the political philosophers of the seventeenth and eighteenth centuries. He was interested in science and philosophy and was a member of the American Philosophical Society, which he served as vice-president from 1769 to 1775. Though of considerable wealth and interested in a number of Philadelphia mercantile houses and in land promotions in the West, he was driven by vanity to seek political office as the road to power and influence. The withdrawal of the Quakers from official positions in the government opened the way for his election as assemblyman in 1756, a post which he held continuously until 1776 with the single exception of the year 1764–65. His somewhat cold and austere nature did not win him the votes of the electors and he was kept in office primarily by the effective functioning of the Quaker political machine—although he himself was not a member of any Philadelphia meeting.

In the Assembly he took a principal part in the legislative work arising out of the war with France and at once assumed a position of party leadership. His public career up to 1766 was that of a colonial politician and provincial statesman of ability. While he supported the war, he never lost an opportunity to advance the interests of his province and of the aristocratic merchant class to which he belonged. In the hope of relieving the strain on Pennsylvania's resources caused by the war, he joined with Benjamin Franklin [*q.v.*] in an attempt to tax the Penns' located but unimproved lands and ultimately, with Franklin, petitioned the Crown to substitute royal control for the proprietary government. This move, coupled with their activity in suppressing the Paxton riots and their continued denial of additional representation to the western counties, cost Galloway and Franklin their seats in the election of 1764.

With the reorganization of the British colonial system, Galloway appeared in the rôle of an imperial statesman and, while he jealously guarded the self-governing rights won by the colonies, he clearly saw the problems of empire. From 1766 to 1775, he was annually elected to the speakership of the Assembly, a position of almost autocratic power. As chairman of the Assembly's committee to correspond with the agents of the colony in London he endeavored to restore harmony between the colonies and the mother country. He sympathized with the government's desire to raise a revenue in America but disapproved of parliamentary taxation and of many of the restrictions on American commerce. His legalistic mind compelled him to accept parliamentary supremacy, but he believed that certain parliamentary powers were being exercised unconstitutionally over the colonies. Recognizing the existence of a large radical element in America, he nevertheless believed that the problem was basically constitutional and could be solved by a written constitution for the empire. He was selected to be a delegate to the First Continental Congress (1774), and agreed to serve on being permitted to draft the instructions of the delegation. His chief contribution to the Congress was a plan for an imperial legislature which would provide the empire with a written constitution. The plan, though accorded a favorable reception, was later rejected and all reference to it expunged from the minutes. Galloway refused to be a delegate to the Second Congress and severely arraigned the First, in *A Candid Examination of the Mutual Claims of Great Britain and the Colonies* (1775). His feeling that all grievances would ultimately be redressed upon orderly petition gave him only contempt for the disorders of the time, and his conservative stand on the questions of the day earned him popular suspicion.

Fearing for his safety in Philadelphia, he retired to the country, hoping to remain neutral in the impending conflict. Though he was passionately attached to his native soil, his conscience, legalism, and pride forbade his going over to the American cause, which he believed to be unjust. Threatened, and in the belief that he could thereby assist in restoring a disorganized government and rescue America from herself, he fled to Howe, who found his services invaluable in the Philadelphia campaign. Upon the occupation of the city he became civil administrator, with the titles of superintendent of police and of the port. Upon the capture of Philadelphia by the Continental forces, in 1778, he went to England with his daughter and there became the spokesman of the American Loyalists. He testified before Parliament on the conduct of the war (*The Examination of Joseph Galloway, Esq. . . . before the House of Commons,* 1779) and published pamphlets attacking Lord Howe and others for their incompetence (*Letters to a Nobleman, on the Conduct of the War in the Middle Colonies,* 1779, and *A Letter to the Right Honourable Viscount H—e, on his Naval Conduct in the American War,* 1779). To the very close of the Revolution he worked to bring about an accommodation between the mother country and the colonies on the basis of a written constitution, and labored to demonstrate the value of the imperial connection. (See his *Historical and Political Reflections on the Rise and Progress of the American Rebellion,* 1780, and *Cool Thoughts on the Consequences to Great Britain of American Independence,* 1780.)

The treaty of peace came as a severe shock to the Loyalists, and Galloway voiced their despair and chagrin at the failure of British arms (*Observations on the Fifth Article of the Treaty with America,* etc., 1783; *The Claim of the American Loyalists Reviewed and Maintained upon Incontrovertible Principles of Law and Justice,* 1788). His estates in America were confiscated and he became largely dependent upon his British pension. In 1793 his petition to the Pennsylvania authorities for permission to return was refused. His thoughts then turned to religion, and he published some tracts, including: *Brief Commentaries upon such Parts of the Revelation and other Prophecies as Immediately Refer to the Present Times* (1802), and *The Prophetic or Anticipated History of the Church of Rome, Written and Published Six Hundred Years Before the Rise of that Church; in which the Prophetic Figures and Allegories are Literally Explained* (1803). His last years were devoted to the service of fellow Americans in England and to literature. He died after twenty-five years of exile, and was buried in the churchyard of Watford, Hertfordshire.

[E. H. Baldwin, in *Pa. Mag. of Hist. and Biog.,* July–Dec. 1902; Penn MSS.—especially Penn Letter-Books, Penn Official Correspondence, and Penn Additional Miscellaneous Manuscript Letters—in the possession of the Hist. Soc. of Pa.; R. C. Werner, "Diary of Grace Growden Galloway," *Pa. Mag. of Hist. and Biog.,* Jan. 1931; *Votes and Proc. of the House of Representatives of the Province of Pa.* (6 vols., 1752–76); *Minutes of the Provincial Council of Pa.* (10 vols., 1852); *Pa. Archives,* esp. 1 ser. (1852) and 7 ser. (1906); *The Writings of Benjamin Franklin* (10 vols., 1905–07), ed. by A. H. Smyth; contemporary Philadelphia newspapers; brief references to Galloway in the *Gentleman's Magazine* (London), Nov. 1780, and Sept. 1803, pp. 847, 887, and in the *Monthly Review* (London), Aug. 1779 and Oct. 1780; W. S. Mason in *Proc. Am. Antiq. Soc.,* Oct. 15, 1924; C. P. Keith, *The Provincial Councillors of Pa.* (1883), pp. 226–35; M. C. Tyler, *The Lit. Hist. of the Am. Revolution* (1897), I, 369–83; W. H. Siebert, *The Loyalists of Pa.* (1920); C. H. Lincoln, *The Revolutionary Movement in Pa., 1760–76* (1901); E. C. Burnett, *Letters of Members of the Continental Cong.,* vol. I (1921).] R. C. W.

GALLOWAY, SAMUEL (Mar. 20, 1811–Apr. 5, 1872), educator, congressman, was of Scotch-Irish ancestry. The first Galloway came to America from Northern Ireland and settled in Gettysburg, Pa., and about the same time the Buchanans, another Scotch-Irish family, settled in the same neighborhood. James Galloway, the father of Samuel, married a Buchanan. Galloway received his early education in Gettysburg, but when he was seventeen or eighteen years old, upon the death of his father, he moved to Greenfield, Highland County, Ohio. In 1829 he entered Miami University, from which institution he graduated four years later at the head of his class. He then began the study of law at Hillsboro, Ohio, but abruptly abandoned his legal studies to enter Princeton Theological Seminary as a student. He remained only a year (1836) at Princeton and then, possibly on account of financial difficulties, began teaching. He was appointed professor of Greek in his alma mater, but ill health compelled him to resign within a year. Upon his recovery, he resumed his teaching, first in Hamilton, Ohio, then at Miami University, 1837–38, and later as professor of classical languages at Hanover College, Hanover, Ind., 1838–40. During this period he was in great demand as a lecturer upon education and temperance. He was by nature deeply religious and for many years was undecided whether to select the ministry or the law for his life-work. In 1841, however, he decided to return to Ohio and resume his study of law. In 1842 he was admitted to the bar and the following year formed a partnership with Nathaniel Massie at Chillicothe. His analytical mind, sound logic, careful preparation, and clear and forcible delivery soon brought him recognition. In 1843 he was married to Joan Wallin of Cincinnati and in the same year was elected secretary of state; in 1844 he moved to Columbus. As secretary of state (1844–50) he was *ex-officio* superintendent of schools. Because of his Calvinistic educational traditions and his association with Horace Mann and Calvin E. Stowe [*qq.v.*], he became an enthusiastic advocate of popular education. His reports to the legislature dwelt upon the deplorable condition of the common schools in Ohio and embodied many valuable suggestions looking toward reform. Through Galloway's efforts the standard of teaching in the state was raised; teachers' institutes were organized; district and county superintendents were appointed to supervise the work; educators were inspired with new vigor, and the public was awakened to the needs of education. Within ten years the school system of Ohio was completely reconstructed.

When the question of slavery began to agitate the country, Galloway allied himself with the anti-slavery men, although he preferred working within the Whig party to joining any of the avowedly anti-slavery political parties. In 1854 he was elected to Congress, where he added to his reputation as an orator. A trenchant address on Kansas (Mar. 17, 1856; *Congressional Globe*, 34 Cong., 1 Sess., App., pp. 210–12), was highly commended for its keen satire and vigorous argument at home and abroad, but Galloway was defeated for reëlection by Samuel S. Cox [*q.v.*]. He thereupon resumed his legal practise and took an active interest in the affairs of the Presbyterian Church. During the Civil War he was in close relations with President Lincoln and Secretary Stanton, both of whom frequently consulted him. He was appointed judge advocate of Camp Chase, the only federal office he ever held. After the war he practised law, and in 1871 his name was suggested for the governorship. His failure to receive the nomination, which went to Rutherford B. Hayes, was a keen disappointment to him. He died the following year, in Columbus.

[Washington Gladden, in *Ohio Archæol. and Hist. Pubs.*, IV (1895), 263–78; Wm. A. Taylor, *Centennial Hist. of Columbus and Franklin County, Ohio* (1909); *A Hist. of Educ. in Ohio* (1876), published by the Ohio General Assembly; J. J. Burns, *Educ. Hist. of Ohio* (1905), p. 410; Chas. Robson, *The Biog. Encyc. of Ohio in the Nineteenth Century* (1876); *Princeton Theol. Sem. Biog. Cat.* (1909); obituaries in *Cincinnati Times and Chronicle* and *Cincinnati Commercial*, Apr. 6, 1872, and in *Am. Educ. Monthly*, Mar. 1873.]

R. C. M.

GALLUP, JOSEPH ADAMS (Mar. 30, 1769–Oct. 12, 1849), physician, was born in Stonington, Conn., the son of William and Lucy (Denison) Gallup, and was christened Joadam. At the age of six he was taken by his family to Hartland, Vt. His father was prominent in the political movements that led to the independence of the state, and, "Whig to the core," was a strong supporter of the Revolution. Joseph studied medicine and, at twenty-one, began practise at Bethel, Vt. Later he studied at Dartmouth Medical College from which, in 1798, he received the degree of M.D. In the fall of 1799 he undertook general practise at Woodstock where he also conducted a drug business. He was active in the formation of medical societies, including the Vermont State Medical Society, incorporated in 1813. Of the latter he became president in 1818, holding that office for eleven years. In 1821 he became professor of the theory and practise of medicine at the Vermont Academy of Medicine, recently established in Castleton. The following year he was elected president of the corporation, serving as such and as professor till 1825, in which year he became professor of materia medica in the medical school at Burlington. After acting in that capacity for one year, his next interest was the founding of a clinical school of medicine at Woodstock. This enterprise was the creature of his heart, his zealous purpose being to give students bedside instruction in the treatment of disease. To that end he established an infirmary in which free treatment was given during the lecture season. This important innovation in medical teaching dates from 1827. In connection with the school he also published for a year or so the *Domestic Medical and Dietetical Monitor or Journal of Health.* His *Sketches of Epidemic Diseases in the State of Vermont* was published in Boston in 1815. A more elaborate work was his *Outlines of the Institutes of Medicine* (2 vols., 1839). An advertisement in the *Vermont Journal* for Jan. 11, 1803, suggests his primacy in inoculating for cow-pox in his community, and he had the credit for being the fourth surgeon in the United States to perform ovariotomy. Village annals reflect him as a man of strong character and great initiative. In our day he would doubtless have been described as "temperamental"; but if he was strict and stern in discipline, he was himself "amenable to correction if applied in the right way."

Dissensions having arisen in the Woodstock faculty, Dr. Gallup withdrew in 1834, whereupon he removed to Boston, remained there a few years, and then returned to Woodstock, where he died Oct. 12, 1849. He was buried in Hartland. His wife, whom he married in September 1792, was Abigail Willard.

[H. S. Dana, *Hist. of Woodstock, Vt.* (1889); W. H. Crockett, *Hist. of Vt.* (5 vols., 1921–23); F. G. Cox, *Illustrated Hist. Souvenir of Bethel, Vt.* (1895); J. D. Gallup, *The Geneal. Hist. of the Gallup Family* (1893); *Gen. Cat. of Dartmouth Coll. and the Associated Schools, 1769–1910* (1910–11); C. S. Caverly, in H. A. Kelly and W. L. Burrage, *Am. Medic. Biogs.* (1920).]

G. A. B—r.

GALLY, MERRITT (Aug. 15, 1838–Mar. 7, 1916), clergyman, inventor, was of Scotch ancestry, the son of David K. and Anna (Wilder) Gally. He was born near Rochester, N. Y., in which town his parents settled a year after Merritt's birth. His father, a Presbyterian clergyman, died when the boy was six years old. When his mother married a second time five years later, young Gally, then eleven years old, became a printer's "devil." He was particularly attracted to the engraving side of the business, and by close observation within five years he had mastered the engraver's art and was doing most of this work for his employer. He also worked for a time with his stepfather, a skilled mechanic, thus gaining some experience in the mechanical field. Determined to have a more liberal education, he entered the University of Rochester in 1859 and worked his way through college, earning money by engraving, and graduated with the degree of B.A. in 1863. Immediately thereafter he entered Auburn Theological Seminary, graduating in 1866. He was ordained by the Presbytery of Lyons, N. Y., on Mar. 11, 1867, during the succeeding year had a parish in Marion, N. Y., and then for two years was pastor of a church in Rochester. At the end of this brief ministry he returned to his first love, the printing trade. In 1869 he patented a platen job-printing-press which combined in one machine a number of features tending to excellence in job-printing work. He had it manufactured in Rochester under a licensing agreement, and it was widely sold under the name "Universal." In 1873 Gally transferred his business office to New York and contracted with the Colt Fire Arms Manufacturing Company of Hartford, Conn., for the manufacture of his press, receiving royalties until the expiration of the patent in 1886. Many improvements were incorporated in the "Universal" by the Colt Company during the life of the Gally patent, and after the expiration of the patent that company continued to manufacture the press without Gally, whereupon he instituted legal proceedings to prevent it but was defeated after a bitter contest. Subsequently he arranged with the National Machine Company, Hartford, to make and sell his presses, which were sold during the succeeding years under the names "Hartford" and "National"; a year before his death, he sold all of his patent rights to this concern.

Gally's financial success was based almost entirely on his printing-press patents but his inventive genius was applied in other directions as well; in all, he acquired a total of fifty patents, involving over 500 claims. In 1872 he was granted two patents for a composing machine or linotype introducing the wedge for justification. In 1873 he devised a method for converting in machinery variable into invariable velocity without affecting the source of power. During this decade, too, he experimented with and patented a system of multiplex telegraphy as well as philosophical apparatus, and turned his attention to automatic musical instruments. He invented in 1876, and undertook to manufacture, a machine for slotting paper used in controlling the pneumatic action of self-playing instruments; he invented a back vent system for tubular church organs and the counterpoise pneumatic system for player pianos. In 1888 he perfected a device for automatically loading and exposing photographic plates and later patented a telephone repeater for long-distance transmission. For the last twenty years of his life he lived more or less in retirement at his home in Brooklyn, N. Y. The University of Rochester conferred the honorary degree of M.A. on him in 1873 and that of Sc.D. in 1904. On Aug. 15, 1866, he had married Mary A. Carpenter of Rye, N. Y., who with one son survived him.

[*Inland Printer,* June and Sept. 1916; *Am. Printer,* Mar. 20, 1916; obituary in *Brooklyn Daily Eagle,* Mar. 9, 1916; *Who's Who in America,* 1903–05; *Gen. Cat. Univ. of Rochester, 1850–1911* (1911); Patent Office records.]

C. W. M.

GÁLVEZ, BERNARDO de (July 23, 1746–Nov. 30, 1786), captain-general of Louisiana and the Floridas, belonged to a family that during his lifetime was one of the most distinguished in the colonial service of Spain. He was born in the village of Macharaviaya in the province of Málaga, the son of Matías de Gálvez and Josefa Gallardo Madrid, both of the ancient nobility but at the time of their son's birth greatly impoverished (*Diccionario Geográfico, Estadístico, Histórico, de la Isla de Cuba,* Madrid, 1863, II, 381–82). Bernardo served in the army in Portugal (1762), in New Spain against the Apaches, in Algiers under Alejandro O'Reilly, and in the military school at Avila. Sent to Louisiana as colonel of the fixed regiment, he was appointed governor and intendant of the province by a royal decree of July 10, 1776, and entered upon his duties Feb. 1, 1777. The war that soon broke out with England afforded ample opportunity for the exercise of his talents, and his powerful family connections (his uncle, José de Gálvez, was colonial secretary under Charles III) obtained generous recognition of his services and the full support of the government for his undertakings. By espousing Felícitas de St. Maxent, the daughter of a prominent Louisiana family, he identified himself with the Creoles and assured himself of their cooperation in the impending crisis.

In the two years of his administration preceding Spain's entry into the war he did all that he could to weaken the British in that quarter of the world, supplying the American frontiersmen with arms through the agency of Oliver Pollock and seizing British ships that had been carrying on a profitable contraband trade with Louisiana. When war came, he boldly rejected the advice of his cautious counselors and undertook a vigorous offensive. In three campaigns he reduced every British post in West Florida, thus making it possible for Spain to obtain both Floridas in the peace settlement of 1783 and to control the mouth of the Mississippi and the Gulf of Mexico. In 1779 he took Baton Rouge, Manchac, and Natchez on the east bank of the Mississippi, and in 1780 and 1781 respectively Mobile and Pensacola on the Gulf.

The conquest of Pensacola is deservedly the most famous episode of his career. So formidable were its defenses that he had to obtain reinforcements from Havana. When these were not forthcoming promptly, he went to Havana in person and, as the nephew of the colonial secretary, got what he wanted. When he was overtaken on his way to Pensacola by a storm that crippled his fleet, he returned to Havana nothing daunted and organized another expedition. Upon the arrival of the fleet before Pensacola, the admiral, who was independent of Gálvez, refused to cross the bar under the guns of the British fort, alleging that to do so would be to court certain destruction. Unable to coerce or persuade him, Gálvez shamed him into compliance by running the gauntlet in a small ship, the *Galveztown,* that belonged to his own Louisiana forces. This feat was commemorated when he was made Count de Gálvez and Viscount de Galveztown, for on his coat of arms was emblazoned the ship *Galveztown* with the proud inscription *"Yo Solo"* ("I alone"). The siege was finally ended by the explosion of a powder magazine that opened a breach in the fortifications and compelled the surrender of the British garrison (May 9, 1781). Gálvez then sailed for Santo Domingo to take part in a joint Franco-Spanish expedition against Jamaica.

In 1783 and 1784 he was in Madrid giving advice to his government in regard to Louisiana, the Floridas, and the American frontier. His influence was increased by the honors that he had won as a result of the West Florida campaign. These included promotion to the rank of major-general, his Castilian title of nobility, and appointment as captain-general of Louisiana and the Floridas. He retained the latter office upon his promotion to the captaincy-general of Cuba and, by special dispensation, even after his elevation to the viceroyalty of New Spain (1785) as successor to his father, Matías de Gálvez.

His name is associated with several important measures and episodes in the history of Louisiana and the Floridas. He aided in obtaining the commercial cedula of 1782 and in shaping the policy of Spain in regard to Indian affairs, immigration, the boundary dispute with the United States, and the navigation of the Mississippi River. In 1784 he transferred St. Mark's from East to West Florida and subordinated the commandants of Pensacola and Mobile to the governor of Louisiana. In the winter of 1784–85 he consulted with Diego de Gardoqui at Havana and gave him supplementary instructions for his negotiation with the United States. In 1785 he received the thanks of Congress for releasing some American merchants imprisoned at Havana (Archivo General de Indias, 146–3–11, Gálvez to Sonora, Mexico, Apr. 26, 1786, No. 574), and in the same year he ordered the summary expulsion of the Georgia commissioners who had come to Natchez to establish Bourbon County. He died in Mexico the last of the following November.

[There is apparently no justification for the statement of Charles Gayarré, *Hist. of La.* (4th ed., 1903), III, 164–66, that Gálvez was under suspicion of treason at the time of his death; see H. H. Bancroft, *Hist. of Mexico* (1883), III, 394–99. For his career see Alcée Fortier, *Hist. of La.* (1904), II, 56–109; *La. Hist. Quart.,* Jan. 1917; "Spanish Correspondence concerning the American Revolution," *Hispanic Am. Hist. Rev.,* Aug. 1918; "Papers Relating to Bourbon County, Ga.," *Am. Hist. Rev.,* Oct. 1909; A. P. Whitaker, *The Spanish-American Frontier* (1927), *passim*; S. F. Bemis. *Pinckney's Treaty* (1926), pp. 74–78; J. F. Yela Utrilla, *España ante la Independencia de Los Estados Unidos* (Lérida, Spain, 1925), vol. I, *passim.*] A. P. W.

GAMBLE, HAMILTON ROWAN (Nov. 29, 1798–Jan. 31, 1864), lawyer, judge, governor, was born in Winchester, Va., the son of Irish immigrants, Joseph Gamble and Anne Hamilton. He was educated at Hampden-Sidney College. Admitted to the Virginia bar at eighteen, he followed the familiar course westward, arriving in the Territory of Missouri in 1818. After successful administration of a judicial office, he served as secretary of state, but retired to devote his entire time and attention to his profession. He was a recognized authority in important land and title suits, and had extensive practise before the state and federal appellate courts. In 1827 he was married to Caroline J. Coalter. Reëntering politics in 1846, he served one term in the legislature, refusing a second term. The Whig state convention of 1850, however, insisted upon nominating him for the supreme bench, and he was elected by a large majority in a Democratic state (*Missouri States-*

man, Sept. 26, 1851). From 1851 to 1854 he served as the presiding justice, his opinions being marked by brevity, learning, and conservatism. In the case of *Scott, a Man of Color* vs. *Emerson* (1852; 15 *Mo.,* 576), Dred Scott's first unsuccessful suit for freedom, he rendered a dissenting opinion, holding that "a master who takes his slave to reside in a State or Territory where slavery is prohibited, thereby emancipates his slave" (*Ibid.,* p. 590). This view was in accord with eight earlier Missouri precedents. In 1854 he resigned because of ill health and definitely retired from political and professional life, removing to Norristown, near Philadelphia. Early in 1861, the political situation became so critical in Missouri that Gamble returned to that state and declared that "going out of the Union would be the most ruinous thing Missouri could do." He was elected in February a member of the state convention, called to consider the relation of the state to the Union. In this body he was the leader of the Conditional Unionists, those who favored compromise and who refused to pledge the state to secession. He was chairman of the committee on federal relations, whose report declaring that "there is at present no adequate cause to impel Missouri to dissolve her connection with the Federal Union" was adopted by the convention. In June 1861, upon the flight of the secessionist state officials, the convention assumed constituent powers, declared vacant the administrative and legislative offices, and selected Gamble as provisional governor. He organized two separate forces of the militia and secured from the Lincoln administration money and equipment to sustain them. Despite the dangerous conflicts of opinion over military policy, he was able in 1863 truthfully to say that no successful invasion of the state had occurred and that lawlessness and disorder had been materially reduced. He was unable, however, to solve the most difficult problem with which the provisional government had to deal, that of emancipation. By the end of 1862 the Unionist party in Missouri had divided into two bitterly hostile factions which respectively advocated and opposed the immediate abolition of slavery. Gamble, essentially conservative, in his message of Dec. 30, 1862, discussed in general terms a plan for gradual, compensated emancipation which he recommended to the consideration of the legislature (*Journal of the Senate of Missouri,* 22 Gen. Assem., 1 Sess., p. 24). When in the following year the convention adopted a gradual emancipation plan, the Radicals, open in their opposition to Gamble, denounced it and demanded the Governor's resignation. He was willing to resign, but would not be forced out of office, and he was supported by men of moderate views. His health had long been frail, and in January 1864, after a short illness, he died. Despite obvious mistakes, his administration of the provisional government had succeeded in its chief objectives. The supremacy of the federal government had been maintained in Missouri; the state had been saved for the Union; free labor had definitely triumphed over slavery.

[*In Memoriam: Hamilton R. Gamble* (1864); *Mo. Hist. Rev.,* Oct. 1910; *The Messages and Proclamations of the Govs. of the State of Mo.,* vol. III (1922); *Jour. and Proc. Mo. State Convention* (5 vols., 1861–63); obituaries in *Missouri Republican* (St. Louis), Feb. 1, 2, 1864.]

T. S. B.

GAMBRELL, JAMES BRUTON (Aug. 21, 1841–June 10, 1921), Baptist clergyman, editor, educator, son of Joel Bruton and Jane (Williams) Gambrell, was born in Anderson, S. C., and died in Dallas, Tex. When he was about a year old his family moved to Mississippi, and there he grew up, attending country schools. He became a Confederate soldier in 1861, and, chiefly as a scout, spent more than two years in the Army of Northern Virginia. On one of his expeditions in Nansemond County he met Mary Tom Corbell, and some months later, January 1864, eluding the Federal guards, he made his way to her home and the two were married. During the latter part of the war he was a captain in the West. Afterward he lived in Virginia, and then returned to his home in Mississippi and taught school for a while before being ordained in 1867 as a Baptist preacher. In the early seventies he was pastor of a church in Oxford, the seat of the University of Mississippi, where he took several courses of study. After preaching at various small towns, he was editor, 1878–93, of the Mississippi *Baptist Record.* During 1893–96 he was president of Mercer University in Macon, Ga., and thereafter till 1918—except for his four or five years' editorship of the *Baptist Standard*—he was corresponding secretary of the Baptist General Convention of Texas. In that state, in the nineties, "the most awful denominational war ever waged in the South" was raging (McDaniel, *post,* p. 70). The new recruit from Mississippi and Georgia was not long in making himself felt. He had an eye for victory, he spoke a language understood by the citizenry, and he knew how to amass funds. About 1915 he assumed the leadership of the newly merged educational and missionary activities of his denomination in Texas, and from 1918 till his death he was a professor in the Southwestern Baptist Theological Seminary in Fort Worth. In the last months of his life, while president of the Southern Baptist Convention, he visited Europe as a fraternal delegate to various gatherings of his codenominationalists. For all his force as an organizer, it was as a speaker and writer that he made his unique place in the minds of his contemporaries. His publications include *Ten Years in Texas* (1909), and *Parable and Precept* (1917). He was a blunt, plain fellow, racy and penetrating, given always to homely analogy. He opposed schemes for church union, he thought war as justifiable as surgery (*Parable and Precept*, p. 23), and he did not always avoid either dogmatism or platitude. He was undoubtedly sincere, however, and it is likely that not many have exceeded him in the force which he brought to bear upon the shaping of life in Texas.

[G. W. McDaniel, *Memorial Wreath* (1921); J. M. Carroll, *Hist. Tex. Baptists* (1923); *Univ. of Miss. Hist. Cat. 1849–1909* (1910); *Who's Who in America 1920–21*; *Quart. Bull. of Mercer Univ.*, June 1911; *Dallas Morning News*, June 11, 1921.] J. D. W.

GAMMON, ELIJAH HEDDING (Dec. 23, 1819–July 3, 1891), Methodist Episcopal clergyman, manufacturer, philanthropist, began life on Gilmore Pond Plantation, now Lexington, Me., the son of Samuel H. and Melinda (Quint) Gammon. His father was a poor farmer, and Elijah left home at seventeen to make his own way in the world. Soon afterward he was converted and began studying for the ministry, supporting himself in the meantime by teaching. At the age of twenty-four he was received into the Maine Conference of the Methodist Church and stationed at Wilton where he received a salary of $100 a year. Here in 1843 he married Sarah J. Cutler. After serving other churches in Maine, in 1851 he was prompted by a severe bronchial affection to go to Illinois in the hope of improving his health. He first settled at Ross Grove, De Kalb County, and opened a private school; but in 1852 he was admitted to the Rock River Conference and put in charge of the church in St. Charles. In 1853 he was appointed to the Jefferson Street Church, Chicago; in 1854, to Batavia; and from 1855 to 1858 he was presiding elder of the St. Charles District. By this time his bronchial trouble so interfered with his work that he decided to retire from the active ministry.

Entering business, he became a pioneer promoter of farm machinery in the Middle West, his sagacity, foresight, energy, and assurance making him one of the leading manufacturers and distributers in his field, and enabling him to acquire a large fortune. He first connected himself with Newton & Company of Batavia, and when the partnership expired in 1861, having had a vision of the great future for harvesting machinery, he established a large distributing house in Chicago, forming a partnership with J. D. Easter. Seeing the possibilities in the harvester devised by Charles W. and William W. Marsh [*qq.v.*], Easter and Gammon secured the exclusive right to its sale in six western states, and in the face of many difficulties, succeeded in bringing it into wide use. In 1868 they dissolved partnership, dividing the territory they held under the Marsh patents. Gammon then took James P. Prindle into partnership and in 1869 acquired an interest in the Plano shops controlled by the Marshes and Lewis Stewart. In 1870 Prindle retired and with William Deering [*q.v.*] Gammon formed the firm of Gammon & Deering, which became sole owner of the Plano plant. Gammon sold his interest to Deering in 1879, but in 1880, the latter having moved the business to Chicago, Gammon, William H. Jones, and others, formed the Plano Manufacturing Company, which took over the old shop and was soon numbered among the most important concerns engaged in the building of twine-binding harvesters. Of this company Gammon was vice-president at the time of his death. In his later years he established a home in Batavia where he engaged in the banking business. His first wife had died in 1855, and in 1856 he had married Mrs. Jane Prindle Colton.

He never lost his interest in the church and remained a member of the Rock River Conference as long as he lived. Much of the wealth which he acquired he devoted to religious and educational purposes. He gave liberally to the Maine Wesleyan Seminary, and to the Garrett Biblical Institute, of which he was long a trustee; but his chief benefaction was the establishment and endowment of the Gammon Theological Seminary, Atlanta, Ga., an institution to train colored men for the ministry of the Methodist Episcopal Church. To this he gave $250,000 during his lifetime, and by the provisions of his will it received from his estate almost as much more.

[Memoir of Gammon by R. I. Fleming, in *Minutes . . . of the Rock River Annual Conference of the M. E. Ch.* (1891), reprinted in *Minutes of the Annual Conferences of the M. E. Ch.* (1891); *Farm Implement News* (Chicago), Aug. 1891; *Northwestern Christian Advocate* (Chicago), July 8, 1891; *Christian Advocate* (N. Y.), July 30, 1891; Robt. L. Ardrey, *Am. Agric. Implements* (1894); *Encyc. of Biog. of Ill.*, vol. I (1892); family data from relatives, through the courtesy of President F. H. Clapp of Gammon Theol. Sem.] H. E. S.

GANNETT, EZRA STILES (May 4, 1801–Aug. 26, 1871), Unitarian clergyman, was born in Cambridge, Mass., the son of Rev. Caleb Gannett, for nearly forty years steward of Harvard College, and his second wife, Ruth Stiles, daughter of President Ezra Stiles [*q.v.*] of Yale College. His father was a slow, dignified, exact, trustworthy person with a taste for mathematics, and his mother a refined, sensitive, deeply religious woman who had read the Bible through twenty-two times. Ezra grew up a sober-minded, conscientious boy with scholarly proclivities. He prepared for college at Phillips Academy, Andover, and at the age of fifteen entered Harvard, graduating with first honors in 1820. After a period of hesitation during which he contemplated taking up the study of law and taught in a private grammar school at Cambridgeport, he decided to become a Unitarian minister and enrolled in the Harvard Divinity School. He finished the course there in 1823, and on May 27, 1824, accepted an invitation to become assistant to Dr. William Ellery Channing [*q.v.*] at the Federal Street Church, Boston, where he was ordained, June 30, 1824. With this church, which later moved to a new edifice on Arlington Street, he was associated as assistant and, after Channing's death, as pastor during the remainder of his life. On Oct. 6, 1835, he married Anna Linzee Tilden of Boston, who died on Christmas Day 1846.

For more than forty years he not only ministered faithfully to the needs of his parish but was conspicuous as well among the New England proponents of liberal religion. He lived a life of unselfish, enthusiastic activity, although a sense of duty beyond his power to perform inclined him to habitual somberness and self-reproach. Gifted with reasoning faculties of a high order, the ability to express ideas in clear and cogent language, an eloquence which sprang from intensity of feeling, and no little executive talent, he exerted a strong influence as preacher, lecturer, editor, and administrator. The year after his ordination he was active in organizing the American Unitarian Association for which he is said to have written the constitution, and of which he was the first secretary, serving for six years. Later (1847–51) he was its president. In 1834 he was instrumental in the formation of the Benevolent Fraternity of Churches for the Support of the Ministry-at-large, which became the principal Unitarian missionary society of Boston. As secretary he directed its early work, and from 1857 to 1862 was its president. He assisted Henry Ware, Jr. [*q.v.*] in the editorship of the *Christian Register,* and in 1831 started the *Scriptural Interpreter* which he conducted until 1835. Broken in health, he went to Europe in 1836, returning in 1838. In 1840 he suffered a paralytic stroke which deprived him of the use of his right leg, but he was soon active again, and the click of his short crutch-canes became a familiar sound on the Boston streets. A conservative Unitarian, with a tenacious belief in the miraculous mission and superhuman authority of Christ, he vigorously opposed the Transcendental movement, his lectures expounding "old-fashioned Unitarianism" drawing large audiences. From 1839 to 1843 he edited the *Monthly Miscellany of Religion and Letters,* and from 1844 to 1849 he was co-editor of the *Christian Examiner.* To the latter he contributed some notable articles on Theodore Parker and Transcendentalism. He was an advocate of temperance, education, and peace, was opposed to slavery, but was wholly unsympathetic toward the Abolitionists. To the activities of the Civil War he gave little support, but on the bronze bas-reliefs of the Soldiers' Monument, Boston Common, his face appears in the Sanitary Commission group. Death came to him in a railroad wreck on the evening of Aug. 26, 1871, while he was on his way from Boston to Lynn to fill a preaching engagement.

[Wm. C. Gannett, *Ezra Stiles Gannett* (1875), with an appendix containing a long list of printed sermons, addresses, essays, and magazine articles; *Heralds of a Liberal Faith,* vol. III (1910), ed. by Samuel A. Eliot; *Services in Memory of Ezra Stiles Gannett, D.D.* (1871); John R. Dix, *Pulpit Portraits, or Pen Pictures of Distinguished American Divines* (1854); Geo. W. Cooke, *Unitarianism in America* (1902); *Unitarian Rev.,* May 1875; *Monthly Religious Mag.,* Dec. 1871; E. E. Hale, in *Old and New,* Oct. 1871; *Liberal Christian,* Sept. 9, 1871; *Christian Register,* Sept. 2, 1871; *Boston Transcript,* Aug. 28, 1871.] H. E. S.

GANNETT, HENRY (Aug. 24, 1846–Nov. 5, 1914), geographer, was born in Bath, Me., the son of Michael Farley and Hannah (Church) Gannett. He attended the city schools until he entered Harvard University in his twentieth year. He graduated from the Lawrence Scientific School (Harvard) with the degree of B.S. in 1869, and the next year he received from Harvard the degree of M.E. In 1874 he married Mary E. Chase of Waterville, Me. His first work was in astronomy at the Harvard Observatory, but he refused the post of astronomer to the Hall North Polar Expedition in 1871, accepting by preference the appointment as topographer to the Hayden Survey, with which he accomplished much pioneer work, mostly in Colorado and Wyoming. In 1882, he became chief geographer of the United States Geological Survey under J. W. Powell, director, and here he remained until his death. His powers of organization were marked and many of the methods inaugurated by him have continued. He was called to special work as geographer of the tenth, eleventh, and twelfth censuses of the United States, and his assignments of the nearly 2,000 enumeration districts for the first of these simplified and clarified the work of the Census Bureau. His peculiar contribution was a statistical atlas. He was assistant director and statistician for the Philippine Census of 1903 and later for the Cuban and Porto Rican censuses. The confusion in the use of place names which he observed during his early days with the Geological Survey led him, with others, to attempt to give authority to geographic designations. This effort resulted in the establishment, in 1890, of the official United States Board of Geographic Names, now the United States Geographic Board; and of this he was chairman for twenty years. He had a peculiar interest in names of places as is shown in his "Geographic Dictionaries" for a number of states (*Bulletins 115–118,* 1894), gazetteers of Porto Rico and Cuba (*Bulletin 183* and *192,* 1901 and 1902), and "The Origin of Certain Place Names in the United States" (*Bulletin 197,* 1902), all published by the United States Geological Survey.

In the broader and more scientific study of geography, so strongly advocated by Gannett, it is not strange to find him with other leaders of geographic thought attempting to find a medium of exchange for their beliefs and discoveries. To this end, he aided in the formation of the National Geographic Society (1883) of which he was the president at the time of his death, and was one of the founders of the Geological Society of America and the Association of American Geographers. He allied himself with many organizations for the spread of geographic knowledge, especially such as covered the scope of his own peculiar interests—cartography, statistics, and applied geography. From 1903 to 1909 he was geographer and editor for the National Conservation Commission. His work was characterized by a zeal for exactitude and a desire that his labors and those of his colleagues and co-workers should be widely known and used. The maps of the United States Geological Survey came to their high perfection under his guidance, and writers of his life and work refer to him as the "father of American map making." Many sections of the West were virgin country when in 1872 he entered upon his work under Hayden, and consequently his task was in part that of a discoverer and designator of many mountains, lakes, and plains. As chief geographer of the Survey he not only organized the work of the field parties but visited them in the field and to a large degree supervised the translation of the field records into topographic maps. In addition to his other writings, which included many contributions to the *Bulletins* of the Geological Survey, Gannett published four works directed toward the education of the public: a *Commercial Geography* (1905) in conjunction with C. L. Garrison and E. J. Houston; *The United States* in vol. II (1898) of Stanford's Compendium of Geography and Travel; *Physiographic Types* (2 vols., 1898–1900); and *Topographic Maps of the United States showing Physiographic Types* (1907).

[N. H. Darton, "Memoir of Henry Gannett," in *Annals Asso. Am. Geographers,* vol. VII (1917); S. N. D. North, "Henry Gannett," in *Nat. Geog. Mag.,* Dec. 1914; obituary notice in the *Bull. Am. Geol. Soc.,* Jan. 1915; *Who's Who in America,* 1912–13; *Harvard Univ. Quin. Cat.* (1925).] R. M. B.

GANNETT, WILLIAM CHANNING (Mar. 13, 1840–Dec. 15, 1923), Unitarian clergyman, was born in Boston, Mass., the son of Rev. Ezra Stiles Gannett [*q.v.*] and Anna Linzee (Tilden) Gannett. At the age of sixteen he enrolled in Harvard College from which he graduated in 1860. After teaching for a year at Newport, R. I., he entered the Harvard Divinity School, but later withdrew and went South to work among the freedmen. He served first at Port Royal, S. C., and after Sherman's army had captured Savannah, in that city. Some of his observations during this period are recorded in an article entitled, "The Freedmen at Port Royal," which appeared in the *North American Review* for July 1865. In June of that year he went abroad, and spent the following winter studying in Germany. Upon his return he published, "Serfdom and the Emancipation Laws in Russia" (*North American Review,* July 1867). Resuming work at the Harvard Divinity School, he graduated in the class of 1868.

Entering the Unitarian ministry, he held brief pastorates in Milwaukee (1868–70) and East Lexington, Mass. (1871–72). The next two or three years were spent principally in writing *Ezra Stiles Gannett,* a biography of his father, published in 1875. This work not only gives an interesting picture of one of the leading early Boston Unitarians, but contains as well a scholarly account of the rise of New England Unitarianism. He was pastor at St. Paul, Minn. (1877–83), and at Hinsdale, Ill. (1887–89). On Nov. 3, 1887, he married Mary Thorn Lewis of Philadelphia. In 1889 he took charge of the Unitarian church in Rochester, N. Y., continuing as pastor until 1908, and as pastor emeritus for the remainder of his life.

Certain ministerial peculiarities, weakness of voice, and impairment of hearing prevented him from achieving prominence as a preacher. His writings were widely read, however, and among Unitarians he came to be regarded as one of the stanchest defenders of individual freedom in matters of religion. An uncompromising individualist, he would not tolerate the slightest creedal interference with liberty. In the struggle between the conservatives and the liberals of the Western Conference, waged in the eighties, he helped win the day for those who opposed even the suggestion of a dogmatic test for membership. He was one of the founders of the *Pamphlet Mission for Freedom, Fellowship, and Character in Religion,* begun in Chicago, March 1878, the name of which was changed the following September to *Unity,* and he long cooperated with Jenkin Lloyd Jones [*q.v.*] in its guidance. His numerous publications include sermons, pamphlets, booklets, and studies designed for help in literary and religious education. Among them are: *The Faith that Makes Faithful* (1887), a volume of sermons prepared in collaboration with Jenkin Lloyd Jones, which had an extraordinary sale both in the United States and in England; *A Year of Miracle* (1882); *The Childhood of Jesus* (1884); *Studies in Longfellow, Whittier, Holmes, and Lowell* (1898); *Of Making One's Self Beautiful* (1899); *A Wicket Gate to the Bible* (1907); and *The Little Child at the Breakfast Table . . . Little Prayers for Morning, Bed-Time, and Household Thanksgivings* (1915), in the arrangement of which he was assisted by Mrs. Gannett. His intellectual radicalism was mellowed by a deep mystical sense which gave beauty to his character and found expression in poems and hymns. With Frederick L. Hosmer [*q.v.*] he published *The Thought of God in Hymns and Poems* (three series, 1885, 1894, and 1918). Several of his hymns have come into general use. He was also one of the editors of *Unity Hymns and Chorals* (1880), a revised edition of which was issued in 1911.

[*Who's Who in America,* 1920–21; *Unity* (Chicago), Mar. 6, 1924; *Christian Register,* Jan. 3, 1924; *Nation* (N. Y.), Jan. 23, 1924; *Unitarian Year Book,* 1924–25; *Harvard Grads. Mag.,* Mar. 1924; *Harvard College: Report of the Class of 1860* (1880); Geo. W. Cooke, *Unitarianism in America* (1902); *Democrat and Chronicle* (Rochester, N. Y.), Dec. 16, 1923.]

H. E. S.

GANO, JOHN (July 22, 1727–Aug. 10, 1804), Baptist clergyman, was a descendant of François Gerneaux, a Huguenot, who, in peril of life after the revocation of the Edict of Nantes (1685), escaped from Guernsey with his family in a vessel he himself purchased, and became an early settler in New Rochelle, N. Y. The patronymic was soon changed to Gano. A son, Stephen, married Ann Walton, and their son, Daniel, married Sarah, daughter of Nathaniel Britton of Staten Island. These were the parents of John Gano, their third child, who was born at Hopewell, N. J. His early years were spent on the family farm. He had some private instruction in the classics from neighboring ministers, and was given the privilege of attending classes at Princeton although not matriculated there. His *Memoirs* give some details of three evangelizing journeys southward. After the first, to Virginia, he was ordained, May 1754, becoming pastor at Morristown, N. J., where he baptized Hezekiah Smith [*q.v.*]. On the second, he preached at Charleston, S. C., George Whitefield being among his hearers. After his return from this journey, he married, probably late in 1755, Sarah Stites of Elizabeth-town, whose sister later married James Manning [*q.v.*]. While on the third of these journeys, he accepted the pastorate of the church at Yadkin, N. C., remaining until the Cherokee war led him to take his growing family back to New Jersey.

In 1762 Gano became pastor in New York, helping in the reorganization of the Baptist church there and serving it for over a quarter of a century. The church was small, but it frequently contained young men who later rose to eminence. Gano was active in the Philadelphia Association, and is reckoned among the founders of Rhode Island College (Brown University). When his church was broken up by the British military occupation of Manhattan, he became chaplain in the Continental Army, most of the time serving Gen. James Clinton's brigade. He was under fire at White Plains and moved about with the brigade, the most distinctive service of which, perhaps, was with the Sullivan expedition into the Susquehanna region of southern New York. On the occasion of the proclamation at Washington's headquarters, Newburgh, of the cessation of hostilities, he was assigned to offer the prayer (*Memoirs of Major General Heath,* 1798, p. 371). This seems to be the chief objective support to the tradition in the Gano family that he was on intimate terms with Washington.

At the end of 1783 Gano returned to his church. Soon it was in a flourishing condition again, and Gano's ability was recognized by his selection in legislative acts as a regent of the University of the State of New York (1784), and as a trustee of King's College, revived as Columbia (1787). Factional opposition with resultant inadequacy of support brought this New York pastorate to an end. There was much of the pioneer in Gano, who felt the religious destitution of the frontier, and in 1788 went to Kentucky. His career there was doubtless a disappointment and was marked by many tribulations. Mrs. Gano met with an accident and soon died. Shortly after, on a preaching tour into North Carolina, he met and married the widow of Thomas Bryant. In 1798, following a fall, he suffered a paralytic stroke; he partially recovered but his public services thereafter were limited. One son, Stephen [*q.v.*], became an eminent clergyman, while another, Maj.-Gen. John Stites Gano, played a rôle of some significance in the military history of the Northwest Territory, especially in Ohio.

[*Biog. Memoirs of Rev. John Gano . . . Written Principally by Himself* (1806), continued and edited by his son, Stephen Gano; see also R. A. Guild, *Early Hist. of Brown Univ.* (1897); W. B. Sprague, *Annals Am. Pulpit*, vol. VI (1860); L. C. Barnes, *The John Gano Evidence of George Washington's Religion* (1926).] W. H. A.

GANO, STEPHEN (Dec. 25, 1762–Aug. 18, 1828), Baptist clergyman, was the fourth child of Rev. John Gano [*q.v.*] and his first wife, Sarah (Stites) Gano. He was born in New York soon after the beginning of his father's pastorate there. The Revolution interrupted his preparation for college, and he entered upon the study of medicine under his maternal uncle at Cranbury, N. J. After four years of training, he was appointed surgeon's mate in the Continental Army, June 1779, and the next year enlisted on a privateer, *L'Insurgent*. Late in life he wrote for his children a brief account of his hardships, involving two shipwrecks, being marooned on an uninhabited island, and confinement in chains on a prison ship. These three years of adventurous service for his country were passed before Gano reached his twentieth birthday. Subsequently, he resumed the practise of medicine, at Tappan, N. Y., and on Oct. 25, 1782, married Cornelia Vavasour, daughter of Capt. Josiah Vavasour of the British navy.

The following year, he united with his father's church, where he was ordained on Aug. 2, 1786. Following his second marriage in 1789, to Polly Tallmadge, he visited his father in Kentucky, and was active in the formation of the first Baptist church in the Northwest Territory (Jan. 20, 1790), near Hamilton, Ohio. After serving at Hudson and several other places in New York, he was invited in 1792 to supply the Baptist church at Providence. He was not formally elected pastor till Mar. 1, 1796, but the Warren Association *Minutes* from 1793 onward rightly designate him as minister of that church. In the history of this venerable church, Gano's pastorate—lasting until his death—still stands as the longest and as one of great importance. Technically it had been a "Six Principle" church and Gano himself had been "under hands." Becoming convinced that the rite was not based upon Scriptural authority, he induced the church to abandon the practise. His pastorate was marked by frequent revivals; he baptized many students and some who became eminent leaders. He also made numerous evangelizing journeys and participated in many of the broader movements of a religious and community nature. From 1794 till 1827 he was a valued member of the Providence school committee; from 1794 till his death, a trustee of Rhode Island College (Brown University), which conferred the degree of A.M. upon him in 1800. For nineteen successive years, he was moderator of the Warren Association, and he was one of three delegates from New England to the meeting in Philadelphia which organized the Baptist Triennial Convention. He was a man of rather liberal views; while not reaching the position of open communion, he did not adhere to the prevailing restricted communion of his denomination and would baptize those who preferred to unite with other than Baptist churches. His second wife died in 1797, and on July 18, 1799, he married Mary Brown of Providence, who survived less than two years. On Oct. 8, 1801, he married Mrs. Joanna Lattine.

[Gano's narrative of his life, written in 1826 at the request of his children, is printed in *Am. Monthly Mag.*, July 1894, having also appeared in the *New York Chronicle*, I (1849), 193–204. A fuller sketch is H. M. King, *Life and Labors of Rev. Stephen Gano, M.D.* (1903); a short sketch, "The Two Ganos," appeared in the *Baptist Memorial and Monthly Chronicle*, Jan. 1843. See also W. B. Sprague, *Annals Am. Pulpit*, vol. VI (1860).] W. H. A.

GANSEVOORT, LEONARD (July 1751–Aug. 26, 1810), lawyer, politician and judge, was baptized at Albany, N. Y., July 14, 1751. He was a son of Harmen and Magdalena (Douw) Gansevoort, a brother of Peter Gansevoort [*q.v.*], and a descendant of a prominent Dutch family of Albany, most of the members of which for three generations had been brewers and merchants in the town. He studied law in New York City, and after being licensed in 1772, began his practise in Albany, where with his wife, Hester Cuyler, he occupied a prominent social position. His career as a lawyer and local politician was interrupted by the outbreak of the Revolutionary War; he became a member of the Albany Committee of Correspondence, and served as its treasurer until November 1775. When the Second Provincial Congress of New York convened in New York City on Dec. 6, 1775, he was one of the twelve deputies elected to it by the Albany Committee. During the three sessions of this congress, and during the Third Provincial Congress, May 18 to June 30, 1776, he busied himself in various capacities with the manifold emergency problems, both constitutional and military, raised by the war. The Fourth Provincial Congress, assembling on July 9, changed its name to "The Convention of the Representatives of the State of New York." From Apr. 18 to May 14, 1777, Gansevoort was president *pro tempore* of this body, and signed the first state constitution, adopted on Apr. 20. In an undated letter to his brother Peter he wrote: "The Spirited Exertions of our Convention (without arrogating any Dignity to myself) has been such that our State has acquired the first Rank not only with Congress but with every thinking Man that loves his Country and Mankind." On May 8, 1777, he was appointed by the Provincial Congress county clerk of Albany, and in the following year represented Albany in the state Assembly. In 1779 he served as county treasurer of Albany, and in 1780 as city recorder. After the Revolution he bought the handsome country house known as Whitehall, a mile and a half from Albany, where with much ceremony he entertained the political leaders of the state, as well as many national figures. He was prominent in local and state politics for many years. In 1786 he was appointed a state commissioner to the Annapolis Convention, but did not attend, and two years later, after a second term in the Assembly, was a member of the Continental Congress. When Philip Schuyler became United States senator from New York, Gansevoort substituted for him in the fourteenth session of the state Senate in 1791, and continued to serve until 1793. In 1794 he was appointed by Gov. Clinton colonel of light cavalry. From 1794 to 1797 he was county judge of Albany. In November 1796 he returned to the state Senate, where he was an influential figure until 1802. During the last decade of his life (1799–1810) he served as judge of the court of probates, which held appellate jurisdiction over the surrogates' courts.

[Manuscript Sketches by Leonard Gansevoort, Jr., and M. Matilda Ten Eyck in the Gansevoort-Lansing MSS. in the N. Y. Pub. Lib.; Leonard Gansevoort's letters to his brother Peter in the Military Papers of General Peter Gansevoort, Jr., in the same collection; indexes of E. A. Werner, *Civil List and Constitutional Hist. of the Colony and State of N. Y.* (1888); *Minutes of the Albany Committee of Correspondence, 1775–1778* (2 vols., 1923), ed. by Jas. Sullivan; *N. Y. in the Revolution as Colony and State: Supp.* (1901), ed. by F. G. Mather; *Calendar of Hist. MSS. Relating to the War of the Revolution in the Office of the Sec. of State* (2 vols., 1868); *Colls. on the Hist. of Albany* (4 vols., 1865–70), ed. by Joel Munsell, vols. I and II; *Minutes of the Commissioners for Detecting and Defeating Conspiracies in the State of N. Y., Albany County Sessions* (3 vols., 1909–10), ed. by V. H. Paltsits, II, 821; Jonathan Pearson, *Contributions for the Geneal. of the First Settlers of the Ancient County of Albany* (1872), p. 51.]

E. M., Jr.

GANSEVOORT, PETER (July 1749–July 2, 1812), Revolutionary soldier, was born in Albany, N. Y., and baptized on July 16, 1749. He was the son of Harmen and Magdalena (Douw) Gansevoort, and a brother of Leonard Gansevoort [*q.v.*]. Appointed major of the 2nd New York Regiment June 30, 1775, he saw his first active service under Gen. Richard Montgomery [*q.v.*] in Canada. He was commissioned lieutenant-colonel Mar. 19, 1776, and placed in command of Fort George in the summer of that year. He was made colonel of the 3rd New York, Nov. 21, 1776, and in the following spring began the noteworthy part of his military career with his appointment to the command of Fort Schuyler (Fort Stanwix), at the site of the present city of Rome, N. Y. It was the year of Burgoyne's invasion from Canada, and an essential part of the British project was the cooperation of a force under St. Leger, which, according to the plan, would approach via Lake Ontario and the Mohawk Valley, converging upon Albany in unison with Burgoyne. Fort Schuyler, garrisoned by about 750 men, stood on the line of march. St. Leger, at the head of a mixed body of soldiers—mainly Tories and Indians—about 1,700 in number, under partisan leaders Col. John Johnson, John Butler, and the famous Mohawk chief, Joseph Brant [*qq.v.*], advanced from Oswego by way of Oneida Lake, and invested Fort Schuyler early in August. Col. Gansevoort, in anticipation of an attack, had written to Gen. Schuyler on July 4, asking for reinforcements, ammunition, and supplies. He disregarded the British commander's manifesto, with its mingled threats and promises, and on Aug. 6 dispatched Col. Marinus Willet [*q.v.*] on a sortie from the fort, in an effort to cooperate with Gen. Herkimer [*q.v.*], who, marching to the relief of Fort Schuyler, was checked in the battle of Oriskany that same day and himself sustained a mortal wound. Following this partial success, St. Leger sent envoys to Gansevoort with a summons to surrender; they were led blindfolded into his presence, and a stern refusal was given. The same answer was returned to a written demand. Food and ammunition were running low, however, and the officers Willet and Stockwell were dispatched secretly to obtain aid from Schuyler. Gansevoort had resolved, as a last resort, to cut his way through at night, when on Aug. 22 the siege was raised. Benedict Arnold with a volunteer force was advancing up the Mohawk Valley, and had sent ahead a captured Tory who spread such an exaggerated account of Arnold's numbers that the Indians and St. Leger fled in confusion toward Lake Ontario, leaving behind their artillery, tents, and military stores. A picturesque incident of the siege was the improvising of a flag, made out of stripes of white, cut from ammunition shirts, blue from a captured British cloak, and red from odds and ends (Stone, *post*, p. 229), and on the site of the fort there is now a tablet bearing the inscription: "Here the Stars and Stripes were first unfurled in battle."

After the siege, Gansevoort was in temporary command at Albany in October 1777, and received the thanks of Congress. On Jan. 12, 1778, he was married to Catherina Van Schaick. Reappointed commandant of Fort Schuyler, he passed a large part of the year 1778 in forced inaction, until he was relieved in November. His request to take charge of Cherry Valley was refused, and he was troubled by spying and desertions. Under orders from Gen. Sullivan in the year following, he surprised the lower Mohawk "castle," and took the prisoners to Albany, where they were later released. He was in command at Saratoga in 1780, and in 1781 was very active at Albany; attempts were made to seize both him and Schuyler. He was in correspondence with Gov. George Clinton and others, shared in the preparations to meet St. Leger's expected invasion, and at the end of the year tried in vain to suppress an insurrection of troops northeast of Albany. He had retired from the line, but was commissioned brigadier-general of militia Mar. 26, 1781. Following the war he held appointments as major-general of militia in the western district, Oct. 8, 1793; military agent of the northern department, Apr. 29, 1802; and brigadier-general of the United States Army, Feb. 15, 1809.

[Jonathan Pearson, *Contributions to the Geneal. of the First Settlers of the Ancient County of Albany* (1872); C. E. Fitch, *Encyc. of Biog. of N. Y.* (1916), pp. 26–27; *Calendar of Hist. MSS. Relating to the War of the Revolution in the Office of the Sec. of State* (2 vols., Albany, 1868); W. L. Stone, *Life of Joseph Brant* (2 vols., 1838), and *The Campaign of Lieut.-Gen. John Burgoyne and the Expedition of Lieut.-Col. Barry St. Leger* (1877); Hoffman Nickerson, *The Turning Point of the Revolution* (1928); *Jours. of the Mil. Expedition of Maj.-Gen. John Sullivan* (1887); Berthold Fernow, *N. Y. in the Revolution* (1887).] E. K. A.

GANSS, HENRY GEORGE (Feb. 22, 1855–Dec. 25, 1912), Roman Catholic clergyman, composer, was born in Darmstadt, Germany, and was only six weeks old when his parents, George and Elizabeth (Ganss) Ganss, emigrated to America. They settled at Lancaster, Pa., where the father became a butcher. Educated in the parochial schools, and at St. Vincent College, Latrobe, Pa., young Ganss graduated in 1876 with the degree of doctor of music. In 1878 he was ordained to the priesthood of the Roman Catholic Church. For thirty years he was an obscure parish priest in small churches in central Pennsylvania, yet the force of his character, his scholarship, and his ability as a musician made him an influence felt throughout the church and the musical world. While stationed at Milton, Pa. (1881–90), he not only built a new church, but conducted a band which took first honors in a contest of 100 bands at Atlantic City. He was also the director of the Williamsport Oratorio Society.

Transferred to Carlisle in 1890, he found a congregation of fewer than thirty-five families worshiping in a little frame church. He turned all his energies again into building, with the result that there rose an ideal small church, perfect in all its appointments and equipped with an organ for which Ganss himself had raised funds by his lectures and writings. At the Easter and Christmas services he played the organ which he had earned, led the choir and orchestra in the rendition of the mass which he had composed, and came down to the pulpit to preach a scholarly and convincing sermon. He took an absorbing interest in the cause of the American Indians, whom he had an opportunity to study at the Carlisle Indian School. In the Indian Missions he labored with zeal and his work was recognized by Cardinal Gibbons, who appointed him financial agent of the Catholic Indian Missions. While on a pilgrimage to Rome he secured the permission of Leo XIII to compile a Catholic Hymnology, but failing health and increased absorption in his writing prevented him from carrying out his plans.

His ecclesiastical music, of which there is a considerable library, was composed before the *Moto Proprio* of Pius IX confined the church to Gregorian plain chant. His work was influenced by the Vienna school of Mozart, Beethoven, and Haydn. It was florid and brilliant but essentially sound. Since his compositions were readily sung and tuneful they were not only widely adopted in the church but were favorites with choral societies. His better-known work included his prize naval hymn, "The Banner of the Sea," commemorating the heroism of the American sailors in the disastrous Samoan hurricane of 1889; a papal hymn, "Long Live the Pope," translated into twenty-five languages; First Mass in D (with orchestra), Second Mass in D (with orchestra), Fourth Mass in F, and Requiem in

D Minor. He was the author of: *History of St. Patrick's Church, Carlisle, Pa.* (1895); *A Critical Review of Mariolatry* (1895); *Mariolatry: New Phases of an Old Fallacy* (1897); and of ten pamphlets dealing with Luther and Reformation subjects, Anglican Orders, and Indian questions. He contributed to the *American Catholic Quarterly Review,* the *American Ecclesiastical Review,* the *Catholic World,* the *Messenger,* the *Ave Maria,* and the *Catholic Encyclopedia,* for which he wrote the article on Martin Luther. As a writer he was a militant controversialist but at the same time a scholar and a gentleman. All his writing was the result of careful and exhaustive study. His library of 5,000 volumes contained some eight hundred titles on Luther. In 1910 he returned to his early home, Lancaster, as rector of St. Mary's Church. Here he died on Christmas Day, 1912, in his fifty-eighth year.

[*Records Am. Cath. Hist. Soc. of Phila.,* June 1914; *St. Vincent College Journal,* XXII, 265; *Cath. News,* Dec. 28, 1912; *Phila. Record,* Dec. 26, 1912; certain family data from a sister, Miss Elizabeth Ganss.]

G. I. C.

GANTT, HENRY LAURENCE (May 20, 1861–Nov. 23, 1919), engineer, industrial leader, was born in Calvert County, Md., the son of Virgil and Mary Jane (Steuart) Gantt. As a boy he displayed marked analytical ability. He attended the McDonogh School in Baltimore County and entered Johns Hopkins University, from which he was graduated at the age of nineteen with the degree of B.A. For three years he taught at the McDonogh School, and then entered Stevens Institute of Technology where he was graduated as a mechanical engineer in 1884. The specialization of his life's work began in 1887 when he became associated with Frederick W. Taylor [*q.v.*], pioneer in scientific industrial management, at the Midvale Steel Company. This association continued for some three years, or until Taylor severed his connection with that firm. Gantt was associated with several firms thereafter until 1897, when he again joined Taylor, first at the Simonds Rolling Machine Company and two years later at the Bethlehem Steel Company. Here he threw all of his abilities and energies into the installation and development of scientific methods of industrial operation; and perfected his task-and-bonus system of wage payment. In 1902 he left Taylor and his work, and opened an office as consulting engineer. One of his major contributions to management engineering and industry was a professional paper, "Training Workmen in Habits of Industry and Cooperation," presented in 1908 to the American Society of Mechanical Engineers, in which he boldly declared that industrial workers were human beings, not machines, and that the policy of driving workmen must give way to a policy of leading. Taylor objected vigorously to this paper, and its presentation brought a break in their personal friendship which was never healed, though Gantt afterward referred to Taylor with great admiration as one who had spent much of his life in trying to establish a basis on which the relations between employer and employee could be made mutually satisfactory (*Industrial Leadership,* p. 28).

At the hearing before the Interstate Commerce Commission in 1910 over an increase in railroad freight rates, Gantt was one of the principal witnesses for the government, developing in his testimony the possibilities of economies in railroad operation that would come from better management. These hearings brought to the American public the first knowledge of the new methods that were in process of development. The years that followed were filled with the struggle of the newer ideas with the old. As consulting engineer, Gantt had as his professional clients some of the most progressive concerns in the United States.

In the course of this work, he wrote his *Work, Wages and Profits* (1913) in which he elaborated his ideas of industrial management and demonstrated his methods of ascertaining the costs of idle men, plant, and equipment. This was followed by *Industrial Leadership* (1916), addresses delivered before the seniors of the Sheffield Scientific School, Yale University, when the World War was demonstrating the need of efficient leadership in war and industry. When the United States declared war on Germany he offered his services and his organization to the government. As a result of this war work he devised a method of visual control of work known as the "Gantt Chart" which was adopted by the United States Shipping Board and the Emergency Fleet Corporation as well as by the Ordnance Department of the United States Army. It is to-day the most widely used analytical presentation of the mechanism of management, and a description by Wallace Clark, *The Gantt Chart* (1922), has been translated into the languages of all industrial nations.

Gantt was essentially a leader, possessed of creative power, high purpose, courage, independence, and tireless energy. His associates had a strong feeling of loyalty to him and made every effort to carry through his plans and win his approval. He never spared himself and he always bore the brunt of hostile criticism during the years of general antagonism to scientific management. He never compromised his high standards of honesty and professional ethics. Though very modest in evaluating his own work, he was vigorous in speech and action to the point of brusqueness when attacking conditions that needed to be improved or remedied. The last year of his life, the first after the close of the World War, was devoted to developing the thought that business and industry must render essential service if they are to survive. In a little book, *Organizing for Work* (1919), published about three months before his death, he enunciated the principle that "the community needs service first, regardless of who gets the profit, because its life depends upon the service it gets." His amplification of this fundamental he expressed thus: "In other words, we have proved in many places that the doctrine of service which has been preached in the churches as religion is not only good economics and eminently practical, but because of the increased production of goods obtained by it, promises to lead us safely through the maze of confusion into which we seem to be headed, and to give us that industrial democracy which alone can afford a basis for industrial peace." He married, Nov. 29, 1899, Mary Eliza Snow, who with a daughter survived him. The single line on his tombstone in Mount Hebron Cemetery, Montclair, N. J., selected by his wife, sums up the motive of his life: "I am among you as he who serveth."

[*Trans. Am. Soc. Mech. Eng.*, XL, 1120 (1920); *Who's Who in America*, 1918–19; *Sen. Doc. 725*, 61 Cong., 3 Sess., IV, 2794 (1911); obituary in *N. Y. Times*, Nov. 25, 1919; personal acquaintance.]

L. P. A.

GARAKONTHIE, DANIEL (*c.* 1600–1676), Iroquois chieftain, friend of the French, was an Onondaga and is thought to be identical with the Sagochiendaghte, a title applied to the head councilor not only of his tribe but of the Iroquois Confederacy, which had its chief council house among the Onondaga. As chief councilor or Sagochiendaghte, he visited Montreal with the embassy of 1654 which came seeking peace. This embassy, which seems to have been the result of Iroquois reverses in the West (L. P. Kellogg, *French Régime in Wisconsin and the Northwest,* 1925, pp. 96–99), was a welcome surprise for the harassed French colonists. In token of their good faith the Iroquois left hostages, among whom was Garakonthie; and it was doubtless at this time that he conceived a strong admiration for French persons and customs. Two years later he returned to Montreal with two rescued prisoners, one of whom was Adrien Jolliet (*Jesuit Relations,* XLI, 255; XLIV, 109).

In a hazardous attempt to make peace, Canada sent to the Iroquois country in 1657 a colony of over fifty Frenchmen, who settled on the Onondaga canton and were destined for capture and torture when in March 1658, by a curious ruse, they made their escape. It is stated, although without positive evidence, that the colony was warned by Garakonthie. He does not appear in the *Jesuit Relations* under his personal name until 1661, when Father Simon le Moyne visited the Iroquois. The chief village of the Onondaga at this time was two miles from the present Manlius, N. Y., on what is known as Indian Hill. Garakonthie and all his warriors went out to meet the Jesuit priest and paid him signal honors. The chief announced himself publicly as the protector of the French, and had near him nineteen captives whom he had rescued from the several Iroquois tribes. He arranged his own cabin as a chapel for the use of the priest, and after a council in which he announced his purpose to unite Onontio (the Indian term for the governor of Canada) and Sagochiendaghte, accompanied Le Moyne to Canada with nine of the rescued captives. The next year he brought as many more to Montreal and despite continued attacks on the colonists by hostile war parties, chiefly from the Mohawk tribe, was received with great honor, loaded with gifts, and returned to his country still more favorably inclined to the French.

In 1664, on a new errand of mercy to Montreal, he was defeated en route by French allied Indians, Algonquian and Montagnais. Nevertheless he refused to take vengeance and made overtures of peace. The next year Father le Moyne died, and Garakonthie on a visit to Quebec in December 1665, delivered an oration of marked eloquence to the spirit of his departed friend. Peace with the Iroquois was finally made in 1667, after the governor had invaded the Mohawk country. During all the period of hostilities, the Onondaga chief had remained true to his purpose. He was called the "Father of the French" and had rescued over sixty white captives from death and torture. On a visit to Quebec during the winter of 1669–70 he declared himself a convert to Christianity and asked for baptism. This ceremony was performed by Bishop Laval in the cathedral at Quebec. The governor, Rémy de Courcelles, stood as godfather, giving in baptism his own name of Daniel; the daughter of the intendant, Mademoiselle Bouteroue, was godmother. Thenceforward the proselyte was firm in his new faith; and he learned to read and write in order to use the sacred books. On a visit to New Netherland (lately become New York), he entered the Protestant church and falling on his knees repeated the Catholic prayers taught him by the Jesuits. Just before his death, at Onondaga, he gave three feasts in which he besought his people to listen to the Jesuit teachings, and when he died he asked to be buried in the French manner. One of the things for which he was noted was his opposition to the sale of liquor in his country. Since the Jesuit missions had, on the whole, little success with the chiefs and warriors of the tribes, the adherence and conversion of a well-known chief like Garakonthie was much exploited. Charlevoix, the Jesuit historian, said of him: "Garakontié, by birth and education a savage, had a noble natural manner, a disposition of much sweetness, a superior genius with much integrity and uprightness of character. His bravery in war, his dextrous diplomacy, his lively spirit in council had acquired for him the greatest esteem in his nation." He was called by the writer of the *Relation* of 1661 "a man of excellent intelligence, a good disposition, fond of the French."

[*The Jesuit Relations and Allied Documents* (73 vols., 1896–1901), ed. by R. G. Thwaites; Thos. Donohoe, *The Iroquois and the Jesuits* (1895), ch. xxii; T. J. Campbell, *Pioneer Priests of North America* (1908), I, 95–100; P. F. X. de Charlevoix, S. J., *Hist. and General Descr. of New France,* transl. by J. G. Shea, III (1868), 41–44, 85, 152, 196.] L. P. K.

GARCELON, ALONZO (May 6, 1813–Dec. 8, 1906), physician, was born in Lewiston, Me., the son of a local farmer, Col. William Garcelon, and Mary Davis. As a boy he worked on his father's farm, and was educated at several private schools. Bowdoin College gave him a degree in arts in 1836. He had paid his way by teaching while going through college and after graduation was principal of Alfred Academy and later of a school at Fryeburg, Me. At the latter town he began to read medicine with Dr. Abiel Hale. Having saved money, he took a course of lectures at Dartmouth Medical College and attracted the attention of the professor in surgery, Reuben D. Muzzey, by the excellence of his dissections. In 1838 Muzzey was called to fill the chair of surgery in the Medical College of Ohio, Cincinnati, whither Garcelon followed him, graduating from the latter institution in 1839. After six months' service as interne in a Cincinnati hospital he returned to his native city to enter into a practise which lasted for sixty-seven years. He is said to have been the first in Maine to operate for mastoid disease and goitre. In addition to his extensive practise, he found time to engage in many local enterprises. He retained his interest in agriculture and operated a farm; built the first cotton-mill in Lewiston; was instrumental in bringing railway connections to the city and was for a time president of the Androscoggin Railroad; took part in the formation of Androscoggin County; was a pioneer in road-making and in the construction of a central highway for the territory east of Lewiston; and with his brother-in-law, William H. Waldron, founded in 1847 the *Lewiston Falls Journal,* of which for some years he was editor. Although a Bowdoin man, he seems to have been much more interested in the local Bates College and Maine State Seminary than in his alma mater. He was active in the formation of the Maine Medical Association and the local county society; he joined the American Medical Association in 1853 and missed but one meeting, that of 1905, held in Oregon. At the outbreak of the Civil War he was at once made surgeon-general of Maine. He served in the first battle of Bull Run, during the Peninsular campaign, and at Antietam. Invalided home for malaria, upon his recovery he rejoined his command and finished four years of service.

Although greatly interested in politics, Garcelon refused to become an organization man. Originally a Whig, he went over to Jackson after his nullification pronouncement but his anti-slavery sympathies later made him a Free-Soiler and then a Republican. He was elected to the state House in 1853 and again in 1857, while in the interim he served as a state senator. The tactics of the Republicans during the Reconstruction period drove him once more into the Democratic fold, and in 1868 he ran unsuccessfully for election to Congress. In 1871 he was elected mayor of Lewiston and in 1879 became the only Democratic governor in the history of Maine. There were three tickets in the field, and as there was no election by the people he was chosen by the legislature. After his governorship he seems to have retired from public life; but, although he gave up some of his other activities, he remained in active medical practise to the last. It is said of him that owing to his many years of constant attendance at the meetings of the American Medical Association he had a larger acquaintance among physicians than any other man in the country. At the session at New Orleans in 1903, when ninety years of age, he was presented with a loving cup by one hundred members of the Association while at the same time the trustees gave him a gold-headed cane. He was a trustee himself from 1882 to 1901 and in the latter year also served as vice-president. Throughout his life he had been exceptionally healthy, and his death in 1906 was due neither to old age nor to any ailment, but to accidental asphyxiation by illuminating gas while he was visiting his daughter at Medford, Mass. Although he read numerous papers at society meetings—delivering one on preventive medicine shortly before his death—none of them was reprinted, and he wrote no major work. He was married twice: in 1841 to Ann Augusta Waldron of Dover, N. H., who bore three sons and a daughter and died in 1857; and in 1859, to Olivia N. Spear, by whom he had one daughter.

[*Jour. Am. Medic. Asso.*, May 16, 1903, and Dec. 15, 1906; *Boston Medic. and Surgic. Jour.*, Dec. 13, 1906; *N. Y. Medic. Jour.*, Dec. 15, 1906; W. L. Burrage in H. A. Kelly and W. L. Burrage, *Am. Medic. Biogs.* (1920); *Lewiston Saturday Journal*, Dec. 8, 1906.]

E. P.

GARCÉS, FRANCISCO TOMÁS HERMENEGILDO (Apr. 12, 1738–July 18, 1781), Spanish missionary-explorer, was born at the Villa Morata del Conde in the kingdom of Aragon, the son of Juan and Antonia Maestro Garcés. His early education he received through the aid of an uncle, Mosen Domingo Garcés, and at the age of sixteen he took holy orders. In 1763, at the age of twenty-five, he was ordained a priest and became a candidate for admission to the College of Santa Cruz de Querétaro in Mexico, there to prepare for mission work among the Indians. In 1768 he was sent as a missionary to the Province of Sonora. His assignment was to San Xavier del Bac, the most northerly mission post and the one most exposed to attack by the Apaches. From this post between 1768 and 1774 he made four expeditions (*entradas*) to points along the Gila and Colorado Rivers. His first and second *entradas* (1768, 1770) took him among the Pimas and his third (1771) among the Yumas on the Colorado. On these expeditions he was convinced of the feasibility of reaching Upper California by routes from Sonora, which conviction was shared by the commander of the *Presidio* at Tubac, Juan Bautista de Anza [*q.v.*]. Accordingly in 1774, Anza, accompanied by Garcés and another religious, Juan Díaz, set forth with a military escort. The expedition proceeded to the Gila-Colorado junction and thence to the mission of San Gabriel in Upper California. From San Gabriel, Garcés returned to the Colorado, Anza passing on to Monterey. In 1775, at the request of Anza, Garcés was permitted by the viceroy to accompany the former on an expedition to California. On this expedition Garcés stopped on the Colorado and made from it important explorations. He descended the river to its mouth, returned up its course, and proceeded to San Gabriel. He next attempted to reach Monterey by a northerly route which took him past the modern Bakersfield to the vicinity of Tulare Lake, but returned to the Colorado River with the intention of proceeding to Moqui (Arizona). This he accomplished, and from Moqui retraced his course to the Colorado and thence went to his mission at San Xavier del Bac. The leader of the Indians at the Gila-Colorado junction was Salvador Palma. He was friendly to Garcés and to the Spaniards and, hoping that he would be showered with gifts, entreated that missions and a *presidio* be established in his country. In 1780 Garcés and Juan Díaz, accompanied by an escort and a group of settlers, reached the Colorado and began the founding of two pueblo missions, La Purísima Concepción and San Pedro y San Pablo de Bicuñer. The expected gifts, however, were not bestowed, and the Indians were grievously disappointed. On July 17 and 18, 1781, under Palma's leadership, the two pueblos were attacked, and Díaz, Garcés, and the Spanish commander of Upper California, Rivera y Moncada, who had arrived at the Colorado, were put to death.

[Elliott Coues, *On the Trail of a Spanish Pioneer; The Diary and Itinerary of Francisco Garcés 1775–76* (2 vols., 1900); C. E. Chapman, *The Founding of Spanish California* (1916); I. B. Richman, *California under Spain and Mexico* (1911); C. A. Engelhardt, *The Missions and Missionaries of California*, vol. II (1912).]

I. B. R.

GARDEN, ALEXANDER (*c.* 1730–Apr. 15, 1791), naturalist, and physician, was the son of Rev. Alexander Garden of Birse Parish, Aberdeenshire, Scotland. He was unusually well grounded in languages, philosophy, mathematics, and the natural sciences, studied under the celebrated Dr. John Gregory at Edinburgh, and was a pupil of Charles Alston, director of the botanical gardens there. In 1753 he graduated with the degree of M.D. from Marischal College, Aberdeen. Soon afterward he went to South Carolina where, in Prince William Parish, he entered into practise and built up a large and fashionable clientele. On Dec. 24, 1755, he was married to Elizabeth Peronneau. He rendered notable service in the smallpox epidemic of 1760 and is said to have amassed a considerable fortune from his practise.

From the first he took an interest in the fauna and flora of South Carolina, partly as an adjunct to the practise of medicine. His health was never good, and in 1754 he was obliged to take a trip northward, going as far as central New York state. Here he met Cadwallader Colden [*q.v.*], philosopher and botanist as well as lieutenant-governor, and saw in his library the first of the Linnæan books that were infusing new life into natural science. On his return he stopped in Philadelphia to visit the enthusiastic Quaker botanist, John Bartram [*q.v.*]. In 1755 he accepted Gov. Glen's invitation to join an expedition to the Cherokee country, which probably took him to the neighborhood of Caesar's Head, in the Blue Ridge Mountains of Greenville County, S. C. His report on the plants and minerals of this expedition was communicated to scientists in England, but apparently was never printed. Soon after his arrival in Charleston, he had begun to correspond with John Ellis, the British naturalist, and by him was encouraged to write to Linnæus. Garden's first letter to the Swedish scientist (dated Mar. 15, 1755) was a diffident and respectful bid for friendship. No reply was received to this or the following letter, but three years later he had an encouraging note. Thereafter for many years his correspondence with Linnæus and Ellis was voluminous and learned; and being well preserved, it forms a delightful and historically precious document in the annals of eighteenth-century science. He was also a correspondent of Thomas Pennant and Peter Collinson in England, Gronovius in Holland, John Clayton [*q.v.*] in Virginia, Colden in New York, and Bartram in Pennsylvania. He sent his friends great quantities of plant specimens, fish, reptiles, and amphibians, with elaborate notes, of which they made excellent use. He also endeavored to propose various new species and genera, some of them justifiable, but was rather discouraged in his attempts by the European naturalists, to whose authority he bowed. He was the discoverer of the vermifugal properties of pink-root (*Spigelia marilandica*), and communicated this intelligence to Linnæus in 1770. He also discovered some remarkable animals, such as *Amphiuma means,* the Congo snake, and the anomalous batrachian called mud eel, *Siren lacertina.* Of these he sent specimens to Europe, and was instrumental, too, in sending the first electric eels. By 1771 he had gained sufficient confidence to dispute with Ellis and Linnæus, and to-day science will support him against these more famous authorities in the belief that the Florida cycad, *Zamia,* is not a fern, that the Carolina jessamine is not a *Bignonia,* and the palmetto not a *Yucca.* Linnæus rewarded his disciple's devotion by having him elected in 1763 a member of the Royal Society of Upsala, a gratifying honor to one who felt himself entirely lonely and unappreciated in his favorite pursuits in a colony too raw for learned interests. He was somewhat piqued by a certain patronizing air on the part of the Royal Society of London toward his manuscripts, but in 1773 accepted a fellowship in that body; and in 1775 his paper, "An Account of the *Gymnotus electricus,*" was read before the Society by Ellis (*Philosophical Transactions,* LXV, 102).

As the storm of the Revolution gathered, Garden sided with his King, and was one of the congratulators of Cornwallis after the battle of Camden. He was banished and his property confiscated by the Act of Feb. 26, 1782, and although in 1784 his property was restored, less an amercement of twelve per cent, he never returned to America. Sea-sickness on the voyage to England in 1783 seriously injured his health; he was already succumbing to tuberculosis. In the hope of recovery he visited Scotland, France, and Switzerland, suffering physically from a round of social activities, though they were grateful to one long deprived of honors and learned intercourse. He assumed the duties and honors of vice-president of the Royal Society, but failing strength soon confined him to his home in Cecil Street, London, where he died, attended by the women of his family. Before his death he is said to have prepared papers on his natural history observations in South Carolina, but unfortunately for science these have not been traced. In person he was apparently a typical Georgian gentleman, refined, metaphysical, proud, touchy, choleric, often intolerant, "fond of good company and particularly of refined female society" (Ramsay, *post,* p. 472). He never forgave his son, Maj. Alexander Garden [*q.v.*], for taking up arms in the Revolutionary cause. The flower *Gardenia* was named in his honor by Ellis.

[See J. E. Smith, *A Selection of the Correspondence of Linnæus and Other Naturalists* (1821); articles "Garden" and "Gardenia" in Abraham Rees's *Cyclopædia,* vol. XV (1819); David Ramsay, *Hist. of S. C.* (1809); P. J. Anderson, *Fasti Academiæ Mariscallanæ,* vol. II (1898); footnote by J. H. Barnhart appended to J. K. Small, "Seminole Bread," in *Jour. N. Y. Bot. Garden,* July 1921, p. 126; Wilson Gee, "South Carolina Botanists," in *Bull. Univ. of S. C.,* Sept. 1918, which is inaccurate in some details; *S. C. Hist. and Geneal. Reg.,* Apr. 1901; *Statutes at Large of S. C.,* IV (1838), 519, 624, V (1839), 631, 634. Some accounts confuse Garden with contemporaries of the same name, since there were several Alexander Gardens of Scotch origin living in Charleston in the middle of the eighteenth century.]

D. C. P.

GARDEN, ALEXANDER (Dec. 4, 1757–Feb. 24, 1829), Revolutionary soldier, author, was born in Charleston, S. C., the son of Dr. Alexander Garden [*q.v.*], the naturalist, and his wife Elizabeth Peronneau. From 1771 to 1775 he was kept at Westminster School, London. Thence he went to college, receiving the M.A. degree from the University of Glasgow in 1779. The same year he was admitted to Lincoln's Inn. He does not appear, however, to have practised law. "His heart from the earliest dawn of the Revolution was devoted to the cause of his country" (*Anecdotes*, p. 2), and while still in school he often declared his wish to aid the Americans (A. S. Salley, Jr., *Journal of the House of Representatives of South Carolina, 1782,* 1916, p. 99), but his father, a stanch Loyalist, forbade his return to America. In 1780, however, he returned to South Carolina and entered the American forces as cornet in Lee's Legion, of Greene's army. The next year he became aide-de-camp to the General, with rank of major (*South Carolina Historical and Genealogical Magazine,* January 1928, p. 23), and he saw active service until the evacuation of Charleston in December 1782. His father, prior to his departure from the state, had left in trust for his son 1,689 acres of land near Goose Creek, a few miles from Charleston. This property was not molested in the confiscation act of February 1782, and it could have been only the petition and service of the son which caused his father's name to be transferred from the confiscation list to that of those amerced twelve per cent (see *Statutes at Large of South Carolina,* vol. IV, 1838, pp. 519, 624–26, and vol. VI, 1839, pp. 613, 634). In 1784 he married Mary Anna Gibbes, and evidently became a planter. He had no children, but adopted his wife's nephew, Alester Gibbes, who took the name Garden and became his heir (Will, Charleston court-house). In 1784 he was elected to the Assembly and served one term. Casual references in his *Anecdotes* tell something of his travels. After the recovery of Charleston, his health being "much impaired," he went to Philadelphia and visited the interior of Pennsylvania and part of New Jersey; he was in England in 1792, again went north in 1817, and in 1826 visited in Virginia. In 1808 he became a member of the South Carolina Society of the Cincinnati; from 1814 to 1826 he was vice-president, and from that time to his death, president. He was in demand for eulogies and orations; he made addresses for the Cincinnati on the deaths of Moultrie and C. C. Pinckney, the eulogy on Pinckney being published at Charleston in 1825. The works for which he is remembered, however, are his *Anecdotes of the Revolutionary War in America* (1822) and *Anecdotes of the American Revolution . . . Second Series* (1828), both published by subscription in Charleston. For the first he had about a thousand subscribers and for the second, about seven hundred. His announced and very apparent purpose was to stimulate the patriotism of youth, but the treatment, while highly laudatory, is not altogether uncritical. The characters and incidents are chiefly South Carolinian, but there is also other material, picked up during his trips north and abroad. The volumes are a valuable source for the Revolution; they are entertainingly written, and bear out the author's claim to his maxim, "With mirth and laughter let old wrinkles come" (Conclusion, *Second Series*). "An abridged and vitiated edition" (Salley, *post*) of both volumes was issued in Brooklyn in 1865, under the editorship of Thomas Warren Field [*q.v.*].

[See Garden's *Anecdotes*; E. A. Jones, *Am. Members of the Inns of Court* (London, 1924), pp. 84–85; A. S. Salley, Jr., in *S. C. Hist. and Geneal. Mag.,* Apr. 1901, pp. 126–27; *The Original Institution of the General Society of the Cincinnati* (1880). Jones states that Garden returned to Glasgow to take the M.D. degree, but is probably confusing him with the son of the Rev. Alexander Garden of St. Thomas's Parish—see R. F. Clute, *Annals of St. Thomas* (1884), pp. 14, 32, 61, 100.]

R. L. M—r.

GARDENER, HELEN HAMILTON (Jan. 21, 1853–July 26, 1925), author, first woman member of the United States Civil Service Commission, was Alice Chenoweth by birth, the daughter of Rev. Alfred Griffith and Katherine A. (Peel) Chenoweth. She was born in Winchester, Va., and through her father was descended from a Welsh ancestor who settled in Maryland about 1700. She was graduated from the Cincinnati, Ohio, high school, from the Ohio State Normal School in 1872, and in 1873–74 was principal of the Ohio Branch State Normal School. At twenty-two she married Charles Selden Smart, who died in 1898. Three years later she was married to Col. Selden Allen Day, U. S. A. Like her father, who had broken away from political and religious traditions, she was independent in her thinking. She also demanded a substantial basis for her ideas and after her brief teaching experience studied biology, medicine, and sociology in New York. Becoming a friend of Robert G. Ingersoll, she spent her Sunday evenings in his home for years and probably through his influence became agnostic and wrote in defense of agnosticism. In addition to her writing she lectured on sociological subjects at the Brooklyn Institute of Arts and Sciences and in university extension courses. Early in her career she adopted the name Helen Hamilton Gardener, by which she was thereafter known, in private as well as public life. As an editor of the *Arena* she contributed articles on humanitarian and feminist subjects. Two volumes of her essays were published as *Men, Women and Gods* (1885), and *Facts and Fictions of Life* (1893). Her first stories, written for *Belford's Magazine.* drew a complimentary letter from Oliver Wendell Holmes. Several novels followed: *Is This Your Son, My Lord?* (1890), dealing with the double moral standard; *A Thoughtless Yes* (1890); *Pray You, Sir, Whose Daughter?*

(1892); *Pushed by Unseen Hands* (1892); and *An Unofficial Patriot* (1894). The last is a story of a Virginian who, leaving the Episcopal church to become a Methodist minister, freed his slaves, removed to Indiana, and joined the Union army. It is to a large extent the story of her own father's life and is considered her best novel. Under the title *Griffith Davenport, Circuit Rider,* it was dramatized by James A. Herne [*q.v.*]. Though she wrote with a directness and a vigor derived from deep feeling for her themes, her narrative style is without subtlety or distinctive art.

As an advocate of woman's suffrage Helen Gardener was associated with Susan B. Anthony, Anna Howard Shaw, and Elizabeth Cady Stanton. In the National American Woman's Suffrage Association she was known as the "Diplomatic Corps," having won, as vice-chairman of its congressional committee, the respect and support of senators and congressmen. She also held in the association the office of vice-president. Before the International Council of Women, assembled by the National American Woman's Suffrage Association at Washington, D. C., in March 1888, she read her paper, "Sex in Brain," which was prepared after fourteen months of biological study. It was prompted by statements of Dr. W. A. Hammond, surgeon-general of the United States, supporting the contention that brains of men and women are structurally different. To disprove this, Mrs. Gardener consulted many brain specialists and studied in the laboratory of Dr. E. C. Spitzka of New York before writing her paper. Her conclusion was that no general differences in weight or complexity of convolutions can be detected between brains of males and females. At sixty-seven, after ill health had made her fear that her work was over, she was appointed United States civil service commissioner by President Wilson, Apr. 13, 1920. In suffrage activities and as commissioner, she was so strictly non-partisan that many of her friends did not know her political preferences. She died in the summer of 1925 at Walter Reed Hospital, in Washington. According to her direction, no religious service was held at her funeral, which took place at her home on Lamont Street. Instead, friends and colleagues spoke of her life and work. By her will she left her brain to Cornell University for research.

[*Who's Who in America,* 1899–1900, 1924–25; Rena B. Smith, "Commissioner Helen H. Gardener," the *Business Woman,* Jan. 1923; Cora Rigby, "The Diplomatic Corps," the *Woman Citizen,* May 2, 1925, J. W. Papez, "The Brain of Helen H. Gardener," *Am. Jour. Physical Anthropol.,* Oct.–Dec. 1927; the *Woman Citizen,* Sept. 5, 1925; *N. Y. Times,* July 27, Aug. 4, Sept. 3, 1925; information from Mrs. Helen Gardener Colton, of Washington, D. C., a great-niece of Helen Gardener.]

S. G. B.

GARDINER, Sir CHRISTOPHER (fl. 1630–1632), sojourner in the Massachusetts Bay Colony, is one of the minor mysteries of American history. The spot-light plays on him luridly for about three years. Before and after is darkness, yet few relatively obscure characters have appeared more often in American fiction and poetry than he and "his wench." He arrived in Massachusetts about a month before the ships bringing the Puritans in June 1630. Gov. Bradford of Plymouth wrote that he brought a "servant or 2, and a comly yonge woman, whom he caled his cousin, but it was suspected, she (after ye Italian maner) was his concubine" (*History of Plimoth Plantation,* 1899, pp. 352 ff.). He built a house about seven miles from Boston and was unmolested for some months. Then the storm broke. His presence was a puzzle to the Puritans. He said that he was connected with the family of Stephen Gardyner, Bishop of Winchester, but no one knows yet of what family he came. He also asserted that he had traveled widely and had been made a Knight of the Holy Sepulchre. At any rate his title was recognized by officials in England. He was a man of education and apparently had a university degree or two but whence derived is unknown. He said that he had come to the colony merely to retire from the world. Presently, however, word came from Isaac Allerton, agent of the colony in London, that he had met not one but two wives of the Knight, one of whom he had deserted in Paris and the other in London, and that they were now living together, the one calling for his return and conversion, the other for his destruction. The Massachusetts Court of Assistants then (Mar. 1, 1631) ordered that he be sent to England as a prisoner. Gardiner fled to the woods. A reward being offered for his capture, some Indians took him to Bradford at Plymouth, who shipped him to Winthrop at Boston, together with an incriminating note-book showing him to be a Papist.

While he was in jail, a packet of letters arrived for him from Maine in care of Winthrop, who opened and read them. They included one from Sir Ferdinando Gorges which proved that Gardiner was his agent. Undoubtedly he had acted as such from the beginning and his purpose in settling near Boston had been to watch the actions of the Puritans. Winthrop prudently decided to drop the matter and Gardiner was free to go. There was now no reason for his remaining. His mistress, Mary Grove, had been arrested and questioned when he had first fled, but nothing could be got from her, and with grim Puritan humor it was ordered that she be shipped to the other two wives in Old England. The sentence was not carried out, and a certain Thomas Purchase from Brunswick, Me., coming to Boston, married her, and all three went back to Brunswick for the winter. Gardiner remained there with them until the following summer, consoling himself in the long winter, as transpired in a law suit nine years later, with a stolen warming pan. By Aug. 15, 1632, he had appeared at Bristol, England, and in the effort of Gorges to break the Massachusetts charter before the Privy Council in January 1632/3, Gardiner was one of the star witnesses against the colony. Then all becomes a blank. The Knight and his lawfully wedded wives disappear; and history records only the death, many years after, of Mary Grove, the "known harlot," who lived the rest of her life a respectable married woman on the Androscoggin and became "the little lady with golden hair" of Longfellow's poem.

[The best account is that by C. F. Adams in *Proc. Mass. Hist. Soc.*, I ser., XX (1884), 60–88. He has a shorter account in his *Three Episodes of Mass. Hist.*, I (1892), 250–68. For contemporary accounts, see Wm. Bradford, *Hist. of Plimoth Plantation* (1899), pp. 352 ff.; letters from Thos. Wiggin, in *Mass. Hist. Soc. Colls.*, 3 ser., VIII (1843), 320–24; Gov. Dudley's letter in Alex. Young, *Chron. of the First Planters of the Colony of Mass. Bay* (1846), p. 333.] J. T. A.

GARDINER, JAMES TERRY (May 6, 1842–Sept. 10, 1912), engineer, was born in Troy, N. Y., the son of Daniel and Ann (Terry) Gardiner, both of New England ancestry. With little education he achieved success as a surveyor, a pioneer in the field of public health, and a leader in the coal industry. He studied for a short time at both Rensselaer Polytechnic Institute and the Sheffield Scientific School. He was little more than a boy, however, when he secured a position on the Brooklyn Water Works; and he was under twenty when he became an inspector of the United States Ordnance Corps in 1861. During the Civil War he gained considerable experience through the construction of the earthworks around the harbor of San Francisco. On the conclusion of peace he became chief topographer of the United States Geological Survey of the Fortieth Parallel and continued with the survey until 1873, establishing the elevations of various datum points on the Great Lakes and in the Rocky Mountains. In 1876 he was appointed director of the state survey of New York. His address at the annual meeting of the American Public Health Association on "The Relations of Topographical Surveys and Maps to Public Health Studies," Oct. 6, 1876, was subsequently published by that organization in *Public Health—Reports and Papers* (1877). He also made a special report on the preservation of the scenery of Niagara Falls (1879). From 1880 to 1886, he was a member of the state board of health and was largely instrumental in establishing proper sewerage systems throughout the state. His reputation and influence, however, were more than local.

As early as 1875 he had made a report on the coal and iron fields of Colorado; and after serving as president of the Street Railroad & Lighting Company of St. Joseph, Mo. (1892–95), he became vice-president of the coal companies of the Erie Railroad. In 1899 he was elected president of the Mexican Coke & Coal Company. Although he seems to have made no technical contribution to the industry, he was a successful executive and administrator and served acceptably as director of a number of coal companies, railroads, and other subsidiary enterprises. In all these undertakings he was noted for his versatility and for his readiness to sense the larger implications of the problem with which he was concerned. In 1868 he married Josephine Rogers, who died four years later; in 1881 he married Eliza Greene Doane, daughter of Bishop William Croswell Doane, of Albany, N. Y.

[C. E. Robinson, *The Gardiners of Narragansett* (1919); Stephen Terry, *Notes on the Terry Families in the U. S.* (1887); *Who's Who in America*, 1912–13; obituaries in *Engineering and Mining Jour.*, Sept. 14, 1912, and *Albany Evening Jour.*, Sept. 11, 1912.] R. P. B—r.

GARDINER, JOHN (Dec. 4, 1737–Oct. 15, 1793), lawyer, was the eldest son of Silvester Gardiner [*q.v.*] and his first wife, Anne Gibbins (or Gibbons). Born in Boston, in his early years he attended the local schools there, but in 1748 was sent to England to complete his education. In 1752 he matriculated at the University of Glasgow, where he graduated M.A. in 1755. He was admitted as a student at the Inner Temple Jan. 23, 1758, reading in the chambers of Charles Pratt, who subsequently as Lord Camden became Lord Chancellor. Called to the English bar June 5, 1761, and joining the Welsh Circuit, Gardiner achieved a measure of success in assize work and in London circles was known as an ardent Whig. Making the acquaintance of Wilkes, Churchill, and other extreme radicals, he became a strong advocate of their cause, and was retained as counsel for Wilkes on his trial, also appearing in a like capacity for the latter's supporters, Breadmore and Meredith. In 1766 he was offered the chief-justiceship of New York and two years later (1768) accepted appointment as attorney-general of the island of St. Christopher in the West Indies, taking up his residence there the same year with his wife. His avowed Whig sympathies, however, impelled the British government to remove him from office (see *The Argument or Speech of John Gardiner Esqre., Barrister at Law who stood Committed by the Pretended Assembly of this Island for a Pretended Contempt,* St. Christopher, 1770). He continued in practise for some years on the Island, but in 1783 returned to Boston, being there naturalized as a citizen by special act of the legislature in February 1784. He quickly came to the front at the Boston bar, at the same time participating in the local political controversies. In 1786 he removed to Pownalboro in the District of Maine. Here he practised law and was elected to the Massachusetts General Court as representative of the town in 1789. All his life a zealous advocate of reform and somewhat of a free lance, he occupied a conspicuous place in the public eye by reason of the bold stand he took in reference to current questions. When residing in Boston he had been instrumental in handing over the Episcopalian King's Chapel to the Unitarians, and when he was a member of the General Court he vehemently advocated the repeal of the existing laws against theatres. His speech, in favor of public dramatic performances, delivered in the House on Jan. 26, 1792, was published in pamphlet form in that year together with his "Dissertation on the Ancient Poetry of the Romans." His one outstanding legislative achievement was the abolition of entails and the repeal of the law of primogeniture in Massachusetts. He was also a strenuous advocate of simplicity in the procedure of the courts and abrogation of the technicalities of "special pleading." His pertinacity in prosecuting these and other changes in the existing law caused him to be known as "the law reformer" throughout the commonwealth. In his early days an advanced Whig, in his later years a convinced Republican, tenacious in his convictions, eloquent in their expression, an accomplished lawyer and somewhat of a wit, he seemed destined for high office, but his career was cut short by drowning when the *Londoner,* the vessel in which he was traveling to Boston for the purpose of attending the legislature, was wrecked off Cape Ann. Gardiner was married (*c.* 1764) to Margaret Harries, daughter of George Harries, of Haverfordwest, Wales. Their son John Sylvester John Gardiner [*q.v.*] was for twenty-five years rector of Trinity Church, Boston.

[E. A. Jones, *Am. Members of the Inns of Court* (1924), p. 85; J. H. Stark, *The Loyalists of Mass.* (1910), pp. 313–15; W. T. Davis, *The Bench and Bar of Mass.* (1895), I, 239–40; T. C. Amory, *Life of Jas. Sullivan* (1859), I, 270; C. E. Robinson, *The Gardiners of Narragansett* (1919); B. E. Packard, *An Address . . . before the Kennebec Hist. Soc. . . . on John Gardiner* (1923); H. W. Foote, *Annals of King's Chapel* (1896), II, 147, 189.]

H. W. H. K.

GARDINER, JOHN SYLVESTER JOHN (June 1765–July 29, 1830), Episcopal clergyman, was born at Haverfordwest, Wales, the son of John [*q.v.*] and Margaret (Harries) Gardiner. His father was a native of Boston, Mass., but having studied law in London at the Inner Temple, was admitted to the English bar and in 1768 accepted the appointment of attorney-general of the island of St. Christopher in the British West Indies. There he settled with his wife and infant son. From his fifth to his ninth year the younger John lived in Boston with his grandfather, Silvester Gardiner [*q.v.*], one of the most eminent physicians of his day and the founder of the town of Gardiner, Me. At this time he attended Master Lovell's school. He then studied in England under the famous educator, Dr. Samuel Parr, whose strict discipline and thorough classical training helped form the leading traits of Gardiner's character and mind. Returning to St. Christopher in 1782, Gardiner came to Boston the following year with his father, who even when holding office under the Crown had openly and warmly defended the principles of the Revolution, and there took up the study of law with his father and with Judge William Tudor. His interest soon turned to divinity, however, and after serving as lay reader at Pownalboro, Me., he was ordained deacon in New York City on Oct. 18, 1787, and priest on Dec. 4, 1791, by Bishop Provoost. His first church was in the parish of St. Helena, Beaufort, S. C. In 1792 he was elected assistant to Dr. Samuel Parker of Trinity Church, Boston, on the Greene Foundation. On Sept. 24, 1794, he married Mary Howard (*Boston Marriages, 1752–1809,* 1903, p. 465). Finding his income insufficient for his needs, he taught a large classical school in conjunction with his parish work, and with such ability that in the words of Dr. Doane, his successor at Trinity, "From the establishment of his school the revival, in this community, of classical learning may be dated." Becoming the rector of Trinity Church upon the death of Dr. Parker in 1805, he dispensed with an assistant for twenty years in order that the capital of the Greene Foundation might accumulate. At the same time he continued to teach a select class of boys in his own house, although he gave up his large school. "The events of Dr. Gardiner's ministry melt together into one smooth and even flow of prosperous life," says Bishop Phillips Brooks, but "the enduring monument of his performances" was the completion in 1829 of a new church, the services in which he lived only long enough to begin.

As a clergyman he was a devoted adherent of the Church of England doctrines and was contemptuous of those who worshipped without liturgy. As a preacher he sought to win rather than alarm his hearers to the attainment of virtue and faith. In politics he was a friend of England and a bitter enemy of France, his opinion of the French revolutionists being vigorously expressed in his pamphlet, *Remarks on the Jacobiniad* (1795). His knowledge of the Greek and Latin classics was profound and he also read Italian and French. The hospitality and kindness of his nature counteracted a somewhat blunt and uncompromising manner and a decided frankness in his likes and dislikes, which might otherwise have made him enemies. In April 1830 he sailed for England, hoping to restore his health which was failing under his unceasing devotion to duty. After a stormy voyage he arrived at Liverpool much exhausted and died peacefully in the presence of his wife and daughter at Harrowgate on July 29, 1830. He was president of the famous Anthology Club from its foundation Oct. 3, 1805, until his withdrawal in 1810, and as such helped to conduct the *Monthly Anthology and Boston Review,* the forerunner of the *North American Review.* He was also one of the founders of the Boston Athenæum. Many of his sermons and addresses delivered between 1802 and 1824 have been published.

[C. E. Robinson, *The Gardiners of Narragansett* (1919); Josiah Quincy, *Hist. of the Boston Athenæum with Biog. Notices of Its Deceased Founders* (1851); G. W. Doane, *The Voice of the Departed: a Sermon Preached in Trinity Ch., Boston on Sunday Sept. 12, 1830* (1830); Phillips Brooks, *Hist. Sermon at Consecration Services of Trinity Church, Boston, Feb. 9, 1877* (1877); *Trinity Church in the City of Boston: An Historical and Descriptive Account* (1888); W. B. Sprague, *Annals Am. Pulpit,* vol. V (1859).]

S. H. P.

GARDINER, LION (1599–1663), colonist, military engineer, was of English stock. In 1635 he was serving in the army of the Prince of Orange in the Low Countries, with the special work of designing fortifications. While on that service he met and married Mary Wilemson of Woerdon, Holland, and became friendly, at Rotterdam, with the Rev. Hugh Peter, John Davenport [*qq.v.*], and others interested in New England colonization. By them he was persuaded to emigrate to Connecticut under a contract with the patentees of the Earl of Warwick, proprietors of the new colony to be planted there. He was to remain four years, to design and erect the defenses for the settlements, and apparently to have charge of the military protection of the colony. In return, he and his family were to have free transportation and he was to receive a salary of £100 a year. The group interested in the project included Lord Brooke, Lord Saye and Sele, and George Fenwick [*q.v.*]. Gardiner and his wife arrived in Boston Nov. 28, 1635, and his knowledge was at once requisitioned by the Massachusetts Bay government, which employed him to design and build a new fort at the harbor. Early in the spring of the following year he took his wife and went to Saybrook, the settlement of the Warwick patentees at the mouth of the Connecticut River, where, as called for in his contract, he built a fort and remained four years. During his stay and while responsible for the safety of the small settlement, the Pequot War broke out. Gardiner was not at all in sympathy with the somewhat stupid course pursued by Massachusetts which brought on the war. "You come hither to raise these wasps about my ears," he protested to Endecott, "and then you will take wing and flee away." The fort was attacked by the savages in the spring of 1637 and well defended by Gardiner. When a joint expedition set out against the Indians in May he was given authority with Mason and Underhill to plan the campaign, which culminated in the great fight at Mystic, May 26, the razing of the Pequot fort, and the extermination of the greater part of the tribe.

On Apr. 29, 1636, Gardiner's son David was born, the first white child born in the settlement, and on Aug. 30, 1638, his daughter Mary. In order, probably, to provide for his family, he bought the Isle of Wight, now called Gardiner's Island, from the Indians, and moved his family there upon the termination of his contract with the proprietors of the Saybrook Colony. There in 1641 his daughter Elizabeth was born. Later he received a grant from the agent of the Earl of Stirling and Gov. Nicoll confirmed the title to the island to Gardiner's son David in 1665 and in 1686 Gov. Dongan erected it into a manor, with full legal manorial rights. The property remains intact in the family to-day. In 1649 Gardiner was one of the purchasers of a tract of about 30,000 acres on which Easthampton now stands, and in 1653 he moved over to Long Island and settled on the main street of the new village. There with his family he lived a peaceful life until his death at the age of sixty-four, exerting a most important influence over the Indians, largely through his close friendship with Wyandanch.

[Gardiner is mentioned by Winthrop and Bradford but the main source of information is his own "Relation of the Pequot Warres" first printed in *Mass. Hist. Soc. Colls.*, 3 ser. III, 131–60. Errors in the introduction to this narrative were corrected by Alexander Gardiner in *Mass. Hist. Soc. Colls.*, 3 ser. X, 185. The best edition of the *Relation* is that published by the Acorn Club (Hartford, 1901). Many of Gardiner's letters have been printed in the Winthrop Papers, *Mass. Hist. Soc. Colls.*, 4 ser. VII, 5 ser. I. Additional information about the family may be found in C. C. Gardiner, *Lion Gardiner and his Descendants* (1890) and *The Papers and Biog. of Lion Gardiner* (privately printed, 1883).]

J. T. A.

GARDINER, ROBERT HALLOWELL (Feb. 10, 1782–Mar. 22, 1864), agriculturist, public benefactor, was born at Bristol, England, son of Robert and Hannah (Gardiner) Hallowell, Loyalist refugees. His father, collector of customs at Boston, had left the city when the British army evacuated it in 1776. On his mother's side Robert was descended from George Gardiner who settled at Aquidneck, R. I., in 1638. The Hallowells seem to have come originally to Connecticut from Devonshire, England. In 1787, at the age of five, Robert inherited the large estate of his maternal grandfather, Dr. Silvester Gardiner [*q.v.*], on the Kennebec River in Maine. The Hallowell family having returned to Boston in 1792, the boy attended for brief periods the Boston Latin School and Phillips Academy at Andover. Later he studied privately with an excellent classicist and at Derby Academy in Hingham. He graduated from Harvard in 1801, second in his class. After two years in England and France observing agricultural and manufacturing methods he embarked upon the management of his estate, assuming the surname Gardiner to comply with his grandfather's will. The young proprietor broke the entail by which the estate was held, believing such arrangements to be un-American and undemocratic. On June 25, 1805, he married Emma Jane Tudor.

He was greatly interested in the advancement of agriculture. The farm which he had reserved as a home he developed as a model by the introduction of superior breeds of animals, improved machinery, and valuable fruits and grains. He fostered agricultural societies. He conceived and took the lead in founding the Gardiner Lyceum, established at Gardiner in 1821 and incorporated in 1822, by which he sought to provide a vocational technical school which would meet needs not served by the traditional liberal education of the time. The Lyceum gave instruction in "mathematics, mechanics, navigation, and those branches of natural philosophy and chemistry which are calculated to make scientific farmers and skilful mechanics." It appears to have been the forerunner of American agricultural and technical schools, and also to have been the first institution of its kind to receive grants of public money from a state legislature. After a few years of prosperity, waning interest caused the withdrawal of state aid. Gardiner for a time was the main support of the institution, which came to an end in 1832 when he gave it up because of financial reverses. A leader in the upbuilding of his local community, he was also active in the missionary and educational work of the Protestant Episcopal Church. When the Sunday-school movement was started, he founded such a school in his own church at Gardiner, Me. He was a member of the Maine House of Representatives in 1822, an overseer of Bowdoin College 1811–41, and a trustee, 1841–60. For eleven years, 1846–55, he served as president of the Maine Historical Society, to the *Collections* of which he made several contributions. His death occurred in his eighty-third year.

[See S. L. Boardman, "The School at Gardiner, Me.," in L. H. Bailey, *Cyc. of Am. Agric.*, vol. IV (1909). The same volume contains a memoir written by a grandson. An extended account of Gardiner by George Burgess appears in *Me. Hist. Soc. Colls.*, vol. VII (1876). See also William Willis in *Me. Hist. Soc. Colls.*, vol. V (1857); C. L. Robinson, *The Gardiners of Narragansett* (1919); *U. S. Literary Gazette*, Aug. 15, 1825; *Boston Daily Advertiser*, Mar. 25, 1864.]

R. H. G.

GARDINER, SILVESTER (June 29, 1708–Aug. 8, 1786), Loyalist physician and landowner, a descendant of George Gardiner (1600–1645) who sailed from Bristol to Boston on the *Fellowship* (June 1637), and seventh child of William Gardiner, cordwainer, by his wife Abigail Remington, was born in South Kingston, R. I. He was a sickly child and was educated privately at Boston by his brother-in-law, the Rev. James MacSparran [*q.v.*], a classical scholar who tutored a few of the sons of the more wealthy colonists. As Silvester showed early an aptitude for medicine, MacSparran encouraged this bent, and made it possible for him to study for eight years abroad, beginning about 1727. In London Gardiner came under William Cheselden, surgeon to St. Thomas's Hospital, from whom he learned to do the lateral operation for kidney stone. He studied also in Paris, but disliked that city. On returning to Boston (*c.* 1735) he soon found himself engaged in an extensive and lucrative practise, and his marriage to the daughter of a wealthy Boston physician proved no obstacle to his advancement (Webster, *post*, p. 5). Feeling that drugs were then improperly dispensed in Boston, he established his own apothecary shop at the "Sign of the Unicorn and Mortar" on Winter and Tremont Streets (*Boston Gazette*, June 19, 1744), the venture proving so profitable that he opened similar shops in Meriden and Hartford, Conn. Meanwhile his fame as a surgeon had spread, and on Oct. 8, 1741, he successfully removed in the presence of the "Medical

Society of Boston" a large stone from the kidney of a boy of six (*Boston Weekly News-Letter,* Nov. 5–13, 1741). In his only medical publication, which was issued as a broadside in March 1761, he proposed the foundation of a hospital for smallpox. This work is entitled: *To the Freeholders and other Inhabitants of the Town of Boston* (reprinted in *Proceedings of the Massachusetts Historical Society,* 1 ser., IV, 1860, pp. 325–28).

In 1753 Gardiner began his activities in developing land in Maine. Under the charter of the Kennebec Company, of which he was the chief promoter, title was gained to land extending for seven miles on each side of the Kennebec River and inland for fifty miles from the mouth. He invested large sums in settling this area (about 100,000 acres), and the towns of Pittston and Gardiner were built by him. These activities soon involved him in legal dispute, and in 1767 six controversial pamphlets appeared at Boston in which the facts of one of his suits, that against James Flagg, were variously set forth. Others appeared in 1770.

Gardiner was energetic and public-spirited, with broad and liberal views. He built a large house and lavishly entertained many of the important persons of his time. During the events preceding the Revolution he established himself as an ardent Loyalist, and when Washington took command of the Continental Army at Dorchester, Gardiner's property had already been confiscated. He was forced to flee to Halifax in ignominious circumstances. From there he went to New York, where he remained till October 1778, when he embarked for England. On arrival in London he applied for subsistence to Lord George Germain, at whose recommendation he was given a yearly allowance of £150 from the Treasury (*Coke,* p. 218). Early in 1785 he returned to America and settled in Newport, R. I. After some trouble he eventually recovered a small part of his land in Maine, but his house and apothecary shop had been destroyed, and his library of 500 volumes sold at auction by William Cooper in 1778–79 (Hanson, *post,* p. 88). He died suddenly of fever, in 1786, and was buried at Trinity Church, Newport. A portrait by Copley is still in the family. Gardiner was married three times: first, on Dec. 11, 1732, at King's Chapel, to Anne, daughter of Dr. John Gibbins (or Gibbons), who bore him six children, their eldest son being John Gardiner [*q.v.*]; second, about 1772, to Mrs. Love Eppes (baptized Abigail), widow of William Eppes and daughter of Benjamin Pickman of Salem; and third, on Feb. 18, 1785, to Catherine Goldthwait, forty-five years his junior. There were no children by his last two marriages.

[Sources include: L. M. and C. M. Gardiner, *Gardiner Hist. and Geneal.* (1907); C. E. Robinson, *The Gardiners of Narragansett* (1919); Wilkins Updike, *The Hist. of the Episc. Ch. of Narragansett* (2nd ed., 1907), ed. by Daniel Goodwin; J. W. Hanson, *Hist. of Gardiner, Pittston and West Gardiner . . . with Geneal. Sketches of Many Families* (1852); H. S. Webster, *Silvester Gardiner* (Gardiner, Me., Hist. Ser. No. II, 1913); R. F. Seybolt, "Lithotomies Performed by Dr. Gardiner, 1738 and 1741," *New Eng. Jour. of Med.,* Jan. 16, 1930; E. L. Gilmore, *Hist. of Christ Ch., Gardiner, Me.* (1893); *Me. Hist. Soc. Colls.,* II (1847), 405; J. H. Stark, *The Loyalists of Mass.* (1910); *The Royal Commission on the Losses and Services of American Loyalists 1783 to 1785. Being the notes of Mr. Daniel Parker Coke, M.D.* (Roxburghe Club pub., Oxford, 1915), ed. by H. E. Egerton; E. A. Jones, *The Loyalists of Mass.* (1930); H. W. Foote, *Annals of King's Chapel* (2 vols., 1882); *Hamilton's Itinerarium, 1744* (1907); *Newport Mercury,* Aug. 14, 1786. In the British Museum there is an undated MS (Add. 15493) of fifty-eight pages entitled "Observations on Newfoundland" said to have been written by "Silv. Gardiner."]

J. F. F.

GARDNER, CALEB (Jan. 24, 1739–Dec. 24, 1806), merchant, Revolutionary "hero," was born in Newport, R. I., the son of William and Mary (Carr) Gardner and a descendant of George Gardiner who was an inhabitant of Newport in 1638. Following the New England maritime tradition he went to sea when young, rising to command and then coming ashore to engage in trade. It seems probable that he was connected with the slave-trade to some extent. He became one of the most prominent and prosperous residents of Newport during the last quarter of the century. In 1775, he was first captain in Col. William Richmond's regiment of militia; in 1776 as major and then lieutenant-colonel of the 1st Rhode Island Regiment, he was active in the construction of the Newport defenses. He was elected deputy from Newport in the General Assembly in 1777 and in 1779 was a member of the Rhode Island council of war. A year later, after being reëlected to the Deputies, he was promoted to the Assistants, the upper house. His chief claim to fame was his piloting of the French fleet into Newport. It has been stated that this was during D'Estaing's visit in 1778, but it actually occurred in 1780 when De Ternay arrived with a fleet convoying Rochambeau's transports. The Newport residents had kept their regular pilots cruising for weeks on the lookout for the fleet, but the French sighted none of them and arrived at Newport on July 11. Gardiner, accompanied by several other gentlemen, rowed out to the *Duc de Bourgogne,* De Ternay's flagship, and piloted her through the difficult passage himself. It is said he later received a reward from Louis XVI for this service. Gardner was one of three men who purchased the hulls of the British frigates sunk in 1778 with the prospect of salvaging them. He was later commissioned to rebuild the lighthouse destroyed by the British when they evacuated Newport in 1779. After the Revolution, he was an assistant in the General Assembly in 1787–90 and in 1792. He served as French vice-consul and was president of a bank and a warden of Trinity Church. He was married three times: to Sarah Ann Robinson, June 3, 1770; to Sarah Fowler, Apr. 17, 1788; and to Mary, daughter of Gov. John Collins, Oct. 20, 1799. He owned a negro boy named Newport Gardner who became noted for his education, was later freed, and went to Liberia in 1825.

[C. E. Robinson, *The Gardiners of Narragansett* (1919), pp. 25, 66; *The Biog. Cyc. of Representative Men of R. I.* (1881); G. C. Mason, *Reminiscences of Newport* (1884), pp. 77, 154–59; E. M. Stone, *Our French Allies* (1884), p. 290; *Records of the Colony of R. I.*, vol. VII, 1770–76 (1862), pp. 201, 403, 456, 599; *Records of the State of R. I.*, vol. VIII, 1776–79 (1863), pp. 218, 616; vol. IX, 1780–83 (1864), pp. 3, 58, 702; vol. X, 1784–92 (1865), pp. 239, 280, 479; *R. I. Hist. Soc. Colls.*, VI (1867), 153.] R. G. A—n.

GARDNER, CHARLES KITCHEL (June 24, 1787–Nov. 1, 1869), soldier, journalist, was born in Morris County, N. J., the son of Thomas Gardner, a veteran of the Revolution, and his wife, Sarah Kitchel. He was descended from John Gardner who is said to have come from London to New Jersey in 1680. When Charles was but four years old, his family moved to Newburgh on the Hudson, where he received his early training. In 1808, while studying medicine under Dr. Hosack, he received an appointment as ensign in the 6th Regiment of Infantry, United States Army, and turned his attention toward a military career. He rose to be adjutant-general and is said to have refused a brevet of lieutenant-colonel. In September 1815, at the instigation of Maj.-Gen. Ripley, with whom he had a personal quarrel, he was arrested and court-martialed. He was found guilty of conduct unbecoming an officer and a gentleman and of disrespectful conduct and language, but not guilty of cowardice or neglect of duty. The court criticized Ripley's conduct, saying "Where the principal charges . . . have related to events long elapsed . . . and the present occasion of the arrest was a personal difference . . . the discipline of the army would not have suffered by his [Ripley's] obeying the dictates of delicacy" (*Daily National Intelligencer*, Feb. 23, 1816). Gardner was recommissioned adjutant-general of the Army of the North and in that capacity signed the Division Orders of May 22, 1816, for the light artillery and infantry in his division to be permanently designated by the first letter of the alphabet, which he claims (*Dictionary*, p. 85) inaugurated the present system in the United States army.

He resigned from the army in March 1818 and married Ann Eliza McLean. The couple took up their residence in New York City, where Gov. DeWitt Clinton [*q.v.*] appointed Gardner police justice and later deputy commissioner-general. In 1819 he published a *Compend of the United States System of Infantry Exercise and Manoeuvres*, and in the following year, *Regulations for Light Infantry and Riflemen.* In June 1820 he edited the first number of the *Literary and Scientific Repository, and Critical Review* (New York), which publication continued until May 1822. His next journalistic venture was the *New York Patriot*, the first number of which appeared May 28, 1823. It was generally believed that John C. Calhoun and Henry Wheaton [*qq.v.*] were responsible for the organization of this paper. Intended to supplant the *National Advocate*, which was thought disloyal to Republican principles, it was made the organ of Tammany Hall. Maj. Mordecai Manuel Noah [*q.v.*], the able and relentless editor of the *National Advocate*, launched a counter attack, seized upon Gardner's political record, charged him with turning from Clinton to the army group of Calhoun, and made many allusions to the court martial. The editorial battle was stiff and amusing. Gardner assumed an air of injured innocence and aloofness in the face of the ruthless attacks by Noah. The *Patriot* and the *National Advocate* were finally bought by Thomas Snowden, and the *Patriot* was discontinued Dec. 31, 1824.

The remainder of Gardner's career seems to have been made up of political appointments. In 1829, he became senior assistant postmaster-general and from 1836 to 1841 was auditor of the treasury for the Post-Office Department. On Sept. 3, 1842, he was appointed secretary of the board of commissioners to settle claims arising under the treaty with the Cherokee Indians, and on Jan. 17, 1844, was removed from office. From 1845 to 1849 he was postmaster at Washington, D. C. In 1853, as the fruit of four years' labor, he published *A Dictionary of all Officers . . . in the Army of the United States . . . 1789–1853* (2nd edition, 1860). He next became surveyor-general of Oregon (November 1853–January 1856), and then returned to Washington to become a clerk in the Treasury Department. He retired in 1867 and died two years later. His wife survived him some seven years.

[Records in the Adjutant-General's Office and in the Bureau of Indian Affairs; Louis H. Fox, "New York City Newspapers, 1820–50, A Bibliography," in *Papers Bibliog. Soc. of America*, vol. XXI (1927); *Daily Na-*

tional Intelligencer (Washington, D. C.), Feb. 23, 1816; Frederic Hudson, *Journalism in the U. S.* (1873), pp. 312–14; *Evening Star* (Washington), Oct. 23, Nov. 2, 1869; *The Biog. Encyc. of N. J. in the Nineteenth Century* (1877); *Court Martial . . . of Maj. Chas. K. Gardner* (1816); inscription on the Gardner monument, Congressional Cemetery, Washington.]

F. W. S.

GARDNER, HENRY JOSEPH (June 14, 1818–July 21, 1892), governor of Massachusetts, was born in Dorchester, Mass., the son of Dr. Henry and Clarissa (Holbrook) Gardner. He was a descendant of Richard Gardner, a resident of Woburn, Mass., in 1642, and a grandson of Henry Gardner (1730–1782), the first treasurer and receiver general of Massachusetts and a member of the Provincial Congress. Graduating at the Phillips Exeter Academy in 1831, Gardner entered Bowdoin College, but did not remain to secure a degree, preferring to go into business. Starting in the dry-goods firm of Denney, Rice & Gardner, in Boston, he ultimately became the controlling force in the corporation, the name of which was changed to Henry J. Gardner & Company. He retired from this occupation in 1876 and during the remainder of his life was resident agent of the Massachusetts Life Insurance Company.

In 1850 he entered municipal politics as a member of the Boston Common Council, of which he was president in 1852 and 1853. He was a representative in the General Court, 1851–52, and a delegate to the Massachusetts constitutional convention of 1853. With the sudden rise of the American, or Know-Nothing, party in Massachusetts, Gardner, who had hitherto been a Whig and an anti-slavery man, rapidly became prominent in its councils. Although it held no public meetings and kept out of the newspapers, this party, based on a fear of Roman Catholic domination and of foreign influence in the United States, attracted large numbers of citizens into its ranks. Gardner, who was an astute politician and a shrewd judge of men and motives, organized "with great skill and success the knave-power and the donkey-power of the Commonwealth" (G. F. Hoar, *Autobiography of Seventy Years,* 1903, I, 189–91). In the autumn of 1854, he was the Know-Nothing candidate for governor, receiving 81,000 votes to 26,000 for the Whigs and 13,000 for the Democrats. In the same campaign, his party elected all but two members of the legislature and every member of Congress from Massachusetts—the most amazing political landslide in the history of the state. In 1855, running against Julius Rockwell, the Republican nominee, Gardner was again successful; and in 1856, when his candidacy was endorsed by the Republicans, he won a third victory. He was finally defeated in 1857 by Nathaniel P. Banks [*q.v.*], a Republican, the Know-Nothing movement having run its course.

Contrary to the expectations of his enemies, Gardner was a rather conservative governor. During his three terms in office, he did little that was sensational, although he fulfilled pledges by having a "reading and writing clause" inserted in the Naturalization Act, by reforming the election laws, and by supporting alien pauper and homestead acts. He disapproved of the Personal Liberty Bill in 1855, but it was passed by the legislature over his veto (J. F. Rhodes, *History of the United States from the Compromise of 1850,* vol. II, 1900, p. 77). After his defeat, he was never again a factor in Massachusetts affairs, and at the time of his death he had been forgotten by all except a few historians. Gardner was married, on Nov. 21, 1843, to Helen Elizabeth Cobb, daughter of Richard and Elizabeth (Wood) Cobb, of Portland, Me., by whom he had four sons and three daughters. He died of cancer at his home in Milton, Mass.

[*Obit. Record Grads. Bowdoin Coll. . . . for the Decade ending 1 June 1899* (1899); F. A. Gardner, *Thos. Gardner, Planter . . . and Some of his Descendants* (1907), p. 3; G. F. Tuttle, *The Descendants of Wm. and Elizabeth Tuttle* (1883), p. 310; G. H. Haynes, "A Know-Nothing Legislature," *Ann. Report, Am. Hist. Asso. . . . 1896* (1897), I, 177–87; E. L. Pierce, *Memoir and Letters of Chas. Sumner,* vol. III (1893), *passim*; H. G. Pearson, *The Life of John A. Andrew* (2 vols., 1904); *Dorchester Births, Marriages, and Deaths to the End of 1825* (1890); *Boston Daily Advertiser,* Nov. 22, 1843; obituary in *Boston Transcript,* July 22, 1892.]

C. M. F.

GARDNER, ISABELLA STEWART (Apr. 14, 1840–July 17, 1924), art collector, social leader, took life-long pride in her descent from Robert Bruce and Mary Stuart. Her father, David Stewart, a New York importer and mine owner, had married Adelia Smith, of Long Island Puritan ancestry. They lived at 20 University Place, New York City, where Isabella was born, the oldest of four children. The household discipline was religiously rigid; at Fenway Court are preserved the now amusing Sunday-school books of Isabella's childhood, the literary pabulum on which "a daughter of the Renaissance" was nourished. The summers of the Stewarts were passed at a Long Island farm where the girl, shapely and energetic, acquired a life-long zest for outdoor sports. She was taught by private teachers until it was determined to place her in a school at Paris, "to finish." Among her friends at this finishing school was Julia Gardner of Boston. On her return to America, Isabella visited the Gardner home, where Julia's brother, John Lowell Gardner, fell in love with her. The engagement and subsequent marriage were conventionally proper, although the Boston legend persists, that "Belle Stewart jumped out of a boarding-school window and eloped with Jack Gardner." They were married at Grace Church, New York, Apr. 10, 1860 (*New York Herald,* Apr. 12, 1860). Mr. Stewart had already built a house for them at 152 Beacon St., Boston, which they occupied after a brief wedding journey.

During the Civil War, which Isabella afterward said she was too young to remember, the Gardner's home régime was as humdrum as any other. The monotony of long evenings in which the young people played backgammon was interrupted by the birth of a son June 18, 1863. The child died Mar. 15, 1865, however, and the mother was prostrated with a grief from which she never recovered though in time she sought relief in social activities that dazzled the city. Her baby lost, she henceforth mothered all the world that was gay, clever, and socially minded. She emerged from her mourning an enchanting hostess. "Effervescent, exuberant, reckless, witty, she did whatever she pleased, and the men, the gayest and most brilliant of them, she captivated. Her figure was perfect, her complexion marvellous, her grace incomparable" (Carter, *post,* p. 29). While many of the stories told in Boston about "Mrs. Jack" are either false or distorted, they reflect the state of excitement in which she kept her fellow townsmen. She was alive to the value of publicity, and she did not contradict a good story about herself, be it true or otherwise. Her good-natured, complacent husband not only never thwarted her social ambitions but rather abetted them.

Mrs. Gardner's interest in the arts of design, which finally motivated her greatest project, Fenway Court, began in 1867 when she visited Copenhagen and saw Thorwaldsen's sculptures. Amid feverish social enterprises she began buying works of art from local art dealers. She attended lectures by Charles Eliot Norton, professor of art at Harvard. She painted a little in water-colors, illustrating, for example, her journal of travel in Egypt and Palestine. Artists, musicians, and literary workers thronged her salon. In 1880 the Gardners, to have a better music room, bought an adjoining house at 150 Beacon St. That accession accelerated the collecting of art treasures with which to fill the additional rooms. Fired by Prof. Edward S. Morse's lectures on Japan, the Gardners started in May 1883 on a trip around the world. Thus began an avid collecting of orientalia. It vivified Mrs. Gardner's appreciation of Whistler, on whom she called in London and from whom she acquired important works. In the eighties and nineties the Gardner music room in Beacon St. resounded with the best music and conversation of contemporary Boston. Gericke, Paderewski, and many other celebrated musicians frequented it. George Proctor, organist at the age of fifteen in the Church of the Redeemer, had attracted Mrs. Gardner's attention; his career as pianist she followed like a brooding mother during the rest of her life, and in his pupils she took keen interest. The art collection, meantime, was growing by the accession of Italian, Flemish, and Spanish masterpieces; of works by English pre-Raphaelites; of paintings by Sargent, Zorn, and others. An acquaintance with Bernhard Berenson greatly aided the Gardners in acquiring art works of unique interest. The lady of the house, however, continued to shock Boston convention by attending prize fights, and conversing familiarly with John L. Sullivan, pugilist, and with Sandow, the strong man. She liked to know unusual people, whatever their social background.

On Dec. 10, 1898, Mr. Gardner dropped dead at the Exchange Club. His will proved that he had implicit confidence in his wife's taste and judgment, and that they had together planned to create an art museum. Mrs. Gardner bought land at Fenway and Worthington St., Boston, on Jan. 31, 1899. A Boston tradition that she literally starved herself to save funds for the contemplated museum is absurd. It is true, however, that she reduced her establishment and devoted all her time and available means to the enterprise. It was incorporated as the Isabella Stewart Gardner Museum in the Fenway, Limited, and an Italianate structure, destined to house important paintings and sculptures, many of which were brought in free of duty, was erected and first opened to the public on Feb. 23, 1903. Mrs. Gardner's many friendships and social contacts made her Italian palace worthy of its historic mission, for not only local writers, musicians, and artists, but many visiting celebrities were entertained against a regal background which the hostess had established, in some passages by work of her own hands.

In 1921 she bought her last old master, a madonna by Giovanni Bellini. She had had a paralytic stroke from which she partly recovered. Her mind remained clear and active; her daily routine was maintained, this including a brief afternoon drive. In July 1924 Boston was alive with a convention whose decorations and regalia greatly amused her. She ordered her car for a second trip downtown in the same day. The unusual exertion and excitement brought on a heart attack from which she died. Her will established Fenway Court "as a museum for the education and enjoyment of the public forever." It so stands, with no legal possibility of changes or additions to the collections. It is the donor's monument. On it a remarkable woman had lavished much of the affection which would normally have gone out to her child.

[Morris Carter, *Isabella Stewart Gardner and Fenway Court* (1925); "Mrs. Gardner's Venetian Palace," in *Harper's Bazar,* July 1903; "An Interesting Step Forward in Art," in *Century Mag.,* Apr. 1903; "Mrs. Gardner and Her Masterpiece," by E. W. Perkins, in *Scribner's Mag.,* Mar. 1925; "A Daughter of the Renaissance," in *Lit. Digest,* Mar. 27, 1926; *Boston Transcript,* July 18, 1924.] F. W. C.

GARDNER, JOHN LANE (Aug. 1, 1793–Feb. 19, 1869), soldier, was born in Boston, the son of Robert Gardner. He was appointed third lieutenant in the 4th Infantry, May 20, 1813, and promoted to second lieutenant, Mar. 28, 1814. He served on the northern frontier through the War of 1812, partly with his regiment and partly as aide to Brig.-Gen. Thomas A. Smith. He was wounded, Mar. 30, 1814, at the La Colle Mill affair, where Wilkinson suffered ignominious defeat. At the close of the war he was transferred to the artillery, and in 1818 was promoted to first lieutenant. For the next eleven years he was on duty in Washington in the office of the quartermaster-general, and for a short time afterward was quartermaster at West Point. In 1825 he married Caroline, daughter of Charles Washington Goldsborough. His captaincy in the artillery dated from Nov. 1, 1823. Returning to regimental duty in 1830, he commanded his company in the Florida War and on garrison duty until he was promoted to major, Oct. 13, 1845. He was the author of a little book published anonymously in 1839, entitled *Military Control, or Command and Government of the Army.* His regiment, the 4th Artillery, served chiefly as infantry during the Mexican War. He commanded it in Scott's campaign from Vera Cruz to the city of Mexico, and for his conduct at Cerro Gordo and Contreras was twice brevetted. After the war he commanded the district of Florida and was promoted to lieutenant-colonel, Aug. 3, 1852. In 1860 he was commanding Fort Moultrie, in Charleston Harbor. He "had done good service in the War of 1812 and in Mexico," wrote Abner Doubleday, who served under him; "but now, owing to his advanced age, was ill fitted to weather the storm that was about to burst upon us. In politics he was quite Southern, frequently asserting that the South had been treated outrageously in the question of the Territories, and defrauded of her just rights in other respects. He acquiesced, however, in the necessity of defending the fort should it be attacked; but as he lived with his family outside of the walls, he could not take a very active part himself" (*Reminiscences of Forts Sumter and Moultrie in 1860–61,* 1876, pp. 18–19). The government left him with scanty instructions, so that he was reluctant to take any decisive measures for defense. He did, however, see to it that his post was well provisioned, and he recommended a substantial increase in the garrison. An attempt to transfer a stock of ammunition from the Charleston Arsenal to Fort Moultrie caused the secretary of war, John Floyd [*q.v.*], to supersede him by Maj. Robert Anderson [*q.v.*], who was a Southerner by birth. Gardner was promoted to colonel July 23, 1861, and was retired on Nov. 1 of that year, but performed some further duty, on recruiting and the like. He was brevetted brigadier-general in 1865. He died at Wilmington, Del.

[F. B. Heitman, *Hist. Reg. and Dict. U. S. Army* (1903), I, 446; G. V. Henry, *Military Record of Civilian Appointments in the U. S. Army* (1870), I, 205–06; *Official Records (Army),* 1 ser., vol. I; *Wilmington Daily Commercial,* Feb. 19, 1869.] T. M. S.

GAREY, THOMAS ANDREW (July 7, 1830–Aug. 20, 1909), horticulturist, was born in Cincinnati, Ohio, the son of Dr. Samuel and Margaret Wringer Garey. His father came of Dutch ancestry; his mother of Pennsylvania German stock. After spending his early youth in Hagerstown, Md., where he obtained a common-school education, he moved in 1847 to Iowa, and from thence he set out in 1849 by ox team for the West. Although his ultimate destination was California, he stopped on the way in New Mexico, and on Oct. 27, 1850, at Albuquerque, he was married to Louisa J. Smith, a native of Massachusetts. After about a year at Albuquerque and six months in Arizona, he and his wife pushed on to San Diego, Cal., arriving in 1852. Soon, however, they moved to El Monte, in Los Angeles County, where they remained for several years. In 1865 Garey bought seventy-two acres of land on what is now South San Pedro St., in Los Angeles and there he developed an extensive citrus nursery. This was in the early days of the citrus industry in southern California, when the demand for orange and lemon trees was increasing. In one year (1873) his sales of fruit trees, mostly citrus, amounted to about $75,000; in a period of three years they totaled around $175,000. He became one of the outstanding personalities in the development of the citrus industry, and in 1882 published a written study, *Orange Culture in California,* which was the first book on the subject to appear in the state. He introduced into California several varieties of citrus-fruits, and was largely instrumental in the dissemination of others, including the Mediterranean Sweet and St. Michael oranges. The name of the former was first applied by Garey; it had been originally received by him erroneously identified as a shaddock. Perhaps the variety with which his name is the most intimately linked is the Eureka lemon, which became one of the two principal varieties grown in California. Though it was developed from the seed of a Sicilian lemon, imported about 1858, it was Garey who, beginning its propagation in 1877–78, disseminated it first as "Garey's Eureka."

Garey was greatly interested in community affairs. He helped to found the towns of Pomona and Artesia; and in his honor the council of Santa Barbara County in 1887 named the town of Garey where he later engaged in the nursery business. For many years he acted as president of the Los Angeles Pomological Society. He was master of the Los Angeles Grange, and an overseer of the state Grange. He was also a charter member of the Good Templars, and took an active part in other local organizations. He accumulated considerable property at times; met with repeated reverses, but recouped his fortunes. In his later life he became an ardent Spiritualist. At the time of his death he was survived by his wife and three of their eight children.

[L. H. Bailey, *Standard Cyc. of Horticulture,* III (1915), 1576; the *Los Angeles Times,* Aug. 21, 22, 1909; information as to certain facts from W. A. Spaulding, Los Angeles, Cal.; C. S. Pomeroy, Riverside, Cal.; A. T. Garey, a grandson, Santa Maria, Cal.]

H. P. G.

GARFIELD, JAMES ABRAM (Nov. 19, 1831–Sept. 19, 1881), soldier, congressman, president of the United States, was the last of the chief executives to be born in the typical American environment of the log cabin. He was preceded by at least six Garfields born in America, his immigrant ancestor having come to Massachusetts Bay with Winthrop (E. G. Porter, in *Proceedings of the Massachusetts Historical Society,* XIX, 1882, p. 83). They were all "hungry for the horizon," and in successive generations they made the cabin and its attributes a part of the family inheritance (G. F. Hoar, *Eulogy upon . . . James Abram Garfield,* 1882, p. 9). Abram Garfield, the father of James, was married in 1820 to Eliza Ballou, of old Rhode Island ancestry. He moved with his family to Ohio, and in 1827, when there were already three children, took a contract to be worked out in the construction of the Ohio Canal; but he abandoned this occupation and became a pioneer farmer in Cuyahoga County in time to welcome to his cabin his last child, James Abram, to become a member of the Disciples of Christ, and to die of a sudden "ague" in 1833. His widow became the man of the family and steered her children through poverty and uncertainty to an honored independence. It was a life of hardship for all of them, and Garfield knew every kind of frontier work, and nothing of that leisure and security that come from economic freedom. Before he was thirty he had scraped together an education, exhausted the intellectual offering of the Western Reserve Eclectic Institute (later Hiram College), joined the Disciples church, worked his way into and through Williams College with the class of 1856, and served as teacher and even principal of the Institute at Hiram. Young for the position, he had as advantages nearly six feet of height, great breadth of shoulders, and a "round German-looking face," which he generally obscured with a heavy beard. He married, on Nov. 11, 1858, Lucretia Rudolph, his childhood playmate, fellow student, and pupil. In the following year he was elected to the Ohio Senate as a Republican; and when in 1861 the crisis of the Civil War came he was a leader who upheld the right of the federal government to coerce a state.

His power of debate, already ripe, increased by his efforts as lay-preacher in his church, and his oratorical style, more florid than it was to be later in his life, made Garfield a useful agent in raising troops and stimulating enlistments. In the summer of 1861 he helped assemble a regiment, the 42nd Ohio Volunteer Infantry, that contained many of his Hiram students; and of this he became lieutenant-colonel, and then colonel. He had no military experience to warrant his appointment to a line command but he possessed what was rare among citizen officers of the Civil War, a willingness to study and an ability to understand books. With a manual before him he made his recruits into soldiers; and he looked and acted his part so well that a few days after he and his regiment joined Maj.-Gen. Don Carlos Buell in Kentucky he was given a brigade and was sent to the Big Sandy to confront Humphrey Marshall, a West Pointer commanding the Confederate army there (F. H. Mason, *The Forty-Second Ohio Infantry: A History,* 1876). At Middle Creek, on Jan. 10, 1862, he won a victory that seemed important because of the scarcity of Union successes, and gained the rank of brigadier-general of volunteers. In April, with his new rank, he fought at Shiloh on the second day; and in the following winter he sat at Washington upon the famous court of inquiry in the Fitz-John Porter case (*Senate*

Executive Document No. 37, 46 Cong., 1 Sess.). Bad health had brought him in from the field, but, his condition improving, he was reassigned to active duty and joined Rosecrans's Army of the Cumberland early in 1863. Here, with an option before him, he chose to be chief of staff rather than to command a brigade; and in this capacity he served through the Chickamauga campaign, winning high praise from subsequent military historians because of his comprehension of the duties of a staff officer (Whitelaw Reid, *Ohio in the War: Her Statesmen, her Generals, and Soldiers,* 1868). He organized a division of military information that was far ahead of prevailing American military practise. For five months the army of Rosecrans remained at Murfreesboro, Tenn. It finally advanced, contrary to the almost unanimous judgment of its officers, chiefly because Rosecrans was convinced by Garfield of the wisdom of the action. In the engagement at Chickamauga that followed, on Sept. 19, 20, 1863, Thomas was the hero and Rosecrans was discredited; while Garfield, chief of staff, gained wide repute for both courage and good sense. He was made a major-general of volunteers, dating from Chickamauga, as a reward; but he was through with fighting, as other opportunities had come to him. In December 1863, he took his seat in the Thirty-eighth Congress as representative from the 19th Ohio district.

The military successes of Garfield in the spring of 1862 made him a prominent political figure in northeastern Ohio, where anti-slavery radicalism had long maintained Joshua R. Giddings in Congress. Giddings had been displaced in 1858 by John Hutchins, whose retirement now was made easier by a new apportionment law passed after the census of 1860. Garfield, young and popular, nominated while he was in the service, was elected by a heavy majority. He did not take his seat until his military services had been rewarded by promotion; and it has been suggested that he surrendered his major-generalcy in December 1863 only because Lincoln believed that major-generals were easier to procure than Administration-Republican representatives. Eight times more, after 1862, Garfield came before the Republican convention of his district, sometimes after Democratic alterations in its boundaries had made Republican success highly doubtful, and once after the breath of scandal had endangered his future; every time he gained the nomination to succeed himself, and every time his people elected him to Congress. He was by nature a student, by training an orator, and by experience became a finished parliamentarian. His industry and his careful personal habits gave him other advantages, which he seized as they appeared. When Thaddeus Stevens passed off the stage of politics in 1868, James G. Blaine and Garfield knew they were ready to become the congressional leaders of their party (G. F. Hoar, *Autobiography of Seventy Years,* 1903, I, 239); and when, in 1876, Blaine was translated to the Senate, Garfield had no real rival in the House.

The committee assignments of Garfield indicate the development of his interests. He took an important place on the committee on military affairs when he appeared in 1863, for he was fresh from the battlefield and the war was yet to be won. In later sessions he served on the committee on appropriations and the committee on ways and means. He developed and trained an interest in public finance that was so sound as to endanger his political prospects. When the Northwest was carried away by the "Ohio" (greenback) idea, and advocated the issuance of irredeemable paper money, Garfield stuck to the promise of a resumption of specie payments. He was too lukewarm on the subject of the protective tariff to suit all of his Republican constituents, for northeastern Ohio contained many factories that were in a period of rapid expansion between the Civil War and the panic of 1873. But his independence of thought caused him less trouble than did two of the scandals of a period full of scandals. He was named in the memorandum book of Oakes Ames [*q.v.*] as one of the congressmen who had accepted stock in the Crédit Mobilier Company. This Garfield denied, and the proof was far from being complete (*House Report, No. 77,* 42 Cong., 3 Sess.); yet the suspicion remained an available weapon for his enemies throughout his life. In the case of the DeGolyer paving contract there was no doubt about the underlying fact. He did accept a retaining fee for services rendered to a company ambitious to furnish the City of Washington with wooden-block pavement (*Nation,* July 1, 1880, p. 5). The interpretation placed upon the episode by his critics was that while a member of Congress he took pay from a company seeking favors from the government of the District; his answer was that he had no connection with the District government by which the paving award was to be made, and that his services were not to be differentiated from those which congressmen and senators were continually performing when they practised the profession of law in the federal courts. Both of these scandals were before his constituents when he appeared for reëlection in 1874, but he surmounted them.

When the Republican party was thrown into the minority in the House after the election of 1874, Garfield and Blaine were its most effective leaders, and worked together with no more suspicions and jealousies than were to be expected. When the latter became senator from Maine in 1876, Garfield became the Republican candidate for speaker and was leader of the minority for the rest of his service in the House. He had taken an active part in the canvass for Hayes, and had gone to Louisiana as one of the "visiting statesmen" to watch the count of votes. He was active in framing the compromise legislation that settled the electoral contest, and served as a member of the electoral commission, where he voted for Hayes on every count. His natural desire to take John Sherman's place as senator from Ohio, when the latter went into the cabinet, was repressed at the request of Hayes who wanted him to remain as Republican leader in the House; but in 1880 there was no such obstruction and the legislature elected him to succeed Allen G. Thurman for the term of six years after 1881. His name, said the *Milwaukee Sentinel* (Jan. 10, 1880), "is exceptionally clean for a man who has been engaged for twenty years in active politics." He never sat in the Senate. On the day that his term would otherwise have begun he was inaugurated as president of the United States.

At the time of Garfield's election to the Senate, John Sherman might easily have sought the post for himself, for he expected to be out of the cabinet after Mar. 4, 1881. But Sherman desired the Republican presidential nomination of 1880, and efforts were made to induce Garfield to promise support in exchange for Sherman's support for the senatorship. Garfield seems to have refused to make a bargain, although he let it be known that his attitude towards Sherman's candidacy would be affected by Sherman's treatment of his. After his election he still declined to pledge support to Sherman, but on Jan. 26, 1880, he wrote: "I have no doubt that a decisive majority of our party in Ohio favors the nomination of John Sherman. He has earned this recognition" (*Cincinnati Gazette*, Jan. 28, 1880). As the spring advanced, the substantial unanimity of Ohio for Sherman brought Garfield into the movement. He went to the Chicago national convention as head of the delegation and manager for Sherman, and on the floor attained a commanding position because of the soundness of his case and the skill with which he managed it. Blaine and Grant were the leading rivals of Sherman for the nomination, and the "Stalwart" leaders who directed the fight for Grant took unsound positions in insisting upon the unit rule for state delegations, and upon the right of state conventions to instruct district delegates how they should vote. Garfield conducted the fight for the freedom of the delegate and blocked the paths of both Grant and Blaine but could not procure a majority for his own candidate. On the thirty-fifth ballot sixteen of the twenty Wisconsin votes were shifted to Garfield, and on the next roll call the nomination was made unanimous in a stampede. The Grant forces, led by Conkling, Cameron, and Logan, never forgave Garfield for his opposition; Blaine, who could not have been nominated, was grateful for the defeat of Grant; Sherman laid his failure to the stubbornness of Blaine and only late in life came to believe that Garfield had been disloyal to him. James Ford Rhodes agrees with Sherman's later opinion, writing that "apparently the thought of his [Garfield's] trust was overpowered by the conviction that the prize was his without the usual hard preliminary work" (*History of the United States from Hayes to McKinley, 1877–1896*, 1919, p. 126). But no evidence of importance has been produced to show that the management of Sherman's cause was anything but loyal; and historical proofs are incapable of determining whether under any circumstances it was ethical for the manager of Sherman to accept the nomination for himself.

In the canvass of 1880 the followers of Blaine and Sherman gave good support to the ticket, but those of Grant sulked, the leaders offering little more than a formal pledge of devotion to the party. Roscoe Conkling [*q.v.*], in particular, was outraged and held aloof. The nomination from his own following of Chester A. Arthur as vice-president gave him no pleasure. The selection of Marshall Jewell [*q.v.*] to be chairman of the national committee was an affront since Jewell had been summarily dismissed by Grant from the office of postmaster-general in 1876. On Aug. 5 Garfield made a pilgrimage to New York to sit with a meeting of the national committee, in the hope that the New York wing of the party might be persuaded to help the ticket, but Conkling could not be induced even to meet him. He distrusted, says his nephew and biographer, "Garfield's imperfect memory of a private conversation" (A. R. Conkling, *The Life and Letters of Roscoe Conkling,* 1889, p. 611). In September, however, Conkling, Cameron, and Grant finally decided to recognize the candidate and made a western trip; in connection with this, Grant presided and Conkling spoke at a rally in Garfield's old district at Warren, Ohio, and they paid a visit of formal courtesy to Garfield at his Mentor farm. What they said to the candidate and what he said to them played a large part in the later political controversy as the "Treaty of Mentor," but cannot be documented. Garfield at least wrote in his diary, "I had no private conversation with the party" (T. C. Smith, *post*, p. 1032). The "Stalwarts" later chose to say that he promised them "fair" treatment as the price of support; and they insisted throughout his presidency that it was for them to determine in what fair treatment consisted. The canvass progressed somewhat more smoothly after this. On Oct. 20 a New York weekly, *Truth*, printed what pretended to be a letter from Garfield to one H. L. Morey in which he advocated the importation of cheap Oriental labor for employment in factories. The Democratic national committee gave wide circulation to this document, in spite of its instant denunciation as a fraud; and Hancock and English, the Democratic candidates, secured five of the six electoral votes of California, where the feeling against the Chinese was strong. But Garfield and Arthur nevertheless carried the country with a plurality of about 10,000 popular votes, and with 214 electoral votes, against 155.

Garfield resigned from the House early in November. He surrendered the Senate seat as well, thus enabling John Sherman to return in 1881 to his old post as senator from Ohio. The President-Elect remained at Mentor, entrenched behind his "snow works" (*Cincinnati Gazette*, Nov. 16, Dec. 13, 1880), keeping up the hard-wood fires in his grates, smoking his large, thick cigars, and listening with non-committal patience to every one who came to see him. All the political leaders came, Conkling as well as Blaine, but the major appointments were kept guarded until Garfield was ready to transmit them to the Senate after his inauguration on Mar. 4, 1881. He attempted to build a conciliation cabinet, but the appointment of James G. Blaine at its head as secretary of state caused it to be regarded by the "Stalwart" element in the party as a triumph for him. Continuously from the moment when Garfield asked Blaine to take the post, he was the recipient of letters of counsel from the latter. Much of the advice was good and some of it was taken. For the treasury, Garfield, appreciating the usual western "jealousy of Eastern financial leadership" (*Harper's Weekly*, Mar. 26, 1881, p. 194), selected Senator William Windom of Minnesota, whom Sherman guaranteed as faithful to sound money and hostile to monopolies. Robert T. Lincoln, secretary of war, was a Grant man before the convention of 1880, but was appointed chiefly because of the tradition that he represented. William H. Hunt, who began life as a Southern Whig, became secretary of the navy. The selection of Wayne MacVeagh of Philadelphia as attorney-general involved an interesting situation, since he was at once a vigorous anti-Cameronian in Pennsylvania politics, and a son-in-law of old Simon Cameron. MacVeagh was known as a reformer, and was angered when Garfield named for assistant attorney-general William E. Chandler, a warm partisan of Blaine. Chandler, however, failed of confirmation by the Senate. Thomas L. James of New York, a Conkling man, had been postmaster of New York City, and became postmaster-general with a suspicion already lodged in his mind that the postal service needed purification. Senator Samuel J. Kirkwood of Iowa took the Interior department.

The doubts that had kept the "Stalwarts" lukewarm during the canvass, and had impelled Conkling to minatory counsels after election, were intensified as the winter of 1881 advanced. On Feb. 11, with Arthur in the chair and Grant among those present, a commemorative dinner was given at Delmonico's in New York to Stephen W. Dorsey [*q.v.*]; and at this it was made to appear that to him as secretary of the national committee was due the credit for the victory of the Garfield ticket. His sharp strategy in carrying Indiana was specially commended. But Garfield's recognition of the "Stalwarts" was less than they expected, or at least desired. On Mar. 23 he sent to the Senate a long list of minor nominees, including men of his own choice for the difficult New York custom-house posts that had occasioned Hayes so much trouble. Conkling took this as an open declaration of war against his friends, and as a violation of pledges that had been given him as the price of his support. He relied upon "senatorial courtesy" to accomplish the rejection of the distasteful nominees, advancing once more the theory that had been fought out with Hayes, that federal appointments within a state must be personally acceptable to the senator from that state. Garfield met the issue with more stubbornness than he usually displayed, telling John Hay, "They may take him [Robertson, the nominee for collector of the port] out of the Senate head first or feet first; I will never withdraw him" (*New York Tribune*, Jan. 11, 1882).

The political battle soon shifted to the Post-Office Department, where Garfield and James had inherited a corrupt situation of old standing. The practise had been allowed to develop whereby rings of contractors in Washington received as lowest bidders scores of "star routes"—where the mails were carried by stage or rider rather than by railroad or steamboat. They then sublet the actual performance to local carriers, whom they paid what the service was worth, and by collusion later secured an unwarranted increase in the compensation to themselves. Ex-Senator Dorsey was heavily involved in "star route" contracts, as was the second assistant postmaster-general, Thomas J. Brady, in whose office the compensations were arranged. An investigation of Brady's work was under way in 1880 when he had asked for a deficiency appropriation of about $1,700,000. It had for a time appeared that the attacks were only the usual Democratic nagging of a Republican administration; but James brought to Garfield a report from the field workers of the department that uncovered more scandal than could be denied or concealed. Brady was dismissed on Apr. 20, 1881, and a list of ninety-three suspected "star routes" was given to the press (*Annual Report of the Postmaster-General,* 1881, pp. 467, 516). The dismissal of Brady and the incidental involvement of Dorsey in charges of fraud came while the Senate was delaying the confirmation of the appointees of Mar. 23. Attempts were made to scare off the investigation, by suggestions that Garfield knew all about the frauds, had connived at them, and had been aware that a share of the plunder had found its way to the Republican campaign fund which Dorsey had administered so skilfully the preceding summer. (Much of Dorsey's campaign correspondence was printed by him in the *New York Herald,* Dec. 18, 1882.) The reply of Garfield to this intimidation was to direct the preparation of the cases to be brought against the conspirators, and to withdraw all other nominations for New York positions except those for the custom-house, so as to emphasize his determination to maintain the independence of the president in matters of appointment. On May 4, however, a letter written Aug. 23, 1880, was made public (*New York Herald,* May 5, 1881), showing that Garfield had then inquired of Jay A. Hubbell, chairman of the Republican congressional campaign committee, how the departments were doing, and expressed the hope that Brady would help as much as possible.

It had been easier for opponents of Garfield to delay action on his appointments because the control of the Senate was insecure for several weeks after the inauguration. Accordingly, the Republican caucus, anxious not to break with the President and not to lose the aid of the votes influenced by Conkling, proceeded slowly in determining party policy. The public reactions respecting the "star route" frauds, and party bosses, and the hobbling theory that underlay Conkling's demand, determined the outcome of the contest. When it became quite clear that Garfield would not surrender, the caucus agreed to confirm. Conkling, with his New York colleague as trailer, resigned his seat upon the issue, and appealed to the New York legislature for a vindication which he did not receive. The two New York vacancies again threw the control of the Senate in doubt, but they transferred the turmoil from Washington to Albany, and gave to Garfield a release from the excitement and pressure that he had been under for two months. He now allowed Blaine to show the hand of the administration in foreign matters, issuing a call for a conference of the American republics to meet in Washington in 1882, and taking up where Hayes and Evarts had left it the contention with England that the Clayton-Bulwer Treaty of 1850 was no longer adequate (Alice F. Tyler, *The Foreign Policy of James G. Blaine,* 1927, pp. 38–41, 165).

Before either of these matters could be pushed to a conclusion, there came an enforced hiatus in the administration. On July 2, while at the Washington railroad station en route for a northern trip and a visit to his college, Garfield was shot by Charles J. Guiteau, an erratic if not crazy lawyer and a disappointed office-seeker, who declared loudly that his was a political crime, that he was a "Stalwart" and wanted Arthur to be president. For eleven weeks Garfield was nursed at the White House, and then at Elberon, N. J., a summer resort where his family was in residence. The official bulletins from his physicians were numerous, but hardly revealed from day to day whether he was incapacitated or not, in the meaning of the Constitution. He never left his sick-bed, however; and on Sept. 19, 1881, he died. The friends of the murdered President raised a handsome fund for the support of his widow and the five children who survived him. One of the latter, James Rudolph Garfield, was to have a distinguished career in politics, serving as secretary of the interior from 1907 to 1909; a second, Harry Augustus Garfield, became president of Williams College and United States fuel administrator during the World War.

Garfield's tragic death silenced the voice of criticism and gave the tone to many laudatory biographies. Not enough of his administration had been revealed for any estimate of it to be possible. He had failed to bring about the harmony that both good nature and selfish interest had urged him to attempt. Whether he could have managed to rule without "Stalwart" support is uncertain. Up to the moment of his accidental nomination for the presidency his career, to an unusual degree, resembles that of a typical successful parliamentary leader in a country possessing responsible government and the cabinet system. He would in England have been in line for Downing Street and the office of premier. In the United States such talents as his could obtain their chance only by accident.

[In addition to the *Cong. Record,* where the speeches of Garfield's long career are to be found, and to the newspapers which gave him abundant space, and to his obituaries, among which the address by Jas. G. Blaine in the hall of the House of Representatives, Feb. 27, 1882, *Cong. Record,* 47 Cong., 1 Sess., p. 1465, is the most distinguished, there are many eulogistic biographies of the campaign type. Probably the best of these is Burke A. Hinsdale, *The Republican Text-Book for the Campaign of 1880: A Full Hist. of Gen. Jas. A. Garfield's Pub. Life* (1880). Garfield's speeches were collected by Hinsdale and published as *The Works of Jas. Abram Garfield* (2 vols., 1882–83). The personal papers, which Garfield preserved in great number, were carefully arranged immediately after his death but were not worked over for nearly a generation, when they were entrusted to Prof. Theodore C. Smith, of Williams College. They include extensive diaries and a large collection of letters. The resulting biography by Professor Smith, *The Life and Letters of James Abram Garfield* (2 vols., 1925), one of the best presidential biographies in existence, is adequate for all reasonable needs.] F. L. P—n.

GARLAND, AUGUSTUS HILL (June 11, 1832–Jan. 26, 1899), attorney-general, son of Rufus and Barbara (Hill) Garland, was born in Tipton County, Tenn. In 1833 his parents moved to Miller County, Ark., where his father died. His mother subsequently took up her residence at Washington, the county seat of Hempstead, and in 1837 was married to Thomas Hubbard. Augustus was educated in a private school at Washington and attended St. Mary's College at Lebanon, Ky., but graduated from St. Joseph's College at Bardstown, Ky., in 1849. On returning to Arkansas he taught school for a time in Sevier County. He studied law with his stepfather, and was admitted to the bar in 1850. Six years later he moved to Little Rock and formed a partnership with Ebenezer Cummins. In 1860 he was admitted to practise before the United States Supreme Court. He was elected to the convention of 1861 as a representative of Pulaski County. He had been a Whig in politics and was now a candidate for presidential elector on the Bell-Everett ticket. He opposed secession but in the second session of the convention, after the bombardment of Fort Sumter, voted with the majority. He was one of the five delegates elected by the convention to the Provisional Congress. In November 1861 he was chosen representative of the third (southern) district in the first Confederate Congress and continued to serve until 1864, when he was sent to the Senate to succeed Charles B. Mitchell, deceased. On leaving the Senate in March 1865, Garland hurried back to Arkansas, where he was asked by Gov. Flanagin [*q.v.*] to open negotiations with Gen. J. J. Reynolds for recognition of the Confederate state government. On July 15, 1865, he secured a pardon from President Johnson and at once applied for reinstatement of his license to practise before the Supreme Court, which he had secured in 1860. An Act of Congress, Jan. 24, 1865, had debarred all who could not take the iron-clad oath—that he had never borne arms against the United States or accepted office in a government hostile to it. Garland, assisted by Reverdy Johnson and Matthew H. Carpenter, contended that the act was unconstitutional since it was in the nature of a bill of attainder and was *ex post facto.* He also contended that, even if the act were constitutional, his disability had been removed by the pardon of the President. Justice Stephen J. Field, speaking for a majority of the court, accepted both views and ordered that he be reinstated (*Ex parte Garland,* 4 *Wallace,* 333–39). Another important case which Garland helped to win was that of *Osborn* vs. *Nicholson,* establishing the validity of contracts for the sale of slaves as against a clause in the Arkansas constitution of 1868 forbidding collection on such contracts (13 *Wallace,* 654–64).

In 1867, after the Democrats had captured the legislature of the state, Garland was elected to the United States Senate, but was not allowed to take his seat. He continued to practise law in Little Rock until the overthrow of the Carpet-Bag régime and the adoption of the new constitution, when he was elected governor. He was inaugurated Nov. 12, 1874. He found that "there was not enough money in the treasury to buy sufficient wood to build a fire in the governor's office." His chief problems were to finance the state, which he did partly by issuing bonds and by providing a sinking fund, and to put an end to the practise of guaranteeing railroad bonds. A legislative committee reported the state debt to be $17,752,196, of which $13,563,567 had been incurred by the Carpet-Bag régime, and of this $4,378,544 could not be accounted for. The debt was reduced by $7,157,145 in 1877 by a decision of the supreme court that the railroad bonds had not been legally issued. Yet Garland opposed repudiation and later stumped the state in opposition to the Fishback amendment forbidding payments of all bonds.

He was again elected to the United States Senate to succeed Powell Clayton and this time he took his seat (Mar. 4, 1877). Soon after he entered Congress he introduced a bill for a commission to investigate the effects of the tariff and lost no opportunity to work for tariff reform. He also supported civil service reform. Following the overflow of 1882, he introduced a bill giving the Mississippi River Commission (created in 1879) authority to construct and repair levees on the Mississippi, holding that it was a matter of national concern and should not be left to the states. On Mar. 9, 1885, he resigned to become attorney-general in President Cleveland's cabinet. While holding this office he and several other public officials and prominent men became the subject of a congressional investigation for their connection with the Pan-Electric Telephone Company. The investigation threatened to expose a scandal of the first magnitude, but Garland's explanation of his connection with the affair was accepted by President Cleveland and a majority of the congressional committee (G. F. Parker, *Recollections of Grover Cleveland,* 1909, pp. 304–05; *House Miscellaneous Document No. 355, House Report No. 3142,* 49 Cong., 1 Sess.). When he retired from the cabinet he resumed the practise of law and spent most of his time in Washington. He was stricken while arguing a case before the Supreme Court and died in a few minutes. His body was taken to Little Rock and interred in Mount Holly Cemetery. In 1853 he married Virginia Sanders, who died in 1877. He wrote one little book, *Experience in the Supreme Court of the United States* (1898), which closes with a poem of two pages, and he collaborated with Robert Ralston on *A Treatise on the Constitution and Jurisdiction of the United States Courts* (2 vols., 1898).

[Josiah Shinn, *Pioneers and Makers of Ark.* (1908); Farrar Newberry, *A Life of Mr. Garland of Ark.* (1908); John Hallum, *Biog. and Pictorial Hist. of Ark.* (1887), I, 380–96, which is hostile toward Garland; obituaries in the *Arkansas Democrat* (Little Rock) and the *Evening Star* (Washington, D. C.), Jan. 26, 1899; *Jour. of Convention of the State of Ark.* (1861); *Jour. of the Cong. of the Confed. States* (7 vols., 1904–05); *Appletons' Ann. Cyc.*, 1874–77, 1885; D. T. Herndon, *Outline of Executive and Legislative Hist. of Ark.* (1922); *Ann. Reports of the Attorney-General,* 1885–88; T. S. Staples, *Reconstruction in Ark.* (1923); D. Y. Thomas, *Ark. in War and Reconstruction, 1861–74* (1926).]

D. Y. T.

GARLAND, LANDON CABELL (Mar. 21, 1810–Feb. 12, 1895), educator, university president, the son of Spotswood and Lucinda (Rose) Garland, was born at his father's home, "The Grove," Nelson County, Va. He was descended through both his father and mother from people of wealth, social distinction, and public usefulness. When at sixteen he was ready for college, his Methodist parents, suspicious of "free thought" at the state university, sent him to the Presbyterian school, Hampden-Sidney. He remained there three years, graduating in 1829. His plan was to become a lawyer, and upon being appointed professor of natural science at Washington College, now Washington and Lee University, he accepted the appointment with the determination that after a year or so he would return to law. He stayed on till the fall of 1832, however, organizing a laboratory method of instruction while there, and then went to Randolph-Macon College where from 1832 to 1836 he was professor of natural philosophy, and from 1836 to 1846, president. The move from Washington College cost him dearly both in salary and in the severance of friendships, but the call was to a Methodist school just being put upon its feet, and as a loyal denominationalist he felt that he could not disregard it. During his time at Randolph-Macon he administered the college, taught mathematics, wrote a text-book on trigonometry, and formed an intimate and lasting friendship with his predecessor as president, Stephen Olin [*q.v.*]. In December 1835 he was married to his third cousin, Louisa Frances Garland, a great-niece of Patrick Henry. Because of a breakdown in health he resigned from the presidency, and retired to the home of his father, intending when he had recovered to carry out his early plan to be a lawyer. After refusing requests from several colleges to become their president, including one from William and Mary, he went, however, in 1847 to teach at the University of Alabama. He was president there from 1855 to 1865, and after the buildings were demolished by Federal troops in the final spring of the Civil War, he undertook for a while to raise funds sufficient to restore them. From 1867 to 1875 he taught at the University of Mississippi. In 1868, at the instigation of Holland N. McTyeire [*q.v.*], then a bishop, but a former student of his at Randolph-Macon, he wrote for the *Christian Advocate* of Nashville, a series of articles favoring a more thoroughly educated ministry, and advocating as a means to that end, one central theological seminary for the entire Methodist Episcopal Church, South. Since many Methodists believed that education was not unmixed with danger, and that the idea of a central training place for ministers did too much violence to the principle of local self-government, there was a great conflict. Before long, however, his plan for a section-wide seminary was incorporated with a plan for a section-wide university to be established at Nashville, and when in 1875, as a result of the friendship between Bishop McTyeire and Cornelius Vanderbilt, Vanderbilt University was established, it had McTyeire as president of its Board of Trust, and Garland as its first chancellor. Until the death of Bishop McTyeire in 1889, these two worked in a harmony so close that it was hard to know which of them was first responsible for any given policy. The progress of the University was most gratifying, but in 1893 the chancellor resigned from his executive duties, and devoted himself wholly to teaching, continuing almost to the day of his death. His "special field" in scholarship was, he said, mathematics, but at various times he taught physics, astronomy, philosophy, and literature, and he prided himself also on a knowledge of Greek, Latin, music, and theology. He was unassuming, meticulous, and devout; gracious, if slightly ceremonial, in manner; and forceful, if slightly plain, in public speech. He was an eager sportsman, a hunter and fisher who seldom missed his game even when he was around eighty; yet, says the notice of him published in the *Christian Advocate* at the time of his death, "He loved all animal life, was the avowed friend of every good dog, and felt a deep interest in birds." During a cold spell he was careful every day to feed the sparrows about his house. "St. Francis of Assisi could not have been tenderer."

[*A Register of the Officers and Students of the Univ. of Ala., 1831–1901* (1901); *Hist. Cat. of the Univ. of Miss., 1849–1909* (1910); Richard Irby, *Hist. of Randolph-Macon Coll., Va.* (1898); *Cat. of the Officers and Alumni of Washington and Lee Univ., Lexington, Va., 1749–1888* (1888); L. S. Merriam, *Higher Education in Tenn.* (1893); O. P. Fitzgerald, *Eminent Methodists: Landon Cabell Garland* (1896); *Nashville American*, Feb. 13, 1895; *Christian Advocate* (Nashville), Feb. 21, 1895.]

J. D. W.

GARLICK, THEODATUS (Mar. 30, 1805–Dec. 9, 1884), surgeon, sculptor, and pioneer in pisciculture, was the son of Daniel Garlick, a farmer of Middlebury, Vt., and Sabra Starkweather Kirby, daughter of Abraham Kirby of Litchfield, Conn. When he was eleven years old, with his elder brother Abner he walked from Middlebury to the home of another brother, Rodolphus, at Elk Creek, now Gerard, Erie County, Pa. From him he learned the trade of blacksmith. Later he acquired the art of stone-cutting from Abner, who had settled in Cleveland, whither Theodatus went in 1818. After a few years in Cleveland he went back to Vermont, returning in 1823 with his father and family to live at Brookfield, Trumbull County, Ohio. Deciding to study medicine, he there entered the office of Dr. Ezra W. Gleason, and subsequently that of Dr. Elijah Flower where he continued for four years, acting as stone-cutter and blacksmith in the mornings and studying in the afternoons. Having saved some money, he was finally able to graduate from the medical school of the University of Maryland in 1834. After a few months in the office of Dr. N. R. Smith, professor of surgery in that school, he returned to Ohio and practised for eighteen years in Youngstown with surgery as his specialty. At the end of this period he entered into partnership with Dr. Horace A. Ackley of Cleveland. Here he soon acquired a high reputation for surgical skill, especially in the field of plastic surgery, performing many notable operations requiring both exceptional aptitude and intrepid self-confidence. His mechanical skill was a professional asset. He invented new splints and procedures in the treatment of fractures, and fashioned surgical instruments unexcelled by any manufactured in his day. Artistic gifts which he possessed were also utilized in his calling, for he made excellent models of surgical and pathological anatomy, duplicates of which are in the medical colleges of Cleveland, Cincinnati, Charlestown, and elsewhere.

His interests and achievements were many and diverse, however. He took much pleasure in making medallions in wax, and busts. These include five medallions of professors at the University of Maryland; bas-reliefs of Andrew Jackson and Henry Clay, who gave him sittings; a full-length miniature of Chief Justice Marshall, made from a portrait; and life-size busts of Judge George Tod of Ohio, and Prof. J. P. Kirtland who had been his preceptor in natural science. Photography was another of his diversions, and he constructed a camera with which he took daguerreotypes, photographing for the first time, in 1840, a person not in direct sunshine. Another interest which had practical results of value was fish culture. He carried on experiments in the artificial breeding of trout on Dr. Ackley's farm which are said to have been the first of their kind in America. An account of this work, *A Treatise on the Artificial Propagation of Certain Kinds of Fish, with the Description and Habits of Such Kinds as are the Most Suitable for Pisciculture,* was published in 1857, a second edition of which was issued by the Kirtland Society of Natural Sciences in 1880. A paper read by him before this society, Feb. 6, 1873, on the "Hybridization of Fish" was published with other papers in a pamphlet the following year.

His first two wives were daughters of his early medical instructor, Dr. Elijah Flower; his third wife, whom he married in 1845, was Mary A. Chittenden of Youngstown, Ohio. He died in 1884 from a disease of the spinal nerves which had attacked him twenty years earlier. A *Biography of Ephraim King* written by Garlick was published by the Western Reserve Historical Society as Tract No. 58, January 1883.

[See *The Biog. Cyc. and Portrait Gallery . . . of the State of Ohio,* vol. III (1884); *Western Reserve Hist. Soc.,* vol. II (1888), Tract No. 67; H. E. Henderson, in H. A. Kelly and W. L. Burrage, *Am. Medic. Biogs.* (1920), states that an autobiography in pencil is in the possession of his daughter.]

A. P. M.

GARMAN, CHARLES EDWARD (Dec. 18, 1850–Feb. 9, 1907), for more than a quarter of a century teacher of philosophy at Amherst College, was born at Limington, Me., where his father, Rev. John Harper Garman, was minister of the Congregational church. His mother was Elizabeth Bullard, daughter of Nathan and Nancy Russell Bullard, of Medway, Mass. In a home where deep religious feeling existed, the boy laid the foundation of a thorough knowledge of the Bible and became familiar with the theological arguments that were used in the denominational controversies of the time. After attending Lebanon Academy, in Maine, and the high school at Athol, Mass., he entered Amherst in the class of 1872. He soon attracted attention, first in the natural sciences and later in philosophy, by his remarkable memory and brilliant scholarship. He was awarded various prizes, among them the one in philosophy, which subject was taught by Prof. Julius H. Seelye [*q.v.*], later the president of the college. From Seelye, Garman received the inspiration that determined his later career. In 1876, after several years of marked success as principal of the high school at Ware, Mass., he entered Yale Divinity School, primarily to study philosophy. He was at once recognized as a scholar with a keenly analytical mind, a masterly power of synthesis, and an ardent love of truth. At the end of his course, in 1879, he was awarded the Hooker Fellowship, which provided for two years of graduate study. At the end of the first year, however, he accepted the position of Walker Instructor in Mathematics in Amherst College. His work included an elective course in philosophy. The next year he was appointed instructor in that subject and the following year, 1882, associate professor. In 1892, he became professor of mental and moral philosophy. For one term, in 1884, he also taught his subject at Smith College. On Aug. 24, 1882, he was married to Eliza N. Miner, daughter of Dr. David W. Miner of Ware, who had taught with him in the high school.

At Amherst his success was immediate and enduring, even though he was handicapped for many years by ill health, which developed soon after he began teaching. His students recognized in him not merely a teacher and a philosopher but also a friend. His view of philosophy led him to see each student as a personal problem, and to him the main purpose of a course in his field was to aid the student in choosing between the materialistic and the spiritual view of life, guiding him through such reconstruction of his religious and social beliefs as an idealistic philosophy might make necessary. The details of his methods in the classroom and of the subject matter of his course changed somewhat through the years, but his aim remained the same. This earnestness of purpose, added to his ability as a teacher, exerted a profound influence upon those who studied under him. In 1906 thirteen of his former pupils contributed articles on philosophical and psychological subjects to a volume with the title *Studies in Philosophy and Psychology* which they published in commemoration of his completion of twenty-five years as a teacher of philosophy in Amherst College. A far greater expression of the appreciation and gratitude of his students came after his death, the following year, in the tributes that were paid to him by hundreds of men in various professions and occupations.

To his teaching he brought a wide range of knowledge and a remarkable power of illustration. His classroom method consisted mainly in presenting problems and forcing the student to face and to think his way through them. An important feature of his system was the use of a series of printed pamphlets, loaned to the students, in which the problems were formulated. He considered this practise superior to the use of text-books, since it provided the student with the problem but not the solution. He made no effort to write for publication, preferring to devote his time and strength to teaching. After his death, however, some of his pamphlets, lectures, addresses, and letters were published in the memorial volume noted below. A philosopher of the Neo-Hegelian school, Garman displayed originality in his application of its teachings to the great problems of ethics and religion. He considered that life consists in the right estimate of values and that such estimate involves a long struggle, both of the individual and the race, toward the ideal of the State, in which are included man's relations to God as well as to his fellow men. To Garman there was no such thing as political ethics apart from divine ethics. His course culminated in the doctrine that the law of service is the ideal for both human and divine action, and that Christianity, in its essential elements, is the historical manifestation of that law and the adequate solution of the problem of evil.

[Eliza Miner Garman, with the cooperation of the class of 1884, Amherst College, *Letters, Lectures and Addresses of Charles Edward Garman* (1909); private correspondence; personal recollections of the writer.]

W. L. R.

GARMAN, SAMUEL (June 5, 1843–Sept. 30, 1927), zoölogist, was born in Indiana County, Pa., where his parents, Benjamin and Sarah Ann (Griffith) Garman, were settlers. In his later years he told inquirers that "hardly a distinct recollection of childhood or a village school is left to me; all are lost or vague and dreamlike." He left home when a mere boy and drifted westward where he had a part in surveying the routes for the Union Pacific Railroad. He fought Indians and shot game for food for the working crews during those months. Finally his desire for education led him to the Illinois State Normal University at Normal, Ill., where he was graduated in 1870. For two years he tried teaching, in 1870–71 as principal of the Mississippi State Normal School and in 1871–72 as professor of natural sciences, in Ferry Hall Seminary, at Lake Forest, Ill. Not finding in teaching the career he desired and being keenly interested in natural history, he made his way to California in 1872 and at San Francisco came under the captivating spell of Louis Agassiz. This was the turning point of his life, for he went East with Agassiz and became one of his devoted pupils. He served faithfully in connection with the famous summer school of natural history which Agassiz established at Penikese Island and at the same time he began that association with the Museum of Comparative Zoölogy at Harvard University which continued throughout his life. In 1874 he accompanied Alexander Agassiz on a scientific expedition to Lake Titicaca, South America, and he was also at times associated with him in his voyages for the exploration of the sea in the West Indian region. But little by little, Garman became completely absorbed in his work as curator of fishes at the Museum in Cambridge, and as the years passed he was less and less inclined to make journeys or even to mingle with his fellow scientists. He thus gradually became a recluse and was little known even to many of his colleagues. The study of sharks, and their near relatives, the skates and the rays, became his chief interest and he rapidly made for himself a reputation as one of the world's foremost authorities on that important group. He published altogether some fifty papers on fishes, and others of less importance on reptiles and amphibians. His reports on the deep-sea fishes collected by the *Albatross* and on the sharks collected by the *Blake* brought him international fame among zoölogists, but his most important contribution to this field, and his last great work, is his memoir, *The Plagiostomia* (*Sharks, Skates and Rays*), published in 1913.

On Sept. 2, 1895, Garman was married to Florence Armstrong of St. John, N. B., and one daughter was born to them. In 1898, Harvard awarded him, in recognition of his scientific work, the degree of B.S., and in 1899, this was followed by an M.A. In 1921 he was made a member of the Linnean Society of London. Although absorbed in his occupations at the Museum, Garman loved his garden at Arlington Heights, where he made his home, and by his work there with his flowers and bees kept himself in good physical condition throughout his long life.

[D. S. Jordan and T. Barbour, "Samuel Garman," in *Science*, Mar. 2, 1928; *Who's Who in America*, 1926–27; obituaries in *Proc. Linnean Soc. of London*, Nov. 1928, by G. H. Parker, and in *Boston Evening Transcript*. Oct. 1, 1927.] H. L. C.

GARNET, HENRY HIGHLAND (1815–Feb. 13, 1882), educator, clergyman, was the son of George and Henny or Henrietta Garnet, who later changed her name to Elizabeth. He was born a slave, at New Market, Kent County, Md., escaped from bondage in 1824, and subsequently made his way to New York, where he entered school in 1826. He was one of the persons of African blood on account of whose matriculation a mob broke up the academy at Canaan, N. H., in 1835. His education was continued, however, under Beriah Green [*q.v.*] at Oneida Institute, Whitestown, N. Y. The intelligent and versatile Presbyterian minister, Rev. Theodore S. Wright of New York, with whom Garnet established an acquaintance, probably became the dominant influence in directing him to the gospel ministry. After finishing his education, he divided his time between preaching and abolition agitation in the employ of the American Anti-Slavery Society. While he did not neglect the ministry, he viewed the anti-slavery platform as his important post of duty. He easily took rank among the foremost negro Abolitionists, and his fame spread throughout the country. He held this position until 1843, when he delivered before a national convention of the free people of color at Buffalo, N. Y., a radical address calling upon the slaves to rise and slay their masters. This utterance caused consternation in that body, and the frightened majority of the representatives voted not to endorse the sentiments expressed therein. The chief opposition to Garnet's appeal in the convention came from Frederick Douglass [*q.v.*], who was then rapidly coming to be the most influential leader of his race. He also opposed the establishment of a press to promote emancipation when it was urged by Garnet, although Douglass himself resorted to it later and became one of the most popular of anti-slavery editors. This convention marked the highest point reached in the leadership of Garnet and the beginning of his comparative decline as a result of the increasing fame of Douglass.

Garnet thereafter found more time to devote to Christian work. From 1843 to 1848 he served as pastor of the Liberty Street Presbyterian Church in Troy, N. Y., and in 1852 he was sent as a missionary to Jamaica by the United Presbyterian Church of Scotland. A few years later, however, he returned to New York to assume the pastorate of the Shiloh Presbyterian Church made vacant by the death of the Rev. Theodore S. Wright. In 1864 he went to Washington as pastor of the Fifteenth Street Presbyterian Church, where he did much for the relief of the distressed during the Civil War and later assisted Federal functionaries in working out their policy with respect to the freedmen. On Feb. 12, 1865, he preached a sermon in the House of Representatives commemorating the passage of the Thirteenth Amendment to the Constitution (*A Memorial Discourse,* 1865). Although he had strongly opposed colonization at the beginning of his career, near the close of his life he began to manifest much interest in Africa. In 1881 he was appointed minister to Liberia. He reached there on Dec. 28, but died on Feb. 13, of the following year. His wife was Julia Williams, whom he married in 1841.

[W. M. Brewer, "Henry Highland Garnet," in the *Jour. of Negro Hist.*, Jan. 1928; S. W. Williams, *Hist. of the Negro Race in America,* vol. II (1883); C. G. Woodson, *The Negro in Our Hist.* (1922); H. H. Garnet, *A Memorial Discourse* (1865), with introduction by J. M. Smith, "Sketch of the Life and Labors of Rev. Henry Highland Garnet"; W. J. Simmons, *Men of Mark* (1887); *Nat. Convention of Colored People; Proceedings* (1847); *N. Y. Tribune,* Mar. 11, 1882.]

C. G. W.

GARNETT, ALEXANDER YELVERTON PEYTON (Sept. 19, 1819–July 11, 1888), physician, the son of Muscoe and Maria Willis (Battaile) Garnett, and nephew of the first James Mercer Garnett [*q.v.*], was born at "Prospect Hill," the home of his parents on the Rappahannock River, Essex County, Va. He was educated by private tutors and at the University of Pennsylvania, from which he graduated with the degree of M.D. in 1841. He immediately applied for a commission in the medical corps of the navy, was found to be qualified, and was commissioned an assistant surgeon. In 1848 the naval vessel to which he was attached paid a visit to Rio de Janeiro, at which time he met Mary E. Wise, eldest daughter of Henry A. Wise [*q.v.*], minister to Brazil, subsequently well known as governor of Virginia. Their friendship ripened into affection and culminated in marriage on June 13 of the same year, in Washington, D. C. In 1851 Garnett resigned from the navy to engage in private practise in Washington. He acquired a highly desirable clientele of patients, and became one of the outstanding general practitioners of the city. At the outbreak of the Civil War he offered his services to the cause of the Confederacy, became one of the prominent medical officers with the Confederate forces, was in charge of two of the military hospitals in Richmond, and was personal physician to President Jefferson Davis.

In 1865, broken in health and with shattered fortune, he returned to Washington. The fact that he very quickly reëstablished his practise and within a short time again became one of the leading general practitioners, notwithstanding that the environment was one of hostility and bitterness engendered by the Civil War, bespeaks the character of the man. His latter years were spent in general practise as a family physician and as a consultant with the younger group of medical practitioners of Washington, who appreciated fully his comprehensive knowledge of disease in general as well as his superior abilities as a diagnostician. Throughout life he was intensely interested in civic affairs and actively and aggressively supported all proposals having in view the betterment of social conditions. The esteem in which he was held was evidenced by numerous appointments to membership on boards of directors of charitable institutions and hospitals in the city of Washington, professorships in the local medical schools, and a number of other honors, including election to the presidency of the American Medical Association.

Garnett came to be recognized as one of the most ardent, fearless, and resolute supporters of the movement to improve the standards of professional ethics in the medical profession, and throughout one of the most bitterly contested and acrimonious investigations that has ever occurred in the Medical Society of the District of Columbia his convictions and ideals remained unshaken. Among his publications, which were comparatively few, may be mentioned, "Observations on the Sanitary Advantages of Tide-Water Virginia" (*Transactions of the American Climatological Association,* vol. IV, 1877) and "Observations on the Potomac Marshes at Washington as a Pathogenic Agent in the Production of the So-Called Malarial Fever," read before the National Health Association in November 1881 and published the following year in *Gaillard's Medical Journal.* He was in poor health during the summer of 1888 and went to Rehoboth Beach, Del., to recuperate. On the evening of his arrival the exertion of climbing the stairs to his chamber overtaxed his heart, which was diseased, and he died of heart-failure within a few minutes.

[S. C. Busey, *Personal Reminiscences and Recollections of Forty-Six Years Membership in the Medic. Soc. of the Dist. of Columbia* (1895); D. S. Lamb and others, *Hist. of the Medic. Soc. of the Dist. of Columbia 1817–1909* (1909); *Louisville Medic. News*, Dec. 22, 1877; *Jour. Am. Medic. Asso.*, July 21, 1888; J. B. Hamilton, *Remarks . . . on the Death of Dr. Garnett* (1888), repr. in part in *Jour. Am. Medic. Asso.*, Aug. 11, 1888; W. B. Atkinson, *A Biog. Dict. of Contemporary Am. Physicians and Surgeons* (1880); J. M. Garnett, *Geneal. of the Mercer-Garnett Family of Essex County, Va.* (1910); *Evening Star* (Washington), July 12, 1888; records in the possession of Garnett's grand-daughter, Mrs. Harry S. Venn, Washington, D. C.]

J. F. S.

GARNETT, JAMES MERCER (June 8, 1770–Apr. 23, 1843), legislator, agriculturist, and educator, the second child of Muscoe Garnett and his wife, Grace Fenton Mercer, was born at "Mount Pleasant," Essex County, Va., and brought up at his father's seat "Elmwood," on the Rappahannock. Muscoe Garnett was a planter of distinction, who served his county as a member of the Committee of Safety during the Revolution; his wife was a daughter of John Mercer of "Marlborough," Stafford County, an eminent lawyer and author of *Mercer's Abridgment of the Laws of Virginia* (1737). As was the custom among the better families, their son was educated at home. He married his first cousin, Mary Eleanor Dick Mercer, daughter of Judge James Mercer of Fredericksburg, on Sept. 21, 1793. Elected to the Virginia legislature in 1799, he joined the rising Democrats in opposition to the Alien and Sedition Acts and became the friend of James Madison and John Taylor of Caroline. He went to Congress in 1805, serving for two terms and following John Randolph in his break with Jefferson. He served with that erratic leader on the jury which indicted Aaron Burr and won from him the uncertain praise: "In Congress he never said an unwise thing or gave a bad vote" (Powhatan Bouldin, *Home Reminiscences of John Randolph of Roanoke*, 1878, App., p. 289).

Retiring to his acres in 1809, he became one of the leaders in the struggle to restore the declining agricultural life of the Old South. He thought, as did John Taylor, that the tariff was a burden on those who farmed, and carried on with Matthew Carey [*q.v.*] spirited arguments in public print on this subject, Garnett writing as "Cornplanter" in the *Spirit of Seventy-Six*, a paper published in Georgetown, D. C., about 1811. From the Fredericksburg Agricultural Society—of which he was president, 1817–37—came one of the first protests against the tariff, declaring it "a tax highly impolitic in its nature, partial in its operation, and oppressive in its effects" (*Remonstrance of the Virginia Agricultural Society of Fredericksburg*, Jan. 3, 1820). He became a member of the anti-tariff convention which met at Baltimore in 1821 and wrote its address, coming back into politics to enter the Virginia legislature during the sessions of 1824–25 on the wave of resentment which arose against the centralizing tendencies of the period. In 1831 he attended an anti-tariff convention at Philadelphia.

In addition to being president of the Fredericksburg Agricultural Society for twenty years, Garnett had a hand in founding the Virginia State Agricultural Society and was chosen as the first president of the United States Agricultural Society on its formation. He wrote widely on agricultural subjects and delivered numerous addresses to agricultural societies all over the section, urging the importance of agricultural organization and cooperation, advocating the selection of better seed, the wider saving and use of capital in agriculture, crop rotation and the use of fertilizers to restore the soils (see especially: *American Farmer*, June 16, 1820, July 6, 1821, May 3, 10, Dec 6, 1822; *Farmer's Register*, Jan. 1, 1837). He was a member of the Virginia constitutional convention of 1829–30, preparing and publishing before the meeting of that body a series of *Constitutional Charts, or Comparative Views of the Legislative, Executive and Judiciary Departments in all the States in the Union, including that of the United States*, in order to save the members' time and to give them the fullest knowledge upon which to act. In the convention he was not active, but in general took the conservative side, opposing enlargement of the basis of suffrage and favoring greater influence for the owners of lands and slaves.

In the early 1820's financial reverses led him to open at his home a school for young ladies where he taught English composition, and his wife and daughters other subjects. In connection with this work he wrote and delivered a series of lectures—one each quarter—which were later gathered together and published, a second edition, enlarged, appearing under the title, *Seven Lectures on Female Education*, in 1824. In these papers he pointed out the obstacles to education in faulty early home training and the weakness in the prevalent methods of education which "drove" the students to work and incited them by "envious rivalship." He advocated a wider education for woman, so that she would be not only better prepared for marriage, but also equipped to enter an independent career in case no person worthy of her affections should appear. His school gained wide recognition and students came not only from all parts of Virginia but from other states as well. It was closed when his wife's health failed, but he soon opened a school for boys in its place, continuing himself to teach composition, and hiring outside teachers for the other branches. As in the early part of his career he had been an active promoter of improvement in agricultural methods, so now he began to advocate improvement in methods of education (*An Address on the Subject of Literary Associations to Promote Education,* 1854). He called attention to the fact that the best talent was being absorbed by the law, politics, and physics, while the education of "the rising generation . . . is generally left to . . . any who list," many of whom use teaching as "a mere stepping stone to some other profession, to be abandoned as soon as possible for almost anything else that may 'turn up.'" To better conditions, he asked for the establishment of a state school system with standard text-books, qualified teachers, and prescribed courses of study. In his seventy-third year he died at "Elmwood," where he was buried.

[J. M. Garnett, *Biog. Sketch of Hon. Jas. Mercer Garnett . . . with Mercer-Garnett and Mercer Geneals.* (1910); A. O. Craven, "The Agricultural Reformers of the Ante-Bellum South," *Am. Hist. Rev.*, Jan. 1928; *Biog. Dir. Am. Cong.* (1928).] A. O. C.

GARNETT, JAMES MERCER (Apr. 24, 1840–Feb. 18, 1916), philologist, was born at the home of his great-uncle, Charles Fenton Mercer, at Aldie, Loudoun County, Va., son of Theodore Stanford Garnett and his wife Florentina Isidora Moreno. Following a rather nomadic childhood—his father was a civil engineer—he spent four years at the Episcopal High School, near Alexandria, and then entered the University of Virginia where he further proved his brilliance as a student, took his master's degree at nineteen, and engaged actively in extracurricular pursuits: among other things he assisted in organizing there what is said to have been the first Young Men's Christian Association incorporated within the precincts of a college. After teaching for a year he returned to the University, served in the "Southern Guard" composed of students, and in July 1861 enlisted as a private in the Rockbridge Artillery of "Stonewall" Jackson's brigade. When paroled at Appomattox, after fighting throughout the war, he was captain of artillery and ordnance officer of Grimes's (formerly Rodes's) division, II Corps, Army of Northern Virginia. (His Civil War diary, chiefly concerned with Gen. Early's Shenandoah Valley campaign, was published in the *Southern Historical Society Papers,* vol. XXVII, 1899.)

He resumed his teaching after the war, and in 1869–70 spent a year at the Universities of Berlin and Leipzig studying classical philology. On his return he was chosen principal of St. John's College, Annapolis, Md., and held this office, with the professorship of history and of English language and literature, until 1880, when he resigned. For two years he conducted a school of his own at Ellicott City, Md. In 1882 he was appointed professor of English language and literature in the University of Virginia and continued as such until 1893, when, the English teaching being divided between two chairs, he was made professor of English language alone. He resigned this position three years later, moved to Baltimore, and, after filling for one session a vacancy in the chair of English literature at the Woman's (now Goucher) College, devoted himself to private teaching, writing, and the affairs of the Protestant Episcopal Church, in which he had long been zealously interested.

He was an accurate, painstaking, and erudite scholar, though the amount of his published work was not large. He edited *Selections in English Prose from Elizabeth to Victoria* (1891), *Hayne's Speech, to which Webster Replied* (1894), *Macbeth* (1897), and *Burke's Speech on Conciliation with America* (1901); wrote most of the two-volume history, *The University of Virginia* (1904), prepared under his supervision; and contributed occasional articles or reviews to magazines and philological journals. His most important works were his metrical translations from the Anglo-Saxon, *Beowulf* (1882) and *Elene; Judith; Athelstan, or the Fight at Brunanburh; and Byrhtnoth, or the Fight at Maldon: Anglo-Saxon Poems* (1889). His *Beowulf,* a strictly literal version, was the first American translation of the poem and was accorded a flattering reception. It was most favorably reviewed by the German critics; was commended by English and American authorities; and was cordially welcomed by American schools and colleges, passing through four editions (Chauncey B. Tinker, *The Translations of Beowulf,* 1903). As a teacher he was less successful. He failed to fire the imaginations of his students, and his own rich scholarship, culture, and exacting ideals did not serve to make him indulgent of the limitations of their knowledge.

He married, Apr. 19, 1871, Kate Huntington Noland, of Middleburg, Loudoun County, Va. During his later years he prepared biographical sketches of a number of his distinguished relatives, notably his grandfather, James Mercer

Garnett, and his first cousin, M. R. H. Garnett [*qq.v.*], and in 1910 published a *Genealogy of the Mercer-Garnett Family.*

[Garnett's own genealogical writings; P. A. Bruce, *Hist. of the Univ. of Va.* (5 vols., 1921–22). J. M. Garnett, P. B. Barringer, and Rosewell Page, *The Univ. of Va.* (2 vols., 1904); C. W. Kent, in *Alumni Bull. of the Univ. of Va.*, 3 ser. IX, 276–78 (Apr. 1916); J. W. Bright, in *Am. Jour. Philology*, Apr.–June 1916; *N. Y. Times*, Feb. 20, 1916.] A. C. G., Jr.

GARNETT, MUSCOE RUSSELL HUNTER (July 25, 1821–Feb. 14, 1864), statesman, was born at "Elmwood," Essex County, Va., the descendant of two prominent Virginia families, and the son of James Mercer Garnett, Jr., and Maria Hunter. His father, eldest son of the first James Mercer Garnett [*q.v.*], died early, and the precocious, serious, and ambitious boy was educated by his maternal kin and by tutors until he was seventeen. After a successful session at the University of Virginia, he devoted two years to an elaborate scheme of private studies before returning to the University to study law. In 1842 he was admitted to the bar, and commenced practise at Loretto, Essex County. He continued his self-education systematically, reading, writing occasional reviews, and building a reputation for eloquent and scholarly oratory, with the intention of qualifying himself for a political career. In 1850 he published *The Union, Past and Future: How it Works and How to Save it,* a forceful pamphlet arraying the economic disadvantages of the Union to the South and protesting against Northern efforts toward governmental centralization. The earliest able philosophical exposition of the relations of slavery to the federal government, it created wide-spread interest and contributed to his election to the state constitutional convention that fall. After serving (1853–56) in the Virginia House of Delegates, where he headed the committee on finance and figured conspicuously in debate, he was elected to Congress in November 1856, from the First Virginia District; and was reëlected to the Thirty-fifth and Thirty-sixth Congresses. Already twice a delegate to Democratic national conventions, he had become known as one of the most brilliant Southern statesmen, a strict constructionist, and an uncompromising defender of slavery. In Congress he was active in tariff and retrenchment legislation—he resembled his distinguished uncle, R. M. T. Hunter [*q.v.*], in his talent for financial matters—but the speeches in which he challenged Northern infringements of the Constitution and encroachment upon the rights of the South furnish better evidence of his fearlessness, cogent logic, and ardent temperament. He was a strong advocate of Virginia's secession, holding during the winter of 1860–61 that such a step would be "the best possible mode of preventing war and reconstructing a Union of equality" ("Biographical Sketch," p. 83). Withdrawing from Congress when Virginia seceded, he was chosen in May 1861 to fill a vacancy in the Virginia convention, and in November was elected to the First Confederate Congress. Although he eagerly supported the conduct of the war, at his own request being transferred from the committee on ways and means to that on military affairs, he was defeated for reëlection by the soldier vote. Before his term ended he contracted typhoid fever in Richmond, and died soon after reaching his home in Essex County. He was survived by his wife, Mary Picton Stevens, of Hoboken, N. J., whom he had married July 26, 1860. His public career loomed larger in promise than it appears in retrospect; but there is little doubt that his learning, ability, and integrity might have won him, had he lived longer, the highest political honors within Virginia's bestowal.

[J. M. Garnett, "Biographical Sketch of Hon. Muscoe Russell Hunter Garnett," in *Wm. and Mary Coll. Quart.*, July–Oct. 1909, reprinted as a pamphlet, 1909, with extracts from his writings; J. M. Garnett, *Geneal. of the Mercer-Garnett Family* (1910); *Cong. Globe*, 34–36 Cong., esp. 36 Cong., 2 Sess., pp. 411–16; E. G. Swem and J. T. Williams, *A Reg. of the Gen. Assembly of Va. 1776–1918* (1918); obituary in *Richmond Enquirer*, Feb. 15, 1864.] A. C. G., Jr.

GARNETT, ROBERT SELDEN (Dec. 16, 1819–July 13, 1861), Confederate soldier, was born at "Champlain," Essex County, Va., of stock distinguished alike in military and civil affairs. His father, Robert Selden Garnett, a brother of the elder James Mercer Garnett [*q.v.*], represented Virginia in Congress for ten years; his mother, Olympia Charlotte, was the daughter of the French general, Jean Pierre DeGouges. He graduated from the United States Military Academy in 1841, served during that winter with the 4th Artillery on the Canadian border, and was commissioned second lieutenant. From July 1843 to October 1844 he was assistant instructor in infantry tactics at West Point. As aide-de-camp to Gen. Wool, 1845, and to Zachary Taylor, 1846–49, he participated in the military occupation of Texas and fought through the Mexican War, his services and gallantry at Palo Alto, Resaca de la Palma, Monterey, and Buena Vista winning him promotion to first lieutenant and the brevets of captain and major. After peace was declared, he was transferred to the infantry and promoted captain, serving another year in Texas before being detailed to the Military Academy, 1852–54, as commandant of cadets and instructor in infantry tactics. In 1855 he was commissioned major and sent to the Northwest, where he commanded the Puget Sound and Yakima expeditions, and remained on duty until 1858 when he went to Europe on leave. He had married, the preceding year, Mary Neilson, of New York City.

Returning from abroad when the Civil War broke out, he resigned from the United States army and entered the service of Virginia. He was appointed adjutant-general of the state troops, and allotted the task of organizing this heterogeneous force into an army. Early in June he was commissioned brigadier-general and given command of the Confederate troops operating in northwestern Virginia. Circumstances were against him from the start of his campaign. Sentiment in that part of the state was against the Confederacy; he lacked cavalry and guns, and had serious difficulty obtaining supplies. He saw that his little army could not hope to accomplish much against the overwhelming enemy forces; but, undaunted, he established headquarters at Laurel Hill, entrenching half of his troops there and half at Rich Mountain under Pegram. When the Federal attack dislodged the Confederates from Rich Mountain, Garnett was compelled to abandon Laurel Hill. He saved his army, outnumbered more than six to one by McClellan's men, by a most masterly retreat, but was himself instantly killed while directing the conduct of his rear guard after the sharp engagement at Carrick's Ford, on Cheat River. He was a brave and skilful officer, of whom the South expected much, but who did not have opportunity to fulfil the promise of his military training.

[*Official Records* (*Army*), 1 ser., vol. II; G. W. Cullum, *Biog. Reg.* (3rd ed., 1891); C. A. Evans, ed., *Confed. Mil. Hist.* (1899), vol. III; H. M. Price and C. T. Allen, "Rich Mountain in 1861," *Southern Hist. Soc. Papers*, vol. XXVII (1899); J. M. Garnett, *Geneal. of the Mercer-Garnett Family* (1910).] A. C. G., Jr.

GARRARD, JAMES (Jan. 14, 1749–Jan. 19, 1822), governor of Kentucky, Baptist clergyman, was a native of Stafford County, Va., a member of a family of considerable local importance. His father, William, was county-lieutenant of Stafford County, and James in 1781 held the rank of colonel in the Stafford County regiment of the Virginia militia (W. P. Palmer, *Calendar of Virginia State Papers*, II, 1881, 43). How much actual fighting the young Garrard saw during the Revolution it is impossible to ascertain, but it is certain that his military life was interrupted by a year in the House of Delegates, 1779, when he represented Stafford County. In 1783, accompanied by his wife, Elizabeth Mountjoy Garrard, whom he had married on Dec. 20, 1769, and their seven children, he removed to Kentucky, where he settled on Stoner Creek in the present county of Bourbon, then Fayette. Here three years later he built his residence, "Mt. Lebanon," where he lived until his death. For many years after his removal to Kentucky Garrard's interests seemed to vacillate between religion and politics. He had been a member of the Baptist Church in Virginia, and soon after coming to Kentucky he helped organize, in 1787, the Cooper's Run church near Mt. Lebanon. For ten years he was one of the ministers of this church, and seems to have been active not only in his work here but also in the organization of Baptist congregations in other parts of Kentucky. In 1785 he was elected as representative of Fayette County in the Virginia House of Delegates. One apparent result of his second service in the Virginia legislature was the creation of Bourbon County out of Fayette and the establishment of Mt. Lebanon as the temporary county seat (W. E. Henning, *The Statutes at Large*, XII, 1823, 89–90). He also represented Fayette and then Bourbon County in the conventions which marked Kentucky's prolonged struggle for statehood, and was a member of the convention which made the first constitution, but he seems not to have played a leading part in any of these meetings.

In 1796 Garrard was one of four candidates for the governorship of Kentucky. He was chosen over Benjamin Logan by the electoral college on the second ballot, although Logan had received a plurality of the votes on the first. The doubtful constitutionality of this election caused considerable discontent and had its influence in bringing about a revision of the constitution a few years later (Charles Kerr, *History of Kentucky*, 1922, I, 316). Garrard's popularity with the Kentucky legislature was attested by the fact that his name was given to a newly created county; his popularity with the people was shown by his election as governor by popular vote at the conclusion of his first term in 1800. During his eight years as governor, however, he did not display unusual ability. As a Republican leader he followed Jefferson in denouncing the Alien and Sedition laws, and used his influence in securing the adoption of the Kentucky Resolutions of 1798. In one of his messages to the legislature he brought considerable ridicule on himself by advocating an increase of importations up the Mississippi as a measure for remedying the defective paper currency in Kentucky.

While governor, Garrard fell very much under the influence of his secretary of state, Harry Toulmin, a Unitarian. He came to have very pronounced Unitarian views and succeeded in spreading his ideas in his own congregation at Cooper's Run. As a result he was dropped from the church and from the Baptist Association in 1803. This act closed Garrard's ministry, and closed also his connection with the Baptist Church. His fellow Baptists seem always to have deplored his political ambitions but never lost faith in his integrity. In fact his popularity throughout Kentucky seems to have been due more to his probity than to his ability. After 1804 Garrard lived quietly at his home without holding or seeking further office. Upon his death the Kentucky legislature erected a monument in his honor at Mt. Lebanon. He was survived by twelve children, one of whom, James, played a prominent part in Kentucky history and is often confused with his father.

[The records of Stafford County were destroyed by fire and consequently very little is known of the Virginia branch of the Garrard family. Garrard's official journals and papers are preserved in the office of the secretary of state of Kentucky at Frankfort. For further reference see E. G. Swem and J. W. Williams, *A Reg. of the Gen. Assembly of Va., 1776–1918* (1918); A. R. des Cognets, *Gov. Garrard, of Ky.: His Descendants and Relatives* (1898); Lewis and R. H. Collins, *Hist. of Ky.* (rev. ed., 1874), I, 366; Mann Butler, *A Hist. of the Commonwealth of Ky.* (1834), p. 295; J. H. Spencer, *A Hist. of Ky. Baptists* (1885), I, 133–34; *Ky. Gazette* (Lexington), Jan. 31, 1822.]

R. S. C.

GARRARD, KENNER (*c.* Sept. 1, 1828–May 15, 1879), soldier, was born in Kentucky while his mother was on a short visit from the family home in Cincinnati, Ohio. His father, Jeptha Dudley Garrard, was a lawyer of high standing, and his great-grandfather, James Garrard [*q.v.*], militia officer of the Revolution, was twice elected governor of Kentucky. His mother was Sarah Bella Ludlow (1802–1882), whose father, Israel Ludlow, was early a landed proprietor of Cincinnati. Young Garrard entered Harvard University with the class of 1848, but left in his sophomore year to enter West Point from the state of Ohio. Graduating in 1851, eighth in his class, he received assignment to the 4th Artillery, but a year later he transferred to the 1st Dragoons, and after much frontier service, was captured, Apr. 23, 1861, by Texas troops not yet affiliated with the Confederacy. After parole, and short service in the office of the commissary-general and as instructor and commandant of cadets at West Point, he was exchanged, and immediately received appointment as colonel, 146th New York Volunteers. He participated with his regiment in the battles of Fredericksburg, Chancellorsville, and Gettysburg; and for gallant services at Gettysburg where he commanded a brigade after the death of its commander, he was brevetted lieutenant-colonel in the regular army. Shortly after, on July 23, 1863, he was appointed brigadier-general of volunteers. He took part in the Rapidan campaign—participating in combats at Rappahannock Station and at Mine Run; was in charge of the cavalry bureau at Washington; and early in 1864, was transferred to the Army of the Cumberland to command the 2nd Cavalry Division in the operations of Sherman's army. He received the brevet of colonel, July 22, 1864, for meritorious services in the expedition against Covington, Ga. In December of the same year he was assigned to the 2nd Division, XVI Army Corps, which he commanded until the end of the war. He took part in the battles before Nashville—receiving the brevet of major-general of volunteers for conspicuous gallantry, and of brigadier-general in the regular army for gallant and meritorious services. He also had an important part in the operations against Mobile, personally leading a storming column in the capture of Blakeley, Ga., Apr. 3–9, and participated in the movement against Montgomery, Ala., Apr. 13–27, 1865. On Mar. 13, 1865, he was brevetted major-general in the regular army for gallant and meritorious services throughout the war. He commanded the District of Mobile until mustered out of the volunteer service, Aug. 24, 1865; and was assistant inspector-general, Department of the Missouri, until he resigned from the army, Nov. 9, 1866. Returning to Cincinnati, Garrard devoted much time to the management of his large real-estate interests, and, declining to enter politics, to the promotion of the welfare of the city. He served on various local administrative commissions, was director of the Musical Festival, and was an active member of the Historical and Philosophical Society of Ohio. His sudden death, the result of intestinal complications, was a shock to the community in which for thirteen years he had exerted an influence for good. He was buried at Spring Grove Cemetery, Cincinnati, Ohio.

[*Official Records (Army)*; *Battles and Leaders of the Civil War*, vol. IV (1888); J. D. Cox, *Atlanta* (1909), and *The March to the Sea* (1906); Whitelaw Reid, *Ohio in the War* (1868), I, 852; *Tenth Ann. Reunion Asso. Grads., U. S. Mil. Acad.* (1879); G. W. Cullum, *Biog. Reg. . . . U. S. Mil. Acad.*, vol. II (1891); A. R. des Cognets, *Gov. Garrard, of Ky.: His Descendants and Relatives* (1898); *Times* (Cincinnati), May 15, 1879; *Cincinnati Enquirer*, May 16, 1879. Date of birth is taken from a statement, in Garrard's handwriting, in records at the U. S. Military Academy, that on July 1, 1847, he was eighteen years and ten months of age.]

C. D. R.

GARREAU, ARMAND (Sept. 13, 1817–Mar. 28, 1865), French novelist of Louisiana, was born in France at Cognac, the son of Louis Armand Garreau and Marie Rose Dumontet of

Saint-Pierre, Martinique. His father served under Moreau and practised law. Garreau received a classical education as a preparation for teaching, then taught in the department of Gironde. In November 1838 he was married to Marie Anais Boraud. Emigrating to America, he opened a school in New Orleans, and in addition to teaching contributed extensively to the French newspapers of New Orleans, especially *La Revue de la Semaine*. He studied local history and wrote a voluminous novel entitled "Louisiana," which appeared in 1849 in *Les Veillées Louisianaises*. It abounded in local color and dramatic situations and narrated the story of the inhabitants of Louisiana who revolted against the Spanish rule in 1768. Upon the proclamation of the Second Republic, Garreau returned to France and established himself at Barbezieux. He became a printer and publisher and founded in 1850 a newspaper, *Le Narrateur impartial*, for which he wrote prose and verse. He published a complete novel, *Ogine, Chronique Angoumoisine du Xe Siècle,* which appeared in 1852, and began a second, "La Maison maudite." In the meanwhile his friend Paul Coq published in Paris an illustrated edition of "Louisiana" in *La Semaine*. In 1854 Garreau discontinued his daily to establish, with the cooperation of H. d'Aussy, the monthly *Légendes et Chroniques de l'Angoumois, de la Saintonge et des provinces limitrophes* in which he completed "La Maison maudite" under the title of "La Grotte maudite" and began "Le Canal des moines." Continuing his chronicles of Southern France in the form of novels, he wrote *Leudaste* (1854), a novel of life in Gaul under the Merovingian kings, and *Chronique du XVIe Siècle, 1548: Les Peteaux* (1854), a story of a revolt against the salt tax.

Persecuted by the local officials of the Second Empire, Garreau was forced to go to Paris, where for a time he studied law and taught school in Saint-Denis, but in 1858 he was again teaching in New Orleans. He continued his literary activities by writing for *Les Cinq Centimes, L'Indépendant, Le Courrier de Bruges,* and *L'Estafette du sud.* He died in New Orleans at the age of forty-seven, survived by his widow and six children. In his writing Garreau followed the romantic lead of Hugo, Musset, and Dumas père. He was endowed with a fervid imagination but complained that he was unable to discipline his style, that his pen was too facile, that he confused history and drama, and that he could not organize his work. He championed the cause of unfortunates, was a bitter foe of bigotry, and a sincere admirer of revolutions.

[Jules Pellisson, "Armand Garreau," in *La Revue de Saintonge & d'Aunis,* Dec. 1, 1909; Charles Testut, *Portraits littéraires de la Nouvelle-Orléans* (1850); E. Fortier, in *Mémoires, premier congrès de la langue française au Canada* (1914); Ruby van Allen Caulfeild, *The French Lit. of La.* (1929); *L'Abeille de la Nouvelle-Orléans,* Mar. 29, 1865.]
L. C. D.

GARRETSON, JAMES EDMUND (Oct. 18, 1828–Oct. 26, 1895), dentist, oral surgeon, author, a son of Jacob M. and Mary A. (Powell) Garretson, was born at Wilmington, Del., and received his early education at the Wilmington Classical Academy. In 1850 he became student-assistant to Dr. Thacher, a dentist of Wilmington; practised dentistry for a time at Woodbury, N. J.; graduated from the Philadelphia College of Dental Surgery in 1856, and in the same year established himself permanently in the practise of dentistry in Philadelphia. He also studied medicine in the University of Pennsylvania, receiving the degree of M.D. in 1859; in which year, Nov. 10, he married Beulah Craft, by whom he had two daughters. He served as a demonstrator in the Philadelphia School of Anatomy for several years, and became a member of the faculty of that institution in 1862. For a time during the Civil War he was in the military hospital service. From 1874 till his death he was connected with the Philadelphia Dental College, at first as instructor in clinical surgery. He became professor of anatomy and surgery there in 1878 and dean of the faculty in 1880. He was also professor of clinical surgery in the Medico-Chirurgical College of Philadelphia, and president of the Medical and Chirurgical Society of that city in 1883. He is generally recognized as the originator of oral surgery as a specialty of dentistry, and in that specialty there can be no doubt that he was the most skilful and eminent practitioner of his day. The outstanding feature of his technique, in which he differed from his predecessors, was the avoidance, so far as possible, of external incisions and consequent scarring of the face. Many extensive operations confined entirely to the interior of the mouth were performed by him at the Hospital of Oral Surgery, Philadelphia Dental College. He was the first surgeon to employ the dental engine as modified for surgical operations (1882); and its subsequent employment in certain operations, especially within the brain case, resulted from his demonstrations of its utility. Beginning in 1855, he contributed more than a hundred articles to dental journals, most of them relating to diseases of the mouth and oral surgery. In 1869 he published *A Treatise on the Diseases and Surgery of the Mouth, Jaws and Associated Parts,* which appeared in subsequent editions, revised and expanded, as *A System of Oral Surgery*

(1873, 1881, 1884, 1890, 1895). In its field it was the first systematic work and the only standard text-book for many years. It was translated into Japanese in 1887.

Garretson's parents were Methodists, while his wife's family belonged to the Society of Friends; and he regularly accompanied his wife to the meetings of the latter sect at Darby near Philadelphia, but never became a Quaker. From an early age he was greatly interested in spiritism, Platonism, Rosicrucianism and transcendental philosophy in general, and throughout his life devoted much time and energy to writing and lecturing on such subjects. Under the *nom de plume* of John Darby he published: *Odd Hours of a Physician* (1871); *Thinkers and Thinking* (1873); *Two Thousand Years After* (1876); *Hours with John Darby* (1877); *Brushland* (1882); *Nineteenth Century Sense* (1887); *Man and His World* (1889). The last-named book consists of *Two Thousand Years After,* and a series of philosophical lectures delivered by him in 1888 before the Garretsonian Society of Philadelphia, founded and named in his honor. An interesting writer and lecturer, and a deeply religious man with a mystic turn of mind, he strove to harmonize the nebulous theories of transcendentalism with the solid facts of science. In 1891 he established a summer home at Lansdowne, Pa., where he died in his sixty-eighth year. His remains were incinerated at the Germantown Cemetery, and his ashes were interred in the Friends' burying-ground at Upper Darby. On May 5, 1930, a statue of him was unveiled at the Dental Department of Temple University, Philadelphia.

[*Dental Cosmos,* Nov. and Dec. 1895, and July 1930; Phila. *Times and Register,* Nov. 9, 1895; B. L. Thorpe in C. R. E. Koch, *Hist. of Dental Surgery,* vol. III (1910); *Index of the Periodical Dental Literature,* 1839–95 (1923–27); the *Dental Review,* Dec. 1895; *Papers of the Hist. Soc. of Del.,* XIX (1897), 10–23; Phila. *Public Ledger,* Oct. 28, 29, 1895; family records.]

L. P. B.

GARRETT, EDMUND HENRY (Oct. 19, 1853–Apr. 2, 1929), painter, illustrator, etcher, author, was born in Albany, N. Y. His parents, Anthony and Eliza A. (Miers) Garrett, moved from Albany to Boston, Mass., while he was still an infant. He inherited pronounced artistic tastes from his father's family. His paternal grandfather was François Grenier of Bordeaux; the patronymic was changed to Garrett when the family emigrated to America. Edmund studied in the public schools of Boston until he reached the age of sixteen, and after graduation he took up wood-carving as a trade for the ensuing four years; then, at the age of twenty, he began drawing illustrations for newspapers and magazines. Having married Marietta Goldsmith of Roxbury, in 1877, he resolved to become a painter. His first finished painting was made in 1879 and was exhibited in the Museum of Fine Arts, Boston. Then, with his wife, he started for Paris, continuing his art training at the Julian Academy, under Jean Paul Laurens, Gustave Boulanger, and Jules Lefebvre. During a sojourn of several years in France, the young couple traveled extensively, visiting Italy, Spain, Holland, and England. On their return to America they settled in Winchester, Mass., subsequently moving to Cambridge, then to Brookline, and finally to Needham.

Garrett's versatility was shown by the variety of his artistic activities. He began as a woodcarver; made illustrations for newspapers, magazines, and books; painted both in oils and watercolors; etched book-plates; lectured; designed title-pages, initials, and coats-of-arms; and wrote and illustrated several of his own books. *Elizabethan Songs* (1891) contained more than twenty illustrations for the verses of Herrick, Ben Jonson, and their contemporaries; *Three Heroines of New England Romance* (1894) carried over sixty drawings illustrating the stories of Priscilla Mullins, Agnes Surriage, and Martha Hilton; and *Victorian Songs* (1895) was ornamented with twenty full-page photogravures characteristic of his fertile fancy and his pithy talent as a draftsman. In 1896 he published a translation of Prosper Merimée's *Carmen* with his original illustrations. *Romance and Reality of the Puritan Coast* (1897) treated of the picturesque north shore of Massachusetts Bay. The drawings in this volume were in his best vein. In like manner he recorded in his *Pilgrim Shore* (1897) a jaunt along the south shore from Boston to Plymouth. Among the other books which he illustrated were Keats's *Eve of St. Agnes* (1885), Lowell's *Vision of Sir Launfal* (1891), Bulwer's novels, Drake's *Culprit Fay* (1893), and the romances of Alexandre Dumas.

Garrett made several visits to England, where he painted many charming water-colors of gardens, castles, manor houses, street scenes, and quaint villages. His most interesting lecture, accompanied by unusually artistic lantern slides, was on the old baronial halls and mansions of England. He spent many of his summers on Cape Cod. To his work as an illustrator he brought a fine appreciation of the subject matter and spirit of the text as well as a competent technical equipment. Much of his work was in pen and ink, which he employed somewhat in the manner of an etcher, suggestively and with a special feeling for the significance and charm of line. The pictorial effectiveness of his drawings was due in part to the stenographic character of his vignettes. Garrett died at his home in Needham, Mass., in his seventy-sixth year, leaving a widow and two sons.

[*Who's Who in America,* 1926–27; S. R. Koehler, "The Works of Am. Etchers: Edmund Henry Garrett," *Am. Art Rev.,* July 1881; E. H. Garrett, *Book-Plates Selected from the Works of Edmund H. Garrett* (1904); "Edmund Garrett's Tudor Decorations," *Am. Mag. of Art,* Oct. 1916; *Boston Transcript,* Apr. 3, Sept. 28, 1929; newspaper articles of the eighties and nineties.]
W. H. D.

GARRETT, JOHN WORK (July 31, 1820–Sept. 26, 1884), railroad executive, banker, was born in Baltimore, the second son of Elizabeth Stouffer and Robert Garrett [*q.v.*]. After two years at Lafayette College in Pennsylvania, he became associated at the age of nineteen with his father and brother in the former's commission house. His seventeen years of training in the diversified operations of the firm proved a valuable preparation for his subsequent career. During the fifties the Baltimore & Ohio Railroad, in which he was a stockholder, was involved in serious difficulties. The necessity of raising more money than the initial three millions (held adequate in 1827 to carry the line to the Ohio River) led to contentions concerning the representation on the board of directors for Maryland, for Baltimore City, and for the individual stockholders, who, though owning a majority of the stock, constituted a minority on the board. Young Garrett prepared such a challenging report on the finances for a subcommittee of which he was chairman, that on Nov. 17, 1858, on the motion of Johns Hopkins, the largest individual stockholder, he was elected president of the railroad. He at once inaugurated new policies, in which economy was strongly stressed, and despite the general financial crisis, his first annual report showed a gain in net earnings. The second year the results were even more remarkable. Supported by this ample vindication of his views, he pressed the reorganization of the board which partially freed the road from political control.

Although sympathetic with his Southern friends, Garrett from the beginning of the Civil War supported the Union. His loyalty was apparently a matter of the head as well as the heart, for he calculated the inevitability of Confederate defeat by superior Northern resources. The importance of his adherence to the Northern cause cannot be overestimated, for the leading Maryland Confederates always held him responsible for their inability to seize Washington. He was sometimes able to give the government the first intimation of hostile movements and received the warmest appreciation of his services from Lincoln, yet the benefits were not all one-sided, for his loyalty and ability saved his railroad from government seizure. Stretching as it did along the theatre of war, twice crossing Confederate territory, the Baltimore & Ohio became a main objective for Southern attack. Only the extraordinary skill and energy of its president prevented its abandonment. Night and day the young official worked, now in a cabinet meeting, now with a reconstruction gang, occasionally escaping capture only because of his rough work clothes. The first military rail-transport movement of history, that of the transfer of 20,000 men from the Potomac to Chattanooga in 1863, was a monumental triumph for Garrett and early railroad management. Meanwhile his efficient management raised profits to a huge figure.

With the return of peace, Garrett first replaced the war damages and then resumed his plans for extending and perfecting the system, securing ultimately direct routes to Pittsburgh and Chicago, and arranging for an independent line into New York. To restore Baltimore as a seaport huge wharves were built at Locust Point to accommodate the ocean liners of the North German Lloyd, with which company he had entered into an alliance, and a system of elevators was erected. The Baltimore & Ohio Company became a self-contained unit by building its own sleeping and dining cars, setting up large hotels in the Alleghanies, creating its own express company, and fostering a separate telegraph company. Garrett's active mind had envisaged a line to New Orleans, extending even across the Southwest to California. In 1880 he was at the height of his success, ruling the railroad and politicians with an iron hand, but such control was not attained without battle. The desperate rate-war with the other trunk lines, lasting until they began to form pools in self-defense, was followed by a bitter and costly rivalry with the Pennsylvania over the Eastern route. Next the charge of discrimination against local shippers had to be met. Then, the necessity, as Garrett conceived it, of controlling the state legislature required constant care and watchfulness. Finally, in 1877, when wages were cut to reduce expense, there came the first great railroad strike. Garrett was already succumbing to the drain upon his energy of twenty-five years of unremitting toil, when the accident which cost the life of his wife, Rachel Harrison, completed his surrender. Though he was a large man physically, always giving the impression of determination and vigor, his intimate letters reveal him as kindly and affectionate.

[J. T. Scharf, *Hist. of Baltimore City and County* (1881); C. C. Hall, ed., *Baltimore, Its Hist. and Its People* (1912); M. P. Andrews, *Hist. of Maryland* (1929); Paul Winchester, *The Baltimore and Ohio Railroad* (2 vols., 1927); Edward Hungerford, *The Story of the Baltimore and Ohio Railroad* (2 vols., 1928); Theo. F. Lang, *Loyal W. Va. from 1861 to 1865* (1895); *Official Records (Army)*; *Ann. Reports . . . of the Baltimore and Ohio Railroad Company*, 1859–84; various reports, pamphlets, and documents of the Baltimore & Ohio Company; and the Robt. Garrett Papers in the Lib. of Cong.] E. L.

GARRETT, ROBERT (May 2, 1783–Feb. 4, 1857), merchant, financier, born at Lisburn, County Down, Ireland, combined the industry and Calvinistic principles of his Scotch mother, Margaret MacMechen, with the generous spirit of his Irish father, John Garrett. Though he was only seven years old when his family emigrated to America, the death of his father placed some responsibility on his young shoulders when his mother bought a farm in Cumberland County, Pa. A move in 1798 merely transferred the family to another farm in Washington County. At sixteen he experienced his first venture into the business world when he accompanied his elder brother on a trading expedition among the Indians. They were forced by the intensely cold weather to spend the winter in an Indian hut near the Ohio River, an experience which gave Robert an enduring interest in the development of the West. Shortly after 1800 he went to Baltimore and became a clerk for four years in a produce and commission house. Later he formed the partnership of Wallace & Garrett, which afforded him further experience in handling the western trade. In 1812, when this partnership was dissolved, he moved back to Middletown, Pa., but returned finally to Baltimore about 1820. He opened a business house which soon assumed the name of Robert Garrett & Sons. Before long he made himself an important factor in the wholesale grocery, produce, forwarding, and commission business. Although he was brought into competition with some of the strongest local firms of Baltimore, he was able to hold his own. He appreciated the strategic advantage of Baltimore's geographical position in lying nearer the frontier than any other seaport, and resolved to capture western trade by developing superior transportation facilities for the farmers of the West. The slow method of shipping produce by pack horses over the Alleghany Mountains he improved upon by establishing fast wagon trains which ran day and night over turn-pikes and plank-roads connecting with the Pennsylvania Canal. When the project of the Baltimore & Ohio Railroad began to materialize, he came to its support and invested heavily in its stock. To meet the demands of the frontier trade, he established direct connections with Latin America at the same time seeking an outlet for American products in Europe. For greater convenience the house developed its own banking operations and became the American correspondent for such firms as George Peabody & Company of London and other houses abroad, winning for itself a position as one of the leading houses of the city. The operations in finance gradually overshadowed the commission and shipping business.

Entering loyally into the enterprises for the expansion of his adopted city, Garrett took active part in developing local business interests. He became a director of the Baltimore Water Company, the Gas Company, and the Shot Tower Company. Already a director of the Savings Bank of Baltimore, he became in 1836 one of the organizers of the Western Bank, serving in this capacity until his death. In 1847, to meet the needs of another portion of the city, he played a leading part in founding the Eutaw Savings Bank, serving it as director throughout the remainder of his life. Keeping constantly in mind the desirability of attracting the western trade to Baltimore, he purchased first the Eutaw House, in order to provide comfortable hotel accommodations in the city, and five years later the Wheatfield Inn, which he replaced by a new hotel in the vicinity of the jobbing trade. Shortly after the close of the Mexican War he built the *Monumental City*, the largest steamship so far constructed in Baltimore, to link the trade of that city with the trade of San Francisco. On May 19, 1817, he was married to Elizabeth Stouffer, daughter of Henry Stouffer, who was long prominent in Baltimore as a merchant and member of the city council. It was to their son, John Work Garrett [*q.v.*], that the father's mantle descended.

[A great quantity of business letters and some family letters have been preserved in the Lib. of Cong., as the Robert Garrett Papers. The files of the *Baltimore American* and *Sun* yield bits of information, as well as fairly full obituary notices. See also Geo. W. Howard, *The Monumental City* (1873); J. Thos. Scharf, *Hist. of Baltimore City and County* (1881); and R. H. Spencer, ed., *Geneal. and Memorial Encyc. of the State of Md.* (1919).] E. L.

GARRETT, THOMAS (Aug. 21, 1789–Jan. 25, 1871), Abolitionist, son of Thomas and Sarah Price Garrett, both Quakers, was born on a farm in Upper Darby, Pa. In the early twenties, with his wife, Mary Sharpless, and their children, he moved to Wilmington, Del. There he set himself up as a hardware merchant and tool-maker. In 1827 his wife died and shortly afterward he was married to Rachel Mendenhall. During a pursuit to recover a free colored woman kidnapped from his father's home, he became convinced that his special mission was to help slaves escape. As early as 1818 he joined the Pennsylvania Abolition Society. In time his Wilmington home became widely known as a refuge for slaves. With the sentiment of a slave state bitterly hostile to him, with his house constantly under surveillance, with a ten-thousand-dollar reward placed by Maryland for his arrest, it is a tribute to his shrewdness that he so long escaped the penalty of the law. Although scurrilously attacked in the press, threatened, and warned by friends to leave, he was not prosecuted until 1848 when certain slave-owners brought suit against him before Chief Justice Taney for assisting seven slaves to escape, and ultimately secured his conviction. The fine, because of his recent business reverses, swept away all his property but did not deter him from continuing his activities in behalf of the negroes. With the assistance of his friends, he was able to rebuild his business handsomely although he was then over sixty years of age. By the time the Emancipation Proclamation had been issued he had helped about 2,700 slaves to escape.

In April 1870 the negroes participated in the Wilmington celebration over the Fifteenth Amendment by drawing Thomas Garrett through the streets in an open barouche, heralded by a transparency labeled "Our Moses." Upon his death some months later several of his colored friends bore him on their shoulders to his resting-place in the Friends' burying-ground. He was interested in many reform movements; his last important public appearance was as presiding officer of a suffrage meeting. The dominating traits of his character were an utter fearlessness which overawed even his slave-holding enemies, an honesty so upright that he refused to allow his lawyer to misrepresent him in pleading for leniency, great resourcefulness in an emergency, and a genuine love for his fellow men.

[*Delawarean* (Dover), Jan. 21, 1850; scrap-book of letters, clippings, etc., compiled by Helen S. Garrett; W. L. Garrison, "The New Reign of Terror in the Slaveholding States for 1859–60," *Anti-Slavery Tracts*, n.s., no. 4 (1860); W. H. Siebert, *The Underground Railroad from Slavery to Freedom* (1898); R. C. Smedley, *Hist. of the Underground Railroad in Chester and the Neighboring Counties of Pa.* (1883); Wm. Still, *The Underground Railroad* (1872); U. S. Circuit Court (Delaware District), Docket, Equity and Law in the Court's Archives, Wilmington, 1846–48; *Wilmington Daily Commercial*, Jan. 25, 1871; Henry Wilson, *Hist. of the Rise and Fall of Slave Power in America*, vol. II (1874).]

E. L.

GARRETT, WILLIAM ROBERTSON (Apr. 12, 1839–Feb. 12, 1904), educator, historian, was born in Williamsburg, Va., the son of Dr. Robert Major and Susan Comfort (Winder) Garrett. He was a Phi Beta Kappa student at the College of William and Mary where in 1858 he received the M.A. degree. Following his graduation he studied law at the University of Virginia. His practise of law at Williamsburg was interrupted by the outbreak of the Civil War. He volunteered as a private in April 1861 and was shortly elected captain of the Williamsburg-Lee Artillery. In this capacity he served in the Peninsular campaign and fought in the battle of Williamsburg (May 5, 1862) with such bravery as to win the official commendation of Gen. J. E. B. Stuart and Gen. James Longstreet. Upon the expiration of his enlistment he assisted in raising a battalion of partisan rangers in middle Tennessee of which he was made adjutant. This battalion in 1863 became a part of the 11th Tennessee Regiment of Cavalry and served under Gen. Forrest, then under Gen. Wheeler, and again under Gen. Forrest. Garrett was promoted to the captaincy of Company B of this regiment in February 1865. A few weeks later he surrendered with it at Gainesville, Ala. The remainder of his life was devoted to educational work. Returning to Williamsburg he became master of the grammar school of the College of William and Mary. In 1868 he removed to Giles County, Tenn., where he began a five-year term as president of Giles College and principal of Cornersville Academy. In this year also, on Nov. 12, he married Julia Flournoy Batte of Pulaski. He was successively superintendent of schools for Giles County (1873–75), associate principal and professor of mathematics in Montgomery Bell Academy in Nashville (1875–91), state superintendent of public instruction (1891–93), and principal of Garrett Military Academy (1893–95). In 1895 he was appointed professor of American history and in 1899 dean of Peabody College for Teachers, holding both positions until his death. In the course of his long residence in Tennessee he became an increasingly important figure in the educational life of the state and of the South. He gave much time to the organization and development of teachers' institutes in middle Tennessee and was at various times president of the Tennessee State Teachers' Association, president of the Tennessee Public School Officers' Association, secretary of the Inter-State Teachers' Association, one of the editors of the *Southwestern Journal of Education*, and in 1891 president of the National Education Association. He organized the Watkins Institute Night School in Nashville, founded for the benefit of laboring men. In his later years his time was occupied with teaching and writing history. He edited the *American Historical Magazine* (devoted largely to Tennessee history) from its establishment in 1896 until Peabody College in 1902 discontinued support of it. His most important writings were: "The South as a Factor in the Territorial Expansion of the United States," in *Confederate Military History,* vol. I (1899); *History of Tennessee* (1900), in collaboration with Albert V. Goodpasture; and *The Civil War from a Southern Standpoint* (1905), in collaboration with Robert A. Halley.

[*Official Records (Army)*, 1 ser. XI, LI; J. B. Lindsley, ed., *Mil. Annals of Tenn. Confederate* (1886), pp. 690–720; *Peabody Coll. Bull.,* Sept. 1903; *Who's Who in America,* 1903–05; Albert V. Goodpasture, "Wm. Robertson Garrett," in *Am. Hist. Mag.,* Apr. 1904; obituary in *Confed. Veteran,* Mar. 1904; information as to certain facts from members of Garrett's family.]

P. M. H.

GARRETTSON, FREEBORN (Aug. 15, 1752–Sept. 26, 1827), itinerant minister of the Methodist Church, and one of those to whom its establishment and early growth in America may be chiefly credited, was born near the mouth of the Susquehanna, in Maryland, of which state his grandfather, Garrett, had been one of the first settlers. His parents, John and Sarah (Hanson), were well-to-do, and he received a good elementary education. Both had died by the time he was twenty-one, and the management of the household numbering a score, white and black, had passed to him. He was a mystic who dreamed dreams and heard voices to which he attributed divine origin. His religious state, fostered by the Church of England, did not satisfy him, and coming under the influence of Robert Strawbridge, Francis Asbury, Daniel Ruff, and others, in 1775, after long inner agitation, he experienced a genuine Methodist conversion. Prompted by a sudden impulse, although till then, he says, he had never suspected slave-keeping was wrong, he freed his slaves. A passion for souls took possession of him. "Brother Garrettson," wrote Asbury, "will let no man escape a religious lecture that comes in his way." Though he fought against the call, he finally became an itinerant preacher, joined the Baltimore Conference of 1776, and for more than fifty years went hither and thither making converts and establishing churches.

From 1775 to 1784 he traveled in Maryland and neighboring states. Conscientiously opposed to oaths and war, though loyal to the American cause, he refused to take the oath of allegiance, and was subjected to much physical violence, and once was imprisoned. Undaunted he pursued his course when other Methodists went into retirement. Thomas Coke, on his arrival in 1784, found him "all meekness and love, and yet all activity." He was the "arrow" that went through the South summoning the preachers to the "Christmas Conference" of 1784, at which the Methodist Church in the United States was organized, and he himself was ordained. Here he volunteered for missionary work in Nova Scotia, where in the face of diverse hardships he labored from the spring of 1785 to that of 1787, exerting an influence there "almost equal to that of Wesley in Europe and Asbury in the United States" (J. M. Buckley, *A History of Methodists in the United States,* 1896, p. 307). Upon his return Wesley requested that he be made superintendent of the Methodist societies in Nova Scotia and the West Indies. For reasons unknown, and much to his astonishment, the Conference refused. (See Jesse Lee, *A Short History of the Methodists in the United States of America,* 1810, p. 126, and Nathan Bangs, *The Life of the Rev. Freeborn Garrettson,* 1829, p. 183.) The remaining forty years of his life were years of almost incessant travels, as presiding elder, Conference missionary, or preacher at large. While he frequently journeyed east and south, the extension of Methodism in New York State was his most signal achievement.

He was a man of some means, and on June 30, 1793, married Catharine Livingston, daughter of Judge Robert R. Livingston [*q.v.*], head of a noted and wealthy New York State family. The Garrettsons established a home on the east bank of the Hudson at Rhinebeck, which became a famous resort for Methodist preachers. Asbury, who frequently visited it, called it "Traveler's Rest." He said that if Garrettson did as much good with his temporal ability as he had with his spiritual, he would be "blessed by the Lord and by men" (*Journal,* II, 233). This Garrettson did, never accepting any salary, and being generous in his gifts. One of his last acts was a bequest to the Missionary and Bible Society, of which he was a founder, sufficient "to support a single missionary until the millenium." His success as a preacher was due to his earnestness, sincerity, and directness of appeal, rather than to oratorical gifts, for he had a harsh, high-keyed voice, and was colloquial in manner. In the counsels of the church his influence was perhaps second to none. Wesley's correspondence with him displays fatherly affection, and at his request Garrettson prepared a journal of his early labors. Wesley died before receiving it, but it was published in 1791, *The Experience and Travels of Mr. Free-*

born Garrettson. Aggressively opposed to slaveholding, he issued in 1820, *A Dialogue Between Do-Justice and Professing-Christian,* in which he favors colonization, and suggests legislation providing for gradual emancipation. Besides one or two sermons and addresses, he also published, *A Letter to the Rev. Lyman Beecher, Containing Strictures and Animadversions on a Pamphlet entitled an Address . . . for the Education of Indigent Pious Young Men for the Ministry* (1816).

[Bangs's *Life* cited above is based on Garrettson's printed and manuscript journals. Ezra S. Tipple, *Freeborn Garrettson* (1910), is a compact sketch based in part on manuscripts and letters in the library of Drew Theological Seminary. See also *Journal of Rev. Francis Asbury* (1821); *Meth. Mag.*, Mar. 1828; and G. G. Smith in *Meth. Rev.* (Nashville), Mar.–Apr. 1895.]
H. E. S.

GARRIGAN, PHILIP JOSEPH (Sept. 8, 1840–Oct. 14, 1919), Catholic prelate, son of Philip and Alice Garrigan, was born in Cavan, Ireland, from which place in 1844 his parents emigrated to Boston, and thence to Lowell, Mass. Here the boy attended the grammar and high schools, and after working a few years entered St. Charles' College, Ellicott City, Md., from which he was graduated in 1862. He then studied theology at the Provincial Seminary of Troy, N. Y., and was ordained, June 11, 1870. He served two years as a curate of St. John's Church, Worcester, before he was called back to Troy as director of the Seminary. In 1875, he was made rector of St. Bernard's Church, Fitchburg, Mass. Here he displayed unusual administrative ability and keen interest in parochial education, and won local distinction as a preacher. Although a permanent pastor, in 1889 he accepted the invitation of Rector J. J. Keane [*q.v.*] to serve as vice-rector of the newly established Catholic University of America. Chosen as a Northerner who might popularize the University in Catholic circles of New England, Garrigan proved an able executive who calmly went his way during an era when the new institution was subject to bitter criticism, and stood loyally by Keane in the controversy which led to the latter's "deposition." He also aided materially in the foundation of Trinity College, a neighboring school for the higher education of women. Frequently nominated for bishoprics, he was finally named by Leo XIII as first bishop of Sioux City, Iowa (Mar. 21, 1902), in the metropolitan province of Dubuque over which Keane ruled as archbishop.

Consecrated by Bishop Thomas D. Beaven in the Springfield cathedral on May 25, Garrigan immediately set forth for his diocese, which included twenty-four counties in the rich agricultural section of northwest Iowa. Again he stood out as a financial administrator, though not without an appeal as a courtly, personable gentleman who was intensely interested in civic and state affairs. Under his direction the diocese made notable progress: the number of priests increased from 95 to 140 and churches and missions from 116 to 143; Trinity College for boys was established (1913); three hospitals were opened at Sioux City and Fort Dodge; and a score of parochial schools were built, as well as an orphanage, a foundling asylum, and a model House of the Good Shepherd for wayward girls. Since there was nothing picturesque in his solid work, however, he attracted little attention beyond the confines of the state. He is said never to have recovered from the poisoned soup served by an anarchistic chef at the great banquet in honor of Mundelein's installation as archbishop of Chicago. He was then an old man, but he continued to carry on for three years and took a rather active part in the various patriotic movements during the World War.

[*Am. Cath. Who's Who* (1911); *Cath. Univ. Bull.*, July 1902; *The Cath. Encyc. and its Makers* (1917); annual Cath. directories; J. J. McCoy, *Hist. of the Cath. Ch. in the Diocese of Springfield* (1900); L. McCarty, *Hist. Souvenir of Catholicity in Sioux City* (1907); *Springfield Republican*, May 26, 1902; *Western World* (Des Moines, Iowa), Oct. 16, 23, 1919; *Sioux City Tribune*, Oct. 14, 1919; *Sioux City Jour.*, Oct. 15, 1919; and information furnished by friends and a niece of the bishop.]
R. J. P.

GARRISON, CORNELIUS KINGSLAND (Mar. 1, 1809–May 1, 1885), financier, was of Huguenot stock. His paternal ancestor, Isaac Garrison, who was naturalized at New York in 1705, was an emigrant from Montauban, Guyenne, France. Some of the family settled in New Rochelle, but one branch moved up the Hudson River to Putnam County, N. Y., and there acquired an extensive estate, called Garrison's. His great-grandfather, Beverly Garrison, moved to Fort Montgomery, Orange County, where his father, Oliver Garrison, who married Catherine Schuyler Kingsland, resided, and where he was born. In Cornelius's infancy his father suffered serious financial losses, in consequence of which the son's education was neglected and at an early age he was dependent upon his own resources. He was bright and energetic, however, and though, when he was thirteen years old he commenced to earn his living by working as a cabin boy on a Hudson River sloop, he continued to attend school during the winter months. In 1825 he went to New York City where he remained for three years, devoting himself to the study of architecture and engineering. Moving subsequently to Canada, he entered the employ of the Upper Canada Company, was engaged in planning and constructing important public works in Ontario, and attained the responsible position of general manager of all the company's Canadian business. In 1833 he resigned, owing to the apparent imminence of war between Great Britain and the United States, and on his return to the United States, settled at St. Louis. His experiences on the Hudson River in his youth caused him to turn his attention to the urgent need for the improvement of the transportation facilities of the Mississippi, and for some years he was engaged in designing, building, and running steamboats, and in organizing regular freight services to New Orleans and other ports. These enterprises, in spite of occasional heavy losses of boats and cargoes, placed him in affluent circumstances.

At the commencement of the "gold" rush to California in 1849 Garrison proceeded to Panama and, considering it the important strategic point in the long journey to the gold fields, established a commercial and banking house there. His foresight was justified by the great success of his venture and in 1852 he went to New York City in order to establish a branch. While he was there the Nicaragua Steamship Company intrusted to him the management of their Pacific agency at San Francisco at a salary of $60,000 per annum. On his arrival in San Francisco in March 1853 he found his employers' affairs in great disorder, but within a short time he had reorganized the office, revitalized its services, and brought the organization to a high standard of efficiency and prosperity. His outstanding achievement, however, was in municipal affairs. Having made a marked impression on the people from the first, he was elected mayor only six months after his arrival. His tenure of office was remarkable for the permanent civic reforms which he brought about. In the forefront of his program he placed the suppression of the notorious public gambling halls and the closing of theatres on Sunday. He also advocated reform of the school system, provision for better schoolhouses, industrial schools for juvenile delinquents and an extension of the basis of taxation. Before he relinquished office public gambling had been ended—never to reappear, and all his schemes for better government and efficient administration had been carried into effect, rendering his mayoralty one of the most memorable in the city's history. At the same time he ardently supported the Pony Express transcontinental mail service, the projected Pacific railroad and telegraph line, and strenuously advocated a transpacific steamship service with the Orient and Australia. Chief of his financial enterprises was the banking firm of Garrison & Fretz, which became one of the strongest banks in California. In 1859 he decided to return to the East, and on his departure was presented with a gold dinner service as a mark of gratitude and respect from the citizens of San Francisco. Settling in New York City, he again entered into the shipping business on a large scale—hence his title "Commodore"—initiating a steamship service between New York and Brazil and promoting extensive trading operations with other countries of South America. He also became largely interested in public-utility corporations, particularly the Pacific Railroad of Missouri and the Wheeling & Lake Erie. He became president of the former upon its sale under foreclosure in 1876 and subsequent reorganization as the Missouri Pacific. Possessing a large fortune, his financial operations were of great variety and magnitude. Toward the end of his life he suffered losses, which caused him temporary embarrassment, but before his death, which occurred in New York City, he had extricated himself from his chief difficulties.

Garrison was married, on Aug. 1, 1831, to Mary Noye Re Tallack, daughter of William Re Tallack. On Oct. 10, 1878, he was married to Letitia Willet Randall. Endowed as he was with extraordinary foresight and intense energy and imagination, all his ventures were characterized by boldness of conception and pertinacity of prosecution. He rendered invaluable aid to the cause of the Union during the war, in large part gratuitously. His strong moral principles and his unassailable integrity induced confidence which was never misplaced, and his Old-World courtesy made him universally popular.

[C. W. Baird, *Hist. of the Huguenot Emigration to America* (1885), II, 143; W. W. Spooner, ed., *Hist. Families of Ameica* (1907), II, 304; Frank Soulé and others, *The Annals of San Francisco* (1855), p. 744; *Appletons' Ann. Cyc.* (1885); *N. Y. Geneal. and Biog. Reg.*, Jan. 1906; *N. Y. Tribune*, May 2, 1885.]

H. W. H. K.

GARRISON, WILLIAM LLOYD (Dec. 10, 1805–May 24, 1879), reformer, was born in Newburyport, Mass., the fourth child of Abijah and Frances Maria (Lloyd) Garrison, who had emigrated to the United States from Nova Scotia early in the nineteenth century. His father, a sea-captain, was intemperate in his habits and deserted his family before William was three years old. Placed under the care of Deacon Ezekiel Bartlett, the boy had a meager schooling, and in 1818 was apprenticed for seven years to Ephraim W. Allen, editor of the Newburyport *Herald*, in the office of which he developed into an expert compositor and wrote anonymously for the paper. When his apprenticeship was completed, he became on Mar. 22, 1826, editor of the local *Free Press*, in which he printed the earliest poems of John Greenleaf Whittier, who was to be his lifelong friend. After the *Free Press* failed, Garrison sought employment in Boston as a journeyman printer, and in the spring of 1828, joined Nathaniel H. White in editing the *National Philanthropist,* devoted to the suppression "of intemperance and its kindred vices." It bore witness to his reforming propensities by attacking lotteries, Sabbath-breaking, and war. At this period he met Benjamin Lundy [*q.v.*], a Quaker, whose influence turned his attention to the evils of negro slavery. Soon Garrison went to Bennington, Vt., to conduct the *Journal of the Times,* an Anti-Jackson organ. He returned in March 1829 to Boston, where, on Independence Day, in the Park Street Church, he delivered the first of his innumerable public addresses against slavery. Later in the summer he was in Baltimore, cooperating with Lundy in editing the weekly *Genius of Universal Emancipation.*

Although Garrison was far from being the first American Abolitionist, he was one of the earliest to demand the "immediate and complete emancipation" of slaves; and it was to this movement that his energies, for the next thirty years, were to be principally devoted. In the *Genius of Universal Emancipation* he wrote more and more vehemently, until, having accused Francis Todd of engaging in the domestic slave-trade, he was sued for libel and found guilty. Unable to pay his fine, he was imprisoned for seven weeks in the Baltimore jail, being released on June 5, 1830, through the intervention of the philanthropist, Arthur Tappan. During the ensuing autumn he lectured in eastern cities, and finally, after issuing a prospectus, founded his famous periodical, the *Liberator,* "in a small chamber, friendless and unseen." He and his partner, Isaac Knapp, virtually without resources, printed the paper on a hand-press from borrowed type, and it appeared every Friday. The motto heading the first number, dated Jan. 1, 1831, was "Our country is the world—Our countrymen are mankind," and its leading article was a manifesto ending, "I am in earnest—I will not equivocate—I will not excuse—I will not retreat a single inch—and *I will be heard."* The subscription price was only two dollars a year, but the circulation was never over 3,000, and there was usually an annual deficit.

Garrison was a philosophical non-resistant, trusting in peaceful means to attain his ends, but his pacifism was of a militant type. Unwilling to resort to the ballot, he voted but once in his lifetime, and he relied on the power of moral principles for the conversion of his opponents. He had no practical method for abolishing slavery, but confined himself to denouncing it as an institution. In his condemnation of slave-owners, he was irrepressible, uncompromising, and inflammatory, and even his supporter, Thomas Wentworth Higginson, did not try to defend him against the charge of "excessive harshness of language." In its early numbers the paper had a plain title; beginning with the seventeenth issue, however, it bore a rude cut of a slave auction near the national capitol, which goaded Southerners into a fury, and they threatened Garrison with bodily harm. But nothing could daunt him. Even when the state of Georgia set a reward of $5,000 for his arrest and conviction, he was imperturbable, and, without making any distinctions or admitting any explanations, continued to pour out a torrent of invective against all those who had anything to do with slavery.

The need for effective organization was met in 1831 by the formation of the New England Anti-Slavery Society, the constitution for which was drafted in part by Garrison. He was elected corresponding secretary and in 1832 became a salaried agent for spreading its doctrines. His *Thoughts on African Colonization* (1832) was a small but forceful pamphlet, undermining the work of the American Colonization Society, the plans for which he had formerly approved. In early May 1833 Garrison sailed for England to solicit funds for a manual-labor school for colored youth. He made many friends, including Daniel O'Connell and George Thompson. After an absence of nearly five months he landed in New York in season to attend unofficially a gathering called for organizing an anti-slavery society in that city. On Dec. 4, 1833, in Philadelphia, he met with fifty or more delegates to form the American Anti-Slavery Society. Its declaration of principles, phrased largely by Garrison, announced that its members, rejecting "the use of all carnal weapons for deliverance from bondage," relied for the destruction of error only upon "the potency of truth." Although Garrison was elected foreign secretary, he soon resigned and would accept no other important office in the society.

In 1835 the English Abolitionist, George Thompson, came to the United States on a lecture tour and was met in many places with enmity. On Oct. 21, the Boston Female Anti-Slavery Society held a meeting, at which a mob of several thousand persons assembled, expecting to tar-and-feather Thompson. The latter, however, had been warned, and the crowd, searching for a victim, seized Garrison, dragged him with a rope around his neck through the streets, and might have used him more roughly but for the courageous intervention of Mayor Theodore Lyman. Garrison spent the night in the Leverett Street jail and in the morning withdrew from the city for several weeks. Meanwhile the opposition to slavery was growing.

Efficient though he was as a propagandist, Garrison had a talent for antagonizing even his supporters. He was a natural autocrat who demanded from his followers implicit belief in all his views. "You exalt yourself too much," wrote Elizur Wright, one of his most loyal friends. He could not endure moderation, and in his self-righteous manner he was often very irritating. His wayward mind was so receptive of radical ideas, and he advocated reforms with such promiscuity that he was accused by his enemies of picking up "every infidel fanaticism afloat." Because of his desire to link abolitionism with other reform movements, he lost some of his influence with sincere anti-slavery people. The appearance of Sarah and Angelina Grimké as speakers at their meetings was distasteful to the more conservative Abolitionists, who did not favor woman's rights. The indifference of many clergymen to the slavery issue soon brought Garrison into open conflict with orthodox churches, which he characterized vividly as "cages of unclean birds, Augean stables of pollution." He eventually denied the plenary inspiration of the Bible and was conspicuously unorthodox. In November 1840 he attended a meeting of the "Friends of Universal Reform," described by Emerson as distinguished by "a great deal of confusion, eccentricity, and freak." He denounced theatres as "deep and powerful sources of evil," and he came out vigorously against the use of tobacco, capital punishment, and imprisonment for debt.

A decisive schism in the anti-slavery ranks developed over Garrison's opposition to concerted political action. The movement for the formation of a third party took shape ultimately in what was known as the "New Organization," and conflicting groups came to be known as the "Old Ogs," of which Garrison was still the leader, and the "New Ogs" (E. E. Hale, *Memories of a Hundred Years,* II, 1903, 129). Although Garrison for some years postponed defection, he could not prevent the nomination in 1839 of James G. Birney for president by the Liberty party. At a meeting of the American Anti-Slavery Society in May 1840 in New York, Garrison and his adherents, coming from Boston in a specially chartered boat, packed the gathering and won a temporary victory. At the World's Anti-Slavery Convention, held the following June, in London, he refused to participate in the proceedings when he found that women were excluded.

At least as early as 1841, Garrison became a disunionist, and publicly called upon the North to secede from a compact which protected slavery. This appeal drew an emphatic protest from the American Anti-Slavery Society; but the Massachusetts organization, in January 1843, under pressure from Garrison, resolved that the United States Constitution was "a covenant with death and an agreement with hell" and "should be annulled." Later in the same year Garrison was elected president of the American Anti-Slavery Society, which passed by a large majority an expression of disunion sentiments prepared by him. Actually, however, he was losing ground. Times were changing, and the fight against slavery was being carried on by more practical men. Garrison naturally disapproved of the annexation of Texas and of the Mexican War. In the summer and autumn of 1846, he was in England for a third visit, addressing reform gatherings. In August 1847 with the negro, Frederick Douglass, he took a lecture tour beyond the Alleghanies, meeting with some rowdyism, but debating night after night against defenders of the Union. In twenty-six days he spoke more than forty times. He was often exposed to wretched weather, and his health, never very good, was seriously impaired.

The compromise measures of 1850 were to Garrison a "hollow bargain for the North" (Swift, *post,* p. 276), and he condemned Webster's Seventh of March Speech as "indescribably base and wicked," "infamous," and "dishonorable." One consequence of Webster's utterance was a strong reaction against Garrison and the anti-slavery disunionists. At the annual meeting of the American Anti-Slavery Society on May 7, 1850, a disorderly mob headed by Isaiah Rynders interrupted the proceedings, but the coolness of Garrison averted bloodshed. In the following year the Society could not obtain the use of any suitable hall in New York and was obliged to seek a haven in Syracuse. Unable to secure declarations against slavery from Father Mathew, the Irish temperance advocate, and from Kossuth, the Hungarian patriot, Garrison denounced them abusively.

On Independence Day in 1854, at Framingham, Mass., Garrison, at an abolitionist gathering, publicly burned the Constitution of the United States, crying, "So perish all compromises with tyranny!" He did not favor the formation of the Republican party, but continued to urge the peaceful separation of the states. As a non-resistant, he could not justify John Brown's uprising. During the five years preceding the Civil War, he suffered much from a bronchial affection and from financial troubles, which curtailed his activities considerably. When secession took place in 1860–61 Garrison welcomed the event as an opportunity for allowing the Southern states to reap the fruits of their folly, maintaining that any attempt to whip the South into subjection was "utterly chimerical." Toward Lincoln, Garrison was at first rather cold, and he criticized what he thought to be the President's uncertain policy; but he also prevented Abolition societies from openly condemning the administration. He soon recognized the significance of the Emancipation Proclamation of September 1862, and the meeting of the American Anti-Slavery Society in December 1863, at Philadelphia, produced a reconciliation between the two factions of Abolitionists.

After the conclusion of peace, in April 1865, Garrison went to Charleston, S. C., with the once execrated George Thompson for his stateroom companion. As the guest of the government he went to attend the ceremonies at the raising of the Stars and Stripes over Fort Sumter. In a brief address, he declared, "I hate slavery as I hate nothing else in this world. It is not only a crime, but the sum of all criminality." As he stood by the grave of Calhoun in the cemetery of St. Philip's Church, he laid a hand upon the tombstone and said solemnly, "Down into a deeper grave than this slavery has gone, and for it there is no resurrection."

In January 1865 Garrison had moved that the American Anti-Slavery Society dissolve, but his proposal was rejected. He did, however, decline a twenty-third term as its president, and was succeeded by Wendell Phillips. He felt that his great task had been accomplished; and, after the ratification of the Thirteenth Amendment, he prepared a valedictory editorial for the *Liberator,* locked the form in type, and sent the final number to the press on Dec. 29, 1865. The paper had been published continuously for exactly thirty-five years.

Garrison had married, on Sept. 4, 1834, Helen Benson, daughter of a retired merchant of Brooklyn, Conn., and had settled in Roxbury, Mass., in a house called "Freedom's Cottage." Seven children were born to them, of whom two died in infancy. In December 1863 Mrs. Garrison, whose systematic management and tactful ways had brought order into her husband's chaotic affairs, was stricken with paralysis and lived for several years more as a helpless invalid. A few months later, Garrison moved to a more retired residence on Highland Street, in Roxbury, where he found "port after stormy seas." Two painful accidents greatly hampered his physical activity, but he made in 1867 another voyage to England, where he was greeted as a hero. On his return, he became an intermittent contributor to the New York *Independent.* In 1868 a testimonial fund of more than $30,000 was raised among his admirers and presented to him. Although his vitality was diminished, he never ceased to be a crusader, and he fought unceasingly for prohibition, woman's suffrage, justice to the red man, and the elimination of prostitution. It seemed to be his mission to act as "an antidote to American complacency." On Jan. 28, 1876, his wife died of pneumonia. In the next year, on his last visit to England, he was so enfeebled that he could appear only occasionally in public. On Oct. 13, 1878, in the office of the Newburyport *Herald,* he set type for three of his sonnets on the sixtieth anniversary of the beginning of his apprenticeship as a printer. A disease of the kidneys soon prostrated him, and he died in New York, at the home of his daughter, Helen Garrison Villard. He was buried in the Forest Hills Cemetery, in Boston. In appearance he was slightly under six feet in height and erect in bearing. His spectacles, which he began to wear before he was twenty, relieved the sharpness of his face and gave him a mild and benevolent expression. Lowell wrote of him,

> "There's Garrison, his features very
> Benign for an incendiary."

As a speaker, he was described by Higginson as "usually monotonous, sometimes fatiguing, but always controlling." In his household he was cheerful, patient, and hospitable, but he was inclined to procrastinate and was always unsystematic. His sense of humor was not well developed. Although he suffered from chronic illness, he could endure long hours of drudgery, and he was rarely in low spirits. He cared little for nature, but he always enjoyed sacred music and wrote no small amount of verse, moralistic in tone, but highly imaginative. His *Sonnets and other Poems* was published in 1843.

Garrison was an extremist, incurably optimistic, often illogical, and extraordinarily persistent. Seldom has individualism been more vehemently asserted than in his protests against social and moral orthodoxy. He was without perspective or a sense of proportion, and could be astonishingly credulous. He had implicit faith in pills and nostrums of all kinds, was keenly interested in phrenology, clairvoyance, and spiritualism, and was frequently deceived by charlatans. Opinion regarding him has differed widely. To some he has been the high-minded idealist who provided the chief impetus for the Abolition movement. By others he has been regarded as an impractical fanatic, who accomplished some good in a disagreeable way. His importance as a dominating figure in starting the campaign against slavery is conceded, but he inspired more than he led and the actual task of freeing the negro was carried through by better balanced leaders. He was a perplexing blend of contradictory qualities, of shrewdness and gullibility, of nobility and prejudice, who will be remembered chiefly for his courage in upholding a righteous cause when it was unpopular.

[The standard, although too extravagantly laudatory, life of Garrison, is *Wm. Lloyd Garrison, 1805–1879: The Story of his Life Told by his Children* (4 vols., 1885–89). The best short biography is Lindsay Swift's *Wm. Lloyd Garrison* (1911), in the American Crisis Biographies. John Jay Chapman's *Wm. Lloyd Garrison* (1913) is so strongly eulogistic as to be useless for those desiring to form a fair estimate of Garrison's character. A complete file of the *Liberator* may be found in the Boston Athenæum. Among other books to be consulted are Henry Wilson, *Hist. of the Rise and Fall of the Slave Power in America* (3 vols., 1872–77); Oliver Johnson, *Wm. Lloyd Garrison and his Times* (1880); John J. Currier, *Ould Newbury* (1896), pp. 681–86; O. G. Villard, *Some Newspapers and Newspaper-Men* (1923), pp. 302–15; Gilbert Seldes, *The Stammering Century* (1928), pp. 239–47; Thos. W. Higginson, *Contemporaries* (1899), pp. 244–56.]

C. M. F.

GARRISON, WILLIAM RE TALLACK (June 18, 1834–July 1, 1882), financier, son of Cornelius Kingsland Garrison [*q.v.*], and Mary Noye Re Tallack. He was born at Goderich, Ontario, Canada, but as an infant he was taken by his parents to St. Louis, Mo., where his youth was spent. He was educated in the local schools, then in 1853, upon his father's appointment as Pacific agent for the Nicaragua Steamship Company, he moved with his family to San Francisco. His first financial experience was obtained with the banking firm of Garrison & Fretz, and subsequently he became associated with all of the elder Garrison's extensive mining, banking, and marine enterprises in California. Combining a natural aptitude for business with an alert mind and a precocious intuition he quickly attained a leading position in business circles in San Francisco, and on his father's return to the East in 1859 he assumed charge of all their joint interests on the Pacific Coast. Five years later he took up his residence in New York, and from that time until his death actively identified himself with the transportation interests of the country. Joining his father in his New York shipping business, he expanded the latter's coast-wise services, became president of the Garrison line to Brazil, and, as the Commodore grew older, gradually relieved him of the management of his heavy marine investments. When the Pacific Railroad of Missouri, which in 1876 passed into the hands of the elder Garrison, was reorganized as the Missouri Pacific, he became vice-president of the new company, for a time served as acting president, and practically guided its operations until its sale in 1880 to Jay Gould. He was also for some years president of the Wabash Railroad.

Garrison's most important achievement in the field of transportation was in connection with New York City's rapid-transit problems. The New York Elevated Railroad Company operated a short line which was totally inadequate to meet requirements, while the Gilbert Elevated Railway Company held a charter under which it had been unable to finance operations owing to the panic of 1873. In 1875 the state legislature created the board of commissioners of rapid transit, which organized the Manhattan Railway Company to build a road in case the two existing companies failed to afford relief within a reasonable time. Garrison and his father both invested in its stock. Then, through the New York Loan and Improvement Company in which he held a preponderant interest, he contracted in 1876 to build and equip the line of the derelict Gilbert company (later the Metropolitan Elevated Railway Company) on terms which gave him control of the latter. He also became its president. Three years later he promoted and carried through the scheme under which the Manhattan company leased for 999 years the property and rights of the New York and Metropolitan companies, thus effecting a complete and permanent unification of the elevated railroads and paving the way for their subsequent extension and successful operation. For a short time after the consolidation he was president of the Manhattan company and continued a director until his death, which occurred at Long Branch, N. J., from injuries sustained in the Parker's Creek railway accident.

Garrison's financial operations were characterized by a breadth of view seemingly incompatible with but invariably accompanied by a remarkable grasp of detail which contributed largely to the success of his ventures. His knowledge of human nature was intuitive, his memory unfailing, his industry prodigious. Throughout his career he was distinguished for courtesy, straightforward dealing, and a transparent honesty. Apart from his business enterprises he was chiefly known for his support of the cause of higher education, and was particularly interested in the development of Washington and Lee University. He was married, in 1865, to Mary

Elizabeth Estill, daughter of James Madison Estill of Kentucky.

[J. B. Walker, *Fifty Years of Rapid Transit, 1864 to 1917* (1918); obituary notices in *N. Y. Times* and *N. Y. Tribune*, July 2, 1882.] H. W. H. K.

GARRY, SPOKANE (1811–Jan. 13, 1892), American Indian missionary, teacher, peace advocate, was born at the "Spokane fishery," now in Spokane County, Wash. His father, Illim-Spokanee', was head chief of the Sin-ho-man-naish tribe, a band later known simply as Spokane Indians. In 1825 the boy was one of several Indian youths of his age selected from the neighboring tribes by Gov. Simpson of the Hudson's Bay Company and sent across the Rocky Mountains to the Red River Missionary School at Upper Fort Garry (now Winnipeg, Manitoba, Canada) to be educated and Christianized at the expense of the company. Thenceforth he was known as Spokane Garry, having been named after Nicholas Garry, then deputy governor of the company. At the school he was converted and learned to read and speak both English and French. In the spring of 1832 he returned to his people, started a native school, and introduced a form of Christian religious worship which spread with amazing rapidity. Tucker (*post*) suggests that the journey of the five western Indians to St. Louis in 1832, in search of the white man's Book of God, was inspired by his teachings.

Garry became in effect the chief of the upper and middle bands of the Spokane Indians, and for nearly sixty years was a leader among the tribes of the Columbia River basin. So far as his influence was felt among his people it was always in the interest of harmony and progress, and to his teachings may be largely attributed the peaceful settlement of northeastern Washington and northern Idaho by invading white settlers. He also restrained several of the Columbia River tribes from joining Chief Joseph of the Nez Perces in 1877. In later life he strove earnestly to protect his people in the possession of the remnant of their lands against the aggressions of the whites, and he concluded all public utterances on the subject with the statement: "This land was all mine, and my people's." His education and natural ability made him the recognized equal of his white contemporaries. In March 1887 he signed the treaty for the relinquishment of the land claims of the upper and middle bands of Spokane Indians. He died in poverty, dispossessed of his lands, with the treaty yet unratified by Congress, and the moneys and consideration, promised thereunder to him and his people, yet unpaid. In person he was a short, stocky man, of homely features but of determined mien. His lodge in early days always contained sugar, coffee, tea, and other supplies which some of the first white settlers lacked, and many of the pioneers in the vicinity of his home were under obligation to him for assistance given them on their arrival in his country. A substantial granite monument was erected to his memory in Greenwood Cemetery, Spokane, Wash., in 1925.

[Wm. S. Lewis, *The Case of Spokane Garry*, Bull. of the Spokane Hist. Soc., Jan. 1917, contains a bibliography; Sarah Tucker, *The Rainbow of the North* (1851); *N. Y. Tribune*, Jan. 15, 1892.] W. S. L.

GARTRELL, LUCIUS JEREMIAH (Jan. 7, 1821–Apr. 7, 1891), lawyer, politician, brigadier-general, was descended from a family of Scotch origin, which is believed to have settled originally in Maryland, from which colony his grandfather, Joseph, emigrated to Georgia at an uncertain date. He settled in Wilkes County, where his son, Joseph, Jr., became a prominent planter and merchant, married the daughter of Dr. Josiah Boswell, and became the father of Lucius Jeremiah Gartell. The latter's name appears as a matriculate, but not a graduate, of the University of Georgia, in the class of 1843. He also attended Randolph-Macon College in Virginia, and read law in the office of Robert Toombs. He was admitted to the bar in Lincoln County in 1842, after one year of practise became solicitor-general of the Northern Circuit, and in 1854 moved to Atlanta. His political career began in 1847 with his election to membership in the General Assembly. He was a Whig, but of the extreme state-rights wing, and within a short time switched over to the Democratic party. In the legislature of 1849 he was one of the radical, Pro-Southern, pro-slavery leaders, and was the author of a set of strongly worded resolutions against the pending settlement of the slavery controversy in Congress. Subsequently when the coalition Union party, consisting of moderate Democrats and Whigs, was organized for the purpose of committing Georgia to Clay's compromise measures, Gartrell championed the ultra Southern-rights view and stumped the state against Toombs, Stephens, and Cobb. Entering Congress in 1857, he took the radical Southern view-point, strongly advocated secession, and resigned when Georgia seceded in 1861.

On the outbreak of the war he organized the 7th Georgia Regiment and was elected its colonel. His regiment participated in the first battle of Manassas (in which engagement his son was killed), and received honorable mention in the report of Gen. Joseph E. Johnston. In October 1861 Gartrell became a member of the Confederate Congress, but on the expiration of one term returned to the field and was commissioned brigadier-general (1864). His service was largely in South Carolina in opposing Sherman's march. After the war he resumed the practise of law in Atlanta. He became noted as a criminal lawyer, perhaps having no superior in Georgia in that variety of practise. He was counsel for the Republican governor, Rufus Brown Bullock [*q.v.*] when criminal action was brought against the latter. Gartrell was a leading member of the Georgia constitutional convention of 1877. His last political effort was to enter the contest for the governorship in 1882 against Alexander H. Stephens [*q.v.*], who defeated him. A contemporary has described him as large, powerful, robust, full of animal spirits, and a ready debater. He was thrice married: first, in 1841, to Louisiana O. Gideon, by whom he had six children; second, in 1855, to Antoinette T. Burke, to whom five children were born; and third, about 1888, to Maud Condon of Greenville, Ala., who survived him.

[I. W. Avery, *Hist. of Ga., 1850–80* (1881); L. L. Knight, *A Standard Hist. of Ga. and Georgians,* vol. V (1917); W. J. Northen, *Men of Mark in Ga.,* vol. III (1911); R. H. Shryock, *Ga. and the Union in 1850* (1926); *Official Records* (*Army*); *Atlanta Constitution,* Apr. 8, 1891.] R. P. B—s.

GARVIN, LUCIUS FAYETTE CLARK (Nov. 13, 1841–Oct. 2, 1922), physician, member of the legislature, and governor of Rhode Island, was born in Knoxville, Tenn. Only by chance of birth, however, was he a Southerner. Except for a certain courtliness of manner, which is traditionally held to be a Southern attribute, he was in every sense a New Englander. His mother, Sarah Ann Gunn, was the daughter of Dr. Luther Gunn of Pittsfield, Mass.; his father, James Garvin, was a native of Bethel, Vt. A teacher of unusual gifts, the latter had left the North to become a professor in East Tennessee College, (now University of Tennessee). In 1846, at the age of thirty-seven, he died of fever. His widow with her two sons moved to Greensboro, N. C., where Lucius, the younger boy, became a pupil in the Friends' School. Here he prepared for Amherst College, from which he was graduated with distinction in 1862. In November of that same year he joined the Union army as private in Company E of the 51st Massachusetts Regiment, seeing service in North Carolina and probably fighting against some of his boyhood friends and neighbors.

On his discharge in 1863 he decided to adopt his grandfather Gunn's profession, and spent a short time as assistant in the office of Dr. Sylvanus Clapp of Pawtucket, R. I., later entering the Harvard Medical School, from which he was graduated in 1867. He began his active practise at once in Lonsdale, a Rhode Island mill village, which was to be his home for the rest of his life. As a physician he achieved a good measure of success, though of necessity the majority of his patients were people of small means, and he never attained any degree of wealth. This, however, was of small concern to him, since his tastes were of the simplest.

From his college days he had been keenly interested in economic and social problems, and about 1881 he came upon Henry George's book, *Progress and Poverty.* It converted him immediately and without reserve to the theory of Single Tax. He was naturally a man of warm enthusiasms, and now, undeterred by ridicule and discouragements, he became the eager champion of an idea which he believed to be the solution of the most pressing problems of the day. For his own aggrandizement he would never have sought public life, but anxious to be heard, he henceforth made himself an active figure in the public life of Rhode Island. Allying himself with the Democratic party, in 1883 he was elected to the General Assembly. Here he served thirteen terms, as well as three terms as state senator. Five times he was Democratic candidate for Congress—in 1894, 1896, 1898, 1900, and 1906—and four times for governor—from 1901 to 1905. He was successful in only two elections, serving as governor for the years 1903 and 1904, but that a Democrat could win at all in a state so strongly Republican as Rhode Island is in itself a tribute to Garvin's personality and reputation.

His devotion to the cause of Single Tax did not deter him from being the untiring advocate of less radical reforms. His career as a legislator was marked by constant agitation for measures intended to increase the welfare of the workingman. He won his two elections as governor at a time when the evil of boss control was a particularly flagrant feature of the Republican party. His unquestioned integrity made him the natural choice of those who wished a change of régime, but unfortunately, since the governor in Rhode Island has little power, a hostile Senate was able to nullify his efforts for betterment. He was nevertheless glad, as a self-appointed preacher of a cherished doctrine, to use the conspicuous platform which the governorship afforded him. He never missed an opportunity to speak or write in behalf of Single Tax, and between the years 1903 and 1918 contributed a number of articles on topics connected with Single Tax, labor problems, and state government to the *Independent,* the *Arena,* the *North Amer-*

ican Review, the Providence Journal, and other periodicals. His interest in public affairs did not abate with the years, and he also remained active in his profession. He served as state senator in 1921–22, and was a candidate for reëlection at the time of his death which came very suddenly at the age of eighty-one.

Garvin was twice married: on Dec. 23, 1869, to Lucy Waterman Southmayd of Middletown, Conn., who died in 1898; and on Apr. 2, 1907, to Sarah Emma Tomlinson of Lonsdale, R. I.

[*Who's Who in America*, 1920–21; *Amherst Coll. Biog. Record* (1927); *R. I. Medic. Jour.*, Feb. 1923; *Public*, Nov. 17, 1911; *Providence Sunday Jour.*, July 30, 1911; *Providence Jour.*, Oct. 3, 1922.] E. R. B.

GARY, ELBERT HENRY (Oct. 8, 1846–Aug. 15, 1927), corporation lawyer, financier, was born near Wheaton, Ill., the youngest of the three children of Erastus and Susan (Vallette) Gary. Both the Garys and Vallettes were of New England colonial stock and both families had migrated to Du Page County, Ill., in the decade of the thirties, Erastus Gary from Pomfret, Conn., and Jeremiah Vallette, the father of Susan, from Stockbridge, Mass. Industrious, ambitious, honest, and with high ideals, these transplanted New Englanders insisted upon the best from their children and enforced their moral tenets with a strict discipline. Although Erastus Gary became a prosperous and influential citizen in the new community, his son experienced early in life the arduous regimen of work on a pioneer farm, an experience which endowed him with excellent health and a robust physique. At the outbreak of the Civil War, he was a student at the Illinois Institute, a Methodist college at Wheaton, which his father had helped to found. Unable to enlist because of his youth he pursued a desultory education until 1864 and then served two months in the army, after which he taught school for a term. At the suggestion of his uncle, Henry Vallette, he began in 1865 to read law in the firm of Vallette & Cody in Naperville, and in the following year entered the Union College of Law in Chicago from which he graduated in 1868 at the head of his class. After three years as clerk of the superior court he again became associated with his uncle in the firm of Van Armen & Vallette, and later with his elder brother under the firm-name of E. H. & N. E. Gary. Upon the inclusion of his old preceptor, Judge Cody, the firm became Gary, Cody & Gary. Keenly alive to the main chance and industrious to the last degree, Gary soon built up a wide practise. His cases became increasingly lucrative, and he began to appear as counsel and to sit on the board of directors of important railway and industrial corporations. Finally in 1898, however, he deserted the law and accepted the presidency of the Federal Steel Company. In the meantime he had acted as first mayor of Wheaton, for he still maintained his residence in the town where he had spent his boyhood; he had served two four-year terms as county judge (1882–90); and he had been elected president of the Chicago Bar Association (1893–94). When he finally moved to New York in 1898 to take up his duties as president of the Federal Steel Company he had reached the forefront of the Illinois bar.

Gary's interest in steel had developed gradually through his directorship in the Illinois Steel Company, and through his work in organizing the American Steel & Wire Company and the Federal Steel Company in 1898. The latter had been backed by J. P. Morgan & Company, and Gary's work in constructing this corporation had so impressed the elder Morgan that he turned over to Gary the major work in organizing the United States Steel Corporation, the largest industrial corporation which the world had yet seen. Although Gary was fifty-five years old when this corporation was formed he dominated its policies until the day of his death, acting as chairman of the executive committee until that committee was abolished in 1903, and then as chairman of the board of directors, 1903–27, and after 1907 as chairman of the finance committee. In dealing with the public his policy was one of candor. In his relations with the government he made an effort to keep within the law and to conduct the business in such a way as to avoid criticism. Within the industry itself he followed a policy of cooperation rather than of ruthless competition, a procedure which he promoted by founding the American Iron and Steel Institute and by means of the "Gary dinners." Toward the stockholders he followed a conservative but fair dividend policy, and toward labor one of high wages and social amelioration, though he insisted upon the open shop. The prosperity of the company, his popularity with the stockholders, and the clean bill which his company received from the Supreme Court in 1919 in the anti-trust suit which the government instituted against the corporation, demonstrate his success. In his latter years he was looked upon as the outstanding champion of the open shop. His unwillingness to negotiate with organized labor led to the strike of 1919 and brought upon him the bitter criticism of humanitarians. In his defense it should be said that he had very early introduced schemes for pensions and the purchase of stock by employees and had encouraged in the subsidiary companies various schemes of employee welfare-work, and when he finally became convinced that public sentiment demanded it, he made a real effort to abolish the twelve-hour day.

Although a product of the economic life of the nineteenth century, Gary surpassed many of his business colleagues in his integrity and consideration for the public interests. His biographer paints him as a knight errant who came out of the West to preach high business ethics to the more unscrupulous Easterners, and his conduct of the steel corporation lends some strength to this view. Certain qualities possessed by Gary made him an ideal executive—perfect self-control, unfailing tact, and extraordinary patience in dealing with conflicting points of view. On the other hand he was somewhat vain, quite devoid of humor, and approached his work with an almost pathetic seriousness. It is said that he refused to play cards because he believed it below the dignity of the head of the United States Steel Corporation. In appearance he was slightly below middle height and meticulous in dress to the point of foppishness. He was fond of reading homilies to his subordinates, probably a hangover from the days when he taught a young ladies' Bible class in the Wheaton Methodist Episcopal church, but he usually practised what he preached (Cotter, *post,* p. 51). Until he left Wheaton he was an ardent church member, and in later life he built a new church for the congregation at Wheaton in memory of his parents. The municipal church and other institutions of Gary, Ind., the steel town which was built by the corporation and named after him, were also the recipients of large donations from the aged capitalist. Shortly before his death he asserted that he believed in "all" of the Bible, "not a little piece here and a little piece there, not some garbled kind of new book that somebody had created for these modern times" (*Elbert Henry Gary: A Memorial,* p. 25). He was married twice: to Julia Graves of Aurora, Ill., on June 23, 1869, by whom he had two daughters; and after her death in 1902 to Emma Townsend of New York, on Dec. 2, 1905.

[Ida M. Tarbell, *The Life of Elbert H. Gary* (1925), is undiscriminatingly laudatory and is concerned chiefly with an account of his business life. In Arundel Cotter, *The Gary I Knew* (1928), there is some inkling of his personality. See also *Elbert Henry Gary: A Memorial* (1927). The public press gave rather full biographies of Gary and usually editorial comment on his life in the issues of Aug. 16, 1927, as did the *Iron Age,* Aug. 18, 1927.] H. U. F.

GARY, JAMES ALBERT (Oct. 22, 1833–Oct. 31, 1920), manufacturer, politician, postmaster-general, was born in Uncasville, Conn., the son of James Sullivan and Pamelia (Forrist) Gary. He was descended from John Gary who emigrated from England in 1712 and settled in New Hampshire. The father, with a background of experience in New England cotton-mills, in 1838 moved his family to Maryland where some years later he helped to establish the Alberton Manufacturing Company, manufacturers of cotton-duck, on the Patapsco River. In 1857 he became the sole owner. Young James was educated at the Rockhill Institute, Ellicott City, Md., and at Allegheny College (B.A., 1854). From the age of thirteen he worked six months of the year in his father's factory. In 1856 he was married to Lavinia W. Corrie, by whom he had a son and seven daughters. Five years later he entered a partnership with his father under the name of James S. Gary & Son, and the business continued to expand, doubling its capacity after the floods of 1866 and 1868. In 1870, upon the death of his father, he took over the entire management of the firm. Later he moved to Baltimore, where he became president of the Citizens National Bank and of the Merchants & Manufacturers Association, vice-president of the Consolidated Gas Company, and director of several financial institutions. He was also for some time chairman of the board of trustees of the Brown Memorial Presbyterian Church and of the Enoch Pratt Free Library.

In his later life, Gary's chief interest, aside from his business, was the Republican party, which he supported consistently. Before the Civil War he had worked with the Whigs, who had in 1858 nominated him for the state Senate, without success. Throughout the war he supported the Unionist party. In 1870 and in 1872 he was defeated as the Republican candidate for representative in Congress for the 5th district. In 1879 he made an active campaign as the Republican candidate for governor, but was defeated. In the Republican conventions, state and national, from 1872 to 1896, Gary had great influence. In 1872 he was elected chairman of the state delegation over the opposition of J. A. J. Creswell, the state boss; in 1876 he swung to Hayes on the second ballot and thereafter was an intimate of both President Hayes and Secretary Sherman; in 1880 he was elected national committeeman. He supported Sherman for the presidential nomination, but later swung most of the Maryland delegates to Garfield. Under Garfield and Arthur his influence was lessened, but he still controlled appointments of the Baltimore postmaster and some positions in the customs house. In 1883 he became chairman of the state central committee. In 1884 he supported Arthur for the nomination until almost the end. Four years later he swung from Sherman to Harrison and controlled considerable patronage under the administration of the latter, whom he supported for renomination in 1892. In 1896 he withdrew as national committeeman, but was made a member of the finance committee. As a result of his activities in the election, McKinley made him postmaster-general in 1897. Ten pages of his annual report were devoted to arguments in behalf of postal savings, in which he said he had been interested for many years. Shortly after the outbreak of the Spanish-American War, he resigned, fearing the strain on his health and not wishing to give up his business connections. His death occurred at his home in Baltimore.

[J. T. Scharf, *Hist. of Baltimore City and County* (1881); H. E. Shepherd, ed., *Nelson's Hist. of Baltimore* (1898); *A Hist. of the City of Baltimore: Its Men and Institutions* (1902); *Geneal. and Biog. of Leading Families of the City of Baltimore* (1897); *Vital Records of Foxborough, Mass., to the Year 1850* (1911); the *Sun* and *News* (Baltimore), Nov. 1, 1920.]

W. C. M.

GARY, MARTIN WITHERSPOON (Mar. 25, 1831–Apr. 9, 1881), Confederate soldier, was born at Cokesbury, Abbeville County, S. C. He was the third son of Dr. Thomas Reeder and Mary Anne (Porter) Gary. His mother was a descendant of John Witherspoon [*q.v.*]. He attended Cokesbury Academy where he was a popular student and captain of the Fencibles, a military company in the school. In 1850 he entered South Carolina College but was forced to leave in 1852, "in consequence of an unsuccessful attempt to induce the Faculty to do away with the Commons Hall" (Charleston *News and Courier*, Apr. 11, 1881). This was the so-called "biscuit rebellion." Gary then entered Harvard, graduating in 1854. He returned to South Carolina and studied law under Chancellor J. P. Carroll at Edgefield, was admitted to the bar in 1855, and was soon a very successful criminal lawyer.

Gary was a member of the South Carolina legislature in 1860 and a leader of the secession movement. After the ordinance was enacted he went into the military service as captain of the Watson Guards, which became Company B of the Hampton Legion. He commanded the legion at first Manassas after Col. Hampton was wounded and Lieut.-Col. Johnson was killed. When the legion was reorganized he was made lieutenant-colonel of infantry, a battalion of eight companies, and when it was filled he became colonel of the regiment. He participated in the battles around Richmond, at second Manassas, Boonsboro, Sharpsburg, Fredericksburg, Suffolk, Chickamauga, Bean's Station, Campbell's Station, and Knoxville. The legion was then ordered mounted and served as cavalry. Gary commanded the contingent on the north side of the James River. After the fight at Riddle's Shop in June 1864 he was made brigadier-general, his brigade including the Hampton Legion, 7th South Carolina, 7th Georgia, and 24th Virginia regiments. He led his men in all the fighting on the north side of the James during the siege and was the last to leave Richmond. After the surrender of Lee, he cut his way through the Federal lines and joined President Davis at Greensboro. Taking command of about two hundred men of his brigade he escorted Davis and his cabinet to Cokesbury, S. C., where one of the last meetings of the Confederate cabinet was held at the home of Gary's mother.

After the war Gary resumed the practise of law at Edgefield, and also prospered as a planter. In 1876 he and Gen. M. C. Butler were the foremost defenders of the "straightout policy" and the nomination of Gen. Wade Hampton for governor. They advocated white supremacy and no compromise with the negroes. In the same year Gary was elected state senator from Edgefield County and served four years, declining reëlection. He was a candidate for the United States Senate, but was defeated by Gen. Butler in 1877 and by Gov. Hampton in 1879. His friends urged his candidacy for governor in 1880, but his break with Hampton in 1878 had destroyed his availability. He was of a hasty and violent disposition, used bold and sometimes profane language, had opposed the payment of the Reconstruction debts, and championed a usury law. He was a stump speaker of the most effective type. Thin, erect, and bald-headed, he was often called the "bald eagle." He was never married.

[Walter Allen, *Gov. Chamberlain's Administration in S. C.* (1888); U. R. Brooks, *Butler and His Cavalry* (1909), and *Stories of the Confederacy* (1912); J. A. Chapman, *Hist. of Edgefield County* (1897); C. A. Evans, ed., *Confed. Mil. Hist.*, vol. V (1899); J. S. Reynolds, *Reconstruction in S. C.* (1905); F. B. Simkins, *The Tillman Movement in S. C.* (1926); Yates Snowden, *Hist. of S. C.*, vol. II (1920); the *State* (Columbia, S. C.), Oct. 15, 1909; *Press and Banner* (Abbeville, S. C.), Nov. 7, 1923, Jan. 21, 1926.]

S. S. M.

GASKILL, HARVEY FREEMAN (Jan. 19, 1845–Apr. 1, 1889), inventor, engineer, was the only child of Benjamin F. and Olive Gaskill and was born on his father's farm on the Slayton Settlement Road in Royalton, N. Y. Until he was sixteen years old he attended the local district schools and did what work he could about the farm. Farming, however, never appealed to him, possibly because he was rather frail. Invention, on the other hand, early seemed to be his forte, as evidenced by the fact that when he was thirteen years old he devised a revolving hay-rake which proved to be a very practical farm implement. Gaskill's father at the time was in no position to commercialize his son's invention, which was not patented, but it is said that the idea was subsequently developed with considerable financial success. In 1861 Gaskill moved with his parents to Lockport, N. Y. Here he was a student in the Lockport Union School for a year or two and then entered the Poughkeepsie Commercial College, from which he graduated in 1866. Returning to Lockport, fully intent upon a business career, he first entered his uncle's law office and devoted considerable time to the study of business law, then was made a member of the firm of Penfield, Martin & Gaskill whose business was the manufacture of a patent clock. Later he was actively interested in a planing-mill combined with a sash-and-blind factory. In both of these industrial undertakings he applied his inventive genius mainly to the improvement of the mechanical equipment. He also devised a clothespin and a horse-drawn hay-rake, but brought neither of them to a manufacturing stage. On July 16, 1873, he joined the Holly Manufacturing Company in Lockport as a draftsman. This firm was engaged in the manufacture of pumping machinery for waterworks, and immediately upon entering its employ Gaskill turned his attention to the improvement of steam-pumps. His talent quickly brought him to the attention of the company's officers and he was given every opportunity to apply his genius. At that time, waterworks pumping machinery was made in the United States principally by two concerns—the Holly Manufacturing Company and the Worthington Pump & Machinery Company. Competition between these two for supremacy and business was keen. Both concerns, however, were aware of the growing demand for higher steam economy and larger pumping capacity and in the Holly Company the task for designing equipment to meet this demand fell to Gaskill. This he accomplished in 1882, when the Gaskill pumping engine appeared. It was the first crank and fly-wheel high duty pumping engine built as a standard for waterworks service. It gave a fairly high steam economy, had larger pumping units, was extremely compact and convenient, and was lower in cost than the preceding types. The Gaskill engine was quickly accepted nationally and gave the Holly Company advantage over its competitor, until the Worthington high duty engine appeared. Meanwhile Gaskill was made in turn engineer and superintendent of his company in 1877, a member of the board of directors and vice-president in 1885, and would eventually have become president but for his untimely death. In addition to his connections with the Holly Company, he was active as a director or an officer of several other manufacturing concerns, public utilities, and banks, and was also a member of the American Society of Mechanical Engineers. He was married, on Dec. 25, 1873, to Mary Elizabeth Moore of Lockport, who survived him.

[C. A. Hague, *Pumping Engines for Water Works* (1907); *Engineering News*, Apr. 6, 1889; *Trans. Am. Soc. Mech. Engineers*, vol. X (1889); obituary in Lockport paper, Apr. 1, 1889; correspondence with Lockport Public Library.] C. W. M.

GASS, PATRICK (June 12, 1771–Apr. 30, 1870), explorer and author, was the last survivor of the Lewis and Clark expedition to the Pacific Ocean, 1804–06. He was the son or grandson of Henry Gass, early settler of Sherman's Creek Valley, then Cumberland, now Perry County, Pa. The Gass family were Scotch-Irish and restless frontiersmen. When Patrick was an infant they removed from his birthplace, Falling Springs, Pa., to Maryland. Patrick was soon sent to his grandfather's for schooling, but reported that he attended school only nineteen days; he did, however, learn to read and write. In 1782 the family moved across the mountains to the Youghiogheny River and three years later to Catfish Camp, now Washington, Pa. There in 1792 his father was drafted to garrison a frontier post and Patrick took his place. The next year he took a trip to New Orleans, returning to his home near Wellsburg, Va. (now W. Va.), by way of Cuba and Philadelphia. After this he was apprenticed to a carpenter. In 1803 he was in the regular army, stationed at Kaskaskia; he joined Lewis and Clark as a private but on the death of Charles Floy was chosen, Aug. 20, 1804, by the suffrages of his mates, a sergeant. He kept a journal and upon his return was the first one of the expedition to publish an account of the memorable journey. His notes were revised by a Wellsburg schoolmaster, David McKeehan, and the volume appeared in 1807, with many quaint illustrations.

Gass was in the War of 1812, with Jackson against the Creeks, and, in 1814, on the northern frontier, taking part in the battle of Lundy's Lane. After the war he returned to Wellsburg, where he lived in shiftless fashion until 1831 when he married Maria Hamilton, who bore him seven children and died in 1846. In 1855 he was one of a delegation to Washington, seeking for better pensions. They were not granted and he lived on his ninety-six dollars a year, aided by his children and friends. In his later life he joined the Campbellites, being baptized in the Ohio River. He was short, broad-shouldered, sinewy, and deep-chested. Lewis wrote for him (Oct. 10, 1806) a testimonial that he was noted for manly firmness and fortitude, and that he was entitled to the highest confidence. He was indeed a loyal, faithful subordinate; his worst vice was a fondness for liquor, which he overcame in his later life.

[Gass's *Jour. of the Voyages and Travels of a Corps of Discovery under the Command of Capt. Lewis and Capt. Clarke* ran through several editions: Pittsburgh, 1807; London, 1808; Philadelphia, 1810, 1811, 1812; Dayton (Ohio), 1847. The book was translated into French (Paris, 1810) and into German (Weimar, 1814). Jas. K. Hosmer reëdited it (Chicago, 1904). This last edition is prefaced by a life of Gass. The journal is very straightforward, somewhat dull, but as the earliest published record of the expedition had great vogue. See also John G. Jacob, *The Life and Times of Patrick Gass* (1859) and J. H. Newton, *Hist. of the Pan-Handle, W. Va.* (1879), pp. 46–49, the dates in the latter, however, being incorrect.] L. P. K.

GASSON, THOMAS IGNATIUS (Sept. 23, 1859–Feb. 27, 1930), Catholic priest and educator, was born at Sevenoaks, Kent, England, to Henry and Arabella (Quinnell) Gasson of the county gentry. His father was of Huguenot extraction, while his mother's family was rooted in the Kentish aristocracy. Privately tutored, the boy's English education was completed at St. Stephen's School, Lambeth, London. In 1872, he went to the United States to visit relatives, and studied under private tutors in Philadelphia. Two years later he was received into the Catholic Church by Rev. Charles Cicaterri, S. J.; and the following year, Nov. 17, he entered the Society of Jesus and commenced his novitiate. In 1877, he took simple vows and began his classical studies at the Jesuit juniorate in Frederick, Md., where he remained until 1880, and then for three years continued his philosophical courses in the College of the Sacred Heart, Woodstock, Md. He was instructor in Loyola College, Baltimore, from 1883 to 1886, and in the College of St. Francis Xavier, New York, from 1886 to 1888. In the latter year he was ordered to the Imperial Royal University of Innsbruck, Austria, for theology, canon law, and church history. Here, on July 26, 1891, he was ordained by the prince-bishop of Brixen in the Tyrol. Returning to the United States, in 1892, he taught in the Jesuit juniorate at Frederick, Md. (1892–94), until he was transferred to Boston College as professor of ethics and political economy and as preacher at the neighboring Church of the Immaculate Conception. In 1907, he became president of Boston College, which largely through his vision and efforts was removed to University Heights and rebuilt on an imposing scale. In 1914, he was ordered to Georgetown University, Washington, D. C., to teach sociology and legal ethics and to act as dean in an endeavor to reorganize the graduate school. Here, as in Boston, he left his mark on his college and won a place in the social and civic life of the community. In 1923, he was superior of the lay retreat house at Mt. Manresa, Staten Island, and the following year was called to Montreal to aid in the reorganization of the Society, which was divided into French and English speaking sections, and to assist in the development of Loyola College. It was there that he died, but his remains were brought to the Immaculate Conception Church in Boston for the final rites and were buried in the cemetery of Holy Cross College in Worcester. Father Gasson's influence was exerted through his work as a beloved teacher and as an administrative officer; he left no literary remains beyond an occasional article in *Donahoe's Magazine*, the *Catholic World*, and the Jesuit publications.

[*Am. Cath. Who's Who* (1911); *Who's Who in America*, 1924–25; *Boston Transcript*, *Evening Star* (Washington), and *Montreal Gazette*, Feb. 28, 1930; *Mosher's Mag.*, July 1899; *Loyola Coll. Rev.*, 1926; materials submitted by associates in the Society of Jesus.] R. J. P.

GASTON, JAMES McFADDEN (Dec. 27, 1824–Nov. 15, 1903), surgeon, teacher, was the son of Dr. John Brown Gaston, of a colonial Huguenot family, and Polly Buford (McFadden) Gaston, of Scotch descent. He was born near Chester, S. C., on the Gaston plantation, "Cedar Shoals," and received his early education in the neighborhood and at Russell Place in Kershaw district. He obtained his B.A. degree from the College (later University) of South Carolina in 1843, and pursued his medical studies with his father at home, at the University of Pennsylvania, and at the Medical College of South Carolina, where he received his M.D. degree in 1846. After practise with his father in Chester County until 1852, he moved to Columbia, S. C., where on Nov. 2 of the same year he married Sue G. Brumby, daughter of Prof. Richard T. Brumby of the state university. In the first years of the Civil War he served as chief surgeon to the South Carolina forces under Brig.-Gen. M. L. Bonham. He accompanied the latter to Richmond, and when the troops were removed to Manassas he was assigned medical director of the department under Brig.-Gen. Beauregard. After the battle of Manassas, at his own request, he was transferred to the 3rd Brigade, South Carolina Volunteers, under Brig.-Gen. Richard Anderson. He was later promoted chief surgeon of his division and participated in the Virginia and Pennsylvania campaigns. Returning to Gen. Beauregard's command, he was sent to establish a general hospital at Fort Gaines, Ga. He was subsequently in charge of a hospital at Fort Valley, where he remained on duty until the close of the war.

Carpet-bag rule in Carolina proved unbearable to Gaston, and in 1865 he went to Brazil to select a home for his family, and to report on the country as a possible refuge for a colony from his native state. His report, *Hunting a Home in Brazil* (1867), led to a migration of many Carolina planter families to that country. Gaston settled first in São Paulo. He attended lectures at the Imperial Academy of Medicine, and receiving an *ad eundum* degree in 1873, moved to Campinas, Brazil, where he was so successful that the Emperor offered him a surgical command in the army. This he declined, and in 1883 he returned to the United States and began practise in Atlanta, Ga. Appointed in 1884 professor of the principles and practise of medicine in the Southern Medical College in Atlanta, he served in that capacity and was known as the leading surgeon and teacher of the South for almost twenty years. His ability as a speaker and as an executive led to his election to the chairmanship of the surgical section of the American Medical Association (1891–92), presidency of the Southern Surgical and Gynecological Association (1891), presidency of the American Academy of Medicine (1895), and to prominent positions in other medical organizations. His professional writings include significant papers on appendicitis, surgery of the gall-bladder and ducts, ovariotomy, and yellow-fever inoculation. He was the first surgeon to demonstrate the feasibility of cholecyst-enterostomy by the use of elastic ligature on dogs, and one of the earliest to appreciate the value of tincture of iodine as a local antiseptic. A bold operator, he always reported his untoward results with absolute fidelity.

Gaston's activities extended beyond his professional interests. In 1885 he patented an airship motor, but was dissuaded from developing the project by friends and colleagues who feared that his ideas might excite doubts concerning his mental balance. He was the father of ten children, most of whom made Brazil their permanent home. He died, aged seventy-nine, at his home in Atlanta, and was buried in Westview Cemetery.

[*Who's Who in America,* 1901–02; H. A. Kelly and W. L. Burrage, *Am. Medic. Biogs.* (1920); *Jour. Am. Medic. Asso.,* Nov. 28, 1903; *Atlanta Constitution,* Nov. 16, 1903; information as to certain facts from Gaston's daughter, Mrs. T. B. Gay, Atlanta, Ga.]

C. G. D.

GASTON, WILLIAM (Sept. 19, 1778–Jan. 23, 1844), jurist, was born in New Bern, N. C. His father, Alexander Gaston, a native of Ireland and a descendant of the French Huguenot, Jean Gaston, had been a surgeon in the British navy before settling in New Bern in 1765. There in 1775 he married Margaret Sharpe, an English woman of Catholic parentage. In 1781, Dr. Gaston, who was an ardent Whig, was murdered by a band of Tories, in the presence of his wife and two children, Jane and William. Thereafter the great object of Margaret Gaston's life was the education of her son. Her deep piety and rare intellectual and moral qualities made an indelible impression upon his mind and character. Trained in the Catholic creed as a child, "after arriving at mature age," he later declared, "I deliberately embraced, from conviction, the faith which had been instilled into my mind by maternal piety."

In 1791 Gaston was enrolled as the first student of Georgetown College, in the District of Columbia; two years later, because of ill health, he withdrew and in 1794 entered the College of New Jersey from which he was graduated in 1796, with the highest honors of his class. Returning to New Bern, he studied law under François Xavier Martin [*q.v.*], afterwards distinguished at the bar of North Carolina, Mississippi, and Louisiana. Admitted to the bar in 1798, Gaston took over the practise of his brother-in-law, John Louis Taylor [*q.v.*], who had just been elevated to the bench.

In politics Gaston was a Federalist. Between 1800 and 1832 he served four terms in the state Senate and seven in the House of Commons. He drafted many of the state's most important statutes, including that regulating descents of inheritances, and served as chairman of the joint legislative committee which in 1818 framed the act establishing the supreme court of North Carolina. He had also a brief but brilliant career in national politics. In 1808 he was a presidential elector, and from 1813 to 1817 served in Congress. His speeches in support of the Bank of the United States and in opposition to the Loan Bill, which proposed to entrust the president with $25,000,000 for the conquest of Canada, won for him a national reputation, while his speech in reply to Clay's "defense of the previous question" has been frequently reprinted as a masterpiece of parliamentary oratory. (The last reprint was in the *Congressional Record,* 67 Cong., 2 Sess., pp. 2086–90.) Gaston was a caustic critic of the administration's war policies, and was charged with a want of patriotism, to which he retorted with great indignation: "I was baptised an American in the blood of a murdered father." In 1817 he voluntarily retired from Congress and never again entered national politics, declining in 1840 the offer of the United States senatorship and in 1841 the offer of a seat as attorney-general in Harrison's cabinet.

There developed in North Carolina a strong popular opposition to the state supreme court, established by the act of 1818, and numerous efforts were made to abolish it. In 1832 the death of the chief justice raised the question anew, and the bar of the state, with great unanimity, urged the election of Gaston as the only means of gaining for it the public confidence. The thirty-second article of the state constitution, however, forbade any person who should "deny the Truth of the Protestant religion," to hold a civil office in the state, and Gaston promptly raised the question of his eligibility. Many eminent lawyers, both within and without the state, including John Marshall, gave as their opinions that, whatever may have been the intention of the authors of the provision, it did not, as worded, disbar Catholics and since this view coincided with his own, Gaston agreed to accept the appointment. He was, accordingly, elected by the General Assembly in 1833 by a vote just short of unanimity.

In 1835 Gaston was a delegate to a constitutional convention held to purge the constitution of its most glaringly undemocratic provisions. Among them was the thirty-second article. As a rule Gaston pursued a liberal course in the convention, especially on questions of representation and suffrage. He favored an amendment making population the basis of representation in the Commons, and unsuccessfully opposed an amendment which deprived free negroes of the vote. On the proposal to abolish the religious qualifications for office-holding, he made the greatest effort of his life, and won a notable personal triumph, for although the convention declined to follow him all the way, it agreed to substitute the word "Christian" for the word "Protestant" in the thirty-second article. This was Gaston's last service in a parliamentary body; he preferred the work of the bench to that of the forum.

Gaston served on the supreme court from 1833 to 1844. His opinions, published in volumes XV to XXXVIII, inclusive, of the North Carolina *Reports*, display profound learning, clarity of reasoning, and vigor of expression; they are also distinguished for their broad humanitarian spirit. As a judge, he sought to mitigate as far as possible the harshness of the slave code. His two great opinions on this subject are *State* vs. *Negro Will* (18 *N. C. Annotated*, 121) and *State* vs. *William Manuel* (20 *N. C. Annotated*, 144). In the former, modifying a previous decision of the court, he held that malice was not to be presumed as a matter of law in the case of a slave who killed his master, or one standing in his master's stead, in defense of his own life against an unlawful assault; in the latter, he held that a manumitted slave was a citizen of the state. Justice Curtis, in his dissenting opinion in the Dred Scott Case, cited Gaston's opinion in *State* vs. *William Manuel* as "sound law."

Gaston's reputation was national. His services as a speaker were in constant demand throughout the country and two of his occasional addresses—one delivered at the University of North Carolina in 1832 and the other at the College of New Jersey in 1835—were especially noteworthy. He was a trustee of the University of North Carolina for forty-two years. He was married three times. By his first wife, Susan Hay, who died within a year of her marriage, he had no children. To his second wife, Hannah McClure, were born two daughters and a son, Alexander. His third wife was Eliza Worthington, by whom he had two daughters. He died suddenly in Raleigh, and was buried in New Bern.

[*Addresses at the Unveiling and Presentation of the Bust of Wm. Gaston by the N. C. Bar Asso.* (1915); W. D. Lewis, ed., *Great Am. Lawyers*, vol. III (1907); W. H. Battle, "Life and Character of Wm. Gaston," *N. C. Univ. Mag.*, Apr. 1844, reprinted in W. J. Peele, ed., *Lives of Distinguished North Carolinians* (1898); S. A. Ashe, *Biog. Hist. of N. C.*, vol. II (1905); Robt. Strange, *Life and Character of Hon. Wm. Gaston* (1844); E. F. McSweeney, *Gastons* (privately printed, 1926); R. B. Creecy, in *N. C. Univ. Mag.*, Oct. 1858; M. E. Manly, *Ibid.*, Nov. 1860; W. B. Hannon, "Judge Wm. Gaston: Statesman and Jurist," *Jour. Am. Irish Hist. Soc.*, X (1911), 253-58; C. A. Hanna, *Ohio Valley Geneals.* (1900); J. Fairfax McLaughlin, "Wm. Gaston: The First Student of Georgetown Coll.," *Proc. Am. Cath. Hist. Soc. of Phila., Records*, VI (1895), 225-51.]
R. D. W. C.

GASTON, WILLIAM (Oct. 3, 1820-Jan. 19, 1894), lawyer, governor of Massachusetts, was born in Killingly, Conn., the son of Alexander and Kesia (Arnold) Gaston. Through his great-grandfather, an emigrant to America in the eighteenth century, he was descended from Jean Gaston, a French Huguenot who fled from France to Scotland about 1640. Through his mother, he was descended from Thomas Arnold, who settled in New England in 1636. Alexander Gaston, a well-to-do merchant and a member of the Connecticut legislature, sent his son to academies at Brooklyn and Plainfield, both in Connecticut, and from there to Brown University, where he graduated with honors in 1840. He began the study of law with Judge Francis Hilliard, of Roxbury, Mass., completing his preparation under Charles P. and Benjamin R. Curtis of Boston. In 1844 he opened an office in Roxbury. Although he was almost immediately successful in his profession, he also interested himself in politics, first as a Whig and later as a Democrat. He was a member of the legislature in 1853, 1854, and 1856; city solicitor from 1856 to 1860; mayor of Roxbury in 1861 and 1862; state senator in 1868; an unsuccessful candidate for Congress in 1870; and mayor of Boston (after Roxbury had been annexed to the city) in 1871–72. In 1873 he was defeated for the mayoralty by Henry L. Pierce and was then nominated for governor, only to be beaten by the Republican nominee, William B. Washburn. In the autumn of 1874, Gaston was once more the Democratic standard-bearer and was victorious over the Republican candidate, Thomas Talbot, by a majority of nearly 8,000. He was the first Democrat to occupy the governor's chair after it had been vacated by George S. Boutwell in 1852.

As governor, Gaston conducted a conservative administration, showing himself to be "more of a patriot than a partisan" (*Boston Post,* Jan. 20, 1894). He also made excellent appointments. Even his opponents spoke of him with respect, referring to him as a "moderate Democrat." His popularity, however, was not sufficient to overcome the normal Republican majority in the state, and he was defeated in the autumn of 1875, for a second term, by Alexander H. Rice, the Republican candidate. As soon as the year closed, he returned to the practise of his profession and never again ran for office.

In 1865 Gaston had formed the law partnership of Jewell, Gaston & Field, in which he remained, with some changes in his associates, for the remainder of his life. Although he had little taste for criminal practise, he became one of the leading trial lawyers of the state and is said to have had more cases during his career than any lawyer in New England. He was president of the Boston Bar Association and head of the Massachusetts Bar Association, and was rigid in support of the ethical principles of his profession. He was married on May 27, 1852, to Louisa Augusta Beecher, daughter of Laban S. Beecher, a lumber merchant. He had one daughter and two sons, one of whom, William Alexander, became his father's law partner. He died in Boston and was buried in Forest Hills Cemetery. Though he was reserved and rather shy in manner, he was the embodiment of dignity and grace. Uniformly kind and courteous, he was a most companionable man, and in spite of the firmness with which he maintained his opinions, made very few enemies.

[W. T. Davis, *Bench and Bar of the Commonwealth of Mass.* (1895), I, 385; *New-Eng. Hist. and Geneal. Reg.*, July 1894; C. A. Hanna, *Ohio Valley Geneals.* (1900); *Boston Transcript,* Jan. 19, *Boston Post,* Jan. 20, 1894; information as to certain facts from acquaintances of Gaston.]

C. M. F.

GATES, FREDERICK TAYLOR (July 2, 1853–Feb. 6, 1929), Baptist clergyman, business executive, and architect of great philanthropic enterprises, was born in Maine, Broome County, N. Y., the son of Rev. Granville and Sarah Jane (Bowers) Gates. "All our ancestral lines," he says in *Our American Ancestry* (1928), a privately printed work showing long painstaking research, "run back practically unbroken to the Puritan and Pilgrim settlement of New England." On his father's side he was descended from George Gates, born in England in 1634, who as a boy came to Hartford, Conn., consigned to Capt. Nicholas Olmstead, whose daughter, Sarah, he married; on his mother's side, from George Bower(s) who was a freeman of Plymouth, Mass., in 1637. Rev. Granville Gates was pastor of small Baptist churches in New York state from 1854 to 1867, in connection with which he showed ability to build up feeble interests; and from 1867 to 1885, was first missionary and then superintendent of missions under the American Baptist Home Missionary Society in Kansas. Frederick, supporting himself in part by serving as clerk in store and bank, prepared for college and graduated from the University of Rochester in 1877, and from the Rochester Theological Seminary in 1880. In the latter year he was ordained to the Baptist ministry, and became pastor of the Central Church, Minneapolis. On June 28, 1882, he married Lucia F. Perkins of Rochester, N. Y., who died the following year; and Mar. 3, 1886, he married Emma Lucile Cahoon of Racine, Wis. In 1888 he resigned his church and undertook the raising of an endowment for Pillsbury Academy, a Baptist school in Minnesota, in which task he displayed exceptional ability to plan and execute a financial campaign. Upon the organization of the American Baptist Education Society, that same year, he was appointed its corresponding secretary. He at once made a thorough study of Baptist educational interests in all parts of the country, and decided that the first great need was an institution of learning of high grade in Chicago. Ever since the passing of the old University of Chicago in 1886, such an institution had been in the minds of some, including Thomas W. Goodspeed and William R. Harper [*qq.v.*], who had interested John D. Rockefeller in the project. Secretary Gates secured for it the indorsement of the Education Society; gave the matter such publicity as to reveal that the denomination throughout the land was favorable; arranged for a conference of leading Baptist educators and laymen of wealth and influence who formulated a clear-cut plan for the institution which won Rockefeller's approval; and was instrumental in raising the million dollars, of which Rockefeller gave $600,000, which insured the establishment of the University.

Their contacts inspired Rockefeller's confidence in him, and when Gates was making one of his Western trips Rockefeller asked him to look into some investments which he had recently made. His report disclosed such extraordinary ability to get at facts, analyze them, and draw sound conclusions, that in 1893 Rockefeller invited him to become associated with his interests. Through this connection he was able to render great and varied service. He became the guiding force in many of Rockefeller's enterprises, notably in connection with his iron-ore projects in Minnesota. These he was primarily instrumental in developing, including the mines, the railroads, and the great fleet of ore-bearing vessels, which were later turned over to the United States Steel Corporation. In all his business relations he was governed by the same high principles of justice, fair dealing, and economic efficiency which guided his private life.

It was in the field of education and philanthropy, however, that he did his greatest work. He continued active in behalf of the University of Chicago, serving for many years as a trustee; but contributed in a much broader way to the educational upbuilding of the country through the General Education Board, the first of the Rockefeller foundations, set up without restriction as to race or creed for the purpose of supporting schools and colleges throughout the United States. Of this he was long the president, and almost to the end of his life, a trustee. It was under his leadership that the Board embarked upon the tasks of aiding the higher educational institutions in building up endowment funds, and of assisting in the intensive development of a small number of leading medical schools. Believing that the study of the causes and prevention of disease offers the greatest field of service to mankind, he conceived the idea of the Rockefeller Institute for Medical Research. The child of his own brain, it became the interest nearest his heart. From its founding until his death he was president of its board of trustees. The large number of appeals for aid for a variety of causes which came into Rockefeller's office from near and far, Gates studied, analyzed, and classified, and it was he who developed the principles and policies which led to the establishment of the Rockefeller Foundation, chartered to advance the well-being of mankind throughout the world. Thus through a happy conjunction with the philanthropic purposes and large vision of Rockefeller, he was able to create in rapid succession a group of institutions all directed to the common end of increasing knowledge and promoting happiness.

He was a vivid, vigorous personality, an innovator by temperament, zealous and even insistent in expressing his convictions and urging the principles in which he believed, but cooperative in action and kind and sympathetic in his personal relations. His death occurred in his seventy-sixth year, while he was visiting a daughter in Phoenix, Ariz.

[See Thos. W. Goodspeed, *A Hist. of the Univ. of Chicago* (1916); John D. Rockefeller, *Random Reminiscences of Men and Events* (1909); *Who's Who in America*, 1928–29; *N. Y. Times*, Feb. 7, 1929; *A Service in Memory of Frederick Taylor Gates* (1929); John D. Rockefeller, Jr., "Remarks at the Memorial Service to Mr. Gates held at the Rockefeller Institute, May 15, 1929." In 1912 Gates published *The Truth about Mr. Rockefeller and the Merritts.* See also Paul De Kruif, *Seven Iron Men* (1929).]

H. E. S.

GATES, GEORGE AUGUSTUS (Jan. 24, 1851–Nov. 20, 1912), educator, was born at Topsham, Vt., the son of Hubbard Gates, a miller, who moved to East St. Johnsbury, and died in 1861. His mother, Rosetta Gates, a graduate of Newbury Seminary, after the death of her husband opened a millinery shop to support the three children. George was educated at St. Johnsbury Academy and at Dartmouth College, where he received the degree of B.A. in 1873. After two years as principal of the Vermont Morrisville Academy he entered Andover Seminary and was graduated in 1880, having meanwhile tutored in Boston and spent two years in travel and study abroad. Because of his modern views he was refused ordination by an ecclesiastical council at Littleton, N. H., presided over by President Bartlett of Dartmouth, who ten years later made amends by bestowing upon him the degree of D.D. Called to a union church at Upper Montclair, N. J., he was ordained by a council headed by Lyman Abbott. In 1882 he married Isabel Smith of Syracuse.

After a successful ministry of seven years, Gates accepted the presidency of Iowa (now Grinnell) College in 1887. He came to this task without the training of the professional educator, but with a vigor and independence of mind and conviction, a transparent honesty of heart, a shining idealism, a persuasive power of speech, and a winning manliness and sympathy which made him a power in public relations as well as within college walls. His Friday morning chapel talks were events which those who heard them never forgot. His judgment of men was fine and sure, and he strengthened the faculty by attracting to Grinnell a group of young instructors of unusual ability. The most conspicuous educational event of his administration was the founding of the chair of "Applied Christianity," which expressed a new idea in the teaching of religion. His deep interest in the practical application of religious teachings also inspired his affiliation with the *Kingdom,* a weekly on which he collaborated with H. W. Gleason, John Bascom, Josiah Strong, Jesse Macy, John R. Commons, and Washington Gladden. A fearless crusader, he assailed the "unscrupulous methods" by which a "book trust" introduced its publications into the schools, and gave publicity to his attack through his book, *A Foe to American Schools* (1897).

During his thirteen years in Iowa, Gates was offered the presidency of two state universities and two Eastern colleges, but he declined out of loyalty to the task which he had assumed at Grinnell. Due to his wife's health, however, he felt obliged to seek a mountain climate, and in 1900, to the deep regret of his associates and students, he laid down his work at the college. For the following ten months he was pastor of the First Congregational Church at Cheyenne, Wyo. During this brief residence he set in motion moral forces which overcame the stubborn resistance of politicians and secured the repeal of a state law licensing gambling. Though he declined overtures from the American Missionary Association School at Talladega, Ala., from Fisk University, and from Washburn College, Kansas, partly because they seemed climatically unsuitable, he accepted the call to the presidency of Pomona College, Claremont, Cal., and began his service there in December 1901. Again, as at Grinnell, his public service far transcended the bounds of his official relations, and all problems of vital public interest in Southern California enlisted his virile cooperation. After seven years of intensive work at Claremont, he felt it necessary to seek release from increasing burdens and spent the first half of 1909 on a trip to Australia and New Zealand. On his return he was urged once more to become the head of Fisk University at Nashville, Tenn. The appeal to his chivalric missionary spirit was too strong to be resisted, and in September 1909 he began his last brief period of work as an educator. Injured in a serious railway accident early in 1912, he attempted with indomitable courage to resume his work, but the effort ended in physical and mental collapse. A leave of absence in the mountains gave him sufficient energy to officiate at the Fisk Commencement in June. He then sought further restoration at Winter Park, Fla., but repeated cerebral attacks sapped his vitality and his despondency over the hopelessness of his situation led him to take his own life. He was buried at Grinnell, Iowa.

[Isabel S. Gates, *The Life of Geo. Augustus Gates* (1915); *Who's Who in America,* 1910–11; C. B. Sumner, *The Story of Pomona Coll.* (1914); *Gen. Cat. Dartmouth Coll. 1769–1900* (1900); *Fla. Times-Union* (Jacksonville), Nov. 21, 1912.] J. S. N.

GATES, HORATIO (*c.* 1728/29–Apr. 10, 1806), Revolutionary soldier, was born at Maldon, Essex, England, the son of Robert and Dorothy (Parker) Gates. Robert Gates has been variously set down as a revenue officer, an army officer, a clergyman, and a greengrocer; his wife was probably a housekeeper to the Duke of Leeds. Horatio Gates was apparently named for his godfather, Horace Walpole. He entered the British army at an early age, as he was a lieutenant with the troops under Gen. Edward Cornwallis, in Nova Scotia, in 1749–50 (Journal in Gates Papers, *post*). He was married to Elizabeth Phillips on Oct. 20, 1754 (certificate by the chaplain, dated "Halifax 2 Aug., 1757," Gates Papers). When the news of Washington's defeat at Great Meadows reached London, the Duke of Newcastle asked Gates to express his opinion as to what should be done. The latter's refusal to do so, on the ground that it would be impertinent, is an interesting commentary upon both his reputation and character (Horace Walpole, *Memoires of the Last Ten Years of the Reign of George the Second,* 1822, I, 347). On Sept. 30, 1754, he was commissioned captain in the "Independent Company of Foot doing duty in New York." In 1755, Gates's company joined Braddock's army in Virginia. He was present at the action of July 9, before Fort Duquesne, when the British were routed and Braddock was fatally wounded. He was himself severely wounded in this battle. On Apr. 28, 1758, he was at Fort Herkimer, in the Mohawk Valley, when the general of that name defended his post against a combined attack of French and Indians. During the next two years he was on duty at Oneida, Fort Hunter, Pittsburgh, Fort Ticonderoga, and Philadelphia.

Late in 1761, he joined Gen. Monckton at New York, and sailed with him on the conspicuously successful expedition for the conquest of Martinique. He was chosen by Monckton, who had apparently become his intimate friend, to go to London with the news of the victory. He reached England in March, and on Apr. 24, 1762, was commissioned a major in the 45th Regiment. Gates went out to join his command in New York, but as there was no vacant majority in the regiment, returned to London. On Oct. 27, 1764, he was appointed to the 60th or Royal American Regiment then at New York, but gained a leave of absence to stay in England until the spring of 1765. On May 8, because he still did not wish to return to America, he was permitted to exchange his majority in the 60th for retirement on half pay. Then settling at Bristol, he lived there until 1769, when he moved to Devonshire. On receiving a letter from his old comrade in arms, Washington, advising him about land in Virginia, he and his wife and son, Robert Gates, sailed from Bristol in August 1772, and took up land in Berkeley County (now W. Va.). For the next three years he lived quietly upon this Virginia plantation, "Traveller's Rest," taking no particular part in public life beyond accepting Lord Dunmore's offer of a lieutenant-colonelcy in the Virginia militia and serving in 1774 as a "gentleman justice" of the county court.

Gates's espousal of the patriot cause in 1775 seems partly explained by his personal revolt against the English caste system. There is some evidence that he was sensitive about his rather humble origins. Probably because of the patronage of Walpole, he had done better in the Seven Years' War than might have been expected of one of his birth. As a Virginia planter and an old friend of Washington, he had no difficulty in gaining the position in society which the Old World had denied him. One need not be surprised, then, to find Gates commissioned as adjutant-general of the Continental Army, with the rank of brigadier-general, as early as June 17, 1775. By July he was in the camp at Cambridge, Mass., organizing the miscellaneous units which made up the American forces besieging Boston. Here, probably, he was at his best, a capable administrator, an indefatigable worker, and a loyal supporter of the efforts of the Commander-in-Chief. After the evacuation of Boston, Congress appointed him, now a major-general (commissioned May 16, 1776) to take command of the troops which on the failure of the Canadian expedition were withdrawing toward Crown Point. A conflict of jurisdiction at once arose between Gates and Schuyler, who was in command of the northern department. Congress settled this, on July 8, 1776, in favor of Schuyler while the troops were south of the border. Gates remained at Fort Ticonderoga until December 1776, when, under Schuyler's directions, he repaired to Philadelphia to assume command of the troops in that city. In February 1777 Congress desired that he resume his office of adjutant-general, but on Mar. 25 ordered him back to Ticonderoga to "take command of the army there." This displacement of Schuyler led to much ill-feeling, and on May 15, 1777, the Board of War agreed to restore Schuyler to command of the northern department and give Gates his choice, either of serving under Schuyler, or resuming the office of adjutant-general. No sooner had he been directed to repair to headquarters in July, than, on Aug. 4, 1777, he was again ordered by Congress to command the northern army, this time to relieve Schuyler (Ford, *Journals*, V, 448, 526; VII, 136, 202, 364; VIII, 540, 604).

This shuffling of commanders was done in the face of the impending invasion by the British army under Burgoyne. Gates was finally in supreme command in the north when the two armies met in the late summer of 1777. Historical accounts of the Saratoga campaign have given abundant reasons for the American victory other than the military skill of Horatio Gates (H. Nickerson, *The Turning Point of the Revolution,* 1928; C. H. Van Tyne, *The War of Independence,* 1929, II, 370–441). The fierce fighting at Freeman's Farm and Bemis Heights served to bring out Benedict Arnold [*q.v.*] as the most dramatic figure on the American side. Gates and Arnold quarreled in September over what the latter regarded as Gates's lack of initiative and inclination to slight his services. By mid-October Gates had Burgoyne in his grasp, when news arrived that Clinton had made a desperate effort to relieve Burgoyne from the south and had captured Forts Clinton and Montgomery on the highlands of the Hudson. Negotiations looking toward the capitulation of Burgoyne's army were already under way. Burgoyne refused an unconditional surrender. Gates's army outnumbered the British more than two to one, but he feared lest Clinton strike at the arsenals in Albany, and he was not sufficiently confident of his own troops to risk another major engagement. The Convention of Saratoga, signed Oct. 17, 1777, therefore provided for the return of the British army to England under promise that it would not serve again in the war, though it was to be subject to exchange.

The severe criticism of Gates for his delay in notifying Congress and Washington of the all-important victory at Saratoga is certainly not fair, as he wrote to President Hancock the day after the surrender, and sent the messages by his adjutant, Wilkinson. The latter did not start south until Oct. 20, consumed three days getting to Esopus, delayed two days at Easton, took three days more to cover the forty-two miles between Easton and Reading, where he halted to gossip about a matter which was to make much trouble for Gates, and did not reach York, Pa., where

Congress was sitting, until Oct. 31 (James Wilkinson, *Memoirs of My Own Times,* 1816, I, 323–33). Gates can hardly be blamed, save perhaps for choosing Wilkinson in the first place. As to his delay in notifying Washington, it should be remembered that Gates did not know where Washington was after the Brandywine campaign, and so requested Congress to forward the dispatches to him, and especially the letter announcing the surrender. Inasmuch as Wilkinson's dispatches had to be relayed back across the state from York to the neighborhood of Philadelphia, delay was inevitable. Congress voted Gates its thanks and ordered a medal struck in commemoration of the victory over Burgoyne, Nov. 4, 1777. Meantime, a serious difference of opinion arose between Washington and Gates, when the latter refused to return the Continental troops demanded by the former (Sparks, *Correspondence of the American Revolution,* II, 27–38).

Although Gates, after Saratoga, expressed his feeling that the infirmities of age were creeping upon him and was determined that this should be his last campaign, Congress on Nov. 27 elected him to the Board of War and appointed him its president. This position kept him with Congress at York through a part of the winter of 1777–78. Meantime, the real evils of Wilkinson's dilatory trip in October began to come to light. After Brandywine some member of Congress wrote a fawning letter to Gates insinuating that Washington was a failure, Gates a hero, and that something should be done about it. On Oct. 11 Gen. Thomas Conway [*q.v.*] seems to have written to Gates expressing his disgust with the mismanagement of the war, his intention to resign, and some insolent criticism of Washington. According to Wilkinson, Gates gave this letter such publicity that every one at his headquarters knew all about it. When he subsequently learned from Conway that Washington was aware of the letter and also of his indiscretion in showing it about, he did not wait to hear from Washington, but wrote at once to the latter complaining that the letter had been stolen from him and asking Washington's aid in finding the culprit. Washington replied on Jan. 4, 1778, in a most dignified fashion, saying he had the information via the Wilkinson-McWilliams-Stirling route and that all it meant to him was that Conway was his enemy. Instead of letting the matter rest, Gates felt called upon to write another lengthy letter to Washington in which, besides venting his spleen on the supposed betrayer of his confidence, he now called the offensive passages a forgery. Washington then pointedly asked why, if the letter was a forgery, Gates had not said so at first, instead of worrying about finding who had looted his files. Moreover, said Washington, if the original is so inoffensive, why not produce it? This neither Gates nor Conway was ever willing to do. Certain members of Congress at the time, notably Benjamin Rush and Gen. Thomas Mifflin [*qq.v.*], were engaged in a plan to supersede Washington with Gates. When the matter got confused with the game of "hunting the letter," the various participants in the Conway Cabal sought cover, and the effort to elevate Gates failed through the inability of the participants to face the withering and honest scorn of the Commander-in-Chief (Sparks, *Writings of Washington,* V, 483–518). It is difficult to establish the fact that Gates actually shared in a conspiracy to secure Washington's position, but he knowingly let his friends in Congress do so.

Wilkinson's indiscretions led to a duel between him and Gates, which took place on Sept. 4, 1778, near White Plains, N. Y. After three rounds of pistols flashing in the pan, and the participants firing into the air, the two shook hands. On Apr. 15, 1778, Gates was again appointed to command the northern department, and took up his headquarters at Fishkill on the Hudson. During the summer of 1778 he tried to get Washington to let him displace Sullivan in the Rhode Island expedition, but "the General did not think proper to supersede an officer of distinguished merit by a doubtful friend" (Greene to Sullivan, July 23, 1778; William L. Clements Library). On Oct. 22, 1778, he was sent to Boston to take command of the troops in the eastern department. He remained there through the winter of 1778–79. His functions in the eastern department seem to have been confined largely to getting supplies. On Oct. 27, 1779, he was at Newport and reported the withdrawal of the British from Rhode Island. Thence he rejoined Washington on the Hudson in December 1779.

In the winter of 1780 Gates retired to his plantation in Virginia. On June 13 he was directed by Congress to take command of the army in the southern department where, because of the surrender of Lincoln at Charleston, the patriot cause was in desperate straits. He reached Hillsborough, then the capital of North Carolina, on July 19. He tarried there to get in touch with the Revolutionary leaders in that state, particularly the leaders of the North Carolina troops and the partisan corps, who still had plenty of fight in them. By August he was on the banks of the Peedee and on the 15th encamped with his army at Rugeley's Mill, near Camden, S. C. Cornwallis and the British were directly in front of him, and it was obvious that a conflict could not be avoided. He chose his ground with considerable skill and care, as Greene afterward attested, and secured the agreement of all his general officers that a battle must be fought. There is reason to believe, however, that his general officers were opposed to his getting into such a position in the first place (Edward McCrady, *The History of South Carolina in the Revolution, 1775–1780*, 1901, p. 674). On Aug. 16 occurred the battle of Camden, one of the most disastrous of the war, for the militia, who composed more than half of his army, ran like sheep. The Maryland troops, the backbone of his Continentals, stood firm, while Gates and the North Carolina general, Richard Caswell, strove in vain to rally the fugitives. The extent of the rout is attested by the fact that on the evening of the day of the battle, Gates reported the affair from Charlotte, N. C., seventy miles from the field. His report of the battle is a thoroughly dignified document, which has abundant supporting evidence. The causes of disaster were the virtual starvation of the troops for weeks beforehand, the reliance on raw militia, and the utter lack of cavalry in the face of Cornwallis's excellent equipment in this branch of the service (Gates to Caswell, Aug. 22, 1780, *Magazine of American History*, October 1880, pp. 304–05, and to the president of Congress, Aug. 20, 1780, Gates Papers; *The State Records of North Carolina*, XV, 1898, pp. 160–62).

On Oct. 5, upon receiving the news of the disaster, Congress turned upon its erstwhile favorite and voted that an inquiry be made into his conduct, and that Washington appoint another commander of the southern department until that inquiry be held (Ford, *Journals*, XVIII, 906). Gen. Nathanael Greene relieved Gates at Charlotte on Dec. 2, but soon found that the reorganization of the southern army was enough work without the additional task of holding an inquiry. Moreover, such a court required the presence of more general officers than could be spared from their duties elsewhere. Greene treated Gates with the utmost kindness. Despite the absence of proper witnesses and generals, Gates was willing that the court of inquiry be held anyway, but Greene, upon the unanimous advice of the general officers, declined to hold it (Greene to Gates, Dec. 6, 1780, Clements Library). Gates therefore withdrew to his plantation, where he was waited on by a committee of four, Patrick Henry, R. H. Lee, Lane, and Thomas Nelson, from the Virginia House of Delegates, who assured him that the House had voted unanimously, on Dec. 28, 1780, that his previous glorious services were such as could not be obliterated by any reverse of fortune. Throughout the year 1781 Gates remained at "Traveller's Rest," writing constantly to Washington and to Congress requesting that the inquiry into his conduct be held. In April he went personally to Philadelphia to press his demand. Washington then wrote Gates, on May 12, 1781, that no court could proceed until charges were preferred, and that he, for one, had no intention of making such charges. Congress thereupon resolved, on May 21, 1781, that their previous act demanding the inquiry did not operate as a suspension of Gates from his command in the line, and that he might go to headquarters and assume such command as Washington might indicate. Gates, however, left Philadelphia and retired once more to Virginia, where he was when Washington passed by on his triumphant march to Yorktown. A year later, on Aug. 5, 1782, Gates again demanded either exoneration or a court martial, and Congress generously responded by repealing its resolve of Oct. 5, 1780, and by ordering Gates to take such command in the main army as Washington should direct. Gates, his self-respect restored, set out for headquarters and during the remainder of the war was with Washington at the cantonment at Newburgh, where he nobly seconded the Commander-in-Chief's efforts to quell the mutiny and discontent among the badly treated Continentals (Ford, *Journals*, XXIII, 466; XXIV, 311).

In 1783 he returned once more to his Virginia home, and there was made president of the state Society of the Cincinnati, on Oct. 9, 1783. In 1784 he and Washington were requested by the General Assembly to bring about cooperation with Maryland in regard to inland navigation and communication with western waters, and drew up a report (Dec. 28, 1784, Clements Library), though the illness of Gates made it necessary for Washington to act alone (Sparks, *Writings of Washington*, IX, 82; Gaillard Hunt, *The Writings of James Madison*, II, 1901, pp. 104–05). In 1784, shortly after the death of his first wife, Gates fell in love with Janet Montgomery, the widow of Gen. Richard Montgomery. The lady however declined his suit (correspondence in the Bancroft Collection, New York Public Library). On July 31, 1786, he married Mary Vallance of Washington County, Md., who brought her husband a fortune of several hundred thousand dollars, most of which was used in caring for the less fortunate Revolutionary soldiers (*Magazine of American History*, November 1884, p. 469). His son by his first wife had died in 1780. Gates continued to reside in Virginia until 1790, when, his old doubts as to social inequality besetting him, he emancipated his slaves and moved to New York. There he took up his residence at "Rose Hill Farm," a place which to-day would be bounded by Twenty-third and Thirtieth Streets and Second and Fourth Avenues. He served one term in the New York legislature, 1800–01. He died at "Rose Hill" on Apr. 10, 1806. His widow survived him until 1810.

Gilbert Stuart's portrait of Gates shows a man with a strong but narrow face, eyelids drooping at the corners, and a chin that is apparently large, yet a trifle receding. His character seems as contradictory as his face. At times vigorous, and full of real ability, at other times he seems to have been wavering and indecisive. There can be no doubt that he was exceedingly unpopular among many of the best officers in the army. He had many good friends in Congress, but some of these fell away from him after they knew him better. His letters show him to have been a stanch Whig, with decidedly liberal views. Sometimes his letters are philosophical to the point of dreaminess. Yet there can be no question of the tenacity with which he adhered to what he regarded as a moral point.

[The Gates Papers, which cover almost the whole of his life, were kept intact by his widow, and by her will were left to Joel Barlow in the hope that he would write an impartial history of the Revolution. Barlow, however, died two years later, and most of the papers then found their way to the N. Y. Hist. Soc., where they are at present. Other collections of related MSS. are in the Lib. of Cong., and the Wm. L. Clements Lib., Ann Arbor, Mich. Jas. Thacher's sketch in *A Mil. Jour. During the Am. Revolutionary War* (1823), pp. 539–48, is one of the earliest attempts at a biography of Gates. Isaac J. Greenwood, "Maj.-Gen. Horatio Gates," in the *New-Eng. Hist. and Geneal. Reg.*, July 1867, is chiefly valuable for reprinting the will of Mrs. Gates. J. A. Stevens, "The Southern Campaign of 1780," in *Mag. of Am. Hist.*, Oct. 1880, prints Gates's correspondence during that period. *The Hist. of the Rise, Progress, and Establishment of the Independence of the U. S. of America: Including an Account of the Late War* (3 vols., 1789) was written by Wm. Gordon, a personal adviser of Gates who probably had access to his papers. Reference should also be made to W. C. Ford, ed., *Jours. of the Continental Cong.* (25 vols., 1904–28), and *The Writings of Geo. Washington* (14 vols., 1889–93); E. C. Burnett, ed., *Letters of Members of the Continental Cong.*, vol. I–IV (1921–28); Jared Sparks, ed., *The Writings of Geo. Washington* (12 vols., 1834–37), and *Correspondence of the Am. Revolution; Being Letters of Eminent Men to Geo. Washington* (4 vols., 1853); Peter Force, *Am. Archives* (9 vols., 1837–53); *Pub. Papers of Geo. Clinton* (10 vols., 1899–1914); B. Tarleton, *A Hist. of the Campaigns of 1780 and 1781* (1787); Chas. Stedman, *The Hist. of the Origin, Progress, and Termination of the Am. War* (3 vols., 1794); Henry Lee, *Memoirs of the War in the Southern Dept. of the U. S.* (2 vols., 1812); *B. F. Stevens Facsimiles of MSS. in European Archives Relating to America* (24 portfolios, 1889–95); *Calendar of Emmet Coll. of MSS.* (N. Y. Pub. Lib., 1900). Obituaries were published in the N. Y. *Evening Post*, Apr. 10, 1806; *N. Y. Herald*, Apr. 12, 19, 1806, the latter of which was several times reprinted.]

R. G. A—s.

GATES, JOHN WARNE (May 8, 1855–Aug. 9, 1911), promoter, speculator, captain of industry, was born near Turner Junction, now West Chicago, Ill., the son of Asel Avery and Mary (Warne) Gates. He received his schooling at the village academy and at North-Western College, Naperville, where he graduated from a six months' commercial course in 1873 (letter from the Registrar, North Central College, Naperville). At nineteen he had saved enough to buy a half-share in a village hardware store and at twenty-one to marry Dellora Baker, of St. Charles, Ill. The manufacture of barbed wire for fencing was an industry just then beginning to have some importance because of the opening of wide tracts of western land, on which rail-fencing could not meet the ravages of fire, wind, and cattle. Gates saw here a field for business enterprise, and, with an audacity that deserved success, sought out Isaac L. Ellwood in 1878 and offered to take a partnership in his wire-manufacturing concern. Ellwood was sufficiently impressed to hire him as a traveling salesman at twenty-five dollars a week. Finding that the Texas ranchers to whom he tried to sell the wire were sceptical of its usefulness, Gates rented a tract at San Antonio, built a corral of the wire, and issued a challenge to the ranchers to let their best Texas steers test its endurance. The wire emerged the victor and orders came rushing in. It was a display of salesmanship that was symbolic in inaugurating his business career. Feeling that where he had tapped so copious a source of profits he had a right to more than the drippings, he turned from salesman to entrepreneur and decided to fill the orders himself. He found a partner with some capital and set up his manufacturing plant in St. Louis. This enterprise involved him in legal complications with Ellwood, but Gates exhausted his opponent by ingeniously moving his plant from one side of the river to the other to avoid the service of injunctions, and they finally reached an agreement. He then turned his attention to the art of "putting-together," as he phrased it, the various wire interests. A series of consolidations starting in 1880 led finally in 1898 to the formation of the American Steel & Wire Company of New Jersey, with a capitalization of $90,000,000. The series of steps by which this was accomplished was traced by himself in 1902 in his testimony on the witness stand in *Parks* vs. *Gates* (*New York Times,* Mar. 17, 1902). Each successive consolidation bought up the stock of the previous one at more than its par value and issued its own stock at considerably more than the appraised value of the constituent properties. It is, however, a testimony to his shrewd financing and to the upward swing of conditions in the wire industry, that, even after the "watering" process, the stock rose in value on the Exchange.

The American Steel & Wire Company was his greatest industrial achievement and with it he became the head of the wire industry of the country. But he was of that new type of captain of industry whose principal activity consisted not so much in the working out of the technical and managerial arrangements of a particular enterprise as in the floating of a variety of new enterprises and the gathering of capital for them. His chief talent lay in promotion. His geniality, his contagious enterprise, his ready flow of talk, his masculine tastes for hunting, gambling, and traveling, and the tradition of financial success that attached to any one who joined the "Gates band-wagon" gave a persuasiveness to any project that he proposed. He was overbrimming with energy: he was, in the words of his secretary, "a great boy with an extraordinary money sense annexed." In addition, he had an intuitive knowledge of how to adapt the methods of his approach to the particular individual. These talents found their best expression in the steel industry. In 1894 Gates had succeeded Jay C. Morse as president of the Illinois Steel Company as Morse's personal choice. This company supplied the iron and steel rods out of which the wire of the Consolidated Steel & Wire Company was made, and Gates managed to pull it out of the non-dividend-paying class of enterprises and make it yield profits. When Carnegie expressed an intention of retiring from his interests it was Gates who saw more clearly than any one else the possibilities of a huge steel combination. While Frick, Gary, and Moore in 1899 discussed terms for such a merger, Gates "hovered around the negotiators" (Tarbell, *post,* p. 108) and broached the idea of a billion-dollar corporation. He participated in the formation of the Republic Iron & Steel Company, and in 1906 he was part of the syndicate which took over the Tennessee Coal & Iron Company in an effort to break the impact of the impending panic.

To the general public Gates was best known as "Bet-you-a-million Gates" because of a reputed audacity of conviction that sought always concrete expression. He denied using the phrase and it is true that, although known as a plunger, he actually relied heavily on the advice of expert technicians like William R. Walker and spread out an elaborate network for gathering information, even using detectives, before he acted. But at the point where inevitably there was a gap between the facts and the decision he showed the utmost daring. And he was certainly somewhat open in his expressions of an aleatory philosophy. A fatal passion for speculation and a restlessness of imagination conditioned the greater part of his business activity. In 1896 he managed a speculative operation of some importance in Chicago gas; in 1897 he was reputed to have cleared twelve million dollars in Wall Street in connection with his wire interests; he was charged by some with having precipitated something of a panic in 1900 through his operations. It was chiefly as a marauder that he was known and feared on the Exchange. Once an unfortunate speculation in the Chicago Grain Exchange wiped out his fortune, but he kept quiet about it, maintained a brave front lest his credit fail, and managed in a short time to retrieve his losses. One of his boldest exploits, carried off with the greatest éclat, led eventually to disaster. At a time when J. P. Morgan needed the Louisville & Nashville Railroad in connection with a consolidation he was managing, Gates secretly gained control of it and resold it to Morgan for a fancy price. Morgan, according to the version published by Gates's private secretary, pretended to be amused, extended Gates a good deal of credit on collateral, manipulated a drop in the price of the securities, and then dictated his terms. The terms were that Gates was to forsake the New York Stock Exchange for good. Whatever the authenticity of his account Gates did retire from New York in his prime. He chose Port Arthur, Tex., at that time a town of less than ten thousand, as his next field of operations. There he invested in the Spindletop Oil Field and organized the Texas Company as an independent concern. He owned a large portion of the real estate of the town and controlled its industries. Though his operations were now on a small-town scale, he showed an undiminished zest for them. He was like a Napoleon banished to St. Helena and reduced to organizing the warfare of the islanders. But he talked, gambled, invested, and promoted as though he were still in New York. He died in Paris, Aug. 9, 1911. He left no dynasty.

Gates was one of the most vigorous and colorful figures in American finance. His significance may be said to lie chiefly in the application of the rough qualities of the frontier to the realm of Big Business. He was intuitive and resourceful rather than intellectual—*David Harum* was the only book he ever mentioned as having read. Later in life he added the veneer of the plutocrat: he maintained a hunting castle near Paris and in his New York apartment he hung Corots and Meissoniers. With as high an endowment of natural gifts as any business man of his day, he fell short of genuine business leadership by the lack of a mature sense of public responsibility.

[O. A. Owen, the private secretary of Gates for eight years, has written two informative articles in the *Saturday Evening Post*: "Bet-you-a-million Gates," Nov. 7, 1925, and "The Superman and his Secretary," Dec. 19, 1925. Brief accounts of his activities in the steel industry are contained in Ida M. Tarbell, *The Life of Elbert H. Gary* (1925), and in H. N. Casson, *The Romance of Steel* (1907). Obituary notices appeared in the *Iron Age*, vol. LXXXVIII, Aug. 10, 1911, and in the *N. Y. Times* and *N. Y. Tribune* for the same date. See also *Current Lit.*, vol. LI, Sept. 1911, "Gates the Gamester"; the *World's Work*, vol. XXII, Oct. 1911, "The Modern Pirate"; and *Everybody's Mag.*, vol. X, Jan. 1904, "John W. Gates: The Forgetful Man," by E. M. Kingsbury.] M. L.

GATES, Sir THOMAS (d. 1621), governor of Virginia, was born at Colyford, Colyton parish, Devonshire (R. N. Worth, *A History of Devonshire*, 1886, p. 70). He is first noticed as a lieutenant in the fleet which sailed under Drake in September 1585 to avenge the wrongs of Queen Elizabeth on the King of Spain, and which captured Cartagena, burned St. Augustine, Fla., and carried back to England the ill-fated Roanoke colonists. In the years which followed, Gates served under Essex. He commanded a company of English soldiers in Normandy in 1591; he served in the expedition which harried the coast of Spain in 1596 and took part in the capture of Cadiz, and he was there knighted by Essex (W. A. Shaw, *The Knights of England*, 1906, II, 93). In the following year he took part in an attack on the Azores. In February 1598/9 Gates and his company were sent into Ireland. After the execution of Essex, Gates commanded a company of English soldiers in the Low Countries. Meanwhile, on Mar. 14, 1597/8, he had been admitted to Gray's Inn (Joseph Foster, *Register of Admissions to Gray's Inn, 1521–1889*, 1889).

Probably as a result of his voyage under Drake, Gates became interested in the plans to colonize Virginia. He was the first named of the grantees in the charter of Apr. 10, 1606, to the Virginia and Plymouth Companies, and invested £2,000 in the Virginia Company. On Apr. 14/24, 1608, the States General of the Netherlands granted him leave of absence from his company for one year to colonize Virginia. From this time until his death, Gates's chief interest was Virginia. In 1609 the reorganized Virginia Company planned an expedition under Gates, to be followed by a second expedition under Lord De La Warr [*q.v.*], and appointed De La Warr general, Gates lieutenant-general, and Sir George Somers admiral. On June 2, 1609, Gates left Plymouth, and six days later Falmouth, with eight ships and a pinnace, carrying five hundred men and women, bound for Virginia. On July 25 the *Sea Adventure,* which carried Gates, Somers, William Strachey [*q.v.*], and Capt. Newport [*q.v.*], was separated from the other vessels in a storm. It failed to reach Virginia, and for ten months the belief prevailed in England and Virginia that the vessel had been lost at sea. The passengers and crew of the *Sea Adventure,* however, after bailing and pumping for three days and four nights, had landed in the Bermudas. They found the islands rich, offering an abundance of fish and wild swine, healthful, and pleasant, and remained there ten months while two cedar pinnaces were under construction. On May 10, 1610, the company set sail from the Bermudas, and in about two weeks arrived in Virginia. It was Strachey's account of this adventure which suggested the writing of *The Tempest* to Shakespeare.

Gates took over the government of Virginia from Percy. He found the colonists in a deplorable condition and decided to carry them back to England. On June 7 they embarked but on the following day they met Lord De La Warr, just arriving from England, who turned them back, took over the government from Gates, and dispatched Somers to the Bermudas and Gates to England for supplies. Gates left Virginia in July and in September 1610 was in England. There he worked to attract settlers from England and Holland to Virginia and to gain support from the Company for the Colony. Plans for another expedition under his leadership were soon under way. In February 1611 he obtained a second leave of absence from the States General, who agreed to maintain his company in Holland and to keep the place of captain open but refused to pay him during his absence. Toward the end of May 1611 he sailed with three ships, three caravels, 280 men and twenty women, 100 cows and 200 swine. He took his wife and daughters with him at this time, thus indicating an intention to remain in Virginia, but Lady Gates died on the voyage and upon arrival in Virginia Gates sent his daughters back to England. About the first of August he was at Jamestown. There he found that Lord De La Warr had turned the government over to Percy and sailed for home. Percy, in turn, had given way to Dale in May 1611. Gates now resumed the government. It was a discouraging time, but he laid the foundations for the prosperity of the colony. Under him Dale founded Henrico.

In the spring of 1614 Gates once more went to England, where he took an active part in the affairs of the Virginia Company. In 1618 he seems to have planned to return to Virginia but in 1619 and 1620 he disposed of sixty shares of his stock in the Company and in January 1621 was at The Hague. He died in the Low Countries, probably before April 1621. His eldest son, Anthony, seems to have been dead in 1632. A second son, Thomas, took part in expeditions against Cadiz in 1626, and Ré and Rochelle in 1627, and was killed at Rochelle. In 1637 two daughters of Sir Thomas Gates, Margaret and Elizabeth, and Margaret, the widow of Anthony Gates, petitioned for money due Capt. Thomas Gates for his services in the expeditions against Cadiz, Ré, and Rochelle, in order that they might have the means to go to Virginia to claim the estate of their father. At various times the heirs attempted to recover the estate of Sir Thomas Gates in Virginia and about 1640 there was before the Governor and Council of Virginia a motion to grant Edmund Dawber, son-in-law and administrator of the estate of Sir Thomas Gates, 8,000 acres of land, half of which was to be free from quit-rents.

[Sources include: *Calendar of State Papers, Domestic Ser., 1611–18* (1858); *Calendar of State Papers, Colonial Ser.,* America and the West Indies, 1574–1660 (1860); *Acts of the Privy Council of England, Colonial Ser.,* vol. I (1908); *The Records of the Va. Company of London* (2 vols., 1906), ed. by S. M. Kingsbury; *Jours. of the House of Burgesses of Va., 1619–1658/9* (1915) and *Minutes of the Council and General Court of Colonial Va.* (1924), both ed. by H. R. McIlwaine. The most notable account of the wreck is Strachey's letter, probably seen in MS. by Shakespeare; it was published in *Purchas his Pilgrimes,* vol. IV (1625). This, with accounts by other members of the party, is reprinted in *Memorials of the Discovery and Early Settlement of the Bermudas or Somers Islands* (2 vols., 1877), ed. by J. H. Lefroy. See also *The Historye of the Bermudaes or Summer Islands* (1882), ed. by Lefroy; *Travels and Works of Capt. John Smith* (2 vols., 1910), ed. by E. A. Arber and A. G. Bradley; E. D. Neill, *Hist. of the Va. Company of London* (1869); Alexander Brown, *The Genesis of the U. S.* (2 vols., 1890).]
I. M. C.

GATLING, RICHARD JORDAN (Sept. 12, 1818–Feb. 26, 1903), inventor, the third son of Jordan and Mary (Barnes) Gatling, was born in Hertford County, N. C., where the first Gatling emigrating from England settled about 1700. His father was a well-to-do planter and apparently possessed considerable mechanical ability, for he invented a cotton-seed sowing machine and a machine for thinning cotton plants. Gatling, still in his teens when his father perfected these devices, is said to have assisted him. Upon completing the studies taught in the county schools, Gatling himself began to teach school at the age of nineteen, but after a year opened a little country store. Business presumably was not very brisk and he brooded over various inventions; in the course of the year 1838 he devised a screw propeller, but when he attempted to have it patented he found that John Ericsson had anticipated him. He then became interested in the improvement of agricultural implements, and in 1839 perfected and patented a rice-sowing machine. Five years later he went to St. Louis, Mo., to have this machine manufactured, as well as a wheat drill operated on the same principle. In the winter of 1845 he contracted smallpox when on a business trip by river-steamer from Cincinnati to Pittsburgh. The boat was held fast in the ice for two weeks, and he could get no medical attention. Upon his recovery he studied medicine in the Medical College of Ohio at Cincinnati, simply to be able to take care of himself and his family. Although he never practised he was ever afterward addressed as "Doctor."

Meantime his business continued to thrive to such an extent that in the fifties he undertook to manufacture agricultural implements not only in St. Louis but also in Springfield, Ohio, and in Indianapolis. He continued too with his inventions and secured patents for a hemp-breaking machine in 1847 and 1860, and in 1857 he invented a steam-plow. In 1861, when war clouds were gathering, his thoughts turned to ordnance and ballistics, in September 1862 he patented a marine steam ram, and on Nov. 4, 1862, he obtained patent no. 36,836 for a rapid-fire gun which came to be known as the Gatling gun and gained for him a world-wide fame. Even in this day of automatic pistols the thug still speaks of his "Gat." The year that the patent was granted Gatling had the first gun made in Indianapolis. Although it was crude, it had a firing capacity of 250 shots a minute. Working diligently to improve it, the inventor was rewarded three years later, on May 9, 1865, with a second patent. With these improvements, twelve guns were manufactured by the Cooper Fire-Arms Manufacturing Company in Philadelphia (Winborne, *post*; Moore, *post*) in 1865 and submitted to the War Department for test. So satisfactory were the results that in 1866 the gun was officially adopted for the United States army, and an order for one hundred given to Gatling. These were made by the Colt Patent Fire Arms Manufacturing Company at Hartford, Conn. Briefly described, the Gatling gun consisted of a group of rifle barrels arranged lengthwise around a central shaft and the whole revolved by suitable gears and by a hand crank. Cartridges were automatically and successively fed into the barrels, the hammers of which were so arranged in connection with the barrels that they were kept in a continuous revolving movement by turning the hand crank.

Ordinarily the gun had ten barrels with ten corresponding locks which revolved together. For the next thirty years Gatling applied himself to the task of perfecting his invention and at the same time, in order to secure contracts for the gun, he personally supervised and conducted many tests in the countries of Europe and South America. When he had so improved the gun that it was capable of firing 1,200 shots a minute, he sold the patent rights to the Colt Fire Arms Company. In 1870 he established his residence in Hartford.

Before selling his patent rights he had invented in 1886 a new gun-metal composed of an alloy of steel and aluminum. This was followed by an extensive series of experiments on large gun-castings which led him to believe that a cast-steel gun could be produced which would have the same ratio of energy to weight of gun as a built-up gun, and which would stand the test of continued firing. He thereupon approached the federal government to secure a subsidy to test his theory with full-size cannon, and in 1897 Congress appropriated $40,000 for this purpose. The following year an 8-inch gun was built under Gatling's direction in Cleveland, but in the trials, Jan. 4, 1899, at Sandy Hook, the gun burst. He always contended that the gun-breech had been maliciously weakened during its manufacture. Following this disappointment Gatling, now eighty years old, turned his attention again to agricultural implements and in 1900 invented a motor-driven plow. A company was subsequently organized in St. Louis to manufacture it but just as the final arrangements were being perfected, he contracted grippe and died Feb. 26, 1903. For his inventions he received many honors both at home and abroad. He was for six years president of the American Association of Inventors and Manufacturers. He married Jemima T. Sanders of Indianapolis in 1854, who with two sons and a daughter survived him.

[C. B. Norton, *Am. Inventions and Improvements in Breech-Loading Firearms* (1882); B. B. Winborne, *The Colonial and State Hist. of Hertford County, N. C.* (1906); W. F. Moore, *Representative Men of Conn., 1861–94* (1894), pp. 314–18; *Sci. American*, Mar. 7, 1903; *N. Y. Times* and *Hartford Times*, Feb. 27, 1903; *Indianapolis Sentinel*, Mar. 2, 1903; *Who's Who in America*, 1899–1900; Patent Office records.]

C. W. M.

GATSCHET, ALBERT SAMUEL (Oct. 3, 1832–Mar. 16, 1907), linguist, and ethnologist, the son of Rev. Karl Albert and Mary (Ziegler) Gatschet, was born at Saint Beatenberg, Switzerland. Attending the schools of Neuchâtel and Bern and early showing an aptitude for linguistics, he entered the University of Bern and subsequently completed his study courses in the University of Berlin, giving special attention to Greek and doctrinal criticism. Returning to Bern, he set out on his long career as a writer on scientific subjects, especially linguistics. In 1868 he emigrated to America and for several years taught languages in New York, during the same period also industriously writing articles in several languages on his favorite subject. Being interested in Indian languages, he entered this comparatively new field, where soon his work attracted the attention of Maj. J. W. Powell, who in 1877 appointed him as ethnologist in the United States Geological Survey. This began Gatschet's field work, in the course of which he gathered linguistic and other data on more than a hundred tribes. At this period there were in America few students of Indian languages and perhaps none trained as Gatschet was by rigorous European methods. In 1879 on the organization of the Bureau of Ethnology he became a member. These were prolific years for the work on the linguistic classification of the Indian tribes. The arrangement of the tribes into families speaking distinct languages published by Powell in the *Seventh Annual Report of the Bureau . . . 1885–86* (1891) was in most part due to the work of Gatschet. Years also of office work preparing the results of the collected data for publication were required. Gatschet's major publications, technical in character, number seventy-two, which together with many smaller articles published in the United States and abroad, and hundreds of linguistic, ethnographic, and bibliographic notes and reviews appearing in various literary and scientific journals, show that his life was a busy one. Adumbrating the studies that were to follow was his first work *Ortsetymologische Forschungen als Beiträge zu einer Toponomastik der Schweiz* (Bern, 1867), a philologic study of Swiss place-names and their derivations. The papers written in America are generally short, highly compressed presentations of results accomplished and display his ability to say much in a few words. *The Klamath Indians of Southwestern Oregon*, however, is a quarto in two volumes, each of 711 pages (*Contributions to North American Ethnology*, 1890), an exhaustive and outstanding work. *A Migration Legend of the Creek Indians* formed No. 4 of Brinton's Library of Aboriginal American Literature (1884); a second volume was published with the title "Tchikilli's Kasi'hta Legend in the Creek and Hitchiti Languages" (1888), vol. V of the *Transactions of the St. Louis Academy of Science.* These publications represent only a small part of Gatschet's great collection of Indian texts, vocabularies, and other data in the archives of the Bureau of American Ethnology. "When philology shall take its proper place as the essential basis of anthropology," said his colleague, James Mooney, of Gatschet, "his name will stand with those of his distinguished countrymen, Gallatin and Agassiz, in the front rank of American science." Gatschet completely disregarded his personal appearance and presented a rather uncouth figure, but those who knew him were impressed by his thoroughness, honesty, and the loyalty of his friendship. He was married late in life (September 1892) to Louise Horner of Philadelphia. They had no children.

[Obituary by James Mooney in *Am. Anthropologist,* July 1907; *Who's Who in America,* 1906–07; *Evening Star* (Washington, D. C.), Mar. 16, 1907; personal recollections.]

W. H.

GAUL, WILLIAM GILBERT (Mar. 31, 1855–Dec. 21, 1919), painter, and illustrator, son of George W. and Cornelia A. (Gilbert) Gaul, was born at Jersey City, N. J. After studying in the public schools of Newark, N. J., and at the Claverack Military Academy, he immediately took up the study of drawing and painting in New York, becoming a pupil of L. E. Wilmarth at the school of the National Academy of Design, 1872–76, and of John G. Brown, as well as in the Art Students' League of New York. Both Wilmarth and Brown were genre painters, and their disciple naturally turned to the same line of work, his early motives being popular and sentimental figure pieces; but it was only when he began to specialize in military subjects that he found his vocation and won public favor. In addition to his work in painting, much of his time and thought was given to illustration. His pictures of Civil-War episodes were spirited, dramatic, excellent in drawing and characterization. Since he was but an infant at the time of these events, the vivid visualization of the stirring scenes of battle, march, and camp, superior to the pictorial efforts of most of the earlier painters who had been eye-witnesses, is evidence of a striking imaginative force. He traveled far in quest of materials, spending much time in the Far West at army posts and on Indian reservations, going also to Mexico, the West Indies, Panama, and Nicaragua. Uniforms and arms of many kinds were to be seen in his studio. The historic accuracy of each detail was studiously sought, and the models who posed as soldiers were fit types of the men who fought in the Civil War. "The Captain," for instance, is a perfect military type, as living as any figure produced by Detaille or De Neuville.

His work as illustrator was in constant demand. The war papers published in the *Century Magazine* kept him busy, and three of his paintings were used as frontispieces in *Battles and Leaders of the Civil War* (4 vols., 1887–88). His illustrations of the life of the cowboy and the Indian were popular. A series of twelve of his drawings, made to illustrate his own account of his travels in Mexico, Central America, and Jamaica, was exhibited at the World's Columbian Exposition, Chicago, in 1893. He was made an associate of the National Academy of Design in 1879, and became an academician in 1882. He exhibited several of his most interesting war pictures in the eighties and nineties, notably his "Charging the Battery," "Saving the Colors," "Silenced," "Holding the Line at all Hazards," "With Fate Against Them," "Guerillas Returning from a Valley Raid," and "Taking the Ramparts." All of these canvases were remarkable for energy of action, actuality, truth to conditions such as place and period, and, above all, their spirit of belligerency. Gaul was fairly entitled to the distinction of being the most capable of American military painters. He is represented in the Toledo Museum of Art, the Peabody Institute, Baltimore, and the Democratic Club, New York. Medals were awarded him by the American Art Association, New York (1882), the Paris Exposition (1889), the Chicago Exposition (1893), and the Buffalo Exposition (1902). He was married late in life, September 1898, to Marian, daughter of Vice-Admiral G. A. Halstead, R. N. He died at the age of sixty-four, at his home in New York, after a long illness.

[Jeannette L. Gilbert, "A Painter of Soldiers," *Outlook,* July 2, 1898; G. P. Lathrop, "An American Military Painter," *Quart. Illustrator,* Oct.–Dec. 1893; Samuel Isham, *The Hist. of Am. Painting* (1905); Joseph Pennell, *Modern Illustration* (1895); *Kunts für Alle,* Oct. 1, 1892, Feb. 1, 1898; *Who's Who in America,* 1914–15; *Am. Art Annual,* vol. XII (1915) and vol. XVI (1919); *N. Y. Times,* Dec. 22, 1919; *Am. Art News,* Dec. 27, 1919.]

W. H. D.

GAUT, JOHN McREYNOLDS (Oct. 1, 1841–Dec. 19, 1918), lawyer, and churchman, was descended from Scotch-Irish ancestors who, coming originally to Pennsylvania, had migrated to Virginia and some generations later, into Tennessee. His great-grandfather was one of those who fought at King's Mountain. Born in Cleveland, Tenn., the son of John Conaway Gaut, a prosperous lawyer, and his wife, Sarah Ann McReynolds, young Gaut was prepared for college at the local academy and graduated at Rutgers in 1866, with the degree of B.A. He began to practise law in Nashville, Tenn., in the following year and with that city, significant for religious clearing-house activities and for religious publications, he was identified for the rest of his life. He was married on May 5, 1870, to Michal M. Harris, daughter of the proprietor of the *Nashville Banner,* and after her death some sixteen months later, he married (Oct. 25, 1876) Sallie Crutchfield of Chattanooga. Gaut was a member of the Nashville city council, 1873–74, and a special judge of the state supreme court in 1881. He was a trustee of the University of Nashville, which later became George Peabody College for Teachers. As an advocate of highway improvement he worked with the state legislature for the public purchase of toll-roads from private interests and the termination of the toll-road system.

A Cumberland Presbyterian and an elder in his local church, he was an important factor in developing the publishing business of his denomination, and served as president and general manager of its Board of Publication from 1870 to 1901. He was the author of numerous contributions to religious journals and of a pamphlet, *Cumberland, or the Story of a Name* (1901). He attained national prominence as the result of the union, or reunion, between the Cumberland Presbyterian Church and the Presbyterian Church in the United States of America in 1906. His legal services were utilized in the contests over property precipitated by a minority group which, refusing to enter into union, continued the name and organization of the Cumberland Presbyterian Church. This litigation involved cases in a dozen states and before the United States courts, with the issues upheld by Gaut receiving almost entire success. In these cases many important questions of law relating to churches and church unions were settled, and Gaut won recognition among his associates as an authority on the law in its relation to church organizations and property. He became general counsel for the Presbyterian Church in the United States of America in 1906 and served as a member of the judicial commission of that denomination from 1908 to 1911. Gaut was a lover of nature and lived for forty years at his country place just outside Nashville, called "Alamo" from its surroundings of poplar trees. He died in 1918, in his seventy-eighth year.

[See *Who's Who in Tenn.* (1911), p. 419; *Who's Who in America,* 1918–19; W. T. Hale and D. L. Merritt, *A Hist. of Tennessee and Tennesseans,* V (1913), 1504; *Minutes of the Gen. Assembly of the Cumberland Presbyt. Ch.,* 1901; *Nashville Banner,* Dec. 19, 1918. A list of the leading church cases in which Gaut participated is contained in 247 *U. S. Reports,* 2, and a summary of the litigation, by Gaut himself, in *Minutes of the Gen. Assembly of the Presbyt. Ch. in the U. S. A.,* 1919, pp. 340–49.]

H. C. N.

GAY, EBENEZER (Aug. 15, 1696–Mar. 18, 1787), clergyman, for nearly sixty-nine years pastor of the First Parish, Hingham, Mass., was the son of Nathaniel and Lydia (Lusher) Gay, and grandson of John Gay who came to America about 1630, settled in Watertown, Mass., and later was one of the founders of Dedham, in which town Ebenezer was born. At the age of eighteen he graduated from Harvard College. While preparing for the ministry he taught the grammar schools of Hadley and Ipswich, and on Dec. 30, 1717, was called to the church in Hingham, where he was ordained and installed on June 11, 1718. The following year, Nov. 3, he married Jerusha, daughter of Samuel and Hannah (Rogers) Bradford, great-grand-daughter of Gov. William Bradford. Eleven children were born to them.

During his extraordinarily long pastorate in Hingham he became one of the most respected and influential of the New England clergy. Although broad-minded, tolerant, amiable, and peace-loving, he had a strength of character, soundness of judgment, and genius for leadership which made him a dominating personality. As a conciliator and adviser he was held in high esteem. Enthusiasm and superstition formed no part of his religious character (*Massachusetts Gazette,* Boston, Mar. 30, 1787). Theologically he was an Arminian, if not an Arian, and although he was not controversial in his preaching, he is numbered among the early Congregationalists who were the forerunners of the Unitarian movement in New England. He was opposed to revivals, creeds, and articles of faith, and was sympathetic toward free inquiry. Revelation, he believed, must be subjected to the test of reason. To his influence, it is said, Jonathan Mayhew's adoption of liberal views was due. Politically he was a Loyalist, but though his sentiments were well known, he behaved with such discretion during the Revolution that he was not molested and retained the friendship of those who differed from him. In appearance he was medium-sized, dignified, and after middle age, patriarchal. His portrait reveals a huge mouth and peculiarly shaped jaw which give to his face an ugly and cynical aspect, yet it is said that a benevolent expression illumined and redeemed it. So well did he retain his mental vigor throughout his ninety years and more, that he was preparing to preach as usual on the Sunday morning when death came to him. On his eighty-fifth birthday he delivered a sermon from the text, "And now, lo, I am four score and five years old" (Judges, xiv, 10), which was published under the title, *The Old Man's*

Calendar (1781), and reprinted several times in this country, and in England and Holland. Among his other published writings are a sermon before the Ancient and Honorable Artillery Company, 1728; one delivered on the arrival of Gov. Belcher, 1730; one before the military companies of Hingham, 1738; the Massachusetts election sermon, 1745; sermon at the Convention of the Congregational ministers of Massachusetts, 1746; sermon on the death of Jonathan Mayhew, 1766; and the Dudleian Lecture at Harvard, on natural and revealed religion, 1759.

[F. L. Gay, *John Gay of Dedham, Mass., and Some of His Descendants* (1879); Solomon Lincoln, Jr., *Hist. of the Town of Hingham* (1827); Wm. B. Sprague, *Annals Am. Pulpit*, vol. VIII (1865); *Hist. of the Town of Hingham, Mass.* (3 vols., 1893); Geo. W. Cooke, *Unitarianism in America* (1902).] H. E. S.

GAY, SYDNEY HOWARD (May 22, 1814–June 25, 1888), journalist, author, the son of Ebenezer and Mary Alleyne (Otis) Gay, was born in Hingham, Mass. His mother was a niece of James Otis and his father a grandson of Rev. Ebenezer Gay [*q.v.*]: an ancestry which he said was the best part of himself. He entered Harvard College as a freshman in 1829, but poor health caused him to withdraw two years later. The degree of B.A. was conferred upon him, however, in 1833. After a period of idleness he entered the counting-house of Perkins & Company, in Boston, where he remained two years. He traveled in the West and then began the study of law in the office of his father in Hingham. A study of history and of ethics had turned his attention to slavery. Convinced that slavery was "absolutely and morally wrong," he gave up the law, for he could never take an oath to support a constitution which upheld the institution.

He went to Boston and became a member of that group of Abolitionists led by Garrison. "This handful of people," he said, "to the outside world a set of pestilent fanatics, were among themselves the most charming circle of cultivated men and women that it has ever been my lot to know." In 1842 he lectured for the American Anti-Slavery Society and the following year went to New York as editor of the *American Anti-Slavery Standard*. He married Elizabeth Neall in 1845. During this period he was an active agent of the "underground railroad." After an editorship of fourteen years, he decided that the anti-slavery cause no longer demanded all his attention and in 1857 he joined the staff of the *New York Tribune*. Appointed managing editor in 1862, he occupied that position until the summer of 1865 when broken health caused his resignation. During the war his services were of great value to the Union; Henry Wilson said that the man deserved well of his country who kept the *Tribune* a war paper in spite of Greeley. In 1867 he was asked to become managing editor of the *Chicago Tribune*; he accepted and remained in Chicago until the great fire of 1871. The following spring he returned to New York and from 1872 to 1874 was a member of the editorial staff of the New York *Evening Post* under William Cullen Bryant.

In 1874 Bryant, then eighty years old, was asked to undertake a history of the United States; to this he agreed with the understanding that Gay would be its author. Bryant's only contribution was a preface to the first volume; he died before the second appeared, but the publishers, with little justification, retained his name. Though wanting a sense of proportion, the four volumes were based largely on research and were very readable. In 1884 Gay's *James Madison*, a severe though sympathetic study from the Federalist point of view, was published in the American Statesmen Series. He wrote the chapter on "Amerigo Vespucci" for Justin Winsor's *Narrative and Critical History of America* (vol. II, 1886), contributed occasionally to the *Critic*, and was engaged on a life of his friend Edmund Quincy, when he died of paralysis in 1888.

[Waldo Higginson, *Memorials of the Class of 1833 of Harvard College* (1883); "Hingham Genealogies," by Geo. Lincoln in vol. II of *Hist. of the Town of Hingham, Mass.* (1893); F. L. Gay, *John Gay of Dedham, Mass., and Some of His Descendants* (1879); *Critic*, June 30, 1888; *Boston Post* and *N. Y. Tribune* for June 27, 1888.] F. M—n.

GAY, WINCKWORTH ALLAN (Aug. 18, 1821–Feb. 23, 1910), landscape-painter, came of a family long prominent in Eastern Massachusetts. He was born at West Hingham, the son of Ebenezer and Mary Alleyne (Otis) Gay. His brother, Sydney Howard Gay [*q.v.*], was an editor, author and historian; his nephew, Walter Gay, a well-known painter. His great-grandfather, Rev. Ebenezer Gay [*q.v.*], was a noted Unitarian clergyman. Young Allan Gay was allowed, at the age of seventeen, to go to West Point and study under Robert W. Weir, professor of drawing in the United States Military Academy. There he obtained a sound foundation. In 1847 he went to France and continued his studies under Constant Troyon in Paris. The formation of the sober and personal style which was to be the distinctive mark of Gay's work was in a large measure due to the influence of this French master. After leaving the Paris atelier Gay visited Italy, Switzerland, and Holland; then, returning to the United States in 1850, he established himself in Boston, there to remain for the greater part of his professional life. He was one of the first American painters to introduce to his compatriots the revivifying spirit of the landscape movement in France which was destined to make such a deep impression upon American painting and taste.

After living and working in Boston for twenty-four years, he went to Egypt in 1874 and spent a winter on the Nile. The following year he exhibited several works at the National Academy. In 1877 he held an exhibition in Boston which contained over a hundred pictures, including landscapes painted in Egypt, Holland, Italy, and America. Later in the same year he traveled to the far East, there to stay for a period of five years. He passed one winter in China, sketching in the vicinity of Hong Kong, Canton, and Macao; and one winter in India; the remainder of the time he spent in Japan, where he made lengthy sojourns at Tokio, Yokohama, and Kioto, as well as in a number of interior towns. His return home was made by way of Europe, with a stop of two years or so in Paris on the way. Soon after arriving in Boston he placed on exhibition a large collection of paintings which described with exceptional completeness and fidelity the life, landscape, flora, and architecture of Japan. All the picturesque aspects of the country were shown with remarkable veracity and charm.

The last few years of his life were passed in retirement at his native place, West Hingham, Mass., where he died at the ripe age of eighty-nine. He was never married. He had a long career of happy work, though in Samuel Isham's opinion he did not attain the measure of fame he deserved. His work was marked by simplicity and truth, and it combined breadth with delicacy. He owed much to the French school, but his manner and method were quite personal, and his pictures have the permanent virtues of modesty and understatement.

[F. L. Gay, *John Gay of Dedham, Mass., and Some of His Descendants* (1879); H. T. Tuckerman, *Book of the Artists* (1867); W. A. A. Otis, *Geneal. and Hist. Memoir of the Otis Family in America* (1924); Samuel Isham, *The Hist. of Am. Painting* (1905); E. C. Clement and Laurence Hutton, *Artists of the Nineteenth Century* (1880); *Am. Art Annual*, Feb. 26, 1910; *Who's Who in America*, 1910–11; *Boston Transcript*, Feb. 24, 1910.]
W. H. D.

GAYARRÉ, CHARLES ÉTIENNE ARTHUR (Jan. 9, 1805–Feb. 11, 1895), historian, was born in New Orleans of Spanish and French descent. His great-grandfather Don Esteban Gayarré came to Louisiana with Ulloa in 1766 as royal comptroller and commissary, and the family continued to play an important part in the affairs of the colony. Don Esteban's grandson Don Carlos married Marie Elizabeth, youngest daughter of Étienne de Boré [*q.v.*]. Their son Charles Étienne (christened Carlos Esteban) spent his childhood on Boré's sugar plantation, gaining his education at a near-by school for the sons of rich planters. In 1825 he graduated with distinction at the College of Orleans (New Orleans), and in the next year, at the age of twenty-one, published an influential pamphlet opposing—chiefly because of its proposed abolition of capital punishment—the criminal code prepared by Edward Livingston. During 1826–29 Gayarré studied law in the office of William Rawle of Philadelphia and was admitted to the Philadelphia bar. After his return to New Orleans, he published in 1830 an *Essai historique sur la Louisiane,* in two volumes, largely a translation of Martin's *History of Louisiana.* Covering the period to 1815, the work was considered so valuable by the legislature that 600 copies were distributed to the various school boards of the state. Elected in the same year by an almost unanimous vote to represent New Orleans in the legislature, Gayarré was appointed, in 1831, assistant attorney-general and, in 1832, presiding judge of the city court of New Orleans. His promising political career reached its climax in his election to the United States Senate in 1835 but was then broken into by ill health which compelled his immediate resignation. He went at once to France for medical treatment and remained there until October 1843. Soon after his return he married Mrs. Annie Sullivan Buchanan of Jackson, Miss., who died without issue in 1914.

During this long stay abroad he began his *Histoire de la Louisiane* (published in two volumes, 1846–47), written in French in order to preserve the exact form of the original documents; it was little more than a series of extracts strung together on a thread of narrative, coming down only to 1769. After this piece of rather arid scholarship, Gayarré went to the other extreme of over-popularization in his *Romance of the History of Louisiana* (1848), a work of mingled history and fiction, which he later ill-advisedly incorporated with a slight change of title as the first volume of his larger *History,* begun in 1851. With the second and third volumes, *Louisiana: its History as a French Colony* (1852) and *History of Louisiana: The Spanish Domination* (1854), Gayarré at last came into his own and succeeded in uniting historical accuracy with vivid narrative and description.

Meanwhile he had resumed his political career: he was elected to the state legislature in 1844; and in 1846, after reëlection to the legislature, was appointed secretary of state, an office which then included the superintendency of public education, and which, together with that of treasurer, constituted a "Board of Currency" with control over the banks of the state. Gayarré filled this important office acceptably, being reappointed in 1850; during his incumbency he persuaded the legislature to purchase numerous foreign documents as the foundation of a state library. In 1853 he was defeated, probably by fraudulent votes, as an independent candidate for Congress; in his *Address to the People of the State on the Late Frauds Perpetrated at the Election* (1853) he gave good reasons for believing that as many as 2,000 out of the 6,000 New Orleans votes were spurious. Still smarting over this injustice, he wrote in 1854 *The School for Politics,* a remarkably mirthless satiric novel. He took part in the formation of the Know-Nothing party in Louisiana, but in June 1855 was excluded as a Roman Catholic from the general council of the party in Philadelphia. Therewith his political aspirations ended. He supported the Confederacy at the outbreak of the Civil War but early came to realize the hopelessness of its cause and in 1863 advocated (in an address read that year and printed in the following) the emancipation and arming of the slaves. His inherited fortune was lost during the war and the rest of his days were passed in poverty. In this period of gloom, however, he completed his four-volume series with his *History of Louisiana: The American Domination* (1866), produced a brilliant psychological study in *Philip II of Spain* (1866), and wrote two artless but interesting novels—the largely autobiographical *Fernando de Lemos: Truth and Fiction* (1872) and *Aubert Dubayet or the Two Sister Republics* (1882), a tale of the American and French revolutions. He served as reporter of the decisions of the supreme court of Louisiana, 1873–76. For twenty-eight years, 1860–88, he was president of the Louisiana Historical Society. Both before and after the Civil War he was distinctly the leader in the notable literary efflorescence of Louisiana, and at his death it was generally recognized that the state had lost its foremost citizen.

[*La. Hist. Soc. Pubs.,* vol. III, pt. 4 (Mar. 1906), Gayarré Memorial Number containing papers by Henry Renshaw, John R. Ficklen, Alcée Fortier, H. Garland Dupré, Jas. S. Zacharie, and Wm. O. Hart; C. E. A. Gayarré, *Hist of La.,* in four volumes (1903 ed.), containing sketch by Grace King and bibliography by Wm. Beer; Grace King, *New Orleans, the Place and the People* (1895), and *Creole Families of New Orleans* (1921); Alcée Fortier, ed., *Louisiana* (1909), I, 491–92; *The South in the Building of the Nation* (1909), XI, 391; E. A. and G. L. Duyckinck, *Cyc. of Am. Lit.* (1875), II, 226–31; "Biographical Sketch of Hon. Charles Gayarré," in *La. Hist. Quart.,* Jan. 1929, being a reprint of a pamphlet (1889) thought to be by Gayarré himself; New Orleans *Daily Picayune,* Feb. 11, 12, and *Times-Democrat,* Feb. 11, 1895.]

E. S. B—s.

GAYLE, JOHN (Sept. 11, 1792–July 21, 1859), governor of Alabama, was born in the Sumter District, S. C., the son of Matthew and Mary (Reese) Gayle. He was of English-Scotch ancestry, his forebears having settled in Virginia in the early colonial days. He attended Newberry Academy and graduated from South Carolina College in 1815. In this same year he made a visit to his parents, who had several years previously settled near what is now Mount Vernon, Ala., and subsequently became a permanent resident of that state. His family later moved to Monroe County and founded a plantation near Claiborne. Soon after going to Alabama young Gayle entered upon the career that became fashionable for graduates of South Carolina College. He resumed the study of law, which he had begun in South Carolina in the office of Abraham Giles Dozier, under the guidance of Judge Abner S. Lipscomb. When his course of study was finished he plunged into politics. He was appointed by President Monroe in 1818 to the first Council of the Alabama Territory. The following year he was elected solicitor of his circuit. During the next twelve years he served four terms in the legislature, sat upon the bench as circuit judge and justice of the state supreme court, and found time and opportunity to develop a lucrative law practise. He won recognition as a barrister and legislator when pleading and oratorical argumentation were highly prized arts. During his service in the legislature, 1829, he was elected speaker of the House over former Gov. Thomas Bibb of Lawrence County.

In 1831 he entered the gubernatorial race as a pro-Union, Jackson Democrat, and was elected decisively over Gov. Samuel B. Moore and Nicholas Davis, the latter a prominent planter and legislator. Two years later he was reëlected without opposition. Gayle's administration was unusually colorful. Under his leadership Alabama rejected the doctrine of nullification, then being espoused by South Carolina, the Governor "upholding the Union in a manner worthy of Daniel Webster or John Marshall." Presently (1833), however, a crisis arose between the state and the United States government over the removal of the Creek Indians that seemed to play havoc with the Governor's and the state's reputation for zeal for the Union. Gayle boldly defended the rights of the state in the controversy; so boldly, indeed, that the Huntsville *Democrat* called him "the wildest and worst of nullifiers." This conflict weakened Union sentiment in Alabama, and cooled Gayle's ardor for President

Jackson. At the end of his term, he moved to Mobile and resumed the practise of law. Gradually he drifted into the ranks of the rising Whig party. In 1836 he was made presidential elector on the Judge White ticket, and in 1840 he became a Harrison elector. In 1841 some of his Whig friends, eager to retire Senator William R. King, nominated Gayle, without his knowledge, it is said, for the senatorship. They were unsuccessful, however, the vote standing, Gayle 55, King 72. In 1847 Gayle was elected to Congress on the Whig ticket, and two years afterward President Taylor appointed him federal district judge. He occupied this position until his death.

Gayle was a man of sterling character, and is reputed to have been one of the ablest speakers and writers in the state. He was calm, judicious, urbane, and affable. His warm heart led him, while governor, into a liberal use of the pardoning power, and his generosity induced him to assist others to the hurt of his own fortunes. He was married, Nov. 14, 1819, to Sarah Ann Haynesworth, the sixteen-year-old daughter of Richard Haynesworth, a prominent Clarke County planter. To this union six children were born, one of whom, Amelia, became the mother of William Crawford Gorgas [*q.v.*]. Mrs. Gayle died in 1835, and four years later, Nov. 1, 1839, Gayle married Clarissa Stedman Peck of Greensboro, by whom he had four more children.

[*Trans. Ala. Hist. Soc.*, IV (1904), 141–65; W. Brewer, *Alabama* (1872); Wm. Garrett, *Reminiscences of Public Men in Ala.* (1872); three manuscripts, "Extracts from the Journal of Sarah Haynesworth Gayle," sketch of Gov. Gayle by Amelia Gayle, and "Genealogy of the Gayle Family," all in the possession of Miss Mary Gorgas of Tuscaloosa, Ala.; T. H. Jack, *Sectionalism and Party Politics in Ala.* (1919); A. B. Moore, *Hist. of Ala.* (3 vols., 1927); T. M. Owen, *Hist. of Ala. and Dict. of Ala. Biog.* (1921), vol. III; *Mobile Daily Register*, July 22, 23, and *Mobile Advertiser*, July 22, 1859.] A. B. M.

GAYLER, CHARLES (Apr. 1, 1820–May 28, 1892), playwright, was born on Oliver Street, New York, the son of C. J. Gayler, a dealer in crockery and hardware and builder of fireproof safes. After attending for a few years an academy in Suffield, Conn., he became at sixteen a school-teacher in Dayton, Ohio, pored over law books in his spare hours, was admitted to practise, and traveled the circuits in Ohio and perhaps in Indiana and Illinois. Having little knowledge of law or aptitude for it, he soon drifted into politics, obtained several minor positions in Dayton, and became an ardent supporter of Henry Clay, for whom he made stump speeches and wrote campaign songs. Then he turned to journalism for a livelihood, becoming for a short period editor of the Cincinnati *Evening Dispatch.* In 1846 he married Grace Christian. For some reason no longer known his editorial career came to a sudden end; he is said then to have turned actor and to have performed the title rôles in *Hamlet, Othello,* and *Richelieu* in Ohio theatres on the James W. Bates circuit. In 1849 his first play, *The Buckeye Gold Hunters,* was produced by Bates at the National Theatre in Cincinnati and was performed for ten weeks. Its success was due to Gayler's exploitation of contemporary material, and that remained one of his characteristic devices. His *Bull Run, or The Sacking of Fairfax Courthouse,* to take one instance, was produced in New York on Aug. 15, 1861, while some Union survivors of the battle, according to a contemporary joke, were still running. Gayler, encouraged by the success of his first venture into the drama, moved to New York, which he made his headquarters for the remaining half of his life. At one time or another he was a theatrical manager; he wrote reviews for the *Tribune* and the *Herald* and did miscellaneous literary work for several magazines. He was best known as a playwright. In all he was reputed to have written nearly four hundred tragedies, comedies, melodramas, and operettas, but the actual number was probably around two hundred. He usually disposed of these pieces outright to the producers, his regular price being two hundred dollars a play. His total revenue from this source, he said late in life, was only $35,000. None of his plays is now remembered. His last two, *Lights and Shadows of New York* and *Fritz, Our German Cousin,* were perhaps his most popular. Gayler was well liked by his journalistic and theatrical associates; he had no professional jealousy; though by no means rich he was generous to those less fortunate than himself. He was decidedly handsome, six feet tall, erect and stalwart, with flowing hair and beard. To visitors at Pfaff's Restaurant he was sometimes pointed out as Walt Whitman. His home was at Bowsonville, L. I. During his last years several benefits were given for him. He died after a long illness at his daughter's home in Brooklyn and was survived by his wife and four of their eight children. He was buried in Greenwood Cemetery.

[*N. Y. Herald* and *N. Y. Times,* May 29, 1892; *Brooklyn Daily Eagle,* May 29, June 2, 1892; *Appletons' Annual Cyc.,* 1892; portrait and sketch, partly fictitious, in *Frank Leslie's Illustrated Newspaper,* May 9, 1868.] G. H. G.

GAYLEY, JAMES (Oct. 11, 1855–Feb. 25, 1920), engineer, metallurgist, inventor, was born at Lock Haven, Pa., the son of Samuel Alexander and Agnes (Malcolm) Gayley. His father, a native of the north of Ireland and a Presbyterian minister, accepted a parish at West Nottingham, Md., shortly after young Gayley was born, and it was there that he was reared. He prepared for college at West Nottingham Academy and entered Lafayette College at Easton, Pa., from which he was graduated with the degree of E.M. in 1876. Immediately thereafter he accepted a position with the Crane Iron Company at Catasauqua, Pa., and served for three years as the company's chemist. In 1880 he went to St. Louis, Mo., as superintendent of the Missouri Furnace Company, and two years later resigned that position to assume the management of blast furnaces of the E. & G. Brooks Iron Company at Birdsboro, Pa. In 1885, when but thirty years of age, he was made superintendent of blast furnaces of the Edgar Thomson Steel Works at Braddock, Pa., which was then owned by Carnegie Brothers & Company, Ltd., and which subsequently became the Carnegie Steel Works. Here he continued for the succeeding fifteen years, becoming in turn manager of the Edgar Thomson plant and, in 1897, managing director of the Carnegie Steel Company. During this fifteen-year period his brilliant career as an iron and steel maker gained for him the title of "father of modern American blast furnace practise." Beginning in 1891, he instituted economies, especially in the matter of fuel consumption in blast furnaces, introducing a number of appliances of his own invention. Among these were the bronze cooling-plate for furnace walls, patented in 1891; a casting apparatus for use with the Bessemer converter, patented in 1896; and the "dry air" blast, the latter developed and perfected through a number of devices extending over the period of years from 1894 to 1911. The dry air blast, application of which is not restricted to blast furnaces, was probably the most important of Gayley's inventions. Its use resulted in important fuel economies, and a uniformity of blast-furnace product previously unattainable. Gayley was the first to design and install charging bins for the raw materials and he also installed, while at the Edgar Thomson Works, the first compound condensing engine for supplying air blast to a blast furnace. When the United States Steel Corporation, which included the Carnegie Steel Company, was formed in 1901, Gayley was made first vice-president and was put in charge of the department of raw materials and their transportation. For eight years he served in this capacity, installing the first mechanical ore unloader at the ore docks of the Carnegie Steel Company, at Conneaut, Ohio, on Lake Erie, and designing and patenting an ore vessel adapted to the use of such unloaders. He resigned from the United States Steel Corporation in 1909, and retired from active business, although in the succeeding twelve years before his death he served as president of the American Ore Reclamation Company and the Sheffield Iron Corporation, with offices in New York City.

Gayley was one of "Carnegie's boys" whose fortunes were made with the merger of Carnegie Steel in the United States Steel Corporation. His wealth was still further enlarged by the royalties on his inventions. For his valuable contributions to American blast-furnace practise he received the Elliott Cresson Medal of the Franklin Institute in 1908, and the Perkins Gold Medal of the American Society of Mechanical Engineers in 1913. Gayley was a member of the American Institute of Mining Engineers, its president in 1904, and a director and president of the board from 1905 to 1913. He was also a member of the American and British Iron and Steel Institutes. He was a trustee of Lafayette College from 1892 till the time of his death and in 1902 presented to his alma mater Gayley Hall of Chemistry and Metallurgy. He made many important contributions to technical literature, practically all of which appeared in the *Transactions of the American Institute of Mining Engineers.* Among these were: "A Chilled Blast-Furnace Hearth"; "Development of American Blast-Furnaces, with Special Reference to Large Yields"; "The Preservation of the Hearth and Bosh-Walls of the Blast Furnace"; and "The Application of Dry Air Blast to the Manufacture of Iron." Gayley was married in February 1884 to Julia Thurston Gardiner of St. Louis, Mo., from whom he was later divorced. At the time of his death in New York City he was survived by her and by three daughters.

[*Trans. Am. Inst. Mining and Metallurgical Engineers,* vol. LXVII (1922); *Iron Trade Rev.,* Mar. 4, 1920; *Who's Who in America,* 1918–19; obituary in *N. Y. Times,* Feb. 26, 1920; Patent Office records.]

C. W. M.

GAYLORD, WILLIS (1792–Mar. 27, 1844), agricultural editor and writer, was born in Bristol, Conn., the son of Lemon Gaylord and Rhoda Plumb. In 1801, when he was nine years old, his father took his family to Otisco, Onondaga County, N. Y., where he is credited with being the third settler. As no schools were at that time established in the village, the boy received his educational training at home and through reading. He was a natural student and took advantage of every opportunity to extend his education, reading with avidity any books that chance brought within his reach. At twelve, he had a severe illness which resulted in a curvature of the spine, crippling him for the remainder of his life and while still young he was further handicapped through an accident to his arm which rendered it entirely useless and caused him severe suffering for many years. Being unable to engage in active pursuits, he turned his attention to study and to literary work. Among his early efforts was a history of the War of 1812 which he wrote in 1816–17. He was unable to get it published, but the rebuff did not discourage him from continuing to write. He later became a regular contributor to the press. He wrote on a variety of subjects, scientific, religious, and literary, but his most valuable work was in the field of practical and scientific agriculture, which became the chief interest of his later years. He began writing about 1833 for the *Genesee Farmer,* published by Luther Tucker [*q.v.*] at Rochester, N. Y., became assistant editor in 1837 and later senior editor. In January 1840, after the death of Jesse Buel [*q.v.*], well-known editor of the *Cultivator,* Albany, N. Y., the *Genesee Farmer* was combined with the *Cultivator,* and Gaylord continued in the capacity of editor until his death.

Through his paper and writings he did much to advance the agriculture of his day, particularly that of New York State. While there were several agricultural writers of the state who were as well or better qualified to discuss a single topic, he is said to have had no equal in his ability to discuss clearly and correctly every department of agricultural science. He was joint author with Luther Tucker of *American Husbandry; Being a Series of Essays on Agriculture* (2 vols., 1840), compiled principally from the *Cultivator* and the *Genesee Farmer.* His treatise on "Geology as Connected with Agriculture" was published in the *Transactions of the New-York State Agricultural Society, for the Year 1841* (1842) and also as No. 11 of the Tribune Publications (1843). His "Treatise on Insects Injurious to Field Crops, Fruit Orchards, Vegetable Gardens, and Domestic Animals," published in the New-York State Agricultural Society *Transactions,* for 1843, was the prize essay of the Society for that year. His series of articles entitled "Dictionary of Terms used in Agriculture" ran in the *Cultivator* from January 1840 to December 1843, but was completed only through the letter "M" at the time of his death. A number of his articles on meteorological subjects appeared in the *American Journal of Science* (see especially the issues of October 1839 and October 1840). His other agricultural writings are in large part contained in the *Genesee Farmer,* 1833–39, the *Cultivator,* 1840–44, and the New-York State Agricultural Society *Transactions,* vols. I–IV (1842–45). Gaylord was practical and judicious in his views, and possessed a happy faculty of communicating them to others. He was placable and forgiving in his temper, modest, disinterested, and unprejudiced. Unprepossessing in personal appearance, he possessed a rich, melodious voice, was a fascinating conversationalist, and notwithstanding his ill health, was always cheerful and uncomplaining. He died after an acute illness of thirty-three hours, at "Lime Rock Farm," Howlet Hill, Camillus, N. Y. He never married.

[Joshua V. H. Clark, *Onondaga* (1849), II, 340–44; *Cultivator,* May 1844, pp. 137–39; Wm. Gaillard, *The Hist. and Pedigrees of the House of Gaillard or Gaylord* (1872), p. 43; *Trans. N. Y. State Agric. Soc.,* IV (1844), 61–62.] C. R. B.

GAYNOR, WILLIAM JAY (Feb. 23, 1849–Sept. 10, 1913), jurist, mayor of New York City, was born and brought up in extreme poverty on a farm near Oriskany in Oneida County, N. Y. His mother, Elizabeth (Handwright) Gaynor, was of English ancestry, and his father, Kieron K. Gaynor, of Irish. In his early life William was educated for the priesthood, attending the Whitestown Seminary, the Assumption Academy, and finally the Christian Brothers College in St. Louis, which he entered as a novice. Abandoning the plan of taking orders at this time, he was admitted into the lay brotherhood of the order, taking the name of Brother Hadrian Mary. In 1867, as a member of that order, he went to the Isthmus of Panama, and thence to Mexico and on to San Francisco, where he remained until 1869. This year he abandoned the order and renounced Catholicism. He resumed his itinerant career as a teacher in the public schools of Boston and then left for Utica to take up the study of law.

In the late seventies he settled temporarily in Flatbush, L. I., where he began his legal practise. Virtually single-handed he fought for town reform, effected a reorganization of town government, and gained an enviable reputation in his term of a year as police commissioner. Removing to Brooklyn in 1885, Gaynor revealed the activities of a private water company as "a spoliation of the funds of the city" and compelled the city officials to collect the tax arrears from the elevated railroads. His activities brought him an offer of the nomination for mayor, which he declined. In 1893 he was elected a judge of the supreme court of New York. His victory was a serious blow to the Brooklyn political ring. John Y. McKane, Coney Island political leader, and a considerable group of his henchmen, were, as a result of Gaynor's vigilance, sent to the penitentiary for election frauds. Although by

1894 his radical views respecting municipal reform had attracted much favorable comment, Gaynor refused to become a candidate for the gubernatorial nomination on the Democratic ticket in that year. In like manner he declined the convention's nomination for judge of the court of appeals. In 1905 he was designated a member of the appellate division of the second department; and in 1907, as the candidate of all parties, he was reëlected to the supreme court of the state. His services on the bench commanded the respect of the legal profession. His judicial pen "was accurately described as 'trenchant.' Erroneous conceptions of substantive law, errors in pleading and practice, were treated with surgical directness" (Woodin, *post,* p. 102). Especially vigorous were his pronouncements upon various phases of the law of libel and slander, clearly establishing the proper place of "malice" in libel actions (16 *Misc.* 186; 23 *Misc.* 168; 42 *Misc.* 414), the nature of privileged communications (42 *Misc.* 441), and the scope of fair criticism (45 *Misc.* 441, 444–45; 113 *App. Div.* 510, 513–14). In 1909 he resigned from the bench to become mayor of New York City.

He was nominated on the Tammany ticket. The following which he had attracted by his strong denunciation of surface-railway manipulations and his emphatic declaration in favor of the construction of the subways by the city itself, were sufficient to give him a plurality of more than 70,000 over his opponent, despite the fact that the rest of his ticket was beaten (New York *Sun,* Nov. 3, 1909). Though by no means pliable to Tammany's purposes, Gaynor and his administration were bitterly assailed by the press. The revelation of the corruption of a police lieutenant, Becker, was a severe blow to his theories of police reform; and despite his campaign record in favor of city ownership of subways, the contracts were awarded to private corporations. In August 1910 a discharged city employee attempted to assassinate the Mayor on the deck of an ocean liner as he was about to leave for Europe. The bullet which was fired passed through his throat and was never extracted (New York papers, Aug. 9, 10, 1910). During the critical period of his convalescence Gaynor exhibited exemplary patience and fortitude. A short time later the Democratic party urged him to run for governor; but to Gaynor his position as mayor was bigger than the governorship and second only to the presidency (letters to John A. Dix and James Creelman, Sept. 25, 26, 1910, *Letters and Speeches,* pp. 32, 34, 35). His term as mayor was brought to a close by his sudden death on board the steamship *Baltic,* Sept. 10, 1913, about six hundred miles off the Irish coast.

Gaynor was one of the most unconventional and picturesque characters in American public life. Blunt, vigorous, he stood on his own feet in the political arena and took no orders. Although generous and placable by nature, he was at the same time hot-tempered, brusque in manner, and pitiless in his scorn. His unconventional methods won for him a host of bitter enemies. Beneath the mask of the terrible antagonist, however, there was the scholar, the philosopher, and the dreamer, who enjoyed to the full the simple pleasures of walking (*Independent,* June 1, 1911), the friendship of little children, and the literary companionship of his favorites, Epictetus and Cervantes. Gaynor was a master of the art of Anglo-Saxon prose. "The most expressive words are short words . . . the simple way is the best," he once wrote (*Letters and Speeches,* p. 5). His letters reveal both his hostility to the corruption of the press—a fact which explains in part the merciless newspaper lampoons to which he was constantly subjected—and his desire for neighborly tolerance. "The world does not grow better by force or by the policeman's club," he once said (*Ibid.,* p. 314). Shortly before his death, he engaged in a series of attacks on the "divinity of courts," or the power to declare laws unconstitutional. "The first duty of government, the prime duty of government," he once declared, "is distributive justice to all" (*Ibid.,* pp. 235, 243, 244, 263 ff.). He was married twice: first to a Miss Hyde, from whom he was later divorced, and in January 1886 to Augusta Cole Mayer, who with seven of their eight children survived him.

[*Some of Mayor Gaynor's Letters and Speeches* (1913); Glenn W. Woodin, "Contributions of Mr. Justice Gaynor to the Law of Libel and Slander," *Bench and Bar,* July 1917, pp. 102 ff.; volume of newspaper clippings relating to his political campaign for the mayoralty in 1909, in N. Y. Pub. Lib.; biographical sketch in the evening *Sun* (N. Y.), June 26, 1911; Henry Clews, *Address of the Memorial Meeting in Commemoration of the Late Wm. Jay Gaynor,* Sept. 23, 1913 (1913); *Who's Who in America,* 1910–11; *Nineteenth Ann. Report Am. Scenic and Hist. Preservation Soc.* (1914), pp. 543–69; obituaries in *N. Y. Times,* Sept. 12, 1913, and other N. Y. papers; family data from Gaynor's daughter, Mrs. W. S. Webb, Jr.]

R. B. M.

GAYOSO DE LEMOS, MANUEL (*c.* 1752–July 18, 1799), Spanish official in Louisiana, was admirably fitted by temperament and training to execute his government's policy in the conflict with the United States over the Mississippi Question. A natural diplomat, he was equipped by schooling in England with a thorough knowledge of the English language, and his conduct and correspondence give evidence of unusual zeal, sagacity, and breadth of vision. In 1773 he began four years of service with the Lisbon Regiment. In 1787, while holding the rank of lieutenant-colonel of infantry and attached to the Spanish embassy in Lisbon, he was summoned to Madrid where, on Nov. 3, 1787, he was commissioned governor of the newly created District of Natchez under the orders of the governor of Louisiana (Archivo Histórico Nacional, Madrid, Sección de Estado, legajo 3889, expediente no. 5). Although instructed to proceed at once to his post, he did not arrive in Louisiana until April 1789. In that year he was promoted to the rank of colonel. Before his departure from Spain he was married, with the King's permission, to Teresa Margarita Hopman y Pereira, who died shortly after their arrival in America. His first duty at Natchez was to carry out the new Spanish policy of inducing the American frontiersmen to settle on Spanish soil. That the policy failed was not his fault, for Americans as well as Spaniards were impressed by his ability, intelligence, and lavish hospitality. Another duty was to promote an intrigue looking toward the separation of the West from the United States. In this connection he carried on an extensive correspondence with James Wilkinson [*q.v.*]—who once said that he would willingly sacrifice one arm if he might embrace Gayoso with the other—and in 1795 executed a commission to confer with the Kentucky conspirator, Sebastian, at the mouth of the Ohio River. He contributed to the northward extension of the Spanish frontier by building forts at Walnut Hills (1790–92) and Chickasaw Bluffs (1795). In 1793 he persuaded the Southern Indians, in a congress at Walnut Hills, to form a confederacy and enter into a defensive alliance with Spain against the United States. As he was about to surrender Natchez to the United States in accordance with the Treaty of San Lorenzo (1795), he was required by a secret order from Madrid to suspend evacuation. This involved him in a controversy (1797–98) with Andrew Ellicott [*q.v.*], United States boundary commissioner, which was terminated by a final order from the court to evacuate. Gayoso had become a brigadier-general in 1795. In 1797 he married Margaret Watts, the daughter of a planter living in the Natchez district, and on Aug. 5 of that year he took possession of the government of Louisiana (Archivo General de Indias, Audiencia de Santo Domingo, legajo 2566, Santa Clara to Alvarez, Sept. 3, 1797, no. 17), succeeding the Baron de Carondelet [*q.v.*]. In this post, which he occupied until his death, he devoted his attention mainly to excluding Americans from settlement in Louisiana while encouraging their commerce with it; to fomenting the Indian trade; and to putting the province in a state of defense against an expected invasion from the United States. He enjoyed the reputation, rare among Spanish colonial officials, of never having used his office for personal gain. He died bankrupt.

[J. A. Robertson, *La. under the Rule of Spain, France and the U. S.* (1911), I, 269–89; Chas. Gayarré, *Hist. of La.* (3rd ed., 1885), III, 358–405; I. J. Cox, *The West Fla. Controversy* (1918), see Index; A. P. Whitaker, *The Spanish-American Frontier* (1927), see Index.]

A. P. W.

GEAR, JOHN HENRY (Apr. 7, 1825–July 14, 1900), governor of Iowa, representative, senator, the son of Rev. Ezekiel Gilbert and Miranda (Cook) Gear, both of pioneer New England families, was born at Ithaca, N. Y., where his father was a missionary to the Indians. In 1836 the family sought the "New West." After two years at Galena, Ill., in the year that the Iowa Territory was organized (1838), they removed to the frontier post of Fort Snelling, where the father became chaplain. John Henry's limited school opportunities were supplemented by his father's instruction. At eighteen, ready to start out into the world for himself, he journeyed to Burlington, then the capital of the Territory. Here he became a clerk in a wholesale grocery house, thus beginning a connection which led to partnership and ultimate ownership. Traveling for this house, he laid the basis of a state-wide acquaintance. In addition to his mercantile enterprise he was actively engaged in promoting local railroads. In 1852 he married Harriet S. Foot, a native of Vermont.

Though for single terms alderman (1852) and mayor (1863) of Burlington, Gear's real political career began with his election, in 1871, to the state House of Representatives, in which he served three terms. In 1874, with the House equally divided between Republicans and Anti-Monopolists, he was chosen speaker on the 137th ballot. His reëlection to that position two years later was the first instance of such succession in the state's history. His legislative service made him an outstanding leader of the regular Republicans and their successful candidate for governor in 1877 and 1879. His terms were noted for retrenchment, economy, and attempted administrative reorganization to such a degree that he was given the popular sobriquet, "Old Business." A temporary check came in 1882 with his defeat for the United States senatorship by James F. Wilson, but in 1886 he was elected to the national House. He was reëlected in 1888, defeated in the "landslide" of 1890, and again returned in 1892. In the interim (1892–93) he served as assistant secretary of the treasury. His congressional service, in committees rather than on the floor, centered on the tariff; he was active in framing the McKinley Bill and in opposing the Wilson Bill. In 1894, after one of the most notable struggles in Iowa politics, he attained his long-sought goal, the senatorship. His senatorial work dealt mainly with transportation problems. He waged a successful contest for reëlection with A. B. Cummins [*q.v.*] but died before his new term began. Without qualities of brilliance, he owed his large measure of political success to untiring industry, strict integrity, and a remarkable facility in making and keeping friends.

[Wm. H. Fleming, "Gov. John Henry Gear," *Annals of Iowa*, Jan. 1903; D. E. Clark, *Hist. of Senatorial Elections in Iowa* (1912); *Jour. of the House of Representatives of . . . the State of Iowa*, 14–16 General Assemblies; *Messages and Papers of the Govs. of Iowa*, vol. V (1904), ed. by B. F. Shambaugh; Walter Geer, *Geneal. of the Geer Family* (1914); *Biog. Dir. Am. Cong.* (1928); *Iowa State Register* (Des Moines), July 15, 1900.] E. D. R.

GEARY, JOHN WHITE (Dec. 30, 1819–Feb. 8, 1873), soldier, territorial governor of Kansas, governor of Pennsylvania, was born near Mount Pleasant, Westmoreland County, Pa., the son of Richard and Margaret (White) Geary. His father, a descendant of a Shropshire family one of whose members had originally settled in Franklin County, Pa., had been an ironmaster, but he had failed at this business and had sought to support his family by keeping a school. When John was a student at Jefferson College, Canonsburg, Pa., his father died, leaving him an accumulation of debts. He was forced to leave college, temporarily at least, and his career for the next few years was varied; he taught school, was a clerk in a store, studied civil engineering and law, was admitted to the bar, and went to Kentucky on a surveying expedition. While in the Blue-Grass state he was sufficiently successful in land speculation to pay off his father's debts. His engineering experience then brought him a position as assistant superintendent and engineer of the Allegheny Portage Railroad.

Geary had been interested in military affairs for more than ten years and when but sixteen had been appointed a lieutenant in the militia. At the outbreak of the Mexican War he was captain of the "American Highlanders" attached to the "Cambria Legion" and he and his company volunteered, joining the 2nd Pennsylvania Infantry at Pittsburgh, where he was elected lieutenant-colonel. The regiment arrived at Vera Cruz Apr. 11, 1847, via New Orleans and the Lobos Islands and participated in Scott's advance to the city of Mexico. Since Col. Roberts, commander of the regiment, was in bad health much of the time, Geary had the responsibility of directing maneuvers. In the attack on Chapultepec he led the assault upon the fortress, and he was placed in charge of this work upon its capture. After the capture of the city he remained there on duty until the end of the war, being elected colonel of his regiment on the death of Roberts.

When President Polk was called upon to organize California he chose Geary to establish the postal service, and on Jan. 22, 1849, appointed him postmaster of San Francisco and mail agent for the Pacific Coast. Geary and his wife, Margaret Ann Logan, whom he had married in 1843, arrived in San Francisco in April, but as President Polk had been succeeded by President Taylor, the new postmaster had hardly begun his service when his Whig successor arrived. He was not at a loss for employment, however, for within eight days he was elected "first *alcalde*" of San Francisco. Shortly the military governor, Brig.-Gen. Riley, appointed him "judge of first instance." Occupying these offices, he was the chief civil officer of the city, executive and judicial, and when American forms were adopted, in 1850, he became the first mayor. He was active in making California a free state and was chairman of the Democratic Territorial Committee. Since Mrs. Geary's health was failing, however, he returned with her to his Pennsylvania farm in 1852 and after her death the next year he remained in his old home.

Geary declined President Pierce's offer of the governorship of Utah, but when Kansas fell into anarchy he accepted the governorship of that territory. He was well qualified for the difficult post, for his whole person commanded respect. He was six feet five and a half inches tall, well built, and carried himself with military precision. Furthermore, he had been promised the full military support of the government. When he arrived in Kansas, Sept. 9, 1856, he found a condition of virtual civil war, because the contending forces had been confident that the army bill would fail in Congress and thus make necessary the withdrawal of federal troops from the Territory. The bill had passed, however, and Geary's first act was to disband the pro-slavery militia which his immediate predecessor had called out. He then proceeded to substitute United States troops, organize his own militia, and arrest an irregular band of free-state sympathizers. Within three weeks marked by vigorous activity he could report "Peace now reigns in Kansas," in time to give this message sufficiently wide circulation to aid in Buchanan's election. Geary continued his vigorous activities as impartially as he could, endeavoring to protect Kansas from both factions. Becoming convinced that Lecompte the chief justice, Clarke the Indian agent, and Donalson the marshal, were flagrantly pro-slavery, he asked the President to remove them. Pierce did so and the enmity of the pro-slavery group focussed itself upon the Governor. He got along fairly well, however, until the meeting of the legislature, Jan. 12, 1857. This body was overwhelmingly pro-slavery and acted in open hostility to the Governor, automatically disregarding his vetoes. His life was threatened, a seeming attempt to assassinate him failed, and his secretary was beaten and then arrested for murder. Just as these things occurred, Gen. Persifor F. Smith declared himself unable or unwilling to supply Geary with more troops, and a letter arrived from William L. Marcy, secretary of state, asking Geary to explain some discrepancies between his charges and Lecompte's reply; in the meantime as the Senate had not confirmed the appointment of Lecompte's successor, the judge was still serving. This cumulation of difficulties discouraged Geary, and on Mar. 4 he resigned, straightway leaving the Territory and going to Washington to report to Buchanan.

Four years of retirement on his Westmoreland farm, during which he married Mrs. Mary (Church) Henderson in 1858, were broken by the guns of Sumter. When the news of that event reached Geary's locality he set up a recruiting office immediately and in a few days was made colonel of the 28th Pennsylvania. He was ordered to Harper's Ferry, where on Oct. 16, 1861, he was under fire at Bolivar Heights and was wounded. The next March he captured Leesburg, and shortly thereafter he was made brigadier-general. Badly wounded at Cedar Mountain, Aug. 9, 1862, he had to return to his home for a while, but he was back in command of a division at Chancellorsville and distinguished himself at Gettysburg. In the fall of 1863 he was sent with the XII Corps under Hooker to join Grant in Tennessee and was active in the operations there culminating at Lookout Mountain and Missionary Ridge; at Wauhatchie, Oct. 28, 1863, he participated in a sharp engagement in which his son was killed. He accompanied Sherman on his famous march to the sea, was military governor of Savannah after its capture, and shortly before the end of the war was made major-general by brevet.

After the Civil War, Pennsylvania politics were marked by a struggle between Curtin and Cameron for control of the National Union or Republican party. Shrewdly realizing the advantages of Geary's military fame and his wide popularity, Cameron's forces made Geary, now a Republican, the party candidate for governor and elected him. He served two terms, from Jan. 15, 1867, to Jan. 21, 1873. Supremely self-confident, he pursued his downright, opinionated way and had many a battle with the legislature; of 9,242 bills passed he vetoed 390. He was active in trying to reduce the debt of the state and in safeguarding the treasury; toward the latter end he sought to promote a plan for lending state funds to private enterprise so that large balances might earn money for the state and not prove tempting to the treasurer. He sought in vain to persuade the legislature to adopt a more careful and orderly procedure, and successfully recommended the calling of a state constitutional convention. He advocated a general railroad law, the regulation of insurance, state control of gas companies, protection against accident in the mines, and safeguards for the public health, but on the other hand urged that taxes be shifted from business to land, especially because this change would aid Pennsylvania business in its competition with that of other states. His headstrong and erratic course, often marred by violent fits of temper, won him a number of enemies, and he barely escaped defeat at the end of his first term, but the state machine and his own popularity, especially with the veterans, saved him. He acquired presidential ambitions as 1872 approached, and in the Labor Reform convention of that year he led on the first ballot but was defeated by David Davis. Within three weeks after his retirement from the governorship he was suddenly stricken and died.

[The most authoritative sketch of Geary is that in *Lives of the Governors of Pa.* (1872), by Wm. C. Armor, who was closely associated with him. *Memorial Addresses on the Death of Gov. John W. Geary* (1873) and *In Memoriam* (Phila., 1873) contain some biographical material. His secretary, John H. Gihon, prepared an account, *Gov. Geary's Administration in Kans.* (1857), which is largely a series of quotations from his official records. These are found completely published in *Trans. Kans. State Hist. Soc.*, vols. IV and V (1890, 1896). See also *A Sketch of the Early Life . . . of Maj. Gen. John W. Geary, Candidate of the National Union Party for Gov. of Pa.* (1866); *Inaugurals and Messages of Gen. John W. Geary, 1867–73* (n.d.); *Daily Patriot* (Harrisburg, Pa.), Feb. 10, 1873. His diary kept during the Mexican War, his scrap-books, and a few papers are in the possession of his family.]

R. F. N.

GEDDES, JAMES (July 22, 1763–Aug. 19, 1838), civil engineer, was born of Scotch ancestry near Carlisle, Pa. In 1794 he moved to the region of Syracuse, Onondaga County, N. Y., where he became one of the pioneers in the salt industry. The township of Geddes was named for him. In 1799 he was married to Lucy Jerome, daughter of Timothy Jerome of Fabius, N. Y. After studying law, he was admitted to the bar. In 1800 he was made a justice of the peace, and in 1809 he was appointed judge of the county court and of the court of common pleas. Becoming interested in public affairs, he was elected to the Assembly in 1804, to the Thirteenth Congress, serving 1813–15, and again to the Assembly in 1822. During his first term at Albany, Simeon DeWitt, surveyor-general of New York, broached to him the possibility of constructing a canal from the Great Lakes to the Hudson River. Since the suggestion touched his imagination, he visited various sections of the state to secure information and launched a campaign to arouse interest in the undertaking. Moreover, although he had received only an elementary education and was entirely without technical training, having used a level on one occasion only, he himself ran the first survey in 1808, under appointment from the surveyor-general. His report to the legislature, Jan. 20, 1809, established the fact that a canal could be constructed without difficulty along a route essentially the same as that later adopted for the Erie Canal. His report included, also, surveys of routes suggested for canals from Oneida Lake down the Oswego River to Lake Ontario, and from Lake Erie to Lake Ontario around Niagara Falls.

After the War of 1812, when work on the New York canals was begun, Geddes was engaged by the Canal Commissioners of New York as one of the four "principal engineers" to construct the Erie and Champlain Canals, tasks to which he devoted the years 1816–22. Though his work during this period on the Western Division of the Erie Canal and on the Champlain Canal, which he apparently completed, did much to establish the commercial supremacy of New York state, Geddes was noted as a discoverer and promoter of new waterways throughout the East, and was called upon by other states as well as by the federal government for assistance. In 1822, for the State of Ohio, he surveyed a canal from the Ohio River to Lake Erie; in 1827, for the federal government, he examined the routes for the Chesapeake & Ohio Canal; in 1828 he was engaged in Pennsylvania; and in 1829, although he had declined to investigate the feasibility of a route between the Tennessee and Alabama Rivers, he reported on a canal in Maine from Sebago Lake to Westbrook.

[Elkanah Watson, *Hist. of the Rise, Progress, and Existing Condition of the Western Canals in the State of N. Y.* (1820); G. C. Haines, *Pub. Docs., Relating to the N. Y. Canals* (1821); *Laws of the State of N. Y. in Relation to the Erie and Champlain Canals* (2 vols., 1825); N. E. Whitford, *Hist. of the Canal System of the State of N. Y.* (2 vols., 1905); reports of the local companies with which Geddes was associated; his *Map and Profile of the Champlain Canal,* etc. (1825), his report to the Secretary of War on the Chesapeake & Ohio Canal (1828); M. S. Hawley and George Geddes, "Erie Canal Papers," *Buffalo Hist. Soc. Pubs.,* vol. II (1880); H. W. Hill, "An Historical Review of Waterways and Canal Construction in New York State," *Ibid.,* vol. XII (1908); Joshua V. H. Clark, *Onondaga* (1849), II, 45 ff.; C. B. Stuart, *Lives and Works of Civil and Military Engineers of America* (1871), pp. 36–47; *Biog. Dir. Am. Cong.* (1928).] R. P. B—r.

GEDDES, JAMES LORAINE (Mar. 19, 1827–Feb. 21, 1887), soldier, college administrator, was born in Edinburgh, Scotland, the son of a British officer, Capt. Alexander Geddes, and of Elizabeth (Careless) Geddes. When he was ten, his father, who had become deeply religious, feeling that he should seek a simpler and more wholesome environment for the rearing of his family, emigrated to Canada. The provincial surroundings were not to young James's liking, however, and at sixteen, by working his passage, he returned to relatives in Scotland. Soon after, in 1845, he visited a soldier uncle in India and entered the British military academy at Calcutta. After two years of study he joined the Royal House Artillery and had seven years of active duty under Gough, Napier, and Campbell. For this service he was awarded a medal, and upon his decision to rejoin his family he was made a colonel of Canadian cavalry. While in Canada, Oct. 14, 1856, he was married at St. Thomas, Ont., to Margaret Moore. The Canadian service was not congenial, and in October 1857 he resigned his commission and removed to Iowa, settling on a farm in Benton County, near Vinton. Wholly inexperienced in farming, he supplemented his income by teaching a country school. He was thus engaged when the outbreak of the Civil War brought a new opportunity.

Before the war began he had been drilling a local company, which upon the organization of the 8th Iowa Infantry became its Company D. When the company was mustered, Sept. 16, 1861, he was commissioned captain, one week later was advanced to lieutenant-colonel, and on Feb. 7, 1862, was promoted to a colonelcy and the command of the regiment. Its initial service was with Frémont in Missouri, but its first real fighting came at Shiloh, Apr. 6, 1862, where the 8th Iowa was one of the regiments called to the support of Prentiss in his crucial buffer position. This reorganized division by holding the "hornet's nest," until after severe losses it was forced to surrender at the end of the day, helped to preserve the main army for its triumph on the morrow. Col. Geddes, himself among the wounded, was highly commended by Prentiss for his part in the action. He was exchanged in time to be in the fighting at Vicksburg and Jackson, acquitting himself so creditably that, in October 1863, he was placed in charge of a brigade. After brief service in Texas the brigade was transferred to Memphis, Tenn., where Geddes served with tact and efficiency as provost-marshal of the district. His last important engagement was in the Mobile campaign in which his brigade had a conspicuous part in the capture of Spanish Fort. For this achievement he was made brevet brigadier-general, June 5, 1865. He resigned from the service on June 30.

Soon after the war he was called to the superintendency of the Iowa Institution for the Education of the Blind, where for two years (June 1867–July 1869) he dealt with problems of administration and instruction conscientiously and intelligently. He was interested from the first in the state's land-grant college at Ames, and became its steward in 1870. The next year he was appointed professor of military tactics and engineering, and to the duties of this position those of vice-president and deputy treasurer were soon added. His teaching was most notable in connection with the launching of military instruction in a land-grant college. His training, enthusiasm, and high military ideals enabled him to achieve gratifying results in skill and discipline under serious limitations. In November 1882, a board unfavorable to the existing administration among other measures of reorganization discontinued Geddes's services. This action led to great protest from students and other friends throughout the state, and a new board in December 1884 appointed him college treasurer and recorder, and later, June 1886, college land agent also. He held these positions until his death, which was occasioned, in his sixtieth year, largely by war disabilities.

Slender, erect, elastic of step, with sharp, clear-cut features, Geddes appeared the true soldier; his personality exemplified the ideal military gentleman. Without relaxing his dignity, he had a kind, modest, considerate manner that won the respect and affection of soldiers and students, fellow officers and colleagues. His interests, developed by travel and wide reading, were broad and tolerant. He was an amateur artist of some talent and a writer of war songs better in form and more restrained in sentiment than the average of such productions. On May 18, 1875, his first wife died, and on Apr. 14, 1876, he married Elizabeth Evans of Vinton, Iowa.

[Scrap-book of newspaper clippings in possession of Geddes's daughter, Mrs. W. B. Niles of Ames, Iowa; MSS. in history files of Iowa State College; *Official Records (Army)*, 1 ser., vols. X, XXIV (pt. 2), XXXI (pt. 3), XXXII (pt. 2), XLIX (pt. 1); *Roster and Record of Iowa Soldiers in the War of the Rebellion*, vol. I (1908); A. A. Stuart, *Iowa Colonels and Regiments* (1865); S. H. M. Byers, *Iowa in War Times* (1888); biennial reports of the Inst. for the Education of the Blind (1868) and of the State College (1871–87); files of the college magazines: the *Aurora*, 1873–87, and the *College Quarterly*, 1878–80; *Iowa State Register* (Des Moines), Feb. 22, 1887.]

E. D. R.

GEERS, EDWARD FRANKLIN (Jan. 25, 1851–Sept. 3, 1924), turfman, was born in Wilson County, Tenn., son of William T. and Emily (Woolard) Geers. As a mere boy on his father's farm he became a local celebrity as a trainer and driver of horses. He conducted a public training stable at Nashville in 1875, and one at Columbia from 1876 to 1889. In 1880 he married Mrs. Pearl (Smith) Neeley. His first trip North was in 1877 when he gave Alice West a record of 2:26, the first trotter he drove under 2:30. In 1879, with Mattie Hunter, he twice lowered the record for pacing mares, the second time, to 2:16½. At both Nashville and Columbia he was patronized by Campbell Brown, and from 1889 to 1892 he was employed by Brown at Ewell Farm. Thus Geers became interested in the Hal family of pacers which Brown was breeding. Going North in 1889, he took Brown Hal on the Grand Circuit and made him the champion pacing stallion with a record of 2:12½. With Hal Pointer, the gelded half-brother of Brown Hal, he won numerous contests during each of several Grand Circuit seasons and in 1892 made him the world's pacing champion with a record of 2:05¼; later lowered to 2:04½. In 1892 Geers was employed to train and drive for C. J. Hamlin of Village Farm, near Buffalo, N. Y., at a salary of $10,000 a year, the largest ever received up to that time by one of his profession. Leaving Hamlin ten years later, he settled at Billings Park, Memphis, which was his headquarters for the rest of his life, his chief patron there being F. G. Jones.

For twenty years Geers was the leading race driver of the world, winning hundreds of races and more than a million dollars in purses and stakes. In 1894 he made Robert J. the world's champion as a pacer, by driving him to a record of 2:01½; he brought out and first raced Star Pointer, 1:59¼, the first light-harness two-minute horse; he won the world's trotting championship in 1900 with The Abbot, 2:03¼. He drove to their records sixty-six trotters in the 2:10 list, the fastest being The Harvester, 2:01, the champion trotting stallion of his day (1910), and he also gave their best records to sixteen pacers in the 2:05 list. At Toledo, Ohio, in 1918 he won the first race in history in which all the heats were paced below 2:00, Miss Harris M. taking the first heat in 1:58¼ and Single G., Geers up, the next two in 1:59½, 1:59¾.

As a race driver, campaign manager, and turf tactician he was equally notable. Personally he was modest, generous, and honest. Because of his taciturnity he was long known as "The Silent Man from Tennessee." He was instantly killed while driving in a race at Wheeling, W. Va., and in 1926 his admirers throughout America erected a monument in his honor in Geers Memorial Park, Columbia, Tenn.

[*Ed Geers' Experience with Trotters and Pacers* (1901), an autobiography; J. T. Moore, "A Hist. of the Hals," *Trotwood's Mo.* (1905–1907), and other articles in the same periodical; *Nashville Tennesseean*, Sept. 6, 1924, and Oct. 10, 1926; *Everybody's Mag.*, Jan. 1921; *Collier's*, Mar. 27, 1926; the *Outlook*, Sept. 17, 1924, *N. Y. Times*, Sept. 4, 1924; newspaper articles and letters in Tenn. State Lib., Nashville; information from Miss Emma Geers, Lebanon, Tenn., Allen Campbell, Spring Hill, Tenn., and J. L. Hervey, ed. of *Horse Rev.*, Chicago.]

J. D. A.

GEMÜNDER, AUGUST MARTIN LUDWIG (Mar. 22, 1814–Sept. 7, 1895), violin-maker, and his brother George (Apr. 13, 1816–Jan. 15, 1899), were pioneers in the development of quality violin-building in the United States. Their father, Johann Georg Heinrich Gemünder (1782–1863), violin-maker to the Prince of Hohenlohe, was their first teacher in the art. August Gemünder left his birthplace, Ingelfingen, in Württemberg, to emigrate to America in 1846. After some months in Springfield, Mass., he went to Boston, where he was joined by his brother George, and from there, in 1852, they went to New York. The success of the brothers was rapid and deserved. From the sixties to the eighties their violins were winning medals in expositions in Paris, Vienna, and London, as well as in Philadelphia and New Orleans, and their name was outstanding in their field. August Gemünder made violins in his New York shop which August Wilhelmj and Adolf Brodsky took pleasure in using in concert, and according to Sarasate, August's copy of his Amati was in all respects equal to the original. The fact that the Gemünder-made Cremonas were often thought to be Amatis is sufficient evidence of their quality.

George Gemünder also made violins in which power, quality, and responsiveness of tone closely approached the best work of the older Italian masters. In their faithful reproduction of the fine models of the great Italian violin-builders, and especially in the varnishing and finishing of their instruments, the brothers were so successful that even experts often mistook their copies for eighteenth-century models. In one case the quality of the Gemünder workmanship resulted in a peculiar injustice to its makers. When George sent a "Kaiser" violin which he had built on the Guarnerius pattern to the Vienna Exposition of 1873, the judges were so struck with the beauty of the instrument that they decided it must be an original Guarnerius and not a copy. George Gemünder was a pupil of Jean Baptiste Vuillaume, and it was in his workrooms in Paris that, in 1845, he repaired Ole Bull's wonderful "Gasparo da Salo" violin with such skill as to win the highest praise from the artist. The elder Gemünder wrote a brief article, "Fine Violins" (*Weekly Review of Music and Drama*, Oct. 18, 1884), and his brother was the author of a pamphlet study, *George Gemünder's Progress in Violin Making* (1881), which contained an autobiographical sketch. It had appeared in German in 1880. August Gemünder died in New York in 1895, his brother four years later, but the firm which he founded was continued by three of his sons. As violin-makers the Gemünders had no contemporary superiors.

[References for August Gemünder: *Music Trade Rev.*, Sept. 14, 1895; *N. Y. Times*, Sept. 8, 1895; for George Gemünder: *Musical Record*, Feb. 1, 1899; *N. Y. Times*, Jan. 17, 1899; W. L. von Lütgendorff, *Die Geigen- und Lautenmacher* (Frankfurt, 1904).]

F. H. M.

GEMÜNDER, GEORGE (April. 13, 1816–Jan. 15, 1899). [See GEMÜNDER, AUGUST M. L.]

GENET, EDMOND CHARLES (Jan. 8, 1763–July 15, 1834), the first minister of the French Republic to the United States, was the only son of Marie Anne Louise Cardon and Edmé Jacques Genet, for many years *premier commis* of the bureau of interpretations of foreign affairs at Versailles. His four talented sisters were appointed to posts of honor in the household of Marie Antoinette and the oldest, Henriette, who became celebrated later as Madame Campan, was first lady in waiting to the Queen. Genet, who was a precocious child, was given the best educational advantages under tutors and his learned father. At the age of twelve he gained recognition in Sweden, France, and England for his translations from Swedish into French. At fourteen he was made a secretary in his father's office, where he translated many of the documents of the American Revolution. In 1780 young Genet studied at Giessen and spent some months in Berlin studying law. He then went to Vienna in the secretariat of Baron de Breteuil and returned to Paris in September 1781, just in time to assume the office left vacant by the death of his father. In the foreign office he was again brought into contact with the affairs of the young American Republic; he later boasted that it was he who bore to Vergennes tidings of the surrender of Cornwallis.

Genet was sent to England in 1783 as acting secretary of the legation with Count de Moustier to secure information that might prove useful in connection with the contemplated treaty of commerce between Great Britain and France. Many intellectual interests besides the linguistic demands of his position in the department of foreign affairs made these years, 1781–87, happily busy ones for Genet. He was keenly on the alert for new ideas in regard to the use of steam in industry and transportation, made hobbies of agriculture and botany, and was interested in mineralogy and scientific expeditions. He kept up an active correspondence with scientific and liberal-minded intellectuals like La Rochefoucauld and Condorcet, and was a member of many learned bodies. At the death of Vergennes, Genet's bureau was abolished in a policy of retrenchment. Friends at Court soon secured for him appointment as secretary to the Comte de Ségur, minister to the Court of Catherine II. He went to Russia in the early fall of 1787, stopping over at Warsaw where he was introduced to King Stanislaus Poniatowski. Thus by the time he was twenty-five Genet had made the rounds of the most important courts of Europe. Ségur quitted St. Petersburg in October 1789 and Genet was left as *chargé d'affaires* of France. His revolutionary sentiments and his adherence to the Constitution of 1791 made him obnoxious to Catherine. He was forbidden to appear at Court and put under surveillance. On news of the events of June 20, 1792, in Paris, he was expelled from Russia. He left St. Petersburg on July 27, and on his arrival in Paris was received cordially by the Girondist ministry as one who had suffered for liberty at the hands of the autocratic Catherine. They planned to utilize him as an evangel of their faith. First they sent him on a temporary mission to Geneva. Then (Nov. 19, 1792) he was appointed minister plenipotentiary to the United States, but was held in Paris by the Girondists until the day of the King's execution in the hope that Louis XVI and the royal family could be sent with him to America.

Genet arrived at Charleston, S. C., on Apr. 8, 1793, aboard the French frigate *l'Embuscade* and was fêted by Gov. William Moultrie, Commodore Gillon, an old friend of the Genet family, and other high dignitaries who gave him encouragement in his plans. He fitted out four privateers in Charleston and then started to Philadelphia by way of Camden, Salisbury, Richmond, and Baltimore. The people of the back country attested in demonstrative fashion their sympathy with France, but the cold caution of the cities, the neutrality proclamation that had met him en route, and the zeal for peace and prosperity that was evident on every hand, convinced Genet that he could not hope for active American participation in the war on the side of France. He still expected, however, to press the right of France under the treaties of 1778 to fit out privateers in American ports and bring her prizes into them. These same treaties were causing Washington and his advisers grave concern, and had occasioned sharp disagreements. George Hammond, the British minister, was in Hamilton's confidence and protested vigorously the depredations on British commerce by the French privateers. Genet consorted with Jefferson, the known friend of France, and his coterie of intellectual and rather radical friends. From his arrival in Philadelphia until the decision of Washington and his advisers early in August to ask for his recall, Genet was the storm center of American politics. Supporters of the administration finally succeeded in discrediting him by publishing the charge that he had threatened to appeal from Washington to the people.

In the midst of these party factions in the declaredly neutral republic, Genet tried unremittingly to carry out his instructions. He sent the botanist André Michaux [*q.v.*] to Kentucky to make common cause with the disaffected element there for an expedition down the Mississippi to wrest Louisiana from Spain. In South Carolina he worked with the aid of restless and dissatisfied leaders like Stephen Drayton and Alexander Moultrie to take Florida from Spain. When the French fleet, leaving Santo Domingo to the double devastation of revolutionary and racial conflicts, came to New York, he planned to send it to recapture St. Pierre and Miquelon for France and to help his emissary Henri Mézières stimulate Canada to revolt. But mutiny in the fleet, the activities of the hostile South Carolina legislature against Drayton and Moultrie, and the lack of funds to enable Clark to start his expedition down the Mississippi before the arrival of Genet's successor, Fauchet, made these energetic enterprises abortive.

Following the news of his recall Genet increased his activities, but to no avail. The sagacious maneuvers of Federalist leaders had turned the tide of popular support from him to Washington. His passionate communications, his insistence, and his maladroit efforts had turned the Republican leaders from active support of him to a silent ignoring of his presence. The repudiated minister, however, had stimulated the organization of local clubs, variously termed Democratic or Republican societies, that soon radiated into almost every state. These became vehicles for the expression of local grievances and contributed no little to the articulation of the growing Republican party. They were Genet's real though unwitting bequest to the democratic movement.

When his successor arrived in February 1794, Genet bought a small farm on Long Island, and on Nov. 6 he married Cornelia Tappen Clinton, daughter of Gov. George Clinton of New York. He later became an American citizen. About 1800 he moved to a farm in Rensselaer County, N. Y., where he spent more than three decades in peaceful if not always calm retirement. He busied himself with farming, scientific agricultural studies, and industrial mechanics. After the death of his wife he married, on July 31, 1814, Martha Brandon Osgood, daughter of Samuel Osgood, former postmaster-general of the United States. An intermittent correspondence with his sister, Madame Campan, was his only link with France. On the coming to power of Louis Philippe, however, he sought some remunerative appointment from him in America.

[The Genet Papers in the Lib. of Cong. include letters to and from Genet, rough drafts of his dispatches, and portions of his memoirs, as well as official documents. Published portions of his memoirs are in M. D. Conway, trans. by Félix Rabbe, *Thomas Paine et la Révolution dans les Deux Mondes* (1900). Published portions of his correspondence are in the *Ann. Report Am. Hist. Asso., 1896,* I (1897), 930–1107; *1897* (1898), pp. 569–679; *1903,* II (1904), 201–86; *Am. Hist. Rev.,* July 1913, pp. 780–84; *Am. State Papers, Foreign Relations,* vol. I (1832). Meade Minnigerode, *Jefferson Friend of France, 1793: The Career of Edmond Charles Genet* (1928) has much data from the Genet Papers but its conclusions are untenable. The sketch by Genet's descendant, L. F. F. Genet, in the *Jour. of Am. Hist.,* vol. VI (1912), is written from a partisan family point of view. Brief obituaries appeared in the *New-York Daily Advertiser* and the *Evening Post,* July 17, 1834, and in the *Courrier des États-Unis,* July 19, 1834.] M. H. W.

GENIN, JOHN NICHOLAS (Oct. 19, 1819–Apr. 30, 1878), hatter, and merchant, was born in New York City. His grandfather, whose name he bore, emigrated to America from Labeurville in the Verdun district of France as a commissary clerk in Rochambeau's expedition in 1780, settled on Long Island, and married Ann Tournier, of French-Canadian extraction. Genin came into prominence in the forties partly because his hat shop adjoined the famous Barnum's Museum and partly through his own methods of advertising. In 1845 he brought out a booklet, *An Illustrated History of the Hat from the Earliest Ages to the Present Time.* In that day such an enterprise attracted far more attention than it would have done at a later period. Encyclopedias were few, and the general public had little access to information of the kind which the young hatter put into his little treatise. Genin achieved his success as a self-advertiser, however, largely by exploits outside the field of his own calling. The outstanding publicity feat of his career was his purchase of the first choice of seats sold at auction for the concert which launched Jenny Lind's tour under the auspices of P. T. Barnum in 1850. He bid $225 for the seat and the next morning every important newspaper in the United States noted the fact and alluded to Genin as a hatter. Barnum later stated that the transaction laid the foundation of Genin's fortune (*Struggles and Triumphs,* 1869, 294–95). At any rate it gave a New York hatter a national reputation. It is hardly to be doubted that Barnum, who was on the most friendly terms with his Broadway neighbor, had advised Genin in the matter. It was reported at the time that the two men were brothers-in-law, but Barnum took pains to deny the rumor.

Some of the streets of lower New York, where traffic was heavy, were so overlaid with mud and filth that the paving stones had not been visible for years. The city authorities did nothing to remedy the situation. Genin at his own cost hired men to work at night to remove the accumulation and in a short time laid bare whole blocks of street pavement on Broadway, thus confounding the municipal street-cleaning department and greatly enhancing his personal prestige as a public-spirited citizen at comparatively slight expense, since he was largely reimbursed by public subscription. He could have had a mayoralty nomination, but political preferment was not the end he had in view.

Genin was among the first of the New York retail merchants to make wide use of novel advertising methods. He built up a large clothing business, obtaining the patronage of both men and women, and also specialized in children's apparel. In time his shops took on some of the aspects of the twentieth-century department store. Because of his early use of paid newspaper advertising and his spectacular methods of drawing attention to his business, he may be regarded as a pioneer in the application of publicity to salesmanship.

[*Selections from the Writings of the late Thos. Hedges Genin* (1869) gives a brief outline of the ancestry of the family. See also *Ballou's Pictorial Drawing-Room Companion,* June 2, 1855. The episode of the Jenny Lind concert seat is related in the *N. Y. Herald,* Sept. 9, 1850, and also in M. R. Werner's *Barnum* (1923), pp. 159–60.] W. B. S.

GENTH, FREDERICK AUGUSTUS (May 17, 1820–Feb. 2, 1893), chemist, born in Wächtersbach, near Hanau, Hesse-Cassel, Germany, was the son of Georg Friedrich and Karoline Amalie (Freyin von Swartzenau) Genth, and was christened Friedrich August Ludwig Karl Wilhelm. His parents were educated persons and early in life he was instructed in natural science. Leaving the Gymnasium at Hanau in 1839, he studied chemistry and other sciences till 1845 in the Universities of Heidelberg, Giessen, and Marburg. Among his teachers were Gmelin, Fresenius, Kopp, Liebig, and Bunsen. He received the Ph.D. degree from Marburg in 1845 and was soon appointed an assistant to Bunsen. In 1848 he emigrated to the United States and opened an analytical laboratory in Philadelphia. He soon gave it up, however, for a mining position in North Carolina, which he held for a year. He then reopened his analytical laboratory in Philadelphia, August 1850, and for about twenty years devoted himself to research, commercial analysis, and the laboratory instruction of special students. In 1872 he succeeded Charles M. Wetherill as professor of chemistry in the University of Pennsylvania. Here he remained till 1888, when he resigned and for a third time opened his private laboratory.

As an analytical chemist, Genth was without a peer in accuracy and industry. He was an expert in mineral chemistry, and readily grasped the structural relations of minerals. Perhaps the best example of this work was his paper on "Corundum, its Alterations and Associated Minerals" (*Proceedings of the American Philosophical Society,* Sept. 19, 1873). Of his 102 investigations published in American and German journals from 1842 to 1893, over seventy were on mineral topics. Many of the papers were comprehensive. The more than twenty minor studies contained details of new methods of analysis or descriptions of new minerals. Genth discovered twenty-three new mineral species, one of which, genthite or nickelgymnite, was named for him. His non-mineral chemical papers numbered about thirty. One group, dealing with fertilizers, arose from his work as chemist of the Pennsylvania Board of Agriculture. His most important chemical paper was a study of the ammonia-cobalt bases. It was begun in 1847; a preliminary paper was published in 1851; and subsequently it was developed jointly with Wolcott Gibbs [*q.v.*]. It was issued in 1856 as a monograph by the Smithsonian Institution and was also published in the *American Journal of Science* (May–November 1857). This perplexing work was continued by other investigators, but to Genth belongs the credit of initiating and sharing one of the finest chemical investigations ever made in the United States.

As a teacher, Genth was inspiring to ambitious or faithful students, but merciless to the indifferent or evasive. Personally, he was most agreeable and cordial. He was married in 1847 to Karolina Jäger, by whom he had three children, and in 1852 to Minna Paulina Fischer, by whom he had nine children. Early in his career he was elected a member of the American Philosophical Society, American Chemical Society (president 1880), National Academy of Science, American Academy of Arts and Sciences, and American Association for the Advancement of Science.

[G. F. Barker, "Frederick Augustus Genth," in *Proc. Am. Phil. Soc.,* Dec. 1901, and, with bibliography, in *Nat. Acad. Sci. Biog. Memoirs,* vol. IV (1902); *Jour. Am. Chem. Soc.,* Golden Jubilee Number, Aug. 20, 1926; E. F. Smith, *Chemistry in America* (1914), pp. 261–63; *Press* (Phila.), Feb. 4, 1893.] L. C. N.

GENUNG, JOHN FRANKLIN (Jan. 27, 1850–Oct. 1, 1919), college professor and writer on rhetoric and Biblical literature, was born at Willseyville, Tioga County, N. Y., the son of Abram C. and Martha (Dye) Genung. His father, a descendant of Jean Guenon, a French Huguenot who came to New Amsterdam in 1657, was a farmer and carpenter-builder. Brought up in a self-sufficient household, which supplied its own food, shoes, clothing, physical comforts, and spiritual satisfactions, John Franklin with his twin brother, George Frederick, early learned habits of independence, industry, and thorough craftsmanship. From the academy at Owego, he entered the junior class at Union College, graduating in 1870. The influence of Professor Tayler Lewis was decisive in making the young man a student of literature, particularly of the Bible. He completed his course at Rochester Theological Seminary in 1875, was ordained in the Baptist ministry, and held for three years a pastorate at Baldwinsville, N. Y. He officiated at the American Chapel in Leipzig while studying for his Ph.D. at the University, and was pastor for one year at Westport, N. Y., after his return from Germany. Meanwhile, May 15, 1880, he had married Florence M. Sprague of Oswego, N. Y.

His real career began with his appointment in 1882 as instructor of English language in Amherst College, where he became associate professor (1884), professor of rhetoric (1889), of literary and Biblical interpretation (1906), and professor emeritus (1917). Immediately upon taking up his college duties he prepared for his students a small manual of selections for rhetorical analysis, which grew through successive stages into *The Working Principles of Rhetoric* (1901), a masterly treatment of the philosophy of composition based on years of sound reading and ripe deliberation, and still unsuperseded in its class. His Biblical studies bore fruit in a translation and commentary on the Book of Job, *The Epic of the Inner Life* (1891); *Ecclesiastes, Words of Koheleth* (1904); *The Hebrew Literature of Wisdom in the Light of Today* (1906); *A Guidebook to the Biblical Literature* (1919), and many articles in Biblical encyclopedias and reviews. As an interpreter of modern literature he is best represented in *Tennyson's In Memoriam* (1884), a rewriting of his doctoral dissertation; *Stevenson's Attitude to Life* (1901); and *The Idylls and the Ages* (1907). He was the first editor of the *Amherst Graduates' Quarterly* (1911–18) and at the time of his death was engaged in writing a history of Amherst College. His genial and deeply spiritual nature is well shown in an article on his dog Caleb, "My Lowly Teacher" (*Harper's Magazine*, May 1911), and in his posthumous book, *The Life Indeed* (1921).

Always the gentlest of teachers, Professor Genung was noted for his kindliness and wit. His classes were both a haven of refuge for the unthinking many and a source of lasting inspiration for the few students capable of appreciating his fine scholarship and rich stores of wisdom. Outside the classroom he touched the life of the community in many ways. His evening readings from Tennyson and Browning were largely attended by students and townspeople alike. As a devoted musician he played the viola in the college orchestra and organized weekly concerts of chamber music in his own home. He served for years as a member of the town planning board and was active in support of the local Baptist church. He was capable of designing a house, engrossing and illuminating a manuscript, and writing both words and music of a hymn or college song. Habits of early rising and earnest application enabled him to perform a prodigious amount of work in spite of the loving deliberation that he gave to every detail, yet he always had time for a walk with his dog before breakfast or for a cheerful hour after supper with students or colleagues, lovers of music or good reading. Two songs for which he wrote the words, "The Soul of Old Amherst" and "Memory Song," form a traditional part of the Commencement exercises at the college of his adoption.

[M. J. G. Nichols, *Genung-Ganong-Ganung Geneal.* (1906); *Rochester Theol. Sem. Gen. Cat.* (1910); *Who's Who in America*, 1918–19; memorial articles by J. M. Tyler, John Erskine, and others, *Amherst Grads. Quart.*, Feb. 1920—Tyler's article is reprinted as introduction to *The Life Indeed*; G. F. Whicher, "Genung's Rhetoric," *Nation* (N. Y.), Nov. 22, 1919; *Boston Transcript, Springfield Republican*, Oct. 2, 1919.]

G. F. W.

GEORGE, HENRY (Sept. 2, 1839–Oct. 29, 1897), economist, reformer, was born in a little brick house in Philadelphia, on the east side of Tenth St., south of Pine. His paternal grandparents were Richard George, a shipmaster of Philadelphia, born in Yorkshire, England, and Mary Reid of Philadelphia. His maternal grandparents were John Vallance, an engraver, born in Glasgow, Scotland, and Margaret Pratt, born in Philadelphia. Henry George's father was Richard Samuel Henry George, born in New Brunswick, N. J., in 1798, who married as his second wife Catherine Pratt Vallance. Henry was the second child and oldest boy of ten children. He thus belonged to middle-class stock, of English and Scotch blood, with a tradition of Welsh. His father was a robust personality, of alert mind and common sense. He had been a dry-goods merchant in New Orleans and then a clerk in the custom-house at Philadelphia. In 1831 he had entered the business of publishing and selling religious books, which he carried on for seventeen years, returning then to the custom-house as ascertaining clerk. His mother had conducted a small private school before her marriage. Both parents were strongly religious, the mother excessively so. The father was a vestryman in St. Paul's Episcopal Church. Henry George from early childhood went to numerous services regularly, and heard family prayers morning and evening. This religious atmosphere doubtless strengthened certain native qualities—idealism and his sense of justice. The tone of many passages in his writings is suffused with exalted spirituality. Also, in this evangelical upbringing, may be found one clue to the doctrinaire quality of his mind.

His schooling was brief and uneventful. He attended Mrs. Graham's private school, on Catherine St., until nine, spent a year in the Mount Vernon Grammar School, and a short and disappointing period in the Episcopal Academy. His happiest school experience was with Henry Y. Lauderbach, who prepared him for high school. In the high school, he said later, he was "for the most part idle"; in less than five months he persuaded his father to put him to work, and before his fourteenth birthday he became errand boy for Samuel Asbury & Company, at two dollars a week. He afterwards did clerical work in the office of a marine adjuster. Though he had left school forever, his reading was unusually wide and fervid. His strong love of verse, inherited from his mother, remained a characteristic all his life. He courted his wife over Dana's *Household Book of Poetry;* he prefaced his day's work on *Progress and Poverty* with a half-hour of poetry read to his children; and constantly his prose fell into cadences akin to blank verse. His reading was supplemented by popular scientific lectures at the Franklin Institute.

Much of his free time he spent about the waterfront. His grandfather had been a sea-captain, his father loved the water, and the boy set his mind on a voyage. Not long before, he had an altercation with his father, and left home, but returned repentant at night. The father now had the sense to let Henry have his fling, and consented to his sailing as foremast boy in the *Hindoo,* an old East Indiaman, bound for Melbourne and Calcutta. A daguerreotype taken just before he sailed in 1855 shows clear-cut, somewhat wilful features, and dark hair thick and wavy. He kept a diary during the whole voyage, recounting every incident in lively language. After a hundred and thirty-seven days the land of Australia was sighted. This was his first contact with a country newly populated by a gold rush. He saw Melbourne briefly, but remembered "its busy streets, its seemingly continuous auctions, its crowds of men with flannel shirts and long high boots, its bay crowded with ships" (Henry George, Jr., *The Life of Henry George,* p. 32). Two months later, early in December 1856, the *Hindoo* made her way up the Hoogly branch of the Ganges to Calcutta. The boy wrote an account in his journal of the contrasting scenes of poverty and riches—contrasts which may have recurred in his thoughts afterwards.

On reaching home in April 1856, he was unable to find work and thought of going to sea again; but after six months he entered the printing-office of King & Baird to learn typesetting. He was identified with printing and publishing in one way and another for the rest of his life; the printer's case and newspaper offices gave him no small part of his education. His polemic qualities were apparent at this period. He was high-strung and impetuous. After nine months at King & Baird's, he quarreled with the foreman and quit. There followed a period of idleness, interspersed with occasional work. Once he turned strike-breaker. Then he went as an able seaman on a topsail schooner to Boston and back. Hearing of the good wages paid in Oregon, he resolved to make his way to the West. He was given the berth of steward on the U. S. lighthouse ship *Shubrick,* which sailed from Philadelphia, Dec. 22, 1857, through the Straits of Magellan for San Francisco. Thither his cousin, James George, had brought his family and Ellen, his wife. They now interceded with the commander of the *Shubrick* to permit Henry to leave the ship before expiration of his time. Receiving news of unemployment in Oregon, and finding no work in San Francisco, he determined to seek his fortune at the newly discovered placer gold-mines on the Frazer River. Unable to proceed at once to the diggings on account of floods, he worked for a time in a miner's supply store that his cousin had opened at Victoria, but fell out with his employer. News from the mines proving disappointing, he borrowed money for a steerage passage back to San Francisco, resolved if nothing opened there to take to the sea for life. Soon after arrival, December 1858, through a Philadelphia printer-friend whom he met, he got work setting type. He received sixteen dollars a week, and paid nine for board and room at the What Cheer House, a men's temperance hotel, which contained a library of several hundred good books. Though he did not read it until years afterwards, it was here that Henry George first saw Adam Smith's *Wealth of Nations.* Work becoming slack, he lost his job, struck out into the interior on a fruitless gold-prospecting expedition, returned to San Francisco with renewed thoughts of the sea, but relinquished these forever when he got work as a compositor on the *Home Journal,* at boy's wages of twelve dollars a week. Through the influence of a friend, he dropped the disbelief in religion which had been growing upon him, and joined the Methodist Church. On coming of age, he joined the Eureka Typographical Union, and soon was foreman at thirty dollars a week. When the *Home Journal* changed hands, he turned to "subbing" on the dailies, and then joined with five other printers in the publication of a small daily of their own, the *Evening Journal.* He worked himself into rags for this venture, only to sell out for the promise of a pittance when he realized that a paper not in the Associated Press and so unable to get the quick news service over the new transcontinental telegraph could not hope to compete with its rivals.

He was in debt and without work. A year before he had fallen in love with Annie Corsina Fox, daughter of Maj. John Fox, of the English army, and Elizabeth A. McCloskey, whose parents were from Limerick and County Clare. She had been born in Australia and had recently come to San Francisco from a convent school at Los Angeles. His ardor in courtship routed another to whom she was engaged, but the uncle who was her guardian disapproved of George because of his poverty. The two had violent words, and Henry George and Annie Fox determined to marry at once. The marriage took place on Dec. 3, 1861, despite the fact that he was penniless and had to borrow decent clothes for the ceremony. Now began heart-breaking years for the young couple. They moved to Sacramento, where the husband did "subbing" on the *Union*. If he got a few dollars ahead, he was apt to put them in a mining venture which brought assessments rather than dividends. The birth of his first child, November 1862, made matters harder. Twice he was discharged for disputes with his foreman. Drifting back to San Francisco, after trying to solicit newspaper subscriptions and to sell clothes-wringers, he joined with two friends in a job-printing office. He even printed cards and labels in exchange for meal, wood, and milk. His wife pawned her trinkets. The second child was born in the midst of this destitution. The doctor had said that mother and child were starving. George stopped the first well-dressed man he met on the street and asked him for five dollars. If the stranger had not been moved by his story, Henry George said later, he was prepared to knock him down. These desperate years gave him a burning personal knowledge of poverty which was reflected in all he afterwards wrote and did. For a time he tried to sell carriage-brakes. Most men would have found these difficult circumstances in which to begin a program of self-improvement in writing, but he set about it. Thus this spring of 1865 marked a turning point in his career. He wrote on a variety of topics for practise or for publication in obscure journals, one of them the *Californian,* to which Bret Harte and Mark Twain were contributors. His style from the first had been clear, natural, and interesting, but as he wrote more it gained in ease and effectiveness.

Though physically removed from the struggle, he was deeply sympathetic with the Union in the Civil War; a newspaper article on the assassination of Lincoln, deposited anonymously in the editor's box of the paper on which he was setting type, opened a way for further paid writing. He joined an abortive filibustering expedition to liberate Mexico from Maximilian, but luckily never got away from San Francisco. In the summer of 1865 the family moved back to Sacramento, and it was here, in a debating society, that a speech in favor of protection converted him from a protectionist to a free trader. The latter view afterwards became a central tenet in his economic philosophy. In November 1866 George returned to San Francisco as printer on the newly established *Times,* and was quickly promoted to reporter, editorial writer, and then managing editor, in the last position earning fifty dollars a week and something for outside correspondence. Unable to increase his salary, he left the paper in October 1868. At this time appeared in the *Overland Monthly,* October 1868, the first of his articles which anticipated his thesis. The long-awaited transcontinental railroad was about to be completed. "What the Railroad Will Bring Us" took the view that increasing population and business activity would result in greater wealth for the few and greater poverty for the many. "The tendency of the new era . . . will be to a reduction both of the rate of interest and the rate of wages, particularly the latter." He saw that the pioneer prosperity of California was due to the fact that the "natural wealth of the country was not yet monopolized—that great opportunities were open to all." Late in 1868 he revisited the East as agent for the San Francisco *Herald,* seeking to get the paper admitted to the Associated Press. This being refused, he established an independent news service, but this was discontinued because of the jealousy of the Associated Press. Yet this stay in the East was of primary importance in his own mental development, for in New York City which, particularly in the eyes of a frontiersman, represented the height of civilization, and should have exhibited social adjustment, he was struck with the "shocking contrast between monstrous wealth and debasing want." Why did progress have its twin in poverty? He resolved to devote his life to discovering the cause of this anomaly in an otherwise harmonious natural scheme.

Returning to California, George became editor of the newly established Oakland *Transcript,* a Democratic paper. Disgusted with Grant as president, he had given his allegiance to the Democratic party. The railroad had just been completed to Sacramento, and extension to Oakland was imminent. Land speculation was rife. One day while riding into the hills about Oakland, he stopped to talk to a passing teamster, and was told the enormous prices of agricultural land. Suddenly it came to him that here was the answer to the question he had asked himself in New York—why advancing wealth entailed advancing poverty. He saw then that "with the growth in population, land grows in value, and the men who work it must pay more for the privilege. I turned back, amidst quiet thought, to the perception that then came to me and has been with me ever since" (Henry George, Jr., *The Life of Henry George,* 1900, p. 210). The rest of his life was given to explaining and proclaiming this thesis. In the fall of 1869 he became a candidate for the California Assembly, but was defeated by the influence of the Central Pacific Railroad, subsidies to which he had opposed. In the summer of 1871, after four months' work, he published a forty-eight page pamphlet, *Our Land and Land Policy,* which contained the essentials of the philosophy which he afterwards expanded: that every man has a natural right to apply his labor to land; that when land is in private ownership and he must pay a rent for the privilege of working land, he is robbed of some of his labor; that taxes should be laid upon land values only, thus taking for the community what the community has produced, and relieving industry and enterprise of the incubus which other taxes represent. A thousand copies of this pamphlet were sold, but George saw that "to command attention the work must be done more thoroughly." In December 1871 he became partner and editor in publishing the *Daily Evening Post,* which exposed public abuses. After four years the paper was given up to its creditors. He was now without a means to broadcast his views. He determined upon an important piece of writing, nevertheless, and for support persuaded his friend, Gov. Irwin, to appoint him state inspector of gas meters. He took office in January 1876. In the summer of this year he spoke in behalf of Tilden in the presidential campaign in California, and gained some reputation as an orator. In the spring of 1877 he was mentioned for the chair of political economy about to be established in the University of California, and was invited to deliver a lecture on "The Study of Political Economy" before the students of the University (printed in the *Popular Science Monthly,* March 1880). He charged the orthodox economists with upholding the rich and damning the poor, pled that the science had been complicated contrary to its nature, and made sharp sallies against conventional education. He believed it was his forthrightness which prevented his being tendered a chair in the University. His oration on the Fourth of July at the San Francisco civic celebration marked an advance in his thought. He spoke now not of California but of mankind, declaring that republican institutions must break down under an inequitable distribution of wealth. He now determined to employ his leisure to give his answer to the problem which had "appalled and tormented" him—why want goes with wealth. He started the writing of *Progress and Poverty* on Sept. 18, 1877, during the depression following the panic of 1873. There were labor troubles and riots throughout the country, and particularly in San Francisco. He first intended to write a magazine article giving the solution for industrial depressions, but finally decided to give full expression to the ideas which he had had in mind since the writing of *Our Land and Land Policy.* The work was early interrupted by several public lectures on the same subject, including his most famous address, "Moses," and by his participation in the election of delegates to the state constitutional convention. Though he was defeated, he led the Democratic ticket. The manuscript which he finally completed by the middle of March 1879 was a definitive and elaborated statement of the thesis, that as all men have an equal right to apply their labor to natural resources, economic rent is robbery, and, by the necessity of paying economic rent, labor, capital, and enterprise receive less return than is their due. To cure this condition, it is not necessary to distribute land; it is necessary only to take economic rent in taxation, abolishing all other contributions to government. This will insure the smooth working of natural economic laws, which, thus freed, will make for an equitable sharing of wealth; monopoly, being grounded in appropriation of land values, will disappear, and so economic society will not be subject to the recurrent seizures called industrial depressions.

His main contentions had been anticipated in part by the writings of Quesnay and the Physiocrats, of Spence, Ogilvie, Paine, and Dove, in the eighteenth century, and those of James and John Stuart Mill, Marx, Spencer, and others in the nineteenth century; but when George formulated his ideas in *Our Land and Land Policy* (1871), he knew nothing of these earlier works. He did not give the works of the classical economists a careful reading until he began his *Progress and Poverty*; though when he did so, he was confirmed in his views by the Ricardian exposition of rent. He was not only perfectly original, but he accomplished a synthesis and gave his message a singular force and beauty. The manuscript was sent to various publishers, but all declined to publish it. Then his friend, William M. Hinton, still in the printing business, offered to make plates of the book and from these an author's edition of 500 copies was published in 1879. Finally the Appletons offered to bring out the regular edition if furnished the plates. It appeared early in 1880.

Now began the career of Henry George as a propagandist. In August 1880 he moved to New York, and eked out a living by lecturing and magazine writing while the book, which began with tardy notice, gained recognition from reviewers and gathered sales here and abroad. In 1881 he published *The Irish Land Question,* which resulted in his sailing for Ireland (October 1881) as correspondent for the *Irish World* of New York. He remained abroad almost a year, writing and speaking in Ireland and England, and always in close association with leaders of the Irish Land League. His books were now published in large cheap editions and he became a public figure. On his return to New York he was tendered a welcoming meeting by workingmen at Cooper Union and a brilliant dinner at Delmonico's. For *Frank Leslie's Illustrated Newspaper* he wrote the series of articles afterwards published as *Social Problems* (1883). He refused proposals to start newspapers in New York and London, but he agreed to lecture in England under auspices of the Land Reform Union, and sailed in December 1883 on what proved to be a triumphal tour. At the invitation of the Scottish Land Restoration League he made another successful lecturing tour of Great Britain at the end of 1884. His *Protection or Free Trade* was published in book form early in 1886.

In the fall of this year he ran for mayor of New York City, backed by most of the labor organizations and a large number of liberals. The campaign was spectacular and fierce. Because he injected the issue of thorough-going social betterment into the campaign, he was branded as a dangerous fanatic by the Tammany and reform Democrats, whose candidate was Abram S. Hewitt. His social-welfare program, nevertheless, brought ardent support to his candidacy. Though Hewitt was elected with 90,552 votes, George came next with 68,110; while Theodore Roosevelt received 60,435. George lacked party machinery, particularly watchers at the polls, and he believed that he was counted out. Immediately after the campaign he urged the adoption of the Australian ballot system which he had advocated for fifteen years. Then followed the organization of Land and Labor Clubs throughout the country to support his principles. He began publication of a weekly, the *Standard,* which in the first numbers was filled with news of the case of Dr. Edward McGlynn [*q.v.*], pastor of St. Stephen's Catholic Church, who was excommunicated, George's followers maintained, because he espoused the doctrine of what now came to be known as the "Single Tax." George was defeated for secretary of state on the United Labor Party ticket in 1887. The years 1888 and 1889 witnessed two more trips to the British Isles, where he spoke to audiences ever better acquainted with his views. He paid a long visit to Australia in 1890, lecturing incessantly and laying the foundation for later applications of the single-tax doctrine there. On his return the first national conference of single-tax men was held in New York.

Late in this year he suffered a stroke of aphasia, and went to the Bermudas to recuperate. In the spring of the next year he was able to begin work on *The Science of Political Economy,* finally published in 1897. It was interrupted by the writing of *An Open Letter to the Pope* (1891) in reply to Leo XIII's encyclical, *The Condition of Labor;* and by *A Perplexed Philosopher* (1892), his castigation of Herbert Spencer for changing his views regarding land and its taxation. George's *Standard* ceased publication in August 1892, following dissensions in the staff, and a declining circulation. He campaigned for Bryan in the presidential election of 1896, believing the gold standard to be the expedient of privilege. In the autumn of 1897 he was for a second time a candidate for mayor of New York, now running as an independent Democrat. The attempt was ill-advised. He was broken in health and he knew the campaign endangered his life, but he believed duty called. Contrary to first resolve, he spoke four or five times a night. His last speech, in the Central Opera House, the night of October 28, showed his great weariness. He succumbed to a stroke of apoplexy at the Union Square Hotel early in the following morning. His body lay in state in the Grand Central Palace, where a hundred thousand persons, it was said, passed before the bier. Public services were held in this hall, and private services in his house at Fort Hamilton, Father McGlynn taking part in both. Henry George was buried beside his daughter Jenny in Greenwood Cemetery, Brooklyn.

[*The Life of Henry George* (1900), by Henry George, Jr.; *The Science of Political Economy,* and to a less extent *Protection or Free Trade,* contain autobiographical references. See also L. F. Post, *The Prophet of San Francisco: Personal Memories and Interpretations of Henry George* (1930) and *An Account of the George-Hewitt Campaign* (1886). The best statement of his principles is in *Progress and Poverty,* which provoked a large controversial literature. For the progress of George's ideas, see A. N. Young, *The Single Tax Movement in the United States* (1916); Joseph Dana Miller, *Has the Single Tax Made Progress?* (pamphlet reprint from *Dearborn Independent*); C. W. Huntington, *Enclaves of Single Tax,* 1921 and following years. R. A. Sawyer, *Henry George and the Single Tax* (1926) contains a list of manuscripts in the New York Public Library and a full bibliography of his writings and of publications concerning him and his works.] B. M.

GEORGE, HENRY (Nov. 3, 1862–Nov. 14, 1916), journalist, was the eldest child of Henry George [*q.v.*], founder of the single-tax movement, and Annie Fox. He was born in Sacramento, Cal., when his parents were enduring the first of many years of bitter poverty. When he had completed the public grammar-school course in San Francisco, whither the family had moved, the father considered that the son had had enough formal education and made him his amanuensis. Henry George was engaged at this time in writing his *Progress and Poverty.* The boy helped with the copying of the manuscript, at the same time studied shorthand, and for years thereafter was his father's intimate clerical helper. When the manuscript of the study was completed, in 1879, he entered a printing-office, learning to set type as his father had done. In 1880 the family moved to New York, and the next year Henry George, his wife and two daughters, sailed for Ireland, to be gone a year. It was decided that the son should become a reporter on the *Brooklyn Eagle,* where a place had been made for him by Andrew McLean. His father chose this in preference to sending him to Harvard because of his distrust of academic learning. The son in after life followed rules for writing which his father gave him at that time—to make short sentences, use small words, avoid adjectives, and shun "fine writing." In 1883–84 he accompanied his father as secretary on a lecturing tour of Great Britain.

When the Henry George organ, the *Standard,* started publication in New York in 1887, young George became correspondence editor, an important post on a paper intended to be the bellwether of a movement. The next year, when his father went to England again, he became the paper's managing editor; but the *Standard* was already declining, and the son was unable to prevent disaffection in the staff. He had gone through the New York mayoralty campaign with his father in 1886, and again was constantly at his side in the second mayoralty campaign in 1897. When his father died of apoplexy five days before the election, he was nominated to carry the banner of the Jeffersonian party, but received, naturally, only a courtesy vote. Later in the same year, on Dec. 2, 1897, he was married to Marie M. Hitch, of Chicago.

George served as Washington correspondent of the Philadelphia *North American,* New York *World,* and *New York American.* In 1906 he went to Japan as correspondent for an American syndicate, and made a similar trip around the world in 1909. In this year he took part in the British budget campaign and visited Count Leo Tolstoy, who had been an admirer of his father. In 1910 he was elected to Congress from the 17th New York District, winning on an anti-tariff platform in a district normally heavily Republican. He was reëlected in 1912. He will be longest remembered for his *Life of Henry George* (1900), a first-rate biography. *The Menace of Privilege* (1905) applied the single-tax doctrine to the abolition of monopolies of the day; *The Romance of John Bainbridge* (1906) undertook to novelize the life of his father, but with little success. He was unnecessarily burdened with the sense of responsibility for carrying on the single-tax movement, which was well established apart from the further efforts of any one person.

[J. D. Miller, in *Land and Freedom,* Sept.–Oct. 1929; Louis F. Post, in the *Public,* Nov. 17, 1916; the *Single Tax Rev.,* Nov.–Dec. 1916; *N. Y. Times,* Nov. 15, 1916. His own *Life of Henry George* contains some autobiographical references.] B. M.

GEORGE, JAMES ZACHARIAH (Oct. 20, 1826–Aug. 14, 1897), soldier, jurist, United States senator, was born in Monroe County, Ga., the son of Mary Chamblis and Joseph Warren George. The latter died in the early infancy of the child, who was brought in 1834 by his mother and stepfather to Noxubee County, Miss. Two years later the family moved to Carroll County, which, with the exception of the years from 1872 to 1887, was George's residence until his death. Aside from such training as the old-field schools afforded, he was self-educated. He participated in both the Mexican and Civil wars, serving in the former as a private in the regiment of Col. Jefferson Davis. He entered the Civil War with the rank of captain and was advanced to colonel. Though brave, he did not have a distinguished military career, owing partly to the fact that he was twice captured and spent a total of twenty-five months on Johnson's Island. During a period of ill health he also served as brigadier-general of state troops.

George was admitted to the bar shortly after his return from the Mexican War and, the following week, was married to Elizabeth Young of Carrollton. In 1854 he was elected reporter of the supreme court of Mississippi and was reëlected in 1860, publishing ten volumes of Mississippi *Reports,* covering the decisions of the court between 1855 and 1863. After the Civil War, he resumed the practise of law. In addition he prepared a *Digest of the Reports* (1872), comprising all the decisions of the supreme court through 1870. This was a careful piece of work in spite of the perplexing questions troubling the courts as a result of war and reconstruction. In 1872, with Wiley P. Harris, he formed a law partnership in Jackson which was preëminent in the state in its day. His leadership in the restoration of native white supremacy in Mississippi and in the overthrow of Gov. Ames brought him great popularity in the state, but these things made him an unavailable candidate for a seat in Congress. In 1879, however, he was appointed to the bench of the supreme court of Mississippi. His ranking associates accorded him the signal honor of at once choosing him chief justice. Though in this office but two years, he rendered a number of important decisions, all marked by their clarity and thorough preparation.

From Mar. 4, 1881, until his death, George

represented Mississippi in the United States Senate. The unifying thread of his senatorial career was his leadership in the defense of his state and the South from federal interference. His authorship of the minority report of the judiciary committee, and his skill in debate, were chiefly responsible for the defeat of the "Bill to Provide for Inquests under National Authority" (*Congressional Record,* 50 Cong., 1 Sess., pp. 8942–51). In addition to being the only Democrat to have an important share in the framing of the Sherman Anti-Trust Law of 1890, he wisely, though unsuccessfully, sought to exempt agreements among workingmen from the operations of the act. Finally, he defended the constitution of Mississippi of 1890 against the vigorous assaults which were made against it. He had participated in the convention which framed this constitution, and had written the clause dealing with the right of suffrage. This clause was the chief point of attack in the Senate, and it was successfully and ably defended by Senator George. In the last few years of his life, he prepared *The Political History of Slavery in the United States* (1915). Death cut short his full plan for the work, and the part he finished was not published until some years after his death. George's strength lay in a great knowledge of law and human nature, and an honest use of this knowledge. His skill as a lawyer made him a force to be reckoned with, but he was chiefly impelled to his activities by an understanding of and love for the common man, which was warmly reciprocated. He is remembered as the "Great Commoner" of Mississippi.

[George's *Pol. Hist. of Slavery* contains a brief biography; his private papers are in the custody of his son, J. W. George, Greenwood, Miss. Other material is to be found in the *Official Records (Army)*; the *Commercial-Appeal* (Memphis, Tenn.), Aug. 15, 1897; the *Cong. Record,* 55 Cong., 2 Sess., pp. 3657–66, 5195–5207; and the *Miss. Hist. Soc. Pubs.,* vol. VII (1903), vol. VIII (1904).] C. S. S.

GERARD, JAMES WATSON (1794–Feb. 7, 1874), lawyer, philanthropist, was of Scotch and French descent. His father, William Gerard, born in Banff in the Highlands of Scotland, was a member of a French family which had fled thither to escape religious persecution. He emigrated about 1780 to New York City, where he married Christina Glass and became a prosperous merchant. There his son, James Watson Gerard, was born. The younger Gerard obtained his early education from private tutors. Entering Columbia College while yet a boy he graduated in 1811, being third in his class and distinguishing himself in mathematics and the classics. On the outbreak of the War of 1812, he enlisted and served in one of the volunteer companies raised for the purpose of defending New York City. On the conclusion of the war he entered the office of George Griffin, one of the leading New York lawyers, and was admitted to the bar in 1816. He had read widely, and was instrumental in forming a debating society called the Forum, in whose discussions he, with Fessenden, Hoffman, and other brilliant juniors constantly participated. His first retainer was on behalf of a boy fourteen years old who was indicted for the theft of a canary, and the circumstances of the case—it being the accused's first offense—made so strong an impression upon him that he determined to take steps to assist in the reformation of junior offenders. He joined the Society for the Prevention of Pauperism, and was a prime mover in the appointment of a special committee which investigated the subject of juvenile delinquency. He strongly advocated the creation of an asylum for youthful criminals where they would be safe from contamination by hardened convicts, and procured the incorporation, on Mar. 29, 1824, of the Society for the Reformation of Juvenile Delinquents, whose House of Refuge, built shortly, was the first institution of its kind in the country. As a member of the board of managers, Gerard contributed powerfully to its successful operation. Though he was now enjoying an extensive practise at the bar, he continued to devote much of his time and means to social reform, identifying himself with all movements having for their object the amelioration of distress, the advancement of the best interests of the city, and efficient administration. *Inter alia,* he induced great reforms in the police system and was the first to advocate the wearing of uniforms by policemen. In 1854, having always been a consistent opponent of slavery, he took a leading part in the agitation against the passage of the Kansas-Nebraska Bill. His greatest services in his later years were rendered in the cause of popular education. For twenty years, first as a school trustee and later as inspector of the fifth school district, he was indefatigable in raising the standard of public educational training. Though on more than one occasion offered the position of commissioner of the Board of Education, he uniformly declined that and all other public office, maintaining that he could do more effective work as inspector than in any other capacity. After his retirement from legal practise in 1869 he devoted all his time to the improvement of educational methods.

As a lawyer, he had an uneventful career, distinguished only by a steady advancement to the headship of the New York bar. Industry and perseverance were his chief characteristics, but he was an advocate by instinct and became the leading jury lawyer of his time. Charles O'Conor said that "his powers of persuasion were marvellous." Indefatigable in the preparation of his cases, gifted with an intuitive knowledge of human nature, and knowing when to stop in addressing a jury, "he tried more causes than any other member of the profession and . . . he tried them more successfully than any other. At *nisi prius* he was unrivalled" (*Proceedings of the Bar,* p. 8). He married on Oct. 3, 1820, Elizabeth, daughter of Increase Sumner, chief justice of the supreme judicial court and governor of Massachusetts.

["Genealogical and Biographical Sketch of the Late James W. Gerard," by J. W. Gerard, Jr., in *N. Y. Geneal. and Biog. Record,* July 1874; *Proc. of the Bar of N. Y. in Memory of James W. Gerard* (1874); *Prominent Families of N. Y.* (1897), ed. by L. H. Weeks; *N. Y. Times,* Feb. 8, 1874; *N. Y. Herald,* Feb. 10, 1874.]
H. W. H. K.

GERHARD, WILLIAM WOOD (July 23, 1809–Apr. 28, 1872), Philadelphia physician, was the great-grandson of Frederick Gerhard, a follower of the Moravian faith, who emigrated to Berks County, Pa., from Hesse-Darmstadt (Germany) in 1737, and the eldest son of William Gerhard of Philadelphia by his wife, Sarah Wood of Salem County, N. J., a gentlewoman of Irish descent. As a youth he was industrious and fond of books, and in 1823 entered Dickinson College, Carlisle, graduating in 1826 (A.B.). He then returned to Philadelphia to study medicine with Dr. Joseph Parrish [*q.v.*], under whose guidance he obtained his M.D. from the University of Pennsylvania in 1830. His thesis on the endermic application of medicaments (*North American Medical and Surgical Journal,* vols. IX–X, 1830), attracted wide attention. In 1831 he went to Paris, where he followed Chomel, Andral, and Louis and had opportunity to study the Asiatic cholera epidemic of 1831–32, which he later described with C. W. Pennock (*American Journal of the Medical Sciences,* August 1832). A large part of his two years abroad was spent observing diseases of children, which at that time had been little studied. Based upon the material collected at Paris he published a series of important papers on the pathology of smallpox (*Ibid.,* February 1833), pneumonia in children (*Ibid.,* August and November 1834), and his well-known study of tuberculous meningitis, "On Cerebral Affections of Children" (*Ibid.,* February and May 1834), which was the first important contribution to the subject since the disease was described by Whytt in 1768. Gerhard's fame, however, rests upon his paper published in 1837, in which typhus was for the first time clearly distinguished from typhoid fever: "On the Typhus Fever, which Occurred at Philadelphia in . . . 1836 . . . showing the Distinction between this Form of Disease and . . . Typhoid Fever with Alteration of the Follicles of the Small Intestine" (*Ibid.,* February and August 1837). Employing the numerical method which he had learned from Louis in Paris, he meticulously analyzed the records of 214 cases all personally studied during the epidemic of 1836, and, finding no evidence of intestinal lesions, declared positively that the disease differed fundamentally from the typhoid fever of Louis (with which he was also intimately familiar). The conclusion was quickly accepted in America where the influence of Louis had already made itself felt, but in England the separation of the two diseases was not accredited until Sir William Jenner's paper on the subject was issued in 1849. Gerhard made only one other important contribution to medical literature. This was his paper on epidemic meningitis published in 1863.

During his student days Gerhard served at the Philadelphia Alms House, and from 1834 to 1868 he was resident physician at the Pennsylvania General Hospital. He also taught the Institutes of Medicine (physiology) at the University of Pennsylvania (1838–72), but, according to Stillé, "from about 1850 Gerhard suffered from disease within the cranium [arteriosclerosis], which, although it did not render him a paralytic or an imbecile, extinguished every spark of his ambition, and caused a permanent halt in his acquisition of knowledge. He repeated over and over his old lectures, but added to them nothing new" (Osler, "Stillé," *post*). In his early days as a clinical teacher he was much sought after for instruction in diseases of the heart and lungs, on which subject he wrote two books (*On the Diagnosis of Diseases of the Chest,* 1836; *Lectures on the Diagnosis, Pathology and Treatment of the Diseases of the Chest,* 1842), the second of which passed through four editions (4th, 1860). He was plain and direct as a lecturer, stimulating his hearers more by his simplicity than his rhetoric. Personally he was distant and devoid of strong personal attachments, but as a worker he was singularly assiduous, observant, and meticulous. In 1850 he married the daughter of Maj. William A. Dobbyn, by whom he had three children.

[The best biography is that by Thomas Stewardson, in *Trans. Coll. Phys. of Phila.,* n.s. IV (1874), 473–81. See also F. H. Garrison, *Introduction to the Hist. of Medicine* (4th ed., 1929), pp. 440–41; Wm. Osler, "The Influence of Louis on American Medicine," *Johns Hopkins Hosp. Bull.,* Aug.–Sept. 1897, and "Alfred Stillé,"

Univ. Pa. Medic. Bull., June 1902, both of which are reprinted in Osler's *Alabama Student* (1908); obituary in *Public Ledger* (Phila.), Apr. 29, 1872.] J. F. F.

GERHART, EMANUEL VOGEL (June 13, 1817–May 6, 1904), German Reformed theologian, college president, was born at Freeburg, Snyder County, Pa., the son of the Rev. Isaac and Sarah (Vogel) Gerhart and great-grandson of Peter Gerhard, who came to Pennsylvania from Alsace in 1730 and settled in Bucks County. After preliminary instruction by his father he was sent in 1833 to the Classical Institute of the Reformed Church at York, but by the time of his graduation in 1838 the Institute had moved to Mercersburg and become Marshall College. He continued his studies in the Mercersburg Theological Seminary, supporting himself meanwhile by teaching. In both college and seminary he was strongly influenced by his teacher, Frederick Augustus Rauch. He was licensed to preach in October 1841 and ordained at the Grindstone Hill Church near Chambersburg in August 1842. The following May he became pastor at Gettysburg, ministering in German and English to four congregations until July 1, 1849, when he went to the First Reformed Church of Cincinnati to labor among the unchurched Germans of that city. While stationed there he made missionary journeys on horseback through parts of Kentucky, Ohio, Indiana, and Wisconsin. When in 1851 the Ohio Synod opened a theological seminary in connection with Heidelberg College at Tiffin, Ohio, Gerhart was made president and professor of theology. A few years later his alma mater merged with Franklin College at Lancaster, Pa., and on July 26, 1854, he was elected president of Franklin and Marshall College, John Williamson Nevin and Philip Schaff having previously declined the office. On taking charge in 1855 he found that the college had few students, no money, and little prospect of either. Resolutely he set to work, traveling up and down the country to plead for students and financial support. At one time he barely saved the buildings of the two literary societies from being attached by the sheriff. His untiring devotion brought Franklin and Marshall through the panic of 1857 and the hard times that followed and through the greater crisis of the Civil War, thus assuring the survival of the institution. In the meantime Nevin expressed a willingness to assume the presidency, and the trustees, eager to secure the prestige of his name, gave Gerhart a testimonial of regard and gratitude and created for him the title of vice-president. He continued, however, to occupy the chair of philosophy and was probably too selfless to resent the ingratitude of the trustees. In 1868 he was elected president and professor of systematic theology in the Mercersburg Theological Seminary, which in 1871 was moved to Lancaster. There he taught indefatigably until a week before his death at the age of eighty-seven. During all these years he was one of the leaders of his denomination, acting regularly as a Synodical delegate from 1843 to 1902, serving as president of the Ohio, the Eastern, and the General Synod, and contributing frequently to the *Mercersburg Review*, the *Reformed Church Review*, and other religious papers. He influenced strongly the doctrinal and liturgical development of the German Reformed Church and was the most eminent of the later proponents of the "Mercersburg theology." In his eightieth year, while a delegate to the Pan-Presbyterian Alliance at Glasgow, in 1896, he amazed his traveling companions by his energy and endurance. In manner he was always dignified and unruffled, in speech deliberate and meticulously logical.

He published *An Introduction to the Study of Philosophy* (1858), *Prolegomena to Christian Dogmatics* (1891), and *Institutes of the Christian Religion* (vol. I, 1891; vol. II, 1894)—the latter a work of great learning but repetitious and cumbersome in style. He edited a volume of Rauch's sermons, *The Inner Life of the Christian* (1856) and the "Triglot" edition in Latin, German, and English of the *Heidelberg Catechism* (1883).

He was married three times: on Jan. 3, 1843, at Hagerstown, Md., to Eliza Rickenbaugh, who died in January 1864; in August 1865 to Mary M. Hunter, widow of Frederick S. Hunter of Reading, Pa., who died the following year; and on Dec. 29, 1875, to Lucia, daughter of the Rev. Ashabel Cobb of New Bedford, Mass., who survived him.

[*Franklin and Marshall Coll. Obit. Record,* June 1904; article by E. N. Kremer in the *Reformed Ch. Rev.*, Oct. 1904; J. H. Dubbs, *Hist. of Franklin and Marshall Coll.* (1903); *Who's Who in America*, 1903–05.] G. H. G.

GERICKE, WILHELM (Apr. 18, 1845–Oct. 27, 1925), musician, conductor, was born in Gratz, Styria, of parents who, though not wealthy, sympathized with their son's musical ambitions. He went to Vienna at the age of seventeen, where he studied with Felix Dessoff at the Vienna Conservatorium from 1862 to 1865. Soon thereafter he began his career as an operatic conductor in Linz. By 1874 he was assistant conductor at the Vienna *Hofoper,* and in 1880 he succeeded Brahms as the conductor of the famous *Gesellschaftsconcerte,* and also took over the leadership of the *Singverein.* At the *Hofoper* he conducted the first performance of Goldmark's *Königin von Saba* (1875), and the first Vienna performance of Wagner's *Tannhäuser* in the Paris version, playing the piano score at sight on his first meeting with Wagner. His gifts had already made a name for him, and in spite of a disagreement with Jahn, he might have continued at the *Hofoper.* It so happened, however, that Col. Henry L. Higginson of Boston, when in the Austrian capital in the fall of 1883, heard Gericke conduct a performance of *Aïda* which so impressed him that he determined to secure his services for the Boston Symphony Orchestra.

Accepting Col. Higginson's offer, Gericke emigrated to Boston in 1884 and succeeded Georg Henschel as director of the Boston Orchestra. On his arrival he found himself confronted with a state of affairs which could not but shock an artist accustomed to the finished performances demanded of the metropolitan European orchestras. Rehearsals were not taken very seriously, and much music of a lighter type was included in the symphony repertory. Gericke, with his concept of what a first-rate orchestra should be, at once set to work to bring the organization to the proper standard. With untiring energy, and despite much adverse criticism, he succeeded in achieving his purpose. Thus his pioneer work in American orchestral development and his establishment of the highest ideals in the symphonic field constitute his merited claim to recognition. He was at first much censured for the "heaviness" of his programs, and himself declared in 1887, when Brahms's Third and Bruckner's Seventh symphonies drove his audience out of the hall by the hundreds, that "during the last movement we were more people on the stage than in the audience." The next year he nearly emptied the house with a performance of Strauss's symphonic poem, "Aus Italien." In 1889 ill health obliged Gericke to relinquish his baton and return to Vienna. There he resumed the direction of the *Gesellschaftsconcerte,* resigning the position in 1895. In 1898 he returned to America to conduct the Boston Symphony (which Nikisch had directed during his absence), and continued with the organization until 1906, when he retired to private life in Vienna. During his incumbency of the directorship he had brought from Europe and had added to his orchestral forces some very notable musicians, including Franz Kneisel, Bernhard Listemann, Louis Svečenski, and Alwin Schroeder.

In spite of his almost uninterrupted activity as a conductor, Gericke found time to write an operetta, *Schön Hannchen* (1865), a requiem, a concert overture for orchestra, several chamber-music selections, and more than a hundred songs and choruses. Though associated with the Vienna *Hofoper* for a decade when it was at the height of its glory, and though he had there won a special reputation as a conductor of "die elegante französische *Spieloper,*" he will be principally remembered for his connection with the Boston Symphony Orchestra.

[M. A. De Wolfe Howe, *The Boston Symphony Orchestra, An Hist. Sketch* (1914), chs. iii, v; *Music,* Mar. 1899; *Who's Who in America,* 1906–07; the *Vienna Neue Freie Presse,* Oct. 31, 1925; *N. Y. Times,* Oct. 30, Nov. 15, Nov. 29, 1925; *Musical America,* Nov. 7, 1925.]

F. H. M.

GERONIMO (June 1829–Feb. 17, 1909), a warrior of the Chiricahua Apaches and the most famous of all Apaches, was born in southern Arizona. His Indian name was Goyathlay, "one who yawns"; the name by which he is commonly known (the Spanish for Jerome) was given by the Mexicans. His father was Taklishim, "the gray one," and his mother was known as Juana. From his youth he took an active part in the bloody raids of Cochise, Victorio, Mangas Coloradas (Red Sleeves), and other chiefs. Though not a Chiricahua by birth he assumed virtual leadership of the tribe, the last hereditary chief, Naichi (Nachez), being content to serve as his lieutenant. The forced removal of the Chiricahuas from the southern reservation to San Carlos, on the Gila, in 1876, started him on another raid, but by May of the following year he was settled in his new home, an industrious farmer. After a brief foray in 1880 he was brought back, but his next effort, two years later, lasted until May 1883, when Crook captured him.

On May 17, 1885, with a considerable following, he started out on the last, the bloodiest, and the most spectacular campaign of his career. For ten months, hotly pursued by Crook's troopers, he raided the outlying settlements, leaving a trail of death and destruction. Followed into Mexico, he was at last surrounded, and on Mar. 27, 1886, again surrendered to Crook. Two nights later, however, with a part of his band, he escaped. Crook was relieved by Miles, who energetically continued the pursuit. A small force under Capt. H. W. Lawton apprehended Geronimo on the Bavispe River, Mexico, in August, and Lieut. Charles B. Gatewood, who was well acquainted with the savage leader, induced him to treat for peace. Returning with the soldiers, he surrendered his band to Miles at Camp Bowie, Ariz., Sept. 4. They were sent as prisoners of war to Fort Pickens, Pensacola; later transferred to Mount Vernon, Ala., and still later to Fort Sill, Okla., where in time they became prosperous farmers and stock-raisers. Geronimo, after several attempts at escape and continued efforts to induce the government to return him to Arizona, apparently became reconciled to his lot. He was converted to Christianity, and in the summer of 1903 he joined the Dutch Reformed Church. He was taken to the St. Louis World's Fair and the Buffalo and Omaha expositions, and on Mar. 4, 1905, was a conspicuous figure in the inaugural procession of President Roosevelt. In 1906 he dictated his autobiography, a highly imaginative production largely given to a justification of the Apache character in its savage state. He died of pneumonia in the hospital at Fort Sill.

Geronimo was of medium height, stockily built, with a tremendous girth of chest and of great strength. Miles, who characterized him as one of the most cruel of savages, says that he was bright and resolute-looking and that his every movement indicated power, energy, and determination. For many years a spirited controversy was waged over the circumstances of surrender, Geronimo and his supporters asserting that Miles and the government had violated promises as to the treatment of the prisoners and Miles maintaining that the surrender was unconditional.

[Jas. Mooney and Cyrus Thomas, *Handbook of Am. Indians* (1907); *Geronimo's Story of His Life* (1906), ed. by S. M. Barrett; John G. Bourke, *On the Border with Crook* (1892); Nelson A. Miles, *Personal Recollections and Observations* (1896); Anton Mazzanovich, *Trailing Geronimo* (1926), ed. by E. A. Brininstool; Chas. H. L. Johnston, *Famous Indian Chiefs* (1909); *N. Y. Times*, Feb. 18, 1909; *Proc. of the Annual Meeting and Dinner of the Order of Indian Wars of the U. S.*, 1929; Britton Davis, *The Truth about Geronimo* (1929).]

W. J. G.

GERRISH, FREDERIC HENRY (Mar. 21, 1845–Sept. 8, 1920), surgeon, anatomist, was born in Portland, Me., the son of Oliver Gerrish, jeweler, and Sarah Little, niece of Dr. Timothy Little, an early Maine anatomist. He was educated in the public schools of his native city and at Bowdoin College where he received a degree in arts in 1866 and one in medicine in 1869. After taking a course in microscopy in New York he settled in Portland and was for a time assistant to the surgeon, William Warren Greene, although he began his own career as a general practitioner. He joined the faculty of the Portland School for Medical Instruction and in 1872 began to lecture on materia medica and therapeutics at the Bowdoin Medical College. In 1873 he was made a lecturer on the same subjects at the University of Michigan and the following year he was made professor, but in 1875 he resigned to assume a professorship at Bowdoin. Beginning in 1876 he wrote many papers, for the most part on subjects relative to the welfare of the medical profession and community, but very few of these were reprinted. In 1878 he brought out a booklet, *Prescription Writing,* which went through seven editions in ten years. With the development of the use of antiseptics he began to take a greater interest in operative medicine and in 1881 published *Antiseptic Surgery,* a translation from the French of Lucas-Championnière. In the following year he became professor of anatomy at Bowdoin.

Gerrish's activities were wide-spread. From 1885 to 1889 he served as president of the Maine State Board of Health. In 1887–88 he was elected president of the American Academy of Medicine. As early as 1892 he had published a paper on the remedial uses of hypnotism and became so great an enthusiast on mental therapy that he was credited with the statement that it could cure anything beyond the province of surgery; but this is probably an exaggeration since he not only retained his membership in the American Therapeutic Society but served as its president in 1908–09. By 1895 he was so well-known as a surgeon—although he had taken up this branch of medicine rather late in his career—that he contributed the article on surgery of the lymphatics to F. S. Dennis's *System of Surgery* (1895–96); and in 1907 he contributed a similar article to W. W. Keen's *Surgery* (1906–21). He became so distinguished as an anatomist that he was asked by his colleagues to edit a work by American anatomists. The result was *A Text-book of Anatomy by American Authors* (1889, 1902) to which Gerrish contributed about two-thirds of the entire text. In 1905 he was made professor of surgery at Bowdoin. Upon his resignation from this chair in 1911 he was made professor emeritus, though he held the chair of medical ethics from 1911 to 1915. He was one of the contributors to the symposium, *Psychotherapeutics* (1910), and in 1917 published his last study under the title *Sex Hygiene.* In 1879 he was married to Emily Manning Swan.

Gerrish was endowed with an unusual but rather disharmonic personality. He was a precisian, a stickler for form, and an idealist, yet he possessed a keen sense of the ridiculous and in his own circle was one of the most humorous and fun-loving of men. An agnostic in matters theological, he adhered to a high standard of personal morality and had an almost spinsterish aversion to certain foibles and petty vices. He had a great capacity for making enemies and was regarded by many as pedantic, conceited, arrogant, and domineering. In controversy he could be very bitter and sarcastic. He labored for the good of his profession and for the advancement of its standing in such matters as higher education, hospital facilities, sanitation, and trained nursing. The objects of his particular interest were the Maine General Hospital and Bowdoin Medical College. He was a pioneer, certainly as far as his own community was concerned, in antiseptic surgery, psychotherapy, and social and moral prophylaxis; and very early in his career he advocated marital continence save for procreation.

[*Boston Medic. and Surgic. Jour.*, Nov. 18, 1920; *Jour. Am. Medic. Asso.*, Sept. 25, 1920; H. A. Kelly and W. L. Burrage, *Dict. of Am. Medic. Biog.* (1928); *Obit. Record of the Grads. of Bowdoin Coll. for the Year Ending 1 June, 1921* (1922); *N. Y. Times*, Sept. 9, 1920.] E. P.

GERRY, ELBRIDGE (July 17, 1744–Nov. 23, 1814), statesman, was born at Marblehead, Mass., third of the twelve children of Thomas and Elizabeth Gerry. His father was a native of Newton Abbot, Devonshire, who came to New England in 1730 as master of a vessel, married Elizabeth Greenleaf, the daughter of a Boston merchant, and settled at Marblehead, where he built up a mercantile business and became commander of the local fort. Elbridge Gerry entered Harvard College in 1758 and was placed twenty-ninth in a class of fifty-two, with which he graduated in 1762. He then joined his father and two elder brothers in business at Marblehead, shipping dried codfish to Barbados and Spanish ports in their own vessels, which returned with bills of exchange and Spanish goods. In May 1772 he was elected representative to the General Court, where he met Samuel Adams and fell completely under his influence. Their ample correspondence during the next two years shows that Adams regarded Gerry as a young man of parts who was worth encouraging in the cause; and Gerry developed an even keener scent than his master for tyranny. A town meeting was held at Marblehead on Dec. 1, 1772, instigated by the circular letter and resolves of Adams's Boston Committee of Correspondence. Thomas Gerry was moderator of the meeting, Elbridge and Thomas Gerry, Jr., were on the committee that drafted the fiery resolves which were adopted, and all three were members of the local committee of correspondence then and there appointed.

Gerry was reëlected to the General Court in May 1773, and promptly placed on the standing committee of correspondence. Early in 1774 his political activities were interrupted by a local brawl. A mob burnt to the ground an isolation hospital for smallpox which Gerry and other prominent citizens had built at their own expense; and public opinion protected the guilty parties from punishment. Gerry and the entire committee of correspondence resigned in disgust. When the Boston Port Bill began to be enforced, however, Marblehead became a leading port of entry for patriotic donations, and Gerry with Col. Azor Orne consented to see to the handling and forwarding of these stores to Boston (*Massachusetts Historical Society Collections*, 4 ser. IV, 1858, pp. 27–226). In August 1774, Gerry was elected to an Essex County convention, and in October to the first Provincial Congress, which appointed him to the executive Committee of Safety. Reëlected to the second Provincial Congress and reappointed to the second Committee of Safety early in 1775, he coöperated with Adams and Hancock in conducting measures of preparedness that bore fruit on the day of Lexington and Concord. During the evening of Apr. 18, 1775, the Committee of Safety held a session at Menotomy (Arlington) on the road from Cambridge to Lexington. Gerry warned Hancock, who proceeded to Lexington after the meeting, that the British scouts were about. Gerry himself, however, went to bed in the Menotomy tavern, and just had time to escape into a cornfield in his nightclothes when a file of men from Lieut.-Col. Smith's detachment began to search the house (Allen French, *The Day of Concord and Lexington*, 1925, p. 102). In the session of the Provincial Congress after the fight, and continuously as member of the Committee of Safety and chairman of the Committee of Supply, Gerry took an active and important part in drafting a narrative of the "massacre," in raising troops, and in procuring all manner of munitions and supplies for the provincial army and materials for fortification. His mercantile connections and interests made this his natural assignment, and he prosecuted the work with energy, economy, and efficiency. On June 7 he was appointed to a committee "to consider the expediency of establishing a number of small armed vessels, to cruise on our sea coasts" (*Massachusetts Historical Society Collections*, LXXVII, 1927, p. 20), but on July 11 James Warren complained of Gerry's "want of faith and ardor" in not "setting up for a naval power" (*Ibid.*, LXXII, 1917, p. 81). Gerry later claimed the joint paternity with James Sullivan of an act of Nov. 1, 1775, to issue letters of marque and establish prize courts; but he was not a member of the committee upon whose report the bill was based (*Ibid.*, LXXVII, pp. 23-

25). He refused an appointment as admiralty judge of the province, and continued his important work in the supply department until Jan. 25, 1776, when he left with John Adams for Philadelphia, as delegate to the second Continental Congress. The association thus formed developed into a firm friendship, although Gerry's character more resembled that of Jefferson, whom he first met on a visit to New York about 1764, and who also became his lifelong friend.

Gerry, at thirty-one, was a spare, dapper little gentleman with pleasant manners, *"rempli de petites finesses"* according to a French observer (Farrand, *post*, III, 233), and a great favorite with the ladies. He had a broad forehead which was soon furrowed with care, a long nose and a habit of contracting his eyes which gave him an unnaturally stern expression. He took his seat in Congress on Feb. 9, 1776, and on the 17th was appointed to the standing committee of five commonly called the Treasury Board, which had oversight of Continental finance until superseded by a new Board in 1779, to which Gerry refused election. He was frequently president of the old Board, and always one of its most industrious members, especially in the detailed examination of accounts. He was an early advocate of separation from "the prostituted Government of G. Britain" (Burnett, *post*, I, 468) and was present on July 4, 1776, but left Philadelphia, worn out by his labors, before the engrossed copy of the Declaration had been signed. On July 21 he wrote to the Adamses to subscribe his name to the document, but actually signed it himself after his return to Congress on Sept. 3 (H. Friedenwald, *The Declaration of Independence*, 1904, pp. 141, 147). He also signed the Articles of Confederation.

Gerry continued to interest himself, both as a member of the committee on the commissary and as private merchant, in the important business of army supplies. He directed his brothers how to route their ships, informed them what commodities were needed, sent instructions about the manufacture of tents and gunpowder, shipped fish to Spain on Continental account, received army supplies in return, and stimulated his friends in Massachusetts to greater exertion (*New-England Historical and Genealogical Register*, July 1876, pp. 312–13). As the war continued, and many members of Congress retired, the value of Gerry's experience increased; and his faithful attendance when colleagues took vacations often gave him double duty. He was constitutionally jealous of standing armies and militarism, but was an early advocate of long-term enlistments for a new model army. On the subject of pensions he vacillated. He was frequently appointed on committees to visit the army, and his correspondence with Washington was friendly, but he was also a supporter of Conway (*Journals of Congress*, Oct. 3, 1777; Apr. 10, 28, and June 11, 1778). In foreign policy he saw eye to eye with John Adams, opposed the French alliance and the consular convention of 1782, supported Arthur Lee, and desired the recall of Franklin whom he believed to be corrupted by France. Nevertheless, Gerry was an implacable enemy to England. As a Marblehead man, he naturally showed a keener interest in the fisheries than any of his colleagues. In the spring of 1779 he proposed, as a condition of peace, the retention of fishing rights on the coasts of Nova Scotia and Newfoundland; but was forced to concede that fisheries should not be *sine qua non*.

Although a merchant himself and a furnisher of supplies, he frowned on profiteering. A delegate to the New Haven price-fixing convention of 1778, he endeavored to enforce on others and personally observed himself their schedule of fair prices. This subject led up to a quarrel between Gerry and Congress on a point of privilege. On Feb. 19, 1780, Congress was debating an estimate of supplies to be furnished by the several states. Gerry moved to recommit that part of the report in order to reduce the Massachusetts quota and restore the price schedule to the 1778 level. Congress voted his motion out of order and refused to record the ayes and noes on the point of order. At this last denial, Gerry took great offense and declared that personal privilege and the rights of his state had been infringed. When satisfaction was not given, he returned to Boston and laid his complaint before the state legislature. While endeavoring to obtain vindication or redress he absented himself from Congress, of which he was still nominally a member, for over three years, during which he engaged successfully in trade and privateering (S. R. Gerry Manuscripts; Tucker Manuscripts, Harvard College Library, II, 214). In state politics he belonged to the anti-Hancock faction, and declined the Governor's appointment as justice of the peace lest he seem to condone the prevalent "idolatry." He also declined two appointments by the General Court to a vacancy in the state Senate, but served in the lower house. He was ever faithful to the Spartan ideals of 1776, extolled republican simplicity, and deplored, "Vanity, Vice and Folly" (S. Adams Manuscripts, Jan. 8, 1781). He was liberal enough to declare the drama not inconsistent with republican virtue, but when the practical issue arose in Boston,

Gerry yielded to the firm prohibition of stage plays by Samuel Adams.

Upon his return to Congress, Gerry was one of the oldest and most experienced members. After peace was concluded he exerted himself successfully to reduce the standing army, and unsuccessfully to abolish the Order of the Cincinnati, which he feared would usurp the powers of Congress. He paid considerable attention to the Northwest Territory, in which he was financially interested. On two occasions he took issue with his state. When Massachusetts refused to ratify the impost amendment on the ground that the grant of half-pay to officers violated ancestral principles, Gerry drafted a reply, pointing out that the country had pledged its faith to the officers three years before. On the second occasion he took the opposite line. In April 1784, he presented a report to Congress in which he declared that "unless the United States in Congress assembled, shall be vested with powers competent to the protection of commerce, they can never command reciprocal advantages in trade" (*Journals of the American Congress,* IV, 1823, p. 393). Yet when a year later Massachusetts formally made that suggestion, Gerry and his colleagues refused to lay it before Congress, on the ground that a convention on commerce would allow "the friends of an Aristocracy" to promote a change of government "which would require a Standing Army, and a numerous train of pensioneers and placemen to prop and support its exalted administration" (C. R. King, *The Life and Correspondence of Rufus King,* I, 1894, pp. 64–65). Gerry's last appearance in Congress was on Nov. 2, 1785; in February or March 1786 he took his seat in the Massachusetts House of Representatives to which he had been elected the previous spring.

Gerry's work in Congress was that of an industrious and conscientious business man. His colleagues appreciated his gentlemanliness, profited by his attention to detail, and never questioned his integrity: qualities which were conspicuous throughout his life. On the other hand, he frequently changed his mind, sometimes for personal reasons, and showed an "obstinacy that will risk great things to secure small ones" (*The Works of John Adams,* VIII, 1853, p. 549). He proved lacking in a sense of humor and showed an habitual suspicion of the motives of others. As an orator he was hesitating and laborious. It would have been better for his fame as for his fortune had he retired from public life and devoted himself to business at the end of the war, for he was of the considerable number of patriots who, though useful as agitators and organizers of victory, carried the "stern republicanism" of the 1770's into a period of different problems that required other qualities.

On Jan. 12, 1786, Gerry married Ann Thompson, the daughter of a New York merchant. At the same time he retired from business with a comfortable fortune invested in government securities and real estate; and in May 1787 he purchased a confiscated Loyalist estate in Cambridge, later the "Elmwood" of James Russell Lowell. Shays's Rebellion drew him closely to other members of the merchant class. Completely reversing his attitude of the year before, he refused to attend the Annapolis Convention in 1786 on the ground that its competence was too restricted; and he accepted an appointment to the Federal Convention of 1787. There he was one of the most experienced and active members but not among the most useful. He began as an advocate of a strong centralized national government, but ended by opposing the Constitution because it did not square with theoretical republicanism. He combined aversion to democracy with jealousy of power, and solicitude for "the commercial and monied interest" with fear of tyranny. He made several freak proposals, such as limiting the army to two or three thousand men, and having the state governors elect the president; and there was much truth in a colleague's statement that he "objected to everything he did not propose" (Farrand, *post,* III, 104). The inconsistency of Gerry made a bad impression on his colleagues. He continually preached compromise in the Convention, but opposed the Constitution as "full of vices" (*Ibid.,* II, 478). He was chairman of the committee that prepared the "great compromise" but disliked the compromise itself. He came out early in favor of the Virginia plan. Oliver Ellsworth accused him publicly of opposing ratification because his motion for redeeming the Continental currency failed. Gerry denied having made any such motion, and the journals bear him out; but he did propose that the federal government be required to discharge both federal and state debts at par (*Ibid.,* II, 356). He publicly declared himself "not possessed of more of the securities than would, by the interest, pay his taxes" (*Ibid.,* II, 413); but the treasury archives record sufficient government securities in Gerry's name to have yielded him about $3,500 a year (C. A. Beard, *An Economic Interpretation of the Constitution of the United States,* 1913, p. 97), and he was writing his brother in 1786 about buying and selling government paper (S. R. Gerry Manuscripts). There seems no reason to doubt the sincerity of Gerry's fear that the Constitution would fail to secure liberty, but it is likely that he expected ratification to fail, when Anti-Federalists would naturally be rewarded for their prescience. The list of objections which Gerry communicated to the state legislature on Oct. 18, 1787, and which were published with augmentations as *Observations on the New Constitution, and on the Federal and State Conventions. By a Columbian Patriot* (1788), were wholly from the popular angle. The "Columbian Patriot," although not elected to the Massachusetts ratifying convention, was invited to take a seat there in order to answer questions. Abusing his guest privilege by proffering information unasked, he was declared out of order, took offense, and refused again to sit. Rufus King then robbed Gerry's published objections of much of their force, by showing that some of them applied equally well to the government of Massachusetts.

Gerry's policy regarding the Constitution cost him several friends and left him in a gloomy frame of mind, expecting a civil war and feeling ill-used by the public. On the other hand, his "stern republican" attitude appealed to the yeomanry. A meeting of Anti-Federalists brought forward his name for governor, but he polled only a slight vote, and Hancock was reëlected. The next year came a new opportunity. Gerry was elected to Congress early in February 1789, at the second polling in his district, after declaring his intention to support the Constitution. He early distinguished himself by a long speech in favor of putting the treasury in commission, believing it unsafe in a republic for "a single officer to have the command of three or four millions of money." He observed that heads of departments were given "such amazing powers as would eventually end in the ruin of the Government" (*Annals of Congress,* 1 Cong., 1 Sess., pp. 387, 389). The absence of a bill of rights had been one of Gerry's leading objections to the Constitution, and Samuel Adams wrote him that Congress ought not to adjourn before proposing one. Yet Gerry surprised his friends by declaring "the salvation of America depends upon the establishment of this Government, whether amended or not. . . . It is necessary to establish an energetic Government" (*Ibid.,* 1 Cong., 1 Sess., p. 445). Gerry thereupon so vigorously supported Hamilton's reports on public credit, including the assumption of state debts, that he was considered a leading champion by the Federalists (W. P. and J. P. Cutler, *Life, Journals, and Correspondence of Rev. Manasseh Cutler, D.D.,* 1888, I, 458–61) and gave his friend Jefferson some distress. Although one of his insuperable objections to the Constitution had been the implied power of Congress to create corporations, he spoke warmly in favor of the Bank charter, and subscribed for thirty shares of the United States Bank. In the Second Congress, to which Gerry was elected in opposition to Nathaniel Gorham, he was singularly silent. In 1793, having refused to stand for reëlection, he retired to cultivate his farm and educate his "young and numerous family."

During his four years' retirement, Gerry began to suspect that the Federalists were aiming at tyranny and a British alliance. He voted for John Adams as presidential elector in 1797, but wrote to James Monroe that his recall from Paris proved the existence of a "deep system . . . to disgrace republicanism" (*New-England Historical and Genealogical Register,* October 1895, p. 436). President Adams appointed him a member of the famous "X. Y. Z. mission" on June 20, 1797, against the advice of his cabinet, because he trusted Gerry and wished a non-party man joined with Marshall and Pinckney. It was an unsuitable choice, because Gerry was so obsessed with the idea that war with France would lead to a British alliance and aristocracy that he was willing to go to almost any lengths in order to prevent a formal breach. Landing in Holland on Sept. 18, 1797, Gerry joined his colleagues in Paris on Oct. 4. Talleyrand, well acquainted with the new-comer's "known attachment to France and conciliatory disposition," decided to negotiate with him alone, and shelve his colleagues (Mémoire of Feb. 15, 1798, Archives des Affaires Étrangères, Correspondance Politique, États-Unis, XLIX, 174). Gerry, when this was broached to him by Talleyrand, made the grave error of promising to keep this proposition and subsequent communications from the French minister a secret from his colleagues. By Mar. 18, when Talleyrand made his propositions openly, he had practically detached Gerry from Pinckney and Marshall, so that when they decided to leave, Gerry determined to stay; and there was a painful scene between him and his colleagues before their departure. Gerry remained because Talleyrand persuaded him that France would declare war if he left, but he refused to negotiate without further powers. Yet his mere presence in Paris was everywhere misunderstood, and played Talleyrand's avowed game of preventing an inconvenient rupture while the privateering continued (*Correspondance Diplomatique de Talleyrand: Le Ministère de Talleyrand sous le Directoire,* 1891, edited by G. Pallain, p. 309). Gerry misjudged the situation both in France and at home. The Directory had no intention of declaring war, but made no better offers to Gerry than to his colleagues. The President, instead of sending Gerry full powers, published the "X. Y. Z. dispatches" and recalled him. On receiving this order, on May 12, 1798, Gerry at once asked for his passports, which he did not obtain until July 15, when Talleyrand had given up trying to inveigle him into a negotiation. Gerry later claimed that his presence in Paris prevented war, since he brought home the text of two conciliatory decrees on neutral trade which afforded the President a new basis of negotiation; but the Directory had other channels of communication, and the new decrees were occasioned by the news of the war fever in America, and a report of Victor du Pont (*Proceedings of the Massachusetts Historical Society,* XLIX, 1916, pp. 63-65).

Gerry sailed from Havre on Aug. 8, and arrived at Boston on Oct. 1, 1798. The Federalists by agreement snubbed him; but in conversation he advised every one to rally around the administration, and a wily unsigned letter from Jefferson, begging him to come out with a public vindication like Monroe's (Jan. 26, 1799, *The Writings of Thomas Jefferson,* Memorial Edition, X, 1903, pp. 74-86), remained unanswered for two years. Annoyed by Secretary Pickering's severe criticisms of his conduct, Gerry attempted to vindicate himself in two statements which he sent to the President, and which, by Adams's advice, he did not publish. His whole conduct on the "X. Y. Z. mission" was entirely honorable, but egregiously mistaken.

Henceforth Gerry was generally regarded in Federalist circles as a "Jacobin" and suffered the social ostracism that was the price of political heterodoxy in Massachusetts. The Republicans, on the contrary, regarded him as the man who showed up a Federalist hoax, and prevented war with France. They nominated him in 1800 for governor of Massachusetts. He gave the Federalists a close race, being the only Jeffersonian ever to carry Boston, but was defeated. Thrice more defeated and by increasing margins in 1801-03, he refused to run again, but as presidential elector on the winning ticket in 1804 had the pleasure of casting his vote for Jefferson. In 1810 the Republicans turned somewhat reluctantly to Gerry as a candidate for governor. He was then sixty-five years old, and not popular; he never made any pretense of loving the common people, and refused to attend caucuses as below his dignity. His opponent, Christopher Gore, had even stronger aristocratic traits, however, and Gerry was elected governor in April 1810. His first administration was uneventful. A bare Federalist majority in the Senate prevented the passage of reform legislation, and Gerry himself declined to remove Federalists from office, although a Republican council made a clean sweep possible. This moderation fairly earned him a reëlection in April 1811, with a Republican majority in both houses. His second administration opened to the taste of his party, with an address castigating the Federalists as secessionists, rebels, and traitors. Apparently he had taken alarm at some Boston Federalists' resolutions threatening nullification of the Non-Intercourse Act. These "treasonable" resolves furnished a pretext if not a reason for purging the public service of Federalists. According to his biographer, Gerry's "reluctant share" in that proscription "caused him many of the most painful moments of his life" (Austin, *post,* II, 307), and several intended victims were spared by him; but on the other hand, additional places were created by reorganizing the judicial system. In his Thanksgiving Day proclamation of 1811, Gerry unwisely criticized Federalist clergymen, some of whom refused to read it. By the end of the year he was receiving a torrent of bitter criticism and invective, including an anonymous letter threatening to burn his house and tar-and-feather the owner, which he made the subject of a special message to the legislature. He also communicated a list of 253 newspaper libels on the government, and attempted to get the law of libel altered, so that contempt of the governor would be equivalent to contempt of court.

The measure that made his second administration immortal was the famous Gerrymander Bill of Feb. 11, 1812 (*Acts of Massachusetts,* V, 517, repealed June 16, 1813). This was a redistricting of the state in such a way as to give to the Republicans state senators in excess of their voting strength. The method was by no means new (E. C. Griffith, *The Rise and Development of the Gerrymander,* 1907, pp. 31-55), but had never been carried to such an extreme. Essex was divided into one compact two-member district including the stalwart Federalist towns, and an absurdly shaped three-member district running around the edge of the county, in which the heavy Republican vote of Marblehead was calculated to quench Federalist majorities in the eleven other towns. A map of Essex County was produced at a Federalist gathering, where Gilbert Stuart or Elkanah Tisdale sketched in head, wings, and claws on the grotesque district, remarking "That will do for a salamander," at which some wit exclaimed, "Gerrymander!" A popular caricature representing the district as a winged monster, with Gerry's profile against its back, gave wide currency to the name (*New-*

England Historical and Genealogical Register, October 1892, pp. 374–83). The act worked so well that in the spring election of 1812, although 51,766 votes were cast for Federalist candidates for state senators as against 50,164 Republican votes, only eleven of the former party were elected, as against twenty-nine of the latter. But at the same election of April 1812 Ex-Gov. Strong defeated Gerry by a majority of twelve hundred in a total vote of over one hundred thousand. A continuance of the moderate policy of Gerry's first administration would probably have kept Massachusetts in the nationalist and Republican column during the War of 1812, and saved the state from a policy that disgraced it in the eyes of the country.

Gerry's defeat, however, took him to Washington. On June 8, 1812, within two weeks of his leaving the governor's chair, the Republican congressional caucus nominated him for the vice-presidency, on the ticket with Madison. The notification reached Gerry on June 15, followed shortly by news of the declaration of war. He at once declared that the country had been too long at peace, and was "degenerating into a mere nation of traders" (Austin, *post,* p. 375). He became unduly alarmed over the truculent attitude of the Federalist press, urged the authorities to arrest the editors, and warned President Madison that the Federalists would seize the castle in Boston Harbor, welcome a British landing force, raise the standard of rebellion, and declare secession. The Madison-Gerry ticket was chosen in November though it failed by a large majority to carry Massachusetts. Vice-President Gerry took the oath of office at his Cambridge residence on Mar. 4, 1813, and presided over the opening session of the Senate on May 24, when he made a warlike oration, predicting the speedy conquest of Canada. Although in his seventieth year and frail in health, he entered into the social life of Washington with great zest. Contrary to the usual practise, he did not relinquish his chair in the Senate at the end of the session of 1813, lest the factious Senator William B. Giles [*q.v.*] become president *pro tempore* and consequently succeed to the presidency in the event of the death both of President Madison, who was severely ill at the time, and of Gerry himself (*American Historical Review,* October 1916, pp. 95–97). Some sixteen months later Gerry's death occurred. On the morning of Nov. 23, 1814, proceeding to the Senate chamber in his carriage, he was seized with a hemorrhage of the lungs and died within twenty minutes.

Gerry had been well-to-do in 1800, but had since suffered severe losses, and left heavy debts which consumed all his estate except the mansion house (Gerry-Townsend Manuscripts). Congress paid for his burial in the Congressional Cemetery, but the House rejected a bill introduced by Senator Christopher Gore and passed by the Senate, for paying the Vice-President's salary to his widow during the remainder of his term of office. Three sons and four daughters survived him. One son was provided for in the army, another in the navy, and a third, Elbridge Gerry, Jr., in the Boston custom-house. Mrs. Gerry lived until 1849, the last surviving widow of a "Signer."

[*The Life of Elbridge Gerry* (2 vols., 1828–29) by his son-in-law, Jas. T. Austin, is a useful work, but unduly reticent about portions of Gerry's career. In S. E. Morison, "Elbridge Gerry, Gentleman-Democrat," *New Eng. Quart.,* Jan. 1929, pp. 6–33, will be found references for many statements made in this article; see also "Two Signers on Salaries and the Stage, 1789," *Proc. Mass. Hist. Soc.,* Oct. 1928–June 1929. Manuscript letters of Gerry are in many autograph collections, especially that of the Pa. Hist. Soc. A remnant of the family papers (Austin collection) is in the writer's possession; another is in the hands of Ex.-Sen. Peter G. Gerry; a third, the Gerry-Townsend MSS., in the N. Y. Pub. Lib.; a manuscript Letter-Book of 1797 to 1803 is owned by Mrs. Townsend Phillips of N. Y. The Samuel Adams MSS. in the Bancroft Collection contain important unpublished correspondence with Adams. Worthington C. Ford printed a number of Gerry's letters to Jefferson, Madison, and Monroe in the *New-Eng. Hist. and Geneal. Reg.,* Oct. 1895, Jan. 1896; and a number of letters to his wife, mostly of 1813–14, in *Proc. Mass. Hist. Soc.,* XLVII, 1914. The Samuel Russell Gerry MSS. in the Mass. Hist. Soc. and the letter-books of S. R. and Thomas Gerry in the Marblehead Hist. Soc. afford much information on Gerry's commercial activities. The Chamberlain MSS. and general manuscript collections of the Boston Pub. Lib. contain records of the Provincial Congress Committee of Supplies and Gerry's contract book of 1775–76. The Pickering MSS. in the Mass. Hist. Soc. contain many letters by and about Gerry, and John Marshall's journal of the X. Y. Z. negotiation. See also *Jours. of the Continental Cong. 1774–1789* (26 vols., 1906–28); E. C. Burnett, *Letters of Members of the Continental Cong.,* vols. I–IV (1921–28); Max Farrand, *The Records of the Federal Convention of 1787* (3 vols., 1927); *Am. State Papers, Foreign Relations,* vol. II (1832); *The Jours. of Each Provincial Cong. of Mass. in 1774 and 1775* (1838); and published writings of contemporary statesmen, especially John Adams and Rufus King.]

S. E. M.

GERRY, ELBRIDGE THOMAS (Dec. 25, 1837–Feb. 18, 1927), lawyer, philanthropist, was a grandson of Elbridge Gerry [*q.v.*] and son of Hannah Green (Goelet) and Thomas Russell Gerry, an officer in the United States navy. Born in New York City, his early education was obtained privately, his parents being in affluent circumstances, and, on the death of his father, when he was yet a child, his mother devoted herself to his upbringing, the influence which she was thus able to exercise having a marked effect on his later career. Entering Columbia College in 1853, he there made a reputation as an epicure, athlete, and scholar and graduated in 1857 with honors.

He then read law in the office of William Curtis Noyes and on his admission to the bar in 1860 commenced practise in New York City, associating himself with Noyes and later with Judge W. F. Allen and Benjamin Vaughan Abbott [*q.v.*]. From the outset his family connections assured him success which was confirmed by his high character and innate ability, and he was soon in the enjoyment of an extensive practise. In 1867 he was elected a delegate to the New York state constitutional convention, where, though not specially identified with any outstanding projects for reform, he took a prominent part in the proceedings. On Dec. 3, 1867, he was married to Louisa Mathilda, daughter of Robert J. and Louisa M. (Storm) Livingston of New York.

In 1870, induced thereto by Henry Bergh [*q.v.*], he became legal adviser to the American Society for the Prevention of Cruelty to Animals. The nature of the work which this position entailed appealed strongly to his humanitarian instincts, and he applied himself with ardor to the task of surmounting the legal and other difficulties which beset the pioneer stages of the Society. In 1874 a pitiable case of cruelty to a child was brought to the attention of Bergh and Gerry and it was disclosed that abused children had not then as much protection as animals, since there was no special organization or government department to see that their rights were enforced. This discovery led to the institution, Dec. 15, 1874, of the New York Society for the Prevention of Cruelty to Children—the first of its kind in the world—incorporation of which was obtained in 1875, Gerry attending to the required formalities, including enabling legislation (see New York Laws of 1875, ch. 130). Becoming standing counsel to the Society, he procured the passage of much supplemental legislation extending the sphere of protection. All the various phases of child rescue, children's shelters, prosecution of offenders, and caring for juvenile delinquents, were exhaustively studied by him; and the immensity and intricacy of the work was such that he gradually withdrew from law practise and devoted himself almost entirely to the interests of the Society. In 1879 he became president, and for the following twenty-two years molded the policy and directed the activities of the Society to such an extent that it was popularly described as "Gerry's Society." He had to contend with bitter opposition from unexpected quarters, his interference in what were described as purely family matters was resented, even his motives were misrepresented and "he was described in print and pictured in cartoon as bent on destroying the dearest rights of every citizen. He was represented as a zealot who would tear children from their parents merely to gratify an officious and meddlesome disposition" (New York *Sun,* Feb. 19, 1927). He never wavered, however, in the pursuit of his ideals, cheerfully shouldering the heavy financial obligations involved, and when he relinquished office in 1901 the Society was recognized as one of the most effective agents for good in the country, and organizations of a similar nature had been established throughout the world. In 1902 he compiled a *Manual of the New York Society for the Prevention of Cruelty to Children.*

Despite his preoccupation with child welfare, his services were requisitioned in other fields of social endeavor and reform. In 1886 he acted as chairman of the commission appointed by the New York legislature to consider the most humane and practical method of carrying into effect the sentence of death in capital cases, which resulted in the substitution of the electric chair for hanging. In 1892 he was chairman of the New York City commission to consider the best way of caring for the insane. Among other positions of public trust which he held were those of trustee of the General Theological Seminary, 1877–1913; governor of New York Hospital, 1878–1912, and trustee of the American Museum of Natural History, 1895–1902. In addition to numerous Reports which were printed in the publications of the Society for the Prevention of Cruelty to Children, he contributed articles on humanitarian and fraternal subjects to the *North American Review* and *Purple and Gold.* He traveled extensively, but his chief recreation was sailing. He was an enthusiastic member of the New York Yacht Club and commodore from 1886 to 1893. His later years were spent principally at Newport, R. I.

[David McAdam and others, *Hist. of the Bench and Bar of N. Y.* (1899), II, 161; *N. Y. Geneal. and Biog. Record,* July 1927; *Who's Who in America,* 1926–27; S. H. Coleman, *Humane Society Leaders in America* (1924), *passim,* esp. pp. 65–87; lengthy obituary notices in the *Sun* (N. Y.), Feb. 18, 1927, and *N. Y. Times* and *World* (N. Y.), Feb. 19, 1927; editorial in the *Sun,* Feb. 19, 1927.]

H. W. H. K.

GERSTER, ARPAD GEYZA CHARLES (Dec. 22, 1848–Mar. 11, 1923), surgeon and pioneer in modern surgical technique, was born at Kassa, once in Hungary but now in Czecho-Slovakia, the son of Nicholas Gerster—descendant of Swiss settlers—and Caroline Schmidt Sándy, and the brother of the prima donna Etelka Gerster. He was educated in public and private schools of his native town and did not have a classical training, a deficiency which he largely overcame in later years by private study. Having taken a degree in medicine from the University of Vienna in 1872, he was about to settle in Kassa when he was called to the colors as an army surgeon. When he was finally placed on the reserve list he was appointed pathologist at the Kassa City Hospital. Since he had an uncle in Brooklyn, N. Y., and had read much about America, he conceived the idea of settling in the United States, which notion was regarded by all his friends and associates as incomparably foolish. He arrived in New York on Mar. 9, 1873, having made the acquaintance on the boat of his future wife, Anna Barnard Wynne of Cincinnati. For the first few years he was engaged in general practise in Brooklyn. (The story that he was the first physician to specialize in surgery is an error; James Wood, as Gerster himself stated, *Recollections,* p. 191, was the first to enjoy that distinction.) The new antiseptic technique which was gradually being adopted tended to make specialization practicable if not almost necessary, however, and after removing from Brooklyn to New York Gerster practised surgery exclusively. He received in 1878 the appointment of attending surgeon to the German (later Lenox Hill) Hospital and two years later a like appointment to the Mount Sinai Hospital, being one of the few Gentiles to be thus honored. In 1882, with John A. Wyeth, he was made surgeon to and professor of surgery in the new New York Polyclinic, retaining this chair until 1894. Having espoused the new technique inaugurated by Lord Lister, he became distinguished as a teacher; among his pupils were William J. and Charles H. Mayo. In 1902 he refused a tentative offer of the chair of surgery in the University of Budapest. He served as president of the American Surgical Association in 1911–12, and in 1916 he was appointed professor of clinical surgery at Columbia University.

Gerster was the first in America to publish a text-book on the new surgery, *Rules of Aseptic and Antiseptic Surgery* (1888). Not only was it revolutionary in content, but the mechanical work was ultramodern; it contained some of the earliest of half-tone pictures, made from the author's own plates. This epoch-making book went through three editions in two years, and was then allowed to lapse because the author believed that it had done its work. As a practitioner, Gerster was described as a physician first and surgeon next, which means that he was a superior diagnostician, that he often declined to operate, and that he excelled on post-operative care. His avocations were many; he was a linguist, a musician, an artist who excelled in etching and painting in oil, a writer and antiquarian who was honored with the presidency of the Charaka Club. His medical writings, with the exception of his text-book, were limited to clinical and historical papers. In 1917 he published his much-read autobiography, *Recollections of a New York Surgeon.*

[In addition to Gerster's autobiography see appreciation by Dr. Wm. J. Mayo, in *Surgery, Gynecology and Obstetrics,* Apr. 1928; *N. Y. Times,* Mar. 12, 1923.]

E. P.

GERSTLE, LEWIS (Dec. 17, 1824–Nov. 19, 1902), California pioneer and capitalist, was born of Jewish stock at Ichenhausen, Bavaria. In 1847 he came to the United States, working his way across the Atlantic as a deck boy. He settled for a short time in Louisville, Ky., where he became a pedler. In 1849 he went to New Orleans, and the next year to California via Panama. He first started a fruit-stand but soon entered the gold-mines near Georgetown, El Dorado County, as a day-laborer. Here he met Louis Sloss, another Bavarian, and a friendship and business partnership were formed which lasted fifty years and made both men wealthy and well known in the world of finance. Leaving the mines, they first opened a wholesale grocery business in or near Sacramento, then moved to San Francisco and became mining-stock brokers. The firm (Louis Sloss & Company) also became the most extensive buyer of wool and manufacturer of sole leather on the Pacific Coast.

After the purchase of Alaska (1867), Gerstle's firm and two others acquired the rights and privileges of the old Russian American Company. These three firms were the nucleus of the Alaska Commercial Company, in the creation of which Gerstle was active and prominent. Almost immediately (1870), the Alaska Commercial Company acquired, from the United States, the exclusive right for twenty years of seal fishing on the islands of St. Paul and St. George. In return for this monopoly, the Company paid the government a yearly rental and a royalty upon each seal captured. The Company, as a part of its agreement, established trading-posts, schools, and churches in various parts of Alaska, and in numerous other ways contributed greatly to the development of the country. Under Gerstle's leadership the Company established a line of ocean steamers between San Francisco and Alaska, and put into operation more than a score of large river boats on the Yukon and steamers plying between Nome and Dawson. For many years, and up until his death, Gerstle was president of the Company, and its successful operations formed the basis of his considerable fortune.

His business interests, however, were not confined to Alaska. He was one of the original promoters of the Union Iron Works in San Francisco, the San Joaquin Valley Railroad, the Pioneer Woolen Mills, and many other manufacturing enterprises. In the late eighties, he coöperated with Senator Warner Miller of New York in the launching of a company to build the proposed Nicaragua Canal. He was a director of the Nevada National Bank, the Union Trust Company, and the California-Hawaiian Sugar Company. For a few months, he was treasurer of the University of California (Aug. 12–Nov. 19, 1902), filling the place made vacant by the death of his partner Sloss. Gerstle held extensive blocks of real estate in the business portions of San Francisco. He devoted much time and study to charitable work, and all worthy charities shared generously in his wide benefactions; but he was especially interested in aiding orphans and the aged and feeble. For a time he was a director of the Hebrew Asylum and Home Society. Of the Jewish faith, he was a member of Congregation Emanu-El in San Francisco. He had a residence on Van Ness Ave., but spent most of his last years at a beautiful suburban-place in San Rafael. Despite his almost four-score years, he could be described by a contemporary at the time of his death as "a most magnificent type of vigorous manhood, active, energetic, firm and resolute," still displaying the "qualities which have characterized all his acts since early youth" (*San Francisco Chronicle*). In 1858 he went East, and married Hannah Greenebaum of Philadelphia, a sister of his partner's wife and a native of Bavaria. She and seven children survived him.

[Brief sketches of Gerstle appear in Bailey Millard, *Hist. of the San Francisco Bay Region* (1924), III, 53–55; *Jewish Encyc.*, V, 641; and a more extended sketch, in the *San Francisco Chronicle*, Nov. 20, 1902. On the early history of the Alaska Commercial Company see H. H. Bancroft, *Hist. of Alaska, 1730–1885,* XXXIII (1886), 637–59, 746–47; "Fur Seal Fisheries of Alaska," *House Report No. 3883,* 50 Cong., 2 Sess. (1889); *Reply of the Alaska Commercial Company to the Charges of Gov. Alfred P. Swineford, of Alaska, against the Company in his Annual Report for the year 1887* (pamphlet; n.p., n.d.).]

P. O. R.

GETTY, GEORGE WASHINGTON (Oct. 2, 1819–Oct. 1, 1901), Union soldier, was born in Georgetown, D. C., the son of Robert and Margaret (Wilmot) Getty. He graduated from West Point in 1840, was commissioned second lieutenant in the 4th Artillery, and promoted first lieutenant in 1845. With Scott's army in the Mexican War, he fought at Contreras, Molino del Rey, Chapultepec, and the capture of the city of Mexico, and was brevetted captain for gallant conduct in action. In 1848 he married Elizabeth Graham Stevenson, at Staunton, Va. He was engaged in the hostilities against the Seminoles in Florida in 1849–50, and again in 1856–57. At the outbreak of the Civil War he was serving on the frontier at Fort Randall, Dakota Territory, as a captain in the 4th Artillery, having been promoted to that rank in 1853. In the Peninsular campaign of 1862, with the temporary rank of lieutenant-colonel, he commanded four batteries, engaged in the siege of Yorktown and the battles of Gaines's Mill and Malvern Hill. He also fought at South Mountain and Antietam. Appointed brigadier-general of volunteers, Sept. 25, 1862, he continued with the Army of the Potomac during the campaign and battle of Fredericksburg. In March 1863 he was assigned to the command of a division at Suffolk, Va., holding the line which prevented approach to Norfolk and Hampton Roads from the south. In April Suffolk was vigorously attacked by the Confederates, who, after the failure of their first attempts, settled down to regular siege operations, in the course of which Getty distinguished himself (Apr. 19, 1863) by personally leading a storming column in the successful assault on Battery Huger at Hill's Point. The siege was raised early in May. For some time after, Getty was engaged in the construction of an intrenched line covering Norfolk and Portsmouth; and then, in early July, he commanded an expedition to the South Anna River, which was planned in view of the absence of the main Confederate army on the Gettysburg campaign. He was promoted major in the regular army, Aug. 1, 1863, his rank and assignment as brigadier-general of volunteers remaining unchanged. He was acting inspector-general of the Army of the Potomac during the early part of 1864, and was then assigned to a division of the VI Corps, which he commanded at the battle of the Wilderness, where he was severely wounded, and at the siege of Petersburg. Early's advance on Washington caused Grant to detach the VI and XIX Corps, which reached the city at the very time that Early was preparing his attack, and put an end to all danger of his entering the capital. The VI Corps becoming a part of Sheridan's Army of the Shenandoah, newly organized for the purpose of permanently clearing the Valley, Getty commanded his division, and occasionally the Corps, throughout the campaign, fighting at Winchester, Fisher's Hill, and Cedar Creek. He took part in the final operations of the Army of the Potomac around Petersburg and in the pursuit of Lee's army until the surrender. He was appointed colonel of infantry in the regular army, July 28, 1866, and mustered out of the volunteer service, Sept. 1,

1866. He was transferred to the 3rd Artillery in 1871. The post and the artillery school at Fort Monroe were under his command for six years. He was a member of the board which in 1878–79 reinvestigated the case of Fitz-John Porter and reversed the findings of the court martial which in 1863 had dismissed the unfortunate general from the army for alleged misconduct at the second battle of Bull Run. Getty retired from active service Oct. 2, 1883, and spent the remainder of his life on a farm near Forest Glen, Md. In his old age, as always, he was a constant reader of military works until failing sight limited such study. He was a dignified, courteous, modest soldier.

[G. W. Cullum, *Biog. Reg.... U. S. Mil. Acad.* (3rd ed., 1891), II, 41–43; *Ann. Reunion, Asso. Grads. U. S. Mil. Acad.*, June 10, 1903; *Official Records (Army)*, 1 ser. XI (pt. 2), XVIII, XXI, XXVII (pts. 2, 3), XXIX (pt. 2), XXXIII, XXXVI (pts. 1, 2, 3), XL (pts. 1, 2), XLIII (pts. 1, 2), XLVI (pts. 1, 2, 3); the *Evening Star* (Washington), Oct. 2, 3, 1901.]

T. M. S.

GEYER, HENRY SHEFFIE (Dec. 9, 1790–Mar. 5, 1859), lawyer, United States senator, was born in Frederick, Md., the son of John Geyer, a native Prussian, and Elizabeth (Sheffie) Geyer. He received a common-school education, and after having studied under his uncle, Daniel Sheffie, began the practise of law at the age of twenty-one. Shortly thereafter he took part in the War of 1812, during which he was promoted to a first lieutenancy and became regimental paymaster of the 38th Infantry. Immediately following the war he moved to the frontier village of St. Louis, where he quickly won distinction at the bar. In 1818 he was elected to the territorial legislature, and, although not a member of the famous constitutional convention, nevertheless, by virtue of being the principal author of Missouri's "Solemn Public Act," he played a prominent part in her struggle for statehood. He cleverly pointed out that the ostensible obligation imposed upon Missouri by Congress through this act did not, in reality, constitute a surrender of proslavery principles. Geyer was thrice a member and twice speaker of the Missouri House in the twenties, and held his fourth and last seat in that body in 1834–35. He effected the major share of the revision of Missouri's statute law in the sessions of 1825 and 1835. During his forty-three years of practise he achieved notable success in untangling the intricacies of land-title litigation, and in the handling of jury trials and chancery cases. In the important land case of *Strother* vs. *Lucas* (6 *Peters*, 763), his brilliant argument caused Chief Justice Marshall surprise at finding "so much learning come from west of the Mississippi River" (Darby, *post*, p. 375), while his overpowering logic in the famous Darnes murder trial (1840) won the highest praise from Rufus Choate.

When the Anti-Benton Democrats in the legislature saw that their favorite, Col. Stringfellow, could not muster sufficient votes to defeat "Old Bullion," they switched their support to Geyer, a Whig, who held principles nearer to their proslavery views than those held by Benton, and elected him on the fortieth ballot (1851). At Washington, Geyer, in common with most Western senators, devoted much of his time to the urging of petitions from groups of his constituents requesting federal land grants, to be used chiefly for the purpose of building railroads. Atlantic seaboard senators consequently attacked the Westerners as "land pirates." Geyer replied that the old states also had a taste for spoils, but his chief retort was to introduce more land-grant petitions from Missouri. When the proposed Pacific railroad was designated to go by way of Chicago and miss Missouri, he charged that the whole scheme was a Wall Street conspiracy. The extreme proslavery leaders in Missouri bitterly assailed him for his silence during most of the debate on the Fugitive-Slave Bill, but he partially retrieved himself by condemning Seward's "higher law" doctrine, and by making the greatest speech of his senatorial career in defense of the so-called "Border Ruffians." In this he contended that the Missourians had a far better right to shape the affairs of Kansas than those week-old Kansan Yankees subsidized by that child of the devil, the Emigrant Aid Society. Although, like many strict constructionists, he opposed the Kansas-Nebraska Bill as subversive of the constitutional rights of the South, Geyer was not in theory a secessionist. He was the leading attorney for the defendant slave-owner in the Dred Scott case, and practically all the arguments, principal points, and citations elaborated in Taney's decision were made by Geyer. Despite his long political career, his chief eminence was as a lawyer. He was married three times: on Jan. 1, 1818, to Clarissa B. Starr; on Apr. 26, 1831, to Joanna (Easton) Quarles; and on Feb. 12, 1850, to Jane (Stoddard) Charless.

[W. V. N. Bay, *Reminiscences of the Bench and Bar of Mo.* (1878); F. L. Billon, *Annals of St. Louis in its Territorial Days from 1804 to 1821* (1888); John F. Darby, *Personal Recollections* (1880); T. T. Gantt, *Memorials and Speeches* (1885); W. B. Stevens, *Centennial Hist. of Mo.* (1921), vol. II; T. H. S. Hamersly, *Complete Regular Army Reg. of the U. S.* (1880); Samuel Treat Papers, Jefferson Memorial Library, St. Louis; contemporary newspaper accounts.]

H. E. N.

GHERARDI, BANCROFT (Nov. 10, 1832–Dec. 10, 1903), naval officer, was born in Jackson, La. His father, Donato Gherardi, an Italian by birth, emigrated to the United States about 1825 and became an instructor in Greek and Latin at the Round Hill School of George Bancroft [*q.v.*]. His mother, Jane Bancroft, was a sister of the historian, who while secretary of the navy appointed his nephew in 1846 an acting midshipman. Young Gherardi, after a few months in school, was ordered to the *Ohio* and served on that vessel in the war with Mexico on the west coast of that country. In 1850–51 he was attached to the *Saranac* of the Home Squadron. Entering the Naval Academy in the fall of 1851, he graduated in June of the following year and was warranted passed midshipman. Ordered to the *St. Louis,* he cruised in the Mediterranean and was present when his commander, Duncan N. Ingraham [*q.v.*], made the memorable assertion of American rights at Smyrna. Soon after his promotion to a lieutenancy in 1855, he was sent to the *Saratoga* of the Home Squadron. At the outbreak of the Civil War he was with the *Lancaster* of the Pacific Squadron.

In 1862, while acting as executive officer of the *Chippewa* of the North Atlantic Blockading Squadron he was promoted lieutenant-commander, and in September of that year he was ordered to the *Mohican,* which ship was employed in searching for Confederate commerce-destroyers in the North and South Atlantic oceans. In the fall of 1863 he joined the West Gulf Blockading Squadron and commanded the *Chocura* until transferred in May 1864 to the *Port Royal.* Gherardi saw active service in the Gulf or on the Mississippi until the close of the war. He was chiefly employed in routine blockade duties, but on Aug. 5, 1864, he participated in the battle of Mobile Bay, under Farragut. During the first part of the battle the *Port Royal* was lashed to the *Richmond,* but later when cast off from her companion she chased three of the enemy's gunboats. Her commander was highly commended for his "cool and courageous conduct."

During the decade succeeding the war, Gherardi was chiefly employed on shore: with navigation and equipment duties at the Philadelphia navy-yard, 1867–70, and with duties on the receiving ship *Independence* at the Mare Island navy-yard, 1871–74. In 1867 he was commissioned commander; and in 1875, captain, to take rank from Nov. 9, 1874. After taking command of the *Pensacola,* the flagship of the North Pacific Squadron, he was, on Aug. 12, 1876, sentenced to suspension for two years for "causing punishment forbidden by law to be inflicted on persons in the Navy" (*General Orders . . . 1863–87,* 1887, no. 217)—a sentence that on Feb. 3, 1877, was remitted. In 1878–81 he commanded the receiving ship *Colorado,* and in 1881–83 the *Lancaster,* flagship of the European Station, being present at the bombardment of Alexandria. Later Gherardi was, successively, president of the Naval Examining Board, governor of the Naval Asylum, and commandant of the New York navy-yard. In 1884 he was promoted commodore; and three years later, rear-admiral, serving while in the latter grade as commander-in-chief of the North Atlantic Squadron, 1889–92, and occupied chiefly in protecting American interests in West Indian and Central American waters. During the Haitian revolution he secured a prompt and equitable settlement of differences between the combatants that was highly creditable to his diplomacy. In 1893 as commander of the "naval review fleet" consisting of thirty-five men-of-war drawn not only from the American navy but from the navies of nine foreign powers, he had the leading part in a naval celebration on the Hudson River in commemoration of the discovery of America. He was retired on Nov. 10, 1894. In January 1872 Bancroft was married to Anna Talbot Rockwell of San Francisco. He died at his home in Stratford, Conn., leaving two sons.

[See Record of Officers, Bureau of Navigation, 1846–1903; Navy Register, 1849–94; *Official Records* (*Navy*), 1 ser. vols. VI, XX–XXII; letters of Capt. Walter R. Gherardi to C. O. Paullin, Feb. 1929; *Who's Who in America,* 1901–02; M. A. DeW. Howe, *The Life and Letters of George Bancroft* (2 vols., 1908); *N. Y. Times,* Dec. 11, 1903. According to Howe, *supra,* p. 17, Gherardi was originally named Aaron Bancroft, presumably for his maternal grandfather.] C. O. P.

GHOLSON, SAMUEL JAMESON (May 19, 1808–Oct. 16, 1883), jurist, Confederate soldier, was born in Madison County, Ky., and moved with his father's family to northern Alabama. His early education was limited to that which he gained from the country schools of the period, but he was naturally studious and ambitious and had acquired a wide knowledge by the time he attained his majority. After studying law at Russellville, Ala., under Judge Peter Martin, he was admitted to practise in 1829. He settled at Athens, the county seat of Monroe County, Miss., in 1830 and was married in 1838 to Miss Ragsdale. In 1835 he was elected to the state House of Representatives from his county and served also in the sessions of 1836 and 1839. After the death of Congressman David Dickson he was elected as a Democrat to fill the unexpired term ending Mar. 4, 1837. A special session of Congress was called in 1837 before the time of the regular election in Mississippi, and a special election was ordered at which Gholson and J. F. H. Claiborne were elected over S. S. Prentiss and E. L. Acee. At the following regular election Claiborne and Gholson were defeated by Prentiss and Word, but they made a contest claiming their seats under the special election. In the debates on this contest Gholson had a heated encounter with Henry A. Wise of Virginia which caused a hurried adjournment of the session. A duel was prevented by John C. Calhoun and other friends. Gholson declined to be a candidate when the questions arising out of the contest were referred to the popular vote in 1838.

Appointed by President Van Buren judge of the United States district court of Mississippi on Feb. 13, 1839, he served as federal judge for twenty-two years. He opposed the repudiation of the Union Bank bonds in 1841, and in 1843 sought an alliance with S. S. Prentiss, his former Whig opponent, in the hope of defeating repudiation. Gov. John A. Quitman was brought before Gholson when arrested by the United States marshal for complicity in the Lopez filibustering expedition against Cuba, and was released on his word of honor without bond. Gholson was of the opinion that Quitman was the governor of a sovereign state and not subject to indictment and arrest on the authority of the courts of the United States. He presided over the Democratic state convention of 1860, and was a member of the constitutional convention of 1861 which passed the ordinance of secession.

On the withdrawal of Mississippi from the Union, he resigned from the federal bench, enlisted as a private in the Monroe Volunteers, and was elected captain of the company, which later became Company I, 14th Mississippi Infantry. He was promoted colonel and brigadier-general of state troops in 1861. At Fort Donelson he was wounded in the right lung and captured with his command. In 1863 he was made major-general of state troops. The next year he accepted a commission as brigadier-general in the Confederate army, and was given command of a brigade of cavalry. He lost his left arm from wounds received in an engagement at Egypt, Miss., Dec. 27, 1864. After the war he resumed the practise of law at Aberdeen, Miss. He was a member of the state House of Representatives in 1865 and 1866 and served as speaker. He was a prominent figure in the political life of the state during the Reconstruction period, and on the restoration of home rule was called on to represent his county in the legislature of 1878. He died at his home in Aberdeen on Oct. 16, 1883, and is buried there.

[*House Jours. of the Miss. Legislature*; *Records of the U. S. Court of Miss.*, 1839–60; *Jour. of the Miss. Constitutional Convention of 1861* (1861); *Confed. Mil. Hist.* (1899), vol. VII; Jas. D. Lynch, in *Bench and Bar of Miss.* (1881); Dunbar Rowland, *Mississippi* (1907), vol. I, *The Official and Statistical Register of the State of Miss.* (1908), and *Hist. of Miss., The Heart of the South* (1925); Natchez *Democrat*, Oct. 24, 1883.]

D. R.

GHOLSON, THOMAS SAUNDERS (Dec. 9, 1808–Dec. 12, 1868), jurist, statesman, was born at Gholsonville, Brunswick County, Va., the son of Maj. William and Mary (Saunders) Gholson, and a descendant in the fourth generation from Anthony Gholson of Brunswick County—presumably the first of the line in America. After attending secondary school in Oxford, N. C., he entered the University of Virginia, where in 1827 he was graduated. He studied law and for some years practised his profession in Brunswick County, winning a reputation as an excellent lawyer and a speaker of unusual eloquence, and marrying meanwhile, May 14, 1829, his first cousin, Cary Ann Gholson. In 1840 he removed to Petersburg and formed a law partnership with his brother, James Hubbard Gholson, which continued until the latter's death in 1848, after which he formed a partnership with James Alfred Jones of Mecklenburg County and Richmond (J. E. Saunders, *Early Settlers of Alabama,* 1899, p. 374). He participated in various important cases, both civil and criminal, perhaps the most famous of which was his prosecution of William Dandridge Epes for the murder of Francis Adolphus Muir, in Dinwiddie County, which created great interest in Southside Virginia. In 1844 he was appointed a visitor of the College of William and Mary. He served as president of the Bank of Petersburg, and founded and aided in the support of a public library in that city.

Gholson became judge of the 5th judicial circuit in Virginia in 1859, and continued through the April term, 1863 (L. C. Bell, *The Old Free State,* 1927, vol. I, p. 344), following which he was elected a member of the Second Confederate States Congress, where he favored a vigorous military policy, advocated inclusive conscription, and protested successfully against the use of negro troops (*Journal of the Congress of the Confederate States of America,* 1905, vol. VII). After the war he formed a cotton and tobacco commission house in Liverpool, England, with his son-in-law, Col. Norman Stewart Walker. He died suddenly, of heart-failure, at Savannah, Ga., while returning to Virginia after a visit to England to look after his new business interests. He was buried at the historic Blandford Church, Petersburg, of which he had formerly (1843) been a vestryman (P. Slaughter, *History of Bristol Parish,* 1879).

Little can be ascertained of his life or personality, save for family traditions of his hospitality, his gentle disposition and keen humor, and his modesty, which led him to shun notoriety of any kind. His career was not dramatic or conspicuous enough for his name to appear frequently in the newspapers of his time; and, although he was a figure of considerable local prominence, even his death—occurring in a strange city, in the troubled days of Reconstruction—evoked but brief comment from the press.

[Gholson's only son, the Rev. John Yates Gholson, died without issue; such accounts of his life and achievements as were in the possession of his daughter, Georgiana Gholson Walker, were destroyed by fire about 1910. Fire likewise destroyed many of the records of Brunswick County, long the seat of the Gholsons, and of the Petersburg Public Library, thus cutting off two possibly important sources of information.] A. C. G., Jr.

GHOLSON, WILLIAM YATES (Dec. 25, 1807–Sept. 21, 1870), jurist, and author, was born in Southampton County, Va., of a family prominent in Southern judicial history. His father, Thomas Gholson, Jr., represented Virginia in Congress from 1808 to 1816, dying as the result of a wound received in the War of 1812; his mother was Ann Yates, grand-daughter of a president of the College of William and Mary. He graduated from Nassau Hall (now Princeton University), and subsequently studied law under the celebrated instructor, Chancellor Creed Taylor, near Farmville, Va. On his twentieth birthday he married the Chancellor's niece, Ann Jane Taylor, and settled on his plantation near Gholsonville in Brunswick County. Three years after his wife's death in 1831 he moved to Pontotoc, Miss., was admitted to the bar, and speedily acquired a considerable practise. He helped to establish the University of Mississippi, and was one of its earliest trustees. On May 21, 1839, he married Elvira, only child of Daniel W. Wright, at one time judge of the Mississippi supreme court.

In 1844 he freed his slaves and moved to Cincinnati, Ohio, where he opened law offices and was shortly afterwards appointed city solicitor. For a time he was in partnership with James P. Holcombe, later professor of law at the University of Virginia and a member of the Confederate Congress. In May 1854, when the new superior court of Cincinnati was organized, Gholson, who had "achieved a professional reputation hardly second to any lawyer in the State" (Reed, *post,* I, 70), was elected as one of the three jurists to occupy its bench. Here he had opportunity further to demonstrate, along with the depth and range of his abilities, his intellectual integrity and courage, his lofty moral nature, and his dignified, courteous bearing. The tribunal formed by him and his fellow judges, Bellamy Storer and Oliver M. Spencer—themselves leaders of the Cincinnati bar—is said never to have been equaled in the annals of the court. After five years of service he was appointed by the governor, Nov. 8, 1859, to fill an unexpired term as justice of the supreme court of Ohio. He was afterwards elected for a full term, but failing health compelled him to resign, Dec. 1, 1863, and he returned to his practise of the law.

His life was one of unremitting industry. A man of great intellectual power, cultivated, studious, keen of perception, and possessing the gift of forceful statement, he won reputation early in his career as an effective political speaker; in later life he amused himself in his leisure hours with the labors of authorship. He was one of the compilers of a *Digest of the Ohio Reports* (1867), edited several editions of *A Compendium of Mercantile Law* by J. W. Smith, and published addresses on the payment of the public debt and on the Reconstruction of the Southern states. "The embodiment of clear legal logic," as he has been called, his judicial opinions rank high for learning and accuracy. "He knew nothing of the parties but their names on the docket; nothing of the cause but from the evidence; nothing of the result and its consequences but the judgment which the law pronounces," wrote a successor on the bench (Manning T. Force in Reed, *post,* I, 28)—an opinion shared by another distinguished contemporary at the Cincinnati bar, Mr. Justice Stanley Matthews, who, speaking further of Gholson's kindness and patience, added, "He loved jurisprudence as a systematic science, for its logic, but never forgot that it was vitalized by the spirit of justice."

[G. I. Reed, *Bench and Bar of Ohio* (1897), vol. I; C. T. Greve, *Centennial Hist. of Cincinnati* (1904), vol. I; J. E. Saunders, *Early Settlers of Ala.* (1899); *Cincinnati Commercial,* Sept. 23, 1870; information supplied by Edward Gholson, Esq., Librarian of the Cincinnati Law Library Asso., and by L. B. Hamlin, Esq., Librarian of the Hist. and Phil. Soc. of Ohio, Cincinnati.] A. C. G., Jr.

GIBAULT, PIERRE (April 1737–1804), Roman Catholic missionary, was the eldest son of Pierre and Marie Saint-Jean Gibault of Montreal, and was christened on Apr. 7, 1737 (Dunn, *post,* p. 23). His great-grandfather had emigrated to Quebec from Poitiers, France, about the middle of the seventeenth century. After completing his education at the Seminary of Quebec, Pierre served for a short time at the cathedral. In 1768, in response to the call for helpers by Father Sebastian Meurin, who was in charge of the Roman Catholic missionary activities in the Illinois country, he was sent thither by Bishop Oliver Briand of Quebec. Accompanied by his mother and sister, he took up his residence at Kaskaskia, the chief Illinois settlement. Missions at Ste. Genevieve and St. Louis were included in his parish. Having been made vicar-general of the Illinois country in 1769, he also visited Vincennes where he found much vice and disorder. Through his influence, a new church was erected in that village.

After the capture of Kaskaskia by Virginia militia July 4, 1778, the generous attitude of the commander, George Rogers Clark [*q.v.*], towards the church served to stir up the enthusiasm of the French for the American cause. To Father Gibault, who asked permission to conduct the usual services in his church, Clark replied that he had nothing to do with churches except to protect them from insult. The effect of this conduct upon the minds of the villagers was magical and they readily took the oath of allegiance to the commonwealth of Virginia. In a conference, Father Gibault undertook to gain the allegiance of the French at Vincennes, assuring Clark that while he had nothing to do with temporal affairs, "he would give them such hints in the Spiritual way that would be very conducive to the business." The priest, accompanied by a Dr. Jean Laffont and a few companions, set out for Vincennes carrying an address prepared by Clark to the inhabitants of that village. The mission was completely successful, winning also the friendship of the Indian tribes of the region. After the capture of Vincennes by the British Lieutenant-Governor Hamilton, Gibault assisted Clark in securing volunteers among the French for the expedition which recaptured that post. For his patriotism Father Gibault received the thanks of the governor and Assembly of Virginia. He later disclaimed responsibility for the submission of Vincennes, and declared he had done nothing further than to counsel peace and union and attempt to prevent bloodshed. His willingness thus to shift all responsibility for leadership to Laffont was due to the demand on the part of Bishop Briand in 1780 that he should appear at Quebec to answer the charge of treason made by British officers. There is no evidence to show that this order was ever enforced. During 1785 he established his residence at Vincennes. After four years, he removed to Cahokia. For his losses during the Revolution, in 1790 he petitioned Gov. Arthur St. Clair to assign him a grant of Seminary land. Following the effective protest of Bishop Carroll of Baltimore against the alienation of church property to an individual clergyman, Gibault crossed the Mississippi to Spanish territory and settled at New Madrid, where he was parish priest until his death early in 1804.

["Kaskaskia Records 1778–1790," ed. by C. W. Alvord, *Ill. State Hist. Lib. Colls.*, vol. V (1909); J. A. James, "George Rogers Clark Papers," *Ibid.*, vol. VIII (1912); *Cath. Hist. Researches*, II, 54–60, 117–19 (Oct. 1885, Jan. 1886); *Am. Hist. Rev.*, Apr. 1909; J. P. Dunn, "Father Gibault: the Patriot Priest of the Northwest," *Trans. Ill. State Hist. Soc., 1905* (1906); J. A. James, *The Life of George Rogers Clark* (1928); John Law, *The Colonial Hist. of Vincennes* (1858); P. L. Peyton, "Pierre Gibault, Priest and Patriot of the Northwest," *Records Am. Cath. Hist. Soc. of Phila.*, Dec. 1901; J. D. G. Shea, *Life and Times of the Most Rev. John Carroll* (1888); John Rothensteiner, *Hist. of the Archdiocese of St. Louis* (2 vols., 1928); Louis Houck, *A Hist. of Mo.* (3 vols., 1908), II, 298–303.]

J. A. J.

GIBBES, ROBERT WILSON (July 8, 1809–Oct. 15, 1866), physician, author, scientist, was born in Charleston, S. C. His father was William Hasell Gibbes [*q.v.*]; his mother was Mary Philp Wilson of Charleston. After graduating from the South Carolina College at Columbia in 1827, he became an assistant to Thomas Cooper [*q.v.*] in the department of chemistry, geology, and mineralogy. In 1830 he received the degree of M.D. from the Medical College of the State of South Carolina at Charleston, but continued at South Carolina College until 1834, when he resigned to give his time to the practise of medicine and to his other interests. As a physician he gained a national reputation, and even in his earlier years acquired a certain prestige. His treatise "On Typhoid Pneumonia, as it Occurs in the Neighborhood of Columbia, S. C." (*American Journal of Medical Science,* October 1842), opposing the use of the lancet in such cases, is said to have revolutionized the treatment of the disease, while Gen. Hampton is quoted as having said that Gibbes saved him $5,000 a year in slaves (Selby, *post,* p. 19).

Gibbes devoted himself with some enthusiasm to a variety of subjects. In 1846 he published the *Memoir of James De Veaux,* an interesting biographical study. The *Documentary History of the American Revolution* (3 vols., 1853–57) was the result of years of painstaking collecting and editing. His many contributions to the best contemporary periodicals show the wide range of his interests, and are written in a style notably simple and direct in a day of literary pomposity. Several of his scientific papers were published by the Academy of Natural Sciences and in the *Smithsonian Contributions to Knowledge.* His scientific collections, planned as the nucleus of a museum, included specimens of paleontology, mineralogy, conchology, and ornithology. He also possessed a remarkably fine art gallery. All these collections were destroyed in the burning of Columbia in 1865. In 1852 he was forced in the settlement of a debt to take over a newspaper, the *South Carolinian,* and a publishing business. He retained active editorship of the paper until 1858 and continued to own it until the destruction of the plant in the fire of 1865. Actively Democratic, the daily was the vigorous opponent of its Know-Nothing contemporary. In a political controversy, involving the reporting of the meetings of city council, Gibbes was ejected from the council chamber. He brought suit against the mayor and city marshal, and the case was widely heralded as a test of the freedom of the press. The modest damages awarded him were claimed as a vindication of the rights of the press. He was twice mayor of Columbia and throughout the Civil War he served as surgeon-general of South Carolina. His business interests included the ownership of the Saluda factory, a plant which manufactured cotton shirting. He was married on Dec. 20, 1827, to Carolina Elizabeth Guignard. They had twelve children, nine of whom survived their parents. Four of their sons were in the active service of the Confederacy and one was a Confederate agent to England. The last years of Gibbes's life were darkened by sorrow, ill health, and financial reverses, and he died a prematurely old man.

[H. S. Holmes, "Robt. Gibbes, Gov. of S. C., and Some of his Descendants," *S. C. Hist. and Geneal. Mag.,* Apr. 1911; *In Memoriam, Dr. Robt. W. Gibbes* (1866); M. La Borde, *Hist. of the S. C. Coll.* (1859); J. A. Selby, *Memorabilia and Anecdotal Reminiscences of Columbia* (1905); Michael Tuomey, *Report on the Geol. of S. C.* (1848); *Rights of Corporators and Reporters* (1857); Dunbar Rowland, *Jefferson Davis* (1923), VI, 446; Frank Leslie's *Illustrated Newspaper,* Sept. 5, 1857, Feb. 2, 1861; *Hist. Mag.,* vol. X (1866), supp. no. 5, p. 160.]

A. R. C.

GIBBES, WILLIAM HASELL (Mar. 16, 1754–Feb. 13, 1834), lawyer, was born in Charleston, S. C., the son of William and Elizabeth (Hasell) Gibbes. His grandfather, Robert Gibbes, was governor of the province from 1710 to 1712 and at one time its chief justice. His father, William Gibbes, was one of a secret committee of five members of the Council of Safety, appointed in 1775 by Charles Pinckney, to gather munitions against the impending Revolution. The son, having earlier read law under John Rutledge, was in England studying in the Inner Temple in 1774. When the news of the "Intolerable Acts" was received, a group of thirty Americans living in England protested in a petition to the House of Commons, and in a memorial direct to the King. Gibbes was among the sixteen South Carolinians who signed the document. When the Revolution broke out, he was refused a passport, but escaped to the Bermudas. Thence he made his way to Philadelphia and then to South Carolina, where he became a captain-lieutenant of the Ancient Artillery. He served in the sieges of Charleston and Savannah. When Charleston surrendered, its citizens were put on parole and confined to the limits of the city. In August 1780 Cornwallis ordered the arrest, and transportation to St. Augustine, of a group of the leading citizens. No particular complaint was lodged against them, but in spite of that fact, they were sequestered in St. Augustine until the close of the war. Gibbes was in this group, which also included Christopher Gadsden [*q.v.*].

At some time before 1783, Gibbes was admitted to the bar, and was in that year elected master-in-equity, a position which he held until 1825. His services in the office have been described as "important and valuable" (O'Neall, *post,* II, 214). In 1811 he was impeached by the legislature on charges growing out of the sale of thirty-five slaves, through the master's court. Gibbes was represented by William Drayton and Keating Simons. The prosecuting attorney was Charles Pinckney. Gibbes was acquitted by a large majority on every charge. From 1825 until his death in 1834 he apparently engaged in the private practise of law. An account book, showing the record of the administration of his estate, indicates that he was a man of large means, and his personal letters show him to have been a man of deep piety and of strong family affections. He was twice married: first, on Aug. 29, 1772, to Elizabeth Allston, by whom he had ten children; and second, on Jan. 21, 1808, to Mary Philp Wilson, who had four children. Five children survived him, of whom Robert W. Gibbes [*q.v.*], physician and publisher, his eldest child by his second wife, was the best known. Gibbes was buried in St. Philip's churchyard in Charleston.

[J. B. O'Neall, *Biog. Sketches of the Bench and Bar of S. C.* (2 vols., 1859); Edward McCrady, *The Hist. of S. C. under the Royal Govt., 1719–76* (1889), and *The Hist. of S. C. in the Revolution* (1901); H. S. Holmes, "Robt. Gibbes, Gov. of S. C., and Some of his Descendants," *S. C. Hist. and Geneal. Mag.,* Apr. 1911; M. L. Webber, "Parish Reg. of St. James' Santee," *Ibid.,* July 1915; *Charleston Courier,* Dec. 12, 1811, Feb. 21, 1834. There are a number of letters, several account books, a portion of a diary, and a detailed family record in an old family Bible, all in the possession of Dr. J. Heyward Gibbes, Columbia, S. C. The impeachment may be followed through the S. C. Senate *Journal,* beginning with Nov. 29, 1811.]

A. R. C.

GIBBON, JOHN (Apr. 20, 1827–Feb. 6, 1896), soldier, was born near Holmesburg, Pa., now within the boundaries of the city of Philadelphia, the third son of Dr. John Heysham Gibbon who upon attaining his majority dropped the final "s" from his family name, and of Catharine (Lardner) Gibbon. A few years later, Dr. Gibbon removed with his family to Charlotte, N. C., and it was from that state that young Gibbon received his appointment to the United States Military Academy in 1842. Graduating in 1847, he was commissioned in the artillery and sent to duty in Mexico, where, however, active operations had ceased before his arrival. He had a taste of Indian warfare in Florida in 1849, against the Seminoles, followed by garrison duty in the West and five years at West Point, teaching artillery practise. Here he prepared *The Artillerist's Manual,* adopted by the War Department in 1859 and published in 1860. On Oct. 16, 1855, he married Frances North Moale, daughter of Samuel Moale of Baltimore. He had been promoted first lieutenant in 1850. He was now (1859) promoted captain, and joined his battery in Utah, whence he marched back to Fort Leavenworth a few months later, at the beginning of the Civil War. Though a Southerner by adoption, and though three of his brothers joined the Confederate army, he remained loyal to the Union. He was ordered to Washington in October 1861 and served for some months as chief of artillery of McDowell's Division. He seems to have had a natural talent for dealing with the volunteer soldier, whose possibilities, as well as limitations, he appreciated from the first; and his success during the period of organization and training brought him appointment as brigadier-general of volunteers, May 2, 1862, and assignment to the command of what later became famous as the "Iron Brigade." He led it at the second battle of Bull Run, at South Mountain, and at Antietam, and was then advanced to the command of a division. At Fredericksburg he was severely wounded, and was absent from duty for more than three months. He was again wounded on the third day at Gettysburg, in which battle he commanded the II Corps twice when Gen. Hancock was temporarily ordered to another part of the field. After his recovery he commanded a draft depot until he was able to rejoin the army in the field, in the spring of 1864. As a division commander he took part in all the heavy fighting of the Army of the Potomac that year—the Wilderness, Spotsylvania, and the rest. He was promoted major-general of volunteers, June 7, 1864. After the fight at Reams's Station, in August, he issued an order depriving three regiments, whose colors had been captured, of the privilege of carrying colors until they should regain it by their behavior in future battles. In this action he was sustained by his superiors, but it caused considerable controversy, both in and out of the army, which was ended only upon the restoration of their colors to all three regiments in recognition of their gallant conduct at Hatcher's Run, in October (*Official Records, Army,* 1 ser., XLII, pt. 3, pp. 493–500, 542–44). In January 1865, he was given the new XXIV Corps, in the Army of the James, commanded it in the final operations against Lee's army, and was one of the commissioners designated to arrange the details of the surrender. He was mustered out of the volunteer service, Jan. 15, 1866, and appointed colonel of one of the new regiments of infantry of the regular army, July 28, 1866. His service after the Civil War was chiefly in the West, and included much Indian fighting. He commanded the expedition, in 1876, which rescued the survivors of Custer's command and buried the dead at Little Bighorn. In 1877, after a march of 250 miles he attacked and defeated the Nez Percé Indians under Chief Joseph, whose fast friend he afterward became. He was made brigadier-general, July 10, 1885. As commander of the Department of the Columbia he was called upon (1885–86) to maintain the peace during the threatened anti-Chinese outbreak in Seattle (C. B. Bagley, *History of Seattle,* 1916, II, 455–77). In 1885 he wrote his *Personal Recollections of the Civil War,* which remained in manuscript until 1928. "They are written in a straightforward, frank, soldierly fashion and tell only what the writer himself saw" (*American Historical Review,* January 1929). In 1891 he retired from active service. He died at Baltimore, and was buried in Arlington National Cemetery. At the time of his death he was commander-in-chief of the Loyal Legion.

[G. W. Cullum, *Biog. Reg.* (3rd ed., 1891), II, 323–24, and IV, 71; *Asso. Grads. U. S. Mil. Acad., Ann. Reunion,* 1896; *Official Records (Army)*, ser. I, vols. XII (pt. 2), XIX (pt. 1), XXI, XXV (pts. 1, 2), XXVII (pts. 1, 3), XXXVI (pts. 1, 2, 3), XL (pts. 1, 2, 3), XLII (pts. 1, 2, 3), XLVI (pts. 1, 2, 3), LI (pt. 1); I. R. Pennypacker, "Military Historians and History," *Pa. Mag. of Hist. and Biog.*, Jan. 1929; *Evening Star* (Washington, D. C.), Feb. 7, 1896; editorial in Portland *Oregonian,* Feb. 8, 1896; family history from Miss Frances M. Gibbon, daughter of Gen. Gibbon.]

T. M. S.

GIBBONS, ABIGAIL HOPPER (Dec. 7, 1801–Jan. 16, 1893), philanthropist, Abolitionist, prison-reformer, the third child of Isaac Tatem Hopper [*q.v.*] and Sarah Tatum, was born in Philadelphia. Being the child of Quaker parents, she was a birthright member of the Society of Friends, and at the "Separation" in 1827, she threw in her lot with the Hicksite branch. She was carefully educated at home and in the Quaker day-schools of the period. When about twenty years old she set up a school of her own in Philadelphia for the elementary education of the children of Friends, in which she continued to teach for ten years. In 1830 she moved to New York and became the head of a Friends' School in that city.

She was married in the Friends' Meeting-House, New York City, Feb. 14, 1833, to James Sloan Gibbons [*q.v.*] of Philadelphia, a native of Wilmington, Del. After their marriage they lived in Philadelphia until 1835 when they moved to New York City, which became their permanent residence. Both were devoted Abolitionists and they made their home a refuge for escaping slaves. They also identified themselves completely with all the lines of humanitarian work which were carried on by Mrs. Gibbons's father. Both Isaac Hopper and James Sloan Gibbons were disowned as members of the Society of Friends in 1842 by the New York Monthly Meeting, of the Hicksite branch, on account of their anti-slavery activities, whereupon Mrs. Gibbons went to the same meeting in June of that year and publicly read her resignation of membership, and resignations in behalf of four of her minor children, giving her reasons for withdrawal from the religious Society in which she had been born. Until her death, however, she remained loyal to the ideals and the way of life of the Quakers.

Becoming interested in some homeless German children in her neighborhood, she set about the establishment of an industrial school which she conducted for twelve years. She worked for a large part of her life to improve the conditions of the poor, the crippled, and the blind children in the city poor-house at West Farms, now Randalls Island, and as a major interest took up the work of prison reform, in which her father had been a prime mover. She made weekly visits to the Tombs and became the wise helper and counselor of the noted matron of that period, Flora Foster. She brought to this work tender sympathy balanced by sound judgment, and rare talent for administration and management. When the Civil War began, she offered herself as nurse and helper in the camps and hospitals, and served with few intermissions from 1861 to 1865. During the anti-draft riots, her home in New York was one of those picked out by the mob for destruction. The house was completely sacked and many papers and articles of great value were destroyed. As soon as the war was over, she helped to start a "Labor and Aid Society" to assist the returning soldiers to find employment and new opportunity. She assisted in establishing the Protestant Asylum for Infants, and was president of the New York Committee for the Prevention of State Regulation of Vice. Her most important humanitarian work, however, was done through the Women's Prison Association, of which she was for many years the efficient president. A "Home" was established by the Association in which discharged prisoners could live while they were finding their way back to normal life again. It was through her efforts also, that provision was made for arrested women to be searched by persons of their own sex. With much right can she be called "the Elizabeth Fry of America."

[S. H. Emerson, *Life of Abby Hopper Gibbons: Told Chiefly Through her Correspondence* (2 vols., 1896); L. M. Child, *Isaac T. Hopper, A True Life* (1853); R. P. Tatum, *Tatum Narrative 1626–1925* (1925); *Charities Rev.*, May 1893; *Friends' Intelligencer and Jour.*, Jan. 28, 1893; *Boston Evening Transcript*, Jan. 25, 1893; *N. Y. Times*, Jan. 17, 18, 1893; *N. Y. Tribune*, Jan. 19, 1893.]

R. M. J.

GIBBONS, JAMES (July 23, 1834–Mar. 24, 1921), Roman Catholic prelate, was born on Gay Street, Baltimore, Md., within the parish of the Cathedral in which he was to preside for forty-three years as archbishop. His parents, Thomas and Bridget Gibbons, had emigrated from Ireland a few years before his birth. The father came of a family of small farmers near Westport, County Mayo. In Baltimore he was employed in a clerical capacity by a firm of importers and seems to have developed considerable ability in business. The mother of the future Cardinal, born Bridget Walsh, was strong, energetic, courageous, and of deep piety. James was her eldest son, the fourth of six children. She held him in her arms when he was three years old to see Andrew Jackson passing in a procession in Baltimore. The health of Thomas Gibbons failed in 1837 and the family returned to Ireland, where he bought land at Ballinrobe, a village near Westport, and became a farmer. There James began his education in a private classical school, in which he made rapid progress, showing special fondness for English literature. When he was thirteen years old his father died, and five years later the mother returned to the United States with her children, settling in New Orleans. There James became a clerk in a grocery store the owner of which was William C. Raymond. His services were so satisfactory that Raymond offered him promotion and became his firm friend for life. In his first summer in New Orleans he had a long illness from yellow fever.

Under the spell of a mission sermon delivered in January 1854 by the Rev. Clarence Walworth, young Gibbons decided to study for the priesthood. Cherishing affection for his native state, he chose to pursue his studies there and in the autumn of 1855 he entered St. Charles College, near Baltimore. He was at the head, or near the head, of all his classes throughout his residence there. Fellow students were warmly attached to him and called him *dominus*. His slender physique was strengthened by fondness for outdoor sports. He was graduated in three years on account of exceptional progress and entered St. Mary's Seminary, Baltimore, to begin his final preparation for the priesthood. A severe illness from malaria prostrated him and he feared for a time that he would be unable to continue his theological studies. After a slow recovery he took high rank as a student, especially in philosophy. On June 30, 1861, he was ordained to the priesthood in the Baltimore Cathedral by Archbishop Kenrick.

His first service as a priest was as assistant at St. Patrick's Church, Baltimore, where he remained but six weeks, being sent at the end of that time to take charge of St. Bridget's Church in the suburb of Canton, then a mission of St. Patrick's. A few months later St. Bridget's was made an independent parish and Gibbons soon showed unusual powers in developing its work. Partisan feeling in the Civil War, just beginning, ran high. He took no part in the controversies, but his sympathies were with the Union, though he had a warm admiration for the Southern people. One of his brothers was a Confederate soldier. Forts McHenry and Marshall, near St. Bridget's, had been strongly garrisoned. A vagrant private soldier attacked Gibbons with a club, but he knocked the man down and subdued him. On another occasion an intruder of Herculean size took possession of his house in his absence, but he defeated the man with an umbrella as a weapon. As chaplain at Fort McHenry he ministered to Federals and Confederates alike. Besides these duties he served another church, St. Lawrence's. His arduous work, combined with fasting on Sundays until he had celebrated late masses, impaired his health, but he regained vigor partly by taking long walks, a practise which he continued throughout his life. He established a parochial school at St. Bridget's and built a rectory.

His success attracted the attention of Archbishop Spalding, who had succeeded to the See of Baltimore, and he was invited in 1865 to become the Archbishop's secretary. After much hesitation, he accepted. The prelate conceived a warm affection and admiration for him. He was made assistant chancellor of the Second Plenary Council of Baltimore in 1866, and in his preparations for it, lightening the burden of his superior, he showed for the first time some measure of the great capacity which was to distinguish him. Though only thirty-two years old, he was nominated as head of the new Vicarate Apostolic of North Carolina, the establishment of which resulted from the Council's labors. On Aug. 16, 1868, he was consecrated Bishop of Adramyttum, the youngest of all the 1,200 Catholic bishops. In North Carolina, the future Cardinal received some of the strongest of the impressions which helped to shape his career. He made long journeys, establishing new churches, and making converts. His work brought him into much contact with non-Catholics, who were attracted by his winning personality, broad tolerance, and rare intellectual force. He was received as an honored guest in the homes of leading citizens of the state. Where there was no Catholic church he preached in court-houses, Masonic lodge rooms, and even in Protestant churches the use of which was offered to him. He studied the non-Catholic viewpoint in order that he might make his appeal with hopefulness. While he was serving this vicarate, the Ecumenical Council of the Vatican was called, of which he was the youngest member. He remained silent in the presence of his elders during the sessions in Rome in 1870 when the doctrine of the infallible teaching office of the Pope was being debated. The American prelates did not question the truth of the doctrine, but there was doubt among them of the opportuneness of declaring it. On the final vote only two were recorded in the negative. Bishop Gibbons voted *placet*. During this trip abroad he was impressed with the difficulties of the relations between Church and State in Europe as compared with the American system. A diary of the Council which he kept, published in the *Catholic World* (February to September 1870), attracted much attention.

When the bishopric of Richmond was vacated in 1872, Bishop Gibbons, already recognized as one of the ablest and most popular of the younger churchmen in America, was appointed to it. In the new post he showed even a fuller measure of his developing powers, administering the diocese with vigor, and attaining a high place in the esteem of people of all creeds. In 1876 he wrote *The Faith of our Fathers* (1877), a book which leaped almost at once into popularity and of which 2,000,000 copies were circulated in his lifetime. Written with literary grace, it is a remarkably clear and interesting exposition of Catholic doctrine, much of it set forth in the guise of temperate replies to the objections against the Church which are most commonly urged. It was translated into a dozen languages.

While in Richmond, Gibbons was called frequently to assist Archbishop Bayley, who had succeeded Spalding in Baltimore. In 1874 Bayley wrote to him that he intended to propose him for coadjutor archbishop with the right of succession. The modest Bishop demurred at first on the ground that he was unfitted for such a high post, and he was persuaded to accept only after two years had elapsed. He was appointed coadjutor in May 1877, and in October of the same year Bayley died. Gibbons, at the age of forty-three years, thus became the head of the oldest archdiocese in the United States, from which influences of great importance to the Church have radiated since the days of Archbishop John Carroll. Non-Catholics vied with Catholics in welcoming the new Archbishop to Baltimore with public celebrations. He was the first native of the city to be appointed to the See. Following his natural bent, he soon identified himself thoroughly with the life of the community, taking an active part in movements of a humanitarian and civic character. Washington being in the diocese of Baltimore, he made frequent visitations there and soon acquired a wide acquaintance among public men. He had met Andrew Johnson when that President attended the closing exercises of the Second Plenary Council of Baltimore, and he came in personal contact with every subsequent President down to Harding. Some of them, especially Cleveland, Roosevelt, and Taft, were his warm friends. When Garfield was assassinated in 1881 he issued a circular letter to the clergy of the diocese expressing horror at the deed. In the same year, at a time when the observance of Thanksgiving Day was far from general, he issued perhaps the first official direction by a prelate of the Catholic Church for celebrating the festival. With leading men of Baltimore he cooperated in the preparation of elaborate fêtes which marked the 150th anniversary of the city in 1880. In the same year he visited Rome and had his first meeting with Leo XIII, whose general views, he found, were like his own in many respects. There developed between them a mutual affection and sympathy which bore abundant fruit in subsequent years. They shared the belief that the power of hereditary governments was declining and that the future of the Catholic Church was to be largely among democratic peoples, whose reasonable aspirations ought to be considered by churchmen in a spirit of intimate understanding. One of the most signal achievements of Gibbons was in the organization and conduct of the Third Plenary Council of Baltimore, over which, by appointment of Leo XIII, he presided in 1884 as Apostolic Delegate. The decrees of the Council have guided the Catholic Church in the United States since, in a period when it has expanded faster here than in any other part of the world. Besides framing ecclesiastical regulations, the Council took a strong stand in support of American civil institutions, for which Gibbons worked ardently. Another outcome was the establishment of the Catholic University at Washington, of the board of trustees of which he was the head from its beginning until his death. He called the University his child and cherished it for many years with the solicitude of a father.

Leo XIII commended him highly for his work in presiding over the Council and a year after the death in 1885 of Cardinal McCloskey [*q.v.*] of New York appointed Gibbons the second American Cardinal. He received the red biretta June 30, 1886, the twenty-fifth anniversary of his ordination to the priesthood, which was made the occasion of a large celebration in Baltimore, in which state and city officials and non-Catholics joined. Nearly the whole American hierarchy gathered for the ceremonies. In the press his appointment was hailed on the ground that he had become thoroughly identified with American life and institutions and that he interpreted the spirit of his country. Going to Rome to receive the red hat, he delivered at his installation in his titular church, Santa Maria in Trastevere, Mar. 25, 1887, a pronouncement whose echoes were heard widely. He declared that the great progress of the Catholic Church in the United States was due in large part to American liberty. He expressed gratitude that he was a citizen of a country "where the civil government holds over us the ægis of its protection, without interfering with us in the legitimate exercise of our sublime mission as ministers of the gospel of Christ" and added: "Our country has liberty without license and authority without despotism." While in Rome, the Cardinal applied himself energetically to obtaining ecclesiastical support for the labor movement. The hierarchy of Canada had condemned the Knights of Labor, which then had a membership of 500,000 in the United States, on the ground of its secrecy. Cardinal Gibbons had summoned Terence V. Powderly, the head of the order, to Baltimore, and had received from him assurances that the secrecy was imposed by means of a pledge, not an oath, and that it did not prevent Catholics from manifesting everything in the confessional, the object of the secrecy being to prevent proscription by employers. Sympathizing deeply with labor's aspirations, he obtained after protracted efforts in Rome the assurance that the Knights would not be condemned in the United States, and the ban in Canada was lifted later. His plea against condemnation, addressed to the Prefect of the Propaganda, was perhaps the strongest document he ever wrote. A copy of it was obtained secretly by a newspaper and when published it was widely acclaimed in the United States and abroad. Gibbons enlisted himself also to prevent ecclesiastical condemnation of Henry George's book *Progress and Poverty* (1879), and succeeded in the face of many obstacles. His view was that discussion of labor and economic questions ought not to be stifled.

When he returned to Baltimore in June 1887, a popular ovation was given him there as a representative of American principles and a powerful champion of labor. He brought a cordial message from Leo XIII to President Cleveland. Later in the year, the fiftieth anniversary of Leo's priesthood was observed and the President, at the Cardinal's suggestion, sent to the Pontiff as a gift a handsomely bound copy of the Constitution of the United States. Cleveland consulted Gibbons about many things, including his message to Congress in 1887 advocating a reduction of the tariff. He had a high regard for the Cardinal's judgment on public questions and his penetrating knowledge of civic conditions. The celebration in 1889 of the centennial of the Catholic Hierarchy in America was marked by a week of imposing observances in Baltimore, organized by Gibbons, in which the Church's complete identification with American institutions was emphasized. A Congress of Laymen was held in connection with the celebration. When, in the last decade of the nineteenth century, Archbishop Ireland of St. Paul was criticized for some experiments which he made in cooperation with the public-school authorities at Faribault and Stillwater, Minn., he was sustained by Gibbons and obtained indorsement from Rome. When, about the same time, the "Cahensly movement" for the appointment of Catholic bishops in the United States on the basis of national groups of immigrants or descendants of immigrants gained ground, Gibbons opposed it with all his talents and resources. He was in favor of early blending of the immigrants with the native population and especially opposed the transplantation of European divisions to this country. In a sermon in Milwaukee he declared that "God and our country" should be the watchword of all in America, regardless of origin. The Cahensly plan failed after memorable controversies, and President Harrison warmly felicitated Cardinal Gibbons on its defeat, considering that it had threatened the solidarity and permanence of the system of government of the United States. A further controversy over Americanism developed from perversions which became current in Europe as the result of a translation into French of the *Life of Father Hecker* (1891) by the Rev. Walter Elliott. Leo XIII addressed to Gibbons a letter on that subject in which he ended the disputes with a reaffirmation of Catholic doctrine concerning the unity of faith. After the death of Leo in 1903, Gibbons hurried to Rome and became the first American to take part in the election of a Pope. Through the exercise of his good offices Cardinal Sarto, who had been reluctant to accept election, was induced to do so, and was elevated as Pius X.

In 1911 Gibbons, his place now secure as one of the foremost citizens of his country no less than as one of the foremost ecclesiastics of the world, received at a celebration in Baltimore of his jubilee as Cardinal honors never before accorded to any American churchman. At a public meeting in the largest hall in the city, densely crowded, addresses eulogizing his services to religion and country were made by President Taft, Ex-President Roosevelt, Elihu Root, James Bryce, and the highest officials of Maryland and Baltimore. The President dwelt on the general benefit of the example set by his patriotism, and Roosevelt said that he embodied what was highest and best in American citizenship. In reply, the Cardinal urged the preservation of the Federal Constitution and obedience to the public authorities in the exercise of their functions.

Gibbons was not identified with any political party but exercised freely his rights as a citizen in the discussion of policies. He ardently sought national harmony and the orderly development of the institutions of the country. After the Spanish-American War he did much to bring about pacification in the Philippines by arranging for the purchase of the "Friar Lands" by the United States. He aided in adapting the Catholic Church in the newly acquired American possessions to the altered régime. His efforts in marshaling Catholic influence against Socialism in the United States was a force in checking its growth. He opposed the election of federal senators by popular vote, the prohibition amendment to the Constitution, and the initiative, referendum, and recall of public officials. When America entered the World War in 1917 he became president of the National Catholic War Council, which consolidated Catholic efforts, and he helped to urge subscriptions to the Liberty Loans. Throughout the war, though he was past eighty years old, he gave the fullest support to the United States with all his official and personal prestige and at its close he warmly received a kindred spirit when Cardinal Mercier visited the United States.

He continued active labors, even preaching, almost to the end of his life. His position for a third of a century as a brilliant ecclesiastic, the ranking prelate of the Catholic Church in the United States, and as a citizen whose patriotism was undoubted, exhibiting judgment, breadth of view, and vision in his public utterances, was unique in the history of the country. His greatest influence was shown as a far-sighted leader and administrator and in promoting the spirit of religious toleration. To the attainment of the latter object he devoted the full resources of his dauntless spirit and rare intellect. He had the faculty of winning men by his singularly attractive personality. Of medium height, slender and graceful, with a well-shaped head and an expressive countenance, his appearance denoted in a marked degree benignity, power, alertness, and frankness. Few men had more devoted friends. As a preacher he had a magnetic manner and a clear, sweet voice with unusual carrying power. The Baltimore Cathedral was always thronged when he delivered his monthly sermons, and in its crypt, at his death, his body was laid. Besides *The Faith of Our Fathers* (1877), previously mentioned, his published works include, *Our Christian Heritage* (1889), *The Ambassador of Christ* (1896), *Discourses and Sermons* (1908), and *Retrospect of Fifty Years* (1916).

[A. S. Will, *Life of Cardinal Gibbons, Archbishop of Baltimore* (2 vols., 1922), for which the Cardinal supplied much of the material; A. E. Smith and V. de P. Fitzpatrick, *Cardinal Gibbons, Churchman and Citizen* (1921); J. T. Reily, *Collections in the Life and Times of Cardinal Gibbons* (7 vols., 1890–1903); *N. Y. Times*, Mar. 25, 1921. Source material is also found in numerous articles written by Cardinal Gibbons for magazines.] A. S. W.

GIBBONS, JAMES SLOAN (July 1, 1810–Oct. 17, 1892), Abolitionist, author, was born in Wilmington, Del., the son of William [*q.v.*] and Rebecca (Donaldson) Gibbons. His father was for years the Nestor of Delaware physicians and was an influential member of the Society of Friends. Respect for learning, sound business judgment, deep religious feeling, Quaker simplicity of manners, and sympathy for the poor and the oppressed were all part of the family tradition. After attending a Friends' school, Gibbons became a dry-goods merchant in Philadelphia, prospered, became known as an opponent of negro slavery, and in 1833 married Abigail Hopper, daughter of Isaac Tatem Hopper [*q.v.*], the Quaker philanthropist. In 1835 he moved to New York. There he was one of the organizers of the Ocean Bank and of the Broadway Bank and was cashier of the former for many years. He wrote frequently for magazines and newspapers on banking and finance and was the author of *The Banks of New York, their Dealers, the Clearing House, and the Panic of 1857* (1859), a clear and readable explanation of contemporary banking practise, and *The Public Debt of the United States* (1867), in which he advocated a substantial reduction in federal taxes. Under the pseudonym of Robert Morris he published a pamphlet on the *Organization of the Public Debt and a Plan for the Relief of the Treasury* (1863), in which his chief proposal was a 20 per cent export tax on gold, and a volume of didactic essays entitled *Courtship and Matrimony, with Other Sketches from Scenes and Experiences in Social Life* (1879); but as an author he is remembered only for his war song, "We are coming, Father Abraham, three hundred thousand strong," which appeared first in the New York *Evening Post* of July 16, 1862, and won immense popularity by reason of its swinging lines and its patriotic and sentimental appeal. Gibbons took a prominent part in the work of the American Anti-Slavery Society and was one of the chief supporters of the *National Anti-Slavery Standard*. At one time he mortgaged his furniture in order to keep the paper alive. For their connection with this paper he and his father-in-law, together with Charles Marriott, were disowned in 1842 by the New York Meeting of Friends, but until his health failed two years before his death Gibbons continued to attend the Friends' meetings. He is said to have begun the movement that resulted in Arbor Day. During the draft riots of July 13–16, 1863, his house on Lamartine Place was sacked by the mob, his papers destroyed, and his own life endangered. His wife, Abigail Hopper Gibbons [*q.v.*], who was nine years his senior, was his partner in all his philanthropic work. She, with two of their six children, survived him.

[*Narrative of the Proceedings of the Monthly Meeting of New-York and their Subsequent Confirmation by the Quarterly and Yearly Meetings in the Case of Isaac T. Hopper* (privately printed, 1843); W. P. and F. J. Garrison, *William Lloyd Garrison: The Story of his Life Told by his Children* (1885); N. Y. *Evening Post*, Oct. 18, 1892; *N. Y. Daily Tribune*, Oct. 19, 1892; *Friends' Intelligencer and Journal*, Oct. (Tenth Month) 29, 1892; S. H. Emerson, *Life of Abby Hopper Gibbons* (2 vols., 1896).] G. H. G.

GIBBONS, THOMAS (Dec. 15, 1757–May 16, 1826), lawyer, politician, steamboat operator, was plaintiff in the famous case of *Gibbons* vs. *Ogden* and was also responsible for one of the first disputed elections to Congress. He was the sixth of the eight children of Joseph and Hannah (Martin) Gibbons, and was born just outside Savannah, Ga., where his father had settled about two years earlier, having come originally from New Providence in the Bahamas. During the Revolution Thomas Gibbons was a Loyalist, while his father and brother were patriots. Thus the Gibbons property was saved during both the British occupation and the anti-Tory reaction. Thomas was accused of betraying the Americans at Charleston in 1780 but Gen. Lincoln cleared him of this charge. After the peace he soon became one of the outstanding lawyers of Georgia, making, it is said, $15,000 a year from his practise in addition to the income from his plantation. In 1791, he was a campaign manager for Anthony Wayne, who defeated James Jackson for reëlection from the First Georgia District. Gibbons had been too active, there were "more votes than voters," and Jackson contested the returns. In his speech at the congressional hearing on Mar. 13, 1792, he spared Wayne who was apparently innocent, but attacked "this person, Gibbons, whose soul is faction, and whose life has been a scene of political corruption" (*Annals of Congress,* 2 Cong., 1 Sess., p. 461). Wayne was unseated and Gibbons challenged Jackson to a duel in which several shots were exchanged without damage to either party. Neither this episode, however, nor his Tory record, prevented "Lawyer Gibbons" from serving as mayor of Savannah in the years 1791–92, 1794–95, and 1799–1801. He then became federal judge for the Georgia district. About 1810, he purchased as a summer residence an estate in Elizabethtown (now Elizabeth), N. J. In 1817, he acquired a little steam ferry, the *Stoudinger,* and in 1818, the *Bellona,* of which Cornelius Vanderbilt was captain. Gibbons ran them first from Elizabethtown Point up the Raritan to New Brunswick, connecting with the steamers of Aaron Ogden [*q.v.*], sometime senator and governor of New Jersey, who operated a ferry line from Elizabethtown Point to New York City. The New York legislature in 1803, with renewals in 1807, 1808, and 1811, had granted to Robert R. Livingston and Robert Fulton [*qq.v.*] the exclusive right of steam navigation in state waters. They had assigned the rights between New York and New Brunswick to John R. Livingston. Ogden, backed by the New Jersey legislature, had unsuccessfully opposed the New York monopoly, and in 1815 had purchased from the latter, Livingston, the right to operate a ferry between Elizabethtown Point and New York. In 1818 Gibbons broke with Ogden and boldly started to run his own ferries from Elizabethtown to New York, competing with Ogden's *Atalanta.* Ogden thereupon secured an injunction on Oct 21, 1818, from Chancellor James Kent of New York. Gibbons appealed, arguing that his federal coasting license was enough to permit the running of the ferry, but the injunction was upheld by Kent on Oct. 6, 1819 (Chancery Reports, 4 *Johnson,* 150), and by the state court of errors on Apr. 27, 1820 (17 *Johnson,* 488). Thereupon *Gibbons* vs. *Ogden* was carried to the Supreme Court of the United States which refused to accept jurisdiction in 1821 (6 *Wheaton,* 449) but finally heard the case in the February term of 1824 (9 *Wheaton,* 1). Gibbons, thoroughly aroused, spared no expense; he secured the legal services of Daniel Webster and Attorney-General William Wirt, and made a provision of $40,000 in his will to carry on the case if he should die before it was settled. The case gave Chief Justice Marshall the opportunity for one of his most famous decisions. Gibbons won the verdict, and the New York monopoly, with all others of its kind, was declared null and void. In thus throwing open American waterways this opinion of Marshall's, according to his biographer, A. J. Beveridge, did "more to knit the American people into an indivisible nation than any other one force in our history excepting only war" (*Life of John Marshall,* vol. IV, 1919, pp. 429–30). The cost of litigation ruined Ogden, but he had had one morsel of satisfaction while it was in progress. At the time they first quarreled, Gibbons had gone to Ogden's home and by insulting him tried to force a challenge from him. Instead of giving him satisfaction in a duel, Ogden sued the irascible Georgian for trespass and won a verdict of $5,000. Belligerent to the end, Gibbons left a will stipulating in strong terms that his son-in-law, whom he did not like, should never get a cent of his property. He died in New York City, probably a millionaire.

[See T. Gamble, *Savannah Duels and Duellists* (1923), pp. 41–45, 57–71, with portrait on p. 58; Georgia Revolutionary and state records; *Proc. N. J. Hist. Soc.,* IX (1862), 118–34; E. F. Hatfield, *Hist. of Elizabeth, N. J.* (1868), pp. 654–57; *Niles' Register,* July 1818; *Savannah Republican,* May 27, 1826. Family papers are in the possession of Mrs. Ellen Fanshawe of Morristown, N. J.] R. G. A—n.

GIBBONS, WILLIAM (Apr. 8, 1726–Sept. 27, 1800), lawyer, was born in Bear Bluff, S. C. After having studied law in Charleston, he removed to Georgia, was admitted to the bar, and opened an office in Savannah. Early espousing the Revolutionary cause, he became a leader in fomenting opposition to the Crown. When the news of the battle of Lexington reached Georgia, Gibbons was one of a group of six men who broke into the King's powder magazine in Savannah (May 1775), thus definitely committing themselves to rebellion. He was a member of the Provincial Congress in July 1775, was a member of the Committee of Safety in December of that year, and, in 1777–81, a member of the executive Council created by the Provincial Congress. He took no part in the actual fighting of the Revolution, being fifty years of age when the war began, but was active in the political and administrative aspects of the struggle. In 1783 he was a member of the state House of Representatives and was elected speaker. After peace was made he was named as a delegate to the Continental Congress and served two years (1784–86). On the expiration of his term he returned to Georgia and resumed the practise of law, serving in the state House during 1785–89 and 1791–93, and being speaker during the sessions of 1786 and 1787. His other public services were as associate justice of the court of Chatham County and as president of the state constitutional convention of 1789. He was regarded by his contemporaries as a great lawyer. The large income received from his practise was judiciously invested in rice plantations and he became one of the leading planters of his region.

[C. C. Jones, *Biog. Sketches of the Delegates from Ga. to the Continental Congress* (1891); S. F. Miller, *Bench and Bar of Ga.* (1858), II, 102; *Biog. Dir. Am. Cong.* (1928).] R. P. B—s.

GIBBONS, WILLIAM (Aug. 10, 1781–July 25, 1845), physician, was born during a visit of his parents to Philadelphia, the youngest of the thirteen children of James and Eleanor (Peters) Gibbons, and the fourth in descent from John Gibbons, who emigrated under William Penn's auspices in 1681 from Warminster in Wiltshire and acquired a tract of land in what later became Chester County, Pa. His father lived as a farmer, surveyor, conveyancer, and teacher at Westtown, Chester County, and was famous for his extensive knowledge of ancient and modern languages. He showed great solicitude for the education of his son, who, after studying medicine privately, was sent to the University of Pennsylvania, where he was much influenced by Benjamin Rush, formed an enduring friendship with William Darlington, and received the degree of M.D. in 1805. His *Inaugural Essay on Hypochondriasis* (1805) he dedicated to his former teachers, Dr. Jacob Ehrenzeller of West Chester and Dr. John Vaughn of Wilmington. In subject and in style the essay reflects the young doctor's interest in literature, although it makes no reference to Burton's *Anatomy of Melancholy.* On May 14, 1806, Gibbons married Rebecca, youngest daughter of David Donaldson of Wilmington, Del., and the next year he was persuaded to move to that place and take over the practise of his teacher Vaughn, who had recently died. For the remaining thirty-eight years of his life, he lived in Wilmington, rising to eminence in his profession and exerting a beneficent influence over the cultural life of the region. Like his father, he was a devout Quaker. In 1822 he published *Truth Advocated in Letters Addressed to the Presbyterians,* an answer to the attacks of a local clergyman, E. W. Gilbert, whose zeal outran his manners. When Gilbert fell desperately sick Gibbons was called in as a last resort and saved his opponent's life. Some years later, when Gibbons published an *Exposition of Modern Scepticism* (1829) to counteract the propaganda of Robert Dale Owen and Frances Wright D'Arusmont, Gilbert, now the doctor's admiring friend, read the pamphlet to his congregation. Gibbons was much interested in the emancipation and education of the negroes; he was the first president of the State Temperance Society and of the Delaware Academy of Natural Sciences. Sharing his father's aptitude for languages, he learned to read Latin, Greek, Hebrew, French, and German. He gave much attention to horticulture, and made his orchard and garden a refuge for birds. In 1824 he began the publication of a religious paper, the *Berean,* which he continued through four volumes. To Israel Daniel Rupp's *Original History of the Denominations* (1844) he contributed the chapter on the Hicksite Friends. Though noted for the cheerfulness and even sprightliness of his conversation, he was opposed to novel-reading and to music in connection with religious services. Like his second son, James Sloan Gibbons [*q.v.*], he was an amateur meteorologist. Thirteen of his fourteen children survived him. His widow founded the Wilmington Home for Aged Women. Two sons, Henry and William Peters, attained distinction as physicians and botanists in California; Henry was also the organizer of the Female Medical College of Pennsylvania (see articles on Bartholomew Fussell and Ann Preston).

["Biog. Notice, Written by one of his Sons," appended to *Review and Refutation* (1847); *Trans. Am. Medic. Asso.*, XXIX (1878), 657–59; J. S. Futhey and Gilbert Cope, *Hist. of Chester County, Pa.* (1881); J. T. Scharf, *Hist. of Del.* (1888); *Gen. Alumni Cat. Univ. of Pa.* (1922); *Friends' Intelligencer,* II, 141 (Eighth month 2, 1845).] G. H. G.

GIBBS, GEORGE (Jan. 7, 1776–Aug. 5, 1833), friend of science, son of "that high-minded, open-handed citizen . . . the merchant prince of Newport, Mr. George Gibbs," and of his wife, Mary

Channing, was the third of that name in a line reaching back to James Gibbs, who emigrated from England to Bristol, R. I., about 1670. Born thus into an atmosphere of wealth, he early went abroad and by personal effort and extensive purchases amassed a collection of minerals comprising some 12,000 (other accounts say 20,000) specimens. This collection, brought to Newport in 1805, was the largest and most valuable yet seen in the United States. Attracted by its fame, Benjamin Silliman the elder, then in the early days of his professorship at Yale, obtained permission to examine the collection, and paid his first visit to it in 1805 or 1806, at a time when Gibbs was again in Europe. On the latter's return, Silliman made his acquaintance, and, as he says in his Journal (*Life,* I, 219), "acquired a scientific friend and a professional instructor and guide." This friendship had important results for Yale, for in 1810, Gibbs, unsolicited, offered to deposit his famous collection in the College. Here, arranged in cases in two rooms in South Middle College, it attracted wide attention, and drew many visitors, not only from New Haven, but from all over the country (*Ibid.,* p. 257). In 1825, Gibbs finally offered the collection for sale at $20,000, giving Yale the first option. Silliman and the college authorities were unanimous in feeling that it must not be lost. A public meeting was called, followed by a personal canvass led by President Day. The amount needed was raised, and the collection became the property of Yale; it still remains one of her great treasures.

The friendship between these two men had another important result. In the early years of the century, American scientific periodicals were few and irregular. The *American Mineralogical Journal,* started in 1810 by Dr. Archibald Bruce [*q.v.*] of New York, had published four numbers, but the failing health of its founder made continuance unlikely. In 1817, at a chance meeting on board the steamer *Fulton* in Long Island Sound, Gibbs urged upon Silliman the duty of starting a new journal of science. "Although . . . many reasons, public and personal, concurred to produce diffidence of success, the arguments of Col. Gibbs, whose views on subjects of science were entitled to the most respectful consideration, and had justly great weight, being pressed with zeal and ability, induced a reluctant assent" (*American Journal of Science,* vol. L, 1847, p. iii, quoted by E. S. Dana in 4 ser., XLVI, p. 15, July 1918). Hence to Gibbs belongs the credit of giving the initial impetus which led to the founding of the *American Journal of Science,* still one of the world's leading periodicals.

Personally, Col. Gibbs (the title by courtesy) was "a man of culture and brilliant conversational powers, and famous for his generous hospitality." Though apparently not college-trained, he received the M.A. degree from Rhode Island College (now Brown University) in 1800, and from Yale eight years later. In 1822 he was vice-president of the New York Lyceum of Natural History, and presented to that institution the great "Gibbs meteorite" from Texas, which later came to Yale as a memorial of him. His publications were limited to four short papers.

His home was presided over by his wife Laura, daughter of Oliver Wolcott [*q.v.*]. Their three sons, George [*q.v.*], Oliver Wolcott [*q.v.*], and Alfred, continued the record of family achievement. Gibbs died at the age of fifty-seven on his estate, Sunswick Farms, near Astoria, L. I.

[G. P. Fisher, *Life of Benjamin Silliman* (1866); Benjamin Silliman, obituary of George Gibbs in *Am. Jour. Sci.,* Jan. 1834; Mary E. Powel, "Some of Our Founders," *Bull. Newport Hist. Soc.,* Apr. 1915; Chandler Wolcott, *Wolcott Geneal.* (1912).]
C. S.

GIBBS, GEORGE (July 17, 1815–Apr. 9, 1873), ethnologist, son of Col. George [*q.v.*] and Laura (Wolcott) Gibbs, and the brother of Oliver Wolcott Gibbs [*q.v.*], was born at Sunswick, near Astoria, L. I. He received his early education at the Round Hill School at Northampton, Mass., then conducted by George Bancroft, the historian. Lacking the necessary political favor he was unable to enter West Point and at seventeen was taken by an aunt to Europe for two years of study and travel. Returning to America he entered Harvard in 1834 and began the study of law. In the same year he published at Cambridge *The Judicial Chronicle,* a list of the judges of the common law and chancery in England and America. He graduated from Harvard in 1838 and entered the law office of Prescott Hall in New York, but his interests were never in the law and he practised only enough to secure a simple livelihood. His interest in politics led him to a study of the career of his grandfather, Oliver Wolcott [*q.v.*], former secretary of the treasury, and of the period in which he lived, and in 1846 he published in two volumes the *Memoirs of the Administrations of Washington and John Adams.* Gibbs confessed that he "felt himself not only the vindicator, but in some sort the avenger of a bygone party and a buried race" and in his editorial contribution there was no effort made to conceal his bias against the Republicans. The *Memoirs* consist chiefly of letters to and from Wolcott and are of great importance for the history of the Federalist party and of early American politics.

With the discovery of gold in California in 1848 Gibbs's spirit was fired. He gave up the law and marched overland with the Mounted Rifles from St. Louis to Oregon, settling at Columbia. His activity in Whig politics secured him the collectorship of the port of Astoria during the administration of President Fillmore; later he settled upon a ranch in Washington Territory near Fort Steilacoom, where he devoted himself to the study of the languages and traditions of the Northwest Indians. During a long period he was attached to the United States Government Commission as geologist in laying the Northwest boundary, and in 1857, as a member of the Northwest boundary survey, he contributed a lengthy report on the natural history and geology of the region. When he returned to New York in 1860 he intended remaining only a few months, but with the outbreak of the war he volunteered his services to the North. His health prevented his serving in the army, but he became an important member of the Loyal National League and of the Loyal Publication Society. During the latter part of his life he lived in Washington, D. C., where his extensive knowledge of the northwest Indians was often employed by the Smithsonian Institution. With J. G. Shea he translated Marie Charles Pandosy's *Grammar and Dictionary of the Yakama Language* (London, 1862), and in 1863 he published three contributions to the study of the Indian languages: *Alphabetical Vocabularies of the Clallam and the Lummi*; *Alphabetical Vocabulary of the Chinook Language*; and *A Dictionary of the Chinook Jargon, or, Trade Language of Oregon.* During the same year he prepared for the Smithsonian Institution, under whose auspices his other contributions had been made possible, his *Instructions for Research Relative to the Ethnology and Philology of America,* and three years later he gave them his *Notes on the Tinneh or Chepewyan Indians of British and Russian America* (1867). In 1871 he married Mary Kane Gibbs, his cousin, and moved to New Haven, Conn., where he died two years later.

[John Austin Stevens, *Memorial of Geo. Gibbs* (1873); *Harvard Univ. Quin. Cat.* (1925); *Morning Jour. and Courier* (New Haven), Apr. 11, 1873; information as to certain facts from private sources.]

F. M—n.

GIBBS, JAMES ETHAN ALLEN (Aug. 1, 1829–Nov. 25, 1902), inventor, was born in Rockbridge County, Va., the son of Richard and Isabella (Poague) Gibbs. He was descended from Dr. John Hirpin, a Huguenot physician, who emigrated to Milford, Conn., in 1715, and was a great-grandnephew of Ethan Allen. His father, a wool-carder, had emigrated in 1816 from Connecticut to Fairfax County, Va., where he tried to establish a machine-carding business. Being unsuccessful he went to Rockbridge County, Va., where he was engaged in his trade when his son was born. Young Gibbs after securing a mediocre schooling went into business with his father and the two continued until 1846 when their mill was destroyed by fire. Gibbs then went to Mill Point, Pocahontas County (now in West Virginia) and attempted to develop a wool-carding business with a machine of his own design. He was unsuccessful, however, and turned to farming. In the early 1850's his attention was directed to the sewing-machine. The pictures he saw in advertisements did not indicate the way in which the sewing-machine did its work and Gibbs, out of curiosity, set to work to solve the mystery in his own way. After a number of months he produced a shuttle sewing-machine with a lever oscillating in a vertical plane. This in itself was not a basic invention but it had two original features: it pulled off a definite quantity of needle thread proportionate to the length of the stitch (anticipating the later-day automatic tensions), and it fed the work positively between two corrugated surface lamps. Gibbs patented these features in 1856 and early in 1857 patented several chain and lock stitch machines which proved to be the forerunners of his important invention of June 2, 1857, for twisted loop rotary hook machine. Shortly after obtaining this patent, Gibbs formed a partnership with James Willcox of Philadelphia, Pa., and in 1858 the Willcox & Gibbs sewing-machine was placed on the market. After making the machine themselves for a few years, the partners interested the Brown & Sharpe Manufacturing Company of Providence, R. I., in manufacturing it for them, which organization has been making it ever since. Thereafter while Willcox looked after sales, Gibbs attended to further improvement of the device. By his efforts his basic patent was reissued in 1858 and at its expiration in 1872 was extended to 1878. In addition he made a number of other sewing-machine improvements (twenty-five all told) and patented a lock and a clutch-driven bicycle. During the Civil War, although Willcox sided with the North and Gibbs engaged in the manufacture of gunpowder for the Confederate army, Willcox maintained Gibbs's interest in the partnership inviolate and at the close of the struggle the two joined hands as though nothing had happened. Gibbs retired from active business about 1890 and, after traveling for a time both in the United States and abroad, settled on his farm in Rockbridge County, Va., where he had made his home since

1862. About the land on which he lived a village gradually grew up, and when the Baltimore & Ohio Railroad was built from Harrisonburg to Lexington and a depot established at the village, Gibbs suggested for it the name "Raphine," which is the Greek form of the verb "to sew." He was twice married: first, in 1883, to Catherine Givens of Nicholas County, W. Va., who died in 1887, and second, in 1893, to Margaret Craig of Craigsville, W. Va. When he died in Raphine he was survived by his widow and by three daughters of his first wife. He was the last male member of his family in America.

[Waldemar Kaempffert, *Popular Hist. of Am. Invention* (2 vols., 1924); E. W. Byrn, *The Progress of Invention in the 19th Century* (1900); O. F. Morton, *Hist. of Rockbridge County, Va.* (1920); *Frank Leslie's Chimney Corner*, Sept. 21, 1872; *Sewing Machine Times*, Dec. 10, 1902; *N. Y. Tribune*, Nov. 29, 1902; correspondence with Brown & Sharpe Mfg. Co., Providence, R. I.; Patent Office records.] C. W. M.

GIBBS, JOSIAH WILLARD (Apr. 30, 1790–Mar. 25, 1861), Orientalist, philologist, and teacher, was born in Salem, Mass., and was descended from Robert Gibbs, fourth son of Sir Henry Gibbs of Honington, Warwickshire, who came to Boston about 1685. His father and grandfather, each named Henry Gibbs, were graduates of Harvard College, but it was fated that Josiah should go to Yale. His father had died in 1794; and as his mother, Mercy (Prescott) Gibbs, had several near relatives living in New Haven, he was sent there to college, and graduated in the class of 1809. While in college he showed unusual ability as a scholar, and in 1811 he was called from Salem to a tutorship at Yale, which he held for four years. Going then to Andover, he studied Hebrew and other Oriental languages with Moses Stuart, in whose family he resided for a time. He also continued the theological studies begun in New Haven, where he had been licensed (in 1814) to preach, though he rarely made use of this privilege. Gibbs was able to give some help in the preparation of Stuart's most important work, the *Hebrew Grammar,* which appeared in 1821. This was mainly a translation of the German textbook of Wilhelm Gesenius, the true founder of modern Hebrew grammar and lexicography. Gibbs now undertook to translate Gesenius's *Hebräisches und Chaldäisches Handwörterbuch über das Alte Testament* (ed. of 1815), for there was as great need of a Hebrew dictionary as there had been of a grammar. The resulting work, entitled *Hebrew and English Lexicon of the Old Testament including the Biblical Chaldee,* was published at Andover in 1824. It was an admirable achievement, and remained the standard lexicon in this country until it was superseded in 1836 by Robinson's work. It was reprinted in London in 1827. He published an abridgment in 1828, which received a second edition four years later.

In the fall of 1824 Gibbs accepted an appointment at Yale College as lecturer in Biblical literature and college librarian. Two years later he was promoted to the rank of professor of sacred literature in the recently established Divinity School. Gibbs next set himself to translate Gesenius's more elaborate *Lexicon Manuale Hebraicum et Chaldaicum,* which appeared in Germany in 1833. Working in his minutely painstaking way, rearranging the material to some extent, verifying and correcting the references, and occasionally adding his own comments and illustrations, he had printed 432 pages (nearly through the letter *cheth*), about one-third of the whole, when his undertaking was brought to an untimely end by the publication, in 1836, of Edward Robinson's less elaborate but excellent translation of the same lexicon. This was a staggering blow, from which Gibbs never fully recovered. The printed sheets, the fruit of so great labor and expense, were destroyed, only a few sets being preserved. These give clear testimony to their author's intimate acquaintance with Hebrew and the cognate languages, and to his extraordinary accuracy and painstaking. From this time on, he devoted himself to the study of comparative philology, following generally in the footsteps of German scholars. He was, as Dwight in his *Memories* says of him, a true philologist, a lover of words; and in this branch of learning he became the leading American scholar of his time. Three small volumes of his studies were published in New Haven during the years 1857–60. Excessively modest and retiring, he was generally in the background when he might well have been prominent. As one of the first members of the American Oriental Society (founded in 1842) he contributed to each of the first five volumes of its *Journal.* He also published many brief articles in the *American Journal of Science and Arts,* the *Bibliotheca Sacra,* the *New Englander,* and other journals.

As a teacher, his strong point was his reputation for absolute fairness. His teaching was generally informing rather than inspiring. His characteristic tendency to leave in balance the two sides of any question led one of his eminent colleagues, Nathaniel W. Taylor, to say jocosely, "I would rather have ten settled opinions, and nine of them wrong, than to be like my brother Gibbs with none of the ten settled." Nevertheless the influence of his scholarly attitude of mind, no less than that of his published works, made itself strongly felt in the future development of the studies in which he was a pioneer. He married, on Sept. 30, 1830, Mary Anna Van Cleve, of Princeton, N. J. One of their five children, Josiah Willard Gibbs [*q.v.*], became a celebrated scientist. Gibbs died in his seventy-first year.

[F. B. Dexter, *Biog. Sketches Grads. Yale Coll., 1805–15* (1912), pp. 250–56, with a complete list of Gibbs's publications; G. P. Fisher, "Discourse Commemorative of Josiah Willard Gibbs, LL.D.," printed in the *New Englander* for July 1861; W. L. Kingsley, *Yale College,* II (1879), 37–40; Timothy Dwight, *Memories of Yale Life and Men* (1903), pp. 265–77; J. W. Gibbs, *Memoir of the Gibbs Family* (1879).]

C. C. T.

GIBBS, JOSIAH WILLARD (Feb. 11, 1839–Apr. 28, 1903), mathematician, and physicist, was born in New Haven, Conn., lived in that city throughout his life except for a period of study in Europe, and died there. He came of a distinguished, cultivated, and learned family. His father, Josiah Willard Gibbs [*q.v.*], was a graduate of Yale in 1809 and professor of sacred literature in the Yale Divinity School from 1824 to 1861. His mother, Mary Anna Van Cleve, was a daughter of Dr. John Van Cleve, a graduate and trustee of Princeton. As a student in Yale College Gibbs took prizes in mathematics and Latin, and was graduated in 1858 with high standing. He continued his studies in New Haven and was awarded the doctorate of philosophy in 1863, after which he was appointed tutor in the college where he taught Latin for two years and natural philosophy for a third year. In 1866 he went to Europe and studied in Paris (1866–67), in Berlin (1867–68), and in Heidelberg (1868–69). During this period he came under the influence of several of the most distinguished mathematicians and physicists of the world. In 1869 he returned to New Haven where two years later, in 1871, he was appointed professor of mathematical physics in Yale College. He served in that capacity for thirty-two years, until his death. As his lectures dealt with advanced topics, there was little opportunity for undergraduates to profit by his teaching during a period when the standard classical type of collegiate curriculum was almost universal. Despite a world-wide reputation, he did not draw graduate students to New Haven; in 1902 he remarked that during the thirty years of his professorship he had had only about half a dozen students really equipped to profit by his courses. Gibbs's influence on science thus came not from the impetus given by the master to a group of young apprentices, nor much from the light shed over immediate colleagues, but chiefly from his writings. In 1884 he declined the offer of a professorship in the newly established Johns Hopkins University; it is interesting but futile to ask whether his immediate influence in America would have been greater had he accepted.

From the commencement of his professorship, if not earlier, to 1879 Gibbs devoted himself to the development and presentation of his theory of thermodynamics. The general basis of this science had been firmly laid during the preceding decades through the discovery of the law of the conservation of energy, including heat as energy (*i.e.,* the first law of thermodynamics); and the law of the dissipation or degradation of energy, or increase of entropy (*i.e.,* the second law of thermodynamics); and those laws had been worked out mathematically with applications to homogeneous substances. The first two scientific papers which he wrote made an exhaustive study of geometrical methods of representing by diagrams, either in the plane or in three dimensions, the thermodynamic properties of such homogeneous substances ("Graphical Methods in the Thermodynamics of Fluids," in the *Transactions of the Connecticut Academy of Arts and Sciences,* vol. II, 1873, pp. 309–42, and "A Method of Geometrical Representation of the Thermodynamic Properties of Substances by Means of Surfaces," *Ibid.,* II, 382–404). Although these papers exhibited the care of his workmanship, which had also been a characteristic of the writings of his father, they were in no way so remarkable as to foreshadow his future place in science. Nevertheless, they undoubtedly gave him a point of view without which he might not have been able to accomplish his later striking results. The second of these two early papers riveted the attention of England's leading physicist, J. C. Maxwell, upon Gibbs as a rising master. Maxwell constructed with his own hands a model illustrating a portion of this work and sent a plaster cast of the model to Gibbs. No greater compliment could have come at the time and the cast was carefully cherished, as indeed it still is.

In 1876 the first half of Gibbs's great memoir "On the Equilibrium of Heterogeneous Substances" appeared in the *Transactions of the Connecticut Academy of Arts and Sciences,* to be followed in 1878 by the second half in the same journal (vol. III, 1874–78, pp. 108–248, 343–524). In 1879, from this point of view regarding equilibrium, he approached the problem of formulating the fundamental principles of dynamics and discussed the vapor densities of a number of substances. His subsequent contributions to thermodynamics (see "Electrochemical

Thermodynamics," in *Report of the British Association for the Advancement of Science,* 1886, pp. 388–89, and "Electro-Chemical Thermo-Dynamics," *Ibid.,* 1888, pp. 343–46), though not unimportant, may be regarded as merely the incidental notes of a scientific man. This great contribution on heterogeneous substances led L. Boltzmann many years later to describe its author as the greatest synthetic philosopher since Newton.

The achievement of Gibbs in the great memoir may perhaps be suggested by analogy, if one recalls that starting from a few axioms or laws of space there was built up step by step a whole body of geometric proof concerning the straight line, triangles, circles, polygons, including the mensuration of plane figures, and extending on to planes, spheres, and figures in three-dimensional space, to culminate in the mensuration of cylinders, cones, and spheres. Now if one should start with the axioms and the theorems of the first book of the plane geometry, which deals with lines and triangles, and then of his own genius develop by logical procedure all the rest, he would be accomplishing what Gibbs did in starting with the known thermodynamic theory of homogeneous substances and working out from it, including the formulation of the appropriate definitions, the theory of the thermodynamic properties of heterogeneous substances.

It was this work on the equilibrium of heterogeneous substances which provided the basic theory for that great new branch of science, more recently developed, known as physical chemistry, though at the time of its publication no one, unless it be Gibbs himself, recognized its basal importance, because at that time there was no such science worthy of the name. Some ten years after the completion of the memoir in the *Transactions of the Connecticut Academy,* Wilhelm Oswald, perceiving its importance, translated it into German and published it in book form, so that it might become more readily available, partly as an interpretation of past experimental investigation but more as a guide to experiments which had still to be performed. A French translation appeared in 1899 by Le Chatelier. It was many years before some of Gibbs's theoretical developments were experimentally verified; and if past history may be taken as a guide, it may be confidently affirmed that to-day, fifty years after the publication of the second half of the paper, suggestions remain which have by no means been exhausted by experimenters.

From 1880 to 1884 Gibbs seems to have busied himself with modifying the work of Hamilton in quaternions and of Grassmann on geometric algebra into a system of vector analysis especially suited to the needs of mathematical physicists. This system he printed privately, for his friends and for his students, in two parts; the first in 1881, the second in 1884. Suggestive articles were published in *Nature* during 1891 and 1893: "On the Rôle of Quaternions in the Algebra of Vectors" (Apr. 2, 1891); "Quaternions and the Ausdehnungslehre" (May 28, 1891); "Quaternions and the Algebra of Vectors" (Mar. 16, 1893); and "Quaternions and Vector Analysis" (Aug. 17, 1893). The work in its entirety was not published, however, until the time of the Yale Bicentennial celebration (1901) when Gibbs was finally persuaded to permit the compilation, and publication by a pupil, of a text-book founded upon the pamphlet of 1881–84 and upon his lectures (E. B. Wilson, *Vector Analysis*). His reluctance was probably due to a feeling that, useful as his system of vector analysis might be, it was after all not important as an original scientific contribution. Even the privately printed pamphlet involved him in a discussion with aggressive supporters of the system of Hamilton; and although many thought he had at the time the better of the argument, years elapsed before history settled the matter in favor of his or some essentially similar system, as contrasted with either of those from which he started, so far as concerns use by the mathematical physicist for whom he had elaborated it.

From 1882 to 1889, except for the completion of the second part of the vector analysis, Gibbs seems to have given his attention chiefly to theories of optics, developing one of his own, electrical rather than electromagnetic. The distinguishing characteristic of his treatment of light is the same as that of his treatment of thermodynamics; namely, an unusual reliance upon logic combined with an unexampled freedom from special hypotheses concerning the detail of the constitution of matter. As he was able to get so much of the behavior of heterogeneous systems in equilibrium out of the two fundamental laws of thermodynamics with appropriate definitions and without special chemical hypotheses, so he built his theory of light chiefly upon the hypothesis that light is a periodic disturbance propagated through media which in their structure are fine-grained compared with the wave length of the light. He set forth his theory in articles contributed to the *American Journal of Science*: "Notes on the Electromagnetic Theory of Light" (April, June 1882 and February 1883); "A Comparison of the Elastic and Electrical Theories of Light with Respect to the Law of Double Refraction and the Dispersion of

Colors" (June 1888); and "A Comparison of the Electric Theory of Light and Sir William Thomson's Theory of a Quasi-labile Ether" (February 1889). The weaknesses of the method are inevitable concomitants of its strength: one gets the general relations which must hold irrespective of the details of the constitution of matter, but one loses the special, and often both important and interesting, facts which depend on those details.

Throughout the nineties Gibbs published little of importance. Of what he was most seriously thinking there is no record. One might be tempted to say that it was his great and last work, *Elementary Principles in Statistical Mechanics,* published in the Yale Bicentennial series in 1902, were it not for the fact that much of this work is known to have been presented in lectures quite early in the nineties; indeed, as early as 1884 he read a paper, of which only a brief abstract remains, containing the fundamental formula of statistical mechanics. In truth, little seems to be known of Gibbs's ways of work except such as can be derived from the finished form of his publications. The notes he left at his death were very meager and for the most part were reminders of what he had wished to treat in some of his classroom lectures. It seems almost certain that he composed the very difficult *Statistical Mechanics* in about a year, from practically no notes whatsoever but from ideas which he had carried in his head for some years.

A noteworthy general characteristic of his writing was the perfection of his English style, brief, precise, free from dogmatic statements; not given to ornamentation or even to intercurrent illustration of his meaning sufficiently concrete to afford the realistic dilution comfortable to the common scientific mind; involved when and only when the unavoidable complexities of the phenomenon under discussion prevented any simpler statement from being exact; fascinating in its inexorable logic. Easy reading Gibbs certainly is not, but those who think they sense unnecessary difficulties may rest assured that they are in the presence of a masterly statement, the significance of which they have as yet not fully penetrated.

Gibbs died at the age of sixty-four. During his later years, he never seemed robust and appeared often afflicted with minor ailments. His figure was spare, and his voice not strong, but his head was impressive and his smile ingratiating. It is not without interest that, although his father lived to be seventy-one, his grandfather died at forty-seven, and his great-grandfather at fifty. Apparently he lived out his life. It is possible, however, that the very intensity of the work on the statistical mechanics somewhat sapped his small reserve of strength. During the period of its composition he could be seen at work in his office on the second floor of the old Sloan Laboratory morning, afternoon, and evening. The work on statistical mechanics was finished in the summer of 1901; in June 1902, while generously helping the author of this biography to formulate his plans of study for the next year, Gibbs mentioned something of his own program of work in the ensuing years. He remarked that, were he to live to be as old as Methuselah, he would continue to study for some time, but that as no such span of life was to be expected, he should turn himself immediately to the publication of what was already worked out. Three things were on his mind: first, a reëdition with considerable amplification of his work on thermodynamics; second, some developments of multiple algebra on which, though he had written but one short essay in 1886, he had an original point of view and in which he was keenly interested; third, a revision of the method used in his theory of orbits, published in 1889 and applied by two of his pupils and colleagues to actual calculation, which had recently been reprinted verbatim in the leading German compendium on theoretical astronomy. He chose as the most important the extension of his thermodynamics. Among his papers, found ten months after his death, were nine lines which may best be interpreted as titles of intended supplementary chapters, with a brief sketch of some of the first and some of the fourth—nothing else. As was apparently his custom, all the details had been carried in his head and the projected contributions were lost with him.

The courses of lectures which he was in the habit of giving toward the end of his life were five: vector analysis, multiple algebra, thermodynamics, theory of light, and theory of electricity. Not all of these were offered in any one year and their content was not always the same. In the main, however, it may be said that the vector analysis covered a great portion of his pamphlet of 1881–84 with some material from his treatment of orbits, or some discussion of the motion of the gyroscope (or spinning top), or of the geometrical principles of crystallographic analysis by vectorial methods. The course on thermodynamics never exhausted the contents of his great memoir and sometimes included hints of his future work on statistical mechanics. In the theory of light he followed his own papers in establishing the fundamental formulas from which he proceeded to discuss the usual topics in reflection, refraction, and dispersion. The courses on multiple algebra and on electricity were too brief to indicate how originally his mind may have been working in these fields. Although he was not an experimental physicist, his lectures showed a keen appreciation of the significance of crucial experiments. His hearers could perceive the realism that underlay his abstract thinking.

Gibbs received honorary degrees from Williams, Princeton, Erlangen, and Christiania. The American Academy (Boston) early recognized him with the award of its Rumford Medal (1880); the Royal Society of London elected him a foreign honorary member and awarded him in 1901 its Copley Medal. He was a member of the National Academy of Sciences, a vice-president of the American Association for the Advancement of Science, a member of the American Philosophical Society, and a foreign honorary member or correspondent of a large number of European learned societies. He never married, but lived in the home of his colleague Addison Van Name, long librarian of Yale University, who had married one of his sisters. His life was spent in this home and at his office, with summers in the mountains, many of them at Intervale, N. H. Toward the close of the day he could often be seen walking quietly about the streets in the neighborhood of the college just to take the air while returning home from his office. He went about little, was rarely seen at the Graduates' Club where his colleagues would often congregate of an evening, but as rarely missed a meeting of the mathematical and physical clubs, or colloquia of the faculties and advanced students, to whom he would listen with every indication of interest and on whose papers he would make the keenest, though always the kindliest of comments. His personality was unassuming, self-contained, and dignified, without the least trace of austerity. His tastes were simple. He would give generously of his time and thought to the simple family and household problems, to the encouragement of earnest students in their work, and to regular university duties. For many years, until his death, he filled the position of secretary and treasurer of the board of trustees of the Hopkins Grammar School at which he had prepared for college. He attended church regularly. He was too busy and too retiring in disposition, however, to take any prominent part in social, religious, and political events. He had none of the peculiarities of conduct which the popular mind associates with genius. He was broad-minded and tolerant. Without the slightest suggestion of boastfulness or conceit, he gave the impression of knowing what it was worth while for him to do and of being happy in the feeling that to do it was worth while. Without his genius he would still have been the type of scholar and of gentleman that any university would esteem as a member of its staff; it is good that to such a one there was added the highest type of genius. The scientific world has been and still is writing the biography of Gibbs's mind in expounding, amplifying, and applying his ideas.

[A sympathetic account of Gibbs's life to which every biographer must be indebted was printed by his pupil and colleague Henry A. Bumstead in the *American Journal of Science,* Sept. 1903. It has been reprinted, with some additions, in his collected works, of which two editions have appeared: *The Scientific Papers of J. Willard Gibbs* (1906), and *The Collected Works of J. Willard Gibbs* (1928), the latter including all of his published writings. A commentary, in two volumes, intended to aid the student of Gibbs's works, is in preparation. See also J. W. Gibbs, *Memoir of the Gibbs Family* (1879), and *Obit. Record Grads. Yale Univ.* (1903), p. 237.] E. B. W.

GIBBS, OLIVER WOLCOTT (Feb. 21, 1822–Dec. 9, 1908), chemist, was born in New York City, the second son of Col. George Gibbs [*q.v.*], mineralogist and horticulturist, and Laura Wolcott Gibbs, daughter of Oliver Wolcott [*q.v.*]. His childhood was spent at Sunswick, near Astoria, L. I., his family home; at Boston, where he lived with an aunt for four years, attending Mr. Leverett's school; and at Newport. Then for several years he attended the grammar school of Columbia College. When he graduated from college in 1841, he had already published a scientific contribution on the use of carbon electrodes in batteries. After an assistantship with Robert Hare [*q.v.*] in Philadelphia, he entered the College of Physicians and Surgeons in New York, in order to qualify himself as a teacher of chemistry in a medical school, and in 1845 he received the degree of M.D. For the next three years he studied in Europe under Rammelsberg, Rose, and Liebig in Germany, and under Laurent, Dumas, and Regnault in Paris, which gave him an unusual perspective in his chosen field.

After Gibbs's return to America in 1848 he was an assistant professor for a year at the College of Physicians and Surgeons, and also gave a series of lectures at Delaware College in Newark, Del. In 1849 he received an appointment as professor at the Free Academy (now the College of the City of New York). He was married in 1853 to Josephine Mauran. In 1863 he moved to Cambridge to hold the Rumford professorship in Harvard College. For eight years he had charge of the chemical laboratory of the Lawrence Scientific School, inspiring his students with true zeal for research and introducing in this country the laboratory methods of research which he had learned in Europe. After 1871, when the chemical instruction in the Scientific School was combined with that of Harvard College, Gibbs lectured on the spectroscope and on thermodynamics. In 1887, upon becoming professor emeritus, he retired to his estate at Newport, where he erected a private laboratory. Here, with several assistants, he continued his researches for ten years.

While Gibbs investigated a wide variety of problems, his chief work was with inorganic compounds, analytical methods, and physiological chemistry. With the collaboration of F. A. Genth [*q.v.*] he conducted classical researches into the nature of the complex compounds of cobalt and helped to build the foundation of one of the most useful of modern chemical theories. His work on the platinum metals was of similar importance. A later series of remarkable investigations established the nature of the complex acids formed by vanadium, tungsten, molybdenum, phosphorus, arsenic, and antimony. In the development of new analytical procedures the electrolytic determination of copper and nickel presented a new and powerful analytical method. Gibbs's sand-filtering device may be said to have been the prototype of the useful, every-day devices perfected by Munroe and Gooch. The use of the spectroscope in chemical investigations also interested him. His early medical training especially fitted him for his researches with his associates, Hare and Reichert, upon the toxic effect of several series of organic compounds upon animals. Thus an unusually wide domain of chemistry and physics received his attention. By nature a pioneer, he often presented an incomplete sketch of his investigations, but one which served as a trusted map in new fields.

In addition to his academic and research activities, Gibbs found time for other interests. With true patriotic spirit he gave his services to the Sanitary Commission during the Civil War. He made important reports on instruments for physical research and several on tariff questions. He was a founder of the National Academy of Sciences, a fellow of the American Academy of Arts and Sciences, an honorary member of the American Philosophical Society and of the German, English, and American Chemical Societies, a corresponding member of the Royal Prussian Academy, and of the British Association for the Advancement of Science. He was president of the National Academy from 1895 to 1900 and of the American Association for the Advancement of Science in 1897, and rendered distinguished service as a member of the Rumford Committee of the American Academy from 1864 to 1894. It was largely through his recognition and appreciation of the fundamental significance of the work of J. Willard Gibbs [*q.v.*] that the Rumford Medal was awarded the Yale physicist in 1880. As associate editor of the *American Journal of Science* he made many abstracts of contemporary physical work. He also wrote a series of reviews of American chemical research for the *American Chemical Journal.*

Wolcott Gibbs was highly regarded in scientific circles and esteemed by his students. Broad in vision, liberal, enthusiastic in spirit, tireless in energy, devoted to his work and his friends, he impressed all who knew him with his positive character and striking personality. Two memorials bear witness to his achievements: the portrait bas-relief wrought upon the great doors of the west entrance of the Capitol at Washington, and the Wolcott Gibbs Memorial Laboratory, erected at Harvard University in 1912 through the generosity of students and friends, of whom Morris Loeb, assistant at Newport, was the chief donor.

[F. W. Clarke, "Biog. Memoir of Wolcott Gibbs," in *Nat. Acad. of Sci. Biog. Memoirs,* vol. VII (1913), with bibliography; E. W. Morley, in *Proc. Am. Phil. Soc.,* Oct.–Dec. 1910; T. W. Richards, *Berichte der Deutschen Chemischen Gesellschaft,* Apr. 21, 1910, also with bibliography; a short autobiographical note in *Science,* Dec. 18, 1908; Morris Loeb, in *Proc. Am. Chem. Soc.* (1910), p. 69; *N. Y. Times,* Dec. 10, 1908.] L. P. H.

GIBBS, WOLCOTT [See GIBBS, OLIVER WOLCOTT, 1822–1908].

GIBSON, GEORGE (October 1747–Dec. 14, 1791), Revolutionary soldier, was born at Lancaster, Pa., of Scotch-Irish and French-Huguenot parentage, the son of George and Elizabeth (de Vinez) Gibson. Little information concerning his early life and training is extant, though his ability to speak French, German, Spanish, and Delaware-Indian languages bears evidence of his education. When about fifteen years old he became an apprentice in a Philadelphia mercantile house and later made several voyages to the West Indies as a supercargo. He left Philadelphia to join his brother, John Gibson [*q.v.*], and his brother-in-law, Captain Calender, at Fort Pitt, to engage with them in the Indian trade. His residence at Fort Pitt ended when a trading adventure to the British posts in Illinois under his personal direction came to grief. He then returned to eastern Pennsylvania where in 1772 he married Anne West, a daughter of Francis West, and rented a farm and mill near Carlisle in Cumberland County. In 1774 he was again in the Ohio Valley, participating in Dunmore's War, and in 1775, at the outbreak of the Revolution, he organized a company of frontiersmen for service in the West. He commanded the company and played the fife. Later his command was attached to Col. Hugh Mercer's brigade then stationed at Williamsburg, Va., where the turbulent and undisciplined frontiersmen found British "redcoats" scarce, but remedied the situation by engaging in fistic combats with other Colonials quartered near.

Gibson participated in minor engagements in Virginia during 1775 and 1776 until he was selected as agent to negotiate the purchase of powder from the Spanish at New Orleans for the use of Virginia and Continental troops. He left Fort Pitt July 19, 1776, with about twenty-five men disguised as traders, and after a perilous journey made in flatboats down the Ohio and Mississippi Rivers, reached New Orleans about the middle of August. The purchase of 10,000 pounds of powder was made through Don Galvez, the Spanish governor, who obligingly placed Gibson under arrest to allay the suspicions of British agents and then aided his escape with the consignment of powder. During 1777–78 Gibson served under Gen. Washington and Gen. Lee in campaigns around New York and in New Jersey, with the rank of colonel, but he was relieved from active service in 1779 and placed in charge of the American prison camp at York, Pa., where he remained until the signing of peace. He then kept to his farm at Carlisle until 1791, when he joined St. Clair's ill-fated expedition as lieutenant-colonel in command of the 2nd Regiment. In the engagement with British renegades and Indians in the Black Swamp region along the Wabash River, Gibson was twice wounded and after the battle was carried to Fort Jefferson, about thirty miles distant, where he died. He was the father of the jurist, John Bannister Gibson [*q.v.*].

[Manuscript biographical sketch of Geo. Gibson by Wm. Plumer, N. H. Hist. Soc.; Anthony Wayne MSS., Hist. Soc. of Pa.; Wm. Irvine MSS., Hist. Soc. of Pa.; Washington Papers, Correspondence with the Military, Lib. of Cong.; *Pa. Archives, 2* ser., *passim*; *Notes and Queries* (Harrisburg), 3 ser. III (1896), p. 421; *House Report 345*, 24 Cong., 1 Sess.; Thos. P. Roberts, *Memoirs of John Bannister Gibson* (1890).] T. D. M.

GIBSON, JOHN (May 23, 1740–Apr. 16, 1822), frontier soldier, secretary of the Indiana Territory, was born at Lancaster, Pa., the son of George and Elizabeth (de Vinez) Gibson and the brother of George Gibson [*q.v.*]. Of his childhood and early training there is no record though in later life he exhibited a superior knowledge of Indian dialects and a studied English diction. At the age of eighteen he began his military career as a participant in the Forbes expedition (1758) which resulted in the capture of Fort Duquesne from the French. On the close of the campaign Gibson settled at Fort Duquesne (renamed Fort Pitt) as an Indian trader. This commercial enterprise met with obstacles in 1763, when, at the outbreak of Pontiac's War, Gibson, with two or three companions, was captured by the Indians near the mouth of Big Beaver Creek on the Ohio River. Some of the captives were put to death, but Gibson is said to have been saved, Pocahontas fashion, by an Indian squaw, and carried as a prisoner to the Great Kanawha River in southwest Virginia. During the year spent as a captive he was given the sobriquet "Horse-head." He may also have acquired an Indian wife, described as a sister or sister-in-law of Logan [*q.v.*], the Mingo warrior. When Col. Bouquet [*q.v.*] secured his release in 1764 Gibson once more returned to Fort Pitt to engage in the Indian trade. In 1774 he took part in the campaign against the Shawnees, Mingoes, and Delawares known as Dunmore's War. Logan's classic but much questioned speech, an incident of Dunmore's War, was made to and reported by Gibson (Papers of Thos. Jefferson, ser. I, folio vii, nos. 153 and 198; ser. V, folio i, no. 4, in the Library of Congress), who probably supplied the flowery eloquence. The following year Gibson aided in the negotiations with the Indians which resulted in the Treaty of Pittsburgh, signed after the outbreak of the Revolution. He was named western agent for Virginia in 1775 and became a warm protagonist for the claims of that state to the territory lying between the Monongahela and Ohio Rivers known as West Augusta. As a member of the Western Pennsylvania Committee of Correspondence he was active during the early stages of the war in securing peace with the Indians, making a tour of the Ohio tribes for that purpose. He then entered the Continental service, serving under Washington in New York and during his retreat southward, until transferred to the western department. In 1776 he was made lieutenant-colonel, and the next year he was promoted colonel, which rank he held until the end of the war. During 1779 he was commandant at Fort Laurens (Bolivar, Ohio), and the next year, while aiding Baron Steuben who was in Virginia raising troops for Gen. Greene, he was named second in command of George Rogers Clark's proposed expedition into the Northwest territory, but Gen. Brodhead [*q.v.*], the commandant at Fort Pitt, negatived the plan by refusing to release Gibson's regiment. Gibson secured his revenge when he took a prominent part in the ousting of Gen. Brodhead at Fort Pitt in 1781, and procured the command for himself until relieved by Gen. William Irvine the following year. At the close of the war he took up his residence in Allegheny County, Pa., where he served as a judge of the court of common pleas and major-general of militia. He was a member of the convention which drafted the constitution of 1790, and with Gen. Richard Butler [*q.v.*] negotiated the purchase for Pennsylvania of the "Erie Triangle" (1789) from the Iroquois Confederacy. During the Whiskey Rebellion (1794) he was an active adherent of the government, and thereby made so many enemies that he was given the "passport and guard" by his less loyal neighbors. After receiving President Jefferson's appointment as secretary of the Indiana Territory Gibson reached Vincennes in July 1800, and in the absence of the governor, W. H. Harrison [*q.v.*], he began the organization of the territorial government, and prepared the first census report. He retained the office of secretary until 1816, but again served as acting governor during the critical period of the War of 1812. He gave invaluable aid to Gov. Harrison at the council of Vincennes with Tecumseh, and sent an expedition that relieved Capt. Zachary Taylor from a perilous position at Fort Harrison (November 1812). On the formation of the new state government Gibson returned to Pennsylvania. He died at Braddock's Field in 1822, survived by his wife, Ann Gibson.

[R. G. Thwaites and Louise P. Kellogg, *The Revolution on the Upper Ohio, 1775–77* (1908), and *Doc. Hist. of Dunmore's War* (1905); Washington Papers, Correspondence with the Military, in the Lib. of Cong.; Logan Esarey, ed., *Messages and Letters of Wm. Henry Harrison* (2 vols., 1922); *Pa. Archives*, 2 ser., IV (1876); "Executive Jour. Ind. Territory," in *Ind. Hist. Soc. Pubs.*, vol. III, no. 3 (1900); E. B. O'Callaghan, ed., *Docs. Relative to the Colonial Hist. of the State of N. Y.*, VIII (1857), 464; Louise P. Kellogg, *Frontier Retreat on the Upper Ohio, 1779–81* (1917); Thos. Jefferson, *Notes on Va.* (1801); C. A. Hanna, *The Wilderness Trail* (2 vols., 1911); Thos. P. Roberts, *Memoirs of John Bannister Gibson* (1890); W. W. Woollen, *Biog. and Hist. Sketches of Early Ind.* (1883); *Olden Time*, Feb. 1847; *W. Va. Hist. Mag.*, Jan. 1903; *Western Pa. Hist. Mag.*, Oct. 1922; *Ind. Mag. of Hist.*, Mar. 1917; *Pittsburgh Gazette*, Apr. 19, 1822.]

T. D. M.

GIBSON, JOHN BANNISTER (Nov. 8, 1780–May 3, 1853), jurist, was the son of Col. George Gibson [*q.v.*] and Anne West of Scotch-Irish descent. Born at Westover Mills, Pa., he passed his youth in that neighborhood, his early education being obtained from his mother, who, after her husband's death, lived on the homestead and built a schoolhouse, where she taught the children of the vicinity. In 1795 he entered the grammar school attached to Dickinson College, Carlisle, matriculating two years later at the latter institution. On leaving college he studied law at Carlisle with Thomas Duncan, subsequently a judge of the supreme court of Pennsylvania, and was admitted to the Cumberland County bar, Mar. 8, 1803. During the following two years his course was unsettled and he practised successively at Carlisle and Beaver, Pa., and Hagerstown, Md., but in 1805 returned to Carlisle. At the bar he achieved but a small measure of success. Lacking magnetism, he was an indifferent advocate, unable to convince a jury or impress a judge. When not engaged in conference or in court he was wont to practise on the violin in his office, in which occupation the majority of his business hours were spent, and he seems to have acquired a local reputation for indolence. In 1810, however, he was elected Democratic representative of Cumberland County in the state legislature, and in that arena displayed an activity which astonished his intimates and gave evidence of hitherto unsuspected ability. Serving only during the sessions 1810–11, 1811–12, he procured the passage of an act abolishing the right of survivorship among joint tenants, led the opposition to the impeachment of Judge Thomas Cooper, consistently advocated internal improvements on a large scale, and was during his last session chairman of the committee on the judiciary. He was named president judge of the newly organized 11th judicial district of the court of common pleas, July 16, 1813, by Gov. Snyder. The appointment was not warranted by his mediocre career as a practising lawyer, and the absence of records relative to his tenure of this office renders it impossible to generalize, but that he proved efficient may be surmised from his promotion, June 27, 1816, by Gov. Snyder to an associate justiceship of the supreme court of the state. This apparently aroused his ambition, drawing forth all his dormant intellectual powers, and during his subsequent thirty-seven years' continuous service on the supreme-court bench he established himself as the dominating figure of the Pennsylvania judiciary, distinguished alike for his breadth of view, his independence and originality, and the masterful opinions wherein he displayed a facility for forcible exposition and an instinct for grasping the crucial points of the most difficult problems which marked him as one of the greatest jurists of his time. Appointed chief justice May 18, 1827, by Gov. Shultze on the death of Tilghman, he was confirmed in that office at the ensuing election of 1828. He resigned Nov. 19, 1838, immediately before the state constitution of 1838 went into effect, and was at once reappointed by Gov. Ritner, the effect of this move being that he was secured in the longest, instead of the shortest, tenure of his office under the new law, which provided for the expiration of existing judges' commissions at intervals of three years in order of seniority as of Jan. 1, 1839. His action was unquestionably open to the severe comment to which it was subjected by the press and he afterwards realized that he had made a mistake, though the high motives which prompted the inception of the scheme by his admirers and its acceptance by him were admittedly in the best interests of the state (see Roberts, *post,* 130–34). In 1851, when by virtue of a further constitutional amendment the entire supreme-court bench was retired and new judges balloted for, "the old Chief," as he was familiarly termed, was nominated and elected an associate justice, although then over seventy years old and physically incapable of participating in the conflict. He died two years later in Philadelphia, and was buried at Carlisle, his home since 1805 with the exception of three years at Wilkes-Barre whilst on the common-pleas bench.

His judicial record is written at large in seventy volumes of the Pennsylvania Reports from 2 *Sergeant and Rawle* to 7 *Harris.* Over six thousand cases came before him for hearing and he delivered reasons for judgment in upwards of twelve hundred, excluding circuit and *nisi prius* cases of which no record has been preserved. It is matter for regret that many of them are badly reported; nevertheless his decisive influence upon the development of the state law can be clearly traced. His opinions range over the whole legal field, but professional judgment accords the greatest respect and authority to those dealing with constitutional problems. Preëminent among these is *De Chastellux* vs. *Fairchild* (3 *Harris,* 18), where, thrusting aside precedent, he laid down the limits of the legislative power in phrases the accuracy of which has never since been challenged. "The legislature," said he, "has no power to order a new trial, or to direct the court to order it, either before or after judgment. The power to order new trials is judicial; but the power of the legislature is not judicial. It is limited to the making of laws; not to the exposition or execution of them. . . . It has become the duty of the court to temporize no longer, but to resist, temperately, though firmly, any invasion of its province, whether great or small" (*Ibid.,* 20–21). Two other cases affecting vital public interests were *The Commonwealth* vs. *Green and Others* (4 *Wharton,* 531), dealing with the Presbyterian Church troubles of 1837—his opinion in which was a masterpiece of cold unbiased dissection—and *Donoghue* vs. *the County* (badly reported in 2 *Barr,* 231), arising out of the Philadelphia riots of 1844, in which by his interpretation of the principle that every man's house is his castle, he settled for all time the common law of Pennsylvania as to riots, and, incidentally, effectively ended the lawlessness which had been sporadic for years in Philadelphia. Bred up, as he was wont to assert, in the school of Littleton and Coke, his mastery of the intricate technicalities of real property law was demonstrated in three outstanding cases: *Lyle et al.* vs. *Richards* (9 *Sergeant and Rawle,* 322), *Hillyard* vs. *Miller* (10 *Barr,* 326), and *Hileman et al.* vs. *Bouslaugh* (1 *Harris,* 344). His opinion in this last case stands out as one of the very rare instances in the United States Reports where the Rule in Shelley's Case is dealt with, and he discusses its application with a clarity, boldness, and knowledge of all the authorities and commentators unequaled in American courts. At his best when the court was sitting *in banc,* he was less successful at *nisi prius,* and jury trials were always irksome to him.

In his opinions he avoided where possible any survey of precedents, seeking rather to found his decision upon principles. Couched in terse, vigorous language, startlingly epigrammatic at times, his reasons for judgment were distinguished by their clarity and brevity—and the longer he remained on the bench the briefer they tended to become. "He said neither more nor less than just the thing he ought . . . in language which could never afterwards be paraphrased" (Chief Justice Black, 7 *Harris,* 12). Beyond his reported opinions and an occasional anonymous review for the *American Law Register,* the only literary compositions which can be traced to his pen are "Some Account of the Rev. Charles Nisbet, first President of Dickenson [*sic*] College" (in the *Port Folio,* January 1824), and a sketch of the life of Judge Thomas Cooper in the *Encyclopaedia Americana* (vol. XIV, supplement, 1847, p. 203).

Apart from the law, his interests were extensive and his range of knowledge remarkable. A profound student of Shakespeare, he read widely in French and Italian literature in his leisure, and he had more than an amateur acquaintance with medicine and the fine arts. He was also a skilled mechanic, an expert piano tuner, and a competent dentist, devising a peculiar plate for his own teeth with complete success after professional assistance had failed him. Above all, however, his chief recreation was music, particularly the violin. He married, Oct. 8, 1812, Sarah Work, daughter of Col. Andrew and Barbara (Kyle) Galbraith of Carlisle, who, together with five of their eight children survived him.

[The chief authority is *Memoirs of John Bannister*

Gibson (1890), by his grandson, T. P. Roberts, which also contains an account of his ancestry so far as it is known. His professional record is exhaustively reviewed in W. A. Porter, *An Essay on the Life, Character and Writings of John B. Gibson, LL.D.* (1855) and S. D. Matlack, "John Bannister Gibson," in W. D. Lewis, ed., *Great Am. Lawyers,* III (1907), 353, the latter being the more balanced appraisal. See also *U. S. Monthly Law Mag.,* Mar. 1851; D. P. Brown, *The Forum* (1856), I, 418; G. J. Clark, *Life Sketches of Eminent Lawyers* (1895), I, 34; John Hays, "Address on Presentation of a Bust of Judge Gibson on behalf of his Grandson, Thomas P. Roberts, Esq.," *Proc. Hamilton Library Asso., Carlisle, Pa.* (1911). An unfavorable and severely critical estimate of Gibson will be found in Owen Wister, "The Supreme Court of Pennsylvania," *Green Bag,* Jan. 1891.] H. W. H. K.

GIBSON, PARIS (July 1, 1830–Dec. 16, 1920), Montana pioneer, senator, was born at Brownfield, Me., the son of Abel and Ann (Howard) Gibson. His ancestors on both sides emigrated to America before the Revolution. He was given a thorough education, and graduated from Bowdoin College in 1851. He at once entered politics, being a member of the Maine legislature in 1854, but upon the death of his father took charge of the home farm. He was married to Valeria Goodenow Sweat on Aug. 23, 1858. That year he went to Minneapolis, Minn., then a town of about 2,000 people, where he built a flouring-mill, the first in the city. Then he started construction of the North Star Woolen Mills, whose product was soon widely known. Within a few years he made a fortune but lost most of it in the panic of 1873. In 1879 he moved to Fort Benton, Mont., and engaged in sheep-raising. Here again he was a pioneer, for his was the first large band of sheep in northern Montana. In following his sheep over the country he came upon the Great Falls of the Missouri. He said later that at that time he saw in them only beauty for he did not know the great possibilities of water-power in developing electricity (*The Founding of Great Falls, and Some of its Early Records,* n.d), but he soon formed a plan for an industrial city and sought the aid of James J. Hill [*q.v.*] who had recently acquired the St. Paul & Pacific Railroad. Hill promised support, and Gibson began to acquire land on the site of his proposed city, and to get title to the power sites and neighboring coal deposits. In 1887 the first trains were run into the new town. Gibson, who served as its first mayor, planned the city on a large scale and with an elaborate park system, and forty years later, with a population of 35,000, Great Falls, Mont., has felt no cramping and no need for revision of the original plans.

For the remainder of his life Gibson was closely connected with the development of the water-power, coal-mining, railroad-building, and sheep-growing of northern Montana. He was an influential member of the Democratic party but his political activities were rarely of partisan character. He was a member of the convention (1889) that framed the constitution of Montana, and a member of the first state Senate (1891). In 1893 when a bill for providing for higher education was before the Senate he argued passionately but in vain for the consolidation of all branches of higher education into one university. In 1901 he was elected United States senator to complete the term of William A. Clark [*q.v.*] who had resigned in 1900. His work in the Senate lasted only four years. He took an active part in conservation and urged the repeal of the Desert Land Act, the Timber Claim Act, and the "commutation clause" of the Homestead Act (*Congressional Record,* 58 Cong., 2 Sess., pp. 3603 ff.). He knew from observation and experience how the large cattle companies and lumber companies were using these laws to get title to large parts of the public domain, and thus robbing the *bona fide* homesteader of his chance to get a good home. He urged that all agricultural land should be held for the true settler, and that the government should hold its timber until it was needed. His efforts commanded the approval of President Roosevelt, but were not accepted by the Senate. He was effective, however, in furthering other plans for conservation, and was a steady friend of reclamation. In 1904 when the Republicans obtained control of the state legislature, he failed of reëlection to the Senate. He did not formally retire from control of his extensive business until he was eighty-five, and took an active interest in the University of Montana until the time of his death.

[*Progressive Men of the State of Mont.* (Chicago, 1901); Tom Stout, *Mont.: Its Story and Biog.* (3 vols., 1921); A. L. Stone, *Following Old Trails* (1913); *Who's Who in America,* 1918–19; *Biog. Dir. Am. Cong.* (1928); *Gen. Cat. Bowdoin Coll.* (1912); *Rev. of Revs.* (N. Y.), Nov. 1903; *Rocky Mountain Mag.,* Sept. 1900; obituary in *Anaconda Standard,* Dec. 17, 1920.]

P. C. P.

GIBSON, RANDALL LEE (Sept. 10, 1832–Dec. 15, 1892), lawyer, sugar-planter, statesman, soldier, son of Tobias and Louisiana (Hart) Gibson, was born at "Spring Hill," Woodford County, Ky., while his parents were on a visit from their home in Terrebonne Parish, La. His great-grandfather, John Gibson, emigrated from England in 1706, and settled in Middlesex County, Va. Later he removed to the Great Peedee River in South Carolina. His grandfather, Rev. Randall Gibson, a soldier in the Continental Army, settled (after the war) in the central part of Warren County, Miss., and is credited with having founded Jefferson College near Natchez.

His father went shortly after his marriage to Louisiana and soon became a prominent sugar-planter in Terrebonne Parish. His mother was the daughter of Col. Nathaniel Hart of "Spring Hill," whose family was among the earliest settlers in Kentucky and was closely connected with the Clays, the Prestons, and other prominent families of that state. Randall Lee Gibson received his early education at the hands of a private tutor at "Live Oaks," his father's plantation, and in the schools of Terrebonne Parish, La., and of Lexington, Ky., where his father long maintained a summer residence. In 1849 he entered Yale College. Upon the completion of his course in 1853 he studied law in the office of Clark & Bayne in New Orleans and was graduated from the law department of the University of Louisiana in 1855. He then spent several years abroad, studying in Germany, traveling in Russia, and serving as attaché to the American embassy in Madrid for six months. On his return home he began the practise of law and engaged in sugar-planting in Thibodaux, Lafourche Parish, La. On the outbreak of the Civil War he enlisted in the service of the Confederacy, serving first as aide-de-camp on the staff of Gov. Thomas O. Moore. In March 1861 he was made captain in the 1st Regiment, Louisiana Artillery, and in August he was made colonel of the 13th Regiment, Louisiana Infantry. He took part in the battle of Shiloh, commanding the Louisiana brigade after Gen. Adams was wounded, and participated in the battles of Perryville, Murfreesboro, and Chickamauga. He was made brigadier-general on Jan. 11, 1864, fought in the Atlanta and Nashville campaigns, and finished his military career with a gallant defense of Spanish Fort near Mobile. In all of these engagements he was especially commended for skill and bravery by his superior officers.

After the war Gibson began the practise of law in New Orleans, first in partnership with Edward Austin and later with his brother, McKinley Gibson. He ran for Congress as a Democrat in 1872 and claimed the election but was not allowed to take his seat. He was elected in 1874 and again in 1876, 1878, and 1880. In 1882 he was elected by the state legislature of Louisiana to the United States Senate and was reëlected in 1888. He died before his second term expired. In the disputed presidential election of 1876 he was one of the four who offered objections before Congress against the recognition of the Hayes electors from Louisiana, and when the decision of the electoral commission favoring those electors was presented to Congress, he offered the objections of eighteen senators and one hundred and fifty representatives. Later he was active in getting President Hayes to order the removal of the United States troops from Louisiana. Because of his interest in improving the navigation of the Mississippi River he was largely influential in getting Congress to adopt in 1878 the plan of James B. Eads for constructing jetties at the mouth of the river for the purpose of keeping the channel open to the Gulf of Mexico. He was also active in urging in 1879 the creation of the Mississippi River Commission to look after the further improvements of the navigation of the river and to protect adjacent lands from overflow. He was opposed to the Greenback craze in the late seventies and early eighties, and although the Louisiana legislature passed a resolution instructing him to support "rag money" measures in the Senate, he refused to be bound by these instructions.

Gibson was the chief agent of Paul Tulane in the founding of Tulane University of Louisiana. After a first-hand study of the universities of Europe, he projected a plan by which in 1884 the University of Louisiana in New Orleans was transferred to the Tulane board of administration and was renamed Tulane University of Louisiana. At Tulane's request Gibson was chosen as the first president of the board of administration and continued in that position until his death. He served also on the boards of administration of the Howard Memorial Library in New Orleans, the Smithsonian Institution, and the Peabody Education Fund. He was married on Jan. 25, 1868, to Mary Montgomery, daughter of R. W. Montgomery, of New Orleans. She died in 1887. He was a man of extensive reading, a ready debater, logical and accurate in his speech, but with little of the oratorical flourish that characterized many of the public men of his time. Though decidedly aristocratic in his bearing, he was always courteous and gentle, and in the society of his friends was very companionable and entertaining. He died in Hot Springs, Ark., whither he had gone for his health, and was buried in Lexington, Ky. He was survived by three sons.

["Memorial Addresses on the Life and Character of Randall Lee Gibson," *Sen. Misc. Doc. 178,* 53 Cong., 2 Sess.; *Obit. Record Grads. Yale Univ. 1890–1900* (1900); *Yale Coll. Class of 1853* (1883); Alcée Fortier, *Louisiana,* I (1914), 473; E. W. Fay, *The Hist. of Educ. in La.* (1898), pp. 181–84.] E. M. V.

GIBSON, WALTER MURRAY (1823–Jan. 21, 1888), adventurer, politician, was born at sea while his parents were emigrating from Northumberland, England, to the United States. After a childhood in New York and New Jersey, he became an orphan at the age of fourteen and began a career of wandering. He lived for a time with Indians, settled long enough near Pendleton, S. C., to marry a Miss Lewis and have three children, drifted to New York after his wife's death, and in 1844 was a commission merchant there. After successful Californian speculations in 1849, he visited Central America, and on his return bought a schooner which he hoped eventually to command as Guatemalan admiral. But the plan failed and he set sail in his vessel with the hope of selling her abroad. In 1852 he reached Sumatra, where a native revolt against Dutch rule promised a market. At first Dutch East India officials welcomed him as a wealthy yachtsman, but his vessel's warlike design, his partiality for the company of semi-independent native princes, and his loose talk about liberty aroused suspicions which led to his imprisonment on a flimsy charge of treason. Confined at Batavia for nearly sixteen months, he studied Dutch and Malay, invented ingenious machines, and explained Christianity to heathen prisoners. After a protracted trial, he was sentenced to exposure in the pillory and twelve years forced labor, but escaped on Apr. 24, 1853. Reaching Washington, he persuaded Secretary of State Marcy to support his claim for damages against the Dutch government. He attracted popular attention by lectures and a fascinating but fantastic book recounting his adventures (*The Prison of Weltevreden,* 1855). Stimulated by a desire to attack the Dutch commercial monopoly in the East Indies, August Belmont, United States minister to the Netherlands, virtually threatened war in September 1854 if Gibson were not compensated. The Dutch presented a direct refusal though the affair later aided Belmont in negotiating a convention for establishing consulates in the Dutch colonies. After attacking both minister and secretary and unsuccessfully petitioning Congress for settlement of his exorbitant claim, Gibson went to Utah, embraced Mormonism, and inspired Brigham Young with a grandiose scheme for selling the Salt Lake Territory to the United States and transplanting the Mormon colony to the Hawaiian Islands. He was sent to Hawaii in 1861 to execute the plan. There he bought large estates which he retained in his own name when expelled from the church three years later. Becoming master of the native language, he published in it a newspaper, the *Nuhou,* which advocated a policy of "Hawaii for the Hawaiians." When the predominant foreigners split into "merchant" and "missionary" factions, he adroitly stepped into the premiership on May 19, 1882. Using with consummate skill all the arts of contemporary American politicians, he maintained himself in office for five years. He pleased both king and people by staging extravagant pageants and undertook a fatuous "Primacy of the Pacific" foreign policy which aimed at protectorates over the archipelagoes of Oceania. This ended in fiasco when Germany protested activities in the Samoan Islands and Hawaiian envoys proved themselves bibulous satyrs. Meanwhile the foreign factions, united by venomous hatred of Gibson and his régime, magnified every scandal of the administration, used Kalakaua's fondness for military display to obtain permission for arming a citizen guard, and finally on June 30, 1887, made a show of force which cowed the king into dismissing his premier and granting a new constitution. Gibson was arrested, but no charge could be proved against him and he was permitted to leave the country on July 5, escorted to his ship by a mob which threatened lynching. Arriving at San Francisco a month later, he spoke in high terms of the new constitution and ministry, giving reporters an impression of quiet urbanity. A year later he died without revisiting Hawaii. Honored by Hawaiians, whether of royal or common blood, he was execrated by the wealthy foreigners. An adventurer who combined broad culture, personal charm, and brilliant abilities with an unstable and romantic imagination, he was too impractical to be a successful statesman.

[*House Report 307,* 34 Cong., 1 Sess.; *Current Lit.,* Mar. 1900, p. 196; P. A. van der Lith, *Encyc. van Nederlandsch-Indië* (4 vols., 1894–1905), vol. II; W. M. Gibson, *Address to the Hawaiian People* (1876); W. D. Alexander, *Hist. of the Later Years of the Hawaiian Monarchy* (1896); *Cong. Record,* 53 Cong., 2 Sess., pp. 309–12; Queen Liliuokalani, *Hawaii's Story* (1898); F. L. Clarke, "Pol. Revolution in the Hawaiian Islands," *Overland Monthly,* Mar. 1888; *San Francisco Chronicle* and *N. Y. Herald,* Aug. 1887, especially Aug. 7; *San Francisco Chronicle,* Jan. 24, 1888.]

W. L. W—t, Jr.

GIBSON, WILLIAM (Mar. 14, 1788–Mar. 2, 1868), surgeon, was born in Baltimore, Md., one of twin boys. He attended St. John's College, Annapolis, and later went to Princeton, where he studied for some time but did not graduate. He began the study of medicine with Dr. John Owen of Baltimore and later was a student in medicine at the University of Pennsylvania for a time. After a return to Princeton he went to Edinburgh where he took his degree in medicine in 1809, the title of his thesis being *"De Forma Ossium Gentilitia."* For his thesis, which dealt with certain phases of ethnology, he used material from the museum of Alexander Monro. In Edinburgh he studied with John Bell; later in London he became associated with Sir Charles Bell, who apparently was warmly attached to him and who took him as a private pupil. He also attracted the attention of Sir Astley Cooper, the great surgeon of Guy's Hospital, and seems to have had the opportunity of seeing a number of the wounded soldiers who were brought home after the battle of Corunna. In addition to his strictly professional pursuits he studied painting, music, botany, and ornithology.

After Gibson's return to America in 1810 he established himself in Baltimore and soon became engaged in organizing a medical department in the University of Maryland. Upon the completion of the project in 1811 he became professor of surgery at the early age of twenty-three. He seems to have acquired a reputation rapidly. Certainly he did not lack originality and courage, for in 1812 he tied the common iliac artery for aneurism, the first time it was done in America. One of his successful surgical deeds was the extraction of foreign material from the shoulder of Gen. Winfield Scott who had been wounded at the battle of Lundy's Lane near Niagara Falls, and had suffered from the wound for some time. In 1828 he ligated the subclavian artery, also a brave undertaking for those days. He held the chair in surgery at the University of Maryland until 1819, when he was called to Philadelphia to the chair of surgery in the University of Pennsylvania, in which he succeeded Dr. Physick. Those were the days of peripatetic teachers in American medical schools.

In Philadelphia Gibson had a long and successful career, holding an important position in the profession, and occupying the chair of surgery until 1855. His principal publication was *The Institutes and Practice of Surgery,* which went through several editions. The first edition, published in 1824, was intended as a guide to his students in following his lectures, but as additions were made to each edition the work developed into a treatise on surgery. His most striking surgical success was the performance of a Cesarean section twice on the same patient who lived for fifty years after the first operation. In 1815 Gibson again visited Europe and apparently was present at the battle of Waterloo where, it is stated, he received a slight wound. After a later trip he published two books: *Sketches of Prominent Surgeons of London and Paris* (1839), and *Rambles in Europe in 1839* (1841).

A man of wide learning, Gibson occupied a high place in his profession and did much to advance the knowledge and practise of surgery. Probably part of his success was due to the influence of his association with Sir Charles Bell and Sir Astley Cooper, for he must have shown evidence of ability to have attracted their attention at such an early age. He had the courage to publish his failures and his frankness appears to have surprised some of his contemporaries. In his teaching his lectures are said to have been characterized by clearness and accuracy of thought while his artistic training enabled him to make diagrams and illustrations of unusual merit. He was also widely versed in classical literature, and there are accounts of his remarkable memory of Latin verse, especially of Ovid, Horace, and Virgil. He was married twice, his first wife being Sarah Hollingsworth, whom he married in Baltimore. He had eight children of whom one son, Charles Bell Gibson (1816–1865), was professor of surgery at the Medical College at Richmond, Va. He died at Savannah, Ga., in his eightieth year.

[Jos. Carson, *A Hist. of the Medic. Dept. of the Univ. of Pa.* (1869); *Autobiog. of Samuel D. Gross* (1887); H. A. Kelly and W. L. Burrage, *Am. Medic. Biogs.* (1920); the *Press* (Phila.), Mar. 4, 1868.]

T. M.

GIBSON, WILLIAM HAMILTON (Oct. 5, 1850–July 16, 1896), artist, naturalist, was born in Sandy Hook, Newtown, Conn., the son of Edmund Trowbridge Hastings and Elizabeth Charlotte (Sanford) Gibson of Brooklyn, N. Y. He was a descendant of John Gibson, who settled in Cambridge before 1634, and a great-great-grandson of Richard Dana [*q.v.*]. He was educated at the Gunnery in Washington, Conn., and at the Brooklyn Polytechnic Institute, where his indifference to general learning was offset by a gift for drawing and a passion for nature study. His father, a broker of New York, died in 1868, and Gibson was thrown upon his own resources. He first opened an insurance office in Brooklyn. As he watched a draftsman at his board, however, his early ambitions were revived, and with a naïve self-confidence which frustrated all adverse counsel, he purchased drawing materials and set himself up as an artist. Considering his inexperience, his success was amazingly quick. John G. Shea published his early drawings in *Frank Leslie's Boys' and Girls' Weekly* and *Frank Leslie's Chimney Corner,* and encouraged him to write texts to accompany them. Later he contributed botanical sketches to the *American Agriculturist* and to Appletons' *American Cyclopædia,* and illustrations to *Hearth and Home,* at the same time building up an odd-job trade with various lithographers, for whom he cut anything from mammoth charts to picture puzzles. His first mature opportunity came in 1872 from Appletons, who sent him to Rhode Island and later to Connecticut to sketch the countryside. His drawings were published as "Providence and Vicinity" and "The Connecticut Shore of the Sound" in W. C. Bryant's *Picturesque America* (2 vols., 1872–74).

Gibson was known to the general public as the author and illustrator of a long and varied succession of nature articles which appeared in *Harper's, Scribner's,* and the *Century* magazines over a period of nearly twenty years. The first of these to indicate the direction of his career was published in *Harper's Magazine* for August 1878, as "Birds and Plumage," for which Helen S. Conant supplied the text. This was followed by "Snug Hamlet and Hometown," "A Winter Idyl," "Springtime," and "An Autumn Pastoral"—sketches of New England throughout the seasons—which appeared in *Harper's Magazine* from August 1879 to November 1880, and were published in book form as *Pastoral Days; or, Memories of a New England Year* (1881). Later articles were reprinted as *Highways and Byways, or Saunterings in New England* (1883); *Strolls by Starlight and Sunshine* (1891); *Sharp Eyes* (1892); *Our Edible Toadstools and Mushrooms* (1895); *Eye Spy* (1897); *My Studio Neighbors* (1898); *Blossom Hosts and Insect Guests* (1901); and *Our Native Orchids* (1905).

As a popularizer of nature study Gibson achieved considerable success. His acute observation compensated for his lack of scholarly training, and his personal approach and informal treatment created in his readers an illusion of sharing that intimacy with nature which he himself enjoyed. Although his magazine articles consumed most of his time, he conducted several lecture courses and contributed annually to the exhibitions of the American Water Color Society, of which he became a member in 1885. He had married Emma Ludlow Blanchard, the daughter of Charles A. S. Blanchard, on Oct. 29, 1873, and with her spent the winters in Brooklyn, working over the material he collected in New England during the summers. He died of apoplexy at his summer home in Washington, Conn.

[M. C. C. Wilson, *John Gibson of Cambridge, Mass., and his Descendants* (1900); J. C. Adams, *Wm. Hamilton Gibson, Artist-Naturalist-Author* (1901); and "Wm. Hamilton Gibson," *New Eng. Mag.*, Feb. 1897; the *Critic*, July 25, 1896; *Appletons' Ann. Cyc.*, 1896; *N. Y. Tribune*, July 17, 1896.] C. P. M.

GIDDINGS, JOSHUA REED (Oct. 6, 1795–May 27, 1864), Abolitionist, was for twenty years a militant anti-slavery congressman from the Western Reserve of Ohio. His relentless attacks on slaveholders, marked by exaggeration and bitterness, and his severe, uncompromising attitude were in a large measure the inheritance of a pioneer, provincial ancestry. George Giddings emigrated from St. Albans, Hertfordshire, England, to Ipswich, Mass., in 1635. His descendants moved in succession to Lyme and to Hartland, Conn., and then to Tioga Point (now Athens), in Bradford County, Pa. Here Joshua Reed Giddings was born, the youngest of the children of Joshua and Elizabeth (Pease) Giddings. When he was six weeks old the family moved to Canandaigua, N. Y., only to move again ten years later to Ashtabula County, Ohio. His father had made large purchases of land, and the family was forced to toil long hours to carry the debt and wrest a living from the soil. The boy found little time to attend school. In the War of 1812 he enlisted as a substitute for his brother and saw a short service against the Indians in northwestern Ohio. For several years thereafter he divided his time between teaching school and farm work, interrupted by nine months' private study of mathematics and Latin in the home of a country parson. On Sept. 24, 1819, he was married to Laura Waters, daughter of Abner Waters, an emigrant from Connecticut. He studied law in the office of Elisha Whittlesey at Canfield, Ohio, in 1821 was admitted to the bar, and then engaged in an eminently successful general practise at Jefferson, Ohio, until 1838. Meanwhile, in 1826, he served one term in the Ohio House of Representatives.

In 1838 Giddings was elected to the federal House of Representatives as a Whig. He threw himself into John Quincy Adams's struggle over the right of Congress to receive anti-slavery petitions, and in the early years of his incumbency he carried on a crusade in Congress for freedom of debate on all matters touching slavery and for a denial of the power of the federal government to tax the people of the free states for the support of slavery. He vigorously opposed the annexation of Texas and the Mexican War in the belief that they were conspiracies to extend the institution. For attempting during the negotiations with Great Britain over the *Creole* case to put the House of Representatives on record as opposed to any federal measures in defense of the coastwise slave-trade, he was censured in resolutions which passed by a vote of 125 to 69. He resigned his seat in Congress in order to appeal to his constituents, and was triumphantly reëlected.

President Polk's compromise with Great Britain over the Oregon boundary seemed to Giddings an attempt to avoid a war which might threaten the life of slavery. With the nomination of Taylor in 1848 he broke definitely with the Whigs and joined the Free-Soil party. In 1854, upon the repeal of the Missouri Compromise, he joined the Republicans. By this time he had formulated an anti-slavery program which included the dedication of all national territories to freedom, opposition to disunion, and the use of the war powers of the President, if war came, to emancipate the slaves of the Southern states. Lincoln was his messmate in Washington in 1847–48, and a careful student of his speeches in Congress (Albert J. Beveridge, *Abraham Lincoln,* 1928, II, 19). Thus it may be that Giddings's greatest influence upon the course of American history was exerted in the evolution of Lincoln's ideas, or at least in the preparation of public opinion for Lincoln's leadership. Owing to a breakdown of his health in April 1858, Giddings was not renominated in his congressional district in the following campaign. He took an active part in the Republican convention of 1860, however, as he had in the convention of 1856, and in 1861 President Lincoln appointed him consul-general to Canada, at which post he served for the remainder of his life. Following his death in Montreal he was buried in Jefferson, Ohio. In addition to his printed speeches and essays he left two published works: *The Exiles of Florida* (1858), and *The History of the Rebellion* (1864). If a man is to be known by the company he keeps, Giddings should be associated politically with John Quincy Adams, William Lloyd Garrison, Wendell Phillips, Charles Sumner, and John G. Palfrey. His severe attitude toward those who did not share his views regarding slavery was a result of a moral earnestness and an inflexible purpose. In private life he revealed quite different traits. He loved sports, music, and children, and his letters to his own children reveal a charming understanding, sympathy, and mutual confidence.

[*The Life of Joshua R. Giddings* (1892), by Geo. W. Julian, a son-in-law, is the best biography, though written with obvious bias. Part of the extensive Giddings correspondence has been preserved in the Lib. of Cong.; part is in the possession of the Ohio State Archeol. and Hist. Soc. at Columbus, Ohio. For Giddings's attitude on slavery the best printed sources are his *Speeches in Congress* (1853) and the series of articles, later reprinted in the Julian biography, which first appeared in 1843 in the *Western Reserve Chronicle* over the name *Pacificus.* His annual addresses to his constituents were published in the *Ashtabula Sentinel.* For further reference see M. S. Giddings, *The Giddings Family* (1882); and the article by B. R. Long in the *Ohio Archeol. and Hist. Quart.,* Jan. 1919.] E. J. B.

GIDEON, PETER MILLER (Feb. 9, 1820–Oct. 27, 1899), pioneer pomologist of the northern Mississippi Valley, was the son of George and Elizabeth (Miller) Gideon, of German and English-Welsh descent respectively. George Gideon served in the War of 1812 as an ensign in Leslie's division, Virginia militia, enlisting from Leesburg, Loudoun County. About 1817 he emigrated to Champaign County, Ohio, settling first at Millerstown, named for his wife's family, and then moving on to a farm near Woodstock, where Peter was born. The boy's schooling was "the three R's, with the rod not spared," but at home he read for himself Gibbon's *Decline and Fall of the Roman Empire,* the Bible, and Josephus. During his boyhood the family moved westward once more, to Clinton, Ill., and there on Jan. 2, 1849, Peter was married to Wealthy Hull. In 1858, with his wife and two children, he removed to Minnesota and took up a claim of 160 acres on "Gideon's Bay," Lake Minnetonka. There, challenged by the rigor of the climate, for forty-one years he bent his efforts toward developing varieties of fruit hardy enough to withstand the northern winters. Time and again a killing frost destroyed his work, but, indomitable, he always began once more, with enlarged knowledge. After many setbacks he produced from seed of the Siberian crab a full-sized apple the introduction of which "proved a boon to the Northwest" (Bailey, *post*) and marked an epoch in American apple-growing. The "Wealthy," named for his wife, had its first published notice in the *Western Farmer* in 1869. Though not ironclad in cold endurance and therefore not successful in the coldest portions of the Old Northwest, it was far superior in quality to most of the Russian varieties being introduced in the North at about the same time, proved dependably productive, and was attractive in appearance throughout a wide climatic range. It had, however, too delicate a skin to be a "long keeper," and during the rest of his life Gideon sought by blending to evolve a fruit with as fine a flavor and a tougher outside. In the course of his efforts to attain his ideal he originated several new varieties, chief among them "Peter," which closely resembles "Wealthy," and "Gideon," which though beautiful and productive, is of most importance as a vigorous, cold-enduring stock for other varieties. Three crab-apples which he developed, "Florence," "Martha," and "Excelsior," also became popular in his region. For several years he was in charge of the state experimental fruit farm established in 1878 on a tract adjoining his own. He described some of his work in a paper, "Growing Hardy Fruits," published in the *Proceedings* for 1885 of the American Pomological Society, and contributed "Our Seedling and Russian Apples" to the *Annual Report* for 1887 of the Minnesota State Horticultural Society. He distributed many thousands of seedlings in the state.

Gideon was a strong man with a clear brain and believed in keeping himself so. He used no liquor or tobacco, drank no tea or coffee, was temperate in eating—almost a vegetarian. His interests ranged beyond his horticultural work. The occult appealed to his imagination. In religion he was a product of the Old and New Testaments, while he disclaimed doctrinal adherence to either. In pioneer days his best friends and neighbors were the orthodox ministers with whom he exchanged opinions and farm implements. A temperamental non-conformist, he usually stood alone or with the unpopular minority. He was an early advocate of abolition, prohibition, woman's suffrage. Beards on men he detested, and was outspoken to the wearers. Horse-racing at fairs he deemed vicious. Prayers at the opening of secular meetings he objected to, and was not content to let the majority prevail. On the other hand, generosity was one of his strong characteristics; he delighted to give away his fruit, and heaped the measure when he sold it. He and the "Wealthy" are commemorated by a monument erected in 1912 by the Native Sons of Minnesota in the Gideon Memorial Park on his homestead at Lake Minnetonka.

["In Memoriam: Peter M. Gideon" and other notices, in *Trees, Fruits and Flowers of Minn.* (1900); *Minn. Hist. Soc. Colls.*, vol. XII (1908), see Index; G. W. Warner and C. M. Foote, *Hist. of Hennepin County* (1881), see Index; L. H. Bailey, *Standard Cyc. of Horticulture*, III (1915), 1577; *Minneapolis Tribune*, Oct. 28, 1899; personal material from a daughter, Mrs. Florence Gideon Webster of Los Angeles.]

W. A. T.

GIESLER-ANNEKE, MATHILDE FRANZISKA (Apr. 3, 1817–Nov. 25, 1884), author, reformer, educator, was born in Westphalia at Lerchenhausen on the Ruhr, the daughter of Karl and Elisabeth (Hülswitt) Giesler. Her girlhood was spent on the estate and in the neighboring castle of Blankenstein, of which her father was Domänendirektor. She enjoyed passionately the outdoor life and romantic scenery of the region, was carefully educated under Catholic auspices, and was married at the age of nineteen to the Gerichtsrat Alfred von Tabouillot. The marriage proved a mistake and was soon dissolved, but a long struggle ensued in the courts before she secured the custody of her infant daughter. Meanwhile she turned to literary work: *Des Christen Freudiger Aufblick zum Himmlischen Vater: Gebete und Betrachtungen* (Wesel, 1839); *Heimathgrüss* (Wesel, 1840), a patriotic anthology, with contributions of her own; *Damenalmanach für das Jahr 1842* (Wesel, 1842); *Der Meister ist da und Rufet Dich: Ein Vollständiges Gebet- und Erbauungsbuch für die Gebildete Christkatholische Frauenwelt* (Borken and Wesel, 1843); *Oithono, oder Die Tempelweihe* (Wesel, 1844), a four-act drama produced at Münster and in the author's honor in Milwaukee in 1882; *Michel Angelo* (Münster, 1845), a German version of a story by Alexandre Dumas; *Der Erbe von Morton Park* (Wesel, 1845), a translation of Ellen Pickering's *The Expectant*; *Produkte der Rothen Erde* (Münster, 1846), a selection of Westphalian writings, including some of her own; and *Das Weib im Konflikt mit den Sozialen Verhältnissen* (1846). During this development from a writer of pious books to a pioneer of German feminism, she abandoned dogmatic religion and became a freethinker. On June 3, 1847, she married Fritz Anneke (born at Dortmund Jan. 31, 1818; died in Chicago Dec. 8, 1872), whose liberalism had cost him his lieutenancy in the Prussian artillery. They removed to Köln and joined the revolutionary movement.

While Anneke was spending eleven months in prison awaiting trial for treason, their first child was born and Frau Anneke started two papers, the *Neue Kölnische Zeitung* and the *Frauenzeitung,* which were quickly suppressed by the police. At liberty again, Anneke joined the revolutionary forces in Baden and the Palatinate, his wife accompanying him as a mounted orderly. Carl Schurz [*q.v.*], who was Anneke's aide-de-camp, describes her at this time as "a young woman of noble character, beauty, vivacity, and fiery patriotism" (*Reminiscences,* I, 1907, 197). They were in the battle of Ubstadt June 23, 1849, were forced back on Rastatt, and amid general confusion were compelled to flee. They reached Zürich in safety and thence emigrated to the United States, settling in Milwaukee, where Mrs. Anneke soon made her appearance as a lecturer. Five children were born to them in America. From 1852 to 1858 they lived in Newark, N. J., where Anneke edited the *Newarker Zeitung* and Mrs. Anneke the *Frauenzeitung.* She also gave considerable aid to the cause of woman suffrage by lecturing on that and related subjects and was highly esteemed by Susan B. Anthony and other leaders of the movement. From 1860 to 1865 she was in Switzerland as a newspaper correspondent, while her husband served as an artillery staff officer under Gen. John A. McClernand and for three months as colonel of the 34th Wisconsin Infantry. Later he was war correspondent for the *Augsburger Allgemeine Zeitung* and after the war secretary of the Deutsche Gesellschaft of Chicago. At Jena, in 1863, Mrs. Anneke published a novel, *Das Geisterhaus in New-York.* In 1865 she founded a girls' school, the Milwaukee Töchter Institut, and conducted it for the rest of her life. It enjoyed a high reputation and a wide influence among liberal Germans in the Middle West. Until late in life she continued to write much prose and verse. To the end, in spite of bereavements and severe illness, she retained her youthful idealism and her enthusiasm for various humanitarian causes.

[C. Herrmann Boppe, "Mathilde Franziska Anneke" (Vortrag gehalten vor der Freien Gemeinde, Milwaukee, Jan. 1885, in MS.); "Mathilde Franziska Anneke," *Romanbibliothek zur Kleinen Kölnischen Zeitung*, no. 146 (Köln, 1886), pp. 583–84; Wilhelm Hense-Jensen, *Wisconsin's Deutsch-Amerikaner* (2 vols., 1900–02); Regina Ruben, *Mathilde Franziska Anneke* (Hamburg, 1906); A. B. Faust, biographical notice and reprint of "Memoiren einer Frau aus dem Badisch-Pfälzischen Feldzug," *German-Am. Annals*, May–Aug. 1918; *Official Records (Army)*, 1 ser. X, XXIII, 3 ser. I; information as to certain facts from Mrs. Anneke's daughter, Mrs. Hertha Anneke Sanne.] G. H. G.

GIFFORD, ROBERT SWAIN (Dec. 23, 1840–Jan. 15, 1905), landscape-painter, etcher, illustrator, was born in the township of Gosnold, Mass., on the island of Naushon, the largest of the Elizabeth Islands, lying between Buzzard's Bay and Vineyard Sound. His father was William Tillinghast Gifford, sailor, pilot, fisherman, at one time skipper of the yacht *Fawn*, owned by Robert Swain, son of William Swain, then a part owner of Naushon, for whom the future artist was named. Swain Gifford's mother was Annie (Eldridge) Gifford, daughter of Stephen Eldridge of Dartmouth, Mass. His birthplace was a humble little house in an isolated spot with a tiny garden and a few gnarled trees about it. Thence the family moved to the mainland, about two years after his birth, and settled in Fairhaven, Mass., a suburb of New Bedford. Here his boyhood years passed uneventfully in study, work, and play.

In spite of delicate health, Gifford was fond of outdoor life; he spent much of his leisure time in sailing and in sketching along the shore. For a short time he was employed in the railroad yard. The idea of becoming a painter, which was vaguely forming in his mind, assumed a more serious character when he made the acquaintance of two men, both marine painters, then living in New Bedford and occupying the same studio—William Bradford and Albert van Beest. The lad was allowed to frequent their studio, and he took them out on the bay in his catboat. His association with them stirred his ambition; they gave him his first practical instruction in drawing from nature. Later he met Walton Ricketson, who was living at Brooklawn, the home of his father, Daniel Ricketson, the local historian of New Bedford. Walton, who was just beginning work as a sculptor, arranged a corner in his studio where young Gifford could paint. In the Gifford household it had by now become obvious that the boy's heart was set upon art as a vocation, but the problem of ways and means loomed large, and his parents had some thought of making a carpenter of him. Ricketson now intervened and suggested that the youth should paint a certain number of pictures and see if there were any buyers for them. This test being agreed to, Gifford did so, and much to the surprise of all concerned, the pictures were sold. With the earned money in his pocket the young artist set out for Boston in 1864 and began his professional career. He was then twenty-four. At first his work was dry and literal, but it gained in quality with experience, becoming increasingly atmospheric and lyrical. From the outset his paintings were welcomed in the exhibitions and found a ready market.

He remained in Boston two years, going to New York in 1866. He was elected an associate of the National Academy in 1867, and academician in 1878. He served for nearly thirty years as teacher in the various art classes maintained by the Cooper Union, and was esteemed and loved by his students. One of them, Frances Eliot, daughter of Hon. T. D. Eliot, a well-known jurist, became his wife in 1873. In 1869 Gifford had made a long journey to the Pacific Coast, mainly to gather material for W. C. Bryant's *Picturesque America* (2 vols., 1872–74). He sketched in Washington, Oregon, and California, and from these sketches several of the most important of the landscapes of that period were painted. In 1870 he made an extensive tour abroad, visiting England, France, Spain, Italy, Morocco, and Egypt. Four years later, in company with his wife, herself a painter of merit, he started on a similar trip, which included Corsica, Algeria, and many parts of North Africa seldom visited by tourists. The pair pitched their tent in the great desert, and were entertained by Arab chiefs in the wilds of the Atlas Mountains. S. G. W. Benjamin tells of an over-night sojourn with a haughty chieftain who had decorated the interior of his dwelling with the heads of twelve men suspected of organizing a conspiracy for the overthrow of the prince. Such pictures as the "Halt in the Desert," the "Palms of Biskra," "Evening in the Sahara," and "The Oasis of Filiach" may be cited as characteristic examples of Gifford's Oriental compositions. About a decade later Gifford made still another visit to the Old World, this time with two artist companions. After this he divided his time between the New York studio and his summer home at Nonquitt, Mass., with the exception of a voyage to Alaska in 1899 with the scientific party made up by E. H. Harriman. This trip of three months took the party along the coast from Seattle to Bering

Strait, and Gifford made many studies of the northern scenery. He had some exciting experiences and narrow escapes in hazardous mountain ascents and sailing among the ice floes.

At Nonquitt, a summer resort on the shore of Buzzard's Bay, a few miles south of New Bedford, Gifford found the most congenial subjects for his landscape work, and painted most of the pictures which will be regarded as representative. Typical examples, such as "Dartmouth Moors," are in a low tone, and are melancholy in sentiment. They are impressive, spacious, solidly constructed, and many of them reveal the somber beauty of autumn on the marshes and among the dunes. Isham suggests that Gifford may have derived from his first teacher, Van Beest, something of the gravity of the old Dutch painters, which reappears in "the long brown sweeps of moorland or seashore under a sky of broken gray clouds." Although Gifford was serious, he was genial and sociable, and extremely popular. His character and distinguished ability won the admiration of his colleagues, and his success shows that good art work was not without recognition in his time. His death occurred in New York, in the winter of 1905.

[The best estimate of Gifford's work is the monograph by S. R. Koehler in the *Am. Art Rev.,* Aug. 1880, together with an account of his etched work in the same issue. Another good study is Cooper Gaw's "Robt. Swain Gifford, Landscape Painter," in *Brush and Pencil,* Apr. 1905. See also S. G. W. Benjamin, *Our Am. Artists* (1879); Howe and Torrey, "Some Living Am. Artists," *Art Interchange,* June 1894; G. W. Sheldon, *Am. Painters* (1879); *Illustrated Cat. of Oil Paintings and Water Colors of the late R. Swain Gifford, N. A.* (1906), a catalogue of the pictures exhibited at the Am. Art Galleries; Z. W. Pease, *Hist. of New Bedford* (1918), I, 378; H. E. Gifford, *Gifford Geneal.* (cop. 1896); the *Standard* (New Bedford), Jan. 16, 28, 1905; *Sun* (N. Y.), Jan. 17, 1905.] W. H. D.

GIFFORD, SANFORD ROBINSON (July 10, 1823–Aug. 29, 1880), landscape-painter, was born at Greenfield, Saratoga County, N. Y., the son of Elihu Gifford and Eliza Robinson Starbuck Gifford. His father was the owner of extensive iron-works at Hudson, N. Y., to which place the family moved in 1824, when the boy was about a year old. At Catskill, just across the Hudson River, Thomas Cole and Frederick E. Church were working at the time of Gifford's boyhood, and it was but natural that he should be interested in them; indeed his artistic aspirations were first aroused by contemplation of the works of Cole. He entered Brown University in 1842, but remained there only two years, for he then definitely determined to devote himself to landscape-painting. With this purpose in view he proceeded to New York and enrolled himself as a pupil of John Rubens Smith, a water-colorist and son of John Raphael Smith, the well-known English engraver. The instruction received from Smith was the only technical training he ever had, though he was always a student, with a mind open to the teachings of nature and the masters of art.

How rapidly his talent developed is shown by his election as an associate of the National Academy of Design in 1851 and his election as an academician in 1854. He set out upon the first of several foreign tours in 1855, when he visited the art museums of the chief European capitals, but found nothing in the art schools that made him wish for their training. He spent the summer sketching in England, Scotland, and Wales, and after a run on the Continent passed the winter in Paris. During the following summer, 1856, he made a long pedestrian tour through Belgium and Holland, went up the Rhine to Switzerland, and thence over the Alps into Italy. Worthington Whittredge, who met him in the course of this trip, and went up the Rhine with him, recounts his direct and original comments on the scenery. Gifford spent the winter of 1856–57 in Rome, where he lived in modest style in a street leading from the Pincian Hill and commanding a view of the city and the dome of St. Peter's. In the spring and summer of 1857 he made a sketching trip through the Abruzzi and in the neighborhood of Naples, and later went to Austria. He returned to New York in September 1857 and took a studio in the old Tenth-Street building, which he retained to the end of his life. He made a second journey to Europe with Jervis McEntee in 1859.

At the outbreak of the Civil War Gifford joined the 7th New York Regiment and served in the ranks through the campaigns of 1861 and 1863–64. A few pictures from his hand record his impressions of military life, but this field was not of a nature to accord with his artistic ideals. Again in 1868 he went to Europe and spent two years, painting in Italy, Sicily, Greece, Syria, Egypt, and Turkey. Some of his most characteristic canvases are "Tivoli," "Palermo," "The Golden Horn," "Venetian Sails," "Leander's Tower," "Lago Maggiore," and others, several of which were exhibited at the Centennial Exposition in 1876. In these landscapes he gave the fullest expression to his feeling for light and color. They are, as his friend John F. Weir has said, interpretations of the sentiments of nature rather than of her superficial aspects. Added to the early influence of Thomas Cole there is discernible more than a trace of the visionary and scenic manner of Turner, though without the abandon and fire of Turner's late period.

In 1870 Gifford started on a painting trip to the Rocky-Mountain region with his friends Whittredge and Kensett, but an unexpected opportunity to join Col. Hayden's exploring party in a horseback expedition through the Indian country of Colorado and Wyoming led him to desert his artist companions. He had a liberal share of the typical artist's independence and curiosity, and his interest in new places and people was inexhaustible. His wide experience as a traveler had taught him the advantage of roving with a minimum of impedimenta. Thus, when he departed for a sojourn of two years abroad, his own luggage was a light satchel hung by a strap over his shoulder. He left without telling anybody where he was going, and when he came home he walked into his studio and set to work with as little ado as if he had merely been away for the week-end. Though he was well-to-do, he shunned luxury or display and lived in an almost ascetic manner. As he told McEntee: "I have lived a frugal life in order to provide for an independent old age and to be able to help a friend." The testimony of all who were close to him is emphatic as to the simplicity, unselfishness, and nobility of his character. His chief recreation was fishing. He sought many remote waters for this sport—those of the Catskills, the Berkshire Hills, the wildernesses of Maine and Canada, the Middle West, and the Adirondacks; he even went to Alaska. He did not marry until 1877, when he was fifty-four. Three years later his health became impaired, and on the advice of his physician he went with his wife to the Lake-Superior region to recuperate. The hoped-for improvement was not realized. His condition became worse. He returned to New York in a very feeble state, and at the end of a few weeks he died of pneumonia, in the fifty-eighth year of his age.

Gifford's work was mainly differentiated from that of his contemporaries by its emotional content, its glowing color and romantic cast. He was more intent upon the phenomena of air and light than the other men of the Hudson River school; his perception of values was more subtle. His landscapes are sunny, cheerful, and sweet; his palette, though of no great depth, agreeable. The subjective nature of his art sets it apart from realism and gives it a personal note. It is the self-expression of a sensitive poetic artist. The recognition which his work received was generous. His landscapes were bought by the most discriminating amateurs of the time, and his patrons included Edwin Booth, J. Taylor Johnston, Marshall O. Roberts, R. M. Hoe, R. M. Olyphant, R. L. Stuart, and James L. Claghorn. His "Villa Malta" hangs in the National Gallery, Washington; "Sunset on the Lake" is in the Art Institute of Chicago; "Lago Maggiore" belongs to the New York Public Library; and the Metropolitan Museum of Art owns "Tivoli," "Lake George," "Near Palermo," and "Kaaterskill Clove."

[*The Gifford Memorial Meeting of the Century Asso.* (1880) contains a portrait, a catalogue of Gifford's pictures on view at the club, and addresses and verses by several of his friends. *The Memorial Cat. of the Paintings of Sanford Robinson Gifford, N. A.* (1881), of the Metropolitan Museum of Art, N. Y., contains a biographical and critical essay by John F. Weir, and lists over seven hundred works. The voluminous catalogue of the Gifford sale collection in New York, 1881, was issued in two parts. For other references see H. E. Gifford, *Gifford Geneal.* (cop. 1896), issued in two parts; Samuel Isham, *Hist of Am. Painting* (1905); G. W. Sheldon, *Am. Painters* (1879); H. T. Tuckerman, *Book of the Artists* (1867); C. E. Clement and Laurence Hutton, *Artists of the Nineteenth Century* (1880); S. G. W. Benjamin, *Our Am. Artists* (1879); *Am. Art Rev.*, Oct. 1880; *N. Y. Tribune,* Aug. 30, 1880.]

W. H. D.

GIHON, ALBERT LEARY (Sept. 28, 1833–Nov. 17, 1901), naval surgeon, was born in Philadelphia. He received his preliminary education at Central High School in that city, and graduated in medicine from the Philadelphia College of Medicine and Surgery in 1852, at the age of nineteen. In 1853–54 he was professor of chemistry and toxicology in the college, then on May 1, 1855, he entered the navy as an assistant surgeon. In 1856, while serving on the China station, he took part in the battle on the Pearl River, near Canton. Two years later he was ordered home, assigned to the *Dolphin* of the Brazil Squadron, and sent on the Paraguay Expedition. In 1860, ranking passed assistant surgeon, he was ordered to the naval hospital in New York, then on Aug. 1, 1861, he was promoted surgeon and assigned to duty on the *St. Louis.* Most of his Civil War service was in European waters. The war over, he spent two years at the Portsmouth, N. H., Navy Yard, following which he was assigned to the *Idaho,* store-ship of the Asiatic Squadron, on which he was shipwrecked in 1869. On Nov. 7, 1872, he was promoted medical inspector, and as such served in the Navy Department in Washington, as fleet surgeon on the European station, and as surgeon of the Naval Academy. He was commissioned medical director Aug. 20, 1879, and served in the naval hospitals at Washington, Mare Island, and New York. He became senior medical director with the rank of commodore in 1895 and on Sept. 28 of that year he was retired from active duty with the same rank. It was a disappointment to him and to many of his friends that he had not been made surgeon-general of the navy. He lived in robust health and vigor until Nov. 14, 1901, when he suffered an apoplectic stroke which proved fatal in a few days. He had married, on Apr. 3, 1860, Clara Montford Campfield, of Savannah, Ga., who with two sons survived him.

Gihon was prominent in many medical, sanitary, and climatological associations. He was at one time president of the American Academy of Medicine, president of the American Health Association, vice-president of the Association of Military Surgeons, and a member of numerous American and foreign medical, historical, and scientific societies. At various times he was honored by the Portuguese, British, and French governments for services rendered their sailors in distress. In person he was very pleasant and versatile. Possessing notable gifts as a speaker and writer, he wrote many papers and addresses on naval hygiene, public health, and sanitary reform. His *Practical Suggestions in Naval Hygiene* (1871), although written before the modern age of bacteriology and therefore of little value as to the real causes or prevention of specific diseases, is interestingly written and reveals keen observation and thorough appreciation of such major sanitary faults as overcrowding, overwork, personal uncleanliness, brutality, poor ventilation, poor rations, promiscuity, all too common in the navy at that time, and of their evil effects. His attributing an outbreak of yellow fever to rotting chips of wood left on shipboard for years was no less intelligent than the guesses made by many leaders of the profession.

[H. A. Kelly and W. L. Burrage, *Am. Medic. Biogs.* (1920); *Buffalo Medic. Jour.*, Dec. 1901; *Jour. Am. Medic. Asso.*, Nov. 23, 1901; *Who's Who in America*, 1901–02; *N. Y. Times*, Nov. 18, 1901; U. S. Navy Registers, 1856–1902.]

P. M. A.

GILBERT, ANNE HARTLEY (Oct. 21, 1821–Dec. 2, 1904), character actress, dancer, was born in Rochdale, Lancashire, England, the daughter of a printer, Samuel Hartley, and his wife, formerly a Miss Colborn. As a small child she accompanied her family to London. When she was about twelve years old she obtained the reluctant consent of her parents to enter the ballet school of Her Majesty's Theatre in the Haymarket, where she paid for her training by playing super in mob scenes. Her first public appearances as a dancer were at Her Majesty's and Drury Lane. By dint of hard work she moved up the ranks of the ballet to the "second four" and the "first four," but did not become a solo performer until after her marriage, in 1846, to George H. Gilbert, a dancer-manager. Together they traveled through England and Ireland on barnstorming tours, and within three years had saved enough to retire into private life as emigrant farmers. After five weeks on a sailing vessel, they reached Staten Island on Oct. 21, 1849, proceeded to Wisconsin, part of the way in a prairie wagon, and settled on the edge of the wilderness. Their agricultural venture was unsuccessful. By 1850 they were back on the stage in the frontier town of Milwaukee. The following year they went to Chicago, and later to Cleveland, Louisville, and Cincinnati. While they were in Chicago Gilbert fell through a stage trap, and was so badly injured that although he was later able to work as prompter and stage manager, he was obliged to give up dancing altogether. Mrs. Gilbert had already begun to supplement dancing with minor acting parts, and as it became apparent that she was well qualified as a character actor, she was given opportunity to develop her gift. Most of her western experience was with Lewis Baker and John Ellsler, for whom she specialized in elderly parts. She was given several offers in eastern theatres, but refused them all until 1864, when she became "first old woman" in Mrs. John Wood's Olympic. She made her New York début on Sept. 19 of that year, as Baroness Frietenhorsen in *Finesse*. After Mrs. Wood's retirement, Mrs. Gilbert joined George Wood's Company, leaving it in 1867 to join Barney Williams, under whose management she appeared as the Marquise St. Main in the first American production of *Caste*.

For thirty years, from 1869 to 1899, Mrs. Gilbert acted in Augustin Daly's company, excepting only a short interlude when she played at Palmer's Union Square Theatre. For most of these years, James Lewis, who had also been in Mrs. Wood's Company, played opposite her in comedy parts. They, with John Drew and Ada Rehan, were known as the "Big Four," and during their long years together developed an unrivaled ensemble technique. Most of the time they played in Daly's theatres in New York, but made several tours of England, France, Germany, and the American provinces. Of the many parts which Mrs. Gilbert acted with this group, the Baroness de Cambrai in *Frou-frou,* Hester Dethridge in *Man and Wife,* Curtis in *The Taming of the Shrew,* and the duenna in *Cyrano de Bergerac* were among her most unusual successes. After Daly's death in 1899, she acted under Frohman's management in support of Annie Russell, then starred for a time in *Granny,* a play written for her by Clyde Fitch. She died suddenly after the company was moved to Chicago. During her long career she had played with some of the most famous actors of her time; with Edwin Forrest as the queen in *Hamlet,* with Edwin Booth as Lady Macbeth, and with the younger Wallack as both Goneril and Regan.

Her attitude toward her work insured her success. No part was too difficult or too insignificant for her to accept, and upon every rôle she concentrated all her energies. In reference to this, she said, "I believe . . . that an actor who is not willing to try everything, and able to do most of it, is not worth his salt" (Martin, *post,* p. 26). Although she was competent in tragic parts, it was to comedy that her angular body and homely face were best adapted. Because of her acute sense of time and her facial and bodily discipline, she acquired a rare technical excellence, and to the end of her life she retained a vitality and originality which marked her work as definitely distinguished.

[Charlotte M. Martin, ed., *The Stage Reminiscences of Mrs. Gilbert* (1901); T. A. Brown, *A Hist. of the N. Y. Stage* (3 vols., 1903); Wm. Winter, *The Wallet of Time* (2 vols., 1913); J. F. Daly, *The Life of Augustin Daly* (1917); *N. Y. Tribune,* Dec. 3, 1904.]

K. H. A.

GILBERT, CHARLES HENRY (Dec. 5, 1859–Apr. 20, 1928), zoölogist, was born in Rockford, Ill., the son of Edward Gilbert (originally Gellert), a Bohemian, and Sarah Bean, a native of Massachusetts. During his childhood his parents moved to Indianapolis, where he received his early education. He entered Butler University at Irvington, a suburb of Indianapolis, where he studied under David Starr Jordan, with whom, in the summer of 1876, he made a study of the fishes of Georgia. After receiving the degree of B.S. in 1879, Gilbert followed Jordan to Indiana University. There he received the degree of M.S. in 1882, and Ph.D. in 1883, serving from 1880 to 1884 as assistant in natural sciences and modern languages. From 1884 to 1889 he was professor of natural history at the University of Cincinnati. He then returned to Indiana University as professor of zoölogy. In 1891 he became professor of zoölogy at Leland Stanford, Jr., University, a position which he held until his retirement as professor emeritus in 1925. He was an excellent teacher, developing in his students an unusual initiative and independence, and much of his best teaching was done in the Stanford Journal Club, where he was associated with advanced workers. His own research was marked by care and exactness; he never trusted others for matters of fact which he could verify himself.

Gilbert took part in many intensive investigations of the fishes in the waters of the United States and certain areas of the Pacific. From 1880 he was assistant to the United States Fish Commission, working with Prof. Jordan under the direction of Spencer Fullerton Baird and G. Brown Goode [*qq.v.*]. With Jordan he prepared a *Synopsis of the Fishes of North America* (1882), and numerous other reports. He had charge of the explorations of the Fish Commission's steamer *Albatross* in the deep seas of the North Pacific, Hawaii, and Japan (1889–1906), and from 1909 to 1927 he carried on special investigations of the salmon fisheries of British Columbia and Alaska, making critical studies of the five species of salmon in those regions. Failing health forced him in 1927 to give up all active research. He had married, Aug. 7, 1883, Julia R. Hughes of Bloomington, Ind., who died in 1916. He was a courteous, courageous, lovable though critical man, devoted to his associates and students, and a great favorite with the fishing fraternity. A list of his papers to 1917 is to be found in Bashford Dean, *A Bibliography of Fishes,* Volume I (1917) and Volume III (1923). Most of his reports are contained in the *Bulletins* and *Reports* of the Fish Commission and Bureau of Fisheries, 1880–1927, and *Reports* of the British Columbia Commissioner of Fisheries, 1913–24.

[D. S. Jordan, "Chas. Henry Gilbert, Teacher, Naturalist, and Explorer," *Stanford Illustrated Rev.,* July 1928, and *The Days of a Man* (2 vols., 1922); *Science,* June 29, 1928; *Who's Who in America,* 1928–29; the *San Francisco Examiner,* Apr. 22, 1928.]

D. S. J.

GILBERT, ELIPHALET WHEELER (Dec. 19, 1793–July 31, 1853), Presbyterian clergyman, college president, was the oldest of ten children born to Elisha and Ellen (Vanderpoel) Gilbert, and a descendant of Jonathan Gilbert who settled in Hartford, Conn., in 1645. He was born in what is now New Lebanon, Columbia County, N. Y. His elementary education was provided by his grandfather, Elisha Gilbert, who came to New York from Hebron, Conn., about 1770, and his secondary and collegiate training was secured at Union College, where he graduated in 1813. He attended the Princeton Theological Seminary from 1814 to 1816, but did not graduate. Licensed to preach in 1817, he was ordained by the Presbytery of New Castle in 1818, having been called to the pastorate of the Second Presbyterian Church in Wilmington, Del. In 1829 a schism occurred in his congregation over the question of building another church edifice and a majority of the members organized a new congregation, which, with Gilbert as its pastor, established itself at Hanover (now Sixth) and King Sts. under the name of Hanover Street Church. Gilbert remained as pastor of this church until April 1834.

In the meantime he had been appointed one of thirty-three trustees of a proposed college at Newark, Del., and on Apr. 11, 1833, he was chosen permanent president of the board. The next year, Sept. 23, he was elected president of Newark College, which, with two professors, had opened its doors on May 8, 1834. Entering upon his new duties as an educator the latter part of October, he remained head of the school for less than a year, resigning because he disapproved of a lottery which had been authorized for its support. Recalled by the Hanover Street Church in October 1835, he served it as pastor for about five years. In the controversy which divided the Presbyterian Church in the late thirties, he was strongly on the side of the New School. On Oct. 12, 1840, he was again called to the presidency of Newark College, and he accepted on the condition that the lottery scheme be abandoned. His second connection with the institution, beginning in May 1841, lasted almost six years and was known as the "golden age" of its early period. In 1843 the legislature changed the name to Delaware College; since 1921 it has been known as the University of Delaware. According to one of his students, David Hayes Agnew [*q.v.*], Gilbert "had an intellectual face, was always interesting in the chapel and excellent as a disciplinarian."

In the spring of 1847 he accepted a call to the Western Presbyterian Church, Philadelphia, where he remained until his death. He also served for a time as co-editor with Rev. Benjamin J. Wallace of the *Presbyterian Quarterly Review.* He is said to have been "a man of clear mind and of decided views; skilled as a controversialist, yet of such courtesy to his opponents, that when the joust was over they were among the first to sit down in his tent. He was 'mighty in the Scriptures' and studied them with constant care." He was married twice: first, on Oct. 21, 1819, to Lydia Munro of Wilmington, who died in 1843; and during his second connection with Newark College, to Mary Ann Singer of Philadelphia.

[J. B. Bloss, *One of the Gilbert Family of New England* (1902); W. B. Sprague, *Annals Am. Pulpit,* vol. IV (1859); *Presbyterian Reunion: A Memorial Volume, 1837–1871* (1870); *Remains of Wm. S. Graham with a Memoir* (1849), ed. by George Allen; B. J. Wallace, *The Tenderness of God* (1853), funeral sermon in memory of the Rev. E. W. Gilbert, D.D.; G. J. Porter, *Hist. Discourse* (1876), delivered at the First Presbyterian Church, Newark, Del., July 22, 1876; L. P. Powell, *The Hist. of Educ. in Del.* (1893); Lafayette Marks, *Centennial Address* (1872); Princeton Theol. Seminary *Biog. Cat. 1909*; *Encyc. of the Presbyt. Ch.* (1884), ed. by Alfred Nevin; *The Presbyt. Quart. Rev.,* Dec. 1853; *Delaware Republican* (Wilmington), Aug. 4, 1853; legislative papers concerning Del. Coll., State Archives, Dover, Del.]

G. H. R.

GILBERT, GROVE KARL (May 6, 1843–May 1, 1918), geologist, son of Grove Sheldon Gilbert and his wife Eliza Stanley, was born in Rochester, N. Y. The family was of English ancestry, descendants of John Gilbert who settled in Dorchester, Mass., in 1630. The father was a portrait-painter in moderate circumstances and the boy's early education was gained largely in the public schools, in which he is reported to have made a good record. He graduated from the local high schools in 1858 and entered the University of Rochester to graduate in 1862. Of a studious and quiet nature, he excelled particularly in mathematics and Greek, though, from his course in later life, one is led to infer that this trend toward the classics was due more to the poor showing given to the sciences in the college curriculum than to a natural taste in that direction. His later development of geological tendencies was doubtless due to the personal influence of H. A. Ward, who assumed the chair of geology and natural history at the university shortly before his graduation, and who founded the unique establishment known first as "Cosmos Hall" and later as "Ward's Scientific Establishment" of Rochester.

After a brief and not unusually successful attempt at teaching, Gilbert entered Ward's employ. His duties consisted mainly in preparing and arranging collections in natural history for teaching and museum purposes. So far as it went, this was good training, for it gave him a wide range (though without great depth) of knowledge of materials and forms in the organic and inorganic world. He remained with Ward for five years, when he sought and obtained an appointment as a volunteer on the geological survey of Ohio, under J. S. Newberry. Here he became associated with Edward Orton, R. D. Irving, and others who later were prominent in geological circles. This was in July 1869, and marks his entrance upon his career as a geologist. Though the state geologist was himself a native of Ohio, Newberry was also professor of geology in Columbia College, and in connection with his dual duties brought Gilbert to New York to assist in the preparation of his reports in the winter of 1870. Here he came into contact with various eastern geologists, including B. Silliman, W. P. Blake, O. C. Marsh, and others, the extent of whose influence can at least be surmised. With this seemingly somewhat meager training in field work, Gilbert sought, and through the influence of Prof. Newberry, secured in 1871, an appointment on the newly established survey west of the 100th meridian under Lieut. G. M. Wheeler. These surveys were largely for military purposes, and the opportunities were none too good for detailed work; in fact, it was little more than reconnaissance work conducted under military regulations. Nevertheless it was profitable, and it gave Gilbert glimpses of problems and unrivaled opportunities for their solution.

The winter of 1872 Gilbert spent in Washington, where he was brought into association with Prof. Baird, of the Smithsonian Institution, Maj. J. W. Powell, fresh from his Grand Cañon experiences, and others of this period, the result of which was to settle definitely his more than half-formed determination to follow a scientific career. He remained with the Wheeler survey until Sept. 30, 1874, when he entered into a contract with Powell, director of the second division of the geological and geographical surveys, which lasted throughout the continuance of Powell's leadership, and was continued under the consolidated surveys until his death in 1918. His earliest monographic work while with Powell included his study in 1876 of the laccolithic structures of the Henry Mountains in Utah, a unique and at that time little-known type of mountain formation. Later, under the reorganization of 1879, he brought out what he is credited with considering his *magnum opus,* the monograph on the extinct Lake Bonneville, of Nevada and Utah. In 1884 he was appointed to take charge of the Appalachian Division, and from 1889 to 1892 was chief geologist of the United States Geological Survey. For this position he had little liking, which seriously interfered with work more adapted to his abilities. Among his later and more popular studies, mention should be made of those on the life history of the Niagara River and recent earth movements in the region of the Great Lakes. An unusual problem of his later years, most discreetly handled, was that offered by the "Coon Butte" crater in Arizona, and its semblance to the craters of the moon. The study afforded an admirable illustration of the deliberate, detailed, and judicial manner in which he approached a problem, though after presenting all the facts he at times left the reader to draw his own conclusions. His last publication related to the transportation of débris by streams, and had particular reference to the results of hydraulic mining in California.

Disliking controversy, and rarely entering upon sensational fields, Gilbert was unquestionably one of the best balanced and most philosophical of American geologists. He was a member of the National Academy of Sciences, American Society of Naturalists, Geological Societies of America and Washington, a foreign member of the Geological Society of London, the American Academy in Rome, the Geographic Society of Berlin and a corresponding member of the Bavarian Royal Academy of Sciences and the Geographic Society of Leipzig. He was the recipient in 1899 of the Wollaston medal of the London Geological Society; the Walker Grand Prize of the Boston Society of Natural History; the Hubbard medal of the National Geographic Society, and the Charles P. Daly medal of the American Geographical Society. He was married on Nov. 10, 1874, to Fannie L. Porter of Cambridge, Mass., who died in 1899, leaving two sons.

[W. M. Davis, "Biog. Memoir, Grove Karl Gilbert," *Memoirs Nat. Acad. Sci.,* vol. XXI (1926), and "Grove Karl Gilbert," *Am. Jour. Sci.,* Nov. 1918; W. C. Mendenhall, "Memoir of G. K. Gilbert," *Bull. Geol. Soc. America,* Mar. 1920, with full bibliography; H. L. Fairchild, "Grove Karl Gilbert," *Proc. Rochester Acad. Sci.,* May 1919.] G. P. M.

GILBERT, HENRY FRANKLIN BELKNAP (Sept. 26, 1868–May 19, 1928), composer, was born in Somerville, Mass., the son of Benjamin Franklin and Therese Angeline (Gilson) Gilbert. Among his ancestors were Humphrey Gilbert of Ipswich (1640), and Lieut. Ezekiel Belknap of Revolutionary fame. His uncle, James L. Gilbert, wrote the well-known ballad "Bonnie Sweet Bessie." John Gibbs Gilbert [*q.v.*], the Boston actor, was a cousin. His father, a bank clerk, was also a church organist, singer, and composer of anthems; his mother was a professional singer. At the age of ten, under the inspiration of Ole Bull's playing, he determined to study violin, and after some preliminary instruction he studied at the New England Conservatory and under Emil Mollenhauer. He organized a musical club which during the late eighties held weekly orchestral performances under his direction. While playing at a hotel in the White Mountains he met Mrs. Emma Stowe, a musical enthusiast. Through her influence his parents were persuaded to allow him to begin lessons with Edward MacDowell, with whom he had studied composition (1888–92). He had already become more interested in composition than in the violin. MacDowell proved a sympathetic guide and was himself influenced by Gilbert's enthusiasm for folk-music. Outside of the musical field Gilbert had other intense intellectual interests, especially in the natural sciences. He was an omnivorous reader and an enthusiastic collector of various kinds of natural-history specimens. His chief interest, however, was always music. In 1893 he visited the World's Fair in Chicago, where he made an intensive study of Oriental music; in 1895 he took his first trip abroad; and in 1901 he made a second trip to Paris, traveling across on a cattle-boat in order to hear Charpentier's *Louise.* After this time he devoted his whole effort to composition.

Gilbert experienced great financial difficulties, and to make both ends meet he held various positions, chiefly in music-printing firms. He did some of his first composing in a barn in Quincy, Mass., where he lived for some time. His greatest productive period dates from his marriage to Helen Kalischer, June 4, 1906, and his enjoyment of a congenial home life. The chief events which brought his work to the attention of the public during his lifetime were the performance of his "Comedy Overture" (planned as the overture for an opera on the subject of Uncle Remus) by the Boston Symphony Orchestra, April 1911; the commissioned composition of the "Negro Rhapsody" for the Norfolk Festival, 1913; the production of his native American ballet, *Dance in Place Congo,* at the Metropolitan Opera House in New York, April 1918; the production of the major portion of the music for the Plymouth Tercentenary Pageant, 1920; the performance of the "Symphonic Piece" by the Boston Symphony Orchestra, 1926; the invitation from the International Music Exposition at Frankfurt to appear there in the summer of 1927 as one of America's foremost composers; and finally the ovation accorded him at the premier of his "Nocturne, from Whitman," introduced by Pierre Monteux with the Philadelphia Symphony Orchestra, March 1928.

His compositions, written for piano, voice, and orchestra, fall naturally into three groups. The first reveals Gilbert's free experimentation under European influences. It includes "Celtic Studies," a group of songs (1895); and a symphonic prologue for Synge's *Riders to the Sea;* and culminates in the "Salammbo's Invocation to Tanith" (about 1901), which made his reputation in Russia, where he became a favorite American composer. Under the influence of Dvorák's symphony, *From the New World,* Gilbert became interested in utilizing native American material. The "Negro Episode," his first orchestral work based on negro rhythms, was praised by Massenet and heralded in France as the first appearance of autochthonous American orchestral writing. This was followed by the "Comedy Overture" (1905), *Dance in Place Congo* (1906), "Americanesque" (1909), "Negro Rhapsody" (1912), and "American Dances in Rag-Time Rhythm" (about 1915). The compositions of Gilbert's last period were written in a mature original style which showed an artistic assimilation of racy national characteristics, not based on either negro or Indian rhythms. These he attempted to make expressive of American optimism, youthfulness, and buoyancy. They include an opera, *The Fantasy in Delft* (1915), and several compositions for full orchestra, the chief of which are "Symphonic Piece" (1925), "Jazz Study" (1924), "Strife" (1910–25), and the "Nocturne, from Whitman" (1925). His last composition was a suite for chamber orchestra, composed on a commission from the Elizabeth Sprague Coolidge foundation. His most popular songs were the "Pirate Song" and the "Fish Wharf Rhapsody," sung by David Bispham.

Gilbert's career was largely self-made. Over three-quarters of his time he spent in gaining a livelihood. He worked also under the severe handicap of a pronounced congenital heart disease, and was able to prolong his life only by force of will and by a careful husbanding of his strength. He made a unique contribution to the evolution of music as the first articulate American composer whose work was wholly indigenous. As he himself said: "It has been my aim from the first to write some American, and un-European music: music which shall smack of our home-soil, even though it may be crude." He wrote many articles on his favorite theme, most of which appeared in the *New Music Review* and the *Musical Quarterly.*

[R. S. Gale, "A Young Composer," *Bellman,* Aug. 6, 1910; Arthur Farwell, "Wanderjahre of a Revolutionist," *Musical America,* Apr. 10, 1909; E. C. Ranck and H. K. Moderwell, "Henry Gilbert; Unusual Composer," *Boston Transcript,* Apr. 25, 1914; Olin Downes, "An Am. Composer," *Musical Quart.,* Jan. 1918; "An Am. Composer's Triumph in Russia," *Current Opinion,* May 1916; E. C. Ranck, "The Mark Twain of Am. Music," *Theatre Mag.,* Sept. 1917; Isaac Goldberg, "An Am. Composer," *Am. Mercury,* Nov. 1928; P. D. White and H. B. Sprague, "The Tetralogy of Fallot," *Jour. Am. Medic. Asso.,* Mar. 29, 1929; *Boston Transcript,* May 21, 1928.]

C. J. F.

GILBERT, JOHN GIBBS (Feb. 27, 1810–June 17, 1889), actor, the son of John Neal Gilbert and Elizabeth Atkins, was born in Boston, Mass. As a boy, working behind the counter of his uncle's dry-goods store, he developed a strong interest in the stage and attended the theatre regularly. Finally he studied the part of Jaffier in *Venice Preserved* until he felt able to present himself to the manager of the Tremont Theatre stock company to ask for a hearing. He did so well at his trial that the manager cast him in the part. Following his début on Nov. 28, 1828, he was offered a permanent position in the company and stayed with the theatre until the following year when the manager of the Camp Street Theatre of New Orleans offered him a better place. He then played in New Orleans and the Mississippi River towns until 1834, when he came back to the Tremont Theatre, remaining there, with one brief exception, until the theatre closed. Part of the time he was actor-manager. While he was in Boston he began to excel in the characterizations of elderly men with which his name later became associated. In 1847 he went abroad to study the acting of certain well-known Europeans. He was invited to play Sir Robert Bramble at the Princess in London and was so well received that he was engaged for the following season. He profited much by his year abroad, having the advantage of observing the work of the artists of the Théâtre Française in Paris, as well as that of Macready in London, for whom he conceived a great admiration. On his return to the United States he played at the Park Theatre in New York, which was destroyed by fire in 1848, then went under Hamblin's management at the Bowery Theatre in a company which included Wallack the younger. In the next few years he played at the Howard Athenæum in Boston, at the Chestnut Street Theatre in Philadelphia, and at the Boston Theatre, at the opening of which, in 1854, he gave the dedicatory address and played Sir Anthony Absolute, regarded as his finest impersonation. He remained in Boston for four years, playing a variety of parts ranging from Caliban to Bottom. He then acted in Philadelphia until Wallack the elder, who had opened his theatre at Thirteenth St. and Broadway in New York City in 1861, asked him to join the company. He made his début with that company on Sept. 22, 1862, and remained with it until the theatre was closed in 1888. Thereafter he played in Joseph Jefferson's company, and at the time of his death was appearing in *The Rivals* with Jefferson and Mrs. John Drew. A certain hardness that marred his earlier work disappeared with the years, though his manner off stage was always somewhat formal and lacking in real humor. William Winter regarded him as unsurpassed in certain parts, such as that of Sir Anthony. His first wife, Maria Deth Campbell, to whom he was married in 1836, died in 1866. In 1867 he was married to Sarah H. Gavett. He had no children.

[Wm. Winter, *A Sketch of the Life of John Gilbert* (1890); T. A. Brown, *A Hist. of the N. Y. Stage* (3 vols., 1903); F. E. McKay and C. E. L. Wingate, eds., *Famous Am. Actors of Today* (1896); W. W. Clapp, Jr., *A Record of the Boston Stage* (1853); Wm. Winter, *The Wallet of Time* (2 vols., 1913).] K. H. A.

GILBERT, LINDA (May 13, 1847–Oct. 24, 1895), philanthropist, daughter of Horace Gilbert, was born in Rochester, N. Y. When she was four years old her parents moved to Chicago where Linda was sent to a convent, and later attended the academy of Our Lady of Mercy. When she was about ten, on her way to and from school, she daily passed one of Chicago's jails. The despairing faces in the windows aroused uncommon interest and resolve in the child's mind. One prisoner asked her to bring him a book. This she did, and, learning that prisoners were not furnished reading matter, she determined to remedy that condition. Accordingly when she became a young woman she established in Chicago the first county jail library. It consisted of 4,000 miscellaneous books. She then set herself to providing libraries for as many jails as possible and to assisting prisoners in whatever way she could, soon becoming known as the "Prisoners' Friend." Beginning work in New York City in 1873, she devoted much attention to the Ludlow Street jail and The Tombs. News of her constructive work traveled to Europe and she received offers of financial help from Italy, France, and Germany, providing she would extend her work to those countries. She refused, saying that there was far more to be done in America than she could hope to accomplish. Having inherited a small fortune, she was free to use the money to advance her cause, but felt that more money was needed and that it was part of society's duty to care properly for its prisoners and to provide for their rehabilitation when they were released. In 1876 she established and incorporated in New York State, the Gilbert Library and Prisoner's Aid Society. Its purpose was to provide prison libraries and to assist ex-convicts to obtain employment. It carried on this work until 1883. She also wrote many articles for the press, advocating prison reforms and the duty of the public to ex-convicts. Having a fondness for mechanics, she invented several small devices, among them a wire clothespin. In 1876, she published *Sketch of the Life and Work of Linda Gilbert*. It consists chiefly of many case records designed as an appeal to the public for funds with which to carry on her work. She died at her home in Mt. Vernon, N. Y.

[F. E. Willard & M. A. Livermore, *A Woman of the Century* (1893); the *Sun* (N. Y.), Oct. 28, 1895; the *World* (N. Y.), Oct. 26, 1895; *Frank Leslie's Illustrated Newspaper*, Apr. 17, 1875.] M. S.

GILBERT, RUFUS HENRY (Jan. 26, 1832–July 10, 1885), physician, inventor, was born in Guilford, N. Y., a son of William Dwight Gilbert, a jurist. His early education was that obtained in the typical "academy" of the time; then, to satisfy his interest in medicine, he became an apprentice to the local druggist. This work did not appeal to him especially and in a short time he entered a machine-shop in Corning, N. Y., where he continued for six years and became a skilled mechanic. His nights and leisure moments he devoted to the study of classical literature and mathematics. For some unknown reason, upon the completion of his machinist's "time," Gilbert entered the office of a physician in Corning and devoted a year to the study of medicine. He then proceeded to New York City and entered the College of Physicians and Surgeons where his proficiency quickly attracted the attention of the dean, Dr. Willard Parker, who made him an assistant. His financial means were limited, however, and after another year, but before completing his course, Gilbert returned to Corning and began the practise of medicine, specializing in surgery. With the performance of a number of difficult operations his fame spread, but the subsequent demands for his professional services so affected his health that after several years he was compelled to give up his practise entirely. He went to Europe to rest and while there studied hospital management both in London and Paris. In the course of this work he became deeply impressed with the preponderance of hospital cases of people living in the densely populated tenement districts of these cities. He ascribed the cause to lack of sunlight and air and from that belief developed his conclusion that cheaper and more rapid transportation facilities would be a most effective means of improving public health. After partially regaining his health, and imbued with his new transportation idea, Gilbert returned to New York. The Civil War had just broken out, however, so he offered his services and was appointed surgeon to the Duryée Zouaves. Again his surgical skill brought him fame and promotions. In the battle of Big Bethel he performed the first surgical operation under fire. Later he was made medical inspector of Fortress Monroe, and still later, medical director of the XIV Army Corps. Before he left the army he had attained the rank of lieutenant-colonel.

With the close of the war Gilbert's health was again so undermined that he could not continue his professional work. He had not, however, forgotten his transportation idea and as a first step toward its consummation he took the position of assistant superintendent of the Central Railroad of New Jersey. While engaged in remodeling this road and gaining considerable renown, he began giving serious attention to his own transportation scheme for New York City, and as soon as his particular work was completed he resigned to devote his whole attention to a system of rapid transit. He worked first on a pneumatic-tube system and obtained two patents in 1870. Armed with these patents he succeeded in having the New York legislature pass an act incorporating the Gilbert Elevated Railway Company on June 17, 1872. He then endeavored to raise capital with which to build his road, but the financial depression following the panic of 1873 interfered. The necessary funds were not forthcoming until in 1876 when the New York Loan and Improvement Company, under an agreement which practically gave it control of the undertaking, contracted to build and equip the line. Work was commenced in March 1876, but property owners on Sixth Avenue, horse-car companies, and others, by injunction proceedings, delayed construction, and one and a half years more passed before these suits were disposed of. The road was finally completed from Trinity Church to Fifty-ninth Street in April 1878, and opened for public travel on June 6. Almost the next day Gilbert was forced out of the management of the company and eventually was locked out of the directorate entirely. Extensive litigations were instituted without any satisfaction to Gilbert and he died at the age of fifty-three, a poor and broken man. He was twice married: first, to the daughter of Justice Maynard of the New York supreme court; and second, to the daughter of J. W. Price of New York, who with two children survived him.

[*Sci. American*, Feb. 2, 1870, May 18, 1878, Aug. 1, 1885; *Official Records (Army)*; *N. Y. Times* and *N. Y. Tribune*, July 11, 1885; *Medic. Record*, July 18, 1885; J. B. Walker, *Fifty Years of Rapid Transit* (1918); Patent Office records.] C. W. M.

GILBERT, WILLIAM LEWIS (Dec. 30, 1806–June 29, 1890), capitalist, was born at Northfield in the town of Litchfield, Conn., the second child and only son of James and Abigail (Kinney) Gilbert. He spent his youth on his father's farm and received his education at the village school. As a young man he taught several winters in a near-by district school, but failing of reappointment, went to Bristol, Conn., where, in company with his brother-in-law, he made parts of clocks. The dozen years he spent there and at Farmington allowed him to become thoroughly conversant with the technique of clock manufacture and to bring out his unusual business ability. In 1841 he went to Winsted, Conn. With his partners, Lucius Clarke and Ezra Baldwin, he purchased the Riley Whiting clock factory, an organization which he was to dominate until his death almost a half century later. This business, originally established by Samuel and Luther Hoadley and Riley Whiting in 1807, and the oldest clock-manufacturing company in the United States in continuous operation, was conducted under various names until finally incorporated in 1871 as the William L. Gilbert Clock Company.

Gilbert concerned himself little with mechanics

or invention; his success was founded upon his business skill, and there were few enterprises in the community in which he did not share financially. Perhaps the most successful of these was the private banking house of Gilbert & Gay which carried on a large business in "western loans" and which continued its activities even after Gilbert became president of the Hurlbut National Bank. Always interested in any project conducive to the advancement of Winsted, he was one of the leading promoters of the Connecticut Western Railroad, was for many years its treasurer, and was president at the time of its incorporation with the Central New England. Although little occupied with politics, he was elected in 1848 and 1868 to the Connecticut legislature, first as a Whig and then as a Republican.

The fortune, estimated at over a million dollars, which Gilbert accumulated, was in part made possible by his own simple tastes and rigid economy. Giving himself almost wholly to business, he made few social contacts. Behind the forbidding exterior, however, was a character dominated by a desire to serve his community. His anonymous charities were many and he was particularly interested in helping young men toward financial independence. In line with this policy he determined to leave the bulk of his estate for the "improvement of mankind, by affording such assistance and means of educating the young as will help them to become good citizens" (Gilbert's will). With the exception of a grant of $48,000 to the town of Winchester to build a tunnel for the improvement of its water supply, of some $50,000 for the Gilbert Academy and Industrial College at Winsted, Baldwin township, La., and $12,000 for a parsonage and library at Northfield, Conn., most of his property went to found two institutions. One was the William L. Gilbert Home for Friendless Children at Winsted; the other was the Gilbert School, a private institution at the same place, supported by its own endowment, which provided free educational facilities for the children of Winchester township. The bequest for the latter institution insisted upon the establishment of a library in connection with the school which should be open to the citizens of the town. In 1835 Gilbert married Clarinda Hine of Washington, Conn. After her death in 1874 he was married to Anna Westcott of New London in 1876. He died at Oshawa, Ontario, Canada, while on a trip made to inspect a children's home.

[*Hist. of Litchfield County* (1881), pp. 227–28; W. J. Pape, *Waterbury and the Naugatuck Valley* (1918), I, 406, 415–17; W. D. Godman, *Gilbert Acad. and Agric. Coll.* (1893); the *Winsted Herald*, July 4, 1890; *Hartford Courant* and the *Evening Citizen* (Winsted), June 30, 1890.]

H. U. F.

GILCHRIST, ROBERT (Aug. 21, 1825–July 6, 1888), lawyer, attorney-general of New Jersey, the son of Robert and Frances (Vacher) Gilchrist, was born in Jersey City, N. J., to which place his father emigrated from the north of Ireland early in the nineteenth century, and where in 1840 he was elected first clerk of Hudson County. Robert obtained his early education at Russell's private school in Jersey City and at Crane's Academy in Caldwell, N. J. His classical studies, he informs us, consisted of "a little Latin and no Greek." He read law in the office of Isaac W. Scudder, with whom he became a partner upon his admission to the bar in 1847. In 1859 he was elected a member of the New Jersey Assembly. At the first call for troops in 1861, he entered the service as a captain in the 2nd New Jersey Volunteers, remaining in the army until 1865. Originally a Whig, Gilchrist joined the Republican party in 1860, but at the close of the Civil War he disagreed so strongly with the Republicans in their policy of reconstruction that he went over to the Democratic party. In 1866 he ran for Congress in the 5th district; he was defeated, however, by the Republican candidate, George A. Halsey. In 1869 he was appointed attorney-general of New Jersey by Gov. Randolph to fill the unexpired term of George M. Robeson, who had become a member of Grant's cabinet. He was reappointed for a full term in 1873 by Gov. Parker, but resigned in 1875 and unsuccessfully sought the nomination of Democratic candidate for the United States Senate. He declined an appointment as justice of the supreme court of the state and also the office of chief justice. He had an extremely lucrative law practise.

Gilchrist is remembered principally as an authority on constitutional law. As attorney-general, one of his most important decisions concerned the right of negroes to vote in New Jersey. The question was submitted by the mayor of Princeton on the eve of a local election. Gilchrist very promptly replied: "The Thirteenth Amendment made all the colored people who were before in slavery free. If a free colored native was not a citizen before, the text of the Fourteenth Amendment makes him so. . . . As a practical, present question of the hour, the right of the colored man to vote, if he is otherwise qualified, should be treated as settled in his favor" (*Newark Daily Advertiser*, Apr. 4, 1870). Gilchrist was one of the commissioners appointed to revise the state constitution in 1873, though he resigned before the work was completed. He drew up New Jersey's riparian-rights act, which became a principal source of income for the state public-school fund, and was also one of the counsel for the state in the suit which tested its constitutionality (35 *N. J. Equity,* 181). Finally, it was through his influence that the United States secured the sum of $1,000,000 left by Joseph L. Lewis for partial liquidation of the national debt. He married Fredericka Beardsley of Oswego, N. Y., daughter of Samuel R. Beardsley, an adjutant-general on the staff of Gen. Meade. She is known as the author of *The True Story of Hamlet and Ophelia* (1889).

[*The Biog. Encyc. of N. J. of the Nineteenth Century* (1877); C. H. Winfield, *Hist. of the Land Titles in Hudson County, N. J.* (1872); W. H. Shaw, *Hist. of Essex and Hudson Counties, N. J.* (1884), II, 1064–65; F. B. Lee, *N. J. as a Colony and as a State* (4 vols., 1902); W. E. Sackett, *Modern Battles of Trenton* (1895); the *Journal* (Jersey City), July 7, 10, 1888.]

J. E. F.

GILCHRIST, WILLIAM WALLACE (Jan. 8, 1846–Dec. 20, 1916), composer, and conductor, was the son of William Wallace and Redelia Ann (Cox) Gilchrist. He was born in Jersey City, N. J., but removed with his parents in 1857 to Philadelphia, where he began the study of music under H. A. Clarke, at the University of Pennsylvania. Clarke, a Canadian from Toronto, and an able and well-educated musician, was "professor of the science of music" at the University at the time, and gave his eager and apt pupil a thorough training. When Gilchrist was still young, however, the Civil War broke out. Before it had ended his father's business was ruined and he was left dependent upon his own resources. After trying in succession law and business, and finding neither satisfactory, he decided to devote all his energies to music. On June 8, 1870, he was married to Susan Beaman, the daughter of Rev. E. A. Beaman, and in September 1871 they moved to Cincinnati. There Gilchrist played and sang in local Swedenborgian churches, and taught singing. Returning to Philadelphia a year later, he became choirmaster of St. Clement's Church, remaining there until 1877, when he was appointed organist and choirmaster of Christ Church (Swedenborgian), in Germantown. In 1882 he became a teacher at the Philadelphia Musical Academy. He was the founder of the Philadelphia Symphony Society and the Philadelphia Mendelssohn Club, both of which he conducted for a number of years. As an organist and composer of outstanding merit, he probably ranked as Philadelphia's best-known and most prominent musician. This was the more to his credit since, unlike many other American composers of his day, he had never studied abroad, and yet made a notable place for himself as a writer in the larger forms of music. His original compositions, however, like those of some of his contemporaries, while meritorious and often scholarly, may be said to reflect standard contemporary European rather than distinctively American impacts.

Gilchrist was a brilliant contrapuntist, and wrote several excellent choral cantatas. He won two prizes given by the Abt Singing Society of Philadelphia and three given by the Mendelssohn Glee Club of New York. The Cincinnati Festival prize, which he won in 1882, was a setting for the Forty-sixth Psalm, for soprano solo, chorus, and orchestra. In this work the themes were unimportant, but developed with much canonic skill. Like others of the composer's choral works —"Ode to the Sun," "Journey of Life," and "The Uplifted Gates"—it was conventional in cast. One of the most spontaneous of his choral works was "The Legend of the Bended Bow." Though many of his songs, sacred and popular, are not devoid of lyric charm, they are somewhat trite in character, for most of them bear the impress of his early training in hymn-singing. In his later songs, the influence of Schumann and Franz is sometimes noticeable. His orchestral and chamber-music compositions, which were probably his best works, included two symphonies, in C and D; a suite for piano and orchestra; a nonet; a quintet; and a trio, for strings and wind. All were classic in style. Rupert Hughes has praised in particular the nonet in G minor and the piano quintet. Of the Andante of the last work he says: "It ranges from melting tenderness to impassioned rage and a purified nobility. The piano part is highly elaborated, but the other instruments have a scholarly, a vocal, individuality" (*post,* p. 209). Gilchrist died in Easton, Pa., at the age of seventy.

[Rupert Hughes, *Am. Composers* (rev. ed., 1914), pp. 196–210; the *Musical Courier,* Dec. 28, 1916; *Musical America,* Dec. 30, 1916; *Public Ledger* (Phila.), Dec. 21, 1916; information as to certain facts from the composer's daughter, Miss Anna R. Gilchrist, Philadelphia, Pa.]

F. H. M.

GILDER, JEANNETTE LEONARD (Oct. 3, 1849–Jan. 17, 1916), newspaper correspondent, editor, and critic, daughter of the Rev. William Henry and Jane (Nutt) Gilder and sister of William Henry and Richard Watson Gilder [*qq.v.*], was born at Flushing, L. I., where her father was conducting a school for girls. When, after various changes of residence, he became an army chaplain at the opening of the Civil War, the Gilders established themselves at Bordentown, N. J. Jeannette attended school there, and had a term or two in a girls' boarding school in southern New Jersey; but her formal education ended at the age of fifteen. For about a year after the death of her father in 1864 she worked in the office of the state adjutant-general at Trenton, first at transcribing records for an historian of the state troops, later, as a regular clerk. She had brief experiences in an accountant's office, as an employee in the United States Mint at Philadelphia, and as copyist in the office of the registrar of deeds at Newark, N. J., besides attempting such odd jobs as coloring stereoscopic views. Her leaning toward journalism had always been strong, and she began her real career with work on the *Newark Morning Register,* founded by her brother, first as a volunteer writer, but ultimately as a regular member of the staff. She also served as Newark correspondent of the *New York Tribune.* After her brother Richard became associate editor of *Scribner's Monthly* she was for a little while his assistant, and she afterward conducted literary, dramatic, and musical columns in the *New York Herald.* In her literary column, "Chats about Books," she adopted the plan of having an American family, faintly reminiscent of the famous Parley group, discuss in their conversations the latest publications. She was also general and literary New York correspondent for various journals, at one time writing six separate weekly letters over different signatures, besides her work for the *Herald.* In 1881 she and her brother Joseph ventured their small savings in founding in New York the *Critic.* After the gradual withdrawal of her brother she succeeded to full editorial control, which she exercised until the *Critic* was merged in the revived *Putnam's* in 1906. During the later years of her life she conducted a literary brokerage business, and edited and published the *Reader.* Most of her adult life was spent in New York City, and it was there she died. During her active career of fifty years she compiled several volumes, among them, with J. B. Gilder, *Authors at Home* (1888); she was an occasional contributor to magazines, and she attempted several plays, including *Quits,* produced in Philadelphia in 1876 by F. F. Mackey, *Sevenoaks,* written for J. T. Raymond, and *A Wonderful Woman,* for Rose Eytinge. None of these achieved great success, and none of her published writings can be said to live, though as editor and newspaper correspondent, and even as literary critic, she was a figure of note and influence in her day. She had a sense of humor, and a quick perception of the potential anecdote in a trivial incident or bit of conversation. In 1900 she published *The Autobiography of a Tomboy* and in 1904, *The Tomboy at Work*; in the latter she gave entertaining glimpses of celebrities whom she knew. Her literary criticisms were clever and incisive rather than profound.

[Miss Gilder's reminiscent volumes, both of which are probably true to fact in the main but which are confusing because some persons and periodicals appear under their own names, while others are disguised; *Who's Who in America,* 1914–15; J. R. Tutwiler, in *Women Authors of Our Day in their Homes* (1903), ed. by F. W. Halsey; *Dial,* Feb. 3, 1916; *Nation* (N. Y.), Jan. 27, 1916; *N. Y. Times* and N. Y. *Evening Post,* Jan. 18, 1916.]
W. B. C.

GILDER, RICHARD WATSON (Feb. 8, 1844–Nov. 18, 1909), editor, poet, public-spirited citizen, was born in Belle Vue, Bordentown, N. J. The earliest Gilders in America had come, as he believed, from Kent via Barbados, and settled probably in Delaware. It is known that his great-grandfather was a farmer of that state. His grandfather, a "measurer" of Philadelphia, was chairman of the Board of Builders of Girard College. His father, William Henry Gilder, was a minister of the Methodist Church who is said to have done some earlier editorial work in Philadelphia, and who at the time of Richard's birth was conducting the Belle Vue Female Seminary at Bordentown. His mother, Jane Nutt, was the daughter of a major in the War of 1812. In 1848 the elder Gilder sold his school at Bordentown and bought another at Flushing, L. I., and here Richard secured his early education, the only boy in a school for girls. At the age of twelve or thirteen the future editor engaged in the amusement, not uncommon with bookish boys, of publishing a paper of his own. The school at Flushing proved unprofitable, and the father returned for a time to preaching, serving charges at Redding and Fair Haven, Conn.; but he soon started another school, at Yonkers, N. Y., where his young son gave some assistance as a teacher. At the opening of the Civil War he became an army chaplain, and the family returned to Bordentown. There is no detailed record of Richard's schooling during this time of frequent family changes, but he must have received some disciplinary training, and he developed an aptitude for writing. For a short time at Bordentown he read law. In 1863 he secured the reluctant consent of his mother and joined the 1st Philadelphia Artillery, a volunteer company which saw a little service at the time of the Confederate invasion of Pennsylvania. Years afterward he discovered that this brief experience entitled him to membership in the Grand Army of the Republic, and he is said to have prized the insignia of that organization above most of his other honors.

After the death of his father in 1864 it was necessary for him to aid in the family support, and he became paymaster on the Camden & Amboy Railroad, and afterward reporter on the

Newark Daily Advertiser, which he left to join in founding the *Newark Morning Register.* He also began writing for *Hours at Home,* and for some months in 1869–70 he edited this magazine in New York and at the same time kept his connection with the *Register* in Newark. In November 1870, *Hours at Home* was merged in the newly founded *Scribner's Monthly,* of which J. G. Holland [*q.v.*] became editor, and Gilder assistant. He performed the duties of a managing editor, conducted a department, "The Old Cabinet," and had charge of the art features of the magazine. This last responsibility was an important one, since *Scribner's Monthly* and its successor, the *Century,* were leaders in developing magazine illustrating to a point never before attained by a general literary periodical. Through Helen Hunt, afterwards Mrs. Jackson, Gilder met in 1872 Helena de Kay, a grand-daughter of Joseph Rodman Drake and at the time a student of painting at Cooper Institute. In the same year he became acquainted with Rossetti's translation of the *Vita Nuova,* and this work, together with his growing love for the young artist, inspired the sonnets published in *Scribner's Monthly* in 1873, and included in the collection, *The New Day* (title-page date 1876) issued in October 1875. From his boyhood he had been writing verse, but none of his early productions is of note; and it is doubtful if any of his later poems excelled the best of these love sonnets. On June 3, 1874, he was married to Helena de Kay.

With the acceptance of the position on *Scribner's Monthly* Gilder began his life-work, and almost immediately after their marriage the home of the Gilders became a center of intellectual and artistic life. For nearly fifteen years they lived in The Studio, 103 East Fifteenth St.; in 1888 they removed to a house in the neighborhood of Washington Square, now 13 East Eighth St.; and at the time of Gilder's death they were abandoning this for an apartment at 24 Gramercy Park. For ten years they had a summer home at Marion on Buzzard's Bay, and later a farm in the Berkshires. While Mrs. Gilder maintained nothing that could be called a salon, her home always attracted a variety of interesting and often distinguished people. Among those who frequented The Studio in the early days were La Farge, Saint Gaudens, Stanford White, Joseph Jefferson, Madame Modjeska, and many of the leading writers of New York. Here Whitman, at a time when most people looked at him askance, received a welcome which he recalled years later with almost effusive appreciation. It was here that the Society of American Artists was founded in 1877, and the Author's Club in 1882; and here were entertained a long list of men and women distinguished in art and literature, both American and foreign. Later, Grover Cleveland and his wife became intimate friends of the Gilders, and were often guests both in the city and at Marion.

In 1879 the family went abroad for a year, largely on account of Gilder's health, which had suffered from overwork. For some time Dr. Holland had been unable to carry the full responsibilities of editor-in-chief, and his assistant's duties had been correspondingly increased. In 1881 he died, just as *Scribner's Monthly* came to an end and was succeeded by the *Century*—nominally a death and a rebirth, practically only a change of name. Gilder succeeded to the editorship, a position that he held for the rest of his life. A man of sounder literary taste and less inclined to sentimentality than his predecessor, he had something of a journalist's sense of what the public wanted, yet had too much integrity to cater to lower tastes. As the Civil War receded in time he saw the desirability of having it treated in adequate literary fashion by actual participants, and arranged for a series of papers, "Battles and Leaders of the Civil War," written by Northern and Southern survivors, and the serial publication of Nicolay and Hay's "Abraham Lincoln: A History." A plan for the publication of Grant's *Memoirs* was frustrated when Mark Twain secured the book for another firm. These special articles were of course in addition to the usual contents of a literary magazine, in the selection of which the editor showed sound and yet catholic taste.

With his earnest devotion to ideals, a great capacity for work, and a willingness to be helpful even when he was imposed upon, Gilder was drawn into an active part in many civic and social movements. In 1882, with an article in the *Century* for August, he joined the attack on Luigi P. di Cesnola [*q.v.*], director of the Metropolitan Museum of Art, whose competence and artistic integrity were questioned by some New York artists and antiquarians. He was president of the Fellowship Club, an organization of artists and writers; the most active member on various committees connected with the Washington Centennial celebration in 1889 and the subsequent permanent construction of the Washington Memorial Arch; president of the Free Kindergarten Association; an ardent worker for international copyright, for civil service reform, and for better city government. Perhaps his most notable single public service was as chairman of the Tenement House Committee, appointed by the governor of New York in 1894. After making a careful personal investigation into tenement conditions in New York City he spent much time in Albany in the interest of recommended legislation. An incident of this investigation was a controversy involving the Corporation of Trinity Church, which owned several antiquated buildings and protested some of the recommendations of the committee as unreasonable and confiscatory. The list of his varied activities in his later years and of the boards and committees on which he served is too long to be repeated. As examples may be mentioned service in Anti-Tammany municipal campaigns; writing, speaking, and organizing in favor of the free importation of works of art; and the writing of the inscriptions for the buildings of the Pan-American Exposition at Buffalo in 1901. He had earlier been a Republican, but he supported Cleveland in his three successive campaigns for the presidency, and was often referred to as one of the chief Mugwumps. A natural conservative, with an Easterner's view of economic matters, he strongly opposed Bryan in 1896, and, though a low-tariff man, supported McKinley as the best way of making his opposition effective. During his later years he was in great demand as a speaker on commemorative occasions and at universities and colleges, choosing such subjects as "Certain Tendencies in Current Literature," "The Citizen and the Nation," "A Literary Man's Estimate of Grover Cleveland," "Literature and Diplomacy." He received at various times honorary degrees from Dickinson, Harvard, Princeton, Yale, and Wesleyan.

Writing in 1905 to a friend who had evidently asked for biographical data Gilder listed the honorary degrees he had received and some of the more important positions he held, adding, "I dare say I am various other things that I cannot remember, but if you can state on positive evidence that I am a poet, I would rather that than all the rest put together." On another occasion he wrote of "The Vanishing City," with a self-satisfaction that he rarely expressed, "Strike me dead, but I wouldn't so much mind showing this to Keats!" He wrote verse as time permitted throughout his life, but more prolifically in his later years; usually publishing first in periodicals, and bringing out frequent small volumes, besides more comprehensive collections in 1894 and 1908. His volumes of verse were: *The New Day* (1876, 1887); *The Poet and His Master* (1878); *Lyrics and Other Poems* (1885); *The Celestial Passion* (1887); *Lyrics* (1887); *Two Worlds* (1891); *The Great Remembrance and Other Poems* (1893); *Five Books of Song* (1894); *"For the Country"* (1897); *In Palestine and Other Poems* (1898); *Poems and Inscriptions* (1901); *A Christmas Wreath* (1903); *"In the Heights"* (1905); *A Book of Music* (1906); *The Fire Divine* (1907); *Poems* (1908). The decorative illustrations for some of these were furnished by Mrs. Gilder. Most of his poems were short, the longest being "The Great Remembrance," something more than two hundred lines of iambic pentameter read before the Society of the Army of the Potomac at a reunion in Boston in 1893. He was at his best in the sonnet and simple lyric measures, and many of his pieces, as was fitting for an editor and a publicist, deal with current events or pay tribute at an appropriate moment to men and women of his time. Much of his work was happily phrased, but he hardly caught the popular ear, and few of his lines are generally familiar to-day; nor did he often attain quite the flawlessness of form that makes the poets' poet. Prose volumes were: *Lincoln the Leader, and Lincoln's Genius for Expression* (1909), and *Grover Cleveland, a Record of Friendship* (1910). As his public services were those of a devoted citizen worker rather than those of an office-holding statesman, so his most notable contribution to the development of American literature was not his own writings, but his admirable services for more than a third of a century as editor of a great literary magazine.

If Gilder's personality is to be judged by the number, the variety, and the devotion of his friends, he must have been the most lovable of men. He seems, however, to have been at times a good, or at least a persistent, hater. Long after Di Cesnola was dead and the directorship of the Metropolitan Museum had passed into hands that he approved, he could go out of his way in a personal letter to recall his accusations of "liar, falsifier, and fraud" (*Letters,* p. 453); and a few months before his death, when the Corporation of Trinity Church was being urged to preserve St. John's Chapel, Varick Street, as an interesting specimen of colonial architecture, he burst forth in a tirade reviving memories of the tenement controversy in which he had engaged nearly half a generation before, and anathematized the trustees as

> "Guardians of a holy trust
> Who, in your rotting tenements,
> Housed the people, till the offence
> Rose to the Heaven of the Just."
> (*Evening Post,* Dec. 14, 1908).

In the author's later years the duties of his vocation and of his avocations pressed hard upon him, and his health became more and more precarious. He took respites abroad in 1895–96 and in 1900, and was often forced to be absent from his office for considerable periods at other times. He remained active, however, and delivered a public address only two weeks before his death, which occurred at the home of a friend in New York City.

[The chief source of detailed information regarding Gilder's life is the so-called *Letters of Richard Watson Gilder* (1916), edited by his daughter, Rosamond Gilder, a confused, inadequate, and inaccurate filial tribute. The *Century* for March 1911 contains a brief but well-written sketch, "Life-Work and Homes of Richard Watson Gilder," by Maria H. Lansdale. Many short commemorative and critical notices appeared at the time of his death and after the publication of the *Letters* in 1916; see especially *N. Y. Times* and *Evening Post*, Nov. 19, 1909; *Nation* (N. Y.), Nov. 25, 1909; Brander Matthews in *No. Am. Rev.*, Jan. 1910; and the *Century*, Feb. 1910.] W. B. C.

GILDER, WILLIAM HENRY (Aug. 16, 1838–Feb. 5, 1900), journalist, was born in Philadelphia, a son of the Rev. William Henry Gilder and Jane (Nutt) Gilder, and a brother of Richard Watson and Jeannette Leonard Gilder [*qq.v.*]. His early life, uneventful, is obscure. At the outbreak of the Civil War he enlisted as a private in the 5th New York Infantry (Apr. 19, 1861). On Nov. 15, 1862, he was transferred and became a second lieutenant in Company H, 40th New York Infantry (Mozart Regiment); he was promoted to lieutenant in January and to captain and assistant adjutant-general in February following. On May 29, 1863, he was again transferred, to Company D of the 40th Regiment. Wounded at Gettysburg and discharged, he reenlisted on Jan. 27, 1864, and the following October was wounded at Hatcher's Run. After the war he went to Newark, N. J., and, although he had an aptitude for mathematics and was a skilled draftsman, he drifted into journalism. In 1878, as a correspondent for the *New York Herald*, and second in command, he accompanied Lieut. Frederick Schwatka on an expedition to King-William Land to discover the bodies or the records of the Sir John Franklin expedition. Schwatka and Gilder left New York June 19, 1878, and wintered with the natives near Chesterfield Inlet on Hudson Bay. A detailed search of the continental coast-line yielded nothing, but they determined to cross Simpson Strait to King-William Land to continue the investigation. The party was absent from the original base of supplies almost a year and during this time traveled 3,251 miles, the longest sledge journey then on record. This expedition, while contributing nothing to geographic knowledge, was daring in its conception and remarkable in its execution. It established the loss of the Franklin party, gathered relics and remains, and recovered a few of the records of the last survivors. Gilder's articles in the *Herald* describing the investigation were collected and published in 1881 under the title of *Schwatka's Search*.

In 1881 James Gordon Bennett organized an expedition to search for the *Jeannette* which, under G. W. De Long [*q.v.*], had sailed in 1879 on a voyage of discovery through Bering Strait. Near Herald Island the *Jeannette* entered the ice pack from which it never escaped. Cut off from the world it drifted with the pack for many months until it was crushed and destroyed in June 1881. In this same month the relief expedition, commanded by Lieut. Robert M. Berry, sailed from San Francisco on the *Rodgers*; Gilder accompanied it as correspondent for the *Herald*. After a long cruise in the Arctic Ocean and an exploration of the islands of Herald and Wrangel, the *Rodgers* was itself destroyed by fire at St. Lawrence Bay in Eastern Siberia. Berry ordered Gilder to proceed along the coast to Nizhni-Kolymsk and thence to Irkutsk to telegraph news of the loss of the *Rodgers*. At Nizhni-Kolymsk he learned of the destruction of the *Jeannette* and shortly afterward he met a courier carrying sealed reports of George W. Melville [*q.v.*] who had discovered the bodies of the De Long party and the records of the expedition. Gilder's enthusiasm was greater than his scruples: he broke open the sealed reports and forwarded the news to the *Herald* (Melville, *In the Lena Delta*, pp. 367–68). After a hazardous journey across Siberia to Nizhni-Novgorod Gilder returned to America. *Ice Pack and Tundra* (1883) is a collection of his articles, illustrated by many of his own drawings, describing this expedition.

He later visited the island of Borneo for Bennett and represented the *Herald* in China when the French took Cochin. Gilder returned to Newark as editor of the *Sunday Standard* when it was purchased by Thomas C. Barr. After its failure he went to Trenton and edited the *Sunday Times* for Barr. When this had failed he joined the staff of the *New York Journal*. In the last years of his life he devoted much of his time to magazine writing.

[Detailed account of arctic experiences in *Schwatka's Search* (1881) and *Ice Pack and Tundra* (1883); George W. Melville, *In the Lena Delta* (1885); F. C. Floyd, *Hist. of the Fortieth (Mozart) Regiment, N. Y. Volunteers* (1909); Frederick Phisterer, *N. Y. in the War of the Rebellion* (3rd ed., 1909); *Letters of Richard Watson Gilder* (1916), ed. by Rosamond Gilder; *Newark* (N. J.) *Evening News*, Feb. 6, 1900; A. W. Greely, *Handbook of Polar Discoveries* (4th ed., 1909); information from J. B. Gilder.] F. M—n.

GILDERSLEEVE, BASIL LANNEAU (Oct. 23, 1831–Jan. 9, 1924), philologist, university professor, author, editor, was born in Charleston, S. C., and died in Baltimore, Md. On his father's side he was of English stock. The first known representative of the name in America was Richard Gildersleeve who was born in 1601 in County Suffolk, England, and arrived, *c.* 1635, in Massachusetts Bay. The Massachusetts atmosphere, however, was apparently as little to his liking as the discarded regimen of the Stuarts. He therefore tried the two Connecticut colonies but settled permanently at New Hempstead, L. I., during the Dutch régime, and died before 1685 under the English government of New York, which of all four experiments provided "the constitutional form most nearly resembling the government from which he had fled some fifty years before" (Andrews, *post,* p. 709). The secular rigor of this doughty Puritan reappears, converted into Calvinistic vigor, in the father of Basil Gildersleeve, the Rev. Benjamin Gildersleeve, seventh in this line of descent and son of Lieut. Finch Gildersleeve (1751–1812), of Putnam County, N. Y., who fought in the patriot army through the Revolution. Benjamin Gildersleeve was born in New Canaan, Conn., in 1791; was graduated in 1814 from Middlebury College; and taught for three years in Mount Zion Academy, Ga. After one year at Princeton Theological Seminary, he was editor of four leading Presbyterian organs in succession, in Georgia, South Carolina, and Virginia. He removed from Georgia to Charleston, S. C., in 1827 and on Aug. 13, 1828, married Emma Louisa Lanneau, daughter of Bazile Lanneau who, with his mother, had been brought to Charleston from his Acadian birthplace when the British in 1775 deported the French inhabitants of Nova Scotia. Lanneau, left an orphan at ten, made his own career and won the esteem of his adopted city. He took part with the patriot army in the Revolution, was for years a member of the state legislature; and was one of the founders of the French Protestant church in Charleston.

Thus on both sides Gildersleeve inherited energy and independence of character. From the Gallic strain on the distaff side, it may be conjectured, came, at least in part, the irrepressible wit which, as on a palimpsest, remained uneffaced beneath the heavier Teutonic script of a later hand. The first fourteen years of his life in which, as he states, "all that came after lay implicit," included an education conformed to no rules of pedagogy and innocent of modern psychology with its "self-expression" as a prior lien in place of duty. Until about thirteen he had no school training except the daily tasks under his strenuous father. The boy was no mere passive recipient. At four he could read and he celebrated his fifth birthday by completing the Bible "from cover to cover." The field of letters was now before him and he browsed widely. As Shakespeare, by his father's creed, was immoral, he read him outside the house and, as occasion permitted, smuggled in the new Waverley novels. His own account of his home-made education is suggestive: "Latin I learned at a tender age, and I 'got through' Cæsar, Sallust, Cicero, Virgil, and Horace before the time when boys of to-day have fairly mastered the rudiments. . . . Of Greek I learned enough to make out the New Testament. . . . French I picked up after a fashion" (*Forum,* February 1891, p. 611). He was also making versions, in prose and verse respectively, of portions of Plato and the Anacreontics. Even in the years of his mature teaching he habitually wrote out in advance accurate translations in prose and verse and he recommended to advanced students the making of careful metrical versions of the Greek poets in order to realize the artistry of the original text. Incidentally, it may be noted, one of Gildersleeve's lifelong diversions was the writing of verse on subjects serious or humorous.

At the age of fourteen he had one year of conventional training under an able drill-master and entered the College of Charleston. In 1845, however, while still a freshman, he transferred his activity to his father's editorial office in Virginia, acquiring technical knowledge which later proved invaluable. After one year at Jefferson College, Pa., he was sent to Princeton and was graduated, in 1849, before he was eighteen. Owing to his precocity in Latin and Greek, college tasks seemed light and he devoted his leisure to reading English, French, German, Italian, and Spanish literature. But, fundamentally conscientious as boy and man, he graduated with high honor even in the higher mathematics, fortunately required of all comers, and received his visé as "a young gentleman well qualified to conduct the classical studies and, indeed, any of the studies of youth preparing for college." The following year he was classical master in the foremost school in Richmond and, incidentally, perfected his own mastery in writing Greek and Latin. Perhaps at this period he formed the habit of translating into Greek, sentence by sentence as uttered, the sermons of which he was an otherwise reluctant auditor. He used to recommend this practise as a peculiarly rewarding means of grace.

Already in college Gildersleeve, through Carlyle, had been introduced to Goethe, "the most important of all the teachers I ever had," as he calls him. Goethe's magnetic influence was added to the lure, then undisputed, of German university training. In the summer of 1850 Gildersleeve sailed for Bremen and spent three years in Europe, chiefly in study at the Universities of Berlin, Bonn, and Göttingen. To his great teachers, from Böckh to Ritschl, and to Germany in general he acknowledges his indebtedness, in no uncertain terms, "for everything professionally in the way of apparatus and of method, and for much, very much, in the way of inspiration" (*Forum,* February 1891, p. 615). This generous tribute is just but it is not the whole story. Admirers of what was most vital in Gildersleeve's personality would lay greatest stress on his native endowment and on his familiar participation, begun in boyhood, in the great thought of great literatures, English and foreign, modern and ancient. After only five semesters of intensive study in German universities he received his degree of Ph.D. at Göttingen in 1853. The title of his doctor's thesis was, *De Porphyrii Studiis Homericis Capitum Trias* (1853). During the next three years at home he continued his philological studies, wrote articles, and, *inter alia,* nearly completed a novel. He also "tasted the salt bread of a tutorship in a private family." To this latter experience he adverted later when reading with his seminar Lucian's *Hireling Professors,* the pungent tractate that had aroused a fellow feeling in Erasmus and many another scholar. In 1856 he was appointed professor of Greek at the University of Virginia, and, during the lean years from 1861 to 1866, he was also professor of Latin. Thus, just before his twenty-fifth birthday, began his career as university professor which continued without interruption, except for his service in the Confederate army, until his retirement from active teaching in Baltimore in 1915. The Civil War came and Gildersleeve, enlisting in the cavalry in 1861, spent his summer "vacations" in the army. In 1864 he joined the staff of Gen. Gordon and was put *hors de combat* for five months by a severe wound. His bodily wound healed but the devastating memories of the war remained. Later, in Baltimore, his Northern students shared with his Southern compatriots the admiration for a soldier's courage, of which they were continually reminded by the choliambic rhythm in his majestic gait. After the war, in 1866, he married Eliza Fisher Colston of Virginia, the gracious hostess who presided over his household until his death. Gildersleeve's mental vigor, it may be noted, reappeared in their son's originality as a student in mathematics. Their daughter continued the Graeco-Roman tradition by marrying Gardner M. Lane, son of George M. Lane, professor of Latin at Harvard, a student contemporary at Göttingen of Gildersleeve and his intellectual congener in brilliant wit and classical scholarship.

The earlier years at the University of Virginia, externally devoted to inspiring generations of students, were also years of intensive occupation with the original texts, unhampered by the latest ephemeral commentaries often, indeed, inaccessible in the South of the sixties, and Gildersleeve refrained from premature publication. Later, however, the natural urge for self-expression, stimulated by financial pressure, called forth essays of permanent value and much editorial writing. The first books that he published were in the field of Latin. In 1867 he issued the first edition of his *Latin Grammar* (revised edition in 1872; 3rd edition, revised and enlarged, with the co-operation of Prof. Gonzalez Lodge, in 1894). The fresh and vigorous presentation of facts in this grammar, with the vivid translation of Latin examples, constitutes a liberal education in Latin and English. The Gildersleeve Latin Series was completed in 1875 by the addition of a *Latin Primer, Latin Reader,* and *Latin Exercise-Book* (editions 1871 and 1875), and, in the same year, the publication of his annotated edition of the satires of *Persius* was again a reminiscence of his collateral professorship of Latin.

When the Johns Hopkins University opened in 1876, Gildersleeve was one of the small band of creative scholars who accepted the task of developing a great school of graduate work and research. He was University Professor of Greek from 1876 to 1915. In this embryo university, as he liked to recount, he was put by President Gilman into an empty room and told to "radiate!" The bare room was soon occupied by graduates of diverse colleges. Some of these were callow, others already mature, but, whatever their previous training, the fortunate members of his Greek seminary, year after year, were confronted with a new vision, shining across wide vistas in literature and language. As in his more personal teaching, where a "mistake" was a "crime," so in the wider sweep of his seminary courses an ineluctable exactitude prevailed. No vagueness was acceptable. No unverified reference was legal. Paradoxically, however, he indulged himself in a rapid fire of allusions which sometimes shot over the heads of his bewildered, yet devoted, hearers. In spite of this he stimulated more than he discouraged and, as net effect in after years, his former students, though far removed in space and time, were conscious of his actual presence, ready to challenge any inadequacy or inaccuracy in their written or spoken word.

While he continued to "shape the ends" of generations of rough-hewn graduates he was also exerting an ever-widening influence through the printed word upon the world of classical scholars. In 1877 appeared his *Justin Martyr,* "un véritable trésor d'observations grammaticales, attestant l'étendue, la précision, l'originalité de son savoir" (Reinach, *post,* p. 43). In 1885 (2nd ed., 1890) was published: *Pindar, Olympian and Pythian Odes.* This exact and brilliant interpretation became forthwith a landmark in the study of Pindar. *Essays and Studies,* published in 1890, is a collection of four "Educational Essays" and nine "Literary and Historical Studies." Two-thirds are republications which required only slight revision, and the varied subject matter, with the wealth of learning sufficiently veiled under his brilliant style, naturally appealed to a wider, less esoteric audience than was the case with the bulk of his technical publications. *Syntax of Classical Greek,* Part I, appeared in 1900. This was the forerunner of his long-looked-for *magnum opus,* planned as the orderly summation of his life-work as grammarian. Part II was published in 1911 with the cooperation of Prof. C. W. E. Miller. The rest of the work remained unpublished at the time of his death, but Gildersleeve's exposition of Attic syntax, as itself one of the high manifestations of Greek art, is amply documented in print. Through the first thirty-six volumes of the *American Journal of Philology* there is a long procession of monographs and articles, major and minor, devoted specifically to this, his favorite field. In the 144th number of the *Journal* (October–December 1915), the "Indiculus Syntacticus," prepared under Gildersleeve's supervision to assist future investigators in correlating his results and methods, comprises nearly five pages of bald titles.

In 1880 Gildersleeve founded the *American Journal of Philology* and edited it for forty years, with Prof. Miller as assistant editor after October 1915. Catholic in its content, the *Journal* is a monument to the range as well as the depth of Gildersleeve's knowledge. It became a clearing-house for American scholars. His personality pervaded the pages of the *Journal.* His verdict was one to be reckoned with. He did not confine himself to conventional discussion and his uncurbed satire occasionally engendered resentment, but his fearless criticism had a tonic effect upon contemporary scholarship. As each quarterly appeared, his readers habitually turned first to the Editor's "Brief Mention" to enjoy his wit, to be stimulated by his penetrating appraisal of contributions in all allied fields of literature or philology. In No. 168 (October–December 1921), appeared an *"Index Scoliodromicus"* which gives twelve and a half pages of titles as a register of the extra-syntactical matters treated of by him in the long series of volumes.

When the *Journal* had just come of age in 1901, his own seventieth birthday was commemorated by the publication of *Studies in Honor of Basil L. Gildersleeve* (1902), a volume of 511 pages containing forty-four technical contributions by former pupils. The portrait frontispiece reproduces his Zeus-like personality at its best: there is a mellower light in the undimmed eyes; the fires of satire are, for the moment, banked. The fine portrait, painted in 1896 and now hanging in "Gilman Hall" at Homewood, is an adequate presentation of Gildersleeve in his later, but continuously virile, years. Inseparable, in fact, from his invincible scholarship was his imposing physical personality. His tall and well-proportioned figure was the normal support for his Olympian head with the dominating eyes, humorous or devastating as the occasion demanded.

He was the recipient of many honorary degrees and an honorary member of the Cambridge (England) Philological Society; the Archaeological Society of Athens; the Philological Syllogos of Constantinople; the Society for the Promotion of Hellenic Studies; a corresponding fellow of the British Academy; a fellow of the American Academy of Arts and Sciences; a member of the American Academy of Arts and Letters; the American Philological Association; the Archaeological Institute of America; and the Managing Committee of the American School for Classical Studies in Athens. To him was accorded the almost unique honor of a second election to the presidency of the American Philological Association. He was president in 1878 and *praeses iterum* in 1909. His two presidential addresses (*Princeton Review,* May 1879; *Transactions and Proceedings, American Philological Association,* XL, 1909) envisage the range and character of philological activity in America through half a century.

The range of his own multifarious activities may be inferred from the bibliographies of his published work but the following items must be added even to this condensed sketch: *The Spiritual Rights of Minute Research* (1895), an address delivered at Bryn Mawr College, was cited by Théodore Reinach when he explained with Gallic clarity the reasons why Gildersleeve's work will live, and "son nom restera inscrit dans le Livre d'or des grands philologues"; "Oscillations and Nutations of Philological Studies," an address delivered before the Philological Congress in Philadelphia, 1900 (*Johns Hopkins University Circulars,* April 1901), was worthy of the important occasion and became a permanent possession of his audience. The Introduction on Herodotus prefixed to Henry Cary's translation, *The Histories of Herodotus* (1899), was distinguished by Gildersleeve himself as "probably my best essay." It merits the attention of historians generally. Two small books, finally, have made an appeal for different reasons to widely different circles of readers. They are: *Hellas and Hesperia* (1909), three lectures at the University of Virginia, on the Barbour-Page foundation, and *The Creed of the Old South, 1865–1915*, reprinted from the *Atlantic Monthly* of January 1892, with another contribution, made in September 1897, "A Southerner in the Peloponnesian War."

Adequately to represent Gildersleeve's human traits of character and the brilliant facets of his scholarship would require space enough to make citation from many sympathetic characterizations by associates and friends—by Professors Miller, Scott, Shorey, and others—and especially from Théodore Reinach's intimate appraisal. Gildersleeve himself in his autobiography, "Formative Influences" (*Forum*, February 1891), speaks frankly of the narrowing isolation of his earlier life as compared with its enrichment in subsequent years. It is, perhaps, due to this factor that the parallax of his self-consciousness must be reckoned with in so many of his later deliverances, grave or gay. In closing his autobiographical sketch (*op. cit.*), he gives this self-diagnosis: "If one day it shall be said of me that I was not slothful in business, fervent in spirit, let nature be credited with the fervor; the diligence is due to the early domination of a creed which itself is dominated by the 'stern daughter of the voice of God.'"

[Autobiographical material includes "Formative Influences," mentioned above; "Professorial Types," in *The Hopkinsian*, 1893; "The College in the Forties," *Princeton Alumni Weekly*, Jan. 26, 1916. Biographical material has been found in manuscript letters, Berlin Univ. documents, etc., loaned by L. L. Mackall, Esq.; *Who's Who in America*, 1922–23; C. M. Andrews, "A Biographical By-Path Through Early New England History," *New Eng. Mag.*, Feb. 1893; W. H. Gildersleeve, *Gildersleeves of Gildersleeve, Conn.* (1914); *The Abridged Compendium of Am. Geneal.*, vol. III (1928), 76–77, pub. by F. A. Virkus & Co. Notable appreciations are those by Théodore Reinach, in *Bull. de l'Asso. Guillaume Budé* (Paris), July 1924; J. A. Scott and others, in *Proc. Am. Philological Asso.*, LVI (1925), xix–xxxii; C. W. E. Miller in *Am. Jour. Philology*, Jan.–Mar. 1924 and *Indogermanisches Jahrbuch*, 1924–25 (1926); Paul Shorey, Wm. M. Thornton and others, in *Johns Hopkins Alumni Mag.*, Jan. 1925; the *Sun* (Baltimore), Jan. 10, 1924. For bibliographies of Gildersleeve's work, see in addition to the *"Indiculus Syntacticus"* and the *"Index Scoliodromicus"* mentioned above, the *Alumni Bull. Univ. of Va.*, Apr. 1924, and *Selections from Brief Mention* (1930) with an introduction and complete bibliography (pp. xxx–liii) by C. W. E. Miller.] F. G. A.

GILES, CHAUNCEY (May 11, 1813–Nov. 6, 1893), clergyman of the Church of the New Jerusalem, editor, author, was born in Charlemont, Mass., eldest of seven children of John and Almira Avery Giles. His father was a descendant of Edward Giles, freeman of Massachusetts Bay in 1634, and his mother, of Christopher Avery who settled in Gloucester, Mass., before 1642. Chauncey grew up as a hard-working New England boy, attended the Mt. Anthony Academy in Bennington, Vt., and Williams College, and although not completing the course he in 1876 received the degrees of B.A. and M.A. as of the class of 1836. On Sept. 8, 1841, he was married to Eunice Lakey, daughter of Abner Forbes and Lucy (Pomeroy) Lakey, of Palmyra, N. Y. He conducted successful schools in Vermont, New York, and Ohio towns, and gained the reputation of being pedagogically in advance of his time as a teacher, especially in the naturalness of his methods and his facility in illustration. As early as 1844, the writings of Emanuel Swedenborg were brought to his attention, and appealing to him as consistent and reasonable, they became the controlling interest of his life. In 1853 with his family, he removed from Pomeroy, Ohio, to Cincinnati, to become pastor of the Church of the New Jerusalem in that city. He made the change at the age of forty, without theological training, his personal experience and the power of the new doctrines, and the methods which had made him a successful teacher, serving him in good stead. Particularly interested in the doctrine of the substantial reality of the human spirit and its faculties, and of the spiritual world, in whose atmosphere the spirit lives even now, and into which it comes with full consciousness when the earthly body is laid aside at death, he dealt with it in a series of lectures. These were later published as *Lectures on the Nature of Spirit, and of Man as a Spiritual Being* (1867), and had a wide sale. Other books by him are: *Heavenly Blessedness* (1872); *The Incarnation, Atonement and Mediation of the Lord Jesus Christ* (1896); *Six Lectures on Our Children in the Other Life* (1872); *Perfect Prayer* (1883); *Progress in Spiritual Knowledge* (1895); *The Sanctity of Marriage* (1896).

Forty years of pastoral service were divided between Cincinnati (1853–64), New York City (1864–78), and Philadelphia (1878–93). In New York editorial work was added to the pastoral, and from 1871 to 1878 he was sole editor of the *New Jerusalem Messenger* (now *New Church Messenger*), the organ of the General Convention of the New Jerusalem, writing himself a large part of its contents. In Philadelphia he began printing his discourses from week to week, a custom which resulted in the publication of a little weekly periodical, the *Helper*. He also wrote stories for children, among them, *The Magic Spectacles; a Fairy Story* (1868), and *The Wonderful Pocket, Chestnutting, and Other Stories* (1868). He was also elected to various ecclesiastical offices of importance, and while pastor in Cincinnati served for several years as president of Urbana University. From 1875 to 1893, the last eighteen years of his life, he was president of the General Convention of the New Jerusalem.

[C. G. Carter, *The Life of Chauncey Giles as Told in His Diary and Correspondence* (1920); J. A. Vinton, *The Giles Memorial* (1864); E. M. and C. H. T. Avery, *The Groton Avery Clan* (1912); biog. sketch in *New Ch. Rev.*, Jan. 1894, reprinted as introduction to *Progress in Spiritual Knowledge*; *New Ch. Messenger*, Nov. 15, 1893; the Phila. *Press*, Nov. 7, 1893.]

W. L. W—r.

GILES, WILLIAM BRANCH (Aug. 12, 1762–Dec. 4, 1830), statesman, the youngest child of William and Ann (Branch) Giles, was born in Amelia County, Va. He was sent first to Hampden-Sidney College and then, with a slave, to Princeton, where he graduated in 1781. He studied law under George Wythe at William and Mary, and in 1786 was admitted to the bar. Occupied as a practising lawyer, with his headquarters at Petersburg, Va., until he entered Congress on Dec. 7, 1790, he gained considerable professional success, particularly in British debt cases, in which he represented the creditors and a nationalistic point of view. From almost the beginning of his congressional career, however, he identified himself with the opposition to Hamilton's centralizing policies. He contributed to the Jeffersonian cause great skill in debate and a rash audacity which led at times to grave discomfiture. He introduced the famous resolutions inquiring into and condemning Hamilton's conduct of the treasury (Jan. 23, Feb. 27, 1793), which resulted in the overwhelming victory and apparent vindication of that statesman. He bitterly opposed Jay's Treaty, ungraciously objected to the tone of adulation in the answer to Washington's last message to Congress, and was a prime mover in the passage of the resolution which led to the revelation of the X. Y. Z. Papers, so disastrous to Republican fortunes. Completely unsuccessful in his Anti-Federalist activities, in which he was more zealous than his own party leaders, he resigned from Congress in October 1798 and was elected to the Virginia General Assembly. Here he supported the Resolution of 1798 and Madison's Report of 1799. He went so far in his hostility to the administration as to declare, probably for political effect, that he was favorable to disunion (Anderson, *post*, pp. 70–71).

Following the victory of Jefferson, Giles returned to Congress in 1801 and became administration leader. He strongly championed the repeal of the Judiciary Act of 1801, and again excelled his revered leader in partisanship. Because of ill health, he did not stand for reëlection in 1802, but in November 1804 entered the Senate, where he continued his loyal support of Jefferson and his war on the judiciary. In the impeachment of Justice Chase, he sought to establish a theory of impeachment which would permit of the subsequent removal of Marshall. He actively favored the election of Madison in 1808, but soon passed into the opposition. He vented his hostility chiefly against Gallatin, whom he now detested, and later against Monroe. From 1809 he was a "War Hawk," advocating governmental vigor as strongly as he had denounced it in the days of Hamilton and John Adams, and during the War of 1812 he was a leader of the "malcontent junto," bitterly opposing the administration. In March 1815 he retired with what grace he could and, though he was a member of the Virginia House of Delegates for the session of 1816–17, remained practically aloof from politics until 1824, when he launched the first of many literary assaults on Monroe, Clay, and John Quincy Adams in the name of state rights. In 1826 he returned to the Virginia Assembly, where he championed the well-known resolutions of 1827 against the tariff and internal improvements. Elected governor in 1827, he served until 1830 and continued to inveigh against federal usurpations. A number of his speeches and pamphlets, chiefly falling within the last stage of his career, were published in 1829 under the title, *Political Miscellanies.* Though opposed to the calling of the Virginia constitutional convention of 1829–30, he was a member of it. Here he stood for conservatism against reform, for Tidewater against the West, thus proving at last disloyal to Jefferson, the only statesman he had consistently supported.

All the other political leaders of his generation, Washington, Hamilton, the two Adamses, Madison, Monroe, Gallatin, and Clay, not to mention John Marshall, felt at one time or another the weight of his bludgeon. Personal animosities frequently marred the clarity of his political judgment and rendered his career erratic and essentially destructive. His unusual ability as a debater is attested by the analogy drawn by John Randolph and others between him and Charles James Fox (T. H. Benton, *Thirty Years' View*, I, 1854, pp. 682–83). Like Patrick Henry and Henry Clay, he learned more from men than books. Unprepossessing in person and with no graces of oratory, he was a formidable fighter in a legislative assembly. Not without demagogy, he voiced the discontent of his district and state until he came at last to support local privilege. History has not been kind to him, but must at least recognize his courage and ability. He was twice married: in 1797 to Martha Peyton Tabb, and on Feb. 22, 1810, to Frances Ann Gwynn; and left issue. Death came on Dec. 4, 1830, at his spacious home in Amelia, "Wigwam," among constituents who had always been loyal.

[D. R. Anderson, *William Branch Giles: A Study in the Politics of Va. and the Nation* (1914), is a scholarly work, favorable to Giles, and dealing chiefly with his political career. It has a valuable bibliography and reproduces a miniature and portrait. The *Annals of the Cong. of the U. S.*, 1790–98, 1801–02, 1804–15, are indispensable. For sidelights on aspects of Giles's career, see also *Am. Hist Rev.*, Oct. 1916, pp. 96–97; Jan. 1931, pp. 336–42. For an obituary and long memoirs, see *Richmond Enquirer*, Dec. 9, 16, 18, 1830.] D. M.

GILL, JOHN (May 17, 1732–Aug. 25, 1785), journalist, was born in Charlestown, Mass., the third of five children. He was the son of Capt. John and Elizabeth Abbot Gill, and the grandson of Lieut.-Col. Michael Gill, an immigrant from Dover, England. The boy was apprenticed to the Boston printer, Samuel Kneeland, whose daughter Ann he afterward married (January 1756). On Apr. 7, 1755, Gill and Benjamin Edes began to publish the *Boston Gazette and Country Journal*, in continuation of the second paper in Boston, started in 1719, but they did not confine their activity to the newspaper. Evans in his *American Bibliography* lists more than 150 of their imprints. Some were merely broadsides and pamphlets—sermons, polemics, and the like—but occasionally they printed books, among which were a Latin text-book, various religious imprints, and Volume II, numbers 2 and 3 (1755) of Prince's *Annals of New-England*. They were for several years official printers. After 1764 their imprints were increasingly propagandic, reflecting the character of their journal, for the *Gazette* became so prominent as an organ of the radicals that in September 1774 the British soldiers were urged to remember "those trumpeters of sedition, the printers Edes and Gill." Their office was a gathering place of the leaders and from it the Boston Tea Party set forth. Gill seems to have confined his activities to his business: his only connection with public affairs was as a member of the committee to demand the removal of the troops after the Massacre.

In April 1775 the partnership was dissolved, Edes escaping with printing materials to Watertown, where he continued the *Gazette*. Gill remained in town and was arrested on Aug. 4 "by martial authority" for "printing treason, sedition and rebellion," but was, on Oct. 2, "so far liberated as to walk the Town" (Peter Force, *American Archives*, II, 1840, 712). On May 30, 1776, after the siege, he started the *Continental Journal and Weekly Advertiser*, a colorless sheet in comparison with the ante-bellum *Gazette*, since it was primarily a newspaper with extracts from other prints, including some from "Jemmy Rivington's lying Gazette." During the war, however, it bore the caption: "The Entire Prosperity of Every State depends upon the Discipline of its Armies," and when not concerned with the ever-pressing questions of paper money, taxation, or price fixing, it gave emphasis to the need of supporting the military effort. Under the new state constitution the paper was conservative, supporting Bowdoin's candidacy for the governorship in 1785. Gill became official printer again, continued the line of pamphlets, and for over a year ran in the paper a reprint of Robertson's *History of America*. He disposed of the *Journal* on Apr. 28, 1785, as a protest against the state stamp act, "not choosing to submit to a measure which Britain artfully adopted as the foundation of her intended tyrany in America." He died insolvent, leaving a numerous issue.

[I. B. Wyman, *The Geneals. and Estates of Charlestown* (1879); J. T. Buckingham, *Specimens of Newspaper Lit. with Personal Memoirs, Anecdotes, and Reminiscences* (1850), I, 165–96, 308–12; C. S. Brigham, "Bibliog. of Am. Newspapers," pt. III, *Proc. Am. Antiquarian Soc.*, Apr. 1915.] D. M. M.

GILL, LAURA DRAKE (Aug. 24, 1860–Feb. 3, 1926), educator, pioneer in vocational placement, was of early Massachusetts stock, the daughter of Elisha and Huldah (Capen) Gill. She was born in Chesterville, Me., while her father, who was threatened with tuberculosis, was living there on a farm. He returned to Massachusetts when Laura was six years old and on May 1, 1873, he died. An aunt, Bessie T. Capen, principal of a girl's school in Northampton, helped Laura to secure an education. She graduated from Smith College in 1881 and then joined the faculty of Miss Capen's school, where she taught mathematics for seventeen years. Smith awarded her a master's degree in 1885, and between 1890 and 1893 she did graduate work in mathematics at the University of Leipzig, at Geneva, and at the Sorbonne.

The outbreak of war with Spain afforded her an opportunity to show the rare organizing gift for which she became widely known. Weary of teaching, she was one of the first women to register for executive service under the Red Cross, and sailed on the adventurous voyage of the *Lampasas* in charge of the first party of nurses dispatched to Cuba. She was later detailed to Chickamauga to select and place nurses in the Leiter General Hospital, and to Montauk Point, L. I., for similar work. At all other times, she had charge of the transportation of nurses to and from New York. At the close of the war, she helped to organize the schools of Cuba under Gen. Leonard Wood, and undertook educational and relief work for the Cuban Orphans' Society. Her qualities as executive and teacher won her in 1901 appointment as dean of Barnard College, where she remained for seven years. During her term of service she secured through Mrs. A. A. Anderson a gift of three city blocks; recognized the need of dormitories and planned the first, Brooks Hall, begun in 1907; established the degree of Bachelor of Science; and inaugurated the Student Council. Her interest in vocational opportunities for women, awakened during her work with nurses, was deepened by her experiences at Barnard, and also by the problems of college women seeking professional advancement, which came to her notice during her presidency of the Association of Collegiate Alumnae. The tinder was ready for the spark when, toward the close of 1909, Dr. Susan Kingsbury, then of the Women's Educational and Industrial Union, Boston, consulted her about the reorganization of their old business and domestic agency. The following January saw her in Boston, laying down lines for the first vocational bureau for college women. She was uncompromising in her effort to hold trained women to the highest standard of scholarship and business efficiency, and indefatigable in her attempts to find freer scope for the native abilities of applicants, secure them better remuneration, and swing them into the service of social and civic movements where they were needed. After leaving Boston in 1911, she was engaged for two years in organization work at the University of the South, Sewanee, Tenn., which institution had given her in 1907 the degree of Doctor of Civil Law. She did similar work at Trinity College, Durham, N. C. During the World War she was a special agent in field organization, United States Employment Service, Department of Labor. Later, she became interested in work for mountain boys. She spent the last seven years of her life at Pine Mountain Settlement, Ky., and at Berea College, where, while serving as house-mother and teacher, she died.

[C. A. Hayden, *The Capen Family* (1929); L. L. Dock and others, *Hist. of Am. Red Cross Nursing* (1922); *Cat. of Officers, Grads. and Non-Grads. of Smith Coll.* (1925); *The Smith Alumnæ Directory*, May 1926; *Columbia Univ. Quart.*, Mar. 1908; *Who's Who in America*, 1924–25; *N. Y. Times*, Feb. 5, 9, 1926.]
M. B. H.

GILL, THEODORE NICHOLAS (Mar. 21, 1837–Sept. 25, 1914), zoölogist, "master of taxonomy," was born in New York City, of English and New York Dutch descent, the son of James Darrell Gill and Elizabeth (Vosburgh) Gill. He was a great-grandson of Judge Nicholas Gill, a native of Yetson in Devonshire, who served as a judge in admiralty in Newfoundland. A youth of brilliant promise, destined by his father for the ministry, Theodore was first thoroughly grounded in the classics; but since this profession did not appeal to him, he took up the study of law. Another field of activity irresistibly attracted him, however, the study of natural science, too unremunerative to be sanctioned by his family. From his boyhood he had been fascinated by the fish displayed in the New York Fish Market. Later, as a not-too-enthusiastic student of the law he kept a horse's skull under his desk, to be studied in leisure moments. Although his desire to become a naturalist ran counter to his father's wishes and to worldly wisdom, he persisted in his purpose and secured a scholarship from the Wagner Free Institute of Science in Philadelphia. Encouraged by the scientists with whom he thus came into contact, he prepared a paper on the fishes of New York which was accepted and published in the *Annual Report* (1856) of the Smithsonian Institution, when the author was only nineteen. The following year he visited Washington and met at the Smithsonian Prof. Joseph Henry, Spencer Fullerton Baird [*qq.v.*], and others with whom he was later to be associated. In 1858 he went with the D. Jackson Stewart Collecting Expedition to the West Indies, especially Barbados and Trinidad. In the fresh waters of the latter island he discovered three peculiar fishes then new to science. His reports were published in the *Annals* of the New York Lyceum of Natural History (vols. VI and VII, 1858–59). After a trip to Newfoundland in 1859 to settle the estate of his grandfather, he returned to Washington, where through Baird's influence he was appointed a member of the group who were preparing reports on the zoölogical findings of the Northwestern Boundary Survey. Some of Gill's preliminary notes appeared in the *Proceedings* of the Academy of Natural Sciences at Philadelphia. In 1861 he became a member of the Smithsonian staff and from the following winter up to 1866 had charge of the library of the Institution. When this great collection of scientific books was placed in the Library of Congress, he went with it, and ultimately became senior assistant librarian of Congress, a post he retained until 1874. From 1860 till his death he was also connected with Columbian (George Washington) University, first as adjunct professor of physics and natural history, from 1884 to 1910 as professor of zoölogy, and thereafter as professor emeritus. Though he was not a particularly gifted lecturer or classroom teacher, his discourses were meaty and highly appreciated.

Despite a profound interest in systematic zoölogy and particularly in fishes, mollusks, and mammals, Gill was never a field worker. For upwards of fifty years he kept his quarters in the Smithsonian, which from 1874 on he seldom left during working hours. He described numbers of new fishes from Museum examples, deriving his ideas of the forms not preserved in the National Museum from accounts given by other authors. In his special field he read everything and forgot nothing. In matters of classification (taxonomy) he was easily first in the world. His published memoirs on fishes alone (as reported in Dean's *Bibliography*) number 388 titles. There is no ichthyological group of importance not treated with some degree of completeness, and always with clarifying result. Five of the most important of his papers are: "Synopsis of the Fresh Water Fishes of the Western Portion of the Island of Trinidad, W. I." (1858); "Arrangement of the Families of Mollusks" (1871); "Arrangement of the Families of Mammals" (1872); "Arrangement of the Families of Fishes" (1872); "A Comparison of Antipodal Faunas" (1893). For several years, beginning in 1898, he edited the *Osprey,* a small ornithological magazine. He also contributed many articles to leading American encyclopedias and lexicons. Yet he seemed to have a fixed dislike for the tedium of continuous writing, such as is demanded in long papers or books. At one time he arranged with Dr. Elliott Coues [*q.v.*] for the preparation of a joint treatise on American mammals. His own part was to consist largely of revision and criticism. But his manuscript was never ready, and Dr. Coues said to the author of this sketch: "I will never write another word in partnership with Gill to save his immortal soul";—and he never did.

Though he rarely left Washington, Gill was an honorary member of scientific societies throughout the world. He made his only visit abroad in 1901, when he represented the Smithsonian Institution and the National Academy of Sciences at the 450th anniversary, the "Ninth Jubilee" celebration, of the foundation of the University of Glasgow. His work, books, social intercourse with friends, and society meetings filled his life. He never married. He "was most highly esteemed and was widely known to biologists throughout the world, as a man of deep and accurate learning, particularly in the study of his specialty, ichthyology. A man of phenomenal memory, familiar with many languages, he was a veritable encyclopedia of science and knew how to make plain to the layman its technical phraseology" (*Annual Report, Smithsonian Institution, 1915,* 1916, p. 27). At his quarters in the Smithsonian he most hospitably received all young naturalists who coveted his personal acquaintance or desired aid from his universal store of biological knowledge. His expression was friendly—often mildly quizzical—and his natural impulse was always toward kindly criticism. He died in Washington in his seventy-eighth year.

[Memoir by Wm. H. Dall, *Nat. Acad. Sci. Biog. Memoirs,* vol. VIII (1916), with bibliography of Gill's writings; *Who's Who in America,* 1912–13; T. S. Palmer, in *Auk,* Oct. 1915; F. A. Lucas, in *Am. Museum Jour.,* Jan. 1915; *Science,* Oct. 16, 1914; Bashford Dean, *A Bibliog. of Fishes* (3 vols., 1916–23); *Evening Star* (Washington, D. C.), Sept. 25, 1914; personal acquaintance.]

D. S. J.

GILLAM, BERNHARD (Apr. 28, 1856–Jan. 19, 1896), political cartoonist, was born in Banbury, Oxfordshire, England, the seventh of the fourteen children of John Sewell Gillam, artist and inventor, and his wife, Lucy Clarke. In 1866 he emigrated with his parents to America, and settled in New York. Aside from three years' training in the schools of Williamsburg, N. Y., he was practically self-educated. In drawing, his favorite activity from early childhood, he had no lessons until he was grown. While he was still in his teens he entered a lawyer's office as copyist, with the intention of reading law. The work proved dull, however, and when he came of age, he gave it up to study engraving. He had begun to sell his drawings in 1876. They were of a humble order—show cards for window display, illustrations for serials in weeklies, and sketches for newspapers. For a time he had ambitions to be a portrait-painter, and through the kindness of Henry Ward Beecher, an early subject, he found a few people to sit for him. His first drawings to indicate his own artistic idiom, however, were his caricatures in *Leslie's Weekly* and the *New York Graphic.* After their appearance his career was determined, and he continued until his death a political cartoonist. During the Garfield campaign he worked with Thomas Nast on *Harper's Weekly.* The following year, 1881, he was engaged by *Puck,* in which his caricatures of Blaine appeared during the campaign of 1884. Although he was himself a Republican, voted for Blaine (Maurice and Cooper, *post*, p. 277), and during the same campaign suggested satires of Cleveland for *Judge*, his series of cartoons in *Puck* from Apr. 16 to Oct. 29, showing Blaine as the "tattooed man," was "probably the most far-reaching . . . ever drawn . . . and did dreadful damage to the Republican candidate" (Seitz, *post*, p. 294).

In 1886, with the reorganization of *Judge*, Gillam became part owner, along with W. J. Arkell, whose sister Bartelle Arkell he married in 1889. During the following ten years, while he was director-in-chief and a contributing member of the staff, *Judge* became a powerful factor in the molding of political opinion. Gillam's cartoons for the campaigns of 1888 and 1892, stressing the perils of Democratic free trade, and the need of Republican protection, included "Easter Eggs—Both Addled," Mar. 31, 1888; "The Modern Exodus from the Land of Free Trade Bondage to the Land of Protection and Plenty," Apr. 21, 1888; "Mud-Slingers," reminding the public that Cleveland had sent a substitute to the war, June 2, 1888; "The Declaration of Dependence," with Cleveland surrendering American industries to England, July 7, 1888; "The Protectionist Pilgrim's Progress," Sept. 22, 1888; "Trying to Raise McGinty [free trade] from the Bottom of the Sea," July 16, 1892; "The Political Columbus who will NOT land in '92," showing Cleveland in the ship *Democracy*, Oct. 8, 1892; and "Benjamin 'Where Am I At,'" Nov. 19, 1892. The last was intended to celebrate the expected Republican victory, but by skilful last-minute touches was altered to commiserate the defeat. Gillam's cartoons were done in color, and given double-page space in the center of the magazine. He brought to his drawings a small fund of literary knowledge, a thorough acquaintance with contemporary politics, and a trenchant wit. In 1893 he removed from his home in Brooklyn to Canajoharie, N. Y. He died there of typhoid fever at the age of thirty-nine, in the home of his father-in-law, Hon. James Arkell.

[*Judge*, Feb. 1, 1896; *Leslie's Weekly*, Jan. 30, 1896; *N. Y. Herald* and *N. Y. Tribune*, Jan. 20, 1896; *Appletons' Ann. Cyc.*, 1896; A. B. Maurice and F. T. Cooper, *The Hist. of the Nineteenth Century in Caricature* (1904); D. C. Seitz, *The "Also Rans"* (1928); W. J. Arkell, *Old Friends and Some Acquaintances* (1927), pp. 73–76; New York directories; information as to certain facts from Gillam's sister, Laura Louisa Gillam.] C. P. M.

GILLEM, ALVAN CULLEM (July 29, 1830–Dec. 2, 1875), soldier, the son of Samuel J. Gillem, was born in Jackson County, Tenn. He was educated at the United States Military Academy where in 1851 he graduated eleventh in a class of forty-two. He married Margaret Jones of Hampton, Va. After ten years of service, against the Seminole Indians (1851–52), in garrisons, and on the Texas frontier, at the beginning of the Civil War he was commissioned captain, and assigned to duty with a brigade under Gen. George H. Thomas. In the following Kentucky campaign, at Shiloh, and at Corinth, he won the commendation of his superior officers. As colonel of the 10th Tennessee Volunteers (1st Middle Tennessee Infantry) he was provost-marshal of Nashville and engaged in minor operations in that vicinity. On June 1, 1863, he was appointed adjutant-general of Tennessee, then under the military governorship of his close friend, Andrew Johnson, and at Johnson's earnest solicitation he was made brigadier-general of volunteers (Aug. 17, 1863). A year later, under Johnson's orders, he undertook a campaign against Confederate supporters in eastern Tennessee. In a series of engagements he was successful, notably at Greeneville, where Gen. John H. Morgan, commanding Confederate raiders, was killed. Badly routed near Morristown, he reorganized his forces and took part in successful raids into southwestern Virginia and western North Carolina. For gallant and meritorious services in these campaigns he was successively and rapidly brevetted lieutenant-colonel, colonel, brigadier-general, and finally, Apr. 12, 1865, major-general, United States Volunteers. In the meanwhile, as vice-president of the convention of January and as a member of the legislature of April 1865, he had taken a prominent part in the reorganization of civil government in Tennessee. For more than a year after the war ended he commanded the district of East Tennessee, and on Sept. 1, 1866, was mustered out of the volunteer service with the rank of colonel in the regular army. Under the congressional plan of reconstruction, on Jan. 9, 1868, he was appointed to command the Fourth Military District (Mississippi and Arkansas). His administration of this office was characterized by a decided relaxation of the rigors of the military rule of his predecessor, Gen. Ord, by a general refusal to interfere with the civil authorities, and by marked improvement in political and economic conditions. He was severely criticized by the radicals for his refusal to support their demands and shortly after Johnson's retirement from the presidency, and to the general regret of the conservative whites, he was transferred to the Texas frontier. He commanded troops in the Modoc campaign (1873). On sick-leave he returned to his home, "Soldier's Rest," near Nashville, where he died.

[G. W. Cullum, *Biog. Reg. Officers and Graduates*

U. S. Mil. Acad. (3rd ed., 1891); W. W. Clayton, *Hist. of Davidson County, Tenn.* (1880), p. 460; J. W. Garner, *Reconstruction in Miss.* (1901), pp. 182–228; *Official Records (Army)*; obituaries in Nashville *Daily American,* Dec. 3, 1875; *N. Y. Times,* Dec. 5, 1875.]
P. M. H.

GILLESPIE, ELIZA MARIA [See ANGELA, MOTHER, 1824–1887].

GILLESPIE, MABEL (Mar. 4, 1867–Sept. 24, 1923), labor leader, was of Quaker origin. She was born in St. Paul, Minn., the daughter of James and Ida (Scott) Gillespie, but passed her girlhood in the home of an aunt, Mrs. Sarah Esther Staples, in Concord, Mass. Between 1898 and 1900 she was a student at Radcliffe College. She began her public work as a secretary of the Boston Associated Charities; and as a resident of Denison House, one of the early college settlements, she familiarized herself with social and industrial conditions. Becoming vitally interested in the problems of women wage-earners, in 1903, when the first Women's Trade Union League was organized in Boston, she allied herself with its work. Her first big task was in connection with women workers in the Fall River textile-strike of 1903–04. Soon after the collapse of the strike, she was called to Buffalo as executive secretary of the Child Labor Committee and of the Consumers' League. For the latter, about 1907, she made a state-wide survey of the canning industry in New York, working between twelve and sixteen hours a day for four months as a cannery hand, in order to get first-hand knowledge of conditions. In 1909 she returned to Boston as executive secretary of the Boston Women's Trade Union League, and was soon an outstanding figure in the unionizing of the women workers of the city. She helped to organize the garment-workers, laundry-workers, textile-workers, clerks, teachers, professors, office-employees and office-building cleaners. In the organization of the telephone operators in 1912, she gave outspoken support to the girls, and was backed by the state branch of the American Federation of Labor, thus bringing women, probably for the first time, to the fore in the labor movement. When agitation for minimum-wage legislation began in Massachusetts, Governor Foss appointed her labor's member on the first Minimum Wage Commission in America. According to one of her colleagues, Prof. A. N. Holcombe, "she was the active proponent of the law before its enactment and to her knowledge and courage was due such success as the administrators of the law obtained in America." She was the first woman elected to the executive committee of the state branch of the American Federation of Labor, and was made vice-president in 1918. A dynamic force in the early stages of the organization of women workers in Massachusetts and the enactment of social-service laws in their behalf, she rarely spoke in public, preferring to work through her many influential associations. She stirred up interest in Massachusetts in the eight-hour day law, gathering data and preparing arguments, while another appeared as spokesman. She provided much of the impetus for the Trade Union College (1919), probably the first attempt to start a school for labor people, and she helped the university men heading the enterprise to secure their students. She served on the administrative committee of the Bryn Mawr Summer School for Women Workers, opened in 1921. To her office at the Trade Union League, Boston, came men and women from churches, colleges, and clubs, seeking light on industrial problems. She died suddenly of heart trouble at the dressmaking shop of which she was manager.

[*Boston Transcript, Boston Post,* Sept. 25, 1923; *Half a Hundred Radcliffe Women* (1922); Alice Henry, *Trade Union Women* (1915); *Procs. of the . . . Conventions of the Nat. Women's Trade Union League,* 1909–22; letter from Prof. A. N. Holcombe.]
M. B. H.

GILLESPIE, WILLIAM MITCHELL (1816–Jan. 1, 1868), civil engineer, educator, was born in New York, the only child of James and Ann (Waldron) Gillespie. His father, of Scotch ancestry, came to New York from Kingston, Ontario, and became a prosperous merchant tailor. His mother was of Dutch descent. After graduating in 1834 from Columbia College, Gillespie continued his studies at the École des Ponts et Chaussées and resided in France and Italy for a number of years. On returning to the United States he published *Rome: As Seen by a New-Yorker in 1843–44* (1845), an honest, sensible book crammed with information about what to see, hear, eat, and drink in Rome. For a short time, according to Edgar Allan Poe, Gillespie was connected with a periodical called the *New World.* Poe describes him in the "Literati of New York City" (*Godey's Magazine and Lady's Book,* May 1846, p. 199) as five feet seven inches tall, with hazel eyes and dark, curling hair, nervous and even fidgety, awkward in disposing his hands, feet, and hat, but vivacious, intelligent, and companionable. In later life he was noted as a talker. "In the formation of his opinions he acknowledged no superior, reverenced no external authority, followed no precedent, accepted no tradition, and took no counsel of custom or example" (*New York Daily Tribune,* Jan. 4, 1868). With this faith in his own intellectual processes went a keen nose for cant and pretense and a fine scorn for ready-made opinions. From 1845 until his death Gillespie was the first professor of civil engineering in Union College at Schenectady, N. Y. Foreseeing the gigantic part that engineering skill must play in the development of the country, he insisted that an acquaintance with its principles should be included in a liberal education, and he also maintained that the engineer should be familiar with the humanities. He proved to be an unusually effective teacher. His two treatises, *A Manual of the Principles and Practice of Road-Making* (1847) and *A Treatise on Land-Surveying* (1855; privately printed, 1851), were quickly recognized as useful works in their field and held their place until long after his death. He translated a portion of August Comte's *Cours de Philosophie Positive* as *The Philosophy of Mathematics* (1851). His volume, *A Treatise on Leveling, Topography, and Higher Surveying* (1870) appeared posthumously. In 1859 he received the degree of LL.D. from Columbia College. On Apr. 7, 1864, he married Harriet Emily Bates of Scarsdale, N. Y. His last years were a valiant struggle against disease. After his return in 1867 from a visit to France he lost the use of his voice and delivered his lectures by whispering his remarks to an assistant, who in turn would repeat them to the class. His malady was finally diagnosed as tuberculosis, but Gillespie refused to yield to it, predicted his speedy recovery, and could not be prevailed on to take to his bed. He died suddenly at his parents' home in New York while sitting down to remove his shoes.

[A. Van V. Raymond, *Union Univ.*, I (1907), 216–20, with portrait; information from Gillespie's son, T. Waldron Gillespie, of "Monte Unde," Mariel, Cuba, and from M. H. Thomas, Curator of Columbiana, Columbia University; obituary in *N. Y. Tribune*, Jan. 4, 1868.] G. H. G.

GILLET, RANSOM HOOKER (Jan. 27, 1800–Oct. 24, 1876), Democratic politician, was born at New Lebanon, N. Y., the son of Capt. John Gillet, a veteran of the Revolution, and Lucy Gillet, his wife. His parents moved in 1802 to a farm in Saratoga County, where young Ransom grew up, working on his father's farm in the summer, and lumbering in the pine-forest during the winter. In 1819 he removed to St. Lawrence County, where he was employed to teach school during the winter and attended the St. Lawrence Academy during the summer. In 1821 he began to read law in the office of Silas Wright [*q.v.*] at Canton, and after a brief period set up his practise at Ogdensburg, having been taken into partnership by Wright. His association with this important Democratic political leader was the beginning of a relationship which lasted till Wright's death in 1847, and did much to define Gillet's political principles and to shape his political career. In 1825 he was married to Eleanor C. Barhydt.

From 1827 to 1837 he was brigade-major and inspector of the local brigade of militia. He became postmaster of Ogdensburg in 1830, and served till 1833. In the meantime he had his first taste of national politics, attending the first National Democratic Convention in 1832. In the same year he was elected to Congress, serving two terms. In Congress he spoke but little, but was on terms of intimacy with James K. Polk, whose candidacy for speaker he supported vigorously in 1835, and with whom he claims to have had much influence in the make-up of the congressional committees. In 1837 he accepted appointment from President Van Buren as commissioner to treat with the Indian tribes in New York, and held this post till 1839. In 1840 he attended the Democratic nominating convention, and was influential in drawing up a series of resolutions which constituted the platform of that year, and which were reiterated by every Democratic convention till 1864.

In private life during the Harrison-Tyler régime, Gillet again appeared in Washington with the advent of the Polk administration. He had hoped for an important office, and was strongly backed by Wright, but was given the relatively insignificant post of register of the treasury. In 1847, however, he received the solicitorship of the treasury, holding this post until the autumn of 1849. Again retiring because of the Whig victory, he was appointed clerk to the attorney-general in 1855, and solicitor to the court of claims in 1858. The defeat of the Democrats in 1860 ended his political career. Gillet remained stanchly Democratic in his political principles, and was severely critical of the Lincoln administration throughout the period of the war. After 1864 he spent most of his time at Lebanon Springs, N. Y., where he occupied himself with writing. Three books appeared from his pen, *Democracy in the United States* (1868), a piece of partisan history, written with an eye to the campaign of 1868; *The Federal Government* (1871), an elementary work on the structure of the government; and *The Life and Times of Silas Wright* (2 vols., 1874), a large part of which consists of Wright's speeches and correspondence.

During his years at Washington, he was active at the bar. He was counsel for Amos Kendall in an important case in which the latter sought to recover counsel fees for his services to the Cherokee Indians, and he acted, curiously enough against Kendall, in the suit of Samuel F. B. Morse against Henry O'Reilly, in which the validity of the Morse patents was in question. Gillet was counsel for O'Reilly, and prepared the brief in the case for the Supreme Court (15 *Howard,* 61; *National Intelligencer,* Dec. 28, 1852). He took over Edwin M. Stanton's practise when Stanton became secretary of war. As writings amply testify, he was a sincere but narrow partisan. Bred in the atmosphere of Democracy, he remained constant to his political creed. His abilities, to judge from his speeches and writings, were hardly more than moderate. On the other hand, he left a memory of personal kindliness and public benefaction in the town in which he spent much of the last part of his life.

[C. E. Fitch, *Encyc. of Biog. of N. Y.,* vol. VI (1923), p. 123; Franklin Ellis, *Hist. of Columbia County, N. Y.* (1878); publisher's notice in Gillet's *Democracy in the U. S.,* passing references in his *Life and Times of Silas Wright,* and the obituaries in the Washington *Evening Star,* Oct. 25, and the *N. Y. Times,* Oct. 26, 1876. A number of Gillet's briefs are in the N. Y. Pub. Lib.] D. P.

GILLETT, EZRA HALL (July 15, 1823–Sept. 2, 1875), clergyman, author, and educator, son of Ely Hall and Mary (Williams) Gillett, was born in Colchester, Conn. On his father's side, he was descended in the seventh generation from Jonathan Gillett, who came to the Massachusetts Bay Colony from England in 1630, and in 1636 settled in Windsor, Conn.; and on his mother's, from Robert Williams who settled in Roxbury about 1638. He prepared for college at Bacon Academy, Colchester, Conn., then tutored for two years, and was admitted to the junior class at Yale in 1839. Graduating in 1841, he entered Union Theological Seminary, where he remained until 1845, the last year as a graduate student. He was ordained into the ministry of the Presbyterian Church (New School) Apr. 16, 1845, was pastor of the First Presbyterian Church of Harlem, N. Y., from 1845–70, and professor of political science at the University of the City of New York, now New York University, from 1870 until his death. The arduous duties of a long and successful pastorate did not stifle the devotion to scholarly interests, which had been stimulated during his graduate year at Union Theological Seminary. Here, while serving as assistant librarian, he acquired a lasting interest in the library which at a later time he was greatly to augment by beginning the McAlpin Collection of British History and Theology.

At New York University his duties included instruction in political science, constitutional and international law, and, at times, moral science and ancient history. Contact with the Van Ess Collection in the Union Theological Seminary Library aroused an interest in sixteenth-century German, which resulted in his earliest printed work, a translation of Luther's commentary on the epistles of Peter and Jude, which appeared in 1859. Of his numerous published writings, the most important work was *The Life and Times of John Huss* (2 vols., 1863), which was published in three successive editions, and led to his appointment as official historian of the Presbyterian Church. His *History of the Presbyterian Church in the United States of America* (2 vols., 1864, second edition, 1875) was followed by *Life Lessons* (1864), *England Two Hundred Years Ago* (1866), *Ancient Cities and Empires* (1867), and *God in Human Thought* (2 vols., 1874). He married Maria Huntington Ripley, of Brooklyn, Oct. 15, 1851, and after her death in 1853, he married, June 19, 1854, Mary Jane Kendall, of Saratoga Springs, by whom he had two sons and one daughter.

["Descendants of Jonathan Gillett," in *The New-Eng. Hist. and Geneal. Reg.,* Apr. 1893; L. E. Gillett, *Gillett and Allied Families* (1828); *Alumni Cat. of the Union Theolog. Seminary in the City of N. Y., 1836–1926* (1926); *Alumni Cat. of Union Theolog. Seminary* (1926); *Semi-Centennial Hist. and Biog. Record of the Class of 1841 in Yale Univ.* (1892); *Universities and Their Sons: N. Y. Univ.* (1901), ed. by J. L. Chamberlain; *Obit. Records of Grads. of Yale Coll.* (1876); the *Presbyterian,* Sept. 11, 1875; *N. Y. Tribune,* Sept. 3, 1875.] M. S. B.

GILLETTE, FRANCIS (Dec. 14, 1807–Sept. 30, 1879), statesman, was a descendant of Jonathan Gillett, who settled in Windsor, Conn., about 1636. Francis Gillet (or Gillette as he signed himself) was born in Bloomfield, then a part of Windsor, the son of Ashbel and Achsah (Francis) Gillet. When he was six years old his father died. Between the boy and his stepfather there was no sympathy, a situation which embittered his formative years. Gillette received his preparatory education at Ashfield, Mass., where his mother was then living, and was graduated from Yale College in 1829. He was an excellent student, the unanimous choice of his classmates for valedictorian, and a member of Phi Beta Kappa. In 1834 he married Eliza Daggett Hooker, a descendant of Thomas Hooker. He had begun the study of law, but because of ill health, was obliged to abandon it and take up the life of a farmer on the family estate in Windsor. There he remained until 1852 when he purchased a farm in Hartford. Twice he was sent to the Connecticut House of Representatives, in 1832 from Windsor and in 1838 from Bloomfield. As a member of the Assembly, he identified himself with the anti-slavery group. In 1838, supporting an amendment to erase the word "white" from the state constitution, he professed to find "the length of the nose" as valid a qualification as color for political rights (*Columbian Register*, New Haven, May 26, 1838).

In 1841 he became the first candidate of the Liberty party for governor. Repeatedly, during the twelve years following, he received the Abolitionist or Free-Soil nominations and was as often defeated. In 1854, however, his long association with minority parties bore fruit, when a coalition of Whigs, Free-Soilers, and temperance men elected him United States senator to complete the unexpired term of Truman Smith. He reached Washington barely in time to vote against the Kansas-Nebraska Bill. During his brief stay in the Senate (May 24, 1854–Mar. 3, 1855), he delivered one formal speech on the slavery issue (*Congressional Globe*, 33 Cong., 1 Sess., pp. 1616–18). In Connecticut he was actively interested in the formation of the Republican party, whose first organ, the Hartford *Evening Press*, knew him as a silent partner. To the temperance movement, as well as the anti-slavery crusade, he lent his vigorous support. He was an incorporator of the American Temperance Life Insurance Company, now the Phoenix Mutual. He devoted his efforts, also, to the cause of education, and gave sympathy and cooperation to Henry Barnard [*q.v.*], who was laboring to reform the Connecticut schools. When the State Normal School was established in 1849, Gillette became chairman of the Board of Trustees and held that office until 1865. He embodied qualities common to many New Englanders of his day, a reforming spirit and a passion for minority causes. His interest in abolition, temperance, and education, though sometimes a bit combative, was sincere and unselfish (*Hartford Courant*, Oct. 1, 1879), and he was the antithesis of the professional politician and office-seeker.

[H. R. Stiles, *The Hist. and Geneals. of Ancient Windsor, Conn.*, vol. II (1892), contains the Gillet genealogy and a long biographical footnote on Francis Gillette (p. 293). See also J. H. Trumbull, *Memorial Hist. of Hartford County* (1886), I, 516, 611, II, ch. iii; *Obit. Record Grads. Yale Coll.*, 2 ser. (1880); *Biog. Dir. Am. Cong.* (1928); obituary in *Hartford Courant*, Oct. 1, 1879.]

D. E. O.

GILLIAM, DAVID TOD (Apr. 3, 1844–Oct. 2, 1923), surgeon, gynecologist, was born in Hebron, Ohio, the son of emigrants from Virginia, William and Mary Elizabeth (Bryan) Gilliam. On the outbreak of the Civil War in 1861, when he was seventeen, he enlisted on the Federal side and was made a corporal in the 2nd West Virginia Loyal Cavalry. He fought under Garfield in Kentucky and then for a time served as a recruiting officer at Wheeling. Later he fought in Crook's command and was wounded and captured by the Confederates in Virginia but managed to escape to Ohio. In 1863 he was discharged from the army as incurably ill. He recovered, however, and began to study in a business school at Cincinnati, but having decided to become a physician, he enrolled in the Medical College of Ohio (Cincinnati), and took the degree of M.D. in 1871. He began to practise in Nelsonville, Ohio, where he settled with his wife Lucinda Ellen, the daughter of Judge Thomas Mintun, whom he had married in 1866. In 1877, however, he was called to serve as pathologist to the Columbus Medical College and in this connection he prepared a text-book of pathology. He resigned in 1879 to accept the chair of physiology at Starling Medical College, but having devoted himself to the practise of gynecology and obstetrics, in 1885 he was made professor of these subjects in the same school, and taught there for many years. He was gynecologist to several Columbus hospitals and upon the creation of the medical department of Ohio State University received the title of professor emeritus of gynecology in that institution. He was regarded as an excellent teacher. In 1899 he devised the so-called Gilliam operation for the relief of backward displacement of the uterus by shortening the round ligaments, an operation which gave him an international reputation. He also devised a new technique for cystocele operation and for the cure of urinary incontinence in the female, the Gilliam operating table, and several new instruments. During 1905–06 he served as vice-president of the American Association of Obstetricians and Gynecologists. Gilliam had a literary style superior to that of many medical writers. In addition to numerous articles in periodicals, he published several books: *The Pocket Book of Medicine* (1882); *The Essentials of Pathology* (1883), and *A Textbook of Practical Gynecology* (1903; 5th ed., 1916). He also prepared an article, "Medical Ohio," for the *History of Ohio* (5 vols., 1912), edited by E. O. Randall and D. J. Ryan, and wrote two pieces of fiction, *The Rose Croix* (1906) and *Dick Devereux: A Story of the Civil War* (1915). He died of cerebral hemorrhage in his seventy-ninth year.

[Sketch by Gilliam's son and associate, Earl M. Gilliam, in H. A. Kelly and W. L. Burrage, *Dict. of Am. Medic. Biog.* (1928); *Who's Who in America*, 1918–19; *Jour. Am. Medic. Asso.*, Oct. 20, 1923; *Ohio State Jour.* (Columbus), Oct. 3, 1923.]

E. P.

GILLISS, JAMES MELVILLE (Sept. 6, 1811–Feb. 9, 1865), astronomer, was born in Georgetown, D. C., the third child and oldest son of George and Mary (Melville) Gilliss, and a descendant of Thomas Gilliss, a Scotchman, who settled on the Eastern Shore of Maryland at some time prior to 1668. He entered the navy as midshipman at the age of fifteen and in 1831 received the grade of passed midshipman. His scientific impulses, he was accustomed to say, were roused to active vigor soon after his examination by remarks to the effect that there was not an officer in the navy capable of conducting a scientific enterprise. In 1833 he applied for leave of absence and entered the University of Virginia, but excessive study injured his eyes and, unable to continue there, he returned to duty. In 1835 he studied in Paris for some six months. Ordered to Washington and assigned to the Depot of Charts and Instruments in 1836, on June 14, 1837, he was put in charge of this establishment, which, under Lieut. Charles Wilkes [*q.v.*], had grown to the pretentiousness of a wooden building fourteen feet by thirteen, located on Capitol Hill, and housing a 4-inch transit instrument. In September 1838 he undertook to make the astronomical observations in Washington necessary to the evaluation of the longitude observations of the Wilkes exploring expedition, which embarked that month. "From that time," he said, "till the return of the expedition in June, 1842, I observed every culmination of the moon, and every occultation visible at Washington, which occurred between two hours before sunset and two hours after sunrise" ("Report on the Erection of a Depot of Charts and Instruments," *Senate Document 114,* 28 Cong., 2 Sess.). He also carried on the duties of the office in regard to instruments, charts, and magnetic and meteorological observations. Becoming aware of discrepancies in the few star catalogues in his possession, he filled in his time observing 1,248 stars in the belief that "the mites which I could add to the data for more correctly locating 'the landmarks of the universe' would not be entirely unworthy of collection" (*Senate Document 172,* pt. 1, 28 Cong., 2 Sess., p. 65). Gilliss had practically no library through which to draw on the experience of others and very few colleagues with whom he could consult, but endowed with remarkable keenness of sight and hearing and conscientious in his attention to detail, with the simple instruments in his ill-adapted building he made observations seldom equalled for accuracy.

In 1841 the inadequacy of the existing building and equipment for astronomical research was urgently pointed out by Gilliss to the Board of Naval Commissioners, whose recommendation, with the endorsement of the Secretary of the Navy, was laid before the President in December 1841. The following August an act of Congress provided for the establishment of a naval observatory at Washington. Gilliss was ordered to prepare plans for the building and secure the instruments. He visited Europe in the interest of the observatory, returning in March 1843; by September 1844 the building was finished, the instruments were mounted and adjusted, and a library had been procured. Gilliss was keenly disappointed when his successor as superintendent of the Depot of Charts and Instruments, Lieut. Matthew F. Maury [*q.v.*], was assigned to the superintendency of the Observatory; nevertheless he bore his disappointment bravely, remarking to his associates that "an officer must obey orders and not find fault with them" (Gould, *post,* p. 156). During the subsequent months he prepared his "Astronomical Observations" of 1838–42 for the press, and they were published in 1846 (*Senate Document 172,* pt. 1, 28 Cong., 2 Sess.). The establishment of this, the first observatory in the United States devoted entirely to research, together with the publication of the first volume of astronomical observations to be issued in America and the preparation of the first catalogue of stars, set an example the importance of which it would be difficult to overestimate.

In 1847 Gilliss advocated an expedition to South America to observe Venus and Mars, in cooperation with northern observatories, for the purpose of a new determination of the solar parallax. The expedition, of which he was put in charge, was authorized by Congress—largely, it would seem, out of deference to the resolutions of approval by the learned societies of the country—and was the occasion of the first order, to Henry Fitz [*q.v.*], for an American-made lens of considerable size. Gilliss located his southern station at Santiago, Chile, and, with two assistants, continued his observations of Venus and Mars from 1849 to 1852. Again his spare time was filled with reobservation of the stars of La Caille's Catalogue, and with 33,000 observations of 23,000 stars within 24–1/5° of the South Pole. Furthermore, many observations of earthquakes were made and reduced, and magnetic and meteorological observations were a regular part of the daily program. The success of the undertaking to determine the solar parallax depended, of course, on the simultaneous observations in both hemispheres. When Gilliss returned to Washington with boxes full of data gathered in three years of unremitting labor he found that practically nothing had been done in the northern hemisphere. The expedition resulted, however, in the establishment of a permanent observatory in Santiago.

In 1855 the Naval Retiring Board placed Gilliss on the "reserved list" on the ground that twenty years had elapsed since his last sea service. This action made him feel unnecessarily humiliated. By order of the Secretary of the Navy, however, he was retained at full pay to complete his report on the Santiago investigations. The report included, besides astronomical and meteorological observations, a treatise on "Chile: Its Geography, Climate, Earthquakes, Government, Social Conditions, Mineral and Agricultural Resources, Commerce, etc." Only four of the six volumes planned were published (*House Executive Document 121,* 33 Cong., 1 Sess.). In 1858 Gilliss went again to South America, crossed the Peruvian desert to Olmos, and in the intervals of intermittent fever observed the solar eclipse (*Smithsonian Contributions to Knowledge,* vol. XI, article 3, 1859). In 1860 he observed another eclipse in Washington Territory (*Report 1860* of the Coast and Geodetic Survey).

At the outbreak of the Civil War, when Maury resigned his commission to enter the service of the Confederacy, Gilliss was at last put in charge of the Naval Observatory. At first his duties included that of equipping the vessels of the navy with charts and instruments, in which connection he was able to stimulate greatly the production of American lenses and instruments. In spite of the confusion of the war, at the Observatory instruments were put in condition, astronomers were added to the staff, and purposeful order was brought out of chaos. Other astronomical institutions began to give their cooperation; the reduction of the accumulated mass of fourteen years' crude observations was started; and rapid publication was provided for. The volumes had begun to appear when Gilliss died, very suddenly, of apoplexy. He had married, in December 1837, Rebecca Roberts, daughter of John Roberts of Alexandria, Va.

[B. A. Gould, in *Nat. Acad. Sci. Biog. Memoirs,* I (1877), 137–79; G. A. Weber, *The Naval Observatory: Its Hist. Activities, and Organization* (1926); C. O. Paullin, in *Columbia Hist. Soc. Records,* vol. XXV (1923); *Astronomische Nachrichten,* Mar. 19, 1865; *National Intelligencer* (Washington, D. C.), Feb. 10, 1865.]

R. S. D.

GILLISS, WALTER (May 17, 1855–Sept. 24, 1925), printer, was born in Lexington, Ky., the son of Thomas Handy and Catherine Isabella (Le Grand) Gilliss, of Scottish and French Huguenot stock. During his boyhood the family moved to New York City. When he was fourteen, Walter, with an elder brother Thomas, set up a small hand-press in an upper room of their home, and began printing business cards for neighboring tradespeople. Two years later, in 1871, Thomas having died, Walter and his eldest brother, Frank Le Grand, entered the printing business in earnest, under the firm-name of Gilliss Brothers, with an office at 48 Nassau St. They later took in as partner their youngest brother, Morton Melville. The firm soon did a flourishing business, printing several important periodicals, including the *Art Interchange* and the first numbers of *Life*; and in 1884 to the partnership was added Arthur B. Turnure, editor and proprietor of the *Art Age,* one of the earliest trade papers devoted to the art of printing.

The early nineties saw the firm's triumphs in overcoming difficulties presented in the printing for Harper & Brothers of Lew Wallace's *Ben Hur* (1891) with numerous marginal illustrations, and of illustrated editions of G. W. Curtis's *Prue and I* (1892) and Henry James's *Daisy Miller* (1892), these books being among the first examples of successful half-tone printing on hand-made paper in this country. In 1892 the firm issued the first number of *Vogue,* set in Caslon type, thus leading in the revival in the United States of that famous letter. Two years later the Gilliss Press adopted its device with the significant motto, in Tuscan, "Trifles make perfection, but perfection is no trifle." The device, first used in Part II of *Transactions of the Grolier Club,* appeared in nearly three hundred books, each bearing witness to Walter Gilliss's scrupulous care and classic taste. The books, printed for various publishing houses, private individuals, universities and institutions, include eighteen of William Loring Andrews's beautiful volumes, some sixty for the Metropolitan Museum of Art, and several for the Grolier Club and the Society of Iconophiles. The Gilliss Press ceased the actual manufacture of books in 1908, Walter Gilliss devoting himself thenceforth to designing the typography of works entrusted to him, and to supervising every detail of their making. From 1911 until his death he was also typographical adviser to Doubleday, Page & Company. During this time he produced his masterpiece, and one of the most difficult pieces of book-making undertaken in America, *The Iconography of Manhattan Island,* by I. N. P. Stokes, published by Robert Dodd, the first volume of which appeared in 1915.

Walter Gilliss excelled chiefly in his ability to form a mental picture of his page and to give instructions for sizes and kinds of type, leading, and other details with a certainty of results, which seldom called for alteration; and in addition to the exercise of this faculty he took untiring pains in perfecting margins, spacing, impression, and registration, thus creating that excellence and beauty of detail for which his books are distinguished. He was a master in the design of title-pages and in his use of ornament, wherein he showed a marked French influence. In his Introduction to Gilliss's own *Recollections,* Henry W. Kent writes: "As sure a craftsman as De Vinne [*q.v.*], though less a scholar, in his individuality of style, in his impeccable workmanship, in his correctness in what constitutes taste in printing, and above all in his elegance, which again is taste, Gilliss's name is to be written with those of the few great printers we have produced." In addition to *Recollections of the Gilliss Press* (1926) and to a few contributions to technical books and magazines, he wrote and printed privately three small volumes: *The Story of a Motto and a Mark* (1902), *A Printers' Sun Dial* (1913), and *A Few Verses and Songs by Walter Gilliss* (1916).

Aside from his work and his devotion to his brother Frank, his great interests were the Grolier Club, of which he was secretary for twenty years, and St. Thomas's Church. He was sincerely religious, and possessed a fine sensitiveness to beauty and a simple, old-time dignity. One of his most prized possessions was a cup presented by the staff of the Gilliss Press to his brother and himself "as a token of appreciation and gratitude from the Boys out of whom they made Men."

[Gilliss's *Recollections of the Gilliss Press,* published after the author's death by the Grolier Club, to which he had presented the manuscript; *Walter Gilliss, 1855–1925* (1925), a collection of tributes, privately printed by Frank LeG. Gilliss; *Gazette of the Grolier Club,* Apr. 1926, *N. Y. Times,* Sept. 26, 1925; personal recollections.]

R. S. G.

GILLMAN, HENRY (Nov. 16, 1833–July 30, 1915), scientist, United States consul, author, was born in Kinsale, Ireland, of Irish and English ancestry. His father, Edward, was a son of Henry Gillman of Belrose and Rock House; his mother, Eleanor Mandeville, a daughter of Capt. John Hackett, H. B. M. 8th Light Dragoons. A line of descent from Adam Winthrop, lord of the manor of Groton in Suffolk and grandfather of Gov. John Winthrop of the Massachusetts Bay Colony, linked him to America's beginnings. He was educated under private tutors and at Hamilton Academy, Bandon, County Cork, with a view to taking orders in the Established Church, but in 1850 emigrated with his parents to America, settling in Detroit, Mich. There he became first assistant in the United States Geodetic Survey of the Great Lakes and married (Dec. 7, 1858) Mary Julia, daughter of Hiram Reeve and Mary (Lyons) Johnson of Detroit. They had four children. Mrs. Gillman died in 1878.

As leader of topographic and hydrographic parties (1851–69) Gillman thoroughly enjoyed the woods and waters of the young, western country, filling his notebooks with precise reports on a wide variety of topics. He gave to his descriptions a literary value that made him a welcome contributor to scientific publications. *Marked for Life,* a volume of poems, appeared in 1863. From 1870 to 1876 he was assistant superintendent of construction for the 10th and 11th lighthouse districts on the Northern Lakes. Elected a fellow of the American Association for the Advancement of Science (1875), he was sent as member-at-large for America to attend the International Congress of Americanists at Luxembourg (1876) where he read a paper on the osteological remains of the mound-builders (*Compte-rendu, 1877,* vol. I, 1878). His most important contribution to science was the discovery of certain peculiarities in the bones of the mound-building Indians, especially the flattening of the tibia known as platycnemism (see *Annual Report . . . Smithsonian Institution, 1873,* 1874). The later destruction of numerous mounds which he had discovered and explored added to the value of his researches. He was one of the first to emphasize the importance of Isle Royale as a field for scientific investigation.

From April 1880 until the summer of 1885 he was librarian of the Detroit Public Library. Appointed United States consul at Jerusalem in 1886, he continued his researches in archeology and botany in his new environment. He supervised the photographing of the texts of the *Didache* or *Teaching of the Apostles,* published in 1887 by the Johns Hopkins University, and the "Epistles of St. Clement," which appeared as Part I (1890) of Volume I of a posthumous edition of Bishop Lightfoot's *The Apostolic Fathers.* His stand against the expulsion of the Jews from Palestine by the Turks was upheld by several European powers and the exclusion laws were modified. On a vacation trip to Italy (1890) he was received with marked cordiality by the Pope, in recognition of assistance rendered the first American pilgrimage to the Holy Land. He returned to America in 1891, making his home with a son in Detroit and finding enjoyment in the leisure for writing that he had long craved. *Wild Flowers and Gardens of Palestine* (1894), *Hassan, a Fellah* (1896), *Vericourt Westhrop and Issue* (1903), and numerous scientific and other papers occupied the working hours of his later years.

[Papers and journals in possession of Dr. Robert W. Gillman, including autobiographic draft of sketch for *Who's Who in America*; A. W. Gillman, *Searches into the Hist. of the Gillman or Gilman Family* (London, 1895); death notice in the *Detroit Free Press*, Aug. 2, 1915.]

G. B. K.

GILLMORE, QUINCY ADAMS (Feb. 28, 1825–Apr. 7, 1888), soldier, military engineer, came of Scotch-Irish ancestry, his forebears having emigrated to Massachusetts in the early part of 1700. His grandfather, Edmund Gillmore, moved from Massachusetts to Lorain County, Ohio, in the year 1770, and there his father, Quartus Gillmore, was born in 1790. At Black River, Lorain County, young Gillmore was born, his mother being Elizabeth Reid. He was given the rudiments of an education at home, then in his fourteenth year he was sent to the Norwalk Academy where he was noted for his proficiency in mathematics. After teaching school for three years, and attending the Elyria high school for two summers, he won an appointment to West Point through his fine scholarship, and was graduated at the head of his class in 1849. He was immediately commissioned second lieutenant of Engineers. His early duties included the construction of fortifications at Hampton Roads, Va., and service at West Point as assistant instructor of practical military engineering, as well as treasurer and quartermaster of the Academy. He was also, for a time, in charge of the Engineer District of New York City. He was promoted first lieutenant, July 1, 1856, and captain, Aug. 6, 1861.

Gillmore's Civil War service was brilliant. He was chief engineer of the Port Royal Expedition, 1861–62, being in the engagement at Hiltonhead, S. C., Nov. 7, 1861, and in command of the troops investing Fort Pulaski, Ga., Apr. 10–11, 1862. For gallant and meritorious services in the capture of this fort, he was brevetted lieutenant-colonel. On Apr. 28, 1862, he was promoted brigadier-general of volunteers, and until April 1863 commanded various areas in Kentucky and West Virginia. On Mar. 30, 1863, he defeated Gen. Pegram at Somerset, Ky., and was brevetted colonel for gallantry. From June 12, 1863, until late in the same year, he commanded the X Army Corps and the Department of the South—having been promoted major-general of volunteers, July 10, 1863; and was engaged in important offensives against Charleston, S. C., the reduction of Morris Island, and the taking of Fort Sumter. Early in 1864 he was transferred with his corps to the James River, where he took part in the engagements near Bermuda Hundred (May 5–June 17), the battle of Drewry's Bluff (May 13–16), and the reconnoissances before Petersburg (June 9). In the summer of the same year, while defending the city of Washington against Gen. Early's raid, Gillmore was seriously injured by a fall from his horse. During his convalescence his services were utilized as president of the board of testing Ames's wrought-iron cannon, and in an inspection of fortifications from Cairo, Ill., to Pensacola, Fla. In the following year he commanded the Department of the South, resigning his volunteer commission on Dec. 5, 1865. For gallant services in the capture of Fort Wagner, he was brevetted brigadier-general, Mar. 13, 1865; and for similar service in the assault on Morris Island, major-general in the regular army.

After the termination of the Civil War, Gillmore served on many important boards and commissions. Perhaps his most important service was as president of the Mississippi River Commission (1879). He was the author of a number of professional books and treatises, most of which were published by the Corps of Engineers: *Official Report to the United States Engineer Department, of the Siege and Reduction of Fort Pulaski, Ga.* (1862); *Practical Treatise on Limes, Hydraulic Cements, and Mortars* (1863); *Engineer and Artillery Operations Against the Defenses of Charleston Harbor in 1863* (1865); *Report on Béton-Aggloméré; or, Coignet-Béton* (1871); *Report on the Compressive Strength, Specific Gravity, and Ratio of Absorption of Various Kinds of Building-Stone* (1874); *Practical Treatise on Roads, Streets, and Pavements* (1876); *Report on Experiments with the Seely and Bethell Processes for the Preservation of Timber* (1879); and *Notes on the Compressive Resistance of Freestone, Brick Piers, Hydraulic Cements, Mortars, and Concretes* (1888). He gained wide reputation as an artillerist as well as an engineer through his successful use of rifled cannon for breaching masonry walls at Fort Pulaski during the Civil War, causing a sensation throughout the world in proving many modern fortifications vulnerable to artillery. He died at Brooklyn, N. Y., leaving a widow, formerly Mrs. Bragg, and four sons by a former wife, Mary Isabella O'Maher, whom he married immediately after graduation from West Point. Interment was at West Point, with high military honors.

[Gillmore's services are outlined in General Orders No. 5, Headquarters Corps of Engineers, Apr. 10, 1888, printed in and supplemented by a sketch in the *Ann. Reunion, Asso. Grads. U. S. Mil. Acad.*, June 11, 1888. See also *Battles and Leaders of the Civil War*, vol. IV (1888); the *Army and Navy Jour.*, Apr. 14, 1888; G. W. Cullum, *Biog. Reg. . . . U. S. Mil. Acad.*, II (ed. 1891), 367–70; *N. Y. Times*, Apr. 8, 1888. Information as to certain facts was supplied by Gillmore's grandson, Gen. Q. A. Gillmore, New York City.] C. D. R.

GILLON, ALEXANDER (Aug. 13, 1741–Oct. 6, 1794), South Carolina merchant, naval officer, and financial agent abroad during the Revolution, was born in Rotterdam, Holland, the son of Mary Gillon. According to Joseph Johnson (*post*, pp. 127 ff.), who knew him, he came of a well-to-do family, had some mercantile training in London, spoke several languages, and was "a man of a very fine personal appearance and of a very acute, well-cultivated mind." In December 1764 he commanded the brigantine *Surprize*, owned in Philadelphia (*Pennsylvania Magazine of History and Biography*, July 1903, p. 354), and the next year in this and other vessels was engaged in British trade out of Charleston. He married Mary Cripps, a Charleston widow, July 6, 1766, and with his stepson John Splatt Cripps and Florian Mey established a mercantile business which in ten years gained him an estate worth £30,000. A hot revolutionist, he was a member of the provincial congress, 1775–77, and captain of the "German Fusiliers"; and in June 1778, as volunteer officer with the Connecticut privateer *Defense* and sloop *Volant*, which he helped fit out, he aided in capturing two British privateers off Charleston. In 1775–76 he imported munitions for the Continental Congress, and was about to close a larger contract (*Journals of the Continental Congress*, 1777) when he was made commodore in the South Carolina state navy, Feb. 16, 1778, with authority to sell products and borrow money abroad and purchase three frigates. He reached France in January 1779, but his schemes aroused Franklin's suspicions and hostility, and he made little progress through what Henry Laurens called "his fervor for accomplishing everything by force of his own powers" (Adams, *Works*, IX, 498). Finally, May 30, 1780, on promise of one-fourth share in prizes, he secured from the Chevalier Luxembourg, as French agent, the new frigate *L'Indien*, built in Holland for American use and first promised to Paul Jones, which he renamed *South Carolina* and manned with Americans from British prisons and French marines. In June 1780 he was enticing seamen from Jones's ships at L'Orient, and intriguing with Arthur Lee to keep Landais in command of the *Alliance*, declaring himself "senior naval officer in Europe" and hoping ultimately to secure this vessel also. Jones, intensely indignant, called him "the Red Ribboned Commodore," and through Franklin balked his plan. The *South Carolina* was interminably delayed. Gillon was overwhelmed by debts, and to secure funds sold part of his purchase of naval stores to J. Laurens, agent of Congress, for £10,000. The money, however, was not paid, and the goods, not yet on board, went across later. John Adams, diplomatic representative in Holland, declared the whole affair villainously ill-managed, though earlier he had said Gillon's "industry, skill, and perseverance merited every assistance" (*Works*, VII, 416, May 8, 1781). Gillon was no doubt overweening, extravagant, and self-seeking, but not demonstrably corrupt. At last, Aug. 19, 1781, the *South Carolina* left the Texel. There was much confusion on board, and during a storm Capt. Barney, a passenger, had to take command. The frigate captured three prizes in the North Sea, stopped at Corunna, and reached Havana Jan. 12, 1782, with five sugar prizes worth $91,500. Gillon now joined Gov. Cagigal of Cuba in an expedition against the Bahamas, with the *South Carolina*, sixty-one Spanish transports, and three Philadelphia privateers. The islands surrendered May 6 without resistance, but Gillon never received the $60,000 promised for his aid. Arriving in Philadelphia May 28, he was detained through court proceedings by Luxembourg's agents. His ship, sailing for Charleston in December, was captured by the British. On the whole venture the Commodore, his backers, and his creditors lost heavily. South Carolina was long vexed with the "Luxembourg Claims," not settled till 1814. Gillon, who seems to have suffered little in reputation, became subsequently a leader in South Carolina anti-Loyalist agitation, and held numerous public offices, being a delegate to Congress in 1784; a member of the South Carolina Assembly, 1786–88; and congressman, 1793–94. After his first wife's death in 1787 he was married again, Feb. 10, 1789, to Ann, daughter of Henry Purcell, rector of St. Michael's, Charleston, and had a son and two daughters. He died on his estate, "Gillon's Retreat," on the Congaree River.

[See Jos. Johnson, *Traditions and Reminiscences, Chiefly of the American Revolution in the South* (1851); U. B. Phillips, "The South Carolina Federalists," *Am. Hist. Rev.*, Apr.–July 1909; D. E. H. Smith, "Commodore Alexander Gillon and the Frigate South Carolina," *S. C. Hist. and Geneal. Mag.*, Oct. 1908, and "The Luxembourg Claims," *Ibid.*, Apr. 1909; also "Records from the Bible belonging to Alexander Gillon," *Ibid.*, July 1918, and letters from Gillon in the same periodical, Jan., Apr. 1900 and Jan., Apr., July 1909. See also I. M. Hays, *Calendar of the Papers of Benj. Franklin in the Lib. of the Am. Phil. Soc.* (5 vols., 1906–08); C. F. Adams, *The Works of John Adams*, vols. VII (1852) and IX (1854); *Jours. of the Continental Cong.*, 1775–82; C. H. Lincoln, *A Calendar of John Paul Jones MSS. in the Lib of Cong.* (1903); C. O. Paullin, *The Navy of the Am. Revolution* (1906); G. W. Allen, *A Naval Hist. of the Am. Revolution* (2 vols., 1913); L. F. Middlebrook, "The Frigate South Carolina," *Essex Inst. Hist. Colls.*, July 1921–Jan. 1930; and, on the Bahamas expedition, W. S. Robertson in *Ann. Report Am. Hist. Asso. for . . . 1907* (1908), I, 240.]
A. W.

GILMAN, ARTHUR (June 22, 1837–Dec. 27, 1909), author, educational executive, one of thirteen children of Winthrop Sargent and Abia Swift (Lippincott) Gilman, was born in Alton, Ill. Back through six generations to Edward Gilman who came to Hingham, Mass., from Norfolk, England, in 1638, his forebears were prominent citizens of New Hampshire and Ohio. His mother, grandmother, and great-grandmother are described as women of unusual intelligence and cultivation. His early education was gained in private schools in St. Louis, Mo., and Lee, Mass. When his father moved to New York City, in 1849, Arthur was sent to Chrestomathic Institute at Rye, N. Y. In 1851 he attended Mr. Leggett's school in New York City. He joined his father's banking firm in 1857 and in 1860 (Apr. 12) married Amy Cooke Ball, of Lee, Mass. Two years later his health—always delicate—failed, and he moved to Lee for a country life. Here he became actively interested in public education, serving twice on the local school committee. In 1865 he traveled in England, gathering data which he incorporated in *The Gilman Family* (1869). He also prepared a text-book, *First Steps in English Literature* (1870), which ran through many editions. In 1872, he moved to Cambridge, Mass., where he served the Riverside Press as literary adviser for many years. He was married a second time, on July 11, 1876, to Stella Houghton Scott. There were four children by his first marriage and three by his second.

Gilman wrote, edited, or collaborated in the preparation of a long series of histories, including Lothrop's Library of Entertaining History (1880–85); the Story of the Nations Series, published by G. P. Putnam's Sons (1885–1904); *Boston Past and Present* (1873); *Theatrum Majorum: The Cambridge of 1776* (1876); *The Story of Boston* (1889); *The Cambridge of Eighteen Hundred and Ninety-Six* (1896); Though he had not received the academic training of a scholar, his high standard of accuracy, combined with his literary skill, gave him an honorable position among American historians. He was the first to use the Ellesmere Manuscript as the basis for an edition of Chaucer's Canterbury Tales (*The Poetical Works of Geoffrey Chaucer,* 3 vols., 1879), and prepared the Complete Index for Harper's edition of *The Complete Works of Samuel Taylor Coleridge* (7 vols., 1884).

His important and permanent work, however, was in the higher education of women. In 1878 it occurred to his wife and to him that Harvard College instruction might be repeated to women, with identical standards and examinations. President Eliot gave the idea prompt endorsement; the professors approached were generously willing to repeat their courses for small remuneration. Seven ladies, carefully chosen, "who did not represent a 'cause' or who would not be looked upon as advanced or in favor of co-education," signed the first announcement of "Private Collegiate Instruction for Women," by Harvard teachers. In 1879 twenty-seven young women registered. The organization was simple. The professors were ultimate authority on academic matters. The seven ladies held monthly meetings and raised money. The center of the organization, however, was the executive secretary, Arthur Gilman. To his tact in launching the idea and to his wise handling of the detailed management of the experiment, looked at askance by the community, is largely due the success of the "Harvard Annex" and its growth into Radcliffe College. Upon the incorporation of the college in 1893 he became its regent. In 1886, he had founded the Gilman School for Girls. This full life of activity in intellectual pursuits and human obligations was made possible by his quick sense of humor, his genuine interest in individuals, his optimistic, devout, and lovable nature.

[The most trustworthy accounts of Gilman are those in a privately printed volume of the Mass. Biog. Soc. (Boston, 1909), and the *Cambridge Hist. Soc. Pubs.,* vol. V (1911). *The Gilman Family* (1869) contains his own short account of his life up to that year. His *Annual Reports* as secretary, through the early years of Radcliffe College, are invaluable for an understanding of his character. There are autobiographical records in the possession of the family. See also *Who's Who in America,* 1908–09; A. W. Gillman, *Searches into the Hist. of the Gillman or Gilman Family* (1895); E. Noyes, *A Family Hist. in Letters and Docs., 1667–1837, Concerning the Forefathers of Winthrop Sargent Gilman* (2 vols., 1919); E. M. H. Merrill, *Cambridge Sketches by Cambridge Authors* (1896); *Harvard Grads. Mag.,* May 1910; obituaries in N. Y. *Evening Post* and *Boston Transcript,* Dec. 29, 1909.] C. H. B.

GILMAN, ARTHUR DELEVAN (Nov. 5, 1821–July 11, 1882), architect, was a descendant of Edward Gilman, a native of Hingham, Norfolk, England, who came to Massachusetts in 1638. Arthur Gilman was born in Newburyport, Mass., his parents were Arthur Gilman (1773–1836), a prosperous Newburyport merchant, and his third wife, Elizabeth, daughter of Joseph and Rebecca Marquand and widow of Samuel Allyne Otis. He attended Trinity (then Washington) College, Hartford, Conn., but left in 1840, during his junior year. He gave early evidence of an interest in architecture in a paper entitled "Architecture in the United States" (a review of Edward Shaw's *Rural Architecture,* 1843, in the *North American Review,* April 1844). The following winter, 1844–45, he gave twelve lectures on architecture for the Lowell Institute, Boston, which were so well received that they were repeated before a second audience. Thereafter he spent some time in travel and study abroad, returning to begin practise as an architect in Boston. On Apr. 27, 1859, he married Frances Juliet, daughter of Henry Raynor of Syracuse, N. Y. During his early years of practise in Boston he was connected with the project for filling in the Back Bay district and widening Commonwealth Avenue. His first important building was the Arlington Street Unitarian Church, dedicated in 1861; his most important work, the Boston City Hall, designed in association with Gridley J. F. Bryant, 1862–65. On May 13, 1867, he was employed to prepare plans for the New York State Capitol at Albany. These, made in association with Edward Hale Kendall, he presented on Aug. 1 of that year, but they were not accepted. On Aug. 14, Gilman and Thomas Fuller were instructed to make designs which, on Nov. 13, 1867, were accepted by the Capitol Commissioners and the Commissioners of the Land Office and on Dec. 7, by the Governor. After 1868 he made New York his headquarters. There in association with Edward Hale Kendall, and with George B. Post as consulting architect, he designed the building for the Equitable Life Assurance Society, at 120 Broadway. It was the first office building in New York to have elevators. At the same time Gilman was the architect of St. John's Episcopal Church at Clifton, Staten Island (1869–71), and for a short time (1871–73) he lived on Staten Island.

Gilman is important as one of the first American architectural eclectics. In his *North American Review* article his passionate rebellion against the classic revivals was already evident; he termed the United States Capitol and the Boston State House "those flaunting and meretricious edifices" and called Stuart and Revett's *Antiquities of Athens* (1837), "that inexhaustible quarry of bad taste." He quoted Pugin and praised the Gothic but reserved his enthusiasm for the architecture of the Italian Renaissance and to a lesser degree that of ante-Revolutionary Boston. In the Arlington Street Church this combination of tastes appears: the exterior is Georgian but the interior based, according to the architect, "as closely as possible upon the church of Sta. Annunziata at Genoa" (Justin Winsor, *Memorial History of Boston,* vol. IV, 1883, p. 484). St. John's Church at Clifton, Staten Island, is, on the other hand, an unusually charming version of the current Gothic revival, unassuming and without the extravagances of detail that so frequently mar similar work. The Boston City Hall and the New York and Boston Equitable Buildings bear witness to Gilman's fondness for Renaissance detail. Working in a vernacular new to him and uncommon at the time anywhere, he floundered hopelessly; but the small scale and monotony of the recurrent engaged columns and windows on every floor set an example the popularity of which at the time and later was attested by numberless imitations.

[*Vital Records of Newburyport, Mass.* (2 vols., 1911); Arthur Gilman, *The Gilman Family* (1869), pp. 98, 145, 191; catalogues of Washington College, Hartford, 1838–40; *Docs. of the City of Boston for the Year 1866* (1867), vol. I, no. 21½; "Annual Report of the New Capitol Commissioners," *Docs. of the Senate of the State of N. Y.,* 1870, no. 13; *Plans and Description of the Equitable Building, Boston* (1874); J. J. Clute, *Annals of Staten Island, N. Y.* (1877), p. 272; H. K. Smith, *Hist. of the Lowell Inst., Boston* (1898); I. K. Morris, *Morris's Memorial Hist. of Staten Island,* II (1900), 306; *The First Fifty Years of the Equitable Life Assurance Soc., N. Y.* (1909), p. 47; obituaries in *Boston Transcript* and *World* (N. Y.), July 17, 1882.]

T. F. H.

GILMAN, CAROLINE HOWARD (Oct. 8, 1794–Sept. 15, 1888), writer, was born in Boston, Mass., the daughter of Samuel Howard, a shipwright, and Anna (Lillie) Howard, a first cousin of Samuel Breck [*q.v.*]. Her father died when Caroline was three years old, and her mother retired with her children to the country, living for brief periods in several New England towns before settling in Cambridge, Mass. Hence, Caroline remembered her early education as a perpetual passing from school to school. During these years, however, her poetical and religious tendencies began to appear. She wrote out the multiplication table in rhyme, and committed her school themes to verse. At sixteen she was confirmed in the Episcopal Church at Cambridge, and at eighteen she sacrificed little luxuries to buy a Bible with wide margins on which she wrote her deliberate religious convictions during several months of study. When she was sixteen, one of her early poems, "Jephthah's Rash Vow," was printed in a newspaper without her knowledge, an occurrence at which, she says, she wept bitterly. Nevertheless, in July 1817 another poem, "Jairus's Daughter," was published with her full consent in the *North American Review.* In December 1819 she was married to Samuel Gilman [*q.v.*], and with him settled in Charleston, S. C., where he had just been appointed minister of the Second Independent Church. In 1832 she began to edit one of the earliest children's papers in the United States, the *Southern Rosebud,* which in the following year became the *Southern Rose,* a magazine for older readers, and in 1839 was discontinued because of the failure of the editor's health. Many of her contributions to this paper were collected and republished. The first of her volumes, *Recol-*

lections of a Housekeeper (1834), humorously described the little vicissitudes of early married life. She attributed its great popularity to the fact that "it was the first attempt, in that particular mode, to enter into the recesses of American homes and hearths." Other books followed in quick succession: *Recollections of a Southern Matron* (1836); *The Poetry of Travelling in the United States* (1838), gracefully humorous sketches of Northern and Southern life; *The Letters of Eliza Wilkinson during the Invasion of Charleston* (1839), which she edited, one of the most pleasing memoirs of the Revolutionary period; *Ruth Raymond* (1840); *Oracles from the Poets* (1844), which went through many editions; *Verses of a Life-time* (1849); *A Gift Book of Stories and Poems for Children* (1850), comprising several volumes for children previously published; *Oracles for Youth* (1852). She also wrote a memorial of her husband, Samuel Gilman (1860); and, in collaboration with her daughter, Mrs. Caroline Gilman Jervey, *Poems by Mother and Daughter* (1872). Her last poem was written just before her ninetieth birthday. After the death of her husband, she remained in Charleston until 1870, when she returned to Cambridge. At the time of her death, in her ninety-fifth year, she was making her home with a daughter in Washington, D. C. Mrs. Gilman considered herself primarily a writer for children. Her prose was of an unaffected and light-hearted character, and her poetry dealt with the beauties of nature and domestic affection, qualities which appealed to the sentiments of the time and which made her one of the most popular women writers of her day.

[Mary Forrest (Julia Deane Freeman), *Women of the South Distinguished in Literature* (1861); Mary I. Tardy, *Living Female Writers of the South* (1872); Arthur Gilman, *The Gilman Family* (1869); E. A. Alderman and J. C. Harris, *Lib. of Southern Lit.*, vol. IV (1909); E. L. Pierce, *The Lillie Family of Boston* (1896); *Critic* (N. Y.), Sept. 22, 1888; *Evening Star* (Washington, D. C.), Sept. 15, 1888.] S. H. P.

GILMAN, DANIEL COIT (July 6, 1831–Oct. 13, 1908), university president, author, and publicist, fifth of the nine children of William Charles and Eliza (Coit) Gilman, was born in Norwich, Conn. His ancestors on both sides were originally from Wales, though they had long been settled in Norfolk, England. Edward Gilman emigrated in 1638 from Hingham to a settlement of the same name on Massachusetts Bay. Daniel's father was a prosperous business man of Norwich, Conn., and his mother was the daughter of a retired merchant of the same place. William Gilman was a man noted for public spirit and practical benevolence, and for his rare judgment in gathering about him competent fellow workers. A daughter said that Daniel was more like his father than any other of the children (Franklin, *post*, p. 4). Gilman was trained in Norwich Academy, where Timothy Dwight was a schoolmate. He entered Yale College in 1848, when Theodore Dwight Woolsey was president and Benjamin Silliman, Denison Olmsted, James Dwight Dana, and James Hadley were professors. Here he formed an intimate friendship with his fellow student, Andrew D. White. The lives of these two men were henceforth to interact. After taking his degree at Yale in 1852, Gilman studied for a few months at Harvard College, living in the home of Prof. Arnold Guyot, who interested him in geography in a way that was to influence his whole life.

In December 1853, Gilman and Andrew D. White sailed for Europe as attachés of the American legation at St. Petersburg. After an absence of two years, Gilman returned to America. "As yet, no plan of life had shaped itself for him" (Franklin, *post*, p. 39), though many paths enticed, especially the ministry. Destiny, however, was training him in a mysterious way for the creative task awaiting him in Baltimore. To friends, his course in these early years seemed to beat about; but it is clear to the student of his life that Gilman was grounding himself in educational experiences that would enable him as a pioneer to blaze a new path for higher learning in America. Significance therefore attaches to whatever his hand touched in this engendering period. For the next seventeen years, his life revolved around Yale. Prof. James D. Dana enlisted him to draw up a plan for what was to become the Sheffield Scientific School. This was published in 1856 as a pamphlet, with the title, *Proposed Plan for a Complete Organization of the School of Science Connected with Yale College*; and Gilman's notes on the European schools of science, published the same year, disclose how fruitful were his observations abroad (Chittenden, *post*, I, 69–70). In the new school, he served as librarian, as secretary, and as professor of physical and political geography. As a member of the New Haven Board of Education, he got an insight into the problem of public schools. In 1859 he announced in his report the establishment of a high school in New Haven. From his educational watch-tower, he perceived at once the significance of the Morrill Act (1862) in quickening scientific study by the founding of agricultural and mechanical colleges, and particularly its bearing upon the Sheffield Scientific School. The latter, as a result of Gilman's efforts, was the first institution to put into actual use the funds derived from the Morrill Act. When Senator Morrill visited New Haven in order to see with his own eyes the first fruit of his planting, he was the guest of Gilman, to whom he recounted the history of his bill.

In 1867 Gilman was called to the presidency of the University of Wisconsin, just as Andrew D. White was entering upon that office at Cornell. But feeling that his time was not yet come, he declined this call, as well as one in 1870 to the presidency of the University of California. Upon a second call, however, in 1872, Gilman became president of the University of California. On his way thither he visited President White; discussed with Gov. Baker of Indiana the plan of Purdue University, and at Urbana studied the formative plan of the University of Illinois. With Louis Agassiz, who happened to be in San Francisco when Gilman arrived, he pondered the place of science in American schools. Demagogic agitation at first beset the path of the University of California. Gilman recorded: "The University of California is nominally administered by the Regents; it is virtually administered by the legislature" (Franklin, *post,* p. 178). The impression Gilman created on the Pacific Coast was happily summarized by John Knox McLean: "He was endowed with an extraordinarily sharp, quick and unerring discernment, first of measures and men, and next of ways and means, not merely as to things in themselves nor yet as to their latent values—he had all that and more. With it all was allied the more fruitful sense of how to extract those values, and how, once extracted, to set them into active productiveness" (*Ibid.,* p. 124).

Hindered by politics at Berkeley, Gilman in April 1874 jotted down the following observations, perhaps for use as the basis of a statement to the regents and public in California: "A wealthy citizen of Baltimore, who died a few months since, has left his fortune for the good of his fellow men. One large portion is devoted to a hospital; another to the maintenance of a University. Nearly seven millions of dollars are consecrated to these two objects. The trustees whom he selected are responsible neither to ecclesiastical nor legislative supervision; but simply to their own convictions of duty and the enlightened judgment of their fellow men. They have not adopted any plan nor authorized, as I believe, any of the statements which have been made as to their probable course—but they are disposed to make a careful study of the educational systems of the country, and to act in accordance with the wisest counsels which they can secure. Their means are ample; their authority complete; their purposes enlightened. Is not this opportunity without parallel in the history of our country?" (*Ibid.,* p. 179). The trustees of the Johns Hopkins University in their search for an executive sought the advice of Presidents Eliot of Harvard, White of Cornell, and Angell of Michigan. In his address at the twenty-fifth anniversary of the Johns Hopkins University, Angell said: "And now I have this remarkable statement to make to you; that, without the least conference between us three, we all wrote letters, telling them that the one man was Daniel C. Gilman of California. That is one of the few acts of my life which I have never regretted" (*Johns Hopkins University, Celebration of the Twenty-fifth Anniversary,* 1902, p. 133).

On Jan. 30, 1875, Gilman accepted the presidency of the new institution, writing from California. The same day he jotted down this note, which may be regarded as the first sketch of the Johns Hopkins University: "The minimum income will be $200,000 per year. Reserving of that $45,000,—for library, apparatus and administration,—we shall have $155,000 for instruction. This would pay four professors, say $6,000 each (= $24,000); twenty, at salaries ranging from $4,000 to $5,000, averaging $4,500 (=$90,000); twenty (adjuncts) on time appointments, three, four, or five years, average $2,000 (= $40,000); total $154,000. We could doubtless much increase numbers by paying less prices; but I think we should pay good salaries as such things go" (Franklin, p. 192). Gilman's conception was clear and complete from the start. "Everywhere," he said, "the real efficiency of a college is admitted to consist, not chiefly in buildings nor in sites, nor in apparatus, but in the number and character of the teachers. We must discover and develop such men as have unusual ability." Turning his back upon buildings and sites, he began the search for personality plus science. The twelve months which he devoted to the discovery of the men who were to do a unique piece of creative work in Baltimore are the most critical and impressive in his career. In accomplishing this task, he drew upon all of his previous experiences in America and in Europe. An example or two must suffice. In the summer of 1875, at West Point, Gilman asked Gen. Michie, "who there was that could be considered for our chair of physics. He told me there was a young man in Troy . . . full of promise. 'What has he done?' I said. 'He has lately published an article in the *Philosophical Magazine,*' was his reply, 'which shows great ability.' . . . "Why did he publish it in London,' said I, 'and not in the

American Journal?' 'Because it was turned down by the American editors,' he said, 'and the writer at once forwarded it to Prof. Clerk Maxwell, who sent it to the English periodical'" (Gilman, *The Launching of a University,* p. 15). Gilman wired at once for an interview with Henry A. Rowland, and afterward wrote in his little notebook: "Rowland of Troy—25 years. $1600 now paid—work not apprec'd—w'd like chance to work. sent papers to N. H. [New Haven]—thrice rejected—'too young to publish such.'" Gilman continued the hunt for potential teachers in Europe, where he consulted Clerk Maxwell of Cambridge, Jowett and Bryce of Oxford, Herbert Spencer and Tyndall at the famous X Club in London, Mahaffy of Dublin, Lord Kelvin of Glasgow, von Holst of Freiburg, and Gneist and Ranke of Berlin. Dr. J. B. Hooker pointed him to J. J. Sylvester for mathematics, and Huxley singled out for him H. Newell Martin for biology. In Williams College he found his chemist, Ira Remsen, a young man recently returned from Germany; and from the University of Virginia he called Basil L. Gildersleeve for Greek.

What wrought the change between the previous activities of these men in their several spheres and the creative character of their efforts in Baltimore? There was of course the coordinating mind of Gilman himself; and there was the emphasis upon graduate studies, facilitated by the fact that the students attracted to Johns Hopkins were already somewhat grounded in culture and specialized in scholarly purpose. But the chief transmuting cause was the freedom of thinking and teaching upon which Gilman insisted from the very start. This condition constituted the springtime that called forth in the Johns Hopkins group all the creative energies of their minds and methods. It may be said with historical accuracy that Gilman founded the University upon the principle, "the truth shall make you free." Exhilaration was in the very atmosphere. One of the first students, Josiah Royce, felt these quickening forces. He records: "The beginning of the Johns Hopkins University was a dawn wherein ''twas bliss to be alive.' Freedom and wise counsel one enjoyed together. The air was full of noteworthy work done by the older men of the place, and of hopes that one might find a way to get a little working-power one's self" (*Scribner's,* September 1891, p. 383). To what extent Gilman was the glass that focused these various rays of light may be inferred from a letter he wrote on Oct. 1, 1876. "One by one the professors, associates, and fellows have been assembling and I have heard their confidential stories of hope, and regret, and desires and aims—till I seem to myself to be a great repository of secrets. . . . Tuesday evening we assemble and meet together. . . . Our main rooms are all in order. . . . Our library is well begun. Books and instruments arrive by every steamer, and before next Sunday the wheels will all be in motion. The result of years and months of planning will soon appear" (Franklin, p. 413).

The opening gun of the University in that American centennial year was the address by Huxley. Gilman records: "This was the storm-signal," especially as there was no opening prayer. A letter from a New York divine complained: "It was bad enough to invite Huxley. It were better to have asked God to be present. It would have been absurd to ask them both" (*The Launching of a University,* pp. 22–23). Huxley reëchoed Gilman's central thought in staking all upon personality. "It has been my fate to see great educational funds fossilise into mere bricks and mortar in the petrifying springs of architecture, with nothing left to work the institution they were intended to support" (*American Addresses,* 1877, p. 121). Many lands and ages contributed to the achievement of the University, for Gilman was familiar with like institutions in Europe and in America; but all of their results were passed through the experience and thinking of Gilman himself, so that the ultimate product bore the stamp of his own personality rather than any particular university system which one might label German, or English, or American. Research was the soul of the whole organism. No effort was made to attract students in large numbers, since capacity for creative investigation, the spirit of discovery, was the prerequisite.

After twelve years of work and waiting, the Johns Hopkins Hospital was to be opened in May 1889. It is a tribute to the organizing power of Gilman that, though he was not a member of the medical profession, his direction was felt to be essential in establishing the Hospital, and "in putting the medical school upon a true university basis." He threw himself with such energy and decision into the task of organizing the Hospital that he was on the point of breaking down, suffering from neuralgia and sleeplessness for the only time in his life. As a result, he was given a year's leave of absence, during which he traveled in the Orient, returning in July 1890. In the Hospital board, which was separate from that of the University, a proposal had been put forward that the Hospital should begin the work of medical instruction. This ran counter to all of Gilman's ideals and actual plans for a medical school as an essential part of the

University in spirit, methods, and standards. The crisis called forth from him a paper that evinces the dynamic in his nature. He took his stand on this sentence in Johns Hopkins's mandatory letter: "Bear constantly in mind that it is my wish and purpose that the Hospital shall ultimately form a part of the Medical School of that University for which I have made ample provisions by my will" (Franklin, p. 265). Gilman told how the trustees of the University had for fifteen years been working toward the founding of the medical school, and the public had looked forward to the event "as an epoch in medical education." Then he laid down "the principle which should govern both boards of Trustees. All that belongs to medical instruction should be under the control of the University; all that belongs to the care of the sick and suffering, and all that concerns admission to clinical opportunities, or to residence within the walls of the Hospital, belongs to the Hospital. A joint committee can easily adjust all questionable points if the fundamental principle is agreed upon" (*Ibid.*, p. 266). Those who are familiar with the achievements of both the medical school and the hospital will recognize the educational statesmanship in the course that he pursued.

There is no need to stress Gilman's patience under the financial disaster which overtook the University when the Baltimore & Ohio Railroad suspended dividends on the common stock, which formed the bulk of the endowment. The medical school, which was thus deferred for seventeen years, opened in 1893, with a half-million dollar endowment, given in part by Miss Mary E. Garrett on condition that women should be admitted to its privileges. The first four professors—William H. Welch, William Osler, William S. Halsted, and Howard A. Kelly—were grouped by Sargent in the painting which Miss Garrett presented to the University. The medical school was open only to graduates of colleges, and the entrance requirements seemed absurdly high at a time when most medical students shunned colleges altogether. Thus in the character of the teachers, their vital connection with the University, and in the high standards of admission, the medical school is regarded as Gilman's second great contribution to the educational development of America.

In 1896 Gilman declined a call to be city superintendent of the schools of New York, although great pressure was brought to bear upon him by Seth Low, Mayor Strong, and others. Gilman had now nearly completed his sixty-fifth year, and this call to a new work was a tribute to the confidence which his organizing mind inspired in the educational leaders of the country. His seventieth birthday and his service for a quarter of a century as president of the University virtually coincided. He therefore decided to retire. In 1902, on an impressive public occasion, Woodrow Wilson, then professor at Princeton, presented to Gilman "an address of affection and congratulation," with the signatures of more than a thousand of the alumni and faculty of the University. "If it be true," said Wilson, "that Thomas Jefferson first laid the broad foundation for American universities in his plans for the University of Virginia, it is no less true that you were the first to create and organize in America a university in which the discovery and dissemination of new truth were conceded a rank superior to mere instruction, and in which the efficiency and value of research as an educational instrument were exemplified in the training of many investigators" (*Johns Hopkins University, Celebration of the Twenty-fifth Anniversary,* 1902, pp. 37–42).

As in youth, so in age, Andrew D. White impinged upon Gilman's career. While American ambassador to Germany, he first disclosed to Gilman in a letter from Berlin, May 20, 1901, the projected Carnegie Institution of Washington. In the first interview with Gilman and Dr. Billings, Carnegie asked them to prepare a plan embodying their ideas of what should be done, saying to Gilman, "You must be President." Into this novel project for the advancement of research and the encouragement of unusual talent, to which Carnegie had given a vast sum, Gilman threw himself with his old-time energy. He surveyed again the field of science in America and Europe. Finding, however, that he did not have a free hand in unifying the forces of the Institution, he resigned at the end of three years. "You have," wrote Mr. Carnegie, "given the Institution a splendid start" (Franklin, p. 4).

During the period of almost thirty years of Gilman's presidency of the Johns Hopkins University and the Carnegie Institution of Washington, he was engaged in a multitude of other activities. Owing to his eminence in geography, President Cleveland made him, in 1896, a member of the United States Commission to Investigate and Report upon the True Divisional Line between Venezuela and British Guiana (*Report and Accompanying Papers,* 9 vols., 1896–97). In 1879 he was made president of the American Social Science Association. In 1882 he was one of the original trustees of the John F. Slater Fund, succeeding, in 1893, Rutherford B. Hayes as its president—an office that he continued to hold until his death. In 1893 he was made a trustee of the Peabody Education Fund. He was president of the National Civil Service Reform League from 1901 to 1907. In the domain of organized charity his energies were enlisted from the start, thanks to the instinct he inherited from his father; hence his guidance was naturally sought by the Russell Sage Foundation, of which he became a trustee. He was likewise a member of the General Education Board.

It was in the place of his birth, Norwich, Conn., that Gilman died, on Oct. 13, 1908. Suddenly the end came, upon the day after his return from one of his happiest journeys in Europe. Of his personal appearance, a friend, a member of the "'91 Club," writes: "One remembers a man above middle height, with a well-developed frame, and broad, though slightly stooping shoulders; the head with extraordinary breadth of brow, square rather than dome-like, eyes keen and penetrating, everchanging, full of insight and sympathy. His walk was quick, and there was energy in all his movements; his eyes especially bright and full of hearty greeting" (Franklin, p. 422). Despite the sweep of his sympathies, his habit of personal reserve made one respect the zone that encompassed the inner core of his being. This quality appeared in his letters, as well as in his conversation. Dr. Welch points out, however, that "he rejoiced exceedingly in any good work or any distinction of any member of the staff, and half the pleasure of any such distinction was to share it with our president" (*Daniel Coit Gilman, First President of the Johns Hopkins University*, 1908, p. 33). His summers were usually spent at Mount Desert, Me., where, delighting in an inner circle of friends, he would engage upon some definite literary task, such as *The Life of James Dwight Dana* (1899), or his "Introduction" to De Tocqueville's *Democracy in America* (1898). The impression he made upon the group in Maine is summed up in the remark of one of his Northeast Harbor friends: "He touched so many things, and to everything he touched he gave life" (Franklin, p. 417). Among his other published works were: *A Historical Discourse, Delivered in Norwich, Conn., . . . at the Bicentennial Celebration* (1859); "Inaugural Address," in *Addresses at the Inauguration of Daniel C. Gilman as President of the Johns Hopkins University* (1876); *James Monroe* (1883); *University Problems in the United States* (1898); and *The Launching of a University* (1906). He was editor-in-chief of *The New International Encyclopædia* (1902).

Gilman was twice married: first, on Dec. 4, 1861, to Mary Ketcham of New York City, who died in 1869; and second, on June 13, 1877, to Elisabeth Dwight Woolsey, who survived him by fourteen months, dying in 1910. Of the first marriage there were two daughters. Two fitting memorials to him are the Gilman School of Baltimore, and the Gilman School of Northeast Harbor.

[Arthur Gilman, *The Gilman Family, Traced in the Line of the Hon. John Gilman, of Exeter, N. H.* (1869); *D. C. Gilman, First President of the Johns Hopkins Univ., 1876–1901* (1908); Fabian Franklin, *The Life of D. C. Gilman* (1910); *Record of the Class of 1852, Yale Coll.* (1878); *Fasciculi of the Memorial Symposium of the Class of Yale 1852 . . . D. C. Gilman* (1910); A. P. Stokes, *Memorials of Eminent Yale Men*, I (1914); R. H. Chittenden, *Hist. of the Sheffield Sci. School of Yale Univ.* (2 vols., 1928); *Autobiography of Andrew D. White* (2 vols., 1905); obituaries in Baltimore *Sun, N. Y. Times*, Oct. 14, 1908. Gilman's official correspondence is on file at the Johns Hopkins Univ., and his private letters are in the possession of Miss Elisabeth Gilman.]

S. C. M.

GILMAN, JOHN TAYLOR (Dec. 19, 1753–Aug. 31, 1828), financier, office holder, politician, and probably the ablest member of a family long prominent in New Hampshire affairs, was the eldest son of Nicholas and Ann (Taylor) Gilman of Exeter, N. H., and a descendant of Edward Gilman of Hingham, England, who came to Massachusetts in 1638. His father was a shipbuilder and merchant, and with the outbreak of the Revolution became state treasurer. After a common-school education, John was associated with his father in business and later served under him as clerk in the treasurer's office, thus gaining experience in accounting and financial matters which stood him in good stead in later years. In 1775 he had a short period of service in the militia, but his work during the war was largely civilian in character. He was a member of the legislature in 1779–81, served on the Committee of Safety, and in 1780 attended a conference of state delegates at Hartford to discuss the conduct of the war. He was several times elected to the Continental Congress, but his actual attendance was limited to a few months in 1782–83.

In June 1783 he succeeded his father, who had died earlier in the year, in the treasurership, and remained in that office for the next five years. From 1788 to 1790 and again for a few months in 1791 he was a member of the federal board of commissioners for the settlement of accounts between the United States and the individual states. He had in the meantime served in the New Hampshire convention for ratifying the Federal Constitution and had been an earnest and influential advocate of that action. Throughout his life he was a consistent Federalist, and, unlike his brothers Nicholas [*q.v.*] and Nathaniel, stood by the party when its fortunes declined. In 1791 he was reappointed treasurer, remaining in office until elected governor in 1794. He held the governorship from 1794 to 1805 and again from 1813 to 1816, his fourteen years constituting the New Hampshire record of service in that office.

For some years following his first election he encountered only scattering opposition, but in 1799–1800 the banking policy of the Governor and his Federalist supporters gave great offense, and opponents organized a strong, coherent party. There was but one chartered bank in the state, the New Hampshire Bank, of Portsmouth. The state held stock in this institution and Gilman was its president. When a group of political opponents led by John Langdon [*q.v.*] applied for a charter they were not only refused, but a law was passed intended to check banking operations by unincorporated organizations. This combination of politics and finance, no rarity in American party history, gave a great impetus to the growing Republican movement. The Governor was charged with lobbying in the interests of the New Hampshire Bank and also with permitting the use of the state deposits for speculative purposes (*Political Observatory,* Walpole, N. H., Feb. 9, 16, 1805). In any case his majorities dwindled steadily, and in 1805 he was decisively beaten by John Langdon. The legislature had fallen under Republican control the preceding year and for the first time since the establishment of the state government the governor made free use of the veto power on its measures. His service as governor was without striking incident and his messages dealt largely with matters of administrative routine.

He was less active in public affairs for the next eight years but served two terms in the legislature. Defeated for the governorship in 1812, a year later he began another period of three years in the executive office. The political campaigns of the war period were exceedingly bitter and majorities narrow. He was opposed to the war, but promptly met the federal requisitions for the defense of Portsmouth, and inasmuch as New Hampshire sent no official delegates to the Hartford Convention in 1814, due to the Republican control of the Council, he escaped some of the obloquy visited upon the governors of Massachusetts and Connecticut. Late in life, however, the implacable Isaac Hill [*q.v.*] assailed him with charges of disloyalty.

In 1816, just as the Dartmouth College dispute began to grow acute, he left office. He had received the degree of M.A. from the college in 1794 and LL.D. in 1799. In addition to his *ex officio* service while governor, he had been a trustee by election since 1807. While protesting against the removal of President John Wheelock [*q.v.*], he refused to support the University faction and maintained a neutral position. His decision not to resign as trustee of the College, however, was of great tactical value to those who supported the College interests, since he would undoubtedly have been replaced by an active opponent. He retired in 1819 when the victory of the college in the United States Supreme Court had been won. He was also a trustee and benefactor of Phillips Exeter Academy.

He is described as a man of fine appearance and dignified manners, "who wore the old-fashioned cocked hat of the revolution with an ease and dignity not unbecoming his high station" (William Plumer, Jr., *Life of William Plumer,* 1857, p. 387), but because of good living and lack of exercise, he became exceedingly corpulent in his last years. He was three times married: on Jan. 13, 1776, to Deborah, daughter of Nathaniel and Dorothy (Smith) Folsom, who died on Feb. 20, 1791; on July 5, 1792, to Mary, sister of his deceased wife and widow of Caleb G. Adams, who died Oct. 15, 1812; and on Dec. 29, 1814, to Mrs. Charlotte (Peabody) Hamilton.

[Sketch by Wm. Plumer, in *Early State Papers of N. H.*, vol. XXII (1893), pp. 830–35; Arthur Gilman, *The Gilman Family* (1869); E. S. Stackpole, *Hist. of N. H.* (1916), II, 287, 382–85; C. H. Bell, *Hist. of the Town of Exeter, N. H.* (1888); J. K. Lord, *A Hist. of Dartmouth Coll.* (1913); obituary in *N. H. Patriot and State Gazette* (Concord), Sept. 8, 1828.] W. A. R.

GILMAN, NICHOLAS (Aug. 3, 1755–May 2, 1814), politician, a son of Nicholas and Ann (Taylor) Gilman and a brother of John Taylor Gilman [*q.v.*], was born at Exeter, N. H. He attended the common schools of that town and on the outbreak of the Revolution entered the army. He was commissioned captain in the New Hampshire line, afterwards transferred to the staff of the adjutant-general, and served until the close of the war, when he returned to Exeter and soon became active in local politics. In 1786 he is reported to have turned his military experience to advantage by organizing and commanding a detachment of local militia during the paper money disturbances which threatened to develop into actual insurrection. He was a delegate to Congress, 1786–88, and together with John Langdon [*q.v.*] represented New Hampshire in the Constitutional Convention of 1787. They did not reach Philadelphia until July 21, when the most important work of the Convention had been completed. Gilman, while making no definite contribution to the Constitution, fully realized the importance of its adoption, and his correspondence shows great anxiety at the failure of New Hampshire to ratify promptly (*State Papers,* XXI, 835–61, *passim*). There was no chance, he declared, to formulate a constitution which could meet all possible objections, and should the one proposed be rejected the country would inevitably drift into chaos and bloodshed. He was an investor in Continental securities and his viewpoint was that of the commercial and financial leaders who gave such strong support to ratification. As a Federalist, Gilman served as representative in the new Congress, 1789–97, but neither during this period of service in the House nor in his later years in the Senate did he take part in debate, and almost his only appearance in the somewhat scantily reported proceedings of the era is in a brief plea for a post office in his native town (*Annals of Congress,* 2 Cong., 1 Sess., pp. 356–57). In the seven years intervening between his retirement from the House and his election to the Senate he was less active in public affairs, but served in the state Senate in 1804–05. His loyalty to the Federalist party had begun to waver, and in 1802 President Jefferson appointed him a commissioner in bankruptcy. In that year he was defeated in a contest for the United States senatorship, but two years later was elected as a Jeffersonian Republican and remained in the Senate until his death, which occurred in Philadelphia while he was on his way home from the capital. His long career in the public service indicates considerable political ability, but as far as can be judged he was never a popular character. The French minister who made some shrewd comments on the members of the Congress of 1788 described him as *"peu aimé par ses collègues"* (Farrand, *post,* III, 232). He never married and, according to William Plumer (*post,* p. 803), "for a New Hampshire man, was wealthy." It was his good fortune to be associated with great men and great events throughout his career, but his reputation was derived from that association rather than from his personal contributions to history.

[*Early State Papers of N. H.,* vols. XXI (1892) and XXII (1893), sketch by Wm. Plumer in vol. XXI, pp. 802–04; Arthur Gilman, *The Gilman Family* (1869); C. H. Bell, *Hist. of the Town of Exeter, N. H.* (1888); C. A. Beard, *An Economic Interpretation of the Constitution of the U. S.* (1913), pp. 93–95; Max Farrand, *The Records of the Federal Convention of 1787* (3 vols., 1911); obituaries in *Aurora and General Advertiser* (Phila.), May 4, 1814; *National Intelligencer* (Washington), May 6, 1814; *Constitutionalist* (Exeter, N. H.), May 10, 1814.] W. A. R.

GILMAN, SAMUEL (Feb. 16, 1791–Feb. 9, 1858), clergyman and author, was born in Gloucester, Mass., the son of Frederick Gilman, a native of Exeter, N. H., and of Abigail Hillier (Somes) of Gloucester. His father had been a prosperous merchant but suffered severe losses in 1798 from the capture of his vessels by the French and died a few years thereafter. When, shortly after her husband's death, Mrs. Gilman removed to Salem, she entered her young son in a little academy kept by the Rev. Stephen Peabody at Atkinson, N. H. His experiences there Gilman later vividly described in his "Reminiscences Pertaining to a New England Clergyman at the Close of the Last Century" (*Christian Examiner,* May 1847). Entering Harvard in the fall of 1807, he graduated in 1811, and thereafter was engaged for several months as clerk in a Boston bank; "a counter jumper by day," he wrote, "and a gentleman by night" (Foote, *post,* p. 11). In November 1811, he returned to Harvard as a resident graduate, and after a year of study there taught school in Boston until 1817, and then acted as tutor in mathematics at Harvard until 1819. His heart was set on the ministry, however, and after some experience preaching as a candidate, on Dec. 1, 1819, he was ordained minister of the Second Independent Church of Charleston, S. C., which, under Gilman's predecessor, the Rev. Anthony Forster, had just embraced Unitarianism.

Gilman's poetical ability had for some time been recognized. He had composed the class poem at his graduation, had published *Monody on the Victims and Sufferers by the Late Conflagration in the City of Richmond, Virginia* (1812), was engaged in translating Florian's *Galatea* in 1815, and in 1817 contributed unsigned translations in verse of satires from Boileau to the *North American Review.* He continued his literary work in connection with his parish duties and conscientiously did five or six hours of reading or writing every day. His writing included prose as well as poetry, and his reading, which comprised both English and German works, was extensive in the fields of theology, history, and literature. What he considered the best of his publications he collected in *Contributions to Literature* (1856), which included *Memoirs of a New England Village Choir* (1829), "Ode on the Death of Calhoun," said to have been sung at Calhoun's funeral, the reminiscences of Rev. Stephen Peabody and his wife, and other pieces in prose and poetry. Towards the end of his life Gilman was considered the leading literary figure in Charleston with the possible exception of his wife, Caroline (Howard) Gilman [*q.v.*], daughter of Samuel and Anna Howard, of Boston, whom he married in December 1819. Every two or three years they returned for a visit to New England, and it was on one of these trips that his most famous poem, "Fair Harvard," was written at a few hours' notice for the 200th anniversary of that college held on Sept. 8, 1836. As a preacher Gilman was kindly and persuasive but not particularly striking or original. Though singularly guileless and childlike, he was a man of strong character, a sturdy advocate of temperance, yet so genial and lovable that he was held in unusual affection by a host of friends both within and without his parish. For sixteen years he was chaplain of the Washington Light Infantry of Charleston. His death came unexpectedly at Kingston, Mass., while he was visiting his son-in-law, the Rev. C. J. Bowen, and he was buried in Charleston, S. C.

[Gilman letters and MSS. in Harvard Coll. Lib.; H. W. Foote, *An Address on Samuel Gilman* (1916), given at the dedication of the Gilman Memorial, Apr. 16, 1916, in the Unitarian Church, Charleston, S. C.; *News and Courier* (Charleston), Apr. 17, 1916; A. D. Andrews, *Sixteen Years Chaplain, Friend, and Counsellor of the Washington Light Infantry of Charleston, S. C.—The Rev. Samuel Gilman, D.D.* (1875); W. B. Sprague, *Annals Am. Pulpit*, vol. VIII (1865); Arthur Gilman, *The Gilman Family Traced in the Line of Hon. John Gilman, of Exeter, N. H.* (1869); *Southern Literary Messenger*, Apr. 1858; *Charleston Daily Courier*, Feb. 10, 11, 13, 18, 1858; *Boston Transcript*, Feb. 11, 1858; *N. Y. Tribune*, Feb. 13, 1858.] S. H. P.

GILMER, FRANCIS WALKER (Oct. 9, 1790–Feb. 25, 1826), lawyer, author, and educational diplomatist, the youngest of the ten children of Dr. George Gilmer and Lucy Walker, and the grandson of Dr. Thomas Walker [*q.v.*], was born at "Pen Park," Albemarle County, Va. Christened Francis Thornton, he called himself Francis Walker after the death of his uncle of that name in 1806 (Trent, *post*, p. 27). During his minority he was able to realize little on the property left him by his father at the latter's death in 1792, so his early education was almost entirely neglected. He learned French, however, from Martha Jefferson Randolph, with whose children he played, and devoured indiscriminately the books left by his father, including medical works in Latin. During 1808–09, he attended school at Georgetown, D. C., and in 1810 took a degree at William and Mary, where he was regarded as a prodigy in learning. The following year, he began to read law in Richmond under the tutelage of the eminent William Wirt, who had married his sister. After some procrastination, due partly to feebleness of health and partly to instability of purpose, he settled down, in 1815, to two years of practise in Winchester, Va. Here he exercised his genius for friendship in association with a very able group of lawyers, manifested his literary proclivities by publishing anonymously his sparkling *Sketches of American Orators* (1816), engaged in animated correspondence with many eminent men, including Joseph Corrèa de Serra, Jefferson, and Du Pont de Nemours, and made some translations from the French at the latter's instance. Moving to Richmond, he attained considerable success at the bar, and, as reporter for 1820–21, he published *Reports of Cases Decided in the Court of Appeals of Virginia* (1821).

In 1824, after having declined the offer of the professorship of law in the new University of Virginia, he undertook at Jefferson's request a unique mission to Great Britain to procure professors, books, and equipment for that institution. As a result of his negotiations, there came to Virginia five foreign scholars, among them Robley Dunglison [*q.v.*], who gave a certain international flavor to the young university and aroused some forebodings in patriotic minds. Though several of these men remained only a short time, their appointment was one of the most interesting experiments in the annals of higher education in America. The considerable measure of success which was achieved by his mission redounds greatly to the credit of the young plenipotentiary, who wrecked his already feeble health by his long and arduous journey. Returning to America, he aided Jefferson in further academic negotiations and finally accepted the professorship of law. His untimely death, Feb. 25, 1826, prevented his entering upon its duties.

Gilmer's story is one of peculiar poignancy. Regarded in his day as the rising star of Virginia, he was unable, chiefly because of infirmity of body and will, to realize upon his promise. He left a few bits of brilliant writing, chief among them his *Sketches, Essays and Translations* (1828), one notable contribution to the intellectual advancement of his commonwealth, and a memory of high character, incomparable conversational ability, and rare personal charm, which served to heighten the contrast with his brief and relatively futile career. He died unmarried and lies buried at "Pen Park," under a pathetic inscription of his own composition.

[Excellent accounts of Gilmer and his British mission are given by W. P. Trent, "Eng. Culture in Va.," *Johns Hopkins Univ. Studies in Hist. and Pol. Sci.*, 7 Ser., nos. V, VI (1889), and P. A. Bruce, *Hist. of the Univ. of Va.*, I (1920), 342–76. Many of the manuscript letters on which these studies are based are in the library of the Univ. of Va. Gilmer's own work, *Sketches, Essays and Translations* (1828), contains a brief biographical sketch, attributed to Wirt. *Original and Miscellaneous Essays, By a Virginian* (1829), a work which has been attributed to Gilmer, could not have been written by him. For genealogical material, see J. G. Speed, *The Gilmers in America* (1897), and G. R. Gilmer, *Sketches of Some of the First Settlers of Upper Ga.* (1855).] D. M.

GILMER, GEORGE ROCKINGHAM (Apr. 11, 1790–Nov. 16, 1859), governor of Georgia, congressman, author, was a conspicuous member of the settlement of Virginians established just after the Revolution on Broad River in upper Georgia. His great-grandfather, George Gilmer, a young Scotch physician, emigrated to Williamsburg, Va., and married there in 1732. His children became farmers in the Valley of Virginia. Thomas Meriwether Gilmer, a grandson, married Elizabeth Lewis in 1783, before his twenty-first year, and a few months later joined the movement to the Broad River. Here in the thrifty agricultural community he prospered. Of his nine children, George R. Gilmer was the fourth. Frail from birth, the boy during his early life was subject to the hardships of primitive farm life and irregular schooling. In 1804 he was sent to Dr. Moses Waddel's academy, where he spent four profitable years. Through the academy by his eighteenth year, he taught a neighborhood school for a while, visited his relatives in Virginia, and entered the law school of Stephen Upson in Lexington. A brief interlude to his law practise came in 1813, when he was sent as first lieutenant in command of an expedition against the Creek Indians. In 1818 he was elected to the legislature, and two years later to Congress. In 1822 he married his Virginia cousin, Eliza Frances Grattan, and in 1824 he was again elected to the state legislature. After two years of successful law practise in Lexington he was returned to Congress, 1827–29, served as governor, 1829–31, spent a third term in Congress, 1833–35, and was again governor, 1837–39. In all his public relations he revealed strong common sense, and proved himself conscientious and able. He was aligned with the Troup party in local politics, defended slavery, and took a strong stand for states' rights, especially in connection with the Cherokee Indian question. Having taken a keen interest in natural science, he left a valuable collection of minerals, an extensive library for the day, and a collection of miscellaneous curios. He was long a trustee of the University of Georgia, and left to it several bequests—notably the Gilmer Fund for the training of teachers. He amused the invalidism of his declining years by writing *Sketches of Some of the First Settlers of Upper Georgia* (1885), commonly called "Gilmer's Georgians," in which he revealed with ingenuous frankness the intimate facts and foibles of the associates of his earlier days. Though he had been prominent in state affairs, it was as the author of this book that he came to be best known. Its publication brought consternation to so many eminent families that, it is said, attempts were made to buy up and destroy the whole edition.

[Gilmer's *Sketches,* reprinted in 1926, contains a substantial autobiography. See also W. J. Northen, ed., *Men of Mark in Ga.,* II (1910), 26–29; U. B. Phillips, *Ga. and State Rights* (1902), published as vol. II of the annual reports of the Am. Hist. Asso. for the year 1901; L. L. Knight, *Georgia's Landmarks, Memorials and Legends* (2 vols., 1913–14); *Daily Chronicle and Sentinel* (Augusta, Ga.), Nov. 19, 1859.]

J. H. T. M.

GILMER, JOHN ADAMS (Nov. 4, 1805–May 14, 1868), member of Congress, was born in Guilford County, N. C. His father, Robert Gilmer, a Revolutionary soldier, a farmer and wheelwright, and his mother, Anne Forbes, were both of Scotch-Irish stock. His education began at an old-field school which he attended for a few months in winter; for the rest of the year he worked on the farm. At seventeen he began to teach and later he studied for two years at an academy in Greensboro. He then taught three years in South Carolina, studied law under Archibald D. Murphy, and, licensed in 1832, began practise. His rise was slow but he finally built up the largest practise in his part of the state. On Jan. 3, 1832, he was married to Juliana Paisley, the daughter of William P. Paisley, a well-known Presbyterian minister. Except for a brief service as county solicitor, he held no office but always he had an active interest in politics as a rather partisan Whig. In 1846 he began a membership of ten years in the state Senate. As a legislator he was the champion of state aid to railroads and an unvarying opponent of agitation of the slavery question. He acquired such a reputation and so much personal popularity that in 1856 the Know-Nothing party, into which North Carolina Union Whigs had generally gone, nominated him for governor. In a hopeless contest, he stumped the state against Gov. Thomas Bragg, gave an excellent account of himself and, though defeated, increased the popular confidence which was already his. He was a rather engaging political figure. Tall and strongly built, full of driving force and with every mark of a passionate temper, well-controlled, he was clearly a fighter; but he had a frank and cordial manner, a keen sense of humor, and a broad and ready wit. He could win attention anywhere, even from opponents.

In 1857 Gilmer was elected to Congress, where he rapidly gained influence, and in 1859, having been reëlected, he was, during the long deadlock over the speakership, for much of the time his party's candidate for the office. As one of the outstanding Southern Unionists he had won Northern support by his opposition to the admission of Kansas under the Lecompton constitution. He had also worked actively to prevent the injection of the slavery question into the discussion of the speakership. During this last term, he was chairman of the committee on elections. In the final session he was an unyielding opponent of secession and a strong advocate of compromise. At his own expense he sent into North Carolina in February more than one hundred thousand copies of anti-secession speeches and documents. He was a close friend of Seward who, with several others, urged Lincoln to appoint him to the cabinet. The President finally authorized Seward to offer him a place and invited Gilmer to visit him at Springfield (J. C. Nicolay and John Hay, *Abraham Lincoln: A History,* III, 1890, 283–85, 362–64). Gilmer, after an unsuccessful attempt to induce Lincoln to restate his position with respect to the South, declined to accept. But he urged upon Seward the policy of withdrawing all troops from Southern forts and of leaving the revenue laws unenforced, believing that this would save the Union (Frederic Bancroft, *Life of William H. Seward,* 1900, II, 120, 122, 545–49).

Gilmer was elected to the secession convention of North Carolina, and though he normally acted with the conservatives, he was committed to the war and there was no turning back. He was elected to the Confederate Congress in 1863 and served from May 2, 1864, until the downfall of the Confederacy. He was chairman of the committee on elections, and a member of the ways and means and of numerous special committees. After the war, he supported Johnson's policies and was a delegate to the National Union Convention of 1866.

[John Livingston, *Portraits of Eminent Americans,* I (1853), 343–56; *Journals of the Senate and House of Commons . . . of N. C.,* 1847–55; *Jour. of the Convention of the People of N. C. . . . 1861* (1862); *Jour. of the Cong. of the Confed. States of America,* vol. VII (1905); J. H. Wheeler, *Reminiscences and Memoirs of N. C. and Eminent N. C. Families* (1884), pp. 192–93.] J. G. deR. H.

GILMER, THOMAS WALKER (Apr. 6, 1802–Feb. 28, 1844), statesman, was born at "Gilmerton," Albemarle County, Va., to George—"the only male member of Dr. Gilmer's family not distinguished for talents"—and Elizabeth (Hudson) Gilmer. He was passably educated by tutors, studied law, settled in Charlottesville, Va., and soon became known for his energy, ambition, legal talent, and rectitude. At twenty-four he married Anne Baker, of Shepherdstown, Va. In 1829 he was elected to the Virginia legislature, where he successfully opposed the rechartering of the state banks and did such valuable work on committees that Gov. Floyd appointed him commissioner to prosecute Virginia's Revolutionary claims upon the federal government. He supported Jackson in 1828, editing the *Virginia Advocate* in his interest so brilliantly as to elicit the cordial approval of John Randolph, but condemned the President's proclamation against South Carolina and asserted the right of secession as a last resort. In 1833 he was reëlected as an exponent of state's rights and strict construction. When Jackson removed the deposits, Gilmer again bitterly assailed the administration and joined with other influential Democrats in forming the Whig party. Defeated for the legislature in 1834 on account of his opposition to Jackson, he was reëlected in 1835 and again in 1838 and 1839, serving as speaker of the House of Delegates during his last two terms and winning recognition, through his industry and eloquence, as "the most prominently useful member of the house" (Gilmer, *post,* p. 26).

Gilmer was elected governor of Virginia, Feb. 14, 1840, on a Whig and conservative platform, and entered actively upon his duties. His administration was marked by his controversy with Gov. Seward of New York. When Seward a second time refused the demand of the Virginia Assembly for the extradition of three men charged with slave-stealing in Virginia, the Assembly passed a law imposing restrictions on commerce between the two states. Three days later Seward demanded that Virginia surrender a felon wanted in New York, whereupon Gilmer replied that the fugitive would be surrendered when Virginia's criminals were returned for trial. The Virginia legislature declining to sustain Gilmer's stand, in March 1841 he drew up an able vindication of himself and resigned the chair. He was immediately elected to Congress by the Whigs, taking his seat on May 31, 1841. His assiduity in ferreting out abuses, in demanding the strictest governmental economy, and in recommending reforms in the civil service won him the sobriquet of Retrenchment Gilmer. From the first he resisted Clay-dictation and the chartering of a national bank, became one of that "corporal's guard" which stanchly supported President Tyler, and ultimately came to be considered the spokesman of the administration in the House. His activity in advocating the annexation of Texas led Thomas H. Benton to condemn his famous "Texas letter" unjustly as part of a scheme to win Calhoun the presidency (*Thirty Years' View,* II, 1856, 581–87), but Gilmer simply found in the Tyler program an agency to carry through a project which he had cherished since visiting Texas in 1837. On Feb. 15, 1844, he was appointed secretary of the navy. Within two weeks he was killed by the explosion of the gun on board the steamer *Princeton.* "What his indomitable energy would have done," wrote his colleague, Gov. Gilmer of Georgia—a none too amiable critic of his kinsfolk—"strengthened and directed as it was by purity of purpose and clear, strong, vigorous intellect, none can say. Judging by what he did, he would, if he had lived, have been the first man of his country as he was of his name" (*post*, pp. 26–27). The tributes of John Randolph, John Tyler, Henry A. Wise, and others who knew him well, bear out this estimate.

[J. G. Speed, *The Gilmers in America* (1897); L. G. Tyler, *Letters and Times of the Tylers*, vol. II (1885); John Tyler, "The Dead of the Cabinet," in *Southern Lit. Messenger*, Aug. 1856; G. R. Gilmer, *Sketches of Some of the First Settlers of Upper Ga.* (1855); M. V. Smith, *Virginia, 1492–1892. . . . With a Hist. of the Executives of the Colony and of the Commonwealth* (1893); H. A. Wise, *Seven Decades of the Union* (1872); *Tyler's Quart. Hist. and Geneal. Mag.*, Apr., July, Oct. 1924, Apr. 1925; obituaries and accounts of the *Princeton* disaster in leading newspapers. There is an excellent portrait of Gilmer in the Virginia State Library at Richmond.]

A. C. G., Jr.

GILMOR, HARRY (Jan. 24, 1838–Mar. 4, 1883), Confederate soldier, was born near Baltimore, Md., the son of Robert and Ellen (Ward) Gilmor. His father was the grandson of Robert Gilmor, who came from Scotland to the Eastern Shore of Maryland in 1767, removed to Baltimore in 1779, and built up an extensive shipping business. His mother was a daughter of William H. Ward, of Wilmington, Del., a descendant of William Ward, who was established in Cecil County, Md., prior to 1683. Young Gilmor was privately educated, spent some time in farming in Wisconsin and Nebraska, and then returned to assist in farming his father's place. He also served in the local militia. His family, strong secessionists, were under surveillance in the early days of the Civil War, and he himself was arrested and detained for two weeks, on suspicion which he justified soon after his release. Determining to join the Confederate army, he managed to cross the upper Potomac, and enlisted under Ashby. In March 1862 he was commissioned captain of Company F, 12th Virginia Cavalry. From then until near the end of the war he served in the Shenandoah Valley and in Maryland, with an occasional incursion into Pennsylvania, and proved himself one of the most enterprising and daring of Confederate raiders. Though engaged in some of the greater battles, as a member of a considerable force, he usually operated with a small number of men, carrying on partisan war after the manner of Marion and Sumter. Captured while on a secret visit to his family near Baltimore, in September 1862, he was naturally held as a spy, but was eventually offered for exchange as an ordinary prisoner of war, and in February 1863 returned to duty with his company. He was soon after commissioned major of a newly organized battalion, later known as the 2nd Maryland. In one of his most famous raids, in February 1864, he cut the Baltimore & Ohio Railroad near Harper's Ferry, and was subsequently tried by court martial as a result of the wholesale robberies committed upon passengers by his men. He was acquitted, as having given no sanction to theft, and as having taken reasonable measures to prevent it.

When Early made his dash on Washington, in July 1864, Gilmor covered the army by raiding to the east, going even beyond Baltimore and destroying the railroad bridge over the Gunpowder River by running a burning train upon it. Here he captured Gen. Franklin, who was returning to the North, disabled by a wound received in Louisiana, but the prisoner made his escape the same night. It was Gilmor who burned the town of Chambersburg, Pa., soon after, most reluctantly obeying imperative orders from his superiors. In a cavalry skirmish a little later he received a severe wound which indirectly caused his death nearly twenty years after. He was back in active service in the autumn, and served until his capture in February 1865, when Gen. Sheridan wrote: "He is an energetic, shrewd, and unscrupulous scoundrel and a dangerous man. He must be closely watched, or he will escape" (*Official Records, Army*, XLVI, pt. 2, p. 442), an unfair estimate of his character, but good evidence of the annoyance he caused the Union commander. In his official report, Sheridan refers to him as "Harry Gilmor, who appeared to be the last link between Maryland and the Confederacy, and whose person I desired in order that this link might be severed" (*Ibid.*, XLIII, pt. 1, p. 56). After the war Gilmor engaged in business in Baltimore, and was police commissioner of that city from 1874 to 1879. His wife was Mentoria Nixon Strong, daughter of Jasper Strong, an officer of the army from 1819 to 1823, and afterwards a planter in Florida.

[*Four Years in the Saddle* (1866) is Gilmor's own account of his experiences in the war. See also *Official Records (Army)*, 1 ser. XXXIII, XXXVII (pt. 1), XLIII (pt. 1), XLVI (pts. 1, 2); and the *Sun* (Baltimore), Mar. 1, 5, 1883.]

T. M. S.

GILMORE, JAMES ROBERTS (Sept. 10, 1822–Nov. 16, 1903), writer, unofficial emissary of President Lincoln, the son of Turner Fales and Mary A. Gilmore, was born in Boston, Mass. Although destined for college, he deserted his preparations for it and entered business, to become at twenty-five the head of a new firm which conducted a shipping and cotton business in New

York City. Apparently his career was very successful, for in 1857 he retired from business with a competency. The Civil War found him relatively unemployed and in possession of a knowledge of Southern conditions which he had derived from his frequent business trips to that region. His facile command of language completed the background of his literary qualifications. His first venture was the *Continental Monthly,* a periodical devoted to anti-slavery propaganda. Although its publication gave Gilmore a great deal of rather flatulent self-satisfaction, it was suspended after Lincoln issued the Emancipation Proclamation. Meanwhile his flood of books had begun. The first, *Among the Pines* (1862), professed to be a true picture of life in the Southern states. It was followed rapidly by six other rather colorless volumes, the last of which, *On the Border,* appeared in 1867. During these years also, Gilmore contributed random articles to the *New York Tribune.*

It was logical that Greeley and Gilmore should cherish the same implacable distrust of Lincoln. In 1863 Gilmore was therefore an understandable choice as an emissary to Gen. Rosecrans to determine whether he was a candidate whom the *Tribune* might support for the presidential nomination in the following year. It was on this journey that Gilmore met James F. Jaquess [*q.v.*], the Methodist parson-colonel who wanted to go to Richmond and convert Jefferson Davis to peace. Almost against his will, Gilmore became associated with this zealous project. At Rosecrans's request, he went to Washington, outlined Jaquess's hopes to Lincoln, and aided the Colonel in obtaining a furlough for his purpose. This visit was not without other result, for it converted Gilmore into an admirer of the President.

When the Jaquess mission failed, Gilmore was too busy writing and lecturing to devote his attention immediately to remedies, but in April 1864 he interviewed Lincoln, and according to his own stories, he persuaded the President to permit a second attempt. Although neither Jaquess nor Gilmore could carry credentials as representatives, Lincoln drew up a statement of peace terms to guide their conversation. These included the perpetual abolition of slavery and the immediate recognition of the supremacy of the Union. In return for this surrender, Lincoln proposed a compensation to the slaveholders of $500,000,000, the restoration of the states to the Union with all their rights, and an amnesty to those engaged in the rebellion. Finally in the first part of July, Gilmore and Jaquess were passed through the lines and transported to Richmond. Once there it was difficult to secure an interview with Jefferson Davis because they were wholly unaccredited, but they finally persuaded or deceived the Confederate President into a willingness to see them, and on the evening of July 17 the conference took place in the old Customhouse.

Gilmore's later narratives of the prelude to this interview conceal by flippancy and the dimness of recollection the motive which led to the dispatch of the mission. Probably both Lincoln and he hoped that it would produce some statement of Confederate war aims so extreme that it could be used in the North to stem the growing clamor of the peace partisans. If such were their hopes, they were not disappointed. Davis vigorously denied that slavery was the barrier to a reconciliation between the nations, insisting rather that the point at issue was the right to self-government. When the interview was over, Gilmore was apprehensive that they would not be allowed to return, but on July 21, he made his report to President Lincoln in safety. It now remained to get the news before the public. Under the pseudonym "Edmund Kirke," Gilmore published a card on July 22, in the *Boston Transcript,* containing the high lights of Davis's ultimatum, and followed it with a longer account in the September and December issues of the *Atlantic Monthly.* With Jaquess, he visited some northern governors, and the two made several speeches to secure further publicity. It is not unlikely that the results of the mission had some minor influence upon the presidential campaign of 1864.

After the war, Gilmore married Laura Edmonds, the daughter of Judge John W. Edmonds of New York. His fortune was so diminished that he reëntered business in 1873, but in spite of this employment, he kept himself in practise with incidental writing. In 1880 he published *The Life of James A. Garfield,* a campaign biography which had an extensive sale, and in 1881, with Lyman Abbott, he edited *The Gospel History.* In 1883 he was able again to retire and devote his time solely to writing and lecturing. His chief interest in both fields was history diluted for popular consumption. Although he gave a course of lectures at the Lowell Institute, most of his addresses seem to have been delivered to societies interested in genealogy or local history. Of his later literary productions, *John Sevier as a Commonwealth-Builder* (1887) is typical. He died at Glens Falls, N. Y.

[J. R. Gilmore, *Personal Recollections of Abraham Lincoln and the Civil War* (1808), and "A Suppressed Chapter of Hist.," *Atlantic Monthly,* Apr. 1887; *Official Records (Army),* 1 ser. XL (pt. 3); *Official Records (Navy),* 2 ser. III; E. C. Kirkland, *The Peacemakers of 1864* (1927); *Literary World,* Nov. 14, 1885; *Boston Transcript, Albany Evening Jour.,* Nov.

17, 1903; *Outlook*, Nov. 28, 1903. The Glens Falls *Times*, Nov. 7, 1903, states that Gilmore was survived by his second wife. Possibly his first wife was Amelia Harris, whose marriage to a James R. Gilmore was noted in the *Boston Transcript*, Aug. 1, 1851.]

E. C. K.

GILMORE, JOSEPH ALBREE (June 10, 1811–Apr. 17, 1867), governor of New Hampshire, business man, was born at Weston, Vt., the son of Asa D. and Lucy (Dodge) Gilmore. The death of his father deprived him of opportunity for more than a common-school education. He became a clerk in Boston, afterward entering business for himself, and in 1842 he moved to Concord, N. H., where he established a wholesale grocery. He had married Ann Page Whipple of Dunbarton, N. H., on July 10, 1832. In 1848 he became deeply interested in railroad matters and was appointed construction agent of the Concord & Claremont Railroad. He was among the successful pioneer railroad men of New England and in 1856 became superintendent of the Concord Railroad, which, after the consolidation of various local lines, had a total of 175 miles—more impressive at that time than in the later era of giant interstate systems. He held his position with the Concord Railroad until failing health obliged him to resign Aug. 11, 1866. In his personal business affairs he was inclined toward speculative ventures and eventually met severe financial losses.

Gilmore was a member of the Whig party but did not hold public office until after that organization had disintegrated. In 1858 and 1859 he was elected to the New Hampshire Senate as a Republican and served as president during his second term. After the outbreak of the Civil War he rendered valuable service and support to Gov. Goodwin and Gov. Berry. In 1863 he received the nomination for the governorship, in spite of considerable opposition due to his railroad connections, and after a campaign so close that final choice was made by the legislature, he was elected. He stated in his message of 1864, following a decisive reëlection by popular vote, that when he first took office he was "but a poor politician and no orator" and that he had a popular minority of more than five thousand to remind him that he had yet to gain the confidence of his fellow citizens.

This confidence he proceeded to win by a vigorous and successful attack on the administrative problems created by the war, a policy which caused serious clashes with the legislature but which earned him an honorable place among the war governors. His experience had been in business rather than in politics and as chief executive he displayed both the merits and defects of his training. His message to the legislature summoned in special session, August 1864, to meet war emergencies, is characteristic. Bluntly criticizing that body for numerous shortcomings, he denounced the military bill of the preceding session as "crude, incomprehensible, and unsatisfactory," and the finance bill as "utterly inadequate." He concluded with the vigorous exhortation: "Throw aside partizan feeling and do your utmost to repair the immense injury which your hasty and injudicious legislation has inflicted on the people of this state." Since he had the support of public opinion and his proposals were, for the most part, sound and feasible, the legislature provided him with most of the authority necessary to carry out his designs. When his administration came to an end in 1865, his health had already begun to fail, and he was obliged to relinquish further public activity when he retired from office. His contemporaries describe him as vigorous, self-confident, and determined, qualities which were indispensable for the conduct of war-time office.

[F. S. Osgood, "Robt. and Jas. Gilmore . . and their Descendants" (1925), MS. in the Lib. of Cong.; Otis F. R. Waite, *N. H. in the Great Rebellion* (1870); E. S. Stackpole, *Hist. of N. H.* (4 vols., 1916); Hobart Pillsbury, *N. H.: A Hist.* (1927), vol. II; *Appletons' Ann. Cyc.* (1867); the *N. H. Statesman* (Concord), Apr. 19, 1867; Gilmore papers, N. H. Hist. Soc.]

W. A. R.

GILMORE, JOSEPH HENRY (Apr. 29, 1834–July 23, 1918), Baptist minister, hymnwriter, university professor, son of Joseph Albree [*q.v.*] and Ann (Whipple) Gilmore, was born in Boston, Mass., and died in Rochester, N. Y. His father, a native of Vermont, became at length a merchant in Boston, and, in New Hampshire, a railway promoter, a state senator, and governor (1863–65). Joseph Henry was graduated from Phillips Andover Academy in 1854, from Brown University in 1858, and from the Newton Theological Institution in 1861. On May 10, 1861, he married Mary Josephine Parkhurst of Newton Center. The next year, while preaching for a short time in Philadelphia, he wrote almost impromptu, somewhat as a relief from his depression over the Civil War, the hymn, "He Leadeth Me." From 1862 to 1864 he was minister in Fisherville, later called Penacook, N. H. There on Thanksgiving Day 1863 he preached the sermon *Hath God Forgotten to be Gracious?* (1864), in which he declared that he had no more pity for the war-victims of the South than for any "lost soul that might have salvation for the asking." During 1864–65 he became private secretary to his father and at the same time editor of the Concord *Daily Monitor.* His wife having died, he on Sept. 21, 1865, married Lucy Ann Brown of Fisherville. From 1865 to 1867 he preached in Rochester, from 1867 to 1868 he taught Hebrew in the Rochester Theological Seminary, and from 1868 to 1908, when he was retired, he was professor of rhetoric, logic, and English in the University of Rochester. He published many text-books, usually scarcely more than pamphlets setting forth in skeleton form the content of courses given by him in the university or elsewhere. Perhaps the most notable of his books, besides *Outlines of Logic* (1876), *The Outlines of Rhetoric* (1877), *Outline Studies in English and American Literature* (1891), and *Outlines of English and American Literature* (1905), were *The Art of Expression* (1875), *A Syllabus of English and American Literature* (1876), *English Language and Its Early Literature* (1878), *English Literature* (1880), as No. 23 of the Chautauqua text-books, and *Familiar Chats about Books and Reading* (1892). He published also *He Leadeth Me and Other Religious Poems* (1877), *Wedlock* (1881), an anthology of poems about marriage, and a series of books containing selections suitable for declamation, *The Primary School Speaker* (1881), *Intermediate Speaker* (1882), and *The Academic Speaker* (1883). From 1870 to 1878 he was an editorial writer for the *Examiner*, New York. He was at times an acting-executive of the university, and his influence in that position, as well as in his position as head of one of the more important departments, was exerted effectively toward establishing extension courses, and opening larger educational opportunities to women.

[G. H. Moses, *N. H. Men* (1893); *Hist. Cat. of Brown Univ. 1764–1904* (1905); *Rochester Theological Seminary Gen. Cat. 1850 to 1910* (1910); F. S. Osgood, "Robt. and Jas. Gilmore . . . and their Descendants" (1925), MS. in Lib. of Cong.; J. L. Rosenberger, *Rochester, the Making of a Univ.* (1927); *Who's Who in America, 1918–19*; *Rochester Democrat and Chronicle*, July 24, 1918; the *Watchman-Examiner*, Aug. 1, 1918.]
J. D. W.

GILMORE, PATRICK SARSFIELD (Dec. 25, 1829–Sept. 24, 1892), bandmaster, was born in a hamlet near Dublin, Ireland. He was intended for the priesthood, but showing no inclination for it, he was put to work as a boy in a shop in Athlone. He was far more interested in the regimental band of this garrison town, however, whose conductor eventually put him through a course of harmony and counterpoint, than in his work. When the Irish regiment in Athlone was transferred to Canada, Gilmore, by that time an excellent cornetist, accompanied it. Before he was twenty-one he left Canada to establish himself as a military band leader in Salem, Mass., and later he established his reputation in Boston with his famous "Gilmore's Band," which he took on extensive tours through the United States. In 1861 he accompanied the 24th Massachusetts Regiment to the field as its bandmaster, and in 1863 was put in charge of all the army bands in the Department of Louisiana. In New Orleans, in 1864, he originated the "monster band concert," an aberration of musical good taste peculiar to the period. Held to celebrate the inauguration of Gov. Hahn, it united a chorus of five thousand adults and children, and an orchestra of five hundred pieces supported by drummers, trumpeters, and artillery. At the "National Peace Jubilee" (1869), and the "World Peace Jubilee" (1872), both in Boston, he further indorsed the idea that "if eighty musicians make good music, eight hundred must make music ten times as good" (L. C. Elson, *The National Music of America*, 1900, p. 310). At the first of these monstrous musical festivals Gilmore conducted an orchestra of one thousand performers, plus a chorus of ten thousand, and "a bouquet of artists, forty strong." In the second, orchestra and chorus were doubled, and their din was increased by a battery of cannon, electrically fired, and half a dozen church bells, with members of the Boston Fire Department in full uniform beating out the "Anvil Chorus" on fifty anvils. In spite of their vulgarity these Gilmore monster jubilees, as Elson says, "planted the seeds of good music in hundreds of villages where they had not existed before" (*Ibid.*, p. 311).

After his second Jubilee, Gilmore left Boston for New York, and though he used bells, cannon, and anvils at his Chicago Jubilee of 1873, he later declared that he was through with "tornado choruses." In New York he was for a number of years bandmaster of the 22nd Regiment, New York National Guard, making tours with his men in the United States, Canada, and Europe. Though he always had a taste for the sensational in music, he was a splendid drillmaster, and his performances never lacked brilliancy. When Manhattan Beach was first opened in the eighties, it was Gilmore who, with young Sousa, Victor Herbert, and Anton Seidl, drew the multitudes thither. His personality was not the least factor in his success. As a composer he left military band numbers, dance-pieces, and songs, which were popular in their day, and from New Orleans he brought the patriotic air, "When Johnny comes marching home again," the words of which he wrote under the *nom de plume* of Louis Lambert. While he was in St. Louis, conducting his band at the Exposition of 1892, he died suddenly, leaving his wife and one daughter.

[L. C. Elson, *The Hist. of Am. Music* (1904); G. P. Upton, *Musical Memories* (1908); P. S. Gilmore, *Hist. of the Nat. Peace Jubilee and Great Musical Festival* (1877); the *Metronome*, Sept., Oct. 1907, and Anniversary Supp., Feb. 1910; *St. Louis Globe-Democrat*, *N. Y. Herald*, Sept. 25, 1892.] F. H. M.

GILMOUR, RICHARD (Sept. 28, 1824–Apr. 13, 1891), Roman Catholic prelate, was born in Glasgow, Scotland, of covenanting parents, John and Marian (Callender) Gilmour, who emigrated to Pictou, Nova Scotia, in 1829 but soon settled as farmers near Cumbola, Schuylkill County, Pa. While attending the village school, Richard, influenced by Irish associates, turned toward Catholicism. About 1840 he was studying Latin and Greek under Father Patrick Rafferty of Fairmount and two years later he entered the Catholic Church with the approval of his mother, who afterwards followed in his foot-steps as finally did also his father. In 1843, Gilmour entered the seminary at Pittsburgh from which in 1846 he transferred to Mount St. Mary's College, Emmitsburg, Md. Here in 1848 he received the master's degree, and on completion of his theological studies was ordained, Aug. 30, 1852, by Bishop Purcell, who assigned him to a church at Portsmouth, Ohio, from which he attended a number of missions. In 1857, he was promoted to the rectorship of St. Patrick's Church, Cincinnati, where he built a school and became aggressively interested in parochial education. Called to a professorship in Mount St. Mary's of the West, Cincinnati (1868), he had taught for only a year when he was assigned to St. Joseph's Church, Dayton. Here by prudent management he quelled racial disorders and blotted out a deficit. This facility for compromising differences between Irish, German, and French peoples and their pastors led the bishops of the Cincinnati province to nominate him to the See of Cleveland where racial strife had tormented Amadeus Rappe into resignation. Gilmour was named bishop by Rome, Feb. 15, 1872, and was consecrated by Archbishop Purcell on Apr. 14.

An aggressive man with the zeal of a convert, an able apologist, a virile writer, and a zealous upholder of episcopal prerogatives, Gilmour ruled his diocese with a strong hand and aroused some sectarian hostility in a locality which was still Puritan in tone. His pastorals urging united Catholic action, construction of schools, and compulsory parochial school attendance embittered Edwin Cowles of the *Cleveland Leader,* whose prejudice was more highly colored by the conversion of his daughter. The Bishop answered attacks in kind in the *Cleveland Press* or in his own organ, the *Catholic Universe,* founded in 1874, which under the editorship of Manly Tello developed into a leading Catholic weekly paper. With the aid of the Catholic Central Association (1875–93), Gilmour won religious freedom for prisoners in penal institutions, 1875, and, by appealing a case through various courts until the state supreme court reaffirmed a previous satisfactory decision, the exemption of Catholic school properties from local taxation (1883; *Gilmour* vs. *Pelton,* 5 *Ohio Decision Reprints,* 447). In a sense, he freed Catholic citizens of an inferiority complex and gave them leadership before lay leaders were developed. His interest in Catholic education was evidenced by the compilation of a *Bible History* (1869), and a series of readers, a primer, and a spelling-book (1874–89), which went through a number of editions. He established about forty parochial schools, fostered a number of academies under teaching sisterhoods, and aided the Jesuits in founding St. Ignatius College in Cleveland. Through immigration, especially Slavic, the population of the diocese grew rapidly and Gilmour's era saw an increase in churches and in priests as well as a relative increase in the number of charitable institutions.

His rule was not without its share of internal difficulties. Somewhat suspicious of the religious, he insisted that the property of charitable institutions supported by the diocese be held in episcopal hands, which insistence resulted in appeals by the religious to Rome. A rigid disciplinarian, he had some trouble with pastors who were compelled to build schools; and, at least in the case of the removal of P. F. Quigley of Toledo, he found himself reversed by Rome. While his attitude as expressed in an address on "The Irish Question" (February 1882) satisfied conservatives, he was unnecessarily bitter in condemnation of the local units of the Irish Land League and unduly suspicious of harmless Irish societies and their organ, the *Celtic Index.* In his hostility to the *Catholic Knight,* organ of the Knights of St. John, he actually made mere subscription a reserved offense, and thus finally forced Joseph J. Greeves to sell this paper as well as his *Catholic Standard* of Toledo (1893). A prominent figure in the Third Plenary Council of Baltimore (Nov. 9–Dec. 7, 1884), Gilmour insisted on being accredited as a representative of the hierarchy as a check upon Bishops Moore and Dwenger [*qq.v.*], whom he suspected of being too weak to obtain papal approval of the Council's *Acta et Decreta.* When Rome did approve of this legislation, Gilmour claimed considerable credit for defending the independence of the American hierarchy. Never strong of body, he succumbed in St. Augustine, Fla., while on a health-seeking visit, and was buried in Cleveland with a eulogy by Bishop McQuaid [*q.v.*], with whose views he had been in harmony.

[*Cath. Encyc.*, IV (1908), 56; J. G. Shea, *The Hierarchy of the Cath. Church in the U. S.* (1886); F. J. Zwierlein, *The Life and Letters of Bishop McQuaid* (3 vols., 1925–27); G. F. Houck and M. W. Carr, *A Hist. of Catholicity in Northern Ohio and in the Diocese of Cleveland* (2 vols., 1903); E. M. Avery, *A Hist. of Cleveland and its Environs* (3 vols., 1918); obituary in *Cleveland World*, Apr. 14, 1891.] R. J. P.

GILPIN, CHARLES SIDNEY (Nov. 20, 1878–May 6, 1930), negro actor, was born in Richmond, Va., the youngest of the fourteen children of Peter and Caroline (White) Gilpin. His father was a laborer in a steel-rolling-mill, and his mother was a trained nurse in the Richmond City Hospital. Until he was twelve, Gilpin attended the St. Francis School for Catholic colored children, then went into the office of the *Richmond Planet* as printer's devil. Although he appeared on the stage as early as October 1890, for many years he was unable to make a living as an actor and supported himself by printing, with only intermittent participation as a song and dance man in restaurants, in variety theatres, and in fairs. From time to time he also appeared in vaudeville as a minstrel. He did not definitely become an actor until 1903, when he signed with the Canadian Jubilee Singers of Hamilton, Ontario. From that time he played continually. In 1905 and 1906 he was with Williams and Walker's *Abyssinia* Company and Gus Hill's Smart Set, and in 1907 became a member of the Pekin Stock Company of Chicago, which offered him his first opportunity as a dramatic actor. From 1911 to 1913 he toured again, this time with the Pan-American Octette, then joined the *Old Man's Boy* Company, in which he played until the latter part of 1914, when he went into vaudeville. In 1916 he settled in New York and became manager of the Lafayette Theatre Company in Harlem, the first negro dramatic stock company in the city of New York.

Gilpin's first appearance in a Broadway cast was as William Custis, the negro clergyman, in the American production of John Drinkwater's *Abraham Lincoln,* which opened Dec. 15, 1919. This was followed by his selection for the rôle of Brutus Jones in Eugene O'Neill's *Emperor Jones,* a part for which he was obliged to compete with white actors. The play opened at the Provincetown Playhouse on MacDougal Street Nov. 1, 1920, was taken up-town to the Princess Theatre, Jan. 29, 1921, and ran almost continually until 1924, with many subsequent revivals. It offered Gilpin the greatest emotional part of his life. In the character of an ex-convict ruler, pursued through the jungle by his island tribe, he carried six of the eight scenes entirely alone, his fright increasing with the crescendo of the approaching tom-tom. He played with all the eloquence and power of his race, and "provided one of the major theatrical sensations of the season" (Burns Mantle, *The Best Plays of 1920–21,* 1921, p. 299). He was one of ten to receive Drama League awards on Mar. 6, 1921, for the greatest contributions to the theatre during the preceding year, and in the same year was given a Spingarn medal by the National Association for the Advancement of Colored People.

In 1926 Gilpin lost his voice, and was forced to retire from the stage, reappearing only occasionally for revivals of *Emperor Jones.* In June 1929, while playing in Woodstock, he suffered a breakdown. He died the following year in Eldridge Park, a suburb of Trenton, N. J., and was quietly buried in Lambertville. Friends in New York, hearing of his death, conducted a second funeral on a lavish scale, June 1, 1930, and had him buried with full honors in Woodlawn Cemetery. He had married Florence Howard in February 1897.

[J. J. Boris, *Who's Who in Colored America,* 1928–29; *Who's Who in America,* 1928–29; *Theatre Mag.*, Jan. 1921; *Century Mag.*, May 1921; *Am. Mag.*, June 1921; *N. Y. Times,* Nov. 7, 1920, May 7, June 2, 1930. Controversy over Drama League award in *N. Y. Times,* Feb. 17, 18, 19, 21, 22, and Mar. 7, 1921.] C. P. M.

GILPIN, EDWARD WOODWARD (July 13, 1803–Apr. 29, 1876), jurist, was born at Wilmington, Del., where his father, William Gilpin, who had married Ann Dunwoody, was engaged in business. He was of English ancestry, tracing his descent from Joseph Gilpin, who emigrated to America about 1695 and settled at New Castle, Del. When Edward was still in his infancy his father failed in business, the home was broken up, and he spent his youth with his paternal grandfather, who operated a paper-mill on the Brandywine River. He attended the local schools; then, at seventeen, being compelled to earn his own living, he obtained employment as clerk in a store at Wilmington. In 1821 he rejoined his father in Philadelphia and was apprenticed to a tanner and currier. A year later he returned to Wilmington, where, after continuing his trade for a short time, he became a clerk in his brother's store. These avocations were extremely distasteful to him, and though he continued to work in the store, he commenced to read law, subsequently entering the office of Senator John Wales, as a student. He was admitted to the bar, Oct. 3, 1827, and commenced practise in Wilmington. His early experiences had given him a practical acquaintance with the business world which was of great assistance to him, and he soon obtained a good connection. No details of his professional progress are available, but in the course of a few years he acquired a leading position at the Wilmington bar, and his ability was recognized throughout the state. He was appointed attorney-general of Delaware, Feb. 12, 1840, by Gov. Comegys, and within two months of assuming office was afforded a striking opportunity of exhibiting a rigid adherence to principle regardless of race and color. He caused a prominent citizen to be indicted on a charge of kidnapping a negro, and procured a court ruling that the evidence of the latter was admissible, though there were white persons present participating in the crime (*The State* vs. *James Whitaker,* 3 *Harrington,* 549). His action created a sensation since it ran counter to all tradition and precedent, but the decision held good. On the expiration of his term in 1845, he was reappointed by Gov. Stockton, and retained office till 1850, when he retired and resumed private practise at Wilmington.

In 1857 Gov. Causey, with the approval of the bar and the public, appointed Gilpin chief justice of Delaware, a position which he occupied for nearly twenty years. His record upon the bench more than justified the high opinions which had been held of his legal ability. Possessing a keen analytical mind, quick to grasp with unerring instinct the crucial points of the most involved cases, a sound lawyer who never permitted the merits of a case to be obscured by technicalities, and an indefatigable worker, he inspired confidence by his independence and by the scrupulous care with which he considered every argument presented to him. Though by temperament tenacious of a conclusion when once arrived at, he always preserved an open mind and on more than one occasion "was known in the afternoon to come into Court and frankly reverse the rulings of the morning" (Lore, *post,* p. 13). The dignity with which he guided proceedings before him was equaled only by the severity with which he met any action which he thought might detract from the respect which was his due. His opinions, couched in clear concise language and distinguished by their logical precision, have been conceded an authority unsurpassed by the opinions of any other occupant of the Delaware bench. In political life he was a supporter of Henry Clay and affiliated himself with the Whig party, but was always inclined to hold independent views, and ardently upheld the Union cause. He was married on Mar. 15, 1842, to Eleanor Adelaide La Motte, daughter of Daniel La Motte. He died very suddenly at Dover, Del., while holding court.

[J. Painter, *The Gilpin Family* (1870); Chas. B. Lore, "The Life and Character of Edward W. Gilpin," *Papers of the Hist. Soc. of Del.,* vol. XXXIV (1902); J. M. McCarter and B. F. Jackson, *Hist. and Biog. Encyc. of Del.* (1882), pp. 546–48; H. C. Conrad, *Hist. of the State of Del.* (1908), III, 541–42; *Daily Gazette* (Wilmington), May 1, 1876.]
H. W. H. K.

GILPIN, HENRY DILWORTH (Apr. 14, 1801–Jan. 29, 1860), United States attorney-general, Philadelphia lawyer, author and editor, brother of William Gilpin [*q.v.*], was born of English Quaker stock, the son of Joshua and Mary (Dilworth) Gilpin. His father, a Philadelphia merchant, married while on a trip to Europe, and Henry was born at his mother's home in Lancaster, England. His parents soon after took their son to the United States but in 1811 they returned to England and for four years the boy attended the school of Dr. Hamilton at Hemel-Hempstead, not far from London. Returning to Philadelphia he entered the University of Pennsylvania from which he graduated in 1819. That same year he entered the office of Joseph R. Ingersoll to read law. From his "commonplace-book" it is evident that at this period of his life he had acquired a bookishness and facility with the classics which were to be distinguishing characteristics throughout his life. When he completed his law studies he was admitted to the bar in 1822; he had already been initiated into business as secretary of the Chesapeake & Delaware Canal Company. He began the practise of law but meanwhile maintained an active literary interest. In 1825 he became editor of the *Atlantic Souvenir,* an annual gift book, and three years later he brought out the second edition of John Sanderson's *Biography of the Signers to the Declaration of Independence.* He was also a frequent contributor to the *American Quarterly Review* and the *Democratic Review,* and was especially apt in the preparation of biographical notices.

In the meantime, under the patronage of George M. Dallas [*q.v.*], he had made his début in politics by writing a pamphlet, *A Memorial of Sundry Citizens of Pennsylvania, relative to the Treatment and Removal of the Indians,* in which he defended the policy of the United States government. When Dallas resigned as attorney for the eastern district of Pennsylvania to go to the United States Senate, Jackson appointed Gilpin as his successor, Dec. 30, 1831. For the next ten years Gilpin held public office and was interested in western investments, especially in Illinois. While he was serving as district attorney, Jackson appointed him government director of the Bank of the United States in 1833. In spite of the fact that feeling in Philadelphia was very bitter on this subject, Gilpin remained a loyal Jacksonian and his pen was active in preparing documents for the government directors in defense of their position. When Congress met he was twice rejected by the Senate for continuance in this directorship; his appointment as governor of the territory of Michigan met a like fate. His service as district attorney, however, was permitted to continue, and in 1837 he published a volume of *Reports of Cases Adjudged in the District Court of the United States for the Eastern District of Pennsylvania, 1828–36.* That same year he was appointed solicitor of the Treasury and removed to Washington where Van Buren further honored him by calling him to his cabinet as attorney-general in 1840. While in Washington he argued the Amistad case (15 *Peters,* 518) against John Quincy Adams and many cases arising under the Florida treaty. He had not abandoned his literary interests; in 1840 he published in three volumes *The Papers of James Madison* and in the next year the *Opinions of the Attorneys-General of the United States.*

With the coming of Harrison and Tyler, Gilpin retired from politics permanently. He had married on Sept. 3, 1834, Eliza (Sibley) Johnston, widow of Senator Josiah S. Johnston of Louisiana, and with her he settled down in Philadelphia to a life of luxurious literary ease, broken only by an extensive trip to Europe in the fifties. He maintained an establishment noted for its great library, and devoted himself to the congenial occupation of classical scholarship. He became president of the Pennsylvania Academy of the Fine Arts; was vice-president of the Historical Society of Pennsylvania; a director of Girard College; and trustee of the University of Pennsylvania. Unfortunately his body was not equal to the confining life prescribed by his literary tastes and after a tedious period of physical decline he died, leaving his fortune to the patronage of art and history.

[Eliza Gilpin, *A Memorial of Henry D. Gilpin* (1860); "Henry D. Gilpin," *U. S. Mag. and Democratic Rev.*, Dec. 1840; F. W. Leach, "Old Philadelphia Families," in the *North American* (Phila.), May 24, 1908; Jacob Painter, *The Gilpin Family* (1870). An interesting "commonplace-book" which Gilpin kept in his early life is in the possession of Thos. L. Montgomery, of the Pa. Hist. Soc.]

R. F. N.

GILPIN, WILLIAM (Oct. 4, 1813–Jan. 20, 1894), first territorial governor of Colorado, Indian fighter, and a brother of Henry Dilworth Gilpin [*q.v.*], was one of the most interesting characters to enter the gold region of the Rockies in the early days. His parents, Joshua and Mary (Dilworth) Gilpin, were of Quaker stock and lived in Brandywine, Pa., where William was born. The boy was sent to England for his elementary education. After his return to America he attended and was graduated in 1833 from the University of Pennsylvania. He entered West Point July 1, 1834, only to resign in good standing Feb. 15, 1835. He then read law for a time in Philadelphia. For many years thereafter he led a restless and eventful life, alternately engaged in warlike and peaceful pursuits. He started on his career as a soldier in the Seminole War of 1836, serving first as second lieutenant by appointment of President Jackson, a friend of the family. Later he was promoted first lieutenant but resigned from the army in April 1838 and went to St. Louis, where he edited the *Missouri Argus.* As a reward for his political services he was appointed chief clerk of the state House of Representatives. After this experience he settled down to the practise of law at Independence, Mo., but the call of adventure was too strong for him. In 1843 he accompanied Frémont's expedition on its way to the Pacific and traveled about on the coast in search of excitement and knowledge. As a major in Doniphan's regiment of Missouri volunteers he fought in the Mexican War and in 1847–48 engaged in Indian fighting in the Rockies. He retired from military life a lieutenant-colonel of volunteers and returned to a relatively quiet life at Independence. It is said, however, that he occasionally traveled between Missouri and the eastern states and that he often lectured. During this period also he produced an extraordinary book, *The Central Gold Region,* first published in 1860. It was the work of a visionary. Gilpin saw the Valley of the Mississippi as the future home of civilization, and Denver, then so young, as its capital city. By means of quaint maps and more quaint argument he proved this thesis to his own satisfaction. Later the book was reissued with the grandiose title *Mission of the North American People* (1873). In 1890 he published *The Cosmopolitan Railway,* in which he proposed uniting the world under the leadership of the United States by a system of railroads, one of which was to connect America to Asia at the Bering Strait.

Gilpin's adventurous life reached its climax when he arrived in Denver in May 1861 as first governor of the newly organized Territory of Colorado. Under his direction judicial districts were laid out, the first territorial legislature was convened, and the first census taken. His great task was to save the district for the Union. Late in the autumn he organized the 1st Regiment,

Colorado Volunteers. The cost of the equipment of the soldiers, as well as their pay, was met by the governor by the issuance of drafts upon the national treasury. When these where repudiated by the treasury, Gilpin's reputation suffered, though the drafts were honored in later years. After a serious wrangle he was recalled in March 1862. He lived in Denver for the remainder of his life. On Feb. 12, 1874, he married Mrs. Julia Pratte Dickerson of St. Louis. It is said that he was connected with a huge Spanish land grant in the San Luis Valley and adjacent New Mexico, from which he realized a comfortable fortune.

[H. H. Bancroft's *Hist. of the Life of Wm. Gilpin* (1889) contains much excellent material but is at times inaccurate. Gilpin's activities in the organization of the regiment of volunteers are described in W. C. Whitford's *Col. Volunteers in the Civil War* (1906). Colorado histories contain accounts of the life of Gilpin. See also Henry Simpson, *The Lives of Eminent Philadelphians* (1859), p. 409; C. K. Gardner, *A Dict. . . . of the Army of the U. S.* (1853), p. 192; the *Denver Republican* and *Rocky Mountain News* (Denver), Jan. 21, 1894. The date of his birth is uncertain, though it is clear that the one usually given, 1822, is wrong. Whitford gives 1813, which would appear to be correct.] J. F. W.

GINN, EDWIN (Feb. 14, 1838–Jan. 21, 1914), publisher, philanthropist, was born on a farm in Orland, Me., the son of James and Sarah (Blood) Ginn. He attended school intermittently, but his persistent ill health induced his parents to place him as a cook in a logging camp at the age of twelve. At fourteen he shipped on a fishing schooner bound for the Grand Banks of Newfoundland. On his return he attended the local high school, supplementing his training at the seminary at Bucksport. Then by "teaching winters, working on the farm and going to Grand Banks summers" he was able to finish his preparation for college at Westbrook Seminary. At twenty he entered Tufts College and graduated in the class of 1862, although he was handicapped by an affliction of the eyes which made it necessary for friends to read his lessons aloud to him for weeks at a time. Shortly after obtaining his degree, he became a traveling book-agent; but in 1867 he opened a publishing house of his own in Boston, soon admitting his brother Frederick as a partner under the firm-name of Ginn Brothers. In 1876 D. C. Heath joined the company, which after 1881 was known as Ginn, Heath & Company. When this partnership was dissolved in 1885, the name of Ginn & Company was adopted. As a publisher, Ginn was highly successful, and seemed to have a gift for picking popular school texts. Among the well-known projects which he sponsored were Hudson's editions of Shakespeare's plays, Wentworth's text-books in mathematics, Allen and Greenough's Latin Series, Goodwin's Greek grammars, the Athenæum Press Series, the National Music Course, by Luther Whiting Mason, and many others.

Although he was an unusually active business man, Ginn had many hobbies. He was fond of music and installed a fine organ in his home. As an employer, he was the first in Boston to inaugurate a system of profit-sharing among his employees. Another of his projects was "Charlesbank Homes," a five-story fireproof structure containing more than five hundred rooms which he built to provide cheap housing for the poor. His desire for world peace led him, in 1909, to set aside the sum of one million dollars for that purpose. Thus in July 1910 the International School of Peace was incorporated under a distinguished group of trustees, of whom Ginn was the first president. Six months after its incorporation the organization became the World Peace Foundation. It assumed an important function in spreading information on international affairs and in endeavoring to promote good-will among mankind, especially through the publication of a series of World Peace Foundation pamphlets, covering various phases of foreign politics. Ginn married, in 1869, Clara Glover, by whom he had three children. After her death in 1890, he married, in 1894, Marguerita Francesca Grebe, of Philadelphia, by whom he had a son and a daughter. In the latter part of his life, he had a beautiful home in Winchester, Mass. On Dec. 15, 1913, he suffered a paralytic stroke, which was followed by pneumonia. After lying unconscious for five weeks, he died and was buried in the Wildwood Cemetery, in Winchester. A high-minded idealist, he fortunately had the practical qualities which earned him the means of putting many of his theories into actual operation.

[Edwin Ginn, *Outline of the Life of Edwin Ginn, Including his Preparation for the Publishing Business* (1908); *In Memory of Edwin Ginn, 1838–1914, Memorial Service at the South Cong. Ch., Boston* (1914); *Who's Who in America,* 1912–13; the *Publisher's Weekly,* Jan. 31, Feb. 28, 1914; *Independent,* Feb. 2, 1914; *Boston Transcript,* Jan. 21, 1914; *Boston Herald,* Jan. 22, 1914; information as to certain facts from members of the Ginn family.] C. M. F.

GINTER, LEWIS (Apr. 4, 1824–Oct. 2, 1897), tobacconist, philanthropist, was born in New York City of old Knickerbocker stock. The family, whose name was originally Guenther, settled in Manhattan some time during the eighteenth century. Lewis's parents were probably John Ginter, a grocer at the corner of Greenwich and Canal Sts., and his wife Elizabeth.

Self-educated for the most part, with no college training, young Ginter accompanied a friend to Richmond, Va., in search of work in 1842, and there soon displayed his characteristic initiative by starting a house-furnishings store on his own account. His business prospered and by the early fifties he had become an "importer of fancy goods" as well as a dry-goods wholesaler trading extensively with village and country merchants. After he had formed a partnership with John F. Alvey, the firm of Ginter & Alvey specialized in silk, linen, and white goods, and Ginter himself went to Europe yearly to buy. Shortly before 1860 his nephew, George Arents, obtained an interest in the firm, which became known as Ginter, Alvey & Arents. It enjoyed an enviable reputation and earned the handsome profit of $40,000 in 1860.

Shortly after the Civil War began, Ginter closed his business and joined the Confederate army as quartermaster (earning the rank of major) under Gen. Joseph R. Anderson in the Army of Northern Virginia, where his frequent activity in battle won him the title of "the fighting commissary." After his parole in April 1865, he became associated with a brokerage firm in New York which failed during the crisis of "Black Friday" (Sept. 24, 1869). This adversity, a blessing in disguise, directed Ginter into the tobacco business in which he made his fortune.

The desire to return to Richmond encouraged him to form a partnership with John F. Allen of that city in 1872. They began in a small way by manufacturing smoking and chewing tobacco and cigars, and Ginter, with his earlier mercantile experience, traveled extensively to put their goods on the market. In the face of sharp competition, he caught the eye of customers by handsome lithographed labels and attractive designs of packing, and cultivated their taste by the high quality of the product. More important, however, was the firm's venture, in 1875, into the manufacture of cigarettes—then a foreign product of the weed and one still untried with Virginia tobacco. Ginter introduced under the name "Richmond Gem" paper-rolled cigarettes made from the virgin leaf, which enjoyed rapidly increasing popularity.

In the early eighties the firm became Allen & Ginter, whose Gem Tobacco Works erected on Cary Street in 1881 were mentioned frequently in the trade journals of the day. Associated with them were John Pope and later Thomas F. Jeffress, both intimates of Ginter's for many years. Ginter appreciated the influence upon the public mind of pointed advertisements at a time when modern scientific advertising was yet unborn. Richmond Gem cigarettes, Opera Puffs, and Virginia Brights became bywords among smokers whose taste had been cultivated by Allen & Ginter, while the more conservative devotees of the pipe found contentment in Old Rip, and Richmond Gem Curly Cut. The first factory began operation with twenty unskilled girls; by 1888 the new plant employed over one thousand skilled women and girls, and cigarette production had increased from 100,000 per month to 2,000,000 per day. The activity of the firm's agents extended throughout the United States and into the leading marts abroad.

Meanwhile the competition among the principal cigarette manufacturers—Allen & Ginter, W. Duke & Sons, Kinney Tobacco Company, William S. Kimball & Company, and Goodwin & Company—was growing so bitter that they were forced to combine for their own advantage. In 1890, after several unsuccessful attempts to merge, Ginter succeeded in negotiating an outright sale of all the businesses to the American Tobacco Company, organized for that purpose. It was capitalized at $25,000,000 and incorporated in New Jersey after Virginia had disallowed a previous charter. Allen & Ginter acquired stock amounting to $7,500,000 in the new corporation, of which Ginter was a director until shortly before his death.

The income which he enjoyed during the ensuing years enabled him to turn his efforts increasingly towards beautifying Richmond, developing her suburban area near "Westbrook," his country estate, and supporting numerous charitable organizations. One of his finest undertakings was the construction of the Jefferson Hotel, opened in 1895 at a cost of $1,350,000. Ginter was a quiet, unassuming man, widely read and widely traveled, a lover of nature and art. He never married. He joined the Episcopal Church a few years before his death in 1897, and was a member of the Masonic order. The provisions of his will bespoke his broad interests in the public welfare and so great was the demonstration at his funeral that the Richmond *Times* declared, "Never before in the history of Richmond did so many of the people do honor to one of their fellow-citizens." He was buried in Hollywood Cemetery, Richmond.

[The city directories of Richmond contain notices of Ginter's mercantile and manufacturing enterprises. Trade journals (*c.* 1888–97) and pamphlets on Richmond by Andrew Morrison (*c.* 1888–93) include brief articles on Allen & Ginter. The Richmond *Times* (Oct. 3 and 6, 1897) prints a detailed account of his life and work and of his funeral; and upon this information the sketch in L. G. Tyler, *Men of Mark in Va.* (1906–09), V, 154–63, is apparently largely based. The *State* (Richmond, Oct. 3–5, 1897) publishes a similar account. The recollections and scrap-book of Thomas F.

Jeffress of Richmond afford some additional information. For Ginter's part in the formation of the American Tobacco Company, see U. S. Commissioner of Corporations, *Report . . . on the Tobacco Industry* (1909), vols. I and II, *passim.*] L. J. C.

GIRARD, CHARLES FRÉDÉRIC (Mar. 9, 1822–Jan. 29, 1895), zoölogist, physician, was born at Mülhausen, Upper Alsace, and received his education at Neuchâtel, Switzerland, where he came under the influence of Louis Agassiz, at first as pupil and then as assistant. When Agassiz came to the United States in 1847, he brought Girard with him, and the young man remained at Cambridge with him until the fall of 1850. In 1849 his first scientific paper, "On the Genus *Cottus*," was published in the *Proceedings of the Boston Society of Natural History* (Vol. III), and this was soon followed by others along the same line. But his interest was by no means confined to fishes, and during those brief years in Cambridge, he published several important papers on flatworms, and one on echinoderms.

In the fall of 1850, when Spencer F. Baird was made assistant-secretary of the Smithsonian Institution, he gave Girard the opportunity to become associated with him in the plans and work which resulted in the establishment of the United States National Museum in 1857. During the decade before the Civil War, Girard published more than 170 notices, papers, and reports, dealing with a large variety of animals. The catholicity of his taste was most surprising, for while fishes and reptiles became his chief interest, he wrote of quadrupeds, spiders, centipedes, insects, and worms as well. The decade was notable for explorations in the far west, particularly in connection with the surveys of the Mexican boundary and for a transcontinental railway, and Girard was looked to for reports on the fishes and most of the reptiles collected by the exploring parties. Some of these reports were made in collaboration with Baird but even in such cases, the work was chiefly Girard's; the most important are: "Researches Upon the Cyprinoid Fishes Inhabiting the Fresh Waters of the United States, West of the Mississippi Valley," which appeared in 1856 in the *Proceedings of the Academy of Natural Sciences*; "Herpetology," of the Wilkes exploring expedition, written wholly by Girard but published in joint authorship with Baird in 1858, a quarto volume of 500 pages with a folio atlas of 32 plates; and "Fishes," another quarto volume of 385 pages with 76 plates, which appeared in Vol. X of the *Reports of Explorations and Surveys . . . for a Railroad from the Mississippi River to the Pacific Ocean* (1859).

During these busy years in Washington, Girard became, in 1854, a naturalized citizen of the United States and also completed a medical course at Georgetown College, which gave him the degree of M.D. in 1856. In 1860 he decided to visit Europe and in 1861 was awarded the Cuvier Prize by the Institute of France. While in Paris, the troubles leading to the Civil War in the United States came to a head and Girard found his sympathies on the side of the South. Having accepted a commission from the Confederacy to supply its army with drugs and surgical instruments he found difficulty in returning to the United States. He finally succeeded in reaching the South and made a tour through Virginia and the Carolinas in the summer of 1863. He published at once in Paris an account of this trip, *Les États Confédérés d'Amérique visités en 1863* (Paris, 1864). With the close of the war, finding life in Washington no longer attractive, he returned to Paris and entered upon a career in medicine to which he devoted the next twenty years. In 1870 he was chief physician to one of the military ambulances during the siege of Paris and as a result published in 1872 an important paper on the etiology of typhoid fever, *L'Ambulance Militaire de la rue Violet, No. 57* (Paris, 1872). In 1888, his interest in zoölogical research reviving, he published two papers on fishes and a bibliography of his own writings. The next three years witnessed the appearance of eight additional papers, the last of which, an important report on North American flatworms, was his final contribution to science. Having never married and being a man of retiring habits and great industry, he was content to live quietly in seclusion at Neuilly-sur-Seine near Paris, until he died in 1895.

["The Published Writings of Dr. Charles Girard," by G. B. Goode, in *Bulletin No. 41*, U. S. Nat. Museum (1891); article by D. S. Lamb, in H. A. Kelly and W. L. Burrage, *Am. Medic. Biogs.* (1920).] H. L. C.

GIRARD, STEPHEN (May 20, 1750–Dec. 26, 1831), merchant, financier, philanthropist, was born in Bordeaux, France, the second child and oldest son of a family of ten. His father, Pierre Girard, served with distinction in the Royal Navy, was made a burgess of the city and captain of the port. His mother, Odette Lafargue, of the neighboring parish of St. Remy, died when Stephen was twelve, leaving him a half orphan. It has been suggested (McMaster, *post*, p. 2) that he was probably born blind in his right eye, and that his education, which he paid for partly out of his earnings, was for this and other reasons scanty. At the age of fourteen he went to sea as a cabin boy, and after six voyages, chiefly to Santo Domingo, he was in 1773 licensed to act as captain, master, or pilot, despite the fact that he was not yet twenty-five years old and had not served the usual term of two years in the navy. In 1774 he made his first independent voyage as officer of a ship sailing from Bordeaux to Port-au-Prince. His own venture in the enterprise was unsuccessful and he found himself in debt. After collecting what he could he sailed for New York with a consignment of sugar and coffee. At the first opportunity he paid his obligations to his Bordeaux creditors, but for the remainder of his life he avoided doing business on credit and never returned to his native city. On the other hand he retained a sincere affection for it, and frequently aided and befriended the unhappy political refugees from France.

In New York he entered the employ of the shipping firm of Thomas Randall & Son, making several voyages, first as mate, and then as captain. Apparently he traded on a small scale for himself; gradually accumulated a little capital, and became master and half owner of the vessel, *La Jeune Babé*. As a result of a rough return voyage from St. Pierre in the early summer of 1776, and the risk of capture by the British, he put into Philadelphia, then the largest city in the colonies and the first in trade. The war for independence had begun and the Declaration of Independence followed within a month after Girard's arrival in Philadelphia, but he did not interest himself greatly in the political controversy. On the other hand the risks of commerce during the first years of the war forced him to abandon it temporarily for merchandising. He was thus enabled to settle down, and in 1777, he married Mary Lum, the daughter of a ship-builder. He bought a modest home in Mount Holly, N. J., where they lived together happily for a time, but Mrs. Girard's mind became affected, and he placed her in the Pennsylvania Hospital, where she died in 1815. These circumstances, together with his partial blindness, account in large measure for Girard's somewhat lonely and self-centered life.

After the departure of the British from Philadelphia he returned to the city, took the oath of allegiance to the Commonwealth of Pennsylvania, and became a free citizen of that state. He established himself on North Water Street on the Delaware and again turned his attention to foreign trade especially to the West Indies though later to Europe and Asia as well, despite the risks of the wars of the French Revolution and Napoleon. It was a business that called for the most careful planning, resourcefulness, and courage. Girard's instructions to his captains and supercargoes and the detailed statements and reports he demanded of them reveal a thrilling story of the romance of commerce in those stormy years. Some of his ventures were complete losses, but on the whole, by dint of unusual business acumen and foresight, coupled with an industry and persistency that would not be denied, he recouped himself by altogether extraordinary profits from others. At one time or another he was the owner of eighteen vessels, though six was the largest number he owned at any one time. Characteristically, he named the finest after the philosophers of his native France: *Montesquieu, Rousseau, Voltaire.* To him commerce was a subject of vast speculative possibilities to which he brought not alone great industry and initiative but more particularly a knowledge of the sea markets, and political conditions, acquired through personal experience and careful study of the reports of his agents. It is little wonder that he became rich, or that his interest in commerce continued to the last. At his death he had three fine ships at sea and one building on the ways at Philadelphia.

His commercial ventures, however, were of such a nature that he had time for other interests. Partly through capital acquired in trade he gradually became interested in real estate, insurance, and banking. Always a strong supporter of the First United States Bank, he served on a committee of five in 1810, to draw up a memorial petitioning Congress to renew the Bank's charter which was about to expire. When Congress refused and the Bank was forced to close its doors, Girard bought the building and other assets and started the "Bank of Stephen Girard" as a private venture with an initial capital of $1,200,000. In his banking business as in commerce he rapidly built up a remarkable system of credit not only in other cities of the United States but also abroad. Business contacts with many small banks and with the federal treasury were established and his relations with Baring Brothers of London greatly expanded. As a result he found himself in a position to render valuable patriotic service at the outbreak of the War of 1812, and presently became a man of prominence in national affairs. The government loan was a dismal failure, when Girard with David Parish, and John Jacob Astor of New York, arranged with Secretary Gallatin to take over the unsubscribed portion and dispose of it to the public. Although they acted mainly as intermediaries on a percentage basis, their action at the critical moment had a powerful effect in restoring the public confidence, and a dangerous financial crisis was averted.

In the depression that followed the war the

plan for a national bank was revived, and A. J. Dallas, the secretary of the treasury, naturally turned to Girard for counsel. He was appointed by the Treasury Department one of the five commissioners to receive subscriptions for the bank stock and elected president of the commission. Again, however, the public was in a doubtful mood. No buyers were found for $3,000,000 of the stock of the new bank till Girard came forward and subscribed for the entire amount. This action made possible the prompt organization of the Second United States Bank, which was effected at a stockholders' meeting in Girard's banking house on Oct. 28, 1816. Girard was sent his commission as one of the five government directors of the Bank by President Madison, but he soon became dissatisfied with the management, withdrew from the Board, gradually sold his stock, and again turned his attention to his own private bank.

In addition to his important activities in the commercial and financial life of the nation, Girard played a remarkable rôle as a citizen of his adopted city. He served the city officially in various capacities. During the terrible yellow-fever epidemic of 1793, in which 4,031 persons died between the 1st of August and the 9th of November, he not only gave liberally of his time and money to the suffering and dying, but with Peter Helm he volunteered to act as superintendent at the fever hospital at Bush Hill. Girard took charge of the interior of the hospital. This involved the care of patients, and "for sixty days," wrote one biographer, "Stephen Girard performed both day and night the duty of receiving, nursing, and caring for those stricken with the fever" (Herrick, *post*, p. 41). His private and other business had, of course, to be neglected. To the protests of some of his friends he replied: "The duties imposed on me in my capacity as a citizen prevent me from answering at the proper time the letters written me by my friends" (McMaster, I, 216). In the subsequent outbreaks of the epidemic he very naturally assumed a leading part in the preventive measures.

Later in life he bought a farm in South Philadelphia, which, although agriculture was quite foreign to his earlier interests, became a source of great satisfaction to him. He gave to it the same practical and scientific attention that he did to his other business. As his commercial activities decreased he became more and more interested in his farm. "At my age," he wrote, "the sole amusement which I enjoy, is to be in the country constantly busy, in attending to the work of the farm generally, and also to my fruit trees, several of which, say about 300, I have imported from France, and I hope will be useful to our country" (*Ibid.*, II, 410). Standard dictionaries on agriculture which he used constantly stood side by side with the works of Voltaire on the shelves of his small library. He never tired of work and study, finding relaxation in the change from one kind of work to another. "To rest is to rust" was a favorite saying with him. "When death comes for me, he will find me busy, unless I am asleep. . . ." "If I thought I was going to die to-morrow, I should plant a tree nevertheless to-day" (Herrick, pp. 108–09). To these ideas he adhered steadfastly until his death. An accident in December 1830 made it difficult for him to take up his routine work, but he managed it again during the following summer, only to succumb to an attack of pneumonia of which he died in December 1831. The newspapers of the day paid glowing tribute to his life and work. The city officials, charitable and other societies, and thousands of citizens attended the funeral. "So large a funeral, it is believed," remarked the *National Gazette* (Dec. 29, 1831), "was never before known in this city." He was buried in the cemetery of Holy Trinity Parish but the body was later removed and placed in the sarcophagus in the main building of Girard College.

For some years before his death Girard had devoted much thought to the disposition of his estate and in 1826 he made his will, bequeathing $140,000 to relatives and to different charities in which he was interested; $300,000 to the Commonwealth of Pennsylvania for internal improvement; $500,000 to the City of Philadelphia, and the residue in cash and real estate, amounting to over $6,000,000, in trust to the City for educating poor white orphan boys. "Never before," said McMaster, "had a private citizen of the United States bequeathed so vast a sum for the public good" (*post*, Preface, p. v). A determined effort to set the will aside was made by certain of the heirs and the case of *Vidal et al.* vs. *The City of Philadelphia* (2 *Howard*, 127) has become a classic in American legal history, contributing not a little to the clarification of the law of charities. The Supreme Court upheld the validity of the will and the beautiful buildings of Girard College stand to-day as a unique monument to the sagacity, philanthropy, and genius of its founder.

Summarizing Girard's life and work, E. A. Duyckinck, in his *National Portrait Gallery of Eminent Americans*, wrote in 1862: "Work was his religion . . . there is something grand in the onward steps of the poor cabin boy, maimed in sight, rude in his person, a stranger in his speech, unhappy in his married life, overcoming the disadvantages of fortune to pursue his far-sighted, intelligent career as a prosperous merchant, building up a vast estate—not for his own luxurious enjoyment, but to enrich his adopted city, and bless, by its kindly support, successive generations of the fatherless and dependent."

[Girard's voluminous correspondence and papers, to which access may be had only by special permission from the Board of City Trustees of Phila., in whose custody they are; Customs House Records of Phila., for the period, now for the most part at the Univ. of Pa.; J. B. McMaster, *Life and Times of Stephen Girard, Mariner and Merchant* (2 vols., 1918), an authoritative biography; C. A. Herrick, *Stephen Girard, Founder* (1923), a popular but scholarly presentation of Girard's life and work written with a fine appreciation of Girard's character and times, by the president of Girard College; Stephen Simpson, *Biog. of Stephen Girard* (1832), a somewhat hostile account by the cashier of Girard's bank, disappointed in his expectation to succeed his father; H. A. Ingram, *The Life and Character of Stephen Girard* (1884), an appreciation by a descendant; *National Gazette* (Phila.), Dec. 27, 1831.]

W. E. L.

GIRARDEAU, JOHN LAFAYETTE (Nov. 14, 1825–June 23, 1898), Presbyterian clergyman and theologian, oldest of the six children of John Bohun and Claudia Herne (Freer) Girardeau, was born on James Island, near Charleston, and died in Columbia, S. C. His grandfather, John Girardeau, a soldier in the Revolution, was descended from Jean Girardeau who around 1700 emigrated to America to escape religious persecution in France. The boy's parents did not themselves join the church until after his birth, but they both grew up in a strong Presbyterian tradition. His mother died when he was seven, and three years later he was sent to Charleston to the school of the German Friendly Society. At fourteen he entered the College of Charleston and at eighteen he was graduated. During 1844–45, tutoring at the home of Thomas Hamlin, some eight miles from Charleston, he became engaged to his fifteen-year-old pupil, Penelope Sarah Hamlin, whom he married in 1849. From 1845 to 1848 he studied at the Columbia Theological Seminary. Licensed to preach in 1848, he officiated at one country church or another, preaching alternately—first to white and then to negro congregations—until 1853, when he took charge of a negro church in Charleston. In the time remaining before 1860 the membership of this church advanced from 48 to 600, with some 1,500 regular attendants. His eloquence, learning, and piety were soon generally recognized, and his congregation was augmented by a number of influential white persons, who, though continuing to worship regularly with the negroes, built a new church and assumed the costs of its operation. Aside from his routine duties, the minister conducted frequent revivals, made missionary trips into the low-coast rice plantations, and advocated the creation of churches specially for negro members.

Throughout the Civil War, Girardeau served as a chaplain on duty with troops actually on the line of battle. From April to July 1865 he was held captive by the Federals, but soon afterward he returned to Charleston, and, ousted from his church by Northern missionaries, preached at large until April 1866. Then, still holding the name at least of his old church—Zion—he again became pastor of a regular congregation. Soon afterward, solicited by his black flock to come back to them, he ministered to them also for a time, then submitted to the new order, completely divorcing the ecclesiastical organizations of the two races. In 1875 he became professor of didactic and polemic theology at the Columbia Seminary, a position which he held until 1895, when in accord with his theory that one should not teach when beyond seventy, he resigned. During these twenty years, he was a faithful and effective teacher, a zealous writer of controversial articles for church papers, a determined opponent—until 1890, when he reversed himself—of church as contrasted with state education, and a vindictive crusader against Darwinism. He also wrote several books, the most notable, *The Will in its Theological Relations* (1891), being an exposition of his belief that Truth lies somewhere midway between free-will and predestination.

[J. L. Martin, *Dr. Girardeau's Anti-Evolution* (1889); G. A. Blackburn, *The Life Work of John L. Girardeau* (1916), bibliography, p. 364; H. A. White, *Southern Presbyt. Leaders* (1911); *News and Courier* (Charleston), June 24, 1898.]

J. D. W.

GIRSCH, FREDERICK (Mar. 31, 1821–Dec. 18, 1895), bank-note engraver, was born in Büdingen, a suburb of Darmstadt, the capital of the Grand Duchy of Hesse. After receiving some instruction in drawing from Carl Seeger, an artist of his native town, he entered the Royal Academy of Darmstadt where he continued his studies. The Revolution which upset Central Europe in 1848 caused him to leave Germany and go to Paris, where he again took up his studies. Almost immediately the French capital also was disturbed by the wave of revolution, and in 1849 the artist emigrated to the United States. Landing in New York, he at once received commissions for engravings from the *New-Yorker Criminal-Zeitung,* for which publication he engraved the premium plates—given with subscriptions to the paper—"Die Helden der Revolution," and "Niagara Falls." These are large folio plates engraved in line, and display a thorough knowledge of technique but do not show any marked individuality so far as their artistic features are concerned. They are typical of their period, however, and at least the equal of any similar productions. During the Civil War Girsch's attention was directed to bank-note engraving, for which field he was singularly well fitted. Among the designs made by him for this purpose, are "De Soto Discovering the Mississippi," on the ten-dollar notes, and the head of Liberty, on the fractional currency of that period. He engraved a plate 12 x 14 inches, entitled, "The Legion of Honor," which President Lincoln proposed to give to soldiers who served in the war, but the latter's untimely death frustrated the plan. During the last few years of his life, Girsch engraved for his own pleasure a large plate entitled "Grand Ma's Toast," and another, which bore the title, "The Gipsy Girl." He died at his home, Mount Vernon, N. Y.

[See D. M. Stauffer, *Am. Engravers upon Copper and Steel* (1907); *N. Y. Herald*, Dec. 20, 1895. The engraver's large plate, "Niagara," is in the collection of the N. Y. Hist. Soc.] J. J.

GIRTY, SIMON (1741–Feb. 18, 1818), known as "the Great Renegade," was born near Harrisburg, Pa., the son of Simon and Mary (Newton) Girty. In 1751 his father was killed by an Indian, and two years later his mother married John Turner. Of her four sons by Girty, three —Simon, James, and George—were to gain an evil notoriety by their alliance with the savages. Simon, though illiterate, was early regarded as capable and talented. From 1759, when he was surrendered after a three years' captivity among the Indians, until 1774, he seems to have been employed as an interpreter about Fort Pitt. As a scout he served with Simon Kenton in Dunmore's War. In the spring of 1776 he was employed as an interpreter for the Continental Congress, and though shortly afterward discharged for "ill behavior," was regarded as loyal and was otherwise employed in the common defense.

With Alexander McKee, later to attain rank in the British militia, and five others, he deserted the American cause and fled, Mar. 28, 1778, from the vicinity of Pittsburgh. Reaching Detroit in June, he was employed by Lieut.-Gov. Hamilton as an interpreter, a post he retained, directly or indirectly, till near the close of his life. Active in the many forays of troops and Indians against the settlers, his conduct was characterized by savage malignity and atrocious acts of cruelty. Though he was influential in saving the life of Simon Kenton and is credited with saving several other lives, he encouraged the torture of captives, and at the burning at the stake of Col. William Crawford, in June 1782, as well as at a number of other burnings, he was a delighted spectator. On the close of the war, he received a pension. In 1784 he married Catharine Malott, a captive, and established a home near the present Amherstburg, on the east side of the Detroit River. His work, however, kept him almost constantly among the Indian tribes in the Ohio country, where he strongly opposed all efforts toward peace with the Americans and took an active part in many battles, including those of St. Clair's defeat and Fallen Timbers. With the British surrender of Detroit in 1796 he returned to his Canadian home, and when Harrison invaded Canada in 1813 he fled to a Mohawk village. In 1816, broken with dissipation, crippled with rheumatism, and totally blind, he again returned. His wife, who because of his drunkenness and cruelty had left him in 1797, ministered to his last wants. He died near Amherstburg.

Girty was five feet nine inches in height, with a heavy frame, short neck, and full, round face. In his prime he had strength, agility, and great endurance. His character was a complex of many contradictions.

[The numerous fictions that have invested Girty's career are critically examined in C. W. Butterfield, *Hist. of the Girtys* (1890). See also Thos. Boyd, *Simon Girty, the White Savage* (1928).] W. J. G.

GIST, CHRISTOPHER (*c.* 1706–1759), explorer, soldier, was born in Maryland, one of the three sons of Richard and Zipporah (Murray) Gist, who were married in 1705. His grandfather, Christopher Gist (or Guest), who came from England, died in Baltimore County in 1691. His father was surveyor of the western shore of Maryland and one of the commissioners who plotted the town of Baltimore. Practically nothing is known of the son's early life and training, but his writings and maps indicate that he was well educated, and it is probable that he early gained experience in exploration and surveying. In 1750 he was living with his family near Daniel Boone, on the Yadkin, in northern North Carolina. Appointed by the Ohio Company to explore the Ohio River lands as far as the present Louisville, he set out from Cresap's post, near Cumberland, Md., on Oct. 31 of that year. Reaching Shannopin's Town (now Pittsburgh), he crossed the Ohio, examining the country as far as the mouth of the Scioto. He then crossed to Kentucky, and after exploring in various directions, made his way to the Yadkin. Here he found that his family, because of Indian depredations, had fled to Roanoke, where he joined them. In the following winter he explored the country south of the Ohio from the Monongahela to the Great Kanawha.

About 1753 he decided to make his home in the wilderness near the present Brownsville, Pa., but seems not to have remained there. He was at Will's Creek, Md., in November of that year when Maj. George Washington arrived on a mission from Gov. Dinwiddie, and on Nov. 15 the two started for Fort Duquesne on the celebrated journey in which Gist twice saved Washington's life. He was with Washington also in the defeat of Coulon de Jumonville, May 28, 1754, and in the surrender of Fort Necessity, July 4 following. In the Braddock campaign he served as guide to the General, and with two sons took part in the disastrous battle of July 9, 1755. Later he raised a company of scouts, of which he seems to have been made captain. In 1756 he went to the Cherokee country in East Tennessee in the vain effort to enlist Indians for service, and for a time was an Indian agent in that locality. He died of smallpox, in either South Carolina or Georgia.

Gist was married to Sarah Howard, but when or where is not known. He had five children. One of his three sons was Nathaniel, who had a number of descendants. Gist was a man highly regarded for his many capabilities, his probity, and his courage. He was the first white American to make a careful exploration of the Ohio River lands in southern Ohio and northeastern Kentucky, preceding Daniel Boone in the latter region by eighteen years. His reports, though brief, show a keen observation both of topography and of the customs of the natives, and his plats and surveys have been praised as "models in mathematical exactness and precision in drawing."

[*Christopher Gist's Jours.*, etc. (1893), ed. by W. M. Darlington; *First Explorations of Ky.* (1898), ed. by J. S. Johnston, being Filson Club Pubs., no. 13; *The Writings of George Washington* (1889–93), ed. by W. C. Ford, esp. vols. I and II; *Md. Hist. Mag.*, Dec. 1913.]

W. J. G.

GIST, MORDECAI (Feb. 22, 1742/43–Aug. 2, 1792), Revolutionary soldier, came from a family which had been locally prominent in Baltimore County, Md., since Christopher Guest, the ancestor, had immigrated thither about 1682. Several members of this family, notably another Christopher, had, by their exploits, foreshadowed the future military career of Mordecai; and Thomas Gist, brother of this second Christopher [*q.v.*] and father of Mordecai, was a training officer in the Revolutionary War when his son won all his laurels. The latter was born near Reisterstown, Md., where Thomas Gist had settled with Susannah Cockey, his wife. He received an elementary education at a local parish school and somewhat later entered business in Baltimore, where he had shipping interests during the Revolution (William Sterrett to M. Gist, Sept. 1 and 2, 1778; John Sterrett to M. Gist, Nov. 16, 1778; Manuscript Division, Library of Congress). In December 1774 he was chosen captain of the "Baltimore Independent Company," one of the first of those volunteer military organizations which heralded the rapid approach of the war. One year later he wrote to a member of the Maryland Convention petitioning a military office. This letter is a typical expression, and breathes the spirit of the warrior patriot (Blakeslee, *post*). The request was granted, and on Jan. 14, 1776, he was commissioned second major in Gen. Smallwood's 1st Maryland Battalion. Gist's Revolutionary career is marked by successive promotions. He was in the battle of Long Island, August 1776, and then covered the retreat of Washington through New Jersey. He was promoted to the rank of colonel on Dec. 10, 1776. The following year he took part in the battle of Germantown. Uneventful skirmishes in Maryland protecting the state from British raiders occupied his time for the next few years, and on Jan. 9, 1779, he attained the rank of brigadier-general. Shortly afterwards he took a prominent part in the battle of Camden, winning a meed of praise from the dying De Kalb, who was mortally wounded in this disastrous engagement (Friedrich Kapp, *Leben des Amerikanischen General Johann Kalb,* 1862, p. 289; J. Spear Smith, *Memoir of the Baron de Kalb,* 1858, p. 26). He was also mentioned in a resolution of Congress of Oct. 14, 1780, for his bravery and good conduct during that action. During the remainder of the war he was given the difficult task of recruiting and supplying the army for the southern district. His letters from the field during this period are filled with indignation at the selfish provincialism of state officers. He himself suffered financially because of this attitude (*Maryland Historical Magazine,* December 1909, pp. 369–72). It was certainly this type of American who won the Revolution. His mind was seemingly cast for this one end, and his whole life was conditioned by the times. His universe was very simple, and right and wrong could be specific and well-defined terms in his ethics. Love of country was to him seemingly the end of earthly existence. Wife and children were of secondary consideration. Superficially this attitude of mind may be observed in the naming of his sons. The first, called Independent, was born Jan. 8, 1779, the only child of Gist's second wife, Mary Sterrett, whom he married Jan. 23, 1778. His first wife was Cecil Carnan. After peace was signed he settled in Charleston, S. C., where the same year he married his third wife, Mrs. Mary Cattell, widow of Capt. Benjamin Cattell. His second son, States, was born in 1787. Gist remained in South Carolina until his death.

[K. W. Blakeslee, *Mordecai Gist and His Am. Progenitors* (1923), though laudatory, seems to be accurate as to details. A complete genealogy of the Gist family may be found in the *Md. Hist. Mag.*, 1913. There is a collection of Gist papers in the Md. Hist. Soc. Archives, from which a small group of photostats has been made for the Lib. of Cong. There is much material in the Continental Congress and Washington Papers in the Lib. of Cong.] C. W. G.

GIST, WILLIAM HENRY (Aug. 22, 1807–Sept. 30, 1874), governor of South Carolina, was born in Charleston, S. C., the son of Francis Fincher Gist and a descendant of a family distinguished in the early history of Maryland. His grandfather, William, was a brother of Christopher Gist [*q.v.*]. At an early age William Henry Gist moved with his parents to Union District, S. C. He attended the South Carolina College but withdrew in 1827 during his senior year, because he and his classmates were dissatisfied with boarding conditions. Although he studied law, he early abandoned that profession in order to manage the extensive planting interests of his family. He was married twice: in 1828 to Louisa, daughter of George Bowen, and after her death, to Mary, daughter of William Rice. A controversy over some remarks about a lady led to a duel in which Gist killed his opponent, Samuel Fair. Early in life Gist became an ardent Methodist, contributing liberally to the support of that church and advocating radical restrictions upon the manufacture and sale of liquors. He was elected president of the Methodist State Sunday School Convention.

It was inevitable that a man of his wealth and moral firmness should receive political recognition. From 1840 to 1844 he represented Union District in the lower house of the state legislature. He served in the state Senate from 1844 to 1856. In 1848 he was elected lieutenant-governor but failed to qualify for that office, preferring his seat in the Senate. In 1858 the state-rights party in the legislature elected him governor, and he served in that office from Dec. 13, 1858, to Dec. 17, 1860. As governor he bent his efforts toward the accomplishment of the most fateful decision ever made by South Carolina, the withdrawal of that state from the Federal Union. In a series of messages to the legislature he prophesied the inevitability of secession, and when the election of Lincoln became likely he changed words to action. Oct. 5, 1860, he addressed confidential letters to the governors of all cotton states except Texas announcing that South Carolina would probably secede and asking their cooperation. On Oct. 12, just after Lincoln's election seemed assured, he called the legislature into extra session to elect presidential electors and intimated that some action might be necessary "for the safety and protection of the State." When the legislature met on Nov. 5, the day before the presidential election, the governor recommended that it remain in session during the crisis and that in the event of Lincoln's success a convention of the people should be called and the armed forces of the state strengthened. Seven days later the resolution for the calling of the secession convention was passed. In his farewell message Gist confidently hoped that "by the 25th of December no flag but the Palmetto will float over any part of South Carolina." His wish was almost literally gratified. On Dec. 20 he and the other delegates to the convention signed the famous ordinance of secession. His public career was completed as a member of the Executive Council of South Carolina, a body created by the convention to strengthen the defenses of the state. The remainder of his life was passed in retirement at "Rose Hill," his spacious country home in Union District, where he died.

[Miss Margaret Gist, York, S. C., has compiled the records of the family; Mrs. R. P. Harry, Union, S. C., has a scrap-book on Gov. Gist; his public career is traced in S. W. Crawford, *The Genesis of the Civil War: The Story of Sumter* (1887), and in John G. Nicolay and John Hay, *Abraham Lincoln, A Hist.*, vol. II (1890); a sketch of him by R. Means Davis is in *Garnet and Black, Published by the Students of the S. C. Coll.*, 1901.] F. B. S.

GLADDEN, WASHINGTON (Feb. 11, 1836–July 2, 1918), Congregational clergyman, widely known as a proponent of the application of Christian principles to social problems, was born in a little hamlet in central Pennsylvania called Pottsgrove. He was a descendant of the New England Gladdings, his great-grandfather, Azariah Gladding, a Revolutionary soldier, having been born in Norwich, Conn. His grandfather, Thomas Gladden, was a shoemaker of Southampton, Mass., from which place his father, Solomon, a school teacher, wandered to Pennsylvania where he married Amanda Daniels of Owego, N. Y. Solomon Washington, as he was originally named, was their first-born. After graduating from college he seems to have dropped the "Solomon."

When he was six years old his father died, and he was brought up on the farm of his uncle, Ebenezer Daniels, near Owego. At sixteen he entered the office of the *Owego Gazette* where he worked at the case and wrote local news. In 1855 opportunity was afforded him to study at the Owego Academy, and the following year he enrolled as a sophomore at Williams College. He taught school during winter vacations, and was college reporter for the *Springfield Republican.* In his senior year he published *Songs of Williams* (1859), contributing thereto "The Mountains, the Mountains!" which has become the accepted college song.

After his graduation in 1859, he taught the principal public school in Owego for a few months, but was soon licensed to preach by the Susquehanna Association of Congregational Ministers. On Dec. 5, 1860, he was married to Jennie O. Cohoon, a former schoolmate in the Owego Academy. His earliest pastorates were at the First Congregational Methodist Church, Brooklyn (1860–61), where he was ordained Nov. 15, 1860, and at Morrisania, N. Y. (1861–66). By frequenting the lecture rooms of Union Seminary and by reading he added to his theological equipment. The writings of Frederick W. Robertson and Horace Bushnell [*q.v.*] emancipated him from "the bondage of an immoral theology" and gave him a practical gospel to preach. In 1866 he became pastor of the Congregational church in North Adams, Mass., where he remained until 1871. While here he began his life-long contribution to periodical literature, defending Bushnell's views in the New York *Independent,* and writing for the new *Scribner's Monthly.* He also published the first of his numerous and widely read books, *Plain Thoughts on the Art of Living* (1868), which reveals his interest in the ethical questions of everyday life, and his ability to write in a plain, virile style. Here, too, industrial conditions suggested the problems which were to be one of his major concerns. In 1871 he joined the editorial staff of the *Independent,* a connection which he severed in 1875, because he felt that the prevailing advertising policy, which it followed, was not entirely honest. That year he took charge of the North Congregational Church, Springfield, Mass., which he served until December 1882, also editing (1878–80) *Sunday Afternoon, a Magazine for the Household,* renamed (September 1879) *Good Company.* He then accepted a call to the First Congregational Church, Columbus, Ohio, where he remained as pastor and pastor-emeritus till his death. From 1904 to 1907 he was moderator of the National Council of the Congregational Churches. He was a frequent preacher and lecturer at the universities, and through his writings was well known in England. During a visit there at the time of the Spanish-American War he spoke extensively on the "Causes of the War, and the Reasons for Friendship between England and America."

He was a man of wide reading rather than of profound scholarship, of practical rather than philosophical turn of mind. Although fearless in acting upon his convictions, he was in general conciliatory and mediating rather than polemic; hence he had the respect and confidence of opposing parties. He did much to popularize the results of Biblical criticism and modern theological views in such books as *Burning Questions* (1890), *Who Wrote the Bible* (1891), *How Much Is Left of the Old Doctrines* (1899), and *Present Day Theology* (1913). His prominence and influence were chiefly due, however, to his exposition of the fundamental principles of religion and his extensive application of them to social relations. He was an early apostle in this country of what has come to be known as the "social gospel," and he remains one of the sanest. Among his first books were *Being a Christian* (1871), *The Christian Way* (1877), and *Working People and their Employers* (1876). In the last he acknowledged the right of labor to organize, and advocated the identification of capital and labor through some application of the principle of cooperation. His social views are more fully set forth in *Applied Christianity* (1886), *Tools and the Man: Property and Industry under the Christian Law* (1893), *Social Salvation* (1902), *The Church and Modern Life* (1908). While favoring government ownership of public utilities, he was opposed to socialism as a system, maintaining that the present social order can be Christianized by application of the fundamental Christian principle, "Thou shalt love thy neighbor as thyself." The Church's chief business, he maintained, is to effect this transformation, not by the use of force, or the indorsement of any particular economic program, but by inspiring individuals with a love of justice and the spirit of service. He recognized the need of greater cooperation among the churches and his *Christian League of Connecticut* (1883) helped to create church federations. He was actively interested in municipal reform, and served on the city council of Columbus from 1900 to 1902, while his little book, *The Cosmopolis City Club* (1893), stimulated the formation of civic organizations. His fairness, scrupulousness, and fearlessness were demonstrated by his opposition to the anti-Catholic crusade of 1893–94, and by his widely discussed condemnation of the American Board of Commissioners for Foreign Missions for soliciting a gift of $100,000 from the president of the

Standard Oil Company, money which he characterized as "tainted," and an act which, as he viewed it, made the Church a partner with plunderers (see "Shall Ill-Gotten Gains Be Sought for Christian Purposes?" *The New Idolatry,* 1905, p. 57). His practical nature was not without a strain of mysticism and an appreciation of poetry. In 1912 he published *Ultima Veritas and Other Verses,* and his hymn "O Master, let me walk with Thee" is widely used in public worship. Of his more than thirty books he considered *Where Does the Sky Begin?* (1904), a volume of sermons, the best.

[Gladden's *Recollections* (1909) is an interesting account of his life and times. *Who's Who in America,* 1918–19, contains a very full but not altogether accurate bibliography. See also *Cong. Year-Book, Statistics for 1918*; *Congregationalist,* July 11, 1918; *Outlook,* July 17, 1918; *Survey,* July 13, 1918; *Ohio State Jour.* (Columbus) and *N. Y. Times,* July 3, 1918.] H. E. S.

GLADWIN, HENRY (Nov. 19, 1729–June 22, 1791), British soldier, was the son of Henry and Mary (Dakeyne) Gladwin, of Stubbing Court, Derbyshire, England. He was commissioned lieutenant in the 48th Regiment of foot on Aug. 28, 1753, and thereafter sailed for America, where his regiment joined Braddock's force in the march to Fort Duquesne. On the fatal 9th of July, 1755, when Braddock was ambushed by the French and Indians, Gladwin was wounded, but managed to retreat with the defeated army. His conduct so commended itself to Colonel (later General) Thomas Gage, that when, in 1757, there was organized the new 80th Regiment, Gladwin was made captain therein (Dec. 26, 1757) and Gage became colonel. In 1760 Gladwin went with part of the regiment to the relief of Fort Niagara, and during Gage's absence commanded the regiment. Amherst gave him the rank of major in 1759, but his commission is dated Dec. 13, 1760 (Army List, 1761). In 1761 he was sent with a detachment of 300 men to garrison the post at Detroit, newly taken over from the French. Thither he went accompanied by Sir William Johnson [*q.v.*], but a severe illness in the summer of 1761 sent Gladwin back to England. There on Mar. 30, 1762, he married Frances, daughter of the Rev. John Berridge, an evangelical preacher. He returned to his command at Detroit in August, but by December was at Fort William Augustus.

In the winter of 1762–63 he returned to the post at Detroit, where he was stationed when Pontiac's War broke out in May. In this organized Indian effort to hold back the oncoming tide of English expansion, Gladwin successfully defended one of the two major posts which managed to escape the destruction and slaughter of the year 1763. His brilliant defense of Detroit became the central theme of Francis Parkman's *History of the Conspiracy of Pontiac* (1851). By November of 1763, Pontiac's power was practically at an end, but Gladwin's letters show that he had to be very much on his guard during the winter of 1764. In August, reinforcements finally got through to Detroit and Gladwin was permitted to return to England. He attained his lieutenant colonelcy Sept. 17, 1763. After his defense of Detroit, he was carried in the Army Lists as "Deputy Adjutant General in America," until 1780, but never returned to that country. Upon the disbanding of the 80th Regiment after the French and Indian War, he went on the half-pay list, and so remained for the rest of his life. He declined to serve in the War for American Independence, although made a colonel Aug. 29, 1777, and major-general Nov. 20, 1782. He died at his country seat, Stubbing Court, near Chesterfield in Derbyshire, and was buried at Wingerworth Church.

[Almost the only biographical research on Gladwin has been done by Charles Moore, who published the results of his investigations in "Henry Gladwin and the Siege of Detroit," *Harper's Mag.,* June 1897, and "The Gladwin Manuscripts," *Mich. Pioneer and Hist. Soc. Colls.,* XXVII (1897), 605–87. Parkman's *Conspiracy of Pontiac* needs some correction; Parkman himself admitted to Dr. Moore that he knew very little of Gladwin. Most of Gladwin's dispatches and papers relating to the siege of Detroit did not come to light until 1930, when they were found in the Gage Papers, Wm. L. Clements Lib. Amherst had turned most of his papers in this matter over to Gage, and Gage had kept them with his own. See also, "The Bouquet Papers," *Mich. Pioneer and Hist. Soc. Colls.,* vol. XIX (1892); "Bouquet Collection, Calendar," in *Report on Canadian Archives* (1890), by Douglas Brymner; *Diary of the Siege of Detroit* (1860), ed. by F. B. Hough; *Jour. of Pontiac's Conspiracy* (1912), ed. by M. A. Burton; W. L. Jenks, "Diary of the Siege of Detroit," *Mich. Hist. Mag.,* July 1928; Jos. Tilley, *The Old Halls, Manors and Families of Derbyshire,* III (1899), 245–46; obituary in *Gentleman's Mag.,* July 1791, p. 682. Other Gladwin sources are in the Burton Hist. Coll., Detroit.] R. G. A—s.

GLASS, HUGH (fl. 1823–1833), was a trapper of the far west whose unique career has been widely celebrated. According to George C. Yount, who talked with him at the Bear River rendezvous in the winter of 1828–29, he had been a sailor and on being taken prisoner by Jean Lafitte was forced to join the pirate's band. On the Texas coast he escaped, only to be captured by Indians; but his life was spared, and while visiting St. Louis with a delegation of the tribe he regained his freedom. His documental history begins with the spring of 1823, when he joined Ashley's second Missouri River expedition. He was in the two battles with the Arikaras and about Aug. 15 joined Andrew Henry's party on its return to the mouth of the Yellowstone. While proceeding somewhat apart from his companions he was attacked by a grizzly bear and so terribly injured that his death was momentarily expected. This episode, with its sequel, has been variously related in prose and verse (*Missouri Intelligencer,* June 18, 1825; John G. Neihardt, *The Song of Hugh Glass,* 1915, and elsewhere). Henry, pressed for time, left the wounded man in charge of two trappers and resumed his march. These trappers, who according to tradition were James Bridger [*q.v.*], then nineteen years old, and a certain Fitzgerald, took from Glass his rifle and equipment and rejoined the party, reporting him dead and buried. Glass, however, slowly regained strength, and after some days began crawling toward Fort Kiowa, more than a hundred miles away, which eventually he reached and where he gradually recuperated. In the winter, vowing revenge for the wrong done him, he joined an expedition to Henry's new post at the mouth of the Bighorn. Here he found Bridger, whom on account of his youth Glass readily forgave. Months later, at Fort Atkinson, he came upon Fitzgerald. His resentment had now cooled, however, and on recovering his favorite rifle he declared the account closed. His subsequent adventures carried him to New Mexico and thence on trapping tours over a wide range of the West. In trapper talk he was the hero of many desperate encounters with the savages. A man of many eccentricities—one of which was his habit of marching and camping at some distance from his fellows—he was highly esteemed for his integrity, truthfulness, and dauntless courage. He is believed to have been killed by Blackfeet on the upper Yellowstone in the early spring of 1833.

[See "The Chronicles of Geo. C. Yount," ed. by C. L. Camp, *Cal. Hist. Soc. Quart.* (Apr. 1923); also "James Clyman, His Diaries and Reminiscences," *Ibid.,* June 1925. The Howe, Chittenden, and Cooke versions of the grizzly-bear episode are given by J. C. Alter in *James Bridger* (1925).] W. J. G.

GLEASON, FREDERIC GRANT (Dec. 18, 1848–Dec. 6, 1903), composer, musician, music-critic, was born in Middletown, Conn., the son of Frederic L. Gleason, a banker and an excellent amateur flutist, and Martha Willard. He showed a talent for music early in life and at sixteen attempted to write a Christmas oratorio. It was his father's wish that he enter a theological seminary and study for the Congregational ministry, but he offered some resistance, and was finally allowed to turn to music instead. After studying with Dudley Buck in Hartford, Conn., Gleason went to Europe in 1869, and there studied with Moscheles, Richter, Plaidy, Lobe, Loeschhorn, Weitzmann, and Haupt. He did not return until, at the age of twenty-seven, he felt that he was thoroughly equipped for the career he had chosen. The record of his subsequent activities is one of consistent hard work as an organist and composer. After acting as organist in churches in Hartford and New Britain, Conn., he was appointed in 1877 teacher of piano, organ, composition, and orchestration at the Hershey School of Music in Chicago. He was elected examiner, director, and fellow of the American College of Musicians in 1884, president of the Chicago Manuscript Society in 1896, president-general of the American Patriotic Musical League in 1897, and from 1900 until his death he was director of the Chicago Auditorium concerts. In addition to these various musical activities he found time to act as a music-critic for Chicago papers, notably the *Tribune.* On Oct. 19, 1887, he was married to Mabel Blanche Kennicott of Chicago.

Gleason's outstanding works are a setting of "The Culprit Fay" for soli, chorus, and orchestra; two symphonic poems, "Edris" and "The Song of Life"; and the text and music of two grand operas, *Otho Visconti,* and *Montezuma.* The overture to *Otho Visconti* was performed in the *Gewandhaus,* Leipzig, in 1892, and at the World's Fair in Chicago by Theodore Thomas's orchestra. His lesser works include a number of songs, sacred and secular choral numbers, piano pieces, a sonata, theme and variations for organ, and a piano concerto. In both of his dramatic works he tried "to combine the melodic element of Italian opera with the richness of harmonization characteristic of the modern German school and the leit-motif idea of Richard Wagner—combining the lyric and dramatic elements in due proportion" (Mathews, *post,* p. 188). He also employed the same scheme in his cantata, "The Culprit Fay." Yet his creative processes were intellectual rather than inspirational. He wrote at a time when the most distinguished of German composers were slavishly imitating Wagner in every detail of his creative procedure, and when the Wagnerian road seemed the only one to take in operatic composition. Despite his conscientiousness and industry, his mastery of counterpoint, and his very considerable technical skill, his operas and symphonic works may be said to deserve the verdict that they were "too deep and dry for the general hearer." Hamilton, in his mention of Gleason, lays the stress on his symphonic, not his operatic compositions (*post,* p. 266). Gleason was a valuable pioneer of good music in the West but, aside from scholarly quality, his works, like those of other American composers of his generation, are now somewhat outmoded. He ranks among the nineteenth-century creators of American music who played a worthy minor part in the development of American composition. When he died he left several scores in manuscript, with the proviso that they were not to be publicly performed until a half-century after his decease.

[J. P. White, *Geneal. of the Descendants of Thos. Gleason of Watertown, Mass.* (1909); Rupert Hughes, *Am. Composers* (1914); W. S. B. Mathews, *The Great in Music* (1900), pp. 186–89; E. E. Hipsler, *Am. Opera and Its Composers* (1927); C. G. Hamilton, *Outlines of Music Hist.* (1908); *Music,* Jan. 1898; *Musical Courier,* Dec. 16, 1903; *Chicago Tribune,* Dec. 7, 1903.]

F. H. M.

GLENN, HUGH (Jan. 7, 1788–May 28, 1833), Santa Fé trader, merchant, army contractor, was born in Berkeley County, Va. (now W. Va.), the son of Hugh Glenn, a native of Scotland. His early life is somewhat shrouded in mystery. On Mar. 17, 1816, he was married in Greensburg, Pa., to Mary Gibson, by whom he had one child, Hugh Gibson Glenn. Like most adventurous Virginians who pressed forward to the constantly advancing frontier, he sojourned in Kentucky, where he was commissioned major of the 19th Regiment of Kentucky Militia from Madison County. One entry gives the date as 1803, but other entries in the same record indicate that his appointment was in 1809, or later. Ultimately he settled in Cincinnati, Ohio, which became his legal abode, and where, according to a history of Hamilton County, he was captain of a company recruited at the outbreak of the War of 1812. From 1814 to 1817, Glenn and his partner, Jacob Fowler, furnished supplies to the northwestern army. On Jan. 20, 1817, he entered into another contract with the federal government (in which he was described as being "of Kentucky"), to furnish provisions at various military posts, and rations to such Indians as visited these posts. These transactions amounted to nearly $200,000 and included supplies furnished forts Harrison, Belle Fontaine, Osage, Clark, Crawford, Edwards, Armstrong, and Belle Point (later Fort Smith). It appears that he personally conducted the provisions to their destination, as Maj. Long reported having met him on the Upper Mississippi in July 1817, when Glenn was taking supplies to the garrison at Prairie du Chien.

Glenn entertained Long's party at Cincinnati in May 1818, and Nuttall the following November. He was introduced to Nuttall as "lately sutler to the garrison of Arkansa." Long's party again met Glenn in September 1820 at his trading house near the mouth of the Verdigris River. Here, on Sept. 21, 1821, he joined Jacob Fowler in a trading expedition to Santa Fé. Glenn was given command of the party composed of twenty men. In the following January he took four of the party and proceeded in advance to Santa Fé, the others lingering at the base of the mountains on the Arkansas, under command of Fowler. Being well received by the Mexicans and getting permission from them to hunt and trade, he sent word for Fowler to bring on the rest of the party. Concluding their enterprise, the party started back to the United States on June 1, 1822. Glenn arrived in St. Louis about July 17, where he sold the furs obtained on the journey to the American Fur Company for $3,705.61. The Glenn-Fowler expedition was the first to go to Santa Fé by way of the Verdigris, and was the first successful expedition from the United States to the Mexican provinces. Glenn himself was said to be a gentleman in manner and in fact. He died at Cincinnati, Ohio, where he was buried in the old Preteman Cemetery.

[*Reg. of the Ky. State Hist. Soc.,* May 1924; H. A. and K. B. Ford, *Hist. of Hamilton County, Ohio* (1881), p. 82; W. A. Brice, *Hist. of Fort Wayne* (1868), p. 290; *Am. State Papers, Mil. Affairs,* vol. II (1834); *Sen. Doc. 13,* 19 Cong., 1 Sess.; *House Doc. 184,* 35 Cong., 1 Sess.; Office of Indian Affairs, Letter Book D, p. 306; S. H. Long, *Voyage in a . . . Skiff to the Falls of St. Anthony in 1817* (1860), p. 65; Edwin James, *Account of an Expedition from Pittsburgh to the Rocky Mountains* (2 vols., 1823); Thos. Nuttall, *Jour. of Travels into Arkansa Territory* (1821); *The Jour. of Jacob Fowler* (1898), ed. by Elliott Coues; Thos. James, *Three Years Among the Indians and Mexicans* (1916), ed. by W. B. Douglas; account books of the American Fur Company, Mo. Hist. Soc.; probate and county court records, Callaway County, Mo.; information as to certain facts from Glenn's great-grandson, Judge Allen B. Glenn, Harrisonville, Mo. James's characterization of Glenn is contrary to those of Glenn's contemporaries, and is therefore not to be relied upon.]

S. M. D.

GLIDDEN, CHARLES JASPER (Aug. 29, 1857–Sept. 11, 1927), telephone pioneer, motorist, aviator, was born at Lowell, Mass., the son of Nathaniel Ames and Laura Ellen (Clark) Glidden. He was descended from Charles Glidden who came to Boston from Bideford, Devon, about 1660, and moved to New Hampshire in 1664. At fifteen the boy entered the employ of the Northern Telegraph Company at Lowell as telegraph messenger boy, then after a brief service with the Franklin Telegraph Company at Springfield, Mass., he became manager of this company's office at Manchester, N. H. He also served as New Hampshire correspondent for Boston newspapers, and acquired a wide acquaintance in northern New England. When the Atlantic and Pacific Telegraph Company was organized in 1873, Glidden was appointed its manager at Manchester, a position which he held until 1877. In the preceding year he had directed for Alexander Graham Bell over the Manchester-Boston telegraph lines a successful test of the possibility of long-distance telephony. That experiment determined his career.

Having installed several private telephone lines at Manchester, Glidden in 1877 suggested to the Bell Company the project of organizing at Lowell a telephone exchange system. It was agreed that if fifty subscribers could be secured the exchange might start. Glidden energetically canvassed the city for the first telephone exchange list to be compiled anywhere. The exchange thus organized was sold in 1879 to a syndicate composed of Glidden, William A. Ingham, and others who obtained the exclusive right to use the telephone in Lowell and the surrounding towns. Under the style of the Lowell District Telephone Company they installed one of the first multiple switchboards, and though it was a crude device compared with the central energy boards of a later day, the company gave generally satisfactory service. In this primitive exchange much of the technique of telephone traffic was developed under Glidden's supervision. It was his discovery that girls' voices carry better than men's over the wires, which led to the use of women as telephone operators.

Following the successful installation of the telephone system at Lowell, Glidden, Ingham, and their associates opened exchanges in 1879 at Fitchburg and Worcester. In the next year they established systems at several places in New Hampshire and Maine. Their Massachusetts companies outside of Boston were the nucleus from which the present New England Telephone & Telegraph Company was created. In 1883 the syndicate, of which Glidden was secretary and principal executive, extended its operations into Ohio, Minnesota, Arkansas, Texas, and other states under the firm-name of the Erie Telephone & Telegraph Company. The main offices continued to be at Lowell. Early in the twentieth century the Erie telephone companies were sold to the Bell organization on terms advantageous to the Lowell group. Glidden found himself with leisure and means to devote the rest of his life to motoring and aviation, in which, successively, he became interested. The family home was removed, in 1902, to Brookline, Mass., whence Glidden organized the first round-the-world motor tour, covering 46,528 miles in 39 countries, in many of which an automobile had not been seen before. In 1905 he established the Glidden trophy for the American Automobile Association, which became the chief touring trophy in the United States. The newspaper and magazine descriptions of his own journeyings were terse and matter-of-fact. They also reveal one of the secrets of his success in business and pleasure-seeking—his meticulously careful provision against accidents and emergencies. In aeronautics he was equally active. Before the commercial future of the airplane was assured he made forty-six balloon ascensions, and was prominently associated with the early air meets at Squantum, Mass. His "Aerial Navigation Company," chartered to operate airships between Boston and New York, was based on premature expectations, but during the World War a sudden development of aviation seemed to justify Glidden in hoping to "see airplanes used in an individual capacity as commonly as are motor cycles now" (*Lowell Courier-Citizen,* Sept. 13, 1927). He served in the aviation section of the Signal Officers' Reserve Corps from 1917 to 1919, was president of the World's Board of Aeronautical Commissioners, incorporated in 1921, and edited the *Aeronautical Digest* from October 1921 to February 1924. Death, due to cancer, interrupted his ambitious plans for further participation in aviatorial technique and finance. He had married, July 10, 1878, Lucy Emma Cleworth, of Manchester. His integrity, and his direct, forceful personality brought him respect and popularity even while he was known to be a hard bargainer, alert to guard his personal interests.

[A sketch, presumably autobiographical, of Glidden's career to 1897 appeared in the Courier-Citizen's *Illustrated Hist. of Lowell and Vicinity* (1897), pp. 474–75. See also G. W. Chamberlain and L. G. Strong, *The Descendants of Chas. Glidden of Portsmouth and Exeter, N. H.* (1925); F. W. Coburn, *Hist. of Lowell and its People,* I (1920), 373–75, and *Moses Greeley Parker, M.D.* (1922), pp. 104–18; the *New Eng. Mag.,* Jan. 1904, for an Arctic Circle motor trip; *Who's Who in America,* 1924–25; the *N. Y. Times* and *Boston Transcript,* Sept. 12, 1927.]

F. W. C.

GLIDDEN, JOSEPH FARWELL (Jan. 18, 1813–Oct. 9, 1906), farmer, inventor, capitalist, was born in Charlestown, Sullivan County, N. H. He was the son of David and Polly (Hurd) Glidden, both natives of New Hampshire, and a descendant of Charles Glidden who came to Boston about 1660. In his early childhood his parents moved to a farm in Orleans County, N. Y. Here he grew to manhood as a typical farmer's boy. He went to the local district schools, though his attendance was limited after reaching his teens to a few months in the winter. Then, with college in mind, he studied at Middlebury Academy, Vt., and in the seminary in Lima, N. Y. After teaching school for several years he returned to his father's farm, his interest in farming being greater than he had realized, and for eight years he remained at home. Anxious for a farm of his own but not having the necessary funds to purchase one, he started out in 1842 with two threshing machines of rather crude construction, offering his services and those of his machines to farmers and employing himself otherwise out of harvest season. For two years he worked his westward way into Michigan and Illinois. Shortly after reaching De Kalb County in Illinois he purchased six hundred acres of land just outside of De Kalb village. From time to time thereafter he acquired more land until his holdings totaled 1,500 acres including his original purchase where he had erected a house. Besides farming he began raising fine cattle, and later, with a friend, purchased 180,000 acres of land in Texas and stocked it with 15,000 head of cattle.

While attending the county fair in De Kalb in 1873 with his friends Jacob Haish [*q.v.*] and Isaac L. Ellwood, Glidden stopped to examine an exhibit of barbed wire recently invented by Henry M. Rose. Apparently improvements in this form of fencing occurred to him, for after experimenting for some months he applied for a patent on Oct. 27, 1873. Two months later, while his patent application was being considered, his friend Haish also made application for a patent for an improvement in barbed wire, and when informed of Glidden's invention, challenged its priority. Interference proceedings then followed, and after a delay of over a year a decision was rendered on Oct. 20, 1874, in favor of Glidden. On Nov. 24, 1874, he was granted patent No. 157,124. The important feature of his patent was the novel method of holding the spur wires in place; and when subsequently wire fencing incorporating this feature was placed on the market, it proved to be superior to other forms of barbed wire. It is still in active demand after more than half a century. It is, too, the sole survivor of hundreds of early styles. Its nearest ranking competitor was the famous "S" barbed wire, invented in 1875 by Jacob Haish and subsequently marketed by him. While the Glidden-Haish patent suit was in process, Glidden applied for and was granted a second patent on May 12, 1874; and following the settlement of the interference, he received a third patent on Aug. 22, 1876. Both of these inventions were concerned with improvements in barbed wire, and in neither did Glidden claim to be the originator of the spurs or prongs characteristic of such fencing. In 1875, after Glidden had unsuccessfully offered a half-interest in his barbed-wire patents to a neighbor for $100, a second neighbor, Isaac L. Ellwood, risked $265 for this same half-interest. They then formed a partnership known as the Barb Fence Company, and proceeded to manufacture barbed wire in De Kalb. A year later, however, Glidden was induced to sell his remaining half interest to the Washburn & Moen Manufacturing Company of Worcester, Mass., for $60,000, plus a large royalty for the life of the patent.

From this time on his only interest in barbed wire was the collecting of his royalties which he continued to draw until 1891, building up a large fortune, although he appeared occasionally as a witness in the barbed-wire infringement litigations which continued for more than twenty years. His only business interests other than his farms and ranches in Illinois and Texas were the De Kalb National Bank, of which he was vice-president from its organization in 1883, the De Kalb Roller Grist Mill, of which he was the owner, and the Glidden Hotel of which he was builder and proprietor. He served as sheriff of De Kalb County in 1852, and was the last Democratic official to be chosen for this office. Glidden was twice married: first, in 1837, to Clarissa Foster, in Clarendon, N. Y. After the death of Mrs. Glidden and her three children, he married Lucinda Warne of De Kalb in 1851, who with one daughter survived him.

[*Biog. Record of De Kalb County, Ill.* (1898); Geo. W. Chamberlain, *The Descendants of Chas. Glidden of Portsmouth and Exeter, N. H.* (1925); *Farm Implement News* (Chicago), Apr. 1887, Oct. 18, 1906. See also Arthur G. Warren, "Barbed Wire; Who Invented It?" in the *Iron Age*, June 24, 1926; C. G. Washburn, *Industrial Worcester* (1917); records and correspondence from Industrial Museum, American Steel & Wire Company, Worcester, Mass.; Patent Office records.]

C. W. M.

GLOVER, JOHN (Nov. 5, 1732–Jan. 30, 1797), Revolutionary soldier, the son of Jonathan and Tabitha (Bacon) Glover, was born at Salem, Mass., but moved early in life to Marblehead. He progressed through the various occupations of shoemaker, fish vender, and merchant, to the position of a man of wealth. One of the business ventures in which he was interested, along with Elbridge Gerry [*q.v.*] and some others, was the building of a smallpox hospital for the inoculation of patients. The project was sponsored by the town of Marblehead, but after protests were made by conscientious objectors the town withdrew its approval, in spite of which the promoters completed the building and opened it for business on Oct. 16, 1773. Opposition became so violent, however, that the proprietors were forced to close it, and finally on Jan. 26, 1774, the building was burned by an angry mob.

Glover first came into prominence in the revolutionary movement as a member of the Marblehead committee of correspondence appointed at the suggestion of the Town of Boston after the circulation of its statement, "The Rights of the Colonists," of 1772. His military interest up to the time of the Boston Tea Party had been secondary to his other activities, but because of his training and experience as an officer in the local militia he soon became prominent when the colonies turned to force. He was an ensign as early as 1759, captain-lieutenant in 1762 under Col. Jacob Fowle, and in 1773 captain of a company in the regiment commanded by Col. John Gallison of Marblehead. In April 1775, after the Massachusetts Provincial Congress had voted to raise an army of 13,000 men for the defense of the province, the Committee of Safety commissioned Glover to safeguard the town of Marblehead from the spying of the British frigate *Lively,* lying off the harbor. About this time Glover set to work to recruit volunteers in case they should be needed for defense of the town, and was ordered by the Committee of Safety to hold his forces ready to march at a moment's notice. Shortly thereafter the Provincial Congress, on the recommendation of the Committee, commissioned him colonel of the 21st Regiment and stationed him at Marblehead until June, when he was ordered to Cambridge to join the forces there. Washington, soon after assuming command in July, placed him in charge of equipping and manning armed vessels for the service of the colonies, then sent him with his regiment to defend Marblehead and afterward Beverly in anticipation of a British attack. After the British evacuation of Boston, he was ordered to New York with his regiment, now reorganized as the 14th Continental Regiment, and attached to Gen. Sullivan's brigade. When the retreat of the American forces from Long Island began, Glover was entrusted with the entire command of the vessels for transporting the troops. In October his forces, stationed on a hill near White Plains, were attacked by the enemy, whom they routed, but they finally had to join the main army on its retreat. His next service was the transportation of Washington's army across the Delaware at Trenton, when his own troops, after crossing, led the advance. In February 1777 he was promoted to brigadier-general and as such he served in the campaign against Burgoyne, after whose surrender he was given charge of conducting prisoners to Cambridge.

From Cambridge Glover was ordered to Rhode Island to help in the attempt to recapture Rhode Island proper. The Americans attacked Newport but were forced to abandon the siege because of the failure of the French fleet to arrive. In the spring of 1779 Glover succeeded Gen. Sullivan in the command of the Providence department, and in June left Providence to join the main army. While his brigade was stationed at West Point he served, in the summer of 1780, as a member of the court which sentenced André. After Washington's departure for Virginia, Glover's troops were among those which remained at West Point for the winter and spring to defend the Hudson Highlands. He was dispatched to Massachusetts early in 1782 to take charge of mustering recruits. Because of failing health, however, he was forced to retire from active service, and in July 1782 Congress placed him on the half-pay establishment. After the war he served as selectman of Marblehead, 1787–92; as a member of the Massachusetts convention to ratify the Federal Constitution, 1788; and as a representative in the General Court, 1788–89. On Oct. 30, 1754, he had married Hannah Gale of Marblehead, who died in 1778, and on Mar. 1, 1781, he married Mrs. Frances Fosdick of Boston. He died in Marblehead in his sixty-fifth year.

[Samuel Roads, Jr., *The Hist. and Traditions of Marblehead* (1880); *New-Eng. Hist. and Geneal. Reg.,* July 1865, pp. 213–15, July 1868, pp. 284–85, July 1876, p. 332; Jared Sparks, *The Writings of George Washington* (1839), IV, 399 and vols. V and VI, *passim*; "The Heath Papers," *Mass. Hist. Soc. Colls.,* 5 ser. IV (1878), 7 ser. IV and V (1904–05); Wm. Upham, in *Essex Inst. Hist. Colls.,* vol. V (Apr.–June 1863); F. A. Gardner, in *Mass. Mag.,* Jan.–Apr. 1908; N. P. Sanborn, *Gen. John Glover and his Marblehead Regt. in the Revolutionary War* (1903); *Vital Records of Marblehead* (1904).]
V. F. B.

GLOVER, SAMUEL TAYLOR (Mar. 9, 1813–Jan. 22, 1884), lawyer, was of Virginia stock. The son of John and Fanny (Taylor) Glover, he was a descendant of Richard Glover who came from England in 1635, settled in Virginia, and became a wealthy planter. About 1825 John Glover moved with his family from Virginia to Harrodsburg, Mercer County, Ky. His son's youth was spent on a farm, but he also received an academic education, graduating at Bardstown College with highest honors. He had taken up the study of law in his spare moments and in 1835 moved to Knox County, where he was admitted to practise. Two years later, however, he went to Missouri, was admitted to the bar of that state, and settled at Palmyra, Marion County. This was the center of the 2nd judicial district and he soon acquired an extensive clientele in Marion and the adjoining counties and became the undisputed leader of the district bar. In 1849, desiring a larger field of opportunities, he once more moved, this time to St. Louis, where he practised until his death. He confined himself to his profession taking little part in public or municipal affairs, until the emergence of the slavery question. He had identified himself with the emancipation policy from his youth up, despite the overwhelming preponderance of pro-slavery sentiment in the states where he had lived, and in 1860 he was a prominent supporter of Edward Bates [*q.v.*] in his candidature for the Republican nomination for president at the Chicago convention of that year. The situation was tense in St. Louis for some months prior to and after the outbreak of the Civil War. Glover was appointed a member of the "Committee of Safety" at a mass meeting which adopted the platform of "unalterable fidelity to the Union under all circumstances," and he took a leading part in the events which retained Missouri within the Union. After the close of the war he gave a signal example of adherence to principle by refusing to take the oath of loyalty which the Constitution of 1865 required, *inter alia,* of all lawyers. He was indicted for practising without having taken the oath, and demurred to the indictment on the ground that the provisions respecting oaths were unconstitutional. His contention was sustained (*The Murphy and Glover Test Oath Cases,* 41 *Mo.,* 339). Thereafter he abstained from participation in politics—emerging on only one occasion when his name was unsuccessfully placed before the Democratic caucus in connection with the United States Senate—and confined himself to his law practise, becoming the recognized head of the St. Louis bar. He was preëminent as counsel, the *Reports* showing that during his career he was retained in thirty cases in the Supreme Court of the United States, thirty-five cases in the court of appeals, and no less than 410 in the Missouri supreme court. Well versed in the law of real property and crimes, an expert in commercial law, and esteemed the best constitutional lawyer of his time in the West, he was noted in court for his clear forcible arguments and his infinite resourcefulness. Fluent of speech, he was capable of rising to real eloquence, though owing to a nervousness which he could never overcome, he often weakened his addresses by stammering. Another serious defect was an infirmity of temper which occasionally became uncontrollable. His failure to achieve more success in public life may be ascribed to a lack of magnetism which precluded him from ever becoming a popular politician. To his intimate friends he could unbend and on such occasions he would shine by his brilliance and geniality, but to the crowd he appeared cold and his forgetfulness of names and faces was apt to be embarrassing. He was married on June 28, 1843, to Mildred Ann Buckner, a native of Louisville, Ky.

[Anna Glover, *Glover Memorials and Geneals.* (1867); *Hist. of the Bench and Bar of Mo.* (1898), ed. by A. J. D. Stewart, p. 120. *Encyc. of the Hist. of Mo.* (1901), ed. by H. L. Conard, III, 65; *Am. Law Rev.,* Jan.–Feb. 1884; and *Proc. Fourth Ann. Meeting Mo. Bar Asso.* (1884), p. 125.]

H. W. H. K.

GLOVER, TOWNEND (Feb. 20, 1813–Sept. 7, 1883), the first man to hold an official entomological position under the United States government, was an Englishman by birth. His paternal grandfather was Samuel Glover, a merchant of Leeds, England, and his mother was Mary Townend of Leaming Lane, Yorkshire. His father, Henry Glover, was in business at Rio de Janeiro at the time of Townend's birth. His mother died when he was six weeks old, and he was sent to relatives in England. Six years later his father died while still abroad, and Townend was educated in England by his relatives, who wished him to study for the ministry or to go into commercial life. He was fond of nature, however, was a natural draftsman, and preferred a different career from either of those suggested by his relatives. When he was twenty-one, therefore, on coming into his father's fortune, he went to Germany to study art under Mattenheimer, the Inspector of the Münich Art Gallery. He became rather proficient, preferring still life in oil, but later made rather remarkable water-colors of flowers and insects. After two years in Germany, he returned to England and established a studio.

In 1836 he came to America, and remained in this country for the rest of his life. He traveled extensively for a time, finally settling at New Rochelle, N. Y. There, in September 1840, he married Sarah T. Byrnes. He was especially fond of orchard work, learned to model fruits, and made a large collection of such models, which he exhibited at different fairs. In the winter of 1853–54, he took his collection to Washington, as a result of which visit he received an appointment in the Bureau of Agriculture of the Patent Office to collect "statistics and other information on seeds, fruits and insects." He traveled extensively in the South and made many important observations on insects. With the exception of an interval of two years and a half, when he went to the Agricultural College of Maryland to teach entomology, he remained with the government agricultural service until 1878. He wrote the bulk of the articles concerning insects published in the *Annual Reports,* and, aside from museum duties, occupied himself in the preparation of a great illustrated work on the insects of the United States. For this project, he etched on copper plates many excellent illustrations. Prints were made from a number of these plates, and sets may be found in a few of the libraries of the United States, but the work as a whole was never completed and published. His health failed in 1878, and he was succeeded in office by C. V. Riley [*q.v.*]. After a few months, Glover retired to Baltimore where, until his death, he lived with his adopted daughter, Mrs. Hopper. His plates were bought by the government just before he died, and are in the possession of the Smithsonian Institution.

Glover was something of a figure in his day, but now is remembered chiefly as the earliest government entomologist. He was an eccentric man, and although he made very many interesting observations his reports were printed badly and at present are seldom consulted, although many early important statements of fact are to be found in them. As early as 1865 he called attention to the great danger to the United States occasioned by the accidental introduction of new insect pests through the importation of foreign seeds and plants. Had government action in regard to the matter been taken at that time, a majority of the most dangerous pests to agriculture that have since established themselves in this country would have been excluded.

[C. R. Dodge, "The Life and Entomological Work of the late Townend Glover," *U. S. Dept. Agric., Div. of Entomology, Bull. No. 18* (1888), with bibliography of 64 numbers; *Psyche*, Nov.–Dec. 1883, p. 115; *Canadian Entomologist*, Sept. 1883, p. 178; Baltimore *Sun*, Sept. 8, 1883.] L. O. H.

GLYNN, JAMES (June 28, 1801–May 13, 1871), naval officer, was born in Philadelphia, Pa., and appointed midshipman from Virginia, Mar. 4, 1815. In his letter applying for this rank (Navy Department Library, Personnel File) he states that his father "fought and died at New Orleans"; he was probably James Anthony Glynn of Richmond, Va., who is said by his sister to have been connected with the navy at that time. The son entered the gunboat service at New Orleans about 1810, and served afterward, 1812–15, as acting midshipman in the *General Pike* and *Superior* on Lake Ontario. Commodore Chauncey recommended him as of "correct habits and honorable feelings." On sea and shore duty, chiefly on the Atlantic coast and in European waters, Glynn rose to lieutenant, 1825, and to commander, 1841. He was on the California coast in the Mexican War, and in 1848, commanding the sloop *Preble*, joined the East India Squadron under Commodore Geisinger. Here, in a career not otherwise distinguished, he gained some note by his rescue of a number of American seamen held captive in Japan. Upon news of them from the Dutch at Nagasaki, Glynn was ordered there from Hong Kong, sailing Mar. 22, 1849, in the face of bad weather and with poor charts, and arriving Apr. 17. The next day he anchored close to the town under the guns of the shore defenses, where he was immediately encircled by a cordon of boats. In interviews with Japanese officials he adopted an assured and severe manner, insisted on prompt action, and secured the delivery of the sailors on Apr. 26. Thirteen of them, including nine Kanakas, had deserted from the whaler *Lagoda* in June preceding. The fourteenth was a half-breed Indian, Ranald MacDonald [*q.v.*], who had landed from another whaler for adventure. In his report Geisinger credits Glynn's accomplishment as "probably the first instance" of our successful negotiations with the island empire. Impressed with the possibility of opening relations with Japan, and the need of a coaling base there for the China trade, Glynn, upon returning to New York in January 1851, laid his views before the government, and published them in a press letter dated Feb. 24, addressed to the firm of Howland & Aspinwall. He thus helped pave the way for the naval mission to Japan, intrusted first, in June 1851, to Commodore J. H. Aulick and later to Commodore Perry. In 1855 Glynn was put on the reserved list, but was restored in 1858 with back pay. In January 1861, he went to Pensacola in the *Macedonian*, and subsequently cruised in the Caribbean against Confederate raiders until Jan. 6, 1862. He was then retired as captain, and had no further service except as lighthouse inspector in 1865. In 1867 he was made a commodore (retired). After a year in Europe, 1869–70, he died at his home in New Haven. He was survived by his wife, Anne (Stoddard) Glynn, to whom he was married after retirement, and whose family lived at Geneva, N. Y.

[Glynn's service record, with dates, is in L. R. Hamersly, *Records of Living Officers of the U. S. Navy and Marine Corps* (ed. of 1870). On the Japanese episode, see "Early American Visitors to Japan," by C. W. Stewart, and "Early Naval Voyages to the Orient," by C. O. Paullin, *Proc. U. S. Naval Inst.*, XXXI (1905), 953–58, and XXXVII (1911), 249–55; *Senate Ex. Doc. No. 59*, 32 Cong., 1 Sess., pp. 2–63; and "American-Japanese Intercourse Prior to the Advent of Perry," by I. Nitobé, in *Ann. Report Am. Hist. Asso. . . . 1911* (1913), I, 131–40.] A. W.

GLYNN, MARTIN HENRY (Sept. 27, 1871–Dec. 14, 1924), editor, congressman, governor of New York, was born of humble Irish parents, Martin and Anne (Scanlon) Glynn, in the village that is remembered as the birthplace of Martin Van Buren, Kinderhook, Columbia County, N. Y. He was educated in the public schools of his native town and subsequently at St. John's College, Fordham University, where he was graduated in 1894, the honor man of his class. After serving for a time on the reportorial staff of the Albany *Times-Union,* he became its managing editor in 1895, and later editor and publisher. He also took up the study of law and was admitted to the bar in 1897, but journalism and politics left him little time to devote to his legal practise.

Glynn's entry into politics took place in 1898, when, at the age of twenty-seven he was elected to represent the Albany district in Congress. Although he served but a single term, and was an unsuccessful candidate for reëlection in 1900, he attracted considerable notice by his assiduous sponsorship of labor legislation. President McKinley appointed him on the National Commission of the Louisiana Purchase Exposition at St. Louis, and he served as vice-president of that body from 1901 to 1905. As comptroller of the State of New York, to which office he was elected in 1906 as the nominee of the Democratic party and the Independence League, Glynn first attracted statewide attention and gained a distinguished reputation as an administrator and a practical economist. His prudent requirement that all state depository banks give surety company bonds instead of personal bonds to protect state funds, proved most effective during the panic of 1907, when the state did not lose a single dollar. His election in 1912 as lieutenant-governor was his reward for his two years of competent service as comptroller. He became governor on the removal of William Sulzer from office, Oct. 17, 1913, and served until Dec. 31, 1914. In his brief administration he secured the passage of the workmen's compensation law and the act of abolishing party conventions and substituting statewide primaries. He continued Gov. Sulzer's investigation of the state departments, which brought forth further revelations of corruption and mismanagement. Glynn's astute financial ability was evidenced by the substantial reduction of state taxes under his administration and the establishment of a land-bank system to finance farm operations. Notwithstanding this record, he was defeated in 1914 by the Republican candidate, Charles S. Whitman, and ran behind his ticket.

Glynn's reputation as an orator was national. His voice was unusually rich in quality and his thoughts were clothed in felicitous diction. His supreme oratorical effort was his speech as temporary chairman of the Democratic Convention at St. Louis in 1916, in which he claimed that the United States was "constrained by the tradition of its past, by the logic of its present and by the promise of its future to hold itself apart from European warfare" (*Official Report of the Proceedings of the Democratic National Convention,* 1916, p. 16). From his keynote was coined the Democratic slogan, "He kept us out of war." This speech has been called the most effective contribution to the literature of that campaign and the slogan, the greatest single factor in effecting the reëlection of Wilson (*Outlook,* Nov. 15, 1916; *New York Times,* Dec. 15, 1924). Without holding any elective office, Glynn, in the last decade of his life, rendered distinguished service in state, federal and international affairs He served as a member of President Wilson's Federal Industrial Commission, 1919–20, and was appointed by Gov. Smith in 1919 one of the two special commissioners to investigate and report on certain phases of the high cost of living. In a notable report the commissioners urged that the dairy industry be regulated as a public utility ("Message from the Governor Transmitting Report of . . . the Commission on High Cost of Living," *Legislative Document No. 29,* Albany, 1920). While abroad in 1921 Glynn performed important services in aid of peace between Ireland and England. It was through his efforts that Lloyd George invited De Valera to come to London to settle the Irish question without "exacting promises or making conditions" (*New York Times,* Oct. 7, 1923). According to the testimony of Lloyd George, it was Glynn who took the British premier's views to the Irish leaders, and it was this exchange that made possible the Irish Free State.

Glynn was married Jan. 2, 1901, to Mary C. E. Magrane, daughter of P. B. Magrane of Lynn, Mass. Throughout his last years of illness he patiently supervised the publication of his newspaper. He was a man of culture, an indefatigable student, a conversationalist of rare charm, possessed of a sympathetic and companionable nature. He died in Albany.

[J. H. Manning, *New York State Men,* no. 243 (1925); J. J. Walsh, "Martin H. Glynn, First Catholic Governor of New York," *Cath. World,* Feb. 1925; *Biog. Dir. Am. Cong.* (1928); *Who's Who in N. Y.,* 1924; *N. Y. Times,* Dec. 15, 1924.] R. B. M.

GMEINER, JOHN (Dec. 5, 1847–Nov. 11, 1913), Catholic priest and publicist, was the son of Sebastian and Caroline (Fritsch) Gmeiner of Baernau in Bavaria who emigrated to Milwaukee, Wis., in 1849. At the age of twelve years, John entered the preparatory department of St. Francis de Sales Seminary from which he advanced to the major seminary. Ordained by Bishop John Henni on June 10, 1870, he was assigned to St. Boniface's Church, Germantown, Wis. The next few years (1873–83) found him teaching at the preparatory seminary or serving German congregations at Holy Trinity in Milwaukee, at the Cathedral, at Cassville, Platteville, Oshkosh, and Waukesha. In addition he edited the *Columbia* (1873–76), through which he familiarized himself with the German-American press and the status of Germans in the Middle West. In 1883, he became a professor in St. Francis de Sales Seminary from which he was later called by Archbishop Ireland to a similar position in the Theological Seminary of St. Thomas at St. Paul, Minn. After 1889 he served for short terms in minor parishes at Mendota, St. Paul, South St. Paul, and Buffalo, Minn., until in 1902 he was sent to a German parish in Springfield, Minn.

Father Gmeiner was a conscientious student, an authority upon German emigrants and the language question, and an able preacher especially in his native tongue. He delivered an address on "Primitive and Prospective Religious Union of the Human Family" at the Parliament of Religions held in Chicago (Sept. 11–27, 1893) which aroused the interest of Archbishops Gibbons, Ireland, and Feehan. Father Gmeiner took a strong stand on the German question declaring in opposition to Cahenslyism: "I do not believe in any possibility of perpetuating here on American soil for many generations to come, the German language, German customs, and German patriotism." Unburdened with views brought from Germany, he urged the Germans to be content and to remember that they were fairly, if not favorably, treated in the Catholic Church, which, however, could not be expected to serve as a literary club to foster peculiar linguistic tastes (*The Church and the Various Nationalities*). In *The Church and Foreignism* (1891), he expressed a stout Americanism which caused many Germans to criticize his "Americanisirungs Evangelium," but which merited Archbishop Ireland's approval. In addition to a number of sound philosophical and historical articles in *Acta et Dicta,* the *Catholic World,* and other religious reviews, Father Gmeiner was the author of a number of books and brochures: *Die Katholische Kirche in den Vereinigten Staaten* (1875); *Sind wir dem Weltende Nahe?* (1877); *Modern Scientific Views and Christian Doctrines Compared* (1884), which was favorably reviewed in Catholic periodicals and by a number of bishops; *The Spirits of Darkness and their Manifestations on Earth, or Ancient and Modern Spiritualism* (1886); *Emanuel—The Savior of the World* (1880, 1888); *The Church and the Various Nationalities in the United States; Are German Catholics Unfairly Treated?* (1887); and *Mediaeval and Modern Cosmology* (1891).

[Material has been drawn from Gmeiner's books and personal information, as well as from his articles in *Acta et Dicta,* July 1908, the *Catholic World,* Oct. 1885, Mar. 1886, Dec. 1887, May and Nov. 1888, Apr. 1889. See also *Who's Who in America,* 1914–15; the *Catholic Bulletin,* St. Paul; *Sadler's Catholic Directory*; *The Official Catholic Directory*; A. N. Marquis, *The Book of Minnesotans* (1907); *St. Paul Pioneer Press,* Nov. 12, 1913; *Minneapolis Morning Tribune,* Nov. 12, 1913.]

R. J. P.

GOBRECHT, CHRISTIAN (Dec. 23, 1785–July 23, 1844), engraver and die-sinker, was a son of the Rev. John Christopher Gobrecht, pastor in the German Reformed Church, and Elizabeth Sands. He was born in Hanover, York County, Pa., where his father had a charge, and early in life was apprenticed to a clock-maker in Manheim, Lancaster County. Not long after he began his apprenticeship his master died. Relieved of his indenture, he went to Baltimore, where he soon established himself as an engraver of ornamental work for clocks and watches, including dials and maker's name-plates. He is said to have been almost entirely self-taught. Subsequently he abandoned watch and clock engraving and devoted himself to the business of general engraving. At first his work consisted of engraving headings for newspapers, and type-punches for type-founders. Eventually he deserted this work and became a writing- and seal-engraver and die-sinker. About 1811 he removed to Philadelphia, where he was employed in 1816 by Murray, Draper, Fairman & Company, bank-note engravers. In 1826 he is known to have furnished designs and models of dies for the United States Mint, in Philadelphia (Stewart, *post,* p. 87), and in 1836 he was appointed assistant engraver of the Mint. Four years later he was appointed engraver of the Mint, remaining in that position until his death.

Early in his career Gobrecht invented a medal-ruling machine, by means of which a medal could be copied and engraved. The machine was used by its inventor on only one production, a portrait of Alexander I, of Russia. It was found, in cases of high relief, greatly to distort the features. In addition to his abilities as an engraver, he was a most ingenious mechanic. Sometime between 1816 and 1821 he "invented and manufactured a reed organ, made of an assemblage of metallic tongues placed in a case and operated with a bellows and keys" (Darrach, *post,* p. 356). At the time Maezel's automatons were being exhibited, he invented a speaking doll, and later a camera lucida. He also produced engravings for calico printers, and dies for book-binders. He engraved the brass dies for em bossing the Morocco covers of the *Boston Token,* from 1831 to 1836, as well as the eagle cover of the Philadelphia *Token.* Among the medals he engraved were the Charles Willson Peale medal, the Franklin Institute medal, and the medal of the Massachusetts Charitable Mechanic Association. Gobrecht died in Philadelphia and was buried in Monument Cemetery. He had married, on May 31, 1818, Mary (Hamilton) Hewes, the widow of Daniel Hewes.

[G. G. Evans, *Hist. of the U. S. Mint* (1885); F. H. Stewart, *Hist. of the First U. S. Mint* (1924); Henry Simpson, *Eminent Philadelphians* (1859); Chas. Gobrecht Darrach, "Christian Gobrecht, Artist and Inventor," *Pa. Mag. of Hist. and Biog.*, July 1906; *North American* (Phila.), July 25, 1844.] J. J.

GODBE, WILLIAM SAMUEL (June 26, 1833–Aug. 1, 1902), mine operator, Mormon convert and later a leading dissenter, was born in London, England. His father, Samuel Godbe, a physician by training, turned to a more congenial profession and became a teacher and composer of music. His mother, Sarah La Riviere, was the daughter of a French nobleman who escaped to London during the Revolution and there became a court violinist and instructor in dancing to the Queen. Early in life the son was brought under the tutelage of his father and uncles, but while still a boy, he bound himself to a ship's captain, lived the adventurous life of a sailor, saw interesting bits of the world, then settled in Hull to complete his apprenticeship with a ship's chandler. Here he capitulated to Mormon missionaries bearing reports of a land of promise in America and became a convert to the new faith. Leaving London as a sailor, he crossed the ocean to New York, and then worked and walked his way to Salt Lake City, finally arriving in the fall of 1851. In the following years he developed a prospering merchandise business, and as a commercial agent for the people, brought supplies to the territory from more or less distant posts.

Although Godbe in his earlier years adhered to the dictates of the Mormon Church, and is said to have accepted and practised polygamy (Whitney, *post*, II, 329), in his more mature years he opposed not only the marriage system, but in general the restrictions imposed upon the life and thought of the Mormon people by their religious leaders, especially in those matters which he believed to be strictly temporal. Conscious of the cultural value of wealth, and believing that the mineral deposits in the surrounding mountains could be of great value to the people of Utah, he chafed particularly under the Church's edict that its members should not tap those resources. Through the pages of a modest paper, the *Utah Magazine*, which he began to publish in 1868, he openly advocated the development of a mining industry. For this heresy he was disfellowshipped in October 1869. Despite the fact that he faced ruin at the hands of a hostile community unwilling to patronize his business, he replaced the *Magazine* with a daily, the *Salt Lake Tribune*, and published it—at a loss—for two years. It became the organ of the growing Liberal party, which Godbe championed, and which developed in opposition to the church party. Thus the "Godbeite Movement," as it was known, was merely a phase of the problem of separatism in Utah.

Meanwhile Godbe had become interested in mining. Having secured options on some claims in the Sweetwater region of Wyoming, where gold had been discovered, he bought a quartz mill in San Francisco, had it shipped to San Pedro, then hauled it by wagon to the mines, a distance of more than a thousand miles. In 1871 he organized in London the Chicago Silver Mining Company, capitalized at £75,000, and on his return, opened and operated mines at Dry Canyon, Utah. Later, at mines at Rush Lake and near Frisco, Utah, he erected and operated smelting furnaces. In 1879–80 he organized the Bullionville Smelting Company which bought the Raymond & Ely tailings at Bullionville, Nev., and produced more than a million dollars' worth of bullion. During the years which followed his activities widened. From 1880 to 1886 he was interested in the development of the gold placers at Osceola, Nev., where thirty-eight miles of ditches and flumes were constructed, but drought brought failure to the venture. In 1882 he took hold of antimony mines in southern Utah from which he shipped the metal to the railroad by means of ox teams. Three years later he organized the Pioche (Nev.) Consolidated Mining & Smelting Company, which acquired among others the Raymond & Ely and Meadow Valley silver mines, adding later those at Jack Rabbit. It was while these were in operation that Godbe urged the development of railroad facilities for the mines, but the silver legislation and the general depression of 1893 halted all operations which were in progress at the time. Godbe was married in Salt Lake City on Nov. 10, 1856, to Mary Hampton, daughter of Benjamin and Patience (Schull) Hampton. He died at the home of one of his sons in Brighton, Utah. In his business relations he displayed unusual vision and acumen; in personal relations he was kindly, gentle, and dignified.

[H. H. Bancroft, *Hist. of Utah* (1890), pp. 647–51, 658; E. W. Tullidge, *The Hist. of Salt Lake City* (n.d.); Noble Warrum, ed., *Utah Since Statehood*, vol. III (1919); O. F. Whitney, *Hist. of Utah* (4 vols., 1892–1904); R. N. Baskin, *Reminiscences of Early Utah* (1914), pp. 80–82; John Hampton, Jr., *Hampton Hist.* (1911), pp. 182–83; *Tullidge's Quart. Mag.*, Oct.

1880, pp. 14–77; *Salt Lake Tribune*, Aug. 2, 1902; information as to certain facts from M. C. Godbe, Salt Lake City, Utah.] M. B. P.

GODDARD, CALVIN LUTHER (Jan. 22, 1822–Mar. 29, 1895), inventor, was born in Covington, Wyoming County, N. Y., the son of Levi and Fanny (Watson) Goddard and a descendant of English and Scotch ancestors who settled in New England in the seventeenth century. His youth was passed mainly on his father's farm. He acquired a meager education and secured a bit of experience in business by buying and selling wool and metal in the Rochester markets. When he was nineteen years old he desired a better education, went to Geneva, N. Y., in the spring of 1841 to attend a preparatory school, and in the autumn of that year entered Yale College. He took the full classical course and graduated with the class of 1845. His straitened circumstances during these four years necessitated an economy of living which is said to be without parallel in the history of Yale. It is said that for three of the four years in college he lived chiefly on Graham crackers and water at an expense not exceeding $15 a year, and maintained a perfect physical condition by strenuous walks for which he gained the sobriquet of "Steamboat Goddard." For a year following his graduation he taught in a classical school in New York City and then became a clerk in a burring-machine manufacturing establishment in that place, continuing in that capacity for eight years. In 1854 he gave his attention to devising better methods than those in use for the thorough cleansing of wool. A considerable proportion of both foreign and domestic wools contain, among other extraneous matters, burs which become embedded in the locks of wool on the sheep and by their wiry hooks cling to the wool with such tenacity that if not removed before carding and spinning, they cause constant breakage of the yarn and are even visible and felt in the finished goods. Goddard set about designing special machinery to extract these burs and succeeded in perfecting and patenting a "burring picker," a machine which not only cleansed the wool from dust and other extraneous substances but removed the burs whole. Upon obtaining his patent (1866), he organized a company and began the manufacture of burring machines in New York City. He subsequently devised the steel ring and solid packing burring machine and feed rolls as attachments to carding machines. These devices he also manufactured in his plant at Second Avenue and 22nd Street. His success was immediate, and his machines were soon recognized as wholly indispensable to the proper manufacture of woolen fabrics. He continued his manufacturing activities in New York until 1875 when his business was transferred to Worcester, Mass., where he directed its affairs until his death. Goddard was the recipient of many medals for his inventions, including the special gold medals of the World's Fairs, at London (1862) and Paris (1867). He married Gertrude Griggs Quimby, daughter of Amos and Abby Quimby, of Milton, N. Y., on Dec. 19, 1846. Of their four children, two survived him at the time of his death in Worcester.

[J. Leander Bishop, *Hist. of Am. Manufactures*, vol. II (1864); *Obit. Record Grads. Yale Univ. 1890–1900* (1900); records of the Class of 1845, Yale College; Patent Office records; *Worcester Sunday Spy*, Mar. 31, 1895.] C. W. M.

GODDARD, JOHN (Jan. 20, 1723/4–July 1785), cabinetmaker, was born in Dartmouth, Mass., the third child of Daniel Goddard, shipwright, and his wife, Mary Tripp. He was a member of the third generation of his family in New England. After his birth his parents removed to Newport, R. I., where in due time John was apprenticed to a cabinetmaker—probably Job Townsend, who left notable examples of his craftsmanship. Shortly after he was twenty-one, young Goddard was made a freeman of the colony, Apr. 3, 1745. On Aug. 7 of the following year he married Job Townsend's daughter, Hannah. Of their children two sons, Stephen and Thomas Goddard, followed their father's trade. In 1764 Goddard and Job Townsend were appointed "viewers of joiners' lumber."

Familiar from childhood with fine wood work, Goddard developed such skill in design and execution that by the early 1760's he was recognized as the leading cabinetmaker in Newport. His shop was on Washington Street, near the waterfront. In 1763 he counted among his customers Moses Brown of Providence and one of his brothers, and Gov. Stephen Hopkins. Newport at that period was important as a center of cultivation and art. Working in the heavy mahogany of Santo Domingo, at that time supplanting walnut as a material for fine furniture, Goddard produced some pieces which for stateliness remain unequaled. He was noted especially for his secretaries and knee-hole desks or "buro tables," but he made almost all kinds of furniture necessary for a dwelling, including tables and leather, common, and cherry chairs. He is identified with the development of the "block front," the most distinctively American product in wood work, especially when the block was surmounted by the shell. Of this front—which he called "swell'd," although the contour is quite other than that now so named—he was probably the originator, perhaps together with his father-in-law. Certainly he brought the style to a perfection beyond which there could be no progress. His masterpieces remain the despair and admiration of later American generations; some of them are still held in Rhode Island as most precious heirlooms, and the few minor examples coming on the market have commanded large prices.

With the British occupation of Newport during the Revolution, the continuity of Goddard's trade was interrupted and the records of his work were largely lost. In 1782 the firm of Goddard & Engs opened a sales warehouse in Providence, "on the wharf of Mr. Moses Brown" (*Providence Gazette,* June 15, 1782, quoted by Isham, *post*). Three years later Goddard died in Newport, leaving his tools to his sons and "all my stock of Mahogony [*sic*] and other Stuff to be worked up" by them, "for the Support and benefit" of his wife and minor children.

[N. M. Isham, "John Goddard and His Work," in *Bull. R. I. School of Design,* Apr. 1927; T. H. Ormsbee, *Early Am. Furniture Makers* (1930); W. A. Dyer, "John Goddard and His Block-Fronts," *Antiques Mag.,* May 1922; C. M. Stow, "John Goddard, Stubborn Master Craftsman," *Antiquarian,* Feb. 1927; L. V. Guild, *The Geography of Am. Antiques* (1927); L. V. Lockwood, *Colonial Furniture in America* (3rd ed., 1926); Wallace Nutting, *Furniture Treasury* (1928); *Vital Records of Dartmouth, Mass., to the year 1850* (1929); *Vital Record of R. I.,* vol. IV, Newport County (1893), p. 32; *Newport Hist. Mag.,* Jan. 1882, and "John Tripp of Portsmouth R. I. and Some of His Descendants," *Ibid.,* July 1883; "Friends Records, Newport, R. I.," *R. I. Hist. Mag.,* Oct. 1886; *Providence Gazette,* July 16, 1785; *U. S. Chronicle* (Providence, R. I.), July 21, 1785.]
W.N.

GODDARD, LUTHER MARCELLUS (Oct. 27, 1840–May 20, 1917), jurist, was the son of Edwin P. Goddard, a native of Connecticut, who married Marie Fillmore, second cousin of President Fillmore, and was for a time a farmer and miller at Palmyra, Wayne County, N. Y. He was born at Palmyra and spent his youth there attending the public school and working for his father during vacations. In 1854 the family moved to Abingdon, Ill., where he completed his education at Hedding College and commenced the study of law. In 1862 he accompanied his parents to Leavenworth, Kan., shortly afterwards joining a freighting outfit with which he traveled to Denver, Colo. For a time he had contemplated entering the ministry, but on his return to Leavenworth he resumed his legal studies and in 1864 entered the Law Department of the University of Chicago (*Catalogue,* 1864–65). He was admitted to the bar by the supreme court of Illinois in June 1865 and returned to Leavenworth, where he commenced practise. In 1868 he was appointed deputy county attorney, for Leavenworth County, serving as such for two years, and in 1871 was elected a member of the Kansas state legislature, in which capacity he distinguished himself by introducing a bill to confer the suffrage upon women. In 1872 he was elected county attorney and held that position for two terms.

The mining industry in Colorado was at this period in its initial stages of development, and, anticipating wider opportunities, Goddard moved in 1878 to Leadville, where he opened a law office, at the same time interesting himself in mining operations. In 1880 he was elected a member of the Leadville school board and he was its president for three years. In 1882 he was elected judge of the district court of the 5th judicial district of Colorado. He had incurred the bitter hostility of a small element of the populace, and a determined attempt was made to oust him from the bench, petitions being presented to the legislature alleging that in the course of the election he had been guilty of bribery and other high offenses. A legislative committee appointed to hear the charges having exonerated him, *quo warranto* proceedings were taken in the supreme court, which were also unsuccessful. As a last resource his antagonists filed a petition with the supreme court asking for his disbarment, which after a full hearing was refused (11 *Colo.,* 259). In 1888 he was reëlected as district judge and in 1892, before his term as such expired, was nominated by the Populist and Democratic parties and elected a justice of the supreme court of Colorado. This necessitated his removal to Denver, where he thenceforth resided. Having been reëlected for a second term in 1896, he remained on the supreme-court bench till January 1901, when he retired and resumed active practise in Denver. He was president of the state Bar Association in 1904–05. He was again appointed to the supreme-court bench by Gov. Peabody in 1905, when the personnel of the court was enlarged, and served until his term expired on Jan. 1, 1909, when he again resumed practise. His judicial opinions were distinguished by their clarity and conciseness. When he ascended the bench the statutes and regulations dealing with prospecting and the location of mining claims and their subsequent development were in a rudimentary condition, and it was largely due to his common-sense decisions and the masterly opinions which accompanied them that the law on the subject was made to fit new conditions and assumed its present form.

Holding strong opinions on most questions of the day, and fearless of consequences in discharging what he conceived to be his duty, he made some bitter enemies in the course of his public career, but in private life he appeared to great advantage, possessing great social charm, spontaneous humor, and an inexhaustible stock of anecdote and story. He was married in 1881 to Mrs. Anna Elizabeth (Westcott) Miller, at Leadville.

[See *Colo. Bar Asso. Report,* 1917, p. 208; J. C. Smiley and others, *Semi-Centennial Hist. of the State of Colo.* (1913) II, 422; *Hist. of Colo.* (5 vols., 1927), vol. IV; *Who's Who in America,* 1914–15; *Rocky Mountain News,* May 21, 1917. *Trial of Judge Luther M. Goddard, including Legislative, Quo Warranto and Disbarment Proceedings,* reported by H. B. Johnson (Denver, 1888) contains an extremely prejudiced review of the efforts made to remove him from the bench, prepared by his leading accusers.] H. W. H. K.

GODDARD, PAUL BECK (Jan. 26, 1811–July 3, 1866), physician, anatomist, pioneer in photography, was born in Baltimore, Md. After his graduation from Washington (Trinity) College, Hartford, Conn., in 1828, he entered the Medical School of the University of Pennsylvania, from which he received the degree of M.D. in 1832. He settled in Philadelphia, where he practised his profession for a time but subsequently became an assistant to Dr. Robert Hare [*q.v.*], professor of chemistry in the University of Pennsylvania. Later he was professor of anatomy in the medical department of the same institution. While he was assistant to Hare, news was received of Daguerre's discovery that pictures could be produced with the sun and a sensitized plate as the agents. Goddard at once began to take a deep interest in the experiments being made in the new art. The slowness of Daguerre's method caused many failures in the experiments, and finally Goddard discovered that by using the vapor of bromide on the silvered plate the process could be much accelerated. This discovery, which was the basis of all future progress in the photographic art, he described before the American Philosophical Society in Philadelphia, in December 1839, exhibiting some of his results (*Proceedings,* vol. III, 1843, p. 180). In 1840 he was made a member of the Society. Describing Goddard's work, Julius F. Sachse said in a lecture before the Franklin Institute: "It was this discovery which solved the question of time exposure, perfecting Daguerre's process and thereby making possible its universal application in the various arts and sciences. . . . It was during this series of experiments with bromine that Doctor Goddard succeeded in obtaining several good views instantaneously in the open air, which were the first instantaneous pictures ever made by the heliographic process" (*Journal of the Franklin Institute,* April 1893, p. 278).

Goddard published many medical works, among them: *Plates of the Cerebro-Spinal Nerves, with References* (1837); *Plates of the Arteries, with References* (1839); an edition of T. B. Curling's *Practical Treatise on the Diseases of the Testis and of the Spermatic Cord and Scrotum* (1843); an edition of Erasmus Wilson's *System of Human Anatomy* (1843); *The Anatomy, Physiology and Pathology of the Human Teeth, with the Most Approved Methods of Treatment* (1844), in collaboration with Joseph E. Parker; an edition of F. J. Moreau's *Practical Treatise on Midwifery* (1844); *The Dissector, or Practical and Surgical Anatomy,* by Erasmus Wilson (1844); the iconographic portion of P. Rayer's *Theoretical and Practical Treatise of Diseases of the Skin* (1845); *A Practical Treatise on the Diseases Peculiar to Women,* by Samuel Ashwell (first American edition, 1845); another edition of Wilson's *Dissector* (1851); Philip Ricord's *Illustrations of Syphilitic Disease* (1851). He died in Philadelphia, in 1866, and was buried in Laurel Hill Cemetery, Philadelphia. His claims to the discovery of bromine as a photographic agent have been ignored by some British writers on the subject, and the credit erroneously given to John Frederick Goddard, a London optician who made, independently, the same discovery and announced it Dec. 12, 1840, in the *Literary Gazette* of London.

[*Proc. Am. Phil. Soc.,* vol. X (1869); "Early Daguerreotypes in the U. S.," *British Jour. of Photography,* July 9, 1920; M. A. Root, *The Camera and the Pencil* (1864), p. 352; A. Brothers, *Photography* (London, 1899); H. A. Kelly and W. L. Burrage, *Dict. of Am. Medic. Biog.* (1928); *North American and U. S. Gazette* (Phila.), July 6, 1866.] J. J.

GODDARD, PLINY EARLE (Nov. 24, 1869–July 12, 1928), ethnologist, was born in Lewiston, Me., the son of Charles W. and Elmira A. (Nichols) Goddard. His father was a market-gardener, florist, and Quaker preacher. The boy attended the Oak Grove Seminary at Vassalboro, and then followed the headmaster to Oakgrove Seminary, Union Springs, N. Y., where he graduated in 1889. He then entered Earlham College from which he received the degree of B.A. in 1892 and of M.A. four years later. Meantime he taught in the Richmond Square Academy in Lewisville, Ind., at the Lowell Institute in Lowell, Kan., and in a public school at Sulphur Springs, Ind. While his fortunes were at a low ebb in 1896–97 he began to read about the American Indian, and finally secured an appointment as lay missionary under the auspices of the Woman's Indian Aid Association of Philadelphia to the Hupa Indians of California. Here he became greatly interested in ethnology. Unassuming, friendly, and inured to hardships, he won the good-will of the Indians and was given every opportunity to learn their language and lore. Realizing the need of formal training for ethnographical research, he determined to undertake postgraduate study. His linguistic studies among the Indians secured his admission to the University of California, the personal interest of President Benjamin Ide Wheeler, and finally an instructorship in the newly instituted department of anthropology. The University awarded him the degree of Ph.D. in 1904. He was assistant professor from 1906 to 1909, when he became assistant curator of anthropology in the American Museum of Natural History in New York; and in this institution he was curator of ethnology from 1914 to his death.

The printed works representing Goddard's contributions to Indian language and culture consist of papers on special subjects rather than large monographs. First of these is "Life and Culture of the Hupa" (*University of California Publications: American Archæology and Ethnology,* vol. I, no. 1, 1903), "a work conceived and executed in isolation and manifesting all Goddard's special genius as ethnologist and writer in purest form" (Kroeber, *post*). This was followed in 1904 by "Hupa Texts" (*Ibid.,* vol. I, no. 2); in 1905 by "The Morphology of the Hupa Language" (*Ibid.,* vol. III); and by "The Phonology of the Hupa Language" (*Ibid.,* vol. V, no. 1) in 1907. These works marked him as an outstanding authority in Athapascan. His seventy publications, mostly intensive, uniformly valuable studies predominantly on Indian languages, are to be found in the publications of the University of California, in the *American Anthropologist,* and in the publications of the American Museum of Natural History. Works that had a wide popular educational influence are: *Indians of the Southwest* and *Indians of the Northwest Coast* (Handbooks of the American Museum of Natural History, nos. 2 and 10, 1913; 3rd ed. 1922 and 1924). He was editor of the *American Anthropologist* from 1915 to 1920, and founder and co-editor with Franz Boas of the *International Journal of American Linguistics.* At the time of his death he was secretary of the Organizing Committee of the International Society of Americanists. In general his contributions to science were produced as a labor of love. Kroeber considered him one of the most vivid personalities in American anthropology. In 1893 he married Alice C. Rockwell of Palmyra, Mich., who was a student with him in Earlham College. Six children were born to them.

[Franz Boas in *Science,* Aug. 17, 1928; A. L. Kroeber in *Am. Anthropologist* (Jan.–Mar. 1929), a model of keen analysis; J. McK. Cattell and J. Cattell, *Am. Men of Science* (1927); *Who's Who in America,* 1928–29; personal acquaintance.] W. H.

GODDARD, WILLIAM (1740–Dec. 23, 1817), printer, journalist, was born in New London, Conn., son of Dr. Giles Goddard, postmaster at that place, and his wife Sarah Updike, daughter of Lodowick Updike, of English and Dutch ancestry. He may have been first apprenticed in 1755 to the printing-trade in New Haven under John Holt, in James Parker's plant; but he soon removed to Parker's printery in New York City. In 1761 he was a journeyman there with Samuel Farley (Thomas, *post,* I, 305). About July 1, 1762, he opened a printing-office in Providence, R. I., becoming the pioneer printer of that city, and on Oct. 20 of the same year, established the *Providence Gazette; and Country Journal.* Lacking support, he suspended the journal on May 11, 1765 (No. 134). By the summer of 1765, having left his press in charge of his mother, he had found employment with John Holt at New York City. In August he returned, temporarily, to Providence and printed, on Aug. 24, 1765, an "extraordinary" number of the *Gazette,* in connection with the Stamp Act agitation, but the newspaper lay moribund until resumption on Aug. 9, 1766 (No. 135), upon the repeal of that act, and then the imprint was "Sarah Goddard & Company." Goddard had sent Samuel Inslee to his mother as "an assistant," but Inslee retired with the issue of Sept. 19, 1767, and then John Carter, who had just left Benjamin Franklin's plant at Philadelphia, became a partner until the issue of Nov. 12, 1768, which he published alone. Mrs. Goddard died in 1770. Meanwhile, William Goddard had printed on Sept. 21, 1765, on Parker's press at Woodbridge, N. J., the *Constitutional Courant,* a patriotic sheet that caused a sensation when sold on the streets of New York. In June 1766 he opened a printery at Philadelphia in partnership with Joseph Galloway and Thomas Wharton [*qq.v.*], hiring one of Franklin's old presses. He began the *Pennsylvania Chronicle, and Universal Advertiser* on Jan. 26, 1767, as the organ of the Anti-Proprietary party, but soon the partnership was broken by disagreements. Goddard continued the paper alone, or with other partnership, until its expiration on Feb. 8, 1774 (No. 368). While Galloway and Wharton became Tories, Goddard clung to the Whig cause in the American Revolution. His Philadelphia ventures led to violent controversy and his language descended to "downright blackguardism" and rose at times "as shrill as a fish-wife's curse" (Wroth, *post,* p. 126), but his stormy career here, as elsewhere, viewed at large, showed him the doughty champion of his age for the liberty of the press and right of public criticism. Even financial disaster did not deter him (*Ibid.,* pp. 128–40). Meanwhile, in the spring of 1773, Goddard had gone to Baltimore as its pioneer journalist, bought out the press and printing equipment of Nicholas Hasselbach, deceased, Baltimore's pioneer printer, and established his business. On Aug. 20, 1773, he established the *Maryland Journal; and the Baltimore Advertiser,* and May 10, 1775, it was continued by his sister, Mary Katherine, under her name. It became a semi-weekly on Mar. 14, 1783, and on Jan. 2, 1784, Goddard resumed the editorship. On May 25, 1785, he was married, at Cranston, R. I., to Abigail Angell (1758–1845), daughter of Gen. James Angell. In 1785 he took Edward Langworthy as a partner but soon dissolved the partnership, and continued alone until Aug. 7, 1789, when he took James Angell, his brother-in-law, as a partner, continuing until Feb. 22, 1793. After that date Angell was the sole publisher. While at Baltimore Goddard established an independent postal system, "which was afterwards taken over by the Continental Congress, and exists to-day as the United States Post Office" (Wroth). His last years, from 1793, were spent in retirement on his wife's farm at Johnston, R. I., where, besides farming, he enjoyed a quiet life and in social company was "the soul of conviviality" (*Proceedings of the American Antiquarian Society,* n.s., XXXI, 1921, p. 97). Isaiah Thomas, who knew him, said of him (*post,* I, 202): "As a printer he was ingenious and enterprising," and "few could conduct a newspaper better"; while as an editor he was "capable" and "his talents were often drawn into requisition."

[The principal sources are L. C. Wroth, *A Hist. of Printing in Colonial Md. 1686–1776* (1922); Isaiah Thomas, *Hist. of Printing in America* (2nd ed., 2 vols., 1874); H. F. Carroll, *Printers and Printing in Providence, 1762–1907* (1907), pp. 5–12, xxxvi; G. P. Winship, *R. I. Imprints, 1727–1800* (1915); C. R. Hildeburn, *A Century of Printing: The Issues of the Press in Pa.,* vol. II (1886); C. S. Brigham, "Bibliography of American Newspapers," in *Proc. Am. Antiq. Soc.,* n.s. XXV (1915), 158, XXXI (1921), 97, XXXII (1922), 152, XXXIV (1925), 102; C. W. Opdyke, *The op Dyck Geneal.* (1889); A. F. Angell, *Geneal. of the Descendants of Thomas Angell* (1872). The best file of the *Providence Gazette* is in R. I. Hist. Soc.; of the *Pa. Chronicle* in Hist. Soc. of Pa. and N. Y. Pub. Lib., and *Md. Jour.* in Md. Hist. Soc.] V. H. P.

GODDU, LOUIS (Oct. 1, 1837–June 18, 1919), inventor, was born in St. Césaire, Canada, the son of Henry A. and Esther (De Lorge) Goddu, both of whom were French Canadians. His very early life and youth were spent on his father's farm, and until he was twelve years old he attended the district school near his home. During this time he gave noticeable evidence of mechanical ability, and about 1850 his parents sent him to Montreal and engaged him as an apprentice in a machine-shop. Goddu remained in Montreal approximately eight years and acquired great skill as a machinist as well as a well-rounded knowledge of mechanical principles and practises. He also took up and learned the shoemaker's trade. On reaching his majority, he left Canada for Northampton, Mass., in search of greater opportunity. For four years he was employed in one of the shoe factories there, becoming eventually an operator of a shoe-sewing machine patented a few years earlier by Lyman Blake. This renewed contact with machinery revived Goddu's interest in mechanics, and he began thinking and working not only on improvements for the Blake machine but also on machinery for other phases of the shoe-making process. Throughout the period of the Civil War he devised and patented machines for pegging and stitching shoe soles, but had very little success in selling or introducing them. In 1865, however, he moved with his family to Lowell, Mass., and there met and became intimate with Gordon McKay, one of the pioneers in the introduction of machinery into the shoe industry. McKay was then particularly interested in bringing about the solution of the problem of nailing shoe soles by machine, and seeing in Goddu a real inventive genius, he hired him and purchased his more promising patents. For some six years Goddu worked for McKay in Lowell, and then moved to Winchester, Mass., where McKay's metallic fastening interests centered. Here Goddu spent the rest of his life, eventually becoming one of the foremost inventors of shoe machines, particularly those which handled tacks, nails, or metals. His greatest series of inventions, probably, were those having to do with the improvements of a soling machine using screw-thread wire. His first machine of this type was devised about 1876. It included a coil of wire held in a revolving kettle suspended from the ceiling. The weight of the kettle gave sufficient pressure to worm the screw-cut wire into the leather sole. In the course of his life Goddu obtained about three hundred patents, 137 of which were for machines which filled important places in shoe production at the time. He was also the inventor of an oil burner for power plants and patented a machine for improved wire nails used in building. For the latter invention he was awarded a gold medal at the World's Columbian Exposition, held at Chicago in 1893. Goddu was a life member of the Mechanics Charitable Association and was at one time park commissioner of Winchester. He married in 1860, in Montreal, Canada, Rosanna Roy, a native of that city, and at the time of his death in Winchester was survived by four sons and three daughters.

[Waldemar Kaempffert, *Popular Hist. of Am. Invention* (1924), vol. II; *Boston Globe,* June 19, 1919; *Boston Transcript,* June 20, 1919; correspondence with Lynn Hist. Soc.; Patent Office records.] C. W. M.

GODEFROY, MAXIMILIAN (fl. 1806–1824), painter, architect, military engineer, though born outside of France, was taken there at an early age. According to his own statement he entered the "Corps du Génie" at seven, and later served as "gendarme de la Garde du roi" and as "Capitaine du Cavalie et du Génie." Though the nature of his subsequent activities is uncertain, before he emigrated to the United States in 1805 he had been three times wounded and had served for six months as prisoner of state (Godefroy to Jefferson, Jan. 10, 1806; Jefferson Papers, Library of Congress, vol. CLV). In 1806 he was teaching architecture, drawing, and fortification "au Collège de Baltimore" (presumably St. Mary's Seminary, Sulpician). In the following year he designed the chapel of St. Mary's Seminary, the first church of the Gothic Revival to be executed in America. (The original design is preserved by the Maryland Historical Society.) He used French Gothic forms, not wholly understood. In 1811 and 1813 he exhibited in Philadelphia a number of projects. For the competition for the Washington Monument in Baltimore, in 1813, he submitted a triumphal-arch design of restrained classic character (preserved in the City Library, Baltimore). In 1814 he designed the First Presbyterian Church, which, like his Commercial and Farmer's Bank, has long vanished. When Baltimore was threatened by the British in the same year, Godefroy was employed in devising the fortifications, which successfully sustained the attack of Sept. 12, and later he designed the Battle Monument erected by the city.

In 1815, after the destruction of the Capitol in Washington, when the reappointment of B. H. Latrobe, its former architect, was under discussion, Godefroy was approached indirectly to take the post, but replied to the President with the most generous recommendation and praise of Latrobe. From July to September 1816, he was in Richmond, Va., designing the Court House (later destroyed) and the formal terraces of the Capitol grounds, as well as proposed internal changes in the Capitol itself (*Virginia Argus,* July 27, 1816). His chief surviving work is the Unitarian Church in Baltimore, begun in 1817. The façade has an arched loggia crowned with a pediment of relief-sculpture by Capellano. The interior, subsequently remodeled, had originally a Roman dome (shown in J. H. Hinton's *History and Topography of the United States,* ed. 1842, II, 526, and in a model preserved by the University of Michigan).

Godefroy had collaborated with B. H. Latrobe since 1815 on preliminary drawings for the Exchange group in Baltimore, for which their design was accepted in 1816 over that of Joseph Ramée. Difficulties arising in this collaboration led to a breach in their relations in 1817, and they were arrayed against one another in the later stages of the work and in the competition for the United States Bank in Philadelphia in 1818. Always despondent in temper, Godefroy gradually became embittered, and sailed from Baltimore for London, after writing adieux to Thomas Sully on Aug. 22, 1819. In London from 1820 to 1824 he exhibited several watercolors, landscapes, and architectural views of American subjects (Algernon Graves, *The Royal Academy of Arts,* III, 1905). His scene from the battle of Poltava, exhibited in 1821, was identical in title with one by C. Godefroy in the Paris Salon of 1833.

[An early account of Godefroy is included in Wm. Dunlap's *Hist. of the Rise and Progress of the Arts of Design in the U. S.* (1834), II, 379, and certain references to him are scattered in C. G. Herbermann's *The Sulpicians in the U. S.* (1916), and J. T. Scharf's *Hist. of Baltimore City and County* (1881). The Poppleton Plat of Baltimore illustrates some of his lost buildings. The chief sources for this article are the unpublished letters of Godefroy in the Dreer Collection in the Pa. Hist. Soc., and of Latrobe in the collection of Gamble Latrobe. The Peabody Institute in Baltimore preserves one of Godefroy's genre paintings, and a plate engraved by him, "Première assemblée du Congrès," is listed in *The Frederic R. Halsey Coll. of Prints,* pt. I (1916), No. 685. A portrait of Godefroy by Rembrandt Peale was deposited in the gallery of the Md. Hist. Soc. in 1925. His name has appeared in different forms and spellings, and in one case, at least, he signed himself "J. Max. M. Godefroy." For his possible relation to or identity with C. Godefroy or Jean Godefroy (1771–1839), or Godefroy, architect (b. about 1760), see these rubrics in the Thieme-Becker *Allgemeines Lexikon der Bildenden Künstler,* vol. XIV (1921).]

F. K.

GODEY, LOUIS ANTOINE (June 6, 1804–Nov. 29, 1878), publisher, was born in New York City, of French parents, Louis and Margaret Godey, who had left their home in Sens and had come to America during the French Revolution. He had little formal education, but found in books and printing-offices a practical training school. He became self-supporting at fifteen. At his death he left a fortune of over a million dollars. He began his long career in Philadelphia sometime in the 1820's as clerk and "scissors editor" for Charles Alexander on the *Daily Chronicle*. In 1830 the two men became joint proprietors of a new venture—the *Lady's Book*. Although Godey is best known as publisher of this periodical, later *Godey's Lady's Book,* he was connected with a number of other Philadelphia publications. With Joseph C. Neal and Morton McMichael he established, in 1836, a successful weekly, the *Saturday News and Literary Gazette*. He and McMichael were partners in a publishing house that issued the *Young People's Book, or Magazine of Useful and Entertaining Knowledge* (1841), and the *Lady's Musical Library* (1842), a periodical supplying the fashionable music of the day. He was also interested in the *Lady's Dollar Newspaper,* and, from 1852 to 1867, in *Arthur's Home Magazine*.

Alexander soon gave up his connection with the *Lady's Book* and Godey assumed entire control of its policies. In the beginning he modeled it frankly upon a popular English periodical for women, filling it with material "selected" from foreign magazines, and depending for feminine favor largely upon a page of music and attractive colored fashion plates. With shrewd business insight he soon realized the wider possibilities of such a publication in a country where women of "the domestic circle" were becoming increasingly important as readers. He ceased to borrow from foreign sources and began to print, and pay for, the work of American women writers. In 1837 he bought out the *Ladies' Magazine* of Boston, and placed its correct and highly respected editor, Mrs. Sarah Josepha Hale [*q.v.*], at the head of his own periodical. By 1843 he could announce a number "entirely the production of lady writers," and assure his readers that the *Lady's Book* was the only magazine in the world "consecrated to the promotion of those pure virtues and moral influences which constitute woman's mission." As the prosperity of the publication increased, Godey attracted to his pages, by means of liberal payments, the best-known of American writers, men as well as women; in 1845 he began to copyright his material. In his own department, "Godey's Arm Chair," he commented on and advertised the many innovations and "embellishments" of his periodical. By 1858 its circulation had reached 150,000. He remained sole proprietor of the paper until 1877 when his two sons temporarily took over the business. At the end of that year he disposed of his interests to a publishing company and retired, confidently appealing to three generations of readers to acknowledge "the purity of the magazine and its eminent fitness for family reading."

Godey's personal life was uneventful. He visited Europe three times, but for the most part he lived quietly in Philadelphia. On Aug. 31, 1833, he married Maria Duke, the daughter of well-to-do parents. Five children of this marriage lived to maturity and gave him their devoted affection. Many of his employees remained with the *Lady's Book* for long years of service and found in him a generous and considerate friend. He was a genial and unostentatious man, amiably tolerant, but conservative in all his instincts. He read widely and was on familiar terms with many contemporary men of letters. He took no part in political life, but knew intimately most of the public men of his time. He was respected by his fellow citizens as an able and honorable business man, and liked for his personal qualities. Edgar Allan Poe once said of him, "No man has warmer friends or fewer enemies." In the columns of the *Lady's Book* his name came to be a synonym for self advertising, but it was the magazine and not the man that he eulogized. Publishing a successful periodical for "the elevation of American womanhood" was his great adventure. Ill health compelled him to spend his winters in St. Augustine for several years before he definitely retired, but in the end his death came suddenly as he sat reading in his own home. He finished a chapter in *Anne of Geierstein,* put his ribbon marker in place, and closed the volume. The book slipped gently from his hand to the floor. He had lived through a turbulent period of American history, but violence played no part in his life.

[J. T. Scharf and T. Westcott, *Hist. of Phila.* (1884); E. P. Oberholtzer, *Philadelphia* (1912); F. L. Mott, *Hist. of Am. Magazines* (1930); Algernon Tassin, "The Magazine in America," *Bookman,* May 1915; R. F. Warner, "Godey's Lady's Book," *Am. Mercury,* Aug. 1924; A. H. Smyth, *Phila. Mags. and their Contributors* (1872); obituaries in *Phila. Inquirer, Public Ledger,* and *North American* for Nov. 30, 1878; files of *Godey's Lady's Book*; information furnished by a representative of the family.] B. M. S.

GODFREY, BENJAMIN (Dec. 4, 1794–Apr. 13, 1862), sea-captain, merchant, financier, philanthropist, was born in Chatham, Mass., and ran away to sea when he was nine years old. His first voyage took him to Ireland, where he stayed nine years. During the War of 1812 he served in the United States navy and learned navigation. Later he was captain of a merchantman, sailing from Chatham to Spain, Italy, and the West Indies, but he lost his ship during a storm in the Gulf of Mexico. He then set up as a merchant at Matamoros, Mexico, near the mouth of the Rio Grande, accumulated a fortune of $200,000, and was transporting it on pack-mules to the States when he was waylaid by brigands and robbed of the whole amount. He began again in New Orleans, prospered, and moved in 1832 to Alton, Ill., where the next year he and Winthrop S. Gilman, later a banker in New York, began a storage and commission business. In their warehouse Elijah Parish Lovejoy [*q.v.*] stored his printing-press before the fatal attack of Nov. 7, 1837. Godfrey was shrewd, daring, and tenacious, and life on the seas and in remote trading ports had made him somewhat high-handed. In 1835, using means that were reprehensible even though within the law, he and his partner secured control of the newly chartered state bank and proceeded to lend money freely to themselves and their friends. Within a few years Godfrey, Gilman & Company, as drawers, discounters, and indorsers, received $800,748 from the bank. They used this money in a reckless attempt to divert the upper Mississippi trade from St. Louis to Alton, but their scheme to corner the lead market failed disastrously, and the panic of 1837 hastened the final reckoning. Godfrey and Gilman resigned their positions in the bank, which had lost by their bad judgment $1,000,000 and all prospects of future usefulness; and the legitimate business interests of Alton, damaged also by the acquittal of Lovejoy's murderers, suffered in consequence for years. Meanwhile, in the heyday of his prosperity, Godfrey, who was much impressed with the necessity for proper educational facilities for girls, had founded Monticello Female Seminary at Godfrey, a few miles north of Alton, had selected Theron Baldwin [*q.v.*] as the first principal, and had given the institution $110,000. He was a trustee of the school until his death and always solicitous of its welfare; to him almost as much as to Baldwin belongs the credit for the high standard that it maintained from its opening in 1838. Godfrey was also the projector and president of the Alton & Sangamon Railroad, now a link in the Chicago & Alton, which was chartered in 1847 and completed to Springfield in 1852. While the line was building, he lived in a car and followed the work as it advanced. In 1853 citizens of Alton presented him with a silver pitcher with representations in repoussé of the first train on the railroad and of the original building of the Seminary. He was twice married, the second time to a Miss Pettit of Hempstead, L. I. He died at his home in Godfrey, Ill.

[N. Bateman and P. Selby, *Hist. Encyc. of Ill.* (1900, and other eds.); W. T. Norton, *Centennial Hist. of Madison County, Ill., and its People* (1912); H. R. Congdon, "Early Hist. of Monticello Seminary," *Trans. Ill. State Hist. Soc.*, 1924; G. W. Dowrie, *Development of Banking in Ill., 1817–63* (1913).]

G. H. G.

GODFREY, THOMAS (1704–December 1749), glazier, mathematician, and inventor of the mariner's quadrant, known as Hadley's, was born in Bristol Township, Philadelphia, the son of Joseph Godfrey, farmer and maltster. While Thomas was still in his infancy, his father died. Later his mother remarried, and the boy was apprenticed to a glazier. He glazed the windows of the State House, now Independence Hall, Philadelphia, when it was built. Employed on a similar work at "Stenton," the home of James Logan, governor of Pennsylvania, he displayed his natural genius for mathematics, astronomy, and optics, and was encouraged by his employer in his love of the sciences. In 1730 he invented and made a quadrant for ascertaining latitude, which he claimed was a more certain instrument than Davis's quadrant, then in general use on British vessels. Davis's quadrant required greater exactness and speed on the part of the observer, and resulted in a high percentage of error in the observations. This caused vessels frequently to miss the Island of Barbados altogether, obliging them to run down a thousand miles farther to Jamaica (*American Magazine,* Aug. 1758). When Franklin started in business in Philadelphia, he rented part of his house to Godfrey, who became one of the original Junto, though he did not long remain in the society. "He knew little out of his way, and was not a pleasing companion," Franklin wrote of him (John Bigelow, ed., *The Life of Benjamin Franklin,* 1902, I, 183). "Like most great mathematicians I have met with, he expected universal precision in every thing said, or was for ever denying or distinguishing upon trifles, to the disturbance of all conversation." He was described by the Rev. William Smith, editor of the *American Magazine,* as "a man of no education, but perhaps the most singular phenomenon that ever appeared in the learned world, for a kind of natural or intuitive knowledge of the abstrusest parts of mathematics and astronomy" (*American Magazine,* July 1758, p. 475).

Early in the year 1730 Godfrey began to apply himself to the improvement of Davis's quadrant transferred to the Mariner's Bow. Having completed his invention, he entrusted it to Joshua Fisher, of Lewistown, who first tried it in Delaware Bay. Subsequently it was given to Capt. Wright, who carried it to Jamaica where "he showed and explained it to several Englishmen, among whom was a nephew of Hadley's" (Watson, *post,* I, 529). In 1734 Godfrey wrote a letter to the Royal Society, which was about to reward its vice-president, James Hadley, who had given notice of his invention of a quadrant, similar to that devised by the Philadelphian. Gov. Logan of Pennsylvania, who was regarded as the foremost mathematician then in America, wrote to the secretary of the Royal Society the whole history of Godfrey's invention, and claimed for him some substantial recognition. Rev. William Smith, nine years after Godfrey's death, insisted that justice had been denied the Philadelphian (*American Magazine,* August 1758), but later accounts assert that the Royal Society sent Godfrey household furniture to the value of £200 as his reward. Godfrey died in December 1749 and was buried on the farm in Bristol Township where he was born, but in 1838, through the efforts of John F. Watson, his body, together with the remains of the other members of the family buried there, was removed to Laurel Hill Cemetery, Philadelphia. Still later, a small obelisk, properly inscribed, was placed over the plot, largely through the efforts of the Mercantile Library of Philadelphia. One of Godfrey's sons was Thomas [*q.v.*], poet and playwright.

[J. F. Watson, *Annals of Phila.* (2 vols., 1844); Harold E. Gillingham, "Some Early Phila. Instrument Makers," *Pa. Mag. of Hist. and Biog.,* vol. LI (1927); "An Account of Mr. Thos. Godfrey's Improvement of Davis's Quadrant, Transferred to the Mariner's-Bow," communicated to the Royal Society of London and published in the *Philos. Trans., No. 435,* Dec. 1734; the *Pa. Gazette,* Dec. 19, 1749.] J. J.

GODFREY, THOMAS (Dec. 4, 1736–Aug. 3, 1763), poet, playwright, was born in Philadelphia, Pa., the son of Thomas Godfrey [*q.v.*], inventor of the quadrant. Owing to the older Godfrey's death in 1749, the son became apprenticed to a watchmaker, but his natural talent for verse brought him to the attention of William Smith, the first provost of the College, Academy and Charitable School of Philadelphia. According to John Galt (*Life and Studies of Benjamin West,* 1816), Smith introduced West to Godfrey, who was "a pupil of his own," and, while the lists of students of the Academy and the Charitable School are incomplete, it is probable that Godfrey attended one or both of them, making up the deficiencies of his earlier education. Under the inspiring influence of the first provost of the College of Philadelphia, Godfrey became a member of the group of young men, among them Benjamin West and Francis Hopkinson, the first native poet-composer, who were founding the arts of painting, music, and drama in the Colonies. Smith also secured Godfrey's release from his indentures to the watchmaking trade and, in May 1758, obtained from the governor of Pennsylvania a commission for Godfrey as ensign in the Pennsylvania militia. Godfrey took part in the campaign against Fort Duquesne, apparently with the rank of lieutenant, though he did not see very active service, being stationed in a garrison on the frontier. At the end of the campaign, he accepted a position as factor in Wilmington, N. C.

Godfrey's lyric and narrative verse, which was printed in the *American Magazine,* edited by Smith, or in the newspapers, was purely tentative work. His love songs were in the mode of the Cavalier poets, his pastorals had a certain sprightliness, and his one poem to be published in book form during his lifetime, *The Court of Fancy* (1762), had passages of imaginative power. But, as he himself pointed out, it was imitative of Chaucer and Pope, and its main interest lay in its superiority to anything else of its kind that had been written in the Colonies up to that time. His real claim to remembrance lies in his *Prince of Parthia,* the first drama written by a native American to be produced upon the professional stage. It was important chiefly because it was no mere closet drama. Godfrey definitely wrote it for the American Company of actors and was inspired to the writing of it by his associations. Under Smith's provostship, the College of Philadelphia defied the prejudices of the Quaker element by giving amateur dramatic productions at Commencement and other occasions. Such a production as *The Masque of Alfred,* given in 1756, must have had its influence upon Godfrey, for his patron wrote many of the words and his friend, Francis Hopkinson, composed the music. He may indeed have taken part.

In 1754, when David Douglass brought the reorganized American Company to Philadelphia, Godfrey undoubtedly saw their performances, for influences of their repertory are found in his play. He must have begun its production in Philadelphia, for in a letter to Provost Smith, dated Nov. 17, 1759, he told of his finishing the drama in North Carolina, and of his fears that it would be too late for Douglass's season. His fears were well grounded, and the play lay in Douglass's hands for eight years. In the meantime Godfrey had died in Wilmington, of a fever. His *Juvenile Poems on Various Subjects. With the Prince of Parthia, a Tragedy,* was published through the efforts of Smith and Godfrey's fellow poet, Nathaniel Evans, in 1765. The play was produced by Douglass on Apr. 24, 1767, at the Southwark Theatre, in Philadelphia, according to advertisements in the *Pennsylvania Journal* and *Pennsylvania Gazette*. It was a romantic tragedy, laid in Parthia about the beginning of the Christian era. Godfrey's plot was largely his own, outside of a general resemblance to the royal murders which were recorded in the history of Parthia. His dramatic models were Shakespeare, Beaumont, and Ambrose Philips. The play is well constructed, the blank verse is varied and forcible, and when the drama was revived by undergraduates at the University of Pennsylvania in 1915, its acting qualities were apparent. Benjamin West's portrait of Godfrey, once in the possession of Richard Penn Smith, seems to have disappeared, and there is no sufficient evidence to prove that the sketch in the possession of the Historical Society of Pennsylvania is really Godfrey.

[Contemporary accounts of Godfrey are given by Nathaniel Evans in the Introduction to *Juvenile Poems . . . With the Prince of Parthia* (1765); and William Smith in the *Am. Mag.*, Sept. 1758. *The Prince of Parthia* is very rare. It was first reprinted by the present writer in *Representative Am. Plays* (1917), and in the same year by Archibald Henderson in separate form, with a valuable introduction. For the play, see Moses Coit Tyler, *A Hist. of Am. Lit. During the Colonial Time* (rev. ed., 1897), II, 244–51; G. O. Seilhamer, *Hist. of the Am. Theatre* (1888), I, ch. xviii; A. H. Quinn, *Hist. of the Am. Drama from the Beginning to the Civil War* (1923), pp. 16–27. See also F. H. Williams, "Pa. Poets of the Provincial Period," *Pa. Mag. of Hist. and Biog.*, Apr. 1893.] A. H. Q.

GODKIN, EDWIN LAWRENCE (Oct. 2, 1831–May 21, 1902), editor, though born in Ireland was of English stock on both sides. The name goes back at least to the twelfth century, when a small colony of Englishmen settled on the coast of Wexford, Ireland, in what was called the Barony Forth. Godkin's mother, Sarah Lawrence, came from a family of Cromwellian settlers. Thus he could truthfully write in 1878, when declining to reply to a magazine article by Goldwin Smith, "I am an Irishman, but I am as English in blood as he is" (Ogden, *post*, I, 1). This double strain of residence and race always marked him. His father, the Rev. James Godkin, was a man of parts and power. In addition to active work as a dissenting clergyman he was at different times in charge of two newspapers, one in Londonderry and one in Dublin, and also served occasionally as Irish correspondent of the London *Times*. He early associated himself with the cause of Home Rule for Ireland, and was a prolific controversial writer. Knowing Ireland minutely, he made economic and political investigations in nearly every county, so that he not only won repute and regard among his fellow countrymen, but became a highly useful man for English Liberals to consult. More than once he was a source of information to Gladstone. Toward the end of his life he was in receipt of a literary pension from the Gladstone government. He died May 23, 1879.

James Godkin's first child, Edwin Lawrence, was born at Moyne, County Wicklow, in the house of his grandmother, Mrs. Anthony Lawrence. There the larger part of his childhood was passed and all of his holidays as a schoolboy. A delicate and precocious boy, he divided his time between outdoor sports and passionate, sometimes furtive, reading of books. At the age of seven he was sent to a preparatory school at Armagh. When he reached the age of ten, though he still lacked robust health, it was decided to find a school for him in England. In 1841 he was entered at Silcoates School at Wakefield, near Leeds, where he remained for more than four years. He then studied for a time at home with an uncle, the Rev. John Edge. Later he went to the Classical Department of the Royal Belfast Academical Institution. In 1846 he became an undergraduate of Queen's College, Belfast. He took his degree in 1851, after an academic career not highly distinguished but showing promise. He displayed marked intellectual ability, along with a disinclination to apply himself steadily to the required work of the college. His sister's recollection of her brother at the age of twenty was of "a very handsome, refined, delicate-looking young man—witty, brilliant, charming, proud, with a fiery temper, but lovable and affectionate" (Ogden, I, 12).

Shortly after graduation, Godkin went to London to enter himself as a law student in Lincoln's Inn, but the impulse to journalism and to politics, honestly in his blood, tended to pull him away from the legal profession, and he soon obtained employment in John Cassell's publishing house. It is known that he wrote for *Cassell's Illustrated Family Paper,* and was for a time its sub-editor, though none of his contributions are surely to be identified. It was Cassell who published his first book, *The History of Hungary and the Magyars: From the Earliest Times to the Close of the Late War* (1853). This was doubtless prompted by Kossuth's visit, which caused a great stir of sympathy in England. Though Godkin in later life made light of its "rhetoric," and its "fearfully profound" philosophical reflections, the book showed a comprehensive knowledge of the material and a fine gift of narrative, and was a remarkable production for a youth of twenty-two. It contained clear premonitions, both in thought and style, of the writer that was to be. The work was not without honor in the country to which it was dedicated.

In 1854 Godkin traveled in Hungary and had a welcome from revolutionists who had heard of his history. Hungarian admirers presented him at that time a sword which is still preserved.

For two years after 1853, he served as correspondent of the London *Daily News* in the Crimea, gaining from his experiences an extraordinary grasp of military theory, and, at the same time, a hatred of war which often showed in his burning language about it. The invitation to this service doubtless came to him in consequence of his book about Hungary, and of a letter which he had written to the *Daily News* concerning the claims of the Greeks to Constantinople. It was regarded by him and his family as a high honor as well as a great opportunity, and he set off for his new work in fine spirits. The mission was hard and at times dangerous, but Godkin performed it with great fidelity and industry. His letters to the *Daily News* were not confined to military operations, and were so meritorious as to win him not only commendation and reward from his editor but public recognition in various forms. After his return he delivered lectures on the war in Belfast and elsewhere. For a time he did editorial work on the *Northern Whig* of Belfast. His employers soon offered him the editorship—no small compliment to a young man of twenty-five—but he broke off in order to fulfil a purpose long cherished to go to America, reaching his destination in November 1856. In New York he studied for a time in the office of David Dudley Field, and on Feb. 6, 1858, was admitted to the bar, but, although he appeared as counsel in at least one case of record, he does not seem to have sought practise.

He had brought with him from England useful introductions, and soon made valuable acquaintances. Chief among his early friends was Frederick Law Olmsted [*q.v.*], whose fascinating letters from the South, first published in the *New York Times,* confirmed Godkin in his own plan to make similar travels on horseback, still keeping up his connection with the London *Daily News.* Writing to that journal about the South and later about American public life was a form of unconscious preparation for the work as an editor which he was soon to take up. In 1857 he spent some time in New Haven where he was admitted to the homes, among others, of President Woolsey and Samuel Edmond Foote. To the elder daughter of the latter, Frances Elizabeth, Godkin became engaged in 1858, and to her he was married on July 29, 1859. She was noted for her uncommon beauty, intellectual superiority, and striking social gifts.

As Godkin's power and promise as a writer on public affairs became better known, various proposals were made to him to take a newspaper position. Olmsted in particular tried to induce him to go to San Francisco to establish a new daily in that city, but Godkin felt himself too ignorant about California and the West to make that venture, besides preferring to live in the East. For some time he cherished a project to found a weekly which suddenly came to fruition in 1865. James Miller McKim of Philadelphia had raised a fund to establish a newspaper especially devoted to the interests of the freedmen. Hearing of Godkin's plan, he offered to join forces with him. Charles Eliot Norton obtained in Boston further subscriptions to the stock, so that the *Nation* was launched July 6, 1865, with a capital of $100,000, distributed among forty stockholders. From the first, the *Nation* under Godkin's editorship had a program much broader than advocacy of a single cause. While giving due attention to the problems growing out of the abolition of slavery, it proposed the widest and most informed comment upon literature, art, music, and public affairs. Its published list of regular or occasional contributors reads like an enumeration of the men of light and leading of that time. Nothing of exactly that tone had before appeared in the United States. From its very beginnings the *Nation* commended itself by its range of scholarship, breadth of view, and high moral tone, and it became, according to James Bryce, "the best weekly not only in America but in the world" (Bryce, *post,* p. 372). Its influence on thinking people long remained out of all proportion to its circulation figures. It was especially influential with the choicer spirits among college undergraduates. Such an undertaking, so conducted, necessarily cost money, and before the first year was over the original capital was nearly exhausted. This condition, together with the embarrassments arising out of so large a number of stockholders, brought the financial affairs of the paper to a crisis. The problem was solved by Godkin's cancelling his contract as editor, taking over the property himself, and forming a new Nation Association under the title of E. L. Godkin & Company.

In 1881 a larger journalistic opportunity came to him. In that year Henry Villard bought the New York *Evening Post* and, with a disinterestedness rare in proprietors, turned over its control absolutely to its editors. These were, at first, Carl Schurz, who was chief, Horace White, and Godkin. The latter linked up the *Nation* with the new company, and it thereafter appeared as the weekly edition of the *Evening Post,* duplicating the editorial matter by selection. In 1883

Schurz withdrew, and Godkin was made editor-in-chief, a position which he held until his retirement, owing to ill health, on Jan. 1, 1900. The change to a daily newspaper necessarily had an effect upon Godkin's political writing. If it lost something of deliberateness and mature judgment, it gained in ardor and dash and the power to drive home the force of argument by repetition, in varied form, day after day. His chief reputation as an editor was created by his valiant service to right thinking and sound politics as editor of the *Evening Post.* Coming after famous editors who had conducted newspapers as personal organs, allied with political parties, and often seeking political advancement themselves, Godkin by his entire independence and treatment of great public questions without fear or favor won for himself a unique place in American journalism. His influence upon the press and public opinion was intensive. He touched immediately only small circles, but from them his individual impress extended to wider groups. Once, when he was remarking on the limited circulation of the *Evening Post,* a prominent Western journalist said that he ought to know how, when big questions came up, other editors waited to get his point of view. They might not agree with it, they might attack it, but they realized that it had to be reckoned with.

To his work as editor he brought an almost unequaled equipment. In history and economics and political theory he was broadly read, and his mind was always full of apt citations and anecdotes. As a writer he had a most original and illuminating humor, with the faculty of being interesting even when he was dealing with the driest subjects. Into the large public movements of his time he threw himself with unquenchable zeal and fearless independence. Though he had strongly sympathized with the Union cause in the Civil War and inclined to the Republican party, as editor of the *Nation* he denounced the Carpetbag régime in the South, assailed the corruption of Grant's administration, and deplored the circumstances of the accession of Hayes to the presidency. As editor-in-chief of the *Post,* he led in 1884 the Mugwump revolt against Blaine, whom he attacked in parallel columns of damning quotations (Nevins, *post,* pp. 461–62). Cleveland he greatly admired and in general continued to support, though he bitterly assailed the President's Venezuela message as marking submission to the "Jingoes" (Ogden, II, 202). An implacable foe of "Silverism," he advocated a moderate tariff and deplored territorial expansion. Impregnated in his youth with the animus of the great Liberal movement in England, he always remained in sympathy with it and hoped that its enfranchising spirit, if not all its methods, might be imitated in his adopted country. "His views," says Bryce, "were definite, not to say dogmatic, and as they were confidently held, so too they were confidently expressed. He never struck a doubtful note" (*post,* p. 367).

When important issues were at hazard, Godkin's pen knew no brother. He was sometimes accused of disloyalty to friendship, but though a friend of Plato, he was a greater friend of the truth as he saw it. Abram S. Hewitt, speaking at the centenary celebration of the *Evening Post,* said that its motto under Godkin's direction had always seemed to him to be, "Whom the Lord loveth, He chasteneth." Yet causes always stood larger in Godkin's mind than personalities. Proof of this he gave notably in his long struggle for civil-service reform. To it he brought stores of knowledge and experience; infinite resources of raillery and ridicule; with noble indignation at the way in which the spoils system was degrading American public life. But it was always the great improvement of the public service which he worked for constructively, more than for pulling down the reputation of any man. Though his foreign birth was sometimes flung at him (Bryce, *post,* p. 372; Rhodes, *post,* pp. 276 ff.), Godkin became thoroughly steeped in American life. With every phase of it, his insatiate intellectual curiosity prompted him to seek acquaintance. In even the freakish and bizarre and vulgar he found much to enjoy. It was his delight to seize upon current slang and give it a humorous twist. His gift for pungent and biting phrase was unexcelled. During his long fight against corruption in New York City, he once wrote that the two things which Tammany leaders most dreaded were honest labor and biography. Accordingly he caused to be printed many of their biographies (Nevins, *post,* pp. 481 ff.; see *Evening Post,* Apr. 3, 1890), with the result that he was several times summoned for criminal libel, though none of the suits was ever pressed to trial. Godkin's eye for a suggestive title was also uncommonly keen. An article which he wrote about the Beecher-Tilton case was headed, "Chromo Civilization." That was a half-battle word.

He believed wholeheartedly in democracy, and followed its developments and even its vagaries, with close and intense concern. About Socialism he wrote with acute perception of its weaknesses and dangers, yet with philosophic tolerance for its successive experiments. He used often to say that he would like to come back to earth fifty years after his death in order to see how democracy was getting on. Toward the end of his life, when the shadows of ill health and approaching night were about him, he became somewhat despondent about the future. His correspondence with Lord Bryce at that time revealed a certain amount of pessimism on either side. The Englishman was gloomy about his own country, though very hopeful for the United States, while the American was confident that England would soon right herself, although he felt discouraged about America. At last, Godkin's "ancient humor" came to his rescue, as this exchange of ideas went on, and he wrote to Bryce: "Do come over soon, and we'll lie under a tree at Dublin while you abuse Great Britain and I abuse the United States."

Godkin had three children. A son, Lawrence, was born May 31, 1860; a daughter, Lizzy, in 1865; and another son, who died in infancy, in 1868. A cruel blow fell on the family in 1873 when the daughter died. Mrs. Godkin never recovered from it, passed through a period of invalidism, and herself died Apr. 11, 1875. These successive shocks made New York distasteful to Godkin, and thereafter he lived in Cambridge for more than two years, while still directing the *Nation.* This fact gave rise to the saying that the *Nation* was the best New York paper edited in Cambridge. On June 14, 1884, he was married to Katherine Sands, who survived him. His health was seriously crippled in 1900, and he spent some time recuperating in Dublin, N. H., and at Lenox, Mass., but in May 1901 he sailed for England. There he passed a year in comparatively good health, writing occasional letters to the *Evening Post,* full of his old verve and humor, but he gradually failed and on May 21, 1902, he died at Greenway House, Brixham, on the River Dart. He was buried in the old Hazelbeach Churchyard at Northampton, England.

Godkin's engaging personality and extraordinary ability as a writer were attested by the friendships and admiration which for years flowed in upon him from the best in America and in England. He was an intimate in the family of Charles Eliot Norton; was in frequent correspondence with James Russell Lowell and William and Henry James, to whom he was closely bound; and was in touch with the leading men in the professions and in literature and public life, both of New York and Boston. Among Englishmen he had troops of friends, from Lord Bryce down. In 1897 Oxford conferred upon him the degree of D.C.L. His personal charm, though unsuspected by the public, was of the highest, making him a great favorite in the social circles in which he moved, though he was always fastidious about accepting invitations and was impatient of time expended in mere feasting and chatter. He wrote many articles over a period of thirty years for the *North American Review,* the *Atlantic,* the *Century, Scribner's,* the *Forum,* and other magazines. His published books, in addition to *The History of Hungary,* were: *Reflections and Comments* (1895), *Problems of Modern Democracy* (1896), *Unforeseen Tendencies of Democracy* (1898). Both in the *Nation* and in the *Evening Post* his pen came to be recognized as a "power in the State." Never seeking or holding a paid office, he faithfully served his day and generation, and left a name which has worthily passed into the best tradition of American journalism.

[*Life and Letters of Edwin Lawrence Godkin* (2 vols., 1907), edited by Rollo Ogden, which contains a list of Godkin's writings; "Random Recollections," by Godkin himself, published in the *Evening Post,* Dec. 30, 1909; Semi-Centennial Number of the *Nation,* July 8, 1915, which contains articles by James Bryce, W. C. Brownell, Henry James, Henry Holt, A. V. Dicey, and others; Jas. Bryce, in *Studies in Contemporary Biog.* (1903); J. F. Rhodes, "Edwin Lawrence Godkin," in *Atlantic Monthly,* Sept. 1908, repr. in *Hist. Essays* (1909); V. L. Parrington, *Main Currents in Am. Thought,* III (1930), 154–68; Allan Nevins, *The Evening Post: A Century of Journalism* (1922); Gustav Pollak, *Fifty Years of American Idealism: The New York Nation 1865–1915* (1915); obituaries in the *Nation,* May 22, 1902, the *Evening Post,* May 21, 1902, the *N. Y. Times,* May 22, 1902, the *Times* (London), May 23, 1902.] R. O.

GODMAN, JOHN DAVIDSON (Dec. 20, 1794–Apr. 17, 1830), anatomist, naturalist, editor of the first medical journal published west of the Alleghanies, was born at Annapolis, Md., the son of Capt. Samuel Godman, a Revolutionary officer, and Anna (Henderson) Godman. His mother died before he was two years old, and his father before he was five. After the death of his mother he was cared for by an aunt who died when he was about six years old. He then lived with a sister in Baltimore, Md. In the winter of 1811–12 he served as an apprentice to a Baltimore printer, and during this apprenticeship he developed the first symptoms of tuberculosis, the disease which eventually caused his death. In 1814, at the time the British fleet was in Chesapeake Bay, he joined the flotilla commanded by Joshua Barney [*q.v.*] and was present at the bombardment of Fort McHenry. He began the study of medicine in 1815 with Dr. William N. Luckey in Elizabethtown, Pa.; later he completed his studies under the direction of Dr. John B. Davidge of Baltimore, and graduated from the University of Maryland in March 1818. During his student days he served as demonstrator in anatomy and for a time gave the lectures in anatomy. After graduation he began the practise of medicine in New Holland, Lancaster County, Pa., but after a few months removed to a small village near Baltimore. He made this move because he expected to be appointed professor of anatomy in the University of Maryland. Failing to receive the appointment, Godman went to Philadelphia determined to establish himself as a lecturer in anatomy and physiology. He at once began to attract attention, and soon Dr. Daniel Drake invited him to come to Cincinnati as professor of surgery in the Medical College of Ohio. He left for Cincinnati on Oct. 6, 1821, having on the same day married Angelica Kauffman Peale, a daughter of Rembrandt Peale.

Disgusted with the intrigue and bickering which arose in the faculty, Godman resigned his position at the end of the first term. He did not leave Cincinnati immediately, however, but remained to edit the first issues of the *Western Quarterly Reporter of Medical, Surgical and Natural Science,* which made its initial appearance in March 1822. In October 1822, he returned to Philadelphia and the following year became the second to assume charge of the Philadelphia School of Anatomy. In 1825 he was on the editorial board of the *Philadelphia Journal of the Medical and Physical Sciences.* Two years later, largely through his influence, the name of the journal was changed to the *American Journal of the Medical Sciences.* In 1826 he had been offered the chair of anatomy in Rutgers Medical College in New York City, but before the end of the second session his tuberculosis had become so active that he was compelled to resign. After spending the early months of 1828 in the West Indies without benefit, he returned, took a house at Germantown, Pa., and devoted his remaining days to literary work.

In 1824 Godman published his *Anatomical Investigations* in which he gave a detailed description of the various fasciae of the human body. His *magnum opus* was his three-volume *American Natural History* (1826–28). This was the first original treatise on the subject, and a valuable addition to the scientific literature of the country. The writing of the natural-history section of the *Encyclopaedia Americana* (1829–33) was assigned to him, but he did not live to complete the task. From early youth he was intensely interested in the study of nature, and embraced every opportunity to increase his knowledge. At the time he lived near Baltimore his home was in that part of Anne Arundel County, Md., which is situated between the Patapsco and Severn Rivers, and Chesapeake Bay. Here, during his rambles through the woods and along the banks of the rivers and bay, he began those observations which he continued after his removal to Germantown by walks through Turner's lane and along the banks of the Wissahickon and Frankford creeks. It was during his last illness, when he was too weak to leave his bed, that he published a series of sketches in the *Friend,* a weekly Philadelphia magazine, in which he described in a charming manner the observations he had made during his various rambles. These sketches are considered the gem of his literary publications. In 1833 they were issued as a separate publication under the title of *Rambles of a Naturalist.* In the year before his death he had assembled a number of his papers which he published as *Addresses Delivered on Various Public Occasions.*

[Thos. Sewall, *An Eulogy on Dr. Godman* (1830); Daniel Drake, in *Western Jour. of the Medic. and Physic. Sci.,* Jan., Feb., Mar. 1831; S. D. Gross, *Lives of Eminent Am. Physicians and Surgeons* (1861), pp. 247–66; *Autobiog. of Samuel D. Gross, M.D.,* I (1887), 44–46; E. F. Cordell, *The Medic. Annals of Md.* (1903); P. S. Godman, *Some Account of the Family of Godman* (1897).]

W. S. M.

GODWIN, PARKE (Feb. 25, 1816–Jan. 7, 1904), editor, author, the son of Abraham and Martha (Parke) Godwin, was born in Paterson (originally Totowa or Totawa), N. J., where his family had been of some prominence. His great-grandfather, Abraham Godwin, had kept a tavern in or near Totowa in the middle of the eighteenth century (William Nelson, *History of the Old Dutch Church at Totowa,* 1892, p. 27) and with three sons, one of them Parke's grandfather, had fought in the Revolution. His father had served as a lieutenant in the War of 1812. Something of his early family history is embodied in *The First Settlers of Totawa,* which he printed privately in 1892. He was graduated from Princeton in 1834, read law at Paterson, and went to Louisville, Ky., where he was admitted to the bar and opened a law office. Before acquiring a practise he returned to New York City, being, according to one account, too much disturbed by the presence of slavery to remain. In a New York boarding house in 1836 he met William Cullen Bryant and began an acquaintance that led to both professional and personal relationships. Bryant offered him a position on the New York *Evening Post,* a journal with which Godwin was intermittently connected for forty-five years; and on May 12, 1842, he was married to Bryant's eldest daughter, Fanny. He contributed articles, largely on economic and social subjects, to J. L. O'Sullivan's *United States Magazine and Democratic Review.* He was one of the New Yorkers who sympathized with the social movements being advocated in New England during the early forties, especially Brook Farm. Though never a resident, he is said to have given this venture hearty support, and to have written the first address in favor of "association"; and he later edited the *Harbinger,* organ of the disciples of Fourier, who became increasingly important in the movement. He also published *Democracy, Constructive and Pacific,* and *A Popular View of the Doctrines of Fourier* (both 1844). He always retained his idealism, although, when he died, the fact that he had been prominent in these transcendental experiments full sixty years before appealed to the imagination and probably led commentators to lay undue stress upon this part of his career. In politics he became first a Free-Soil Democrat, then a Republican. During the presidential campaign of 1860 he was active both in writing and in speaking. His faith in Lincoln was unwavering, and from a once-famous interview with the President he brought back to doubting New York Republicans the personal message that an emancipation proclamation was being delayed only until a favorable moment.

In 1853 he became associated with C. S. Briggs and George William Curtis in the editorship of the newly founded and short-lived *Putnam's Monthly Magazine.* His volume of *Political Essays* (1856) was gathered from his contributions to *Putnam's.* Besides his work for the journals mentioned, and others, he compiled a *Hand-Book of Universal Biography* (1852), later revised as *The Cyclopaedia of Biography* (1866, 1878). He projected a history of France, of which only the first volume, bringing the narrative to 843 A.D., was published (1860). He also edited the works of William Cullen Bryant (4 vols., 1883–84), and accompanied them with a biography (2 vols., 1883). He was in demand as a speaker on memorial occasions, and his *Commemorative Addresses* (1895) contains his utterances on G. W. Curtis, Edwin Booth, Bryant, and others. Evidence of his general literary interests may be found in his translations, made during the transcendental period, of the first part of *The Autobiography of Goethe* (2 vols., 1846–47), which he edited, and Zschokke's *Tales* (2 vols., 1845); in *Vala, A Mythological Tale* (1851) associated with the life of Jennie Lind; and in *A New Study of the Sonnets of Shakespeare* (1900), published when he was eighty-four years old. *Out of the Past* (1870) was a collection of literary and critical papers contributed to various journals—the first as early as 1839. A similar collection of political and social papers, promised in the preface of this volume, seems never to have been issued.

Godwin acquired a financial interest in the New York *Evening Post* in 1860. Both before and after that date he was close to Bryant in the editorial conduct of the paper. After the death of Bryant in 1878 he became editor-in-chief. Differences of opinion as to policies had long existed between Bryant and Godwin on the one hand, and Henderson, business manager and half owner, on the other; and a controversy that had smouldered while the veteran editor lived became active at his death. After three somewhat troubled years of editorship, Godwin closed his connection with the *Post* in 1881, when the paper was sold to the Villard interests. He soon became editor of the *Commercial Advertiser,* a position that he held until he retired from active routine duties. The list of his books and the known amount of his journalistic work would seem sufficient to refute the charge of laziness made by some of his acquaintances; though it must be remembered that his active career covered a period of nearly seventy years. Godwin's hair and beard are said to have become snowy white at a comparatively early age, and in his impressive portraits both appear as profuse as those of his distinguished father-in-law. A public-spirited citizen, member of many social and civic organizations, a patron of the opera and of other arts, he was long a familiar and a notable figure in New York, and in his later years seemed the most important if not the sole remaining link between the twentieth century and the literary past of Irving, Cooper, Willis, Poe, and their contemporaries.

[See *Who's Who in America,* 1903–05; obituary notice in the New York *Evening Post,* Jan. 7, 1904; Allan Nevins, *The Evening Post: A Century of Journalism* (1922); Wm. Nelson and C. A. Schriner, *Hist. of Paterson and its Environs,* II (1920), 65–67; Eugene Benson, "Parke Godwin, of the Evening Post," *Galaxy,* Feb. 1869; W. W. Clayton, *Hist. of Bergen and Passaic Counties, N. J.* (1882), p. 524.] W. B. C.

GOEBEL, WILLIAM (Jan. 4, 1856–Feb. 3, 1900), legislator, governor of Kentucky, was born in Carbondale, Pa., and was the eldest of the four children of William Goebel, a cabinet-maker, and his wife, Augusta Greenaclay, both of whom were natives of Germany. The Goebel family removed to Kentucky about 1863 and settled in Covington. After attending the public schools in Covington, William took a course in the Hollingsworth Business College. His father then apprenticed him to a Cincinnati jeweler, but he shortly abandoned this trade and began the study of law with former Gov. John W. Stephenson in Covington, but after a few months entered the Cincinnati Law School where he was graduated in 1877. After his graduation from law school he enrolled as a special student at Kenyon College, Gambier, Ohio, but the death of his father forced him, after two months, to withdraw in order to support the family. He practised law independently for a few years, was for five years a partner of John G. Carlisle [*q.v.*], then entered the law firm of Stephenson and remained a member of it until the death of the latter.

Goebel's political career began in 1887 when he was elected as a Democrat to the Kentucky Senate from Kenton County. To this position he was reëlected four times in succession, serving continuously until his nomination for governor in 1899. During the entire period of his legislative service he encountered bitter opposition within his own party. This political animosity resulted, among other things, in his killing John Sandford, a prominent banker and politician, in Covington in April 1895. On his examining trial he pleaded self-defense and was released, the grand jury subsequently refusing to indict him. His long service in the Senate made him an influential force in Kentucky legislation. He identified himself with the reform element and is generally credited with the passing of much of the reform legislation of the period, particularly that relating to taxation and the regulation of railroads. In the latter connection he aroused the enmity of the Louisville & Nashville Railroad. He was also the sponsor of the Goebel Election Law of 1898 which was bitterly denounced.

In 1899 he was a candidate for the Democratic nomination for governor, and secured the nomination in the Louisville convention by a series of shrewd political maneuvers which greatly increased the number of his enemies and divided his party. The resulting campaign was probably the most exciting in the history of the state, and resulted in the election, on the face of the returns, of his Republican opponent, William S. Taylor, by a small majority. Goebel charged fraud and contested the election before the legislature which was Democratic in both branches. While the contest was in progress he was shot by an assassin, Jan. 30, 1900, but before his death the legislature declared him legally elected governor. His death brought Kentucky to the verge of civil war, but in the end quiet was restored and the lieutenant-governor, J. C. W. Beckham, took office.

Goebel was not an orator but had a talent for vituperation and biting speech. He was taciturn and reserved and had practically no intimate friends outside his own family. He owed his success to unusual skill as a politician and to a courage that seemed to have no limit. His integrity was questioned by his opponents but no one doubted his success as an organizer. He probably inspired a greater amount of loyalty in his supporters and of personal hatred on the part of his opponents than any other figure in Kentucky politics. He never married.

[The best summary of Goebel's career is in the Louisville *Courier-Journal,* Feb. 4, 1900. The killing of Sandford and the Goebel assassination are described in L. F. Johnson, *Famous Ky. Tragedies and Trials* (1916). His gubernatorial campaign is depicted (somewhat luridly) by R. E. Hughes, F. W. Schaefer, and L. F. Williams, *That Kentucky Campaign* (1900). See also *Cincinnati Commercial Tribune,* Feb. 4, 1900; T. S. Duke, *Celebrated Criminal Cases of America* (1910), pp. 509–15; Chas. Kerr, W. E. Connelly, and E. M. Coulter, *Hist. of Ky.,* II (1922), 1008–13, 1080; Caleb Powers, *My Own Story* (1905); *Jour. of . . . the Senate of . . . Ky.,* 1900.]

R. S. C.

GOERZ, DAVID (June 2, 1849–May 7, 1914), Mennonite clergyman, organizer, was the eighth of twelve children, only three of whom reached maturity, born to Heinrich and Agnes Goerz at Neu Bereslow, near Berdiansk on the Sea of Azov, South Russia. His father, a German Mennonite colonist, was apprenticed to a blacksmith in his youth and later was an overseer holding a responsible position at Kertch, then at the village of Schardau, in the Mennonite colony east of the Molotschnaya. Here David attended the village school and later became an outstanding student at the Ohrloff Vereinsschule, preparing to teach and preach as was his mother's wish. He had to earn part of his way through school. At sixteen he took up surveying. At eighteen he was baptized and began six years of teaching. On June 21, 1871, when he was just past twenty-one, he married Helen Riesen, daughter of a Prussian cabinetmaker. She became the mother of his nine children and his lifelong helpmeet. At twenty-four Goetz emigrated to America, settling temporarily at Summerfield, Ill., where he taught two years. Soon he became secretary of the Mennonite Board of Guardians which was instrumental in locating thousands of immigrants in Central Kansas. In February 1875 he founded in Summerfield a German paper, *Zur Heimath,* which in December of that year he removed to Halstead, Kan., where he also started a bookstore and prospered financially. He identified himself with Mennonite Conference work in 1876 and was either secretary or moderator of the district for many years. In 1878 he was ordained as a Mennonite minister. Two years later he organized the Mennonite Mutual Fire Insurance Company, the first in Kansas. His poetical and musical inclinations led him to help in the preparation of a German church hymnbook. He was interested in the cause of higher education, was one of the organizers of the Bethel College Corporation and for many years served it as secretary, treasurer, and solicitor. In 1893, when the school opened, he removed to a residence on the campus at Newton, Kan., where in 1896 he started and edited the *School and College Journal.* He organized and became pastor of the campus church in 1897. Two years later the Conference sent him to India to distribute a large shipment of corn in the famine area and to investigate foreign-mission possibilities. He located the field around Champa, where the Mission to the Lepers was later established. There the need of suffering humanity was burned into his soul and he vowed, if brought safely home, to devote his energies to establishing an institution of mercy. He lived to see the Bethel Deaconess Home and Hospital, Newton, Kan., become a reality in 1908. He was a dreamer, but his visions always took practical shape.

Naturally reticent, he had but few intimates. Though he was deeply attached to his family, his urge to serve was so insistent that he left home and traveled from coast to coast seeking support for good causes. Facile of pen and forceful of speech, a hard driver of self and of others, he either repelled or convinced. He could brook no opposition, and he had no successor. In 1910 his iron nerves gave way. To regain his health he and his wife traveled abroad. On their return they removed to California, where he died and was buried in Hollywood Cemetery.

[*Bundesbote-Kalender* (1915); *Mennonitisches Lexikon,* vol. II (1928); C. H. Smith, *The Mennonites* (1920); *A Biog. Hist. of Central Kansas,* II (1902), 1080–81; *Kansas: A Cyc. of State Hist., Suppl. Vol. of Personal Hist. and Reminiscences,* Part II (1912), p. 1270; C. H. Wedel, *Sketches from Ch. Hist. for Mennonite Schools* (1920); H. S. Bender, *Two Centuries of Am. Mennonite Lit.* (1929); obituary in *Der Herold* (Newton, Kan.), May 14, 1914; personal acquaintance; statements from relatives.] C. E. K.

GOESSMANN, CHARLES ANTHONY (June 13, 1827–Sept. 1, 1910), chemist, teacher, was born in the little town of Naumburg, in Hesse-Cassel, Germany, the son of Heinrich and Helena Henslinger-Boediger Goessmann. He was christened Karl Anton. As a boy he was trained in the schools of Naumburg and Fritzlar and then, becoming interested in pharmacy, he spent several years as apprentice and assistant pharmacist in the towns of Gudensberg, Göttingen, Mainz, and Fulda. In 1850 he matriculated at the University of Göttingen. Influenced by the renowned chemist and teacher, Friedrich Woehler, who had been a fellow student with Goessmann's father at Marburg, the young pharmacist decided to become a chemist. In 1852 he received his Ph.D. degree and for the next five years remained with Woehler at Göttingen as assistant. At the same time he carried on important investigations in organic chemistry, the results of which, published in some twenty papers, established his reputation as one of the promising young chemists. As an instructor at Göttingen, he won the friendship of two American students, one of whom, J. H. Eastwick, was instrumental in his emigrating to America, for in 1857 Goessmann accepted an invitation to become chemist of the sugar refinery of Eastwick Brothers in Philadelphia. Three years later he was asked by Prof. George H. Cook, of Rutgers College, and state geologist of New Jersey, to join in an investigation of the salt deposits at Syracuse, N. Y. This led to his acceptance of a permanent position as chemist of the Salt Company of Onondaga, which he held until the end of 1868. Thus, for the first twelve years of his stay in America, he was associated with the small group of chemists who were applying a knowledge of chemistry to rapidly developing industries. In this field his investigations in connection with sugar-refining and with salt deposits and refining were of the first order and ranked him as one of the leading American chemists. For the two years, 1862–64, during the period of his connection with the salt industry, he was also professor of chemistry at Rensselaer Polytechnic Institute. On Oct. 22, 1862, he was married to Mary Anna Clara Kinny, of Syracuse.

In 1868, William S. Clark, another of Goessmann's Göttingen students, who had been elected president of the newly established Massachusetts Agricultural College at Amherst, offered the professorship of chemistry in this new institution to his former instructor. Goessmann accepted, and for forty years remained in active service, finding his real life-work in helping to shape the policies of this new type of college, and to develop in the experiment station the practical application of chemistry to the solution of problems in agriculture. During the first years in his new position, he was also chemist to the Massachusetts State Board of Agriculture and state inspector of fertilizers, as well as analyst to the State Board of Health. When the Massachusetts State Experiment Station was established in 1882, he was made director and chemist, retaining the latter position until his retirement in 1907. He was the first chairman, in 1880, of the organization which in 1884 became the Association of Official Agricultural Chemists, and president of the American Chemical Society in 1887. In 1907 the Carnegie Foundation granted him a pension on which he retired from active service. The titles of papers and reports which he published number over two hundred, and deal with various phases of agricultural chemistry: sugar,

sugar cane, soils, plant nutrition, fertilizers, and animal feeding.

[*Chas. Anthony Goessmann* (1917), published by the Corporation and the Associate Alumni of the Mass. Agric. Coll., contains a bibliography of Goessmann's publications and a list of articles about him. See also the *Ann. Reports of the . . . Mass. Agric. Coll.*, 1869–1911; *Am. Chem. Jour.*, Nov. 1910; *Proc. Am. Chem. Soc.*, 1910; *Springfield Republican, Boston Transcript*, Sept. 2, 1910.] J. S. C.

GOETHALS, GEORGE WASHINGTON (June 29, 1858–Jan. 21, 1928), engineer, administrator, soldier, will chiefly be recorded in history as builder of the Panama Canal. He was born in Brooklyn, N. Y., of Dutch parentage, the son of John Louis Goethals and Marie Le Barron, who emigrated to the United States by way of Ghent about the year 1850. After attending the Brooklyn public schools, he entered the College of the City of New York, intending to become a physician. He worked his way through three years of college by running errands and doing odd jobs of bookkeeping. Attracted by notice of a cadetship at West Point, he wrote President Grant on the subject, but received no reply. Later, Representative "Sunset" (S. S.) Cox, hearing of Goethals's high scholarship, gave him the coveted appointment to the Military Academy, from which institution he graduated June 15, 1880, second in a class of fifty-two members. While at the Academy, he was well liked, was president of his class, and rose to the rank of cadet captain.

His service in the Engineer Corps of the army covered all grades from second lieutenant to colonel, inclusive, and among his more important details were: engineer officer, Department of Columbia (1882–84); improvements on the Ohio River (1884–85); instructor and assistant professor of civil and military engineering, United States Military Academy (1885–89); improvements on the Cumberland and Tennessee Rivers, completion of the Muscle Shoals Canal, and construction of the Colbert Shoals Lock (1889–94); assistant to the chief of engineers (1894–98); chief engineer, I Army Corps, and the campaign in Porto Rico (1898); instructor in practical military engineering at the United States Military Academy (1898–1900); river and harbor works, Block Island to Nantucket, and fortifications of Narragansett Bay and New Bedford (1900–05); General Staff (1903–07); and construction of the Panama Canal (1907–14).

In January 1880, when Goethals was still a West Point cadet, Ferdinand de Lesseps had begun the construction of a sea-level canal across the Isthmus of Panama. Until 1898–99, when the project was finally abandoned, the French had struggled against tropical disease, administrative mismanagement, and a defective organization. From 1899 to 1901, the United States through a Canal Commission undertook investigation of the feasibility of an interoceanic canal —considering all possible routes through Central America. On June 28, 1902, an Act of Congress, and in 1904, ratification of a treaty with the Republic of Panama, made the building of the Panama Canal possible. The first chief engineer, John F. Wallace [*q.v.*], resigned after a year of service, and his successor, John F. Stevens, decided to retire late in March 1907. Immediately, President Roosevelt appointed Goethals, then a lieutenant-colonel and serving on the General Staff, as Stevens's successor, and in the selection of Goethals, after the retirement of two chief engineers, the President realized the necessity of a certain permanence of policy in the construction of the Canal, and of complete control by the chief engineer of every activity in and near the Canal Zone, unhampered by political or other considerations. The commission form of Canal Zone government was abolished, and all responsibility for success or failure rested on the shoulders of Goethals alone. Ultimately, the administration of the Panama Canal became that of one-man control.

Many difficulties confronted the new chief engineer. The appointment of an army man was not altogether popular with Canal employees. There were many insinuations that objectionable militarism in canal methods would follow (*Scribner's Magazine*, March 1915, pp. 270–75). From the start, this initial prejudice required tactful and intelligent handling. Furthermore, employees to the approximate number of thirty thousand and of many nationalities must needs be housed, fed, amused, and kept in health in a climate which had hitherto been considered the worst in the world. To this end, there were constructed on a mammoth scale offices, sleeping-quarters, kitchens, messes, machine-shops, cold-storage plants, schools, hotels, clubs, and recreation centers. An efficient, self-sustaining supply department was created, and an accounting department capable of auditing the collection and disbursement of funds—not alone of Canal expenditures proper, but of the Panama Railroad Company and of an immensely diversified commissary. A complete judicial system was instituted, with its own law-courts, police, jails, and penitentiary. A very important department of sanitation under William C. Gorgas [*q.v.*] had been at work since 1904 in the effort to eliminate the causative sources of yellow-fever and malarial infections—not merely within the Canal

Zone but in the neighboring Republic of Panama. As if these difficulties were not enough, labor troubles occurred, involving hours of labor and wages; and the vast and complicated problem of lock construction was for a time overshadowed in importance by discouraging recurrence of slides in Culebra (Gaillard) Cut, where the excavation for the Canal penetrated the Continental Divide. By persistent, patient, intelligent study and labor on the part of Goethals and his assistants, however, these gigantic engineering problems, as well as those involving personnel, were met and overcome. In this connection, Goethals was always generous in praise for those who preceded him. Of the work of the De Lesseps Company he said: "Much that was of inestimable value had been learned from the French and from their experience, and that they builded well so far as they went is the consensus of opinion"; and again, with respect to the initial work of John F. Stevens, he stated: "We were fortunate in falling heir to the organization that had been perfected for excavating Culebra Cut, for no one not thoroughly familiar with railroad transportation and not possessed of organizing ability, could have succeeded in this part of the work—the one part for which our previous training had not fitted any of us" (*Scribner's Magazine,* May 1915, p. 533).

Asked what part of the Canal work he considered the most difficult, his invariable reply was "the problem caused by the 'human element'" (*Ibid.,* June 1915, p. 724). It became the custom of the Chief Engineer to devote a part of each day, but especially Sunday mornings, to hearing complaints of employees, no matter how trivial or unimportant; and to encouraging a feeling among subordinates that he was always accessible, and sympathetic to their worries. Also, by constant personal visits, often unexpected, to all parts of the great Canal project, Goethals gained a wonderfully intimate, first-hand knowledge, not alone of engineering difficulties, but of the daily life of his army of workers—their joys, sorrows, amusements, ambitions, and mental as well as physical reactions to all phases of the problem of the Panama Canal. His grasp of multifarious details was considered by subordinates uncanny; there appeared to be no triviality, however insignificant, that was not stored away in the Chief Engineer's memory.

Thus, little by little, an organization was built up, which, in team-work and *esprit de corps,* has probably never been surpassed. Every employee, from the Chief Engineer down, believed in the Canal, and each gave the work his best personal effort (*Independent,* Dec. 18, 1916, p. 481), but "at the head was always General Goethals, giving to the outer world throughout those long years the impression of complete efficiency, serenity, and calm confidence in the success of the undertaking" (*Nation,* Feb. 1, 1928, p. 111). Starting in a certain atmosphere of opposition if not hostility, Goethals ended his construction days on the Isthmus of Panama with the respect and even veneration of most of his helpers; to many of them he had become a hero.

The Panama Canal was practically completed in 1913, and in August 1914 was opened to the commerce of the world. Goethals remained on the Isthmus as governor of the Canal Zone until the latter part of the year 1916, having meanwhile, on Mar. 4, 1915, been made a major-general in the United States army by special act of Congress in recognition of his accomplishment. On the same date, he received the "Thanks of Congress." On Nov. 15, 1916, he was, at his own request, transferred to the army retired list, and about the same time served as chairman of the board to pass upon the Adamson Act, which threatened to precipitate a great railroad strike. In 1917, for a few months only, he was state engineer of New Jersey. From April to July of that year he served as general manager of the Emergency Fleet Corporation and, as such, fought strenuously against the project of building a great number of wooden ships, as well as the cost-plus policy of President Wilson (*Scientific American,* Aug. 11, 1917, p. 94). Unable to agree with his superior, he submitted his resignation, and on Dec. 18, 1917, was recalled to active duty as acting quartermaster-general. In January 1918 he was given the additional duty of director of purchase, storage, and traffic, and as such directed not alone the purchase, storage, and transport of all supplies, but the movement of all troops within the United States and overseas. In this position, according to Maj-Gen. Peyton C. March, chief of staff during the World War, Goethals developed into one of the greatest supply men produced in any army, allied or enemy (Gen. Peyton C. March, *New York Times Magazine,* July 1, 1928, and *Literary Digest,* July 26, 1919, p. 71).

On Mar. 4, 1919, Goethals voluntarily returned to the army retired list and to the active practise of his profession—until the year 1923 as head of the firm of George W. Goethals & Company and thereafter under his own name. He served as consulting engineer on many important works such as the Inner Harbor Navigation Canal at New Orleans, the Columbia Basin Irrigation Project, the East Bay Municipal Utility District of Oakland, Cal., and the Lake

Worth Inlet District in Florida. The New York-New Jersey Port and Harbor Development Commission selected him as its chief consulting engineer, and he continued as such with the Port of New York Authority created by the legislatures of the two states, until his death (Hodges, *post*).

In appearance, Goethals was above medium height, erect and soldierly except for a slight stoop of the shoulders, impassive of features and unsmiling. He possessed, however, a keen sense of humor. Stern of purpose and in many respects a martinet, he had a driving power that carried all before it. In 1918 he was awarded the Distinguished Service Medal for conspicuous service in reorganizing the army's quartermaster department; France made him a commander of the Legion of Honor; Great Britain, an honorary Knight Commander of the Order of St. Michael and St. George; and the Chinese government bestowed upon him the Grand Cordon of the Order of the Striped Tiger, Second Class. In addition, he received many other honors, medals, and honorary degrees. He was a member of a number of clubs, societies, and associations.

In the summer of 1927, failing health forced him to give up active work, and he retired to Vineyard Haven, Mass., which he had considered his home since 1894. Although he returned to his New York office in the fall, for a time, his illness progressed, and on Jan. 21, 1928, he died of cancer. His death was a distinct shock to his many engineering and military friends throughout the world. Funeral services were held in the Chapel of the United States Military Academy at West Point, and interment was in the historic cemetery overlooking the Hudson River. His widow, Effie Rodman of New Bedford, Mass., to whom he had been married in 1884, with their two sons, survived him.

[War Department records; information from Lieut.-Col. George R. Goethals relating to his father's genealogy and boyhood; J. B. Bishop and Farnham Bishop, *Goethals: Genius of the Panama Canal* (1930); J. B. Bishop, "Personality of Gen. Goethals," *Scribner's Mag.*, Feb. 1915; "The Building of the Panama Canal," *Ibid.*, Mar.–June 1915, in which Goethals gave his own story of the construction of the Canal; W. C. Gorgas, *Sanitation in Panama* (1915); *Current Hist.*, May 1928; Wm. R. Scott, *The Americans in Panama* (1912); J. S. Heald, *Picturesque Panama* (1928); Arthur Bullard, *Panama* (1914); *Engineering News-Record*, Jan. 26, 1928; memoir by Gen. H. F. Hodges, U. S. A., in *Trans. Am. Soc. Civil Engineers*, vol. XCIII (1929); valuable biographical sketch by Gen. J. P. Jervey, U. S. A., in the *Military Engineer*, Mar.–Apr. 1928.]

C. D. R.

GOETSCHIUS, JOHN HENRY (Mar. 8, 1718–Nov. 14, 1774), Reformed Dutch clergyman, whose truculent personality left its mark on the Church of his generation, was born in Switzerland at Berneck (Bernegg) in the Canton of St. Gall, the third of the eight children of Maurice and Esther (Werndli) Goetschy. Members of his family had been citizens of Zurich for several centuries. His father, an able but eccentric Reformed clergyman, was deposed at Saletz in 1733 because of some immorality but continued to wield considerable influence. On Oct. 4, 1734, he left Zurich as the leader of several hundred emigrants, whose vague intention was to find a new home in the Carolinas. After suffering many privations and vicissitudes the company reached Rotterdam, where Goetschy managed to secure a commission as missionary in Pennsylvania. On May 29, 1735, with his family and followers, he arrived, ill and weary, at Philadelphia, and the next day he died. His seventeen-year-old son, thus thrown on his own resources, took to preaching to the German Reformed settlers in Philadelphia and the back country, and for the next five years he was a thorn in the side of John Philip Boehm [*q.v.*], whose congregations he invaded with scant regard for church order or even for common decency. The Presbytery of Philadelphia refused his application for ordination, but Goetschy continued not only to preach and catechize but to perform ministerial acts. By ignorantly taking sides with Boehm's antagonists he succeeded in doing a great deal of unintentional mischief. His activities embraced Skippack, Old and New Goshenhoppen, Great Swamp, Egypt, Saucon, Maxatawny, Moselem, Oley, Berne, and Tulpehocken congregations. In 1739 the Synods of Holland forbade the Pennsylvania churches to countenance unordained ministers on pain of losing the support of the Synods. Goetschy then resorted to the Rev. John Philip Dorsius of Neshaminy, under whom he read theology for one year. On Apr. 7, 1741, Dorsius, Theodorus Jacobus Frelinghuysen [*q.v.*], and Gilbert Tennent [*q.v.*], acting on their own initiative, ordained him; and Bernardus Freeman [*q.v.*] installed him as pastor of the Dutch churches at Jamaica, Newtown, Success, and Oyster Bay on Long Island. As the names of his supporters indicate, Goetschius (he had now Latinized his name) had joined the Coetus party, who, combining personal ambition with real insight into the needs of the Church, were struggling to wrest the control of the Dutch churches in America from the Classis of Amsterdam. Their opponents, who were strong on Long Island, were known as the Conferentie party, and the controversy between them was long and bitter. The opposition frequently locked Goetschius out of his churches, compelling him to hold his services in barns or under large trees. At one time, to prevent his preaching, the chorister gave out the 119th Psalm to be chanted by the congregation—a proceeding that would have lasted nearly a whole day, but Goetschius mounted the pulpit and, with his stentorian voice, preached the singers down. He was a stocky little man, ready of wit and not averse to a good fight. The Conferentie party disputed the validity of his ordination and finally made him submit in 1748 to reëxamination and reordination. In that year he moved to New Jersey as colleague pastor at Hackensack and Schraalenburgh, where, with diminishing need for belligerence, he lived till the end of his life. On Aug. 26, 1750, he married Rachel Zabrowisky of Bergen County; their descendants are still numerous in that vicinity. In his later years Goetschius had the reputation of a man of learning; he trained several candidates for the ministry and was one of the first trustees of Queen's (later Rutgers) College. From time to time he preached at New Paltz, N. Y. He published one sermon, *De Onbekende God, or The Unknown God—Acts 17:23* (New York, J. P. Zenger, 1743), in which he affronted his hearers by addressing them, characteristically, as Paul had addressed the Athenian idolaters. His influence on the Reformed Dutch Church was strong and generally beneficial.

[W. J. Hinke, *Life and Letters of the Rev. John Philip Boehm* (1916) and *Hist. of the Goshenhoppen Reformed Charge* (1920); J. Schoonmaker (grandson), article in W. B. Sprague, *Annals Am. Pulpit,* IX, Pt. II (1869), pp. 15–17; *Eccl. Records State of N. Y.* (7 vols., 1901–16), see index volume; T. B. Romeyn, *Hist. Discourse Delivered on Occasion of the Re-Opening and Dedication of the First Ref. (Dutch) Ch. at Hackensack, N. J.* (1870); *Records of the Ref. Dutch Churches of Hackensack and Schraalenburgh, N. J.,* Pts. I and II (Holland Soc. of N. Y., 1891); W. H. S. Demarest, *A Hist. of Rutgers Coll. 1766–1924* (1924); B. C. Taylor, *Annals of the Classis of Bergen* (1857).]

G. H. G.

GOETZ, GEORGE WASHINGTON (Feb. 17, 1856–Jan. 15, 1897), metallurgist, was born in Milwaukee, Wis. His father, August William Goetz, was from Worms, on the Rhine, and his mother, Augusta (Stoltze) Goetz, a native of Erfurt, in Thuringia. His attendance at school met with more or less interruption, owing to the financial circumstances of his family. At ten his interest in the natural sciences was keenly awakened by the lectures, illustrated by experiments, at the Engleman private school. His mother, noticing his own faculty for experimentation, thereupon placed entirely at his disposition a small room which served as his chemical and physical laboratory. After three years at the Engleman School, he was obliged, on account of the expense, to return to the public school. One year at high school and a brief term at the University of Wisconsin ended his preliminary education. In 1870 he went to work as telegraph operator in the office of the Milwaukee Iron Company. In Nelson P. Hulst, at that time chemist of the company, he found a most appreciative friend, in whose chemical laboratory he spent much time absorbing with avidity both chemical and technical information. At the same time he was reading Draper, Ganot, and Tyndall; taking mathematical lessons at night in exchange for lessons in telegraphy; and centering his interest in the metallurgical operations of the plant. When, in 1876, Dr. Hermann Wedding visited the iron works, he met young Goetz and immediately took an interest in him. After inquiring about the school of mines at Berlin, Goetz arranged to go there for study, and left for Berlin in the fall of 1876. The following summer Wedding invited him to his home in the Harz Mountains where he was privileged, under the doctor's guidance, to visit the metallurgical establishments in that vicinity. Goetz commenced his metallurgical career with the Otis Steel Company in 1881 and was given charge of their open-hearth steel department. In 1882 he was again in Europe, studying mechanical-puddling, and upon returning had charge of that work, then new, at the Otis plant. When in England he met Thomas, the inventor of the basic steel process, with whom he spent two months at Hörde, Westphalia. In 1890, having won the foremost rank as an iron and steel metallurgist, through his pioneer work in several important improvements in his particular branch, such as the application of gas analysis, mechanical-puddling, and the basic process, which he was the first to use successfully in America, he established at Milwaukee a complete metallurgical laboratory and was consulting metallurgist for the Illinois Steel Company, the Wellman Iron & Steel Company, the Westinghouse Company, the Krupp Company of Germany, and others. In 1885, 1888, 1890 and 1894 he was in Europe, investigating iron and steel problems and gas fuel. Toward the close of his life he took up in some degree, non-ferrous metallurgy, working in the Rocky Mountain states and Lake Superior regions, but he obtained no substantial results. In 1886, at Berlin, Germany, he married Elsie Luedecke, whose acquaintance he had made at the home of his friend Hermann Wedding. Her devoted care and inspiration did much to prolong his life but could not avert the untimely end. She and their three children survived him.

[Nelson P. Hulst, "Biog. Notice of Geo. W. Goetz," *Trans. Am. Inst. of Mining Engineers*, vol. XXVII (1898); *Engineering and Mining Jour.*, Mar. 6, 1897; the *Milwaukee Jour.*, Jan. 16, 1897; an unpublished biography in the possession of Goetz's family.]

R. C. C.

GOFF, EMMET STULL (Sept. 3, 1852–June 6, 1902), horticulturist, was born at Elmira, N. Y., the son of Gustavus A. and Mary (Stull) Goff. His boyhood was spent on a New York farm. He attended the public schools and later the Elmira Free Academy from which he graduated in 1869. For the next thirteen years he was engaged in a fruit-growing and farming project near Elmira in which he was associated with his father and brother. On Oct. 2, 1880, he was married to S. Antoinette Carr. The opportunity for a professional career came to him in 1882 when he was appointed horticulturist of the New York Experiment Station at Geneva, N. Y. For seven years he carried on investigations relating to the culture of many different plants of economic importance. By reason of the reputation which he gained through his excellent work there he was appointed to the newly created position of professor of horticulture and horticulturist of the experiment station of the University of Wisconsin. He entered upon his duties at Wisconsin in 1889 and continued them actively until his death in 1902. This new position afforded him a chance to show that his abilities were not limited to the carrying on of investigational work, and while he is best known for the high character of his researches, he was equally proficient as an instructor.

Goff's researches included phases of economic entomology, plant pathology, plant physiology, as well as horticulture. In all of these fields, he made noteworthy contributions. The testing of varieties was one of the lines of work to which the experiment station was expected to devote a considerable part of its efforts. Out of the data secured through such tests, Goff developed a systematic classification of the various common vegetables. He was not a mere laboratory investigator, however. His studies always followed lines in which the results might be directly used to help the agriculturist. This was especially true of his experiments in the use of fungicides and insecticides. He displayed his ability to work out new methods of utilizing the available information on a particular subject in his conception of the kero-water pump, a device for mechanically mixing kerosene and water to be used in the control of sucking insects, and in his development of the tar-paper-disc method of controlling cabbage maggots. His investigation of the nature and extent of root development in plants contributed largely to the knowledge of this important phase of plant production and gave a scientific basis for the formulation of certain cultural practises. Possibly his most notable research was his study of the differentiation of the flower buds of fruit plants, which, though it remained unfinished at his death, elicited the praise of botanical and horticultural scientists in general. He contributed three excellent books to horticultural literature: *Lessons in Commercial Fruit Growing* (1902); *Principles of Plant Culture* (1897); and *Lessons in Pomology* (1899). The first, a model of its kind, was adopted as a text-book in a number of agricultural colleges and secondary schools, and in spite of the rapid advances in horticultural knowledge, held its place for an unusually long time.

[L. H. Bailey, ed., *Cyc. of Am. Agric.*, vol. IV (1909); R. G. Thwaites, *The Univ. of Wis. Its Hist. and Its Alumni* (1900); the *Madison Democrat*, June 7, 1902; reports of the N. Y. Experiment Station, 1882–88; reports of the Wis. Experiment Station, 1881–1901.]

J. G. M.

GOFF, JOHN WILLIAM (Jan. 1, 1848–Nov. 9, 1924), jurist, was born in County Wexford, Ireland, and emigrated to the United States when a child. His youth was spent in New York City amid poverty. So straitened were his circumstances that he had to forego attending school owing to the necessity of working for a living. He joined the night classes at Cooper Union, however, and studied to such purpose as to acquire a competent education, though he could never be described as a scholar. In 1865 he entered the office of Samuel G. Courtney, at one time United States district attorney, and after serving as a junior clerk for some years, studied law and was admitted to the New York bar. He had associated himself with the Fenian organizations, and many of his compatriots became his clients. A short time after his admission to the bar he acquired considerable notice owing to his connection with what became known as "Goff's Irish Rescue Party." One O'Reilly, convicted of treason in Ireland, having escaped to the United States, planned an attempt to rescue some comrades who had been transported to Australia, and Goff took a leading part in chartering a New Bedford whaler for the purpose. (See New York *Evening Post*, Feb. 1, 1913.)

In 1888 he became assistant district attorney for New York City, and, subsequently, was nominated on the Independent Citizens' ticket for the office of district attorney, but failed of election. The contest had been signalized by gross frauds on the part of election officials and Goff was instrumental in procuring indictments against many adherents of the Democratic and Republican parties in respect to it. In 1893 the state Senate, in consequence of allegations of grave scandals involving the police force in New York City, appointed a committee, known as the Lexow Committee, to investigate the administration of the police department of the city, including the charges of corruption which had been freely made, and at the request of the New York citizens' association and chamber of commerce, Goff was retained as its counsel. During the lengthy inquiry which followed, he displayed great ability. The chief charges of blackmail and bribery were clearly substantiated, and as a result, many of the higher officials and a large number of the rank and file were disgraced. As a reward for his services, Goff, in November 1894, was elected recorder of the city and county of New York on the Political Reform ticket for a period of twelve years, and was the last to hold the office. In November 1906 he was elected a justice of the supreme court of New York, 1st District, for a fourteen-year term, and continued to sit on the bench till Jan. 1, 1919. He retired prior to the completion of his term owing to his having reached the prescribed age limit. In the course of his judicial services, which extended over a period of twenty-five years, he presided over some of the more celebrated criminal trials of the time. Among them were those of Walter Langerman, Dago Frank, Marie Barberi, Gyp the Blood, and Lefty Louie. At the first trial of Police-Lieut. Becker for the murder of Herman Rosenthal in 1912, which also took place before him, a unique point of law was raised by counsel for the accused, who held that it was a mistrial by reason of the judge's being over the statutory age. An investigation of the county records of Wexford, however, showed that the objection had no foundation in fact. At the outset of his career, Goff was not profoundly learned in the law, and after his admission to the bar his professional and other interests precluded any extended study, but he possessed a remarkable understanding of human nature, which contributed not only to his many successes in jury trials but was of material advantage to him on the bench. He was one of the best cross-examiners of his day, and though he was not eloquent, his speeches were always forcible, clear, and persuasive. He was married, on May 26, 1881, to Catherine O'Keefe of New York City.

[*Who's Who in America*, 1922–23; *The Asso. of the Bar of the City of N. Y., Year Book*, 1925; the *Green Bag*, Nov. 1897; *N. Y. Times*, Nov. 10, 1924; court and other official records; information as to certain facts from John W. Goff, White Plains, N. Y.]

H. W. H. K.

GOFFE, WILLIAM (d. 1679?), regicide, was the son of Stephen Goffe, rector of Stanmer in Sussex, and the brother of Stephen Goffe who became chaplain to Henrietta Maria. He learned the trade of dry salter in London. Later he married Frances, the daughter of Edward Whalley [*q.v.*], with whom he was destined to be closely associated. On the outbreak of the Civil War he entered the army and rose to the rank of colonel. He was a member of the High Court of justice appointed by Parliament to try Charles I, and signed the death warrant of the King. On May 19, 1649, he was given an honorary M.A. by the reformed University of Oxford. He fought in the battles of Dunbar and Worcester. He was a member for Yarmouth of Cromwell's Parliament of 1654, in the following year was appointed major-general for Sussex, Hampshire, and Berkshire, and in 1656 was elected to Parliament from Hampshire. He was a strong supporter of the house of Cromwell. He would have accepted Cromwell as King in 1657, and was made a member of Cromwell's House of Lords. On the death of the lord protector, he transferred his allegiance to Richard Cromwell, who, in 1658, granted him lands in Ireland to the value of £500 per annum. On Apr. 16, 1660, the Council of State issued a warrant for the apprehension of Goffe, who, accompanied by his father-in-law, Edward Whalley, fled to New England. From this time until the death of Whalley in 1674 or 1675 the careers of the two men are identical. They were at Boston and its vicinity from July 27, 1660, to Feb. 26, 1660/61; at New Haven and its vicinity from Mar. 7, 1660/61, to Aug. 19, 1661; and in Milford from Aug. 19, 1661, to the fall of 1664. On Oct. 13, 1664, they left New Haven for Hadley, Mass., where they were received into the home of the Rev. John Russell. There Whalley died in 1674 or 1675. Shortly after this, according to tradition, Goffe suddenly appeared to the inhabitants of Hadley and rallied them to the defense of their town from an attack of the Indians during King Philip's War. In 1676 he removed to Hartford, where he lived with either Capt. Thomas Bull or his son, Jonathan Bull, under the name of T. Duffell. His presence in Hartford was reported to Gov. Andros at New York, and in 1680 Andros complained to Gov. Leete of Connecticut. On June 10, 1680, the latter ordered a search for Goffe to be made in Hartford and on the following day the governor and assistants of Connecticut wrote Andros that he had not been found. Goffe's wife and children had remained in England, living with the wife of William Hooke, the sister of Whalley. Much of the knowledge of the careers of Whalley and Goffe in New England is derived from the correspondence of Goffe and his wife. This correspondence ceased in 1679 and it seems probable that Goffe died in Hartford at about that time.

["Mather Papers," *Mass. Hist. Soc. Colls.*, 4 ser., vol. VIII (1868); "Jour. of Col. Goffe," *Proc. Mass. Hist. Soc.*, Dec. 1863; *Calendar of State Papers, Domestic Series*; *Calendar of State Papers, Colonial Series*; Jos. Foster, *Alumni Oxonienses, 1500–1714* (4 vols., 1891–92); *Acts and Ordinances of the Interregnum, 1642–60* (3 vols., 1911), ed. by C. H. Firth and R. S. Rait; W. Cobbett, *Parliamentary Hist. of England*, vol. III (1808); Thos. Carlyle, *The Letters and Speeches of Oliver Cromwell* (3 vols., 1904); *Clarke Papers* (4 vols., 1891–1901), ed. by C. H. Firth; John Nalson, *A True Copy of the Jour. of the High Court of Justice for the Trial of King Chas. 1st* (1684); *The Memoirs of Edmund Ludlow* (2 vols., 1894), ed. by C. H. Firth; F. B. Dexter, "Memoranda Respecting Edward Whalley and Wm. Goffe," *Papers of the New Haven Colony Hist. Soc.*, II (1877), 117–46; Thos. Hutchinson, *The Hist. of the Colony of Mass. Bay*, vol. I (1764), and *The Hutchinson Papers* (2 vols., 1865); Sylvester Judd, *Hist. of Hadley* (rev. ed., 1905); David Masson, *The Life of John Milton* (7 vols., 1859–94); Mark Noble, *The Lives of the English Regicides* (2 vols., 1798); Ezra Stiles, *A Hist. of Three of the Judges of King Chas. I* (1794); L. A. Welles, *The Hist. of the Regicides in New England* (1927). *The Dict. of Nat. Biog.* contains a more detailed account of Goffe's career in England.]

I. M. C.

GOFORTH, WILLIAM (1766–May 12, 1817), physician, pioneer, probably the first to vaccinate west of the Alleghanies, was the son of Judge William Goforth, a distinguished pioneer of Kentucky and Ohio. His mother was probably Catharine Meeks, who is recorded as having been married to a William Goforth in New York on May 16, 1760. The younger William was born in New York City, studied medicine with Dr. Joseph Young and Dr. Charles McKnight, the latter a surgeon and at that time a public lecturer, and just after he had reached his majority, accompanied his brother-in-law, Gen. John Stites Gano, down the Ohio to Kentucky, landing on June 10, 1788, at Maysville, then called Limestone. He settled first at Washington, Ky., the second largest town in the district, and there he married the daughter of Rev. William Wood, pastor of the Baptist church. For eleven years Goforth practised at Washington. In 1799 he moved to Columbia, Ohio, a small village near Cincinnati where his father had settled, and in 1800 to Cincinnati, then a village of 750 inhabitants. There he took Daniel Drake [*q.v.*] into his house as a student. In 1801, having received cowpock from Dr. Benjamin Waterhouse, who had received it from England in 1800, he made what are believed to be the first vaccinations in the Northwest Territory, his pupil being one of the first to be vaccinated. For a short time after 1802 Goforth had as his partner Dr. John Stites, recently come from the East, but in 1804 Stites was replaced by young Drake. Goforth was then putting on his books from three to six dollars' worth of business a day, although, according to Drake, the Doctor's extremely unmethodical habits in money matters rendered only about a fourth of that amount collectible. For Drake's tuition, Goforth received from the young man's father $400, a large sum when the regular fee for a physician's visit was twenty-five cents. In June 1804 Goforth was commissioned surgeon-general of the 1st (Gano's) Division of the Ohio Militia. The following year he signed with his military title the diploma which he gave to Drake, the first medical diploma issued in the Northwest Territory. He also helped Drake financially when the latter set out for further study in Philadelphia. Like his more famous pupil, Goforth had a keen interest in natural science. In 1803, at considerable expense, he dug up at Big Bone Lick, Ky., a collection of prehistoric fossil bones, which he turned over to an English adventurer, Capt. Thomas Ashe, who took them to England, claimed all the credit for their discovery, and kept the proceeds of their sale for the Liverpool Museum.

For seven years Goforth was the leading physician of Cincinnati. He was tall, of good figure, enthusiastic, sanguine, with an alert mind. An ardent Mason, he usually embellished his signature with some of the emblems of Masonry. His manners were distinguished; he was meticulous in his attire. Every morning he had his hair done and powdered by the barber, then, dressed in all the elegance possible, with gloved hands and carrying a gold-headed cane, he sallied forth on his daily visits. His manners were courteous and polite and, as they sprang in part from great kindness of heart and he was especially courteous to the poor and humble, he was popular with all classes. In 1807, being a great admirer of the French, he went to New Orleans by flatboat, becoming there a parish judge and a member of the convention which drafted the first constitution of the state of Louisiana. During the British attack upon New Orleans he served as surgeon of a volunteer regiment. In May 1816, however, having tired of New Orleans, he embarked with his family on a keel boat for Cincinnati, where he disembarked eight months later. He resumed his practise there, but in the following spring he died from liver disease contracted during his voyage on the river.

[Daniel Drake, *Discourses Delivered by Appointment before the Cincinnati Medic. Lib. Asso.* (1852), p. 38, and *Pioneer Life in Ky.: A Series of Reminiscential Letters* (1870), ed. by C. D. Drake; E. D. Mansfield, *Memoirs of the Life and Services of Daniel Drake*

(1855); Otto Juettner, *Daniel Drake and his Followers* (cop. 1909); *Names of Persons for whom Marriage Licenses were Issued by the Secretary of the Province of N. Y. Previous to 1784* (1860); *Quart. Pub. Hist. and Phil. Soc. of Ohio,* XV (1920), 13; Thomas Ashe, *Memoirs of Mammoth, and Various other Extraordinary and Stupendous Bones* (Liverpool, 1806), *Travels in America* (1808), II, 179, 191, 204, 258, and *Memoirs and Confessions of Capt. Ashe* (1815), II, 198 ff.; *Hist. of Cincinnati and Hamilton County, Ohio* (1894); A. G. Drury, in H. A. Kelly and W. L. Burrage, *Dict. of Am. Medic. Biog.* (1928); obituary in *Liberty Hall and Cincinnati Gazette,* June 2, 1817.]

A. P. M.

GOING, JONATHAN (Mar. 7, 1786–Nov. 9, 1844), Baptist clergyman, missionary secretary, and educator, was born in Reading, Windsor County, Vt., the son of Capt. Jonathan and Sarah (Kendall) Going, and a descendant of Robert Gowinge, who, having emigrated from Edinburgh, is listed in 1644 among the freemen of Dedham, Mass. The home in which Jonathan grew up was respectable though not distinctly religious. His early education was in the public schools, but he prepared for college in the academy at New Salem, Mass., entering Brown University in 1805. Converted in his freshman year, he was baptized by Rev. Stephen Gano [*q.v.*]. After his graduation in 1809, he pursued theological studies for a while under President Messer of the University. He then returned home, where his influence led to the conversion of his parents, his sister, and his three brothers who, like himself, entered the Baptist ministry. When he was ordained at Cavendish, May 9, 1811, there was no other college-educated Baptist minister in Vermont. The following August he married Lucy Thorndike of Dunstable, Middlesex County, Mass. After a little more than four years as pastor in Cavendish, he was called to Worcester, where he served for sixteen years with marked ability. He was among the founders of Worcester Academy and of Newton Theological Institution; he became a trustee of Brown University and an original trustee of Amherst College. His activities in behalf of the weaker churches led to the organization of the Massachusetts Baptist State Convention.

In 1826, Rev. John M. Peck [*q.v.*] spent a night at Going's home in Worcester and for the next five years they were in frequent correspondence. During the summer of 1831 the two traveled hundreds of miles in Missouri, Illinois, Kentucky, and Indiana. Before they separated, they had "agreed on the plan of the American Baptist Home Mission Society" (Rufus Babcock, *Memoir of John Mason Peck, D.D., Edited from His Journals and Correspondence,* 1864, p. 219). At a meeting of the Baptist Missionary Society held in Boston the plan was indorsed and Going was advised to devote himself to the new enterprise. Resigning his pastorate, he threw all his great ability into the task. In April 1832, he was elected corresponding secretary and for the next five and a half years did a great constructive work. Besides much traveling and extensive correspondence, he edited a weekly periodical in the interest of the home mission cause, the *American Baptist and Home Missionary Record.*

In 1837 Going was elected president of the college at Granville, Ohio, later called Denison University. Here he spent his last seven years, devoting himself to the educational problems that clustered about a frontier college and to the denominational interests of the state. His health had been somewhat impaired by overwork, but he still had the prestige of a stalwart body, a well-founded reputation for homely humor, and a recognized administrative ability, perhaps seen at its best in institutional organization. In this field his advice and participation were frequently sought. A few discourses, including his presidential inaugural, reports, and papers connected with the home-mission enterprise, constitute his printed works.

[The fullest account of Going's career is in *Baptist Home Missions in North America* (1883), edited by H. L. Morehouse. See also W. B. Sprague, *Annals Am. Pulpit,* vol. VI (1860); Isaac Davis, *Hist. Discourse on the Fiftieth Anniversary of the First Bapt. Ch. in Worcester, Mass.* (1862); Henry Crocker, *Hist. of the Baptists in Vt.* (1913); *Memorial Vol. of Denison Univ.* (1907); Edmund Turney, *The Prospect of Death an Incentive* (1845); *Christian Watchman* and *Baptist Record,* Nov. 1844.]

W. H. A.

GOLDBECK, ROBERT (Apr. 19, 1839–May 16, 1908), pianist, composer, educator, and musical author, was born at Potsdam, Prussia. There is no record of his parentage, except that his mother was a sister of the eminent teacher and composer, Louis Köhler, who, recognizing the boy's musical precocity, began early to give him thorough training in piano and harmony. After he had acquired a local reputation, some influential townspeople, notably Alexander von Humboldt, enlisted the interest of the King of Prussia by giving the fourteen-year-old lad a concert appearance, graced by the King's presence. In this way funds were provided for sending him to Brunswick to study advanced piano playing and composition with Litolff, with whom he remained four years. He then went to Paris, and though not yet nineteen years old, he was admitted into the most exclusive society by the aid of letters of introduction from von Humboldt. Among the distinguished people who took an interest in him was Alexandre Dumas, the elder, who introduced him to Berlioz, Halévy, Auber, and other musicians. He remained in Paris three years enjoying considerable popularity, not only because of his pianistic achievements, but because of his ingratiating manner. Through Humboldt's influence again he made his London début at Devonshire House, Piccadilly, under the patronage of the Duke of Devonshire. In 1861 he established himself in New York, but in 1867 he went to Boston to assist Eben Tourjée in founding the New England Conservatory, remaining there until 1868, when he took up his abode in Chicago. There in 1873 he began to publish *Goldbeck's Monthly Journal of Music,* but gave up its publication to go to St. Louis as director of the Harmonic Society and codirector and teacher in the Beethoven Conservatory. In 1880 he founded his own school, the St. Louis College of Music. Evidently for the purpose of enlarging his sphere as a teacher, he began (Apr. 15, 1882) to publish another monthly journal, *Goldbeck's Musical Instructor,* which was really a course of instruction in piano, harmony, and voice. Later it became *Goldbeck's Musical Art,* and in 1893 it was revived as the *Musical World.*

Goldbeck was a restless individual, not long contented in one place, though he lived in St. Louis four different times. In 1885 he went to New York, but as Köhler died in 1886 and had willed him his Conservatory at Königsberg, Goldbeck went abroad to take charge of it. He remained only until 1891, when he returned to St. Louis, and there, after many wanderings, he died in 1908. He was an indefatigable worker; besides his teaching and concertizing, he wrote an *Encyclopedia of Music Education* (3 vols., 1903), published in London, a work on harmony, and several graduated courses for piano, voice, and 'cello. As a composer he was prolific. Though his largest contribution was for pianoforte, he wrote a number of chamber, church, and choral selections, as well as two piano concertos, the second of which was performed several times. Three of his orchestral works, "Mexican Dances," "Forest Devotion," and "Leaping Marionettes," were played by Theodore Thomas in Chicago, St. Louis, and on tour. Several operas were not performed, though an early operetta, *The Soldier's Return,* and one of his best operas, *Newport,* were performed in London in 1856 and 1889 respectively. Most of his compositions are now almost forgotten. He was three times married. His third wife, Elise F. Haenschen, who survived him by several years, was an excellent pianist, who appeared often in recital and with orchestra.

[Ernst C. Krohn, *A Century of Missouri Music* (1924); F. O. Jones, ed., *A Handbook of Am. Music and Musicians* (1886); the *Étude,* July 1908; information as to certain facts from Mr. Krohn.] F. L. G. C.

GOLDBERGER, JOSEPH (July 16, 1874–Jan. 17, 1929), medical research worker, was brought to the United States at the age of six by his parents, Samuel Goldberger and Sarah Gutman, Jewish immigrants from Austria. Settling in New York, the father engaged in the grocery business, sending the son Joseph to the public schools and later to the College of the City of New York (1890–92). His medical education was obtained at Bellevue Hospital Medical College where he graduated in 1895. Following an internship in Bellevue Hospital (1895–97), and two years of private practise in Wilkes-Barre, Pa., he was appointed assistant surgeon in the United States Public Health Service in 1899. Early assignments took him to Tampico and Vera Cruz, Mexico, in relation to yellow fever and typhus. At different times he contracted both diseases. His penchant for research brought him to the Hygienic Laboratory at Washington in 1904, the remainder of his career being devoted to investigations in connection with that institution. His early studies included those of dengue in the South and of straw-mite itch in New Jersey. He devoted some time to the investigation of parasitic trematodes, studied diphtheria carriers, and devised media for the isolation of the cholera vibrio. In his investigation of typhus in Mexico he had demonstrated that the disease can be transmitted by the head louse as well as by the body louse.

In 1913 he was appointed director of the field pellagra investigation for work in the Southern states. He early became the leading exponent of the theory that pellagra is a nutritional disease induced by an unbalanced diet. For a decade he and his coworkers made observations and experiments upon the diets of inmates of various public institutions in Georgia, Mississippi, and Alabama, where pellagra was present. They proved conclusively that diets which included fair amounts of fresh meat and milk will prevent pellagra and clear up the disease when present. It was further shown that diets with the generally accepted standards of protein, fat, and carbohydrate and high in caloric value are not protective from pellagra unless there is present the element contained in fresh meat and milk. Goldberger gave to this element, apparently a heretofore unrecognized vitamin, the name "P-P factor." He further showed that this factor was plentifully contained in both fresh and dried yeast. In order to disprove the theory of an infective origin of pellagra, Goldberger in 1916 carried out a series of experiments on animals and humans which failed completely to produce the disease. The details of this long pellagra campaign, which practically freed Southern public institutions of the disease, are recorded in articles published in the *Public Health Reports* from 1914 to 1925. Goldberger was a member of the American Public Health Association, the Association of American Pathologists and Bacteriologists, and of the American College of Physicians. He was a frequent contributor to the programs of medical meetings, where he advanced his views with an intransigeance which won him much ill will, though this uncompromising attitude was at variance with his usual gentle speech and manner. He was married on Apr. 19, 1906, to Mary Humphreys Farrar of New Orleans, by whom he had four children. He died in the Naval Hospital at Washington from a malignant tumor of the kidney.

[R. C. Williams, "Jos. Goldberger, M.D.," *Archives of Pathol.*, Feb. 1929; *Jour. Am. Medic. Asso.*, Jan. 26, 1929; *Who's Who in America*, 1928–29; *Evening Star* (Washington, D. C.), Jan. 17, 1929; *N. Y. Times*, Jan. 18, 19, 1929.]
J. M. P.

GOLDER, FRANK ALFRED (Aug. 11, 1877–Jan. 7, 1929), historian, was born near Odessa in southern Russia. In 1880 his parents, Joseph and Minnie Golder, emigrated to the United States and settled in Bridgeton, N. J. After attending the public schools of Bridgeton and Georgetown College in Kentucky, Golder entered Bucknell University, from which he was graduated in 1898. The next year he went to Alaska where he spent three years on a lonely island settlement as a United States commissioner and teacher in a government school. These years among Aleuts and half-breed fishermen had an important effect upon his career. He became greatly interested in the country and in the Aleuts and their myths, many of which he collected and subsequently published, and he returned to the United States with a determination to write the history of Alaska. In the pursuit of this aim, he entered Harvard College where he received the B.A. degree in 1903. In the graduate school he continued his researches in Alaskan history which eventually took him to the Bibliothèque Nationale and the Archives de la Marine in Paris and gave him his doctorate in 1909. These studies changed his point of view in respect to Alaskan history and diverted his historical interests from research in the American field to that of Russia. In 1914, after further researches in St. Petersburg, he published *Russian Expansion on the Pacific 1641–1850*, a work which was promptly recognized in America and Europe as one of the most valuable studies of Russian activities in the Pacific. Meanwhile, beginning in 1908, he had held teaching appointments at the University of Missouri, Boston University, the University of Chicago, and the State College of Washington.

In 1914 the Carnegie Institution selected Golder to investigate the sources for the study of American history in the Russian archives. The results of this investigation he published in his *Guide to Materials for American History in Russian Archives* (1917), and in a number of papers on Russian-American relations in the *American Historical Review.* At this time also he secured an important collection of unpublished letters of John Paul Jones which in 1927 he brought out under the title *John Paul Jones in Russia.* The continuance of his studies in Russia was made temporarily impossible by war conditions and early in 1915 he returned to the United States to the history faculty of the State College of Washington, where he had held an appointment since 1910. In January 1917 he sailed from Seattle for Russia to undertake further investigations in the archives under the auspices of the Carnegie Institution and the American Geographical Society. He reached Petrograd in time to witness the exciting scenes of the March Revolution, and he remained in Russia during that eventful summer watching and recording in his diary the rising tide of revolution which culminated in the Bolshevik *coup d'état* of Nov. 7. At the request of the American ambassador, he went to Vladivostok to accompany the Stevens Railway Commission across Siberia and on its tours of inspection in European Russia. Despite these semi-official duties, he found time to work in the archives and to make a further valuable contribution to the history of the North Pacific in his edition of papers relating to Bering's explorations published under the title *Bering's Voyages* (2 vols., 1922–25).

Golder left Russia a few weeks before the Bolshevik uprising, returning to the United States where, a few months later, he joined Col. House's Inquiry Commission as a specialist on Russian affairs. In 1920 he returned to eastern Europe to collect materials for the newly established Hoover War Library at Stanford University, and the following year he joined the history faculty at Stanford but remained in Europe as a member of Hoover's American Relief Administration. During the great Russian famine he rendered invaluable service as an official of the relief organization; hundreds of Russian scholars owed their lives to his untiring labor. On the withdrawal of the commission from Russia,

Golder returned to Stanford where he was appointed director of the Hoover War Library and professor of history, and where he was engaged in research on the Russian Revolution at the time of his death. In addition to the works mentioned, Golder wrote *On the Trail of the Russian Famine* (1927), in collaboration with Lincoln Hutchinson; chapters in *The Pacific Ocean in History* (1917), by H. M. Stephens and H. E. Bolton; and parts of *The Russian Revolution* (1918), compiled by A. I. Petrunkevitch, S. N. Harper, R. J. Kerner, and himself. He also contributed numerous papers on Alaska and Russian-American relations to other publications. The works which he edited include S. F. Platonov's *History of Russia* (1925); *Documents of Russian History* (1927); and *The March of the Mormon Battalion* (1928), taken from the journal of Henry Standage.

[Unpublished diaries, letters, and reports in the Hoover War Library contain a record of Golder's observations and experiences in Europe from 1914 to 1926. There are also a fragmentary diary and a few miscellaneous papers relating to his Alaskan sojourn. *Harvard Coll. Class of 1903* (1928) contains a short autobiographical sketch and the *Stanford Illustrated Rev.*, Feb. 1929, has an article by R. H. Lutz. Other brief accounts of his career are contained in the *Am. Hist. Rev.*, Apr. 1929, and the *Jour. of Modern Hist.*, June 1929.] H. H. F.

GOLDSBOROUGH, CHARLES (July 15, 1765–Dec. 13, 1834), congressman, last Federalist governor of Maryland, was born at "Hunting Creek," near Cambridge, Md. His father was Charles Goldsborough, a member of the prominent Eastern Shore family and half-brother of Robert Goldsborough [*q.v.*]; his mother was Anna Maria (Tilghman) Goldsborough. His early education was obtained at home or in the neighborhood. Later he attended the University of Pennsylvania where he received the degree of B.A. in 1784 and that of M.A. in 1787. He also studied law and was admitted to the bar in 1790. On Sept. 22, 1793, he married Elizabeth, daughter of Judge Robert Goldsborough of Talbot County, by whom he had two children. After her death, he married in 1804 his cousin Sarah Yerbury Goldsborough, daughter of Charles Goldsborough of "Horn's Point" and grand-daughter of Robert Goldsborough, the Revolutionary leader. She lived until 1821 and bore him fifteen children.

Goldsborough early became active in politics as a Federalist, and was elected to local offices. From 1791 to 1795 and from 1799 to 1801 he was in the state Senate. In 1804 he was elected to Congress from his home district, a Federalist stronghold, and was regularly returned until 1817. He was one of three Maryland congressmen to vote against the declaration of war in 1812. On Dec. 14, 1818, the Federalist legislature elected him governor. One of the principal problems of his administration was the building of roads to connect Maryland with the West. In accordance with a resolution of the legislature in 1817, he rendered a report, recommending the revision of methods of calculating tolls, the joining of existing turnpikes so as to connect Baltimore with the National Road at Cumberland, state ownership of turnpikes, and the establishment of a board to investigate the possibility of roads and a canal to the West (*Executive Communication to the General Assembly of Maryland at December Session 1818 on the Subject of Turnpike Roads,* 1819). Another serious question was the democratization of the state government. Up to this time, Maryland had been Federalist, but the Republicans had been growing steadily in strength and claimed that a fair distribution of representation would put the state in their control. In the session of 1818 the Federalists had a majority in joint session, and had defeated a bill to increase the representation of Baltimore. The election of Goldsborough without popular approval had started an agitation for the popular election of the governor. Much, therefore, turned upon the election of Oct. 4, 1819. In this sharp contest, the Republicans won a majority of the joint session, and consequently, Goldsborough had to retire from the governorship on Dec. 20 following. He also withdrew entirely from public life, and resided on his estate at Shoal Creek, near Cambridge, Md., until his death.

[J. T. Scharf, *Hist. of Md.* (1879); H. E. Buchholz, *Govs. of Md.* (1908); *Md. Hist. Mag.*, June 1915; *Biog. Dir. Am. Cong.* (1928); *Gen. Alumni Cat. Univ. of Pa.* (1917).] W. C. M.

GOLDSBOROUGH, LOUIS MALESHERBES (Feb. 18, 1805–Feb. 20, 1877), naval officer, was born at Washington, D. C., the son of Charles Washington and Catharine (Roberts) Goldsborough. His father, of the well-known Maryland family (G. A. Hanson, *Old Kent,* 1876), was chief clerk of the Navy Department and author of *The United States' Naval Chronicle* (1824). The boy received a midshipman's warrant in 1812, but saw no service until 1816. In 1823–24 he was acting lieutenant and in 1825 received a lieutenant's commission. Shortly thereafter he was given leave of absence to study in Paris and also visited Switzerland and Italy. While serving in the Mediterranean (1827–29), he commanded four boats that recaptured an English brig from pirates. In 1830 he was given charge of the newly created Depot of Charts and

Instruments at Washington, established in pursuance of a plan which he himself had suggested to the Secretary of the Navy; in this capacity he served a little more than two years. On Nov. 1, 1831, he was married to Elizabeth Gamble Wirt, daughter of William Wirt [*q.v.*]. Three children were born to them. In 1833 Goldsborough led a band of German emigrants to Wirt's estates near Monticello, Fla.; he commanded a steamboat expedition and later a company of mounted volunteers in the Seminole War. He then returned to the navy. Made commander in 1841, he was stationed at Portsmouth, N. H., 1843–46. In 1845 he published *A Reply by L. M. Goldsborough to Attack made upon the Navy of the United States* and some time later (probably 1848), a *Letter to the Secretary of the Navy Concerning Assimilated Rank* (n.d.). During the Mexican War, he commanded the *Ohio,* and led an attack on Tuxpan. He was senior naval member of a commission which explored California and Oregon, 1849–50, was superintendent of the Naval Academy, 1853–57, being made captain in 1855, was at the Washington Navy Yard for a time, and commanded the Brazil Squadron, 1859–61.

On Sept. 23, 1861, he took command of the Atlantic Blockading Squadron (in spite of a law retiring officers after forty-five years' service). When it was divided, Oct. 29, he retained command of the North Atlantic Blockading Squadron. He commanded the fleet which early in 1862, with 12,000 troops under Gen. Burnside [*q.v.*], attacked the coast of North Carolina, capturing Roanoke Island (Feb. 7–9) and destroying a Confederate fleet. These achievements won him the "thanks of Congress" and the consequent right to fifty-five years' service before retirement. He soon returned to the James, where the *Monitor* and the *Merrimac* had fought in his absence. When the latter reappeared (Apr. 11 and May 8), with the approval of the Navy Department he avoided a fight. Ordered to assist in the Peninsular campaign, he told McClellan that he could neither control the James nor take Yorktown, because his first duty was to watch the *Merrimac.* After the capture of Yorktown, the James River flotilla was strengthened, and the President ordered the military and naval forces to cooperate in an advance toward Richmond. After the destruction of the *Merrimac* on May 11, the flotilla attacked Drewry's Bluff, eight miles from Richmond, but was repulsed on May 15. Assistant Secretary Fox still hoped the navy would take Richmond, but Goldsborough was convinced that the navy could do nothing further until the army by a land attack had reduced the defenses at the Bluff. McClellan, who was not ready then, was later ordered to abandon the campaign, and on July 6, the James River flotilla was made an independent command, under Commodore Charles Wilkes [*q.v.*]. This action on the part of the Navy Department and attacks upon him in the press made Goldsborough think his usefulness was ended, and at his own request he was relieved on Sept. 4, 1862. He had been made a rear-admiral, July 16, 1862, and he performed important administrative duties at Washington until 1865, when he took charge of the European Squadron, with orders to look for Confederate cruisers. His retirement was due in 1867, but in response to his wife's personal pleas and in the face of opposition from naval officials, was postponed by order of the President. He was again stationed in Washington during 1868–73, and then retired.

[Goldsborough's official papers are in the N. Y. Pub. Lib., and his letters to his wife in the Lib. of Cong. See also *Confidential Correspondence of Gustavus Vasa Fox* (2 vols., 1918–19), ed. by R. M. Thompson and Richard Wainwright; *The Diary of Gideon Welles* (3 vols., 1911); *Official Records (Navy)*; *House Ex. Doc. 27*, 40 Cong., 1 Sess.; *House Ex. Doc. 40*, 40 Cong., 2 Sess.; *Notes upon the Case of Rear Admiral L. M. Goldsborough* (1867) and *Notes upon the Naval Service of L. M. Goldsborough* (n.d.), published at the time of the retirement controversy; G. A. Weber, *The Naval Observatory* (1926); *Battles and Leaders of the Civil War* (4 vols., 1887–88); J. T. Headley, *Farragut and Our Naval Commanders* (1867); R. W. Neeser, *Statistical and Chronological Hist. of the U. S. Navy* (1909); Park Benjamin, *The U. S. Naval Academy* (1900); *Evening Star* (Washington), Feb. 20, 1877.]

W. C. M.

GOLDSBOROUGH, ROBERT (Dec. 3, 1733–Dec. 22, 1788), lawyer, member of the Continental Congress, was born at "Horn's Point," near Cambridge, Md. His parents were Charles Goldsborough, a prominent lawyer and planter and later secretary of the province of Maryland, and Elizabeth (Ennalls) Goldsborough, of a distinguished family of Dorchester County. The Goldsborough family was descended from Nicholas Goldsborough, who settled in Maryland about 1670 and is said to have been a descendant of a Sir Richard who owned the manor of Goldesburgh in Yorkshire in the time of Henry III. Young Robert received his legal training at the Middle Temple, Westminster, which he entered Dec. 2, 1752. He was called to the English bar on Feb. 8, 1757. Returning to Maryland with his wife, Sarah Yerbury, daughter of Richard Yerbury of Bassinghall Street, London, whom he had married on Mar. 27, 1755, he practised law with such success that he was, by 1767, "at the top of the profession" and "possessed of a considerable fortune." Gov. Sharpe had made him sheriff of Dorchester County; he had been elected to the House of Delegates in 1764, and appointed attorney-general in 1766. The governor desired also to make him a member of the council, but when finally the approval of Lord Baltimore was received, Goldsborough refused the office and resigned the position of attorney-general (1768). The Maryland convention that met on June 22–25, 1774, elected him one of the delegates to the Continental Congress. He was present at the early sessions of the Congress and was chosen on the committee to state the rights of the colonies, but seems to have taken little part in proceedings. He was also present at the session of May 1775. In that year he was a delegate from Dorchester to the Maryland convention, signed the "Association of the Freemen of Maryland" (July 26), and was elected to committees to consider defense and to write to Virginia. He was also chosen a member of the council of safety and of the delegation to Congress (Aug. 14), but was not among the delegates chosen on July 4, 1776. Elected to the convention which met on Aug. 14, 1776, to frame a constitution for Maryland, he was made a member of the committee to adopt a plan of government. He was elected one of the first senators under this constitution, but was inactive until 1781, when he supported measures to protect the Eastern Shore from British and Tory raids. In 1788 he was chosen a delegate from Dorchester to the convention which ratified the Federal Constitution (*Maryland Journal and Baltimore Advertiser,* Apr. 15, 1788), but apparently did not attend. He died a few months later on the estate where he was born.

[H. F. Thompson and A. S. Dandridge, in *Md. Hist. Mag.,* June 1915; *Archives of Md.,* ed. by W. H. Browne, vols. IX (1890), X (1892), XIV (1895); J. T. Scharf, *Hist. of Md.* (1879); R. H. Spencer, *Thomas Family of Talbot County, Md., and Allied Families* (1914); *Biog. Dir. Am. Cong.* (1928); E. A. Jones, *Am. Members of the Inns of Court* (1924); G. A. Hanson, *Old Kent* (1876); obituary in *Md. Jour. and Baltimore Advertiser,* Jan. 16, 1789.] W. C. M.

GOLDSMITH, MIDDLETON (Aug. 5, 1818–Nov. 26, 1887), physician, surgeon, was born at Port Tobacco, Md., the son of Dr. Alban and Talia Ferro Middleton Smith of Virginia. His father, an eminent surgeon and teacher, had his name changed to Goldsmith by act of the New York legislature. Throughout his boyhood in Virginia, and later in Kentucky, where his father was professor of surgery in the Kentucky School of Medicine at Louisville, Goldsmith indicated an unusual interest in natural history and medicine, and early became his father's assistant and prosector. After attending Hanover College, Indiana, in 1837 he accompanied his father to New York City, and studied at the College of Physicians and Surgeons, in which the elder Goldsmith conducted lecture courses. He graduated in 1840 and soon after sailed as ship's surgeon on a voyage to China and India, where he studied ophthalmia. On his return he entered his father's office. Together they are said to have introduced in America the practise of lithotrity, a method of crushing bladder stones, for which operation they became widely known. With Doctors Markoe, Sayre, Le Conte, and others he founded the first alumni association of the College of Physicians and Surgeons and contributed largely to its first *Transactions.* At this time he assisted Audubon in the dissection and classification of specimens for the *Birds of America.* He also held the position of coroner's physician, in which capacity he made daily autopsies, and when they failed to satisfy his scientific zeal, dissected the bodies of paupers to be buried in Potter's Field, now Washington Square. As a result of these practical researches, and the perfection of the microscope, which was then coming into use, he developed an enthusiastic interest in anatomical pathology, and with his friends, Dr. J. C. Peters and Dr. Lewis A. Sayre, he founded, in 1844, the New York Pathological Society, probably the first pathological society in the world. In the same year he was called to the chair of surgery in Castleton Medical College, in Vermont, where he remained ten years. He was president of the Vermont State Medical Society in 1851, and in 1854 removed to Rutland. In 1856 he accepted the chair of surgery in the Kentucky School of Medicine at Louisville, which his father had formerly occupied, and in the following year became dean of the college. During his residence in Louisville he was called far afield for consultation and operation, especially for eye conditions and stone in the bladder.

When the Civil War broke out Goldsmith became brigade surgeon in the Army of the Cumberland and took part in many engagements, including Shiloh. He became medical director in Gen. Buell's army at Shiloh, and later inspector of hospitals in Grant's army at Corinth and finally surgeon-general of all military hospitals in Kentucky and the Department of the Ohio. At length he was put in charge of the general army hospital at Jeffersonville, Ind., which at times housed as many as five thousand wounded. During his service he became interested in the nature of gangrene, erysipelas, and pyemia, scourges of the hospitals of his day, and devised a bromine treatment for gangrene which checked its ravages in the hospitals under his charge, and was generally adopted. He published his observations in a pamphlet of ninety-four pages entitled *A Report on Hospital Gangrene, Ery-*

sipelas, and Pyaemia as observed in the Departments of the Ohio and the Cumberland: With cases appended (1863). In this paper, written more than three years before Lister had begun his experiments, he pointed out that the various treatments in use for these three infections had but one thing in common, their antiseptic powers. Since chlorine was injurious to the lungs and too caustic for general use, he employed bromine, which, he said, "was respirable without injury or inconvenience." He was thus a pioneer in antiseptic surgery.

At the close of the war, finding Louisville hostile to his outspoken Unionism, he returned to Vermont, and for the remaining years of his life resided in Rutland. He abandoned regular practise, but continued as consulting surgeon and a valuable expert witness. In 1880 he published a treatise on gall-stones. He established the Rutland Free Dispensary, and in 1878, as special commissioner, carried on an able investigation of the state insane asylum, which resulted in its improvement and reform. Until his death he retained an active interest in all new developments within his profession, especially the germ theory of disease, which he had so early apprehended. His library, reputed to be the largest medical collection in Vermont, was bequeathed at his death to the New York Academy of Medicine. He was an impressive man, "neat and even showy in his dress" (*Medical Record,* p. 497); a fair Latin and Greek scholar; especially fond of Hesiod's "Theogony" and "Works and Days"; a great lover of the out-of-doors; and an enthusiastic fisherman, hunter, and botanist. He drew up the game laws of Vermont, which served as models for other states, and established experimental farms for raising cattle, sheep, grain, and potatoes. He was married in June 1843 to Frances Swift, daughter of Henry Swift of Poughkeepsie, N. Y., whom he survived but a few days. He left two daughters.

[John C. Peters, "Biog. Sketch of the late Middleton Goldsmith, M.D., LL.D.," in the *Medic. Record* (N. Y.), May 5, 1888, was reprinted separately in 1889 under the title *In Memoriam: Middleton Goldsmith.* See also the *Medic. Record* (N. Y.), Dec. 10, 1887; and H. A. Kelly and W. L. Burrage, eds., *Am. Medic. Biogs.* (1920).] A. P. M.

GOLDTHWAITE, GEORGE (Dec. 10, 1809–Mar. 16, 1879), Alabama jurist, United States senator, son of Thomas and Anne (Wilson) Goldthwaite, was born in Boston, Mass., whither his mother moved after her husband had deserted her and returned to England. Though she was a woman of superior intellect and culture, she supported her family by keeping a boarding-house. George received his preparatory education in the Boston Latin School and at the age of fourteen entered West Point. During his fourth year there he and some of his friends were ejected because of persistent hazing. They offered their services to the Greek revolutionists, but instead of going to Greece, Goldthwaite went to Montgomery, Ala., and began life, according to himself, with five dollars and a "flee-bitten horse." He read law under his older brother, Henry [*q.v.*], was admitted to the bar at eighteen, and established himself at Monticello, Pike County. After several years of successful practise in this little village he returned to Montgomery and formed a partnership with his brother-in-law, John A. Campbell. In 1843 he was elected circuit judge and held this position until 1852 when he was elected justice of the state supreme court. Four years later he was made chief justice of this court, but resigned after thirteen days to accept an unusual legal opportunity as attorney for the huge Cowles estate. In 1866 he was elected circuit judge again, but was disqualified for this office by the Reconstruction acts of Congress in 1868. In 1851 he had been appointed one of the committee of three selected to prepare the code of laws of Alabama which was accepted by the legislature in 1852.

When the national crisis of 1850 came, Goldthwaite opposed secession. Though a large planter—he owned plantations in Texas and in the Mississippi Delta—he was not deeply sympathetic with the institution of slavery. He represented Alabama in the Nashville Convention and used his influence on behalf of compromise, but when he reported the work of the Convention to a large assemblage in Montgomery he said, "If the assertion of just rights brings disunion, let it come!" Though he remained a conservative down to 1860, he followed Alabama into secession and served it for three years as adjutant-general. He is said to have been Gov. A. B. Moore's chief adviser. Elected to the United States Senate in 1870 upon the crest of a premature "White man's movement" in state politics, he gained a reputation for calmness, conservatism, and discreet conduct, which made him an ideal man for Alabama at this critical time. He retired at the end of his term because of ill health. He was married on Nov. 30, 1835, to Olivia Price Wallach of Washington, D. C. Four sons and two daughters were born to them.

[Willis Brewer, *Alabama* (1872); J. W. DuBose, *The Life and Times of Wm. Lowndes Yancey* (1892); Wm. Garrett, *Reminiscences of Public Men in Ala.* (1872); Charlotte Goldthwaite, *Descendants of Thos. Goldthwaite* (1899); T. M. Owen, *Hist. of Ala. and Dict. of Ala. Biog.* (1921), III, 672; B. F. Riley, *Makers and Romance of Ala. Hist.* (n.d.); *The South in the Building of the Nation* (1909), vol. XI; *Mobile*

Daily Reg., Mar. 19, 1879; *N. Y. Tribune*, Mar. 18, 1879; information as to certain facts from Goldthwaite's grand-daughter, Miss Olivia Arrington, Montgomery, Ala.] A. B. M.

GOLDTHWAITE, HENRY BARNES (Apr. 10, 1802–Oct. 19, 1847), Alabama jurist, was the son of Thomas and Anne (Wilson) Goldthwaite, and a brother of George Goldthwaite [*q.v.*]. He was born in Concord, N. H., but moved with his mother in early childhood to Boston, where he received a public-school education. At the age of thirteen he went to Richmond, Va., with his brother Robert, and worked in a dry-goods store for two years. Then he removed to Montgomery, Ala., where he was for a short time a clerk in the store of his brother John. From selling dry-goods he turned to reading law in the office of Nimrod E. Benson, and upon his admission to the bar, formed a partnership with Benjamin Fitzpatrick, then a promising young lawyer. For several years he edited a newspaper in conjunction with his law practise. His newspaper affiliations led him inevitably into politics, for newspapers in that day were expected to speak aggressively, if not authoritatively, upon political questions. At that time, too, the rivalry between the popular leaders and the "Georgia machine" in Alabama gave political journalism a rare opportunity. In 1825 Goldthwaite was elected solicitor of his circuit. Four years later he represented Montgomery County in the legislature. His legislative career terminated abruptly the following year when he was defeated for reëlection. He then moved to Mobile where he achieved distinction as a lawyer.

In 1836 he was elected as a Democrat to the bench of the state supreme court without opposition, and was reëlected in 1842. Under the promptings of the Democrats, who yearned to take the Mobile district away from the Whigs, he resigned and made the race for Congress against James Dellet of Monroe County, a classical scholar and stump speaker extraordinary. Goldthwaite himself could charm his hearers with his superior logic, striking personality, and cutting style. The campaign was colorful, and, true to custom, people from far and near came to hear the battle of words. Dellet won with a small majority. The next legislature returned Goldthwaite to the supreme-court bench over the distinguished C. C. Clay [*q.v.*]. He served in this capacity until 1847 when he was struck down by yellow fever. At this time he was being seriously considered for an appointment to the United States Supreme Court. On Apr. 10, 1839, he was married to Eliza Witherspoon, and by her had four sons.

[Charlotte Goldthwaite, *Descendants of Thos. Goldthwaite* (1899); Willis Brewer, *Alabama* (1872); Wm. Garrett, *Reminiscences of Public Men in Ala.* (1872); T. M. Owen, *Hist. of Ala. and Dict. of Ala. Biog.* (1921), III, 675; *The South in the Building of the Nation* (1909), vol. XI; *Reg. and Jour.* (Mobile), Oct. 21, 1847; information as to certain facts from Miss Olivia Arrington, Montgomery, Ala.] A. B. M.

GOMPERS, SAMUEL (Jan. 27, 1850–Dec. 13, 1924), labor leader, was born in a London tenement. His father, Solomon Gompers, was a workingman, a cigar maker by trade, and the earliest recollections of young Samuel were of laboring people and their problems. A few years prior to the birth of Samuel his grandfather had emigrated to London from Holland, where the family had lived for many years. Samuel's mother, Sarah Rood, also came from Holland to England where she married his father. From the age of six to ten the boy attended a Jewish free school, but his parents were too poor to permit him to continue after he was old enough to work, so he was taken from school and at the age of ten apprenticed to a shoemaker. A few months later he ended his shoe-making career and was apprenticed by his father to a cigar maker. During the sixties the Civil War stimulated the interest of many English people in America. The elder Gompers decided that the New World offered advantages for economic betterment and in 1863 he landed in New York with his family. They settled on the East Side and Gompers followed his trade of cigar making. Samuel assisted his father for several months after landing and then started out on his own initiative as a journeyman cigar maker. In 1864 he joined the Cigarmakers' Union. "All my life," he said in his autobiography, "I had been accustomed to the labor movement and accepted as a matter of course that every wage-earner should belong to the union of his trade. I did not yet have a conscious appreciation of the labor movement. My awakening was to come later" (*Seventy Years of Life and Labor,* I, 33). He was married, at the age of seventeen, to Sophia Julian, a young working girl.

Although Gompers's formal education ceased at the age of ten, his thirst for knowledge was insatiable, and soon after his arrival in New York he began to spend much of his spare time at Cooper Union, attending lectures and engaging in debates. He early became interested in the fraternal movement and joined the Odd Fellows and the Foresters. The most significant of his experiences, however, was his life as a cigar maker in the factories in and about New York City. It was in the cigar shop that he tested his theories on his fellows and acquired thereby what he called his "intuitions." The little shops of skilled cigar makers of those days were schools of economic research, and it is not surprising that out of one of them came the model for the American Federation of Labor. The room was very quiet, work was paid for by the piece, and there were no rules against talking. "In fact," said Gompers, "these discussions in the shops were more like public debating societies or what we call these days 'labor forums'" (*Seventy Years,* I, 81). Papers, magazines, and books were purchased from a fund to which all contributed, and while the others worked one would read aloud for an hour or longer, his fellows turning over to him a definite number of cigars to make up his lost time. Gompers's voice was strong, and he always read more than his period. From the *Sun* he absorbed his "ideas of style, sentence structure, and the use of words. Charles A. Dana's editorials were in themselves a daily stimulus to my mind," he added, though Gompers "more often than not disagreed with the editorial policy" (*Ibid.,* I, 80). The workers subscribed for several labor papers, and Gompers read to them all the German writings of Marx, Engels, Lassalle, and others that he could lay hands on. Into the shop came the Socialist exiles from Europe, and one of these, Ferdinand Laurrell, to whose memory Gompers dedicated his autobiography, the latter considered his best teacher. Laurrell was a Swede who had been a leader in the Marxian Socialist organization of the Scandinavian countries. When Gompers came to him with "some wild plans . . . for human betterment," Laurrell kept on working, did not miss a word, and then, said Gompers, "point by point he replied. Soon my self-confidence began to ebb, and I began to feel physically smaller as Laurrell systematically and ruthlessly demolished my every statement. By the time he had finished I vowed to myself, 'Never again will I talk that stuff—but I will find principles that will stand the test'" (*Seventy Years,* I, 73).

Laurrell translated and interpreted for him the Communist Manifesto "paragraph by paragraph," and "this insight into a hidden world of thought aroused me," Gompers wrote, "to master the German language in order that I might read for myself." Laurrell taught him the true Marx, as Gompers declared; not the Marx of the afterward Socialist party, but the Marx of trade unionism and labor's own struggle for betterment, and gave to Gompers the standards that guided him in all new problems: "Study your union card, Sam, and if the idea doesn't square with that, it ain't true" (*Seventy Years,* I, 74–75). Laurrell advised him to go to the meetings of the Socialists: "Learn all they have to give," he said, "read all they publish, but don't join." Gompers did not join, owing, he stated, "to the influence of Laurrell who kept holding me back from alliance with any movement that had been associated with radicalism." At those meetings, however, he met "a group of the finest men it has ever been my good fortune to meet in any circle of life." They were refugees from Europe, and Gompers was admitted to their inner circle, *die Zehn Philosophen,* which included the Irish refugee J. P. McDonnell, who had spent several years in the office of Karl Marx in London, and P. J. McGuire, his old schoolmate at Cooper Union and a member of the Marxian International. From this little group, said Gompers, "came the purpose and the initiative that finally resulted in the present American Labor movement—the most effective economic organization in the world. We did not create the American trade union—that is a product of forces and conditions. But we did create the technique and formulate the fundamentals that guided trade unions to constructive policies and achievements" (*Seventy Years,* I, 85–87).

Although local cigarmakers' unions had existed in New York City as early as 1864, they had collapsed during the period of business depression after 1873. In 1877, however, the cigar makers made a desperate recovery and carried on a prolonged strike against the tenement-house sweating system. The strike was a disastrous failure. The unions had no funds, no discipline, no inducement to hold together as militant organizations during periods between strikes or periods of business depression. In such times they became mere debating societies, dwindling down until only the theoretical debater on cooperation, socialism, anarchism, and labor politics held the floor. Gompers and Strasser took the lead in reorganizing the cigar makers. Strasser was given the ambitious title of international president, by which was meant traveling organizer for North America, and Gompers remained president of Local 144, continuing to work in the shop but also organizing unions out of hours. They accomplished four things: they made the international officers supreme over the local unions; they increased the membership dues to unheard-of amounts in order to build up a fund; they concentrated the control of that fund in the national officers, and they adopted, or prepared to adopt, sickness, accident, and unemployment benefits. This was the beginning of militant, persistent unionism in America. The cigarmakers' union became the model for all others, and when twenty years afterward, in the last decade of the century, another depression like that of 1873–79 took place, Gompers could report to the Federation of Labor that, for the first time in history, the unions had weathered the storm.

In 1881, after other unions had copied the cigarmakers' union of 1877, came the next step, the "Federation of Organized Trades and Labor Unions of the United States of America and Canada." Gompers was chairman of the Committee on Constitution, and it was in his committee that the final plan of organization was worked out. This federation was reorganized in 1886 as the American Federation of Labor. The principles of organization adopted were entirely different from those of any other labor movement in the United States or any other country. There were to be no "dual unions"—only one union could be accepted for each trade in all North America; no local unions were to be admitted—such unions must enter their own International Union and get what representation they could through their national unions; the delegates from each international union were to cast as many votes as were proportionate to the number of its members; local or city trades assemblies and federations (composed of local unions of the several trades) were to have each only one vote; each national union was to be completely self-governing over its own locals and free from domination by the Federation.

Gompers was elected president of the new labor organization, and until his death in 1924, with the exception of one year, he was the official head of the American labor movement. The power that he exerted in that movement may be expressed as "moral," a term which, in his interpretation, signified the organized consent of collective action on which the American Federation of Labor was founded. Moral influence meant the belief that drastic methods would not bring education and solidarity; that it was persuasion, not domineering, that unionized. One of the national unions had disciplined a radical agitator, whose rebellious following broke up the union's meetings. The national officers, in despair, called in Gompers. He announced his intention of talking with the revolutionist. The officers protested. Discipline was at stake. Why recognize rebellion? But after Gompers's conference with the rebel, the union was again united.

Gompers's "moral influence" with the executives of each national union was founded on their knowledge that no "dual union" would be allowed to displace them. No "dual union" can be admitted to the Federation. There must be but one union for all North America for each trade or industry. A thousand independent unions are eligible to the British Trade Union Congress. The American Federation of Labor admits less than 150. In England, as Dr. Perlman has pointed out, there is a class psychology which unites all the unions against all the employers. In America, however, dual unionism means that either one or the other union furnishes strikebreakers for the employer. Dual unions did arise, and some of them became powerful. Gompers was not always able to bring them together; but he did not yield to them.

In another direction "moral power" was Gompers's substitute for the weakness of labor in competition with business men. He had seen in New York scores of cooperative stores, cooperative workshops, and other cooperative business enterprises undertaken by the unions, especially the Knights of Labor. These "substitutes for capitalism" broke down under the incapacity of organized labor to enforce discipline when it became the employer of labor. No one understood better than Gompers the limits beyond which the organization of labor could not go. It could not lift itself as a body out of manual labor and become a body of business men or professional men. For this reason Gompers was always against "theorizers" and "intellectuals" in the organization of labor. They were "industrially impossible." Amid all the differences in America of religion, of race, of language, of politics, there was only one direction toward which labor could unite—more wages, more leisure, more liberty. To go further than this was to be misled by theorists, idealists, and well-meaning but "fool" friends of labor. Labor could have "moral power" only when it struggled for better homes, better living, better citizenship, by its collective action. In the exposition of this point of view Gompers was the best of theorizers and the greatest "intellectual" of them all.

It was this firm conviction that labor never could displace the capitalist in the management of business that made it possible for Gompers to enter into negotiations with capitalists, and even to disregard the outcries from his own ranks against his membership in the National Civic Federation along with the most noted, and even alleged anti-unionistic, of capitalists. He held that labor was always right. Up to the very last ditch he defended and appealed for help, even for those who afterward were convicted of dynamiting and murder. This may seem like a paradox to many, but this policy of his was merely the result of an experience with the courts gained in boyhood and during the collective struggles of organized labor and his belief that misrepresentations, false accusation, and misuse of the courts all too frequently occur.

He knew full well the weakness of labor in business, and he knew equally well its weakness in politics. He penetrated the underlying fact of American political parties, that they are great, cooperative institutions of professional politicians and bosses competing for control of government and political jobs, and not organizations of citizens based on principles of public welfare. Organized labor never could compete with these unions of political experts, and a labor party was, at least in this country, as politically impossible as producers' cooperation and socialism were industrially impossible. What, then, should organized labor do in politics? Simply bargain for immunity from interference by legislatures, courts, and executives, so that it could use its own collective moral and economic power to bargain collectively with the capitalists.

Only for one year, 1895, did the American Federation of Labor fail to choose Samuel Gompers as its president. Dissatisfaction of union members as a result of the prevailing business depression coupled with an unusual showing of strength by the Socialistic membership resulted in the election of John McBride. In the 1896 convention of the Federation Gompers was again a candidate for the presidency and succeeded in defeating McBride. With the expansion of the American Federation of Labor Gompers became, as its head, an important public figure. Crises in labor matters and his innumerable public speeches kept him constantly before the public. Just prior to the outbreak of the war he was appointed by President Wilson to serve on the Council of National Defense. During the war, in order to demonstrate that American labor stood solidly behind the government, he organized a War Committee on Labor composed of representatives of organized labor and of employers. He became an implacable foe of pacificism and combated it publicly on every occasion. At the Peace Conference he was appointed by President Wilson as a member of the Commission on International Labor Legislation. After the war he was plunged into the struggle of American labor to maintain its wartime gains. Despite his advanced age he continued his manifold activities without check until 1924. At the convention of the Federation in that year it was apparent that he had only a short time to live and within a few days after the close of the convention he died.

He was primarily a man of action, but in the course of his long career as official spokesman of American labor he frequently wrote in defense of labor's policies or to explain their significance to the members of the Federation. These writings will be found principally in the files of the *American Federationist,* the official publication of the American Federation of Labor. Gompers's published books are: *Labor in Europe and America* (1910); *American Labor and the War* (1919); *Labor and the Common Welfare* (1919) and *Labor and the Employer* (1920), compiled and edited by Hayes Robbins; *Out of Their Mouths: A Revelation and an Indictment of Sovietism* (1921), with the collaboration of W. E. Walling; and *Seventy Years of Life and Labor* (2 vols., 1925). Of these works the last is the most significant, being Gompers's own account of his life in the labor movement. This autobiography is more than a book of reminiscences; it is a source book to which the student of labor must necessarily turn for an authoritative account of the rise and growth of American trade unionism.

Gompers himself was conscious that his two strong qualities were his dramatic instinct and what he called his "intuition." The former he connected with his keen love of music and the opera, and declared that he nearly became a musician. What he meant by "intuition" was a highly intellectual method of experimental research in testing out all the theories he came upon and measuring just how far they would work or not work. His "intuitions" were not the mere internal "hunches" of a Bergson's philosophy, but the slow thinking and intense concentration of mind upon experiments and theories which characterize great scientists and inventors. In this way he evolved his economic philosophy. "At no time in my life," he wrote in his autobiography, "have I worked out definitely articulated economic theory" (*Seventy Years,* II, 17–18). He reached his conclusions gradually, "after discarding proposals to which I temporarily subscribed." And, contrasting himself with the "intellectuals" whom he always distrusted and opposed when they attempted to guide the labor movement, he said, "These facts I knew intuitively and have turned them about in my mind during the decades I have been in the movement, but it is an understanding that those outside of the movement rarely grasp" (*Ibid.,* II, 24, 27).

He prided himself upon his physical stamina. "I never got tired and never gave any thought to my body for it never demanded my attention," he wrote, and quoted the family saying: "The Gompers are built of oak" (*Seventy Years,* I, 495). In his personal life he followed a philosophy of freedom: "no inhibitions, no restrictions, but to allow natural inclination to take its course."

Even in his last years, "his doctors vainly endeavored to make him see the need of diet and physical discipline" (*Ibid.*, II, 529–30). One of nine children and the son of one of six, Gompers spent his early youth in a family group of which his grandfather was patriarch. He had to a marked degree the family consciousness of the Hebrew. All his life he was surrounded by kinsmen among whom a strong loyalty prevailed. His wife bravely bore the hardships occasioned by his refusal to abjure his union principles, even during the cigarmakers' strike of 1877–78, when at one time, save for the help of his mother and brothers, his family would have been without food. Five of Gompers's children, three sons and two daughters, lived to maturity. His wife died in 1920 and in 1921 he married Grace Gleaves Neuscheler, who survived him.

[Additional material on the life and work of Gompers will be found in L. S. Reed, *The Labor Philosophy of Samuel Gompers* (1930); J. R. Commons and associates, *Hist. of Labour in the U. S.* (2 vols., 1918); T. V. Powderly, *Thirty Years of Labor* (1889); annual convention proceedings of the American Federation of Labor; labor periodicals and newspapers, both conservative and radical. See also *Who's Who in America*, 1922–23, for certain specific details, and obituary in the *N. Y. Times*, Dec. 14, 1924.]

J. R. C.

GONZALES, AMBROSE ELLIOTT (May 29, 1857–July 11, 1926), newspaper publisher and writer of negro dialect stories, was born on a plantation in Colleton County, S. C. His father was Ambrosio José Gonzales, a Cuban patriot in exile, and his mother was Harriet Rutledge Elliott, of a family long established in the South Carolina low country. The ravages of the Civil War and the fall of the Confederacy having left the family destitute, young Ambrose early in life became accustomed to hard work. Scarcely in his teens, he entered manfully into the task of helping his family reëstablish the ancestral home which had been destroyed by Sherman's men. His formal schooling consisted of a few months at the public school in Beaufort, S. C., and one year at a private school in Virginia. At sixteen he learned telegraphy and went to Grahamville, S. C., a small station on the Charleston & Savannah Railway, where he worked four years. Something of his aspirations and genius is indicated by the fact that while there he and his brother, N. G. Gonzales, "printed" with pen and ink a small "newspaper," the *Palmetto*. Each issue totaled two copies, but those two had a remarkable circulation throughout the village.

After working several years as a telegraph operator in New York City and a few months in New Orleans, Gonzales returned to South Carolina and served as a traveling correspondent on the Charleston *News and Courier*. His brother was working for the same paper. Both took an interest in politics, and both had ideas as to what type of leadership the state needed to set it back on the road to progress. When, in 1890, Tillman was elected governor, many of the ablest men in the state felt that affairs had become intolerable. They believed that there was now as much necessity for redeeming the state from a certain white element as there had once been for redeeming it from the negro. With the moral and financial support of such men, Gonzales and his brother began in 1891 to publish the *State*, at Columbia, S. C. The paper's outspoken opposition to lynching, its plea for child-labor laws, better schools, compulsory-education laws, and its fight for wholesome politics won for it a high esteem among liberal people, but made many bitter enemies for its editors. In 1903, N. G. Gonzales, because of his strenuous newspaper campaign against the Tillman régime, was shot down by Lieut.-Gov. James H. Tillman, nephew of Ben Tillman and candidate for governor. Ambrose Gonzales then assumed the additional responsibilities incurred by his brother's death, continued, with another brother, William Elliott Gonzales, to publish his paper, and lived to see it achieve a national reputation. In 1922 he suffered a stroke which impaired his strength and affected his speech. It was after this time, however, that he produced the works upon which his claim to literary recognition rests. His friends had long since urged him to enlarge a newspaper contribution which he had made years before in the form of negro dialect stories. Drawing upon newspaper sketches previously published, and writing a great many more that he had been wanting to write, he produced four volumes of stories in the unusual dialect of the low-country or Gullah negroes: *The Black Border* (1922); *With Aesop Along the Black Border* (1924); *The Captain* (1924); and *Laguerre, a Gascon of the Black Border* (1924). Because of his intimate knowledge of these negroes, Gonzales not only succeeded admirably in portraying the humor and the pathos of their simple lives, but he also compiled a glossary and philological commentary, appended to his first book, which constitute one of the few accurate studies of the Gullah dialect.

[Probably the best source for Gonzales's life up to 1903 is the foreword which he wrote for his brother's posthumously published book: *In Darkest Cuba* (1922). The lives of the two were so closely interwoven that in writing his brother's biography he was also largely writing his own. This foreword was reprinted in the *State*, July 12, 1926, which contained in the same issue other biographical articles. See also Yates Snowden and H. G. Cutler, eds., *Hist. of S. C.* (1920), vol. IV.]

G. B. J.

GOOCH, Sir WILLIAM (Oct. 21, 1681–Dec. 17, 1751), colonial governor of Virginia, was born at Yarmouth, England, the son of Thomas Gooch and his wife, Frances, the daughter of Thomas Lone of Worlingham, Suffolk. He entered the English army at an early age and served with distinction under Marlborough in Europe, being present at the battle of Blenheim. His wife was Rebecca, the daughter of Robert Staunton, of Hampton, Middlesex, whose name, according to tradition, has been perpetuated in the town of Staunton, Va., established during her residence in the colony. Gooch assumed his duties as lieutenant-governor of Virginia on Sept. 8, 1727, following the brief acting-governorship of Robert Carter [*q.v.*]. He was received with favor by the colonists and before long was awarded £300 by the Council from the quit-rents, and £500 by the House of Burgesses from the provincial revenues. At the outset of his career he took a sincere interest in colonial affairs. When British merchants opposed the building of a lighthouse at Cape Henry, because of the tax on ships which would be imposed to pay for it, when they petitioned the Board of Trade for a repeal of the law imposing a tax on imported liquors and slaves, and again when they petitioned the same body for a law which would make land in the colonies liable for all debts, Gooch stanchly defended the colonists before the Board of Trade. He was especially emphatic in urging the repeal of the act of Parliament prohibiting the importation of tobacco stripped from the stalk, since it involved shipping unnecessary but taxable bulk. For the convenience of the colonists, also, he urged the use of inspector's notes on tobacco in warehouses as a form of currency. When some of the planters objected to the law of 1730, requiring the inspection of tobacco and the destruction of "trash," he wrote *A Dialogue Between Thomas Sweet-Scented, William Oronoco, Planters, both men of good Understanding, and Justice Love-Country, who can speak for himself. . . . By a sincere Lover of Virginia* (1732). It was a homely fable, setting forth in simple terms the economic benefits of a tobacco which would bring better prices and a higher value to inspector's notes.

In 1740 Gooch raised four hundred men in Virginia to assist the British forces in their attack on Carthagena, New Grenada, on the northern coast of South America. Upon the unexpected death of Alexander Spotswood [*q.v.*], appointed to the command of the battalions, Gooch assumed the command. He was seriously wounded in the campaign and also contracted the fever. Writing to the Bishop of London, in September 1741, he reported, "I am still weak in my knees, and very lame." For the defense of the colonists against Indians on the frontier, ne negotiated with the Six Nations the Treaty of Lancaster (July 1744), which insured a protection for colonists on the northern and western borders of the colony.

Gooch took a great interest in the state of the Church in Virginia. He reported regularly to the Bishop of the Diocese of London, who had jurisdiction of the Church in the American colonies, and urged upon the Assembly the passage of legislation for the promotion of religion and morality. A man of exemplary character himself, he gave careful thought to the character of the men whom he recommended to the Bishop for ordination. Though he deplored the prevalence of free-thinking in the colony, he was tolerant toward dissenting denominations. He accompanied his letters to the Bishop with Barbados sweetmeats, Madeira wine, "much improved by passing through this hott Climate," and promises of Virginia "Hamms." Throughout his administration he enjoyed the good will and loyalty of the colonists, and was many times the subject of public expressions of regard by the legislature. In August 1736, after he had served the colony for nine years, the speaker of the House of Burgesses addressed him in terms of unqualified respect: "You have not been intoxicated with the Power committed to You by His Majesty; but have used It, like a faithful Trustee, for the Public Good, and with proper Cautions. . . . You never propose Matters, without supposing Your Opinion subject to the Examination of Others, nor strove to make other Mens Reason blindly and implicitly obedient to Yours" (*Journals of the House of Burgesses, 1727–40*, p. 242).

On Nov. 4, 1746, Gooch was created a baronet and in the following year was promoted major-general in the British army. At his death his brother Thomas, Bishop of Ely, succeeded to the baronetcy, though the Bishop was the elder brother. When the Governor resigned his office in 1749, because of declining health, it was to the regret of the colonists. He had been an able and energetic executive, whose force was always tempered by tact. He died in Bath, England, and was buried in Yarmouth, survived by his wife. His only son, William, had died in Virginia. In her will the Lady Rebecca left to the College of William and Mary a large folio Bible, bound in four volumes, and a gilt sacrament cup, subsequently transferred to the Bruton Church.

[P. S. Flippin, *Wm. Gooch, Successful Royal Gov. of Va.* (1926), reprinted from the *Wm. and Mary Coll. Quart. Hist. Mag.*, Oct. 1925, Jan. 1926, and *The Royal Government in Va.* (1919) in the Columbia University Studies in History, Economics and Public Law; "The Virginia Clergy: Gov. Gooch's Letters to the Bishop of London," in the *Va. Mag. of Hist. and Biog.*, July,

Oct. 1924, Jan. 1925; W. L. Grant and J. Munro, *Acts of the Privy Council of England, Colonial Series*, vol. III (1910); H. R. McIlwaine, *Jours. of the House of Burgesses of Va., 1727–40* (1910), *1742–49* (1909); L. G. Tyler, *Encyc. of Va. Biog.* (1915), I, 60–61; Geo. Chalmers, *An Introduction to the Hist. of the Revolt of the Am. Colonies* (1845), II, 161–62, 198–202; Chas. Campbell, *Hist. of the Colony & Ancient Dominion of Va.* (1860), pp. 414–49; manuscript materials in the Lib. of Cong.] P. S. F.

GOOD, ADOLPHUS CLEMENS (Dec. 19, 1856–Dec. 13, 1894), Presbyterian missionary to Africa, naturalist, was born in a log house at West Mahoning, Pa., the second of five sons of Abram Good, a German farmer, and his wife, Hannah Irwin, of Scotch-Irish descent. When the boy was thirteen the family moved to Glade Run, where he grew up. He entered the Glade Run Academy at sixteen, graduated at Washington and Jefferson College in 1879, and at Western Theological Seminary in 1882. While in college he did much toward self-support, and was noted for his splendid physique, his serious, manly deportment, and his versatility, by which he was characterized through life. He was ordained in June 1882 by the Presbytery of Kittanning and before the end of the year was at Baraka on the Gabun River in the French Congo, fifteen miles north of the equator. Here he began active missionary work and preached his first sermon in the native tongue within ten months after his arrival. On June 21, 1883, he was married to Lydia B. Walker, who with one son survived him.

When the mission at Baraka was closed by the government under the requirement that all religious and educational work should be conducted in the French language, a new station was opened in 1885 at Kangwe, 150 miles inland on the Ogowai River, just south of the equator. Here for seven years Good made constant journeys into the hinterlands by boat, established churches, and organized a successful and lasting work. In 1892, however, fearing that the mission would be closed by the government, the Presbyterian Board turned it over to French Protestant missionaries, and Good began work in the Bulu country in German territory north of the French Congo. After the mission was planted at Efulen, he made a journey of 300 miles, on which he visited numerous villages, encountered great hardships, and penetrated farther inland than any previous white explorer. On a second journey in the fall of 1894 he was seized with a fever, but was able to reach Efulen where he died. In addition to his unusually effective missionary work, he prepared a Bulu primer, revised the translation of the New Testament and hymn-book into Mpongwe, and translated the Gospels into Bulu. He was also an indefatigable naturalist and probably added more to our knowledge of the insect forms of Africa than any other single collector. His collections of *Lepidoptera*, embracing forty-seven species and seventy-two genera new to science, have been described in twenty-nine papers by various authors, and his *Coleoptera* probably embrace over 1,000 species previously unknown. He also collected some valuable birds and mammals.

[Ellen C. Parsons, *A Life for Africa* (2nd ed., 1900), is an authentic biography, to which is appended "The Scientific Labors of Rev. A. C. Good," by W. J. Holland, and Good's "Superstitions and Religious Ideas of Equatorial West Africa," reprinted from an earlier work. See also *Woman's Work for Woman*, Mar. 1895; *The Church at Home and Abroad*, Feb., Mar., June 1895; A. I. Good, *The Chief's First White Man* (1917); Newton Donaldson, *Hist. of the Class of 1879, Washington and Jefferson Coll.* (1921).] F. T. P.

GOOD, JAMES ISAAC (Dec. 31, 1850–Jan. 22, 1924), German Reformed clergyman, historian, was third in descent from Jacob Guth of Zweibrücken in Rhenish Bavaria, who landed at Philadelphia Sept. 9, 1765, and lived successively in Lancaster, Lebanon, and Berks counties. Guth taught the Reformed parish school at Bern Church in Berks, read the services in the absence of a minister, and was a candidate for ordination at the time of his death in 1802. His sons, Joseph and Philip Good, were members of the state legislature. Three of Philip's sons—William A., Jeremiah Haak [*q.v.*], and Reuben—became German Reformed clergymen. William A. Good (1810–1873) studied theology under the Rev. Lewis Mayer at York and was the first superintendent of public instruction in Berks County, holding office for six years. His wife was Susan B. Eckert; their son, James Isaac, was born at York, where his father was then pastor.

Good graduated with honors from Lafayette College in 1872 and from Union Theological Seminary three years later. He was ordained pastor of Heidelberg Church at York June 16, 1875; was pastor of Heidelberg Church in Philadelphia 1877–90, and of Calvary in Reading 1890–1905. From 1890 to 1907 he was professor in Ursinus School of Theology, where he taught several subjects, served as dean 1893–1907, and supported six or more students each year out of his own income. In 1898 he effected the removal of the School to Philadelphia. When Central Theological Seminary was opened at Dayton, Ohio, in 1907, he became its professor of church history and liturgics. Until his death he regularly spent the first semester at Dayton and the second at Ursinus, where he now taught church history to undergraduates. He was president of the board of foreign missions of the Reformed Church in the United States 1893–1924, president of the General Synod 1911–14, president of the Western Section of the Reformed Alliance, and vice-president of the World Alliance of Reformed and Presbyterian Churches. As chairman of the Western Section's committee on relations with churches in Europe, he cheered and aided the needy Reformed churches on the Continent. He was the last prominent leader of the anti-liturgical party in his denomination and a thorough conservative, believing "about as firmly in the infallibility of the Heidelberg Catechism as in the infallibility of the Bible. . . . Of progressive revelation, historical development, evolution, divine immanence, and a social gospel, he had no thought, save to condemn them as sceptical innovations and evidences of decadent faith. His was a static universe with a static God working in a miraculous way" (G. W. Richards, *post*, p. 208). His chief work, however, was in church history. In 1879 he made his first trip to Europe and, while seeking information about his ancestors, became interested in the history of the Reformed Church. For the next quarter of a century he went abroad every summer to collect books, copy manuscripts, and visit places associated with great events of the past. Later he turned to the history of the Reformed Church in the United States and made himself the foremost scholar in that field. To other students he gave generous assistance. Possessing ample means, he was able to gather a notable historical library, which he bequeathed to Central Theological Seminary. The Harbaugh Manuscripts he gave to the General Synod. In Holland, aided by Prof. William J. Hinke, he secured complete transcripts or photographs of all documents relating to the Reformed Church in Pennsylvania. Of his books, over twenty in number, the more important are: *The Origin of the Reformed Church in Germany* (1887); *History of the Reformed Church of Germany, 1620–1890* (1894); *Early Fathers of the Reformed Church* (1897); *History of the Reformed Church in the United States, 1725–92* (1899); *Aid to the Heidelberg Catechism* (1904); *History of the Reformed Church in the U. S. in the Nineteenth Century* (1911); *History of the Swiss Reformed Church since the Reformation* (1913); and *The Heidelberg Catechism in its Newest Light* (1914). His historical writings are strongly colored by his theological convictions. His first publication, a thirty-three page *Essay on the Works and Language of Pope* (Easton, Pa., 1872), reveals his indebtedness to his teacher, Francis Andrew March [*q.v.*]. He edited with W. J. Hinke the *Minutes and Letters of the Coetus of the German Reformed Congregations in Pennsylvania, 1747–92* (1903) and was chairman of the German Reformed half of the committee that edited the *Hymnal of the Reformed Church* (1920). The quantity of work that he accomplished as pastor, professor, and author is remarkable even for a scholar of Pennsylvania German origin. Flowers and pictures were among his principal delights. He never married. The end of his busy, happy life came in Philadelphia; he did a full, satisfactory day's work, went to bed eager for the morrow, and died in his sleep.

[G. W. Richards, "The Rev. Jas. I. Good, D.D., LL.D., as a Church Historian," *Papers of the Am. Soc. of Ch. Hist.*, 2 ser., VIII (1928), 199–209; memoirs by G. W. Richards, G. L. Omwake, and W. J. Hinke in *Ref. Ch. Rev.*, Apr. 1924, pp. 113–18, 118–21, 152–67; the last slightly revised and with a portrait in *Jour. Presbyt. Hist. Soc.*, Oct. 1924; *Ref. Ch. Messenger*, Jan. 24, 31, Feb. 7, 1924; *Phila. Inquirer*, Jan. 23, 1924; *Who's Who in America*, 1922–23; *Biog. Cat. Lafayette Coll. 1832–1912* (1913); *Alumni Cat. Union Theol. Sem., N. Y., 1836–1926* (1926); information from Pres. G. L. Omwake of Ursinus Coll., and Prof. Wm. J. Hinke of Auburn Theol. Sem.] G. H. G.

GOOD, JEREMIAH HAAK (Nov. 22, 1822–Jan. 25, 1888), German Reformed clergyman, uncle of James Isaac Good [*q.v.*], was born at Rehrersburg, Berks County, Pa., the son of Philip Augustus and Elizabeth (Haak) Good. When he was ten years old his father died, leaving him to be reared by his uncle, Joseph Good of Reading, who was in comfortable circumstances and made ample provision for the boy's education. After attending the Reading Academy, he entered the preparatory department of Marshall College at Chambersburg in 1836 and graduated in 1842 as valedictorian of the class. He stayed at Mercersburg for four more years, studying theology under Philip Schaff and John Williamson Nevin and teaching in the preparatory department of the college. On May 2, 1846, he was licensed to preach by the Mercersburg Classis. His first charge was at Lancaster, Ohio, October 1846–October 1847, where he also taught a school. On Dec. 23, 1846, he married Susan Hubbard Root of Granville, Ohio, who survived him. From 1847 till 1853 he lived in Columbus, where he started a church paper, the *Western Missionary* (later the *Christian World*), in 1848, and continued to edit it for some years until the pressure of other work compelled him to give it up. In 1850 Heidelberg College was founded at Tiffin by the Ohio Synod of the German Reformed Church, and Good was elected professor of mathematics. His brother, Reuben Good, was at the same time made head of the preparatory department. The rest of his life was spent in the service of the college and of the theological seminary affiliated with it. He was professor in the college till 1869, when he was elected professor of dogmatics and practical theology and president of the seminary. Good accepted the new post, although the salary was less than he had been receiving. For nineteen years he was treasurer of the Ohio Synod. He supplied a number of congregations—the First Reformed, Grace, St. Jacobi's (German), Bascom's, and Salem—in and near Tiffin, and was the founder and for a long time the pastor of the Second Reformed Church of Tiffin. He published *The Reformed Church Hymnal* (1878), an edition of the *Heidelberg Catechism* (1879), *The Children's Catechism* (1881), *Prayer Book and Aids to Private Devotions* (1881), and *The Church Member's Handbook* (1882), and wrote a great deal for church papers. He was a doughty opponent of the "Mercersburg School," holding tenaciously to the old doctrines and cultus of his church, although his own instruction in theology had been under the leaders of the new school. His robust health finally gave way, and in 1887 he was made professor emeritus. He died at Tiffin within less than a year of his retirement and was buried there in Green Lawn Cemetery.

[H. Harbaugh, D. Y. Heisler, W. M. Deatrick, *The Fathers of the Reformed Ch. in Europe and America*, vol. VI (1888); *Franklin and Marshall Coll. Obit. Record*, vol. I, no. 1 (1897); J. I. Good, *Hist. of the Reformed Ch. in the U. S. in the 19th Century* (1911); G. W. Williard, *The Hist. of Heidelberg Coll.* (1879); *Reformed Ch. Messenger*, Feb. 15, 1888.] G. H. G.

GOOD, JOHN (Dec. 20, 1841–Mar. 23, 1908), inventor, manufacturer, was born in County Roscommon, Ireland, and was left fatherless in very early infancy. His mother, after struggling along for a few years, hopefully emigrated to the United States and settled in Brooklyn, N. Y. For a time he attended a parochial school, then, at the age of twelve, he went to work in a ropewalk—an establishment where rope was made by hand. In the course of four years, after he had gained a thorough knowledge of rope-making, he turned to the machinist's trade. He served a four-year apprenticeship with James Bulger in Brooklyn and then returned to the ropewalk of Henry Lawrence & Sons, Brooklyn, this time as foreman. At that time (1861) every operation of rope-making was done by hand, and Good with his four years' experience with machinery began to apply his knowledge in an effort to devise rope-making machinery to replace the hand operations. He experimented continuously at home and in his spare time for eight years, and was then rewarded by receiving his first patent on Oct. 5, 1869, for a machine called a breaker, designed to draw flax and other fibers into slivers. Although it was a labor-saving device, Good was unable to induce any cordage manufacturers to buy the machine. He, therefore, in 1870, established a machine-shop of his own in Brooklyn and manufactured his breaker there. He also sold the patent rights to Samuel Lawson & Sons of Leeds, England, who introduced the breaker in the British Isles. Within a few years his breaker had replaced the old hand operation in every hard-fiber rope plant in the world. For fifteen years, from 1870 to 1885, Good continued the manufacture of his breaker, patented and manufactured other rope-making machines, and built up an enormous business. On Oct. 7, 1873, he was granted a patent for his famous "nipper" for a spinning-jenny, and for the first time rope-yarn was spun without cutting. This was done by means of rollers. He also devised a regulator for his hemp-drawing and spinning machine, patented on June 15, 1875, and made a third improvement on this same machine with a "measuring stop motion," patented Feb. 10, 1885. In addition to these inventions, between 1885 and 1900 he obtained many patents for other modifications of his "breakers," "nippers," "spreaders," and "regulators."

Until 1885 Good had confined his attention wholly to the manufacture of rope machinery, but in that year he began the construction of a large rope plant at Ravenswood, L. I., preparatory to entering the field of cordage manufacture. He also acquired manufacturing sites and erected two plants near London, England. In these he planned to manufacture what he called "new-process" rope, based on the patent No. 330,315 granted to him on Nov. 10, 1885. He had devised a method of making a rope so much stronger than that which had formerly been made that lower quality and cheaper grades of fiber could be used and still yield a product ample in strength for any need. All rope sizes could be made, too, of hemp, sisal, or jute. Before his factories were ready, however, the rope manufacturers of the United States formed a combination or association for the purpose of controlling the manufacture and sale of rope and twine. Instead of entering the association when his plants were ready to begin operations in 1888 he accepted an offer of $150,000 annually to keep them closed. Upon the termination of this agreement a second and similar contract could not be arranged. Good thereupon made a contract in 1891 with the National Cordage Company to manufacture cordage and machinery exclusively for that company for the consideration of $200,000 annually. In April 1892 this contract was canceled and Good became an aggressive competitor in the cordage industry but went down in 1897 with the industrial depression which did not end until after the Spanish-American War. In 1898 the John Good & Jennings Patent Machine Cordage Company (later the John Good Cordage Company), was organized with Good as president, but this, too, passed out of existence. Good not only managed his various enterprises but continued with his experimental work as well. His inventions in rope-making machinery involved well over one hundred patents, the last of which was granted after his death, and constituted the basis of the machinery for manufacturing cordage in fully seventy-five per cent of the factories of the world. On Apr. 19, 1888, he received the title of "Count of the Holy Roman Empire," an honor conferred upon him by His Holiness the Pope for his benefactions to the Catholic Church. He was married on June 1, 1881, to Julia E. Durand of Brooklyn, who with two sons and a daughter survived him.

[*Cordage Trade Jour.*, Apr. 2, 1908; *Brooklyn Daily Eagle*, Apr. 20, 1888, Mar. 24, 1908; Chauncey M. Depew, ed., *One Hundred Years of Am. Commerce* (1895), vol. II; Patent Office records.] C. W. M.

GOODALE, GEORGE LINCOLN (Aug. 3, 1839–Apr. 12, 1923), botanist, educator, son of Stephen Lincoln Goodale [*q.v.*] and his wife, Prudence Aiken Nourse, was born in Saco, York County, Me. There, in an atmosphere of Puritan restraint but of wholesome enjoyment, he grew up, acquiring a lively practical interest in a great variety of affairs. In 1860 he graduated from Amherst College, where he had been associated with Edward Tuckerman, the foremost American student of lichens, and after a year as assistant in chemistry there, he entered upon the study of medicine, first in Portland, Me., and then in the Harvard Medical School. While he was a medical student he took part in the scientific survey of Maine authorized by the state legislature. He received the degree of M.D. in 1863 from both Harvard and Bowdoin, and began to practise his profession in Portland. After three years, in the interest of his health he took the long journey to California via Panama, returning to Maine not only restored in body, but with a broadened conception of the vegetation of the earth. In December 1866 he was married to Henrietta Juel Hobson of Saco. They had five children, only two of whom lived to maturity. For four years, 1868–72, he taught in Bowdoin College and its medical department; and during this time, with C. F. Brackett, he founded and published (1870–72) the *Bowdoin Scientific Review*. By the publication of his first botanical papers in the reports of the state survey (1862 and 1863) he had attracted the attention of Dr. Asa Gray [*q.v.*], and in 1872 he was called to Harvard as instructor in botany. In this modest position his usefulness was so appreciated that larger opportunities came to him. In 1873 he became assistant professor and in 1878 was appointed full professor of botany; the following year there were added to his duties the curatorship of the Botanical Museum and the Botanic Garden, which he held for thirty years; and in 1888 he succeeded Asa Gray as Fisher Professor of Natural History. He developed a lecture method characterized by finish, dignity, and clarity; his elementary courses became popular both with students preparing to be professional botanists and with general audiences. He lectured at the Harvard Summer School, at the Lowell Institute, and at Cooper Union in New York, and was one of the first to illustrate his lectures by means of lantern slides. To the hitherto almost exclusively taxonomic interest in plants, Goodale added interest in the morphological and physiological questions which have since so stimulated the study of nature. An early pupil of Pfeffer, he was the author of the first "physiological botany" in America, published in 1885 as Volume II of *The Botanical Text-Book* of Asa Gray. Having seen plant physiology well started, he attempted similarly to arouse interest in economic botany and for the new Botanical Museum, completed in 1890, he made collections of specimens and of models designed to cultivate public interest in the practical as well as scientific aspects of plant life. By extensive travels to the sources of tea, coffee, sugar, rubber, and other plant products of economic importance, he made personal and professional acquaintance with the leaders in the related industries, convincing them of the mutual importance and value of botany and plant industry. The evidences of the confidence which he inspired include a number of honorary degrees from various universities, his election to the presidency of the American Association for the Advancement of Science (1890), membership in the National Academy of Sciences, and his success in securing funds for carrying on the many considerable botanical projects which he conceived and inspired. The Botanic Garden of Harvard University was administered with an originality and understanding quite unusual for so small a garden; the Botanical Museum, which houses the laboratories of structural, physiological, and cryptogamic botany and draws thousands to its exhibition rooms, the Ware Collection of Blaschka Glass Models of plants, and the sugar experiment station in Cuba illustrate Goodale's diversity of interest and his solicitude to increase the interest of the public in botanical science. In

1909 he retired, becoming Fisher Professor Emeritus and honorary curator of the Botanical Museum, in which he continued to take an active interest until his death.

[Memoir by B. L. Robinson, in *Nat. Acad. Sci. Memoirs*, vol. XXI (1926), which contains other references and a list of Goodale's publications; *Who's Who in America*, 1921–22; *Harvard Grads. Mag.*, Sept. 1923; *Science*, June 8, 1923; *Boston Transcript*, Apr. 12, 1923.] G. J. P.

GOODALE, STEPHEN LINCOLN (Aug. 14, 1815–Nov. 5, 1897), agriculturist, was born at South Berwick, Me., the son of Enoch Goodale and his wife Lucy, daughter of Stephen and Lydia (Foster) Lincoln. The year after his birth, the family moved to Saco, Me., where Enoch Goodale established himself as a druggist, selling also chemicals and books. Stephen helped in the store, which was frequented by physicians, and in response to his early environment developed an interest in science, particularly chemistry. He attended the public schools and at thirteen entered Thornton Academy. After a three years' course, although he had a keen taste for study and investigation, he followed a life-long practical bent and went into business with his father. In 1837, when he was twenty-two, this business came under his control. On Sept. 23, 1838, he married Prudence Aiken Nourse of Bangor, Me. Since leaving school he had maintained his habits of study, his chief interests being pharmacy (chemistry) and agriculture, and when some three years after his marriage he bought a place in Saco he began at once to use the extensive grounds surrounding his house for the cultivation and scientific study of trees and shrubs. He eventually developed a collection which has been called one of the finest, if not the very finest, in the state. "For forty years he carried on experiments in the application of science to plant life, agriculture, forestry, fruit and flower culture, and artificial fertilizers" (Boardman, "Goodale," *post*, p. 90).

His interest in scientific agriculture led to his election in 1856 as first secretary of the reorganized State Board of Agriculture, a position which he occupied with great satisfaction to the Board and the State for seventeen years. His work was much more than secretarial, it was broadly educational. His first report, for the year 1856, contained 134 pages, 115 of which were written entirely by himself. In view of the newness of agricultural discussion from the standpoint of science, it was a remarkably discriminating review of such scientific knowledge in the fields of chemistry, botany, forestry, vegetable and fruit growing, and animal husbandry as seemed to be applicable to agricultural practise. It is typical of the author's efforts in behalf of agriculture during the next sixteen years. In his succeeding reports, most of which he wrote himself, he continued his educational work by discussing the newer phases of knowledge in their relation to agriculture, treating of such subjects as the dairy, fruit culture, and the principles of breeding. In 1861 he published *The Principles of Breeding: or, Glimpses at the Physiological Laws Involved in the Reproduction and Improvement of Domestic Animals,* which was used as a text-book in some of the agricultural colleges.

Goodale was much interested in the founding of Maine's land-grant college, the State College of Agriculture and the Mechanic Arts, later the University of Maine, which for ten years he served as trustee. While some of his views as to what the "Farmer's College," as he termed it, should be and do are now discarded, there is little doubt but that his influence was a noteworthy factor in preparing the state to welcome it. He had an important part in the scientific and agricultural surveys of Maine and carried on an extensive correspondence with scientists in Germany and England. While he was secretary of the Board of Agriculture he also managed an extensive nursery, was president of the Saco and Biddeford Savings Institution, and was president, manager, and chemist of the Cumberland Bone Company, manufacturers of fertilizer. Saco was his residence throughout his life, and there he died in his eighty-third year. His oldest son, George Lincoln Goodale [*q.v.*], also active in the fields of applied science and scientific education, was for many years professor of natural history at Harvard.

[S. L. Boardman, "Stephen Lincoln Goodale: His Life-Work in Behalf of Maine Agriculture," *Fortieth Ann. Report of the Secretary of the Board of Agric., 1897* (1898), pp. 88–110, and *Agric. Bibliog. of Me.* (1893); *Reports* of the Board, 1856–72; *Daily Kennebec. Jour.* (Augusta, Me.) and *Lewiston Saturday Jour.*, both Nov. 6, 1897; information as to certain facts from Robert L. Goodale, M.D., Boston, Mass.] W. H. J.

GOODALL, HARVEY L. (May 28, 1836–Mar. 28, 1900), journalist and founder of the pioneer livestock market paper, was born at Lunenburg, Essex County, Vt. He spent his boyhood on a farm and enjoyed only limited educational advantages but read with eagerness all the books he was able to procure. At the age of sixteen he left home fired with a desire to see the world. He shipped as a sailor to Europe, where he tramped the roads for some months without funds or friends. Becoming homesick, he returned to the United States and found employment in a New England cotton-mill. He subsequently studied stenography, was an official reporter during two sessions of the Pennsylvania Senate, and then engaged in newspaper work in Harrisburg, Pa., Lancaster, Pa., Philadelphia, and New York, successively. About 1858 he went to London for the purpose of publishing a daily paper on board the *Great Eastern,* then about ready to enter the service. When this scheme was defeated by an explosion on board the vessel which delayed its departure for some months, Goodall accepted the treasurership of a large circus, with which he toured Europe. He returned to the United States by way of Havana and arrived in New Orleans while the Louisiana state convention was in the act of passing the secession resolutions. Despite the imminence of war, however, he succeeded in getting a boat for the North, and on his arrival at Alton, Ill., enlisted (July 20, 1861) in the 2nd Illinois Cavalry, in which as a non-commissioned officer he served for three years.

After the close of the war he again engaged in newspaper work at Cairo, Ill., where he published the Cairo *Daily Times* until 1868. A year later he went to Chicago and established the weekly *Sun,* maintaining also an office for the printing of market circulars and miscellaneous job work. Impressed with the importance of the livestock industry of the West and Northwest, of which Chicago had become the focus and distributing point, he decided to issue a livestock market paper in place of his weekly market circulars. This paper, which he called the *Drovers Journal,* was published at the Union Stock Yards and was first issued on Jan. 11, 1873. The first livestock market paper ever published, it soon won for itself an important place in the livestock industry and was of great service in making known the facilities of the Union Stock Yards. A daily edition was started in January 1877 and a semiweekly edition was also published. Goodall maintained a branch office of the *Drovers Journal* in Liverpool for a year or two in the early eighties, but closed it when unfavorable restrictions upon the importation of American cattle made it unnecessary. To the end of his life, however, he continued to publish the Chicago editions of the *Drovers Journal* and the *Sun,* which had become a daily. In 1900 he died of heart trouble. The *Drovers Journal* was carried on for some years by his wife, Ellen F. Sullivan, whom he had married in 1883. Goodall was a generous man of upright character, scrupulously honest and conscientiously just in all his dealings.

[D. W. Wood, *Chicago and its Distinguished Citizens, or the Progress of Forty Years* (1881), pp. 314–18; *Chicago Daily Drovers Jour.,* Mar. 29, 1900; L. H. Bailey, *Cyc. of Am. Agric.,* IV (1909), 578; *Breeder's Gazette,* Apr. 4, 1900; *Chicago Tribune,* Mar. 29, 1900.]

C. R. B.

GOODALL, THOMAS (Sept. 1, 1823–May 10, 1910), manufacturer, originated the horse blanket and introduced into the United States several English methods of making the coarser woolens. Born at Dewsbury, Yorkshire, England, the youngest son of George and Tabitha Goodall, he lost his father when he was six months old and his mother before he reached the age of three. For eleven years he was an apprentice in a woolen-mill. At seventeen he was virtually in charge of the business, buying the wool and other supplies and disposing of the product. The week after he came of age he went into business for himself and prospered moderately. In 1846 he emigrated to the United States, and found employment in Connecticut, Massachusetts, and Rhode Island. On Apr. 29, 1849, he married Ruth, daughter of Jerry Waterhouse, a manufacturer of South Hadley, Mass. He settled at Troy, N. H., in 1852 and engaged in the manufacture of satinets and beavers. One freezing, blustery day, while watching a farmer struggle to fasten a blanket over a horse, he conceived the idea of making a blanket especially for horses. During the Civil War he also supplied blankets to the army and navy. In 1865 he sold his horse-blanket factory, which was still the only establishment of its kind, and returned with his family to England, intending to enjoy a long vacation. He was the sort of man, however, to whom a "vacation" is usually a brief interval preceding a more profitable enterprise. Soon he was engaged in exporting lap robes, then somewhat of a novelty, to the United States and Canada, traveling back and forth across the Atlantic in search for the best markets. Encouraged it is probable by the Wool and Woolens Act of 1867, he came to Sanford, Me., in October of that year and for $15,500 bought an old flannel factory and a grist-mill and sawmill, thereby obtaining all the water privileges of the Mousam River. Two sets of cards and ten looms, manned by fifty operatives, were in motion early the next year, and Sanford entered the first stage of its transformation from a hamlet of thirty dwellings and a grocery into a humming New England mill town. The Sanford Mills were the first in the United States to make carriage robes and kersey blankets. Goodall managed the business with shrewd sense and a thorough knowledge of manufacturing processes. Not the least of his achievements was the training of his three sons, who, in 1874, with Amos Garnsey, Jr., and Lucius C. Chase of Boston, formed the partnership of Goodall & Garnsey to manufacture plain and fancy blankets. On Oct. 1, 1881, the sons organized Goodall Brothers, the first company in the United States to make mohair car and furniture plushes and mohair carriage robes. On Apr. 4, 1885, Goodall & Garnsey and Goodall Brothers were consolidated with the Sanford Mills, and Thomas Goodall retired formally from the business, although he continued to watch its affairs with keen interest. He lived in a handsome residence in Sanford, had a summer home on the sea-wall at Old Orchard, and passed the winters in Florida. From his retirement he watched his sons organize in succession the Sanford Light & Water Company, the Goodall Worsted Company, the Mousam River Railway (from Sanford to Springdale), the Sanford National Bank, the Sanford Power Company, the Sanford & Cape Porpoise Railway, and the Maine Alpaca Company. In 1900 the original enterprise, the Sanford Mills, employed 750 operatives and turned out $1,000,000 worth of goods each year, while the annual product of its offshoot, the Goodall Worsted Company, was valued at $1,500,000. Sturdy and sound of body, looking like a man of sixty in spite of his seventy-seven years, Goodall kept his health till early in 1910, when the death of his wife so weakened him that he himself died three months later.

[E. Emery, *The Hist. of Sanford, Me., 1661–1900* (1901); brief obituaries in *Daily Kennebec Jour.* (Augusta, Me.), and *Daily Eastern Argus* (Portland, Me.), May 12, 1910; letter from his son, Louis Bertrand Goodall, July 12, 1928.] G. H. G.

GOODE, GEORGE BROWN (Feb. 13, 1851–Sept. 6, 1896), naturalist, author, administrator, was born in New Albany, Ind., the son of Francis Collier and Sarah Woodruff (Crane) Goode. He was of mixed Colonial descent, numbering among his ancestors John Goode of Virginia and Jasper Crane of New England, both of whom settled in America in the seventeenth century. In 1857 he removed with his parents to Amenia, Dutchess County, N. Y., where he prepared for college, and later entered Wesleyan University in Middletown, Conn., from which he graduated in 1870. For a short time thereafter he attended Harvard, studying natural history under Louis Agassiz, but was recalled to Wesleyan in 1871 to take charge of the new Orange Judd Museum of Natural History. The following year he met Spencer F. Baird [*q.v.*], then assistant secretary of the Smithsonian Institution, in charge of the National Museum, also United States fish commissioner, who became interested in him, and in 1873 provided openings for him in both projects under his direction. For several summers Goode was employed in the Atlantic Coast explorations of the Fish Commission, and in the winters divided his time between Wesleyan and the National Museum. In 1877 he definitely left Wesleyan, and accepted an appointment to serve with Baird in the Smithsonian. By degrees he took over a large part of the rapidly expanding duties in the control of the National Museum and the United States Fish Commission, both of which began or were developed as extensions of the Smithsonian Institution. In 1887 he became assistant secretary of the Smithsonian, and on the death of Baird, assumed the position of United States fish commissioner until January 1888.

Goode's first important technical paper was his *Catalogue of the Fishes of the Bermudas* (1876), an excellent study of local fauna. Numerous other studies followed, usually presented in monographic form. To him, the use of scientific knowledge for the promotion of human wealth and comfort was entirely legitimate and praiseworthy. Particularly in *The Natural and Economical History of the American Menhaden* (1879) does his absorption with the economic aspect of ichthyology become apparent. The value of the menhaden, as fertilizer or as food for its kind, received from him the same careful attention as problems of pure science. His weightiest paper, *Oceanic Ichthyology* (1895), prepared with the help of T. H. Bean [*q.v.*], is a study of all the deep-sea fish at that time known. It included, along with the results of previous expeditions, the records of the American explorations in the steamers *Blake, Albatross,* and *Fish Hawk,* and added one hundred and fifty-six new species of fish to the catalogue of Atlantic fauna. *American Fishes* (1888) was his only attempt at popular writing. Besides presenting in readable form an accurate discussion of food and game fish, it contained pertinent comments on fish by poets and philosophers from Aristotle to Thoreau.

In the later years of his life, Goode devoted himself to museum administration, a task for which he was particularly suited. His theories of management are set forward in two publications: "The Museums of the Future," *Annual Report of the Board of Regents of the Smithsonian Institution* (1891) and "The Principles of Museum Administration," *Annual Report of the Museums Association* (1895). As a museum executive he was also called upon to conduct several important expositions, in all of which he stressed the educational significance of the material on exhibit. He supervised the Smithsonian exhibits in the Philadelphia Centennial Exposition in 1876, served as United States commissioner at the Fisheries exhibitions in Berlin, 1880, and at London, 1883, and was concerned with the Columbian Historical Exposition of

1892–93, The World's Columbian Exposition of 1893, and many minor local expositions. His talent for organization was also given rein in his survey of American fisheries for the tenth census of 1880. Under his direction experts were sent to all parts of the coast and inland waters of the country in an attempt to make a general evaluation of the actual and potential aquatic resources of the United States. The results of the several reports he published as *The Fisheries and Fishery Industries of the United States* (7 vols., 1884–87).

Goode was also particularly interested in the historical and biographical phases of natural history. The *Origin of the National Scientific and Educational Institutions of the United States,* published in the April 1890 *Proceedings* of the American Historical Association, of which he was a founder, *An Account of the Smithsonian Institution* (1895), and *The Smithsonian Institution 1846–96* (1897) were his best-known historical treatises. His sympathetic sketches of the lives of intellectual pioneers of America, including one of Thomas Harriott of Roanoke, the first to publish in English a treatise on American natural history, constituted a valuable contribution to the literature of American science. His own family record, which he published in 1887 as *Virginia Cousins* has been considered a model genealogical monograph. Goode's work as a whole was marked by fairness and accuracy. He was slow to enter into controversy, and quick to admit and correct errors. His genial disposition made him a particularly happy organizer, and at his death he was sincerely mourned. He was survived by his wife, Sarah Lamson Ford Judd, the daughter of Orange Judd [*q.v.*], and by four children.

[*Virginia Cousins* (1887); *Ann. Rep. of the Board of Regents of the Smithsonian Institution . . . 1897,* pt. II (1901); *Nat. Acad. Sci., Biog. Memoirs,* vol. IV (1902); *Leading Am. Men of Sci.* (1910); *Science,* Sept. 18, Nov. 6, 1896; the *Evening Star* (Washington), Sept. 7, 1896.] D. S. J.

GOODE, JOHN (May 27, 1829–July 14, 1909), lawyer and statesman, was born in Bedford County, Va., of substantial stock, the son of John and Ann M. (Leftwich) Goode, and a descendant of the John Goode who settled in Virginia in the seventeenth century. After graduating from Emory and Henry College in 1848, he attended the Lexington Law School, and in April 1851 was admitted to the bar and commenced to practise at Liberty, Va. His election, six months later, to the state legislature marked the beginning of a public career of half a century, during which he was to champion his people's rights and do his duty without fear or favor. On July 10, 1855, he married Sallie, daughter of R. A. Urquhart, of Isle of Wight, Va.

When he had finished his work as a member of the Virginia Secession Convention he enlisted in the ranks of the 2nd Virginia Cavalry, fought at First Manassas, and subsequently was called to the staff of Gen. Jubal Early. While at the front he was elected to represent the Bedford district in the congress of the Confederacy, and served until the dissolution of that body. After the war he moved to Norfolk, and for fifteen years engaged assiduously in law and politics, participating in a number of celebrated Virginia criminal cases, and, an eloquent speaker and debater, taking an active part in state and national campaigns. He served in the Virginia legislature in 1866, in the "Whig and Democratic Convention" at Richmond (1867–68), as Democratic national committeeman from 1868 to 1876, and was elected seven times a delegate to Democratic national conventions. In November 1874 he was elected to Congress from the 2nd Virginia district, which he represented, wrote James Barron Hope, "in a manner worthy the best days of Virginia" (*Norfolk Landmark,* July 10, 1880). During the Forty-fourth Congress he was appointed to the committee on banking and currency, and participated in the discussion growing out of the Hayes-Tilden contest; during the two succeeding Congresses he was chairman of the committee on education and a member of the committee on naval affairs. Defeated for reëlection, he moved to Washington, D. C., and practised his profession there until shortly before his death. In May 1885 he was appointed solicitor-general of the United States, retaining the office until August 1886, when the Senate, by a strictly party vote, refused to confirm his nomination. During President Cleveland's second term, he served on the Chilean Claims Commission. In July 1898 he was made president of the Virginia Bar Association; but probably the highest honor conferred upon him was his election, without opposition, to the presidency of the Virginia Constitutional Convention of 1901–02, which position he filled with the wisdom, moderation, and fidelity that characterized the performance of his numerous lesser public trusts.

Goode was a fine specimen of the old-school Southern gentleman, his classical features, massive brow, open and expressive countenance bespeaking character no less plainly than his vitality and manly bearing indicated unusual physical strength. His integrity, simple but devout faith, and cultivation of intellect were matters of common knowledge. It was said at his death that no man living knew more of the history of his time, state and national, or of the leading men—practically all of whom he had known—of the preceding fifty years. His more important addresses are included in his autobiographical *Recollections of a Lifetime* (1906). Besides this scholarly and penetrating, though loosely connected, series of impressions of men and events, possessing narrative interest as well as genuine historical worth, he wrote for the Richmond *Times-Dispatch* a series of articles on "The Civilian Leaders of the Confederacy," but never published them in book form.

[*Recollections of a Lifetime, by John Goode of Va.* (1906); G. B. Goode, *Va. Cousins* (1887); L. G. Tyler, *Men of Mark in Va.* (1907), III, 143–45; W. W. Old, in *Report of the Twenty-First Ann. Meeting of the Va. State Bar Asso.*, XXII (1909), 69–81; obituaries in the Richmond *Times-Dispatch* and Norfolk *Virginian-Pilot* of July 15, 1909, and in the Washington *Evening Star* of July 14, 1909. See also *Norfolk Landmark* of July 10, 1880 (editorial) and July 15, 1909; *Who's Who in America*, 1908–09.] A. C. G., Jr.

GOODELL, HENRY HILL (May 20, 1839–Apr. 23, 1905), educator, college president, the son of Rev. William Goodell [*q.v.*], missionary to Turkey, and of Abigail Perkins Davis, his wife, was born in Constantinople. At the age of seventeen he was sent to the United States. He prepared for college at Williston Seminary, Easthampton, Mass. Graduating at Amherst in the class of 1862, he hastened to offer his services in the field and was commissioned second lieutenant, 25th Connecticut Volunteers, on Aug. 16, 1862. He was promoted first lieutenant, Apr. 14, 1863, and made aide-de-camp on the staff of Col. Bissell of the 3rd Brigade, 4th Division, XIX Army Corps, July 8 of the same year. He served in the battles of Irish Bend and Vermillion, at the siege of Port Hudson, in the Têche campaign and at Donaldsonville and was mustered out at Hartford, Conn., Aug. 26, 1863. On leaving the army he spent nearly a year in the study of modern languages, and from 1864 to 1867 was teacher of modern languages and gymnastics in Williston Seminary.

In 1867, at the opening of the Massachusetts Agricultural College, he was elected professor of modern languages and English literature, and during the next twenty years he taught in addition such branches as military tactics, the natural sciences, rhetoric, elocution, and history. He also created the college library and for many years filled the office of librarian. In 1886 he was chosen to the presidency of the college, a position he filled most acceptably until his death in 1905. He combined with that office the directorship of the Experiment Station, and the editorial supervision of its reports and all its bulletins. During his administration the scope of the institution was extended, the resources greatly augmented, the course of study broadened, and the standard of scholarship raised; in 1896 the doors were first opened to women. Eminently successful as an administrator, Goodell possessed a natural aptitude for teaching, bringing to his work a well-trained mind and a forcefulness which imparted itself to his students. He was a miracle of energy, a man of generous instincts, and ever anxious to do his duty wherever duty called him. No one ever appealed to him in vain for aid or advice. His rare tact and skill in dealing with men was well known, and perhaps nowhere better shown than as chairman of the executive committee of the Association of Agricultural Colleges and Experiment Stations, a position in which his influence was felt far beyond his own college. He was a frequent lecturer, especially before agricultural and horticultural societies. He wrote with facility and rapidity, and extremely well. Besides his annual reports, covering the years 1887–1905, he was the author of some twenty biographical sketches and addresses.

Goodell was prominently identified in many ways with the welfare of the town of Amherst. In 1885–86 he represented the district in the General Court. He was always especially interested in the public library and for many years was chairman of its book committee, editing the annual reports and preparing the catalogues. For a quarter of a century he served as a vestryman of Grace Church and as parish clerk. On Dec. 10, 1873, he was married to Helen Eloise Stanton, daughter of John Stanton of New Orleans. He died on shipboard, returning from Florida, whither he had gone for the benefit of his health.

[Calvin Stebbins, *Henry Hill Goodell* (1911), with selections from Goodell's addresses; *Amherst Record*, Apr. 26, 1905; *Obit. Record Grads. Amherst Coll.*, 1905; F. Tuckerman, in *Mass. Agric. Coll. Alumni News*, III (1905), 25, V (1907), 42; W. E. Stone, in the same journal, IV (1906), 39; W. P. Brooks, in *Forty-third Ann. Report, Mass. Agric. Coll.* (1906); *College Signal*, May 3, 1905; *Amherst Coll. Biog. Record* (1927); *Who's Who in America*, 1901–02.] F. T.

GOODELL, WILLIAM (Feb. 14, 1792–Feb. 18, 1867), missionary in the Near East for forty-two years, was the second of twelve children born to William and Phebe (Newton) Goodell in a two-room farm house in Templeton, Mass. He was a descendant of Robert Goodell, or Goodale, who came from Suffolk County, England, and settled in Salem, Mass., in 1634. His parents lived a life of poverty, patience, meekness, and faith; his father, he says, being "full of the millennium and of the missionary spirit long before the existence of the 'Missionary Herald,' or of the American Board, or of the 'Panoplist.'"

Determined to get an education but with no means of support assured, in 1811 William strapped his trunk on his back, and walked the sixty miles to Phillips Academy, Andover. Here, since he soon demonstrated his strength of character and intellectual ability, his financial needs were supplied from funds provided by one of the trustees, Lieut.-Gov. Phillips, and, during his last year, by money derived from the sale of two fat oxen sent him from Vermont by a great-uncle, Solomon Goodell, an early benefactor of the Connecticut Missionary Society and of the American Board of Commissioners for Foreign Missions. Graduating from Dartmouth College in 1817, where he had supported himself by teaching, he entered Andover Theological Seminary. After the completion of his course there in 1820, the better to prepare himself for the missionary field, he attended medical lectures at Dartmouth for a few months; then for a year traveled in the West as agent for the American Board. At the annual meeting of the Board held at New Haven in 1822 he was ordained, Sept. 12, and on Nov. 19 of the same year he was married to Abigail Perkins Davis, daughter of Hon. Lemuel Davis of Holden, Mass.

On Jan. 21, 1823, he and his wife arrived at Malta en route for Jerusalem where they expected to establish themselves. Except for one visit (1851–53), he was not to return to America until in his seventy-fourth year he went home to spend his last days. After nine months' preparatory study at Malta, unfavorable conditions in Jerusalem making it inadvisable for him to go there, he repaired to Beirut where, with others, in the face of obstacles and persecution, he established a mission. War conditions forced him to retire to Malta in 1828, and for three years he superintended the mission press. In April 1831 he received instructions from the American Board to go to Constantinople and establish a new mission with special reference to the Armenians; and that city became his permanent residence. Here, in 1834, he was joined by Harrison Gray Otis Dwight [*q.v.*]. Although never robust physically, Goodell was otherwise eminently fitted for his work, being an excellent scholar and linguist, of sanguine temperament, brave-hearted, sagacious, tactful, tolerant, and humbly and sincerely religious. During his long career he continued his work through war, pestilence, persecutions, and plots against his life. Perhaps as much as any individual he laid the foundation for the American Board's work in Turkey. One of his greatest services was a translation of the Bible into Armeno-Turkish. In this work he was greatly assisted by native scholars, notably Bishop Dionysius and Panayotes Constantinides. The New Testament was issued in 1831 from the press at Malta, and the Old Testament, from the press at Smyrna in 1842. The final revised edition of the translations appeared in 1863. In 1865 he returned to America and died in less than two years at the home of his son, William Goodell, M.D., Philadelphia. His wife and seven other children survived him, one of them being Henry Hill Goodell [*q.v.*]. During his only furlough in America he published *The Old and the New; or The Changes of Thirty Years in the East* (1853), and after his death there appeared (1870) a volume of his evangelistic sermons in Armenian.

[E. D. G. Prime, *Forty Years in the Turkish Empire; or, Memoirs of Rev. William Goodell, D.D.* (1876); E. M. Bliss, *The Encyc. of Missions*, vol. I (1891); *Missionary Herald*, May 1867, Dec. 1867; H. H. Jessup, *Fifty-three Years in Syria* (2 vols., 1910), vol. I; J. K. Greene, *Leavening the Levant* (1916); J. S. Dennis, *Centennial Survey of Foreign Missions* (1902); H. O. Dwight, *The Centennial Hist. of the Am. Bible Soc.* (1916); G. T. Chapman, *Sketches of the Alumni of Dartmouth Coll.* (1867); *Twenty-sixth* and *Twenty-seventh Ann. Report, Am. Bible Soc.* (1842, 1843); *Eclectic Mag.*, May 1862; *Hours at Home*, Aug. 1867; Phila. *Press*, Feb. 22, 1867.]

H. E. S.

GOODELL, WILLIAM (Oct. 25, 1792–Feb. 14, 1878), reformer, was born in Coventry, Chenango County, N. Y., where his parents, Frederic and Rhoda (Guernsey) Goodell, were among the first settlers. He was descended from Robert Goodell, or Goodale, who settled at Danvers, Mass., in 1634. Delicate in childhood, he spent much of his time indoors with his mother, who encouraged his interest in literature, particularly poetry, and in composition. Shortly after her death, in his eleventh year, he went to live with his grandmother Goodell in Pomfret, Conn. Here he remained five years, attending the common school, working on the farm, and enjoying the use of two large libraries. Important in his intellectual and moral development was the influence of his grandmother, a strong-minded woman with advanced ideas on some of the social evils of her day. William hoped for a college education, but was disappointed, and at eighteen, his health much improved, he entered the employ of a mercantile firm in Providence, R. I. On Jan. 1, 1817, he sailed as supercargo in a ship bound for East Indian, Chinese, and European markets. Returning to the United States in 1819, he reëntered business in Providence, Wilmington, N. C., and Alexandria, Va. On July 4, 1823, he married Clarissa C. Cady, daughter of Josiah Cady of Providence. Upon the failure of his commercial venture in Alexandria, he found employment in New York City where he was active in promoting the Mercantile Library Association, of which he became a director in 1827. In that year he gave up business and removed to Providence to become editor of a reform weekly, the *Investigator and General Intelligencer,* which soon drifted into temperance reform. In 1829 this paper became connected with the *National Philanthropist* of Boston and in 1830 was removed to New York, where, as the *Genius of Temperance,* it continued to assail various evils. To arouse interest and gain subscriptions, Goodell was frequently forced into the lecture field. During these same years he also published the *Female Advocate* to further the movement for the moral reform of unfortunate women, as well as the *Youth's Temperance Lecturer,* one of the earliest temperance papers for children. In 1833 he helped to organize the American Anti-Slavery Society and began to publish the *Emancipator,* in the name of C. W. Denison. In 1834 the paper, appearing under Goodell's name, became the Society's organ. Two years later he spoke effectively before the Massachusetts legislature in behalf of the Massachusetts Anti-Slavery Society and against the appeal of certain Southern states for legislation restraining the anti-slavery agitators. The same year (1836) he took charge of an anti-slavery paper in Utica, N. Y., the *Friend of Man,* which he edited for six years in Utica and Whitesboro. Here he also published for a year the monthly *Anti-Slavery Lecturer* and began (1842) the *Christian Investigator.* Meantime he lectured widely and, in 1840, helped organize the Liberty Party. In 1843 he was induced to set up in Honeoye, N. Y., his ideal church, based upon temperance, anti-slavery, and church union principles. He entered the ministry without seeking or desiring formal ordination, and was very successful, being "a man of tender and exquisitely sympathetic nature." In 1847, feeling that the Liberty Party's program of opposition to slavery was too narrow, he left that party to found the Liberty League, which, with a platform of opposition to slavery, tariffs, land monoply, the liquor traffic, war, and secret societies, nominated Gerrit Smith for president. While at Honeoye, Goodell wrote extensively on slavery, notably *Views Upon American Constitutional Law, in its Bearing Upon American Slavery* (1844), *The Democracy of Christianity* (2 vols., 1849), *Slavery and Anti-Slavery: A History of the Great Struggle in Both Hemispheres* (1852), and *The American Slave Code, in Theory and Practice* (1853). In 1854 he settled in New York to edit the *American Jubilee,* later the *Radical Abolitionist,* which, enlarged and published as the weekly *Principia,* continued until abolition was effected. Unlike Garrison, Goodell thought it possible under the Constitution to do away with slavery and was a believer in both the Constitution and the Union. Following the war, he wrote for reform and religious papers, and occasionally preached. In 1869 he was among the organizers of the National Prohibition Party. The next year he removed to Janesville, Wis., to be near his two daughters, and there he passed the remaining years of his life, retaining to the end an active interest in religion and reform.

[*In Memoriam, William Goodell, Born in Coventry, N. Y., Oct. 25th, 1792. Died in Janesville, Wis., Feb. 14th, 1878* (1878); *The U. S. Biog. Dict. and Portr. Gallery of Eminent and Self-Made Men: Wis. Vol.* (1877), pp. 193–95; Henry Wilson, *Hist. of the Rise and Fall of the Slave Power in America* (1872), I, 232 ff., 408–21, 555; W. P. and F. J. Garrison, *Wm. Lloyd Garrison* (4 vols., 1885–89), I, 91; obituary in *Wis. State Jour.* (Madison), Feb. 18, 1878.] W. R. W.

GOODENOW, JOHN MILTON (1782–July 1838), Ohio jurist, congressman, was born in Westmoreland, Cheshire County, N. H., of Puritan stock. His formal education was limited to the common schools, over one of which he presided for a time. He undertook to manage a country store with results financially unfortunate. In 1811 he removed to Canton, Ohio, where he studied law. On admission to the bar in 1813, he commenced practise at Steubenville, Ohio. In the same year he was married to Mrs. Sarah Lucy (Wright) Campbell. He was later married a second time, but the date, and the name of his second wife, have not been found. His life as an attorney was strenuous, for he followed the circuit judge on his quarterly rounds throughout the eastern part of the state. The circuit judge was the conservative Benjamin Tappan [*q.v.*], and with him Goodenow developed a bitter quarrel. When he failed in an attempt to secure a county office, he claimed that Tappan had traduced him, and brought suit against the judge, for slander (*Goodenow* vs. *Tappan,* 1 *Ohio Reports,* 60). The quarrel shortly took a new course. Judge Tappan, in the case of *Ohio* vs. *Lafferty* (Tappan, *Reports,* 81), held that crimes under the English common law should be held as crimes by Ohio courts in the absence of specific state legislation. In opposition to this view Goodenow wrote an able treatise, *Historical Sketches of the Principles and Manners of American Jurisprudence in Contrast with the Doctrines of the English Common Law on the Subject of Crimes and Punishments* (1819; copy in Law Library, Western Reserve University). His reasoning was generally approved by Ohio judges and Tappan's ruling was not accepted. Ohio to this day has no common-law crimes, as such, a fact for which Goodenow is to some extent responsible (42 *Ohio*

State Reports, 386). In 1817 he was appointed collector of internal revenue for the sixth district. In 1823 he was a member of the Ohio House of Representatives.

Defeated for Congress in 1826 by his brother-in-law John C. Wright, Goodenow was victorious over Wright in the Jackson landslide of 1828. He took his seat in December 1829, but resigned in April 1830 before the end of the first session because of his appointment as a justice of the supreme court of Ohio. He was forced by ill health to resign from the bench shortly after he had taken up his duties. In 1832 he removed to Cincinnati, where he was elected presiding judge of the court of common pleas. His irascible disposition made him unpopular with the lawyers, however, and he held the office for only two years. In 1835 he set up an office at St. Clairsville, where he practised with small success. He felt that his services to the Democratic state machine had not been fittingly rewarded, and in his embitterment emigrated to Texas in November 1837. His health failed him, however, and in the following year he determined to return to Ohio, but died at New Orleans before he had completed the journey. He was buried in Cincinnati. Goodenow is described as tall and slender, with a physique which denoted feebleness but which was capable of great exertion. His life is a study in frustrations in which ill health and unruly temper played their parts. His contemporaries admitted that his achievements did not give a just measure of his talents.

[*Western Law Monthly* (Sept. 1863), pp. 169 ff.; W. T. Utter, "Ohio and the English Common Law," *Miss. Valley Hist. Rev.*, Dec. 1929; Curtis Wright, *Geneal. and Biog. Notices of Descendants of Sir John Wright of Kelvedon Hall, Essex, England* (1915); *The Biog. Encyc. of Ohio of the Nineteenth Century* (1876); *Biog. Dir. Am. Cong.* (1928); *Ohio Statesman* (Columbus), July 24, 1838.]

W. T. U.

GOODHUE, BENJAMIN (Sept. 20, 1748–July 28, 1814), United States senator, merchant, was born at Salem, Mass., the fourth son of Benjamin and Martha (Hardy) Goodhue, and a descendant of Deacon William Goodhue of Ipswich, who landed in Massachusetts about 1636. After his graduation from Harvard in 1766 he became a merchant in Philadelphia. During the Revolution he was again in Salem, becoming part-owner in one or two privateers and one of the volunteers from that town in the Rhode Island expedition in August 1778. His first appearance in state politics was in 1779–80, when he was a member of the constitutional convention. From 1780 to 1782 he represented Salem in the General Court, and in 1783 and again from 1785 to 1788, he was a state senator from Essex County. In 1789 his district sent him to Congress, in which body he served as their representative for almost eight years. He was a stanch Federalist and a defender of Jay's Treaty. When George Cabot resigned from the Senate in 1796, Goodhue was chosen to fill his place. He supported the Alien and Sedition bills, but broke with the administration when President Adams nominated his son-in-law, Col. Smith, to the offices of brigadier- and adjutant-general. At this time Adams and his cabinet were at odds, and it should be remembered that Goodhue was a cousin of Timothy Pickering, the secretary of state. It is doubtful if Adams ever forgave Goodhue for not taking his side in that controversy.

In November 1800 Goodhue resigned from the Senate and returned to Salem. He was twice married: first, on Jan. 6, 1778, to Frances Richie of Philadelphia, and second, on Nov. 25, 1804, to Anna Willard of Lancaster, Mass. His son Jonathan, a merchant in New York, survived him. At the time of his death William Bentley commented in his *Diary* (IV, 1914, p. 271): "His habits since his return [to private life] have given him no influence in society & as he rose gradually to public notice so he insensibly passed away from all his former friendships, & notice, being habitually & publicly intemperate. . . . Mr. Goodhue while in health had a good person, a taciturnity, but his manners were not forbidding & he regarded the public Institutions of Life and Religion. His Friendships were in little circles, but his civilities everywhere enough to get no enemies from neglect. As a merchant unimpeached, he was for consolidating, as he called it, our Republican Institutions, & if they had consolidated into a European form he would not be in opposition."

[The Goodhue papers, Essex Inst., Salem, Mass.; Pickering MSS., Mass. Hist. Soc.; *New-Eng. Hist. and Geneal. Reg.*, Jan. 1851; D. H. Hurd, *Hist. of Essex County, Mass.* (1888), vol. I; *Birth, Marriage and Death Reg. . . . of Lancaster, Mass.* (1890); G. W. Allen, "Mass. Privateers in the Revolution," *Mass. Hist. Soc. Colls.*, vol. LXXVII (1927); Octavius Pickering and C. W. Upham, *Life of Timothy Pickering* (4 vols., 1867–73); Geo. Gibbs, *Memoirs of the Administrations of Washington and John Adams* (2 vols., 1846); H. C. Lodge, *Life and Letters of Geo. Cabot* (1877); C. R. King, ed., *The Life and Correspondence of Rufus King* (6 vols., 1894–1900).]

L. S. M.

GOODHUE, BERTRAM GROSVENOR (Apr. 28, 1869–Apr. 23, 1924), architect, was born of prosperous old New England stock, at the family homestead in Pomfret, Conn. He was the son of Charles Wells Goodhue and Helen Grosvenor (Eldredge) Goodhue. From his mother, who sketched and painted, he derived a love of drawing and a precocious ability. From her, also, he first learned the stories of St. Augustine and St. Francis, which probably gave the original stimulus to his love and knowledge of the Middle Ages. He had little formal schooling, but read and sketched insatiably. Long days in the woods had their part in leading him to blazon on the walls of his boyhood attic studio the motto, so significant for his romanticism: "Art pre-exists in Nature, and Nature is reproduced in Art." At fifteen he went to New York to enter the office of Renwick, Aspinwall & Russell. James Renwick had designed Grace Church and Saint Patrick's Cathedral; his office was doubtless the best place in America to learn Gothic detail. Goodhue was no ordinary office boy. Reading and drawing at night, he soon gained a reputation among the draftsmen not only for his independence of thought, but for his fabulous facility—in spite of his left-handedness—with pen and ink. Slight, blond, blue-eyed, red-cheeked and debonair, he was ambitious to excel, even in the boyish consumption of beer. A "whimsical, humorous, baffling quality . . . wove a veil of mockery and persiflage over a real and powerful sincerity" (Whitaker, *post*, p. 31). Goethe was his God.

While still in Renwick's office, at twenty-one, Goodhue entered several of the open competitions then in vogue, including that for designs for the Cathedral of St. John the Divine in New York, and even won the competition for a cathedral in Dallas. This was the occasion for a new alliance. In Boston, Ralph Adams Cram and Charles Francis Wentworth, a few years Goodhue's senior, had begun the practise of architecture in 1880, devoting themselves chiefly to churches. To the young firm of Cram & Wentworth he brought the Texas commission, destined to prove illusory, and entered its employ at the close of 1889 as head draftsman of the little office. Later he was taken into the partnership. On the death of Wentworth the firm became, as it remained for many years, Cram, Goodhue & Ferguson. The influences under which their style was formed were from the contemporary phase of the Gothic revival in England as represented particularly in the work of Sedding, from High Church ritualism, and from the Arts and Crafts movement of William Morris and Walter Crane, concerned with the revival of handicraft in the sympathetic and functional use of materials. Essentially all these tendencies were phases of a romanticism which expressed itself characteristically in an evanescent magazine, the *Knight Errant,* for which Goodhue designed the cover, in Morris's tradition, in 1891. This is but one of many examples of Goodhue's work in book design, in which he was active at that period. It led him to design two fonts of Roman type, the Merrymount (cast in 1896 for *The Altar Book . . . of the American Church* of D. Berkeley Updike) and the well-known Cheltenham. Many of his page borders, title-pages, and book-plates, much prized by collectors, reveal the influence of Morris, although, as time went on, Goodhue's virtuosity led him to experiment also in other styles.

With the literary activity and fervor of Cram, appealing for a return to beauty and sacrifice in the church, with the magical draftsmanship in which Goodhue clothed his Gothic fantasy in design, their firm flourished and took the lead in ecclesiastical architecture. Their first success was won in alliance with the High Churchmen. They took up the ritual arrangements and the traditional forms of the English church as they had been cut off by Henry VIII. All Saints', Ashmont (Boston), their earliest triumph, built in 1892, shows a free use of the forms of this last phase of English Gothic, with walls of brown, seam-faced granite (a material they brought into honor), and windows of rich clear glass, heavily leaded in contrast to the naturalistic opalescent windows of John La Farge [*q.v.*]. Other striking works of the early period were St. Stephen's, Cohasset, Mass., romantically situated on its bold ledges, and St. Stephen's, Fall River, with its deep western arch divided by great canopied mullions.

Goodhue could now satisfy his romantic urge to travel. He was drawn by the picturesque to Quebec, to Mexico (his book *Mexican Memories* appeared in 1892), to Germany, to Persia, to China. Half-fanciful recollections of these journeys, in text and drawings sometimes published in current magazines, are some of his most characteristic creations—the dream cities which rose so magically under his pen: Traumberg and Monteventoso and Xanadu, cities of domes and towers, rising on lofty rocks or cliffs washed by the sea. Their forms like their names were chosen for romantic appeal: the Gothic of the North, with its chivalry and mysticism, feudal Italy, the mysterious East. Some such dream cities Goodhue was to build at West Point and at San Diego.

The first period of his work culminated in the buildings at West Point, won in competition in 1903. The precipitous site favored the victory of Gothic, castellated design. In the development of the plans the chapel fell particularly to Goodhue, who mantled it with superb ruggedness. The motive of the front of St. Stephen's was there effectively devoloped. The group gave a powerful impetus to the adoption of Gothic forms in collegiate work generally.

The execution of the work at West Point led to Goodhue's establishment in New York. He had married, on Apr. 8, 1902, Lydia T. Bryant of Boston, and now built himself a characteristic house in the metropolis. There many churches now came to the firm, of which the two offices became increasingly independent until the final dissolution of the partnership in 1913. Thus Goodhue had the major responsibility in the detail of St. Thomas's on Fifth Avenue, and the later New York churches are to be assigned entirely to him. In St. Thomas's Goodhue achieved a measure of romance even on a prosaic street corner. The plan of the church, in which Cram still had a part, is designed with extreme skill to produce a rich variety of effects of mass and space within the constricted rectangle of the site. The front, unsymmetrical with a bold tower on the outer corner, is suggestive of the French flamboyant churches, but freely conceived. The great carved reredos rising the full height of the tall nave, with tier upon tier of saints in their canopied niches, is of inspiring beauty and grandeur. In such designs Goodhue was at his best, the romanticist still felt free to be himself.

In the South Church, the Chapel of the Intercession, and St. Vincent Ferrer in New York, Goodhue repeated and varied his now characteristic formulae for the high-shouldered urban church. In the last, a new influence, that of Sir Gilbert Scott's work at Liverpool Cathedral, is apparent. After his first sight of this Goodhue redesigned completely his proposed Cathedral of Maryland in Baltimore, with bolder scale and less traditional details. In the designs for the chapel for the University of Chicago, Byzantine elements mingled with the Gothic; in St. Bartholomew's in New York, in which Stanford White's round-arched portal was to be incorporated, Goodhue played freely with Romanesque and Byzantine forms. These were but the first steps in a development which was to carry him away from historical forms, into a struggle for freedom of expression which was to occupy the last years of his life.

From the early days, although classic form repelled him as a *fait accompli,* he had occasionally worked in it admirably, especially in its romantic Spanish phases—in that baroque so akin to Gothic. Soon after the American occupation of Cuba he did Trinity Church in Havana (1905), and other little Spanish churches there, the forerunners of his California houses and of the exposition of 1915 in San Diego. There he threw a great arched causeway across a deep ravine and piled up at the end picturesque masses of dome and tower. The front of the Gillespie house at Montecito, most truly classic of his works, is a calm proscenium, backing the terraced garden.

As Goodhue grew older, he became dissatisfied with his romanticism. Even within the Gothic, he came to appreciate, "the essence of the French cathedral plan is logic" (Whitaker, *post,* p. 20). He grew dissatisfied with his medievalism. Daily experience convinced him that "Mediæval Gothic is now impossible, . . . and the Gothic we do to-day, if it is to be vital, and beautiful, and true, and good . . . must be of our own times." At first he did not mean "that we must abandon . . . any of the old materials." "Steel-framing and reinforced concrete are good enough things in their way . . . but just because we have such materials is no reason why we should throw away stone and oak" (*Ibid.,* pp. 22–23). By 1918, however, at least he had come to a different emphasis, holding, in a letter to Paul Cret, "that while architecture should represent a decent reverence for the historic past of the art, . . . we should only ignore our rightful heritage for the most compelling reasons." One of these compelling reasons was the invention of the steel frame, or reinforced-concrete construction, which to his mind did "abrogate practically all known forms." "I assure you," he added, "I dream of something very much bigger and finer and more modern and more suited to our present-day civilization than any Gothic church could possibly be" (*Ibid.,* p. 27). Thus, though realizing himself "too conservative wholly to abandon the language of ornament" to which he was accustomed, he moved toward the camp of the logicians and modernists.

Paradoxically, yet naturally enough, as Goodhue moved toward "modernism," he moved also toward classicism—the classicism of calm and ordered masses and spaces. The force of late-Victorian rationalistic theory overbore romanticism in his thought; the force of the classic spirit in the great body of contemporary American work overbore romanticism in his practise. When he commenced to do government buildings he had to make concessions, and he approached the task with a heavy heart. At least he would criticize the *fait accompli,* he would rationalize the classic. Unconsciously he would Gothicize it as well.

In the competition for the great war memorial in Kansas City, his design, like the winning design of H. Van Buren Magonigle, was of vast block-like masses, colonnades reduced to lowest terms, in which the suggestion and the proportions only were classical, the general disposition picturesque. The chief element was a background for colossal sculptured figures, recalling somewhat the massive German monuments of the imperial period.

Among his executed works of the last period the most significant are the Nebraska Capitol and the National Academy of Sciences. The capitol is a composition of gaunt and simple masses, the broad base, marked by continuous horizontal lines, contrasting sharply with the lofty tower of multiplied and unbroken verticals. The logic for which the designer strove is, to be sure, mostly apologetics. In the general disposition, the practical functions of the tower are an afterthought. In spite of Goodhue's eagerness that his buttresses should really butt, they only seem to do so. Mass and line are the essentials of the building, and its impressive merits are in these, not in structural truth. Details of "style," however, largely occupied the designer. It is, as Goodhue said, "a sort of Classic" although the elimination of many horizontal cornices from the competitive design makes it also a sort of Gothic or Byzantine. Especially in the interior the effect is sometimes not vitally unified in form.

The same expurgated classicism prevails in the building of the American Academy of Sciences in Washington. Downcast at first at the requirement of conformity to the established character of the surroundings, he strove to vitalize old formulae by elimination of columnar elements, by refinements of profiling and restraint of sculptured ornament. Beautiful in material and detail, the building yet suffers from the broken rhythm of its short façade. The forms, but hardly the spirit, of the classic are there.

Once he had accepted steel, Goodhue dreamed of a skyscraper which, by office rental, would bear the cross far above the city. Essentially his tower for the site of the old Madison Square Garden was the tower of the Nebraska Capitol on a still vaster scale. It was a scheme of soaring lines, and of vast corner buttresses, which tended to destroy the rental on which the whole was predicated. It was a glorious vision of form, based on a contradiction in terms. The vision has remained. It gleams often in Hugh Ferriss's paper-cities of the future, and is palely reflected in more than one executed building.

In the final estimate of Goodhue's work there must be taken into account, beside the intrinsic quality of his works, the question of leadership. We must recognize that in the great movements on the stage of the world he made but a dilatory entrance, and that his steps were halting and uncertain. Essentially he was a belated romanticist and eclectic. The Gothic revival abroad had pretty well run its course of a century and a half before his advent. Augustus Welby Pugin, whom he admired, and whom he resembled in facility, preceded him by two generations. Even in America powerful Gothic work had been done a half century earlier by John Haviland, Richard Upjohn, and Renwick. Supremely impressionable, Goodhue veered, in his middle years, with every wind that blew, from Spain, from Byzantium, from Persia. His turn to the logic of function, his attempt to express modern material, came a generation after that of Louis H. Sullivan, Frank Lloyd Wright, and Otto Wagner, themselves not so much pioneers as consummators of a half century of speculation and experiment. Goodhue's work must be regarded as representing not a transition but a tardy compromise. Whether the future held for him a new unity, a more vitally creative modernity, we cannot know. He was cut off in the prime of his energies, at fifty-five, by his death on Apr. 23, 1924.

[Goodhue's early buildings are discussed by Montgomery Schuyler in "The Works of Cram, Goodhue and Ferguson, 1892–1910," *Architectural Record,* Jan. 1911. His drawings are reproduced in two folios: *A Book of Architectural and Decorative Drawings by Bertram Grosvenor Goodhue* (1914), which includes reprintings of his travel fantasies, and an important paper by H. Ingalls Kimball on his work on book design; and *Bertram Grosvenor Goodhue, Architect and Master of Many Arts* (1925), ed. by C. H. Whitaker, containing notices and photographs of buildings. See also *The Work of Cram and Ferguson, Architects, Including Work by Cram, Goodhue and Ferguson* (1929); *Jour. of the Am. Inst. of Architects,* May, June, Aug., Sept. 1924; *Architectural Record,* May 1924; and the *N. Y. Times,* Apr. 24, 26, 1924, and June 29, 1930. Goodhue contributed as an expert to Sylvester Baxter's *Spanish-Colonial Architecture in Mexico* (2 eds., 10 and 12 vols., 1901), for which the plans were drawn by him.] F.K.

GOODHUE, JAMES MADISON (Mar. 31, 1810–Aug. 27, 1852), lawyer, newspaper editor, was born at Hebron, N. H., the son of Stephen and Betsey (Page) Goodhue. He was graduated from Amherst College in 1833. After teaching, reading law, and farming in New York and Illinois, he went to Platteville, Wis., where he married Henrietta Kneeland, Dec. 22, 1843. The young couple settled in Lancaster, Wis., where Goodhue practised law and wrote a novel of life in the mining regions, *Struck a Lead,* which was published in the *Galena Gazette* and later in book form (1883). Finding his true sphere in journalism, he bought the local paper, the *Wisconsin Herald,* in 1845, and edited it until April 1849. Meanwhile he was watching developments in Minnesota. As soon as he learned that the new territory was to be established, which would mean the possibility of obtaining public printing, he loaded a printing-press on a steamboat and went up the Mississippi to St. Paul, the designated capital. On Apr. 28, 1849, before the territorial officers arrived, he issued the first newspaper printed in Minnesota. It was called, not the *Epistle of St. Paul,* as he had at first planned, but the *Minnesota Pioneer.*

Avoiding party politics, Goodhue used his keen wit and real literary talent to promote immigration to Minnesota. His paper had wide circulation and effectively advertised the territory. He described the regions adjacent to St. Paul, extolled the products of Minnesota soil, praised the climate, answered numerous questions from prospective settlers, and urged the opening of Indian lands to settlement. In the frontier community he was outstanding, a broad and bulky figure moving about the settlement, delivering his papers himself and in the process gathering news for the next issue, enlivening dull minds, and delighting keen ones with his spontaneous and never-ending humor. His critical faculties were sharp, and he made effective use of satire in attacking conditions or individuals that he did not like. He called attention to the "free school in St. Paul"—the waterfront and docks where children ran wild; he criticised the sprawling formlessness of the growing city; he condemned speculation in town-lots; and in 1851 he wrote so vitriolic an editorial against absentee office-holders as to involve himself in a knifing and shooting affray with the brother of one of the office-holders.

In 1851, with the making of the Sioux treaties which opened to settlement the lands west of the Mississippi, Goodhue's dreams for the expansion of the new territory began to come true. He accompanied the commissioners on their trip up the Minnesota River to Traverse des Sioux, where the first treaty was negotiated, and his daily news-letters, published in the *Pioneer* and twice reprinted elsewhere, spread before the reader a colorful panorama of frontier life and Indian character, shot through with shrewd and illuminating comment. Unfortunately he did not live to see that phenomenal expansion which by 1858 had made a new state from the territory he had first known as a fringe of white settlement east of the Mississippi, but his vigor and charm had so impressed themselves on Minnesota citizens during his three short years in the territory, that the legislature of 1853 perpetuated his memory in the name of Goodhue County.

[Files of Goodhue's papers are in the libraries of the Wisconsin and Minnesota historical societies. See also E. D. Neill, "Obituary of Jas. M. Goodhue," *Minn. Hist. Soc. Colls.,* I (1872), pp. 197–204; J. H. Stevens, "Recollections of Jas. M. Goodhue," *Ibid.,* VI (1894), pp. 492–501; J. F. Williams, "A Hist. of the city of St. Paul, and of the County of Ramsey, Minn.," *Ibid.,* vol. IV (1876); Jonathan Goodhue, *Hist. and Geneal. of the Goodhue Family* (1891), pp. 62, 63, 119, 120.] S. J. B.

GOODLOE, DANIEL REAVES (May 28, 1814–Jan. 18, 1902), Abolitionist, author, was born in Louisburg, N. C., the son of Dr. Kemp Strother and Mary Reaves (Jones) Goodloe. He attended a local academy for some years and was then apprenticed to a printer in Oxford, N. C. True to the adage, he never thereafter got far away from printer's ink, beginning his journalistic career as soon as he reached his majority by publishing the *Examiner* in Oxford. It soon failed and he went to Tennessee and attended a school in Mount Pleasant. In 1836 he volunteered for service against the Creek Indians in Alabama. They soon made peace and his company then volunteered for the Seminole War and served in Florida. The pension Goodloe later received for this service supported him in his old age. Returning to North Carolina, he studied law under Robert B. Gilliam and was admitted to the bar but was unsuccessful in practise. He was offered a nomination to the legislature but declined because he was out of harmony with the people of the state on the subject of slavery, and finally in 1844 drifted to Washington where Senator Willie P. Mangum secured for him a position with the *Whig Standard,* of which he shortly became editor. That soon failed, and he edited the *Georgetown Advocate* and later the *Christian Statesman* until 1852 when he was made assistant editor of the *National Era,* an anti-slavery paper established in 1847 to advocate the principles of the Liberty party. When Gamaliel Bailey, the founder and editor, died, Goodloe succeeded him and held the position until the outbreak of the war caused the collapse of the paper. Into its columns he brought writers of distinction, such as Grace Greenwood, Mary Mapes Dodge, Harriet Beecher Stowe, and Mrs. Southworth.

While he was still an apprentice, his reading in the *Richmond Whig* and *Richmond Examiner,* both advocates of emancipation in Virginia, of the debates on the subject, had converted him to anti-slavery views; and he quickly became a full-fledged Abolitionist. In 1844 he published in the *New-York American* an anti-slavery article, the first of a considerable number which came from his pen. After the suspension of the *National Era* he was Washington correspondent for the *New York Times* until 1862, when President Lincoln appointed him chairman of the commission to carry out the compensation provision of the act emancipating slaves in the District of Columbia. From the close of 1863 he did editorial work on the *Washington Chronicle,* and later in 1865 President Johnson appointed him United States marshal for North Carolina. He supported Johnson's policy of restoration until 1866 when he became convinced that it was not sufficiently drastic. He accordingly signed the call for the Southern Loyalist convention, and, advocating congressional reconstruction, joined in the organization of the Republican party in the state in 1867. He was violently opposed, however, to the proscriptive tendencies of the Carpet-baggers and of certain native leaders, such as Holden, whom he disliked and distrusted, and he soon parted company with them. In 1868 he bitterly opposed the ratification of the "Carpet-bag" constitution and was an independent candidate for governor against Holden. Later he went again to Washington where he was a free-lance writer, but finally returned to Louisburg, N. C. He suffered a stroke of apoplexy in 1900 but survived it two years. He died in Warrenton, N. C., and is buried there.

Goodloe's most important writings include the *New-York American* article of 1844, later published as a pamphlet entitled, *Inquiry into the Causes which have Retarded the Accumulation of Wealth . . . in the Southern States* (1846); *The South and the North: Being a Reply to a Lecture . . . by Ellwood Fisher* (1849); *Is it Expedient to Introduce Slavery into Kansas?* (1855); *The Southern Platform* (1858); *Federalism Unmasked* (1860); *Emancipation and the War* (1861); "Resources and Industrial Condition of the Southern States" in *Report of the Commissioner of Agriculture, 1865* (1866); *Letter of Daniel R. Goodloe to Hon. Charles Sumner on the Situation of Affairs in North Carolina* (1868); *The Marshalship in North Carolina* (1869); *The Birth of the Republic* (1889); and *A History of the Demonetization of Silver* (1890). He wrote (Bassett, *post,* p. 56) the history of Reconstruction in North Carolina which appeared without credit in Samuel S. ("Sunset") Cox's *Three Decades of Federal Legislation* (1885). During 1894–95 he wrote a series of articles on the same subject for the Raleigh *News and Observer.* A close friend of Greeley and Raymond, he wrote constantly for the *New York Tribune* and the *New York Times.* Goodloe was attractive and genial, generous to a fault, unswervingly courageous, charitable, and tender-hearted. He had a genius for friendship and held the affection and confidence even of political enemies.

[J. S. Bassett, "Anti-Slavery Leaders of N. C.," *Johns Hopkins Univ. Studies in Hist. and Pol. Sci.,* ser. XVI, no. 6 (1898); S. B. Weeks in *Southern Hist. Asso. Pubs.,* vol. II (1898); *News and Observer* (Raleigh, N. C.), Jan. 26, 1902.]

J. G. deR. H.

GOODLOE, WILLIAM CASSIUS (June 27, 1841–Nov. 10, 1889), Kentucky politician, the son of David Short Goodloe and his wife Sallie Ann Lewis Clay Smith, was born at "Castle Union" in Madison County, Ky., the country residence of his grandfather, Col. John Speed Smith. He came of prominent Kentucky and Virginia ancestry; his grandfather was a congressman and his great-grandfather, Green Clay, a general in the War of 1812. Some four years after William's birth his father established himself as a merchant in Lexington, Ky.; he also served at various times as major-general of the Kentucky militia, United States revenue agent, supervisor of internal revenue, and United States pension agent. William, after a period in the private schools at Lexington, entered Transylvania University and was about to graduate when he withdrew, in May 1861, to become private secretary to his great-uncle Cassius M. Clay [*q.v.*], recently appointed minister to Russia. In the summer of 1862 he returned to the United States and entered the Union army. His military career was "neither extensive nor arduous." He was given a commission as captain and served for a time on the staff of his kinsman, Green Clay Smith, who was in command of the post at Lebanon, Ky.; later, he served on the staff of Gen. Nelson. He never rose above the rank of captain, his title of "Colonel" being the honorary title quite commonly bestowed upon Kentuckians with and without military experience. In January 1864 he withdrew from the army, and in the same year, after a brief study of law, was admitted to practise at Lexington. On June 8, 1865, he was married to Mary E. Mann of Mannville, R. I., who bore him six children.

Goodloe helped organize the Republican party in Kentucky, and in 1867 began the publication at Lexington of the *Kentucky Statesman,* a Republican newspaper. Defeated in this year as a candidate for the state House of Representatives, he ran again in 1871 and was elected, although by a very doubtful majority. In 1873 he was elected to the state Senate. After the close of the readjustment era in Kentucky and the resumption of Democratic control of state politics, Goodloe did not again hold an elective office. Defeated in 1875 as a candidate for attorney-general and again the following year as a candidate for United States senator, he was appointed in 1878 minister to Belgium, where he remained for two years. Resigning in 1880, he returned to Kentucky and devoted the remainder of his life to the upbuilding of the Republican party in the state. He was an effective public speaker and his oratorical efforts in the various campaigns undoubtedly contributed to the increase of the Republican vote. Like his great-uncle, Cassius M. Clay, whom he resembled in many ways and whose career he seems to have consciously imitated, Goodloe was a man of bitter tongue, of arrogant disposition, and of unfailing courage. He made many enemies even in his own party, and his career was a stormy one, marked by bitter altercation and occasional violence. One of these personal disputes resulted in his death. In July 1889 he was appointed a collector of internal revenue and in November of the same year was killed in the post office at Lexington in one of the most sensational fights in the history of Kentucky. His opponent, Armistead M. Swope, who also was killed in the fight, was Goodloe's personal and political enemy and his rival for the leadership of the Republican party in the state.

[H. Levin, *The Lawyers and Lawmakers of Ky.* (1897); Wm. H. Perrin, *Hist. of Fayette County, Ky.* (1882), pp. 606–12; *Courier-Journal* (Louisville, Ky.), Nov. 10, 1889; L. F. Johnson, *Famous Ky. Tragedies and Trials* (1916); *Biog. Encyc. of Ky.* (1878); *Louisville Commercial,* Nov. 9, 10, 11, 1889.] R. S. C.

GOODMAN, CHARLES (1796–Feb. 11, 1835), stipple-engraver, lawyer, was born in Philadelphia, Pa., the son of John and Mary (Roach) Goodman. His father, a whitesmith, became a member of the Pennsylvania legislature and later prothonotary of the district court of Philadelphia. Charles Goodman's career as an engraver was brief but distinguished. In his youth he was placed with David Edwin [*q.v.*], under whom he became an accomplished stipple-engraver. One of his early works, a portrait of Charles Stewart, appeared in the *Analectic Magazine* for December 1815. When not quite of age he formed a partnership with Robert Piggot [*q.v.*], and although most of the plates produced by the pair were inscribed "C. Goodman & R. Piggot," making it difficult to differentiate their work, some were inscribed by Goodman alone. Among the earliest works engraved by the partners were the portraits of Peyton Randolph, after Peale, and Samuel Adams, after Copley, which appeared in *Delaplaine's Repository of the Lives and Portraits of Distinguished American Characters* (2 vols., 1815). While they concerned themselves mainly with small plates, a few larger engravings are known to have been made by them, among them a folio print of President Monroe, published Dec. 15, 1817. Their other works included portraits of the Rev. G. H. E. Muhlenberg, after Peale; Rev. Joseph Pilmore, after Neagle; Dr. N. Chapman, after Sully; a plate after J. L. Krimmel's picture "Departure for Boarding School" (*Analectic Magazine,* November 1820); and another, after Alexander Rider, entitled "Kidnapping." Many of their plates appeared in the *Port Folio* as well as the *Analectic.*

In 1819 the partners, both still young, decided to change their professions. Goodman began the study of law, and his friend, Piggot, to prepare for the ministry. Both students continued to engrave occasionally. Goodman was admitted to the bar on May 14, 1822, and on Dec. 14, 1824, he was married to Margaret Thatcher, in St. John's Evangelical Lutheran Church, Philadelphia, which his father was mainly responsible for founding. As an engraver, he reflected considerable credit upon his preceptor, Edwin. His work displayed a great deal of the delicacy and skill observable in Edwin's productions, and he was adventurous enough to aspire to engrave something more than mere heads. A portrait of Benjamin Franklin, in the *Analectic,* June 1818, is an excellent example of his work, and shows him to have been a worthy successor of Edwin. He was represented in the exhibition of "one hundred notable American engravers," held in the New York Public Library in 1928, by two examples, one of which was his portrait of John Wesley, described by Fielding. After he began the practise of law, he took an active interest in movements for the improvement of his native city, his interest arising from the fact that his father was a popular politician, and prominently identified with similar works. He died, at a relatively early age, in Philadelphia.

[D. McN. Stauffer, *Am. Engravers* (1907), pp. 108–09, and for a check list of plates, pt. II, pp. 189–96; W. S. Baker, *Am. Engravers and their Works* (1875), pp. 72–73, 136–37; J. T. Scharf and Thompson Westcott, *Hist. of Phila.* (1884), vols. I and II; Mantle Fielding, *Am. Engravers* (1917), with check list supplementary to Stauffer; J. H. Martin, *Martin's Bench and Bar of Phila.* (1883). The date of Goodman's death was taken from *Poulson's Daily Advertiser,* Feb. 12, 1835; facts regarding his marriage were gleaned from the manuscript records of St. John's Lutheran Church, Phila., in the Pa. Hist. Soc. Henry Simpson, *The Lives of Eminent Philadelphians* (1859), contains an account of his father.] J. J.

GOODMAN, KENNETH SAWYER (Sept. 19, 1883–Nov. 29, 1918), playwright, was born at Chicago, Ill., the son of William Owen and Erna (Sawyer) Goodman, and grandson of Senator Philetus Sawyer of Wisconsin. He was educated in the public schools of Chicago, at the Hill School, where he was associated in dramatic activities with Edward Sheldon, and at Prince ton, where he graduated with the class of 1906. At Princeton he was a leader in the organization of the Senior Council, a winner of the Baird Poetry Prize, on the editorial board of the *Nassau Literary Magazine,* and editor of the *Tiger.* On leaving Princeton he returned to Chicago and managed the local interests of the Sawyer-Goodman lumber company. At the same time he carried on his literary work, which absorbed more and more of his time, turning definitely to the dramatic field with a special concentration on the form of the one-act play. The association of his father with the Art Institute led Kenneth Goodman into the dramatic activities there. He played in some of the productions of the Donald Robertson Players, the forerunners of the civic-drama movement in Chicago, and wrote his first plays, in collaboration with Thomas Wood Stevens, for the annual festival productions of the Institute. These were published in 1914 as *Masques of East and West* following a number of local printings, beginning in 1911, of dramatic works under the imprint of the Stage Guild, an organization in which Goodman was the leading spirit.

In 1912 he was active in the organization of the Chicago Theatre Society, and wrote for its production a translation of Paul Ernest Hervieu's *La Course du Flambeau.* His first volume of original plays, *Quick Curtains,* was published in 1915. This included "The Game of Chess," which had been very successfully produced by B. Iden Payne in his Chicago season of 1912–13, with Walter Hampden and Whitford Kane in the major parts, and his first play, "Dust of the Road," many times performed by various community-theatre organizations. All these plays were written for immediate production, and were at once in demand by various little theatres both in England and America. One of the harlequinades, "A Man Can Only Do His Best," was given at the Gaiety Theatre, Manchester, in 1914; and one of the plays written with Ben Hecht, "The Hero of Santa Maria," was among the early successes of the Washington Square Players in New York. This volume was followed by *More Quick Curtains* in 1920. In 1925, seven years after Goodman's death, a volume of plays written in collaboration with Ben Hecht was published under the title, *The Wonder Hat.* At the outbreak of the war, Goodman took an active interest in the navy-recruiting problem, was commissioned first lieutenant, and became senior aide to Commander William Moffett, at Great Lakes Station. While in this service he contracted pneumonia and died after a brief illness. He married Marjorie Robbins on June 12, 1912, and left two children. His interest in the drama, and in the artistic progress of Chicago, prompted his parents to give to the Art Institute the splendid Kenneth Sawyer Goodman Memorial Theatre, which was opened to the public in 1925.

[The prefaces to *Masques of East and West* (1914), *Quick Curtains* (2nd ed., 1923), and *More Quick Curtains* (1923) contain comments on Goodman by Percy MacKaye, Thos. Wood Stevens, and B. Iden Payne, respectively. See also *Fifth Year Record, Class of 1906, Princeton Univ.* (1912); *Princeton Alumni Weekly,* Dec. 18, 1918; and the *Chicago Tribune,* Nov. 30, 1918. Information as to certain facts was supplied by members of Goodman's family.] T. W. S.

GOODNIGHT, CHARLES (Mar. 5, 1836–Dec. 12, 1929), cattleman, came of a line of pioneers. Early in the eighteenth century his great-grandfather, Michael Goodnight, emigrated from Germany to Rockbridge County, Va. His son, Isaac, was born in Kentucky. Among Isaac's prodigious family of twenty-one children was one named Charles, who, in 1825, married Charlotte Collier, and soon thereafter emigrated to Macoupin County, Ill., where their son, the future cattleman, was born. While the second Charles was still a child, his father died. His mother remarried, and in 1846 the family moved to Texas, settling upon the Milam County frontier, where Charles was thrown into contact with border Indians. He entered the cattle business in 1856, at the age of twenty, and in 1857 moved to Palo Pinto County, on the northwest Texas frontier. There he joined companies of independent rangers, or minute men, as scout and guide against the Indians. He was under Capt. J. J. Cureton at the Pease River fight in 1860. With the outbreak of the Civil War he joined the Frontier Regiment of Texas Rangers; he participated in many Indian fights, and became a noted guide. It is doubtful if any other Texas frontiersman so thoroughly mastered the technique of open-country scouting.

In 1866 he located, on the Pecos River, the first Texas cattle ranch in southern New Mexico. Two years later he established another ranch on the Apishapa, in Colorado, and in 1870 located a permanent range on the Arkansas, four miles above Pueblo. Meantime, with Oliver Loving, he had laid out the Goodnight Cattle Trail from Belknap, Tex., to Fort Sumner, N. Mex. (1866), and blazed an extension into Wyoming known as the Goodnight-Loving Trail. In 1875 he laid off the New Goodnight Trail from Alamogordo Creek, N. Mex., to Granada, Colo. That year, the reverses of the late panic and the fact that the ranges were over-stocked prompted him to trail back to Texas. With a herd of 1600 cattle he crossed 300 miles of wilderness and in 1876 settled in the Palo Duro Canyon in the

Texas Panhandle, 250 miles from a railroad. The following year he blazed his last cattle trail, from the JA Ranch in the Panhandle to Dodge City, Kan.

In this year, 1877, he formed a partnership with John George Adair, of Rathdair, Ireland, and began the development of the great JA Ranch, which soon embraced nearly a million acres of land and almost a hundred thousand head of cattle. On that range Goodnight took a herd of longhorned cattle, and, bringing in Shorthorn and Hereford stock for breeding, developed it in the course of eleven years into one of America's finest beef herds. In the late seventies he roped three buffalo calves from which he raised a large herd, thereby preserving the buffalo of the southern plains. He crossed the buffalo with Polled Angus cattle, and produced the first herd of cattalo—a new breed of stock. Because of his extensive experiments as a breeder, he was sometimes referred to as the "Burbank of the range." Goodnight actively fought outlaws for nearly forty years; he treated with the Comanche tribe under Quanah [*q.v.*], and he made friends with the Kiowas and the Pueblos of Taos. In 1880 he conceived the first Panhandle stockmen's association, to fight organized lawlessness. During the eighties this organization paid many of the local officials, employed its own counsel, prosecuted cow thieves and outlaws, and suppressed attempts at vigilante methods. It introduced pure-bred cattle, systematized range work, and policed the trails, practically revolutionizing the Panhandle cattle country. Goodnight dominated its policies and battles throughout its existence. He joined with other cow men in establishing and supporting the first frontier schools and later, at the town of Goodnight, founded one of the pioneer educational institutions of west Texas, the Goodnight College, which in 1917 became a public high school.

In 1871 he had married Mary Ann Dyer. After her death in 1926, he married, Mar. 5, 1927, at the age of ninety-one, Corinne Goodnight of Butte, Mont., who, although her name was the same, was not related to him. A child of this marriage, his only child, did not survive. Goodnight died at ninety-three, generally recognized as the most representative cowman that the West has known. Until the last day of his life he was vigorous and fiery in mental faculty. He died holding the truth to be above orthodox creeds; hating hypocrisy, liars, and cow thieves. He was massive of frame, quick of movement, and powerful of physique. His tremendous head, set forward on his broad shoulders, was crowned with a great shock of hair. From beneath shaggy brows his eyes flashed and burned into every man he faced. His strong frame sloped to the hips, and his legs bowed out in great curves to conform to the lines of a cow horse. He was awkward upon the ground, but at supreme ease in the saddle. Like most frontiersmen, he had no time to write, but toward the end of his life he dictated his reminiscences.

[The most important sources are the collections of MSS. in the files of J. Evetts Haley and the Panhandle-Plains Hist. Soc., Canyon, Texas, where are to be found two volumes of "Recollections of C. Goodnight"; "Correspondence"; and Haley's MS. "Life of Charles Goodnight." Supplementary data are contained in James Cox, *Hist. and Biog. Record of the Cattle Industry and the Cattlemen of Texas* (1895); J. G. McCoy, *Hist. Sketches of the Cattle Trade of the West and Southwest* (1874), pp. 380–86; J. M. Hunter, *The Trail Drivers of Texas* (ed. of 1925); J. E. Haley, "Goodnight's Indian Recollections" in *Panhandle-Plains Hist. Rev.*, 1928; personal reminiscences in *Pioneer Days in the Southwest* (1909); H. T. Burton, *A Hist. of the JA Ranch* (1928), with bibliography, also pub. in *Southwestern Hist. Quart.*, Oct. 1927–July 1928; J. F. Dobie, "Charles Goodnight—Trail-Blazer" in *Country Gentleman*, Mar. 1927; J. W. Freeman, *Prose and Poetry of the Livestock Industry of the U. S.*, I (1905), 58–65; *Kansas City Star*, Mar. 27, 1927; obituaries in *Tucson Daily Citizen*, Dec. 12, 1929, and *Dallas Morning News*, *Houston Post-Dispatch*, *San Antonio Express*, all of Dec. 13, 1929.]

J. E. H.

GOODNOW, ISAAC TICHENOR (Jan. 17, 1814–Mar. 20, 1894), educator, Kansas pioneer, was born in Whitingham, Vt., the son of William and Sybil (Arms) Goodnow. He attended the local schools and at the age of fourteen became a merchant's clerk. At twenty he entered the Wesleyan Academy, Wilbraham, Mass., for four years of study, and then (1838) became professor of natural sciences at the Academy. On Aug. 28, 1838, he was married to Ellen D. Denison. In 1848 he accepted a position as professor of natural sciences at the Providence Conference Seminary and moved from Wilbraham to East Greenwich, R. I. Since 1840, when he had voted for James G. Birney, he had been outspoken in his opposition to the extension of slavery, and in 1854 he became vitally interested in the project of the New England Emigrant Aid Company to send Free-Soil colonists to Kansas. Resigning his professorship, he devoted himself for several months to raising a company of some 200 emigrants, who left Boston in March 1855 and founded the town of Manhattan, Kan. Goodnow was a member of the committee which selected the townsite. He was one of the representatives of Manhattan in the Free-State convention held at Lawrence in August 1855, and in April 1858 was a member of the convention which drew up the Leavenworth Constitution. In 1857 he had returned to the East to solicit funds for the establishment of a Methodist church in Manhattan, and secured $4,000. Encouraged by this success, he took a leading part, together with his brother-in-law, Joseph Denison, and Washington Marlatt, in the founding of Bluemont Central College. In the interest of this institution Goodnow again visited the East, and raised $15,000 in cash and a library of some two thousand miscellaneous volumes. The college was chartered by the territorial legislature in 1858 and the cornerstone laid at Manhattan in 1859. Goodnow was elected to the first state legislature, in November 1861, and secured the passage of a bill locating the state university at Manhattan. The bill was vetoed by Gov. Charles Robinson, however, and the university established at Lawrence, but a year later, when the Morrill Act made possible the establishment of a state agricultural college, the offer by the trustees of Bluemont Central College of their building, land, and equipment as the nucleus for such a school, was accepted, and in September 1863 the Kansas State Agricultural College was opened at Manhattan. In 1862 and again in 1864 Goodnow was elected state superintendent of public instruction, in which capacity he was *ex officio* a regent of the Agricultural College. In 1866 he was made agent to dispose of some 82,000 acres of land belonging to the college, and before 1873, when he relinquished the office, had sold about 42,000 acres. He was subsequently appointed land commissioner of the Missouri, Kansas & Texas Railway, which office he held for seven years. During that time he sold land amounting to more than $1,500,000. The last ten or twelve years of his life he spent quietly at his home near Manhattan, where he died.

[J. D. Waters, *Columbian Hist. of the Kan. State Agric. Coll.* (1893); *Industrialist* (pub. by the State Agric. Coll.), Mar. 24, 1894; *Portr. and Biog. Album of Washington, Clay, and Riley Counties, Kan.* (1890); *Trans. Kan. State Hist. Soc.*, vols. IV (1890), V (1896), 141–42; W. E. Connelley, *A Standard Hist. of Kansas and Kansans,* IV (1918), 1853–54; D. L. Wilder, *Annals of Kan.* (1876); J. D. Baldwin and Wm. Clift, *A Record of the Descendants of Capt. George Denison* (1881); E. W. Arms, *A Geneal. Record of the Arms Family* (1877); David Sherman, *Hist. of the Wesleyan Acad. at Wilbraham, Mass.* (1893); obituaries in *Central Christian Advocate*, Apr. 11, 1894, *Zion's Herald,* Apr. 4, 1894.]
M. S.

GOODRICH, ALFRED JOHN (May 8, 1847–Apr. 25, 1920), musical theorist, teacher, writer, was born at Chilo, Ohio, the son of Luther Alfred Goodrich, a teacher of piano and voice, and Dolly (Healy) Goodrich. In his early childhood his family removed to California and there he obtained his general education in the public schools of Sacramento and San Francisco. He began the study of music with his father, who taught him for one year, after which he was entirely self-taught. He began to compose in both large and small forms early in his career. It was his ambition to become a concert pianist, but through excessive practising he injured a finger, which probably caused him to give up his pianistic aspirations and to devote himself to teaching piano and voice. Gradually he developed a larger and keener interest in the teaching of various aspects of the theory of music. This finally became his main work and induced him to write a series of books which set forth his views on harmony and related subjects.

In 1866, at the age of nineteen, Goodrich went to New York and taught theory of music at the Grand Conservatory. Eight years later he was married to one of his earliest students, Florence Ada Backus, who was a gifted musician, an excellent theorist, and later a composer of music for children. In 1876 he went to the Fort Wayne (Ind.) Conservatory, after which, for two years, he was musical director of Martha Washington College at Abingdon, Va. Following this connection he taught in Chicago for about ten years, and then he was called to the Beethoven Conservatory of St. Louis as vocal director. In 1910 he went to Paris, where, with the exception of a trip around the world during the period of the Great War, he remained until his death. There is no record that he ever taught there. Among his compositions, some of which were youthful works, are two string quartets; a trio, performed both in New York and Chicago; a sonata; two concert overtures; a cantata; a well-written suite for piano; a volume of songs; a hymn for soprano, invisible chorus, and orchestra; and a number of piano compositions. When he heard a performance of Tschaikowsky's Fifth Symphony, it caused him to throw a bundle of his early compositions into the fire. His wife, however, succeeded in rescuing the piano suite from the flames.

Goodrich was a man of lofty ideals, precise in manner and speech, and rather distinguished in appearance. He was an earnest and successful teacher, especially of harmony, and was one of the first to discard the figured-bass system and to teach the importance of appealing to the ear in harmony study. As a keen analyst of the works of the great masters, he was much freer in his statement of rules for the student's guidance in harmonic procedure than were the text-books of his period. As he himself was largely self-taught, his text-books were intended for use either with or without a teacher. His published works include: *Music as a Language* (1881); *The Art of Song* (1888); *Complete Musical Analysis* (1889); *Goodrich's Analytical Harmony* (1893); *Theory of Interpretation*

(1899); and *A Guide to Practical Musicianship* (1900), republished in 1906 as a *Guide to Memorizing Music.* A work on "Synthetic Counterpoint" was still unpublished in 1929. He also contributed numerous articles on musical subjects to magazines and newspapers.

[*Who's Who in America,* 1908–09, 1910–11; Rupert Hughes and Arthur Elson, *Am. Composers* (rev. ed., 1914); *Musical America,* May 29, 1920; information as to certain facts from Goodrich's sister-in-law, Mrs. Marian A. Young, Providence, R. I.] F. L. G. C.

GOODRICH, BENJAMIN FRANKLIN (Nov. 4, 1841–Aug. 3, 1888), physician, industrialist, was born in Ripley, N. Y., the ninth child of Anson and Susan (Dinsmore) Goodrich and sixth in descent from the colonist William Goodrich, who died in Wethersfield, Conn., in 1676. He attended the typical academies of the time in the towns of Westfield and Fredonia, near his birthplace, and also in Austinburg, Ohio. On the completion of this elementary schooling, at the age of seventeen he began the study of medicine with John Spencer, a practising physician of Westfield. A year later he entered the Cleveland Medical College (the medical department of Western Reserve College), where he graduated in February 1861. Three months later he was awarded a state certificate of assistant-surgeon. On Oct. 29, 1861, he enlisted as a private in Company I, 9th New York Cavalry and on Nov. 5 was promoted to hospital steward. On May 20, 1862, he was discharged to accept an appointment as contract surgeon with the Army of the Potomac. He was assigned to a battalion of engineers and attached to headquarters, where he served until November 1862, when he entered the University of Pennsylvania to take a course of lectures in surgery. He was commissioned assistant surgeon, 9th New York Cavalry, in July 1863, and remained in the army until the fall of 1864, when he resigned. He then established himself as a practising physician in Jamestown, N. Y., but a little over a year later gave up his profession, never to resume it, and with a lawyer friend as a partner, went into the real-estate business in New York City. In 1867, through one of their transactions, the partners came into control of the Hudson River Rubber Company at Hastings-on-the-Hudson, which had been engaged in the manufacture of rubber goods under a licensed agreement with Charles Goodyear [*q.v.*]. Neither Goodrich nor his partner, J. P. Morris, knew anything about rubber, but in the hope of securing some financial benefit from their acquisition, they bought out the stockholders with $5,000 of Morris's money and organized a new company. Goodrich, as president, took complete charge of the business. During 1867 and part of 1868 he operated the plant and endeavored to sell its product, learning as he went along and becoming a stanch believer in the future of rubber. Competition, however, was extremely keen; handicapped by worn-out mechanical equipment, his factory could not turn out a satisfactory product, and the partners were forced to abandon it. Goodrich, however, had by no means lost his interest and soon prevailed upon Morris to buy another small rubber factory, offered for sale in 1868 at Melrose, N. Y. This venture, even with $10,000 invested in it by Morris, was also unsuccessful. By 1869 the two partners were losing money. In looking about for a suitable location for a plant, farther away from their New England competitors, Goodrich came upon an advertisement by the Board of Trade of Akron, Ohio, inviting the establishment of manufactories in that town. A visit to Akron convinced him of the desirability of transferring his rubber business to that place, and after an inspection of his Melrose plant by the president of the Akron Board of Trade, during which Goodrich called into play all of the selling strategy at his command, he was not only permitted to settle in Akron but was advanced money with which to move his equipment from Melrose and erect his factory. On Dec. 31, 1870, a new firm, Goodrich, Tew & Company was formed, three of the four members being related to Goodrich by marriage. A two-story building was completed by the spring of 1871 and the first manufactured products were sold in May of that year. These consisted largely of fire hose, billiard cushions, and belting. During the next ten years Goodrich found it extremely difficult to keep his company alive. Lack of working capital and confidence of the local people in his undertaking prevented his acquiring either an adequate supply of raw materials or a proper working force. The company was reorganized in 1874 as Goodrich & Company and new members added to the firm, but with only temporary success. When collapse seemed inevitable, about 1879, Goodrich, still enthusiastic, again called upon his selling strategy and from George W. Crouse secured, for the first time, adequate financial backing. The B. F. Goodrich Company was thereupon incorporated, May 10, 1880, with Goodrich as president, and from that time forward success crowned his efforts. In 1881 he took over the duties of manager in addition to those of president, but the increased work proved too great a strain on his health and he died seven years later at Manitou Springs, Colo. He was married on Nov. 4, 1869, to Mary

Marvin of Jamestown, N. Y., who with two sons and a daughter survived him.

[L. W. Case, *The Goodrich Family in America* (1889); *The Growth of an Ideal* (1918), pub. by the B. F. Goodrich Company; *India Rubber Rev.*, Apr. 1925; F. Phisterer, *N. Y. in the War of the Rebellion* (3rd ed., 1909); S. A. Lane, *Fifty Years and Over of Akron and Summit County* (1892); *Mil. Order of the Loyal Legion of the U. S. Commandery of Ohio, Circular No. 18, Ser. of 1888* (1888); *Akron Daily Beacon*, Aug. 4, 1888.] C. W. M.

GOODRICH, CHARLES AUGUSTUS (Aug. 19, 1790–June 4, 1862), Congregational clergyman, author, was born in Ridgefield, Conn., the fourth of the ten children of the Rev. Samuel and Elizabeth (Ely) Goodrich and a grandson of the Rev. Elizur Goodrich [*q.v.*]. The Goodriches, a family of ministers, were of English origin and had been settled in Hartford County for five generations. As Charles showed a predilection for the ministry, he received conscientious instruction from his father and was sent, despite the strain on the family resources, to his father's college, Yale. Upon his graduation in 1812 he read theology under the Rev. Andrew Yates [*q.v.*] in East Hartford and after preaching for some months at Saratoga Springs, N. Y., was settled July 15, 1816, as a colleague of the Rev. Samuel Austin [*q.v.*] in the First Congregational Church of Worcester, Mass. He was ordained Oct. 9, 1816, his father delivering the sermon. On June 24, 1818, he married Sarah, daughter of the Rev. Benoni Upson, by whom he had seven children. A protest against Goodrich, begun by a busybody outside the congregation, grew *forte* and *accelerando* into the most violent quarrel in the church history of Worcester. The objection to him seems to have had both a doctrinal and a political basis. Although a stanch conservative by all ordinary standards, Goodrich was not an extreme Calvinist of the Hopkinsian stamp, and he was inclined also to credit Thomas Jefferson with a moderate amount of virtue. These aberrations nearly wrought his undoing. Though an ecclesiastical council cleared him of all charges brought against him, the long, arduous conflict wore down his never robust health; he asked for his dismissal and received it Nov. 4, 1820. He returned to his native county and made his home in Berlin for the next twenty-eight years. Thereafter, until his death, he lived in Hartford. Though he preached and even engaged in politics —he was a state senator in 1838—his chief occupation was the writing of children's books and informational works of various kinds. For such tasks he had some of the aptitude of his brother, Samuel Griswold Goodrich [*q.v.*], for whom he did some work. He was, in fact, a moon to Peter Parley's sun. The most popular of all his numerous books was the *History of the United States of America* (1822) which, constantly revised and brought down to date, went through more than 150 editions. *A Child's History of the United States* (improved from the 21st ed., 1846) was another favorite. His *Lives of the Signers of the Declaration of Independence* (1829; 8th ed., 1840) was translated into German as *Lebensbeschreibungen sämmtlicher Unterzeichner der Unabhängigkeits-Erklärung* (Sumneytaun [*sic*], Pa., 1842) by Enos Benner, who also published a revised edition in 1858. Other characteristic volumes are *Cabinet of Curiosities, Natural, Artificial, and Historical* (2 vols., 1822); *Pictorial and Descriptive View of All Religions* (1829); *Outlines of Modern Geography on a New Plan* (1827); *Stories on the History of Connecticut* (1829); *The Universal Traveller* (1837); and *The Family Tourist* (1848). No bibliographer has compiled a list of all his books and their numerous editions.

[G. L. Rockwell, *Hist. of Ridgefield, Conn.* (1927), p. 503; L. W. Case, *The Goodrich Family in America* (1889); M. S. Beach and others, *Ely Ancestry* (privately printed, 1902); *Obit. Record Grads. Yale Coll.*, 1862; F. B. Dexter, *Biog. Sketches Grads. Yale Coll.*, vol. VI (1912); Samuel Goodrich, *The Duty of a Gospel Minister* (2nd ed., Worcester, 1816; sermon preached at his son's ordination); Wm. Lincoln, *Hist. of Worcester, Mass.* (1837), containing a list of pamphlets relating to Goodrich's pastorate; S. G. Goodrich, *Recollections of a Lifetime* (2 vols., 1856); *Diary of Thomas Robbins, D.D. 1796–1854* (2 vols., 1887); *Diary of Isaiah Thomas 1805–28* (2 vols., 1909); *Roll of State Officers . . . of Conn., 1776–1881* (1881), p. 290.] G. H. G.

GOODRICH, CHAUNCEY (Oct. 20, 1759–Aug. 18, 1815), lawyer, United States senator, eldest son of Rev. Elizur [*q.v.*] and Catharine (Chauncey) Goodrich and brother of the younger Elizur Goodrich [*q.v.*], was born at Durham, Conn. He grew up in a home which represented the best standards of New England culture of that period, graduated with distinction at Yale in 1776, and taught for a time in the Hopkins Grammar School, New Haven. From 1779 to 1781 he was a tutor at Yale and at the same time studied law. After admission to the bar he settled at Hartford where he soon established a considerable practise. His first wife, Abigail Smith, died in September 1788 and on Oct. 13, 1789, he married Mary Ann Wolcott, thus establishing an alliance with one of the families which had long exercised a dominating influence in Connecticut affairs. By inheritance, training, profession, and social position he was fully qualified for membership in that Federalist politico-ecclesiastical oligarchy which governed the state until 1818. In 1793 he became a member of the state legislature and a year later was elected to Congress. A stalwart Federalist, he revealed in his correspondence with his brother-in-law, Oliver Wolcott [*q.v.*] during these years both the statesmanship and the limited vision which characterized so many leaders of that party (George Gibbs, *Memoirs of the Administrations of Washington and John Adams, Edited from the Papers of Oliver Wolcott, Secretary of the Treasury,* 2 vols., 1846). Goodrich remained in Congress until 1801, and his speeches on the Jay Treaty (*Annals of Congress,* 4 Cong., 1 Sess., pp. 717–25) and on the Foreign Intercourse Bill (*Ibid.,* 5 Cong., 1 Sess., pp. 931–41) disclosed a high order of ability.

After resigning from Congress in 1801 he resumed the practise of law at Hartford, reëntering politics as a member of the Council in 1802 and serving until 1807 when he was elected to the United States Senate. As senator he was praised by the Federalists for his sturdy opposition to the Embargo and other restrictive policies of the Republican majority, and criticized by the Republicans as an obstructionist of questionable loyalty. In 1813 he was elected lieutenant-governor of Connecticut and resigned from the Senate. A year earlier he had been elected mayor of Hartford and he retained both local offices until his death. His health had begun to fail, but he took a prominent part in the Hartford Convention of 1814. Theodore Dwight, a contemporary, in his history of that ill-starred gathering remarks of Goodrich (*post,* p. 428), "Rarely has any individual passed through so many scenes in public life with a higher reputation, and a more unimpeachable character." His shortcomings were those of the local group and sectional school of political thought to which he belonged.

[See L. W. Case, *The Goodrich Family in America* (1889); G. H. Hollister, *The Hist. of Conn.* (2 vols., 1855), esp. II, 634–38; F. B. Dexter, *Biog. Sketches Grads. Yale Coll.,* III (1903), 609–11; *Conn. Mirror* (Hartford), Aug. 21 and 28, 1815; Theodore Dwight, *Hist. of the Hartford Convention* (1833); R. J. Purcell, *Conn. in Transition 1775–1818* (1918).]

W. A. R.

GOODRICH, CHAUNCEY (Sept. 10, 1798–Sept. 11, 1858), bookseller, horticulturist, was born in Hinsdale, Berkshire County, Mass., the fourth of the nine children of Elijah Hubbard Goodrich by his second wife, Mabel Nicholson, and the fifth in descent from William Goodrich, who emigrated from Suffolk to Connecticut about 1643 and settled in Wethersfield. In his early years work on the farm alternated with attendance at school; later he engaged in teaching; and at nineteen he left home and found employment at Hartford, Conn., in the publishing house of Oliver D. Cooke. After six years of varied service, including a good deal of itinerant bookselling for the firm, he set up a business of his own at Castleton, Vt., in 1823 and moved it further north four years later to Burlington, where he lived for the rest of his life. In 1828 he married Arabella Marsh of Hartford, Vt., one of whose brothers was President James Marsh [*q.v.*] of the University of Vermont. She died in 1835, leaving Goodrich with two daughters. To selling books he in time added printing and publishing. His press work was sufficiently good to secure contracts for him from publishers in New York and Philadelphia; under his own imprint he issued a number of substantial works, including the statutes of Vermont, the first American edition of Coleridge's *Aids to Reflection* (1829), *The Friend* (1831), and *The Statesman's Manual* (1832), and many volumes of history, philosophy, and theology, as well as schoolbooks. The business yielded him a living but did not make him rich.

His work as a horticulturist was more significant than his publishing; no man did more than he to encourage and improve fruit growing in Vermont and northern New York. On his farm he maintained nurseries to provide his fellow citizens with hardy varieties of trees and bushes. He went up and down the state preaching the moral and monetary value of gardens and orchards; "By their *fruits* ye shall know them," was, he declared, his favorite text. He was one of the leading organizers and supporters of the Champlain Horticultural Society, which performed a useful work for that whole section of the country. He himself was the author of *The Northern Fruit Culturist, or The Farmer's Guide to the Orchard and Fruit Garden* (Burlington, 1849; 2nd ed., corrected and enlarged, 1850). It is a simple, practical guide to the subject, couched in clear, persuasive language; not for nothing was its author a distant relative of Peter Parley. The homely flavor of the book is well exemplified by such characteristic pieces of advice as, "Do your own grafting, and teach your sons and *daughters* to assist you" (p. 33), and, "No boy should be allowed to eat apples, who is not prompt to handle worms' nests without mittens" (p. 75). Goodrich was a devout Episcopalian, having been converted to that creed while living in Hartford. Out of his limited income he gave generously to the work of his church and to the support of promising students at the University of Vermont.

[L. W. Case, *The Goodrich Family in America* (1889); D. W. Marsh, *Marsh Geneal.* (1895); Nathan Crosby, *Annual Obit. Notice of Eminent Persons for 1858* (1859); J. E. Goodrich, article in L. H. Bailey, *Cyc. of Am. Agric.* (4th ed., 1909), IV, 579; A. M. Hemenway, *The Vermont Hist. Gazetteer,* I (1868), 647.]

G. H. G.

GOODRICH, CHAUNCEY (June 4, 1836–Sept. 28, 1925), American Board missionary to China, was born on a farm in Hinsdale, Berkshire County, Mass., and was the third of six sons of Elijah Hubbard and Mary Northrup (Washburn) Goodrich. He was a nephew of Chauncey Goodrich, 1798–1858 [*q.v.*], bookseller of Burlington, Vt. Reared in a Christian home, the younger Chauncey at twelve decided to become a minister, and during his sophomore year at college, a foreign missionary. After preparatory studies at Hinsdale Academy and the Union High School, Burlington, Vt., he entered Williams College, where he ranked high as a scholar and was prominent in student activities. Graduating in 1861, he spent a year at Union Theological Seminary in New York, then entered Andover Theological Seminary, where he graduated in 1864. He was ordained in the Congregational Church at Hinsdale on Sept. 21 of the same year, and early in 1865 sailed for China. On July 22, 1925, he celebrated his sixtieth anniversary as a missionary, being at the time the oldest Protestant missionary in China.

He acquired the language rapidly and began preaching in Chinese at Tung Chou, near Peking, within about a year after his arrival. He became a very active and efficient missionary, was secretary of the North China Mission, and overseer of the Mission Press. After 1873, however, his principal activities were in the fields of education and translation. He was professor of astronomy and Christian evidences at the North China College at Tung Chou (later North China Union College and in 1915 affiliated with Peking University) and in the Gordon Memorial Theological Seminary at the same place, of which he was dean for twenty-five years, he taught such subjects as Old Testament history, church history, homiletics and pastoral theology. He was also overseer of a boys' school in Peking which grew in his day from a school of twelve pupils to one of over six hundred.

His first translation was that of a portion of the Gospels into Mongol. He was the leading spirit of a committee of five who translated the entire Bible into Mandarin. This vast work required twenty-nine years of incessant labor; was completed in 1918 and published the following year. With Dr. Henry Blodgett he edited the Chinese *Hymn Book* (1877), of which he was also musical editor. For this work, of which there have been several editions, he translated many hymns from the English and composed many others in Chinese. In 1891 (new edition, 1923) he published *A Pocket Dictionary (Chinese-English) and Pekingese Syllabary* containing 10,000 characters, and in 1898 (new edition, 1916), *A Character Study of the Mandarin Colloquial,* containing 39,000 sentences, both of which are aids of permanent value to the study of the Chinese language. Goodrich had a fine physique and enjoyed uninterrupted good health. His forehead was well shaped, his voice was clear and resonant, and he spoke Chinese with a great degree of perfection. He was a man of genial and lovable nature and a faithful and inspiring teacher and preacher. On Sept. 10, 1864, he married Abbie Ambler of Green River, N. Y., who died at Tung Chou, Sept. 1, 1874. On May 31, 1878, he married Justina Emily Wheeler of Seymour, Conn., who died at Tung Chou, Sept. 4, of the same year. On May 13, 1880, he married Sarah Boardman Clapp, who became his strong co-worker and sympathetic adviser throughout the latter part of his life. Of his four children, a son and a daughter of the last marriage survived him.

[*Report of the Class of 1861 Williams Coll.,* 1887 and 1915; *Who's Who in America,* 1924–25; J. H. Hewitt, *Williams Coll. and Foreign Missions* (1914); Williams Coll., *Alumni Obit. Record,* 1925–26; *Congregationalist,* Dec. 17, 1925; *Missionary Herald,* Dec. 1925, June, and Aug., 1926; *Chinese Recorder,* July, Oct., Nov. 1925; much information furnished by his son.]

F. T. P.

GOODRICH, CHAUNCEY ALLEN (Oct. 23, 1790–Feb. 25, 1860), clergyman, educator, and lexicographer, son of Elizur Goodrich, 1761–1849 [*q.v.*], and Anne Willard Allen, was born in New Haven, Conn. After graduating from Yale College in 1810, he was rector of Hopkins Grammar School, New Haven, and from 1812 to 1814, tutor at Yale, during which period he studied theology under President Timothy Dwight [*q.v.*]. At the latter's suggestion, to supplement the meager aids to the study of Greek, he prepared a text-book, *Elements of Greek Grammar* (1814), based chiefly on the work of the Dutch scholar, Caspar Frederick Hachenberg, which went through several editions and was used for almost a quarter of a century. On Sept. 27, 1814, he was licensed to preach by the New Haven Association of Ministers, and after supplying several churches he accepted a call to the Congregational church, Middletown, Conn., where on July 24, 1816, he was ordained and installed. On Oct. 1, 1816, he married Julia Frances (originally Frances Juliana), daughter of Noah Webster [*q.v.*]. The following year, however, his health having proved unequal to the demands of the ministry, he resigned to assume the duties of the newly founded professorship of rhetoric at Yale. Religion still continued to be his major interest, and he was foremost among those who made possible the establishment of a theological department at Yale in 1822. Purchasing the *Christian Spectator* in 1828, he edited it as the *Quarterly Christian Spectator* until 1836, making it the exponent of the "New Haven theology" as promulgated by Dr. Nathaniel Taylor [*q.v.*], professor of didactic theology in the theological department. In 1838 he proposed the establishment of a professorship for the training of students in preaching and pastoral work, and gave $5,000 for that purpose. The first appointee having declined, he himself was transferred to the office and served therein until his death. By assisting Professor Eleazer Fitch in the pastoral work of the college, through weekly meetings for the students which he conducted, and as a consultant on spiritual matters, he exerted a notable influence on the religious character of the institution. He was also a strong supporter of the temperance movement, and was prominent in organized missionary activity.

In spite of his many duties and although not always in the best of health, he was able to do considerable writing and editing. He prepared *Lessons in Greek Parsing* (1829) and *Lessons in Latin Parsing* (1832), which were widely used. He contributed a chapter on "Revivals of Religion" to Robert Baird's *Religion in the United States of America* (1844). The same year he issued a four-page pamphlet, *Can I Conscientiously Vote for Henry Clay?*, an anonymous defense of a Christian's support of that statesman; and in 1849 he attacked anonymously Horace Bushnell's *God in Christ,* in a publication entitled, *What Does Dr. Bushnell Mean?* He published in 1852 *Select British Eloquence,* an octavo of nearly a thousand pages, containing speeches, biographical sketches and notes. For years he spent much time on Webster's *Dictionary,* editing an abridgment in 1829 which had been prepared under his supervision by Dr. Joseph E. Worcester [*q.v.*]. Assisted by several colleagues, he made a thorough revision of the original *Dictionary* in 1847. Among his contributions to the work as a whole were the synonyms, a treatise on the principles of pronunciation, and a memoir of the author. His death, occasioned by cerebral hemorrhage, occurred at New Haven in his seventieth year.

[F. B. Dexter, *Biog. Sketches Grads. Yale Coll.,* vol. VI (1912), gives list of publications including contributions to periodicals. See also T. D. Woolsey, *A Discourse Commemorative of the Life and Services of the Rev. Chauncey Allen Goodrich, D.D.* (1860); L. W. Case, *The Goodrich Family in America* (1889); Timothy Dwight, *Memories of Yale Life and Men* (1903); *The Semi-Centennial Anniversary of the Divinity School of Yale College* (1872); A. P. Stokes, *Memorials of Eminent Yale Men* (2 vols., 1914); *Two Centuries of Christian Activity at Yale* (1901), ed. by J. B. Reynolds, S. H. Fisher, and H. B. Wright; obituaries in *Congreg. Quart.,* Apr. 1860, and *Boston Transcript,* Feb. 28, 1860.]

H. E. S.

GOODRICH, ELIZUR (Oct. 26, 1734–Nov. 22, 1797), Congregational clergyman, was born in Wethersfield, Conn., the sixth child of David and Hepzibah (Boardman) Goodrich, and a descendant of William Goodrich who came from England and settled in Wethersfield about 1643. He prepared for college under Rev. James Lockwood, graduated from Yale in 1752, studied theology, was tutor at Yale in 1755, and the following year became pastor of the Congregational church, Durham, Conn., where he was ordained Nov. 24. Here he remained until his death, at which time he was recognized as one of the most stalwart and able representatives of the established order. He was an excellent scholar and devoted much time to the interpretation of difficult passages in the Scriptures. His interest in mathematics and astronomy was almost equally keen. He computed the eclipses of each year and wrote a notable account of an Aurora Borealis display. To augment his meager salary, he began to prepare boys for college, and nearly three hundred passed under his instruction. In 1776 he was elected to the Corporation of Yale College. "No man living probably so well understood the interests of our University," Timothy Dwight [*q.v.*] stated in his funeral discourse on Goodrich, "or for more than twenty years took so active and important a part in its concerns." He and Ezra Stiles [*q.v.*] received an equal number of votes for the presidency of Yale in 1777, and it was through his exertions in Stiles's behalf that the latter was finally elected. He was repeatedly chosen a member of the Conventions of Delegates from the Synod of New York and Philadelphia and the Association of Connecticut (1766–75), the first of which was called because of alarm over the report that diocesan bishops would be stationed in each of the colonies either by Act of Parliament or the agency of the Church of England. For these conventions he drew up a number of reports, including one in 1774 on the subject of religious liberty in Connecticut. (See *Minutes of the Convention of Delegates,* etc., 1843, and *Historical Magazine,* July 1868.) He urged participation in the Revolution as a religious duty, and at one election more than a thousand citizens registered a protest against a supposed weakness in Gov. Trumbull's administration by voting for Parson Goodrich. He married, Feb. 1, 1759, Catharine Chauncey of Durham. Among their seven children were Chauncey [*q.v.*], lawyer and United States senator, and Elizur [*q.v.*], congressman, jurist, and educator. Chauncey Allen Goodrich [*q.v.*], lexicographer,

Charles Augustus Goodrich [*q.v.*], author, and Samuel Griswold Goodrich [*q.v.*], better known as Peter Parley, were their grandsons.

[The date of birth is that given by Chauncey A. Goodrich in W. B. Sprague, *Annals Am. Pulpit,* vol. I (1857); vital records of Wethersfield printed in *New-Eng. Hist. and Geneal. Reg.,* Jan. 1864, p. 53, give Oct. 18. In addition to these references, see: L. W. Case, *The Goodrich Family in America* (1889); Wm. Chauncey Fowler, *Memorials of the Chaunceys* (1858); D. D. Field, *A Statistical Account of the County of Middlesex in Conn.* (1819); T. Dwight, *A Discourse Preached at the Funeral of Rev. Elizur Goodrich, D.D.* (1797); F. B. Dexter, *Biog. Sketches Grads. Yale Coll.,* vol. II (1896), which lists five published sermons.]

H. E. S.

GOODRICH, ELIZUR (Mar. 24, 1761–Nov. 1, 1849), lawyer, politician, and educator, the second son of Rev. Elizur [*q.v.*] and Catharine (Chauncey) Goodrich and brother of Chauncey Goodrich, 1759–1815 [*q.v.*], was born at Durham, Conn. He attended Yale College and on July 5, 1779, was a member of the company of students which resisted the advance of a British raiding party. He was severely wounded in this encounter. At his graduation in 1779 he was awarded the Berkeley Scholarship. Elected a tutor in the college in 1781, he taught for the next two years, studied law, and in 1783 began practise in New Haven. He was a man of wide reading and culture, became learned in the law, and also built up a considerable practise. He was in many respects an admirable representative of Federalist leadership in "the Land of Steady Habits." Office-holding was a steady habit of his own. Beginning in 1789 as member of the city council, he was connected with the government of New Haven, in various capacities, for about twenty-five years, serving as mayor from 1803 to 1822. In May 1795 he began a period of seven years in the legislature, where he served both as clerk and as speaker. In 1803 he was elected to the Council, which, composed of the ablest and most dependable party leaders, was one of the most powerful political machines in the history of state government. He remained a member until 1818. In addition to these legislative activities, he was probate judge of New Haven, 1802–18, and chief judge of the county court, 1805–18. The constitutional convention of 1818 which reformed the old charter government of the state and substituted a more modern and democratic constitution, practically ended his political career. This same year his wife, Anne Willard Allen, whom he had married in 1785, died, and for some time thereafter he lived with different members of his family in Hartford, Utica, and Washington, but returned to spend his last years in New Haven.

Goodrich had made a brief incursion into national politics as a member of the Sixth Congress, but resigned in 1801 to accept from President Adams the lucrative post of collector of the port of New Haven. President Jefferson, however, turned a cold and suspicious eye on the transaction. His prompt removal of the incumbent in favor of one of his own supporters, the resultant Federalist uproar, and the President's defense of the action, give the episode a unique importance in the history of American civil service (C. R. Fish, *The Civil Service and the Patronage,* 1905, pp. 32–58). Elizur Goodrich's connection with Yale was one of the most interesting and useful of his activities. He was professor of law from 1801 to 1810, *ex officio* member of the corporation from 1809 to 1818, and secretary from 1818 to 1846.

[L. W. Case, *The Goodrich Family in America* (1889); G. H. Hollister, *The Hist. of Conn.* (1855), II, 638–40; F. B. Dexter, *Biog. Sketches Grads. Yale Coll.,* IV (1907), 115–17; R. J. Purcell, *Conn. in Transition* (1918); obituary in *Hartford Courant,* Nov. 3, 1849, repr. from New Haven *Journal and Courier,* Nov. 2, 1849.]

W. A. R.

GOODRICH, FRANK BOOTT (Dec. 14, 1826–Mar. 15, 1894), author, journalist, and playwright, was born in Boston, Mass., the son of Samuel Griswold Goodrich [*q.v.*], better known as Peter Parley, and his second wife, Mary Boott. He graduated from Harvard in 1845, and in 1851, when his father was appointed United States consul at Paris, accompanied the family to France. He lived in Paris from 1851 to 1855. By reason of his father's position, and his own social and literary associations, he was able to keep in touch with the leading figures and events of the period which saw the *Coup d'État* of 1852, and Louis Napoleon's marriage and elevation to the throne. In a series of letters contributed to the *New York Times* over the signature Dick Tinto and published in 1855 as his first book, under the title *Tricolored Sketches in Paris,* he gave a vivid and readable account of life and incidents in that city as he saw them. Returning from Paris in 1855, he settled in New York and became active in its literary circles. He capitalized his experiences in France by writing *The Court of Napoleon, or Society under the First Empire* (1857), which was followed quickly by *Man Upon the Sea; or a History of Maritime Adventure, Exploration and Discovery* (1858), and *Women of Beauty and Heroism from Semiramis to Eugénie* (1859), both superficial, hastily written books, intended to catch the popular fancy. He was also interested in dramatic writing, and collaborated with some of the best-known dramatists of the time. Prominent among the plays in which he had a share were two with Frank L. Warden, *Fascination,* performed Jan. 2, 1857, at Tripler Hall and revived several times in the years 1888–90, and *Romance after Marriage, or The Maiden Wife,* a comedy in three acts developing a situation in Octave Feuillet's *La Clé d'Or,* performed at Wallack's Theatre in November 1857; *The Dark Hour before Dawn,* with John Brougham [*q.v.*], published in 1859; and *The Poor of New York,* with Dion Boucicault. This last play had a conspicuous success, from which Boucicault, especially, profited. In 1859 Goodrich married Ella Schmidt, daughter of a Southern physician long resident in New York. In 1860 there appeared *The Greatness and Decline of César Birotteau,* the first of a projected series of translations of the novels of Balzac, in which Goodrich collaborated with Orlando Williams Wight. This volume was followed in the next year by *The Petty Annoyances of Married Life, The Alchemist,* and *Eugénie Grandet.* The series was then discontinued, to be resumed in 1886 by a Boston publishing house. During the Civil War, Goodrich was a stanch supporter of the Union. At the end of the war, stung by criticisms of the people of the North, he compiled in refutation a volume known as *The Tribute Book, a Record of the Munificence, Sacrifice, and Patriotism of the American People during the War for the Union* (1865). His eyesight began to fail shortly after this period, and his literary production dwindled. He spent some years traveling abroad. In 1871 he republished his *Women of Beauty and Heroism* under the new title *World Famous Women, a Portrait Gallery of Female Loveliness, Achievement, and Influence; from Semiramis to Eugénie,* and in 1873 issued, under the title *Remarkable Voyages,* a new edition of the popular *Man Upon the Sea.* His literary style was easy and clear, but his books were superficial and without permanent value. In his later years his eye trouble caused him to relinquish all idea of further literary work. He was a man of great dignity, brilliant conversational power, and a wide range of interests. He had independent means, and lived quietly in and near New York, enjoying the esteem of a small circle of intimate friends. He died at Morristown in his sixty-eighth year, leaving no children.

[S. G. Goodrich, *Recollections of a Lifetime* (2 vols., 1856); L. W. Case, *The Goodrich Family in America* (1889); *Harvard Grads. Mag.*, June 1894; T. A. Brown, *A Hist. of the N. Y. Stage* (3 vols., 1903), I, 437, II, 179, 499, 501, 636; obituary in *N. Y. Times*, Mar. 22, 1894.]

L. H. H.

GOODRICH, SAMUEL GRISWOLD (Aug. 19, 1793–May 9, 1860), author and publisher, best known under his pen name, Peter Parley, was the son of the Rev. Samuel and Elizabeth (Ely) Goodrich. He came of a notable Connecticut family; his grandfather, Elizur Goodrich, his cousin Chauncey Allen Goodrich, and his brother Charles Augustus Goodrich [*qq.v.*] were clergymen of distinction in their day; his uncles, Chauncey and Elizur Goodrich [*qq.v.*], were prominent lawyers and the former, a United States senator. He was born at Ridgefield, where his father was pastor of the First Congregational Church. Because of financial inability, and perhaps partly because as a child he showed little interest in study, his parents gave him only an elementary education. Later, when his own theory of books for children may have colored his recollections, he records that he received *Mother Goose* "with no real relish," and speaks of Hannah More's "Moral Repository" as "the first work that I read with real enthusiasm" (*Recollections,* I, 166, 172). At the age of fifteen he left home to become a merchant's clerk, first at Danbury, then at Hartford. A plan to work his way through college was discouraged by his parents, but he carried out various schemes for self-education. He served with the state militia at New London in the War of 1812, started at Hartford a pocketbook factory which soon failed, and in 1816 entered with a friend on a publishing venture. In 1818 he married Adeline Gratia, daughter of Senator Stephen Row Bradley [*q.v.*] of Vermont. She died June 24, 1822.

The publishing business underwent various changes and vicissitudes; his memoirs dwell on the financial losses. At this time he began to publish school and juvenile books, a few of which he wrote himself. In 1823 he went abroad and met a number of literary celebrities, including most of the Edinburgh group and Hannah More, now a woman of nearly eighty. In 1826 he was married to Mary Boott of Boston and removed to that city. Here he published, and except for two years edited, *The Token,* probably the best in a literary way of the American giftbook annuals, though not the most showy or elaborate. It was in *The Token* that many of Hawthorne's tales first appeared. The idea of the Peter Parley books is said to have been suggested to Goodrich by his visit to Hannah More. The first of them, *The Tales of Peter Parley about America,* was published in 1827 and was followed by more than a hundred other volumes to which Goodrich affixed the Parley name, besides spurious imitations in both England and America. In these books a kindly and omniscient old gentleman is represented as talking to a group of priggishly inquiring children, and instruction is given a thin sugar-coating of fiction.

They met the educational needs of the time and sold by the million. In 1833 he founded *Parley's Magazine* for children, which he sold the following year, and in 1841 he established *Robert Merry's Museum,* another juvenile periodical. He retained the editorship until 1850 and a connection with the magazine until 1854.

Goodrich was always interested in public affairs, though he took no active part in politics until the later thirties of the century, when (1837) he served in the Massachusetts legislature. He was a stanch Federalist and a defender of the Hartford Convention, in which some of his relatives took part; later he was an intense admirer of Webster. From 1851 to 1853 he was United States consul at Paris, and as he had also been in Paris in 1848 he was able to write piquantly his observations both of the Revolution of that year and of the *Coup d'État* of 1852. After his removal from the consulate he visited Italy; on his return to the United States he lived in New York City and remained active in business almost until his death. He was a man of intense convictions, a strong, somewhat wordy, controversialist, and his criticisms of men and policies both at home and abroad are often picturesque. Besides the Peter Parley books and other juvenile and educational works he issued two volumes of his poems (*The Outcast and Other Poems,* 1836; *Poems,* 1851) and some miscellaneous work. His *Recollections of a Lifetime,* two rambling volumes of interesting material, appeared in 1856. Much controversy has arisen over the claim of Goodrich to the authorship of works that he published, and particularly to that of some of the Peter Parley books. For many years he had little use of his eyes and could work only with the aid of readers and amanuenses; and no man even with full command of his powers could have written all the works that bear the Parley name. It is well known that Hawthorne compiled one of the books (*Peter Parley's Universal History on the Basis of Geography,* vol. II, 1837), and friends of Samuel Kettell [*q.v.*], one of Goodrich's assistants, went so far as to maintain after that author's death that he was the real Peter Parley. Goodrich, while admitting that he employed help, insisted that all work was done in accordance with his own detailed plans, and was put in final shape by himself. His *Recollections* (II, 537) contains a "List of Works of which S. G. Goodrich is the Editor or Author," with some notes, and the following statistical summary: "I thus stand before the public as the author and editor of about one hundred and seventy volumes—one hundred and sixteen bearing the name of Peter Parley. Of all these, about seven millions of volumes have been sold: about three hundred thousand volumes are now [1856] sold annually." Among works published too late to be listed in the *Recollections* are *Thousand and One Stories of Fact and Fancy, Wit and Humor, Rhyme, Reason and Romance* (1858) and *Illustrated Natural History of the Animal Kingdom* (1859).

[The chief source of information concerning Goodrich is his *Recollections of a Lifetime*; but the autobiographical detail in this work is rather scant after the chapters that deal with the author's early years. An extended but unreliable sketch is found in L. W. Case, *The Goodrich Family in America* (1889). The list of Goodrich's works from the *Recollections* is reprinted in full in S. A. Allibone, *A Critical Dict. of Eng. Lit. and Eng. and Am. Authors,* vol. I (1858); a list of his works based on Roorbach's *Bibliotheca Americana* (1852 and supplements) is given in E. A. and G. L. Duyckinck, *The Cyc. of Am. Lit.* (rev. ed., 1875), II, 110–13. See also sketch accompanying review of Goodrich's *Poems* (1851) in *Internat. Monthly Rev.,* Jan. 1851; F. L. Mott, *A Hist. of Am. Magazines* (1930); obituary in the *Evening Post* (N. Y.), May 11, 1860, repr. in *Littell's Living Age,* Apr.–June 1860.] W. B. C.

GOODRICH, SARAH [See GOODRIDGE, SARAH, 1788–1853].

GOODRICH, WILLIAM MARCELLUS (July 21, 1777–Sept. 15, 1833), organ builder, a descendant of William Goodridge who became a freeman of Watertown, Mass., in 1642, was the second of nine children born to Ebenezer and Beulah (Childs) Goodridge of Templeton, Mass. In young manhood he changed the traditional spelling of the family name to "Goodrich" and adopted "Marcellus" as a middle name. He early showed mechanical ability and, through seeing a small organ built at Templeton by a Mr. Bruce, became interested in organ construction. At the age of twenty-one he obtained employment in the shop at Milton, Mass., of Benjamin Crehore, a famous maker of pianofortes and other musical instruments. In 1799 he set up for himself in Boston. He constructed a duplicate of J. N. Maelzel's panharmonicon, a combination of wind instruments played mechanically after the mode of the modern orchestrion, and in 1809, by agreement with the inventor, traveled through the countryside exhibiting it. Since Maelzel's original instrument had been lost at sea, Goodrich's duplicate was later sent to Europe for exhibition. In 1809, also, Goodrich moved to East Cambridge, where his factory was for many years a landmark at Otis and Fifth Streets. With him were associated his brother-in-law, Thomas Appleton, a well-trained cabinetmaker, and for a time Ebenezer Goodrich, a younger brother, who, after a family disagreement, established his own shop for the manufacture of reed organs. Among the apprentices of William Goodrich were Elias and George Hastings, initiators of the important firm of organ builders later known as Hook & Hastings.

The first organ built under Goodrich's direction was one for the Catholic Cathedral in Franklin Street, Boston. This was followed by a succession of church organs, some of which were still in use in the next century. "I have seen organs built by him," an organist and organ builder wrote in 1906, "which were of excellent tone in the flue work; but the reeds were very unmusical" (Clarke, *post*). An example of the work Goodrich was often called upon to do, and of the compensation which he received, may be cited from H. W. Foote's *Annals of King's Chapel* (vol. II, 1896, p. 404): "May 6, 1824, the wardens agreed with William Goodrich, then the principal organ builder in Boston, to repair the organ, insert an adequate number of sub-bass pipes and put the instrument 'into the most perfect condition' for three hundred dollars, which sum was to be paid in part by a deed of pew No. 56, valued at one hundred and seventy-five dollars."

For some time Goodrich's sister, Sarah Goodridge [*q.v.*], kept house for him. In February 1822 he was married to Hannah Heald, but they left no children. His death, in his fifty-seventh year, was due to apoplexy.

[For Goodrich see: L. W. Case, *The Goodrich Family in America* (1889), p. 371; E. A. Goodridge, *The Goodridge Geneal.* (1918); W. H. Clarke, "American Pioneer Organ Builders," *Musician,* Feb. 1906; H. C. Lahee, "Organs and Organ Building in New England," *New Eng. Mag.,* Dec. 1897; Arthur Gilman, *The Cambridge of Eighteen Hundred and Ninety-Six* (1896), p. 342; obituaries in *Boston Transcript* and *Boston Daily Advertiser,* Sept. 16, 1833. For Benjamin Crehore, piano maker, from whom Goodrich learned his trade, see A. K. Teele, *The Hist. of Milton, Mass.* (1887), pp. 149 and 378.] F. W. C.

GOODRIDGE, SARAH (Feb. 5, 1788–Dec. 28, 1853), miniature painter, was the sixth of the nine children of Ebenezer Goodridge, a farmer and mechanic of Templeton, Mass., and his wife Beulah Childs. She was descended from William Goodridge, an English emigrant who was admitted freeman to Watertown, Mass., in 1642. Until she was seventeen she remained, for the most part, in Templeton, where she received the customary district-school training. Thereafter she alternated between her father's home and those of her brothers and sister. Her artistic talent manifested itself early, and before she was able to buy paper she drew sketches of her family and companions on birch bark. Since the esthetic advantages of rural New England were negligible, she had little instruction, for examples only crude wood cuts, and was necessarily in the main self-taught. For a few months she attended a boarding school in Milton, where she had gone to keep house with her brother William [*q.v.*]. Later she accompanied him to Boston, and had a few drawing lessons from a man in his household. After teaching for two summers in the Templeton school, she returned to Boston in 1812, where she lived with her sister, Mrs. Thomas Appleton, and began her career as an artist. The following summer she was again in Templeton, making portraits of her friends at the rate of fifty cents for a life-size crayon drawing, and $1.50 for a sketch in watercolors. She resumed her residence in Boston that fall in the home of her second brother, with whom she remained for two years. For a time she devoted herself to oils, but after studying with an artist from Hartford, who taught her all he knew of painting on ivory, she abandoned everything in favor of miniatures.

While she was in Boston it was her good fortune to meet Gilbert Stuart, who became interested in her work and invited her to take her unfinished miniatures to his studio for criticism and suggestions. During the years from 1820 to 1824 when she enjoyed his informal instruction, her work gained both sureness and delicacy. At his request she painted a miniature of him in 1825, with which he was sufficiently pleased to have it preserved in a bracelet with his own and his wife's hair. An engraving from it was cut by A. B. Durand [*q.v.*] for *The National Portrait Gallery of Distinguished Americans* (vol. I, 1834), and she herself made two replicas of it. Her other miniatures included Isaiah Thomas, a painting which, according to his friend Rev. George Allen, "should be known as the best likeness" of him (*Proceedings of the American Antiquarian Society,* n.s. XII, 1898, p. 341), and of which a steel engraving by Henry W. Smith was included in the second edition of Thomas's *History of Printing in America* (1874); Christopher Columbus Baldwin; Gen. Henry Lee; Russell Sturgis (after Stuart); Daniel Webster (*c.* 1826), of which many replicas were made; and Gen. Knox. The last was a copy of Stuart's only miniature, which he painted for her as an example in technique. Although Sarah Goodridge never attained the fragile loveliness of some of her contemporaries, her work, by reason of its directness and simplicity, was unusually forceful.

She twice visited Washington, D. C., in 1828 and in 1841, but although she was well received, she found Boston a more congenial and profitable city. During the years of her residence there, she painted about two miniatures a week, supported her mother for the last eleven years of her life, nursed a paralytic brother for two years, and reared her orphaned niece. Her best work was done before 1840, but she continued with unflagging energy until 1850, when the failure of her eyes compelled her to retire. In 1851 she removed with her sister's family to Reading, Mass. She died of paralysis during a Christmas visit in Boston.

[The best account of Sarah Goodridge's life was written by her sister, Mrs. Ephraim Stone, for G. C. Mason, *The Life and Works of Gilbert Stuart* (1879). Further material may be found in H. B. Wehle, *Am. Miniatures* (1927); Theodore Bolton, *Early Am. Portrait Painters in Miniature* (1921); A. H. Wharton, *Heirlooms in Miniatures* (1898); L. W. Case, *The Goodrich Family in America* (1889); E. A. Goodridge, *The Goodridge Geneal.* (1918); C. L. Nichols, "The Portraits of Isaiah Thomas," *Proc. Am. Antiq. Soc.*, n.s. XXX (1920), 251 ff.; *Boston Daily Atlas*, Dec. 29, 1853.]

C. P. M.

GOODRIDGE, WILLIAM MARCELLUS [See GOODRICH, WILLIAM MARCELLUS, 1777–1833].

GOODSELL, DANIEL AYRES (Nov. 5, 1840–Dec. 5, 1909), Methodist bishop, son of Buel and Adeline (Ferris) Goodsell, was born in Newburg, N. Y., and died in New York City. His father, an itinerant Methodist minister, was poor, but Daniel attended the University of the City of New York (now New York University), and graduated in 1859. The same year he entered the Methodist ministry, and in June 1860 he was married to Sarah F. Loweree of Flushing, L. I. He preached at various churches in eastern New York, and by 1876 attained enough prominence to be made delegate to the quadrennial Methodist General Conference, an office which he thereafter filled regularly. From 1880 to 1887 he was literary editor of the New York *Christian Advocate,* and in 1888, the time of his elevation to the bishopric, he was secretary of the Methodist board of education. His breadth of mind caused him to emphasize—too strenuously for many of his followers—the unity of all Christianity; brought him into such fraternity with his codenominationalists in the South that in 1905 he was head of the joint commission which prepared the Methodist Hymnal; and carried him in 1907 to the point of condemning the church proscriptions against dancing, theatre-going, and card playing. This disposition to tolerance made him particularly valuable as an ecclesiastical ambassador, and much of the time after 1888 he was traveling, not only throughout America, but in Europe and the Orient as well. He was also an active writer, and in addition to his many magazine articles he published three books: *Nature and Character at Granite Bay* (1901), a pleasing group of out-of-door essays and character-studies; *The Things Which Remain* (1904), an address for young ministers, listing the elements of traditional Christianity which he believed would necessarily survive any process of scientific scrutiny; and *Peter the Hermit* (1906), a cursory sketch of the crusader made on the basis of several already existing portraits.

[N. Y. Univ., *Gen. Alumni Cat. 1833–1905* (1906); *Who's Who in America,* 1908–09; *Christian Advocate* (N. Y.), Dec. 9, 1909; *N. Y. Times,* Dec. 6, 1909.]

J. D. W.

GOODSPEED, THOMAS WAKEFIELD (Sept. 4, 1842–Dec. 16, 1927), clergyman, educational leader, was the grandson of Jason Goodspeed of Rhode Island who settled in Caldwell, N. Y., and there married Isabella, daughter of Stephen Millard of Rhode Island. Their son Stephen Goodspeed, born in Glens Falls, N. Y., married Jane Johnson, the daughter of a miller of Queensbury, N. Y. Thomas was the fifth of their seven children. The boy's schooling in Goodspeedville, near Glens Falls, and in Avon, Fulton County, Ill., where the family settled in 1855, was supplemented by study with his brother, Edgar, pastor of the Central Baptist Church in Poughkeepsie, N. Y. In the winter of 1857–58 Thomas joined his brother's church and began to think of entering the ministry. By March of the latter year he was in the preparatory department of Knox College, and in 1859 he entered the old University of Chicago. After three years he transferred to the University of Rochester, where in 1863 he received the degree of A.B. In September he entered Rochester Theological Seminary and during the following summer in Avon, Ill., he had his first experience as a preacher. At the beginning of 1865 he became pastoral supply of the North Baptist Church, Chicago, and was ordained in March. Graduated from Rochester in 1866, he assumed his first pastorate in Quincy, Ill., June 1, 1866. On Sept. 4, 1866, in the Baptist Church of Panton, Vt., he was married to Mary Ellen Ten Broeke, by whom he had two children. In 1871 he became his brother Edgar's associate in the Second Baptist Church of Chicago. In succeeding his brother on the board of trustees of the Baptist Union Theological Seminary, the course of his whole life was changed, leading him into what he regarded as his real work. Accepting appointment on Nov. 4, 1875, as special agent of the seminary, he resigned his position as associate pastor Dec. 4, 1875, and although for a short time he served as pastor of the Baptist Church in Morgan Park, he resigned definitely in 1879 and thereafter gave all of his time to the educational work of his denomination. In something over thirteen years he raised not less than half a million dollars in new funds.

Deeply stirred by the closing of the old University of Chicago in 1886, Goodspeed undertook to establish a new Baptist college in Morgan Park. In July 1888, however, he declined an invitation to lead the "Provisional University Committee" because he had learned of other developments. His association with John D. Rockefeller in establishing the Baptist Union Theological Seminary led him to correspond with Rockefeller regarding education in Chicago, and according to Frederick Taylor Gates [*q.v.*], corresponding secretary of the American Baptist Education Society, these letters led Rockefeller to decide to found an institution in Chicago. Gates had independently concluded that a college was needed there. Meanwhile William Rainey Harper [*q.v.*], who had left the Baptist Union Theological Seminary to become a professor in Yale University, had been in conference with Rockefeller and in communication with Goodspeed. When Harper on Oct. 13, 1888, reported to Goodspeed a conversation with Rockefeller and urged that it would be a pity if the Morgan Park plans interfered with a larger program, Goodspeed immediately placed all his facts in Harper's hands and induced Gates to abandon his campaign. Harper believed that Rockefeller would establish in Chicago a university with graduate and professional schools. Goodspeed understood that he intended to found a college. Gates suggested the wisdom of beginning with a college, even if a university were to be the ultimate creation. Goodspeed then wrote a report embodying his conception of Rockefeller's intentions. This report was approved in March 1889 by the American Baptist Education Society. Rockefeller then offered to give the new institution $600,000 provided others gave $400,000. On June 10, 1889, Goodspeed officially began his work for the society, and he and Gates worked together to raise the required sum.

On July 9, 1890, at the first meeting of the board of trustees of the new university, of which he was one of the six incorporators, Goodspeed was made secretary of the board. For nearly twenty-three years he served in this position, earnestly cooperating with President Harper and then with President Judson and the trustees in developing the financial strength of the university. From 1894 until his death he was secretary of the board of trustees of the Baptist Union Theological Seminary and of Rush Medical College. He served also on the boards of Frances Shimer Academy (1895–1914), the Chicago Baptist Hospital (1895–1900), and the Chicago Manual Training Association (1897–1913). Retiring from active service in 1912 with the title of corresponding secretary of the board of trustees, he began to write his reminiscences, but interrupted this task to prepare a history of the university for its quarter-centennial celebration. The work appeared in 1916 as *A History of the University of Chicago,* and was followed by *The University of Chicago Biographical Sketches* (2 vols., 1922–25); *A History of the Hyde Park Baptist Church, 1874–1924* (1924); *The Story of the University of Chicago 1890–1925* (1925); and *Ernest De Witt Burton* (1926). At the time of his death he had almost finished his biography of William Rainey Harper, posthumously published in 1928.

[The above sketch is based upon Goodspeed's unpublished reminiscences. For general reference see W. A. Goodspeed, *Hist. of the Goodspeed Family,* vol. I (1907); *Who's Who in America,* 1926–27; Chicago *Tribune,* Dec. 17, 1927.] D. A. R.

GOODWIN, DANIEL RAYNES (Apr. 12, 1811–Mar. 15, 1890), college president and divine, was born in North Berwick, Me., the son of Samuel and Anna Thompson (Gerrish) Goodwin, and brother of Ichabod Goodwin [*q.v.*]. He was descended from Daniel Goodwin, who was in Kittery, Me., in 1653. He was sent to the academy at South Berwick and to Limerick Academy, and in 1832 he graduated from Bowdoin College at the head of his class. After teaching for one year at Hallowell, Me., he went to Andover Theological Seminary, but in 1835 he returned to Bowdoin as tutor in modern languages under his old teacher, Henry W. Longfellow. Later in the same year, when Longfellow resigned, Goodwin succeeded to the professorship and spent some two years in study abroad. He remained at Bowdoin until 1853, not only teaching the modern languages but also serving as librarian for fifteen years. On Jan. 2, 1838, he was married to Mary Randall Merrick, by whom he had four daughters and two sons. Early in the forties he began his connection with the Episcopal Church, and was confirmed at Gardiner. In spite of a very considerable prejudice which prevailed in Maine against the Episcopal Church, he was ordained deacon in 1847 and priest in 1848, and helped to organize the church in the college town. His reputation, both as a scholar and teacher, and as a churchman, led to his election in 1853 as president of Trinity College at Hartford, Conn., where he also acted as professor of modern languages, and later of moral and intellectual philosophy. He exerted his influence to raise the standard of study and of discipline, and won the respect and regard of faculty and students alike. In 1860 he became provost of the University of Pennsylvania. In his inaugural address he stressed the importance of physical training and athletics, in which he took a lifelong interest. His administration was noteworthy also for intellectual vigor. But a real conservative at heart, he did not approve of adding a scientific department under the conditions then existing, and this led to his retirement from office in 1868. At Philadelphia as at Hartford he had strengthened and improved both scholarship and discipline. For the remaining years of his life he was connected with the Philadelphia Divinity School, as dean from 1868 until 1883, and as professor of systematic divinity from 1865 until his death in 1890. Not only in his own diocese but in the General Conventions of the Church he was perhaps the most influential leader of his time of the Evangelical party. He wrote much, both on philosophical and theological subjects. In person he was a man of noble and winning aspect, tall and dignified, with finely cut features and piercing eyes. He had an eager interest in men and in the new social problems of the day, though he was by temper and disposition conservative.

[An excellent biographical sketch is that by John Vaughan Merrick in the *Proc. Am. Phil. Soc.*, July–Dec. 1890, with bibliography. See also T. M. Clark, *Evangelical Principles and Men* (1890), a memorial discourse on the character and services of Goodwin; *Tenth Ann. Festival of the New Eng. Soc. of Pa. . . . Dec. 22, 1890*; J. S. Goodwin, *The Goodwins of Kittery, York County, Me.* (1898); *Obit. Record of the Grads. of Bowdoin Coll.*, 2 ser., no. 1 (1890); *Living Church*, Mar. 29, 1890; *Public Ledger* (Phila.), Mar. 17, 1890.]
K. C. M. S.

GOODWIN, ELIJAH (Jan. 16, 1807–Sept. 4, 1879), minister of the Disciples of Christ, pioneer preacher in Indiana and Illinois, editor, was born in Champaign County, Ohio, the son of Aaron Goodwin by his second wife, Mary Chapman. His parents soon migrated to the "American Bottom," Illinois Territory, about twelve miles east of St. Louis, but after three years of fever and ague they decided to return to Ohio. On the journey back, however, they were attracted by prospects in Indiana Territory, and finally settled near what is now Washington, Daviess County. Here Elijah grew up under primitive surroundings, working on the farm, getting a little schooling, and eagerly reading whatever books he could obtain, which happened to be chiefly religious. His mother was a "shouting Methodist," who believed it a sin to quench the spirit, and Elijah imbibed the idea that there were no truly religious people in the world but Methodists. When, however, certain preachers of the "Christian" persuasion came to the neighborhood, he was attracted by their doctrines, and joined a church of their order about four miles from his home. At the age of seventeen he began to preach and at once impressed the older ministers with his fervor and ability. In the fall of 1825 the Indiana Christian Conference licensed him. Cutting loose from all worldly affairs and receiving little remuneration except the pleasure of seeing sinners converted, he carried on evangelistic work from house to house and from county to county. In 1827 the Indiana and Wabash Conferences appointed him to travel among their churches, and in this office he was accustomed to cover a circuit of 600 miles every eight weeks. Probably no one did more to establish "Christian" churches in southwestern Indiana, and in some of the neighboring counties in Illinois than did he. On Aug. 5, 1828, he married Jane Moore Davis. After a preaching tour through five counties of Tennessee, he established his home on his father-in-law's farm in Gibson County, Ind. He became pastor of the church at Union, carried on evangelistic work, taught school, ran a store, and was tax collector. During this period he became a Campbellite. From 1840 to 1847 he devoted himself wholly to religious work, making preaching tours in Kentucky as well as in Indiana and Illinois. In one year, he records, "I traveled 2,925 miles, and preached 450 sermons, and baptized 108 persons."

In 1847, having purchased a half interest in the *Christian Record*, a monthly periodical, he moved to Bloomington, Ind., where he edited and published this magazine jointly with Rev. J. M. Mathes. The following year he became connected with the movement which resulted in the establishment of North Western Christian University, now Butler University, Indianapolis, and he severed his connection with the *Record*. In January 1849 he put forward a plan for a state missionary society, and in the fall of that year the Indiana Christian Home Missionary Society was formed. From 1849 to 1851 he was pastor at Madison, Ind., and from 1851 to 1854 of the churches at Bloomington and Clear Creek. During the next two years, as agent for North Western Christian University, opened in 1855, he canvassed the state to secure needed funds. He was one of the board of commissioners which organized the institution; was from the beginning a member, and twice president, of its board of directors; and was for ten years its treasurer. From 1856 to 1859 he was pastor in Indianapolis. In the latter year he became sole proprietor of the *Christian Record*, then published in that city, and edited it until it was merged with the *Christian Standard* in 1866. On Feb. 16, 1863, his wife died, and on June 19, 1864, he married Marcia M. Bassett, editor of the *Christian Monitor.* His activities in behalf of the University occupied much of his time until 1871 when he took charge of a mission church in Philadelphia. A brief pastorate (1872–74) in Newport, Ky., followed. The next two years he was in Indianapolis, where he assisted his wife in editing her paper. At Oskaloosa, Iowa, to which place he moved in 1877, his health failed, and he died near Cleveland, Ohio, whither he had gone in hope of receiving benefit from mineral springs there. A volume of sermons, *The Family Companion: or a Book of Sermons on Various Subjects both Doctrinal and Practical,* was published by him in 1856.

[James M. Mathes, *Life of Elijah Goodwin* (1880), is largely autobiographical. See also J. S. Goodwin, "The Goodwin Families in America," *Wm. and Mary Coll. Quart. Hist. Mag., Supp.* (1897); F. D. Power, *Sketches of Our Pioneers* (1898); Errett Gates, *The Disciples of Christ* (1905); *Christian Standard,* Sept. 27, Oct. 11, 1879; Madison Evans, *Biog. Sketches of the Pioneer Preachers of Indiana* (1862); *Indianapolis Jour.,* Sept. 5, 1879.] H. E. S.

GOODWIN, HANNIBAL WILLISTON (Apr. 30, 1822–Dec. 31, 1900), clergyman, inventor, was born in Taughannock on the shores of Lake Cayuga, in Tompkins County, N. Y., the son of George and Cynthia Williston (Gregory) Goodwin. After attending the district schools he entered Union College in Schenectady, N. Y., and graduated in 1848. The succeeding autumn he matriculated in the Yale Law School at New Haven, Conn., but within a few months gave up this study and entered the General Theological Seminary of the Episcopal Church in New York City. He was graduated from this institution in 1851, and following his ordination was appointed rector of Christ Church at Bordentown, N. J. In 1854 he accepted a call to St. Paul's Church, Newark, N. J., and for the succeeding five years served this parish. From there he went to Trenton, N. J., and organized Trinity Parish, but after a year he was required to relinquish the work because of illness. Hopeful of regaining his health, he moved with his family to San Francisco, Cal., in 1860, and for seven years resided there, serving as rector of Grace Church. The California climate proved very beneficial. By 1867 Goodwin had so fully recovered that he returned to the East, again settled in Newark, and accepted the rectorship of the House of Prayer. For the next twenty years he conducted this office faithfully and arduously, but because of rather delicate health he gave it up upon reaching the retirement age of sixty-five years. For the remainder of his life he had no active charge.

Goodwin had always been an ardent advocate of the religious education of the young through the use of pictorial illustrations of Scriptural events. While rector of the House of Prayer he secured a stereopticon outfit but found that to have suitable illustrations he would have to make them himself. This led him to take up the study of photography and eventually to undertake experiments, in a small way, in order to find a substitute for glass upon which to make photographic negatives. The idea was not original with him, nor was he a technician, but his interest was aroused, and by working diligently for upwards of ten years he developed a process and product and applied for a patent for a "Photographic Pellicle" on May 2, 1887. A little later Henry M. Reichenbach of the Eastman Dry Plate Company applied for and on Dec. 10, 1889, received patent no. 417,202 for the "manufacture of flexible photographic films." The Patent Office thereupon declared an interference between the two patentees and a bitter fight was precipitated. Goodwin had little difficulty in proving that he was the original inventor of the celluloid photographic film, but he was involved in over twelve years of expensive litigation to break down the Dry Plate Company's efforts to prevent the issuance of a patent. He eventually obtained patent no. 610,861 on Sept. 13, 1898, a little over two years before his death. He died as a result of a fractured leg and attendant shock and was survived by his wife Rebecca and two children.

[John S. Goodwin, *The Goodwins of Delaware Water Gap, Pa., and Tompkins County, N. Y.* (1898); U. S. Nat. Museum records; correspondence with General Theological Seminary, N. Y. City, and Union College, Schenectady, N. Y.; Patent Office records; obituaries in *Newark Evening News, Newark Daily Advertiser,* Dec. 31, 1900; *N. Y. Times,* Jan. 1, 1901; the *Churchman,* Jan. 12, 1901.] C. W. M.

GOODWIN, ICHABOD (Oct. 8, 1794–July 4, 1882), merchant, financier, politician, brother of Daniel Raynes Goodwin [*q.v.*], was born on a farm in North Berwick, Me. His parents, Samuel and Anna Thompson (Gerrish) Goodwin, were of old colonial stock, but without large means. After attending an academy in South Berwick, Ichabod became a clerk in the office of Samuel Lord, a merchant in Portsmouth, N. H. Later he was promoted to the post of supercargo on a merchant vessel, where he learned navigation. For some years he followed the sea as master and part owner of various craft. About 1832, after twelve years at sea, he became a merchant in Portsmouth, engaging in the foreign carrying-trade with considerable financial success. He had already, on Sept. 3, 1827, married Sarah Parker Rice, the daughter of William Rice, a wealthy Portsmouth merchant. Since New Hampshire was entering a period of important internal development, there were opportunities in various fields for a man of Goodwin's resources and ability. In addition to engaging in sundry local manufacturing and financial enterprises, he became an active participant in early railroad enterprises. He was the first president of the Eastern Railroad, holding office for about twenty-five years, and a member of the first board of directors of the Portland, Saco & Portsmouth Railroad Company, serving as president of the latter from 1847 to 1871.

Like a majority of New England business leaders of the period, Goodwin was a stalwart Whig. He took an active part in politics and attended several national conventions as delegate-at-large from New Hampshire. Between 1838 and 1856 he served six terms in the legislature as representative of Portsmouth, was a member of the constitutional convention of 1850, and several times an unsuccessful candidate for Congress. A natural conservative, he remained with the Whig party during its moribund years and in 1856, as its last candidate for the governorship, polled some 2,000 scattered votes. He then joined the Republican party and was elected governor in 1859 and 1860. His inaugural message, especially those sections dealing with the transportation problems of the state, shows a wide acquaintance with business affairs. In his second message he suggested that railroad consolidation would be necessary for the relief of both stockholders and the public, a remedy he lived to see generally applied throughout New England.

The crisis of 1860–61 gave Goodwin an opportunity to perform notable services for both state and nation. In his message of 1860, though he was inclined to make light of threats of disunion as of common occurrence in presidential election years, he announced that New Hampshire, at any cost, would stand by the Union and the Constitution. When the war opened in the spring of 1861 he acted with great promptness and vigor. Confronted with an almost empty treasury, and reluctant to summon the legislature in special session because of further expense and the danger of delay, he borrowed $680,000 on his personal responsibility, gathered men and supplies to meet the first call for troops, and in addition exerted an inspiring influence on the people of his own and neighboring states. His acts, many of them undoubtedly extra-legal, were validated by the next legislature (June 1861), and he was able to turn over the machinery of government to his successor, Nathaniel S. Berry, in good running order. After his retirement from office he continued in business for some time. With advancing age he gradually curtailed his activities although he retained the presidency of several Portsmouth enterprises, including two banks, to the end. His work as war governor, together with his various public services in Portsmouth, account for the high reputation he enjoyed for many years throughout the state and New England generally.

[Frank Goodwin, "Hon. Ichabod Goodwin," *Granite Monthly,* May 1880; J. S. Goodwin, *The Goodwins of Kittery, York County, Me.* (1898); Otis F. R. Waite, *N. H. in the Great Rebellion* (1870); *Concord Daily Monitor,* July 5, 1882; *Portsmouth Jour.,* July 8, 1882; *Unit. Rev.,* Aug. 1882.]

W. A. R.

GOODWIN, JOHN NOBLE (Oct. 18, 1824–Apr. 29, 1887), lawyer, politician, was born in South Berwick, Me., the son of John and Mary (Noble) Goodwin. He attended Berwick Academy, graduated from Dartmouth College in 1844, returned home to read law in the office of John Hubbard, and was admitted to the bar in 1848. In 1854 he was a member for York County of the state Senate. In November 1857 he married Susan Howard Robinson of Augusta. In 1860, by a majority of almost fifteen hundred, he was elected to Congress as a Republican. He made friends but did little to distinguish himself in Washington, and in the election of 1862 he came out a paltry but decisive 127 votes behind his Democratic rival. When Congress in the course of its last sittings passed a bill to organize Arizona as a territory, although at this time it contained something less than six hundred American-born residents, John A. Gurley of Ohio was appointed governor, and Goodwin chief justice, of the territory. Gurley died before the party of officials could set out for the West, and President Lincoln thereupon named Goodwin to the vacant governorship. On Dec. 27, 1863, Goodwin and his cavalcade entered Arizona; and two days later, at Navajo Springs, the territory was formally organized. Although he owed his appointment solely to political considerations, Goodwin proved to be a conscientious, capable, and popular governor. Doubts about his personal character were quickly dispelled, for though a New Englander he was no Puritan. His tact and judgment were displayed to best advantage in his handling of the political situation, which was rendered delicate by the fact that many, probably most, of the residents were Southern sympathizers. Goodwin appointed a number of them to office, and by centering public attention on the welfare of the territory rather than on the war in the East he managed to conciliate factions and to maintain a stable government. He also showed real ability and diplomacy in guiding the work of the first legislature. He made a tour of the territory to study its needs at first hand and was interested in a railway enterprise. His capital he established at Prescott, which was named in honor of the historian. In 1865 Goodwin was sent to Washington as representative of Arizona in the Thirty-ninth Congress and after the expiration of his term of office took up the practise of law in New York City. He never returned to Arizona. He died at Paraiso Springs, Cal., whither he had gone to seek relief from the gout. His son brought the body back to Augusta, Me., for burial.

[*Biog. Dir. Am. Cong.* (1928); G. T. Chapman, *Sketches of the Alumni of Dartmouth Coll.* (1867); *Daily Eastern Argus* (Portland, Me.), Apr. 30, 1887; H. H. Bancroft, *Hist. of the Pacific States,* vol. XII (1888); T. E. Farish, *Hist. of Ariz.,* vols. II–V (Phoenix, Ariz., 1915–18).] G. H. G.

GOODWIN, NATHANIEL CARLL (July 25, 1857–Jan. 31, 1919), actor, was born in Boston, the son of Nathaniel Carll and Caroline (Hinkel) Goodwin. His early education was at the Abbott school for boys on the Little Blue Estate in Farmington, Me., where, as a "slight, delicate youth, with peculiar flaxen hair, round blue eyes, and a complexion as fair as a girl's," he won a prize for declamation. He was then apprenticed to a Boston dry-goods house, but spent much time cultivating a natural gift for mimicry, and haunting the theatres. Finally his father let him study with an old actor in Boston, and then Stuart Robson got him a job as Ned the newsboy in *Law in New York,* at the Howard Athenæum, Boston, where he first appeared in 1873. He also gave his imitations of other actors. He next went to New York, and in 1875 and 1876 appeared in vaudeville at Tony Pastor's and elsewhere. He was also cast in *The Littlest Rebel* with Minnie Palmer, and in *Evangeline.* On June 24, 1877, he married Eliza Weatherby, an actress who had come to America with the Lydia Thompson Blondes. With her he appeared in a series of burlesque entertainments known as *Froliques,* acted in *The Black Flag* at the Union Square Theatre, and played for a short time with Harrigan and Hart. He was engaged as low comedian for the Cincinnati Dramatic Festival, in 1883, playing such rôles as the grave-digger in *Hamlet.* Others in the company were Barrett, McCullough, and Mary Anderson. This established his reputation, and in the following decade he starred successfully in a series of light comedies, farces, and musical pieces. His greatest success at this time was *A Gilded Fool,* by Henry Guy Carleton. His first wife died in 1887. In September 1893 he produced *In Missoura,* by Augustus Thomas, in which he played a realistic rôle, touched with quaint pathos. Later he revived *David Garrick,* and in 1896 he was the Sir Lucius in Jefferson's famous "all-star" revival of *The Rivals.* Following this engagement he made a tour to Australia, taking with him Maxine Elliott as his leading woman. In October 1888 he had married Mrs. Nellie Baker Pease of Buffalo, but the union had not been successful and divorce proceedings were under way when he left for Australia. There was much baseless but unpleasant gossip in the newspapers, and after his return to America, on Feb. 20, 1898, he married Miss Elliott. With her as co-star, he made a series of productions which were among the most successful of his career, including especially *The Cowboy and the Lady,* and *Nathan Hale* by Clyde Fitch (1899), and *When We Were Twenty-One* by H. V. Esmond (1900). In 1901 he produced *The Merchant of Venice,* at the Knickerbocker Theatre, New York, acting Shylock to Miss Elliott's Portia. The production was ambitious, but the play lay beyond the powers of either star, and was a failure. Shortly thereafter Miss Elliott went her own way as an independent star, and Goodwin never again succeeded in recapturing the success of his earlier days. In 1904 he played Bottom in a production of *A Midsummer Night's Dream* which opened the New Amsterdam Theatre, New York, and in 1912, after a series of failures, he came back to New York as Fagin in an "all-star" revival of *Oliver Twist.* Otherwise his appearances were artistically negligible during these years, though the plays produced included Jacobs's *Beauty and the Barge,* Alfred Henry Lewis's *Wolfville,* and *The Genius* by the De Mille brothers.

In 1908 Miss Elliott was divorced from Goodwin, and on Nov. 8, 1908, in Boston, he married Edna Goodrich, who was then his leading woman. In his autobiographical book he sets forth his various marital difficulties, which in this case, according to his account, included the pursuit of his wife to London in quest of his watch. In 1911 she secured a divorce. On May 24, 1913, he was married to Marjorie Moreland and was divorced from her in 1918. That same year he returned to the New York stage, not as a star but merely as one member of the company playing Jesse Lynch Williams's comedy, *Why Marry?* Under the restraint of another's management, he gave a brilliant and delightful performance, and when the play went on tour he was everywhere warmly acclaimed. But due to the shock of the removal of his right eye some months earlier, his system had broken down, and he died rather suddenly, on the morning of Jan. 31, 1919. His popularity "on the road" was still so great that the play *Why Marry?,* hitherto successful, no longer attracted, and the tour had to be closed. Goodwin was said to be about to marry for the sixth time when he died. He was buried from the home of his aged parents, in Roxbury, Mass.

The New York *Evening Post* spoke of Goodwin as "wayward, impulsive and reckless." He was. Of medium stature, with blue eyes, a wide, merry mouth, and a genial wit, in his early years he was equally attractive as an entertainer on or off the stage, and this perhaps was his undoing, since it led him to take his stage career too lightly, while his social life became too prominent. He loved to gamble, whether on horses or mining stock, and he loved wine, women, and song. Once, in Brooklyn, he appeared intoxicated on the stage, so the play had to be stopped, and the next night he was forced publicly to apologize (*New York Tribune,* Mar. 7, 1895). During the early days of his marriage with Miss Elliott, they maintained a lavish summer home at Shooters Hill, Kent, England. One cannot escape a certain sympathy with this genial, easy-going, and democratic actor amid the alien guests his beautiful and socially aspiring wife gathered into their home. The situation contained more elements of genuine satirical comedy than most of the plays he put upon the stage. In later years, Goodwin was broken by his failures in Shakespearian rôles for which he had never really prepared himself; his constant and publicly aired matrimonial difficulties did his serious reputation no good; and he became coarsened both in face and figure. The publication of his amusing but tasteless book in 1914 did not help matters. But he never quite lost the affections of those who had known him as the delightful comedian of the eighties and nineties, and when his last rôle was one of dignity and distinction, in a brilliant modern comedy, there was general rejoicing.

[J. S. Goodwin, *The Goodwins of Kittery, York County, Me.* (1898); *Nat Goodwin's Book* (1914); *Who's Who on the Stage* (1906); N. Y. *Evening Post,* Jan. 31, 1919; leading morning papers, Feb. 1, 1919.]

W. P. E.

GOODWIN, WILLIAM WATSON (May 9, 1831–June 15, 1912), Hellenist, the son of Hersey Bradford Goodwin and Lucretia Ann Watson, was born at Concord, Mass., where his father was associated with Dr. Ezra Ripley in the ministry of the Congregational (Unitarian) Church. He was descended from Christopher Goodwin, who was in Charlestown in 1642, and from Myles Standish of Plymouth. Both his parents died during his infancy, and he was reared in Plymouth by his grandmother, Lucretia Burr (Sturges) Watson. The adjacent Clark's Island, granted to his ancestors by royal charter, remained his summer home throughout his life, and he was an expert yachtsman. He was taught his first Greek by his uncle, Benjamin Marston Watson, and entered Harvard in 1847. There, as he often liked to recall, he pursued the rather meager curriculum of a small provincial college, occasionally relieved, however, by the lectures of Louis Agassiz, Asa Gray, Henry W. Longfellow, and others. He spent two additional years as a graduate student in Cambridge, but in 1853 he went to Göttingen, where the great classical philologists of the day were Schneidewin and K. F. Hermann. After studying also in Bonn and in Berlin, he received the degree of Ph.D. from Göttingen in 1855. His dissertation, *De Potentiae Veterum Gentium Maritimae Epochis apud Eusebium* (1855), dealt with sea power in antiquity, an important subject in itself, and noteworthy as treated by one who was to win fame as a grammarian and an interpreter of literature rather than as a historian.

After visiting Italy and Greece, Goodwin returned to Cambridge in 1856, and began his long career as teacher and officer of Harvard College. First tutor in Greek and Latin, then in Greek alone, he succeeded C. C. Felton in 1860 as Eliot Professor of Greek Literature, a chair founded by the father of President Eliot, and held by Goodwin until he resigned in 1901. Even then, as professor emeritus, he continued his lectures on Plato and Aristotle, and from 1903 to 1909 was a member of the Board of Overseers of the University. For over forty years he was prominently engaged in forwarding the processes which transformed Harvard from a college to a university, his one guiding principle being that scholarship should be raised and maintained at a high level. He opposed all measures, like the reduction of the college course from four years to three, which he thought implied a lowering of standards; on the other hand, he often renounced his own naturally conservative instincts when convinced that the cause of learning would thereby be benefited. In 1866–67, when the faculty numbered only twenty-one persons, Goodwin joined the liberal majority which reduced the required studies in the sophomore year to seven hours a week, with elective studies amounting to six hours a week. While he voted to give up compulsory Greek for sophomores, in order that the elective system might have free play for older students, he opposed with resourcefulness, frank speech, and forceful leadership the substitution of other subjects for Greek in the requirements for matriculation. Though he was not a controversialist by nature, his convictions were decided, and with wit, sarcasm, and a clear marshaling of facts and precedents he fought the battle for Greek, which waged until 1896. In debates into which his opponents often injected acrimony, he was never known to lose his temper, although he could often see that the fight was a losing one. As he told his chief opponent, President Eliot, he "had been set to guard a gate," and he guarded it well.

When, at the early age of twenty-nine, Goodwin found himself a full-fledged professor, he showed his zeal for higher standards by the publication of his *Syntax of the Moods and Tenses of the Greek Verb* (1860), the book which parted company at once with the somewhat limp and flabby methods of Greek study in America and with the metaphysical concepts in which Greek syntax had become involved in Germany. Upon this work he concentrated his exact and thorough reading of the Greek authors, his deep insight into meanings theretofore misapprehended, his fine knowledge of English idiom, his power of scientific classification, and a certain sturdy common sense which was part of his New England inheritance. This work was greatly enlarged in 1890, but it had been done so well in the beginning that he was not obliged to retract anything of importance. He also published *An Elementary Greek Grammar* (1870 and subsequent editions). In 1861, he had revised and republished C. C. Felton's translations of the *Birds* and *Clouds* of Aristophanes, and two years later the same author's *Panegyricus of Isocrates*. In 1870 he published in five volumes a revised translation of *Plutarch's Morals*. At a time when good text-books were rare, he brought out a *Greek Reader* (1871), excellent for its selections and for the judicious notes thereon, and *Selections from Xenophon and Herodotus* (1877). In collaboration with J. W. White, his younger colleague, he prepared *The First Four Books of Xenophon's Anabasis* (1880), which has since appeared in many editions. The constitutional, legal, and artistic achievements of the Greeks also interested Goodwin profoundly. Greek law and legal procedure were the subjects of one of his frequently-repeated courses, and his intimate knowledge of them, as well as of the tangled history of fourth century (B. C.) politics, gave peculiar authority to his editions of *Demosthenes on the Crown* (1901 and 1904) and *Against Midias* (1906). He wrote also on "The Relation of the πρόεδροι to the πρυτάνεις in the Athenian Senate," and on "The Value of the Attic Talent in Modern Money" (*Transactions of the American Philological Association*, XVI, 1885). His favorite dramatist was Aeschylus, and no one who listened to his translation of the *Agamemnon* could doubt Goodwin's appreciation of the beauty and ethical import of that drama. His critical method is admirably illustrated in his paper "On the Text and Interpretation of certain passages in the Agamemnon of Aeschylus" (*Ibid.*, VIII, 1877). Other papers in the English *Journal of Philology* and articles in Liddell and Scott's *Greek-English Lexicon* (1883) exhibit his exactitude and lucidity in exposition.

Unlike many Greek scholars of his own and earlier generations, Goodwin early saw the advantage, if not the necessity, of visiting Greece. He became one of the founders of the Archæological Institute of America (1879), and was the first director of the American School of Classical Studies in Athens (1882–83). The result was a paper of the first importance on "The Battle of Salamis," first published in the *Papers of the American School of Classical Studies in Athens* (vol. I, 1885), and later in the *Harvard Studies in Classical Philology* (vol. XVII, 1906). In recognition of the quality of his scholarship he received many honorary degrees from American and foreign universities and was elected to membership in many learned societies.

Goodwin was among the first to admit women of advanced training to his courses. Becoming one of the incorporators of the Society for the Collegiate Instruction of Women and later of its successor, Radcliffe College, he served on various of its governing boards until his death. His home life was one of rare sweetness and dignity. He was twice married happily. By his first wife, Emily Jenks of Philadelphia, he had two sons, one of whom died in infancy. The other, Charles Haven, died a year after his graduation in 1888. In his memory Goodwin founded one of the best endowed scholarships in his university. His second wife, Ellen Chandler, whom he married in 1882, died in 1914. The virtues of his ancestors were reflected in his own frank and simple bearing, his clear, though somewhat hurried, speech, his forthright and upright life. Upon the solid qualities of his Pilgrim ancestry, which had given him a reticence and a poise not unlike the reticence of his own Greeks, he superimposed a culture that was cosmopolitan, a purity of word and action that made him, as President Eliot said, "a model of the vigorous, high-minded, happy scholar."

[*Harvard Grads.' Mag.*, Sept. 1912; *Proc. Am. Phil.*

Soc., vol. LII (1913); *Proc. Am. Acad. Arts and Sci.*, vol. LIII (1918); *Proc. Mass. Hist. Soc.*, vol. XLVI (1913); Harvard Univ., Minutes of the Faculty of Arts and Sciences, Oct. 29, 1912; *Boston Transcript*, June 17, 1912; personal acquaintance.] C. B. G.

GOODYEAR, CHARLES (Dec. 29, 1800–July 1, 1860), inventor, was born in New Haven, Conn., the son of Amasa and Cynthia (Bateman) Goodyear. He was of the fourth generation descended from Stephen Goodyear, who succeeded Gov. Eaton as leader of the company of London merchants which founded the New Haven colony in 1638. Running true to type, Charles's father was a hardware manufacturer and merchant. He specialized more or less in farming tools, such as hay forks and scythes, of his own invention, but also manufactured metal and pearl buttons. In this environment young Goodyear grew up, attended the local public schools, and divided his time between the factory, store, and farm which his father owned. While still young he indicated a desire to continue his studies and enter the ministry, but his father, convinced that Charles possessed good business ability, placed him at the age of seventeen in the hardware store of the Rogers brothers in Philadelphia to learn merchandising. Here Goodyear remained until he came of age, and then he returned to New Haven to become his father's business partner. For five years father and son worked together in building up their business, the former constantly at work devising new and improved tools for home and farm use, while the latter attended to the sales, contributing occasionally an idea for a new product, but showing no particular interest in developing it. During this time, too, on Aug. 24, 1824, young Goodyear married Clarissa Beecher of New Haven.

In 1826 Charles Goodyear moved to Philadelphia where he opened a hardware store, handling chiefly the products of his father's manufactory. Four years later both father and son were bankrupt because of their unusual liberality in extending credit to retail dealers as well as individual customers. Charles, too, was broken in health, and his outlook for the future was far from pleasant. He did not take advantage of the bankrupt laws but partially held off creditors by giving them interests in newly invented hardware products. Even so, both father and son owed many thousands of dollars. As a matter of fact, time and again for the next thirty years until his death, Goodyear was thrown into prison for failure to pay some debt. In 1834, while on a business trip to New York, he chanced to see the store sign of the Roxbury India Rubber Company and stopped in. He was particularly interested in an inflated rubber life-preserver which he saw in the window, and on examining it, observed that the inflating valve was rather crude. Believing that a better valve to be made by his father might be the means of repaying some of their debts, Goodyear applied himself to the task of designing one and within a few days again stopped at the Roxbury store with his model. The manager, however, upon seeing it, was more impressed with Goodyear's potential ingenuity than the actual example of it. He intimated that it would be more to Goodyear's material benefit were he to perfect a process of curing India rubber in such a way as to prevent it from sticking, melting, and decomposing in summer. Goodyear then learned of the difficulties faced by the American India rubber companies because of this failure of the rubber goods which they made and sold. The industry had come into existence in 1830 and had experienced a mushroom growth for four years and then collapsed with losses in excess of $2,000,000.

Much impressed, Goodyear went back to Philadelphia, and began optimistically to experiment with rubber. His first tests were made in jail, where he was committed for debts immediately upon his return. He plunged into the task literally with no other tools than an unusually sanguine and determined nature and a firm belief in the future for rubber. He began by kneading into the raw rubber (he could purchase this for practically nothing, since the market had collapsed) every conceivable material. Magnesia seemed to give the most promising results, and in the winter of 1834–35, with money advanced by a friend, and using the kitchen of his home as a work shop, he coated cloth with his "gum elastic," made shoes with it, and stored them away. With the coming of hot weather, however, his product fared no better than that of the defunct rubber companies, for it, too, melted. Undaunted, he continued to mix and knead his raw product with liquids and inert materials for the whole year of 1836 without a single encouraging result. By this time his funds as well as the patience of his friends were exhausted and one by one his personal belongings and household effects found their way to the pawn shops.

In the spring of 1837 Goodyear found a home in the country near New Haven for his family and after establishing them there and relying upon the charity of friends and neighbors to feed them, he went to New York to experiment further. One friend gave him a room and another (a druggist) supplied him with rubber and chemicals with which he again set to work. Shortly thereafter he experienced some encouraging results and obtained Patent No. 240 on

June 17, 1837. In this he claimed to destroy the adhesive properties of rubber by superficial applications of the metals—nitric acid with copper or bismuth being especially recommended. He also claimed the use of lime with the gum to bleach it. With this process patented, Goodyear obtained another financial backer. Then renting an abandoned rubber factory on Staten Island, he began making samples of useful and ornamental articles—toys, maps, surgical bandages, and even clothing. To prove the value and wearing qualities of this latter product he made and wore a suit and shoes. This act, incidentally, led some one to remark of him, "If you meet a man who has on an India rubber cap, stock, coat, vest and shoes, with an India rubber money purse without a cent of money in it, that is he" (*Gum-Elastic and Its Varieties,* p. 110). Capitalists, however, could not be inveigled into investing in rubber and Goodyear's efforts to introduce his process commercially were unsuccessful. Again he and his family were destitute; they were then living on Staten Island, N. Y. Friends and relatives pleaded with him to give up his interest in rubber and go back to the business he knew, but to no avail. Instead, with a small loan of money, Goodyear took his family back to New Haven, while he went on to Roxbury, Mass., where the rubber industry had started and where the abandoned rubber factories with their valuable machinery still stood. There he met E. M. Chaffee, the original champion of rubber, and John Haskins, one of the factory managers, and through their kindness was allowed to use the idle equipment. Then by his patented process, in the winter of 1837–38 he made and sold shoes, piano covers, table-cloths and the like, and for a time was able to support his family in comfort. He had not yet discovered, however, the process of vulcanizing rubber upon which the industry was later founded.

Early in 1838 Goodyear met Nathaniel M. Hayward [*q.v.*] of Woburn, Mass., a former employee of one of the rubber companies, who was about to patent his discovery that sulfur spread on rubber eliminated its stickiness. Goodyear naturally was much interested in this and during that year employed Hayward to experiment further with sulfur. It was arranged between them, too, that Goodyear be made assignor to Hayward's patent, granted Feb. 24, 1839. The Hayward process consisted of dissolving sulfur in oil of turpentine and mixing it with the rubber and then treating that product with Goodyear's patented acid and metal coating. This was the starting point of vulcanization, which consists in mixing sulfur and rubber and heating it for a number of hours. Up to this time heat had been the cause of the failure of all of Goodyear's rubber products, both melting and decomposing them, but shortly after acquiring Hayward's patent and while engaged in an animated argument with a group of men in his room, Goodyear accidentally dropped a mass of the sulfur and rubber mixture which he had in his hand on top of the red-hot stove. To his astonishment the mass did not melt, as he expected, and while it was charred a bit, there was not a sticky place on it. With five years of experimenting back of him Goodyear felt positive that he had solved the mystery of rubber. This was true, for he had discovered the process which afterwards came to be known as "vulcanization."

With his family in dire need, Goodyear struggled on in experimentation—now with various mixes and baking temperatures—and made samples which remained elastic at all temperatures. He went further and produced "hard" rubber as well as "soft," but with each month of work he found himself isolated. Friends and relatives would have nothing to do with him, no one would listen to him, and two years passed before a single person would believe him. Three years more he struggled with the problems of proper mix and heat to obtain a uniform product. For this he occasionally received some money from his wealthy brother-in-law, William C. de Forrest, and eventually from the Rider brothers in New York. The cost of these experiments exceeded $50,000, all of which Goodyear borrowed but never was able to repay. Finally he had perfected his process to such a degree that he applied for and received his celebrated Patent No. 3,633 on June 15, 1844. This patent was reissued in two divisions, on Dec. 25, 1849, and again on Nov. 20, 1860, and was extended for seven years from June 15, 1858. While it was an immensely valuable patent, Goodyear reaped but a small share of the profits. The reason for this was that he was a most poverty-stricken man, heavily in debt, and was obliged to sell licenses and establish royalties at a price far below the real value of the rights conveyed. Daniel Webster, whose fee was $25,000 for defending in 1852 the patent rights of companies operating under licenses from Goodyear, received more money than Goodyear ever acquired for himself and his family.

Having established the rubber industry in the United States, Goodyear went to Europe in 1851 with his family to extend his patent. As an advertisement he designed a magnificent exhibit at the great international exhibition in London which cost him $30,000. Everything in the exhibit was of rubber—furniture, floor-covering, jewelry, books. Again in 1855 at the Exposition Universelle in Paris he spent $50,000 for a similar exhibit. For this Napoleon conferred upon him the Grand Medal of Honor and the Cross of the Legion of Honor. He borrowed money for both exhibitions. He obtained loans also to secure his foreign patents, which were granted in all countries except England. Here Thomas Hancock had received a patent for vulcanizing rubber in 1843. Goodyear brought suit for infringement but lost (July 1855). In addition to these activities he succeeded in selling manufacturing licenses in England, France, and Germany, and before he returned to the United States a rubber industry in Europe employing 60,000 hands had been established. He found time, too, to write a book, *Gum Elastic and Its Varieties* (2 vols., 1853). It was bound in India rubber, and a few copies "designed for public libraries," were printed on India rubber tissue. After remaining abroad about eight years, during which time his wife died and he married Fanny Wardell of London in 1854, Goodyear returned with his family to America. So poor was he at the time that he was compelled to pawn his wife's jewelry to pay boat passage. For a time thereafter he again flourished, took up his experiments, and discovered new uses for rubber. While he claimed in his patents nearly five hundred uses for his product, he overlooked rubber tires. About the beginning of 1860 his health began to fail seriously. He had never been robust, and his many years of deprivation now told on him. In this state he was completely overcome by the sudden death of a favorite daughter and died in a hotel in New York while on his way to his daughter's bedside. Instead of a rich estate he left to his widow and six children debts approximating two-hundred thousand dollars.

[*Gum-Elastic and Its Varieties* contains considerable autobiographical material. Other sources include: James Parton, *Famous Americans of Recent Times* (1867); B. K. Peirce, *Trials of an Inventor: Life and Discoveries of Chas. Goodyear* (1866); E. W. Byrn, *The Progress of Invention in the Nineteenth Century* (1900); B. W. Kaempffert, ed., *A Popular Hist. of Am. Invention* (1924), I, 163–70; Grace Goodyear Kirkman, *Geneal. of the Goodyear Family* (1899); Geo. Iles, *Leading Am. Inventors* (1912); *N. Y. Tribune*, July 2, 1860; Nat. Museum and Patent Office records.]

C. W. M.

GOODYEAR, CHARLES (Jan. 1, 1833–May 22, 1896), industrialist, was born in Germantown, Pa., the son of Charles [*q.v.*] and Clarissa (Beecher) Goodyear. William Henry Goodyear [*q.v.*] was his youngest brother. His father, originally a hardware merchant, became so engrossed in a determination to find a way to vulcanize rubber that he gave up every opportunity to earn money and instead trusted to the charity of his friends and relatives to keep his wife and children from starving. This was the environment in which Charles was reared, living in poverty first in the country outside of Philadelphia, then in New Haven, where he obtained an elementary education, on Staten Island, N. Y., in Europe for a number of years, and finally in New York City. As he grew up he helped his father, as did his mother, brothers, and sisters, with his many experiments and in the making of rubber goods of one sort or another. After his father had secured his famous patent and had sold licenses to manufacturers, Charles assisted him in this business and carried it on alone after the elder Goodyear's death in 1860. Meanwhile, however, Howe had invented the practical sewing-machine and Charles was amongst those who saw the possibility of its application to the manufacture of shoes. Even before his father's death he had become interested in the shoe-making business in Philadelphia, and at the opening of the Civil War was president of the American Shoe-tip Company.

Thus launched in the shoe industry and possessing a clear-cut picture of the course of its future development—a complete machine-made shoe—Goodyear kept a sharp lookout for possible ideas which might be of value. In 1864 he made his first accession by purchase—a machine to stitch light "turned" soles, invented by Auguste Destouy. He then organized the Goodyear Shoe Machinery Company to make and sell this device. In 1867 he purchased another patented shoe-sewing-machine, invented by Christian Dancel, and employed Dancel as his factory superintendent. Ever alert for men or ideas, he employed a second mechanical expert named Mills in the same year. Although leading shoe manufacturers looked upon his idea as a mere chimera, he went ahead and organized a company in England in 1870 and then reorganized his New York firm in 1871 as the Goodyear Boot & Shoe Machinery Company. During the succeeding years his experts made progress in creating machines, which were marketed, but they were never sold in sufficient quantity to offset the enormous costs of experiment. Dancel, too, by 1874 had developed the rudiments of the perfect machine, but it was not until 1885 that Goodyear's dream was even partially realized. Being a genius for organization, Goodyear obtained the help of Jonathan Munyon, who brought about a consolidation with Goodyear's competitor Gordon McKay, by which, after 1880, McKay took care of the turned-shoe business and Goodyear the welt-shoe business. Munyon likewise had a genius for putting the products of the two on the market, and from that time on, both businesses flourished. Goodyear finally retired in 1888 and spent the remaining eight years of his life between his Florida, North Carolina, and New York homes. He was married to Mary Henrietta Colt of New Haven, Conn., July 14, 1858, who with three sons and four daughters survived him.

[Grace Goodyear Kirkman, *Geneal. of the Goodyear Family* (1899); B. W. Kaempffert, *A Popular Hist. of Am. Inventions* (2 vols., 1924); F. A. Gannon, *Shoemaking Old and New* (1911); F. J. Allen, *The Shoe Industry, Old and New* (1916); *Shoe and Leather Reporter,* May 28, 1896; *N. Y. Times, N. Y. Tribune,* May 23, 1896.] C. W. M.

GOODYEAR, WILLIAM HENRY (Apr. 21, 1846–Feb. 19, 1923), archeologist, curator, author, was born in New Haven, Conn., the youngest son of the inventor, Charles Goodyear [*q.v.*], and his wife, Clarissa Beecher. He spent six boyhood years in England and France, gaining a cosmopolitan background which he broadened at Yale by specializing in history. After his graduation in 1867, he went to Heidelberg and later to Berlin for further study in history and Roman law. The accident of ill health sent him to Italy, where he became deeply interested in Roman and medieval antiquities. He returned to Berlin to study under the eminent archeologist, Karl Friederichs, whom he accompanied to Cyprus in 1869 when the latter went to negotiate for the Di Cesnola finds. Goodyear returned through Syria, Greece, and Italy, studying the monuments. At Pisa in February 1870, he made important discoveries which determined his life-work. Taking his cue from Ruskin's notes on architectural "refinements" at Pisa, he subjected the cathedral group to a searching survey with foot rule and plumb-line, bringing to light an amazing number of subtle irregularities—bends, leans, curves in lines and surfaces supposedly straight—which he was able to demonstrate could not be due to accident or settling, but must be the result of the architect's reasoned esthetic intent. In August 1874 he published the results in *Scribner's Monthly,* under the title, "A Lost Art," promulgating the theory that until Gothic tradition was discarded during the Renaissance, mathematical regularity in the great buildings of history was the exception rather than the rule.

Twenty years elapsed before Goodyear had the financial means to pursue investigations necessary to prove the wide distribution of refinements, to trace their historic continuity from remote classic antiquity to the Renaissance, and to restore them to vitality in modern building design; ut he never abandoned his purpose. In the interim he embarked upon the long career of teaching, writing, and educational lecturing which, extending over thirty-five years, did so much to awaken in America some sense of artistic values. His knowledge of Cypriote antiquities won him in 1882 a curatorship at the Metropolitan Museum. Eight years later he was called to the Museum of the Brooklyn Institute of Arts and Sciences where he remained at the head of the department of fine arts from its organization until his death. During his museum years he gained, according to Conrow, an extensive grasp of historic painting, Greek and modern sculpture, ceramics, jade, and ancient glass, and a scholarly grasp of classic and American archeology, ethnology, and anthropology. At his suggestion the Children's Museum of the Brooklyn Institute was established in 1899 and in 1902 he helped to found the American Anthropological Association. Meanwhile from his pen had come *A History of Art* (1888); *Roman and Medieval Art* (1893); and *Renaissance and Modern Art* (1894).

In 1891, at the close of a research trip to Egypt, Goodyear completed his *Grammar of the Lotus,* tracing the origin of Greek ornament to the symbols of the sun-worshipers. By 1895 financial backing was assured for the long-delayed survey of the architectural monuments of Europe which he carried out between that year and 1914. Using as detectives camera and plumb-line, he gathered with infinite pains survey proofs of refinements in Egyptian, Greek, Roman, Byzantine, and Gothic buildings. With the publication of the data in American and foreign technical journals, and with the exhibition here and abroad of enlarged survey photographs, many eminent authorities were convinced not only of the structural and therefore purposed character of the irregularities, but of their effectiveness in enhancing the apparent size of structures as well as the interest and vitality of the architecture. Goodyear's catalogues for the survey exhibitions in Rome and in Edinburgh in 1905 are, according to Porter, among his most important utterances on the subject, and in general the pronouncements of learned societies and critics indicate that he largely won his case for deviation as the traditional practise in the architecture of all but modern times. By the rediscovery of this fundamental principle, repairs begun upon St. Mark's, Venice, and projected for the Leaning Tower of Pisa were checked, and refinements were incorporated in such modern buildings as the Cathedral of St. John the Divine in New York, the Columbia University Library, the Albright Art Gallery, Buffalo, N. Y., and the

Art Museum in Fairmount Park, Philadelphia. At the time of his death Goodyear was engaged in drawing together in definitive book form his widely scattered papers on refinements. The introductory volume, *Greek Refinements,* was published in 1912. For the publication of the remainder of his studies a fund was subscribed by friends of the Architectural Research and the Brooklyn Museum. Goodyear was thrice married: on June 30, 1871, to Mrs. Sarah M. Sanford; on Feb. 1, 1879, to Nellie F. M. Johns, and on Jan. 1, 1897, to Mary Katharine Convert.

[W. S. Conrow, "Wm. Henry Goodyear: An Appreciation," *Brooklyn Museum Quart.,* July 1923; Russell Sturgis and A. L. Frothingham, *A Hist. of Architecture,* III (1915), 60–62; A. Kingsley Porter, review of *Greek Refinements, N. Y. Times,* Apr. 5, 1914; G. H. T. Middleton, "Deliberate Deception in Ancient Buildings," the *Nineteenth Century,* Mar. 1897; C. E. Norton, *Hist. Studies of Church Building in the Middle Ages* (1880), p. 321; Russell Sturgis, ed., *A Dict. of Architecture and Building,* III (1902), pp. 263–68; *Jour. of the Royal Inst. of British Architects,* June 1906, Nov. 1907; Antonio Taramelli, in *L'Arte,* Jan.–Apr. 1900; *Gazzetta di Venezia,* Nov. 9, 1903; *Yale Univ. Obit. Record,* 8 ser., no. 3 (1923); *Brooklyn Daily Eagle,* Feb. 19, 20, 1923; *N. Y. Times,* Feb. 20, 1923.]

M. B. H.

GOOKIN, DANIEL (1612–Mar. 19, 1686/7), colonist, soldier, magistrate, was the third son of Daniel Gookin of Carrigaline, Ireland, and his wife Mary Byrd, daughter of Canon Richard Byrd of Canterbury Cathedral. The father had lived in Kent and the younger Daniel may have been born in Kent, England, or County Cork, Ireland. The father was much interested in colonial ventures, Virginian and New England, but they proved unprofitable. The earliest glimpse which we have of the son was when he was eighteen years old, living temporarily on his father's plantation in Virginia near Newport News. In February 1634/5 young Daniel was granted 2,500 acres on the south side of the James River. In 1639 he was in London and on Nov. 11 of that year a license, in which he was described as a widower, was issued for his marriage to Mary Dolling. Since Edward Johnson later spoke of him as a Kentish soldier (*post,* p. 230), it is possible that he may have seen military service during this stay in Europe. Early in 1641, with his wife and infant son, he went to Virginia intending to settle there, on his Nansemond plantation. He was at once made a burgess and represented Upper Norfolk in the Assembly beginning January 1641/2. He held other offices, including that of captain of the train bands, and in 1642 received a grant of 1,400 acres additional. He was an ardent Puritan and one of the signers of the "Nansemond Petition" praying the Elders of the Church in Massachusetts to send clergy to Virginia. After the passage of the Act of Conformity (March 1642/3), Gookin decided to leave Virginia and took up lands in Maryland near the present Annapolis. He soon determined to emigrate to Massachusetts and arrived in Boston with his family May 20, 1644, being admitted to the First Church May 26 and made a freeman on May 29. He settled at Roxbury, but little is known of him for the next three or four years, except that he was one of the founders of the free grammar school there and made at least one visit to Virginia. He appears to have been engaged in the intercolonial coasting trade. In 1648 he moved to Cambridge and was granted 500 acres there in 1649. He was made captain of the train band, a post he held for nearly forty years, and in 1649 was elected deputy to the General Court. The next year he was in England, but was deputy again in 1651 and in 1652 was chosen Assistant, being chosen to that office every year, except 1676, for thirty-five years. He was again in England in 1655 when he saw Cromwell and was appointed by him to push the matter of Jamaican settlement from New England, although Gookin did not approve of the venture. After a visit to Massachusetts, he returned to England, 1658, and was made collector of customs and afterward "Deputy Treasurer at War" at Dunkirk, but was at Cambridge again by 1660. He engaged in land deals, was one of the projectors and proprietors of the new town of Worcester; held various local offices; and became sergeant-major of the regiment of Middlesex and in 1681 major-general of all the forces of the colony. He was greatly interested in the welfare of the Indians and his efforts on their behalf were second only to those of Eliot. In 1656 and again in 1661 he was "chosen to be ruler over the praying Indians," and his defense of them during King Philip's War, when the frenzy of the people was directed against them as well as against the enemy, made him extremely unpopular in Massachusetts. In 1680 he came out strongly as a strict constructionist of the charter and was opposed to sending agents to England and to obeying the laws of trade. His wife died Oct. 27, 1683, and he married within two years Mrs. Hannah (Tyng) Savage. He wrote three books, none of which was published until long after his death. These works included "An Historical Account of the Doings and Sufferings of the Christian Indians of New England" (*Transactions and Collections of the American Antiquarian Society,* vol. II, 1836), "Historical Collections of the Indians in New England" (*Massachusetts Historical Society Collections,* 1 ser., I, 1792), and an unfinished History of New England, which has been lost.

[F. W. Gookin, *Daniel Gookin, 1612–1687* (1912); J. W. Thornton, "The Gookin Family," in *New-Eng. Hist. and Geneal. Reg.*, Oct. 1847, Apr. 1848; *Ibid.*, Jan. 1853, p. 59; Edward Johnson, *A Hist. of New-England,* etc. (1654), reprinted in *Johnson's Wonder-working Providence, 1628–51* (1910), ed. by J. F. Jameson.]

J. T. A.

GOOLD, WILLIAM A. (Nov. 5, 1830–Dec. 19, 1912), Alabama coal-miner, prospector, and operator, was born near Glasgow, Scotland. He was the son of James Goold, a coal-miner, and Jeannette (Smith) Goold. At the age of ten he deserted the schoolroom for the coal-mine and entered upon a long life of association with the coal trade. In 1852 he emigrated to America and settled in the Pennsylvania coal-fields. For two years he plied the coal trade in Pennsylvania, Maryland, and Virginia, making enough money to send for his wife and son, who were still in Scotland. At this time there was considerable coal-mining activity in Alabama. Sensing possibilities in this new field, Goold went South in 1854 and leased the Hewell mines near Tuscaloosa, where he made the first coke produced in the state. Thus began one of the most romantic careers in the history of the coal industry in Alabama. For more than fifty years he tramped the vast mineral solitudes of the state, and probed and prospected for adventure and wealth. In 1855 the Tuscaloosa mines failed and Goold became manager of mines at Montevallo. Two years later he opened the Raglan mines in St. Clair County and shipped large amounts of coal down the Coosa and Alabama Rivers. During the Civil War he opened mines in the Cahaba field, near Helena, from which he shipped large quantities of coal to the Confederate iron works at Selma. Burned out by the Wilson raiders, he entered the cotton-brokers' business at Selma, failed, and then resumed coal-mining and coking in Shelby County in the "Goold seam."

In 1871 he took to the woods again. During the next thirty years the call of the rugged black-jack and scrubby pine ridges kept this small, slightly built, wiry man tramping and grubbing for hidden treasures. He covered the vast mineral region from the Coosa River to the Tennessee, opening several mines of his own and prospecting and managing mines for large coal companies organized in the district. His most notable achievement, however, was tapping the Browne seam in the Warrior field, which contained a vast quantity of first-class coking coal, and from which the first coke pig iron in Alabama was made. To the well-known Pratt Coal & Coke Company, organized to exploit the Browne seam, Goold sold his small property for a pittance. He assisted in opening the Pratt mines, then plunged into the woods again, prospecting for himself and for companies in the Birmingham and Sheffield districts, and managing mines for them. "Uncle Billy" Goold, as he was called, knew the history of Alabama's coal and iron industry and told many thrilling stories of its checkered course. The stubborn hills he loved yielded him fair wealth, but he lost it in his last mine, in Tuscaloosa County. At eighty-two he lay down to rest, a quaint, jovial, and canny old Scotchman.

[Ethel M. Armes, *The Story of Coal and Iron in Ala.* (1910); *Jefferson County and Birmingham, Ala.* (1887), ed. by J. W. Dubose; T. M. Owen, *Hist. of Ala. and Dict. of Ala. Biog.* (1921), vol. III; the *Age-Herald* (Birmingham), Dec. 20, 1912; information as to certain facts from Goold's son, William Goold, Acmar, Ala., and R. F. Lovelady, Birmingham, Ala.]

A. B. M.

GORDIN, JACOB (May 1, 1853–June 11, 1909), American-Yiddish playwright, was born in Mirgorod, Poltava, Russia. He was the son of rich and educated parents, Michael and Ida Gordin, and had the advantage, rare with Jews of that day in Russia, of a good private-school education. Before he emigrated to America in 1891, he was a teacher, a journalist, and a dramatic critic. He was a great admirer of Tolstoy, and the fact that he was born in Gogol's native town may have had an added influence in Russianizing his literary tastes, for even though his reputation was achieved as a Yiddish playwright, he remained much more characteristically Russian than Russian-Jewish in his approach both to life and to the theatre. In fact, the qualities of his playwriting can hardly be fully appreciated without a knowledge of the Russian theory of the theatre and of acting. Yet his plays were immediately successful, and his influence was profound on the people who attended the Yiddish theatres which flourished on the lower East Side of New York during the last years of the nineteenth century and the beginning of the twentieth, and which were considered by distinguished critics of the time to be far superior to the regular Broadway theatre in playwriting and acting. The Thalia Theatre, with which he was connected, was the most literary of the group, and was associated with the acting of Bertha Kalich. At the People's Theatre Jacob Adler appeared in his dramas.

Gordin's first play, *Siberia,* was also the first thing he had written in Yiddish. It was produced in 1892, and was followed by about thirty-five other original plays, forty-three adaptations and free translations, and twelve one-act plays. Among the best-known of these are: *The Jewish King Lear*; *God, Man and the Devil*; *Mirele Efros*; *The Wild Man*; *The Jewish Priest*; *Sol-*

omon Kaus; *The Slaughter*; *The Jewish Queen Lear*; and a dramatization of the *Kreutzer Sonata* which was later adapted by Langdon Mitchell and produced in English by Harrison Grey Fiske in 1907. He was, too, the author of numerous short stories, essays, and newspaper articles, and even for a short time early in his career, edited a Russian newspaper in New York. He wrote for the theatre at a time when a stark realism was considered the finest form of drama, and many of his plays bear the mark of a realism so heightened as to approach caricature, especially those which deal with life in the Ghetto. In performance this effect was increased by the interpolation of clownish interludes, out of all relation to the plays themselves, to which he seriously objected, but which were the custom in the Yiddish as in other folk theatres. Gordin never attempted literally to interpret his people, believing that that was not a dramatist's vocation. He often said, "I am not a Jewish writer; I am merely a writer writing for Jews" (*American Hebrew, post,* p. 173). A dramatic figure himself, he achieved great personal popularity and influence in his district. He had eleven children, five daughters and six sons. He founded the "Educational League," a cultural society, before which he often lectured and to which he devoted much time and effort. After his death a journalist, writing of him, said, "There was never a coarse word, or lewd expression, or any frivolous game, or show talk in his presence" (*Ibid.*, p. 172). He died in Brooklyn at the age of fifty-six.

[Hutchins Hapgood, *The Spirit of the Ghetto* (1902); Bernard G. Richards, article in the *Am. Hebrew,* June 18, 1909; Judith Herz, article in the *New Era Illustrated Mag.*, Dec. 1903; *N. Y. Dramatic Mirror,* June 19, 1909; *Theatre Mag.*, July 1909; "The Shakespeare of the Ghetto," *Literary Digest,* July 3, 1909; *N. Y. Times,* June 12, 1909. Gordin's works were collected and published in Yiddish in 1910.]

E. J. R. I.

GORDON, ANDREW (Sept. 17, 1828–Aug. 13, 1887), pioneer missionary of the United Presbyterian Church in India, the fifth child of Rev. Alexander Gordon and Margaret (Martin) Gordon, was born in Putnam, Washington County, N. Y., where his father, a native of Montrose, Scotland, was pastor of the United Presbyterian Church. His mother died when he was a little more than four years old, and his father, when he was barely seventeen. During his boyhood he was obliged to work in order to help support the family, but by attendance at country schools and a short period of study at an academy in Johnstown, Fulton County, N. Y., he managed to prepare himself for Franklin College, New Athens, Ohio, from which he graduated on Sept. 25, 1850. He attended the theological seminary at Canonsburg, Pa., and on Nov. 2, 1853, he was licensed to preach by the Albany Presbytery. In the meantime, May 18, 1852, he had married Rebecca Campbell Smith of New Athens.

In May 1853 the Associate Presbyterian Synod, assembled at Pittsburgh, resolved to establish a mission in India, and at its meeting in Albany the following year elected J. T. Tate and Gordon as its missionaries. The former declined the appointment, but after much hesitation Gordon decided to undertake the enterprise single-handed, and on Aug. 29, 1854, in the Charles Street Church, New York, he was ordained "to preach the Gospel in North India." With this rather indefinite commission, accompanied by his wife and small daughter, he set sail for Calcutta on Sept. 28, arriving there Feb. 13, 1855. So long and tedious was the voyage, Gordon wrote, that "our child outgrew her clothes. New garments became old and were worn out. The events of the voyage faded from memory in the monotonous past." After a further journey of some 1,700 miles in a wagon drawn by coolies, he arrived in Siälkot, in the Punjab, which he had finally chosen as the seat of the mission. Here, more or less isolated, and for some time feebly supported, he succeeded in establishing an increasingly important work. Thirty years later its agencies comprised eight organized churches, theological and literary institutions, and numerous schools. During this period Gordon was in the United States from 1865 to 1875, having been invalided home, but while here was actively engaged in behalf of missions. After his final return from the field in 1885, he wrote a full and vivid account of the history of his enterprise under the title *Our India Mission* (1886), two chapters of which deal with the Sepoy mutiny. He entered the sanitarium at Clifton Springs, N. Y., because of failing health, but a week before his death was taken to Philadelphia, where he died in the home of a friend and was buried in West Laurel Hill Cemetery.

[H. O. Dwight, H. A. Tupper, E. M. Bliss, *The Encyc. of Missions* (2nd ed., 1904); *Phila. Inquirer,* Aug. 15, 1887; *United Presbyterian* (Pittsburgh), Aug. 25, Sept. 29, 1887; Crisfield Johnson, *Hist. of Washington County, N. Y.* (1878); information from the Board of Foreign Missions of the United Presbyterian Church of North America; and Gordon's *Our India Mission,* above.]

H. E. S.

GORDON, GEORGE ANGIER (Jan. 2, 1853–Oct. 25, 1929), Congregational clergyman, author, was the son of George and Catherine (Hutcheon) Gordon. He was born, of farming ancestry, on the estate of Pitodrie, of which his father was overseer, in the parish of Oyne, Aberdeenshire, Scotland. In his boyhood he worked on the farm and obtained an elementary education in local schools. Emigrating to America, he reached Boston on July 13, 1871, and for three years he worked at various manual trades. True to his Scottish upbringing, he promptly sought out a Presbyterian church. Rev. Luther H. Angier, the pastor of the church which he selected, discerning the young man's mental and spiritual promise, encouraged him to study for the ministry and secured his admittance on Sept. 16, 1874, to the Congregational theological school in Bangor, Me., from which he graduated in 1877. During the summers of 1875 and 1876 he acted as minister of a small missionary parish in Temple, Me., which ordained him as its pastor on June 20, 1877. His ministry here was brief, for his keen intellectual interests prompted him to further study. Again through the good offices of Mr. Angier (whose surname he adopted as his own middle name) he was enabled to enter Harvard College as a special student in the autumn of 1878. Here he attracted the attention of President Eliot and Professors James, Palmer, and Goodwin, and, after two years, was admitted to the senior class, receiving in 1881 the degree of B.A., with honors in philosophy. On Aug. 1, 1881, he became pastor of the Second Congregational Church in Greenwich, Conn., where he remained until called to the Old South Church in Boston. He was installed as its pastor on Apr. 2, 1884, and served until his death, although his active duties ceased in 1927. On June 3, 1890, he married Susan Huntington Manning, daughter of his predecessor in the ministry of Old South Church.

The Council convened to advise upon Gordon's installation in Boston was not unanimous in its approval of him. Some of its members were startled by the "heresies" of the young candidate, and for several years he was regarded as a dangerous radical in Congregational circles. But the utter sincerity of his character, his power as a preacher, and the success of his ministry gradually wore down opposition. His loyalty to Harvard was firm and constant. He served on the first board of preachers, under the voluntary system, 1886–90, again as university preacher, 1906–09, as a member of the board of overseers and as president of the alumni association. Various colleges testified to his learning and ability by bestowing upon him their honorary degrees.

Gordon was a philosopher who knew how to preach, and a theologian with religious insight and fervor. Philosophically, he was influenced most deeply by Plato, Aristotle, and Kant; theologically, he reasoned "through man to God." Beginning his sustained thinking at a time when Idealism prevailed, and in a region where the influence of Emerson was strong, he accepted the philosophical principle of Unity but added to it the antithetical principle of Difference, thus maintaining a concrete unity in diversity, instead of a simple, abstract unity. Holding both principles equally valid, he enshrined both in the being of God and so defended on philosophical grounds the doctrine of the Trinity. Afterward, he descended from this high level to that of a "social" or "domestic" Trinity, but his first important book, *The Christ of To-day* (1895), contains his most notable contribution to theological thought. Strenuously upholding the doctrine of the Trinity (he once humorously referred to himself as "the only Trinitarian left in New England"), he differed fundamentally from the Unitarians to whom in other respects he was closely allied, while his emphasis upon man's free moral agency, which might stand out forever against the divine love, separated him from the Universalists, notwithstanding his "new theodicy."

He was not a "popular preacher," for he held himself above topics of transient interest and never condescended to sentimentalism or triviality. He chose rather to deal with themes of eternal moment—the moral sovereignty of God, the tragic grandeur of Humanity, and individual responsibility to God—which he treated with mental resonance and moral passion. His was preëminently a teaching ministry to thoughtful men and women, and from his commanding position as minister of Old South Church he was the outstanding champion of religious freedom and theological progress in American Congregationalism. Despising sham and sensationalism, he was quick to recognize genuine intellectual promise and encourage with generous words of sympathy and appreciation many an obscure young clergyman whose frank expression of unconventional opinions had excited suspicion and distrust. His principal publications, in addition to the volume mentioned, include: *The Witness to Immortality in Literature, Philosophy and Life* (1893); *Immortality and the New Theodicy* (1897); *The New Epoch for Faith* (1901); *Ultimate Conceptions of Faith* (1903); *Through Man to God* (1906); *Religion and Miracle* (1909); *Revelation and the Ideal* (1913); *Aspects of the Infinite Mystery* (1916); *Humanism in New England Theology* (1920); *Unto Victory* (1927).

[G. A. Gordon, *My Education and Religion: An Au-*

tobiog. (1925); J. W. Buckham, *Progressive Religious Thought in America* (1919), pp. 86–142; *Twenty-fifth Anniversary Report of the Secretary of the Class of 1881 of Harvard Coll.* (1906); *Book of the Fortieth Year . . . Fortieth Anniversary of the Installation of Geo. A. Gordon . . . as Minister of the Old South Ch. in Boston* (1924); F. G. Peabody, memoir in *Proc. Am. Acad. of Arts and Sci.*, vol. LXIV, no. 12 (1930); *Our Heritage, Old South Ch., 1669–1919* (1919); the *Congregationalist* (Boston), Nov. 14, 21, Dec. 12, 1929; *Who's Who in America*, 1928–29; *Boston Transcript*, Oct. 25, 26, 1929.] W. W. F.

GORDON, GEORGE BYRON (Aug. 4, 1870–Jan. 30, 1927), archeologist, was born at New Perth, Prince Edward Island, Canada. He was the son of James and Jane McLaren Gordon, and, as the names attest, of Scotch ancestry. After attending the schools of his native country, he studied at the University of South Carolina. From 1890 to 1893 and again from 1901 to 1903 he was a student at Harvard University, receiving at the end of that time the D.S. degree in anthropology. Meanwhile, from 1894 to 1900 he was the chief of the Harvard archeological expedition to Honduras in Central America. The expedition's main field of work was at Copan, the ruins of which formed the subject of a number of his publications. In 1903 he was called to the University Museum in Philadelphia as assistant curator in the department of anthropology, and in the following year he became curator of the department and lecturer in anthropology in the University of Pennsylvania. The second of these positions he held until 1907, when he became assistant professor of anthropology. In 1915 he withdrew from teaching to devote his whole time to the Museum. He had been appointed director of the Museum in 1910, having been selected for this position with the hope that he could coördinate and reorganize its work. In this he was eminently successful, holding the directorship until early in 1927, when his tragic death resulted from a fall which fractured his skull.

Gordon's scientific interests were confined to anthropology until 1910. His special field of research was American anthropology. As curator of the anthropological section of the Museum he led an expedition to Alaska, thus gaining a first-hand knowledge of the far North similar to that which he had previously gained of the South. When he became director of the Museum, his interest at once broadened, and he devoted his energies to the task of making it a record of the history of mankind. Shortly after he became director, Charles Custis Harrison became president of the Museum's board, and the two worked together toward this end. Expeditions were sent to Egypt, Palestine, and Babylonia, in each of which countries notable work was begun. Not only was the Museum enriched from these sources, but a section of Chinese Art was added. The results of Gordon's studies appeared in book form as: *Researches in the Uloa Valley* (1898); *Caverns of Copan* (1898); *The Hieroglyphic Stairway, Ruins of Copan* (1902); *The Serpent Motive in the Ancient Art of Central America and Mexico* (1906); *The Book of Chilam Balam of Chumayel* (1913); *In the Alaska Wilderness* (1917); *Baalbek* (1919); and *Rambles in Old London* (1924). In addition to these works he contributed numerous articles and reviews to the *American Anthropologist*, the *Museum Journal*, and other periodicals. While Gordon possessed many attractive personal qualities, he found it difficult to cooperate in enterprises of which others were leaders, and had the reputation of being an exacting master. Like many Canadians, he was not entirely in sympathy with his American surroundings, and during the World War he did what he could to arouse Canada to do her share in preserving the British Empire.

[C. C. Harrison, memoir in the *Museum Jour.* (Phila.), Mar. 1927; *Who's Who in America*, 1926–27; *Museums Jour.* (London), Mar. 1927; *Am. Jour. of Archeol.*, July–Sept. 1927; *Pub. Ledger* (Phila.), Jan. 31, 1927.] G. A. B—n.

GORDON, GEORGE HENRY (July 19, 1823–Aug. 30, 1886), Union soldier, author, son of Robert and Elizabeth (Carlisle) Gordon, was born in Charlestown, Mass. When he was five years old his mother, then a widow, moved to Framingham, Mass. After graduating from Framingham Academy he entered West Point July 1, 1842, graduated in 1846, and became brevet second lieutenant in the Mounted Rifles. Then, following a short service in Jefferson Barracks, Mo., he was sent to Mexico, where he engaged in all the battles fought by Gen. Scott. He participated in the siege of Vera Cruz in March 1847, was wounded the following month in the battle of Cerro Gordo, and fought in the battles of Contreras and Chapultepec. For bravery at Cerro Gordo he was brevetted first lieutenant. He took part in the capture of Mexico City in September 1847 and two months later was severely wounded in a hand-to-hand engagement with two guerrillas near San Juan Bridge. After his recovery he was on frontier duty in Washington (1850–51) and at Fort Scott, Kan. (1853–54).

Gordon resigned in October 1854 and returned to Massachusetts. After attending Harvard Law School for two terms in 1855–56 he was admitted to practise in 1857. Having foreseen the probability of civil conflict, in April 1861, when news of the attack on Fort Sumter came to Boston, he immediately began to raise the regiment which became the 2nd Massachusetts Infantry. It was modeled upon the plan of the regular army and quickly became noted for its efficiency, bravery, and discipline. He was appointed colonel May 24, 1861. Although he was strongly recommended for appointment as a brigadier, he did not receive advancement until June 9, 1862, following his distinguished services in the retreat of Gen. Banks in the Shenandoah Valley. He was engaged in the battles of Winchester, Cedar Mountain, Chantilly, South Mountain, and Antietam. Early in 1863 his health failed but he had recovered enough to command a division in the siege of Suffolk and in the expedition toward Richmond. Late in 1863 he was engaged in operations around Charleston Harbor, S. C., and in July of the following year he was entrusted with keeping communications open by White River with Gen. Steele in Arkansas. In March 1865 he was placed in command of the Eastern District of Virginia and continued until relieved because of ill health in June 1865. He was brevetted major-general of volunteers Apr. 9, 1865.

Gordon had married Mary Elizabeth Scott in June 1864. When he was mustered out in August 1865 he returned to the practise of law in Boston. He was one of the founders of the Military Historical Society of Massachusetts and devoted the last years of his life to the military history of the Civil War. His *Brook Farm to Cedar Mountain . . . 1861–62* (1883), *History of the Campaign of the Army of Virginia . . . from Cedar Mountain to Alexandria, 1862* (1879), and *War Diary of Events . . . 1863–1865* (1882), form a continuous and valuable history of the campaigns with which he was associated. His strong opinions and trenchant criticisms which hindered his promotion in the army are evident in these volumes. He possessed a sense of humor and a large fund of anecdotes, but though his narrative is vivid and animated, he frequently wrote too much.

[Autobiographical materials in his own writings; Alonzo H. Quint, *Record of the Second Mass. Infantry, 1861–65* (1867); J. H. Temple, *Hist. of Framingham, Mass.* (pub. by the town, 1887); Geo. W. Cullum, *Biog. Reg. . . . U. S. Mil. Acad.* (3rd ed., 1891); *Official Records (Army)*; *Eighteenth Ann. Reunion. Asso. Grads. U. S. Mil. Acad.*, 1887; *Boston Transcript*, Aug. 31, 1886.]

F. M—n.

GORDON, GEORGE PHINEAS (Apr. 21, 1810–Jan. 27, 1878), printer, inventor, the son of Phineas and Mary (White) Gordon, was born in Salem, N. H., where the family had resided for a hundred years or more, and where his grandfather had been a tavern-keeper and the first postmaster. He received his primary education in Salem and subsequently attended an academy in Boston. Early in life he became an actor but presumably for the reason that he gained but little livelihood in this profession, he settled in New York and became an apprentice in the printer's trade. After completing his apprenticeship he opened a small job-printing office of his own in New York and operated it for a number of years. His early experiences in news offices and press rooms and his knowledge of the limitations which the available press equipment possessed, caused him around 1835 to begin to experiment in the construction of improved presses for card printing. He continued experimenting for more than fifteen years before he applied for any patents, the first one of which was granted him in 1851. While his job press had many defects he quickly made improvements and began to manufacture it, calling it the "Yankee" job press. A year or two later he introduced a second job press, called the "Turnover," from its method of manufacture, and in 1854 he brought out a press called the "Firefly," which was fed with strips of cards and could turn out approximately 10,000 cards an hour. About 1858 he invented the so-called "Franklin" press which was very successful and which subsequently became known as the "Gordon." It was extremely strong and well put together, and found its way into hundreds of offices for a great many years thereafter. This press had a rotating ink-distributing disk within which another ink disk revolved in the contrary direction. Both moved very slowly. An excellent distribution of ink was thus effected as the inking rollers passed over an entirely new surface every time they reached the disks.

Gordon built all told more than a hundred kinds of presses. At first he had them constructed in Rhode Island, but in 1872 he established works in Rahway, N. J., with offices in New York. He resided alternately in Rahway and Brooklyn. Apparently he never lost his interest in the stage, for in 1874 he built in Rahway a magnificent opera house for that city which unfortunately was destroyed by fire ten years later. In the course of his business career he secured over fifty patents for his inventions of presses and accumulated a large fortune. He suffered from ill health during the last few years of his life and at the time of his death he was living in Norfolk, Va., where he had gone to recuperate. He was twice married: first in 1846 to Sarah Cornish, and second in 1856 to Lenore May, who with a daughter by his first wife survived him. He was buried in Greenwood Cemetery, Brooklyn, N. Y.

[Edgar Gilbert, *Hist. of Salem, N. H.* (1907); *Am. Cyc. of Printing* (1871); W. W. Pasko, ed., *Am. Dict. of Printing and Bookmaking* (1894); 50 *N. J. Equity*, 397; *N. Y. Times*, Jan. 28, 1878; *Brooklyn Daily Eagle*, Jan. 30, 1878; Patent Office records.] C. W. M.

GORDON, GEORGE WASHINGTON (Oct. 5, 1836–Aug. 9, 1911), soldier, lawyer, politician, the son of Andrew and Eliza K. Gordon, was born in Giles County, middle Tennessee. Having grown to maturity, partly in Texas and Mississippi, the young man completed his education under Bushrod R. Johnson at the Western Institute of Nashville in 1859 and took up the work of surveying. Within two years the Civil War was precipitated, and he entered the service of his state. His first assignment was as drill-master of the 11th Tennessee Infantry. He joined this outfit at its rendezvous shortly after it was organized, and marched with it into East Tennessee, where he saw service under Gen. Zollicoffer and Gen. Kirby-Smith. In a short time he was elected captain of Company I, then he was promoted to the lieutenant-colonelcy and later to the command of the regiment (December 1862). Joining Bragg's army, he participated in the battles of Murfreesboro, Chickamauga, and Missionary Ridge. He followed Johnston to Atlanta and was promoted to the rank of brigadier-general after the battle of Kenesaw Mountain. After the fall of Atlanta, he followed Hood to middle Tennessee and in the bloody battle of Franklin, where every brigade commander except himself was killed, he was wounded and captured within the Federal lines. He is said to have been the youngest and one of the most dashing of the Confederate brigadiers.

When the conflict was over, Gordon was still a young man of twenty-nine. Though a battle-scarred veteran of many campaigns, he started life over by taking up the study of law at Cumberland University at Lebanon, Tenn. Having completed his preparation, he entered upon the practise of his profession at Pulaski, but soon removed to Memphis, where he labored unobtrusively for a number of years. Meanwhile he acquired a large plantation in Mississippi. The quality of the man was manifested when an epidemic of yellow fever struck the town in 1873 and Gordon remained to work with the stricken sufferers. It was not until 1883 that he began to take part in public life. In that year he became a state railway commissioner, and two years later was appointed to a post in the Department of the Interior, serving for four years as Indian agent in Arizona and Nevada. He returned to Memphis in 1889, and was made superintendent of the city schools in 1892. In 1906 he was elected to the United States House of Representatives, the last Confederate brigadier to sit in Congress. He was twice reëlected and during his three terms, he served on the committee on military affairs. He attended to all of his official duties with scrupulous conscientiousness, and is said to have written all his letters, never having accustomed himself to dictating them. In 1910 and again in 1911 he was elected commander-in-chief of the United Confederate Veterans. At a reunion of this body, he suffered an exposure from which he failed to recover. He was survived by his second wife, Minnie Hatch, to whom he was married in 1899. His first wife, Ora S. Paine, whom he had married on Sept. 5, 1876, died in New York on their wedding journey. It seems that he never went out of his way to promote his own fortunes. Such men rarely have their names written among the great. In time of conflict he rose rapidly by reason of his efficient courage; in time of peace he rose slowly by reason of his unassuming ability.

[J. T. Moore and A. P. Foster, *Tenn., the Volunteer State* (1923), II, 131–32; *Who's Who in Tenn.* (1911), p. 313; *Official Records (Army)*; J. B. Lindsley, *The Mil. Annals of Tenn.* (1886), 290 ff.; "Memorial Addresses Delivered in the House of Representatives and the Senate of the U. S.," *House Doc. 1474*, 62 Cong., 3 Sess.; *Confed. Mil. Hist.* (1899), VIII, 309–10; *Commercial Appeal* (Memphis), Aug. 10, 1911.] T. P. A.

GORDON, JAMES (Dec. 6, 1833–Nov. 28, 1912), special agent of the Confederacy, senator from Mississippi, was the son of Robert Gordon, a native of Scotland, and Mary Elizabeth Walton, of Amelia County, Va. He was born at Cotton Gin Port, an early settlement on the Tombigbee River in Monroe County, Miss. The following year, his parents moved into what is now Pontotoc County, Miss. In this frontier country, Robert Gordon amassed a large fortune in land and slaves, and erected a stately house, "Lochinvar." James Gordon, the only son and heir of this fortune, was educated at St. Thomas Hall, Holly Springs, Miss., at La Grange College, Alabama, and at the University of Mississippi, where he received his bachelor's degree in 1855. In 1856 he was chosen to represent his county in the state legislature, and on Feb. 7 of the same year, celebrated his marriage to Carolina Virginia Wiley, of Oxford, Miss.

When the Civil War began, Gordon raised the first company of cavalry to leave the state, arming and equipping his men from his own purse. After the battle of Seven Pines, he returned and recruited the 2nd Mississippi Regiment of Cavalry, of which he was made colonel. He participated in thirty-three engagements, probably distinguishing himself chiefly at the battle of Corinth. There his command was in the van of the Confederate attack, and, after the battle, covered the retreat of Van Dorn to Holly Springs. In 1864 he was sent to England as a special agent of the Confederate government. After arranging for the purchase of a privateer, he started his eventful return. He was captured the day he landed at Wilmington, N. C., and placed on a prison ship at Old Point Comfort, but escaped the following month. Finally reaching Canada, he established contact with his wife's uncle, Jacob Thompson, Confederate agent, with headquarters at Montreal. Unfortunately, he also met John Wilkes Booth. After the assassination of Lincoln, Gordon was suspected of implication in the crime, and a large reward was offered for his apprehension. He met the issue by securing a pass, entering the United States, and defending his reputation with complete success. He then returned to Mississippi and remained out of public view until the close of Reconstruction. In 1878 and 1886 he was in the lower house of the state legislature, and beginning with 1904, served two terms in the state Senate. From Dec. 27, 1909, to Feb. 22 of the following year, he filled the unexpired term of Anselm J. McLaurin in the United States Senate. He used this rather unpromising situation to secure national attention by his apt and well-received speech on retirement from the Senate. He was a frequent contributor to newspapers and such magazines as *Forest and Stream; American Field,* and the *London Field,* generally using the pen name, Pious Jeems. In addition to his article on "The Battle and Retreat from Corinth" (*Publications of the Mississippi Historical Society,* IV, 1901), he published a short volume of verse under the title, *The Old Plantation and Other Poems* (1909). Lacking his father's business sagacity, he lost his patrimony, but he walked away from his estate whistling. He partially recovered from this financial disaster and spent the last part of his life at Okolona, Miss. On Apr. 28, 1904, he had married Ella Narcissa Neilson, of Oxford, Miss.

[*Who's Who in America,* 1912–13; *Biog. and Hist. Memoirs of Miss.* (1891), I, 805–07; *Official and Statistical Reg. of the State of Miss.,* 1912; *Miss. Hist. Soc. Pubs.,* III–VI (1900–02); *Official Records (Army)*; the *Commercial Appeal* (Memphis), and the *Daily Democrat* (Natchez), Nov. 29, 1912.] C. S. S.

GORDON, JOHN BROWN (Feb. 6, 1832–Jan. 9, 1904), soldier, statesman, was born in Upson County, Ga., although shortly before his birth his parents, the Rev. Zachariah Herndon Gordon and Melinda (Cox) Gordon, were living in Wilkes County, N. C. His great-great-grandfather, Adam Gordon, emigrated from Aberdeenshire, Scotland, about 1760 and settled near Fredericksburg, Va. Adam's son, Charles Gordon, moved to North Carolina and became prominent in the civic affairs of that state; and Charles's son, Chapman Gordon, was a soldier in the American Revolution. John matriculated in the University of Georgia and was a member of the class of 1853, but did not graduate. Studying the law privately, he was admitted to the bar and practised for a while in Atlanta. The outbreak of the Civil War found him engaged in developing coal mines in the mountains of extreme northwest Georgia where the state touches Tennessee and Alabama. He was only twenty-nine years of age and his life up to this time had been without noteworthy events.

Though destined to become the most important military figure in the history of Georgia, Gordon was wholly without training or experience in martial affairs when he was elected captain of a company of mountaineers. This company, the "Raccoon Roughs," was accepted by the governor of Alabama and was soon at the front in Virginia. Gordon in September 1854 had married Fanny Haralson, of Lagrange, Ga. She went to the war with her husband and was his companion throughout the struggle. Under fire, Gordon's personality and genius for war speedily asserted themselves. He was promoted rapidly and in less than two years became a brigadier-general (Nov. 1, 1862). In May 1864 he was promoted major-general and near the end of the war he became a lieutenant-general, being one of the three Georgians to reach that rank. He commanded the II Army Corps and one wing of Lee's army at Appomattox. He participated in the battles of Seven Pines, Malvern Hill, Chancellorsville, Gettysburg, Spotsylvania, and Petersburg. In an official report D. H. Hill spoke of Gordon as the "Chevalier Bayard of the Confederate Army."

Returning to Georgia on the conclusion of the war, Gordon resumed the practise of law in Atlanta. He was still a young man, thirty-three years of age, and, with the prestige of his military record and his outstanding ability as a popular leader, naturally entered politics. In 1868 he accepted the nomination for governor from the revived Democratic party, but was defeated by R. B. Bullock [*q.v.*], the Republican candidate. During these troublous times Gordon was in the thick of the fight to secure the restoration of home rule in Georgia, and when the Reconstruction period was over he was rewarded by a United States senatorship. In the contest for this coveted post he defeated Alexander H. Stephens and Benjamin H. Hill. As a senator (1873–80) he was regarded as an able representative of the state. Charges, later given currency (New York *Sun,* Dec. 29, 30, 1883), that he had been a mainstay of Collis P. Huntington [*q.v.*] in the latter's efforts to protect his Pacific railroad interests against legislative action, went unanswered and were generally regarded in Georgia as unimportant (Arnett, *post,* p. 30; Felton, *post,* pp. 79–143). Shortly after his reëlection in 1879, however, Gordon resigned (1880), under circumstances which led to much criticism, and entered the employ of the Louisville & Nashville Railroad. Gov. Alfred H. Colquitt [*q.v.*] appointed as his successor for the unexpired term Joseph E. Brown [*q.v.*]. These two men and Gordon comprised what has been described as the "new triumvirate" of Georgia Democracy and in general represented the rising commercial and industrial, rather than the agrarian, spirit. Gordon denied charges of bargain and corruption and six years later was elected governor, serving four years (1886–90). On the expiration of his term the legislature again elected him to the United States Senate, where he served from 1891 to 1897.

More than any other Georgian, Gordon fired the imagination of his native state. For nearly forty years he was the idol of the people. In physique, bearing, and manner he was courtly and impressive. From the organization of the United Confederate Veterans in 1890 to his death he was the commander-in-chief. In 1903 he published his *Reminiscences of the Civil War.* This volume gives a detailed account of the major battles in which he participated, but it is more notable because of its entire lack of sectional rancor and its uniform generosity and fairness toward friend and foe alike. Gordon died on Jan. 9, 1904, at Miami, Fla.

[See *Official Records (Army)*; *Battles and Leaders of the Civil War* (4 vols., 1887–88); *Confed. Mil. Hist.* (1899), I, 702–05; Bernard Suttler, in *Men of Mark in Ga.,* vol. III (1911); Mrs. Wm. H. Felton, *My Memoirs of Ga. Politics* (1911); Huntington letters, in N. Y. *Sun,* Dec. 29, 30, 1883; A. M. Arnett, *The Populist Movement in Ga.* (1922); Thos. G. Jones, eulogy in *Confed. Veteran,* July 1904; *Atlanta Constitution,* Jan. 10–14, 1904. The date of Gordon's birth is usually given as July 6, 1832, but in the memorial edition of his *Reminiscences* (1904), the date Feb. 6, 1832, appears in the introduction, as also in *Who's Who in America,* 1903–05.]

R. P. B—s.

GORDON, LAURA DE FORCE (Aug. 17, 1838–Apr. 6, 1907), lawyer, editor, suffragist, was born in North East, Erie County, Pa., the daughter of Abram and Katy (Allen) De Force. Although largely self-educated, she gave evidence early in life of literary and oratorical ability, appearing as a lecturer when only fifteen years of age. In 1862 she was married to Dr. Charles H. Gordon, a native of Scotland, who served as a captain in the 3rd Rhode Island Volunteer Cavalry, assigned to duty in the Department of the Gulf. Mrs. Gordon accompanied her husband to the South, living for some time in New Orleans. After the war they crossed the plains in a wagon train to White Plains, Nev., where Mrs. Gordon was the first white woman. They soon removed to California and in 1870 settled in Lodi, then Mokelumne. Ten years later Mrs. Gordon was divorced from her husband. She had not long remained idle after her arrival in the state. At first she edited a woman's department in the *Narrow Gauge,* a short-lived, semi-weekly published in Stockton, Cal. The same year, 1873, she began her career as a publisher, issuing, on Sept. 22, the first number of a semi-literary newspaper, the *Stockton Weekly Leader.* This venture met with such success that she was encouraged to attempt the publication of a daily paper and on May 1, 1874, there appeared the *Daily Leader* of Stockton. Since a woman editor at that time was a novelty, the paper received much notice in the state and its able editing brought it respect and patronage. It supported the Democratic party, the success of which, in 1875, induced Mrs. Gordon to move the paper to Sacramento, where after a short time she sold it.

In 1878, while attending the meetings of the state legislature as a reporter, Mrs. Gordon was active in securing the passage of a bill permitting women to practise law in the state. The same year the legislature founded the Hastings College of Law as a part of the state university. Mrs. Gordon and another woman student applied for admission but were refused. They took the matter to the courts and were granted admission, insuring the right of women to register as students in the educational institutions of the state thereafter. Not only was Mrs. Gordon one of the first two women to be admitted to the bar in California (1879), but she was also one of the first two to be admitted to practise before the Supreme Court of the United States (Feb. 3, 1887). In addition to her legal work, she carried on an active campaign for woman's suffrage, speaking and writing tirelessly in its favor all of her life. She was the author of a guide book, *The Great Geysers of California and How to Reach Them* (1877), but has no other volumes to her credit. The last years of her life were devoted to farming in San Joaquin County, Cal. Having no children, she adopted a nephew. She died, after a short illness, of bronchial pneumonia, the result of a cold contracted on a pleasure trip.

[*A Woman of the Century* (1893), ed. by Frances E. Willard and Mary A. Livermore; *Stockton Independent,* Apr. 6, 1907; *San Francisco Examiner* and *San Francisco Chronicle,* Apr. 7, 1907; *An Illustrated Hist. of San Joaquin County, Cal.* (1890), pp. 163 ff.; pp. 562 ff.; information as to certain facts from Mrs. Gordon's nephew and niece.]
B. R.

GORDON, WILLIAM (1728–Oct. 19, 1807), author, clergyman, born at Hitchin, Hertfordshire, England, was educated for the dissenting ministry under the learned Dr. Zephaniah Marryatt in London. He began his ministry in 1752 in an Independent Church in Ipswich and remained there until 1764 when he quarreled with a leading member of the church who employed his workmen on Crown business on Sunday. He then succeeded Dr. David Jennings in the Old Gravel Lane Church in Southwark. His political sympathies were with the colonists; he had already been in correspondence with several of the colonial leaders and in 1770 he resigned his pastorate and emigrated to America (*Proceedings of the Massachusetts Historical Society,* VII, 1863–64, 291–97). On July 6, 1772, having already preached to the society a year, he was ordained as pastor of the Third Congregational Church at Roxbury, Mass. In the same year he published at Boston a *Plan of a Society for Making Provision for Widows,* a pamphlet advocating old age pensions. He was a vigorous partisan of independence and in 1775 was made chaplain to both houses of the Provincial Congress assembled at Watertown. Congress possessed great confidence in him and voted him a good horse and access to the prisoners of war. He was commissioned to obtain the letters of Gov. Hutchinson which Congress learned were in the hands of a Capt. McLane of Milton. In 1776, "struck with the importance of the scenes that were opening upon the world," he determined to write an adequate history of the Revolution. To this end he tirelessly collected his materials. He conducted a vast correspondence, interviewed generals and statesmen, consulted manuscript collections, borrowed letters and memoranda, and in his wide travels became a familiar figure in council and camp. But he was rash and devoid of restraint; he was "somewhat vain, and not accurate nor judicious; very zealous in the cause, and a well-meaning man, but incautious" (C. F. Adams, *Works of John Adams,* II, 1850, 424). He delivered the election sermon before the General Court on July 19, 1775, and the first independence anniversary sermon on July 4, 1777, both of which were published and widely circulated. Early in 1778 he delivered a pungent attack against Article V of the proposed constitution and was summarily dismissed from both houses.

When Gordon was ready to publish his history he thought it necessary to return to England because of the objections in America to an impartial history of the Revolution. Accordingly he returned to London in 1786 and lived with John Fields, the noted apothecary, whose sister, Elizabeth, he had married. He was surprised to find in England prejudices similar to those he had left America to escape. A friend told him that his history could not be printed according to his manuscript, that it was too bold, too favorable to the Americans, and filled with statements which the English law would regard as libels. The manuscript was then revised by several hands and much original material was omitted. At length, in 1788, *The History of the Rise, Progress, and Establishment of the Independence of the United States of America* was published in four volumes. An American edition appeared in New York the following year in three volumes, and a second American edition in 1794. Gordon realized £300 from the sale of the *History.* For more than a hundred years it was considered to be an authority of the very first importance but at length it was discredited and shown to be chiefly a plagiarism from the *Annual Register* (O. G. Libby in *Annual Report of the American Historical Association for the Year 1899,* I, 367–88). Gordon in 1789 secured a congregation at St. Neots in Huntingdonshire. He returned to Ipswich in 1802 and lived in great poverty until his death.

[The article in the *Dict. Nat. Biog.* is inadequate and inaccurate. See M. C. Tyler, *Lit. Hist. of the Am. Revolution,* II (1897), 423–28; J. S. Loring in the *Hist. Mag.,* Feb., Mar. 1862; H. Niles, *Principles and Acts of the Revolution in America* (1822), pp. 482–83; R. L. Hine, *Hist. of Hitchin* (1929); *Monthly Repository* (London), Dec. 1807. Manuscript materials include letters at the Hist. Soc. of Pa., and a biography, "Life of the Rev. Wm. Gordon" (1810), by Jas. Conder, in Williams Lib., Gordon Square, London.]
F. M—n.

GORDON, WILLIAM FITZHUGH (Jan. 13, 1787–Aug. 28, 1858), lawyer and statesman, born at Germanna, Orange County, Va., of Scotch-Irish ancestors who had been prominent in Revolutionary Virginia, was the second son of James Gordon of Orange, who married his first cousin, Elizabeth Gordon. His primary education was completed in the neighborhood old-field school, but in his thirteenth year he was sent to learn the mercantile business in Fredericksburg. His intellectual development was such that in a few years he was able to teach school long enough to obtain sufficient funds for a two-year course at Spring Hill Academy. Returning to Fredericksburg in 1807 he worked as a law clerk, meanwhile studying law, was admitted to the bar and practised one year at Orange Court House, but moved in 1809 to Albemarle County. He was chosen attorney for the commonwealth in 1812, but resigned before his term expired to continue his general practise. During the War of 1812 he served as private in the Virginia militia; later the Assembly named him successively brigadier-general and major-general. After the war he returned to his practise, and in 1818 was elected to the House of Delegates, where, save for one session, he was a member continuously until 1829, his most important work in this body being his energetic support of Jefferson's projected state university.

In the Virginia Constitutional Convention of 1829–30 Gordon was conspicuous as the framer of the successful compromise measure fixing the representation in the two houses of the General Assembly on "the mixed basis" of population and taxation. He was elected to the Virginia Senate for the 1829–30 session, but resigned to succeed William Cabell Rives in the House of Representatives, where he served in the Twenty-first, Twenty-second, and Twenty-third congresses, from Jan. 25, 1830, to Mar. 3, 1835. The most notable event of his congressional career was his introduction, on June 20, 1834, of a bill providing for the establishment of an independent treasury. The idea was not entirely a new one (D. R. Dewey, *Financial History of the United States,* 1903, p. 235), nor was it enacted during Gordon's incumbency, but the bill represented the first step toward the separation of bank and state (E. M. Shepard, *Martin Van Buren,* 1888, p. 283) which became an actuality under Van Buren's policy.

Always an extreme state-rights Democrat, Gordon, in protest against "Jacksonian Democracy," became a Whig, and as such was defeated in the elections for the Twenty-fourth Congress. In 1837 he followed Calhoun in the return to the Van Buren Democrats, but his days of active politics were over, and he retired to his law practise and to his agricultural activities at "Edgeworth," his home in Albemarle County. Only once again did he appear before the public, when in 1850 he was one of the leading figures in the Southern Convention at Nashville. Both as statesman and citizen he sustained a reputation for honor and integrity. He also stood high at the bar, where his dignity and courtesy combined with his "persuasive arts of conciliation and of personal appeal" to make him an able advocate. He was twice married: first, on Dec. 12, 1809, to Mary Robinson Rootes, and, second, on Jan. 21, 1813, to Elizabeth Lindsay.

[Armistead C. Gordon, *Wm. Fitzhugh Gordon* (1909), and *Gordons in Virginia* (1918); *Proc. and Debates of the Va. State Convention of 1829–30* (1830); P. A. Bruce, *Hist. of the Univ. of Va.* (5 vols., 1920–22); John R. Tucker, "Reminiscences of Virginia's Famous Judges and Jurists," the *Times* (Richmond), Feb. 8, 1895.]

J. C. W.

GORDON, WILLIAM WASHINGTON (Jan. 17, 1796–Mar. 20, 1842), lawyer, railroad president, was the son of Ambrose and Elizabeth (Meade) Gordon. Ambrose Gordon, a native of Monmouth County, N. J., served under Col. William Washington in the Southern campaigns of the Revolution as a lieutenant of cavalry. He moved to Georgia about 1790 and on account of his war services received various grants of land from the state. He settled in Augusta, but he owned a plantation in Screven County, where his eldest son, William Washington Gordon, was born. In due time young Gordon received an appointment to the United States Military Academy at West Point and was the first Georgian to be graduated (1815). He became an aide to Gen. Gaines, but resigned in October 1815 to study law under James M. Wayne of Savannah, afterward associate justice of the Supreme Court of the United States. He made Savannah his home and in 1818 began the practise of law there. His vision, however, was broader than the four walls of a lawyer's office, and his interests widened accordingly to include some of the movements which were developing in the state.

During the third decade of the nineteenth century the foundation of the Georgia railway system was laid with the construction of the Central Railroad of Georgia and the Georgia Railway. The Charleston and Hamburg Railway, extending from the South Carolina coast to Augusta, Ga., began operation in 1833. It threatened ruin to Savannah's trade with upper Georgia, the main artery of which had been the Savannah River, navigable to Augusta. Gordon and his associates determined to save Savannah's primacy as the port of outlet for Georgia's principal export crop, cotton, by constructing a railroad from the coast to Macon, situated in the heart of Georgia and in the center of the cotton-producing area. Following this idea, they obtained a charter from the legislature in 1833 authorizing the construction of the Central Railroad of Georgia. Two years later the charter was amended in such a way as to give the railroad banking privileges. This amendment was put through the legislature by Gordon who had been elected to the legislature largely for the purpose of working for the railroad.

The road as laid out called for 190 miles of track. Gordon, trained in engineering at West

Point, was fitted to manage this enterprise, and was chosen first president of the railroad. At the close of 1836 a beginning of construction was made, but owing to the crises of 1837 and 1839, the road progressed slowly. In October 1838 Gordon reported that the road had begun to operate a passenger train and that some cotton was being transported. By May 1839 seventy-six miles of track had been laid. Stage coaches connected the end of the road with Macon. In 1842 difficulties multiplied—the company could not sell bonds: the price of cotton fell to starvation levels; great freshets washed away the roadbed; and contractors could with difficulty be kept at work when money due them was not forthcoming. The strain on the officials of the road was severe. Gordon actually met his death in the effort to keep the enterprise going, finally succumbing in 1842, a year and a half before the road reached Macon. So excellent had been his administration of the road's affairs that the construction costs were lower by half than the average of other railroads built in the United States at that time. After his death an impressive monument was erected in his honor by the Central of Georgia in Savannah.

Gordon was married, in 1826, to Sarah Anderson Stites, of Savannah. His son, W. W. Gordon, a graduate of Yale, was a captain in the Confederate army and served with the rank of brigadier-general in the Spanish-American War.

[Wm. J. Northen, ed., *Men of Mark in Ga.*, II (1910); L. L. Knight, *A Standard Hist. of Ga. and Georgians* (1917); Geo. W. Cullum, *Biog. Reg. . . . U. S. Mil. Acad.* (3rd ed., 1891); U. B. Phillips, *Transportation in the Eastern Cotton Belt* (1908); *Savannah Daily Republican*, Mar. 21, 23, 26, 28, Apr. 5, 1842.] R. P. B—s.

GORDY, JOHN PANCOAST (Dec. 21, 1851–Dec. 31, 1908), educator, historian, philosopher, was born near Salisbury, Md., the son of Elijah Melson and Martha Ellen (Shepard) Gordy. His scholastic record was prophetic of the career which he followed throughout his life. At seventeen, after attending the schools in the neighborhood of Salisbury, he began to teach. At twenty he became the principal of a small academy in Farmington, Del., and two years later he was appointed vice-principal of an academy in Dover. At the end of another two years he entered Wesleyan University from which he was graduated in 1878 with special honors in English literature, logic, psychology, and ethics. Following his graduation he served until 1882 as tutor in metaphysics, then went abroad for travel and study. He received the degree of Ph.D. from the University of Leipzig in 1884. Returning to the United States, he was professor of philosophy and pedagogy at Ohio University at Athens, 1886–96, then at Ohio State University, 1896–1900. In 1901 he was called to New York University as professor of the history of education and of American history, a position which he held until his death in New York City in 1908. He was an enthusiastic teacher. He threw himself into the work of lecturing with a passion which emphasized but which did not obscure the salient points he desired to bring out. Consequently his courses were popular and at the same time stimulative in a marked degree. His treatment of American history was somewhat narrowly political and his interest in the subject, both as a writer and teacher, was secondary to his primary concern with the fields of philosophy and education.

Gordy's one important work in the field of history and politics was his *History of Political Parties in the United States,* in two volumes, published in 1895 and republished in two subsequent editions. Although it displayed no great originality in treatment, and lacked an adequate analysis of the social and economic forces giving rise to party movements, it served a useful purpose as a general compendium of American party history. He intended to continue this work in a number of volumes, but his absorbing duties as an educator and then his sudden death prevented the completion of the project. The remainder of his publications were in the fields of philosophy and education. They included a *History of Modern Philosophy* (1887), translated from the German of Kuno Fischer; *Lessons in Psychology* (1890), revised and enlarged in later editions; *Rise and Growth of the Normal School Idea in the United States* (1891); and *A Broader Elementary Education* (1903). These, too, were useful works, though in pedagogy, as in history, Gordy was inclined to be encyclopedic rather than closely scientific, and wrote with a somewhat unwarrantable dogmatism. He was married on Mar. 27, 1884, to Eugenie Day, of Dresden, Germany. They had one daughter, Gwendolen, whose death in 1908 led them, by mutual compact, to take their own lives.

[*Alumni Record of Wesleyan Univ., Middletown, Conn.* (1911); Ohio Univ. and Ohio State Univ. catalogues; *N. Y. Times,* Jan. 1, 1909; information as to certain facts supplied by members of Gordy's family.] M. S. B.

GORGAS, JOSIAH (July 1, 1818–May 15, 1883), soldier and teacher, was the son of Joseph and Sophia (Atkinson) Gorgas. The progenitor of the family in America was a Dutchman who came hither in 1680 and according to tradition was descended from a Spaniard who settled in Holland when Spain ruled the Low Countries. Josiah was born in Dauphin County, Pa., in which section of the country his more immediate ancestors had resided. His family was poor and the boy began early to earn his own living, working for a time in a printing-office. Desiring both an education and an army career, he managed to obtain an appointment to West Point, where he graduated in 1841, ranking sixth in a class of fifty-six. He was assigned to ordnance service as second lieutenant and stationed at Watervliet Arsenal, N. Y. In 1845 he was sent abroad for a year to study the ordnance and arsenals of the European armies. When he returned he was again stationed at Watervliet, but early in 1847 was sent with General Scott's expedition to Vera Cruz. He participated in the siege of that city and was left there in charge of the ordnance depot until July 1848. During the next twelve years he was stationed at various arsenals, being promoted in 1855 to a captaincy. While in command of the Mount Vernon Arsenal, near Mobile, he married, December 1853, Amelia, daughter of John Gayle [*q.v.*], former governor and congressman, and at that time United States district judge of Alabama. His Southern marriage and associations, together with a conservative temperament which induced a deep dislike of the Abolitionists, caused him to sympathize strongly with the South in the sectional controversies; and on Apr. 3, 1861, he resigned his commission and went to Montgomery, the seat of the Confederate government. On Apr. 8 he was appointed a major in the Confederate service and was assigned to duty as chief of ordnance.

Within a week war had begun, and Gorgas faced the stupendous task of providing arms and munitions for the Confederate forces. He found the situation alarming. In the captured arsenals and in the possession of the several states were about 15,000 rifles, many of them old, and about 130,000 smooth-bore muskets, most of which had been altered from flint-locks to percussion. In addition there were perhaps some 90,000 ancient flint-lock muskets which might be made serviceable. Even of these inferior weapons, however, there were not enough to arm the volunteers. There were no infantry accoutrements, and practically no cavalry arms or equipments. The deficiency in artillery was even more serious. Though some 429 cannon of all sizes were found in the fortifications along the coast, they were mostly of old design and short range. The few field batteries available were of light caliber, and were mostly old iron guns dating back to the War of 1812. There was but little small-arms ammunition. Worst of all, there was not a single manufacturing arsenal in the Confederate States; and there was but one foundry, the Tredegar Works at Richmond, that could cast cannon. In all the South there were but two insignificant powder mills and one of them had been closed.

Two things were necessary: to rush importations from abroad, and to provide for the manufacture of arms and munitions in the Confederacy itself. Agents were hurried to Europe, but it was not until the beginning of 1862 that anything arrived from that source. Thereafter, small arms, cannon, and raw material for munitions filtered through the blockade; but the chief reliance of the armies was upon local manufactures and captures from the Federals. Gorgas not only displayed extraordinary administrative ability but, proving himself a rare judge of men, gathered about him a remarkable group of subordinates. With a small amount of machinery captured at Harper's Ferry, he established an armory in Richmond for making rifle-muskets and another at Fayetteville, N. C., for making rifles. Despite the difficulty of procuring machinery and finding skilled workmen, he set up arsenals at Charleston, Augusta, Macon, Atlanta, Columbus, Selma, Baton Rouge, Little Rock, and other places. He caused a cannon foundry and a central laboratory to be established at Macon. An excellent powder-mill was built at Augusta by one of his ablest subordinates, Col. George W. Rains [*q.v.*]. Lead was mined, under contract, near Wytheville, Va., a small amount of copper in East Tennessee, and iron chiefly in Virginia and Alabama. Saltpetre (potassium nitrate), used in making powder, was imported or made from the nitrous earths of caves and artificial beds. In 1862 a separate nitre and mining bureau was organized under the energetic direction of Col. Isaac M. St. John [*q.v.*], who had begun the work under orders from Gorgas. Gorgas found it necessary to scatter his establishments over the country, because railway transportation was too weak to carry the raw materials to a central point. By 1863 he had the ordnance bureau operating with high efficiency. Although the heaviest guns in the coast fortifications had been brought from England, and the best of the small arms and field artillery had been captured from the Federals, he had brought about a steady improvement in the products of the foundries and armories. An ample supply of excellent powder was being furnished the armies. During 1864 the internal weakness of the Confederacy imposed heavy burdens upon him, but Gorgas was able to supply arms and ammunition to the very end of the struggle. In the course of the war he was promoted to lieutenant-colonel, then to colonel, and finally, on Nov. 10, 1864, to brigadier-general.

The collapse of the Confederacy left Gorgas impoverished and without a profession. Going to Alabama he became the manager of the Brierfield Iron Works, but in 1869 joined the teaching staff of the partly resuscitated University of the South at Sewanee, Tenn., as head master of the junior department. When the University was more fully restored in 1870, he became professor of engineering and in 1872 was made vice-chancellor. Elected president of the University of Alabama in 1878, he resigned a year later because of ill health and accepted the lighter duties of librarian. He lived in Tuscaloosa until his death. The oldest of his six children was William C. Gorgas [*q.v.*], surgeon in the United States army.

[Sources include: G. W. Cullum, *Biog. Reg. Officers and Grads. U. S. Mil. Acad.* (3rd ed., 1891); Marie D. Gorgas and Burton J. Hendrick, *William Crawford Gorgas: His Life and Work* (1924); unsigned sketch in *Southern Hist. Soc. Papers*, XIII (1885), 216–28; "Notes on the Ordnance Department of the Confederate States," by Gorgas himself, *Ibid.*, vol. XII (1884), and recollections of the ordnance bureau by other officers, in the same journal: II (1876), 56–63, XVI (1888), 286–89, XXVI (1898), 365–76, XXXVII (1909), 1–20; *Official Records (Army)*; G. R. Fairbanks, *Hist. of the Univ. of the South at Sewanee, Tenn.* (1905); W. G. Clark, *Hist. of Educ. in Ala. 1702–1889* (1889); obituary in *Times-Democrat* (New Orleans), May 20, 1883; unpublished official papers in the "Confederate Archives" of the Adjutant-General's Office, Washington. Gorgas kept a diary which is in the possession of a member of the family and is soon to be published. A carbon copy of this diary, as far as Dec. 1864, is in the MSS. Division of the Lib. of Cong.] C. W. R.

GORGAS, WILLIAM CRAWFORD (Oct. 3, 1854–July 3, 1920), sanitarian, surgeon-general of the United States army, was the son of Josiah Gorgas [*q.v.*]. His mother was Amelia Gayle, daughter of Judge John Gayle [*q.v.*], a former governor of Alabama, and William was born at the old Gayle home, Toulminville, near Mobile. His father was an officer of ordnance in the United States army, who, though Northern born, had become through marriage and association a thorough Southern sympathizer. Giving up his commission just before the opening of the Civil War, he was appointed major and chief of ordnance in the Confederate forces, being promoted through the intermediate grades to brigadier-general. In the capital city of the Confederacy, young William spent the four stirring years of the war and with his mother saw the entrance of the Federal troops, after his father accompanied Jefferson Davis in his evacuation of the city. Following a short time spent in Baltimore, the family moved to Brierfield, Ala., where the father for four years was manager of a blast furnace. In 1869, the University of the South was opened at Sewanee, Tenn., and General Gorgas was made its head. Up to this time the boy's education had been quite irregular. He had had the advantages of a private school conducted by a Mrs. Munford in Richmond, but there had been too many distractions for satisfactory progress. He spent six years at the Sewanee school and in 1875 graduated with the degree of bachelor of arts.

From his youthful experiences Gorgas had acquired a desire for a military career. All means of obtaining for him an appointment to West Point were exhausted without success and he decided, against his father's wishes, to get into the army by way of a medical degree. He entered Bellevue Hospital Medical College in New York in 1876, graduating in 1879 after three years of financial difficulties. Following an interneship at Bellevue Hospital, in June 1880 he was appointed to the Medical Corps of the United States Army. For nearly two decades Gorgas's life was that of the average army doctor of the period. Following several years in Texas posts and a tour of duty in North Dakota, he spent practically the entire decade preceding the Spanish-American War at Fort Barrancas, in Pensacola Bay, Fla. Shortly after the beginning of his army career he went through an epidemic of yellow fever at Fort Brown, Tex., and was himself stricken. Thereafter, being an immune, he was frequently drafted for service where yellow fever existed, which fact accounted for his long service at Fort Barrancas in a section long notorious for its epidemics. To Gorgas, as to others, the disease was a riddle. There was no understanding its suddenness of appearance, its puzzling choice of victims, and the inutility of ordinary means of prevention.

Following the occupation of Havana by American troops in 1898, Gorgas was placed in charge of a yellow-fever camp at Siboney. It is significant of the view of the disease then current that he recommended the destruction by fire of the village with all the equipment of the camp. The recommendation was carried out. Later in the same year, he was appointed chief sanitary officer of Havana. After five years of civil war the city was in a highly insanitary condition. Though yellow fever was infrequent, it was, as always, the chief concern. Gorgas cleaned up the city, applying to yellow-fever control the generally accepted methods—segregation of the sick, quarantine of infected localities, and general cleanliness. Though a friend of Dr. Carlos J. Finlay [*q.v.*] and familiar with his theory of the mosquito transmission of yellow fever, Gorgas placed no credence in this idea. Despite the improved sanitary condition of Havana, the yellow-fever situation, instead of improving, became worse. Following the proof furnished by the board of which Walter Reed [*q.v.*] was the head that the *Stegomyia* mosquito was the carrier of yellow fever, the mystery was largely solved. The *Stegomyia,* since more accurately named *Aëdes Aegypti,* was the common mosquito pest of the city. It is a highly domesticated insect, breeding in all kinds of water containers in and around habitations. Depriving the mosquito of breeding places was the plan adopted for control of the insect. The task was not easy, but within a few months Gorgas had not only freed Havana of its mosquitoes, but had permanently rid the city of yellow fever. His success in Havana brought him an international reputation as a sanitarian.

The years 1900 to 1904 saw the gradual development of plans for digging the Panama Canal. The need of a sanitary expert in its planning and construction was apparent. Gorgas was moved from Havana to Washington in 1902 and in March of the following year, Congress raised him to the grade of colonel in recognition of his Cuban achievement. For two years he studied the canal problem, reviewing the French experience at the isthmus and making visits to the Suez Canal and to Panama. In 1904 the actual work at the isthmus commenced. Gorgas with his staff of assistants arrived in June of that year. He early encountered administrative difficulties. Despite the knowledge that the French failure had been due to disease, the American administration was disinclined to support adequate measures for preventing a repetition of that experience. The first Canal Commission, headed by Admiral John G. Walker [*q.v.*], had strongly in mind the prevention of graft and extravagance. Expenditures for sanitary improvements were regarded as falling under the latter head. It required a visitation of yellow fever, starting in November 1904, to obtain for Gorgas any support for his work. He began the application to the Canal Zone of the measures which had been so successful at Havana. Again the mosquito was to be deprived of breeding places and cases of yellow fever segregated and protected from mosquitoes. The problem at Panama was more difficult than at Havana and results far less prompt. It was well into 1905 before yellow fever had been stamped out, and in the meantime determined efforts were in progress to discredit Gorgas's work and to supplant him. It is probable these would have been successful had it not been for the interest aroused by a report issued by Dr. Charles A. L. Reed of Cincinnati to the American Medical Association, in which the obstructive hand of Commissioner Carl E. Grunsky was so largely featured (*Journal of the American Medical Association,* Mar. 11, 1905). Though the Reed report was followed by the discharge of the Walker Commission and the appointment of one headed by Theodore P. Shonts [*q.v.*], Gorgas's troubles were not over. Yellow fever was still prevalent and the new commissioners were dissatisfied that the first interest of the sanitary service was the destruction of mosquitoes rather than the cleaning up of the cities of Panama and Colon. A recommendation from the new commission for the removal of Gorgas, however, was disapproved by President Roosevelt, and active support of his work was directed. In November 1906 the President made a visit to Panama and shortly afterward Gorgas was made a member of the commission charged with construction of the Canal. For a time he had very nearly a free hand, but after the reorganization of the commission in 1908, with Col. George W. Goethals [*q.v.*] as chairman and chief engineer, he was again hampered. Goethals, given unusual powers by executive order, ruled the Canal Zone with despotic control. He was free in criticism and centered his attacks upon the expense of the sanitary work. Despite, however, the difficulty due to lack of cooperation from the chief commissioner, Gorgas not only rid the Canal Zone of yellow fever, but he made the cities of Panama and Colon models of sanitation comparable in healthfulness to any in the United States. In the meantime his reputation had extended until he was generally regarded as the foremost sanitary expert of the world. In 1913 he was asked by the Transvaal Chamber of Mines to visit South Africa and make recommendations for the control of pneumonia among the negro mine workers. While engaged in this work, he was notified of his appointment, January 1914, as surgeon-general of the army, with rank of brigadier-general. He returned to the United States in April to take up his new duties, and the following year was made a major-general. The recently organized International Health Board enlisted him as an adviser, and in 1916 sent him with a staff of assistants for a tour of South and Central America with a view to continuing the fight on yellow fever in these sections. Following this trip, a plan for the elimination of yellow fever was adopted and Gorgas was made director of the work.

April 1917 brought the United States into the World War and put a stop for the time to Gorgas's public health activities. He served as head of the medical service of the army until after the Armistice, when having reached the age for retirement he was again available for work with the International Health Board. He was commissioned to investigate the presence of yellow fever on the west coast of Africa and in May 1920 sailed with his staff for London. After attending the meeting of the International Hygiene Congress in Brussels, he returned to London, where he experienced a stroke of apoplexy, and died a month later in the Queen Alexandria Military Hospital at Millbank. The funeral was held in St. Paul's Cathedral, and the body returned to the United States to rest in Arlington National Cemetery. He had been the recipient of many honors and had been decorated by a number of foreign governments. During his last illness he was visited by King George and knighted.

As the man who made possible the construction of the Panama Canal, Gorgas's name will be forever linked with that gigantic work. His achievement at Havana, which first gave him fame, is overshadowed by his later and greater success. He published *Sanitation in Panama* (1915) but wrote comparatively little, leaving his work to speak for itself and to be reported upon by others. Physically he was somewhat more than average height. He conserved to the end the trim figure which early athletic habits had given him. His portraits show a fine oval face with firm mouth and humorous eyes. His hair was deep black in youth. In later years his heavy crown of white hair and his white moustache contributed much to a distinguished appearance. Temperamentally he was mild, amiable, and optimistic. To a pliability of temperament was added a quiet determination and persistence. It was this combination of seemingly opposing qualities that carried him successfully through his Panama difficulties. He was married in 1885 to Marie Cook Doughty of Cincinnati, Ohio.

[M. C. Gorgas and B. J. Hendrick, *William Crawford Gorgas: His Life and Work* (1924), an intimate biography furnished by his wife; F. H. Martin, in *Surgery, Gynecology and Obstetrics*, Oct. 1923, and *Maj. Gen. Wm. Crawford Gorgas* (pub. by the Gorgas Memorial Institute in 1924); Robt. E. Noble, in *Am. Jour. Pub. Health*, Mar. 1921; J. F. Siles, in *Am. Jour. Tropical Med.*, Mar. 1922; V. C. Vaughan, in *Jour. Laboratory and Clinical Med.*, Aug. 1920, and in *Pa. Medic. Jour.*, Nov. 1920; M. W. Ireland, in *Science*, July 16, 1920; *British Medic. Jour.*, July 10, 1920; *Sanidad y Beneficencia* (Habana), Apr., May, June 1921; *Cronica Medico-Quirurgica de la Habana*, June 1921; *Who's Who in America*, 1920–21; London *Times*, July 5, 10, 24, 1920; additional references and bibliography of Gorgas's writings in the *Index-Cat. of the Lib. of the Surgeon General's Office, U. S. Army*.]

J. M. P.

GORHAM, JABEZ (Feb. 18, 1792–Mar. 24, 1869), silversmith and merchant, born at Providence, R. I., was the son of Jabez and Catherine (Tyler) Gorham and a descendant of John Gorham, of Northamptonshire, England, who settled at Plymouth, Mass., in 1643. When he was fifteen years old his father died, and thereafter he had no opportunity for schooling. Providence was then a center for the manufacture of silverware and gold-plated jewelry, and young Jabez was apprenticed to Nehemiah Dodge, who had been one of the pioneers in that industry. At the age of twenty-one, with four other young men, Gorham formed a jewelry firm, which continued five years. At the end of that time, he joined with Stanton Beebe in a like venture that lasted until 1831. No record remains of Gorham's personal skill as a craftsman; in salesmanship he is known to have succeeded. Most of his stock was retailed by the Yankee peddlers of the period, and he was able to hold his own against the competition of other New England producers in the Boston market.

Until about 1825 such articles as spoons and forks were made by American silversmiths only on special order. Gorham was one of the first to see a future in silverware production. At the end of his partnership with Beebe, in 1831, he and H. L. Webster, another silversmith who believed there was a market for such goods, undertook the manufacture of spoons, forks, and later thimbles and a few other small articles. They were the first silversmiths to use machinery in this industry (J. L. Bishop, *History of American Manufactures from 1608 to 1860,* 1864, II, 714). In 1842 Gorham, having withdrawn from the partnership with Webster, bought the silverware part of the business and formed a new firm with his son, John Gorham, as junior partner. Five years later, the elder Gorham retired; the son continued the industry, and in 1865 the Gorham Manufacturing Company was incorporated by the State of Rhode Island. Gorham was married first, Dec. 4, 1816, to Amey Thurber, who died Nov. 26, 1820; and second, Apr. 16, 1822, to Lydia Dexter, who survived him. He represented Providence in the General Assembly of Rhode Island and in 1842–44 was a member of the Providence Common Council. As a young man he had been a captain of a militia company. In politics he was a Whig and in his later years a Republican.

[Georgiana Guild, "Notes on the Providence Line of the Gorham Family," *New-Eng. Hist. and Geneal. Reg.*, Apr. 1900; S. G. C. Ensko, *Am. Silversmiths and Their Marks* (privately printed, 1927); J. B. Bowditch, in *State of R. I. and Providence Plantations at the End of the Century: a Hist.*, vol. III (1902), ed. by Edward Field; J. F. P. Lawton, "Gorham Manufacturing Company," *New England States*, vol. IV (1897), ed. by W. T. Davis; *Representative Men and Old Families of R. I.*, vol. II (1908); W. A. Greene, *Providence Plantations for Two Hundred and Fifty Years* (1886); *A Modern City, Providence, R. I., and Its Activities* (1909), ed. by Wm. Kirk.]

W. B. S.

GORHAM, JOHN (Feb. 24, 1783–Mar. 27, 1829), chemist and physician, son of Stephen and Molly (White) Gorham, was born in Boston, and made that city his home throughout his life. His early education was obtained at Exeter, N. H., and his academic training at Harvard, from which he received the degrees of B.A. in 1801, M.B. (bachelor of medicine) in 1804, and M.D. in 1811. Soon after gaining his first medical degree, he went to London and took private lessons in experimental chemistry with Friedrich Accum, who at that time was the most noted teacher of chemical manipulation in Europe. Later he studied chemistry with Thomas Hope at the University of Edinburgh. In London he became acquainted with Benjamin Silliman [*q.v.*], who was also a student of Accum's. Each man on his return to the United States taught chemistry with conspicuous success, Gorham at Harvard and Silliman at Yale. Gorham continued his medical studies at Harvard, one of his teachers being Dr. John Warren [*q.v.*], whose daughter, Mary, he married on June 2, 1808. In 1809 he was appointed adjunct professor of chemistry and materia medica, and when Aaron Dexter resigned as Erving Professor of Chemistry and Mineralogy in 1816, Gorham succeeded him. The latter appointment must have been regarded as a significant scientific event, because Gorham delivered a formal inaugural address ("Address Delivered on the Induction of John Gorham, M.D., As Erving Professor of Chemistry in Harvard University, December 1816," *New England Journal of Medicine and Surgery,* January 1817), and soon afterward John Adams, Ex-President of the United States, wrote a long letter to Gorham setting forth in grandiloquent language the opportunities for chemists to make discoveries which would benefit humanity. Realizing the necessity for an adequate text-book adapted to the needs of college students, Gorham wrote *The Elements of Chemical Science* (2 vols., 1819–20), dedicated to Aaron Dexter, his teacher and former colleague. It was one of the first systematic text-books on chemistry written by an American and published in this country, and was a standard work for many years. Although Gorham's regular duties as a teacher and a physician were onerous, he found time to prepare and publish several original papers in chemistry, the more important of which are: "Analysis of Sulphate of Barytes from Hatfield, Mass" (*Memoirs of the American Academy of Arts and Sciences,* vol. III, pt. 2, 1815), "Indigogene" (*New England Journal of Medicine and Surgery,* April 1817), "Chemical Examination of a Quantity of Sugar Supposed to Have Been Intentionally Poisoned" (*Ibid.,* July 1817), and "Chemical Analysis of Indian Corn" (*Ibid.,* Oct. 1820). He was one of the projectors of the *New England Journal of Medicine and Surgery* and for fifteen years was one of its editors. He was a Fellow of the American Academy of Arts and Sciences and a member of the Massachusetts Medical Society, serving the latter as librarian (1814–18) and as recording secretary (1823–26). His work as Erving Professor of Chemistry ceased in 1827, when he was succeeded by John W. Webster [*q.v.*]. Gorham was an accomplished teacher and was especially helpful to his students, often assisting them personally in their studies. His work as a chemist-physician exerted a dynamic influence on the development of chemistry at a time when this science was struggling for a permanent place in American educational institutions.

[Harvard Univ., *Quinquennial Cat., 1636–1925* (1925); W. L. Burrage, *A Hist. of the Mass. Medic. Soc.* (1923); *New-Eng. Hist. and Geneal. Reg.,* Oct. 1898; *A Report of the Record Commissioners of the City of Boston, containing Boston Births from A.D. 1700 to A.D. 1800* (1894); *Chemistry in Old Boston* (pamphlet, 1928); Benj. Silliman, Jr., *Am. Contributions to Chemistry* (1875), reprinted from the *Am. Chemist,* Aug.–Sept. and Dec. 1874; Jas. Jackson, *An Address Delivered at the Funeral of John Gorham* (1829); *Am. Jour. of Arts and Sci.,* III (1821), pp. 331–41; *Boston Medic. and Surgic. Jour.,* Mar. 31, Apr. 7, 1829; *Am. Jour. of the Medic. Sci.,* IV (1829), pp. 538–39; *Columbian Centinel* (Boston), Mar. 28, 1829.]

L. C. N.

GORHAM, NATHANIEL (May 1738–June 11, 1796), business man and statesman, was born in Charlestown, Mass., and was baptized in the First Church there on May 21, 1738. The eldest of the five children of Nathaniel and Mary (Soley) Gorham, he was descended from John Gorham, born in England, who emigrated to Massachusetts and in 1643 married Desire Howland, daughter of John Howland of the *Mayflower.* When he was about fifteen, Nathaniel was apprenticed to Nathaniel Coffin, a merchant of New London, whom he served until 1759, when he returned to Charlestown and engaged in business on his own account. He appears to have prospered early and became one of the leading men of Massachusetts both as business man and as statesman. In 1763 he married Rebecca Call, by whom he had nine children. He was a member of the "Ancient" Fire Society, one of the benevolent organizations which included the "best people"; and was one of the incorporators of the Charles River Bridge (1785). From the beginning of the Revolutionary period he took an active part in public affairs, serving as a member of the colonial legislature from 1771 to 1775; as a delegate to the Provincial Congress, 1774–75; and as a member of the Board of War from 1778 until its dissolution in 1781. He was also a delegate to the state constitutional convention of 1779–80, a member of the state Senate in 1780, a member of the state House from 1781 to 1787, being speaker in 1781, 1782, and 1785. On July 1, 1785, he was appointed judge of the Middlesex court of common pleas. He was a member of the Council, 1788–89. In addition to his activity in state politics, he sat in the Continental Congress in 1782, 1783, and 1785–87, being elected president of the Congress June 6, 1786, and was a delegate to the Federal Constitutional Convention of 1787, in which he served for some weeks as presiding officer in the Committee of the Whole after his election to that position on May 30. A contemporary sketch of Gorham, written at the time by William Pierce, says: "Mr. Gorham is a merchant in Boston, high in reputation, and much in the esteem of his countrymen. He is a Man of very good sense, but not much improved in his education. He is eloquent and easy in public debate, but has nothing fashionable or elegant in his style;—all he aims at is to convince, and where he fails it never is from his auditory not understanding him, for no Man is more perspicuous and full . . . [He] is . . . rather lusty, and has an agreeable and pleasing manner" (Farrand, *post,* III, 88). He took part frequently in the debates and was in favor of a seven-year term for the president, of long terms for senators, of extensive powers for Congress, and of the appointment of judges by the executive. He believed in a strongly centralized government but that, even so, the country was too vast to remain undivided for more than a century and a half (*Ibid.*). The following year he was a member of the Massachusetts state convention at which the Federal Constitution was adopted.

At the end of the Revolution, in settlement of a boundary dispute, New York had ceded to Massachusetts a vast tract of land known as the Genesee Country. In order to realize on these holdings, Massachusetts in April 1788 sold the lands, 6,000,000 acres, to Oliver Phelps of Windsor, Conn., and Nathaniel Gorham, who had formed a partnership rather than bid against each other. It is probable that the partnership was in reality a syndicate including others, among them Robert Morris of Philadelphia, but the purchase was in the names of Phelps and Gorham. The purchase price was $1,000,000 to be paid in three annual instalments in the scrip of Massachusetts, known as the "consolidated securities," which had fallen much below par. In July 1788, not without complications, the purchasers succeeded in extinguishing the Indian title to the eastern part of the enormous domain, some 2,600,000 acres, and in the next two years large amounts of land were sold to settlers, sometimes whole townships at a single sale. Various business difficulties were encountered, however, among them an uncontemplated rise in the price of the scrip which made the cost much greater than the purchasers had expected. By 1790 a large part of the property had been sold, but Phelps and Gorham were unable to meet their payments and, as far as Massachusetts was concerned, compromised matters by surrendering all the western lands title to which was still encumbered by Indian claims. Gorham's resources were insufficient to tide him over the crisis and he became insolvent. He succumbed to the strain and died of apoplexy. He had never visited the vast domain which he had attempted to settle but his son Nathaniel became an early pioneer there. Another, Benjamin, entered public life and represented Massachusetts in Congress for several terms. A daughter, Lydia, married John Phillips and was the grandmother of Phillips Brooks.

[*Rochester Hist. Soc. Pub. Fund Ser.*, VI (1927), 297; *The Records of the Federal Convention of 1787* (3 vols., 1911), ed. by Max Farrand; *The Debates in the Several State Conventions on the Adoption of the Federal Constitution,* ed. by Jonathan Elliot, vol. II (1861); T. T. Sawyer, *Old Charlestown* (1902); J. F. Hunnewell, *Records of the First Church in Charlestown, Mass.* (1880); Amos Otis and C. F. Swift, *Geneal. Notes of Barnstable Families* (1880), vol. I; W. G. Sumner, *The Financier and the Finances of the Am. Revolution* (1891), vol. II; Orsamus Turner, *Hist. of the Pioneer Settlement of Phelps and Gorham's Purchase* (1851), and *Pioneer Hist. of the Holland Purchase* (1849); J. F. Hunnewell, *A Century of Town Life* (1888); P. D. Evans, "The Pulteney Purchase," *Quart. Jour. N. Y. State Hist. Asso.*, Apr. 1922.] J. T. A.

GORMAN, ARTHUR PUE (Mar. 11, 1839–June 4, 1906), United States senator, was born at Woodstock, Howard County, Md., the son of Peter and Elizabeth A. (Brown) Gorman. His grandfather, John Gorman, emigrated from Ireland to Harrisburg, Pa., in 1800 and removed to Old Town, Baltimore County, Md., as a cattle drover. His other grandfather, John R. Brown, belonged to a well-known colonial Maryland family. When Gorman was six years old his parents moved to a place near Laurel, which they called "Fairview." Here his father, a contractor, furnished granite for public buildings and for the Baltimore & Ohio Railroad. In 1852 the boy was appointed a page in the House of Representatives. He attracted the attention of Stephen A. Douglas, who secured his transfer to the Senate chamber and took him into his own household as friend and private secretary. Gorman accompanied Douglas on the famous Lincoln debate tour. Advanced to messenger, assistant doorkeeper, and assistant postmaster, he finally became postmaster of the Senate. After the Civil War, in the controversy between the Senate and President Johnson, Gorman's sympathies were with the President, and he lost his position as Senate postmaster in 1866. Johnson rewarded him, however, with an appointment as collector of internal revenue. In this office Gorman was successful in collecting $150,000 arrears, and made something of a name for himself. Removed in 1869 by the new administration, he was elected in that same year to the Maryland House of Delegates, where he served until 1875, being speaker during the last two years. At the close of the legislative session of 1872, he was appointed president of the Chesapeake & Ohio Canal Company, of which he had been a director since 1869, and this new position, one of great political influence, enabled him to secure his hold upon the Democratic party in Maryland. Elected state senator in 1875 and reëlected in 1877 and 1879, he was elected United States senator in 1880, to succeed William Pinkney Whyte. He was reelected in 1886 and in 1892. As chairman of the National Executive Committee in 1884, he successfully conducted Cleveland's campaign and in recognition of his services was practically given the distribution of federal patronage in Maryland during Cleveland's first term. When the federal elections measure (Force Bill) was under consideration in 1890, the Democrats were in a hopeless minority. Gorman secured the aid of the Silver Republicans to defeat the bill in return for Democratic support of the free coinage measure, for which achievement he was given a silver service bought by popular subscription of persons all over the state. Although he was opposed to Cleveland's renomination and was himself prominently mentioned as a presidential possibility in the National Democratic Convention of 1892, once the candidate had been chosen Gorman became head of the committee that managed the campaign. During his third term as senator he took a leading part in recasting the Wilson Tariff Bill. The Senate amendments, for which he was largely responsible, placed coal, sugar, and iron ore on the duty list, whereas the President had favored free raw materials. Representative Wilson, the author of the original bill, read to the House a letter from Cleveland referring to "the abandonment of Democratic principle" exhibited in the Senate's action. To this letter Gorman replied by a speech in the Senate, in the course of which he made a personal attack upon the President (*Congressional Record,* 53 Cong., 2 Sess., p. 7801). During his last two terms Gorman was the outstanding Democratic leader and chairman of the caucus. The Republican victories of 1895 and 1896 were followed by his defeat in 1898, but the triumph of his enemies was of short duration, for on Mar. 4, 1903, he began his fourth term as senator and was immediately chosen caucus chairman and minority leader. His last public service was as state director of the Washington Branch of the Baltimore & Ohio Railroad, when he made a report which led to the sale of the state's stock. Hardly any one in public life had more devoted friends or more implacable enemies. Death came to him at his Washington residence from a sudden heart attack after an illness of almost six months. He was survived by six children and his wife, who when he married her was a widow, Mrs. Hattie (Donagan) Schwartz, daughter of Dr. James Donagan of Reading, Pa.

[*Who's Who in America,* 1906–07; Paul Winchester, *Men of Maryland Since the Civil War* (1923); Baltimore *Sun,* June 5, 1906; "Arthur Pue Gorman: Memorial Addresses," *Sen. Doc. 404,* 59 Cong., 2 Sess.; J. G. Pearre, "Arthur Pue Gorman," published in the *Cincinnati Enquirer,* Apr. 27, 1902, at the time when Gorman was being groomed as a presidential possibility; R. M. McElroy, *Grover Cleveland, the Man and the Statesman* (1923).]

H. F. W.

GORMAN, WILLIS ARNOLD (Jan. 12, 1816–May 20, 1876), lawyer, soldier, second territorial governor of Minnesota, was the only son of David L. and Elizabeth Gorman, both of Irish descent. He was born near Flemingsburg, Ky. In 1835 he removed with his parents to Bloomington, Ind. He studied law and was admitted to the bar but soon ventured into politics; in 1837 and 1838 he was clerk and in 1839–40 enrolling secretary, of the Indiana Senate, and for three terms, 1841–44, a member of the Indiana House of Representatives. The law school of Indiana University was opened in 1842 at Bloomington and Gorman was granted its degree of LL.B. in 1845. At the outbreak of the Mexican War he enlisted as a private, was chosen a major in the 3rd Indiana Regiment, and was seriously injured at Buena Vista. When his regiment's term expired he returned to Indiana only to enlist again and be chosen colonel of a new regiment which participated in the capture of Huamantla and in the battles of Atlixco, Puebla, and Tlaxcala. In 1848 he was governor of Puebla.

From 1849 to 1853 he was a Democratic representative in Congress from Indiana, and in 1852 he actively supported Pierce for the presidency. As a reward, he was appointed governor of Minnesota Territory, whither he moved in May 1853. "Gifted with a fine and strikingly handsome person, with an impressive manner, with great natural endowments as an orator, and with much force and energy of character" (St. Paul *Pioneer-Press,* May 21, 1876), he soon became a leader in territorial politics. As governor he was also superintendent of Indian affairs and negotiated several treaties, under one of which he removed the Sioux from near St. Paul to the upper Minnesota River. He believed that in granting land for railroads the Territory should reserve at least three per cent. of gross earnings in lieu of general taxation, and to his stand is due Minnesota's system of taxing railroads. While admittedly honest as an official, Gorman was not averse to making money through political maneuvers. A bill was introduced in the legislature to remove the capital from St. Paul to St. Peter where the St. Peter Company, in which he was a stockholder, promised to erect territorial buildings. The measure passed both houses and Gorman would have signed it, but the chairman of the committee on enrolled bills disappeared with the bill and the session ended before he was found.

In 1857, at the end of his term, Gorman began practising law in St. Paul. As delegate to a constitutional convention he took an active part in the Democratic branch after partisan feeling had split the convention into two groups holding separate sessions. He was opposed to a proposition, coming up in both wings, to seek boundaries different from those provided by Congress, although the change might have benefited him financially. He was a member of the conference committee appointed to make one constitution out of the Democratic and Republican drafts, and at a meeting of the committee, construing a remark of a Republican member as a personal insult, he broke his cane over that gentleman's head. The incident did not injure him politically for in 1859 he was elected to the state legislature and in 1860 was a candidate for presidential elector on the Douglas ticket. At the outbreak of the Civil War, he was commissioned colonel of the 1st Minnesota Volunteers. For gallantry at the battle of Bull Run he was made brigadier-general in September 1861. He served also at Ball's Bluff, South Mountain, and Antietam. In 1862 he commanded a military division in Arkansas. Mustered out in 1864, he resumed his law practise in St. Paul in partnership with Cushman K. Davis [*q.v.*], his aide during much of the war. In 1869 he became St. Paul's city attorney and held that position until his death.

Gorman was twice married: in January 1836, to Martha Stone of Bloomington, Ind., who died in 1864, and on Apr. 27, 1865, to Emily Newington of St. Paul.

[Eulogy by Cushman K. Davis, in *Minn. Hist. Soc. Colls.*, vol. III (1880); J. H. Baker, "Lives of the Governors of Minnesota," *Ibid.*, vol. XIII (1908); E. D. Neill, *Hist. of Minn.* (4th ed., 1882); W. W. Folwell, *A Hist. of Minn.* (1921); *Pioneer-Press and Tribune* (St. Paul and Minneapolis), May 21, 1876; date of birth from tombstone in Oakland Cemetery, St. Paul.]

L. B. S.

GORRIE, JOHN (Oct. 3, 1803–June 16, 1855), physician, pioneer in mechanical refrigeration, was born in Charleston, S. C. Although he is said to have been of Scotch-Irish descent, the fact that his parents came from the West Indies and that he was of dark complexion with black hair and eyes lends probability to the belief of those who knew him that he was of Spanish extraction. His early education was received in the schools of Charleston and he graduated from the College of Physicians and Surgeons, New York City, in 1833. After a few months in Abbeville, S. C., he settled at Apalachicola, Fla., then an important cotton port, where he continued to reside until his death. He was soon the leading physician of that city and from the very beginning of his residence was prominent in civic affairs. In 1834 he was made postmaster, which office he held for four years; from 1835 to 1836 he was a member of the city council as well as treasurer of the city; and in 1837 he was elected mayor. In 1839 he gave up public office to devote his whole attention to his profession.

About this time he conceived the idea of artificially cooling the air of sick rooms and hospitals with the hope of curing and preventing fever, and, under the *nom de plume* of Jenner, he wrote in 1844 a series of eleven articles bearing on the subject ("On the Prevention of Malarial Diseases," *Commercial Advertiser,* Apalachicola). Becoming more and more engrossed in refrigeration projects, finally, about 1845, he gave up his practise entirely, in order to devote his whole time to them. From the problem of artificially cooling air he passed to that of artificially freezing water, or ice-making, and by 1850 had succeeded in accomplishing this feat on a small scale and with machinery of his own design. Having no capital, he went to New Orleans where he secured from a Bostonian the necessary funds to apply for a patent on his process. This patent, no. 8080, was granted May 6, 1851, and is said to be the first United States patent on mechanical refrigeration (letter, June 18, 1898, from Commissioner of Patents to Acting Assistant Secretary, United States National Museum). The principle of Gorrie's invention was the same as that incorporated in many of the commercial mechanical refrigerators now in use, namely, the absorption of heat accompanying the expansion of air. While he succeeded in making ice publicly in Apalachicola with his small equipment, Gorrie was quite anxious to secure the necessary funds to build a plant on a large commercial scale. After exhausting all means for securing financial help in many cities in the South, he returned to Apalachicola, became melancholy, suffered a nervous collapse from which he was unable to recover, and died at the age of fifty-two. In the year preceding his death, 1854, he published *Dr. John Gorrie's Apparatus for the Artificial Production of Ice in Tropical Climates.* In recognition of his invention the Southern Ice Exchange erected a monument to his memory at Apalachicola, which was unveiled on April 30, 1900; and on Apr. 30, 1914, there was unveiled in Statuary Hall in the United States Capitol at Washington a statue of Gorrie, one of the two statues presented by the State of Florida. In May 1838 he married Mrs. Caroline (Myrick) Beeman.

[*Ice and Refrigeration,* May 1897, June 1900, Aug. 1901, June 1914; U. S. National Museum records; *Jour. Am. Medic. Asso.,* Nov. 14, 1908; W. Kimball, "Reminiscences of Alvan Wentworth Chapman," in *Jour. N. Y. Botanical Garden,* Jan. 1921.] C. W. M.

GORRINGE, HENRY HONEYCHURCH (Aug. 11, 1841–July 6, 1885), naval officer, was born in Barbados, son of an English clergyman for many years rector of the established church at Tobago. Removing to the United States in early youth, Henry entered the merchant service and in the summer of 1862 joined the United States navy as acting master's mate. Assigned to the upper Mississippi, he fought through the war in Porter's flotilla, with frequent promotions for courage and ability. From September 1863 to January 1865, he commanded the small gunboat *Cricket,* Porter's flagship in the Red River campaign, which during the hot action at Deloach's Bluff, Apr. 26, 1864, was struck thirty-eight times in four minutes, suffering thirty-one casualties in a crew of fifty. He was among those commended for special ability in this campaign (*Official Records, Navy,* XXVI, 77, and D. D. Porter, *Incidents and Anecdotes of the Civil War,* 1885, pp. 242 ff.). After the war he stood fourth in examination for lieutenant in the regular service, and on January 13, 1869, was commissioned lieutenant commander to date from Dec. 18, 1868. After commanding the *Portsmouth,* 1869–71, in the South Atlantic Squadron, he served three years in the Hydrographic Office, preparing several volumes of sailing directions for the South Atlantic. Similar work then took him on an enjoyable Mediterranean cruise in the paddle-wheeler *Gettysburg,* during which he visited Turkey, Egypt, and the African coast, gathering data for four volumes of sailing directions, and incidentally contributing several excellent travel letters to the New York *Nation.* When in 1879 the Khedive of Egypt presented the obelisk, Cleopatra's Needle, to the United States, and W. H. Vanderbilt offered to finance its transportation, Gorringe, who was keenly interested in the gift, volunteered to take complete charge of its removal from Alexandria to New York. Granted six months' leave, with a trusted subordinate, Lieut. (later Rear Admiral) Seaton Schroeder [*q.v.*], he sailed in August 1879. Overcoming diplomatic obstacles and engineering difficulties with equal persistence, he lowered the monolith, sixty-nine feet long and weighing 220 tons, with machinery of his own devising; transported it in a caisson to a drydock in Alexandria; inserted it in the steamer *Dessoug,* purchased from the Egyptian government, through a hole made in the bow; secured it with heavy timbers; and on July 20, 1880, arrived with it in New York. From Ninety-sixth Street, North River, to Central Park the obelisk was moved in iron channels, with cannon balls as rollers, and was elevated on its original pedestal and foundation stones, Jan. 22, 1881. A full account of the transportation appears in Gorringe's elaborately illustrated folio, *Egyptian Obelisks* (1882). For a man with only a sailor's training and with limited facilities and funds—the total cost was $103,732—the accomplishment appears incredible; but, as Schroeder states, Gorringe had not only mechanical genius but "unlimited self-confidence; never was it 'Can this be done?' but only 'How shall this be done?'" (*A Half Century of Naval Service,* 1922, p. 76). Subsequently his services were in demand as a consulting engineer. Becoming interested in ship-building, he engaged in press criticism of the government's shipping policy. His furlough had been several times extended, and a sharp interchange of notes with the secretary of the navy, W. E. Chandler [*q.v.*], on his outside activities ended in his resignation, Feb. 21, 1883. (For these letters, see *Army and Navy Register,* Mar. 3, 1883.) He then organized and became manager of the American Shipbuilding Company, which began operations in Philadelphia but soon went into receivership. During efforts at reorganization, Gorringe suffered a fall from a train in December 1884 which injured his spine and caused his death six months later in New York. He was unmarried. According to his closest service friend, Admiral Schroeder, "He had such sterling qualities as to endear him to any one who could pierce the crust of an unfortunate sensitiveness. . . . He enlisted as a seaman and worked his way to command by sheer bravery and capacity."

[In addition to sources cited in the text, see *Official Records* (*Navy*), 1 ser., vols. XXV, XXVI; *Army and*

Navy Register, Mar. 3, 1883, July 11, 1885; *Proc. U. S. Naval Inst.,* vol. XII, no. 1 (1886), p. xvi. L. R. Hamersly, *Records of Living Officers of the U. S. Navy and Marine Corps* (3rd ed., 1878); *Army and Navy Jour.,* July 11, 1885; *N. Y. Tribune* and *N. Y. Herald,* July 7, 1885.] A. W.

GORTON, SAMUEL (*c.* 1592–1677), colonist, founder of the "Gortonites," was born of a good family at Gorton, three miles from Manchester, England. Owing to confusion between two children of the same name, his birth has sometimes been assigned to the year 1600 but it is probable that he was the child baptized Feb. 12, 1592/3. Although he himself said he had not been to school it is evident that he learned much, probably from tutors, and could read the Bible in the original tongues. When he was about twenty-five, probably, he was in London engaged in the business of finishing cloth. Although brought up in the Church of England he developed heterodox opinions and emigrated to Massachusetts in the belief that that colony practised religious toleration. In 1637 he arrived in Boston with his wife, Mary Maplet, and at least one child. His views very soon brought him into conflict with the authorities, who were already dealing with the Antinomian controversy, and within two months he was tried for teaching heresy, convicted, fined, imprisoned, and banished. From Boston he went to Plymouth but fared no better there. He embroiled himself in a religious dispute with Ralph Smith, a Plymouth minister whose house he had leased, and Smith had him haled to court. After trial, Gorton was fined and ordered to find sureties for his good behavior. He seems also to have been banished and in any case left the colony in the winter of 1638 and went with a few followers to Aquidneck (Rhode Island). On Apr. 30, 1639, he took part in organizing the government of Portsmouth. Soon he was again in trouble with the Coddington government at Newport and was publicly whipped. He next took refuge with Roger Williams at Providence but it is said he never was admitted an inhabitant there. He then bought land and settled at Pawtuxet, but again got into disputes with the colonists and, having refused to present himself at Boston at the order of the Massachusetts authorities, moved once more, this time to Shawomet. He had bought the land from Miantonomo but in June 1643 two of the inferior sachems contested his claim and the validity of the purchase and applied for relief to the court at Boston. He was summoned to Boston by a court order of Sept. 7, 1643, and when he did not go, Massachusetts sent forty soldiers and captured him, together with several companions, though they were living outside the jurisdiction of that colony. They were taken to Boston, where they were tried for blasphemy and for being enemies "of all civil authority among the people of God" (*Records of the Governor and Company of the Massachusetts Bay,* II, 51). They were condemned to imprisonment at hard labor in irons, Nov. 3, and released and banished Mar. 7, 1644. Gorton went first to Portsmouth and then to England to seek redress. He obtained from the Earl of Warwick a letter of safe conduct ordering Massachusetts to leave him unmolested in "the land called Narragansett Bay," and after his return in May 1648 he lived peaceably for the rest of his life at Shawomet, which he renamed Warwick. His troubles or advancing age appear to have sobered him, and he became a dignified and useful citizen. On Sundays he preached to the colonists and Indians and among other civil offices he performed the duties of representative of Warwick in the Assembly in 1649, 1651, 1652, 1655–57, 1659, 1660, 1662–66. He was at one time a judge in the highest court, served several times in the upper house, was chosen many times to audit the town books, and at his death was a member of the town council while his son Samuel was treasurer.

Before his death Gorton attained a clear and dignified literary style, as shown in his letter of defense to Morton (printed by Thomas Hutchinson, *The History of the Colony of Massachusetts-Bay,* 1764, I, 549). His earlier style, however, in his controversial works, was incoherent and often vituperative. Among his religious beliefs, he denied the doctrine of the Trinity, although he declared Christ to be God and the only proper object of worship; he denounced a "hireling ministry" and denied the fitness of men who were paid, claiming that each man should be his own priest; he would do away with all outward ordinances; and taught a conditional immortality dependent upon individual character (Schaff-Herzog, *post*). He also held that by union with Christ one partook of the perfection of God, and denied the actual existence of heaven or hell. His publications include the following: *Simplicities Defence against Seven-Headed Policy* (1646), a vindication of his course in New England (reprinted in the *Rhode Island Historical Society Collections,* vol. II, 1835, and in Peter Force's *Tracts,* vol. IV, 1846), replied to by Edward Winslow [*q.v.*]; *An Incorruptible Key Composed of the CX Psalme* (1647); *Saltmarsh Returned from the Dead* (1655); *An Antidote Against the Common Plague of the World* (1657). He also left some manuscripts now in the possession of the Rhode Island Historical Society, notably a commentary on the

Lord's Prayer containing his latest religious beliefs. Gorton would never have considered himself the founder of a sect, but he had followers who called themselves Gortonites and persisted as a distinct group for nearly a century. He died at Warwick between Nov. 27 and Dec. 10, 1677. He had had three sons and at least six daughters.

[Accounts of Gorton include Adelos Gorton, *The Life and Times of Samuel Gorton* (privately printed, 1907), which is uncritical, but contains citations of almost all available sources; Gordon Goodwin, in *Dict. Nat. Biog.*, with bibliography; J. M. Mackie, "Samuel Gorton," in Jared Sparks, *The Lib. of Am. Biog.*, 2 ser., vol. V (1845); *The New Schaff-Herzog Encyc. of Religious Knowledge* (1909), vol V. Contemporary references occur in *Winthrop's Jour.* (2 vols., 1908), ed. by J. K. Hosmer; *Records of the Gov. and Company of the Mass. Bay*, vol. II (1853); Nathaniel Morton, *New England's Memoriall* (1669); Charles Deane in *New-Eng. Hist. and Geneal. Reg.*, July 1850.]

J. T. A.

GOSNOLD, BARTHOLOMEW (fl. 1572–1607), navigator, colonizer, was the eldest son of a Suffolk squire of Grundisburgh, Anthony Gosnold, by Dorothy Bacon, his wife. The year of his birth is unknown but a will of 1572 contains unmistakable mention of him. For a time, obeying a family tradition, he attended Cambridge University, where he matriculated as a pensioner of Jesus College in 1587 but probably took no degree. The assertion (Alexander Brown, *The Genesis of the United States,* 1890, II, 904) that Gosnold served Sir Walter Raleigh in one or more expeditions to America is as baseless as it is unlikely, for his kinsmen, Henry and Robert Gosnold, were bound by close ties to the Earl of Essex, Raleigh's bitter enemy, and Raleigh considered Bartholomew's voyage in 1602 a grievous infraction of his American patent. About 1596 he was married, probably to Catherine, daughter of Sir Thomas Barrington, a Puritan of Essex interested in maritime affairs. Six children were born to him and baptized at Bury St. Edmunds, where apparently he made his home. The Earl of Southampton, a warm friend of Essex, in 1602 contributed largely to fitting out a ship to be commanded by Gosnold, who with thirty-one others embarked in a small vessel, the *Concord,* sailing from Falmouth Mar. 26, 1602. Emulating Verrazano, he set a western course across the Atlantic and after sighting the Azores made a landfall on the southern Maine coast near Cape Porpoise, then stood southward and, having landed at the tip of a foreland to which he gave the name of Cape Cod, skirted its outer shore and doubled Monomoy Point. The *Concord* continued her explorations, traversing Nantucket Sound and passing through Muskeget Channel. An islet, now No Man's Land, Gosnold named Martha's Vineyard in honor of his eldest child. The appellation was afterward transferred to the larger island which bears it to-day. Elizabeth's Isle, the modern Cuttyhunk, was selected as a base and a little fort erected. On the lookout for a passage through the continent to the South Sea, Gosnold examined the coast of the mainland from West Island to Narragansett Bay, apparently sighting Point Judith. Verrazano had preceded him in this region long before. The desire of his companions to return to England destroyed Gosnold's hope of establishing a small trading-post, and loading his ship with furs, cedar, and sassafras, obtained by friendly trade with the Indians, he set sail on June 17 and anchored before Exmouth July 23, 1602. Gabriel Archer and John Brierton [*q.v.*]—both members of the expedition—then prepared favorable narratives of the voyage, Brierton's being published in 1602. Raleigh considered Gosnold an interloper and asked Cecil's aid in confiscating the cargo. The sequel is uncertain. Gosnold now for some years busied himself with interesting English merchants and others in an American settlement. His relative Edward-Maria Wingfield was one of the grantees of the Virginia charter of 1606, and his brother Anthony Gosnold a subscriber to the stock of the Company. They accompanied him when on Dec. 20, 1606, he sailed from the Thames as vice-admiral of the fleet in command of the *God Speed,* which carried fifty-two of the original pioneers bound for the projected settlement. The fleet made land at Cape Henry Apr. 26, 1607. The sealed instructions, which now were opened, nominated Gosnold a member of the local council for the colony, and charged him to search the country for minerals and to explore the river in hope of finding a passage. Gosnold's sound judgment opposed the selection of the dank island in the James River as the site for the settlement, but Wingfield, now president, overruled him and there Jamestown was founded. In June, as a councilor, Gosnold signed the first report drawn up for the information of the home authorities (Neill, *Virginia Vetusta,* pp. 25–27), but on Aug. 22 following, during an epidemic of malarial fever, he died. He was buried with military honors. The loss of his amiable but sturdy leadership was a notable misfortune for the struggling colony.

[Biographical data are found in Jas. Savage, *Geneal. Dict. of the First Settlers of New England,* II (1860), 283; *New-Eng. Hist. and Geneal. Reg.*, vols. LVI–LIX (1902–05), especially Oct. 1902, p. 403, July 1903, pp. 310–13, and Oct. 1904, p. 396; John and J. A. Venn, *Alumni Cantabrigienses,* II (1922), 242; *Harleian Soc. Pubs.* XIII (1878), 148; and *Bury St. Edmunds: St. James Parish Register,* vol. I (1915), being Vol. XVII of the Suffolk Green Books. The accounts of Gosnold's voyage by Gabriel Archer and John Brierton were included in *Purchas his Pilgrimes* (5 vols., 1625–26); other reprintings of them may be found in *Mass. Hist. Soc. Colls.*, 3 ser., vol. VIII (1843), and C. L. Levermore, *Forerunners of the Pilgrims*, vol. I (1912); Brierton's was reprinted separately in 1903 and in H. S. Burrage, *Early English and French Voyages* (1906). See also Wm. Strachey, *The Historie of Travaile into Virginia Britannia* (1849), ed. from the original MS. by R. H. Major; *Capt. John Smith . . . Works, 1608–31* (1884), ed. by Edward Arber; Wm. Stith, *The Hist. of the First Discovery and Settlement of Va.* (1747); Jeremy Belknap in his *Am. Biog.*, II (1798), 100–23; E. D. Neill, *Hist. of the Va. Co. of London* (1869) and *Virginia Vetusta* (1885); article on Gosnold by J. K. Laughton in *Dict. Nat. Biog.*; B. F. De Costa, "Gosnold and Pring," in *New-Eng. Hist. and Geneal. Reg.*, Jan. 1878; C. E. Banks, "Martin's or Martha's?—What is the Proper Nomenclature of the Vineyard," *Ibid.*, Apr. 1894; Fulmer Mood, "Martha Gosnold and Martha's Vineyard" and "Richard Hakluyt and John Brierton," *Ibid.*, July, Oct. 1929; *Old Dartmouth Hist. Sketches*, no. 1 (1903).] F. M—d.

GOSS, JAMES WALKER (Dec. 29, 1812–Nov. 26, 1870), minister of the Disciples of Christ, educator, was born in Albemarle County, Va., the third and oldest son of Rev. John Goss and Jane Walker. The elder Goss had been a tutor in the family of Gov. James Barbour [*q.v.*], and later became a Baptist minister. James was educated by his father, private tutors, and in a local academy. He planned to study medicine, but after spending part of one year at the University of Virginia he forsook medicine for the ministry, and in 1832 was licensed to preach by the Baptists. On Sept. 29, 1835, he married Jane Ashley Grigsby, daughter of Joseph Grigsby. A venture in financing an apothecary establishment at Charlottesville resulted in his bankruptcy and the sacrifice of his property to satisfy the creditors. He again turned to the ministry and as a result of reading Alexander Campbell's *Christian Baptist* came to see, as he thought, "the true light." His Campbellite views created a division in his congregation, and in 1836 he helped to form a Christian church in Charlottesville. The Baptists excluded him from their communion, and, spurred on by the personal antagonisms resulting from the controversy, he began his work as a minister of the Disciples with energy, making preaching tours and establishing churches in neighboring counties without remuneration. He did more than any other to lay the foundation and promote the early growth of the Churches of Christ in Virginia. He aided in the publication of the *Christian Publisher* 1836–40, the first periodical published by the Disciples of the Alleghanies, and from 1843 to 1845 he was its sole editor and publisher, its name having been changed to the *Christian Intelligencer*. After 1845 he was interested primarily in education. He established a school for girls in 1851 at Gordonsville, Va., which in 1856 was moved to Albemarle County and renamed Piedmont Female Academy. He conducted it until 1867 when he went to Hopkinsville, Ky., to take charge of the Southern Kentucky Female Institute. Stricken with paralysis two years later and forced to return to Virginia, he died at Piedmont, near Charlottesville, in 1870. He was a man of unusual energy, somewhat better educated than his contemporaries among the Disciples, and possessed an indomitable will that led him to sacrifice much to propagate a faith that had "only the Bible as its text-book."

[*Christian Examiner* (Richmond), Jan. 2, Apr. 1, Aug. 1, 15, Sept. 15, Oct. 1, 1871; F. A. Hodge, *The Plea and the Pioneers in Va.* (1905); Edgar Woods, *Albemarle County in Va.* (1901).] T. D. M.

GOSTELOWE, JONATHAN (1744–Feb. 3, 1795), cabinetmaker, was born in the old township of Passyunk, now a part of Philadelphia. His father, George Gostelowe, is said to have emigrated from Sweden about 1729. His mother, Lydia, according to her tombstone in Christ Church Graveyard, Philadelphia, was a native of Northamptonshire, England. Jonathan learned his trade as a joiner in his native city, where there were several prominent furniture makers in the middle of the eighteenth century, but it is not known who was his master. His advertisements in the newspapers show that he worked in mahogany and in walnut, and made bureaus, dining and Pembroke tables, bedsteads, card tables, and chairs. It is also surmised that he made clock cases for Edward Duffield, whose daughter Mary he married on June 16, 1768. Identified specimens of his craftsmanship include a walnut serpentine bureau, a chest-on-chest, and a communion table and an elaborately carved font which he presented to Christ Church, Philadelphia, in 1789. His work as a cabinetmaker displays considerable originality at a time when many Americans were following the designs of English leaders in the craft. All of Gostelowe's surviving pieces depend for their merit more upon graceful but substantial lines than upon elaboration or ornament. His label is one of the half dozen of early American cabinetmakers that are known to exist.

During the Revolution he was first a major in an artillery corps and then commissary of military stores in Philadelphia under Robert Towers, chief commissary general of military stores for the Committee of Safety. After the Revolution Gostelowe retained his interest in military matters, became captain of a company in the 3rd Battalion, Pennsylvania Militia, in 1783–84, and subsequently, 1787, a lieutenant in an artillery battalion in the same force. He was elected chairman of the Gentlemen Cabinet and Chair Makers in Philadelphia in 1788, and headed their contingent in the historic Federal Procession held in that city on July 4, 1788. His first wife had died two years after their marriage, and on Apr. 19, 1789, he married Elizabeth Towers. He retired from business in 1793 and died in 1795. He was buried in Christ Church Graveyard.

[C. W. Brazer in *Antiques*, June, Aug. 1926; Robert Towers MSS., in the library of the Hist. Soc. of Pa.; *Pa. Archives*, 6 ser.; *Dunlap's Am. Daily Advertiser*, Feb. 14, 1795; records of Christ Church, Phila.; Benjamin Dorr, *A Hist. Account of Christ Church, Phila.* (1841); J. T. Scharf and T. Westcott, *Hist. of Phila.* (1884), I, 449.]

J. J.

GOTTHEIL, GUSTAV (May 28, 1827–Apr. 15, 1903), rabbi, was born in Pinne, Prussia, the son of Bernhard and Bertha (Adersbach) Gottheil. His secular education culminated in the Universities of Berlin and Halle, and his Jewish studies were guided by Solomon Plessner and by such outstanding savants as Zunz and Steinschneider. Samuel Holdheim, with whom he served as assistant preacher in the Berlin Reform Synagogue from 1855 to 1860, ordained him as rabbi. He began a thirteen-year ministry in the Manchester Congregation of British Jews in 1860, and at its completion he accepted the call to become assistant rabbi to Samuel Adler [*q.v.*] in Temple Emanu-El, New York. Eighteen months later, Adler was made rabbi emeritus, and Gottheil became the rabbi of the congregation, a position which he filled for twenty-three years, until at the age of seventy-two he retired as rabbi emeritus. His wife, Rosalie Wollman, by whom he had two daughters and three sons, died Dec. 15, 1893.

Gottheil was a notable organizer. In 1873 he founded the Emanu-El Preparatory School (later merged into the Hebrew Union College of Cincinnati), a school which gave the preliminary training to several men who subsequently became prominent in the American Rabbinate. He was one of the founders and a president of the Jewish Publication Society of America established in 1888; he organized the Association of Eastern Rabbis; and was one of the founders of the New York Board of Jewish Ministers. In 1889 he organized the Emanu-El Sisterhood of Personal Service. Though this was not the first American synagogue organization of women for philanthropic purposes, yet Gottheil's gift for organization, and the attractive name, Sisterhood, made it a model which was rapidly copied by synagogues throughout the city and the country. His relations with his Christian colleagues were most cordial. As one of the founders of the New York State Conference of Religion, he assisted in editing its *Book of Common Worship* (1900). He held a memorial service in his Temple for Henry Ward Beecher, and took part in the memorial service for Phillips Brooks. Following in the footsteps of his orthodox predecessor, Gershom Mendes Seixas [*q.v.*], who in the early years of the century more than once occupied the pulpit of St. Paul's Church, Gottheil not infrequently occupied Christian pulpits. In the Parliament of Religions of the World at the Columbian Exposition in 1893, he was one of the representatives of Judaism. The general recognition accorded him as religious spokesman of the Jews brought out his gift for suave but fearless Jewish apologetics, in which his careful diction, his dignity, wit, and natural tact lent their persuasive force. None took offense when he made such pointed remarks as "In ancient times, the Jews refused to eat with publicans and sinners; in modern times, publicans and sinners refuse to eat with Jews."

Among Gottheil's published works are *Moses versus Slavery* (Manchester, 1861); *Prayers and Meditations for the House of Mourning* (1890); *Morning Prayers* (1889), a compilation of devotional thoughts called *Sun and Shield* (1896). He also published "Anti-Semitism in Europe" in *Zionism and Anti-Semitism* (1904), prepared in collaboration with Max S. Nordau. Indicative of his liberalism is his collection of non-Christological *Hymns and Anthems Adapted for Jewish Worship* (1887) later made the basis of the *Union Hymnal* (1897), and the *Union Prayer-Book* (2 vols., 1895), in the preparation of which he had a determining part.

Gottheil's influence was extensive. The orthodox Jewish masses, who opposed his religious views, were attracted by his espousal of Zionism. For Reform Jewry he combined the Jewish, the English, and the German cultures then needed for the transition from German to American standards. His liberalism brought him close to Christian circles. All elements alike esteemed his kindly sympathy, generosity, pastoral geniality, and sense of human understanding.

[F. H. Vizetelly, in *Jewish Encyc.*, vol. VI; *N. Y. Times*, Apr. 16, 1903; *Jewish Chronicle* (London), May 1 and 15, 1903; I. S. Moses, in *Year Book of the Central Conf. of Am. Rabbis*, vol. XIII (1903); *Reformer and Jewish Times* (N. Y.), Oct. 25, 1878; *Am. Hebrew* (N. Y.), Apr. 17, 24, 1903; *Jewish Comment* (Baltimore), Apr. 17, 24, 1903; *Reform Advocate* (Chicago), Apr. 25, 1903; *Who's Who in America*, 1901–02.]

D. de S. P.

GOTTSCHALK, LOUIS MOREAU (May 8, 1829–Dec. 18, 1869), pianist, composer, was born in New Orleans, La., the eldest of seven children. His father, Edward Gottschalk, was a wealthy and cultured English broker born in

London, but not of Jewish ancestry, as has been generally stated. He emigrated to America at the age of twenty-five and settled in New Orleans, where he married Aimée Marie de Bruslé, a Creole of rare charm and beauty. Her family, of noble French lineage, had migrated from the island of Santo Domingo, where her grandfather, the Chevalier Antoine de Bruslé, had been governor of the northern province. Her father, Theodat Camille de Bruslé, was a captain in the British West India army, but when the British abandoned the island, he fled to Jamaica. There he married a refugee of French and Spanish noble birth, and with her he settled in New Orleans. Moreau (named for his mother's uncle, Moreau de l'Islet) very early manifested a talent for music. When he was about three years old, his mother, an accomplished singer, discovered him at the piano, picking out the melody of an aria she had just been practising. At four he began to study piano with Letellier and violin with Miolan, and later, also with Letellier, he became acquainted with the mechanism of the organ. At eight, such had been his progress in music that he played at a benefit for Miolan.

On the urgent recommendation of Letellier, Edward Gottschalk decided to send his son to Paris, and in May 1842 the thirteen-year-old boy sailed for Havre in care of the ship's captain. In July he entered the private school of Monsieur and Madame Dussert in Paris. He studied piano with Hallé and then with Stamaty, and harmony with Maledan. Later he became the pupil and close friend of Berlioz. He progressed rapidly in his studies and through family connections he was introduced to the best French society, where he became a great favorite. At his first Paris appearance in the Salle Pleyel *non payant,* in April 1845, he attracted the attention of Chopin, who predicted a great future for him. Meantime his father had suffered losses and Moreau decided to assist him by concertizing. In 1846–47 he gave a series of concerts with Berlioz at the Italian Opera and in 1850 he successfully toured Savoy, Switzerland, and the French provinces. At the invitation of the Queen of Spain he played in Madrid in November 1851, where he had the greatest ovation he had yet received. The Queen conferred upon him the order of Isabella the Catholic, and, in 1856, the title of Chevalier of the Royal Order of Charles III. In 1853, following his triumph in Paris, he returned to America and gave a most successful concert in the ball-room attached to Niblo's Garden, New York (Feb. 11). After the concert Barnum offered him twenty thousand dollars and his expenses for one year's concertizing under his management, but he refused the offer on the advice of his father, who considered Barnum only a showman. Although he was unfavorably received in Boston, his playing was so popular in New York that in the winter of 1855–56 he gave eighty concerts there. Following this brilliant season he wasted six years in the West Indies, returning to New York in 1862. During the next three years he gave more than eleven hundred concerts in the United States and Canada, after which he toured California, Panama, and South America, all under the management of Max Strakosch. In 1869 he went to Rio de Janeiro, Brazil, where he organized a huge festival, but on Nov. 26 he was taken sick while playing his own favorite composition, "Morte." He was removed to Tijuca, where he died a month later. He was buried in Rio with great pomp, but later his remains were brought to New York and placed in Greenwood Cemetery after a service in St. Stephen's Church, Oct. 3, 1870.

Gottschalk was a prolific composer. During his lifetime, and for several decades after his death, his compositions, largely in bravura style, enjoyed great popularity, but later they were almost totally forgotten. Probably the best known were "Last Hope," "Tremolo Étude," and "Bamboula." As a pianist, he was one of the greatest of his period; he was decidedly the best American performer. He had a brilliant technique and an appealing quality of tone, tinged with deep melancholy. Undoubtedly his fascinating performance of his own compositions, which he always featured, contributed greatly to their popularity. Though he was a notable interpreter of Beethoven, he seldom performed this master's works, choosing to please rather than to educate an unsophisticated public. He was endowed with a most lovable personality. He was modest and generous almost to extravagance, and possessed an ingratiating presence. Like his father, he was a proficient linguist, speaking five languages fluently. Though English was his mother tongue, he thought and wrote in French and nearly all of his compositions bore French titles.

[Gottschalk's diary is contained in *Notes of a Pianist* (1881) edited by his sister, Clara Gottschalk Peterson, and translated from the French by her husband, Robt. E. Peterson. Octavia Hensel's *Life and Letters of Louis Moreau Gottschalk* (1870) is entertaining but inaccurate. Information as to certain facts was supplied by Clara Aimée Gottschalk, a niece of the pianist. For short notices see Henry Didimus, "Biog. of Louis Moreau Gottschalk," *Graham's Mag.*, Jan. 1853, republished separately (1853), and the *N. Y. Times,* Oct. 4, 1870.]

F. L. G. C.

GOUCHER, JOHN FRANKLIN (June 7, 1845–July 19, 1922), philanthropist, college president, born at Waynesburg, Greene County,

Pa., was the son of Dr. John and Eleanor (Townsend) Goucher. Graduating from Dickinson College in 1868, he received several offers to enter business in Pittsburgh, where he had spent much of his early life. These he declined, and in 1869 entered the Methodist Episcopal ministry in the Baltimore Conference. During the twenty-one years of the active pastorate that followed Goucher was conspicuous in the building of fifteen churches, including the Harlem Park, the Strawbridge, and the First Church of Baltimore. On Dec. 24, 1877, he married Mary Cecelia Fisher, daughter of an old Maryland family of Pikesville, whose wealth made possible the numerous Goucher philanthropies. Goucher's most notable work was in the Woman's College of Baltimore (now Goucher College) and in the vast system of Methodist schools and missions in the Far East. His rôle in the history of the Woman's College has been subject to two widely entertained misapprehensions: that he was the founder of the college and that he was its first president. The idea of a college for women seems to have been due to John B. Van Meter; and was adopted in March 1883 by the Baltimore Conference to celebrate the centennial of the organization of the Methodist Episcopal Church in America. Contributions were received from many sources, but it was through the gifts of Henry Shirk and especially of Goucher, whose early donations totaled $75,000, that the college was made possible. It was opened in 1888 under the presidency of William H. Hopkins, who served until Sept. 1, 1890, when Goucher assumed the duties. He succeeded in gathering an able faculty, in protecting its more liberal members from the sometimes narrow views of the Baltimore Conference, and in building up the physical equipment of the college to meet the needs of its rapid growth. As a president Goucher had definite faults. He was deficient in financial abilities. He undertook an extensive building program while neglecting the endowment funds. This lack of financial vision was aggravated by the fact that he was often an absentee president. These long and frequent absences were necessitated by his educational projects in Europe and the Far East. Himself enthusiastic and generous, he was convinced that such a noble work as the college would never lack the necessary funds. This conviction, however, could do little to balance the annual budgets, with the result that when he resigned the presidency in 1908 the college was virtually bankrupt. In 1910, in recognition of the services of Goucher and his wife to the institution, the trustees changed its name to Goucher College. The Gouchers made further gifts, but their liberality had already threatened to exhaust their resources.

Throughout his long career Goucher was vitally interested in the Methodist schools and missions of the Far East. At one time his own funds maintained 120 primary vernacular schools in India. Large sums were spent in educational efforts in Korea and West China. It was estimated in 1904 that he had already spent a quarter of a million dollars for foreign missions. Among his many efforts the most important was the furthering of higher education in China and Japan; he was especially interested in the Anglo-Japanese Methodist College in Tokio, to which he made substantial donations.

Goucher's publications, *True Education* (1904), *Young People and World Evangelization* (1905), *Christianity and the United States* (1908), and *The Growth of the Missionary Concept* (1911), are slender both in bulk and in importance. The last of these, and the most substantial, comprised lectures delivered on the Nathan Graves Foundation at Syracuse University.

[*Who's Who in America, 1922–23*; C. H. Fahs in *Missionary Rev. of the World*, Nov. 1922; *Baltimore: Its Hist. and Its People* (1912), vol. III; *The Woman's College of Baltimore City—Articles of Incorporation, Constitution, By-Laws and Organization* (1886); *Christian Advocate* (N. Y.), July 27, 1922; *Minutes of the Baltimore Conference of the M. E. Ch.*, 1923; private information.] F. M—n.

GOUDY, WILLIAM CHARLES (May 15, 1824–Apr. 27, 1893), lawyer, of Scotch ancestry, the name being variously spelled Goudy, Gowdy, and Goudie, was the son of Robert Goudy, a printer who had emigrated from County Tyrone, Ireland, to Washington County, Pa., and there married Jane Ansley, also of Scottish descent. He was born in Indiana, where his parents had settled shortly after their marriage. In 1833 the family proceeded to Jacksonville, Ill., where he attended the public schools and graduated in 1845 from Illinois College. Although he had worked as a printer in his father's office he did not pursue that vocation after leaving college but became a school-teacher at Decatur, Ill., and read law in his spare moments. He studied for some months at Springfield in the office of Stephen T. Logan, a partner of Abraham Lincoln, and was admitted to the Illinois bar in 1847. The following year he commenced practise at Lewistown, Fulton County, and engaged actively in Democratic politics. He became state's attorney for the 10th judicial district in 1852, but resigned in 1855 to attend to his growing private practise. In 1856 he was elected state senator from Fulton and McDonough counties, and served till the end of 1861. During this period he acquired a reputation as a legislative draftsman and became a friend of Stephen A. Douglas, to whom he gave unwavering support in his last political struggles. He had in 1859 removed to Chicago, the extent of his law practise and the character of his retainers prompting him to take this step, and at once assumed a leading position at the bar. He was an unsuccessful candidate for delegate to the constitutional convention of 1862, and in the following year, when the death of Douglas made a vacancy in the Illinois representation in the United States Senate, he was nominated by a large section of the Democratic party but failed of election. From this time forward he gradually withdrew from politics and confined himself to the law, though in 1868 he was a delegate to the National Democratic Convention, and late in life became a friend and adviser of Grover Cleveland.

For thirty years he was one of the most prominent lawyers in the Middle West and held briefs during that period in almost every important case. His initial successes were gained as an expert in real property law, a subject upon which he was later regarded as perhaps the highest authority in the United States. As his practise extended, however, he became equally expert in commercial and constitutional law. In consultation he was extremely cautious, preferring safety to brilliance and invariably advising against speculative litigation. As an advocate he overlooked nothing. His speeches went directly to the salient points, and his arguments, prepared with the utmost care, were extremely compact. From 1886 until his death he was general counsel to the Chicago & North Western Railway. He was retained in much heavy railroad litigation, particularly when questions of constitutional law were involved. He was counsel for the defendants in the *Wabash, St. Louis & Pacific Railway Company* vs. *Illinois* (118 *U. S.*, 557). Among other notable cases in which he appeared were *Kingsbury* vs. *Buckner* (58 *Ill.*, 310; 70 *Ill.*, 514; 134 *U. S.*, 650), involving the ownership of the Ashland Block in Chicago, in which he received a fee of $75,000; and the Story Will litigation.

Somewhat reserved in manner, he was never a striking figure, his outward appearance and demeanor giving no indication of his intellectual strength and forensic ability. His secretiveness and brevity of utterance caused F. B. Wilkie to describe him as "a sort of locomotive enigma," but he enjoyed the unbounded trust of his clients, high and low. In 1849 he married Helen M. Judd, daughter of S. Corning Judd of Lewistown.

[Ensley Moore, "A Notable Illinois Family," *Ill. State Hist. Lib. Pub. No. 12* (1908); F. B. Wilkie, *Sketches and Notices of the Chicago Bar* (1871); *Bench and Bar of Chicago* (1883); *Chicago Legal News*, Apr. 29, 1893; *Daily Inter Ocean* (Chicago), Apr. 28, 1893; G. J. Clark, *Life Sketches of Eminent Lawyers* (1895).]

H. W. H. K.

GOUGE, WILLIAM M. (Nov. 10, 1796–July 14, 1863), writer on financial subjects, was born in Philadelphia, Pa. In 1823 he and Stevenson Smith became proprietors and editors of the *Philadelphia Gazette*, but in a few years Gouge retired. He reported the debates of the Delaware Convention for revising the constitution of the state, printed in 1831, and in 1833 published *A Short History of Money and Banking in the United States, Including an Account of the Provincial and Continental Paper Money, to Which Is Prefixed an Inquiry into the Principles of the System with Considerations of Its Effects on Morals and Happiness*, a second edition of which was issued in 1835. With an introduction by William Cobbett, it was reprinted in London under the title, *The Curse of Paper-Money and Banking* (1833), the history of colonial and continental currency being omitted. An abridgment also appeared in *La Revue Universelle*, Brussels (J. R. McCulloch, *The Literature of Political Economy*, London, 1845). He was at this time an uncompromising opponent of banks, paper money, and corporations. Banking, he affirmed, simply takes loanable money out of the hands of the owners and places it under control of irresponsible corporations. The *History* is of value, however, because of the detailed description it gives of the organization of state banks and the abuses associated with their management. During the secretaryship of Levi Woodbury [*q.v.*], 1834–41, he was appointed clerk in the Treasury Department and remained connected with it for many years, compiling some of the most valuable reports which up to that time the Department had issued. He also wrote *An Inquiry into the Expediency of Dispensing with Bank Agency and Bank Paper in Fiscal Concerns of the United States* (1837). In 1841 he was editor of the *Journal of Banking*, published in Philadelphia, which suspended operations, however, after one year. In this was again reprinted *A Short History of Paper Money and Banking in the United States*. In contributions to this journal his opposition to banks was somewhat modified, and he apparently took the position that notes issued against real commercial paper could not be overissued. Bank issues over and above this demand, however, he believed would inflate the currency and thus raise prices and lead to an unfavorable balance of trade. In 1852 he published *Fiscal History of Texas, Embracing an*

Account of the Revenues, Debts and Currency from 1834 to 1851–52, with Remarks on American Debts. In May 1854 James Guthrie [*q.v.*] secretary of the treasury, appointed him special agent "to examine the books, accounts, and money on hand in the offices of all the assistant treasurers of the United States, except at San Francisco, and designated depositories." In his "Report on the Public Depositories" (*Senate Executive Document No. 2*, 33 Cong., 2 Sess., pp. 255–75) he approved the independent treasury system whereby fiscal operations of the government would be separated from banks. In 1857–58 he was one of the two accountants of the state banks of Arkansas, the other being A. H. Rutherford, and in 1858 was published *Report of the Accountants of the State Bank of Arkansas.* Gouge died in Trenton, N. J., in his sixty-seventh year.

[R. H. I. Palgrave, *Dict. of Political Economy,* vol. II (London, 1896); J. T. Scharf and T. Westcott, *Hist. of Phila.* (1884), II, 1168, III, 1977; *Bankers' Mag. and Statistical Reg.* (N. Y.), Sept. 1863; *Phila. Inquirer,* and *Trenton Daily State Gazette,* both July 16, 1863.] D. R. D.

GOUGH, JOHN BARTHOLOMEW (Aug. 22, 1817–Feb. 18, 1886), temperance lecturer, was born at Sandgate, Kent, England, the son of John Gough, a veteran of the Peninsular War, receiving an annual pension of twenty pounds. His mother, Jane, was for twenty years a schoolmistress in the village school, at that time an important position. John was first instructed at home but was later sent to the seminary of a Mr. Davis at Folkestone. There, while still a pupil, he became the teacher of two classes, one in spelling and the other in arithmetic. His father once took him to a prayer-meeting at which the venerable William Wilberforce spoke. The evangelist took an especial interest in the lad, presented him with an autographed book, and spoke so many friendly and encouraging words to him that they registered an indelible impression.

Although his parents were poor, when he was twelve years of age they paid ten guineas to an acquaintance, David Mannering, to take the boy to America. For two years he worked on Mannering's farm in Oneida County, N. Y., but at fourteen with only half a dollar in his pocket he went to New York City to seek his fortune. Here he learned the book-binding trade, and as soon as he was earning three dollars a week he sent for his father, mother, and sister to join him. His mother and sister came at once but his father stayed behind in order to save his pension. Owing to a financial depression which began soon after the arrival of the mother in 1833, John lost his position. In the resulting hardships his mother died and he began to dissipate and drink. In 1839, after having acted low comedy parts on the stage without much success, he set up a book-binding shop of his own at Newburyport, Mass. On Dec. 18 of that year he married Lucretia Fowler, but his wife and first child both died during one of his ten-day periods of drunkenness. His condition now became steadily worse until he was unemployed, homeless, a confirmed drunkard, and at the age of twenty-five, a victim of delirium tremens.

In 1842, moved by some kind words from a stranger who talked with him on a public street, he promised to sign the total-abstinence pledge. At the temperance meeting at which he took the vow, he told the story of his experiences and soon was in much demand as a speaker. Within five months he had violated his pledge but immediately announced the fact and continued temperance work. About three years later while in New York he drank with a friend and spent a week in a drunken debauch. He immediately made a complete public confession and the church of which he was a member forgave him. From that time on he never violated his pledge and remained an ardent worker for the cause of temperance.

On Nov. 23, 1843, he was married in Worcester, Mass., to Mary Whitcomb. During this year, the first of his lecture work, he traveled 6,840 miles, gave 383 addresses, and received $1,059 out of which he paid all expenses. The fruits of his activity were 2,218 pledges. He soon became one of the most accomplished platform orators in America, and at the height of his career such was the demand for his services that he received an average of about $175 for each lecture. By 1853 his fame had so spread that the London Temperance League called him to England. Here his audiences were largely hostile, but on a second trip in 1857–60 he was received with great enthusiasm, as he was also in 1878. Shortly before his death Gough estimated that in all he had delivered more than 9,600 lectures to over nine million people. In his library he had the signatures of more than 140,000 persons whom he had personally induced to take the pledge. This number, however, does not include all those who signed the pledge at his meetings, for he reported that up to 1853 alone, these totaled 215,179. He continued lecturing to the last, dying in the midst of a speaking tour at Frankford, Pa.

Gough made a unique impression because his career was dramatic in the extreme, and because he possessed rare speaking ability. Both friend and foe attest the fact that he had a fine musical voice which was under perfect control. As he willed he could make his audience respond with laughter or with tears. One does not find clear-cut analysis or argument in his speeches, but rather an appeal to the emotions. He never had much enthusiasm for a national prohibition law, but directed all his energies toward the reform of individuals. His publications include, *Autobiography of John B. Gough* (1845); *The Autobiography of John B. Gough with a Continuation of His Life to the Present Time* (1859); *The Farewell Oration of John B. Gough, in Exeter Hall* (London, 1860); *Orations Delivered on Various Occasions by John B. Gough* (1859); *Autobiography and Personal Recollections of John B. Gough* (1869); *Sunlight and Shadow or Gleanings from My Life Work* (1880); *Platform Echoes: or, Leaves from My Note-Book of Forty Years* (1885).

[*Goffiana; A Review of the Life and Writings of John B. Gough* (1846); *Memorial Meeting in Honor of the Late John B. Gough Held in Chickering Hall, N. Y. City, Sunday Mar. 7th 1886* (1886); Carlos Martyn, *John B. Gough, the Apostle of Cold Water* (1893); *Andover Rev.*, May 1886; W. H. Daniels, *The Temperance Reform and Its Great Reformers* (1878); J. G. Woolley and W. E. Johnson, *Temperance Progress of the Century* (1903); E. H. Cherrington, *Standard Encyc. of the Alcohol Problem* (1926); Honoré W. Morrow, *Tiger! Tiger! The Life Story of John B. Gough* (1930); *Boston Transcript*, Feb. 19, 1886.] J. D.

GOULD, AUGUSTUS ADDISON (Apr. 23, 1805–Sept. 15, 1866), physician, conchologist, son of Nathaniel Duren Gould [*q.v.*] and his wife, Sally Prichard, was born in New Ipswich, N. H. His father was originally a farmer but later became well-known as a conductor and teacher of music. The boy's early years were largely spent in helping till the farm, only a small part of his time being available for school attendance. At the age of sixteen, however, he was able to enter Harvard College from which he graduated in 1825. His college life was a period of struggle against poverty, but it was in these years that he developed a taste for natural history, botany first attracting his attention. Following his graduation from Harvard, he spent a year as a private tutor in Maryland. He then returned to Boston, began the study of medicine, was an interne in the Massachusetts General Hospital, and in 1830 received the degree of M.D. from the Harvard Medical School. His early years as a physician were again a struggle with poverty, but he eventually became one of the leading medical men of Massachusetts.

It is as a naturalist, and particularly as a conchologist, however, that Gould is chiefly known and honored. With the exception of Thomas Say [*q.v.*], the father of American conchology, perhaps no one had greater influence in developing the study of that science. From 1833 until his death he was a constant contributor to the scientific journals of his time, principally upon molluscan topics, but also on insects, *Crustacea*, and general zoölogy. With Louis Agassiz he was a joint author of the *Principles of Zoology*, published in 1848. Chief among Gould's contributions to American science must be placed his *Report on the Invertebrata of Massachusetts* (1841), embracing descriptions, with figures, of the land, fresh water, and marine *Mollusca* of the New England states. The beautiful illustrations are all from Gould's pen. For many years this report was the only work available to students of American *Mollusca* and its value in encouraging a study of this subject is beyond estimate. Another of his important works was the study of the mollusks obtained by the United States Exploring Expedition under the command of Charles Wilkes ("Mollusca and Shells," *United States Exploring Expedition . . . Under the Command of Charles Wilkes, U. S. N.*, vol. XII, 1852), illustrated by many beautiful figures in a folio atlas. The work contains, besides the descriptions of new species, valuable observations on geographic distribution, former extent of continents determined by land species, and environmental notes, subjects at that time barely touched upon by conchologists. In *The Terrestrial Air-Breathing Mollusks of the United States, and the Adjacent Territories of North America* (1851–78) by Amos Binney, Volumes I and II of which Gould edited, he performed a vast service to students of American land shells, introducing such subjects as principles of classification, geographic distribution of genera and species, geological relationships, and anatomical structures. Among his other published works are *Otia Conchologia: Descriptions of Shells and Mollusks from 1839 to 1862* (1862) and *The Naturalist's Library; Containing Scientific and Popular Descriptions of Man, Quadrupeds, Birds, Fishes, Reptiles, and Insects* (1851). He also collaborated with Frederic Kidder and others in preparing *The History of New Ipswich* (1852).

Personally Gould was of genial disposition, easily making friends and holding them. His wife, whom he married on Nov. 25, 1833, was Harriet Cushing Sheafe, daughter of Henry and Lucy (Cushing) Sheafe. Those who had the privilege of meeting him in his home, surrounded by his family, were greatly impressed by his kindliness and generous impulses. He was honored by membership in many societies. In addition to the societies of his profession, he was an early member of the Boston Society of Natural History and for several years its president, an original member of the National Academy of Sciences, the American Academy of Arts and Sciences, and of many others at home and abroad. He died of Asiatic cholera, at the age of sixty-one years.

[Jeffries Wyman, in *Proc. Boston Soc. Nat. Hist.*, vol. XI (1868), and in *Nat. Acad. Sci. Biog. Memoirs*, vol. V (1905), both with bibliography; *Am. Jour. Sci.*, Nov. 1866; *Proc. Am. Acad. Arts and Sci.*, VII (1868), 300; T. T. Bouvé, in *Anniversary Memoirs of the Boston Soc. of Nat. Hist.* (1880); W. H. Dall, "Some American Conchologists," in *Proc. Biol. Soc. of Washington*, vol. IV (1888).] F. C. B.

GOULD, BENJAMIN APTHORP (June 15, 1787–Oct. 24, 1859), schoolmaster, merchant, brother of the poet Hannah Flagg Gould and father of the astronomer Benjamin Apthorp Gould [*qq.v.*], was born in Lancaster, Mass., the fourth of the ten children of Benjamin and Griselda Apthorp (Flagg) Gould, and the fifth in descent from Zaccheus Gould, who emigrated from Bucks to New England about 1638 and settled finally at Ipswich (Topsfield), Mass. Benjamin Gould fought with the patriot soldiers at Lexington and Bunker Hill, witnessed Burgoyne's surrender at Saratoga, and was captain of the main guard at West Point when Arnold escaped and André was captured. Like so many Revolutionary soldiers, he was reduced to poverty. Benjamin Apthorp Gould, accordingly, had a long, hard struggle for an education. Most of his boyhood and youth was spent in Newburyport and its vicinity, where he gained some experience as a teacher. At the age of twenty-three he was able, at last, to enter Harvard College, where he took high rank, especially in Latin and Greek. Some months before his graduation in 1814, at the suggestion of President Kirkland, he was appointed to the principalship of the Boston Public Latin School, and with the consent of the college authorities he entered at once upon his duties. Years of poor instruction and poor discipline had brought the Latin School to a sorry state, and its trustees were agreed that a man sufficiently young to adapt himself to its peculiar conditions was needed to rehabilitate it. Gould proved to be that man. His gift for teaching was something akin to genius; his pupils revered him; and under his administration the Latin School became famous. A remarkable number of his pupils attained distinction in later life. Gould himself was a member of the American Academy of Arts and Sciences and was well at home in the humanities. He prepared an excellent revision for use in American schools of Alexander Adam's *Latin Grammar* (1825), and his annotated editions of *Ovid* (1827), *Horace* (1828), and *Virgil* (1829) were the first schoolbooks of the kind to be edited in this country. On Dec. 2, 1823, Gould married Lucretia Dana, daughter of Nathaniel and Lucretia (Dana) Goddard. Overwork and confinement told on his health so that in 1828 he felt obliged to resign from the Boston Latin School, but his warm interest in education remained unabated. He was the first president of the Latin School Association and was a trustee of Dummer Academy in Newbury. For a number of years he was a member of the Boston school committee. He was also a member (1834–37) of the Common Council. After his retirement he became a merchant, acquired a number of ships, and engaged extensively and successfully in the Calcutta trade. His integrity, culture, and liberality made him one of the distinguished Bostonians of his generation. His wife and their two sons and two daughters survived him.

[Joseph Palmer, *Necrology of the Alumni of Harvard College 1851–52 to 1862–63* (1864); *Cat. of the Boston Public Latin School, with an Hist. Sketch by Henry F. Jenks* (1886); B. A. Gould, *The Family of Zaccheus Gould of Topsfield* (1895); *Proc. Am. Acad. Arts and Sciences*, V (1862), 4; *Boston Transcript*, Oct. 25, 1859; *Boston Herald*, Oct. 25, 26, 1859.] G. H. G.

GOULD, BENJAMIN APTHORP (Sept. 27, 1824–Nov. 26, 1896), astronomer, was born in Boston, Mass., the son of Benjamin Apthorp Gould [*q.v.*] and Lucretia Dana Goddard. He fitted for college at the Boston Latin School and graduated from Harvard in 1844, where under the teaching of Benjamin Peirce [*q.v.*] he acquired a keen interest in mathematics. After graduation he taught for a year in the Boston Latin School, and then went abroad firmly resolved to devote his life to scientific pursuits with a view to the development of science in his own land. A year at Berlin and another at Göttingen imbued him with the spirit of German scholarship. Contacts with Gauss, Bessel, Encke, and Argelander strengthened his ambition, and he returned to America in 1848 fired with zeal to emulate these masters. Fortunate in birth and education, physique, and natural ability, he was well equipped for the forty-eight years of clear-visioned and unremitting labor which he gave to his chosen science.

To meet his financial needs, he tutored at Cambridge in French, German, and mathematics. In the hope that its establishment would "be hereafter referred to as an era for astronomy in America" he founded in 1849 the *Astronomical Journal*, which he conducted until the outbreak of the Civil War compelled him to suspend publication. From 1852 to 1867 he was in charge of the longtitude department of the United States Coast Survey. He was quick to see the advantage of the telegraphic method and adapted it to the work of the Survey, obtaining the longitude of Washington from Greenwich over the first transatlantic cable. Meanwhile, from 1855 to 1859, he was director of the Dudley Observatory, Albany, N. Y., and in 1858 moved to that city. A bitter controversy over the management of the institution arose between some of the trustees and Gould, which had wide publicity. This trouble brought his connection with the observatory to an end in 1859, and he returned to Cambridge. (For synopsis of the controversy, see *Memoirs of the National Academy of Sciences,* XVII, 158–60.) The need of accurate star positions in the work of the Coast Survey led Gould to the formation of a "standard catalogue," in which for the first time systematic corrections were applied to the various catalogues used, *Standard Mean Right Ascensions of Circumpolar and Time Stars, Prepared for the Use of the U. S. Coast Survey* (1862). He also reduced and published the observations of fixed stars made by Joseph D'Agelet at Paris in 1783–85 (*Memoirs of the National Academy of Sciences,* vol. I, 1866). In 1861 he married Mary Apthorp Quincy, daughter of Josiah Quincy [*q.v.*], a talented woman, whose sympathy and cooperation were a great aid to him in his subsequent work. With her financial assistance he erected a private observatory near Cambridge, from which he made observations of the positions of stars near the north celestial pole. Her death occurred in 1883 and his "Cordoba Zone Catalogue" is dedicated to her, "Who bravely endured privation, exile and afflictive bereavement [two of their five children were drowned in South America in 1874] that it might be worthily finished, but who has not seen its completion." During the Civil War, as actuary to the United States Sanitary Commission, he made and published an extensive series of observations on the heights, ages, and peculiarities of the soldiers. In 1866 he became interested in the problem of determining accurate star positions from photographic plates and undertook the measurement and reduction of Rutherfurd's photographs of the Pleiades and of Praesepe (see *Memoirs of the National Academy of Sciences,* vol. IV, 1888).

Gould's greatest work, however, was his observations of the stars in the southern heavens. He envisioned a great catalogue extending to the southern sky the work of Bessel and Argelander on the northern sky. Planned at first as a private expedition, the project developed into the establishment of a national observatory at Córdoba in the Argentine Republic. Ground was broken in 1870. Impatient at the enforced delay in commencing his catalogue observations, he started on the determination, largely with the naked eye and field glasses, of the magnitudes, or brightness, of the southern stars. This was carried through to completion and published as "*Uranometria Argentina*" (*Resultados,* vol. I, 1879). Charts accompanied the catalogue. Regular observation with the meridian circle was started in 1872. Gould's plans contemplated the observation in zones of all the brighter stars between 23° and 80° south declination; the repeated observation of a large number of these stars to form a general catalogue of very accurate positions; the continuation of Argelander's and Schönfeld's *Durchmusterungen,* or identification catalogues; the photography of clusters; and a spectroscopic survey of the southern stars. Gould brought with him a corps of enthusiastic but untrained assistants. With unfaltering devotion and energy the main part of the program was carried out in fifteen years. The zone-catalogues give the positions of 73,160 stars and the general catalogue, of 32,448 stars. That so many observations could be made and reduced and the results largely printed in this short time is astounding. The *Durchmusterung* was carried out by his successors; the spectroscopic plan had, for sheer lack of time, to be abandoned; the plates of the southern clusters were taken at Córdoba and brought back to America, and their measurement and reduction occupied much of the last ten years of Gould's life. The results of his work in South America were published in *Resultados del Observatorio Nacional Argentino en Córdoba* (15 vols., 1879–1896).

Broken in health he returned home to stay in 1885; the following year he reëstablished his *Astronomical Journal* which was under his editorial charge until his death. Making his home in Cambridge, he was active in scientific, historical, and social organizations. Before going to South America he had become a Free and Accepted Mason, and later had acted as an official intermediary between the Masons of North and South America. He became deputy grand master of the grand lodge of Massachusetts, but declined the office of grand master. Many honors were conferred upon him, both at home and abroad. His death was the result of a fall on Thanksgiving Day 1896.

[*The Family of Zaccheus Gould of Topsfield* (1895), compiled by Gould himself; *Popular Astronomy,* Jan. 1897; G. C. Comstock in *Memoirs of the Nat. Acad. of Sci.,* vol. XVII (1924), is accompanied by a bibliography of Gould's numerous publications; *Astronomische Nachrichten,* Feb. 4, 1897; *Observatory,* Jan. 1897; *Monthly Notices Royal Astronomical Society,* Feb. 1897; *Boston Transcript,* Nov. 27, 1896. The introductions to the various volumes of the *Resultados del Observatorio Nacional Argentino en Córdoba* give much insight into Gould's character.] R. S. D.

GOULD, EDWARD SHERMAN (May 11, 1805–Feb. 21, 1885), author, was born at Litchfield, Conn., the fourth son among the nine children of Judge James Gould [*q.v.*] and his wife, Sally McCurdy Tracy. From his father, at one time head of the Litchfield Law School and a judge of the state supreme court, he derived his literary precision and taste. He was an honor student at the Litchfield Female [*sic*] Academy in 1818.

For some time Gould followed a varied career of writing in New York. He was married, but his wife and two sons deserted him. In 1836 he delivered a series of lectures under the title, "American Criticism on American Literature," decrying superficial and callow American standards of authorship and pointing to the merits of British literature. He published these lectures the same year in a booklet, *Lectures Delivered Before the Mercantile Library Association* (1836). His labors included the writing of novels, sketches, comedies, translations, and critical texts. In 1843 he published *The Sleep-Rider; or, The Old Boy in the Omnibus,* a short novel of adventure; and in 1850 edited *Forecastle Yarns,* written by a sailor brother, John W. Gould. His *John Doe and Richard Roe; or, Episodes of Life in New York* (1862), a series of sketches presenting realistically the atmosphere of the metropolis, appeared first in serial form, and are typical of the author's journalistic ventures in periodicals such as the *Knickerbocker Magazine,* the *Literary World,* and the *Mirror.* In the same spirit as his novels is *"The Very Age!"* (1850), a comedy of manners. He also published a number of translations from the French. In 1867, his *Good English; or, Popular Errors in Language* undertook to correct current stylistic and philological errors; to it was appended a lecture on "Clerical Elocution" delivered before the Divinity School of the Protestant Episcopal Church in Philadelphia. *Good English* reflects upon *The Dean's English: A Criticism on the Dean of Canterbury's Essays on the Queen's English,* by a Briton, G. Washington Moon, and it drew from Moon a stern reply in *Bad English Exposed: A Series of Criticisms on the Errors and Inconsistencies of Lindley Murray and Other Grammarians* (4th ed., 1871), in which he found Gould the more culpable because he was one who had "long been recognized in America as an authority in matters of literary and philological criticism." Although some of his criticism may have been minute and unwarranted historically, Gould showed himself unquestionably a purist of good taste. His work was praiseworthy for its refinement and scope. Particularly in his critical rather than his creative labors he rendered excellent service towards raising the standards of American writings. In his eightieth year he was killed by a runaway horse in New York City. He was buried at Litchfield.

[G. C. Woodruff, *A Geneal. Reg. of the Inhabitants of the Town of Litchfield, Conn.* (1845); P. K. Kilbourne, *Sketches and Chronicles of the Town of Litchfield, Conn.* (1859); Emily N. Vanderpoel, *Chronicles of a Pioneer School* (1903) and *More Chronicles of a Pioneer School* (1927); A. C. White, *The Hist. of the Town of Litchfield, Conn.* (1920); *N. Y. Times,* Feb. 22, 1885; *New Haven Evening Register,* Feb. 23, 1885.] L. L.

GOULD, ELGIN RALSTON LOVELL (Aug. 15, 1860–Aug. 18, 1915), economist, reformer, was born at Oshawa, Ontario, the eldest son of John T. and Emily Adelaide (Cronk) Gould. His grandfather, Joseph Gould, emigrated to Ontario from England about 1830 and bought large tracts of land; his mother's ancestors were early Dutch settlers in Dutchess County, N. Y. Gould graduated from Victoria College (later federated with the University of Toronto) in 1881, and studied at the Johns Hopkins University 1881–86, receiving the Ph.D. degree in 1886. Tall, handsome, and vigorous, he was an enthusiastic student and an able debater and writer. He became a citizen of the United States in 1885 and was married Sept. 27, 1887, to Mary Hurst Purnell of Baltimore. His study, "Local Government in Pennsylvania," appeared in 1883 (*Johns Hopkins University Studies in History and Political Science,* vol. I, no. 3). His most important research, done in Europe for the United States Department of Labor from 1887 to 1892, consisted of studies of production costs, wages, and family budgets for the sixth and seventh *Annual Reports* of the Commissioner of Labor. Gould summarized the results of these studies in "The Social Condition of Labor" (*Johns Hopkins University Studies,* vol. II, no. 1, 1893). While in Europe he collected material also for his reports, *The Gothenburg System of Liquor Traffic* and *The Housing of the Working People* (Fifth and Eighth Special Reports of the United States Commissioner of Labor, 1893 and 1895). His *Popular Control of the Liquor Traffic* (1895) urged the adoption of the Gothenburg system in the United States. He was a lecturer at the Johns Hopkins University 1892–97 and at Columbia University 1901–02. He was professor of statistics in the University of Chicago for one year, 1895–96. In 1896 he organized the City and Suburban Homes Company of New York, a limited-dividend corporation designed to provide comfortable housing at moderate prices, of which he was president until his death. He was president for some time of the Thirty-fourth Street National Bank, helped establish the Morris Plan system of banks, and was a leader in reform movements in New York City. One of the organizers of the Citizens Union in 1897, he helped elect Mayor Low in 1901, was city chamberlain during Low's administration, was vice-chairman of Gov. Hughes's commission to revise the City Charter in 1907–08, and was active in the League for Political Education, the City Club, St. Bartholomew's Church, and other organizations. He was a member of the International Institute of Statistics and of various economic and statistical associations. As a scholar, executive, and man of affairs, he rendered notable service to the common life. While on a visit to Glacier National Park in August 1915, he was kicked by a horse and died six days later on a train near North Bay, Ontario, Canada.

[*Elgin Ralston Lovell Gould: A Memorial* (League for Political Education, 1916); Henry Bruere, memorial address, *Phi Beta Kappa Key*, Jan. 1916; *Banquet to R. Fulton Cutting and Elgin R. L. Gould . . . Jan. 7, 1902* (privately printed, 1902); *Who's Who in America*, 1914–15; *N. Y. Times*, Aug. 19, 1915; information from Mrs. E. R. L. Gould of New York.]

H. S. W.

GOULD, GEORGE JAY (Feb. 6, 1864–May 16, 1923), financier and railroad executive, was the son of Jay Gould [*q.v.*] and Helen Day (Miller) Gould. After attending a private school he elected to enter business instead of going to college, and was trained carefully by his father to handle competently the Gould fortune. On his father's death in 1892 he was given almost complete control of his estate. He was then but twenty-eight years old, rather shy, unaggressive, and unprepossessing. Although not powerful physically he was keenly interested in all kinds of sports, including boxing, fencing, fishing, hunting, yachting, and tennis. He did much to popularize polo in the United States, having his own playing field and a string of ponies (G. J. Gould, "Polo and the Business Man," *Independent*, June 2, 1904). He was a director of the opera, backed a musical comedy, had a game preserve in North Carolina, a lodge in the Berkshires, and belonged to numerous clubs. His country home, "Georgian Court," at Lakewood, N. J., was one of the show places of the country; when it was built in the late nineties it was probably the most magnificent private residence in the United States (*Harper's Bazar*, Dec. 30, 1899, and Mar. 3, 1900; *Munsey's Magazine*, June 1900).

The main properties which he controlled after the death of his father were the Western Union Telegraph Company, the Manhattan Elevated Railroad, the Missouri Pacific, the Texas & Pacific, the International & Great Northern, and the Wabash. The four western railroads were the basis of what was known as the "Gould system," and both Gould and his co-trustees agreed, partly for sentimental reasons, that they should be retained and made secure. In the process of consolidating the position of his existing lines, he was drawn into a policy of expansion until he eventually had plans for a railroad from ocean to ocean. This concept was apparently not originally his, but was forced upon him piecemeal because of individual circumstances. In the East it seemed desirable from a competitive view-point that the Wabash have a terminal on the coast instead of at Buffalo. The project was furthered by the desires of the president of the Wabash and by the encouragement of Carnegie and other steel men who periodically became dissatisfied with the dominance of the Pennsylvania Railroad at Pittsburgh. Local roads were bought and an entirely new line constructed from Toledo by way of Pittsburgh to Baltimore. The entrance to Pittsburgh was one of the most expensive bits of construction ever completed, costing $380,000 a mile for sixty miles. The whole project was opposed bitterly by the Pennsylvania Railroad, which went to the extreme of destroying the Western Union poles and wires on its right of way because the Western Union was another Gould property.

While Gould was occupied with his eastern plans he found it necessary to devote much of his funds and attention to the West. The Gould roads had long suffered from the lack of a proper outlet to the Pacific, but about 1900 the situation became worse. A fight with Harriman over the Colorado Fuel & Iron Company had antagonized Harriman, and consequently the Union Pacific discriminated against the Missouri Pacific. Gould's reply, in the winter of 1900–01, was to buy the Denver & Rio Grande, which gave the Gould line a through road as far as the end of the Union Pacific at Salt Lake. The next move was made by Harriman who in 1901, shortly after the death of Huntington, bought the Southern Pacific, and was therefore able to divert traffic from the Gould roads both in the north and in the south. Gould's only recourse was to charter the Western Pacific and start building his own line to San Francisco. Although the Western Pacific was a well-built road and was finally completed in 1911, its construction helped Gould but little. His resources had been extended to the limit by his struggles both east and west and by unusually large family expenditures. Other factors, such as the opening of the Panama Canal and the panic of 1907, further weakened him. The opposition, headed by Harriman and Kuhn, Loeb & Company, took away road after road, most of which were by this time bankrupt. Gould had lost control of the majority of his roads by 1912; the last one, the Denver & Rio Grande, finally went in 1918.

With the collapse of his plans, Gould sought more and more to withdraw from active business management. He was harassed continually by law suits of all kinds, ranging from the efforts of a musical-comedy producer to collect damages for alleged breach of contract to a family action for an accounting of the Jay Gould estate. This latter suit was brought in 1916 and Gould was removed by the court as chief executor and trustee in 1919, chiefly for confusing personal and estate funds. The suit dragged on until 1927 and was advertised as the most expensive piece of private litigation ever presented. In the midst of these troubles Gould seems to have sought consolation outside of his home. On Sept. 14, 1886, he had married Edith M. Kingdon, an actress by whom he had seven children. In the winter of 1913–14 he met Guinevere Jeanne Sinclair, who appeared in the unsuccessful musical play, *The Girl in the Film.* After the failure of the play Miss Sinclair adopted the title of Mrs. Sinclair and occupied an apartment in New York; some time later she moved to an estate at Rye, N. Y. Her three children, born in 1915, 1916, and 1922 were acknowledged by Gould in his will as his own. After Mrs. Gould died on Nov. 13, 1921, Gould married Miss Sinclair (May 1, 1922). His daughter Gloria later testified that he lived with his first wife until her death. The newly married couple took their honeymoon in Europe, renting an estate in Scotland, where presumably they expected to reside permanently. While at Mentone, France, Gould contracted pneumonia, and died on May 16, 1923.

[The best general account of Gould's activities is that by B. J. Hendrick, "The Passing of a Great Railroad Dynasty," in *McClure's Mag.*, Mar. 1912. The Goulds have been described in a number of magazine articles, mostly laudatory, of which E. M. Gilmer, "The Goulds," *Cosmopolitan Mag.*, May 1909, is a fair example. See also *N. Y. Times,* July 12, 13, 15, 1922, and May 17, 1923; C. M. Keys, "The Overlords of Railroad Traffic," *World's Work*, Jan. 1907; H. T. Newcomb, "The Recent Great Railway Combinations," *Review of Reviews* (N. Y.), Aug. 1901. The best account of Gould's entrance to Pittsburgh is given in J. L. Cowan, "Freeing a City from a Railroad's Control," *World's Work,* Jan. 1905. The situation in the West, with the story of the building of the Western Pacific, is told most impartially in *Interstate Commerce Commission Reports,* vol. CXIII (1927); from the standpoint of the railroad it is given in the pamphlet *Story of the Western Pacific Railway* (n.d.); the view of a stockholder in the Denver & Rio Grande is given by Ernest Howard, in *A New Story of Am. Railroad Wrecking* (n.d., probably 1918) and *Wall Street Fifty Years after Erie* (1923).] R. E. R.

GOULD, GEORGE MILBRY (Nov. 8, 1848–Aug. 8, 1922), physician, ophthalmologist, editor, author, was born at Auburn, Me., the son of George Thomas and Eliza Ann (Lapham) Gould. He was a descendant of Robert Goold, a native of Somersetshire, England, who emigrated to Hull, Mass., in 1665. In his eighth year he moved with his father to Salina, Athens County, Ohio, and there was educated at the public schools. In 1861, before he was thirteen, he enlisted as a drummer boy in the 63rd Ohio Volunteers and served for eighteen months, being discharged on account of ill health; again, in 1864, he enlisted in the 141st Regiment of Ohio Volunteers and served until the disbandment of the regiment. After graduating from Ohio Wesleyan University in 1873, with the degree of B.A., he attended the Harvard Divinity School, receiving the degree of S.T.B. in 1874, and then studied at the Universities of Paris, Leipzig, and Berlin. Upon his return to the United States he acted for a year as pastor of a Unitarian church in Chillicothe, Ohio, then opened a book and art store in the same town. On Oct. 15, 1876, he was married to Harriet Fletcher Cartwright of Pomeroy, Ohio. In 1885, at the age of thirty-seven, partly in order to discover the cause of his persistent ill health, he relinquished his business career and entered Jefferson Medical College, Philadelphia. The following year, in collaboration with L. W. Fox, he published *A Compend of the Diseases of the Eye* (1886). He received the degree of M.D. in 1888 and at once began practise in Philadelphia, specializing in ophthalmology and particularly in the correction of refraction. In the first year of his practise he devised the cemented bifocal lenses which have since been so widely used. From 1892 to 1894 he was ophthalmologist to the Philadelphia Hospital.

His professional life was tempestuous. His theories and contentions, particularly in connection with the effects of eye-strain, which he held to be one of the great fundamental causes of ill health, both physical and mental, were regarded by his contemporaries as not only radical but false, though they are to-day widely accepted; while his brusqueness and inclination to use harsh language in characterizing what he regarded as harmful opposition to his teaching (especially in regard to the consequences of eye-strain), together with his justifiable criticism of the imperfect procedures of many refractionists, antagonized a number of his fellow specialists and of neurologists. Nevertheless he had devoted friends and ardent admirers both in and out of his profession. He was president of the American Academy of Medicine in 1895 and a speaker at the Congress of Arts and Sciences at the St. Louis Exposition in 1904.

In 1887 he wrote to Lafcadio Hearn [*q.v.*], who was at that time in the West Indies, an expression of his great admiration of certain of Hearn's translations. Hearn replied, and a long correspondence ensued which resulted in the removal of Hearn to the United States. When he called at the doctor's office in Philadelphia he was invited to become a guest at Gould's house, an invitation which he readily accepted. It would be difficult to conceive two characters more widely different than those of the physician, dogmatic and scientific by nature, and the irresponsible, unmoral dreamer. It is possible that Gould was interested in Hearn merely from a scientific standpoint, and he made every effort to reform the latter's erratic and erotic character, but he frequently expressed his admiration of Hearn's literary attainments and there is no doubt that he treated his guest with the utmost kindness and consideration. In 1908, after the publication of Elizabeth Bisland's uncritical biography of Hearn, he issued an analytical volume, *Concerning Lafcadio Hearn,* with a bibliography by Laura Stedman.

He had a marked literary gift, and it was perhaps for his contributions in the fields of medical lexicography and medical journalism that he was most widely known during his lifetime. In 1890 he published *The Student's Medical Dictionary* (11th ed., 1900), which was followed by *A Pocket Medical Dictionary* (1892), *A New Medical Dictionary* (1894, many subsequent editions), *An Illustrated Dictionary of Medicine, Biology and Allied Subjects* with a supplement entitled *A Dictionary of New Medical Terms* (both 1894), *An American Year Book of Medicine and Surgery* (1896–1905), and *A Cyclopedia of Practical Medicine and Surgery* (1900). He published also a number of works on various phases of ophthalmology. He was editor of the *Medical News,* 1891–95, and of the *Philadelphia Medical Journal,* 1898–1900. In the latter year he published *Suggestions to Medical Writers* and in 1901, with the avowed purpose of founding a school of medical journalism, established *American Medicine,* which he edited until 1906. He also published a volume of poems, *An Autumn Singer* (1897), and two semi-philosophical works: *The Meaning and the Method of Life* (1893) and *The Infinite Presence* (1910), "a search for religion in biology." His literary and psychological interests found expression in the six volumes of *Biographic Clinics* (1903–09), in which he interpreted such famous personalities as De Quincey, Carlyle, and George Eliot in the light of his favorite theory of eye-strain. He edited *The Jefferson Medical College of Philadelphia* (2 vols., 1904), a history, and in collaboration with Laura Stedman, grand-daughter of the poet, prepared the *Life and Letters of Edmund Clarence Stedman* (2 vols., 1910). In 1917 he married Miss Stedman as his second wife. Gould practised in Philadelphia from 1888 to 1908, in Ithaca, N. Y., from 1908 to 1911, and then in Atlantic City, N. J., where he died.

[For Gould's career see sketch by Mrs. Gould and other articles in *Jour. Am. Medic. Editors' Asso.,* June 1925; *Bibliog. of the Contributions of George M. Gould, M.D., to Ophthalmology, General Medicine, Literature, Etc.* (1909); *N. Y. Medic. Jour.,* June 15, 1921; *Who's Who in America,* 1921–22; *Am. Medicine.* Aug., Sept. 1922; *Medical Life,* Nov. 1922; *N. Y. Times,* Aug. 9 and 10, 1922; *Am. Jour. Ophthalmology,* Jan. 1923; *Trans. Am. Ophthalmol. Soc.,* vol. XXI (1923). On Gould's relations with Hearn see, in addition to biographies of Hearn, the *N. Y. Times Book Review,* Aug. 17, Oct. 12, 1930, and *Books* (*N. Y. Herald Tribune*), Aug. 17, 1930.]

G. C. H.

GOULD, HANNAH FLAGG (Sept. 3, 1789–Sept. 5, 1865), poet, sister of the first Benjamin Apthorp Gould [*q.v.*], was born in Lancaster, Mass., the fifth child of Benjamin and Griselda Apthorp (Flagg) Gould. In 1808 she removed with her parents to Newburyport, where she lived for fifty-seven years in unbroken, uneventful contentment. In person she was tall and of somewhat masculine proportions and features. She never married. She was her father's housekeeper and devoted companion in his old age and was noted for her piety, charity, hospitality, vivacity, and wit. Although she possessed a knack for versifying, she did not begin to cultivate it until in her mid-thirties, when she set the town laughing with her mock epitaphs on local celebrities. She then began to contribute to magazines and annuals. Her friends collected these fugitive pieces, secured copies of others still unpublished, and presented her with her first published volume, *Poems* (1832). It proved unexpectedly successful and was republished in 1833, 1835, and 1836, when a second volume was added. The two volumes were reprinted in 1839, and a third was issued in 1841. For twenty years she was a popular writer. She is said to have composed her pieces while busy with household tasks or enjoying a walk along the banks of the Merrimac. They are invariably short and usually treat religious or patriotic themes, domestic incidents, nature, or child life. Her control of language and meter was at first uncertain and never remarkable, but her readers were pleased with her good humor, sprightly fancy, and orthodox sentiments and did not miss the presence of genuinely poetic qualities. Her simplicity and sincerity were also real merits. She was at her best in her nature poems for children, some of which, such as "The Frost" and "The Pebble," found their way into school readers and became widely known. Her later publications were: *The Golden Vase: A Gift for the Young* (1843; 1844); *Gathered Leaves* (1846), a volume of prose; *New Poems* (1850); *The Diosma: A Perennial* (1851), in part a compilation, in part original; *The Youth's Coronal* (1851); *The Mother's Dream, and Other Poems* (1853); *Hymns and Other Poems for Children* (1854); and *Poems for Little Ones* (1863). To this list may be added *The Rising Monument* (Newburyport, 1840), a broadside poem on the Bunker Hill Monument; *The Mermaid's Cave* (1832), with music by C. E. Horn; "an original hymn" sung at most of the memorial services in Newburyport during her lifetime; and several other items, chiefly occasional poems. She died in Newburyport and was buried in New Hill (later part of Highland) Cemetery.

[Biographical data: B. A. Gould, *The Family of Zaccheus Gould of Topsfield* (1895); J. J. Currier, *Hist. of Newburyport, Mass.*, (2 vols., 1906–09); Sidney Perley, *The Poets of Essex County, Mass.* (1889); *New-Eng. Hist. and Geneal. Reg.*, Jan. 1866, p. 79; *Boston Transcript*, Sept. 6, 1865; *Daily Herald* (Newburyport), Sept. 7, 8, 1865. Contemporary reviews and notices: *New Eng. Mag.*, May 1832, and Apr. 1833 ("Literary Portraits, No. V: Miss H. F. Gould"); *Am. Monthly Rev.*, July 1832; *North Am. Rev.*, Oct. 1835; *Southern Literary Messenger*, Jan. 1836 (by E. A. Poe); *Baltimore Literary Monument*, Nov. 1838 ("Our Female Poets").] G. H. G.

GOULD, JAMES (Dec. 5, 1770–May 11, 1838), jurist, born at Branford, Conn., where his great-grandfather, Dr. Richard Gould of North Taunton, Oakhampton, Devonshire, had settled about 1700, was the son of William Gould, a well-known physician of that town, by his second wife, Mary Foote, widow of Timothy Johnson. His early education was obtained in the common schools, under the heavy handicap of defective eyesight. Strenuous application, however, enabled him in 1787 to enter Yale College, where he graduated in 1791 with high honors. He then became a school-teacher in Wethersfield, Conn., and later in Baltimore, Md., but returned to Connecticut early in 1793 and entered the law office of Judge Chauncey at New Haven. In September of that year he accepted a position as tutor at Yale. In 1795 he resumed his legal studies, entering the law school which Tapping Reeve [*q.v.*] had established in 1784 at Litchfield. In 1798 he completed the course and was admitted to the bar. The same year the appointment of Reeve as a judge of the superior court of Connecticut rendered it necessary for him to seek assistance in the tutorial work and management of the law school, which he had hitherto conducted alone, and at his request Gould became his colleague, at the same time continuing to practise. For a number of years they remained thus associated, and when Reeve finally withdrew in 1820 Gould assumed sole charge. In politics a Federalist, he was in May 1816 appointed a judge of the superior court and court of errors. In 1818 a new constitution was framed which involved a complete change in the court system, and as a consequence he was retired from the bench in the following year. He did not resume active practise but devoted his energies henceforth to the affairs of the law school, continuing to lecture until growing physical infirmity compelled him to close the school in 1833.

As a practitioner he was careful and competent, though not distinguished. He found office work somewhat irksome and was always seen to best advantage as an advocate. With no pretension to eloquence or humor, his arguments were invariably logical, clothed in simple, clear, forcible language, and noted for their brevity. His short tenure of judicial office did not afford him any opportunity of influencing the jurisprudence of the state. As a teacher of law, however, he was preëminent. Always a student, he had a profound knowledge of the common law and was "the impersonation of its genius and spirit" (Chief Justice Church, *post*, p. 52). In addition he possessed the art of imparting his knowledge to his pupils in language so simple and unambiguous that the difficulties of the subject seemed to disappear. He read his lectures so slowly that not a word was lost, every student being able to make a verbatim note, and then the discussion of the various points took place, in which his critical scholarship had full play. "In the more abstruse subjects of the law, he was more learned than Judge Reeve, and as a lecturer more lucid and methodical" (*Ibid.*, p. 56). His *Principles of Pleading in Civil Actions* (1832) was an expansion of one of his courses of lectures and is a good example of his style and method. Handsome, genial, and refined, he has been described as "an accomplished gentleman of the old school" (*Law Reporter, post*). On Oct. 21, 1798, he married Sally McCurdy, eldest daughter of Gen. Uriah Tracy of Litchfield.

[*New Haven Colony Hist. Soc. Papers*, II (1877), 332; F. B. Dexter, *Biog. Sketches Grads. Yale Coll.*, vol IV (1907); D. C. Kilbourn, *The Bench and Bar of*

Litchfield County, Conn. (1909); S. E. Baldwin, "James Gould," *Great Am. Lawyers,* II (1907), 455; *Law Reporter,* June 1838; Samuel Church, "Address on the Occasion of the Centennial Celebration, 1851," *Centennial Celebration held at Litchfield, Conn., Aug. 13 and 14, 1851* (1851).] H. W. H. K.

GOULD, JAY (May 27, 1836–Dec. 2, 1892), financier, christened Jason by his parents, was born at Roxbury, N. Y., the son of John Burr and Mary (Moore) Gould, who owned a poor hill farm. On his father's side he was descended from Nathan Gold, of Bury St. Edmunds, England, who emigrated to Milford, Conn., in 1647 and some three years later settled in Fairfield, Conn. On his mother's side he was of Scottish descent. By determined effort, working for a blacksmith and later as clerk in a country store, he obtained some education in an academy and learned the rudiments of surveying. With this equipment he showed a precocious knack in money-making. Between his eighteenth and twenty-first years he helped prepare maps of Ulster, Albany, and Delaware counties in New York, Lake and Geauga counties in Ohio, and Oakland County in Michigan, and in 1856 he published a volume of local history, *History of Delaware County, and Border Wars of New York.* At twenty-one, an undersized, keen-witted, unscrupulous young man, he had saved $5,000. With Zadock Pratt, a New York politician, he opened a large tannery in northern Pennsylvania, and shortly prevailed upon a New York leather merchant, C. M. Leupp, to assist him in obtaining full control of it. His business relations with both men were sharp to the point of knavery, and his enemies always declared that his speculations were partly responsible for Leupp's suicide in 1857. Abandoning the tannery, after a brief career in 1859–60 as leather merchant at 39 Spruce St., New York, he began speculating in small railways. A profitable deal in bonds of the Rutland & Washington was followed by his managership of the Rensselaer & Saratoga and investments in other lines.

Gould's operations first became spectacular when in October 1867 he and James Fisk [*q.v.*] joined the directorate of the Erie Railroad, of which Daniel Drew [*q.v.*] was treasurer and controlling agent. In the titanic and scandalous battle with Cornelius Vanderbilt which followed, Gould supplied the strategic imagination while Drew contributed low cunning and Fisk impudence. Defying a court injunction, they broke Vanderbilt's attempted corner by flinging 50,000 shares of Erie upon the market (March 1868). Gould and his fellow conspirators were promptly forced to flee to Jersey City, whence he descended upon Albany to buy the passage of a bill legalizing the recent issue of Erie stock and forbidding a union of the Erie and New York Central. Lavish bribes secured this legislation. A peace was then patched up with the Vanderbilt interests, and Drew retired from the Erie leaving Gould and Fisk in absolute control. A series of sensational operations followed. The Gould-Fisk partnership, reinforced by the addition of Peter B. Sweeney and William M. Tweed as directors, looted the Erie by huge stock-watering measures; carried out a daring raid on the credit, produce, and export markets of the nation in the fall of 1868; and attempted a year later to corner the gold market, bringing about the disastrous panic of Black Friday (Sept. 24, 1869). The result was an avalanche of popular anger. Litigation over the sale of fraudulent Erie stock was begun, and following Fisk's death and the overthrow of the "Tweed ring," Gould was ejected from his control of the Erie on Mar. 10, 1872, Gen. John A. Dix [*q.v.*] taking his place.

His destructive activities were now to be succeeded by operations with at least some constructive elements. Possessing a fortune which has been estimated at $25,000,000 (Gustavus Myers, *post,* II, 337), Gould was in a position to undertake ambitious strokes. He turned to the West. Buying large blocks of Union Pacific Railroad stock, he became a director in 1874 and remained in virtual control until 1878, meanwhile buying control of the Kansas Pacific. In 1879 he also bought control of the Denver Pacific, Central Pacific, and Missouri Pacific. By threatening to extend the Kansas Pacific to Salt Lake City to connect with the Central Pacific, thus forming a new transcontinental railroad in competition with the Union Pacific, he compelled the Union Pacific to consolidate with the Kansas Pacific at par. Soon afterward he sold his Kansas Pacific stock, thus clearing a sum which Henry Villard placed at ten millions (R. I. Warshow, *post,* 151). He retained possession of the Missouri Pacific and increased its efficiency. By 1890 he owned the Missouri Pacific system (5,300 miles), the Texas & Pacific (1,499), the St. Louis Southwestern (1,222), and the International & Great Northern (825), or one-half of all the mileage in the Southwest. His system, at a time when practically all Southwestern traffic was carried to St. Louis or Kansas City, was the only real competitor of the Santa Fé (S. F. Van Oss, *American Railroads as Investments,* 1893, p. 551). Meanwhile, Gould had extended his dealings into other fields. He owned the New York *World* from 1879 to 1883; became part owner of the New York elevated railways in 1881 and practically full owner in 1886; and bought control of the Western Union Telegraph Company. Working almost to the end, and remaining the same cold, astute, unscrupulous man, without friends and caring for no diversions except books and gardening, he died of tuberculosis in his fifty-seventh year. He had married Helen Day Miller early in life, and his sons, especially George Jay Gould [*q.v.*], succeeded to the control of his property.

[R. I. Warshow, *Jay Gould: The Story of a Fortune* (1928), is a thin and unsatisfactory biography. It is supplemented by Murat Halstead and J. F. Beale, Jr., *Life of Jay Gould* (1892); Trumbull White, *The Wizard of Wall Street and his Wealth* (1892); Gustavus Myers, *Hist. of the Great Am. Fortunes* (1910), II, 281 ff., III, 61 ff.; Meade Minnegerode, *Certain Rich Men* (1927), pp. 135 ff.; and C. F. and Henry Adams, *Chapters of Erie* (1871). For Gould's later railway operations, see "Report of the U. S. Pacific Railway Commission of 1887," *Sen. Ex. Doc. 51*, 50 Cong., 1 Sess.; Nelson Trottman, *Hist. of the Union Pacific* (1923); and Stuart Daggett, *Chapters on the Hist. of the Southern Pacific* (1922). For genealogy see E. H. Schenck, *Hist. of Fairfield* (1889), I, 370–71. See also obituary articles in the *N. Y. Times*, Dec. 3, 1892.]

A. N.

GOULD, NATHANIEL DUREN (Nov. 26, 1781–May 28, 1864), conductor, teacher of music, was born at Bedford (not Chelmsford as stated in several publications), Mass., a son of Reuben and Mary (Gould) Duren. His father was a great-grandson of John Durrant who had settled in Billerica, Mass., by 1659; his mother came of a Chelmsford family, descended from Thomas Gould who was living in Salem Village, N. H., in 1662. Reuben Duren was a builder whose high-steepled churches were famous, and who successfully constructed over Pawtucket Falls in the Merrimac River, at the site of the present Lowell, a bridge, including an arch of wide span, generally thought impossible of completion. Since Reuben and Mary Duren had many children, Nathaniel was sent when he was ten years old to live with his mother's brother, Nathaniel Gould of New Ipswich, N. H., farmer, constable, surveyor, amateur musician appointed by town meeting to "raise the tune on the Sabbath." The boy, whose name was legally changed from Nathaniel Gould Duren to Nathaniel Duren Gould, showed marked proficiency in music and penmanship and good scholarship in other subjects. At sixteen he taught a district school and began to give music lessons. He had mastered every instrument then customarily played and had convinced himself that anybody, adult or child, could be taught to sing. When the Middlesex Musical Society, said to have been the second singing society of its kind in America, was formed in 1805 in adjacent Massachusetts towns, Gould was chosen its conductor. Ten years later he founded at New Ipswich the Hubbard Society, named after Prof. John Hubbard of Dartmouth College, whose concerts were held, in respect of musical quality, as second only to those of the Händel and Haydn Society of Boston. Gould also directed a military band which had wide celebrity in New England. In addition to his musical activities he engaged in trade, and took a prominent part in public affairs. He represented New Ipswich in the legislature from 1809 to 1812 and again in 1814–16, and was a selectman in 1817, 1818, and 1820. In 1812 he became a deacon in his church, and from 1817 to 1824 he was a trustee of the New Ipswich Academy. On Nov. 15, 1801, he had married Sally Prichard. Of their children born at New Ipswich, Augustus Addison [*q.v.*] attained distinction as a naturalist, and Charles Duren, as a Boston publisher in the firm of Gould & Lincoln. During his thirty years' service to music in southern New Hampshire Deacon Gould "exerted a decided influence in favor of temperance and religion, at a time when musicians, almost without exception, were tipplers and scoffers" (Kidder and Gould, *post*, p. 382). He removed in 1820 to Boston, where he continued in a larger field to teach and conduct throughout New England. He joined the Händel and Haydn Society Oct. 3, 1820 (Perkins and Dwight, *post*). For ten years he made his headquarters in New York where, as in Boston, he was a pioneer "in the field of juvenile instruction even before [Lowell] Mason entered it" (Elson, *post*, p. 86). After his return to Boston, he carried on his historic researches which were summarized in his *Church Music in America*, published by A. N. Johnson in 1853. He had previously published *Penmanship or the Beauties of Writing* (1822); *Social Harmony or A Compilation of Airs, Duetts, and Trios* (1823); *Musical Prosody* (1830); *National Church Harmony . . . Music Arranged for the Organ and Piano Forte* (1832); and *The Sacred Minstrel; A Collection of Psalm Tunes, Chants, etc.* (1839). He continued his useful activities well into old age, dying in Boston in his eighty-third year.

[C. H. Chandler and Sarah F. Lee, *The Hist. of New Ipswich, N. H.* (1914); Frederic Kidder and A. A. Gould, *The Hist. of New Ipswich* (1852); H. A. Hazen, *Hist. of Billerica, Mass.* (1883); B. A. Gould, *The Family of Zaccheus Gould of Topsfield* (1895), pp. 343–44; S. P. Cheney, *The Am. Singing Book* (1879); L. C. Elson, *The Hist. of Am. Music* (1925); C. C. Perkins and J. S. Dwight, *Hist. of the Händel and Haydn Soc. of Boston, Mass.*, vol. I (1883–93); *Boston Transcript*, May 30, 1864.]

F. W. C.

GOULD, ROBERT SIMONTON (Dec. 16, 1826–June 30, 1904), Texas jurist, teacher, was born in Iredell County, N. C. His father, Daniel Gould, was a Presbyterian minister, a native of New Hampshire. His mother, Zilpha (Simonton) Gould, was born in North Carolina, and evidently possessed the sturdy qualities of her Scotch-Irish parentage. Her husband died when her son Robert was only seven years old, and the widow established a college boarding-house at Tuscaloosa, Ala., the seat of the state university, on the meager profits of which she supported her sons until they had completed their college education. Gould attended the University of Alabama from 1840 to 1844, graduating at the age of eighteen. The next year he began the study of law, a career which was interrupted by his election as a tutor in mathematics. In 1849 he obtained a license to practise law and opened an office in Macon, Miss., in partnership with the former governor, Joshua L. Martin. In 1850 he moved to Centerville, Texas, and three years later was elected district attorney of the 13th judicial district. Declining reëlection, he returned to private practise, in which he seems to have been successful. In 1855 he married Lenna Barnes, a native of Alabama. The confidence of his neighbors was attested by his election to the convention of 1861, in which he voted in favor of the ordinance of secession. He had, in the meantime, been elected judge of his home district, but resigned almost at once to enter the Confederate army as a captain. He was soon a major, in command of a force of his own, called "Gould's Battalion," and after participating in a number of battles and being severely wounded, he emerged from the war a colonel.

In 1865, a widower with a daughter to support, he returned to his long-neglected practise and was almost immediately elected to the position of district judge which he had resigned four years before. Within the year, his pronounced Southern sympathies proved distasteful to the military authorities and he was removed on the charge of hindering reconstruction. Considering his removal illegal, he did not resume his practise, but spent the next three years in the attempt to make a precarious living on his farm near Centerville. In 1870 he once more commenced the practise of law, this time in Galveston, and four years later he was appointed by Gov. Coke an associate justice of the supreme court of Texas. He was elected to the same office under the constitution of 1876, and in 1881, upon the resignation of Justice Moore, became chief justice for the remainder of the term. His judicial career was almost at an end, however, for he was not renominated by the Democratic convention of 1882. He had made himself a master of the difficult subject of community property, and his decisions in this field became precedents of great importance. Notable among them are those in the cases of *Yancy* vs. *Batte* (48 *Texas,* 46), *Johnson* vs. *Harrison* (48 *Texas,* 257), and *Veramendi* vs. *Hutchins* (48 *Texas,* 531).

Gould had none of the arts of the politician and was not a good popular speaker, but he had a clear mind and the tastes and inclinations of a scholar. With his distinguished record and a personality which is still remembered for its winsome qualities, he was unusually well fitted to become a teacher and leader of young men, and when the University of Texas was opened at Austin, on Sept. 15, 1883, he was made a member of the law-school faculty. He developed a special interest in the Roman law, a subject of unusual importance in the Southwest, and for more than twenty years he was the central figure in a school in which many of the lawyers of Texas have been trained. He died at Austin in his seventy-eighth year.

[Memorial address by R. L. Batts, in the *Alcalde,* vol. II, 883–90; J. D. Lynch, *The Bench and Bar of Texas* (1885), pp. 312–14; 98 *Texas Reports,* i–x; *Proc. . . . Texas Bar Asso.,* 1904; *Austin Statesman* and *Houston Post,* July 1, 1904.] R. G. C.

GOULD, THOMAS RIDGEWAY (Nov. 5, 1818–Nov. 26, 1881), sculptor, was born in Boston, Mass. His parents were John Ridgeway Gould (1778–1826) and his wife, Ann Ridgeway. Left fatherless at eight, Thomas and his three brothers began in boyhood to support themselves and their mother. Thomas eventually became the Boston representative of a mercantile firm established in New Orleans by his brother, John M. Gould. In his early thirties, an amateur without any instruction other than hints from artist friends, he modeled his first figure, in the studio of Seth Wells Cheney [*q.v.*]. When the Civil War ruined his business, he turned to sculpture for support. A cultivated, interesting man, he found financial success almost immediately within the circle of his own acquaintances. In a little Boston studio he produced busts of John A. Andrew, Civil War governor of Massachusetts; of Ralph Waldo Emerson (this bust is now owned by Harvard University); of the elder Booth, to whom he later paid a tribute by his book, *The Tragedian; An Essay on the Histrionic Genius of Junius Brutus Booth* (1868). Both the elder Booth and his son Edwin were Gould's personal friends. In 1863 he exhibited colossal heads of Christ and Satan in the Boston Athenæum. These works won high praise from H. T. Tuckerman, a noted art critic of the day; and even from James Jackson Jarves, usually a caustic critic of American art. Other lauded pieces were "Michael Angelo," "Imogen,"

"Childhood." The unanimity of the critics was amazing. Fortified by their approval, Gould went with his family to Italy in 1868, and opened a studio in Florence. Here, within a year, he modeled his most noted work, "The West Wind," a female figure lightly draped in a starry-belted skirt. Several marble replicas were made; the original passed to the Mercantile Library, St. Louis, Mo. Interest in the piece was heightened by press controversy (1874) concerning a false charge that except for the drapery, it was copied from Canova's "Hebe." It was duly admired at the Centennial Exhibition of 1876, but later judgments have been less favorable. "He demonstrates in every line of this childish work his utter inability to conceive an artistic whole," wrote Lorado Taft in 1903 (*The History of American Sculpture,* p. 189).

The attention attracted by "The West Wind" brought many orders to Gould, who therefore took a larger studio in Florence. Having begun sculpture too late, he now produced it too rapidly. Among his works were a "Cleopatra" and an "Undine," both sent to Boston. His Shakespearean subjects included a high relief of a bearded, helmeted, plumed head called "The Ghost in Hamlet," a "Timon of Athens," and an "Ariel," the latter owned by the daughter of Edwin Booth. His bronze statue of John Hancock, made for the Centennial celebration at Lexington, Mass., was placed in Lexington's Town Hall in 1875. The same year saw the erection of his statue of John A. Andrew in the cemetery at Hingham, Mass., the commission coming from the Grand Army of the Republic. His nine-foot bronze figure of King Kamehameha I is in front of the Government Building, Honolulu, and his "Ascending Spirit" in the Gould lot in Forest Hills Cemetery near Boston. His last work, a "Puritan" for the Common at Cambridge, Mass., was unfinished at his death, and was completed by his son Marshall Gould. After a visit to the United States in 1881 he returned to Italy and died in Florence, in November of that same year, survived by his wife, Rebecca (Sprogell) Gould, and by their two sons, a sculptor and an architect. Gould himself was a man of culture and sterling worth; his drawings and sketches had both force and poetic feeling, but his sculpture was based on too frail a foundation of knowledge and skill to have lasting value, except as eloquent testimony to the taste of the times.

[H. T. Tuckerman, *Book of the Artists* (1867); J. J. Jarves, *Art Thoughts* (1869); S. G. W. Benjamin, *Art in America* (1880), following in substance Benjamin's illustrated article in *Harper's Magazine,* Apr. 1879; *Bryan's Dict. of Painters and Engravers* (5 vols., 1903–05), II, 264; B. A. Gould, *The Family of Zaccheus Gould of Topsfield* (1895); *Boston Transcript,* Nov. 29, 30, 1881. Information as to certain facts from Charles Stratton, Esq., of Boston.]

A. A.

GOULDING, FRANCIS ROBERT (Sept. 28, 1810–Aug. 22, 1881), Presbyterian clergyman, author, was born in Midway, Liberty County, Ga., a community settled by New England Puritans transplanted to South Carolina in 1695 and to Georgia in 1752. His father, Thomas Goulding, educated in New Haven, was a Presbyterian clergyman and theologian. His mother, Ann Holbrook, of Wolcott, Conn., was a daughter of Nathan Holbrook, a Revolutionary patriot. Francis spent his early childhood partly at Midway and partly at Savannah, but at twelve went with his family to live in Lexington. At nineteen he was graduated from the state university and at twenty-two from the Theological Seminary in Columbia, S. C., of which his father was president. Having entered the ministry, he was married in Savannah in 1833 to Mary Wallace Howard, upon whose solicitation and for whose first use, it is said, Lowell Mason composed the music for the hymn, "From Greenland's icy mountains." He preached in Sumter County, S. C., in Greensboro and Washington, Ga., became an agent of the American Bible Society, and preached again, in Eatonton and (1843–51) in Bath, Ga. While in Eatonton in 1842, he constructed—four years before Howe's invention was patented—a sewing-machine, but, while satisfied of its usefulness, made no application for a patent, laying the device aside, he said, in order that he might attend "to weightier duties" (Rutherford, p. 193). In 1844 he published a story of devout juvenility called *Little Josephine,* and in 1852, after countless revisions, *Robert and Harold,* later entitled *The Young Marooners on the Florida Coast.* Before 1869 the book is said to have gone through six editions in England, in 1890 it was translated into French, and by 1919—when it was last published—it had gone through at least ten editions in the United States. In 1853 he moved to Kingston, Ga., opened a school for boys, and began work on a volume about the instinct of birds and beasts. Here his wife died; and in 1855, having married Matilda Rees, he moved with her to her estate at Darien, not far from his birthplace. Here he again took up his ministry. During the Civil War he served unofficially, it seems, as a chaplain, and then, his library having been burned by Union troops, he went to Macon, where he taught a school for girls, compiled a *Soldiers Hymn Book,* and wrote a series of articles called "Self Helps and Practical Hints for the Camp, the Forest, and the Sea." After the war, impoverished and unable to preach because of a throat affection, he turned to writing. *Marooner's Island,* published serially in 1867 and in book form in 1869, went through as many as three editions, but nothing else that he wrote was widely popular. *Sal-o-quah or Boy Life Among the Cherokees* (1870), *Sapelo or Child-Life on the Tide-Water* (1870), *Nacooches, or Boy Life from Home* (1871) constituted a series called the Woodruff Stories, in memory of a boyhood friend, Lorenzo Woodruff. By 1869 he was living in the hill country at Roswell, Ga., genial, hard put for money, and tortured by asthma. It was here that death came to him.

[James Stacy, *Hist. of the Midway Congregational Church* (Newman, Ga., rev. ed., 1903); J. W. Davidson, *Living Writers of the South* (1869); M. L. Rutherford, *The South in Hist. and Lit.* (1907); E. A. Alderman, J. C. Harris, *The South in the Building of the Nation* (1909), vol. XI; W. J. Northen, *Men of Mark in Ga.*, vol. II (1910); Gen. Cat. Univ. of Ga. 1785–1906 (1906).]
J. D. W.

GOUPIL, RENÉ (*c.* 1607–Sept. 29, 1642), missionary, a lay brother of the Society of Jesus, was a native of the province of Anjou in France. In his youth he entered the Jesuit novitiate at Paris with a view to studying for the priesthood, but, after a few months, ill health obliged him to leave the novitiate. He seems to have studied medicine and, when his health was restored, he left France for Canada, where he arrived in 1640. For two years he gave his services to the Fathers as a *donné* and, at the request of Father Isaac Jogues [*q.v.*] who had come from the Huron missions to get supplies, Goupil was assigned to accompany him on the return journey. The party of about forty, four Frenchmen and the rest Hurons, left Three Rivers on Aug. 1, 1642. The next day they were ambushed and captured by the Iroquois. Most of the Hurons were killed. Jogues, Goupil, and William Couture, another *donné,* were condemned to slavery and for some time were in constant danger of death. The hands of the prisoners had been so badly mutilated that they had to be fed by others. Even the Indians were moved to pity. On Sept. 29, the Feast of St. Michael, Goupil was killed, in the village of Ossernenon, near what is now Auriesville, N. Y. The immediate cause of his death was the exasperation of an old man who saw the captive making the sign of the cross over his grandchild. Two Indians followed Jogues and Goupil as they went to pray in the near-by woods and ordered them back to the village. Near the gate one of them split Goupil's skull with a tomahawk. He fell with the name of Jesus on his lips. On the journey to Ossernenon Goupil had pronounced the vows of the Society of Jesus. Jogues found his body in the torrent and covered it with stones, hoping later to bury it. When he sought it, it had disappeared. Only the next spring did he find the head and some gnawed bones. These he secreted, but was unable to take them with him when he escaped in 1643. Goupil is honored by the Catholic Church as a martyr for the Christian Faith with the title of "Saint." After prolonged investigation his beatification, together with that of seven other Jesuits, took place on June 21, 1925. He was canonized by Pope Pius XI on June 29, 1930.

[Jogues's letters and account of Goupil's life and martyrdom have been reprinted in *The Jesuit Relations and Allied Documents,* ed. by R. G. Thwaites, vol. XXVIII (1898). They have been utilized by J. J. Wynne, *The Jesuit Martyrs of North America* (1925); see also M. J. Scott, *Isaac Jogues, Missioner and Martyr* (1927).]
J. C.

GOVAN, DANIEL CHEVILETTE (July 4, 1829–Mar. 12, 1911), Confederate soldier, was born in Northampton County, N. C., the son of Andrew Robison and Mary Pugh (Jones) Govan. The family fled to America from Govan, Scotland, after the Jacobite uprising of 1745. Daniel's father was a congressman from South Carolina in 1822–27. Soon after leaving Congress he moved to North Carolina, then to Somerville, Tenn., about 1830, and later, on the removal of the Chickasaw Indians (1832), he settled in Marshall County, Miss. Young Daniel was prepared for college by a private tutor and was a member of the senior class at the University of South Carolina in 1848, although he apparently did not graduate. The next year, with a kinsman, Ben McCulloch [*q.v.*], he joined the gold rush, traveling overland to California by the Southern route. In 1850, when McCulloch was elected sheriff of Sacramento, Govan served as his deputy. Two years later he returned to Mississippi and became a planter. In December 1853 he married Mary F. Otey, daughter of Bishop J. H. Otey [*q.v.*]. He moved to Arkansas and settled in that part of Phillips County which is now included in Lee County. Here he engaged in planting until the beginning of the Civil War, when he at once raised a company which became a part of the 2nd Arkansas Regiment, of which he was made lieutenant-colonel. He took part in the campaigns in Kentucky, Tennessee (Shiloh), Mississippi, around Chattanooga, and Atlanta, rising to the rank of brigadier-general. In the last-named campaign he captured the 16th Iowa Regiment with its colors. Nearly twenty years later, Sept. 26–27, 1883, he was invited to attend a reunion of the regiment and returned the flag. Before the fall of Atlanta, Govan and his regiment were captured (Sept. 1,

1864), but he was soon exchanged. He followed Hood [q.v.] back to the west and advised against the attack at Franklin, where his division commander, P. R. Cleburne [q.v.], was killed. After the battle of Nashville the remnant of the army joined Gen. Joseph E. Johnston [q.v.] in North Carolina and there Govan surrendered to Sherman. He then returned to his plantation and continued there until 1894, when he accepted from President Cleveland an appointment as Indian agent at a post in the state of Washington. In 1896 Mrs. Govan died and two years later Govan returned to Tennessee. He lived in that state and in Mississippi, with one or another of his fourteen children, until his death. In 1878, at the request of a friend, he wrote a brief "History of Cleburne's Division," printed in the first volume of Fay Hempstead's *Historical Review of Arkansas* (1911). He was one of the four men Cleburne had in mind when he said: "Four better officers are not in the service of the Confederacy" (*Official Records, Army,* 1 ser., XXXI, pt. 2, p. 759). Govan was a member of the Episcopal Church. On hearing of his death Capt. Irving A. Buck, Cleburne's adjutant-general, wrote: "I regard him as one of the best soldiers it was my good fortune to know—a true Christian gentleman, a noble patriot, a loyal and uncompromising friend."

[C. A. Evans, *Confed. Mil. Hist.,* X (1899), 400; *Biog. and Hist. Memoirs of Eastern Ark.* (1890), pp. 594–95; *Official Records (Army)*; I. A. Buck, *Cleburne and His Command* (1908); information from Govan's niece, Mrs. Bettie Govan Burke; obituaries in *Commercial Appeal* (Memphis), Mar. 13, 1911, and *Confederate Veteran* (Nashville), Sept. 1911.] D. Y. T.

GOVE, AARON ESTELLUS (Sept. 26, 1839–Aug. 1, 1919), educator, was born at Hampton Falls, N. H., son of John Francis Gove, a village blacksmith, and Sarah Jane Wadleigh. He was descended from John Gove, who came to Massachusetts from England some time before 1650, through his son, Edward, who settled in New Hampshire in 1665. Although Aaron's parents gave him the middle name Estellus, he never used it after his boyhood days. In 1847 the Goves moved to Boston and the boy entered school a pupil of Master Page. Later they went West and established a home at Rutland, Ill. At fifteen Aaron, a quiet, studious, taciturn youth, began teaching. Attending the State Normal School between teaching terms, he was graduated with the second class in 1861. In August of that year he enlisted as private in the 33rd Illinois Regiment. Steadily promoted, he was brevetted major for bravery in action at Vicksburg. After the Civil War he had charge of schools at Rutland and at Normal, Ill., until 1874 when he became superintendent of schools in Denver, Colo. On Feb. 13, 1865, he married Caroline Spofford of North Andover, Mass., daughter of Farnham and Lydia Spofford.

For thirty years he superintended the schools of Denver, retiring in 1904 to enter the service of the Great Western Sugar Company as their legislative representative and adviser. It was he who dictated the educational article in the state constitution of Colorado in 1876, and for a generation he was recognized as the educational leader of the state. Significant of the quality of his work is the fact that in the early eighties John D. Philbrick, representing the federal Bureau of Education, visited the Denver schools and wrote a report published by the commissioner which gave them a nation-wide reputation for buildings, organization, and efficient administration. Gove was president of the National Education Association (1887–88), and was one of the founders of the National Council of Education. He established and edited the *Illinois Schoolmaster* and the *Colorado School Journal,* and he was founder and president of the Colorado Education Association. Thrifty of speech, unsparing of thought, Gove more than any other educator shaped school policies in Colorado for a generation. Among Colorado school men his leadership was never questioned. Schoolmaster, he liked best to be called; he was indeed a master of schools. He never wrote a textbook, but the Reports of the National Education Association during the period of his career chronicled his utterances and school men throughout the nation sought and followed his counsel.

[*Colo. School Jour.,* Sept. 1919; W. F. Stone, *Hist. of Colo.,* IV (1919), 110–12; Frank Hall, *Hist. of the State of Colo.,* vol. IV (1895); *Hist. of the City of Denver, Arapahoe County and Colo.* (1880), pp. 451–52; *Portr. and Biog. Record of Denver and Vicinity, Colo.* (1898); *Hist. of Colo.* (5 vols., 1927), pub. under supervision of the State Hist. and Natural Hist. Soc.; *Report of the Commissioner of Educ. for the Year 1882–83* (1884); *The Jour. of Proc. and Addresses of the Nat. Educ. Asso.,* 1884, 1887–92, 1894–1903; *Addresses and Proc., Internat. Cong. of Educ.* (1903); W. H. Gove, *The Gove Book, Hist. and Geneal. of the Am. Family of Gove and Notes of European Goves* (1922); I. H. Elliott and V. G. May, *Hist. of the Thirty-third Regiment Ill. Veteran Volunteer Infantry in the Civil War* (1902); *Who's Who in America,* 1918–19; *Rocky Mountain News* (Denver), Aug. 2, 1919.] H. M. B.

GOWANS, WILLIAM (Mar. 29, 1803–Nov. 27, 1870), bibliophile and publisher, was born in Scotland, county of Lanark, a son of vigorous Scotch peasantry. All the schooling he ever had was in the parish school near the Falls of the Clyde. Life on the farm was distasteful to the boy and his father's decision to emigrate to the

United States in 1821 brought a welcome change. A short residence in Philadelphia was followed by some five years in Crawford County, Ind. He and Abraham Lincoln, without knowing each other, must have been flat-boatmen on the Ohio and Mississippi at about the same time. When Gowans was about twenty-five years old he went to New York and tried his hand at various occupations, including gardening, news vending, and stone cutting. In 1830 he played a minor part with Edwin Forrest at the Old Bowery Theatre. At length he set up a bookstall on Chatham Street, consisting simply of a row of shelves, protected at night (or in the daytime when the owner was peddling or attending book auctions) with wooden shutters, an iron bar, and a padlock. In later years he testified that the first person to lend him substantial encouragement in his new line of business was James Harper (J. H. Harper, *The House of Harper,* 1912, p. 49). He also recounted the pleasure that was his as a boarder for several months (*c.* 1837) in the family of Edgar Allan Poe (*New York Evening Mail,* Dec. 10, 1870). For the rest of his life he was ever identified with books, not books with pages uncut and luxurious bindings, but second-hand and rare volumes, and "unconsidered trifles and remnants." His locations were many, and for a brief period he set up as a book auctioneer, but from 1863 to the end of his life he was the "Antiquarian of Nassau Street" with his shop at No. 115 on that thoroughfare. Like Bulwer's Covent Garden friend, he was a bookseller who preferred to buy rather than sell. When a would-be patron complained that his price for a book was too high, he said, "Well, we will make it higher," at the same time placing the volume on a shelf out of reach. His books filled the store floor, basement, and sub-cellar, the treasures in the depths discoverable only with the aid of a small tin sperm-oil lamp. "Books lay everywhere in seemingly dire confusion, piled upon tables and on the floor, like Pelion on Ossa, until they finally toppled over, and the few narrow alleys which had originally been left between the rows became well-nigh impassable" (W. L. Andrews, *post,* p. 13). His executors sold at auction some 250,000 bound volumes after eight tons of pamphlets had been sold as waste paper.

Gowans did some publishing from time to time, his earliest production being a reprint of the English edition (1701) of Dacier's translation of Plato's *Phaedo* in 1833. Between 1842 and 1870 he issued twenty-eight catalogues of his books. These catalogues are full of "his antiquarian reminiscences, his quaint and shrewd opinions, and curious speculations." Other worthwhile publications were the historical reprints known as *Gowans' Bibliotheca Americana* (5 vols., 1845–1869). Not without self-revelation is a sketch he wrote of a fellow bibliophile, "Reminiscences of Hon. Gabriel Furman" (Gabriel Furman, *Notes, Geographical and Historical, Relating to the Town of Brooklyn, on Long-Island,* 1865, pp. xxv–xxxiv). He married in middle life Susan Bradley of New York, who died in 1866 leaving no children.

[W. L. Andrews, in *The Old Booksellers of N. Y. and Other Papers* (1895); obituaries in *N. Y. Evening Mail,* Dec. 1, 1870; N. Y. *Evening Post,* Nov. 28, 1870, N. Y. *Sun* and *N. Y. Tribune,* Nov. 29, 1870, *Nation,* Dec. 1, 1870; *Catalogue of the Books Belonging to the Estate of the Late Mr. William Gowans* (16 pts., 1871); portrait in *Gowans' Bibliotheca Americana.*]

A. E. P.

GOWEN, FRANKLIN BENJAMIN (Feb. 9, 1836–Dec. 14, 1889), lawyer, railroad president, prosecutor of the Molly Maguires, was born at Mount Airy (Philadelphia), the son of James Gowen who emigrated to the United States from Ireland in 1811, and Mary (Miller) Gowen, a daughter of James Miller of Mount Airy. Upon his arrival, James Gowen settled in Philadelphia, where he became a successful merchant, acquiring a moderate fortune on which he retired to a farm at Mount Airy. He became noted throughout the state of Pennsylvania as a breeder of shorthorn cattle. Early in his youth Franklin Benjamin Gowen was sent to a Catholic school at Emmitsburg, Md., and from this institution he was transferred to the Moravian school at Lititz, Lancaster County, Pa., where he finished his formal education. He became a clerk in a store at Lancaster at the age of nineteen and two years later accepted the superintendency of a furnace at Shamokin, Pa. Here he became acquainted with the vast resources of the anthracite coal fields, which had much to do with his later career. For a time he engaged in mining as a member of the firm of Turner & Gowen. He was admitted to the bar in May 1860 and acquired an extensive and lucrative practise. In 1862 he was elected district attorney of Schuylkill County. He was elected a member of the constitutional convention of Pennsylvania in 1872 and took a conspicuous part in the work.

The most dramatic happening of his life was his work as counsel for the Commonwealth of Pennsylvania in the prosecution of the Molly Maguires. This famous secret society had terrorized the anthracite coal regions for twenty years. Everybody knew when he undertook the work that he risked his life, because he was dealing with a band of successful, experienced murderers. He put detectives on the case, one of whom lived and worked among the members of the secret society for three years, ultimately becoming a member of the organization. Upon the testimony of this man, and corroborating evidence gathered by Gowen himself, he procured the conviction and execution of a number of the leaders and broke up the organization.

In 1870 he was elected president of the Philadelphia & Reading Railroad, for which he had been counsel since 1864. His administration of the road was marked by great ability, but his record is marred by the fact that the Company encountered financial difficulty during his administration. This was due, at least in part, to his policy of tying up the anthracite coal-mines with the Philadelphia & Reading Railroad. He planned, as he said in a report to stockholders, "to secure—and attach to the Company's railroad—a body of coal-land capable of supplying all the coal-tonnage that can possibly be transported over the road." The pursuit of this policy brought disaster. The Company defaulted on the interest of its obligations in 1880, and the road was placed in the hands of receivers by the United States circuit court. Gowen continued to direct operations and the management of its finances, however, and it was later restored to the stockholders. Shortly afterward it passed through a second period of receivership. Many of the properties which he acquired during the period of expansion subsequently became immensely profitable.

After his resignation from the presidency of the Reading, Gowen practised law and acquired a position of preëminence. In December 1889 while in Washington, D. C., to appear before the Interstate Commerce Commission in behalf of one of his clients, he committed suicide in his room at a hotel, by firing a bullet into his brain. No satisfactory explanation could be found for his act; he was fifty-three years of age, in good health, at the height of his mental powers, well-to-do, and enjoying the respect of his contemporaries.

[Obituaries in *Public Ledger* (Phila.), Dec. 16, 1889; *North American* (Phila.), Dec. 16, 1889; *Sun* (Balto.), Dec. 16, 1889; *Report of the Case of the Commonwealth vs. John Kehoe et al. . . . with the Testimony and Arguments of Counsel in Full, Stenographically Reported by R. A. West* (1876, Miners' Journal Book and Job Rooms, Pottsville, Pa.); F. P. Dewees, *The Molly Maguires* (1877); *Speeches of Mr. Franklin B. Gowen and Others Concerning the Phila. & Reading Railroad Company; Delivered at a Public Meeting . . . at the Cannon St. Hotel, London, on Thursday, the 10th of Nov., 1881* (London, 1881); J. T. Scharf and T. Westcott, *Hist. of Phila.* (1884), III, 2187.]

W. C. P.

GRABAU, JOHANNES ANDREAS AUGUST (Mar. 18, 1804–June 2, 1879), Lutheran clergyman, was born in Saxon Prussia at Olvenstedt near Magdeburg, the elder of the two children of Johann Andreas and Anna Dorothea (Jericho) Grabau. The father, a farmer, bestowed care and love on his son's education until his unexpected death in 1822 left the family in grief and distress. Assisted by his teachers and by a small stipend, Grabau completed the course in the Dom-Gymnasium in Magdeburg and matriculated at Michaelmas 1825 in the University of Halle, where he studied for five years. After teaching for four years in Magdeburg and Sachsa, he was elected pastor of St. Andreas in Erfurt Mar. 3, 1834, and was ordained June 17 in the Barfüsser Kirche. On July 15 he married Christiane Sophie Burggraf, who with two sons and a daughter survived him. In 1836 he announced that as a strict Lutheran he could no longer use the Union liturgy, and when his superiors failed to persuade him he was deposed from office and forbidden to enter his church. He conducted services in private houses in defiance of the authorities until he was arrested Mar. 1, 1837, and imprisoned at Heiligenstadt. In September he escaped. With his rescuer, Capt. Heinrich K. G. von Rohr, who had been dismissed from the Prussian army for opposing the Union, he made his way about the country visiting sympathizers as far away as Stettin. On Sept. 21, 1838, he was captured and remanded to prison. Finally he received permission to emigrate; Von Rohr gathered a company of one thousand with Grabau as their pastor; and in June and July 1839 they sailed from Hamburg in five ships. Grabau and the greater part of the company settled in Buffalo in October. There he was pastor of the Dreifaltigkeits-Kirche for almost forty years. A notable pastor and preacher, he was too often tactless, opinionated, and headstrong in dealing with other ministers of his denomination, and in consequence he failed to realize his dream of a great Lutheran synod that would conform in doctrine to the Book of Concord, as he understood it, and in government to the old Saxon and Pommeranian church ordinances. In 1840, with Von Rohr as his first pupil, he opened a school, later known as Martin Luther Seminary, to train candidates for the ministry. On July 15, 1845, Grabau, Von Rohr, and three other clergymen met at Milwaukee and organized the Synod of the Lutheran Church Emigrated from Prussia, which soon became known as the Buffalo Synod. In 1853–54 he and Von Rohr visited Germany to confer with Wilhelm Löhe on matters of doctrine. From 1842 until 1866 he carried on a fierce controversy with C. F. W. Walther [*q.v.*] and other theologians of the Missouri Synod on the subject of ordination, the ministry, and the church. The Missouri Synod made the controversy into a war of extermination against Grabau and his followers, set up rival congregations, and rejoiced when the Buffalo Synod split into three factions in 1866. The largest faction, consisting of Christian Hochstetter and eleven other pastors, promptly allied themselves with the Missourians; Von Rohr continued at the head of his party until his death in 1874; and Grabau, with a few pastors still loyal to him, kept open his seminary, started a new paper, *Die Wachende Kirche,* to take the place of the old *Informatorium,* which remained in Von Rohr's possession, and was elected *Senior Ministerii* of the new Buffalo Synod. The last years of his life were peaceful. He edited a hymn-book for his Synod and had a liturgy ready for publication at the time of his death. Violent and irascible when engaged in theological controversy, he was at all other times gentle and mild of manner, though relentless in his demands on his own body, mind, and conscience.

[J. A. Grabau, *Lebenslauf des Ehrwürdigen J. An. A. Grabau* (Buffalo, 1879); Ernst Denef, "Geschichte der Buffalo Synode," in *Die Wachende Kirche* (North Tonawanda, N. Y., 1920–29); H. R. Grabau, article in *Luth. Cyc.* (1899); W. A. Grabau, *Die Geschichte der Familie Grabau* (Leipzig, 1929); information as to certain facts from Profs. Ernst Denef and Herbert C. Leupold, formerly of Martin Luther Seminary.]

G. H. G.

GRÄBNER, AUGUST LAWRENCE (July 10, 1849–Dec. 7, 1904), Lutheran theologian, historian, was born at Frankentrost, Mich., the son of Johann Heinrich Philipp and Jacobine (Denninger) Gräbner. His father (1819–1898), born at Burghaig near Kulmbach in Upper Franconian Bavaria, studied under Wilhelm Löhe at Neuendettelsau, and emigrated to the United States in 1847 as pastor of a congregation of twenty-two families who bought government land in Saginaw County, Mich., and established the poetically named colony of Frankentrost. Since his father was a member of the Lutheran Synod of Missouri, Gräbner entered Concordia College at Fort Wayne, Ind., in 1865 and Concordia Seminary at St. Louis in 1870, but illness kept him from completing both his academic and his theological course. He was already a promising scholar, steeped in Tacitus, Dante, and Luther, and profoundly influenced by his chief preceptor, Carl Ferdinand Wilhelm Walther [*q.v.*]. In 1872 he became a teacher in the Lutheran High School at St. Louis. On Aug. 14, 1873, he married Anna, daughter of his teacher, Prof. Gottlieb Schaller of Concordia Seminary. Gräbner was professor in Northwestern College at Watertown, Wis., 1875–78, and in the Wisconsin Synod's newly opened theological seminary in Milwaukee, 1878–87. When he went to Milwaukee he was ordained as assistant pastor of St. Matthew's Church and also assumed the editorship of the Synod's *Gemeindeblatt.* In 1887 on the death of his father-in-law he succeeded to the professorship of church history in Concordia Seminary, and after the retirement and death of Prof. C. H. R. Lange in 1892 he also lectured in English on dogmatics and kindred subjects. He published *Dr. Martin Luther: Lebensbild des Reformators* (1883), an edition of Chemnitz's *Enchiridion* (1883), *Johann Sebastian Bach* (1886), *Half a Century of Sound Lutheranism in America* (1893), *Herr, Ich Warte auf Dein Heil* (1895), *Outlines of Doctrinal Theology* (1898), and several minor writings. His most enduring work is the *Geschichte der Lutherischen Kirche in America, Erster Theil* (1892), which brings the story down to 1820 and was left uncontinued at his death. Gräbner had all the requisites of a historian except fairness. Because of their alleged doctrinal aberrations he treated several venerable figures of the past with undeserved asperity, and he made a few minor errors, but the work as a whole is sound and even brilliant. (For the worst that a hostile critic can make of it see the *Lutheran Church Review,* April and July 1893.) In January 1897 Gräbner issued the first number of the *Theological Quarterly,* of which he was not so much the editor as the author, for the paucity of contributors compelled him to write the contents of each number practically unassisted. The seven volumes that appeared during his lifetime are a monument to his varied learning, unbudgeable orthodoxy, and literary power. He wrote excellently in both English and German, read avidly in thirteen languages, and seemed to aspire to universal scholarship. For years he allowed himself but five hours a night for sleep; he was reputed to have read ten thousand books. In 1902 he paid an official visit to the Lutheran churches of New Zealand and Australia, arbitrated their quarrels, and returned home by way of Europe. In October 1903, immediately after the celebration of the twenty-fifth anniversary of his ordination, his health broke, and after a painful illness of fourteen months he died in St. Louis and was buried in Concordia Cemetery. His wife and eleven of their twelve children survived him.

[*Who's Who in America,* 1906–07; *Concordia Cyc.* (1927); *Der Lutheraner,* Dec. 20, 1904, Jan. 3, 17, 1905; *St. Louis Globe-Democrat,* Dec. 8, 1904; Theo. Gräbner, *Lutherische Pioniere: II, Die Frankenkolonien des Saginawtales* (1919); portrait in *Theol. Quart.,*

Jan. 1905; additional data supplied by Gräbner's son, Prof. Theo. Gräbner of Concordia Seminary.]

G. H. G.

GRACE, WILLIAM RUSSELL (May 10, 1832–Mar. 21, 1904), international merchant, capitalist, steamship owner, concessionaire, was a highly successful pioneer in economic imperialism. He came from a good family in Queenstown, Ireland, being the son of James and Ellen Mary (Russell) Grace. His boyhood ambition was to gain a commission in the Royal Navy but this was blocked by his father, who had risked life and fortune supporting Venezuela's struggle for independence. William ran away to sea and roved about the world for two years, then his father bought him an interest in a Liverpool firm of ship chandlers. Bored with that, he went to Callao, Peru, where his father helped to place him in a similar firm. His brother, Michael P. Grace, joined him and the firm evolved from Bryce & Company, through Bryce, Grace & Company to Grace Brothers & Company. Their fortunes and their influence in Peru increased steadily. Shortly after 1860 William was forced, on account of his health, to give up his residence in Peru, but he left Michael to attend to the family interest there. On Sept. 11, 1859, he had married Lillius Gilchrist, daughter of a Thomaston, Me., shipbuilder. For a while he drifted around Ireland and other countries, but in 1865 he settled in New York City where he organized W. R. Grace & Company. It was originally formed to serve as correspondent for Grace Brothers & Company of Callao.

When Peru built its railway system under Meiggs auspices, the Grace concerns secured contracts for practically all the supplies. Grace became a confidential adviser to the Peruvian government, and between 1875 and 1879 he handled the business of arming and equipping the Peruvian army. Through his efforts, also, a large part of the navy was purchased. The firm furnished Peru with most of its munitions and secured additional ships during the war with Chile in 1879. The unsuccessful outcome of the war left Peru with an unstable government and a debt of some $250,000,000. The bondholders, especially in England, grew restive, and this gave Grace a chance for his master stroke. By the Grace-Donoughmore Contract of 1890, he practically secured a mortgage on the nation, taking over the national debt and receiving tremendous concessions in return. The Peruvian Corporation, Ltd., formed to manage the concessions, was nominally directed by Lord Donoughmore and a board composed largely of British bondholders, but Grace was the power behind the scenes. In return for assuming two bond issues, the company received outright the valuable silver mines of Cerro de Pasco; the entire output of the guano deposits; five million acres of land containing valuable oil and mineral deposits; as well as the lease of two railways for sixty-six years, and the right to build and hold in perpetuity another road, with generous land grants for construction. In exploiting these concessions the company did much to develop the country's resources, but Grace did not limit his attention to Peru. In 1895 the Grace companies united under a Virginia charter as William R. Grace & Company (*New York Tribune,* Jan. 11, 1895). The firm opened offices in practically every country of Latin America and in importing, exporting, and banking it established world-wide contacts. Extending into Chile, the company developed nitrate properties, cotton and sugar mills, and traction, light, and power companies. Grace had already, in 1891, organized the New York & Pacific Steamship Company, and later the Grace Steamship Company.

In 1880 the "Pirate of Peru" became the first Roman Catholic mayor of New York City. Opposing Tammany, he conducted a reform administration, attacking patronage, police scandals, and organized vice, breaking up the Louisiana Lottery in New York and reducing the tax rate. He was elected for a second term in 1884, on an independent ticket. In 1897 he founded the Grace Institute to give women and girls a practical education in stenography, dressmaking, and the domestic arts. He died in 1904, survived by his wife, two sons and three daughters.

[John Thompson, "A Career of Romantic Achievement," *World's Work,* May 1904; L. H. Weeks, ed., *Prominent Families of N. Y.* (1897); the *N. Y. Geneal. and Biog. Record,* July 1904; Henry Hall, *America's Successful Men of Affairs,* vol. I (1895); *Who's Who in America,* 1903–05; the *Statist* (London), Jan. 18, Feb. 1, 8, 15, 22, Mar. 29, 1890; *Memoria de Hacienda y Comercio presentada al Congreso Constitucional de 1890, por el Ministro del Ramo* (Lima, Peru, 1890); *Eighteenth Ann. Gen. Report of the Council of the Corporation of Foreign Bondholders,* 1890; R. W. Dunn, *Am. Foreign Investments* (1926); Peter Hevner, *A One-sided Hist. of Wm. R. Grace, the Pirate of Peru* (1888); *N. Y. Herald, N. Y. Times,* Mar. 22, 1904.]

R. G. A—n.

GRACIE, ARCHIBALD (Dec. 1, 1832–Dec. 2, 1864), Confederate soldier, was born in New York City, the son of Archibald Gracie and Elizabeth Davidson Bethune, of Huguenot descent. His grandfather, Archibald Gracie, emigrated from Scotland to Petersburg, Va., where he became a prominent merchant. Later removing to New York City, he became known as a merchant, banker, and pioneer advocate of public-school education. Young Archibald was educated in Heidelberg, Germany, and at West

Point. Following his graduation from the Military Academy in 1854 he was stationed at Fort Vancouver, Wash., and at Fort Dalles, Ore., taking part in the Snake River expedition in 1855. He was stationed at Fort Boise, Idaho, when he resigned his commission, May 31, 1856, to enter business with his father, then a merchant in Mobile, Ala. On Nov. 19, 1856, he was married at Elizabeth, N. J., to Josephine Mayo, the daughter of Edward C. Mayo, of Richmond, Va.

Gracie joined the Washington Light Infantry company of Mobile and became its captain. When the Civil War broke he chose to stay with his company, and under orders from Gov. Moore he seized the United States arsenal at Mount Vernon before Alabama seceded. This company became a unit in the 3rd Alabama Infantry, which was the first body of Alabama troops to be mustered into service. With this organization he saw service in Virginia. On July 12, 1861, he was promoted major of the 11th Alabama. In the spring of 1862 he raised a regiment of his own, the 43rd Alabama, of which he was elected colonel, and was assigned to Kirby-Smith's corps, then operating in eastern Tennessee. Later in the same year he led an expedition across the Cumberland Mountains, attacking and capturing Fort Cliff, which was defended by Tennessee Unionists. He continued with his regiment during the Kentucky campaign and was in command of Lexington during the Confederate occupation. Commissioned brigadier-general in November 1862, he took part in the engagement at Chickamauga, where his brigade lost in two hours more than seven hundred killed and wounded. He was wounded in an engagement at Bean's Station, but recovering, he rejoined his brigade and served under Gen. Beauregard in the campaign of May 1864. From June until his death in December he was in the trenches at Petersburg, where he won the admiration of Gen. Lee. On Dec. 2, while peering through a telescope at the enemy's lines, he was instantly killed. After the surrender his remains were interred in the family vault in New York City. He was soon to have received his commission as major-general and has been accorded that rank on a brass tablet in the library at West Point.

[W. Brewer, *Ala.: Her Hist., Resources, War Record, and Public Men* (1872), pp. 426–27; T. M. Owen, *Hist. of Ala. and Dict. of Ala. Biog.* (1921), III, 686; L. A. Shaver, *A Hist. of the Sixtieth Ala. Regiment, Gracie's Ala. Brigade* (1867); A. Gracie, *The Truth about Chickamauga* (1911); *Official Records (Army)*; *Confed. Mil. Hist.* (1899), VII, 412–15; Geo. W. Cullum, *Biog. Reg. . . . U. S. Mil. Acad.* (3rd ed., 1891); *Confed. Veteran*, Aug. 1897; *Richmond Whig*, Dec. 3, 1864. Gracie is commemorated in Francis O. Ticknor's poem, "Gracie, of Alabama."]

A. B. M.

GRADLE, HENRY (Aug. 17, 1855–Apr. 4, 1911), physician, was born in Friedberg, a suburb of Frankfurt-am-Main in Hesse-Nassau, the son of Bernard and Rose Schottenfels Groedel. His father emigrated to America in 1859 and established himself in the tobacco business in Chicago. The son remained in Germany with his mother who removed to Darmstadt where he was educated in the academy. His mother died in 1866, and two years later, his preliminary education completed, he joined his father in Chicago. Entering the medical department of Northwestern University, he was graduated in 1874 at the age of nineteen. After an interneship in Mercy Hospital he spent three years in postgraduate study in Heidelberg, Vienna, Paris, Berlin, and Leipzig. He was chiefly interested in physiology and in diseases of the eye, ear, nose, and throat. From Koch he received an introduction to the budding science of bacteriology, and upon his return to Chicago he was subjected to much ridicule for his advocacy of the bacterial origin of diseases. In 1883 he published *Bacteria and the Germ Theory of Disease*, the first book in the English language dealing with this subject, and the first American medical work to be translated into the Japanese language. Establishing himself in general practise, he began a teaching career at Northwestern University which lasted nearly thirty years. He was professor of physiology from 1879 to 1883, professor of general etiology, clinical ophthalmology and otology from 1893 to 1896, and professor of ophthalmology and otology from 1896 to 1906. In the meantime he had given up general practise and had become one of the busiest men in his specialty in Chicago, having built up a clientele devoted to him on account of his personality, his interest in his cases, and his exceptional operative skill.

Throughout his career Gradle was a profound student of periodic medical literature, not only in English, but in French and German. He contributed many articles on ophthalmic and related subjects to American and German medical periodicals and in addition to his early book on bacteriology wrote a text-book on *Diseases of the Nose, Pharynx and Ear* (1902). He had a remarkably retentive memory for literary citations and a gift for extemporaneous speech in the most correct English. He was a member and one-time president of the Chicago Ophthalmological Society and a member of the Heidelberger Ophthalmological Society. His death, caused by a recurrent cancer of the bladder, occurred in Santa Barbara, Cal. He left his library to the John Crerar Library of Chicago, together with a fund for the purchase of journals relating to his specialty. He had married, on Aug. 31, 1881, Fanny Searls, by whom he had two sons.

[Casey A. Wood, ed., *Am. Encyc. and Dict. of Ophthalmol.*, vol. VII (1915); *Who's Who in America*, 1910–11; *Jour. of the Am. Medic. Asso.*, Apr. 15, 1911; information as to certain facts from members of Gradle's family.] J. M. P.

GRADY, HENRY WOODFIN (May 24, 1850–Dec. 23, 1889), orator, journalist, first of the three children of William S. and Anne Elizabeth (Gartrell) Grady, was born in Athens and died in Atlanta, Ga. His father, a North Carolinian largely of Irish ancestry, emigrated to Georgia about 1846. His mother, whose origins were in the main Scotch, was related to many families which had long been prominent around Athens. At the beginning of the Civil War, the elder Grady, made captain of the Highland Guards, organized and equipped his company and went off to Virginia. Promoted to colonel, he was killed at Petersburg. The most persistent legends about the boyhood of Henry Grady state that he was alert, sympathetic, loyal, and affectionate. He attended local schools, joined the Methodist Church in 1865, together with his fiancée, Julia King, and in 1868, without ever having had to leave Athens, graduated from the University of Georgia—hale and lovable, clever at speaking and writing, remarkable for his aversion to the exact sciences. Three years later, after a course in law (1868–69) at the University of Virginia, he returned to Georgia, and was married to Julia in 1871. As a student, over the signature King Hans—made up from his fiancée's name and his own—he had written several gossipy communications for the *Atlanta Constitution,* and soon after he left Charlottesville he went to Rome, Ga., to edit a paper called the *Courier.* There, forbidden by his employer to denounce corruption in local politics, he instantly bought the two other papers of the town, combined them, and next day, as editor-publisher of the *Daily-Commercial,* fulminated as he desired. The paper soon collapsed. In 1872 he went to Atlanta and with two other men as blithe and high-minded as himself founded the *Atlanta Herald.* This paper, also, in spite of fitful energy and of journalistic ethics that would shock high-minded young men less ebullient than its editors (Dugat, *post,* p. 25), soon reached the whirlpool it was inevitably bound for and took with it all that was left of Grady's patrimony. For a while he wrote for the *Constitution* and the *Augusta Chronicle.* Then, offered the editorship of the *Wilmington Star* and having before him the necessity for decision, he followed a premonition and went to look for work in New York. A trial piece which he wrote for the *New York Herald* was found acceptable, and he returned to Atlanta as special reporter for that paper 1876–77. In 1879 Cyrus W. Field, whom he had met through Gen. John B. Gordon, lent him $20,000 and with this he bought a fourth interest in the *Constitution.* He was a born journalist, but up till that time an engaging boyishness, which in personal matters indeed he never outgrew, had retarded him in business. His new power on the *Constitution* sobered him. He had an unerring sense for news, a zeal for ordered progress, and a faculty for writing in accord with popular taste even when he was pleading a cause so right that it was in advance of popular sanction. With these abilities he went far to shatter the post-bellum despair which kept much of the South still in its spell; he encouraged the development of local resources and the diversification of crops, and convinced his readers of the need for manufacturing and for a logical adjustment of the negro question. All of this constituted a doctrine which became inescapably clear once it was pronounced. The result of it was soon evident throughout the South, and particularly in Atlanta, which became in a sense the capital of the new movement. Grady was suddenly famous. Invited to address the New England Club of New York City, he spoke there in December 1886, with all the frankness, passion, and magnanimity he was master of, his great but brief speech, "The New South," declaimed incessantly ever since by aspiring young orators throughout America. The effect was immediate. Civil War animosities were becoming tiresome the country over, and people were glad to be told by so authentic-seeming a prophet that the continued holding of them was more evil than good. Here and there it was said that he was a renegade trimming himself for high politics, but in general his sincerity was unquestioned, and he had to contend only with the clamor raised on all sides to hear him personally declare his creed. Among the best-known of his other orations, all re-stating in general the principles of his editorials, are the following: "The South and her Problems" (Dallas, October 1887), "The Solid South"—a necessity, he said (Augusta, November 1887), "The Farmers and the Cities" (Elberton, Ga., June 1889), "Against Centralization" (University of Virginia, June 1889), and "The Race Problem in the South" (Boston, December 1889). A teetotaler and prohibitionist, he was sentimental, pious, and even in his theorizing quite conventional in his attitude toward fundamental social problems, but when he came home from Boston after a speech on the race problem, and it was apparent that the pneumonia he had contracted there would be the death of him, the country was most justly moved. It was losing an accepted leader of driving power, integrity, sweetness, and unmeasured promise.

[F. H. Richardson, *A Fruitful Life* (1890); *Joel Chandler Harris' Life of Henry W. Grady . . . A Memorial Volume* (1890); J. W. Lee, "Henry Woodfin Grady," in *Lib. of Southern Lit.*, vol. V (1909); W. J. Northen, *Men of Mark in Ga.*, vol. III (1911); R. F. Terrell, *Study of the Early Journalistic Writings of Henry W. Grady* (1927); G. Dugat, *Life of Henry W. Grady* (1927); Dudley Miles, "The New South," Bk. III, ch. IV, *The Cambridge Hist. Am. Lit.*, vol. II (1918); E. D. Shurter, *The Complete Orations and Speeches of Henry W. Grady* (1910); T. R. Crawford, "Early Home of Henry W. Grady," *New England Mag.*, June 1890; *Life and Labors of Henry W. Grady* (1890); O. Dyer, character sketch in H. W. Grady's *The New South* (1890); Edna H. L. Turpin, "Henry W. Grady," in H. W. Grady's *The New South and Other Addresses* (1904); *Atlanta Constitution*, Dec. 23, 24, 1889.]

J. D. W.

GRAEBNER, AUGUST LAWRENCE [See GRÄBNER, AUGUST LAWRENCE, 1849–1904.]

GRAESSL, LAWRENCE (Aug. 18, 1753–*c.* Oct. 12, 1793), Catholic missionary priest, was born at Ruemannsfelden in the Bavarian Forest, the son of Lorenz Graessl (or Graessel). On completion of his classical studies, he entered the Jesuit novitiate where he was a student when the Society of Jesus was dissolved in 1773. Later ordained as a secular priest, he was engaged in parochial duties and as a tutor in Munich when the aged Father Ferdinand Farmer [*q.v.*], pastor of St. Mary's Church in Philadelphia, urged him to come to Pennsylvania where the German Catholics required a younger pastor able to preach in their native tongue. Fired by the appeal, Graessl wrote from Munich (Aug. 1, 1786) to his parents that he had enlisted for missionary work. Writing again to them from London (Aug. 3, 1787), he described his journey and begged their prayers that he might not fail. His letters are both courageous and sad, for the presentiment of death was always with him. He arrived in Philadelphia in October 1787, and Father John Carroll [*q.v.*] appointed him an assistant at St. Mary's to care for the German communicants as the late Father Farmer had arranged. Some of the Germans who were insistent on having as their pastor Father John Charles Heilbron, a Capuchin, who had come to the country uninvited, seceded and established Holy Trinity Church. To avoid difficulties, Graessl was sent on missions throughout Pennsylvania, Delaware, and New Jersey for a twelvemonth during which he suffered much fatigue but gloried in his ability to hear confessions in French, English, German, Dutch, and Spanish.

In March 1788 he was stationed at St. Mary's as curate to Francis Beeston, a recently arrived English priest, and his name is found as one of the incorporators of the church (Sept. 13, 1788), though much of his time was spent on the missions. In the winter of 1789, Carroll visited Philadelphia and met the young German priest whom he described as "a most amiable ex-Jesuit." Two years later, Graessl represented Philadelphia at the first provincial synod in Baltimore (Nov. 9, 1791) and apparently won favor with the bishop and his fellow priests for his learning and sanctity. Bishop Carroll, realizing that the Church would be placed at a decided disadvantage if he should die suddenly, applied to the Holy See for a division of his diocese or the appointment of a coadjutor with the right of succession. To the latter alternative Rome agreed, and Cardinal Antonelli ordered the bishop to take the advice of the older and wiser priests in selecting a successor. The choice fell on Graessl, and his name was sent to Rome for ratification, though the formal appointment did not arrive until two months after his death. In a final letter to his parents (June 19, 1793), Graessl informed them of his selection and his readiness to carry on, though he warned them that he was dying of consumption and urged them to bid his Bavarian friends farewell. Ill as he was, he devoted himself to his parishioners during the fatal weeks of the plague of yellow fever in which Philadelphia lost over 4,000 citizens including ten physicians and eight ministers, and the Catholic congregations lost 335 members and three priests. Father Graessl succumbed and was buried in St. Joseph's. Known as a scholar, he was a worthy trustee of the College of Philadelphia.

[J. L. J. Kirlin, *Catholicity in Phila.* (1909); J. G. Shea, *A Hist. of the Cath. Ch. within the Limits of the U. S.*, vol. II (1888); Peter Guilday, *The Life and Times of John Carroll* (2 vols., 1922); *U. S. Cath. Hist. Mag.*, Jan. 1887; *Records of the Am. Cath. Hist. Soc. of Phila.*, *passim* and especially IV (1893), 244–459 for minute book of St. Mary's Church; *Am. Cath. Hist. Researches* (1884–1912), *passim*; *Federal Gazette and Phila. Daily Advertiser*, Oct. 12, 1793.]

R. J. P.

GRAFF, FREDERIC (May 23, 1817–Mar. 30, 1890), civil engineer, was born at Philadelphia, Pa., the son of Frederick [*q.v.*] and Judith (Swyer) Graff. The father, because he felt that his own experience as an engineer had been one of more anxiety than profit, decided that his son should have a business career. Accordingly, the latter, after the completion of his schooling, was placed with a hardware firm to learn that business. He soon found this work not to his liking and began the study of engineering with his father and in spite of him. In 1842 he became an assistant engineer in the water department of Philadelphia and five years later, at his father's death, succeeded him as chief engineer of the department. Graff held this position from 1847 to 1856 and from 1866 to 1872, and has the distinction of being the first chief engineer elected to the water department after it was made an independent bureau at the time of the consolidation of Philadelphia in 1854. As chief engineer, he directed the reorganization of the department which combined the various district works with the principal city works, and planned and directed the construction of the Corinthian Avenue Reservoir, the Belmont Reservoir on George's Hill, the reservoir in the city park, and the rebuilding of the Fairmount Dam. The effect of his work was to remodel the old decentralized system of water-supply into a modern unified system suitable for a metropolitan district of the size of Philadelphia, with a planned provision for expansion in pace with the future growth of the city. As chief engineer of the water department and a park commissioner, Graff, in 1851, recommended the establishing of a park upon the Schuylkill River, for which he prepared maps and plans. This recommendation was acted upon, and during his service as a commissioner the East Side Park lands were purchased and improved and subsequently developed into the Fairmount Park System. From 1873 to 1877, Graff was associated with Henry R. Worthington of Philadelphia and New York, designer and manufacturer of water-works machinery; and for the remaining years of his life engaged in practise as a consulting engineer. In these connections he made trials of pumping machinery and reports upon water-supply systems for many of the larger cities in the East, including those of Cambridge, Mass., Brooklyn, N. Y., Providence, R. I., and Washington, D. C., and established a reputation as one of the leading water-works engineers of his time. His standing in the profession was recognized by his election to the office of president of the American Society of Civil Engineers in 1885 after he had served as a director of the Society for several years. He was also president of the Engineers' Club of Philadelphia (1880) and was for three years a vice-president of the Franklin Institute. He was a joint author of the "Report of the Committee on the Preservation of Timber" in the *Transactions of the American Society of Civil Engineers,* vol. XIV (1885), in which volume also appears his presidential address. His paper, "The History of the Steam Engine in America," is printed in part in the *Journal of the Franklin Institute,* October 1876. Graff married Elizabeth Mathieu of Philadelphia. No children survived him. He died at Philadelphia.

[See sketch by John Bogart in *Proc. Am. Soc. Civil Engineers,* vol. XVII (1891); Emile Geyelin, in *Report of Proc. of the Eleventh Ann. Meeting of the Am. Water Works Asso.* (1891); *Jour. Franklin Inst.,* June 1890; obituary in Phila. *Press,* Mar. 31, 1890. The younger Graff seems to have spelled his first name without the final "k" which his father retained.] F. A. T.

GRAFF, FREDERICK (Aug. 27, 1774–Apr. 13, 1847), engineer, was the third in America of a line of builders, contractors, and engineers. His grandfather, Jacob Graff, arrived in Pennsylvania from Germany in 1741. His father, also christened Jacob, established the family fortunes on a firm basis; and Frederick, born in Philadelphia, was followed in his profession by Frederic [*q.v.*], his son. In 1797 he began his apprenticeship as a draftsman on the Philadelphia Water Works, with which he was connected during the rest of his life. In 1805, four years after the first system, in Centre Square, was opened, he was appointed superintendent. This system, to the success of which he contributed materially, was the first steam-power water-works in the United States. From the Schuylkill the water was raised fifty feet and, after flowing through a brick tunnel six feet in diameter, was again raised thirty-six feet to the reservoir from which it was distributed by wooden mains throughout the city. The boiler, an ingenious device made of five-inch pine planks secured with braces and stay bolts, contained a cast-iron fire-box and a number of flues. Part of it has been preserved by the Franklin Institute, of which Graff became a member in 1826. (A description by Frederic Graff, Jr., of the machinery used in this system was published in the *Journal of the Franklin Institute,* April 1853.)

Graff's most notable achievement was the construction at Philadelphia of an efficient hydraulic system. Except possibly for the works at Bethlehem and Bellefonte, Pa., it was the pioneer system of its kind in America. As early as 1810 Graff and John Davis were instructed to examine all possible sources of supply. They selected Mount Morris, now Fairmount, as the site for a new reservoir. At first they used a steam-power plant; but before the undertaking was completed, in 1822, Graff had projected the hydraulic development which he carried out with such tenacity, skill, and judgment. The crib dam which he erected on the river was thirteen feet in height and over 1,250 feet in length; and the eight breast wheels were sixteen to eighteen feet in diameter. For this innovation Graff was almost entirely responsible. With practically no data on which to base his calculations, he designed the mains, over 113 miles of which were laid by 1842, the connections, stop-cocks, and fireplugs. Since they were constructed of iron, he encountered many obstacles in the process of manufacture; but he surmounted all of them in such a manner as to establish his reputation throughout the United States. He remained chief engineer of the Water Department until his death, when he was succeeded by his son Frederic Graff, Jr. His wife was Judith Swyer.

[Memoir of Frederic Graff, Jr., in *Jour. of the Franklin Inst.*, June 1890; *Ann. Report of the Chief Engineer of the Water Dept. of the City of Phila. for the Year 1875* (1876); paper by Emile Geyelin on the growth of the Philadelphia Water Works in *Report of Proc. of the Eleventh Ann. Meeting of the Am. Water Works Asso.* (1891); obituary in the *North American* (Phila.), Apr. 14, 1847.] R. P. B—r.

GRAFFENRIED, CHRISTOPHER, Baron de (1661–1743), Swiss adventurer and colonizer, was born in Bern, being the only child of Anton de Graffenried, Lord of Worb, by his first wife, Catherine Jenner. A restless youth, constantly at odds with his father who was critical of his extravagances, he nevertheless made friends with those high in political and social life. After a period of Continental travel and study, he visited England about the year 1680. There, through Christopher Monck, second Duke of Albemarle, he secured introductions at the Court of Charles II. He was unsuccessful in negotiating a marriage, however, and went to France, where he was well received at the Court of Louis XIV. In 1683 he returned to Bern, and the following year married Regina Tscharner. In 1702 he became bailiff of Iferton, in Neuchâtel.

Falling into financial straits, Graffenried relinquished his office in 1708 and decided to retrieve his fortune in America. His interest in the Province of Carolina was intensified by conversations with Franz Ludwig Michel who was negotiating with the Canton of Bern in behalf of a company organized by Georg Ritter to take emigrants from Switzerland to North Carolina. In the hope of establishing mining operations in that region Graffenried went to London and in 1709 received a grant of 5,000 acres from the Lords Proprietors of North Carolina and was appointed Landgrave. When Michel arrived in London shortly afterward he and Graffenried pooled their resources, their aim being to secure additional tracts of land on which both Swiss emigrants and German Palatines then in exile in England could be colonized. To this end Graffenried secured an option on 100,000 acres, and in 1710 his interests were definitely merged with those of Michel and the Ritter Company. Thereupon transportation to North Carolina of ninety-two Palatine families (about 650 persons) was undertaken, the journey to America being under the personal guidance of John Lawson [*q.v.*], surveyor-general of Carolina. Later in the year 1710 a company of 156 Swiss were brought over by Graffenried.

The lands assigned for the colony lay between the Neuse and Trent Rivers, and there a town was laid out, called New Bern. Misfortune attended the colony from the beginning. About one-half of the Palatines died at sea, the labor of those who survived was exploited by Lawson, and supplies were so insufficient that Graffenried, after his arrival, had to mortgage his lands to Thomas Pollock of North Carolina and ultimately lost them. The settlers did not receive the small allotments promised them. The government of North Carolina was in a state of confusion, and proper protection was not given the colonists against the Indians. In 1711, when the Tuscaroras revolted, the Palatine and Swiss settlers suffered greatly by death and destruction of property. At the beginning of the conflict, Graffenried was captured but was ransomed and thereupon negotiated a truce, which was soon broken. After the first period of the conflict he visited Gov. Spotswood of Virginia seeking military aid and also lands in that province. He secured a patent for lands on the upper Potomac in the vicinity of the present Washington, where he hoped to find silver mines and whither also he hoped to transport the New Bern settlers. Since in this project he did not have the support of Michel, he returned to North Carolina, and, his resources being exhausted, he left the colony in 1713, and returned to his native Bern. There he spent his remaining years. Of his thirteen children, one son, Christopher, emigrated to Virginia and became the progenitor of the American branch of the family.

[T. P. de Graffenried, *Hist. of the de Graffenried Family* (1925); Wolfgang Friedrich von Mülinen, "Christoph von Graffenried, Landgraf von Carolina, Gründer von Neu-Bern," *Neujahrsblatt herausgegeben vom Historischen Verein des Kantons Bern für 1897* (Bern, 1896); V. H. Todd, *Christoph von Graffenried's Account of the Founding of New Bern* (1920); *The Colonial Records of N. C.*, vol. I (1886).] W. K. B.

GRAFLY, CHARLES (Dec. 3, 1862–May 5, 1929), sculptor, youngest of the eight children of Charles and Elizabeth (Simmons) Grafly, was born in Philadelphia, Pa., of German ancestry on his father's side, and with a distinctly artistic strain from his Dutch mother. The family circumstances were modest. In boyhood he went to the public school, but even then the lure of form drew him. At seventeen he apprenticed himself as carver in Struthers's stone yard, where important work was being done for the city. "He helped to carve countless bits of sculpture on the Philadelphia City Hall" (family letter). At twenty-two he entered the Pennsylvania Academy of the Fine Arts. There he profited much by courses in painting, modeling, and dissection under Thomas Eakins and Thomas Anshutz and thus prepared himself for his studies in Paris, begun in 1888. At the Académie Julien, he had the instruction of Chapu in sculpture. Later he entered the École des Beaux-Arts, remaining there until he went home in 1890. That year he showed in the Salon his heads of St. John and of Daedalus; the Daedalus was bought by the Pennsylvania Academy and cast in bronze for its permanent collection. Returning to Paris, he won honorable mention at the Salon of 1891 for a life-size nude female figure, *"Mauvais Présage,"* now in the Detroit Museum of Art. In 1892 he taught modeling in the Pennsylvania Academy and in Drexel Institute. Having created ideal figures as well as portrait-busts, he soon began to establish a reputation as a sculptor of imaginative groups, as a portraitist, and as a teacher. In 1893 his works won a medal at the Columbian Exposition, and he became a charter member of the National Sculpture Society. His fellow artists already recognized his sincerity, imagination, and skill.

His marriage on June 7, 1895, to Frances Sekeles of Corinth, Miss., was followed by another sojourn in Paris, a period of intense intellectual and artistic activity. His skilful hand tried in vain to keep pace with his teeming ideas. Much effort was given to a heroic fragment, "Vulture of War," now in the St. Louis Museum. On his return home Philadelphia became the principal scene of his endeavor, though after he established a summer home near Gloucester, Mass., and built a spacious studio in 1904, much large work was accomplished there also.

Grafly's symbolism has often been discussed. The "Symbol of Life," his small bronze group of 1897, showed a man and woman striding together, the man holding a scythe-handle, the woman an ivory globe with springing wheat. The work was largely conceived and was modeled with selective realism. It pleased many and puzzled all. Less enigmatic, yet with Grafly's characteristic style, was the later small bronze, "From Generation to Generation," a youth and a grandsire pausing before a winged dial, a feature afterward used in his clock for the Pennsylvania Company's Bank. In his monumental "Fountain of Man," the most original of the decorative sculptures at the Pan-American Exposition in Buffalo (1901), symbolism certainly loomed too large. Critics said that for full enjoyment of the work a commentary was needed. Grafly tried to show the dual nature of man's soul in the guise of an inscrutable two-headed, double-bodied form, mysteriously swathed; it arrested attention and was the climax of an imposing ensemble. This strange entity was upheld by the "Senses," five strong figures circling above a basin supported by four crouching groups, in each of which a primeval man and woman typified conflicting forces of the soul.

Thereafter his symbolism became less recondite. At the St. Louis Exposition (1904), his "Truth," a beautiful life-size nude, revealing herself within a shell, was an easily understood allegory. His "France" and "Great Britain" on the New York Custom House (1904) were straightforward enough. Equally clear in meaning is his "Pioneer Mother Monument," one of the sights of the Panama-Pacific Exposition (1915). The chief feature of this work, designed for a location in San Francisco, is a woman of valiant type. Clad in frontier garb and wearing a sunbonnet, she presents to the nation her two children. Accepting at its face value this colossal bronze group, the public at once understood its message. Grafly's mind turned naturally toward symbolic expression. The crowning work of his maturity is the General Meade Memorial in Washington, D. C., a heroic marble monument which engaged his mind from 1915 to 1925. Here, interweaving the real and the ideal, he grouped around the dominant figure of the Gettysburg hero, four nobly modeled forms representing chivalry, loyalty, fame, progress, with "War" standing behind, flanked by two stalwart male figures representing energy and military courage, ready to join with the other four in emerging from the shadow of "War's" wings. Consummate knowledge of the resources of sculpture was needed to bring this complex design into a fine simplicity, a perfection of detail, an adequate characterization. As a work of art it makes an instant impression on the visitor at the Mall, where it stands not far from Shrady's Grant. Grafly's task was trebled by the fact that in this work he was bound to satisfy not only his own exacting standards but the demands of the state of Pennsylvania and the requirements of the federal government. It speaks well for him that he carried the undertaking through to a happy end. The experts of the Federal Art Commission were prompt to recognize the beauty and significance of the completed group. In characterization and simplicity the sculptor considered his statue of former President Buchanan (1927), in Lancaster, Pa., "one of his finest works, if not the finest after the Meade Memorial" (family letter). An earlier bronze statue, the General Reynolds (1901), is a colossal feature of the Smith Memorial, Fairmount Park, Philadelphia.

Grafly was probably the foremost American sculptor of male portrait-busts. In this field he created a gallery of masterpieces. Artists and other professional men gladly became his sitters. Among these were Paul Bartlett, Frank Duveneck, Joseph De Camp, George Harding, Childe Hassam, William Paxton, Edward Redfield, Elmer Schofield, Thomas Anshutz, Herman Kotzschmar, and Edward H. Coates. He cared little to have his subjects "pose" before him. With his mastery of construction he "caught the likeness" as they walked at ease about his workshop. His portraits for the Hall of Fame, New York University, are naturally less vivid than such works as his Duveneck (Carnegie Institute, Pittsburgh) or his Paxton (Museum of Fine Arts, Boston); nevertheless, his Farragut (Hall of Fame, 1927), is a noble realization. His portrait studies of women are not numerous. His bust of his mother won him a silver medal at Atlanta, Ga., and that of his wife is one of his most sensitive productions. He excelled in modeling the female nude, and his beautiful line drawings from the nude were highly commended.

In 1892 he was called to the chair of sculpture at the Pennsylvania Academy of the Fine Arts and, to prepare himself, visited art centers abroad. Twenty-five years later he took a like position in the Boston Museum of Fine Arts. He had the communicative gift and the large view which unite to make a teacher. He taught with pleasure and with conscience, since in his teaching as in his sculpture, imagination and integrity worked in harmony. It was not Grafly's purpose to make disciples. Among his pupils to attain distinction are Laessle, Polasek, Manship, not one of whom imitates him. Several of his "boys" won the coveted fellowship of the American Academy in Rome. Abhorring the superficial, Grafly had an outspoken contempt for what he called "union-suit sculpture"—the sleek sculpture of ignorance masquerading as impressionism. He was familiar with all the crafts tributary to the art, which he so loved that he watched his every work diligently throughout all its stages, at times casting a bust with his own hands rather than trust it to the plaster moulder, and often giving long days of labor to the finish of his bronzes and marbles. He was equally adept in rendering exquisite detail and in the harder task of creating those broad planes which sweep aside all insignificant detail. His end was tragic. He was struck down by an automobile; the operation performed in an effort to save his life was unsuccessful, and he died in the Philadelphia Graduate Hospital, leaving a widow and one daughter.

[See *Who's Who in America,* 1928–29; *Am. Art Annual,* 1917; *Fairmount Park Art Asso.* (1922), with portrait and outline of biography; Lorado Taft, *Modern Tendencies in Sculpture* (1921), and *The Hist. of Am. Sculpture* (rev. ed., 1930); V. C. Dallin, article in *New England Mag.,* Oct. 1901; J. E. D. Trask, article in *Art and Progress,* Feb. 1910; Anna Seaton-Schmidt, article in *Am. Mag. of Art,* Dec. 1918; *N. Y. Times,* May 6, 1929. Grafly's work was often noted and illustrated in the daily press and in art journals, especially during the exposition years 1901, 1904, and 1915, and during the progress of the Meade Memorial. The *Sunday Star* (Washington, D. C.), Oct. 18, 1925, has an article on that Memorial. Clippings and illustrations in the library of the Metropolitan Museum of Art give interesting data. A discriminating estimate of Grafly, signed S. H., is in the *Studio,* Feb. 15, 1906.] A. A.

GRAFTON, CHARLES CHAPMAN (Apr. 12, 1830–Aug. 30, 1912), Episcopal bishop, son of Joseph and Anna Maria (Gurley) Grafton, was born in Boston, Mass., and died in Fond du Lac, Wis. His father, descended from Salem ancestors of English extraction, was a major in the War of 1812 and afterwards surveyor of the port of Boston. His mother was the daughter of John Ward Gurley, first attorney-general of Louisiana. Charles attended the Boston Latin School 1843–46, and entered Phillips Academy, Andover, from which—because of eye-trouble, it is said, he soon withdrew to study at home under a private tutor. In 1863 he was graduated in law at Harvard. Confirmed in the Episcopal Church in 1851 and already a laboriously earnest Christian, he found himself increasingly drawn toward the High Church principles enunciated in England by Pusey. He determined to enter the priesthood and to that end, soon after his graduation, went to Baltimore and put himself under the tutelage of Bishop W. R. Whittingham, an ecclesiastic whose views were more in accord with his own than were those of the Bishop of Massachusetts. He was made deacon in 1855 and appointed assistant at Reisterstown, Md.; later he engaged in missionary activities in Baltimore. In 1858 he was ordained priest and the following year became a curate of St. Paul's Church, Baltimore, and chaplain of the deaconesses of the Maryland diocese. At Harvard he had been an Abolitionist, but by the time of the Civil War his position was more that of a conservative Unionist. Going to England at the conclusion of the war, he associated himself with one or two others in establishing the Society of St. John the Evangelist, known as the "Cowley Fathers," an order inspired by the ideals of monasticism. Later he organized the first great London mission and acted as chaplain in a cholera hospital. From 1872 to 1888 he was rector of the Church of the Advent in Boston, achieving a degree of success indicated by the fact that during those years he baptized half as many converts as were baptized into all the other nineteen Episcopal churches in the city. One of his dearest interests was the Sisterhood of the Holy Nativity, which he founded in 1888, resigning his church and going to Providence where the mother house was established. The next year he became Bishop of Fond du Lac, Wis. Here he raised endowments, built churches, inaugurated seminaries and schools —most notably Grafton Hall, a school for girls, instituted religious orders and houses, and in general administered the affairs of his realm with great energy and sagacity. In the early 1900's, in pursuance of his life-long concern with Eastern Christianity, he visited Russia, and upon returning did what he could to bring about a coalition between Eastern Orthodox, Anglican, and Old Catholic communions. Among the most important of his many books are: *Plain Suggestions for a Reverent Celebration of the Holy Eucharist* (1898); *Pusey and the Church Revival* (1902); *Christian and Catholic* (1905), devoted to religious essays; *A Catholic Atlas* (1908), ecclesiastical lore presented chart-fashion; *A Journey Godward of a Servant of Jesus Christ* (1910), personal reminiscences; *The Lineage of the American Catholic Church Commonly Called the Episcopal Church* (1911); and *Meditations and Instructions* (1923). *The Works of Rt. Rev. Charles C. Grafton,* in eight volumes, edited by Talbot Rogers, appeared in 1914. Personally Grafton was distinguished in appearance and manner, suave in his contacts, consciously, if never complacently, as true a medieval Prince of the Church as Wisconsin ways would warrant.

[H. W. Belknap, *The Grafton Family of Salem* (1928); *Harvard Univ. Quinquennial Cat.* (1919); *Who's Who in America,* 1912–13; *Churchman,* Sept. 7, 1912; *Milwaukee Sentinel,* Aug. 31, 1912.]

J. D. W.

GRAHAM, CHARLES KINNAIRD (June 3, 1824–Apr. 15, 1889), Union soldier, civil engineer, was born in the city of New York. He entered the navy as a midshipman in 1841, served in the Gulf Squadron during the war with Mexico, and resigned in 1848. He studied both law and engineering and elected to follow the latter profession, although he qualified to practise law and was duly licensed. He was one of the surveyors employed in laying out Central Park and in 1857 became constructing engineer at the Brooklyn navy yard, where he built the dry docks and landings. On the report of the bombardment of Fort Sumter he immediately enrolled for military service, taking some four hundred of the navy-yard workmen with him. He was appointed major of the 1st Regiment of the "Excelsior Brigade," raised by Daniel E. Sickles, promoted lieutenant-colonel, and then appointed colonel of the 5th Regiment of the same brigade, pending acceptance for federal service. The regiment was mustered in Oct. 15, 1861, and designated as the 74th New York. Graham was mustered out in April 1862 but was reappointed in May and served through the Peninsular campaign, fighting at Fair Oaks, Malvern Hill, and in other battles. Invalided home, he was employed on recruiting duty until well enough to return to service in the field. In March 1863 he became brigadier-general of volunteers, with rank antedated to Nov. 29, 1862. He commanded a brigade of the III Corps at Chancellorsville and Gettysburg. On the second day at Gettysburg he was wounded in the head during the heavy fighting in the Peach Orchard, was captured, and was sent as a prisoner to Richmond, where he remained until exchanged in September 1863. In November he joined Butler's Army of the James, where he was assigned to the command of the naval brigade and of the flotilla of army gunboats. With these he made many expeditions up the James and in adjacent waters, on one of which he burned the house, near Fredericksburg, of the brother of the Confederate secretary of war, James Alexander Seddon. For this the responsibility rests on Butler, who ordered it, as he reported, in retaliation for the burning of Montgomery Blair's house by Early. Graham was mustered out Aug. 24, 1865, and resumed the practise of his profession in New York. He was chief engineer of the dock department, 1873–75, surveyor of the port, 1878–83, and naval officer of the port, 1883–85. At the time of his death, which took place at Lakewood, N. J., he was engineer for the New York board of commissioners for Gettysburg monuments. He had survived his wife, Mary Graham, less than a year.

[*Circular No. 18* (Nov. 25, 1889) of the N. Y. Commandery, Mil. Order of the Loyal Legion; *Official Records (Army)*, I ser., XI (pts. 1, 2), XXV (pt. 1), XXVII (pt. 1), XXXIII, XLII (pt. 3), XLIII (pt. 1); *N. Y. Times,* Apr. 16, 1889; unpublished documents in the War Department.]

T. M. S.

GRAHAM, DAVID (Feb. 8, 1808–May 27, 1852), lawyer, author, was born in London, England, where his parents were temporarily staying while on their way from the north of Ireland to the United States. His father, David Graham, was a Presbyterian clergyman and a man of much culture. Having become involved in some political troubles, he had been compelled to emigrate, and eventually he took his family to New York City. The son received an excellent education at home from his father, and also studied law with the latter, who, having abandoned the ministry, had been admitted to the bar and was practising in New York City. On his admission to the New York bar in 1829, the younger Graham entered into partnership with his father, and from the first gave evidence of possessing unusual ability. As a student, he had been intensely interested in the highly technical and involved system of pleading and practise of the courts, and in 1832 he published *A Treatise on the Practice of the Supreme Court of the State of New York* (republished in 1834). Though he was only twenty-four years old at the time he displayed a complete mastery of the subject. The work was received with enthusiasm by the profession and took the place of all existing books on practise until superseded by the code of procedure promulgated in 1850.

In 1832 Graham was chosen to serve on a committee to draft a new city charter, and in 1834 he was elected an alderman of the city of New York. In the latter year also he published *A Treatise on the Law of New Trials in Cases Civil and Criminal,* which passed through several editions. His practise increased rapidly, and as counsel he was constantly requisitioned in cases of exceptional difficulty, but despite the heavy demands on his time he prepared *A Treatise on the Organization and Jurisdiction of the Courts of Law and Equity in the State of New-York,* which appeared in 1839. Shortly thereafter he appeared as corporation counsel in the series of actions, brought against the city of New York for damages resulting from the destruction of buildings when an attempt was made to stay the progress of the great fire of 1835, and successfully defended his clients (*2 Denio,* 461). It was, however, in the criminal courts that his legal ability and exceptional powers of advocacy were best demonstrated. The reputation which he had acquired through his brilliant defense of Ezra White on a sensational charge of murder had been enhanced by his conduct of Bishop Onderdonk's case in 1844, but his defense of Mary Bodine, indicted for the murder of her brother's wife and child, established him as the ablest criminal lawyer of his time. The evidence was entirely circumstantial and on the first trial the jury disagreed. On the second trial she was found guilty, but the conviction was quashed on appeal on exceptions to the judge's rulings. The third trial lasted a fortnight and resulted in an acquittal after a remarkable address to the jury by Graham. Appointed in 1848 by the legislature one of the commissioners on practise and pleadings, he drafted much of the resultant code of civil procedure, though he dissented from some of the conclusions (*Dissent from Portions of the Code of Civil Procedure as Reported Complete by the Commissioners,* 1850).

Graham's health, never robust, finally gave way in 1851, necessitating his retirement from practise. He went to Europe in the hope that a change of climate would prove beneficial but shortly afterward died at Nice. Though not a profound lawyer, he had a thorough grasp of underlying principles and a knowledge of their practical application which few of his contemporaries could equal. In the courts he was supreme. An expert cross-examiner, his handling of witnesses was masterly; no emergency ever found him unprepared. His addresses were always distinguished for their beauty of language and close reasoning, and he seemed to exercise a magnetic influence in his appeals to a jury. His courtesy was proverbial, and he was never known to lose control of his temper under any circumstances. Early in life, as a Whig, he took an active part in politics, being an ardent supporter of Clay and Webster, but he never aspired to public office, and in his later years took no part in public life.

[The source material for the details of Graham's career consists chiefly of reports of cases in which he was engaged, and similar official documents. Sketches of his life are to be found in D. McAdam and others, *Hist. of the Bench and Bar of N. Y.* (1897), I, 335; *Green Bag,* Aug. 1894; *Law Reporter,* July 1852; *N. Y. Times, Evening Mirror* (N. Y.), June 19, 1852.]

H. W. H. K.

GRAHAM, EDWARD KIDDER (Oct. 11, 1876–Oct. 26, 1918), president of the University of North Carolina, was born at Charlotte, N. C., the son of Archibald and Elizabeth Owen (Barry) Graham, both parents being members of families which have given to the state distinctive leadership in the fields of education and government. He attended the city schools and Carolina Military Institute of Charlotte. He entered the University of North Carolina in 1894, and graduated in 1898, being second in his class and the winner of the senior oratorical prize. After teaching one year in a private school in Charlotte, he returned to the University in 1899 as librarian, and before the end of the year became an instructor in the English department, which he served as instructor (1899–1902), associate professor (1902–04), and professor (1904–13). He became dean of the college of liberal arts in 1909, acting president in 1913, and president in 1914. He received in 1902 the degree of M.A. from Columbia College, where he spent a second year in graduate study in 1904–05.

Both as a teacher and as an executive, Graham achieved special distinction. From his class in English composition, in which subjects for discussion and themes were drawn from the everyday life of the state, scores of men went directly into teaching, journalism, law, or business, deeply impressed by his conceptions of citizenship, democracy, and culture. The deanship afforded him new opportunities for extending the work of the classroom. In his stimulating chapel talks, he developed his conceptions of student conduct on what has been characterized as the most democratic, self-governing campus in America. Chapel became a constructive training ground for informed citizenship, and the remarkable advance in education, health, public welfare, highway construction, and industry which North Carolina made in the two decades between 1910 and 1930 was due in large measure to the ideas to which Graham gave vivid expression as dean. In notable addresses throughout the state he insisted that the civilization of the state could be advanced only by intelligent work on the part of the entire people, all effort being shot through with fine feeling. In this way only, in Graham's opinion, could a cultured democracy be wrought out.

His term of service as acting president and president was a brief five years. It was long enough, however, for him to win state-wide acceptance of the ideas which he had been developing as teacher and dean. In December 1914, largely as a result of his leadership, every village, town, and city in North Carolina spent three entire days in the consideration of community problems. In the same year Graham established in the University the department of rural economics and sociology, stimulated the founding of the North Carolina Club, a faculty-student organization for the consideration of state problems, and provided for the publication of the University *News Letter,* a weekly publication which has devoted itself steadily to the study of North Carolina economic and social questions. He placed the division of extension upon a firm basis, provided for the holding of important institutes concerned with health, education, editorial policies, highway construction, and public welfare, and developed the idea advanced in his inaugural address, that a state university was not a thing apart, but the best instrument yet devised through which a state could serve itself. In this respect he broke from the conception of a university held by the more conservative eastern institutions, but in so doing, he won the instant approval and support of the state, and gave to the University a social-mindedness which has been one of its most distinctive characteristics since his death.

When the United States entered the World War, Graham anticipated the organization of the Students Army Training Corps by establishing a training unit on the University campus long in advance of the national organization. Consequently, when the latter was perfected, he logically became the regional director for the South Atlantic states. His death from influenza, which swept the country in the fall of 1918, was truly "in the line of duty." His wife, Susan Williams Moses, to whom he was happily married on June 25, 1908, died on Dec. 22, 1916, leaving a son.

Though frail in physique, Graham was commanding in appearance and spoke with grace and power. Among his vigorous and convincing presidential reports may be cited: *The University of North Carolina Record. The President's Report,* December 1916, and December 1917. His *Education and Citizenship, and other Papers* was published posthumously in 1919.

[*Univ. of N. C. Record,* January 1919; R. D. W. Connor, "Edward Kidder Graham," in H. W. Odum, ed., *Southern Pioneers in Social Interpretation* (1925); *Who's Who in America,* 1918–19; *Raleigh News and Observer,* Oct. 27, 1918.] L. R. W.

GRAHAM, GEORGE REX (Jan. 18, 1813–July 13, 1894), editor, publisher, was born in Philadelphia, the elder child of a shipping merchant who lost his money and died poor just as his son, aged fifteen, was to enter the law office of Charles Jared Ingersoll [*q.v.*]. The orphaned boy and his sister Mary then found an asylum with a prosperous maternal uncle, George Rex, on a farm in Montgomery County, Pa. In 1832 he returned to Philadelphia and apprenticed himself to a cabinetmaker. With ardent literary and forensic ambitions, he pored at night over Addison, Burke, and Blackstone, and got himself introduced to Judge Thomas Armstrong, who consented to direct his legal studies. To comply with the bar regulations he worked for one year as a clerk in Armstrong's office, meanwhile rising daily at 4:00 A. M. so as to work at his trade in the early morning as well as after hours. On Mar. 27, 1839, he was admitted to practise. Two months later, however, he became assistant editor of Samuel C. Atkinson's *Saturday Evening Post* and at the same time bought from his employer a small magazine, the *Casket.* Before the end of the year he also married Elizabeth Fry of Germantown. In November 1840 he paid William Evans Burton [*q.v.*] $3,500 for the *Gentleman's Magazine.* Combining his two subscription lists, in January 1841 he issued the first number of *Graham's Magazine* to 5,500 subscribers.

At one time or another Charles J. Peterson, Edgar Allan Poe, Rufus Wilmot Griswold, Emma Catherine Embury, Ann Sophia Stephens, Robert Taylor Conrad, Joseph Ripley Chandler, and Bayard Taylor [*qq.v.*] were on the staff, but Graham was his own editor and determined his own policies. In place of the insipid, jejune, even stale provender then usual, he offered his readers an entirely fresh, appetizing, and varied diet of fiction, light essays, verse, biography, travel, art criticism, book notices, and editorial chat, with a mezzotint every month by the popular John Sartain [*q.v.*], a colored fashion plate, and later one or more other engravings. With canny understanding he made *Graham's* the kind of men's magazine that appeals most strongly to women. He secured contributions from a galaxy of favorite writers by paying them with unprecedented liberality. This, his greatest innovation, compelled a general increase in magazine rates and made the "Graham page" the standard unit of measure. His success was immediate. In March 1842 he claimed 40,000 subscribers, and for some time the magazine yielded an annual profit of $50,000.

By nature Graham was amiable, generous, and optimistic. Grown suddenly rich, he took a mansion on Arch Street, kept a handsome carriage, and played the host to statesmen, authors, and foreign notables, but his lavishness has been exaggerated. His house adjoined that of a wine merchant, Elijah Van Syckel, and as the two families were intimate a doorway was cut through the party wall. Van Syckel, however, did not use his home for a warehouse, and the door did not facilitate the delivery of wine for Graham's dinners. But his prosperity was short. With Robert Montgomery Bird [*q.v.*] and Morton McMichael he bought the Philadelphia *North American* and merged with it the *United States Gazette*. He was interested in the *Evening Bulletin* and speculated in mining stocks and Pennsylvania mountain land. Financial difficulties overwhelming him, he neglected his magazine and began to drink heavily. In August 1848 he was forced to assign *Graham's* to Samuel D. Patterson & Company, though he remained its editor. Recouping some of his losses, he bought it back in March 1850, but his energies had abated, and the magazine did not flourish. In December 1853 he sold out for good.

His career was ended, although his life was not half over. After 1857 his name disappeared from *McElroy's Philadelphia Directory,* which had listed him as connected with the *Saturday Evening Mail.* In 1870, in New York, he was beggared by a stock swindle. A place was found for him on the Newark, N. J., *Daily Journal,* but although his habits were good, his mind was sluggish and his will feeble. His wife died the next year. For a while he lived with a nephew at St. Cloud, Essex County, N. J. In 1880 cataracts were removed from both his eyes and his sight partially restored. Pensioned by several wealthy Philadelphians, he was cared for by Frank Wilfred Baldwin of the Orange, N. J., *Chronicle* until 1887, when he was committed to the Orange Memorial Hospital. To visitors he would talk, serenely and with evident pleasure, of the great men he had known in early life, dwelling especially on his relations with Longfellow and Poe. He died in the hospital and was buried in Laurel Hill Cemetery, Philadelphia.

[C. J. Peterson, "George R. Graham," *Graham's Mag.,* July 1850, pp. 43–44; J. H. Martin, *Bench and Bar of Phila.* (1883), p. 272; John Sartain, *The Reminiscences of a Very Old Man* (1899); E. P. Oberholtzer, *Phila.: A Hist. of the City and its People* (n.d.); F. L. Mott, *Hist. of Am. Magazines 1741–1850* (1930); *Publishers' Weekly,* XLVI (1894), 123; *Critic,* July 21, 1894; *Newark Advertiser,* July 14, 1894; N. Y. *Sun, Times, Herald,* and *Tribune,* July 14, 1894; *Evening Bulletin* (Phila.), July 16, 1894; information from Gertrude Wilson Powell (Mrs. Lyman P. Powell), and Wm. J. Proud, Supt. of Laurel Hill Cemetery.]

G. H. G.

GRAHAM, ISABELLA MARSHALL (July 29, 1742–July 27, 1814), philanthropist, early promoter of charitable organizations in New York City, was born in the shire of Lanark, Scotland, the daughter of John and Janet (Hamilton) Marshall. She grew up in Elderslie, near Paisley, and in the latter place she sat under the preaching of Rev. John Witherspoon [*q.v.*], afterward president of the College of New Jersey. She had good educational advantages, attending for seven winters an excellent school conducted by Mrs. Betty Morehead. In 1765 she became the second wife of Dr. John Graham, a physician of Paisley. He was appointed a surgeon of His Britannic Majesty's 60th, or Royal American Regiment, and in 1767 Mrs. Graham accompanied him to Canada. They were first in Quebec, then in Montreal, and spent four years at Fort Niagara on Lake Ontario. In 1772 they went with the regiment to the island of Antigua where the following year Dr. Graham died. Mrs. Graham was left with three daughters, the oldest not more than five, and shortly a son was born. She took her family back to Scotland and for a time lived at Cartside. Later she removed to Paisley where she taught a small school, and finally at the suggestion of friends she took charge of a boarding school in Edinburgh. Eminently successful in this enterprise, upon the advice of Dr. Witherspoon and others she came to New York in 1789 and established a school for young women, which soon achieved a high reputation.

She was a woman of earnest Scotch piety, given to good works, always devoting a tenth of her income to religious and charitable purposes. While in Edinburgh she suggested the idea of poor persons putting aside a penny a week to constitute a fund to help contributors when sick. This "Penny Society" developed into the Society for the Relief of the Destitute Sick. Similarly in New York she interested herself in improving the condition of the poor. In November 1797 the Society for the Relief of Poor Widows with Small Children, said to be the earliest organization of its kind in America, was formed at her home; and she became its directress. After 1798, when she gave up teaching, she devoted practically all her time to philanthropic work. Of her children only two were now living, Isabella, the wife of Andrew Smith, a merchant, and Joanna, the wife of Divie Bethune, another merchant, prosperous and benevolent, who wrote and printed tracts for Mrs. Graham's widows, "imported Bibles for her to distribute" and "replenished her charity purse when exhausted." Rev. George Washington Bethune [*q.v.*] was his son. With one or the other of these daughters Mrs. Graham lived during the remainder of her life. On Mar. 15, 1806, she presided at a meeting in the city hall at which the Orphan Asylum Society, probably the first in the United States, was organized. The following year an asylum was built. When in 1811 the Magdalen Society was formed Mrs. Graham was made president of the board of ladies intrusted with the internal management of Magdalen House, an office which she held until her death. She was active in the organization of the Society for the Promotion of Industry Among the Poor (1814), and just before her death started a Sunday-school for adults in the village of Greenwich. Much of her correspondence and many devotional exercises written by her were published by her daughter, Mrs. Bethune, under the title, *The Power of Faith: Exemplified in the Life and Writings of the Late Mrs. Isabella Graham, of New-York* (1816), the biographical portions being supplied by Divie Bethune. It went through numerous editions here and abroad. An abridgment, *The Life of Mrs. Isabella Graham,* was issued in 1839, and an enlargement of the first edition in 1843. Mrs. Bethune also edited *The Unpublished Letters and Correspondence of Mrs. Isabella Graham* (1838).

[In addition to the works mentioned above, see John M. Mason, *Christian Mourning: a Sermon Occasioned by the Death of Mrs. Isabella Graham* (1814); E. P. Belden, *New-York, Past, Present, and Future* (1849); Martha J. Lamb, *Hist. of the City of New York,* vol. II (1881); B. J. Lossing, *Hist. of New York City* (1884); N. Y. *Evening Post,* July 27, 1814.] H. E. S.

GRAHAM, JAMES (d. January 1700/01), public official in the city and province of New York, was the son of John and Isabella (Auchinlick) Graham and was probably born in Scotland. He arrived in New York Aug. 8, 1678, in the same ship with Gov. Andros. He had been trained in the law and there are indications that Andros advised his coming believing he might make very good use of him in his government. He was commissioned by the governor as one of the six aldermen of the city of New York, Oct. 30, 1680, and in 1683 William Penn sought his assistance on a commission deputed to buy the upper Susquehanna Valley from the Indians. When Gov. Dongan granted to the city of New York a charter of greater privileges (1683), Graham was the first appointee to the newly created office of recorder, taking a place "on ye Bench on ye Right hand of ye Mayor" (*Minutes of the Common Council,* vol, I, p. 118). Later, as attorney-general of the province he was destined to subscribe to that same Dongan charter the attestation: "The Attorney General hath perused this Pattent and finds Nothing Contained therein prejudicial to his Majesties Interest." On Feb. 5, 1684, the court of general sessions was established and Graham was one of the judges at the first session. The same year Gov. Dongan appointed him clerk of the first court of chancery to be established in New York. In 1687, after grave malfeasance had been discovered in connection with the collection of customs, the governor appointed Graham one of two emergency men to farm the revenues. Recommendation for compensation was made later to the committee of trade and transportation because of the resulting improvement in the revenue.

In April 1691 Graham became by unanimous choice speaker of the first General Assembly of the province of New York (*Assembly Journal,* vol. I, p. 2), and with only two interruptions he continued as speaker for eight years. He had also been a member of the governor's council on different occasions. It was inevitable that he should be arrayed in 1689 against the usurpers, Leisler and Milborne, and so temporarily he shared with his friend Andros incarceration in Boston. Later, on Gov. Sloughter's arrival, he was able to bring about the execution of the usurpers, but when the Leislerians got the ear of the new governor, Lord Bellomont, in 1700, he was again out of favor. His capability in drafting state papers is evidenced in his appeal to the King to repeal the Bolting Act (*Minutes of the Common Council,* vol. II, pp. 32–54), and in his argument offered to Bellomont for New York as the chief port of entry (*Documents Relative to the Colonial History . . . of New York,* vol. IV, pp. 382–84). Graham was married in 1684 to Elizabeth Windebank and had two sons and four daughters. His landed estate in Ulster County and elsewhere was considerable. On his Morrisania manor, where he later died, he had on Sept. 5, 1698, "one overseer two white servants and 33 slaves."

[E. B. O'Callaghan, ed., *Docs. Relative to the Colonial Hist. of the State of N. Y.,* vols. I (1856), II (1858), III (1853), IV (1854), and *Calendar of Hist. MSS. in the Office of the Secretary of State* (2 vols., 1866); *Minutes of the Common Council of the City of N. Y.* (1905), vols. I and II; *Calendar of Council Minutes, 1668–1783* (1902); *N. Y. Geneal. and Biog. Record,* Apr. 1928; W. S. Pelletreau, ed., *Early Wills of Westchester County, N. Y.* (1898); C. M. Andrews, *Narratives of the Insurrections, 1675–90* (1915); J. R. Brodhead, *Hist. of the State of N. Y.* (2 vols., 1853–71); manuscript letters of Bellomont in the N. Y. Hist. Soc.]
A. E. P.

GRAHAM, JAMES DUNCAN (Apr. 4, 1799–Dec. 28, 1865), army officer, father of William Montrose Graham [*q.v.*], was the grandson of John Graham, who came from Scotland in 1736 and settled in Virginia, and the son of Dr. William and Mary Campbell Graham. Dr. Graham served in the 2d Virginia Regiment in the Revolutionary War, and each of his four sons who grew to maturity found his career as an officer in the United States army and was breveted for distinguished service. James Duncan Graham was born in Prince William County, Va., graduated from West Point in 1817, and was assigned to the 1st Artillery. From 1819 to 1821 he served as first assistant to Maj. Stephen H. Long on his expedition to the Rocky Mountains. This determined his career; his particular interest thenceforth was in topographical engineering. For several years he was assigned to topographical duty and on July 7, 1838, was commissioned major, Corps of Topographical Engineers. In 1839 he was the astronomer of the surveying party that fixed the boundary between the United States and the Republic of Texas. In the steps leading toward a settlement of the controversy over the northern boundary of Maine he was detailed commissioner for the survey and exploration of the boundary (1840–43) and later served as principal astronomer and head of the scientific corps on the part of the United States for the joint demarcation of the United States and the British provinces. In this arduous service (1843–47) he showed exceptional ability, in recognition of which he was breveted lieutenant-colonel. He was then detailed to direct the resurvey of Mason and Dixon's line. In 1850–51, as principal astronomer and head of the scientific corps he surveyed part of the Mexican border. Because of this latter service Mount Graham in southeastern Arizona was named for him (F. H. Hodder, ed., *Audubon's Western Journal: 1849–50,* 1906, p. 155). For ten years beginning with 1854 he had duty on the Great Lakes, and for most of that time he was the superintending engineer of harbor improvements. During the period of this duty, after most careful scientific observations covering several years, he discovered the existence of a lunar tide on the Great Lakes (1858–59). He was promoted lieutenant-colonel, Topographical Engineers, on Aug. 6, 1861, was given the same rank in the Corps of Engineers two years later when the two corps were combined, and was promoted colonel, Corps of Engineers, on June 1, 1863. His last duty was that of superintending engineer of sea-walls in Boston Harbor, having charge of the repair of harbor works from Maine to the Chesapeake. He met his death in consequence of exposure in a severe storm on the coast of Massachusetts while inspecting a sea-wall which had just been completed under his direction. He was twice married: on July 6, 1828, to Charlotte Hustler Meade, sister of Gen. George Gordon Meade; and later to Frances Wickham of Richmond, Va. He was a constant student, not only of his own profession, but in art, science, and letters.

[Geo. W. Cullum, *Biog. Reg. . . . U. S. Mil. Acad.* (3rd ed., 1891); Edwin James, *Account of an Expedition from Pittsburgh to the Rocky Mountains . . . under the Command of Maj. Stephen H. Long* (2 vols., 1823); *Report of Lieut. Col. J. D. Graham . . . on Mason and Dixon's Line* (2nd ed., 1862); *Sen. Doc. 121,* 32 Cong., 1 Sess.; *Sen. Doc. 16,* 34 Cong., 3 Sess.; *Sen. Doc. 1,* 36 Cong., 2 Sess.; *Ex. Doc. 1,* 38 Cong., 1 Sess.; Graham's library, letters, and collection of paintings, for the most part still in the possession of his grandchildren.]
C. S. A.

GRAHAM, JOHN (*c.* 1718–November 1795), Loyalist, was born in Scotland and emigrated to Georgia in 1753 expecting to inherit a relative's fortune. Disappointed in his expectations, he engaged in trade in Savannah for a dozen years, and was in "great business" in 1760 when he first met Gov. James Wright. Probably in 1755 he married Frances Crooke, a grand-daughter of Robert Cunningham of South Carolina. He was appointed a member of the Council in August 1763, on Wright's recommendation, and soon became receiver of moneys from the sales of lands out of the 2,500,000 acres ceded by the Creeks and Cherokees. His income from this source averaged £2,000 a year. Quitting business for agriculture, by 1776 he had developed three large plantations, had accumulated 262 slaves, and was deriving from his property a gross produce of £2,700 annually. His troubles began with his opposition in August 1775 to sending delegates to the Continental Congress. On Jan. 19, 1776, the governor and Council were arrested but were paroled the next day. Fearing rearrest, Graham hid in the swamps until he escaped to the man-of-war *Scarborough* in the Savannah River. In March he received his commission as lieutenant-governor, a new office without salary. His vessel, *Inverness,* and its cargo were burned by revolutionists, who also destroyed 400 barrels of his rice and his house in Savannah. By releasing three Whig prisoners he obtained permission from the Council of Safety on May 1 to leave Georgia with the privilege of returning, but he had to give a bond of £10,000 and pledge his property as security for his creditors. On May 13 he sailed for England. In his memorial to Lord George Germain after his arrival he stated that he had left at the mercy of his enemies a fortune of £50,000 sterling, chiefly in slaves, and requested that he be given a salary from the beginning of his lieutenant-governorship. The King granted him £300 without back pay. With other fellow officials he remained in England until after the British reduction of Georgia.

Returning to Savannah in July 1779, Graham witnessed d'Estaing's siege. With Gov. Wright he lived in a tent outside of the town. A year later he was at Augusta with 100 men, enforcing the disqualifying act by disarming Whigs and exacting security for their good behavior. In January 1782 he personally received from Lieut.-Gen. Alexander Leslie at Charleston the superintendency of Indian affairs for the Mississippi region with a salary of £500 per annum, £110 a year for rents and office supplies, and perquisites of about £500 annually. The appointment was confirmed by the Crown. When the British and Loyalists evacuated Charleston in July 1782 Graham removed with more than 200 slaves to East Florida, where he received five grants of land of 500 acres for himself and each of his four sons. Clearing and settling three plantations, he placed Lieut.-Col. John Douglas, a fellow refugee from Georgia, in charge, obtained Leslie's permission to go to England for his health's sake, and named Douglas deputy-superintendent of Indian affairs. Graham sailed about Nov. 1, 1782. A year later his claim for his losses in Georgia was heard in London and he was allowed £400 a year. In order to supplement this income he became a merchant in London. In November 1786 he presented his East Florida claim and was awarded something more than a thousand pounds. He served as an executor for his brother James, who had plantations in both Georgia and Florida, and as joint agent in London of Georgia Loyalists for prosecuting their claims. He died at Naples, Italy.

[D. P. Coke, *The Royal Commission on the Losses and Services of Am. Loyalists, 1783 to 1785* (1915), ed. by H. E. Egerton; W. H. Siebert, *Loyalists in East Fla., 1774–85* (2 vols., 1929) published by the Fla. State Hist. Soc.; Conveyances, 1751–61 (Ga. Dept. of Archives and Hist., Atlanta), vol. C, pt. 1, p. 174; Will of Heriot Crooke, *Ibid.*; *Colonial Records of Ga.* (1907), vols. VIII, IX, X; *Ga. Hist. Soc. Colls.*, vol. III (1873), vol. V, pt. 1 (1901); *Acts of the Privy Council, Colonial Series, 1745–66* (1911), *1766–83* (1912); *Hist. MSS. Commission Report on Am. MSS. in the Royal Inst. of Great Britain*, vols. I–IV (1904–09); *S. C. Hist. and Geneal. Mag.*, Oct. 1918; *S. C. Gazette and Pub. Advertiser,* June 11, 1786.]

W. H. S.

GRAHAM, JOHN (1774–Aug. 6, 1820), diplomat, was born at Dumfries, Prince William County, Va., of an influential and wealthy family, prominent in the commercial life of that port in its most ambitious day. He was the son of Jane Brent and Richard Graham, "one of the earliest land adventurers on the Ohio River" (S. P. Hildreth, "History of an Early Voyage on the Ohio," *American Pioneer,* March 1842, p. 102), and brother of George Graham, acting secretary of war under Madison and Monroe. His wife was Susan Hill, the daughter of Clement and Eleanor (Brent) Hill of Prince Georges County, Md. He graduated from Columbia College in 1790 and emigrated to Mason County, Ky., which in 1800 he represented in the legislature, his commanding person, prepossessing countenance, and agreeable manners having soon helped to call to public notice his industry and obvious talents. From Aug. 31, 1801, until February 1803, when he resigned, he was attached to the American Embassy at Madrid, first as secretary of legation and later as chargé d'affaires. On Dec. 12, 1804, President Jefferson appointed him secretary of the Territory of Orleans. He soon made himself indispensable to Gov. Claiborne, won his confidence and esteem "as a man and an officer," and in time took over the internal correspondence of the territory. When Jefferson was notified of Aaron Burr's designs in the western country, he sent Graham, who was then in Washington, as his confidential agent "to enquire into Burr's movements, put the Governors, etc., on their guard, to provide for his arrest if necessary, and to take on himself the Government of [upper] Louisiana" (A. E. Bergh, *The Writings of Thomas Jefferson,* 1905, vol. 1, p. 462). Proceeding to Marietta, he obtained from the unsuspecting Blennerhassett the information he desired and, after warning him—fruitlessly—against further complicity and rousing Ohio and Kentucky, hastened on to intercept Burr; but, arriving at Nashville one day too late, found his quarry flown.

The next year Madison, as secretary, invited him to become chief clerk in the state department. He served in this capacity from July 1, 1807, to July 18, 1817, collaborating with Secretary Monroe in developing the nation's policies towards the Central and South American countries, and performing his duties so creditably that when Madison retired from the presidency one of the few letters of recommendation which he wrote to his successor set forth his sense of Graham's "great merit." From Mar. 4 to 10, 1817, he acted as secretary of state *ad interim*. In July 1817 President Monroe appointed him, with Cæsar Augustus Rodney and Theodorick Bland, a special commission "to obtain information of the actual condition and political prospects of the Spanish provinces which were contending for independence." The findings of this commission Graham embodied in an exhaustive report. He was named minister plenipotentiary to Portugal (to reside in Brazil), Jan. 6, 1819, but the climate proved too severe, and, after less than a year at Rio de Janeiro, he returned with his family to Washington, where he died.

Madison, who knew Graham intimately, commented upon him "as among the most worthy of men, and most estimable citizens; as adding to a sound & discriminating judgment, a valuable stock of acquirements adapted to public affairs; and to both, a purity of character, a delicacy of sentiment, and an amenity of temper & manners, exceeded in no instance to which I could refer" (G. Hunt, *The Writings of James Madison*, VIII, 1908, 390). Monroe, who had also worked with Graham and had known him from youth, referring to this tribute, wrote, "It gives me pleasure to concur in every sentiment expressed of him by Mr. Madison, and on the most thorough conviction that nothing is said that is not fully merited" (S. M. Hamilton, *The Writings of James Monroe*, VII, 1902, 17–18).

[*Official Letter Books of W. C. C. Claiborne* (1917), ed. by Dunbar Rowland, vols. III, IV, and VI; J. J. Coombs, *Trial of Aaron Burr* (1864); Jas. Parton, *The Life and Times of Aaron Burr* (1858); I. J. Cox, "Monroe and the Early Mexican Revolutionary Agents," *Ann. Report of the Am. Hist. Asso. for the Year 1911*, vol. I (1913); W. B. Chilton, "The Brent Family," *Va. Mag. of Hist. and Biog.*, Jan. 1911; *The St.-Mémin Coll. of Portraits* (1862), published by Elias Dexter; *Nat. Intelligencer* (Washington, D. C.), Aug. 7, 29, 1820.]

A. C. G., Jr.

GRAHAM, JOHN ANDREW (June 10, 1764–Aug. 29, 1841), lawyer, author, was the grandson of John Graham, an Edinburgh clergyman and near connection of the Marquis of Montrose, who, emigrating in 1718, became in 1732 the first minister in that part of Woodbury which is now Southbury, Conn. His father, Andrew Graham, a prominent surgeon, married Martha Curtiss and resided at Southbury, where he was born. He received an excellent classical education at the hands of a private tutor and in 1781 entered the law office of Edward Hinman at Southbury. On his admission to the Connecticut bar in 1785 he moved to Vermont and opened a law office at Rutland. Practising chiefly in the court of common pleas, he soon acquired an extensive business and in 1790 was admitted to the bar of the supreme court of the state. In October 1794, as delegate from Rutland, he attended the Episcopal Convention of Vermont, at which the selection of a bishop was the chief matter of business. On his nomination his friend and relative, Rev. Samuel Peters, was elected, and since the latter was then in England, Graham was dispatched thither as diocesan agent to procure, if possible, the consecration of Peters in England. He displayed great diplomacy and resource on this mission but in the end was unsuccessful. Returning to Vermont in November 1795, he made his report, then in 1796 he betook himself again to England, where he remained for the next three years. During this time he wrote *A Descriptive Sketch of the Present State of Vermont* (1797), became well known in literary and political circles, and was an intimate friend of Horne Tooke. When he returned to the United States, he resumed practise in Rutland, but in 1803 went to Washington, D. C., finally making his home in New York City.

Admitted to the New York bar in 1805, Graham practised chiefly in the criminal courts, where he soon acquired a wide reputation through his spectacular eloquence and versatility. Of good presence, always respectful to the court, extremely effective in eliciting the sympathy of the jury and having a ready command of picturesque language, he became one of the most popular advocates in New York. His protest against the practise of examining in private, and without the aid of counsel, a person accused of crime, and subsequently using the testimony as evidence against him at his trial, created a sensation and led to an amendment of the code by the legislature. (See the *Report of Hiram Maxwell's Case . . . with the Speech and Doctrine Advanced by John A. Graham*, 1823.) In 1812 he published his *Speeches Delivered at the City-Hall of the City of New York, in the Courts of Oyer and Terminer, Common Pleas and General Sessions of the Peace*, which, despite a considerable strain of somewhat tinseled rhetoric, shows him to have been an impressive speaker. He also wrote *Memoirs of John Horne Tooke, Together with his Valuable Speeches and Writings: also,*

Containing Proofs Identifying him as the Author of the Celebrated Letters of Junius (1828). He was twice married: first to Rachel Freeman Hodges of Clarendon, Vt., and second to Margaret Lorimer, daughter of James Lorimer of London, England.

[Wm. Cothren, *Hist. of Ancient Woodbury, Conn.*, I (1854), 545–52; C. L. Williams, *Statistics of the Rutland County Bar* (1847), p. 17; *The Correspondence of John A. Graham with His Grace of Canterbury, when on his Mission as Agent of the Church of Vt.* (1835); A. D. Hodges, Jr., *Geneal. Record of the Hodges Family in New England* (3rd ed., 1896), p. 215; A. M. Hemenway, *Vt. Hist. Gazetteer*, III (1877), p. 1013; *N. Y. Evening Express*, Aug. 30, 1841.]

H. W. H. K.

GRAHAM, JOSEPH (Oct. 13, 1759–Nov. 12, 1836), Revolutionary soldier, was born in Chester County, Pa. His father, James Graham, of Scotch-Irish descent, emigrated from County Down, Ireland, in 1733 and settled in Berks County, Pa. His mother, Mary (McConnell) Barber Graham, James Graham's second wife, some time after the death of her husband in 1763 removed to the vicinity of Spartanburg, S. C., and then settled in Mecklenburg County, N. C., about 1768. Joseph Graham was educated at Queen's Museum, Charlotte. In 1778 he enlisted in the 4th Regiment of the North Carolina Continental Line and served for a year as quartermaster-sergeant. Relieved of service he volunteered again in 1780 and was appointed adjutant of a militia regiment. Later he became captain of a company of mounted infantry. During this period he saw active service in North Carolina and in South Carolina. He was in command of the reserve during the spirited defense of Charlotte in September 1780, which delayed the advance of Cornwallis, and won from the British the title for the town of "Hornet's Nest." He received nine severe wounds from which it took him two months to recover, but he resumed his service and remained until March 1781. In August of that year he organized a company of dragoons and soon afterward became major. He served near Wilmington until November 1781, when his service finally ended. He had participated in fifteen minor engagements and showed excellent capacity as a soldier.

After the close of the war Graham engaged in tobacco planting and at intervals held public office. He was commissioner to collect and sell government property and was for a time sheriff of his county. In 1788 he was a delegate to the convention called to consider the Constitution of the United States and voted against ratification. He was also a delegate to the Convention of 1789, in which he voted for ratification. In neither did he participate in the debates. From 1788 to 1794, while he was still a young man, he sat in the state Senate, where he displayed a particular interest in internal improvements and public education. Later, during the years 1814–15, he was a member of the Council of State. In 1813 and again in 1823 he ran for Congress, but was both times defeated. He was one of the first members of the board of trustees of the University of North Carolina and served in that capacity until his death.

In 1787 Graham was married to Isabella Davidson, the daughter of John Davidson of Mecklenburg County. In 1795 he acquired an interest in an iron mine, furnace, and forge at Vesuvius Furnace in Lincoln County, and moved there with his family. The business was highly profitable and he acquired a considerable fortune. From the close of the Revolution until his death he took an active interest in military matters, and in 1802 he outlined an elaborate plan for a state military school, with a four years' course of study, and submitted it to the legislature. When in January 1814 President Madison called on the governors of North Carolina and South Carolina for two regiments to reinforce Jackson in the Creek War, Gov. Hawkins nominated Graham to command the brigade. He was appointed, but owing to the failure of the war department to furnish supplies, the departure of the brigade was delayed and when it reached Jackson the battle of Horseshoe Bend was over.

Beginning in 1820 Graham wrote for Archibald D. Murphey, who was collecting material for a history of North Carolina, a series of letters and articles which constitute a valuable record of Revolutionary warfare in western North Carolina and in South Carolina. His account, based on memory, of the adoption of the much disputed Mecklenburg Declaration of Independence is one of the chief reliances of the proponents of the authenticity of the Declaration.

[Wm. A. Graham, *Gen. Jos. Graham and his Papers on N. C. Revolutionary Hist.* (1904); G. W. Graham, *The Mecklenburg Declaration of Independence* (1905); J. H. Wheeler, *Hist. Sketches of N. C.* (1851), II, 233–37, 268–69; Wm. H. Hoyt, ed., *Papers of Archibald D. Murphey* (1914); *N. C. Standard* (Raleigh), Dec. 7, 1836.]

J. G. de R. H.

GRAHAM, SYLVESTER (July 5, 1794–Sept. 11, 1851), reformer, was born in West Suffield, Conn. He was the grandson of John Graham (University of Glasgow, 1714), a clergyman and physician, who emigrated to Boston in 1718 and settled in that part of Woodbury which is now Southbury, Conn., and the youngest child of the seventy-two-year-old John Graham (Yale, 1740), also a clergyman and physician, by his second wife Ruth. After his father's death in 1796 he was reared successively by various relatives to the detriment of his health and education. He worked as a farm-hand, clerk, and teacher, until, threatened by the reappearance of tubercular symptoms, he decided to prepare for the ministry. He studied languages at Amherst Academy, Amherst, Mass., during the quarter ending Nov. 13, 1823, but left because fellow students circulated reports derogatory to his character. During a long subsequent illness he was nursed by two Miss Earls, one of whom became his wife in 1826 and with several children survived him. Soon thereafter, according to Horace Greeley, himself an intermittent Grahamite, he was preaching in New Jersey, and in 1831 he was stated supply at Berkshire Valley, Morris County, N. J.

Although Graham was connected with the Presbytery of Newark until 1834, in 1830 he was made general agent for the Pennsylvania Temperance Society. During six months of lecturing he studied human physiology, diet, and regimen. In 1830–31 he delivered addresses on these subjects in Philadelphia which he repeated in New York in June 1831 and then found himself launched on a lecture career which took him up and down the Atlantic Coast states. He advocated bread at least twelve hours old, made of the whole of the wheat unbolted and coarsely ground, and also recommended hard mattresses, open bedroom windows, cold shower baths, looser and lighter clothing, daily exercise, vegetables, fresh fruits, rough cereals, pure drinking water, and cheerfulness at meals. In 1832–33 he lectured on the cholera, publishing his discourse as *A Lecture on Epidemic Diseases Generally and Particularly the Spasmodic Cholera* (1833). In 1832 he edited Luigi Cornaro's *Discourses on a Sober and Temperate Life* and in 1834 his lectures on chastity, subsequently published in Germany, were published in London as *The Young Man's Guide to Chastity. The Aesculapian Tablets of the Nineteenth Century* (1834) consisted of testimonials by his followers. His lectures on comparative anatomy, on the Biblical mention of the use of flesh and wine, and his lectures for colored people were added to his repertoire in 1836–37. Everywhere his frankness met with opposition. The prudish were shocked by his common-sense talks to mothers; trouble was precipitated by his *Treatise on Bread and Bread-Making* (1837), advocating home-made bread instead of the adulterated bakers' product, and in Boston he was attacked by a mob of bakers and butchers. But while he was the subject of jokes, lampoons, and caustic editorials and was apostrophized by Emerson in his journal as the "poet of bran bread and pumpkins," the millers barreled Graham flour, Graham boarding houses sprang up, and his adherents showered him with gifts. To combat opposition to Grahamism, David Cambell edited the *Graham Journal of Health and Longevity* (April 1837–December 1839) and in 1839 Graham himself published his most ambitious work, *Lectures on the Science of Human Life* (2 vols., republished, with biographical sketch, 1858). After 1840 his influence as the eloquent popularizer of a workable system of personal hygiene waned. In 1841 he began to issue his Biblical lectures in quarterly instalments. Of the four volumes projected, he completed only one, *The Philosophy of Sacred History* (1855), edited after his death by H. S. Chubb. His health failed steadily, and he died at his home in Northampton, Mass., after submitting to stimulants, a dose of Congress water, and a tepid bath.

[J. H. Trumbull, *Memorial Hist. of Hartford County, Conn., 1633–1884* (1886), II, 392, 413–14; F. B. Dexter, *Biog. Sketches of the Grads. of Yale Coll. 1701–45* (1885), pp. 648–49; *Minutes, Gen. Assembly Presbyt. Ch. in the U. S. A.*, 1831, p. 229, 1832, p. 393, 1833, p. 544, 1834, p. 111; *Springfield Republican*, Sept. 12, 1851; information from R. S. Fletcher, librarian of Amherst Coll.]

M. W. G.

GRAHAM, WILLIAM ALEXANDER (Sept. 5, 1804–Aug. 11, 1875), lawyer, statesman, the eleventh child and youngest son of Joseph [*q.v.*] and Isabella (Davidson) Graham, was born near Vesuvius Furnace in Lincoln County, N. C. He was educated in the private schools in the neighborhood, at Dr. Muchat's Classical Academy at Statesville, and at the Hillsboro Academy. Entering the University of North Carolina in the summer of 1820, he graduated with high honor in 1824. He studied law under Chief Justice Thomas Ruffin at Hillsboro, obtained his county court license in December 1826 and his superior court license a year later, and settled at Hillsboro for the practise of his profession. In the course of a decade he was a recognized leader of that bar. His public life commenced as member of the House of Commons in 1833. He was continuously a member of that body, serving twice as its speaker, until his election as United States senator, Nov. 24, 1840. His career as legislator was marked by an earnest and intelligent advocacy of internal improvements and public education. In politics he was a Whig, and soon he became a leader of his party. In November 1840 he was elected for the unexpired term of Senator Strange, but since the General Assembly of North Carolina of 1842–43 was Democratic, he was retired to private life on Mar. 4, 1843. On Dec. 7, 1843, he was unanimously nominated for governor by the Whig convention in Raleigh and was elected the following August by a substantial majority. He retired from that office at the end of his second term in January 1849. In both terms he demonstrated his superior ability as an administrator, particularly in the building and financing of railroads. In the summer of 1849 President Taylor offered him his choice of the missions to Russia and Spain. He refused to accept either, but at the death of Taylor and the reorganization of the cabinet by his successor Fillmore, he was tendered and accepted the secretaryship of the navy. During his encumbency of this office he was a moving spirit in four measures of far-reaching importance: namely, the reorganization of the coast survey; the reorganization of the personnel of the navy; the exploration of the Amazon; and the expedition to Japan. The third was suggested to him by M. F. Maury, and the fourth by Commodore M. C. Perry.

In June 1852 Graham was nominated for the vice-presidency by the Whig National Convention at Baltimore, with Gen. Winfield Scott as his chief. He then resigned his seat in the cabinet. The result of the election was foredoomed; it was not a Whig year. At the end of the Fillmore administration Graham returned to North Carolina with a reputation as man and statesman as extensive as the country itself. Thenceforward until his death he was distinctly a leader of the moderates. Throughout the hot debate that led up to secession he was strongly in favor of preserving the Union. He condemned secession not only as a political heresy, but as essentially suicidal to the best interests of the South. So strong was his position before the country at large that he received the support of a number of delegates for nomination for the presidency by the Constitutional Union party in 1860, and after the general election in the fall of that year the New York and Pennsylvania electors were strongly urged to cast their ballots for him in the electoral college, as the only means to avert the impending dissolution of the Union. But when war came he ceased to be a Union man. Five of his sons were devoted to the cause, but all of them became officers in the armies of the South. He was elected to the Senate of the Confederacy in February 1864 and took his seat in May of that year. Here he worked to secure the opening of negotiations looking to peace without independence, and, after the failure of the Hampton Roads conference, he urged action on the part of individual states—an utterly hopeless scheme. He was elected by the General Assembly of 1866 to the United States Senate, but was not allowed to take his seat. For the remainder of his life he was a loved and trusted adviser of the people of the state. He was one of the original trustees of the Peabody Fund and took an active interest in its management until his death. He died suddenly at Saratoga Springs, N. Y., while acting as an arbitrator in the dispute as to the dividing line between the states of Maryland and Virginia. On June 8, 1836, he was married to Susannah Sarah Washington of New Bern, N. C. Of their ten children, seven sons and one daughter survived him. His memory in North Carolina is perpetuated in the name of a county and of one of the smaller cities of the state.

["Addresses at the Unveiling of the Bust of Wm. A. Graham by the N. C. Hist. Comm.," *N. C. Hist. Comm. Pubs.*, Bull. no. 7 (1910); Montford McGehee, *Life and Character of the Hon. Wm. A. Graham* (1877); S. A. Ashe, *Hist. of N. C.*, vol. II (1925); Cornelia P. Spencer, *The Last Ninety Days of the War in N. C.* (1866); Kemp P. Battle, *Hist. of the Univ. of N. C.* (2 vols., 1907–12); Wm. A. Graham, *Gen. Jos. Graham and his Papers on N. C. Revolutionary Hist.* (1904); *Morning Star* (Wilmington, N. C.), Aug. 12, 1875.]

F. N.

GRAHAM, WILLIAM MONTROSE (Sept. 28, 1834–Jan. 16, 1916), soldier, born in the District of Columbia, came of a distinguished family. His father was Col. James Duncan Graham [*q.v.*]; an uncle, Lieut.-Col. William Montrose Graham, for whom he was named, was killed while leading his regiment at Molino del Rey, Mexico. His mother was Charlotte (Meade) Graham. Graham's wife, to whom he was married at Fortress Monroe, Va., Sept. 4, 1860, was Mary Brewerton Ricketts, daughter of Maj.-Gen. James B. Ricketts and of Harriet J. Pierce Ricketts, daughter of Col. Benjamin K. Pierce, and a niece of President Franklin Pierce. He received his early schooling at Hallowell's Academy, Alexandria, Va., at Mt. St. Albans, Washington, D. C., and at Bolmar Academy, Westchester, Pa. At the age of nineteen he went with the Stevens Expedition as assistant astronomer. Two years later he was commissioned second lieutenant in the army and was assigned to the 1st Artillery. Almost immediately he saw active service against the Seminole Indians in Florida, 1855–56, and on the Texas frontier, 1856–61, where he participated with credit (1859–60) in operations against the Mexican bandit Cortinas and his marauders along the Rio Grande. Shortly after the beginning of the Civil War he was promoted captain, Oct. 26, 1861, and assigned to the command of Light Battery K, 1st Artillery. He took part with distinction in Gen. McClellan's entire Peninsular campaign, for which service he received the brevet of major. Subsequently, he was brevetted lieutenant-colonel for gallantry at Antietam, and colonel for distinguished services at Gettysburg, and during the years 1863–65 commanded the 2nd Brigade, Horse Artillery, Army of the Potomac, until ordered on mustering and disbursing duty at Concord, N. H.

On Mar. 13, 1865, he was awarded the brevet of brigadier-general for gallant and meritorious services throughout the Civil War, and later in the same year was assigned to command the 2nd District of Columbia Infantry as a colonel of volunteers. In the period following the Civil War, Graham passed through two serious epidemics of yellow fever, at Jackson Barracks, La., in 1867, and at Key West in 1873, and took part in 1869 in a punitive expedition from Fort Riley, Kan., against hostile Indians on the Republican River. He became major, 4th Artillery, in 1879; lieutenant-colonel, 1st Artillery, in 1887; colonel, 5th Artillery, in 1891; and a brigadier-general in 1897. As a general officer his first assignment was to command the Department of Texas, and the outbreak of the Spanish War in 1898 found him commanding the Department of the Gulf with headquarters at Atlanta. He was promptly appointed a major-general of volunteers Mar. 4, 1898, and commanded the II Army Corps at Falls Church, Va., and later at Camp Meade, Pa. He was retired from active service under operation of law Sept. 28, 1898, but was retained on active duty under his volunteer commission until Nov. 30. In 1916 he was promoted to the rank of major-general on the retired list. He died at Wardour, Annapolis, Md., at the home of one of his daughters, and was interred with military honors in the Congressional Cemetery, Washington, D. C. Studious, devoted to his profession, possessing a keen sense of humor, Graham combined lofty ideals of duty and rigid discipline with a chivalrous attitude towards subordinates, which marked him as an outstanding officer of the old army. He was survived by his wife, two sons, and three daughters.

[W. L. Haskin, *The Hist. of the First Regiment of Artillery from its Organization in 1821 to Jan. 1st, 1876* (1879), has been largely drawn upon for incidents with which Graham was connected, supplemented by T. F. Rodenbough and W. L. Haskin, *The Army of the U. S.* (1896); W. H. Powell, *Records of Living Officers of the U. S. Army* (1890); *Jour. of the Mil. Service Inst.*, July-Aug. 1916; F. B. Pierce, *Pierce Geneal.* (1882); and F. B. Heitman, *Hist. Reg. and Dict. of the U. S. Army* (1903). Short but interesting sketches appeared in the *Post* (Washington, D. C.), and *Army & Navy Reg.*, Jan. 22, 1916, and information as to certain facts has been furnished by members of Graham's family.] C. D. R.

GRANGER, FRANCIS (Dec. 1, 1792–Aug. 28, 1868), American political leader, was born in Suffield, Conn., the second of the three sons of Gideon [*q.v.*] and Mindwell (Pease) Granger. His father was for thirteen years postmaster-general in the administrations of Jefferson and Madison. Francis entered Yale College at the age of sixteen and graduated in 1811. When his father removed to Canandaigua, N. Y., in 1816, the son followed and began the practise of law. In 1817 he married Cornelia Rutson Van Rensselaer, daughter of Jeremiah Van Rensselaer of Utica, a well-to-do Federalist. Granger was elected to the state Assembly in 1825 as a follower of Gov. Clinton, won a following, and when reëlected in 1826 received thirty-three votes for speaker, but was not chosen. The opportunity now presented itself for him to extend his popularity. With the Anti-Masonic excitement sweeping New York, Granger made himself one of the conspicuous figures of the movement and thus became associated with Thurlow Weed, who was just rising into prominence. He was chairman of a select committee of the legislature that recommended more stringent laws against kidnapping, and of a legislative joint committee of investigation with power to visit the seat of the excitement, hear witnesses, examine papers, and make a report. The committee's recommendations were rejected, but Granger won considerable prominence. His political strength was augmented at this time by his advocacy of a canal in Chenango County. In 1828 he was nominated by the National Republicans for lieutenant-governor, and by the Anti-Masons, who held a separate convention, for governor. After some consideration he accepted the first of these nominations, but was defeated in the election. The next year he returned to the Assembly. In 1830 he was the unanimous choice of both the Anti-Masons and the National Republicans for governor, and he was nominated again in 1832. Both times he was defeated, and in 1834 his candidacy was not renewed, William H. Seward being nominated in his stead.

Granger was by this time closely associated with the rising Whig party. He was elected to Congress as a Whig in 1834, but played a relatively inconspicuous rôle. In 1836 he was nominated on the Anti-Masonic ticket for vice-president, and by the Whigs of Massachusetts for the same office. The election was thrown into the Senate, where Granger received sixteen votes, against thirty-three for Richard M. Johnson. He now returned to Congress, serving two more terms in the House. During this period he joined John Quincy Adams in opposing Southern restriction on the right of petition and earned the hostility of the slave-holders. He was a supporter of Harrison's candidacy in 1840, and on the victory of the Whig ticket was appointed postmaster-general. His nomination was opposed by Southern members of the Senate but was confirmed. After the succession of Tyler to the presidency, and the rupture between the President and the Whig leaders, Granger accompanied most of the other members of the cabinet into retirement. Reëlected to Congress to fill a vacancy, he served until Mar. 3, 1843, but thereafter resisted every effort to bring him back into public life, even declining the offer of a foreign mission.

His views on the slavery question were now becoming more conservative. Though opposed to the annexation of Texas, he broke with Weed on slavery in 1845, and was a partisan of the Compromise measures of 1850 and a strong supporter of the Fillmore administration. He presided over the Whig convention of 1850, having been put in the chair, as Weed confesses in his *Autobiography* (II, 186), because that was where he could do the least harm. When the convention adopted resolutions praising William H. Seward, Granger retired from the hall. He and the conservative Whigs held a separate convention, but made no nominations for the state officers. Granger at this time gave the name to a faction of his party, the Silver Grays, so called from the flowing gray hair of their leader. Again retiring into private life, he emerged for the Peace Conference of 1861. In this convention he appeared as an ardent advocate of compromise. He was by now thoroughly conservative and had voted the Bell-Everett ticket in 1860. His part in the Conference was not very effective. From 1861 till his death he lived in retirement at Canandaigua.

[J. N. Granger, *Launcelot Granger of Newbury, Mass., and Suffield, Conn.: A Geneal. Hist.* (1893); *Autobiog. of Thurlow Weed* (2 vols., 1884), ed. by his daughter, Harriet A. Weed; *Wm. H. Seward: An Autobiog., from 1801 to 1834* (3 vols., 1891), ed. by F. W. Seward; De Alva S. Alexander, *Pol. Hist. State of N. Y.* (3 vols., 1906–09); F. B. Dexter, *Biog. Sketches Grads. Yale Coll.*, vol. VI (1912); J. D. Hammond, *Hist. of the Pol. Parties in the State of N. Y.* (3 vols., 1852); L. E. Chittenden, *A Report of the Debates and Proc. in the Secret Sessions of the Conference Convention, for Proposing Amendments to the Constitution of the U. S., Held at Washington, D. C., in Feb., A. D., 1861* (1864); obituary in *Buffalo Commercial Advertiser*, Aug. 31, 1868.]

D. P.

GRANGER, GIDEON (July 19, 1767–Dec. 31, 1822), lawyer, politician, and office-holder, a descendant of Launcelot Granger who was a taxpayer at Ipswich, Mass., in 1648, was born in Suffield, Conn. He was the second child of Gideon and Tryphosa (Kent) Granger, the former a graduate of Yale (1760) and a well-to-do lawyer and local politician. The younger Gideon was prepared for college by his pastor and graduated at Yale in 1787. He was admitted to the bar in 1789, began practise in Suffield, and on June 14, 1790, married Mindwell Pease of that town. One of his three children was Francis Granger [*q.v.*]. In 1792 he was elected to the legislature and, with the exception of two sessions, represented Suffield in that body for the next nine years. He took a prominent part in the adoption of the Common School Law of 1795, an enactment of considerable significance in educational history, the authorship of which is generally attributed to him. He early showed signs of a mild liberalism which made him the object of suspicion to the "high-toned Federalists" of the state, and his contributions published under the pseudonym of Algernon Sidney in the *American Mercury* of Hartford are among the first evidences of opposition to the rule of the famous "Standing Order." By 1798 he was definitely aligned with the Republicans and was an unsuccessful candidate for Congress. Two years later he gave vigorous support to Jefferson in the presidential contest. As a leader of the Republican minority in such a Federalist stronghold as Connecticut he had little chance of advancement in elective offices; accordingly in November 1801 he accepted President Jefferson's offer of the postmaster-generalship. He was on cordial terms with the President, whose letters indicate that Granger was entrusted with important party responsibilities in Connecticut, including distribution of the patronage.

As postmaster-general, Granger proved a successful administrator at a time when, owing to the western movement, the acquisition of Louisiana, and the rapid growth of population, the problems of the service were becoming increasingly difficult. He was also a pioneer in the practise of separating political opponents from the post-office payroll, although during his service the spoils system was still somewhat rudimentary. He held office until Mar. 17, 1814, when his resignation was forced by President Madison because of a disagreement in regard to the appointment of a Philadelphia postmaster, and also, probably, because of some suspicion regarding his loyalty to the President in the election of 1812. After resigning office he resumed the practise of law and moved to Whitestown (now Whitesboro), N. Y., where he engaged in professional business connected with the Phelps and Gorham land purchase. In 1816 he decided to settle at Canandaigua and the following year established his permanent residence there. He had for some time been an admirer of DeWitt Clinton and was especially interested in the Erie Canal project. He served in the New York Senate in 1820–21 in order to give further support to the construction of the canal. He might well have had a further career in New York politics but in 1822 his health began to fail and he died at Canandaigua after suffering intensely for several months.

He was the author of several political pamphlets which were widely circulated in New England for campaign purposes and are still frequently encountered in old libraries. Of these, *A Vindication of the Measures of the Present Administration* (1803) is a general defense of the Jefferson administration, with special emphasis on its economy and fiscal reform; *An Address to the People of New England* (1808) defends the Embargo, but is mainly an earnest plea for the Union, pointing out the disastrous effects in New England should dismemberment result from Federalist disloyalty; and *The Address of Epaminondas to the Citizens of the State of New York* (1819) is a defense of DeWitt Clinton's governorship. His writings, although occasionally somewhat heavy in style, indicate a keen, constructive intellect and a wide range of political and economic information.

[See F. B. Dexter, *Biog. Sketches Grads. Yale Coll.*, vol. IV (1907); J. N. Granger, *Launcelot Granger of Newbury, Mass., and Suffield, Conn.: A Geneal. Hist.* (1893); W. E. Rich, *The Hist. of the U. S. Post Office to the Year 1829* (1924), which contains interesting information on Granger's services as postmaster-general, based on official reports and unpublished material in the government archives and the Lib. of Cong.; *N. Y. Advertiser,* Jan. 11, 1823. *The Writings of Thomas Jefferson* (10 vols., 1892–99), ed. by P. L. Ford, contain some of the President's letters to Granger. Some of the latter's correspondence is preserved in the Jefferson Papers in the Lib. of Cong.] W. A. R.

GRANGER, GORDON (Nov. 6, 1822–Jan. 10, 1876), Union soldier, was born in Joy, Wayne County, N. Y., the son of Gaius and Catherine (Taylor) Granger. He was descended from Launcelot Granger, a taxpayer at Ipswich, Mass., in 1648. Entering West Point in 1841, he was graduated in 1845 and was commissioned a second lieutenant in the 2nd Infantry, but a year later was transferred to the newly organized Regiment of Mounted Riflemen (now the 3rd Cavalry). Accompanying Scott's army in the Mexican War, he was present at the siege of Vera Cruz, the battles of Cerro Gordo, Contreras, Churubusco, and Chapultepec, and the taking of the city of Mexico. His subsequent service before the Civil War was practically all on the western frontier, involving some minor Indian hostilities. He was promoted first lieutenant in 1852 and captain in 1861. He fought at Wilson's Creek in August 1861, and his conduct there secured him appointment in September as colonel of the 2nd Michigan Cavalry. In the operations against New Madrid and Island No. 10 during the spring of 1862 and in the advance upon Corinth, he commanded a brigade, having been appointed brigadier-general of volunteers early in the campaign (Mar. 26, 1862). He was made major-general of volunteers, Sept. 17, 1862, and commanded a division in garrison and in minor operations in Kentucky and Tennessee until the summer of 1863, when he joined Rosecrans's army for the campaign which culminated in the battle of Chickamauga (Sept. 19 and 20). "Had Granger never rendered any other service to the nation than he did on that illustrious occasion," said Gen. T. J. Wood, "he would have been justly entitled to its lasting gratitude"; and Gen. G. W. Cullum adds, "Granger's heoric bravery on that momentous Sunday afternoon in its inspiring influence was worth a thousand men." When the whole right of the Union army was swept away, leaving Thomas, the "Rock of Chickamauga," precariously holding the position with his single corps, Granger, without orders, left the pass he was guarding several miles in the rear, and hurried forward with all available troops. Attacking furiously with two brigades he drove back the Confederate troops on the right, who were already closing around Thomas's corps. Between three o'clock and sunset those two brigades lost forty-four per cent. of their strength; some regiments, muskets empty and cartridge boxes empty, were at last fighting only with the bayonet; but Thomas held his ground till nightfall, the army was saved from total wreck, and to Granger belongs no small share of the credit. During the remainder of the operations around Chattanooga, including the battle of Missionary Ridge, he commanded the IV Corps. He commanded sometimes a corps and sometimes a division in the relief of Knoxville, the operations against Fort Gaines and Fort Morgan, Ala. (August 1864), and the taking of Mobile (April 1865). He was mustered out of the volunteer service on Jan. 15, 1866, appointed a colonel of infantry in the regular army on July 28, 1866, and served as such until his death, which took place ten years later at Santa Fé, where he was stationed in command of the District of New Mexico. In 1869 he married Maria, daughter of Dr. Joseph P. Letcher of Lexington, Ky. Granger was outspoken and rough in manner, kindly and sympathetic at heart. His independence occasionally came near to insubordination, and at ordinary times he lacked energy. It was only in dire emergency that he would show the best of which he was capable. Therefore, "great in battle" (Gen. Rosecrans's phrase) though he was, Grant distrusted him, and was unwilling to give him an important command. Chickamauga is his greatest glory.

[G. W. Cullum, *Biog. Reg.* (3rd ed., 1891), II, 237; J. N. Granger, *Launcelot Granger of Newbury, Mass., and Suffield, Conn.: A Geneal. Hist.* (1893); Gen. T. J. Wood in *Seventh Ann. Reunion Asso. Grads. U. S. Mil. Acad.* (1876), p. 55; *Battles and Leaders of the Civil War* (1887–88), vol. III; Archibald Gracie, *The Truth About Chickamauga* (1911); *Official Records (Army)*, 1 ser., vols. III, VIII, X (pt. 1), XVI (pt. 1), XXIII (pt. 1), XXX (pts. 1, 2), XXXI (pts. 1, 2), XXXIX (pt. 1), *Daily New Mexican* (Santa Fé), Jan. 11, 12, 13, 1876.] T. M. S.

GRANT, ALBERT WESTON (Apr. 14, 1856–Sept. 30, 1930), naval officer, was born at East Benton, Me., of Scotch-English ancestry, the son of E. B. Grant and his wife, a Miss Stuart of Massachusetts. His boyhood was spent at Stevens Point, Wis., where in his infancy the family settled as pioneers. At seventeen he won a competitive appointment as midshipman, and in 1877 graduated from the Naval Academy, where with his powerful physique he was prominent in athletics and captain of the crew. Up to 1898 his career followed routine lines of alternate sea and shore duty, with promotion to ensign in 1881 and lieutenant in 1893. During the Spanish-American War he served in the battleship *Massachusetts,* which operated in the search for Cervera's squadron and the Santiago blockade, though at the final battle she was withdrawn for coaling. From September 1898 to 1900 he was in the *Machias.* Then, after promotion to lieutenant commander, 1900, and two years as instructor at the Naval Academy, he was in the Far East as executive of the *Oregon,* 1902–03, and commander of the *Frolic,* 1903–05. While in charge of instruction in seamanship at the Naval Academy, 1905–07, he prepared a book on tactics, *The School of the Ship* (1907), long used there as a text-book. After completing the War College course in October 1907, he commanded the *Arethusa,* 1907–08, and was then, despite his juniority for such duty, selected by Admiral Robley D. Evans as chief of staff in the world cruise of the fleet, 1908–09, in which position he was retained by Evans's successors. After his promotion to captain, 1909, he commanded the flagship *Connecticut* for a year. He was subsequently commandant of the Philadelphia Navy Yard until November 1912 and after brief service in charge of the Atlantic Reserve Fleet was sent to Newport News in July 1913, for inspection work on the *Texas,* then building, which he commanded in 1914–15. His most notable work in the navy was as commander of the submarine flotilla of the Atlantic Fleet during the pre-war period from June 1915 to July 1917, with promotion to rear admiral in September 1915 and additional duty in charge of all submarines. With characteristic zeal he threw himself into the task of building up the efficiency of boats and personnel, organized a training school for officers, established the submarine base at New London and the Panama base at Coco Solo, and in 1916 strongly urged before Congress increased submarine construction limited to larger types of 750–800 tons (*Hearings Before the House Committee on Naval Affairs,* 1916, pp. 1553–1678). From July 1917, he commanded Battleship Force 1, Atlantic Fleet, with the temporary rank of vice admiral, and during Admiral Mayo's inspection tour abroad, September–December 1918, he commanded the fleet in the western Atlantic, receiving the Distinguished Service Medal after the war. The western fleet was then the backbone of the navy, from which trained personnel were drawn for activities in every field. From March 1919 until his retirement on Apr. 14, 1920, Grant was commandant of the Washington Navy Yard. He had great energy and mental grasp, was "a horse for work," possibly over-inclined to supervision of detail (though his rigid insistence on attention to watertight integrity doubtless saved the *Minnesota* when hit by a mine off Virginia in 1918), kindly and humorous beneath a rough and bluff manner, thoroughly dependable, with talent for mechanics and special knowledge in the fields of electricity, submarines, and torpedoes. He was married, May 6, 1886, to Florence Southall Sharp of Norfolk, Va., and had three sons. After retirement he engaged in engineering business in Philadelphia, where his death, from a stomach ailment, occurred at the naval hospital. He was buried at Norfolk.

[*Who's Who in America,* 1930–31; obituary notices in *Army and Navy Jour.,* Oct. 4, 1930; *Army and Navy Reg.,* Oct. 4, 1930; *N. Y. Times,* Oct. 2, 1930; information as to certain facts from naval officers and members of the family.] A. W.

GRANT, ASAHEL (Aug. 17, 1807–Apr. 24, 1844), physician, missionary to the Nestorians, was born in Marshall, N. Y. He was the son of William and Rachel (Wedge) Grant, and a descendant of Matthew Grant who came from England to Dorchester, Mass., about 1630, and later was one of the founders of Windsor, Conn. As a youth Asahel worked on his father's farm, frequently with a book tied to the plow-handle. An injury to one of his feet, inflicted when he was cutting wood, removed his father's objections to his studying for a profession, since it handicapped him for agricultural labors. Accordingly, he set about preparing himself to become a physician, and after two or three terms in a near-by academy and a brief course in chemistry at Hamilton College, he began the study of medicine under Dr. Seth Hastings of Clinton, N. Y. Later he spent a year with Dr. Douglass of Utica. On Aug. 23, 1827, he married Electa Spafford Loomis, a native of Torrington, Conn., and soon afterward established himself in the township of Braintrim, Pa. After four years his wife died, leaving him with two sons, and he removed to Utica, N. Y., where he acquired from an older physician a large practise which he successfully maintained. An elder in the Presbyterian church, and deeply interested in religious work, he finally decided that he was more needed abroad than at home, and in October 1834 he offered his services to the American Board of Commissioners for Foreign Missions. Having expressed a preference for work among the Nestorians, he was assigned to that field, and sailed from Boston May 11, 1835, accompanied by his second wife, Judith (Lathrop) Grant, adopted daughter of Dr. William Campbell of Cherry Valley, N. Y.

The Nestorians, survivors of an ancient Christian sect, inhabited the district of Oroomiah (Urumiah) in western Persia, and the Kurdistan mountains. In 1833 the American Board had appointed Rev. Justin Perkins [*q.v.*] to labor among them, in the hope that the Nestorian church might "exert a commanding influence in the spiritual regeneration of Asia." When Grant arrived in October 1835 the two established the mission at Oroomiah. Dr. Grant's dispensary was at once crowded with patients, many of them from remote places. Both the poor and the nobility, Moslems and Nestorians, sought his services. The zeal with which he carried on his work was intensified by his belief that the Nestorians were the remnant of the lost tribes of Israel. The reasons for this conviction he set forth in *The Nestorians; or, The Lost Tribes: Containing Evidence of Their Identity; an Account of Their Manners, Customs, and Ceremonies; Together with Sketches of Travel in Ancient Assyria, Armenia, Media, and Mesopotamia; and Illustrations of Scripture Prophecy* (1841). While its arguments have not been accepted, the book is of value as a descriptive work. In 1839 Grant made a perilous journey into the almost inaccessible hills of Kurdistan, where he was cordially received by the patriarch, Mar Shimon. In 1840, his wife having died the year before, he returned to America with their four-year-old son, but, after a six months' stay, went back to Persia to establish a mission for the mountain Nestorians. Ashitha was chosen as a center, and a building was erected sufficient to accommodate the missionary families and a school. Subject to great hardships and in constant peril of his life, Grant traveled among the wild tribes of the mountains. His work was brought to an end in 1843, however, by an attempt of the Turks in conjunction with the Kurds to subjugate the Nestorians, who stubbornly refused to seek any alliances. A massacre occurred in which thousands of the Nestorians were slaughtered. Grant escaped to Mosul, where he ministered to the refugees until, in the spring of 1844, he sickened and died.

[Thos. Laurie, *Dr. Grant and the Mountain Nestorians* (1853), reviewed by J. L. Dimon in the *New Englander*, Aug. 1853; Justin Perkins, *A Residence of Eight Years in Persia Among the Nestorian Christians* (1843); A. H. Grant, *The Grant Family* (1898); Julius Richter, *A Hist. of Protestant Missions in the Near East* (1910); E. M. Bliss, *The Encyc. of Missions* (1891), vol. I; *Report of the Am. Board of Commissioners for Foreign Missions* (1844), p. 139; *Missionary Herald*, Aug. 1844.]

H. E. S.

GRANT, CLAUDIUS BUCHANAN (Oct. 25, 1835–Feb. 28, 1921), Michigan jurist, was born at Lebanon, York County, Me., the son of Joseph and Mary (Merrill) Grant. His earliest paternal American ancestor was James Grant, who came from England in 1645 and settled at Berwick, Me. Grant prepared for college at the Lebanon Academy and in October 1855 entered the University of Michigan. He was graduated from the literary college in 1859 with high honors and became a teacher of classics and later principal in the Ann Arbor High School. The outbreak of the Civil War wrought a definite change in his life. In 1862 he organized a military company and was elected its captain. The company was assigned to the 20th Regiment of Michigan Infantry. Grant was commissioned major, June 20, 1864, and colonel of the regiment, Dec. 20, 1864. He was present at the siege of Vicksburg and went to Virginia with Gen. Grant for the final campaign of the war. After being mustered out he returned to the University of Michigan to study law. He had been married on June 13, 1863, to Caroline L. Felch, daughter of the former governor, Alpheus Felch [*q.v.*], and upon his admission to the bar in 1866, he began the practise of law at Ann Arbor in partnership with his father-in-law. He was elected recorder in 1866, served as postmaster of Ann Arbor from 1867 to 1870, and was also a member of the board of education. From 1870 to 1874 he was a member of the Michigan House of Representatives. He was elected a regent of the University of Michigan in 1871, serving 1872–80. In 1873 he removed to Houghton and formed a law partnership with Joseph H. Chandler. From 1876 to 1878 he was prosecuting attorney of Houghton County.

In 1881, upon the creation of the 25th Judicial District, he was elected its first circuit judge and served until 1889, being so energetic in his campaign for the prosecution of law-breakers that when he left the bench no district in the state had a better reputation for law-observance. In the spring of 1889 he was elected a justice of the Michigan supreme court, a position he held for twenty years. He was chief justice in 1898, 1899, and 1908. As a member of the supreme court he threw all of his influence toward a broad construction of the provision in the Michigan constitution giving to the board of regents of the University of Michigan independent control of the affairs of the University. In 1910 he returned to the practise of law. He retired from active professional duties in 1913 and died some eight years later at St. Petersburg, Fla. Grant was notable in the history of Michigan by reason of the length, variety, and character of his service. The dominant note of his character was fearlessness. He was a champion of law and order and delivered hundreds of addresses on that subject.

[G. I. Reed, *Bench and Bar of Mich.* (1897); B. A. Hinsdale, *Hist. of the Univ. of Mich.* (1906); 216 *Mich. Reports* (Cooper); *Mich. Biogs.* (1924), I, 344; B. M. Cutcheon, comp., *The Story of the Twentieth Mich. Infantry* (1904); *Mich. Official Dir. and Legis. Manual,* 1909–10; *N. Y. Times,* Mar. 1, 1921; personal information from a daughter, Mrs. Chester D. Barnes.]

E. S. B—n.

GRANT, FREDERICK DENT (May 30, 1850–Apr. 11, 1912), soldier, son of Ulysses S. Grant [*q.v.*] and Julia (Dent) Grant, was born at St. Louis, Mo., while his father was a first lieutenant in the 4th Infantry. As a boy he saw considerable active military service, for he frequently accompanied his father in the field, notably in the Vicksburg campaign, where he received a slight bullet wound and later contracted an illness which was very nearly fatal. He entered West Point as a cadet in 1866, graduated in 1871, and was commissioned second lieutenant in the 4th Cavalry. He was on leave of absence for a year and a half, during which time he visited Europe, before joining his regiment on the Texas frontier. After a few months there he was detailed as aide to Lieut.-Gen. Sheridan—an assignment which at that time carried with it the pay and the temporary rank of lieutenant-colonel, and which he continued to hold until his resignation from the army in 1881. His regular station was in Chicago, at the headquarters of the Division of the Missouri, but he was in the field with the Yellowstone expedition in the summer of 1873, and with the Black Hills expedition in the summer of 1874. He married, Oct. 20, 1874, Ida M. Honoré, daughter of Henry Hamilton Honoré of Chicago. His promotion to first lieutenant dated from June 28, 1876. In 1878–79 he accompanied his father in his journey around the world. He resigned from the army in 1881, being then a first lieutenant in the 4th Cavalry, and in 1886 became president of the American Wood Working Company. President Harrison appointed him envoy extraordinary and minister plenipotentiary to the Austro-Hungarian Monarchy in 1889 and he served at Vienna until 1893, when his successor was appointed by President Cleveland. From 1895 to 1897 he was commissioner of police of New York City. He was mustered into the volunteer service in the Spanish-American War, May 2, 1898, as colonel of the 14th New York Infantry, and on May 27, 1898, was appointed brigadier-general of volunteers. He commanded a brigade in camp at Chickamauga Park, Ga., and after the termination of hostilities was stationed for some months in Porto Rico. Transferred to duty in the Philippines, he arrived at Manila in June 1899, and for nearly three years commanded a brigade in Luzon, operating against insurgents engaged in guerrilla warfare for a great part of the time. In April 1902 he took command of a brigade in Samar and Leyte, where he established civil government. Soon afterward he returned to the United States and took charge of the Department of Texas. Meanwhile, he had been appointed a brigadier-general in the regular army, Feb. 18, 1901, and on Feb. 6, 1906, he became major-general. After leaving Texas, he held other territorial commands, with headquarters at Chicago or New York; commanded the "blue army" in the Manassas maneuvers of 1904; and was in charge of the troops at the Jamestown Exposition of 1907. He died in New York and was buried at West Point.

[G. W. Cullum, *Biog. Reg.* (3rd ed., 1891), vol. III and *Supp.*, vol. V (1910); *Asso. Grads. U. S. Mil. Acad. Ann. Reunion,* 1912, pp. 149–52; *N. Y. Tribune,* Apr. 13, and *N. Y. Times,* Apr. 13 and 14, 1912.]

T. M. S.

GRANT, GEORGE BARNARD (Dec. 21, 1849–Aug. 16, 1917), inventor, mechanical engineer, the son of Peter Grant, a ship-builder, and his wife, Vesta Capen, was born in that part of Gardiner, Me., then known as Farmingdale. He was a great-grandson of Capt. Samuel Grant, one of the pioneers in the settlement of Maine, and was descended from Peter Grant of Inverness, Scotland, who with his three brothers came to Massachusetts Bay Colony from Plymouth, England, on the ship *Mary and John,* in May 1630. On his mother's side he was descended from Barnard Capen, who came from England about 1630 and in 1633 was granted land in Dorchester, Mass., where he died in 1638. George Barnard Grant prepared for college at Bridgton (Me.) Academy, studied for three terms in the Chandler Scientific School of Dartmouth College, and in 1869 entered the Lawrence Scientific School of Harvard College, where he completed the four years' course in three years, receiving the degree of B.S. with the class of 1873.

He had a strong scientific and mechanical mind and while a student at Harvard devoted much study to the invention of a calculating machine which would save time and labor in arithmetical computations involving addition, subtraction, multiplication and division. During his college course he published "On a New Difference Engine," in the *American Journal of Science* (August 1871) and took out his first patents with reference to calculating machines, one in 1872 and another in 1873. After his graduation he continued his study in this line, in which he was one of the pioneers in America, but was hampered by lack of funds to construct the machine embodying his invention, until through the efforts of Prof. Wolcott Gibbs [*q.v.*], Fairman Rogers of Philadelphia assumed the financial responsibility for the construction of the machine, which was duly completed and exhibited at the Centennial Exposition in Philadelphia in 1876. This calculating machine, known as "Grant's Difference Engine," was about five feet in height by eight feet in length; it weighed nearly 2,000 pounds and consisted of some 15,000 pieces; its cost was about $10,000, most of which was contributed by Rogers, who provided that the machine should be a donation to the University of Pennsylvania. In connection with Grant's development of the calculating machine he placed on the market two models, the first called the "Barrel," or "Centennial" model, which was shown at the Centennial Exposition together with the Difference Engine, and the other a "Rack and Pinion" model, of which 125 were sold. Both of these models were sturdy and reliable in operation and their use did much to break down the then prevalent deep-seated prejudice against the use of calculating machines in business.

Shortly after his graduation, as a result of his calculating-machine work, he started a machine-shop for gear-cutting in the old Waverly House in Charlestown, Mass., and became one of the founders of the gear-cutting industry in the United States. He later moved his shop to Boston and incorporated his business under the name of "Grant Gear Works Inc.," which he conducted as long as he lived, and which was continued under the same name after his death; he also established two other gear-cutting shops, one in Philadelphia, incorporated under the name of "Philadelphia Gear Works Inc.," which he conducted until he disposed of it in 1911, and the other in Cleveland, Ohio, incorporated under the name of "Cleveland Gear Works Inc.," which he disposed of after a few years.

From a financial point of view his business success was made in gear-cutting and gear-cutting machinery, in connection with which he took out various patents. He never ceased to study the problems of calculating machines, however, and during the last years of his life he conducted considerable experimental work in connection with the development of such machines. His publications include *Chart and Tables for Bevel Gears* (1885), *A Handbook on the Teeth of Gears . . . with Odontographs* (1885), and "Odontics, or the Theory and Practice of the Teeth of Gears" (*American Machinist,* Apr. 17, 1890–Dec. 25, 1890), later published separately as *A Treatise on Gear Wheels.* He was a resident of Malden, Mass., first in that part known as "Linden," in 1878, and in that part known as "Maplewood" in 1882. He moved his residence to Lexington in 1887, and later to Pasadena, Cal., but became a resident of Lexington again before his death. He traveled widely in both America and Europe, and in addition to his work in mechanical lines devoted much time, by way of avocation, to the study of botany. He died, unmarried, in Pasadena, Cal.

[C. A. Hayden, *The Capen Family* (1929); *Vital Records of Gardiner, Me., to the Year 1892* (2 vols., 1914–15); J. W. Hanson, *Hist. of Gardiner, Pittston, and West Gardiner* (1852); obituary in *Boston Transcript,* Aug. 18, 1917; information from Grant's stepbrother, Edwin A. Bayley, Esq., of Boston.] L. L. L.

GRANT, JAMES BENTON (Jan. 2, 1848–Nov. 1, 1911), metallurgist, banker, and governor of Colorado, was born on a plantation in Russell County, Ala. He was a son of Dr. Thomas McDonough Grant and Mary Jane (Benton) Grant. In January 1865, while still a boy, he joined the Confederate army. The close of the war found his family in reduced circumstances, but an uncle, James Grant, a lawyer of Davenport, Iowa, undertook to educate his nephews, and in December 1870 James went to Davenport. He soon entered the Iowa State College of Agriculture, later spent a year at Cornell University studying civil engineering, and in 1874 went to the School of Mines at Freiberg, Saxony, where he studied mining and metallurgy for two years. Equipped for his life-work, he traveled round the world seeking a place in which to practise his profession and selected Colorado. After an unfortunate start in 1876 in Clear Creek and Gilpin counties, he went to Leadville and in partnership with his uncle built the Grant Smelter. It opened for business on Oct. 1, 1878, with James Benton Grant as manager. With the growth of mining in Leadville the smelter prospered and its manager became a well-known citizen. On Jan. 19, 1881, he was married to Mary Matteson Goodell of Springfield, Ill. The smelter in Leadville was burned in 1882 and Grant moved to Denver, where, after a merger with the Omaha Smelting Company of Nebraska, the Omaha & Grant Smelter was opened in 1883. In 1899 the new company was consolidated with others to form the American Smelting and Refining Company, the largest of its kind in the United States. Grant was a director of the new concern. Although his capital was largely invested in smelting, he had a substantial interest in Leadville mines and was one of the engineers who launched the Yak Tunnel in the same district. He was also one of the organizers, in 1884, of the Denver National Bank and became its first vice-president, which position he held until his death.

In 1882 Grant was induced, after much persuasion, to run for governor on the Democratic ticket. In his favor he had means, personal popularity, and a reputation for absolute integrity. On the other hand he was young, a Democrat in a Republican state, and an ex-Confederate soldier in a Union district. The Republican and Greenback-Labor parties made unfortunate nominations, however, and Grant was elected, the first Democratic as well as the youngest governor of Colorado. His administration has been characterized as "a quiet, strong, tranquil government, almost without striking incident" (Frank Hall, *History of the State of Colorado,* 1891, III, 37). This was the beginning and end of his career in high political office; he had no ambitions in that direction. Throughout his residence in Denver, however, he was interested in educational matters. In 1891 he was elected a member of the Denver Board of Education, was chosen its president the following year, and ably filled that position from 1892 to 1899. He served also as one of the trustees of the University of Denver from 1884 to 1904, and was one of the organizers of the Colorado Scientific Society. In 1902 heart trouble caused him to curtail his activities. While maintaining his business interests in an advisory capacity, he spent a large part of the remainder of his life in the open, hunting, fishing, and watching over his ranch at Littleton. His death occurred at Excelsior Springs, Mo., in his sixty-fourth year.

[*After Forty Years: Hist. and Biog. Sketches of the Founders and Directors of the Denver Natl. Bank* (1924); *Portr. and Biog. Record of the State of Colo.* (1899); and *Semi-Centennial Hist. of the State of Colo.* (1913), vol. II; *Denver Post,* Nov. 2, 3, 4, 1911; *Denver Republican* and *Rocky Mountain News,* Nov. 2, 1911.]

J. F. W.

GRANT, JOHN THOMAS (Dec. 13, 1813–Jan. 18, 1887), Georgia capitalist, railroad builder, was descended from Daniel Grant, born in Virginia in 1716 of Scotch progenitors, who moved to Wilkes County, Ga., after the Revolution. That county had but recently been laid off and was on the frontier. Daniel Grant is said to have erected there the first Methodist Church in Georgia and the first school-house in the county. That he was an unusual man, far in advance of his fellow citizens, is indicated by the fact that he emancipated his slaves. His grandson, Daniel, married Lucy Crutchfield and settled in Greene County, where their son, John Thomas Grant, was born.

When John was a lad the family removed to Athens, Clarke County, so that the boy might be educated at the University of Georgia. His course was completed in 1833. The year following his graduation he was married to Martha Cobb Jackson, a grand-daughter of Gov. James Jackson. In 1844 he moved to Walton County, where he acquired a huge tract of land and developed one of the greatest plantations in ante-bellum Georgia. He owned 2,000 acres and more than a hundred slaves. His career, however, was rather that of a builder and promoter than a planter. He correctly visualized the future importance of railroads, threw himself with great energy into the new industry, and executed large building contracts for railways in Georgia, Alabama, Tennessee, Mississippi, Louisiana, and Texas. As a pioneer in this field he became rich and powerful, and merits an honorable place in the economic history of the South. He never entered politics, except to serve one term (1856) in the state Senate as a senator from Walton County. When his work was interrupted by the Civil War, he became an aide with the rank of colonel on the staff of his friend, Gen. Howell Cobb. At the close of hostilities, Grant and his son, William D. Grant, who had been a captain in the Confederate army, moved to Atlanta, where they became prominent among the business men who made that city an important commercial, financial, and manufacturing center. The Grants resumed the work of railroad building and became large holders of real estate in the city. Grant was a man of culture, a talented musician, and a patron of literature and the arts. He was a member of the Presbyterian Church and his purse was always open to worthy causes. He died in Atlanta in his seventy-fourth year.

[*Memoirs of Ga.* (2 vols., 1895); L. L. Knight, *A Standard Hist. of Ga. and Georgians* (6 vols., 1917); *Cat. of the Trustees, Officers, Alumni, and Matriculates of the Univ. of Ga.* (1906); *Atlanta Constitution*, Jan. 19, 20, 1887.] R. P. B—s.

GRANT, LEWIS ADDISON (Jan. 17, 1829–Mar. 20, 1918), Union soldier, was born at Winhall, Vt., the youngest son of James and Elizabeth (Wyman) Grant. His father and mother were both of Massachusetts stock. The boy's public-school instruction was supplemented by attendance at the Leland and Gray Seminary, of Townshend, and the Chester Academy. Then followed several years of school-teaching at places as widely separated as Washington, N. J., and Harvard and Boston, Mass., during which he studied law. In 1855 he was admitted to the Windsor County bar and two years later to practise before the Vermont supreme court. At Bellows Falls he entered into partnership with H. E. Stoughton and the firm soon had an extensive practise.

In the first year of the Civil War Grant volunteered and on Aug. 15, 1861, was commissioned major of the 5th Vermont Infantry. Within a few months after his regiment reached the front he was promoted lieutenant-colonel (Sept. 25) and a year later, colonel (Sept. 16, 1862). At Fredericksburg he was wounded while commanding the Vermont brigade. At the battle of Salem Heights, Va., May 3, 1863, he led his command over the enemy's breastworks and captured three battle flags. For this act he was awarded the Congressional Medal of Honor, May 11, 1893. Gallantry in action during the campaign before Richmond and in the Shenandoah Valley resulted in his promotion to brigadier-general Apr. 27, 1864, and major-general by brevet on Oct. 19 of the same year. In the battle of Cedar Creek (Oct. 19, 1864) he commanded a division. He was again wounded at Petersburg, Apr. 2, 1865. During the course of the war he led his regiment in six battles, his brigade in twenty. Having been honorably discharged, Aug. 24, 1865, in 1866 he was appointed lieutenant-colonel of the 36th Infantry in the regular army, but declined the commission because of his preference for civil life.

After the war he removed from Vermont to Chicago and in 1867 to Des Moines, Iowa, where he engaged in the business of placing loans on real estate. Later he settled at Minneapolis, where he continued in the practise of his profession. In 1890 the post of assistant secretary of war was tendered him at the instance of the Secretary, Redfield Proctor, who had served as a regimental commander under Grant in the Civil War. Grant accepted the appointment and held the office during the remainder of the Harrison administration and for some months after Cleveland's inauguration in 1893, several times serving as acting secretary. He was twice married: On Mar. 11, 1857, to S. Augusta Hartwell of Harvard, Mass., who died in 1859, and on Sept. 9, 1863, to Mary Helen Pierce of Hartland, Vt.

[L. S. Hayes, *Hist. of the Town of Rockingham, Vt.* (1907); O. F. R. Waite, *Vermont in the Great Rebellion* (1869) containing Grant's report of the battle of Fredericksburg; G. G. Benedict, *Vermont in the Civil War* (2 vols., 1886–88); F. B. Heitman, *Hist. Reg. and Dict. U. S. Army* (1903), vol. I; *Official Records (Army)*; *Who's Who in America*, 1914–15; *Minneapolis Morning Tribune*, Mar. 20, 1918.] W. B. S.

GRANT, PERCY STICKNEY (May 13, 1860–Feb. 13, 1927), clergyman of the Protestant Episcopal Church, was born in Boston, Mass., the son of Stephen Mason and Annie Elizabeth Newhall (Stickney) Grant. "All my people," he once testified, "immigrated from England in the 1630's, except one (John Grant) who came in 1707. There is nothing but colonial blood in my family. As a boy, too, I came under old-time American influence. I attended the public schools of Boston, and prepared for college at the Roxbury Latin School, founded in 1645." It was while he was a student at Harvard, from which he graduated in 1883, that Grant decided to enter the ministry, mainly "through a desire to be helpful." His father attended a Baptist church, where young Grant taught a negro Sunday-school class when he was fourteen years old. Dissatisfied with Baptist theology, he thought of joining the Congregationalists, "but I was much given to political history," he said in later years, "and cared a great deal about historical connections. About that time I came into touch with a professor from Trinity College, Hartford, who told me that if I was looking for a church that had a place in history, the Episcopal Church was the one I wanted" (*New York Times*, Feb. 14, 1927). Accordingly, he entered the Episcopal Theological School at Cambridge, at the same time continuing his studies at Harvard, and in 1886 received from the former institution the degree of B.D., and from the latter the degree of M.A. In the month of his graduation he was ordained deacon in the Protestant Episcopal Church. This same year he began his ministry in Fall River, Mass., where in May 1887 he was ordained priest. Here, in spite of numerous calls, he remained seven years as assistant minister of the Church of the Ascension (1886), and minister of St. Mark's (1887–93), during the last three years of which period he was also rector at Swansea. He became noted and greatly beloved for his work among the textile operatives. In 1893 he was invited to New York City and it was said, when he went away, that "not St. Mark's only, but all Fall River was his church."

In October 1893 he entered upon his ministry of thirty-one years as rector of the Church of the Ascension, Fifth Avenue and Tenth Street, New York. This church, possessed of a building of singular beauty and a constituency of wealth and culture, had long been a stronghold of fashionable orthodox churchmanship; but it had fallen on evil days. "I came to a bankrupt parish in a bankrupt neighborhood," said Grant. "Everybody was moving up town." As the parish members moved out, however, the common people moved in. Looking at his empty pews, the new rector thought of his worker-friends in Fall River and made the brave decision "to address not a little group of old parishioners, but the whole city of New York." Already, as a condition of his coming, he had stipulated that the church be a free church. Pews were surrendered as private property, and thrown open to the public. The Sunday morning services were shortened in favor of sermons on subjects of the day. The afternoon vespers, attended by two or three dozen forlorn souls, were transformed into musical services. Dark and empty on Sunday nights, the church was opened to the people for informal revivalistic meetings, which in 1907 were placed in charge of Alexander Irvine, socialist, who developed them into the famous Ascension Forum. The rector's policy was a success. Contributions to the church mounted from $18,000 to $65,000 a year. Debts were paid off and an endowment fund raised. Fifty-one separate extra-religious organizations in the parish made it a center of activity day and night. On Sunday mornings large congregations assembled to hear brave, free preaching; in the afternoons overflowing audiences gathered to listen to great music; in the evenings the church was packed with motley throngs of Christians and Jews, Protestants and atheists, socialists, communists, and radicals of every description, to hear experts talk on political or economic subjects. Questions and discussions lasted often until midnight.

In his early years Grant enjoyed the favor of his church authorities. Bishop Henry C. Potter [*q.v.*] admired the brilliant young rector, and in 1899 took him as his companion on a trip around the world. Bishop David H. Greer [*q.v.*] sustained him, though Grant was now openly attacking the divorce laws of the church, criticizing the House of Bishops for its conservatism, and looming as the militant leader of a radical wing among the clergy. After Greer's death the atmosphere changed. Grant had become a social as well as an ecclesiastical heretic. He was fighting with labor for improved working conditions and recognition of labor unions. He was doing unconventional things—participating in strikes, welcoming the unemployed to his church, expressing sympathy with extremists of the syndicalist and I. W. W. variety. During the World War, though no pacifist, he championed free speech, opposed the Espionage Act, organized demonstrations in favor of amnesty for political prisoners, stood by a Tolstoyan agitator, Bouck White, and shocked the nation by comparing a crowd of "red" deportees on the S. S. *Buford* with the Pilgrims on the *Mayflower.* In 1919 Bishop Charles S. Burch struck at Grant by attacking his forum. Attempts at adjustments failed, and two years later the forum closed. In this same year (1921) Grant resumed his battle against the divorce laws of the church, and dramatized the issue by announcing his engagement to Mrs. Rita de Acosta Lydig, a woman twice divorced. Bishop William T. Manning refused his consent to the marriage and announced that no clergyman over whom he exercised control would be allowed to perform the ceremony. On Jan. 14, 1923, Grant preached a sermon regarded as heretical on doctrinal grounds. Bishop Manning demanded retraction or withdrawal from the ministry. Grant published a long reply deemed unsatisfactory by the Bishop, but the controversy ended. Assailed now from without and within, blocked in his personal as well as ecclesiastical relations, in failing health, Grant resigned his church in June 1924, and retired to his country home at Bedford Hills. Here on Feb. 8, 1927, he was stricken with appendicitis, and five days later, at the Westchester Hospital, Mount Kisco, he died suddenly in his sleep.

Percy Stickney Grant was a rare combination of priest and prophet; he reverenced the tradition and historical continuity of his church, yet flamed with a passion for justice and liberty. He was an aristocrat in the elegance of his dress and bearing, his love of beauty and refinement, his exquisite culture, but a democrat in his belief in the common man. He was a poet who sought gladly the seclusion of his library, yet an untiring champion of righteousness who heeded every call on behalf of the outcast and oppressed. His publications reveal the wide range of his spirit: *Ad Matrem and Other Poems* (1905); *The Search of Belisarius* (1907); *Observations in Asia* (1908); *Socialism and Christianity* (1910);

The Return of Odysseus, A Poetic Drama (1912); *Fair Play for the Workers* (1918); *Fifth Avenue Parade and Other Poems* (1922); *Essays* (1922); *The Religion of Main Street* (1923). In 1908–09, he was University Preacher at Harvard, and in 1919 was chosen Phi Beta Kappa poet at Harvard. He died unmarried.

[*Who's Who in America*, 1926–27; *Class of 1883, Harvard Coll. Thirtieth Anniversary 1883–1913*; *Sixth Report* (n.d.), and other class reports; *N. Y. Times* and *Herald Tribune*, Jan. 20, 26, 1923; June 21, 1924, Feb. 14, 1927; N. Y. *Evening Post*, Feb. 1, 1923.]

J. H. H.

GRANT, ULYSSES SIMPSON (Apr. 27, 1822–July 23, 1885), general of the armies, president of the United States, was the descendant of a long line of hard-working, undistinguished Grants, of whom the earliest in America, Matthew Grant, landed in Massachusetts with his wife, Priscilla, in 1630. The progeny of this Puritan clung to New England until Capt. Noah Grant, having served throughout the Revolution, emigrated to Pennsylvania in 1790 and later to Ohio. The Captain's second son, Jesse Root Grant, learned the trade of tanner and established himself at Point Pleasant, Ohio, where in 1821 he married Hannah Simpson, the daughter of a farmer. She had youth, strength, and health, and stood in need of them during the years of hard work and meager comforts that followed. In their little two-roomed frame cabin the future president was born. He was baptized Hiram Ulysses Grant. His youth was spent at Georgetown, Ohio, whither the family moved when he was a year old.

From his mother he seems to have inherited many of the traits that distinguished him. She was a silent, undemonstrative, religious woman, of great common sense and good judgment. The father, Jesse Grant, was an aggressive, hard-working person whose shrewdness and thrift were rewarded, in the passage of time, by business successes. Almost entirely self-taught, he desired for his children the educational opportunities that had been denied him. From the time he was six years old until he was seventeen, young Ulysses regularly attended school, but this did not exempt him from labor. Detesting the tannery, he was set to work on his father's farm. Like many silent people, the boy had no difficulty in understanding and in securing the obedience of dumb animals. His love of horses amounted to a passion. At seven he was hauling wood with a team; at eleven he was strong enough to hold a plow; thereafter, until seventeen, he writes, "I did all the work done with horses" (*Personal Memoirs*, I, 26). During these years he developed the qualities that later marked him—fearlessness, self-reliance, resourcefulness, determination. In person he was rather short but sturdy and well-muscled; he was modest, reticent, clean-minded, and did not use profanity; he abhorred hunting and the taking of animal life.

In the winter of 1838–39, Jesse Grant applied for and received for his son an appointment to the United States Military Academy. The information roused no enthusiasm in the boy. In due time, however, he departed and, after several wonderful days in Philadelphia and New York, registered at West Point as Ulysses Hiram Grant. He had transposed his given names, fearing that his initials "H. U. G." would make him an object of ridicule. At West Point he was informed that his congressman had reported his name as Ulysses Simpson Grant. Failing to obtain a correction from the authorities, he accepted uncomplainingly the designation bestowed upon him (Edmonds, *post*, pp. 35–37; Wilson, *post*, pp. 7, 21–22). No high lights marked Grant's four years at West Point. Throughout this time he held a place near the middle of his class, though his work in mathematics was above average. As a rider he had no peer among the cadets, but in other respects he was colorless. Quiet, unobstrusive, as tidy as necessary, "Sam" Grant sought neither honors nor popularity. He had no intention of remaining in the army.

Upon graduation in June 1843, the best rider at West Point requested a commission in the cavalry but, as there was no vacancy in that arm, he reported for duty with the 4th Infantry. He served two years in Missouri and Louisiana, and in September 1845 joined Gen. Taylor's small but efficient army at Corpus Christi, Tex. Later it moved to the Rio Grande River where a conflict with the Mexicans occurred. With the Mexican War, Grant was never in sympathy (*Personal Memoirs*, I, 53). Nevertheless, he took part actively in all of Taylor's battles except the last, Buena Vista. At Monterey he participated, as the only mounted man, in the charge of his regiment and repeatedly distinguished himself, making at one time a dash, mounted, through the city held by the enemy to obtain ammunition for the troops. For Taylor, Grant conceived a great admiration (*Ibid.*, I, 100). He saw this rough and ready Indian fighter, individualized by bluntness, lack of ostentation, and by the uniform success of his operations, advance from a seat in the saddle to the president's chair. Unconsciously perhaps, he seems to have patterned his own habits and dress on those of Taylor (Coolidge, *post*, p. 30). After Monterey, Grant, with his regiment, was transferred to Gen. Scott's army, and as regimental quartermaster made the long march from Vera Cruz to Mexico city. He took part in the hand-to-hand fighting at Molino del Rey and in the attack on the gates of the capital city, receiving mention in division orders and in brigade and regimental reports for bravery. From the war Grant emerged a first lieutenant and brevet captain, but no less averse to a military life than he had always been.

As soon as his regiment was settled in its new station in Mississippi he obtained leave and, on Aug. 22, 1848, married Julia Dent, to whom he had become engaged shortly after graduation. The wedding journey ended at his new station, Sackett's Harbor, N. Y., where the southern bride with unimpaired cheerfulness made the best of a northern winter. The year 1852 witnessed his departure with his regiment for the Pacific coast by way of the Isthmus of Panama, a region so infested with disease that Mrs. Grant, who in 1850 had given birth to a son, did not make the journey. The transit of the Isthmus was a nightmare. Mules could not be obtained. Delays occurred. Cholera broke out and many died. Grant, the quartermaster, buried the dead, cheered the living, and by his energy and resourcefulness prevented a greater loss of life. From the mushroom, San Francisco, the regiment was ordered to Fort Vancouver, near the present city of Portland. Here Grant remained until September 1853, when promotion to a captaincy took him to Humboldt Bay, Cal. No place more dreary than this tiny frontier settlement can be imagined. With little to do, lonely as only the inarticulate can be lonely, hungry for his wife and children whom he saw no prospect of supporting on his pay, Grant at times drank more than he should have done (Coolidge, p. 35; Edmonds, p. 74; Meade, *post,* II, 162–63; W. C. Church, in *Army & Navy Journal,* June 6, 1908). A warning from his commanding officer was followed by his resignation, which was promptly accepted by Jefferson Davis, then secretary of war (Old Records Section, Adjutant General's Office).

In July 1854, after eleven years of service, Grant was out of the army, out of money, without an occupation, and a long way from home. Late in August he joined his family in St. Louis. In the six years that followed he was successively farmer, real-estate agent, candidate for county engineer, and clerk in a custom house. In none of these occupations was he successful. Finally, after a visit to his father, he was given a clerkship in a leather store conducted by two of his brothers at Galena, Ill. He did not, however, remain very long. The turn in the tide had arrived. Following the bombardment of Fort Sumter in April 1861 and Lincoln's call for volunteers, Grant presided at a mass-meeting in Galena. He declined the captaincy of a company but announced that a war would find him in the service.

There followed a period of about six weeks during which he strove without success to find in the military hierarchy a place that befitted his training and experience. He was successively drillmaster of the Galena company, clerk in the state adjutant-general's office, and mustering officer. He wrote to the adjutant-general at Washington requesting the command of a regiment but never received a reply. He spent two futile days in Cincinnati cooling his heels in the outer office of George B. McClellan, then considered the coming man. Finally, in June, Gov. Yates appointed him colonel of the 21st Illinois Volunteers. In a few days Grant had the regiment in camp at Springfield, hard at work. In a month it was ordered to Mexico, Mo., where, in August, much to Grant's surprise, he was appointed brigadier-general (*Personal Memoirs,* I, 254; Wilson, p. 86; Woodward, *post,* p. 189).

In 1861 Illinois and the states west of the Mississippi constituted what was known as the Western Department, under the command of Maj.-Gen. John C. Frémont. The latter, in September, placed the new brigadier in charge of a district with headquarters at Cairo, Ill. Throughout the next two months recruits poured in until Grant had nearly 20,000 men. The Confederate Gen. Polk had converted Columbus, Ky., about twenty miles south of Cairo, into a strong fortification which controlled the traffic on the Mississippi. Across the river lay Belmont, a Confederate camp. Early in November, Frémont directed Grant to make a demonstration down the river toward Columbus. By converting this demonstration into an attack on Belmont, Grant nearly ruined a promising career. Having defeated the enemy on landing, his 3,100 boisterous recruits got out of hand and began to loot the captured camp. Meanwhile the Belmont garrison, reenforced from Columbus, had been rallied and interposed between the Union troops and their boats. Grant fired the tents to regain the attention of his men. They reformed, forced their way through the enemy, and, under heavy Confederate fire, piled pell-mell into the boats which hastily pulled out. Their commander was the last to embark (Badeau, *post,* pp. 17–18; *Personal Memoirs,* I, 273, 279; *Battles and Leaders,* I, 351).

At this time the Confederates under Gen. Albert Sidney Johnston held the West Tennessee border and protected their great supply depot at

Nashville by a line from Bowling Green, Ky., westward to Columbus. The flanks were strongly held, but the center was lightly guarded by Fort Donelson on the Cumberland River and Fort Henry on the Tennessee. Grant proposed to Gen. Henry W. Halleck, who had succeeded Frémont, the capture of Fort Henry (*Personal Memoirs,* I, 287). He purposed to penetrate Johnston's vulnerable center, capture the forts, and cut in two the enemy's forces. In making this proposal, he was probably unaware that, since November 1861, Gen. Buell at Louisville had repeatedly urged upon both McClellan and Halleck, without success, a similar movement in connection with a land movement against Nashville (*Official Records, Army,* 1 ser., VII, 451, 457, 487, 520, 527, 531). The recurrence of these recommendations caused Halleck to study the situation. Appreciating that the capture of the forts would cause the abandonment of Columbus, a place too strong to attack, he acceded to Grant's second request of Jan. 28, in which Commodore A. H. Foote [*q.v.*] joined (*Official Records, Army,* 1 ser., VII, 121; Badeau, p. 27; Wilson, pp. 103–04; Woodward, p. 215).

Preceded by gunboats, the expedition of 17,000 men started up the Tennessee five days later. Fort Henry surrendered to the gunboats, whereupon two of them steamed twelve miles upstream and destroyed the Memphis and Ohio bridge. Donelson, twelve miles eastward, was Grant's next objective. Heavy rains delayed his start until Feb. 12, but by the 13th his army had invested the fort, then held by about 17,000 men. Foote attacked with the gunboats on the 14th, but was so roughly handled that he withdrew. In the freezing dawn of Feb. 15, Grant, at the request of the wounded Foote, boarded the flagship for a conference. While this was in progress the Confederates attacked heavily and by 9:00 A. M. had driven back and broken the Union right and most of the center. The road was open for their escape.

While returning to his headquarters from the flagship, Grant was informed of the situation. A gallop along the line determined his conduct. With his right and center in confusion, he decided, with rare courage, to attack with his left. His order to Gen. C. F. Smith to assault at once was magnificently executed. By nightfall the Union troops had possession of the entire outer line of Confederate trenches. The fate of the garrison was sealed. Gen. Simon B. Buckner on the following morning requested an armistice. Grant replied: "No terms except an unconditional and immediate surrender can be accepted. I propose to move immediately upon your works" (Badeau, p. 48). So Buckner, who in 1854 had loaned Grant the money to rejoin his family (Wilson, pp. 77–78; Coolidge, p. 37; Edmonds, p. 78), surrendered over 14,000 men to his former classmate. When the telegraph announced this victory, the North became frantic with joy. President Lincoln at once named Grant a major-general of volunteers and the Senate promptly confirmed the nomination.

Buell's advance into Tennessee with about 37,000 effectives and Grant's control of the Tennessee determined the Confederates to seek a union of their forces south of that river. About 40,000 effectives were concentrated at Cornith, Miss., to crush Grant's army before it could be reënforced by Buell. A brief misunderstanding between Halleck and Grant, early in March, resulted in the replacement of the latter by Gen. C. F. Smith. On Mar. 17, Grant was reinstated (*Personal Memoirs,* I, 327; Badeau, I, 60, 65; *Official Records, Army,* 1 ser., X, pt. 2, pp. 3, 5, 6, 15, 17, 32; Woodward, pp. 225–27). While Smith commanded, he took the army up the Tennessee River, established headquarters at Savannah, and began operations for the capture of Corinth. When Grant rejoined, he retained the headquarters at Savannah, for no apparent good reason, and ordered the concentration at Pittsburg Landing of all his forces (about 38,000 men), except General Lew Wallace's division of 5,000 which was left at Crump's Landing, five miles below Pittsburg.

Although both Grant and his chief lieutenant, Sherman, were aware that the numerically superior Confederate army was only twenty-two miles distant, no intrenchments were constructed about the Union camp, no line of defense was established, no adequate system of reconnaissance instituted, no plan of action prepared. From Mar. 17, when Grant reassumed command, to Apr. 6, when Johnston's army attacked, the Union commander was in ignorance of the movements of his foe. Grant says: "When all reinforcements should have arrived I expected to take the initiative by marching on Corinth. . . . I regarded the campaign . . . as an offensive one and had no idea that the enemy would leave strong intrenchments to take the initiative" (*Personal Memoirs,* I, 332). Less than one and a half miles from Sherman's headquarters, Johnston's soldiers formed line of battle on the afternoon of Apr. 5, and, without discovery, slept all night on their arms. That afternoon Grant had said: "There will be no fight at Pittsburg Landing; we will have to go to Corinth" (*Official Records, Army,* 1 ser., X, pt. 1, p. 331). That evening he had sent a telegram to Halleck: "I have scarcely the faintest idea of an attack (general one) being made upon us, but will be prepared should such a thing take place" (*Ibid.,* X, pt. 1, p. 89). Before 6:00 A. M. on the 6th, the Confederates attacked. Notwithstanding desperate efforts, the Union lines were forced steadily back.

Grant, breakfasting at Savannah nine miles from the battle-field, heard the roar of the guns and hastened to Pittsburg Landing. On the battle-field he rode from division to division, encouraging officers and men, but otherwise exercising no influence on the combat (*Personal Memoirs,* I, 343). He sent an urgent appeal to Buell and ordered Lew Wallace to march to the battle. Johnston was killed about 2:30 in the afternoon. Beauregard, his successor, issued an order at 5:30, suspending the attack. At this time the leading regiments of Buell's army were moving into position on the heights above the landing to repel Confederate attacks. Grant spent the stormy night of Apr. 6 on the river bank, nursing a swollen ankle. Lew Wallace arrived about 7:00 P. M. on his extreme right. Three divisions of Buell's army took position on the left. With 25,000 fresh men in line, there was no question as to the outcome of the struggle when it opened on the following morning. Resisting stubbornly, the Confederates were driven back all day and by nightfall were in full retreat toward Corinth. There was no pursuit.

No battle fought in the West ranks with Shiloh in severity. No major battle displayed less generalship, and none more courage on the part of the enlisted men. Doubtless, on the night of Apr. 6, Grant, sitting under a tree in the rain, reviewed in his mind the things he had left undone. The results of this mental castigation became evident in the next campaign. In the storm of denunciation that followed, the captor of Donelson offered no excuses. Lincoln refused to relieve him, saying: "I can't spare this man—he fights."

During the remainder of 1862, Grant, at Corinth, devised plans for taking Vicksburg, the capture of which would give the Union army control, not only of the Mississippi, but also of the Confederacy's only remaining railroad leading east from that river. In November, Grant with 30,000 men marched south from Memphis in his first effort to take Vicksburg. Sherman's force was to cooperate by moving down the Mississippi. Sherman was defeated. Grant's movement was halted when the enemy cut his railroad line of communications and burned his supply depot at Holly Springs, Miss. Back again in Memphis, he began on Jan. 20, 1863, the formation of the second expedition. In this, several projects were attempted, all of which contemplated the cutting of waterways for placing the troops, by boats, south of Vicksburg, without encountering the Confederate river batteries.

Convinced, by the end of March, of the impracticability of these schemes, Grant decided to march the army, west of the river, to a point below the fortifications and then transport it by steamers to the eastern bank. Rear Admiral David D. Porter [*q.v.*] undertook to run the batteries with his iron-clad gunboats and transports and then place them at Grant's disposal. The plan was successfully carried out. On Apr. 30 the invading force, consisting of 20,000 men, landed at Bruinsburg. It was one of the boldest movements in modern warfare (Wilson, p. 169). Abandoning his communications, Grant had placed his numerically inferior force in the heart of a hostile country. Behind him was a wide river controlled above and below his landing place by the enemy; between him and Memphis, his base, were Johnston's and Pemberton's armies. Knowing that he must live off the country he immediately sent out foraging parties. Before the three days' rations carried by his men had been consumed, ample supplies were on hand, and the army did not thereafter lack food.

Shiloh showed Grant at his worst; Vicksburg showed him at his flawless best. He skilfully interposed his army between the forces of Johnston and Pemberton and struck quickly and vigorously. With his right he defeated Johnston and drove him out of Jackson; with his left he defeated Pemberton at Champion's Hill. Pemberton withdrew to the fortifications of Vicksburg on May 20, to emerge therefrom as a prisoner of war. The garrison never had a chance. The surrender took place on July 4, 1863. When, ten days thereafter, Port Hudson fell, the Mississippi was Unionist from source to mouth. The Confederacy was cut in two.

During the months of the campaign, Grant had been denounced by the newspapers and would perhaps have lost the confidence of Lincoln but for the favorable reports of Charles A. Dana [*q.v.*], who "probably saved Grant's career" (Woodward, pp. 291–93; J. H. Wilson, *The Life of Charles A. Dana,* 1907, p. 193). Now, after the completion of one of the most brilliant military operations in American history, he was again acclaimed and promoted, this time to major-general in the regular army; and again, as at Corinth, his army was scattered. In September, by Halleck's direction, he ordered four divisions, under Sherman, eastward to cooperate with Rosecrans in the relief of Chattanooga. Before these started, Rosecrans had been badly defeated at Chickamauga and penned in Chattanooga while Bragg, perched on Missionary Ridge and Lookout Mountain, in control of all approaches waited for the Union army to starve into surrender.

In this plight the Administration turned to Grant. Secretary of War Stanton met him en route to Louisville in October, conferred on him command of all the territory from the Alleghanies to the Mississippi except the southwestern section, and enabled him to replace Rosecrans by Thomas (*Personal Memoirs,* II, 17–19; Wilson, pp. 184–85). Grant proceeded to Chattanooga, where he found the Union army not only perilously close to starvation but almost without shoes and clothing for the coming winter. Acting on plans that had been prepared before his arrival (Coppée, *post,* pp. 165–68; Edmonds, p. 197, note; *Battles and Leaders,* III, 717–18), Grant, within five days, had opened communications with his base at Nashville. The army was soon reclothed, well fed, and supplied with ammunition.

As soon as Sherman arrived at Bridgeport on Nov. 14, Grant fixed Nov. 23 for the execution of his plan for attacking Bragg. Accordingly, Thomas on that day took Orchard Knob, the right of the Confederate outpost line. On the 24th, Hooker captured the point of Lookout Mountain and Sherman seized the extreme right of Missionary Ridge. When, the following morning, Thomas attacked the Confederate center, his men, as directed, captured the first line of rifle pits; then, without orders, in a tremendous burst of patriotic fervor, swept up Missionary Ridge to its summit and drove their enemies from the field. Pursuit begun by Sherman was halted by Grant when Bragg's defeated army, the only obstacle between the Union forces and Atlanta, intrenched at Dalton, Ga.

A gold medal, the thanks of Congress, and the grade of lieutenant-general, the latter to carry with it the command of the armies of the United States, were bestowed on Grant, together with the adulation of a grateful nation. He was undeniably the man of the hour. Repeatedly urged to become a candidate for the presidency, he invariably refused, stating that he had but one desire—to end the war (Woodward, pp. 307–08; Coolidge, p. 142). Lincoln sent for him, wanting to judge for himself what manner of man Grant was. He saw a short, round-shouldered, rather scrubby-looking man in a tarnished major-general's uniform, with clear, resolute, blue eyes, a heavy jaw, and an inscrutable face partially covered by rough, light-brown whiskers which served to conceal its strength (Badeau, II, 20; Coolidge, p. 146). Lincoln liked him, believed in him, and remained his steadfast friend.

When Grant became general-in-chief, the Union forces stood in need of nothing so much as unity of plan and coordination of effort. The new leader supplied both. For the first time since the beginning of the war a plan of action was prepared that covered the concerted movements of all the Union forces. In his letter of Apr. 4, 1864, to Sherman (*Personal Memoirs,* II, 130), Grant proposed three simultaneous major movements: that of Meade's Army of the Potomac against Lee's army; that of Butler's Army of the James against Lee's communications and Richmond; that of Sherman's Army of the Tennessee against Johnston's army and Atlanta (Wilson, p. 223). For these he had available about 253,000 men. Grant's policy, to which he consistently adhered, was to use the greatest number of troops practicable against the armed forces of the enemy; to hammer those forces and their resources until by mere attrition, if in no other way, there should be nothing left to them but submission. On May 4 all the armies moved. Throughout the campaigns that followed, Grant, from his headquarters with the Army of the Potomac, kept in touch with them, directing and coordinating their operations toward the common end.

Meade's army crossed the Rapidan and bivouacked the night of May 4 in the Wilderness. Meade hoped to pass its tangled depths before Lee could intercept him, but that alert foe had decided that the Union army should fight in a locale where the terrain compensated for his weakness. He had 65,000 men to Meade's 118,000. When Meade, early on May 5, moved southward, he was struck in flank by Lee. For two days the opponents, in the desperate battle that ensued, swayed back and forth through the dense forest, without material advantage to either. Undeterred by his appalling losses (17,666, *Battles and Leaders,* IV, 248), Grant then determined to march by Lee's right flank and interpose between him and Richmond. Sherman called this decision "the supreme moment of his [Grant's] life" (*Battles and Leaders,* IV, 248). But Lee, informed of the movement, beat his opponent to the objective—Spotsylvania Court House.

At Spotsylvania, after another bloody conflict, and again after North Anna, Grant repeated successfully his tactics of passing by Lee's right. When Lee, however, only twenty miles from Richmond, assumed an intrenched position past Cold Harbor to the Chickahominy, Grant realized that his former tactics would no longer avail, that he must attack Lee in front or abandon the campaign north of the James. A break through Lee's center would probably result in the capture of Richmond and possibly in the disintegration of Lee's army. So Grant attacked at Cold Harbor and lost nearly 6,000 men in an hour (Steele, p. 502; *Battles and Leaders,* IV, 148). Satisfied that he could not drive Lee from his intrenched position, he called off the attack and, on the night of June 12, withdrew from Lee's front to cross the James River. The Wilderness campaign was ended. The terrific losses of the Army of the Potomac were made up by heavy reënforcements, but in the public mind Grant's prestige was lowered (Woodward, p. 325). He had not defeated Lee during the entire campaign and had been regularly outmaneuvered (Meade, II, 202), yet his policy of attrition had worn down his enemy and robbed him of the initiative. After the battle of the Wilderness, Lee did not again assume the offensive.

In conception and execution, the withdrawal from Lee's front and the movement across the James was a brilliant military achievement. The army began its silent march after dark on June 12. By midnight of the 16th it was south of the river. Lee was completely deceived and for four days lost his foe (*Battles and Leaders,* IV, 541; Lee, *post,* p. 348). Finally realizing what had occurred, he brought his army south of Richmond. The long-drawn-out siege of Petersburg was on—a siege made necessary by the failure of the left wing, under Butler, to capture Petersburg and invest Richmond during the progress of the Wilderness campaign (Adams, *post,* pp. 269–75; Coolidge, p. 170; Wilson, p. 223; Woodward, pp. 318–19, 346–48). From June 18, 1864, to Apr. 2, 1865, the Army of the Potomac invested Petersburg, sapping, mining, assaulting, cutting Lee's avenues of supply and sending out flanking expeditions far to the west. In this long siege the Confederate commander, having the advantage of interior lines, was able to meet every attack that Grant made with a force large enough to stop it. But the siege was doing its work. The Confederate army stood desperately in need of food and transportation. Sherman's men, marching through Georgia, found it a land of plenty while Lee's heroic army was starving in the trenches.

Sheridan's victory at Five Forks on Apr. 1, 1865, marked the beginning of the end. On the following day Grant assaulted the Confederate right, breaking it and forcing it back. That night Lee's army abandoned Petersburg and Richmond and marched westward, hoping to join Gen. Joseph E. Johnston's army. Grant paralleled the march and sent Sheridan's cavalry far ahead to carry on a running fight and cut off Lee's retreat. At Appomattox Court House, Sheridan stood across Lee's path. The end was at hand. On Apr. 9, 1865, Lee surrendered the Army of Northern Virginia on Grant's terms, which were so considerate and magnanimous that they were never questioned by the Confederate chieftain (*Personal Memoirs,* II, 483–94). Seventeen days later Johnston surrendered his army to Sherman. The Civil War was over.

Grant's greatness lay in his ability to visualize the war in its essentials. He saw that as long as the Confederacy was an undivided unit its military forces and resources could be shifted to any point where they were needed. He saw, furthermore, that no great success could result from the capture of localities, that success could come only by the destruction of armies. As general-in-chief his strategy was sound: to cut the Confederacy into fragments; to engage all its armies at the same time so that one could not reënforce another; to destroy those armies by following them wherever they might go and by pounding them to pieces. To these principles he adhered and by them he won.

[*Personal Memoirs of U. S. Grant* (2 vols., 1885–86); *Official Records* (*Army*); Old Records Section, Adjutant-General's Office; A. Badeau, *Mil. Hist. of Ulysses S. Grant* (3 vols., 1868–81); Jas. G. Wilson, *General Grant* (1897); W. C. Church, "The Truth about Grant," *Army and Navy Jour.*, June 6, 1908; F. S. Edmonds, *Ulysses S. Grant* (1915); L. A. Coolidge, *The Life of Ulysses S. Grant* (1922); W. E. Woodward, *Meet General Grant* (1928); J. F. C. Fuller, *The Generalship of Ulysses S. Grant* (1929); J. H. Smith, *The War with Mexico* (2 vols., 1919); *Battles and Leaders of the Civil War* (4 vols., 1887–88); J. C. Ropes, *The Story of the Civil War* (4 vols., 1894–1913); J. F. Rhodes, *Hist. of the U. S.*, vols. III–V (1893); C. F. Adams, "Some Phases of the Civil War," in *Studies Military and Diplomatic* (1911); M. F. Steele, *Amer. Campaigns* (1922); H. Coppée, *General Thomas* (1893); Fitzhugh Lee, *General Lee* (1894); Jas. Longstreet, *From Manassas to Appomattox* (1896); George Meade, *Life and Letters of George Gordon Meade* (1913).]
C. A. B.

The subsidence of conflict left Grant in command of the army of the United States, in a position under the President and the Secretary of War which was never clearly defined. He had been transferred rapidly from volunteer and temporary status to a commission in the permanent establishment; and in 1866 Congress revived the rank of general, unused since 1799, in the certainty that President Johnson would nominate Grant for the post. Trusting Grant more completely than it did the President, the radical Congress in the following year blocked removals from office by the Tenure of Office Act and required that all army orders must pass through the office of the commanding general. Johnson was as ready to give as Grant was to accept the position, for he was at the moment courting Grant. He forced him, in the month after the appointment, to join the presidential party in the memorable "swing round the circle," hoping to gain popularity from citizens who saw Grant on the same platform with himself. Grant declined to be ordered on a mission to Mexico for the President, and tried, but without skill, to avoid giving the prestige of his own name to Johnson's plans.

Demobilization, a shapeless affair, took place under Grant. The policing of the western border and the protection of the construction camps of the continental railroads came under his control; yet he was convinced that the whole Indian policy of the United States was corrupt and wrong. His most delicate duty, however, was in connection with the administration of the Reconstruction acts, passed over Johnson's veto and enforced by the army until such time as Congress was ready to declare the Confederate states restored. Grant had toured the South for the President, and thought the "mass of thinking men of the south" were willing to accept the result of the war (*Senate Executive Document No. 2,* p. 106, 39 Cong., 1 Sess.); but he supported Stanton who had become anathema to Johnson. Protesting the suspension of Stanton, Grant assumed the duties of secretary of war *ad interim,* Aug. 12, 1867. For the next five months he was his own superior officer, for he retained the actual command as general. But he enraged Johnson by surrendering the secretaryship to Stanton after the Senate had declined to concur in the latter's dismissal. Johnson raised an issue of personal veracity (R. W. Winston, *Andrew Johnson,* 1928, p. 418), asserting that Grant had promised not to surrender the office but to force a case for judicial interpretation of the Tenure of Office Act. The merit of the issue seems beyond historical determination, but it ended the relations of the two men. Grant never forgave the President, and upon the occasion of his own inauguration in 1869 declined to ride in the same carriage with his predecessor (H. Garland, *Ulysses S. Grant,* 1920, p. 385).

The course of events of the spring of 1868 made Grant the inevitable nominee of the Republican party for the presidency. He had become the rallying figure for the opponents of Andrew Johnson, and was already the outstanding character in American life. He had no real party affiliation. Only once had he voted for president, and that time for James Buchanan, "because I knew Frémont" (L. A. Coolidge, *Ulysses S. Grant,* 1917, p. 270). But he embodied the forces that maintained the Union. Without enthusiasm he allowed himself to be nominated by the Republicans. He disliked politics as he disliked war; he had no vindictive spirit toward the soldiers who had sustained the Confederacy, but he had no intention of permitting the defeated leaders to direct the policy of the United States. He was aware that election would mean retirement from the comfortable salary and allowances of the general of the army (nearly $25,000 a year) and an exchange of a life post for the presidency, which meant eight years at most. He accepted the nomination in a brief note, four words of which have constituted his contribution to American opinion: "Let us have peace." His companion on the ticket was a popular Indiana politician, Schuyler Colfax.

Grant was elected president in 1868, losing the electoral votes of only eight states, though the popular majority was much smaller than these figures would indicate. He had taken no active part in the canvass and he admitted no one, not even his wife, to his confidence after election. The official family that he set up in the Executive Mansion was like an army headquarters, where work was done with military aides and orders were expected to receive in time of peace the same respect that they had commanded in time of war. Grant was in no sense a militarist, but the only way he knew how to work was the way of a commanding general. He picked his cabinet officers to suit himself, and so clumsily that the group had to be reorganized before it could function. The state department he gave to a personal friend, Elihu B. Washburne, to gratify his pride; he allowed a military aide, John A. Rawlins, to appropriate the war department to reward himself (J. H. Wilson, *The Life of John A. Rawlins,* 1916, p. 351); he picked a great merchant with whom he had dined well, Alexander T. Stewart, to fill the treasury post, only to discover that his appointee was legally incompetent. The other places he passed around with no reference to the existence of a party that fancied it had a right to rule, or to popular sense of fitness in appointment; and he could not understand or forgive criticism of himself because of this.

He and his family enjoyed life in the White House. All four of the children were there part of the time, though Frederick Dent Grant [*q.v.*] graduated at West Point in 1871, went to Europe, and was then on active duty. The military guard that had remained on duty since Lincoln's time was dispensed with, and the mansion was opened to family and friends. A former mess sergeant became the butler until Mrs. Grant rebelled. There was a "spare room" for the casual guest. Mrs. Grant's father, Col. Frederick Dent, still an unreconstructed Southerner but meticulously polite, was commonly much in evidence. The correspondents around the offices led him on to tell them how the General was a good Democrat but did not know it. Grant's own old father, Jesse, was sometimes there, though more often he was at his post-office at Covington, Ky., where Grant found him and left him. The vacations were likely to be spent in a cottage at Long Branch, where Grant kept out of ballrooms and took his keenest pleasure in driving in a light carriage behind a span of spirited horses. He did not care who gave him the horses. The old rumors about his excessive drinking hovered about him periodically, but most of the testimony is unreliable and none suggests that any of his official acts was ever affected by intoxication.

The financial status of the government was at the front among the problems of the Grant administrations. The Democratic party, in the preceding canvass, had made an appeal to the debtor farmers of the West and South, with an offer of greenbacks as a painless way of paying off the war debt. Earliest of the important bills to receive Grant's signature was one to establish the public credit by declaring a policy of ultimate redemption of legal-tender notes in coin. Steps were taken promptly to fund the confused mass of Civil War securities, and to baffle the gamblers in gold. These latter, on "Black Friday" (Sept. 24, 1869), thought they had cornered the gold on the market and "fixed" the President by extending favors to his hangers-on (R. H. Fuller, *Jubilee Jim, The Life of Col. James Fisk, Jr.*, 1928, p. 361; *New York Herald,* Oct. 8, 1869; *House Report No. 31,* 41 Cong., 1 Sess.). Grant ruined their hopes by releasing from the treasury such a flood of gold that it broke the corner. The financial collapse of 1873 increased the difficulty of currency deflation, for it was easy to array the debtor classes against any measure tending to appreciate the currency. But Grant vetoed an inflation bill in the following spring (Apr. 22, 1874), and signed on Jan. 14, 1875, an act setting January 1879 as the date for the resumption of specie payments.

For almost the whole of Grant's term of office Hamilton Fish [*q.v.*] was secretary of state. The two men never developed a friendly intimacy, yet Grant in general supported Fish in a firm and wise foreign policy. The attempt to annex the Dominican Republic in 1869, which produced a disastrous breach with Charles Sumner, was Grant's own venture, though it may have been the idea of political profiteers. He never receded from a belief in its wisdom, beaten though he was. Controversies with the British were cleared after the surrender of the latter on the *Alabama* claims, in the Treaty of Washington, May 8, 1871. Neutrality was maintained in spite of provocation given by Spain during her suppression of the Ten Years' War in Cuba.

The enforcement of the Fourteenth Amendment was attempted only half-heartedly and without success. Northern opinion reached its crest of militancy against the South in the spring of 1868. After the failure of the impeachment proceedings against Johnson there was never again adequate backing for a comprehensive interference with the gradual reëstablishment of home rule at the South. Midway in Grant's first term began the terrorism of the negro electorate that deterred the negroes from exercising their right to vote. Despite the Force Acts of 1870–71, the Southern states elected white officers and advanced along the process of consolidation in Democratic ranks that ended in a Solid South by 1876. Grant came, by 1880, to fear the election as president of one of the Confederate leaders who had tried to wreck the Union, but as president himself he saw the impossibility of permanent coercion.

Out of the Western and Northern moderate opinion there developed a Liberal Republican movement based on a belief in the unwisdom of Reconstruction and a demand for a reform in the administration of the national government. Its first objective, which was unattainable, was the defeat of Grant for renomination and reëlection in 1872. Horace Greeley, who received incongruous nominations from both the Liberal Republicans and the Democrats, was easily defeated. Grant again stayed out of the canvass. "I am no speaker," he wrote, "and don't want to be beaten" (A. R. Conkling, *Life and Letters of Roscoe Conkling,* 1889, p. 435). The storm of scandal broke around his head before he was reelected, and panic soon followed. A conviction was being driven home that as president he was a failure. "What wretched work.... They are tearing the government to pieces," Gideon Welles had written (*Americana,* April 1912, p. 403); "Can you really believe that the maker of the first Grant Cabinet ... is fit for a President? I cannot," asserted Greeley before he was himself nominated (W. B. Parker, *The Life and Public Services of Justin Smith Morrill,* 1924, p. 239). The *New York Tribune* (July 24, 1885) at Grant's death still believed that "the greatest mistake of his life was the acceptance of the presidency." "The crisis came," said the *Nation* (Mar. 9, 1876), "when an ignorant soldier, coarse in his taste and blunt in his perceptions, fond of money and material enjoyment and of low company, was put in the Presidential Chair."

The personal criticisms of Grant during his second term were galling to him, for he knew no way of dramatizing a simple personal honesty, and his power of speech and pen was totally inadequate in a fight with fluent and impassioned reformers. He sometimes replied to opposition with destruction. Sumner denounced the Dominican project and prevented the ratification of the treaty; whereupon Grant forced his deposition as chairman of the Senate committee on foreign relations (R. Cortissoz, *Life of Whitelaw Reid,* 1921, I, 190; S. Welles, *Naboth's Vineyard,* 1928, I, 392), and recalled his friend Motley from the post of minister to Great Britain. Grant was capable of letting go without a word the most dependable of his advisers—Hoar, Jewell, Bristow. Yet, craving association, he had room in his entourage for Conkling, the Camerons, and Zach Chandler. He believed the prosecution of his private secretary, Orville F. Babcock, was only a disguised attack upon himself, and did not lose confidence in Babcock's integrity until long after most other Americans. Conkling, to whom among others he offered the chief justiceship after Chase died, had a nicer sense of the needs of the office than did Grant and declined it. Yet the final choice, Morrison R. Waite, was good. Grant's critics long alleged that he packed the Supreme Court after its first legal-tenders decision (*Hepburn* vs. *Griswold,* Feb. 7, 1870, 8 *Wallace,* 603), by appointing Bradley and Strong, thus procuring a reversal in the second legal-tenders case, but the evidence for this seems unconvincing (Charles Warren, *The Supreme Court in United States History,* 1922, III, 238; *American Historical Review,* April 1929, p. 532).

The breath of personal scandal has not touched Grant in any plausible form, but it struck so close to him and so frequently as to necessitate the vindication of his honor by admitting his bad taste in the choice of associates. Babcock was under suspicion of improper interest in the Dominican matter (S. Welles, *Naboth's Vineyard,* 1928, I, 400), long before he was smirched by his connection with the whiskey ring. Grant allowed himself to appear in public as the guest of Jim Fisk. Belknap, his secretary of war, was proved to have accepted graft money from a post trader; and Grant by letting him resign protected him from the consequences of a successful impeachment. The accumulating criticisms that Grant incurred threw him into the arms of those who did not criticize, and these were not the best leaders in the nation or the party.

As the second term approached its end there was suggestion of a third. Grant, in a somewhat cryptic letter (*New York Herald,* May 31, 1875), declined to be a candidate. He could not see why his fellow citizens did not desire him to continue in the presidency, and his wife resented the fact that they did not; but he accepted retirement without complaint. He had some achievements, after all. He had inherited a situation with Great Britain that was full of threat, and left it with American esteem satisfied and Anglo-American relations more harmonious than they had ever been. He had brought the United States through the factional hazards that followed the attempt to remove a president, through the financial and moral uneasiness of a period of deflation and the panic of 1873, and through the uncertainties of an electoral contest that might have blossomed into another civil war (A. Badeau, *Grant in Peace,* 1887, p. 256). There were trying days during the electoral count. It was uncertain until a few hours before Mar. 4, 1877, whether Grant would have a successor, and there was a possibility that he would be called upon to face a new crisis. The conviction that he would not have any hand in a *coup d'état* helped to prevent one.

Grant left office with a few thousand dollars saved from his salary, and a craving to see Europe. With a family party, he sailed from Philadelphia in May 1877 for Liverpool and the foreign world. He embarked as a private citizen, but he landed as a world figure with whom the chamberlains of the European courts were uncertain how to act; for to treat him as a simple commoner would be grotesque, whereas he had no rank that would establish him in any rigid sequence of court precedence. It was left for his son Jesse to put Queen Victoria in her place (J. R. Grant, *In the Days of My Father General Grant,* 1925, pp. 224–27), but it took a long time for the European governments to assimilate ex-presidents with their own ex-royalties. For more than two years the Grants went from capital to capital, with an increasing baggage train of gifts and souvenirs, and an increasing need for a fortunatus purse (J. R. Young, *Around the World with General Grant,* 1879). As the tour approached its end, a longing for home stimulated its progress, to Grant's political disadvantage.

Hayes had failed to get along with his party, and neither sought nor could have obtained a renomination. The friends of Grant were desirous for a return of the "good old days." The murmurings of labor presaged to the nervous a possible industrial revolt, and there was clamor, much of it inspired, for a "strong" man at the helm of state. The political advisers of Grant urged him to delay his return until the eve of the campaign of 1880, when his renomination might be accomplished on a wave of friendly publicity. He came back, instead, in the autumn of 1879, and the spreading third-term boom excited a stronger wave of opposition. At the Chicago convention in 1880 the faithful old guard, 306 strong, stood firm for Grant, and later struck off a medal to celebrate their loyalty; but they did him no good, for a coalition of his opponents defeated him by agreeing upon Garfield as the candidate.

The last phase of Grant's life was saddened by lack of means, by positive misfortune, by calumny, and at last by sickness until death. He took up his residence in a house in East Sixty-sixth St., New York, in August 1881, and lived with gratitude upon the income from a fund of $250,-000 which some of his admirers placed in trust for him. The securities in which this was invested proved unreliable, and the income failed him (Woodward, *Meet General Grant,* 1928, pp. 476, 490). He went into business and was exploited. The failure of the brokerage firm of Grant & Ward (May 6, 1884) threw him into bankruptcy and humiliation. He had earlier used his swords and souvenirs as security for a loan which had been swallowed up. An attempt was made by his friends to care for him by reviving the office of general, which he had vacated upon entrance to the presidency, but political opposition delayed this until it was almost too late. On his last day in office President Arthur signed the revival bill, and it was left to a Democratic president, Cleveland, to deliver the commission that carried a salary for life.

The life was short. A dangerous cancer of the throat was wearing Grant away, though he was fighting the disease in order to carry to completion the only civil task that he had learned how to do well. In 1884 he wrote for the publishers of the *Century Magazine* an article (February 1885) on the battle of Shiloh. This paid him handsomely and was an immediate success, whereupon was conceived another Cæsar's *Commentaries* to be written by the victor of the Civil War. He set to work upon the *Personal Memoirs,* writing in the sickroom and in the quiet of the house at Mount McGregor where he was taken to die. Mark Twain, then in business as a publisher of subscription books, waited for the copy, to put upon the market one of the most successful of American books. The family of Grant received nearly $450,000 from this literary endowment (A. B. Paine, *Mark Twain: A Biography,* 1912, II, 816); but he himself died, simply and greatly, before he could know of its triumph. He was buried at last in a great mausoleum of granite on Riverside Drive in New York City.

[Grant was not a bookish man, and he wrote as little as possible until he compiled the *Personal Memoirs of U. S. Grant* (2 vols., 1885–86). There is no considerable collection of his manuscripts, and the printed salvage from his letters is fragmentary: J. G. Cramer, ed., *Letters of Ulysses S. Grant to his Father and his Youngest Sister, 1857–1878* (1912); J. G. Wilson, ed., *Gen. Grant's Letters to a Friend* [Elihu B. Washburne] *1861–1880* (1897). The many biographies are rarely more than compilations from his *Personal Memoirs,* enriched with fragments from the two works by his military aide, Adam Badeau, *Mil. Hist. of Ulysses S. Grant* (3 vols., 1868–81); and *Grant in Peace* (1887). The best of these biographies is W. E. Woodward, *Meet General Grant* (1928). Others not already listed in the previous bibliography are: J. S. C. Abbott, *The Life of Gen. Ulysses S. Grant* (1868); W. C. Church, *Ulysses S. Grant and the Period of Nat. Preservation and Reconstruction* (1897); Hamlin Garland, *Ulysses S. Grant. His Life and Character* (1898, new ed., 1920); Owen Wister, *Ulysses S. Grant* (1900); Chas. King, *The True Ulysses S. Grant* (1914). Better than any of the biographies for the period of his presidency are: J. F. Rhodes, *Hist. of the U. S.,* vols. VI–VII (1893); E. P. Oberholtzer, *A Hist. of the U. S. Since the Civil War* (3 vols., 1917–26); and C. G. Bowers, *The Tragic Era* (1929), a spirited brief for Andrew Johnson by an eloquent Democratic historian.]

F. L. P—n.

GRANT, ZILPAH POLLY [See BANISTER, ZILPAH POLLY GRANT, 1794–1874].

GRASS, JOHN (1837–May 10, 1918), a chief of the Blackfoot (Sihasapa) Sioux, was born in a camp on the Grand River, South Dakota. The surname Grass (Pezhi or Piji) is dynastic and was borne by his father and his grandfather, both of whom were with the Sioux allies in the expedition under Col. Henry Leavenworth against the Arikaras in 1823. At some time young Grass was baptized and received into the Catholic church, according to tradition by Father De Smet, who christened him John. He early distinguished himself in battle, and at seventeen, for exploits performed against the Crows and the Mandans, he received his warrior name, Mato Watakpe (Charging Bear), which also had been borne by his ancestors. About the same time, to prove his endurance, he underwent the extreme ordeal of the sun dance. Though he was later to become one of the leading exponents of a peace policy, he probably took part in some of the conflicts with the whites in the fifties and sixties. Fanny Wiggins Kelly, in an account of her captivity among the Sioux in 1864, mentions him as Jumping Bear and gratefully credits him with having saved her life on one occasion and with having subsequently aided in effecting her ransom.

Grass in his youth became noted as an orator,

and in the agitation against the whites during the early seventies he made full use of his powers. He strongly opposed war, which he declared would be ruinous, and urged upon his people the necessity of gradually abandoning the chase for more settled occupations. Though his counsels for the time went unheeded, after the conflict of 1876–77 his prestige returned; and a few years later, with the adherence of Gall, the former war chief, to his side, his influence became dominant. At Fort Yates, on the Standing Rock Agency, he served for many years as the chief justice of the Court of Indian Offenses, an office which he held at his death, and he took part in many treaty councils with the whites. He stoutly defended the rights of his people, and as an Indian commissioner at the council of 1888, relative to the cession of certain lands in the present South Dakota, brought the proceedings to a close because of a belief that the government commissioners were seeking an unfair advantage. A new commission, headed by Charles Foster, former governor of Ohio, in the following year, offered more favorable terms, and Grass, though for a time demanding further concessions, in the end led his people to accept the proposed treaty. On the entry of the United States into the World War he advised the young men to enlist; and his grandson, Albert Grass (Walking Elk), killed at Soissons, was one of the first of the American Expeditionary Force to fall in battle. Grass died, after a winter's illness, at his home south of Fort Yates and was buried in the local Catholic cemetery. He was six feet, two inches tall, of stalwart frame, with features expressive of high intelligence and resolute will. As a judge he was regarded as stern but just. As an orator he stood with the first among his people, and as a councilor, fitted for his part with strong native sense and an exceptional skill in argumentation, he had no superior. "He struck me," wrote Foster, "as an intellectual giant in comparison with other Indians," and James McLaughlin, in 1910, mentioned him as "the ablest orator and most influential surviving chief of the Sioux."

[Doane Robinson, "John Grass," in *S. D. Hist. Colls.*, I (1902), pp. 154–56; James McLaughlin, *My Friend the Indian* (1910); Fanny Wiggins Kelly, *Narrative of My Captivity Among the Sioux Indians* (1872); *Bismarck* (N. D.) *Tribune*, May 15, 1918; information as to certain facts from Lieut.-Col. A. B. Welch, Mandan, N. D., an adopted son of Grass.] W. J. G.

GRASSELLI, CAESAR AUGUSTIN (Nov. 7, 1850–July 28, 1927), manufacturing chemist, philanthropist, was one of the captains of industry who made Cleveland a manufacturing center. He may be said to have inherited his occupation. His forefathers living at Torno on Lake Como, Italy, were "chemist-druggists and perfumers"; his grandfather, Jean Angelo Grasselli, was a chemist of Strasbourg; his father, Eugene Ramiro Grasselli, emigrated from Strasbourg to the United States in 1836 and three years later he settled in Cincinnati and established a small chemical manufacturing plant. Before leaving Europe he had married Frederica Eisenbarth of Württemberg. Caesar Augustin was born in Cincinnati, the fifth in a family of nine children, three sons and six daughters. He attended local private schools, and after school hours served an apprenticeship in his father's works. In 1867 he moved with his family to Cleveland, whither they had been attracted by the development of the oil industry. At twenty-one he was married to Johanna Ireland, the daughter of a Cincinnati merchant, and two years later he entered into partnership with his father, whose death in 1882 threw added responsibilities upon the young chemist. In 1885 the Grasselli Chemical Company was incorporated with a capital of $600,000, and Caesar Augustin was elected president. After thirty years in this position he became chairman of the board of directors and his son, Thomas, succeeded to the presidency. In the period of the father's administration the valuation of the company's property had risen to more than thirty million dollars, and its activities expanded to fourteen widely scattered manufacturing plants with distributing stations in strategic centers for the marketing of the company's products. Grasselli was an aggressive, resourceful chief at a time when a manufacturer had to be ready to meet complex problems of production, selling, transportation, and finance. As the industrial revolution developed new opportunities, the Grasselli company turned to new fields of production. In 1904 it began the manufacture of zinc or spelter and became one of the largest producers of this metal in the country.

Grasselli's eminent success in business brought him actively into other corporations. He was one of the founders in Cleveland of the Broadway Savings and Trust Company and also of the Woodland Avenue Savings and Trust Company, of both of which he was president until their merger with the Union Trust Company in 1921. He was a patron and trustee for many years of the Western Reserve Historical Society. In the later years of his life he gave liberally in time and money to various Cleveland charities. The old family home on Fifty-fifth Street was given to the Cleveland Society for the Blind to be the Grasselli House, and after the death of his wife in 1910 the family home at South Euclid became Rose-Mary, the Johanna Grasselli Home for

Crippled Children. In recognition of his distinguished career in business, church, and charities King Victor Emanuel III in 1910 made him a knight of the Order of the Golden Crown of Italy, and in 1921 a commander of the same order. In 1923 Pope Pius XI conferred on him the decoration of commander of the Order of St. Gregory the Great. His most striking characteristics were an exceedingly sensitive sense of honor in all his relations, and a kindliness which was the substratum of all his life.

[*Who's Who in America*, 1926–27; Western Reserve Hist. Soc., *Trans.-Ann. Report*, no. 110 (1929); *The Cleveland Directory of Directors*, 1907; *Cleveland Plain Dealer*, July 29, 1927.] E. J. B.

GRASTY, CHARLES HENRY (Mar. 3, 1863–Jan. 19, 1924), editor, publisher, newspaper owner, was one of the many sons of Methodist manses to achieve distinction in journalism. He was born in Fincastle, Va., the son of the Rev. John Sharshall Grasty and Ella Giles Pettus. In 1876 he entered the University of Missouri, but he was compelled for financial reasons to leave in 1880 without graduating. He became a reporter on the *Kansas City Times* and at twenty-one he was made the managing editor of the paper—a position which he held for five years. On May 29, 1889, almost immediately after leaving the *Times*, he was married to Leota Tootle Perrin of St. Joseph, Mo. From his savings in newspaper work and from some profitable investments in Kansas City real estate, he was able in 1892 to secure the controlling interest in the *Baltimore* (Md.) *News*. He was soon waging war on the political corruption found in the city, and in this work he was aided by Fabian Franklin who was associated with him as editor of the paper after 1895. In 1908 he concluded sixteen years of successful management when the *News* was sold to Frank A. Munsey for a handsome purchase price. For a brief period he remained as general manager of the *News* and then went to St. Paul as editor and controlling owner of the *St. Paul Dispatch* and the *Pioneer Press*. His year in that city (1908–09) was not happy. At its close he sold the paper to its old owners and went to Europe with his family. Returning to the United States he secured in 1910 control of the *Sun* in Baltimore and at once enlarged the Sunday *Sun* and added the *Evening Sun*. At the same time he renewed his old attacks on the political machine. The fight of the *Sun* to secure the Democratic convention of 1912 for Baltimore was more successful and in the nomination of Woodrow Wilson, Grasty played a prominent part. He had seen presidential timber in Wilson while the latter was still president of Princeton University. His crusading campaigns so affected his health that in July 1914 he sought recuperation in Europe and in October of that year severed all connection with his paper. Even while abroad he could not break away entirely from newspaper work and became a war correspondent for the Associated Press, an organization of which he had been a director from 1900 to 1910. Upon his return to the United States in 1916, he served as treasurer of the *New York Times*, but the business desk chafed him as long as critical events were taking place in Europe and he went back with Gen. Pershing in 1917 with a roving commission as a special editorial correspondent of the *Times*. After brief service in the Paris office of the *Times*, he began a series of tours along the war front which led to many interviews with military and diplomatic leaders and entitled him to a permanent place in a journalistic hall of fame. The judgment that he was "the ablest all-round newspaper man in America" (Baltimore *Sun*, Jan. 20, 1924) had substantial foundation, for he was familiar with every detail of newspaper technique. Editor, publisher, and newspaper owner, the rôle he loved best of all was that of a reporter of stirring events; and in that rôle he died in London.

[For obituaries see the *N. Y. Times* and the Baltimore *Sun*, Jan. 20, 1924. The more striking of his interviews with war leaders may be found in *Flashes from the Front* (1918). Tributes to him may be found in H. E. Warner, *Songs of the Craft* (1929) and in a memorial volume, *Charles H. Grasty, 1863–1924*.] J. M. L.

GRATIOT, CHARLES (1752–Apr. 20, 1817), pioneer trader, was born in Lausanne, Switzerland, the son of Huguenot parents, David and Marie (Bernard) Gratiot. He received some schooling in Lausanne, and at seventeen was sent to his mother's brother in London, who in turn sent him to a brother in the fur trade in Montreal. Arriving in that city in May 1769, he remained in the employ of his uncle for six years. He then took a partner, and on means advanced by his uncle made a trading venture to the west, but returned sixteen months later after suffering heavy losses. In 1777 he joined with two partners, under the firm name of David McCrae & Company, and again went west. In December he opened a store in Cahokia, in the present Illinois, the other partners establishing themselves in Kaskaskia. He formed the acquaintance of George Rogers Clark [*q.v.*], on his invasion of the Illinois towns the following July, became strongly attached to him, and with Jean Gabriel Cerré and Father Gibault [*qq.v.*] rendered many services to the American cause. Early in 1781 he moved to St. Louis, and by his marriage, June 25, to Victoire, the half-sister of Col. Auguste

Chouteau [*q.v.*], allied himself with the wealthiest and most powerful family in Upper Louisiana.

The McCrae partnership appears to have been dissolved before Gratiot left Cahokia. His affairs prospered, and to extend his trade connections he traveled repeatedly to New Orleans, to the Atlantic seaboard, and to Europe. It is said that he was the first resident of St. Louis to visit Philadelphia (1783–84). On one of these journeys, possibly that of 1793–95, he formed the connection with John Jacob Astor [*q.v.*] that was to continue till his death. With his fur trading he combined the operation of a distillery, a tannery, and a salt works and he also dealt extensively in land. It was on his portico, with himself as interpreter, that the formal transfer of Upper Louisiana was made on Mar. 10, 1804. He was the first presiding justice of the court of quarter sessions of St. Louis; on the incorporation of the village as a town, in 1809, he was elected a trustee. He continued actively in business until his death.

Though not the wealthiest of the St. Louis traders, Gratiot was the most widely known, and he brought the frontier fur center to the attention of the world. He was a man of exceptional initiative, energy, and persistence. He had a good knowledge of law and a logical mind; often in litigation, he prepared his own briefs, with an equal skill in the use of French and English, and is said to have won all his cases. Though the value of his services to Clark has been variously appraised, there is no dispute as to his sincere and active friendship for the American cause. His son Charles was one of the four French youths appointed by Jefferson to West Point immediately after the transfer of Louisiana. He graduated as an engineer; in 1819–29 planned and erected the defenses of Hampton Roads, including Fortress Monroe, and from 1828 to 1838 was chief engineer of the army with the brevet rank of brigadier-general.

[Wm. Hyde and H. L. Conard, *Encyc. of the Hist. of St. Louis* (1899), vol. II; F. L. Billon, *Annals of St. Louis in Its Early Days,* etc. (1886), and *Annals of St. Louis in Its Territorial Days* (1888); J. T. Scharf, *Hist. of St. Louis City and County* (1883); H. M. Chittenden, *The Am. Fur Trade of the Far West* (1902); G. W. Cullum, *Biog. Reg.* (3rd ed., 1891), vol. I.]

W. J. G.

GRATZ, BARNARD (1738–Apr. 20, 1801), merchant, was born in Langensdorf, Upper Silesia, the son of Solomon Gratz. He emigrated to Philadelphia in 1754 from London, England, where he had served in the counting-house of his cousin, Solomon Henry. Upon his arrival in Philadelphia he entered the employ of David Franks, a leading fur-trader. After four years he determined to venture into business for himself as a merchant. Relinquishing his position to his brother Michael [*q.v.*], he formed a partnership with Benjamin M. Clava which lasted for a year. Thereafter he conducted the business alone until, some time later, he associated himself with his brother in an enterprise conducted at Fourth and Market Streets, and became one of the so-called "merchant venturers" who did great pioneer service in opening up to settlement and trade that territory which became the states of Ohio, Kentucky, Indiana, and Illinois.

Barnard Gratz and his brother Michael were among the signers of the Non-Importation resolutions adopted on Oct. 2, 1765, by "the merchants and other citizens of Philadelphia" as a remonstrance against the Stamp Act. When the definite break with the mother country came, the Gratz brothers cast their lot with the revolutionists. Barnard took the oath of allegiance to the Commonwealth of Pennsylvania and to the United States as a free nation on Nov. 5, 1777. He is the first recorded president or "parnas" of the Mickveh Israel congregation, the third Jewish congregation to be organized in the United States. He laid the corner-stone of the first synagogue erected in Philadelphia, June 16, 1782, and participated in its dedication on Sept. 13 of that year. In 1783 he was one of a committee who entered a protest against the clause in the constitution of Pennsylvania which required that every member of the Assembly should take the oath of allegiance to Pennsylvania, declaring that "The Scriptures of the Old and New Testaments were given by divine inspiration." This requirement debarred Jews from serving as members of the Assembly, and the clause was later amended. Similarly, while residing in Baltimore he joined in the agitation to repeal the constitutional requirement that all office-holders in the state of Maryland must declare their allegiance "upon the true faith of a Christian." This agitation continued for twenty-nine years and in 1825 the clause was finally changed. Gratz married on Dec. 10, 1760, Richea, the daughter of Samson Mears or Myers. She died less than five years later, leaving two daughters, one of whom did not live to grow up. The other, Rachel, married Solomon Etting of Baltimore, the first Jew to hold office in the state of Maryland. While visiting at her home, Gratz died.

[*B. and M. Gratz, Merchants in Phila. 1754–1798* (1916), ed. by W. V. Byars; H. S. Morais, *The Jews of Phila.* (1894); *Letters of Rebecca Gratz* (1929), ed. by David Philipson.]

D. P—n.

GRATZ, MICHAEL (1740–Sept. 8, 1811), merchant, was born in Langensdorf, Upper Silesia, the son of Solomon Gratz. Like his brother Barnard [q.v.], he served his apprenticeship in the London counting-house of his cousin, Solomon Henry, which he entered in 1756. Faraway India had come within the ken of venturesome traders and Michael, following the lure of this distant land of new opportunities, sailed from London in 1757. His expectations must have been disappointed for he remained in India little more than a year. Returning to London either late in 1758 or early in 1759, in April of the latter year he set sail for America in order to join his brother, Barnard. Upon his arrival in Philadelphia he entered the employ of David Franks as had his brother five years previously. It was not long before the brothers formed a partnership, known as B. & M. Gratz. They "adventured" in the coast trade between New Orleans and Quebec and in the country west of Lancaster, Pa., the frontier town of that day. Through the influence of Joseph Simon, the leading merchant of Lancaster, whose daughter, Miriam, Michael married on June 20, 1769, the brothers obtained valuable business connections and secured large tracts of land in Virginia, western Pennsylvania, Ohio, Indiana, Illinois, and Kentucky, their holdings in the last named state including the famous Mammoth Cave territory. Among other ventures the Gratz brothers ran a line of steamboats from the Forks of the Ohio (Pittsburgh) down the river into Kentucky and Indiana. As stanch patriots they were very helpful in securing needed supplies for the colonies, notably Virginia, by running the British blockade.

During the Revolution Michael Gratz had removed to Virginia, where he took the oath of allegiance to that state in 1783 (Thompson Westcott, *Names of Persons who took the Oath of Allegiance to the State of Pennsylvania,* etc., 1865). The first Philadelphia directory, published in 1785, contains the name of Michael Gratz and describes him as "merchant, Fourth between Market and Chestnut." He continued actively in business until 1798 when his health began to fail and his sons Simon and Hyman succeeded to the business. Among his twelve children was the well-known philanthropist, Rebecca Gratz [q.v.]. Michael was buried in the old cemetery on Spruce Street between Eighth and Ninth, where rest so many of the pioneers of the Jewish community of Philadelphia.

[*B. and M. Gratz, Merchants in Phila., 1754–1798* (1916), ed. by W. V. Byars; H. S. Morais, *The Jews of Phila.* (1894); *Letters of Rebecca Gratz* (1929), ed. by David Philipson; *Poulson's Am. Daily Advertiser,* Sept. 9, 1811.]

D. P—n.

GRATZ, REBECCA (Mar. 4, 1781–Aug. 29, 1869), philanthropist, daughter of Michael [q.v.] and Miriam (Simon) Gratz, was born in Philadelphia. In 1801, being then in her twenty-first year, she was elected secretary of the "Female Association for the Relief of Women and Children in Reduced Circumstances." She helped found the Philadelphia Orphan Society in 1815; she was elected secretary of this society in 1819 and served in this capacity for forty years; upon her retirement in 1859 the Board of Managers in an eloquent testimonial to her worth and work wrote that to her "much of its prosperity is due, while to her dignity, grace and noble personal qualities the managers have always yielded the tribute of their warm admiration and personal regard." She founded in 1838 the Hebrew Sunday School Society, the first institution of its kind in the United States, and served as the president until 1864, when owing to her advanced age she resigned in her eighty-third year. The society is still in a flourishing condition and through its agency religious education is imparted to Jewish children in a number of schools supported by its funds. Along this same line of endeavor was her service in inspiring the foundation of the Jewish Foster Home for the housing and education of orphan children. The first suggestion for such an institution was made in a letter to the *Occident,* a monthly magazine published in Philadelphia. This letter, dated 1850 and signed "A Daughter in Israel," was attributed to her. Five years later the idea here suggested was realized largely through her efforts in the foundation of the Jewish Foster Home.

Her fame rests chiefly upon the generally accepted tradition that she was the original of the famous character Rebecca in Sir Walter Scott's novel *Ivanhoe.* It was through Washington Irving that she was brought to Scott's attention. Irving's fiancée, Matilda Hoffman, was an intimate friend of Rebecca Gratz, who was with her during her last illness and whom Irving met frequently in the sick room. Upon a visit to England not long after the death of Miss Hoffman, Irving met Scott. Upon Scott's informing him that he was contemplating writing a novel with Jews among the principal characters, Irving told him about the lovely Philadelphia Jewess. That Irving's description influenced Scott in his delineation of Rebecca appears from some words in a letter addressed by Scott to Irving in 1819 after the appearance of *Ivanhoe.* Scott wrote, "How do you like your Rebecca? Does the Rebecca I have pictured compare well with the pattern given?" In a letter written by Rebecca Gratz on Apr. 4, 1820, to her sister-in-law, Mrs. Benjamin Gratz, of Lexington, Ky., she speaks of Scott's heroine as her namesake. Her brief last will and testament reads: "I, Rebecca Gratz of Philadelphia, being in sound health of body and mind, advanced in the vale of years, declare this to be my last will and testament. I commit my spirit to the God who gave it, relying on His mercy and redeeming love, and believing with a fine and perfect faith in the religion of my fathers. Hear, O Israel, the Lord our God is one Lord. . . ."

[David Philipson, ed., *Letters of Rebecca Gratz* (1929); H. S. Morais, *Eminent Israelites of the Nineteenth Century* (1880), and *The Jews of Phila.* (1894); *B. and M. Gratz, Merchants in Phila. 1754–98: Papers of Interest to Posterity and to the Posterity of their Associates* (1916), ed. by W. V. Byars; S. A. Mordecai, *Recollections of my Aunt Rebecca Gratz* (1893); Gratz Van Rensselaer, "The Original of Rebecca in *Ivanhoe*," *Century Mag.*, Sept. 1882; Joseph Jacobs, "The Original of Scott's Rebecca," *Am. Jewish Hist. Soc. Pubs.*, vol. XXII (1914); M. M. Cohen, "An Old Phila. Cemetery, the Resting Place of Rebecca Gratz," *Phila. Hist.* (City Hist. Soc. of Phila.), vol. II, no. 4 (1920); H. F. Barnes, *Charles Fenno Hoffman* (1930).]
D. P—n.

GRAU, MAURICE (1849–Mar. 14, 1907), theatrical and operatic impresario, was born in Brünn, Austria, of Jewish parents, by whom he was taken at the age of five to New York City. After an education in the city public schools, he attended the Free Academy, since called the College of the City of New York. His graduation in 1867 was followed by studies in the Columbia School of Law and an apprenticeship in a New York law firm. By 1872, however, his entire interest had become absorbed in the activities of an uncle, Jacob Grau, a well-known theatrical and musical manager, in whose opera house he had often sold librettos. In that year, in association with Charles A. Chizzola, he demonstrated unusual ability in the management of a tour by Mlle. Aimée, the French singer, and very shortly afterward gained his first financial success by clearing $60,000 on the tour of Anton Rubinstein, the pianist, and Henri Wieniawski, the violinist. During the next three years, before severing connections with Chizzola in 1875, the younger manager was engaged in a variety of activities: he organized the English opera company of Clara Louise Kellogg [*q.v.*]; he introduced to the American public Tommaso Salvini; he managed three opera-bouffe and operetta companies; and brought back to this country the distinguished Italian tragedienne, Adelaide Ristori. In 1879 he conducted as an independent manager, and with great financial success, the tour of a celebrated French opera company. These early activities of Grau have tended to be obscured by the more important events during the years of his association with Henry Eugene Abbey [*q.v.*] and John B. Schoeffel, an association begun in May 1882 and extending over a period of many years. Although his firm managed the American tours of such outstanding European actors as Bernhardt, Irving, Terry, Benoît-Coquelin, Jane Hading, Mounet-Sully, and Réjane, its fame is due more to its activities in connection with the Metropolitan Opera during one of its most brilliant periods. When the Metropolitan Opera House opened its doors for the first time on Oct. 22, 1883, Abbey was serving as manager, and Grau as business manager. The winter and spring seasons resulted in a financial catastrophe for the managers, and it was not until almost eight years later, on Dec. 14, 1891, that Grau and Abbey resumed the direction of the house. This second venture was more successful. Subsequent seasons at the Metropolitan were good, but losses on outside theatrical ventures kept the managers financially distressed. At the end of the 1895–96 season, creditors took over the direction of the Metropolitan and there was a confused transitional period of management, until in 1898, after the death of Abbey and the withdrawal of Schoeffel, Grau emerged as managing-director in charge of the Maurice Grau Opera Company. From the fall of 1898 until the spring of 1903, when ill health forced him to retire, Grau directed the activities of the Metropolitan on a magnificent scale. It was "probably," writes Henry Krehbiel in *Chapters of Opera,* "the most brilliant operatic government that the world has ever known from a financial point of view, and its high lights artistically were luminous in the extreme" (p. 277). During the period when he shared the direction with Abbey and Schoeffel, and still more during his later years of autocracy, he established the hitherto undared policy of casting as many as five stars in the same production. He introduced and developed many operatic singers whose names are now famous. He insisted that operas should be sung in the language of the original libretto, and, although prejudiced at first against German opera, he was soon convinced of its marketability, and gave to it the same careful attention and sumptuous production that he gave to the better known French and Italian works. After retiring, he lived in Croissy-Chatou outside of Paris.

[T. A. Brown, *Hist. of the N. Y. Stage* (3 vols., 1903); H. E. Krehbiel, *Chapters of Opera* (1909); biographical sketch by Chas. Seymour in *Farewell tour 1900–01 Mme. Sarah Bernhardt—M. Coquelin, under the direction of Mr. Maurice Grau* (1900), issued as a special number of *Le Théâtre* (without date and without page numbers); the *Nation,* Mar. 21, 1907; *Theatre Mag.*, May 1907, and May 1920; *Who's Who in America,* 1906–07; *N. Y. Times,* Mar. 15, 1907.]
E. M., Jr.

GRAUPNER, JOHANN CHRISTIAN GOTTLIEB (Oct. 6, 1767–Apr. 16, 1836), musician, was born in Verden, Hanover, Prussia, the seventh child of Johann Georg and Anna Maria Agnesa Schoenhagen Graupner. Though he played several instruments, he followed in the footsteps of his father and became an excellent oboe player in a regiment at Hanover. Desiring a larger sphere of activity, however, at his own request he received an honorable discharge. This parchment certificate was signed at Hameln Apr. 8, 1788, and on the reverse side his birth date was given as Oct. 6, 1767, and his baptismal date as Oct. 9, 1767. Soon after his discharge he went to London, and three years later when Haydn assembled an orchestra, the largest in existence at that time, he was chosen first oboist (1791–92). Here he developed an intense admiration for the composer. The following year he went to Prince Edward Island, but finding scarcely any demand for his services, in 1795 he went to Charleston, S. C. There he played in a theatre orchestra and on Apr. 6, 1796, he was married to Mrs. Catherine Comerford Hillier, a distinguished English opera-singer, daughter of a London attorney. With his wife he soon went to Boston, where he made his first American solo appearance in the Boston Theatre in 1796. His wife had already made her successful debut there in 1794. He played the oboe in the Federal Street Theatre but at once planned to form an orchestra for concert performances, the first of its kind in America. As early as 1800 he had opened a music store at 6 Franklin Street, where he also had a music-hall and gave lessons. He not only sold instruments, but he published music, engraving and printing it himself. In 1807 he became an American citizen.

Gathering together both amateur and professional instrumentalists, as well as vocalists, Graupner organized the Phil-harmonic Society in 1810 or 1811. He was its first and only president, and the meetings, which were semi-social, were held Saturday evenings in Graupner's Hall and later in Pythian Hall in what was then Bond Street. The society began with less than twelve members, among whom were the Russian and English consuls, both violinists. Besides being an oboist, Graupner played the violin, double-bass, German flute, clarinet, and the piano sufficiently well to fill in these parts when necessary, and he gave lessons on these instruments. The baton was not then used in orchestra-conducting, but Graupner directed from the double-bass. At first he ventured only on symphonies by Gyrowetz, and as the orchestra gained in skill he undertook the simpler symphonies of his idol, Haydn. As other foreign musicians settled in Boston, the ensemble improved and under his leadership the Phil-harmonic was said to be the finest among contemporary American orchestras. Its last concert took place at the Pantheon, Boylston Square, Nov. 24, 1824.

Meantime choral work in Boston had received an impetus when a festival celebrating the Peace of Ghent was held in King's Chapel on Washington's birthday, 1815. This made so deep an impression that it became evident that the time was ripe for a permanent choral society. Accordingly Graupner, Thomas Smith Webb, and Asa Peabody sent out a notice for a meeting to be held on Mar. 30, 1815, at which the Handel and Haydn Society was organized. Its first concert took place in King's Chapel on Dec. 25, 1815. The chorus, under the direction of its president, T. S. Webb, numbered nearly one hundred, of whom twenty were women. Accompaniments were furnished by an orchestra of twelve players, trained by Graupner, and an organ. The program consisted of selections from Haydn's *Creation* and from Händel's *Messiah,* probably the first attempt at oratorio performance in this country.

Graupner gave many concerts with his wife and also wrote a pianoforte method, *Rudiments of the Art of Playing on the Pianoforte* (2nd ed., 1825), containing pieces by Domenico Scarlatti, Corelli, Bach, Cherubini, and Pleyel, as well as some compositions of his own. All of his children were musical, and a son, John Henry Howard Graupner, whom he had trained as a pianist and engraver, had charge of the music-engraving department of the Oliver Ditson Company for many years. He died at 1 Province House Court, and according to the records of Trinity Church his funeral took place there on Apr. 20, 1836.

[Letter, dated Oct. 29, 1906, to Allan Brown, Allan Brown Library, Boston, Mass., from Graupner's granddaughter, Catherine Graupner Stone, authenticating disputed dates, especially those of birth, death, and burial; letter to Allan Brown from Seymour H. Stone, Graupner's great-grandson; Philip Hale's program notes in the 1909–10 program book of the Boston Symphony Orchestra, giving historical facts about the Graupner family; L. C. Elson, *The Hist. of Am. Music* (1904); J. S. Dwight, "Hist. of Music in Boston," in *The Memorial Hist. of Boston,* vol. IV (1883), ed. by Justin Winsor; W. A. Fisher, *Notes on Music in Old Boston* (1918); O. G. T. Sonneck, *Bibliog. of Early Am. Music* (1905), and *Early Concert-Life in America, 1731–1800* (1907); F. S. Ritter, *Music in America* (1883).]

F. L. G. C.

GRAVENOR, JOHN [See ALTHAM, JOHN, 1589–1640].

GRAVES, JAMES ROBINSON (Apr. 10, 1820–June 26, 1893), Baptist minister, and controversialist, was born in Chester, Vt., youngest of the three children of Zuinglius Calvin and Lois (Schnell) Graves. On the Graves side of the house he was mainly of French extraction, and on the Schnell side mainly German. His mother, left a widow when he was an infant, was able to give him only meager schooling. At fifteen he joined the Baptist church, and at nineteen went with his mother and sister to Ohio, whither they had been preceded by his brother Zuinglius Calvin Graves [*q.v.*]. After two years as principal of the Kingsville Academy, he removed in search of a more healthful climate to Jessamine County, Ky. There he took charge of the Clear Creek Academy, and in constant gloomy self-depreciation studied assiduously for four years with the view of fitting himself for the ministry. In 1844 he was ordained, in 1845 he established himself in Nashville, Tenn., as head of a classical and mathematical academy, and in 1846 he assumed the editorship of the weekly *Tennessee Baptist,* a position which involved his editing also a monthly, a quarterly, and an annual. Indirectly it led to his establishing the Southwestern Publishing House (1848) and the Southern Baptist Sunday-School Union—both suspended by the Civil War—and after the war, to his establishing the Southern Baptist Publication Society. He is also to be credited with inaugurating the first Ministers' Institute among Tennessee Baptists and for procuring funds to launch the Mary Sharp College for women at Winchester, Tenn. As a minister he was sufficiently eloquent to command the attention of a congregation throughout a three-and-a-half-hour sermon, and to convert before he was thirty years old some thirteen hundred people. Beginning in 1850, he agitated the doctrine that Baptist ministers could not indorse the ordination of persons who did not regard immersion as a requisite for Christianity. This test, he maintained, was an "Old Landmark" of the Church. The idea was taken up widely, and at last, becoming a "movement," seriously threatened Baptist unity. *Old Landmarkism; What is It?*, written by him, appeared in 1880. In 1855 he published his *Great Iron Wheel or Republicanism Backwards and Christianity Reversed,* a series of letters which had shortly before appeared in his Nashville paper. This book, comprising nearly six hundred pages of matter, addressed to Bishop Joshua Soule [*q.v.*] of the Methodist Church, is a truculent and dogmatic tirade against the Methodist denomination, but it accorded well with the ecclesiastical temper of that era, whether Baptist or Methodist. The attack and the rebuttal it inspired, *The Great Iron Wheel Examined, or its False Spokes Extracted and an Exhibition of Elder Graves, its Builder* (1856), by W. G. Brownlow [*q.v.*], sold in incredible numbers, the Graves book running to as many as 50,000 copies. The two of them offer what is perhaps the classic recorded example of sectarian asperity in the United States. A revised edition of Graves's work, *The New Great Iron Wheel* (1884), is no less drastic. Of the many doctrinal debates in which he took part, the one which occurred about 1875 at Carrollton, Mo., is the most memorable. Supported by a group of expert linguists, theologians, and polemics, he arrayed himself against Methodists in general and the Rev. Jacob Ditzler in particular in a debate which was published in 1,175 pages as the *Graves-Ditzler or Great Carrollton Debate* (1876). In 1883 he published what he considered his most important book, *The Work of Christ in the Covenant of Redemption; Developed in Seven Dispensations,* describing the pre-millennarial reign of Jesus, and showing how various days of the week may be thought of as typifying the various ages of history. Besides the books already mentioned, he published others of a religious character, and edited numerous theological works. About 1870 he left Nashville for Memphis. Among his activities there, in addition to his vocation of ministerial publisher and book-dealer, was a debate with a Methodist preacher in which he maintained that supernatural visitations are to be attributed to the vagaries of fallen angels (*Ford's Christian Repository,* June 1900, pp. 351–52). He was married three times: first, in 1845 to Florence Spencer, sister of his brother's wife, and the second and third times to two daughters of Dr. George Snider of Mississippi, Lou and Georgie Snider.

[*Dr. Z. C. Graves and the Mary Sharp College, 1850–96* (1926); J. H. Borum, *Biog. Sketches of Tenn. Bapt. Ministers* (1880); J. H. Spencer, *A Hist. of Ky. Baptists,* vol. II (1886); J. J. Burnett, *Sketches of Tennessee's Pioneer Bapt. Preachers* (1919); *Memphis Appeal-Avalanche,* June 27, 1893; *Public Ledger* (Memphis), June 27, 1893; information from the Rev. O. L. Hailey, Nashville, Tenn.] J. D. W.

GRAVES, JOHN TEMPLE (Nov. 9, 1856–Aug. 8, 1925), journalist, orator, was born at Willington district, Abbeville County, S. C., the son of James Porterfield Graves, a general in the Confederate army, and Catherine Floride (Townes) Graves. He was descended from John Temple Graves, a colonel in the Revolutionary army, and from William Calhoun, an elder brother of John C. Calhoun. He was a member of the class of 1875 of the University of Georgia, but did not graduate. After leaving the university he taught school for a time and on Apr. 17, 1878, he was married to Mattie Gardner Simpson of Sparta, Ga. In 1880, more for his own amusement, apparently, than anything else, he wrote and published an account of a local political combat. The ornate manner of his writing proved exactly to the taste of his fellow Georgians, and he was from that time a marked man. About 1882 he went to Jacksonville, Fla., where for five years he was editor first of the *Daily Florida Union* and later of the *Florida Herald*. During this time he went into politics, became Democratic elector-at-large in 1884, and suddenly found himself one of the best-known men in the state. In 1887 he returned to Atlanta and became for one year editor of the *Atlanta Journal*. Then, in a search for editorial independence, he removed to Rome, Ga., and edited the *Tribune of Rome*. Here his wife died, and on Dec. 30, 1890, he was married to Anne E. Cothran. The *Tribune* prospered, but the owners and the editor could not agree in politics, and in 1890 the editor resigned. In 1888 he had been Democratic elector-at-large from Georgia.

Graves's address on the death of Henry Grady (1889) brought him so wide a reputation as a public speaker that he became a lecturer. He acquired such popularity that by 1908 he had spoken from as many as 1,900 platforms. Meanwhile he resumed his newspaper activities. From 1902 to 1906 he was editor of the *Atlanta News* and afterward, until the fall of 1907, of the *Atlanta Georgian*. He was widely, and apparently with some justice, blamed for his part as editor of the *News* in fanning the racial animosity which exploded in the Atlanta riots of September 1906. In the spring of 1907 he created further notice by advocating that Roosevelt be made the presidential candidate of all parties. In the following year he was himself the candidate of the National Independence party for the vice-presidency. From 1907 to 1915 he was editor of the *New York American*, and during the period from 1915 almost to the time of his death, he wrote special articles for the Hearst papers and also for a while edited the *Palm Beach Post* and the *Hendersonville* (N. C.) *Times*. He wrote: *A History of Colleton, S. C.*, and *The Winter Resorts of Florida* (1883), and was coeditor of a collection of oratory, *Eloquent Sons of the South* (2 vols., 1909). He opposed monopolies and war, and in 1923, as a herald of peace, he went about the country delivering his speech "Armageddon." In religion he was a Presbyterian elder who took the Bible literally. With regard to the negro question, a favorite theme, he believed that the only way to settle the issue was to transport all negroes back to Africa. He died at his home in Washington after several months of ill health.

[A. D. Candler and C. A. Evans, *Georgia* (1906), vol. II; W. J. Northen, *Men of Mark in Ga.*, vol. IV (1908); J. P. De Graffenried, *Hist. of the De Graffenried Family* (1925); Benjamin Brawley, *A Social Hist. of the Am. Negro* (1921); *Who's Who in America, 1924–25*; "An Oratorical Editor," *Outlook*, Aug. 19, 1925; *Evening Star* (Washington, D. C.), Aug. 8, 1925; *Atlanta Constitution* and *N. Y. Times*, Aug. 9, 1925.]

J. D. W.

GRAVES, ROSEWELL HOBART (May 29, 1833–June 3, 1912), for more than fifty years a missionary of the Southern Baptist Convention in South China, was a native of Baltimore. His father, John James Graves, of old New England stock, was a physician, and served in the Maryland legislature and as a city official of Baltimore. His mother, Anna Jane Baker, combined a deeply religious nature with marked literary ability. From the time when, at the age of fifteen, Graves joined the Seventh Baptist Church of Baltimore, then under the pastorate of the famous Dr. Richard Fuller [*q.v.*], he devoted much time to religious activities. In the year of his graduation from St. Mary's College (B.A. 1851) he decided to enter the ministry, and a few years later he took the further step of determining to be a missionary. Appointed, in 1855, to China, for some months he studied medicine under his father's direction and at the University of Maryland. He acquired theological training under the direction of Dr. Fuller, and in 1856 he was ordained to the Baptist ministry.

In 1856 he sailed for China and in August of that year arrived in Canton, which for the remainder of his long life was to be the center of his work. The language gave him some trouble, and for years he struggled with ill health, but by diligent application he became master of the one and by care and determination he largely overcame the other. In 1864 he was left the only representative of his mission board in South China. From then until his death, as the senior member of his mission, which later grew to large proportions, he had a marked influence upon its policies. During his earlier years he gave much time to itinerant preaching throughout the region, and helped to bring into existence Christian groups as far west as Kwang-si. During his middle and later years he more and more centered his attention upon training Chinese preachers and upon literary activities. The Graves Theological Seminary, in Canton, rose out of his efforts, with himself as its first head, and he was the author of scores of religious books and pamphlets in Chinese, the total circulation of which ran into the millions, and, in English, of *Forty Years in China, or China in Transition* (1895). He was one of the organizers of the China Baptist Publication Society, helped in the revision of the translation of the Scriptures into the literary language, and devised a widely used system of phonetic writing for the Cantonese dialect.

He was married three times, in 1863 to Mrs. Eva M. Gaillard (died 1864), the widow of a colleague, in 1872 to a boyhood friend, Jane W. Norris (died 1888), and in 1890 to a missionary to the Chinese in the United States, Mrs. Jane Lowrey Sanford, who survived him.

[A partially completed biography, in manuscript, by R. E. Chambers (in possession of the Board of Foreign Missions of the Southern Baptist Convention), based largely on Graves's diaries and letters; anonymous biographical sketches in the *Chinese Recorder,* May 1913, and the *Foreign Mission Journal,* July 1912; annual reports of the Board of Foreign Missions in the Southern Baptist Convention *Proceedings.*] K. S. L.

GRAVES, ZUINGLIUS CALVIN (Apr. 15, 1816–May 18, 1902), college president, was born in Chester, Vt., eldest of the three children of Zuinglius Calvin and Lois (Schnell) Graves. Frail, as a child, he spent most of the time between his fifth and sixteenth years on a farm belonging to his uncle, and it was during this time that he forsook the traditional Congregationalism of his mother and joined the Baptists. Returning to Chester, he pursued his schooling at Ludlow. He supported himself meantime by teaching district school, and—licensed to preach though never ordained—by serving as supply pastor at the Ludlow Baptist Church. Soon after completing his high-school course, he went to Ashtabula, Ohio, where he successfully conducted an academy for four years before succeeding his younger brother, James Robinson Graves [*q.v.*], as principal of an academy in Kingsville, Ohio. In July 1841, he was married to Adelia C. Spencer, sister of Platt Spencer, author of the Spencerian system of writing. In December 1850, he removed to Winchester, Tenn., to become first president of the Mary Sharp College, an institution for the higher education of women lately organized there largely through the efforts of his brother. Shaping the courses of the new college after those of Brown and the University of Virginia, he maintained a degree of scholastic integrity almost unique at that time among women's schools in the United States, and by 1861 it was admitting yearly more than three hundred young women, representing twelve different states. The Civil War closed the college for about two years, but Graves opened it again soon after the war, working for a while without a salary, and adapting himself and his educational aims to the demands of the new era. From 1891 to 1893, he was president of Soule College in Murfreesboro, Tenn., and during 1893 he taught at Boscobel College, a Baptist institution for women, situated in Nashville. Toward the latter part of 1893 there were high prospects for the reorganization of Mary Sharp College, and the old president went down to Winchester to take charge, the Boscobel seniors following him in a body so that they might receive their diplomas at his hands. His wife died in 1894, and the financial stringency of the times succeeded, by June 1896, in starving Mary Sharp College quite out of existence. Forlorn and detached, constantly becoming deafer, he lived out his remaining days in retirement.

[*Dr. Z. C. Graves and the Mary Sharp College, 1850–96* (1926); J. H. Borum, *Biog. Sketches of Tenn. Bapt. Ministers* (1880); Wm. Cathcart, *The Bapt. Encyc.* (1881); J. J. Burnett, *Sketches of Tennessee's Pioneer Bapt. Preachers* (1919); *Nashville Banner,* May 19, 1902; information from the Rev. O. L. Hailey, Nashville, Tenn., Dec. 5, 1928.] J. D. W.

GRAVIER, JACQUES (May 17, 1651–Apr. 23, 1708), known to his generation as the apostle to the Illinois Indians, was born at Moulins in central France. Educated in a Jesuit college, he performed his novitiate at Paris (1670–72), after which he was sent as instructor to several provincial towns. In 1684 he returned to Paris for advanced studies, and the next year was designated for the mission field in Canada. He spent one year at the mission of Sillery and was then ordered to the western field, where during 1687–88 he was stationed at St. Ignace on the Straits of Mackinac. In the latter year he was sent to aid Father Allouez [*q.v.*] among the Illinois. After the death of Allouez in 1689, Gravier was made vicar general of the Illinois mission, then located among the Kaskaskia and Peoria tribes on the Illinois River. During the first years he ministered both to them and to the Miami, among whom Allouez had died. In 1693 the Illinois mission was established on Lake Peoria, whither the French fort was removed at this time. The Peoria Indians were less easily influenced than the Kaskaskia; among the latter the great chief Rouensa became a Christian at the solicitation of his daughter, who had come under Father Gravier's influence (L. P. Kellogg, *Early Narratives of the Northwest,* 1917, p. 351). During nine months of 1693 the missionary baptized over two hundred Indians; the first baptism recorded was that of the child of Michel Aco [*q.v.*], Hennepin's companion on his Mississippi voyage, and the daughter of Rouensa. The register of this baptism is still extant (*Transactions of the Illinois State Historical Society for the Year 1904,* p. 394).

When Gravier had been several years among the Illinois he was removed to St. Ignace where for about three years he officiated as the Superior of the western missions. The Illinois mission, however, held his heart and in 1699 or 1700 he was allowed to return thither. He found his neophytes, with all the tribe of the Kaskaskia, about to remove to the river that now bears their name, in order to be in communication with the French of Louisiana. Father Gravier opposed the removal, but to no effect. He then resolved to visit in person the new colony at the mouth of the Mississippi and set forth from Peoria Sept. 8, 1700, for the long perilous voyage down the great river. His account of the tribes along the banks, as well as the flora and fauna of the lower Mississippi, is accurate and interesting. Arrived the last day of the year at Biloxi, he formed a friendship with Sieur de Bienville [*q.v.*], and remained in the Louisiana colony until 1702.

In that year, having returned to his mission on Lake Peoria, he found the Indians averse to his ministrations, and hostile to all French occupation. In the summer of 1705 he was attacked by an enemy Indian and severely wounded. The Jesuits at Kaskaskia sent a party to their comrade's relief; this rescuing group was besieged in the mission house, but Gravier finally made an escape. Since his wounds did not heal, in 1706 he went to Louisiana for medical treatment, and after some months voyaged to Paris. Later thinking himself sufficiently healed he returned to America, but soon after his ocean voyage died from the effects of his wounds, at the French post of Mobile. Gravier was a fervent Jesuit and a devoted missionary, and is considered to be the true founder of the Illinois mission. He reduced the language of that tribe to grammatical structure, and wrote an Illinois grammar now in Harvard University library.

[The chief source is *The Jesuit Relations and Allied Documents*, ed. by R. G. Thwaites, vols. LXIV, LXV, LXVI (1900); Gravier's narrative is published in J. G. Shea, *Early Voyages Up and Down the Mississippi* (1861). See, by the same author, *The Cath. Ch. in Colonial Days*, being vol. I (1886), of *The Hist. of the Cath. Ch. in the U. S.*; and *Hist. of the Cath. Missions Among the Indian Tribes of the U. S. 1529–1854* (1855), also C. W. Alvord, "The Illinois Country," *The Centennial Hist. of Ill.*, vol. I (1920); John Rothensteiner, *Hist. of the Archdiocese of St. Louis* (2 vols., 1928).]

L. P. K.

GRAY, ASA (Nov. 18, 1810–Jan. 30, 1888), botanist, was born at Sauquoit, Oneida County, N. Y., the eldest of the eight children of Moses Gray, a thriving farmer and tanner, by his wife, Roxana Howard. His parents, of Scotch-Irish and English descent, had migrated from central Massachusetts. Gray attended a school at Clinton, nine miles from his home, and transferred in 1825 to Fairfield Academy, in Herkimer County, where from James Hadley, father of James Hadley [*q.v.*], the philologist, he received his first lessons in natural science. During the winter of 1827–28 his attention was drawn to botany by the article on that subject in Brewster's *Edinburgh Encyclopædia.* He bought the *Manual of Botany* by Amos Eaton [*q.v.*], studied it till spring, though "out of all reach either of a greenhouse or of a potted plant" (*Letters,* I, 14), and sallied forth one memorable April day to discover and identify an early specimen of *Claytonia Virginica.* He continued as Hadley's pupil in the Fairfield Medical School 1829–31 and profited during the long vacations by association with Dr. John F. Trowbridge of Bridgewater. About this time, also, he began a correspondence with Lewis Caleb Beck [*q.v.*], for whom he acted later as substitute lecturer, and with John Torrey [*q.v.*], so soon to become his friend and master. He graduated M.D. Jan. 25, 1831, though not yet of age, but did not take up the practise of medicine. Heart and mind he was already dedicated to the study of botany.

His next eleven years were busy, happy, and impecunious. Having delivered a course of lectures on botany at the Medical School in May and June 1831, he used the forty dollars proceeds for an excursion to Niagara Falls and the Finger Lakes region. From 1832 to 1835 he taught science in Bartlett's High School at Utica. In the summer of 1832 he journeyed down the Unadilla into Pennsylvania, called on Louis David de Schweinitz [*q.v.*] at Bethlehem, explored Sussex County, N. J., and Orange County, N. Y., and accompanied Torrey, whom he now first met, on a trip to Tom's River, N. J. The next summer he botanized again in the Jersey tidal marshes and pine barrens. He collected plants and minerals along the Black River in New York in the late spring of 1834, lectured in Hadley's place at Hamilton College in the summer, and, securing a furlough from Bartlett, spent the following autumn and winter as Torrey's assistant in New York. Living in their home, he enjoyed the privilege of daily association with Torrey, while his taste, manners, and general culture improved under the influence of Mrs. Torrey. Scientific and literary stimulus also came in abundance from his friendship with John Carey, an able New York botanist. He had already begun to issue, in a small edition, his *North American Gramineæ and Cyperaceæ* (pt. I, 1834; pt. II, 1835), each part containing a hundred species and illustrated by dried specimens. This, his first independent publication, was praised by William Jackson Hooker as "among the most beautiful and useful works of the kind that we are acquainted with. The specimens are remarkably well selected, skillfully prepared, critically studied, and carefully compared with those in the extensive and very authentic herbarium of Dr. Torrey" (*Letters,* I, 45). In December 1834 he read before the New York Lyceum of Natural History his first two scientific papers. Late in 1835 he removed permanently to New York to be near his friend Torrey. His *Elements of Botany* appeared in 1836, and that summer he was appointed botanist of a projected government exploring expedition, command of which was eventually given to Lieut. Charles Wilkes [*q.v.*], but Gray was so vexed by delays and changes in personnel that he resigned before it sailed. Meanwhile he had become curator of the Lyceum of Natural History and was collaborating with Torrey on their *Flora of North America* (vol. I, 1838–40; vol. II, 1841–43)—"a work justly esteemed as second alone to De Candolle's *Prodromus Regni Vegetabilis* as a contribution to a knowledge of the vegetation of the globe" (J. D. Hooker, *post,* p. xv). Having accepted the professorship of botany in the University of Michigan, then organizing, he sailed for Europe in November 1838 to purchase books for the University and to study the type-specimens of American plants in various herbaria, a task made necessary by the advance of the *Flora.* He was abroad a year, visiting England, France, Italy, Austria, Bavaria, and Switzerland. The trip was in every way successful and laid the foundation of his lifelong friendship with so many European botanists. Returning to the United States, in the summer of 1841 he joined John Carey and James Constable on a trip to the Valley of Virginia and the mountains of North Carolina. He never assumed his duties at the University of Michigan. In 1842 the first edition was published of his *Botanical Text-Book,* long a standard work. With its lucid text and telling illustrations from pen-drawings by Isaac Sprague, it early set in American botany an admirable standard. It became the model for numerous imitations, and its definitions did much to unify the interpretation and application of technical terms in America and in other English-speaking countries. In its sixth edition (1879) it was finally renamed *Structural Botany.* That summer he accepted the Fisher professorship of natural history in Harvard University, thus bringing his *Wanderjahre* to a close. With forty-five years of unbroken health and activity still before him, he was now the acknowledged leader of American botanists.

No misfortunes or uncertainties marred the happiness of his long life. On May 4, 1848, he married Jane Lathrop Loring, daughter of Charles Greeley Loring [*q.v.*], who shared sympathetically in his work and survived him to edit his autobiography and letters. He traveled a good deal: to Europe in 1850–51, 1855, 1868–69, 1880–81, and 1887; to Florida in 1875; to California in 1872 and, with Joseph Dalton Hooker for a companion, in 1877; to California and Mexico in 1885. He created the Harvard department of botany and trained many of the eminent botanists of the next generation. He maintained a constant and friendly correspondence with scientists throughout the world, and at his house in the Botanical Garden, built originally for William Dandridge Peck and once occupied by Thomas Nuttall [*qq.v.*], he entertained them on their visits to Cambridge. He was one of the founders of the National Academy of Sciences, president 1863–73 of the American Academy of Arts and Sciences, president in 1872 of the American Association for the Advancement of Science, and a regent 1874–88 of the Smithsonian Institution. In all he accepted membership, regular, corresponding, foreign, or honorary, in sixty-six learned and scientific societies, ranging in degree from the Royal Society of London to the Polk County Agricultural Society of Iowa. Everywhere he seems to have been beloved for his simplicity, good humor, and friendliness as well as revered for qualities that made him one of the great botanists of the world.

His productions during these forty-five years fall into several distinct groups. To the *American Journal of Science* he contributed an unbroken series of reviews, bibliographical notes, news items, and short biographies that, taken together, constitute an authoritative, detailed, and readable history of botany extending over a period of half a century. This work, alone, was an extraordinary accomplishment; both his reviews and his biographies are masterpieces in their kind. He wrote frequently for the *Nation* and with less regularity for other periodicals. He also produced five important text-books—*First Lessons in Botany and Vegetable Physiology* (1857; 1868); *How Plants Grow* (1858); *Field, Forest, and Garden Botany* (1868; 1870); *How Plants Behave* (1872); and another *Elements of Botany* (1887)—which did immense service in popularizing the subject. In the field of plant geography Gray was a pioneer and master. Of his contributions to this department the most famous was the monograph on the botany of Japan and its relations to that of North America and other parts of the north temperate zone (*Memoirs of the American Academy of Arts and Sciences,* vol. VI, 1859). "In it, by a comparison of the floras of Eastern and Western America with one another and with Japan, and of all with the Tertiary flora of North America, Gray has outlined the history of the vegetation of the north temperate zone in relation to its past and present geographical features, from the Cretaceous period to the present time" (J. D. Hooker, *post,* p. xvii). Probably this work did more than any other one production of his to give Gray his world-wide reputation. His greatest achievement, however, was his elaboration of the descriptive botany of North America. Most of his more than three hundred and fifty books, monographs, and shorter papers deal with portions of this vast subject. Among these the most notable were the *Manual of the Botany of the Northern United States* (1848; Gray's last revision, 1867; later editions by his Harvard successors)—the most widely used of all his books; *Genera Floræ Americæ Boreali-Orientalis Illustrata* (vols. I and II, 1848–49); and *Synoptical Flora of North America* (vol. II, pt. I, 1878; vol. I, pt. II, 1884; 2nd ed. of both parts, 1886; reissued with corrections, 1888; vol. I, pt. I, Fascicles i and ii, 1895–97). He also elaborated the collections gathered on the Wilkes Expedition, of which he had once been the appointed botanist. This work (*United States Exploring Expedition during the Years 1838–42,* vol. XV, 1854–57; vol. XVII, 1874) is, in the judgment of Benjamin Lincoln Robinson, "one of the most extensive and remarkable contributions ever made by an American investigator to world science." Gray was fortunate to live in just the period during which the vast and diversified flora of more than half a continent was being brought to light by scientific exploration. An almost overwhelming quantity of material assembled by government expeditions and surveys and by countless private collectors was referred to him for scientific elaboration. In such work Gray was at the height of his genius. "The botanist is yet to be born who could write a more clear, accurate, and compact account of the flora of any country," wrote Farlow (*Smithsonian Report, post,* p. 773), and this seeming hyperbole merely states the fact. It is quite apparent that Gray owed much to his remarkable command of literary expression. He himself quoted approvingly the dictum of George Bentham that "the aptness of a botanical description, like the beauty of a work of the imagination, will always vary with the style and genius of the author" (*Scientific Papers of Asa Gray,* 1889, I, 119). His own style, sober but relieved by gleams of humor, was a marvel of clarity, proportion, and precision. The two volumes of *Scientific Papers,* edited after his death by Charles Sprague Sargent [*q.v.*], are good literature as well as good science.

On Sept. 5, 1857, Charles Darwin wrote Gray the famous letter in which he first outlined his theory of the evolution of species by means of natural selection, and to Gray, as to Hooker and Lyell, he sent one of the three advance copies of the *Origin of Species.* Gray became Darwin's chief American advocate, and Darwin prized him as one of his most influential supporters and most searching critics. To the discomfiture of some of Darwin's militantly agnostic disciples, Gray insisted on describing himself as "in his own fashion a Darwinian, philosophically a convinced theist, and religiously an acceptor of the 'creed commonly called the Nicene,' as the exponent of the Christian faith" (*Darwiniana,* 1876, p. vi). At the time this looked very much like carrying water on both shoulders. Gray appears now, however, to have been wiser than his generation; his contention that "variations . . . are evidently not from without but from within—not physical but physiological" looks forward to the discoveries of Mendel and De Vries. His essays on evolution and its implications were collected in *Darwiniana* (1876) and in 1880 he published two lectures, delivered at Yale Divinity School, on *Natural Science and Religion.*

In 1872 George Lincoln Goodale [*q.v.*] relieved him of his teaching duties, and in 1873 Charles Sprague Sargent succeeded him as director of the Botanical Garden, but Gray retained the Fisher professorship and kept at work until his death. On his birthday in 1885, one hundred and eighty American botanists united to send him letters of congratulation and to present him an eleven-inch silver vase embossed with figures of plants associated with his name and studies—*Grayia polygaloides, Shortia galacifolia,* and eleven others. On his last visit to England he received honorary degrees from Oxford, Cambridge, and Aberdeen. He died at his home in Cambridge one month after a paralytic stroke. Characteristically, his last act was a letter to a fellow-botanist, gently upbraiding him for coining a superfluous plant name. He was buried in Mount Auburn Cemetery.

[Jane Loring Gray, *Letters of Asa Gray* (2 vols., 1893), with a bibliography, a fragment of autobiography, etc.; Jas. Dwight Dana and Wm. Gilson Farlow [*qq.v.*], memoirs and bibliography, *Ann. Report of the Board of Regents of the Smithsonian Inst. . . . to July 1888* (1890); Wm. G. Farlow, another memcir, *Nat. Acad. Sci. Biog. Memoirs,* vol. III (1895); *Am. Acad. Arts and Sci.: Memorial of Asa Gray* (1888); *In Memoriam: Asa Gray* (1888), funeral sermon, etc.; unsigned memoir by Geo. Lincoln Goodale in the *Nation,* Feb. 2, 1888; Chas. Sprague Sargent, *Asa Gray* (reprint of article in the N. Y. *Sun,* Jan. 3, 1886); Chas. Reid Barnes [*q.v.*], "Asa Gray," *Botanical Gazette,* Jan. 1886; Wm. G. Farlow, memoir, *Ibid.,* Mar. 1888; C. V. Riley, "Personal Reminiscences of Dr. Asa Gray," *Ibid.,* July 1888; editorial and obituary, *Boston Transcript,* Jan. 31, 1888; J. D. Hooker, memoir, *Proc. Royal Soc. London,* vol. XLVI (1890); John Merle

Coulter [q.v.], chapter in *Leading Am. Men of Science* (1910), ed. by D. S. Jordan; Francis Darwin, *The Life and Letters of Charles Darwin* (2 vols., 1888) and *More Letters of Charles Darwin* (2 vols., 1903); Leonard Huxley, *Life and Letters of Sir J. D. Hooker* (2 vols., 1918); G. L. Goodale, "The Development of Botany since 1818," in *A Century of Science in America with Special Reference to the Am. Jour. of Science 1818–1918* (1918); G. F. Wright, "The Debt of the Church to Asa Gray," *Bibliotheca Sacra*, July 1888; Gamaliel Bradford, *As God Made Them* (1929); *The Development of Harvard Univ.* (1930), ed. by S. E. Morison; B. L. Robinson, "Asa Gray," *Science*, July 17, 1925, "Portraits in the Gray Herbarium," *Harvard Alumni Bull.*, Mar. 5, 1931, and letter to editor, May 9, 1931, parts of which have been used freely in the composition of this article.] G. H. G.

GRAY, ELISHA (Aug. 2, 1835–Jan. 21, 1901), inventor, was born at Barnesville, Belmont County, Ohio, the son of David and Christiana (Edgerton) Gray. His father, who had emigrated from Pennsylvania and had married there, was rather unfortunate financially and the family lived modestly on the farm, the children attending the public schools. Before Elisha had completed his studies his father died suddenly and he was compelled to find work. He first tried blacksmithing but found that he was not strong enough to carry on that trade. He then took up carpentry and boat-building and was working at these trades when one of the professors of Oberlin College encouraged him to try to get a college education. Gray was then twenty-two years old and by doing carpentry work to earn his way, he was able to spend three years in the preparatory school and two years in the college. His particular interest during his college course lay in the physical sciences and by the time of his leaving this interest narrowed to electrical mechanisms. Ill health, brought on by overwork while in college, greatly restricted his activities for the succeeding five years, but during the six years after 1867 he invented an automatic self-adjusting telegraphic relay, a telegraph switch and annunciator for hotels, a private telegraph line printer, and a telegraphic repeater. In 1872 he moved to Chicago where he maintained his residence throughout his life and organized with E. M. Barton the firm of Gray & Barton out of which grew the Western Electric Company. He continued in the firm for about two years and then retired to devote his whole time to electrical researches. Gray's interest at this time lay in the development of a system of electro-harmonic telegraphy for transmitting musical tones as a means of increasing the number of messages capable of being sent simultaneously over a single wire. He obtained two patents for the system July 27, 1875. As he progressed in this, the idea of transmitting vocal sounds came to him and after experimenting for some time he filed a caveat (a confidential report of an invention which is not fully perfected) in the United States Patent Office on Feb. 14, 1876. That very day, but a few hours earlier, Alexander Graham Bell filed a patent application for a speaking telephone, thus anticipating Gray. With the subsequent formation of the Bell Telephone Company and the introduction of the telephone as a competitor of the telegraph, the Western Union Telegraph Company acquired Gray's as well as Edison's telephone patents and a bitter infringement battle followed, extending over several years and involving the most malicious accusations of malpractise both within the Patent Office and outside. Bell's patent of Mar. 7, 1876, was sustained, but the Gray-Bell controversy, in the minds of many people, has never been satisfactorily settled. Gray never fully recovered from this disappointment but he continued for the balance of his life to invent electrical devices and amassed about seventy patents. For some of these the financial return to him was quite large but he spent all in further research work. Probably his most important invention in his later years was the telautograph, patented in 1888 and 1891. By this electrical mechanism facsimile writing or drawing could be transmitted to distant points almost instantaneously. Gray had developed the invention by 1893 and at the World's Fair in Chicago that year he transmitted writing through wire resistances equivalent to 250 miles. The telautograph came into general use in banks and railway stations, and was adaptable to a variety of industrial uses. At the time of his sudden death near Boston, Mass., Gray was engaged in experimentation with under-water signaling to vessels at sea. Besides numerous articles which appeared in technical journals, he published *Experimental Researches in Electro-Harmonic Telegraphy* (1878) and *Nature's Miracles* (3 vols., 1899–1900). In 1893 he was organizing chairman of the first International Electrical Congress, held in Chicago. He was decorated by the French government and was the recipient of honorary degrees from several colleges in the United States. His wife was M. Delia Shepard of Oberlin, Ohio, whom he married about 1865 and who with a son survived him.

[The *Am. Inventor*, Feb. 1, 1901; *Electrical Rev.*, Jan. 26, 1901; E. W. Byrn, *Progress of Invention in the Nineteenth Century* (1900); T. A. L. Du Moncel, *The Telephone, Microphone and Phonograph* (1879); *Electrical World and Engineer*, Jan. 26, 1901.]
C. W. M.

GRAY, FRANCIS CALLEY (Sept. 19, 1790–Dec. 29, 1856), Harvard benefactor, traced his descent from William Gray, a pioneer maker of shoes at Lynn, Mass., whose grandson, William

Gray [q.v.], settled at Salem, Mass., entered the shipping business, and prospered exceedingly. He married Elizabeth, daughter of John Chipman of Marblehead, and Francis Calley was their sixth child. Born at Salem, he attended the public schools there, proceeding in due course to Harvard College, where he graduated in 1809. In August 1809 he accompanied John Quincy Adams, the newly appointed minister to Russia, in the capacity of unpaid secretary to the United States legation at St. Petersburg. After spending four years abroad he returned in 1813, studied law in Boston, and was admitted to the Massachusetts bar in 1814. He did not, however, engage in active practise but, taking up his residence in Boston, devoted himself to public affairs and literary pursuits. By family tradition a Federalist, he became in 1822 a representative of Boston in the General Court, and by successive reëlections continued such until his election as senator from Suffolk County in 1825, which position he filled in 1826, 1828, 1829, 1831, and 1843. He was also elected a member of the Executive Council in 1835. Since he did not possess a strong political instinct, his legislative career was undistinguished.

In 1826 Gray was elected a fellow of Harvard. It was a critical period in the history of the college in that receipts were not meeting expenditures and upon him and his colleagues devolved the responsibility of remedying the situation. To this task he devoted himself whole-heartedly both in council and by public appeal, and when he retired in 1836 radical retrenchments and reforms had freed the college from financial embarrassment. Gray never married, and by virtue of recommendations contained in his will, Harvard became the beneficiary of a considerable portion of his estate, including a choice collection of 3,000 engravings, together with $16,000, the income of which was to be applied in connection with the collection, as well as an additional $50,000 with which to establish and maintain a museum of comparative zoölogy. His relatives, William Gray and John Chipman Gray [q.v.], were also benefactors, and the family name was perpetuated in Gray's Hall, a dormitory built by the University in 1863. In addition to numerous contributions to the *North American Review* and other periodicals Gray wrote "Remarks on the Early Laws of Massachusetts Bay, with the code adopted in 1641, and called the Body of Liberties" (*Massachusetts Historical Society Collections*, 3 ser., vol. VIII, 1843) and *Prison Discipline in America* (1848).

[Details of the family history appear in Edward Gray, *Wm. Gray of Salem, Merchant* (1914), and Abner Forbes, *The Rich Men of Mass.* (2nd ed., 1852). His career is outlined in Wm. T. Davis, *Bench and Bar of the Commonwealth of Mass.* (1895), and more fully in an obituary notice in the *Boston Daily Advertiser*, Dec. 30, 1856. For particulars of his Harvard benefactions see *Harvard Univ., Ann. Reports of the President*, 1856–57, 1857–58; and *Harvard Univ.* (1900), ed. by Joshua L. Chamberlain, pt. 2, p. 92; *Cat. of the Coll. of Engravings Bequeathed to Harvard Coll. by Francis Calley Gray* (1869).]

H. W. H. K.

GRAY, GEORGE (May 4, 1840–Aug. 7, 1925), jurist, was the great-grandson of William Gray who, leaving Belfast early in the eighteenth century, settled in Kent County, Del. His grandfather, Andrew Gray, moved to New Castle County, in 1808, and his father, Andrew Caldwell Gray, who married Elizabeth, daughter of Frederick Scofield of Stamford, Conn., was a capitalist and lawyer practising at New Castle, where he himself was born. Obtaining his early education in the local schools, he went in 1857 to the College of New Jersey, now Princeton University, graduating in 1859. He then studied law in his father's office, spent a year at the Harvard Law School, and was admitted to the Delaware bar in 1863. He practised at New Castle, then at Wilmington, his father's various industrial and railroad interests furnishing him at the outset with opportunities of advancement. A strong Democrat, he engaged actively in local politics and was a delegate to the National Democratic Convention of 1876. He had become the recognized leader of the local bar when Gov. Hall in 1879 appointed him attorney-general of Delaware. In this position he displayed great energy and efficiency, and despite his corporation affiliations no outside influences were permitted to interfere with enforcement of the law. Reappointed in 1884 by Gov. Stockley, he resigned Mar. 16, 1885, on his election as United States senator. He remained in the Senate for fourteen years, being reëlected in 1887 and 1893 and serving till March 1899. A masterly speech in which he had nominated Bayard for the presidency at the National Democratic Convention at Cincinnati in 1880 had made him known nationally, and in the Senate he took rank as one of the leaders of his party. He declined to enter Cleveland's administration as attorney-general of the United States, but gave the President invaluable support on the floor of the Senate. In 1896 he refused to follow Bryan on the currency question and actively supported the nominees of the Gold Democrats. During the latter portion of his term he served on the committee on foreign relations. Though President McKinley was a political opponent, he had a high regard for Gray's diplomatic temperament and ability and appointed him a member of the Joint High Commission which met at Quebec in August 1898 to adjust outstanding difficulties between the United States and Canada. Later in the same year he appointed him one of the United States commissioners to negotiate peace with Spain. In the deliberations which resulted in the Treaty of Paris he took a prominent share, and though he opposed in principle the acquisition of the Philippines he declined to dissociate himself from his colleagues on that point. On his retirement from the Senate in 1899 he was appointed by McKinley judge of the United States circuit court for the 3rd circuit, a position which he retained till 1914.

Possessing an eminently judicial mind, Gray combined a thorough knowledge of legal principles and practise with a capacity for applying that knowledge to concrete cases, and his decisions were rarely reversed. His later reputation rests principally, however, on his extra-judicial labors which were varied and responsible. In November 1900 he was nominated by McKinley as a member of the Permanent Court of Arbitration at The Hague, an appointment which was continued by Presidents Roosevelt, Taft, and Wilson. In October 1902 he was appointed by President Roosevelt chairman of the commission to arbitrate between the operators and the miners during the anthracite coal strike in Pennsylvania, the successful accomplishment of which was perhaps the outstanding feature of his career. Later on he was equally effective in terminating labor troubles in Alabama and Illinois. In 1903–04 he acted as the third of the three members of the commission of arbitration between the United States and the Dominican Republic and in 1909–10 was a member of the tribunal in the North Atlantic Coast Fisheries arbitration between Great Britain and the United States at The Hague. His last public services were as chairman of the United States delegation to the Pan-American Scientific Congress in 1915, and as a member of the American-Mexican Joint Commission in 1916. The last years of his life were spent in retirement at Wilmington. He was married in 1870 to Harriet L. Black, daughter of Dr. Charles H. Black of New Castle. She died in 1880 and on Aug. 8, 1882, he was married to her sister, Margaret J. Black. An able lawyer, a far-sighted politician, strong in his convictions, but ever amenable to argument, his chief characteristics were an unimpeachable integrity, a desire to render service, and an open mind, readily receptive of fresh impressions, which softened political animosities and caused Republican and Democrat alike to entrust him with missions of the utmost delicacy and responsibility.

[H. C. Conrad, *Hist. of the State of Del.*, III (1908), 1009; W. L. Bevan and E. M. Williams, *Hist. of Del., Past and Present*, III (1929), 196–98; *Harper's Weekly*, Mar. 3, 1894; the *Green Bag*, June 1908; *Case and Comment*, July 1899; *Who's Who in America*, 1924–25; the *Evening Jour.* (Wilmington), Aug. 8, 1925.]

H. W. H. K.

GRAY, GEORGE ALEXANDER (Sept. 28, 1851–Feb. 8, 1912), cotton manufacturer, was born in Crab Orchard township, Mecklenburg County, N. C., the youngest child of George Alexander Gray and Mary Wallace, daughter of Robert Wallace, whose parents had emigrated from Ireland. His paternal grandparents were Ransom Gray, of Mecklenburg, a soldier in the Revolution, and Narcissa Alexander, daughter of Col. George Alexander, who came to North Carolina from Pennsylvania. In 1853 the father gave up farming and moved his family of nine to the Rock Island cotton factory near-by and within a few years moved on to another little mill in Stowesville. Here, in June 1859, the father died suddenly of apoplexy. The mother, who was remarkable for her courage and contrivance, now had a hard struggle. The older children worked, but George, only eight years old, was his mother's companion and special pet. In 1861, with the outbreak of the Civil War, George too entered the factory, but the mill soon closed, and the Grays moved to Caleb Lineberger's cotton factory at what was called "Pinhook" on the South Fork of the Catawba River. George began work here as a sweeper boy at ten cents for a twelve- to fourteen-hour day. Shortly afterward he had an accident in the factory in which his arm was broken in three places, and he narrowly missed suffering an amputation. The proprietor of the mill persuaded his mother to send the boy to school during his convalescence, and this one year comprised the whole of his formal education. He had a turn for machinery and made it his study. Given more and more responsibility, he became assistant superintendent of the mill and did everything from supervising spinning and weaving to replacing buckets in the little breast wheel.

When Gray was only nineteen, he became superintendent of the Woodlawn cotton-mill. A few years later, in 1878, he was engaged by the Oates brothers to equip and operate the Charlotte Cotton Mills, the first plant in what later became a textile center. After conducting this factory for four years, he was employed by Col. R. Y. McAden to start his mill at McAdenville. In 1888, having saved a little money, he went to Gastonia, then a tiny settlement at the junction of the Southern Railroad and a smaller road, and with the assistance of R. C. G. Love and J. D. Moore he organized the first mill in the district, the Gastonia Cotton Manufacturing Company.

Confident that Gastonia, with cheap fuel, abundant labor, raw material, and good transportation, would some day become an important seat of cotton manufacturing, he set about fulfilling his prophecy. In 1893 with G. W. Ragan and R. C. Pegram he built the Trenton mill, and three years later with John F. Love he erected the Avon mill. This plant was significant because it was the first mill at Gastonia to run on fine yarns and sheeting. Then followed other promotions in quick succession—the Ozark mill, 1899; the Loray, 1900; the Gray mill, built entirely by himself, 1905; and the Clara, Holland, and Flint mills, 1907. Gray was president of most of these factories, and only two mills were built in the town in his lifetime without his assistance. He also helped organize the Wylie mill at Chester, S. C.; the Scottdale at Atlanta; and the Mandeville at Carrollton, Ga.

Gray was one of the first Southerners to bring technical proficiency to cotton manufacture in the South. Other enterprises had had to rely upon Northern advice and assistance. He constantly strove for smoother, better-controlled power, and in successive mills installed the latest steam-engines. In 1905 he operated the first electrically driven mill in the Carolina Piedmont and then abandoned his steam-driven generator as soon as he could get hydro-electric power from Great Falls. He hailed this and similar hydro stations as foretelling a new day in manufacture. It is said he could walk through a great room throbbing with spindles or looms and detect by the sound a defectively operating machine in a remote corner. He prescribed for himself strict discipline in his hard-working daily life but he was not without a sense of humor. Nervously energetic, he made up his mind quickly, acted forthwith, and knew no relaxation (aside from reading Shakespeare and Burns) except in added superintendence of his mills. He joined the Methodist church in Gastonia and for the rest of his life was devoted to its service. In appearance he was small and thick-set, with bushy eyebrows and a penetrating, sparkling glance that nobody forgot. He gave the impression of one of his own whirring spindles. At his death he was survived by his wife, Jennie (Withers) Gray, and eight of their ten children.

[S. A. Ashe, ed., *Biog. Hist. of N. C.*, VII (1908), 122–29; *Gastonia Gazette*, Feb. 9, 1912; C. W. Patman, "Geo. A. Gray: An Appreciation of a Remarkable Career," *Knit Goods*, Mar. 1912; Broadus Mitchell, "Some Southern Industrialists," *Va. Quart. Rev.*, Jan. 1929; autobiographical material in an article by Gray, "A Visit to Great Falls," in *Charlotte Daily Observer*, Apr. 5, 1908.]

B. M.

GRAY, HENRY PETERS (June 23, 1819–Nov. 12, 1877), portrait- and genre-painter, was born in Greenwich Street, New York City, the son of George W. Gray, merchant, and the grandson of Harry Peters, owner of a farm in Manhattan, east of Broadway, subsequently the site of Vauxhall Gardens. The boy was sent to a school in Clinton, N. Y., and on returning home at the age of nineteen he became a pupil of Daniel Huntington, president of the National Academy of Design, with whom he studied for about a year, 1838–39. So rapidly did he develop that in 1839, at the age of twenty, he exhibited five paintings at the National Academy. In 1840 he went to Europe and passed some eighteen months assiduously studying and copying the works of the old masters in the museums of Italy, more especially the works of the Venetian school. In 1843 he was married to Miss Clark, an artist, who became president of the New York Association of Women Painters. Soon after his marriage he visited Boston and painted many portraits there. On his second trip abroad in 1845 he was accompanied by his wife. After his return to New York in 1846 his reputation grew apace and he was kept busy painting portraits. He took an active part in the affairs of the National Academy, to which he had been elected in 1842, was a member of the council, vice-president in 1861, and president in 1869. In 1871 he made his third visit to Italy, with his family, and this time he remained nearly four years, making a long sojourn in Florence, where he took a studio and was a prominent figure in the American colony. It was at this time that he painted "The Origin of Our Flag," one of his most ambitious compositions, which became the property of Thomas B. Clarke of New York, and "The Flower of Fiesole," which was exhibited at the National Academy in 1875, and which is considered one of his best works. After 1874 he confined himself to painting portraits. His "Venus and Paris" and "Pride of the Village" were shown at the Paris Exposition of 1867.

During the period of a third of a century when Gray was before the public he was deemed one of the most accomplished figure-painters of America. The sort of subjects he painted may be described as classical genre. His motives were derived from mythology and history, with occasional excursions into the field of moral and religious symbolism. He was one of the most perfect types of the academic painter that America has produced. His work had all the merits, and avoided some of the common defects, of the academic school. It was conceived, composed, and executed strictly in accordance with the canons of the Venetian school; and, so far as derivative art may be flawless, it was so. Indeed, his work was faultily faultless. His portraits were much admired, and his many sitters included a number of personages well known in the New York of the middle nineteenth century. "History will certainly assign to him a permanent and most honorable place among the earlier American painters," said a writer in the *Evening Post* the day after his death. His "Greek Lovers," "The Wages of War," and "Cleopatra Dissolving the Pearl" belong to the Metropolitan Museum of Art, New York; his "Cupid Begging his Arrow" is in the Pennsylvania Academy, Philadelphia; and his "Judgment of Paris" is in the Corcoran Gallery, Washington.

[D. O'C. Townley, "Living Am. Artists," in *Scribner's Monthly,* Aug. 1871; Henry T. Tuckerman, *Book of the Artists* (1867); C. E. Clement and L. Hutton, *Artists of the Nineteenth Century and their Works* (2 vols., 1879); *N. Y. Tribune* and *Evening Post,* Nov. 13, 1877; Samuel Isham, *Hist. of Am. Painting* (1905); J. D. Champlin and C. C. Perkins, eds., *Cyc. of Painters and Paintings* (4 vols., 1886–87); Thieme-Becker, *Allgemeines Lexikon der Bildenden Künstler,* vol. XIV (1921); *Illustrated Cat. of Paintings in the Metropolitan Museum of Art, N. Y.* (1905).] W. H. D.

GRAY, HORACE (Mar. 24, 1828–Sept. 15, 1902), Massachusetts jurist, justice of the Supreme Court of the United States, was born in Boston, Mass., the eldest child of Horace and Harriet Upham Gray. He was the grandson of Lieut.-Gov. William Gray [*q.v.*] and an elder half-brother of John Chipman Gray [*q.v.*]. He was prepared for college in Boston at private schools, but during the latter part of his youth the family lived in a country suburb where there was opportunity for rambles and sport. In 1845 he was graduated from Harvard College, but probably on account of his extreme youth, he had not yet attained distinction as a scholar. After leaving college, he took a trip to Europe. His chief intellectual interest was in natural history, but in 1847, while he was in Europe, his father, who had been a wealthy man, met with financial reverses. The son returned home and in February 1848 entered the Harvard Law School. His ability, industry, and enthusiasm soon won him a place among the best scholars in the school. He there learned with his fellow student, C. C. Langdell [*q.v.*], to study law by an examination of all decided cases bearing upon the point immediately under consideration. This method he followed through life, and his judicial opinions are characterized, unduly in the opinion of some, by a critical and chronological examination of all important decisions bearing upon the question at issue.

After leaving the law school, Gray studied in Boston in the offices of Sohier & Welch and of John Lowell prior to his admission to the bar in 1851. Soon afterward, on the illness of Luther S. Cushing, reporter of decisions of the supreme judicial court, Gray served as a temporary substitute, preparing the last volume of Cushing's *Reports,* and in 1854 he was appointed to the office. The position of reporter at that time was regarded as one of great importance and often served as a stepping-stone to the bench. The reporter was allowed to engage in private practise, and Gray was counsel in a number of important cases. He also took an active interest in the political conflicts which engaged the country shortly before the outbreak of the Civil War. The influence of his social circle and of his own temperament, naturally conservative, might have been expected to draw him to the side of the Whigs, but he was an original Free-Soiler; and, as a Republican, he was an unsuccessful candidate in 1860 for the nomination of attorney-general for Massachusetts. After 1861 his legal advice was frequently sought by Gov. John A. Andrew on the legal problems arising from the war. On Aug. 23, 1864, Gov. Andrew appointed Gray an associate justice of the supreme judicial court. He was then thirty-six years old, the youngest man ever made judge of that court. By the death or resignation thereafter of five of the judges then on the bench, he became senior associate justice in the short period of five years; and on the death of Chief Justice Chapman was himself appointed chief justice on Sept. 5, 1873. During his tenure of office the members of the court not only sat together to hear appeals but individually conducted trials of cases in the first instance. The training thus gained in deciding questions of fact Gray deemed throughout his life as of great importance for the appellate work to which in his later life he was almost exclusively confined. He remained on the Massachusetts bench for eighteen years and during that period wrote far more than his share of the published opinions of the court. He was gifted with a remarkable constitution and a quickness in reading that enabled him to take in a printed page almost at a glance, as well as a memory that retained what he read.

The distinction of Gray's work in the Massachusetts court naturally led to his appointment in 1881 as a justice of the Supreme Court of the United States. There he sat for the remainder of his life, lending strength to the Court by his profound knowledge of the common law and his wise judgment. If he did not attain the reputation of his colleague Miller, on constitutional questions, or that of his colleague Bradley, on problems demanding acute analysis, he was preëminent in his knowledge of former decisions, and of the history and development of legal doctrine. He was actively engaged in the work of the Court until 1902. On Feb. 3 of that year, after sitting in court, he had an apoplectic shock from which he never recovered.

While Gray was a judge in Massachusetts, and to a lesser extent after his appointment to the Supreme Court of the United States, he was frequently regarded as a martinet. Undoubtedly he was a strict disciplinarian who would not brook even slight offenses against proper decorum in court. This characteristic, however, was not due to a harsh or impatient temper. He was of genial disposition, and, except where the dignity of the court was in question, he was a patient man. The key to his conduct, and, indeed, to his whole life, is found in an undeviating devotion to what he deemed the duties of his office. His serious work was largely confined within the limits of his judicial labors. Before he went on the bench he wrote for Josiah Quincy's *Reports* an elaborate appendix on writs of assistance and notes on slavery in Massachusetts and England. He also delivered an address on Chief Justice Marshall at Richmond in 1901. But for the most part both the amount of work which his office required and his views of judicial propriety restricted such activities.

Though his working hours during most of his life exceeded those of most men, Gray was fond of congenial society. He was also a great reader of miscellaneous literature. Biography, books of travel, and especially books relating to birds and animals, he read with avidity. The tastes which had seemed at one time likely to lead him to devote his life to natural science continued, and he often spent a portion of his vacation in fishing or duck shooting. In appearance he was one of the most striking men of his time. He was six feet and four inches tall and, unlike most very tall men, all his proportions were on the same large scale. His massive head, his large but finely shaped hands, and the great bulk of his frame, all seemed to mark him as belonging to a larger race than his fellows. His face in repose was serious, but he relished a joke or good story that did not infringe on the rather strict boundaries which he thought should limit humorous conversation. He remained unmarried until 1889. On June 4 of that year he was married to Jane Matthews, the daughter of his friend and colleague Stanley Matthews, who had recently died.

[Geo. F. Hoar, memoir in *Proc. Mass. Hist. Soc.*, 2 ser., vol. XVIII (1905), and tributes by C. F. Adams and Solomon Lincoln, *Ibid.*, vol. XVI (1903); Samuel Williston, "Horace Gray" in *Great Am. Lawyers*, vol. VIII (1909), ed. by W. D. Lewis; *Proc. of the Bar and of the Supreme Judicial Court of Mass. in Memory of Horace Gray, Jan. 17, 1903* (1903); *Proc. Am. Acad. of Arts and Sci.*, June 1904; *Boston Transcript* and *Evening Star* (Washington, D. C.), Sept. 15, 1902.]

S. W.

GRAY, ISAAC PUSEY (Oct. 18, 1828–Feb. 14, 1895), Union soldier, governor of Indiana, minister to Mexico, was born in Chester County, Pa. His parents, John and Hannah (Worthington) Gray, of Quaker descent, moved from Pennsylvania to Ohio in 1836. Gray's formal education was limited to the common schools, though he early acquired the habit of home reading. His first responsible position was a clerkship in a store in New Madison, where he soon became a partner and a few years later the sole proprietor. During this period he used his spare time reading law. In 1850 he was married to Eliza Jaqua, daughter of an old resident of the county, and five years later he removed with his family to Union City, Ind., where he continued his mercantile business and also the study of law. Within a few years thereafter he entered upon the practise of law and soon was recognized as a leading member of the Indiana bar, his practise extending to the Supreme Court of the United States. After the outbreak of the Civil War, on Sept. 4, 1862 he was commissioned colonel of the 4th Indiana Cavalry, but resigned, due to ill health, Feb. 11, 1863, before his regiment got into action. In June of the same year he was commissioned colonel of the 106th Regiment of "Minute Men" and took part in the attempt to capture Gen. Morgan. Mustered out of this service on July 17, he was commissioned captain of the Union City Guards of the Randolph Battalion of the Indiana Legion, but this office he also resigned Nov. 13, 1863.

Immediately following the war Gray entered upon his political career. In 1866 he became the Republican candidate for Congress against George W. Julian who had long represented the district in the national House of Representatives. He proved himself a skilful political organizer and although he was defeated the vote was exceedingly close, Julian winning by but 915 majority. Two years later he was elected to the state Senate where he sat four years. While serving as president *pro tempore* of that body he was largely responsible for the ratification of the Fifteenth Amendment of the United States Constitution. Indiana was the last state to vote on the Amendment and her vote was necessary to assure adoption. The state Senate had a Republican majority, but the Democrats were bitterly opposed to the Amendment and tried to defeat it by absenting themselves from the Senate chamber, thus preventing a quorum. Gray, by leaving the chair and locking the doors to the chamber and counting the Democratic members in the lobby as present, declared a quorum and thus the Amendment was declared passed.

In 1872 Gray identified himself with the Liberal Republican movement, was a member of the Cincinnati convention which nominated Horace Greeley for the presidency, and was a member of the national committee of that short-lived party. In 1874 he declined the nomination of the Democrats for attorney-general, but two years later he accepted their nomination for lieutenant-governor on the ticket with "Blue Jeans" Williams and was elected. Gov. Williams died in office, Nov. 20, 1880, and Gray filled out the term. In 1881 he was the Democratic nominee for senator and in 1884 was nominated governor on the Democratic ticket and was elected by a large majority. He was chosen by the Indiana legislature to succeed Benjamin Harrison as United States senator in 1887 but declined the election. In the national campaign of 1888 in Indiana his friends started a Gray boom for the vice-presidential nomination, but it collapsed. Four years later, with Daniel W. Voorhees and Joseph E. McDowell, he was largely responsible for carrying the state for Grover Cleveland (Buley, *post,* p. 42), and in March 1893 he was appointed by the President United States minister to Mexico —one of the first diplomatic appointments made by Cleveland in his second term. Two years later he died in Mexico after a short illness. President Diaz and his cabinet with the entire diplomatic corps accompanied the body to the train and the flags on all government buildings were placed at half-mast. For the honors paid their minister the United States Congress passed a resolution of thanks to the Mexican government. Gray was a man of rugged and positive character and exceptional native ability and represented much that was best in the public life of his time.

[*A Biog. Hist. of Eminent and Self-Made Men of the State of Ind.* (1880), vol. I; F. M. Trissal, *Pub. Men. of Ind.: A Pol. Hist. from 1860 to 1890* (1922); J. P. Dunn, *Ind. and Indianans* (1919), vol. II; O. B. Carmichael, "The Campaign of 1876 in Ohio," *Ind. Mag. of Hist.,* Dec. 1913; R. C. Buley, "The Campaign of 1888 in Ind.," *Ibid.,* June 1914, *A Portrait and Biog. Record of Delaware and Randolph Counties, Ind.* (1894); *Indianapolis Jour.,* Feb. 15, 16, 1895; *Indianapolis Sentinel,* Feb. 15, 16, 17, 1895.] W. W. S.

GRAY, JOHN CHIPMAN (July 14, 1839–Feb. 25, 1915), lawyer, author, educationalist, was born at Brighton, then a suburb of Boston, Mass. He was the grandson of Lieut.-Gov. William Gray [*q.v.*], a merchant and ship-owner of Salem, Lynn, and Boston, and the son of Horace Gray of Boston, also a merchant. His mother was Sarah Russell Gardner, the daughter of Samuel Pickering Gardner. After attending the Boston Latin School, Gray proceeded to Harvard College where he graduated in 1859, fifth in his class. He then entered the Harvard Law School, graduated LL.B. in 1861, and continued his studies there until January 1862, when he entered the law office of Peleg W. Chandler [*q.v.*]. On Sept. 18, 1862, he was admitted to the Suffolk County bar. He was a strong supporter of the Union and was commissioned second lieutenant in the 41st Massachusetts Volunteer Infantry, Oct. 7, 1862. Placed on the staff of Brig.-Gen. Gordon at Harper's Ferry, he served for a year in that capacity with the Army of the Potomac and in the Peninsular campaign. In 1863 he became assistant adjutant-general, assistant judge-advocate and secretary to Gordon. In July 1864 he was appointed judge advocate with the rank of major on the staff of Gen. Foster and later served in the same capacity on the staff of Gen. Gillmore, commanding the Department of the South. On the termination of the war he returned to Boston and commenced practise there in partnership with John C. Ropes [*q.v.*]. In 1866 he assisted in the founding of the *American Law Review* and in conjunction with Ropes edited the first four volumes (1866–70). Appointed a lecturer in the Harvard Law School, Dec. 4, 1869, he retained this position by successive reappointments till Mar. 18, 1875, when he became Story Professor of Law. On Nov. 12, 1883, he was transferred to the Royall Professorship of Law, a place which he held for twenty-nine years, resigning Feb. 1, 1913. He had been for nearly forty years a member of the faculty and on his retirement was appointed Royall Professor Emeritus. He had on more than one occasion been offered a judgeship, but always declined to sever his connection with the law school.

Gray's tenure of office coincided with the rise and development of the modern system of legal education and the substitution of the case system for the formal lecture course. He was not a pioneer in adopting the new method; for some years he adhered to the time-honored practise of following carefully prepared lectures, but later, on becoming convinced of the superior advantages of discussing only case law in class, he completely changed his method, identified himself whole-heartedly with the new movement, and became its most brilliant exponent. At first his range of subjects was wide, including bankruptcy, federal court procedure, evidence, conflict of laws, and property, and later, for a short time, constitutional law. In course of time, however, he confined himself to the law of property, particularly real property, on which subject he became the foremost authority in the United States. As a teacher he was never pedantic or abstruse but always sought to place himself on a level with his students, a task which his clarity of thought and simplicity of speech rendered easy.

Gray continued to practise law throughout his connection with the law school by special arrangement with the governing body. He believed that by maintaining contact with actual legal business and litigation he would be a more efficient teacher. Associated with John C. Ropes and subsequently with Judge Loring, his firm enjoyed an extensive practise, but he confined his attention to consultations, opinions, and appellant court briefs, his temperament not being suited to jury litigation. He was frequently retained in important contests beyond the confines of Massachusetts, one of which was a suit relative to the will of Benjamin Franklin (150 *Pa.*, 437). Since his cases dealt largely with real property, charitable trusts, and quasi-public educational corporations, they were never of a sensational order, and the public in general knew little of his supreme legal attainments.

Gray's contributions to legal literature, though few, were of outstanding excellence. His first two works, *Restraints on the Alienation of Property* (1883) and *The Rule against Perpetuities* (1886), dealt with certain phases of property law which had not previously been adequately expounded, and the last-named at once took its place as the standard text on its subject. It was not only accepted as authoritative in the United States, but enjoyed an equal, perhaps higher, reputation in the British courts. As an auxiliary to his law-school courses he compiled *Select Cases and Other Authorities on the Law of Property* (6 vols., 1888–92), which was adopted as a prescribed text in the leading law schools throughout the country. In 1908–09 as Carpentier Lecturer at the Columbia School of Law he delivered a course of lectures published in 1909 as *The Nature and Sources of the Law.* The work immediately attracted attention by reason of the attractive manner in which Gray had discussed problems of analytical jurisprudence and had contributed new lights on the threadbare subject of sovereignty. He also wrote articles for various legal periodicals and assisted Albert G. Browne as reporter of the decisions of the supreme judicial court contained in the *Massachusetts Reports,* volumes 100–11. On June 4, 1873, he was married to Anna Sophia Lyman Mason, the daughter of Rev. Charles Mason, rector of Grace Church, Boston, and granddaughter of Jeremiah Mason. His elder half-brother, Horace [*q.v.*], was chief justice of the supreme judicial court of Massachusetts and later associate justice of the United States Supreme Court. Gray's correspondence with his family and friends during the Civil War has been edited by Worthington Chauncey Ford under the title *War Letters, 1862–65, of John Chipman and John Codman Ropes* (1927).

[Roland Gray, *John Chipman Gray* (1917) contains a biographical sketch and reprints of a number of articles including those found in the *Am. Law Rev.*, Mar.–Apr. 1906; *Harvard Law Rev.*, Apr. 1915; *Harvard Grads.' Mag.*, June 1915; *Law Quart. Rev.*, July 1915; *Mass. Law Quart.*, Feb. 1916; *Cambridge Hist. Soc. Pubs.*, vol. X (1916); and *Proc. Am. Acad. Arts and Sci.*, vol. LI (1917).] H. W. H. K.

GRAY, JOHN PURDUE (Aug. 6, 1825–Nov. 29, 1886), physician, alienist, and pioneer in the modern management of insanity, was born in Center County, Pa., the son of Peter B. Gray, a farmer and Methodist minister, and Elizabeth Purdue, the daughter of a physician. His premedical education was obtained at Bellefonte Academy and at Dickinson College (A.M. 1846). He graduated in medicine from the University of Pennsylvania in 1849 and at once secured the position of resident physician at Blockley Hospital in Philadelphia under Dr. Benedict, whose protégé he seems to have been. In 1851, when the latter was made medical superintendent of the New York State Lunatic Asylum at Utica, Gray accompanied him as third assistant physician, was promoted the following year to second assistant, and finally, when Benedict was forced to resign for personal reasons, he became, in 1853, first assistant and acting medical superintendent at the early age of twenty-eight. Later in the same year he accepted the position of medical superintendent to the Michigan State Lunatic Asylum at Kalamazoo, but in 1854 he was persuaded to return to Utica as full medical superintendent and held this position up to the time of his death. On Sept. 6, 1854, he was married to Mary B. Wetmore, the daughter of Edmund A. Wetmore of Utica.

Gray had been made assistant editor of the *American Journal of Insanity* in 1852 and two years later he succeeded to the full editorship. In 1874 he was given the chair of psychological medicine and medical jurisprudence in Bellevue Hospital Medical College and in 1876 was appointed to the same chair in the Albany Medical College, resigning both posts in 1882. As a forensic expert and medical witness he was widely known and figured in many prominent cases. He examined for insanity one of the assassins of

Lincoln (Payne) and aided the government in the prosecution of Guiteau. His writings were limited to papers on phases of insanity. He was the leading alienist of his day in America and is conceded to have done more than any other one man in bettering the condition of the insane. Regarding the insane man as physically rather than mentally ill, he gave his patients fresh air and exercise and as far as possible abolished mechanical restraint and solitary feeding. He also revolutionized asylum construction, introducing steam heat and forced ventilation. When in 1879 he toured Europe he found some of his innovations in use. He paid much attention to the microscopic study of the brain of the insane and his asylum became a sort of postgraduate school for the training of alienists. He was made an honorary member of several European societies of alienists and at one time he was president of the Association of Medical Superintendents of American Institutions for the Insane. In a sense he was a medical martyr. In 1882 he was shot in the face by a man later pronounced insane, and although technically the wound was not serious, his health failed from that period and he was obliged to spend much of the last two years of his life in the South or abroad. On resuming his duties his final collapse soon took place.

[W. G. Tucker, "John Purdue Gray," *Ann. Report of the Regents of the Univ. of the State of N. Y.* (1889); J. B. Andrews, memoir in *Am. Jour. of Insanity,* July 1887; *Medic. Record,* Dec. 4, 1886; M. D. Raymond, *Gray Geneal.* (1887); *N. Y. Tribune,* Nov. 30, 1886.] E. P.

GRAY, JOSEPH W. (Aug. 5, 1813–May 26, 1862), journalist, was born of Puritan stock at Bridport, Addison County, Vt. During his early childhood, his parents, Urel and Betsey Case Gray, moved to Madrid, N. Y., where he attended a rural school. He studied later in the institutes at Potsdam and Gouverneur founded by the New York State Association for Teachers. In 1836 he began to teach in the public schools of Cleveland, then just incorporated as a city. After teaching three or four years in Cleveland and in Cuyahoga County, he read law and opened his own office. He left Cleveland to practise in Michigan but returned shortly and with his brother Admiral N. Gray purchased the *Cleveland Advertiser,* a Democratic evening daily, Jan. 1, 1842. The name of the paper was changed to the *Plain Dealer,* "a name that exactly suited the outspoken, trenchant style of J. W. Gray" (Orth, *post,* p. 513). Taking an active interest in politics, he was considerably responsible for reviving the Democratic party in the state of Ohio, then dominantly Whig. He was a good paragrapher, possessed striking wit, and rarely let his paper go to press without a few epigrammatic stabs denouncing the Whigs and calling upon the Democrats to save the country. During the fifties he gathered a distinguished staff on the *Plain Dealer* including such men as J. B. Boughton, later a New York editorial writer; David R. Locke [*q.v.*], editor of the *Toledo Blade* and author of *The Nasby Papers* (1864); William E. McLaren [*q.v.*], later Protestant Episcopal bishop; A. M. Griswold, journalist, humorist, and lecturer; James D. Cleveland, later a leading lawyer; George Hoyt, journalist and artist; and Charles F. Browne [*q.v.*] who adopted his famous pen-name "Artemus Ward" while on the *Plain Dealer* staff.

Gray was appointed postmaster of Cleveland in 1853 by President Pierce and held the position until 1858 when he was removed for his refusal to advocate the Lecompton Constitution. In 1858 he ran unsuccessfully for Congress on the Democratic ticket. He was a delegate to the Charleston-Baltimore convention of the Democratic party in 1860 and as a close friend of Stephen A. Douglas fought for his nomination for the presidency. Though he had suffered the loss of the sight of one eye in 1858 he remained at work through the campaign of 1860 and the stirring events which followed. Because of his politics, his newspaper became unpopular when the Civil War began but following the leadership of Douglas, Gray gave the Union his full support. He died somewhat suddenly from after-effects of the injury to his eyes. He had been in charge of the *Plain Dealer* during the period when American journalism was changing rapidly with the introduction of steam presses, railroads, and the telegraph. Keeping pace with these changes he increased the circulation of the paper to 40,000 in 1860. He was a pioneer in illustrated journalism, especially in the use of cartoons. Upon his death he was survived by his wife, Catherine Foster of Cleveland, and two sons and a daughter.

[George Hoyt, "Old Plain Dealer Days," in the *Cleveland Plain Dealer,* Aug. 24, 1902, gives an excellent account of Gray. See also *Ibid.,* May 27, 1862, May 23, 1916; S. P. Orth, *A Hist. of Cleveland, Ohio* (1910), I, 513–14; Gertrude Van R. Wickham, *The Pioneer Families of Cleveland, 1796–1840* (1914), II, 605–06; *Cleveland, Past and Present* (1869); *N. Y. Times,* May 29, 1862.] D. W. M.

GRAY, ROBERT (May 10, 1755–1806), navigator, fur-trader, and discoverer, commanded from 1789 to 1793 the *Columbia,* the first vessel to enter the Columbia River. He was probably the great-grandson of Edward Gray who settled in 1643 in Plymouth, Mass., married a niece of Gov. Winslow of the Plymouth colony, and whose son Edward in 1680 removed to Tiverton in Rhode Island where Robert Gray was born. As a young man he took an active part in the naval service of the Revolutionary War and at its close was recognized as a competent navigator. A little later six energetic citizens of Boston and vicinity resolved to link the China trade with the nascent fur-trade of the Northwest coast of America. In pursuance of this plan the ship *Columbia* under Captain John Kendrick [*q.v.*], who also commanded the expedition, and the sloop *Lady Washington* under Robert Gray sailed from Boston in September 1787. Throughout the voyage Gray was the driving force. By his energy, determination, and daring, the little ninety-ton sloop gathered the cargo of sea-otter skins with which the *Columbia*, to whose command he had been transferred, began her return voyage, July 30, 1789, from the Northwest coast by way of China. On Aug. 10, 1790, with a salute of thirteen guns, the ship dropped anchor in Boston Harbor, having sailed almost forty-two thousand miles and carried the American flag for the first time around the world. She had shown to Boston a new source of wealth, even though her voyage had not been remunerative.

After being refitted, the *Columbia* left Boston in September 1790 and arrived at Vancouver Island in June 1791. Gray was in command and was also a part owner in the venture. After the season's trade to the northward he wintered in Clayoquot Sound, where he built the *Adventure*, the second vessel launched on the Northwest coast. The following spring, while seeking trade to the southward, he made his discoveries of Gray's Harbor and the Columbia River. Prior to that time the so-called "River of the West" or "River Oregan" of Jonathan Carver had been merely a name upon the maps. Spanish and English navigators—Heceta, Meares, and Vancouver—had glanced at its "sortie" and passed on; but on May 11, 1792, Gray sailed his vessel through the line of foaming water and seething breakers that guarded the long-sought river. The season's trading completed, he sailed for China, homeward bound; and on July 20, 1793, after another world-encircling voyage, the *Columbia* anchored off Long Wharf, Boston, to a salute of eleven guns. Little did he realize that his discovery would give to his country the foundation of a claim to Old Oregon and would make his ship, *Columbia*, as well known as the *Constitution*. On Feb. 3, 1794, Gray was married to Martha Atkins of Boston, and settled down to a quieter life as the master of coasting vessels operating out of that port. They had five children, four daughters and one son; but the son died in infancy. In the summer of 1806, while on a voyage to Charleston, S. C., Gray died of yellow fever. It is believed that he was buried at sea.

[*House Report 456*, 29 Cong., 1 Sess.; *House Report 502*, 30 Cong., 1 Sess.; *Senate Doc. 335*, 32 Cong., 1 Sess.; *New England Mag.*, June 1892; F. W. Howay, "Captains Gray and Kendrick: The Barrell Letters," *Wash. Hist. Quart.*, Oct. 1921; "John Boit's Log of the Columbia" and "Remnant of Official Log of the Columbia," *Quart. of the Ore. Hist. Soc.*, Dec. 1921; "Letters Relating to the Second Voyage of the Columbia," *Ibid.*, June 1923; S. E. Morison, *The Maritime Hist. of Mass., 1783–1860* (1921); M. D. Raymond, *Gray Geneal.* (1887). Manuscript sources include Robt. Haswell's logs of the first and second voyages of the *Columbia*, in the Bancroft Library, Berkeley, Cal., and John Hoskins's log of the second voyage of the *Columbia* in the library of the Mass. Hist. Soc.]

F. W. H.

GRAY, WILLIAM (June 27, 1750, o.s.–Nov. 3, 1825), merchant, lieutenant-governor of Massachusetts, father of Francis Calley Gray [*q.v.*], was born in Lynn, Mass., the oldest son of Abraham and Lydia (Calley) Gray. When he was a small boy, his father, a shoemaker in humble circumstances, moved to Salem, where the lad was apprenticed to Samuel Gardner. Later he entered the counting-house of Richard Derby and at the age of twenty-eight started business for himself. At this period he signed his name "William Gray, Tertius," to distinguish himself from several other William Grays in Salem. In 1775, as a member of the Salem militia, he made a forced march with his company to Lexington, arriving too late for the battle. On June 6 of the following year he was commissioned second lieutenant, but there is no record that he had any further Revolutionary service. His business ventures proved to be highly profitable, and he was the owner of a number of privateers during the Revolution. He was one of the first New England merchants to enter the trade with Russia, India, and China. Timothy Pickering, writing on Nov. 29, 1799, said of him, "William Gray of Salem is a man of unspotted character and for mercantile talents and extent of business, the first merchant in the United States." From 1801 to 1807, when Salem's prosperity was at its height, he employed annually about 300 seamen, and before 1815 he had owned at least 113 vessels. When he moved to Boston in 1809, he was the owner of fifteen ships, seven barks, thirteen brigs, and one schooner, and his estate was estimated at $3,000,000.

Like most of the able and well-to-do people of New England at that period, Gray had originally been a Federalist. For some years he was a selectman and in 1788 he was a delegate to the state convention held to consider the Federal Constitution and voted for ratification. In 1792 he was an unsuccessful candidate for state senator, and in 1804, when the Jeffersonians were gaining strength, he was defeated as a candidate for representative, but in 1807 he was chosen as a Federalist senator from Essex County and was reëlected in the following year. In June 1808, however, although the Embargo was vigorously opposed by the New England merchants, Gray came out openly in its favor, thus incurring the enmity of his associates and bringing upon himself social ostracism. He published a vindication of his conduct in the *Salem Gazette* (Aug. 12, 1808), but party spirit was running so high that he felt it wise to move to Boston, where he resided during the remainder of his life.

Having deserted the Federalists, Gray was induced in 1810 to run for lieutenant-governor on the Republican ticket, with Elbridge Gerry, and was elected by a small plurality. During the campaign "all the virulence of invective" was heaped upon him. He was reëlected in 1811 but because of ill health declined a nomination in 1812. During the war with England he consistently supported the Madison administration, subscribing with extraordinary liberality to all the government loans. He was defeated as Republican candidate for lieutenant-governor in 1814 and 1815 and declined a nomination for the governorship in 1816. He was also badly beaten for senator from Suffolk County in 1818, 1819, and 1820, but was chosen as a delegate to the constitutional convention of 1820. In 1816 he had been unanimously elected president of the Boston branch of the Bank of the United States and served for the six following years. His last public appearance was as chairman of a public dinner in Faneuil Hall, Mar. 4, 1825, to celebrate the election of John Quincy Adams to the presidency. He died not long afterward, leaving an estate of more than a million dollars. He was married, Mar. 29, 1782, to Elizabeth Chipman, the daughter of Hon. John Chipman and Elizabeth (Brown) Chipman, of Marblehead. They had ten children of whom six survived their parents. Gray was a man of simple tastes, indefatigably industrious, scrupulously honest, and very generous. His portrait by Gilbert Stuart, painted in 1807, shows a rugged, plain face, marked by determination and good nature.

[Edward Gray, *Wm. Gray, of Salem, Merchant* (1914) is the best account of Gray. See also S. E. Morison, *The Maritime Hist. of Mass.* (1921).]

C. M. F.

GRAYDON, ALEXANDER (Apr. 10, 1752–May 2, 1818), author, born at Bristol, Pa., was the son of Alexander Graydon by his second wife, Rachel Marks, of German and Scotch descent. In 1730 his father had emigrated from Ireland to Philadelphia where he became a merchant and lawyer, and a figure in the coffee-houses. Young Alexander was first sent to the school conducted by David James Dove [*q.v.*] and at the age of eight entered the College and Academy of Philadelphia. In his youth he acquired a veneration of truth and justice that afterwards "prevented his becoming a patriot, in the modern acceptation of the word" (*Memoirs*, p. 29). For a time he sighed for the ladies and aspired with some success to be a rake. At the age of sixteen he reluctantly began the study of law, a profession for which he was unfitted by his indolence, his dislike for litigation, and his indifference to worldly gain. Having dissipated himself in poetry, metaphysics, and wine, Graydon went to York to recuperate. After six months he returned to Philadelphia improved in health though unaltered in disposition. He "still affected the man of pleasure and dissipation and had a sovereign contempt for matrimony" (*Ibid.*, p. 107). Although he became an accomplished fencer and a great frequenter of taverns, he indulged in no excesses of wine or debts.

At the outbreak of the Revolution he joined the volunteers in Philadelphia, but was revolted by the persecution of the Loyalists, Doctor Kearsley and Isaac Hunt [*qq.v.*]. Congress commissioned him a captain on Jan. 6, 1776, and he spent the winter recruiting and drilling his battalion. In May he was sent with a sum of money in specie to General Schuyler at Lake George and returned in time to join in the movement of the army to New York. His regiment assisted in covering the retreat of the army from Long Island to New York. He was later stationed at Fort Washington and was taken prisoner at the Battle of Harlem Heights. The British treated him well and sent him to New York whence he was removed in January 1777 to Long Island. After a captivity of eight months he was paroled and returned to Philadelphia. He was officially exchanged in the spring of 1778 and married a Miss Wood of Berks County. Though he did not actively participate in politics, Graydon was elected prothonotary of the newly formed county of Dauphin in 1785 and moved to Harrisburg. He was one of the earliest and most conspicuous advocates in Pennsylvania of the adoption of the Federal Constitution and was elected a member of the state convention. Graydon, to whom the principles of Gallic republicanism and the new democracy were repugnant, supported the Federalists and was dismissed from office in the proscription that followed the election of Gov. Thomas McKean [*q.v.*].

He then retired to his small farm near Harrisburg with his second wife, Theodosia Pettit, whom he had married Dec. 16, 1799. He had contributed articles to John Fenno's *Gazette* and the "Notes of a Desultory Reader" to the *Port Folio,* when he published in 1811 at Harrisburg his *Memoirs of a Life, Chiefly Passed in Pennsylvania Within the Last Sixty Years; with Occasional Remarks upon the General Occurrences, Character, and Spirit of the Eventful Period.* The volume was issued under a changed title and with an introduction by John Galt in Edinburgh in 1822, achieving a second edition in 1828. Two years before his death Graydon returned to Philadelphia where he hoped to become a publisher and to devote his time to literary pursuits. Though he had himself suffered from political intolerance, his *Memoirs* are free from any deforming bias. A rich sense of humor, wealth of anecdote, shrewd observation of character and of opinion, and at times considerable literary charm have made his book one of the best-known and most valuable historical sources for the period.

[Information regarding Graydon's mother and brother William may be found in *Notes and Queries* (Harrisburg, 1893, 1894); Alexander Graydon, *Memoirs of his own Time,* ed. with intro. by John Stockton Littell (Phila., 1846); *Port Folio* (Phila.), July 1818; *Phila. Mo. Mag.,* Apr. 1829; *Poulson's Am. Daily Advertiser* (Phila.), May 4, 1818.]

F. M—n.

GRAYSON, WILLIAM (1736?–Mar. 12, 1790), Revolutionary soldier, member of the Continental Congress, United States senator, was born in Prince William County, Va. His father, Benjamin Grayson, married the twice-widowed Susana Monroe, aunt of James Monroe [*q.v.*], and William was the third child and third son of their four children. He attended the College of Philadelphia (now the University of Pennsylvania) and is said to have attended the University of Oxford and to have studied law in London, but his name does not appear in Joseph Foster's *Alumni Oxonienses, 1715–1886* (1887–88) or in E. A. Jones's *American Members of the Inns of Court* (1924). The outbreak of the Revolution found him engaged in the practise of law at Dumfries, Va. On Aug. 24, 1776, he was commissioned lieutenant-colonel and aide-de-camp to Gen. Washington. Promoted colonel in January 1777, he took part in the battles of Long Island, White Plains, Brandywine, and Germantown. At Valley Forge, in the spring of 1778, he served on the commission appointed by Gen. Washington to arrange for the exchange of prisoners with Sir William Howe, and later testified at the trial of Maj.-Gen. Charles Lee [*q.v.*] regarding the confusion prior to the battle of Monmouth. He retired from the army in April 1779 and later became a commissioner of the Board of War (December 1779). Resigning in September 1781, he practised law at Dumfries until in 1784 he was elected to the Virginia House of Delegates (1784–85, and 1788) and to the Continental Congress (1785–87). Taking his seat in Congress in March 1785, he was active in the debate preceding the passage of the Land Ordinance of May 20, 1785 (*Journals of Congress,* Apr. 26–May 20, 1785). He was much interested in the development of the western country and Manasseh Cutler [*q.v.*] found his influence of value in procuring the enactment of the Ordinance of 1787 (W. P. and J. P. Cutler, *Life, Journals and Correspondence of Rev. Manasseh Cutler,* 1888, I, 293–94). Grayson was not the author, as is alleged (*Annals of Congress,* 15 Cong. 2 Sess., col. 1225), of the anti-slavery clause in the Ordinance, though he approved it as a voluntary concession to Northern and Eastern opinion; Nathan Dane [*q.v.*] may have added the clause upon Grayson's suggestion (Bancroft, *post,* II, 115, 431). It was agreed to by the Southern members, Grayson wrote to Monroe (*Ibid.,* II, 437), in order to prevent "tobacco and indigo from being made on the northwest side of the Ohio," and for "several other political reasons"—meaning, principally, a settlement of the Mississippi question in accordance with Southern interests (Stone, *post*). This argument Grayson developed in the Virginia convention of 1788. Free navigation of the Mississippi, he declared, in opposing the ratification of the Federal Constitution, would be safer under the Articles of Confederation. He feared that the North, using the treaty-making power, would yield the Mississippi to Spain, and by preventing development of the Mississippi country, assure to itself a permanent position of dominance. Following the passage of the first tariff act in 1789 he wrote to Patrick Henry predicting that the South would prove to be the "milch cow of the Union" (L. G. Tyler, *The Letters and Times of the Tylers,* I, 1884, 170). After ratifying the Constitution, Virginia, in a repentant mood, elected Grayson and Richard Henry Lee, both Anti-Federalists, to the United States Senate. Grayson died at Dumfries during the second session of Congress. Skilled in debate, he loved the sport of dialectics, and is said to have excelled "in fascinating manners, in humor, in wit," and "in an almost unrivalled play of the intellectual powers" (Grigsby, *post,* IX, 169, 199). He married Eleanor Smallwood, sister of William Smallwood [*q.v.*].

[Hugh B. Grigsby, "Hist. of the Va. Federal Convention of 1788," *Va. Hist. Soc. Colls.,* n.s., vols. IX and X (1890–91); *Tyler's Quart. Hist. and Geneal. Mag.,* Jan., Apr. 1924, Jan. 1925, Oct. 1926; *Wm. and Mary Coll. Quart.,* July 1907; Geo. Bancroft, *Hist. of the Formation of the Constitution of the U. S. A.* (2 vols., 1882); J. A. Barrett, *Evolution of the Ordinance of 1787* (1891); F. D. Stone, in *Pa. Mag. of Hist. and Biog.*, Oct. 1889; *Md. Hist. Mag.*, June 1927; *Proc. of a General Court-Martial, Held . . . for the Trial of Maj.-Gen. Lee* (1778), p. 41; F. B. Heitman, *Hist. Reg. of Officers of the Continental Army* (1893); *Va. Independent Chronicle and General Advertiser* (Richmond), Mar. 24, 1790.] F. E. R.

GREATHOUSE, CLARENCE RIDGEBY (*c.* 1845–Oct. 21, 1899), journalist, lawyer, diplomat, was born in Kentucky, the son of Dr. Ridgeby Greathouse, an early emigrant to California. In 1870 he went to San Francisco. He practised law with Louis T. Haggin, then, upon the latter's retirement, in the firm of Greathouse & Blanding—finally Wallace, Greathouse & Blanding. He was also active in local politics as a Democrat and in 1883 he became the general manager of the San Francisco *Examiner,* a Democratic daily. He continued in this position until 1886, when he was appointed consul-general at Kanagawa (Yokohama), Japan. Upon the confirmation of his appointment he left Washington May 31, 1886, and served successfully at his post for four years. At this time events and conditions in Korea were largely an enigma and a challenge to discovery to most foreigners in the Far East. Korea was also the one Asiatic country in which American influence and American participation in governmental affairs was at least the equal of that of any other Occidental nation. The successive American representatives in the Korean capital succeeded in so impressing the Korean King with the friendly and disinterested nature of the policy of their government that he was led to secure a comparatively large number of American advisors and on Sept. 12, 1890, Greathouse was engaged to serve as legal advisor to the Korean government. At that time there were eight Americans serving in Seul in various advisory capacities. The extent of American influence in Korea displeased the Chinese, but despite positive suggestions by the Chinese Resident against the employment of further foreign advisors, on Jan. 3, 1891, the Korean government gazetted Greathouse as a vice- president of the home office and gave him charge of matters pertaining to foreign legal affairs. Gen. Charles Le Gendre [*q.v.*] at this time was a vice-president of the same office as foreign advisor to the King.

It is difficult to evaluate the work accomplished by Greathouse during his eight years in Korea. It is certain, however, that he secured the confidence of the King, and that for a time he was given complete charge of the trial of important political cases. He is also said to have acted as head of the Korean post-office department, but since during most of his service this department was weak and struggling he cannot be said to have accomplished much in this direction. His legal knowledge was often called upon in the drafting of conventions, in the constant negotiations with foreign representatives in Seul, and in the revising of Korean law and the reorganizing, at least on paper, of the Korean judicial system. His best-known work was in connection with the trial of the Koreans implicated in the murder of the Queen of Korea by Japanese and Korean conspirators on Oct. 8, 1895. After the King had escaped from his Japanese and Korean captors to the safety of the Russian legation, he asked Greathouse to supervise the investigation into the circumstances surrounding the death of the Queen. Greathouse attended all sessions of the court, examined the witnesses, and had the trials conducted in a thoroughly modern manner. It was owing to his influence that the trials were free from the gross faults which customarily disfigured the proceedings of all Korean courts, and that for general approximation to Western notions of justice and integrity they were in every way remarkable. During the last few years of his life Greathouse acted as confidential advisor to the King on foreign affairs. As far as the records show, he was never married; his mother remained with him until his death. While he was in Japan he secured the services of a young Goanese, H. A. Dos Remedios, as his secretary. When he went to Korea he took his assistant with him and Dos Remedios came practically to occupy the position of son as well as secretary, although he was never officially adopted. Greathouse died in Seul while still in the service of the government of Korea.

[The only trustworthy sources on the life of Greathouse are in the archives of the Department of State, and in the former American legation in Seul, Korea. Unfortunately, these are very meager. For printed sources see the *Korean Repository,* Mar. 1896, and the *Examiner* (San Francisco), Nov. 18, 1899.] H. J. N.

GREATON, JOHN (Mar. 10, 1741–Dec. 16, 1783), Revolutionary soldier, was born at Roxbury, Mass., the son of John and Catherine (Lenton) Greaton, or Graeton. His father was the last landlord of the famous Greyhound Tavern and was also a trader, dealing in West Indian goods, with stores in Roxbury and Boston. The younger John likewise was a trader, a fact which probably accounts for his early interest in the Revolutionary movement. He joined the Sons of Liberty and was chosen on Dec. 26, 1774, one of a committee of fifteen in Roxbury to carry into effect the non-importation agreement. He had been elected lieutenant of the militia in the first parish of Roxbury, Nov. 18, 1774, and in that capacity or another was actively engaged in the battle of Lexington, along with friends and neighbors. When the Continental Army was raised he enlisted and from the very first bore a conspicuous part in the war. He was rapidly promoted, becoming major, then lieutenant-colonel, and on July 1, 1775, colonel of Gen. Heath's regiment. During the siege of Boston he did spectacular work in destroying and carrying away British supplies assembled at various places for the use of the army garrisoned there. After service in these preliminaries, he went on the expedition to Canada and with the rest of his regiment suffered intensely from the hardships of that campaign. On Jan. 1, 1776, he was commissioned colonel of the 24th Continental Infantry. Upon his return he joined Washington's army at Morristown where he remained through the Trenton and Princeton campaign. He was with Nixon's brigade in the campaign against Burgoyne, then became senior officer at Albany and for a time commander of the northern department. His further promotion was bound up in the jealousies and diplomacies of the Continental Congress, and the resolve making him a brigadier-general was not finally passed by Congress until Jan. 7, 1783.

During the month of December 1782, while his promotion was under serious consideration, Greaton was among those officers who were beginning to feel the seriousness of the failure of Congress to pay the troops and keep its promises to them. He was one of five officers of the Massachusetts line, who, together with officers from Connecticut, New York, New Jersey, New Hampshire, and the general hospital, presented a memorial to Congress reporting the dissatisfaction in the army (*Journals of the Continental Congress,* XXIV, 291–93). They suggested commuting the half-pay for life already pledged for full pay for a certain number of years, or for a sum in gross. Several months later Congress adopted their suggestion, and offered the officers full pay for five years. Shortly after this decision the army was disbanded and Greaton returned to his home at Roxbury, where he died in December 1783, having commanded his regiment throughout the war. Greaton was married in 1760 to Sara Humphreys, by whom he had several children, among them a son, Richard Humphrey Greaton, who was an ensign in his father's regiment and later a captain in the United States army, and a daughter, Ann, who married Samuel Heath, son of General Heath.

[F. S. Drake, *The Town of Roxbury* (1878); W. E. Thwing, *Hist. of the First Church of Roxbury, Mass.* (1908); *Mass. Soldiers and Sailors of the Revolutionary War, a Compilation from the Archives,* vol. VI (1899); F. B. Heitman, *Hist. Reg. of Officers of the Continental Army* (1914); *Jours. of the Continental Congress*; Washington Papers, Lib. of Cong., vol. I; "Heath Papers," *Mass. Hist. Soc. Colls.,* 5 ser. IV (1878), 7 ser. IV, V (1904, 1905); death notice in *Boston Evening Post and General Advertiser,* Dec. 20, 1783.]
V. F. B.

GREATON, JOSEPH (Feb. 12, 1679–Aug. 19, 1753), Jesuit missionary and first Catholic pastor in Pennsylvania, was born in London of a gentle family, whose safety in days of persecution lay in its obscurity. He entered the Society of Jesus, July 5, 1708, and after the usual training, probably on the Continent, was professed and ordained, Aug. 4, 1719, for the English and colonial missions. About 1720, he departed secretly for Maryland. Here he resided on a Jesuit-owned manor in Anne Arundel County and quietly celebrated mass in private chapels and in homes, going as far as Conewago, Lancaster, Chester, and Philadelphia. In 1729, he went to reside permanently in Philadelphia whose growth, due to a heavy German and Ulsterite immigration which contained some Catholics, he foresaw.

His residence on the northwest corner of Front and Walnut Streets proving too small for his twenty-two Irish and seventeen German communicants, Father Greaton purchased through John Dixon, a Catholic surgeon-barber, a lot on Walnut Street between Third and Fourth Streets. Here was erected St. Joseph's Church, which the pastor decorated with valuable paintings spirited out of England, of which three are said to be preserved (the "Ecce Homo," "St. Ignatius," and "St. Francis"). In 1734, despite the guarantees of Penn, Lieutenant-Governor Patrick Gordon laid complaints before the Council and sought to prevent Catholic worship as contrary to English law; but apparently neither the Council nor the home government was interested enough to take action, though the public character of the "popish" church was noticed in London prints (*Grub-street Journal,* July 7, 21, 1737). Father Greaton's congregation grew, so that in 1741 he was given an assistant, Henry Neale, S. J., while the Pennsylvania Germans were attended by the Jesuit fathers Wapeler and Schneider. During King George's War, the Catholic congregation was suspected of French sympathies and annoyed by the non-Quaker colonists. In 1750, the Quakers actually protected the Catholic chapel from a Presbyterian mob. Otherwise, Father Greaton's pastorate was uneventful. Growing old, he assigned the church to his successor, Robert Harding, S. J. [*q.v.*], and retired to Bohemia, Md., where he served in a less arduous capacity until his death.

[J. L. J. Kirlin, *Catholicity in Phila.* (1909); J. G

Shea, *Hist. of the Catholic Ch. in the U. S.*, vol. I (1886); *Catholic Encyc.*; D. H. Mahony, *Hist. Sketches of the Catholic Churches and Institutions of Phila.* (1895); *U. S. Catholic Mag.*, Apr. 1845; *The Am. Catholic Hist. Researches* (1884–1912), index volume; *Records of the Am. Catholic Hist. Soc. of Phila.* (1887–1926), *passim*; Henry Foley, S. J., *Records of the Eng. Province of the Soc. of Jesus*, vol. III (1878); *Phila. Directory*, 1785.]
R. J. P.

GREELEY, HORACE (Feb. 3, 1811–Nov. 29, 1872), editor, political leader, was born at Amherst, N. H., the third child of Zaccheus Greeley and Mary Woodburn his wife, the former being of English and the latter of Scotch-Irish stock. The father made a scanty living by farming and day labor, first at Amherst, later at Westhaven, Vt., and finally in Erie County, Pa. Greeley's irregular schooling ended at fourteen, when he was apprenticed to Amos Bliss, editor of the *Northern Spectator* at East Poultney, Vt. But he was a precocious lad, who gained much from his mother's repetition of British traditions, ballads, and snatches of history, the family copies of Shakespeare, Campbell, and Byron, and the omnivorous reading possible in a newspaper office and the town library of East Poultney. When the *Northern Spectator* died in June 1830, he walked most of the way to the Erie County home, and after a short stay with his still-struggling parents found employment as a printer at Jamestown and Lodi, N. Y., and Erie, Pa. Finding his prospects poor, he set out, with about twenty-five dollars and his personal possessions tied in his handkerchief, for New York City, where he arrived in August 1831. He was twenty years old, "tall, slender, pale, and plain," as he later described himself, with an "unmistakably rustic manner and address," and equipped with only "so much of the art of printing as a boy will usually learn in the office of a country newspaper" (*Recollections*, p. 84). Obtaining board and room for two dollars and a half a week, he sought work in vain for several weeks before accepting the eye-ruining job of setting up a New Testament in agate with notes in pearl.

A succession of employments, including some typesetting for the *Evening Post*, from which William Leggett discharged him because he wanted only "decent-*looking* men in the office," enabled Greeley to save a small sum, and in January 1833 to form a partnership with a printer named Francis V. Story, who when drowned the following July was succeeded by Jonas Winchester. During 1833–34 the firm printed from 54 Liberty St., two lottery organs called *Sylvester's Bank Note and Exchange Manual* and the *Constitutionalist*, and did a job-printing business. But Greeley was far more than a printer. His fingers itched for the pen, and he was shortly contributing paragraphs to the two journals and to newspapers. He soon gained reputation in press circles, and a dubious tradition states that James Gordon Bennett offered him a partnership in starting the *Herald*. One reason for distrusting the tradition is that Greeley and Winchester had already, on Mar. 22, 1834, founded a weekly literary and news journal called the *New Yorker*. This periodical, well printed, avoiding political partisanship, containing full abstracts of foreign and domestic newspapers, and selected tales, reviews, and pieces of music, was edited largely with shears; but there were original contributions by Greeley, R. W. Griswold, Park Benjamin, and Henry J. Raymond (F. L. Mott, *History of American Magazines, 1741–1850*, 1930, pp. 358–60). It gained steadily in circulation. At the end of one year it had 4,500 subscribers; at the end of three years, 9,500. But the "cash principle" not yet being applied to the magazine business, it still lost money. Greeley suffered great mental anguish from his constant struggle with debt. "My embarrassments were sometimes dreadful," he wrote; "not that I feared destitution, but the fear of involving my friends in my misfortunes was very bitter" (Parton, *post*, p. 172). He had married on July 5, 1836, Mary Youngs Cheney, who was born in Cornwall, Conn., but was a schoolteacher for a time in North Carolina. However great his worries over his magazine, it shortly gave him a wide reputation.

The failure of the *New Yorker* was fortunate for Greeley in that literary and non-partisan journalism was not his real forte. To add to his income he wrote constantly for the *Daily Whig* and other newspapers, and in 1838 accepted from Thurlow Weed, William H. Seward, and other Whig leaders the editorship of a campaign weekly, the *Jeffersonian*. It ran for one year, obtained a circulation of 15,000 and exercised real influence. Greeley's salary of $1,000 was less important than the political friendships he formed. He struck Seward as "rather unmindful of social usages, yet singularly clear, original, and decided, in his political views and theories" (F. W. Seward, *Autobiography of William H. Seward . . . with a Memoir of his Life*, 1877, p. 395). In 1840 the Whig leaders called upon him to edit and publish another weekly. The result was the *Log Cabin*, begun May 2, which gained an unprecedented success. Of the first issue 48,000 copies were sold, and the circulation swiftly rose to almost 90,000. Greeley not only edited it and the *New Yorker* simultaneously, but made speeches, sat on committees, and helped manage the state campaign. He thought later that few men had contributed more to Harrison's victory than he (*Recollections,* p. 135). Ceasing after the election, the *Log Cabin* was revived on Dec. 5, 1840, as a general political weekly, and continued till it and the *New Yorker* were merged in the *Tribune.* Greeley's apprenticeship was now completed.

Though in 1841 twelve dailies were published in New York City, no penny paper of Whig allegiance existed. Nor was there any newspaper standing midway between the sensational enterprise of Bennett's *Herald* and the staid correctness of Bryant's *Evening Post.* Greeley, now fully trusted by his party, with a large popular following and a varied practical experience, saw the opportunity. With a capital which he estimated at two thousand dollars, one-half in printing materials, and with one thousand dollars borrowed from James Coggeshall, he launched the *New York Tribune* on Apr. 10, 1841. His object, he stated later, was to found "a journal removed alike from servile partisanship on the one hand, and from gagged, mincing neutrality on the other" (*Recollections,* p. 137). For some days the prospect was dubious; his first week's receipts were ninety-two dollars, the expenses $525 (*Ibid.,* p. 140). Then, thanks to the *Tribune's* sterling merits and the *Sun's* bitter attacks, subscriptions poured in rapidly. The paper began its fourth week with an edition of 6,000, and its seventh with 11,000, after which progress was slow. Success had been fairly assured when during July Greeley formed a partnership with a far more practical man, Thomas McElrath, who for ten years gave the establishment efficiency and system and Greeley entire independence. On Sept. 20 the *Log Cabin* and *New Yorker* were merged into the weekly *Tribune.* Greeley, assisted with great ability by H. J. Raymond, labored tirelessly, his average day's writing in the early years according to Parton being three columns of close print. As funds accumulated, however, the staff was increased, till by 1846 the *Tribune* was the best all-round paper in the city, and Greeley had time for additional pursuits.

The *Tribune* set a new standard in American journalism by its combination of energy in newsgathering with good taste, high moral standards, and intellectual appeal. Police reports, scandals, dubious medical advertisements, and flippant personalities were barred from its pages; the editorials were vigorous but usually temperate; the political news was the most exact in the city; book reviews and book-extracts were numerous; and as an inveterate lecturer Greeley gave generous space to lectures. The paper appealed to substantial and thoughtful people and when its price was raised, on Apr. 11, 1842, to nine cents weekly or two cents daily it lost fewer than two hundred subscribers. Greeley stamped it with his individual and then highly radical views. He was an egalitarian who hated and feared all kinds of monopoly, landlordism, and class dominance. Believing that all American citizens should be free men politically and economically, he sought means of increasing this freedom. At first he turned to Fourierism. Through the influence of Albert Brisbane [*q.v.*], he not only allowed a Fourierist association to publish first daily and then tri-weekly articles on the front page of the *Tribune* (1842–44), but also advocated the formation of Phalanxes, conducted a newspaper debate on the subject with Raymond (1846), and invested in the North American Phalanx at Red Bank, N. J. He espoused the agrarian movement for the free distribution of government lands to settlers as a guarantee against capitalist tyranny, attacked the railway land grants as fostering monopoly, assailed the heartlessness of corporations which exploited their workers, and in general inveighed against the fierce acquisitive competition of the day. Wage slavery in the forties distressed him as much as bond slavery. "How can I devote myself to a crusade against distant servitude," he wrote an anti-slavery convention in 1845, "when I discern its essence pervading my immediate community" (*Tribune,* June 20, 1845)? Newspapers, he wrote, should be "as sensitive to oppression and degradation in the next street as if they were practised in Brazil or Japan." His thinking seemed inconsistent when it included high-tariff doctrines, but he never favored protection as more than a temporary means to an end. "Protection is the shortest and best way to real Free Trade," he wrote in 1851 (*Tribune,* June 23, 1851). He opposed capital punishment, urged freedom of speech and of the mails for Abolitionists, advocated the restriction of liquor-selling, and supported cooperative shops and labor unions, himself becoming in 1850 first president of the New York Printers' Union. Though no believer in woman's suffrage, he sympathized with other parts of the woman's rights crusade.

Greeley's devotion to such social aims made the *Tribune* more than a mere financial success; it became a great popular teacher, champion, and moral leader, and a vehicle for the ideas and experiments of constructive democracy. It required an able and liberal staff, and he drew to the Nassau Street office a versatile group. Margaret Fuller was literary reviewer and special writer from 1844 to 1846, living for a time in Greeley's Turtle Bay home. Charles A. Dana joined Greeley in 1847, acting as city editor, foreign correspondent, and managing editor. Bayard Taylor, after contributing travel letters, became a staff member in 1848. George Ripley was made literary assistant in 1849, raising the literary department to high influence. In the fifties the staff included James S. Pike, Washington correspondent and editorial writer; Solon Robinson, agricultural editor; W. H. Fry, music critic; C. T. Congdon and Richard Hildreth. To the energy of Dana, Pike, and the city editor, F. J. Ottarson, the paper owed its prompt and full intelligence. By 1854 it employed fourteen local reporters, twenty American correspondents, eighteen foreign correspondents, and a financial staff under George M. Snow (Parton, pp. 391–411). During the late fifties the *Tribune* attained a national influence far surpassing that of any rival. Its total circulation on the eve of the Civil War, daily, weekly, and semi-weekly, was 287,750. This covered the whole country outside the South. The power of the paper was greater than even this circulation would indicate, for the weekly was the preeminent journal of the rural North, and one copy did service for many readers. As James Ford Rhodes has said, for great areas the *Tribune* was "a political bible." Many elements entered into its influence, but the greatest was the passionate moral earnestness of Greeley himself, his ability to interpret the deeper convictions of the Northern public, and the trenchant clarity and force of his editorials.

The effort which the *Tribune* had expended in the forties on numerous causes was concentrated in the fifties upon the Free-Soil movement. Greeley objected to slavery on both moral and economic grounds. At first he held mild views, but his opinions underwent a steady intensification. He opposed the Mexican War, indorsed the Wilmot Proviso, and in 1848 supported Zachary Taylor as the only candidate who could prevent Cass's election to the presidency. Two years later he showed coolness to the compromise measures, declaring to the South that he would let "the Union be a thousand times shivered rather than that we should aid you to plant slavery on free soil" (*Tribune,* Feb. 20, 1850). The fight over the Kansas-Nebraska Bill aroused Greeley to his greatest eloquence. His editorial, "Is It a Fraud?" (Feb. 15, 1854), was a magnificent answer to the Democratic claim that the measures of 1850 had involved a recognized repeal of the Missouri Compromise. He advocated "determined resistance" to the execution of the Kansas-Nebraska Act and assisted Gerrit Smith, Eli Thayer, and others in arming the Kansas Free-Soilers. He applauded forcible resistance to the Fugitive-Slave Act as the best method of obtaining its repeal (June 3, 1854). Having declared in 1852 that "if an anti-slavery Whig must give up his anti-slavery or his Whiggery, we choose to part with the latter," Greeley was among the first editors to join the Republican party, and attended the national organization meeting at Pittsburgh, Feb. 22, 1856. He was disgusted with Seward because he failed to seize the leadership of the "uprising of the Free States" (*Tribune,* Nov. 9, 1854), and warm in his advocacy of Frémont's candidacy for the presidency. In the critical year 1857 his union of moral fervor with shrewd practicality is seen at its best. Of the Dred Scott decision he said, it "is entitled to just so much moral weight as would be the judgment of a majority of those congregated in any Washington bar-room" (*Tribune,* Mar. 7, 1857), and he praised John Brown while condemning his raid. He insisted, however, upon the importance of the Union, showing no patience with Garrison's secessionist views, and he strongly attacked Know-Nothingism. He sought only the attainable. In 1854 he had dissolved, through political pique, his alliance with Thurlow Weed and Seward, and in 1860 was a free agent. As a delegate from Oregon at the Republican National Convention he joined with the Blairs to defeat Seward by urging the nomination of Edward Bates of Missouri, but on the night before the balloting advised the Massachusetts delegates to support Lincoln.

In these decades Greeley's restless energy was expended in numerous directions, some ill-advised. Though not of rugged health, he seemed indefatigable, sleeping but five or six hours daily, writing much, traveling widely, making speeches, and attending political conferences. For three months in 1848–49 he was a member of Congress, where he introduced a homestead bill and aired the scandal of excessive mileage payments. During 1851 he was in Europe for three months, acting as juryman at the Crystal Palace Exhibition, testifying before a parliamentary committee, and hastily touring the Continent. On entering Italy his first observation was characteristic—that the country badly needed subsoil ploughs. Revisiting Europe in 1855, he derived much amusement from a two days' incarceration on a debt charge in a Paris prison. In the summer of 1859 he made a journey to the Pacific Coast, toured California, and returned by way of Panama. These travels furnished material for newspaper letters and the volumes, *Glances at Europe* (1851) and *An Overland Journey from New York to San Francisco in the Summer of 1859* (1860). In addition to these writings he published a volume of lectures called *Hints Toward Reforms* (1850), and edited a compilation from official records entitled *History of the Struggle for Slavery Extension or Restriction in the United States* (1856). For years he was a constant lecturer before lyceums, young men's associations, and rural groups, appearing in some winter seasons twice a week. Far less creditable was his thirst for political office. He would have welcomed reëlection to Congress in 1850, would have stooped to take the lieutenant-governorship in 1854, and in 1861 was bitterly disappointed by his failure to secure Seward's seat in the United States Senate. In 1863, again a candidate for the Senate, he was again defeated by Thurlow Weed's opposition. He was an unsuccessful candidate for the House of Representatives in 1868 and 1870, and for the state comptrollership in 1869, but won a seat in the state constitutional convention of 1867. These political adventures by no means enhanced his dignity or influence.

Few Americans were more intimately in the public eye than he, and none commanded such a mixture of admiration with affectionate amusement. The oddity of his appearance, with his pink face of babylike mildness fringed by throat-whiskers, his broad-brimmed hat, white overcoat, crooked cravat, shapeless trousers, and white socks, his shambling gait and absent-minded manner, was exaggerated by every caricaturist. His squeaky voice and illegible handwriting became themes of familiar humor. His eccentricities of manner, which sometimes shocked precise men like Bryant, his naïveté on many subjects, and his homely wisdom on others, appealed to the millions. Some of his phrases, like "Go West, young man," were universally current. By signing many editorials and by frequently appearing in public he gave his work a direct personal appeal unusual in journalism, and his private life was the subject of much curiosity. He cared nothing for money, and though in later years he received $10,000 annually, this and most of his *Tribune* stock slipped from him. His charities were endless, and some impostors received thousands of dollars from him (*Proceedings at the Unveiling of a Memorial to Horace Greeley,* 1915, p. 95). Buying in 1853 a fifty-four acre farm in Chappaqua, N. Y., he spent many week-ends there, interesting all *Tribune* readers in his swamp reclamation and crop experiments, and finally publishing *What I Know of Farming* (1871). Of the seven children born to him, only two daughters, Gabrielle and Ida, lived to maturity; the bereavements made Mrs. Greeley neurasthenic; her housekeeping was characterized by Margaret Fuller as "Castle Rackrent fashion"; and though Greeley's devotion never wavered, his home life was comfortless. He made and kept many friends, especially among women who, like the Cary sisters and Elizabeth Cady Stanton, valued him for his inner and not outer qualities.

The Civil War brought Greeley new tests of sagacity and firmness, which he failed to meet as creditably as he did all tests of courage and patriotism. From the beginning he was accused of vacillation, though his position had more consistency than appeared on the surface. His primary demand was that no concessions be made to slavery. He sternly opposed the Crittenden Compromise, preferred disunion to any "complicity in slavery extension," and, once hostilities opened, regarded the extinction of slavery as an irrevocable object. His doctrine in 1861 was that if a real majority of Southerners wished to go from the Union they should be allowed to do so, but that the revolt was one of "a violent, unscrupulous, desperate minority, who have conspired to clutch power" (*Recollections,* p. 398; *Tribune,* Nov. 9, 16, 1860; Nov. 19, 1861). When war began he supported it with energy, though the unfortunate cry, "Forward to Richmond!" (June 28, 1861), was raised by Dana, not by Greeley. He quickly allied himself with the radical anti-slavery element led by Sumner, Stevens, and Chase, opposing the President's policy of conciliating the border states and demanding early emancipation. Though other newspapers accepted the modification of Frémont's emancipation order, Greeley did not, insisting that Congress or the President resort to a general liberation of slaves. His editorial on emancipation, "The Question of the Day" (*Tribune,* Dec. 11, 1861), declared that "rebels" should have been warned at the outset that they would lose their slaves, that they had no rights to consideration, and that the Union could not "afford to repel the sympathies and reject the aid of Four Millions of Southern people." His rising impatience with Lincoln's policy culminated in his famous signed editorial, "The Prayer of Twenty Millions" (Aug. 20, 1862). This arraigned Lincoln as remiss in executing the Confiscation Act, as unduly influenced by "certain fossil politicians hailing from the Border Slave States" (the Blairs), and as offering a "mistaken deference to Rebel slavery." On Sept. 24 the *Tribune* hailed Lincoln's Emancipation Proclamation as recreating a nation. Greeley's radicalism involved his journal in bitter warfare with not only the Democrats but also with the Seward-Weed moderates, and the fight extended to state politics. In 1862 he was acclaimed the principal leader of New York Republicans, but his poor judgment of men and fluctuating principles caused him to lose influence in political circles (DeA. S. Alexander, *A Political History of the State of New York,* III, 1909, p. 91).

Greeley's popular reputation and influence were injured in 1864 by his hesitation to support Lincoln and in 1864–65 by his peace activities. He favored postponing the Republican National Convention on the ground that the party was not united behind Lincoln (letter to N. Y. *Independent,* Feb. 25, 1864), and declared that Chase, Frémont, Ben Butler, or Grant would make as good a president, while the nomination of any of them would preserve the salutary one-term principle (*Tribune,* Feb. 23, 1864). As late as Aug. 18 he believed that Lincoln was already beaten, and wrote a friend that "we must have another ticket to save us from utter overthrow" (N. Y. *Sun,* June 30, 1889). Not until Sept. 6 did he state in the *Tribune* that "we fly the banner of Abraham Lincoln for the next Presidency," one dubious story asserting that this announcement followed Lincoln's private offer to appoint Greeley his next postmaster-general.

Even more ill-advised was Greeley's course in regard to peace. During 1863 he advocated mediation by a foreign power, and communicated on the subject with C. L. Vallandigham and the French minister, telling Raymond, "I'll drive Lincoln into it" (J. F. Rhodes, *History of the United States,* 1893, IV, 222). In July 1864, he attempted to bring about direct peace negotiations. He wrote to Lincoln that he had learned that two emissaries from Jefferson Davis were in Canada with "full and complete powers for a peace"; declared that "our bleeding, bankrupt, almost dying country also longs for peace; shudders at the prospect of fresh conscriptions, of further wholesale devastations, and of new rivers of human blood"; and urged Lincoln to make a frank offer of peace (J. G. Nicolay and John Hay, *Abraham Lincoln: A History,* 1890, IX, 186). Lincoln shrewdly prevailed upon the reluctant Greeley to go to Niagara Falls to open the negotiations. Greeley exceeded his instructions, but found that the Confederates were without proper powers from their government and asked for further directions. When Lincoln thereupon closed the affair with the ultimatum that he would gladly consider any official proposition which embraced the restoration of peace, the integrity of the whole Union, and the abandonment of slavery, Greeley sent him a reproachful letter, for he believed that the President should have left the door open (Greeley, *The American Conflict: . . . Its Causes, Incidents, and Results,* II, 1866, p. 664). On Aug. 9 he wrote Lincoln that if the "rebellion" could not be promptly crushed the nation faced "certain ruin," begging him to make a fresh peace effort, and making the astounding proposal that if peace could not be made, there be an armistice for one year, "each party to retain, unmolested, all it now holds," and the blockade of the South to be lifted (Nicolay and Hay, IX, 196–97). These and similar views, expressed publicly and privately, created a wide-spread feeling that Greeley's judgment and nerve were deplorably weak.

Greeley's radical political views extended to Reconstruction. Believing in full negro equality, he indorsed not only the Fourteenth but also the Fifteenth Amendment and favored the congressional policies. In 1866 he was again a lion of the state Republican convention, controlled by anti-Johnson radicals. But the intemperate zeal with which the *Tribune* supported Johnson's impeachment owed more to John Russell Young, the managing editor, than to Greeley, then absent on a final Western trip. Greeley was also liberal enough to favor general amnesty, and called, as in his fine speech at Richmond on May 14, 1867, for the erasure of all sectional antagonism. He seconded the movement this year for Jefferson Davis's release from Fortress Monroe, and on May 13 signed his bond in Richmond. Noisy attacks followed, thousands of subscribers to Greeley's two-volume compilation, *The American Conflict,* cancelled their orders, the weekly *Tribune* lost more than half its circulation, and an effort was made in the Union League Club to reprimand him. The *Tribune* rejoiced in Grant's election, and for two years supported him with uniform cordiality. But, because of his support of the one-term principle and for two other reasons, one rooted in disapproval of Grant's public policies and the other in New York state politics, Greeley steadily cooled toward Grant. As a leader of the Reuben E. Fenton wing in New York politics, he viewed with hostility the rise of the Conkling-Cornell machine under Grant's protection, and resented what he felt to be Grant's unfair apportionment of federal patronage. Conkling's defeat of the Greeley-Fenton group in the state convention of 1871 led to an open split. At the same time Greeley became convinced that the Grant administration was demoralized and corrupt, indifferent to civil-service reform, mistaken in its Santo-Dominican policy, and illiberal toward the South. On May 6, 1871, the *Tribune* expressed doubt of the wisdom of renominating Grant; on Sept. 15 it declared flatly against renomination. When independent Republicans pressed the movement for a new party in the congressional session of 1871–72, Greeley encouraged them. He wrote a friend on Mar. 13, 1872, that he would carry the fight against Grant to its bitter end, though "I know how many friends I shall alienate by it, and how it will injure the *Tribune,* of which so little is my own property that I hate to wreck it" (J. Benton, ed., *Greeley on Lincoln, with Mr. Greeley's Letters to Charles A. Dana and a Lady Friend,* 1893, p. 211). His career was approaching its tragic climax.

Before the Civil War the *Tribune* had been Horace Greeley; after the war there was no such close identity. The paper had become a great institution of which his control was but partial. Disbursements by 1871 exceeded a million dollars annually, the whole staff approached 500, and the stock was held by twenty proprietors (Greeley's anniversary article, *Tribune,* Apr. 10, 1871). Both Greeley's influence and that of the *Tribune* diminished after the war; the rise of the Associated Press, the multiplication of good local newspapers, and the disappearance of the great slavery issue, reduced their power. Personal editorship was declining. But from time to time Greeley still wrote editorials with his old fire, in what E. L. Godkin called "an English style which, for vigor, terseness, clearness, and simplicity, has never been surpassed, except, perhaps, by Cobbett" (Rollo Ogden, *Life and Letters of Edwin Lawrence Godkin,* 1907, I, 255).

As the Liberal Republican movement first developed, Greeley discouraged mention of his name for the presidency; but as the revolt spread and there seemed a likelihood of successful coalition with the Democrats, his lifelong desire for political advancement made him receptive. The reform element in the movement favored Charles Francis Adams or Lyman Trumbull; the politicians who were promoting a coalition favored David Davis or Greeley (A. K. McClure, *Old Time Notes of Pennsylvania,* 1905, II, 334). When the convention met in Cincinnati on May 1, Greeley had astute supporters, notably Whitelaw Reid and William Dorsheimer, on the scene. The contest narrowed to a struggle between Adams and Greeley, the managers of the latter sprung an effective stampede, and to the consternation of Schurz and other reformers, Greeley was nominated, with B. Gratz Brown as associate. The convention refused to make either nomination unanimous and many delegates departed, feeling with Samuel Bowles that the ticket had been made by a combination of political idiots and political buccaneers (G. S. Merriam, *The Life and Times of Samuel Bowles,* 1885, II, 212). Greeley was indorsed by a dispirited Democratic national convention at Philadelphia in July and some state coalitions were effected, but many Democrats bolted because of his former abuse of the party. The low-tariff element represented by the *Nation* was disaffected, while Schurz joined Greeley only after a reproachful correspondence with him. In an exceptionally abusive campaign, Greeley was attacked as a traitor, a fool, an ignoramus, and a crank, and was pilloried in merciless cartoons by Nast and others; he took the assaults much to heart, saying later that he sometimes doubted whether he was running for the presidency or the penitentiary. In answer to the "bloody-shirt" argument, he brought forward as his chief issue a plea for the reconciliation of North and South by the removal of all political disabilities and the union of both sections for common reforms. In his letter of acceptance he eloquently expounded the idea that both sides were "eager to clasp hands across the bloody chasm" (*Tribune,* May 22, 1872). Retiring from his editorship, he made an active speaking campaign in Indiana, Ohio, and Pennsylvania, his addresses to the huge crowds being notable for their intellectual strength (James G. Blaine, *Twenty Years of Congress,* II, 1886, p. 534). The October elections made it clear that he could not be successful in November. Yet the magnitude of the defeat was a surprise. Greeley carried only six border and Southern states and received only 2,834,125 of the popular vote against 3,597,132 cast for Grant. Among the chief factors in this disaster were the elaborate Republican organization, the distrust of Greeley by most financial interests, the impossibility of reconciling many Democrats, and the wide popular feeling that his judgment of both men and policies was hopelessly weak. Yet his candidacy had results of permanent value in actually doing much to close the "bloody chasm."

The tragedy of Greeley's death immediately followed the election. After his exhausting campaign tour he had watched with little sleep by the bedside of his wife, who died Oct. 30. He was profoundly hurt by the feeling that he was "the worst beaten man who ever ran for high office." The final stroke came when, on returning to the *Tribune,* he found that the reins there had passed firmly into the hands of Whitelaw Reid, who had no intention of surrendering them, and that he had practically though not nominally lost the editorship which had been his lifelong pride (Charles A. Dana, "The Last Blow," N. Y.

Green

Sun, Nov. 30, 1872). His mind and body both broke, and he died insane on Nov. 29. A shocked nation paid him in death the tribute he had never received while living. His funeral in New York on Dec. 4 was attended by the President, Vice-President, cabinet members, governors of three states, and an unequaled concourse of spectators. His failings were forgotten, while the services he had done the republic as its greatest editor, perhaps its greatest popular educator, and certainly one of its greatest moral leaders, were universally recalled.

[Greeley wrote an autobiography, *Recollections of a Busy Life* (1868; new eds., 1873, 1930), which offers not only a narrative of the main facts in his career, but also a frank revelation of the forces which influenced his tastes and thought, and which is admirable in its simplicity and concreteness. The best biographies are: W. A. Linn, *Horace Greeley: Founder and Editor of the N. Y. Tribune* (1903); James Parton, *The Life of Horace Greeley, Editor of the N. Y. Tribune* (1855, 1869, 1872, etc.); and L. D. Ingersoll, *The Life of Horace Greeley, Founder of the N. Y. Tribune* (1873). Some new facts are added in Don C. Seitz, *Horace Greeley, Founder of the N. Y. Tribune* (1926). Among treatments from a special point of view are Chas. Sotheran, *Horace Greeley and Other Pioneers of Am. Socialism* (1892), and F. N. Zabriskie, *Horace Greeley, the Editor* (1890). An estimate of Greeley's place in the history of American thought may be found in Vernon L. Parrington, *Main Currents in Am. Thought,* II, 1927, pp. 247–57. The recollections of associates may be found in C. T. Congdon, *Reminiscences of a Journalist* (1880); C. A. Dana, "Greeley as a Journalist," in E. C. Stedman and E. M. Hutchinson, *A Lib. of Amer. Lit.,* VII (1889); and J. C. Derby, *Fifty Years Among Authors, Books, and Publishers* (1884). Lives of John Hay, C. A. Dana, and Whitelaw Reid, and E. D. Ross, *The Liberal Republican Movement* (1919) should also be consulted. The state of N. Y. published in 1915 the *Proc. at the Unveiling of a Memorial to Horace Greeley at Chappaqua, N. Y., Feb. 3, 1914.* The files of the *N. Y. Tribune* are indispensable to a study of his life.]

A. N.

GREEN, ALEXANDER LITTLE PAGE (June 26, 1806–July 15, 1874), Methodist minister, was born in Sevier County, Tenn., one of the sixteen children and youngest of the seven sons of George and Judith (Spillmon) Green. His father, born in Maryland or Virginia soon after the arrival of his parents from England, fought on the side of the colonists in the Revolution. Both he and his wife, whom he married in 1776 when she was fifteen, were austerely puritanical Methodists. When Alexander was only a few years of age his parents removed to North Alabama, and there he grew up, working on the farm and attending country schools. When he was nine years old he was converted and at sixteen became a class-leader. In 1824 he was admitted to the Tennessee Conference on trial and was ordained elder in 1827. Though harried by frontier conditions in general and by Baptists and schismatics, he was soon the means of bringing some 200 new members into his communion. After serving on several circuits, his success was marked enough for him to be sent in 1829 to Nashville, which, for the most part, with such intermissions as were required by the itinerancy provision of his church, he always thereafter thought of as his home. On Oct. 19, 1831, he was married to Mary Ann Elliston, who at fourteen had recently been graduated from the Nashville Female Academy. He was a delegate to the quadrennial General Conferences of his church from 1832 to 1844, with the exception of the one in 1840. At that time he was in disfavor because of his belief that the Methodists of Canada, then about to form an organization of their own, should be compensated for the contributions which they had made to the agencies of the Methodist Church in America at large. Four years later, the Southern Methodists followed the Canadians in separation. At that time the fact of the former restitution, which he had prominently advocated, was a considerable element in the decision by the courts that the withdrawing brethren were entitled to a part of what had previously been held in common. Among the chief of these holdings were the publishing houses. When in 1854 the Supreme Court of the United States ordered a *pro rata* division, Green was largely influential in having the Southern Methodist publishing houses located in Nashville. During the Civil War he spent much of his time in Alabama. At the General Conference of 1866, where he was on such important committees as those to amend the *Discipline,* and to supervise ecclesiastical books and periodicals, he proposed and partly carried through a series of reforms in church administration. His major interest during the latter part of his life was the publication house he had brought to Nashville. He was a man who knew how to get along in this world as well as how to prepare for the next one —prosperous in business and an enthusiastic sportsman. Emphasizing as a preacher the emotional at the expense of the philosophic, he was "not bookish," it is said, "in his science, mechanics, or grammar" (Green, *post,* p. 203). He said that he had heard preachers of his acquaintance surpass Milton in describing "angels, devils, rivers, and serpents," and he thought none too well of Shakespeare. In spite of all his deviation from the established canons of literary taste he, however, set great store by education, and was an important figure in the inauguration of Vanderbilt University.

[Charles Elliott, *Hist. of the Great Secession from the M. E. Ch.* (1855); A. H. Redford, *Hist. of the Organization, M. E. Ch. South* (1871); J. B. M'Ferrin, *Hist. of Methodism in Tenn. 1783–1840* (3 vol., 1869–73); W. M. Green, *Life and Papers of A. L. P. Green*

(1877); W. W. Sweet, *The M. E. Ch. and the Civil War* (1912); *Republican Banner* (Nashville), July 16, 1874.]
J. D. W.

GREEN, ANDREW HASWELL (Oct. 6, 1820–Nov. 13, 1903), lawyer, the son of William Elijah Green and his third wife, Julia, daughter of Oliver Plimpton, traced his descent from Thomas Green of Leicester, England, who emigrated to Massachusetts Bay about 1635 and settled in that portion of Malden which is now included in Melrose and Wakefield. He was born at Worcester, where his father was practising law, was educated at the Academy there, and prepared himself for West Point. Abandoning his purpose to enter the army, he became a clerk in a mercantile firm in New York. He subsequently determined to study law and in 1842 entered the office of Samuel J. Tilden [*q.v.*]. After his admission to the New York bar in 1844, he continued in association with Tilden, ultimately becoming his partner.

For many years he was actively connected with municipal affairs. In 1854 he was appointed a member of the Board of Education, becoming president in 1856. During the six years he served on the board he made an exhaustive study of the public-school system then in vogue, acquiring a complete mastery of the subject. When in April 1857 the legislature passed an act for the regulation and government of Central Park under eleven persons, Green was named one of the commissioners. The following September he was appointed treasurer, and, the next year, president. On Sept. 15, 1859, the board created the office of comptroller of the park and placed Green in that position, the entire executive management being vested in him. So efficient was his guidance that the legislature empowered the board to lay out the northern end of Manhattan Island, and to devise plans for the improvement of the Harlem River and Spuyten Duyvil Creek. Green's reports suggested in broad outline practically all the immense improvements which were carried to completion during the ensuing half century, including Riverside Drive and Fort Washington, Morningside, and Pelham Bay parks. He envisaged Central Park as the center around which should be grouped all the major institutions of science, art, and education in the city, in partial fulfilment of which the locations of the Metropolitan Museum of Art and the American Museum of Natural History were determined. The Brooklyn bridge project had his hearty support and the Washington bridge across the Harlem River was an outcome of his plans. He continued comptroller of the park until the Tweed charter of 1870 removed the members of the board from office.

In September of the following year, at the suggestion of William F. Havemeyer [*q.v.*] and Samuel J. Tilden, he was appointed deputy comptroller of New York City by Comptroller Richard B. Connolly. After the election of Nov. 7, when the Tweed ring was ousted, Green became comptroller. The city finances were in the utmost confusion, but before he retired from office in December 1876 he had retrieved the situation and put the municipality on a safe financial basis. In 1880 he again became a park commissioner but resigned on finding that he was not being accorded support in carrying further his policy of improvements. He served on the state commission to revise the tax laws in 1881, and two years later was appointed by Gov. Grover Cleveland a member of the Niagara Park Commission, continuing to hold that position for nearly twenty years, during the last fifteen of which he was president.

More than twenty years previously he had conceived the idea of merging New York City and the municipal areas adjacent thereto, thus creating one central metropolitan authority in lieu of the five existing municipalities. For a long time he was the lonely advocate of the project, but ultimately on his petition the state legislature, May 8, 1890, authorized a commission to look into the matter. Gov. David B. Hill [*q.v.*] nominated him as a member, and he became president. The commission, indorsing his views, prepared a scheme of consolidation, which on being submitted to the communities concerned was approved, and the bill incorporating Queens, Kings, Richmond, and New York counties, including the Bronx, as the City of New York was passed in 1897, the consolidation taking effect Jan. 1, 1898. In recognition of his prolonged and successful effort in this behalf, a gold medal was presented to him inscribed, "The father of Greater New York."

He was a member of the New York constitutional convention of 1894. In 1895 he secured the incorporation of the American Scenic and Historic Preservation Society. He was a trustee under the will of his partner Samuel J. Tilden, who bequeathed his fortune for the purpose of providing a public library in the City of New York, and it is credibly averred that to Green's influence the bequest may be attributed. Subsequently he was a powerful factor in procuring the union of the Astor and Lenox libraries with the New York Public Library. In his eighty-fourth year he was murdered on the steps of his house by an insane negro, who had mistaken him for another person.

[R. H. Greene, "Andrew Haswell Green," *N. Y. Geneal. and Biog. Record,* Apr. 1904; John Foord, *The Life and Public Services of Andrew Haswell Green* (1913); Samuel Sweet Green, *Andrew Haswell Green, a Sketch* (1904); Samuel Stillman Greene, *A Geneal. Sketch of the Descendants of Thos. Green[e] of Malden, Mass.* (1858); E. H. Hall, "A Short Biog. of Andrew Haswell Green," *Ninth Ann. Report, 1904, of the Am. Scenic and Historic Preservation Soc.* (1904); *N. Y. Times,* Nov. 14, 1903.] H. W. H. K.

GREEN, ASA (Feb. 11, 1789–*c.* 1837), physician, author, bookseller, was born in Ashby, Mass., the third son of Oliver Green and Dorothy Hildreth. Since he was one of nine sons and daughters, it is likely that the practical note in several of his novels has autobiographical significance. Despite the large family, he had the advantages of education; he received the A.B. degree at Williams College in 1813, and the M.D. degree from Brown University in 1822 and from Berkshire Medical Institution in 1827. At college he is said to have had "a good reputation as a scholar" and to have been "distinguished for wit and vigor of thought." Such an estimate is very reasonable in the light of his subsequent literary efforts. He practised medicine in Lunenburg, Townsend, and North Adams, Mass.; but at the same time he published two small newspapers—the *Berkshire American,* established first at Pittsfield and moved in 1827 to North Adams, Mass., and the *Socialist,* started in 1828, a fact which is doubtless indicative of dissatisfaction with his profession. Both journalistic ventures failed, however, although in comment upon the first Green was described as "a ready writer, deservedly popular, well-educated, and having both tact and talent" (*History of Berkshire County,* 1885, p. 484), and in remarks upon the second the paper itself was said to evince "good literary taste and a humorous style of composition" (*Ibid.,* p. 489).

It appears that shortly after these failures Green went to New York and entered upon a career as author and bookseller. *The Life and Adventures of Dr. Dodimus Duckworth, A. N. Q.* (1833) is a sportive, burlesque novel about a quack doctor; the tale is probably an intentional thrust at abuses of the medical profession in his generation. *Travels in America by George Fibbleton, Exbarber to His Majesty the King of Great Britain* is scarcely less restrained as a satire on the Rev. Isaac Fidler's *Travels in America* and as a reply to Mrs. Trollope, "the most severe castigator of American manners." In the same humorous vein is *"A Yankee Among the Nullifiers,"* also published in 1833, in its good-natured picture of opposition in the South towards the North. A volume displaying more realistic tendencies, agreeably pert, is *Perils of Pearl Street* (1834) in which three business failures of an ambitious country youth in New York have graphic portrayal. Probably Green's own experiences are the background. A final book, *A Glance at New York* (1837), presents in a similarly humorous way the harsh realities of a great commercial city. What has been written of Green as a struggling journalist is applicable to him as an author; his novels are facile, self-respecting, humorous. In such a volume as *Travels in America,* the form and spirit tend to be that of the picaresque novel with its loosely connected scenes and roguish character, and in others a realistic method and atmosphere, with a humor varying from the genial to the burlesque, are manifest. He is a novelist representative of the early background of American prose fiction particularly in aspects of virility and healthy satire.

[Ezra S. Stearns, *Hist. of Ashburnham, Mass., from the Grant of Dorchester, Canada, to the Present Time, 1734–1886* (1887); *Hist. of Berkshire County* (1885); D. D. Field, *Hist. of the County of Berkshire, Mass.* (1829); E. A. and G. L. Duyckinck, *Cyc. of Am. Lit.* (rev. ed., 1875); *Hist. Cat. of Brown Univ., 1764–1914* (1914); *Gen. Cat. of Officers and Grads. of Williams Coll.* (1910).] L. L.

GREEN, ASHBEL (July 6, 1762–May 19, 1848), Presbyterian clergyman, eighth president of the College of New Jersey, was born at Hanover, N. J., where his father Jacob Green [*q.v.*] was long the Presbyterian minister. His mother was Elizabeth Pierson, grand-daughter of Abraham Pierson [*q.v.*], the first president of Yale College. As a boy he was instructed chiefly by his father and at the age of sixteen began a three-year period of teaching which was interrupted somewhat by militia service in the Revolutionary War. Entering the junior class of the College of New Jersey in 1782, he graduated the next year with first honors. After serving as a tutor for two years, he was appointed professor of mathematics and natural philosophy.

While teaching he had studied theology under Dr. John Witherspoon [*q.v.*], and in February 1786 he was licensed to preach by the Presbytery of New Brunswick. In May 1787 he was ordained and installed as colleague to Rev. James Sproat [*q.v.*] at the Second Presbyterian Church, Philadelphia. Six years later he became principal minister of the church, and so continued till 1812, rising to a position of influence both in the city and in his denomination. For eight years, beginning in 1792, he was elected chaplain to Congress, with Bishop William White [*q.v.*]. His many-sided leadership in the general work of his denomination began in 1788 when he was a member of the Synod which adopted the constitution of the Presbyterian Church. His record of office-bearing attests his great ability for organization, management, and finance, and his devotion to missions and education. For more than twenty years, between 1790 and 1839, he was a member of the General Assembly. As stated clerk from 1790 to 1803 he was its executive officer, and in 1824 he was moderator. Practical wisdom and strength and dignity in debate gave him remarkable authority in its proceedings. He wrote many of the important documents of the Assembly, one of them being the historic declaration against slavery formulated in 1818. He was prominent in the formation of the administrative boards of the Church and a member of all of them. As chairman of a committee of the General Assembly appointed for that purpose he composed the "plan" of Princeton Theological Seminary, the greater part of which is still in force. He was president of its board of directors from its foundation in 1812 until 1848. For ten years he managed its financial affairs and then procured the organization of a board of trustees, upon which he served until his death. In 1812 he was elected president of the College of New Jersey. During his ten years' incumbency the student body doubled and the teaching staff was strengthened. He was reputed to have been the first college president to introduce the study of the Bible into the curriculum. His presidency, however, was a rather troubled one, there being several violent outbreaks of disorder, against which rigid discipline and criminal process were employed. In 1822 a disagreement with the trustees, combined with physical infirmities, moved him to resign his office.

The remainder of his life was spent in Philadelphia. For twelve years he edited the *Christian Advocate,* a monthly magazine, writing much of it himself. He was active in church organizations and in many others, religious, philanthropic and educational. By urging ecclesiastical proceedings against Albert Barnes [*q.v.*] for false teaching, and by articles in the *Advocate,* he combated what with somewhat narrow judgment he considered intolerably dangerous errors in doctrine and polity. He preferred to see the church divided rather than these views prevail, and he worked shrewdly and uncompromisingly for the Old School victory which in 1837 produced such a division. Besides many sermons and addresses, and contributions to the *Christian Advocate,* he published *Discourses Delivered in the College of New Jersey, together with a History of the College* (1822); *Lectures on the Shorter Catechism* (1829); "Sketch of the Life of Rev. Jacob Green, A.M.," in the *Advocate* (1831–32); *A Historical Sketch or Compendious View of Domestic and Foreign Missions in the Presbyterian Church of the United States* (1838); *Lectures on the Shorter Catechism* (2 vols., 1841), a part of which had been published under the same title twelve years before. He also edited Witherspoon's *Works* (1800–01), and left in manuscript a valuable biography of him, which is preserved in the library of the New Jersey Historical Society at Newark, N. J.

Green was a striking figure, with his good looks, courtly old-time dress, and stately manners. Much honored for his character, abilities, and achievements, he was not popular. The self-esteem so amusingly evident in his autobiography created a rather consequential demeanor and made him dogmatic in the expression of his opinion, while his course in church controversy gave him a reputation for intolerance and rigor. He was, however, a man of sincere faith and devout life, never mean or petty, candid, kindly and generous. He would have won high place in any field requiring masterful leadership and power to get things done. He married in 1785 Elizabeth Stockton of Princeton (died 1807), in 1809 Christiana Anderson (died 1814), and in 1815 Mary McCulloh of Philadelphia. His son Jacob [*q.v.*], professor in Jefferson Medical College, was a distinguished chemist.

[*The Life of Ashbel Green* (1849), ed. by J. H. Jones, which is largely autobiographical; S. S. Greene, *A Geneal. Sketch of the Descendants of Thos. Green[e] of Malden, Mass.* (1858); W. B. Sprague, *Annals Am. Pulpit,* vol. III (1859); *Minutes of Gen. Assembly of Presbyt. Ch. U. S. A., passim* (containing documents relative to Princeton Seminary); Presbyterian *Digest* (1923); *Gen. Cat. of Princeton Univ. 1746–1906* (1908); *The Presbyt. Ch. in Phila.* (1895), ed. by W. P. White and W. H. Scott; E. H. Gillett, *Hist. of the Presbyt. Ch. in the U. S. A.* (2 vols., 1864); R. E. Thompson, *A Hist. of the Presbyt. Churches in the U. S.* (1895); John Maclean, *A Hist. of the College of N. J.* (2 vols., 1877); J. F. Hageman, *Hist. of Princeton and its Institutions* (2 vols., 1879).]　R. H. N.

GREEN, BARTHOLOMEW (Oct. 12, 1666–Dec. 28, 1732), printer, journalist, was born in Cambridge, Mass., the son of Samuel Green [*q.v.*] by his second wife, Sarah Clark. He served his father and assisted his half-brother Samuel when the latter managed Sewall's press in Boston after 1682. When Sewall was released from the license in 1684, the Greens continued to print, and on his brother's death, in July 1690, Bartholomew assumed charge. He was burned out two months later and rejoined his father in Cambridge, where his name shares in some dozen of the elder's last imprints. When the father retired in 1692 Bartholomew returned to Boston, undoubtedly taking the material of the Cambridge establishment. Printing ceased in Cambridge for a century, and Green continued to print for the college. Though several of his Boston works are of 1692, yet the permit "to Set up his Press . . . within . . . Boston" is dated June 6, 1693. He remained the chief printer in New England for "near Forty Years," enjoying the patronage of Government during the whole period. John Allen's name is on some of the imprints, but there was no formal partnership. Green printed the *Boston News-Letter* from the start, Apr. 24, 1704, except for the period Nov. 10, 1707–Oct. 1, 1711, and succeeded Campbell as publisher on Jan. 7, 1723. It was not his policy to print all the news; he announced on Mar. 7, 1723, that he intended to publish "those Transactions only, that have no Relation to any of our Quarrels, and may be equally entertaining to the greatest Adversaries" and to "extend his Paper to the History of Nature among us." On Jan. 5, 1727, he promised up-to-date news, instead of carrying on "a Thread of Occurencies of an Old Date." His "Philosophical Transactions" were usually accompanied by moral or religious reflections; piety was his outstanding trait. "He began to be Pious, in the Days of his Youth; And he wou'd always speak of the wonderful Spirit of Piety that then prevail'd in the Land, with a singular Pleasure" (*Boston Weekly News-Letter,* Jan. 4, 1733). He was a follower of the Mathers and was involved in their quarrel with Colman in 1700, printing Mather's unlicensed pamphlet but refusing to print the reply without an imprimatur, and then putting out a handbill justifying his stand. He became a deacon of the South Church Apr. 17, 1719, and may have been a tithing man in 1703, but was excused from serving as clerk of the market in 1709. Green was married in 1690; his wife Mary bore him nine children by 1706; she died Mar. 26, 1709. On June 16, 1710, he married Jane Toppan, presumably a niece of Samuel Sewall, who performed the ceremony and recorded the birth of the first son of his "cousin Green"; but a Toppan genealogy says that this niece died in 1728. By his second wife he had two more children, yet when he died, "after a long and painful Languishment of a Sore that broke inwards" (*Boston Weekly News-Letter,* Jan. 4, 1733), his will mentioned only the widow and four children. His printing establishment was valued at £126. The *News-Letter* passed to his son-in-law John Draper [*q.v.*].

[Isaiah Thomas, *Hist. of Printing in America* (2nd ed., 1874); J. T. Buckingham, *Specimens of Newspaper Literature, with Personal Memoirs, Anecdotes and Reminiscences,* I (1850), 23–27; Chas. Evans, *Am. Bibliog.*, vols. I and II (1903–04). His birthdate is often given as Oct. 26, 1667.]

D. M. M.

GREEN, BENJAMIN EDWARDS (Feb. 5, 1822–May 12, 1907), lawyer, diplomat, and promoter, was born at Elkton, Ky., the son of Duff [*q.v.*] and Lucretia Maria (Edwards) Green. His father, as editor of the *United States Telegraph,* settled in Washington in 1825, and there Benjamin grew up. Graduating from Georgetown College in 1838, he studied law at the University of Virginia and began practise in New Orleans. On July 10, 1843, through the influence of Calhoun, he was commissioned secretary of the legation in Mexico, and upon the withdrawal of Waddy Thompson [*q.v.*], the minister, he became chargé d'affaires, which post he held (Mar. 9–Sept. 1, 1844) until Wilson Shannon [*q.v.*] was appointed minister. He managed skilfully the negotiations concerning the boundary dispute, the claims convention, and the disastrous Mier expedition (*Senate Document No. 1,* 28 Cong., 2 Sess., pp. 52–91) during the delicate and critical period in which the United States was drifting into war with Mexico. In 1845 he returned to Washington, practised law, and engaged in railroad enterprises, and, securing a contract to build the U. S. S. *Powhatan* and repair other ships, joined Simon Cameron and A. Mehaffey in the Gosport (Va.) Iron Works. In 1846, as "Democrat," he wrote on the Oregon question for the Washington *Daily Union.* After the Mexican War he was employed by the Mexican government to aid in arranging the indemnity payments promised by the United States. In 1849 President Taylor sent him on a secret mission to the West Indies intended to be a preface to the purchase of Cuba. He was also provided with plenipotentiary powers to treat with the Dominican Republic for the establishment of a naval station on its coast, but except for securing from Hayti the recognition of United States consular officers without reciprocal obligation on the part of the United States, his mission was unsuccessful. Upon his return to the United States, he settled in Dalton, Ga., organized the Dalton City Company (1850), and devoted himself to the industrial development of the state. Among the enterprises in which he was interested were the Dalton & Morganton and the Dalton & Jacksonville railroads, the Central Transit Company, the Cherokee Iron Foundry, the Texas Land Company, and others in which his father was engaged. During the Civil War he was manager of the Washington County (Tenn.) Iron Works, under contract with the Confederate government. On July 26, 1866, he was married to Lizzie Waters of Lexington, Ky.

After the war he became solicitor and general manager of the American Industrial Agency, a company organized to provide Northern and European capital for the agricultural rehabilitation of the South, and after the failure of this venture, he organized a company to encourage immigration to the South from the northwestern states and Germany. He was interested in a company for the construction of a canal across Florida connecting the waters of the Atlantic Ocean and the Gulf of Mexico. He was secretary to the Crédit Mobilier of America and published its *Prospectus* (1873) and a history of the company in the *New York Herald* (Feb. 6, 1873). He played an important rôle in politics as an opponent of the state "Ring," over the signature "Granger" contributed articles on the Greenback movement to the *Terre Haute Express*, and was largely instrumental in the calling of the Georgia state convention of the Greenback party in 1880 (C. T. Parker to Green, July 5, 1880).

Deeply interested in finance and currency, he wrote a number of works on political economy. He published the *Opinions of John C. Calhoun and Thomas Jefferson on the Subject of Paper Currency* (Philadelphia, n.d.), and his own translation of B. A. G. de Cassagnac's *History of the Working and Burgher Classes* (1871), adding a long introduction (also published separately as *The Irrepressible Conflict Between Labor and Capital*, 1872) in which he discussed the economic causes of the Civil War. He was editorial writer for the *Dalton Citizen* and in 1868 he became editor of the *People's Weekly* of Washington. In 1886 he contributed to the *Southern Historical Society Papers* (XIV, 226–41) "Calhoun-Nullification Explained," and in 1901 he published *Shakespeare and Goethe on Gresham's Law and the Single Gold Standard.* He died at his home, "Greenhurst," near Dalton, leaving a number of unpublished manuscripts, notable among which are the following: "Ordinances in Relation to Lands and Water Courses," translated from the Spanish and containing the laws in force in Mexico in 1844; "The Evolution of a Georgia Cracker," an account of social and economic conditions in Georgia in the fifties; "Alexander H. Stephens on Harrison and Tyler —Sectional Parties"; "Lincoln's Entrance into Richmond in 1865"; and "United Hearts," a biographical and historical account of the period from the election of Tyler through the free silver controversy.

[See A. S. Salley, Jr., "The Calhoun Family of S. C.," *S. C. Hist. and Geneal. Mag.*, Apr., July 1906; R. T. Green, *Geneal. and Hist. Notes on Culpeper County* (1900); Duff Green, *Facts and Suggestions*, etc. (1866); *House Report No. 354*, 33 Cong., 1 Sess.; *House Report No. 142*, 33 Cong., 2 Sess.; obituaries in *Atlanta Georgian (and News)* and *Atlanta Jour.*, May 13, 1907, and *Atlanta Constitution*, May 14, 1907. In addition to these sources there are Green's unpublished works and his correspondence in private hands in Chapel Hill, N. C.]

W. L. W—t., Jr.
F. M. G.

GREEN, BERIAH (Mar. 24, 1795–May 4, 1874), reformer, was born at Preston, Conn., the eldest of six children of Beriah and Elizabeth (Smith) Green, who removed to Pawlet, Vt., about 1810. He graduated from Middlebury College with the class of 1819, receiving valedictory honors, and went to Andover Seminary to prepare himself for the missionary service of the American Board of Commissioners for Foreign Missions. To eke out his slender resources, he undertook to teach at Phillips (Andover) Academy. Within the year, however, his eyes and health began to fail, and he left the seminary. His health gradually returning, he married, Jan. 21, 1821, Marcia Deming of Middlebury, Vt., and for a short time afterward was in the service of the American Board on Long Island and at Lyme, Conn. Ordained on Apr. 16, 1823, he became pastor of the Congregational church at Brandon, Vt. Three years later, Mar. 31, 1826, his wife died, leaving two children, and on Aug. 30 of that year he married again, his second wife being Daraxa Foote, also of Middlebury, who with her seven children survived him. In 1829 he accepted a call to the distinctly "orthodox" church of Kennebunk, Me., but the next year left to take the chair of sacred literature in the theological department of Western Reserve College. In Cleveland, Green's hostility to American slavery, first specifically awakened in 1822 and growing with his belief that the Christian doctrines should be more practically applied to everyday life, came to a crisis, and on four consecutive Sundays he preached in the college chapel sermons in which he "haled American slavery to the bar of the Christian religion." These powerful sermons attracted wide attention, and in December 1833 he was made president of the convention in Philadelphia at which the American Anti-Slavery Society was formed. The same year he accepted the presidency of the Oneida Institute at Whitesboro, N. Y. Here he attempted to maintain a school of high character where manual should be combined with mental labor, where Hebrew and the Greek scriptures should be substituted for the regular Greek and Latin classics, and where students of every color and nationality should mingle as equals. This position he held until 1843, shortly before inadequacy of support forced the Institute to close. His interpretation of Calvinism proved to be so radically different from that of surrounding clergy that one after another of the orthodox pulpits were closed to him. For a time also his prominence as an Abolitionist told on his position and popularity. In 1837 the Presbyterian church in Whitesboro divided on the question of slavery, and the Abolitionist faction established a Congregational church, of which Green was pastor from 1843 to 1867. He published two volumes, *The Miscellaneous Writings of Beriah Green* (n.d., *circa* 1841) and *Sermons and Other Discourses with Brief Biographical Hints* (1860), as well as some thirty-five pamphlets, mostly on theological and abolitionist subjects, including *The Martyr: A Discourse in Commemoration of the Murder of the Rev. Elijah P. Lovejoy* (1838) and *Sketches of the Life and Writings of James Gillespie Birney* (1844). Intellectually Green was a man of considerable originality. He had strong convictions, but an intensely practical character which probably was responsible in no small measure for the modification of his early theological views. His activities as an Abolitionist attest his moral courage. For the last twenty-five years of his life he lived in virtual retirement. He died suddenly in his eightieth year while speaking against the local liquor traffic in the Town Hall at Whitesboro.

[Autobiographical material in Green's *Sermons and other Discourses* (1860); pamphlet, *Beriah Green* (1874), by his son, S. W. Green; P. H. Fowler, *Hist. Sketch of Presbyterianism within the Bounds of the Synod of Central N. Y.* (1877); *Fiftieth Anniversary of Whitestown Seminary, June 20, 1878* (1878); reminiscences of Green in J. B. Grinnell, *Men and Events of Forty Years* (1891).] W. R. W.

GREEN, DUFF (Aug. 15, 1791–June 10, 1875), journalist, politician, industrial promoter, son of William and Lucy Ann (Marshall) Green, was born in Woodford County, Ky. His great-grandfather, Robert Green, settled in Virginia about 1712 and served Orange County as justice of the peace, member of the House of Burgesses, and sheriff. William, grandson of Robert and father of Duff, served, when a youth of fifteen, under Gen. Morgan at the battle of Cowpens. Duff Green attended a neighborhood school, studied at home under his mother, and then received a classical training at the Danville Academy. He taught in the Elizabethtown Academy and meanwhile studied medicine. He enlisted as a private in the War of 1812, saw service at Vincennes and Fort Harrison under Gen. William H. Harrison, and was promoted to a captaincy. On Nov. 26, 1813, he married Lucretia Maria Edwards, daughter of Benjamin and sister of Gov. Ninian Edwards [*q.v.*] of Illinois. To them were born eleven children, one of whom, Benjamin Edwards Green [*q.v.*] was closely associated with some of his father's later enterprises.

After the war, Green became a merchant in Kentucky, but in 1816 went to Missouri to survey public lands. He engaged in land speculation, built up a large mercantile business at St. Louis with branches at St. Charles, Franklin, and Chariton, secured a contract for carrying the mails, served as postmaster of Chariton, which town he founded, established the first stage-coach line west of the Mississippi River (*Facts and Suggestions,* 1866, p. 27), and yet found time to study law. He was admitted to the bar and built up a large and lucrative practise. He became active in territorial politics and bitterly opposed any restrictions being placed on Missouri's entrance into the Union. At a political rally at Franklin his toast was, "The Union—It is dear to us but liberty is dearer" (*Missouri Historical Review,* October 1920, p. 5). He was one of the most influential members of the Missouri constitutional convention and represented Howard County in both houses of the state legislature. He served on the Indian frontier as brigadier-general of the first Missouri brigade; and in 1823 purchased the *St. Louis Enquirer,* with which he supported Jackson in the presidential election of 1824.

The following year he removed to Washington where he purchased the *United States Telegraph,* and violently assailed Adams's administration on the "corrupt bargain" charge, advocating Jackson and reform. As printer to Congress (1829–33), a member of the "Kitchen Cabinet," and editor of the Jackson organ, Green became one of the most influential leaders of the Democratic party. He was fearless and independent, however, and opposed Jackson in the Eaton imbroglio and the choice of Van Buren as Jackson's successor. When the break came between Jackson and Calhoun, Green followed the latter (whose son had married Green's daughter), thus losing both his position in the party and the government printing. Though a radical state-rights advocate, he was a moderate nullifier and continually warned Calhoun against the extreme views of McDuffie and Hamilton. He strove to build up a political and economic union of the South and West by calling attention to their common interests on tariff and internal improvements.

Green attacked Jackson for usurping dictatorial powers and supported Clay for the presidency in 1832. He first urged Calhoun's nomination in 1836, then shifted to the Harrison camp, and finally supported White through the *United States Telegraph Extra.* He relinquished the editorship of the *Telegraph* in 1836, though he continued as publisher until the death of the paper the following year, and founded the *Reformer,* a state-rights, reform journal which he abandoned in 1838. He founded the *Pilot* (Baltimore) in 1840, supported Harrison, and was largely responsible for Tyler being placed on the Whig ticket. Tyler rewarded him by offering him a choice of administration posts, but Green asked instead to be sent to England and France as the unofficial representative of the United States. He was cordially received by the free traders, Cobden, Hume, McGregor, and by other governmental officials of England. Through personal contacts and his writings (*inter alia,* "The United States and England," *Great Western Magazine,* London, September 1842) he aided in molding public opinion favorable to the reduction of duties, a commercial treaty, direct trade with the South, a modification of England's attitude toward slavery and the interest of the United States in Texas, and the settlement of the Oregon and boundary disputes (Green Manuscripts, Chapel Hill).

Returning to the United States, in January 1844 Green established in New York the *Republic,* a radical free-trade, civil-service, and postal-reform journal, and renewed his activities for the Southern cause. He advocated emigration to Texas (Green to Houston, Jan. 19, 1844) and Santo Domingo (letter dated Mar. 23, 1847) with the idea of their ultimate acquisition, internal improvements to tie up the South and West, and the publication of Southern school books and a Southern review. Tyler appointed him consul at Galveston, Tex., in 1844 and sent him to Mexico with the view of acquiring Texas, New Mexico, and California. Failing in this project, Green tried to foment a revolution so that the United States might intervene. When the Mexican War came he offered to recruit a regiment to be placed under Governor Henderson of Texas (Green to Henderson, May 16, 1846). After the war he acted as agent of the United States in making payment to Mexico under the treaty of Guadalupe Hidalgo.

Green was engaged in numerous industrial enterprises. He bought and developed vast tracts of coal and iron lands in Virginia and Maryland and contracted to build a portion of the Chesapeake & Ohio Canal (Green to Everett, Mar. 17, 1844); was interested in channel and harbor improvements; built a portion of the East Tennessee & Georgia Railroad; secured charters from the Georgia, Alabama, Mississippi, Louisiana, and Texas legislatures for a Southern Pacific railroad and arranged with the Mexican Government for its extension to the west coast, raised funds through the Pennsylvania Fiscal Agency, and was ready to begin construction when the Civil War began; was consulted while in Paris (1842) by Nicholas I of Russia concerning a Trans-Siberian railroad, and after the Civil War organized the Sabine & Rio Grande, the Selma, Rome & Dalton, and other railroads. Among the industrial agencies he organized were the Union Potomac Company (Virginia, 1836), the Union Company (Maryland, 1839), and the American Land Company (Maryland, 1840), the Jonesboro Iron Works (Tennessee, 1861), the Planters Insurance Trust and Loan Company (Georgia, 1861), the Maryland Industrial Agency (Maryland, 1867), and the Mississippi American Industrial Agency (Mississippi, 1867). For a short while in 1857 he published a weekly, the *American Statesman,* in Washington.

While neither a slave-holder nor a secessionist, Green was sent by Buchanan (1860) to Springfield to consult Lincoln about his attitude toward secession. Green believed that his "allegiance to the Federal government was subservient to . . . [his] allegiance to the State and . . . acquiesced in and acknowledged the authority of the State" (Green to Robert J. Walker, 1865). During the war he conducted iron works in Alabama and Tennessee for the Confederacy, and was several times in consultation with Davis and other Confederate leaders concerning the foreign and financial policies of the Confederate States. In 1861 he published *Facts and Suggestions on the Subjects of Currency and Direct Trade* and *The Treasury Notes of the Confederate Government,* and in 1864, *Facts and Suggestions Relative to Finance and Currency.* In 1865 Lincoln gave him private audience at Richmond concerning peace (J. G. Nicolay and John Hay, *Complete Works of Abraham Lincoln,* 1905, VI, 87–89). His last years were spent at his home, "Hopewell," near Dalton, a town which he had founded, engaged in writing on financial and economic subjects, and in organizing the agencies previously mentioned to raise capital and secure labor for the economic reconstruction of the South. Among his later published works are *Facts and Suggestions, Biographical, Historical, Financial, and Political* (1866); *A Memorial and a Bill Relating to Finance, National Currency, Debt, Revenue, etc.* (1869); and, *How to Pay Off the*

National Debt, Regulate the Value of Money and Maintain Stability in the Values of Property and Labor (1872).

Green was independent and self-assertive, a man of strong beliefs and firm convictions. He inspired loyalty among friends and supporters and fear and hatred among his enemies. The former bestowed upon him such encomiums as "the able and fearless advocate of the rights of the people," "high minded and sagacious," "bold and faithful champion"; the latter censured him as "infamously notorious" and "an impudent blackguard" (*United States Telegraph*, Mar. 13, 1829), but even they respected him (Biddle to Green, Apr. 29, 1841). His long life was devoted to what he considered the rights of the people, the defense of the political rights of the South in the Union, the organization and development of a free and independent press, and the economic and industrial development of the nation.

[Green's own work, *Facts and Suggestions* (1866); a collection of his letters in the Lib. of Cong., and a much larger collection of his MSS. in private hands at Chapel Hill, N. C.; Wm. M. Paxton, *The Marshall Family* (1885); R. T. Green, *Geneal. and Hist. Notes on Culpeper County, Va.* (1900); Green letters in *Southern Hist. Asso. Pubs.*, vol. VII (1903); W. B. Bryan, *A Hist. of the National Capital*, vol. II (1916); obituary in *Atlanta Constitution*, June 11, 1875.]

F. M. G.

GREEN, FRANCES HARRIET WHIPPLE (September 1805–June 10, 1878), author, reformer, was born in Smithfield, R. I., the daughter of George Whipple. Her ancestors were among the earliest settlers in the state. She was educated in the district schools and later at a private school in Providence, giving evidence of a retentive memory and creative literary ability. By 1830 she had attracted considerable attention by her poetic contributions to Rhode Island papers, and had edited herself the *Original*, containing sketches of local interest, many of them her own. From 1830 on she devoted herself to one cause after another, temperance, labor, suffrage, abolition, spiritualism, being "unfortunately for her personal comfort, . . . ever on the unpopular side of every question in Rhode Island" (Rider, *post*, p. 30). In *The Envoy, From Free Hearts to the Free* (1840) and in *Shahmah in Pursuit of Freedom; or, The Branded Hand* (1858) she attacked slavery. As editor and publisher of the *Wampanoag and Operatives Journal* of Fall River (1842–43), she turned her attention to the education, assistance, and encouragement of the female operatives in the manufacturing districts. Displaying an equal interest in the laboring classes was her novel *The Mechanic* (1841). In *Might and Right, by a Rhode Islander* (1844) she showed herself to have been a violent partisan of Thomas Dorr and an ardent supporter of his demands for a more liberal suffrage in Rhode Island. Perhaps her most popular work was the *Memoirs of Elleanor Eldridge* (1838), followed by *Elleanor's Second Book* (1839), the actual story of a colored woman who had suffered from legal injustice. A student of botany all her life, she published, in collaboration with Joseph W. Congdon, a *Primary Class-Book of Botany*, enlarged and republished in 1855 under the title: *Analytical Class-Book of Botany*. In addition to the above works she contributed many articles to the serial publications of her day, and in these most of her poetry appeared. Of her verse, her best poem, according to Griswold, was *Nanuntenoo, a Legend of the Narragansetts*, of which three cantos were published in Philadelphia in 1848. "The Dwarf's Story," appearing in the *Rhode Island Book* (1841), Griswold describes as a "gloomy but passionate and powerful composition" (R. W. Griswold, *The Female Poets of America*, 1849, p. 123).

On July 1, 1842, Frances Whipple was married to Charles C. Green, an artist of Springfield, Mass. This marriage proved unhappy, however, and in 1847 they were divorced. Shortly afterward Mrs. Green became interested in spiritualism, and for a time made her home with S. B. Brittan in New York City, contributing to his paper, the *Univercoelum and Spiritual Philosopher*, and assisting him in editing the *Young People's Journal of Science, Literature and Art*. Later she contributed to Brittan's spiritualist magazine, the *Shekinah*. About 1860 she removed to California where in 1861 she married William C. McDougall and, as Frances H. McDougall, made her last literary effort, *Beyond the Veil* (1878). She died in Oakland, Cal. Possessing "a disposition admirably tempered by thorough culture and mature reflection, a loving and hopeful philosophy of life—softened and sustained by every tender affection—she was yet invincible in her resistance of every form of evil" (Brittan, *post*).

[S. S. Rider, *Bibliog. Memoirs of Three R. I. Authors* (1880); S. B. Brittan, "Mrs. Frances H. Green M'Dougall," *Banner of Light* (Boston, Mass.), Aug. 24, 1878; *San Francisco Chronicle*, June 11, 1878.]

W. R. W.

GREEN, FRANCIS (Aug. 21, 1742 o.s.–Apr. 21, 1809), Loyalist, philanthropist, was the second son of Benjamin and Margaret (Peirce) Green and a descendant of Percival Green who came to Boston in 1635 and settled in Cambridge, Mass., in 1636. Benjamin Green was secretary to the British forces at the siege of Louisbourg and was later president of the Council of Nova Scotia. Francis was born in Boston and after attending private school entered Harvard. Soon after his entrance, his father secured for him a commission (July 2, 1755) as ensign in the 40th Regiment, with the understanding that he might have leave of absence to complete his college work. The French War intervened and Francis had to join his regiment at Halifax in 1757. The next year he was at the siege of Louisbourg, and after its capture remained in garrison there until 1760 when he was transferred to Quebec. In this year, despite the interruption to his studies, he was granted his degree by Harvard. The 40th Regiment marched to Crown Point in June 1761 and proceeded thence to New York where they were embarked for the West Indies, arriving in time to participate in the siege of Havana. Green was commissioned lieutenant on Sept. 30. Within a few years, however, he decided to give up his military career and while in England in 1766 sold his commission. Returning to Boston, he established himself as a merchant and on Oct. 18, 1769, was married to his double cousin, Susannah, daughter of Joseph and Anna (Peirce) Green.

In the dispute with England preceding the Revolution, he was an opponent of the unlimited power of taxation by the British Parliament but remained loyal to the Crown. His opinions were well known and on a business trip through Connecticut he was twice threatened as a Tory and driven out with violence from Windham and Norwich (1774). He was one of the Addressers of General Gage and became thoroughly obnoxious to the Patriot party. On Nov. 1, 1775, during the siege of Boston, he was appointed captain of the third company of Loyal Associated Volunteers. Ten days later his wife died, and in March of the following year, when the town was evacuated by the British, he took his three surviving children to Halifax. He was made a magistrate there, but in 1777 went to New York. The next year he was among those proscribed and banished by Massachusetts. In 1779, with Philip Dumaresq who had also been a merchant in Boston, he fitted out the war vessel *Tryon,* 16 guns, and in 1780, at his own expense, equipped the sloop *Carleton* as part of the refugee fleet under George Leonard. He also cooperated with Leonard in equipping the *Restoration.* Going to England in 1780, he resided there until June 1784, when he emigrated to Nova Scotia. He served as sheriff of Halifax County for three years, as senior judge of the court of common pleas, and as first joint treasurer of the province. In 1785 he married Harriet, daughter of David Mathews, president of the Council of Cape Breton and formerly mayor of New York. They had six children, four born in Nova Scotia and two in Medford, Mass., where Green settled after his return to the United States in 1797. He died at Medford.

Green's son Charles, a child by his first wife, was a deaf mute. He was sent by his father to Thomas Braidwood's school in Edinburgh, and there, with great success, was taught to speak. Green visited the institution a number of times and became much interested in methods of instruction for the deaf and dumb. In London, in 1783, he published anonymously a dissertation on the subject entitled *Vox Oculis Subjecta, a Dissertation on the Most Curious and Important Art of Imparting Speech and the Knowledge of Language, to the Naturally Deaf and (Consequently) Dumb.* In 1801 he published, also anonymously, an English translation of Abbé de l'Epée's work on the subject, *Institutions des Sourds et Muets,* and from 1803 to 1805 published articles and translations in the *New England Palladium* and other Boston newspapers under the pseudonym "Philocophos." He was a complete master of his subject as far as knowledge went at that time, and was the first American writer on it. His translation of De l'Epée's work has been twice republished, in London in 1819 and in the *American Annals of the Deaf* (vol. XII) in 1860. He helped to establish a school for deaf mutes in London and endeavored, though unsuccessfully, to establish one in America.

[Alexander Graham Bell, "A Philanthropist of the Last Century Identified as a Boston Man," *Proc. Am. Antiq. Soc.,* n.s. XIII (1900), with additional references; *Boston Births . . . 1700–1800* (1894), p. 246; S. A. Green, *An Account of Percival and Ellen Green and Some of Their Descendants* (1876); Lorenzo Sabine, *Biog. Sketches Loyalists Am. Rev.* (2 vols., 1864); E. A. Jones, *The Loyalists of Mass.* (1930); *Proc. Mass. Hist. Soc.,* 2 ser. II (1886), 239; J. H. Stark, *The Loyalists of Mass.* (1910); obituary in *Columbian Centinel* (Boston), Apr. 22, 1809.] J. T. A.

GREEN, FRANCIS MATHEWS (Feb. 23, 1835–Dec. 19, 1902), hydrographer, was the son of Mathews Wylly Green and Margaret Augusta (Gilchrist) Green, and a grandson of Francis Green [*q.v.*] and Harriet (Mathews) Green. He was born at Boston, Mass. When the Civil War began in 1861 and he joined the volunteer navy as a master at the age of twenty-six years, he had already experienced seven years of sea service since the completion of his schooling at the English High School of Boston in 1854. From 1861 to 1866 he was constantly employed in the North Atlantic and Gulf of Mexico blockading squadrons. In the middle of December 1868 he was made a lieutenant commander in the regular navy. He continued in the routine duties of that service, mainly on shipboard, until 1872, when his interest in professional marine hydrography was recognized by his engagement under the United States Hydrographic Office to prepare a volume of sailing directions relating to the West Indies (published in 1877 as *The Navigation of the Caribbean Sea and Gulf of Mexico,* vol. I). In the course of this employment, finding that a large part of the coast to be described had not been surveyed, he conducted a survey (1874) in the U. S. S. *Fortune* from which, taken together with coördinate operations by the U. S. S. *Wyoming,* the Mexican coast from the Rio Grande to Vera Cruz was charted, and also the harbor of Alvarado.

Before the age of the electric telegraph, determination of longitude was attended with much uncertainty. It was known that the longitudes of various places in the West Indies and Central America did not harmonize: the starting points upon which they depended had been determined in general by the observation of moon-culminations which subjected them to a probable error of two or three seconds of time. Faced with the need of adjusting these longitudes, Green prepared himself by becoming a skilful astronomical observer, and when, upon the completion of the West Indian submarine cables, the Hydrographic Office organized an expedition for the determination of longitude in the West Indies and Central America by the exchange of telegraphic time signals, he was appointed to lead the expedition. In 1876 he published *The Determination of Secondary Meridians by the Electric Telegraph,* as No. 5 of the Practical Papers of the United States Hydrographic Office, and the following year, *Report on the Telegraphic Determination of Differences of Longitude in the West Indies and Central America* (1877), later summarized in *Telegraphic Determination of Differences of Longitude in the West Indies and Central America* (1883). In 1877 he was selected to lead another expedition to determine the longitudes of the principal places on the east coast of South America by the exchange of time signals over the transatlantic cables from Europe and the submarine cables between Para in northern Brazil and Buenos Aires in Argentina. In 1881 he led an expedition of the same nature to China, Japan, and the East Indies. In collaboration with Lieutenant Commander Charles H. Davis [*q.v.*] and Lieut. J. A. Norris he prepared *Telegraphic Determination of Longitudes on the East Coast of South America* (1880) and *Telegraphic Determination of Longitudes in Japan, China, and the East Indies* (1883). Altogether there were directly determined by these three expeditions about thirty secondary meridians which, for many generations, had been used as starting points for surveys and chronometric measurements of meridian distance. Many more positions were related by dependence upon those that were directly determined, so that these expeditions resulted in a large addition to the accurate knowledge of the earth's surface. Green also published *A List of Geographical Positions for the use of Navigators and Others* (1883) and papers on "Geography" in the *Annual Report of the Board of Regents of the Smithsonian Institution* for the years 1882–84 (1884–85).

In subsequent years, Green reached the grade of commander and spent some time in educational employment as captain of the Pennsylvania schoolship *Saratoga.* He reached the statutory age for retirement from the navy in 1897 and, in the years immediately preceding his death, gave service as an editorial contributor to the *Century Dictionary.* He died in Albany, N. Y., during a temporary visit from his home in Boston. He was married, at Beverly, Mass., Sept. 1, 1870, to Elizabeth S. Cushing.

[T. H. Hamersly, *Gen. Reg. of the U. S. Navy and Marine Corps for One Hundred Years* (1882); reports of Green's various surveying expeditions included in reports of the secretary of the navy, *House Ex. Doc. No. 1,* pt. 3, 43 Cong., 2 Sess., *Ibid.,* 45 Cong., 2 Sess., *Ibid.,* 47 Cong., 1 Sess.; W. S. Hughes, *Founding and Development of the U. S. Hydrographic Office* (1887); S. A. Green, *An Account of Percival and Ellen Green and Some of their Descendants* (1876); *Who's Who in America,* 1901–02; *Boston Transcript,* Dec. 22, 1902.]

G. W. L.

GREEN, GABRIEL MARCUS (Oct. 19, 1891–Jan. 24, 1919), mathematician, was born in New York City, of German parents, and was educated in the public schools. He graduated from the College of the City of New York, in 1911, and then entered Columbia University, receiving his A.M. degree in 1912 and his Ph.D. degree in 1913. He won two prizes for mathematical ability and another for highest rank in all college subjects. After completing his studies at Columbia he taught mathematics for a year in the College of the City of New York and in 1914 was appointed to an instructorship at Harvard. Two years later he was about to be made an assistant professor when his career was cut short by a fatal attack of pneumonia. He never married.

At Columbia he had come under the influence of Prof. Kasner, who was then paying special attention to projective differential geometry, and it was in this field that he wrote his doctor's dissertation, *Projective Differential Geometry of Triple Systems of Surfaces* (Lancaster, Pa., 1913), and did most of his subsequent work. It is interesting to recall Legendre's statement concerning the youthful Abel's investigation of elliptic functions—how the young, almost unknown Norwegian anticipated in a brief time the proposed publication of Legendre's life-work. Prof. Wilczynski (*post,* pp. 2–3) records a similar anticipation: "I had been engaged for some time in studying this very subject [projective differential geometry] and was very nearly ready to prepare my results for publication. I wrote to Green, asking him for some of the details of his work, not suspecting that it had been published already, and to my great astonishment received, a few days later, his printed thesis. This thesis made it quite unnecessary for me to publish my own work on the subject." Green lived long enough to publish only sixteen papers of any moment; these, however, were sufficient to reveal his genius in mathematics as a whole as well as in the domain of pure geometry. No American of his years in recent times had given greater promise in this field, and the sudden termination of his labors was a loss felt by all mathematicians of the United States. Like so many mathematicians he was an accomplished musician and was especially fond of the piano. As Prof. Wilczynski has said of him: "His touch was delicate and his musical intuition fine. Music was a form of expression especially well adapted to his emotional and idealistic temperament. . . . His expression, always sensitive and often serious, had in it a characteristic undertone of cheerfulness and joy, the joy of a man whose faith in life had not been destroyed, and whose belief in his own powers had not been broken."

[E. J. Wilczynski, short biog., and complete bibliog., *Bull. Am. Math. Soc.,* Oct. 1919; death notices, *Ibid.,* Mar. 1919; *Am. Math. Monthly,* Feb. 1919; *Science,* Feb. 14, 1919; *Boston Transcript,* Jan. 25, 1919.]

D. E. S.

GREEN, HENRIETTA HOWLAND ROBINSON (Nov. 21, 1834–July 3, 1916), financier, was born at New Bedford, Mass., the daughter of Edward Mott Robinson and Abby Slocum Howland, both of Quaker stock. Her father acquired an independent fortune as a partner in the house of Howland, which amassed great wealth in whaling and the China trade during a long period preceding the Civil War. Much of the daughter's childhood and many of her later years were passed with a maiden aunt, Sylvia Ann Howland, who was reputed the richest woman in New Bedford, her wealth having also come from the shipping and trading interests of the Howland family. By way of formal education the girl attended a Friends' school on Cape Cod and later Mrs. James Lowell's School in Boston. Notwithstanding a rather somber background and rearing, she was no stranger to social gaiety. In 1860, when she was twenty-five, her mother died, and three years later, when her father left New Bedford because of business interests in New York City, she accompanied him. Her father died in 1865 and by his will she received about $1,000,000 outright and a life interest in nearly $5,000,000 more. About the same time her aunt, Sylvia Ann Howland, died in New Bedford, leaving her a life interest in a residuary estate of perhaps a million and a half. Knowing that she was heir-at-law as the only living person in the fourth generation from Gideon Howland, she made claim to absolute inheritance of her aunt's property. This claim was not sustained by the courts, and as plaintiff in legal proceedings against the trustees under the will admitted to probate, she presented an earlier will (1862) in which she was the chief beneficiary. It contained a strange compact between her aunt and herself to the effect that neither could make a later will without consulting the other. Much litigation followed, but before the case was finally decided a settlement was made out of court.

Before her father's death Hetty had become engaged to Edward Henry Green, fourteen years her senior, who had long been engaged in the Philippine silk trade. The marriage took place in 1867. While the couple were living abroad, a son and a daughter were born to them. The father and mother entered into an arrangement under which each remained wholly independent of the other in all financial matters. Returning to the United States, she became a successful operator in the Stock Exchange. Her handling of the great interests in her charge was eagerly watched by men familiar with large affairs. She negotiated several successful "bull" movements on the New York Stock Exchange, notably in Louisville & Nashville, Philadelphia & Reading, and Georgia Central Railroad stocks. Her business in Wall Street was chiefly confined, however, to the lending of money. Foreseeing the money stringency of 1907, she converted extensive investments into cash and was prepared to meet the heavy demands of that panic period, with a resulting profit to others as well as to herself. Meanwhile she retained and extended her holdings in railroad, government, and municipal bonds, but did not confine her investments to those classes of securities. After her death it was found that she had over $5,000,000 invested in Chicago real estate. She had long been reputed the richest woman in the United States.

"Hetty Green," as she was popularly known for nearly forty years, was partly the victim of a newspaper tradition, partly of her own eccentricities. Her native shrewdness, intensified by single-handed combat with the financial powers of her time, steeled her personality for conflict and perhaps subordinated the more ordinary womanly traits. The newspapers always over-emphasized those peculiarities in her conduct that seemed to indicate a grasping and penurious disposition. Like every person known to have great wealth, she was annoyed by importunities from strangers and to avoid them adopted a simple and obscure manner of life. A keen New England wit, rather than humor, was always with her. Asked why she had taken out a license to carry a revolver, she replied: "Mostly to protect myself against lawyers. I'm not much afraid of burglars or highwaymen." After her husband's death in 1902, she lived with her daughter in a modest Hoboken apartment and intermittently in New York City, where she died at the age of eighty-one, survived by a son and a daughter, to whom her estate of over $100,000,000 descended.

[Obituaries in N. Y. papers of July 4, 1916; *N. Y. Times*, July 9, 1916; W. M. Emery, *The Howland Heirs* (1919), "The Howland Will Case," *Am. Law Rev.*, July 1870; Boyden Sparkes and S. T. Morse, *Hetty Green: A Woman who Loved Money* (1930); Franklyn Howland, *A Brief Geneal. and Biog. Hist. of Arthur, Henry, and John Howland and Their Descendants, of the U. S. and Canada* (1885).] W. B. S.

GREEN, HENRY WOODHULL (Sept. 20, 1804–Dec. 19, 1876), jurist, brother of John Cleve Green [*q.v.*], was a member of one of the oldest New Jersey families. His father, Caleb Smith Green, a farmer in Hunterdon (later Mercer) County, N. J., married Elizabeth, daughter of Aaron Van Cleve of Batavia, N. Y., and he was born in Maidenhead (now Lawrenceville), N. J. He spent his youth on his father's farm and his early education was procured at the academy which became the Lawrenceville School, whence he proceeded to the College of New Jersey in 1818, graduating there in 1820. He then took up the study of law with Charles Ewing at Trenton, and, when the latter became chief justice in 1824, completed his course at the law school in Litchfield, Conn. He was admitted as an attorney at Trenton in November term 1825 and became a counselor in February 1829. Since Trenton was the county seat, he commenced practise there, and thenceforward, until his elevation to the bench twenty-one years later, the record of his career at the bar presents a story of continuous advancement and uninterrupted success. He did not confine himself to any particular branch of law. His capabilities were first displayed in local trials before a jury, following which he was entrusted with briefs in the court of chancery and the supreme court. Appellate work followed in a natural sequence. In a short time he became recognized as one of the leading members of the state bar and was retained in almost every case of importance, more particularly when intricate points of law were involved. In 1832 he had been elected recorder of the city of Trenton, and in 1837 he was appointed reporter of the court of chancery, a position which he retained for seven years. In this capacity he published *Reports of Cases determined in the Court of Chancery of the State of New Jersey, 1838–45* (3 vols., 1842–46). These reports (2–4 *N. J. Equity*) have a very high standing with the profession.

In 1842 Green was elected as a Whig to represent Mercer County in the Assembly, but served only one term, having no inclination for political life. He was a delegate to the National Whig Convention at Baltimore in 1844, however, and there nominated Frelinghuysen for vice-president. In the same year he was elected a delegate from Mercer County to the convention which was called to revise the New Jersey constitution. The task involved heavy responsibilities inasmuch as the existing constitution was a makeshift production of the Provincial Congress of 1776. Green took a leading part in the proceedings, during the course of which he strenuously opposed the election of judges. In 1845 he became a member of the commission appointed to collate and revise the New Jersey statutes. The result of their labors appeared as *Statutes of the State of New Jersey Revised and Published under the Authority of the Legislature in 1847*.

On Nov. 2, 1846, Green was appointed by Gov. Stratton chief justice of the supreme court of New Jersey and was reappointed at the end of his first term. In March 1860, eight months prior to the expiration of his second term, he was appointed chancellor and ordinary or judge of the prerogative court and continued as such till May 1, 1866, when his health, gradually weakened by over-work, broke down and he resigned. In 1864, on the death of Chief Justice Taney, President Lincoln had offered him the position of chief justice of the Supreme Court of the United States, but failing health had compelled him to decline its responsibilities. In all he held judicial office for nearly twenty years. Though his record as chancellor was distinguished, his reputation will rest mainly upon his work as chief justice. He came to the bench endowed with a remarkable legal instinct and logical faculty, fortified by wide reading which a tenacious memory enabled him to utilize to the utmost. He also possessed a strong personality which made him the dominating figure when presiding in the supreme court or the court of errors and appeals. In rare instances were his decisions reversed and he almost invariably carried his colleagues with him in his disposition of a case. "His manner was very dignified and impressive. His tall form and strong frame, his massive head, stern features and—though one would imagine otherwise—even his long and rather shaggy reddish hair gave him an air of command and judicial dignity" (Keasbey, *post,* p. 512). Though he enjoyed unbounded respect and confidence as a judge, he was never popular. His ingrained austerity of demeanor, his outspoken dislike of mediocrity, and his somewhat hasty temper repelled familiarity or close friendships. On Mar. 22, 1831, he was married to Emily Augusta Ewing, the daughter of Chief Justice Ewing. She died in 1837 and on Jan. 2, 1840, he married her sister, Susan Mary Ewing.

[E. F. and W. S. Cooley, *Geneal. of Early Settlers in Trenton and Ewing, "Old Hunterdon County," N. J.* (1883); E. Q. Keasbey, "Henry Woodhull Green," in *Great Am. Lawyers,* vol. IV (1908), ed. by W. D. Lewis; *N. J. State Bar Asso. Year Book,* 1904–05; *Proc. N. J. Hist. Soc.,* 2 ser., vol. IV (1877).]

H. W. H. K.

GREEN, HORACE (Dec. 24, 1802–Nov. 29, 1866), laryngologist, the first American physician to specialize in diseases of the throat, was born in Chittenden, Vt., the youngest of the nine children of Zeeb and Sarah (Cowee) Green. His father, a soldier in the Revolution, was descended from Thomas Green who emigrated to Massachusetts Bay about 1635. Among his ancestors also were a number of physicians and apothecaries. Green studied medicine with his brother, Dr. Joel Green of Rutland, attending at the same time the Medical School at Middlebury (known later as Castleton Medical College), where he received his M.D. degree in 1825. After graduation he formed a partnership with his brother but had opportunity in the winter of 1830–31 to visit Philadelphia and attend medical lectures there. In 1835 he removed to New York City, where with the exception of several brief interruptions he practised until the end of his life. He spent several months in Europe in 1838, when he came under the influence of Louis, but he did not remain long enough to learn Louis's painstaking methods. He went abroad a second time in 1851.

Green is remembered chiefly for the acrimonious controversy which arose in 1846 after the publication of his *Treatise on Diseases of the Air Passages: Comprising an Inquiry into the History, Pathology, Causes and Treatment, of those Affections of the Throat called Bronchitis, Chronic Laryngitis, Clergyman's Sore Throat.* It was the first systematic work ever published on that subject and went into a fourth edition in 1858. Green's seemingly innocuous statement that it was possible to introduce a probang into the larynx and in this way apply local medication was attacked furiously, his opponents characterizing the procedure as not only quite impracticable but dangerous to life (the laryngoscope had not yet been invented). Unfortunately, Green had laid himself open to criticism by saying that medication applied in this way would cure a great variety of intractable pulmonary and laryngeal diseases, tuberculosis among them. His knowledge of pathology was not wholly sound, being probably based upon the imperfectly comprehended teachings of Louis (Wright, *post,* p. 203). In pointing out, however, the value of applying solutions of silver nitrate locally in catarrhal inflammation of the pharynx and larynx he made a fundamental contribution. Marshall Hall, the English physiologist, at first skeptical of Green's claims, became convinced after seeing experiments carried out upon the larynx of dogs (*Northwestern Medical and Surgical Journal,* 1854, n.s. ii). So rancorous were the attacks on Green that he was compelled to resign from one New York medical society and narrowly missed expulsion from the Academy of Medicine, but in spite of this professional jealousy he built up a large practise. He contributed extensively to medical journals and was the author of *Observations on the Pathology of Croup* (1849) and of a *Practical Treatise on Pulmonary Tuberculosis, embracing its History, Pathology and Treatment* (1864). From 1840 to 1843 he was professor of medicine and president of Castleton Medical College, and in 1850 he became one of the founders of the New York Medical College, where he was also professor of medicine, occupying the chair until his retirement in 1860. In 1854 he founded the *American Medical Monthly,* which was, however, short-lived. He was married twice: on Oct. 20, 1829, to Mary Sigourney Butler of Rutland, Vt., who died Aug. 17, 1833; and on Oct. 27, 1841, to Harriet Sheldon Douglas of Waterford, N. Y. He had one child by his first wife, and ten by his second. In deportment he was urbane and kindly. He spent the winters of 1863–64 and 1864–65 in Cuba for his health. He died at his country residence at Sing Sing (Ossining), N. Y.

[S. S. Greene, *Geneal. Sketch of the Descendants of Thomas Green[e] of Malden, Mass.* (1858); *Triennial Cat. Castleton Medic. Coll.* (1829); W. S. Miller, article in *Bull. Johns Hopkins Hospital,* Aug. 1919, with portrait, and briefer account in H. A. Kelly and W. L. Burrage, *Am. Medic. Biogs.* (1920); Jonathan Wright,

Hist. of Laryngology and Rhinology (2nd ed., 1914); Sam. W. Francis, article in *Medic. and Surgic. Reporter*, Jan. 26, 1867; *Bull. N. Y. Acad. Med.*, Jan. 1867; *N. Y. Medic. Jour.*, Jan. 1867; *N. Y. Times*, Dec. 3, 1866; D. B. St. John Roosa, *Medic. Times*, Apr. 1901.] J. F. F.

GREEN, JACOB (Feb. 2, 1722–May 24, 1790), Presbyterian clergyman, a descendant of Thomas Green who came to New England about 1635, and the son of Jacob and Dorothy (Lynde) Green, was born in Malden, Mass. When Jacob the younger was little more than a year old his father died, and when he was seven, his mother having married again, he was taken to live in Killingly, Conn. After attempting to learn a trade under several masters, he prepared for college and entered Harvard, from which he graduated in 1744. While a student he was greatly influenced religiously by the preaching of Whitefield and Gilbert Tennent [*qq.v.*]. After his graduation he taught school in Sutton, Mass., and in 1745 he was licensed to preach. In November of the following year he was ordained and installed pastor of the Presbyterian church, Hanover, Morris County, N. J., a relationship which continued until his death.

He performed his pastoral duties faithfully but also engaged in numerous other activities. Because his salary was too small for the support of his family, the parish voted that "Mr. Green practice Physick if he can bair it and the presbytery approve it" (E. D. Halsey, *History of Morris County, New Jersey*, 1882, p. 198), and for thirty years he ministered extensively to the physical welfare of the people. In 1774 he built a school-house and taught Latin to eight scholars. He also drafted wills and settled estates, carried on farming, and ran a grist-mill and distillery. "If I somewhat increased my worldly estate," he is reported to have said, "I also increased sorrow and incurred blame, in all things except the practice of physick" (*Christian Advocate*, February 1832, p. 52). In 1748 he became a trustee of the newly founded College of New Jersey, serving for sixteen years. For eight months (1758–59) he acted as vice-president and was in charge of the institution.

He took advanced ground on the question of slavery, and incurred the wrath of neighboring slaveholders. Before the War of Independence he outspokenly upheld the colonists' cause, and published in 1776 a pamphlet, *Observations on the Reconciliation of Great Britain and the Colonies, by a Friend of American Liberty.* During the war, proximity to the British lines exposed him to danger, but he refused to leave his home for safety. When the Continental paper money was issued he published in the *New Jersey Journal* (November–December 1779) "Letters on Our Paper Currency," pointing out the inevitable effect of such an issue, and proposing a plan for the liquidation of this currency similar to that which was finally adopted. He was a member of the Provincial Congress of 1776, and chairman of the committee to draft the constitution of the state. This instrument, reported after two days and adopted a week later, remained in force till 1844.

In 1780 Green led a group of four ministers who, objecting to the control exercised over churches and ministers by presbyteries and the synod, withdrew from the Presbyterian Church and formed what soon was called The Associated Presbytery of Morris County. In their organization Presbyterian views regarding the ministry were combined with Congregational polity. The movement for the formation of "associated presbyteries" flourished during thirty years, chiefly in New York State, and then passed away. Besides the writings mentioned, he published sermons, and other pamphlets, including *An Inquiry into the Constitution and Discipline of the Jewish Church* (1768), and *A Vision of Hell, and a Discovery of Some of the Consultations and Devices There in the Year 1767* (1776), which went through several editions. He married in June 1747 Anna Strong of Brookhaven, Long Island (died 1756), and in October 1757 Elizabeth Pierson of Woodbridge, N. J., granddaughter of Abraham Pierson [*q.v.*], first president of Yale College. One of his ten children was the distinguished clergyman Ashbel Green [*q.v.*].

[Sources include Ashbel Green, "Sketch of the Life of Rev. Jacob Green, A.M.," *Christian Advocate*, Aug. 1831–May 1832; *The Life of Ashbel Green* (1849), ed. by J. H. Jones; S. S. Greene, *A Geneal. Sketch of the Descendants of Thos. Green[e] of Malden, Mass.* (1858); W. B. Sprague, *Annals Am. Pulpit*, vol. III (1859); Richard Webster, *A Hist. of the Presbyt. Ch. in America* (1857); E. H. Gillett, *Hist. of the Presbyt. Ch. in the U. S. A.* (2 vols., 1864); John Maclean *Hist. of the Coll. of N. J.* (1877), vol. I; *Princeton Univ. Gen. Cat.* (1906); M. C. Tyler, *The Lit. Hist. of the Am. Revolution* (1897), II, 294; J. F. Tuttle, "The Rev. Jacob Green," *Proc. N. J. Hist. Soc.*, 2 ser. XII (1893). The opinions of the organizers of the Associated Presbytery are stated in the pamphlet *A View of a Christian Church and Church Government* . . . by the Associated Presbytery of Morris County (1781), probably written by Green.] R. H. N.

GREEN, JACOB (July 26, 1790–Feb. 1, 1841), teacher, chemist, naturalist, was born in Philadelphia, where his father, Ashbel Green [*q.v.*], was pastor of the Second Presbyterian Church. His mother was born Elizabeth Stockton. As a boy he was interested in botany. At the age of seventeen he graduated from the University of Pennsylvania and two years later published, in collaboration with Ebenezer Hazard, *An Epitome of Electricity and Galvanism* (1809). Turned aside from medicine by the crude surgery of the day—his M.D. from Yale in 1827 was honorary—he studied law, was admitted to the bar, and began to practise. Nevertheless, he continued his scientific pursuits, published a *Catalogue of the Plants Indigenous to the State of New York* (1814), and in 1818 was made professor of chemistry, experimental philosophy, and natural history in the College of New Jersey, of which his father had become president. He resigned his position in 1822, accepted three years later the first professorship in chemistry at Jefferson Medical College in Philadelphia, and held it until his death. Some of his lectures were published as *Electro-magnetism* (1827). In 1828 he visited England, France, and Switzerland, where, as he delightfully details in *Notes of a Traveller* (3 vols., 1830), he made many congenial acquaintances among scientists. On his return he finished a *Text-book of Chemical Philosophy on the Basis of Turner's Elements* (1829), which was followed by a *Syllabus of a Course in Chemistry* (1835) and *Chemical Diagrams* (1837). Besides these text-books, his papers in scientific journals indicate that his principal researches were in the same field as his teaching, but he also found time for studies in other branches of science. Thus his *Astronomical Recreations* (1824) was a popular elaboration on the basis of his own "evening rambles." His best-known contribution to biology was the paleontological *Monograph of the Trilobites of North America* (1832), but he also described living species of mollusks, salamanders, and lizards from the eastern United States and the Hawaiian Islands (see Nickles, *post*). In addition, he was attracted by some aspects of ethnology and described (*American Journal of Pharmacy,* 1834) beads, metals, and pottery known to and used by the aborigines of North America. His work as an educator was perhaps his greatest service to his contemporaries; he evidently was popular with his students, and several have testified to the inspiration of contact with him; but his actual additions to knowledge are rather desultory, perhaps because of his wide interests. Even as a chemist he was better known for his scholarly but popular presentation of compiled data than for the fundamental value or accuracy of his original contributions. His last treatise was *Diseases of the Skin* (1841). He was the recipient of four honorary degrees. He died, unmarried, in Philadelphia.

[E. F. Smith, *Jacob Green, 1790–1841, Chemist* (1923), with portrait; S. S. Greene, *A Geneal. Sketch of the Descendants of Thos. Green[e] of Malden, Mass.* (1858); J. M. Nickles, *Geologic Lit. on North America,* vol. I (Bull. 746, U. S. Geol. Survey, 1923); *North American and Daily Advertiser* (Phila.), Feb. 2, 1841; J. W. Holland, *The Jefferson Med. Coll. of Phila. 1825–1908* (1909); *Cat. Officers and Alumni Rutgers Coll. 1766–1916* (1916); *Gen. Cat. Princeton Univ. 1746–1906* (1908).] H. B. B.

GREEN, JAMES STEPHENS (Feb. 28, 1817–Jan. 19, 1870), representative and senator from Missouri, was born near Rectortown, Fauquier County, Va., son of James S. and Frances Ann Green. At nineteen he accompanied his father and brothers to Alabama, but soon moved to Missouri, first to Ralls County and subsequently, about 1836, to Lewis County, where he and his brother Martin E. Green (later brigadier-general in the Confederate army) purchased a sawmill. After several years of operating the mill, during which time he married Elizabeth Reese, augmented his common-school education as best he could, and read law, he was in 1840 admitted to the bar. He opened an office in Monticello and, in partnership with his brother-in-law, Addison Reese, speedily built up a large and lucrative practise. He married for his second wife, Nov. 28, 1847, Mary Evans of Fayette, Mo. (Fayette *Missouri Democrat,* Nov. 29, 1847).

He entered politics early, under the auspices of Thomas H. Benton [*q.v.*], demonstrating his remarkable power and adroitness as a stump speaker when the Democrats nominated him presidential elector on the Polk and Dallas ticket in 1844, and winning further prestige by his activities in the state constitutional convention of 1845. He represented Missouri in the Thirtieth and Thirty-first Congresses, attracting notice by his forceful support of the Administration's Mexican policy; and in 1848 served as counsel for his state in the Missouri-Iowa boundary controversy before the Supreme Court. As his experience widened he opposed the Free-Soil school and planned, led, and prosecuted the revolt against his political mentor in 1849 which broke Benton's hold upon Missouri Democracy and is still remembered as one of the most aggressive and successful of American political struggles. He did not offer himself for reëlection in 1850 (*Biographical Directory of the American Congress,* 1928), and in 1852 was defeated by his Whig opponent. President Pierce appointed him chargé d'affaires to Colombia, May 24, 1853, and on June 19, 1854, named him minister resident. He never presented his credentials, however, having found the service uncongenial, but resigned, in August 1854, and, returning to Missouri, resumed the practise of law. After a victorious campaign for Congress, 1856, in which he helped release the state from Know-Nothing domination, before he could take his seat the legislature elected him to succeed David R. Atchison [*q.v.*] in the United States Senate. Here he served from Jan. 12, 1857, to Mar. 3, 1861, plunging into the Kansas contest with his maiden speech, in which he effectively defended Buchanan against Douglas's savage attack, and bearing so conspicuous a part in the fight upon "squatter sovereignty" and in the drawn-out debates over "an imaginary negro in an impossible place" that for a time he occupied a more prominent position in the public eye than perhaps any of his fellow senators. He soon came to be recognized as one of the ablest exponents of Breckinridge Democracy in the Senate, and succeeded Douglas as chairman of the important committee on territories. He presented the majority report of this committee favoring the admission of Kansas as a state under the Lecompton constitution; later, when the acts organizing Colorado, Dakota, and Nevada as territories were passed by a unanimous Senate, with no introduction of the slavery issue, it was he who prepared and reported the bills.

From the day of Lincoln's inauguration, which terminated his public career, Green's fortunes declined. Summarily arrested by Federal troops at the outbreak of the war, he was released on parole, July 5, 1861. After a visit to Washington he was captured by Confederate troops but was released in August 1862. A tendency to intemperance in drink now grew upon him and in a few years brought about his death. "No man among his contemporaries had made so profound an impression in so short a time," wrote James G. Blaine (*Twenty Years of Congress,* 1884, I, 272); "he had peers, but no master, in the Senate." He was one opponent whom the belligerent Douglas most disliked to meet, and with reason: there were few who could approach him in debate, his logic, careful preparation, readiness, repartee, and irony making him an exceedingly dangerous antagonist. While seldom eloquent, his style was smooth and convincing; his manner courteous, but fearless and assured. His tall, spare figure, intellectual face, and clear voice lent him a commanding presence and appearance not unlike those of Henry Clay, whom he was thought to resemble.

[Richard Edwards and M. Hopewell, *Edwards's Great West and Her Commercial Metropolis* (1860); J. F. Green," *Mo. Hist. Rev.,* Oct. 1926; W. V. N. Bay, *Reminiscences of the Bench and Bar of Mo.* (1878); *Cong. Globe,* 35 and 36 Congs.; *Hist. of Lewis, Clark, Knox, and Scotland Counties, Mo.* (1887); W. B. Stevens, *Centennial Hist. of Mo.,* vol. II (1921).]

A. C. G., Jr.

GREEN, JOHN (Apr. 2, 1835–Dec. 7, 1913), ophthalmologist, the son of James and Elizabeth (Swett) Green, was born at Worcester, Mass., the third in descent from Dr. John Green who was a member of the Massachusetts General Court in 1777. Samuel Swett Green [*q.v.*] was his younger brother. Never a robust child, he did not enter into the strenuous physical exercises of his companions, nor, on the other hand, did his precollege years give any indication of unusual scholarship. Endowed with an accurate and retentive memory as well as intellectual curiosity, he habitually listened to the recitations of the class above him, paying scant attention to the assigned work, and thus earned for himself an inconspicuous place as a student. From the public schools of Worcester, he entered Harvard College at the age of sixteen. By the time he had reached his senior year he determined not to postpone his medical studies but undertook, successfully, to complete the senior work at college concurrently with his first year of medicine, graduating with the degree of A.B. in 1855, S.B. in 1856, and A.M. in 1859. In 1858 he had finished the requirements of the course in medicine, but because he considered the standards of the course too low, he refused to accept the degree until 1866, by which time his objections had been removed. Having been admitted in 1858 a fellow of the Massachusetts Medical Society, which entitled him to practise, he spent the next two years in professional study in London, Paris, Berlin, and Vienna. In 1861 he began the practise of medicine in Boston, filling the position of attending physician and surgeon to the Boston Dispensary. During the Civil War he served as acting assistant surgeon, United States army, in the Army of the Tennessee, taking care of the wounded after the battle of Pittsburg Landing, and at Frederick, Md., after the battle of Antietam. Through contacts he made in St. Louis during his connection with the Western Sanitary Commission, he was attracted to that city and decided to settle there to practise ophthalmology, for which he had prepared himself by a year of special study (1865) in London, Paris, and in Utrecht with Donders and Snellen. In 1868 he was married to Harriet Louisa Jones, of Templeton, Worcester County, Mass.

No one can estimate how much influence Green contributed to furthering the cause not only of the medical sciences in St. Louis, but of other branches of learning and the arts. So versatile was his genius, so profound his comprehension of problems in the arts and in sciences unrelated to his own, that the impact of his mind upon the leaders in education and culture was a constant stimulus to progress in their departments. His greatest accomplishment was to bring ophthalmology into recognition in St. Louis as a science in itself. When he began special practise, the general surgeon was still operating for cataract. Vigorously he stressed the importance of the specialist's trained hand for this most delicate procedure. He contended against the carelessness of the general practitioner in dealing with diseases of the eye, and with equal vigor sought to educate his patients in regard to the consequences of their own neglect. The stress of these unremitting efforts upon a constitution not robust, and the drain upon his nervous energy entailed by his own tireless and exacting researches were probably the chief factors in developing in him a certain brusqueness of manner. But his sympathies were always with the poor and his professional services were rendered without charge in unnumbered instances. He had a genius for making friends and together with his gifted wife attracted to his home the most brilliant and progressive minds of the community.

Green taught ophthalmology first as a lecturer, from 1874 to 1886; then as professor, from 1886 to 1889; thereafter until 1911 as special professor, and always—except for two years—in connection with what is now the Washington University School of Medicine. His service in the wards of the hospitals covered a period of almost forty years. Among his contributions to the science of ophthalmology were subjective tests for astigmatism, ratios for the gradation of optotypes, a method of mounting test lenses, formulae for solutions of atropin and of atropin and cocaine, a method for treating the lacrimal duct, an improvement in orbital evisceration and one of the best and most humane of the many operations for entropion. He died in St. Louis of pneumonia in his seventy-ninth year, active and productive to the end.

[A. E. Ewing, article in *Trans. Am. Ophthalmol. Soc.*, vol. XIII, pt. III (1914), containing complete bibliography of Green's publications; *Am. Jour. Ophthalmol.*, Apr. 1914; J. L. Lowes, article in *Harvard Grads.' Mag.*, Mar. 1914; S. S. Greene, *A Geneal. Sketch of the Descendants of Thos. Green[e] of Malden, Mass.* (1858); *St. Louis Globe-Democrat*, Dec. 8, 1913.]

H. J. H.

GREEN, JOHN CLEVE (Apr. 4, 1800–Apr. 29, 1875), China merchant, financier, philanthropist, brother of Henry Woodhull Green [*q.v.*], was born in Maidenhead (now Lawrenceville), N. J., the son of Caleb Smith and Elizabeth (Van Cleve) Green. He was descended from William Green who came from England and settled near Trenton about 1700, and from Jonathan Dickinson [*q.v.*], first president of the College of New Jersey (Princeton). He was one of the first class to enter what became the Lawrenceville School, then, after further schooling in Brooklyn, he entered the employ of N. L. & G. Griswold, prominent New York merchants with extensive foreign trade. Compromising between the New England quarterdeck and the New York counting-house systems of training young merchants, he spent some ten years (1823–35) at sea as supercargo of Griswold ships, frequently visiting South America and China. He married Sarah, the daughter of George Griswold, junior partner of the firm. In 1833, while in Canton as agent for the Griswolds, he accepted an invitation to join the firm of Russell & Company, the most powerful American house in the China trade. A year later he was head of the firm. When the end of the East India Company's monopoly added the lucrative opium trade to the previous tea and textile business, he grew rich along with the company. It was here that he commenced his long intimacy with John M. and Robert B. Forbes [*qq.v.*]. In 1839 he retired three months after Commissioner Lin at Canton launched his attack on the opium trade. R. B. Forbes, who succeeded him as head of the company, has implied that Green, then head of the chamber of commerce at Canton, signed the agreement to abstain from the opium trade all the more readily since he was giving up his active connection with the firm. In any case he returned to New York with an ample fortune, which he continued to increase by combined shrewdness and caution. He continued for some time as consignee of Chinese tea cargoes and also became a director of the Bank of Commerce and president of the Bleecker Street Savings Bank. The most important source of the money which he accumulated, however, was investment in railroads. In 1846 he was the heaviest financial backer of his old Canton partner, J. M. Forbes, who purchased and became president of the Michigan Central Railroad. He also supported Forbes in gaining control of the Chicago, Burlington & Quincy system, continuing as a director in that road and the New Jersey Central until his death. The dividends from these investments frequently reached fifteen per cent., and Green was probably worth three millions by 1870. His three children having died young, he made very generous gifts to philanthropic and educational institutions while he still lived. He was one of the founders of the Home for Ruptured and Crippled, served long as governor of the New York Hospital, and contributed heavily to the Deaf and Dumb Asylum. He is particularly remembered, however, for his very liberal gifts to three educational institutions near his old home. In response to a request made by the treasurer of Princeton, he gave the college about a half-million dollars, its largest benefaction up to that time, which saved it from a critical financial situation; secured the present northeast corner of the campus; and financed the construction of three buildings which were rated as the finest in their day. He also endowed three chairs in science and financed a school of civil engineering, augmenting these donations by the terms of his will. For some twenty-five years he was a trustee of the Princeton Theological Seminary, where he endowed a chair in church history, built a professor's house, and made further gifts. The Lawrenceville School, which he had attended as a boy, received even more from him and later from his estate, and was thus enabled to inaugurate the house system and to attract a faculty which gave it a high place among American preparatory schools. Portraits of him in the trustees' room at Princeton and at the Lawrenceville School show a tall, erect figure with clean-cut features characterized by high cheek-bones and an aquiline nose. R. B. Forbes called him a man of "great experience and uncompromising ability," while J. M. Forbes more than once referred to him as cautious and "tender hearted." He was a devoted Presbyterian. He died in New York City and was buried in the Ewing Cemetery near Trenton.

[*Necrol. Report . . . Princeton Theol. Sem.*, 1877, pp. 5–7; J. Maclean, *Hist. of the Coll. of N. J.* (1877), I, 10–16; J. F. Hageman, *Hist. of Princeton and its Institutions* (1879), II, 314–15; R. B. Forbes, *Personal Reminiscences* (ed. 1878), pp. 142–49, 159, 161; Sarah Forbes Hughes, *Letters and Recollections of John Murray Forbes* (1899), I, 71, 72, 78, 87, 119, II, 133; H. G. Pearson, *An American Railroad Builder, John Murray Forbes* (1911), pp. 29, 62, 88, 90, 177; H. V. Poor, *Manual of the Railroads of the U. S.*, 1868–69, 1875–76; E. F. and W. S. Cooley, *Geneal. of Early Settlers in Trenton and Ewing, "Old Hunterdon County," N. J.* (1883); *State Gazette* (Trenton), Apr. 30, 1875, and the history of Lawrenceville by R. J. Mulford, in preparation. Greene's will is on file in the office of the secretary of state in Trenton.]
R. G. A—n.

GREEN, JONAS (1712–Apr. 11, 1767), printer, journalist, baptized Dec. 28, 1712, was the great-grandson of Samuel Green [*q.v.*], the Cambridge, Mass., printer who succeeded the pioneer printers of English America, in 1649, and the fifth son of Deacon Timothy Green and Mary Flint of Boston. His father, a printer, removed in 1714 to New London, Conn., and here Jonas learned his trade. Subsequently he worked for a brother in the firm of Kneeland & Green, of Boston, and while in that city issued one book with his imprint, the first Hebrew grammar printed in America (1735), by Judah Monis. Going to Philadelphia, he worked for both Benjamin Franklin and Andrew Bradford [*qq.v.*], and on Apr. 25, 1738, he was married in Christ Church to Anne Catherine Hoof, born in Holland. They had six sons and eight daughters, eight of the children dying in infancy. In 1738 he removed to Annapolis, Md., where he became public printer to the Province. His earliest known imprints in Annapolis are of 1739. Here, on Charles Street, Jan. 17, 1745, he established the *Maryland Gazette*, second of that name, which was continued by him, his wife, his sons, or his grandson, until Dec. 12, 1839. When the Stamp Act of 1765 went into effect Green headed his issue of Oct. 10 (No. 1066) as "Maryland Gazette, Expiring: In uncertain Hopes of a Resurrection to Life again." On Jan. 30, 1766 (No. 1067), it appeared as "The Maryland Gazette, Reviving." During the war period from Dec. 25, 1777, the paper was suspended until publication was resumed by Green's two sons on Apr. 30, 1779. From October 1758 to 1766 Green had William Rind, a former apprentice and journeyman, as his partner on the newspaper. Two other known employees were Thomas Sparrow, Maryland's first engraver, and William Poultney, a binder. Green was not a versatile publisher; his business, aside from his newspaper, being principally political and governmental printing. His typographical masterpiece was Thomas Bacon's *Laws of Maryland* (1765). Isaiah Thomas (*post*, I, 321) said of his printing that it "was correct, and few, if any, in the colonies exceeded him in the neatness of his work." Regarding his newspaper Thomas said (*Ibid.*, II, 156) it was as good as "any paper then printed on the continent." In Annapolis Green was an alderman, vestryman of St. Anne's Parish, postmaster many years, an auctioneer at public sales, clerk of entries at horse-races, secretary of the lodge of Masons, and secretary of the Tuesday Club, a convivial professional club of gentlemen, in which he was dubbed "P.P.P.P.P.," meaning poet, printer, punster, purveyor, and punchmaker. As a social being he seems to have been "a whimsical, good-natured man, quick of wit, kindly and obliging, the friend and comrade of all his little world" (Wroth, *post*, p. 81). He died on Apr. 11, 1767, at his residence in Annapolis. His widow at once assumed the conduct of the printing business and the *Gazette*, assisted by her son William (d. 1770). She died on Mar. 23, 1775, and the family tribute in the *Gazette* (Mar. 30) referred to her as of a "mild and benevolent Disposition" as well as "an Example to her Sex."

[The principal source, thoroughly documented, is

L. C. Wroth, *A Hist. of Printing in Colonial Md.* (1922); see also Isaiah Thomas, *Hist. of Printing in America* (2nd ed., 1874); C. S. Brigham, "Bibliog. of Am. Newspapers," *Proc. Am. Antiq. Soc.*, Apr. 1915; *New-Eng. Hist. and Geneal. Reg.*, Jan. 1862, Apr. 1874; J. L. Bass, *Flint Geneal.* (1912). Virtually a complete file of the *Gazette* is in the Md. State Library.]

V. H. P.

GREEN, JOSEPH (1706–Dec. 11, 1780), merchant, author, was born, presumably in Boston, some time in 1706 and probably attended the South Grammar School (John Rowe, *Letters and Diary,* 1903, p. 169). He graduated from Harvard in 1726 and became a merchant and, for a time at least, a distiller. Well known in Boston society, and by the marriages of his brothers and sisters connected with several prominent Boston families—Wheelwrights, Bulfinches, and others—he belonged to the Fire Club and to a French Club, the members of which met to talk in French. He married, probably after 1742, an unidentified Elizabeth, who outlived him; but no children, if any were born, were alive when he died. Green had a pew in the First Church and for a time served on its standing committee (A. B. Ellis, *History of the First Church,* 1881, p. 332). As the Revolution approached he became a Loyalist, and did not sign the non-importation agreement of 1769. In 1774, after some hesitation, he joined in an address from the merchants to Governor Hutchinson, protesting against the course of the patriots and against the "Solemn League and Covenant" suspending commercial intercourse with Great Britain. In the same year his appointment as a counsellor of the province testified to the government's confidence in his loyalty. His house was defaced by the patriots and, refusing the appointment, in 1775 he took refuge in London. He was named in the act of banishment passed in Massachusetts in 1778. He died in London. Known in his own day as a wit and poet he is interesting to-day as a layman in literature at a time when in Boston there were not many such. Some of his occasional verse, most of it satirical, is at least as good as that of any of his American contemporaries. A mock epitaph (E. A. and G. L. Duyckinck, *Cyclopædia of American Literature,* rev. ed., 1875, I, 130) written on him early in his life is revealing:

> "Siste Viator, here lies one,
> Whose life was whim, whose soul was pun,
> And if you go too near his hearse,
> He'll joke you, both in prose and verse."

Green wrote much that cannot now be identified. He probably contributed to the *New-England Weekly Journal* and had a hand in satires against Governor Belcher (John Adams, *Works,* 1850, II, 182). Other writings safely to be called his are: "The Poet's Lamentation for the Loss of His Cat, which He Used to Call His Muse" (*London Magazine,* 1733; Duyckinck's *Cyclopædia,* 1855 edition, I, 122–23); a parody on a hymn by Mather Byles (*American Museum; or Universal Magazine,* 1790, VIII, Appendix I, pp. 1–2); *Entertainment for a Winter's Evening* (1750; 1795); *The Grand Arcanum Detected* (1755); lines on a picture of John Checkley (S. L. Knapp, *Biographical Sketches,* 1821, p. 135; *Collections of the Massachusetts Historical Society,* LXXI, 125); a poem to a niece about a gift to him (*Proceedings of the Massachusetts Historical Society,* VIII, 394). Among the pieces more or less dubiously ascribed to Green are: *The Dying Speech of Old Tenor* (1750); *A Mournful Lamentation for the Sad and Deplorable Death of Mr. Old Tenor, a Native of New England* (1750; *Proceedings of the Massachusetts Historical Society,* XLIII, 1910, pp. 255–60); *An Eclogue Sacred to the Memory of the Rev. Dr. Jonathan Mayhew* (1766); "Epitaph on John Cole" (*Massachusetts Magazine,* September 1789, p. 585); "Extempore on the Fourth Latin School Being Taken Down to Make Room for Enlarging the Chapel Church" (Samuel Kettell, *Specimens of American Poetry,* 1829, I, 138).

[A. H. Thwing, "Inhabitants and Estates of the Town of Boston" (a manuscript card index at the Mass. Hist. Soc.); the books cited above; *Pubs. Col. Soc. Mass.*, XVII (1915), 220–21; *Mass. Hist. Soc. Colls.*, 5 ser., II (1877), 70–73 and LXXI (1914), 125; *Proc. Mass. Hist. Soc.*, 1 ser. VIII (1866), *passim,* XI (1871), 392–94, 2 ser. X (1896), 164; letters (MS.) of Joseph Barrell at the Mass. Hist. Soc.; Samuel Curwen, *Jours. and Letters* (ed. of 1864); John Eliot, *Biog. Dict.* (1809); W. C. Ford, *Broadsides and Ballads Printed in Mass. 1639–1800* (1922); *Gentleman's Mag.* (London), Dec. 1780; R. W. Griswold, *Poets and Poetry of America* (16th ed., 1855); Thos. Hutchinson, *Diary and Letters* (2 vols., 1883–86), *passim,* and *Hist. of Mass. Bay,* III (1828), 258; J. H. Stark, *Loyalists of Mass.* (1910), pp. 137–40; M. C. Tyler, *A Hist. of Am. Lit.* (1878), II, 48–51.]

K. B. M.

GREEN, LEWIS WARNER (Jan. 28, 1806–May 26, 1863), Presbyterian clergyman, prominent as an educator in Kentucky and Virginia, was born in the former state near the town of Danville. He was of Scotch-Irish ancestry, the twelfth and youngest child of Willis and Sarah (Reed) Green, and a descendant of Robert Green, who, coming from England, *c.* 1712, settled in what is now Culpeper County, Va. Both his parents died when he was young, and he was brought up by his oldest brother, Judge John Green. He was first instructed by Duncan F. Robertson and Joshua Fry, noted Kentuckian teachers, and at the age of thirteen was sent to a classical school at Buck Pond, Woodford County, conducted in the home of Dr. Louis Marshall [*q.v.*], brother of the Chief Justice. After spending three years at Transylvania University, he transferred to the newly founded Centre College, and was a member of the first graduating class (1824), which consisted of Green and one other. For a time he studied law, and then turned to medicine. In February 1827 he married Eliza J. Montgomery, who died two years later. Finally deciding to enter the ministry, he studied first at Yale, then at the Theological Seminary, Princeton, leaving there in 1832 to become professor of belles-lettres and political economy in Centre College. He was licensed to preach by the Presbytery of Transylvania, Oct. 4, 1833, and was ordained by the same body, Oct. 6, 1838. In April 1834 he married Mrs. Mary Lawrence, daughter of Thomas Walker Fry of Spring House, Ky. On leave of absence in Germany (1834–36), he studied at Berlin, Halle, and Bonn.

His rather exceptional educational advantages, his abilities as a public speaker, his attractive personality, and his adherence to orthodox Presbyterian doctrines, which had not been shaken by his contact with German scholarship, made him a natural candidate for responsible academic positions in his section of the country. In 1838 he was appointed by the Synod of Kentucky professor of Oriental and Biblical literature in the theological seminary then connected with Hanover College, Ind., but the next year he returned to his old chair at Centre College with the additional duties of vice-president, and colleague-pastor of the Danville Presbyterian Church. In May 1840 the General Assembly elected him professor of Oriental literature and Biblical criticism at the Western Theological Seminary, Allegheny, Pa. After seven years here he became pastor of the Second Presbyterian Church, Baltimore, but was soon elected president of Hampden-Sidney College where he had a successful administration, 1848–56. In the latter year when Transylvania University was reorganized, he was chosen head of that institution, but the withdrawal of state support caused him to resign in 1857. On Jan. 1, 1858, he became president of Centre College, the affairs of which he was ably managing at the time of his death.

[LeRoy J. Halsey, *Memoir of the Life and Character of Rev. Lewis Warner Green, D.D.* (1871), which contains twenty-nine sermons; A. F. Lewis, *Hist. of Higher Education in Ky.* (1899); Lewis and R. H. Collins, *Hist. of Ky.* (1874), vol. II; Robt. and Johanna Peter, *Transylvania University* (1896), being Filson Club Pubs. No. 11; *Presbyterian* (Phila.), June 13, 1863.] H. E. S.

GREEN, NATHAN (1787?–1825), privateersman, was a resident of Salem, Mass. Local records suggest that he may have been the son of Capt. John and Patty (Sampson) Green or of a senior Nathan Green. It is probable that he followed the sea from boyhood. He married Thankful Goodale of Salem on July 15, 1813. The only fully recorded part of his life is the period during which he was in command of the *Grand Turk,* which shared with the *America* of Salem under James W. Chever [*q.v.*] the distinction of being the most successful privateer in the War of 1812. The *Grand Turk,* the third of that name, belonged to thirty owners, principally from Salem, and made three cruises between Feb. 16, 1813, and June 9, 1814, under the command of Holton J. Breed. She returned from her third voyage badly battered after a lively but unprofitable action with the British packet *Hinchinbroke.* Thereupon the command was given to Green, who sailed from Salem on the fourth voyage Aug. 6, 1814. Cruising principally around the Scilly Islands and the Bay of Biscay, the *Grand Turk* made eight prizes, burned four other vessels, and stopped twenty-three neutrals, returning to Salem Nov. 17, 1814. The fifth voyage, which gave Green his particular reputation, started from Salem Jan. 1, 1815. He headed for Brazil and learned that there were eight British ships at Pernambuco. He captured two prizes, on one of which were found fourteen nail kegs containing some $17,500 in gold. On Mar. 10, however, the *Grand Turk* nearly came to grief. Chasing an apparent merchantman, Green suddenly found her to be an English frigate which turned and started in pursuit. The privateer was one of the fastest vessels afloat, but the wind suddenly died, whereupon both ships sent out boats with sweeps to tow them. Another frigate appeared, and the combined British crews nearly outrowed the exhausted Americans who were within gunshot part of the time. On the third day a breeze enabled the *Grand Turk* to escape. A week later the two frigates appeared again while the *Grand Turk* was taking on the valuable cargo of a captured brig, but quick work on Green's part saved both privateer and prize. Finding that the Treaty of Ghent was about to be ratified, Green returned to Salem, arriving on Apr. 28, 1815. The proceeds of this fifth voyage totaled some $73,000. Half of this went to the owners, and the rest, after expenses were deducted, to the officers and crew proportionately. Green's share was probably more than $4,000 for the cruise of less than four months. The only apparent further record of Green states that he was drowned at New York early in 1825. His two daughters died in infancy, a son was born after his death.

[*Vital Statistics of Salem, Mass., to the Year 1850,*

I (1916), 388, III (1924), 446, V (1925), 299; *Essex Register* (Salem), Apr. 29, 1815, and Feb. 24, 1825; *Salem Gazette,* Feb. 25, 1825; R. E. Peabody, *The Log of the Grand Turk* (1926), pp. 197–212 and Appendix.]
R. G. A—n.

GREEN, NORVIN (Apr. 17, 1818–Feb. 12, 1893), physician, legislator, president of the Western Union Telegraph Company, was born in New Albany, Ind., but removed in early youth to Breckenridge County, Ky. His parents, Joseph and Susan (Ball) Green, were of Virginia ancestry. He attended the country schools and worked on his father's farm until his father's bankruptcy forced him to make a living for himself. At the age of sixteen he opened a grocery store on a flatboat and traveled down the Ohio and Mississippi selling supplies to the lumbermen on the banks. Later he secured employment as a wood-cutter and by this work earned the money for a medical education. He first studied with Dr. Mason of Carrollton, Ky., and later entered the Medical College of the University of Louisville, where he graduated in 1840. In this same year he married Martha English of Carrollton and entered upon the practise of medicine in Henry County. His practise was interrupted by two terms in the Kentucky House of Representatives, 1850 and 1851–53. The records are too meager for a judgment of his ability as a physician or legislator, but in neither capacity did he achieve any great distinction. He was always known as "Doctor" Green even after he abandoned medicine, and his political preferment shows that he enjoyed the confidence of his neighbors. He was a presidential elector on the Pierce ticket in 1852 and the next year was appointed one of the commissioners for locating the new Federal Building at Louisville.

The year 1853 also marks the time when Green definitely turned his back on medicine and politics and engaged in the business career which was to bring him his reputation. In this year the two rival telegraph lines from Louisville to New Orleans—the People's, and the New Orleans & Ohio—were consolidated after a period of ruinous competition, and the consolidated lines were shortly leased for operation to a number of men, of whom Green was one. Previous to this he had been an active member of the New Orleans & Ohio Company. After a period of failing business the Louisville-New Orleans lines were reörganized as the Southwestern Telegraph Company with Green as president. Under his management the Southwestern Company became prosperous, but Green had wider ambitions. He was one of the first to conceive the idea of a national consolidation of telegraph companies, and in 1857 he took the first steps toward realizing his ambition by initiating the consolidation of the six leading telegraph lines in the United States. This resulted in the formation of the North American Telegraph Company. In 1866 the process was completed by the formation of the Western Union, embracing all the lines in the United States. Green served as vice-president of it until 1878, when he became the president and continued in that capacity until his death. With the beginning of his telegraph interests Green moved to Louisville and maintained his home there until his death, although for the last thirty years of his life he spent most of his time in New York. He was a prominent figure in Louisville and in 1867 was elected as one of the representatives from that city in the Kentucky House of Representatives. From 1870 to 1873 he was president of the Louisville, Cincinnati, & Lexington Railway. To the November 1883 number of the *North American Review* he contributed an article on "The Government and the Telegraph."

[J. S. Johnston, *Mem. Hist. of Louisville* (2 vols., 1896); Lewis and R. H. Collins, *Hist. of Ky.* (2 vols., 1874); *Courier-Journal* (Louisville), Feb. 12, 13, 1893.]
R. S. C.

GREEN, SAMUEL (1615–Jan. 1, 1701/02), printer, emigrated to Massachusetts from England with his parents, Bartholomew and Elizabeth, about 1633, and settled in Cambridge. After the retirement of Stephen Day [*q.v.*] and his son, he became manager of the press which President Dunster of Harvard College had acquired by marriage with the widow of Josse Glover. Isaiah Thomas was of the opinion that Green had served no apprenticeship; Green himself wrote in 1675, "I was not [before] used unto it." Nevertheless, his was the only printing office in the English colonies until 1665; outside of Cambridge and Boston he had no competition until 1685; and he continued in business until 1692. In 1654 the Society for the Propagation of the Gospel in New England sent over "iron worke and letter for printing." This press was placed under Green's management also, and the publication of Eliot's Indian translations begun. In 1660 the Society sent over Marmaduke Johnson and a special set of type. Eliot's Indian Bible, completed in 1663, was the greatest of Green's books and probably owes much of its excellence to Johnson, who was trained in the art. Upon Dunster's forced resignation in 1654, Green sold his press to Harvard College, and about 1670 the Society's press was also placed under academic control. With some interruptions Green continued as the college printer. He was also printer for the Colony through

1691, and his editions of *The Book of the General Lawes and Libertyes concerning the Inhabitants of Massachusetts,* together with several editions of the *Bay Psalm Book,* are, after the various Indian books, his chief works. The list of his known imprints number about 275. From 1652 he was for many years clerk of the writs for Middlesex County, and he was town clerk from 1694 to 1697. He was also a considerable landholder. His chief avocation, however, was the militia service, in which he was very active. A sergeant as early as 1653, he rose in rank slowly, did not become captain until he was seventy-five years of age, remaining in office the rest of his life. Green was twice married. His first wife, Jane Banbridge, died on Nov. 16, 1657; and he became the husband of Sarah Clark (1644–1707) Feb. 23, 1662/63. He is supposed to have had nineteen children, and he founded a veritable clan of printers, beginning with his three sons, Samuel, Bartholomew [*q.v.*], and Timothy.

[Isaiah Thomas, *Hist. of Printing in America* (2nd ed., 1874); L. R. Paige, *Hist. of Cambridge, Mass.* (1877); Wilberforce Eames, *Bibliographic Notes on Eliot's Indian Bible* (1890); C. A. Duniway, *Development of Freedom of the Press in Mass.* (1906); Chas. Evans, *Am. Bibliog.*, vol. I (1903).] D. M. M.

GREEN, SAMUEL ABBOTT (Mar. 16, 1830–Dec. 5, 1918), physician, antiquarian, librarian, author, was born at Groton, Mass., the fourth of the six children of Dr. Joshua and Eliza (Lawrence) Green. He was descended in the eighth generation from Percival and Ellen Green who came to Boston in 1635 and settled in Cambridge the next year. He spent his boyhood in Groton where he was fitted for college at Lawrence Academy, an institution early endowed by his kinsmen of the Lawrence family. After his graduation from Harvard College in 1851 he studied medicine with Dr. Jonathan Mason Warren of Boston and graduated from the Harvard Medical School in 1854. Meanwhile he attended a course of lectures in the Jefferson Medical College of Philadelphia in 1851 and 1852 and was a surgical house pupil in the Massachusetts General Hospital in 1853. In 1854 he made a long voyage in a sailing vessel, necessitated by the state of his health, then resumed his medical studies in Vienna. On his return to the United States in 1855 he began the practise of medicine in Boston, where, excepting for the Civil War period, he spent the rest of his professional life. His war record, and he was the first physician in the state to enter the army medical service, began with his commission as assistant-surgeon of the 1st Regiment, Massachusetts Volunteers, May 25, 1861. On Sept. 2, 1861, he was commissioned surgeon of the 24th Regiment, and served as a staff officer under Generals Stevenson, Foster, Hawley, Terry, and Kautz. He organized and had charge of the hospital ship *Recruit* during the Burnside expedition against Roanoke Island, which left Annapolis in January 1862, was in charge of the hospital steamer *Cosmopolitan* on the coast of South Carolina, and was chief medical officer on Morris Island during the siege of Battery Wagner. In October 1863 he was sent as a surgeon to St. Augustine and Jacksonville, Fla. Brevetted lieutenant-colonel of volunteers for distinguished services in the field during the campaign of 1864, he served finally, from April to July 1865, as acting staff-surgeon in Richmond.

After the war Green again took up his medical practise in Boston and served the community in many capacities. He was city physician, 1871–82; trustee of the Boston Public Library, 1868–78, and acting-librarian, 1877–78; and mayor of Boston, 1882. Outside his medical practise his most absorbing interest was his connection with the Massachusetts Historical Society, in which his membership began in 1860. He was the "keeper of the cabinet" in 1861; a member of its council from 1860 to 1918; its librarian from 1868 to 1918; and its vice-president from 1895 to 1914. During his incumbency he found time to write several works on the history of his native town, Groton, and continued his interest in Lawrence Academy which he served for many years as a member of the board of trustees and to which he gave the bulk of his estate as residuary legatee. He never married.

[C. P. Greenough, memoir in *Proc. Mass. Hist. Soc.*, vol. LIV (1922); S. A. Green, *An Account of Percival and Ellen Green and Some of their Descendants* (1876); *Who's Who in America,* 1918–19; *Boston Post, Boston Transcript,* Dec. 6, 1918.] J. H. T.

GREEN, SAMUEL BOWDLEAR (Sept. 15, 1859–July 11, 1910), horticulturist and educator, was born in Chelsea, Mass., the son of Thomas and Anna (Marden) Green. His father, at one time mayor of Chelsea and for forty years a wholesale flour dealer in Boston, was of English descent; his mother came of Dutch stock. The New Hampshire farm where young Samuel spent his summers was probably responsible for his early decision to become a farmer. His father stipulated that the boy be educated for the calling, and he matriculated at the Massachusetts Agricultural College, from which he received the B.S. degree in 1879. Before he was twenty he became superintendent of Vine Hill Farm, West Hartford, Conn., where he directed some nineteen workers in dairying and fruit raising. During the next two years he worked for a market gardener, a seedsman, and a nurseryman; for three years more he was superintendent of the horticultural department at the Houghton Farm Experiment Station at Cornwall, N. Y.; then he was foreman successively in nurseries in Brighton and in Newton, Mass. In 1886 he was made superintendent of the horticultural department at the Massachusetts Agricultural College, where he carried on the practical work of the nursery, greenhouse, and market garden maintained for the instruction of students. On his twenty-eighth birthday he was married to Alice C. Hazelton of Wellesley Hills, Mass., and in the following spring, 1888, he was appointed horticulturist to the Minnesota Agricultural Experiment Station. Four years later he became professor of horticulture and subsequently of horticulture and forestry in the University of Minnesota. During his long years as a teacher, Green never forgot the problems of the practical farmers. In 1890 he was secretary of the Minnesota State Horticultural Society; from 1892 to 1910 he was a member of its executive board, and from 1907 to 1910 its president. He was president of the board of administration of Farmers' Institutes of Minnesota and for many years a member of the executive committee of the Minnesota Forestry Association. The year 1900 he spent on leave for the study of forestry and horticulture in the principal countries of Europe. In 1904 at the Louisiana Purchase Exposition in St. Louis he managed the horticultural and forestry exhibits of all the state experiment stations and agricultural colleges of the United States.

In addition to these varied activities, he served the horticultural interests of the state in research and experiment, in teaching, and in writing. His more important works, some of them textbooks, were: *Amateur Fruit Growing* (1894); *Vegetable Gardening* (1896); *Forestry in Minnesota* (1898); *Principles of American Forestry* (1903); *Farm Wind-Breaks and Shelter Belts* (1906); *Popular Fruit-Growing* (1909). He was also one of the editors of *Farm and Fireside* from 1888 until his death. In the spring of 1910 he was appointed dean of the new Department of Forestry of the University; but on July 11 of that year he suffered a stroke of apoplexy and died. He was an indefatigable worker and a natural leader. His activities brought him into contact with people from all over the state and gained for him a wide circle of admirers. Characteristic of the man is his safeguarding of the "fruit list" of the horticultural association, in which varieties of fruit suitable for planting in Minnesota were recommended—he would include no new variety without careful testing over some period of years.

[The issue of the *Minnesota Horticulturist* for Sept. 1910 is a memorial number devoted to Green. See also *Forty Years of the Univ. of Minn.* (1910), ed. by E. B. Johnson; H. B. Hudson, *A Half Century of Minneapolis* (1908); *The Book of Minnesotans* (1907); *Who's Who in America*, 1910-11; *Am. Lumberman*, July 16, 23, 1910; *Farm and Fireside*, Aug. 10, 1910; *Minneapolis Morning Tribune*, July 12, 1910.] S. J. B.

GREEN, SAMUEL SWETT (Feb. 20, 1837–Dec. 8, 1918), librarian, born in Worcester, Mass., was descended from four progenitors who were *Mayflower* passengers. He also traced his descent from Thomas Green who emigrated to Massachusetts Bay about 1635 and settled in Malden. Three direct ancestors and an uncle, brother, and nephew were physicians. His father James, an apothecary, orphaned at six, unschooled after twelve, and his mother, Elizabeth Swett, managed to give their three sons a full collegiate and professional education at Harvard; John [*q.v.*] in medicine, Samuel in divinity, James in law. Samuel was so devoted to his mother that, giving up marriage, he cared for her until her death at ninety-three. He graduated from Harvard in 1858, spent three years in illness at home, and graduated from the Divinity School in 1864, with an "unsaleable theology," weak eyes, and delicate health. Until he was thirty-three he was much of an invalid. He preached a few sermons, tried banking for six years, and in 1871 was unexpectedly given charge of the Worcester Free Library. Hereupon, in work for which he was singularly adapted, his physical troubles vanished.

The library, founded by his uncle in 1859, had fallen into neglect. Within a year he brought it into the public notice. He began to work actively with the local schools; he sought loans from other libraries when they were needed; and he encouraged factory workers to visit the library. He taught his staff never to allow a reader to leave the building with his questions unanswered; an unsatisfied reader was a dissatisfied customer. His was the first sizable New England library to open on Sunday (Dec. 8, 1872), an example almost immediately followed by the Boston Public Library. These things, now mere commonplaces, but innovations then, attracted much attention in England, France, and Germany. In 1876 Green was prominent in the Philadelphia library conference which started the modern library movement. He was one of the seven incorporators of the American Library Association and was for the next seventeen years very active in its proceedings, serving twice as a vice-president and in 1891 as its president. In

1890 the governor of Massachusetts appointed him on the new State Library Commission, the first of its kind in America, on which he served almost nineteen years. In the summer of 1893 he presided over the World's Congress of Librarians in Chicago. Resigning his active librarianship in January 1909, he devoted the remaining nine years of his life to writing. The library directors made him librarian emeritus and gave him office room and the service of his favorite secretary for an hour daily. He spent his mornings at the library until within ten days of his death. In addition to his various activities as a librarian he maintained many connections with learned societies here and abroad. His publications, in a plain, rugged, forceful style, include: *Library Aids* (1881); *Libraries and Schools* (1883), a collection of papers and speeches by himself and others; *The Public Library Movement in the United States* (1913); many articles in the American Antiquarian Society's *Proceedings,* and numerous professional papers in the *Library Journal.*

[*Samuel Swett Green* (1926), by Robert K. Shaw, Green's successor; autobiographic sketches in the *Lib. Jour.*, Dec. 1913, and in the class books of the Harvard class of 1858; Z. W. Coombs, *Samuel Swett Green* (1909); Samuel Stillman Greene, *A Geneal. Sketch of the Descendants of Thos. Green[e] of Malden, Mass.* (1858).]
F. W. A.

GREEN, SETH (Mar. 19, 1817–Aug. 20, 1888), pioneer fish culturist, was born in a section of Monroe County, N. Y., later included in the city of Rochester. His father, Adonijah Green, conducted a tavern at Carthage on the Genesee River. As a boy Green exhibited a preoccupation with unprofitable wanderings in the woods and along the streams and a confirmed addiction to fishing. He received a common-school education and then established a fish stall in the old Rochester city market. On Feb. 14, 1848, he married Helen M. Cook. It was probably about 1837 that he first thought of hatching trout and salmon by artificial means and began the experiments that continued for the rest of his life. His efforts resulted in the location of trout ponds near Caledonia, N. Y., about 1864. In 1868 he was appointed to the New York State Fish Commission and later became the superintendent of fisheries. In 1875 he established a hatchery adjacent to his own, which had been acquired by the state. In 1867 he undertook the propagation of shad near Holyoke, Mass., at the solicitation of officials of four of the New England States. Using methods that have since been superseded, he was successful in hatching several million young shad. His successful transportation in 1871 of live shad from the Atlantic to the Pacific coast was the first step toward establishing this species in a new habitat in greater abundance than now prevails in its original home and probably was of greater economic benefit than his attempts at artificial propagation.

He also experimented with the hatching of salmon, sturgeon, whitefish, striped bass and other fish in cooperation with the State of New York and the United States Fish Commission. He was a prolific writer and dozens of his reports and papers appear in the publications of the American Fish Culturists Association (later American Fisheries Society), in whose activities he was prominent. In 1870 he published *Trout Culture,* and in 1879, in collaboration with his lifelong friend R. B. Roosevelt, he expanded it into the more complete *Fish Hatching and Fish Catching.* He also published *Home Fishing and Home Waters* (1888). His lifelong skill in angling led him to contribute articles on this subject to sportsmen's periodicals. He received several medals from American and European societies.

Green was a practical fish culturist and popularizer of methods rather than the discoverer of new principles. The process of artificially fertilizing and incubating fish eggs had been a subject for experiment in Europe during the previous century, and the basic possibilities were well understood. In the United States his work was antedated by that of Garlick and Ackley, who in 1853 hatched trout and published a treatise on the work, and by Ainsworth, whose experiments in 1859 were of much help to Green. The fact remains, however, that he made fish breeding a recognized art of practical significance in this country instead of a subject for inconsequential experiments. He was superintendent of fisheries of the state of New York and was actively at work until his death.

[*Buffalo Morning Express,* Aug. 20, 26, 1888; Wm. F. Peck, *Hist. of Rochester and Monroe County, N. Y.* (1908), I, 93; *Landmarks of Monroe County, N. Y.* (1895); Thaddeus Norris, *Am. Fish Culture* (1868); J. H. Slack, *Practical Trout Culture* (1872); J. H. Thompson, "The Father of Am. Fish Culture," *Am. Angler,* July 1917; *Proc. Am. Fisheries Soc.,* 1872–88, *passim.*]
M. C. J.

GREEN, THOMAS (Aug. 25, 1735–May 1812), printer, editor, was born in New London, Conn., the son of Samuel and Abigail (Clark) Green, a great-great-grandson of Samuel Green [*q.v.*], the publisher of Eliot's Indian Bible, and a grandson of Timothy Green, father of Jonas Green [*q.v.*], who was appointed official printer for Connecticut in 1713 (*Colonial Records,* V, p. 477). Descended from such a line, he naturally entered the trade. He received his early training in New London, but it is not known whether his instructor was his grandfather, his father, or any one of three uncles who were printers. After the death of his grandfather in May 1757, Thomas went to New Haven, where he entered the employ of James Parker & Company, printers of the *Connecticut Gazette.* In September 1761 he married Desire Sanford. Three years later, as the father of two children, he was anxious to establish an office of his own. Looking over the surrounding country, he selected Hartford for the enterprise, as that town was the most important one in Connecticut without a newspaper. In the autumn of 1764 he established himself on Main St., over the shop of an Irish barber, James Mookler, and began, Oct. 29, the *Connecticut Courant.* Green acted also as bookseller, stationer, and bureau of general information. Advertisements of his stock in trade listed a miscellaneous collection of articles, ranging from Bibles to sealing-wax. In 1767, apparently believing that prospects for success were brighter in New Haven than in Hartford, he began to make arrangements to return there. The control of the *Courant* was transferred to an associate, Ebenezer Watson. In New Haven Green began another paper, *The Connecticut Journal and New Haven Post Boy,* the first number of which appeared Oct. 23, 1767. About 1799 Thomas Green, Jr., was taken into partnership with his father. The elder Thomas retired in 1809 and died in May 1812. Green was a conservative editor. The papers under his control flourished in advertisements and in news but did not contain, compared with most American journals of the period, a great mass of political or party propaganda. Editorials, in the strict sense of the word, were noticeably few. Because of his moderation during the Revolution, Green was once accused of being a Tory. After 1789 the *Journal* was mildly Federalist. The *Courant* has had a continuous existence to the present day, now being called the *Hartford Courant*; after reorganization the second paper has continued as the *New Haven Journal Courier.* Practically nothing is known of Green's personality or of his family life. He was married three times. Abigail, his second wife, died Sept. 20, 1781, and on Mar. 21, 1782, he married Abigail Miles, who survived him.

[A. C. Bates, article in *Papers of the New Haven Colony Hist. Soc.,* vol. VIII (1914); G. E. Littlefield, *Early Boston Booksellers* (1900) and *The Early Mass. Press* (1907); Isaiah Thomas, *Hist. of Printing in America* (2nd ed., 1874); *The Literary Diary of Ezra Stiles,* II (1901), 549. Files of the *Connecticut Courant* and the *Connecticut Jour.* are available in the Yale Univ. Library, and in the Conn. Hist. Soc.] J. M. M.

GREEN, WILLIAM (Nov. 10, 1806–July 29, 1880), lawyer, traced his descent from William Green, a member of the body-guard of King William III, whose son, Robert, emigrated to Virginia about 1712. His grandson, Col. John Williams Green, rose to eminence as chancellor and judge of the Virginia court of appeals, married Mary Brown, Dec. 24, 1805, and resided at Fredericksburg, where their eldest son, William, was born. He attended private schools in Fredericksburg and Spotsylvania County, but his education was principally received at the hands of his father, who, it is credibly alleged, relearned Greek in order to teach it to his son. He also studied law with his father and was admitted to the bar in 1827 before he was twenty-one years old. He then removed to Culpeper County where he commenced practise. In 1829, when his practise was yet small, he added to his income by engaging in literary work, contributing articles on a variety of subjects to the *Culpeper Gazette* and the *Southern Literary Messenger,* but he soon became favorably known by reason of his steady application to business and the scrupulous care with which he prepared his cases. As a result he attracted the major part of the legal work within the counties of Rappahannock, Orange, Louisa, and Culpeper, which comprised his circuit, giving him an opportunity to display that profound knowledge of the law which later placed him indisputably at the head of the Virginia bar.

From early youth Green had been systematic in his studies, ranging through all branches of the law, and owing to his retentive memory, assisted by his invariable practise of daily annotating his text-books and reports, he was always prepared for any point which might unexpectedly arise in the course of a trial or argument. In consequence of this, he was frequently retained in cases before the court of appeals, and his appellate practise increased to such an extent that in 1855 he removed to Richmond. From that time forward until his death, he was admittedly *facile princeps* at the Virginia bar. He was retained on behalf of John Brown, after the latter's conviction for treason in 1859, to apply to the supreme court of appeals for a writ of error, and, though the writ was refused, his argument displayed acquaintance with all the learning bearing upon the law of treason, ancient and modern. His finest effort, however, was made in a case which was devoid of all popular appeal, inasmuch as it involved an abstruse point of real property law; namely, whether a devisee took by purchase or as heir under the operation of the rule in Shelley's case (*Moon* vs. *Stone,* 19 *Grattan,* 130). The court was so impressed by his argument that it was ordered to be printed in full in the *Report,* where it occupied 127 pages. It also received unstinted praise in English legal circles.

Green never participated actively in public affairs, but, actuated by a strong sense of duty, served the Confederate government during the Civil War in the Department of the Treasury, and, subsequently, officiated as a judge of the court of conciliation for the city of Richmond. In 1870 he was appointed professor of law at Richmond College and as such conducted the first law classes held there, but pressure of counsel work soon compelled him to resign. Thenceforward he confined himself to his law practise, employing his leisure in writing articles on professional topics and in the preparation of material for projected works on legal, historical, and kindred subjects. He was married on Apr. 6, 1837, to Columbia E. Slaughter, the daughter of Samuel Slaughter of Culpeper County, Va. His published writings, with the exception of *The Genesis of Certain Counties in Virginia from Cities and Towns of the Same Name* (n.d), and an essay on "Lapse, Joint Tenants and Tenants in Common," which appeared as an appendix to B. B. Minor's edition (1852) of Wythe's *Decisions,* consist entirely of articles contributed to various periodicals, chiefly legal, the most remarkable of which was that on *"Stare Decisis"* in the *American Law Review,* September 1880. Among his papers at his death were found the incomplete manuscript of a profound work on practise, to which he had devoted twenty years of unremitting labor, an extensive collection of notes for a projected "History of Executive, Legislative and Judicial Administration in Virginia," and material for new editions of the works of Lord Bolingbroke and Butler's work on *nisi prius.* Contemporary testimony is unanimous as to his intellectual power and incomparable legal knowledge, and it would appear to be corroborated by such reports of his arguments as are available and his scattered writings. Armistead C. Gordon says that he was considered a "living encyclopædia of unusual knowledge," but points out that he has been criticized as possessing no creative faculty or power of original thought.

[Philip Slaughter, *A Brief Sketch of the Life of Wm. Green* (1883); Armistead C. Gordon, *Virginian Portraits* (1924); *Va. Law Jour.,* Sept.–Oct. 1880; *Am. Law Rev.,* Sept. 1880; the *State* (Richmond), and *Richmond Dispatch,* July 30, 1880.] H. W. H. K.

GREEN, WILLIAM HENRY (Jan. 27, 1825–Feb. 10, 1900), Hebrew scholar, was born at Groveville, N. J., son of George Smith Green and Sarah Kennedy. His father was a brother of John Cleve and Henry Woodhull Green [*qq.v.*]. One of his ancestors was Rev. Jonathan Dickinson [*q.v.*], first president of the institution now known as Princeton University, and many others were ministers or elders in the Presbyterian church. He graduated from Lafayette College in 1840, remained there for two years as tutor, and then entered Princeton Theological Seminary. A year there was followed by another year of teaching at Lafayette and two more years as a student at the Seminary, where he graduated in 1846. For three years he was instructor in Hebrew at the Seminary. He was ordained by the Presbytery of New Brunswick on May 24, 1848, and from 1849 to 1851 was pastor of the Central Presbyterian Church in Philadelphia. In 1851 he was elected professor of Biblical and Oriental literature in Princeton Theological Seminary, and here he remained active until his death. In 1859 he became professor of Oriental and Old Testament literature, and later, as senior member of the faculty, he acted for seventeen years as president of the Seminary. In 1868 he declined the presidency of the College of New Jersey (now Princeton University). In 1891 he was moderator of the Presbyterian General Assembly. Through all the years of its activity he was chairman of the Old Testament section of the American Bible Revision Committee. He married twice, Mary Colwell in 1852, and Elizabeth Hayes in 1858. He was tall and dignified, earnest and austere, controlled by an active sense of duty, personally unassuming. As a teacher of Hebrew he was accurate, methodical, and eminently successful. His *Grammar of the Hebrew Language* (five editions) first appeared in 1861. A practical rather than a philosophic or comparative work, it was characterized by clarity and conciseness of statement, and, after Ewald, marked an advance over Gesenius, especially in the grouping of vowels and in the avoidance of classical nomenclature and methods.

The year 1873 was the exact bisector of his academic and scholarly career. In the years that followed he no longer taught Hebrew grammar, and the language became in his hands more and more a tool of exegesis and criticism. This trend was partly a product of his own intellectual development, and partly a product of the controversy that is associated with the term Higher Criticism. By temperament, training, and conviction he was unable to accept in any measure the Graf-Wellhausen theory, or any other hypothesis that questioned the historical truth, the unity, or the Mosaic authorship of the Pentateuch. In 1863 he had published *The Pentateuch Vindicated from the Aspersions of Bish-*

op Colenso. This was the forerunner of a long series of writings attacking radical criticism and defending the traditional, a series that began with *Moses and the Prophets* (1882), went on to *The Hebrew Feasts* (1885), *The Higher Criticism of the Pentateuch* (1895), *The Unity of the Book of Genesis* (1895), ended with a *General Introduction to the Old Testament* (1898), and included scores of journal articles and public addresses. In controversy he was keen, merciless, learned, and well equipped. If there were discrepancies or contradictions in the Old Testament, they were only apparent and could be explained, and he was most adroit and resourceful in explaining them, although his explanations must occasionally have been a strain on his own better judgment. Nothing less difficult than the slaughter of 500,000 soldiers on one side in a single battle between Jewish tribes could bring forth even the admission that there might have been an error in textual transmission. He was generally recognized as the scholarly leader in America of the ultraconservative school of Biblical criticism.

[Accounts of Green's life and scholarly work by his colleague John D. Davis were published in the *Presbyterian and Reformed Review,* July 1900, and the *Biblical World,* June 1900. See also: *Who's Who in America,* 1899–1900; *Press* (Phila.), May 6, 1896, Feb. 11, 1900; N. Y. *Observer,* Apr. 30, 1896; *Prof. William Henry Green's Semi-Centennial Celebration, 1846–96* (1896); J. F. Stonecipher, *Biog. Cat. of Lafayette Coll. 1832–1912* (1913); *Princeton Gen. Cat. 1746–1906* (1908).]
H. H. B.

GREENE, ALBERT GORTON (Feb. 10, 1802–Jan. 3, 1868), poet, jurist, book collector, was born in Providence, R. I., the eldest of the four children of John Holden and Elizabeth (Beverly) Greene. He was a Rhode Islander "from way back," being eighth in descent from Samuel Gorton [*q.v.*] and John Greene, the doughty founders of Warwick. His father, an architect, built the First Congregational Church, which was long famous for its graceful spire. After his graduation in 1820 from Brown University, Greene studied law under John Whipple and was admitted to the bar in 1823. In 1824 he married Mary Ann, daughter of Capt. Benjamin Clifford and sister of John Henry Clifford [*q.v.*], who later became governor of Massachusetts. When Providence was organized under a new charter in 1832, Greene gave up his practise of law in order to devote himself to municipal affairs. He was clerk of the city council 1832–67, clerk of the municipal court 1832–57, and justice of that court 1858–67. He was an expert at drafting ordinances and framing acts, his most notable accomplishment in that field being the original Rhode Island school bill. As a magistrate, by his integrity, tact, fairness, and learning, he won and held the respect and affection of his fellow citizens.

Primarily he was a man of letters, more at ease in his study than in court or on the street. At the age of sixteen he wrote one of the most popular of American humorous poems:

> "Old Grimes is dead; that good old man
> We never shall see more:
> He used to wear a long, black coat
> All buttoned down before."

The poem is a worthy addition to that genre of which Goldsmith's "Elegy on Mrs. Mary Blaize" and Cowper's "John Gilpin" are the best-known examples. Greene realized that he had no serious pretensions to the name of poet and never published a collection of his verse. To *The Rhode-Island Book* (Providence, 1841), edited by Anne C. Lynch (Mrs. Botta), he contributed "To the Weathercock on our Steeple," "The Baron's Last Banquet," "Old Grimes," "Stanzas" ("Oh think not that the bosom's light"), and "Song of the Windmill Spirits." Other poems of his are to be found in the pages of *The Literary Journal and Register of Science and the Arts* (Providence, 1833–34), which he edited with ability but was compelled to relinquish for lack of financial support. His "Adelheid" was once fairly well known; he himself probably cared most for an "Ode on the Death of the Rev. Dr. William E. Channing." From 1854 to 1868 he was president of the Rhode Island Historical Society. He was the editor of Capt. Thomas Dring's *Recollections of the Jersey Prison-Ship* (Providence, 1829; N. Y. 1831; Morrisania, N. Y., 1865). Greene was greatly interested in the industrial arts and had a wide knowledge of manufacturing processes. His love of painting and sculpture, fostered by his father, was strong; unable, like most Americans of his generation, to see the originals, he made a notable collection of engravings. His private library, which he not only collected but read, numbered 18,000 volumes and 2,000 pamphlets, and was especially rich in English poetry and drama, American elementary school books, and American poetry. In the last department it was unrivalled; it is now embodied in the Harris Collection of American Poetry at Brown University. His wife died in 1865; in 1867 illness made his retirement necessary; and he spent his last days in the home of his daughter, the wife of the Rev. Samuel White Duncan of Cleveland, Ohio. There,

> "Undisturbed by anxious cares,
> His peaceful moments ran;
> And everybody said he was
> A fine old gentleman."

His death came with merciful suddenness an hour or two after he had taken his customary morning stroll.

[See G. S. Greene and Louise B. Clarke, *The Greenes of R. I.* (1903); Adelos Gorton, *Life and Times of Samuel Gorton* (privately printed, 1907); *Hist. Cat. Brown Univ. 1764–1904* (1905); *Cat. of the Private Library of the late Hon. Albert G. Greene* (auctioneer's cat., N. Y., 1869); J. C. Stockbridge, *Cat. of the Harris Collection of American Poetry* (1886); *The Biog. Cyc. of Representative Men of R. I.* (1881); S. G. Arnold, *Greene-Staples-Parsons: An Address delivered before the R. I. Hist. Soc.* (1869); G. W. Curtis, notice in "Editor's Easy Chair," *Harper's Magazine*, Nov. 1868. Five of Greene's poems are accessible in R. W. Griswold, *Poets and Poetry of America* (16th ed., 1856).]
G. H. G.

GREENE, CHARLES EZRA (Feb. 12, 1842–Oct. 16, 1903), civil engineer, educator, was born in Cambridge, Mass. His father, Rev. James Diman Greene, was a descendant of James Greene, admitted a freeman of Malden, Mass., in 1647; his mother, Sarah Adeline, was the sister of Edward Henry Durell [*q.v.*] and the daughter of Daniel Meserve Durell, chief justice of the New Hampshire court of common pleas. After attending the Cambridge High School and Phillips Exeter Academy, Charles entered Harvard, graduating with the degree of A.B. in 1862. Following a period of employment in rifle factories at Millbury and Worcester, Mass., he served some nine months as a clerk in the quartermaster's department, Readville, Mass., and on Jan. 5, 1865, was commissioned first lieutenant and appointed quartermaster of the 7th Regiment of colored troops, with which he saw service in Virginia and Texas. Resigning his commission in August 1866, he studied civil engineering at the Massachusetts Institute of Technology and in 1868 received the degree of B.S. After practical experience in his profession as assistant engineer on the Bangor & Piscataquis Railroad, as assistant engineer on federal river and harbor improvement projects in Maine and New Hampshire, and as a member of the firm of Greene & Danforth of Portland, he was appointed city engineer of Bangor, Me. On Sept. 12, 1872, he married Florence Emerson of Bangor, and in October of that year he was elected to the chair of civil engineering at the University of Michigan. From this time until his death his home was at Ann Arbor. In 1895–96 the College of Engineering was made an independent department, and Greene became its first dean.

In addition to his university work, he continued to practise as a consulting engineer. In 1879–81 he was chief engineer of the Toledo, Ann Arbor & Northern Railway; in 1881–82, in charge of construction of the Wheeling & Lake Erie Railroad bridge at Toledo, and the following year, consulting engineer for the Cherry Street bridge there. He designed and superintended the construction of the Ann Arbor Water Works in 1885, and the following year designed the water-works for Pontiac and Ypsilanti. In 1890 he planned the sewer system of Ann Arbor. He was consultant from time to time on the Washington Monument and Congressional Library projects, of which his cousin Bernard Greene was engineer in charge. He was vice-president of the Farmers and Mechanics' Bank of Ann Arbor for some years, and a director in other local companies.

In his first professional publication, a pamphlet issued in 1873, Greene sought to apply graphical methods of analysis to the problems of roof trusses. The value of the graphical methods of solution had not yet been recognized by the profession, and the paper, first prepared as a thesis at the Massachusetts Institute of Technology, had been rejected by the faculty of that institution (Merrick, *post*). Nevertheless, throughout his career Greene continued to develop graphic methods as applied to structural frames, bridges, and arches, and ultimately had the satisfaction of seeing his theories adopted and his works acknowledged as authorities in their field. He was an associate editor of *Engineering News* in 1876–77 and published numerous papers in that journal. His *Graphics for Engineers, Architects, and Builders,* with the sub-title, *Trusses and Arches,* was issued in three parts, "Roof Trusses" (1876), "Bridge Trusses" (1879), and "Arches" (1879), and is his most notable work. The last two parts set forth an original method of graphical analysis which had been widely used. In 1891 he published *Notes on Rankine's Civil Engineering, Part II,* and in 1897 his last book, *The Action of Materials Under Stress, or, Structural Mechanics.*

As a teacher, Greene "sought to convince, to reach the reasoning faculty, and to train the judgment rather than the memory" (*Michigan Alumnus,* December 1903); notable for his power of clear elucidation, "he would get an idea from his mind into the minds of his hearers with just the accuracy with which he would throw an actual bridge across an actual chasm" (*Ibid.,* November 1903). As dean, he displayed both kindliness and executive ability. During his administration the Engineering College grew rapidly and was brought to a position of high rank among technical institutions. He died suddenly, at Ann Arbor, in his sixty-second year, survived by his wife, a son, and a daughter. The son, Albert Emerson Greene, followed his father's profession and was one of his successors in the chair of civil engineering.

[Obituary and Minutes of the University Senate in *Mich. Alumnus,* Nov. and Dec. 1903; *Who's Who in America,* 1903–05; sketch by H. B. Merrick in *The Michigan Technic,* 1904; B. A. Hinsdale, *Hist. of the Univ. of Mich.* (1906); *Harvard Univ., Class of 1862, Report* (1912); *New-Eng. Hist. and Geneal. Reg.,* Jan. 1883; *Engineering News,* Oct. 29, 1903; *Detroit Free Press,* Oct. 17, 1903.] L. M. G.

GREENE, CHRISTOPHER (May 12, 1737–May 14, 1781), Revolutionary soldier, was born at Warwick, R. I., the second son of Philip and Elizabeth Wickes Greene. He was a member of the Greene family famous in that region since its early history, descendants of John Greene, surgeon, who emigrated from Salisbury, England, to Boston in 1635, moved to Providence and finally to Warwick. Christopher Greene appears to have been a business man of many interests, for he was associated with relatives in the operation of extensive works built on the south branch of the Pawtuxet River—forges, anchor works, dams, and sawmills. He became a freeman in 1759, and a member of the Rhode Island legislature in 1771 and 1772, representing the town of Warwick. His share in the Revolution began when he was chosen lieutenant in the "Kentish Guards," established by the Rhode Island legislature in 1774, and marched with them in April 1775 when news of Lexington alarmed the country. In May 1775 the legislature organized an army of observation and defense, consisting of fifteen hundred men, armed, equipped and officered, and appointed Greene major of the regiment of King's County and Kent under Col. James Mitchell Varnum. Shortly thereafter Greene's regiment marched to join other New England troops stationed outside Cambridge.

Greene volunteered to go with Benedict Arnold's expedition to Canada and was commissioned lieutenant-colonel in command of the first battalion. He was with the forces which went by boat up the Kennebec, then marched through the woods to the St. Lawrence, suffering perilous hardships. They reached the vicinity of Quebec about Nov. 10, but the fatal assault on that city which ended in the death of Gen. Montgomery and the capture of most of the patriot troops did not come until Dec. 31. Greene was held prisoner at Quebec until August 1777, when he was released by exchange. Upon his return he was promoted to the rank of colonel of the 1st Rhode Island Infantry, and in October he was placed in command of Fort Mercer on the Delaware, just below and nearly opposite Philadelphia. With Fort Mifflin it guarded the approach to the city, and because of its strategic position was bound, if held, eventually to cause the evacuation of Philadelphia by the British. Scarcely had he reached the fort with his tired troops when it was attacked on Oct. 22 by Col. (Count) Donop with twelve hundred Hessians. Greene's troops numbered only a few hundred, but they finally forced the Hessians to retreat with heavy losses. For this gallant defense the Continental Congress voted Greene a sword. Transferred to Rhode Island in January 1778, he took part in the Battle of Rhode Island on Aug. 29, 1778, in command of his famous Rhode Island regiment of negro troops recruited from slaves freed for patriotic service. In 1781 he was appointed to the command on the lines in Westchester County, N. Y., with his headquarters on the Croton River. Here he was surprised on May 14, 1781, and was killed. On Jan. 6, 1757, he had married Ann Lippitt, by whom he had several children.

[The best life of Greene is M. S. Raymond, "Col. Christopher Greene," *Mag. of Hist. with Notes and Queries,* Sept.–Oct. 1916. See also *Records of the Colony of R. I. and Providence Plantations in New England,* vol. VII (1862); F. V. Greene, *The Revolutionary War* (1911); *Correspondence of the Am. Revolution* (1853), vol. II, ed. by Jared Sparks; "Heath Papers," *Mass. Hist. Soc. Colls.,* 5 ser., vol. IV (1878), 7 ser., vols. IV and V (1904–05); G. S. Greene and Louise B. Clarke, *The Greenes of R. I.* (1903); J. N. Arnold, *Vital Records of R. I.,* vol. I (1891).] V. F. B.

GREENE, DANIEL CROSBY (Feb. 11, 1843–Sept. 15, 1913), missionary, was born at Roxbury, Mass., the son of David Greene and Mary Evarts, a sister of William M. Evarts [*q.v.*]. He came of "typical New England Puritan stock" and also had a background of tradition of the American Board of Commissioners for Foreign Missions which both his father and his maternal grandfather, Jeremiah Evarts [*q.v.*], had served as secretary. He attended Dartmouth College and received his A.B. degree in 1864. After teaching for two years in Wisconsin and Illinois, he entered the Chicago Theological Seminary but left it after one year to complete his course at Andover. On his graduation from Andover, in 1869, he was married to Mary Jane Forbes, a teacher at Mount Holyoke Seminary. The same year, with his wife, he entered the service of the American Board and became the founder of its Japan Mission. His service in Japan, from November 1869 to September 1913, coincided approximately with the "Meiji (Enlightened Rule) Era" (1868–1912) of the Emperor Mutsuhito. Of this notable transition from feudal to modern Japan, Greene was throughout a close and sympathetic observer.

After a few months in Tokio, the Greenes established themselves in Kobe, where, after four years' effort, temporarily retarded by the old edicts against Christianity—a church was organized. This was the beginning of the Kumi-ai (Associated, or Congregational) churches. In 1874 Greene was transferred to Yokohama to serve on a committee of missionaries, with Japanese associates, to prepare what became the standard Japanese version of the New Testament. On this committee he successfully urged the adoption of a style intelligible not merely to a select group of scholars but to the people at large. When a revision of this version was undertaken in 1910, he was made chairman of the new committee.

In 1881 Greene was appointed to Kyoto, where he played a most important part in the development of the Doshisha, the school founded by Niishima. During the years which followed he took a keen interest in the problems of treaty revision and extraterritoriality and upheld Japan's claims for justice. Deeply interested also in contemporary religious thought, he spent some months of his next furlough in Germany. On his return to Japan in 1890 he was assigned to Tokio, the intellectual as well as the political center of the Empire, where he entered upon his congenial task of "relating the Christian movement in a helpful way to the general social and political development of the Empire." One phase of this work was his editorship of the annual volume originally entitled *The Christian Movement in its Relations to the New Life in Japan,* the first issue of which appeared in 1903. In his relations with Japanese Christians, he took a liberal attitude toward new movements of thought among them, even if he did not wholly approve them. He sympathized with Japanese aspirations for autonomy in their religious activities, and he was willing that the missionary should assume an advisory, rather than an authoritative, position. He contributed much toward good relations between Japan and the United States and interested himself even in the matter of having men of good character sent out to the Far East in the consular and diplomatic services. He was an active member and president (1894, 1900–03) of the Asiatic Society of Japan and contributed valuable papers to its *Transactions.*

[*A New-Englander in Japan, Daniel Crosby Greene* (1927), by Greene's oldest son, Evarts B. Greene, is an unbiased characterization of the father's life and work based largely on the father's correspondence. An annotated copy, indicating sources in some detail, is in the library of Andover Theological Seminary, Cambridge, Mass. Other sources include the *Congregationalist,* July 24, 1913, Sept. 25, 1913; *Outlook,* Sept. 27, 1913; the *Japan Weekly Mail* (Yokohama), Supp., Sept. 20, 1913; and the *Trans. Asiatic Soc. of Japan,* Nov. 1914.]

E. W. C.

GREENE, EDWARD LEE (Aug. 20, 1843–Nov. 10, 1915), botanist, was born in Hopkinton, R. I., the son of William and Abby (Crandall) Greene. About 1855 his parents moved to Illinois and thence to Wisconsin, settling near Janesville, where Edward picked up Norwegian from his neighbors and made friends with a Swedish naturalist, Thure Ludwig Theodore Kumlien (see the memoir in *Pittonia,* I, 250–60). His attendance at Albion Academy was interrupted by three years' service (Aug. 21, 1862–July 13, 1865) as a private in the 13th Wisconsin Infantry. Since the regiment was detailed for garrison, guard, patrol, and picket duty, Greene, with the *Class-Book of Botany* by Alphonso Wood [*q.v.*] in his blanket-roll, was able to botanize through Kentucky, Tennessee, and Alabama and emerged from the war blithe and unscathed. Though not of college rank, Albion Academy conferred degrees and in 1866 gave its returned pupil a Ph.B. After teaching for a few years, Greene went in 1870 from Decatur, Ill., to Colorado, collected plants for Asa Gray and George Engelmann, and, though of Baptist and Quaker antecedents, entered Jarvis Hall, the Episcopal seminary conducted at Golden City by Bishop George Maxwell Randall. Ordained in 1873, he ministered to congregations at Pueblo, Colo., Vallejo, Cal., and Georgetown, Colo., and traversed as a missionary large tracts of Wyoming, Colorado, New Mexico, Arizona, and California. In 1882 he was made rector of St. Mark's, Berkeley, Cal., but, persuading himself that his ordination was invalid, he resigned in 1885 and became a Roman Catholic layman. He was instructor in botany at the University of California, 1885–86, assistant professor, 1886–90, and professor, 1890–95. Students, drawn to him by his originality and independence, thought him delightfully irregular. Well-formed physically, with a shock of hair turned white as cotton in early life, his was a striking figure set off by regular and handsome features and a noble bearing. Every student remembered his beneficent and disarming smile, his play of wit, and his strong relish for humor. In 1895 he resigned. Gifted with an unusual measure of self-esteem and with a wider field knowledge of the North American flora than was possessed by any other botanist of his day, he removed to Washington, where he was professor of botany in the Catholic University of

America, from 1895 to 1904, and an associate of the Smithsonian Institution (1904–14).

His more important separate publications were: *West American Oaks* (Pt. I, 1889; Pt. II, 1890), with illustrations by Albert Kellogg and George Hansen [*qq.v.*]; *Pittonia: A Series of Papers Relating to Botany and Botanists* (5 vols., 1887–1905); *Flora Franciscana* (Pts. I–IV, 1891–97; incomplete); *Manual of the Botany of the Region of San Francisco Bay* (1894); *Plantæ Bakerianæ* (1901; incomplete); *Leaflets of Botanical Observation* (2 vols., 1903–09); and *Landmarks of Botanical History* (Pt. I, to A.D. 1562, 1909; never continued), published by the Smithsonian Institution. In this last work his most eager interests centered. To developing at Washington his ideas as to new species and nomenclature he bent for twenty years the full energies of a powerful mind and an unwasting enthusiasm, supplemented by a mastery of the English tongue remarkable for its purity, persuasiveness, and Biblical strength. Disregarding almost entirely the effects of climatic and edaphic influences, he thought of species as immutable and so was able to discover some three thousand new ones, but only a small proportion of them have been accepted by other botanists. Asa Gray reviewed his early writings with unmistakable distrust (*American Journal of Science,* CXXX, 320–21, CXXXIII, 426, CXXXIV, 493–94); and until he left California he was subject to constant and bitter attack in *Zoe* (see especially Katharine Brandegee, "The Botanical Writings of Edward L. Greene," April 1893). Greene's assertion, however, of the right of a botanist to publish his results without first submitting specimens or manuscript to Asa Gray may well prove, in historical retrospect, his most significant effort in behalf of North American botany. He never answered his opponents and never changed his views, and there were other botanists who admired both the man and his work. Greene never married. In 1914 he transferred his herbarium and library, rich in type-specimens and in rare botanical works, to Notre Dame University in return for a modest annuity. He died in Providence Hospital, Washington, after a long, wasting illness and was buried at Notre Dame, where he had planned to spend his remaining years. *Greenella,* an herb discovered by him in southern Arizona, was named in his honor by Asa Gray. Except Thomas Nuttall, no other botanist in North America has had so long, picturesque, and dramatic a career.

[*Who's Who in America,* 1899–1915; autobiographical chapter in *Some Roads to Rome in America* (1909), ed. by G. P. Curtis; H. H. Bartlett, "The Botanical Work of E. L. Greene," *Torreya,* July 1916, with portrait; J. N. Rose, "E. L. Greene," *Botanical Gazette,* Jan. 1916; J. A. Nieuwland, obituary, *Am. Midland Naturalist,* Nov. 1915; C. S. Sargent, *The Silva of North America,* VIII (1895), 84; *Roster of Wis. Volunteers, War of the Rebellion, 1861–65,* I (1886), 767; *Extracts from Personal Letters on the Landmarks of Botanical History* (n.p., n.d.); W. L. Jepson, memoir, *Newman Hall Review,* I (1918), 24–29; Daniel Cleveland Correspondence (MS.).]

W. L. J.

GREENE, FRANCES HARRIET WHIPPLE [See GREEN, FRANCES HARRIET WHIPPLE, 1805–1878].

GREENE, FRANCIS VINTON (June 27, 1850–May 15, 1921), soldier, historian, and engineer, was born in Providence, R. I., the youngest son of George Sears Greene [*q.v.*] and his second wife, Martha Barrett Dana, daughter of Hon. Samuel Dana of Boston. He was a brother of George Sears Greene, Jr., and of Samuel Dana Greene [*qq.v.*]. His early education was received at Trinity School, in New York, and Burlington College, N. J. Entering West Point in 1866, he graduated in 1870 at the head of his class, was commissioned in the 4th Artillery, and served for two years at coastal forts in the South. He was transferred to the Corps of Engineers in 1872 and was engaged for four years upon the survey of the Canadian boundary, being promoted to first lieutenant in 1874. After a period of duty in the office of the secretary of war, 1876–77, he was sent abroad to observe and report on the Russo-Turkish War then in progress. From June 1877 to December 1878 he was with the Russian headquarters in the field, being present at the battles before Plevna, at Shipka Pass, and elsewhere, and for courage in action was decorated with the orders of St. Anne and St. Vladimir. On his return to the United States he was employed for some time in the preparation of his report, which, after its submission to the War Department, was published in 1879 under the title of *The Russian Army and Its Campaigns in Turkey in 1877–78.* It immediately became and still remains the standard work on the subject, and is studied as constantly in foreign armies as in that of the United States. On Feb. 25, 1879, Greene was married, in Washington, to Belle Eugénie, daughter of Henry Chevallié of Richmond, Va., whose first American ancestor came to America from France in 1790. For six years he was in charge of public works in the city of Washington, as assistant to the engineer commissioner, and was then an instructor in practical military engineering at West Point for a short time. He had been promoted captain in 1883. Resigning from the army, Dec. 31, 1886, he became vice-president and afterward president of the Barber Asphalt Paving Company, engaged in an industry which was then in its infancy. He joined the New York National Guard as a major in 1889, and had become a colonel before the war with Spain. He entered the volunteer army as colonel of the 71st New York Infantry, May 2, 1898, but served with it only a few days, being appointed brigadier-general of volunteers on May 27, 1898. In charge of the second expedition to the Philippines, he arrived at Manilla on July 17, commanded a brigade in the trenches and at the attack and capture of the city, and was senior member of the commission which drew up the terms of capitulation of the Spanish army. He was appointed major-general of volunteers, Aug. 13, 1898. In the next month he returned to the United States and was soon sent to Havana, having been selected as governor of the city. This assignment he declined, but he prepared a comprehensive report (*New York Times,* Jan. 1, 1899) on the condition of the city, which served as the basis for the extensive works of rehabilitation carried out during the American occupation. He resigned from the volunteer army, Feb. 28, 1899, and after serving as chairman of the committee appointed to examine into the canal question in New York (see *Documents of the Assembly of the State of New York, 1900,* No. 79), became managing director of the New Trinidad Lake Asphalt Company. From 1903 to 1904 he was police commissioner of the city of New York. "He lost no time in forcing the fight against graft and incompetency. He dismissed many high officers, shook up the bureaus, transferred idle wardmen to patrol duty, established military discipline, and in a few months raised the police army to a state of discipline it had not known before. It soon became a vigilant, efficient, dependable force" (*New York Times,* May 17, 1921). He has been called the best commissioner the city ever had. From 1905 to 1915 he lived in Buffalo, where he was president of the Niagara, Lockport & Ontario Power Company and the Ontario Power Company. After his withdrawal from active practise he returned to New York and there spent the remainder of his life. He was an active director of the New York Institution for the Instruction of the Deaf and Dumb from 1893 and its president, 1919–21. His reputation as a military historian rests chiefly upon his notable work on the Russo-Turkish War, but in addition to numerous short articles he wrote several other books, including: *Sketches of Army Life in Russia* (1880); *The Mississippi* (1882), in Scribners' series, Campaigns of the Civil War; a biography, *General Greene* (1893), in the Great Commanders Series; *The Revolutionary War and the Military Policy of the United States* (1911); *Our First Year in the Great War* (1918). Of his personal characteristics his friend, Gen. Tillman, said: "He was of very striking and attractive physical appearance and of impressive personality, a man of wide reading and general culture. His mind worked with astonishing rapidity; though remembering all details and considering every factor of the problems before him, his conclusions were always lucidly set forth and shown to rest only on the principles involved" (Tillman, *post,* p. 76). He had six children—four daughters and two sons, one of whom, Warwick Greene (1870–1929), was director of public works in Manila for several years, served as a major and lieutenant-colonel in the World War, and was chief of a mission sent to Finland and neighboring countries in connection with the peace settlement.

[There is an excellent brief biography by S. E. Tillman in *Fifty-third Ann. Report Asso. Grads. U. S. Mil. Acad.* (1922), pp. 69–78. Greene's military career in the Philippines is adequately treated in F. E. Chadwick, *The Relations of the U. S. and Spain: The Spanish-American War,* vol. II (1911). See also G. W. Cullum, *Biog. Reg.* (3rd ed., 1891), vol. III, and Supp., vols. V (1910) and VI (1920); G. S. Greene and Louise B. Clarke, *The Greenes of R. I.* (1903), pp. 615–18; *Army and Navy Jour.,* May 21, 1921; *N. Y. Times,* May 16 and 17, 1921; *N. Y. Tribune,* May 16, 1921.]

T. M. S.

GREENE, GEORGE SEARS (May 6, 1801–Jan. 28, 1899), soldier and civil engineer, the son of Caleb Greene and his wife Sarah Robinson, daughter of Thomas and Sarah (Wickes) Greene, was descended from John Greene, who came to America in 1635, was one of the founders of Warwick, R. I., and established a notable family. (See sketch of William Greene, 1695/96–1758.) Caleb Greene was a shipowner, whose once prosperous business was ruined by the Embargo and the war. It was intended that his son George, born at Apponaug, R. I., should enter Brown University, but lack of money made this impossible, and instead he went to New York where he found work. He was appointed a cadet at West Point in 1819, graduated in 1823, and was commissioned in the artillery. Returning to the Military Academy immediately, to teach mathematics, he remained there for nearly four years, except for a few months when he was teaching at the Artillery School at Fort Monroe. Leaving West Point finally in 1827, he served for several years at various artillery posts in New England. On July 14, 1828, he was married, at Pomfret, Conn., to Elizabeth Vinton, who died in 1832. He was promoted to first lieutenant in 1829. Resigning from the army, June 30, 1836, he took up engineering as a profession, engaging particularly in railroad construction. On Feb. 21, 1837, he married Martha Barrett

Dana, daughter of Hon. Samuel Dana. At the outbreak of the Civil War he was engineer in charge of the Croton water-works extension and the Croton Reservoir in Central Park, New York. He was appointed colonel of the 60th New York, Jan. 18, 1862, and served with his regiment in the neighborhood of Washington until appointed brigadier-general of volunteers, Apr. 28, 1862. He was then assigned to a brigade under Gen. Banks, in the Shenandoah Valley, and commanded it in action for the first time at Cedar Mountain in August. At Antietam, by virtue of seniority, he commanded a division, and then resumed command of his brigade, which was reorganized in April 1863 so as to be composed entirely of New York regiments. He fought at Chancellorsville, and with great distinction at Gettysburg. With the XII Corps he arrived on the battlefield at Gettysburg late in the afternoon of the first day's fighting, was posted at Culp's Hill, on the extreme right of the Union line, and helped to resist the Confederate attacks of the second day. That evening the entire corps, with the exception of Greene's brigade, was withdrawn in order to strengthen the Union left, and for a time this brigade bore the whole brunt of the renewed attacks of the Confederates, who could have placed themselves across the Union line of communications if the Culp's Hill position were carried. The safety of the army, therefore, depended upon Greene's brigade, until, little by little, it was strengthened by troops sent from other commands. It was again in action on the third day of the battle. In September, the XII Corps was transferred to Tennessee and Greene served with it in the early part of the Chattanooga campaign. He was severely wounded, however, at Wauhatchie, Oct. 28, 1863, being shot through the face, and saw no further field service until 1865. His wound made necessary a difficult operation in May 1864, and when he had recovered sufficiently to be fit for duty of any kind he was employed on courts martial. He commanded a brigade in the North Carolina campaign of March and April 1865, and marched in the great review at Washington. After being mustered out of the volunteer service, Apr. 30, 1866, he resumed the practise of his profession in New York, where he did extensive work in connection with the water supply, the elevated railways, and the laying out of new streets. He was engaged on important engineering operations elsewhere, also, notably the planning of the sewerage system of Washington and the construction or extension of water-supply systems in Detroit, Troy, and Yonkers. He was one of the founders of the American Society of Civil Engineers, and its president from 1875 to 1877. His interests were not confined to professional matters. He was an active member, and for some time president, of the New York Genealogical and Biographical Society; he collected the bulk of the material for a genealogical account of the Greene family, which was completed and published after his death (G. S. Greene and Louise B. Clarke, *post*), and he was deeply interested in the affairs of the United States Military Academy, of which he became the "oldest living graduate," a distinction in which he took the keenest delight. In 1894, by virtue of a special act of Congress, he returned to the regular army as a first lieutenant, the rank which he held at the time of his resignation in 1836, and was placed on the retired list. Harsh in manner and a strict disciplinarian, he was not a man to win immediate affection, but those under him soon learned to appreciate his ability and his rigid sense of justice. He died at Morristown, N. J., where he had resided since 1883, and was buried at Warwick, R. I. Two of his sons, George Sears and Francis Vinton Greene [*qq.v.*], attained distinction in their father's profession, and a third son, Samuel Dana Greene [*q.v.*], as executive officer of the *Monitor* in her fight with the *Merrimac.*

[W. F. Fox and others, *In Memoriam, George Sears Greene* (1909); G. S. Greene and Louise B. Clarke, *The Greenes of R. I.* (1903), based on the material collected by Greene and containing a biographical sketch of him by his son, F. V. Greene; R. H. Greene, in *N. Y. Geneal. and Biog. Record*, Apr. 1899; G. W. Cullum, *Biog. Reg.* (3rd ed., 1891), I, 301–03, IV, 24; *Mil. Order of the Loyal Legion . . . State of N. Y., Circ. No. 14* (1900); *Trans. Am. Soc. Civil Engineers*, vol. XLIX (1902); O. O. Howard, in *Thirtieth Ann. Reunion Asso. Grads. U. S. Mil. Acad.* (1899), 135–43; *Official Records (Army)*, 1 ser. XII (pt. 2), XIX (pt. 1), XXV (pt. 1), XXVII (pt. 1), XXXI (pt. 1); *N. Y. Tribune*, Jan. 29, 1899.] T. M. S.

GREENE, GEORGE SEARS (Nov. 26, 1837–Dec. 23, 1922), civil engineer, eldest son of George Sears Greene [*q.v.*] and Martha Barrett (Dana) Greene, and brother of Samuel Dana and Francis Vinton Greene [*qq.v.*], was born at Lexington, Ky. Although he entered Harvard College in 1856, he left without a degree in order to study engineering under his father. During his apprenticeship he served as assistant engineer on the Croton aqueduct, on various railroads in Cuba, and with several mining companies on Lake Superior. His first important contributions to the theory and practise of his profession were made in connection with his topographical surveys of Westchester County, New York, and of Long Island. As a result of his experience he devised a drifting head for transits, which has proved especially valuable, and introduced other changes in surveying instruments which have since become standard. He was married, Apr. 23, 1862, to his cousin, Susan Moody Dana. In 1875 he became engineer-in-chief of the department of docks, New York City, a position which he held for twenty-two years and in which he brought to completion his most notable works. These were the design and construction of the sea wall surrounding the greater part of Manhattan Island and the building of the wharves and piers in the Chelsea Improvement on the North River between Charles Street and Twenty-third Street. Both of these undertakings involved novel and difficult problems. The mud was deeper than any that had been previously encountered, making it impossible to drive piles to a hard bottom. To meet this situation Greene developed a radical and highly successful method of construction based upon the theory that the sustaining power of piles depends partly upon their "skin resistance," or the friction of the mud against their sides. The fact that this scheme permitted a slight movement of the structures resting upon the piles led to public alarm and open criticism of his work, but its success was recognized by the experts appointed to examine it. Their report (contained in the *Twelfth Annual Report of the Department of Docks,* 1882, pp. 37–45) made clear the magnitude of Greene's achievements and the brilliant manner in which he utilized cement in under-water construction. During the latter part of his career he practised in New York as a consulting engineer. From 1911 to 1914 he was a member of the board of advisory engineers of the State Barge Canal. He was also a director, treasurer, and vice-president of the American Society of Civil Engineers.

[G. S. Greene and Louise B. Clarke, *The Greenes of R. I.* (1903); *Trans. Am. Soc. Civil Engineers,* vol. LXXXVIII (1925); *Who's Who in America,* 1922–23; *Engineering News-Record,* Jan. 4, 1923; *N. Y. Times,* Dec. 24, 1922.]

R. P. B—r.

GREENE, GEORGE WASHINGTON (Apr. 8, 1811–Feb. 2, 1883), author, educator, born at East Greenwich, R. I., was the son of Nathanael Ray and Anna Maria (Clarke) Greene, the grandson of Gen. Nathanael Greene [*q.v.*], and a descendant of John Greene, surgeon, who came from Salisbury to New England in 1635. At the age of fourteen he matriculated at Brown University but because of poor health withdrew in 1827 and went to Europe. With the exception of one year in 1834 as principal of Kent Academy at East Greenwich he lived abroad until 1847. He met by accident at an inn in Southern France Henry Wadsworth Longfellow and there began an intimate friendship that was to influence his career profoundly. From that meeting with Longfellow, literature became the inspiration, the guide, and the comfort of his life (Dedication, *Life of Nathanael Greene,* vol. I, 1867). He began his historical career by writing essays for the *North American Review,* the first of which appeared in 1835. From 1837 to 1845 he was United States consul at Rome. While there he wrote his one-volume *Life of Nathanael Greene* (1846) in Jared Sparks's Library of American Biography. In 1848 he became instructor in modern languages at Brown University and while there he published several text-books of French and Italian. In 1850 a volume of his *Historical Essays* was published. On Feb. 9, 1852, he was married to Catharine Van Buren Porter, daughter of an old New England family, and removed to New York City where he devoted himself to lecturing and writing. A collection of his articles, *Biographical Studies,* appeared in 1860 and his *Historical View of the American Revolution,* a series of popular lectures first delivered before the Lowell Institute, was published five years later.

Greene had in early youth determined to write an adequate biography of his distinguished grandfather. To that end he traveled widely collecting documents and interviewing those who might reminisce about the General. "Among all who had known him I found but one opinion both of his greatness and of his goodness, of the vigor and depth of his mind, of the warmth and purity of his heart" (*Life of Nathanael Greene,* vol. I, p. vii). The earlier volume for Sparks had been written from the common printed authorities; now he worked in the family papers, containing hundreds of letters and documents. "Every page I read confirmed my original opinion, and strengthened my first intention" (*Ibid.,* p. viii). In 1866 he wrote a lengthy and labored pamphlet, *Nathanael Greene: An Examination of the Ninth Volume of Bancroft's History,* attacking Bancroft's statements concerning his grandfather. To this Bancroft effectively replied in his letter to the editor of the *North American Review,* published in April 1867. The first volume of the long-expected *Life of Nathanael Greene* appeared in 1867, the second and third volumes in 1871. Two factors seriously impaired the value of the *Life*: Greene agreed heartily with his friend Washington Irving that "care should be taken to vindicate great names from the pernicious erudition . . . which, in the name of learned research, goes prying about the traces of history, casting down its monuments, and marring and mutilating its fairest trophies," and Greene was the devoted grandson of an eminent grandfather. Thus a mistaken sense of patriotic duty and the adulation of ancestor worship disfigured the labors of many years.

In 1871 Greene was invited to become lecturer in American history in the new Cornell University. He accepted and for a year held the first chair of American history to be established in the United States. But his library was more congenial than the classroom; his lectures quietly read from manuscript lacked any distinctly didactic quality. Some years earlier he had edited *The Works of Joseph Addison* (5 vols., 1854; 6 vols., 1891). Now he wrote and published *The German Element in the War of Independence* (1876) and *A Short History of Rhode Island* (1877). He had always been of delicate health and he spent the last years of his life in the quiet seclusion of his home at East Greenwich.

[G. S. Greene and Louise B. Clarke, *The Greenes of R. I.* (1903); *Landmarks of Tompkins County, N. Y.* (1894), ed. by J. H. Selkreg; *Hist. Cat. Brown Univ. 1764–1904*; *Providence Jour.* and *N. Y. Times*, Feb. 3, 1883; letters of Longfellow to Greene, in *Life of H. W. Longfellow* (2 vols., 1886), ed. by Samuel Longfellow.]

F. M—n.

GREENE, NATHANAEL (July 27/Aug. 7, 1742–June 19, 1786), Revolutionary general, was born at Potowomut (Warwick), R. I., the son of Nathanael Greene by his second wife, Mary Mott. His ancestors had emigrated in 1635 from Salisbury, England, to Massachusetts, whence they had soon been driven to Rhode Island by religious persecution. The younger Nathanael Greene early displayed an aptitude for study and a proficiency in mathematics. His reading was guided by Ezra Stiles [*q.v.*], afterward president of Yale, Lindley Murray, and possibly Henry Knox, the Boston bookseller. He worked at his father's iron foundry at Potowomut until 1770, when he moved to Coventry to take charge of the family forge there. In 1765 Greene was admitted as a freeman of Warwick. From 1770 to 1772 and again in 1775 he served as deputy to the General Assembly. He was brought up as a member of the Society of Friends, but on Sept. 30, 1773, he was "put from under the care of the meeting" because he had attended a military parade. On July 20, 1774, he married Catharine Littlefield.

Although a vigorous and energetic man, Greene had from early childhood a stiff knee, which rendered him somewhat sensitive and quick to resent insults. In October 1774, when in the face of the impending struggle with Great Britain he helped to organize a militia company, known as the Kentish Guards, he was made to feel the force of his infirmity. His fellows refused to allow him to act as an officer. His character is attested by his willingness to serve in the ranks. Upon the arrival of the news of Lexington the Kentish Guards set out for the scene of conflict, but they were recalled by the Loyalist governor. Greene and three others, however, pushed on to Boston. On Apr. 22, 1775, in spite of the governor, the Rhode Island Assembly approved the raising of 1,500 men, and appointed Greene on a committee to consult with Connecticut. In May the Assembly voted to organize three regiments, and appointed the erstwhile private to be brigadier in charge of them. The regiments were promptly raised and by June 3 Greene had them at the camp in Jamaica Plain, where several other regiments were assigned him. On June 22 Greene was chosen a brigadier-general in the Continental Army. He served through the siege of Boston, where he was conspicuous for his talent in gathering and conserving military supplies and for his services in removing intercolonial jealousies. After the evacuation of Boston by the British in March 1776 he was put in command of the army of occupation of that city.

On Apr. 1, he took his brigades by way of Providence and New London, and thence by sea, to New York. In May he assumed charge of the defenses of New York, but, although he made plans with great care and skill, the execution of his orders left much to be desired. While the British attack on Long Island in the late summer of 1776 was at its height Greene was seriously ill for three weeks, but after the defeat of the Americans he retired with the rest of the army above New York. After the battles at Harlem, he was given command of the troops in New Jersey, with headquarters at Fort Constitution (Fort Lee). He had been promoted on Aug. 9, 1776, to be a major-general in the Continental Army. On Oct. 12 he conducted an attack on the British camp at Staten Island, but was called back to the general headquarters by Howe's landing on Throgg's (Frog's) Neck. This move and the resulting battle at White Plains seriously threatened Fort Washington, on the Hudson. Washington determined to defend this post, but on Nov. 16 it was stormed and captured by the British, and the evacuation of Fort Lee necessarily followed. Historians are inclined to blame Greene for the mistaken advice not to evacuate Fort Washington (Van Tyne, *post*, p. 258).

On the famous Christmas Eve of 1776, when Washington stunned his foe at Trenton, Greene led the left column, the position of which insured not only the defeat but also the capture of the Hessian detachment. He then withdrew with the army to its winter quarters at Morristown, N. J. In March, when Congress was manifesting some discontent with the conduct of the war, Washington, who had already begun to lean heavily upon Greene, sent him to Philadelphia to confer with Congress (*Journals of the Continental Congress,* Mar. 20, 21, 24, 1777). He then returned to the army and spent the rest of the spring skirmishing with British outposts in northern New Jersey. When it was expected that Howe would take the British troops north from New York to cooperate with the oncoming army of Burgoyne from Canada, Greene was sent with Knox to examine the passes in the highlands of the Hudson.

In July 1777 it was rumored in camp that a French officer, DuCoudray, was to be made a major-general, with a commission antedating Greene's, and be placed in charge of all the artillery. This threatened introduction of an outsider who would rank them so enraged the American generals in the field that Greene, Henry Knox, and John Sullivan all sent letters to Congress, threatening to resign if such an injustice were committed. Congress, embarrassed by loose promises evidently made in their name by Silas Deane, envoy to France, and at the same time offended at the bold action of the three generals, sent their letters to Washington, demanding that he reprimand them for their attempt to bully the government, and further demanding an apology from them. John Adams wrote Greene privately, advising him to apologize. Greene resolutely refused to do so. Congress meantime yielded to the threat of the generals (*Journals,* July 7, 1777; Burnett, *post,* II, 403–05).

Greene's skilful disposition of his troops after Brandywine insured the safe withdrawal of the army and saved the artillery. In the subsequent battle of Germantown, he led the left column. The darkness of an early morning attack and the atrocious condition of the roads delayed his arrival on the field, but there is no evidence to support Bancroft's contention that Washington blamed Greene for this and, in any case, the discomfiture of the Americans was due to other causes. In November 1777 Greene was directed to try to hold the forts on the Delaware, but was unable to effect anything so he returned with his troops to the main army, then going into winter quarters at Valley Forge.

In the winter of 1777–78, a serious attempt was made in Congress to displace Washington in favor of Gates. Among the malcontents was Quartermaster-General Thomas Mifflin [*q.v.*], whose own sins were patent by this time. In Mifflin's absences from his post, Washington had tended to rely more and more upon the energy and sagacity of Greene in matters of supply. When the "Conway Cabal" failed of its purpose, Greene was in a position to call attention to the sad condition of the quartermaster's department. On Feb. 25, 1778, he reluctantly consented to become quartermaster-general himself, and on Mar. 2 was so appointed by Congress. Mifflin continued to act as quartermaster until this date, though he had resigned the previous November. Greene stipulated that the appointment of subordinates should be in his own hands, and particularly that the transport service should be reorganized. He further insisted upon the appointment of John Cox and Col. Charles Pettit, tried and trusted friends, as assistant quartermasters-general. The bill reorganizing the department contained a provision that Greene should be responsible for the conduct of subordinates (*Journals,* Mar. 2, 1778). This was to make trouble later. Greene at once established a system of supply depots so as to draw upon the fertile middle states for forage and upon New England for manufactured goods which came in through the port of Boston. He further insisted upon monthly returns from his deputies.

When the British evacuated Philadelphia in June 1778, Washington, whose army was now recovered from the winter at Valley Forge and supplied by the skill of Greene, pursued the British into New Jersey. Resuming for the moment his command in the line, Greene led the right at the battle of Monmouth on June 28, 1778. When Sir Henry Clinton retreated to New York, Greene moved with the army back to the old posts in the highlands of the Hudson. In July an expedition from New England under Sullivan was planned to drive the British from Rhode Island. Greene went to his old home to assist in the preparations for the attack. The withdrawal of Count D'Estaing, however, left the Americans alone outside Newport. Sullivan, advised by Greene, withdrew to the northern part of the island, where the emboldened British attacked them but were decisively defeated on Aug. 29, 1778. Greene commanded the right in this exceedingly bloody battle. As there was much discontent because of the failure of the French fleet, and as more supplies were needed from Boston, where D'Estaing had put in, Greene went thither in September. Here he had to act the part of the diplomat in urging the French to continue with the plan, at the same time concealing the American resentment at D'Estaing's conduct. By October he was back in Rhode Island organizing the production and shipment of quartermaster supplies. In the winter of 1778–79, headquarters were at Middlebrook, N. J., where, thanks to the exertions of Greene, the suffering was not so acute as the previous winter. The extent of his activity may be judged by his administration of over $50,000,000 in the year 1779 alone (*Journals of the Continental Congress,* XV, 1432). During the winter of 1779–80, the severest of the war, headquarters were at Morristown, N. J. The following summer there was a period of maneuvering without any great battle. Greene's excellent dispositions rendered the army more mobile, and Clinton's only attempt, against Rhode Island, was promptly halted by Washington's threat against New York.

In their desperate effort to display efficiency, in the spring of 1780, Congress listened once more to the now jealous Mifflin, and decided again to reorganize the quartermaster's department. The administration of vast sums of money by Greene obviously gave opportunity for dishonesty and embezzlement on the part of his subordinates. Although Mifflin had complained at being held too strictly accountable for such peculation during his own administration of the department, he nevertheless allowed Congress to attack his successor on this score. Green replied to this chicanery with honest scorn, which only enraged the politicians. On Mar. 27, 1780, Mifflin and Timothy Pickering [*q.v.*] presented a new plan for the quartermaster's department, which did not remove the old fault of trying to hold the quartermaster-general personally and financially liable for the acts of his subordinates, but did take away from Greene his two trusted officers, Cox and Pettit. Asked to comment upon it, Greene responded in such vigorous fashion that he only added oil to the flames cf jealousy. He demanded a vote of confidence, which the Committee promptly recommended but Congress refused him. Following the adoption of the new plan by his enemies in Congress on July 15, 1780, Greene flatly declined to continue as quartermaster-general. Congress was so angered that after the acceptance of his resignation on Aug. 3, an effort was made to expel him from the army altogether. This failed, however, despite a fierce turmoil in Congress in which angry words passed. Pickering was appointed his successor. Returning to headquarters after a foraging expedition, Greene was royally welcomed by his old companions and especially by the Commander-in-Chief (Greene to Wm. Greene, Sept. 3, 1780, W. L. Clements Library).

In September 1780, when Washington left headquarters on the Hudson to confer with Rochambeau at Hartford, Greene was left in supreme command of the Continental Army. It was during this absence that the plot of Benedict Arnold [*q.v.*] came to a head. Greene was the president of the board of general officers who sent the unfortunate André to the gallows, and he took over the command of the post at West Point, vacated by Arnold. After the crushing defeat at Camden, S. C., however, Congress suspended Gates from his command until a court of inquiry could be held into his conduct, and begged the Commander-in-Chief to choose a successor. Washington promptly chose Greene (Oct. 14, 1780) and the latter set out for his greatest campaign.

It was clear to Washington and Greene that Gates's disaster had been largely due to his failure adequately to provide and safeguard his supplies. Greene therefore stopped in Philadelphia for nine days, en route to his new command. The extent of his work in those few days is astonishing. A medical department and engineers, supplies, artillery, clothing, horses, and every detail of equipment, were provided for by him. A chastened Congress gave him all possible help, on paper. All troops raised, or to be raised, between Delaware and Georgia were allotted to his army. President Joseph Reed of Pennsylvania, his warm personal friend, opened the state arsenals to him. Greene emphasized the need of horses, for transport and for cavalry, as it was the lack of the latter which had deprived Gates of an adequate intelligence service. He then pushed south and stopped six days at Richmond, where he arranged for similar cooperation with the all-important Gov. Thomas Jefferson of Virginia (Jefferson to Greene, Feb. 18, 1781, Clements Library). Upon entering North Carolina, he at once made provision for the construction of batteaux for adequate water transportation. Stopping in Hillsboro, then the seat of the patriot government in North Carolina, he made sure of the cooperation of the various state organizations. On Dec. 2 he joined Gates at Charlotte, to complete the reorganization of the shattered army. The inquiry into the conduct of Gates was postponed, and ultimately given up altogether (see Gates, Horatio). The work of organizing and equipping a practically destitute army was enough for the ablest of generals (Greene to Congress, Dec. 28, 1780, Clements Library). Greene profited by Gates's failure and secured the warm cooperation of the partisan corps, under Francis Marion, Thomas Sumter, and Andrew Pickens. In Daniel Morgan, Otho Williams, and William Washington he found able subordinates, and the legion of Henry Lee proved invaluable for securing military intelligence. Greene's tact and ability in handling these brilliant but independent men was in marked contrast to the conduct of his predecessor.

In December 1780 he moved his small army to Hicks Creek on the Pedee. He then outwitted Cornwallis by dividing his force. During the bewilderment of the British commander, one division of the patriots under Morgan gained a brilliant and profitable victory over the redoubtable Tarleton at Cowpens (Jan. 17, 1781). The enraged Cornwallis determined to put an end to Greene, burned his baggage, and started out to find and punish the impudent commander. Greene then gave a classic example of the American military policy in the Revolution, which was to retreat as far as the British would pursue, and when the enemy, drawn far from his base, was obliged to return, to turn also and follow him (Greene to Lafayette, July 17, 1781, Clements Library). Cornwallis was clearly the stronger, and the two armies raced for the River Dan. The foresight of Greene in preparing the batteaux two months earlier enabled him to reach the north side of the river, while Cornwallis on the opposite bank was helpless to pursue. Cornwallis then turned and retreated south. Greene at once recrossed the Dan and was at his heels. The Continental forces caught up with the British commander at Guilford Court House (near modern Greensboro, N. C.) and a fierce battle ensued. The British gained a Pyrrhic victory on Mar. 15, 1781, but Greene was able to draw off his troops ten miles and was ready to begin again. On Apr. 6 he started around to the west of Cornwallis, forcing the British to retire to the southeast. Greene, instead of following them, made a rapid march to the south and by the 20th he had his army once more in front of Camden, S. C. From this post the British commander, Lord Rawdon, made a violent sortie, and at Hobkirk's Hill (Apr. 26, 1781) the British gained another expensive and useless victory. Greene again withdrew his troops a few miles to the north, and after reforming them started once more for Camden. Rawdon did not wait for him, but fled with his troops to join Cornwallis and the patriot army entered Camden in triumph. At the end of this phase of the campaign, despite two apparent defeats, the Americans held precisely the post they sought.

Greene then sent out detachments which cut off and captured the British posts at Fort Granby, Fort Watson, and Fort Motte. Lee was detached with an expedition which went to Georgia and recaptured Augusta. In May, Greene besieged the important British post at Ninety-Six, S. C., but as this was relieved by Rawdon on June 19 he was obliged to raise the siege. Again it was a Pyrrhic victory for the British, as Rawdon was at once obliged to retreat with the rescued garrison and Greene occupied the post. He then withdrew his army for the month of July 1781 to the hills of the Santee, to avoid the summer fevers. On Aug. 22 he set his army in motion once more, headed for the one remaining British outpost at Eutaw Springs, S. C. On Sept. 8 he caught the British under Stuart at that place and inflicted a severe defeat upon them, so that Stuart fled with the remnant of his force toward the British base at Charleston. Greene retired to the hills, refreshed his army, and started for that city. In December the British had been cleared out of practically every position in South Carolina save Charleston, which the army under Greene was besieging. Meantime, Cornwallis had surrendered his army at Yorktown and the war was practically over. Greene was obliged, however, to exert heroic measures to keep his army together before Charleston for another year, as the British did not evacuate that town until Dec. 14, 1782.

The South Carolina legislature met at last and voted Greene 10,000 guineas, most of which he had to expend on his own army. He was also obliged to pledge much of his personal fortune, and he became involved with a contractor, John Banks, whose paper he had to indorse personally to keep the army from starvation (Banks Papers, Clements Library). His warning to the muddling Continental Congress brought no more response than did Washington's similar letters from Newburgh. In 1783 he started north to revisit his Rhode Island home and repair the wreck of his fortunes. He met Washington at Trenton and together they visited Congress at Princeton. After a visit to Coventry, R. I., he again returned to the South, where the bankruptcy of Banks involved Greene in debts he could not pay. He therefore sold his South Carolina estates, and moved to a plantation in Georgia which had been voted him by the grateful people of that state. He went back and forth between Georgia and Rhode Island every year for the remainder of his life. In 1785 he established himself near Savannah at Mulberry Grove, the confiscated estate of the Loyalist lieutenant-governor, John Graham. He died there on June 19, 1786, and was buried in the cemetery of Christ Episcopal Church, Savannah. In 1902 his remains were removed from the cemetery and reinterred beneath the Greene monument in Johnson Square, Savannah. He had five children, George Washington, Martha Washington, Cornelia Lott, Nathanael Ray, and Louisa Catherine. His widow, who on June 28, 1796, was married to Phineas Miller, survived until 1814.

[Wm. Johnson, *Sketches of the Life and Correspondence of Nathanael Greene* (2 vols., 1822), and G. W. Greene, *The Life of Nathanael Greene* (3 vols., 1867–71), are based upon a study of the Greene manuscripts, but are *ex parte* biographies and must be used with extreme care. The Greene manuscript collection was kept together for many years, as recorded by J. F. Jameson in *Pubs. R. I. Hist. Soc.*, III, no. 3, Oct. 1895. Sold in 1894 to J. A. Garland, they were purchased from him in 1905 by Jos. F. Sabin. Sabin sold a small part of the collection, and in 1926 the residue was purchased by Wm. L. Clements, who has since reassembled in the W. L. Clements Lib., Ann Arbor, Mich., most of the missing documents, and added hundreds not in the original collection. A smaller collection, covering the years 1778–79, is in the Lib. of the Am. Philos. Soc., Philadelphia, see *Calendar of the Correspondence Relating to the Am. Revolution of Brig.-Gen. George Weedon, . . . and Maj.-Gen. Nathanael Greene* (1900). Others are in the Lib. of Cong. and the private collection of Lloyd W. Smith of Morristown, N. J. Some of his letters are published in *R. I. Hist. Soc. Colls.*, VI (1867); *Year Book 1899, City of Charleston, S. C.* (1900), App.; Jared Sparks, *Correspondence of the Am. Revolution* (4 vols., 1853); *Sou. Hist. Asso. Pubs.*, XI, 186–207, May 1907. See also Jared Sparks, *The Writings of George Washington* (12 vols., 1834–37); W. C. Ford, *The Writings of George Washington* (14 vols., 1889–93); *Jours. of the Continental Cong., 1774–1789*, vols. I–XXVII (1904–28); E. C. Burnett, *Letters of Members of the Continental Cong.* (4 vols., 1921–28); Peter Force, *Am. Archives*, 4 ser., vol. VI (1846); 5 ser., vols. I–III (1848–53); H. B. Carrington, *Battles of the Am. Revolution* (1876); C. H. Van Tyne, *The War of Independence* (1929). The dates of Greene's birth and death are established in *The Remains of Maj.-Gen. Nathanael Greene* (1903). For genealogical information, see G. S. Greene and Louise B. Clarke, *The Greenes of R. I.* (1903).] R. G. A—s.

GREENE, NATHANIEL (May 20, 1797–Nov. 29, 1877), translator, editor, and politician, was born in Boscawen, N. H., a descendant of John Greene, one of the founders of Warwick, R. I. (see William Greene, 1695/96–1758), and the son of Nathaniel and Ruth (Fowler) Greene. He was christened Peter, but in early manhood took the name of his father by authority of the Massachusetts legislature. His father died in 1812, leaving the family in meager circumstances. A memoir of Franklin had already decided the boy's career, and at the age of twelve he had walked to Concord and become an apprentice in the office of the *New Hampshire Patriot*, edited by Isaac Hill [*q.v.*]. Chiefly by persistent reading and his practise as a printer, he obtained an education. Connections followed with the *Concord Gazette*, the *New Hampshire Gazette* published at Portsmouth, and the *Merrimack Intelligencer*, published at Haverhill, Mass., where, when he was about twenty, he set up for himself with the *Essex Patriot*. In the winter of 1817–18 he was married to Susan Batchelder, daughter of Rev. William Batchelder. His ability and enterprise were noticed in Boston, and a group of Democratic politicians, headed by David Henshaw, the principal party organizer in the state, invited him to establish the *American Statesman* (later the *Boston Statesman*) in that city. The first number appeared on Feb. 6, 1821. For many years thereafter Greene played an important rôle in the politics of the city and the state. The Henshaw and Theodore Lyman factions of the party were rivals for patronage favors and in the end the more aristocratic faction lost. Having shrewdly promoted the interests of Andrew Jackson throughout the administration of John Quincy Adams, Greene reaped a substantial reward in his appointment as postmaster at Boston, an office which he held from 1829 to 1841 to the general approbation of the public, and again from 1844 to 1849 by designation of President Tyler. In August 1831 the *Statesman* ceased to be the party organ and the *Morning Post*, managed by Greene's younger brother, Charles G. Greene, superseded it. For a time the *Statesman* was issued as the weekly edition of the *Post*. Meanwhile Greene had been cultivating his knack as a linguist, acquiring a working knowledge of French, Italian, and German. In 1836 he published a translation of Luigi Sforzozi's *History of Italy*; and the following year, two volumes of *Tales from the German* of K. F. van der Velde. The latter translation was praised by W. H. Prescott in the *North American Review* (January 1838) for its spirit and fluency and the fact that certain passages had been modified to be acceptable to "our severer standard of morals." With his translation of *The People's Own Book* (1839), he is said to have introduced the French reformer, H. F. Robert de Lamennais, to American readers. In 1843 he issued a collection, *Tales and Sketches: From the Italian, French, and German.* With the end of his postmastership he retired from public life and went abroad for a long period, living much of the time in Paris, writing verse under the name "Boscawen," sending correspondence to Boston papers, and doing other literary work. A volume, *Improvisations and Translations*, the contents of which had originally appeared in the *Boston Post*, was published in 1852. He returned to Boston some years before his death and lived quietly and almost unknown at the Coolidge House in Bowdoin Square.

[C. G. Coffin, *The Hist. of Boscawen and Webster* (1878); G. W. Chase, *The Hist. of Haverhill, Mass.* (1861); A. B. Darling, *Political Changes in Mass., 1824–48* (1925); *U. S. Mag. and Dem. Rev.*, Nov. 1847; G. S. Greene and Louise B. Clarke, *The Greenes of R. I.* (1903); obituaries in *Boston Transcript*, Nov. 30, *Boston Globe* and *Boston Post*, Dec. 1, 1877, of which the last mentioned is the best.] F. L. B.

GREENE, SAMUEL DANA (Feb. 11, 1840–Dec. 11, 1884), naval officer, was born at Cumberland, Md., of New England parentage. His father, Gen. George Sears Greene [*q.v.*], was a native of Rhode Island; his mother, Martha Barrett Dana, of Charlestown, Mass. On Sept. 21, 1855, he entered the navy as an "acting midshipman on probation at the Naval Academy" and graduated in 1859, seventh in a class of twenty which included Alfred T. Mahan [*q.v.*]. Promoted midshipman and ordered to the *Hartford* on his graduation, he served on that ship in the East Indies and did not return home until after the outbreak of the Civil War and after his promotion to a lieutenancy on Aug. 31, 1861.

Greene's claim to fame is based upon his connection with the *Monitor,* the first Federal ironclad and one of the most celebrated vessels of modern times. During her career of a little less than a year he served as her only executive officer, under five different commanders; he stood on her deck when she was launched and left it a few minutes before she sank. In the early part of her engagement at Hampton Roads with the *Merrimac* on Mar. 9, 1862, Greene, then twenty-two years of age, had charge of the turret and also of the guns, every one of which he pointed and fired until he took command of the vessel when Lieut. J. L. Worden [*q.v.*], her commander, was wounded. On the retreat of the *Merrimac,* Greene, after firing a few parting shots at her, withdrew to the *Minnesota,* which he had orders to protect. The next day he was superseded as commander by a superior officer. He was subsequently criticized for permitting the *Merrimac* to escape. His conduct, however, was in accord with the orders of both President Lincoln and Assistant Secretary Fox, which confined the *Monitor* to a defensive rôle (W. C. Church, *The Life of John Ericsson,* 1890, I, 287). Worden recommended him to the department for advancement and commended him for the "great courage, coolness, and skill" with which he handled the guns, and for his earnest devotion to duty throughout the engagement (*Battles and Leaders,* I, 729).

Greene was with the *Monitor* when she moved up the James River in connection with McClellan's advance upon Richmond and participated in her hard-fought action against Fort Darling. He was also with her when she foundered off Hatteras on the night of Dec. 30–31, 1862. His meritorious conduct during this disaster was called to the attention of the Navy Department and of the commander-in-chief of the North Atlantic Blockading Squadron by his superior officer. In 1863–64 he was employed as executive officer of the *Florida* in chasing blockade-runners, and during the last year of the war in a similar capacity on the *Iroquois,* which was engaged in searching for Confederate commerce-destroyers. He was promoted lieutenant-commander from Aug. 11, 1865; and commander, from Dec. 12, 1872. For more than half of the period between 1866 and 1884 he was attached to the Naval Academy, serving, at different times, as instructor in mathematics, head of the department of astronomy, navigation, and surveying, assistant in charge of building and grounds, and senior aid to the superintendent. In 1868–71 he saw service with the Pacific Squadron. He commanded the *Juniata* of the European station, 1875–76; the training ship *Monongahela,* 1876–77; and the *Despatch* on special service, 1882–84.

His death, which was by his own hand, occurred at the Portsmouth navy-yard where he was stationed as executive officer. The cause assigned for this act was anxiety over an article on the engagement between the *Monitor* and *Merrimac* that he was preparing for publication. On Oct. 9, 1863, he was married to Mary Willis Dearth of Bristol, R. I., who died in 1874. The eldest of the three children born of this marriage, Samuel Dana Greene, Jr. (1864–1900), entered the Naval Academy and graduated in 1883 at the head of his class. On Nov. 8, 1876, Greene married Mary Abby Babbitt, also of Bristol. He was a brother of Gen. Francis Vinton Greene [*q.v.*], George S. Greene, Jr. [*q.v.*], and Maj. Charles T. Greene.

[Sources include Record of Officers, Bureau of Navigation, 1846–88; Navy Register, 1855–85; *Official Records (Navy)*, 1 ser., vols. VII–IX; Greene's paper, "In the 'Monitor' Turret," published in the *Century Mag.*, Mar. 1885, and included in *Battles and Leaders of the Civil War* (1887), I, 719–29. See also G. S. Greene and Louise B. Clarke, *The Greenes of R. I.* (1903); *Proc. U. S. Naval Inst.*, vol. XI (1885), vol. XLIX (1923); *Concord Evening Monitor,* Dec. 12, 1884.] C. O. P.

GREENE, SAMUEL STILLMAN (May 3, 1810–Jan. 24, 1883), educator, author of textbooks, the eighth of eleven children of Ebenezer and Sybil (Hitchcock) Greene, was born and passed his boyhood on his father's farm in Belchertown, Mass. He was descended from Thomas Green, who came to America about 1635 and in 1651 was a resident of Malden, Mass. Samuel's parents, educated in Leicester Academy, a school of high rank in Massachusetts, gave their children an endowment of rugged health and mental energy. The household had, in Samuel's childhood, a touch of pedagogical atmosphere. His father, known as "Master" Greene, taught the district school, and an older brother, Rev. John Greene, kept a private school. At an early age Samuel showed a fondness for study, and mastered without aid, according to family tradition, a Latin grammar, Pike's *Arithmetic,* and a geometry. He attended brief terms of district school and spent one winter under his brother's instruction. At nineteen he was employed to teach a district school in his native town. For his services he was "boarded 'round" and the sum of ten dollars a month was paid to his father, because Samuel was under age. He entered Brown University in 1833, paying his expenses by teaching school, and was graduated with the degree of A.B. in 1837, valedictorian of his class. After graduation he taught for three years in Worcester Academy, and on Aug. 29, 1839, was married to Edna Amelia Bartlett of Worcester. In 1840 he was appointed superintendent of public schools in Springfield, Mass., the first position of its kind in the state. From 1842 to 1849 he taught in the public schools in Boston, first in the English High School, and for five years as master of the Phillips Grammar School. In 1849 he assumed the duties of another pioneer post as agent of the Massachusetts State Board of Education, the first office of the kind in the United States. He was a contemporary and associate of Horace Mann [*q.v.*].

In 1851 he became superintendent of schools of Providence, R. I., and at the same time held the position of professor of didactics at Brown University. In 1852, with others, he opened a private normal school in Providence, which in 1853 was given support by the city and in 1854 taken over by the state, as the Rhode Island Normal School, now Rhode Island College of Education. Greene was regarded as the founder of this institution. His wife had died in 1851, and on Aug. 10, 1854, he married Mary Adeline Bailey of Salem, Mass.

In 1855 he was appointed professor of mathematics and civil engineering at Brown University, in 1864 transferred to the chair of natural philosophy and astronomy, and in 1875 transferred again, to the chair of mathematics and astronomy. Although identified with Brown University for more than thirty years, he continued to be actively interested in the problems of elementary education. He was president of the Rhode Island Institute of Instruction, 1856–60, president of the National Teachers' Association, 1864–65, and president of the American Institute of Instruction, 1869–70. His progressive ideas regarding teaching were embodied in text-books which made his name a household word. Published, for the most part, between 1848 and 1878, they sold at an average rate of 50,000 copies a year. Among the best known were: *Greene's Analysis: A Treatise on the Structure of the English Language* (1848), revised and enlarged as *An Analysis of the English Language* (1874); *Greene's First Lessons in Grammar* (1848); *The Elements of English Grammar* (1853), an abridgment of which was published with the title: *Greene's Introduction: An Introduction to the Study of English Grammar* in 1856; *A Grammar of the English Language* (1867); and *An Introduction to the Study of English Grammar* (1868), not to be confused with the earlier work issued under a similar title. He also prepared and published, in 1858, *A Genealogical Sketch of the Descendants of Thomas Green[e] of Malden, Mass.* He died in his seventy-third year.

[Greene's *Geneal. Sketch,* mentioned above; Reuben Guild, "Sketch of the Life of Prof. Samuel S. Greene," in *Baptist Quart. Rev.,* Apr.–June, 1883; T. W. Bicknell, *A Hist. of the R. I. Normal School* (1911); T. B. Stockwell, *A Hist. of Pub. Educ. in R. I.* (1876); *Hist. Cat. Brown Univ.* (1905); *Fifty-fourth Ann. Meeting, Am. Inst. of Instruction, 1883* (1884); *Jour. of Educ.,* Feb. 8, 1883; *Brunonian,* Jan. 27, 1883; *Providence Jour.,* Jan. 25, 26, 1883; records in the possession of R. I. Coll. of Educ.; letters, etc., the property of Greene's daughter, Mrs. R. B. Comstock of Providence.]

J. L. A.

GREENE, WILLIAM (Mar. 16, 1695/96–February 1758), colonial governor of Rhode Island, was the son of Samuel and Mary (Gorton) Greene and a great-grandson of John Greene, founder of the family in America. The latter, a son of Richard Greene of "Bowridge Hill," Dorset, England, was by calling a surgeon, and in 1635 emigrated from Salisbury in Wiltshire to Massachusetts. He settled first at Salem, but in 1637 moved to Providence, where he became one of the original proprietors. He assisted in the founding of the town of Warwick, and at various times represented it in the Rhode Island General Assembly. His son John was deputy-governor of Rhode Island from 1690 to 1700, and his son Samuel, father of William, was at various times between 1704 and 1719 a deputy in the Assembly. William's mother, Mary, was a grand-daughter of Samuel Gorton [*q.v.*].

William Greene was a practical surveyor, and in 1728, 1736, and 1741 aided in fixing the line between Rhode Island and Connecticut. On July 15, 1740, he was elected deputy-governor of the colony and served until May 1743, when he became governor, succeeding Richard Ward [*q.v.*]. During the period of his incumbency the struggle between France and Great Britain for North America was at its height. Governor Shirley of Massachusetts and Admiral Sir Peter Warren, commander of the British naval forces in American waters, both complained to Greene that Rhode Island was not contributing its share of men and money (*Correspondence,* I, 324, 420; *Records,* V, 183, 186), but Greene replied, with truth, that Rhode Island, despite its slender population (three thousand men capable of bearing arms), had cheerfully ordered three hundred able-bodied soldiers to be sent to join His Majesty's land forces, as also one hundred seamen in the sloop *Tartar* to join the naval forces (letter to Warren, July 1746, *Records,* V, 183–85). Writing to the colonial agent in London he commented further, "our Small Government have got their Men Ready much Sooner than the Massachusetts and a Greator proportion not withstanding they so often Complain of us" (*Correspondence,* II, 2). Nevertheless, he was compelled to hearken to the just reproach of the British Admiralty that Rhode Islanders were carrying on illicit trade with the enemy under cover of flags of truce. In May 1745 Greene was succeeded in the governorship by Gideon Wanton, but he again held office in 1746–47 and from 1748 to 1755. In the boundary dispute with Massachusetts, 1746–47, he stood resolutely for the interests of Rhode Island and secured the cession to it of the towns of Cumberland, Warren, Bristol, Little Compton, and Tiverton, a territory claimed by Massachusetts but covered by the original Rhode Island charter of 1663. Greene's third term was marked by a contest over paper money in which, supported by the Newport merchants, he vigorously opposed the further emission of bills of credit as "unjust and unreasonable," dangerous to trade, unfair to creditors, and likely to lead to the forfeiture of the colonial charter (*Correspondence,* II, 116–29), although, at the direction of the Assembly, he later instructed the agent in London to use every effort to prevent the passage of an act by Parliament prohibiting the issue of bills by the Colony (*Ibid.,* II, 134–35). Opposition to the control of the government by the Newport faction had been growing for some time, and in 1755 Greene was defeated for the governorship by Stephen Hopkins [*q.v.*] of Providence. In 1757, however, he was reelected, but he died early in the next year, at Warwick.

Greene was married on Dec. 30, 1719, to his second cousin, Catharine Greene, great-granddaughter of the first John Greene and daughter of Benjamin Greene, familiarly called "Tobacco Ben." On her mother's side she was a granddaughter of Randall Holden. She bore her husband six children, of whom one son, William [*q.v.*], became the second governor of the State of Rhode Island.

[See S. G. Arnold, *Hist. of the State of R. I. and Providence Plantations* (2 vols., 1859–60); Edward Field, *State of R. I. and Providence Plantations* (3 vols., 1902); G. S. Greene and Louise B. Clarke, *The Greenes of R. I.* (1903); J. R. Bartlett, *Records of the Colony of R. I.*, vols. IV and V (1859, 1860); *The Correspondence of the Colonial Governors of R. I., 1725–75* (2 vols., 1902), ed. by Gertrude S. Kimball. The date of Greene's death is given variously as Feb. 22, 23, and 25, 1758.]

I. B. R.

GREENE, WILLIAM (Aug. 16, 1731–Nov. 29, 1809), second governor of the State of Rhode Island, was born at Warwick, R. I., one of the six children of Gov. William [*q.v.*] and Catharine (Greene) Greene. In 1758 he married his second cousin, Catharine Ray, daughter of Simon and Deborah (Greene) Ray of New Shoreham, Block Island. He was elected deputy from Warwick to the Rhode Island General Assembly in 1773, 1774, 1776, and 1777. In May 1776 when Rhode Island proclaimed its independence of Great Britain, he was one of the signers of the declaration. On July 18, 1776, the Declaration of Independence by the Continental Congress having meanwhile been proclaimed, Greene was appointed one of a committee to visit certain persons suspected of treason and demand papers relating to disputes between the Independent States of America and Great Britain. The same year he was made first associate justice of the superior court of Rhode Island and in February 1777 became chief justice. On Dec. 10, 1776, and again in 1777 he was appointed a member of the Council of War. In May 1777 he was made speaker of the Rhode Island House of Deputies. In December of that year, in response to the recommendation of Congress that the states name commissioners to meet at New Haven to regulate prices of commodities, William Greene and Jabez Bowen were named commissioners from Rhode Island. In May 1778 Greene was elected governor to succeed Nicholas Cooke, and served eight successive years. It is said that while he was governor he was accustomed, during the sessions of the Assembly, to walk from Warwick to Providence (more than ten miles) every morning and home again in the afternoon.

In October 1778, distress in Rhode Island from want of provisions was so extreme that by request of the Assembly, Governor Greene wrote to the General Assembly of Connecticut, asking that the embargo on exportation of provisions might be so far modified as to permit their entry into Rhode Island. In January 1779 he sent similar pleas to the delegates in Congress, to Connecticut, and to Governor Clinton of New York. In October of that year he protested against the Massachusetts embargo on foodstuffs.

Greene showed liberality toward British sympathizers in Rhode Island, forbidding their molestation after the withdrawal of the enemy. In 1779 the manuscript records of the Town of

Newport were seized by the British and afterwards lost. The Governor complained of the matter to General Washington, who lent his aid, and the records were recovered. In 1780, on the occasion of the battle of Springfield, N. J., Washington wrote to Greene highly commending the Rhode Island troops who had sustained the brunt of the attack. In July of that year the French fleet under Admiral De Ternay, bringing six thousand troops under the command of the Count De Rochambeau, arrived at Newport, whereupon the Governor convened the Assembly, and addresses of welcome to the French general and admiral were prepared, and arrangements were made for a public dinner to be given at a future day to all the French officers. In 1782, Rhode Island withstood the impost act passed by Congress, a course which in 1783 brought from Congress a new impost, which had, in the main, the approval of the delegates Arnold and Collins. In 1786 Greene was succeeded as governor by John Collins [*q.v.*], leader of the paper-money party, and retired to Warwick. In 1796 he was an unsuccessful candidate for Congress, and in 1802 he was nominated for the governorship by the Federalists against Arthur Fenner [*q.v.*], a Republican, but was again defeated. He died at Warwick in his seventy-ninth year. Ray Greene, the oldest of his four children, was a United States senator from 1797 to 1801.

[S. G. Arnold, *Hist. of the State of R. I.*, vol. II (1860); Edward Field, *State of R. I. and Providence Plantations* (3 vols., 1902); G. S. Greene and Louise B. Clarke, *The Greenes of R. I.* (1903); *Records of the Colony of R. I.*, vol. VII (1862); *Records of the State of R. I.*, vols. VIII–X (1863–65); obituary in *Providence Gazette*, Dec. 2, 1809.] I. B. R.

GREENE, WILLIAM CORNELL (1851–Aug. 5, 1911), mining promoter, was born at Chappaqua, Westchester County, N. Y. His restless temperament showed itself early and sent him, still in his teens, westward in quest of adventure. He spent some desultory years as a government contractor in Kansas and then in Colorado, and in 1877 became a cowpuncher on the frontier rim of Arizona, finding at length the adventure he had sought in repelling the raids of the Apache Indians and the depredations of cattle rustlers. Because of his skill in improvising a volunteer force for these expeditions and his exploits at their head the title he acquired of "Colonel Bill" became the symbol of a far-spread border reputation for prowess. Since, however, cowpunching offered more adventure than profit, Greene prospected for a mine in the Bradshaw Mountains and when the boom came to Tombstone, Ariz., at the turn of the decade he went there and worked as a miner. After the boom he married and bought a small ranch in the San Pedro Valley near Hereford. In the nineties he became convinced that a fine tract of grazing land in the state of Sonora, known as La Cananea, contained mineral deposits. He filed mining claims and, with the aid of some Arizona capital, obtained possession of this land, which at the time an American syndicate was using for ranching. On May 26, 1899, he formed the Cobre Grande Copper Company and succeeded in selling a block of 31,000 shares of its stock to J. H. Costello, a Pennsylvania capitalist, who was placed in charge of operations. Several months later Greene ousted Costello by means of a Mexican court order, and formed a new company, the Cananea Consolidated Copper Company, a Mexican corporation, to which he transferred the property. He then persuaded a group headed by Thomas W. Lawson [*q.v.*], who at that time was organizing the Amalgamated Copper Company, to give him financial backing. Lawson was to honor drafts by Greene on short-term notes up to $1,000,000 for the development of the property, and was to receive in return an option on a controlling block of shares in the newly formed Greene Consolidated Copper Company, at one-third of par. It was Greene's contention later that Lawson, after honoring drafts for $135,000, refused to honor any more and called in the outstanding notes. Greene narrowly avoided losing his property, and the experience embittered him against Lawson and against the Eastern money power which the latter symbolized. In 1900 Greene moved to New York with his second wife, Mary Proctor, and set up his offices in Wall Street somewhat in the grand manner. With a capacity to persuade such Wall Street leaders as Gates, Hawley, Huntington, and Weir to sit on his boards of directors he combined a knowledge of promoting methods which would appeal to the small investor. His talent for writing prospectuses amounted to genius. For several years his fortunes prospered. In 1903 the Gates-Hawley interests made a systematic attack on Greene Consolidated stock, but Greene withstood the onslaught and several months later copper ore estimated at $100,000,000 was discovered on his properties. He immediately extended his corporate organization and in 1904 formed additional companies to capitalize the Cananea bonanza—the Greene Gold-Silver Company and the Greene Consolidated Gold Company. He bought a large section of Sonora for cattle ranching; bought mines and holdings in the Sierra Madre Mountains, organizing the Sierra Madre Land & Lumber Company; secured control of a railroad tapping the Sierra

Madre holdings, and built one to his Cananea holdings. At about this time the Cananea mining camp was producing copper to the value of $10,000,000 a year.

At the height of his prosperity, Greene was at the head of companies with a capitalization of $100,000,000, of which it was estimated that his personal holdings amounted to something less than half. In the general decline of stock values during the "Lawson panic" of 1904 he was severely affected, however, since he had been speculating heavily in the securities of his companies. In addition to the general effect of market conditions it seems clear that in several quarters in Wall Street there were groups who were not unwilling to aid in his fall, although his own belief that there was an organized conspiracy of Eastern financiers bent on defeating him, an impetuous Westerner untrained in the artifices of the Stock Exchange, seems too laborious an interpretation of the situation. His aggressiveness and the informality of an outsider which characterized his actions, while they had won him support at first, finally invited attack. He carried over into Wall Street the Wild-West characteristics of bluff heartiness, braggadocio, and gun-toting which he had found effective in Arizona, where he had once shot a man on the street whom he suspected of having done him an injury. A remark that Lawson had made about him in his articles in *Everybody's* entitled "Frenzied Finance" precipitated a sequence of accusation and recrimination carried on through paid advertisements in the newspapers, in which each spared no epithets and even threatened personal violence when he should meet the other. Greene's border reputation as a gunfighter made Wall Street uneasy for the safety of Lawson, but an actual meeting of the two in Boston was anticlimactic and resulted in reconciliation.

Greene's financial situation, however, responded neither to bluster nor reconciliation. His fall, once begun, was extremely rapid. A group intent upon getting control of the Cananea properties did its best to keep him from repairing his losses by borrowing. Finally in 1906, he capitulated to Thomas F. Cole, John D. Ryan, and the Amalgamated Copper interests, which had already acquired the Cananea Central mine. The result was the formation of the Greene-Cananea Consolidated Copper Company, with an authorized capitalization of $60,000,000, the Greene stock being exchanged for the new at 1 : 1½ shares. Greene was to remain the head of the new company, but within three months after its formation he was divested of all actual power, and in February 1907 he was dropped from the board of directors. The panic of 1907 disposed of most of the rest of his fortune. He made a trip to Japan in a last effort to obtain new capital but failed and returned to Cananea. He was still the owner of several large Mexican cattle ranches and in managing them he spent the last years of his life. He died at Cananea.

[J. H. McClintock, *Arizona* (3 vols., 1916), II, 603–05; *Who's Who in America*, 1910–11; *Engineering and Mining Jour.*, June 9, 16, Oct. 6, Dec. 22, 1906, Jan. 5, Feb. 23, 1907, Aug. 19, 1911; *N. Y. Times*, *N. Y. Tribune*, Aug. 6, 1911.]

M. L.

GREENER, RICHARD THEODORE (Jan. 30, 1844–May 2, 1922), educator, lawyer, the first person of African descent to receive a degree from Harvard College, was the son of Richard Wesley Greener and Mary Ann Le Brun. He was born in Philadelphia, but moved to Boston when he was five years old. He attended a grammar school in Cambridge, prepared for college at Oberlin, and Phillips Academy, Andover, Mass., and entered Harvard. Graduating in 1870 at the age of twenty-six, he began his career as the principal of the male department of the Institute for Colored Youth in Philadelphia. After remaining two years in this position, he served as a principal of the Summer High School of Washington, D. C., for part of a year, then entered the office of the United States attorney for the District of Columbia. For a while in 1873 he was an associate editor of the *New National Era* of Washington, but in that year accepted the chair of mental and moral philosophy and logic in the University of South Carolina, which he held until 1877, when the Wade Hampton legislature closed the door of the institution to members of his race. On Sept. 24, 1874, he was married to Genevieve Ida Fleet, by whom he had seven children. Greener assisted with the instruction in Latin, Greek, international law, and constitutional history of the United States, and in 1875 was university librarian. He also served on the commission to reconstruct the school system of the state, completed the law course of the University of South Carolina, and took an active part in politics, although he never sought election to any office. He was admitted to the bar in South Carolina in 1876 and in the District of Columbia the following year. In 1877 he became an instructor in the law department of Howard University, and dean in 1879. In 1880 he gave up his deanship to become a law clerk in the office of the first comptroller of the United States Treasury, but served in this capacity only two years. In 1882 he settled down to practise law in the District of Columbia.

Greener came into prominence as a leader of

his race in 1879 when he took issue with Frederick Douglass [*q.v.*], who was advising the restless freedmen in the South not to migrate to the West, but to remain where they were, that in their large numbers they might some day wield political power. Greener, insisting that migration would be a remedy for the disorders of the South, urged the freedmen to go West and take up fertile land. He considered it a promising sign, too, that the negro had learned to flee from persecution. (See articles by Douglass and Greener in *Journal of Social Science,* May 1880.) By 1884 he had become a prominent figure in politics, having participated in several national campaigns as a Republican. In 1885 he was appointed secretary of the Grant Memorial Association in the State of New York, and a few months later Mayor Grace of New York City appointed him chief examiner of the municipal civil-service board, which office he held until 1890. He later served as consul at Bombay, India, and in 1898 was appointed United States commercial agent at Vladivostok, Siberia. He retired from foreign service in 1905, and thereafter made his home in Chicago until his death. Greener was a fluent speaker. He did not take rank with John M. Langston and Frederick Douglass, but there were few others of his race who could compete with him in forceful and logical presentation of facts. He published no extensive works, but his well-prepared lectures and addresses covered a wide range, embracing almost every aspect of local and national life as it influenced the status of the freedmen.

[W. J. Simmons, *Men of Mark* (1887); C. G. Woodson, *A Century of Negro Migration* (1918), pp. 138–40; A. A. Taylor, *The Negro in S. C. During the Reconstruction* (1924), p. 104; *Tenth Report of the Class of 1870 of Harvard Coll., Fiftieth Anniv.* (1920); *Who's Who of the Colored Race* (1915); *Who's Who in America,* 1910–11; *Chicago Daily Tribune,* May 4, 1922.] C. G. W.

GREENHALGE, FREDERIC THOMAS (July 19, 1842–Mar. 5, 1896), congressman, governor of Massachusetts, was born in Clitheroe, Lancashire, England, the only son among the seven children of William and Jane (Slater) Greenhalgh. His father, who was a cloth printer, emigrated to Lowell, Mass., in 1855, to take charge of the printing department in the Merrimack Manufacturing Company. Shortly after his arrival, he changed the spelling of his name to Greenhalge. Frederic, after making a good record in the Lowell public schools, entered Harvard College in 1859. Because of financial difficulties and the illness of his father, he was obliged to withdraw at the close of his junior year; but he was awarded his degree by Harvard in 1870, "as of the class of 1862." After some experience as a tutor and as a teacher in a small school in Chelmsford (near Lowell), he was accepted in March 1862 as a law student in the office of Brown & Alger. His studies were interrupted by a few months of service with the Commissary Department in the Union army, but ill health prevented his being given a commission, and he returned home, convalescing from malaria, in April 1864. In 1865, he was admitted to the Middlesex bar and soon afterwards formed the law firm of Howe & Greenhalge.

His political career began with his election in 1868 to the Lowell Common Council. In 1872–73 he was a member of the school board; he was justice of the police court from 1874 to 1884; and served two terms, 1880–81, as mayor of Lowell. He was an unsuccessful candidate for the state Senate in 1872, and was a delegate to the Republican National Convention in 1884. In 1885 he served in the Massachusetts legislature but was defeated for reëlection. In the autumn of 1888, he was chosen as representative from the 8th district to the Fifty-first Congress, in which he was a member of the committee on the civil service, the committee on elections, and the committee on revision of the laws. Although he showed much ability as a debater and was renominated by his party, he was defeated for a second term.

At the state Republican convention, Oct. 8, 1893, Greenhalge was nominated for governor by acclamation, and in the election was victorious by a majority of more than 35,000 over his Democratic opponent, John E. Russell. He was subsequently elected by large majorities for two additional terms, in 1894 and 1895. In the gubernatorial chair he showed himself fearless and independent, gaining the respect of the people by his intelligent vetoes. On Feb. 20, 1894, when a mob of more than five thousand unemployed marched from a mass meeting on Boston Common to the State House, he made an effective speech in which he promised to aid them, and afterwards, when threatened by Morrison I. Swift, their leader, showed such firmness and courage that Swift became "noticeably less belligerent" (*Boston Transcript,* Mar. 5, 1896). He wore himself out by over-conscientiousness in attending to his official duties, and died of a disease of the kidneys while still in office.

He was married in 1872 to Isabel Nesmith, daughter of John Nesmith, former lieutenant-governor of Massachusetts; they had four children. Greenhalge was a trustee of the Rogers Hall School, Westford Academy, and the Lowell General Hospital, as well as trustee and president of the Lowell Savings Bank. He was an alert and active man, fond of outdoor life, especially walking, and he greatly enjoyed his summer home at Kennebunkport, Me. That he had no small literary gift is evidenced by some of the poems printed after his death in his biography. Socially he was very attractive, although he never failed to maintain his dignity. Politically, he matured rather slowly, but he grew steadily in prestige and influence, and he was never more highly regarded by men of both parties than at the time of his death.

[J. E. Nesmith, *The Life and Work of Frederic Thomas Greenhalge, Gov. of Mass.* (1897) is the official biography and presents a full, if somewhat eulogistic, account of his career. See also *Representative Men of Mass.* (1898); and obituary in the *Boston Transcript,* Mar. 5, 1896. An excellent bust of Greenhalge, in marble, by Samuel Kitson, was presented to the state by citizens of Lowell.] C. M. F.

GREENHOW, ROBERT (b. 1800–Mar. 27, 1854), physician, scientist, linguist, historian, was born in Richmond, Va., son of Robert Greenhow, who was a son of John Greenhow, merchant of Williamsburg, and an immigrant from England. His mother was Mary Ann Wills Greenhow, who lost her life in the Richmond theatre fire in 1811. Robert was graduated in 1816 from the College of William and Mary after which he studied medicine in New York City under David Hosack [*q.v.*], and his distinguished pupil, John W. Francis [*q.v.*], receiving his M.D. degree at the College of Physicians and Surgeons, New York, in 1821. He then completed his medical education in Paris, making the acquaintance in Europe of many famous men including Lord Byron. He ostensibly practised medicine in New York City from 1825 to 1828 and also lectured on chemistry before a New York literary and scientific society. In 1828 he was appointed translator to the Department of State at Washington, where he remained until 1850 when he removed to California. In August 1852 he was appointed law officer to the United States land commission in California and two years later died in San Francisco from injuries received in a fall. His wife was Rose O'Neil Greenhow of Washington, D. C., an alleged Confederate spy during the Civil War, who with four daughters survived him.

Greenhow excelled as a linguist, being especially proficient in French and Spanish. As translator for the state department it was his duty to become familiar with all documents bearing on special problems in America's foreign relations, which led him, in 1835, to prepare his first book, *The History and Present Condition of Tripoli.* In 1839, the Oregon question being in course of agitation in and out of Congress, he prepared at the request of Senator Lewis F. Linn [*q.v.*], head of a congressional committee on American claims to the Oregon Territory, a treatise on the geography and history of the Northwest coast of America which was published by order of Congress. Five years later that work was enlarged, partly rewritten, and published as *The History of Oregon and California.* It was brought out in London in 1844 and in America in 1844 and 1846. Greenhow also prepared a history of the Spanish colonies within the United States, which was privately printed in 1856. In 1848 he read before the New York Historical Society a critical paper on the supposed labors of Archbishop Fénelon among the Iroquois. He assembled bits of evidence from widely divergent sources, and, while recognizing their imperfection, thought they justified a belief that the celebrated Bishop of Cambray, in his youth, had actually spent some years in the wilds of North America. At a later time it was found that the Fénelon who was a missionary in America was the bishop's brother.

The authorship of the *History of Oregon and California* constitutes Greenhow's chief claim to consideration as a historian. It is a pioneer work, for which the materials had to be quarried from the original sources in the form of journals of explorers, who wrote in Spanish, French, and English; the diplomatic acts and correspondence of various nations, and a wide range of literary and historical works. Greenhow was devoted to the source method of study, refusing to accept the statement of a secondary writer where a first-hand witness could be found, and making a careful independent translation of such as were in languages other than English. He was violently attacked by Falconer for alleged unfairness to England in his discussion of the Oregon question, but the Englishman's argument was vitiated by innumerable errors due to faulty research as well as biased reasoning. On the whole, despite the circumstances of national partisanship under which the book was produced, it must be accounted a valuable compendium of authentic material on its subject. The style is pure, elevated, and has an epic swing, and the notes, which are numerous, supply much valuable information about the sources used. There are seventy-five pages of "Proofs and Illustrations" after the manner of Robertson's *America* and other substantial works.

[The biographical notices of Greenhow are meager and imperfect. New York directories prove his residence there as a physician. An obituary notice in the daily *Alta California*, Mar. 28, 1854, gives an account of his death and most of what is known of his life. Information as to certain facts has been supplied by Miss Mary T. Greenhow, Richmond, Va.] J. S.

GREENLEAF, BENJAMIN (Sept. 25, 1786–Oct. 29, 1864), educator, author of mathematical text-books, was born in Haverhill, Mass., a descendant of Edmund Greenleaf who came to America from England in 1635 and settled in what is now Newburyport, Mass. His parents were Caleb and Susanna (Emerson) Greenleaf, the latter born in Methuen, Mass., July 2, 1761, being the daughter of William and Abigail Emerson. Obliged to work upon his father's farm as a boy, he had so little schooling that at fourteen he did not know the multiplication table. Soon, however, an eagerness for knowledge dwarfed almost every other interest. He procured books wherever he could, and read them by fire-light and candle-light. "If ever I offered up an earnest prayer," he is reported to have said, "it was for rainy days, that I might betake myself to my books" (Barrows, *post*, p. 20). Not until he was nineteen did he begin to prepare for college. During the next five years he studied for a time at the academy in Atkinson, N. H., and taught school. In 1810 he entered the sophomore class of Dartmouth College where he distinguished himself in mathematics. After his graduation in 1813 he became principal of the grammar school in his native town, but the following year he was appointed preceptor of Bradford Academy, Bradford, Mass.

This school, which during the eleven years of its history had maintained a precarious existence under numerous principals, now became a popular and efficient institution. A man of originality and progressive tendencies, Greenleaf also displayed marked peculiarities. He was careless in his dress, and indifferent to the ordinary rules of politeness. Some portion of his body was always in motion, so nervous and restless was he; a fact that gave to his utterances a certain dramatic quality. He had long black hair which he braided behind into a queue. His discipline, according to a pupil, was "an odd mixture of ridicule, sarcasm, and moral suasion, with a wholesome seasoning of corporal punishment" (*Ibid.*, p. 29). When he inflicted the latter it was with whatever instrument was nearest at hand. His essential goodness and ability, however, caused him to be respected and liked, and made him eminently successful as a schoolmaster. He taught the classics faithfully, if not with enthusiasm: his interest was in mathematics and the natural sciences. After more than twenty years as preceptor, he resigned in 1836, and the academy became a school for girls.

His influence as an educator extended far beyond his classroom. He was among the first to give popular illustrated lectures on subjects in chemistry, physics, geology, and astronomy; and although he dispensed with such aids himself, his experience in teaching enabled him to prepare a series of text-books in arithmetic, algebra, geometry, and trigonometry, which had wide and long popularity. The earliest and perhaps the most famous of these, the *National Arithmetic,* appeared in 1836. In 1837, 1838, and 1839, he was a member of the Massachusetts legislature, where he advocated the establishment of normal schools, and was chairman of a committee that recommended geological and natural history surveys of the state, which were later made. In 1839 he founded and became the head of the Bradford Teachers' Seminary, which position he held until 1848. His later years were spent in work upon his text-books, in making calculations for almanacs, and in general activities in behalf of education. He was married, Nov. 20, 1821, to Lucretia Kimball, by whom he had nine children.

[Elizabeth A. Barrows, *A Memorial of Bradford Academy* (1870); *New-Eng. Hist. and Geneal. Reg.,* Jan. 1865; G. T. Chapman, *Sketches of the Alumni of Dartmouth Coll.* (1867); J. E. Greenleaf, *Geneal. of the Greenleaf Family* (1896); *New Eng. Mag.,* May 1903; J. M. Greenwood and Artemas Martin, "Notes on the Hist. of Am. Text-Books on Arithmetic," *House Doc. No. 5,* 55 Cong., 3 Sess., I, 835; obituary in *Boston Journal,* Oct. 31, 1864.] H. E. S.

GREENLEAF, HALBERT STEVENS (Apr. 12, 1827–Aug. 25, 1906), industrialist and public official, was born in Guilford, Vt., the son of Jeremiah and Elvira Eunice (Stevens) Greenleaf, and a descendant of Edmund Greenleaf who emigrated from Suffolk, England, to Massachusetts about 1635, settling at what is now Newburyport. Jeremiah Greenleaf (1791–1864) was a school-teacher and the author of several works well-known in their day, including *Grammar Simplified* (1820), which went through twenty-odd editions, *The Self-Taught Latinist* (1825), a *Family Gazetteer* (8th ed., 1843), and a *New Universal Atlas* (1840). Halbert received a common-school education, supplemented by some training in a local academy. From his nineteenth to his twenty-third year he taught school during the winter months, and during one season worked in a country brickyard. At twenty-three, he made a six months' sea voyage in the whaling ship *Lewis Bruce,* serving as a common sailor. Shortly after his return from the sea, he married on June 24, 1852, Jane Frances Brooks of Bernardston, Mass., and in September of that year settled at Shelburne Falls. After a few months as a day-laborer in a cutlery establishment, he went to work in the gimlet and bit manufactory of Sargent & Foster. The senior member of this firm, James Sargent, became his fast friend, and Greenleaf was made business manager and then a member of the firm. In the meantime he was commissioned a justice of the peace (March 1856), and became the captain of a local military company. In 1859 he went to Philadelphia to join the firm of Linus Yale, Jr., & Company which was engaged in the manufacture of locks, but in 1861 he returned to Shelburne Falls, and established the Yale & Greenleaf Lock Company of which he became business manager. He enlisted in the Union army in August 1862, as a private soldier, entering the 52nd Massachusetts Regiment. He was commissioned captain of Company E on Sept. 12, and a month later, Oct. 13, was unanimously elected colonel. He was soon afterwards ordered into service with Gen. Banks in the Department of the Gulf. Here he distinguished himself in several encounters, and bore a conspicuous part in the assault on Port Hudson and in the subsequent siege operations.

At the expiration of his term of service, he accepted the command of the government steamer *Colonel Benedict* on the lower Mississippi, and soon after the close of the war took charge of the extensive salt works on Petite Anse Isle, St. Mary's Parish, La. In 1867, at the invitation of James Sargent, who had invented a chronometer type of lock and had set up his business in Rochester, N. Y., in 1864, he became a member of the firm of Sargent & Greenleaf, in that city. The firm prospered, and made locks of all kinds during the rest of Greenleaf's life.

Greenleaf became active in politics fairly late in life. He stumped for Gen. Hancock in 1880, and organized a local marching club. In 1882 he was elected to Congress as a Democrat by a plurality of over 6,000 in a strongly Republican district. In 1884 he failed of reëlection, though he ran far ahead of his ticket. Again becoming a candidate in 1890, he was elected in the Democratic reaction of that year, but by a slender majority. He did not take much part in debate in his two terms in Congress, though in the first session of the Fifty-second Congress he made a cogent speech on the reduction of the wool duty (*Congressional Record,* 52 Cong., 1 Sess., pp. 2789–94). He interested himself in pensions, serving in the 48th Congress on the pension committee. His orientation on two major problems of a later period is shown by his votes for the creation of a committee on the alcoholic liquor traffic and for the creation of a committee on woman's suffrage. Mrs. Greenleaf was an ardent suffragist and a close friend of Susan B. Anthony. Greenleaf's last political campaign was for the mayoralty of Rochester in 1894. His opponent was George W. Aldridge, already rising into prominence as the Republican boss of Monroe County. Greenleaf made a good run, but in the last days of the fight the charge was made that he was a member of the A. P. A. (American Protective Association). He at once categorically denied any such connection, but the denial was of no avail, and this political canard had much to do with his defeat. In 1895 he was stricken with paralysis. He was able to pay some attention to his business, however, and lived eleven years longer, dying on Aug. 25, 1906, at Charlotte, N. Y.

[W. F. Peck, *Semi-Centennial Hist. of the City of Rochester* (1884), pp. 705–08; J. F. Moors, *Hist. of the Fifty-Second Regt. Mass. Vols.* (1893); J. E. Greenleaf, *Geneal. of the Greenleaf Family* (1896); for the mayoralty campaign of 1894, R. M. Gordon, "George W. Aldridge," MS. in the library of the Univ. of Rochester; obituary in Rochester *Democrat and Chronicle,* Aug. 26, 1906.]

D. P.

GREENLEAF, MOSES (Oct. 17, 1777–Mar. 20, 1834), map-maker and author, brother of Simon Greenleaf [*q.v.*] and eldest of the five children of Moses and Lydia (Parsons) Greenleaf, was born in Newburyport, Mass. In 1790, the family, long prominent in local affairs, moved to New Gloucester in the District of Maine. Here Moses attended the short-termed elementary school where he showed proficiency in mathematics and English. From 1799 to 1806 he kept a general store, first in New Gloucester and later in Bangor, then, this business proving unsuccesful, turned his attention to real estate, in which he had been interested for several years. Entering into a partnership agreement with William Dodd of Boston, owner of a township in Maine later called Williamsburg, he commenced in 1810 the actual settlement of the town in fulfilment of his contract by moving thither with his family. He had married Persis Poor of Andover, Me., Feb. 11, 1805. The remainder of his life was devoted to the task of procuring settlers for the interior of Maine. He surveyed roads; he located stone and mineral deposits; he secured a charter for the Piscataquis Canal & Railroad Company (1833); and, most important of all, through his publications he made his unrivaled knowledge of Maine's resources public property.

His *Map of the District of Maine from the Latest and Best Authorities* (1815) was a great improvement over previous maps, both in detail and in engraving. The volume accompanying it, *A Statistical View of the District of Maine; More Especially with Reference to the Value and Importance of the Interior: Addressed to the Consideration of the Legislators of Massachusetts* (1816), had a two-fold purpose: to give prospective purchasers of land information concerning the interior of Maine, and to give the legislators information and suggestions on which to base legislation affecting settlement and the welfare of settlers. The book created a feeling of optimism regarding the ability of the District to finance its own destinies, and was influential in promoting the separation of Maine from Massachusetts, a step which Greenleaf, though a Federalist, heartily approved. At the time of the separation in 1820, the plates of the 1815 map were brought up to date, and a new map issued. Greenleaf continued the collection of data, and in 1829 published the *Map of the State of Maine with the Province of New Brunswick* and its accompanying volume, *A Survey of the State of Maine, in reference to its Geographical Features, Statistics, and Political Economy.* The latter work, in most respects a development of the earlier volume, is one of the most important books relating to the history of the State of Maine. An atlas, containing six maps and a diagram, published at the same time to illustrate the book, is of value in the study of the northeastern boundary and the land grants in Maine. Notwithstanding generous legislative support of both ventures, Greenleaf lost money on his publications. He went on, however, with the collection of data, intending at the proper time to produce another map. In 1844, by correcting the plates of the 1829 map, his heirs carried out this intention as best they could. From 1812 to 1816, Greenleaf was justice of the peace for Hancock County and when Piscataquis County was organized in the latter year, he was appointed justice of its court of common pleas. He prepared a valuable treatise on Indian languages, published in 1824 in *The First Annual Report of the American Society for Promoting the Civilization and General Improvement of the Indian Tribes Within the United States.*

[E. C. Smith, *Moses Greenleaf, Maine's First Map-Maker* (1902), containing a short biography, documents, a bibliography of the maps of Maine, and a reprint of Greenleaf's treatise on Indian languages; Jonathan Greenleaf, *A Geneal. of the Greenleaf Family* (1854); J. E. Greenleaf, *Geneal. of the Greenleaf Family* (1896); discussion by Benjamin Rand of Greenleaf's *Statistical View,* in *North Am. Rev.,* Sept. 1816; *Eastern Argus* (Portland, Me.), Mar. 26, 1834.]

R. E. M.

GREENLEAF, SIMON (Dec. 5, 1783–Oct. 6, 1853), lawyer, author, brother of Moses Greenleaf [*q.v.*], was born at Newburyport, Mass., with which place his family had been connected for nearly a hundred and fifty years, his American ancestor, Edmund Greenleaf, originally of Ipswich, Suffolk, England, having settled there in 1635. His father, Moses Greenleaf, married Lydia, daughter of Rev. Jonathan Parsons of Newburyport, and resided in that town. In 1790, when Simon was seven years old, his parents moved to New Gloucester, Me., leaving him with his grandfather, Jonathan Parsons, to enjoy the superior educational facilities which Newburyport then provided. He attended the Latin School there, obtaining a thorough classical training, and when he was sixteen rejoined his parents at New Gloucester. In 1801 he entered the law office of Ezekiel Whitman [*q.v.*], later chief justice of Maine, and in June 1806 he was admitted to the Cumberland County bar. On Sept. 18 of the same year he married Hannah Kingman, daughter of Capt. Ezra Kingman of East Bridgewater, Mass.

He had commenced practise in Standish, a short distance from Portland, but six months later removed to Gray, where, being the only lawyer in the neighborhood, he enjoyed an extensive connection. The times, however, were not litigious and for a period of twelve years he devoted his leisure to an intensive study of the common law, reading widely and deeply, and obtaining a familiarity with the source material which no other practitioner of his time possessed. In 1818 he removed to Portland, whither his reputation for learning had preceded him, and at once took his place among the leaders of the bar there. On the establishment of the supreme judicial court, June 24, 1820, following the admission of Maine as a state, he was appointed reporter. As such he prepared and published *Reports of Cases Argued and Determined by the Supreme Judicial Court of the State of Maine,* vols. 1–9 (1820–32). Notable for their clear yet concise captions and admirable abstracts of the arguments, their accuracy has never been impugned, and they have always been highly valued by the profession. A second edition was called for shortly prior to Greenleaf's death. For some years before becoming reporter he had been engaged in compiling *A Collection of Cases Overruled, Denied, Doubted or Limited in their Application,* which he published in 1821. Concurrently with his court duties he continued in practise, being mainly engaged in counsel work, where his attractive personality, profound legal knowledge, and compelling logic made him particularly effective. His resignation in 1832 was prompted by a realization that his official duties prevented his giving adequate attention to his increasing retainers. In 1833, Justice Joseph Story [*q.v.*], Dane Professor of Law at Harvard, offered Greenleaf the Royall Professorship of Law at that institution, which had become vacant through the death of Ashmun, and he accepted. Removing to Cambridge, he was associated with Story in the law school for thirteen years, and on the death of the latter, succeeded him in the Dane Professorship. His health, however, gradually became seriously impaired, and he was compelled to resign in 1848, whereupon he was appointed emeritus professor.

To the efforts of Story and Greenleaf is to be ascribed the rise of the Harvard Law School to its eminent position among the legal schools of the United States. In temperament and intellect the two professors were essentially unlike. Story was quick, brilliant, picturesque; Greenleaf was deliberate, thorough, impressive. The former aroused enthusiasm, the latter evoked a desire for learning. "Story prepared the soil, and Greenleaf sowed the seed" (*Law Reporter*, November 1853, p. 414). Each was the antithesis and yet the complement of the other, and under their dual leadership, the school achieved a nation-wide reputation. As a lecturer, Greenleaf was systematic, meticulously exact, and practical, vouchsafing little indication of the wealth of learning from which his lectures were constructed. Giving freely of his time to the elucidation of their individual difficulties and assisting in their activities, he enjoyed the respect and confidence of his pupils in an extraordinary degree. While engaged in tutorial work he prepared what was originally intended as a textbook on evidence, published in 1842 as *A Treatise on the Law of Evidence.* The profession at once hailed it as the ablest extant work on the subject, distinguished alike for its deep learning, clarity of style, and practical utility. He added a second volume in 1846, and a third in 1853. In its completed form it came to be regarded as the foremost American authority, and passed through numerous editions under successive editors. After his retirement, Greenleaf's health improved, and in addition to completing his work on evidence he published *Cruise's Digest of the Law of Real Property, Revised and Abridged for the Use of American Students* (7 vols. in 5, 1849–50), which in the United States entirely superseded the English original.

Allied, politically, with the Federalist party, he was in 1816 an unsuccessful candidate in Cumberland County for the Massachusetts Senate, but was elected in 1820 to represent Portland in the first Maine legislature, where he took a leading part in framing the initial legislation of the new state. When his term expired he retired and thereafter had neither the time nor the inclination to participate actively in public life. In addition to the books already mentioned he was the author of *A Brief Inquiry into the Origin and Principles of Free Masonry* (1820); "A Brief Memoir of the Life and Character of the Hon. Prentiss Mellen, LL.D., late Chief Justice of Maine" (17 *Maine Reports,* 467); and *Examination of the Testimony of the Four Evangelists by the Rules of Evidence Administered in Courts of Justice, with an Account of the Trial of Jesus* (1846). He was a frequent contributor to periodicals, several of his articles being republished in pamphlet form, as were also his inaugural discourse as Royall Professor of Law in Harvard University (1834) and *A Discourse Commemorative of the Life and Character of the Hon. Joseph Story* (1845).

[J. E. Greenleaf, *Geneal. of the Greenleaf Family* (1896); Wm. Willis, *A Hist. of the Law, the Courts, and the Lawyers of Me.* (1863), p. 522; W. T. Davis, *Bench and Bar of the Commonwealth of Mass.* (1895); *Law Reporter,* Nov. 1853; *Boston Post,* Oct. 8, 1853.]

H. W. H. K.

GREENLEAF, THOMAS (1755–Sept. 14, 1798), printer, journalist, was born at Abington, Mass. A descendant of Edmund Greenleaf who settled at Newburyport, Mass., in 1635, he was the fourth child and second son of Joseph Greenleaf and Abigail Payne, youngest daughter of Rev. Thomas Payne. His father was a justice of the peace for Plymouth County, Mass., who had "some talents as a popular writer," which he devoted to the patriot cause by contributions to Isaiah Thomas's *Massachusetts Spy.* One of his papers brought him into special disfavor with the royalist government and caused his dismissal from office. In 1773 he purchased an outfit and established a printery in Boston, which was managed by his son who had been taught the printing art in the Boston shop of Isaiah Thomas. In the brief period before the war put an end to the business the Greenleaf printing-house issued a few pamphlets and volumes, and continued (July 1774–March 1775) the *Royal American Magazine, or Universal Repository of Instruction and Amusement,* which Isaiah Thomas had begun. In 1785 Thomas Greenleaf removed to New York City, where in September he became manager for Eleazer Oswald of the *New-York Journal, or the Weekly Register.* Greenleaf became owner of the paper on Jan. 18, 1787, and modified its title to the *New-York Journal, and Weekly Register.* On Nov. 19, 1787, it became a daily newspaper, with the title, *New-York Journal, and Daily Patriotic Register.* The last daily issue was July 26, 1788, and the coördinate weekly or country paper was continued from July 3, 1788, with a modified title, until May 4, 1790. After that date it became a semi-weekly, with title, *New-York Journal, & Patriotic Register,* under which it was published until Dec. 28, 1793 (vol. XLVII, no.

104), when it adopted the name, *Greenleaf's New-York Journal,* continuing as a semi-weekly. On Oct. 13, 1791, Greenleaf was married to Ritsana or Anna Quackenbos (1767–1845), a daughter of Johannes and Catherina DeWitt Quackenbos and a grand-niece of Gov. George Clinton. They had three daughters and a son. On May 11, 1795, Greenleaf established the *Argus, & Greenleaf's New Daily Advertiser.* He supported Aaron Burr's party against the Federalists, and did not spare even "the venerable Washington" from "a great degree of virulence" (Thomas, II, 119). In September 1798, during a devastating scourge of the yellow fever which was raging in New York City and Philadelphia, his apprentices forsook him and two-thirds of his customers fled the city. From "a too sedulous attention" to his duties, and already weakened by "a slow wasting consumption," he fell a victim to the disease and died on Sept. 14. An obituary in his own newspaper extolled him for his domestic, neighborly, and friendly virtues, and characterized him as "a warm friend to Civil and Religious Liberty, unawed by persecution or prosecution." "He loved his country; and, if at any time . . . he dipped his pen in gall, and exercised it with unusual severity," it was because he hated "political apostacy" and wanted "to preserve the Constitution from encroachment." In the judgment of Isaiah Thomas, he was "well acquainted with the business, enterprising, and amiable in manners" (*Ibid.,* II, 119–20).

His widow continued her husband's papers until Mar. 8, 1800, when the *Argus* came to an end and the *New-York Journal* was sold to David Denniston.

[Isaiah Thomas, *Hist. of Printing in America* (2nd ed., 1874), I, 174 and II, 119, faulty with respect to the history of Greenleaf's newspapers; C. S. Brigham, "Bibliography of American Newspapers," *Proc. Am. Antiq. Soc.,* XXVII (1917), 383 ff., 434 ff., 448 ff.; J. E. Greenleaf, *Geneal. of the Greenleaf Family* (1896), pp. 196–97; *The Quackenbush Family in Holland and America* (1909), pp. 89, 108, 143; obituary in *Greenleaf's New-York Journal, & Patriotic Register,* Sept. 16, 1798 (No. 4226), with the inner pages in mourning borders, copied with adjustments in the *Independent Chronicle: and the Universal Advertiser* (Boston), Sept. 20–24, 1798, and other newspapers.]

V. H. P.

GREENOUGH, HENRY (Oct. 5, 1807–Oct. 31, 1883), architect, painter, author, brother of Horatio and Richard Saltonstall Greenough [*qq.v.*], was born in Newburyport, Mass., the fifth of the eleven children of David and Betsey (Bender) Greenough. After attending George Barrell Emerson's school at Lancaster, he entered Harvard College in 1823 but left in his junior year because of his father's financial losses. During the next three years he helped manage the family properties, drew plans for several buildings, and was a teacher in Mr. Greene's School at Jamaica Plain. In 1829, through the influence of his friend Washington Allston [*q.v.*] he received the commission to design the Orthodox Church in Cambridge. His health declining, he sailed that autumn for Marseilles and joined his brother Horatio in Italy. For the next three and a half years he made his headquarters in Florence, studying painting under Prof. Bezzuoli at the Royal Academy of Fine Arts, with Thomas Cole, John Cranch, John Gore, and S. F. B. Morse among his fellow students. Returning to Boston in 1833, he reassumed the management of the family affairs and redeemed them, after his father's death in 1836, from an apparently hopeless confusion. On Mar. 18, 1837, he married Frances Boott, by whom he had two sons. In 1844, upon Allston's death, he was employed to clean and prepare for exhibition Allston's huge unfinished picture, "The Feast of Belshazzar." At the request of Richard Henry Dana, he wrote for the *Boston Post* (June 10, July 25, 1844) two notable articles on the coloring and composition of the picture. In 1845 he sailed with his wife and child for Italy and spent nearly five years in Southern Europe. During 1848–49 the Greenoughs saw much of Margaret Fuller, the Brownings, and their friends. They returned to Boston in July 1850, and Greenough was soon engaged in designing the Cambridgeport Athenæum. In 1852, working with Italian fresco painters whose temperament and language he thoroughly understood, he superintended the decoration of the Crystal Palace in New York. In *The Industry of All Nations: An Illustrated Weekly Record of the Crystal Palace Exhibition* (1853; numbers XI and XII), he explained his theories of decoration. During the rest of his life he designed many houses in Boston and Cambridge. He was so indiscreet as also to write and publish two novels, *Ernest Carroll* (1859) and *Apelles* (1860). The first deals with the life of art students in Florence; in the course of the story John Ruskin is burned in effigy, but otherwise the story is dull and choked with exposition. *Apelles* is even worse—ancient Greek life glimpsed through a Bowdlerizing fog of Boston romanticism.

[Frances Boott Greenough, *Letters of Horatio Greenough to his Brother Henry Greenough* (1887); *New-England Hist. and Geneal. Reg.,* Apr. 1863; *Vital Records of Cambridge, Mass.* (2 vols., 1914–15); *Harvard Quinquennial Cat. 1636–1915* (1915); *Louis Agassiz: His Life and Correspondence* (2 vols., 1885), ed. by Elizabeth C. Agassiz; L. L. Noble, *The Course of Empire . . . and Other Pictures of Thomas Cole* (1853); Geo. Carstensen and Chas. Gildermeister,

New York Crystal Palace (1854); Alexander McKenzie, *Lectures on . . . the First Church in Cambridge* (1873).] T. F. H.

GREENOUGH, HORATIO (Sept. 6, 1805–Dec. 18, 1852), sculptor, was born in Boston, Mass., fourth of the eleven children of David and Betsey (Bender) Greenough, and fifth in descent from William Greenough (1639–1693), an English sea-captain, who had settled in Massachusetts. David Greenough was a well-to-do merchant, and his sons, among whom were Henry and Richard Saltonstall Greenough [*qq.v.*], were reared in an atmosphere of culture. Horatio was a healthy, athletic boy with much personal charm. He stood high in his classical studies, was poor in mathematics, won a prize for memorizing English poetry. His love for shaping things was apparent from his childhood. A marble figure of Phocion in his father's garden stimulated him to try carving, at first in soft chalk, later in solid plaster, and by the time he was twelve he had produced a collection of miniature busts copied from engravings. An interested neighbor introduced him to William S. Shaw [*q.v.*], director of the Boston Athenæum, who saw in his chalk carvings "the germ of a great and noble art" (Dunlap, *post,* II, 414), and gave him *carte blanche* to the fine-arts room. The boy had tried, but without success, to learn clay modeling out of the *Edinburgh Cyclopedia*; Solomon Willard explained the process to him; M. Binon, a French sculptor then in Boston, gave him further counsel and let him model by his side; Alpheus Cary, the stone-cutter, showed him how to carve in marble, thus enabling him to execute his little bust of Bacchus. His progress was such that his father no longer objected to the amount of time he devoted to his artistic pursuits and insisted only that he graduate from Harvard. Joseph G. Cogswell [*q.v.*], the librarian, lent him drawings and documents; Dr. Parkman of Boston, who later assisted him to travel, gave him the foundation of his anatomical knowledge; Washington Allston [*q.v.*], whom he met through the family of Richard Henry Dana [*q.v.*], was attracted to him and guided his art studies. "Allston," wrote Greenough to Dunlap, "was to me a father, in what concerned my progress of every kind. He taught me first how to discriminate, how to think, how to feel" (*Ibid.,* II, 421). While still in college, learning of proposals for Bunker Hill Monument, young Greenough made and presented a wooden model for an obelisk 100 feet high, which was at first chosen, afterward to be rejected in favor of Solomon Willard's design for a shaft 220 feet high (Justin Winsor, *Memorial History of Boston,* 1880–81, IV, 477).

He graduated from Harvard in 1825. Toward the end of his senior year, the university authorities, recognizing his bent, permitted him to embark for Europe in a sailing vessel bound for Marseilles, and later sent him his diploma. From Marseilles he went by land to Rome, where he began the serious study of his art. "Until then," he later wrote, "I had rather amused myself with clay and marble than studied" (Dunlap, II, 422). Like other students, he had the kindly aid of Thorwaldsen. In his first year abroad he modeled several busts, life-size; also a figure of "Abel," never put into final material. His roommate, the painter Robert W. Weir [*q.v.*], afterward Whistler's instructor at West Point, wrote that Greenough overworked, that after a long day of endeavor he would often rise in the night to study some project. Malaria overtook him before the close of his first year in Rome, and he returned to the United States. Here, his health being restored, he modeled from life an excellent likeness of President John Quincy Adams (now in the New York Historical Society) as well as other portraits, including one of Chief Justice Marshall. In 1828 he returned to Italy to put the plaster casts of these busts into marble, spent three months in Carrara to familiarize himself with the processes of stone carving, then settled in Florence, which, because of its climate and artistic advantages, he had chosen as a permanent dwelling-place.

One of his early commissions was a small marble group called "Chanting Cherubs," ordered by J. Fenimore Cooper [*q.v.*]. The subject of this work was frankly borrowed from the Madonna del Trono in the Pitti Palace, a picture attributed to Raphael or his school. Cooper said that aside from the idea, the sculptor had little aid from the original, and added, "Perhaps the authority of Raphael was necessary to render such a representation of the subject palatable in our day. . . . I hope that the peculiarity of its being the first work of the kind which has come from an American chissel, as well as the rare merit of the artist, will be found to interest the public at home" (*New-York American,* Apr. 30, 1831). "Fenimore Cooper," Greenough later wrote, "saved me from despair after my second return to Italy." At first, the American public was hostile to the "Chanting Cherubs" because of the nudity of the infants. A whirlwind of protest greeted them. Greenough, though sick at heart, made a spirited defense, and a similar work, "The Child and the Angel," was later accepted without moral indignation.

At Cooper's suggestion, Greenough spent the winter of 1831 in Paris, chiefly for the purpose of modeling a bust of Lafayette. The old hero, then seventy-four, was satisfied with the bust already made of him for posterity by the French sculptor, David d'Angers, and some persuasion from Cooper was needed to induce him to pose for the young American. Greenough's portrait was successful enough, though perhaps not altogether what Cooper declared it to be, the best likeness ever made of Lafayette. The general himself tactfully called one work his American bust and the other his French bust, without publishing his own preference. That winter Greenough made other portraits, including Cooper's, and broadened his views through contact with French art. After his return to Florence, spurred by his active imagination and by the sympathetic appreciation of American travelers abroad who gave him small commissions, he produced several groups, busts, and figures. Tuckerman relates that having received some anonymous financial aid in 1833 which he believed to be from Boston, he modeled and sent home a bas-relief, showing a dejected artist whose flickering lamp is renewed with oil poured by a hand out of the clouds.

In 1833, as the result of efforts in his behalf by Cooper and others, Greenough was awarded a government commission for a statue of Washington to be placed in the United States Capitol. The opportunity called forth all his idealism and patriotism, and for nearly eight years he gave himself body and soul to what he looked upon as the crowning work of his career. His design took shape as a colossal, half-draped, marble figure of Washington seated, the right arm uplifted in majesty, the left extended in conciliation. When at last the work reached the Capitol in 1843 the entrance had to be widened temporarily to admit it. Designed especially for indoor placing, it was to have been set under the dome, but its tremendous weight shook the floor, and it was speedily withdrawn to an outside position, facing the eastern front of the building. The reception accorded his masterpiece brought Greenough bitter disappointment. However highly extolled by a few enthusiasts, it had little appeal to the public except as a subject for gibes and witticisms. The change of location was unfortunate. "I have treated the subject poetically," the sculptor wrote, "and I confess I should feel pain at seeing it placed in direct and flagrant contrast with everyday life" (*Letters, post*, p. 180). Had he expected the statue to be placed outdoors, he would have adopted an historic treatment, "Washington on horseback, and in his usual dress," and would have been careful to avoid ridges and pockets in which rain and snow might collect to cause disintegration of the stone. Deterioration later became so evident that the work was removed to the Smithsonian Institution, where in spite of its obscure position and indifferent lighting the thoughtful observer will conclude that this, the first colossal group in marble by an American, deserved a better fate than to become, in the bitter phrase of its creator, "the butt of wiseacres and witlings."

A second colossal group by Greenough, "The Rescue," was placed on a buttress of the Capitol portico. He began it about the time of his marriage in 1837 to Louisa Gore of Boston, and worked on it intermittently until 1851. Because of slow quarrying methods, there was a delay of four years before he could obtain Seravezza marble of the dimensions required; and two of the figures in the group were entirely remodeled at the eleventh hour. "The Rescue" shows a pioneer family of father, mother, and child, with a dog as innocent bystander, saved from an attacking Indian by the father's heroism. The group has a definite sculptural intention aside from its anecdotal interest; the composition is thoughtfully studied; there are passages of good, even sensitive modeling. Among the faults noted by modern criticism is the patchwork effect of the whole; the group seems too easily divisible into three sections—the mother and child, the father and Indian, and the dog. Greenough's works were chiefly in marble. The two great compositions for Washington were the most significant; a second series included a dozen or more portraits of famous sitters, and a third, a score of idealistic pieces in bas-relief or in the round, made for private ownership.

In 1851 political troubles in Florence led Greenough to give up the pleasant studio he had built on the Piazza Maria Antonia and return to the United States. Making his home in Newport, R. I., he entered upon a year of intense activity. He planned an imposing Cooper monument for the vicinity, formed a project to execute, with H. K. Brown [*q.v.*], the equestrian statue of Washington afterward made by Brown with the assistance of J. Q. A. Ward; wrote essays, and delivered lectures on art. After his quiet sojourn in Italy, the more exhilarating atmosphere wrought unduly upon his nervous system; he fell ill of what was diagnosed as brain fever, was taken to Somerville, Mass., for treatment, and there after a few days he died.

Greenough was a sturdy republican, who had watched with sympathy the republican movement abroad; a firm patriot, yet enjoying intercourse with Europeans and counting among his best friends a Presbyterian pastor, a Franciscan friar, a Hungarian nobleman, and an Italian poet. He was a linguist and a classical scholar, confessing himself unable either in speaking or writing to give up his habit of quotation in various tongues, yet winning general praise as a good talker. He had a genius for friendship. His volume, *Aesthetics in Washington* (1851), is vivid, epigrammatic, and often strangely far-seeing; but his occasional invective is unconvincing. Greenough's importance in the history of American sculpture is due to the influence of his career rather than to the intrinsic merit of his work. Dedicating himself to his art with the utmost earnestness, he did much to dignify it in the minds of his countrymen. The first American sculptor to go to Italy to live, he set a fashion that lasted for half a century.

[Wm. Dunlap, *Hist. of the Rise and Progress of the Arts of Design in the U. S.* (1834); *Letters of Horatio Greenough to his Brother Henry Greenough* (1887), ed. by F. B. Greenough; J. H. Sheppard, "Geneal. of the Greenough Family," *New-England Hist. and Geneal. Reg.*, Apr. 1863; H. T. Tuckerman, *A Memoir of Horatio Greenough* (1853), with a complete list of his works, and *Book of the Artists* (1867); "Greenough the Sculptor," *Putnam's Monthly*, Mar. 1853; Nathaniel Hawthorne, *Italian Notes* (1858); R. W. Emerson, *Journals*, (1909–14); J. J. Jarves, *The Art Idea* (1864); S. G. W. Benjamin, *Art in America* (1880); Lorado Taft, *The Hist. of Am. Sculpture* (rev. ed., 1930).]

A. A.

GREENOUGH, JAMES BRADSTREET (May 4, 1833–Oct. 11, 1901), philologist, was born in Portland, Me., the son of James and Catherine Greenough. He was educated at the Boston Latin School and Harvard College, graduating in 1856. For some years he practised law in Marshall, Mich., and there, on Nov. 26, 1860, married Mary Battey Ketchum, by whom he had two sons. She died on July 19, 1893, and on Dec. 21, 1895, he married Harriet Sweetser Jenks. He took part in the political events of 1860, chiefly by writing verses for campaign songs. In November 1862 he was appointed commissioner of the circuit court in Marshall, and later commissioner of drafting for Calhoun County, Mich.

After a European tour in 1864, he accepted (1865) a post as tutor in Latin at Harvard. He became assistant professor in 1873, and was elected professor of Latin in 1883. Inspired by the work of Bopp and Schleicher in Germany, he studied Sanskrit; he was the first to teach that language and comparative philology at Harvard. Through *Syntax of the Moods and Tenses of the Greek Verb* (1860), by William W. Goodwin [*q.v.*], he was led to a study of Latin syntax, which bore fruit in his *Analysis of the Latin Subjunctive* (1870). This became the source of all subsequent treatments of the Latin moods, anticipating at many points Delbrück's *Conjunctiv und Optativ*. Greenough's criticism of this work in the *North American Review* (October 1871) and Delbrück's appreciative answer constitute a pleasing incident in scholastic comity. In association with Joseph Henry Allen [*q.v.*], he published Allen and Greenough's *Latin Grammar* (1872), by which, in that and later editions, the results of his original studies in syntax became accessible alike to scholars and schoolboys. In the classroom he was eager, vigorous, lucid; his illustrations were taken from all aspects of life, often with comic aptness; but the logical continuity of his exposition was never lost in his discursiveness. His genius for teaching led him to the preparation of much-needed text-books. Alone or in collaboration with others he published editions of Cæsar, Cicero, Virgil, Horace, Livy, Ovid, and Sallust, all revealing his own research. The last edition of the *Cæsar* was largely based on a special exploration of the sites and routes of Cæsar's campaigns in Gaul. Greenough's original monographs and reviews make a long list. He was the chief force which moved his classmates and other friends to found the *Harvard Studies in Classical Philology*. He had a share in planning the organization of advanced studies for women in Cambridge, thus helping to found the institution which later grew into Radcliffe College.

A talented writer of verse, he was also an excellent actor. For private theatricals he produced *The Queen of Hearts* and *Blackbirds*; a Latin version of G. M. Lane's *Lone Fish Ball*; a dramatic adaptation of *The Rose and the Ring*; and an operetta, *Old King Cole*, with Frederic De Forest Allen [*q.v.*]. One of his best known translations is his rendering in Ciceronian Latin of Theodore Roosevelt's *The Strenuous Life*. Toward the end of his life he issued, with G. L. Kittredge, *Words and their Ways in English Use* (1901). He was devoted to the woods and streams of the Canadian seigniory which belonged to him and his elder brother. A brilliant teacher, an entertaining companion, an alert inquirer, he embodied the full scope of the term philologist, as understood by the Greeks. He used to say, "Nothing steadies a man like a few sound prejudices," yet he was never contentious nor dogmatic, and his facile mind was capable of infinite patience in research and thinking.

[*Report of the Harvard Class of 1856*, for the years 1865 (p. 21), 1899 (p. 35); *Memorial of the Harvard Class of 1856* (1906), pp. 117–21; memoir by G. L. Kittredge, in *Harvard Studies in Classical Philology*, XIV

(1903), 1–16; *Boston Transcript,* Oct. 11, 1901; personal acquaintance.] C. B. G.

GREENOUGH, RICHARD SALTONSTALL (Apr. 27, 1819–Apr. 23, 1904), sculptor, brother of Henry and Horatio Greenough [*qq.v.*], was born in Jamaica Plain, a suburb of Boston, Mass., the youngest of the eleven children of David and Betsey (Bender) Greenough. His father carried on a large business in real estate and until just before his death in 1836 was prosperous enough to give his family every opportunity for culture. At one time four of his sons were in Harvard College. Richard very early showed an artistic bent, especially toward music, and sang ballads before he could speak plainly. As a child in Jamaica Plain, he went to the school kept by Mr. Charles W. Greene, and on the removal of the Greenoughs to Boston, he entered the Boston Latin School, remaining there until he was about seventeen. Though fully prepared for college, he declined a college training, perhaps because of his father's financial reverses, and entered the counting-room of two elder brothers, commission merchants in Boston. Here for a short time he worked faithfully, meanwhile giving his leisure to drawing and modeling. His admiration for his brother Horatio, fourteen years his senior, and his own tastes determined his career. In 1837 the brothers in the counting-room, recognizing Richard's ambition, sent him to Florence to study under Horatio's guidance. Because of ill health, he returned in 1838 to Boston, where he regained his vigor and continued his studies.

His first work to gain attention was a bust of William Hickling Prescott, presented by William Prescott to the Boston Athenæum in 1844. Ideal heads and statuettes followed. On Oct. 20, 1846, he married Sarah Dana Loring of Boston, who years later published a three-volume novel, and various stories and poems. The couple went abroad in 1848 and after a few months in Florence established themselves in Rome, where for some years the sculptor successfully busied himself with portrait-busts and several ideal works, notably the "Shepherd Boy and Eagle." On being exhibited in the Boston Athenæum, this group won increasingly favorable notice, until finally several persons contributed altogether $2,000 for its purchase and presentation to the Athenæum. As seen to-day, it appears a straightforward, rather commonplace composition, less than life-size, of a boy crouching under the attack of an eagle whose nest he has robbed. Warmly praised by the critics of the day, it led to a commission for a bronze statue of Franklin, heroic in size, standing on a four-square pedestal of green marble, adorned with bronze bas-reliefs, two of which are by Thomas Ball [*q.v.*]. Henry Greenough was the architect. The placing of this monument in front of the Boston City Hall was made the occasion of a veritable jubilee on a scale remarkable in the city's annals. Greenough thereby reached the summit of his fame. The statue is simple and dignified, and in its surroundings holds its own. The sculptor was less successful in his two statues of John Winthrop, first governor of Massachusetts; in these he showed a grave weakness in his failure to recognize the head as the culminating detail in a portrait statue. The seated marble figure of Winthrop, dated Paris, 1856, is in the rotunda of the chapel at Mount Auburn; a bronze copy of the standing figure of the same subject is in Boston on the grounds of the First Church, and a marble replica, dated 1876, in Statuary Hall at the Capitol, Washington. This second statue is well composed and in most respects well modeled, the treatment of the hands being particularly good. Greenough's small model of an equestrian statue of Washington was not carried out in full size but was cast in bronze. Most of his much-admired portrait-busts have passed into private ownership. Among his later sitters were Bishop Potter and W. W. Astor. His "Carthaginian Maiden," in marble, is owned by the Boston Museum of Fine Arts; a bronze copy was bequeathed to the Athenæum in 1869. Other ideal works in marble are his "Cupid Bound," his "Circe and Ulysses," and his "Psyche." The "Psyche" was shown at the Athenæum in 1849; a replica was placed in the Protestant cemetery, Rome, as a monument to his wife, who died in Austria in 1855.

Like his brothers, Richard Greenough was at home in many lands. He lived and worked in Boston, Mass., in Newport, R. I., in Paris, in Florence, and in Rome, the greater part of his studio life being spent in Rome, where he died at the age of eighty-five.

[J. H. Sheppard, "Geneal. of the Greenough Family," *New-England Hist. and Geneal. Reg.*, Apr. 1863; *Letters of Horatio Greenough* (1887), ed. by F. B. Greenough; *Am. Art in Bronze and Iron* (1903), ed. by W. D. Mitchell, vol. I, no. 3, p. 29; *Memorial of the Inauguration of the Statue of Franklin* (1857), ed. by N. B. Shurtleff, prepared and printed by the authority of the City Council, Boston; C. E. Fairman, *Art and Artists of the Capitol of the United States of America* (1927); H. T. Tuckerman, *Book of the Artists* (1867); Lorado Taft, *Hist. of Am. Sculpture* (rev. ed., 1930); *The Athenæum Centenary: The Influence and Hist. of the Boston Athenæum* (1907).] A. A.

GREENUP, CHRISTOPHER (*c.* 1750–Apr. 27, 1818), lawyer, governor, congressman, was born probably in Loudoun County, Va. He took part in the Revolution and rose in rank to a captaincy. Near the end of the conflict he emigrated to the Kentucky district of Virginia and settled at Frankfort, though he identified himself with Lexington to the extent of buying a town lot there in 1783. He secured a license to practise law in the same year, but he is best known for his political activities, for throughout the next quarter of a century he was almost continuously serving in some political capacity. In 1785 he was appointed clerk of the Virginia court for the district of Kentucky and continued in that position until Kentucky became a state. In this same year he was also elected to represent Fayette County in the Virginia legislature. The problem uppermost for the next seven years in the political life of Kentucky was the effort to secure statehood. Greenup took part in the initial step in that direction, the militia convention held in Danville in November 1784, and served as clerk of the body. He was also a member of the convention held in 1785 and of the one in November 1788 when the Spanish conspiracy was brewing. In the last he was able to steer a course so circumspect that the promoters of the *Western World* years later (1806) were unable to implicate him as a possible conspirator.

With the coming of statehood in 1792 Greenup was first rewarded by being chosen an elector to select the state senators, and then he became one of Kentucky's first two members of the United States House of Representatives. He took his seat at the second session of the Second Congress on Nov. 9, four days late. He was reëlected to the Third and Fourth Congresses, serving until Mar. 4, 1797, when he returned to Frankfort and served for a time as clerk of the Kentucky Senate. In 1804 he was elected governor for the regular term of four years and during his tenure of office assumed an intelligent and progressive attitude on the questions of the day. He rounded out his political career by serving as a Madison elector in 1809 and becoming a justice of the peace in 1812.

His interests were many and diverse: when the Bank of Kentucky was chartered in 1807, he became one of its directors. He was a member of the Danville Political Club; in 1787 he joined the Kentucky Society for Promoting Useful Knowledge; in 1789 he helped to organize the Kentucky Manufacturing Society; in 1801 he was appointed a member of the Kentucky River Company, a body organized to improve the Kentucky River; and in 1811 he helped to conduct a lottery to build a church in Frankfort. He died at Blue Lick Springs in his sixty-ninth year. He had married, in 1787, Mary Catherine Pope, the daughter of Nathaniel Pope of Virginia.

[Lewis and R. H. Collins, *Hist. of Ky.* (2 vols., 1874); T. M. Green, *The Spanish Conspiracy* (1891); Thos. Speed, *The Political Club, Danville, Ky., 1786–90* (1894), Filson Club Pubs. No. 9; William Littell, *Pol. Trans. in and concerning Ky.* (1806), reprinted in Filson Club Pubs. No. 31 (1926); *Reg. of the Ky. State Hist. Soc.*, May 1903, Sept. 1904; *Ky. Gazette*, Nov. 13, 1804; Innes MSS. and Breckinridge MSS., Lib. of Cong.]

E. M. C.

GREENWALD, EMANUEL (Jan. 13, 1811–Dec. 21, 1885), Lutheran clergyman, was born near Frederick, Md., the son of Christian and Mary Magdalena (Smith) Greenwald. He was of Swiss descent, his great-grandfather having emigrated to Pennsylvania to escape conscription. His father, a carpenter whose daily reading was in the Bible and Arndt's *Wahres Christentum,* resolved as the result of a dream to educate his son for the ministry. Emanuel, therefore, studied the ancient languages and theology under the Rev. David Frederick Schaeffer at Frederick, walking the four miles to town every morning and returning in the evening. At the end of five years, when his course of instruction was completed, he had tramped 14,000 miles. This training for the ministry, though deficient on the formal side, was on the practical side excellent. Greenwald was licensed to preach Oct. 18, 1831, stowed his books and clothes in his saddle-bags, and started westward to find himself a charge somewhere beyond the mountains. He dismounted Oct. 27 at New Philadelphia, Ohio, to deliver a letter, preached the next evening to the settlers, and stayed for twenty years. Young, robust, indefatigable in the service of his Master, he established fourteen preaching stations in the surrounding country and for a time visited all of them regularly, conning his sermons on horseback as he forded the Tuscarawas or followed through the forest the blazes cut for him by his parishioners. Living was cheap; for his first year's board he paid thirty-five dollars and taught his host's two sons for an hour a day. He married Lavinia Williams of New Philadelphia Dec. 17, 1834, was ordained at Lancaster, Ohio, June 2, 1836, issued the first number of the *Lutheran Standard* Oct. 24, 1842, and continued to edit it for two years, and was president of the English District Synod of Ohio from 1848 to 1850. During these strenuous years he developed that genius for the pastoral office that made him in Ohio and later in Pennsylvania one of the most beloved of ministers. In 1851 he moved to Columbus to organize an English Lutheran congregation in connection with Capital University, which had been founded in 1850. In order to sustain himself he at the same time resumed the editorship of the *Standard.* As an upholder of confessional Lutheranism he soon found himself engaged in controversy with Benjamin Kurtz [*q.v.*] of the *Lutheran Observer*, who was the leading advocate of the "new measures"; he did the Lutheran Church lasting service at this time by opposing revivals and other innovations of the "American Lutherans." Disagreements also arose nearer home over the management of Capital University and over the language question. Greenwald, by nature peace-loving, found his position growing unbearable and withdrew in September 1854 to Christ Church, Easton, Pa. There he built up a strong congregation by giving intelligent attention to the religious instruction of the younger members. In the controversies that led to the formation of the General Council of the Evangelical Lutheran Church in North America he was again on the conservative side and thought it desirable to find a congregation entirely in accord with his views. In May 1867 he became pastor of Holy Trinity, Lancaster, Pa., where he remained till his death. His work there was the climax of his career. Some idea of his pastoral work may be gained from the fact that in the last year of his life, when he was ill and frail, he made five hundred parochial calls. He organized two new congregations in Lancaster, Grace Church and Christ Church, and found time to write a number of articles, books, and pamphlets of a devotional or didactic character. Among his publications are: *The Lutheran Reformation* (1867); *The Foreign Mission Work of Pastor Louis Harms* (1867); *Meditations for Passion Week* (1873); *A Young Christian's Manual of Devotion* (1873); *Sprinkling the True Mode of Baptism* (1876); *The True Church: Its Way of Justification and its Holy Communion* (1876); *Discourses on Romanism and the Reformation* (1880); *Jesus Our Table Guest: An Order of Family Prayer* (1883). These books are now seldom met with, but they preserve in their simple, dignified English the savor of his godly life and unwavering faith.

[C. E. Haupt, *Emanuel Greenwald, Pastor and Doctor of Divinity* (Lancaster, Pa., 1889); *Daily New Era* (Lancaster), Oct. 17, 1881, Dec. 18, 1884, Dec. 21, 24, 1885; G. W. Sandt, article in *Luth. Ch. Rev.*, Oct. 1918.] G. H. G.

GREENWOOD, GRACE [See LIPPINCOTT, SARAH JANE CLARKE, 1823–1904].

GREENWOOD, ISAAC (May 11, 1702–Oct. 12, 1745), mathematician, was born in Boston, the fifth of the nine children of Samuel and Elizabeth (Bronsdon) Greenwood. His great-grandfather, Miles Greenwood, was a lieutenant and chaplain in Cromwell's army; his grandfather, Nathaniel Greenwood, emigrated to Massachusetts in 1654 and settled at Boston, where he was later chosen a selectman; his father was a merchant, shipbuilder, and man of means. After graduating in 1721 from Harvard College, Greenwood continued his theological studies in London, began to preach, and became an attentive auditor at the scientific lectures of John Theophilus Desaguliers [*q.v.* in *Dictionary of National Biography*], whose discourses on experimental philosophy were popular in the city. He met Thomas Hollis, the benefactor of Harvard College, who was so impressed with his talent and zeal that he proposed to the Harvard Corporation to found a professorship of mathematics with Greenwood as the incumbent. In his later correspondence, however, he expressed concern for Greenwood's habits; and when the Corporation finally decided to appoint him, Hollis was evidently surprised but agreed to approve him if the election were unanimous (Quincy, *post,* II, 11-22). Perhaps the deciding influence was Greenwood's *Experimental Course on Mechanical Philosophy* (Boston, 1726). The election took place on May 12, 1727, when the appointee was only twenty-five years old, and he took up his duties the following February.

His work at Harvard extended through ten years. During this time he published his *Arithmetick, Vulgar and Decimal: With the Application Thereof to a Variety of Cases in Trade and Commerce* (Boston, 1729), the first text-book of its kind to be written in English by a native American. Although it appeared anonymously, its authorship was made known by an advertisement in a Boston paper. He also contributed "A New Method for Composing a Natural History of Meteors" (1728), and "A Brief Account of Some of the Effects and Properties of Damps" (1729) to the *Philosophical Transactions of the Royal Society* (vol. XXXV, p. 390; vol. XXXVI, p. 184). Although his actual attainments were unimposing, he was probably as well trained in mathematics as any American of his time. The stimulating effect of the scientific lectures of Desaguliers in London led him in these years to give a series of popular lectures in Boston on astronomy. He was repeatedly reprimanded for his tendency to dissipation. Although wine drinking was common, excess in that direction could hardly be condoned in a man in his position. He was removed from office in 1738 and spent his closing years as a private tutor. He died at Charleston, S. C.

Greenwood was married July 31, 1729, to Sarah Shrimpton Clarke (1708–76), daughter of Dr. John Clarke, a Boston politician and sometime member of the Harvard Corporation.

They had five children. One son, Isaac, became a dentist and maker of mathematical instruments; and John Greenwood [*q.v.*], a son of this Isaac, became a noted dentist.

[John Eliot, *A Biog. Dict.* (1809); Benj. Peirce, *A Hist. of Harvard Univ.* (1833); Josiah Quincy, *Hist. of Harvard Univ.* (1840); Frederick Greenwood, *Greenwood Genealogies* (1914); I. J. Greenwood, "Brief Memoirs and Notices of Prince's Subscribers," *New-England Hist. and Geneal. Reg.*, Apr. 1860.]

D. E. S.

GREENWOOD, JOHN (May 17, 1760–Nov. 16, 1819), dentist, son of Isaac and Mary (I'ans) Greenwood, was born in Boston, Mass. His father was an ivory-turner and mathematical instrument-maker; his grandfather, Isaac Greenwood [*q.v.*], was at one time professor of mathematics at Harvard College. John's education, as shown by his letters, did not progress far beyond the elementals. He was early apprenticed to an uncle, Thales Greenwood, a cabinetmaker in Portland, Me. On the outbreak of the Revolutionary War his uncle closed his shop and enlisted, while John entered the service as a fifer-boy. When news of the fight at Concord came to him, John took French leave and walked to Cambridge, hoping to get to his parents who were in Boston. He reached the army in time to see something of the battle of Bunker Hill, but failed to get through the lines into the city. His casual desertion seems not to have caused him trouble, for he became a fife-major and took part in a raid against the British lines. In the capacity of a scout he was detailed to the Arnold expedition against Canada, returning to the main army in time to take part in the Trenton campaign. Shortly after that battle his enlistment expired and, tired of soldiering, he refused to reënter the service. He is said to have turned privateersman and may thus have secured the means that enabled him to study dental mechanics and establish himself as a dentist in New York City. At all events he did so establish himself near the end of the year 1784 or the beginning of 1785. His father had dabbled in dentistry and his son reaped the benefit of his experience.

Greenwood's first known advertisement of his claim to professional skill appeared in the *New York Daily Advertiser* of Feb. 28, 1786. In 1806 he went to France to study the latest European dental practises and, on his return, advertised great improvements in methods and apparatus. He is credited with being the originator of the foot-power drill, of spiral springs which held the plates of artificial teeth in position, and the use of porcelain in the manufacture of such teeth. He took casts in beeswax and cut and modeled teeth from "sea-horse" (hippopotamus) ivory. Among his other dexterities was that of replacing decayed teeth by live human molars, supplied by indigent individuals at a price. His most distinguished patient was President George Washington who relied largely upon Greenwood's ability up to the day of his death. Two of the sets of artificial teeth which he made for Washington are still in existence and are remarkable examples of dental skill. Greenwood's career was typically that of the self-taught, mechanical genius who becomes fascinated by his work. He possessed all the strength and weakness of the pioneer in an undeveloped field, but American dentistry is largely in his debt for the impetus in right directions which he gave it, and his methods were fundamentally sound along the lines of mechanics and instrumentation. Washington's confidence would be in itself sufficient evidence of the man's skill, for before he met Greenwood the President had had experience with a number of dentists and was exacting in his demands. Greenwood's health failed at the age of fifty-nine from too close application to work, and he died at his Park Row home, New York City, in 1819. On Mar. 22, 1788, he had married Elizabeth, daughter of William and Jane (Coessart) Weaver.

[Sources include Frederick Greenwood, *Greenwood Genealogies* (1914); Justin Winsor, *Memorial Hist. of Boston* (4 vols., 1880–81); E. C. Kirk, "Pioneer Dentistry in New York," *Dental Cosmos*, Oct. 1906, giving two portrait prints of Greenwood and many facts; *Mass. Soldiers & Sailors of the Revolutionary War* (1899), vol. VI, giving the military record which does not agree with Greenwood's memoirs, compiled by E. Bryan in the *Am. Jour. Dental Sci.*, vol. I (1839), nos. 4 and 5 (the latter are based on Greenwood's recollections many years after the events and are confused and contradictory but must be taken into account); C. R. E. Koch, *Hist. of Dental Surgery*, vols. I (1909) and III (1910), ed. by B. L. Thorpe; material in the records of the S. S. White Dental Mfg. Company, Phila.; *N. Y. Columbian*, Nov. 17, 1819. Dean J. B. Robinson, of the Baltimore College of Dental Surgery, University of Maryland, has the custody of one of the sets of artificial teeth which Greenwood made for Washington, and some of Greenwood's letters; in the Washington MSS., Library of Congress, are a few letters of value on the subject.]

J. C. F.

GREENWOOD, MILES (Mar. 19, 1807–Nov. 5, 1885), Cincinnati ironmaster, was born in Jersey City, N. J. His father, Miles Greenwood of Salem, Mass., was descended from Miles Greenwood, a lieutenant and chaplain in Cromwell's army, through his son Samuel, who settled in Boston, Mass., about 1665 and in 1678 was one of the assistants in charge of the Boston fire-engine. His mother was a Demarest of Jersey City, of Dutch and French Huguenot descent. In 1808 the family moved to New York and later, in 1817, to Cincinnati, Ohio. During the next eight years the boy struggled to support himself and his invalid father by working as a bootblack and bill-poster, by cutting cord wood, and by running a small merchandise store. At the same time he was trying to educate himself. In 1825 he moved with his father to New Harmony, Ind., where he remained four years, working in the community and attending school, first for six months in Illinois, and later in the school started at New Harmony by Robert Owen. In 1827 he went to Pittsburgh, where he obtained work in an iron foundry. The following year he took charge of a factory at New Harmony, but the failure of the New Harmony experiment caused him to return to Cincinnati, where, in 1829, he entered the iron foundry of John and Thomas Bevan. Three years later, in partnership with Joseph Webb, he established on the Miami Canal, the Eagle Iron Works, which in time became the largest iron-manufacturing concern in the old West. The partners commenced operations on borrowed capital and employed ten hands. Later Greenwood bought out the interest of his partner and began to expand the plant. By 1851 the Eagle Iron Works employed 350 hands and manufactured annually goods valued at $360,000. Greenwood's factories made hydraulic presses, steam-engines, iron fronts for buildings, heating apparatus, and an innumerable assortment of small hardwood articles.

The expansion of his business did not deter Greenwood from taking an active interest in civic affairs. As a member of the City Council in 1840 he labored diligently to cut down unnecessary expenses while introducing various improvements in the different departments. As an active member of the Volunteer Fire Department, he recognized the inefficiency of the system and the fact that it was a nursery "where the youth of the city were trained in vice, vulgarity, and debauchery" (Howe, *post,* II, 98). He therefore became an earnest advocate of a paid steam fire department for the city, and undaunted by the opposition which the project encountered both in the City Council and from the volunteer firemen, was active in bringing about its establishment. The first steam-engine, the "Uncle Joe Ross," was constructed at his iron works by Messrs. Shawk and Latta. This was the first steam fire-engine in the United States. It was first called into use in May 1852, when it was driven by Greenwood himself and the steam fire-engine company had a fight with the old volunteers. On Apr. 1, 1853, a paid steam fire department was organized in Cincinnati, and Greenwood became chief engineer. When he was questioned by a deputation from Baltimore regarding the merits of the new fire engine over the old system he characteristically replied: "First, it never gets drunk; second, it never throws brickbats; its only drawback is that it cannot vote" (Greve, *post,* I, 660). He constructed the building for the Ohio Mechanics' Institute and took an active interest in its work. He was also a director of the House of Refuge.

During the Civil War, Greenwood turned his establishment over to the government for war purposes, and in it more than 2,000 bronze cannon, scores of gun-carriages and caissons, and several sea monitors of the first class were made, and 40,000 Springfield muskets were improved by percussioning and rifling. His factories were burned three times by Southern sympathizers and he suffered large financial losses through mistakes made by government engineers in drawing up the plans for the monitors. After the war, in 1867, he performed the duties of county treasurer gratuitously in order that the widowed family of the treasurer, who had died in office, might receive the pay. In 1869 he was appointed by the superior court one of the directors of the Cincinnati Southern Railway and was chosen president of the board. Three years before he died a number of prominent merchants presented him with a thousand dollars in gold as a mark of their esteem. Greenwood was a man of fine physique, able to perform an enormous amount of work. He was twice married: in 1832 to Miss Howard W. Hills, and in 1836 to Phoebe J. Hopson.

[Henry Howe, *Hist. Colls. of Ohio* (2 vols., 1890–91); C. J. Greve, *Centennial Hist. of Cincinnati and Representative Citizens,* I (1904), 660; Chas. Cist, *Sketches and Statistics of Cincinnati* (1851 and 1859); *Cincinnati Past and Present* (1872); *First Ann. Report of the Chief Engineer of the Cincinnati Fire Dept. Under the New Organization* (1854); Frederick Greenwood, *Greenwood Geneals.* (1914); J. F. Brennan, *A Biog. Cyc. and Portr. Gallery of Distinguished Men . . . of Ohio* (1879); *Cincinnati Times-Star,* Nov. 6, 7, and *Cincinnati Commercial Gazette,* Nov. 7, 8, 1885.]

R. C. M.

GREER, DAVID HUMMELL (Mar. 20, 1844–May 19, 1919), bishop of the Episcopal Church, was a native of what is now West Virginia, having been born in Wheeling. His ancestors had emigrated from Ireland toward the close of the eighteenth century and settled in Pennsylvania. His father, Jacob Rickard Greer, went from Carlisle, Pa., to Wheeling, where he married Elizabeth Yellott Armstrong, daughter of an Episcopal rector born in England. David was the second of their six children. His father was a wholesale merchant and he was brought up in comfortable circumstances. At the age of fifteen, having attended the Wheeling schools, he entered Morgantown Academy, and in 1860 became a member of the junior class of Washington College from which he graduated in 1862. For two years he taught in Wheeling, worked in his father's office, and studied law. He then entered the Episcopal theological school at Gambier, Ohio, and on June 27, 1866, he was ordained deacon. From 1866 to 1868 he was in charge of Christ Church, Clarksburg, W. Va. Admitted to the priesthood in the chapel of the Theological Seminary, Alexandria, Va., May 19, 1868, the following October he became rector of Trinity Church, Covington, Ky., an office which he filled until May 1871. On June 29, 1869, he married Caroline Augusta Keith, daughter of Quincy Adams and Priscilla Keith of Covington. After a trip to Europe (1871–72), he began on Sept. 15, 1872, a sixteen-years' rectorship at Grace Church, Providence, R. I.

He rose rapidly to leadership in the diocese and soon became known and esteemed outside its limits. His preaching, deeply religious but eminently practical and fired by his own vital personality, drew large numbers to his church. Although devoted to his calling, he was thoroughly human and without professional self-consciousness. He rarely wore clerical garb on the street, and was friendly to all sects and classes. He was broad in his churchmanship but unpartisan, liberal in his views, and alive to the problem created by modern science; nevertheless he clung to the evangelical theology in which he was reared. The grounds of his faith are set forth in the Bedell Lectures which he delivered at the theological school, Gambier, Ohio, in 1889, published under the title, *The Historical Christ, the Moral Power of History* (1890). His quick initiative, calmness, judgment, and patience made him an able administrator. He was sensitive to the needs of the poor and afflicted, and while in Providence founded the Saint Elizabeth Home for incurables. Calls to other churches were declined until in 1888 he accepted the rectorship of St. Bartholomew's, New York, in which city he again had a conspicuous ministry. One of his notable achievements there was the religious and social work which, supported by his wealthy parishioners, he inaugurated on the East Side through the establishment on East Forty-second Street of St. Bartholomew's Parish House. In 1892 he was called to succeed Phillips Brooks at Trinity Church, Boston, but he felt that his obligations to St. Bartholomew's required him to decline. He would probably have been elected Brooks's successor as bishop, had he not discouraged those who wished to nominate him. A delegate from the Rhode Island diocese to the General Conventions of 1877, 1880, 1883, and 1886, he also represented the New York diocese in 1895, 1898, and 1901. He took a most conservative position on the divorce question, favoring a canon forbidding remarriage even of the "innocent party." In 1893 he published a volume of sermons, *From Things to God,* and in 1895 delivered the Lyman Beecher Lectures on Preaching at Yale, which appeared the same year under the title, *The Preacher and His Place.* In 1898 he published *Visions.* After nearly fifteen years at St. Bartholomew's, he was elected bishop coadjutor of the diocese of New York, and was consecrated, Jan. 26, 1904; becoming diocesan at the death of Bishop Potter in 1908. To the manifold and exhausting duties of this office he gave himself without stint. He carried on the work of constructing the Cathedral of St. John the Divine with zeal, and the liberal policy of its administration was due in no small part to him. He believed thoroughly in non-resistance, and when the World War broke out he vigorously opposed the entrance of the United States into the conflict, but loyally supported the government when the step was finally taken. In May 1919 he entered St. Luke's Hospital to undergo an operation not considered necessarily dangerous, but he was too worn out by his labors to recover, and on May 19, he died.

[C. L. Slattery, *David Hummell Greer* (1921); *Who's Who in America,* 1918–19; *Biog. and Hist. Cat. of Washington and Jefferson Coll.* (1889); obituaries in *N. Y. Times,* May 20, 21, 1919, and other N. Y. papers; *Churchman,* May 24, 31, 1919; *Living Church,* May 24, 1919; *Outlook,* May 28, 1919.] H. E. S.

GREER, JAMES AUGUSTIN (Feb. 28, 1833–June 17, 1904), naval officer, son of James and Caroline (King) Greer, was born in Cincinnati, Ohio. He attended private schools in Dayton where his father, a native of Pennsylvania, was engaged in manufacturing. Entering the navy in 1848 as an acting midshipman, he cruised on board the *Saratoga* and *Saranac.* In the fall of 1853 he was sent to the Naval Academy, where a year later he graduated and was advanced to the rank of passed midshipman. In September 1855 he was warranted master, and a few months later commissioned lieutenant. From 1854 to 1857 he was on board the *Independence* of the Pacific Squadron. This service was followed by tours of duty on board the *Southern Star* of the Paraguay expedition (1858) and the *Sumter* of the African Squadron (1859–60). As a lieutenant on board the *San Jacinto* he commanded the marines who boarded the *Trent* and the cutter which conveyed Mason and Slidell from the British to the American ship. In 1862, the year of his promotion to the grade of lieutenant-commander, he cruised on board the *St.*

Louis in search of Confederate commerce-destroyers.

During 1863–64 Greer served with the Mississippi Squadron, commanding first the *Benton* and later the *Black Hawk,* and participated in the engagements against Vicksburg, the attack on Grand Gulf, and other operations of the squadron, one division of which he for a time commanded. In 1865 he was sent to the Naval Academy where he served as assistant to the commandant of midshipmen, and while there, in the following year, he was promoted commander. After periods of service with the Pacific Squadron and on ordnance duty at the Philadelphia navy-yard, he returned in 1869 to the Academy, remaining until 1873, when he was chosen to command the *Tigress,* one of the two ships sent in search of the *Polaris* wrecked during an Arctic expedition conducted under the auspices of the Navy Department. He made a complete search of Baffin Bay and Davis Strait, salvaged some of the papers and instruments of the ill-fated vessel, obtained information respecting the rescue of the survivors, and returned home after a four-months' cruise. In 1876 while in command of the *Lackawanna* of the Pacific Squadron he was promoted captain and ten years later, after periods of service as captain of the Washington navy-yard, member of the Naval Retiring Board, and president of the Naval Examining Board, he was made commodore. From 1887 to 1889 he was commander-in-chief of the European Station—his last active service—and from 1891 to 1894 he was chairman of the Light-House Board—his last important professional service. He was promoted rear-admiral from Apr. 3, 1892, and retired in that grade on Feb. 28, 1895. His death occurred in Washington. On Nov. 26, 1857, he was married to Mary Randolph Webb, the daughter of a naval officer.

[Record of Officers, Bureau of Navigation, 1846–93; *Reg. of the Officers of the Navy of the U. S.,* 1849–1905; *Who's Who in America,* 1903–05; *Official Records (Navy),* 1 ser. I, XX, XXIV–XXVII; *Report of the Secretary of the Navy,* 1873; *Evening Star* (Washington, D. C.), June 17, 1904.] C. O. P.

GREGG, ANDREW (June 10, 1755–May 20, 1835), farmer, politician, the son of Andrew and Jane (Scott) Gregg, was born of Scotch-Irish ancestry near Carlisle, Pa. His father, a native of Londonderry, Ireland, emigrated to Massachusetts early in the eighteenth century. About 1722 he moved to Londonderry, N. H., whence he went to Delaware, and in 1732 he settled on a farm in southern Lancaster County, Pa., where his first wife died. Less than two years later he married Jane, daughter of William Scott, an emigrant from Armagh, Ireland, and in 1750 he removed to a farm near Carlisle, where Andrew the younger was born. The son received an excellent classical education in Rev. John Steel's Latin School, Carlisle, and at the Academy in Newark, Del. While a student at Newark in the early years of the Revolution he frequently turned out with the militia, but apparently saw no active service. When the British invaded Delaware in 1777 the academy broke up, and young Gregg returned to the Carlisle farm to help his father. In 1779 he set out for Philadelphia on his way to France for his health. His acceptance of an appointment as tutor in the University of Philadelphia altered his plans, however, and for the next four years he remained at that institution. Lured by the West, in 1783 he moved to Middletown, Pa., where he opened a country store. On Jan. 29, 1787, he married Martha, daughter of Maj.-Gen. James [*q.v.*] and Mary (Patterson) Potter of Buffalo Valley, now Union County. Shortly after his marriage he pushed farther into the interior, first to Lewistown, and in 1789 into the fertile Penn's Valley, Center County, to take up farming.

On Oct. 11, 1791, Gregg was elected to the United States House of Representatives. His record of sixteen years in that body reveals him to have been a well-informed man of practical common sense who jealously guarded the interests of his backcountry constituents. A contemporary has described him as being "remarkable for a sound and discriminating mind, agreeable and dignified manners, strict regard for truth, and unbending and unyielding honesty" (Sherman Day, ed., *Historical Collections of the State of Pennsylvania,* 1843, p. 205). He styled himself "a practical farmer" who would never sacrifice "the interests of agriculture to commerce," because they were "so ultimately connected as to be inseparable" (*Annals of Congress,* 9 Cong., 1 Sess., p. 746). A man of strong party predilections, he was identified with the Jeffersonians with whom he generally voted, and invariably he manifested a strong sense of national pride. Aroused by British outrages committed against American commerce, on Jan. 29, 1806, he introduced a sweeping resolution in the House forbidding the importation of all British goods whatsoever, but it was never adopted by the House. The schism of the Pennsylvania Republicans found Gregg following the more conservative Constitutionalists, who, on Jan. 13, 1807, with Federalist assistance, elected him for a single term to the Senate. Conforming to his Jeffersonian affiliations, here he supported the Embargo and Non-Intercourse Acts, and later, the declaration of war against England. From June

26, 1809, to Feb. 28, 1810, he was president *pro tempore* of the Senate. In 1814, desiring better educational facilities for his family, he became a resident of Bellefonte, where he was president of the Centre Bank. On Dec. 19, 1820, he returned to public life as secretary of the commonwealth of Pennsylvania, having been appointed by the Independent Republican governor, Joseph Hiester. In 1823 the Independent Republicans nominated him for governor and the Federalists supported him, but he was overwhelmingly defeated by John Shulze, candidate of the more radical Republicans. The last twelve years of his life (1823–35) were spent in retirement at Bellefonte.

[The principal sources, in addition to those cited above, are an unfinished family sketch written by Gregg and published in W. H. Egle, *Pa. Geneals.; Scotch-Irish and German* (1886); J. B. Linn, *Hist. of Centre and Clinton Counties, Pa.* (1883); *Biog. Record of Central Pa.* (1898); L. A. Morrison, *The Hist. of Windham in N. H.* (1883); *Am. Sentinel* (Phila.), May 25, 1835; *Poulson's Am. Daily Advertiser* (Phila.), May 28, 1835.]

J. H. P.

GREGG, DAVID McMURTRIE (Apr. 10, 1833–Aug. 7, 1916), Union soldier, the son of Matthew Duncan Gregg and Ellen (McMurtrie) Gregg, both of Scotch-Irish ancestry, was born at Huntingdon, Pa. His father, a lawyer and iron manufacturer, was a son of Andrew Gregg [*q.v.*]. David's early life was spent in central Pennsylvania, where he attended private schools before entering the University at Lewisburg (now Bucknell University). While a student there he was appointed, July 1851, a cadet at West Point. Graduating four years later, he began his career as a second lieutenant of cavalry and spent nearly six years fighting Indians in the Far West. The outbreak of the Civil War found him a first lieutenant, but he was immediately promoted captain and stationed with the troops defending Washington. In January 1862 he was appointed colonel of the 8th Pennsylvania Cavalry, which was in March attached to the Army of the Potomac. During that year Gregg served under McClellan in the Peninsular campaign of May and June, covered the movement from Harrison's Landing to Yorktown in August, and from September to November took part in the Maryland campaign, though he obtained leave to marry Ellen Frances Sheaff on Oct. 6. He received merited recognition, Nov. 29, 1862, by being appointed brigadier-general of volunteers. Commanding a division of cavalry, he took part in Stoneman's raid toward Richmond in April and May 1863. As Lee marched northward on his invasion of Pennsylvania, Gregg played an important part for the opposing forces by reporting accurately the movements of the Confederate army and by handicapping the cavalry on which Lee relied for information by a series of engagements paralleling the line of march. At the battle of Gettysburg, Gregg was stationed on the extreme right wing of Meade's army, about three miles east of the town. During the afternoon of July 3, Gen. J. E. B. Stuart with 7,000 Confederate cavalry attempted to turn this flank and attack the Union rear while Pickett was assaulting the center of the line. To meet this attack Gregg could muster only 5,000 men. Fighting a skilful defensive battle, he used his superior artillery with great effect on the advancing enemy, and met each charge with a counter-charge. In the fierce "Sabre Battle" which took place, his troops held their own and at nightfall were still in their original positions. Gregg had repulsed an attack which might have done irreparable damage and had gained one of the most conspicuous cavalry victories of the war. After Gettysburg he participated actively in the pursuit of Lee's army. During Grant's campaign against Richmond in 1864 he commanded the 2nd Cavalry Division of the Army of the Potomac, and on Aug. 1 was brevetted major-general of volunteers for distinguished service, particularly in reconnaissance at Charles City Road. He took part in no further important engagements before resigning his commission on Feb. 3, 1865.

He then lived in Reading, Pa., until February 1874, when President Grant appointed him consul at Prague. Finding consular work distasteful, he resigned in August and returned to Reading. He took an interest in municipal and charitable affairs, was elected auditor-general of Pennsylvania and served efficiently for three years. In 1907 he published *The Second Cavalry Division of the Army of the Potomac in the Gettysburg Campaign.* Endowed with a rare combination of modesty, geniality, and ability, he was universally liked and respected. His victory at Gettysburg was only the most conspicuous among many well-handled engagements. Grant considered him one of the best cavalry officers in the Union army.

[W. H. Egle, *Pa. Geneals.; Scotch-Irish and German* (1886); *Military Order of the Loyal Legion of the U. S. Commandery of the State of Pa.*, circular no. 6, series of 1917; *Official Records (Army)*; H. B. McClellan, *Life and Campaigns of Maj. Gen. J. E. B. Stuart* (1885); George Meade, *Life and Letters of George Gordon Meade* (1913), ed. by G. G. Meade; W. B. Rawle, *The Right Flank at Gettysburg* (1878); F. M. Pierce, *The Battle of Gettysburg* (1914); G. W. Cullum, *Biog. Reg.* (3rd ed., 1891); *Press* (Phila.), Aug. 8, 1916.]

W. L. W—t., Jr.

GREGG, JOHN (Sept. 28, 1828–Oct. 7, 1864), Confederate general, was born in Lawrence County, Ala., where his father, Nathan Gregg, originally from East Tennessee, was one of the early settlers. His mother, Sarah Pearsall, who at the time of her marriage to Nathan Gregg was a widow, Mrs. Camp, was descended from Thomas Pearsall who settled in Virginia shortly after 1630. When John Gregg was about eight years old the family moved to La Grange, Ala., and in 1847 John graduated from La Grange College, an institution which was then flourishing, but which did not survive the war. He taught school after graduation, studied law in Tuscumbia, and in 1851 or 1852 moved to the newly founded town of Fairfield, in Freestone County, Texas. He practised law, and after four years was elected district judge. About this time he married Mary Garth, daughter of Jesse Garth of Alabama. An ardent secessionist, he was a member of the irregularly assembled convention which voted Texas out of the Union, and was then sent to represent the state in the Confederate Congress at Montgomery. The Texas delegates did not arrive until after the adoption of the provisional constitution, but were allowed to sign for their state afterward. Leaving Congress in the summer, Gregg raised the 7th Texas Infantry, of which he became colonel, and was mustered in at Marshall, Texas, in September 1861. His regiment formed part of the garrison of Fort Donelson, and was surrendered with it when Grant captured that place in February 1862. Gregg was exchanged after some months of imprisonment. He was appointed brigadier-general in September 1862, and was assigned to the command of a brigade of Tennessee and Texas troops which suffered defeat at Raymond in the early part of the Vicksburg campaign and then joined Johnston's army, which observed, but could not prevent, the siege and surrender of the city. At Chickamauga, two months later, Gregg's brigade was one of those which were thrust into the gap opened in the Union line and nearly completed the destruction of Rosecrans's army. Gregg, after recovering from a severe wound received here, was assigned to the Texas brigade, formerly Hood's, in Longstreet's corps, and went with it to Virginia when Longstreet rejoined Lee's army. He served through the campaign of 1864 until he was killed in battle before Richmond in October, after five months of almost continuous fighting. The records of the Confederate War Department show that he was awarded $2,750 for a horse killed in action on May 7, and $2,200 for another killed on Sept. 29. The brigade, already famous, enhanced its reputation for hard fighting and suffered terrible losses. Perhaps the greatest day in its history was that of Longstreet's attack in the battle of the Wilderness (May 6, 1864), on which occasion, when Lee, in his anxiety to retrieve a desperate situation, sought to join in the charge of the troops, Gregg's brigade refused to advance until Lee should go back, and then delivered a successful attack which cost it fifty per cent. in casualties.

[J. E. Saunders, *Early Settlers of Ala.* (1899), pp. 200–03; C. E. Pearsall, *Hist. and Geneal. of the Pearsall Family* (1928), III, 1399; S. S. Johnson, *Texans Who Wore the Gray* (1907), pp. 107–08; *Confed. Mil. Hist.* (1899), XI, Tex., 234–36; *Battles and Leaders of the Civil War,* IV (1888), 124–25; *Official Records (Army),* 1 ser., vols. VII, XXIV (pts. 1, 3), XXX (pts. 2, 4), XXXVI (pt. 3), XLII (pts. 1, 2, 3); *Ibid.,* 2 ser., vols. III, IV; unpublished documents in the War Dept.]

T. M. S.

GREGG, JOSIAH (July 19, 1806–Feb. 25, 1850), Santa Fé trader, author, was born in Overton County, Tenn. His parents were Harmon and Susannah (Schmelzer) Gregg, and he was a descendant of William Gregg, an Ulster Quaker who settled in Pennsylvania about 1682. In 1812, after three years in Illinois, the family moved to the region about Fort Cooper, on the Missouri, where two brothers of Harmon had also settled, and in 1825 moved further west to the neighborhood of Independence. Josiah had a fairly liberal education; he knew enough Spanish to enable him to read understandingly the archives of the Southwest, and he somehow acquired a knowledge of medicine and surgery that caused him to be dubbed a doctor, though he never engaged in practise. Ill health prompted him to seek the remoter frontier, and on May 15, 1831, he set out with a caravan from Independence for Santa Fé. His health returned, and he became a trader. During a period of more than nine years he made frequent journeys to Santa Fé, occasionally going on to Chihuahua. He was a close and scientific observer and an avid reader, making copious notes of everything that interested him. In the winter of 1843–44 he finished the manuscript of a book on the Southwestern trade, and in the following spring, with a letter of introduction to John Bigelow [*q.v.*], he journeyed to New York. Through the influence of Bigelow, who became his close friend and to some extent retouched his manuscript, a publisher was soon found, and the book, under the title *Commerce of the Prairies,* was published in two volumes that summer (1844). It had an immediate success. A second edition was published in the following year, a fourth in 1850, and a sixth, under a slightly different title, in 1857, as well as three editions in German in the years 1845–47. In the spring of 1846 he rode 1,200 miles on horseback to join Gen. Wool's army at San Antonio. To Bigelow he wrote that he had some sort of official appointment—"call it govt ag't, interpreter or what you please" (Twitchell, *post,* p. 20). After some months of service in Mexico he returned with Doniphan's army, but was again in Mexico in the spring of 1848. In 1849 he made his last journey to Santa Fé. From there he went to California, reaching the Trinity mines, in the northern part of the state, in the fall. He commanded an exploring party of seven men, which left the mines in November and after terrible suffering crossed the Coast Range to the Pacific. On the march in an effort to return with some of his men to the settlements, Gregg, worn out from hunger and exposure, fell from his horse and in a few hours expired.

He never married. He was a man widely known and greatly esteemed for his many admirable qualities, and he seems to have had no enemies. He was, as Thwaites has written, preëminently the historian of the Santa Fé trade, and his book is a recognized classic of the frontier. In the main it is accurate, though it reveals some curious omissions and an occasional error in its accounts of the early expeditions.

[See R. E. Twitchell, "Dr. Josiah Gregg," *Hist. Soc. of New Mex. Pubs.,* no. 26 (1924); W. E. Connelley, "Dr. Josiah Gregg, Historian of the old Santa Fé Trail," *Proc. Miss. Valley Hist. Asso.,* vol. X (1920); *Doniphan's Expedition* (1907), ed. by W. E. Connelley; annotations by R. G. Thwaites in *Commerce of the Prairies* as reprinted in *Early Western Travels,* vols. XIX–XX (1905); J. T. Lee, "The Authorship of Gregg's *Commerce of the Prairies,*" in *Miss. Valley Hist. Rev.,* Mar. 1930, and "New Found Letters of Josiah Gregg," in *Proc. Am. Antiq. Soc.* for Apr. 1930 (vol. XL, 1931). An account of Gregg's last adventure, by L. K. Wood, one of his party, that appeared in the Humboldt, Cal., *Times,* beginning Apr. 26, 1856, has been several times reprinted verbatim (for one instance see *Ky. State Hist. Soc. Reg.,* Jan., May 1908), or in paraphrase; see O. C. Coy, "Last Expedition of Josiah Gregg," *Grizzly Bear,* July 1916.]

W. J. G.

GREGG, MAXCY (1814–Dec. 14, 1862), Confederate soldier, politician, was born at Columbia, S. C., the son of Col. James and Cornelia (Maxcy) Gregg. His father was a graduate of South Carolina College (later the University of South Carolina) and a lawyer by profession. His mother was a daughter of Jonathan Maxcy [*q.v.*]. Maxcy studied law with his father and was admitted to the bar in 1839. He was an intense Southerner, active in politics, and a leader of the State-Rights party. He was appointed major in Col. M. L. Bonham's regiment of volunteers on Mar. 24, 1847, and ordered to Mexico; but he failed to reach the battlegrounds in time to take part in any of the major engagements. After the war he returned to Columbia and practised law until 1860. "In 1850, when the North violated the Missouri Compromise and swindled the Southern people out of California, Gen. Gregg was early and decided in declaring for secession in a speech" (*Charleston Mercury,* Dec. 15, 1862). He was a leading member of the Convention of Southern Rights Associations in Charleston. In 1857 and 1858 he advocated the reopening of the slave trade as a means of separation from the North. He was a delegate from the Richland district to the South Carolina secession convention and a member of the central committee which framed the ordinance of secession, adopted on Dec. 20, 1860. In this convention he argued that all laws of Congress "fall instantly to the ground on passage of the act of secession." He was the author of a resolution to instruct the governor to appoint postmasters for South Carolina (*Richmond Examiner,* Dec. 25, 1860; *Daily Richmond Enquirer,* Dec. 22, 1860). Gregg was appointed colonel of the 1st Regiment of South Carolina Volunteers, and was busy about Charleston with his forces from Jan. 3, 1861, until the fall of Fort Sumter, after which he served in Virginia. He was made a brigadier-general in December 1861 and was returned to South Carolina. He was under fire with his brigade later at Cold Harbor, Frazier's Farm, Malvern Hill, Cedar Run, Second Manassas, Ox Hill, Harper's Ferry, Sharpsburg, Shepherdstown, and Fredericksburg. He was wounded on the leg at Manassas and had his horse shot from under him at Sharpsburg. He was killed at Fredericksburg.

Gregg won the confidence and admiration of his superior officers. Gen. A. P. Hill spoke of him as the "invincible pillar of my strength"; Gen. Lee said, "In Brigadier-Generals Gregg and Cobb, the Confederacy has lost two of its noblest citizens and the army two of its bravest and most distinguished officers . . ." (*Official Records, Army,* 1 ser., XXI, 555–56). Gen. T. J. Jackson said of him, "Gen. Gregg was a brave and accomplished officer, full of heroic sentiment and chivalrous honor. He had rendered valuable service in this great struggle for our freedom, and the country has much reason to deplore the loss sustained by his premature death" (*Official Records, Army,* 1 ser., XXI, 632). Gregg was unmarried. He was well versed in the classics, especially in Greek literature and philosophy. He was a close student of botany and ornithology and had a large and select library and a well-equipped astronomical observatory at his home in Columbia. He was buried in the yard of the First Presbyterian Church, at Columbia, S. C.

[*Richmond Examiner*, Nov. 2, Dec. 21, 1862; *Charleston Mercury*, Dec. 15, 17, 1862; C. S. Boucher, *S. C. and the South on the Eve of Secession 1852–60* (Washington Univ. Studies, vol. VI, 1919); J. F. J. Caldwell, *The Hist. of a Brigade of South Carolinians Known first as "Gregg's" and subsequently as "McGowan's Brigade"* (1866); C. A. Evans, *Confed. Mil. Hist.* (12 vols., 1899); *Cyc. of Eminent Men of the Carolinas of the Nineteenth Century* (2 vols., 1892); Yates Snowden, *Hist. of S. C.* (5 vols., 1920).]

S. S. M.

GREGG, WILLIAM (Feb. 2, 1800–Sept. 13, 1867), cotton manufacturer, was a descendant in the fifth generation of William Gregg who is believed to have come over to Penn's "lower counties" with the Proprietor in 1682. A later William was born in Delaware, became a frontiersman in Virginia and South Carolina, fought in the Revolutionary War, and married Elizabeth Webb of Philadelphia. Their son William was born near Carmichaels, Monongalia County, in what is now West Virginia. His parents were Quakers, and though he did not unite with the Society of Friends, its principles showed in his character. His mother died when he was four years old and he was brought up to the age of ten or eleven by a kind woman neighbor. He was then taken in charge by his uncle, Jacob Gregg, a prosperous watchmaker and manufacturer of cotton-spinning machinery at Alexandria, Va. The boy began to learn the watchmaker's craft, but Jacob Gregg soon moved to a waterpower on Little River, Ga., midway between Monticello and Madison, where, under the stimulus to home manufactures afforded by the War of 1812, he established a small cotton factory. Here William got his first taste of an industry for which he later did more than any other ante-bellum Southerner. When the little mill was ruined by the peace, which brought a flood of English goods into America, Jacob Gregg placed his nephew with an old friend and fellow-craftsman at Lexington, Ky., under whom the youth resumed his apprenticeship in watchmaking and silversmithing. In 1821 he went to Petersburg, Va., to complete his training with one Blanchard. "His education was thus a practical one of manual dexterity. It is not known that he ever went to school a day in his life." It is reasonable to believe "that his trade . . . gave him a sense of precision and a love of the beautiful which were characteristics throughout his life" (Mitchell, *post*, p. 5). In 1824 he established himself in business in Columbia, the capital of South Carolina, where within a decade he accumulated a comfortable fortune, but was forced to retire on account of ill health. In 1829 he married Marina Jones, of Edgefield District, whom he met in his commercial journeys over the state. Upon his retirement he moved to Edgefield, and, partly as an amusement, bought an interest in the small and poorly conducted Vaucluse cotton factory near-by. In a short time he had reorganized it and put it on a paying basis, and in 1843, in partnership with his brother-in-law, James Jones, acquired full possession of it.

In 1838 Gregg took up his residence in Charleston and became a silent partner in the successful jewelry firm of Hayden, Gregg & Company. It was now that his public life began. Charleston was a focus of the state and of the South—cultural, political, financial. He used his leisure to look about him and reflect upon what he saw. He became convinced that exclusive devotion to a staple agriculture was economically unwise, and that what South Carolina and the whole section needed was to embark in cotton manufacturing. Industrial communities, he believed, by furnishing markets, making up home products, and giving employment to unpropertied whites who were rendered superfluous by negro slavery, would enrich agriculture and be enriched in return. It seems certain that Gregg was influenced in his thought by Henry C. Carey [*q.v.*] of Philadelphia, who, in books, magazines, and newspapers, and in the personal contacts in which Gregg doubtless shared, was preaching American economic development through diversification of occupations and a protective tariff. In 1844 Gregg visited the textile districts of the Middle States and New England, and began writing a series of articles, *Essays on Domestic Industry,* published in the *Charleston Courier,* and appearing in 1845 in pamphlet form. These essays boldly reproached the South for obsession with partisan politics and neglect of native resources. The industrial progress of the North, he contended, should be patterned after rather than disparaged, and he insisted that if the South clung to its old creed of cotton culture, it was inviting ever swifter decline through action of the law of diminishing returns. Though severe in its criticism, Gregg's argument was so clear and persuasive that he gained an active audience, and a subscription was immediately begun to erect a cotton factory in Charleston. He himself, however, undertook to establish a mill in the interior. Forming the nucleus of a company, almost entirely of Charleston capitalists, in 1845, he applied to the legislatures of South Carolina and Georgia for a charter of incorporation. Limited liability was unpopular in the South at this time, being associated in the public mind with speculation bordering on dishonesty. Accordingly Gregg published a pamphlet, *An Inquiry into the Expediency of Granting Charters of Incorporation for Manufacturing Purposes in South Carolina,* which he placed in the hands of legislators. In it he sought to remove fears by showing the difference between industries on the one hand, and ambitious projects of internal improvement and banks on the other. He pointed out, furthermore, that only the cooperation of many investors could bring manufactures into existence in the South. Georgia refused a charter, but South Carolina granted one by a single vote, and in 1846 Gregg began erecting the plant of the Graniteville Manufacturing Company in Edgefield District, near Aiken, on the same Horse Creek which operated the Vaucluse factory. This mill, of nearly 9,000 spindles and 300 looms, was to be an object-lesson. Though lacking formal technical training, he was conspicuously successful in directing all the engineering operations. He used native materials and labor in building a granite factory and upwards of a hundred cottages for operatives, thus bringing into existence the first typical Southern cotton-mill village. He took great care to provide comfortable homes for the workers, believing that only through such communities could the "poor whites" be returned to a decent standard of living. As soon as the plant was completed, country people poured in to seek employment and living quarters, and soon the mill had its 300 operatives and the village 900 inhabitants. Only the first superintendent and a few overseers were brought from the North. The company began actual operation in 1848 with $300,000 capital. Gregg acted as president, and operated the plant. The mill had scarcely gotten under way before it encountered the depression of 1850–51, and though in these years it was not able to pay dividends, it held its own. Once over this difficulty, the company amply justified Gregg's optimism, in the years from 1850 to 1866 paying average dividends in excess of 12½ per cent., and in the last thirteen years of this time almost 15½ per cent.

Other cotton-mills, driven by steam where water-power was not available, now sprang up in the South under the influence of Graniteville, and Gregg acquired a wide reputation as the leading Southern cotton manufacturer. His constant advice was that a Southern mill should specialize in a small range of coarse cloths, and endeavor to sell its product in a national or world market, rather than try to turn out a variety of goods to meet all the demands of local consumption. Factories should not be started without ample working capital, for they should seek to sell their product direct from the mill without the intermediation of commission agencies, which could not be relied upon, he thought, to consult the best interests of the manufacturing company. He wanted the Southern mills to be self-sufficient, and his few differences with his own directors were occasioned by this desire. In 1858 Gregg declared in favor of a protective tariff, particularly for Southern industries—an extraordinary step for a South Carolinian of that day. He represented Edgefield District in the state House of Representatives in 1856 and 1857. His principal speech in the first session was directed against further subsidy by the state of the Blue Ridge Railroad intended to connect Anderson, S. C., and ultimately Charleston, with Cincinnati, Ohio. He believed the whole scheme was promoted by self-seeking Charleston merchants who were not regarding the good of the commonwealth. By the time of Gregg's second term in the legislature, the depression of 1857 had caused almost all South Carolina banks to suspend specie payments. Declaring that the banks were solvent if given time to recover, pointing out that the panic was made in New York, and believing that sudden liquidation would ruin the cotton farmers, Gregg stood out against collection by the state of a high tax on note issues of suspended banks. In the main he won his case, though ably opposed by C. G. Memminger [*q.v.*]. Gregg's speech was interpreted in some quarters as favoring the suspended banks, but in reality he was taking the only means of protecting the community as a whole. In general he was opposed to banks and bank investors, preferring to see money go directly into industrial enterprises. He was an unsuccessful candidate for the state Senate in 1858, after a bitter campaign in which he was unfairly charged with exploiting the workpeople of Graniteville. As a matter of fact, his solicitude for the operatives was one of his chief claims to remembrance. He instituted the first carefully organized welfare work in a Southern factory community, giving affectionate attention to the school (where attendance was compulsory for the children), the library, and the health, recreation, and housing of the villagers. He was a benevolent despot, but was the pioneer in opening the door of social betterment to the poor whites through industrial employment. After 1854 he lived near the mill and was the personal friend of everybody. He was a leader in the organization of the South Carolina Institute for the encouragement of the mechanical arts, and made its third annual address (1851).

He was a delegate from Edgefield to the convention which considered the relation of the people of South Carolina to the government of the United States, and on Dec. 17, 1860, signed the ordinance of secession. That year he had published a series of articles in *De Bow's Review* urging Southerners to put themselves in an economic position of defense. During the Civil War he managed to keep his plant in operation in spite of enormous impressments by Confederate and state governments. As soon as possible after the war he went to the North and to Europe to secure equipment for refitting the mill. He had scarcely set things to rights, however, when the mill-dam broke. As a result of standing waist deep in water, without food or rest, while repairing it, he was taken ill and died within a few days. More than any other man, he was the father of the Southern cotton manufacture.

[Broadus Mitchell, *William Gregg, Factory Master of the Old South* (1928); *Charleston Mercury*, Sept. 23, 1867; Gregg's *Essays on Domestic Industry* (1845), which gives his most important views.]

B. M.

GREGORY, CASPAR RENÉ (Nov. 6, 1846–Apr. 9, 1917), New Testament scholar, was of French extraction. His great-grandfather, René Grégoire, was a French officer, a Protestant, who came to America to serve under Washington in the Revolution. Having married in Santo Domingo and become a planter there, he was killed in an insurrection about 1797, and his young son, Caspar Ramsay Grégoire, was sent to Philadelphia, where he became a ship-captain and ship-owner, and Anglicized his name. The latter's son, Henry Duval Gregory, long the head of a classical school in Philadelphia and later vice-president of Girard College, was the father of Caspar René Gregory. His mother's name was Mary Jones. He was prepared for college at his father's school, and graduated from the University of Pennsylvania in 1864 at the age of seventeen. After three years of teaching and theological study in Philadelphia, he entered Princeton Theological Seminary, from which he graduated in 1870. He continued study and literary work at Princeton until 1873, when, perhaps under incentive from Ezra Abbot [*q.v.*], he went to Leipzig for study, and spent there the rest of his life, serving for thirty-three years as instructor and professor at the University. Before long he was invited to complete the final (eighth) edition of Tischendorf's "Greek New Testament with Prolegomena" for which Tischendorf had left practically no materials. This great work (*Novum Testamentum Græce,* 3 vols., Leipzig, 1884, 1890, 1894) containing, with other vast stores of admirably arranged learning, a catalogue of all known Greek manuscripts of the New Testament, engaged Gregory's main effort for twenty years, and on its publication was at once accepted as an indispensable tool of scholarship. In preparing it he visited all the great and many of the smaller libraries of Europe and made journeys to the East. In the meantime he had been naturalized as a German, and in 1884 became *Privatdocent* at Leipzig, in 1889 *ausserordentlicher Professor,* and in 1891 *ordentlicher Honorarprofessor.* He was a clear, forcible, and interesting teacher of the New Testament. In 1886 he was married at Cambridge, Mass., to Lucy Watson Thayer, daughter of Joseph Henry Thayer [*q.v.*]; they had one son and three daughters.

In the twenty years after the Prolegomena Gregory, whose mind seethed with plans, published many important products of a scholar's industry, partly the fruit of four long journeys to the East. In the course of his studies he probably examined more manuscripts of the New Testament than any other man that ever lived, and he was recognized as a master in Greek paleography and in New Testament textual studies. His ultimate aim was a fresh Greek text of the New Testament. During all these years, moreover, the inner impulse of an earnest and self-denying Christian and the intense loyalty of a foreigner to his adopted country led him to spend endeavor, time, and sentiment on a succession of Christian social undertakings and movements in Germany. A little man, with black hair and, in later years, no hat, a keen eye, delicately cut features and sharp nose, and a pointed beard, alertness and vivacity in his every movement and utterance, unlike either German or American, his cordial ways and sincere goodness made him beloved and admired, perhaps all the more for some oddities and what seemed a certain lack of sense of proportion. He was tough and wiry, extraordinarily capable of long hours at his desk and of heavy physical labor in travel, especially on foot.

In 1914, when the War broke out, he was nearly sixty-eight years old, but within ten days he had by sheer importunity compelled the unwilling recruiting officers to accept him as an enlisted man for active service in the German army. At the front in France he insisted on serving in the trenches; he was finally commissioned lieutenant in an infantry regiment. For some time he was assigned to the hazardous and very arduous duty of seeking out and registering graves of fallen German soldiers, a valuable work for which his vocation had uniquely fitted him. On Apr. 9, 1917, at Neufchâtel-sur-Aisne, then under bombardment, he was lying in bed because of an injury to his knee due to the fall of his horse, and was fatally wounded by a fragment of shell, dying the same day. A public monument has been erected to his memory near his house in Leipzig. Besides the Prolegomena, his chief books are *Textkritik des Neuen Testamentes* (3 vols., 1900, 1902, 1909); *Canon and Text of the New Testament* (New York, 1907); *Die griechischen Handschriften des Neuen Testaments* (1908); *Einleitung in das Neue Testament* (1909); *Die Koridethi Evangelien* (1913), with Gustav Beermann.

[Karl Josef Friedrich, *Volksfreund Gregory: Amerikaner, Pfadfinder, Urchrist, deutscher Kämpfer* (2nd ed., Gotha, 1920), contains much interesting personal detail. *Who's Who in America,* 1916–17; *Princeton Theol. Sem. Bull.: Necrological Report,* Aug. 1918; *Biblical World* (Chicago), Nov. 1911; H. Frankfurth, "Caspar René Gregory, ein Bekenner," *Zeitwende* (Munich), Aug. 1926.] J. H. R.

GREGORY, DANIEL SEELYE (Aug. 21, 1832–Apr. 14, 1915), Presbyterian clergyman, educator, and editor, born in Carmel, N. Y., was of English descent, the son of Horace and Elizabeth (Seelye) Gregory. His great-grandfather, Rev. Elnathan Gregory, a graduate of Princeton in the class of 1757, had been pastor in Carmel from 1761 to 1774. Daniel graduated from the State Normal School, Albany, in 1850 and for three years taught in the public schools. Entering Princeton, he graduated from the college in 1857, and from the theological seminary in 1860, having served as tutor in belles-lettres at the college from 1858 to 1860. On Nov. 5 of the latter year he married Jennie G. Brown of Croton Falls, N. Y., who died in 1866; and in December 1867, Harriet Byram, adopted daughter of D. M. Halliday of New York. Ordained to the Presbyterian ministry in 1861, he held pastorates in Galena, Ill., 1861–63; Troy, N. Y., 1863–66; New Haven, Conn., 1866–69; and South Salem, N. Y., 1869–71.

Withdrawing from the active ministry, he was professor of intellectual and moral philosophy and logic in 1871, and after 1874, of English language and literature, at the University of Wooster, Ohio. In 1878 he was elected president of Lake Forest University and professor of Christian philosophy and the mental sciences, an office which he held until 1886 when he resigned to accept a pastorate at Morgan, Minn. Here he remained until 1889, when, at the request of Dr. Isaac K. Funk [*q.v.*], he joined the editorial staff of the *Standard Dictionary of the English Language* (2 vols., 1893–95), of the first edition of which work he was managing editor. Following its completion, he became co-editor with Dr. Funk of the *Homiletic Review,* in which capacity he served from 1895 until 1904. In January of the latter year, he was appointed general secretary of the American Bible League, and managing editor of the *Bible Student and Teacher.* A man of scholarly mind and wide knowledge of the English language, he brought to his lexicographical work a well-balanced judgment, a keen intellect, and a broadness of interpretation that proved of great value. Strong in his convictions, he was a sturdy champion of the traditional view of the Bible and the doctrines of his faith. His opinions and spirit are revealed in his published works which include, *Why Four Gospels?* (1877); *Christ's Trumpet-Call to the Ministry* (1896); *The Church in America and Its Baptism of Fire* (1896), with S. B. Halliday; *The Crime of Christendom* (1900); *Bible League Primers: No. 1* (1904); "Constructive Studies in John, the Gospel for the Christian," in the *Bible Student and Teacher* (January–July 1908).

[*Who's Who in America,* 1914–15; *Princeton Theol. Sem. Biog. Cat.* (1909); *Gen. Register of Lake Forest College, 1857–1914* (1914); *The College of Wooster, Cat. of the Alumni and Faculty* (1916); *Homiletic Rev.,* June 1915; *Presbyterian* (Phila.), Apr. 22, 1915; N. Y. *Evening Post,* Apr. 15, 1915.] F. H. V.

GREGORY, ELIOT (Oct. 13, 1854?–June 1, 1915), painter and essayist, the son of James Gilbert and Eliza (Morgan) Gregory, was born in New York City. He was descended from Ezra Gregory who settled in Connecticut some time in the eighteenth century. From 1870 to 1872 he attended the Sheffield Scientific School at Yale, and the following year he took a special course at Sheffield, at the same time attending the art school. He received no degree, and in 1876 he went to Paris to study under Carolus-Duran. In 1880 he exhibited a portrait of Longfellow in the Paris Salon, as well as a statue, "Corinne." During the eighties he painted portraits of various Americans, including Admiral Baldwin, his uncle by marriage; Mrs. Astor; Ada Rehan; and August Belmont. His portrait of Gen. George W. Cullum was hung at West Point. After 1890 he devoted more of his time to writing than to painting. He wrote for the New York *Post* a series of essays which he signed "An Idler." Some of these essays were collected and published as *Worldly Ways & Byways* (1898), and a second volume, *The Ways of Men,* appeared in 1900. He also wrote a comedy, *Under the Stars,* and further essays by him appeared in various periodicals as late as 1910. In 1911 he was given the Cross of the Legion of Honor in recognition of his writings on French subjects.

The pen-name that Gregory chose is not without significance. He preferred to live in the fashionable world, and he spent most of his time in New York City, Newport, and France. His paintings and sculpture, though praised at the time when they appeared, were soon forgotten, and his name is not mentioned in most histories of American art. His writing was rather desultory and derives such charm as it has from its suggestion of leisurely culture and intimacy with sophisticated society. He sought to be an arbiter of manners and discussed in his essays such topics as feminine charms, American cooking, the lack of a true social life in this country, the inefficiency of public servants, and the miserable lot of American husbands. He also wrote occasionally on the arts, treating in a light and personal tone such subjects as the first performance of "Cyrano," Madam Calvé at home, Tolstoi's definition of art, and the character of Carolus-Duran. His essays on France and the French led Jules Claretie to say that he would prefer Gregory to any one else as a literary guide to the curiosities of Paris. Gregory was, in short, a devotee of the genteel tradition. Always critical of those Americans who expatriated themselves, he felt it his duty to raise the tone of life in this country by correcting American manners and purifying American taste. Like Edith Wharton, to whom he dedicated his second book, he hoped for an alliance between the arts and so much of an aristocracy as might be found to exist in the United States. His contributions to that cause were, like the man himself, rather mild and perhaps ineffectual.

[*Who's Who in America,* 1914–15; *N. Y. Times,* June 2, 1915; records of Yale University; information as to certain facts from Capt. John F. Jackson, U. S. N., Washington, D. C. There is autobiographical material in some of the essays.]

G. H.

GREGORY, JOHN MILTON (July 6, 1822–Oct. 19, 1898), Baptist clergyman, educational leader, university president, was born at Sand Lake, N. Y., of transplanted New England stock, a son of Joseph G. Gregory, farmer-tanner, and Rachel Bullock. His early education was received in a village school near his home and in Poughkeepsie Academy. He graduated from Union College in the class of 1846 when Eliphalet Nott [*q.v.*] was in mid-career as president. After a brief period of teaching and studying law he was ordained to the Baptist ministry in 1847 and served in pastorates in Hoosick Falls, N. Y., and Akron, Ohio. He made a definite shift to educational work in 1852 when he took charge of a private high school in Detroit, Mich. He joined the newly organized Michigan State Teachers' Association in 1853 and soon became a founder and editor of the *Michigan Journal of Education,* thus inaugurating a progressive career of thirty years of leadership in public education in the Middle West. He was elected superintendent of public instruction for Michigan and by reëlection served from Jan. 1, 1859, until 1864 when he refused reëlection in order to accept the presidency of Kalamazoo College, a position which he held for three years. As superintendent he was *ex officio* a member and secretary of the Michigan state board of education which until 1861 was charged with the management of the Michigan State Agricultural College. First-hand knowledge of the workings of a new land-grant college in its early stages which he gained, together with his experience at Kalamazoo, fitted him for the beginning of his influential career as the first regent (president) of the Illinois Industrial University (now the University of Illinois) after its creation in 1867.

In Illinois, as in other western states where land-grant colleges were established, strong pressure was exerted to insure a "practical" institution for farmers and mechanics. The new regent sensed fully the meaning of this pressure but with the aid of several able members of the board of trustees he formulated clearly his "grand idea" of a new type of tax-supported institution for all the people of the state, "a true University . . . its central educational courses, while equally broad and liberal . . . to be selected to fit men for the study and mastery of the great branches of industry, rather than to serve as introductions to the study of law, medicine and theology" (*First Annual Report of the Board of Trustees,* 1868, 48–49). The next thirteen years he gave enthusiastically to building up a university, not a mere vocational school, in spite of inadequate revenues, public indifference, opposition in the faculty. and disciplinary difficulties with the students. Resigning as regent in 1880, he devoted several years to writing, travel, and incidental public service.

Three times he served on commissions connected with international expositions: as United States commissioner to the Vienna Exposition in 1873; as judge in the educational department of the Centennial Exposition in 1876; and as Illinois commissioner to the Paris Exposition of 1878. In 1881 he served as president of the Illinois State Board of Health, and later for about a year, as general superintendent of the educational work of the American Baptist Home Mission Society, concerning himself largely with schools in the South. Two books came out of these years: *A New Political Economy* (1882) and *The Seven Laws of Teaching* (1884), besides numerous published articles and addresses on educational subjects. Upon the organization of the first United States Civil Service Commission in 1883, he was appointed as one of the three members, resigning in 1885. He then spent five years abroad. He was twice married, in 1848 to Julia Gregory, a cousin, who bore him five children; in 1879 to Louisa C. Allen by whom he had one daughter who became his biographer. His last years were spent in literary, community, and religious work in Maryland, in California, and in Washington, D. C., where he died.

[Allene Gregory's *John Milton Gregory, A Biography* (1923), is a rather emotional and eulogistic volume, based, however, on Gregory's diary and writings. See also Allan Nevins, *Illinois* (1917); reports (1859–64) of the Superintendent of Public Instruction of Michigan; reports (1868–80) of the Board of Trustees of the Illinois Industrial University; *Washington Post*, Oct. 21, 1898.] K. C. B.

GREGORY, SAMUEL (Apr. 19, 1813–Mar. 23, 1872), pioneer in the medical education of women, was born in Guilford, Vt. In 1840 he was graduated at Yale, receiving the degree of A.B. For the next few years he taught evening classes in English in manufacturing towns and in 1847 did at least one piece of hack writing, *Gregory's History of Mexico,* which was issued that year, in paper covers, by F. Gleason of Boston. During Gregory's last year in college he had become interested in anatomy and physiology as a result of lectures delivered to the senior class by members of the medical faculty. He read further for himself along these lines, became interested in mesmerism as applied to the cure of disease, and in addition to his teaching lectured gratuitously in different parts of New England on educational and sanitary subjects. He received his master's degree from Yale in 1845 and after 1853 added an honorary M.D. to his name (*Statistics of the Class of 1840, Yale College,* 1860, p. 29).

During the summer and fall of 1847 he gave some public lectures in behalf of "the medical education of females" and urged the establishment of an institution for that purpose. For the remaining twenty-five years of his life he was active in the promotion of this cause. His primary objects were to educate women in the care of children for whom as mothers they were responsible; to train women in the care of the sick for whom intelligent nursing was necessary; and to give women missionaries some of the fundamentals of medicine that would be of special use to them in the mission field. Later, he included in his scheme the full medical education of women so that they might "become thoroughly qualified Female Physicians, and thus be able to administer to their sex, and to enlighten them in relation to the principles of health, and the means of preventing and relieving sickness and suffering." On Nov. 1, 1848, after due announcement, the Boston Female Medical School, later the New-England Female Medical College, was opened with a class of twelve pupils. It was the earliest school of its kind in the United States. At first there was but one lecturer, Enoch C. Rolfe, M.D., "with occasional assistance by others," but the number was added to year by year, until in 1853 the faculty had seven members. From the beginning Gregory was secretary and chief executive officer, and for a period, professor of chemistry also. He wrote reports, contributed to periodicals, and published a number of pamphlets, one of which—*Letter to Ladies, in Favor of Female Physicians for their own Sex* (1850)—went through several editions and was especially influential in gaining subscriptions. He was also secretary of the Female Medical Education Society, organized Nov. 23, 1848, with a membership of six to sustain the school and secure a hospital. Incorporated Apr. 30, 1850, the Society claimed some fifteen hundred members in 1851. It was reorganized by act of the legislature in 1856, under the name New-England Female Medical College, and a board of trustees was created and empowered to grant the degree of Doctor of Medicine. In 1859 Dr. Marie E. Zakrzewska [*q.v.*] was appointed to organize the clinical department. The school was a somewhat migratory institution, and it was not until 1870 that it was able to occupy a new college building of ample size on land acquired from the city. In 1872 Gregory died in Boston, of consumption. He was unmarried.

Gregory attacked the medical profession in his early pamphlets, *Man-Midwifery Exposed and Corrected* (1848) and *Female Mid-Wifery Advocated* (1848), and thus aroused their antagonism. He considered the microscope "one of those new-fangled European notions," and "pronounced against such innovations as . . . thermometer, test-tubes, etc., as proof of incapacity to recognize the ailments of patients" (*Zakrzewska,* pp. 251, 284). Nevertheless, he built more firmly and wisely than he knew. Two years after his death the school which he founded was merged with the Boston University School of Medicine, which became one of the first co-educational medical schools in the world.

[Published records of the Yale class of 1840; *Obit. Record Grads. Yale Coll.,* 1872; Annual Reports, Cata-

logues, and Announcements of the New-England Female Medical College; Trustees' Records, Secretary's Records of the Female Medical Education Society; *A Woman's Quest: The Life of Dr. Marie E. Zakrzewska* (1924), ed. by Agnes C. Vietor; *Boston Transcript*, Mar. 25, 1872.]
J. P. S—d.

GREGORY, STEPHEN STRONG (Nov. 16, 1849–Oct. 24, 1920), lawyer, the son of Jared C. and Charlotte (Camp) Gregory, of Connecticut ancestry, was born in Unadilla, Otsego County, N. Y. In 1858 his father, a lawyer of considerable capacity, moved to Madison, Wis., and there the son was educated in the public schools and at the University of Wisconsin. Following his graduation in 1870 he spent a year in the law department of the University, taking his LL.B. degree in 1871. On his admission to the Wisconsin bar in that year he opened an office in Madison and practised there for three years. Desiring a wider field, however, he gained admission to the Illinois bar, Sept. 14, 1874, and established himself in Chicago, where he spent the remainder of his life. He had no liking for public life and consistently declined to allow his name to be brought forward as a candidate for office, preferring to retain his freedom of thought and action. The only official position he ever occupied was that of election commissioner for the city of Chicago, which he held for two years (1888–90). With this exception his life was spent in unremitting attention to his professional duties. When he moved to Chicago, though young, he had already acquired a reputation as an advocate, and in a short time he was recognized as one of the ablest members of the Illinois bar. He did not confine himself to any particular branch of the law, but accepted retainers in all the courts, federal and state, and from the first exhibited outstanding qualities as a counsel. His intuitive appreciation of human nature enabled him to deal with witnesses in a masterly manner, his wide knowledge of legal principles and mastery of case law placed him in a class by himself as a trial lawyer, while his extreme accuracy of statement gained for him the confidence of all courts in which he appeared.

In course of time Gregory was briefed in all the important local cases of his day. He represented the city of Chicago in its heavy litigation over the Lake Front before the United States Supreme Court and appeared for the Sanitary District of Chicago in the suit which established its constitutionality. He was also retained in the "Chicago Traction Cases" the complexity of the details of which have probably never been surpassed. Although his practise was almost entirely confined to civil cases, on one occasion he appeared in criminal proceedings which attracted world-wide attention, namely, the Debs case arising out of the Pullman strike, where the accused were indicted for conspiracy to obstruct a mail train on the Rock Island Railroad. Gregory was leading counsel for Debs and the directors of the American Railway Union. It has been well said that his assistance was generally sought in cases of great public interest in which personal rights were assailed (American Bar Association *Journal*, *post*, p. 143). He enjoyed great personal popularity, possessing the confidence and respect of people of all classes. Genial, courteous, enjoying a joke and capable of perpetrating one, he was ever a friend of the younger element, particularly the junior members of the bar. He occasionally contributed articles to the legal periodicals, one of which, "Some Reflections on the German Constitution," reprinted from the *Virginia Law Review* for March 1918, was published in pamphlet form. He took active part in legal organizations and served as president of the Chicago Bar Association, 1900, the Illinois State Bar Association, 1904, and the American Bar Association, 1911. He was married, on Nov. 25, 1880, to Janet M. Tappan of Madison, Wis., who with two sons and a daughter survived him.

[An excellent review of Gregory's career is contained in the Am. Bar Asso. *Jour.*, Nov. 1920. See also *The Bench and Bar of Chicago* (n.d.); *Who's Who in America*, 1918–19; *Chicago Legal News*, Nov. 4, 1899; *Proc. Ill. State Bar Asso.* (1921); *Chicago Tribune*, Oct. 25, 26, 1920.]
H. W. H. K.

GREIST, JOHN MILTON (May 9, 1850–Feb. 23, 1906), inventor, manufacturer, was born in Crawfordsville, Ind., seventh of the eight children of Joseph W. and Ruth Anna (Garretson) Griest. His parents had moved to Indiana from Pennsylvania, where earlier generations of the father's family, spelling their name "Griest," had settled in the early days of the colony. They were Quakers in religion. John's father, still actuated by the spirit of the pioneer, had, during the gold rush, pushed on across the Continent to California, where shortly afterwards he died. Although the family was poor, young John was allowed to go to school until he was fourteen. He then went to work in Plainfield, Ind., selling Wheeler & Wilson sewing-machines. He was apparently an able salesman, for in the course of five or six years his selling territory was extended to cover parts of the states of Indiana, Illinois, and Iowa. His large experience with users of sewing-machines acquainted him with a real demand for additional equipment which would enable the user to do more than straight sewing. Early in the seventies, therefore, he began, in a small way, to manufacture attachments in Delavan, Ill., and shortly thereafter moved to Chicago and organized the Greist Manufacturing Company. Although at that time many patents had been issued for tucking, ruffling, and other sewing-machine attachments, Griest was the first to undertake the refinement of these earlier devices and make them practical. In the course of the succeeding seventeen years his company built up an extensive business based upon his own patented improvements, which numbered close to fifty. In addition to those he himself manufactured, in 1883 Greist sold a number of patents having to do with hemming, tucking, and ruffling to the Singer Manufacturing Company, and three years later he perfected a button-hole attachment which brought his company large contracts from the sewing-machine manufacturers. In 1887 he gave up his Chicago business to establish and manage an attachment department for the Singer company, to which his patents during this period were assigned. In 1889 he resigned from the Singer company and went to New Haven, Conn., where he organized the firm of J. M. Greist & Company, but about a year later moved to Westville, a suburb of New Haven, and established the Greist Manufacturing Company. The demand for his products grew rapidly and in the course of a few years nearly all of the sewing-machine manufacturers and supply houses ordered their attachments from Greist. At the time of his death his establishment employed upward of 350 people. Greist built up a large fortune and five years before his death purchased land in Westville and developed a seven-hundred-acre estate which was his residence, but which was always open as a public park. He was married twice: in August 1870 to Sarah Edwina Murdock, who died on Aug. 14, 1897, and in October 1899, to Mary Fife Woods of Pittsburgh, Pa., who, with two sons and a daughter by his first wife, survived him.

[W. R. Cutter, *Geneal. and Family Hist. of the State of Conn.* (4 vols., 1911); Chicago and New Haven directories; *Sewing Machine Times*, Mar. 10, 1906; *New Haven Evening Register*, Feb. 23, 1906; Patent Office records.]

C. W. M.

GRELLET, STEPHEN (Nov. 2, 1773–Nov. 16, 1855), a recognized minister of the Society of Friends, whose missionary itineraries covered practically all of Europe and the United States and reached up into Canada, was born in Limoges, France, the fifth child of Gabriel Marc Antoine de Grellet and Susanne de Senamaud. As a youth in his native country he was known as Étienne de Grellet du Mabillier. His father was a wealthy manufacturer of porcelain and proprietor of iron works, one-time comptroller of the mint, and an intimate of Louis XVI. Étienne was taught by tutors and attended several colleges, but received his principal scholastic training at the Collège of the Oratorians, Lyons. He displayed keen religious sensibilities, but became skeptical regarding Roman Catholic dogmas. At the outbreak of the Revolution the family estates were confiscated, and his parents barely escaped the guillotine. Étienne and some of his brothers joined the royal forces in Germany, and in 1792 as a member of the King's Horse Guards, he entered France. Later he was made a prisoner of war and sentenced to be shot, but escaped to Amsterdam, from which place with his brother Joseph, he sailed for Demerara, South America, arriving in January 1793. Here they engaged in mercantile pursuits, but in 1795, upon a false report that a French fleet was approaching the coast, they fled to New York. By this time Étienne had become a disciple of Voltaire, but through associations formed in Newtown, Long Island, where he took up his residence, and the reading of William Penn's writings, he was converted to the beliefs and practises of the Friends. In the latter part of 1795 he went to Philadelphia and engaged in business. Here in the fall of 1796 he was formally received into the Society of Friends, and in March 1798 he was duly recorded as a minister of Christ by the Monthly Meeting of the North District, of which he was a member. During the yellow-fever epidemic of 1798, he visited the sick and dying, contracted the disease, and was so sick that his death was judged inevitable and actually reported. In 1799 he removed to New York and on Jan. 11, 1804, married Rebecca Collins, daughter of Isaac and Rachel Collins of that city.

From 1799 on, his career was a series of missionary and philanthropic journeys separated by intervals in which he was able to give sufficient attention to business to provide funds to support him in his far-reaching ministry. He combined the grace, courtesy, and affableness of a French noble with Quaker simplicity, gentleness, sagacity, and calm reliance upon the Divine guidance, and was cordially received by all classes. He served the lowly and stood unabashed before rulers, who listened with respect to his views and recommendations. He not only held religious meetings, but visited mines, hospitals, prisons, and asylums, and sought to ameliorate social conditions generally. His travels in the United States extended north to the Kennebec, south to New Orleans, and westward to Illinois. In the South he held meetings among the slaves, and talked of the wrongs of the slave-system with their masters. Visiting Canada, he preached in his native tongue to Roman Catholics. He made four tours in Europe. The first (1807–08) was confined to France. The second (1811–14) included the British Isles, France, Switzerland, Italy, and Spain. After ministering in Newgate, together with his friend, John Forster, he conferred with Elizabeth Fry and is credited with inspiring her work for the female prisoners there. He was received by the King of Bavaria, with whom he discussed the religious and social conditions of the kingdom, and in London after the "Peace of Paris," he pled with the King of Prussia and the Emperor of Russia for the spirit of peace in the future government of Europe. In 1816 he made a trip to Haiti, and upon his return interested English philanthropists in effecting social improvements there. On his third European tour (1818–20) he was joined in London by William Allen. Besides countries already traversed he visited Norway, Sweden, Finland, Russia, the Crimea, and Greece. Received by Alexander I of Russia, he reported the wretched conditions he had found in prisons and poorhouses. As a result of their discussion of educational methods, *Scripture Lessons for Schools* (1820), compiled by Grellet, Allen, and others, was adopted in Russia. He was also received by the Pope, to whom he suggested needed reforms. This third journey is commemorated by Whittier in his poem "The Christian Tourists" (*Complete Poetical Works,* 1900, p. 147). During 1831–34 he was again abroad. In his later years his activities were lessened by failing health. After 1823 with his wife and one daughter he made his home in Burlington, N. J., where just after the completion of his eighty-second year he died.

[Benj. Seebohm, *Memoirs of the Life and Gospel Labours of Stephen Grellet* (2 vols.; English edition, 1860, American, 1860, French, *Un Quaker Français,* 1873), based on autobiographical material; Wm. Guest, *Stephen Grellet* (English edition, 1880, American, 1881, Japanese, 1887); Frances A. Budge, *A Missionary Life: Stephen Grellet* (1888); Cortlandt Van Rensselaer, *The Fight, Faith and Crown* (1856); *A Testimony* (of Burlington Monthly Meeting) *Concerning Stephen Grellet* (1856); *Christian Observer* (London), July 1862; *London Review,* Apr. 1862; *Eclectic Review* (London), July 1863; R. M. Jones, *The Later Periods of Quakerism* (2 vols., 1921); *Friends' Intelligencer,* Dec. 1, 1855; *N. Y. Tribune,* Nov. 19, 1855.]

H. E. S.

GRESHAM, WALTER QUINTIN (Mar. 17, 1832–May 28, 1895), soldier, jurist, statesman, was a direct descendant of Lawrence Gresham, who in 1759, as a small boy, was sent from his native England to Virginia to live with his uncle under indenture. Lawrence's son, George, was born near Petersburg, Va., Oct. 9, 1776, and in early manhood joined the stream of emigrants pouring into Kentucky, taking his mother and father with him. In 1801 George married Mary Pennington, the only sister of Dennis Pennington, a leading figure in the early history of Indiana, whither George moved his family in 1809. His son, William, the father of the subject of this sketch, was born in Mercer County, Ky., Sept. 17, 1802. On Nov. 3, 1825, he married Sarah Davis, who was born Sept. 15, 1807, near Springfield, Washington County, Ky., and they went to live in a log cabin on land his father had entered near Lanesville, Harrison County, Ind. William Gresham, a cabinetmaker by profession, was elected by popular vote a colonel in the state militia and, while sheriff of Harrison County in 1834, was stabbed and killed by an outlaw whom he was attempting to arrest.

Walter was born on the family homestead near Lanesville and was brought up with his two brothers and two sisters by his mother, who continued to operate the farm with the assistance of her boys and their step-father, Noah Rumley, the boys attending the log schoolhouse in the Gresham woods. The return of his elder brother Benjamin from the Mexican War enabled Walter, then seventeen, to accept the place as minute clerk which Dennis Pennington had arranged for him in the office of his legal guardian, Samuel J. Wright, county auditor. His earnings in this position, and in alternately teaching in the log schoolhouse on the Gresham farm and serving as a clerk in the offices of the clerk of the courts and the clerk of the county, enabled him to attend the Corydon Seminary for two years, until in September 1851 he began a year in the state university at Bloomington. The following September he took up the study of law in the office of Judge William A. Porter. Almost two years spent thus resulted in his admission to the bar on Apr. 1, 1854, on the motion of Judge Porter, and soon afterwards to the formation of a partnership with Thomas C. Slaughter, later circuit judge, which brought him almost immediate success.

Even before his admission to the bar, Gresham became interested in politics. While brought up in an abolitionist environment, he was not an extremist in his opposition to slavery. He believed that the passage of time would bring about the abolition of slavery without violence and with due compensation to the slaveholders, and he used his influence with people of Corydon, the county seat, which was situated on a direct road from the Kentucky border to the north, to curtail the activities of the "underground railroad." When the Kansas-Nebraska Bill, which provided for territorial option on the slavery question, threw the country into a frenzy, Gresham became particularly active against it. In the congressional election of 1854, in addition to helping the management of the campaign of Judge Slaughter against the Democratic incumbent from the 2nd Indiana district, William H. English [*q.v.*], he also became the Anti-Nebraska candidate for prosecuting attorney, but both of the law partners lost the election by a narrow margin.

Debarred from the old Whig party because of its proslavery tendencies, Gresham joined the American or Know-Nothing party and in 1855 was induced to run for county clerk, losing again by a narrow margin. The following year he took an active interest in the organization of the Republican party and even took the stump for its nominee for the presidency, John C. Frémont. On Feb. 11, 1858, he married Matilda McGrain, the daughter of Thomas McGrain, a native of Dublin, Ireland, and his wife, Matilda Reed, the daughter of a Presbyterian minister from the north of Ireland. In 1860 Gresham won his first and only political victory, defeating his Democratic rival for election to the lower branch of the Indiana legislature by sixty votes. Early in 1861, as chairman of the committee on military affairs of the state legislature, he drafted a bill, giving the governor control of the appointment of militia officers theretofore elected by the men, which was defeated in the Senate but was passed before the end of the special session. His opposition to the spoils system and particularly to the displacement of the trustees of the state benevolent institutions for party reasons led to a breach with Gov. Oliver P. Morton which had considerable influence upon his subsequent career. With the outbreak of the Civil War Gresham offered his services to the Governor, but was refused a commission. In keen disappointment he came home to Corydon and organized a company, enlisting as a private and being elected its captain. In August he was commissioned lieutenant-colonel of the 38th Indiana Regiment and in December was promoted colonel of the 53rd Indiana.

Soon the order came to join Gen. Grant's forces in Tennessee and this association proved to be the beginning of a lasting friendship. At the battle of Shiloh, he guarded the station at Savannah and so did not participate in the fighting, but at the siege of Corinth, through the Mississippi campaign and the investment of Vicksburg, he saw active service. On Aug. 11, 1863, upon the recommendation of Generals Grant and Sherman, he was appointed brigadier-general and placed in command of the Natchez district, where he was so successful in dealing with the situation involving cotton speculators and thieves that in the spring of 1864 he was assigned to Sherman's army and was placed in command of the 4th Division of the XVII (Blair's) Corps in the Atlanta campaign. He participated in the battle of Kenesaw Mountain (June 27) and on July 20 at Leggett's Hill before Atlanta was wounded in the knee by a sharpshooter's bullet, a wound which incapacitated him for over a year and from which he never fully recovered.

On Mar. 13, 1865, he was brevetted major-general of volunteers for his gallantry at Atlanta, and in the following November, as soon as he was able to walk with crutches, he opened a law office at New Albany, Ind., in partnership with Judge John Butler of Salem. In 1866 he was the unsuccessful Union party candidate for Congress against Michael C. Kerr, but when the legislature met in January 1867, it elected him state agent for the handling of the state finances in New York, where the state debt was payable. After attending the Republican convention in Chicago in 1868, as delegate-at-large from Indiana, he was again prevailed upon to run for Congress, and again defeated, this time because the 2nd Indiana district had been gerrymandered to insure Democratic victory. He became disgusted with partisan politics and even declined in 1869 appointments proffered by President Grant as collector of the port of New Orleans and United States District Attorney for Indiana, the latter because of his promised support to Gen. Thomas Brown. Grant then appointed him United States district judge for the district of Indiana. He was fast becoming a strong figure among the Republicans and was frequently mentioned as a presidential possibility, along with his rival for Indiana leadership, Gen. Benjamin Harrison. In 1880, when the Republicans were in control of the legislature, he became a candidate for the senatorial nomination, but the strength of Harrison caused him finally to withdraw from the fight.

In April 1883, after the death of Timothy Otis Howe, President Arthur, to block an incipient Harrison presidential boom and with a view to an Arthur-Gresham ticket, offered Gresham the postmaster-generalship by telegraph. The latter accepted and served eighteen months, achieving important reforms, including the reduction of letter postage from three to two cents and the increase of allowable weight from one-half to one ounce, the improvement of foreign postal service, the reëstablishment of fast mails, and the reduction of letter postage to Canada. He was also active in the fight against the Louisiana Lottery, bringing it to a head by excluding the lottery from the mails. On Sept. 25, 1884, on the death of Charles J. Folger, he accepted a stop-gap appointment as secretary of the treasury until Oct. 28, when he was appointed circuit judge of the 7th judicial district to succeed Judge Thomas Drummond, who had previously retired. His fearlessness in decisions is well illustrated in the celebrated Wabash case, when he ordered the removal of one of Jay Gould's friends from the receivership of the railroad.

The delegates to the Republican National Convention of 1884 in Chicago had Gresham's name under consideration and he was the second choice of many, but no votes were cast for him. By 1888, however, he had gained more strength and on the first ballot received 107 votes, with Senator John Sherman in the lead with 229. Benjamin Harrison, fourth on the first, was finally nominated on the eighth ballot. When Harrison was elected, Gresham was mentioned by the press as the logical man to fill a vacancy on the Supreme Court, but he refused to be considered. His hostility to a protective tariff became more and more pronounced, and after the passage of the McKinley law of 1890, he and others announced their opposition. This was so marked that in 1892 he was unofficially tendered the presidential nomination by the Populist party, prior to their Omaha Convention, but he declined, although assured of the support of the leaders in Illinois and Indiana from both major parties. He had supported the Democrat Kerr on a hard-money platform in the congressional election of 1874, but it was not until 1892 that he went over to the Democrats entirely and voted for Cleveland. In February 1893 the President-Elect offered him the secretaryship of state. At first he declined, but he was finally prevailed upon to accept and entered on his duties Mar. 7, 1893. His foreign policy was carried out with firmness uninfluenced by jingoist opposition. In the Hawaiian controversy he advised the President that the treaty of annexation negotiated by Harrison should not be resubmitted to the Senate, on the ground that only the restoration of the legitimate government would satisfy the demands of justice. In the Nicaraguan-British dispute, he brought about the withdrawal of the British ships from Corinto and the extension of the time in which indemnity could be paid for insults done to British subjects, with the result that the money was paid before the expiration of the time and the Mosquito Reserve territorial question was settled. In the difficulty with Spain over the *Alliança,* fired upon by a Spanish gunboat, he sought "peace with honor," receiving a disavowal of any intended discourtesy and an apology from the Spanish government. During the Sino-Japanese War, the American ministers, under Gresham's instructions, were the channels of communication between the warring nations. The Bering Sea Award controversy, the difficulties with Italy over the lynching of Italians in Colorado, the insurrection in Brazil, and many other questions came up for consideration during his incumbency. While he was still holding office, he died in Washington from a complication of diseases, aggravated by pneumonia, and one year after his funeral in Chicago, he was buried in the Arlington National Cemetery. As a man he was "absolutely without personal vanity, modest in his deportment, democratic in his actions" (*New York Times, post*). As a statesman, though he was strong and independent, he lacked a far-reaching knowledge of foreign affairs and left no enduring mark on American foreign policy.

[The most complete life of Gresham is the *Life of Walter Quintin Gresham, 1832–1895* (2 vols., 1919), by his wife. See also Montgomery Schuyler, "Walter Quintin Gresham," in vol. VIII (1928) of *Am. Secretaries of State and their Diplomacy,* ed. by S. F. Bemis; *Papers Relating to the Foreign Relations of the U. S.,* 1893–95; *N. Y. Times, Evening Star* (Washington), May 28, 1895; *Chicago Tribune,* May 28, 29, 1895. The Gresham papers have been deposited in the Lib. of Cong.] H. F. W.

GREW, THEOPHILUS (d. 1759), mathematician, astronomer, is first heard of in 1732, when he published at Annapolis, Md., *The Maryland Almanack for the Year of our Lord God, 1733 . . . By T—— G——, Student in the Mathematics.* During the next quarter-century he became well known throughout the southern and middle colonies for his astronomical calculations. His almanacs, published in New York, Philadelphia, Annapolis, and Williamsburg, Va., enjoyed a wide circulation. In addition he published in the newspapers the solutions of many mathematical problems relating to navigation and surveying. His school-announcements indicate that he was giving instruction in "Arithmetick . . . Merchants Accompts, Algebra, Geometry, Surveying, Gauging, Trigonometry . . . Navigation . . . Astronomy, and all other Parts of the Mathematicks" in Philadelphia as early as 1734. In 1740 he accepted a call to the headmastership of "The Public School of Kent County, in Maryland." Two years later he returned to Philadelphia and again opened a school for the teaching of mathematics. During the next eight years he was frequently called into consultation by various city and colonial land-surveys. His expert advice was sought at the hearings of the long boundary contest between Maryland and Pennsylvania. He was one of the commissioners appointed to represent Pennsylvania at the joint meeting of November 1750 at New Castle, Del. On Dec. 17, 1750, he was appointed first professor of mathematics at the College and Academy of Philadelphia. Apparently, in 1753, the trustees permitted him to carry on a private-venture evening school at the same time, in partnership with Horace Jones, his assistant at the college. His skill in mathematics made him a valued member of Benjamin Franklin's coterie. Provost William Smith, in his "Account of the College and Academy," published in the *American Magazine* for October 1758, refers to him as having "so long been an approved teacher of Mathematics and Astronomy in this city, that I need say nothing to make him better known than he is already." At its first Commencement, May 17, 1757, the college conferred upon him the honorary degree of M.A. in recognition of his scientific attainments. According to the records of Christ Church, Philadelphia, he married Elizabeth Cosins in 1735, Frances Bowen in 1739, and Rebecca Richards in 1747. He died in Philadelphia.

[*American Weekly Mercury,* Oct. 3–10, 17–24, 31–Nov. 7, Dec. 5–12, 1734, Oct. 16–23, 1735; E. L. Clark, *A Record of the Inscriptions on the Tablets and Grave-Stones in the Burial Grounds of Christ Church, Phila.* (1864), p. 424; Chas. Evans, *Am. Bibliog.,* II, 3546, III, 6687–88, 7012, 7206; J. W. Jordan, "Penn *versus* Baltimore: Journal of John Watson, Assistant Surveyor to the Commissioners of the Province of Pa., 1750," *Pa. Mag. of Hist. and Biog.,* Oct. 1914; T. H. Montgomery, *A Hist. of the Univ. of Pa.* (1900); *Pa. Archives,* 2 ser. II (1876), 119, VIII (1878), 107; *Pa. Gazette,* May 29–June 5, 1735, Nov. 6, 1740, May 20, 27, Aug. 26, Sept. 2, Oct. 14, 21, 28, Nov. 4, 18, 25, 1742, Mar. 10, 17, 24, 1743, Sept. 20, 27, Oct. 11, 1744, Nov. 14, 21, Dec. 5, 17, 1751, Jan. 7, 21, 28, 1752, Sept. 20, 27, 1753, Aug. 12, 1756, Nov. 15, 22, Dec. 13, 1759; R. F. Seybolt, "Schoolmasters of Colonial Phila.," *Pa. Mag. of Hist. and Biog.,* Oct. 1928.] R. F. S.

GRIDLEY, CHARLES VERNON (Nov. 24, 1844–June 5, 1898), naval officer, was born in Logansport, Ind., the son of Franklin and Ann Eliza (Sholes) Gridley. He was descended from Thomas Gridley, an early member of the Massachusetts Bay colony. His earlier years were spent in Michigan and it was from that state that he was appointed to the Naval Academy, Sept. 26, 1860. Soon after graduation in 1863, he was assigned to duty on the *Oneida,* and in the following year he took part in the battle of Mobile Bay. In November 1866 he was promoted to the rank of master and ordered to the steam-sloop *Kearsarge* of the South Pacific Squadron. On Feb. 21, 1867, he was commissioned lieutenant. After assignments on board the *Michigan,* man-of-war on the Great Lakes, 1870–72, and the *Monongahela,* of the South Atlantic Station, 1873–74, he served four years, 1875–79, as instructor at the Naval Academy. Following this service he was assigned to the flagship *Trenton,* European Station, 1879–81, promoted commander Mar. 10, 1882, and then served as navigation officer of the Boston navy-yard, 1882–84. From 1884 to 1886 he was in command of the training ships *Jamestown* and *Portsmouth,* served briefly as senior officer of the Cruising Training Squadron, and then spent four years, 1887–91, in light-house inspection service at Buffalo, N. Y. Ordered to the Washington, D. C., navy-yard, 1891–92, he spent the next two years, 1892–94, in command of the cruiser *Marion,* followed by another three years at Buffalo, N. Y., in light-house service. On Mar. 14, 1897, he was commissioned captain and ordered to command the receiving-ship *Richmond* at the Philadelphia navy-yard.

On July 28, 1897, Gridley took command of the *Olympia,* the flagship of the Asiatic Squadron. This was a doubly pleasant assignment, inasmuch as Commodore Dewey [*q.v.*], who later became the flag officer, was not only his superior officer but his personal friend. Shortly before the battle of Manila Bay, May 1, 1898, Gridley was officially pronounced physically unfit for active service. With true bravery and self-sacrifice, he protested this ruling and was permitted to retain his command in spite of the state of his health. When action against the Spanish forces became imminent, Dewey gave his now famous command: "You may fire when you are ready, Gridley" (*Autobiography of George Dewey,* 1913, p. 214). This virtually put upon Gridley the responsibility for beginning the action, a compliment of the highest order. When he had decided that the time was right, he initiated and personally directed the gunfire from his own conning tower. Though the result of the battle was a victory for the American forces, unfortunately it practically ended Gridley's life. Condemned by a medical survey, he started home May 25 but passed away at Kobe, Japan, leaving in the United States his wife, Harriet Frances Vincent, whom he had married on May 1, 1872, two daughters, and a son. Dewey strongly recommended that Gridley be advanced ten numbers in the promotion list as a partial reward for his ability and sound judgment. Finally six numbers were given him. He was buried at Lakeside Cemetery, Erie, Pa., where four guns from the arsenal at Cavite, sent by the United States government, were placed at his grave. He was later honored in having a destroyer named for him. This ship, launched in 1918, was sponsored by his daughter Ruth.

[L. R. Hamersly, *The Records of Living Officers of the U. S. Navy and Marine Corps* (rev. ed., 1894); U. S. Navy registers, 1863–98; *Ships' Data: U. S. Naval Vessels* (1922); A. M. Hall and E. W. Benham, *Ships of the U. S. Navy and Their Sponsors, 1913–23* (1925); R. W. Neeser, *Ship Names of the U. S. Navy* (1921); *Army & Navy Jour.*, June 11, 1898; *N. Y. Tribune*, June 6, 1898; information as to certain facts from R. M. Gridley, Beaver, Pa., and from Gridley's daughter, Mrs. Lewis Buddy, III, Brooklyn, N. Y.]
A. R. B.

GRIDLEY, JEREMIAH (Mar. 10, 1701/02–Sept. 10, 1767), lawyer, sometimes called Jeremy, was born in Boston, the son of Richard and Rebecca Gridley and brother of Richard Gridley [*q.v.*]. Jeremiah graduated from Harvard in 1725, taught school, and studied law. Sometime prior to May 19, 1755, he moved to Brookline where he continued to reside until his death. He was active in the affairs of that town, was often chosen moderator at the town meetings, and represented the town in the General Court in 1755, 1756, and 1757. He was also prominent in the colony's militia and became colonel of the 1st Regiment. He always had strong literary tastes and at one time edited the *Weekly Rehearsal*, which lasted only about a year, the first copy appearing Sept. 27, 1731. Outside of his main career, that of the law, he also had many other concerns. He became interested in maritime affairs and assisted in the formation, June 1742, of the charitable organization then known as the Fellowship Club, composed of ship-masters, incorporated Feb. 2, 1754, as the Marine Society. He was always held in high esteem by its membership and was of great service to them but was never president of the society, as has often been stated. He also became a Free Mason, May 11, 1748, in St. John's Lodge, Boston, of which he became Master in 1754. On Oct. 1 of the following year he was installed as Grand Master of the Masons for all North America and served in that office until his death.

Early admitted to the bar he soon became prominent and later befriended many young members, such as James Otis and John Adams. It has been stated (Washburn, *post*, p. 211) that he was attorney-general in 1742 but that appears to be an error. He was appointed, however, Mar. 25, 1767, serving until he died (*Proceedings of the Massachusetts Historical Society*, 2 ser. X, 1896, p. 290). The most famous case with which he was connected was that involving the legality of the Writs of Assistance in 1761, when he was appointed government counsel. His argument for the government side was dignified and conservative. He admitted that some of the rights of Englishmen were denied if the validity of the Writs were admitted but based his argument on the need of a taxing power vested in the government even though it might over-ride individual rights (Quincy, *post*, p. 481). He was opposed by the fiery eloquence of James Otis. His appearance on the English side in this case does not seem to have interfered, as has sometimes been said, with his popularity. Four years later he was named with Otis and Adams as counsel for the committee of the town of Boston which was to wait on Governor Bernard and secure a reopening of the Courts (*New-England Historical and Genealogical Register*, April 1868, p. 107).

Gridley was evidently a man of ability who enjoyed the high esteem of his community throughout his life. He was a broad-minded, cultivated man, an able lawyer averse to technicalities, and cared little for wealth. His executors had planned a simple funeral but we are told that all classes united to do him honor and that the judges, bar, militia, Masons and others marched to his grave. He had married, date unknown, Abigail Lewis, by whom he had three daughters. The cause of his death was given as "a rising of the lights."

[R. G. F. Candage, "The Gridley House, Brookline, and Jeremy Gridley," *Brookline Hist. Soc. Pubs.*, no. 1 (1903); S. L. Knapp, *Biog. Sketches of Eminent Lawyers, Statesmen and Men of Letters* (1821); Josiah Quincy, Jr., *Reports of Cases Argued and Adjudged in the Superior Court . . . of Mass. Bay* (1865); Emory Washburn, *Sketches of the Judicial Hist. of Mass.* (1840); *Works of John Adams* (10 vols., 1850–56); *Brookline Hist. Pub. Soc. Pubs.*, no. 7 (1896), p. 119; *Vital Records of Brookline, Mass.* (1929), p. 203; *A Report of the Record Commissioners of the City of Boston, Containing Boston Births from A. D. 1700 to A. D. 1800* (1894), p. 11; *Boston Gazette and Country Jour.*, Sept. 14, 1767; *Mass. Gazette and Boston News-Letter*, Sept. 17, 1767.]
J. T. A.

GRIDLEY, RICHARD (Jan. 3, 1710/11–June 21, 1796), soldier, military engineer, was born in Boston, the son of Richard and Rebecca Gridley. He was descended from Richard Gridley, described as "an honest poore man, but very apt to meddle in publike affaires, beyond his calling or skill," who arrived in Boston about 1630 (*A Short Story of the Rise, Reign, and Ruine of the Antinomians, Familists & Libertines, that Infected the Churches of Nevv England*, London, 1644, p. 31). Richard, of the fourth generation, was apprenticed to a Boston wholesale merchant, but having a bent for mathematics, he became a surveyor and civil engineer. While employed in this profession he acquired a skill in drawing later attested by *A Plan of the City and Fortress of Louisburg; With a Small Plan of the Harbour . . . from the Original Drawing of Richard Gridley* (Boston, 1746, and London, 1758), and studied military engineering under John Henry Bastide, a British officer engaged in planning fortifications for Boston harbor and vicinity.

On Feb. 25, 1730, he married Hannah Deming (1708/09–1790), by whom he had nine children. In 1745 he was commissioned lieutenant-colonel and captain of the artillery train of the expedition then preparing to invest Louisburg, the French fortress on Cape Breton island. Commissioned chief bombardier during the siege, he supervised the erection of the British batteries surrounding Louisburg. In 1746 he was employed in drawing plans for a battery and other fortifications in Boston harbor in anticipation of an attack by the French fleet. He accompanied Gov. William Shirley on his journey to the Kennebec in 1752 and built Fort Western (Augusta) and Fort Halifax. Commissioned colonel (1755), he commanded the provincial artillery during the Crown Point expedition, and as chief engineer built Fort William Henry and the fortifications around Lake George. He was blamed by the Earl of Loudoun, British commander-in-chief in America, for opposing the junction of provincial and regular troops. During the second siege of Louisburg (1758) he had charge of army stores and supervised the carpentry work. In 1759 Maj.-Gen. Jeffery Amherst, in response to a request from William Pitt, placed Gridley in command of the provincial artillery, and in this capacity he participated in the battle on the Plains of Abraham and the capture of Quebec. Following the restoration of peace he went to England to adjust his accounts with the War Office. For his services he was granted the Magdalen Islands, with a valuable seal and cod fishery, half pay as a British officer, and 3,000 acres of land in New Hampshire. He lived for several years on the islands. In 1772 Gridley and Edmund Quincy began smelting iron ore at Massapoag Pond in Sharon, Mass. At the outbreak of the Revolution the Massachusetts Provincial Congress commissioned Gridley chief engineer (April 1775) and colonel of artillery with the rank of major-general (May 1775). He constructed the breastworks on Breed's Hill and was wounded in the ensuing battle of Bunker Hill (June 1775). For a few months he held a commission of colonel of artillery from the Continental Congress (Sept. 20–Nov. 17, 1775) but was replaced because of his "advanced age" after a council of officers requested his removal. He was retained as chief engineer of the Continental Army (June 1775–August 1776) and was later engineer general of the eastern department (Jan. 1, 1777–Dec. 31, 1780). In March 1776 he fortified Dorchester heights and following the evacuation of Boston destroyed the British intrenchments on the Neck and strengthened the fortifications in the region of Boston. During 1776 and 1777 he manufactured mortars and howitzers at his furnace in Sharon (*New-England Historical and Genealogical Register,* January 1868, p. 3; *Journals of Congress,* Feb. 14, 1777). When peace was celebrated in Boston at the close of the Revolution he was not invited to participate. His inquiry brought the response: "Because, General, you are not considered . . . a Christian"—Gridley had become a Universalist. He died at his home in Stoughton (now Canton).

[D. T. V. Huntoon, in *New Eng. Freemason* (Boston), May 1874, in *Memorial Services . . . Held in Canton, May 30, 1877, Revere Encampment, Post 94, Grand Army of the Republic* (1877), and *Hist. of the Town of Canton, Norfolk County, Mass.* (1893); *E.* Davis, in *Universalist Quart.* (Boston), July 1876, where it is incorrectly stated that Gridley was twice married; *Am. Archives,* 4 ser. (6 vols. 1837–46); Geo. A. Ward, *Jour. and Letters of Samuel Curwen* (1842), p. 452; C. H. Lincoln, *Correspondence of Wm. Shirley* (1912); R. Frothingham, *Hist. of the Siege of Boston* (1849); I. N. Tarbox, *Life of Israel Putnam* (1876); Jared Sparks, *The Writings of Geo. Washington,* vol. III (1834); *Mass. Soldiers and Sailors of the Revolutionary War,* vol. VI (1899); F. B. Heitman, *Hist. Reg. of Officers of the Continental Army* (1893); *Columbian Centinel* (Boston), Oct. 20, 1790, June 22, 1796.]

F. E. R.

GRIER, ROBERT COOPER (Mar. 5, 1794–Sept. 25, 1870), associate justice of the United States Supreme Court, was born in Cumberland County, Pa., the eldest of eleven children of Rev. Isaac Grier and Elizabeth (Cooper) Grier. Both his father and his grandfather, Rev. Robert Cooper, were Presbyterian ministers. Soon after Robert's birth, the family moved to Lycoming County, where the father farmed, taught school, and preached to three congregations. In 1806 he was called to Northumberland to take charge of an academy, which under his able direction later received a charter as a college. Robert's teacher until he was seventeen was his father. From him he received such thorough instruction in the classics that until his death he read his Testament in the original Greek. In 1812 he graduated from Dickinson College, having entered as a junior only the year before. After serving a year as an instructor at Dickinson, he was called back to Northumberland to assist his father as principal of the academy. In 1815 his father died, and Robert, though only twenty-one years of age, was appointed his successor. In this capacity he taught Greek, Latin, mathematics, astronomy, and chemistry, and in spare intervals studied law. Admitted to the bar in 1817, he practised his profession for a year at Bloomsburg and later at Danville, where his business became so extensive that he was able to support his mother and to give each of his ten brothers and sisters a liberal education. In

1829 he married Isabella Rose, daughter of John Rose, a native of Scotland who had come to America in 1798. The Rose family was one of refinement and wealth, and through his wife Grier subsequently acquired an estate near Williamsport, where, in order to recuperate from arduous judicial labors, he frequently would repair to engage in his favorite recreation of trout fishing. In 1833 he was appointed president judge of the district court of Allegheny County. This office he held until Aug. 5, 1846, when upon nomination of President Polk he was unanimously confirmed by the Senate as associate justice of the Supreme Court of the United States. Two years later he moved from Allegheny City, where he had gone upon his appointment as district court judge, to Philadelphia, where he lived until his death.

Grier's term of service on the Supreme Court covered the period immediately before, during, and immediately following the Civil War. Consequently many questions of great public importance, involving slavery, war, and reconstruction, came before him for decision. Although he was charged by the anti-slavery papers with subservience to slave interests (Warren, *post,* II, 547), his opinions, rendered when public feeling on these matters ran extremely high, seem in retrospect unusually free of bias, and highly judicial in tone and substance. He wrote a concurring opinion in the Dred Scott case and during the Civil War rendered the very strong opinion in the Prize cases upholding the power of the President to establish by proclamation a blockade of the ports of the Confederate States, and after the war he voted with the majority of the Court against the validity of a measure making an oath of non-participation in the Confederate cause a prerequisite to the engagement in certain occupations. Originally a Federalist, he later became a Democrat, but was a stanch Unionist during the Civil War. Until the summer of 1867 he had enjoyed such excellent health that he had never been absent from a single session of the Court, but during that year he became afflicted with partial paralysis, and thenceforth his physical and mental powers gradually declined. Finally, his inability to address himself to the cases before the Court prompted a committee of the Court to wait upon him and advise him of the desirability of retiring. This he decided to do and on Feb. 1, 1870, his resignation became effective.

His opinions are characterized by concision, clarity of statement, and the citation of few but carefully chosen authorities. It has been said that "no other justice of the Court has surpassed the ease, accuracy and finish of his written style" (Veeder, *post*). Although of a modest nature he was fearless in setting forth his views. On one occasion the Court decided to postpone the consideration of a case (the McCardle Case, March 1868) of which Grier thought the interests of the country required an immediate decision. He accordingly entered in the record a vigorous protest against the action of his colleagues. This conduct excited much comment in political circles, being styled on the one hand as, "an unseemly exhibition . . . [and] a breach of judicial decorum" and on the other as an "everlasting memorial" to his honor (Warren, III, 204–06).

On Feb. 23, 1857, Grier wrote a letter to the incoming president, James Buchanan, about the then pending Dred Scott case, detailing to him in confidence the attitude of the various members of the Court and stating what the final decision would be. President Buchanan, therefore, was somewhat disingenuous when he declared in his inaugural address, "To [the Supreme Court's] decision . . . I shall cheerfully submit, whatever this may be . . ." (Warren, *post,* III, 20). Although such a letter now would be highly unethical, at the time it was written it was not so regarded. It appears that Judges Story, Curtis, and perhaps others had on occasion informed relatives or intimate friends of the probable outcome of a pending case.

Grier was over six feet tall, of large frame and great muscular power, but inclined to stoutness. In deportment he was courteous and dignified. He died in Philadelphia.

[*Albany Law Jour.*, Oct. 15, 1870; *Am. Law Rev.*, Jan. 1871; *Western Jurist,* Jan. 1871; *Phila. Inquirer,* Sept. 27, 1870; J. W. F. White, "The Judiciary of Allegheny County," *Pa. Mag. of Hist. and Biog.*, July 1883; V. V. Veeder, "A Century of Federal Judicature," *Green Bag.*, Apr. 1903; F. R. Jones, "Robert Cooper Grier," *Ibid.*, Apr. 1904; H. L. Carson, *The Supreme Court of the U. S.: Its Hist.*, I (1892), 343–45; Charles Warren, *The Supreme Court in U. S. Hist.* (3 vols., 1922); C. E. Hughes, *The Supreme Court of the U. S.* (1928), p. 75; sketches of Robt. Cooper and Isaac Grier in W. B. Sprague, *Annals Am. Pulpit*, vol. III (1858); C. Morris, *Makers of Phila.* (1849), p. 245.]
G. W. G.

GRIERSON, BENJAMIN HENRY (July 8, 1826–Sept. 1, 1911), Union soldier, was born in Pittsburgh, Pa., the son of Robert and Mary (Shepard) Grierson, natives of Dublin, Ireland. He attended an academy at Youngstown, Ohio, taught music there and at Jacksonville, Ill., and for five years was a merchant at Meredosia, Ill. Enlisting in the army as a private in 1861, he was commissioned major in the 6th Illinois Cavalry and promoted to colonel. In the spring of 1862 he engaged in several small raids, routing a force of Confederates at Hernando, Miss. Returning to Gen. Sherman's command he was employed in scouting for a few months, destroying rebel arms, camps, and supplies and pushing the Confederates out of Tennessee. The Cavalry being reorganized, Grierson was assigned to command the 1st Brigade, consisting of the 6th Illinois (his own), the 7th Illinois, and the 2nd Iowa Cavalry. By order of Gen. Grant he left La Grange, Tenn., Apr. 17, 1863, with about 1,700 men and in sixteen days traversed six hundred miles of the enemy's country in a succession of forced marches, fighting and destroying property. Ruining the Vicksburg & Meridian Railroad and the New Orleans & Jackson, and laying waste public property, he reached his goal, Baton Rouge, La., May 2. This raid was immensely helpful to Grant in the Vicksburg campaign, for it upset the enemy's plans, drew forces from vulnerable points, and diverted attention from the main movement against Vicksburg. In referring to it, Grant said, "General Grierson was the first officer to set the example of what might be done in the interior of the enemy's country without a base from which to draw supplies" (Short, *post,* p. 840). President Lincoln recognized the service rendered in this campaign by promoting Grierson to major-general of volunteers "for gallant and distinguished service in his great raid through the heart of the so-called Confederacy." In 1864 Grierson made short raids in Tennessee and Mississippi in an attempt to distract Southern attention from the preparations for Sherman's march. In May 1865 he was actively employed in the campaign against hostile Indians in the Western states and territories, and at various times he commanded the Department of Texas and Arizona and the District of New Mexico. In 1890 he received his appointment as brigadier-general of the regular army and in the same year he was retired. He was twice married: on Sept. 24, 1854, to Alice Kirk of Youngstown, Ohio, who died in 1888; and on July 28, 1897, to Lillian (Atwood) King of Jacksonville, Ill. He died at his summer home at Omena, Mich.

[R. U. Johnson and C. C. Buel, eds., *Battles and Leaders of the Civil War,* vols. III and IV (1888); *Personal Memoirs of U. S. Grant* (2 vols., 1885–86); F. B. Heitman, *Hist. Reg. and Dict. U. S. Army* (2 vols., 1903); Wm. F. Short, *A Hist. of Ill. and Morgan County* (1906), pp. 838–41; *Ill. State Hist. Soc. Jour.,* Oct. 1911; J. S. C. Abbott, "Heroic Deeds of Heroic Men," *Harper's New Monthly Mag.,* Feb. 1865; *Who's Who in America,* 1908–09; *Chicago Daily Tribune,* Sept. 2, 1911.]

J. P. S—h.

GRIERSON, FRANCIS (Sept. 18, 1848–May 29, 1927), author, musician, had the baptismal name of Benjamin Henry Jesse Francis Shepard. His father, Joseph Shepard of Wicklow, Ireland, was descended from an old Cumberland family to which Thomas Shepard [*q.v.*], the founder of Harvard College, belonged. His mother, Emily (Grierson) Shepard, traced her lineage through Robert Grierson, the original of Scott's "Redgauntlet," to Gregor, founder of the Clan MacGregor in the ninth century, and was closely related to Lord Wolseley, Sir James Moncrieff Grierson, and Gen. Benjamin Henry Grierson [*q.v.*], the Union cavalry officer. Francis was born in Birkenhead, Cheshire, and six months later his father emigrated with his family to America, where he became an American citizen, settled in a log-cabin on the Illinois prairie, and later moved to Alton. The stirring period just before the Civil War made on young Francis an indelible impression, to be recorded fifty years later in *The Valley of Shadows,* with accurate recollection of events, characters, and even local dialect. In 1859 his family moved to St. Louis, where in 1861 the boy served as a page on Gen. Frémont's staff. In 1863 his family moved to Niagara Falls, and six years later the youth of twenty-one struck out alone and almost penniless for Paris. With only two years of musical training, he had already, at seventeen, given professional recitals on the piano and had developed remarkable powers of improvisation. Now, unaided by letters of introduction, he succeeded at once in gaining the interest of Auber, director of the Conservatoire, who was much impressed with his talent. Tall and handsome, with Byronic features, "Jesse Shepard," once launched, quickly became the sensation of the day. His playing, weird and mystical, produced a profound effect upon all hearers. His large hands had the astounding span of an octave and a half, "and it is said that at certain wonderful moments, he could add the strangest, most inexplicable voice, that did not follow the music but went along with it, almost independent of it, rising up from out of the middle chords of the piano, faintly at first, and at last filling the room with indescribable and thrilling tones" (Preface to American edition of *The Valley of Shadows,* 1909). Of this voice, which had a range of four octaves, Stephane Mallarmé later said, "It is not a voice, it is a choir!" Of the musician he said, "For the first time in the history of music we now have the real poet of the piano." Grierson's success was the more interesting in that he gave only private performances, save when he was specially invited to sing in Saint-Eustache, Notre Dame, the basilica at Montmartre, and, later, in the Cathedral of Baden, where he sang and played the organ at the same time. His triumphant course took him to London, thence to St. Petersburg, where he was a guest in the Imperial Palace, thence to Berlin, and again to Paris and London. Famous now in the most important European capitals, he rested to an extent upon his laurels, but never entirely abandoned his musical performances, giving them intermittently and with hardly abated power until the very day of his death.

Grierson's even more important literary talent developed late. In the early eighties he was back in America and published a series of essays in the *Chicago Times.* In 1884 he made another trip to Paris; in 1886–88 he was living in San Diego, where certain art-loving citizens aided him to build the "Villa Montezuma," one of the landmarks of the town; in 1889 he was back in Paris, publishing, still under the name of Jesse Shepard, his first book, *La Révolte Idéaliste,* which received letters of commendation from seven academicians, including Sully Prudhomme and Henry de Regnier, because of the purity of its French style and the beauty of its thought. Maurice Maeterlinck greeted the author's mystical soul as *"la plus vraiment fraternelle que j'aie trouvée jusqu'ici."* It was not until ten years later, however, that Grierson, changing his name so that his writing might not be considered the work of a mere musician, definitely settled down, in London, to a literary career. Thus his first book in English, *Modern Mysticism and Other Essays* (1899) did not appear until he was fifty years old. It was followed by *The Celtic Temperament and Other Essays* (1901). In these volumes Grierson showed himself master of an oracular yet lucid and rhythmical style, not a little influenced by the practise of the French Symbolists. He now devoted seven years to the writing of what proved to be his masterpiece, *The Valley of Shadows; Recollections of the Lincoln Country 1858–63* (1909), an uneven but in parts marvellously vivid and beautiful account of the life and spirit of those years in the ominous shadow of the oncoming war. Here he wrote in a freer style which at its best attained an epic and prophetic quality. Other volumes of essays followed: *Parisian Portraits* (1910); *La Vie et Les Hommes,* in French (1911); *The Humour of the Underman* (1911); and *The Invincible Alliance* (1913). As early as 1910 Grierson had pointed out in the *New Age,* to which with Arnold Bennett and H. G. Wells he was a chief contributor, the inevitableness of an approaching war with Germany, and in November 1913 he became so convinced of the nearness of the struggle that he returned, for the last time, to America. He now spent two years in New York, two on lecture tours, and two in Washington, D. C., where he wrote his last important works, *Illusions and Realities of the War* (1918) and *Abraham Lincoln, the Practical Mystic* (1918). After a year in Toronto, and another year in New York, he moved to Los Angeles and settled there for the remainder of his life. His only production during this period was a pamphlet entitled *Psycho-Phone Messages* (1921), really a collection of imaginary utterances on contemporary affairs by various statesmen such as Jefferson, Hamilton, Webster, but generally considered, owing to ambiguous phraseology, to have made claims of Spiritualist mediumship. Grierson, however, was not a Spiritualist, but a philosophical mystic, finding his source of inspiration in an impersonal realm of Spirit accessible to the sub-conscious. He died while sitting at the piano during a recital, passing away quietly, after the closing piece of the evening, with his hands still resting on the keys. His last days were spent in extreme poverty. He was never married but for the final forty-two years of his life was constantly attended by his faithful friend, Lawrence Waldemar Tonner, who acted as his secretary, manager, and personal representative.

[Waldemar Tonner, *The Genius of Francis Grierson* (privately printed, 1927); autobiographical passages in Grierson's writings; description of Montezuma Villa in *Boston Ideas,* Apr. 16, 1928; detailed letter from Mr. Tonner; personal acquaintance. See *Reader's Guide to Periodical Literature* for numerous articles on Grierson's work.]

E. S. B—s.

GRIEVE, MILLER (Jan. 11, 1801–*c.* 1878), journalist, diplomat, was born in Edinburgh, Scotland, third of the four children of John and Marion (Miller) Grieve. The entire family emigrated to America in 1817 and settled in Savannah, Ga. There one of the sons and a son-in-law engaged in shipping, but both died of yellow fever in the epidemic of 1820, and the surviving members of the family moved first to Liberty County and afterward to Oglethorpe County. Miller set up as a lawyer in Lexington. In 1829 he became private secretary to George Rockingham Gilmer [*q.v.*], a neighbor who had just been elected governor. This position he retained for two years only, but it affected his entire life in that it necessitated his definite removal to Milledgeville, then the state capital. In 1833 he was married to Sarah Caroline Grantland, daughter of Fleming Grantland. Her uncle, Seaton Grantland, along with Richard McAllister Orme, had since the early 1820's conducted in Milledgeville a paper named the *Southern Recorder.* Grieve, in the year of his marriage, bought out Grantland, and from then till 1853 dominated the paper, making it—thanks to the force of his logic and the testiness of his phraseology—the unofficial organ of the Whig party in Georgia and a respected vehicle of opinion over the entire country. When in 1831 Gilmer was defeated for a second term as governor, Grieve vowed that his mentor should be reinstated in office, and in fact, so potent was the *Recorder,* that in 1837 this end was achieved. In 1840 the *Recorder* was perhaps the determining factor in Georgia's voting for Harrison and Tyler, and in 1848 for Taylor and Fillmore. During the terms beginning in 1841 and 1843 Grieve represented his county in the state legislature, and there, as chairman of the bank committee, devised means for raising the value of bills on the central bank. He refused the United States ministry to the Argentine Republic offered him by President Taylor, but accepted Fillmore's offer to make him chargé d'affaires in Denmark and was commissioned Aug. 30, 1852. His service in Copenhagen—whither he was accompanied by two young sons and a young nephew—was apparently adequate. Locally he was active, being a captain of the town militia, a promoter of railways, a trustee of public institutions, a benefactor of Oglethorpe University—to the sum of $20,000—and a pillar of Presbyterianism. He spent his last years in retirement in Milledgeville, and died there, leaving many children.

[*Memoirs of Ga.* (2 vols., 1895), I, 266–68; W. J. Northen, *Men of Mark in Ga.,* II (1910), 104–05; A. M. G. Cook, *Hist. of Baldwin County, Ga.* (1925).]

J. D. W.

GRIFFES, CHARLES TOMLINSON (Sept. 17, 1884–Apr. 8, 1920), composer, pianist, teacher, was born in Elmira, N. Y., the third of five children of Wilber Griffes, a manufacturer, and Clara Tomlinson Griffes. His paternal ancestors, though originally Welsh, had lived in America since the Revolution, but his maternal grandfather was born in England. While neither of the parents was musically gifted, theirs was a home of culture, in which there was more than the usual amount of music. One of his older sisters was a violinist; another was a piano teacher and organist who began teaching her brother when he was a small boy. He was not especially precocious musically, but he was an excellent student, particularly strong in languages, fond of poetry and books of travel, and he possessed an unusually retentive memory. He was also fond of water-color painting and pen-and-ink drawing, and his copper-plate etching was so fine that at one time he was strongly advised to follow etching as a profession. As a boy he began to show a marked interest in music, and early in his high-school course he decided to make music his life-work. He studied piano and organ with his sister until he was fourteen; then he became a pupil of Mary Selena Broughton of Elmira College for Women. At eighteen he went to Berlin, on the advice of his teacher, to prepare for the career of a concert pianist. He remained there four years, studying piano with Ernst Jedliczka and later with Gottfried Galston, theory with Klatte and Loewengard, and composition with Philipp Rüfer and Engelbert Humperdinck—the latter probably being most influential in leading him to discover his own ability for composition. He taught some in Berlin and on his return to America in 1908 he accepted a position as teacher of piano, organist, and choirmaster at the Hackley School for Boys, Tarrytown, N. Y., where he remained until his untimely death. Most of his compositions were written at the school or in his summer studio in New York. He was of a retiring disposition and made comparatively few friends, but these few were people who were actively interested in the arts. He died at an age when few composers have reached their full powers of expression and his published compositions total only forty, yet an astonishingly large proportion of these are valuable contributions to the literature of music.

The first works published by Griffes were songs which followed closely the German romantic style which he had absorbed in his student days in Berlin. As he matured, he showed a groping for new forms of expression and a longing for warmer coloring. Though the work of this transitional period was not always beautiful, it was strikingly individual and displayed certainty of workmanship and a positive technique in writing. Gradually he developed a style quite his own, but influenced at times by Oriental idioms. He was an enthusiastic reader of Lafcadio Hearn, and his natural passion for the exotic inspired him to study the music of China and Japan so carefully and to familiarize himself so thoroughly with their people and customs that he was able at will to saturate his music with the atmosphere of the East, as, for example, in his "Five Poems" of ancient China and Japan for voice and piano, in which he used the pentatonic and whole-tone scales. Shortly before his death he attained wide recognition by the Boston Symphony Orchestra's performance, Nov. 28–29, 1919, of "The Pleasure-Dome of Kubla Khan," a symphonic poem after Coleridge (composed in 1912, revised in 1916). His other large works include the "Poem" for flute and orchestra, first played by the Barrère Ensemble in New York, 1918; two sketches on Indian themes for string quartet, played by the Flonzaley Quartet, 1918–19; and a sonata for piano, first performed by the composer at the New York MacDowell Club, 1918. Of his ten piano pieces, several display his style at its best—"Clouds," "The Fountain of the Acqua Paola," "The White Peacock," "The Vale of Dreams." Among his twenty-four published songs at least nine or ten possess qualities of enduring charm, as "The Lament of Ian the Proud," and "Thy Dark Eyes to Mine," settings to poems by Fiona MacLeod; "Symphony in Yellow," and "We'll to the Woods and Gather May."

[Wm. Treat Upton, "The Songs of Chas. T. Griffes," *Musical Quart.*, July 1923; *Fortnightly Musical Rev.*, June 20, 1928; J. T. Howard, *Our Am. Music* (copyright 1930, 1931); *Musical America*, Dec. 4, 1915, May 22, 1920; Philip Hale's program notes in the 1919–20 program book of the Boston Symphony Orchestra; *N. Y. Times*, Apr. 10, 18, Nov. 25, 1920; information as to certain facts from A. Marguerite Griffes, a younger sister of the composer, and from Wm. Treat Upton.]

F. L. G. C.

GRIFFIN, APPLETON PRENTISS CLARK (July 24, 1852–Apr. 16, 1926), librarian, bibliographer, son of Moses Porter and Charlotte Helen (Clark) Griffin, was born at Wilton, N. H., whence the family moved to Medford, Mass., in 1854. His ancestry included Hugh Griffin, the first town clerk of Sudbury, Mass., and, in his mother's line, Samuel Appleton (Ipswich, *c.* 1636); Roger Conant, first governor of the Cape Ann Colony, 1625–26; Henry Prentiss, "planter" of Cambridge, 1640; and John Rogers, fifth president of Harvard College. Leaving the Medford public school, he began work as a "runner" in the Boston Public Library, Dec. 1, 1865. Thenceforth libraries, with occasional help from private tutors, schooled this descendant of Harvard graduates. His entire career of sixty years was spent in the service of four libraries of the scholarly type, to the first of which he gave twenty-eight years and ten months and to the fourth, twenty-eight years and eight months of service.

From "runner," he advanced by gradual steps to "custodian of the shelves," "custodian of the building," and, finally, "keeper of the books," directing the selection, ordering, and classifying of 25,000 volumes of the best literature added annually to one of the most systematic general collections of books in America. He thus acquired a knowledge of literature not to be duplicated in a like period except by one of like powers of absorption and persistence. In the course of fifteen years he stood among the best bibliographers of the country. His elaborate list on the Renaissance (*Bulletin of the Boston Public Library,* July 1879–January 1882), was praised by John Addington Symonds; his "European Origin of the Aryans" (*Ibid.*, April 1890), by Salomon Reinach. The library published many of his lists. In September 1894 his long connection with the Boston Public Library ceased, and he spent the next three years in research and compilation in the Boston Athenæum and in the Lenox Library in New York. For the Athenæum he prepared its elaborate *Catalogue of the Washington Collection* (1897). His *Bibliography of the Historical Publications of the New England States* (1895) was contributed to the Colonial Society of Massachusetts (see its *Publications,* vol. III, 1897), to which he belonged for thirty years. He contributed to *Appletons' Cyclopedia of American Biography* the sketches of Philip Freneau, Robert Fulton, Thomas Gage, and Nathanael Greene. The first edition of his *Bibliography of American Historical Societies* was published by the American Historical Association in 1896, the second edition, greatly enlarged, in 1907.

On Aug. 27, 1897, he was appointed an assistant on the staff then being organized for the Library of Congress, and when in 1900 the division of bibliography was created, he became chief bibliographer. In this position, which he held for eight years, he published over fifty bibliographic lists (more than 3,350 pages), regarded as useful contributions to knowledge. Upon the death in 1908 of Ainsworth Rand Spofford [*q.v.*], he became chief assistant librarian of Congress, which position he held until his death. He was now chief reference officer of the library and the librarian's chief adviser on the selection of books. He was greatly competent in both capacities because of his constant studies in general literature, his accumulated knowledge, his industry, his unusual *flair* for source material submerged beyond the reach of indexes, catalogues, and lists, and his sound judgment as to what material is of real worth in a research library.

Griffin was married on Oct. 23, 1878, to Emily Call Osgood of Cambridge, Mass., who died on Oct. 20, 1924. They had four children. Griffin died in 1926, after an illness of five days, and was buried in Mount Auburn, Cambridge, beside his wife and daughter.

[*Who's Who in America,* 1926–27; publications of the Boston Public Library; *Report of the Librarian of Congress,* 1926; *Library Jour.*, May 1, 1926; *Libraries,* June 1926; *Pubs. Col. Soc. Mass.*, vol. XXVI (1927); *Evening Star* (Washington, D. C.), Apr. 17, 1926; family data.]

F. W. A.

GRIFFIN, CHARLES (Dec. 18, 1825–Sept. 15, 1867), Union soldier, son of Apollos Griffin, was born in Granville, Licking County, Ohio.

He entered West Point in 1843, graduated in 1847, and was commissioned in the artillery. Sent at once to Mexico, he commanded a company under Gen. Patterson on his march from Vera Cruz to Puebla, but the campaign was already nearly over. He was promoted to first lieutenant in 1849, and served mostly on the frontier until 1860, when he was ordered to West Point as an instructor in tactics. His stay there was short, for in January 1861 he was directed to organize a light battery with personnel transferred from the detachments of enlisted men on duty at the academy, and it was immediately moved to Washington. Known at first merely as "the West Point battery," it became Battery D of the 5th Artillery when that regiment was organized, and as such took part in the battle of Bull Run, where Griffin, who had been promoted to a captaincy in April, commanded it. It was heavily engaged, and at last was almost annihilated by a volley at short range from a Confederate regiment which had been allowed to approach, against Griffin's protest, on the assurance of the chief of artillery that it was a body of Union troops. "It seemed as though every man and horse of that battery just laid right down and died right off," said a witness ("Report on the Conduct of the War," pt. II, p. 216, *Senate Report No. 108,* 37 Cong., 3 Sess.). Of its six guns only one was brought away. Until the next spring it remained at Washington. During this time Griffin was married (Dec. 10, 1861) to Sallie Carroll, daughter of William T. Carroll of Maryland. He commanded his battery in the early part of the Peninsular campaign, and then, having been appointed brigadier-general of volunteers, June 9, 1862, was assigned to the command of a brigade of the V Corps, which he held through the remainder of the Peninsular campaign and at the battle of Antietam. At the second battle of Bull Run, his brigade was not engaged, though near at hand, and, as Pope reported, "Griffin himself spent the day in making ill-natured strictures upon the general commanding the action in the presence of a promiscuous assemblage" (*Official Records, Army,* 1 ser., XII, pt. 2, 15). He was relieved from command, pending investigation, but soon restored—not "tried and acquitted," as is often said—and was shortly advanced to the command of a division, with which he fought at Fredericksburg and Chancellorsville. He was absent on account of sickness during most of the Gettysburg campaign, but arrived on the field on the last day of the battle. With his division he went through the whole Virginia campaign of 1864, and on Apr. 1, 1865, the day of Five Forks, was put in command of the V Corps. His commission as major-general of volunteers was dated the next day. He was one of the commissioners appointed to carry out the terms of Lee's surrender. Mustered out of the volunteer service, Jan. 15, 1866, he was appointed colonel of the 35th Infantry, July 28, 1866, and spent the short remainder of his life in charge of the military district of Texas, where he showed great zeal and vigor in carrying out the accepted policy of reconstruction. When yellow fever broke out in Galveston, he refused to leave the place, soon caught the disease, and died there. Arrogant, self-confident, often perilously near to insubordinate, Griffin's was not an attractive personality on the surface. "Quick to resent insult, fancied or real," says a friendly writer, ". . . his nature was bellicose" (Cullum, *post,* II, 331). The picture of a brigade commander on the battlefield loudly demanding "what Pope had ever done that he should be made a major-general" is not a pleasing one. Morris Schaff tells of an occasion when Griffin "blurted out something mutinous" that was overheard by Grant. The latter asked Meade who the offender was, adding, "You ought to arrest him"; to which Meade "soothingly" replied, "It's Griffin, . . . and its only his way of talking" (*The Battle of the Wilderness,* 1910, p. 166). It is usually safe to presume the incompetency of a commander of this type, but Griffin was an exception. If he talked loudly, he also fought well. That he was an able leader of troops is proved by his steady progress upward, commanding a battery, a brigade, a division, and finally a corps, making good in each position before advancement to the next. He was popular, too, with his officers and men; it is to be supposed that he was more considerate of his subordinates than of his superiors. Finally, he was stern in his sense of duty, and the manner of his death was heroic.

[G. W. Cullum, *Biog. Reg.* (3rd ed., 1891), vol. II; *The Biog. Encyc. of Ohio of the Nineteenth Century* (1876); *N. Y. Tribune,* Sept. 16, 1867; *Official Records (Army),* 1 ser., vols. II, XI (pts. 1, 2), XII (pt. 2), XIX (pts. 1, 2), XXI, XXV (pts. 1, 2), XXXVI (pts. 1, 2, 3), XL (pts. 1, 2, 3), XLII (pts. 1, 2, 3), XLVI (pts. 1, 2, 3), LI (pt. 1).] T. M. S.

GRIFFIN, CYRUS (July 16, 1748–Dec. 14, 1810), statesman, jurist, and last president of the Continental Congress, was born in Farnham Parish, Richmond County, Va., of stock that had long been prominent among the Virginia gentry, son of Col. LeRoy and Mary Ann (Bertrand) Griffin. After studying law at Edinburgh University and the Middle Temple, in 1774 he returned to Virginia to practise his profession, accompanied by his wife, formerly Lady Christina Stuart, eldest daughter of the sixth Earl of Traquair, with whom he had made a runaway marriage (1770) while in Edinburgh. He took an interested part in pre-Revolutionary movements, but while asserting the rights of the colonies, hoped for a peaceful issue to the differences with England; and when again in London, on business, addressed to the Earl of Dartmouth, Dec. 30, 1775, a "Plan of reconciliation between Great Britain and her Colonies." He represented Lancaster in the Virginia legislature from May 1777 to May 1778, when he was elected a member of the Continental Congress, but his patriotic spirit chafed at the bickerings and delays of that body and he was distinctly relieved when Congress, Apr. 28, 1780, appointed him judge of the Court of Appeals in Cases of Capture. He presided over this court until 1787, when, its business having dwindled after the conclusion of the war, it was abolished following provision for a more comprehensive federal judiciary; but not before Congress had passed a resolution "expressing their sense of the ability, fidelity, and attention of the judges" (Jameson, *post,* p. 391), and not before it had helped to further the beginnings of the United States Supreme Court by familiarizing the public mind with the idea of a superior tribunal of federal judicature.

Returned to the Virginia Assembly from Lancaster, 1786–87, Griffin was again elected to the Continental Congress and served as its president from Jan. 22, 1788, until its dissolution. He had been one of the judges chosen by the states of Connecticut and Pennsylvania to preside over the provisional court that determined the ownership of the Wyoming Valley (1782); and his services in settling that important controversy may have led President Washington in 1789 to name him one of three commissioners to attend a treaty between the Creek Indians and the state of Georgia. That same year he applied to Washington for "appointment in the diplomatic service or as a judge of the Supreme Court." The legislature of Virginia elected him a member of the Privy Council (*Virginia Argus,* Dec. 28, 1810), but before he could qualify for that office, Washington—presumably seeking to strengthen the new government by a judicious choice, despite the charge of Federalist patronage—appointed him federal judge for the District of Virginia. Before his death at Yorktown twenty-one years later, Griffin had beheld the business of the court mount steadily in quantity and importance, and he had helped preside over two of the most famous cases in the legal history of that period: the trial of James T. Callender for libel and that of Aaron Burr for treason. Accomplished, upright, dependable, industrious, he enjoyed fully the confidence and respect of his age, but after his death his services and standing were undeservedly forgotten. He was neither orator nor author; his work was not that which attracts popular notice; he has had no biographer; but, above all, he has been completely overshadowed by the giants who were his contemporaries.

[E. Alfred Jones, *Am. Members of the Inns of Court* (1924); *Va. Mag. of Hist. and Biog.,* Jan. 1894, Oct. 1911, Jan. 1915; Daniel Grinnan, "Cyrus Griffin," *Va. Law Reg.,* Jan. 1928; E. C. Burnett, *Letters of Members of the Continental Cong.,* vols. I–IV (1921–28); J. F. Jameson, "The Old Federal Court of Appeal," *Papers of the Am. Hist. Asso.,* vol. III (1889). Mary Stuart Young's romantic novel, *The Griffins* (1904), is not dependable biography, but contains some interesting letters by the Frenchman, Brissot de Warville.]

A. C. G., Jr.

GRIFFIN, EDWARD DORR (Jan. 6, 1770–Nov. 8, 1837), Congregational clergyman, college president, was born in East Haddam, Conn., the son of a prosperous farmer, George Griffin, and his wife, Eve Dorr. Upon his graduation from Yale College in 1790 he secured the principalship of an academy at Derby, Conn., intending ultimately to study law, but a serious illness and a fall from a horse precipitated him into the ministry. In New Haven he read theology under the younger Jonathan Edwards, who instilled in him the undiluted Edwardsian Calvinism and the Edwardsian penchant for revivals. He was licensed to preach Oct. 31, 1792; supplied several pulpits in Connecticut until his ordination as pastor at New Hartford, June 4, 1795; married Frances, daughter of the Rev. Joseph Huntington and adopted daughter of Governor Samuel Huntington, May 17, 1796; was assistant to Alexander McWhorter at the First Presbyterian Church, Newark, N. J., 1801–07, and pastor after McWhorter's death 1807–09; and was professor of pulpit eloquence in Andover Theological Seminary, 1809–11, pastor of the Park Street Congregational Church, Boston, 1811–15, and pastor of the Second Presbyterian Church, Newark, N. J., 1815–21. He helped to found the American Bible Society and was active in the United Foreign Missionary Society, his famous sermon on the *Kingdom of Christ* (1805, 1808, 1821) being one of the landmarks in the missionary movement. As a pulpit orator and champion of unyielding orthodoxy he was renowned but hardly popular in every quarter. So disliked was he by the authorities of Harvard College that they resorted to every imaginable shift, including two amendments of their charter, to prevent him from exercising his functions as a member *ex officio* of the board of overseers. At Andover he was criticized for extravagance; in

Boston his strict Calvinism found little acceptance and finally led to a breach in his congregation; and in Newark his opponents managed to affront him by cutting down his salary. At this latter juncture he accepted the presidency of Williams College and was inaugurated Nov. 14, 1821. The Amherst secession had just taken place, and Williams—what was left of it—seemed on the point of dissolution. To Griffin belongs the honor of having saved the college. After a hurried examination he decided that what was needed to put it on its feet was a new professor, a new building, and a revival of religion. Raising $25,000 he employed a professor of rhetoric and built a new chapel (now Griffin Hall), but the third ingredient in his tonic had an effect quite unforeseen. Distracted parents, hearing of the "gracious visitation" at Williams, sent their incorrigible sons to the Berkshire institution to be simultaneously reclaimed and educated. The college was soon so overstocked with young ruffians that order was maintained only by drastic measures. What really preserved the college was Griffin's physical presence, which alone was enough to inspire confidence and even awe. He was six feet three inches tall, weighed 250 pounds, and with his symmetrical proportions, ruddy cheeks, and white hair was strikingly handsome. Though his sermons and addresses were seldom better than mediocre, his polished rhetoric and magnificent voice made them sound like works of genius. Over occasions of ceremony he presided with the aplomb of a Lord Chancellor on the woolsack. In his composition there was a tinge, also, of romanticism; it was he who first directed attention to the natural beauty of the country around Williamstown. In 1836, on account of increasing ill health, he retired; a year later he died of dropsy of the chest at his daughter's home in Newark. His wife had died three months before him.

[W. B. Sprague, *Annals Am. Pulpit*, vol. IV (1859); S. H. Cox, "Personal Reminiscences of Dr. Griffin," in *Presbyt. Quart. Rev.*, Mar. 1858; F. B. Dexter, *Biog. Sketches Grads. Yale Coll.*, vol. IV (1907)—with full bibliography and list of sources; Leonard Woods, *Hist. of the Andover Theol. Sem.* (1885); C. J. Stone, *Geneal. of the Descendants of Jasper Griffing* (1881); L. W. Spring, *A Hist. of Williams Coll.* (1917).]

G. H. G.

GRIFFIN, EUGENE (Oct. 13, 1855–Apr. 11, 1907), electrical engineer, soldier, manufacturer, was born at Ellsworth, Me., the son of George K. and Harriet (Jackson) Griffin. He entered the United States Military Academy in July 1871, and graduated June 16, 1875, standing third in his class. In the same year he was commissioned a second lieutenant of engineers. After a period of service at the School of Application, Willetts Point, New York Harbor, he was assigned to the geographical survey being conducted in Colorado, New Mexico, Arizona, and Texas under Lieut. George M. Wheeler. He was promoted first lieutenant June 30, 1879. In 1883 he returned to West Point as assistant professor of civil and military engineering. During 1885–86, while on the staff of Gen. Winfield Scott Hancock he served as engineer officer of the Division of the Atlantic and the Department of the East. Meanwhile, he had contributed to the literature of his profession two significant papers: *Notes on Military Photography* (c. 1882), in Vol. I of the Professional Papers of the Engineer School of Application, and *Our Sea-Coast Defenses* (1885). The latter is a careful historical study characterized by scientific accuracy and a statesman-like grasp of the problems involved. From June 1886 to March 1888 Griffin was assistant to the engineer commissioner of the District of Columbia. In this capacity, in 1887, he made an investigation of telephone, telegraph, arc light, incandescent light, and electric underground wires in the United States. During this investigation he had visited a number of important cities and inspected several electric railroads and on his return to Washington he prepared a report on electricity as a motive power for street cars (Mar. 16, 1888, *Senate Miscellaneous Document No. 84,* 50 Cong., 1 Sess.), perhaps his most important contribution to engineering literature. This report materially quickened the progress of the traction industry, and had a direct effect on Griffin's career. Invited to become general manager of the railroad department of the Thomson-Houston Electric Company, of which he later became vice-president, he resigned from the army (Oct. 5, 1889) to accept that position. In 1892, when his company was consolidated with the Edison company to form the General Electric Company, he was elected vice-president of the latter corporation and placed at the head of the commercial department. In 1893 he became president of the Thomson-Houston International Electric Company.

It is no exaggeration to say that through his position in these corporations he directed the development of the electric-traction industry in America. In 1887 there were only twenty electric railways in operation in the United States and Canada, and twenty-two under construction. The rolling stock on these roads included only 100 diminutive cars equipped with 10-horsepower motors. Within two years after Griffin became associated with the Thomson-Houston Company, its railroad business increased from practically nothing to over $4,000,000 a year; and for a considerable period it was unable to meet the demands made upon it. By 1904 there were in the United States and Canada 55,000 cars weighing as much as forty-eight tons and equipped with as many as four 200-horsepower motors. In that year Griffin contributed to the *Electrical World* (Mar. 5, 1904) an article on "The Foundation of the Modern Street Railway" which is the best account of his services to the industry. Daring and decisive, analytical but far-sighted, he forecast developments in transportation, particularly in interurban traffic, that a quarter of a century after his death are only beginning to take place.

Griffin was married in 1889 to Almira Russell Hancock, niece and adopted daughter of General Hancock. During the Spanish-American War he organized the 1st Regiment, United States Volunteer Engineers, and commanded it in Cuba and Porto Rico. In 1899, before he was mustered out of service, he was promoted brigadier-general of volunteers. His death, due to apoplexy, occurred at Schenectady. He was buried at West Point. His wife, a son, and a daughter survived him.

[G. W. Cullum, *Biog. Reg.* (3rd ed., 1891); *Asso. Grads. U. S. Mil. Acad., Ann. Reunion*, 1908; *Who's Who in America*, 1906-07; *Proc. Am. Soc. Mech. Engineers*, June 1907; *Electrical World* and *Electrical Rev.*, both of Apr. 20, 1907; *N. Y. Times*, Apr. 12, 1907.] R. P. B—r.

GRIFFIN, SIMON GOODELL (Aug. 9, 1824-Jan. 14, 1902), Union soldier, was born in Nelson, N. H., the son of Nathan and Sally (Wright) Griffin. Both of his grandfathers, Massachusetts men, served in the Revolution. From early childhood he lived with an uncle, Samuel Griffin of Roxbury, working on the farm for most of the year and attending district school for a few weeks each winter, until he was able to get a place as a teacher for the short school sessions. He continued farming between school terms as before, and also studied law, finally securing admission to the bar in 1860. Meanwhile he had been elected to the legislature and had served two years there. At the outbreak of the Civil War he helped to organize a company of the 2nd New Hampshire Infantry, armed with Sharp's breech-loading rifles instead of the regulation musket. He was mustered into the service as captain, June 1, 1861, moved with the regiment to Washington three weeks later, and took part in the battle of Bull Run in July, fighting in Burnside's brigade. While on a visit to New Hampshire for the purpose of urging the equipment of all new regiments with Sharp's rifles, he was offered promotion in one of them and accordingly resigned, Oct. 31, 1861, to be mustered in as lieutenant-colonel of the 6th New Hampshire, Nov. 28, 1861. This regiment was designated to take part in Burnside's expedition to Hatteras and sailed from Annapolis in January 1862. It remained on Hatteras Island, Roanoke Island, and in that vicinity until July, taking part in minor hostilities, including Reno's expedition into Camden County. When the colonel resigned in March, Griffin succeeded to the command of the regiment, and on Apr. 22 was promoted to colonel. In August the regiment joined Pope's army in Virginia, and fought at the second battle of Bull Run. From this time until the end of the war it was a part of the IX Corps, and followed its fortunes, fighting under Burnside in both the east and the west. After the battles of South Mountain, Antietam (where the regiment was one of those repulsed with heavy loss in the attack on the bridge), and Fredericksburg, it was sent to the department of the Ohio, and then to assist Grant before Vicksburg by blocking Johnston's movements for the relief of the city. In October 1863 Griffin, who had been commanding a brigade since May, was assigned to the command of Camp Nelson, Ky. In January 1864, as agent of his state, he visited the New Hampshire regiments in Virginia and North Carolina, in order to assist in the reënlistment of the veteran soldiers whose three-year terms were about to expire. He rejoined his brigade in March. He was appointed brigadier-general of volunteers, May 12, 1864, upon the recommendation of Gen. Burnside, who wrote that he had been "conspicuous for his bravery and gallantry." Gen. Parke had made a similar recommendation the previous summer. Through the Virginia campaign of 1864 he commanded a brigade, fighting in the battles in the Wilderness and the operations against Petersburg. In March 1865 he succeeded to the command of a division and retained it during the pursuit of Lee's army. He was mustered out Aug. 24, 1865, having never been absent a day on account of sickness or wounds, although it is said that two horses were killed and five wounded under him and that seven bullets had passed through his clothes.

Returning to New Hampshire, he engaged in manufacturing in Harrisville until 1873, when he went to Texas and spent some time there, occupied with land and railroad operations, but eventually came back to New Hampshire, settling at Keene. He was a member of the legislature in 1866, 1867, and 1868, being speaker the last two years, and was an unsuccessful candidate for Congress in 1871 and 1873. At the time of his death he had just finished *A History of the Town of Keene,* which was published in 1904. His first wife, Ursula I. Harris, of Nelson, N. H., died not long after their marriage in 1850; his second wife, whom he married Jan. 1, 1863, was Margaret R. Lamson of Keene.

[Sketch by O. Applegate, Jr., in Griffin's posthumous *Hist. of the Town of Keene* (1904); Lyman Jackson, *Hist. of the Sixth N. H. Regt.* (1891); A. B. Crawford in *Granite Monthly,* Jan. 1882; *Official Records (Army),* 1 ser., vols. XXX (pt. 3), XXXVI (pts. 1, 2), XL (pts. 1, 3), XLII (pts. 1, 3), XLVI (pts. 1, 3); *Mil. Order of the Loyal Legion of the U. S. Commandery of the State of Mass.,* circ. no. 11, ser. 1902; *Manchester Union,* Jan. 15, 1902; Griffin's own manuscript narrative, giving his military services in minute detail, in the War Dept. files.]
T. M. S.

GRIFFIN, SOLOMON BULKLEY (Aug. 13, 1852–Dec. 11, 1925), editor, was born in Williamstown, Mass., the third of the four children of Nathaniel Herrick and Hannah Elizabeth (Bulkley) Griffin, and the sixth in descent from Jasper Griffing, a Welshman, who settled in Southold, L. I., about 1675. He was named for his maternal grandfather, Maj. Solomon Bulkley of Williamstown. His father, a Congregational minister, was connected with Williams College for thirty-two years, first as professor of ancient languages and later as librarian. Griffin was a member of the class of 1872 at Williams, but because of weak eyes he did not take all the courses required for graduation. He did become locally famous, however, as an expert first-baseman. In 1872 he began his lifelong service on the *Springfield Daily Republican,* his first salary being twenty-five dollars a month. He was promoted to managing editor on the death of the second Samuel Bowles in 1878 and retained this position for forty-one years. To him, almost as much as to the third Samuel Bowles, belongs the credit for maintaining the *Republican* as the best of American provincial newspapers. At first much of his work consisted of reporting the news of the Connecticut Valley and of western Massachusetts, and for years he wrote the bulk of the editorial matter printed under the caption "State and Local Topics" in the *Sunday Republican.* His wider reputation rested on his political reporting and on his editorials. In 1885 he spent an extended vacation in Mexico, sending home to his paper a series of letters later republished as *Mexico of To-day* (1886). On Nov. 25, 1892, he married Ida M. Southworth of Springfield. He was president of the Hampshire Paper Company of South Hadley Falls, vice-president of the Carew Manufacturing Company of South Hadley, and a director of the Southworth Paper Company of Mittineague. He was an alumni trustee of Williams College, 1910–20, and a permanent trustee for the rest of his life. He succeeded his employer as a member of the advisory board of the Pulitzer School of Journalism in Columbia University. His old-fashioned dignity, simplicity, and solidity of character were incorporated in a stalwart, thick-set body and a bushy, reddish-brown beard. After his retirement in 1919, he wrote a volume of reminiscences, *People and Politics Observed by a Massachusetts Editor* (1923), and at the time of his death had just finished the proofs of a panegyric on *W. Murray Crane: A Man and Brother* (1926). He and Crane had been close friends for many years. Griffin's death came without warning as the result of a heart attack. He was survived by his wife and two sons.

[C. J. Stone, *Geneal. of the Descendants of Jasper Griffing* (privately printed, 1881); *Who's Who in America,* 1924–25; *Springfield Republican,* Dec. 12, 1925.]
G. H. G.

GRIFFING, JOSEPHINE SOPHIE WHITE (Dec. 18, 1814–Feb. 18, 1872), social reformer, born in Hebron, Conn., was the daughter of Joseph White, farmer, and maker of axes, a descendant of Peregrine White [*q.v.*], born on the *Mayflower* off Cape Cod. Her mother, Sophie White, was a sister of Samuel Lovett Waldo [*q.v.*], the artist, and a descendant of Peter Waldo, the founder of the English sect of the Waldenses. In her twenty-second year Josephine married at Hebron, Charles Stockman Spooner Griffing, a mechanic, and in 1842 they moved to Ohio. Interested in the problem of negro slavery and sympathetic with the work of the anti-slavery societies, she and her husband became active in the movement, lecturing and organizing in the West. Their home was a station on the Underground Railroad for slaves escaping to Canada. Hearing the pioneer lecturers on woman's suffrage, in 1848 she became an advocate of this new cause which seemed to her another important step toward freedom for the human race. Working incessantly for this double goal, she was frequently in danger of physical violence. Parker Pillsbury wrote that she "performed labor, made sacrifices, encountered sufferings at the west, not known, probably never will be known to the world" (*Acts of the Anti-Slavery Apostles,* 1884, p. 487). Her work was particularly valuable because of her practical ability and imperturbable calm. Accompanied by her younger sister who gave a musical program, she coated her unpleasant doctrines with entertainment that made them more palatable to her backwoods audiences. It is in line with her character that when the Civil War came she should have been one of the earliest workers in the Loyal League and in the sanitary units, and one of the first, also, to recognize the dimensions of the problems presented by the freed slaves. In 1863 she went to Washington to urge federal aid for these people, advocating a most modern program of education for self-support, colonization on deserted plantations, and emergency relief—with temporary work to avoid pauperization. She labored unceasingly with members of the cabinet and of Congress for the establishment of a bureau to organize and direct her projects. With her daughter she served as a paid agent of the National Freedman's Relief Association of the District of Columbia, after it was organized in March 1863, distributing supplies, establishing industrial training centers, and convoying refugees North for employment. She was also an assistant commissioner of the Freedman's Bureau, for the establishment of which, in 1865, she had labored zealously. After the war, leaders of the woman's suffrage movement declared it unthinkable that the illiterate male negro should be enfranchised and not the intelligent white woman, and in 1867 Mrs. Griffing helped organize the Universal Franchise Association of the District of Columbia and became its president. She was also corresponding secretary of the National Woman's Suffrage Association and her sane work in Washington was most valuable in inspiring respect for her cause.

[Waldo Lincoln, *Geneal. of the Waldo Family* (1902); E. C. Stanton, S. B. Anthony, and M. J. Gage, *Hist. of Woman Suffrage* (3 vols., 1881–87); I. H. Harper, *Life of Susan B. Anthony* (vols. I, II, 1899, vol. III, 1908); *Evening Star* (Washington), Feb. 19, 1872; information from a nephew, Chas. J. Douglas, Boston.]
K. H. A.

GRIFFIS, WILLIAM ELLIOT (Sept. 17, 1843–Feb. 5, 1928), educator, clergyman, and author, was born in Philadelphia, the fourth child of Capt. John Limeburner Griffis, of Welsh ancestry, and his wife, Anna Maria Hess, who was of German-Swiss descent. When he was five years old he entered a dame school, and from 1850 to 1860 was a pupil in the public schools. He had three months' service with the 44th Pennsylvania Regiment in the Civil War and was at the battle of Gettysburg. Having been privately tutored, he entered Rutgers College, from which he graduated in 1869. While here he taught the first Japanese students sent to New Brunswick, N. J., on the advice of Dr. Guido Verbeck [*q.v.*]. When in 1870 a call came from the Fukui clan in western Japan for some one "to organize schools on the American principle and teach the natural sciences," Griffis was selected by the Rutgers faculty for that responsible duty. He accepted the appointment, sailed from San Francisco on Dec. 1, and landed at Yokohama on Dec. 29. After a few weeks in Tokio, he proceeded by boat to Kobe and Osaka, and then across the country to Fukui, where he equipped the first chemical laboratory in Japan. He took great pride in the claim that he was the only foreigner living who as a guest in a daimio's capital in the interior, saw the feudal system of Japan in operation. It was while he was there that the system was formally abolished, and he enjoyed the unique privilege of witnessing in Fukui castle the dignified ceremonies attendant upon that abolition and the farewell of the Prince of Echizen to his retainers. Early in 1872, Griffis was called to Tokio to teach chemistry and physics in what is now the Imperial University, and he remained there till July 1874, when he returned to the United States. During all the rest of his life he spent much time in the great work of interpreting Japan to America with voice and pen. His first book, *The Mikado's Empire* (1876) went into twelve editions, and has been a mine of information about Japan; and *Corea—the Hermit Nation* (1882) has been similarly valuable.

In 1877, Griffis graduated from Union Theological Seminary, New York City, and entered upon the work of the ministry, serving as pastor of the First Reformed Church, Schenectady, N. Y. (1877–86); of the Shawmut Congregational Church, Boston (1886–93); and of the First Congregational Church, Ithaca, N. Y. (1893–1903). It is significant of his vigor and versatility that, in connection with his pastoral work, he kept up varied literary labors and was associated with many learned societies. From 1903, he devoted himself for twenty-five years to writing and lecturing. He wrote with avidity and has to his credit a list of about fifty books and hundreds of articles. Among the former are: *Matthew Calbraith Perry: A Typical American Naval Officer* (1887); *Japan—in History, Folk-lore, and Art* (1892); *The Religions of Japan from the Dawn of History to the Era of Méiji* (1895); *Townsend Harris, First American Envoy to Japan* (1895); *America in the East* (1899); *Verbeck of Japan* (1900); *A Maker of the New Orient, Samuel Robbins Brown* (1902); *The Japanese Nation in Evolution* (1907); *A Modern Pioneer in Korea; the Life Story of Henry G. Appenzeller* (1912); *Hepburn of Japan* (1913); and *The Mikado—Institution and Person* (1915). It is a matter of wonder that he kept himself so well informed upon so many subjects. In the case of European nations, he kept in touch with their affairs by frequent visits. In the case of Japan, it was over fifty years before he visited the country a second time, but, by means of the printed page, by visits from Japanese (some of whom lived in his family), and by correspondence with friends in Japan, he was able to secure reasonably accurate information. On his second visit there, he received many courtesies from Japanese friends and the government. Twice he received Imperial decorations, the Fourth Class and the Third Class Orders of the Rising Sun; and in 1927 he was honored by an audience with the Emperor. He was twice married, first to Katharine L. Stanton, June 17, 1879, who died in 1898; and second, June 28, 1900, to Sarah F. King.

[*The Mikado's Empire* (1876) contains a good record of Griffis's life and work in Japan; his *Sunny Memories of Three Pastorates* (1903) describes his career in the ministry; *Who's Who in America*, 1926–27, contains a fairly complete list of his writings. See also *Cat. of the Officers and Alumni of Rutgers Coll., 1766 to 1916* (1916); *Class of 1869, Rutgers Coll., Hist. to 1916* (1918); *Alumni Cat. of the Union Theol. Sem. in the City of N. Y. 1836–1926* (1926); the *Congregationalist*, May 10, 1928; *Korea Mission Field*, Apr. 1928; *N. Y. Times*, Feb. 6, 1928.] E. W. C.

GRIFFITH, BENJAMIN (Oct. 16, 1688–*c.* Oct. 5, 1768), Baptist clergyman, is perhaps entitled to be called the first official historian of the American Baptists. He was born in the County of Cardigan, South Wales, and had two half-brothers, Enoch and Abel Morgan, the former of whom came to America in 1702 and the latter in 1712. Griffith arrived in 1710, and the next year united with the Welsh Tract Baptist Church, Delaware. In 1720 he moved to what is now Montgomery County, Pa., where he henceforth made his home, living, after 1722, on a farm of 300 acres in the Neshaminy Valley. On Dec. 7, 1720, he married Sarah Miles of Radnor, who survived until Nov. 22, 1752. They joined the Montgomery church, of which Griffith became pastor in 1722, although he was not ordained until Oct. 23, 1725. Here he served until his death. While he had no special oratorical gifts, he was sought as a counselor in matters ecclesiastical, legal, and medical, and he was evidently of great influence in the Philadelphia Baptist Association. In 1743 he published *A Short Treatise of Church-Discipline*, printed by Franklin, which was much used by Baptist ministers and churches; and in 1747, *An Answer to a Pamphlet Entitled "The Divine Right of Infant Baptism,"* probably the work for the printing of which the Philadelphia Association had voted in 1746 "to make a subscription." This Association had kept no formal records, but in 1746 it designated Griffith to "collect and set in order the accounts of the several Baptist churches in these provinces, and keep a record of the proceedings of our denomination in these provinces" and it was further "agreed" that he "should have satisfaction for his trouble" (Gillette, *post*, p. 54). Griffith entered his information concerning the churches and the early affairs of the Association in a carefully written folio volume, at present deposited in the library of the American Baptist Historical Society, now one of the most important source books of early American Baptist history. Morgan Edwards [*q.v.*], who continued this "Association Book," beginning in 1761, was undoubtedly stimulated in, if not to, his important historical work by this earlier enterprise. Griffith died about twelve days before his eightieth birthday, although the epitaph on his tombstone reads, "aged 80 years."

[W. B. Sprague, *Annals Am. Pulpit*, vol. VI (1860); Morgan Edwards, *Materials Towards a Hist. of the Baptists in Pa.* (1770); *Minutes of the Phila. Baptist Asso., from A. D. 1707, to A. D. 1807* (1851), ed. by A. D. Gillette.] W. H. A.

GRIFFITH, GOLDSBOROUGH SAPPINGTON (Nov. 4, 1814–Feb. 24, 1904), philanthropist, was born in Harford County, Md., the son of James and Sarah (Cox) Griffith. His father died as the result of exposure while serving in the War of 1812 when the boy was only a few months old; his mother married again; and in 1826 the family, increased by several children, moved to Baltimore. In order to help in their support, young Griffith at the age of twelve secured a regular position in a tobacco manufactory. The occupation was distasteful to him, however, and he was soon commanding excellent pay as an expert paper-hanger. At the age of twenty-two, having accumulated $500, with a partner who had amassed a similar amount, he opened a paper-hanging and upholstering house. Within a few years he became sole owner and conducted a large business until 1854 when he sold it to his half-brothers that he might devote his entire attention to the carpet-house which he had meanwhile opened.

On May 30, 1839, he married Elizabeth Dürst, whose parents were natives of Switzerland. Becoming an earnest worker in his wife's church, the German Reformed, he served it in many capacities throughout his long life. During an eighteen months' visit in Europe with his wife, he acted as American delegate to the Evangelical Alliance in Lübeck in 1856, and again in Berlin the following year. In 1863, when because of the Civil War the Maryland Sunday

School Union was in danger of extinction, his great success as a Sunday-school teacher and organizer led to his appointment to the presidency, an office to which he was annually reëlected until his death. He was peculiarly fitted by virtue of his unquestioned loyalty to the Union and his sympathy with the South, to undertake the task of administering physical and spiritual aid to the sick and wounded soldiers in the border state of Maryland during the Civil War. On May 4, 1861, a few days after the first shedding of blood, the Baltimore Christian Association was organized at his initiative. His selection as president naturally followed. The effort to supply clothing, hospital supplies, delicacies of food, and religious literature to 60,000 suffering soldiers of both armies taxed his time and abilities to the utmost. When the United States Christian Commission was formed in the following November, the Baltimore organization became an auxiliary to the national body, though maintaining its own identity, and achieved a remarkable work over a wide territory, despite an unsympathetic element in the population. The desire to relieve the desperate distress of the South, which he had seen personally on two visits immediately after the war, and to rehabilitate the thousands of refugees in Maryland impelled him to suggest the formation of the Maryland Union Commission, which he reluctantly consented to head.

Distinguished as Griffith was in Sunday-school circles and for his war work, he is most notable for his labors in behalf of penal reform. He was one of three men to call a meeting in 1860 with a view to organizing the Children's Aid Society, later known, in recognition of a handsome bequest, as the Henry Watson Children's Aid Society. Its object was to care for homeless children and to prevent delinquent children from becoming confirmed criminals by being committed to penal institutions. Griffith was a deeply interested member of the board of managers for years. From the age of nineteen, he had manifested an interest in the welfare of prisoners, carrying on personal religious work among them, and in 1859 he had organized the first prison Sunday-schools ever established. A few years after the war, in 1869, at the suggestion of the penitentiary warden, he summoned a gathering of interested men who founded the Maryland Prisoners' Aid Association, of which Griffith, almost as a matter of course, was elected president. The society soon made its influence felt among managers of penal and charitable institutions throughout the state; in his official capacity Griffith made annual tours of inspection, and neglectful wardens soon felt the lash of his tongue and pen. He played a leading rôle in much remedial penal legislation during the seventies and eighties. A relentless foe of the objectionable features of prison systems in the South, he traveled extensively in that section, fearlessly denouncing the evils he encountered. He represented Maryland at nearly all the national and international prison congresses and was made corresponding member of the *Société Générale des Prisons* of France and of the Howard Association of London.

He was also a pioneer temperance worker, was long associated with the Y.M.C.A., and was one of the incorporators of the News Boys' Home and a founder of the Asylum for Feeble-minded Children. Despite his lack of early formal training, he was a frequent and forceful contributor to religious papers and to the Baltimore newspapers. An indomitable will, and strict economy, enabled him to give away about $200,000 during his lifetime. Inspired by a charity that embraced all men, he labored without any apparent loss of energy until his ninetieth year. Two pamphlets published by him are, *Argument on the Contract Labor System and the Reformation of Convicts* (187–), and *Report on the Penal and Reformatory Institutions of the State of Maryland* (1872).

[G. H. Nock, *The Story of a Great Life* (n.d.); *Biog. Cyc. of Representative Men of Md. and the District of Columbia* (1879); J. T. Scharf, *Hist. of Baltimore City and County* (1881); Baltimore *Sun*, and *Baltimore American*, Feb. 25, 1904.] E. L.

GRIFFITH, WILLIAM (1766–June 7, 1826), lawyer, was born at Boundbrook, N. J., the son of Dr. John Griffith. His early education was obtained at home. When he was eighteen he entered the law office of Elisha Boudinot [*q.v.*], at Newark. In 1788 he was admitted as attorney to the New Jersey bar, in the following year he removed to Burlington to practise his profession, and in 1791 he was admitted to the bar as counselor. He eventually became the state's ablest lawyer on New Jersey land titles. One of his students was Richard Smith Coxe [*q.v.*], who later became his son-in-law. Griffith is best known for his legal writings. He published in 1796, *A Treatise on the Jurisdiction and Proceedings of Justices of the Peace in Civil Suits,* which passed through three editions, and in 1797, *The Scriveners Guide,* both of which works proved valuable to the legal profession. In 1798–99 he published in the *New Jersey State Gazette* a series of fifty-three essays, over the signature of "Eumenes," which were issued in the form of a pamphlet in 1799. These essays were written to demonstrate that the state constitution, adopted hastily on July 2, 1776, was defective in structure and unsound in principle. The author urged the election of a convention to revise the constitution, but his proposition was defeated in the legislature. He was appointed by President John Adams as an associate justice of the third federal circuit, his appointment being one of those confirmed by the Senate at midnight on Mar. 3, 1801, but his court was abolished by act of Congress in December of the same year and he resumed his law practise. In 1812 he invested heavily in the business of wool and woolen manufacture and soon became bankrupt. To recoup his losses he returned to his law practise and to legal writing. He was a member of the Assembly in 1818–19 and again in 1823–24. During the years 1820–24 he published the *Annual Law Register,* containing a reliable account of the officials, laws, and regulations of each of the then twenty-four United States, and a succinct account of the origin, history and practise of the courts of New Jersey. From 1824 to 1826 he served as mayor of Burlington, and in the latter year he was appointed clerk of the United States Supreme Court. Before he could assume his new duties, however, he was stricken with heart disease and died in Burlington. His *Historical Notes of the American Colonies and Revolution from 1754 to 1775,* incomplete at his death, was published posthumously in 1836; another edition was published in 1843.

[L. Q. C. Elmer, "The Constitution and Government of the Province and State of New Jersey," in *N. J. Hist. Soc. Colls.,* VII (1872), 293; W. E. Schermerhorn, *The Hist. of Burlington, N. J.* (1927); J. P. Snell, *Hist. of Hunterdon and Somerset Counties, N. J.* (1881); F. B. Lee, *N. J. as a Colony and as a State* (1902), vol. III; *The Biog. Encyc. of N. J.* (1877); E. M. Woodward and J. F. Hageman, *Hist. of Burlington and Mercer Counties, N. J.* (1883); *True American* (Trenton), June 10, 1826; *Daily National Intelligencer* (Washington, D. C.), June 12, 1826; William Nelson, *Fifty Years of Hist. Work in N. J., 1845–1895* (1898).]
W. G. E.

GRIFFITHS, JOHN WILLIS (Oct. 6, 1809?–Mar. 30, 1882), naval architect, was born in New York City. His father was probably John Griffiths, shipwright in an East River yard. Though the younger Griffiths became one of America's outstanding naval architects, the details of his family and early life remain surprisingly obscure. After a public-school education, he received a thorough training in ship carpentry under his father's direction. His special talents soon made him a draftsman; he served for a while, apparently, at the Portsmouth, Va., Navy Yard and then with Smith & Dimon, prominent New York shipwrights. He first attracted attention in 1836 by a series of original articles on naval architecture in the Portsmouth *Advocate,* and five years later, exhibited at the American Institute in New York the model of a clipper ship embodying some of his novel theories. Early in the forties he delivered before the shipbuilders of New York and other audiences the first formal lecture on naval architecture given in America. This lecture was later expanded into *A Treatise on Marine and Naval Architecture or Theory and Practice Blended in Ship-building* (copyright 1849), which passed through several editions in England and America and was even translated into Dutch. It was closely followed by *The Ship-builder's Manual and Nautical Referee* (2 vols., 1853). His final book was *The Progressive Shipbuilder* (2 vols., 1874–75). He was editor of the *American Ship* from October 1878 until his death. Through his writings Griffiths did more than any one else to put shipbuilding in America on a scientific basis, in place of the "rule of thumb" methods then in vogue. He was not only an influential theorist, however, but a practical designer of ships as well, and one of the first in the United States outside of naval constructors like Joshua Humphreys [*q.v.*], to specialize in designing. Most of his contemporaries, like Donald McKay, Samuel Hall, and Jacob Bell [*qq.v.*], owned shipyards and actually built the ships they designed, just as at that time the architect of a house was generally also the builder. Griffiths, however, with his particular inventive genius and bold originality, was content to draw the plans and let others execute them. He showed amazing versatility in that period of constant innovation, designing outstanding vessels of many sorts—sail and steam, wood and iron, war and commerce. Though the *Ann McKim,* built at Baltimore in 1832, is often called the pioneer clipper, Griffiths is credited with designing the first "extreme clipper ship," the *Rainbow,* 750 tons, launched in 1845 for the China trade. He also designed the *Sea Witch,* 907 tons, launched a year later. To secure increased speed by reducing resistance, he gave these ships slender bows and sterns rising high above the water, concave bow waterlines and "the greatest breadth at a point considerably further aft than had hitherto been considered practicable" (Clark, *post,* p. 65). Conservative skeptics attacked these innovations, questioning the safety of such sharp, slender ships, but they proved to be the fastest afloat and strongly influenced the subsequent development of the American clipper. Griffiths then turned to steamships, where again his influence was important. The first steamships had lines very similar to those of sailing ships, but Griffiths exhibited at the Crystal Palace exposition in London a model with a straight bow and other features later generally adopted. These features were incorporated in the *Arctic, Baltic,* and *Pacific* which he is said to have designed for the ill-starred line of Edward K. Collins [*q.v.*]. During the early fifties, these were the fastest and finest steamships in the world. Griffiths later attempted to cut the transatlantic passage to seven and even to six days. He is said also to have become a special naval constructor in 1858 and as such to have designed the *Pawnee,* a twin screw vessel of remarkably light draft in spite of its heavy armament. His writings and the success of his ships brought him orders from all parts of the world. In addition to designing complete ships, he also developed several important special features including iron keelsons, watertight bulkheads, bilge keels, and triple screws. He developed an improved form of rivet, invented a machine for bending timber to the crooked forms necessary for shipbuilding and designed the *New Era,* 1,140 tons, the first ship built with mechanically bent timbers (1870). One of his last experiments is said to have been a lifeboat steamer, in 1875. During his later years, he was active in the endeavor to revive the declining American merchant marine and was a conservative in his arguments for the use of wood instead of iron in American ships. He died at his home in Brooklyn after a protracted illness.

[Griffiths's own books, cited above, are the best sources for his achievements. A death notice in the *N. Y. Herald,* Apr. 1, 1882, and an obituary in the *Am. Ship,* Apr. 1, 1882, confirm the date of his death. An analysis of his innovations in clipper-ship construction is in A. H. Clark, *The Clipper Ship Era* (1910), pp. 65–67, and in C. G. Davis, *Ships of the Past* (1929), p. 64. His pioneer clippers are described in O. T. Howe and F. C. Matthews, *Am. Clipper Ships* (2 vols., 1926–27), II, pp. 501, 569. Some of his innovations are described in U. S. Patent Office report for 1854, *Sen. Ex. Doc. 42,* 33 Cong., 2 Sess., I, 644, and for 1862, *Ibid.,* I, 177, 335. See also F. C. Matthews, *Am. Merchant Ships* (1930).]

R. G. A—n.

GRIGGS, JOHN WILLIAM (July 10, 1849–Nov. 28, 1927), lawyer, statesman, youngest son of Daniel Griggs and Emeline Johnson, was born on a farm near Newton, Sussex County, N. J. His ancestors, originally English settlers in Massachusetts, founded Griggstown, N. J., in 1733, coming from Gravesend, Long Island, where the progenitor of the New Jersey family owned land in 1672. His mother was the granddaughter of Henry Johnson, a captain in the New Jersey militia in the Revolutionary War. Griggs received his early education at Collegiate Institute, Newton, and entered Lafayette College in 1865. After graduating in 1868, he began the study of law under former Congressman Robert Hamilton, at Newton, and finished in 1871 with Socrates Tuttle, preceptor and father-in-law of Garret A. Hobart [*q.v.*], whose lifelong friend Griggs was. Upon admission to the bar of Paterson in 1871, he formed a partnership with Tuttle.

Early in his professional career Griggs attracted the attention of the political leaders in his county and soon established a reputation as an able campaign speaker. At the age of twenty-six he was elected to the General Assembly and was chairman of the committee on the revision of the laws, being generally credited with authorship of the law of elections. He was reëlected in 1877 and rapidly attained leadership in his party's battles. Defeated for reëlection in 1878, he was appointed counsel to the Board of Chosen Freeholders of Passaic County and from 1879 to 1882 he served as city counsel of Paterson. In 1879 he opened an office for himself and within a few years gained a place of first rank at the bar of New Jersey. In 1882 he was elected to the state Senate, and being reëlected for a second term, served as president of that body in the session of 1886, presiding with dignity and impartiality over the Laverty impeachment trial for the greater part of the session. While in the upper body he displayed signal ability in the passage of legislation to tax the railroads and other corporations, serving as chairman of the joint committee which harmonized the differences between his own and the more radical bill of Gov. Leon Abbett. Having been delegate-at-large to the Republican National Convention of 1888, considered by President Harrison for the Supreme Court, and tendered a judgeship on the highest court of New Jersey by the Democratic Gov. Werts, which he declined, Griggs was clearly one of the outstanding men of his party in New Jersey, and with Garret A. Hobart as his campaign manager, was nominated and elected governor in 1895 by a plurality of 26,900, being the first Republican governor in that state since 1866.

His election brought him immediately into national prominence, and it was but a logical promotion when President McKinley called Griggs from the governorship to his cabinet in 1898 as chief law officer of the government. Few epochs in our history have presented more difficult or delicate legal questions, as the reports of the Supreme Court and the opinions of the attorney-general bear witness. Among the cases decided by the Supreme Court, momentous not only for the constitutional points involved, but for the argument of counsel, the close division of the court, and the vehemence of the opinions rendered on both sides, were the Insular Cases. His able advocacy in these and other important cases gained for him eminent rank as a lawyer, while his opinions as attorney-general and his counsel at the cabinet table placed him among the notable men who have held that office. Before the succession of Roosevelt to the presidency, Griggs resigned to resume the practise of law and was among the first members appointed to the Permanent Court of Arbitration at The Hague, serving thereon from 1901 to 1912. He was an aspirant for the United States Senate in 1902 but did not receive his party's nomination. As head of a firm in New York, he soon built up a lucrative corporation practise. Prior to the dissolution of the Marconi Wireless Telegraph Company he was its president, and at the time of his death he was general counsel and director of the Radio Corporation of America, and of other large corporations. In appearance he was tall, slender, erect, with finely chiseled features, and a proud bearing that bespoke a commanding personality. He was keenly devoted to hunting and fishing, an expert rifle shot, good at golf, and an excellent whist and chess player. Added to his versatility as a sportsman was his reputation as a raconteur of unusual charm. He was married in 1874 to Carolyn Webster Brandt, who died in 1891, and in 1893 to Laura Elizabeth Price, having by them two sons and five daughters.

[W. E. Sackett, *Modern Battles of Trenton, 1868–1913* (2 vols., 1895–1914); Wm. Nelson and C. A. Shriner, *Hist. of Paterson and Its Environs* (1920); J. J. Scannell, *New Jersey's First Citizens and State Guide*, 1923–24; *Green Bag*, Mar. 1898; S. F. Bigelow and G. J. Hagar, *The Biog. Cyc. of N. J.* (n.d.); W. S. Griggs, *Geneal. of the Griggs Family* (1926); J. F. Stonecipher, *Biog. Cat. of Lafayette Coll., 1832–1912* (1913); F. B. Lee, *Geneal. and Memorial Hist. of the State of N. J.* (1910); *N. Y. Times*, Nov. 29, 1927.]

J. T. V.

GRIGSBY, HUGH BLAIR (Nov. 22, 1806–Apr. 28, 1881), historian, was born at Norfolk, Va., of English descent, son of the Rev. Benjamin Porter Grigsby, pastor of the first Presbyterian church organized in that borough, and his wife Elizabeth McPherson. In spite of a delicate physique which forced upon him a regimen of systematic exercise and unflagging prudence, he progressed rapidly under private instruction before spending two years at Yale, where he pursued with distinction, among other subjects, the course in law. Upon the completion of his studies he was admitted to the Norfolk bar, but his increasing deafness caused him to relinquish legal practise, and he embarked in journalism as owner and editor of the Norfolk *American Beacon*. During 1828–29 and 1829–30, when, as he later observed, his editorial labors often compelled him to do the work of three men, he represented Norfolk in the House of Delegates and succeeded Gen. Robert Barraud Taylor as a member of the Virginia Constitutional Convention of 1829–30. Meanwhile, so capably did he conduct the affairs of his newspaper that, when at the end of six years his health made it necessary for him to withdraw, he was able to retire with a competency.

He married, Nov. 19, 1840, Mary Venable Carrington, daughter of Col. Clement Carrington of Charlotte County, Va., and there resided, save for a temporary removal to Norfolk, until his death. At "Edgehill," his wife's patrimonial estate, surrounded by an excellent library, he followed the quiet existence of the scholar and gentleman farmer, studying, enjoying nature, making pets of animals and birds, writing his historical and biographical works, and experimenting eagerly in agricultural engineering. His deafness did not make him a recluse, however: he won friends readily, loved the company of children, and maintained a hospitable establishment. By precept and example he sought to encourage the causes of education and culture in his state, fostered the genius of the sculptor, Alexander Galt, and composed voluminous numbers of graceful letters and occasional chaste, if uninspired, verses. He took a particular interest in the College of William and Mary, served on its board of visitors, and in 1871 was elected its chancellor.

In youth Grigsby evinced an aptitude for biography, and his later writings or addresses were largely concerned with this phase of literature. Devoted to Virginia and, in his day, the acknowledged historian of the state, he was thoroughly familiar with its story from the beginnings and with the history of nearly every native family within its borders. He was an active supporter of the Virginia Historical Society, contributing regularly to its publications and serving as its president from 1870 until his death, at the same time enjoying honorary membership in the historical societies of Pennsylvania and Massachusetts. Of his numerous productions, the chief were his sketches of *The Virginia Convention of 1776* (1855) and *The History of the Virginia Federal Convention of 1788* (2 vols., 1890–91), distinguished in style and diction. His account of *The Virginia Convention of 1829–30* (1854) is likewise valuable. Besides being the authoritative narratives of the proceedings of these three conventions, Grigsby's essays are supplemented by sketches of the men who sat in each body, significant for their pictures of the "second growth" of eminent Virginians as well as for their accurate summaries of the earlier nationally known figures. His other major publications include his *Discourse on the Life and Character of the Honorable Littleton Waller Tazewell* (1860), *The Founders of Washington College* (1890), and *Discourse on the Lives and Characters of the Early Presidents and Trustees of Hampden-Sidney College* (1913). He was an enthusiastic historian, who more than counterbalanced an occasional religious bias or a deficiency in creative imagination by his thoroughness, his grasp of the facts and principles underlying American history, his eloquence, sense of proportion, and fund of anecdote and humor, but especially by his gift for uncovering local material that would doubtless otherwise have perished.

[R. A. Brock, "Biog. Sketch of Hugh Blair Grigsby," serves as the introduction to Grigsby's *Hist. of the Va. Federal Convention* which appeared as volumes IX and X, n.s. (1890–91) of the *Va. Hist. Soc. Colls.* See also W. H. Grigsby, *Geneal. of the Grigsby Family* (1878); *New-Eng. Hist. and Geneal. Reg.*, July 1881; the *State* and *Daily Dispatch* (Richmond), Apr. 30, 1881.]
A. C. G., Jr.

GRIM, DAVID (Aug. 25, 1737–Mar. 26, 1826), tavern-keeper, merchant, antiquarian, was born in Zweibrücken, Bavaria. His father, Philip, with his wife and seven children, of whom David was the youngest, sailed from Amsterdam for New York in July 1739 (Eickhoff, *post, Anhang,* p. 135). He was a Lutheran and in 1750 was interested in the erection of a Lutheran church for "High Germans," his name appearing on a deed of sale for the land upon which it was to be built. David attended the school of the Lutheran community, and for two years, beginning in 1757, was in service aboard the *King of Prussia,* cruising about the West Indies. In 1767 he was an innkeeper at the "Sign of the Three Tuns," Chapel (Beekman) Street (*New-York Journal,* Jan. 29, 1767). Later he was at the Hessian Coffee House, William Street. Naturally, German Protestants patronized his table, and there was a great gathering of the clan in his hostelry on the anniversary of the repeal of the Stamp Act, Mar. 18, 1774 (*Ibid.,* Mar. 24, 1774). He continued his tavern business during the Revolution and his house is spoken of as "the usual Place for the Drawing of Lotteries" (*New York Mercury,* Jan. 31, 1780). By 1789 he had given up tavern-keeping and had become a merchant at 50 Nassau Street (*The New York Directory and Register for the Year 1789*), and for the rest of his life he was successful in business and a man "of affairs and influence" (G. U. Wenner, *The Lutherans of New York,* 1918, p. 19). He joined the German Society of the City of New York when it was organized, Oct. 9, 1784, succeeded Baron von Steuben as president Jan. 21, 1795, and held the office until Jan. 25, 1802 (Eickhoff, *post,* p. 97). He also served for some years as treasurer of the Lutheran church. When, in 1792, the merchants of New York City determined to erect a "handsome brick building" for a Tontine Coffee House, on Wall Street, Grim was appointed to receive competitive plans and to dispose of the old buildings on the site, and it was Grim who collected from subscribers and paid the bills.

Grim is chiefly remembered, however, for activities of quite another sort. In the last years of his life he found amusement in making pen-and-ink sketches of landmarks in the city as he remembered them in his younger days, and in recording reminiscences. When comparison is possible with other sketches or records, his memory appears to have been remarkably accurate, and in many cases his handiwork is actually the sole source of information. Among his sketches are: "Plan and Elevation of the Old City Hall," the only reproduction extant of the City Hall prior to its alteration in 1763; "Part of New York in 1742 showing the site of the present [City Hall] park; the Collect and Little Collect Ponds; and a portion of the west side of Broadway"; "A Plan of the City and Environs of New York as they were in the years 1742–1743–1744"; and the course of the destructive fires of 1776 and 1778. Notes accompany most of the sketches; other notes describe St. Paul's Chapel, the several slips along the East River shore, the negro plot of 1741, and the visit of the Mohawk and Oneida Indians in 1784. Grim was married soon after his West Indian career to a wife who died Oct. 6, 1779 (Rivington's *Royal Gazette,* Oct. 9, 1779). Two daughters, Elizabeth and Catherine, married lieutenants in the regiment of the Margrave of Anspach, quartered in New York during the Revolution; a son, Philip, died before his father. Grim was married a second time, Dec. 24, 1781, to Mary Barwick.

[Anton Eickhoff, *In der Neuen Heimath* (1884); Walter Barrett (J. A. Scoville), *The Old Merchants of N. Y. City* (4 vols., 1863–66); E. B. O'Callaghan, *Names of Persons for Whom Marriage Licenses were Issued by the Secretary of the Province of N. Y., Previous to 1784* (1860); I. N. P. Stokes, *The Iconography of Manhattan Island, 1498–1909* (6 vols., 1915–28); D. J. Valentine, *Manual of the Corporation of the City of N. Y.,* for 1854, 1855, 1856, 1866; *N. Y. Evening Post,* and *N. Y. American,* Mar. 27, 1826.]
A. E. P.

GRIMES, ABSALOM CARLISLE (Aug. 22, 1834–Mar. 27, 1911), Confederate mail-runner, son of William Leander and Charlotte (Wright) Grimes, was born in Jefferson County, Ky., and died in St. Louis, Mo. When he was sixteen, his father, a pilot on the upper Mississippi, put an end to the boy's career as a telegraph messenger, and took him on the *Uncle Toby* as an apprentice. He was licensed a pilot in 1852, and began working the river between St. Louis and St. Paul. In May 1861, applying for a renewal of his license, he became angered by the demand of a naturalized German official that he take an oath of allegiance to the Federal Government, and returned to his home in Hannibal. With him, under like impetus, went his fellow townsman, Samuel L. Clemens. Apprehended there and taken to St. Louis, they escaped and soon afterward joined a nondescript, self-equipped group of ten or twelve Confederate soldiers. Clemens, mounted on a mule named Paint Brush, was their second lieutenant when he was not more essentially occupied with his functions as Punchinello. It was a gusty, roistering troop, sometimes attached to larger units, sometimes traveling independently, occasionally in skirmishes, but oftener at country parties more concerned with love than with war, or engaged in horse-play. Before long, Ab was captured, but escaping, he returned to St. Louis. There, plotting with some women of his acquaintance, he conceived a plan of carrying mail to Confederate soldiers, and in April 1862, with a great batch of letters, he undertook his first run. A few days later, he reached a Confederate camp at Rienzi, Miss., much to the elation of the soldiers there anxious for news from home. He returned to St. Louis, and, his women friends still aiding him, for about two years made trips back and forth, whenever he was not a prisoner. After a few months he was made official mail-carrier and commissioned major, but he was fortunately not obliged to work in a definite military organization. Five seperate times he was captured and confined in Northern territory but always, by disguise and subterfuge, by his own irresistible personality, and by romantic daredeviltry, he managed after a little to escape and reinstitute his runs. Wounded at the time of his sixth capture in 1864, he was tried at St. Louis and sentenced to be hanged, but was temporarily spared because of feigned illness. His sentence was commuted by Lincoln, first to imprisonment for the duration of the war, and later, on condition that he take an oath of allegiance to the United States, to imprisonment till Dec. 1, 1864. He was taken to the Jefferson City penitentiary. Toward the end of November, though the order for his release was already in the hands of the warden, he was on the instigation of that functionary so brutally beaten that he carried the fierce scars of the event with him till his death.

On Mar. 7, 1865, after an engagement of seven years, he married Lucy Glascock of New London, Mo., and they went on a honeymoon trip by boat to New Orleans. Returning he again took up his work as pilot, once ascending the Missouri as far as Fort Benton, Mont., but in general keeping to the more usual destinations along the Missouri and the Mississippi above St. Louis. In 1870 he settled down as a confectioner in Hannibal, but two years later moved to St. Louis and till 1883 worked as a pilot. For many years subsequently he managed a hunting club in Lincoln County, Mo., then conducted a moving-picture show in St. Louis and afterwards worked for the General Compressed Air-Vacuum Cleaning Company. His wife died in 1903, and on Dec. 15, 1905, he married his twenty-year-old ward, Nell Tauke. In 1910–11, on the basis of a diary he had kept he wrote the reminiscences which, edited by M. M. Quaife, were published in 1926 under the title, *Absalom Grimes, Confederate Mail Runner.*

[*St. Louis Globe Democrat,* Mar. 29, 1911; *St. Louis Republican,* Mar. 28, 1911; letter from Health Commissioner of City of St. Louis, to author, July 3, 1928; S. L. Clemens, "The Private Hist. of a Campaign that Failed," *Century,* Dec. 1885; A. B. Paine, *Mark Twain, A Biography* (3 vols., 1912).]

J. D. W.

GRIMES, JAMES STANLEY (May 10, 1807–Sept. 27, 1903), erratic philosopher, was born in Boston. His parentage is uncertain: he was probably the son either of Andrew Grimes and Polly Robbins or of Joseph Grimes and Sally Robbins (*A Volume of Records Relating to the Early History of Boston, Containing Boston Marriages from 1752 to 1809,* 1903). He practised law for a time in Boston and New York City, and was sufficiently prominent in his profession to enjoy the acquaintance of Webster, Choate, Clay, and Van Buren. He then became professor of medical jurisprudence in the Castleton Medical College; he also taught for a period in Willard Institute, which claimed to be the first woman's college established in the United States. Eventually he drifted to the newly founded town of Evanston, Ill., where he resided for the rest of his long life.

His main interest, however, was not in the law but in wide speculative problems of sciences and pseudo-science. Ill-trained, and sharing the interest of his day in occult phenomena, he nevertheless possessed a fearless, original, and absolutely honest mind. He was one of the first American evolutionists, one of the first American investigators of mesmerism to reach constructive conclusions, a stout opponent of superstition in a superstitious age. Like many of his contemporaries, however, he was hampered by ignorance coupled with excessive self-confidence. His attention was attracted at the outset by phrenology; he threw himself into the study of this subject in 1832 and for a number of years was one of its most fervent exponents. Bold, argumentative, gifted with a ready flow of speech and considerable humor, in his leisure moments he roamed the platforms of the Eastern states, delighting equally in lecture and debate. In 1839 he published *A New System of Phrenology,* in which he set forth a different system of classification from the orthodox one of Spurzheim, substituting, for the latter's dichotomy of mental functions into the intellectual and affective, a threefold division into ipseal (self-regarding), social (other-regarding), and intellectual (relation-regarding) activities. O. S. Fowler [*q.v.*], editor of the *American Phrenological Journal,* promptly attacked the heretic in a thirteen-page review, and, although Grimes's system was championed by the important Phrenological Society of Albany (E. N. Horsford, *Report on the Phrenological Classification of J. S. Grimes,* Sept. 3, 1840), it made little headway against Fowler's opposition. Grimes then for a time turned his energies to mesmerism and mental healing and is credited by Woodbridge Riley with having started "the whole tribe of Yankee healers" (*American Thought,* 1915, p. 116). In particular, it was a lecture of his in Poughkeepsie which first aroused the interest of Andrew Jackson Davis [*q.v.*] in the subject of mesmerism. During the next two decades his pen became increasingly active. In 1845 he published *Etherology* (republished in part in 1850), in which he attacked the assertions of Joseph Rodes Buchanan [*q.v.*] that the organs of the brain can be excited by touching the head, and showed himself in advance of his time by ascribing mesmerism to the power of suggestion rather than to the action of an occult fluid; on the other hand, he introduced elsewhere in his system an occult fluid of his own, the universal "etherium," and argued fancifully that the seat of consciousness is to be found in the medulla oblongata. Next appeared *Phreno-Geology* (1851), which Grimes claimed was "the first essay ever published on theistic evolution"; then, *The Mysteries of Human Nature Explained* (1857, republished under a modified title 1875 and 1881), a further study of occult phenomena, giving special attention to the errors of spiritualism; and then, *Outlines of Geonomy* (1858, republished in 1866), a hardy statement of various ingenious theories in regard to the formation of planetary systems and of the earth. In 1860 he made his last appearance on a New England platform in a series of eight debates on spiritualism at the Melodeon in Boston, where he successfully routed his spiritualistic opponent, Leo Miller. Shortly after this he retired to Evanston and sank into forty years of obscurity broken only by the publication of his belated *Phreno-Physiology* in 1893. He would seem never to have lost his self-confidence, however, for at the age of seventy he persuaded an insurance company to change a $4,000 life policy to an annuity policy of $400. Under this second policy he drew over $10,000 before he died twenty-six years later.

[*Chicago Daily Tribune,* Sept. 29, 1903; *Proc. Am. Asso. for the Advancement of Science,* 1903–04; *Great Discussion of Modern Spiritualism between Leo Miller and J. S. Grimes* (Boston, 1860); autobiographical references in Grimes's writings.] E. S. B—s.

GRIMES, JAMES WILSON (Oct. 20, 1816–Feb. 7, 1872), lawyer, legislator, governor of Iowa, and United States senator, was born at Deering, Hillsborough County, N. H., the youngest of eight children. His parents, John and Elizabeth (Wilson) Grimes, were intelligent, independent farmers of Scotch-Irish stock. He entered Dartmouth College in August 1832, at the age of sixteen, but left at the close of the first term of his junior year, in February 1835. In 1845 he was awarded the degree of A.B. as of the class of 1836. After leaving college, he read law in the office of James Walker at Peterborough, N. H., but shortly set forth to seek his fortune in the West. On May 15, 1836, he became a resident of Burlington, Iowa. Here he entered the profession of the law at the age of nineteen and soon became active in public life. In September of that year he acted as secretary of the commission which made two important treaties with the Sac and Fox Indians. The following year he was appointed city solicitor. Elected in 1838 to the first Legislative Assembly of the Territory of Iowa, he served as chairman of the committee on judiciary. He served again in 1843 as a member of the sixth Legislative Assembly, and in 1852 as a member of the fourth General Assembly of the state, where he was a leader in the promotion of railroads. At this time he was listed as a farmer, being interested in stock-breeding and agriculture. He was a charter member of the Southern Iowa Horticultural Society, and for a time served as editor on the staff of the *Iowa Farmer and Horticulturist.* On Nov. 9, 1846, he had married Elizabeth Sarah Nealley. In the practise of law he was associated with Henry W. Starr.

Grimes was a man of commanding presence. "Careless of appearance, and somewhat rough and ungainly in early life, he grew with years in suavity, and grace, and dignity of bearing."

Always, "he abhorred pretension and indirection" (Salter, *post,* p. 390). He had been reared a Whig and later adhered to that party both from preference and from conviction. Nominated for the office of governor by the Whigs, he was elected on Aug. 3, 1854, after an energetic and fatiguing campaign. He stood for the revision of the state constitution and the establishment of banks and advocated better schools, internal improvements, and the enactment of homestead laws which would give to foreign-born settlers the same rights as were granted to native-born. He upheld the inviolability of the Missouri Compromise; and in his inaugural address on Dec. 9, 1854, made it plain that he would do everything in his power to combat the further spread of slavery. Placing "business above politics, and the state above his party," Grimes, with a sense of institutional values, helped to remake Iowa. While he was in office the constitution of the state was revised and the capital removed from Iowa City to Des Moines; the State University was located permanently at Iowa City; schools free to all children were placed on a public-tax basis; a prohibitory liquor law was enacted; a State Historical Society was established; and institutions were created for the care of the insane, the deaf and dumb, and the blind. By the year 1856 he regarded the old parties and old issues as dead; and in that year spoke with force and deep conviction in behalf of the new Republican party, declaring that the great issue before the country was the extension or non-extension of slavery into the territories. It has been said that he, more than any one else, "made Iowa Republican, and allied it with the loyal States" (Salter, *post,* p. 116).

On Mar. 4, 1859, he first took his seat in the United States Senate. He was appointed to the committee on pensions and private land claims; and on Jan. 24, 1861, became a member of the committee on naval affairs, of which he was chairman from Dec. 8, 1864, until the end of his senatorial career. He was instrumental in keeping the Naval Academy at Annapolis, and was one of the first to recognize the necessity of an adequate fleet and the advantages of iron-clad ships. He was also chairman of the committee on the District of Columbia; and in the latter part of his senatorial career served on the committees on patents and the Patent Office, public buildings and grounds, and appropriations. He was associated with a group of men who during the Civil War created a detective service to sift out disloyal persons in the public service and elsewhere.

During the impeachment trial of President Johnson in 1868, Grimes displayed an integrity which cost him his political power and probably hastened his death. Though he considered many of the President's acts as highly deplorable, he did not believe that they constituted "high crimes and misdemeanors" and he seriously doubted the wisdom of a policy of impeachment. The strain of the trial brought on a stroke of paralysis, and when the time came for voting on the impeachment he had to be carried into the Senate chamber. He voted "Not guilty," while James Harlan [1820–1899, *q.v.*], the other senator from Iowa, voted "Guilty." One ballot the other way would have given a two-thirds majority, and the President would have been retired from office. A storm of political abuse broke upon Grimes; even the town of Burlington viewed his conduct with disfavor.

He returned to Congress when it reassembled in December 1868, but his spirit and strength were gone. In April 1869 he was ordered to Europe for a rest. There he suffered another stroke, and on Aug. 11, sent to the governor of Iowa his resignation as senator, to take effect Dec. 6. When he returned to America in September 1871, he found public sentiment once more in his favor. He died a few months later at his home in Burlington.

[B. F. Shambaugh, *The Messages and Proclamations of the Governors of Iowa* (7 vols., 1903–05), II, 3–112; collection of pamphlets from Grimes's library, in the library of the State Hist. Soc. of Iowa; Wm. Salter, *The Life of James W. Grimes* (1876); Eli C. Christoferson, "The Life of James W. Grimes," MS. in the library of the State Hist. Soc. of Iowa; G. T. Chapman, *Sketches of the Alumni of Dartmouth Coll.* (1867); D. E. Clark, *Hist. of Senatorial Elections in Iowa* (1912); *Sioux City Daily Jour.,* Feb. 9, 1872.]

B. F. S.

GRIMKÉ, ANGELINA EMILY (1805–1879). [See GRIMKÉ, SARAH MOORE, 1792–1873.]

GRIMKÉ, ARCHIBALD HENRY (Aug. 17, 1849–Feb. 25, 1930), negro lawyer, author, publicist, son of Henry Grimké of South Carolina and Nancy Weston, a beautiful family slave, was born near Charleston. When his father died, the child was entrusted to the guardianship of his white half-brother. After the Civil War, young Grimké, a boy of sixteen, went North and partly through his own efforts, partly with the help of friends, entered Lincoln University, receiving the degree of B.A. in 1870 and M.A. in 1872. With the aid of his aunt, Sarah Moore Grimké [*q.v.*], he then entered the Harvard Law School and took the LL.B. degree in 1874. The following year he was established in Boston and beginning to practise law. He very soon became a prominent figure in negro affairs, being made president of the local branch of the National Association for the Advancement of Colored People, and later vice-president of the entire organization. On Apr. 19, 1879, he married Sarah E. Stanley of Boston and, once fairly settled, began to develop his natural talent for writing and to contribute articles to the periodical press in the interests of the negro race. From 1883 to 1885 he was the editor of the *Hub,* a Boston paper devoted to colored welfare. This post offered him his opportunity to begin his lifelong crusade against race prejudice, race discrimination, and the double standard of sex morality, of which he himself had been a victim. In the early nineties he published the two biographies for which he is best known in the literary field: *The Life of William Lloyd Garrison, the Abolitionist* (1891), and *The Life of Charles Sumner, the Scholar in Politics* (1892). In connection with these works he produced numerous pamphlets on the history of the anti-slavery movement and a series of special articles for the *Boston Herald,* the *Boston Traveler,* and for the *Atlantic Monthly.* At the same time he became increasingly active as a member of the American Negro Academy, under whose auspices most of his pamphlets and lectures were published, in agitating for a fully operative negro franchise.

In 1894 Grimké was appointed by President Cleveland American consul to Santo Domingo where he served until 1898. Upon his retirement, again in Boston, he turned with fresh zest to the question of the negro vote. In 1899 he addressed an open letter to President McKinley in which he stated the negro point of view with admirable clearness on behalf of the Colored National League. From this time forward, he devoted his best energies to writing and lecturing on the problems of the negro race in connection with his work for the American Negro Academy, of which he was president from 1903 to 1916. In 1919, as a testimonial to his efforts in behalf of negro advancement, he received the Spingarn medal, the highest honor annually bestowed by the National Association for the Advancement of Colored People upon an American citizen of African descent. The body of Grimké's writings is considerable, typical of which are: *Right on the Scaffold, or, The Martyrs of 1822* (1901), a sympathetic life of Télémaque (Denmark) Vesey, leader of the Charleston slave rising of 1822; *The Ballotless Victim of One-Party Governments* (1913), a protest against race-discrimination at the polls; "The Sex Question and Race Segregation," *Papers of the American Negro Academy, 1915* (1916), an indictment of the double standard; *The Ultimate Criminal* (1915), a suggestive tractate on the influence of race discrimination upon negro crime; and *The Shame of America, or, The Negro's Case Against the Republic* (1924). In addition to his lifelong crusade on behalf of his race, Grimké found time for other and varied activities. He was trustee of the Estate of Emmeline Cushing for Negro Education, president of the Frederick Douglass Memorial and Historical Association, treasurer of the Committee of Twelve for Negro Advancement, member of the Authors' Club, London, and member of the American Social Science Association. He died at his home in Washington, where he had lived and worked since 1905.

["A Biog. Sketch of Archibald Grimké," by his daughter, Angelina W. Grimké, in *Opportunity, A Jour. of Negro Life* (N. Y.), Feb. 1925; *Archibald H. Grimké* (1930), by his brother, Francis J. Grimké; *Atlantic Monthly,* July 1904; *Who's Who in America,* 1924–25; *Who's Who of the Colored Race,* 1915; *Who's Who in Colored America,* 1928–29; *Jour. of Negro Hist.,* Apr. 1930; *Washington Herald,* Feb. 27, 28, 1930; *Washington Tribune,* Aug. 23, 1929, Feb. 28, 1930.]
E. M. H.

GRIMKÉ, JOHN FAUCHERAUD (Dec. 16, 1752–Aug. 9, 1819), South Carolina jurist, was the son of John Paul and Mary Faucheraud Grimké of Charleston, S. C., and was of German and French descent. Ht was educated at Trinity College, Cambridge (A.B. 1774), and studied law in the Middle Temple. With twenty-nine other Americans, he petitioned the Lords against the Boston Port Bill. He returned to the colonies in September 1775 and a year later, on Sept. 16, 1776, he was commissioned captain in the South Carolina Continental artillery, rising to lieutenant-colonel. He was deputy adjutant-general for South Carolina and Georgia until made prisoner at the surrender of Charleston, May 12, 1780. After being tried for alleged violation of his parole in March 1781, he considered his parole void and rejoined the Continental Army, remaining until the end of the war. On Oct. 12, 1784, he married Mary Smith of Charleston. They had fourteen children of whom three were Thomas Smith, Sarah Moore and Angelina Emily [*qq.v.*]. Grimké sat in the state House of Representatives five years, serving as speaker, 1785–86. At the same time he held a judgeship, dating from 1783, and in 1799 he became senior associate, virtually chief justice. In 1788 he was intendant of Charleston and a member of the convention which ratified the federal Constitution, voting himself for the Constitution. The following year he was made a presidential elector. He took an active interest in the improvement of internal navigation, lent his support to three companies, and served as president of the Catawba River Company. He died at Long Branch, N. J.

Grimké has been called "a stern, unbending judge." His most important decisions, those regarding seizures by partisan troops during the Revolution, were relatively conclusive. In appeals sittings he occasionally delivered the opinion of the court. Sometimes arbitrary, he was not popular in his up-country circuit, and in 1811 a committee reported impeachment charges against him, but they failed of the requisite two-thirds vote of the House. He did his best work as a legal compiler in the period of legal reform following the Revolution. In 1785 he and Judges Pendleton and Burke were elected a commission "to effect a revisal, digest, and publication of the laws." Their report (1789) was not adopted, but certain recommendations were later passed. This work apparently led Grimké to publish his *Public Laws of the State of South Carolina* (1790 and later editions), "invaluable when published," and superseded only when Thomas Cooper published his *Statutes at Large of South Carolina* (5 vols., 1836–39) in 1836, a work partly based on Grimké's. Cooper, however, was somewhat critical of his omissions. Grimké also published *The South Carolina Justice of Peace* (1788), and *The Duty of Executors and Administrators* (1797). Despite his unpopularity, he contended against legal delays, opposed inheritance by primogeniture, and had a higher opinion of feminine mentality than most men of his day.

[*S. C. Hist. and Geneal. Mag.*, Apr. 1901, July 1902, Jan. 1903, July 1904, Jan. 1908, Apr., July, Oct. 1911, Jan. 1912, Apr. 1912–Oct. 1918, Apr. 1921; J. B. O'Neall, *Biog. Sketches of the Bench and Bar of S. C.* (1859), vol. I; E. A. Jones, *Am. Members of the Inns of Court* (1924); John Drayton, *Memoirs of the Am. Revolution* (1821), I, 110; Wm. Moultrie, *Memoirs of the Am. Revolution* (1802), II, 172–93; *Jour. of the Convention of S. C. which Ratified the Const. of the U. S., May 23, 1788* (1928); *Charleston Courier*, Aug. 21, 1819.]
W. C. M.

GRIMKÉ, SARAH MOORE (Nov. 26, 1792–Dec. 23, 1873) and her sister, Angelina Emily (Feb. 20, 1805–Oct. 26, 1879), anti-slavery crusaders and advocates of woman's rights, were born in Charleston, S. C. Their parents, Judge John Faucheraud Grimké [*q.v.*] and Mary Smith Grimké, were wealthy, aristocratic, and conservative; but Sarah and Angelina early showed signs of dissatisfaction with their environment. Neither social gaiety nor the formalism of the Episcopal Church met their needs; and their tender, reflective natures made them question the institution of slavery. Sarah, the elder sister, greatly influenced Angelina in this revolt, though at the age of thirty Angelina was in advance of her more conservative sister. As a girl Sarah regretted the fact that her sex made it impossible for her to study the law. Contact with her father and her older brother, Thomas [*q.v.*], sharpened her mind and deepened her conscience. But it was her association with Quakers, met on a trip to Philadelphia when she was twenty-seven, that crystallized her discontent with her home. After many trying spiritual experiences, she returned North and became a Friend. Angelina, having experimented with Presbyterianism, followed her sister. Both, however, chafed under the discipline of the orthodox Philadelphia Friends, and Angelina, the more expansive and self-reliant, came especially to resent in them what seemed to her an equivocal attitude on slavery and Abolition. A life of modesty, economy, and charity seemed hollow when she longed for an opportunity to serve humanity. Nor did Sarah find peace; her sensitiveness and lack of self-confidence made her life among the Quakers one of almost intolerable conflict and suffering.

In 1835 Angelina, after much reflection, determined to express her growing sympathy with Abolition and wrote to Garrison, encouraging him in his work. The letter, to her surprise, was published in the *Liberator* (Sept. 19, 1835). Although Sarah and the Philadelphia Friends disapproved, Angelina, having turned the corner, could not go back. Eager to make a more positive contribution to the cause increasingly close to her heart, she wrote an *Appeal to the Christian Women of the South* (1836). In this thirty-six-page pamphlet she urged Southern women to speak and act against slavery, which she endeavored to prove contrary not only to the first charter of human rights given to Adam, but opposed to the Declaration of Independence. "The women of the South can overthrow this horrible system of oppression and cruelty, licentiousness and wrong," she wrote, urging them to use moral suasion in the cause of humanity and freedom. Anti-slavery agitators eagerly seized this eloquent and forceful appeal, enhanced in value by the fact that it came from the pen of one who knew the slave system intimately. In South Carolina, on the other hand, copies of the *Appeal* were publicly burned by postmasters, and its author was officially threatened with imprisonment if she returned to her native city.

After pondering for months, this shy, blue-eyed young woman, courteous and gentle in bearing, took what seemed to her a momentous step. She decided to accept an invitation from the American Antislavery Society to address small groups of women in private parlors. After an inward struggle Sarah also determined to risk the disapprobation of the Friends, and henceforth the sisters were on intimate terms with Abolitionists and aided former slaves. Sarah, on her part, wrote an *Epistle to the Clergy of the Southern States* (1836). Two years later Angelina, in her *Letters to Catherine E. Beecher in Reply to an Essay on Slavery and Abolitionism Addressed to A. E. Grimké* (1838), denounced gradualism. It was at this time that the sisters persuaded their mother to apportion slaves to them as their share of the family estate, and these slaves they at once freed.

From addressing small groups of women it was a natural step to the lecture platform. At first the sisters, timid and self-conscious, spoke only to audiences of women, but as their reputation for earnestness and eloquence grew, it was impossible to keep men away. Their lectures in New England aroused great enthusiasm. The prejudice against the appearance of women on the lecture platform found many expressions; one was the famous "Pastoral Letter" issued by the General Association of Congregational Ministers of Massachusetts, a tirade against women-preachers and women-reformers (*Liberator,* Aug. 11, 1837). Whittier, though he defended "Carolina's high-souled daughters," at the same time urged them to confine their arguments to immediate emancipation (John Albree, ed., *Whittier Correspondence,* 1911, p. 265).

So great was the opposition to their speaking in public that the sisters felt compelled to defend woman's rights as well as Abolition, for in their minds the two causes were vitally connected. Not only the efforts made to suppress their testimony against slavery, but their belief that slavery weighed especially heavily on both the colored and white women of the South, led them openly to champion the cause of their sex. Sarah's *Letters on the Equality of the Sexes and the Condition of Woman* (1838) maintained that "the page of history teems with woman's wrongs" and that "it is wet with woman's tears." She indicted the unrighteous dominion exercised over women in the name of protection; she entreated women to "arise in all the majesty of moral power . . . and plant themselves, side by side, on the platform of human rights, with man, to whom they were designed to be companions, equals and helpers in every good word and work" (p. 45). Angelina, in her *Appeal to the Women of the Nominally Free States* (1837), strongly insisted on women's equal responsibilities for the nation's guilt and shame and on their interest in the public weal. Gradually many of the opponents of slavery were won over to the cause of woman's rights, and the introduction of the question into the anti-slavery agitation by the Grimkés was an important factor in the development of both causes.

On May 14, 1838, Angelina married the Abolitionist, Theodore Dwight Weld. They had one child, Charles Stuart. Since she suffered from ill health after marriage, which made the strain of public lectures seem unwise, she and her sister aided Mr. Weld in conducting a liberal school at Belleville, N. J. Later the family removed to Hyde Park, Mass., where both the sisters died. The latter part of their lives was marked by devotion to their work of teaching and by an indomitable interest in the causes to which both had contributed.

[Catherine H. Birney, *The Grimké Sisters: Sarah and Angelina Grimké* (1885); Theo. D. Weld, *In Memory: Angelina Grimké Weld* (1880), containing sketch of Sarah Moore Grimké; *S. C. Hist. and Geneal. Mag.,* Jan. 1906; E. C. Stanton and others, *Hist. of Woman Suffrage,* vol. I (1881); F. J. and W. P. Garrison, *Wm. Lloyd Garrison, 1805–1879: The Story of His Life Told by His Children* (1885–89); *Woman's Jour.,* Jan. 3, 1874, Nov. 1, 1879; *Boston Transcript,* Oct. 28, 1879; Garrison MSS. in the Boston Public Library.]

M. E. C.

GRIMKÉ, THOMAS SMITH (Sept. 26, 1786–Oct. 12, 1834), educator, reformer, brother of Sarah Moore and Angelina Emily Grimké [*qq.v.*], was born in Charleston, S. C., where his father, John Faucheraud Grimké [*q.v.*], was a wealthy and influential lawyer. His mother, Mary Smith, was a great-grand-daughter of the second landgrave of South Carolina, and her Puritan background partly explains her son's deep religious bent. After studying in the South, Thomas entered Yale College in the fall of 1805 and graduated in 1807. Although he desired to enter the ministry of the Episcopal Church, he yielded to his father's wishes and studied law in the office of Langdon Cheves. For a number of years his law partner was Robert Y. Hayne. He attained eminence at the bar and in politics, even though he often espoused unpopular causes. As a state senator (1826–30), he supported the general government on the tariff question. During the nullification controversy he opposed, boldly and passionately, the state's preparations for military resistance and employed his logic and eloquence in behalf of the Union and of peace (*To the People of the State of South-Carolina,* 1832). He was also a pioneer in the causes of temperance and world peace. In his *Address on the Truth, Dignity, Power and Beauty of the Principles of Peace* (1832), and in a series of vigorous articles in the *Calumet,* the organ of the American Peace Society, he took issue with the advocates of peace who admitted the Scriptural legality of war.

Grimké's educational theories were no less radical than his pacifism. He believed that education must "partake deeply and extensively of the vital spirit of American institutions." Though he was a distinguished classicist, mathematics and the classics found little place in his educational plan, which was essentially utilitarian and religious. As early as 1832 he advocated manual training in the schools and championed science because it promoted the substantial, practical improvement of the people. He also favored the higher education of women. Modern history and modern literature bulked large in his plans. He outlined and himself adopted a reformed orthography which omitted silent letters and emphasized consistency, justifying the system on the ground that it was appropriate for America and for democratic, mass education (*Oration on American Education,* 1835). His piety and his religious fervor were evidenced in his conviction that the Bible should be basic in every scheme of education, from the primary school to the university (*An Essay on the Appropriate Use of the Bible, in Common Education,* 1833). Grimké died while on his way to Columbus, Ohio, in the fall of 1834, and was buried in Columbus. He had married, on Jan. 25, 1810, Sarah Daniel Drayton, by whom he had six sons. His family and friends were devoted to him because of his simplicity and gentleness of manner, his humility of heart, and his intellectual courage.

[In addition to the lectures and addresses mentioned, a small part of his total output, the volume entitled *Reflections on the Character and Objects of all Science and Literature* (1831) is representative. The best contemporary accounts of Grimké are to be found in the *Calumet,* Jan.–Feb. 1835, and in the *Am. Annals of Educ. and Instruction,* Nov. 1835. The "Letter Book" of Wm. Watson, in the possession of Miss Elizabeth Dana, of Cambridge, Mass., contains several important letters from Grimké. Consult also Catherine H. Birney, *The Grimké Sisters, Sarah and Angelina Grimké* (1885); C. B. Galbreath, "Thos. Smith Grimké," *Ohio Archaeol. and Hist. Quart.,* July 1924; F. B. Dexter, *Biog. Sketches of the Grads. of Yale Coll.,* vol. VI (1912); the *S. C. Hist. and Geneal. Mag.,* Jan. 1903; *Charleston Courier,* Oct. 24, 1834; *Southern Patriot* (Charleston), Oct. 27, 1834.] M. E. C.

VOLUME IV, PART 2

GRINNELL - HIBBARD

(VOLUME VIII OF THE ORIGINAL EDITION)

CROSS REFERENCES FROM THIS VOLUME ARE MADE TO THE VOLUME NUMBERS OF THE ORIGINAL EDITION.

CONTRIBUTORS
VOLUME IV, PART 2

Charles G. Abbot . . . . . C. G. A.	Charles Lyon Chandler . . C. L. C.
Thomas P. Abernethy . . . T. P. A.	Alexander W. Chilton . . . A. W. C.
Adeline Adams . . . . A. A.	Barrett H. Clark . . . . . B. H. C.
James Truslow Adams . . . J. T. A.	Jane Clark . . . . J. C.
Raymond William Adams . . R. W. A.	Rudolf A. Clemen . . . . . R. A. C.
Robert Greenhalgh Albion R. G. A.	Ernest W. Clement. . . . . E. W. C.
Edmund Kimball Alden . . E. K. A.	Oral Sumner Coad . . . . . O. S. C.
Gardner W. Allen . . . . . G. W. A.	Frederick W. Coburn. . . . F. W. C.
Horace Newton Allen . . . H. N. A.	Henry Sloane Coffin . . . . H. S. C.
Francis G. Allinson . . . . F. G. A.	Arthur C. Cole . . . . . . A. C. C.
William H. Allison . . . . W. H. A.	R. D. W. Connor . . . . . R. D. W. C.
Katharine H. Amend . . . K. H. A.	Robert Spencer Cotterill . R. S. C.
Benjamin M. Anderson, Jr. B. M. A., Jr.	E. Merton Coulter . . . . E. M. C.
Lewis Flint Anderson . . . L. F. A.	Walter H. Crockett . . . . W. H. C.
John Clark Archer . . . . J. C. A.	Robert E. Cushman . . . . R. E. C.
Frederick W. Ashley . . . F. W. A.	J. Chalmers DaCosta . . . J. C. DaC.
Benjamin Wisner Bacon . . B. W. B.	Harrison C. Dale . . . . . H. C. D.
Horace B. Baker . . . . . . H. B. B.	Arthur B. Darling . . . . . A. B. D.
Ray Palmer Baker . . . . . R. P. B—r.	William W. Davis . . . . . W. W. D.
Thomas S. Barclay . . . . . T. S. B.	Richard E. Day . . . . . . R. E. D.
Viola F. Barnes . . . . . . V. F. B.	Tyler Dennett . . . . T. D.
Clarence Bartlett . . . . C. B.	Alfred L. P. Dennis . . . . A. L. P. D.
George A. Barton . . . . . G. A. B.	Davis R. Dewey . . . . . . D. R. D.
Ernest Sutherland Bates. . E. S. B.	Charles A. Dinsmore . . . . C. A. D.
Adolph B. Benson . . . . . A. B. B.	Frank Haigh Dixon . . . . F. H. D.
Edith R. Blanchard . . . . E. R. B.	William E. Dodd . . . . . . W. E. D.
Arthur R. Blessing. . . . . A. R. B—g.	Elizabeth Donnan . . . . . E. D.
Willard G. Bleyer . . . . . W. G. B.	William Kavanaugh Doty. W. K. D.
Helen C. Boatfield . . . . H. C. B.	William Howe Downes . . . W. H. D.
Ernest Ludlow Bogart . . . E. L. B.	Stella M. Drumm . . . . . S. M. D.
William A. Boring . . . . W. A. B—g.	Edward A. Duddy . . . . . E. A. D.
Witt Bowden. . . . . W. B.	Raymond S. Dugan . . . . R. S. D.
Sarah G. Bowerman . . . . S. G. B.	J. Harold Easterby . . . . J. H. E.
Jeffrey R. Brackett . . . . J. R. B.	Edward R. Eastman . . . . E. R. E.
Benjamin Brawley . . . . . B. B.	Edward Dwight Eaton . . . E. D. E.
Walter C. Bronson . . . . W. C. B.	Walter Prichard Eaton . . W. P. E.
Robert Preston Brooks . . R. P. B—s.	Edward Edelman . . . . . E. Ed—n.
E. Francis Brown . . . . . E. F. B.	Edwin Francis Edgett . . . E. F. E.
L. Parmly Brown . . . . . L. P. B.	William G. Elliott . . . . W. G. E.
Marshall S. Brown. . . . . M. S. B.	Ephraim Emerton . . . . E. Em—n.
Robert M. Brown . . . . . R. M. B.	Eugenia, Sister . . . . . . E.
William Adams Brown . . . W. A. B—n.	Paul D. Evans . . . . P. D. E.
Abram R. Brubacher . . . . A. R. B—r.	Hallie Farmer . . . . H. F.
Paul H. Buck . . . . P. H. B.	William H. Faulkner . . . W. H. F.
Edmund C. Burnett. . . . . E. C. B.	Albert B. Faust . . . . . . A. B. F.
Claude A. Burrett . . . . . C. A. B.	Charles Feleky . . . . . . C. F.
Isabel M. Calder. . . . . . I. M. C.	Daniel M. Fisk . . . . . . D. M. F.
Robert G. Caldwell . . . . R. G. C.	Percy Scott Flippin . . . . P. S. F.
Harry J. Carman . . . . . . H. J. C.	Dixon Ryan Fox . . . . . . D. R. F.
Zechariah Chafee, Jr. . . . Z. C., Jr.	Fabian Franklin . . . . . . F. F.
W. Ellison Chalmers . . . . W. E. C.	John H. Frederick . . . . . J. H. F.

Contributors

John C. French	J. C. F.
Robert D. French	R. D. F.
Claude M. Fuess	C. M. F.
John F. Fulton	J. F. F.
Ralph H. Gabriel	R. H. G.
Francis P. Gaines	F. P. G.
Katharine Jeanne Gallagher	K. J. G.
Eilene Marie Galloway	E. M. G.
William A. Ganoe	W. A. G.
Curtis W. Garrison	C. W. G.
Fielding H. Garrison	F. H. G.
George Harvey Genzmer	G. H. G.
Beatrice Chandler Gesell	B. C. G.
W. J. Ghent	W. J. G.
Howard E. Giles	H. E. G.
Dorothy Burne Goebel	D. B. G.
Edward A. Goldman	E. A. G.
Robert W. Goodloe	R. W. G.
Cardinal Goodwin	C. G.
Armistead Churchill Gordon, Jr.	A. C. G., Jr.
Ross Aiken Gortner	R. A. G.
Virginia Gearhart Gray	V. G. G.
A. W. Greely	A. W. G.
William B. Gregory	W. B. G.
J. G. deR. Hamilton	J. G. deR. H.
Talbot Faulkner Hamlin	T. F. H.
Ralph V. Harlow	R. V. H.
Mary Bronson Hartt	M. B. H.
George C. Harvey	G. C. H.
Earl L. W. Heck	E. L. W. H.
G. L. Hendrickson	G. L. H.
David Jayne Hill	D. J. H.
Homer Carey Hockett	H. C. H.
M. M. Hoffman	M. M. H.
Harry N. Holmes	H. N. H.
John Haynes Holmes	J. H. H.
E. Washburn Hopkins	E. W. H.
Walter Hough	W. H.
James L. Howard	J. L. H.
Leland Ossian Howard	L. O. H.
M. A. DeWolfe Howe	M. A. DeW. H.
William J. Humphreys	W. J. H.
Augustus E. Ingram	A. E. I.
Asher Isaacs	A. I.
Daniel D. Jackson	D. D. J.
Joseph Jackson	J. J.
M. C. James	M. C. J.
Willis L. Jepson	W. L. J.
Claudius O. Johnson	C. O. J.
Edgar H. Johnson	E. H. J.
Peter Leo Johnson	P. L. J.
H. Donaldson Jordan	H. D. J.
James R. Joy	J. R. J.
Louise Phelps Kellogg	L. P. K.
Rayner W. Kelsey	R. W. K.
Fiske Kimball	F. K.
Allen Marshall Kline	A. M. K.
James O. Knauss	J. O. K.
Rhea Mansfield Knittle	R. M. K.
H. W. Howard Knott	H. W. H. K
Morris Knowles	M. K.
Edwin W. Kopf	E. W. K.
William Palmer Ladd	W. P. L.
Herbert S. Langfeld	H. S. L.
Conrad H. Lanza	C. H. L.
Fred V. Larkin	F. V. L.
Kenneth S. Latourette	K. S. L.
Max Lerner	M. L.
John V. Lewis	J. V. L.
Arnold J. Lien	A. J. L.
Paul H. Linehan	P. H. L.
Richard S. Lull	R. S. L.
William O. Lynch	W. O. L.
William G. MacCallum	W. G. M.
Thomas McCrae	T. M.
Arthur S. McDaniel	A. S. M.
Reginald C. McGrane	R. C. McG.
William F. Magie	W. F. M.
Dumas Malone	D. M.
Isaac E. Marcuson	I. E. M.
H. A. Marmer	H. A. M.
Frederick H. Martens	F. H. M.
Alpheus T. Mason	A. T. M.
Emil Mayer	E. M—r.
Bernard Mayo	B. M—o.
Franklin J. Meine	F. J. M.
Clarence W. Mendell	C. W. M—l.
A. Howard Meneely	A. H. M.
Newton D. Mereness	N. D. M.
George P. Merrill	G. P. M.
George L. Meylan	G. L. M.
Raymond C. Miller	R. C. M—r.
Edwin Mims, Jr.	E. M—s., Jr.
Broadus Mitchell	B. M—l.
Catherine Palmer Mitchell	C. P. M.
Samuel Chiles Mitchell	S. C. M.
Carl W. Mitman	C. W. M—n
Frank Monaghan	F. M.
Walter A. Montgomery	W. A. M.
Robert E. Moody	R. E. M.
Edward C. Moore	E. C. M.
G. Andrews Moriarty, Jr.	G. A. M., Jr
Samuel Eliot Morison	S. E. M.
Allan Nevins	A. N.
Lyman C. Newell	L. C. N.
A. R. Newsome	A. R. N.
Robert Hastings Nichols	R. H. N.
Roy F. Nichols	R. F. N.
Harold J. Noble	H. J. N.
Alexander D. Noyes	A. D. N.
Grace Lee Nute	G. L. N.
Ellis P. Oberholtzer	E. P. O.
Thomas Oestreich	T. O.
Frank Lawrence Owsley	F. L. O.

Contributors

Walter Pach . . . . W. P.
William B. Parker . . . . . W. B. P.
Henry B. Parkes . . . . . . H. B. P.
George W. Patterson . . . G. W. P.
Frederic Logan Paxson . . F. L. P.
Charles E. Payne . . . . . C. E. P.
Theodore C. Pease . . . . . T. C. P.
James H. Peeling . . . . . J. H. P—g.
Lawrence Perry . . . . . . L. P.
Frederick T. Persons . . . F. T. P.
A. Everett Peterson . . . . A. E. P.
James M. Phalen . . . . . . J. M. P.
Francis S. Philbrick . . . . F. S. P.
Paul Chrisler Phillips . . . P. C. P.
Ulrich B. Phillips . . . . . U. B. P.
J. Hall Pleasants . . . . . J. H. P—s.
David deSola Pool . . . . . D. deS. P.
Charles Shirley Potts . . . C. S. P.
Edward Preble . . . . E. P.
Richard J. Purcell . . . . . R. J. P.
Arthur Hobson Quinn . . . A. H. Q.
Lowell Joseph Ragatz . . . L. J. R.
Belle Rankin . . . . B. R.
Albert G. Rau . . . . A. G. R.
P. O. Ray . . . . P. O. R.
Lizette Woodworth Reese . L. W. R.
Charles Dudley Rhodes . . C. D. R.
George L. Richardson . . . G. L. R.
Hester Dorsey Richardson . H. D. R.
Irving B. Richman . . . . . I. B. R.
Donald A. Roberts . . . . . D. A. R—s.
David A. Robertson . . . . D. A. R—n.
Edgar E. Robinson . . . . . E. E. R.
William A. Robinson . . . . W. A. R.
Lois K. M. Rosenberry . . . L. K. M. R.
Victor Rosewater . . . . . V. R.
Earle Dudley Ross . . . . E. D. R.
Frank Edward Ross . . . . F. E. R.
Dunbar Rowland . . . . . D. R.
John Ruhräh . . . . J. R.
A. M. Sakolski . . . . A. M. S.
Joseph Schafer . . . . . . J. S—r.
Louis Bernard Schmidt . . . L. B. S.
Herbert W. Schneider . . . H. W. S.
Frank W. Scott . . . . . . F. W. S.
George Dudley Seymour . . G. D. S.
Benjamin F. Shambaugh . . B. F. S.
William Bristol Shaw . . . W. B. S.
Henry D. Sheldon . . . . . H. D. S.
Guy Emery Shipler . . . . G. E. S.
Paul Shorey . . . . P. S.
William Adams Slade . . . W. A. S.
Clara Millerd Smertenko . C. M. S.
David Eugene Smith . . . . D. E. S.
Edgar Fahs Smith . . . . . E. F. S.
W. Roy Smith . . . . W. R. S.
Oscar G. T. Sonneck . . . . O. G. T. S.
John Spargo . . . . J. S—o.
John W. Spear . . . . J. W. S.
Charles Worthen Spencer . C. W. S.
Harris Elwood Starr . . . H. E. S.
Bertha Monica Stearns . . B. M. S.
George M. Stephenson . . . G. M. S.
Wayne E. Stevens . . . . . W. E. S.
George R. Stewart, Jr. . . . G. R. S., Jr.
Margaret B. Stillwell . . . M. B. S.
Donald L. Stone . . . . . . D. L. S.
R. H. Sudds . . . . R. H. S.
William U. Swan . . . . . . W. U. S.
William W. Sweet . . . . . W. W. S.
Edwin P. Tanner . . . . . E. P. T.
John S. P. Tatlock . . . . . J. S. P. T.
Frank A. Taylor . . . . . . F. A. T.
Marten ten Hoor . . . . . M. ten H.
Anthony V. Tesar . . . . . A. V. T.
Holland Thompson . . . . . H. T.
Irving L. Thomson . . . . . I. L. T.
Edward Larocque Tinker . . E. L. T.
Francis J. Tschan . . . . . F. J. T.
Frederick Tuckerman . . . F. T.
Edward Tuthill . . . . . . E. T.
William Treat Upton . . . W. T. U—n.
William T. Utter . . . . . W. T. U—r.
John T. Vance . . . . J. T. V.
John G. Van Deusen . . . . J. G. V-D.
Carl Van Doren . . . . . . C. V-D.
DeForest Van Slyck . . . . DeF. V-S.
Henry R. Viets . . . . . . H. R. V.
Albert T. Volwiler . . . . A. T. V.
John D. Wade . . . . J. D. W.
W. Stewart Wallace . . . . W. S. W.
W. Randall Waterman . . . W. R. W.
Royal B. Way . . . . R. B. W.
Elizabeth Howard West . . E. H. W.
Melvin J. White . . . . . . M. J. W.
W. L. Whittlesey . . . . . W. L. W—y.
George W. Wickersham . . G. W. W.
Robert Wild . . . . R. W.
James F. Willard . . . . . J. F. W.
Samuel C. Williams . . . . S. C. W.
Tyrrell Williams . . . . . T. W.
Walter Williams . . . . . W. W.
James A. Woodburn . . . . J. A. W.
Helen Wright . . . . H. W.
John W. Wright . . . . . . J. W. W.
Nelda E. Wright . . . . . . N. E. W.
Walter L. Wright, Jr. . . . W. L. W—t., Jr.
Donovan Yeuell . . . . . . D. Y.

DICTIONARY OF
AMERICAN BIOGRAPHY

Grinnell — Hibbard

GRINNELL, FREDERICK (Aug. 14, 1836–Oct. 21, 1905), industrialist, engineer, inventor, was born in New Bedford, Mass., the son of Lawrence and Rebecca Smith (Williams) Grinnell. Both his parents were of colonial stock, his father being a descendant of Huguenot ancestors through Matthew Grinnell who came to America at some time prior to 1638 and settled near Newport, R. I. Grinnell's elementary education was obtained at the Friends' School in New Bedford, and at the age of sixteen he entered Rensselaer Polytechnic Institute, Troy, N. Y., where he completed the four-year course in three years, graduating as a civil and mechanical engineer in 1855 at the head of a class of sixty. In the fall of that year, when he was nineteen, he entered the Jersey City Locomotive Works as a draftsman. Three years later he became an assistant engineer of construction on the Burlington & Missouri River Railroad, now part of the Chicago, Burlington & Quincy system. Upon the completion of this road, in about a year, he returned to the locomotive works where he remained until 1860, when he became treasurer and superintendent of the Corliss Steam Engine Works at Providence, R. I. He continued with this company throughout the Civil War, working especially on the installation of steam engines designed by G. H. Corliss [*q.v.*] for war vessels, but in 1865 returned to the Jersey City Locomotive Works as general manager. This manufactory was under lease by the Atlantic & Great Western Railroad, and during his association with it (1865–69) Grinnell, as superintendent of motive power and machinery, designed and built over a hundred locomotives. In 1869 he purchased a controlling interest in the Providence Steam & Gas Pipe Company, which had been in existence for some twenty years and was engaged largely in the manufacture of fire-extinguishing apparatus and the installation thereof in manufacturing establishments, particularly textile mills. Fire-extinguishing apparatus at that time consisted, in the main, of perforated pipe installed along the ceilings of factory rooms and connected with a water-supply system manually operated. Many attempts had been made to devise automatic sprinklers to be used in the water-pipe lines in factories, and in 1874 Henry S. Parmelee of New Haven patented such a device, which through a licensing agreement the Providence Steam & Gas Pipe Company undertook to manufacture. Grinnell with great energy worked thereafter to improve the Parmelee invention and in 1881 patented the automatic sprinkler which today (1931) bears his name. Basically it is a valve sprinkler with deflectors, set in operation by the melting of solder. Besides attending to the business of introducing the sprinkler throughout the world, Grinnell devoted much time to its improvement and between 1882 and 1888 perfected four types of metal-disc sprinklers and in 1890 invented the glass-disc sprinkler which was essentially the same as that in use today. He secured some forty distinct patents for improvements on his sprinklers and besides invented a dry pipe valve and automatic fire-alarm system. In 1893 he brought about the combination of a number of the more important competing sprinkler manufacturers and organized the General Fire Extinguisher Company, with offices and plants in Providence, R. I., Warren, Ohio, and Charlotte, N. C. This company, under his active leadership, became the foremost organization in its field of manufacture. Grinnell retained the management of the whole business until his retirement shortly before his death. He was in addition director of banks in New Bedford and Providence and of several textile manufactories. He was a member of the American Society of Mechanical Engineers and of a number of yachting clubs. In October 1865 he was married to Alice Brayton Almy of New Bedford, who died in 1871 leaving two daughters. Three years later, 1874, he married Mary Brayton Page of Boston, who with their five children and the two daughters of his first wife survived him at the time of his death in New Bedford.

[*Trans. Am. Soc. Mech. Engineers*, vol. XXVII (1906); P. J. McKeon, *Fire Prevention* (1912); Gorham Dana, *Automatic Sprinkler Protection* (1914); *Who's Who in America*, 1903–05; H. B. Nason, *Biog. Record Officers and Grads. Rensselaer Poly. Inst.* (1887); genealogy in W. M. Emery, *The Howland Heirs* (1919); obituaries in *Fire and Water Engineering*, Nov. 4, 1905, *Sunday Telegram* (Providence), and *Providence Daily Jour.*, Oct. 22, 1905.] C. W. M—n.

GRINNELL, HENRY (Feb. 13, 1799–June 30, 1874), merchant and philanthropist, was a son of Capt. Cornelius and Sylvia (Howland) Grinnell, a brother of Joseph and Moses Hicks Grinnell [*qq.v.*], and father of Henry Walton Grinnell [*q.v.*]. Born at New Bedford, Mass., he spent his youth there, obtaining an excellent education at the New Bedford Academy, and in 1818 went to New York City where he became a clerk in the commission house of H. D. & E. B. Sewell. He remained in their employ for seven years, during which time he acquired an intimate knowledge of the shipping business. In 1822 he was married to Sarah Minturn, sister of Robert B. Minturn [*q.v.*]. In 1825 the firm of Fish & Grinnell, in which his brother Joseph was a partner, was dissolved by the retirement of Preserved Fish [*q.v.*], whereupon Henry joined Joseph and their younger brother, Moses Hicks, in forming the new firm of Fish, Grinnell & Company, for the purpose of continuing the business. Compelled by ill health to retire, Joseph Grinnell left the firm, Jan. 1, 1829. Robert B. Minturn took his place and some few years later the business became Grinnell, Minturn & Company. Under the new name the scope of the firm's operations was greatly expanded by its entry into the general shipping business, and though its policy was always extremely conservative, it gradually became one of the strongest mercantile houses in New York City. For twenty-one years Henry Grinnell continued an active member of the firm, his high standard of commercial morality and aversion to speculative ventures being important factors in the increasing prosperity of the business, and when he retired in 1850 he was a wealthy man. For a considerable period he now withdrew entirely from active business, but in 1859 he entered the insurance field and for a number of years was the United States manager for the Liverpool and London Insurance Company.

Grinnell's early connection with the whaling industry had caused him to take great interest in all matters connected with the sea and more particularly the arctic regions and their exploration. He had in consequence awaited the return of the Franklin Polar Expedition with more than ordinary anxiety, and when in 1850 over four years had passed and no tidings had been received of it, he bore the entire expense of fitting out two vessels, the *Advance* and *Rescue*, which under the command of Lieutenant De Haven, sailed from New York in May of that year in search of the lost explorer. Though the main object of the expedition was not achieved, land was discovered beyond Davis Strait and Baffin Bay which was named Grinnell Land. Undaunted by this failure, in 1853 Grinnell placed the *Advance* at the disposition of Elisha Kent Kane [*q.v.*], for a second search, contributing assistance in other respects to Kane. Though this second expedition was equally unsuccessful and the *Advance* was lost, it attained the highest latitude ever reached by a sailing vessel. On later occasions Grinnell manifested his unabated interest in polar explorations, contributing munificently to the voyage of Isaac I. Hayes [*q.v.*] to Ellesmere and Grinnell Lands in 1860 and to the *Polaris* venture of Charles F. Hall [*q.v.*] in 1871. He was one of the founders and president (1862–63) of the American Geographical and Statistical Society and continued actively interested in its progress throughout his life. Noted in business for strength of character and decision, bordering on obstinacy, in private he was always ready to respond to appeals for financial assistance for any meritorious object. He was consistently reticent as to the extent of his contributions to charitable and other public causes and had an extreme aversion to publicity.

[E. K. Kane, *The U. S. Grinnell Expedition in Search of Sir John Franklin* (1854), and *Arctic Explorations: The Second Grinnell Expedition* (2 vols., 1856); C. F. Hall, *Arctic Researches* (1865), see Introduction; C. H. Davis, *Narrative of the North Polar Expedition. U. S. Ship Polaris* (1876); C. R. Markham, *The Lands of Silence* (1921); *Jour. Am. Geog. Soc. of N. Y.*, vol. VI (1876); *N. Y. Tribune*, July 2, 1874.]

H. W. H. K.

GRINNELL, HENRY WALTON (Nov. 19, 1843–Sept. 2, 1920), naval officer, was born in New York City, the son of Henry [*q.v.*] and Sarah (Minturn) Grinnell. After three years (1858–61) at the New York Free Academy (later the College of the City of New York), he entered the United States navy. He was appointed mate, June 1862; acting ensign, November 1862; acting master, 1864; and acting volunteer-lieutenant, 1865. On board the *Monongahela* of the West Gulf Blockading Squadron, he took part in the battles of New Orleans and Mobile Bay. In the former, on Nov. 18, 1863, he distinguished himself by his command of a landing party which materially aided the army (*War of the Rebellion, Official Records, Navy,* 1 ser., vol. XX, pp. 681–82). After the cessation of hostilities, while serving on the *Susquehanna* of the Asiatic Squadron, he declined appointment as ensign in the regular navy and was honorably discharged July 25, 1868. He accepted instead a commission as captain in the Imperial Japanese navy and began to train seamen at the Heigo Naval School. Almost immediately he was appointed inspector-general with the rank of rear-admiral, and served in that capacity from 1868 to 1870. In 1872–73 he was naval adviser to the republic of Ecuador. During the following years, although he did not devote his entire attention to the naval affairs of Japan, as trips to the United States show, he retained his commission and helped to develop the seamanship that defeated China. In the Chino-Japanese War he saw active service at the battle of the Yalu River, the decisive naval engagement of the conflict. When he was honorably discharged at the end of the war, as a vice-admiral, he received a substantial gratuity. Returning to the United States in time to find his country at war with Spain, he reëntered the navy as a volunteer lieutenant and served on board the *Iowa* until peace was declared. Thereafter he lived in retirement at Puntarassa, Fla., and Boston. He had married, in 1874, at Sydney, Australia, Louise I. S. Pratt. In June 1910 he was married to Florence G. Roche of Boston. He died at Saint Augustine, Fla., and was buried at Arlington. Grinnell carried on his family's predilection for exploration by making trips into little-known parts of Asia. One of these he described before a meeting of the American Geographical Society at Cooper Union, June 13, 1871 (*Journal of the American Geographical Society of New York,* vol. III, 1873). The paper, entitled "Journey Through Eastern Mantchooria and Korea," shows both the traveler's love of adventure and the explorer's curiosity concerning native habits and resources.

[The *Cat. of the Alpha Delta Phi* (1899) contains biographical facts supplied by Grinnell himself. See also W. M. Emery, *The Howland Heirs* (1919); *Army and Navy Jour.,* Sept. 11, Oct. 2, 1920; *Boston Transcript,* Sept. 3, 1920; *Fla. Times-Union* (Jacksonville), Sept. 4, 1920.]
D. A. R—s.

GRINNELL, JOSEPH (Nov. 17, 1788–Feb. 7, 1885), merchant and manufacturer, was born at New Bedford, Mass., where his father, Capt. Cornelius Grinnell, coming from Little Compton, R. I., when a boy, had become a prosperous merchant and ship-master. His mother was Sylvia Howland, descended from Henry Howland who was in Plymouth in 1624. The Grinnell family, originally Huguenots of the name of Grennelle, had fled from France to England in 1572 to escape persecution and in 1642 Matthew Grinnell appeared in Portsmouth, R. I. Joseph received a good education at the New Bedford Academy, entered his father's office, where he obtained a thorough mercantile training, and in 1809 was appointed deputy-collector and surveyor of the port. The following year he went to New York City and there, with his uncle, John H. Howland, engaged in the shipping business under the firm name of Howland & Grinnell. Though at the outset the venture was successful, the War of 1812 caused them severe losses and in 1814 the firm was dissolved. The following year with his relative, Preserved Fish [*q.v.*], he established the firm of Fish & Grinnell, acting as New York agents for New Bedford whale-oil merchants.

The new firm made headway rapidly, and in a few years was one of the most substantial commission houses in New York City. In 1825 Fish was able to retire on a competence, whereupon Grinnell induced his brothers, Henry and Moses Hicks [*qq.v.*] to join him as partners, trading as Fish, Grinnell & Company. Three years later, his health gave way and he in his turn retired (Jan. 1, 1829). He spent the next eighteen months in Europe and on his return late in 1830 made his home permanently in New Bedford. Here he entered the shipping business, at the same time engaging in other local commercial and financial undertakings. In 1832 he was elected president of the newly chartered Marine Bank (later known as the First National Bank), which office he held continuously for forty-four years, and in 1841 he became associated with the Boston & Providence Railroad as a director and for five years president. He had also commenced to take an active part in public life and was elected to the governor's council in 1838, 1839, and 1840, but declined a fourth term. In 1843 he was elected a representative from Massachusetts to the Twenty-eighth Congress, and being reëlected to the Twenty-ninth, Thirtieth, and Thirty-first, served continuously in the federal House of Representatives from Dec. 3, 1843, till Mar. 3, 1851, when he retired, having refused a fifth nomination. In the House he was a prominent Whig figure, serving on the committees of post-offices, manufactures, and commerce, and initiating much beneficent legislation concerning inland and maritime transportation.

Following his election to Congress Grinnell had become actively interested in industrial projects. Up to this time New Bedford had been dependent solely upon the whale fisheries for its prosperity and the precarious nature of this industry had impressed him with the necessity of establishing manufactories in order to insure continual progress. He accordingly directed his energies to this object and enlisted the support of leading townsmen. In 1846 a charter for a cotton factory was obtained, the necessary capital was subscribed, conditioned on his becoming president of the new undertaking, and in 1847 the first unit of the Wamsutta Mills was constructed. Thereafter he was continuously engaged in superintending its operations, which were successful from the outset, and brought a new era of prosperity to New Bedford. Under his management its expansion was such that at the time of his death it was composed of six units, with a total of 200,000 spindles and 4,300 looms, employed 2,400 hands, and was capitalized at $3,000,000. In 1869 he paid a second visit to Europe, where he spent six months, but with this exception, the last thirty years of his life were passed in his native town. His mental and physical faculties remained unimpaired to the end despite his advanced age. Cautious in all his dealings, his unfailing common sense contributed much to a career which was characterized by a scrupulous discharge of all obligations. He was twice married: on May 14, 1812, to Sarah Russell of New Bedford, who died July 27, 1862; and on Sept. 19, 1865, to Rebecca (Chase) Kinsman, daughter of Abijah Chase of Salem, Mass. His adopted daughter, Cornelia Grinnell, who was a niece, married Nathaniel P. Willis [*q.v.*].

[Benj. Rodman, *Memoir of Jos. Grinnell* (1863); Z. W. Pease, *Hist. of New Bedford* (1918), III, 463; D. Hamilton Hurd, ed., *Hist. of Bristol County, Mass.* (1883); J. A. Scoville, *The Old Merchants of N. Y. City* (4 vols., 1863–66), somewhat inaccurate; Franklyn Howland, *A Brief Geneal. and Biog. Hist. of Arthur, Henry, and John Howland and Their Descendants* (1885); *Biog. Dir. Am. Cong.* (1928); *Boston Transcript*, Feb. 7, 1885; *N. Y. Tribune*, Feb. 8, 1885.]

H. W. H. K.

GRINNELL, JOSIAH BUSHNELL (Dec. 22, 1821–Mar. 31, 1891), Congregational clergyman, Abolitionist, and commonwealth builder, once described himself as a "pioneer, farmer, and radical." He was born in New Haven, Vt. His father, Myron Grinnell, was a descendant of French Huguenot ancestors who settled in Rhode Island prior to 1640; his mother, Catherine Hastings, was a daughter of a Scotch immigrant. His early life in New England was typical in that it accustomed him to toil, hardship, and moral ideas. When he was sixteen he taught a country school; later he graduated from Oneida Institute, Whitesboro, N. Y. During the summer and fall of 1844 he was agent of the American Tract Society in Wisconsin. Graduating from Auburn Theological Seminary, Auburn, N. Y., in 1847, he became pastor of the Congregational church in Union Village, N. Y., where he remained till 1850. In 1851 he started the First Congregational Church of Washington, D. C., and there he delivered what is said to have been the first sermon against slavery ever heard in that city. Compelled to leave because of his views, he took a pastorate in New York City. While there, Feb. 5, 1852, he married Julia Ann Chapin of Springfield, Mass., and also formed a life-long friendship with Horace Greeley [*q.v.*]. Loss of voice necessitated a change of occupation, and Greeley made to him the remark, "Go West, young man, go West," which has since become historic. He went to Iowa in 1854 and purchased six thousand acres in Poweshiek County. Here he and three others founded the town of Grinnell. A church was started with Grinnell as preacher and largely through his influence Grinnell University was planned. It was well under way when in 1859 Iowa College, founded in 1846 at Davenport by the "Iowa Band" of home missionaries, moved to Grinnell and absorbed it. The institution is now known as Grinnell College. The church and college attracted a high type of settler and the community took on a distinct New England atmosphere. It grew rapidly after 1863 when Grinnell used his influence as a director of the Rock Island Railroad to bring the road through the town.

As early as 1856 his interests and activities became state-wide. He attended the convention which organized the Republican party of Iowa and was chosen to write the address to the voters. The same year he was elected state senator on a platform of "No Liquor Shops; Free Schools for Iowa; No Nationalizing of Slavery" (Grinnell, *post*, p. 117). In the Senate he was chairman of the committee which secured the passage of the Free School Act of 1858 and was one of the sharpest critics of the doctrines involved in the Dred Scott Decision. He soon became known as perhaps the leading Abolitionist of the state. John Brown himself brought a band of escaped slaves to Grinnell's home in 1859, and there wrote part of his Virginia Proclamation. In 1860 Grinnell was a delegate to the convention which nominated Lincoln for president and two years later was himself elected congressman, serving from 1863 to 1867. A warm personal friend of Lincoln, he supported the Administration vigorously. In debate he was relentless toward the opposition, sparing neither sarcasm nor ridicule. He urged the use of colored soldiers in the war and was an ardent supporter of a high protective tariff. The war over, he opposed the readmission of the Southern states until they should give the vote to the black man. In 1867, he lost the Republican nomination for governor. Friendship for Greeley and a conviction of Grant's inadequacy led him to support the former for president in 1872. By so doing he put behind him promotion in his own party. He was a man of wide interests, however, and continued active in the life of his state. He had a pioneer's faith in its future and probably no one did more through speaking and writing to make Iowa known beyond its own borders.

He did much, also, for agricultural development. Wherever farmers were gathered, he urged higher standards in grain growing and stock breeding, and as a practical farmer he led the way by first introducing Devon cattle and Norman and Clydesdale horses into the state. These activities brought him recognition in many state organizations and the presidency of the American Agricultural Association (1885). He early recognized the significance of the railroad. As a builder, promoter, or director he was connected with a number of lines and acted as president and later receiver of the Central Railroad of Iowa. He always remained deeply interested in the church and in education. He served as trustee of Grinnell College for thirty years and was a liberal benefactor of the institution. When in 1882 the college and part of the town were destroyed by a tornado, he hurried East to raise funds. His energy, eloquence, and wide contact with public men never served him better, for he quickly raised forty thousand dollars. He died in 1891 just after having completed his autobiographical reminiscences.

[J. B. Grinnell, *Men and Events of Forty Years* (1891); T. O. Douglass, "The Builders of a Commonwealth," vol. II (MS., copies in libraries of Grinnell College and Univ. of Chicago), and *The Pilgrims of Iowa* (1911); J. L. Hill, *Yankees* (1923); *Annals of Iowa*, Jan. 1896, July 1897, Apr., Oct. 1907; *Iowa State Register* (Des Moines), Apr. 2, 3, 1891.] C. E. P.

GRINNELL, MOSES HICKS (Mar. 3, 1803–Nov. 24, 1877), merchant, shipowner, a son of Capt. Cornelius and Sylvia (Howland) Grinnell, and younger brother of Joseph and Henry Grinnell [*qq.v.*], was born at New Bedford, Mass., and obtained his education at the academy there. He received a commercial training in his father's office and in 1821 entered the employ of William R. Rotch & Company of New Bedford, who were importers and were also interested in the whaling business. His industry and ability enabled him to acquire in a short time an intimate knowledge of the shipping-trade, and he made several voyages as supercargo in the vessels of the firm, visiting Brazil and Europe. In 1824 he went to New York and became associated with Fish & Grinnell, whale-oil merchants, of which firm his brother Joseph was a partner. In 1825, on the retirement of Preserved Fish [*q.v.*], he and Henry Grinnell entered the firm, which then became Fish, Grinnell & Company, but on Jan. 1, 1829, Joseph Grinnell retired and the two continuing brothers joined with Robert B. Minturn [*q.v.*], establishing the firm which later became Grinnell, Minturn & Company. Hitherto operations had been confined to the commission trade, but now the firm entered the shipping business and Moses Hicks Grinnell assumed charge of the new development. Imbued with an ardent desire to see the United States marine again participating in world-wide commerce, he devoted himself with single-minded pertinacity to this object. The firm became agents for a line of packet ships between London and New York and then commenced building its own ships. Wherever trade prospect offered, Grinnell, Minturn & Company's vessels penetrated. In 1850, when Henry Grinnell retired from the firm its commercial reputation was second to none in New York, and to Moses Hicks's inspiration and ingenuity this was in great part due.

Grinnell continued to participate actively in the management of the shipping firm until 1861. His business energies, however, extended to other corporations, including the Phoenix Bank, the Sun Mutual Insurance Company, and the Institution for the Savings of Merchants' Clerks, of all of which he was at one time president. He was also president of the Chamber of Commerce from 1843 to 1848, a commissioner of charities and corrections from 1860 to 1865, and a member of the original Central Park Commission. Throughout his life he took an active interest in national affairs and was elected in 1839 as a Whig representative of New York to the Twenty-sixth Congress, serving till Mar. 31, 1841. He later became a Republican and in 1856 was a presidential elector on the Frémont ticket. On the outbreak of the Civil War he unhesitatingly championed the Union cause, joined the Union Defense Committee, and rendered great services, financial and otherwise, to the administration. In March 1869 President Grant appointed him collector of the port of New York, a position which he retained till July 1870. He then served as naval officer of customs until April 1871, when he finally retired from public life.

In later years possessed of great wealth, Grinnell was always a munificent but unostentatious donor to charities, both public and private. He contributed, with his brother Henry, to the planning and fitting out of the second Franklin Expedition under Kane (1853–55), and assisted generously in relief work during the period of the war, but the full extent of his benefactions was never known. Late in life a friend said of him: "Mr. Grinnell, though white-haired, shows scarcely any encroachment of age. His ruddy complexion, clear eye, erect figure and elastic step betoken firm health and a constitution as robust as ever. Every lineament of his frank face speaks a liberal soul. . . . His friends are legion, his word a bond" (*New York Times, post*). He was married twice: in 1826 to Susan H. Russell, daughter of Gilbert Russell of New Bedford; and in 1836 to Julia Irving, a niece of Washington Irving.

[J. A. Scoville, *The Old Merchants of N. Y. City* (4 vols., 1863–66); *Biog. Dir. Am. Cong.* (1928); *Appletons' Ann. Cyc.*, 1877; *The Diary of Phillip Hone* (2 vols., 1889), ed. by Bayard Tuckerman; A. H. Clark, *The Clipper Ship Era* (1910); *N. Y. Times* and *World* (N.Y.), Nov. 25, 1877; *N. Y. Tribune*, Nov. 26, 1877; *Sun* (N.Y.), Nov. 27, 1877.]

H. W. H. K.

GRISCOM, CLEMENT ACTON (Mar. 15, 1841–Nov. 10, 1912), financier, shipowner, born in Philadelphia, Pa., was the son of Dr. John D. Griscom, a prominent physician, and Margaret (Acton) Griscom, and was descended from Andrew Griscom who settled in New Jersey in 1680. He was educated in the public and private schools of Philadelphia, graduating from the Friends' Academy in 1857 at the age of sixteen. At nineteen he started in business as a clerk with the importing firm of Peter Wright & Sons of Philadelphia, and three years later he was admitted to partnership in the firm. Displaying those talents which later distinguished him, he prevailed upon the firm to purchase their own sailing ships, which proved very profitable. Later, as steam came into general use, the firm purchased more vessels and placed him in charge of this phase of the business. In the meantime he had taken up the study of marine architecture especially in its application to the development of the merchant marine. Through his efforts Peter Wright & Sons became the agents of the American Steamship Company, operating between Philadelphia and Liverpool, which was organized in 1871 and controlled by the Pennsylvania Railroad Company. In the same year the firm became the agents for the International Navigation Company, of which Griscom was made vice-president and in 1888 was elected president. The ships of the International Navigation Company, generally known as the Red Star Line, operated under a Belgian charter (the Société Anonyme Belge-Américaine). In 1884 the company bought the ships of the American Steamship Company (the American Line) and in 1886 the Inman Line was purchased from the British owners. It was at this time that Griscom's training in marine construction came to the fore since he felt that vessels with new improvements were necessary for the prestige of his company. He therefore developed his idea of a vessel with twin screws, transverse bulkheads, and water-tight compartments, which were all revolutionary steps in ship-building. The steamships *City of New York* and *City of Paris* were built with these innovations and became models for later vessels constructed by his own and other companies. Soon afterward he had two additional vessels built, the *St. Louis* and *St. Paul*, in which he developed another improvement, the construction of staterooms in suites.

For many years Griscom had planned on eventually bringing most of the large steamship companies in the transatlantic trade under one head, but it was not until 1902 when he associated himself with J. P. Morgan that the International Mercantile Marine Company was formed and the International Navigation Company merged into it. This brought under one ownership and management five large transatlantic lines whose aggregate fleet comprised 136 vessels with a tonnage of 1,034,884. Griscom was president of this new company for two years and then served as chairman of the board of directors until his death. His other interests were varied. He was a director or officer in numerous banks, railroads, and industrial concerns, and was for several years a member of the board of Trustees of the City Ice Boats of Philadelphia. In 1887 he was one of the delegates representing the United States at the International Maritime Conference for revising the rules of the road at sea, which met at Washington. For many years he made earnest efforts to secure Congressional action in the interests of the American Merchant Marine and greatly regretted that, for operating reasons, it was impossible to have all of the ships of the International Mercantile Marine Company under the American flag. He was a man of pleasing personality and made friends with ease. He also was possessed of tremendous capacity for work and often stayed at his desk for eighteen hours at a stretch. He had splendid health and vigor and when not engaged with his business affairs he was enthusiastically busy with his avocations—yachting and farming. On June 18, 1862, he was married to Frances Canby Biddle of Philadelphia. The later years of his life he spent in semi-retirement on his large estate near Philadelphia where he died after a long illness.

[L. G. Fryburg, *Griscom Family* (1924); *Who's Who in America*, 1912–13; J. W. Jordan, *Colonial Families of Phila.* (1911), II, 1067–73; Dexter Marshall, "Captains of Industry," *Cosmopolitan*, May 1903; Lawrence Perry, "The Head of the Internat. Shipping Corporation," *World's Work*, Dec. 1902; W. L. Marvin, "The Great Ship 'Combine,'" *Am. Monthly Rev. of Revs.*, Dec. 1902; Hans Keiler, *Am. Shipping: Its Hist. and Econ. Conditions* (1913); H. W. Schotter, *The Growth and Development of the Pa. Railroad Co.* (1927), pp. 93, 211; *Illustrated Cat. of the Notable Paintings by the Great Masters, Collected by the Late Clement A. Griscom, Esq.* (1914); *Phila. Enquirer, Public Ledger* (Phila.), Nov. 11, 1912.] J. H. F.

GRISCOM, JOHN (Sept. 27, 1774–Feb. 26, 1852), teacher, chemist, philanthropist, was born at Hancock's Bridge, N. J., the son of William and Rachel (Denn) Griscom, and a descendant of Andrew Griscom, Quaker, who settled in New Jersey in 1680. He attended the country schools near his home, at seventeen began to teach, and after a few months of study at the Friends' Academy in Philadelphia, took charge of the Friends' School at Burlington, N. J. Having become interested in chemistry, he introduced the subject into his classes and began lecturing on the subject. In 1807 he was persuaded to open a school in New York, which, though the support promised by friends failed, became highly successful. Reorganizing it in 1825 as the New York High School for boys, he instituted the Lancasterian system of monitorial instruction. The advantages of low fees, unusually good equipment for study of science, and a new emphasis on gymnastics could not overcome the handicap of untrained instructors and opposition from other schools, and in 1831 the establishment was sold. Griscom then became principal of the Friends' School in Providence, R. I. Finding Quaker simplicity indisposed to accept the "gimcrackeries of science" (*Memoir, post,* p. 256) as essentials of education, and embarrassed by the Hicksite division, he resigned after three years and settled in West Haverford, Pa., with his daughters. He returned to Burlington in 1840, lecturing and serving as superintendent of schools until his death. For the last two years of his life he was nearly blind.

Griscom's lectures, lucidly expressed and illustrated by demonstrations enjoyed by the speaker as much as by his audience, made him, according to J. W. Francis [*q.v.*], "the acknowledged head" of teachers of chemistry (*Memoir,* p. 424). Besides the courses delivered to groups of subscribers, he lectured (1813–20), as professor of chemistry, at Columbia College and in the short-lived medical schools of Rutgers College. His chief service, according to himself, was to be "a trumpetblower" (*Memoir,* p. 400). He published few researches of his own, but his selections and translations from foreign scientific literature, contributed to the *American Journal of Science* and the *Journal of the Franklin Institute* (which for some years he helped edit) kept American students abreast of current thought. He made known the medical properties of cod-liver oil and the value of iodine in treatment of goiter. He was one of the founders of the New York Society for the Prevention of Pauperism and the Society for the Reformation of Juvenile Delinquents and was a leader in the establishment of the House of Refuge, the first reformatory in the country. All his interests are exposed in *A Year in Europe* (2 vols., 1823), in which he relates his visits to scientists, philanthropists, schools, hospitals, and prisons and outlines the needs of institutions at home. Jefferson said the book gave the most satisfactory view of public institutions abroad he had ever read (*Memoir,* p. 152). Griscom was twice married: in 1800 to Abigail Hoskins, who died Apr. 3, 1816; and on Dec. 13, 1843, to Rachel Denn, a cousin. His son, John H. Griscom, became a distinguished physician in New York, and his daughter Abigail married S. J. Gummere [*q.v.*].

[J. H. Griscom, *Memoir of John Griscom, LL.D.* (1859); E. F. Smith, *John Griscom, 1774–1852, Chemist* (1925); B. K. Peirce, *A Half Century with Juvenile Delinquents* (1869); the *Am. Jour. of Sci.*, Jan. 1860; *Am. Chemist*, Aug.–Sept. 1874; *N. Y. Times*, Feb. 28, 1852; *Friends' Rev.*, Mar. 6, 1852.] E. F. S.

GRISWOLD, ALEXANDER VIETS (Apr. 22, 1766–Feb. 15, 1843), Episcopal clergyman, first and only bishop of the Eastern Diocese, was born in Simsbury, Conn., the son of Elisha and Eunice (Viets) Griswold. On his father's side he was a descendant of Edward Griswold, an emigrant from Kenilworth, England, who settled in Wethersfield, Conn., in 1639. His mother's grandfather, John Viets, was a wealthy physician who, coming probably from Germany before 1700, established himself in New York. Later he moved to Simsbury to venture and lose his fortune in the copper-mines there. An uncle, Roger Viets, had been sent to Yale to prepare for the Presbyterian ministry, but while at college he became an Episcopalian, and soon persuaded the rest of the family to follow his example. Alexander's early years were spent on his father's farm, but when he was ten years old, since he displayed more interest in books than in agriculture, his uncle, then rector of the Simsbury parish, took him into his own home. He now assisted in the cultivation of the parish glebe, but had the advantage of his uncle's instruction and library by means of which he secured a good knowledge of the classics and mathematics besides much general information. The impoverishment of his father who endeavored to remain neutral during the Revolution, the removal of his Loyalist uncle to Nova Scotia after the war, and his own early marriage to seventeen-year-old Elizabeth Mitchelson in 1785, prevented him from entering Yale as he had planned. Until he was twenty-eight years old he cultivated a small farm, and read law though without expectation of practising it. Persuaded by his friends who believed his character and abilities fitted him for the ministry, in 1794 he offered himself as a candidate for orders. In 1795 he was made deacon, and later in the same year was ordained priest by Bishop Seabury at Plymouth, Conn. For ten years (1794–1804) he served at the same time the churches in Plymouth, Harwinton, and Northfield, eking out his small salary by farming and teaching. In 1804 he became rector of St. Michael's Church, Bristol, R. I. He was elected bishop of the Eastern Diocese May 31, 1810, and was consecrated at Trinity Church, New York, May 29, 1811. He continued to serve as rector at Bristol until 1830 when he took charge of St. Peter's Church, Salem, Mass., and it was not until five years later that he devoted himself wholly to his episcopal work. His first wife died Sept. 10, 1817, and some ten years afterward he married Mrs. Amelia Smith.

The Eastern Diocese comprised the churches in Massachusetts including Maine, Rhode Island, Vermont, and New Hampshire. In all this territory, when Bishop Griswold took charge, there were only twenty-two Episcopal churches and sixteen officiating clergymen. It was a diocese requiring of its bishop self-renouncing devotion, willingness to endure the hardships of frequent long and exhausting journeys, great faith, much executive ability and tact, and firmness in discipline. All these Bishop Griswold possessed. Through his wise labors, at his death the field comprised a hundred churches and five fully organized dioceses. To him belongs the credit of recreating the Episcopal Church in New England outside of Connecticut. His influence extended beyond his diocese. A pastoral letter issued in 1814 did much to awaken the whole church to missionary activity and stimulate the formation of its missionary organization. In 1838 he became presiding bishop. Humble, unostentatious, and gentle, he was nevertheless firm in the exercise of authority when required, and resolute in matters involving principle. Although never a partisan, he was evangelical and Low Church in his sympathies. In 1827–28 he published in the *Episcopal Register* of Vermont, a series of articles in defense of prayer-meetings, which later appeared in book form under the title *Remarks on Social Prayer-meetings* (1858). In the same periodical, 1828–29, he also published articles on the improvement of the liturgy. Disturbed by the progress of the Oxford Movement, at the time of his death he had just finished *The Reformation, A Brief Exposition of Some of the Errors and Corruptions of the Church of Rome* (1843). He also published *Prayers Adapted to Various Occasions of Social Worship* (1835), and *Discourses on the Most Important Doctrines and Duties of the Christian Religion* (1830), besides several single sermons and addresses. Death came to him suddenly in Boston on the doorstep of the home of Bishop Manton Eastburn who in 1842 had been elected his assistant. Of his fourteen children only one survived him.

[John S. Stone, *Memoir of the Life of Rt. Rev. Alexander Viets Griswold* (1844), is based in part upon autobiographical material, and contains portrait. See also Wm. B. Sprague, *Annals Am. Pulpit*, vol. V (1859); Chas. C. Tiffany, *A Hist. of the Protestant Episc. Ch. in the U. S. A.* (1895), and other church histories; F. H. Viets, *A Geneal. of the Viets Family* (1902); H. R. Stiles, *The Hist. and Geneals. of Ancient Windsor, Conn.*, II (1892), 348–88; *Boston Transcript*, Feb. 16, 1843.]
H. E. S.

GRISWOLD, JOHN AUGUSTUS (Nov. 11, 1818–Oct. 31, 1872), manufacturer and congressman, the son of Chester and Abbey (Moulton) Griswold and a descendant of Edward Griswold who settled in Windsor, Conn., in 1639, was born in Nassau, N. Y. His father was at one time a member of the New York Assembly. Young Griswold entered the hardware house of Hart, Lesley & Warren, of Troy, N. Y., when he was seventeen but left at the end of a year to accept a position as book-keeper for C. H. & J. J. Merritt, cotton manufacturers. After establishing a wholesale and retail drug business, he became an agent for the Rensselaer Iron Works and, later, head of the Bessemer Steel Works, the Rensselaer Iron Works, and other blast furnaces.

As a substantial citizen, well-established socially through his marriage, Sept. 14, 1843, with Elizabeth Hart, daughter of Richard P. Hart, Griswold was elected mayor of Troy on the Democratic ticket in 1855. In 1860 he was an unsuccessful candidate for Congress. Throughout his public career, he was an ardent supporter of the Union; after the fall of Fort Sumter he presided at a mass meeting to raise troops; and he later assisted in the organization of several regiments, one of which, the 21st New York, was known as the Griswold Light Cavalry. An early advocate of armored ships, he and John F. Winslow [*q.v.*] accepted a contract for a number of wooden vessels sheathed with metal. Griswold, with Winslow, and C. S. Bushnell, showed the Naval Board a model of Ericsson's *Monitor,* and, gaining the interest of President Lincoln, agreed to construct and deliver such a "floating battery" within one hundred days, on the understanding that they should assume the entire cost—approximately a quarter of a million dollars—in case the undertaking failed. The *Monitor,* begun in October 1861, was constructed at the plant of T. F. Howland, Greenpoint, Long Island, under Ericsson's direction, but the machinery, plates, and much of the other iron work were manufactured in Troy. The ship was launched on Jan. 30, 1862. On Mar. 9 it defeated the *Merrimac.* As a result of its success, Griswold and his associates built six more vessels of the same type. Their destructiveness affected materially the course of the war. On account of these patriotic activities, Griswold was elected to the Thirty-eighth Congress as a War Democrat. Since he voted for the repeal of the Fugitive-Slave Act, he was returned to the Thirty-ninth Congress only by Republican support. As a member of the Committee on Naval Affairs during his first two terms, he defended the conduct of the war, and in a speech delivered Feb. 4, 1865 (*Congressional Globe,* 38 Cong., 2 Sess., p. 597), attacked the proposal to divide the responsibility of the Navy Department. Upon his reëlection in 1866 he became a member of the committee on ways and means. In 1868 he was an unsuccessful candidate on the Republican ticket for the governorship of New York.

In 1864, in association with Erastus Corning, A. L. Holley [*qq.v.*], Winslow, and Erastus Corning, Jr., Griswold secured control of the Bessemer patents in America. His firm, known after 1868 as John A. Griswold & Company, exerted a profound influence upon the development of the iron and steel industry in the United States. So general was the interest in the plants erected in Troy that the members of the American Association for the Advancement of Science visited the city in 1870 to examine the works. After his defeat for the governorship and his withdrawal from public life, Griswold devoted himself to the promotion of his financial interests in Troy and to the cultural advancement of the city, in which his name has been perpetuated by various organizations.

[*Invitation to the Members of the Am. Asso. for the Advancement of Sci.* (n.d.) ; *The Bessemer Steel Works and the Rensselaer Iron Works* (1870), pub. by John A. Griswold & Company; *The Navy in Congress* (1865) ; F. B. Wheeler, *John F. Winslow, LL.D., and the Monitor* (1893) ; W. C. Church, *The Life of John Ericsson* (1890) ; J. M. Swank, *Hist. of the Manufacture of Iron in All Ages* (1884) ; *Biog. Dir. Am. Cong.* (1928) ; *Monitor,* Sept. 1868; N. B. Sylvester, *Hist. of Rensselaer County, N. Y.* (1880) ; *N. Y. Tribune,* Nov. 1, 1872 ; *Troy Times,* Nov. 1, 2, 4, 1872.] R. P. B—r.

GRISWOLD, MATTHEW (Mar. 25, 1714–Apr. 28, 1799), jurist, governor of Connecticut, was the eldest son of John and Hannah (Lee) Griswold, and was a descendant of Matthew Griswold, who with his brother Edward settled in Connecticut in 1639. He was born at Lyme, Conn., and was a resident of the town for the greater part of his life. His natural abilities were considerable and he seems to have developed them with little aid from others. President Stiles of Yale mentions that he "fitted for College, settled a Farmer, studied Law proprio Marte, bot him the first considera. Law Library in Connect." (F. B. Dexter, *Extracts from the Itineraries and other Miscellanies of Ezra Stiles,* 1916, p. 412). He was admitted to the bar in 1743, began practice in his native town, and on Nov. 10, of the same year, married Ursula, daughter of Gov. Roger Wolcott, of Windsor, Conn.

In 1751 he began his public career as representative of Lyme in the General Assembly, a position which he held until 1759 when he was chosen a member of the Council, the real seat of political power under the charter government. He became a supporter of the colonial cause when the revolutionary movement began and from the days of the Stamp Act agitation until the close of the struggle was prominent among the civil leaders of the state. During the war he was for some time head of the Council of Safety, and in 1779 received the honorary degree of LL.D. from Yale. His most important public activity had commenced in 1769 when he began a period of fifteen years' service as deputy governor, which under the peculiar system then prevailing, as yet unaffected by the salutary influence of the doctrine of separation of powers, involved the responsibility of presiding over the General Assembly when acting in its judicial capacity. Until 1784 that body constituted the highest appellate tribunal of Connecticut. He was therefore for fifteen years chief justice of the state. From 1784 to 1786 he was governor, rendering competent service in the period of post-war depression and dissension. Two years later he closed his public career by presiding over the convention which ratified the federal Constitution. He then retired to his farm at Lyme, a fine example of the sturdy citizenship which governed the New England states in the transition from colonial dependence to membership in the republic. President Stiles gives an interesting glimpse of him and his establishment with its "fine Library of well chosen Books," its herds of cattle and general prosperity, and of the owner "in perfect Health of Body and Mind. Lame yet vigorous. . . ." (*Itineraries,* p. 412).

[F. C. Norton, *The Governors of Conn.* (1905); E. E. and E. M. Salisbury, *Family Hists. and Geneals.* (3 vols. in 5, 1892); G. H. Hollister, *The Hist. of Conn.* (2 vols., 1855); A. B. Allyn, *Black Hall Traditions and Reminiscences* (1908).] W. A. R.

GRISWOLD, ROGER (May 21, 1762–Oct. 25, 1812), lawyer, politician, was the son of Matthew [*q.v.*] and Ursula (Wolcott) Griswold and was born at Lyme, Conn. He graduated at Yale in 1780, studied law in his father's office, was admitted to the bar in 1783, and established himself in practice at Norwich. He remained there until 1798, when he returned to Lyme. On Oct. 27, 1788, he married Fanny, daughter of Zabdiel and Elizabeth (Tracy) Rogers. In 1794 he entered the Connecticut legislature but in September of the same year he was elected to the national House of Representatives and his services in the state government were ended until 1807. He was active in the Federalist party in Congress from 1795 to 1805, first as a defender of the policies of Washington and Adams and later as a virulent critic of those of Jefferson. In both capacities he was a leader in debate and a frequent speaker. He was keen, analytical, and eloquent, but also, at times, dogmatic and intolerant. In February 1798 he acquired great notoriety by a brawl on the floor of the House with Matthew Lyon [*q.v.*] of Vermont, a Republican member described in the gentle verses of Richard Alsop and Theodore Dwight as:

> "a strange, offensive brute
> Too wild to tame, too base to shoot."

This affray, the first serious one of the sort to occur in Congress, and discreditable to both participants, called forth a series of cartoons and satirical pamphlets, still found in old libraries and collections of Americana. (For official record see *Annals of Congress,* 5 Cong., 1 Sess., pp. 1034 ff.)

The tenor of Griswold's congressional speeches shows that he followed the common Federalist course, passing from an enthusiastic nationalism toward sectionalism and an indiscriminate opposition to the majority policies. Of his many able speeches in the House, one of his best was that in opposition to the resolution amending the Constitution with respect to the method of electing the president, afterward embodied in that document as the Twelfth Amendment (*Ibid.,* 8 Cong., 1 Sess., pp. 744 ff.). In 1804 the bitterness of the Federalist leaders resulted in discussion of the project of a northern confederacy, which came to nothing because the mass of New Englanders were either indifferent to alleged grievances or rapidly becoming supporters of Jefferson. Griswold's views appear in a well-known letter to Oliver Wolcott [*q.v.*], Mar. 11, 1804, in which he declared that "the vices of this government are incurable" and, after stating the grievances, concluded that "there can be no safety to the Northern States without a separation from the Confederacy" (Henry Adams, *Documents Relating to New England Federalism,* pp. 354–58).

On leaving Congress in 1805 Griswold resumed his law practice and two years later was appointed to the superior court. In 1809 he left the bench to become lieutenant-governor, and a year later he was supported for the governorship by a faction of the party strong enough to force the election into the legislature, which, however, continued him in second place. In 1811 and again in 1812 he was elected governor by a popular majority. Connecticut was bitterly opposed to the war with Great Britain and Griswold's conduct, later the theme of widespread censure, received both official and popular approval. He refused to place Connecticut militia under the command of federal officers, and this resulted in a constitutional argument, lasting after the Governor's death, Oct. 25, 1812, in regard to the president's military powers and on the meaning of the militia clauses of the Constitution. (See *American State Papers, Military Affairs,* vol. I, 1832, pp. 325–26; also Theodore Dwight, *History of the Hartford Convention,* 1833, which quotes largely from Connecticut official records, pp. 234–74, *passim.*) Though Griswold had the fine qualities of character and leadership which distinguished so many of the leading Federalists, they were largely nullified by his inability to see the trend of democratic development, or to grasp the essential principles of American nationality.

[Griswold can be best studied through his official utterances as congressman and governor. See also F. B. Dexter, *Biog. Sketches of the Grads. of Yale Coll.,* IV (1907), 146–49; David Daggett, *An Eulogium Commemorative of the Exalted Virtues of His Excellency Roger Griswold* (1812); E. E. and E. M. Salisbury, *Family-Hists. and Geneals.* (1892), vol. II; *Conn. Courant* (Hartford), Nov. 3, 1812.] W. A. R.

GRISWOLD, RUFUS WILMOT (Feb. 15, 1815–Aug. 27, 1857), journalist, anthologist, author, was born in Benson, Rutland County, Vt., one of the younger of the fourteen children of Rufus Griswold, a needy farmer and tanner from

Connecticut, by his wife, Deborah Wass, a native of Martha's Vineyard (A. M. Hemenway, *Vermont Historical Gazetteer,* vol. IV, 1882, p. 1176; C. E. Banks, *History of Martha's Vineyard,* vol. III, 1925, p. 495). At the age of fifteen, in a newspaper office at Albany, N. Y., he began a variegated, bustling career, in the course of which he was connected with almost twenty newspapers and periodicals and compiled, edited, or wrote upwards of forty volumes, most of them ephemeral. Several passages in his life are obscure; some books credited to him have never been seen by a reliable bibliographer; and his character is still in dispute.

For several years subsequent to his Albany sojourn he was an itinerant printer and perhaps a sailor. In New York, in March 1837, he married a Caroline Searles and for a few months made his headquarters with her parents. About this time he procured a license as a Baptist minister. Although he revered Jonathan Edwards, detested Jefferson and Thomas Paine, and at one time edited an Anti-Catholic organ, there was little of the minister in his disposition. No record has been found of his occupying a regular charge, and the only confessed witness to his preaching is Edwin Percy Whipple, who testified, "In theology he is all bone and muscle. His sermons are his finest compositions, and he delivers them from the pulpit with taste and eloquence" (*Graham's Magazine,* June 1845, p. 243). He was generally addressed as a clergyman, however, and was commonly referred to as Doctor Griswold. Both a D.D. and an LL.D. of unknown provenance were sometimes attributed to him. From February 1838 to May 1839 he edited the *Vergennes Vermonter.* Allegiance to Henry Clay compelled him to subordinate his Abolition sentiments, but he fought tenaciously against imprisonment for debt and capital punishment. For most of the next eighteen months he was in New York working for Park Benjamin and Horace Greeley. With William Leggett, Rufus Dawes, and several others he established a library in the New York City Prison. In November 1840 he went to Philadelphia to write first for the *Daily Standard* and later for the *Gazette.* He became seriously ill late in 1841 and, while recuperating, applied unsuccessfully for a chaplaincy in the Navy. About this time he made the acquaintance of Edgar Allan Poe.

The year 1842 was the turning point of his career; from then almost until his death in 1857 he was conspicuous and influential. He worked hard and with success to increase public respect for American authors; his contemporaries regarded him as the foremost advocate of "Americanism" in literature. In April appeared his anthology, *The Poets and Poetry of America* (numerous later editions). From May 1842 until October 1843 he was assistant editor of *Graham's Magazine,* in succession to Poe, at a yearly salary of $1,000. In November 1842 his wife died in New York, leaving him with two daughters. Of his various publications the most important in these years were: *The Songs of Béranger in English* (1844); *The Poetical Works of W. M. Praed* (1844; 1852), the first collected edition of Praed; *The Poets and Poetry of England in the Nineteenth Century* (1844; several later editions), memorable for some strange critical pronouncements; *The Prose Works of John Milton* (2 vols., 1845; 1847), the first American edition of Milton's prose; *The Prose Writers of America* (1847; several later editions); and *The Female Poets of America* (1848; several later editions). These and his abundant other work brought him a good if somewhat uncertain income, enabling him to collect an excellent library and to entertain hospitably. He was courted by a horde of minor writers with their eyes on critical favors still to come; another group, nourishing no such hope, constituted a formidable body of enemies. He took pleasure in advancing the reputation of his protégés, among whom were Maria Brooks, Alice and Phoebe Cary, Charles Fenno Hoffman, Charles Godfrey Leland, Richard Henry Stoddard, and Bayard Taylor [*qq.v.*]. In behavior he was at times erratic. He was usually well disposed toward people, but sensitive to criticism and vindictive when provoked. Meanwhile, on Aug. 20, 1845, in New York, he was married reluctantly, almost secretly, to Charlotte Myers, a well-to-do Jewess of Charleston, S. C. The whole affair is wrapped in darkness, but Griswold appears to have been the victim of a hideous fraud, and the marriage was never consummated.

During these years Griswold had several encounters with Poe and treated him, on the whole, with kindness and forbearance. When news of Poe's death reached New York he wrote for the *Daily Tribune* (Oct. 9, 1849) a long and decidedly unconventional obituary signed "Ludwig." Harsh, realistic, and candid, not malevolent, but extenuating nothing, it astonished and incensed the poet's friends, whose indignation rose when it was learned that Poe had named Griswold as his literary executor. Stung by accusations of treachery, bent on justifying the "Ludwig" article at all costs, Griswold sacrificed judgment and honesty to pride. Collecting all the current scandal about Poe, he incorporated the whole mass, together with a good many errors, into his inexcusable memoir (*International Monthly Magazine,* October 1850; Vol. III of *The Works of the Late Edgar Allan Poe,* 1850–56). In his published version of two of Poe's letters he inserted passages fulsomely complimentary to himself. His editorial work on Poe's writings was conscientious though not entirely satisfactory, and it is fairly clear that his rage was directed less against Poe, who fascinated him and whose genius he recognized, than against Poe's over-zealous defenders.

His last years were made miserable by disease, scandal, and domestic trouble. In 1852 he obtained a divorce in Philadelphia on the ground of desertion, and the next year he married Harriet Stanley McCrillis of Bangor, Me., by whom he had one son, William McCrillis Griswold [*q.v.*]. In 1850–52 he edited the *International Monthly Magazine* and in 1852–53 P. T. Barnum's *Illustrated News.* In 1854, during a severe recurrence of his old malady, tuberculosis, he wrote his most substantial work, *The Republican Court, or American Society in the Days of Washington* (1855; with author's last additions and corrections, 1864). In 1855 he secured the release from Moyamensing Penitentiary of George G. Foster, a friend of his Albany days, who had been convicted of forgery. In 1856 a coalition of his enemies attempted to get his divorce set aside, thereby creating an unsavory newspaper scandal. Griswold, who now realized that he was dying, defended himself successfully and published a pitiful *Statement* (Philadelphia, 1856) of his relations with Miss Myers and the other contestants. To the *New York Herald* of Feb. 13, 1856, he contributed a review (also published separately) of the Duyckincks' *Cyclopædia of American Literature,* repaying in full an old score. It is still, perhaps, the most destructive book-review written by an American. He died, lonely and prematurely aged, at his home in New York and was buried in Greenwood Cemetery, his two most extensive projects, a life of Washington and a biographical dictionary, remaining unfinished.

[R. W. Griswold Papers, Boston Pub. Lib.; J. T. Fields Papers, Henry E. Huntington Lib.; W. M. Griswold, *Passages from the Correspondence and Other Papers of Rufus W. Griswold* (1898); Killis Campbell, "The Poe-Griswold Controversy," *Pubs. Mod. Lang. Asso.,* XXXIV (1919), 436–64; J. L. Neu, "Rufus Wilmot Griswold," *Univ. of Texas Bull.,* No. 2538, Oct. 8, 1925 (*Studies in English,* No. 5), pp. 101–65, with full direction to sources.] G. H. G.

GRISWOLD, STANLEY (Nov. 14, 1763–Aug. 21, 1815), clergyman, editor, politician, the son of Shubael and Abigail (Stanley) Griswold, was born at Torrington, Conn. He was descended from Edward Griswold who with his brother Matthew settled in Connecticut in 1639. He served in a militia company in the Revolution, graduated from Yale in 1786, studied theology, and four years later was installed as pastor at New Milford. On Aug. 5, 1789, he was married to Elizabeth Flagg of East Hartford, Conn. Despite the fact that he was an unusually successful preacher (Orcutt, *post,* pp. 264, 268), he was expelled in 1797 by the Litchfield South Ministerial Association, ostensibly on doctrinal grounds, although it was generally believed that his political heresies were more responsible for this action than his alleged disbelief in human depravity or preaching of universal salvation. The case aroused great interest and was the subject of considerable newspaper and pamphlet discussion, but his congregation stood by him loyally and he remained with them five years longer. The apostate continued on his wayward course, however. He supported the Republican demands for Church disestablishment and a new state constitution, preached the sermon at the Wallingford celebration of Jefferson's inauguration in 1801, and made himself offensive to his clerical brethren generally. In 1803 he left the ministry. The *Connecticut Courant,* Feb. 22, 1804, contains the deposition of a Litchfield citizen solemnly setting forth allegations that Griswold had in his hearing expressed approval of the Democratic clubs, spoken highly of the French Revolution, reprobated the British government, declared himself "against a government of force and energy," against the executive power and long terms provided by the Constitution, and had stated that "he considered the present as a vastly improved age and that virtue and patriotism kept pace with information and science." A person with such views could hardly be comfortable in Connecticut, and before this indictment appeared, Griswold had moved to Walpole, N. H., to become editor of the *Political Observatory,* one of the new presses which the Republicans were planting at strategic points in Federalist territory. He edited this publication for about two years. Judged by standards of the day, the paper was ably conducted. "For daring villainy," said a leading Federalist organ, "for effrontery and boldness in falsehood, for ferocious assaults on private character he is hardly inferior to Anthony Pasquin" (*New England Paladium,* Mar. 12, 1805).

In 1805 President Jefferson appointed Griswold secretary of Michigan Territory. He was now swallowed up in the western wilderness, where the Federalists ceased from troubling and Republicans held the offices. After serving as territorial secretary for about three years, he was forced to resign in 1808 as the result of a quarrel with Gov. William Hull. He then established a residence in Ohio and from June 2, 1809, to Jan. 12, 1810, served by appointment as United States senator from that state. In the latter year, Mar. 16, he was appointed judge in the newly organized Illinois Territory. The remaining five years of his life he spent in the arduous duties of a frontier circuit judge along the Ohio and lower Wabash. Where and when he acquired his knowledge of law is obscure, although in all probability his duties required no great legal erudition. In 1815 two New England missionaries who crossed his trail reported that Griswold was "a decided friend of the Bible Society" and much interested in improving religious conditions on the frontier (Mills and Smith, *post*, p. 11). Gov. John Reynolds said of him that he was "a correct, honest man—a good lawyer—paid his debts, and sang David's Psalms" (*post*, p. 337). He died of fever at Shawneetown, Illinois Territory, in the summer of 1815.

[F. B. Dexter, *Biog. Sketches of the Grads. of Yale Coll.*, IV (1907), 476–81, gives a summary of Griswold's career with bibliography, list of works, and miscellaneous references. See also Samuel Orcutt, *Hist. of the Towns of New Milford and Bridgewater* (1882), pp. 256–73; R. J. Purcell, *Conn. in Transition* (1918); S. J. Mills and Daniel Smith, *Report of a Missionary Tour . . .* (1815); John Reynolds, *The Pioneer Hist. of Ill.* (1852), p. 337; and the *Conn. Courant* (Hartford), Sept. 20, 1815.] W.A.R.

GRISWOLD, WILLIAM McCRILLIS (Oct. 9, 1853–Aug. 3, 1899), bibliographer, was born at Bangor, Me., the son of Rufus Wilmot Griswold [*q.v.*] and Harriet Stanley (McCrillis) Griswold. He was fitted for college at Phillips Exeter and graduated from Harvard in 1875. As a child he began his life-long study of periodical literature, so that on entrance into college he already had a large fund of general information, but at second-hand. To the college curriculum he gave only enough attention to win passing marks, spending his time reading in the Cambridge and Boston libraries. Upon graduation, having independent means, he spent several years in European study and travel, contributing pseudonymous articles to American journals. From 1882 to 1888 he was employed in the Library of Congress. At this period Dean E. W. Gurney [*q.v.*], a remarkable judge of character, termed Griswold "one of the few men worth having in a large library." So lacking in power of self-promotion was he, however, that in the Library of Congress his time was wholly occupied in clerical work in the copyright office. He is still remembered there as likable, independent, and methodical, the first to suggest keeping systematic accounts of the copyright fees. The struggle for existence never touched him in full force; therefore he could turn to the labor of love on which he spent the rest of his days, the production of periodical indexes, published at his own expense under the pseudonym "Q. P. Index." Publication began in 1880 with *A General Index to the Nation, Volumes I–XXX,* to the complete surprise of the *Nation's* editors. Thin pamphlet quarterly indexes to the files of the *Revue des Deux Mondes* and many other journals followed. From 1882 to 1885 he issued *Q. P. Index Annual,* and from 1886 to 1889, *Annual Index to Periodicals,* published under his own name after 1887. He also prepared *A Directory of Writers for the Literary Press in the United States* (1884). The usefulness of all these works was impaired by eccentricities in abbreviation and by phonetic deformations, applicable least of all in an index, ranging from new-fangled "fotografy" to old-fashioned "chymistry." These imperfections were increased by Griswold's defective knowledge of the printer's art. His passion, rather than gift, for indexing was also exhibited in *Descriptive List of Novels and Tales* (10 parts, 1890–92). Under the title *The Monograph* he republished serially about sixty biographies by other authors, indexed by Griswold. For twenty years he also contributed, anonymously, to the *Nation:* chiefly book reviews and political editorials. The last index by him was *The Novels of 1897* (1897). The year before he died he saved himself from oblivion by publishing *Passages from the Correspondence and Other Papers of Rufus W. Griswold* (1898), interspersed with the son's explanatory notes and comments. Intended not as an *apologia,* but as a truthful portrait by indirection, this was said by the careful and just biographer George E. Woodberry to have been done "thoroughly, frankly, and with impenetrable justice" (*Nation,* Nov. 17, 1898). It is the work by which William Griswold will be remembered. On Sept. 14, 1882, he was happily married to Anne Deering Merrill, who was singularly in sympathy with him. They had four children. Griswold's death occurred at Seal Harbor, Me.; he was buried in Bangor.

[The most extended account of Griswold's life is a printed memoir by his classmate Thomas Fenton Taylor, distributed to the class in 1899. See also *Harvard Coll. Class of 1875, Secretary's Report No. VIII* (1905), *Report No. IX* (1915) and *Fiftieth Anniversary Report* (1925); *Nation* (N. Y.), Aug. 31, 1899; *Publishers' Weekly*, Sept. 9, 1899; *Library Jour.*, Sept. 1899; *Harvard Grads. Mag.*, Dec. 1899.] F.W.A.

GROESBECK, WILLIAM SLOCUM (July 24, 1815–July 7, 1897), Ohio lawyer, congressman, was born near Schenectady, N. Y., the son of John H. Groesbeck, of prominent Dutch lineage, and Mary (Slocum) Groesbeck. When he was three years old his parents removed to Cincinnati, Ohio, where his father engaged in banking. Groesbeck first attended Augusta College at Augusta, Ky., then Miami University at Oxford, Ohio, graduating with first honors in 1834. He studied law in the office of Vachel Worthington and was admitted to the bar in 1836. During the next two decades he built up a lucrative practice, for he was early conceded to be an unusually gifted attorney, served as a member of the state constitutional convention of 1850–51, and in 1852 was a member of the commission appointed to codify the Ohio code of civil procedure. In politics he was a Democrat. Though he was defeated in 1854 as a candidate for Congress from the 1st Ohio district, in the election of 1856 he was successful and served in the Thirty-fifth Congress. He was a member of the committee on foreign relations and attracted some attention by his debate with A. H. Stephens on the question of the Walker expedition (*Congressional Globe,* 35 Cong., 1 Sess., pp. 249 ff.). In 1858 he failed of reëlection principally because of his stand on the Kansas-Nebraska question, which was thought to be equivocal, and he thereby lost the support of many Anti-Nebraska Democrats. He also lost the German vote in his district, which, under the leadership of Stephen Molitor, solidly supported John A. Gurley, the successful Republican candidate. Groesbeck did not again reach Congress, though in 1864 he was elected to the state Senate.

In 1861, with Salmon P. Chase and Thomas Ewing, Groesbeck was a delegate from Ohio to the Peace Convention. During the war he was recognized as one of the leading Union Democrats of Ohio, and in 1866 he was a delegate to the National Union Convention. The most noteworthy achievement of his career as a lawyer was his service in defense of President Johnson in the impeachment proceedings. He was appointed a counsel in the place of J. S. Black, who had withdrawn, and although his presentation came late in the trial, it was generally conceded to have been the most brilliantly performed part of the case (*Nation,* Apr. 30, 1868; *New York Herald,* Apr. 26, 1868). Arguing that Secretary Stanton held his office under the commission issued during Lincoln's first term, he held that this would have had no force in Lincoln's second administration even if the President had lived. He contended, moreover, that since Johnson's term was legally distinct from Lincoln's, it was absurd to hold that Stanton's removal had in any sense been illegal (*Congressional Globe,* 40 Cong., 2 Sess., Supp., pp. 310 ff.).

Groesbeck became a leader of political liberals following the war and joined the Liberal Republican movement in 1872. A small group who were dissatisfied with Horace Greeley as a candidate nominated Groesbeck for the presidency, but he was given little support in the campaign and in the election received a single electoral vote for the vice-presidency. He was heartily in favor of the reform of the civil service. Recognized as an authority on bimetallism, he served as a member of the monetary commission of 1876 (he favored the remonetization of silver at the ratio of sixteen to one), and two years later he was sent to the International Monetary Conference at Paris, where he advocated the fixing of the ratio between gold and silver by international agreement. Groesbeck's later years were spent quietly at "Elmhurst," his elegant home on the outskirts of Cincinnati. He was a man of considerable wealth because of his investments in Cincinnati real estate. He had married, on Nov. 12, 1837, Elizabeth Burnet, who died in 1889, leaving three sons and two daughters.

[C. T. Greve, *Centennial Hist. of Cincinnati and Representative Citizens* (1904), II, 210–16; *Biog. Cyc. . . . of the State of Ohio,* vol. VI (1895); Geo. I. Reed, ed., *Bench and Bar of Ohio* (1897), vol. I; *Gen. Cat. of the Grads. and Former Students of Miami Univ., 1809–1909* (1909); the *Commercial Tribune* (Cincinnati), July 8, 1897.]

W. T. U—r.

GRONLUND, LAURENCE (July 13, 1846–Oct. 15, 1899), Socialist writer and lecturer, was born in Denmark and was educated in Danish schools. His studies were interrupted by the Danish-German War in which he took part, but later he finished his work at the University of Copenhagen and received the degree of M.A. there in 1865. He then entered upon the study of law, but in 1867, before completing his work, he emigrated to America. He secured a position in the Milwaukee public schools, teaching German, but continued his law course in his spare time, was admitted to the Chicago bar in 1869, and for a number of years was a practising attorney. Interested in social questions, he became convinced of the desirability of the Socialist program through reading Pascal's *Pensées.* Extensive further reading resulted in the publication of his first work, *The Coming Revolution: Its Principles* (1878), which was cast in dialogue form. Six years later he wrote his most important work, *The Coöperative Commonwealth* (1884). In the introduction, he describes its content as, "German Socialism which is presented . . . with this important modification that it has been digested by a mind Anglo-Saxon in its dislike for all extravagancies and in its freedom from any vindictive feeling against *persons,* who are from circumstances what they are." The book forecasts the inevitable downfall of the wage system, founded as it is on the exploitation of labor, but the coming revolution in reality is to be a sweeping evolution. It was the first comprehensive work in English on Socialism, and presented the views of German writers, and especially those of Karl Marx with such modifications as Gronlund felt necessary in order to adapt them to the American environment. The work was widely read and the author was referred to as the "foremost exponent of collectivism among writers of the English language." His passionate interest in the cause of Socialism, and the popularity that came with the wide sale of his book, led him into the lecture field, and he traveled to all parts of the country. For a short time he became editor of a Socialist paper and then took a position in the Department of Labor, but returned to the lecture platform. In 1887 he published *Ça Ira! or Danton in the French Revolution,* and in the same year wrote two tracts, *Insufficiency of Henry George's Theory* and *Socialism vs. Tax-Reform; An Answer to Henry George.* In both of these he attacked with great vigor the single-tax wing of the Socialist Labor Party and urged that neither land reform nor free trade could achieve the necessary abolition of the wage system. In 1888 he was elected a member of the executive committee of the Socialist Labor Party. *Our Destiny, the Influence of Nationalism on Morals and Religion,* which he published in 1891, develops the thesis that in its effort for the abolition of the wage system and the development of the organic unity of national society Socialism is not only an economic program but religious as well. At this time Gronlund started a movement for the secret organization of a society to be known as the American Socialist Fraternity, which was to inspire a few students in each college to harmonize their own programs with the great social destiny, and so hurry the advance of Socialism. His *New Economy; A Peaceable Solution of the Social Problem,* and his paper *Socializing a State,* both published in 1898, advocate first gaining control of the political machinery in order to change eventually the governmental machinery. He joined the staff of the *New York Journal* in charge of the labor section, but died shortly after assuming his duties there. He was married Dec. 24, 1895.

[W. D. P. Bliss and R. M. Binder, *The New Encyc. of Social Reform* (1908); *Who's Who in America,* 1899–1900; A. H. Dodge, *Socialist-Populist Errors* (1894); *N. Y. Jour.,* Oct. 16, 1899; *N. Y. Times,* Oct. 17, 1899.]

W. E. C.

GROS, JOHN DANIEL (1738–May 25, 1812), German Reformed clergyman, educator, philosopher, was born in the Bavarian Palatinate at Webenheim near Zweibrücken, the son of Lorenz and Anna Magdalena Gross, and was baptized June 22, 1738. He matriculated at the University of Marburg Apr. 20, 1759, and at the University of Heidelberg Apr. 21, 1761, and landed at Philadelphia Dec. 4, 1764. Eager to add him to its ranks, since he was a man of scholarly attainments, bore good credentials, and was vouched for by John William Hendel [*q.v.*], the Coetus of Pennsylvania, of which Caspar Dietrich Weyberg was then president, ordained him forthwith instead of first securing the approval of the Dutch Synods. This was the first overt act of the Coetus in the long struggle to free itself from the benevolent but short-sighted supervision of the Dutch church authorities. Gros was pastor of German Reformed congregations at Allentown, Egypt, Jordan, and Schlosser's (now Union) between 1765 and 1770, at Saucon and Springfield, 1770–72, at Kingston, N. Y., 1773–83, in New York, 1783–95, and at Canajoharie, 1796–1800. While in Pennsylvania he was a useful member of the Coetus. Quite naturally he took umbrage when his backwoods parishioners withheld his pay and refused to hear his preaching. He left the province and thereafter was virtually an independent minister. As chaplain of regiments of New York militia he took part in the battles of Oriskany, Sharon, and Jamestown.

In New York he was highly esteemed for his learning. William Hendel, Jr., Philip Milledoler, and other men of future importance studied theology under him, and with the reorganization of King's College as Columbia College in 1784 he was appointed professor of German and geography. His course consisted of a "description of the Globe in respect of all general matters: rise, extent, and fall of ancient empires; chronology as low as the fall of the Roman Empire; present state of the world; origin of the present States and Kingdoms—their extent, power, commerce, religion, and customs; modern chronology." Herbert B. Adams characterized it as "a highly creditable course, the best that the writer has found in the annals of any American college at that early period" (*post,* p. 60). In introducing into America this broader orientation of history in accordance with German rather than English methods, Gros was a forerunner of Francis Lieber [*q.v.*]. He served also as professor of moral philosophy, 1789–95. His course in this department was a marvel of laborious thoroughness, beginning with an introductory study of the nature of man and then following a triple division: the first containing "the law of nature, that is, the natural and invariable principles of justice and equity, by which human conduct ought to be regulated"; the second showing "how those principles are to be applied to the various states of man"; the third exhibiting "the application of these natural principles to the states of the nations of the earth." In 1795 Gros published the text of this course as *Natural Principles of Rectitude for the Conduct of Man in All States and Situations of Life.* He also acted as regent of the University of the State of New York, 1784–87, and as trustee of Columbia College, 1787–92, offices for which he was fitted by a shrewd practical element in his nature. He acquired considerable wealth by purchasing soldiers' land-warrants and bought a farm near Fort Plain, N. Y., whither he retired to spend his last years in philosophic calm. He died in the neighboring town of Canajoharie.

[*Catalogus Studiosorum Marpurgensis* (1909), p. 336; *Die Matrikel der Universität Heidelberg,* IV (1903), 200; I. D. Rupp, *A Collection of Thirty Thousand Names of . . . Emigrants in Pa., 1727–76* (2nd ed., 1876), p. 368; *Eccl. Records State of N. Y.*, vol. VI (1905); *Minutes and Letters of the Coetus of the Ger. Ref. Congregations in Pa., 1747–92* (1903); J. I. Good, *Hist. of the Ref. Ch. in the U. S., 1725–92* (1899); *A Hist. of Columbia Univ. 1754–1904* (1904); J. W. Francis, *Discourse in Commemoration of the 53rd Anniversary of the N. Y. Hist. Soc.* (1857), repub. as *Old New York* (1858, 1866); E. T. Corwin, *A Manual of the Ref. Ch. in America* (4th ed., 1902); H. B. Adams, *U. S. Bureau of Ed. Cir. of Inf. No. 2: The Study of Hist. in Am. Colleges and Universities* (1887); full obituary in N. Y. *Columbian,* June 5, 1812; personal assistance from Prof. Wm. J. Hinke of Auburn Theological Seminary.] G. H. G.

GROSE, WILLIAM (Dec. 16, 1812–July 30, 1900), Indiana legislator, judge, soldier, was born in Montgomery County near Dayton, Ohio, the son of William Grose, a Pennsylvanian, and Mary Hubbell, a native of New Jersey. His grandfathers were soldiers in the Revolution, while his father served under William Henry Harrison in the War of 1812. When William was a small boy his father moved the family to Fayette County, Ind., removing in 1830 to Henry County, where the son attended his last term of school and at twenty began work as a farm hand at eight dollars a month. In December 1836 he was married to Rebecca Needham. Soon after his marriage he began the study of law and was admitted to the bar in 1843. In 1846 he moved to Newcastle where his law practice soon became lucrative. Entering politics, he was in 1852 an elector on the Pierce ticket and in the same year an unsuccessful Democratic candidate for Congress. On the organization of the Republican party he at once identified himself with its activities and was a member of the first Republican National Convention in 1856. In the same year he was elected to the state legislature, declining reëlection two years following. In 1860 he was chosen common pleas judge, which office he resigned at the opening of the Civil War to accept at the hands of Governor Morton the command of the 36th Indiana Volunteer Infantry.

Grose's war record was conspicuous. His regiment was the only part of General Buell's army to take part in the first day's battle at Shiloh and in the second day's battle he became brigade-commander. As the commander of the 3rd Brigade he took part in the battles of Corinth, Perryville, Stone River, Chickamauga, Chattanooga, Lookout Mountain, Missionary Ridge, and all the battles before Atlanta. In July 1864, while in front of Atlanta, he was commissioned brigadier-general. Later his command was transferred to General Thomas's army and he took part in the battles of Franklin and Nashville and in the pursuit of General Hood's army. In June 1865, by order of General Thomas, he was made president of a court-martial in Nashville, Tenn., in which capacity he served until Dec. 31, 1865, when he resigned to return to his home in Newcastle. He had meanwhile, in August 1865, been commissioned major-general of volunteers. In 1866 he was appointed by President Johnson revenue collector of the 5th district and remained in office eight years. From 1884 to 1886 he served as one of a commission of three appointed to supervise the building of three state hospitals for the insane, at Evansville, Richmond, and Logansport, and in 1887 he was elected state senator for Fayette and Henry counties. This was his last public service. In 1891 he published *The Story of the Marches, Battles, and Incidents of the 36th Regiment, Indiana Volunteer Infantry,* an account of the engagements in which his regiment took part. Following the death of his first wife, in 1879, he was married, five years later, to Mrs. Martha Black. He died at his home in Newcastle. A man of commanding stature and presence, deliberate and self-possessed, he was one of the most conspicuous of Indiana's Civil War leaders.

[Geo. Hazzard, *Hist. of Henry County, Ind., 1822–1906* (1906), I, 136–41, 348–51; *A Biog. Hist. of Eminent and Self-Made Men of the State of Ind.* (1880), I, 101, 102; F. B. Heitman, *Hist. Reg. of the U. S. Army* (1890); David Stevenson, *Indiana's Roll of Honor* (2 vols., 1866); the *Indianapolis Jour.*, July 31, 1900; *Indianapolis Sentinel,* Aug. 1, 1900.] W. W. S.

GROSEILLIERS, MÉDART CHOUART, Sieur de (fl. 1625–1684), explorer, was born in France at Charly-Saint-Cyr near Meaux in 1621 or 1625. He was the son of Médard and Marie (Poirier) Chouart. At an early age he entered the service of the Jesuits as *donné* or assistant. In 1637 (or 1641) he went to Canada, where he spent several years in the mission to the Hurons on Manitoulin Island and learned the Huron tongue. Attracted by the fur trade, he left the mission and went to Three Rivers, where on Sept. 3, 1647, he married Hélène, widow of Claude Étienne and daughter of Abraham Martin, after whom were named the Plains of Abraham near Quebec. She died in 1651, and on Aug. 24, 1653, Chouart was married again, to Marguerite, widowed sister of Pierre Esprit Radisson [*q.v.*]. By this marriage he apparently acquired property with which, added to the proceeds of his ventures in furs, he bought land, assuming the title of Sieur des Groseilliers.

In the following year, 1654, he met his brother-in-law Radisson at Three Rivers and in the words of Radisson, the two formed a partnership to "travell and see countreys." Their first journey together may have been one made between 1654 and 1656, since both appear to have been absent from Three Rivers during this interval, but it may have been that made later, between 1658 and 1660. This expedition of 1658–60 took them to the far west (see sketch of Radisson) and, according to the Canadian authority, Benjamin Sulte, was followed (1661–63) by a further far western journey, the record of which, or "booke of annotations," kept by Chouart, was lost. The journey of 1658–60 yielded Groseilliers and Radisson an immense quantity of furs, with which they returned to New France. The expedition had been made without a license from the governor, however, and the furs were therefore confiscated, and heavy fines imposed upon Radisson and Groseilliers alike. They went to Paris to secure remission of the fines, but returned to Quebec without success. Angry and resentful toward the government of New France because of their treatment at its hands, in 1664 they took ship for Port Royal in Acadia and then for Boston in New England. Here they were fortunate enough to meet Col. George Cartwright, royal commissioner of Charles II, and before him they laid a proposal for a voyage to Hudson Bay, in the English interest. Cartwright induced them to accompany him to England. On their way all were captured by a Dutch ship, but after being landed on the coast of Spain, finally reached their destination. Through Cartwright's influence they obtained an audience with King Charles on Oct. 25, 1666, which resulted in the promise to them of a ship with which to make a trading venture to Hudson Bay. Many notable Englishmen, including the Duke of York, Prince Rupert, the Duke of Albemarle, Sir George Carteret, and others, took stock in the enterprise. In the records of the transaction Groseilliers is set down as "Mr. Gooseberry."

The expedition set forth in June 1668, two vessels, the *Nonsuch* and the *Eaglet,* sailing from the Thames for Hudson Bay. In the first Groseilliers was given passage and in the second, Radisson. The *Nonsuch,* with Groseilliers on board, succeeded in finding the bay and reached the south shore (James Bay) on Sept. 29. Here the adventurers were within a hundred and fifty miles of the nearest French settlements. They entered a river (the Nemisco), which they called Rupert's River after their patron, Prince Rupert, and at its mouth they built a stockaded post which they named Fort Charles. On this initial voyage Radisson did not reach Hudson Bay at all, since the commander of the *Eaglet* failed of an entrance and returned to England. Thither the next spring, after a winter spent in Hudson Bay, Groseilliers returned with a cargo of furs, and upon both Groseilliers and Radisson King Charles bestowed medals and gold chains. The success of the expedition resulted in the organization of the Hudson's Bay Company which on May 2, 1670, received a royal charter. In the same year Groseilliers and Radisson accompanied Resident Agent Charles Bayly to the new field and opened a trade on the shores of the Bay.

Beginning with 1674, the adventurous brothers-in-law yielded to overtures by France, their native country, and in 1681 were sent to undertake a trading expedition to Hudson Bay from New France, in the interest of the French. In 1684 and afterward they were again in the service of the English, Radisson becoming a denizen of England and Groseilliers settling down in Canada where, prior to 1698, it is thought, he died.

[*Voyages of Peter Esprit Radisson* (Prince Soc., 1885); ed. by G. D. Scull; G. E. Ellis, "The Hudson Bay Company," in Justin Winsor, *Narr. and Crit. Hist. of America,* vol. VIII (1889); L. J. Burpee, *The Search for the Western Sea* (1908); Agnes C. Laut, *Pathfinders of the West* (1904); Geo. Bryce, *The Remarkable History of the Hudson's Bay Company* (1900); L. P. Kellogg, *Early Narratives of the Northwest* (1917), and *The French Régime in Wis. and the Northwest* (1925); W. W. Folwell, *A Hist. of Minn.,* vol. I (1921); Benjamin Sulte, "Découverte du Mississippi en 1659," *Trans. and Proc. Royal Soc. of Canada,* 2 ser. IX (1903); Cyprien Tanguay, *Dictionnaire Généalogique des Familles Canadiennes,* vol. I (1871); A. E. Adams, "A New Interpretation of the Voyages of Radisson," *Minn. Hist.,* Dec. 1925; N. M. Crouse, *In Quest of the Western Ocean* (1928).]

I. B. R.

GROSS, CHARLES (Feb. 10, 1857–Dec. 3, 1909), educator, historian, was born of Hebrew parentage in Troy, N. Y., the son of Louis and Lottie (Wolf) Gross. With no family traditions of scholarship, he early attracted the attention of his teachers by his scholarly ability and ambition. At Williams College, where he was graduated in the class of 1878, he confirmed the impression of his rare fitness for the scholar's life. With characteristic decision and independence of character he fixed almost immediately on the field of study to which he henceforth devoted himself with unwavering tenacity of purpose, the history of English legal and governmental institutions. After a year of teaching at the Troy Academy he studied in Germany and France, taking the degree of Ph.D. at Göttingen in 1883, and then for five years worked by himself mostly in English libraries and archives. His special interest soon became centered about the early stages of municipal government as related to the associations of merchants and craftsmen. For his doctoral dissertation he had chosen the subject: *Gilda Mercatoria: Ein Beitrag zur Geschichte der Englischen Städteverfassung,* and this firstling of his talent, published in 1883, was later expanded into *The Gild Merchant* (2 vols., 1890), ever since regarded as the standard work on the subject. It at once attracted attention by the freshness and originality of its thought as well as by the thoroughness of the investigations upon which its novel conclusions were based. At the Anglo-Jewish Exhibition at London in 1887 he gave a lecture on "The Exchequer of the Jews of England in the Middle Ages." Through the publication of these and other related studies Gross became known to American scholars, and though he was at the time personally unknown to any one at Harvard he was called thither in 1888 as instructor in history. The experiment justified itself at once. He adjusted himself with unusual readiness to the varied requirements of American academic life, taking his share of elementary teaching and administrative work, but giving also advanced courses in the medieval institutions of England and France. In his teaching he carried on the same principles of careful attention to every detail which marked his study and writing. In addition to other important administrative duties he served for nine years as chairman of the department of history and government. Promoted to assistant professor in 1892, he was made professor in 1901 and the year before his death became the first incumbent of the Gurney Professorship of History and Political Science.

Faithful in the routine of the teacher, he never slackened in his tireless labor of research. His vacations were usually spent in visits to the collections of material for his publications, and twice he thus spent a "sabbatical year." At an early period he began gathering items of bibliography and continued this work to the day of his death, the first result being the substantial volume: *A Bibliography of British Municipal History* (1897), published in the Harvard Historical Studies. He took a keen interest in the conduct of this series and was for many years active in the preparation of the several volumes for the press. He was twice intrusted by the Selden Society with the editorship of important works: first, *Select Cases from the Coroners' Rolls, 1265–1413* (1896), and later, *Select Cases concerning the Law Merchant, A.D. 1270–1638* (1908). The work by which Gross will be chiefly remembered, however, is his monumental *Sources and Literature of English History from the Earliest Times to about 1485.* The first edition in 1900 at once took its place as an indispensable aid to every student of early English history. Immediately after its publication he began collecting new titles, and from these materials a second revised and enlarged edition was prepared in 1915 by his devoted secretary, Addie Frances Rowe, under supervision of a committee of his colleagues. The peculiar value of the volume comes from the fact that it is not only a list of titles as complete as human diligence could make it, but also a discriminating discussion of the more important sources in the light of the author's unequaled control of the whole material.

Gross's personality was a rare combination of extreme reserve with an almost childlike dependence upon friendship. He accumulated learning only to share it. Colleagues and students alike were always welcome to the hospitality of his singularly generous nature. He was married in London, July 15, 1889, to Annie Smith. His domestic life, begun with every promise, was clouded almost throughout by the distressing illness of his wife, a sorrow which he bore without complaint and with unflinching loyalty.

[Minute of the Harvard Faculty of Arts and Sciences, *Harvard Univ. Gazette,* Jan. 7, 1910; Ephraim Emerton, in the *Harvard Grads. Mag.,* Mar. 1910, reprinted from *Proc. Mass. Hist. Soc.,* Vol. XLIII (1910); C. H. Haskins, in *Proc. Mass. Hist. Soc.,* vol. XLIX (1916); Joseph Jacobs, "Charles Gross," *Pubs. Am. Jewish Hist. Soc.,* no. 19 (1910); *Who's Who in America,* 1908–09; *Boston Transcript,* Dec. 3, 1909; personal acquaintance.]

E. Em—n.

GROSS, SAMUEL DAVID (July 8, 1805–May 6, 1884), pioneer, surgeon, teacher, and author, was born on his father's farm near Easton, Pa., the son of Philip and Johanna Juliana

(Brown) Gross. His great-grandparents had come to Pennsylvania in one of the emigrations from the ruined Palatinate. During his country life young Gross studied with care and avidity the fauna and the flora of the section of the state in which he grew up. He knew the calls of all the birds, the habits of all the animals, and acquired the capacity for close observation belonging to woodsmen, a faculty which he believed was of the greatest benefit to him throughout his medical life. Having acquired such knowledge as the country schools could give, he began the study of medicine, as was the custom of those days, under a preceptor. In accordance with this method of instruction the student would learn how to make pills, tinctures, and plasters; would go with the preceptor on his rounds, would help bleed patients and aid in the performance of small operations and in cases of childbirth. When time permitted he would shut himself up in company with a treatise on anatomy and a few dried bones and find out what he could. Gross soon made up his mind that his education was not sufficient to permit him to study medicine thoroughly. He therefore stopped working under his preceptor and attended school in Wilkes-Barre, Pa., completing his general education at the well-known academy at Lawrenceville, N. J. He then began the study of medicine in the Jefferson Medical College, recently started by the noted surgeon Dr. George McClellan [*q.v.*], father of the general.

After his graduation in 1828 he worked daily with McClellan in his dispensary and opened an office of his own on Library Street below Fifth Street. He married, in 1828, Louisa Weissell, a twenty-year-old widow with one child. During his early period in Philadelphia he published several translations from the French and German, which included: *A Manual of General Anatomy* (1828) by A. L. J. Bayle and H. L. G. M. Hollard, *A Manual of Practical Obstetrics* (1828) by Jules Hatin, *A Treatise on the Nature, Cause, and Treatment of Contagious Typhus* (1829) by V. J. von Hildenbrand, and *Elements of Operative Surgery* (1829) by Alphonse Tavernier. The last named was the first treatise on operative surgery published in America and it had a very considerable success. In the autumn of 1830 he issued an original work, *Treatise on the Anatomy, Physiology, and Diseases and Injuries of the Bones and Joints,* a book which was well received by the profession but from which he gained not a single cent. Compelled because of his limited means to abandon practice in Philadelphia, he went to Easton where he practised, studied, and conducted a series of most valuable experiments on dogs relating to gunshot wounds in the abdomen. His observations were cited years afterwards by C. J. Parkes of Chicago in his famous studies on the same subject. Appointed demonstrator of anatomy in the Medical College of Ohio in 1833, he was made professor of pathological anatomy in the Cincinnati Medical College when it was founded by Daniel Drake [*q.v.*] two years later. In 1839 he published his great book, *Elements of Pathological Anatomy,* the first effort ever made in English to present the subject systematically and in carefully connected form. After many refusals, the manuscript was finally accepted by a publisher in Boston. Though the work had a very large sale, Gross received no remuneration for the first edition. It made him famous at home and abroad, however, and by means of subsequent editions remained the chief authority on the subject for over a quarter of a century. After a few years in Cincinnati he was elected in 1840 professor of surgery in the University of Louisville and became the most celebrated surgeon of the South. He was called from there to the University of the City of New York in 1850 to fill the place of Valentine Mott [*q.v.*], but not caring for the city he returned to Louisville after about a year. In 1856 he became professor of surgery in the Jefferson Medical College.

His contributions to medical literature were continuous and important. In 1851 he published *A Practical Treatise on the Diseases and Injuries of the Urinary Bladder, the Prostate Gland, and the Urethra,* which at once became an accepted authority. The last edition of this book, edited by his son, Samuel W. Gross [*q.v.*], appeared in 1876, and was still a standard textbook more than ten years later. In 1854 Gross issued *A Practical Treatise on Foreign Bodies in the Air-Passages,* the first attempt to systematize knowledge on the subject and the third pioneer work he had given to the profession. Since the changes in laryngology destined to be wrought by the bronchoscope were not anticipated, this essay was long regarded as definitive. In 1859 he brought out in two volumes his textbook, *A System of Surgery, Pathological, Diagnostic, Therapeutic and Operative,* the first comprehensive treatment of the subject published in the United States, the greatest surgical treatise of the day, and probably one of the greatest ever written. This book, beautifully written and so clear that any man of reasonable intelligence can understand it, was an immense success. The sixth edition, issued in 1882, contained 2,300 pages and 1,600 illustrations. It is a veritable mine of information and gives evidence of the broadest scholarship and the most complete acquaintance with surgical literature, a philosopher's grasp of all surgical problems, and an immense clinical experience. Translated into several languages, it was read, admired, and praised the world over and had an enormous influence on surgical thought. The personal element is recognizable on every page and no modern book exactly takes its place. At the outbreak of the Civil War, at the request of the government, he wrote *A Manual of Military Surgery* (1861) for the use of army surgeons, which, in 1874, was translated into Japanese.

In 1861 he edited *The Lives of Eminent American Physicians and Surgeons of the Nineteenth Century,* writing several of the articles himself. He also edited medical journals, contributed numerous articles and reviews to periodicals, read valuable papers to societies, participated in important surgical debates, made addresses, and every now and then brought forth a paper of original research.

Gross was one of the greatest of surgeons and was particularly noted for operating for stone in the bladder, patients coming from long distances to obtain the benefit of his services. He was one of the founders and was long the most influential member of the American Medical Association. He founded the Philadelphia Pathological Society, the Philadelphia Academy of Surgery, and the American Surgical Society. He also established the Academy of Surgery prize for original articles, called the Samuel D. Gross Prize, to be contested for every five years. He presided over the International Congress of Surgeons held in Philadelphia in 1876 and was made vice-president of the German Surgical Society. He received the degree of D.C.L. from Oxford University and that of LL.D. from Cambridge and from Edinburgh. Probably the degree of which he would have understood the significance most accurately and would have appreciated most highly was the LL.D. of the University of Pennsylvania which came to him on his deathbed. It is probable that no finer mind was ever devoted to the art and science of surgery. One of the greatest teachers, he was heard by his classes with what may justly be described as reverence. He illustrated important points by striking cases and now and then clinched an idea with an amusing story or an apt historical anecdote, though he never descended into the bawdy. He was one of the first men to insist upon the proper plan of suturing wounds of the intestines and of restoring hopelessly damaged intestines by resection and suturing and of suturing tendons and nerves. He also invented numerous instruments. That he was a philosopher as well as a surgeon is revealed in his two-volume *Autobiography,* which, edited by his sons, appeared in 1887. Active to the last, a short time before his death he cut successfully for stone in the bladder. He died in Philadelphia and his body was cremated.

[J. C. DaCosta, *Opening Address, Jefferson Medic. Coll.* (1901); G. M. Gould, *The Jefferson Medic. Coll. of Phila. . . . a Hist.* (2 vols., 1904); *Hist. of Blockley; a Hist. of the Phila. General Hospital from Its Inception, 1731–1928* (1929), compiled by J. W. Croskey; W. W. Keen, "Address on the Unveiling of the Bronze Statue of the Late Prof. Samuel David Gross, in Washington, D. C.," in *Am. Jour. Medic. Sci.,* June 1897, which is the basis for the sketch in H. A. Kelly and W. L. Burrage, *Am. Medic. Biogs.* (1920); Otto Juettner, *Daniel Drake and His Followers* (1909); *Surgery, Gynecology and Obstetrics,* July 1922; J. W. Holland, *The Jefferson Medic. Coll. of Phila. from 1825 to 1908* (1908); *Press* (Phila.), May 7, 1884; *Medic. Record* and *Medic. News,* May 10, 1884.]

J. C. DaC.

GROSS, SAMUEL WEISSELL (Feb. 4, 1837–Apr. 16, 1889), eldest son of Samuel David Gross [*q.v.*] and Louisa (Weissell) Gross, was born in Cincinnati. He studied medicine for one year at Louisville, then went to Jefferson Medical College, from which he graduated in 1857. After his graduation he became a student of anatomy, surgical pathology, and clinical surgery. He served throughout the Civil War as surgeon, under Buell, Rosecrans, and Grant, and on June 11, 1865, was brevetted lieutenant-colonel of volunteers for faithful and meritorious service. He wrote several important articles embodying his surgical experiences, notably one in which he insisted that instead of relying on pressure to restrain the hemorrhage, as was the usual custom, veins should be ligated just as arteries were. On his return to Philadelphia he soon took a prominent place as a writer of papers and a debater in medical societies. He early became interested in cancer and sarcoma, both of which held his close attention throughout his professional career. He became surgeon to the Philadelphia Hospital, surgeon to the hospital of the Jefferson Medical College, and lecturer on genitourinary surgery at the Jefferson Medical College. On Dec. 28, 1876, he married Grace Linzee Revere of Boston.

He wrote *A Practical Treatise on Tumors of the Mammary Gland* (1880) which is still referred to in every treatise on the subject and the following year published another important book, *A Practical Treatise on Impotence, Sterility, and Allied Disorders of the Male Sexual Organs* (1881). His article on bone sarcoma ranks with that of Auguste Nélaton as a classic, and he broadened and solidified the conception of giant-cell sarcoma. With Moore of London, Banks of Liverpool, and W. S. Halsted [*q.v.*] of

Baltimore he founded and developed the present-day radical operation for cancer. He was one of the unusual surgeons who are able to examine sections from tumors they have removed. Few things pleased him more than to have hours off in an afternoon that he might devote to such microscopic examination. After his father resigned the chair of surgery in Jefferson Medical College in 1882, the younger Gross became professor of the principles of surgery and clinical surgery, while his devoted friend, Dr. John H. Brinton [*q.v.*], became professor of the practice of surgery and clinical surgery. Gross was a great teacher, and like his father drew crowds to his clinics. His demonstrations of a case in which he proposed operating were beautiful and his operations were carried out with dexterity, with precision, and nearly always with success. He was one of the first men in Philadelphia who employed antiseptic surgery.

He died at the height of his powers in the fifty-third year of his age, when he had under way a new edition of his father's famous text-book on surgery, and a surgical treatise of his own on cancer.

[*Hist. of Blockley; a Hist. of the Phila. General Hospital from Its Inception, 1733–1928* (1929), compiled by J. W. Croskey; G. M. Gould, *The Jefferson Medic. Coll. of Phila. . . . a Hist.* (2 vols., 1904); J. C. DaCosta, "Samuel W. Gross," *The Jeffersonian*, Mar. 1915; J. W. Holland, *The Jefferson Medic. Coll. of Phila. from 1825 to 1908* (1908); H. A. Kelly and W. L. Burrage, *Am. Medic. Biogs.* (1928); *Press* and *North American*, both of Phila., Apr. 17, 1889; *Medic. News*, Apr. 20, 1889.]
J. C. DaC.

GROSSCUP, PETER STENGER (Feb. 15, 1852–Oct. 1, 1921), jurist, was born in Ashland, Ohio, the son of Benjamin and Susannah (Bowermaster) Grosscup. His great-grandfather, Paul Grosscup (probably of the family Grosskopf), was a colonial magistrate who served in the state constitutional convention of 1790 and in the Pennsylvania state legislature from 1792 to 1798. He was prepared for college at Ashland and graduated in 1872 at Wittenberg College as valedictorian of his class. After graduating from the Boston Law School in 1873, he settled down in Ashland, where he practised law till 1883, serving as city solicitor during six years of that period. He was the Republican candidate for Congress in 1876, but running in a Democratic district, he was defeated. Two years later, being thrown by reapportionment in the same district with William McKinley, he put the latter in nomination for the seat in Congress, to which he was elected. Grosscup was again defeated for Congress in 1880. In 1883 he removed to Chicago, where he became a law partner of Leonard Swett, who had been a law partner of Abraham Lincoln. During the eighties Grosscup took part in several important criminal cases in Chicago, namely, the Election Conspiracy of 1884, the Ker and Mackin cases and the Hoke Case at Peoria, but his practice was mainly civil, some of the more important litigation involving the Chicago University property, the Storey will case, and the Crawford, Webster, and Kean cases.

In December 1892, President Harrison appointed Grosscup district judge for the northern district of Illinois. He immediately gained a reputation as a judge learned in the law by his dissenting opinion in the case relating to the Sunday closing of the World's Columbian Exposition (56 *Fed.*, 648), his view being upheld by the circuit court of appeals, of which Chief Justice Fuller was the presiding justice. It was during the Chicago railway strike of 1894, however, that he sprang into national prominence and from that time on he was constantly in the public eye. He and Circuit Judge William A. Woods had issued an injunction against Eugene V. Debs and other officers of the American Railway Union, restraining them from interfering with interstate commerce or the transmission of the mails (62 *Fed.*, 828). When the injunction was disobeyed, and mob violence seemed imminent in Chicago, he joined with the district attorney and others in a telegram to President Cleveland calling for federal troops. But not unmindful of the duties of his own office he immediately summoned a grand jury and delivered to them a charge (63 *Fed.*, 436), a classic in forensic English, which did much to restore public confidence in law and order and brought him a national reputation as a fearless judicial officer.

In January 1899, Grosscup was promoted to the circuit court of appeals and in 1905 was made presiding judge. It was while he was serving in that court that the case involving the Standard Oil Company of Indiana came before him, in which the court reversed the decision of District Judge K. M. Landis, who had fined the defendant $29,240,000 for accepting rebates as a shipper in interstate commerce (164 *Fed.*, 376). Although the decision of the court was unanimous, Grosscup's opinion drew a sharp attack in the press from President Roosevelt implying that the result was a miscarriage of justice, to which Grosscup replied that there was no more reason why he should take any notice of the President's criticism than if it came from an ordinary citizen (*New York Times, New York Herald*, July 24, 1908). Grosscup also figured in other outstanding cases, important among which were the Chicago Union Traction Company cases (112 *Fed.*,

607, 114 *Fed.*, 557, 132 *Fed.*, 848); *United States* vs. *James et al.*, involving the right of silence based on the Fifth Amendment (60 *Fed.*, 257); the Beef Trust Case (122 *Fed.*, 529); and the Western Union Telegraph Case (119 *Fed.*, 294), in which he chose "rather, to make precedent" in order to protect a news service not copyrightable. His power of ready analysis and lucid statement, coupled with apt illustrations, served to give his opinions high rank in American judicial literature.

Grosscup did not confine his activities to the bench, for he was an exceedingly able public speaker and writer and delighted in polemics. He delivered several notable addresses on public questions. His debate with Carl Schurz on the subject of territorial expansion, at the Saratoga Conference of the Civic Federation in 1898, in which he took the affirmative, attracted attention throughout the country (*New York Times*, Aug. 20, 1898). But his favorite theme on the platform and in the magazine columns was industrial consolidation. He contended with the constancy of a crusader that the control of trade by the corporations was inevitable and even desirable; that the evils arising therefrom could be prevented by reasonable regulation and a wide distribution of the shares, or a "peopleizing" of the corporations, which he believed was the surest method of combatting socialism. In the Chicago Traction cases, he demonstrated that he was no doctrinaire and that he was capable of leading in the work of reorganizing and coördinating those intricate corporate and municipal interests, but his controversial temperament increasingly tended to impair his influence on the bench. In 1907 he was indicted with the other directors of the Mattoon and Charleston Interurban Railway, following a wreck in which fifteen lives were lost. The indictment was quashed, but the affair gave added color to the charge, repeatedly made, that he was a tool of the corporations, based on his decisions in some of the corporation litigation and in the reorganization of the Chicago Union Traction Company.

He resigned from the bench in October 1911, though not until he had openly defied his critics to produce any evidence of misconduct in office on his part, offering to cooperate in any investigation into his judicial career and private business. He gave as his reason for resigning his desire for more freedom as an individual and as a citizen to take his part in moulding public opinion. Thereafter he continued his rôle of the stormy petrel, espousing the cause of the Progressives in the election of 1912, despite his former tilt with Roosevelt, and defending the Germans for their violation of Belgium's neutrality; but when the United States entered the war he appeared at a public function in New York City on the platform with Joseph H. Choate and pledged his support to the President and the nation as a loyal citizen. He died on board the *Caronia*, while bound for Southampton. Grosscup was married on Dec. 16, 1885, to Virginia Taylor, of Loudonville, Ohio, who died in 1899, leaving one daughter, Mrs. Frank Leslie Moon, who survived him.

[For genealogy and biography see the *Pa. German*, Feb. 1907; I. D. Rupp, *Hist. of the Counties of Berks and Lebanon* (1843), pp. 483–87; *Case and Comment*, June 1911; *The Biog. Cyc. and Portrait Gallery . . . of Ohio*, VI (1895), 1432; J. M. Palmer, ed., *The Bench and Bar of Ill.*, I (1899), 110–11; S. W. Norton, *Chicago Traction : A Hist. Legislative and Pol.* (1907); *Chicago Legal News*, Dec. 16, 1899; *Am. Bar Asso. Journal*, Oct. 1921; *Evening Post* (N. Y.)), Apr. 24, 1917; and the *N. Y. Times*, Oct. 23, 1921. For Grosscup's philosophy see the *Outlook*, Feb. 28, 1903; *McClure's Mag.*, Feb. 1905; *Am. Mag.*, Dec. 1905; and the *North Am. Rev.*, Dec. 1908, Dec. 1909, Mar. 1910, July 1911, Mar. 1912, Mar. 1914, and Dec. 1919.]

J. T. V.

GROSSMANN, GEORG MARTIN (Oct. 18, 1823–Aug. 24, 1897), Lutheran clergyman, was born in Germany at Grossbieberau in Hesse-Darmstadt, the son of Ludwig and Maria Margarete (Rotenhäuser) Grossmann. His father was a teacher. After attending the normal school at Friedberg, Grossmann married Nannie Steppes and engaged for some years in teaching. Becoming interested in missionary work in America that was being directed by William Löhe of Neuendettelsau, he studied theology under Friedrich Bauer at Nürnberg and at the University of Erlangen and offered his services to Löhe, who recognized his pedagogical skill and chose him to conduct a training school for parochial teachers at Saginaw, Mich. Grossmann was ordained at Hamburg by the Rev. J. Meinel and, with his family and some young men who were to be his pupils, reached Saginaw in July 1852 and opened his school. The Lutheran ministers of Saginaw County were members of the Missouri Synod, and Grossmann before long found himself unpleasantly concerned in a controversy between Löhe and the Missouri Synod over the nature of the ministerial office and its relation to the priesthood of believers. He sided with Löhe against the extreme congregationalism of the Missourians, who proceeded to make things so uncomfortable for him that he was compelled to move to a part of the country unoccupied by pastors of that synod. Accordingly, late in October 1853, he and his friend Johannes Deindörfer [*q.v.*] went to Iowa, where they proposed to found a synod that would remain loyal to Löhe and to Löhe's principles. Grossmann settled at

Dubuque, reopened his school, and gathered together a Lutheran congregation, while Deindörfer went some sixty miles northwestward into Clayton County. For the next few years both men had to contend with dire poverty. On Aug. 24, 1854, Grossmann, Deindörfer, and two young clergymen recently sent over by Löhe met in Deindörfer's cabin at St. Sebald in Clayton County and organized the German Lutheran Synod of Iowa. Unpromising as was its beginning, the synod grew, although for a generation it was handicapped by the polemical onslaughts of the Missouri Synod, by some dissension and intrigue within its own ranks, and by the straitened circumstances of its members. Löhe continued to send men and money for its work, however, and as German immigrants poured into the West and Northwest the synod extended its activities east to Lake Erie and west to the Rocky Mountains. Grossmann was its president from 1854 to 1893. He soon transformed his school into a theological seminary, of which he was president until 1874. The brothers Conrad Sigmund and Gottfried Leonhard Wilhelm Fritschel [*qq.v.*] were the other permanent members of the faculty. In 1878, in vacant rooms in an orphanage at Andrew, Jackson County, Iowa, he resumed his training of parochial teachers; two years later the Wartburg Normal College moved into its own quarters at Waverly, where, on a salary of $600 a year and a house, he continued to direct the work until 1894, when the infirmities of old age made it necessary for him to retire. In 1895 he published a small book on *Die Christliche Gemeindeschule*. He died at Waverly after a long illness.

[Johannes Deindörfer, *Geschichte der Evangel.-Luth. Synode von Iowa* (1897); G. J. Fritschel, *Geschichte der Luth. Kirche in Amerika*, vol. II (Gütersloh, Germany, 1897); *Quellen und Dokumente zur Geschichte und Lehrstellung der ev.-luth. Synode von Iowa* (Chicago, n.d.), ed. by G. J. Fritschel; G. J. Zeilinger, *A Missionary Synod with a Mission* (1929); information as to certain facts from Prof. Geo. J. Fritschel of Wartburg Theological Seminary.]

G. H. G.

GROSSMANN, LOUIS (Feb. 24, 1863–Sept. 21, 1926), rabbi, educator, was born in Vienna, Austria, the son of Ignatz and Nettie (Rosenbaum) Grossmann. At the age of ten he came to the United States with his father, who had received a call to officiate as rabbi for Congregation Beth Elohim of Brooklyn, N. Y. Three years later he went to Cincinnati to enter the Hebrew Union College which had been founded the previous year as the rabbinical seminary of the Reform group in America. At the same time he entered Hughes High School, and in 1884, at the University of Cincinnati, he finished his secular education. The same year he graduated from the Hebrew Union College with the degree of Rabbi and in 1888 he received the degree of Doctor of Divinity. From 1884 to 1898 he was rabbi of Temple Beth El, Detroit, Mich., from which pulpit he was called to become associate rabbi of Congregation B'nai Yeshurun of Cincinnati, Ohio, whose rabbi at that time was Isaac M. Wise [*q.v.*], pioneer of American Reform Judaism and founder and president of the Hebrew Union College. Grossmann, in addition to his rabbinical work, served as professor of ethics and Jewish pedagogy at the Hebrew Union College until 1921, when he became professor emeritus.

Though descended from a line of rabbis and ever sincere and earnest as a preacher, his most distinctive work was that of teacher. He left a profound impression on his pupils and did much to inspire them with ideals. He never married, but his love for children made him intensely interested in their welfare and training, and he contributed much to the progress of Jewish religious education. Though himself the product of the *yeshivah*, he was among the first to realize the importance of adapting modern scientific methods to education, and particularly of applying modern psychology to the problem of Jewish religious training. Although a pioneer in the development of the newer principles of education which have become universal today, either because of his own early, unsystematic, *yeshivah* training, or because of the manifold interests that engrossed him, he was not able to put into concrete, usable form his oft-times revolutionary ideas, and consequently much of their value was lost. Two books, *Principles of Religious Instruction in Jewish Schools* (Berlin, 1913) and *The Aims of Teaching in Jewish Schools* (1919), are all that he left on the subject of education.

His other published volumes were mostly sermons and addresses. They include: *Inaugural Sermon Delivered in Temple Beth El, Detroit, Mich., Dec. 6, 1884* (1884); *The Real Life* (1914); *Glimpses into Life* (1922); *Some Chapters on Judaism and the Science of Religion* (1889); *Maimonides* (1890); *Some Addresses and Poems by B. Bettmann* (1904), which he edited. Together with David Philipson, he also edited *Selected Writings of Isaac M. Wise* (1900). He published two services for children for Sabbath and holy days and prepared musical settings for children's services. He was president of the Central Conference of American Rabbis during the trying years of the World War. In his messages to the Conference he predicted many of the problems that religion would be forced to face in the period of reconstruction which was bound to follow the war, and he urged his colleagues to prepare to meet them. His death occurred in Detroit when he was in his sixty-fourth year.

[*Hebrew Union Coll., Jubilee Vol. 1875–1925* (1925); *Yr. Bk. Central Conference of Am. Rabbis*, 1918–19, 1927; *Who's Who in America*, 1926–27; *N. Y. Times*, *Detroit News*, and *Evening Star*, Washington, Sept. 22, 1926.] I. E. M.

GROSVENOR, CHARLES HENRY (Sept. 20, 1833–Oct. 30, 1917), soldier, congressman, son of Peter and Ann (Chase) Grosvenor, was born in Pomfret, Conn. He was descended from John Grosvenor who emigrated to America in the seventeenth century. His grandfather, Thomas Grosvenor, served as colonel of a Connecticut regiment during the Revolution. His father was a major in the War of 1812. In 1838, when Charles was a boy of five, the family moved to Athens County, Ohio. Lacking help from his parents, young Grosvenor obtained an education through his own efforts, by working in a store and teaching school. Later he studied law under the direction of Lot L. Smith, a lawyer of considerable repute, and was admitted to the bar in 1857. On Dec. 1, 1858, he was married to Samantha Stewart. Upon the outbreak of the Civil War he entered upon a distinguished career. Enlisting in the 18th Ohio Volunteers as a private, he rapidly rose to the rank of major. In June 1863 he was promoted lieutenant-colonel, and in March 1865 he was brevetted a brigadier-general of the Department of Georgia. His most active service was in Tennessee. He was in command of a brigade at the battle of Nashville, where he lost 228 men in a fifteen-minute assault, and for a short time he was in command of the post at Chattanooga. After the war he resumed his practice at Athens. In 1866 his first wife died, and on May 21, 1867, he was married to Louise Currier.

In 1873 Grosvenor entered state politics upon his election to the Ohio House of Representatives. Reëlected, he served as speaker of the House from 1876 to 1878. In 1872 and again in 1880 he was a Republican presidential elector, and in the preconvention campaign in the latter year, he ardently supported Blaine. In 1884, upon his election to Congress, he began a noteworthy career in that body, representing the Athens district almost continuously from 1885 to 1907. (He was defeated for election in the landslide of 1890.) He was a strongly partisan Republican and was always assured of appointment to prominent committees when that party was dominant. By nature conservative, he was frequently the butt of the wrath of those espousing "reform" measures. Champ Clark speaks of him, along with Hepburn and Cannon, as one of the three leading debaters in the House, given to the use of a repartee "as savage as a meat-ax, sometimes as bitter as gall" (*post*, II, 320). Despite the asperity of his debating, however, he was popular with his associates, for in private he was most congenial and a brilliant conversationalist. In appearance he was striking, with his "magnificent head of snow-white hair and snowy whiskers reaching clear down to his waist" (*Ibid.*). Because of his penchant for arithmetical prediction of election results he was nicknamed "Old Figgers." He achieved a national reputation as a political speaker and with Champ Clark engaged in public debates before Chautauqua audiences. In the intricacies of state Republican politics in Ohio he was highly involved. He was the Ohio leader of the presidential boom for John Sherman, in 1887–88, and, largely because of his efforts, the Ohio delegation to the Republican convention was instructed for Sherman. Grosvenor himself was not a delegate, being "so offensively Sherman," according to Foraker, who headed the delegation. Since Foraker was only half-hearted in his advocacy of Sherman, he lost Grosvenor's friendship upon the defeat of the candidate at Chicago. In 1896 and 1900 Grosvenor attended the Republican conventions as delegate-at-large. Upon the completion of his duties in Congress he retired to Athens, where he resumed his law practice. He was the author of *William McKinley, His Life and Work* (1901) and *The Book of the Presidents, with Biographical Sketches* (1902).

[Grosvenor's career may best be followed in the files of the *Athens Daily Messenger* which contains, in the issue of Oct. 30, 1917, a lengthy obituary notice. See also *Who's Who in America*, 1914–15; C. M. Walker, *Hist. of Athens County, Ohio* (1869); *The Biog. Encyc. of Ohio of the Nineteenth Century* (1876), ed. by Chas. Robson; and Whitelaw Reid, *Ohio in the War* (1893), vol. I. Numerous references to Grosvenor are to be found in the memoirs of contemporary congressmen, notably Champ Clark, *My Quarter Century of Am. Politics* (2 vols., 1920).] W. T. U—r.

GROSVENOR, EDWIN PRESCOTT (Oct. 25, 1875–Feb. 28, 1930), lawyer, son of Prof. Edwin Augustus and Lillian (Waters) Grosvenor, both of whom survived him, was born at Constantinople, Turkey, where his father was then professor of history in Robert College. With his twin brother, Gilbert Hovey Grosvenor, he entered Amherst College in the fall of 1893 and was graduated with the degree of A.B., *magna cum laude*, in 1897. He taught for the next four years, 1897–1901, for the most part at the Chestnut Hill Academy, in Philadelphia, where he was master of Latin and Greek. Meanwhile, in 1900, he had received the degree of M.A. from Amherst College. In 1901 he entered the Columbia University School of Law and three years later was graduated at the head of a class of 400. During his senior year he was one of the editors of the *Columbia Law Review.* Shortly after Grosvenor's graduation, Henry W. Taft, who had been appointed by Attorney-General Moody special assistant to prosecute the so-called licorice trust for violation of the federal antitrust laws (*United States* vs. *MacAndrews and Forbes,* 149 *Fed.,* 823, 836; 212 *U. S.,* 585), selected him as his assistant. Later, in 1908, Grosvenor was appointed by Attorney-General Bonaparte as special assistant to the attorney-general. He continued to serve in that capacity under Attorneys-General Wickersham and McReynolds until the latter part of 1913. During this period he had a wide experience with the enforcement of the antitrust laws and the laws affecting interstate commerce. He wrote the briefs for the government in fourteen cases of large importance, eight of which were in the United States Supreme Court. His principal achievements were in the criminal proceedings against the night-riders in Kentucky, and in the civil and criminal proceedings against the bathtub trust. The former cases were brought against the members of a tobacco growers' association organized as a protest against the prices for leaf tobacco established by the tobacco trust. The growers agreed not to raise tobacco for a year. To prevent others from producing they rode in bands at night to the plantations of recalcitrants, destroyed crops, flogged planters, burned warehouses, and even took from station platforms and sheds, and destroyed, tobacco which had been delivered to carriers for shipment in interstate commerce. Grosvenor marshaled the evidence, secured indictments, tried the cases and secured the conviction of several well-known citizens who had participated in these lawless acts. During the pendency of these cases he was twice shot at from ambush and once in the court-room. His fearless, able, and successful conduct of these prosecutions established his reputation for vigor and courage. He prepared the brief and argued the case for the government on appeal and secured affirmance of the convictions in the United States circuit court of appeals at Cincinnati.

The so-called "bathtub" trust was a combination of manufacturers and dealers in plumbing supplies, camouflaged under pretended licenses to use certain patent rights. Grosvenor penetrated this disguise, secured convictions of the individual defendants, and won from the Supreme Court a decision which effectively prevents the extension of a patent monopoly beyond the particular invention or process described in it. This decision (*United States* vs. *Standard Sanitary Manufacturing Company et al.,* 226 *U. S.,* 20) constitutes a landmark in the development of the antitrust law. It has been cited many times by the lower federal courts and has been frequently referred to and quoted from in the Supreme Court.

On Jan. 1, 1914, at the invitation of former Attorney-General Wickersham, Grosvenor joined the old established law firm of Strong & Cadwalader, in New York City, which was then reorganized under the name of Cadwalader, Wickersham & Taft, and continued in that association until his death. As a result of his work in the Department of Justice he was recognized as a leader in the field of law referred to. His advice was widely sought and he was retained as counsel in a number of important causes. His candor at times led him with almost brutal sincerity to point out to clients that they were trying to fool not him only but themselves also, in clothing with statements of legal purpose, agreements whose actual objects were to accomplish forbidden ends. He fully understood and was in sympathy with the principles underlying the antitrust laws, but he also was alive to the injustice of over-zealous prosecution by government attorneys, as well as the danger of business men yielding to the temptation to cloak their actual purpose to destroy competition, under the guise of exchanging information for trade purposes. The line of safety is not always easy to trace. But when the Fur Dealers Association, organized and conducted under his advice, was attacked by the government, he successfully defended it and secured from Judge Bondy in the United States District Court (*United States* vs. *Fur Dealers Association,* 5 *Fed.,* 869) a decision which was acquiesced in by the government and which is one of the landmarks of the law affecting trade associations. During the war Grosvenor served in the Military Intelligence Division, office of the chief of staff, with the rank of captain. On Oct. 26, 1918, he was married to Thelma Cudlipp of Richmond, Va., a painter of recognized ability, who with their two daughters survived him. He died of pneumonia after a very short illness at his home in New York.

[*Who's Who in America,* 1928–29; *Amherst Coll.: Biog. Record of the Grads. and Non-Grads. . . . 1828–1921* (1927); *Amherst Grads'. Quart.,* May 1930; *N. Y. Times,* Mar. 1, 1930.]

G. W. W.

GROSVENOR, JOHN [See ALTHAM, JOHN, 1589–1640].

GROSVENOR, WILLIAM MASON (Apr. 24, 1835–July 20, 1900), journalist, publicist, was born in Ashfield, Franklin County, Mass., a descendant of John Grosvenor who emigrated from England to Roxbury, Mass., about 1670. William's father, Rev. Mason Grosvenor, graduated from Yale, married Esther D. Scarborough, of Brooklyn, Conn., and was for many years professor of moral philosophy in Illinois College, Jacksonville, Ill. William entered Yale in 1851, but remained only three years. From 1859 to 1861 he was editor of the *New Haven Palladium.* In the latter year he enlisted in the 13th Regiment, Connecticut Volunteers. He was made adjutant, then promoted to captain, December 1862, was wounded at Port Hudson, and in October 1863 was commissioned colonel of the 2nd Regiment of Louisiana Native Guards (colored). Returning to New Haven in 1864, he was for two years editor of the *Journal-Courier.* In 1866 he became editor of the *St. Louis Democrat,* which position he held, except for a period between 1870 and 1872, until 1875. While in St. Louis, he entered vigorously into the Liberal Republican movement, and with Joseph Pulitzer [*q.v.*] led it to success. As editor of the *Democrat* and personal friend of many prominent Republicans in St. Louis, he was influential in the final overthrow of radical Republicanism in Missouri. His support of Carl Schurz's candidacy for the United States Senate was responsible for Schurz's election. In his campaign Schurz spoke of Grosvenor as his manager. During this period he also wrote a volume filled with arguments and supporting statistics on the tariff, entitled *Does Protection Protect* (1871), answering the inquiry in the affirmative. During 1873–74 he proved statistically the illicit production of whiskey and specifically identified many offenders. His figures and conclusions were furnished the United States government, and on the strength of them Benjamin H. Bristow [*q.v.*], then (1875) secretary of the treasury, secured the indictment of more than a hundred distillers, federal inspectors, and others, and obtained many convictions, thus completely breaking up the St. Louis Whiskey Ring.

From 1875 to 1900 Grosvenor was economic editor of the *New York Tribune,* and a writer of editorials on national and international affairs. With John R. G. Hassard [*q.v.*], the two working independently, he deciphered the famous code telegraphic dispatches having to do with the presidential election crisis of 1876. He was the author of *American Securities* (1885) and edited *Dun's Review* from 1893 until his death. His advice was frequently sought by representatives of the federal government in framing tariff acts and financial measures. During the Homestead strike in 1892, he made and published a detailed statement of wages, hours, production, and cost of living in Homestead that largely affected public opinion. He refused to hold office, and would never accept railroad passes or similar favors, because, as he said, "it might sometime unexpectedly be my duty to heave a brick editorially through the front window of some railroad or public utility office, and my aim is likely to be truer if I haven't a pocketful of passes." During the panic of 1893 he controlled the Electro Matrix Printing Company, personally holding much of the stock. The company was at a standstill for lack of funds that had been subscribed but could not be paid. Probably at the suggestion of David R. Francis [*q.v.*], secretary of the interior, John G. Carlisle [*q.v.*], secretary of the treasury, requested Grosvenor, as an economist and statistician, to come to Washington to advise on the proposition that the United States Treasury issue additional currency and aid in extending credits. Deeming the proposition economically unsound, Grosvenor explained to his family what his advice would be and that it might insure the failure of the enterprise in which he was financially interested. Upon reaching Washington he saw no reason to alter his opinion, advised against the proposed action, and lost a fortune in the subsequent Electro Matrix failure.

Grosvenor was a man of powerful physique. He had a magnificent head and shoulders, wore a 9½ hat, had bristly eyebrows, long hair, and a long beard. He was gifted in music, literature, mathematics, and as a linguist; was one of the most expert amateur billiard players in New York, could carry on three games of chess simultaneously, and played a remarkable game of whist and of tennis. He was a person of uncompromising integrity, a Presbyterian in religious belief, and active in the church of which he was a member. He enjoyed personal acquaintanceship with most of the presidential candidates, cabinet officers, and many of the senators and representatives in Congress during the period of his public life. He was twice married, first to Ellen M. Stone who died in 1867, and in 1870, to Ellen Sage.

[Daniel Kent, "The Eng. Home and Ancestry of John Grosvenor of Roxbury, Mass.," *New Eng. Hist. and Geneal. Reg.*, Apr. 1918; *Obit. Record Grads. Yale Coll.*, 1886; H. B. Sprague, *Hist. of the 13th Infantry Reg. of Conn. Volunteers* (1867); T. S. Barclay, *The*

Liberal Republican Movement in Mo. (1926); *Reminiscences of Carl Schurz* (2 vols., 1907–08); D. C. Seitz, *Joseph Pulitzer, His Life and Letters* (1924); *N. Y. Tribune* and *N. Y. Times,* July 21, 1900; *Commercial and Financial Chronicle* (N. Y.), July 28, 1900; personal letters.] W. W.

GROTE, AUGUSTUS RADCLIFFE (Feb. 7, 1841–Sept. 12, 1903), entomologist, was born at Aigburth, a suburb of Liverpool, England. His father was German by birth and a descendant of Hugo Grotius. His mother was English, a daughter of the Welsh ironmaster Augustus Radcliffe. Grote's parents emigrated to America in 1846 and settled on Staten Island, where they bought a large farm and where his father became interested in real estate and in the building of the Staten Island Railway. The commercial panic of 1857 destroyed the financial prospects of the family, and Augustus, who had been preparing for Harvard College, was obliged for a time to abandon college work. Later he went to Europe and completed his education on the Continent. He was a born naturalist and began to collect specimens as a boy. At the age of twenty-one he published his first papers, on new species of *Noctuidae,* in the *Proceedings* of the Academy of Natural Sciences and of the Entomological Society of Philadelphia. From that time until his death he published extensively. He described more than two thousand new species of American *Lepidoptera* and wrote many papers on other aspects of entomology. While traveling in the Southern states, he became interested in the cotton caterpillar and wrote and lectured about this species. He urged the government to make an appropriation to investigate the causes of the ravages of the insect, without success, though subsequent appropriations were made for the purpose.

In 1873 Grote went to Buffalo, N. Y., and became curator of the Buffalo Society of Natural Sciences. In the bulletins of this society he published many articles and in 1879 began the publication of the *North American Entomologist,* which ceased publication after its first volume. In 1878 he was vice-president and chairman of Section B of the American Association for the Advancement of Science and delivered an address, "Scientific Education," at the St. Louis meeting of that year. In 1884 he returned to Europe and spent the remainder of his life in Bremen and in Hildesheim, the last nine years in the latter place, where he held the position of honorary assistant in the Römer Museum. During these years abroad he was a frequent contributor to American publications and published numerous essays both in English and German, some of them dealing with abstruse philosophical subjects. His published entomological bibliography includes 201 titles. While in Buffalo he wrote a number of essays upon topics wholly unrelated to his special scientific studies. In 1880 he published *Genesis I–II: An Essay on the Bible Narrative of Creation,* followed the next year by *The New Infidelity,* which was subsequently translated into German. In 1882 he published in London a volume of poems, *Rip van Winkle, a Sun Myth, and Other Poems,* the first one of which, dealing with the ghost theory in evolution, is said to have been favorably reviewed by Herbert Spencer. He was an accomplished musician, was organist of one of the Episcopal churches in Buffalo, and composed many pieces of music. He is also said to have attempted the composition of two operas which were never completed. He was a man of vivid personality, and his admirable work in the *Lepidoptera* made him one of the foremost American entomologists of his time. His influence upon the classification was great, and his work was sound and will last. He was twice married. His first wife, whom he married in 1880, died in 1883. His second wife, Minna Ruyter, whom he married in Germany, survived him.

[For a bibliography of Grote's scientific works, see the *Allgemeine Zeitschrift für Entomologie,* vol. IX, 1904, pp. 1–6. Biographical sources include C. J. S. Bethune, "Prof. Augustus Radcliffe Grote," *Thirty-fourth Ann. Report of the Entomol. Soc. of Ontario, 1903* (1904); *Entomol. News,* Nov. 1903; E. O. Essig, *A Hist. of Entomol.* (1931); *N. Y. Times,* Sept. 24, 1903. Grote's collections are in the possession of the British Museum of Natural History.] L. O. H.

GROUARD, FRANK (Sept. 20, 1850–Aug. 15, 1905), scout, was born in the Paumotu Islands in the South Pacific. His father was Benjamin F. Grouard, of Portsmouth, N. H., a Mormon elder and missionary, and his mother a native of the islands. In 1852 the parents with their three sons moved to California. Frank was taken into the family of Addison Pratt, of San Bernardino, who shortly afterward moved to Beaver, Utah. At fifteen the boy ran away from school and home, and at San Bernardino hired out as a teamster with a wagon train bound for Helena, Mont. For the next four years he was variously employed. In January 1869, while working as a mail-carrier, he was captured by a band of Sioux at the mouth of Milk River, Mont. The youth's features and dark skin persuaded his captors that he was an Indian, and his life was spared. For six years he lived with the hostiles, becoming, according to his own statement, closely acquainted with Sitting Bull and Crazy Horse and mastering the Sioux language.

In the fall of 1875, at Camp Robinson, Nebr.,

he joined the whites, and in February 1876, at Fort Laramie, engaged with Gen. George Crook as a scout. He served throughout the campaign, taking an active part in the battles of Powder River (Mar. 17), the Rosebud (June 17), the exceptionally hazardous scouting expedition of Lieut. F. W. Sibley (July), and the engagement at Slim Buttes (Sept. 11). His part in the crisis that resulted in the killing of Crazy Horse at Camp Robinson, Sept. 5, 1877, has been censured as a misrepresentation of the chief's purposes, but his published account asserts that Crazy Horse had planned a massacre of the whites. After the Sioux war he continued as a government scout, stationed usually at Fort McKinney, Wyo. During the Messiah craze of 1890–91 he was attached to the Pine Ridge agency and rendered valuable service in reporting the progress of the ferment among the Sioux. In the spring of 1891 he returned to Fort McKinney. Three years later he told his life-story —a tale in which fact is liberally intermixed with highly wrought fiction—to a journalist, who published it in book form. His last ten years were spent in or about St. Joseph, Mo., where he died. Among his fellow scouts Grouard was treated with some aloofness, his residence among the Sioux prompting the fear that he was secretly aiding the hostiles. Crook, however, trusted him wholly and praised his work in high terms. Bourke regarded him as an exceptional woodsman, and Finerty, the war correspondent, asserted that he deserved to take rank among the foremost of scouts and plainsmen.

[Joe De Barthe, *The Life and Adventures of Frank Grouard* (1894); J. G. Bourke, *On the Border with Crook* (1891); H. W. Wheeler, *Buffalo Days* (1925); J. F. Finerty, *War-Path and Bivouac* (1890); additional information supplied by I. R. Bundy, librarian of the St. Joseph Pub. Lib., and by Jos. Fielding Smith, historian of the Mormon Church.] W. J. G.

GROVER, CUVIER (July 29, 1828–June 6, 1885), Union soldier, born at Bethel, Me., was the son of John and Fanny (Lary) Grover, a brother of La Fayette Grover [*q.v.*], and a descendant of Thomas Grover who emigrated from England to Charlestown, Mass., about 1642. His father was a physician. Prepared for college at the age of fifteen, young Grover refused to go, having determined to become either a soldier or a merchant. Too young to enter West Point, he became a clerk of Eben D. Jordan [*q.v.*] in Boston and for two years was successful in business. In July 1846 he entered West Point and in July 1850 graduated fourth in his class and was made brevet second lieutenant of artillery. In 1853 he was assigned to engineering duty on the exploring expedition through the region now traversed by the Northern Pacific Railroad. In January and February 1854, on snow shoes and with only four men, he made his memorable crossing of the Rocky Mountains in the midst of hostile Indians. His report on the climatic conditions removed many of the objections to the feasibility of a Northern Pacific Railroad (*Senate Executive Document No. 78*, 33 Cong., 2 Sess., I, 498–515). He was made a first lieutenant in the 10th Infantry on Mar. 3, 1855. In the expedition for the reduction of the rebellious Mormons he served with such distinction that when martial law was declared in Utah he was appointed provost marshal of the territory. He became a captain in the 10th Infantry Sept. 17, 1858, and at the outbreak of the Civil War was on frontier duty at Fort Union, N. Mex. Called upon to surrender to the Confederate government, he burned his supplies and by a brilliant forced march reached the Missouri River with his command. He was made a brigadier-general of volunteers on Apr. 4, 1862, and served with the Army of the Potomac in the Virginia Peninsular campaign. For gallant services in the battle of Williamsburg he was brevetted lieutenant-colonel and after the battle of Fair Oaks was brevetted colonel. He participated in the battles of Savage Station, Glendale, Malvern Hill, Bristoe Station, and Second Manassas. From Dec. 30, 1862, to July 1864 he commanded a division of the XIX Corps in the Department of the Gulf. He was engaged in the Shenandoah campaign from August to December 1864 and on Oct. 16 was brevetted major-general for gallantry at the battles of Winchester and Fisher's Hill. On the same day he was wounded at the battle of Cedar Creek. From January to June 1865 he was in command of the District of Savannah. In March 1865 he was brevetted brigadier-general and major-general. When he was mustered out of the volunteer service in August 1865 he was assigned to frontier duty in the West. He was promoted colonel in the 1st Cavalry Dec. 28, 1875. Grover frequently suffered from nervous prostration and a facial neuralgia contracted during the Red River campaign. He was twice married: first, on Aug. 1, 1865, to Susan Flint, who died Sept. 27, 1869; and second, Jan. 28, 1875, to Ella Miller. He died in 1885 at Atlantic City where he had hoped to find improved health.

[Wm. B. Lapham, *Hist. of Bethel, Formerly Sudbury, Canada, Oxford County, Me., 1768–1890* (1891); G. W. Cullum, *Biog. Reg.* (3rd ed., 1891), vol. II; *War of the Rebellion: Official Records (Army)*; *Army and Navy Jour.*, June 13, 1885, reprinted in *Sixteenth Ann. Reunion, Grads. U. S. Mil. Acad.* (1885); *N. Y. Times*, June 8, 1885.] F. M.

GROVER, LA FAYETTE (Nov. 29, 1823–May 10, 1911), lawyer, politician, manufacturer, was born in Bethel, Oxford County, Me., son of Dr. John Grover and Fanny (Lary) Grover. He was a descendant of Thomas Grover who came to Charlestown, Mass., about 1642; a grandson of John, a Revolutionary soldier, and Jerusha Wiley Grover; and a brother of Gen. Cuvier Grover [*q.v.*]. He attended Gould's Academy, Bethel, and had the advantage of two years' college work at Bowdoin College, 1844–46. He studied law under Asa I. Fish at Philadelphia, where he was admitted to the bar in March 1850. Later in the same year, moved by the gold excitement, he shipped around the Horn for California whence he proceeded in August 1851 to Oregon where he had a conspicuous career as a public man. He was first appointed clerk of the United States district court at Salem, then prosecuting attorney of the second judicial district. He was also auditor of accounts with the general duties of secretary to the legislature. In that capacity he edited a volume of documents, *The Oregon Archives* (1853), selected from the archives of the Provisional Government. This is commonly referred to as "Grover's Oregon Archives." It is a useful work, but he omitted a number of significant items, and committed numerous errors in dating, placing, and transcribing those printed, so that the edition leaves much to be desired on the score of accuracy. In 1853 and 1855 Grover was elected a member of the territorial legislature, and in 1854–56, by appointment of the Interior and War Departments, he was auditor of claims growing out of the Rogue River Indian War and the Indian wars of Washington and Oregon. He was a member of the Oregon constitutional convention in 1857 and was a representative from Oregon in the Thirty-fifth Congress, in which he served seventeen days. From 1866 to 1870 he was chairman of the Democratic state committee, and in 1870 was elected governor, being reëlected in 1874. He resigned Feb. 1, 1877, and, by election of the legislature, became a United States senator from Oregon, Mar. 8, 1877, serving one term. Grover was a man of keen, alert mentality, and of excellent training in the law, but his public career is marred by acts of extreme partisanship which made him for many years both feared and hated in Oregon. An example is his attempt as governor to certificate one Democrat as elector in 1876–77. This move, if it had succeeded, would have elected Tilden president. The point at issue was the disqualification of one of the three Republican candidates for presidential elector, John W. Watts, because he was a postmaster. Grover contended that this justified him in certifying E. A. Cronin, a Democrat, the next highest on the list of candidates. Despite the well-known provision of law enabling the electors of a state to fill by appointment such vacancies as may occur in their number, Grover prepared an extended brief supporting his view of the case. which was, of course, reversed by the electoral commission. During the controversy Governor Grover was in danger of mob violence, and when he appeared soon afterward in the United States Senate to take the oath of office he encountered petitions against his seating on the ground of corruption in the election. This opposition he readily overcame and served respectably during his senatorial term. His governorship, however, is the most outstanding feature of his career. In his period, 1871–77, the state was just emerging from the pioneer stage of its existence and, with one transcontinental railroad completed, was anticipating extraordinary development. Grover realized that such expectations were often illusory and, in any event, that a highly speculative scheme of promotion was dangerous. He therefore held a tight hand on state finances, caused the adoption of a policy which brought the state's indebtedness within the constitutional limits, yet provided for the erection of the state capitol and other public buildings, for promoting education through the creation of a state superintendency, and for opening the state university. He also took positive steps to encourage immigration but trusted more to low taxes and a sound industrial development. He is remembered as one of several strong Democratic governors in this Republican state.

For a number of years he was prominent as a woolen manufacturer in Salem. Later he lost his fortune and, old age coming on, he spent the remaining days of his life in such humble retirement that he was almost completely forgotten by the succeeding generation. Those who knew him well describe him as a genial, intelligent, and well-read gentleman of many attractive qualities. He was married in 1865 to Elizabeth, daughter of Thomas Carter of Portland. His death occurred in Portland, and he was buried in Riverview Cemetery.

[See W. B. Lapham, *Hist. of Bethel, . . . Me.* (1891); *Biog. Dir. Am. Cong.* (1928); W. D. Fenton, "Political History of Oregon from 1865 to 1876," *Ore. Hist. Soc. Quart.*, Dec. 1901; *Ibid.*, June 1911; *Morning Oregonian* (Portland), May 11, 1911; *Who's Who in America*, 1910–11. Grover's brief in the Watts-Cronin case was published under the title, *Executive Decision by the Gov. of Ore. in the Matter of Eligibility of Elector of President and Vice President of the U. S. for 1876* (1876).]

J. S—r.

GROW, GALUSHA AARON (Aug. 31, 1822–Mar. 31, 1907), politician, fifth of the six children of Joseph and Elizabeth (Robbins) Grow, of English stock, was born in Ashford, now Eastford, Windham County, Conn. His father died when Galusha was four and his mother took her family to Voluntown, Conn., where her father, a Revolutionary veteran, was a farmer and inn-keeper. Galusha had the usual life of a chore boy with a little schooling in the winter and the activities of his grandfather's tavern for variation. About 1834 his mother, an enterprising woman, decided to go west into Pennsylvania to seek her fortune. Her father gave her some of his property, and thus provided she and her family joined a party which went by boat to Honesdale, Pa., and then overland to the Tunkhannock Valley where settlements were being opened up. Here she bought 400 acres near Glenwood, and twelve-year-old Galusha settled down with his brother to farm this tract. His mother soon opened a store and as business increased the family began to deal in lumber. Galusha made a number of journeys down the Susquehanna to Port Deposit with lumber consignments and at fourteen was entrusted with a schooner-load of lumber to take to Annapolis or further south for sale. In 1838 he attended the Franklin Academy at Harford, Pa., kept by Willard Richardson, and in 1840 entered Amherst College, graduating in 1844 with an enthusiastic interest in politics. He made his political début that year campaigning for Polk and after the campaign began the study of law, first in the office of Governor Cleveland of Connecticut and then with F. B. Streeter, of Montrose, Pa. After his admission to the bar in 1847 he went into partnership at Towanda with David Wilmot [*q.v.*]. In the course of this partnership Wilmot's political fortunes received a temporary check in 1850 when the more conservative Democrats put up a candidate in opposition. In order to prevent a split in the party these two opponents agreed to withdraw in favor of a third man whom Wilmot should name. Grow was the man and he took his seat forthwith in the Thirty-second Congress, as its youngest member.

His frontier experiences had made him familiar with the exactions of land-speculators and the sufferings of the frontiersmen from their rapacity. Also, his study of Blackstone had impressed him with the doctrine that occupation and use provided the only valid claim to the ownership of land. In Congress, therefore, he manifested immediate interest in the question of the public lands. His first set speech was on the subject of man's right to the soil, and he joined the group who were urging that the government be more generous in its policy of land distribution. In his second term he introduced a bill providing that every applicant be given a quarter section, but in the famous homestead controversy of that Congress it was not his measure that passed the House.

Many congressmen with frontier interests, of whom Grow was one, were restive under the control which the conservative element, mainly Southerners, exercised over legislation, and when the question of repealing the Missouri Compromise arose, determined that the time had come for a new alignment. As a result, conferences were held in Washington during the early part of 1854 attended by Democratic and Whig congressmen from the free states for the purpose of making new arrangements for political action. In these conferences Grow was a conspicuous figure. He was imposing, measuring six feet two inches; his strength had been gained as a "bark-spudder" and was considerable. He lacked any sensitivity which might have made another hesitate to bear the brunt of the new struggle, and his habits were reliable for he was a dyspeptic bachelor who lived apart from the convivial world. Consequently, he could be counted on to take the offensive at any time, and this strength and coolness made him one of the most aggravating of the new Republicans, one who could easily goad an impulsive Southerner to desperation and took delight in doing so. Thus equipped, he took his place beside Campbell, Banks, Giddings, and their associates, in the rough and tumble of the turbulent congressional sessions just prior to the Civil War. He won notoriety for his brush with L. M. Keitt [*q.v.*], and on one occasion made use of a bodyguard and was bound over to keep the peace. During these sessions he was also active in defeating various schemes of speculators and in urging the creation of new territories. When secession cleared the House of the Southern members, the Republicans at length could initiate a program, and when the special session of the war Congress came together in July 1861, Galusha Grow was elected speaker. During his term in this office he had the pleasure of seeing the homestead measure for which he had so long labored enacted into law. This was the crowning event in his career, for the Pennsylvania legislature had rearranged the congressional districts so that he now lived in a Democratic stronghold, and he was defeated for reëlection in the disastrous year 1862.

For thirty years he spent his time striving ineffectually to return to politics in the face of

Cameron's hostility. He was a delegate to the Republican National Convention in 1864, 1884, and 1892, served as chairman of the state committee in the late sixties, and in the Hayes Administration declined the Russian mission. He was active in various business enterprises, lumber, oil, and railroads, even going to Texas for four years as president of the Houston & Great Northern Railroad (1871–75). Finally he did succeed in coming back to political prominence. In 1893 William Lilly, congressman-at-large from Pennsylvania, died, and as Grow's biographer says, "Through the accident of Quay being in Florida, tarpon fishing, the organization did not promptly give orders to crush him" (p. 279), and Grow was elected. He served through four Congresses as a picturesque veteran, still actively interested in extending homestead legislation and acquiring new territory; he was a veritable Nestor in the House. Upon his retirement in 1903 Andrew Carnegie placed him upon his pension list and he went back to Glenwood to think over the past and dictate his memoirs. A frontiersman, he had labored earnestly to destroy the frontier and provide opportunity for individuals to develop the resources of the nation.

[J. T. DuBois and Gertrude S. Mathews, *Galusha A. Grow* (1917), partially drawn from Grow's fragmentary autobiography; *Cong. Globe,* 32–37 Cong., *Cong. Record,* 53–57 Cong.; speech on the homestead question, delivered Mar. 30, 1852, in the *Globe,* 32 Cong., 1 Sess., App., pp. 424–28; G. M. Stephenson, *The Political Hist. of the Public Lands, 1840–62* (1917); Edwin Maxcy, "Galusha A. Grow, Father of the Homestead Bill," *Overland Monthly,* July 1908; *Who's Who in America,* 1906–07; *Pub. Ledger* (Phila.), Apr. 1, 1907.]
R. F. N.

GRUBE, BERNHARD ADAM (June 24, 1715–Mar. 20, 1808), Moravian missionary, was born in Thüringen at Walschleben near Erfurt and was educated in his native village and at Jena. Entering the Moravian ministry in 1740, he served some small congregations in Holland and taught in the seminary at Lindheim. He was sent to Pennsylvania in the spring of 1748, was a teacher at Bethlehem for several years, and then volunteered for work among the Indians. In January 1752 he took up his quarters at Meniolágoméka, a village west of Wind Gap in what is now Monroe County. There his clumsiness in wielding an axe nearly cost him a leg, and for weeks he lay in his hut with a board for a bed and a wooden bowl for a pillow. Meanwhile he held daily meetings for the Indians and studied the Delaware language. After six months he was transferred to the mission at Shamokin. In the summer of 1753 he visited the Indian villages along the west branch of the Susquehanna and in the Wyoming Valley. In the autumn of 1753 he conducted a party of settlers from Bethlehem to the recently acquired Wachovia Tract in North Carolina. Returning to Bethlehem the next spring, he married and was assigned to the mission at Gnadenhütten. On the evening of Nov. 24, 1755, hostile Indians burned his mission station on Mahoning Creek and massacred eleven of the occupants. Grube and his converts fled to Bethlehem, where he remained for two years. During 1758–60 he had charge of the mission at Pachgatgoch near Kent, Litchfield County, Conn. In October 1760 he was put in charge of the station at Wechquetanc on Head's Creek in Monroe County, Pa. There he conducted all his services in the Delaware language and wrote his *Dellawaerisches Gesang-Büchlein* (1763) and *Evangelien-Harmonie in die Delaware Sprache Übersetzt* (1763), which were printed at Friedensthal by John Brandmiller, the Swiss clergyman-printer (see *Pennsylvania Magazine of History and Biography,* vol. VI, no. 2, 1882, pp. 249–50 and W. J. Hinke, *Life and Letters of the Rev. John Philip Boehm,* 1916, pp. 127–29). At the outbreak in 1763 of Pontiac's War Grube and his Indian followers found their lives in jeopardy. Every one hated them, the whites being even more murderous than the savage Indians. Boarding up his chapel and huts, he retreated to Nazareth with his converts, later to Bethlehem, and thence to Philadelphia, where he stood a virtual state of siege, the "Paxton Boys" threatening to invade the town and kill the Indians, and the citizens themselves unfriendly. Grube comported himself with bravery and tact and found a powerful friend in Benjamin Franklin. From 1765 until 1785 he was pastor at Lititz in Lancaster County. His wife died here in 1776, and two years later he married again. He officiated at the marriage of John Heckewelder [*q.v.*] July 4, 1780, in Ohio and at that of David Zeisberger [*q.v.*] June 4, 1781, at Lititz. For short periods he ministered to congregations near Nazareth, in Philadelphia, at Paulin's Kill, Warren County, N. J., and at Emaus, Lehigh County, Pa. Honored as one of the patriarchs of his church, he lived his last years at Bethlehem and on his ninety-first birthday tramped, staff in hand, the ten miles to Nazareth to spend the day with old friends who had shared his labors among the Indians.

[G. H. Loskiel, *Hist. of the Mission of the United Brethren among the Indians in North America* (London, 1794), transl. by C. I. La Trobe; Edmund De Schweinitz, *Life and Times of David Zeisberger* (1870); "A Missionary's Tour to Shamokin and the West Branch of the Susquehanna, 1753," *Pa. Mag. of Hist. and Biog.,* Oct. 1915; "Diarium einer Reise von Bethlehem, Pa., nach Bethabara, N. C., von Oct. 8 bis Nov. 23, 1753," ed. by W. J. Hinke, *German-American*

Annals, Aug., Sept., 1905, and Jan. 1906; *Records of the Moravians in N. C.* (4 vols., 1922–30), ed. by Adelaide L. Fries; J. W. Jordan, "Biog. Sketch of Rev. B. A. Grube," *Pa. Mag. of Hist. and Biog.*, Apr. 1901, with direction to MSS.; Oswald Seidensticker, *The First Century of German Printing in America, 1728–1830* (1893).] G. H. G.

GRUENING, EMIL (Oct. 2, 1842–May 30, 1914), pioneer ophthalmologist and otologist, teacher, scholar, was born in Hohensalza, East Prussia, the son of Moritz and Bertha (Thorner) Gruening. He was an earnest student and at the time of his graduation from the Gymnasium intended to become a teacher. In 1862 he emigrated to the United States, mainly because he detested Prussianism and militarism and the then impending compulsory service. He secured pupils in private families, teaching the classics and foreign languages, then, upon the advice of Dr. Willard Parker [*q.v.*], he matriculated in 1864 at the College of Physicians and Surgeons of New York. A year later he enlisted in the 7th New Jersey Volunteer Infantry and participated in the battle of Hatcher's Run and the siege of Petersburg. He was also present at Appomattox at the surrender of General Lee. Honorably discharged, he resumed his studies, graduating from the medical school in 1867. He then spent three years in post-graduate work in London, Paris, and Berlin, under such masters as Von Graefe, Virchow, and Langenbeck. Returning to New York in 1870, he was appointed to the staff of the Ophthalmic and Aural Institute. Later he became personal assistant to Dr. Hermann Knapp, who was chief surgeon there.

In 1878 Gruening was appointed ophthalmic surgeon to the New York Eye and Ear Infirmary, where he served for thirty-four years. The following year he began a twenty-five year service at the Mt. Sinai Hospital, and in 1880 he began a twenty-four year connection with the German (Lenox Hill) Hospital, serving them also as otologist. He was professor of ophthalmology at the New York Polyclinic Hospital for thirteen years. He was an active member of the national medical societies and had the unique honor of serving as chairman of both the American Ophthalmological and the American Otological societies. His contributions to medical literature represented important original investigations in the field of his specialty. To the *System of Diseases of the Eye,* edited by W. F. Norris and C. A. Oliver, he contributed the chapter on "Wounds and Injuries of the Eyeball and its Appendages" (vol. III, 1898). He was one of the first to describe, and to operate successfully upon, brain abscess of otitic origin ("Two Cases of Otitic Brain Abscess; Operation; Recovery," *Mt. Sinai Hospital Reports,* vol. II, 1900), and was also one of the first to call attention to the danger of blindness due to the use of wood alcohol ("Methyl Alcohol Amblyopia," *Archives of Ophthalmology,* July 1910).

His research upon the relation of ocular symptoms in nose affections, as well as his work upon the mastoid, its diagnosis and cure, were genuine contributions to medical science and aided in the development of the infant specialty of otology. He was a skilful operator and devised many new instruments for surgical use. He was also a thorough diagnostician and an ideal teacher and leader of men. Apart from his profession he was passionately fond of music, able in the criticism of art, and devotedly attached to his family and the education of his children. His death occurred at his home in New York City. He had married, in 1874, Rose Fridenberg, who died in 1876. In 1880 he was married to her sister, Phebe, who with four daughters and one son survived him.

[W. B. Marple, article in *Trans. Am. Ophthalmol. Soc.*, vol. XIV (1915); W. H. Wilmer, article in *Arch. of Ophthalmol.*, vol. XLIII (1914); *Am. Jour. of Ophthalmol.*, June 1914; *Laryngoscope,* June 1914; *Annals of Otol., Rhinol., and Laryngol.*, June 1914; *N. Y. Times,* May 31, 1914.] E. M—r.

GRUNDY, FELIX (Sept. 11, 1777–Dec. 19, 1840), criminal lawyer, jurist, politician, was the youngest son of George Grundy who emigrated from England and settled upon the frontier of Virginia. In 1779 the family removed to Pennsylvania, but in the following year they migrated once more, settling this time in central Kentucky. Here the boy received his meager education. He was instructed first by his mother, and then by Dr. James Priestly at the Bardstown Academy. In order to fit himself for his career, he studied law under George Nicholas and was admitted to the Kentucky bar in 1797 at the age of twenty. Two years later he was elected a member of the convention which was called to remodel the constitution of the state. His capable service in this body opened before him a political career, and for some years thereafter he sat in the legislature of Kentucky. It was as a member of this body in 1802 that he opposed and the yet unheralded Henry Clay supported the chartering of a banking corporation. In 1806 the ambitious young politician was appointed to an associate justiceship on the state supreme court of errors and appeals. He was almost immediately promoted to the chief justiceship, but finding the salary inadequate to supply his needs, he resigned in 1807 and moved to Nashville, Tenn., resolved to devote his time to the practice of his profession in a growing community where he would be free from political encumbrances. His reputation had preceded him to his new home and he soon came to be regarded as the most skilful criminal lawyer of the Southwest. It was said at one time that out of 165 capital cases which he had defended, only one execution took place. This success was the result of finesse rather than of legal learning. He would depend upon others to work up the cases in which he was concerned, devoting his own time and attention to the jury. His manner was genial and his bearing distinguished. He knew how to flatter by condescension and to impress by his eloquence, and as a master of pathos he could move juries to tears. A science in his hands became an art, and the gallows was often cheated of its due (J. C. Guild, *Old Times in Tennessee,* 1878, pp. 293–99).

Once having engaged in politics, Grundy was unable to steer clear of the alluring diversion, and in 1811, with war clouds lowering, he permitted himself to be elected to Congress. In 1813 he was reëlected, and during these two terms, as a member of the committee on foreign affairs, he took a leading part in bringing on and sustaining the struggle with England. From 1815 to 1819 he abstained from office; but the appalling panic of the latter year called him again before the people, and he was elected to a seat in the state legislature. In earlier times he had been a champion of relief laws in Kentucky; he now became the champion of relief in Tennessee, fostering a state-owned "bank" or loan office, the object of which was to extend the credit of the government to the debtors in order to enable them to discharge their obligations. In this he was unsuccessfully opposed by Andrew Jackson, yet this bid for popularity did not win for him the dominant position in local politics which he doubtless sought. Jackson read his hand, and though the two men were often afterward associated in politics, they were never intimate. Grundy presently had to accept Jackson's leadership, and Jackson was forced to accept Grundy's support (T. P. Abernethy, "Andrew Jackson and the Rise of Southwestern Democracy," in the *American Historical Review,* October 1927, pp. 66–67).

For six years Grundy served in the legislature, for two years he withdrew from public life, and then in 1827 he ran for Congress in Jackson's home district. He now received the open support of "Old Hickory" against John Bell, but he lost the race. This misfortune was requited as soon as Jackson became president in 1829. On the transfer of John H. Eaton from the Senate to the cabinet, Grundy was selected to fill the vacancy in the Senate (T. P. Abernethy, "The Origin of the Whig Party in Tennessee," in the *Mississippi Valley Historical Review,* March 1926, pp. 506–08). As a member of this body he took an active part in the nullification controversy of 1832. Having always professed state-rights principles, he now manifested considerable sympathy with the stand taken by the South Carolinians; but when Jackson's position became clear, he subsided and tried to smooth over all apparent differences between himself and his chief. In 1833 his term expired and Jackson attempted to secure the seat for Eaton, who had resigned from the cabinet as a result of the storm created by the marriage of the latter to Peggy O'Neill. Tennessee resented the action of the President in the matter, and Grundy was reëlected after a bitter struggle. In spite of these facts, he never ceased to be a supporter of the administration. In 1838 he resigned from the Senate to accept the attorney-generalship in Van Buren's cabinet. It is notable that Jackson had never conferred office upon the most distinguished Tennessean enlisted under his banner. In 1839 Grundy was again elected to the Senate, and he gave up his cabinet post in order to accept the place. He died in 1840 and was buried in Nashville. Early in life he had married Ann P. Rogers, of Kentucky. He was devoted to his family and to his home. As a respected citizen, he was always scrupulously careful of the conventionalities and proprieties of society as he found it.

[The best brief accounts of Grundy's career are to be found in J. W. Caldwell, *Sketches of the Bench and Bar of Tenn.* (1898), pp. 53–60; and in the *U. S. Mag. and Democratic Rev.*, Oct. 1838. Other sources include W. W. Clayton, *Hist. of Davidson County, Tenn.* (1880), pp. 100–02; and J. M. Bright, *An Oration on the Life, Character, and Pub. Services of the Hon. Felix Grundy* (1859).]
T. P. A.

GUE, BENJAMIN F. (Dec. 25, 1828–June 1, 1904), lieutenant-governor of Iowa, journalist, historical writer, the eldest son of John and Catherine (Gurney) Gue, was born in Greene County, N. Y. His father was of French and his mother of English descent. In 1834 his parents removed to a farm near Farmington, in Ontario County, where he grew to manhood. His higher education was limited to two terms in the Canandaigua and West Bloomfield academies. When the family left the farm and separated in 1851, Benjamin went back to his native county where he taught school for one term. Caught by the spirit of the westward movement, he decided to go to the new state of Iowa and after a journey of three weeks he arrived at Davenport, Mar. 22, 1852. On a quarter section of land, in the northwest corner of Scott County, on Rock Creek, he and a younger brother began farming with a plow, a wagon, and a team of horses. They prospered, bought more land, and soon each possessed a farm of his own. On Nov. 12, 1855, Benjamin was married to Elizabeth R. Parker, a young woman who had been teaching school in the vicinity.

Although his parents were Friends, Gue became an active Unitarian, helped to establish the First Unitarian Church of Des Moines, and was one of the founders of the Iowa Unitarian Association. From his Quaker abolitionist parents he early acquired a deep interest in the anti-slavery movement. It was this interest that drew him into politics and led him to serve as a delegate to the convention that met in Iowa City in February 1856 to organize the Republican party in Iowa. In 1857 he was elected to a seat in the lower house of the General Assembly, to which position he was reëlected in 1859. In the legislature he took a leading interest in legislation for the establishment and support of the Iowa State Agricultural College (now the State College of Agriculture). Later (1866) he served as president of the board of trustees of this institution, and in the face of considerable opposition he secured the admission of women on an equality with men. In 1861 he was elected to a seat in the Iowa Senate, which place he held through two regular sessions and one extra session. President Lincoln appointed him postmaster at Fort Dodge in 1864; and in 1865 he was elected to the office of lieutenant-governor.

Gue began his journalistic career in 1864 as editor and publisher of the *Fort Dodge Republican* which he soon rechristened the *Iowa North-West.* Republicanism, temperance, and woman's suffrage were the outstanding policies of his paper. In 1871 he assumed editorial control of the *Iowa Homestead* at Des Moines, and for a few months he was chief editor of the *Daily State Journal.* At this point his newspaper work was interrupted by his appointment (December 1872) to the office of United States pension agent for Iowa by President Grant. Eight years later he and his son acquired the *Iowa Homestead* by purchase. During this period of his editorship of the paper he took part in the Greenback movement and in 1883 indorsed every plank in the party's platform except the one "arraigning the republican party" (Des Moines *Iowa Tribune,* July 18, 1883). The latter part of his life he devoted to the writing of biographical and historical sketches which were printed in the *Annals of Iowa* and in the year before his death he published in four volumes a *History of Iowa from the Earliest Times to the Beginning of the Twentieth Century,* designed to be "a cyclopedia of general information pertaining to Iowa." He died at Des Moines in his seventy-sixth year.

[Gue's *Hist. of Iowa,* vol. IV, pp. 111–12; E. H. Stiles, *Recollections and Sketches of Notable Lawyers and Pub. Men of Iowa* (1916); C. R. Tuttle and D. S. Durrie, *An Illustrated Hist. of the State of Iowa* (1876); Johnson Brigham, article in the *Annals of Iowa,* July 1904; *Pioneer Lawmakers' Asso. of Iowa. Reunion of 1904* (1904); *Reg. and Leader* (Des Moines), June 2, 1904, Jan. 2, 1910. Gue had no middle name; he simply adopted an initial.] B. F. S.

GUÉRIN, ANNE-THÉRÈSE (Oct. 2, 1798–May 14, 1856), in religion Mother Theodore, educator, foundress of the Sisters of Providence of Saint Mary-of-the-Woods, Indiana, was born in Étables, Côtes-du-Nord, France. Her father, Laurent Guérin, was a naval officer in the service of Napoleon and was killed by brigands near Avignon while returning on furlough just before the Russian campaign. Her mother, Isabelle LeFèvre, was a member of a family of the lesser nobility. She attended a private school in Étables and later continued her education under a tutor. In 1823 she entered the community of the Sisters of Providence at Ruillé-sur-Loir, founded by Abbé Jacques Dujarié in 1806. As Sister Theodore, she showed unmistakable signs of her aptitude for the religious life and the work of education. Immediately upon taking her vows she was appointed superior of the establishment at Rennes. After ten years at Rennes, she was transferred to Soulaines, where she received medallion decorations for the excellence of her teaching. There also she pursued a four years' course in medicine and pharmacy under the noted Lecacheur, a course which proved invaluable in her later labors.

In answer to an appeal made to the community at Ruillé-sur-Loir, by Rt. Rev. Célestine de la Hailandière, Bishop of Vincennes, Ind., for sisters for his diocese, six sisters with Mother Theodore as superior set out for America on July 26, 1840. After many hardships, delays, and disappointments, the little company arrived at Saint Mary-of-the-Woods on Oct. 22. Here in the wilderness she established the first academy for young women in the state, chartered in 1846 with powers to confer academic honors and degrees. Upon her death in 1856, she left behind her an institution securely founded, a growing community, a flourishing academy, and a number of thriving schools in various towns of Indiana. Mother Theodore was not only an educator, but an organizer of extraordinary ability. Her extensive correspondence with ecclesiastics, national and local authorities, her carefully kept diaries, annals, and journals of travel, are rich sources of information for the biographer and the historian. And in addition to her rare intellectual qualities, she possessed a deep spiritual nature, a masterful power of training religious educators, and the soul of a missionary.

[*Life and Life-Work of Mother Theodore Guérin* (1904); Clémentine de la Corbinière, *The Life and Letters of Sister St. Francis Xavier* (1917); manuscript annals of the community of St. Mary-of-the-Woods, manuscript memoirs of Mother Mary Cecilia; Mother Theodore's diary, journals of travel, and correspondence.] E.

GUERNSEY, EGBERT (July 8, 1823–Sept. 19, 1903), physician, the son of John Guernsey and Amanda Crosby, was born at Litchfield, Conn., and was descended from superior Puritan stock. He received his education at Phillips Andover Academy and then taught school for a time. In 1843 he was in Europe and on his return began the study of medicine under Valentine Mott [*q.v.*] in the medical department of the University of the City of New York. During his undergraduate period he served as city editor of the *Evening Mirror* under N. P. Willis and G. P. Morris and also worked as a drug clerk to gain some practical experience with pharmacy. After his graduation in 1846 he worked for a time as manager of a large drug firm and then opened an office at Williamsburg, now part of Brooklyn, where he secured the appointment of city physician. He was one of the founders, in 1848, of the *Williamsburg Times* (later the *Brooklyn Daily Times*) and edited it for eighteen months. During this period he also published two elementary school histories of the United States which were extensively used as textbooks. As a result of overwork he suffered a breakdown and gave up his career for the time being to live quietly at Fishkill on the Hudson, where he later established a summer home. In 1850, his health restored, he reëntered practice, this time in New York City, and began to adopt some of the tenets and practices of homeopathy, although he never formally abandoned the old school of medicine and resorted apparently to the new doctrines only when his customary remedies failed to benefit his patients. Owing to the ethics of the period, he was obliged to fraternize with colleagues who made use of homeopathic remedies. Perhaps it was because he could face both ways that he became phenomenally successful as a practitioner.

Having secured in 1851 the appointment as physician to the Home for the Friendless, Guernsey served in that capacity until 1865. In 1853 he published *Homœopathic Domestic Practice,* the title of which is usually given simply as *Domestic Practice,* which went through successive editions and was translated into French, German, Danish, and Spanish. It was followed two years later by the *Gentleman's Handbook of Homœopathy,* a small manual designed especially for travelers. In 1861 he was made professor of materia medica in the New York Homœopathic Medical College and in 1864 he was given the chair of theory and practice which he resigned in 1867. From 1864 to 1868 he was surgeon of the 6th New York Regiment. In 1870 he established the Western Dispensary, known later as the Guernsey Maternity Hospital, which finally merged with the Hahnemann Hospital. He resumed his journalistic activities in 1873 with the establishment of the *Medical Union,* a journal which appeared later as the *New York Journal of Homœopathy,* the *Homœopathic Times,* and the *Medical Times,* and which up to the time of Guernsey's death had published thirty-one volumes. In 1877 Guernsey was the chief instrument in turning the Inebriate Asylum on Ward's Island into the Metropolitan Hospital and was president of its medical board until his death. He was also one of the founders of the Union League Club of New York, the Homœopathic State Insane Asylum at Middletown, N. Y., and several homeopathic training schools for nurses. He was a man of huge bulk and in the latter part of his life suffered from organic heart disease, yet he kept active almost to the end of his life. His character and personality are said to have been memorialized in Bret Harte's tale, *The Man Whose Yoke Was Not Easy,* and higher praise could hardly be awarded. One of his ambitions, as shown by the files of the *Medical Times,* was to bring the homeopathic sect into greater harmony with the main body of practitioners, but he confessed that in this crusade he fell between two stools, sharing the fate of many peace-makers. Nevertheless, he must be credited in part for improving the relations between the two groups. In 1848 Guernsey was married to Sarah Lefferts Schenck, but of their five children only one survived him.

[E. Cleave, *Biog. Cyc. of Homoeopathic Physicians and Surgeons* (1873); *Who's Who in America,* 1903–05; the *Medic. Times,* Oct., Dec. 1903; *Brooklyn Times,* Sept. 19, 1903; *N. Y. Times,* Sept. 20, 1903.] E. P.

GUESS, GEORGE [See SEQUOYAH, 1770–1843].

GUFFEY, JAMES McCLURG (Jan. 19, 1839–Mar. 20, 1930), oil producer, was born in Sewickley township, Westmoreland County, Pa., seventh of the nine children of Alexander and Jane (Campbell) Guffey. His father, an operator of salt works and an early user of natural gas, was a descendant of William Guffey who came to Pennsylvania in 1738 and twenty years later was a member of the pioneer English settlement in Westmoreland County. James went to the "Old Sulphur Springs" school and worked on his father's farm. Later he attended the Iron City Commercial College, a pioneer commercial school in Pittsburgh. At the age of eighteen he entered the office of the superintendent of the Louisville & Nashville Railway at Louisville, Ky., as a clerk. He was next employed by the Adams Express Company in Nashville, Tenn. In 1872 he returned to Pennsylvania and became a salesman of oil-well machinery and supplies at St. Petersburg in Clarion County for the Gibbs & Sterrett Company. This work gave him a large acquaintance in the newly developed oil regions and taught him a great deal about oil and its future possibilities. He accordingly leased land and began to drill. In 1875 he went to the Bradford oil region where later the town of Guffey in McKean County was named for him.

In 1880, together with John H. Galey, he organized the firm of Guffey & Galey, for twenty-five years one of the most courageous firms in oil history. He settled at Titusville, drilling the famous Matthews and Lucas gushers—the latter with a daily capacity of eighty thousand barrels. With Galey he opened pools in Pennsylvania and West Virginia; at one time they were the largest producers in the former state and operated in every oil-producing center. Guffey himself became one of the largest, if not the largest, individual landowner, producer, and operator in the United States. The firm's rich Kansas holdings, consisting of 243,000 acres under lease, were transferred to the Forest Oil Company, then a Standard Oil subsidiary. An additional holding of a million and a half acres in the same state was never developed. The Magnolia Petroleum Company purchased the Texas holdings of Guffey & Galey and became one of the largest producers in that region. The partners organized another firm, the J. M. Guffey Petroleum Company with a capital of $15,000,000, for the purpose of building the first pipe lines and refinery in the South Texas region. This company later became a valuable part of the Gulf Refining Company. In 1900 the firm held a blanket lease on 186,000 acres of the Osage nation in the Indian Territory which it later sold for $1,250,000 to T. N. Barnsdall. Among the famous pools associated with the names of Guffey and Galey were the Spindletop in Texas, the Coalings in California, the Sand Fork and the Kyle in West Virginia, and the McDonald in Pennsylvania.

The kindred fields of gas and coal also won Guffey's interest. In 1883 he turned his attention to the newly discovered natural-gas territory in the Pittsburgh district and opened up many fields. He became vice-president of the Westmoreland & Cambria Natural Gas Company and of the Wheeling Natural Gas Company; president of the Southwest Natural Gas Company, Bellevue Natural Gas Company, and the United Fuel Gas Company—all pioneers. He also had gold- and silver-mining interests in Idaho, mining and real-estate holdings in Colorado, Florida, Nova Scotia, and coal lands in Pennsylvania and West Virginia. Although singularly successful in oil, because of his real-estate holdings he was hard hit in the panic of 1907. His friend Galey, who was in Alaska when the disaster befell him, came to his rescue to the best of his ability and although rated a multi-millionaire at the time, he died, as did Guffey, a relatively poor man.

Guffey's other great interest was in the field of politics. He began his long period of service in the Democratic party at the age of twenty-seven as city clerk in Pithole City, a small oil town in Venango County. In 1878 he made an unsuccessful race for Congress, but thereafter sought no office, refusing the nomination for governor of Pennsylvania in 1898. In 1897, however, he was elected by the state committee as a member of the Democratic National Committee, and he held this important office from 1898 to 1908 and from 1912 onward. He opposed William Jennings Bryan in the latter's third campaign for the presidential nomination, and as a delegate to the Democratic National Convention at St. Louis in 1904 helped to nominate Judge Alton B. Parker. He was also opposed to the nomination of Woodrow Wilson. In his own state he was highly esteemed as an adviser and observer, and served for eight years on Gov. Pattison's staff.

Guffey was married in 1887 to Nancy Elizabeth Cook. They had one child, a daughter. Outliving most of his contemporaries, he was known to the younger generation of men in the oil, gas, and coal fields as a personality endowed with traditions rather than as a person; and he stood for them as the ideal of pioneer daring and attainment.

[*Oil and Gas Jour.* (Tulsa, Okla.), Mar. 27, 1930; *Pittsburgh Post Gazette, Pittsburgh Sun-Telegraph,* and *Pittsburgh Press,* Mar. 20, 1930; *Who's Who in Pa.* (1908); *Hist. of Pittsburgh and Environs* (1922), IV, 301–02; *Hist. of Westmoreland County, Pa.* (1906), vol. III; Sam Hudson, *Pa. and its Public Men* (1909); J. W. Jordan, *Encyc. of Pa. Biog.*, vol. VIII (1917).]

A. I.

GUGGENHEIM, DANIEL (July 9, 1856–Sept. 28, 1930), capitalist and philanthropist, second of the seven sons of Meyer Guggenheim [*q.v.*], was born in Philadelphia. He had entered high school when in 1873 his father, having formed a firm for the manufacture and importation of Swiss embroideries, sent Daniel and his older brother to Switzerland to study the business and act as his deputies in the factory at St. Gall. Daniel remained in Switzerland for eleven years, learning a good deal about the current methods of mercantile management in Europe. Returning to the United States in 1884, he found that the Guggenheim money was rapidly being deflected from laces and embroideries to copper mining and smelting, and every son was needed to help establish the new business and liquidate the old. He took his place easily as the outstanding personality and business intelligence among the seven sons and traveled about with his father from one plant to another, assisting him in the general supervision of the properties. The Guggenheim strategy—the integration of smelting and refining with exploration for and control of the sources of supply, and the establishing of intimate financial relations with producers—was to no small degree the product of Daniel's planning. It was chiefly due to him also that a consolidation with the "Smelting Trust" was effected in 1901 on terms which left to the Guggenheim brothers the control of the reorganized American Smelting & Refining Company. As chairman of the board of directors of this company or as president, until 1919, Daniel Guggenheim was its guiding head during the two decades when it spanned the American continent from Alaska to Chile and extended its operations to Africa; and in the third decade of the century, while he was not the active head of the company, his influence was still dominant. He was also the head of or a director in the ganglion of miscellaneous corporations which, in the Guggenheim plan of operation, clustered about the central enterprise —among others the Guggenheim Exploration Company, the American Smelters Security Company, the Chile Copper Company and the Utah Copper Company.

His policy was a continuation of that which the firm of M. Guggenheim's Sons had found so successful. More and more, however, the trend of the firm was to combine mining operations with processing under a single control. Largely instrumental in this result was the Guggenheim system of forming exploration companies in various parts of the world, to examine mining properties for possible exploitation. The mining survey was elevated to a crucial position in the sphere of operations, and no money was spared in hiring competent engineers for it. Once exploitation was determined upon, the Guggenheim method was rapid and bold. Huge sums were spent in overcoming engineering obstacles. In 1912 a "mountain of copper" in Alaska, whose potentialities were considered staggering, was made accessible by building a railroad over a moving glacier and hauling the cumbersome machinery and the ore over it; in Chile, at Rancaqua in 1908, Chuquicamata in 1911, and later at Potrerillos, huge deposits of low-grade copper ore were finally treated after difficult engineering obstacles were met; the Chuquicamata mine was eighty miles from the sea, at an elevation of 9,500 feet, forty-five miles from a water supply and eighty-five from a source of power. Even more important than these engineering feats was the Guggenheim policy of ruthlessly replacing old production methods and technological processes by new ones. They aimed at mass production, and thus often utilized ore of low-grade content which previous methods had found unprofitable. The supremacy of the Chilean fields in the nitrate industry was challenged in the post-war period by the synthetic process developed during the War. Guggenheim enterprise entered in 1924, however, acquired control of several large English and Chilean companies, discarded the old Shanks process and replaced it with a process involving electric shovels, large concrete tanks, mechanical refrigeration and centrifugal driers, thus making the 8% rather than the 16% ores marginal, cutting labor and fuel costs about 75%, and rendering possible competition with the synthetic producers. There was also a skilful financial reorganization of the nitrate industry; the Chile Nitrate Company was formed to absorb the large number of individual producers, and the Chilean government, in return for removing the export tax on nitrate, was given 50% of the stock.

The international scope of his operations and the success of the industrial reorganizations he effected gave color and dash to Daniel Guggenheim's career. Although he was not primarily a banker or promoter and in the main restricted his operations to mining and metallurgy, he was one of the foremost representatives of American industrial imperialism. He developed tin mines in Bolivia, gold mines in the Yukon regions, diamond fields in the Belgian Congo and Angola, copper mines in Alaska, Utah, and Chile, nitrate fields in Chile, and rubber plantations in the Belgian Congo. Smelting and refining plants were scattered not only over the United States but also close to the mines abroad. Often the success of his operations affected the prosperity of foreign countries, even the stability of governments. His rule over his enterprises was absolute, but it was that of a benevolent monarch. He continued his father's tradition of scrupulous adherence to business ethics, and the episode of the repayment in 1906 of losses to the extent of $1,500,000 which had been incurred by outside investors on the strength of Guggenheim participation in a Canadian mining venture, has become a part of the folklore of Wall Street. Toward his employees his attitude was a liberal and well-meaning paternalism. His avowed labor creed included the passing of social legislation (unemployment, sickness and old age insurance) by the agreement of organized labor and organized capital, and through a similar concord of capital and labor the legislative enactment of industrial democracy including profit-sharing, but with the reservation that the bonuses be given the employees in lump sums at the end of the year, so that they might be saved and not squandered. Testimony before the United States Commission on Industrial Relations in 1915, under the questioning of the commissioners, revealed, however, certain discrepancies between his creed and his policy. He knew very little about actual labor conditions in his plants, not even the approximate wage rate; he was an adherent of the open shop and individual bargaining; he had not instituted any of the industrial-democracy features in his own plants. Nevertheless, his attitude toward labor was undoubtedly liberal for his day. He continued also the tradition his father had set with regard to charity and philanthropy. Many of his charities were anonymous. Among his philanthropies that received notice were the Daniel and Florence Guggenheim Foundation, "to promote through charitable and benevolent activities the well-being of mankind throughout the world"; the subsidizing of free band concerts in New York City; and the Daniel Guggenheim Fund for the Promotion of Aeronautics. The last-named fund, aggregating four or five million dollars, did much to shift the emphasis in aviation from stunt flights to the development of safe and unsensational flying, and thus to make passenger traffic safe and commercially feasible. Guggenheim was married on July 22, 1884, to Florence Schloss. They had three children. He was a member of Congregation Emanu-El, in New York, and for many years a trustee. As he neared the age of seventy, he gradually turned over the management of his affairs to the younger of his two sons, and in his seventy-fifth year he died at "Hempstead House," his country home near Port Washington, Long Island.

[E. P. Lyle, in *Hampton's Mag.*, Feb.–Apr. 1910; F. E. Richter, "The Copper-Mining Industry in the U. S.," *Quart. Jour. of Econ.*, Feb., Aug. 1927; *Fortune*, July 1930; *Liberty*, Nov. 8, 1930; *Bull. Pan-American Union*, June 1929; *Time*, July 28, 1930; "Report of the U. S. Commission on Industrial Relations" (11 vols., 1916), *Sen. Doc. No. 415*, 64 Cong., 1 Sess., vol. VIII; and *Annals Am. Acad. Pol. and Social Sci.*, May 1915; *Commonweal*, Nov. 13, 1929, p. 34; *N. Y. Times*, Sept. 29, 1930.]

M. L.

GUGGENHEIM, MEYER (Feb. 1, 1828–Mar. 15, 1905), financier, was born in Langnau, Switzerland, the son of Simon Guggenheim. He came to the United States at nineteen, meeting and courting on the long voyage his future wife, Barbara Myers. It is said that he started his career by selling shoelaces on the streets of Philadelphia, and then engaged in small merchandising of various sorts. He manufactured stove-polish and lye, then set up a store selling coffee, spices and other commodities for the housewife; finally he invested in railroad stock. Twenty-five years of persistent business effort, in which his acquisitive and inquisitive faculties were happily blended, led in 1872 to the establishment of the firm of Guggenheim & Pulaski, importing chiefly Swiss embroideries. The firm was reorganized in 1881 as M. Guggenheim's Sons, and the four eldest sons, grown to maturity, were taken into the business. It was part of the Guggenheim scheme of things that each son was to be carefully prepared by education and apprenticeship for his rôle in the firm—a process that created eventually one of the most integrated dynastic enterprises American business has seen.

In 1887 a sudden change occurred in Meyer Guggenheim's career which destined his three younger sons to an apprenticeship in smelting instead of embroideries and caused even the first four ultimately to transfer their allegiance to the new enterprise. Through some friends in Philadelphia who owned two Colorado mines—the "A. Y." and the "Minnie"—and wished to sell them, he grew interested in copper mining. He sent one of his younger sons, Benjamin, to Leadville to investigate the mines and Benjamin reported them to be full of water. Guggenheim then made the trip himself. Although the little man from Philadelphia, with the long whiskers parted in the middle, was ridiculed by the hardened veterans of mining, he decided to venture his money. After that decision he was led by the peculiar logic of one commitment after another to throw his entire fortune into mining ventures.

It required but a short time to convince him, however, that although speculative profits might lurk somewhere in a mining bonanza, the field for certain profits and systematic factory organization lay not in the mining but in the processing of metals. Most of the profits of mining, he felt, went to the smelters. He bought $80,000 worth of stock in the Globe Smelter and put his sixth son, Simon, to work at sixty dollars a month as a time-keeper on the slag dumps to learn the business. In 1888 with Edward R. Holden, one of the Globe partners, he formed the Philadelphia Smelting & Refining Company, and built a smelter at Pueblo, Colo., at a cost of $1,250,000. His quick intelligence saw that while competition among smelters for the American ores was severe, the whole product of the Mexican mines, which had to pay heavy freight charges to be shipped to Colorado, could be captured by building a plant in Mexico. In 1891 he sent his son William to Monterey to build the second Guggenheim smelter and the first complete silver-lead smelter in Mexico, and three years later he built another at Aguascalientes, fitting out both plants with a considerable array of welfare devices for the employees. Still dissatisfied because of his dependence on the process of refining, he built a refinery at Perth Amboy, N. J., placing his son Benjamin in charge. He had by this time become so deeply involved in the metallurgical industries that he gave up the importation and merchandising of embroideries and threw all his resources into his new venture. At an age when most men are planning to retire he found himself at the height of his powers. To his abilities must be added, as perhaps his chief resource, the possession of seven sons whom he had trained in business tactics and on whom he could rely—a resource which enabled him to adapt the measure of personal control inherent in individual enterprise to the demands of large-scale enterprise and industrial integration.

The fall in the value of silver in 1893 led to a tightening of conditions in the smelting industry and the formation of the American Smelting & Refining Company. As one of the leaders of the industry Guggenheim had been invited to join the consolidation. He had refused, not so much from public-spirited scruples against a "trust," as from his unwillingness to surrender that direct equivalence between one's business abilities and one's profits that constitutes the psychological basis of individual enterprise. He would not merge his efforts with those of a trust unless he could control it. His demands for control seemed unreasonable, and since they were unconditional the American Smelting & Refining Company, when it was formed in 1899 among eighteen of the largest smelting and refining plants of the country, did not include the Guggenheims. In fact, they were the only company of first importance not included. Guggenheim's decision was crucial, since his defeat in the competitive struggle with the Trust would mean absorption on the conqueror's terms. The struggle that followed brought out every bit of business wisdom that he and his sons possessed. The Guggenheim strategy was to make alliances with the mine-operators, a measure indispensable to a smelting company if it would keep its plants supplied with enough ore for economical processing. The execution of this strategy was considerably aided by the inherent suspicion which the fact of trusthood cast upon the Trust from the very start and which it was not very successful in allaying. Guggenheim capitalized immediately every slip that the Trust made in its relations with the public. When the Trust lowered the price that it paid the mine operators for the gold content of the ore from twenty dollars an ounce to nineteen, Guggenheim offered twenty and eventually forced his competitors to follow suit. When Colorado passed an eight-hour law and the Trust closed down some of its plants as a result, Guggenheim ran his under the new arrangement, although the old conditions were later restored. He helped mine owners over financial difficulties, giving them loans or advances or subscribing to their stock. He managed thus to obtain their friendship and eventually their contracts. Any mine operator disgruntled at the treatment accorded him by the Smelter Trust found the Guggenheims ready to take over his contract. The most important act of the Guggenheims in entrenching themselves permanently in the control of sources of ore supply, however, was the formation in 1899 of the Guggenheim Exploration Company. This new company served a unique function, combining in itself the characteristics of prospector, engineer, promoter, and financial backer. Every new discovery of ore in any part of the world brought a Guggenheim representative to the spot, ready to finish the prospecting, construct the engineering works, or manage a flotation of stock.

Through these means the Guggenheims were so successful in capturing more than their proportionate share of the ore supply for smelting that the Trust finally surrendered in 1901. It offered to absorb the Guggenheim properties under such terms that control by the Guggenheims was assured. It paid them $45,200,000 in stock, which was worth $36,000,000 in market valuation. To effect this it increased its own capital stock from $65,000,000 to $100,000,000. The purchase on the market of additional stock to the nominal value of $6,000,000 gave the Guggenheims control of the company. One of the sons, Daniel [*q.v.*], became chairman of the executive committee and another a member;

four of them sat on the board of directors. Meyer Guggenheim had accomplished his work and had founded his dynasty securely. His sons, under the leadership of Daniel, carried on in the management of the American Smelting & Refining Company the business strategy they had learned from him, and followed also his example of philanthropy in aiding the hospitals and charities of Philadelphia and New York. His death occurred in his seventy-eighth year, at Palm Beach, Fla.

[E. P. Lyle, in *Hampton's Mag.*, Feb.–Apr. 1910, the source for subsequent articles in periodicals; *Fortune*, July 1930; *Liberty*, Nov. 8, 1930; F. E. Richter, "The Copper-Mining Industry in the U. S.," *Quart. Jour. of Econ.*, Feb., Aug. 1927; W. R. Ingalls, *Lead and Zinc in the U. S.* (1908); "Capital and Labor Employed in the Mining Industry," *Report of the Industrial Commission*, XII (1901), esp. 294–305, giving the testimony of the manager of the Guggenheims' Pueblo smelter; obituaries in *Am. Hebrew*, Mar. 24, 1905; *N. Y. Herald*, Mar. 17, 1905.] M. L.

GUIGNAS, LOUIS IGNACE [See GUIGNAS, MICHEL, 1681–1752].

GUIGNAS, MICHEL (Jan. 22, 1681–Feb. 6, 1752), missionary to the Sioux Indians, was a native of Aquitaine, where he was born at Condom in the diocese of Auch. At the age of twenty-one he entered the Jesuit order and in 1716 was sent to reinforce the mission work in New France, which was languishing for lack of new men. After a year's initiation into the difficulties of labor among the Indians, Guignas was sent to the mission at Mackinac, the entrepôt for the western fur trade and the rendezvous of traders and Indians from all the northern regions. One large tribe had never been reached, that of the Sioux, on the headwaters of the Mississippi. In 1727 it was determined by the governor of New France to found a post and a mission in this region and Guignas was one of the two missionaries chosen for this difficult task. Careful preparations were made for the voyage and the missionaries were furnished with astronomical instruments to take observations. Leaving Mackinac Aug. 1, 1727, the expedition passed to the Mississippi by the well-known Fox-Wisconsin route and ascending the great river, built Fort Beauharnois on the northwest side of Lake Pepin, near the present Frontenac, Minn. The missionaries named their mission St. Michel Archange. Guignas was the diarist of the expedition and described the adventures of the party with a lively pen (*Collections of the State Historical Society of Wisconsin*, XVII, 22–28). The next year the garrison was obliged to evacuate the fort because of a French invasion of the Fox country. On Oct. 15, 1728, Guignas and several of the officers and soldiers were captured below the Wisconsin River and kept prisoners for five months during which time they had "much to suffer and everything to fear." Finally Guignas escaped to the Illinois country and recuperated among his brethren at the Kaskaskia mission. Nothing daunted by this experience, he again accepted an appointment to the Sioux country in 1731 when Godefroy de Linctot went to restore the Sioux post. For five years the garrison remained at Fort Trempealeau in Wisconsin, so remote that in 1735 Guignas's colleagues wrote that he had not been heard from for so long it was feared he had been captured and burned. In 1736 the fort was removed to Lake Pepin where Father Guignas had a notable garden. From here he and the French garrison were driven the next year by a revolt of the Sioux; they retreated by way of Lake Superior to Mackinac.

After all these adventures Guignas in 1740 retired to Quebec where he spent the remainder of his life, acting as prefect in 1749. Naturally gentle, he showed uncommon courage in danger, not for a brief moment, but over long periods of time. He was influential with the Indians, who respected him for his bravery and good sense. He did not make many converts among the Sioux, however. His chief ministration was to the soldiers and officers of his posts, who, distant from civilization, appreciated the cultured presence, good advice, and restraining influence of the missionary.

[The chief sources for Guignas's career are the notices in *The Jesuit Relations* (R. G. Thwaites's ed., vol. LXVIII, 1900, p. 329). The French documents in *Wis. Hist. Colls.*, vol. XVII (1906), throw light on his Sioux experience. See also L. P. Kellogg, "Fort Beauharnois," in *Minn. Hist.*, Sept. 1927. J. G. Shea, in *Early Voyages up and down the Mississippi* (1861), says he signed his name Louis Ignace; the Jesuit Records, however, mention him as Michel.] L. P. K.

GUILD, CURTIS (Jan. 13, 1827–Mar. 12, 1911), journalist, author, born in Boston, Mass., was the son of Curtis and Charlotte Louisa (Hodges) Guild and was descended directly from John Guild who emigrated from England to Massachusetts in 1636 and settled in Dedham. His father, who was graduated from Harvard in 1822, had been a prosperous merchant but underwent business reverses; consequently the son, after being prepared at English High School, could not enter college, but became a clerk in the shipping house of Barnard, Adams & Company. At twenty he joined the staff of the Boston *Journal*, transferring in 1849 to the *Evening Traveller*, where he was admitted to partnership in 1856. He had meanwhile become a contributor to the *Knickerbocker Magazine*. He showed himself to be an enterprising journalist and devised, among other things, a display bulletin for his paper. In 1857 he effected a merger of the *Boston Evening Traveller,* the *Boston Daily Atlas,* the *Daily Evening Telegraph,* and the *Boston Chronicle* under the name of the *Boston Morning Traveller* and *Evening Traveller,* with Samuel Bowles [*q.v.*] as editor-in-chief. The enterprise was short-lived, however. Bowles left after a few months and in 1858 the project failed, leaving Guild saddled with debts. On Jan. 1, 1859, he reëstablished himself as the manager and editor-in-chief of the *Commercial Bulletin,* which he described as "a most sensational novelty," giving tabulated stock quotations, reports of markets, and general banking news. It was immediately successful and at various periods was enlarged until it grew to be an influential paper. Guild remained with it until 1898 and came to be recognized as an authority of national reputation on financial matters. His lighter journalistic ventures appeared in book form. *Over the Ocean* (1869) was a compilation of letters which he wrote for the *Bulletin* during a European trip in 1867. It was followed by *Abroad Again* (1877); *Britons and Muscovites* (1888), dealing with experiences in Russia; *A Chat about Celebrities* (1897); and a volume of verse, *From Sunrise to Sunset* (1894).

Guild was well known in Boston as an antiquarian. He organized the Bostonian Society in 1881, was for many years its president, and was a leader in movements for the preservation of such institutions as the old State House and its Common. Familiar with local history, he had a store of quaint anecdotes and entertaining reminiscences and was a felicitous raconteur. The legend under his portrait in the Bostonian Society aptly states: "He loved his Boston as few men do." He collected books, especially first editions, and was a member and president of the Club of Odd Volumes. He was also a member of the New England Historic Genealogical Society and of the Authors' Club of Boston. He was married, on Sept. 22, 1858, to Sarah C. Cobb, daughter of David W. and Abby (Crocker) Cobb, and grand-daughter of Gen. David Cobb, one of Washington's aides. He had two sons, Curtis [*q.v.*] and Courtenay, both graduates of Harvard. Guild was a courtly gentleman, tactful, dignified, and witty, with a pride in his native city and a keen sense of public duty.

[Edwin M. Bacon, memoir in *Proc. Bostonian Soc.,* 1912; *Who's Who in America,* 1910-11; Chas. Burleigh, *Geneal. and Hist. of the Guild, Guile, and Gile Family* (1887); *New Eng. Hist. and Geneal. Reg.,* supp. to issue of Apr. 1912; *Boston Transcript* and *Boston Herald,* Mar. 13, 1911; *Commercial Bull.,* Mar. 18, 1911.]

C. M. F.

GUILD, CURTIS (Feb. 2, 1860–Apr. 6, 1915), governor of Massachusetts, soldier, was born in Boston, Mass., the son of Curtis [*q.v.*] and Sarah Crocker (Cobb) Guild. He was educated at Miss Lewis's School, in Roxbury, the Chauncy Hall School, and at Harvard College, where he graduated with highest honors in 1881. He had served as class orator as well as editor of the *Crimson* and the *Lampoon.* After a tour of Europe, he went through every department of the *Commercial Bulletin,* the financial newspaper founded by his father, and was made a partner in 1884. In 1902, upon the death of his uncle, he became the sole owner and editor. Having been an officer in the Harvard Rifle Corps, in 1891 he joined Troop A of the Massachusetts Volunteer Militia and was elected second lieutenant May 7, 1895. In 1897 he was appointed to the staff of Gov. Roger Wolcott with the rank of brigadier-general. On the day after the blowing up of the *Maine* (Feb. 15, 1898), Guild filed his name as a volunteer in the expected war with Spain and was shortly sent by the Governor on a special mission to Washington to ascertain what was to be required of Massachusetts. In April, after the declaration of war, he became adjutant of the 6th Cavalry, with the rank of first lieutenant, and was promoted lieutenant-colonel and inspector-general, VII Army Corps, later being made inspector-general of the Department of Havana. In these capacities he inaugurated a system of weekly inspection reports, helped break up the "fever camp" at Miami, Fla., prepared camp sites at Savannah, Ga., and reformed slaughter-house practices in Havana. His record won him the commendation of the inspector-general of the army and of the War Department.

Guild entered politics as president of the Republican State Convention in 1895. He was a delegate-at-large to the Republican National Convention of 1896, was made one of its vice-presidents, and was active in securing a gold plank in the platform. He was a campaign speaker in both 1896 and 1900 and was founder and first president of the Massachusetts Republican Club in 1901. He was elected, Nov. 4, 1902, lieutenant-governor of Massachusetts on the ticket with John L. Bates. In 1905 he was elected governor by a plurality of 22,558 votes and was reëlected for two additional terms. As governor he interested himself in labor legislation, especially in behalf of women and children, and urged measures providing for the better sanitation and ventilation of factories, a hospital for the feeble-minded, and new laws for the insane. It has been authoritatively stated that he initiated more legislation than any previous governor, and he unquestionably brought about many reforms. In 1908 he received seventy-five votes for the Republican nomination for vice-president. In 1910 he was sent by appointment of President Taft as special ambassador to the Mexican Centennial, and, on July 21, 1911, as ambassador to Russia. He retired to private life in 1913, after the inauguration of President Woodrow Wilson. He had married, on June 1, 1892, Charlotte Howe Johnson, of Boston. In 1908 he was made a Grand Officer of the Crown of Italy in recognition of legislation effected by him for the protection of immigrants from fraudulent bankers, and in 1909 the University of Geneva, at its 350th Jubilee, gave him the degree of S.T.D. for "services in the promotion of public morality." He also received the Grand Cordon of the Order of St. Alexander Nevski from the Czar of Russia. Guild was a member of the Massachusetts Historical Society, the Society of Colonial Wars, the Order of Foreign Wars, the Sons of the American Revolution, and was an occasional contributor to magazines. He was one of the most efficient and popular governors in the history of Massachusetts.

[Wm. R. Thayer, memoirs in *Proc. Mass. Hist. Soc.*, vol. L (1917), and *Harvard Grads.' Mag.*, June 1915; *Twenty-Fifth Anniversary Report . . . of the Class of 1881 of Harvard Coll.* (1906); Chas. Burleigh, *Geneal. and Hist. of the Guild, Guile, and Gile Family* (1887); *Who's Who in America*, 1914–15; *Boston Transcript*, Apr. 7, 1915; *Commercial Bull.*, Apr. 10, 1915.]

C. M. F.

GUILD, REUBEN ALDRIDGE (May 4, 1822–May 13, 1899), librarian, was born in West Dedham, Mass., the second of the eleven children of Reuben and Olive (Morse) Guild, and the sixth in descent from John Guild, who emigrated from England to Massachusetts in 1636 and settled in Dedham. His father began life as a blacksmith and became a carriage maker, proprietor of a livery stable and omnibus line, undertaker, and superintendent of the village cemetery. For forty years a deacon of the Unitarian church, he yielded at the age of eighty-four to the Baptist principles of his children and was rebaptized by immersion in the Great Pond at Dedham. The younger Guild's first employment was in a variety store opposite his home. Later he was clerk for two years in a Boston drygoods house, attended academies in Wrentham and Worcester, and, since his teachers had all happened to be Brown graduates, entered Brown University. Upon his graduation in 1847 he was appointed assistant librarian and was promoted the next March to librarian in succession to his former teacher, Charles Coffin Jewett, who had been called to the Smithsonian Institution. Guild was already as deeply rooted in Brown University as his ancestors had been in Dedham. Knowing himself settled for life, he married Jane Clifford Hunt on Dec. 17, 1849. By giving readers free access to the shelves, then an almost unheard-of procedure, he did his full share to make Brown a nursery of scholars. He took a prominent part in the Librarians' Convention of 1853 and was one of the founders in 1876 of the American Library Association. His *Librarian's Manual* (1858) was a standard work for many years. In the autumn of 1877 he traveled in England and Scotland. One of the memorable days of his life was Feb. 16, 1878, when the new University Library, made possible by the bequest of John Carter Brown, was dedicated. The next morning he solemnly carried a handsome copy of Bagster's *Polyglot Bible* from the old library and deposited it as Book One on Shelf One in Alcove One of the new building. Subsequently, he catalogued almost unassisted the 48,000 volumes housed there. The warm friend of all Brown men, he was secretary for fifteen years of the alumni association. For seven years he served as a member of the common council of Providence and for fifteen years as a member and secretary of the school committee. He grew learned in the history of the University and of the state in which it is the chief institution of higher education. For the *Publications of the Narragansett Club* he wrote "A Biographical Introduction to the Writings of Roger Williams" (1 ser., vol. I, 1866) and edited "Letter of John Cotton, and Roger Williams's Reply" (*Ibid.*), and Williams's "Queries of Highest Consideration" (*Ibid.*, vol. II, 1867). He was also editor of *Literary and Theological Addresses of Alva Woods* (1868) and William R. Staples's *Rhode Island in the Continental Congress* (1870), and author of *Life, Times, and Correspondence of James Manning* (1864), *History of Brown University* (1867), *History of St. John's Commandery* (1875), *Chaplain Smith and the Baptists; or, Life, Journals, Letters, and Addresses of the Rev. Hezekiah Smith, D.D.* (1885), *Early History of Brown University, 1756–1791* (1897), and of numerous historical and biographical sketches. He was active in the work of the Baptist church. He continued to live in Providence after his retirement in 1893. At his death in his seventy-eighth year he was survived by his wife and four of his six children.

[Chas. Burleigh, *Geneal. and Hist. of the Guild, Guile, and Gile Family* (1887); *Biog. Cyc. of Representative Men of R. I.* (1881); *Proc. Am. Antiq. Soc.*, n.s., XIII (1900), 126–30; *Hist. Cat. Brown Univ. 1764–1904* (1905); *Memories of Brown* (1909), ed. by

R. P. Brown and others; W. C. Bronson, *Hist. of Brown Univ. 1764–1914* (1914); *Providence Daily Jour.*, May 15, 1899.] G. H. G.

GUILFORD, NATHAN (July 19, 1786–Dec. 18, 1854), Ohio educator, the eldest son of Dr. Jonas and Lydia (Hobbs) Guilford, was born in Spencer, Worcester County, Mass. He was descended from William Guilford who emigrated to America about 1648 and settled first in Massachusetts. He attended Leicester Academy, graduated in 1812 from Yale College, and after graduation conducted for a few months a classical school in Worcester. He then entered the law office of Francis Blake of Worcester with the intention of fitting himself for the legal profession. In the fall of 1814 he moved to Lexington, Ky., and during the next year and a half devoted part of his time to teaching. Two years later, while residing in Alexandria, Ky., he formed a law partnership with Amos Kendall [*q.v.*]. They decided to establish themselves in Georgetown, Ky., but in November of that year (1816) Kendall was compelled to withdraw on account of his newspaper and other political activities. Guilford moved to Cincinnati, passed the bar examination in December 1816, and began to practise. On Aug. 29, 1819, he was married to Eliza Wheeler Farnsworth of Woodstock, Vt. His interest in education led him to join with Samuel Lewis and others in advocating free education. In order to advance his ideas Guilford and his brother George established a publishing house with which he was actively associated until about 1840. He also edited for seven years (1818–25) an educational almanac under the pseudonym of Solomon Thrifty. In addition to the usual information found in such works, *Solomon Thrifty's Almanac* contained on each page some statement emphasizing the value of education and the need of public schools in Ohio.

During the winter of 1821–22, Gov. Allen Trimble appointed seven commissioners to devise and report upon a common-school plan for Ohio. Although Guilford was appointed a member of the committee he refused to cooperate with the other members on the ground that their plans were inadequate. Instead in 1822 he published *A Letter on Free Education* urging the establishment of schools supported by general taxation. Since the Assembly was unwilling to risk advanced legislation, an appeal was made to the people and in 1824 Guilford was elected to the state Senate on this platform. With the assistance of Ephraim Cutler of Marietta, he guided the legislature in its authorization, Feb. 5, 1825, of an assessment for educational purposes, of one-half mill on the value of all taxable property, despite the strenuous opposition to the law by the larger tax payers of Cincinnati, the proprietors of private schools, and by the group it was especially designed to assist, namely, the poorer classes whose children were known as charity students. He then devoted himself to the promotion of legislation for the erection of the free public schools of Cincinnati and in February 1829 succeeded in securing the passage of such a law. The schools were placed under the control of a board of trustees, later called the board of education. The earliest meetings of the board were held in Guilford's home and he served as a member until his resignation, July 1832.

Compelled by his educational activities to withdraw gradually from the practice of law, Guilford devoted more attention as a publisher to the improvement of school textbooks. In 1831 he brought out *The Western Spelling Book,* styled "an Improvement on the American Spelling Book, by Noah Webster"; and in 1836 he published *The Juvenile Arithmetic,* which was extensively used. Later, from 1843 to 1847, he was the owner and editor of the *Cincinnati Daily Atlas,* a Whig journal. In 1850 a special act of the legislature authorized the election by popular vote of a superintendent of public schools for Cincinnati. Guilford was elected and held office from April 1850 until June 1852 with an annual salary of five hundred dollars. In his first report he recommended a revision of the textbooks and the classification of schools, and vigorously attacked the verbatim recitation and the strict disciplinary methods then in vogue. Though he was a man of great kindness he was said to be a confirmed deist and lost his position as a result of an argument which arose over the question of the use of the Bible in the schools. In 1854 he was elected city magistrate and was holding that office at the time of his death.

[F. B. Dexter, *Biog. Sketches of the Grads. of Yale Coll.*, vol. VI (1912); I. M. Martin, *Hist. of the Schools of Cincinnati* (1900); J. B. Shotwell, *Hist. of the Schools of Cincinnati* (1902); Wm. T. Coggeshall, memoir in *Am. Jour. of Educ.*, Mar. 1860; *Autobiog. of Amos Kendall* (1872), ed. by Wm. Stickney; Nathan Guilford, Jr., *The Guilford Family in America* (p. p. 1898); H. M. Guilford, *Guilford Geneal.* (1918); *Cincinnati Gazette,* Dec. 20, 1854.] R. C. McG.

GUINEY, LOUISE IMOGEN (Jan. 7, 1861–Nov. 2, 1920), essayist, poet, was born in the Roxbury section of Boston, the only child of Patrick Robert and Janet Margaret (Doyle) Guiney, and was of Irish, Scottish, and English ancestry. Her father, born Jan. 15, 1835, at Parkstown, County Tipperary, was a lawyer with literary tastes. As an officer of the 9th Massachusetts Infantry he took part in thirty-six battles of the Civil War, was wounded desperately at the Wilderness, and was mustered out a brigadier-general by brevet with his health permanently shattered. Removing his hat one March day in 1877, he knelt in the street, crossed himself, and died, leaving his daughter an imperishable image of a brave and noble soul. The memory of him moulded her character, his religious devotion strengthening her devotion, his poetic aspirations flowering in her lyrics, his valor transmuted in her into a spiritual heroism that sustained her through a life of privation and disappointment. Upon her graduation in 1879 from Elmhurst, the convent school of the Order of the Sacred Heart in Providence, R. I., she returned home to eke out her mother's slender resources by hack writing and research. Her first book of verse, *Songs at the Start* (1884), and her first essays, collected in *Goose Quill Papers* (1885), brought her friends in Boston literary circles, and thereafter she wrote fairly steadily and from time to time brought out a small volume of essays or lyrics. Though steadfastly loyal to Hazlitt and Tennyson, her first models, she found in Cavalier England her country of the mind, and in its poetry and biography she became ultimately as learned as any one of her generation. Her own best work—minor, but true and exquisite—is to be found in *A Little English Gallery* (1894), studies of Lady Danvers, Henry Vaughan, George Farquhar, Topham Beauclerk, Bennet Langton, and William Hazlitt, precise in scholarship and opulent in sympathy; in *Patrins* (1897; 1901), the most carefully wrought of her familiar essays; and in *Happy Ending* (1909; enlarged edition, 1927), which contains all of her verse that, after years of revision, she was willing to preserve. She was postmistress of Auburndale, Mass., 1894–97, and later found employment in the catalogue division of the Boston Public Library. Two visits to England had made her long for the time when she might live there, and in 1901 the opportunity came. Thereafter her home was in Oxford and her days divided, rather unequally, between laborious study in the Bodleian Library and foot tours along the Thames or into the Cotswolds. Life so ordered was grateful to her, for she "loved grubbing for facts" (*Letters,* II, 246); her letters to her numerous friends are cheerful and even gay; but deafness, which had begun in her young womanhood, grew steadily oppressive; during the war years she found it increasingly difficult to live; her practice of stinting herself of food and coals in order to buy precious books told ultimately on her health. She experienced, too, the pain of seeing some beloved projects anticipated by the publications of luckier scholars. Her two most ambitious undertakings, a biographical and critical study of Henry Vaughan and a great anthology of Catholic poets from Sir Thomas More to Alexander Pope, enriched by elaborate biographical and bibliographical notes, remained incomplete at her death, which occurred at Chipping Campden, Gloucestershire, after an illness of several weeks. She was buried in Wolvercote Cemetery near Oxford.

[See Alice Brown, *Louise Imogen Guiney* (1921); E. M. Tenison, "A Bibliography of L. I. Guiney," *Bookman's Jour.,* Dec. 1922, Jan. and Mar. 1923, and *Louise Imogen Guiney: Her Life and Works 1861–1920* (1923); *Letters of Louise Imogen Guiney* (2 vols., 1926), ed. by Grace Guiney; numerous unpublished letters, 1883–1908, and holographs of her poems in Louise Chandler Moulton Papers (Lib. of Cong., MSS. Div.); "Letters to Dora Sigerson (Mrs. Clement K. Shorter) and to Mr. Shorter," ed. by Michael Earls, S. J., *Bookman,* Apr. and Aug. 1922, Feb. 1923 (including some not repub. by Grace Guiney); "Letters from Oxford," *Commonweal,* May 7, 14, 1930; J. B. Rittenhouse, "The Charm of L. I. Guiney," *Bookman,* Feb. 1921; Katherine Brégy, chap. in *Poets and Pilgrims* (1925); Edmund Gosse, "A Belated Cavalier," *Silhouettes* (1925); Grace Guiney, "L. I. Guiney: A Comment and Some Letters," *Catholic World,* Aug. 1925; Sister M. Agnes Alma, "American Ideals and L. I. Guiney," *Ibid.,* Aug. 1928. For her father see also: F. B. Heitman, *Hist. Reg. and Dict. U. S. Army* (1903); *Boston Transcript,* Mar. 22, 1877; J. B. Cullen, *The Story of the Irish in Boston* (rev. ed., 1893).]

G. H. G.

GUITERAS, JUAN (Jan. 4, 1852–Oct. 28, 1925), physician, was born in Matanzas, Cuba, to Eusebio Guiteras and Josefa Gener, both from families prominent in Cuba's struggle for independence. He received his early education at the Colegio La Empresa in Matanzas, directed by his uncle, Antonio Guiteras. Following his graduation in 1867, he took up the study of medicine first at the University of Havana and then at the University of Pennsylvania where he obtained his degree of M.D. in 1873. After an interneship in the Philadelphia Hospital, he was appointed to the attending staff of that hospital and pursued the practice of medicine for the following six years. In 1879 he was designated by the United States government as a member of the Havana Yellow Fever Commission. This commission was headed by Dr. Stanford Chaillé of New Orleans and included Maj. George M. Sternberg [*q.v.*] of the army. One of the charges put upon the commission was a study of the pathology of yellow fever and this work was assigned to Guiteras. In 1880 he entered the Marine Hospital Service, in which he served up to 1889, reaching the grade of past-assistant surgeon. During 1884–88 he held the chair of clinical medicine in the Medical School of South Carolina and in 1889 he was appointed to the chair of pathology in the University of Pennsylvania, holding this position until his return to

Cuba in 1899. During the Cuban war for independence (1895) he headed the Revolutionary Committee, in Philadelphia, and his home and his purse were open to his needy compatriots. Following the outbreak of the Spanish-American War he went to Cuba as acting assistant surgeon attached to the staff of General Shafter, and in this capacity participated in the Santiago campaign. After the occupation of Havana by the American troops he was assigned to the Las Animas hospital where all cases of yellow fever were treated. He was designated a member of a board for the diagnosis of the disease, on which he was associated with Maj. W. C. Gorgas [*q.v.*] of the army, Dr. Carlos J. Finlay [*q.v.*], and Dr. Antonio Albertini. This duty brought him into intimate contact with the army board, headed by Maj. Walter Reed [*q.v.*], which was engaged in experimental work upon the transmission of yellow fever. The finding of that board that the disease was transmitted by a mosquito now classed in the genus *Aedes*, was confirmed by Guiteras the following year through independent experiments conducted at Las Animas. Following the methods of the Reed board he succeeded in producing the disease in eight subjects, unhappily with three deaths. Coincident with this work he was carrying out investigations upon the feasibility of immunization by a vaccine. It took but a short time to show that vaccination was not applicable to prevention of this disease. In 1900 he was appointed professor of pathology and tropical medicine in the University of Havana, a position which he filled for over twenty years. The Palma government, with due regard to his talents, named him a member of the Higher Board of Health and director of Las Animas hospital. He was director of public health in Cuba from 1909 to 1921 and president of the National Board of Health and secretary of Public Health and Charities from 1921 to the time of his death. In 1916 he was appointed a member of the yellow-fever commission of the International Health Board of the Rockefeller Foundation.

Guiteras made many valuable contributions to the knowledge of tropical medicine. He is credited with being the first to discover the presence of the *Filaria bancrofti* in the United States and of hookworm disease, yaws, and chappa in Cuba. He wrote the first adequate description of the last-mentioned disease (*Chappa: Acropatia Mutilante,* 1904). After his notable work in confirmation of the mosquito transmission of yellow fever, his principal contribution to the knowledge of that disease was his recognition of the great importance of infantile cases. He pointed out the frequency of the disease in young children and the part these cases played in maintaining its endemicity and in producing immunity to the disease in the adult population of Havana. Among the many Cuban and American medical societies to which he belonged were the American Academy of Public Health and the Association of American Physicians. He wrote extensively for medical periodicals, his earlier contributions being mainly on the subject of yellow fever. His later writings covered a variety of subjects relating to public health and tropical medicine. He founded *La Revista de Medicina Tropical* in 1900 and acted as editor until 1906. He was married on May 5, 1883, to Dolores Gener of Matanzas, which was his home at the time of his death.

[Biographical sketches in: *Rev. Med. Cubana* (Havana), Feb. 1907; *Sanidad y Beneficia* (Havana), 1921; *Who's Who in America,* 1922–23; W. B. Parker, *Cubans of Today* (1919); obituaries in: *Jour. Am. Medic. Asso.,* Nov. 7, 1925; *Lancet* (London), Nov. 21, 1925; *Am. Jour. Pub. Health,* Feb. 1926; *Outlook,* Nov. 11, 1925; *N. Y. Times,* Oct. 29, 30, 1925.] J. M. P.

GULICK, JOHN THOMAS (Mar. 13, 1832–Apr. 14, 1923), missionary, naturalist, writer on evolution, the son of Rev. Peter Johnson and Fanny Hinckley (Thomas) Gulick, and the brother of Luther Halsey Gulick, 1828–1891 [*q.v.*], was born at Waimea, Kauai, Hawaiian Islands, where his father was one of the early American missionaries. The son attended Punahou Academy, Honolulu, and the preparatory department of the University of the City of New York. For a short time in 1849–50 he was a miner in California. He continued his education at Williams College, graduating in 1859, and then studied at the Union Theological Seminary, 1859–61. In 1862 he went to Japan. At Kanagawa, near Tokyo, he supported himself by photography and school teaching, at the same time trying to induce the American Board of Commissioners for Foreign Missions to begin work there. In 1864 he was appointed by the Board missionary to Peking, and the following year he was transferred to Kalgan, North China, a post he occupied until 1875. He then returned to Japan where he continued his work in the mission field, especially in Kobe and Osaka, until 1899. Returning to the United States, he spent the years from 1900 to 1905 at Oberlin, Ohio, where he studied problems relating to evolution and elaborated his most extensive work on that subject for the press.

Gulick's attention had been directed to evolution as early as 1851 and 1852, when he was engaged in collecting species of *Achatinellidæ* or land-snails on the island of Oahu, and he soon became widely known as a student of this group through his descriptions of many new Hawaiian species. His first evolutionary contribution, "On the Variation of Species as Related to their Geographical Distribution, Illustrated by the Achatinellinæ," appeared in *Nature,* July 18, 1872. This was followed by "Diversity of Evolution under one set of External Conditions," published in the *Journal of the Linnean Society* (London, vol. XI, 1873). Other essays on the formation of species through isolation and segregation followed, and the results of these studies concerning the factors of organic evolution were published from time to time in *Nature,* the *American Journal of Science,* and in the *Proceedings of the Boston Society of Natural History.*

Gulick held that nearly all evolution, as we now observe it, is divergent, through the influence of segregation. Portions of his theory of divergence were published in London in the Linnean Society's *Journal* (vol. XX, 1890), and in the United States in the annual report of the Smithsonian Institution for 1891. But the fullest exposition of this hypothesis is given in his contribution: *Evolution, Racial and Habitudinal,* issued by the Carnegie Institution (Publication No. 25, 1905). According to David Starr Jordan (*Science, post*) he was, in the details of his work, far ahead of his time. Even before he had read *The Origin of Species* (1859) he had reached the conclusion that "many genuine species had been derived from descent from one original stock or species." Throughout his life he retained the conviction that between scientific truth and religion there exists a complete harmony, so that he was at all times "a thoroughgoing Darwinian, as well as a Christian Missionary." In 1906 Gulick returned to Hawaii, devoting his later years to the study of social problems. He died in Honolulu, at the advanced age of ninety-one. He was twice married: first, on Sept. 3, 1864, in Hong Kong, to Emily de la Cour, who died in 1875; and, second, on May 31, 1880, to Frances A. Stevens of Osaka, Japan.

[Bibliographies of Gulick's writings on evolution may be found in the Carnegie publication already cited and in the *Cat. of Scientific Papers* (19 vols., 1869–1925), vols. III, VII, and XV, published by the Royal Soc. of London. Other sources of information include the *Honolulu Star-Bulletin,* Apr. 16, 1923; David Starr Jordan, article in *Science,* Dec. 21, 1923; *Obit. Record of Alumni of Williams Coll., 1923–24* (1924); J. M. Cattell and D. R. Brimhall, *Am. Men of Sci.* (1906); "John T. Gulick, A Contributor to Evolutionary Thought," by his son, Addison Gulick, in *Sci. Monthly,* Jan. 1924.]

F. T.

GULICK, LUTHER HALSEY (June 10, 1828–Apr. 8, 1891), missionary, was born at Honolulu, Hawaii, the eldest of the eight children of Rev. Peter Johnson and Fanny Hinckley (Thomas) Gulick. His boyhood was spent in Hawaii, but he was sent to the United States for his education and was graduated from the Medical College of the University of the City of New York in 1850. While a medical student he engaged in city mission work and was ordained to the Congregational ministry at the Broadway Tabernacle in October 1850. On Oct. 29, 1851, he married Louisa Lewis, of Brooklyn, N. Y., and the following month sailed from Boston for Micronesia as a medical missionary under the American Board of Commissioners for Foreign Missions. He did not reach the Caroline Islands until 1852, having stopped in Hawaii to act as chief organizer for the Hawaiian Mission Children's Society. He was stationed at Ponape and Ebon for some years, during which time he published *A Sermon on the Foolishness of Preaching* (1853) and a useful compilation of *Notes on the Grammar of the Ponape Dialect* (1858), reprinted in the *Journal of the American Oriental Society,* volume X (1872). From 1863 to 1870 he was secretary of the Hawaiian Evangelical Association, with general superintendence of its missions. In this capacity his economy of administration and ability as an organizer so impressed the American Board that he was chosen to inaugurate the Board's missions in the Roman Catholic Latin countries of southern Europe (1871). In Spain (1871–73) he recommended establishing the line of mission posts in the northern part of the country that is still maintained by the Board. In Italy (1873–74) he found conditions so unfavorable that upon his suggestion the Board withdrew its missions. He then inspected the stations in Turkey and Bohemia and returned to the United States to aid the Board in arousing interest in missionary work. In 1875 the American Bible Society sent Gulick to the Far East as its agent for the publishing and distribution of Bibles. He founded the Bible House at Yokohama, then turned his attention to China, where he enormously increased the circulation of Bibles by use of colporteurs working under missionary supervision. He edited the *Chinese Recorder and Missionary Journal* (1885–89) and founded the *Medical Missionary Journal.* He died at Springfield, Mass., at the age of sixty-two, after forty years of missionary service, the most distinguished member of a great missionary family.

[*Report of the Hawaiian Missionary Soc.,* 1852–62; *Ann. Report of the Hawaiian Evangelical Asso.,* 1863–70, 1891; *Ann. Report of the Am. Board of Commissioners for Foreign Missions,* 1872–74; *Bible Soc. Record,* 1876–87, Apr. 16, 1891; biographical sketch in the *Friend* (Honolulu), May 1891, reprinted in the *Chinese*

Recorder and Missionary Jour., July 1891; *Missionary Herald*, June 1891; D. MacGillivray, *A Century of Protestant Missions in China* (Shanghai, 1907); *Congreg. Year-Book*, 1892; *Springfield Daily Republican*, Apr. 9, 1891.] F. E. R.

GULICK, LUTHER HALSEY (Dec. 4, 1865–Aug. 13, 1918), specialist in physical education, author, was born in Honolulu, Hawaiian Islands, the fifth of the seven children of Luther Halsey Gulick [*q.v.*] and Louisa Lewis, missionaries. He entered the preparatory department of Oberlin College in 1880, but illness caused him to leave and in 1885 he became a student in the Sargent School of Physical Training, Cambridge, Mass. In 1886 he entered the Medical College of the University of the City of New York and three years later received the degree of M.D. He was married, on Aug. 30, 1887, to Charlotte Vetter of Hanover, N. H. Handicapped by heart trouble and severe headaches, Gulick became intensely interested in physical education and hygiene. He organized the physical training course in the Y. M. C. A. Training School, Springfield, Mass., in 1886, and continued as director until 1903. While engaged in this work he originated the triangle as the emblem of the Y. M. C. A., denoting the physical, social, and spiritual aims of the organization. It was there also that he devised, in collaboration with one of his students, James Naismith, the game of basketball. From 1887 to 1903 he also filled the position of secretary for the physical training department of the Y. M. C. A. International Committee. From 1900 to 1903 he was principal of the Pratt Institute High School, Brooklyn, N. Y., and for the next three years he served as director of physical training in the public schools of New York City. His two outstanding contributions to the New York public schools were the reorganization and coördination of physical education activities and instruction in hygiene, and the organization of the Public Schools Athletic League. In 1907 he organized the child hygiene department of the Russell Sage Foundation and served as director until 1913 when failing health compelled him to resign. After a few months of rest, though his health was but slightly improved, he cooperated with his wife in organizing the Camp Fire Girls movement, serving as president of the group for one year. The last five years of his life were devoted to writing and lecturing on physical education, hygiene, and dancing. He was a popular and stimulating writer and speaker and was always seeking new and better ways of educating the masses in matters of physical education, play, and hygiene.

Gulick filled many offices in organizations devoted to the subjects in which he was interested. He was chairman of the Physical Training Lecture Committee of the St. Louis Exposition, 1904; member of the American Olympic Games Committee, Athens, 1906, and London, 1908; delegate to the Second International Congress on School Hygiene, London, 1907; lecturer on hygiene, New York University, 1906–09; consultant, New York Hospital for Deformities and Joint Diseases, 1907; secretary, American Association for the Advancement of Physical Education, 1892–93; president, American Physical Education Association, 1903–06; organizing secretary, American School Hygiene Association, 1907; president, Public Schools Physical Training Society, 1905–08; and president, Playground Association of America, 1906–09. Besides filling many important offices in national organizations, he edited *Physical Education,* 1891–96; *Association Outlook,* 1897–1900; and the *American Physical Education Review,* 1901–03. His published works include the Gulick Hygiene Series; *Physical Measurements and How They Are Used* (1889); *Physical Education by Muscular Exercise* (1904); *The Efficient Life* (1907); *Mind and Work* (1908); *The Healthful Art of Dancing* (1910); and *Medical Inspection of Schools* (1907), in collaboration with Leonard P. Ayres.

Gulick was impulsive, independent, firm in his convictions, and always ready to defend them regardless of consequences. Born of missionary parents and engaged for many years in religious work, he was fervent in his religious beliefs, but he was liberal in his views and aroused much antagonism and criticism among the fundamentalists in the organization. He was blunt and forceful in the expression of his feelings, particularly when he felt that his opponents were insincere or were placing self-interest above principles. Although much weakened by long illness and pain, he accepted a call from the National War Council in the fall of 1917 to go to France to make a survey of the rapidly growing work of the Y. M. C. A. with the American Expeditionary Forces. He spent two months in France and on his return made a report on the kind of men needed and the training they should receive. This report and the help he gave in carrying out its recommendations greatly enhanced the service rendered by the Y. M. C. A. in France. He was so deeply stirred by what he saw in France that on the return trip he began the manuscript of his best book, *The Dynamic of Manhood* (1917). Unable to rally from the fatigue and overstrain of this trip, he retired to his camp in the Maine woods where he died a few months later. He was survived by his wife, three daughters, and one son.

[F. E. Leonard, *Pioneers of Modern Physical Training* (1915); *Am. Physical Educ. Rev.*, Oct. 1918; *Playground*, Oct. 1918; *Survey*, Aug. 24, 1918; *Boston Transcript* and *N. Y. Times*, Aug. 14, 1918.]

G. L. M.

GUMMERE, FRANCIS BARTON (Mar. 6, 1855–May 30, 1919), philologist, was born at Burlington, N. J., the son of Samuel James [*q.v.*] and Elizabeth Hooton (Barton) Gummere, and the grandson of John Gummere [*q.v.*]. Graduating from Haverford College in 1872, when he was but seventeen years old, he was clerk for a year in an iron foundry and read law for another year in a Philadelphia office before deciding to adopt the family profession of teaching. At Harvard University, where he went for an additional year of study, he came under the spell of Francis James Child [*q.v.*] and remained Child's disciple ever after. He took a second A.B., from Harvard, at the close of the academic year 1874–75 and his A.M. at the same time from Haverford. For the next few years he taught, as his father had done, in the Friends' School, Providence, R. I., and spent his long vacations in Europe. Then he went to Germany for several years of study at Leipzig, Berlin, Strassburg, and Freiburg, and took his Ph.D. at Freiburg in 1881 with an able dissertation on *The Anglo-Saxon Metaphor* (Halle, 1881), that completely upset Rudolf Heinzel's theory, then generally accepted, that Anglo-Saxon poetic style was based on Old Norse models. Subsequently, he was an instructor in Harvard, 1881–82, and headmaster of the Swain Free School in New Bedford, Mass., 1882–87, before entering on his life work at Haverford, where he was professor of English and German, 1887–1909, and professor of English literature from 1909 until his death. There he was completely happy and at home, and wisely declined to consider a call to the University of Chicago in 1895 and to Harvard in 1901. At Haverford he maintained the tradition of teaching established by his father and grandfather, giving courses in early English literature, Chaucer, Shakespeare, Milton, the popular ballads, and Goethe. Meanwhile he became known as a scholar throughout the United States and Northern Europe. He was a member of the American Philosophical Society and president in 1905 of the Modern Language Association of America, and delivered courses of lectures at Northwestern and the Johns Hopkins universities and at the University of California. In 1909 a group of his pupils published a volume of *Haverford Essays* in his honor. In 1907 he suffered a nervous breakdown and lost the use of his right eye, and the next year, while on a tramping expedition through the Virginia mountains, he seriously overtaxed his heart and was compelled thereafter to guard his health. His death ten years later was as unexpected, however, as it was sudden. Gummere was married, Sept. 14, 1882, to Amelia Smith Mott, daughter of Richard Field Mott of Burlington, N. J. She graduated from the Friends' School in Providence in 1878 and in later years produced several noteworthy books on the American Friends and edited the *Journal and Essays of John Woolman* (1922).

His books, besides the dissertation previously mentioned, are: *Handbook of Poetics* (1885); *Germanic Origins* (1892); *Old English Ballads* (1894); *The Beginnings of Poetry* (1901); *The Popular Ballad* (1907); *Lives of Great English Writers* (in collaboration with Walter Swain Hinchman, 1908); *The Oldest English Epic* (1909); *Democracy and Poetry* (1911). Of his shorter writings mention must be made of three articles on the ballad and primitive poetry in *Modern Philology* (June, Oct. 1903; Jan. 1904), his contributions to the Child Memorial Volume (Vol. V, 1896, of the Harvard *Studies and Notes in Philology and Literature*), and to the *Anniversary Papers by Colleagues and Pupils of George Lyman Kittredge* (1913), his edition of Peele's "Old Wives' Tale" in C. M. Gayley's *Representative English Comedies* (1903), and the chapter on ballads in the *Cambridge History of English Literature* (vol. II, 1908). Like his father he wrote poetry for his own delectation; one of his poems, "John Bright," is in E. C. Stedman's *American Anthology* (1900).

Although he was a distinguished prosodist and student of early Germanic life, his name is chiefly associated with his theory of the communal origin of the English and Scottish popular ballads. This theory, deriving ultimately from J. G. Hamann through Herder and Jacob Grimm, he developed with a wealth of learning and much persuasiveness but with something short of perfect success. His esthetic criticism of the ballads will not easily be superseded. Combining Friendly simplicity of manners and obedience to the inner light with an extraordinary extensive and accurate knowledge of ancient and modern literature, Gummere was one of the most highly bred as well as one of the most learned of American Anglists. His contribution to American culture is not to be estimated by the mere extent of his fame.

[J. M. Manly, "Francis Barton Gummere, 1855–1919," in *Modern Philology*, Sept. 1919; Christopher Morley, "In Memoriam, Francis Barton Gummere" in *Haverford Coll. Bull.*, vol. XVIII, No. 2, pp. 29–35; *Quin-*

quennial Cat. . . . Harvard Univ. (1915); *Harvard Coll. Class of 1875, Fiftieth Anniversary Report* (1925); *Biog. Cat. . . . Haverford Coll. 1833–1922* (1922); *Nation*, July 26, 1919; *Who's Who in America*, 1918–19; *Press* (Phila.), May 31, 1919.] G. H. G.

GUMMERE, JOHN (1784–May 31, 1845), mathematician, schoolmaster, was born near Willow Grove, Pa., the son of Samuel and Rachel (James) Gummere. He was a great-grandson of Johann and Anna Gömere, who were driven from their home in French Flanders by religious persecution. Joining a company of Protestant refugees from Crefeld, husband and wife crossed the ocean to Pennsylvania in 1719 and took up a farm, later known as the old "Monastery" property, along the Wissahickon in Germantown. There they both died on the same day in May 1738. Their son, John Gumre, married Sarah Davis and became the father of Samuel Gummere, who was a recorded minister of Friends and at one time postmaster at Stroudsburg. Samuel had, like his son, a mathematical mind. He could solve any problem capable of solution by arithmetic, but beyond arithmetic his education did not go.

John's love of mathematics would not let him rest satisfied with the poor repertory of the country schools. While still a boy, perhaps as young as thirteen, he got possession of the necessary books and taught himself algebra, mensuration, geometry, trigonometry, surveying, and practical astronomy. When he was nineteen he taught a school at Horsham, Pa., for a few terms and then entered the Friends' Boarding School at Westtown, Pa., where for six months he was under the tuition of Enoch Lewis [*q.v.*], whom he always remembered with respect and affection. His own distinguished career as a teacher began at Rancocas, N. J., where he remained for six years. In 1808 he married Elizabeth, daughter of William Buzby, a farmer of Rancocas. He returned to Westtown as a teacher in 1811, and in the spring of 1814 he opened a boarding school of his own at Burlington, N. J. That year also saw him elected to the American Philosophical Society, to whose *Transactions* he contributed various papers, and saw the publication of his *Treatise on Surveying,* which ran through twenty-two editions. His *Elementary Treatise on Astronomy* (1822) was also a deservedly popular textbook. Their author corresponded with Robert Adrain and Nathaniel Bowditch [*qq.v.*], and continued to add to his knowledge until he was considered one of the most eminent mathematicians in the United States. In order to further his studies he learned both French and German. Meanwhile his school became famous and drew pupils from all parts of the Union and from the West Indies. Gummere was himself an ideal teacher, winning both the respect and the affection of his pupils, and taking equal delight in acquiring knowledge for himself and in imparting it to others. He introduced chemistry and "natural philosophy" into the curriculum, sending to London at considerable expense for apparatus and supplies. "In his oral as well as written instruction," wrote Allinson, "he avoided the too common error of over-estimating the supposed attainments of the pupil." In 1833 he gave up his school in order to teach mathematics in the newly established Haverford School. For several years he was superintendent as well as teacher, but in 1843, because of differences over the management of the institution, he and the members of his family withdrew amicably. He and his son, Samuel James [*q.v.*], reëstablished the old school at Burlington. Two years later he died. The philologist Francis Barton Gummere [*q.v.*] was his grandson.

[W. J. Allinson, *Memorials of the Life and Character of John Gummere* (1845); *A Hist. of Haverford Coll. for the First Sixty Years of its Existence* (1892); the *Friend* (Phila.), Sixth mo. 28, 1845.] G. H. G.

GUMMERE, SAMUEL JAMES (Apr. 28, 1811–Oct. 23, 1874), college president, was born at Rancocas, N. J., the son of John [*q.v.*] and Elizabeth (Buzby) Gummere, and was educated in the school conducted at Burlington by his father, who imparted to him his own thorough knowledge of mathematics and astronomy. As his preceptor in languages, William Strong, later a justice of the United States Supreme Court, planted in him an abiding love of literature and so prevented him from becoming one-sided in his interests. After assisting his father for a short time, Gummere went to Providence, R. I., to organize the classical department in the Friends' (later the Moses Brown) School, where he was immediately successful, had Pliny Earle Chase as one of his pupils, and enjoyed the society of Moses Brown and other Rhode Island Friends. In 1834 he returned home to become an assistant teacher in the Haverford School, where his father was now superintendent and his brother William an assistant. The school was small and its faculty by necessity versatile; during this first period at Haverford Gummere gave instruction in mathematics, physics, chemistry, and Latin, but he was well qualified to teach these subjects and several others. In January 1835 he married Abigail, daughter of John Griscom [*q.v.*] of New York and Burlington, who died Sept. 28, 1840. By 1843 the financial difficulties of the school had led to so much disagreement among the trustees that the Gummeres and several other teachers resigned, father and son going back to

Burlington to reopen the old school. On Jan. 9, 1845, Gummere married Elizabeth Hooton Barton, daughter of David Barton of Philadelphia. Francis Barton Gummere [*q.v.*], the philologist, was their son. The year 1854 Gummere spent traveling in England, France, and Switzerland. In 1862 he was recalled to Haverford, which had meanwhile become a college, as principal and professor of mathematics, physics, and astronomy, and two years later he was given the title of president. Although the college was small—it had sixty-one students and four professors in 1863–64—and grew slowly, his administrative duties were sufficiently numerous and worrisome to wear down his normally robust health and cut short his life. As a personality on the campus and in the classroom he left a profound impression on all who met him. Gentle, modest, reserved to the point of self-effacement, he won love by his sheer goodness and admiration by his attainments. His combination of the scientific and the literary temper made him an ideal teacher. Students remembered his lectures for their lucidity and precision. Known the country over as a mathematician and astronomer, in private he cultivated the art of writing Latin verse. After his death one of his compositions, an ode, "*Ad Horologium Meum,*" was found concealed behind the pendulum of his clock. He was a member of the American Philosophical Society, and in 1869 went to Iowa to observe a total eclipse of the sun. Slight of figure but muscular, he was fond of walking, swimming, and skating. In the last winter of his life he appeared on the pond and exhibited the fancy figures dear to the old-fashioned skater. Overwork brought on in the summer of 1874 a breakdown from which he never recovered.

[*A Hist. of Haverford Coll. for the First Sixty Years of its Existence* (1892); I. Sharpless, *The Story of a Small Coll.* (1918); the *Haverfordian,* Mar. 1887; the *Friend* (Phila.), Tenth mo. 30, 1874; *Friends' Rev.* (Phila.), Tenth mo. 31, 1874; letter to author from Gummere's grandson, Richard Mott Gummere, June 21, 1928.]

G. H. G.

GUMMERE, SAMUEL RENÉ (Feb. 19, 1849–May 28, 1920), lawyer and diplomat, was born in Trenton, N. J., the son of Barker and Elizabeth (Stryker) Gummere. He was fifth in line of descent from Johann Gummere (Gömere), a Huguenot who emigrated from French Flanders to Pennsylvania early in the eighteenth century and founded a family which produced a number of well-known educators. Samuel was sent by his father, an eminent lawyer, to Trenton Academy, Lawrenceville School, and Princeton, where he graduated in 1870. After studying law in his father's office, he was admitted to the bar as attorney in 1873 and as counselor three years later. Though a faithful and able student of the law, he never practised in court, but confined himself to office work. He traveled extensively in Europe and from 1881 to 1884 was secretary to the American minister at The Hague. Frequently a guest of Ion H. Perdicaris, a wealthy American resident at Tangiers in Morocco, he joined the latter in visiting the secretary of state to protest against the practice of issuing certificates of American citizenship as carried on profitably but illegally by the United States consulate at Tangiers. As a result, in 1898 Gummere was appointed consul-general for Morocco. In May 1904 his friend Perdicaris was kidnapped by the half-bandit, half-patriot Riffian chief, Raisuli, who asked for a ransom of $70,000. Gummere held the weak Moroccan government responsible for the prisoner's release, and Raisuli then demanded political concessions from the government, in addition to the ransom. After a month of negotiation he felt "further delay undignified, humiliating, and futile" (*Munsey's Magazine, post,* p. 735). An ultimatum, backed by a naval squadron, a threat to land marines, and Secretary of State John Hay's dispatch requiring "Perdicaris alive or Raisuli dead" (*Foreign Relations, post,* p. 503), forced the Moroccan sultan to accept Raisuli's terms and the American was freed. Gummere was officially commended by Hay for his vigorous handling of the incident and in the following year, Mar. 8, 1905, was rewarded by appointment as the first minister of the United States to Morocco. In 1906 he was one of the American representatives in the conference which met at Algeciras to settle European differences regarding Morocco, and his wide knowledge of the local situation was invaluable to the other commissioners. Resigning his diplomatic post in 1909, he took up his residence at Wimbledon in England. After engaging actively during the World War in work among the wounded in both England and France, he died at his Wimbledon home. A diplomat of polish and ability, he was also a brilliant conversationalist and raconteur. He never married.

[*Munsey's Mag.,* Feb. 1905; *Foreign Relations of the U. S., 1904* (1905); *Who's Who in America,* 1916–17; J. C. Guernsey, *The Class of 1870, Princeton Univ., Feb. 1915–Feb. 1916* (1916); *State Gazette,* Trenton, N. J., May 29, 1920.]

W. L. W—t, Jr.

GUNN, FREDERICK WILLIAM (Oct. 4, 1816–Aug. 16, 1881), schoolmaster, son of John N. and Mary (Ford) Gunn, was born on his father's farm in that part of Washington, Litchfield County, Conn., known as Judea, the youngest of eight children. Both his father and mother died when he was ten years old, and thereafter he was brought up under the direction of his oldest brother, John. He was a bright, inquisitive boy, eager to get at the root of things and fond of outdoor life. Having studied previously at a school in Cornwall, Conn., conducted by Rev. William Andrews, he prepared for college at the local academy, Judea, under Rev. Watson W. Andrews, the former's son. At the age of seventeen he entered Yale, graduating in 1837. A few years later he wrote of himself: "I am a non-conformist in many things—in some I stand all alone." The statement was true, and the fact acknowledged was perhaps the principal determining influence in his career. In college he was known as a sturdy, generous youth of pronounced individualism, true to the dictates of his own mind and heart. He did sufficiently well in his studies, but had no ambition to take high rank as a scholar. He read widely in English literature, sought an all-round development, was noted for physical strength and skill, and was fond of fishing and hunting, killing game with a bow and arrow, in the use of which he was an expert. After graduating he returned to Washington. His mother had dedicated him as a child to the ministry, but he had read Carlyle, Emerson, and Theodore Parker, and could not conform to the Calvinistic theology of his place and time. He finally decided to study medicine. In order to earn money he taught school in New Preston, Conn., 1838–39, and in the latter year reopened the academy at Washington. His teaching ability attracted many pupils. The idea of becoming a physician he was forced to abandon, because although he fought to overcome the weakness he could not witness severe pain without fainting. Teaching became his life work. He advocated total abstinence where rum making and selling were considered respectable. The anti-slavery movement was under way, and the general sentiment of the town was opposed to it. Again he took an independent stand, and became prominent in a little group of ardent abolitionists. As a result, he was persecuted as an infidel and fanatic, and his pupils were taken from him. Called back to more tolerant New Preston in 1845, he taught there until 1847, when he went to Towanda, Pa., and opened an academy. On Apr. 16, 1848, he married Abigail I. Brinsmade, daughter of Gen. Daniel B. Brinsmade of Washington. In 1849, the prejudice against him there having waned and the influence of the Brinsmade family being in his favor, he returned to Washington and resumed teaching in the academy. In October of the following year he started the family school, later called "The Gunnery," which became widely known and in which many boys who afterwards attained prominence were educated. He was not a conventional schoolmaster nor did the government of the school conform to prevailing practices. From both Mr. and Mrs. Gunn the boys received home-like care and affection. A large degree of freedom was permitted and self-government was encouraged. The discipline was unique, penalties being fitted to offenses in ingenious ways. Training of the intellect was secondary, and moral and physical development, primary. A knowledge of public events and the duties of citizenship were made almost compulsory. After conducting the school for more than thirty years the master died and was buried in the town of his birth, and former pupils erected a monument to his memory.

[*The Master of the Gunnery* (1887), ed. by W. H. Gibson; John Coleman Adams, *William Hamilton Gibson* (1901), ch. I; *Records of the Class of 1837 in Yale Univ.* (1887); *Hartford Courant* and *New Haven Journal-Courier*, Aug. 18, 1881; *N. Y. Daily Tribune*, Aug. 17, 1881. J. G. Holland in *Arthur Bonnicastle* (1873) describes the Gunnery under title "The Bird's Nest."]

H. E. S.

GUNN, JAMES NEWTON (1867–Nov. 26, 1927), industrial engineer, was born in Springfield, Ohio, the son of Rev. James W. and Mary Catherine (Johnson) Gunn. His boyhood and youth were spent in his native city where he passed through the public schools and continued studying, under private tutors, languages, mathematics, and engineering. In the early 1890's he became connected with the Library Bureau, Boston, Mass., and while with this organization, he developed the use of commercial card indices. He perfected and patented, too, the tab type of index card and the vertical file, both of which are now in universal use. During his service with the Library Bureau, which included several years spent abroad organizing its foreign business, he studied business systemization and became a pioneer in the new field of industrial and production engineering. Upon his return from Europe in 1901 he organized the firm of Gunn, Richards & Company, Business Consultants. As president of this firm, he came into intimate contact with the inner workings of many corporations and came to be recognized as an authority on corporation management. Between 1901 and 1911 he did valuable work for the Regal Shoe Company, Campbell's Soup Company, the Pennsylvania Steel Corporation, and other large organizations. In 1911 he was called upon by the Studebaker Corporation to evolve a cohesive automobile unit out of the old wagon-building concern. In the course of two years as general manager he completely reorganized the company and fulfilled his mission successfully.

Then his services were secured by the United States Tire Company. Being a trained thinker and a minutely critical analyst, he mastered the requirements of this, to him, comparatively strange industry after a few months and was prevailed upon to accept the presidency of the company in November 1915. At the same time he was made assistant to the president of the United States Rubber Company, the parent organization. Gunn's association with these companies continued for eight years, during which time the tire company's sales practically doubled and the net profits increased fifty per cent. He was also active in the general councils of the rubber industry, being a director and a member of the executive committee of the Rubber Association of America. In 1923 he was compelled to give up these associations because of ill health, but he subsequently incorporated his own consulting-engineering business and was quite active during the remaining three years of his life, serving as receiver of the Hodgman Rubber Company and as engineer of Lockwood, Greene & Company. Gunn assisted in the organization of the Harvard Graduate School of Business Administration, and was one of its first lecturers. He represented the Rubber Association on the War Industries Board during the World War and was president of the Lincoln Highway Association for four years. He was married to Mabel Scott of New York, who with three daughters survived him.

[*India Rubber World,* Dec. 1, 1915; *Automobile Topics,* July 13, 1918, June 9, 1923, Jan. 19, 1924, Jan. 26, 1924; *N. Y. Herald Tribune, N. Y. Times,* and *Boston Transcript,* Nov. 28, 1927; correspondence with Rubber Association of America.] C. W. M—n.

GUNNISON, JOHN WILLIAMS (Nov. 11, 1812–Oct. 26, 1853), army engineer, was born at Goshen, N. H., the son of Samuel and Elizabeth (Williams) Gunnison. His father was a farmer, of colonial stock. John had his early education in Hopkinton Academy, N. H. On July 1, 1833, he entered West Point, from which he graduated with high honors four years later, as a second lieutenant of the 2nd Artillery. He served in the Seminole War as an ordnance officer during the winter of 1837–38. In the spring of 1838 he was detached to aid in the transfer of the Cherokees to the Indian Territory, and on the completion of this service he returned to the Seminole campaign as a second lieutenant of topographical engineers. From 1840 to 1849 he was engaged in surveys in Georgia and the lake region of the North and Northwest. In the latter year, as a first lieutenant (appointed May 9, 1846) he was assigned to Capt. Howard Stansbury's party directed to explore a central route to the Pacific and to survey the Great Salt Lake region. The unusual severity of the winter compelled him to remain for much of the time in Salt Lake City, where he made a study of the Mormon religion and people that resulted in the publication in 1852 of a book, *The Mormons, or Latter-Day Saints, in the Valley of the Great Salt Lake.* He returned to Washington in 1850, and from 1851 to the early part of 1853 he was engaged in surveys in the northern lake regions. On Mar. 3, 1853, he was made a captain and shortly afterward was assigned to the exploration and survey of a westward route by way of the Huerfano River, Cochetopa Pass, and the Grand and the Green valleys to the Santa Clara, in southwestern Utah. Leaving St. Louis about the end of June, his expedition reached the Sevier River, near Sevier Lake, southwest of Great Salt Lake, in October. On the morning of the 23rd, while at breakfast in their camp, his party of ten was attacked by a band of Pahvant Indians. Gunnison and six others were killed and their bodies horribly mutilated.

Gunnison was married, Apr. 15, 1841, to Martha A. Delony, of St. Marys, Ga., who with three children survived him. He was highly regarded both for his character and his professional attainments, and the news of his death and the desecration of his body was received with sorrow and indignation throughout the land. Charges were made that a party of Mormons had aided in the crime, and they were supported by Federal Judge W. W. Drummond, in a letter resigning his office and again, more elaborately, in a letter of Apr. 25, 1857, to Gunnison's widow. These charges were, however, discredited by further investigation, and it is generally conceded that the act was committed solely by the Indians in revenge for certain aggressions by parties of emigrants.

[G. W. Gunnison, *A Geneal. of the Descendants of Hugh Gunnison* (1880); G. W. Cullum, *Biog. Reg.* (3rd ed., 1891); H. H. Bancroft, *Hist. of Utah* (1889); J. C. Alter, *James Bridger* (1926); *House Ex. Doc. No. 18,* 33 Cong., 1 Sess.] W. J. G.

GUNSAULUS, FRANK WAKELEY (Jan. 1, 1856–Mar. 17, 1921), Congregational clergyman, was the son of Joseph Gunsaulus, of Spanish ancestry, and Mary Hawley Gunsaulus, his wife, whose forebears were Puritan and who herself was an ardent worker in the Methodist church. He was born in Chesterville, Ohio. From the public schools he went to Ohio Wesleyan University where he was the most popular student of his day. In 1875, after receiving the degree of A.B., he was ordained in the Methodist ministry and began preaching on a Methodist circuit with headquarters at Harrisburg, Ohio. On Sept. 20, 1876, he married Georgiana Long of Holly Meadows, W. Va. As a Methodist preacher he served Worthington, Ohio, 1876–78, and Chillicothe, Ohio, 1879. In this year he entered the Congregational ministry. He was pastor of the Eastwood Church and later the High Street Congregational Church in Columbus, Ohio, 1879–81, minister of the Congregational Church in Newtonville, Mass., 1881–85, during which time he became a friend of Phillips Brooks, and pastor of the Brown Memorial Presbyterian Church of Baltimore, Md., 1885–87. He was pastor of the Plymouth Congregational Church, Chicago, from 1887 until 1899, when he succeeded Newell Dwight Hillis in the pulpit of the independent Central Church, to which for twenty years his preaching drew great crowds. Six feet in height and weighing over two hundred pounds, with a large chest, a firmly set head, and powerful vocal equipment, he had an imposing presence made still more effective by restrained yet dramatic gestures and vocal cadences now exquisite in poetical pathos, now thunderous in prophecy.

One Sunday morning in Plymouth Church, Chicago, the young minister chose as his theme "What I would do if I had a million dollars," a subject used that day by many preachers of the city. Gunsaulus said he would found an institute for technical training where the poorest boy could have an opportunity equal to that of the richest. At the close of the sermon Philip Danforth Armour [*q.v.*] spoke to his pastor about putting into practice what he had been preaching. "If you will give five years of your life," he said, "I will give the money, and we will do it together." Accordingly they established the Armour Institute, later called the Armour Institute of Technology, which was opened in 1893. Gunsaulus was president from the beginning until his death. Without technical training in engineering or education, he was a leader, emphasizing the development of personality and preparation for performance. In 1919 he resigned his pastorate to give all his time and strength to the Institute.

Besides preaching in his own pulpit Gunsaulus gave many lectures throughout the country, including courses at Johns Hopkins University, on "The Messages of the Great English Poets"; at Chicago Theological Seminary, on "The Higher Ministries of Recent English Poetry"; at McCormick Theological Seminary, on "The Influence of Music in the Church"; at Yale Divinity School in 1882, and again in 1911 when he delivered the Lyman Beecher lectures. From 1912 he was professorial lecturer at the University of Chicago. His avocations were collecting paintings, drawings, prints, pottery, textiles, manuscripts, rare books, poetry and music. He was among the earliest to appreciate the work of Josef Israels and Mauve and at one time owned the two Mauves now in the Metropolitan Museum of Art in New York. His collections of Wedgwood and Near-Eastern pottery are in the Gunsaulus Gallery of the Chicago Art Institute which was presented and named by W. H. Miner of New York. His summer lectures were undertaken in part to secure funds wherewith to purchase objects of artistic or historical worth to bestow on educational institutions. One of his gifts to the University of Chicago was Mendelssohn's manuscript of *Elijah,* a significant item, for he found great joy in this music as rendered by his choir and built on it one of his greatest sermons and services. With him the whole service was a single act of worship. He never missed a choir rehearsal and often declared: "This is where I get my sermons." Sometimes he wrote hymns for special occasions. His Christmas card frequently took the form of a Christmas hymn with music by the director of his choir and words by himself.

Books were a special joy to him. He haunted McClurg's rare book section, fondly named by Eugene Field, the "Saints and Sinners Corner" —the saints being the Rev. F. M. Bristol, the Rev. John Stryker, and the Rev. F. W. Gunsaulus. He presented the Gunsaulus Collection of Incunabula to the University of Chicago, and encouraged many others to be generous in donations to the library. By the time he was twenty-three he had published the first of his own books a volume of sermons. His love of music and poetry bore fruit in three volumes of verse: *Loose Leaves of Song* (1888); *Phidias and Other Poems* (1891); *Songs of Night and Day* (1896). His interest in the Renaissance found expression in a historical novel, *Monk and Knight* (2 vols., 1891). Other books were: *Transfiguration of Christ* (1886, 1907); *William Ewart Gladstone* (1898); *The Man of Galilee* (1899); *Paths to Power* (1905); *Paths to the City of God* (1906); *The Higher Ministries of Recent English Poetry* (1907); *The Minister and the Spiritual Life* (1911); *Martin Luther and the Morning Hour in Europe* (1917); *Prayers* (1922).

His main interest always was religion. Dr. S. Parkes Cadman declared him the American divine who best understood and made articulate the religious aspirations of his country. Gunsaulus himself said: "The only pulpit that men respect permanently pours forth the music of redemption." A great cleric, as Dr. Lyman Abbot once declared, must be a great citizen. In Gunsaulus' parish were included not only Central Church, but Chicago, and the nation, and other countries. Long a member of the Political Action Committee of the Union League Club, he showed great common sense and humor in its discussions and activities. He appealed for Cuba's freedom in 1895 and pleaded for fair treatment of the Philippines and Porto Rico in 1900; he rebuked an attempt to raise the religious issue in the Taft campaign of 1908 and during the World War patriotically spoke for American policies. As preacher and civic leader in Chicago for thirty years he held a place like that of Phillips Brooks in Boston or Henry Ward Beecher in Brooklyn.

[*In Memoriam: Frank Wakeley Gunsaulus* (1921); Edgar Bancroft, *Dr. Gunsaulus, the Citizen* (1921); C. H. Dennis, *Eugene Field's Creative Years* (1924); *Who's Who in America*, 1920–21; *Congregationalist*, Mar. 31, 1921; *Chicago Daily Tribune*, Mar. 18, 1921.]

D. A. R—n.

GUNTER, ARCHIBALD CLAVERING (Oct. 25, 1847–Feb. 24, 1907), playwright, novelist, publisher, was born in Liverpool, England, and was brought to New York by his parents when he was six years old. The family soon moved to San Francisco, where he attended the public schools and the recently opened school of mines of the state university. In 1868 he secured a position as civil engineer with the Central Pacific Railroad. Next year he was employed as a chemist in the laboratory of an assayer in San Francisco. Then for several years he was in Utah, first as chemist in a smelting works and then as superintendent of a mine. In 1874 he returned to San Francisco, worked for a year in a stock-broker's office, and then set up a brokerage business of his own. In 1879 he moved to New York, where, except for travel, he remained for the rest of his life.

Just when he first essayed authorship is unknown, but *Found the True Vein* (San Francisco, 1872) appears to be his oldest surviving work. It is a five-act play, with scenes in a Pullman "palace" car and in the depths of a mine, and among the *dramatis personae* are characters similar in type to those that Bret Harte was then beginning to exploit—a stage driver, a Chinese, several miners, and a supercilious young woman from the East. Gunter was also the author of *Prince Karl* (produced at the Boston Museum, Apr. 5, 1886) in which Richard Mansfield scored his earliest success, and of a number of other plays, including *Two Nights in Rome, The Deacon's Daughter, Polly Middles,* and *Fresh, the American.* On Nov. 8, 1886, he married Esther Lisbeth Burns, who was the niece of George Henry Story, the curator of paintings in the Metropolitan Museum of Art. She became the capable manager of the Home Publishing Company, which Gunter had organized to publish his first novel, *Mr. Barnes of New York* (1887). The story deals with the adventures in Europe of a rich and impudent young American. It had been declined by all the large publishers in New York, but when Gunter brought it out at his own risk it scored the most sensational success in the history of American publishing. More than one million copies of the book were sold in the United States; in England it was pirated simultaneously by six different publishers. During the next six or seven years Gunter was the most widely read of American novelists; whoever read novels read the Gunter novels; his books, in their yellow paper covers, seemed almost ubiquitous. After *Mr. Potter of Texas* (1888), *That Frenchman!* (1889), *Miss Nobody of Nowhere* (1890), *Miss Dividends* (1892), *Baron Montez of Panama and Paris* (1893), *The King's Stockbroker* (1894), and *A Princess of Paris* (1894), his vein of story-telling began to run a little thin, and his public declined, but he continued to write at least one novel a year, and died with his pen in his hand. His writing abounds in solecisms and anachronisms, his technique was crude, but the public liked his stories anyway. His success was made without advertising and without assistance from critics.

[*Who's Who in America*, 1906–07; San Francisco directories, 1868–80; *Publishers' Weekly*, Mar. 2, 1907; *San Francisco Chronicle*, Feb. 25, 1907; *N. Y. Times*, Feb. 26, 1907; "Chronicle and Comment" in the *Bookman*, Oct. 1902, May 1907; "The Lounger" in *Putnam's Monthly*, Apr. 1907.]

G. H. G.

GUNTHER, CHARLES FREDERICK (Mar. 6, 1837–Feb. 10, 1920), candy manufacturer and rare-book collector, was the son of John M. and Marie F. Gunther. He was born at Wildberg, in Württemberg, Germany, and came to America with his parents in 1842. They settled in Lancaster County, Pa., but eventually removed to Somerset County. Here the boy, although slightly more than ten years old, became a government mail carrier. He covered his route over the mountains to Johnston and return on horseback, receiving as compensation twenty-five cents a day. In the spring of 1850 the family moved to Peru, Ill. After a brief period of attendance at public and private schools, Gunther, then fourteen, began to earn his livelihood. In rapid succession he was a clerk in a country store, a drug clerk, the manager of the local postoffice, and finally cashier in a local bank. In his capacity as bank cashier he became acquainted with the prosperity which the South was enjoying and in 1860 decided to move thither. He took up his residence in Memphis, Tenn., as the employee of an ice company. The outbreak of the Civil War prostrated business, and Gunther served as steward and purser on an Arkansas River steamer engaged in carrying supplies and transporting troops for the Confederacy until his boat was captured and burned by the Union forces. He was taken prisoner but was soon released and, returning to Peru, secured a position there in a bank. In 1863 he was engaged as a commercial traveler for a wholesale confectionery house in Chicago and five years later he opened his own retail store in that city.

Henceforth, Chicago was his permanent home, and he became integrally connected with its industrial, civic, and artistic growth. In time his name was a synonym for high-grade confectioneries, particularly because of his numerous popular inventions, among which the caramel is best known to the American people. The great fire of 1871 destroyed his business and left him almost destitute of resources. With renewed energy and determination, he reëstablished his business on a more extensive scale in what is now the McVicker Theatre Building. He made his palatial State Street store one of the points of interest for tourists on account of its rare treasures of historical art, and he was one of the first merchants of Chicago to advertise in the news columns of the papers. In 1879 he was a member of the commission organized to tour Mexico with a view toward closer trade relations between the two republics. His civic interests led him to take an active part in politics. He was elected alderman from the second ward on the Democratic ticket and served from 1897 to 1901. From 1901 to 1905 he was city treasurer; and in 1908 an unsuccessful candidate for the Democratic nomination for governor. He brought the old Libby Prison to Chicago for exhibition and was one of the organizers and the first president of the Coliseum Company.

In addition to these varied activities Gunther was an art connoisseur and collector. By shrewd business methods he acquired a notable collection of art treasures and rare books. Before his death he offered his entire collection to the city of Chicago with the proviso that a fire-proof building should be erected for its safe-keeping. The city failed to comply with his request, and the collection went to his widow, Jennie Burnell Gunther, whom he had married in 1869, and to his son. They sold 50,000 historical manuscripts to the Chicago Historical Society, of which Gunther for twenty years was a director, for a sum of $150,000. This collection contains rare Lincoln material as well as material on the early history of Chicago, and some Shakespearian and Napoleonic manuscripts.

[The Gunther collection is described in the *N. Y. Times*, Oct. 27, 1918, and in *Ill. State Hist. Soc. Jour.*, Apr. 1920. See also *Biog. Dict. and Portrait Gallery of Representative Men of Chicago* (1892); *Book of Chicagoans* (1917); *Chicago Daily Tribune*, *Chicago Daily News*, *Chicago Herald and Examiner*, Feb. 11, 1920.] R. C. McG.

GUNTON, GEORGE (Sept. 8, 1845–Sept. 11, 1919), editor, economist, was born in Chatteris, Cambridgeshire, England, the only son of Mathew Gunton, an agricultural laborer, and Ann Middleton. He had only a meager schooling, but his desire for education was early displayed and as a youth he read widely. In 1862, at the age of seventeen, he married Elizabeth Bocock, by whom he had eight children. Well-nigh penniless, in 1874 he emigrated to the United States, leaving his family scattered among relatives. He first settled in Fall River, Mass., where he worked as a weaver, and while there he wrote articles for the *Labor Standard* of Paterson, N. J., under the name of Middleton. In 1875 he was secretary of the Weavers' Union which engaged in an unsuccessful strike. As a consequence he was black-listed and found it impossible to secure work as a weaver. Even his family which had now joined him was ostracized. He attracted the attention of Ira Steward and George McNeill, leaders of the labor movement in New England, and through their intercession with General Butler, he secured work as a laborer in the custom-house and later in the navy-yard. In 1878 the *Labor Standard* and the Fall River *Labor Journal* were merged at Fall River and Gunton was made manager, serving in this position for four years. In 1882 the *Labor Standard* suspended publication and Gunton was again without settled occupation. He devoted a portion of his time to securing an amendment of the ten-hour act passed by the Massachusetts legislature in 1874, whereby the law restricting the labor of women and children was strengthened. In 1880 he ran for the Massachusetts legislature on the Greenback ticket.

In 1883 a labor group persuaded Gunton to edit manuscript material left by Steward. These notes, however, proved to be too fragmentary for editing, but the project gave birth to Gunton's own volume, *Wealth and Progress*, which appeared in 1887 and passed through several editions. In the meantime (1885) he moved to New York and attracted the attention of Rev. Heber Newton, who placed Gunton at the head of an economic society in his church. Through Newton's influence others became interested, and as a result of this backing, the Institute of Social Economics was established in 1890. The following year Gunton became editor of a new magazine known as the *Social Economist,* published under that name until 1896 when it appeared under the title of *Gunton's Magazine,* which continued publication until 1904. In 1899 he was appointed director of economic and sociological work of the national Young Men's Christian Association. In addition to *Wealth and Progress,* he wrote: *Principles of Social Economy* (1891); *Trusts and the Public* (1899); *Outlines of Social Economics* (1900), with Hayes Robbins; and *Outlines of Political Science* (1901), also in collaboration with Robbins.

During the years from 1890 to 1905 Gunton's writings undoubtedly influenced the direction of economic thought in the United States. Human economy rather than money economy was the center of his philosophy. In particular he urged that an increase in the standard of living of laborers together with shorter hours would elevate the wants of laborers which in turn would increase production and thus be beneficial to the manufacturer. While the theory was not consciously accepted at the time by manufacturers, it later received wide acceptance. Gunton did not believe that trusts were an evil for he reasoned that the concentration of capital led to lower prices and this in turn meant higher real wages. Trusts in his opinion did not destroy competition but simply changed the plane of competition.

Gunton separated from his first wife in 1882, and in 1886 he married Mrs. Whipple, a woman of forceful character, who assisted him in establishing a position of influence in New York. This marriage ultimately was dissolved and in February 1904 he married Mrs. Rebecca Douglas Lowe, president of the American Federation of Women. She had considerable wealth, and as the magazine had ceased publication, they lived in Hot Springs, Va. The third marriage also proved unfortunate, however, and in 1915 Gunton moved to New York, where he died. His last work, *Americanization and the League of Nations* (1919), written shortly before his death, had a wide distribution.

[*Who's Who in America,* 1914–15; *Pol. Sci. Quart.,* Dec. 1887, Sept. 1900, Sept. 1901; *N. Y. Tribune,* Mar. 13, 1892; *N. Y. Times, N. Y. Herald,* and *Evening Post* (N. Y.), Sept. 13, 1919; information as to certain facts from Gunton's son, Matthew Gunton, Newcastle, Pa.]

D. R. D.

GURLEY, RALPH RANDOLPH (May 26, 1797–July 30, 1872), philanthropist, was born in Lebanon, Conn., fifth of the seven children of the Rev. John and Mary (Porter) Gurley. He entered Yale with the class of 1818 and before graduating was recognized among the first in his class. Upon leaving Yale he removed to Washington, D. C., where, in 1822, he became an agent of the American Colonization Society, and to this organization he devoted the rest of his life. He was successively agent, secretary, vice-president, and life director. His work as secretary was largely in Washington, where he looked after the correspondence, planned and outfitted the expeditions of the colonists, regulated the affairs of Liberia on the American side of the Atlantic, edited for twenty-five years the organ of the Society, the *African Repository,* and prepared for an even longer time its *Annual Reports.* Besides these duties he wrote for the press on colonization and lectured for the Society in North, West, and South. With the rise of the abolition movement his efforts in behalf of colonization increased, and he even invaded New England to debate publicly with several of the leading abolitionists. Later he crossed the Atlantic to urge the cause of colonization in England, where he engaged in spirited public debates at Egyptian Hall, London. His *Mission to England* (1841), published upon his return, "contains some of the best articles ever penned on the subject of African colonization" (*African Repository,* September 1872, p. 282). "During those years of bitter struggle, between 1830 and 1840, Gurley stands out as the great Colonizationist" (Fox, *post,* p. 74). He was "essentially a peacemaker and lover of the Union" (*Ibid.,* p. 73); the more radical abolitionists considered him pro-slavery; but when the war came he sided with the North. His reputation as a controversialist was high, for he was "blessed with one of the mildest and gentlest of dispositions . . . which was . . . manifested in his placid smile, his mild, benevolent face and gentle manner, which charmed everyone" (*African Repository, loc. cit.*). In person he was tall, and, in the vigor of manhood, remarkably handsome. He thrice visited Liberia. In 1824 he was sent thither for the first time by the Society and the United States government to investigate charges made against Jehudi Ashmun [*q.v.*], who was unofficially acting as governor, and to straighten out existing difficulties in the colony. The latter task he performed satisfactorily, drawing up a "Plan for the Civil Government of Liberia" which was adopted by the people, accepted by the Society, and put into successful operation. His investigation completely vindicated Ashmun and contributed to Ashmun's first appointment as colonial agent for Liberia. Later Gurley became Ashmun's biographer, publishing *Life of Jehudi Ashmun, Late Colonial Agent in Liberia,* in 1835. In 1849 he again visited Liberia under instructions from the United States government, and upon his return made a report on the condition and prospects of the colony, which was printed. Upon the occasion of his final visit in 1867 he was warmly received by the people. Gurley was a licentiate of the Presbytery of the District of Columbia, and, although never ordained or installed over any church, preached widely, his services being eagerly sought for particularly among the colored churches. He also acted for a time as chaplain of the House of Representatives. Among the poor, and particularly among the negro poor, of Washington, his labors were abundant, and to save one negro family from separation he even sacrificed his own library and his home. He died in Washington only three months after the death of his wife, Eliza (McLellan) Gurley, who had come to that city as a bride nearly forty-five years before. Of their thirteen children but two survived their parents.

[Mason Noble, *A Discourse Commemorative of the Life and Character of the Rev. Ralph Randolph Gurley* (1872); *Memorial of the Semi-Centennial Anniversary of the Am. Colonization Soc.* (1867); E. L. Fox, *The Am. Colonization Soc., 1817–40* (1919); *Fifty-sixth Ann. Report, Am. Colonization Soc.* (1873).]

W. R. W.

GURNEY, EPHRAIM WHITMAN (Feb. 18, 1829–Sept. 12, 1886), educator, was born in Boston, Mass., the son of Nathan and Sarah (Whitman) Gurney. His father was superintendent of the Massachusetts General Hospital. After graduation from Harvard College in 1852 he taught for a short time in the school of D. B. Tower on Park Street, Boston, and then opened a classical and scientific school for boys in Cambridge, in connection with Professors George M. Lane and Joseph Lovering [*qq.v.*]. In 1857 he was appointed tutor in Greek and Latin at Harvard College, was advanced to an assistant professorship in 1863, transferred to the department of philosophy in 1867, and in the following year, to the department of history. Made professor in 1869, he received in 1877 the title of professor of history and Roman law, and in 1886, shortly before his untimely death, he was given the McLean Professorship of Ancient and Modern History. His academic career thus illustrates the prevailing character of higher education in America at the time. He was first of all a scholar, grounded in the traditional classical training and prepared to give instruction in any subject within the range of humane learning—classics, philosophy, history, or law. He became a teacher of history because he found there the most obvious opportunity to utilize his wide reading and to satisfy his scholarly tastes. He was an admirable representative of the fast vanishing "donnish" type. He loved learning for its own sake. The college was his world. His happiness was in books and in the human relations growing out of his occupation with them. Though master of an exceptionally easy and lucid style, he was singularly lacking in the impulse to literary production. A ready talker, he never delivered formal lectures either to his students or to the larger public. For two years, 1868 to 1870, he was associated with James Russell Lowell as editor of the *North American Review,* then the most important American literary periodical, but his name does not appear in the list of contributors at any time. The foundation of the New York *Nation* under his friend, E. L. Godkin [*q.v.*], gave him a welcome vehicle for the expression of his thought without the embarrassment of publicity, and for many years he contributed valuable articles of literary and political criticism.

His marriage, Oct. 3, 1868, to Ellen Sturgis Hooper, daughter of Dr. Robert William Hooper, brought him into close association with an important circle of Boston society. He built a commodious house on the outskirts of Cambridge and began there the course of generous hospitality to students, colleagues, and visiting scholars which was to be one of his most notable contributions to the academic life of his day. The coming of Charles William Eliot to the presidency of the university in 1869, marking a decisive epoch in the history of the institution, opened for Gurney new opportunities of usefulness. In the period of transition from the semi-rural college to the all-embracing university no one stood closer to the great leader than he. A personal friendship widened out into mutual confidence and hearty cooperation. In 1870 the office of Dean of the Faculty of Harvard College was created, and Gurney was the first incumbent. His administration established the tradition of an office designed primarily to relieve the president of the many details of personal dealings with students, but capable of development into a powerful agency for good. His interpretation of his function was guided first and always by the imperative claims of scholarship and academic honor. He shared with his brother-in-law, Henry Adams [*q.v.*], the arduous task of building up a department of history based upon the new principle of independent study. In his method of instruction he never departed from the traditional textbook and recitation, but he knew how to lift this dreary routine into the higher air of real reflection and critical discussion. The last years of his life were clouded by domestic sorrow and the slow process of an insidious disease borne with exemplary fortitude.

[Grace W. Edes, *Annals of the Harvard Class of 1852* (1922); *Letters of Chauncey Wright* (1878); the *Nation,* Sept. 16, 1886; *Boston Transcript,* Sept. 13, 1886.] E. Em—n.

GUTHE, KARL EUGEN (Mar. 5, 1866–Sept. 10, 1915), physicist, educator, was born in Hanover, Germany, the third child and the second son in a family of five children born to Otto and Anna (Hanstein) Guthe. He received his early education in the Gymnasium in Hanover and passed his *Abituriensexamen* in 1884. From 1885 to 1887 he attended the Technische Hochschule at Hanover, and then went to the University of Marburg where he completed his academic work and passed the *Oberlehrer* or state teachers' examination in 1889. His thesis for this examination dealt with certain aspects of seismology. The certificate which he received allowed him to teach the several subjects of physics, chemistry, geography, and all of the natural sciences, in the schools of higher learning in Germany. He then went to the University of Strassburg where he held a teaching position and continued his studies. In 1892 he returned for a short time to the University of Marburg and wrote a dissertation upon the mechanical telephone, *Ueber das Mechanische Telephone* (1892), receiving the degree of Doctor of Philosophy.

In the summer of that year he came to the United States, and several years later was made a naturalized citizen. Immediately after his arrival he went to Grand Rapids, Mich., where he shortly married Clara Belle Ware, whom he had met the previous year in Germany. To this marriage three children were born. In the fall of 1892 he went to Ann Arbor, and spent the winter doing research work in the department of physics at the University of Michigan. In 1893 he was appointed instructor in physics, a position which he held until 1900. He spent his Sabbatical leave, from May 1900 until August 1901, studying under Professor Planck at the University of Berlin, and upon his return to Ann Arbor, as assistant professor of physics, he continued his work there until 1903. In this year he went to Washington as associate physicist of the United States Bureau of Standards, but two years later he accepted the position of professor of physics at the University of Iowa. In 1909 he was recalled to the University of Michigan, as professor of physics. Several years later he was instrumental in the organization of the Graduate School and in 1912 was appointed its first dean. Thereafter, he devoted himself to the problems of organization and the development of the policies of this school. In the summer of 1915 while attending scientific meetings in San Francisco he was taken ill and it was found necessary to operate. The first operation was followed after a short period by another, which proved too great a strain, and he died of heart-failure in Ashland, Ore.

As a result of the publication of numerous papers on physics, he came to be recognized as an authority on certain aspects of electricity. Among these papers are: *A Study of the Silver Voltameter* (1904); *On Fibers Resembling Fused Quartz in Their Elastic Properties* (1904); *The Silver Coulometer* (1905); *Experiments on the Heusler Magnetic Alloys* (1906), with L. W. Austin; and *A New Determination of the Electromotive Force of Weston and Clark Standard Cells by an Absolute Electrodynamometer* (1906), all of which appeared as Bureau of Standards Bulletins. He was the author of several textbooks, the first of which, *A Manual of Physical Measurements,* written jointly with J. O. Reed, appeared in 1902. It ran through several editions. In 1903 he published *Laboratory Exercises with Primary and Storage Cells.* Later he was one of several authors who collaborated in *A Textbook of Physics* (1908). With J. O. Reed he published a *College Physics* (1911), and two years later he brought out his last book, *Definitions in Physics* (1913).

[*Who's Who in America,* 1914–15; J. M. Cattell, *Am. Men of Sci.* (2nd ed., 1910); *N. Y. Times,* Sept. 12, 1915; *Science,* Nov. 12, 1915.] G. W. P.

GUTHERZ, CARL (Jan. 28, 1844–Feb. 7, 1907), artist, was born in Schöftland, in the canton of Aargau, Switzerland, the son of a school teacher, Heinrich Gutherz, and his wife, Henrietta Lüscher. In 1851 his father emigrated with his family to America and established terra-cotta works near Cincinnati. With raw material at hand, and under his father's guidance, Carl soon learned to model, but the plant was financially unsuccessful, so it was abandoned, and the family moved on to Memphis, Tenn. Heinrich Gutherz died there, still in early middle life, and young Carl went to work as a mechanical draftsman. Within a few years he had become expert but dissatisfied, so with the money he had saved and with the help of his family, he sailed for Paris for instruction in art. There he studied in the Académie des Beaux-Arts, and later with Pils, Lefebvre, and Boulanger, from whom he learned the best romantic technique of the day. During the Franco-Prussian War he left Paris, studied for a time in Brussels and Antwerp, and then proceeded to Rome, where he painted his first noteworthy picture, "Awakening Spring," which later received an award in the Philadelphia Centennial. In 1872 he returned to Memphis, but removed to St. Louis after two years to teach in Washington University, and to assist Halsey C. Ives in the development of an art department which in 1879 became the St. Louis School of Fine Arts.

In 1884 he returned to Paris for a residence of twelve years, the most productive period of his life. He exhibited annually in the Salon and was awarded the perpetual privilege of hanging his pictures in the exhibitions. His best paintings were shown during this period, including "Lux Incarnationis" (1888), "Arcessita ab Angelis" (1889), "Temptation of St. Anthony" (1890), "Ad Astra" (1891), and "The Evening of the Sixth Day" (1893). He moved in the most respectable art circles and numbered among his intimates Bréton, Boulanger, Lefebvre, and Puvis de Chavannes. By the latter's work he was particularly affected, and began for the first time to interest himself seriously in murals, which, although less pristine, were distinctly reminiscent of those of Chavannes. So successful was he in this new field that in 1895 he was offered the commission to design the ceiling of the House Reading Room in the Library of Congress. He removed to Washington, D. C., the next year to see it accomplished. The legend of the fresco was "The Spectrum of Light," executed in seven panels, each representing in one of the rainbow colors "some phase of achievement, human or divine" (Small, *post,* p. 109), with a central figure illustrating the allegory. Two other important commissions in mural art followed, "Law and Justice" in the Fort Wayne Court House, and in the People's Church of St. Paul, a pictorial delineation of the development of Unitarian theology. As a portrait painter, Gutherz was also moderately accomplished. Among the contemporary figures who sat to him were Gen. Robert E. Lee, Senator Morgan of Alabama, Senator Bate of Tennessee, Justice Bradley, Jefferson Davis, and Susan B. Anthony. His portraits were less successful than his imaginative painting, however, as his true style was not photographic realism, but a poetic and mystical romanticism, in which his preoccupation with allegorical subjects, with diffuse form and roseate luminosity, could have full play. He died in Washington, D. C. He had married, in 1879, Katherine Scruggs, the daughter of Finch Philip Scruggs, a Methodist minister of Alabama.

[Lilian Whiting, "The Art of Carl Gutherz," *International Studio,* Feb. 1905; *Am. Art Ann.,* 1907–08; *Art Rev.,* Mar. 1907; *Who's Who in America,* 1906–07; Herbert Small, *Handbook of the New Lib. of Cong.* (1901); E. H. S. Dunklin, *Scruggs Geneal.* (1912), p. 63; the *Evening Star* (Washington, D. C.), Feb. 8, 1907.] C. P. M.

GUTHRIE, ALFRED (Apr. 1, 1805–Aug. 17, 1882), engineer, was born in Sherburne, N. Y., the oldest child of Dr. Samuel [*q.v.*] and Sybil (Sexton) Guthrie. When he was twelve years of age, they removed to Sacketts Harbor, then a port and military post of some magnitude. Here the elder Guthrie, who, like many early physicians, was something of an inventor and a man of affairs, developed a mining powder, which he exploited commercially, and established a vinegar and alcohol factory. In these undertakings Alfred was apparently associated with his father, under whom he and his brother Edwin studied medicine and chemistry. In the course of his experiments with the distillation of alcohol, the father stumbled upon chloroform, or "chloric ether," as he called it. It is doubtful, however, that Alfred's contribution to this discovery was significant. Nevertheless, since the family possessed an excellent library, he must have been well grounded in the rudiments of medicine, which he practised successfully for a decade.

After the construction of a railroad to the North, with the subsequent diversion of traffic from the water route and the failure of some of his father's schemes, Guthrie's practice fell off noticeably; and in 1845, with the other members of his family, also financially embarrassed, he attempted to retrieve his fortunes in the West. An engineer in fact if not in name, he undertook the design and construction of the hydraulic works on the Illinois & Michigan Canal, utilizing the surplus power to convey the sewage of Chicago to the Mississippi. Although these works, opened in 1848, were used until the seventies, much of the time under his immediate supervision, he is remembered primarily because of his services in connection with the development of a federal system of steamship inspection, to the need of which his attention had been directed by a series of appalling explosions. Beginning his studies in 1851, he examined, at his own expense, over two hundred vessels and prepared a number of charts illustrating the nature of the defects he had observed. Through the public support which he secured for his proposals, he succeeded in having a bill providing for systematic regulation introduced into Congress. When it was passed, in 1852, over the united opposition of both owners and operators, he was placed at the head of the enforcement bureau. As a result, the number of accidents was reduced so notably that even Guthrie's most bitter opponents came to recognize the value of his work. He was twice married: first, on Oct. 2, 1823, to Nancy, daughter of Thomas and Hepzibah (Jewett) Piper, who died July 10, 1855; and, second, on Mar. 31, 1857, to Phoebe, daughter of Chauncey and Eliza (Dunn) Guthrie, who survived him. He died in Chicago.

[The facts regarding Guthrie's career have been gleaned largely from the records of his father's life, from the reports of the Board of Sewerage Commissioners of the City of Chicago, and from his "Memorial . . . Submitting the Results of an Investigation . . . into the Causes of the Explosion of Steam-Boilers," Feb. 6, 1852, *Sen. Misc. Doc. 32*, 32 Cong., 1 Sess. See also H. N. and E. G. Dunn, *Records of the Guthrie Family* (1898); *Engineering News*, Aug. 26, 1882; *Chicago Tribune*, Aug. 18, 1882.] R. P. B—r.

GUTHRIE, GEORGE WILKINS (Sept. 5, 1848–Mar. 8, 1917), lawyer, diplomat, the son of John Brandon Guthrie and Catherine (Murray) Guthrie, and a descendant of Robert Guthrie, a native of Ireland who emigrated to America in 1744, was born in Pittsburgh, Pa. His father was a prominent resident of that city, having twice served it as mayor. Young Guthrie was educated in the public schools and in 1866 graduated from the Western University of Pennsylvania (now the University of Pittsburgh) with the degree of A.B. In 1868 he received the degree of A.M. from the same institution. He then began the study of law in the office of Hon. Robert J. Walker in Washington, D. C., and at the same time entered the law school of Columbian College (now George Washington University) where he received the degree of LL.B. in 1869. Admitted in the same year to the Washington bar and to the bar of Allegheny County, Pa., he began practice in Pittsburgh, at first in partnership with Col. James W. Kerr and later with the Hon. Malcolm Hay. He was early recognized as a leader in the legal profession and was retained in many of the most important civil-law cases in western Pennsylvania. In 1876 he was associate counsel for the Tilden electors in Florida. He took an active part in the affairs of the Democratic party, was one of the secretaries of the National Democratic Convention in 1884 and a delegate to the conventions of 1904 and 1912. He also took a prominent part in municipal affairs, being a member of the Municipal Program Committee of the National Municipal League in 1900. In 1896 he was a candidate for mayor of Pittsburgh, sponsored by the Citizens Municipal League, but failed of election. In 1905, when Pittsburgh was swept by a wave of political and moral reform, he was again a candidate for the mayoralty as leader of the reformers, and on Feb. 20, 1906, was elected for a term of three years by the largest vote ever polled in the city up to that time. He was the third member of his family to hold this office. During his administration he brought about a number of reforms in the municipal government, among them the institution of the municipal civil service, and was responsible for many civic improvements.

In 1912 he was elected chairman of the Pennsylvania State Democratic Committee and was instrumental in developing the campaign which culminated in the nomination of Woodrow Wilson for president of the United States. On May 20, 1913, President Wilson appointed him ambassador to Japan. This appointment came at a time of intense Anti-American feeling in that country, provoked by the California Alien Land Bill. Shortly after Guthrie assumed his duties as ambassador (Sept. 8, 1913) a mob attacked the Japanese Foreign Office in Tokio in demand of stronger action on the part of the Japanese government in the controversy. A very serious situation might have resulted had he not succeeded in convincing the Japanese statesmen that the economic and social problems of California had no real relationship to the good will of the United States as a whole toward Japan, and that the best interests of both nations would in the end be served by a calm consideration of the issues involved. When the World War broke out he assumed the additional responsibility of attending to the affairs of Germany in Japan and handled the problems which arose with great tact. On Mar. 8, 1917, he died very suddenly at Tokio. His body was brought to the United States on a Japanese cruiser as a token of the high esteem with which he was regarded by that government.

Possessed of high civic ideals coupled with extraordinary ability, Guthrie was unusually fitted for public service. He was a prominent Mason and Grand Master of that order in Pennsylvania in 1910–11. He was an officer of several hospitals and charitable organizations and a member of a number of clubs as well as a trustee of the University of Pittsburgh. He was married on Dec. 2, 1886, to Florence J. Howe of Pittsburgh.

[*Who's Who in America*, 1916–17; H. N. and E. G. Dunn, *Records of the Guthrie Family* (1898); obituaries in *Japan Magazine*, Apr. 1917; *Outlook*, Mar. 28, 1917, *Japan Weekly Chronicle*, Mar. 15, 1917; *N. Y. Times*, *Pittsburgh Post*, and other N. Y. and Pittsburgh papers for Mar. 9, 1917.] J. H. F.

GUTHRIE, JAMES (Dec. 5, 1792–Mar. 13, 1869), railroad promoter, secretary of the treasury, was born of pioneer parents in Bardstown,

Ky. His father, Adam Guthrie, a native of Cork, Ireland, came to America at the age of twelve in 1774 and lived for a time with the family of his eldest sister near the headwaters of the South Branch of the Potomac River, in what is now West Virginia. In 1788 he started westward over the mountains to Kentucky, and on the way fell in with the party of Edmund Polk, a veteran of the Revolution, whose daughter Hannah he married. Settling at Bardstown, Nelson County, Ky., he became active in the Kentucky militia and represented his county in the state legislature (1800–08). After a preliminary education in McAllister's Academy, Bardstown, James Guthrie began the study of law with John Rowan, and, admitted to the bar, remained at Bardstown in the practice of his profession until 1820. After two unsuccessful campaigns for the state legislature, he was appointed commonwealth's attorney and removed to Louisville, where he continued to reside until his death. In 1827 he was elected a representative in the lower house of the Kentucky legislature. After four years in that capacity he was elected to the state Senate, representing Jefferson and Bullitt counties, and was continuously reëlected until 1841. He was twice speaker *pro tempore* of the Senate, and in 1835 was the unsuccessful candidate of his party for the United States Senate. In each house he served as chairman of the committees on judiciary, and on internal improvement, his most important work being done in connection with the latter. It was largely owing to his efforts that the state undertook the improvement of its rivers, and incorporated the private companies which built its system of Macadam roads and made the beginning of railway construction between Lexington and Louisville.

During this period Guthrie laid the foundation of his immense fortune by his judicious investments in Louisville real estate, and added to his wealth by his promotion of Macadam roads and of railways. He was the outstanding railway promoter in Kentucky before the Civil War, and was the controlling force in the notorious Portland Canal as well as in many banking institutions. In fact, his success in this field was so spectacular that his reputation as a business man overshadowed his achievements as a legislator. He became the foremost citizen of Louisville, serving as a member of the City Council, organizing the public school system, and founding the University of Louisville, which he served as president until after the Civil War. In 1849 he presided over the convention which made the third constitution of Kentucky.

By 1850 Guthrie's activities as a railroad promoter had brought him into contact with the leading industrial men of the South and had given him a wide reputation as a financier. He attended the Southern conventions which were so common during the forties and exerted an appreciable influence on their deliberations. His outstanding position in the Democratic party and in the business world was given recognition by his appointment by President Pierce in 1853 as secretary of the treasury. On his record Guthrie does not deserve to be ranked as one of the great secretaries, but he was certainly much more than a routine one. He showed himself a ruthless reformer, overhauling the treasury regulations, curbing extravagance, reducing the debt, and weeding out incompetence. He attracted particular attention to himself by his removal of the collector of the Port of New York for using his office for political purposes (*Louisville Daily Democrat,* Oct. 26, 1853). He brought down upon himself a storm of protest by his recommendation that the issue of paper money by state banks should be taxed out of existence.

Upon retiring from the treasury in 1857, Guthrie devoted himself to the promoting and financing of the languishing Louisville & Nashville Railroad. Through his influence the railroad was able to sell its bonds and complete its track. At the outbreak of the Civil War, Guthrie was president of the road, and his attitude in the war was probably determined primarily by his business interests. After a period of apparent vacillation during which, as a member of the Virginia Peace Convention and of the Kentucky Border Conference, he sought a compromise, he made his decision to adhere to the Union and throughout the war placed his railroad at the disposal of the United States government. The service of the Louisville & Nashville Railroad in transporting troops and supplies to the Southwest was one of the deciding factors in the conquest of that region. There was continual friction, but Guthrie was able both to retain the control of his road and to elicit the praise of the Union authorities. He remained a Democrat throughout his career, however; actively supported McClellan in 1864, and after the war was over was elected to the United States Senate as a conservative (*Louisville Daily Democrat,* Jan. 12, 1865), where he became an uncompromising upholder of President Johnson's policies and an unrelenting opponent of the reconstruction measures of Congress. Failing health brought about his resignation in February 1868, and his death followed shortly afterward.

Guthrie was married on May 13, 1821, to Eliza C. Prather of Louisville, who died in 1836. He was survived by his three daughters. In personal appearance he was uncouth and unprepossessing, and was lame for life from a wound received in a personal encounter during his Bardstown days. He was a man of many eccentricities, of a domineering and arrogant personality, and wholly lacking in the usual graces of the politician. His success in business and in politics was chiefly due to his sound judgment and to his reputation for absolute honesty and integrity.

[John Livingston, *Portraits of Eminent Americans*, vol. III (1854); John Savage, *Our Living Representative Men* (1860); George Baber, in *Ky. State Hist. Soc. Reg.*, Jan. 1912; R. S. Cotterill, "James Guthrie, Kentuckian," *Ibid.*, Sept. 1922; *Report of the Debates and Proc. of the Convention for the Revision of the Constitution of the State of Ky.* (1849); Lewis and R. H. Collins, *Hist. of Ky.* (2 vols., 1874); H. Levin, *Lawyers and Lawmakers of Ky.* (1897); J. S. Johnston, *Memorial Hist. of Louisville* (1897); *Hist. of the Ohio Falls Cities and Their Counties* (1882), I, 489; *Daily National Intelligencer* (Washington, D. C.), Mar. 15, 1869; *Frankfort Commonwealth*, Mar. 19, 1869; "The Louisville and Nashville Railroad, 1861–65," in *Am. Hist. Rev.*, July 1924; *Annual Reports of the Secretary of the Treasury*, 1853–57; genealogical information from Rev. Laurence R. Guthrie, Mercersburg, Pa., who has compiled a volume on "American Guthrie and Allied Families."]
R. S. C.

GUTHRIE, SAMUEL (1782–Oct. 19, 1848), chemist and physician, descended from John Guthrie, an emigrant from Edinburgh, Scotland, who died in Litchfield County, Conn., in 1730, was born in Brimfield, Mass., the oldest son of Samuel and Sarah Guthrie. He had little formal education. Besides some years of desultory study of medicine with his father, who was a physician, he took only two courses of lectures, one at the College of Physicians and Surgeons, New York, in 1810–11, and the other at the University of Pennsylvania in 1815. He must have been in practice before the War of 1812. By his father's will he received "one dollar, to be paid . . . when called for," the five volumes of Benjamin Rush's *Enquiries*, and one set of silver catheters. A significant year in his life was 1817, when he moved, with his wife and three children. from Sherburne, N. Y., which had been their home for some years, to Sacketts Harbor, N. Y. Here he lived about thirty years. Northern New York at that time was nearly a wilderness, and Guthrie, being a man of ingenuity, self-reliance, and versatility, plunged into a pioneer's life. In addition to clearing the land, constructing a house, and raising crops, he became a practical chemist. His immediate neighbors, besides calling upon "the doctor" for aid in sickness, knew him as a quiet, taciturn man, who made the best vinegar in the vicinity, distilled a good brand of alcohol, and performed mysterious — often astounding — experiments with apparatus fabricated by himself. To the country at large he was most acceptably known as the inventor and manufacturer of an effective priming powder, called the "percussion pill," and the punch lock for exploding it, which together replaced the flash-in-the-pan type of powder and made the old-fashioned flint-lock musket obsolete. He had a laboratory near his house where he performed experiments, and a mill about a mile away where he manufactured for many years large quantities of this powder and other explosives (*e.g.*, potassium chlorate and mercury fulminate). In 1830 he devised a process for the rapid conversion of potato starch into molasses, and in July 1831 sent Benjamin Silliman [*q.v.*] a description of his process together with a sample of the product. To Silliman he also sent samples of crystallized potassium chlorate, of numerous varieties of powder, of oil of turpentine, and of "spirituous solution of chloric ether." His letters describing these chemical substances were published with editorial comment in the *American Journal of Science* during 1832 and reprinted, probably in the same year, as *The Complete Writings of Samuel Guthrie* (n.d.). The "chloric ether" made by Guthrie in 1831 by distilling chloride of lime with alcohol in a copper still proved to be chloroform, and the discovery antedated slightly the independent discoveries of the same compound made at practically the same time by Soubeiran in France and Liebig in Germany. Guthrie married Sybil Sexton in 1804. The eldest of their four children, Alfred [*q.v.*], removed to Chicago where he attained some distinction as an engineer; the second son, Edwin, captain of a company of Iowa volunteers, was killed in the Mexican War. Samuel Guthrie died in 1848 at Sacketts Harbor, in the house where he had lived for thirty years.

[H. N. and E. G. Dunn, *Records of the Guthrie Family* (1898); Ossian Guthrie, *Memoirs of Dr. Samuel Guthrie and the History of the Discovery of Chloroform* (1887); Victor Robinson, M.D., in *Medical Life* (Guthrie Number), Mar. 1927; E. F. Smith, *Chemistry in America* (1914), Benj. Silliman, Jr., *American Contributions to Chemistry* (1874), reprinted from the *Am. Chemist*, Aug., Sept., Dec. 1874.]
L. C. N.

GUY, SEYMOUR JOSEPH (Jan. 16, 1824–Dec. 10, 1910), portrait and genre painter, was a native of Greenwich, a parliamentary borough of London. He became the pupil of Buttersworth and Ambrose Jerome, London painters, and in 1854, at the age of thirty, emigrated to New York, where he made something of a reputation as a portrait painter at first but eventually determined to devote himself to genre work. His pictures of child life, exhibited from time to time at the National Academy of Design between 1860 and 1900, became deservedly popular. He was elected associate of the Academy in 1861 and was made an academician in 1865. He was also a member of the American Society for Painters in Water-colors, the Artists' Fund Society, and the Century Association. He married Anna M. Barber, daughter of W. W. Barber, an engraver in the United States Mint at Philadelphia. Three of his paintings, "Evening," "Solitaire," and "Supplication," were exhibited at the Centennial Exposition, Philadelphia, 1876. To the Paris Exposition of 1878 he sent "Baby's Bed-Time" and "Learning the Gamut." Two of his works, "Rest" and "Preparing for Tomorrow," were at the Paris Exposition of 1900. For his four genre pictures at the Louisiana Purchase Exposition, St. Louis, 1904, he received a gold medal; he also received a medal at the Buffalo Exposition of 1901. "Out of His Element" went into the Thomas B. Clarke collection and his "Making a Train" into the collection of Mrs. George W. Elkins of Philadelphia. His portrait of his colleague, Charles Loring Elliott, the portrait painter, is in the Metropolitan Museum of Art, New York.

Guy's pictures of children have been called trite and over-elaborated, but the best examples are so genuine in sentiment and so fully in sympathy with the human motive that their merits should far outweigh their defects. They are excellently drawn, and in a number of instances lamp-light or candle-light effects are rendered with striking success. His thorough English training is shown in his exact draftsmanship and choice of subjects; it is also perhaps responsible for his lack of values. For while his color is not unpleasant, it is, in common with most of the British genre painting of the period, quite innocent of those last refinements of relativity which give the greatest distinction to the work of the Dutch "little masters." One of the most characteristic examples of his work is "Making a Train," in the Elkins collection. Few more intelligent or more original pictures of child life by an American hand exist. In the attic bedroom a little girl is trying on a garment that sweeps the floor behind her. The action, posture, and expression of this ingenuous young maiden are full of natural childish grace and charm. The artificial lighting of the interior is cleverly rendered, and the accessories, especially the cross-legged cot-bed in the background, with its patchwork quilt, are triumphs of still-life work.

[*Cat. of the Thos. B. Clarke Coll. of Am. Pictures* (1891); Samuel Isham, *Hist. of Am. Painting* (1905); *Am. Art Ann.*, 1911; *Art Jour.*, Sept. 1875; Chas. M. Kurtz, ed., *Nat. Acad. Notes* (1884); *Evening Post* (N. Y.), Nov. 9, 1877; John F. Weir, *Official Report of the Am. Centennial Exposition* (1876); *Am. Art. News*, Dec. 24, 1910.]
W. H. D.

GUYOT, ARNOLD HENRY (Sept. 28, 1807–Feb. 8, 1884), geographer, was born at Boudevilliers, Switzerland, the son of David Pierre and Constance (Favarger) Guyot. His father's ancestors had come to Switzerland from France in the fourteenth century. In Arnold's boyhood his family moved to Hauterive, near Neuchâtel. Before his education was completed, he had determined upon the ministry as a profession. This was probably the result of his home environment; his ancestors, Protestant since the sixteenth century, were strong and sturdy upholders of religious freedom. On the other hand, his contacts with his fellow students were constantly turning his attention to the natural sciences. Entering the College of Neuchâtel in 1821, he had for a classmate Leo Lesquereux [*q.v.*], the botanist. Later as a student in Germany at Karlsruhe, he became closely associated with Alexander Braun and Carl Schimper, botanists, and with Jean Louis Rodolphe Agassiz [*q.v.*]. His zeal for the ministry and the languages took him to Metzingen, to Stuttgart, and finally to Berlin, but in the Prussian capital he took excursions with Alexander Humboldt in botany and studied psychology under J. W. Hegel, physics and meteorology under H. W. Dove, and physical geography under Ritter. The influence of friends and instructors increased his scientific trend, and definitely turned him from the ministry to the study of the natural sciences. His doctor's thesis was "The Natural Classification of Lakes" (*De Naturali Lacuum Divisione,* 1835). For five years after receiving the doctorate of the University of Berlin (1835) he was in Paris acting as a tutor. During this time Agassiz formulated his theory of glacial epochs, which opened up a new field of investigation and thought, and Guyot's studies and publications between 1838 and 1848 were largely in the field of glaciology. He made frequent trips to Switzerland where, in the field, he subjected the findings of Agassiz to severe tests. His own contributions included the laws of glacial motion, the structure of glaciers, and the movement of morainic matter, and were of the highest importance. In 1839 he was called to the chair of history and physical geography at the Academy of Neuchâtel, and here he remained until the Academy was closed in 1848.

In that year, on the advice and urgent invitation of Agassiz, who had preceded him, Guyot came to America and settled at Cambridge, Mass. During the following winter (January and February 1849) he delivered the Lowell Institute lectures at Boston, published the same year as *The Earth and Man.* This volume, one of Guyot's most significant publications, reflected the influence of Ritter and his own deep insight into the relationships between the earth and its inhabitants, and thrust him into a commanding place among American geographers. For six years he lectured under the Massachusetts Board of Education in institutes and normal schools on geography and methods of teaching it. This work formulated for him a plan of teaching geography which he afterwards incorporated in a series of textbooks. It is probable that these books, published between the years 1866 and 1875, were the first definite attempt at a scientific presentation of geography in American schools, and they were in a large measure the models for textbooks in geography during many succeeding years. In 1854, he accepted the chair of physical geography and geology at Princeton, and here he remained until his death. Among his achievements was the founding of a museum, the first of its kind at Princeton, and to the collection and classification of specimens he devoted much time. His monument at Princeton is Guyot Hall, which houses the museum and the departments of natural science.

In addition to his teaching, Guyot became interested in meteorological and topographic work. Under the direction of the Smithsonian Institution, he began the work of selecting and equipping weather observation stations, particularly in New York and Massachusetts. This work was the genesis of the system of weather stations all over the United States which makes weather maps and weather predictions possible. His topographic work consisted of obtaining by barometric measurements the altitude of significant localities, and from the accumulated data constructing topographic maps of the Appalachian Mountains and, in greater detail, of the Catskill region. His zeal for obtaining altitudes was untiring, and many thousands of heights in the Appalachian system from Maine to South Carolina were measured and recorded.

Guyot's principle of teaching geography was the principle of his own studies, first observation in the field and then deductions from the accumulated facts. He urged that the pupils of the schools should be made familiar with their own environment, and when this was accomplished, the concepts of man's relationships with the earth in distant lands might be the more easily understood. His study of a problem was thorough and his faithfulness to details gave him confidence and power. His teachings and his textbooks emphasized the necessity of a study of the topographic map as an introductory study of any area. This was the beginning of the modern idea in teaching geography.

In his memoir of Guyot James Dwight Dana [*q.v.*] stated that his "special weakness was . . . an unobtrusiveness that disinclined him to assert himself, that made him too easily content with work without publication" (*post,* p. 343), but his writings, although comparatively few and confined in the main to the fields of glaciology, the teaching of geography, and orography, were of value probably because they were the result of laborious search, the fruit of many seasons of field work. He was always deeply religious, and in a volume published in 1884, *Creation, or the Biblical Cosmogony in the Light of Modern Science,* he attempted to correlate his scientific work with the Biblical story of creation. Guyot married in his sixtieth year, July 2, 1867, Sarah Doremus Haines, the daughter of Governor Haines of New Jersey.

[Memoir by J. D. Dana, in *Nat. Acad. Sci. Biog. Memoirs,* vol. II (1886); Louis Favre, in *Bull. de la Société des Sciences Naturelles de Neuchâtel,* vol. XIV (1884); L. C. Jones, *Arnold Guyot et Princeton* (1929) and "Arnold Henry Guyot," in *Faculty Papers of Union Coll.,* vol. I (1930); Charles Faure, "Vie et Travaux d'Arnold Guyot," in *Le Globe: Journal Géographique* (Geneva), vol. XXIII, *Mémoires* (1884); obituaries in *Science,* Feb. 22, 1884, and *N. Y. Tribune,* Feb. 9, 1884.]

R. M. B.

GWIN, WILLIAM McKENDREE (Oct. 9, 1805–Sept. 3, 1885), politician, was the second of the seven children of James and Mary Gwin. His father, a native of Wales, made his way through the mountains from South Carolina to the Cumberland settlement in Tennessee in 1791. He was an Indian fighter and a friend of Andrew Jackson. About 1803 he became an itinerant Methodist preacher, and his son William McKendree, born in Sumner County, Tenn., was named for the Western leader of that denomination. Young Gwin received professional training in both law and medicine, taking his degree in the latter subject at Transylvania University (now Transylvania College), Lexington, Ky., in March 1828. The subject of his thesis was "Syphilis." The twenty-three closely written pages are preserved in the college library at Lexington. After his graduation, Gwin moved to Clinton, Miss., where he practised medicine until 1833. In that year he received from President Jackson an appointment as United States marshal for the district of Mississippi. In 1840 he was elected a member of the lower house of Congress, but served one term only. Financial obligations forced him into private life and he moved to New Orleans, where he received an appointment to superintend the construction of a custom-house in that city. This position he held until Taylor was elected president in 1848, when, as he declared, "determined not to make money, but to devote all my energies to obtaining and maintaining political power" (letter to brother, *Overland Monthly,* August 1891, p. 206), he decided to go to California.

Accordingly, upon his arrival in San Francisco in the summer of 1849, he plunged immediately into the discordant political life of the territory. Traveling extensively and speaking frequently, he urged the formation of a state government. When the constitutional convention met at Monterey in September 1849, he was chosen to represent the San Francisco district. His training and experience together with his native tact qualified him for assuming a position of leadership in such a body. His efforts on behalf of slavery in the convention, which have been greatly exaggerated, were not permitted to interfere with his main purpose—to hasten the formation of a state government and secure his own election to the Senate of the United States. This accomplished, he reached Washington in 1850 before California was admitted to the Union. Following its admission on Sept. 9, his credentials were accepted, and he continued to represent his adopted state until 1861. He has been given credit for establishing a mint in California and for initiating plans to survey the Pacific Coast. Following the outbreak of the Civil War in 1861, he was arrested, by order of General Sumner, while on board a vessel in the Bay of Panama, and was taken to New York, where he was held a prisoner at Fort Lafayette from Nov. 18 to Dec. 2, 1861. He went to Paris in 1863 and was there until June of the following year, during which time he succeeded in interesting Napoleon III in a project for establishing settlers from the South in Sonora and Chihuahua, Mexico. He went to Mexico in 1864 in pursuance of his plan, but Maximilian refused to permit him to carry it into execution, and the scheme failed. In October 1865, on reëntering the United States after a second visit to Mexico, he was arrested again and held a prisoner in Fort Jackson for a period of eight months. He lived twenty years longer, but his public career was over, and at the time of his death in New York he was practically unknown. He was married twice: first to Caroline Sampson, who died before 1834, and second, to Mary Bell. There were two children of his first marriage and four of his second. Gwin possessed a striking personality and was genial and clever, but in his public career gave occasional indications of a willingness to employ subtle intrigue to further his purposes.

["Memoirs on History of the United States, Mexico, and California by Ex-Senator William M. Gwin, Dictated by Himself for the Bancroft Library" (MS., 1878); J. F. H. Claibourne, *Mississippi as a Province, Territory, and State* (1880), both of which must be used with discretion; J. G. Cisco, *Historic Sumner County, Tenn.* (1909); J. B. McFerrin, *Hist. of Methodism in Tenn.*, vol. I (1869); *Overland Monthly,* May, June, Aug., Nov. 1891; H. H. Bancroft, *Hist. of Cal.*, vol. VI (1888); Helen H. Blattner, "The Political Career of William M. Gwin" (MS., master's thesis in the library of the Univ. of Cal.); *War of the Rebellion: Official Records,* 1 ser., XLVIII (pt. 2), L (pt. 2), 2 ser., II, VIII; *Biog. Dir. Am. Cong.* (1928); James O'Meare, *Broderick and Gwin* (1881); obituaries in *N. Y. Times* and *Daily Examiner* (San Francisco) for Sept. 4, 1885; certain information from Gwin's son, W. M. Gwin of San Francisco, and from Mrs. C. F. Norton, librarian of Transylvania College, Lexington, Ky.]

C. G.

GWINNETT, BUTTON (*c.* 1735–May 16, 1777), signer of the Declaration of Independence, was born at Down Hatherley, Gloucestershire, England, the son of Samuel and Anne (Emes) Gwinnett, and was baptized on Apr. 10, 1735. His father, whose ancestors had long lived in Wales, was a clergyman, and his mother was related to people of consequence in Herefordshire. He was married on Apr. 19, 1757, to Ann Bourne of Wolverhampton. For several years before and after 1760 he was engaged in exporting goods to the American colonies, and by September 1765 he had settled in Savannah, Ga., as a merchant. In October of that year he purchased St. Catherine Island, a tract of some thirty-six square miles lying off the coast of Georgia, near the then flourishing port of Sunbury. There he set up as a planter. Sunbury was the "capital" of a group of settlers originally from New England, and it was through them, and especially through his intimate friendship with Lyman Hall, that Gwinnett was brought to an interest in politics. He was a justice of the peace in 1767–68, and in 1769 was a member—though a somewhat laggard one—of the Georgia Colonial Assembly, but afterward for nearly five years, perhaps because of the ceaseless financial worries of his plantation, he seems to have eschewed all public activity. In January 1776 he attended a meeting of the Georgia Council of Safety, and was elected as one of five delegates to the Continental Congress. He arrived in Philadelphia in May, took a respectable part in the sittings of the Congress, signed the Declaration of Independence and left in time to be back in Savannah by late August. It was his ambition to be a general of Georgia troops, but all his machinations were unavailing, and he found it necessary to satisfy himself with his election in October as speaker of the Georgia Assembly and his reëlection as delegate to the Continental Congress.

During the following months he took an important part in the drafting of the first constitution of Georgia and in thwarting the schemes by which Georgia was to be absorbed by South Carolina. In March 1777, upon the sudden death of Gov. Archibald Bulloch, he was commissioned "President of the State of Georgia" and commander-in-chief of the army, positions which he occupied for about two months, when, somewhat inexplicably, he was defeated in his candidacy for reëlection to the governorship by a representative of his own faction in politics. As governor, his affiliation with his "radical" New-England-derived neighbors brought him the enmity of the conservatives. He was opposed particularly by Gen. Lachlan McIntosh [*q.v.*], whose brother he had arrested upon a suspicion of treachery, and whose authority as a soldier was always perilously near clashing with his own authority as governor. The bungling of an expedition of Georgia soldiery upon British strongholds in Florida in the spring of 1777 precipitated an inquiry in the Assembly as to whether the civil authority had hampered the military, or otherwise; in short, as to whether Gwinnett or McIntosh was the more culpable. The inquiry sustained Gwinnett, but McIntosh, in pique, proclaimed his opponent before the Assembly as a "scoundrel and a lying rascal" (Jenkins, p. 152). In the duel which followed next morning on the outskirts of Savannah both men were wounded, and Gwinnett died three days later. He died insolvent, and it is not known where he was buried; his descendants are apparently extinct; there is no trustworthy portrait of him; but of his thirty-six autographs, one, in 1924, was sold at public auction for $14,000.

[C. F. Jenkins, *Button Gwinnett* (1926), an exhaustive biography without formal bibliography but with full references to sources in the text and footnotes; C. C. Jones, *Biog. Sketches of the Delegates from Ga. to the Continental Cong.* (1891); W. G. Charlton, in *Ga. Hist. Quart.*, June 1924, a laudatory sketch; *The Colonial Records of the State of Ga.*, vols. X, XV (1907); *The Revolutionary Records of the State of Ga.*, vol. I (1908).]

J. D. W.

HAAN, WILLIAM GEORGE (Oct. 4, 1863–Oct. 26, 1924), soldier, was born on a farm near Crownpoint, Ind., the son of Nicholas and Anna Marie (Weins) Haan, who had emigrated from Germany in 1850. After elementary preparation at a country school and near-by high school, he received appointment to West Point in 1885 and graduated four years later near the head of his class. Assigned to the artillery, he eventually held all grades from lieutenant to colonel, inclusive. In 1898 he accompanied his battery to the Philippines, and for distinguished conduct in action during the attack on Manila, Aug. 13, 1898, and against insurgents near Manila, Feb. 5, 1899, he received silver-star citations and was recommended for brevet promotion to a captaincy. He was selected as a member of the original General Staff Corps, 1903–06, and during 1903–04 was on important duty in Panama as confidential representative of the government. In the year 1906 he performed meritorious service in connection with the great San Francisco fire and earthquake, as acting chief of staff, Pacific Division. At the outbreak of the World War he was promoted brigadier-general, N. A., and assigned to command the 57th Field Artillery Brigade at Camp MacArthur, Texas; but on Dec. 17, 1917, he was advanced to major-general and to the command of the 32nd Division, largely made up of soldiers from the states of Wisconsin and Michigan. The Red Arrow Division, as it came to be known, was the sixth American division sent overseas, and though at first somewhat disorganized by use as labor and replacement troops, the division took an active part in the defensive-sector operations in Alsace, and in the major offensives of the Marne-Aisne, Oise-Aisne, and Meuse-Argonne. Its most brilliant exploit, perhaps, was the capture of the stubbornly defended Côté Dame Marie. For his services, General Haan was awarded the Distinguished Service Medal (United States) and the Croix de Guerre with Palm (France) and made Commander of the Legion of Honor (France) and Commander of the Order of the Crown (Belgium).

On Nov. 30, 1918, while leading the VII Corps into Germany, he was promoted brigadier-general in the Regular Army. Returning to the United States with his division, he became director of the War Plans Division, General Staff, and with marked ability handled many difficult problems attending army reorganization. He was promoted major-general, U. S. A., July 3, 1920. After his retirement from active service Mar. 31, 1922, he made his home in Milwaukee and engaged in special writing for the *Milwaukee Journal.* An article by him, "The Division as a Fighting Machine," appeared in the *Wisconsin Magazine of History* for September 1920. He died at Mount Alto Hospital, Washington, D. C. Interment, with high military honors and in the presence of a distinguished gathering, was at Arlington; and some five years later, Nov. 9, 1929, an impressive granite monument, erected by General Haan's wartime division, was unveiled by the Governor of Wisconsin with fitting ceremonies. He was survived by his widow, Margaret (Hawes)

Haan, daughter of an officer of the army transport service, whom he had married Aug. 16, 1905. Battery Haan, a defensive work of Fort Bruja, Panama Canal, was named by the War Department in his honor.

[*Ann. Report, Asso. Grads. U. S. Mil. Acad.* (1926); *Badger Legionnaire,* Nov. 10, 1924; *Broadside and Barrage* (Milwaukee), Nov. 1924; *Evening Star* (Washington), Oct. 27, 1924; *Who's Who in America,* 1922–23.] C. D. R.

HAARSTICK, HENRY CHRISTIAN (July 26, 1836–Jan. 26, 1919), pioneer in Mississippi barge transportation after the Civil War, was born at Hohenhameln, Hanover, Germany. During the German immigration of 1849, with his parents, Henry and Christina Haarstick, he arrived in New York after an ocean voyage of forty-nine days. The family went westward along the Erie Canal route and on to St. Louis, reaching their journey's end on July 25, 1849, in the midst of devastation by fire and cholera. Henry attended the Saxony School of the German Evangelical Church, the Wykoff English School, and Jones Commercial College. In February 1853 he entered the employ of the Maloney & Tilton distillery, and in nine years rose to partnership. When in 1862 fire destroyed the property of the firm, Haarstick bought the interests of his partner and rebuilt the plant. Four or five years later, seeing the opportunity in river transportation, he sold the distillery to Card & Lawrence, and in 1869 bought stock in the Mississippi Valley Transportation Company, the only considerable barge line on the river. In the course of the next decade, serving in the capacities of director, vice-president, and finally general manager, he firmly established the concern.

Because of high freight rates on the more speedy railroads, interest revived in cheaper river commerce, asleep since the Civil War. In August 1881, in order to control the eastern outlet for his railroads afforded by the Mississippi, Jay Gould assimilated the Mississippi Valley Transportation Company, in which Haarstick now owned stock to the amount of $600,000, and consolidated it with the St. Louis & New Orleans Transportation Company. A certificate of corporate existence of the resulting St. Louis & Mississippi Valley Transportation Company was issued at Jefferson City, Mo., on Sept. 10, 1881. The board of nine directors was headed by Haarstick and had five members controlled by Gould. Because all competition was overshadowed the cry of monopoly was raised, but this soon quieted as service improved and rates decreased. The company under Haarstick's management commanded thirteen tugs and ninety-nine barges with a capacity of 5,000,000 bushels of grain, owned large elevators at Belmont, Mo., and New Orleans, and maintained floating steam elevators at New Orleans to transfer grain from the barges to ocean vessels. Activities culminated in 1892–93 when 4,200 carloads were transported. Decline due to railroad competition began in 1894, and ten years later Haarstick retired. In his thirty-five years of activity on the river he had seen St. Louis become an important grain market. He was a member of the executive committee of the St. Louis Merchant's Exchange which held a convention, Oct. 26, 1881, to discuss the improvement of the Mississippi and its tributaries, and in 1885 he was elected president of the Merchant's Exchange. After his retirement from business in 1904 he continued as vice-president of the St. Louis Union Trust Company. He died in St. Louis at the age of eighty-two, survived by his wife, Elise (Hoppe) Haarstick, whom he had married in 1861, and by two of their three children.

[Biographical sketches of Haarstick are found in James Cox, *Old and New St. Louis* (1894), and the *Book of St. Louisans* (1906), ed. by J. W. Leonard. Detailed data regarding his business activities are found in the *Daily Picayune* (New Orleans), June–Oct. 1881, Sept.–Nov. 1904; *St. Louis Commercial Gazette,* Sept. 15, 1881; and the *Waterways Journal* (St. Louis), Nov. 5, 12, 1904. Obituaries appeared in the *St. Louis Globe-Democrat,* Jan. 27, 1919, and other St. Louis papers.] V. G. G.

HABBERTON, JOHN (Feb. 24, 1842–Feb. 24, 1921), author, editor, son of Job John and Esther Eliza (Peck) Habberton, was born in Brooklyn, N. Y. When the son was six years old, his father died and he was sent to Illinois to live with an uncle. After a slight schooling he worked in a country store and as a telegraph operator, but in 1859 he returned to New York, where he learned the printing trade. He enlisted as a private in the Union army in 1862 and served through 1865. At the close of the war he secured a position with Harper & Brothers, in whose employ he remained until 1872. He married, Feb. 25, 1868, Alice Lawrence Hastings, the daughter of Dr. Panet Marshall Hastings of Hartford, Conn. In 1872 he ventured into a publishing business of his own but soon failed. Shortly after he embarked upon an editorial career, and from 1874 to 1877 he was literary editor of the *Christian Union,* afterward the *Outlook.* Later he worked on the editorial staff of the *New York Herald,* 1876–93, as literary and dramatic critic. In 1893 he was for a short time editor of *Godey's Magazine* and from 1897 to 1899 he was on the staff of *Collier's Weekly.* His first attempt at sustained fiction was *Helen's Babies* (1876), written at the suggestion of his wife, who said: "The mischief those boys get into would fill a book. Why don't you keep a record for a week or two?" The manuscript was rejected by several publishers but was finally published anonymously and the author's identity was discovered only by accident. This story of the escapades of his own boys was so popular that Habberton rapidly wrote other fiction: *The Barton Experiment* (1877); *The Jericho Road* (1877); *The Scripture Club of Valley Rest* (1877); *Other People's Children* (1877), a sequel to *Helen's Babies*; *Some Folks* (1877); *The Crew of the "Sam Weller"* (1878); *Canoeing in Kanuckia* (1878), in collaboration with Charles L. Norton; *Just One Day* (1879); *The Worst Boy in Town* (1880); *Who Was Paul Grayson?* (1881); *Mrs. Mayburn's Twins* (1882); *The Bowsham Puzzle* (1884); *One Tramp* (1884); *Brueton's Bayou* (1886); *Country Luck* (1887); *Couldn't Say No* (1889); *All He Knew* (1890); *The Chautauquans* (1891); *Out at Twinnett's* (1891); *Well Out of It* (1892); *Honey and Gall* (1892); *A Lucky Lover* (1892); *Phil Fuzzytop* (1900); *Some Boys' Doings* (1901); *Caleb Wright; a Story of the West* (1901); *The Tiger and the Insect* (1902); and *Budge & Toddie; or, Helen's Babies at Play* (1908). He also wrote one play, *Deacon Crankett,* which was performed over five hundred times; a biography, *George Washington* (1884); and edited *Floral Life* in several volumes (1903–08). He is remembered today almost exclusively because of *Helen's Babies,* which has considerable humor of a not remarkable kind, a simple plot involving the love story of the young uncle who spends his vacation in charge of his sister's children, and a pleasant, unaffected style. All his stories deal with ordinary events in everyday life and with ordinary people. Habberton lived many years at New Rochelle, N. Y., and for a time at Westwood, N. J. Just before his last illness he was living at the Soldiers' Home at Kearny, N. J. He died at Mountainside Hospital, Glen Ridge, N. J.

[John Habberton, "My Literary Experiences," *Lippincott's Mag.,* Dec. 1886; *Who's Who in America,* 1918–19; F. H. Hastings, *Family Record of Dr. Seth Hastings, Sr.* (1899); *N. Y. Times, N. Y. Tribune,* Feb. 26, 1921; *Newark Evening News,* Feb. 25, 26, 1921; information as to certain facts from Habberton's son, John L. Habberton, North Caldwell, N. J.]

S. G. B.

HABERSHAM, ALEXANDER WYLLY (Mar. 24, 1826–Mar. 26, 1883), naval officer, merchant, the son of Richard Wylly and Sarah (Elliott) Habersham and great-grandson of James Habersham [*q.v.*], was born in New York City. His father was a lawyer and a representative from Georgia in the Twenty-sixth and Twenty-seventh Congresses. Alexander received his early education from private tutors and was appointed to the United States Naval Academy from Georgia. After his graduation in 1848 he was assigned to the Pacific Squadron and then, 1851–52, was on duty with the Coast Survey. In 1853 he was made acting lieutenant of the store ship *J. P. Kennedy* which sailed that year with the United States surveying and exploring expedition to the North Pacific and China seas, and in 1854, at Hongkong, he was assigned as acting master to the *John Hancock,* another ship in the exploring expedition. Upon his return to San Francisco in October 1855 he learned of his promotion the previous month to the rank of lieutenant. Subsequently, while stationed at the Philadelphia Navy Yard, he published an account of the exploring expedition under the title *My Last Cruise, or Where We Went and What We Saw.* He was assigned to the *Powhatan* of the East India Squadron in 1857 and on May 30, 1860, resigned from the service to engage in business in Japan. He was responsible for one of the first shipments of Japanese tea ever imported into the United States. In 1861 he returned to America, but in December was arrested by Federal authorities as a Southern sympathizer. Upon his refusal to take the oath of allegiance to the United States, on the ground that his allegiance was due to the state of Georgia, he was confined in Fort McHenry, Md., for four months.

At the close of the Civil War he became a partner in the Baltimore firm of Habersham & Barrett, later Smoot, Habersham & Barrett, importers and dealers in teas and East Indian goods. Subsequently he became a member of the firm of Habersham, Kirby & Company, coffee brokers, and in 1870 or 1871 established a coffee and canned-goods brokerage business for himself. At the time of his death he was one of the best-known coffee merchants in the country.

In early life he married Jessie Steele of Annapolis, Md., a grand-daughter of Francis Scott Key [*q.v.*]. They had several children. Habersham died in Annapolis two days after his fifty-seventh birthday.

[J. G. B. Bulloch, *A Hist. and Geneal. of the Habersham Family* (1901); U. S. Naval Acad. Grads.' Asso., *Reg. of Grads., 1846–1916* (1916); E. C. Marshall, *Hist. of the U. S. Naval Acad.* (1862); Baltimore directories; obituary in Baltimore *Sun,* Mar. 28, 1883.]

J. H. F.

HABERSHAM, JAMES (January 1712 o. s.–Aug. 28, 1775), merchant, planter, colonial official, was born in Beverley, Yorkshire, England, the son of James and Elizabeth Habersham, and was baptized on June 26 (or Jan. 26), 1715. As a young man he migrated in 1738 to the infant colony of Georgia, the settlement of which had been begun under James Edward Oglethorpe [*q.v.*] only five years before. Habersham came to the colony in the ship that brought his friend George Whitefield [*q.v.*], the evangelist, successor of John Wesley in Georgia, to establish an orphanage in the new colony. Soon after their arrival Habersham opened a school for destitute children and later cooperated with Whitefield in establishing the Bethesda Orphanage, said to have been one of the first institutions of that sort in America. When Whitefield returned to England in 1741, Habersham took charge of the orphanage. In 1744, however, he resigned that charge to organize the firm of Harris & Habersham, the first and for years the most important commercial enterprise in the colony. The firm carried on a large trade with the Northern colonies, England, and the West Indies, exporting deer skins, rice, indigo, lumber, naval stores, and cattle.

Habersham also developed large farming interests. The proprietary government of Georgia, dominated by Oglethorpe, had forbidden the use of African slaves and sought to direct the energies of the colonists into grape growing and the production of silk. Conditions were unfavorable to these light forms of industry, however, and it became evident to many that Georgia would be forced to follow the example of South Carolina, which had found prosperity in rice production. For this purpose Whitefield and others deemed slaves necessary, and Habersham was one of the most outspoken advocates of the introduction of slaves. On this subject he wrote to the trustees of the colony in 1739 as follows: "Though the people have been as industrious as possible, they are not able to live; for I believe there is not an instance of one planter in the colony who can support his family with his own produce. Besides, the sun is so extremely hot here in the summer, that no white man can stay in the field the best part of the day. All who come to settle here are put into a wilderness, which they have to clear before they can plant it; which is so intolerably costly, with white hands, that I have heard some affirm, that to clear our good land—which is swamp—effectually with them, would cost almost as much as they could buy land for in some parts of England" (Stevens, *post,* I, 292). Eight years later he said, ". . . things have had such a dreadful appearance for some time past, that, rather than see the colony deserted and brought to desolation, and the inhabitants reduced to want and beggary, I really, with the Trustees, would have consented to the use of negroes, and was sorry to hear that they had written so warmly against them" (*Ibid.,* I, 297). When the trustees finally yielded in 1749, Habersham rapidly developed rice plantations. Just before the Revolution he owned 198 slaves and was producing about seven hundred barrels of rice annually, from which he received an income of some $10,000.

In addition to being the first business man of the province and one of the largest planters, Habersham played a leading part in the political life of the colony. He held many offices, the names of which now mean little. A native-born Englishman and keenly appreciative of the disinterested motives which induced the British Crown and many Englishmen to accord to Georgia a measure of support wanting elsewhere, he was a stanch Loyalist in the years leading up to the Revolution. In the new government adopted for Georgia after the colony became a royal province upon the resignation of the trustees or proprietors in 1752, Habersham was appointed a councillor and secretary of the province (1754); in 1767 he became president of the upper house of the General Assembly. When James Wright, the governor, left the province on leave of absence in 1771, Habersham replaced him as "President and Commander-in-Chief of his Majesty's Province of Georgia, Chancellor, Vice-Admiral, and Ordinary of the same for the time being." His appointment was due to the recommendation of Governor Wright, who spoke of him as "a gentleman of property, no Liberty Boy, but a firm friend to Government and a very worthy, honest man." As acting governor, although he did not approve many of the oppressive acts of Great Britain, Habersham resolutely resisted the rising tide of revolutionary spirit, dissolving the General Assembly when it ventured to elect as speaker a man distasteful to the Crown.

His burdens as acting governor, as manager of his own extensive business and properties, and as temporary manager of Governor Wright's eleven plantations, were too much for Habersham's strength. On the return of the Governor in 1773, Habersham, his health much impaired, went North for a change of climate, and died in 1775, in New Brunswick, N. J., in great distress of mind that public affairs should have taken the revolutionary turn he so much dreaded. He was married on Dec. 26, 1740, to Mary Bolton, at Bethesda, Whitefield performing the ceremony. Of the ten children born of this union, three sons survived. They were all educated at Princeton and became ardent patriots, and two of them, Joseph [*q.v.*] and John, were eminent citizens during and after the Revolutionary War.

["The Letters of Hon. James Habersham, 1756–1775," *Ga. Hist. Soc. Colls.*, vol. VI (1904); C. C. Jones, *Hist. of Ga.* (1883); W. B. Stevens, *A Hist. of Ga.* (2 vols., 1847–59); *Hist. Colls. of the Joseph Habersham Chapter, D. A. R.*, vol. I (1902); W. J. Northen, *Men of Mark in Ga.*, vol. I (1907); J. G. B. Bulloch, *A Hist. and Geneal. of the Habersham Family* (1901).]
R. P. B—s.

HABERSHAM, JOSEPH (July 28, 1751–Nov. 17, 1815), Revolutionary patriot, postmaster-general, was born in Savannah, the second son of James Habersham [*q.v.*], the most important business man in colonial Georgia, and of Mary (Bolton) Habersham. In his ninth year he was sent to New Jersey to be educated. In 1768, partly because his health was poor and partly because his father was dissatisfied with his education, he went to England, where for three years he was connected with a mercantile concern. Upon his return to Georgia in 1771, he was set up in business by his father, first with his brother James, and later, in 1773, with Joseph Clay [*q.v.*], a kinsman and for many years a leading merchant of Savannah. The firm name was Joseph Clay & Company.

Joseph Habersham and his two brothers, growing to manhood while the revolutionary clouds were gathering, all ardently espoused the American cause, while their father remained loyal to the Crown. This family division was typical of Georgia. The older colonists generally resisted the revolutionary movement, but were unable to restrain their sons. Young Habersham was a member of the first group that raised the standard of rebellion in Georgia. The occasion was a meeting held on Wednesday, July 27, 1774, at which a committee was set up to prepare resolutions similar to those adopted in other colonies condemning the coercive measures recently enacted by the British Parliament. Habersham was a member of that committee and thereafter he was always in the most advanced group of revolutionists. He was a member of the Council of Safety, and took a leading part in the first overt act of the war—the seizure of the royal powder magazine at Savannah—and in the capture of a vessel from London loaded with military stores. He was a member of the provincial congress which met in Savannah on July 4, 1775, was appointed major of the first battalion of troops raised for the protection of Georgia, and later became a colonel in the Continental Army.

After the Revolution, Habersham was twice speaker of the General Assembly of Georgia; in 1785–86 he was a delegate to the Continental Congress; and in 1788 he was a member of the convention which ratified the Federal Constitution in Georgia. His last public service was as postmaster-general of the United States, a position to which he was appointed by President Washington in February 1795. He held the post during Washington's second term and throughout the administration of John Adams. When Jefferson invited him to become treasurer of the United States he interpreted the tender as a request for his resignation as postmaster and surrendered his portfolio in November 1801. Returning to Savannah, he resumed his commercial career, which had been interrupted by the war, and in 1802 became president of the Branch Bank of the United States, a position which he was holding at the time of his death in 1815. He is said to have raised and exported the first cotton shipped from America.

In May 1776 Habersham married Isabella Rae, whose father was a planter residing near Savannah. Ten children were born to them. Habersham was a man of strong character and positive convictions. His conception of honor and patriotism was high; his temper was quick, but he was tolerant of the opinions of others.

[C. C. Jones, *Hist. of Ga.* (1883), and *Biog. Sketches of the Delegates from Ga. to the Continental Cong.* (1891); sketch by Otis Ashmore in W. J. Northen, *Men of Mark in Ga.*, vol. I (1907); *Hist. Colls. of the Joseph Habersham Chapter, D. A. R.*, vol. I (1902); J. G. B. Bulloch, *A Hist. and Geneal. of the Habersham Family* (1901); *Republican and Savannah Evening Ledger*, Nov. 23, 1815, which gives date of death as Nov. 18.]
R. P. B—s.

HACK, GEORGE (*c.* 1623–*c.* 1665), merchant, physician, colonist, was born in Cologne, Germany, of a Schleswig-Holstein family. He was educated in that city and received his degree in medicine at the university. Emigrating to New Amsterdam, he began his career in the New World with the practice of his profession but gradually abandoned it to form a partnership with Augustine Herrman [*q.v.*] in the Virginia tobacco trade. His wife, Anna Verlett, a sister-in-law of Herrman, was associated in this enterprise. She was apparently a woman of much business sagacity and natural ability and carried on a trade in tobacco under her own name. By 1651 the firm of Herrman & Hack was one of the largest and most successful of the colonial-trading companies dealing in tobacco. Marketing the produce from Maryland and Virginia in New Amsterdam, it had become a formidable rival to the Dutch West India Company. In October of that year, however, the business slowly developed by Herrman and the Hacks received its death blow with the passage by the British Parliament of the Navigation Act, which excluded all but English ships from trade with the English colonies. This measure drove Herrman into bankruptcy and determined Hack to leave New Amsterdam and settle permanently on his estates in Northampton County, Virginia. He was one of the framers and signers of the so-called "Engagement of Northampton" of Mar. 25, 1651, in which the people of that county, though promising "to be true and faithful to the Commonwealth of England as it is now established without Kinge or House of Lords" (*Virginia Historical Register*, vol. I, 1848, pp. 163–65), left no doubt in the minds of the rest of the Virginians that they stood ready to support the rights of the exiled Prince Charles at the first seasonable occasion.

Though Anna Hack carried on a trade in tobacco with Herrman after 1651, George Hack devoted his time to its culture and to the practice of medicine, first in Northampton County, then in Northumberland and Lancaster counties, Virginia, and later in upper Baltimore County, Maryland. The Hacks were formally made naturalized citizens of Virginia in March 1658 and on Sept. 17, 1663, the upper House of Assembly of Maryland ordered the preparation of an act of naturalization of George Hack and his family and of Augustine Herrman. Before naturalization was completed, however, Hack died, on one of his Virginia estates. His will was proved on Apr. 17, 1665. He left two daughters, neither of whom married, and two sons: George Nicholas Hack, the founder of the Norfolk branch of the family; and Peter, for many years a member of the Virginia House of Burgesses, the founder of the Maryland branch. Hack's descendants eventually changed the spelling of the name to "Heck."

[*Va. Mag. of Hist. and Biog.*, Jan. 1898; *Jours. of the House of Burgesses of Va., 1619–1658/9* (1915), ed. by H. R. McIlwaine; *Wm. and Mary Coll. Quart. Hist. Mag.*, Apr. 1900; E. B. O'Callaghan, *Calendar of Hist. MSS. in the Office of the Secretary of State, Pt. I, Dutch MSS.* (Albany, 1865), pp. 128, 129; Berthold Fernow, *The Records of New Amsterdam*, I (1897), 326; *Archives of Md.*, vols. I and II (1883, 1884); *N. Y. Geneal. and Biog. Record*, Apr. 1878, p. 54; J. C. Wise, *Ye Kingdome of Accawmacke* (1911); Maryland land records, Annapolis.]
E. L. W. H.

HACKETT, FRANK WARREN (Apr. 11, 1841–Aug. 10, 1926), lawyer, writer, assistant secretary of the navy, was born and died at Portsmouth, N. H., though he was for over fifty years a resident of Washington, D. C. He was the youngest son of W. H. Y. Hackett, attorney and banker, and Olive (Pickering) Hackett. As a boy in Portsmouth he was an intimate friend of Thomas Bailey Aldrich, who modeled on him the character of Pepper Whitcomb in his famous *Story of a Bad Boy*. Young Hackett was educated at Phillips Exeter Academy, at Harvard College (A.B. 1861, A.M. 1864), and at the Harvard Law School. During the Civil War he held a commission as assistant paymaster in the navy and was assigned to the *Miami*, on which ship he took part in two naval engagements in North Carolina waters, one of them a desperate fight at close quarters with the Confederate ironclad *Albemarle*. Admitted to the bar in 1866, he practised his profession in Massachusetts and New Hampshire until 1871 when he became private secretary to Caleb Cushing, United States counsel in the Geneva arbitration of the *Alabama* claims, assisting the other American representatives throughout the arbitration. On the conclusion of this duty, he returned to the United States and, becoming a resident of Washington, successfully practised law before the court of *Alabama* claims, the United States Supreme Court, and other tribunals. During the eighties and nineties, he was one of an interesting group, including Henry Adams, John Hay, Henry Cabot Lodge, and Theodore Roosevelt, who met frequently at Henry Adams' Washington house.

In 1900 President McKinley appointed Hackett assistant secretary of the navy. While in office (April 1900–December 1901) he chose the personnel of the Schley court of inquiry and was in charge of the department during the crisis growing out of the Boxer Rebellion in China. Concurrently with his other work, he wrote a number of memoirs and historical studies. His most interesting books for the general reader are *The Gavel and the Mace* (1900), which is an accurate and highly amusing account of the course and conduct of the business of Congress, as of the period of Speaker Thomas B. Reed, and his *Reminiscences of the Geneva Tribunal of Arbitration* (1911), which is the authoritative "inside" story of the arbitration of the *Alabama* claims. He had a simple and genial personality, a gift of effective epigram, and was a man of considerable independence of thought and action. Abstemious himself, he regarded the Eighteenth Amendment as contrary to American principles, and one of his last professional acts was the writing of a portion of a brief in a case which tested the validity of that amendment in the Supreme Court. He was one of the founders of St. John's Orphanage in Washington and its secretary for thirty-four years. In 1912 and 1913 he was president of the New Hampshire Historical Society. He suffered a stroke in 1921 which obliged him to retire from all professional activities, but this did not prevent his enjoying a quiet family life until the time of his death. He had married, on Apr. 21, 1880, Ida Craven, youngest daughter of Rear-Admiral Thomas Tingey Craven [*q.v.*]. His widow and two sons survived him.

[*Who's Who in America*, 1922–23; *Harvard Grads.' Mag.*, Sept. 1926; the *Manchester* (N. H.) *Union*, Aug. 11, 1926, and obituary notices in the metropolitan press.]
D. L. S.

HACKETT, HORATIO BALCH (Dec. 27, 1808–Nov. 2, 1875), New Testament scholar, was the grandson of John Hackett, a shipbuilder, who superintended the construction of the Revolutionary frigate *Alliance*, of which Horatio's maternal grandfather, Rev. Benjamin Balch, became chaplain. Richard and Martha (Balch) Hackett had four sons, of whom the second, born in Salisbury, Mass., was named Horatio. Before the boy was six years old his father died. With the aid of relatives he attended Phillips Academy, Andover, 1823–26, where he was among the organizers of the Philomathean Society and was valedictorian of his class. By teaching school and by securing again some temporary financial aid, he was able to take his college course at Amherst, ranking first at graduation in 1830. After leaving Amherst he attended the Andover Theological Seminary, interrupting his course by one year as tutor at Amherst, and graduated in August 1834. The next month, on Sept. 22, he was married to his cousin, Mary Wadsworth Balch. With his wife he went to Baltimore, where he taught in Mount Hope College. As a result of studying the question of the proper subjects of baptism—the mode does not seem to have concerned him at this time—he united with the First Baptist Church of Baltimore. After a year in Maryland he became adjunct professor of the Latin and Greek languages at Brown University, where he gained full professorial rank before he was thirty, but left in 1839 to begin a service of almost thirty years at the Newton Theological Institution. In 1868 he resigned at Newton, intending to press the task of the American Bible Union in Bible translation. After one year, however, he was invited to the chair of Biblical literature and New Testament exegesis at Rochester Theological Seminary and began his work there September 1869. While attending to his regular teaching duties, he was also active as a member of the New Testament Company of the American Bible Revision Committee.

It was during his three decades at Newton that Hackett did his most distinctive work, winning his renown as a New Testament scholar and teacher. Three times he was granted leave of absence to permit trips abroad. On the first, in 1841–42, he visited Germany, where he became acquainted with the leading Biblical scholars, such as Tholuck, Gesenius, Neander, and Hengstenberg. In 1852 a trip to the Levant brought its fruit in his *Illustrations of Scripture; Suggested by a Tour through the Holy Land* (1855). In 1858–59 he spent six months in Athens, making special studies in Greek as an aid to his work in New Testament translation. His most notable exegetical work was his *Commentary on the Original Text of the Acts of the Apostles* (1852, rev. ed., 1858). He contributed some thirty articles to William Smith's *Dictionary of the Bible* (3 vols., 1860–63) and with Ezra Abbot [*q.v.*] edited an American edition of the work (1868–70). In 1845 he published a *Grammar of the Chaldee Language*, translated from the German of G. B. Winer, followed by *The Epistle of Paul to Philemon* (1868), from J. J. van Oosterzee, and *The Epistle of Paul to the Philippians* (1870), from Karl Braune—the last two for the Lange series. He was a firm believer in the scientific exegesis of his day and believed this should be used in all Biblical instruction. Thus he was an advocate of a new translation of the Scriptures, in which work he actively participated both in the Bible Union movement among the Baptists and in the New Testament Company of the American (Westminster) Revision Committee.

[Geo. H. Whittemore, *Memorials of Horatio Balch Hackett* (1876), containing bibliography of Hackett's books and contributions to periodicals; Wm. Cathcart, ed., *The Bapt. Encyc.* (1881); G. B. Balch, *Geneal. of the Balch Families in America* (1897); S. F. Smith, *Hist. of Newton, Mass.* (1880), pp. 563–65; *Proc. Am. Acad. Arts and Sci.*, vol. XI (1876); *Examiner and Chronicle* (N. Y.), Nov. 11, 1875; *Boston Transcript*, Nov. 3, 5, 1875.]
W. H. A.

HACKETT, JAMES HENRY (Mar. 15, 1800–Dec. 28, 1871), early American character actor, was born in New York City. He was the son of Thomas C. Hackett who had settled in America and in 1799 had married the daughter of the Rev. Abraham Keteltas, of Jamaica, L. I., called "the fighting parson." Thomas Hackett's father was of English-Irish birth; his mother was a daughter of Baron de Massau of Amsterdam, and his wife was connected with many Knickerbocker families, so James was born an aristocrat in old New York. He entered Columbia at fifteen but left after a year because of ill health, read law for a few months, and then entered the grocery business in 1817. In 1819 he married Catharine Lee Sugg, noted in New York as a singing actress, and removed to Utica, where a cousin, John Beekman, aided him to establish a business. He remained in Utica till 1825, when he returned to New York City and lost all his money in speculation. His wife thereupon resumed her acting and singing, and Hackett himself, who had evidently amused his friends as an amateur, also tried the stage, appearing in *Love in a Village* as Justice Woodcock, to his wife's Rosetta, on Mar. 1, 1826. The theatre was the famous old Park. He was not greatly successful, and at his next appearance he gave imitations of various actors, notably Edmund Kean, and what we would now call "character impersonations" of an auctioneer and of "Uncle Ben"—a Yankee type. These imitations obviously were what had amused Hackett's friends, and they now amused the public. They suggest that Hackett's talents were, at first, chiefly mimetic; he could "take off" familiar types and dialects, and he was less an actor than a glorified entertainer.

The following October he made a great hit as one of Shakespeare's Dromios, aping Barnes, the other Dromio, so perfectly that the delighted audience couldn't tell them apart. He had also added new imitations and Yankee stories to his repertoire, and with this meager histrionic equipment (which included one attempt to play Richard III in imitation of Kean) he sailed for England. The new-world theatre challenging the old! On Apr. 5, 1827, he appeared at Covent Garden, London, where his Yankee stories and his imitation of Kean were not too greatly appreciated. Back in America, on May 13, 1828, at the Park Theatre, he first acted Falstaff, in *Henry IV,* part one, a character thereafter to be one of his famous rôles. He was, at this period, constantly seeking for novelties, and finding them, evidently, in native types which he could imitate. In 1830 he made a stage version of *Rip Van Winkle* (not the first, to be sure, but one of the most successful before Jefferson). His Rip was not idealized like Jefferson's but was a realistic picture of a Catskill Dutchman. On Apr. 18, 1831, he brought out a prize play "written by a gentleman of this city" (New York) called *The Moderns, or a Trip to the Springs,* which crudely satirized life at Saratoga, and in which Hackett played Melodious Migrate, "a Connecticut School and Singing teacher." The school scene in this play fathered a long line of similar farce, still thriving among rural amateurs. In April 1831 he brought out another prize play, by James K. Paulding, *The Lion of the West, or a Trip to Washington.* Here he played Colonel Nimrod Wildfire, an uncouth Kentuckian from the Border, just elected to Congress. The part became immediately popular, and remained so, and again the play fathered a long line of similar comedies (*vide* C. H. Hoyt's *A Texas Steer*). It is evident from the fact that Hackett offered prizes for these dramas, and from the native character types he portrayed in them, that he was a definite force in the growth of American comedy.

In 1832 he again visited London and also played engagements there in 1840, 1845, and 1851. His Falstaff was well received in England. In 1836 he produced a play of the Revolution, *Horseshoe Robinson,* by Charles Dance, from Kennedy's novel. The next year he produced in New York a dramatization of Irving's Knickerbocker history, made by W. B. Bernard. It was a "colossal failure," being dramatically spineless, but is interesting as showing Hackett's preoccupation with native material. In November 1838, he was at the Park in a list of nine parts which ranged from Falstaff to Paul Pry (converted into a Yankee!) and Rip. At the same theatre on Sept. 30, 1840, he attempted Lear, and on Oct. 21, urged to it in part by his correspondence with John Quincy Adams regarding the character, he appeared as Hamlet. He had the comedian's ambition to be a tragedian, but he was quite evidently unequal to either rôle and could not endure the comparison with such actors as Kean, Macready, and Forrest. Meanwhile, he had tried his hand at management and continued to do so. He was manager of the Astor Place Opera House during the Macready riot in 1849, managed the National (New York), the Howard Athenaeum in Boston, and other houses at various times, and in 1854 brought Mario and Grisi to America. After 1855, he acted but fitfully, and in 1864 friends, on his behalf, sought a consular post for him. His first wife died in 1845, leaving a son, John K. Hackett, who became a noted jurist in New York. On Mar. 27, 1864, he was married again, to Clara Cynthia Morgan, and they had one son, James Keteltas Hackett [*q.v.*]. The father died at Jamaica, L. I., Dec. 28, 1871.

Joseph Jefferson, a keen critic of acting, says in his autobiography that Hackett remained an amateur all his days (*The Autobiography of Joseph Jefferson,* 1890, p. 138). George William Curtis considered his Falstaff "hard and dry" and "devoid of unction," and there was always, here and in England, much difference of opinion concerning it. William Winter gives it high praise, however, as a consistent and well-wrought impersonation of "a stern individuality, latent within the humor and the boisterous conviviality of the man" (*The Wallet of Time,* 1913, vol. I, p. 99). Hackett was a lifelong student of Shakespeare and in 1863 published *Notes and Comments upon Certain Plays and Actors of Shakespeare, with Criticisms and Correspondence*—the correspondence being that between himself and John Quincy Adams. The sardonic or "dry" quality he gave to Falstaff was in part, at least, deliberate. But it was undoubtedly the best Falstaff of its time both in America and England and must have deserved its popularity.

Much more than his Falstaff, however, the racy native character types he depicted, evidently with careful realism of external detail and copious broad humor, were what made him an important figure in our early theatre. Crude as the plays were in which these characters appeared, they helped to pave the way for an indigenous drama to come.

Hackett, in early years at any rate, was said to have been sturdy and handsome in appearance. He had native dignity and a scholarly mind and yet was genial and charming and universally popular as well as respected. The debts he contracted as a young man, he paid off with his early stage earnings, and the rest of his life was given to a conscientious service of the theatre. He founded the first American-born theatrical family, made one of the earliest "American invasions" of London, helped to develop American character comedy into a popular art, did what his talents allowed for the classics, and died ripe in years and popular respect.

[Montrose J. Moses, *Famous Actor Families in America* (1906); Brander Matthews and Lawrence Hutton, *Actors and Actresses of Great Britain and the U. S.* (1886), vol. III; G. C. D. Odell, *Annals of the N. Y. Stage,* vols. III and IV (1928); the *N. Y. Mirror,* June 2, 1832; *Am. Hist. Record,* Mar. 1872; John Durand, "Souvenirs of Hackett the Actor," the *Galaxy,* Oct. 1872, based on an autobiographical sketch furnished by Hackett; biographical sketch by C. J. Foster in Hackett's *Notes and Comments*; *N. Y. Tribune,* Dec. 29, 1871.]

W. P. E.

HACKETT, JAMES KETELTAS (Sept. 6, 1869–Nov. 8, 1926), American actor, son of James Henry [*q.v.*] and Clara C. (Morgan) Hackett, was born on Wolfe Island, Ontario. Two years later his father died, so the son never saw him act. But as a youth, Hackett appeared often in amateur theatricals, and on entering the College of the City of New York with the class of 1891, he became a leading figure in college plays. He founded in 1888 the City College Dramatic Society, served as its manager and leading actor, and throughout his college course received prizes for declamation of poetry and oratory. Frohman relates in his *Memories of a Manager* that Hackett, at this time, spent many evenings in the gallery of the Lyceum Theatre, and though he studied law for a few months after leaving college, he soon forsook that study for the stage, making his début as François in *The Broken Seal,* with A. M. Palmer's stock company, at the Park Theatre, Philadelphia, Mar. 28, 1892. He joined Lotta Crabtree soon after, as her leading man, and then became briefly a member of Daly's company in New York but left it to star in a road tour during the season of 1893–94, playing *The Private Secretary, The Arabian Nights,* and *Mixed Pickles.* Then he joined the Queen's Theatre Stock Company in Montreal, coming again to New York in January 1895 to play the Count de Neipperg in *Madame Sans-Gêne* and later to support Kyrle Bellew and Mrs. James Brown Potter.

In November 1895, Hackett joined the Lyceum Stock Company, Frohman having kept an eye on him ever since his college days, and on Feb. 10, 1896, he took E. H. Sothern's place in *The Prisoner of Zenda,* the reigning romantic drama of the day. Sothern had gone on tour in this play, and Hackett, after going to Boston to study the other's methods of make up and rapid changes, stepped into his shoes in the New York cast. His popular success was great, and Frohman made him leading man of the stock company following the resignation of Herbert Kelcey. The following November, while acting in *The Courtship of Leonie* with a new leading woman, Mary Mannering, recently from England, he fell in love with her, and on May 2, 1897, married her. While with the Lyceum company, he created the rôles in America of George Lamorant in Pinero's *The Princess and the Butterfly* and Nigel Stanyon in R. C. Carton's *The Tree of Knowledge.* The latter play he took on tour as a star but soon abandoned it for Anthony Hope's *Rupert of Hentzau,* produced Nov. 21, 1898, in Philadelphia. The Hope romance was temporarily shelved while Hackett played Mercutio in a production of *Romeo and Juliet* with Maude Adams and William Faversham in the name parts. All three players lacked proper training for such rôles, and the elaborate revival failed. Hackett thereupon returned to romance, taking *Rupert of Hentzau* across the continent. To the Zenda tale he added *The Pride of Jennico,* adapted from a novel by Agnes and Egerton Castle, in 1900, and *Don Caesar's Return,* by Victor Mapes, in 1901.

In 1902 Hackett appeared in a dramatic version of *The Crisis,* then a "best seller," in an effort to get away, if possible, from the romantic school in which he had been reared. But on Dec. 6, 1904, he courted favor in *The Fortunes of the King,* a romantic melodrama about Charles II. In the autumn of 1905, however, at the Savoy Theatre, New York, he produced and acted with much success Alfred Sutro's social drama, *The Walls of Jericho,* his wife playing with him, and the success of the venture was sufficient to enable him to rent a theatre on West Forty-second Street, New York, renaming it the Hackett, and to branch out into management, as his father had attempted to do almost seventy-five years before. But like his father, he was by no means always successful. He failed to attract patronage with Sutro's *John Glayde's Honor,* in 1907–08, and by September 1908 he was once more emerging at his own theatre in a revival of *The Prisoner of Zenda*—already an out-moded play. Among other productions were *Craig Kennedy, John Ermine of Yellowstone,* and *The Bishop's Candlesticks.*

In 1910 Mary Mannering divorced Hackett, and in 1911 he married Beatrice H. Beckley, of London, who had been his leading woman. In 1914 he inherited, rather unexpectedly, a large fortune, said at the time to be $1,200,000. This was left to him by his niece, Mrs. Millicent Hackett Trowbridge of New York, daughter of his half-brother and older than he. She did not approve nor like him, it was reported, but died intestate, and he was next of kin. Relieved by this good fortune of financial worries, he was able to further his personal ambitions and at once produced *Othello* (1914), following it with a production of *Macbeth* which was shown at the Criterion Theatre, New York, in 1916, with sets by Joseph Urban. The "new stage-craft" was then comparatively strange to America, nor was it fully grasped by Hackett himself. None the less, this production was arresting in many ways and marked a step forward in scenic development in America. During the ensuing war years Hackett was conspicuous for his performances of *Out There* and *The Better 'Ole.* After the war, in November 1919, he appeared with the Theatre Guild in New York in the name part of *The Rise of Silas Lapham,* adapted from Howells's novel. In 1920 he took his production of *Macbeth* to London and later to the Odéon in Paris, where it was well received, and he was awarded the Legion of Honor ribbon for it. He did not again act in America, though he returned to the United States in 1924. In November 1926 he was to have acted a scene from *Macbeth* before the King, at Drury Lane, but illness forced him to Paris for treatment, and he died in that city on Nov. 8, 1926.

As a young man Hackett was tall and straight and virile of figure, with dark hair, firm chin, and sharply chiseled features. His early development came at a time when romantic melodrama was the vogue, and he developed the dashing swagger and picturesque appearance and somewhat artificial pose of that artificial type of play. He did it well and became a matinée idol. When ambition led him to more serious impersonations, his lack of voice training was obvious in the classics, and his lack of simplicity, naturalness, and emotional sincerity in modern works. He was sometimes harsh, dry, and stilted. But his *Walls of Jericho* was excellent, and in later years he worked hard, if fitfully, to master the difficulties of Shakespeare. In the story of the American theatre he will be remembered chiefly as one of the leading figures of "cloak and sword" romance, who strutted our stage in the golden nineties and caused great fluttering in the feminine dove-cotes.

[James K. Hackett Scrap Book, Locke Collection, N. Y. Pub. Lib.; *Who's Who in America,* 1926–27; *Who's Who on the Stage* (1906); Daniel Frohman, *Memories of a Manager* (1911); *N. Y. Times,* Nov. 9, 14, 1926.]

W. P. E.

HACKLEY, CHARLES HENRY (Jan. 3, 1837–Feb. 10, 1905), lumberman, philanthropist, of Welsh descent, was born in Michigan City, Ind., the oldest of five children. He was the son of Joseph H. Hackley, a native of New York state, and his wife, Salina Fuller. In early boyhood Charles was taken by his parents to Southport, now Kenosha, Wis. In the spring of 1856 he worked his passage to Muskegon, Mich., on a schooner and thereafter was identified with that place. After three years in the employ of Durkee, Truesdell & Company, first as laborer, then as foreman, and finally as bookkeeper, he organized the firm of J. H. Hackley & Company in partnership with his father. From the time of the organization of this firm, the name of which was changed several times, Hackley's rise was rapid. Between 1880 and 1890 his company was cutting more than thirty million feet of lumber annually (Hotchkiss, *post,* p. 221). As early as 1886 Hackley foresaw the exhaustion of the timber resources of western Michigan and he consequently bought lands in Wisconsin, Minnesota, Louisiana, Florida, Mississippi, South Carolina, and British Columbia (*American Lumbermen,* p. 224). He held at one time or another many public and semi-public offices in Muskegon during the last thirty years of his life. He was city and county treasurer and alderman of his ward, for some time a member of the Board of Public Works, and for many years a member of the Board of Education, serving as its president from 1892 to 1900. He served as director and officer of various banking institutions and when the lumber industry was dying was successful in inducing other industries to establish themselves in Muskegon. He was a delegate to the Republican National Convention in 1892 and 1896.

To the development of Muskegon he contributed generously through his philanthropic gifts. In 1888 he gave $125,000 for the erection and maintenance of a public library, to which he added an endowment of $75,000 in 1891. Next he presented a square in the central part of the city as a public park and then made gifts for the erection of a manual-training school and of a hospital. While these large benefactions were being announced, Hackley erected statues to beautify the city. When he died, it was estimated that his gifts to Muskegon had the value of almost $1,500,000. The total of his gifts, including those made in his will and by his widow, reached more than $4,400,000. He was married on Oct. 3, 1864, to Julia E. Moore of Centerville, N. Y., who with two adopted children survived him.

[*American Lumbermen* (1905); *Who's Who in America,* 1903–05; Emory Wendell, *Wendell's Hist. of Banking and Banks and Bankers of Mich.* (2 vols., n.d.); *The Hackley Pub. Lib. of Muskegon, Mich.* (1891); G. W. Hotchkiss, *Hist. of the Lumber and Forest Industry of the Northwest* (1898); *Muskegon Daily Chronicle,* Nov. 2, 1895, June 10, 1903, and Feb. 10, 1905; *Am. Lumberman,* Feb. 18, 1905; *Grand Rapids Herald,* Feb. 11, 1905; *Muskegon Chronicle,* May 19, 1928.]

J. O. K.

HADDOCK, CHARLES BRICKETT (June 20, 1796–Jan. 15, 1861), educator, was born in Salisbury, later Franklin, N. H., the son of William and Abigail Eastman (Webster) Haddock. His mother was an older sister of Daniel Webster. He was graduated from Dartmouth College in 1816, at the head of his class, and then entered the theological seminary at Andover, Mass., where he remained for two years, receiving ordination as a Congregational minister. In 1819 he was appointed to the Dartmouth faculty as its first professor of rhetoric and oratory. His duties in this position included active association with the college literary societies and with the various prize-speaking contests which formed an important part of the undergraduate life of the time. In 1838 he became professor of intellectual philosophy and political economy, serving until 1850, when President Fillmore appointed him chargé d'affaires to Portugal, where he remained until 1854. He returned to the United States in the same year and resided at West Lebanon, N. H., until his death. In personal appearance, abilities, and temperament he was notable for a marked resemblance to his distinguished uncle. He was in both early and later life an unusually handsome man, of dignified bearing and "courtly manners." He wrote and spoke gracefully and effectively, and was much in demand as a speaker in the college and neighboring pulpits and on formal public occasions. He enjoyed great popularity with the students at a time when faculty relations with the undergraduate body were traditionally stiff and formal. In the opinion of his colleagues, he had all the qualities requisite for a markedly successful public career but deliberately preferred the quiet usefulness of the educator and scholar.

Haddock was nevertheless interested in public affairs and from 1845 to 1848 he was a member of the state legislature. Largely through his efforts the new office of commissioner of common schools was established in 1846 and he became the first incumbent of the position (1846–47). His initial survey of the New Hampshire school system, *Report of the Commissioner of Common Schools* (1847), is notable for keen analysis and breadth of view. In it he stated forcibly the importance of public schools in a democracy and pleaded vigorously for better school-houses, better pay for teachers, and better training for the profession. He was active in developing teachers' institutes for normal training and urged the further establishment of public high schools. He was also an earnest advocate for the building of the railways extending from Concord, N. H., to Burlington, Vt., demonstrating by public addresses their economic benefits to the community and pleading for the issue of company charters with the power of eminent domain. His occasional addresses, magazine articles, and speeches in the legislature were published in 1846 under the title: *Addresses and Miscellaneous Writings.* He was twice married: first, on Aug. 19, 1819, to Susan Saunders Lang, daughter of Richard Lang, and on July 21, 1841, to Caroline (Kimball) Young, daughter of Richard Kimball. A son, Charles Haddock, survived him.

[J. K. Lord, *A Hist. of Dartmouth Coll.* (1913) and *A Hist. of the Town of Hanover* (1928); G. T. Chapman, *Sketches of the Alumni of Dartmouth Coll.* (1867); S. G. Brown, *A Discourse Commemorative of Chas. Brickett Haddock, D.D.* (1861); "Our Diplomatic Servants: Chas. B. Haddock," *Internat. Mag.,* Dec. 1850; *New-Eng. Hist. and Geneal. Reg.,* Apr. 1861; *Boston Transcript,* Jan. 17, 1861.]

D. L. S.

HADDON, ELIZABETH [See ESTAUGH, ELIZABETH HADDON, *c.* 1680–1762].

HADFIELD, GEORGE (*c.* 1764–Feb. 5, 1826), architect, was born in Leghorn, the son of Charles Hadfield, an English or Irish hotelkeeper, and his wife Isabella. His sister Maria was a painter of some distinction, and in 1782 married the miniature painter Richard Cosway (see G. C. Williamson, *Richard Cosway,* 1905, and *Dictionary of National Biography*). Beginning in 1781, Hadfield sent drawings of classical projects to the Royal Academy exhibitions. He studied in the schools of the Academy and received a gold medal in 1784. After working for a time under the architect James Wyatt, he received the traveling studentship of the Academy, and spent the years to 1794 in Rome. His drawings of the temple at Palestrina and other drawings were exhibited at the Academy in 1795 and are preserved by the Royal Institute of British

Architects. In that year, on recommendation of the painter John Trumbull [*q.v.*], Hadfield was invited by the commissioners of the city of Washington to act as superintendent of the Capitol, then under construction. He commenced his duties on Oct. 15. The situation was a difficult one, for the foundations laid by Stephen Hallet [*q.v.*], the first superintendent, were on a plan different from that originally designed, and to the original plan its author, William Thornton [*q.v.*], just appointed one of the commissioners, was determined to return. Hadfield objected both to the part already executed and to the scheme of Thornton's design, and proposed to use the colossal order, with or without an attic, instead of having a high basement. He was overruled by the commissioners, however, and Thornton undertook to furnish drawings which should adapt his design to the existing foundations. The work on the north wing then proceeded, with considerable friction owing to Thornton's academic pedantry and Hadfield's lack of practical experience. In 1798 Hadfield furnished the adopted design for the Treasury and Executive Offices (burned by the British in 1814), but his attempt to assert a professional right to supervise the execution, not recognized by the commissioners, brought notice of his dismissal, May 28, 1798. In 1800 he patented the first machine for brick-making in the United States; in 1803 he served as a councilman of the city of Washington. As time went on he secured other architectural commissions. Thus in 1802 he was employed on Jefferson's recommendation to design the Washington county jail; in 1803 he designed the Arsenal; in 1816–19, Commodore Porter's house; in 1820 the City Hall (finished 1849, refaced with stone 1917); in 1822 the Assembly Rooms, in 1824 the Branch Bank of the United States (demolished 1904). Two other notable works of his planning were the Van Ness mausoleum in Oak Hill Cemetery, on the model of a temple of Vesta, and "Arlington," the house for G. W. Parke Custis, Washington's adopted son. This house, later the home of Robert E. Lee and now preserved in Arlington National Cemetery, has a Doric portico modeled on that of the great temple at Paestum and is one of the earliest and most notable houses of the Greek revival.

Hadfield's story is one of unfulfilled promise. A prize student at the Academy, the brother of Maria Cosway, and the protégé of the Queen and of Lady Chesterfield (who on her death left him a legacy of £1,500), he was expected to achieve a prominent place in his profession. His failure was apparently due in part to the discouragements of his early years in Washington, brought on by his lack of practical experience. One of his contemporaries, B. H. Latrobe [*q.v.*], wrote of him some years before his death: "All that he proposed proved him a man of correct tastes, of perfect theoretic knowledge and of bold integrity. . . . He loiters here, ruined in fortune, temper and reputation, nor will his irritable pride and neglected study ever permit him to take the station in the art which his elegant taste and excellent talent ought to have obtained" (*The Journal of Latrobe,* 1905, p. 133). He died in Washington, unmarried, on Feb. 5, 1826, aged about sixty-two years.

[Wm. Dunlap, *Hist. of the Rise and Progress of the Arts of Design in the U. S.* (2 vols., 1834; rev. ed., 3 vols., 1918); Gordon Goodwin, in *Dict. Nat. Biog.*; Samuel Redgrave, *A Dict. of Artists of the English School* (1874); Glenn Brown, *Hist. of the U. S. Capitol* (2 vols., 1900–02); *Doc. Hist. of the Construction and Development of the U. S. Capitol Building and Grounds* (1904); W. B. Bryan, *A Hist. of the National Capital* (2 vols., 1914–16); Fiske Kimball, *Thomas Jefferson, Architect* (1916), 61, 67, 179; Jonathan Elliot, *Hist. Sketches of the Ten Miles Square Forming the District of Columbia* (1830); H. F. Cunningham, in *Architectural Record,* Mar. 15, 1915; H. F. Cunningham, J. A. Younger, and J. W. Smith, *Measured Drawings of Georgian Architecture in the District of Columbia, 1750–1820* (1914); G. A. Townsend, *Washington Outside and Inside* (1873); obituaries in *National Journal* and *Daily National Intelligencer* of Washington, D. C., Feb. 6, 1826.]

F.K.

HADLEY, ARTHUR TWINING (Apr. 23, 1856–Mar. 6, 1930), economist, president of Yale University, was the son of James Hadley [*q.v.*], professor of Greek in Yale College. On the day of Arthur's birth, a class of undergraduates who were studying under his father waited in vain for their instructor until a scout, sent forth to reconnoiter, returned grinning and wrote on the blackboard, "Unto us a child is born, unto us a son is given." Young Hadley grew up naturally into the academic life. His grandfather had been professor of chemistry in the Fairfield (N. Y.) medical college; and his father, a brilliant philologist, taught at Yale from 1845 until his death in 1872. His mother, Anne Loring, was the daughter of Stephen Twining, steward of Yale from 1819 to 1832. He was prepared for college at Hopkins Grammar School in New Haven and entered Yale at the age of sixteen, in a class characterized by a member of the faculty as "the smartest and wickedest" that had been known in many a year. His career as an undergraduate evinced the versatility of intellect that was so conspicuous in him throughout his life, giving rise eventually to the campus tradition that he could encounter specialists in any field upon their own ground and send them away discomfited. He took prizes in mathematics, English composition, the classics, astronomy, and public speaking; and graduated in 1876 as valedictorian of his class. His interest in debating, which began as a member of the class debating team, persisted all his life, and during the five years that preceded his election to the presidency he found time to coach the teams that met Harvard and Princeton.

After graduation he remained for a year at Yale, studying history and political science, and then went abroad to continue these studies for two years at the University of Berlin, where he was a pupil of Adolph Wagner. In the autumn of 1879 he joined the faculty of Yale College as tutor. During his four years in this position he gave instruction in Greek, logic, Roman law, and German; and it was not until 1883, when he began his term as instructor in political science, that he was permitted to narrow the range of his teaching and to confine himself to his chosen field. From that time until he was made president he devoted himself to the study and teaching of his specialty, serving as professor of political science in the graduate school (1886–91), as professor of political economy in the college (1891–99), and as acting professor of political economy in the Sheffield Scientific School (1890–91). From 1892 to 1895 he served as dean of the graduate school.

His first book, *Railroad Transportation, Its History and Its Laws,* was published in 1885. It was the earliest comprehensive study of the subject to appear in the United States and immediately established him as an authority in the field. It displayed a remarkably full knowledge of the history of railroading and a lively understanding of the problems of rate-making and control. These were matters of more than academic interest, and Hadley's views upon them demonstrated his sound practical sense. His analysis of the mistakes that had been made, both by directors of railroads and by state and national governments, was impartial and scholarly; and while his book made no attempt to lay down a definite program for the future, it afforded a critical study of the immediate problems in the railroad world, in the United States and abroad. The book was recognized in Europe by two Russian translations and a French translation that won Hadley a medal at the Paris Exposition in 1889. The chapter entitled "Competition and Combination in Theory" best reveals the power and clarity of Hadley's thinking. In it he pointed out the fallacy in the theory of Ricardo, that under free competition the value of goods will tend to be proportional to the cost of production. Other economists had observed that this law did not function smoothly in practice; Hadley, going further, declared that in the case of industries with large permanent investments the law was entirely false in theory. "It is not true," he said, "that when the price falls below cost of production people always find it for their interest to refuse to produce at a disadvantage. It very often involves worse loss to stop producing than to produce below cost" (p. 70). This principle is now recognized as a part of fundamental economic theory.

The year of the publication of his first book marked the beginning of Hadley's public career. In May 1885 he was called as expert witness before the committee of the Senate that drafted the Interstate Commerce Law. In June, he was appointed commissioner of labor statistics of the State of Connecticut, and he continued to hold this office until 1887, publishing two reports that extended his reputation as an economist into the fields of statistics and labor problems. In 1886–87 he lectured at Harvard on "Problems of Railroad Administration." From 1887 to 1889 he was associate editor of the *Railroad Gazette,* with special charge of the department of foreign railroads. He had already contributed articles on subjects connected with industry to J. J. Lalor's *Cyclopædia of Political Science* (vol. III, 1884), and he was called upon for the article on railroads for the ninth edition of the *Encyclopædia Britannica* (1886) and for the chapter on the railway in its business relations in Scribner's *American Railway* (1888). He had charge of the department of economics in MacMillan's *Dictionary of Philosophical Terms* (1889) and wrote articles for R. H. I. Palgrave's *Dictionary of Political Economy* (vol. II, 1896, vol. III, 1899).

In the midst of activities that were winning him distinction at home and abroad, Hadley continued to discharge his duties as a teacher with unfailing conscientiousness. He always regarded teaching as work of the first importance, giving the best that was in him to his classes, and he speedily established a reputation as one of the most brilliant and stimulating teachers at Yale. His second book, *Economics—An Account of the Relations between Private Property and Public Welfare* (1896), has been widely used as a textbook. In its clarity of exposition, its breadth of outlook, and its sound common sense, it reflects the author's talents as a teacher of college students, as well as his mastery of economic thought.

On the evening in May 1899 when it became known on the campus that Hadley was to be the next president of Yale, the undergraduates marched to his house to show him their enthusiastic approval. His personality, down to the least of his bewildering mannerisms, was already registered on the memories of hundreds of students. The peculiar inflections of his voice, his manner of turning up his eyes as he came to the end of a period and gathered his thoughts for the next, his eccentric gestures, made with one forearm, and often both, swinging loosely from the elbow, became the peculiar delight of Yale gatherings, at first in the undergraduate classrooms and presently at university functions of every sort. The ability to imitate Hadley was enough to give any Yale man a place in the affections of his classmates, and stories told in the Hadley manner became a part of the stock of college tradition. While students and alumni amused themselves with irreverent additions to the Hadley myth, they listened to the man himself with constantly increasing respect, fascinated by the readiness of his wit, charmed by the wealth of his culture, enriched in their own intellectual lives by the example of his broad and philosophic approach to every subject. Whether he was setting the table on a roar at an alumni dinner, or holding the graduating class in rapt, attentive silence by one of his fine baccalaureate addresses, President Hadley could always command the attention of a Yale audience. His attainments were not solely scholastic, however. He was one of the best whist and chess players in New Haven, was good at tennis, enjoyed walking and mountain-climbing, was keenly interested in football strategy, and argued that baseball would be a better game if played with ten men. Military strategy fascinated him and he was an authority on the strategic side of Napoleon's campaigns (*Yale Alumni Weekly,* Mar. 14, 1930).

Audiences on both sides of the Atlantic were given opportunities to hear him, through the lectureships that he held from time to time during his term as president and after his retirement. He gave the Lowell Institute lectures at Boston in 1902, speaking on "The History of Academic Freedom," and the Dodge lectures at Yale in the same year on "The Responsibilities of Citizenship." In 1906 he delivered the Kennedy lectures on "Standards of Public Morality" before the New York School of Philanthropy. In the following year he was at the University of Berlin as Roosevelt professor of American history, and in 1914 he lectured at Oxford University. As incumbent of the Watson chair in American history he lectured before the Anglo-American Society in London in 1922, and as the first American lecturer on the Watson foundation he delivered lectures on "Economic Problems of Democracy" at London, Birmingham, Manchester, Sheffield, Cambridge, and Oxford. In 1924, he addressed the World Power Conference in London and delivered lectures on the West Memorial Foundation at Carnegie Institute of Technology and at Stanford University. Some of his colleagues on the Yale faculty, taking the view of administrative work commonly held by college teachers, had regretted his election to the presidency. They deplored the termination of his teaching career and were loath to see his time absorbed in duties that would interfere with his progress as an economist. It is true that he met no classes after 1899 and that no more books dealing exclusively with economic matters proceeded from his pen; but in the many audiences that he addressed, he found a new field for his talents as a teacher, and the books and articles he published give evidence that he did not cease to be a scholar when he became president of Yale. His scholarly interests, indeed, seem to have been broadened by his new experiences. The titles of his later volumes are evidence that he no longer thought of himself as an economist addressing students in his field, but as a public teacher with a broader task of instruction to perform. There was little in these later books to attract the attention of the sturdy specialist, but it is probable that they represent the true fruition of his scholarship; for even as an economist, he was never so much interested in new discoveries or theories as in relating the facts of a modern world to the age-old problems of human conduct and human happiness.

The sum of his achievements as president of Yale must be reckoned in terms of his general influence rather than by reference to particular measures that he originated and put into operation. During his administration Yale developed into a great national university. Much of this development was the natural fruition of time, and it is impossible to declare that this step or that in the advance of the university was due to Hadley alone; but those who lived and worked at Yale through that period were keenly aware of his influence, moving steadily in the direction of improved standards, all the way from the graduate school, which grew in importance and vitality throughout his administration, to the freshman year, established as a separate school in his last year as president, with the purpose of furnishing better instruction for incoming students. New enterprises inaugurated during his term of office, including the School of Forestry, the University Press, the *Yale Review,* and Yale-in-China, reflected the highest ideals of the parent institution in scholarship and in public service;

and all the existing schools of the university moved forward under him toward higher standards of usefulness. His administration gave Yale a vastly increased endowment and an unprecedented number of new buildings, including the Bicentennial group, six laboratories, two recitation halls, a new hall for the School of Music, three dormitories, the Bowl and the armory at Yale Field, and the Memorial Quadrangle, which was completed in the last year of his active service.

In 1921, having seen the university through the difficult period of the World War, Hadley retired from the presidency. He still had many interests to keep him occupied, for his service to the university had marked him as a man to be summoned to other duties. He had been chairman of the Railroad Securities Commission, established by Act of Congress in 1910, and of the commission, commonly called by his name, appointed by President Taft in 1911 to investigate conditions of the railroads. The railway valuation act of 1913 arose out of the report of the Hadley commission. His interest in railroads continued throughout his life. He was a director of the New York, New Haven & Hartford Railroad and took great pride in the part he played in restoring its broken fortunes. He was also a director of the New York, Westchester & Boston, of the Atchison, Topeka & Santa Fé, and of the Rutland Railroad of Vermont. At the time of his retirement he was suggested as a candidate for the presidency of the United States (*New York Times,* Apr. 11, 1920); and in 1926 he refused the offer of the Democratic nomination for United States senator from Connecticut because he was a Republican.

His marriage to Helen Harrison Morris, daughter of Luzon Burritt Morris [*q.v.*], governor of Connecticut, took place June 30, 1891, and he and his bride spent the summer of 1891 abroad. They were both enthusiastic travelers and visited Europe together many times. On Dec. 2, 1929, they sailed from New York for a trip around the world on board the *Empress of Australia.* Hadley had always wished to be where he could see the Southern Cross night after night, to visit the Great Wall of China, and to complete the circuit of the globe; and this voyage brought the fulfillment of all three wishes. As the liner drew toward Japan, however, under a north wind and an incessant drizzle, he fell ill with pneumonia and at one o'clock on the morning of Mar. 6 (eleven o'clock A. M., Mar. 5, Eastern standard time), after an illness of but two days, while the ship lay at her pier in Kobe, he died. Funeral services were held in Battell Chapel on the Yale campus, Apr. 11, and he was buried in the Grove Street cemetery in New Haven.

[Sources include material on file in the office of the Secretary of Yale University; *Obit. Record Grads. Yale Univ.* (1930); *Yale Alumni Weekly,* June 7, 1899, Mar. 14, 21, Apr. 25, 1930; Irving Fisher, "Arthur Twining Hadley," in *Economic Jour.,* Sept. 1930; Henry Alloway, "Attic Economist Who Personified Yale," in *Wall. St. Jour.,* June 26, 1930; B. J. Hendrick, "President Hadley of Yale," in *World's Work,* June 1914; *New Haven Journal-Courier,* Mar. 6, 1930; *Who's Who in America,* 1928–29. A full list of Hadley's writings appears in *Reports to President of Yale Univ. for the Academic Year 1929–1930* (1931).]

R. D. F.

HADLEY, HERBERT SPENCER (Feb. 20, 1872–Dec. 1, 1927), attorney-general and governor of Missouri, chancellor of Washington University, was born in Olathe, Kan. His father, Maj. John Milton Hadley, a descendant of Simon Hadley who came from Ireland and settled in Chester County, Pa., about 1712, was born in Indiana of Quaker parents who had migrated thither from North Carolina. He established himself in Kansas shortly before the Civil War and served for four years in the Union Army. His wife, Harriett (Beach) Hadley, was a direct descendant of John Beach, an English Puritan, who settled in Connecticut about 1640. Their son Herbert Spencer Hadley attended the University of Kansas (A.B., 1892) and Northwestern University (LL.B., 1894). From 1894 to 1898 he practised law at Kansas City, Mo., twenty miles from his birthplace. In 1898, as assistant city counsellor, he began a brilliant public career. Later, as prosecuting attorney for Jackson County he attracted more than local attention. From 1905 to 1909 he was attorney-general of Missouri, and from 1909 to 1913 he was the first Republican governor of the state since Reconstruction days. He was sincerely, actively, and prominently identified with the Roosevelt wing of the Republican party. It was partly due to his request that Roosevelt decided early in 1912 again to become a candidate for the Republican presidential nomination (Harold Howland, *Theodore Roosevelt and His Times,* 1912). At the Republican National Convention in June of that year Hadley was the floor-leader of the Roosevelt delegation. After the triumph of the Taft wing, he declined to leave the Republican party but also declined actively to support President Taft. From 1913 to 1917 he practised law at Kansas City. Considerations of health induced him in 1917 to become a professor of law in the University of Colorado at Boulder. While there he published *Rome and the World Today* (1922), a stimulating book on certain phases of Roman law. In 1923 he was called to the chancellorship of Washington University, St. Louis. A few months before his death he was made a trustee of the Rockefeller Foundation.

While attorney-general, Hadley successfully prosecuted the Standard Oil Company for protracted and deceitful violations of Missouri anti-trust laws (*State ex. inf.* vs. *Standard Oil Company,* 194 *Mo.,* 124 and 218 *Mo.,* 1). The prosecution received much publicity because of testimony forced from unwilling witnesses high in the management of the company, including John D. Archbold [*q.v.*]. This bitterly contested case, and other similar cases instituted by Hadley against certain railroad corporations, had some effect in discouraging the questionable practices then prevailing as characteristics of big business. As an educator and university official, Hadley emphasized training for citizenship and a practical application of the social sciences to modern American life. Perhaps his greatest work was in helping to start the current movement for reforming American criminal justice. As a member of the National Crime Commission, he prepared and published a report on reform in criminal procedure, which, in the opinion of Newton D. Baker, "will for years point the way for further progress." The report is printed in the *American Bar Association Journal* for October 1926. Hadley was one of the authors of *The Missouri Crime Survey* (1926), and as a member of the Council of The American Law Institute was largely responsible for the preparation by that organization of a model code of criminal procedure—a four-year undertaking financed by the Laura Spelman Rockefeller Memorial. (The code was adopted by the Institute in May 1930 and published later in the same year with the title, *The American Law Institute: Code of Criminal Procedure.*)

Hadley had a genius for friendship and was noted for winsomeness of manner in all personal contacts. Tall, slender, dignified, courteous, he was a fluent public speaker, rather restrained in style and habitually well-prepared. Officially he revealed a refreshing willingness to cooperate for the public welfare with men of opposite political views, such as Joseph W. Folk, a Democrat, who was governor when Hadley was attorney-general. Although his decision in 1912 not to bolt the Republican party annoyed the extreme supporters of Roosevelt, Roosevelt himself showed no resentment and to his intimate friends said of Hadley: "He will not be with us, but we must not blame him" (W. D. Lewis, *The Life of Theodore Roosevelt,* 1919, p. 367). Hadley never spoke of Roosevelt except with admiration and affection, and at Kansas City in 1916 Roosevelt was entertained in Hadley's home. Hadley was married on Oct. 8, 1901, to Agnes Lee of Kansas City, who with three children survived him.

[*Who's Who in America,* 1926–27; T. M. Marshall, "Herbert Spencer Hadley," *The Washingtonian* (St. Louis), Dec. 1927; W. H. H. Piatt and others, *In Memoriam Herbert Spencer Hadley* (Kansas City Bar Asso., 1928); O. K. Davis, *Released for Publication* (1925), with portrait; Chalmers Hadley, *Notes on the Quaker Family of Hadley* (1916); Walter Williams and F. C. Shoemaker, *Missouri* (1930), vol. IV; *St. Louis Post-Dispatch,* Dec. 2, 1927; newspaper clippings at Mo. Hist. Soc. Lib., St. Louis; personal recollections; comments of Mrs. Hadley.]

T. W.

HADLEY, JAMES (Mar. 30, 1821–Nov. 14, 1872), philologist, the son of James and Maria (Hamilton) Hadley, was born in Fairfield, Herkimer County, N. Y., where his father, James Hadley, was professor of chemistry in the College of Physicians and Surgeons of the Western District of New York. He was descended from George Hadley who emigrated from England and settled in Ipswich, Mass., about 1639. James was sent to Fairfield Academy where he came under the beneficent influence of David Chassell, who seems to have been a greater factor in his development than was any other single man. He later stated that he read Virgil at the age of seven, Livy at eight, and Tacitus at nine; and these authors formed only a slight part of his early reading. An accident when he was quite young left him lame and thus, perhaps, contributed to his studious habits. When he was only sixteen he was made an assistant in the Academy and three years later was admitted to the junior class in Yale College. There he was elected to Phi Beta Kappa and was salutatorian of the class of 1842. The year following the attainment of his bachelor's degree he spent in graduate study, the next two at the Divinity School. He was appointed tutor in Yale College in 1845, after acting in the same capacity for a part of the preceding year at Middlebury College. He was promoted to be assistant professor of Greek in 1848, and when Professor Woolsey retired in 1851, Hadley succeeded him, holding the chair of Greek until the time of his death. On Aug. 13, 1851, he married Anne Loring Twining, the daughter of Stephen Twining of New Haven. Their only child was Arthur Twining Hadley [*q.v.*], later president of Yale University.

The great reputation which Hadley has enjoyed as a philologist rests primarily on the evidence of his colleagues and pupils. His writings, however, cover an extraordinarily broad field. Of the twenty articles published shortly after his death under the editorship of William Dwight Whitney (*Essays Philological and Critical, Selected from the Papers of James Hadley,* 1873) one is "The Greek Genitive as an Ablative Case," another, "Tennyson's Princess," and a third, "On the Hebrew Chronology from Moses to Solomon." In 1860 appeared his *Greek Grammar for Schools and Colleges,* which had a long and distinguished career. His essay on "The Nature and Theory of Greek Accent" had the unusual distinction for that day of being translated into German and receiving in Germany the most cordial welcome. To the *New Englander,* the *American Journal of Science,* and the *Nation,* Hadley was a frequent contributor of notices and reviews. At the time of his death he had just begun work on the revision of the New Testament as a member of the American Commission for the Revision of the Bible. Shortly after his death President Woolsey edited under the title of *Introduction to Roman Law* (1873) Hadley's lectures on this subject given at Harvard and at Yale, which have not yet lost their usefulness. Hadley was considered "the best and soundest" of American philologists by William Dwight Whitney, himself perhaps the outstanding figure in American philology, who said further, in his preface to Hadley's *Essays,* "In extent and accuracy of knowledge, in retentiveness and readiness of memory, in penetration and justness of judgment, I have never met his equal."

[Timothy Dwight, *Memories of Yale Life and Men, 1845–1899* (1903), p. 355; Arthur Twining Hadley, "Biographical Memoir of James Hadley," *Nat. Acad. Sci. Memoirs,* V (1904), 249–54; sketch by W. D. Whitney in *Yale College: A Sketch of Its Hist.* (1879), ed. by W. L. Kingsley; Noah Porter, "In Memoriam: Professor James Hadley," *New Englander,* Jan. 1873; A. P. Stokes, *Memorials of Eminent Yale Men* (1914), I, 336–44; *Biog. Record, Class of 1842, Yale Coll.* (1878); *Obit. Record Grads. Yale Univ.* (1880); *Hartford Daily Courant,* Nov. 15, 1872.] C. W. M—l.

HA-GA-SA-DO-NI [See Deerfoot, 1828–1897].

HAGEN, HERMANN AUGUST (May 30, 1817–Nov. 9, 1893), entomologist, was the first man to hold a chair confined to entomology in any college in the United States. He was born at Königsberg, Germany. His father, Carl Heinrich Hagen, was professor of political economy, technology, and agriculture in the University of Königsberg. His mother was Anna Dorothea Linck. He graduated from the Gymnasium in 1836 and in 1840 took his degree in medicine from the University of Königsberg. His grandfather, Carl Gottfried Hagen, had been a professor of natural history in Königsberg, and he directed the boy's attention toward entomology. Young Hagen became interested early in his career in the dragon-flies, and in 1839, with Professor Rathke, he visited Norway, Sweden, and Denmark, studying the entomological collections and libraries. Curiously enough, his thesis for his doctorate in medicine was on an entomological topic. After graduation he studied in Berlin, Vienna, and Paris, returning to Königsberg in 1843 to begin practice as a physician and surgeon. He became prominent in local affairs, was vice-president of the city council and member of the school board; but during all of the years after his return to his old home he published almost continuously on entomological subjects, mainly upon insects of the *neuropteroid* series, including a study of fossil forms and those found in amber. In 1861, at the special request of the Smithsonian Institution, he wrote the *Synopsis of North American Neuroptera* which really started the study of these forms in the United States. But the work, prepared during his Königsberg residence, that fixed his reputation among entomologists and which proved to be one of the most useful books of the century was his *Bibliotheca Entomologica* which included the entomological literature of the world down to 1862. It was issued in two volumes in 1862 and 1863. It found its way into all entomological libraries and came to be known colloquially as "the entomologists' bible."

In 1867, on the invitation of Louis Agassiz, Hagen came to America to develop an entomological department of the museum of comparative zoölogy at Cambridge, Mass., and in 1870 he was appointed professor of entomology in Harvard College. His work at Cambridge was admirable. He had very few students and devoted most of his time to the building up of the museum. He refused an invitation to take charge of the great entomological collections in Berlin. In 1882 he made a transcontinental journey, visiting California, Oregon, Washington, and Montana, making large collections and many important discoveries. His personal bibliography comprised more than four hundred titles, and he was greatly esteemed by the scientific men of the United States. In Europe he was elected to honorary membership in most of the entomological societies. In fact, he was one of the leading entomologists of the world. He was married in 1851 to Johanna Maria Elise Gerhards. In September 1890 he had a stroke of paralysis but lived for three years after.

[Samuel Henshaw, biographical sketch in *Proc. Am. Acad. Arts and Sci.,* n.s. XXI (1894), 419–23; *Entomol. News,* Dec. 1893; *Deutsche Entomol. Zeitschrift,* 1894, pt. II, pp. 323–25; *Entomologists' Monthly Mag.,* Jan. 1894.] L. O. H.

HAGER, JOHN SHARPENSTEIN (Mar. 12, 1818–Mar. 19, 1890), lawyer, judge, United States senator, was born on a farm near Morristown in Morris County, N. J. Both his father,

Lawrence Hager, and his mother, Mary Sharpenstein, were German Protestants whose forebears had emigrated to New Jersey early in the eighteenth century. He graduated from the College of New Jersey (later Princeton) in 1836, studied law, was admitted to the bar in 1840, and practised in Morristown, N. J. In June of 1849, however, he appeared in San Francisco, and for some time thereafter worked as a merchant and a miner in the northern mines. Returning thence to San Francisco early in 1852, he resumed the practice of law and entered politics, serving in the state Senate in 1853 and 1854. The following year he was elected district judge and held this office until 1861, winning for himself a reputation for fairness and integrity that shielded him in days of bitter criticism. After a period of retirement, during which time he traveled through parts of Europe, Asia, and Africa, he was elected again in 1865 to the state Senate. Within a month of taking office he emphasized his sympathy with the administration by introducing resolutions in praise of the position of President Johnson on Reconstruction. He remained in this office for six years, achieving some notice by his speech in 1870 in opposition to the ratification of the Fifteenth Amendment. For a long period he was chairman of the judiciary committee. He was also chairman of a joint committee to consider bills relating to a state university, and in 1869 he was made a regent of the new institution.

Hager was interested for a time in the organization of the California, Atlantic & Pacific Railway, and in 1872 he stated that he favored giving the Central Pacific a competitor. One of his earliest declarations in the state Senate had been in opposition to monopoly, in particular to railway monopoly. In 1873 he was elected as an Anti-Monopoly Democrat to fill an unexpired term in the United States Senate, where he interested himself in railway grants, Indian affairs, and especially in land titles and the importation of Chinese labor. His anti-monopoly convictions led him into frequent clashes with those speaking for larger railway grants, though he was insistent upon large federal appropriations for public works in San Diego harbor. In the tariff discussions he attempted to provide a protection for the California farmer. At the close of the term of office in 1875 he received a complimentary vote for governor in the Democratic state convention. He was chairman of the resolutions committee of the state convention of 1876 and went as a delegate to the national convention. In 1878 he was chosen to serve as a delegate to the convention to revise the state constitution. Not satisfied with the result, he voted against its adoption.

When President Cleveland came to office in 1885 he made Hager collector of the port of San Francisco. According to one commentator the President in his choice showed "good judgment and great independence," since Hager was a man of "character, capacity and cultivation" not "closely associated with either of two factions in his party." His work as collector of the port gave general satisfaction except for a flurry over the treatment of the Chinese ambassador and his suite in 1886. A resident of California for forty years, he held elective office for more than half of that time. He was always a public figure, yet his reputation rested upon his individual counsel rather than his leadership in debate. Upon a visit in St. Louis in the autumn of 1872, he married Elizabeth (Lucas) Hicks, the daughter of James H. Lucas and widow of Silas Hicks. He died in San Francisco and was buried in Bellefontaine Cemetery, St. Louis, Mo.

[E. D. Halsey, *Hist. of Morris County, N. J.* (1882); O. T. Shuck, *Hist. of the Bench and Bar of Cal.* (1901); *Biog. Dir. Am. Cong.* (1928); the *Daily Alta California* and *Morning Call* (San Francisco), Mar. 20, 1890.]

E. E. R.

HAGGIN, JAMES BEN ALI (Dec. 9, 1827–Sept. 12, 1914), lawyer, rancher, capitalist, was born at Harrodsburg, Ky., where his grandfather, Capt. John Haggin, a native of Virginia, had settled about 1774. His father, Ferah Temple Haggin, was a successful lawyer in Louisville. His mother, Adaline Ben Ali, was the daughter of a Christian Turk who, forced to leave his native country, fled to England, studied medicine, and married an English lady. Later he emigrated to Philadelphia and practised his profession there. James Ben Ali Haggin studied law with his father and was admitted to the Kentucky bar in 1845. For short periods he practised law in St. Joseph, Mo., Natchez, Miss., and New Orleans. Early in 1850, he moved to San Francisco, where he opened a law office and resided during the greater part of the next forty years. After one or two law partnerships of brief duration, he formed a long-lived partnership with Lloyd Tevis [*q.v.*], his brother-in-law. The firm's success brought wealth to the partners and opportunities for successful business ventures. Haggin shrewdly invested in gold, copper, and silver-mining enterprises in California, South Dakota, and Utah. In some instances, he was associated with Senator Hearst of California and with Marcus W. Daly, whose holdings in the Anaconda Copper Company Haggin afterward acquired. It is stated that at one time he owned or controlled over a hundred mines, scattered from Alaska to Peru and Chile.

During the seventies, Haggin (in company with W. D. Carr, whose share Haggin afterward purchased) acquired hundreds of thousands of acres of so-called "desert land" in the Sacramento, San Joaquin, and Kern River valleys, on which he proceeded to develop intensive irrigation projects. These ultimately became highly profitable but roused the hostility of cattle owners, who claimed that grazing lands were impoverished by the diversion of water for irrigation purposes. Irrigation was then in its infancy, and Haggin's legal right to divert the flow of the Kern River was for many years bitterly contested in the courts. Ultimately the legal status of irrigation projects and riparian rights was cleared up in a manner favorable to the irrigation interests. In the early eighties, stock-breeding began to enlist Haggin's interest. Beginning on a small scale near Sacramento, his activities in this line grew rapidly and soon extended to Kentucky, where he developed, near Lexington, an immense horse-breeding estate. As an avocation, he engaged extensively in horse-racing, and between 1881 and 1891 his horses captured most of the great racing trophies East and West.

All that Haggin did was done on a large scale, but only after a studious investigation and careful weighing of each contemplated undertaking. As a result, he never sustained a severe loss nor encountered financial embarrassment. At his death he left an estate of about $15,000,000 which included luxurious residences in San Francisco, New York City, Woodford County, Ky., and Newport, R. I. He made two extended trips to Europe (1858–60, 1865–70), where he spent much time studying economic, political, and social conditions. He was twice married. His first wife was Elizabeth Sanders, daughter of Col. Lewis Sanders of Natchez, who died May 23, 1894. On Dec. 23, 1897, he married Pearl (Margaret?) Voorhies of Versailles, Ky. He died at his summer home in Newport, R. I., after a month's illness, and was buried in Woodlawn, New York City. He was a member of the Protestant Episcopal Church, of numerous city clubs, and of the Democratic party, although he was never active in politics.

[Alonzo Phelps, *Contemporary Biog. of California's Representative Men* (1881), pp. 325–28, contains the longest biographical sketch, with portrait engraving. Haggin's irrigation activities and litigation may be studied in W. M. Morgan, *Hist. of Kern County, Cal.* (1914), Chs. ix, xi; in Haggin's collection of affidavits of residents of Kern County, printed in *The Desert Land Laws of Kern County, Cal.* (1877); and in the *U. S. vs. James B. Haggin, Testimony Taken Before the Register and Receiver of the U. S. Land Office at Visalia, Cal. . . . 1877* (1878), especially pp. 1–32. Haggin's mining, irrigation, and racing successes are interestingly related, with portrait, in S. E. Moffett, "James Ben Ali Haggin," *Cosmopolitan*, June 1902. See also *Who's Who in America*, 1912–13; *Hist. of Ky.* (1928), vol. III; and *N. Y. Times*, Sept. 13, 15, 18, 1914.]

P. O. R.

HAGNER, PETER (Oct. 1, 1772–July 16, 1850), third auditor of the Treasury, known as "the watchdog of the Treasury," was the son of John Valentine and Margaretta (Hanckin) Hagner. His father, born in 1730 near Heilbronn in Württemberg, where he became a master wine cooper, emigrated to America and settled in Philadelphia about 1755. There Peter Hagner was born and in the common schools received his education for the counting-house. For a time he attended the University of the State of Pennsylvania (now the University of Pennsylvania) though he did not graduate. In June 1788 he made an agreement with a Philadelphia merchant, Peter Borger, to serve as an apprentice "to learn the art, trade and mystery of a merchant for a term of two years and one month" (A. B. Hagner, *post*, p. 9). In 1790 he became a clerk in the counting-house of Phillips, Crammond & Company. He was contemplating entering the West India trade when the yellow fever appeared in Philadelphia in December 1793. After a short illness he went to Trenton. There he found himself without employment and was advised by Dolly (Payne) Todd, an old friend, to seek a position in the government offices. James Madison, then a representative in Congress from Virginia and a suitor for the hand of Mrs. Todd, sponsored his application and he secured a clerkship in the office of the accountant of war. This began a career of service in the government that lasted almost fifty-seven years. When the government offices were transferred to Washington in 1799 he was principal clerk in the office of the accountant of war, and later, with the election of James Madison, he was successively appointed temporary accountant of war, additional accountant, and accountant. On Mar. 6, 1817, Hagner became third auditor of the Treasury, a post that had recently been created by Congress. So important did this position become from the number and value of claims settled by the Third Auditor (before the establishment of any court of claims) that John Randolph of Roanoke pausing in a speech to find a phrase to express his sense of the importance of the Emperor Nicholas in the affairs of Europe described him as the "great Third Auditor of nations." Congress twice voted its appreciation of Hagner's services in the settlement of important claims. In January 1845 James Buchanan argued in the Senate that the claim of Mr. Reeside against the Post Office Department should be referred to Peter Hagner, "that official of the Government who, above all others, is distinguished for holding the purse strings of the Treasury tight—who has never suffered a dollar to go out of the Treasury, unless the fitness of the claim has been well established" (*Ibid.*, pp. 42–43). Hagner resigned from his post in 1849 and died the following year. He was twice married. His first wife was Sarah Nichols, whom he married at Christ Church, Philadelphia, Dec. 8, 1799. In 1805 he married Frances Randall, daughter of John Randall, collector of the port of Annapolis.

[Alexander B. Hagner, *A Personal Narrative of the Acquaintance of My Father and Myself with Each of the Presidents of the U. S.* (1915); *Eminent and Representative Men of Va. and the District of Columbia* (1893); *The Biog. Encyc. of Md. and District of Columbia* (1882); *Daily Nat. Intelligencer* (Washington, D. C.), July 17, 1850.] F. M.

HAGOOD, JOHNSON (Feb. 21, 1829–Jan. 4, 1898), soldier, governor of South Carolina, was born in Barnwell County, S. C., the son of Dr. James O. and Indina Allen Hagood, and grandson of Johnson Hagood, lawyer and amateur scientist of local fame. After preliminary education in Richmond Academy at Augusta, Ga., young Hagood entered the Citadel, the state military academy at Charleston, S. C., from which he was graduated in 1847. He then studied law under Judge Edmund Bellinger of Charleston. Admitted to the bar in 1850, he settled in Barnwell, planter as well as lawyer, and in the following year was named by Governor Means deputy adjutant-general of militia, a position which afforded him an opportunity to supervise much training of troops. In the same year he was elected by the legislature commissioner in equity for Barnwell County. On Nov. 21, 1856, he married Eloise B. Butler, the daughter of Senator A. P. Butler. At the outbreak of the Civil War, he was named colonel of the 1st South Carolina Regiment and had a part in the reduction of Sumter. Ordered to Virginia, he was in the first battle at Manassas and then hurried back to aid in the defense of Charleston, serving notably at Secessionville, after which in July 1862 he was made brigadier-general. He remained in the vicinity of Charleston until the spring of 1864 when he was again sent to Virginia, arriving in time to win Beauregard's praise for valor at Walthall Junction in May. His most spectacular exploit was on the Weldon Road in August when at the head of a small detachment he cut his way through a larger encircling body of Federals; but his severest service was in the trenches around Petersburg. At one time, according to his own statement (*Southern Historical Society Papers*, January-December 1888, p. 395), he occupied a section for sixty-five days before he was relieved, losing about 1,500 of his 2,300 men.

Returning to his Barnwell plantation at the close of the war, Hagood immediately manifested intelligent and influential interest in rebuilding the state, particularly in the development of agriculture and education. He was among the first in this period to champion diversified farming, and he practised effectively on his own plantation what he preached to others. In 1869 he was chosen first president of the South Carolina Agricultural and Mechanical Society. Meantime he had entered politics, having run unsuccessfully as Democratic candidate for Congress in the election of 1868. He was a conspicuous figure in both Tax-Payers' Conventions, 1871 and 1874, and was vice-president of the Democratic convention of 1876. Nominated by that group for comptroller-general, he went in with the Hampton ticket in the desperate struggle which marked the end of Reconstruction in South Carolina. Two years later he was renominated without opposition and again elected. With the powerful indorsement of Hampton, Hagood defeated Gen. Martin Evans for the Democratic nomination for governor in 1880, and in the general election he overwhelmed Blair, his Republican opponent. As governor, Hagood had two ambitions: to give the state a business-like administration and to stimulate, as far as possible, the economic life of the people. In both endeavors he realized measurable success. Not interested in reëlection, he withdrew from political life, save for one further venture when in behalf of his friend, General Hampton, he joined the vain fight against the Tilman movement of 1890, after which he enjoyed again the quiet of his Barnwell plantation. But he labored consistently for the causes which were his civic passions, the establishment of a saner agriculture and the perfecting of an adequate educational system. He was twice chairman of the state board of agriculture and was for fourteen years chairman of the board of visitors of the Citadel. To him is due no small share of credit for the material and intellectual progress slowly achieved by his state. He died in Barnwell.

[*Cyc. of Eminent and Representative Men of the Carolinas* (1892), vol. I; Clement A. Evans, ed., *Confed. Mil. Hist.*, vol. V (1899); John S. Reynolds, *Reconstruction in S. C.* (1905); *Southern Hist. Soc. Papers*, Jan.–Dec. 1884, Jan.–Dec. 1885; Yates Snowden, ed., *Hist. of S. C.* (1920), vol. II; *Memoirs of the War of Secession* (1910), from the original manuscripts of Johnson Hagood; *News and Courier* (Charleston, S. C.), Jan. 5, 1898.] F. P. G.

HAGUE, ARNOLD (Dec. 3, 1840–May 14, 1917), geologist, younger brother of James Duncan Hague [*q.v.*], was born in Boston, Mass. His father, Rev. William Hague, a Baptist minister, was the son of a sea-captain in the East India trade who settled at Pelham Manor, N. Y., and married a descendant of French Huguenots, and a grandson of a Baptist minister of Scarborough, England. His mother, Mary Bowditch (Moriarty) Hague, came of a Salem family. When Arnold was twelve years of age the family moved to Albany, N. Y., where he attended the Albany Boys' Academy, from which he graduated at the age of fourteen. In 1857, the family moved to New York City. During the next few years, though urged to enter upon a business course, he fitted for college. In his twenty-first year, having volunteered for service in the Union army and been rejected on physical grounds, he entered the Sheffield Scientific School at Yale. He was admitted to advanced standing in the course in chemistry. Owing to the war, the classes were so reduced that but four were left to graduate. This circumstance was beneficial to the few remaining, however, since it brought them into more direct contact with their instructors than would otherwise have been possible. Among the latter were George J. Brush and James Dwight Dana [*qq.v.*], and among the older students with whom Hague became intimate were O. C. Marsh, Clarence King, and J. Willard Gibbs [*qq.v.*], and others who later became prominent in scientific circles. It was an inspiring atmosphere and must have had an important bearing upon his after life. He was graduated with the degree of Ph.B. in 1863 and again showed his patriotism by attempting enlistment, but was rejected on the same grounds as before. Returning then once more to scientific studies, he spent a year in Göttingen and another in Heidelberg, where he studied in Bunsen's laboratory, devoting his attention mainly to mineralogy and chemistry. A third attempt made about this time to enter the Union army brought him a personal message from the President showing that to him, at least, the use for the scientific man for other purposes than food for powder was already realized. In effect the President said, "Stay where you are: we shall need such as you, later." In the spring of 1865 Hague entered the celebrated *Bergakademie,* or Royal School of Mines in Freiberg, Saxony, and there met for the first time Samuel F. Emmons [*q.v.*], also a student, with whom he formed a firm and lasting friendship. In 1866 he returned home, being then twenty-six years of age and having what was for the time a liberal education in chemistry, mineralogy, and geology. A few weeks later he was offered by Clarence King a position as assistant geologist on the Geological Survey of the Fortieth Parallel, plans for which were then maturing. The offer was promptly accepted. By a coincidence S. F. Emmons also returned from his foreign studies about this time and through the intervention of Hague was given a like appointment. Thus simply the two men who were to remain ever after in close association were started upon their careers. Hague continued with the Fortieth Parallel survey until the completion of the work. He and Emmons were responsible for Volume II, *Descriptive Geology* (1877), of the Report of the survey. After the accomplishment of this work, Hague became government geologist of Guatemala and spent a year examining mines and studying the volcanoes of that country. The year following, at the instance of Li Hung Chang, he went to China to examine the gold, silver, and lead mines of the northern part of the empire. With the reorganization of the United States geological surveys in 1879 under one head and the appointment of Clarence King as director, Hague received once more an appointment as a United States geologist, taking oath of office in April 1880 and serving throughout the remainder of his active career. He passed the summer of 1880 in a study of the Eureka mining district of Nevada, but this work was interrupted by a change in plans incidental to the resignation of King and appointment of J. W. Powell [*q.v.*], and the seasons of 1881 and 1882 were spent in a re-study of the rocks of the Fortieth Parallel survey and other collections in New York. In 1883, under Director J. W. Powell, Hague was appointed geologist in charge of the survey of the Yellowstone National Park. To this work he devoted the rest of his professional life, his particular interests being problems in vulcanology and petrology.

Hague was a man of culture, of quiet demeanor, and always a gentleman however trying the conditions. "Considerate of the feelings of others; temperate in language and habits, by nature reticent and reserved, he was conservative in his opinions, cautious in his judgment and deliberate in action" (Iddings, *post*, p. 45). His standard of work was high, and he never allowed himself to be hurried in the preparation of a report. Indeed in this matter he was over-cautious and often recast his manuscripts many times, occasionally rewriting an entire page because of a change or correction involving but a few words. His most important studies were issued as publications of the Geological Survey, but he also contributed to periodicals. In 1913 his biographical sketch of his friend Emmons was published in Volume VII of the *National Academy of Sciences Biographical Memoirs*. Hague was elected to membership in the National Academy of Sciences in 1885 and represented it on many important occasions. He was an active member of the Committee on Forest Reservations in 1896; a fellow of the Geological Societies of London and America; the American Philosophical Society; the American Institute of Mining Engineers, and other organizations of less importance. On Nov. 14, 1893, he was married to Mary Bruce (Robins) Howe of New York, daughter of George W. Robins and widow of Walter Howe. There were no children from this marriage. His death, which occurred suddenly on May 14, 1917, was apparently due to an injury caused by a fall during the previous winter.

["Memorial of Arnold Hague," by J. P. Iddings, Hague's assistant, in *Bull. Geol. Soc. Am.*, vol. XXIX (1918), with full bibliography of Hague's publications; autobiographical material in Hague's memoir of Emmons, mentioned above; J. S. Diller, "Arnold Hague," in *Am. Jour. Sci.*, July 1917; bibliography in J. M. Nickles, *Geol. Lit. on North America* (1923), being Bulletin 746 of the U. S. Geol. Survey; Wm. Hague, *Life Notes* (1888); *Discourse in Memory of Wm. Hague* (1889); *Obit. Record Grads. Yale Univ.*, 1917; *Evening Star* (Washington), May 14, 1917; personal recollections.] G. P. M.

HAGUE, JAMES DUNCAN (Feb. 24, 1836–Aug. 3, 1908), mining engineer, brother of Arnold Hague [*q.v.*] and son of Rev. William and Mary Bowditch (Moriarty) Hague, was born in Boston, Mass. He was given his preliminary education in private schools and in 1854 entered the Lawrence Scientific School of Harvard University. In 1855–56 he studied in the University of Göttingen, Hanover, and in 1856–58 at the Royal School of Mines at Freiberg, Saxony. From 1859 to 1861 he was a chemist with a South Sea exploring expedition, studying the phosphate deposits of Jarvis, Baker, and adjacent islands. On the outbreak of the Civil War he entered the United States Navy, serving for a year as judge advocate to the fleet stationed at Port Royal, S. C. In 1863 he became superintendent of the Albany & Boston Copper Mine in the Lake Superior region and was also connected with the early developments of the Calumet and Hecla properties. In 1867 he followed his brother Arnold in joining the Geological Survey of the Fortieth Parallel under Clarence King [*q.v.*]. In this connection he continued for three years and to the Report of the survey he contributed the classic third volume, *Mining Industry* (1870). From 1871 to 1878 he was in private employ as a consulting mining engineer, residing in California; after 1879 and until his death his headquarters were in New York. For a number of years he was president of the company controlling the famous North Star Mine of Grass Valley, Cal.

Hague was a fellow of the American Association for the Advancement of Science, the American Academy of Arts and Sciences, the American Geographical Society, the New York Historical Society, the New England and St. Andrew's societies, and numerous other organizations. He was a man of dignified, gentlemanly, and kindly appearance. In April 1872 he married Mary Ward Foote of Guilford, Conn., who died in 1898, leaving him one son and two daughters. He died at Stockbridge, Mass., in his seventy-third year.

[Biographical sketch by R. W. Raymond in *Trans. Am. Inst. Mining Engineers*, vol. XXXIX (1909); obituary notice in *Eng. and Mining Jour.*, Aug. 8, 1908; *Who's Who in America*, 1908–09; *Boston Transcript*, Aug. 4, 1908; *N. Y. Times, Boston Post*, Aug. 5, 1908; full bibliography of Hague's publications in J. M. Nickles, *Geol. Lit. on North America* (1923), being Bulletin 746 of the U. S. Geol. Survey.] G. P. M.

HAHN, GEORG MICHAEL DECKER (Nov. 24, 1830–Mar. 15, 1886), the first Republican governor of Louisiana, congressman, editor, was born at Klingenmünster in Bavaria, Germany, and when a small child was brought to the United States by his widowed mother, Margaretha Decker Hahn, along with four other children. After a short stay in New York, they settled in New Orleans about 1840. The next year the mother died of yellow fever. Young Michael attended the public schools of his adopted city, and after graduating from high school, entered the law office of Christian Roselius, a leading New Orleans lawyer, and at the same time attended lectures in the law department of the University of Louisiana (now Tulane University), from which he received the degree of LL.B. in 1851. While a student he made a living by conducting a real-estate agency and by writing for newspapers. After completing his studies he immediately began the practice of his profession, combining with it the duties of a notary public. When barely twenty-two he was elected to the New Orleans school board, and soon became its president. In the days before the Civil War he was a Democrat, but independent in his political thinking. He was opposed to the Slidell wing of the party in Louisiana, opposed the nomination of Buchanan in 1856, and in 1860 supported Douglas for the presidency. Throughout the controversial fifties he was a bitter opponent of slavery, and in 1860–61 he was a member of a committee which canvassed the state against secession. He omitted the oath of allegiance to the Confederacy in renewing his oath as notary, and when Farragut's fleet arrived at New Orleans he hastened to pledge his allegiance to the United States government.

In December 1862 the two Louisiana congressional districts within the Union lines elected congressmen, and Hahn was chosen to represent the 2nd district, but, with the representative from the 1st district, he was not permitted to take his seat until February 1863. During his short stay in Washington he supported the war measures of President Lincoln and at the expiration of his term he was appointed prize commissioner at New Orleans. In 1864 he purchased the New Orleans *Daily True Delta,* which he edited for some time as a Republican newspaper—the first of two ventures in Republican journalism in New Orleans, for in 1867 he started the *New Orleans Republican,* which he conducted until 1871. In the election of Feb. 22, 1864, he was chosen governor by the Free-State party, one of three groups participating in the election, and proceeded to carry out President Lincoln's mild reconstruction policy. He resigned the governor's office, Mar. 4, 1865, having been elected to the United States Senate, but it seems he never pressed his claim to a senatorial seat because of his opposition to President Johnson's reconstruction policy. During a New Orleans riot, in 1866, he received a gunshot wound which made him a cripple for the rest of his life. In 1871 he gave up his New Orleans newspaper and retired to his sugar plantation in St. Charles Parish, where the following year he laid out the town of Hahnville. On Feb. 15, 1872, he issued the first number of the *St. Charles Herald,* which he published until his death. He was chosen a representative to the state legislature, where he served for a time as speaker, and served also as district judge. In 1884 he was Republican nominee for Congress in the 2nd district of Louisiana, and, in a district usually Democratic, he was elected by 3,000 majority. Not long after he had entered upon his new duties he was found dead at his lodging place in Washington. Hahn was a scholarly man of much ability and was recognized for his integrity and devotion to principle. Because of this he was able to retain the respect of the people although affiliated with a party which was unpopular in the state. Said Congressman Blanchard of Louisiana: "Of all the leading Republicans of Louisiana he was one of the least objectionable."

[*Addresses on the Life and Character of Michael Hahn . . . Delivered in the House of Representatives and in the Senate, 49 Cong., 1 Sess.* (1886); *Maynier's La. Biogs.*, pt. I (1882), pp. 42–46; Mrs. Eugene Soniat, *Biog. Sketches of Louisiana's Govs. from D'Iberville to McEnery, by a Louisianaise* (1885); J. R. Ficklen, *Hist. of Reconstruction in La. (through 1868)* (1910); Ella Lonn, *Reconstruction in La. After 1868* (1918); Alcée Fortier, *A Hist. of La.* (1904), vol. IV; *Evening Star* (Washington, D. C.), Mar. 15, 1886; *Times-Democrat* (New Orleans), Mar. 16, 1886.]

M. J. W.

HAID, LEO (July 15, 1849–July 24, 1924), Roman Catholic bishop and Benedictine abbot in North Carolina, was born near Latrobe, in Westmoreland County, Pa., the fourth of ten children. His father, John Haid, a nurseryman by occupation, came to America from the Duchy of Luxemburg; his mother, Mary A. Stader, was a native of Treves in Germany. Leo began his elementary studies in the local common schools when he was eight years of age. In 1862 he entered the preparatory department of St. Vincent's College, near Latrobe, a school directed by Benedictine monks. The abbey to which the school was attached was the first permanent foundation (1846) of the Benedictine Order in the United States. Haid was attracted to the life of his teachers, and after his school course in 1869 he became a member of that order at St. Vincent's Abbey, and was ordained there Dec. 21, 1872. After his ordination he spent thirteen years at the abbey engaged as a teacher, as secretary of the college, and as chaplain to the students. Gifted with a rare power of inspiring others with his own lofty ideals and with his own zeal, he was signally successful as a teacher, and exercised a marked influence over the young men committed to his care. His energy and sustained power for work soon made him a leading figure in the life of the community.

In 1885 he was elected abbot of Belmont Abbey, a newly formed Benedictine community near Belmont, N. C. The Rev. Dr. Jeremiah O'Connell, a retired missionary of the Carolinas and Georgia, had bought the Caldwell Estate some twelve miles from Charlotte, and with many onerous conditions attached offered it through the future Cardinal Gibbons, then vicar apostolic of North Carolina, to the Benedictine Order for religious and educational purposes. When Haid and his little colony of Benedictines arrived at Belmont, then called Garibaldi, in July 1885, they found a veritable wilderness. The early years of the abbatial life were years of great struggle and poverty. "Among strangers who did not understand our lives, or our object in coming into their midst, without means," said Bishop Haid in an address delivered in 1910, "we were obliged to build and lay the foundations for the future." In spite of forlorn appearances, however, nature had favored the spot, and with the sturdy Benedictine spirit of labor, sacrifice, and prayer the monks set to work.

By a brief dated Dec. 7, 1887, Abbot Haid was appointed vicar apostolic of North Carolina and titular bishop of Messene. On July 1, 1888, he received episcopal consecration from Cardinal Gibbons in the Cathedral of Baltimore. Invested with the double dignity and honor, unique in the United States, of abbot and bishop, he devoted himself with characteristic energy to the upbuilding of his vicariate. He gave special care to the education of priests for North Carolina, and with untiring activity promoted the erection of churches, schools, and charitable institutions in all parts of the state and elsewhere in the South. To mark the twenty-fifth anniversary of his abbacy, Pope Pius X, on June 8, 1910, raised Belmont Abbey to the rank and dignity of a Cathedral Abbey, with an independent territory of its own, and conferred upon the bishop the title of the first abbot-ordinary. At the close of a long episcopate in 1924, he left to his successor a rich inheritance, well ordered and firmly established. Belmont Abbey College had grown to be one of the prominent Catholic educational institutions of the South, and Belmont Abbey was widely known as the center of Catholicism in North Carolina.

[S. A. Ashe, *Biog. Hist. of N. C.*, IV (1906), 153–57; J. S. Bassett, "A North Carolina Monastery," in *Mag. of Am. Hist.*, Feb. 1893; New York *Sun*, Feb. 14, 1886; J. J. O'Connell, in *Catholicity in the Carolinas and Georgia* (1879); *The Cath. Church in the U. S. A.* (1914), III, 260–75; *America*, Oct. 29, 1910; *Cath. World*, Sept. 1924; *Charlotte Observer* and *N. Y. Times*, July 25, 1924.]

T. O.

HAIGHT, CHARLES COOLIDGE (Mar. 17, 1841–Feb. 8, 1917), architect, was born in New York City, the son of Benjamin Isaac Haight, assistant rector of Trinity Church, and Hetty (Coolidge) Haight. He was of the tenth generation in America among the descendants of John Hoyt (or Haight), who settled in Salisbury, Mass., in the middle of the seventeenth century. In 1806 his grandfather, Benjamin, moved from Bedford, Westchester County, N. Y., where his branch of the family had lived, to New York City, and there he became a well-known merchant. Charles Haight graduated from Columbia College in 1861, studied law for a short time, and then enlisted in the 7th Regiment, with which he served in Baltimore in 1862. The same year he was commissioned in the 31st New York Volunteers, serving as first lieutenant and adjutant from October 1862 to December 1863, when he received a captain's commission in the 39th New York Volunteers. Severely wounded at the Wilderness, he retired in November 1864. He then entered the office of Emlen T. Littell, architect, where he remained as a student until he left in 1867 to open his own office.

Haight's earliest important work was the school of mines building, Columbia College, 1874, which, although in the then fashionable Victorian Gothic style, showed much creative promise. Hamilton Hall, 1880, on the Madison Avenue side of the Columbia block, was almost entirely free from Victorian mannerisms and was one of the earliest examples of the adaptation of collegiate Gothic to school architecture in America. It was followed in 1884 by the library and in 1887 by the Trinity parish offices on Church Street in much the same style, the Columbia library being especially noteworthy because of its exposed iron trusses. Other outstanding educational buildings of this period, all revealing the same effort to attain charm, dignity, and an honest expression of their function, were those at Hobart College, Geneva, N. Y., St. Stephen's College, Annandale, N. Y., and the grammar school building at the University of the South, Sewanee, Tenn. Haight also designed several commercial buildings, the largest of which was that for the Lawyer's Title Insurance Company of New York, 1894. Its most striking feature is a graceful tower with a picturesque top.

Three works most perfectly characterize Haight's taste and ability during this period: the General Theological Seminary, New York, 1887–89; the New York Cancer Hospital, 1885–90; and the Havemeyer house, 1890. The first of these is a quiet group of brick and stone buildings around a quadrangle, full of variety, charm, and unforced atmosphere. The Cancer Hospital is picturesquely composed, somewhat after the manner of a French château, but with detail of English flavor. The freest in design is the Havemeyer house, the style of which, although distantly based on Richardsonian Romanesque, is much quieter and less manneristic; it is without doubt one of the most successful adaptations ever made of a picturesque style to city conditions, beautiful in composition and exquisitely refined in detail. The building of Vanderbilt and Phelps halls at Yale, completed in 1898, carried still further the beginning already made of the adaptation of English collegiate Gothic in America. These two buildings were the first of several at Yale which formed the bulk of Haight's later work. A. M. Githens became associated with him in the most of this work which was done under the name of Haight and Githens. The university library was the first of these and was followed rapidly by a large group of halls and laboratories for the Sheffield Scientific School, all in a continually more free English collegiate style.

Haight was an ardent yachtsman and usually spent his summers on the water. In person he was a "gentleman of the old school," dignified and courtly in manner. He was married in October 1870 to Euphemia Kneeland and died at Garrison-on-Hudson in his seventy-sixth year.

[Montgomery Schuyler, *A Rev. of the Work of Chas. C. Haight* (1899), Great Am. Architect Ser., no. 6, supp. to the *Architectural Record;* Morgan Dix, *Hist. of the Parish of Trinity Ch.*, IV (1906), 530; D. W. Hoyt, *Geneal. Hist. of the Hoyt, Haight, and Hight Families* (1871), p. 543; obituary in the *N. Y. Times*, Feb. 9, 1917; appreciation by A. M. Githens in the *Architectural Record*, Apr. 1917; information as to certain facts obtained from Haight's son, Col. C. Sidney Haight.]

T. F. H.

HAIGHT, HENRY HUNTLY (May 20, 1825–Sept. 2, 1878), lawyer, governor of California, was born in Rochester, N. Y., the son of Fletcher Mathews and Elizabeth Stewart (MacLachlan) Haight. He graduated at Yale with the class of 1844 and two years later went with his father, who was a lawyer of some eminence, to St. Louis, where he was admitted to the bar, and where they practised together until 1849. Like so many other Americans in Missouri, Henry Haight left to seek his fortune in California, arriving in San Francisco on Jan. 20, 1850. The gold fever was still carrying thousands to the mines, but Haight took up his residence in San Francisco and entered upon the practice of law, remaining thus occupied until 1867. For a time his partner was James A. McDougall. Later he was joined by his father, Fletcher Haight, who in 1857 and 1859 was an unsuccessful aspirant for the Republican nomination for justice of the state supreme court, and who in 1861 was appointed by President Lincoln United States district judge for the southern district of California. In Missouri both father and son had been interested in the Free-Soil movement, but in California Henry Haight affiliated with the Democratic party, in an inconspicuous way, in the campaign of 1852. He transferred his interest to the Republican party as it came into existence in California, and in 1859 was chairman of the Republican state committee. In 1860 he supported Lincoln but by 1864 he was opposed to the administration and gave his support to the Democratic nominee. Then and later his recurring conviction of the importance of constitutional procedure caused him to shift positions, which gave him with many a reputation for inconsistency, but which to his closer acquaintances evinced "not obliquity, but indecision" (Stebbins, *post,* p. 3).

In 1867 Haight was the candidate of the Democratic party for governor and was elected at the close of an exciting and vigorous campaign. Apparently he devoted much of his thought to national affairs. He opposed the continuance of Chinese immigration, favored an eight-hour day, and violently attacked proposals for negro suffrage. Later he advocated free trade, a specie currency, the exclusive right of each state to regulate its domestic concerns, and opposed all proposals to weaken the Constitution. In transmitting the proposed Fifteenth Amendment to the California state legislature he declared that it would fail of success and that a "military oligarchy" would not long control the "people of remote states." Among the important acts of the period of his governorship was that establishing the University of California, and after his retirement he served as a member of the board of regents. In 1868 he was supported in California as a proper candidate for the presidency and three years later, against his wishes, he was renominated for governor. Again he made his appeal on national grounds, stressing Democratic doctrine, but he was defeated. He resumed the practice of law and in 1878 was elected a delegate to the convention called to revise the state constitution. He did not, however, take his place. On Sept. 2, 1878, he was taken suddenly ill at his office and died in San Francisco on the same day. His wife, Anna (Bissell) Haight, whom he married in St. Louis in January 1855, survived him. A man of good education, decided views, and given to wise and patient counsel, his abiding reputation rested upon his career as a lawyer rather than as governor. As Horatio Stebbins said of him (*post,* pp. 2–3): "The extraordinary thing in him was that there was nothing extraordinary, but a quite symmetrical combination of the usual faculties of men."

[Horatio Stebbins, memorial address in *Bull. of the Univ. of Cal.,* Sept. 1878; W. J. Davis, *Hist. of Pol. Conventions in Cal., 1849–92* (1893); D. W. Hoyt, *Hoyt, Haight and Hight Families* (1871); W. R. Cutter, *Geneal. and Family Hist. of Western N. Y.* (1912), vol. II; *Sacramento Daily Union, Daily Morning Call,* and *Daily Alta California* (San Francisco), Sept. 3, 1878.]

E. E. R.

HAILMANN, WILLIAM NICHOLAS (Oct. 20, 1836–May 13, 1920), leader of the kindergarten movement in the United States, the son of William Alexander and Babette Hailmann, was born at Glarus, Switzerland, a few months before the family removed to Islikon, where the father was employed as a designer of cotton-prints. Earlier generations of the family had contributed to the development of the textile industry in Alsace. Brought up as an only child in a rural environment by a mother who was an admirer of Pestalozzi, and receiving a goodly part of his school education from Pestalozzian teachers, Hailmann was himself largely a product of the new education which he later advocated. At thirteen he was admitted to the polytechnic division of the cantonal college of Zürich, Pestalozzi's native city. Three years later he emigrated to Louisville, Ky., where he maintained himself, first, by teaching the modern languages, and later, by pursuing his major interest, the natural sciences, in the girls' and also in the boys' high school. In 1857 he married the niece of the preceptress of the former, Eudora Lucas. Revisiting Zürich in 1860, Hailmann became intensely interested in the kindergarten education exemplified there. On assuming the directorship of the German-American Academy in Louisville in 1865 he established a kindergarten in connection with the institution. Throughout the rest of his life, whatever his position might be, he, aided by his wife, was persistently active in the dissemination of Froebelian doctrines, in the establishment of kindergartens, in conducting training schools, and in promoting the application of kindergarten principles in the elementary school. In 1866 and again in 1872, he sent his wife to Switzerland to study kindergarten theory and practice.

From 1873 to 1883 Hailmann served as director of German-American academies in Milwaukee and Detroit. During this and the following decade he took an active part in the work of the National Education Association, mainly in the interest of the kindergarten movement. Upon the establishment of a kindergarten section in 1885, he was elected chairman. After serving eleven years as superintendent of schools at La Porte, Ind., 1883–94, he was appointed federal superintendent of Indian schools. Kindergartens were established for Indian children and training schools for kindergarten teachers. Deprived of his position for political reasons against the protest of leading American educators and other prominent citizens, he was elected superintendent of the city schools of Dayton, Ohio, in 1898. From 1904 to 1914 he served on the faculties of the Chicago Normal School and the Cleveland Normal Training School. His failing health requiring a change of climate, he accepted in 1914 a professorship in the Broadoaks Kindergarten Normal School at Pasadena, Cal., which position he retained until his death. In California Hailmann organized the Kindergarten-Primary Council of the West in furtherance of his plan of bridging the gap between the kindergarten and the elementary school. In his honor the Southern California Kindergarten-Primary Club undertook the building up of the William N. Hailmann Memorial Library of the University of California, Southern Branch, as a historical library of child education.

G. Stanley Hall said of Hailmann that he was "by far the most eminent of all men in this country devoted to the interests of the kindergarten" (*Kindergarten and First Grade,* October 1920). The learning, culture, and intellectual vigor which attracted the attention of his fellow workers are reflected in the breadth and perspicuity of his treatment of the problems of child education in his rather numerous, though brief, publications. His expositions of the doctrines of Froebel are among the most lucid in educational literature. His writings include: *Outlines of a System of Object-Teaching* (1867); *Kindergarten Culture in the Family and Kindergarten* (1873); *Twelve Lectures on the History of Pedagogy* (1874); *Letters to a Mother* (1876); *Early Education* (1878); *Four Lectures on Early Child-Culture* (1880); *Primary Helps* (1882); *The Application of Psychology to the Work of Teaching* (1884), awarded the Bicknell Fund prize by the American Institute of Instruction; *Froebel's Education of Man* (1887), a translation and commentary; *Laws of Childhood and Other Papers* (1889); *Constructive Form Work* (1901); and, in collaboration with Frederick Manley, *The English Language* (1903). After the death of his first wife in 1904, he married Helena Kuhn, Dec. 25, 1907.

[Biographical sketch by Barbara Greenwood in *Pioneers of the Kindergarten in America* (1924); *Who's Who in America,* 1916–17; brief biographical sketches in *Kindergarten and First Grade,* Oct. 1920, June 1922; Indian Rights Asso., *Publications,* 2 ser., no. 46 (1898); manuscript sketch of the life of Hailmann by his daughter, Elizabeth E. Hailmann.]

L. F. A.

HAINES, CHARLES GLIDDEN (Jan. 24, 1792–July 3, 1825), lawyer, author, politician, was born at Canterbury, N. H., the youngest of the ten children of Samuel and Hannah (Johnson) Haines. His father had served as a captain of New Hampshire militia during the Revolution. He spent his boyhood on his father's farm, attending the village school in winter. In 1806, at the age of fourteen, he obtained a position as clerk in the office of the secretary of state of New Hampshire at Concord. At this time he began to evince an interest in military affairs and organized a military company of boys, of which he was elected captain. In 1812 he was admitted to Middlebury College, Middlebury, Vt., graduated in 1816, and shortly afterward began the study of law under United States Senator Seymour. While carrying on his law studies he served as assistant editor of the leading journal of Vermont, published in Middlebury, and also as aide-de-camp to the governor of Vermont. In 1818 he removed to New York City and entered the law office of Pierre Van Wyck as a law student and in 1821 was admitted to the New York bar. Long an admirer of Gov. DeWitt Clinton of New York, he became personally acquainted with him and soon after was appointed his private secretary. His duties served to stimulate his interest in politics and he began to take an active part in state affairs, writing on various current topics, particularly the canal question. During his first year in New York he published a pamphlet entitled *Considerations on the Great Western Canal from the Hudson to Lake Erie* (1818), twice republished by the New York Corresponding Association for the Promotion of Internal Improvements, and in 1821 he brought out another work entitled *Public Documents, Relating to the New-York Canals.*

Though writing interfered with his legal work, Haines enjoyed a good practice from the beginning and took particular interest in questions involving federal and state constitutions. In 1824 he was admitted to the United States Supreme Court bar, having been retained as associate counsel in the first hearing of *Ogden* vs. *Saunders* (12 *Wheaton,* 213), a case involving the constitutionality of the New York state bankruptcy law. Henry Clay was one of his associates. Daniel Webster was of opposing counsel. He also appeared in the patent case, *Ex Parte Wood and Brundage* (9 *Wheaton,* 603), involving a motion to grant a writ of mandamus in which the Supreme Court granted the motion in his favor. In 1822–23 he published one of the first law journals in this country, the *United States Law Journal and Civilian Magazine,* and contributed to it editorials and essays. He grasped every opportunity to speak in public, especially on the issues concerning state internal improvements. When in 1824 DeWitt Clinton was removed as state-canal commissioner, Haines, in many speeches, publicly supported Clinton and denounced his removal as unjust, guiding the reaction of the public mind in favor of Clinton. On Sept. 21, 1824, the convention of the People's party, in support of Clinton for governor, met at Utica. Though only thirty-two years of age, Haines exerted a great influence in Clinton's behalf and had the gratification of seeing him elected, in November of the same year, by a majority of thirty thousand. In January 1825 Governor Clinton appointed him adjutant-general of the state, but his untimely death prevented him from assuming the duties of his office. From November 1824 he occupied himself mainly by writing articles on current political matters. Continuous sedentary habits, aggravated by a ruptured blood vessel, had seriously impaired his health and he was forced to seek recovery at Charleston, S. C. Finding recuperation a slow process, he returned to New York and on July 3, 1825, at the age of thirty-three, passed away. His funeral, on July 6, was attended by hundreds of mourners, among whom was the Marquis de Lafayette.

[C. G. Haines, *Memoir of Thos. Addis Emmet, . . . with a Biog. Notice of Mr. Haines* (1829); J. O. Lyford, *Hist. of the Town of Canterbury, N. H., 1727–1912* (2 vols., 1912); A. M. and T. V. Haines, *Deacon Samuel Haines of Westbury, Wiltshire, England, and his Descendants* (1902); *Cat. of the Officers and Students of Middlebury Coll. . . . 1800–1915* (1917); *Mercantile Advertiser* (N. Y.), July 4, 6, 1825; N. Y. *Evening Post,* July 5, 7, 1825.]

W. G. E.

HAINES, DANIEL (Jan. 6, 1801–Jan. 26, 1877), jurist, governor of New Jersey, born in New York City, was the son of Elias Haines and was descended from James Haines (or Hinds) who emigrated to Salem, Mass., in 1637 and later moved to Southold, L. I. His mother was Mary Ogden, the daughter of Robert Ogden and a niece of Gov. Aaron Ogden [*q.v.*]. He received his early education under Dr. Edmund D. Barry, a distinguished teacher, and at the academy in Elizabethtown, N. J. After graduating at the College of New Jersey in 1820, he entered the law office of Thomas C. Ryerson in Newton, Sussex County. In 1823 he was admitted to the bar and began to practise in Hamburg, Sussex County. Despite the fact that he inherited Federalist traditions, he took an active part in promoting the election of Andrew Jackson and was instrumental in securing for Jackson, in the election of 1824, all the votes cast in the small township of Vernon, where he resided. In 1839 he was nominated and elected for one year to the upper house of the legislature. Here he was immediately thrown into a political controversy known as the "Broad Seal War." It was the ability and tact which he displayed in this contest that brought him forward as a political leader of recognized ability, and led to his election, in 1843, as governor. During his term of one year, he brought about the calling of a convention which framed the new constitution of 1844. According to the constitution of 1776, the office of governor carried with it that of chancellor, and Haines's opinions (4 *N. J. Equity*) are held in high regard.

In 1847 Haines was again the Democratic nominee for governor and was elected under the new constitution for a term of three years. During this tenure he devoted his efforts chiefly to two tasks: that of building up the school system of the state, and that of improving state governmental machinery. In 1852 he was appointed an associate justice of the supreme court. Reappointed, he held this office until November 1866. Though his knowldege of the law was not profound, his chief qualification being that of broad and somewhat varied experience, he was a man of sound judgment and honest purpose. In 1860 he supported the Douglas ticket because he believed "that the election of Lincoln as a sectional candidate might precipitate war" (Elmer, *post,* p. 261), but after the attack on Sumter he supported the Union cause to the limit, taking an active part in raising troops. His two sons and a son-in-law volunteered, and one son gave his life in support of the North. Haines was a ruling elder in the Presbyterian Church, a member of the Bible Society and other religious societies, and a trustee of many public institutions. He was especially interested in prison reform and in 1868 he was appointed by the legislature to study prison systems in his own and other states. In 1870 he was sent as a delegate to the National Congress on Penitentiary and Reformatory Discipline at Cincinnati, where he was elected a member of a committee to organize a national reform association and to make preparations for the calling of an international congress which met in London in 1872. He was a delegate to the London conference and for one year (1872) was vice-president of the National Prison Association of the United States. He was twice married. His first wife was Ann Maria Austin of Warwick, N. Y., whom he married on June 28, 1827. She died on Dec. 8, 1844, and on July 6, 1865, he married Mary Townsend.

[John Whitehead, *The Judicial and Civil Hist. of N. J.* (1897); J. P. Snell and others, *Hist. of Sussex and Warren Counties, N. J.* (1881); L. Q. C. Elmer, *The Constitution and Government of the Province and State of N. J.* (1872); G. R. Howell, *The Early Hist. of Southampton, L. I.* (2nd ed., 1887); *Newark Daily Advertiser,* Jan. 26, 1877; *Daily State Gazette* (Trenton), Jan. 27, 1877.] A. T. M.

HAINES, LYNN (Apr. 12, 1876–Oct. 9, 1929), publicist, editor, was born in Waseca, Minn., the son of Caleb and Alice (Nelson) Haines. His early education was obtained in the elementary schools of his native town and St. Paul. In 1899 he entered Hamline University in St. Paul but left to become a reporter for one of the Appleton (Minnesota) newspapers. He showed a natural aptitude for journalism and within a year he was appointed a reporter for a leading St. Paul newspaper and was assigned to cover the political news at the state Capitol. Two years later he was appointed political writer for a syndicate distributing news to the Minnesota newspapers. While writing for the syndicate he made extensive studies of Minnesota state governmental history and procedure and in 1909 he organized the Minnesota Voters' League, an organization created to stimulate and broaden the education of the voters concerning their state government. Toward the close of 1911 he removed to Washington, D. C., to assume his new duties as press correspondent for a St. Paul newspaper. Here he now closely followed the activities of the United States Congress and in 1912 he published *Law Making in America,* an interesting narrative of the 1911–12 session of the Sixty-second Congress, which described the machinery and methods of national legislation. He also wrote and published *The Senate from 1907 to 1912* (1912), which narrated the part which thirty senators (terms expiring Mar. 3, 1913) had played during those years, when the tariff, Canadian reciprocity, and railroad regulation were under discussion. At the same time he published as a pamphlet "The Story of the Democratic House of Representatives," a chapter from his *Law Making in America,* in which he proposed remedies to the conditions in the House retarding the legislative machinery.

In 1914 Haines was elected executive secretary of the newly created National Voters' League, the object and purpose of which was to relate the legislative history of bills, record the attitude of senators and representatives upon pending legislation, and disseminate information directed to improve the personnel of Congress and its procedure. In 1915 he published *Your Congress,* an interpretation of the political and parliamentary influences dominating law-making in the United States, and in February 1916 he became editor of the *Searchlight on Congress,* the monthly publication of the League containing information of general interest concerning Congress. To it he contributed numerous political articles, essays, and reviews, outstanding among which were "How to reform the nominating machinery" (July 1924), and "Who's Who on Woman Suffrage" (July 1919). The *Searchlight* ceased publication in 1927. In 1926 Haines published *Your Servants in the Senate,* a narrative of the Senate during the Harding-Coolidge régime. This proved his most popular book. During the last three years of his life he was in failing health, and on Oct. 9, 1929, passed away, following an operation for appendicitis. In 1904 he had married Byrma Kyes of Minneapolis and after her death he married (1911) Dora Bacheller, who survived him.

[Biographical sources include: the *Evening Star* (Washington, D. C.), Oct. 9, 1929; *Washington Post,* Oct. 10, 13, 1929; *Minneapolis Jour.,* Oct. 9, 11, 1929; *New Republic,* Nov. 6, 1929; information as to certain facts from Mrs. Alton Haines, and from the dean, Hamline Univ. For reviews of Haines's works see the *Am. Pol. Sci. Rev.,* May 1912, May 1916.] W. G. E.

HAISH, JACOB (Mar. 9, 1826–Feb. 19, 1926), contractor, inventor, manufacturer, was born near Karlsruhe, in the Duchy of Baden, Germany, the son of Christian and Christina (Layman) Haish. When ten years old he came with his parents to the United States. After living about ten years on a farm in Pennsylvania the family removed to De Kalb County, Ill. Here Haish obtained a public school education, while helping with the farm work, and also learned carpentry from his father. At twenty he struck out for himself and after working for three years for several farmers he purchased a farm for himself at Pierce, Ill. Poor health, however, forced him to give up his farm in 1851, and to earn a living he turned to carpentry. For two years he worked at his trade in Kaneville, Ill., and then moved to De

Kalb, Ill., where he remained for the rest of his life. He was extremely successful here and in the course of twenty years built up a commanding business as a building contractor and lumber dealer. Around 1873 he became interested in improving barbed wire and applied for his first patent on Dec. 22, 1873, only to discover that a fellow townsman, Joseph F. Glidden [*q.v.*], had applied for a similar patent two months earlier. Haish unsuccessfully challenged Glidden's claim through interference proceedings but obtained three other barbed-wire patents before a decision was rendered late in 1874. He then invented the so-called "S" barbed wire, patented on Aug. 31, 1875, and proceeded to manufacture it in De Kalb. It was popular, had a wide sale, and a reissue of the patent was made Jan. 6, 1880.

In 1876 the Washburn & Moen Manufacturing Company of Worcester, Mass., bought Glidden's patents and then proceeded to obtain control of the entire barbed-wire production of the United States. Haish, backed by the Farmers' Protective Association, refused to sell and precipitated a legal contest which continued from 1876 to 1892. Infringement cases were tried in several federal districts and were carried from lower to higher courts until Feb. 29, 1892, when a decision by the United States Supreme Court was rendered in favor of the Washburn & Moen Company. While Haish failed to establish a legal right to the independent manufacture and sale of barbed wire, he continued to derive a large income from his barbed wire manufacturing machines which he himself used and leased to other manufacturers, including the Washburn & Moen Manufacturing Company. His later activities included the manufacture of plain wire, nails, and staples, woven-wire fencing, and agricultural implements of various kinds. In the course of his life he acquired much real estate both in De Kalb and Chicago. He founded the Barb City Bank in De Kalb, later the Jacob Haish State Bank, of which he was president at the time of his death. His wife was Sophia Ann Brown, daughter of Thomas C. Brown, a farmer of Napersville, whom he married on May 24, 1847.

[Arthur G. Warren, "Barbed Wire: Who Invented It?," *Iron Age*, June 24, 1926; *The Biog. Record of De Kalb County, Ill.* (1898); L. M. Gross, *Past and Present of De Kalb County, Ill.*, vol. II (1907); correspondence and records from Industrial Museum, American Steel & Wire Company, Worcester, Mass.; Patent Office records.]

C. W. M—n.

HALDEMAN, SAMUEL STEMAN (Aug. 12, 1812–Sept. 10, 1880), scientist, philologist, was born at Locust Grove, Lancaster County, Pa., the eldest of the seven children of Henry and Frances (Steman) Haldeman, of Swiss descent. His great-grandfather, Jacob Haldeman, was a member of the Committee of Safety during the Revolution; his grandfather, John B. Haldeman, sat in the General Assembly of Pennsylvania in 1795; a grand-uncle, Frederick Haldimand, held a commission in the British army and later became the first governor-general of Canada.

When Haldeman reached the age of fourteen he was placed under the tutelage of Dr. John Miller Keagy, who had opened a classical school at Harrisburg. From Keagy's school he proceeded to Dickinson College at Carlisle, Pa., where he remained for two years; then, finding the routine of college study irksome, he returned to his home. He had early in life developed a keen interest in the study of natural history and had gathered together a collection of fresh-water shells, insects, birds, and minerals, which he arranged as a museum in his father's barn. To the study of these he again devoted himself until his father, though entirely in sympathy with his scientific bent, decided that it was time for him to turn his attention to some more practical form of employment. He therefore placed the management of a sawmill in his son's hands, and with this Samuel occupied himself for five years.

In 1836 Henry Darwin Rogers [*q.v.*], one of Haldeman's instructors at Dickinson College, and now state geologist of New Jersey, was appointed geologist of Pennsylvania and summoned his former pupil to take in hand the field operations in New Jersey. In the following year Haldeman was transferred to Pennsylvania. In 1835 he had married Mary A. Hough of Bainbridge, Pa., and had removed to Chickies, Pa., where with two of his brothers he became interested in the manufacture of pig iron and where, although he took no active part in the management of the business, he experimented in the use of anthracite for smelting purposes. Upon the completion of his service as assistant in the state survey of Pennsylvania, he returned to his home at Chickies and in 1842 began the publication of his *Monograph on the Freshwater Mollusca of the United States.* In this monograph he described the *Scolithus linearis,* the most ancient of all organic remains found in Pennsylvania. Haldeman's sense of hearing was so marvelously acute that he could differentiate the sounds emitted by insects, and in the *American Journal of Science* for May 1848, he announced the discovery of a new organ of sound possessed by certain of the *Lepidoptera.* He studied exhaustively the American Indian dialects, becoming a recognized authority on this subject, and also devoted much labor to the investigation of English, Chinese, and other languages. While managing his father's sawmill, he developed an intense interest in the study of vocal sounds and later, while on one of his visits to Europe, investigated more than forty varieties of speech and established the boundaries of their vocal repertoire.

He was lecturer in zoölogy at the Franklin Institute in Philadelphia in 1842–43; professor of natural history at the University of Pennsylvania 1851–55; professor of geology and chemistry at the Pennsylvania Agricultural College and professor of natural sciences at Delaware College 1853–58; and was the first professor of comparative philology at the University of Pennsylvania from 1868 until his sudden death in 1880. In 1858 he won, in competition with eighteen European scholars, a prize of £100 offered by Sir Walter Calverley Trevelyan, President of the Phonetic Society of Great Britain, for his essay on "Analytical Orthography," which was later published in the *Transactions of the American Philosophical Society*. He was deeply interested in spelling reform and wrote a number of works on orthography, etymology, and orthoepy. In 1846 he joined the Roman Catholic Church. He died at Chickies, Pa., on Sept. 10, 1880.

Haldeman published, besides numerous papers of a philological and scientific nature: *Elements of Latin Pronunciation* (1851); a revision of R. C. Taylor's *Statistics on Coal* (1855); *Analytic Orthography* (1860); *Tours of Chess Knight* (1864); *Affixes* (1865; rev. ed., 1871); *Pennsylvania Dutch* (1872); *Outlines of Etymology* (1877); *Word-Building* (1881).

[See John Livingston, *Portraits of Eminent Americans now Living*, vol. IV (1854); Alex. Harris, *Biog. Hist. of Lancaster County, Pa.* (Lancaster, 1872); W. H. Browne, obituary, *Am. Jour. Philology*, Dec. 1880; D. G. Brinton, memoir, *Proc. Am. Philosophical Soc.*, XIX (1880–81), 279–85; J. G. Morris, brief eulogy, *Proc. Am. Asso. Advancement of Science*, XXX (1881), 261–63; C H. Hart, memoir, *Penn Monthly*, Aug. 1881 (also separately) with bibliography by Mrs. Eliza Figyelmesy, his daughter; C. H. Hart, another memoir, *Pop. Science Monthly*, July 1882; J. P. Lesley, memoir, *Biog. Memoirs Nat. Acad. Sciences*, vol. II (1886); H. L. Haldeman (nephew), memoir, bibliography, etc., *Records Am. Cath. Hist. Soc.*, Sept. 1898; P. C. Croll, "Prof. Samuel S. Haldeman, LL.D.," *Pa.-German*, July 1905; *Cat. of the Library of Prof. S. S. Haldeman . . . to be Sold at Auction* (1881). For the spelling of Haldeman's middle name see H. L. Haldeman, above.]

G. C. H.

HALDERMAN, JOHN A. (Apr. 15, 1833–Sept. 21, 1908), judge, soldier, legislator, diplomat, was born in Fayette County, Ky., the son of Dr. John A. and Susan Henderson (Rogers) Halderman. After the death of his mother in 1843, his father moved to Carlinville, Ill., and later remarried, leaving his son to live with his mother's family in Kentucky. The youth read law in the office of Col. C. C. Rogers of Louisville, Ky., and was admitted to the bar. In 1854 he went to Kansas and served as private secretary to the first governor of the territory. Later he was appointed judge of the probate court of Leavenworth County. On Oct. 20, 1861, at St. Louis, Mo., he married Anna Dorrien, but his married life proved unhappy, and he was later divorced. During the Civil War he served as major of the 1st Regiment of Kansas Infantry, being mustered in at Fort Leavenworth on May 31, 1861. In July 1861 he was appointed provost-marshal-general of the Army of the West by Gen. Nathaniel Lyon. At the battle of Wilson's Creek, Aug. 10, 1861, after Colonel Deitzler was wounded and disabled, Halderman succeeded to the command of the regiment and was mentioned in general orders and the official report for soldierly conduct. On Apr. 30, 1862, he resigned and was honorably discharged at Lawrence, Kan., in order to organize the northern division of the Kansas state troops. He was appointed major-general of the new unit and served from 1862 to 1864. After the war he lived in Leavenworth and was mayor of the city for two terms. He also served in both houses of the legislature and was a regent of the state university.

On Apr. 16, 1880, Halderman was appointed consul at Bangkok, Siam. A year later he was advanced to consul-general, and on July 13, 1882, his rank was raised to minister resident and consul-general. Owing to the change of administration, he resigned on June 17, 1885. While in Siam he succeeded in introducing postal and telegraphic systems, and in recognition of his efforts he received a vote of thanks from the International Postal Union and was made a commander of the Royal Order of Cambodia by King Norodom and the French government. For suppressing a liquor traffic, conducted under cover of the American flag, he received the decoration of Knight Commander of the Most Exalted Order of the White Elephant. General Grant stated that in his opinion Halderman's career was "one of the highest successes in American diplomacy." His closing years were spent in Washington, D. C. He died at Atlantic City, N. J., and was interred in Arlington Cemetery. Tall, broad-shouldered, and deep-chested, he was a splendid specimen of manhood. It has been said that "no General in the Southwest was more admired by his compeers, or more beloved by his soldiers." In civil life, his personal charm, keen intelligence, and high sense of honor won for him many friends.

[*Report of the Adjutant-Gen. of the State of Kan., 1861–65*, vol. I (1896); *Reg. of the Dept. of State Cor-*

rected to Dec. 1880 (1881) and *Corrected to Aug. 1882* (1882); D. W. Wilder, *The Annals of Kan.* (1886); C. R. Tuttle, *A New Centennial Hist. of the State of Kan.* (1876); *Trans. Kan. State Hist. Soc.*, vol. X (1908); *Leavenworth Times,* Sept. 24, 1908; files of the State Dept., War Dept., and Pension Office. Halderman's middle name is given as "Adams" and "Acoming," but he always signed himself "John A."]

A. E. I.

HALE, BENJAMIN (Nov. 23, 1797–July 15, 1863), educator, born at Newburyport, Mass., was the eldest of the ten children of Thomas and Alice (Little) Hale and a descendant in the eighth generation of Thomas Hale of Hertfordshire, England, who settled in Newburyport about 1637. Graduating from Bowdoin in the class of 1818, he taught a year at Saco Academy. He then entered Andover Theological Seminary only to have his course interrupted by a call to Bowdoin as tutor in 1820. Two years later, however, he received a license to preach in the Congregational Church. In 1823 he was called to the principalship of the Gardiner Lyceum which opened that year with twenty students. At Gardiner the young principal built up an institution modeled closely upon the manual-labor school at Hofwyl, Switzerland, of Phillip E. von Fellenberg, a follower of Pestalozzi. He organized courses in navigation, surveying, chemistry, civil architecture, carpentry, and agriculture. He also established short winter courses in different branches of husbandry, a precedent which was followed by the great majority of agricultural colleges, and experimented with student government. To help meet the need for textbooks for the practical subjects which the school taught, he published in 1827 an *Introduction to the Mechanical Principles of Carpentry,* but by this time the school had passed its zenith and was soon to disappear for lack of student patronage and financial support. Hale therefore accepted in the same year (1827) the professorship of chemistry at Dartmouth. He interested himself also in geology and mineralogy and took the lead in building up what was then an important collection of minerals. The following year he took orders in the Episcopal Church, preached frequently thereafter, and in 1835 published *Scriptural Illustrations of the Daily Morning and Evening Service, and Litany of the Protestant Episcopal Church.* The existence of episcopacy at Darmouth had irritated the Congregational clergy of the state who controlled the institution. Growing resentment gradually came to a head and at the commencement meeting of the board of trustees in August 1835 the professorship of chemistry was abolished secretly and without warning. Hale was not notified of his change of status until after President Nathan Lord and the trustees had left Hanover. Unable otherwise to defend himself, he promptly published a long and remarkable letter concerning the affair, answered by a pamphlet, full of innuendo and erroneous statements, the author and printer of which were not disclosed. Public sympathy both among students and in the community ran strongly in Hale's favor.

On Dec. 21, 1836, Hale was inaugurated third president of Geneva (later Hobart) College, a small Episcopalian institution at Geneva, N. Y. In his inaugural address he displayed his religious liberalism: "I trust I shall not be suspected of any purposes which may be regarded as sectarian; I value my own religious liberty too highly to design any infringement on that of others" (Turk, *post,* p. 19). But he was also an educational liberal, and that fact undoubtedly played an important part in his selection for his new post. Geneva College was already experimenting with a so-called "English course," by which students could obtain a degree by substituting modern languages for the classics, and Hale was in full sympathy with the movement. He proved also to be a wise administrator, and was particularly successful in the management of college finances. The institution was almost bankrupt when he took charge. When failing health compelled him to resign in 1858, the trustees of the institution called attention to "his success in elevating it to its present prosperity," commenting at the same time on "the talent, suavity, zeal, and usefulness that have characterized his presidency." Upon his resignation he returned to Newburyport, where he resided until his death. He had married, Apr. 9, 1823, Mary Caroline King, and was the father of two children.

[An excellent contemporary account of the Gardiner Lyceum during the Hale régime appears in the *U. S. Lit. Gazette,* Aug. 15, 1825. Pamphlets relating to the Dartmouth controversy and containing miscellaneous Hale sermons and addresses may be found in the library of Yale University. Descriptions of Hobart College during the Hale administration will be found in A. D. White, *Autobiography* (1905), I, 17–22; and in M. H. Turk, *Hobart; the Story of a Hundred Years, 1822–1922* (1921). See also R. N. Tappan, *Two Hundred and Fiftieth Anniversary of the Settlement of Newbury* (1885); R. S. Hale, *Geneal. of Descendants of Thos. Hale of Watton, Eng., and of Newbury, Mass.* (1889); and A. D. White, *The Work of Benj. Hale* (1911).]

R. H. G.

HALE, CHARLES (June 7, 1831–Mar. 1, 1882), journalist, consul, politician, was the son of Nathan [*q.v.*] and Sarah Preston (Everett) Hale, and the brother of Lucretia Peabody and Edward Everett Hale [*qq.v.*]. His father was a nephew of the patriot Nathan Hale [*q.v.*], and his mother was a sister of Edward Everett [*q.v.*]. After preparation at the Boston Latin School, Charles went to Harvard College in 1846. Before entering college he had become interested in the South Sea islands and had published in 1845 *A Description of the Washington Islands,* which was compiled from earlier writers. As an undergraduate he brought out *A Vocabulary of the Nukahiwa Language* (1848), the language spoken in the same archipelago. Known at Harvard as a good student and pleasant companion, he graduated in 1850 and immediately entered the office of his father, who was proprietor and editor of the *Boston Daily Advertiser.* In January 1852 he founded *Today: A Boston Literary Journal,* for which he wrote voluminously during the one year before it failed. As junior editor of the *Daily Advertiser* he contributed an exposure of the manner in which Roman Catholic schools were being inspected by the Know-Nothing politicians of the state legislature's nunnery committee. Amplified and republished under the title *"Our Houses are Our Castles"* (1855), the pamphlet called public attention to him and aided in his election as a Republican to the General Court in the fall of 1855. He was reëlected and in 1859 chosen speaker—the youngest member ever to hold that position. In the fall of 1861, owing to a serious illness, he traveled abroad and visited W. S. Thayer, a college classmate who had become consul-general in Egypt. On Thayer's death in 1864 Secretary of State Seward offered the position to Hale, who sold his interest in the *Advertiser* and reached Alexandria in August. There he found that Francis Dainese, the acting consul-general, had broken with the Egyptian government because claims of doubtful validity made by American protégés had not been satisfied. Instructed by Seward to avoid all unnecessary disputes during the critical period of the Civil War, he disavowed the action of Dainese and reëstablished friendly relations. Remaining in Egypt six years, he was active in the development of international tribunals to replace the old consular courts and was considered a favorite of the Khedive Ismail. In 1870 he resigned because of ill health and spent the winter recuperating in England. On his return to Boston in 1871 he was at once elected to the state Senate but resigned in February 1872 to become assistant secretary of state under Hamilton Fish [*q.v.*]. After two years of service, he resigned and again returned to Boston, where he was admitted to the bar on the strength of his experience in presiding over consular courts. His faithful constituents sent him once more to the General Court, this time to the House of Representatives, where he served with distinction on the judiciary committee, but in July 1876 he suffered a complete breakdown as a result of overwork in drafting bills—a task at which he was particularly expert. He accepted reëlection in 1877 with the understanding that he would speak only in emergency. His strength of mind as well as of body gradually declined under repeated paralytic attacks until his death. He was a man of substantial ability and well-trained mind who wrote with clarity but without brilliance. In addition to many editorials in the *Boston Daily Advertiser* between 1850 and 1865, he contributed occasionally to the *American Almanac* and the *North American Review.* He also added a biography of the author to John Sterling's *Onyx Ring* (1856) and collaborated with his father in editing the *Journal of Debates and Proceedings in the Convention of ... Massachusetts, 1820–21* (1853) and with B. K. Peirce in a work with the same title covering the convention of 1788, published in 1856.

[E. E. Hale, *The Life and Letters of Edward Everett Hale* (2 vols., 1917); *Foreign Relations of the U. S.,* 1864–67; F. Dainese, *The Hist. of Mr. Seward's Pet in Egypt* (1867); *Boston Transcript,* Mar. 3, 1882.]

W. L. W—t., Jr.

HALE, CHARLES REUBEN (Mar. 14, 1837–Dec. 25, 1900), Protestant Episcopal bishop of Cairo, Ill., and coadjutor to the Bishop of Springfield, was born in Lewistown, Pa., the son of Reuben C. and Sarah Mills Hale. He was graduated at the University of Pennsylvania (A.B., 1858) and, after a special course of study in preparation for the ministry, was ordained to the deaconate in St. Paul's Church, Philadelphia, Jan. 8, 1860, by the Rt. Rev. Alonzo Potter, Bishop of Pennsylvania. On Oct. 17, 1861, he was advanced to the priesthood by Bishop Potter at Christ Church, Eddington, Pa. He acted as curate at Christ Church, Germantown, and at All Saints' Church, Lower Dublin, Pa., during the years 1861–63. At the end of that time he accepted the position of chaplain in the United States navy, which he held until 1870, devoting a part of his time, in addition to his duties as chaplain, to the teaching of mathematics in the Naval Academy, Annapolis. In 1871 he became rector of St. John's Church, Auburn, N. Y., remaining until 1873, when he left for New York and engaged in the establishment of a mission for Italians in the metropolis. After devoting two years to this service, which enlisted his enthusiasm, he was called to the rectorate of the Church of St. Mary the Virgin, Baltimore, which he accepted. From 1877 to 1885 he was assistant at St. Paul's Church, Baltimore, leaving there to accept the deanship of the Trinity Cathedral, Davenport, Iowa, where he remained until his elevation to the episcopate. At the meeting of the diocesan convention of the Diocese of Springfield, Ill., May 17, 1892, he was elected coadjutor bishop of that diocese, under the jurisdiction of the Rt. Rev. George Franklin Seymour. He was consecrated in Trinity Cathedral, Davenport, July 26, 1892, his consecrators being Bishops Seymour, Perry, Walker, W. A. Leonard, Worthington, and Nicholson.

Hale was a High-churchman of the type characteristic of his day, though he would be known at the present time as an Anglo-Catholic. He was chiefly distinguished for attainments in scholarship. He was an excellent theologian, an expert liturgiologist and widely read in church history. He was a prominent worker, through his books and articles and by personal contact, in the cause of intercommunion, writing extensively on the relationships, historically, of the Episcopal Church and other communions, particularly the Orthodox Greek Church and the Old Catholics, and taking part in negotiations between these communions. In 1858 he was a member of a committee of three, appointed by the Philomathean Society of the University of Pennsylvania, to translate the famous Rosetta Stone, his fellow members being S. Huntington Jones and Henry Morton. In addition to the compilation of extensive documents bearing on intercommunion he wrote: *Innocent of Moscow, the Apostle of Kamchatka and Alaska* (1877, 1888); *The Russian Church* (1880); *England's Duty Toward Egypt* (published in the official report of the Church Congress, Carlisle, England, 1884); *A Visit to the Eastern Churches in the Interest of Church Unity* (1886); *Missionary Relations Between the Anglican and the Eastern Churches* (1894); *Mozarabic Collects* (1881), arranged from the ancient liturgy of the Spanish Church. Hale died in Cairo, Ill. He had married, in 1871, Anna McKnight, daughter of Major McKnight, who died in 1884 leaving no children.

[W. S. Perry, *The Bishops of the Am. Church* (1897); *Who's Who in America*, 1899–1900; *Living Church*, Jan. 5, 1901; *Chicago Tribune*, Dec. 26, 1900.]

G. E. S.

HALE, DAVID (Apr. 25, 1791–Jan. 20, 1849), journalist, was born at Lisbon, Conn., the son of the Rev. David and Lydia (Austin) Hale. He was a nephew of Nathan Hale [*q.v.*] of Revolutionary War fame. He left school at the age of sixteen to be a clerk in a store in Coventry, Conn., and two years later went to Boston to accept a similar position in a commission house. Owing to the business depression caused by the War of 1812, he returned to Coventry where he taught a district school. Later he returned to Boston to assist his cousin, Nathan Hale [*q.v.*], who was editor of the *Boston Daily Advertiser*. In 1815 he again engaged in business as the active partner in an importing and jobbing drygoods firm, but owing to his serious illness in 1817, this business venture proved unsuccessful. He contributed to the *Boston Recorder*, one of the first religious weekly newspapers in this country, and proposed to establish a religious daily paper in Boston. Upon the recommendation of his friend, Gerard Hallock [*q.v.*], he became the business manager of the *New York Journal of Commerce* when it was started in 1827 by Arthur Tappan [*q.v.*], a public-spirited business man prominent in religious and philanthropic activities. When after sixteen months, Tappan had spent nearly $30,000 on the paper, he turned it over to his brother Lewis [*q.v.*], and early in 1829 the latter entered into an arrangement with Hale and Hallock by which, at the end of two years, they became the sole proprietors. Hale did not confine his work to the business department of the paper, but wrote articles and editorials as well.

Under the new managers the *Journal of Commerce* initiated new methods of news gathering (see also biography of Hallock). A semaphore signaling device was set up to announce the arrival of ships, so that the editors and the compositors might be ready to handle the foreign news as soon as the pilot boat owned by the *Journal of Commerce* brought to the office the newspapers from abroad. On occasion Hale would mount a chair in his office or at the Exchange, and read to the assembled merchants the latest foreign news. The publishers also ran expresses with relays of horses from Washington to New York and secured for their paper the president's messages and the proceedings of Congress ten hours or more ahead of the United States mail.

Continuing to carry out the aims for which the paper had been established by Arthur Tappan, Hale and Hallock did not permit the advertisement of theatres, lotteries, or business transacted on Sunday, and no work connected with the editing and publishing of the paper was permitted between midnight on Saturday and midnight on Sunday, with the result that the Monday morning edition appeared an hour late. Hale was an active churchman and took great interest in the Broadway Tabernacle, completed in 1836 as the first strong Congregational church in New York City. When in 1840 the church property was sold on the foreclosure of a mortgage, Hale purchased it, and during his ownership the building was used for large public meetings, lectures, and concerts, as well as for religious services.

Hale was married, on Jan. 18, 1815, to his

first cousin, Laura Hale, the daughter of Richard Hale. She died in 1824 and on Aug. 22, 1825, he married Lucy S. Turner of Boston. Upon his death early in 1849, the *Journal of Commerce* continued under the name of Hallock, Hale & Hallock, David A. Hale, his son, representing the heirs of the estate, and William H. Hallock, son of Gerard Hallock, being admitted to partnership.

[Jos. P. Thompson, *Memoir of David Hale . . . with Selections from His Miscellaneous Writings* (1850), Frederic Hudson, *Journalism in the U. S. from 1690 to 1872* (1873); Wm. H. Hallock, *Life of Gerard Hallock* (1869); E. E. Hale, "Geneal. of the Family of Capt. Nathan Hale," App. to I. W. Stuart, *Life of Capt. Nathan Hale* (1856); Victor Rosewater, *Hist. of Coöperative News-Gathering in the U. S.* (1930); and files of the *Morning Courier*, the *Morning Courier and N. Y. Enquirer*, and the *N. Y. Jour. of Commerce.*]

W. G. B.

HALE, EDWARD EVERETT (Apr. 3, 1822–June 10, 1909), author, Unitarian minister, brother of Lucretia Peabody and Charles Hale [*qq.v.*], was born in Boston, the fourth of his parents' eight children, and died, at eighty-seven, in the house, in the Roxbury district of Boston, in which he had lived for forty years. His father, Nathan Hale [*q.v.*], was a nephew of the young American soldier of the same name whose story is a classic episode in the War of Independence. His mother, Sarah Preston Everett, was a sister of Edward Everett [*q.v.*]. He was fond of saying that he was "cradled in the sheets of a newspaper," and his father's long identification with the *Boston Daily Advertiser*, of which he acquired the ownership in 1814 and was editor for nearly fifty years thereafter, gave abundant color to the remark. When he was about eleven years old, his father suggested his translating, for publication in the *Daily*, an article from a French newspaper. It made no difference that he had never studied French. With the help of a sister and a dictionary he translated the article, which was duly printed (*Life and Letters*, 1917, I, 196). An easy-going journalistic attitude towards writing in general characterized much of his own work throughout life. At a dame school and the Boston Latin School he was made ready to enter Harvard College, as he did, at the age of thirteen. Looking upon school as a "necessary nuisance," he acquired much of his early education from the large, happy, and busy family of which he was a member. The young people made miniature railroad engines and printed books and periodicals of their own composition. Church-going and Sunday school, dancing lessons, frequent contacts with the most stimulating minds of the stirring, homogeneous community—all combined with the more definite processes of schooling to qualify the thirteen-year-old freshman for getting the best out of college. At Harvard he appears to have taken a healthy, all-round interest in the duties and pastimes of his course, gaining some mastery of the classics and English composition, and graduating in 1839, second in his class, a member of Phi Beta Kappa, and class poet. At seventeen his formal education thus stood completed.

It had always been taken for granted that he would enter the Unitarian ministry. Without feeling any positive impulse in that direction, and with a marked disinclination to a formal course in theology, he devoted his first two years out of college to teaching in the Boston Latin School, wrote for the press, and pursued his studies for the ministry under private guidance. Before the end of 1842 he began to preach, and in April 1846 was ordained minister of the Church of the Unity in Worcester, Mass. Ten years later he became minister of the South Congregational Church in Boston—his only other parish for the forty-three ensuing years through which he was to continue his active ministry.

A sketch of "Boston in the Forties"—in his *New England Boyhood and Other Bits of Autobiography* (1900)—helps one to account for the Hale of the fifties and thereafter. Here he depicted the ferments of the little city, of whose inhabitants Emerson was saying that "every man carries a revolution in his waist-coat pocket." What Hale himself said of the leaders in Boston at this time was that they "really believed that they could make the city of Boston the city of God, and they meant to do so," and that they were "men who knew that all things are possible to one who believes" (*Ibid.*, p. 243).

Big of body and spirit, destined to grow, with his aspect of a shaggy prophet and his great, reverberating voice, into the very figure of a seer, Hale was precisely the man to put into action the prevailing beliefs of the Boston in which he came to maturity. Strongly Unitarian in his theological views, honored as a leader in his denomination, he was nevertheless concerned chiefly with the aspects of Christianity on which all could agree. The "New Civilization" for which he labored implied a general betterment of human relationships, social, political, personal. Before the Civil War he threw himself heartily into the work of the New England Emigrant Aid Company, writing a book on Kansas (spelled Kanzas) and Nebraska, and thus virtually beginning his long career of the service of causes through the printed word. As the war approached he drilled with a rifle corps in Boston—but felt, when the contest began, that he could be of most use at home. There he worked tellingly enough in the Sanitary Commission to win for his figure a conspicuous place on one of the bas-reliefs adorning the Soldiers' Monument on Boston Common. What was more important, he wrote at this time, "The Man Without a Country" (*Atlantic Monthly,* December 1863), one of the best short stories written by an American, and representing Hale at his best as a writer of fiction with a purpose.

The intended immediate purpose of "The Man Without a Country" was to influence an impending election. Its larger, long-continued service as a rarely effectual incentive to patriotism was unforeseen. In its blending of fact, none too thoroughly verified, with extravagant fiction, all narrated with a plausibility of detail clearly suggesting the influence of Defoe, it displays to the best advantage its author's method and manner. Four years earlier, in 1859, he had published in the *Atlantic Monthly* the story "My Double; and How He Undid Me," revealing him, equally at his best, in a distinctive vein of humor. These stories, with others, were included in his first volume of fiction, *If, Yes, and Perhaps. Four Possibilities and Six Exaggerations, with Some Bits of Fact* (1868). His many subsequent books were, almost without exception, the work of a religious, humanitarian journalist, keenly perceptive of significances, historic and other, prodigal in illustrations from fact, but much less concerned with minor points of accuracy than with major considerations of meaning. "If a parable teaches its lesson," one can imagine his saying, "what matter if it does not tally at every point with the books of reference?" Especially in two of his books, *Ten Times One is Ten* (1871) and *In His Name* (1873), which he, though probably few others, counted his best, he gave the direction to far-reaching movements—the Lend-a-Hand movement, with its familiar motto of Hale's invention, "look up and not down, look forward and not back, look out and not in, lend a hand," and the I. H. N. and other clubs of organized good-will. Both of these stories appeared in *Old and New,* a monthly magazine which Hale edited from 1870 to 1875. This was a periodical of which one of his friends said that "it would have succeeded had there been anybody connected with it who wanted to make money." Through the press, daily, weekly, and monthly, Hale constantly poured himself forth, turning at times from prose to verse. In the vast bulk of his production three volumes—containing much of autobiography—must be noted: *A New England Boyhood* (1893; reprinted in *A New England Boyhood and Other Bits of Autobiography,* 1900), *James Russell Lowell and His Friends* (1899), and *Memories of a Hundred Years* (2 vols., 1902).

Two honors, one local, one national, were appropriate to the end of his career. When the twentieth century came in, it was Hale who was chosen to read the Ninetieth Psalm from the balcony of the Massachusetts State House to the great silent crowd that assembled on Boston Common during the final hour of Dec. 31, 1900. The national honor was his election, at the end of 1903, as chaplain of the United States Senate. In these final years also he seized every occasion to urge, through speech and print, the cause of international peace. This was but the logical climax of a life-long work for the general well-being of mankind.

His domestic life was happy and spirited. On Oct. 13, 1852, he married Emily Baldwin Perkins, of Hartford, Conn., a grand-daughter of Lyman Beecher [*q.v.*]. Travel, more often in America than in Europe, gave variety to the family routine of Boston in the winter and Matunuck, R. I., in the summer. Up to April in the last year of his life he performed the duties of his chaplaincy at Washington. Then he came back to Boston, where he died, June 10, 1909. His wife, with their one daughter and three of their seven sons, survived him.

[The three autobiographical volumes mentioned above provide many facts in the life of Hale. These are supplemented by the prefaces he wrote for the "Library Edition" of his works (Boston, 1898–1901). *The Life and Letters of Edward Everett Hale,* by Edward E. Hale, Jr. (2 vols., 1917), is the authoritative biography. The Philip Nolan of "The Man Without a Country" is not to be confused with the Philip Nolan [*q.v.*] of history, as Hale explained in "The Real Philip Nolan," *Miss. Hist. Soc. Pubs.,* IV (1901), 281–329.]

M. A. DeW. H.

HALE, EDWARD JOSEPH (Dec. 25, 1839–Feb. 15, 1922), editor, diplomat, was born at "Haymount" near Fayetteville, N. C., the son of Edward Jones Hale, a well-known and able editor, and Sarah Jane Walker. Prepared for college at Fayetteville, he entered the University of North Carolina in 1856 but was compelled by illness to withdraw immediately. He spent the year in travel, and, returning the next year, was graduated in 1860. He at once became associated with his father in the conduct of the *Fayetteville Observer.* On Jan. 15, 1861, he was married to Maria Rhett Hill, of Chatham County. She died many years later and on Dec. 5, 1905, he married Caroline Green Mallett of Fayetteville. Upon the outbreak of the Civil War Hale enlisted in the Confederate army, refusing a commission at first because of his ignorance of military matters. He served from Bethel to Appomattox, at both of which he was present, rising to the rank of major and assistant adjutant-general of Lane's North Carolina brigade. His last promotion was given for "conspicuous gallantry and merit." He was three times wounded in battle. After the close of the war he was in business for a short time in New York City but soon returned to North Carolina and reëstablishd the *Fayetteville Observer,* which he edited with one intermission until 1913.

In 1885 President Cleveland appointed Hale consul at Manchester, where he remained four years. He became widely popular in England, was on terms of friendship with many of the leaders in public life, was elected to many organizations, and was in constant demand as a speaker. At the conclusion of his official service he was sent by the North of England Trust Company to India as a commissioner with large powers to deal with problems connected with the indigo crop and to prepare a report upon them. He handled the matter so satisfactorily that the company urged him to accept a permanent position with it, a proposition which he rejected when he discovered that it involved the surrender of his American citizenship. Before he returned to the United States and to his editorial duties he stopped again in Manchester, served as vice-president of the International Congress on Navigation (1890), and in 1890–91 was American commissioner of the Manchester ship canal. In 1893 he declined appointment as minister to Turkey. He was a leader in civic matters, especially in regard to navigation, and was one of the founders of the National Rivers and Harbors Congress. He made a close study of the problems of the navigation of the Cape Fear River and in 1899 published a scheme for the canalization of Cape Fear which he had worked out with the advice of the most eminent authorities in Europe and which was finally in part adopted by Congress. In politics he was an active Democrat and served as delegate at large to the Democratic national conventions in 1884 and from 1896 to 1912. In 1913 President Wilson appointed him minister to Costa Rica, where he served until diplomatic relations were severed in 1919. He was a man of wide learning and genuine culture, who always impressed a new acquaintance as belonging to an earlier day. A fine example of the "old-fashioned Southern gentleman," he was big-hearted, hospitable, and deeply interested in people as well as in affairs.

[S. B. Ashe, ed., *Biog. Hist. of N. C.,* vol. VIII (1917); *Who's Who in America,* 1920–21; Walter Clark, ed., *Histories of the Several Regiments and Battalions from N. C. in the Great War, 1861–'65* (5 vols., 1901); *News and Observer* (Raleigh), *Charlotte Observer, Fayetteville Observer,* Feb. 16, 1922.]

J. G. deR. H.

HALE, EDWIN MOSES (Feb. 2, 1829–Jan. 15, 1899), physician, was born at Newport, N. H., the son of Dr. Syene Hale, a graduate of Dartmouth, and Betsy (Dow) Hale. He was descended from Thomas Hale, who emigrated from Watton, England, and settled in Newbury, Mass., about 1637. When Edwin was seven, his father removed with the family to Fredonia, Ohio. The boy attended the public schools of the village and at fifteen went to Newark, Ohio, where he learned the printer's trade and became an associate editor of the local newspaper. For a short time he was deputy postmaster of the town. Later he abandoned newspaper work for the study of law. Having been taken down with a severe attack of pneumonia from which he recovered under the treatment of Dr. A. O. Blair, a pioneer homeopath, he became a convert to that school of medicine and entered the Western College of Homeopathic Medicine at Cleveland in its first course in 1850. In 1852 he began the practice of medicine in Jonesville, Mich. Three years later he was married to Abba Ann George, of Jonesville.

After twelve years in Michigan, Hale was called to the professorship of materia medica in the Hahnemann Medical College of Chicago. He had already written his *Monograph upon Gelseminum* (1860), which was his introduction in the profession. In 1870 he was made professor of medical botany and pharmacology; in 1871 special lecturer on the heart; and in 1872 his chair was enlarged to comprehend therapeutics of the new remedies. In 1877 he resigned from Hahnemann and accepted the chair of materia medica in the Chicago Homeopathic College. Hale claimed to have been the first to teach the law of dosage based upon the primary and secondary effects of drugs. Briefly, this was that small doses were indicated when patients exhibited symptoms of the primary effects and large doses for the secondary manifestations. He was a prolific writer. His *New Remedies: Their Pathogenetic Effects and Therapeutical Application in Homœopathic Practice* (1864) passed through five editions, was translated into German, French, and Spanish, and was accepted by homeopaths and eclectics of his period as an authority. Most of the medicines discussed in the work were those derived from the vegetable kingdom of the United States. The work also contained numerous personal studies of the iodides and bromides from the standpoint of homeopathy. Some of his teachings in this line, for a long time neglected, are now (1931) coming into vogue as authoritative. Aside from the *New Remedies,* his important publications include *A Systematic Treatise on Abortion* (1866); *Lectures on Diseases of the Heart* (1871); and *The Practice of Medicine* (1894). He served as assistant editor of the *North American Journal of Homœopathy* from 1860 to 1869 and of the *American Homœopathic Observer* from 1867 to 1874. He retired from active practice in 1890. At the time of his death he had completed the manuscript of the book on "Presenility and Diseases of Old Age."

[E. Cleaves, *Biog. Cyc. of Homœopathic Physicians and Surgeons* (1873); T. L. Bradford, *Homœopathic Bibliog.* (1892), and "Biogs. of Homœopathic Physicians" (1916), in the library of the Hahnemann Medic. Coll., Philadelphia, Pa.; R. S. Hale, *Geneal. of Descendants of Thos. Hale of Watton, Eng., and of Newbury, Mass.* (1889); *Hahnemannian Monthly,* Feb. 1899; *Eclectic Medic. Jour.,* May 1899; *Chicago Tribune,* Jan. 16, 1899.] C. B.

HALE, ENOCH (Jan. 19, 1790–Nov. 12, 1848), physician, was born in Westhampton, Mass., the fifth of the eight children of the Rev. Enoch and Octavia (Throop) Hale. The family was descended from Robert Hale of Kent, England, who settled in Charlestown, Mass., in 1632. His uncle was the patriot, Nathan Hale [*q.v.*] and his brother, Nathan Hale [*q.v.*], for many years edited the *Boston Daily Advertiser.* As a young man, Hale showed signs of a grave pulmonary condition and was sent, therefore, to New Haven, Conn., where he attended the lectures on chemistry of Prof. Benjamin Silliman. From Silliman he acquired a scientific point of view which led to experimental investigations in other fields than chemistry. He began his studies in medicine, his health much improved, under the direction of Jacob Bigelow and John Warren in Boston, and was graduated, M.D., by the Harvard Medical School in 1813. His inaugural dissertation, *Experiments on the Production of Animal Heat by Respiration* (1813), was a creditable piece of experimental work and called forth a refutation by Benjamin C. Brodie (*Medical and Physical Journal,* October 1814) and a "reply" by the youthful Hale (*New England Journal of Medicine and Surgery,* January 1816). Soon after his graduation Hale went to Gardiner, Me., to practise. The same year, 1814, he made some observations on epidemic meningitis, *History and Description of an Epidemic Fever, Commonly Called Spotted Fever* (Boston, 1818), second only in importance to the first description of the disease given by Elisha North [*q.v.*] in 1811. His close associate in Maine was Benjamin Vaughan, the English politician and scientist, who lived at Hallowell, near Gardiner. Vaughan, who enjoyed a large correspondence with the scientific men of England and who had an excellent library, stimulated Hale to further scientific work, especially in meteorology and on the relation between climate and epidemic disease.

In 1818 Hale removed to Boston, where he practised and taught medicine for the rest of his life. He was appointed district physician to the Boston Dispensary in 1819, served on the first staff of the Boston Lying-In Hospital, established in 1832, and was visiting physician to the Massachusetts General Hospital from 1837 to 1848. He won the Boylston Prize for medical dissertations, in 1819 and again in 1821, in the latter year writing an early paper on intravenous therapy. Both contributions were based upon experiments upon himself with various drugs. His next published work, *Observations on the Typhoid Fever of New England* (1839), was the result of the study of patients, over a period of years, at the Massachusetts General Hospital. The importance of the book, historically, lies in the fact that he advised physicians "to abstain from attempting too much by active treatment" (p. 75) at a time when the excessive use of drugs was the accepted practice. Hale was one of the first physicians in Massachusetts, moreover, to realize the important "self-limiting" character of the disease. As a teacher, especially in private instruction in midwifery, he was closely associated with John Collins Warren, George Hayward, and Walter Channing. He was a founder of the Boston Society for Medical Improvement (1828), the leading medical and literary society of its time, and served as recording secretary of the Massachusetts Medical Society (1832–35). Toward the end of his life, in 1846, he strongly upheld the claims of W. T. G. Morton [*q.v.*] as the discoverer of ether anesthesia. Hale was a courteous, scholarly gentleman, honest to a fault. He led an active social and professional life, although never in good health. He was married three times: in 1813 to Almira Hooker, in 1822 to Sarah Hooker, and in 1829 to Jane Murdock. There were no children.

[Walter Channing, *Memoir of the Late Enoch Hale* (1848); *Boston Medic. and Surgic. Jour.,* Nov. 22, 1848; T. F. Harrington, *The Harvard Medic. School* (1905), vol. II; W. L. Burrage, *Hist. of the Mass. Medic. Soc.* (1923); C. M. Holloway, *Nathan Hale: The Martyr-Hero of the Revolution* (1899); *Boston Transcript, Boston Daily Advertiser,* Nov. 13, 1848.] H. R. V.

HALE, EUGENE (June 9, 1836–Oct. 27, 1918), lawyer, politician, legislator, the son of James Sullivan and Betsey (Staples) Hale, was born at Turner, Me. He was descended from Thomas Hale who settled in Newbury, Mass., about 1637. He was educated in the common schools of his native town and at Hebron Academy, studied law, and was admitted to the bar in 1857. Later in life he received honorary degrees from three Maine colleges, Bates, Colby, and Bowdoin. After admission to the bar he began practice at Ellsworth, opening his career in public office as prosecuting attorney for Hancock County. He was active in the Republican organization and a delegate to the national convention of 1868. Elected to the Maine legislature, 1867–68, he displayed that ability on the floor which was destined to make him, eventually, one of the outstanding figures in national affairs.

In 1868 he was elected to Congress and served in the House from Mar. 4, 1869, to Mar. 3, 1879. On Dec. 20, 1871, he married Mary Douglass Chandler, daughter of Senator Zachariah Chandler [*q.v.*] of Michigan, then one of the outstanding figures in Reconstruction politics. Hale earned a recognized place, however, by his own efforts and was soon regarded as an authority on naval affairs and public expenditures, subjects in which he was especially interested throughout his long service in Washington. He was in general a supporter of orthodox Republican policies, and a friend and admirer of James G. Blaine. He was prominent in the latter's forces at the conventions of 1876 and 1880, and the published letters of Mrs. Blaine show the long-standing intimacy existing between the two Maine leaders and their families. During this period he twice declined cabinet posts, President Grant having offered him the Post Office Department in 1874 and President Hayes the Navy Department a few years later. His interests and abilities were distinctly legislative rather than executive.

In 1878 Greenbackism was rampant in Maine, especially in the eastern districts, and Hale was defeated. Local political conditions were so serious, however, that in 1879 he was elected to the legislature and became the leader of the Republican forces in the ugly situation created by the attempt of Greenback-Democratic Fusionists to "count out" a Republican legislative majority in the winter of 1879–80. When this scheme was finally defeated, he headed the legislative committee which conducted an exhaustive investigation. A year later he entered the United States Senate, succeeding Hannibal Hamlin, for what proved to be the first of five full terms (Mar. 4, 1881–Mar. 3, 1911).

A comprehensive survey of Hale's thirty years in the Senate would involve a discussion of most of the great legislative measures and public policies of that period. His record was largely affected by his personal qualities, which were in many respects the antithesis of those of his colleague, William P. Frye [*q.v.*], whose term of service practically coincided with his own. He lacked the enthusiasm and emotionalism which made the latter such a successful campaigner and was probably, as a result, never in as close touch with the great currents of public opinion. He was naturally a conservative, a skeptic on matters of social and political reform, and his Senate speeches show the analytical temperament which frequently forced him into a negative attitude when innovations were involved. He had much the same philosophy of government and economics as Senator Aldrich, with whom he was frequently associated in the popular mind. He was an uncompromising supporter of the high tariff and once described it as the force which "builds up these great hives of human industry throughout our whole country and produces materials for the people at a cheaper rate than could in any other way be produced" (*Congressional Record,* 61 Cong., 1 Sess., p. 1946). While supporting the reciprocity clauses of the McKinley Bill of 1890 as calculated to broaden American markets (*Ibid.,* 51 Cong., 1 Sess., p. 9511), he later became a strong opponent of all tendencies toward freer trade, including concessions to the Philippines, the tariff commission idea, and President Taft's Canadian reciprocity policy.

Hale was at his best in debate on naval appropriation bills, where his mastery of detail, broad knowledge of the subject matter, and constant mental alertness made him a most formidable opponent. In naval affairs he performed constructive work of the utmost importance especially in the early stages of developing the modern fleet. "I hope," he declared in the course of debate, Apr. 9, 1884, "that I shall not live many years before I shall see the American Navy what it ought to be, the pet of the American people." Toward the close of his career, however, the pet, like the camel in the fable, had shown a propensity to crowd the other occupants of the tent; and Hale changed his emphasis. "As I look back upon the years, for the last twenty years, I recall that the more we have done for the military the more they have claimed. It is the theory of the army and the navy that the Government is run for the benefit of those establishments. . . . Every immense appropriation for a war establishment increases the chances for war; but I do not expect that any warning note of this kind will receive much consideration either here or elsewhere. We have caught the infection of war establishments and war expenditures from the

English practice and habit and precedent, which are entirely different from ours" (*Congressional Record,* 61 Cong., 2 Sess., p. 6595).

While the immediate occasion for these last remarks was his opposition to increasing the number of capital ships, a type of construction which he regarded as less effective in proportion to cost and subject to unduly rapid obsolescence, the change in viewpoint is also indicative of his profound dislike of American imperialism resulting from the war with Spain. The latter episode with its accompanying sentimentality and humbug aroused his scorn. "It was not a real war," he declared in the Senate on May 20, 1910; "it stimulated the desire of conquest; it set the country wild; and it has been the source of constant trouble and vexation, and in a way—I will not say a disgrace to us since—but a constant expenditure and a constant burden, which today the people do not believe in and which we would be very glad if we could avoid." At the time, his opposition to the war and resultant expansion for the first time brought him dangerously near defeat by the Maine legislature.

After 1901 Hale became increasingly unpopular in the country at large. He was not in sympathy with the program of the Western Progressive element, and his tariff policy, his dislike for Federal regulatory legislation, his contempt for the clamor against railroads, trusts, and big business generally, and for such alleged reforms as popular election of senators, direct legislation, and similar projects, gave weight to the charge that he stood for an undesirable alliance between government and seekers for special privilege. His relations with President Roosevelt were far from cordial. As the breach between the two wings of the Republican party became wider, his position became increasingly difficult, although by seniority, especially after the death of Senator Allison, his power in the Senate organization reached its height. The prospect of having Hale in the chairmanship of appropriations, of the Republican caucus, and of the committee on committees, contributed to a furious assault by the Progressive press of the country. Ominous signs of revolt appeared in his own state and in April 1910 he announced that he would not be a candidate for reëlection. The remainder of his life was spent in Ellsworth, Me., and Washington, D. C., where his death occurred. He was a member of the National Monetary Commission after his retirement from active politics. Toward the close of his career Hale was described as "a small but superbly constructed man, erect as an admiral, exuding dignity, gravity and autocracy from every pore," his face, with its gray, close-cut, carefully pointed beard, "heavy, solemn and stern" (*Independent,* Feb. 4, 1909, p. 258). Judgment of his career is likely to be determined largely by the individual attitude toward the question which dominated American politics from 1890 on—the proper relationship of business and government. If it should be true, as the *Outlook* remarked, Apr. 30, 1910, that he belonged to a period of bargaining for favors, it cannot be denied that he was a man of great intellectual power, personal honesty, and strength of character.

[There are frequent references to Hale in the periodical and biographical literature of the period. For brief sketches of his career see L. C. Hatch, *Maine: A Hist.* (1919); *Who's Who in America,* 1916–17; *Biog. Dir. Am. Cong.* (1928); *Harper's Weekly,* May 7, 1910; *Current Lit.,* June 1910; *Nation,* Nov. 23, 1916; *Evening Star* (Washington, D. C.), *Portland Press,* Oct. 28, 1918.]

W. A. R.

HALE, HORATIO EMMONS (May 3, 1817–Dec. 28, 1896), ethnologist, was born in Newport, N. H., the son of David Hale, a lawyer, and Sarah Josepha (Buell) Hale [*q.v.*], an author and editor. He was descended from Thomas Hale, an early settler in Massachusetts. Some circumstance of his boyhood training had interested him as a youth in languages, and as early as 1834, close to the time of his entrance into Harvard, he published *Remarks on the Language of the St. John's or Wlastukweek Indians, with a Penobscot Vocabulary.* After his graduation from college in 1837, he found at once an appointment in the scientific corps of the Wilkes Exploring Expedition, and from 1838 to 1842 he sailed the seas collecting linguistic materials in practically new fields. His monumental *Ethnography and Philology* (1846, vol. VI, United States Exploring Expedition) was immediately used as the basis of subsequent papers by his contemporaries, and Daniel G. Brinton [*q.v.*], upon whose shoulders the mantle of Hale fell, regarded it "as indispensable to one who would acquaint himself with Polynesian and American ethnography, the two fields in which it is the strongest" (*post,* p. 25). His opportunities of studying the distribution of languages while on the voyage around the world with Captain Wilkes led him to use the drift of the Polynesian tongue as a clue to the migration of this race. Especially interested in his neighbors, the Iroquois, he investigated their history and discovered that the Tutelo of Virginia spoke a Siouan language ("The Tutelo Tribe and Language," *Proceedings of the American Philosophical Society,* vol. XXI, 1883). The beliefs of the Iroquois about death and the after life he discussed in *The Iroquois Book of Rites* (1883).

In 1854 Hale married Margaret Pugh, the daughter of William Pugh, formerly of Canada. The following year he was admitted to the bar in Chicago and in 1856 he established himself in the practice of law at Clinton, Canada. He still retained his interest in linguistics, however, and published occasional papers. Toward the close of his active career he put out two books: *An International Idiom* (1890), relating to the Chinook jargon, and *The Fall of Hochlega* (1893). He was a conscientious student, recording accurately what he saw and heard, and should be regarded as one who aided in the development of the science of anthropology. A member of the old school, he laid stress on language as a solution to ethnological problems. He was honored as vice-president of the American Association for the Advancement of Science, Buffalo, 1886, president of the American Folk-Lore Society, and member of other learned societies. He was a gentle, kindly man, widely informed, and in his nature uncontroversial. Brinton records (*post,* p. 26) that "in all his writings Mr. Hale was singularly fair and courteous to his contemporaries. He loved science for its own sake. . . . In personal intercourse he was ever kindly and considerate and ready to aid the student freely from the abundant resources of his knowledge."

[D. G. Brinton, article in the *Am. Anthropologist,* Jan. 1897; *Popular Sci. Monthly,* July 1897; *Proc. Royal Soc. of Canada,* vol. XII (1894), for bibliography, and 2 ser., vol. III (1897), for biography; W. S. Wallace, *Dict. of Canadian Biog.* (1926); the *Critic,* Jan. 16, Mar. 20, 1897.] W. H.

HALE, JOHN PARKER (Mar. 31, 1806–Nov. 19, 1873), lawyer, politician, diplomat, was born at Rochester, N. H. He was descended from Robert Hale who settled in Charlestown, in Massachusetts, in 1632. His parents were John Parker and Lydia C. (O'Brien) Hale, the latter the daughter of an Irish refugee who had died in the American service during the Revolution. His father was a successful lawyer but his death in 1819 left the family in straitened circumstances and it was due to the courage and self-sacrifice of his mother that John was enabled to attend Phillips Exeter Academy and Bowdoin College, graduating from the latter in 1827. He then studied law at Rochester and Dover, was admitted to the bar in 1830, and began practice at the latter town, maintaining residence there henceforth. When he left college he had gained a reputation for combined brilliance and laziness. In his profession he came to be known not as a learned, but as a "ready lawyer," possessed of tact and oratorical ability, and remarkably skilled in extricating himself from untenable positions (Bell, *post,* p. 417). He rose rapidly and made a reputation as a successful jury lawyer. It was doubtless due to this fact, as well as to his democratic principles, that he was an advocate of increasing the powers of the jury and making them judges of the law as well as the fact.

Hale's political career began in 1832 with his election to the state legislature. In 1834 he was appointed United States district attorney and held office until removed by President Tyler in 1841. A year later he was elected to Congress. New Hampshire was a Democratic stronghold and Hale followed conventional doctrines. His early speeches have a somewhat demagogic tone, but he showed independence, and shortly before the end of his term, he proposed a limitation of the area open to slavery should Texas be added to the Union. His attitude on the Texas question finally led to a breach with the party when in January 1845 he addressed a letter to his constituents denouncing annexation as promoting the interests of slavery and "eminently calculated to provoke the scorn of earth and the judgment of heaven" (*Exeter News-Letter,* Jan. 20, 1845). In a special convention, the Democrats on Feb. 12 revoked his renomination and solemnly read him out of the party. With the backing of some loyal friends, he proceeded to organize an independent movement. As a result, the New Hampshire legislature in 1846 passed under control of a combination of Whigs and independent Democrats, which on June 9 elected the insurgent Hale to the United States Senate for a six-year term commencing Mar. 4, 1847. It was the most notable anti-slavery success hitherto achieved.

For some time, until joined by Chase and Sumner, Hale occupied a most conspicuous place, and if excluded from all party councils and responsibilities, he was at least free to assail slavery without the restraint which party membership imposed. His most notable speech was probably the one delivered in reply to Webster's address of Mar. 7, 1850, on the territorial question (*Congressional Globe,* 31 Cong., 1 Sess., App. pp. 1054–65). His long speeches, however, are in general inferior to his brief extemporaneous utterances in the course of debate. Avoiding the excesses of some anti-slavery advocates, good humored, witty, and eloquent, he was personally popular, although his sallies occasionally provoked outbursts of wrath among the Southern members. It was during his first term in the Senate that he secured the abolition of flogging in the navy, a reform which he had urged from the time of his appearance in the lower house. His further argument that discipline should be more intelligent and humane, that the navy should offer advantages to the ordinary seaman which would make service attractive to the best grade of young men, rewarding good conduct with promotion and better opportunities (*Ibid.*, 32 Cong., 1 Sess., p. 449), was decidedly in advance of his time. He constantly urged the abolition of the grog ration as well and this was finally brought about in 1862. He himself considered these reforms the outstanding accomplishments of his Senate career, and in deference to his opinion they are recorded on his monument in the State House yard at Concord. In addition to his anti-slavery activity in the Senate, Hale conducted various platform campaigns on the subject and was a well-known lecturer throughout the North. He also appeared as counsel in cases arising under the Fugitive-Slave law, including the famous Anthony Burns case involving Theodore Parker and other eminent Bostonians. His prominence in the anti-slavery cause led to his nomination for the presidency by the Liberty party in 1847, but he withdrew in favor of Van Buren when the Free-Soil party absorbed the Liberty party in 1848. In 1852 he accepted the nomination of the Free-Soilers and polled 150,000 votes.

On the expiration of his first term in the Senate Hale resumed legal practice and for a short time lived in New York. By 1855, however, the anti-slavery coalition again controlled the New Hampshire legislature and after a prolonged contest he was elected to serve out the unexpired term of Charles G. Atherton, deceased. Three years later he was reëlected for a full term. He had become one of the most prominent Republicans in the country, although the influence of his earlier Democratic affiliations was still perceptible, and it was reported that the power of the national party leaders was exerted in his behalf, inasmuch as the legislature was reluctant to break the local precedents which favored rotation. This term, however, added little to his fame, although he was active on the floor and prominent in the adoption of the various measures which at last gave slavery its quietus. During the war he held the chairmanship of the committee on naval affairs. The standard of public morals had relaxed, and in naval matters, to quote Secretary Welles, there had developed a "debauched system of personal and party favoritism" (*post,* I, 482), especially pernicious in the services of construction and supply. There was a navy-yard in New Hampshire, and Hale was admittedly careless, easy going, accommodating, and not over careful as to the character of his professional and political associations. His friends, who have always insisted on his personal honesty, believed that he was imposed upon by unscrupulous and designing parties, and Secretary Welles, that he was trying to use his chairmanship for personal gain and political advantage. Senators Grimes and Foot both expressed disapproval of his conduct and in 1864 when he was a candidate for reëlection the impression was abroad that the leaders in Washington would be glad to see his retirement. Late in 1863 an investigation disclosed that he had accepted a fee from one J. M. Hunt, convicted of fraud against the government, and had appeared on his behalf before the secretary of war. Although exonerated by the Senate judiciary committee of any violation of law, the fact that its report included a bill making such practice illegal in future (*Congressional Globe,* 38 Cong., 1 Sess., pp. 420, 460, 555) told heavily against him and undoubtedly contributed to a decisive defeat by the Republican caucus at Concord, June 9, 1864. His speech on the proposed bill (*Ibid.,* pp. 559 ff.) does not indicate a keen sense of moral values and lends color to the comment of the *Boston Daily Courier,* Jan. 1, 1864, that though he did not mean to be dishonest or dishonorable, "his perceptions were befogged by the atmosphere of fraud, corruption and crime surrounding him in the party to which he is attached."

In March 1865 Hale was appointed minister to Spain although he would have preferred the Paris legation. According to Sumner, "President Lincoln selected Hale out of general kindness and good-will to the 'lame ducks,'" and "wished to break his fall" (E. L. Pierce, *Memoir and Letters of Charles Sumner,* vol. IV, 1893, p. 255). His training and temperament were not suited for such a post, and he was handicapped by ignorance of the language. As far as can be judged by the somewhat meager records in the *Papers Relating to Foreign Affairs* his services were not especially significant. In 1869 he became embroiled in a singularly bitter quarrel with H. J. Perry, secretary of the legation, and in addition to the personal questions involved, the minister was charged with serious moral delinquencies involving the Queen of Spain and with having abused his importation franchise. Hale admitted signing certain compromising documents but pleaded that the secretary had laid them before him without explaining their contents which were in Spanish. He was recalled Apr. 5, 1869, and took leave July 29. His strength had already begun to fail, having been seriously impaired by the famous National Hotel epidemic of 1857, and he spent some further time abroad in a vain quest for health. Returning to New Hampshire in June 1870, he suffered a paralytic stroke soon afterward and his last years were spent in semi-invalidism. His wife was Lucy Lambert of South Berwick, Me.; his daughter, Lucy Lambert Hale, the wife of William Eaton Chandler [*q.v.*]. As a crusader in a humanitarian cause Hale ranked among the great men of the day, but his qualities were not those best calculated to produce constructive legislation or successful administration.

[The New Hampshire Historical Society has a considerable collection of letters and miscellaneous manuscripts relating to John P. Hale. Other sources include *The Hale Statue* (1892), published by the N. H. General Court; E. S. Stearns, *Geneal. and Family Hist. of the State of N. H.* (1908), III, 1044–49; I. W. Stuart, *Life of Capt. Nathan Hale* (2nd ed., 1856); C. H. Bell, *The Bench and Bar of N. H.* (1894), pp. 415–18; *Diary of Gideon Welles* (3 vols., 1911); G. W. Julian, "A Presidential Candidate of 1852," *Century*, Oct. 1896; J. H. Ela, "Hon. John P. Hale," *Granite Monthly*, July 1880; *Boston Transcript*, *N. Y. Tribune*, Nov. 20, 1873; *Independent Statesman* (Concord, N. H.), Nov. 27, 1873.] W. A. R.

HALE, LUCRETIA PEABODY (Sept. 2, 1820–June 12, 1900), author, daughter of Nathan [*q.v.*] and Sarah Preston (Everett) Hale, and sister of Charles and Edward Everett Hale [*qq.v.*], was born in Boston. Her father was editor of the *Boston Daily Advertiser* and her mother, in spite of eleven children, was often his secretary. Writing was the usual thing in the Hale household. Members of the family were frequently called upon for emergency book reviews, essays, or translations. In writing of Lucretia, Ellen Day Hale, a niece, says of her: "She was the delicate member of an extremely strong and vivacious family. Her life had its short intervals of intense action, and its longer periods when she was almost an invalid" (*Bookman, post,* p. 422). She attended Miss Elizabeth Peabody's school and later George B. Emerson's school, where she met her lifelong friend Susan Lyman (Mrs. Peter Lesley), who became the original of the Lady from Philadelphia in the Peterkin stories. Lucretia shared with her brothers and sisters lessons in dancing, painting, and music; and the social life of the Hales included attendance at the Italian opera and the best concerts and plays, as well as gatherings of congenial friends in their own home. On Sundays the family attended the Brattle Street Church. About 1860 the Hales moved from their large house near Boston Common to a small one in Brookline, where the father died in 1863 and the mother in 1865.

Lucretia's first writing to attract attention was a story, "The Queen of the Red Chessmen," published in the *Atlantic Monthly* for February 1858. Her other writings include: *Struggle for Life* (1861), a religious story; *The Lord's Supper and its Observance* (1866); *The Service of Sorrow* (1867); *Six of One by Half a Dozen of the Other* (1872), a novel written with several other authors, including Edward Everett Hale; *Designs in Outline for Art-Needlework* (1879); *Point-Lace: a Guide to Lace-Work* (1879); *More Stitches for Decorative Embroidery* (1879); *The Peterkin Papers* (1880); *The Art of Knitting* (1881); *The Last of the Peterkins, with Others of their Kin* (1886); and *Fagots for the Fireside* (1888), a collection of 150 games. The two Peterkin books constitute Lucretia Hale's claim to literary recognition. The first Peterkin story was told to amuse the daughter of her friend Mrs. Lesley, and the first publication of the earlier stories was in *Our Young Folks.* The invention of the Lady from Philadelphia, whose common sense settled all the problems arising from other people's stupidity, appealed to the satirical vein in both children and adults. In 1867 Lucretia went with her sister Susan to Egypt, where her brother Charles was consul-general of the United States. Their stay lasted for some months and included a horseback journey in Palestine. Two years after her return to the United States, Lucretia settled in Boston and became interested in public affairs concerning women. She taught for a time in a correspondence school, conducted private classes in history, and served as one of the first women members of the Boston School Committee. She wished to live in a social settlement house, but because of her brother Edward's opposition to this idea, she made her home in a small apartment, filled with books and pictures. During her last years she became blind and her mind was impaired. She died in Boston and was buried from the South Congregational Church.

[*Who's Who in America*, 1899–1900; Ellen Day Hale, "Lucretia Peabody Hale," the *Bookman*, June 1925; *Letters of Susan Hale* (1919), ed. by Caroline P. Atkinson; obituary in the *Boston Transcript*, June 12, 1900; information from Miss Ellen Day Hale, Washington, D. C.] S. G. B.

HALE, NATHAN (June 6, 1755–Sept. 22, 1776), hanged by the British, long known as the "Martyr Spy" of the Revolutionary War, and now revered as the ideal youthful hero of the Republic, was born in Coventry, among the hills of Tolland County, Conn. His father, Richard, a descendant of Robert Hale who settled in Cambridge, Mass., in 1632, was a substantial farmer and untiring patriot; his mother, Elizabeth Strong, belonged to a family conspicuous for devotion to public affairs. In their family of twelve children there were nine sons, six of whom took part in the Revolution. As a boy, Nathan doubtless helped with the chores on his father's large farm, but he had time for fishing, swimming, and wrestling. He was prepared for college by the village minister, Rev. Joseph Huntington, an excellent classical scholar, noted for wit and urbanity, from whom Hale may have acquired some of his engaging manners and his interest in the heroes of antiquity. In 1769 he entered Yale. During his course he became one of the most prominent members of Linonia, a secret fraternity devoted to "incitement of literary exertion," the library of which, if he did not found, he organized. He was an omnivorous reader of books of all kinds, but was noted for his physical prowess no less than for his literary and oratorical powers. The marks of a prodigious broad jump which he made on the New Haven Green were long preserved.

After his graduation in 1773 he visited his uncle, Maj. Samuel Hale, preceptor of a Latin School in Portsmouth, N. H., where he doubtless met his cousin Samuel, later an incorrigible Tory and General Howe's Deputy Commissioner of Prisoners. From October 1773 to March 1774 he taught school in East Haddam, Conn.; and from March 1774 to July 1, 1775, in New London. He won all hearts in both places and was a successful teacher. His amazing athletic feats gave him great prestige among men and his handsome person and engaging manner made him popular with the ladies. An outstanding event of his life in New London was a speech in behalf of liberty and independence which he made at the town meeting summoned on receipt of the news of the battle of Lexington. Both his impassioned utterance and his "noble demeanor" deeply impressed the gathering.

He received a lieutenancy at the hands of the General Assembly of Connecticut July 1, 1775, and after two months' recruiting he was at Cambridge with the Continental Army, participating in the siege of Boston. His activities are reflected in his diary and letters, which reveal an alert, serious young officer, keenly interested in everything going on, but with time for social intercourse, for correspondence with family and friends, and for wholesome, manly exercise and sports, all entered into with refreshing zest. On Jan. 1, 1776, he was promoted to a captaincy. When Boston was evacuated in March the colonial army was moved to New York. Hale arrived there on Apr. 30, and before the middle of May, assisted by "sailors and skippers" of his company, he executed the feat of cutting out a sloop loaded with supplies from under the guns of the British man-of-war *Asia*. His natural leadership, resourcefulness, and devotion led Lieut.-Col. Thomas Knowlton to select him as one of the captains of the "Knowlton Rangers."

When "in the darkest hour of the Revolution" Washington deemed it imperative to secure information about the strength and designs of the enemy, he turned to Knowlton, who called upon his captains for a volunteer. At first no one responded but at the second call Hale offered himself for the dangerous enterprise. When an intimate friend, Capt. William Hull, sought to dissuade him, he replied: "I wish to be useful, and every kind of service, necessary to the public good, becomes honorable by being necessary." Intending to assume the rôle of school-master and taking his college diploma as his credentials, he left the camp on Harlem Heights about Sept. 12 and proceeded in a roundabout way to Long Island. Having accomplished his mission, he returned to New York and had almost reached his own picket lines, when, on the night of Sept. 21, he was apprehended as a spy and taken before General Howe, whose headquarters were then in the Beekman mansion. That he was betrayed by his Tory cousin, Samuel, was the belief of the times and of his family. Sketches and other valuable military information having been found on his person, "he at once declared his name, his rank in the American Army, and his object in coming within the British lines." Howe, without the form of a trial, gave orders for his execution the next day. While preparations for the hanging were being made on the morning of Sunday, Sept. 22, he was permitted the hospitality of the tent of Capt. John Montresor, chief engineer of the British forces in America, whose professional interest, since he was accustomed to make such sketches as were found on Hale, led him to befriend the prisoner. Here Hale with great calmness wrote two letters, one to his brother Enoch, and one to Col. Knowlton, who, unknown to his subordinate, had been killed shortly before. He then went forth to the gallows where, it seems clear, he made a "spirited and sensible speech," of which the memorable words, reminiscent of a similar utterance in Addison's *Cato,* "I only regret that I have but one life to lose for my country," were the conclusion. His friend and comrade, Lieut. Elisha Bostwick, describes Hale as "a little above the common stature in height, his shoulders of moderate breadth, his limbs straight & very plump; regular features—very fair skin—blue eyes—flaxen or very light hair which was always kept short—his eyebrows a shade darker than his hair & his voice rather sharp or piercing—his bodily agility was remarkable. I have seen him follow a football & kick it over the tops of the trees in the Bowery at New York (an exercise he was fond of)—his mental powers seemed to be above the common sort—his mind of a sedate and sober cast & he was undoubtedly pious; for it was remarked that when any of the soldiers of his company were sick he always visited them & usually prayed for & with them in their sickness."

[Town Records, Coventry, Conn.; Hale Papers and Hale's Diary, Conn. Hist. Soc., Hartford; Conn. Archives in State Library, Hartford; Linonia Minutes, Yale Univ. Library; U. S. Pension Bureau, Rev. War: Survivor's File No. 10,376, Elisha Bostwick; I. W. Stuart, *Life of Captain Nathan Hale* (1856); H. P. Johnston, *Nathan Hale 1776, Biog. and Memorials* (1914); E. E. Hale, *Nathan Hale* (1881); Stephen Hempstead, "Capture and Execution of Capt. Hale in 1776," *Mo. Republican,* Jan. 18, 1827; F. B. Dexter, *Biog. Sketches Grads. Yale Coll.,* vol. III (1903); M. H. Campbell, *Revolutionary Services and Civil Life of General William Hull* (1848); Frederick Mackenzie, *Diary of Frederick Mackenzie* (2 vols., 1930.)]

G. D. S.

HALE, NATHAN (Aug. 16, 1784–Feb. 8, 1863), journalist, born in Westhampton, Mass., was of English ancestry, a descendant of Robert Hale who settled in Charlestown, Mass., in 1632, and the son of Rev. Enoch and Octavia (Throop) Hale. Nathan Hale [*q.v.*], who was hanged as a spy by the British, was his uncle. After receiving his early education from his father, he entered Williams College, from which he received the degree of A.B. in 1804. For a short time he studied law in Troy, N. Y., and then went to Phillips Exeter Academy, N. H., where he taught mathematics until 1810, in which year he received the degree of A.M. from Dartmouth. Returning to his native state, he completed his law studies in Boston and was admitted to the Suffolk bar in 1810. In 1814 he abandoned the legal profession and began his long career in journalism. After a brief editorship of the *Boston Weekly Messenger,* in the spring of 1814 he purchased the *Boston Daily Advertiser,* the first daily newspaper to be established in that city, which he edited until 1854, when he retired from its active control. To him a newspaper was the means for swaying public opinion as well as for recording events. He applied this belief, however, only to the world of government, business, and political affairs, for he long excluded from his paper news and opinions of books, art, plays, and music. For many years he was a participant in politics and public affairs, taking sides upon all the great questions of the day, in city, state, and nation. He was one of the first American editors to introduce editorial articles as a regular feature, and a file of the *Advertiser* reflects his own political opinions and his attitude towards all the great problems that contributed to the making of history during nearly fifty years. When it is said that the *Advertiser* was first Federalist, then Whig, and finally Republican, that it opposed the Missouri Compromise of 1820, and the Kansas-Nebraska Bill of 1854, it will be seen that Hale supported those parties in their successive incarnations and opposed all measures seeking to extend slavery or to establish it more firmly. His interest in all the leading local movements of his time was no less than his interest in national affairs. He was a member of the Massachusetts House of Representatives from 1820 to 1822 inclusive, of the Senate from 1829 to 1830, and of two constitutional conventions. As acting chairman of the Massachusetts Board of Internal Improvements, he was an early advocate of the establishment and extension of railroads in New England, and he became the first president of the Boston & Worcester Railroad when it was organized in July 1831, holding that position until June 1849. His services as a railroad organizer give him high place in the history of American transportation. He was a leading spirit in other public enterprises, and among his contributions to the betterment of Boston was his work as chairman of the commission that established the Boston water system. His interests seem to have been widespread and in the forwarding of them all his newspaper was a powerful factor.

From time to time, moreover, he engaged in other journalistic undertakings. In 1815, as a member of the Anthology Club, he helped to found the *North American Review*; he was also one of the founders of the *Christian Examiner,* which first appeared in January 1824, and from 1840 to 1846 he published and edited the *Monthly Chronicle.* His series of stereotype maps of New England became a standard geographical authority, and were reprinted from time to time with the necessary additions and revisions. He also published the *Journal of Debates and Proceedings in the Convention of Delegates Chosen to Revise the Constitution of Massachusetts* (1821), and many pamphlets on railroads, canals, and other practical schemes for public improvements. In 1816 he married Sarah Preston

Everett, daughter of Judge Oliver Everett, and sister of Edward Everett [*q.v.*]. Their children were Lucretia Peabody, Charles, Edward Everett [*qq.v.*], Nathan, a journalist, and Susan, an artist. He was a member of the Brattle Square Church and a deacon there for many years.

[Frederic Hudson, *Journalism in the U. S. from 1690 to 1872* (1873); Justin Winsor, *The Memorial Hist. of Boston* (4 vols., 1881–83); S. A. Allibone, *Critical Dict. of Eng. Literature* (1859); S. K. Lothrop, "Memoir of Hon. Nathan Hale, LL.D.," *Proc. Mass. Hist. Soc.*, XVIII (1881), 270–79; Calvin Durfee, *Williams Biog. Annals* (1871), obituary in *Boston Daily Advertiser,* Feb. 9, 1863.] E. F. E.

HALE, PHILIP LESLIE (May 21, 1865–Feb. 2, 1931), figure painter, critic, teacher, born in Boston, Mass., was the son of Rev. Edward Everett Hale [*q.v.*] and Emily Baldwin (Perkins) Hale. He attended the Roxbury Latin School, then, after passing the entrance examinations for Harvard, decided upon the career of a painter. To this end he prepared himself by a course of study at the school of the Boston Art Museum, at the Art Students' League of New York, at the Julian Academy, and at the École des Beaux-Arts, Paris. On his return from France he took a studio in Boston and accepted an appointment as one of the teachers in the school of the Museum of Fine Arts, a position which he held for over thirty years with conspicuous success. He also served for several seasons as a teacher in the schools of the Pennsylvania Academy. His work as a figure painter received recognition in a steadily increasing degree after 1900, and is shown by the awards and honors conferred on him at Buffalo, 1901, St. Louis, 1904, Buenos Aires, 1910, Chicago, 1914, New York, 1916, and Philadelphia, 1916, 1919. In 1915 he was a member of the international art jury at the Panama-Pacific Exposition at San Francisco. Of the many exhibitions held in Boston, those at the Guild of Boston Artists in 1916 and 1919 were most noteworthy. To the first of these exhibitions the Corcoran Gallery, Washington, lent the "Girl with Muff," which took the Harris medal at the Art Institute of Chicago in 1914. "The Madonna of the Porcelain Tub" was also among the outstanding works shown. The exhibition of 1919 contained a group of uncommonly fine drawings in sanguine, silver-point, and pastel. The silver-points, especially, were remarkable for their distinction and delicacy.

On June 11, 1902, Hale married Lilian C. Westcott of Hartford, Conn. She became a talented artist. In 1913 he published *Jan Vermeer of Delft,* a study of a painter for whose work he entertained an ardent admiration. It was an original and valuable contribution to the literature of art, as well as a competent study of the little master's methods and qualities. It is written with gusto in a personal style which is excellent for its clearness and freedom from cant. At various periods Hale acted as art critic for the Boston press, but his heart was not in the work, and he did not take it very seriously. He was unmerciful in dealing with mediocrity, and his sarcasms were stinging. Yet the many young men and women who were his pupils unite in testifying to his personal interest and helpfulness as a teacher. He died at the Baker Memorial Hospital, Boston, in his sixty-sixth year, leaving his widow and a daughter.

[*Who's Who in America,* 1930–31; *Am. Art Annual,* 1929; *Bull. of the Museum of Fine Arts,* Apr. 1931; obituaries in the Boston newspapers of Feb. 3, 1931; *Boston Herald* and *Lowell* (Mass.) *Courier-Citizen,* Feb. 4, 1931.] W. H. D.

HALE, ROBERT SAFFORD (Sept. 24, 1822–Dec. 14, 1881), lawyer, congressman, was born in Chelsea, Vt., the son of Harry and Lucinda (Eddy) Hale, and a descendant in the seventh generation of Thomas Hale who removed from Watton, England, to Newbury, Mass., about 1637. He was graduated from the University of Vermont in 1842 and taught in the academy at Montpelier before returning to Chelsea to begin the study of law. He completed his studies in the office of Augustus C. Hand in Elizabethtown, N. Y., where he established his law practice and his home. He married Lovina Sibley Stone, daughter of Capt. Jeremiah Stone of Elizabethtown. Upon his admission to practice, in Albany, in January 1847, he entered into a partnership with Orlando Kellogg which continued until his election as county judge and surrogate of Essex County in the fall of 1856. After eight years on the bench he engaged in private practice until May 20, 1880, when ill health necessitated his retirement. His practice extended throughout northern New York, where his native ability, erudition, eloquence, and courage gave him distinguished rank in his profession. His scholarly tastes and the breadth of his culture led to his choice as a regent of the University of the State of New York, Mar. 29, 1859, and he served actively with that body during the remaining twenty-two years of his life.

In 1860 Hale was a presidential elector, casting his vote for Abraham Lincoln. In 1865 he was elected to fill a vacancy in Congress and served in the turbulent second session of the Thirty-ninth Congress. Three years later he was appointed special counsel of the Treasury Department before the United States court of claims in the matter of claims for captured and abandoned cotton. In 1870 he was defeated at the polls for the New York court of appeals, in an election which went against his party, but shortly afterward he was called to Washington for the most distinguished service of his career, that as agent and counsel of the United States before the American-British Mixed Claims Commission, 1871–73. His full report indicates that the British claims amounted to about $96,000,000; that the sole responsibility for the United States briefs in these 478 claims rested upon him, and that the awards to the British claimants by the Commission against the United States amounted to only about two per cent. of the claims presented. His last service in Washington was as representative in the Forty-third Congress (1873–75), after which he returned to his home. He was the first president of the village of Elizabethtown in 1875 and in 1876 one of the commissioners of the state topographical survey.

[Robert Safford Hale, *Geneal. of Descendants of Thos. Hale of Watton, Eng., and of Newbury, Mass.* (posthumously published, 1889); *Ann. Report of the Regents of the Univ. of the State of N. Y.* (1883); U. S. Dept. of State, *Papers Relating to the Treaty of Washington*, vol. VI (1874); *N. Y. Times*, Dec. 15, 1881.] A. S. M.

HALE, SARAH JOSEPHA BUELL (Oct. 24, 1788–Apr. 30, 1879), author, editor, mother of Horatio Emmons Hale [*q.v.*], was born in Newport, N. H., on a farm belonging to her great-grandfather, Daniel Buell, one of the proprietors of that settlement. She was the daughter of Capt. Gordon Buell, Revolutionary soldier, and his wife, Martha Whittlesey, who had left their native Connecticut soon after the close of the Revolution to establish a home in a newly settled region of New Hampshire. In this rural community she lived a quiet domestic life for forty years before she began the work that was to make her name a household word in America.

She received her early education largely from her mother to whose teaching she attributed her love for books and her faith in the capacity of women. By an older brother, a student at Dartmouth, she was instructed in Latin and philosophy. In October 1813 she married David Hale, a lawyer of Newport, with whom she continued her education, writing with his encouragement occasional articles which she sent to the neighboring newspapers. When her husband died suddenly, in 1822, leaving her with scanty means to provide for their five children, she determined to try her hand seriously at authorship. She published a little volume of verse, *The Genius of Oblivion* (1823), and sent out numerous poems, signed "Cornelia," to local periodicals. In 1826 one of them won a prize offered by the *Boston Spectator and Ladies' Album*, and in the following year her novel, *Northwood, A Tale of New England*, brought her to the attention of a wider audience. Attracted by this novel the Rev. John Lauris Blake [*q.v.*] offered Mrs. Hale the editorship of a monthly periodical for women about to be established in Boston. She accepted the offer, moved to Boston in 1828, and there, in the columns of the *Ladies' Magazine*, began her active life as writer and promoter of conservative reforms.

Although twenty or more ephemeral periodicals for women had come and gone in America before this time, the *Ladies' Magazine* was the first publication of its kind to have any real significance. Mrs. Hale wrote at least half of every number herself, providing her readers with wholesome sketches of American life, poems, essays, and literary criticism of considerable discrimination. In every issue of the paper she urged her favorite reform, the better education of her own sex, and although she steadily refused to countenance the woman's rights movement, she contended vigorously that women should be permitted to fill places of importance as teachers.

While editing the *Ladies' Magazine* she initiated various benevolent and patriotic activities in Boston, notably the Seaman's Aid Society and women's clubs for raising money to complete Bunker Hill monument. Meantime she published several volumes of prose and verse, among them a little book entitled *Poems for Our Children* (1830), containing the well-known "Mary's Lamb." When, late in her life, a controversy arose about the authorship of this poem, she instructed her son to declare that she had written every poem in the volume (*Century*, March 1904).

In 1837 Louis A. Godey [*q.v.*] bought out the *Ladies' Magazine* and established Mrs. Hale as literary editor of the *Lady's Book*. She carried on her new duties from Boston for several years, but in 1841, her sons educated, she moved to Philadelphia and became completely identified with the new undertaking for the rest of her life. The happy alliance of Godey's advertising ability with Mrs. Hale's gentility, moral principles, and earnest devotion to culture made the *Lady's Book* the best known of all American periodicals for women.

Mrs. Hale contributed freely to its columns, but as time went on she devoted herself more particularly to the departments known as "Literary Notices" and "Editors' Table." Here she guided the taste of thousands of women away from all indelicacy, and carried on decorous conversations with her readers setting forth the duties and privileges of women. She believed that the members of her sex were God's appointed agents for morality in the world, but that they must accomplish their mission through moral influence and not by means of any direct responsibility in public affairs. She continued her campaign for education, urging that colleges of medicine and liberal arts be established for women, and that the teaching in such colleges be entrusted as largely as possible to women. Her articles on this last subject exercised considerable influence on the founder of Vassar College (*Autobiography and Letters of Matthew Vassar,* 1916).

In addition to her work in the magazine Mrs. Hale edited letters, annuals, and anthologies of verse. Volumes of poetry and prose, giftbooks, cookbooks, and other treatises dealing with the home came regularly from her pen. Her most ambitious undertaking was *Woman's Record, or Sketches of Distinguished Women* (1853; 1869; 1876), a volume in which she attempted to illustrate, by means of over fifteen hundred biographical sketches, the history of woman and her influence on society and literature. In all she published thirty-six volumes.

In December 1877 Mrs. Hale, then in her ninetieth year, wrote her final words in the *Lady's Book* and retired from her half-century of editorship. Two years later she died in Philadelphia, serene in the consciousness that she had labored faithfully to elevate her country-women by providing for them in her periodical "a beacon-light of refined taste, pure morals, and practical wisdom."

[Sarah Josepha Hale published brief accounts of herself in the *Ladies' Wreath* (1837); *Godey's Lady's Book,* Dec. 1850, Dec. 1877; *Woman's Record* (1853). Other sources of information are: G. R. Howell, *Geneal. of Descendants of Thomas Hale* (1889); Edmund Wheeler, *The Hist. of Newport, N. H.* (1879); *New-Eng. Hist. and Geneal. Reg.,* July 1879; the *Granite Monthly,* Mar. 1880; obituaries, *Boston Daily Advertiser; N. Y. Tribune, Public Ledger* (Phila.), May 2, 1879; portraits in *Woman's Record* (by W. B. Chambers, engraved for *Godey's Lady's Book* in 1850), and in the *Am. Mag.,* Mar. 1910 (by T. B. Read), accompanying an article by Ida M. Tarbell on "The American Woman."]
B. M. S.

HALE, WILLIAM BAYARD (Apr. 6, 1869–Apr. 10, 1924), clergyman, journalist, was born in Richmond, Ind. He was the son of William Hadley and Anna (Bunting) Hale and claimed relationship with the Hales most famous in American history. With an engaging presence and a promising forensic talent, he was educated for the ministry after studying at Boston University and Harvard and, on ordination in 1893, was assigned as mission priest to the Church of Our Saviour, Middleboro, Mass. He attracted attention early in his career as the author of *An Address in Memory of the Rt. Rev. Phillips Brooks, D.D.* (1893), and as the contributor of radical magazine articles to the *Arena* and was called to speak in different cities. He went in for university-extension work, accountable for his address on "The Making of the American Constitution," delivered before the summer meeting of university students at Oxford in 1895, and in 1897 he published *The New Obedience.* In 1899 he became rector of St. Mary's at Ardmore, Pa., giving in the same year six lectures on "Great Novelists" for the American Society for the Extension of University Teaching. In 1900 he stumped the West for Bryan. Meanwhile parish preaching and family difficulties were grinding on the handsome young rector's high-strung temperament. Feeling need of change, he turned to journalism and in quick succession occupied positions with the *Cosmopolitan, Current Literature,* and the *World,* became managing editor of the Philadelphia *Public Ledger* for four years, and then served the *Times* in New York and as its Paris correspondent. But he did not divest himself of clerical orders until 1909 when he joined the staff of the *World's Work.*

While on the *Times,* Hale spent a week at Roosevelt's elbow in the White House describing graphically the presidential routine in feature stories, assembled in book form in 1908 under the title *A Week in the White House with Theodore Roosevelt.* His next exploit was an interview with Kaiser Wilhelm, sold to the *Century* for $1,000, but suppressed. For nearly two hours the Kaiser walked the deck of the *Hohenzollern* at Bergen with Hale, talking freely "about things American." The *Century's* advance advertisement, on the heels of the same ruler's trouble-breeding London interview, precipitated its withdrawal, "at the request of the author," though the sheets were ready for binding (*New York Times,* Apr. 11, 1924). The whole edition was bought up, taken on a warship into the mid-Atlantic, and burned by German naval officers. During the War, a proof of this "highly indiscreet" statement, said to have been confided to the Harvard University library, disappeared, but the *New York Tribune* broadcast excerpts from a copy held out by an employee of the magazine.

Through his association with Walter Hines Page on the *World's Work,* Hale was called upon to prepare an intimate biography of Woodrow Wilson for serial publication. As *Woodrow Wilson: The Story of his Life* (1912) it won warm approval and acceptance as the official campaign biography. Hale liked to refer to himself as Wilson's biographer. The volume of Wilson's characteristic political addresses, entitled *The New Freedom* (1914), compiled and edited by Hale, includes an introduction by Wilson crediting the work to him in laudatory terms. The selection of Hale to go to Mexico as President Wilson's confidential agent, therefore, was not so wrapped in mystery as it seemed. His report, following a three months' sojourn, undoubtedly determined the refusal to recognize Huerta. Subsequently he visited the revolutionists in Northern Mexico and conferred with Carranza, after which the embargo on arms, which had placed them at disadvantage, was lifted. But by May 1914 Hale was no longer connected with the government, and the ardent attachment between him and the President had cooled, to change in time to open enmity. Hale's final blast of embitterment, *The Story of a Style* (1920), written, as the author explains, in 1919 but held back on account of the President's illness till the physicians reported recovery, and then published with slight revision "in the direction of restraint," acridly belittled and ridiculed Wilson's literary ability.

Hale's sorry day began with his retention as adviser for the German propaganda in this country, organized by Dr. Dernburg, at a salary of $15,000 a year to be paid him direct from Berlin. This employment was prompted, so it is averred (*Saturday Evening Post,* June 22, 1929, p. 12), by a mistaken belief that he held the key to the back door of the White House. In his new capacity, he fulminated numerous special pleas for Germany and arguments against British activities on the seas, often masked behind deceptive names, and headed a movement to stop all export of munitions. Charged with writing the Dernburg speech justifying the sinking of the *Lusitania,* he insisted that he had merely edited it. This brought widespread denunciation upon him. Before the entrance of the United States into the War, Hale's service was transferred to the Hearst papers, at first as correspondent at Berlin, and later as a staff man in New York. In 1918, intercepted Bernstorff cables exposed his previous relations with the Germans. Pilloried by pitiless publicity, the storm broke upon him afresh. Clubs expelled him. Magazines and publishing houses closed to him. Biographical handbooks expunged his name. He had no recourse but to seek cover and for the rest of his life he remained in comparative seclusion, writing little, though his publication attacking Wilson's style was to have been part of a larger work. He died in Munich. He had married, on June 27, 1899, Mabel Jolly, daughter of a wealthy Boston wool merchant. The couple lived together scarcely six months and divorce ensued. On Oct. 5, 1909, he married, in London, Olga Unger, youngest daughter of Emil Unger, a New York banker.

[Hale's books; *Who's Who in America,* 1899–1900, 1916–17; *Who's Who in Pa.* (1904); contemporary newspapers; R. E. Annin, *Woodrow Wilson* (1924); Count Bernstorff, *My Three Years in America* (1920); G. S. Viereck, *Spreading Germs of Hate* (1930); H. A. K. Harris, "William Bayard Hale und Woodrow Wilson," *Deutsche Rundschau,* Oct. 1921; *N. Y. Times,* Apr. 11, 1924.]

V. R.

HALE, WILLIAM GARDNER (Feb. 9, 1849–June 23, 1928), classical scholar, was born in Savannah, Ga., of New England parents, William Bradford and Elizabeth (Jewett) Hale. His boyhood home was Peterboro, N. H., whence he went to Phillips Exeter Academy and to Harvard, where he was graduated in 1870 and where he became a fellow, 1870–71, and then tutor until 1880, with the exception of the year 1876–77, which was spent in study at Leipzig and Göttingen. In 1880 he succeeded Tracy Peck as professor of Latin in Cornell University. He was married on June 13, 1883, to Harriet Knowles Swinburne of Newport, R. I., by whom he had two sons and two daughters.

The influence of such teachers as Goodwin, Lane, and Greenough directed his studies naturally toward the syntax of Greek and Latin. In Leipzig he sought the instruction of Georg Curtius; and in general from Germany he brought back the interests acquired by personal contact with the schools of Curtius and Schleicher. From the points of view thus early assumed he never departed, and in a paper of 1901 he reaffirms his conviction that comparative study is not a whit less important in syntax than in morphology (*Harvard Studies,* XII, 1901, 110), to which he appends the significant note: "An obvious truth, the neglect of which by all but a few workers in the present generation will seem inexplicable to the coming one." For the purposes of creating an Indo-European comparative syntax this direction was deserving of all praise, but as a point of departure for determining and defining the actual facts of Latin usage it has proved less fruitful than was hoped. There is in all of Hale's work a much larger element of theory than now seems necessary, in the elaboration of which he was ingenious and subtle. It resulted in considerable innovations of nomenclature, which have been rather a hindrance than a help to the diffusion of his ideas. His general scheme of Latin syntax is presented in his *Latin Grammar* (with C. D. Buck, who handled the forms), an acute and independent treatment of the subject, but too delicate a mechanism to be operated by the casual teacher of Latin. To the training of teachers and to the practical teaching of Latin Hale devoted much attention, not only in the preparation of his *Latin Grammar* and *First Latin Book,* but also in conducting a very successful teachers' training course, and by giving actual instruction in elementary Latin in the University of Chicago High School. He was skilful and stimulating in using a Socratic form of lecture in which, while himself teaching and directing, his students participated and enjoyed the sensation of reaching conclusions by their own observation. None of his works exercised so wholesome and practical an influence as his pamphlet on *The Art of Reading Latin.* Its purpose is to set forth the method he had devised of teaching students to read Latin at sight in the Latin order of words. Its value is to be estimated less by the originality of the idea than by the skill with which it was presented. In 1892 Hale accepted the position of head of the department of Latin in the new University of Chicago and there remained until his retirement in 1919, after which he made his residence at Stamford, Conn., where he died. Into the movement for the establishment of the American School of Classical Studies in Rome (now a part of the American Academy in Rome) Hale threw himself with great energy, and the success of the campaign was due in large measure to his efforts. He was the first director of the new foundation, and the School was opened under his leadership in the autumn of 1895. During this year, in connection with the paleographical work of his students, Hale discovered in the Vatican Library a manuscript of Catullus, long misplaced and thus effectually lost, which proved to be the starting point of much of the work of the remainder of his life. To this manuscript, which he christened *R,* he accorded a place side by side with the MSS. *O* (Oxford) and *G* (Paris) as a source for the reconstruction of the Verona archetype, from which our text of Catullus is derived. His discovery was variously received. Ellis, the English editor, accepted Hale's conclusions and embodied the results in his Oxford text. German editors have been more skeptical and at best have suspended judgment until the complete description and publication of the manuscript should be available. This discovery led Hale to the ambitious plan of tracing the whole history of the text of Catullus, to which he believed that *R* furnished the key. To this large task he devoted much of the leisure of his later years, leaving the work unfinished at his death.

He had wide acquaintance in America and was the recipient of many academic honors. To his opinions and the causes which he supported weight was lent by the distinction of his personality. Not only in literature but in music and art he possessed well-trained and discerning judgment. He was fond of outdoor life, of the woods, of boating and fishing (which he enjoyed at his summer home on Moosehead Lake), and at least up to the time of his retirement he played a strong game of tennis. He was tall and of fine physique, and up to the last year or two of his life his vigorous appearance belied his years.

The more important of Hale's publications are: *The Cum-Constructions* (pt. I, 1887; pt. II, 1888); *The Art of Reading Latin* (1887); three papers on "The Sequence of Tenses in Latin," *American Journal of Philology,* 1886–88; "The Anticipatory Subjunctive, in Greek and Latin," *University of Chicago Studies in Classical Philology,* vol. I (1895); "The Origin of Subjunctive and Optative Conditions in Greek and Latin," *Harvard Studies in Classical Philology,* vol. XII (1901); "A Century of Metaphysical Syntax," *Congress of Arts and Sciences* (St. Louis, 1904, vol. III, 1906); *A Latin Grammar,* with C. D. Buck (1903); *A First Latin Book* (1907). Concerning MS. *R* of Catullus the first announcement was made in the *Rendiconti della Reale Accademia dei Lincei, Classe di Scienze Morali, Storiche e Filologiche* (Rome), June 21, 1896, and in the *Classical Review,* June 1896. Of several later publications pertaining to it the most important are: "Der Codex Romanus des Catullus," *Hermes,* XXXIV (1899), 133–144; "The Manuscripts of Catullus," *Classical Philology,* III (1908), 233–256; "Stampini and Pascal on the Catullus Manuscripts," *Transactions of the American Philological Association,* LIII (1922), 103–112.

[*Tenth Report of the Class of 1870 of Harvard Coll.* (1920); *Who's Who in America,* 1919–20; *N. Y. Times,* June 24, 1928; C. D. Buck, obituary, *Classical Philology,* July 1928; G. L. Hendrickson, memoir, *Classical Jour.,* Dec. 1928. A portrait, by his daughter, Virginia Hale, hangs in the Classics Building of the University of Chicago.]

G. L. H.

HALL, ABRAHAM OAKEY (July 26, 1826–Oct. 7, 1898), lawyer, politician, journalist, author, was born in Albany, N. Y., the son of Morgan James and Elsie Lansing (Oakey) Hall. His ancestry was for the most part English, his paternal grandfather being a carpenter of Hampshire, England, who married a Welsh woman, emigrated to America, and settled in Albany. On the maternal side he claimed descent from Col. John Oakey, or Okey, as the name was then spelled, one of Oliver Cromwell's aides and a member of the group responsible for sending Charles I to his doom. With the restoration of the Stuarts in 1660, Colonel Oakey escaped to

Holland, where he died. His son Abraham, after whom A. Oakey Hall was named, married a French woman by the name of D'Assigne.

In 1829 when Hall was only three years of age his father, a New York City merchant associated with the firm of P. R. Starr, died of yellow fever. The mother managed by taking boarders to make a livelihood and to send her son to the public schools. At fourteen he entered the University of the City of New York where he paid his way in part by contributing to newspapers and doing odd jobs. An excellent student, he received the degree of B.A. in 1844 and that of M.A. three years later. Ambitious for power and fame, he chose the law for a profession and spent one term at the Harvard Law School, where by his brilliance he made a very good impression. Leaving Cambridge, apparently because of lack of funds, he entered the law office of Charles W. Sanford of New York City where he remained only a short time before going to New Orleans. Here he became a newspaper reporter, an activity which he soon abandoned to continue his law studies in the office of Thomas and John Slidell. In 1849 he was admitted to the New Orleans bar, but two years later returned to New York and was given permission to practise in that state. In 1853 he formed a partnership with Aaron J. Vanderpoel, a former classmate, which afterward became the firm of Brown, Hall, & Vanderpoel.

Hall soon embarked on a political career which if not outstanding was at least notorious. He was appointed assistant district-attorney of New York County in 1851, and was district attorney from 1855 to 1858. Up to this time he had been successively a Whig, a Know-Nothing, and a Republican. In 1862 he was elected district attorney by a combination of Republicans and a Democratic faction headed by Fernando Wood, and served until 1868. It is asserted that during the last six years of his incumbency in this office he sent twelve thousand persons to prison and pigeon-holed more than ten thousand indictments against others. The noted trial of Mrs. Cunningham for the murder of Dr. Burdell during his district attorneyship served to bring him into prominence. Realizing that the dominant power in New York politics was Tammany Hall, he forsook his former associations and in 1864 became a member of that organization. In 1868 Tammany made him mayor to succeed John T. Hoffman who had been elevated to the governorship of the state. During his four years as mayor he acted as the mountebank of the "Tweed ring," covering up ugly facts and unpleasant details by means of a ready wit, clever speeches, and debonair manners. His catering to the Irish and German voters won for him the title "Mayor Von O'Hall." Accused in 1871 of being implicated with Tweed, he stoutly maintained his innocence and refused to resign as mayor. Indicted and brought to trial in December 1872, he conducted his own defense and was acquitted.

From 1879 to 1882 he was city editor of the New York *World*. He gave up this position to go to London where, at the request of his friend James Gordon Bennett the younger, he was for five years London representative of the *New York Herald*. During 1890–91 he served the New York *Morning Journal* in a similar capacity. While in London he was admitted to the English bar and practised in the English courts. In 1889 he sued James Bryce for libel because a chapter on the "Tweed ring" in the first edition of *The American Commonwealth* referred to Hall as one of the culprits. He demanded £10,000 damages, but after pending nine years the case was dropped (*American Law Review*, May–June 1898).

Hall was a lover of literature and something of an author. Among his best works were: *The Manhattaner in New Orleans or Phases of "Crescent City" Life* (1851); *Old Whitney's Christmas Trot* (1857); *Sketches of Travel* (1859); *Horace Greeley Decently Dissected* (1862); *The Congressman's Christmas Dreams and the Lobby Member's Happy New Year: A Holiday Sketch* (1870); *Ballads of Hans York* (1880); and "History of the Tweed Ring" (1898, unpublished). He also aspired to be known as a playwright. *The Crucible* in which he himself played a part in 1878 represents his greatest claim to dramatic distinction. *Loyalina, Brigadier General Fortunio and His Seven Gifted Aides-de-Camp* (1864), *Humpty Dumpty, Fernande,* and *Let Me Kiss Him for His Mother* were among his lesser productions.

Hall craved social distinction, and despite early poverty and almost insuperable obstacles he achieved it. Fearless, level-headed, meticulous in speech and dress, he gained the title "Elegant Oakey." He was a director of the Manhattan Club, 1868–71; president of the Lotus Club, 1870–73, and a member of many other societies. He was married twice: first, to Katharine Louise, daughter of Joseph N. Barnes, by whom he had six children; and second, in 1896, to the widow of Capt. John J. Clifton of Scranton, Pa. He was reared in the Presbyterian faith, later became a Swedenborgian, and in 1898, with his wife, was received into the Roman Catholic Church. He died in New York City.

[Hall's own writings may be profitably supplemented by "A Scrapbook of Clippings Relating to the Career of

A. Oakey Hall" (14 vols., 1857), in N. Y. Pub. Lib.; James Bryce, *The American Commonwealth* (1888), vol. III; John Bigelow, *Life of Samuel J. Tilden* (1895); Elmer Davis, *Hist. of the N. Y. Times* (1921); Gustavus Meyers, *The Hist. of Tammany Hall* (2nd ed., 1917); M. R. Werner, *Tammany Hall* (1928) and article in *New Republic*, May 27, 1931; J. G. Wilson, *The Memorial Hist. of the City of N. Y.*, vol. III (1893); C. F. Wingate, "An Episode in Municipal Government," in *North Am. Rev.*, Oct. 1874, Jan., July 1875; *Every Saturday* (Boston), Oct. 21, 1871; H. L. Clinton, *Celebrated Trials* (1897); obituary notices and editorials in the leading N. Y. papers under date of Oct. 8, 1898, especially the very fair estimate in the *N. Y. Times*.] H. J. C.

HALL, ARETHUSA (Oct. 13, 1802–May 24, 1891), educator, author, was the seventh of nine children of Aaron Hall and his second wife, Sarah Richardson. Her father, after teaching school in various towns in Worcester County, had settled as a farmer in Norwich (now Huntington), Mass., where Arethusa was born. From the time she was nine, she was brought up by her half-sister Apphia, the wife of Sylvester Judd of Westhampton. In 1822 she moved with the Judd family to Northampton, and the following year attended Westfield Academy, but for the most part she conducted her own education, reading and studying with her brother-in-law who was editor of the *Hampshire Gazette*, and becoming a woman of considerable breadth of culture for the times. In 1826 she was made teacher of one of the early academies which antedated the rise of the American high school, at Greenland, N. H., and between 1827 and 1828 she took charge of the "female department" at Haverhill Academy. Injuries received in 1831 during a carriage journey on a rough road made her a partial invalid for some twelve years. During this time she taught for short periods in a number of schools for girls here and there in New England, in 1839 becoming associated for some months with her second cousin, Dr. Samuel Read Hall [*q.v.*], who in 1823 had founded the first normal school in America at Concord, Vt., and was then opening his Teachers' Seminary in the little town of Plymouth, N. H. Dr. Hall was a progressive educational theorist as well as an experienced teacher, and cooperation with him widened Miss Hall's horizon. She was called in 1849 to the faculty of the Brooklyn Female Academy, forerunner of the Packer Institute. Two years later she joined Prof. Alonzo Gray in founding another notable school for girls, the Brooklyn Heights Seminary. In this school, which included primary, junior, and senior departments, she took the seniors under her especial care, giving what she herself later thought to be pioneer courses in the history of English literature and the history of art. She remained assistant principal until Prof. Gray's death in 1860. Not long afterward, failing health compelled her to give up teaching, and she retired upon the little competence she had accumulated. From 1873 to 1890 she passed a part of every winter in the Cambridge home of Francis Ellingwood Abbot [*q.v.*]. Beloved and revered by her friends and pupils, she died at the Judd homestead in Northampton in her eighty-ninth year.

During periods of leisure from teaching she found time to prepare several thoughtful works, all somewhat tinged with the stilted religious expression of her day. The first of these was a translation, *Thoughts of Blaise Pascal* (1846); the second, *A Manual of Morals* (1849), was a book of ethics for children, seeking to impart instruction in "right conformity to the nature of things." While at Brooklyn she prepared *The Literary Reader* (1850), and *Life and Character of the Rev. Sylvester Judd* (1854), a biography of her favorite nephew. Her *Memorabilia of Sylvester Judd, Sr.* (1882) was privately printed in Northampton. In 1875–76 at the request of F. E. Abbot, she wrote her autobiography.

[*Arethusa Hall: A Memorial* (priv. printed, 1892), ed. by F. E. Abbot, contains Miss Hall's autobiography; D. B. Hall, *The Halls of New England* (1883), 391, 444–48, contains some genealogical material collected by herself. The date of her death has been verified by the City Clerk, Northampton, Mass.] M. B. H.

HALL, ARTHUR CRAWSHAY ALLISTON (Apr. 12, 1847–Feb. 26, 1930), bishop of the Protestant Episcopal Church, was born at Binfield, Berkshire, England, the son of Maj. William Thomas Hall, a retired officer of the British army, and Louisa Astley (Alliston) Hall. He was educated at Brighton College and Christ Church, Oxford, receiving the degree of B.A. in 1869 and that of M.A. in 1872. Although trained in the evangelical school of the Church of England, he came at Oxford under the influence of the Tractarians, especially the Rev. Henry Parry Liddon and the Rev. Richard M. Benson. The latter had been instrumental in 1866 in founding the Society of St. John the Evangelist, a revival of the monastic life. Its location at Cowley, near Oxford, led to its members being known as the Cowley Fathers. Young Hall entered the Order as a lay brother after taking his degree. He was ordained deacon by the Bishop of Oxford, Dec. 18, 1870, and advanced to the priesthood on St. Thomas Day, 1871. For two years longer he remained in training at Cowley. In 1874 he was sent to the American branch of the Society and became assistant priest at the Church of the Advent, Boston, Mass., where he remained until 1882, when the Order transferred its headquarters to the Church of St. John the Evangelist in

Bowdoin Street. Father Hall was early recognized as a preacher of great power; he exercised a wide influence in the community, and was frequently called to conduct parochial missions and retreats and to give sermons and addresses, in other parts of the United States and Canada. His tall and striking figure in its monk's habit, his deep and powerful voice, and his fiery earnestness in the pulpit made a profound impression on his hearers. His sermons were characterized by lucid thought and intensely practical counsel. In 1889 he was elected by the Diocese of Massachusetts as a deputy to the General Convention of the Church and was also made a member of its standing committee. His action in 1891 in supporting the election of Phillips Brooks as bishop of Massachusetts was disapproved by the superior of his Order and he was recalled to England.

His seventeen years in New England had won him many friends, who regretted keenly the fact that he had been withdrawn from the American Church. When the death of Bishop W. H. Bissell left a vacancy in the episcopate in the Diocese of Vermont, Father Hall was put forward as a candidate and was elected bishop at a special convention in August 1893. He submitted to the Order of which he was a member the question as to whether he could be released from his vow of obedience to accept the election, and in a General Chapter it was voted that this be done. He therefore accepted the election, and was consecrated in St. Paul's Church, Burlington, Vt., Feb. 2, 1894. His episcopate was marked by energetic and faithful pastoral care and notable growth throughout the diocese. He early took a leading place in the House of Bishops and was a member of many important committees and commissions, including those for the revision of the lectionary and the prayer book, in the work of which he took a prominent part. He served for many years on the committee on constitution and canons of which he was at first secretary and later chairman. His reputation as a canonist was very high and his advice was sought by bishops from all parts of the country, while his intimate knowledge of the spiritual life led to his being sought as director and confessor by large numbers of people both within and without his diocese. He was active in the cause of Christian unity and served as a member of the Commission on the World Conference on Faith and Order by which the Lausanne meeting of 1927 was effected. His literary and scholarly achievements were recognized by several universities. He was a voluminous writer, some of his books attaining a wide popularity. His principal works were: *Meditations on the Creed* (1881), which ran into many editions; *Christ's Temptation and Ours* (1896), the Baldwin Lectures, Ann Arbor, Mich.; *The Use of Holy Scripture in the Worship of the Church* (1903), the Bishop Paddock Lectures, General Theological Seminary, New York; *The Christian Doctrine of Prayer* (1904), the Bohlen Lectures, Philadelphia; *The Relations of Faith and Life* (1905), the Bedell Lectures, Kenyon College, Ohio. His work on *Confirmation* (1900), in the Oxford Library of Practical Theology is considered an authority on the subject. His volume of retreat addresses on *The Virgin Mother* (1894), is a deeply spiritual study of the character of Saint Mary. He also contributed a volume, *The Doctrine of the Church* (1909), to the Sewanee Theological Library. He died in Burlington, Vt.

[*Stowe's Clerical Directory* (1929); *The Living Church*, Mar. 15, 1930; *The Mountain Echo* (Burlington, Vt.), Apr. 1930; *The Cowley Evangelist*, June 1930; *Burlington Free Press and Times*, Feb. 27, 1930; *Who's Who in America*, 1928–29.]
G. L. R.

HALL, ASAPH (Oct. 15, 1829–Nov. 22, 1907), astronomer, was descended through a long line of New England Halls from John Hall, "of New Haven and Wallingford," who came to America in 1632 or 1633, took part in the Pequot War in 1637, settled in New Haven, Conn., about 1640, and moved to Wallingford some thirty years later. Asaph's father, also named Asaph, inherited a large estate when he was nineteen. He attempted to become a merchant but with financially disastrous results, then established a clock-factory at Hart Hollow, in Goshen, Conn., and used to load up his wagon with clocks and travel as far south as Georgia selling the clocks and finally the horse and wagon. He married Hannah C. Palmer, daughter of Robert Palmer, and of their six children Asaph was the oldest. The family lived on a farm in Goshen on the bleak slope of Ivy Mountain. Asaph attended the district school. When he was thirteen his father died on one of the clock-selling trips. All the property was heavily encumbered with mortgages. His mother started a cheese-factory, the boy helping as best he could, but the income was inadequate, and at sixteen Asaph was apprenticed to a carpenter for three years. Later, as a journeyman, he had won a reputation as a skilful house builder.

His father had accumulated a good many books and these he read eagerly. He early developed the tendency to go to original sources for his information. When he became interested in a subject it was his practice to make a list of all the titles that he could find of works dealing with it. Later he referred to textbooks as "intellectual pap, suitable only for babes." During one winter he attended the Norfolk academy, studying algebra and six books of Euclid. After he became twenty-one he began to lay up money out of his wages of a dollar and a half a day for a college education. In 1854, with his savings of three hundred dollars, attracted by a newspaper advertisement, he went to Central College at McGrawville, N. Y. He found some books in the library he wanted to read, learned some mathematics and a little French and Latin, and kept the college buildings in repair. The most important result of his year and a half at this institution was his engagement to Chloe Angeline Stickney of Rodman, N. Y., a fellow student. They were married at Elkhorn, Wis., Mar. 31, 1856, and went immediately to Ann Arbor, Mich., where Hall entered the sophomore class in the University. Professor Brünnow was much impressed with the young man's quickness in grasping the principles of astronomical observation and during the remaining three months of the year gave him special attention. For one reason or another, however, he left college and took charge of the school at Shalersville, Ohio. Then he went to Thomaston, Conn., to resume the practice of his trade as carpenter, but, in pursuance of his ambition to become an astronomer, after a few months there went on to Cambridge and took a position in the Harvard observatory at three dollars a week. In 1858 in connection with a survey in the West, he observed twenty-three moon culminations at a dollar apiece and made computations for farmers' almanacs which brought in a few dollars. An acquaintance assured him he would starve if he persisted in following astronomy. In 1859 his salary was raised to four hundred dollars, however, and he began to send papers, chiefly on the orbits of comets and asteroids, to the journals. In 1862 he went to Washington as aide in the Naval Observatory and in the following year, on the resignation of Professor Hesse, succeeded to the post of professor of mathematics there.

Hall's scientific predilections were peculiarly in line with the work of a national observatory. Other astronomers had announced discoveries which had turned out to be nothing but "subjectivities," and of these he had a wholesome dread. He was an enthusiastic and accurate observer and a keen and accurate mathematician and computer. During his many years at the telescope he made constant use of the micrometer, determining the positions of planets, satellites, asteroids, comets, and stars. His most spectacular observation was his discovery of the two satellites of Mars. All textbooks stated that Mars had no satellites, but after a careful search, on Aug. 11, 1877, Hall found a faint star near Mars which on Aug. 16 he proved to be a satellite (Deimos). The next day, Aug. 17, he saw the other (Phobos) also and on Aug. 17 and 18 established its character. With him observation was followed by elaborate and careful discussion and the resulting improvement of accepted values. Among his five hundred published papers are masterly investigations of the orbits of the various satellites, the mass of Mars, the perturbations of the planets, the advance of Mercury's perihelion, the parallax of the sun, the distances of Alpha Lyræ and sixty-one Cygni, the mass of Saturn's rings, the orbits of double stars, and the solution of the many problems in mathematics which these investigations brought up.

After his retirement from the Naval Observatory in 1891 and the death of his wife in 1892, he bought a piece of land with a house in Goshen. In 1896 he accepted an invitation to give instruction at Harvard in celestial mechanics, but he returned to "Gunstock," as he called his place, for his vacations. In 1901 he was married a second time, to Mary B. Gauthier. His publications continued until September 1906, fourteen months before his death, which occurred at the home of his son Angelo at Annapolis, Md. The eldest of his four sons, Asaph, carried on his work at the Naval Observatory.

[Memoir by G. W. Hill in *Nat. Acad. Sci. Biog. Memoirs*, vol. VI (1909); D. B. Hall, *The Halls of New England* (1883); *Pop. Astron.*, Feb. 1908; *Science*, Dec. 13, 1907; *Astronomische Nachrichten*, Feb. 1908, p. 127; *Evening Star* (Washington, D. C.), Nov. 24, 1907.]

R. S. D.

HALL, BAYNARD RUSH (Jan. 28, 1798–Jan. 23, 1863), Presbyterian clergyman, educator, author, a descendant of Richard Hall, who received grants of land in Maryland in 1663, was born in Philadelphia, Pa. His parents were Dr. John Hall, a surgeon on the staff of General Washington, and Elizabeth Ann Baynard. He was left an orphan at the age of three. By means of a small legacy from a maternal uncle, and by his own toil as a printer, young Hall obtained a liberal education. He graduated from Union College in 1820 and from Princeton Theological Seminary in 1823. In 1821 he was married in Danville, Ky., to a Miss Young, to whom he had been engaged since he was sixteen and whose family had moved from Philadelphia to Kentucky on account of financial losses. In 1823 the Halls turned to the west from Philadelphia to join Mrs. Hall's mother and brother, who were living on the edge of the "New Purchase," a tract of land south and east of the Wabash River obtained by treaty with the Indians in 1818.

In 1820 the Indiana legislature created a state seminary, situated at Bloomington. This was opened to students in May 1824, and Hall became its first principal at a salary of $250 a year. When this seminary received a college charter in 1828 Hall was elected professor of ancient languages, which position he held until 1831. He had been ordained as a Presbyterian minister by the Salem Presbytery in Indiana in 1825. Together with two fellow ministers, George Rush and Isaac Reed, Hall helped to organize, in Reed's cabin, the Wabash Presbytery. Reed, an early Presbyterian missionary in Indiana, had married a sister of Mrs. Hall in Kentucky, and it was largely through Reed's influence that Hall came to Indiana, with a view to his being "on the ground" when the new seminary should open. Hall preached for the Bloomington Presbyterian church from 1826 to 1830, and in October 1826 at Vincennes he helped to organize the Synod of Indiana.

Hall's pioneer experiences gave him the subject of his book, *The New Purchase; or, Seven and a Half Years in the Far West.* It was published under his pen name, Robert Carlton, in 1843, was republished in 1855, and in 1916 the Indiana centennial edition was brought out by the Princeton University Press. The work pictures varied aspects of frontier life, the roads, the modes of travel, the cabin homes and inns; the settler's games, weddings, and "shivarees"; the barbecues, rifle matches, log-rollings, stump speeches, the college exhibitions, and the court trials of the time.

After Dr. Andrew Wylie came to Indiana as the first president of the college in 1828, some college quarrels arose, and Hall found it necessary to leave. From Indiana he went to Bedford, Pa., where he opened an academy in which he taught for seven years, also preaching in the Presbyterian Church. In 1838 he moved to Bordentown, N. J., later to Trenton, N. J., and then to Poughkeepsie and Newburgh, N. Y., in which places he preached and taught school. In 1852 he became principal of Park Institute and pastor of the Reformed Dutch Church at Brooklyn, N. Y., where after some ten years of service, he died. In addition to the *New Purchase,* he was the author of a *Latin Grammar* (1828); *Something for Everybody* (1846), homilies on current customs and morals; *Teaching a Science; the Teacher an Artist* (1848); and *Frank Freeman's Barber Shop: A Tale* (1852).

[Sources: *The New Purchase* (ed. 1916), partly autobiographical; Meredith Nicholson, *The Hoosiers* (1900); D. D. Banta, "Early Sketches of Ind. Univ." (MS., Ind. Univ. Lib.); J. P. Dunn, *Ind. and Indianans,* vol. II (1919), pp. 873–74; *Md. Hist. Mag.,* Sept. 1913; *S. C. Hist. and Geneal. Mag.,* Jan. 1922; *Union Univ. Centennial Cat. 1795–1895* (1895); E. A. and G. L. Duyckinck, *Cyc. of Am. Lit.* (ed. 1875), vol. II; *N. Y. Times,* Jan. 27, 1863.]

J. A. W.

HALL, CHARLES CUTHBERT (Sept. 3, 1852–Mar. 25, 1908), was born in New York City, the son of William Cooper and Jane Agnes (Boyd) Hall. A delicate lad, he received his early education from tutors. Graduating from Williams College at the early age of twenty, he spent two years of theological study at the Union Theological Seminary in New York City and, after a further year of study at the Presbyterian College in London and New College, Edinburgh, was ordained to the Presbyterian ministry in 1875. Following a pastorate of two years at Newburgh, N. Y., he was called to the pastorate of the First Presbyterian Church of Brooklyn, a position which he occupied for twenty years. In 1897 he became president of the faculty of Union Theological Seminary, New York, of which institution he was already a director. During the eleven years of his presidency he served also as professor of pastoral theology (1897–1904) and of homiletics (1904–08). On Aug. 21, 1877, he married Jeanie Stewart Boyd of New Windsor, N. Y., by whom he had three children.

Pastor of one of the most important churches in Brooklyn when only twenty-five, he soon came to occupy a large place in the religious life of that city. An interesting and effective preacher, he influenced men rather by the compelling force of his personality and the warmth of his religious life than by the originality and profundity of his thought. The pastoral contacts formed through his ministry bore fruit in devotional books, of which the best-known is *The Silver Cup* (1909), a collection of children's sermons. A lover of music and himself an organist of no mean ability, he edited, in cooperation with Sigismund Lasar, *The Evangelical Hymnal* (1880). Short of stature, meticulously neat in personal appearance, with a merry eye and personal charm, he had a rare gift of making friends.

He came to the presidency of Union Seminary at the close of a period of controversy with the General Assembly, which had won freedom for the institution at the cost of the severing of many ties. His administration inaugurated a period of reconciliation in which, without the surrender of principle, the constructive aspects of the ministry were emphasized. During his administration the constituency of the seminary was broadened, its interdenominational character was redefined, and plans for its removal from its old site on Lenox Hill to the new site on Morningside Heights were consummated. While he did not himself live to witness its removal, it was his wise policy and tactful administration which made it possible.

Hall also rendered notable service on the foreign field. Going to India in 1902–03 as Barrows Lecturer, he won many friends by his sympathetic understanding of the Eastern mind, revealed in his printed lectures *Christian Belief Interpreted by Christian Experience* (1905). Four years later, against the advice of his friends, yet under a strong sense of duty, he repeated this service, his lectures on the second trip being published under the title *Christ and the Eastern Soul* (1909). The strain proved too great, however, and he came back a broken man, bearing the seed of a disease from which he never recovered. Among his publications, in addition to the works already named, are the following: *Into His Marvellous Light* (1892), *Does God Send Trouble?* (1894), *Qualifications for Ministerial Power* (1895), *The Gospel of the Divine Sacrifice* (1897), *The Redeemed Life After Death* (1905), *The Universal Elements of the Christian Religion* (1905), *and Christ and the Human Race* (1906). He also served as editor of the American edition of *The Expositor*.

[*Union Theol. Sem. Gen. Cat. 1836–1918* (1919); *Who's Who in America*, 1908–09; *Outlook*, Jan. 12, 1907, Apr. 4, 1908; *Presbyterian*, Apr. 1, 1908; *N. Y. Times*, Mar. 26, 1908; correspondence with the family; personal acquaintance.]
W. A. B—n.

HALL, CHARLES FRANCIS (1821–Nov. 8, 1871), Arctic explorer, was born in Rochester, N. H. Of a restless nature, he emigrated westward and finally settled in Cincinnati, Ohio, where he was in turn blacksmith, journalist, stationer, and engraver. He married and had children. Arctic explorations especially interested him, and he followed indefatigably the efforts of John Franklin to discover the Northwest Passage, and studied the reports of the many expeditions sent out to determine his fate. When England ceased to search, Hall endeavored to organize an American expedition, but was still unsuccessful when, in 1859, the fate of Franklin was discovered by McClintock in the voyage of the *Fox*. Hall then determined to solve personally the fate of the retreating party under Crozier, believing that some of them must be yet living as castaways among the Eskimo. Utilizing an American whaler for transportation to Davis Strait, Hall was landed alone with a whaleboat and scant supplies in Frobisher Bay, on July 30, 1860. From his base, Rescue Harbor, 63° N., 65° W., with Eskimo help, he examined the coasts, Meta Incognita, discovered by Frobisher in 1575 and 1578. Obtaining many relics of Frobisher's expeditions, he returned home in 1862, bringing with him Eskimos Joe and Hannah, invaluable and loyal aids. He had become an accurate observer, skilled in Eskimo speech, and an adept in all phases of Eskimo life.

During the next two years he prepared for the press an account of his expedition, published in London as *Life with the Esquimaux* (2 vols., 1864) and in New York as *Arctic Researches, and Life among the Esquimaux* (1865). Encouraged by the success of his first venture, he determined to visit King William Land, where Crozier's party was last seen, and secured the financial support of Henry Grinnell [*q.v.*], who had previously helped finance the expeditions of Elisha Kent Kane and Isaac I. Hayes [*qq.v.*]. In August 1864, with Joe and Hannah, Hall was landed at the north end of Hudson Bay with boat, tent, provisions, and instruments. His researches occupied five years and entailed sledge journeys of more than 3,000 miles. He found several skeletal remains, obtained from the natives many articles of the Franklin party, and secured information from old Eskimos: one of Franklin's ships was said to have made the Northwest Passage and stranded off O'Reilly Island, where natives visited it in 1849. It was said that in July 1848 Crozier, with two sledges and forty men, retreated down the west coast of King William Land, en route to Repulse Bay (Nourse, *post*).

Hall now planned a voyage to the North Pole, and his past success so impressed Congress that on July 9, 1870, an act was passed and on July 12 approved by the president, appropriating $50,000 and authorizing the use of a naval vessel for the voyage. With his two Eskimos and a scientific staff, Hall sailed June 29, 1871, from New York, in the *Polaris*, equipped with supplies for two and a half years. From the Greenland ports were obtained dogs, furs, sleds, and other equipment, and the force was increased by Hans Hendrik and his family. Ice conditions proved to be unusually favorable, and the *Polaris* steamed speedily northward through Kane Sea, Kennedy and Robeson channels, into the Arctic Ocean. She was there turned back by an impenetrable icepack, in 82° 11′ N., 61° W., the most northerly point then reached by any vessel. This was 250 miles north of the point reached by the *Advance* under Elisha Kent Kane [*q.v.*]. Turning south, the *Polaris* was anchored in an unique harbor, an open roadstead in 81° 37′ N., 62° W., sheltered by an enormous berg, 650 x 450 x 300 feet in size. An observatory was built on land, while Hall made a sledge trip to Cape Brevoort, where he saw Grinnell Land to the west, extending above 83° N. On his return he had a stroke of apoplexy and died, Nov. 8, 1871. With his death exploration practically ceased, and in 1872 the *Polaris* turned southward, to be caught in the ice-pack, damaged by storms, and beached near Littleton Island. The party divided during a violent gale, one part wintered in a house built from the ship, and were brought home by the whaler *Ravenscraig*. The remainder suffered the horrors of the ice-pack and after a drift of 1,300 miles were rescued by the sealer *Tigress* off the coast of Labrador. (See Blake, *post.*) The geographic results of the expedition were extensive and important. Kennedy Channel disclosed the way to the North Pole. Greenland and Grinnell Land were extended about three degrees of latitude northward. East of the *Polaris* anchorage were thousands of square miles of vegetation-covered land, far the largest ice-free area of Greenland. (See Davis, *post.*) With similar limited resources no man has surpassed Charles Francis Hall in arctic explorations.

[J. E. Nourse, *Narrative of the Second Polar Expedition Made by Charles F. Hall* (1879), being *Senate Ex. Doc. No. 27*, 45 Cong., 3 Sess.; C. H. Davis, *Narrative of the North Polar Expedition: U. S. Ship Polaris, Capt. Charles Francis Hall Commanding* (1876); Emil Bessels, *Die Amerikanische Nordpol Expedition* (1879); *Arctic Experiences: Containing Capt. George E. Tyson's Wonderful Drift on the Ice-Floe* (1874), ed. by E. V. Blake; J. F. Brennan, *A Biog. Cyc. and Portr. Gallery of . . . Ohio* (1879), p. 140; *Cincinnati Times and Chronicle*, May 10, 1873; *Cincinnati Commercial*, May 11, 1873; *N. Y. Tribune*, May 12, 1873.]
A. W. G.

HALL, CHARLES HENRY (Nov. 7, 1820–Sept. 12, 1895), Protestant Episcopal clergyman, was a Georgian by birth, his parents, Charles and Margaret (Reid) Hall, being residents of Augusta. He traced his descent from Hugh Hall, a planter in Barbados. The latter's son, Hugh, who had been a prominent official there and was often in New England, died at Boston in 1732 (see *New-England Historical and Genealogical Register*, July 1888, pp. 303–06). Charles was educated in the North, preparing for college at Phillips Andover Academy, and in 1842 graduating from Yale College. While in college he became an Episcopalian, and after completing his course began to prepare for the ministry. Without being a member of the theological school, he studied Biblical literature at Andover, Mass., continuing his work at Hartford, Conn., and later at the General Theological Seminary, New York. He was ordained deacon, Aug. 25, 1844, at St. Paul's Church, Red Hook, N. Y. In the spring of 1845, having spent the previous winter in Augusta, he took charge of St. John's Church, Huntington, Long Island, and was ordained presbyter on Nov. 12, in St. James' Church, Fair Haven, Conn. From Easter 1847 to the summer of 1848 he was rector of the Church of the Holy Innocents, West Point, N. Y., serving also as chaplain of the United States Military Academy. For the next eight years he was in charge of St. John's Church, John's Island, S. C. Having many slaves among his parishioners, he assiduously schooled himself to preach with a simplicity and directness which would make the gospel clear to their understanding, and was revered by them as a prophet. On Mar. 2, 1848, he married Annie Maria Cumming of Augusta, who died Nov. 2, 1855, from the effects of an accident.

The last thirty-nine years of his life were spent in Washington, where he was rector of the Church of the Epiphany (1856–69), and in Brooklyn, where he succeeded Dr. Abram N. Littlejohn [*q.v.*] at Holy Trinity, when the latter became bishop of Long Island. Although a Southerner and a Democrat, he was a strong Unionist, and in Washington, preceding and during the Civil War, he ministered to a church divided in its sentiments with great tact and effectiveness. Jefferson Davis occupied a pew there until the secession, after which it was taken by Secretary Stanton. The church was used as a hospital during the war, and it was on one of Henry Ward Beecher's visits to Brooklyn soldiers in Washington that he became acquainted with Hall, and there began the long and intimate friendship between the two which resulted in Beecher's request that this Episcopal rector should conduct his funeral service. On Sept. 10, 1857, he married Lizzie, daughter of George C. Ames of Washington.

In Brooklyn he soon became not only one of the most prominent clergymen but also one of the leading citizens. A man of athletic build and energy, at home everywhere, broad-minded, tolerant, and sympathetic, yet loyal to his own convictions, he was beloved and trusted. He was conspicuous in Masonic circles, served as chaplain of the 23rd Regiment, was civil service commissioner and park commissioner. As a rule he did not bring politics into the pulpit, but he did not hesitate to speak on civic and social reforms. He was an active supporter of Grover Cleveland for president. In addition to his parish duties, he was chairman of the standing committee of the diocese, chancellor of the cathedral, and prominent in the councils of the Episcopal Church. Upon the younger clergy he had a great influence. Always an assiduous student of the Bible, he had published in 1857 *Notes, Practical and Expository, on the Gospels,* two volumes, which came into wide use. In *True*

Protestant Ritualism (1867), he made a virile attack on High Church tendencies as expressed in *The Law of Ritualism* by Bishop Hopkins [*q.v.*]. His volume of sermons, *The Valley of the Shadow* (1878), was criticized because of alleged unorthodox views on future punishment. With S. B. Whitely, he edited the *Hymnal: According to the Use of the Protestant Episcopal Church in the United States of America* (1872); and besides individual sermons and addresses, he published *Spina Christi, Musings in Holy Week* (1874), and *The Church of the Household* (1877). His death occurred in Brooklyn just before the completion of his seventy-fifth year.

[The best sketch of Hall is in the *Brooklyn Eagle*, Sept. 13, 1895; see also: *Biog. Record of the Class of 1842 of Yale College* (1878); *Obit. Record Grads. Yale Univ. 1890–1900* (1900), p. 370; *Churchman*, Sept. 21, 1895; *Outlook*, Sept. 21, 1895.] H. E. S.

HALL, CHARLES MARTIN (Dec. 6, 1863–Dec. 27, 1914), chemist, manufacturer, descended from John Hall who, coming from England some time before 1652, settled at Medford, Mass., about 1675, was born in Thompson, Geauga County, Ohio. His parents, Rev. Heman Basset Hall and Sophronia (Brooks) Hall, by moving to the village of Oberlin gave him the opportunity of securing an education in Oberlin College. He proved himself an excellent student, perhaps taking life too seriously. In spite of his constant burial in books, however, he was well liked by his fellows of the class of 1885. Even before entering college he dreamed of great inventions that should benefit humanity, and his interest was early directed towards chemistry. "My first knowledge of chemistry was gained," he once said, "from reading a book on chemistry which my father had studied in the forties. I still have the book, published in 1841. It is minus the cover and title-page so I do not know the author." At Oberlin it was his good fortune to come under the influence of Prof. F. F. Jewett, trained at Yale and at Göttingen, who was then in charge of the chemistry department of Oberlin College. The lad attracted Jewett's attention before he entered college, through his purchases of "a few cents worth of glass tubing or chemical laboratory test tubes." When he was part way through the regular college course in chemistry, Jewett took him into his private laboratory to work, and discussed his problems with him. A remark of Jewett's turned young Hall's attention toward aluminum. "Speaking to my students," Jewett wrote later, "I said that if anyone should invent a process by which aluminum could be made on a commercial scale not only would he be a benefactor to the world but he would also be able to lay up for himself a great fortune. Turning to a classmate, Charles Hall said, 'I'm going for that metal.'"

At the age of twenty-two Hall discovered the only commercially successful process of making aluminum, succeeding where such giants as Wöhler (who first isolated aluminum in 1827), Rose, Deville, and many others had struggled in vain. It was well known that aluminum could be electrolyzed from fused cryolite but the process was not practicable. Hall's original contribution was the idea that aluminum oxide, dissolved in melted cryolite, could be electrolyzed. An old clay crucible lined with carbon, heated by a plumber's torch, was his first electric furnace, installed in the family woodshed. With carbon electrodes and current from his simple batteries he made his first famous globules of the metal. He had the usual troubles of the inventor. Two groups of financial backers deliberated and declined to invest their funds. He spent a year (July 1887–July 1888) with the Cowles Electric Smelting Company of Lockport, N. Y., but they gave up the option they had taken on his patent, which, applied for July 9, 1886, was not granted until Apr. 2, 1889. At length he secured the financial support of the Mellons and other investors and under the name of the Pittsburgh Reduction Company began to produce fifty pounds of aluminum daily at Kensington, Pa., in November 1888. The Hall process quickly brought the price down to $1.00 and in 1914 to eighteen cents per pound. This achievement made aluminum a common metal and brought it into general use. Since Hall was later unjustly accused of stealing the process (independently discovered by Héroult in France and patented there Apr. 23, 1886) from the Cowles Company, it is important to compare the dates of his service in that company with the proved date, Feb. 23, 1886, of his discovery. His originality was at last approved, Jan. 20, 1893, by a decision of Judge William Howard Taft in a suit to restrain infringement, brought by the Pittsburgh Reduction Company against the Cowles Electric Smelting and Aluminum Company in the United States circuit court for the central district of Ohio (*Decisions, post*).

In 1905 Hall was elected a trusteee of Oberlin. He believed thoroughly in the high ideals of his college and ultimately became its greatest benefactor, bequeathing to it by his will one-third of his estate, a bequest that has grown with the passing years to a value conservatively estimated at fifteen million dollars. His devotion to his mother was shown by a special provision that a great memorial building should be erected in her memory. His love of music was attested by his gift, jointly with F. N. Finney, of a magnificent pipe organ for the chapel, and his love of art by a gift of his choicest rugs, paintings, and Chinese porcelains to the College art collection. In 1911 he received the Perkin medal in recognition of his services to the world. He never married.

[*Decisions of the Commissioner of Patents and of U. S. Courts in Patent Cases, 1894* (1895); *Memorial Volume to Charles M. Hall* (1915); D. B. Hall, *The Halls of New England* (1883); *Jour. of Industrial and Engineering Chem.*, Mar. 1911; *Rev. of Revs.*, June 1911, Apr. 1915; *World's Work*, Aug. 1914; *School and Society*, Jan. 23, 1915; *N. Y. Times*, Dec. 28, 29, 1914.] H. N. H.

HALL, DAVID (1714–Dec. 24, 1772), printer, bookseller, was a native of Edinburgh, Scotland, where he learned the trade of printing. After his apprenticeship he went to London and found work in Watt's printing office, in which William Strahan was employed as a journeyman. When Strahan established himself as a master printer, Hall seems to have been engaged to assist him, for in 1743, when Benjamin Franklin wanted an experienced and reputable journeyman in his Philadelphia printing house, his friend Strahan, subsequently the King's Printer, sent Hall to him. In writing to Strahan (Feb. 12, 1744), Franklin remarked that "Mr. Hall . . . gains ground daily in the esteem of all that know him. . . . He is obliging, discreet, industrious and honest" (*Life of Benjamin Franklin*, edited by John Bigelow, 1905, I, 375). When in 1748 Franklin became very busy with a multiplicity of interests and public affairs, he took Hall, who was his foreman, into partnership; and from that time onward Hall carried on the printing business for the firm of Franklin & Hall and also edited and published Franklin's *Pennsylvania Gazette*. The firm continued until Feb. 1, 1766, when Franklin sold his interest to his partner.

Hall was not alone very long, for in May 1766 he took William Sellers, who had been his journeyman, into partnership, and as Hall & Sellers the firm was continued until Hall's death. Since they had the government printing, including the printing of paper money for the Province of Pennsylvania, the business was lucrative. "Had he not been connected with Franklin," remarks Thomas (*History of Printing*, I, 246), "he might have been a formidable rival to him in the business of printing and bookselling. . . . Hall was well acquainted with the art of printing; and was an industrious workman, of first rate abilities; a prudent and impartial conductor of the Gazette." Franklin's son William disliked Hall and wrote his father in 1766 that Hall was joining hands with the Proprietary party, characterizing him as "a mere snake in the grass" who possessed "no friendship for" Franklin (Bigelow's *Franklin*, I, 511). Franklin expressed a different view in his *Autobiography* (*Ibid.*, I, 291), speaking of Hall as "a very able, industrious, and honest partner," and adding, "He took off my hands all care of the printing-office, paying me punctually my share of the profits. This partnership continued eighteen years, successfully for us both." It is significant that shortly after Hall's arrival in Franklin's shop, the volume which has been judged the finest piece of printing from Franklin's press, Cicero's *Cato Major*, was published (1744). Franklin also enlarged his *Poor Richard's Almanac*, after he had a partner, and other almanacs were printed by the firm of Franklin & Hall, with whom the use of rubrication on almanacs became frequent. Like his partner, Hall conducted a bookselling and stationery shop in connection with his printing business in Philadelphia. He was married Jan. 7, 1748, to Mary Lacock. He died in Philadelphia, Dec. 24, 1772, and was buried in Christ Church graveyard.

[Isaiah Thomas, *Hist. of Printing in America* (2nd ed., 2 vols., 1874); "Wm. McCulloch's Additions to Thomas's Hist. of Printing," *Proc. Am. Antiq. Soc.*, XXXI (1921), 89–247; "Wm. Strahan to David Hall," *Boogher's Repository*, Apr. 1883; "Correspondence between Strahan and Hall," *Pa. Mag. of Hist. and Biog.*, vols. X–XIII (1886–89); W. J. Campbell, *The Collections of Franklin Imprints in the Museum of the Curtis Pub. Co.* (1918).] J. J.

HALL, DOMINICK AUGUSTIN (*c.* 1765–Dec. 19, 1820), federal judge in Louisiana, was a native of South Carolina, according to most accounts (although Gayarré says he was of English birth), and began his legal career in Charleston. In 1801 he was appointed by President John Adams judge of the Fifth United States Circuit, then composed of the districts of North and South Carolina and Georgia, but he retired the following year upon the repeal of the Judiciary Act under which the appointment was made. By act of Congress, Mar. 26, 1804, which provided a temporary government for the newly acquired Louisiana territory, a district court having the powers of a United States circuit court, but consisting of a single judge, was established for the Territory of Orleans. President Jefferson selected Hall as judge of this court, apparently because of his special qualifications, including his command of French and his knowledge of maritime jurisprudence. He arrived in New Orleans in the fall of 1804 and continued to perform the duties of the position until 1813, when, a state government having been formed, he was induced to give up his United States judgeship and accept an appointment as a judge of the supreme court of Louisiana. Since he had long been accustomed to individual modes of decision, he found his new position less congenial than the old, however, and since the vacancy caused by his resignation had not been filled, he applied for and received back his federal judgeship, which he held for the rest of his life.

Hall's relations with Gen. Andrew Jackson in New Orleans during the War of 1812 brought him into national prominence. Jackson had declared martial law, which was submitted to with little objection so long as the enemy was upon the soil of the state. After the British had taken to their ships and newspapers printed accounts of peace, however, people and legislature clamored for the restoration of civil law and the dismissal of the militia. Jackson's refusal to comply with their demands or to relax his vigilance until he was officially informed of peace, involved him in a violent quarrel with people, legislature, governor, and judge. During the progress of the controversy he arrested a member of the legislature, one Louaillier, for writing an objectionable letter. The request of the prisoner's counsel for a writ of *habeas corpus* was refused by the state courts on the ground of no jurisdiction, whereupon the prisoner made his demand of Judge Hall, who willingly complied. Jackson, very angry, ordered the arrest of Hall. About this time a messenger arrived from Washington with an important letter for Jackson and an order to postmasters to facilitate the progress of the bearer of news of peace. When the General broke the seal he found that through an error the wrong letter had been enclosed, and, in spite of the fact that the orders to postmasters made it evident that war was over, he would not relax his martial law. Louaillier, although not in the army or navy, was court-martialed, but acquitted. Jackson, however, set the sentence aside and retained him in prison. Realizing that it would be useless to try Judge Hall by court martial, Jackson sent him out of the city with orders not to return until peace was regularly announced or the enemy had departed from the coast. Official news of peace came next day, and the General immediately revoked martial law and freed his prisoners. The able, popular, but over-punctilious judge, returning to the city thirsting for revenge, summoned Jackson into court to show why he should not be held in contempt for refusal to recognize the court's writ of *habeas corpus.* The General was tried, convicted, and fined $1,000, which he paid at once. After this one notable episode of his career, Hall continued in the routine work of his office for some five years, until his death, which occurred in New Orleans.

[*A Charge Delivered to the Grand Jury of the United States, for the Louisiana District, at the July Term, 1821, By John Dick, Esq., Judge of the United States for That District* (1821); J. S. Bassett, *The Life of Andrew Jackson* (1916), ch. XIII; letter on the Hall episode from Jackson to Amos Kendall, June 18, 1842, printed in *Cincinnati Commercial,* Feb. 5, 1879; *S. C. Hist. and Geneal. Mag.,* Apr. 1909; Chas. Gayarré, *Hist. of La.* (3rd ed., 1885), vol. IV, ch. XII; Alcée Fortier, *A Hist. of La.* (1904), III, 17, 82, 156, 159; notice of Hall's death in the minutes (MS.) of the U. S. District Court, Eastern District of Louisiana, V, 100, in New Orleans.]

M. J. W.

HALL, FITZEDWARD (Mar. 21, 1825–Feb. 1, 1901), picturesque and unique figure in the field of philology, was born at Troy, N. Y., the eldest son of Daniel, a well-to-do lawyer, and Anjinette (Fitch) Hall, who represented distinguished colonial families. Fitzedward's paternal grandfather served as a naval officer in the Revolution and went from Cape Cod to Vermont, where he was judge of the supreme court, and died in 1809; he was a descendant of John Hall of Coventry, England, who came to Charlestown, Mass., in 1630 and settled at Yarmouth some years later. On the mother's side the boy was descended from Thomas Fitch [*q.v.*], whose ancestor came to America in 1637. After preliminary schooling at Walpole, N. H., and in the Rensselaer Polytechnic Institute (graduating in 1842), Fitzedward entered Harvard College as a member of the famous class of 1846 (Child, Lane, and Norton were his classmates) and eventually received from Harvard the degrees of A.M. and LL.D. (1895), though he missed his first Commencement because he had been sent by his father to India to find a brother who had run away to sea. This accident determined Fitzedward's career, for, being wrecked in the Hugli River and detained at Calcutta, he remained there for three years, occupying himself with teaching and newspaper work, and took up the study of the local dialects. Language, always his favorite study, now became his lifework. After drifting to Ghazipur, where he stayed about half a year, he settled down in Benares, Jan. 16, 1850, and was soon made instructor at the local Government College. Three years later he became professor of Anglo-Sanskrit in the same college and occupied this position till July 1855, when he was appointed inspector of public instruction for Ajmere-Merwara. Meantime, in 1854, at Delhi, he had married Amy, the daughter of Lieut.-

Col. Arthur Shuldham. In December 1856 he was transferred as inspector of public instruction to the Central Provinces, with headquarters at Saugor. The next year he helped personally to defend the fort there, during the Mutiny, and then took a vacation of eighteen months, visiting France, England, and his native country. On his way back to India, in 1860, he received from Oxford the degree of D.C.L. In 1862 he left India permanently and became professor of Sanskrit, Hindustani, and Indian jurisprudence at King's College, London. He was also librarian to the India Office and after 1864 acted as examiner for the Civil Service Commissioners, first in Hindustani and Hindi, and then, succeeding Max Müller, in Sanskrit (1880), and a few years later in English. In 1869 he retired to Marlesford, not far from London, where he devoted himself for eight years to the completion of a task begun some years before: the editing of Sir Horace Hayman Wilson's translation of *The Vishńu Puráná* (1864–77), with an enormous mass of new elucidatory material.

Hall's interest, even in boyhood and markedly so in college, had been centered on linguistic phenomena, though he had also studied mathematics and dipped into medicine. In India, from the first, he gave his whole life to philological studies and, while he kept up his collection of English idioms, devoted most of his time to work in Sanskrit, publishing in rapid succession over thirty volumes of translations, texts, and commentaries, at the rate of one or two a year, while performing the onerous duties of inspector of public instruction during part of this time. He was the first American to edit a Sanskrit text—two treatises on Vedanta philosophy, *The Atma-Bodha, with Its Commentary; also the Tattva-Bodha* (1852). He discovered in 1859 new manuscripts of the *Brihaddevata* and *Natyashastra* (poetics), which he edited, and in the same year completed the publication of both the *Surya-Siddhanta* (astronomy) and the famous romance of Subandhu, *Vásavadattá*. These were but the outstanding contributions made during his sixteen years in India. But his interest in India did not cease when he retired. Besides the great *Vishńu Puráná,* he edited Ballantyne's Hindu Grammar (1868), wrote *Benares Ancient and Medieval* (1868), and published a Hindu Reader (1870). This was but one side of his prodigious activity. He soon became as a writer on English philology no less authoritative than he already was in the field of Sanskrit. His countless contributions as editor of the *Oxford English Dictionary* continued to the time of his death, when Dr. Murray recorded in most appreciative terms how great a loss English philology had thereby suffered. Hall also supplied Joseph Wright's *English Dialect Dictionary* with some two thousand linguistic notes. He was an indefatigable contributor of critical linguistic notes and articles to many journals in England and America, notably the *Academy, Spectator, Dial,* and New York *Nation,* besides writing more elaborate theses and books on philological topics, and editing for the Early English Text Society the works of William Lauder and Sir David Lyndesay (1864, *et seq.*). He was a caustic polemic writer and easily dominated opponents both in Great Britain and America. His *Recent Exemplifications of False Philology* (1872) treated Richard Grant White with the same ruthlessness as that later employed in *Doctor Indoctus* (1880) to the discomfiture of Prof. John Nichol of Glasgow. Hall's *Modern English* (1873), his philological articles, such as "On English Adjectives in -able" (*Nation,* Mar. 21, 1877), and a series of papers published in the *American Journal of Philology* (1881, *et seq.*) and in *Modern Language Notes* (1883, *et seq.*), besides the constant casual notes referred to above, united in making him in the last decade of the nineteenth century almost the supreme judge of English usage, one whose verdicts were never questioned with impunity. In the domain of Sanskrit, he wrote understandingly on philosophy, dramaturgy, and astronomy; yet essentially he was neither a philosopher nor a scientist, but a collector of idioms, a critic of linguistic usage, a purist, and a grammarian. His style was too subject to his own criticism to be natural; it was self-conscious and pedantic. He was a better scholar than writer, though as a writer, if somewhat ungainly, he was trenchant and powerful. As an opponent in philological disputes he was aggressive and irritating; but he often seemed to be captious when he only asked for precision. His learning and industry were immense. He had a host of admirers, many warm friends, and some exasperated enemies. Till his death, when he was almost seventy-six, he remained physically and mentally active and if not engaged in writing spent much of his time raising flowers and angling. Before he died he made over to Harvard University his large collection of Oriental books and manuscripts.

[The best account of Hall's life and publications will be found in two articles written by a personal friend in the New York *Nation,* Mar. 21, 1895, and Feb. 14, 1901. The fairest appraisement of him as a scholar and writer appeared in *Mod. Lang. Notes,* Mar. 1901, p. 183, *et seq.* The Sanskrit texts edited by Hall prior to his retirement were published chiefly in the Calcutta *Bibliotheca Indica.* See also: D. B. Hall,

The Halls of New England (1883); Joseph Foster, *Alumni Oxonienses,* vol. II (1888); the *Athenaeum,* Feb. 16, 1901; *Harvard Quinquennial Cat. 1636-1915* (1915).] E. W. H.

HALL, FLORENCE MARION HOWE (Aug. 25, 1845-Apr. 10, 1922), author, lecturer, daughter of Dr. Samuel Gridley and Julia (Ward) Howe [*qq.v.*], was born in Boston, at the Perkins Institution for the Blind, of which her father was the founder and director. She attended several private schools and studied at home with private tutors, some of them foreign refugees. Distinguished foreigners frequently visited the Howes and became part of the children's background. Florence and her brothers and sisters played about the earthworks above Boston Harbor, from which Washington's cannon had forced the British out of Boston. Their summers were passed first at Newport, where Longfellow and Dr. Howe rented a house together, then at Lawton's Valley, R. I. During the Civil War, when the United States Naval Academy was at Newport, Lawton's Valley was the scene of many festivities. At this period Florence met David Prescott Hall, a lawyer, whom she married on Nov. 15, 1871. During the five years of her engagement she occupied herself with charitable work in South Boston.

The first six years of her married life were spent in New York City; then the Halls lived for fifteen years in a country home at Scotch Plains, N. J. Four children made expenses so heavy that Mrs. Hall began writing for newspapers and magazines. She was never successful in story writing but found a market for works of the essay type. Her published volumes include: *Social Customs* (1887); *The Correct Thing in Good Society* (1888); *Little Lads and Lassies* (1898); *Laura Bridgman* (1903), in collaboration with her sister Maud Howe Elliott; *Flossy's Play-Days* (1906); *Social Usages at Washington* (1906); *A Handbook of Hospitality for Town and Country* (1909); *Boys, Girls and Manners* (1913); *Julia Ward Howe and the Woman Suffrage Movement* (1913), selections from her mother's speeches and essays, with an introduction; *Good Form for All Occasions* (1914); *Julia Ward Howe* (1915), with her sisters Laura E. Richards and Maud Howe Elliott; *A-B-C of Correct Speech and the Art of Conversation* (1916); *The Story of the Battle Hymn of the Republic* (1916); *Memories Grave and Gay* (1918); *Manners for Boys and Girls* (1920). Her literary work involved considerable research on a small scale. Her guides to manners and customs are clearly written, with some humor and agreeable didacticism.

In 1893 the Halls moved to Plainfield, N. J., and Mrs. Hall became active in club and suffrage work, in connection with which she often lectured. She was at different times chairman of correspondence for New Jersey of the General Federation of Women's Clubs, vice-president, director, and chairman of the department of education of the New Jersey State Federation of Women's Clubs, president of the New Jersey Woman Suffrage Association, president of the Plainfield Alliance of Unitarian Women, regent of the Plainfield Continental Chapter, Daughters of the American Revolution, leader in the Woman Suffrage party for the 12th Assembly District of Manhattan, and president of the Newport County, R. I., Women's Republican Club. In 1902 she made her first trip to Europe. After the death of her husband in 1907 she made her home with her daughter in a studio apartment in Washington Square, New York, until the daughter's marriage, after which she went to live with her youngest son at High Bridge, N. J., where she died.

[*Memories Grave and Gay,* mentioned above; *Who's Who in America,* 1922-23; Julia Ward Howe, *Reminiscences* (1899); *Letters and Journals of Samuel Gridley Howe* (2 vols., 1906-09), ed. by Laura E. Richards; *N. Y. Tribune* and *N. Y. Times,* Apr. 11, 1922; certain information from Samuel Prescott Hall, Esq., of Washington, D. C., a son of Mrs. Hall.] S. G. B.

HALL, GEORGE HENRY (Sept. 21, 1825-Feb. 17, 1913), painter, was the eldest child of Patten Hall of Manchester, N. H., and his wife, Parthenia Coburn of Dracut, Mass. He was a descendant of Thomas and Mary (Dickey) Hall, emigrants from the north of Ireland who settled in Londonderry, N. H., in the first quarter of the eighteenth century. Patten Hall, a prosperous lumber dealer, died in 1829 and shortly afterward his widow with her three children moved from Manchester to Boston (Dickey, *post*). There George Henry received his education in the public schools. He began to paint as early as 1842. His self-portrait, in the Brooklyn Museum, is dated 1845 (letter, Jan. 25, 1930, from Florence Sparks, Secretary of the Department of Fine Arts). In 1846-47 his name first appeared in the Boston Directory, where he was listed as "artist, 23 Tremont Temple." He was then one of thirty-eight painters practising in Boston. In 1849 he went to Dusseldorf for a year (Clement and Hutton, *post*), and spent some time thereafter at Paris and at Rome, where he may have painted "The Roman Wine Cart." In the early fifties he returned to the United States and settled in New York. He was elected an associate member of the National Academy of Design in 1853. His resignation in 1855 was doubtless due to his again taking up residence abroad. In 1860 he visited Spain where he painted scenes from Spanish rural life. In 1863 he was reëlected an associate member of the Academy and in 1868 a full member. He became one of the most regular exhibitors at the Academy exhibitions, sending such canvases as "Group of Spanish Children" (1868); "Thursday Fair of Seville" (1869); "Young Lady of Seville and her Duenna" (1870). His mode was that of the episodical painting of the middle-nineteenth century. In pursuit of his favorite subjects he painted in Italy in 1872, in Egypt in 1875. A life-long bachelor, he was free to come and go; he lived abroad in the years 1888–91 and again in 1895, this being probably his last visit to Europe (letter from Grace W. Curran, librarian of the National Academy of Design). He exhibited at the National Academy almost continuously down to 1908 when his name appeared for the last time in an Academy catalogue. By his will, after the death of his chief beneficiary, $15,000 of his estate was to go to Columbia University. At the Academy Centennial Exhibition in 1925, he was represented by one painting, a still-life. A popular and successful painter in his early years, he lived to see a vogue of newer methods and viewpoints in art.

[Hall was one of six deceased members of the National Academy eulogized with brief characterization of the services of each by President John W. Alexander at the annual meeting, May 14, 1913 (Minutes of the Nat. Acad. of Design). See C. E. Clement and Laurence Hutton, *Artists of the Nineteenth Century and Their Works* (1885); T. S. Cumming, *Hist. Annals of the Nat. Acad. of Design* (1865), p. 279; *Academy Sketches,* by "Nemo," descriptive of the National Academy exhibition of 1877; H. T. Tuckerman, *Book of the Artists* (1867), p. 482; John Dickey, *Geneal. of the Dickey Family* (1898), p. 234; *Who's Who in America,* 1906–07; *Am. Art Annual,* vol. XI (1914); *Boston Transcript,* Feb. 19, 1913; *N. Y. Times,* Feb. 19, Apr. 18, 1913.] F. W. C.

HALL, GRANVILLE STANLEY (Feb. 1, 1844–Apr. 24, 1924), psychologist, philosopher, educator, was born in Ashfield, Mass., the son of Granville Bascom and Abigail (Beals) Hall and a descendant of John Hall who came from England to Charlestown, Mass., in 1630 and later settled at Yarmouth. On the paternal side his ancestry could be traced to William Brewster and on the maternal, to John Alden. The childhood environment was that of healthy country life, which the boy enjoyed heartily, learning the ways of the animal world around him and mastering the rudiments of the many trades which the farmer of that day was compelled to practise in order to eke out a livelihood. He was strong, sturdy, obstinate, and insatiably curious. The home surroundings were religious and intelligent. The mother was one of the early graduates of the Albany Female Academy, and the father through education, travel, and reading was superior to his economic position.

Stanley Hall, as he was called throughout life in his own family, went rapidly through the district schools, spent a brief period at the Ashfield Academy, and after a year at Williston Academy, at Easthampton, entered Williams College in 1863. Here his fine presence and dominating personality almost immediately found recognition in spite of his extreme poverty. He associated with Hamilton Wright Mabie and Francis Lynde Stetson [*qq.v.*] and completed with credit if not with distinction the curriculum of the college but obtained the more important part of his education from a varied course of reading, mostly in literature and philosophy, which he undertook as a member of a literary club. Young Hall, while admiring the somewhat masterful methods of Mark Hopkins, did not fall under his spell but became an adherent of John Bascom [*q.v.*], who represented a more progressive tendency in philosophy.

His immediate family was profoundly religious, and it was with the purpose of entering the ministry that Hall went to college. Evidently his inquisitive and skeptical tendency had already shown itself, for when in his sophomore year, under the influence of a general college revival, he professed conversion, there was almost ecstatic joy at home. His letters on this occasion, while graphic, are quite conventional, and it is plain that this experience did not mean any considerable change in his development. From this time on he led a Bible class in a neighboring manufacturing village and enrolled among those specifically preparing for the ministry. Upon graduation in 1867 he entered Union Theological Seminary in New York, and taught in a girls' private school to help pay his way. At the seminary he continued to show skeptical tendencies, and after a frank talk with Henry Ward Beecher he decided to leave the seminary and embarked for Germany. He arrived at Bonn in the summer of 1868 and spent more than two years learning German, studying German life, and coming into close contact with philosophical and theological leaders, more particularly with Dorner, the theologian, and Trendelenburg, the philosopher. He found the unconventionality of the students, the *Gemüthlichkeit* of the people, most congenial after the inhibited life of his childhood and youth.

In 1871 he returned to New York heavily in debt, to find that young men trained in German philosophy were not wanted in American colleges. After spending the next year completing his theological course and tutoring in the family of Jesse Seligman, he finally in 1872 secured a position in Antioch College. Here for four years he threw himself with great zest into his work, teaching literature and philosophy, delivering lectures, coaching plays, and preaching in Unitarian churches. He also cultivated close relations with the young Hegelians, led by William T. Harris, at St. Louis, Mo. The publication in 1874 of Wilhelm Wundt's *Grundzüge der Physiologischen Psychologie* aroused him to the possibilities of psychology. He resigned his position at Antioch in 1876 and after two years as an English instructor at Harvard, at the end of which he took his Ph.D. degree, in 1878 he again sailed for Germany, this time confining himself largely to research with Helmholtz in physics, Ludwig in physiology, and Wundt in experimental psychology.

Upon his return to America in 1880 there followed another period of disappointment and discouragement. After a few months, however, he was asked to give a course on pedagogy at Harvard, which was a marked success. A little later there came an opening at the Johns Hopkins University. In 1882 Hall was given a special lectureship and granted a thousand dollars for the establishment of a psychological laboratory. In 1883 he was made professor of psychology and pedagogics. Although William James at Harvard had already organized laboratory work in psycho-physics, the new chair at Johns Hopkins almost from the beginning took the lead in this field. Hall continued his researches in experimental psychology and gathered about him a group of young men—James McKeen Cattell, John Dewey, Joseph Jastrow, Edmund Clark Sanford, and others—many of whom contributed to the development of the sciences in America. In 1887 he founded the *American Journal of Psychology*. Another achievement was the formation in 1891 of the American Psychological Association, of which Hall became the first president.

Hall also engaged in educational writing and criticism. His first study, *The Contents of Children's Minds,* was published in 1883. He followed it with two bibliographical contributions dealing with history and reading and attracted wide attention by an article on "The Moral and Religious Training of Children" in the *Princeton Review* for January 1882. By 1888 he had established himself as perhaps the foremost educational critic in the country, particularly in the field of secondary and higher education. It was this reputation that led to his selection as president of the new foundation established by Jonas Gilman Clark [*q.v.*] at Worcester, Mass.

Clark's original intention was to found another New England college, but Hall persuaded him to establish a very different type of institution, a university devoted to scientific research along the lines embodied by Gilman in the Johns Hopkins, but modeled even more closely than that institution on the German type.

After a year in Europe, Hall went to Worcester and opened the new institution on Oct. 2, 1889. The original faculty of Clark University, while small, contained several men of genius. For a brief period the university was received with wide acclaim and accomplished work of a high order. Very soon, however, misunderstandings arose. The chief cause of the dissension, which almost wrecked the institution, was that Clark never told Hall or the board of trustees, to whom he made over the institution, the exact size of his fortune or his ultimate purposes concerning it. It was assumed that his wealth was comparable to that of Leland Stanford. Consequently all the early plans, discussions, and promises were on a scale which it was impossible to realize afterward. Clark, a business man accustomed to autocratic control, interfered frequently with the details of administration on the material side, thus bringing himself into conflict with the faculty. The new president found himself in a difficult situation, which was made worse by the attacks of the local paper on the supposed practice of vivisection in the biology department. The founder, instead of having the local support and approbation which he had counted upon, became a target for popular criticism. His enthusiasm cooled, and he was inclined to blame the new president for the resulting state of affairs and wished to return to his earlier ideal of a men's college. The board of trustees, however, headed by George Frisbie Hoar, senior senator from Massachusetts, irritated by the founder's lack of confidence in them, stood unanimously by the president. Consequently the annual allowance of money, which the founder had generously given in the first two years over and above the regular endowment fund, became smaller and smaller. The faculty grew discontented, and a crisis was prevented only by the intervention of William Rainey Harper [*q.v.*], who arranged in 1892 to take over the larger part of the staff for the new University of Chicago.

From this date the university lived on the

interest of the endowment already given by the founder, which amounted to only $28,000 a year. The departments continued were mathematics, physics, chemistry, biology, and psychology and education. After Clark's death on May 23, 1900, it was found that he had provided for the establishment, with a separate president, of Clark College, and that his total estate was much smaller than had been surmised. The financial condition of the university was, however, much alleviated. The president continued to have the full support of the board of trustees and resigned his position in 1919 at the age of seventy-five.

Hall was never regarded by his contemporaries as an administrator. His chief interests were in other directions, yet in a trying situation he exhibited many of the qualities of a leader—always correct and courteous in his attitude toward the founder, silent as to the difficulties of the institution, and sure of his own policy. The members of the board of trustees alone understood the situation, and supported him from first to last unanimously. What he might have done if the foundation had realized its original scope one cannot say, but it is probable that he would have shown himself an educational administrator of a high order.

During this same period of stress and strain Hall was devoting himself to the new child-study movement, which his papers previously mentioned had inaugurated. Interest in this aspect of psychology came to focus in a conference on experimental psychology in education at the Columbian Exposition in Chicago in 1893. Hall presided, delivered the opening address, and gathered together from all over the country the men who were interested in the new work. For the next fifteen years this child-study movement was one of the two or three most prominent theoretical interests in teaching circles. Hall's leadership was due largely to his wide and thorough training, to his ability as a public speaker, and to his indefatigable energy in answering thousands of letters and in serving on innumerable committees. A new journal, the *Pedagogical Seminary,* which he founded in 1891, became the organ of the movement. More and more the advanced students who came to Clark specialized in this field. Popular interest was intense; societies for the promotion of child-study were organized in two or three states. Popular magazines were filled with articles, many of them sentimental, some of them silly, but a tribute none the less to the vital interest in the subject.

His own interest culminated in the publication in 1904 of *Adolescence, Its Psychology and Its Relation to Physiology, Anthropology, Sociology, Sex, Crime, Religion and Education.* This large two-volume work, which contained digests of all the literature of the subject, was a vast collection of material in all stages of assimilation bound together by certain fundamental principles or points of view of the author. Portions of the work were suggestive and penetrating; many passages had unusual literary power and appeal. Because of the size of the book and its special vocabulary (Hall had coined more than three hundred new words) the author had considerable difficulty in finding a publisher. However, when once published, more than 25,000 copies were sold in America. Some of the more usable portions were republished in a smaller work entitled *Youth; Its Education, Regimen and Hygiene* (1906), which was largely used in colleges and normal schools.

Beginning in 1893 Hall returned to the classroom as head of the department of psychology. For many years he lectured from six to eight hours a week on a wide range of subjects. Among them were the emotions, genetic psychology, abnormal psychology, adolescence, and educational problems. He also covered the history of philosophy in a three-year cycle, in the first year's work devoting his time largely to the Greeks. Much attention was given to Plato. His attitude toward medieval and much of modern philosophy was skeptical. Hall had little sympathy with the theory of knowledge, regarding it as a mere attempt to obfuscate knowledge. Of modern philosophers he had the least sympathy with Hegel and the most with men like Comte and Spencer, although he was in no sense a disciple of either. He interpreted Schopenhauer sympathetically. As an academic lecturer he was uneven, many of the aspects of the subject with which he had slight sympathy being passed over inadequately. On the other hand, no lecturer could be clearer or more forceful or richer in suggestions in dealing with the topics which suited his own view of life. His great strength as an academic teacher came out in his seminar, which for years met every Monday evening during the academic term. As a popular lecturer to teachers' gatherings and at summer schools he was at his best; free from unction, he carried his large mass of learning easily, frequently tantalizing his audience with allusions far beyond their comprehension but at the same time able in his summaries and conclusions to make the drift of his argument plain.

The publication of *Educational Problems* (2 vols., 1911) marks a definite return of his interest from education to psychology. Previously he had shown a strong interest in the work of

Freud and Pavalov. As a phase of this renewed interest in psychology came his *Founders of Modern Psychology* (1912), in which the term psychology is interpreted generously. The thinkers dealt with are Zeller, Lotze, Fechner, Von Hartmann, Von Helmholtz, and Wundt. The discussion deals as much with philosophy as psychology. In 1917 came the publication of one of his great major interests in the two volumes on *Jesus, the Christ, in the Light of Psychology*. This work, published during the European War, never reached the popularity of some of his other books, but it aroused great discussion. Like the other volumes it is largely made up of digests and discussions of technical literature. Like them, however, it contains many suggestions embodying his fundamental point of view. *Morale the Supreme Standard in Life and Conduct* (1920), was the result of his interest in war activities; and his final contribution in this field, *Senescence: The Last Half of Life* (1922), is also an embodiment of his fundamental point of view, written in his way, but with a breadth and elevation characteristic of his old age.

Retiring from the presidency of Clark University in 1919, he devoted his time to several literary and scientific projects, maintained his connection with his old friends, and lectured occasionally. His chief works of this period were his *Recreations of a Psychologist* (1920) and his autobiography, *Life and Confessions of a Psychologist* (1923), a book of great interest, sometimes inaccurate on minor points, but in two chapters on psychology and education containing excellent summaries of his own contribution and of his evaluation of the movements of his time. After his death it was discovered that he had accumulated a considerable fortune, a large part of which was left to establish a professorship of genetic psychology at Clark University.

Hall was a man of strong physique and great energy. He frequently worked twelve or fourteen hours a day. He rejoiced in physical achievement and mastered many forms of mechanical skill. He was fond of hill climbing. In the physical world as in the mental he had a strong bent toward exploration and experimentation. In both cases he combined boldness with New England caution. Frequently he would throw out startling suggestions, pointing toward the most revolutionary conclusions, but at the same time he almost invariably left a window open behind him through which he might escape from responsibility for the ideas expressed. He was married to Cornelia Fisher of Cincinnati in September 1879 while in Germany. Two children were born to this marriage, Robert Granville Hall and Julia Fisher Hall. Mrs. Hall died in 1890, and in 1899 he married Florence E. Smith of Newton, Mass., who survived him.

His original point of view is better described in a book by George E. Partridge, *Genetic Philosophy of Education* (1912), than in any work of his own. His place in the development of American psychology is much disputed. In education he made a profound impression on his own generation. Because of his personality and of his ideas he influenced the schools of the country more profoundly than any other thinkers except William Torrey Harris and John Dewey. His influence on education extended to foreign countries and at the present time is particularly strong in England.

[Hall left a great abundance of biographical material, including early essays, diaries, notes, and thousands of letters. A selection from these has been prepared for publication by H. D. Sheldon. See also: L. N. Wilson, *G. Stanley Hall, A Sketch* (1914); *G. Stanley Hall Memorial Vol.* (Clark Univ., 1925); E. L. Thorndike, *Biog. Memoir of Granville Stanley Hall 1846–1924* (1928); Lorine Pruette, *G. Stanley Hall: A Biog. of a Mind* (1926).]

H. D. S.

HALL, HAZEL (Feb. 7, 1886–May 11, 1924), poet, daughter of Montgomery George and May Hoppin (Garland) Hall, was born in St. Paul, Minn. When she was a small child, however, her parents moved to Portland, Ore. At the age of twelve she lost the use of her legs, and the remainder of her comparatively short life was spent chiefly in a wheel-chair, her time occupied in sewing. Highly imaginative and emotional, she found expression in the writing of verse, none of which was published until she was thirty. Thereafter she was a frequent contributor to some of the leading periodicals of the country. For a group of needlework poems called "Repetitions," published in May 1921, she received the Young Poet's Prize offered by *Poetry*. She died in Portland before completing her thirty-eighth year.

Her poems are collected in three volumes. The first of these, *Curtains,* appeared in 1921; the second, *Walkers,* in 1923; and the last, *Cry of Time,* after her death, in 1928. The work of one shut in, they are necessarily narrow in range and predominantly subjective. "Brown window-sill," she writes, "you hold my all of skies," and of the walls of her home, "my days are bound within your hold." Curtaining her window with "filmy seeming," and giving free play to her imagination as she plied her needle, she put into song her dreams and fancies. The footsteps of passersby, the linen she monogrammed for a bride, the bishop's cuff she pleated, enabling him to raise his hand in better prayer, were her themes. These, however, and nature, too, when she turned to it, were essentially means by which she expressed the state of her own soul. With noticeable frequency, especially in *Cry of Time,* owing no doubt to physical causes, her subjects are frustration, neglect, grief, the sleep of forgetfulness, and death. She had a genuine, though not strong, lyrical gift, which raised her above the level of the mere versifier. The appeal of her poetry is in a song-like melody and in the moods that it portrays rather than in its thought.

[*Cry of Time* contains an introduction with some biographical material by Louise T. Nicholl. See also *Oregon Daily Journal* and *Morning Oregonion,* both of Portland, May 12, 1924; *Poetry,* July 1924; *Overland Monthly,* Aug. 1924; *Bookman,* Feb. 1929; *Books* (*N. Y. Herald Tribune*), Mar. 3, 1929. Certain information has been supplied by Miss Ruth Hall of Portland, a sister of Hazel Hall.] H. E. S.

HALL, HENRY BRYAN (Mar. 11, 1808–Apr. 25, 1884), engraver, portrait painter, was the head of a family of British-born engravers who came to the United States about the middle of the nineteenth century. He was born in London. Benjamin Smith, one of the engravers of Boydell's *Shakespeare Gallery,* taught him the use of the burin when the boy was articled to him at fourteen. Later Hall helped on plates after Sir Thomas Lawrence, under tutelage of the painter's chosen engraver, Henry Meyer. His first employment after finishing his apprenticeship was with H. T. Ryall, historical engraver to the Crown, with whom he worked four years executing the portrait work in the "Coronation of Queen Victoria," from the crowded canvas by Sir George Hayter. Self-taught, possibly, by his close study of the portrait canvases he engraved, he developed during his London career considerable ability as a portrait painter. He had notable sitters, among them Napoleon III. Later, in America, he painted two brother artists, Thomas Sully and Charles Loring Elliott. He also painted miniatures on ivory.

Hall married in England and lived in a series of dull London suburbs—Stepney Holloway, Camden Town—where several children were born to him. In 1850 he emigrated to America with his namesake, leaving the rest of the family to follow within the year. He came well-introduced, and on his arrival in New York had no difficulty in securing ample commissions for portrait engraving for various publishers. He had already taught his younger brother, George R. Hall (who followed him to America), to engrave, and gradually initiated three of his sons and his daughter Alice into the art, in which they had some individual success. At the close of the Civil War, when the rage for likenesses of soldier heroes inaugurated, according to Weitenkampf (*post,* p. 102), a period of "rank commercialism," Hall went into business with his sons, Henry Bryan Hall, Jr., Alfred Bryan Hall, and Charles B. Hall. The firm, known as H. B. Hall & Sons, had a large business in the engraving and publishing of portraits. After the death of the senior member in 1884, the firm was continued as H. B. Hall Sons and from 1899 was carried on by Charles B. Hall alone.

Hall devoted his personal skill largely to the engraving and etching of portraits of American historical personages, Revolutionary heroes, signers of the Declaration of Independence, many of which were private plates executed for such collectors as Dr. Thomas Addis Emmet [*q.v.*] of New York and Francis S. Hoffman of Philadelphia. Among his best plates were portraits of Washington, of which he engraved not less than twelve, after Trumbull, Stuart, Sharpless, and Peale. Baker cites his self-portrait, done in 1872, as a fine example of his ability as an etcher. He died after a paralytic stroke, in Morrisania, N. Y. His collection of prints and water colors, including many from his own hand, was sold in 1885.

[W. S. Baker, *Am. Engravers and Their Works* (1875); D. M. Stauffer, *Am. Engravers upon Copper and Steel,* vol. I (1907); Frank Weitenkampf, *Am. Graphic Art* (1912); *Catalogue of the Library . . . of . . . Henry B. Anthony. . . . Also the Unique Coll. of Proof Engravings, Water-Colors, etc., of the Celebrated Am. Engraver Henry B. Hall* (1885); *Calendar of the Emmet Coll. of MSS., etc., Relating to Am. Hist.* (N. Y. Pub. Lib., 1900), which lists many of Hall's etchings and engravings; *N. Y. Times* and *N. Y. Tribune,* Apr. 26 and 28, 1884.] M. B. H.

HALL, HILAND (July 20, 1795–Dec. 18, 1885), historian, jurist, and governor of Vermont, descended from John Hall, born in Kent, England, in 1584, who came to New England in 1633 and some five or six years later settled in Hartford, Conn., was born at Bennington, Vt. He was the oldest of the seven children of Nathaniel and Abigail (Hubbard) Hall. His youth was spent on his father's farm in Bennington. He was educated in the common schools of the locality supplemented by one term in the academy at Granville, N. Y., and by private study. He studied law, was admitted to the bar of Bennington County in December 1819, and settled down to the practice of his profession in his native town. He was a representative of his town in the legislature in 1827, clerk of the county court in 1828, and state attorney for the county from 1829 to 1831. In January 1833 he was elected to fill a vacancy in Congress and served till Mar. 3, 1843.

In 1842 he declined to stand for reëlection. During the next decade and a half he filled the offices of state bank commissioner, 1843–46, judge of the supreme court of Vermont, 1846–50, second comptroller of the treasury, 1850–51, and federal land commissioner for California, 1851–54. Up to this time he had been a member of the Whig party, but his anti-slavery principles led him in the middle fifties to identify himself with the rising Republican party. He was a member of the Vermont delegation to the Republican National Convention in 1856, and was nominated as the Republican candidate for governor in 1858. He was elected by a substantial majority, and reëlected for a second term in 1859. At the expiration of his second term as governor he retired from public life, except for a brief service as a member of the famous Peace Convention held on the eve of the Civil War.

Notwithstanding the numerous offices he held, Hall is best known as a historian of his native state. From his early youth history and biography were his favorite studies, and he made the early history of Vermont his special field. In 1859 he became president of the Vermont Historical Society and held the office for six years. Later as chairman of the committee on printing and publication he brought about the publication of the first two volumes of the society's *Proceedings.* In 1868 he published his most important historical work, *The History of Vermont, From Its Discovery to Its Admission into the Union in 1791.* This is an excellent piece of historical research, based upon a careful study of the original documents and showing sound historical scholarship, although the Vermont sympathies of the author are evident in his treatment of New York's claim to jurisdiction over the Vermont settlements. Besides this work, Hall presented a number of carefully prepared papers before various historical societies, and contributed to historical periodicals.

He was married on Oct. 27, 1818, to Dolly Tuttle Davis. They had eight children and lived to celebrate their sixtieth wedding anniversary. Hall died at the home of his son Charles, in Springfield, Mass., in his ninety-first year.

[Two memoirs by Hall's son, Henry D. Hall, in *New-Eng. Hist. and Geneal. Reg.*, Jan. 1887, and in A. M. Hemenway, *Vermont Hist. Gazetteer,* vol. V (1891), pt. III (section relating to Bennington), pp. 83–96; W. H. Crockett, *Vermont,* V (1923), 112–13; M. D. Gilman, *The Bibliog. of Vermont* (1897); D. B. Hall, *The Halls of New England* (1883); *Springfield Daily Republican,* Dec. 19, 1885; *Burlington Free Press and Times,* Dec. 21, 1885.] A. M. K.

HALL, ISAAC HOLLISTER (Dec. 12, 1837–July 2, 1896), Orientalist, descended from John Hall of Coventry, Warwickshire, England, who came to Massachusetts in 1630 and ultimately settled at Yarmouth, was the son of Dr. Edwin and Fanny (Hollister) Hall. He was born at Norwalk, Conn., where his father was pastor of the First Church (Congregational), and lived in that town until 1854, when his father became professor of theology in the seminary at Auburn, N. Y. Isaac graduated from Hamilton College as valedictorian of his class in 1859, and afterward served as tutor there in 1862–63. In 1864 he went to New York, where he took the course of study in the Law Department of Columbia College, graduating in 1865, and practised his profession for the next decade. His was "a queer law office," as a college classmate wrote of him later: "Hall was never seen to read law, but was always poring over some ancient book in some dead language" (Hawley, *post,* p. 21).

It was during this period that George Smith published his remarkable discoveries of Babylonian parallels to the cosmology of Genesis, obtaining among other data the first clews for the decipherment of Cypriote inscriptions. These were followed up by Hall so successfully that he became one of the first to translate an entire Cypriote inscription. This early success determined the interest which was to dominate the remainder of his life. Early in 1875 he established a column headed "Biblical Research" in the New York *Independent* and later in the same year accepted an appointment as instructor in the Syrian Protestant College in Beirut, where he taught until 1877. Here in 1876 he was so fortunate as to discover a Syriac manuscript of the New Testament of about 800 A.D., containing the four Gospels in the Philoxenian version, the Book of the Acts, and several of the Epistles. (See his account of his discovery in the *Journal of the American Oriental Society,* vols. X and XI, 1880, 1885.) This he brought to America upon his return in 1877 and published with three facsimile pages in 1884, also in phototype in the *Williams Manuscript: The Syrian Antilegomena Epistles,* in 1886. From 1877 to 1884 he served as a member of the editorial staff of the *Sunday School Times* published in Philadelphia, meantime so developing his taste for philological and archeological studies as to become an authority on Greek, Phœnician, and Himyaritic inscriptions. The publication of his text of the Syriac New Testament in 1884 established his reputation as "the most thorough Syriac scholar in America." His achievements in the decipherment of Cypriote led to his appointment in that year to a position on the staff of the Metropolitan Museum of Art in New York, assisting Gen. L. P. di Cesnola [*q.v.*] with Greek and Phœnician inscriptions on material in the Cesnola collection. He was appointed curator of the department of sculpture in 1886, in which year he also lectured on New Testament Greek at the Johns Hopkins University, Baltimore—a subject for which his earlier studies in New Testament and Septuagint Greek had fitted him. These had borne fruit in the work entitled *American Greek Testament: A Critical Bibliography of the Greek New Testament as Published in America* (1883).

The most important part of Hall's career was spent in the service of the Metropolitan Museum, where he collaborated with Cesnola in preparing the great illustrated catalogues of Cypriote art. Syriac became more especially his province, however, and in this field he was recognized as the leading American authority, publishing many texts and critical papers, especially in the *Journal of the American Oriental Society* and the *Journal of Biblical Literature.* It was in recognition of these Syriac studies that he was invited to attend the Tercentenary of Dublin University, where the degree of doctor of letters was conferred on him. He also received the honor of the presidency of the American Philological Association, and was vice-president and director of the American Oriental Society, as well as for many years a member of the council of the Society of Biblical Literature and Exegesis. The "Proceedings" of that Society for the year of his death contain a Minute prepared by Dr. William Hayes Ward, which closes with the following judicious tribute: "The careful exactness, as well as the enterprise which characterized Dr. Hall's abundant work, will assure him an honored and permanent record in the annals of American scholarship" (*Journal of Biblical Literature,* vol. XVI, 1897, p. iii). Hall was married on Sept. 5, 1876, to Fannie M. Dederick.

[*The New Schaff-Herzog Encyc. of Religious Knowledge,* vol. V (1909); *Jour. Am. Oriental Soc.,* vol. XVIII (1897), pt. II, p. 145 and, for a partial list of his publications vol. XXI (1902), pt. I; D. B. Hall, *The Halls of New England* (1883); C. A. Hawley, *A Hist. of the Class of '59 of Hamilton Coll.* (1899); L. W. Case, *The Hollister Family of America* (1886); N. Y. *Independent,* July 9, 1896; *N. Y. Times,* July 3, 1896.]

B. W. B.

HALL, JAMES (Aug. 22, 1744–July 25, 1826), clergyman, born in Carlisle, Pa., was the son of James Hall, a Scotch-Irish immigrant who came to America with his father sometime before 1723, and married Prudence Roddy. In 1751 they removed to Fourth Creek in Rowan (now Iredell) County, N. C. In this community of pious Presbyterians, young James Hall frequently heard sermons of missionaries from the Synod of Philadelphia, and was led through their influence into the ministry. He entered the College of New Jersey at Princeton, where he studied theology under Witherspoon, and from which he was graduated in 1774 with distinction. Declining a professorship of mathematics, he returned to North Carolina and was licensed to preach by the Orange Presbytery. In 1776 he accepted a call to the pastorate of Fourth Creek (now Statesville) Church, and two years later was installed as pastor of the united congregations of Fourth Creek, Concord, and Bethany, a parish about thirty miles in length and twenty in width. He resigned the pastorate of the first two in 1790, but continued to serve Bethany until his death in 1826.

During the Revolution, Hall's pastoral labors were frequently interrupted by the war. An ardent patriot, as became a pupil of Witherspoon, he aroused the spirit of independence among his parishioners, and on more than one occasion, during the British invasion, led a company of them into battle, serving as both commander and chaplain. General Greene offered him a brigadier-general's commission, but he declined it. As chaplain he accompanied an expedition against the Cherokee Indians of Georgia and preached to the troops the first gospel sermon ever heard in the Cherokee country. After the Revolution, he was called upon as pastor to combat a lowered moral and spiritual tone that followed in the wake of war, and threw himself into the work with such vigor as to undermine his health. In 1786 he took, with great benefit to his health, a sea voyage from Charleston to Philadelphia to attend the Synod of New York and Philadelphia. There he aided in the organization of the General Assembly of the Presbyterian Church, to which he was subsequently a delegate sixteen times and of which he was moderator in 1803. From 1788 to 1812 he was a regular attendant upon the Synod of the Carolinas and in 1812 was its last moderator. He was active in the organization of the American Bible Society and of the North Carolina Bible Society, and was the first president of the latter.

Dr. Hall's services as a missionary were in such constant demand that in 1790 he resigned the pastorate of Fourth Creek and Concord to give more time to missions. Under commissions of the General Assembly and of the Synod of the Carolinas he performed fourteen long and arduous missions, extending throughout the Carolinas and from Kentucky to Mississippi. In 1800, commissioned by the General Assembly, he established at Natchez the first Protestant mission in the lower Mississippi Valley, of which, in 1801, he published an account in *A Brief History of the Mississippi Territory.* The next year he participated in a great revival which swept over western North Carolina, which he described in *A Narrative of a Most Extraordinary Work of Religion in North Carolina* (1802). Education shared his interest with religion. About 1778 he founded at Bethany an academy called Clio's Nursery. Twenty Presbyterian preachers and many eminent public men were its contributions to the church and the state. Hall sought to promote scientific studies by the establishment at his own home of an Academy of the Sciences, of which he was the director. He was an early patron of the University of North Carolina and was one of the chief promoters of the theological seminary at the College of New Jersey, to which he bequeathed two hundred and fifty acres of land in Tennessee.

Convinced that the responsibilities of a family would hamper his ministerial work, he never married. He was most assiduous in the performance of his pastoral duties, despite the hardships of such service in a frontier community. As a pulpit orator he was distinguished for power rather than eloquence. Above six feet in height, broad-shouldered and muscular, with a massive head and a fine voice, he possessed the physical as well as the intellectual equipment of a great preacher. From early manhood he suffered occasional depressions of mind and spirit, accompanied by a deep conviction of his own sinfulness and of the Divine displeasure, during which times he refrained from his ministerial functions. The last seven years of his life were passed under such a cloud. He was buried in the churchyard at Bethany.

[W. H. Foote, *Sketches of N. C.: Hist. and Biog.* (1846); W. B. Sprague, *Annals Am. Pulpit,* vol. III (1859); Archibald Henderson, "Rev. James Hall, Teacher," *N. C. Teacher,* Jan. 1925; *N. C. Telegraph,* Aug. 11, Oct. 6, 1826, *Raleigh Register,* Aug. 15, 1826.]

R. D. W. C.

HALL, JAMES (Aug. 19, 1793–July 5, 1868), author, jurist, banker, was born at Philadelphia, Pa., the son of John Hall, Revolutionary soldier and member of a family of Maryland planters, and Sarah (Ewing) Hall [*q.v.*], daughter of the Rev. John Ewing [*q.v.*], provost of the University of Pennsylvania. His mother had literary taste and considerable talent, and four of her sons, whose education was largely under her direction, became writers. One, John Elihu [*q.v.*], was for many years editor, and another, Harrison, was publisher of the *Port Folio,* to which she and James and another son, Thomas Mifflin Hall, contributed. James was sent to an academy at twelve, but so disliked school and teachers that he was soon allowed to continue his education at home, where he studied Latin and French and read widely, especially romantic poetry and fiction. He spent two years in a business office, and at eighteen began the study of law, which he interrupted to join the Washington Guards, the first company organized in Philadelphia for service in the War of 1812. In the next year he was made a lieutenant under Winfield Scott. He was in the battles of Chippewa, Lundy's Lane, Niagara, and Fort Erie, and was commended for "brave and meritorious service." At the close of the war in 1815 he was appointed one of five artillery officers to accompany Decatur's expedition against Algiers, but his vessel was too late to be of service. His diary of the trip contains a colorful account of the voyage and of his visit to Gibraltar and Malaga, and many poems. On his return he was stationed at Newport, R. I., and, in 1817, at Pittsburgh, where he had trouble with his superior officer and after a court martial held on Sept. 11, 1817, was cashiered. The President remitted punishment and restored him to his rank. He published his defense in pamphlet form in 1820.

Hall resumed the study of law while in the army, and on being admitted to the bar in 1818 resigned his commission, spent two years mainly in writing and in further study, and in 1820 set out down the Ohio River for Illinois. Self-confident, able, romantic, and ambitious to win distinction, he landed at Shawneetown, then one of the most promising towns in that region. Within twelve years he had contributed in a surprising number of ways to the development of the infant commonwealth. He at once began the practice of law and at the same time became editor and part owner of the *Illinois Gazette.* Small in stature but dignified in bearing, ready and eloquent in speech, he was much in demand as a speaker at public meetings. Within a year he was appointed prosecuting attorney for a circuit that included nine counties, an immense raw and lawless area extending from the Ohio to the Mississippi. After four years of vigorous and effective service he was elected circuit judge for the same number of counties. As prosecutor he displayed energy and courage in attempting to rid the region of the organized gangs of horse thieves, counterfeiters, murderers, and "regulators" which infested it, and he was a just and able judge.

Following the abolition of the circuit system

in 1828, he was appointed state treasurer and moved to Vandalia, the state capital, where he spent perhaps the most active years of his career. He reorganized the financial system of the state, and was a leader in the state agricultural society, first president of the state antiquarian society, officer in the state Bible society, vice-president, with Governor Coles, of the state lyceum, and a trustee of Illinois College. His last address in Illinois, on education, was the principal feature of the first meeting held to plan a state system of free public schools. Meanwhile, he was editor, 1829–32, of the *Illinois Intelligencer,* a leading paper at the state capital, and in 1830 established the *Illinois Monthly Magazine,* the first literary periodical west of Ohio. To this journal he contributed nearly half the contents.

His first wife, Mary Harrison Posey of Henderson County, Ky., whom he had married in 1823, the grand-daughter of Gen. Thomas Posey and of Washington's "charming cousin, the beautiful Miss Thornton," died in 1832; his term as treasurer ended, and early in 1833 he moved to Cincinnati, where he spent the rest of his life. His second wife was Mary Louisa (Anderson) Alexander, a widow, whom he married on Sept. 3, 1839. For two years he edited the *Western Monthly Magazine,* as successor of the *Illinois Monthly Magazine.* It lost most of its subscribers in 1835 because of his vigorous defense of Catholics (May–June 1835) against Lyman Beecher's *A Plea for the West* (1835), and Hall withdrew from the editorship to become cashier of the Commercial Bank. In 1853 he became president of a reorganized bank of the same name.

Always an indefatigable writer of both prose and verse, Hall is remembered chiefly as one of the most important recorders and interpreters of pioneer history, life, and legend in Illinois and the Ohio Valley. He said that the sole intention even of his tales was to convey accurate descriptions of the scenery and population of the country. He was a close and discriminating observer, with a clear and vivid though often sentimental and self-conscious style. He was, moreover, a born controversialist, and much of the material which streamed from his pen to the newspapers and magazines was attack or defense in political, social, or literary debate. Before his removal to Cincinnati, especially while riding his circuit, his life was full of romantic and dangerous adventure. On his way down the Ohio to Shawneetown he wrote a series of letters, published in the *Port Folio* (July 1821–May 1822) and in the *Illinois Gazette.* These, with some additions, were published in book form as *Letters from the West* (London, 1828). Other works by Hall include: *Legends of the West* (1832); *The Soldier's Bride and Other Tales* (1833); *Sketches of History, Life, and Manners in the West* (vol. I, 1834, vols. I and II, 1835); *Statistics of the West at the Close of the Year 1836* (1836, later editions published as *Notes on the Western States, Containing Descriptive Sketches of Their Soil, Climate, Resources and Scenery*); *History of the Indian Tribes of North America, with Biographical Sketches and Anecdotes of Their Principal Chiefs* (3 vols., folio, richly illustrated, vol. I, 1836, 1838; vol. II, 1842, vol. III, 1884), prepared in collaboration with Thomas L. McKenney, with Hall writing most of the text. Of these works probably the most valuable are the *Legends of the West* and the *Sketches of History, Life and Manners.* These and several other titles were very popular, and were published in many editions.

[The best account of Hall, by J. F. Meline, appeared in the *Cincinnati Commercial,* Oct. 16, 1868. See also: W. H. Venable, *Beginnings of Literary Culture in the Ohio Valley* (1891); R. L. Rusk, *The Lit. of the Middle Western Frontier* (1925); *Nation* (N. Y.), Nov. 12, 1868; Esther Shultz, "James Hall in Shawneetown," *Ill. State Hist. Soc. Jour.,* Oct. 1929, and "James Hall in Vandalia," *Ibid.,* Apr. 1930; H. W. Beckwith, *The Land of the Illini*; Davis L. James, "Judge James Hall," *Ohio Archeol. and Hist. Quart.,* Oct. 1909, with a fairly complete bibliography; F. W. Scott, *Newspapers and Periodicals of Ill. 1814–79* (1910); manuscript diary of trip to the Mediterranean in the possession of Hall's son in 1908, when it was seen by the writer; *Trial and Defence of First Lieut. James Hall* (1820); preface to *Legends of the West* (rev. ed., 1853); obituaries in *Cincinnati Commercial,* July 6, 1868, and *Cincinnati Gazette,* July 7, 1868.]

F. W. S.

HALL, JAMES (Sept. 12, 1811–Aug. 7, 1898), geologist and paleontologist, was born of English parentage in Hingham, Mass. He was the eldest son of James and Susanna (Dourdain) Hall, who during their long voyage to America sometime in the first decade of the nineteenth century improved the opportunity for falling in love, and were married soon after reaching Boston. The family was poor and James's education was gained mainly at the public schools. With the aid of private instruction from a friendly young school-master he was fitted for the Rensselaer School (now Rensselaer Polytechnic Institute) at Troy, N. Y., whence he was graduated in 1832. Amos Eaton [*q.v.*], senior professor at the school, was then at his best, arousing an enthusiasm for natural science in all with whom he came in contact. That in the vigorous and youthful Hall he should have discovered an apt and favorite pupil was inevitable. Ebenezer Emmons [*q.v.*], later to play an important part in American geology, was at the school as an instructor, and the summer months of both Hall and Emmons were devoted to field excursions extending as far south as the Coal Measures of Pennsylvania. Almost without funds, but overflowing with vigor and determination, Hall spent the summer immediately after his graduation studying the geology of the Helderberg Mountains southwest of Albany, and returned in the fall to Troy with no definite prospect for the future. Eaton found him a temporary position in the library, however, and brought him to the attention of "the Albany Patroon," Stephen Van Rensselaer, through whose influence he later received an appointment to a subordinate position on the newly organized geological survey of the state. Here he was for a time assistant to Ebenezer Emmons, but the arrangement was unsatisfactory to both men and there quickly developed between them the mutual antipathy which lasted throughout their lives, to their own detriment and that of the cause for which they labored. Upon the resignation of Timothy Conrad, to whom had been assigned the fourth district, Hall was relegated to his place. This particular district had by universal consent come to be regarded as the least interesting of the four into which the state had been divided; nevertheless, through pluck, energy, and ability to see things correctly, Hall produced a report second to none, one which has become a classic in geological literature (*Geology of New York: Part IV, Comprising the Survey of the Fourth Geological District,* 1843). Although it had been expected that the survey would be brought to a close in 1838, Hall and Emmons were given extensions until 1843 in order to complete their work. (See Merrill, *post,* pp. 331–33.) In this year Hall was commissioned to prepare a report on the paleontology of the state, a task in which he was engaged for more than fifty years (*New York State Natural History Survey: Paleontology,* 8 vols. in 13, 1847–94), and from this time until his death he was practically master of the paleontological field and resented most fiercely any intrusion upon his domain. In 1855–58 he was also state geologist of Iowa and during 1857–60, of Wisconsin as well. In both cases there arose serious disagreements between him and the state authorities which interfered with the satisfactory conclusion of the work. He was appointed director of the New York State Museum in 1866 and, in 1893, to the position of state geologist, which was created especially for him.

Hall's lifework lay almost wholly in the domain of stratigraphic geology and invertebrate paleontology. As to its value there can be no question. "No man had caught and interpreted the meaning of the stratigraphic record as he did in his great volume of 1843," wrote John M. Clarke (*post,* p. 549). In but one instance did he break into the dynamic field, that one in a paper on sedimentation and mountain making ("Contributions to the Geological History of the North American Continent," read 1857, published in *Proceedings of the American Association for the Advancement of Science, 1882,* 1883). But for him, wrote Dana, "the geological history of the North American Continent could not have been written" (quoted by Clarke, *post,* p. 551). His influence was world-wide and became especially powerful through his habit of giving employment as assistants in his laboratory to younger men who ultimately themselves rose to distinction. Among those who came thus under his influence were Charles Emerson Beecher, John Mason Clarke [*qq.v.*], C. S. Prosser, Charles Schuchert, and C. D. Walcott. His bibliography is among the largest of the world's men of science; it comprises not less than 10,000 printed pages and is exceeded, if at all, only by that of the celebrated Bohemian geologist, Barrande.

The predominating features of Hall's mental make-up were self-reliance and determination to succeed at all costs. When appropriations failed, as they sometimes did, he carried on his surveys at his own expense. Knowing what he wanted, he went after it; and there was no turning him aside. He was given to occasional outbreaks of almost childish jealousy; made many enemies, and was continually waging bitter wordy wars, but though repeatedly beaten he could not be downed. His vices were those of the strong and self-reliant. He was at once the most admired and the most disliked among all American workers. Hall's portrait in middle life by no means belies his record. It is that of a strong, forceful man whose path it was not safe to cross. In later life, with snow-white beard and hair, his appearance was benign. He was of strong physique and, though given to many complaints of ill health, lived to attend and experience without harm all the discomforts of the Russian Geological Congress in 1897, when he was eighty-six, but died suddenly the following year, in the midst of his labors.

It was one of Hall's peculiarities that he employed no amanuensis, but wrote out his correspondence in a large sprawling hand, with frequent erasures and blottings, then copied it, keeping the original draft for his own record. Nevertheless, he wrote profusely and was apparently at no time too busy to reply to any intelligent and well-meaning correspondent. His work received prompt and widespread recognition. He received two honorary degrees, the Wollaston medal of the Geological Society of London in 1858, the Walker prize of the Boston Society of Natural History in 1884, and the Hayden medal from the Academy of Natural Sciences of Philadelphia in 1890. He was first president of the Geological Society of America; vice-president of the International Congress of Geologists at Paris in 1878, at Bologna in 1881, and at Berlin in 1885, and was a charter member of the National Academy of Sciences.

He was married in 1838 to Sarah Aiken, daughter of John Aiken of Troy, and at that time joined the Catholic Church. Later he ceased to be a communicant. Differences in religious views led to other differences, and he built a separate house for his wife and their four children. He was still thus partially estranged from his family at the time of his death.

[The materials for this sketch are compiled in part from personal recollections but largely from J. M. Clarke, *James Hall of Albany, Geologist and Paleontologist* (1921), and a memoir by J. J. Stevenson in *Bull. Geol. Soc. of America*, vol. X (1899), containing full bibliography of Hall's publications. See also G. P. Merrill, *Contributions to a Hist. of Am. Geol. and Nat. Hist. Surveys* (1920); J. M. Nickles, *Geol. Lit. on North America* (1924), Bull. 746, U. S. Geol. Survey; *Albany Evening Jour.*, Aug. 8, 1898; *N. Y. Times*, Aug. 9, 1898.] G. P. M.

HALL, JOHN (July 31, 1829–Sept. 17, 1898), Presbyterian clergyman, eldest child of William and Rachel (McGowan) Hall, was born in County Armagh, Ireland. His father was a farmer, a man of scrupulous honor, an elder in the Presbyterian Church, and both parents were earnestly religious. There were eight other children in the family. The boy attended the village school, then a classical school some miles distant, and at twelve entered the college at Belfast, graduating in arts in 1846, and in theology in 1849. He helped support himself by teaching in a girls' school. A tide of deep religious feeling was flowing both in Scotland and among the Scotch-Irish in Ulster. Young Hall came under the influence of Dr. Henry Cooke, the leader of the Irish Presbyterian Church, popularly known as "the Cock of the North," and accepted cordially his slightly modified Calvinism with a strict theory of Biblical inspiration—a theology which was the basis of his message ever after. The divinity of that age and place was polemical: Presbyterians battled with Romanism, and with the High Church wing of Episcopacy in the Church of Ireland. John Hall became a life-long militant, evangelical Protestant.

Upon completing his theological course, he was sent as a missionary to Connaught, and served among a wild and poverty-stricken people as school-teacher, pastor, and itinerant preacher. Finding drink an economic and moral menace, he became an ardent advocate of temperance. His reputation as a preacher spread rapidly, and in 1852 he was called to the First Church of Armagh, a leading congregation in North Ireland. In the same year he married a young widow, Mrs. Emily (Bolton) Irwin, the mother of three little boys, and of this marriage there were three sons and one daughter. In Armagh, Hall exercised a vast influence. His congregation, composed both of townsfolk and of farmers from the surrounding district, found him a compelling and moving preacher and a pastor of amazing zeal and fidelity. His tall and commanding presence, his soft rich voice, his solemn and tender manner, his aptness in homely illustration, his conviction of the truth of his gospel, and his utter devotion to his task, made him a force. He toiled indefatigably, writing in prose and verse for various papers, speaking on behalf of temperance and missions, and was recognized as an outstanding figure in the Irish pulpit. In 1858 he was called to Dublin as colleague to Dr. Kirkpatrick in Mary's Abbey, the chief Presbyterian Church at the capital. His ministry drew a large congregation and led to the erection of a new edifice in Rutland Square. He founded and edited a monthly paper, the *Evangelical Witness,* and threw himself into the cause of national unsectarian education. In this he was ahead of most of the leaders of the Irish Presbyterian Church. The government in 1860 appointed him one of the three commissioners of education.

In 1867 he was sent to the United States on a deputation from the Irish Church, and this visit led to his call to the Fifth Avenue Presbyterian Church, New York City, then located at Nineteenth Street and Fifth Avenue. The new minister at once became a foremost figure in the religious life of the country. Beecher spoke of him as "the young Irishman with the golden mouth." He drew crowded congregations Sunday morning and afternoon, and usually preached in some other pulpit at night. He wrote for the *New York Ledger,* edited by his friend and supporter Robert Bonner, and for many religious publications. He continued to serve the cause of education by becoming chancellor of the University of the City of New York (1881–91), then in a precarious plight. He served on many boards, lectured at various colleges, and was sought after to preach on special occasions. With these numerous outside activities he devoted himself to his own people, and for thirty years he built up and held the largest Protestant congregation in the city. To accommodate this company of many hundreds a new church was built at Fifth Avenue and Fifty-fifth Street. His people venerated him with awed affection. He never modified the message of his earliest ministry. The Bible was God's Word and the Shorter Catechism was "an excellent compendium of scriptural truth." He applied it with skill and sympathy to men's needs. He hated sensationalism; he relied little on organization; he had no professional helpers—not even a secretary; but by his preaching and pastoral visitation he drew in, trained in his view of the Christian life, and permanently molded the most influential congregation in the New York of that time. He died while on a visit to Ireland, at Bangor, County Down.

[T. C. Hall, *John Hall, Pastor and Preacher* (1901), a biography by his son, contains all the important facts. His Lyman Beecher lectures to the Yale Divinity School, 1874–75, *God's Word Through Preaching* (1875), give his theory of preaching. See also H. W. Jessup, *Hist. of the Fifth Ave. Presbyt. Ch.* (1909); *Universities and Their Sons, N. Y. Univ.* (1901), ed. by J. L. Chamberlain; *N. Y. Times*, Sept. 18, 1898; *N. Y. Observer*, Sept. 22, 1898.] H. S. C.

HALL, JOHN ELIHU (Dec. 27, 1783–June 12, 1829), lawyer, editor, was the son of John and Sarah (Ewing) Hall [*q.v.*], and a brother of James Hall [*q.v.*]. His father came of a Maryland family descended from Richard Hall who took land rights in Maryland in August 1663 and was elected to the provincial Assembly in 1665. His mother was a daughter of John Ewing [*q.v.*], provost of the University of Pennsylvania; and his wife, Fanny M. Chew, was a member of another notable Philadelphia family. Born in Philadelphia, John Elihu Hall studied at Princeton but did not graduate, read law in Philadelphia, and was admitted to the Pennsylvania bar in 1805. Three years later, in Baltimore, he began the publication of the *American Law Journal* (6 vols., 1808–17), probably the first legal periodical issued in the United States. Its success was remarkable; no English law journal up to that time had shown equal vitality or usefulness. It was quoted in writings by Judge Story and other leading legal writers of the day. Hall also published *The Practice and Jurisdiction of the Court of Admiralty* (1809); *An Essay on Maritime Loans, from the French of Balthazard Marie Émerigon with Notes, to Which is Added an Appendix* (1811); *Tracts on Constitutional Law, Containing Mr. Livingston's Answer to Mr. Jefferson* (1813), a discussion of the New Orleans batture case; and *Office and Authority of a Justice of the Peace in the State of Maryland; to Which is added a Variety of Precedents in Conveyancing* (1815). In politics he was an intense Federalist, and opposed to war in 1812. In that year, July 27–29, he shared in defending Alexander C. Hanson, Jr., publisher of the *Federal Republican*, against an anti-British mob in Baltimore, from which he deemed it fortunate to escape with his life. A little later, in Philadelphia, he published an anonymous pamphlet on the riot, *To the People of the United States* (n.d). In 1813 he was admitted to the bar of the United States Supreme Court.

Meanwhile he had been adventuring in literature. It is said that he had collected and arranged an edition of William Wirt's *Letters of the British Spy*, to which he contributed several letters which won the approval of the author (Simpson, *post*, 467). He had met Tom Moore in Philadelphia in 1804, when Moore's translation of Anacreon was in press in that city, and he corresponded with him for years thereafter. In March 1806 he contributed to the *Port Folio* the "Original Biography of Anacreon" (reprinted, enlarged, April–September 1820), and in 1810 he prefixed to an edition of *Poems by the Late Dr. Shaw* a life of the author with extracts from his diaries. His command of languages, ancient and modern, was unusual. In 1813 he was appointed to a professorship in the University of Maryland, an appointment that ranked him as, *prima facie*, one of the seven most eminent scholars of the city. The following year he was elected a member of the American Philosophical Society.

About this time, led apparently by his mother's literary example and his acquaintance with the poet Moore, Hall turned definitely from a promising legal career to one of less distinction in letters. In 1816 he moved to Philadelphia to become editor of the *Port Folio*, founded by Joseph Dennie [*q.v.*], of which his brother, Harrison Hall, had just become the publisher. The avowed purpose of the new editor was "to vindicate the character of American literature and manners from the aspersions of ignorant and illiterate foreigners" (quotation in Mott, *post*, p. 240). With contributions from himself, from his mother, and from two other brothers, James and Thomas Mifflin Hall, the magazine became almost a family enterprise. Its brilliance had faded since Dennie's death, however; it continued to decline, and after two suspensions was finally discontinued in December 1827. During these years Hall brought out a few works in the legal field, including *Tracts on the Constitutional Law of the United States Selected from the Law Journal* (1817) and *Digested Index to the Term Reports, from 1785 to 1818* (edited by J. B. Moore, American edition by Hall, 2 vols., 1819). He made an attempt to revive his able legal journal in the *Journal of Jurisprudence* (only one volume, Philadelphia, 1821), and published three literary volumes: *The Lay Preacher by Joseph Dennie, Collected and Arranged by John E. Hall* (1817); *The Philadelphia Souvenir: a Collection of Fugitive Pieces from the Philadelphia Press* (1826), with biographical and explanatory notes, and original contributions by the editor; and *Memoirs of Eminent Persons, with Portraits and Facsimiles* (1827). After two years of failing health, he died in 1829, at Philadelphia.

[See L. E. L. Ewing, *Dr. John Ewing and Some of His Noted Connections* (1924); E. P. Oberholtzer, *The Lit. Hist. of Phila.* (1906); Henry Simpson, *The Lives of Eminent Philadelphians* (1859); J. H. Martin, *Bench and Bar of Phila.* (1883); B. C. Steiner, *Hist. of Educ. in Md.* (1894); E. F. Cordell, *Hist. Sketch of the Univ. of Md.* (1891) and *Univ. of Md. 1807–1907* (2 vols., 1907); *Md. Hist. Mag.*, Sept. 1913, p. 299; H. M. Ellis, *Joseph Dennie and His Circle* (1915); A. H. Smyth, *The Phila. Mags. and Their Contributors* (1892); F. L. Mott, *A Hist. of Am. Mags. 1741–1850* (1930); *National Gazette* and *Daily Chronicle*, both of Phila., June 13, 1829.] F. S. P.

HALL, LUTHER EGBERT (Aug. 30, 1869–Nov. 6, 1921), reform governor of Louisiana, born near Bastrop, Morehouse Parish, La., was the only son of Bolling Cass and Antoinette (Newton) Hall. His father, a planter, traced his ancestry back to seventeenth-century Virginia. Since the family was only fairly well off, young Hall occasionally went into the fields between terms in the Bastrop public schools. At sixteen he spent a year at Tulane University, but graduated, in 1889, at Washington and Lee, with valedictory honors. During a year's interruption in his course he taught school and studied law in Bastrop. He returned to Tulane in 1892 for his degree of LL.B., and was immediately admitted to the bar. On Nov. 23, 1892, he married Clara Wendell of Brownsville, Tenn., who bore him two children. After attempting to practise in Alexandria, La., he returned to Bastrop and became the partner of Judge George Ellis. He soon, however, entered the firm of his uncle, Churubusco Newton, and here founded his distinguished legal career. From 1898 to 1900 he filled the unexpired term of State Senator Baird. His election as judge of the 6th congressional district in 1900 and his reelection in 1904 brought about his removal to Monroe, La. In 1906 he was chosen judge of the court of appeals for the northern district of Louisiana, a position covering nine parishes. His continued rise culminated in his election to the supreme court of Louisiana in 1911.

Meanwhile Democratic politics in Louisiana fostered such flagrant bossism that an independent Democratic Good Government League was formed in 1911 under John M. Parker's leadership. Although by temperament and training judicial rather than executive, moved by his fidelity to duty as he saw it, Hall resigned from the supreme court in 1912, without having actually served, in order to become the League's gubernatorial candidate. John T. Michel, thirteenth-ward boss of New Orleans, and James B. Aswell, state superintendent of schools, were both running for the Democratic nomination, but after an extensive tour of the parishes, Hall won the Democratic primary and thus the assurance of election. He was inaugurated on May 20, 1912. Most of his twenty-five platform pledges were redeemed at the first session of the legislature. Improved levees, port development for New Orleans, a conservation commission, reduced executive patronage, public schools freed from politics, and a bonding of the state debt were some of the accomplishments of his administration. In his main battle, however, which was the fight for reassessment of taxation to increase state revenue without further burdening the small property holder, he was defeated. After four stormy years in the governorship, he removed to New Orleans in 1916 to practise law. He became assistant attorney-general of Louisiana in 1918, in which year he was defeated for the United States Senate by E. J. Gay. In August 1921 he was defeated for the Democratic nomination to the supreme court of the state; but asserting that his opponent was not legally qualified, he waged a bitter fight to secure from the courts recognition of his own nomination. His death occurred in the midst of this contest.

[Sketches of Hall are found in H. E. Chambers, *A Hist. of La.* (1925), III, 359; Alcée Fortier, *Louisiana* (1914), I, 488; *Who's Who in America*, 1920–21; *La. Hist. Quart.*, Jan. 1923; but the fullest data are supplied by the New Orleans *Item*, June 22, 1911, and July 28, 1914. This paper was the official organ of Judge Hall during his gubernatorial campaign. Other New Orleans papers to be consulted for the period 1911–21 are the *Times-Picayune* and the *New Orleans States*. The Hall family possesses a collection of dated clippings which fully cover Hall's career. See also obituaries in *New Orleans States* and *Times-Picayune* for Nov. 7, 1921.] V. G. G.

HALL, LYMAN (Apr. 12, 1724–Oct. 19, 1790), statesman, was the son of John and Mary (Street) Hall, citizens of the town of Wallingford, Conn. His father was descended from John Hall who came to Boston in 1633, later moved to New Haven, and about 1670 settled in

Wallingford; his mother was a grand-daughter of Rev. Samuel Street, first pastor of the church in that town. After graduation from Yale in 1747, Hall studied theology under his uncle, Rev. Samuel Hall, and in June 1749 began to preach at Bridgeport, Conn., as a candidate for ordination. Three months later he was ordained by the Fairfield West Consociation, though some members of the congregation protested against his ordination. He was from the first at odds with his congregation, and finally, in June 1751, he was dismissed by the Consociation after a hearing on charges of immoral conduct. The charges were proven and confessed by him, but the Consociation, confident of the sincerity of his repentance, voted that he be restored to good standing in the ministry and he continued for two years to fill vacant pulpits. Meanwhile, however, he decided to abandon preaching, studied medicine, and set up as a practitioner at Wallingford.

In his early thirties he joined a group of New England Congregationalists whose forebears had migrated in 1697 to South Carolina and taken up land at a place which they named Dorchester, near Charleston. About the time he joined them they began another migration and between 1752 and 1756, the entire colony had moved to the "Midway District" on the coast of Georgia, where in 1758 they founded the town of Sunbury. For the purposes of local government, Georgia was divided into parishes, and the Sunbury settlement was the most important part of St. John's Parish. The site of the settlement was unhealthful: the dwellings and plantation quarters were located on the edge of malarious swamps, so that Hall had ample scope for the practice of his professional skill. Being a man of education and polish, of social habits and a well-rounded character, he became a leader in his section.

In the early days of the revolutionary movement Georgia was lukewarm, but St. John's Parish became the center of a revolutionary group. As Governor Wright reported, the head of the rebellion was in that parish, where the trouble was due to "descendants of New England people of the Puritan independent sect" (Jones, *post*, p. 93). Of all these Puritans, Lyman Hall was probably the hottest advocate of the revolutionary cause. When the Provincial Congress failed to join hands with the other colonies, St. John's Parish, under Hall's leadership, held a convention of its own and extended an invitation to the people of the other parishes to join with it in sending delegates to the Continental Congress. Receiving no encouragement, St. John's Parish acted on its own initiative and elected Hall, in March 1775, as a delegate. He was admitted to the Congress and though refraining from voting took part in the debates. When Georgia was finally brought around to the revolutionary cause, Hall retained his seat in the Continental Congress as a member from Georgia and with his colleagues Button Gwinnett and George Walton [*qq.v.*] he signed the Declaration of Independence. When the British subjugated the coast of Georgia in 1778, Hall's residence in Savannah and his rice plantation were destroyed. He thereupon moved his family to the North and resided there until the close of the war. Returning to Georgia with the coming of peace, he made Savannah his home and resumed the practice of medicine. In 1783 he was elected governor of Georgia. In a message to the General Assembly, July 8, 1783, he made a remarkable recommendation, to wit, that a grant of land be set aside for the endowment of a state-supported institution of higher learning. This recommendation led, the following year, to the chartering of one of the first state-supported universities in America, with an endowment of 40,000 acres of land (see sketch of Abraham Baldwin).

After his brief term of office Hall removed in 1790 to Burke County, Ga., where he invested his accumulations in a plantation. There he died, within a few months, in his sixty-seventh year. He was twice married: first on May 20, 1752, to Abigail Burr, daughter of Thaddeus and Abigail Burr of Fairfield, Conn., who died July 8, 1753; second, before he left Connecticut, to Mary Osborn, daughter of Samuel and Hannah Osborn, also of Fairfield. His only son, John, was born of the second marriage.

[F. B. Dexter, *Biog. Sketches Grads. Yale Coll.*, vol. II (1896); C. C. Jones, *The Dead Towns of Ga.* (1878), and *Biog. Sketches of the Delegates from Ga. to the Continental Cong.* (1891); T. P. Hall, *Geneal. Notes: Relating to the Families of Hon. Lyman Hall, of Ga., Hon. Samuel Holden Parsons Hall, of Binghamton, N. Y., and Hon. Nathan Kelsey Hall, of Buffalo, N. Y.* (1886); D. B. Hall, *The Halls of New England* (1883).]

R. P. B—s.

HALL, NATHAN KELSEY (Mar. 28, 1810–Mar. 2, 1874), jurist, was born in that part of Marcellus which is now Skaneateles, Onondaga County, N. Y., the son of Ira and Katherine (Rose) Hall. His father, a New England shoemaker, was descended from John Hall who came to Boston about 1633 and later settled in Wallingford, Conn. Ira Hall moved to Erie County in 1818, but his son Nathan remained at Marcellus with Nathan Kelsey, for whom he was named, until he was sixteen. He then worked on his father's farm, and at his father's trade until 1828, when he entered the law-office of Millard Fillmore, then a struggling young lawyer at Aurora. While studying law, young Hall taught a district school for eleven dollars a month, did odd jobs of land surveying, and acted as clerk in the office of the Holland Land Company. Upon his admission to the bar in 1832 he formed a partnership with Fillmore, who was then practising in Buffalo. During the next decade he held several minor city and county offices, and in 1841 became judge of the court of common pleas for Erie County. A Whig in politics, he was a member of the Assembly in 1845, and of the United States House of Representatives from 1847 to 1849, but refused a renomination. On July 23, 1850, he became postmaster general in Fillmore's cabinet, holding office until Aug. 31, 1852. In that year Fillmore appointed him United States judge of the Northern District of New York, which office he filled with credit until his death. Perhaps his most important opinion was given Sept. 23, 1862, in the case of Rev. Judson D. Benedict, a pacifist who had been arbitrarily arrested by order of the War Department. Hall held that the president could not constitutionally suspend the writ of *habeas corpus,* and ordered the release of the prisoner, who was, however, immediately rearrested and taken by the United States marshal to Washington, out of his jurisdiction (*New York Tribune,* Sept. 24, 26, 1862).

Hall was calm and patient, intensely serious, almost austere; without imagination, fervor, or graces of expression. He was fearless in his interpretation and application of the principles of the law, which was to him a sacred thing. He never played, and, in fact, wore himself out by intense application to the heavy business of his district. His interest in education was keen. He was instrumental in reorganizing the public-school system of Buffalo and served as trustee of several educational institutions. On Nov. 16, 1832, he was married to Emily Paine of Aurora, who with four of their five children predeceased him.

[J. O. Putnam, "Nathan Kelsey Hall," in *Buffalo Hist. Soc. Pubs.,* IV (1896), 285–98; *Biog. Dir. Am. Cong.* (1928); T. P. Hall, *Geneal. Notes: Relating to the Families of Hon. Lyman Hall, of Ga. . . . and Hon. Nathan Kelsey Hall, of Buffalo, N. Y.* (1886); *Albany Law Jour.,* Mar. 7, 1874; *Buffalo Commercial Advertiser,* Mar. 2, 3, 4, 1874; *Buffalo Express,* Mar. 3, 4, 1874.]

H. T.

HALL, SAMUEL (Nov. 2, 1740–Oct. 30, 1807), printer, son of Jonathan and Anna (Fowle) Hall, was born in Medford, Mass., where his ancestor, John Hall, settled about 1675. After serving his term as apprentice to his uncle, Daniel Fowle [*q.v.*], printer of the *New Hampshire Gazette,* he went to Rhode Island and became Anne Franklin's partner in the publication of the *Newport Mercury,* beginning with the issue of Aug. 17, 1762. After Mrs. Franklin's death on Apr. 19, 1763, Hall continued the paper with success until March 1768 when he sold it to Solomon Southwick. In April of that year he established the first printing-house in Salem, Mass., where, on Aug. 2, he began the publication of the *Essex Gazette,* announcing his purpose to promote "a due sense of the Rights and Liberties of our Country." Intensely Whig in sympathy, the *Essex Gazette* was an able agent of the colonial cause. "The country had no firmer friend in the gloomiest period of its history, as well as in the days of its young and increasing prosperity, than Samuel Hall" (Buckingham, *post,* I, 228). When Isaiah Thomas [*q.v.*], printer of the *Massachusetts Spy,* was forced to move his paper from Boston to Worcester, the Provincial Congress persuaded Hall and his brother Ebenezer, who had been his partner since 1772, to accommodate it and the army by moving to Cambridge. Accordingly the *New England Chronicle or Essex Gazette* was founded at Stoughton Hall in May 1775. In April 1776 Hall moved his paper to Boston, calling it the *New-England Chronicle.* In June he sold out to Powars & Willis, who rechristened the paper the *Independent Chronicle.* Five years later, Oct. 18, 1781, he began the publication of the *Salem Gazette,* succeeding Mrs. Crouch's paper of the same name and probably taking over her press and types. The heavy tax on advertising influenced him to discontinue his business in Salem with the issue of Nov. 22, 1785, and with the hope of better opportunities, to establish again a printing-house and paper in Boston. The first issue of his *Massachusetts Gazette* appeared Nov. 28, 1785. In September 1787 he sold it to J. W. Allen, his partner since June. Except for a short period, Apr. 23 to Oct. 15, 1789, when he published in French for J. Nancrède the *Courier of Boston,* he thereafter confined himself to the printing and sale of books, blanks, and pamphlets. As a publisher he is known for his children's books. In 1805 he retired from active business, selling his establishment to Brooks & Edmands.

[Isaiah Thomas, *The Hist. of Printing in America* (2nd ed., 2 vols., 1874); J. T. Buckingham, *Specimens of Newspaper Literature* (2 vols., 1850); G. L. Streeter, in D. H. Hurd, *Hist. of Essex County, Mass.* (1888), vol. I, ch. V; C. S. Brigham, "Bibliography of American Newspapers," *Proc. Am. Antiq. Soc.,* 2 ser., XXV (1915), XXXIV (1924); *Colonial Soc. Mass. Pubs.,* IX (1907); D. B. Hall, *The Halls of New England* (1883); *Vital Records of Medford, Mass.* (1907); *Columbian Centinel* (Boston), Oct. 31, 1807.]

R. E. M.

HALL, SAMUEL (Apr. 23, 1800–Nov. 13, 1870), shipbuilder, was born in Marshfield, Mass., the son of Luke and Anna (Tuels) Hall and a descendant of Adam Hall who emigrated from England to Massachusetts some time before 1725. Since the North River at Marshfield was a shipbuilding center of prime importance, it was natural that Samuel and his brothers should start work in the shipyards after a brief schooling. He served his apprenticeship in the yard of Deacon Elijah Barstow at Hanover near by, and with his two brothers had built several small vessels by 1828. Then he set out with twenty-five cents and a broadax to seek his fortune elsewhere. He went first to Medford, Mass., and then to Camden, Me., but finally returned to the North River where he built vessels on his own account at Duxbury. In 1839, he established a shipyard near the present foot of Maverick Street in East Boston, which was just becoming a shipbuilding center. That same year, he launched the 650-ton *Akbar* for the opium trade of the Forbes family. He later turned out the brig *Antelope* and schooner *Zephyr* for the same trade. His real prominence dates from Oct. 5, 1850, however, when he launched, complete even to spars and rigging, the *Surprise*. This ship, speedy and profitable until wrecked by a drunken pilot off Japan in 1875, was the first clipper built in Massachusetts. During the next three years Hall built a group of clippers surpassed only by those from the near-by yard of Donald McKay [*q.v.*], whose first clipper took the water just two months after the *Surprise*. In 1850, Hall also built the *Game Cock* and *Race Horse*; in 1851, the *R. B. Forbes*; in 1852, the *John Gilpin, Flying Childers, Hoogly,* and *Polynesia*; and in 1853, the *Amphitrite, Mystery, Wizard,* and *Oriental*. The *John Gilpin* participated in "the most celebrated and famous ship-race that has ever been run" (Howe and Matthews, *post,* I, 306), when McKay's *Flying Fish* beat her by one day in a neck-and-neck race from New York to San Francisco in 1852. Most of Hall's clippers were built for Boston ship-owners—Pierce & Hunnewell, the Bacons, and the Forbeses. He built "his masterpiece," the *Wizard,* on his own account and sold her in New York for $95,000. He showed originality and ability in ship designing, but, unlike McKay, who designed all his own ships, had the plans for several drawn by Samuel Pook. Altogether, 110 ships were launched from his yard. He set the style for New England fishing schooners with the *Express* and *Telegraph,* built on fast but sometimes dangerous clipper lines. During the later fifties, he gradually retired from active management of the yard, and its last clipper, the *Florence,* was built under the direction of his son, Samuel Hall, Jr., in 1856. Hall was a public-spirited citizen; he was rewarded with a silver service for his efforts in having water piped to East Boston in 1851. He was president of the East Boston Ferry Company, the Dry Dock Company, and the Maverick National Bank. His first marriage, with Christina Kent, was childless, but by his second, with Huldah B. Sherman, he had two sons and six daughters.

[Ample biographical details of Hall and his family are given in L. V. Briggs, *Hist. of Shipbuilding on the North River, Plymouth County, Mass.* (1889); M. A. Thomas, *Memorials of Marshfield* (1854); W. H. Sumner, *A Hist. of East Boston* (1858), containing a complete list of his ships; A. V. Clark, *The Clipper Ship Era* (1910); O. T. Howe and F. C. Matthews, *Am. Clipper Ships* (2 vols., 1926–27); *Boston Transcript,* Nov. 14, 1870.]

R. G. A.

HALL, SAMUEL READ (Oct. 27, 1795–June 24, 1877), educator, born in Croydon, N. H., was a descendant of John Hall, who, coming from England to Massachusetts some time before 1652, settled in Medford about 1675. The youngest of the numerous family of Samuel Read and Elizabeth (Hall) Hall, he was christened Read Hall, but upon the death of his brother Samuel, he was given that name and the change was legalized by an act of the legislature. During his youth his health was delicate. The loss of his father's property prevented his securing a college education, but he had taken a course of classical study at Kimball Union Academy, Meriden, N. H., and he began to teach school in 1814 in Rumford, Me., where he is credited with having made the first use of blackboards in the United States (W. B. Lapham, *History of Rumford, Oxford County, Me.,* 1890, p. 184). He was early convinced that the entire system of education in the country was defective and that immediate and drastic reform was necessary. While principal of an academy at Fitchburg, Mass., he had studied theology with Rev. William Eaton and in 1822 was licensed as a Congregational minister. In March of the following year he began his missionary labors at Concord, Vt., where, by an understanding with his people, he established a training-school for teachers. It was incorporated in November 1823 as the Concord Academy. There had been in the early decades of the nineteenth century in America, under French and Prussian influence, considerable academic discussion of teacher-training, but Hall took the first practical step by the opening of his normal school. He was also one of the founders of the American Institute of Instruction, the oldest educational association in

America, organized in Boston in 1830. That same year he went to the Phillips Academy at Andover, Mass., as principal of the newly established teachers' seminary. There he was regarded as omniscient and indefatigable. Poor health and dissatisfaction caused him to resign in April 1837, however, and shortly afterward he accepted the appointment as principal of the Holmes Plymouth (N. H.) Academy. When the school was closed in 1840, owing to financial difficulties, Hall accepted the call to a church in Craftsbury, Vt., and became principal of the Craftsbury Academy, to which he added a teachers' department. He left the Academy in 1846 and twelve years later resigned his pastorate to accept the less onerous duties of the church at Brownington, Vt. In 1867 he resigned because of old age and retired to his farm. He did not long remain inactive. From 1872 to 1875 he was pastor of the church at Granby, Vt., and during these latter years he frequently lectured on geology and astronomy. His first wife, Mary Dascomb, whom he married June 17, 1823, died in 1836; his second wife, Mary Holt, whom he married June 6, 1837, survived his death in 1877, as did one of his ten children. He was an inveterate writer of textbooks and published works on geology, geography, arithmetic, grammar, and history. His *Lectures on School-Keeping* (1829) and *Lectures to Female Teachers on School-Keeping* (1832) were early and important contributions to the scientific study of education.

[*Hall's Lectures on School-Keeping* (1929), ed. by A. D. Wright and G. E. Gardner, contains a biographical sketch of Hall as well as a bibliography of his writings and a selected bibliography on his life and writings. See also D. B. Hall, *The Halls of New England* (1883); *Cyc. of Educ.* (1925), ed. by Paul Monroe; Claude M. Fuess, *An Old New England School* (1917); Henry Barnard, *Normal Schools* (1851); *Am. Jour. of Edu.*, Sept. 1858, Mar. 1866; Elbridge Smith, "The Founders of the Institute" in *Lectures Delivered before the Am. Inst. of Instruction at Boston, Mass., Aug. 1867* (1868); *Free Press and Times* (Burlington, Vt.), June 29, 1877.] F. M.

HALL, SARAH EWING (Oct. 30, 1761–Apr. 8, 1830), essayist, was born in Philadelphia, the daughter of the Rev. John Ewing [*q.v.*], and of Hannah (Sergeant) Ewing. At the time of her birth, her father was the pastor of the First Presbyterian Church and a tutor in the College of Philadelphia; later he was provost of the University of Pennsylvania. Her education was mainly acquired at home, where her scholarly father made it "his custom to converse in the most familiar manner, upon serious and instructive topics. . . . His fireside, while it was the scene of hospitality and cheerfulness, was always enlivened with literary and scientific discussion" (*Selections, post,* p. xii). Sarah gained "a critical acquaintance with the principles of grammar, and an extensive knowledge of the ancient classics, by hearing her brothers recite their Latin and Greek lessons, to their father, and by listening to the conversation of learned men, who frequented his house" (*Ibid.*, p. xii). She was also "much addicted to the study of astronomy" and on the whole a notable bluestocking.

In 1782 she married John Hall, son of a wealthy Maryland planter, and for the next eight years lived on a farm beside the Susquehanna in Octorara, Cecil County, Md. About 1790 her husband removed with his family to Philadelphia, where he later became secretary of the Pennsylvania land office and subsequently, in 1799–1801, United States marshal for the district of Pennsylvania. He then engaged in business, not too successfully, and with his family went to Lamberton, N. J., to live, but in 1805 returned to Maryland and in 1811 to Philadelphia, which thereafter was Mrs. Hall's home. There John Hall died in 1826.

Although she was the mother of ten children, Mrs. Hall was a student of current as well as classical literature. From the time she was twenty-eight or twenty-nine, it is said, she remained in her study at night for hours after her family had retired, reading and writing. When Joseph Dennie [*q.v.*] established the *Port Folio* in 1801 she was among the selected group of its contributors—the only other woman in the charmed circle being Mrs. Elizabeth Graeme Ferguson [*q.v.*]. At that time "to write for the *Port Folio* was considered no small honor" (*Ibid.*, p. xvi). During the entire existence of that periodical Mrs. Hall continued to contribute from time to time. In the issue for April 1815 her article ascribing *Waverley* to Walter Scott was reluctantly published, with a long disclaimer by the editor, who declared the novel displayed a style that was "juvenile, crude and incorrect, compared to the acknowledged productions of Mr. Scott" (p. 327). The following year the *Port Folio* passed into the possession of her son Harrison Hall, and from that time until its demise in 1827 was edited by her son John Elihu Hall [*q.v.*]. Two other sons, James Hall [*q.v.*] and Thomas Mifflin Hall, were contributors.

All of Mrs. Hall's writings appeared either anonymously, or over such names as "Constantia" or "Florepha." She had a clear, easy style, and displayed remarkable ability in controversy. Her *Conversations on the Bible* (1818), which was published anonymously, went through five editions, one being issued in England. Some of her essays, such as "On Duelling," "On Female Education," and "Defence of American Women," together with extracts from her letters, were published by Harrison Hall in 1833, in a volume entitled *Selections from the Writings of Mrs. Sarah Hall, Author of Conversations on the Bible.* She died in Philadelphia in her seventieth year and was buried in the burial ground of the Third Presbyterian Church, in that city.

[Memoir of Mrs. Hall by one of her sons, in the *Selections* from her writings; E. A. and G. L. Duyckinck, *Cyc. of Am. Lit.* (rev. ed., 1875), I, 855; A. H. Smyth, *The Phila. Mags. and Their Contributors* (1892); F. L. Mott, *A Hist. of Am. Mags., 1741–1850* (1930); *Poulson's Am. Daily Advertiser*, Apr. 9, 1830.]

J. J.

HALL, SHERMAN (Apr. 30, 1800–Sept. 1, 1879), Congregational clergyman, missionary to the Chippewa Indians, was born in Weathersfield, Vt., the son of Aaron and Sarah (Brigham) Hall. Through his maternal grandmother he was related to the Sherman family of which Roger Sherman, one of the signers of the Declaration of Independence, was a member. After preparation in Phillips Academy he entered Dartmouth College, from which he was graduated in 1828. The year 1831 marked his graduation from Andover Theological Seminary, his ordination at Woburn, Mass., by the Rev. Lyman Beecher, his marriage to Betsey Parker, and his departure for his mission field on Lake Superior under appointment of the American Board of Commissioners for Foreign Missions. At Lapointe, a fur-trading post on Madeline Island, close to the site of an early Jesuit mission on the south shore of Lake Superior, he established a mission of the American Board, the first mission among the Chippewa since the time of the Jesuits. From this outpost the Indians west and south of Lake Superior were visited and mission stations founded among them.

Because of the efforts of the United States government to promote a policy of civilization and education among the Indians by aiding schools at mission posts, Hall's position at the head of one of the largest of the North American mission fields was one of considerable importance. That his work was appreciated by the government is evident in the large grants of money given to his schools. At least two of these were opened on Madeline Island. The resident Indians and some of the numerous bands that came to trade were instructed in the civilized crafts, and a church was built. With great labor and care Hall learned the difficult Chippewa language and between 1833 and 1856 translated or supervised the translation of textbooks, hymns, and portions of the Bible into the native tongue. These translations, printed in the East, were used widely among the Chippewa. Three editions of the New Testament, in the translation of which he was assisted by Henry Blatchford, a native interpreter, were issued during his lifetime.

In 1852 the United States government invited him to become superintendent of a manual-labor school to be established, as an experiment, among the Chippewa Indians concentrated at the junction of the Crow Wing and Mississippi rivers. In November 1854, after a little more than a year's service as missionary and superintendent of the school, he resigned from the position, since the American Board had come to the conclusion that it was no longer expedient to help support a missionary at a place where the good he might accomplish would be offset by the encroaching evils of the frontier. He retired to a farm that he had bought in Sauk Rapids, Minn., and became the pastor of a little Congregational church there. From that time until his death in 1879 he served this small parish, financially aided by the American Home Missionary Society. In the last years of his life he was judge of probate and superintendent of schools.

[Letters written by Hall to the A. B. C. F. M. and to members of his family have been preserved: the first group in the archives of the A. B. C. F. M. in Boston, the second by Ernest W. Butterfield, Esq., of Concord, N. H. Copies of these have been made by the Minn. Hist. Soc. Excerpts from some of Hall's letters were printed in the *Missionary Herald*, esp. Feb., Sept. 1832, Jan. 1834, Aug. 1836, May, Oct. 1842, Sept. 1854; and the *Home Missionary*, esp. July, Sept. 1855, Nov. 1858, Jan., Apr. 1859. Brief biographical sketches may be found in *Home Missionary*, Nov. 1879; S. R. Riggs, "Protestant Missions in the Northwest," *Minn. Hist. Colls.*, vol. VI (1891); and Grace L. Nute, "The Letters of Sherman Hall, Missionary to the Chippewa Indians," in *Minn. Hist.*, Mar. 1926; see also *Congreg. Year Book*, 1880; *Daily Globe* (St. Paul), Sept. 2, 1879.]

G. L. N.

HALL, THOMAS (Feb. 4, 1834–Nov. 19, 1911), inventor, patent attorney, was born in Philadelphia, Pa., of English parentage. After attending the public schools in Philadelphia, he entered the Academy of the University at Lewisburg, Pa. (now Bucknell), in preparation for a business career. After one term, 1852–53, he was honorably discharged in order to enter the ministry. To this end he tutored with the Rev. Dr. Malcolm, a Baptist clergyman of note. Before his ordination, however, he abandoned his theological studies to devote himself to science and mechanics. For a number of years he studied mechanics intensively, at the same time obtaining employment of one sort or another in Philadelphia, St. Louis, Milwaukee, and finally in New York. As early as 1858, while a resident of St.

Louis, he began work on the development of a writing machine, and after nine years of concentrated effort perfected it, being granted United States patent No. 65,807 for a "Typographic Machine" on June 18, 1867. Authorities qualified to write impartially regard this as a pioneer typewriter invention. It was operated from a keyboard by means of finger levers with a connecting link and an individual typebar for each finger lever. It embodied devices anticipating future requirements, such as a stop ring for preventing undue penetration of the paper to yield uniform printing results, an automatic line lock to limit the travel of the carriage when the printing reached the end of the line, and devices for varying the length of movement of the printing surface. The invention indicated a remarkable foresight of the ultimate improvements of the typewriter. Hall immediately organized a company to manufacture the machine, but financial conditions following the Civil War, combined with the fact that the business world was not ready for such a device, soon caused the abandonment of the manufactory. Several machines were made, however. For one exhibited at the Paris Exposition in 1867, an award of merit was granted. In 1873 Hall went to Europe to study mechanisms and mechanics, particularly in the shops of Vienna, St. Petersburg, and Paris. After his return to New York he spent the next five years on typewriter improvements, and in 1880 invented a one-keyed typewriting machine, so light and convenient that it could be readily used by travelers. This machine was manufactured and placed on the market in 1881 as the "Hall Typewriter." It embodied the pantograph principle and was operated with one hand by means of a stylus. Its operation was slow, however, and as a result, the machine was soon succeeded by others incorporating principles that are in favor today. Hall subsequently established himself as a patent attorney in New York City but devoted a great amount of time to mechanical improvements, and before his death invented a number of sewing-machine attachments, an improved mill-grinder, and other machinist's tools. In 1884 the Franklin Institute of Philadelphia awarded him the John Scott legacy medal and award for his typewriter. He was married at the age of twenty-eight, after establishing his residence in Brooklyn, and was survived at the time of his death by two daughters and a son.

[*Who's Who in America*, 1910–11; *Illus. Phonographic World*, Mar. 1892, Mar., June, July 1897; *Typewriter World*, Jan. 1912; *Brooklyn Daily Eagle*, Nov. 20, 1911; *Scientific American*, Dec. 30, 1911; *Appletons' Ann. Cyc. 1890* (1891); C. V. Oden, *Evolution of the Typewriter* (1917); *Evolution of the Typewriter* (1921), prepared by the Royal Typewriter Company; U. S. Museum correspondence.]

C. W. M—n.

HALL, THOMAS SEAVEY (Apr. 1, 1827–Dec. 1, 1880), manufacturer, inventor, descended from John Hall who was in Charlestown, Mass., in 1645 and ultimately settled at Dover, N. H., was born at Upper Bartlett, N. H., the son of Rev. Elias and Hannah (Seavey) Hall. He is said to have attended Middlebury College, Middlebury, Vt. Engaging in the textile industry, with headquarters at Stamford, Conn., he became one of the most prominent woolen manufacturers of New England. In 1866 he retired from business and shortly thereafter, while on a railroad trip, was aboard a train that was wrecked by a misplaced switch. Through good fortune he escaped injury, but in viewing the wreck it occurred to him that such catastrophes should and could be prevented. Accordingly he immediately turned his attention to perfecting a system of signals that would prevent accidents not only from misplaced switches but also from open drawbridges, collisions of trains, and collisions at highway crossings. He analyzed thoroughly the fundamental requirements of the problem and focused his attention almost immediately upon the practical application to it of electric automatic signals. On Feb. 26, 1867, he received patent No. 62,414 for "an alarm or bell to warn those at a distance." That same year he organized the Hall Drawbridge & Signal Company at Stamford. Because sleet, snow, and ice interfered with moving the parts of the signal he had originally patented, Hall devised the electric inclosed disc or "banjo" signal, the initial patent on which, No. 89,308, was granted to him Apr. 27, 1869. This was his most important invention. The signal was controlled by a wire circuit through track treadles—keys or instruments operated by the passage of wheels of passing trains. A very satisfactory electromagnetic device operating a wire-framed disc covered with silk of a suitable color for a day signal, surmounted by a glass or other transparent material of corresponding color for the night signal, was subsequently developed. A kerosene lamp was placed behind the glass to produce the night signal. A number of patents were issued to Hall for the various features of this system. Later, designs were worked out for signals at drawbridges controlled by a circuit controller mechanically operated by the movable draw, thus providing protection in both directions. Lastly, highway-crossing protection was devised, and a patent issued to Hall in 1879 was made effective immediately. The principles developed by Hall still prevail in railroad-signalling practise. His first signal was installed at Stamford in 1868 and the first installation of his automatic block-signalling system was made on the Eastern Railroad of Massachusetts on sixteen miles of road in 1871. Hall was married to Sarah C. Phillips, and at the time of his death in Meriden, Conn., was survived by his widow and a son.

[S. Marsh Young, "Railway Block Signalling," in *General Manager,* Dec. 1892; obituaries in *Railway Age,* Dec. 1880, and *New Haven Evening Register,* Dec. 3, 1880; D. B. Hall, *The Halls of New England* (1883), pp. 152, 161, 729; Patent Office records; correspondence with H. S. Balliet and Henry M. Sperry, New York City.] C. W. M—n.

HALL, WILLARD (Dec. 24, 1780–May 10, 1875), jurist, promoter of public education in Delaware, was born in Westford, Mass., of an ancestry of deacons and ministers. His father was Willis Hall, a descendant of Stephen Hall who was living in Concord, Mass., in 1653; his mother, Mehetable (Poole) Hall of Hollis, N. H. To her he attributed the moulding of his character during the formative years. After three years in the academy at Westford, he entered Harvard College in 1795, graduating four years later with honors. His law reading was completed under Samuel Dana of Groton, Mass., and in March 1803, he was admitted to the bar in Hillsboro, N. H. Dissatisfaction with the crowded condition of his profession in New England caused him to remove to Delaware in April 1803. Carrying letters of introduction from Harrison Gray Otis to James A. Bayard and Cæsar Rodney, he had no difficulty in being admitted to the Delaware bar. He made his home in Dover, and in 1806 married Junia Killen, daughter of the former chancellor of Delaware. She died within a few years, and in 1829 he married Harriet Hilliard. His only child, Lucinda, was born of the first marriage. From 1812 to 1814 he served as secretary of state and in 1816 he was elected on the Republican ticket to Congress, serving two terms as representative, from March 1817 to March 1821. After another term in 1821 as secretary of state, he was elected to the Delaware Senate, taking his seat in January 1823. On May 6 of the same year he was appointed, chiefly on Cæsar Rodney's recommendation, judge of the United States district court of Delaware, in which capacity he served until Dec. 6, 1871, when he retired. He had little taste for legislative duties, and it was in this later period that his life work was accomplished. During his more than forty-eight years on the bench only one of his decisions, that of *United States* vs. *Commandant of Fort Delaware* (1866) was seriously questioned, and the principles governing his decision in this case were similar to those governing that of the United States Supreme Court in the famous *ex parte Milligan* case (4 *Wallace,* 2), decided the same year (summary of case in *American Law Review,* April 1867). He had preëminently the conservative, judicial mind which sought to preserve the sanctity of the common law, but his strict sense of justice operated evenly and without prejudice. Ample leisure from judicial duties afforded him opportunities to give the state his most valuable services. On authorization by the legislature in 1824, he revised the laws of Delaware, completing the task in 1829. He was elected on the ticket of both parties as a delegate to the constitutional convention of 1831, where he was the foremost antagonist of John M. Clayton [*q.v.*] on the issues before that body (*Debates of the Delaware Convention for Revising the Constitution of the State,* Wilmington, 1831).

Hall best deserves recognition, however, as a founder and a tireless advocate of public-school education in Delaware. His ideas were embodied in the school law of 1829, drawn up by him at the request of the legislature but not adopted entire. This law first recognized the principle of general free education, but gave to school districts individually the taxing power for educational purposes. In 1836 he organized the New Castle County School Convention, and through this medium kept the subject constantly before the people. From 1852, when it was organized, to 1870, he was president of the Delaware School Board. The value of his services can hardly be over-estimated, yet his democratic ideas, carried out with relentless logic—such as the decentralization provided for in the law of 1829—were responsible also for retarding influences which brought him into conflict with a progressive group. He was also opposed to a state normal school. After his resignation as judge in his ninety-first year he ceased to take an active part in affairs. He died about four years later at Wilmington, to which place he had removed in 1825.

[The best memoir of Willard Hall is D. M. Bates, "Memorial Address on the Life and Character of Willard Hall," in *Hist. Soc. of Del. Papers,* No. 1 (1879); the best source up to 1852 is a sketch, probably autobiographical, in John Livingston, *Portraits of Eminent Americans Now Living,* II (1853), 421–27. A long letter from Hall to J. M. Clayton, July 1, 1856, on the Kansas troubles (MS. Div., Lib. of Cong.) is revelatory. See also D. B. Hall, *The Halls of New England* (1883), p. 524; *Wilmington Daily Commercial,* May 11, 1875; S. B. Weeks, *Hist. of Public School Educ. in Del.* (1917), being U. S. Bureau of Educ. Bull., 1917, no. 18.] C. W. G.

HALL, WILLARD PREBLE (May 9, 1820–Nov. 3, 1882), lawyer, soldier, lieutenant-governor and governor of Missouri, was born at Harper's Ferry, Va. (now W. Va.), of New England ancestry. He was the son of John and Statira (Preble) Hall. His father, for many years superintendent of the government armory at Harper's Ferry, and the inventor of a breech-loading gun called "Hall's carbine," was descended from Stephen Hall who was in Concord, Mass., as early as 1653 and settled at Stow, Mass., about 1685; his mother, a native of Maine, sister of William Pitt Preble [*q.v.*], traced her ancestry to Abraham Preble who settled at Scituate, Mass., in 1636. Among his progenitors were men of distinction in the law and ministry. Willard Hall was prepared for college in the schools of his native town and in Baltimore and was graduated from Yale College in 1839, at the age of nineteen. In 1840 he removed to Huntsville, Mo., where he studied law under his brother and began the practice of his profession. The following year he settled at Sparta, Mo., and in 1843 made his permanent home in St. Joseph, Mo. In that year he was appointed circuit attorney by Governor Reynolds. His cordial manner won him a large measure of popularity, and in 1844 he was presidential elector on the Democratic ticket, and helped carry Missouri for James K. Polk. Hall was chosen to take the certificate to Washington. When the Mexican War began he was a candidate for Congress, but, notwithstanding, he enlisted as a private in the regiment commanded by Col. A. W. Doniphan [*q.v.*]. When the army took possession of Santa Fé, Gen. Stephen W. Kearny ordered Hall to collaborate with Colonel Doniphan in preparing a code of laws for governing New Mexico. This code survived, in its main features, for more than a generation. While at Santa Fé, Hall was notified of his release from military service on account of his election to Congress. Pending the beginning of the session, he volunteered for the expedition which took possession of California. He served three terms in Congress, where he secured a grant of 600,000 acres of land for the Hannibal & St. Joseph Railroad. He also aided in the passage of acts giving to the State of Missouri swamp and waste lands which helped to endow its public-school system. At the expiration of his congressional career he returned to the practice of law, and was soon recognized as one of the best lawyers in a circuit conspicuous for able men. He opposed the secession of Missouri from the Union, and was elected a delegate to the state convention of 1861. At the first session he became one of the recognized leaders. When Hamilton R. Gamble [*q.v.*] was made provisional governor in July 1861, after Governor Jackson had been driven from the state by Federal forces, Hall was chosen lieutenant-governor, and after Gamble's death in 1864, succeeded him as provisional governor. When his term expired the following year he returned to St. Joseph. There he owned a farm and took great interest in agricultural experiments.

On Oct. 28, 1847, at St. Joseph, Hall was married to Ann Eliza Richardson, daughter of Maj. William P. Richardson, by whom he had four children. After her death he was married a second time, on June 22, 1864, to Ollie L. Oliver, by whom he had two sons and a daughter.

[D. B. Hall, *The Halls of New England* (1883), p. 521; Henry Preble, *Geneal. Sketch of the First Three Generations of Prebles in America* (1868); *Messages and Proclamations of the Govs. of the State of Mo.*, vol. IV (1924), ed. by G. C. Avery and F. C. Shoemaker; W. E. Connelley, *War with Mexico, 1846–47: Doniphan's Expedition* (1907); C. L. Ruth, *The Daily News' Hist. of Buchanan County and St. Joseph, Mo.* (1898); *Missouri Republican*, Nov. 4 and 5, 1882; *Obit. Record Grads. Yale Coll.*, (1883); *A Quarter-Century Record of the Class of 1839, Yale Coll.* (1865); letter of A. W. Doniphan to D. C. Allen, June 22, 1863, in the Doniphan Papers, Mo. Hist. Soc.]

S. M. D.

HALL, WILLIAM WHITTY (Oct. 15, 1810–May 10, 1876), physician, pioneer editor of popular health magazines, was of Scottish ancestry. He was descended from Adam Hall, a native of Ireland, who settled in Pennsylvania about the middle of the eighteenth century. Adam's great-grandson, Stephen, married, it is said, an English woman named Mary Wooley, and their son, William Whitty Hall, was born in Paris, Ky. He graduated from Centre College in 1830 and, with the intention of becoming a missionary, studied both theology and medicine. In 1836 he received the degree of M.D. from Transylvania University, where he had been a pupil of John Esten Cooke [*q.v.*], and was ordained to the Presbyterian ministry. The following year he was a missionary in Texas and for a number of years he preached occasionally, but he gradually abandoned preaching for medicine. He practised in New Orleans and Cincinnati, and in 1851 removed to New York City where he established a consultation practice, "strictly confined to chronic ailments of the throat and lungs" (*Hall's Journal of Health*, January 1854, p. 4). In this field lay his major interest. While resident in Cincinnati he published several technical books in all of which there was a savor of enthusiasm or charlatanry. The first of these was *Consumption a Curable Disease, Illustrated in the Treatment of 150 Cases*, published in Pittsburgh in 1845. Two years later appeared *Observations on the Curability of Consumption by a New, Safe and Painless Method, Illustrated in Selections of 350 Cases* (1847); in 1848, *Bronchitis, Chronic*

Laryngitis, Clergyman's Sore Throat (5th ed.), written in collaboration with one S. W. Hall; and in 1850, *The Nature, Cause, Symptoms and Cure of Diseases of the Throat and Lungs.* Upon his arrival in New York in 1851 he published the first of his works for the general public, a small booklet entitled *Throat-ail, Bronchitis and Consumption,* followed in 1852 by *Bronchitis and Kindred Diseases,* which appears to have been technical and went through four editions, the last in 1870. In 1854 he began to publish a popular periodical, *Hall's Journal of Health,* "to teach man how to avoid disease." This he continued up to the time of his death, and some years thereafter it was absorbed by *Popular Science.* In 1857 he published *Consumption* (2nd ed. 1865), which was followed by: *Health and Disease: A Book for the People* (1859; 2nd ed., 1860); *Sleep* (1861), with an amplification entitled *Sleep or the Hygiene of the Night* (1870); *The Guideboard to Health, Peace and Competence; or the Road to Happy Old Age* (1862); *Health and Disease as Affected by Constipation and Health by Good Living* (1870; 2nd ed., 1873); *How to Live Long* (1875); and *Dyspepsia and Kindred Diseases* (posthumous, 1877). In 1875 he began a new periodical, *Hall's Medical Adviser,* which ceased at his death.

Hall appears to have been an individualist in medical practice and there is no evidence that he ever affiliated with his profession nor, on the other hand, that he ever directly antagonized it. He never weighed more than 125 pounds, and it was his custom to violate one of the rules he laid down for others by working from five in the morning till ten at night. In his sixty-sixth year he fell in a fit on the street, in New York, and died almost at once. He was twice married: his first wife being, it is said, Hannah Mattock of Cincinnati; his second wife, Magdalen Matilda Robertson, daughter of Archibald Robertson [*q.v.*] and sister of Anthony Lespinard Robertson, justice of the superior court of New York City.

[H. A. Kelly and W. L. Burrage, *Am. Medic. Biogs.* (1920); D. B. Hall, *The Halls of New England* (1883), pp. 670–71; *Hall's Jour. of Health,* June 1876; *N. Y. Times* and *Sun* (N. Y.), May 12, 1876.]

E. P.

HALLAM, LEWIS (*c.* 1740–Nov. 1, 1808), actor, theatrical manager, was the son of Lewis Hallam, an actor. When bankruptcy overtook William Hallam, manager of an obscure theatre in Leman Street, London, he sent a company of players to the New World in an effort to retrieve his fortunes. As director of the expedition he appointed his brother Lewis, formerly his first low comedian. The leading lady was Lewis's wife, likewise prominent at the London house. They were accompanied by their son Lewis, who, according to his own statement made in later life, was twelve years old at the time he left a grammar school at Cambridge to join the emigrants. The visitors made their first American appearance at Williamsburg, Va., Sept. 15, 1752, in *The Merchant of Venice.* Several of the colonies had already seen sporadic acting, but with this date begins the continuous history of the American theatre. On this occasion Lewis, Jr., initiated his career by rushing from the stage in tearful panic when the time came for him to speak his one line.

After two years of playing in various cities, including New York and Philadelphia, the company transferred its efforts to Jamaica for the next four years. During this time the elder Lewis Hallam died, and his widow married David Douglass. When the reorganized company returned to America in 1758, Douglass was the manager and a principal actor. Lewis, the younger, was now leading man, assuming such rôles as Hamlet, which he was probably the first to present in this country, and Romeo, which he played at least once to his mother's Juliet. When the imminence of the Revolution forced the American Company, as Douglass's players were now called, to suspend activities early in 1775, they set up again in Jamaica. Hallam had already gone to England, where, it appears, he gave a performance of Hamlet at Covent Garden in 1775. Later he rejoined the troupe in the West Indies. When the war came to an end, the company, much changed, returned to America. Douglass had retired in Jamaica, and Mrs. Douglass had died in or about 1774; consequently Hallam controlled the property. After a very lean year, he entered into a stormy partnership in 1785 with a rival actor and manager, John Henry. For a time there was much moral and patriotic opposition to these so-called British players, but by degrees they gained a substantial following. Beginning in the early nineties they concentrated largely on New York, with occasional visits to Boston and other northern points, the Philadelphia field being now controlled by Wignell and Reinagle. About 1793, his first wife having died after a long separation, Hallam married Miss Tuke, a young and beautiful actress whom he had introduced to the stage. About the same time his son Mirvan made his début, but proved to be an inferior actor.

In 1794 Henry sold his interest in the property to John Hodgkinson, a recent recruit, who, with Hallam's connivance, had done everything in his power to drive Henry from the company. Hallam soon discovered the new partner to be a greater source of discord than the old one. Hodgkinson was greedy for authority and parts for himself and his wife. The Hallams were forced to yield, but bitter enmity was the inevitable consequence. In 1796 William Dunlap was induced to become a third partner in the concern. He endeavored to act as mediator, but peace did not result; indeed the quarrel, aggravated by Mrs. Hallam's persistent intoxication, went so far as to form, on one occasion, an unannounced but highly diverting part of the evening's entertainment. In 1797 Hallam withdrew from the management but continued his connection as a salaried actor. During his final years his favorite rôles were gradually usurped by younger men, until in 1806 Cooper, the new director, refused to reëngage the enfeebled actor. After a few "last and only performances" at Philadelphia, he died in that city.

As a theatrical manager Hallam left much to be desired. Parsimonious, crafty, and quarrelsome, he was often the cause of the troubles in which he found himself. As an actor, however, he was much admired for many years, at one time or another personating creditably nearly every important character in the dramas then current. Of medium height, erect, and slender, he was distinguished by grace and vigor. He was competent in tragedy, comedy, and pantomime, though in tragedy he was too much given to passionless declamation. His forte was high comedy, in which he showed himself an able artist of the old school, not disposed to follow nature, but correct and finished in his manner. Regardless of personal qualities, his place in the original company from London and his half century and more of service make him a conspicuous figure in the early history of the American theatre.

[Most of the facts and some errors about Hallam are to be found in Wm. Dunlap, *A Hist. of the Am. Theatre* (1832). The first American appearance of the Hallam company was announced in the *Virginia Gazette*, Williamsburg, Aug. 28, 1752. See also W. B. Wood, *Personal Recollections of the State* (1855); Chas. Durang, "The Phila. Stage," published serially in the *Phila. Dispatch* from 1854 to 1860; G. O. Seilhamer, *Hist. of the Am. Theatre* (3 vols., 1888–91).]

O. S. C.

HALLECK, FITZ-GREENE (July 8, 1790–Nov. 19, 1867), poet, was descended from Peter Halleck (or Hallock), one of an English congregation who, fleeing from the hard hand of Laud, settled in 1640 on the eastern shore of Long Island. The poet's father, Israel, an Episcopalian, was a Tory in the Revolution, the friend of André, Percy, and Tarleton. After the war he settled as a merchant in Guilford, Conn., where in 1787 he married Mary Eliot, a farmer's daughter, descended from John Eliot, missionary to the Indians and translator of the Indian Bible; her maternal grandfather was William Leete, governor of Connecticut from 1676 to 1683. Fitz-Greene, second child and first son of the marriage, attended the public schools till his fifteenth year, when he was already a voracious reader and facile versifier. In 1811, after six years in a Guilford store, he went to New York and was for eighteen years in the employ of Jacob Barker, a banker; from 1832 to 1849 he was a confidential clerk in the counting-house of John Jacob Astor. His duties during these long terms of service left him leisure for literary and social pursuits; he perfected his knowledge of French, learned to read Italian, Spanish, and Portuguese, and early made the acquaintance of New York men of letters. In 1813 Joseph Rodman Drake [*q.v.*], won by Halleck's saying that it would be heaven "to lounge upon the rainbow and read Tom Campbell," became his close friend, and they collaborated on the poem by "Croaker & Co.," satires on local celebrities, most of which appeared in the *Evening Post* from March to June 1819. Halleck's longest poem, *Fanny,* a satire on social climbers, came out the same year, and was enlarged in 1821. He visited Europe in 1822, writing "Alnwick Castle" and "Burns" during the tour. "Marco Bozzaris" appeared in the *New York Review* for June 1825 and was immensely popular at once, being reprinted in American and British newspapers, translated into French and modern Greek, and spouted by countless elocutionists and school-boys. Halleck collected his poems in a thin volume, *Alnwick Castle, with Other Poems,* in 1827. After "Red Jacket" (1828) he wrote almost no verse for many years; but in 1834 he edited Byron's verse and prose, and in 1840 published two small volumes of *Selections from the British Poets.* When the Author's Club was formed in New York in 1837 with Irving as president, Halleck was chosen vice-president. Many distinguished visitors to the city became his friends, including Dickens, Thackeray, Miss Mitford, the Keans, Lafayette, Joseph and Louis Napoleon, Lord Morpeth (later Earl of Carlisle). In 1847 *The Poetical Works of Fitz-Greene Halleck* appeared. Astor at his death left the poet a small annuity, to which his son added a gift of $10,000; and in 1849 Halleck retired to his native village. He often visited New York, however, his friends sometimes drawing him from his retreat, as when the Century Club in 1854 gave a dinner in his honor, Bryant presiding. He published additional stanzas of "Connecticut" in 1852, and *Young America* in 1865. He died in Guilford in his seventy-eighth year. A monument was erected at his grave there; and in 1877 a statue of him was unveiled in Central Park, New York.

Halleck's personality and manner were very winning. "I have never seen a man," wrote Bayard Taylor, "who was so simply and inevitably courteous." As a talker he was at his best, said Tuckerman, in "a French café in Warren Street," his favorite haunt after business hours; "Halleck's mind, at such times, was like a bubbling spring, . . . he did not play the oracle; . . . not discourse, disputation or dictation, but *conversation,* was his function and delight." Yet he had settled convictions, not of the crowd. He detested the vulgar politician, preferring the soldier, and hence said to Duyckinck at the outbreak of the Civil War, "Thank God we shall now be ruled by gentlemen." The license of the press so disgusted him that he declared Providence "slept on its post . . . when printing was invented." "After uttering something which probably brought my surprise unconsciously into my face," says Taylor, "he would quietly add: 'I am not a republican, you must remember; I am a monarchist.' I should also have supposed him to be a Roman Catholic, from the manner in which he occasionally referred to the Church of Rome; but he expressed, in reality, the feeling of an Anglican Catholic who regretted the separation."

In poetry Halleck's ideal was Campbell; yet his own poems, except for their concise and finished style, show more the influence of Byron and Scott. "Fanny" clumsily tries to reproduce the wit without the wickedness of "Beppo." In "Alnwick Castle" Scott's romance of the feudal age is combined, rather unsuccessfully, with Byron's satiric realism. The irregular stanza of "Marco Bozzaris," the rapid narrative, the passion for liberty and martial heroism, suggest the same great romancers; but the polish of style owes something to Campbell, and the sympathy for a small people struggling to be free is thoroughly American. In "Red Jacket," "Connecticut," and "Young America," Halleck used American material, but with little success except in the first, which draws a true and vivid portrait of an Indian chief. "Burns," simple in language and meter, is one of the best tributes in verse to its subject's genius and warm humanity. The elegy on Joseph Rodman Drake unites depth of feeling with delicacy and restraint of expression. Halleck's satires and album verses may be dismissed with his own words about his share in the "Croaker Poems": "They were harmless pleasantries, luckily suited to the hour of their appearance." His modest estimate of his poetry as a whole doubtless explains why he wrote little and stopped soon; like Gray, he seems to have known that he had not much to say. He was over-rated by his contemporaries because American poetry was poor and American criticism lax in the early nineteenth century; but his best work gives him a secure niche among minor American poets.

[Sources include: J. G. Wilson, *The Life and Letters of Fitz-Greene Halleck* (1869); *The Poetical Writings of Fitz-Greene Halleck* (1869), ed. by J. G. Wilson; W. C. Bryant, *Some Notices on the Life and Writings of Fitz-Greene Halleck* (1869); E. A. Poe, *South. Lit. Messenger,* Apr. 1836; H. T. Tuckerman, *Lippincott's Mag.,* Feb. 1868; E. A. Duyckinck, *Putnam's Mag.,* Feb. 1868; G. P. Lathrop, *Atlantic Monthly,* June 1877; Bayard Taylor, *North Am. Rev.,* July 1877. See also *N. Y. Herald,* Nov. 21, 1867; W. E. Leonard, "Bryant and the Minor Poets," *Cambridge Hist. Am. Lit.,* vol. I (1917), with bibliography; N. F. Adkins, *Fitz-Greene Halleck* (1930).] W. C. B.

HALLECK, HENRY WAGER (Jan. 16, 1815–Jan. 9, 1872), soldier, author, lawyer, capitalist, came of ancestors who served in both the Revolution and the War of 1812. According to family tradition, his father, Joseph Halleck, was a descendant of Peter Hallock of Long Island. His mother was Catherine Wager, the daughter of Henry Wager of Utica, N. Y., a magistrate, who was a close personal friend of Baron Steuben and an elector of Thomas Jefferson. Halleck was born in Westernville, Oneida County, N. Y. At an early age he took such a dislike to enforced farming that he ran away from home in pursuit of an education. His maternal grandfather adopted him and sent him to the Hudson (N. Y.) Academy, whence he went to Union College. He was there elected to Phi Beta Kappa, and was later awarded (1837) the A.B. degree. Appointed to the United States Military Academy at West Point, he became a cadet on July 1, 1835. His ability was demonstrated by his standing as a cadet officer of high rank, as number three in a class of thirty-two at his graduation on July 1, 1839, and as assistant professor of chemistry and engineering during and after his four-year course.

Commissioned as a second lieutenant of engineers, on July 1, 1839, he was sent to his first station at New York Harbor, where he worked upon the fortifications. In the fall of 1844, he accompanied Marshal Bertrand to Europe, where he met Marshal Soult, was introduced at the French Court, and was given permission to visit the fortifications of France. The inspiration of this tour abroad caused him on his return home to write a "Report on the Means of National Defence," which was published by Congress (*Sen-*

ate Document No. 85, 28 Cong., 2 Sess.) and was so highly thought of that he was invited by the Lowell Institute of Boston to deliver twelve lectures. These he published in 1846 under the title, *Elements of Military Art and Science,* a book which was looked upon as authoritative and had a wide circulation among regular and volunteer officers, especially during the Civil War. When the Mexican War broke out in 1846, Halleck, a first lieutenant, was sent on the transport *Lexington* to Monterey, Cal., by way of Cape Horn. During the voyage of seven months, he translated Henri Jomini's *Vie Politique et Militaire de Napoléon,* which he published in four volumes in 1864. In California he filled varied and responsible positions, serving as secretary of state under Generals Mason and Riley, chief of staff of Burton's operations in Lower California, aide-de-camp to Commodore Shubrick, and lieutenant-governor of Mazatlan. For "gallant conduct in affairs with the enemy on the 19th and 20th of November 1846, and for meritorious services in California," he was brevetted a captain on May 1, 1847. After the war he continued as aide to General Riley, was inspector and engineer of light-houses, and acted as member of the board of engineers for fortifications on the Pacific Coast. During this time he took a prominent part in the California constitutional convention (S. H. Willey, in *Overland Monthly,* July 1872). He was promoted a captain of engineers, July 1, 1853, but, because of the cuts in the army after the war and the hopeless future in a profession little rewarded by the government, he resigned from the service on Aug. 1, 1854.

In 1843 he had already declined the professorship of engineering in the Lawrence Scientific School of Harvard. Before his resignation he had completed his study of law, and he became in 1854 head of the leading law firm in California, Halleck, Peachy & Billings, and refused a proffered seat on the state supreme bench and the office of United States senator. His business enterprises, in which he was eminently successful, forbade his acceptance of a restricting desk. He was director-general of the New Almaden quicksilver mine, president of the Pacific & Atlantic Railroad, which ran from San Francisco to San José, and major-general of California militia. His business preoccupation, however, did not prevent his writing. In 1859 he published *A Collection of Mining Laws of Spain and Mexico*; in 1860, a translation of *Fundamental Principles of the Law of Mines* by J. H. N. de Fooz; and in 1861, a treatise, *International Law, or Rules Regulating the Intercourse of States in Peace and War,* which was condensed and used widely as a textbook in schools and colleges. On Apr. 10, 1855, he married Elizabeth Hamilton, the grand-daughter of Alexander Hamilton. From this union was born an only child, Henry Wager Halleck, in 1856.

At the beginning of the Civil War, Winfield Scott, who held a high regard for Halleck's merits, urged President Lincoln to give him advanced rank. Accordingly, on Aug. 19, 1861, he was commissioned a major-general in the regular army. He was ordered to St. Louis, where on Nov. 18, 1861, he succeeded General Frémont in the command of the Department of Missouri. Halleck found the miserable conditions of extravagance, illegal organization, graft, and inefficiency, about which he had been warned by McClellan. With skill and summary restriction of abuses, he coldly and impartially put an end to evil practices in the border state. If Frémont's management of the slavery question had been too radical, Halleck's was too conservative. He was denounced in the press and in Congress by the extreme Abolitionists and pro-slavery secessionists; but he was not swerved from his course by criticism or threats. The successes of his subordinates, Grant and Foote at Donelson, Curtis at Pea Ridge, Pope at Island No. 10, and Grant at Shiloh, brought prestige to Halleck's department, although the victories were attributable rather to the skill of the individual commanders in the field than to Halleck himself. The departments of Kansas and Ohio were added to his command on Mar. 11, 1862, and the whole named the Department of the Mississippi. After bending his efforts toward reorganization, he took the field in person in April. But his labors there were not so meritorious as in the office. With double the number of his opponent's forces, he moved on the enemy cautiously with "pick and shovel," rather than intrepidly with a hundred thousand bayonets. Though Corinth, the objective, was captured, he allowed Beauregard's forces to escape and did not pursue them with vigor. This movement ended Halleck's active campaigning, during which he was known to the soldiers as "Old Brains." About five feet nine inches tall, sturdy and erect, Halleck looked the part of the soldier, but his austerity, aloofness, and scholarly procedure robbed him of that spark of personality which ignites the fire of achievement in others.

Recognizing his characteristics and needing some one to untangle the snarled situation in the eastern theatre, Lincoln called Halleck against his inclination to Washington. On July 11, 1862, he was made military adviser to the President with the title of general-in-chief, an anomalous position which scarcely any one could have filled with credit. Brusque, mathematical, direct, wholly impersonal and impartial, Halleck not only antagonized office seekers and politicians but also his subordinates far away with the forces. He was impatient of McClellan over the very shortcomings he had himself exhibited before Corinth. His counsels to his generals were frequent and often superfluous. His fears for the safety of Washington led him into errors of judgment. At times he appeared to have broken faith with McClellan, Pope, and Hooker over promised troops. Devoting his time to minutiae and the manner of raising soldiers and equipment, he seemingly obscured in his own mind the sound strategy of the main army. His timidity is illustrated in his dispatches to Meade after Gettysburg, which suggested the postponement of an engagement with Lee. Critics blame him in part for the failure to reap the fruits of that decisive battle. Here the picture of Halleck could be painted very black. It is impossible, however, now to reconstruct the difficulties which surrounded Halleck in what he termed his "political Hell" (letter to his wife, Aug. 9, 1862). He had been suddenly inducted into the supreme command of armies hastily assembled from a country that had no idea of training and scientific fighting. He found himself in an impenetrable fog of detail. Knowledge of the battlefield had to be gained mainly from dispatches. Halleck in this transitional period tirelessly worked out plans, which were ordinarily approved because those in power were not as well versed as he. Many orders of the President and Secretary of War were issued in his name when he did not approve of the contents. Being but an office general he had no opportunity to obliterate his mistakes by victories on the battlefield. Too much, however, cannot be said of Halleck's unflinching insistence upon discipline in those early days.

After almost three years of war, his incongruous position was alleviated. An order of Mar. 12, 1864, several days after Grant had been created a lieutenant-general, changed the status of Halleck from that of general-in-chief to chief of staff of the army. Although the new office was more logical and appropriate to the work Halleck had been doing, it was indeed a demotion, but he took the change in good part. Unlike other generals, who asked for relief or resigned when they could not have the positions to which they believed themselves entitled, he pursued his duties with his same unflagging energy. During the last year of the war he remained in Washington with curtailed powers. On Apr. 19, 1865, after Appomattox, he was relieved from the office of chief of staff and three days later was assigned to command the Military Division of the James, with headquarters at Richmond. After the Johnston convention he ordered Meade's army to push forward, to disregard the truce made by General Sherman, and to pay attention to the orders of no one save Grant. By this action, although it was induced by his superiors, Halleck incurred the enmity of Sherman. The breach between the two men was not healed until years later. On Aug. 30, 1865, after the termination of hostilities, Halleck was transferred to command the Military Division of the Pacific with headquarters at San Francisco. From there, on Mar. 16, 1869, he was transferred to command the Division of the South with headquarters at Louisville, Ky. He took up his new duties on June 17, 1869. This was his last assignment, for he died in Louisville on Jan. 9, 1872, in the arms of his brother-in-law, Schuyler Hamilton [*q.v.*]. He was buried in Greenwood Cemetery. Doubtless the great strain of his four years in Washington hastened his end, which was all the more tragic because of his happy domestic life. There was also no little tragedy in his career. He gave up much in entering the army in 1861, but he was not fitted to command and, thrust against his will into a treacherous position, was the victim of his limitations.

[G. W. Cullum, *Biog. Reg. Officers and Grads. U. S. Mil. Acad.* (3rd ed., 1891); Records of the Adjutant-General's Dept., War Dept.; *War of the Rebellion: Official Records (Army)*, see index; *Battles and Leaders of the Civil War* (4 vols., 1887–88); G. W. Richards, *Lives of Gens. Halleck and Pope* (1862); Jas. B. Fry, "Misunderstandings between Halleck and Grant," in *Mag. of Am. Hist.*, Dec. 1886; *Louisville Commercial*, Jan. 10, 1872; *Army and Navy Jour.*, Jan. 13, Feb. 3, 1872; memoir by Jas. G. Wilson, in *Jour. of the Mil. Service Institution of the U. S.*, May–June, Sept.–Oct., 1905; Emory Upton, "The Mil. Policy of the U. S.," *Senate Doc. No. 494*, 62 Cong., 2 Sess.; W. A. Ganoe, *Hist. of the U. S. Army* (1924); *Memoirs of Gen. W. T. Sherman* (2 vols., 1875); *Personal Memoirs of U. S. Grant* (2 vols., 1885–86); *McClellan's Own Story* (1887); Geo. Meade, *Life and Letters of Geo. Gordon Meade* (2 vols., 1913); L. H. Hallock, *A Hallock Genealogy* (1928).]
W. A. G.

HALLET, ÉTIENNE SULPICE (fl. 1789–1796), was one of the first of a long line of French architects who have influenced American design and building. The *Almanach Royal* for 1786 listed him as one of three admitted the previous year to the class of *Architectes Experts-jurés du Roi 1re Colonne*—a class second only to the Academicians. He came to America apparently in connection with the attempt of Quesnay de Beaurepaire, in 1786–88, to found his sanguinely-conceived *Académie des Sciences et Beaux-Arts* at Richmond, with branches in Baltimore, Philadelphia, and New York. In Quesnay's published *Mémoire* (1788) the name of Hallet occurs in the list of *"Patrons à la Nouvelle York."* The outbreak of the French Revolution put an end to the scheme of the Academy, and left Hallet stranded in America.

In 1790 he was living poorly in Philadelphia, then the temporary seat of the federal government. The following year, upon the dismissal of Pierre Charles L'Enfant [*q.v.*] who had been expected to design the public buildings for the new federal capital, Thomas Jefferson [*q.v.*], secretary of state, proposed to conduct a public competition on the lines of those he had come to know in France, and drafted a program of requirements for the Capitol building. Although this program, with the corresponding program for the President's House, was not published until the following March, Hallet had already, before the close of the year 1791, prepared and shown to Jefferson a design for the Capitol. In this first design he created the type which was ultimately to prevail in America: a building with a tall central dome and wings for the two legislative houses. The external forms were those of the current Louis XVI style.

Jefferson, in his design for the Virginia capitol in 1785 had followed a different fundamental conception and fitted the elements within the body of a rectangular classical temple. This idea he probably urged on Hallet, for in the design which Hallet submitted to the judgment of the commissioners of the federal city in July 1792 (along with one for the President's House, now lost) he adopted the temple form. The Virginia capitol had had a portico in front only. Hallet took the final step toward the classical ideal by employing a peristyle, surrounding the whole building with columns. In thus pursuing the initiative of Jefferson, Hallet was far in advance of the trend of literal classicism abroad, where the temple had hitherto only been adopted playfully, as in garden structures.

Although Hallet's temple design did not entirely satisfy Washington and the commissioners, it was the one most favored among those received up to the date fixed (July 15, 1792). Hallet was retained to make revised studies with a guarantee of expenses and encouragement of success, while certain other competitors were authorized to submit further designs. Working now for the commissioners at Georgetown, Hallet produced several further sets of drawings, in some of which, incidentally, he was the first to adopt the form of the classic hemicycle for a modern legislative hall. First he revised his temple design, which had been thought too cramped, but the result, with fifty-foot columns, was judged too expensive. The dilemma of accommodations too small or scale too great caused the abandonment of the temple scheme. Reverting to his original idea, he made two designs with wings and a high dome. The first was regarded as not sufficiently classical. In the second he again followed a suggestion of Jefferson, that the new church of St. Geneviève in Paris (later the Panthéon), with its cruciform plan and monumental temple portico, offered a suitable model for the type.

This design of Hallet's was seen in Philadelphia by a new competitor, William Thornton [*q.v.*], who hastily prepared and submitted a plan with a large central dome, which was recommended by Washington and Jefferson before it was seen by the commissioners, and was awarded the prize. Hallet received the £250 promised as second prize, and additional compensation for the extra designs he had made at the request of the Commission (a total of £500), as well as a lot in the city valued at £100. He had meanwhile made a sixth design, not seen by Washington and Jefferson, in which the dome, likewise with an interior peristyle, had been enlarged and reduced in height. It was placed not over the vestibule, but over the desired conference room on the west, which was now given the form of the ancient Pantheon in Rome.

When Thornton's design was received in Washington, it was subjected to criticism by Hallet and other professionals there on structural and practical grounds. Hallet was then commissioned, at a salary of £400 per year, to prepare a practicable revision of Thornton's plan and to supervise the erection of the building. The name "Stephen Hallette" on the cornerstone laid Sept. 18, 1793, seems to indicate the pronunciation of his name by his American contemporaries. Now arose a misunderstanding, for while the authorities regarded the new design as Thornton's rendered into practical form, Hallet supposed it "owed its adoption to its total difference from the other." It kept the dome over the western conference room, as in his sixth design. Since the recessed front which Hallet proposed in these was disliked, he was led to lay the foundations of the central part of the edifice with a large square open court, not unlike that of the Hôtel de Salm. This action appears to have been a principal cause of his dismissal by the commissioners on June 28, 1794. Certain drawings still required were furnished by him in November and December of that year. His dismissal led to a series of appeals to the President from his wife, Mary Gormain Hallet, by which it appears that three children of theirs had died in Washington, and that the family was in want. Small payments of various claims for services were made, the last on June 19, 1795. Hallet lingered in the city, occupied with the invention of a crane for raising stone and with other models, until August 1796, after which time he drops from sight.

[See Wells Bennett, in *Jour. Am. Inst. of Architects,* July–Oct. 1916, with Hallet's letters and drawings preserved in the Lib. of Cong. and at the Dept. of State; Fiske Kimball and Wells Bennett, *Ibid.,* Mar. 1919, and *Art Studies,* I (1923), 76–92. These articles supersede the earlier discussions of the architects of the Capitol, of which the more notable are: G. A. Townsend, *Washington, Outside and Inside* (1873); J. Q. Howard, in *Internat. Rev.,* Nov. 1874; Glenn Brown, *Hist. of the U. S. Capitol* (2 vols., 1900–02), and *Doc. Hist. of the U. S. Capitol* (1905), being *House Doc. 646,* 58 Cong., 1 and 2 Sess. (1903–04). See also Ch. Bauchal, *Nouveau Dictionnaire Biographique et Critique des Architects Français* (1887).] F. K.

HALLET, STEPHEN [See HALLET, ÉTIENNE SULPICE, fl. 1789–1796.]

HALLETT, BENJAMIN (Jan. 18, 1760–Dec. 31, 1849), owner of packet lines and founder of seamen's Bethels, was descended from Andrew Hallett, who settled on Cape Cod about 1646. Born in Barnstable, Mass., a son of Jonathan and Mercy (Bacon) Hallett, Benjamin served in the Revolution, on board the frigate *Deane* and in the land forces, and at the close of the war turned his attention to the coasting trade. In 1788 he established a packet line between Boston and Albany, a business then thought in danger of being crowded because of the two sloops engaged in it. In 1808 his famous sloop *Ten Sisters* was built in the yard of Richard Hill at Catskill, N. Y., and for many years sailed as a fast packet between New York and Boston. Hallett was an active Christian from his twentieth year and for seventy years a prominent layman of the Baptist denomination. He is said to have been singularly gifted in prayer and exhortation. Shortly after the War of 1812, on the deck of the *Ten Sisters,* anchored in Coenties Slip, New York, he held his first religious service for seamen. This was at the beginning of the movement for religious and social work among seamen later known as the "Bethel Movement." At first it consisted of services on the decks of ships, announced by a special flag displayed at the masthead. The Rev. Gardiner Spring [*q.v.*], pastor of the Brick Presbyterian Church in New York, soon lent his hearty approval and cooperation, but the other New York ministers were not at first in sympathy with the project, and left it entirely to laymen of whom Hallett was one of the leading spirits. After several years of successful work in New York, he took his Bethel flag to Boston. After his retirement to his farm in Barnstable, the work ceased to consist of deck services and was transferred to chapels for seamen—"seamen's Bethels"—which became numerous in Boston, New York, and other cities. Hallett's Bethel flag was then permanently established at the Seamen's Chapel on Central Wharf in Boston. Hallett was a familiar figure in Boston and New York and in his later years presented a patriarchal appearance. He married Abigail Lovell of Barnstable, who died Dec. 5, 1845. Their family consisted of one son, Benjamin F. Hallett [*q.v.*], and twelve daughters. His tombstone records that at his death his living descendants numbered seventy-nine.

[*Christian Watchman and Christian Reflector,* Jan. 17, 1850; Frederick Freeman, *Hist. of Cape Cod,* vol. I (1858); S. L. Deyo, *Hist. of Barnstable County, Mass.* (1890); Amos Otis, *Geneal. Notes of Barnstable Families* (1888), I, 473; Mary Rogers Bangs, *Old Cape Cod* (1920); Wm. Cathcart, *Bapt. Encyc.* (1881); *Boston Daily Jour.,* Jan. 9, 1850; *N. Y. Herald,* Jan. 10, 1850.] F. T. P.

HALLETT, BENJAMIN FRANKLIN (Dec. 2, 1797–Sept. 30, 1862), editor, politician, only son among the thirteen children of Benjamin Hallett [*q.v.*] and Abigail (Lovell) Hallett, was born in Osterville, Barnstable County, Mass. The evangelical piety of his father, a shipmaster remembered for his sponsoring of the Bethel movement among sailors, was probably the decisive factor in the choice of Brown University, then a center of religious orthodoxy and political liberalism, as the place for young Hallett's education. He graduated in 1816 with the stamp of a reformer on him, remained in Providence studying law, and was admitted to the Rhode Island bar in 1819. On June 25, 1822, he married Laura Larned of Providence. He practised his profession intermittently throughout his life and was noted for a readiness to champion cases in which he could argue his favorite theory of the rights of individuals against the encroachments of governments. An avid interest in politics prevented him, however, from devoting the time and study to law necessary to win him eminence at the bar. He became a political editor and a party manager, prominent in the press and omnipresent on committees, a factor ever to be felt in shaping his party's course.

As editor of the *Providence Journal* from 1821 to 1828, he is credited with bringing about the reform of the state supreme court. He then edited the *Daily Advertiser,* in 1829 supporting a movement for free suffrage. He was called to Boston in 1831 to edit the Antimasonic *Boston Daily Advocate.* "As furious as a windmill in a tornado," he readily established himself as the leader of radical Antimasonry in Massachusetts, and when that cause seemed ready for its demise he deliberately and skilfully steered a goodly portion of his party into the ranks of Jacksonian Democracy. For a while opposition to banks and all monopoly became his creed and he fought along these lines with the zeal characteristic of him. When the political scene shifted again, however, and the annexation of Texas became a major issue, Hallett, following the trend within his party, deserted the Van Burenites and in 1838 merged his *Advocate* with the *Boston Post,* organ of his erstwhile rivals. Thereafter party control rather than his earlier liberalism seemed to concern him. The year 1848 found him a "Hunker." The fifties saw him a "Doughface" steering by Southern charts. He was one of the first to support Pierce in 1852 and was rewarded by appointment as district attorney of Boston. He supported Buchanan in 1856 and wrote the Cincinnati platform. In 1860 he was ready to make further concessions to the Southern wing of the party and vigorously supported Breckinridge in the ensuing campaign. He died in September 1862 as the Civil War was demonstrating the irony of his career. The struggle over slavery had clouded his vision and made a conservative and a mere politician out of a man who had been born to reform.

Hallett published a number of his legal arguments in pamphlet form, most notable among them being *The Rights of the Marshpee Indians* (1834) and *The Right of the People to Establish Forms of Government* (1848), his defense of the legality of the Dorr government in the case of *Luther* vs. *Borden* (*7 Howard,* 1). He also published as pamphlets a number of speeches, letters on politics, and Fourth of July orations.

[Files of the *Boston Advocate,* 1831–38; files of the *Boston Post*; *The Proc. of the Mass. Antimasonic Conventions,* 1831–34; *Hist. Cat. Brown. Univ.* (1914); A. B. Darling, *Political Changes in Mass., 1824–48* (1925); W. G. Bean, "Transformation of Political Parties in Massachusetts 1850–60," unprinted doctoral thesis, Harvard Univ. Lib., 1922; obituaries in *Boston Post,* Oct. 1, 3, 1862, and *Providence Jour.,* Oct. 1, 2, 1862.] P. H. B.

HALLETT, MOSES (July 16, 1834–Apr. 25, 1913), Colorado jurist, was the son of pioneer parents, Moses and Eunice (Crowell) Hallett. His father moved from Massachusetts in the early nineteenth century to engage in farming, first in Missouri and then in Galena, Ill. In the latter place the younger Moses Hallett was born. He attended Rock River Seminary and Beloit College, and thence went to Chicago to study law in the office of a practising attorney. He was admitted to the bar in 1858 and practised law in Chicago. Like many of his contemporaries, he was lured to the Rockies in 1860 by the gold fever. He sought his fortune in the mining districts of Clear Creek and Gilpin counties, but his search was unavailing, and he therefore returned to his profession, opening an office in Denver with Hiram P. Bennett. Immediately recognized as a man of ability, he was elected a member of the Council of the third and fourth sessions (1863–65) of the territorial Assembly. It is significant that he served on the judiciary committee during both sessions.

He entered upon his long career as judge in 1866, when President Johnson appointed him chief justice of the supreme court of the Territory of Colorado. He held the office as long as Colorado remained a territory. The chief concern of the inhabitants of that region in the sixties was mining, but the mining law was incomplete and in need of interpretation. Colorado was also a frontier district, and the manners of the people were often as crude as their surroundings. Judge Hallett soon became known as a fearless upholder of the dignity of the court against revolver-carrying frontiersmen. In 1877, after Colorado entered the Union, Hallett was appointed United States district judge in the district of Colorado, and held office until his resignation in 1906. As the years passed his character grew more stern and his rule from the bench more severe. Respected on every hand for his honesty and profound knowledge, he is said to have done more than any other jurist toward clarifying the mining law of the state. Appeals from his judgments were rare. He was quoted in all the texts. Yet personally he was not popular: kindly toward inexperienced young lawyers, he was severe with all others.

He had few interests outside the court room, but when the University of Colorado opened its law school in 1892 he was selected as its first dean. He acted in that capacity and as lecturer on, then professor of, American constitutional law and federal jurisprudence until 1902. He was a trustee of the George W. Clayton estate, and largely under his direction the Clayton College for Orphan Boys was started on its way. In memory of his wife, Katharine (Felt) Hallett, to whom he had been married on Feb. 9, 1882, he erected the Katharine Hallett Home for Nurses at St. Luke's Hospital. Though a stanch Republican and a member of the Episcopal church, he devoted little time to either politics or church affairs. After his retirement from the bench in 1906 he added considerably to his fortune through transactions in real estate. His death removed from the scene one of the best-known and most awe-inspiring figures in Colorado.

[*Semi-Centennial Hist. of Colo.* (1913), II, 395–97; W. F. Stone, *Hist. of Colo.*, III (1918), 29–30; Frank Hall, *Hist. of the State of Colo.*, vol. IV (1895); *Who's Who in America*, 1912–13; *Denver Republican*, Apr. 26 and 28, 1913; *Rocky Mountain News*, Apr. 26, 1913.]

J. F. W.

HALLIDIE, ANDREW SMITH (Mar. 16, 1836–Apr. 24, 1900), engineer, inventor, was born in London, England, the son of Andrew and Julia (Johnstone) Smith. By family consent he adopted the name of his godfather and kinsman, Sir Andrew Hallidie, a Scottish physician of note, which action was afterwards legalized by the California legislature. After acquiring some education and interspersing it with practical experience in civil engineering, particularly surveying, young Hallidie left England for California in 1853, when he was seventeen years old. A fortune in gold was his ambition, but after two years of mining without any real success, he undertook to earn a living as a surveyor and contractor. In the course of his first year he ran lines for water ditches and for roads to mines, and was engaged to build a flume across the Middle Fork of the American River. Before coming to the United States he had had some experience with wire-rope structures, in connection with the business of his father who was engaged in manufacturing wire rope in accordance with certain inventions he had made in 1835. Accordingly, for the American River job Hallidie designed and built a wire suspension structure to carry an open flume three feet wide and two feet deep. The span was 220 feet and when completed was in every way successful. Hallidie was then but nineteen years of age. His reputation was established, however, and in the succeeding twelve years he designed and built at least fourteen wire suspension bridges and flumes in various sections of the Pacific Slope and in British Columbia. Some time in 1857 he decided to manufacture wire rope. The following year he erected a factory in which was produced the first wire rope on the Pacific Coast. This enterprise subsequently developed into the California Wire Works, of which Hallidie was president at the time of his death. In 1867 he invented a rigid suspension bridge, and in the same year perfected a method of transporting freight over canyons and rough surfaces by means of endless wire ropes, which became known as the "Hallidie ropeway." He also made several inventions for the transmission of power by means of rope. The success of his ropeway for the transportation of freight suggested to Hallidie the application of the same principle to the pulling of the loaded streetcars up the steep hillsides of San Francisco streets, which work at the time was being performed by horses. By 1871 he had devised an underground endless moving cable and a mechanical gripping device to be attached to the under side of the streetcars. When the idea was presented to the public it was more or less ridiculed and generally considered visionary, but through the perseverance of Hallidie and a few friends, sufficient money was raised to install the system on one street. The installation was completed on Aug. 1, 1873, and proved so completely successful that other installations were made, not only in San Francisco but in other cities as well, all of which brought fame and fortune to Hallidie. He was a regent of the University of California from its founding in 1868, chairman of its finance committee from 1874 until his death, and acting president during the period between the election and the installation of President Wheeler. He was president of the Mechanics Institute of San Francisco; vice-president of the James Lick School of Mechanical Arts; and much interested in the organization of the Wilmerding School. Though he did not enter politics, he took an active part in municipal affairs, especially in reform movements. He was a founder of the San Francisco Public Library and Art Society and a member of two boards of freeholders formed for the purpose of framing the charter for the government of San Francisco. He served, too, on the Executive Committee of the World's Columbian Exposition, 1892–93. Hallidie was married in November 1863 to Martha Elizabeth Woods of Sacramento, Cal., who with one daughter survived him at the time of his death in San Francisco.

[Memorial of the Board of Regents of the Univ. of Cal., July 24, 1900, printed in the *Univ. Chronicle*, Oct. 1900; R. D. Hunt, *California and Californians*, vol. IV (1926); obituaries in *San Francisco Chronicle* and *San Francisco Call*, Apr. 26, 1900; Patent Office records; U. S. Nat. Museum correspondence.]

C. W. M—n.

HALLOCK, CHARLES (Mar. 13, 1834–Dec. 2, 1917), journalist, author, and scientist, was born in New York City, the son of Gerard Hallock [*q.v.*] and Eliza (Allen) Hallock. His father was a journalist in Boston and New York and was editor of the *New York Journal of Commerce* from 1828 to 1861. Charles Hallock attended Yale, 1850–51, then Amherst College, 1851–52, receiving from the latter the degree of A.B. *extra ordinem* in 1871 (*Amherst College Biographical Record of the Graduates and Non-Graduates,* 1927). On Sept. 10, 1855, he was married to Amelia J. Wardell of New York, the daughter of Oliver T. Wardell. After acting as assistant editor of the *New Haven* (Conn.) *Register* for one year, 1855–56, he joined the staff of the *Journal of Commerce* and continued with it until his father retired in 1861. During the Civil War he lived in Canada, where he was a broker in St. John, New Brunswick, and in Halifax, Nova Scotia, and served on the staff of the St. John *Telegraph and Courier.* On returning to the United States, he became financial editor of *Harper's Weekly* for a year. His outstanding work in journalism, however, was not in daily newspaper work but lay in the founding and the editing for seven years of *Forest and Stream,* an illustrated magazine devoted to hunting, fishing, and outdoor recreation, the first issue of which appeared on Aug. 14, 1873. Later he edited two other similar magazines, *Nature's Realm* (1890) and *Western Field and Stream* (1896–97).

Besides fostering interest in outdoor life through the periodicals which he edited, Hallock was also active in movements for the scientific conservation of natural resources and for the preservation of game. He was one of the founders of the first game preserve in the United States, the Blooming Grove Park Association in Pike County, Pa., established in 1871, and for the two years following served as its secretary. In 1874 he organized the International Association for the Preservation of Game and the next year formulated a series of uniform game laws. In the late seventies and eighties he visited the Middle West, because of his interest in fishing in Michigan and in game preservation in Minnesota. In the latter state he founded the town of Hallock in 1880. In 1883 he made the first successful experiments in growing sunflowers for the oil product and for many years he was engaged in doing field work and in collecting specimens for the Smithsonian Institution.

Hallock's first book, *The Recluse of the Oconee,* was published when he was only twenty years of age. For over half a century he continued to write books, monographs, and pamphlets, most of which dealt with the subjects connected with his activities in outdoor life, including fishing, camping, sport, and travel. A partial list of his publications includes: *A Complete Biographical Sketch of "Stonewall" Jackson* (1863); *The Fishing Tourist: Angler's Guide and Reference Book* (1873); *Camp Life in Florida; A Handbook for Sportsmen and Settlers* (1876); *Vacation Rambles in Northern Michigan* (1877); *Hallock's American Club List and Sportsman's Glossary* (1878); *Hallock's Dog Fanciers' Directory and Medical Guide* (1880); *Our New Alaska; or, the Seward Purchase Vindicated* (1886); *The Salmon Fisher* (1890); *Luminous Bodies Here and Hereafter* (1906); and *Peerless Alaska* (1908). During his last years he contributed to antiquarian and metaphysical magazines. He died in Washington, D. C., in his eighty-fourth year.

[In addition to the *Amherst Coll. Biog. Record,* cited in the text, see *Who's Who in America,* 1918–19; and Hallock's *The Hallock-Holyoke Pedigree* (1906).]
W. G. B.

HALLOCK, GERARD (Mar. 18, 1800–Jan. 4, 1866), journalist, brother of William Allen Hallock [*q.v.*], was born at Plainfield, Mass., the son of Margaret Allen and the Rev. Moses Hallock, for forty-five years pastor of a church at Plainfield, and for forty years a teacher there. Fitz-Greene Halleck and Gen. H. W. Halleck [*qq.v.*] were of the same family. At the age of fifteen, Gerard Hallock prepared for college in seven months and entered Williams College in 1815. After being graduated with honors in the class of 1819, he studied at Andover, and in 1821 opened a private school at Salem, where he taught Hebrew and German. With a loan of $300, secured from David Hale [*q.v.*], he began the publication on Jan. 1, 1824, of a weekly newspaper, the *Boston Telegraph,* which devoted considerable space to religious subjects. On June 2, 1825, he was married to his cousin, Eliza Allen. That same year (1825) he became editor of the *Telegraph and Recorder,* a combination of his own paper with the *Boston Recorder,* one of the first religious weekly newspapers in the country, established by Nathaniel Willis and Sidney E. Morse [*qq.v.*] on Jan. 4, 1816. In 1826 he sold his half interest in this paper to join Sidney E. and Richard C. Morse as joint owner and editor of the *New York Observer,* started by the Morse brothers in 1820 as the first religious newspaper in New York City. He continued as editor of this paper until 1828, when he became editor of the *New York Journal of Commerce.* Early in 1829 he entered into an agreement with Lewis Tappan [*q.v.*] by which he and David Hale were to become, in two years, sole proprietors of the paper.

When the *New York Journal of Commerce* was established in 1827, it joined the Association of Morning Papers, a cooperative organization the members of which shared the annual cost of $2,500 for maintaining rowboats to secure from incoming ships copies of foreign newspapers, which, before the success of the transatlantic cable in 1866, were the chief source of news from abroad. After the *Journal of Commerce* was admitted to the association, its rival, the *Morning Courier,* established the same year, withdrew and began its own news-boat service.

To meet this competition, as well as to avoid accepting news gathered on Sunday, the *Journal of Commerce* obtained a pilot boat at a cost of $3,000 and thereupon was expelled from the association. The three-cornered rivalry resulted by 1831 in the maintenance of six news boats at a cost of $25,000 a year. After the advent of the first popular penny papers, the *Sun* and the *Herald,* the competition increased until 1848, when a new cooperative organization, the Associated Press, was formed, with the *Journal of Commerce* as one of the six members. The following year the Harbor News Association was established and later, because the limited telegraph facilities made greater cooperation essential, the Telegraph and General News associations. Hallock seems to have been the president of all of these organizations, because, when in 1856 they were consolidated into the General News Association of the City of New York, the regulations adopted, which have been called "the Magna Charta of all Associated Presses," provided that he was to continue as president of the new association. Thus Hallock may be regarded as one of the pioneers in the cooperative news-gathering movement.

In assuming the editorship of the *Journal of Commerce,* Hallock stipulated that it should be "conducted according to the original principles upon which it was established, excluding Theatre, Lottery, and all immoral advertisements and notices, strictly observing the Christian Sabbath" (*Life, post,* p. 68). Nor did he permit his editorial policies to be affected by fear of loss of subscribers. On one occasion when it was pointed out to him that his editorials were leading subscribers to stop the paper, he is said to have replied, "I do not consult my subscription list to ascertain my principles" (*Ibid.,* p. 36). In politics he stanchly supported the rights of the South in the fugitive-slave law controversy, opposed the election of Lincoln in 1860, after the election sought to avert war between the states, and as soon as hostilities had begun, urged measures of peace and conciliation. As a result, the paper, together with three other daily papers in New York, was denounced in a grand-jury presentment in August 1861, for "encouraging rebels now in arms against the Federal Government," but action was postponed until the next session of the court. A few days later, the postmaster-general of the United States issued an order excluding from the mails these four papers, because they were regarded as "dangerous from their disloyalty." Thereupon Hallock withdrew from the *Journal of Commerce* and retired to New Haven, Conn., where he died five years later.

[Wm. H. Hallock, *Life of Gerard Hallock* (1869); Jos. P. Thompson, *Memoir of David Hale* (1850); Frederic Hudson, *Journalism in the U. S. from 1690 to 1872* (1873); L. H. Hallock, *A Hallock Geneal.* (1928); "Gerard Hallock, Esq.," *Harper's Weekly,* Oct. 16, 1858; Victor Rosewater, *Hist. of Coöperative News-Gathering in the U. S.* (1930); files of the *Morning Courier,* the *Morning Courier and N. Y. Enquirer,* and the *N. Y. Journal of Commerce.*]

W. G. B.

HALLOCK, WILLIAM ALLEN (June 2, 1794–Oct. 2, 1880), first secretary of the American Tract Society, brother of Gerard Hallock [*q.v.*], was a descendant of English settlers on the eastern end of Long Island. He was born in the rugged town of Plainfield in western Massachusetts, where his father, Rev. Moses Hallock, a Yale graduate, was pastor of the newly organized church. Thither Moses Hallock brought his bride Margaret Allen from Martha's Vineyard. For years he taught pupils in his home, preparing more than three hundred for college, fifty of whom became ministers, seven of whom became well-known foreign missionaries. William, the eldest son, graduated in 1819 with highest honors at Williams College and pursued at Andover Seminary his studies for the ministry. When about to graduate in 1822 he was invited to enter for a time the service of the New England Tract Society which had been organized at Andover ten years before and was in serious need of promotional work. Hallock took up the task with energy, visiting on foot churches in eastern New England and later making journeys to New York, Philadelphia, Baltimore, and Washington. Two years' activity intensified his enthusiasm for religious literature for the masses but gave him a growing conviction that the society, which had changed its name to the American Tract Society and which aimed at a nation-wide work, should not have its center in the secluded village of Andover. Meanwhile the officers of the New York Religious Tract Society, founded in 1812, were considering giving it national scope and appointed a committee to consult the New England society with reference to a union of the two societies. After a public meeting in Boston their proposal was disfavored, but Hallock was so convinced of its importance that he made urgent representations which led to his being sent to New York for further discussion, with the result that the union was effected in May 1825, and Hallock was elected corresponding secretary of the new American Tract Society.

All of the energies of Hallock's long life from this time on were concentrated upon the work of this rapidly growing society, of which he was secretary for forty-five years and emeritus secretary for the ten subsequent years. His "prodigious industry" was the wonder of his associates. He conducted the extensive publishing and missionary correspondence of the society, supervised, in cooperation with an interdenominational committee, all of its publications, standard religious volumes as well as tracts, edited the *American Messenger* (1830–70), organized the society's colportage system, and wrote tracts which had a circulation of hundreds of thousands of copies. In addition to these various activities he wrote several biographies and compiled a *Brief Sketch of the Hallock Ancestry in the United States* (1866). His *Memoir of Harlan Page* (1835) was widely read. On Sept. 1, 1829, Hallock married Fanny Leffingwell Lathrop of Norwich, Conn. After her death in 1867 he was married to Mrs. Mary Lathrop of Brockport, N. Y.

[*Memorial of Rev. Wm. A. Hallock, D.D.* (1882), by Mrs. H. C. Knight, published by the Am. Tract Soc.; Calvin Durfee, *Williams Biog. Annals* (1871); *N. Y. Times,* Oct. 4, 1880; *N. Y. Observer* and *Evangelist* (N. Y.), Oct. 7, 1880.] E. D. E.

HALLOWELL, BENJAMIN (Aug. 17, 1799–Sept. 7, 1877), educator, minister of the Society of Friends, was born in Cheltenham township, Montgomery County, Pa., the son of Anthony and Jane (Shoemaker) Hallowell. His father died when Benjamin was two and a half years old, and he found a home first with his grandfather Shoemaker and later with an uncle. He grew up accustomed to farm work but attended school regularly, where he displayed exceptional aptitude for mathematics. Skilful with tools and eager to learn a trade, at the age of fifteen he was apprenticed to a carpenter and joiner. A fall from a ladder so injured his ankles and back that it was thought he would never be equal to the physical demands of building or farming, and he returned to school in order to fit himself for teaching. In 1817 he became a pupil of John Gummere [*q.v.*] at Burlington, N. J., who awakened in him a keen interest in the natural sciences, which thereafter, together with mathematics, became his major intellectual pursuit.

From 1818 to 1824 he taught at Westfield, N. J., Fair Hill, Montgomery County, Md., and Westtown, Pa. During this period he also made many of the calculations for Gummere's *Elementary Treatise on Theoretical and Practical Astronomy* (1822), and published a revision of Bonnycastle's *Mensuration,* and a key to the same. On Oct. 13, 1824, at the close of the monthly meeting of Friends at Sandy Spring, Md., he married Margaret E. Farquhar, and the following December he opened a school of his own in Alexandria, Va. With the exception of the period 1842 to 1846, when it was in charge of two nephews, he conducted it for nearly thirty-four years. It soon acquired a high reputation, having in 1830 students from fourteen states and territories, and from South America, Cuba, and England. Because of the exceptional training in mathematics it offered, Robert E. Lee and others went there to be prepared for West Point. He also gave much private instruction. During the interim in his management of the school, he bought a farm at Sandy Spring and carried on agricultural experiments; served as professor of chemistry in the medical department of Columbian College, Washington; and from 1845 to 1846 was in charge of a newly established Friends' high school in Philadelphia. In the fall of 1859, having sold his Alexandria school, he became the first president of the Maryland Agricultural College, but in a few months, his health failing, he retired. That same year he was recommended as an approved minister of the Society of Friends by the Alexandria Monthly Meeting, and confirmed by the Fairfax Quarterly Meeting, Virginia.

Well over six feet in height, of massive frame, clothed in Quaker simplicity, dignity, and kindliness, quietly and unselfishly obedient to the principles of his faith, he came to be both revered and beloved, and exerted a wide influence. In him a scientific mind, unusual teaching ability, business sagacity, fervent religious spirit, and philanthropic impulses, were joined. He gave frequent lectures on astronomy, chemistry, and geology, and contributed to the *American Journal of Science.* He was one of the founders of the Lyceum at Alexandria, and of a society, formed in 1827, to secure the legal rights of slaves; for a time he served as city surveyor; he was the first president of the Alexandria Water Company, and devised the water system for that community. His religious activities were numerous and extended. He was prominent in the Sandy Spring settlement of Friends and in the Baltimore Yearly Meeting, a contributor to the *Friends' Intelligencer,* and author of *The Young Friend's Manual* (1867), which contains a statement of the doctrines of the Friends. In 1863 he made a religious tour to the West, traveling 5,920 miles. While absent he heard of General Lee's repulse at Gettysburg, and although the General was his warm personal friend, "My heart," he says, "rejoiced! It was impossible to avoid it. It was an instinctive outburst in favor of right, justice, and freedom." He was one of the leaders in carrying out President Grant's "peace policy" with the Indians, serving as secretary of the General Committee of the Yearly Meetings, to which was intrusted the superintendency of the tribes in Nebraska. He headed the delegation which in 1869 visited that state, and wrote the report which was published that year. During his later days, which were spent in Sandy Spring, where he died and was buried, he wrote an account of his life, which appeared after his death. Among his publications, not already mentioned, were several addresses, *Astronomy* (1869), *Geometrical Analysis* (1872), and *Memoir of Margaret Brown* (1872).

[*Autobiography of Benjamin Hallowell* (1883) contains selections from his religious and educational writings; for Grant's "peace policy" see R. W. Kelsey, *Friends and the Indians* (1917), and *Memoirs of Samuel M. Janney* (1881); obituaries appeared in *Friends' Intelligencer*, Ninth Mo. 15, 22, 1877; *Baltimore American*, Sept. 10, 1877.] H. E. S.

HALLOWELL, RICHARD PRICE (Dec. 16, 1835–Jan. 5, 1904), merchant, abolitionist, descended from John Hallowell who came from Nottinghamshire, England, to Pennsylvania in 1682 or 1683, was born in Philadelphia, the son of Morris Longstreth and Hannah Smith (Penrose) Hallowell. He was a member of the Society of Friends and attended Haverford School (later Haverford College) from 1849 to 1853. Hallowell was a wool commission-merchant during most of his active business life, first in Philadelphia, but after 1857 in Boston. On Oct. 26, 1859, he married Anna Coffin Davis, the marriage taking place in the home near Philadelphia of the bride's grandparents, James and Lucretia Mott [*qq.v.*], of anti-slavery fame. His home after his marriage was at West Medford, Mass. He was for a time a director of the National Bank of Commerce, Boston, a trustee of the Medford Savings Bank, a selectman of the town of Medford, vice-president of the New England Woman Suffrage Association, and treasurer of the Free Religious Association.

His religious and family connections made it natural for him to dedicate himself in early life to the anti-slavery cause. He broke his first business connection in Philadelphia because his firm dealt in slave-made products from the South. He joined the Pennsylvania Society for Promoting the Abolition of Slavery and became an active leader in the anti-slavery agitation in Philadelphia and later in Boston. With others he went to Harper's Ferry in 1859 to receive the body of John Brown after the execution and escort it to North Elba, N. Y., for interment. Departing from the strict peace tenets of the Society of Friends, he became actively engaged early in the Civil War in recruiting for the famous colored regiments, the 54th and 55th Massachusetts Volunteers. He was treasurer of the recruiting fund and later was engaged actively and successfully in securing proper remuneration for the members of these regiments. When feeling was running high on the slavery question he served occasionally as a member of an informal bodyguard for William Lloyd Garrison and Wendell Phillips at public meetings. After the Civil War he spent time and money for the uplift of the colored race and was especially interested in the establishment of schools for colored people in the South. He was a trustee of the Calhoun Colored School, Alabama, from its foundation until the time of his death, and was a manager of the Home for Aged Colored Women in Boston.

Apart from his business and philanthropic interests, Hallowell found time to indulge a taste for historical study. He had a good literary style, and became deeply interested in the early history of Quakerism in New England. In 1870 he published *The Quakers in New England.* His chief work, *The Quaker Invasion of Massachusetts,* which ran through four editions between 1883 and 1887, is a virile defense of the Quakers, a story of their persecutions at the hands of New England Puritans, and a criticism of their critics. A shorter work, *The Pioneer Quakers* (1886), is in the same tone but brings the story down to 1724, about fifty years beyond the limits of the earlier volume. His last publication was a pamphlet entitled *Why the Negro Was Enfranchised* (1903), containing two letters first printed in the *Boston Herald,* Mar. 11 and 26, 1903.

[*Medford Hist. Reg.*, Oct. 1904; *Medford Mercury,* Jan. 8, 1904; *Boston Transcript,* Jan. 5, 1904; *Who's Who in America,* 1903–05; *Biog. Cat. of Matriculates of Haverford Coll., 1833–1922* (1922); J. C. Rand, *One of a Thousand* (1890); W. P. Hallowell, *Record of a Branch of the Hallowell Family* (1893).] R. W. K.

HALPINE, CHARLES GRAHAM (Nov. 20, 1829–Aug. 3, 1868), journalist, poet, born at Oldcastle, County Meath, Ireland, was the son of Nicholas John and Anne (Grehan) Halpine. His father, after a brilliant career at Trinity College, took orders in the Irish Church but devoted himself to literature. For many years, as editor of the *Dublin Evening Mail,* he was influential in Irish Protestant circles. The son matriculated at Trinity College at an early age and for a time studied medicine, then law, devoting his leisure to writing for the press. He finally went into journalism in Dublin but soon removed to London. The death of his father in impoverished circumstances and his own early marriage determined him, in 1851, to emigrate to America. Here he wrote advertisements in verse and became private secretary to P. T. Barnum. In 1852 he joined B. P. Shillaber in Boston as co-editor of the *Carpet-Bag,* a humorous weekly. After a few months he went to New York and became French translator for the *New York Herald.* He published anonymously *Lyrics by the Letter H* (1854), poems that had previously appeared in various newspapers, where, as Fitz-James O'Brien said in reviewing the volume, they ought to have remained. As Nicaraguan correspondent of the *New York Times,* he reported the filibustering expedition of William Walker and, after a short period as Washington correspondent, he became an associate editor of the *Times.* In 1857 he acquired an interest in the *Leader* and became its principal editor; through his political articles and sketches it rose rapidly in circulation and influence. Halpine actively interested himself in politics: in Dublin as a member of the "Young Ireland" group and in America, first as private secretary to Stephen A. Douglas and later as a member of the general committee of Tammany Hall. He successfully led the reform movement against Fernando Wood. He was versatile, impetuous, and of a tremendous and restless energy. His contributions to magazines and newspapers were clever and voluminous and brought him a large income. He was a member of a Bohemian group that included Fitz-Hugh Ludlow and Fitz-James O'Brien. He was a brilliant conversationalist; his stammer sometimes served his wit as when he announced that "Harriet Beseecher Be Stowe" had gone abroad to collect funds for the anti-slavery cause.

At the outbreak of the Civil War he joined the 69th Regiment as a lieutenant and was quickly promoted to the staff of General Hunter, with whom he remained the greater part of the war. He was brevetted lieutenant-colonel of volunteers June 5, 1864, for gallantry and distinguished services at the battle of Piedmont, and at the end of the war received the brevets of colonel and brigadier-general. Under assumed names he wrote effective letters of criticism to many vacillating and lukewarm editors of Northern newspapers. He prepared for Hunter's signature the first order for the enlistment of a negro regiment and overcame many of the objections of the Northern soldiers with his famous poem, "Sambo's Right to be Kilt." In his communications to the press written in the character of an ignorant Irish private, "Miles O'Reilly," he achieved a wide popularity in the North. Failing eyesight forced his retirement from the army, July 31, 1864. Having gained prominence as a reformer of municipal corruption, upon his return from the army he was invited by the Citizens Association to assume the editorship of the *Citizen,* the organ of reform. He built up the Democratic Union, an organization opposed to political corruption. Halpine had frequently held political offices, but in 1866 he ran against Tammany Hall and was elected register of the County and City of New York. *Miles O'Reilly His Book* (1864) was immediately successful and was followed by *Baked Meats of the Funeral* (1866), which included his recollections of the war and miscellaneous essays. He died suddenly in 1868 from an overdose of chloroform taken to relieve insomnia.

[*Poetical Works of Charles G. Halpine* (1869), with biog. sketch and notes by Robt. B. Roosevelt; the *Independent,* Feb. 12, 1903; *N. Y. Herald* and *Tribune* Aug. 4, 1868; *Frank Leslie's Illustrated Newspaper,* Aug. 22, 1868; Horatio Bateman, *Biogs. of Two Hundred and Fifty Distinguished National Men* (1871), I, 219; C. A. Read, *The Cabinet of Irish Lit.* (new ed., 1905), vol. III; Frederick Phisterer, *N. Y. in the War of the Rebellion* (3rd ed., 1912).] F. M.

HALSEY, JOHN (Mar. 1, 1670–1716), South Sea pirate, the son of James and Dinah Halsey, was "a Boston man, of New England." He went to sea while a youth and after a time was in command of small vessels trading with the southern colonies and the West Indies. In 1693 he was master of the sloop *Adventure* plying between Boston and Virginia. He later secured a privateer's commission to prey on French shipping off the Newfoundland banks, and in 1703 it is recorded that he brought into Barbados three barks valued at £1,800, upon which he refused to pay the Lord Admiral's tenths (*Calendar of State Papers: America and West Indies 1704–05,* p. 21). In the summer of 1703 Col. Nicholas Paige, John Colman, Benjamin Gallop, and other leading citizens and merchants of Boston built and equipped as a privateer the *Charles,* a brigantine of some eighty tons burden. In August 1703, while riding at anchor, the ship was seized by the notorious John Quelch and employed in a long piratical cruise which ended in Boston the next June when Quelch and five of his men were hanged. The owners recovered the *Charles* and secured Halsey to command it. Unable to secure a commission in Massachusetts, he went to Rhode Island, and there Governor Cranston, on Nov. 7, 1704, commissioned him "to fight and destroy any privateers or others, subjects and vassalls of France and Spaine, for 12 months if the War continue so long" (*Ibid.,* p. 313). Halsey in June 1705 brought into Rhode Island a Spanish prize valued at £4,000 and precipitated a long quarrel between Governor Dudley of Massachusetts and Governor Cranston. Dudley maintained that Cranston had no authority to commission privateers; Cranston that he had such a right and was determined to exercise it. Although the Rhode Island Assembly under the influence of Colman had passed a resolution on June 19 supporting its governor, four days later the owners humbly petitioned Dudley to have the prize and a new commission (*Ibid.*, pp. 592–93). On June 27 Judge Nathaniel Byfield of the admiralty court adjudged the vessel a prize.

Once again on the high seas, and lured by tales of pirate wealth, Halsey abandoned honest privateering, became a pirate, and sailed for Madagascar. Doubling the Cape of Good Hope, he shaped his course for the Red Sea where he encountered a Dutchman of sixty guns from Mocha. Since he had determined to take only Moorish ships, he was overpowered and confined by his crew, who attacked the Dutch ship. The crew, "perceiving they had catched a Tartar," released him in time to be saved by his courage and seamanship. After a few profitless captures and a narrow escape from the Moorish fleet, they came upon a fleet of four English ships and drove off the convoy. They secured £10,000 from the *Rising Eagle* and £40,000 in money from the *Essex*. Having discharged the *Essex,* they sailed to Madagascar to divide the booty. Some of the English merchants from the *Essex* later returned in the *Greyhound* from India with necessaries to barter with the pirates. They were dismayed to discover that a Scotch ship, the *Neptune,* was also trading with Halsey and his men. A storm having destroyed the pirate fleet, the English merchants persuaded them to seize the *Neptune.* The pirates first took the *Neptune* and then robbed the merchants of the *Greyhound* a second time and ordered them to sea. While the Scotch ship was being fitted by the pirates Halsey died of a tropical fever and was buried with pomp and solemnity. The prayers of the Church of England were read and colors were flying and salutes fired as he was buried in Madagascar in a grave made in a garden of watermelons and protected by palisades from the wild hogs. Halsey was said to have been "brave in his person, courteous to all his prisoners," and to have "lived beloved and died regretted by his own people" (Hayward, *post,* p. 422).

[*Calendar of State Papers: America and West Indies 1704–05, 1706–08*; Capt. Chas. Johnson, *A Gen. Hist. of the Robberies and Murders of the Most Notorious Pirates* (4th ed., 1726, best modern ed. by A. L. Hayward, N. Y., 1926); Philip Gosse, *The Pirates' Who's Who* (London, 1924); Geo. F. Dow and J. H. Edmonds, *The Pirates of the New Eng. Coast 1630–1730* (Salem, Mass., 1923); Howard M. Chapin, *Privateer Ships and Sailors . . . 1625–1725* (Toulon, France, 1926).]
F. M.

HALSEY, THOMAS LLOYD (*c.* 1776–Feb. 2, 1855), consul in Buenos Aires, was the son of Thomas Lloyd Halsey and Sarah (Bowen) Halsey. His father, a prominent and wealthy citizen of Providence, R. I., was French consular agent in Rhode Island during the Revolutionary War. Halsey was born in Providence and was graduated at the College of Rhode Island (Brown University) in 1793. Shortly afterward he entered upon a commercial career, and sometime before 1807 arrived in Buenos Aires. After having been engaged in business there for several years, he was appointed United States consul by President Madison on June 18, 1812, and began to serve in that capacity on Aug. 30, 1814. During his consulate, he busied himself profitably in supplying the army of the United Provinces of the Rio de la Plata with a large amount of arms and ammunition—1,600 guns, 450 barrels, and 25 cases of powder, as well as crystals and soldiers' caps and other equipment which he imported from the United States. Much of this was used by San Martín in his campaigns of 1817 and 1818, which brought about the liberation of southern South America from Spanish rule. Halsey also, in company with Col. John Devereux, guaranteed a loan of 2,000,000 pesos to the Provinces of the Rio de la Plata, which is said to have prolonged the existence of that government, whose supreme director, Pueyrredón, wrote to President Madison on Jan. 31, 1817, expressing his gratitude for this loan. A year later, however, Pueyrredón asked that Halsey be recalled because of his sympathetic relations with José Artigas, opponent of the administration.

Meanwhile, the enterprising consul had become interested in privateers cruising against Spain, and, although the United States was at peace with that country, he sent a number of blank commissions to acquaintances in Baltimore, who filled them in to suit themselves and sent out ships to reap the easy profits of this respectably disguised piracy. For his connection with these activities in violation of the good faith of the United States, his commission as consul was revoked by Secretary John Quincy Adams on Jan. 22, 1818, although he continued to serve until the arrival in Buenos Aires of W. G. D. Worthington, to whom he turned over the consulate in September 1819. The following year he visited the United States in an endeavor to persuade Adams to reappoint him, but without success.

For several years after he ceased to be consul he continued in business in Buenos Aires. He had a large estate outside the city, and imported a number of blooded sheep from the United States, being responsible for the introduction, in 1810, of the Merino breed into Argentina. He was a man of luxurious habits; to indulge his taste for terrapin soup he kept a supply of live terrapins in the cellar of his house. His South American ventures seem to have been extremely profitable. When he returned to Providence in the thirties he was the possessor of a considerable fortune. He was a trustee of Brown University from 1809 to 1839 and was prominent in Providence banking circles in his later years. He died after a dissipated old age, leaving an estate of a quarter of a million dollars, augmented shortly by the settlement of a claim of $100,000 for arms and munitions furnished the Argentine government. To the discomfiture of his sisters and their children, this estate was left in trust for his daughter, Maria Louisa Andrea del Valle, born in Argentina, and at her death the major portion was to go to her eldest son. These provisions of his will gave rise to protracted litigation which was settled out of court in 1898.

[J. F. and E. D. Halsey, *Thomas Halsey of Hertfordshire, England, and Southampton, L. I., 1591–1679, with His American Descendants* (1895); *Hist. Cat. Brown Univ.* (1915); State Dept. records, "Argentina No. 1"; W. R. Manning, *Diplomatic Correspondence of the U. S. Concerning the Independence of the Latin American Nations* (3 vols., 1925); *Memoirs of John Quincy Adams,* IV (1875), 44–47, 70, 88, V (1877), 77, 92–93, 98; C. L. Chandler, *Inter-American Acquaintances* (1915), pp. 68–74; *Agricultural and Pastoral Census of the Nation: Stock-Breeding and Agriculture in 1908,* III (1909), 65–66 (published in both Spanish and English by the Argentine government); M. G. Marshall, *The English in South America* (1878), p. 384; *Providence Daily Post,* Feb. 5, 1855; *Providence Jour.,* Dec. 15, 1898.] C. L. C.

HALSTEAD, MURAT (Sept. 2, 1829–July 2, 1908), journalist, the son of Griffin and Clarissa (Willets) Halstead, was born in Ross Township, Butler County, Ohio. After a short period of preparation under B. W. Chidlaw at Paddy's Run Academy he entered Farmers' College near Cincinnati. While in college he gave evidence of ability in writing and contributed to the newspapers. After several interruptions, during which he taught a district school, he graduated in 1851 and began his journalistic career. He joined the staff of the *Cincinnati Commercial* in March 1853 and a year later purchased a sixteenth interest in the firm. Gradually he assumed the editorial conduct of the paper and in 1865 acquired the controlling ownership. Halstead reported the political conventions of 1856 with considerable success, and his reports of the conventions of 1860 were later published as a book. He witnessed and described the hanging of John Brown near Harper's Ferry. During a part of the Civil War he represented his paper at the front and by his reports established his reputation as a brilliant war correspondent. This reputation was enhanced by his observation of the German armies in the Franco-Prussian War. In 1872 he was a member of a small group of influential Republican editors who supported the nomination of Horace Greeley for president. In the early eighties the *Cincinnati Commercial* was merged with its rival, the *Cincinnati Daily Gazette,* Halstead becoming editor-in-chief. During the presidential election of 1884 he conducted a campaign daily in New York and from his headquarters telegraphed his editorials to Cincinnati. But the *Commercial Gazette* was unable to meet the vigorous and sensational competition of the new *Cincinnati Enquirer.* Halstead remained in the East editing the *Brooklyn Standard-Union* and contributing signed articles to newspapers and magazines. President Harrison in 1889 nominated him as minister to Germany, but the Senate rejected the nomination because of articles he had written denouncing the purchase of senatorial seats. His tremendous energy unimpaired, Halstead, who had written a million words annually for forty years, now devoted himself to the writing of books. In the latter years of his life he produced, with the aid of scissors and paste, more than a score that were sold profitably by subscription. Among these were: *Our Country in War and Relations with all Nations* (1898), *Full Official History of the War with Spain* (1899), *The World on Fire . . . A Strange and Awful History* (1902), and *Pictorial History of the Louisiana Purchase and the World's Fair at St. Louis* (1904). Halstead was vigorous and forceful as a journalist, but as a historian was naïve and garrulous. He was vigorously independent and constantly fought laxity and corruption in public life. He married Mary Banks in 1857, and the simple domestic joys that he found in his large family contributed greatly to the cheerful and optimistic attitude he maintained toward the world.

[Autobiographical materials scattered through his writings; *Rev. of Revs.* (N. Y.), Apr. 1896 and Aug. 1908; *N. Y. Times, Cincinnati Commercial Tribune,* July 3, 1908; *Who's Who in America,* 1908–09; G. S. Merriam, *Life and Times of Samuel Bowles* (2 vols., 1885).] F. M.

HALSTED, GEORGE BRUCE (Nov. 25, 1853–Mar. 16, 1922), mathematician, descended in the sixth generation from Timothy Halsted who came from England about 1660 to settle at Hempstead, Long Island, was born at Newark, N. J. He could point with pardonable pride to the fact that the rolls of the College of New Jersey, at Princeton, bore not only the names of his brother and himself, but also those of his father, an uncle, his grandfather, a great-uncle, and his great-grandfather. His father was Oliver Spencer Halsted and his mother Adela (Meeker)

Halsted, a member of a one-time wealthy family of Charleston, S. C.

Halsted entered Princeton in 1872, and received his bachelor's degree in 1875 and his master's degree in 1878, having led his class throughout his entire course. He then proceeded to the Johns Hopkins University, becoming the first pupil of J. J. Sylvester, who was beginning to lay the foundations for advanced mathematical research in America. Receiving the degree of doctor of philosophy in 1879, Halsted returned to Princeton, for a time, as an instructor in graduate mathematics. From 1884 to 1903 he was professor of mathematics at the University of Texas, and it was there that his most important work was done. For a short period he taught at St. John's College, Annapolis, Md., and for three years, 1903–06, was a member of the faculty at Kenyon College, Ohio. He closed his teaching career at the Colorado State Teachers College, 1906–12, formerly known as the State Normal School. After his retirement he devoted himself for a time to electrical engineering, but in 1918 his health began to fail, and three years later he had to give up all work. He died at Roosevelt Hospital, New York, survived by his wife, Margaret Swearingen, and by three sons.

Halsted's chief interest lay in the field of geometry, and he did much to make the non-Euclidean theories known in the United States. His translations of certain treatises on the subject included: János Bolyai's *The Science Absolute of Space Independent of the Truth or Falsity of Euclid's Axiom XI* (1891), *Girolamo Saccheri's Euclides Vindicatus* (1920), Lobachevskii's *Geometrical Researches on the Theory of Parallels* (1891) and *New Principles of Geometry with Complete Theory of Parallels* (1891), A. V. Vasiliev's *Nicolái Ivánovich Lobachévsky* (1894); and *The Introduction to Lobachevski's New Elements of Geometry* (pamphlet, 1897). He also wrote *Metrical Geometry: An Elementary Treatise on Mensuration* (1881), *Elements of Geometry* (1885), *Elementary Synthetic Geometry* (1892), *Projective Geometry* (in Merriman and Woodward's *Higher Mathematics*, 1896; separately printed, 1906), *Rational Geometry* (1904), and *On the Foundation and Technic of Arithmetic* (1912). He translated Henri Poincaré, *The Foundations of Science and Hypothesis, the Value of Science, Science and Method* (1913), with a special preface by Poincaré and an introduction by J. Royce; and contributed some ninety articles on geometry and on the lives of eminent mathematicians to the *American Mathematical Monthly*. He was a man of ability in his chosen field, but certain eccentricities prevented him from attaining the success, either as a teacher or as a writer, which his powers seemed in his youthful years to promise.

[See L. E. Dickson, in *Am. Math. Mo.*, Oct. 1894; Cristoforo Alasia, in *Le Matematiche*, 1902, Feb.–Mar. and supplement; A. M. Humphreys, in *Science*, Aug. 11, 1922; *Who's Who in America*, 1922–23; W. O. Wheeler, *Descendants of Rebecca Ogden and Caleb Halsted* (1896); *Reviews of Halsted's Rational Geometry* (1905); D. M. Y. Sommerville, *Bibliog. of Non-Euclidean Geometry* (1911); considerable amount of autobiographical material written by Halsted and now in the files of Princeton Univ.] D. E. S.

HALSTED, WILLIAM STEWART (Sept. 23, 1852–Sept. 7, 1922), surgeon, descended from Timothy Halsted, an emigrant from England who settled at Hempstead, Long Island, about 1660, was born in New York City. He was the son of William Mills Halsted and Mary Louisa Haines, daughter of Richard Townley Haines. Sent at ten years of age to a private school, he afterward went to Andover and then to Yale where he graduated in 1874 without having shown any special brilliance or interest in his studies. He was distinguished as an athlete, however, and when football first came into vogue at Yale he was captain of the team which defeated Eton in the game of Dec. 6, 1873. Returning to New York he entered the College of Physicians and Surgeons and graduated in 1877. After a time as interne at Bellevue Hospital he was chosen to organize the medical service in the newly built New York Hospital, which he did with success. In 1878 he sailed for Europe, where he spent two years in study, chiefly in Vienna. Returning to New York in 1880 he plunged into active work in surgery and his advance was extremely rapid. Within five years he was visiting surgeon to several hospitals, including Bellevue and the Presbyterian. He was in charge of the out-patient surgical department of Roosevelt, was demonstrator in anatomy, and held a private quiz which was most eagerly attended.

He was extraordinarily energetic and during this time accomplished what would have exhausted, both physically and mentally, a less powerful man. In the course of these years he developed an operative technique involving complete cleanliness, deliberate action at every step so that extreme care might be observed in the gentle handling of tissues, and perfect control of hemorrhage. His ideas of what tissues could bear without being injured or weakened so as to allow the entrance of infection put his operating on a physiological basis. His operative technique was not Listerism, for Lister trusted almost entirely to the antiseptic dressing of the wound, nor was it exactly a fore-shadowing of the aseptic method, for both of these attend only to the bacteria which might invade the wound. It was rather a method concerned with the preservation of the powers of the patient's tissues to resist, and in its various ramifications and extensions was probably Halsted's greatest contribution to surgery. His second great service was his discovery in 1884 of the possibility of anesthetizing a whole region of the body by injecting cocaine into the nerve. As happened to so many people in the days just after the first production of cocaine, he fell under its influence for a time; but with heroic effort, and sustained by the faith and friendship of Dr. W. H. Welch, he overcame his dependence upon the drug and went to Baltimore to live. At first he worked in Dr. Welch's laboratory, which was built before the completion of the rest of the Johns Hopkins Hospital.

In 1889, when the hospital was opened, he became the acting surgeon and head of the outpatient department, and a year later was made professor of surgery. In the years after he left New York his whole attitude seems to have changed and, from the vigorous operator and quiz-master that nothing could tire, he became, with leisure, a thoughtful, earnest student in the laboratory, concentrated on the larger surgical problems. From the beginning to the end of his surgical work in the Johns Hopkins Hospital he kept this attitude and for thirty-two years he was almost continuously active, as the two large volumes of his published papers show (*Surgical Papers by William Stewart Halsted,* 1924, edited by Walter C. Burket, with a bibliography). He worked especially on the surgery of hernia and of cancer of the breast, on the methods of intestinal suture, on the diseases of the gall-bladder and gall ducts, on the thyroid and parathyroid, and on the surgery of the large arteries and aneurysms, but he was always interested in every other condition that lent itself to surgical treatment and was perhaps especially interested in tuberculosis, for which he earnestly advocated the good effects of continuous open air and sunshine.

On June 4, 1890, he married Caroline Hampton, daughter of Frank and Sally (Baxter) Hampton, and niece of Gen. Wade Hampton [*q.v.*]. She had been head nurse in the new hospital's operating room. Their married life was one of complete mutual devotion. The summers were spent at their place "High Hampton," at Cashiers in the mountains of North Carolina, and there they delighted in the peace and beauty of the mountain country and, for an avocation, cultivated dahlias.

Halsted was never prominent in public life and abhorred every sort of publicity. He made many trips to Europe and visited the clinics of all the great German, Austrian, and Swiss surgeons, among whom he was profoundly respected and admired. He made a point of attending the congresses of the German Surgical Association, of which he was an honorary member. His particular interest, and his third great service to his profession, was finally in the careful training of the young men of his staff and his success is to be realized from the long list of distinguished surgeons who owe everything to his example and stimulus. Whenever it seemed right to him he arbitrarily directed one or other of these young men into a special career. He was rather unapproachable, very critical of men, gifted with a sudden turn of speech that was caustic, but a delightful, witty, and humorous companion for his friends. Toward his patients and perhaps especially the poor, including the mountaineers of North Carolina who were his summer neighbors, he was benevolence and kindness personified.

In 1919 he underwent an operation for gallstones and recovered, but in 1922 he had another attack requiring operation, and this after a short time ended fatally. A month after his death Mrs. Halsted died of pneumonia.

[W. G. MacCallum, *Wm. Stewart Halsted, Surgeon* (1930); Rudolph Matas, J. M. T. Finney, W. H. Welch, in *Bull. Johns Hopkins Hospital,* vol. XXXVI (1925); Harvey Cushing, in *Science,* Oct. 27, 1922; R. Leriche, "L'Œuvre de William Halsted," in *Lyon Médical,* May 3, 1914; *Yale Univ. Obit. Record,* 1923; *Who's Who in America,* 1922–23; *N. Y. Times* and *Sun* (Baltimore), Sept. 8, 1922.]

W. G. M.

HAMBIDGE, JAY (Jan. 13, 1867–Jan. 20, 1924), artist, was born in Simcoe, Ontario, Canada, and was christened Edward John. His parents, George Fowler and Christina Shields Hambridge, had nine children of whom Jay was the eldest. His early education was limited to the public schools of Simcoe and at fifteen he ran away. A fearless adventurer, his first objective was the West. At Council Bluffs, Iowa, he found employment as a surveyor's helper and in 1885 started as printer's devil in the offices of the *Kansas City Star.* On Jan. 1, 1889, he was married to Cordelia Selina De Lorme, of Council Bluffs. After ten years in Kansas, having become a leading reporter, he joined the forces of the *New York Herald.* He had become interested in drawing as an added equipment to reportorial efficiency and studied nights at the Art Students' League. There he met Walter Appleton Clark, the illustrator, with whom he later shared his studio, and, as was his habit, a hard-earned knowledge. Though he was never deeply interested in illustration, he developed a capable and intelligent aptitude and some of his works found their way to the exhibitions of the time (Paris, 1900; St. Louis, 1904). His more absorbing passion, then awakening, was his ambition to discover the technical bases of design.

In 1900 Hambidge succeeded in enlisting the sympathetic interest of Richard Watson Gilder, editor of the *Century,* who sent him to Girgenti to make drawings of the Greek remains. After his return, on Nov. 2, 1902, he read a paper, "The Natural Basis of Form in Greek Art," which advanced his theory of Greek design. In it he set forth the belief that in the symmetrical forms of nature there is a certain "principle of proportion" which is constant and may be expressed mathematically; that this same "principle of proportion" occurs in Greek art; and that the Greeks had this knowledge and used it. Thus he attributed their sense of form to an applied mathematical theory rather than a mere instinct for design. Though the Parthenon measurements of Sir Francis Cranmer Penrose, then head of the Greek department of the British Museum, were at the time regarded as authoritative, Penrose was impressed by Hambidge's theories and urged him to develop them. With such indorsement, Hambidge became completely absorbed in his quest for a verification of his hypothesis. In the development of his theory he established a clear-cut differentiation between what he termed "dynamic" and "static" symmetry. Dynamic symmetry he believed to be a method of obtaining regularity, balance, and proportion in design by diagonals and reciprocals to rectangular areas instead of by the plane figures of geometry, or by measurements of length units—such as the foot and meter—which have been used for the purpose for many centuries. "Static symmetry, as used by the Copts, Byzantines, Saracens, Mohammedans, and the Gothic and Renaissance designers, was based upon the pattern properties of the regular two-dimensional figure such as the square and the equilateral triangle" (*Diagonal,* November 1919, pp. 10–11). In nature and in Greek art, however, this type of mensuration is unsatisfactory, since both show that "the measurableness of symmetry is that of area and not line" (*Ibid.,* December 1919, p. 27). Thus he believed that the classic artists were careful to fix the limits or form of their compositions with exactness, but that within these bounds they worked freely. In this way they were able to carry their creations to any desired perfection of finish without becoming hard or mechanical. Moderns have proceeded in a reverse manner, with a loose regard for limits, which, in part, explains the difference between modern and classic Greek design. When classic Greek design was first measured in modern times it was found that ends and sides of design areas could not be divided into one another without an unending fraction appearing as the result. Investigation has shown that these design areas cannot be reduced to the regular figures of geometry, a fact which suggests that a more subtle system for measurement for design purposes must have been used.

After years of study, years also of struggle, Hambidge was invited to present his findings to the Society for the Promotion of Hellenic Studies at their August meeting in 1914. When this major recognition was prevented by the World War, his strong spirit temporarily broke under the disappointment. The devotion and encouragement of George Whittle, however, gradually overcame his discouragement and in 1916 he started a course of lectures in Whittle's small quarters, continuing them later in the studio of Edward B. Edwards, the designer. The attendance and interest of Robert Henri and George W. Bellows [*qq.v.*] did much to enlist that of other painters. Gradually, too, Hambidge published the results of his work. *Dynamic Symmetry* (copyright 1917), an explanation of the mathematical basis of the theory, was followed by *Dynamic Symmetry: The Greek Vase* (1920), and from November 1919 to October 1920 he published the *Diagonal,* the purpose of which was to disseminate information concerning the theory of dynamic symmetry. Inevitably opposition developed, but his supporters stood by him. To the objection that "formulas are not of use to the free spirit," Bellows replied that "if a thing is made easier by technical understanding, then by so much is it true that having the particular phase made easier, your strength is conserved for those things which yet remain troublesome" (*American Architect,* Dec. 29, 1920, p. 851). Denman W. Ross, of Harvard, and William Sergeant Kendall, of Yale, also supported his theory. Through help from the Trowbridge fund, secured by Kendall, Hambidge was enabled to go again to Athens, and by the generous assistance of L. D. Caskey, the American archeologist, he was further enabled to make his own measurements of the Parthenon and other Greek temples. These final researches resulted in the publication of *Dynamic Symmetry in Composition* (1923) and *The Parthenon and Other Greek Temples: Their Dynamic Symmetry*

(1924). Though the widespread and controversial interest of 1922–23 was stimulating, the hardships attending a winter in Greece coupled with a lifelong struggle against a misapprehending opposition had taken severe toll. On Jan. 20, 1924, while lecturing, Hambidge suffered a stroke and died a few hours after. His last words were an apology to his listeners for interrupting their evening.

[In addition to works mentioned in the text, sources include: the *Diagonal,* Nov. 1919–Oct. 1920; L. D. Caskey, *Geometry of Greek Vases* (1922); Claude Bragdon, "A Dissertation on Dynamic Symmetry," the *Architecural Rev.,* Oct. 1924; A. N. Hosking, *The Artists Year Book,* 1905–06; *Art News,* Jan. 26, 1924; *N. Y. Times,* Jan. 21, 1924; information as to certain facts from members of Hambidge's family; personal acquaintance.] H. E. G.

HAMBLETON, THOMAS EDWARD (May 17, 1829–Sept. 21, 1906), Confederate blockade runner and Baltimore financier, son of Thomas Edward and Sarah (Slingluff) Hambleton of New Windsor, Carroll County, Md., came of a numerous family which had been noted in Talbot County, Md., since the early settlements. He was thoroughly schooled at St. Mary's College, a Catholic institution in Baltimore which educated many Protestants, and after graduation in 1849 he entered into partnership with a Mr. Didier to manufacture agricultural implements (*Matchett's Baltimore Directory,* 1851). On Sept. 15, 1852, he married Arabella, daughter of Maj. Dixon Stansbury. By 1855 he had entered his father's wholesale-drygoods firm as junior partner, and the next year his father retired, leaving the business to his two sons, Thomas and John. At the outbreak of the Civil War, since much of the business was with the South, the brothers transferred their interests to Richmond. Thomas served the Confederacy for a short time as private in the 1st Maryland Cavalry, but was released to aid the cause in the more important business of blockade running. He became allied with the Richmond Importing & Exporting Company, a concern engaged in running the blockade from Wilmington and Charleston. In 1863 he purchased the steamer *Coquette* from the Confederate government and built the steamer *Dare,* which he commanded until the close of the war. The *Coquette* was finally captured near Georgetown, S. C., but the crew escaped.

At the close of the war Hambleton returned to Baltimore and opened a real-estate broker's office but in 1868 entered the stock-brokers' firm which his brother John had established (*Woods Baltimore Directory,* 1867 and 1868). During the rapid expansion of business which followed the Civil War they became associated with many new enterprises, among them the Consolidated Gas Company and the United Railways & Electric Company. For his share in the development of the latter Thomas Hambleton is especially notable. Long before the days of electric cars he foresaw the possibilities of a complete traction system for Baltimore and purchased the People's Line. Seeking more capital, he went to Philadelphia and interested Widener and others in his plans, bought the North Baltimore Railway Company, and organized the Baltimore Traction Company of which he was president. He then absorbed the Citizens', Pimlico & Pikesville, Curtis Bay & Baltimore, and Powhatan companies, thus concentrating about seventy-seven miles of trackage under one concern. Electricity was just being demonstrated as practicable, and when the City & Suburban Railway Company was purchased, the entire system was changed to an electric line. The final merger, not accomplished by Hambleton, but in which he played a part, was made when his line was consolidated with the City Passenger, Baltimore & Northern, and Central systems. Hambleton was also interested in a number of railroads, being a member of the reorganization committee of the Cincinnati, Washington & Baltimore Railroad, and president of the Albany & Northern Railroad at the time of his death. His first wife died on Aug. 25, 1893, and in 1899 he married Mrs. Theodosia L. Talcott, widow of Maj. Charles Talcott.

[*Baltimore, its Hist. and its People* (1912), II, 158–61; *Who's Who in America,* 1906–07; R. H. Spencer, *Geneal. and Memorial Encyc. of the State of Md.,* vol. II (1919); obituaries in the *Baltimore American* and the *Sun,* Sept. 22, 1906.] C. W. G.

HAMBLIN, JOSEPH ELDRIDGE (Jan. 13, 1828–July 3, 1870), Union soldier, descended from James Hamblen who came from London and settled in Barnstable, Mass., in 1639, was the son of Benjamin and Hannah (Sears) Hamblin. In his childhood the family spent four years in Boston where his father was connected with the *Boston Daily Advertiser,* and after Benjamin Hamblin's death in 1837 the widowed mother and her four children returned to that city. Joseph was educated in the Boston public schools. He was employed by a firm of engine builders in Boston and then in New York, and in 1854 became an insurance broker in New York City under the firm name of Rathbone & Hamblin. His interest in military pursuits began about 1851, when he joined the 7th Regiment of the New York National Guard, and was continued during his residence in St. Louis, 1857–61, when he was connected successively with two military organizations. He had a commanding presence physically, being nearly six and a half feet in height and well proportioned. With the outbreak of the Civil War he returned to New York and entered the military service of the United States, Apr. 22, 1861, as adjutant of the 5th New York Volunteers, known familiarly as Duryée's Zouaves. He received his commission as lieutenant on May 10, 1861, and served under General Butler at the battle of Great Bethel, Va. On Aug. 10, 1861, he was commissioned captain and ordered to duty at Baltimore, where he engaged in erecting fortifications. His work excelled, and promotion came rapidly. He was made a major on Nov. 4, 1861, and was transferred to the 65th New York Volunteers, or 1st United States Chasseurs.

During the next seven months, he participated in the battles of Yorktown, Williamsburg, Fair Oaks, Glendale, and Malvern Hill, and on July 20, 1862, was promoted to lieutenant-colonel for meritorious services. He took part in the important battles of Antietam, Fredericksburg, and Chancellorsville, and for meritorious services was commissioned colonel on May 26, 1863.

He commanded his regiment under General Meade in the battle of Gettysburg in July 1863 and in 1864 was with Grant's forces in Virginia, at the Wilderness, Spotsylvania Court House, and Cold Harbor. Later in that year he was with Sheridan in the Shenandoah Valley, serving with distinction at Winchester, Fisher's Hill, and Cedar Creek. Up to this time, he had led a charmed life, escaping uninjured on several occasions when his horse was shot under him, but at Cedar Creek he received a bullet in the right thigh which confined him to the hospital for three months. With this one exception he was constantly on duty from the beginning to the end of the Civil War. On Sheridan's recommendation he was made brevet brigadier-general of volunteers on Oct. 19, 1864. After returning from the hospital, he took part in the battles of Hatcher's Run, Petersburg, and Sailor's Creek. His conspicuous gallantry at Sailor's Creek, Apr. 6, 1865, won for him the commission of brevet major-general, which he retained until he was mustered out of service.

Returning to New York City after the war, he again entered the insurance business as a member of the firm of Rathbone, Greig & Hamblin, and resumed military life in 1867 as adjutant-general of the New York National Guard and chief of staff under General Shaler, his old comrade in arms. Only about a week before his death, he met with his former regiment at the occasion of their anniversary. He was married on Oct. 15, 1868, to Isabella Gray. At the time of his death he was superintendent of agencies for the Commonwealth Fire Insurance Company.

[*Brevet Maj.-Gen. Joseph Eldridge Hamblin 1861–65* (1902), comp. by Deborah Hamblin; *War of the Rebellion: Official Records (Army)*; *Battles and Leaders of the Civil War*, III (1887), 227; *The Shenandoah Campaigns of 1862 and 1864 and the Appomatox Campaign, 1865* (Mil. Hist. Soc. of Mass., 1907); *U. S. Army and Navy Jour.*, for July 9, 1870; *N. Y. Times*, July 5, 6, 1870.]

A. R. B—g.

HAMBLIN, THOMAS SOWERBY (May 14, 1800–Jan. 8, 1853), actor, theatrical manager, was intended for a mercantile life, but after taking part in a school performance of *Hamlet,* he turned to the stage and found employment as super and occasional dancer at the Adelphi Theatre in his native London. In 1815 he was connected with Sadler's Wells Theatre, and on Dec. 26, 1818, he appeared at Drury Lane, where he played secondary parts for a season or two. Then followed an engagement as a leading actor at the Bath Theatre from Nov. 27, 1820, until his dismissal for insubordination in 1823 (John Genest, *Some Account of the English Stage,* 1832, vol. VIII, p. 681; vol. IX, pp. 120, 224). After brief connections with the Brighton and Dublin theatres Hamblin emigrated to America, accompanied by his wife, the actress Elizabeth Blanchard. Here he made his début, Nov. 1, 1825, as Hamlet at the Park Theatre, New York, and for the next five years he starred as a tragedian in various American cities. Though possessing many essentials of success, including a superb figure and a magnificent head, he never ranked with the most popular actors, partly because he was so afflicted with asthma that his husky voice was at times unintelligible and his efforts had the appearance of hard labor.

On Aug. 2, 1830, Hamblin began a more important phase of his career by taking over, in association with James H. Hackett, the management of the Bowery Theatre in New York. Hackett soon withdrew, and with two intermissions Hamblin remained in control until his death. At the outset he stressed standard drama, but after a season or so he began catering to his immediate neighborhood by presenting increasingly spectacular and melodramatic attractions. Aquatic and equestrian plays, performing animals, strong-man acts, and even boxing contests were presented for the delight of those who could not appreciate the more classic offerings of the rival Park. Inevitably the "Bowery Slaughter-House" drew heavily, and its director would have become wealthy had not ill luck persistently dogged him. On Sept. 22, 1836, shortly after he had bought the building outright, it was destroyed by fire at a loss of between $60,000 and $70,000. Hamblin now visited England and acted, with little success, at Covent Garden, London. Returning, he appeared on various New York stages until May 6, 1839, when he opened a new Bowery Theatre, which he had built in a handsome style. Once more the house was burned to the ground, Apr. 25, 1845, at a loss of about $60,000 to the director (*Evening Post,* New York, Apr. 26, 1845). For a few years Hamblin devoted himself to acting, but early in 1848 he again became sole manager of the Bowery, this structure having been erected in 1845. Ambitious to control the first theatre in the city, he also leased the Park, and having refitted it at great expense, opened it on Sept. 4, 1848; but true to its manager's fate, it was totally destroyed by fire, Dec. 16, 1848. Thereafter he confined himself to directing the Bowery until his death from brain fever at the age of fifty-three.

A man of loose morals, Hamblin was divorced by his wife in 1834 (N. M. Ludlow, *Dramatic Life as I Found It,* 1880, p. 725) and was forbidden to remarry while she was alive. After living in turn with two actresses, each known as Mrs. Hamblin, he married the beautiful and gifted actress, Mrs. Eliza Mary Ann (Trewar) Shaw, shortly after his first wife's death in 1849. By his two wives he had several children. An irascible temper led him on one occasion to the *New York Herald* office, where he gave James Gordon Bennett an unmerciful horsewhipping for publishing aspersions against him (T. A. Brown, *A History of the New York Stage,* 1903, vol. I, p. 128). In all his business and professional dealings, however, he was scrupulously honorable. If he did nothing to elevate dramatic taste, he rendered a valuable service by encouraging many promising young actors, whom he brought out at the Bowery; Charlotte Cushman, for example, owed her first New York opportunity to him. But nothing about Hamblin impressed his contemporaries more than the indomitable perseverance by which he triumphed over his singular succession of disasters.

[In addition to the sources cited above, see obituary notice in *N. Y. Herald,* Jan. 10, 1853; records of Greenwood Cemetery, New York; F. C. Wemyss, *Twenty-Six Years of the Life of an Actor and Manager* (1847), pp. 106 ff.; J. N. Ireland, *Records of the N. Y. Stage* (2 vols., 1866–67); G. C. D. Odell, *Annals of the N. Y. Stage,* vols. III–V (1928–31).]
O. S. C.

HAMER, THOMAS LYON (July 1800–Dec. 2, 1846), Ohio legislator, congressman, soldier, was born in Northumberland County, Pa. His father, said to have been a poor farmer, moved to upper New York in 1812, then in 1817 removed to Butler County, Ohio. On the trip west Thomas left the family and after a time settled at Withamsville, Clermont County, to become the teacher of a subscription school. While thus engaged he continued his own education by means of borrowed books, at the same time laying the foundation for his later forensic achievements in the local debating society. Under the direction of Thomas Morris [*q.v.*], of Bethel, he qualified for admission to the bar and began to practise at Georgetown, in Brown County, when barely of legal age. Becoming interested in politics, he served in the state legislature in 1825, 1828, and 1829, occupying the speaker's chair in the lower house during the session of 1829–30. Two years later, as an independent Democrat, he defeated both his friend Morris, the regular candidate, and their Whig opponent, in a contest for a seat in the Twenty-third Congress. He served for three consecutive terms and was recognized as one of the ablest of the Ohio Democrats. In 1840 he presided at the state convention which nominated Gov. Wilson Shannon for reëlection. Thomas Corwin, Shannon's opponent, so totally eclipsed him as a campaign speaker that Hamer was presently put forward as the only champion of his party in the state capable of coping with the great Whig orator. Hamer had none of Corwin's wit, but he was a logical and convincing speaker, and notwithstanding Corwin's election, Hamer's friends accorded to him a full share of the honors of debate.

Hamer loyally supported the Mexican War policy of the Polk administration, enlisting promptly and raising the 1st Ohio Volunteers. Commissioned brigadier-general by the President, he served with distinction under Taylor and became division commander when wounds incapacitated General Butler at Monterey. While thus engaged he was elected to the Thirtieth Congress, but on Dec. 2, 1846, he succumbed to disease. The Ohio legislature sent a deputation to Mexico to act as an escort of honor for the body on its homeward way, and it was interred at Georgetown. Hamer was the most notable Ohioan sacrificed on the altar of the Mexican War, and that his death was a national misfortune, the Whig commander Taylor testified when he wrote of the fallen Democratic general: "His loss to the army at this time cannot be supplied" (*Ohio Statesman,* Jan. 18, 1847). To him was due Grant's appointment to West Point, under circumstances which indicate a magnanimous nature. Grant's father had been Hamer's friend and associate in the old days of the debating society, but a political dispute had led to estrangement. Hesitating to address his former friend on behalf of his son, the elder Grant applied to

Senator Morris, who passed the letter on to Hamer. Hamer gladly made the appointment, and as one consequence the old friendship with the Grants was restored. Possibly this incident colored President Grant's estimate of Hamer as "one of the ablest men Ohio ever produced" (*Personal Memoirs of U. S. Grant,* 1885, I, 33, 103). Hamer was married, early in his career, to Lydia Bruce Higgins, the daughter of Robert Higgins of Virginia. After her death in 1845 he was married to Catherine Johnston, the daughter of Dr. William Johnston of Kentucky.

[The sources of information about Hamer are very meager. The most intimate account is that given in Byron Williams, *Hist. of Clermont and Brown Counties, Ohio* (1913), vol. I, pp. 416 ff. Williams gives the date of Hamer's death as Dec. 3, although most authorities give Dec. 2. Some additional matter appears in *The Hist. of Brown County, Ohio* (1883), pp. 343–52; C. B. Galbreath, *Hist. of Ohio* (1925), II, *passim*; and E. O. Randall and D. J. Ryan, *Hist. of Ohio* (1912), IV, *passim*. Accounts of the proceedings at Columbus and Georgetown upon the receipt of the news of Hamer's death are found in the *Ohio State Jour.*, Jan. 2, 1847. See also "Centennial Anniversary of the Birth of Ulysses S. Grant," *Ohio Archæol. and Hist. Soc.*, July 1922; and R. P. Spalding, *Eulogy upon Gen. Thos. L. Hamer Pronounced before the General Assembly of Ohio . . . Jan. 18, 1847* (1847).]

H. C. H.

HAMILTON, ALEXANDER (1712–May 11, 1756), physician and social historian, was born in or near Edinburgh, Scotland, of a gentle and learned family. His father, Dr. William Hamilton, was professor of divinity and principal of the University of Edinburgh; his cousin, Dr. Robert Hamilton, was professor of anatomy and botany in the University of Glasgow, and of his six brothers, one was Dr. John Hamilton, a prominent physician of Calvert County, Md. After studying with Dr. John Knox, a surgeon of Edinburgh, and attending the colleges of pharmacy in that city, Hamilton sailed for America, settling in Annapolis, Md., in the winter of 1738–39. Here he commanded a respectable practice among the wealthier colonials and supervised the education of others in his profession. Among his students was Thomas Bond [*q.v.*], a native of Maryland, who in 1752 founded the Pennsylvania Hospital in Philadelphia.

Hamilton is better remembered, however, as a social chronicler. Aside from his one medical pamphlet, *A Defence of Dr. Thomson's Discourse* (1752), supporting the practice of inoculation, two of his journals survive to us; the first, his *Itinerarium,* and the second, his history of the famous Tuesday Club. The *Itinerarium,* dedicated to Onorio Razolini in 1744, is the log of a journey into the northern colonies made in the summer of that year. Leaving Annapolis May 30, he traveled on horseback to Philadelphia, thence to New York. After a few days in New York he sailed to Albany in a sloop, remaining about a week, and returning to New York on July 5th. He proceeded by horse to Boston. Following a short visit there and a tour of New England, he returned by way of New York and Philadelphia, reaching Annapolis late in September, after a journey of 1,624 miles. His report of his travels forms an interesting document of observation and opinion, disclosing intimately to the reader the manners of the colonies and of the recorder himself. He was primarily interested, not in the medical men he met, of whom he had a poor opinion, but in the quality of "conversation" in the cities he visited, most of which he considered inferior. Philadelphia he found very solemn since Whitefield had preached there, and dedicated to merchandizing, with no taste for "public gay diversions . . . so conducive to the improvement of politeness, good manners, and humanity" (*Itinerarium,* pp. 25–26). New York was more to his liking, with the bustle of people in the streets, and gaily dressed women well in evidence. In Albany he was exasperated by the preponderance of the Dutch, whose language he deplored, and whose "women in general, both old and young, are the hardest favored I ever beheld" (*Ibid.,* p. 89). Of all the northern cities, Boston pleased him the most, for although it was "not by half such a flagrant sin to cheat . . . as to ride about for pleasure on the Sabbath day," still there was "an abundance of men of learning and parts" and at balls he saw "as fine a ring of ladies, as good dancing, and heard musick as elegant" as he had ever witnessed anywhere. To the rest of New England he was not so complimentary, and as he crossed the bridge on his return, he reports himself as saying "Farewell Connecticut . . . I have had a surfeit of your ragged money, rough roads, and enthusiastick people" (*Ibid.,* p. 209).

In the spring of the next year, as the fellow of Jonas Green [*q.v.*], Hamilton assisted in the founding of the Tuesday Club—"designed for humor, and . . . a sort of farcical Drama of mock Majesty"—of which he was the historiographer, setting down the annals of the club in a mock-serious style, with caricatures of the members from his own pen. His name in the Club was Loquacious Scribble, Esq., and he was known as "a most cheerful facetious companion" who "never failed to delight with the effusions of his wit, humor and drollery" (*Itinerarium,* pp. XXV–XXVI). So much was he the "life and soul" of the organization that it never met after his death. Although reared a Presbyterian, Hamilton served from 1749 to 1752 on the vestry of St. Anne's Anglican Church. He died at Annapolis at the age of forty-four. In 1747 he had married Margaret Dulany, the daughter of Daniel Dulany of Annapolis, who survived him.

[Hamilton's correspondence, "Dulany Papers," Md. Hist. Soc.; *Hamilton's Itinerarium* (1907), ed. by A. B. Hart; G. W. Norris, *The Early Hist. of Medicine in Philadelphia* (1886); H. D. Richardson, *Side-Lights on Md. Hist. with Sketches of Early Md. Families* (1913); manuscript records of the Tuesday Club, Md. Hist. Soc.; *Md. Gazette,* June 2, 1747, May 13, 1756; E. S. Riley, *The Ancient City: A Hist. of Annapolis in Md., 1649–1887* (1887).] H. D. R.

HAMILTON, ALEXANDER (Jan. 11, 1757–July 12, 1804), statesman, was born in the British colony of Nevis, one of the Leeward Islands. His family was good, his father being a Scottish merchant of St. Christopher, the fourth son of Alexander Hamilton of Grange in Ayrshire, and his mother Rachel Fawcett (Faucette), the daughter of a French Huguenot physician and planter of Nevis. She had been carefully educated, had made an unhappy marriage with a Danish landholder of St. Croix named John Michael Levine, had separated from him, and after meeting James Hamilton had made unavailing efforts to obtain complete freedom from her husband. Her union with Hamilton, though legally irregular, was on an irreproachable moral foundation, and she was socially recognized as his wife. But the home was not prosperous. James Hamilton's affairs, as his son later wrote, soon "went to wreck," and Rachel was living apart from him and dependent upon relatives in St. Croix when she died in 1768. Alexander Hamilton was thus practically an orphan at eleven, though his father survived until 1799. After receiving some desultory education from his mother and a Presbyterian clergyman at St. Croix, and learning to speak French fluently, at twelve he had to go to work in the general store of Nicholas Cruger in Christianstadt. From this position he was rescued by his intense ambition for a college education, his brilliancy (particularly demonstrated by a newspaper letter descriptive of a hurricane which swept St. Croix in 1772), and the generosity of his aunts. They sent him to New York in the fall of 1772. After some preliminary training at Francis Barber's grammar school at Elizabethtown, N. J., he entered King's College (now Columbia University) in the autumn of 1773. Already he had formed habits of persistent study which he retained throughout life, while his letters of the time display astonishing maturity.

The preliminaries of the Revolution interrupted Hamilton's college work and gave him opportunities for distinction which he seized with characteristic dash and address. Little weight need be attached to his statement that he temporarily inclined toward the royal side; from the time that he was a guest of William Livingston's at Elizabethtown he accepted the patriot views, and Robert Troup's story that it required a trip to Boston in 1774 to confirm his Whig opinions appears improbable. At a mass-meeting in "the Fields" (now City Hall Park) on July 6, 1774, he spoke against British measures, and at once began writing for Holt's *New York Journal, or General Advertiser* with a vigor which attracted attention. In December 1774, he contributed to the pamphlet war of the day *A Full Vindication of the Measures of Congress from the Calumnies of Their Enemies,* in some 14,000 words, and when the Rev. Dr. Samuel Seabury replied, he continued the debate in *The Farmer Refuted; or, a More Comprehensive and Impartial View of the Disputes Between Great Britain and the Colonies,* this reaching 35,000 words. These anonymous pamphlets showed such grasp of the issues, so much knowledge of British and American government, and such argumentative power, that they were attributed to John Jay, and Dr. Myles Cooper of King's College was incredulous that a lad of seventeen could have written them. Hamilton's position was that of a moderate who loyally defended the King's sovereignty and the British connection but rejected the pretensions of Parliament. His conduct was as restrained as his pen, and there is evidence that he several times acted to allay mob excitement, once (Nov. 26, 1775) protesting to John Jay when a party under Isaac Sears destroyed Rivington's press. But as the Revolutionary movement gained headway he was gladly borne into its full current. Robert Troup's statement that in 1775 Hamilton and he formed a volunteer company called "Hearts of Oak" is probably true; while early in 1776 he applied for the command of an artillery company authorized by the provincial Convention, was examined, and on Mar. 14 received his commission. His skill in drilling his company attracted attention, and Gen. Nathanael Greene is said to have been so impressed that he introduced Hamilton to Washington (G. W. P. Custis, *Recollections and Private Memoirs of Washington,* 1859); it is certain that Lord Stirling made a fruitless effort to obtain him for his staff. During the summer and fall campaign he fought with Washington on Long Island, helped fortify Harlem Heights, commanded two guns at White Plains, and was in the New Jersey retreat, while that winter he shared in the descents upon Trenton and Princeton. Though he thirsted for military glory, promotion would have been slow. It was fortunate for him that Washington, doubtless impressed by the reputation of his pamphlets, made him a secretary, and (Mar. 1, 1777) aide-de-camp, with the rank of lieutenant-colonel. His true weapon was the pen.

As secretary and aide, Hamilton held a position of great responsibility, and his duties were by no means confined to giving literary assistance to Washington. He became a trusted adviser. Since Washington was not only commanding general but virtually secretary of war, an enormous amount of business passed through his headquarters, which Hamilton did much to organize and systematize; while he inevitably came to take minor decisions into his own hands. He complained of the labor, writing that it was hard "to have the mind always upon the stretch, scarce ever unbent, and no hours for recreation." But though he was allowed to take part in a few skirmishing expeditions, and on one of these was the officer who warned Congress to remove from Philadelphia to Lancaster, Washington wisely kept him at his desk. Intercourse with the General, correspondence with Congress and the states, and occasional military missions, gave him an unrivaled opportunity for learning the situation of the army and nation. It was a characteristic of Hamilton's genius that he should not only grasp a state of affairs with lightning speed, but be seized with a passionate desire to offer constructive remedies. Before he had been at headquarters a year he had drafted the first of a series of important reports on the defects of the military system and the best mode of improving it. Among these papers are the report of Jan. 28, 1778, on the reorganization of the army; the report of May 5, 1778, on the work of the inspector-general's office; and the plan for this office as adopted by Congress on Feb. 18, 1779. Hamilton also prepared a comprehensive set of military regulations which he laid before Washington. Meanwhile, he was giving attention not only to the management of the army but to the problem of invigorating the whole government, and in facing this his *flair* for bold political theorizing again awakened.

The growth of Hamilton's political ideas, and the extraordinary ripeness and incisiveness of his thought, are exhibited in his correspondence with a committee of the New York state convention (Gouverneur Morris, Robert Livingston, William Allison), and also with Robert Morris, James Sullivan, James Duane, and other leaders, the whole covering the years 1777–81. He was a stanch believer in representative government, then widely distrusted. In a letter of May 19, 1777, to Gouverneur Morris, he ascribed the supposed instability of democracies to the fact that most of them had really been "compound governments," with a partitioned authority, and declared that "a representative democracy, where the right of election is well secured and regulated, and the exercise of the legislative, executive, and judiciary authorities is vested in select persons, chosen really and not nominally by the people, will, in my opinion, be most likely to be happy, regular, and durable" (*Works,* 1904, IX, 72). But he insisted from the first that his democracy should have a highly centralized authority, armed with powers for every exigency. He sent Robert Morris a 14,000-word letter (Apr. 30, 1781) embodying a systematic treatise on finance as part of this strongly centralized system, and containing a proposal for a national bank; its financial ideas were defective, but as William Graham Sumner said, its statesmanship was superb. Writing to Duane (Sept. 3, 1780), he vigorously exposed the defects of government under the Confederation, condemned the timidity, indecision, and dependence of Congress, and set forth a detailed plan for a revised form of government—a plan, it has been observed, almost exactly paralleled in the very successful Swiss government of later days (H. J. Ford, *Alexander Hamilton,* 1920, p. 92). In this letter he made the first proposal for a constitutional convention, suggesting that Congress should call a representation of all the states, and that this body should grant to Congress "complete sovereignty in all that relates to war, peace, trade, finance"—much more power than it enjoys today, though Hamilton would have reserved all internal taxation to the states. This willingness to entrust to Congress vastly increased authority at a time of general disgust with its inefficiency, vacillation, and corruption, is another proof of Hamilton's political discernment. One secret of his success was his belief in the possibility of a rapid renovation of political instruments.

Meanwhile, Hamilton had allied himself with one of the richest and most influential families of New York by his marriage late in 1780 to Elizabeth, second daughter of Gen. Philip Schuyler. "It is impossible to be happier than I am in a wife," he wrote in 1797, and he was always tenderly devoted to her (*Works,* 1904, X, 260; A. M. Hamilton, *post,* pp. 95 ff.). They had eight children, one of whom was James Alexander Hamilton [*q.v.*]; the first child, Philip, was born Jan. 22, 1782. Hamilton had also detached himself from Washington's staff in a last attempt to gain military distinction. The excuse for this he found in a quarrel in February 1781, when Washington administered a reprimand to his aide because the latter kept him waiting for a few minutes. The manner in which Hamilton resented this entirely proper rebuke, his rejection of Washington's subsequent advances, and his private slurs upon Washington's abilities, do him grave discredit. Unfortunately it was far from the last example of his hastiness and irascibility. Through Washington's magnanimity he was appointed to head an infantry regiment in Lafayette's corps, and at the siege of Yorktown commanded a brilliant attack upon one of the two principal British redoubts. Returning to Albany as hostilities ended, he rented a house, took Robert Troup to live with him, and after less than five months' study was admitted to the bar. His intention, he wrote Lafayette, was "to throw away a few months more in public life, and then retire a simple citizen and good paterfamilias." The public service of which he spoke was a term in the Continental Congress, which he entered in November 1782, finding it the weak flywheel of a deplorably ramshackle government. Chafing at the feebleness he saw all about him, he did what little he could to arouse a greater vigor. His efforts included the composition of the spirited but impotent reply of Congress to the refusal of Rhode Island to consent to the five per cent. impost plan (Dec. 16, 1782; *Works,* 1904, II, 179–223); the introduction that same winter of a resolution asserting the absolute necessity of "the establishment of permanent and adequate funds to operate generally throughout the United States, to be collected by Congress"; and letters to Washington somewhat officiously but shrewdly urging him to preserve the confidence of the army for use in a possible crisis. He would have introduced resolutions calling for a constitutional convention if he had not foreseen their total failure.

Though Hamilton retired from Congress in 1783 to devote himself to the law, opening an office in New York at 58 Wall St., he continued to throw his energies into the movement for a stronger federal government. Part of his legal work involved a defense of federal authority against the excesses of state law. In the noted case of *Rutgers* vs. *Waddington* he maintained that the peace treaty between the United States and Great Britain overrode the laws of New York, and particularly the Trespass Act, under which the widow Rutgers had claimed arrears of rent from a Loyalist who had occupied her property during the Revolution; his masterly argument, of which only the long brief remains, carried the case in the mayor's court, though the legislature formally reaffirmed its authority. He was an alert spectator of the growing confusion of 1784–86, and eager for an opportunity to act. The commercial negotiations of Virginia and Maryland, and the call for a general commercial convention to meet at Annapolis in September 1786, furnished the opening he desired. He secured appointment as one of the two New York delegates to the Annapolis meeting; when it failed to reach an agreement, he saw the possibility of driving home the lesson that commercial harmony was impossible without political unity; and he secured the unanimous adoption of an address recommending that the states appoint commissioners to meet in Philadelphia the following May "to take into consideration the situation of the United States, to devise such further provisions as shall seem to them necessary to render the Constitution of the Federal Government adequate to the exigencies of the Union, and to report an act for that purpose to the United States in Congress assembled." It was one of the most adroit and timely of all his strokes. The timidity of the other delegates made the terms of the call vague, but Hamilton unquestionably looked forward to the adoption of an entirely new Constitution.

In the legislature of 1787, in which the support of the New York business community gave him a seat, he led a spirited but mainly unsuccessful fight against the state laws which contravened the treaty with Great Britain. Late in the session, the bill for New York's complete adherence to the impost measure asked by Congress was brought up, and in its behalf Hamilton made one of his greatest speeches. "I well remember," Chancellor Kent later wrote of the address, "how much it was admired, for the comprehensive views which it took of the state of the nation, the warm appeals which it made to the public patriotism, the imminent perils which it pointed out, and the absolute necessity which it showed of some such financial measure" (William Kent, *Memoirs and Letters of James Kent,* 1898, p. 297). He met defeat in the Assembly, 36 to 21, but he had aroused public sentiment. Seizing the day after the impost vote, he introduced a motion instructing the New York delegates in the Continental Congress to support a constitutional convention, and despite the efforts of Gov. George Clinton's followers to weaken it, carried it in both houses. When the legislature named three delegates to the proposed convention, Hamilton as a federalist was offset by two anti-federalists, Robert Yates and John Lansing. Clinton and his powerful state-rights group took the most hostile attitude toward his labors, declaring that the Articles of Confederation required only slight amendment. But, as Hamilton gained the support of a solid body of merchants and other capitalists, he was able in increasing degree to place the anti-federalists upon the defensive.

Hamilton's rôle in the Constitutional Convention was not of the first importance; his rôle at home in New York was. Because of legal work his attendance in Philadelphia was irregular, his longest stay being from May 27 to June 29; his influence was lessened by the fact that Yates and Lansing could carry the state's vote against him; and his theories of centralization made him an object of distrust to many delegates. On June 18 he introduced his "propositions" for a Constitution, proposing that the senators and the chief executive serve during good behavior, that the governors of each state be appointed by the federal government, and that all state laws be strictly subordinate to national laws (*Works,* 1904, I, 347–69). Naturally they had little influence. During the debates he argued strongly in favor of the popular election of members of the House of Representatives, and in the contest between the small and large states supported the latter, though ready to compromise. At the close of the sessions he made a moving plea for unanimity in signing the Constitution, declaring that no true patriot could hesitate between it and the grave probability of anarchy and convulsion. Since Lansing and Yates had quit the convention, he signed alone for New York. Already (July 24) he had fired the first shot in a fierce war of newspaper essays over the Constitution, attacking Clinton for his hostility. The rejoinders were instant, and he exposed himself to misunderstanding when he signed several of his early articles "Caesar." But rising with characteristic ardor to the occasion, he carried the war into the enemy's camp by planning the "Federalist" series, the memorable first number of which he wrote in the cabin of a sloop while returning from legal work in Albany. Of this truly magnificent sequence of eighty-five expository and argumentative articles, publication of which began Oct. 27, 1787, in the *Independent Journal* and continued for seven months, he wrote at least fifty-one alone, and three more in conjunction with Madison (E. G. Bourne and P. L. Ford, in *American Historical Review,* April, July 1897). By the printing of these papers he accomplished his first preëminent service in the adoption of the Constitution; the second lay in securing the adherence of New York. The state convention which met at Poughkeepsie in June 1788 was found to contain at first forty-six anti-federalists or doubtful men to only nineteen assured federalists. "Two thirds of the convention and four sevenths of the people are against us," wrote Hamilton. But with Jay and Robert Livingston as lieutenants, he led a spectacularly effective fight on the floor of the convention. His opponents argued first for postponement, then for rejection, and then for conditional ratification, but Hamilton overthrew every one of their contentions. Fortunately for history, his irresistible speeches were reported with considerable fulness (*Works,* 1904, II, 3–99). The turning point came with his conversion of Melancthon Smith, and on July 26 the final vote showed a majority of three for the Constitution. This convention offers one of the few outstanding instances in American history of the decision of a deliberate body being changed by sheer power of sustained argument. In political management and general political contests Hamilton was one among several able leaders of his day, and was likely to err through passion or prejudice; but in parliamentary battle he was to have no real equal until the senatorial giants of the generation of Webster and Clay appeared.

The next task was to secure able and loyal officers for the new government, and Hamilton doubtless realized from the outset that he would be one of these. He sat again in the Continental Congress in February 1788, and introduced the ordinance fixing the dates and place for giving effect to the new government. By hard work in the state elections he also carried both branches of the legislature, and thus made it possible to send two federalists, Philip Schuyler and Rufus King, to the United States Senate. Nervous lest Washington refuse to become the first president, he wrote him an insistent letter. He was thus much in the foreground till the new government was organized in April 1789, and when Robert Morris proved unavailable for the Treasury Department, his selection for that post was universally expected. Commissioned on Sept. 11, 1789, he spent the following year at work in New York, removing to Philadelphia in the fall of 1790.

Though he had no practical experience with the management of finances, his labors were marked by his usual rapidity. The organization of a collecting and disbursing force throughout the country had to be carried on simultaneously with the preparation of a plan for placing the public credit upon an adequate basis. No interest had been paid for years on the foreign loans, the domestic debt was heavily and generally regarded as of dubious validity, and paper emissions and partial repudiation had demoralized public opinion. Hamilton's report was ready when Congress met on Jan. 4, 1790, but its delivery was delayed. He had hoped that he would be permitted to present his comprehensive and energetic scheme on the floor of the House, and labor there for its enactment, and he was deeply disappointed when, at the instance of Madison and others who feared his forensic talents, the representatives insisted that he report only in writing. He had to convert his brief for the speech into a written argument which he laid before the House on Jan. 14 (*Works,* 1904, II, 227–89). Unquestionably this famous document is one of the greatest of his state papers, but its originality has often been exaggerated; he drew heavily upon features of the British financial system as it had been developed up to the time of Pitt (C. F. Dunbar, "Some Precedents Followed by Alexander Hamilton," *Quarterly Journal of Economics,* October 1888). Yet in its boldness, grasp, and courage the plan was admirable. Hamilton based his proposals upon the assumption that the government would completely and punctually meet its engagements. It is the opinion of an expert student that nine congressmen in ten had come to the capital with the expectation of scaling down the debt (Edward Channing, *A History of the United States,* IV, 1917, p. 69). But Hamilton argued at length against the general view that a discrimination should be made between the original holders of public securities and actual holders by purchase, many of the latter being speculators who had paid a small fraction of the face value; and he proved the impolicy as well as impracticability of such action. He also argued that the federal government should assume the debts contracted by the states during the war, these having been shouldered for the common cause of independence. His tabulation placed the foreign debt at slightly over $11,700,000, the domestic debt at slightly more than $42,000,000, and the state debts at approximately $25,000,000. Since the interest on these sums would be excessive, he proposed several alternative schemes for funding the debt on a basis that would postpone full interest charges, offering the creditors various options, including part payment in lands and in annuities. To provide the annual revenue of $2,240,000 that he estimated was required by the government, he proposed to levy both import duties and an excise.

Hamilton's plans met fierce opposition, Maclay of Pennsylvania characterizing them as "a monument of political absurdity"; it was argued that they played into the hands of a "corrupt squadron" of "gladiators" and "speculators." Madison argued stubbornly in favor of discrimination between the first holders and the later purchasers of public securities, but was defeated by a vote of 36 to 13. After a sharp debate the bill for the assumption of the state debts was temporarily beaten, but Hamilton finally carried it to success through his famous bargain with Jefferson and Madison for the location of the national capital. The funding and assumption measures, combined in one bill of a more rigid type than Hamilton's original proposals, became law on Aug. 4, 1791. He immediately made use of these achievements to undertake further steps. On Dec. 13, 1790, he presented to the House his plan for an excise on spirits; the next day he offered his elaborate plan for a national bank; and on Jan. 28, 1791, he reported on the establishment of a mint (*Works,* 1904, II, 337–51; III, 388–443; IV, 3–58). All three proposals were accepted. The palpable need for revenue carried the excise bill past bitter opposition; and the bank was established by a law of 1792, though not until Hamilton had clashed with Madison, Edmund Randolph, and Jefferson on the constitutionality of the measure, and had given the first exposition of the doctrine of implied powers to justify his position. As a capstone for his financial and economic structure, he presented to Congress at the winter session of 1791–92 his report on manufactures, a cardinal feature of which was the proposal that protection be given to infant industries by either import duties or bounties. As the successive reports of the Secretary were studied, the scale of his ideas gradually became evident. He was not merely planning a fiscal system, but doing it in such a way as to strengthen the central government and develop the resources of the country, to stimulate trade and capitalistic enterprises, and to bring about a more symmetrical balance between agriculture and industry.

Unquestionably the secretaryship of the treasury represented the climax of Hamilton's career. Dealing with a field so complex and novel, he could not hope to avoid errors and his opponents have since made the most of some of them. Speculation in federal and state certificates of debt became a veritable mania, with general over-expansion, and ended in a panic and business depression. Hamilton miscalculated future interest rates, expecting them to fall though national growth caused them to rise. Not seeing how rapidly wealth would accumulate, he gave the debt too long a tenure. He has also been criticized for instituting a financial system that was too drastic and firm for the day and that placed an unwise strain upon the new government; even though disaster was avoided, he dangerously stimulated political passions, aroused an armed rebellion against the excise, and founded a protective system that has grown to exaggerated proportions. But the best vindication of his measures lies in their results. He created as from a void a firm public credit; he strengthened the government by not merely placing it on a sure financial foundation, but also uniting great propertied interests behind it; and he gave the country a stable circulating medium, more adequate banking facilities, and important new industries. He saw the importance of what he called "energy in the administration" (*Works,* 1904, II, 57), and if only because he went further than any other member of the government in exercising the powers of the Constitution, he must rank as one of the boldest and most far-sighted of the founders of the nation.

Hamilton's natural aggressiveness, his belief that he was the virtual premier of Washington's administration, which led to improper interferences with other departments, and his unnecessary offenses to the susceptibilities of Jefferson, Madison, and others, accentuated the party divisions which sprang naturally from differences in principles. Both he and Jefferson honestly believed that the policy of the other would tend to the destruction of the government and Constitution. They formed also a personal dislike; Hamilton wrote of Jefferson in 1792 that he was a man of "profound ambition and violent passions" (*Ibid.,* IX, 535), while Jefferson assailed Hamilton in private and protested to Washington against the "corrupt squadron" of the Treasury Department (P. L. Ford, *The Writings of Thomas Jefferson,* VI, 1895, pp. 101–09). The struggle between the federalists and anti-federalists, between Hamiltonians and Jeffersonians, was carried on by letters circulated among public men, by efforts on both sides to influence Washington, greatly distressing the latter, by congressional oratory, and by newspaper broadsides. It shortly reached a point of great bitterness, and perhaps proved the unwisdom of Washington's attempt to set up an amalgamation cabinet, representing opposite points of view. The President wrote both secretaries in an effort to moderate their feelings, but without success. Hamilton had encouraged John Fenno [*q.v.*] to establish the *Gazette of the United States* in New York in 1789, and to transfer it a year later to Philadelphia, while in October 1791 the *National Gazette* of Philip Freneau [*q.v.*] appeared under the patronage of Jefferson. Both were soon full of severe articles, with not a few personalities. The assaults on Hamilton culminated in a demand, planned by Jefferson and Madison but presented in the House by William Branch Giles, that he furnish full information concerning the loans which had been effected, their terms, and the application of the proceeds. The scarcely veiled charge of the Republicans was that Hamilton had taken funds raised in Europe, which should have been used to pay debts there, and deposited them in the Bank of the United States in order to extend its "special items" and increase its profits. Giles was indiscreet enough to make still more serious charges. In a series of replies early in 1793, Hamilton completely vindicated himself and routed his accusers, and Giles's nine resolutions of censure were overwhelmingly defeated.

When the French revolutionary wars and the arrival of Genet (Apr. 8, 1793) added fuel to the party flames, Hamilton succeeded in winning Washington to his stand that the administration should show a stricter neutrality between France and Great Britain than most of his party opponents desired. Genet, as Jefferson wished, was received without reservations, and Jefferson's view that the treaty of alliance with France was merely suspended instead of dead was also adopted; but Washington issued what amounted to a proclamation of neutrality and Hamilton followed it with strict instructions to the collectors of customs for enforcement. When the British minister demanded restitution of the British vessels captured by privateers which Genet had illegally fitted out in America, Hamilton's opinion that restitution should be made was adopted by Washington over Jefferson's protests. In this troubled period Hamilton maintained close relations with the British envoy. He succeeded also in having John Jay sent to London to negotiate a treaty covering the commercial and other disputes between Great Britain and the United States, and he carefully controlled Jay's work in the interests of his financial policy at home (S. F. Bemis, *Jay's Treaty,* 1923; for Hamilton's instructions to Jay, see *Works,* 1904, V, 121–31). The breach between Jefferson and Hamilton grew steadily more open and embarrassing until Jefferson's resignation as secretary of state in December 1793, and Jefferson continued to try to discredit the Hamiltonian party by connecting it with speculation at home and British interests abroad. While it is commonly said that Hamilton enjoyed the decisive favor of Washington, there were points in foreign affairs upon which Washington rightly preferred Jefferson's counsel, and some upon which the three men had no real disagreement. Neutrality was a clearly defined American policy before Hamilton ever asserted it, and Jefferson had been fully committed to it. But in home affairs Hamilton's place was secure, and when the Whiskey Rebellion occurred in 1794 he played the chief rôle in its suppression, attending Gen. Henry Lee's punitive force as a superintending official. He regarded the insurrection as an opportunity for the federal government to vindicate its strength. Soon afterward financial pressure, for his office paid only $3,500 a year, caused him to resign (Jan. 31, 1795). Even after he left the cabinet, however, he did much to advise Washington, as in the recall of Monroe from France and the sending of C. C. Pinckney in his stead; and he assisted Washington to give final form to his Farewell Address (Horace Binney, *An Inquiry into the Formation of Washington's Farewell Address,* 1859).

Until his death, Hamilton remained out of civil office. His best work had all been done; his cruellest errors remained to be committed. When Jay returned home with his treaty to meet a storm of criticism, Hamilton brought his pen into play in its behalf, writing two powerful series of newspaper articles signed "Camillus" and "Philo-Camillus." Their ability extorted from Jefferson a remarkable tribute. "Hamilton," he wrote to Madison, on Sept. 21, 1795, "is really a colossus to the anti-republican party. Without numbers, he is an host within himself" (P. L. Ford, *The Writings of Thomas Jefferson,* VII, 1896, p. 32). Though he was the leader of his party in 1796, he showed no aspiration for the presidency, to which because of the hostility of the South his election would have been impossible. He returned with zest to his work at the New York bar of which he was regarded as the foremost member, and where his earnings shortly reached $12,000 a year. A great favorite with the merchants of the city, he was "employed in every important and especially in every commercial case" (*Memoirs and Letters of James Kent,* 1898, p. 317); of insurance business he had "an overwhelming share." He took delight in his leisure for domestic life, building for his large family in 1802–03 a new home, "The Grange," at what is now Amsterdam Avenue and 141st–145th streets. Had he been discreet his pathway might have been fairly smooth, but discretion repeatedly failed him. In 1797 a baseless accusation against his honesty as secretary of the treasury, brought by Monroe and others, forced him to make public confession of his intrigue some years previous with a Mrs. Reynolds; an avowal which had the merit of a proud bravery, for it showed him willing to endure any personal humiliation rather than a slur on his public integrity. From the beginning of John Adams's administration he was on ill terms with the President, partly because of an old mutual dislike, and partly because in 1796 Hamilton had encouraged the Federalist electors to cast a unanimous vote for Adams's running-mate Thomas Pinckney, frankly declaring that he would rejoice if this gave Pinckney the presidency in place of Adams. Hamilton also attempted to maintain a steady influence over the acts of Timothy Pickering and Oliver Wolcott as secretaries of state and the treasury, and succeeded until the President discovered the connection and angrily reorganized his cabinet. To the end of his life Adams cherished resentment over this "intrigue," condemning Hamilton and Pickering (though not Wolcott) in the strongest terms. The natural ill-feeling between two men so unlike in temperament and principles resulted in a series of clashes. Hamilton and Adams disagreed upon the personnel of the diplomatic commission to be sent to France, the former resenting the appointment of Elbridge Gerry; they disagreed upon the Alien and Sedition Acts, which Hamilton with his usual shrewdness condemned as "violence without energy"; and upon the course which was to be pursued when the French Directory, in the X.Y.Z. Affair, outraged American feeling.

When war threatened with France in 1798, Hamilton again entertained dreams of military achievement. Following the passage of a law for raising a provisional army, Washington, who was to command it, suggested Hamilton's appointment as inspector-general with the rank of major-general, his plan being to make his old aide second in command. Gen. Henry Knox forthwith raised the question of precedence, refusing to serve if the generals were ranked according to the order of Washington's published list. Adams acceded to this view, ordering the commissions to be dated to give Knox the first rank. Washington thereupon threatened to resign, and Adams reluctantly yielded. Commissioned as inspector-general on July 25, 1798, Hamilton was busy for several months with plans for organizing a force of 50,000 and for offensive operations against Louisiana and the Floridas. He hoped to effect conquests upon an impressive scale. When suddenly Adams dissipated both the war cloud and these dreams of glory by his wise stroke in dispatching a new minister to France, Hamilton and his supporters were filled with angry consternation. With outward good grace, Hamilton advised his friends in the Senate that "the measure must go into effect with the additional idea of a commission of three," but his inward resentment was extreme. He realized that the French mission, rending the Federalist party in two, had struck it what would probably be its death-blow. A short time later he heard that Adams had accused him of being under British influence. After writing twice to the President and receiving no answer, he rashly gave way to his feelings. In what he called "a very belligerent humor," he wrote a letter harshly arraigning Adams as unfit for the presidency and letting out much confidential cabinet information. Against his friends' protests he circulated it widely, a copy was obtained by Aaron Burr, and the Republicans saw that it went through at least five printings during the year 1800 (*Letter from Alexander Hamilton Concerning the Public Conduct and Character of John Adams, Esq., President of the United States,* 1800). It was a blunder of the first magnitude, and represented so palpable a surrender to personal irritation that it was without excuse.

Yet, after this surrender to petty motives, Hamilton magnificently rose above them during the Jefferson-Burr contest for the presidency in the election of 1800–01, while three years later he was to perform a still more signal service for the Republic. When the Jefferson-Burr tie went to the House, he might have joined other Federalists in attempting to revenge themselves upon Jefferson by throwing the election to his rival, but believing that Burr was an ill-equipped and dangerous man, Hamilton cast his influence into the opposite scale. After Jefferson's election he necessarily played a minor part in national politics, though he watched public affairs alertly and in 1801 joined with some friends in founding the New York *Evening Post* to increase his influence. He trenchantly criticized Jefferson's first message, he supported the acquisition of Louisiana, and he occasionally wrote on other questions. The rising tide of disaffection with the Republican administration in certain New England circles, and the half-covert talk of secession there and in New York, found in him an immovable opponent. When in 1804 Burr again sought the governorship of New York, and it was suspected that if victorious he meant to join the New England malcontents in the formation of a Northern confederacy, Hamilton immediately took the offensive with his old dash. He succeeded in stemming the tide which had set in behind Burr's Independent and Federalist ticket, and the Republican candidate, Morgan Lewis, was easily elected. It was a brilliant achievement, scotching the best hopes of the secessionists. Burr's defeat left him thirsting for revenge, and he found his opportunity in a statement published by Dr. Charles D. Cooper, declaring that Hamilton had called Burr "dangerous" and had expressed privately "a still more despicable opinion of him." A challenge for a duel passed, and Hamilton lacked courage to defy public opinion by rejecting it, though he accepted with the utmost reluctance. The encounter took place on the early morning of July 11, 1804, under the Weehawken heights on the banks of the Hudson, and Hamilton fell mortally wounded at the first shot. He was carried back to the home of William Bayard at 80 Jane St., and after excruciating suffering died the next afternoon. It was the end of both a brilliant career and a dastardly plot against the Union. "The death of Hamilton and the Vice President's flight, with their accessories of summer-morning sunlight on rocky and wooded heights, tranquil river, and distant city, and behind all, their dark background of moral gloom, double treason, and political despair, still stand as the most dramatic moment in the early politics of the Union" (Henry Adams, *History of the United States of America,* 1890, II, p. 191).

Hamilton was below the middle height, being five feet seven inches tall, slender, remarkably erect, and quick and energetic in his movements. His complexion was clear and ruddy, his hair reddish brown, his eyes deep blue, and his whole countenance recognizably Scottish. It was often observed that his face had a double aspect, the eyes being intent and severe, the mouth kindly and winning. Few could resist his captivating traits, and even his enemies acknowledged the charm of his graceful person, frank manners, and lively conversation. He possessed a quick and powerful pride, which Gouverneur Morris somewhat unfairly called vanity. When at work, and he worked almost incessantly, he had a marvelous faculty of concentration; many observers spoke of his ability to reach conclusions as by a lightning flash—to divine them. *"Hamilton avait diviné l'Europe,"* said Talleyrand (*Life, Letters and Journals of George Ticknor,* 1876, I, 261). In his political activities he displayed a taste for intrigue, which he sometimes carried too far. His machinations against Adams in 1796, his confidential correspondence with the British minister while he sat in Washington's cabinet, his proposal to trick the Republicans in 1800 out of New York's presidential electors—a proposal which Gov. Jay quietly set aside as one "which it would not become me to adopt"—can all be counted heavily against him. Apart from this, his character was of the highest stamp, while his patriotism was unquestioned. His power as an orator was the greatest of his time, but it was characteristic of him that he chose to exert it upon select bodies of influential men, not upon the multitude. His abilities as a political leader were surpassed by few, but again he chose to work upon and through small groups rather than upon the masses. His intellect was hard, incisive, and logical, but wanting in imagination and in subtlety.

Hamilton's political principles were clearly formed by the time he was twenty-five, were pursued unremittingly throughout his life, and have probably laid a clearer impress upon the Republic than those of any other single man. He did not believe in the people, but instead profoundly distrusted the political capacity of the common man, believing him too ignorant, selfish, and ill-controlled to be capable of wise self-government. "Take mankind in general, they are vicious, their passions may be operated upon," he said in the Federal Convention (*Works,* 1904, I, 408); and again he referred to the people as a "great beast." He recognized that the ideas and enthusiasms of the time made large concessions to popular and republican government necessary, but he strove to hold them within close bounds. The main instruments of power, he believed, should be kept in the hands of selected groups, comprising those with intelligence and education enough to govern, and those with property interests for government to protect. This implied a concentration of strength in the central government. His belief in a powerful federal authority, springing thus from his political philosophy, was confirmed and made aggressive by his observations of the evils of the Confederation, with its feebleness and its disintegrating emphasis on state rights. At the time of the Federal Convention he believed the complete extinction of all the states desirable but impossible (*Works,* 1904, I, 397 ff.), and the plan which he actually brought forward would have reduced the states to shadows and have placed a tremendous authority in the hands of the federal executive. As a member of the cabinet, he wished to go beyond the words of the Constitution in invigorating the government, and hence proclaimed his doctrine of implied powers; a doctrine which, as developed under Marshall and since, has tremendously strengthened the national as compared with the state sovereignties. Accepting representative institutions, he perceived the necessity of creating an economic element devoted to a strong government and eager to uphold it for selfish as well as patriotic reasons, hence his funding measures and his views in the reports on the national credit and on manufactures. In the *Federalist,* which is a keen study in the economic interpretation of politics, he had remarked: "Every institution will grow and flourish in proportion to the quantity and extent of the means concentrated towards its formation and support"; as administrator he simply gave this principle application. He thought much of governmental strength, but little of liberty. He emphasized national wealth, power, and order, and neglected local attachments and autonomy. He believed in governmental measures for helping whole classes to grow prosperous, but he paid no attention to the aspirations of the individual for greater happiness, opportunity, and wisdom. He was a hard, efficient realist, whose work was invaluable to the nation at the time it was done, but whose narrow aristocratic political ideas needed correction from the doctrines of Jefferson and Lincoln.

[There is still room for a biography of Hamilton making full use of his papers, which were purchased by the government in 1849 and are now in the Lib. of Cong. *Hist. of the Republic of the U. S. of America, as Traced in the Writings of Alexander Hamilton* (6 vols., 1857–60), by his son, John Church Hamilton, is a documentary life on an excessively grand scale. J. C. Hamilton also published a seven-volume edition of the *Works* (1850–51), which is supplemented rather than supplanted by the editions of Henry Cabot Lodge (9 vols., 1885–88; 12 vols., 1904). Two lives strongly biased in Hamilton's favor are Lodge, *Alexander Hamilton* (1882), and J. T. Morse, *Life of Alexander Hamilton* (1876). Still more partisan, and full of dubious if interesting theorizing, is F. S. Oliver, *Alexander Hamilton: An Essay on Am. Union* (1906). More impartiality is shown in W. G. Sumner, *Alexander Hamilton* (1890); James Schouler, *Alexander Hamilton* (1901); and H. J. Ford's thoughtful but often inaccurate *Alexander Hamilton* (1920). In Claude G. Bowers, *Jefferson and Hamilton* (1925), and Francis W. Hirst, *Life and Letters of Thomas Jefferson* (1926), the point of view is frankly hostile to Hamilton. There is material of value in *The Intimate Life of Alexander Hamilton* (1910), by his grandson, Allan McLane Hamilton [*q.v.*], and there are interesting sidelights in E. S. Maclay, *Jour. of Wm. Maclay* (1890). Hamilton's connections with journalism are treated in Allan Nevins, *The Evening Post: A Century of Journalism* (1922). For a study of the background, two books by Charles A. Beard, *An Economic Interpretation of the Constitution of the United States* (1913) and *Economic Origins of Jeffersonian Democracy* (1915), are invaluable. Gertrude Atherton, who published *A Few of Hamilton's Letters* (1903), put much original research into her historical novel upon him, *The Conqueror* (1902). Paul Leicester Ford compiled a *Bibliotheca Hamiltoniana* (1886) which should be brought down to date. Among articles on special phases of his work in technical journals may be cited the following: A. D. Morse, "Alexander Hamilton," *Pol. Sci. Quart.*, Mar. 1890; E. G. Bourne, "Alexander Hamilton and Adam Smith," *Quart. Jour. of Economics,* Apr. 1894; E. C. Lunt, "Hamilton as a Pol. Economist," *Jour. of Pol. Economy,* June 1895; W. C. Ford, "Alexander Hamilton's Notes on the Federal Convention of 1787," *Am. Hist. Rev.*, Oct. 1904. See also the published writings of Washington, Adams, Jefferson, Madison, and Monroe.]

A. N.

HAMILTON, ALLAN McLANE (Oct. 6, 1848–Nov. 23, 1919), physician, alienist, author, cosmopolite, was of most distinguished ancestry. His father, Philip Hamilton, a well-known member of the bar, was a son of Alexander Hamilton, and his mother, Rebecca, was the daughter of Louis McLane [*q.v.*], minister to England and member of Jackson's cabinet. The son was born in the paternal residence at Williamsburg, later a part of Brooklyn, N. Y., and as a boy he attended school in New York and Brooklyn. Later he was sent to the Poughkeepsie Military Institute. He was too young to figure in the Civil War but made the trip to Washington with his father to secure a commission for his older brother Louis and there met Lincoln. In 1865 he made a voyage around the Horn to California. Having registered as a pupil with Dr. Henry B. Sands, he began in 1867 the study of medicine and took his degree at the College of Physicians and Surgeons in 1870, winning two prizes for excellence in studies. He opened an office on East Twenty-eighth Street the following year, but as financial returns were slow he obtained a salaried position as inspector for the board of health and also did newspaper work.

From 1871 to 1880 Hamilton was connected with the Health Department. He speaks of this period as "nine years of slavery," made sordid through the ignorance of tenement dwellers and the greed of politicians. He could have been health commissioner but this would have meant a political assessment of $5,000, and he withdrew his name. He put these years to the best possible collateral use, however, and became a pioneer in the field of neurology. He made himself known to the profession through several textbooks and on his resignation from the health department he secured several hospital and dispensary appointments as neurologist. Soon he was fairly launched in his career as a consulting neurologist and medical witness in mental cases and was one of a very few American physicians who could and did practise in Great Britain. For three years, 1900–03, he was professor of mental diseases at Cornell University Medical College.

Hamilton believed strongly in recreational activity and constant change. He therefore became a great traveler, crossed the Atlantic fifty times, and made long sojourns in Japan, Northern Africa, Italy, and Great Britain, to say nothing of trips to all regions of the United States. His autobiographic work, *Recollections of an Alienist, Personal and Professional* (1916), discusses in the first part his social contacts and the second part his leading professional experiences with celebrities. These he could give without breach of confidence for all were matters of public record. He testified in more than a hundred homicidal cases, in which insanity was a defense, including those of the presidential assassins Guiteau and Czolgosz. His opinions in outside cases are always of interest. His chief writings include: *Clinical Electro-Therapeutics* (1873); *Nervous Diseases: Their Description and Treatment* (1878); *A Manual of Medical Jurisprudence* (1883); *A System of Legal Medicine* (2 vols., 1894); *Railway and Other Accidents* (1904); and *The Intimate Life of Alexander Hamilton* (1910). His medical works were not classics (with the exception perhaps of the *Manual,* which went through three editions in seven years), and the author never seemed greatly concerned with the ultimate future of his writings. He contributed many articles to magazines and for one year, 1875–76, edited the *American Psychological Journal.*

Hamilton died at his summer home at Great Barrington, Mass., following a period of invalidism. He was twice married. His second wife was May (Copeland) Tomlinson of Sioux Falls, S. Dak., whom he married on Mar. 27, 1902. It has been said of him that, although he accomplished a great deal in his life, his performances were not in proportion to his true ability. He was too versatile, too restless, and too far in advance of his time to reap the fullest reward of his accomplishments.

[In addition to Hamilton's *Recollections,* see the *Jour. of Nervous and Mental Disease,* Jan. 1920, May 1921; *Jour. Am. Medic. Asso.,* Nov. 29, 1919; *Medic. Record,* Dec. 6, 1919, Jan. 17, 1920; *Who's Who in America,* 1918–19; *N. Y. Times,* Nov. 24, 1919.]

E. P.

HAMILTON, ANDREW (d. Apr. 26, 1703), governor of East and West New Jersey, deputy-governor of Pennsylvania, deputy postmaster-general of America, was noteworthy as the last proprietary governor of the Jerseys and as the able, but not entirely successful, champion of the rule of the Jersey proprietors against the forces which sought their overthrow. Of his early life little is known save that he was a merchant in Scotland. After the acquisition of East Jersey by the twenty-four proprietors in 1682, Hamilton was one of the Scots who became interested. In 1686 he removed his family to the province and in the next year, upon the return to Scotland of Lord Neill Campbell, the latter named him deputy-governor (*New Jersey Archives,* vol. I, p. 541). When as part of the Stuart policy of establishing an American vice-royalty, the power of Sir Edmund Andros was extended over the Jerseys, Andros continued Hamilton as his own subordinate (*Ibid.,* vol. II, p. 37), but few functions of government were exercised. The situation in East Jersey after the Revolution of 1688 was peculiar. There was no outbreak similar to Leisler's Rebellion in New York, but a large element objected to the restoration of proprietary rule. This opposition to the proprietary régime with its system of quitrents became the central thread in the politics of East Jersey. It was largely the expression of the dislike of the New England settlers to a semifeudal control. Hamilton therefore deemed it wise to sail for England leaving East Jersey to the luxury of no central government. Various efforts to reëstablish proprietary rule came to nothing. But eventually in 1692 the proprietors of both East and West Jersey commissioned Hamilton as governor (*Ibid.*, vol. II, pp. 84–88). By wise moderation he succeeded in having his authority recognized and for five years was able to administer the turbulent Jerseys with excellent results.

Meanwhile the precarious power of the proprietors was being threatened by the Crown, which was viewing all private jurisdictions with disapproval, and in nervous anxiety lest the fact that Hamilton was a Scot should offend the royal authorities, the proprietors removed him. The result was disastrous. Jeremiah Basse [*q.v.*], the new governor, played into the hands of the anti-proprietary groups in New Jersey. In despair the proprietors in 1699 endeavored to reëstablish Hamilton as governor (*New Jersey Archives,* vol. II, p. 301), but the riotous disturbances known as the "East Jersey Revolution" nullified his authority and brought contempt upon the proprietary régime. In consequence the proprietors of both East and West Jersey surrendered their political rights to the Crown, Apr. 15, 1702, though retaining their title to the land. The proprietors endeavored to have Hamilton named as royal governor, but the prize went to Lord Cornbury, governor of New York, who received an additional commission for New Jersey. Meanwhile, William Penn, on his return to England late in 1701, named Hamilton as his deputy in Pennsylvania. His brief administration there was marked chiefly by his efforts to retain a close union between the province and the three lower counties on the Delaware. Returning to visit his family in New Jersey in the spring of 1703, he died at Perth Amboy of a "hectic fever."

Hamilton's most lasting service was his share in organizing the American postal system. In 1692 he was named deputy in America by one Thomas Neale who had received a royal patent to set up a post in the colonies. Hamilton's interest may have been due to his relations with William Dockwra, an East Jersey proprietor who had established a penny post in London. Hamilton induced various American colonies to pass laws establishing uniform rates and otherwise encouraging the post, and in 1698 he presented a valuable report to the English postal authorities. On Neale's death in 1699 the latter's interests passed to Hamilton and one West, an Englishman, who were creditors. They controlled the post till Hamilton's death. Hamilton's son, John Hamilton, was later named postmaster-general for America and served till 1730. The character of Andrew Hamilton was evidently that of the typical Scot, canny, moderate, and diplomatic. He served his principals faithfully and faced difficulties with courage and sense. He was thrice married. His second wife was Anne, the daughter of Thomas Rudyard, a former deputy-governor of East Jersey. His third wife is given in his will as Agnes. John Hamilton, a son by his first wife, was long prominent in New Jersey affairs, a member of the council, and acting governor. Andrew Hamilton of East Jersey may have been connected with the famous Philadelphia lawyer of the same name, with whom he is often confused, but direct evidence is lacking.

[The chief source of information for the public career of Andrew Hamilton is the *N. J. Archives,* 1 ser., I–II (1880–90). A sketch of his life appears in vol. I, p. 509. See also W. A. Whitehead, *East Jersey under the Proprietary Governments* (rev. ed., 1875), p. 226; W. E. Rich, *Hist. of the U. S. Post Office to the Year 1829* (1924); Deborah Logan and Edward Armstrong, *Correspondence between Wm. Penn and Jas. Logan* (1870), vol. I, *passim;* and *Acts of the Privy Council, Colonial Series,* vol. II (1910), *passim.*] E. P. T.

HAMILTON, ANDREW (d. Aug. 4, 1741), an eminent Philadelphia lawyer, whose early life is shrouded in obscurity, seems to have come in the last years of the seventeenth century to Accomac County, Va., where he kept a classical school and acted as steward of an estate. On Mar. 6, 1706, he married the widow of the owner of the estate, Anne (Brown) Preeson, who assisted him to valuable connections in Maryland. At the time of his marriage he was using the name of Hamilton, and two years later bought an estate of 6,000 acres on the Chester River in Maryland. Here he lived for some years, built up a law practice, and served as deputy from Kent County in the Maryland Assembly. In 1712–13 he visited England, was admitted to Gray's Inn, Jan. 27, 1713, and two weeks later was called "per favor" to the bar. Shortly after his return to America he moved to Philadelphia, and in 1717 he was appointed attorney-general of Pennsylvania. He took an important part in public affairs and his legal services were sought more and more by the proprietors. From 1724 to 1726 he was again in England as their agent. On his return to America the proprietors granted him an estate of 153 acres in what is now the heart of Philadelphia, and in 1727 he was appointed recorder of that city and prothonotary of the supreme court, very profitable offices. For twelve years, beginning in 1727, he represented Bucks County in the Assembly and after 1729 was speaker, except for the session of 1733. The Assembly seems to have found his legal and other abilities indispensable, but his course in politics was singularly independent. He was vigorous in opposition to "encroachments" by governors, but he did not ally himself with the so-called anti-proprietary party and throughout his career retained the confidence and esteem of the proprietary family and interests. His independence, versatility, and self-confidence are illustrated by his connection with the erection of the Pennsylvania State House, afterward known as Independence Hall (F. M. Etting, *An Historical Account of the Old State House of Pennsylvania,* 1876). Its site and main architectural features are due to him. In 1737 he was appointed judge of the vice-admiralty court. All these public positions are testimony to his commanding abilities, for his vigorous personality and activity could not fail to make enemies and his generally independent attitude extended to omission of formal adherence to any religious creed. All this may be read between the lines, as well as explicitly, in Franklin's obituary of him in the *Pennsylvania Gazette.*

His title to fame is his successful defense of John Peter Zenger, publisher of the New York *Weekly Journal,* against a charge of seditious libel. Circumstances combined to make this occasion momentous and dramatic. For several years prior to 1735 the conflict between popular and governmental parties in New York had been working toward a crisis. The popular party, led by Morris, Alexander, and Smith, using what was a new weapon in New York politics, an opposition newspaper, seemed to the governmental clique to be making alarming headway. Failing to secure support from the city government and from the grand jury, the provincial government had recourse to a prosecution by the attorney-general "on information" for seditious libel. In April 1735 Zenger's counsel, Alexander and Smith, leaders of the New York bar, attacked the validity of the judges' commissions and were promptly disbarred. Zenger was thus left practically defenseless, for the few remaining New York lawyers were either attached to the court party or too intimidated to be helpful. The issue at stake was, in a very real sense, the freedom of the press as the only orderly means of resistance to an arbitrary and unscrupulous executive. The popular leaders secretly invited Hamilton to undertake Zenger's defense, and his appearance in the case in August 1735 was a surprise to the excited populace and to the hitherto triumphant court. The law of libel and the regular court procedure in such cases at the time confined the functions of the jury to determination of the mere fact of publication, the libelous character of the words being left as a question of law to the judges. The only hope of success lay in persuading the jury, at peril to themselves, to render a "general verdict" on both law and facts. This Hamilton succeeded in doing by a masterly command of the technique of advocacy and by a speech which has been characterized as the "greatest oratorical triumph won in the colonies prior to the speech of James Otis against writs of assistance" (Osgood, *post,* II, 460). This outcome naturally excited great local enthusiasm; Hamilton was presented with the freedom of the city in a gold box. It attracted attention in England also, four editions of the London reprint being required in three months. From the strictly legal standpoint it is probably true that the points for which Hamilton contended were not "good law" at the time in America or England. Sir James Stephen calls the speech "singularly able, bold and powerful, though full of doubtful, not to say bad, law" (*A History of the Criminal Law of England,* 1883, II, 323). Precisely these points, however, were embodied fifty-six years later in Fox's Libel Act. A different result of the trial would probably have throttled, for a time at least, the political press of America. Hamilton died in August 1741 and was buried first at his estate, "Bush Hill," and afterward in the graveyard of Christ Church, Philadelphia. His son James [*q.v.*] was later lieutenant-governor and acting governor of Pennsylvania.

[W. H. Loyd, article in *Great Am. Lawyers,* vol. I (1907), ed. by W. D. Lewis; J. F. Fisher, "Andrew Hamilton, Esq., of Pa.," *Hist. Mag.,* Aug. 1868; E. A. Jones, *Am. Members of the Inns of Court* (1924); Livingston Rutherfurd, *John Peter Zenger: His Press, His Trial, and a Bibliog. of Zenger Imprints* (1904); P. W. Chandler, *Am. Criminal Trials* (1844); L. R. Schuyler, *The Liberty of the Press in the Am. Colonies before the Revolutionary War* (1905); H. L. Osgood, *The Am. Colonies in the Eighteenth Century* (1924); *Pa. Mag. of Hist. and Biog.,* Apr. 1901; *Ibid.,* vol. XX (1896), pp. 405–08.]

C. W. S.

HAMILTON, ANDREW JACKSON (Jan. 28, 1815–Apr. 11, 1875), Unionist leader in Texas during the Civil War and provisional governor, was born in Madison County, Ala., the son of James and Abagail (Bayless) Hamilton. As a boy he was employed in the office of the county clerk, where he learned to read and commenced the study of law. In 1841 he was admitted to the bar, and two years later married Mary Jane Bowen. Moving to Texas in 1847, the Hamiltons established themselves on a farm near La Grange. In 1849 Hamilton, who was an excellent stump speaker, secured appointment as attorney-general of the state. He thereupon removed to Austin, where he continued to reside, identifying himself with the frontier needs and ideals of western Texas. He served a term in the state legislature, 1851–53, as a representive of Travis County, and in 1859, as the result of the Unionist victory of that year which made Sam Houston governor, he was sent to Congress. There, although he was a new member, he received a substantial vote as a compromise candidate for speaker. Again and again, from his Western point of view, he spoke for conciliation, pointing out the economic grievances of the South and the measures by which he believed that the tide of secession might be checked. Even after the withdrawal of the other representatives of Texas, he remained in Congress, returning to Texas in March 1861, to be elected to the state legislature as an avowed Unionist, from one of the few districts in the state which even then commanded a majority against secession. With the outbreak of war, Hamilton was regarded as a traitor to his state. A year later he escaped through Mexico to Washington, where he was promptly appointed by Lincoln and Stanton a brigadier-general and provisional governor of Texas. The remainder of the war he spent largely in New Orleans, waiting for a favorable opportunity to assume the functions of his office. In 1864 he obtained a permit from the President to export cotton from Texas. In spite of the disapproval of Welles, who considered him "a profuse talker, but of questionable capability and sincerity" and later characterized him as "a deceptive, vain, self-conceited partisan" (*Diary*, II, 316, 580), his appointment as provisional governor was confirmed by President Johnson, and he arrived in Galveston in June 1865, to carry out the difficult task of Presidential reconstruction.

His appointments were wise, his relations to the military officers were tactful, and, though he was later blamed for acting as an attorney for persons interested in bonds which the state was seeking to recover, his courage, efficiency, and lack of rancor were generally recognized. Within a year he had brought something like order out of the chaos which followed the war. A constitution had been written in which many of his ideas were incorporated, and in August 1866 he was able to turn over the government of Texas to its duly elected officials. Going to Washington as one of the leaders of a band known as the "Southern loyalists," he was soon, strangely enough, numbered with the opponents of President Johnson and of the policies which he represented, and in this capacity, opposed the recognition of Texas, perhaps because its officers were so largely ex-Confederates.

His decisions as a member of the Texas supreme court, to which he had been appointed in 1866 by military authority, were also eminently conservative, tending as they did to validate all the ordinary acts of Texas during the period of secession. The most important cases in which he rendered a decision were the *Sequestration Cases* (30 *Texas*, 688). He was counsel in the important case of *Ex parte Rodriguez* (39 *Texas*, 705). When the Congressional plan of reconstruction was introduced, including negro suffrage, Hamilton felt that the Northern Radicals had gone far enough, and in 1868 he regained much of his lost popularity by opposing the disfranchisement of the white voters, a measure of which his brother, Morgan Calvin Hamilton, later United States senator, was one of the chief advocates. The conservatives now turned to him as their candidate for governor. Hamilton always believed that he was legally elected, but his selection was set aside by the military authorities in favor of his more radical opponent, who inaugurated the brief but disastrous era of Carpet-bag domination. When the Democrats came into power in 1873, Hamilton was bitterly disappointed and sought to challenge the legality of the election before the courts, but the new administration was too firmly entrenched by Republican mistakes to fear judicial decrees, and it was evident that the career of even a conservative Republican in Texas was ended. His death occurred suddenly two years later.

[C. W. Ramsdell, *Reconstruction in Texas* (1910); Executive Records, Register Book 281, at Austin; Johnson Papers, Lib. of Cong.; *War of the Rebellion: Official Records,* 1 ser., IX, XV, XXVI, XXXIV (pt. 2), XLVIII, 2 ser., IV, VI, VII, 3 ser., II, V; *Cong. Globe,* 36 Cong., 1 Sess., esp. pp. 277, 603, App., p. 240, 36 Cong., 2 Sess., App., pp. 174–78; *Diary of Gideon Welles* (3 vols., 1911); scrapbook of newspaper clippings in the possession of Hamilton's daughter, Mrs. W. W. Mills of Austin; *Biog. Dir. Am. Cong.* (1928); J. D. Lynch, *The Bench and Bar of Texas* (1885); *Galveston Daily News,* Apr. 13, 1875.] R. G. C.

HAMILTON, CHARLES SMITH (Nov. 16, 1822–Apr. 17, 1891), soldier, was born at Western, Oneida County, N. Y., a son of Zane A. Hamilton and his wife, Sylvia Putnam. He was a direct descendant of William Hamilton who came to New England from Glasgow, Scotland, in 1668, was later prosecuted for killing the first whale off the New England coast, and died in 1746 at the age of 103 (J. M. Bailey, *History of Danbury, Conn.*, 1896, p. 67). During Charles

Hamilton's boyhood, his parents moved from Oneida to Erie County, N. Y., and Charles received his early education at the Aurora Academy. He entered the Military Academy at West Point in 1839 and graduated in 1843, a classmate of U. S. Grant. Assigned for service as a lieutenant of infantry, he participated with distinction in the battles of the Mexican War, was grievously wounded at Molino del Rey, and was brevetted captain for gallant conduct. He married Sophia Jane Shepard of Canandaigua, N. Y., in February 1849, and after two years as recruiting officer at Rochester, N. Y., and a period of service in the Indian country, he resigned his commission in 1853, hoping, as did Grant and many others, to gain success in other fields. He settled at Fond du Lac, Wis., and engaged in farming and the manufacture of flour until the outbreak of the Civil War. In the early summer of 1861 he recruited and organized the 3rd Wisconsin Volunteers, and was commissioned colonel of that regiment. He was soon promoted to the rank of brigadier-general and participated in the siege of Yorktown and in the Shenandoah Valley campaign. Then, having been transferred to the West, while in command of a division under Rosecrans he took part in the battle of Iuka in September 1862, and two weeks later at Corinth again distinguished himself by his coolness, bravery, and high soldierly qualities. His own accounts of Iuka and Corinth were published in *Battles and Leaders of the Civil War* (vol. II, 1887). On Grant's recommendation he was promoted to the rank of major-general of volunteers, Sept. 19, 1862. From January to April 1863 he was in command of the XVI Army Corps and the District of West Tennessee, but he felt that he had not been given the command to which his rank, his record, and his talents entitled him, and he therefore resigned his commission on Apr. 13.

Returning to Fond du Lac, he resumed his former business. In 1869, President Grant appointed him United States marshal at Milwaukee, in which office he served eight years. He continued to live at Milwaukee and for many years successfully manufactured linseed oil. In 1878 he became president of the Hamilton Paper Company. He served as a member of the board of regents of the University of Wisconsin from 1866 to 1875, being president of the board, 1869–75, and in that capacity was a successful champion of a liberal state policy in relation to higher education (see especially his *Annual Report* for 1869). He was commander for a time of the Wisconsin department of the Military Order of the Loyal Legion. In 1889, when the national reunion of the Grand Army of the Republic was held in Milwaukee, Hamilton was too feeble to attend, but the survivors of the old 3rd Wisconsin Volunteers marched to his home to pay respect to their first colonel. Less than two years later he died.

[See H. L. Conard, *Hist. of Milwaukee* (1895), I, 383; G. W. Cullum, *Biog. Reg. Officers and Grads. U. S. Mil. Acad.* (3rd ed., 1891); R. G. Thwaites, *Hist. of the Univ. of Wis.* (1900), p. 96; Eben Putnam, *A Hist. of the Putnam Family* (1891); *War of the Rebellion: Official Records (Army)*, 1 ser., V, X, XI, XII, XVII, XXIII, XXIV, XXX, LI, 2 ser., IV, VI; *Milwaukee Jour., Milwaukee Sentinel*, Apr. 18, 1891; *Harpers Encyc. of U. S. Hist.* (1902), vol. V, *sub* "Iuka Springs," vol. II, *sub "Corinth,"* vol. IV, *sub* "Hamilton, Charles Smith"; the last account erroneously refers to him as a grandson of Alexander Hamilton.]

R. W.

HAMILTON, EDWARD JOHN (Nov. 29, 1834–Nov. 21, 1918), philosopher, was born in Belfast, Ireland, the eldest son of Anna (Patterson) and the Rev. William Hamilton. His father was head-master of the Royal Belfast Academical Institution until 1843, when he was sent as a clergyman of the Free Presbyterian Church of Scotland first to Picton, Ontario, and four years later to Cincinnati, Ohio. Hamilton began to be interested in philosophy early in life and under the guidance of his father devoted much time to the study of Thomas Reid and other Scotch thinkers. After several years of preparatory school, he entered Hanover College in Indiana, where in 1853 he obtained the A.B. and later the A.M. degree. Already he showed an independence of thought which was characteristic of his later work. After graduation he attended the Princeton Theological Seminary for a year, then the Union Theological Seminary and the New Albany (Indiana) Theological Seminary. Returning to the Princeton Theological Seminary, he remained from 1856 to 1858. During these years he studied the philosophy of Locke, Hamilton, and John Stuart Mill, in conjunction with his theological work, but he remained the critic and seeker after a system of his own. Immediately after his graduation from the Princeton Theological Seminary, he was ordained in the Presbyterian ministry, Nov. 25, 1858, and sent as pastor to Oyster Bay, Long Island, where he remained for three years.

In 1861 Hamilton returned to Ireland with the twofold purpose of visiting relatives and recovering his strength. During part of his visit he acted as preacher in the village of Dromore West, County Sligo. He returned to the United States in 1863 and was appointed by Governor Parker chaplain of the 7th New Jersey Volunteers. He served in the field until the end of the Civil War, then resumed his theological activities as pastor of the Presbyterian Church in

Hamilton, Ohio. It was during this period that he wrote his first philosophical book, *A New Analysis in Fundamental Morals* (1870), which was undoubtedly inspired by his practical interest in ethical questions. On Sept. 23, 1867, he was married to Eliza (Cleland) Hume of Cincinnati.

The year 1868 marked a definite and important change in his life. Chosen Holliday Professor of Mental Philosophy at Hanover College, he taught there for eleven years, working intensively at the same time in the fields of epistemology, ethics, metaphysics, and logic. The outcome of this study was perhaps his most ambitious book, *The Human Mind* (1883). During the academic year 1882–83, he was acting professor of ethics, economics, politics, and logic at Princeton University, and the following year he was appointed acting professor of intellectual philosophy at Hamilton College. In 1886 he became Albert Barnes Professor of Philosophy and Hebrew at the latter institution and retained the chair until 1891. During these eight years he worked on his two important books in the field of logic and epistemology respectively: *The Modalist; or The Laws of Rational Conviction* (1891), and *The Perceptionalist; or Mental Science* (1899). His epistemological theory, as expressed in *The Perceptionalist,* differs from both idealism and materialism. He believed in the objective reality of space, time, and the universe, and laid stress upon the distinction between thought or concept and belief or conviction. According to his theory of logic, one must include contingency and probability as well as necessity and certainty in a pure logic.

From 1891 to 1894 Hamilton worked on the *Standard Dictionary,* but at the end of that period he returned to academic pursuits and taught for one year, 1894–95, as professor of philosophy at Whitworth College, Sumner, Wash., and for four years, 1895–99, at the University of Washington. In 1899 he took up residence in Plainfield, N. J., to devote himself henceforth to literary work, principally in the field of philosophy. In 1902 he published a comprehensive ethics entitled *The Moral Law, or the Theory and Practice of Duty.* His ethics was not founded upon any existing theories, but the underlying principle was that of the "absolute good." Anxious that the Germans should know and understand his philosophical doctrine, and fearing that a translator might give a misleading meaning to important concepts, he therefore went twice to Germany to work in that language, in 1906–07 to Göttingen, and in 1911–12 to Charlottenburg. In 1911 he published *Perzeptionalismus und Modalismus, eine Erkenntnistheorie,* and in 1912 *Erkennen und Schliessen, eine theoretische Logik auf der Grundlage des Perzeptionalismus und Modalismus.* That he was able at the advanced age of almost eighty to present his logical and epistemological views in a new order and form in a foreign language is evidence of the energy and mental virility of the man. His last work was *Rational Orthodoxy,* published in 1917.

[Martin Klose, short biography in *Erkennen und Schliessen*; *Who's Who in America,* 1918–19; J. H. Dulles, *Princeton Theol. Sem. Biog. Cat.* (1909); *Princeton Theol. Sem. Bull. Necrological Report,* Aug. 1919.] H. S. L.

HAMILTON, FRANK HASTINGS (Sept. 10, 1813–Aug. 11, 1886), surgeon, was the son of Calvin Hamilton, a farmer and owner of a stage route, and his wife Lucinda. He was born in the now obliterated village of Wilmington, Vt., whence his father moved to Schenectady, N. Y., in 1816. He attended Union College, graduated in 1830, then registered as a pupil with Dr. John Morgan of Auburn. Later he took a course of lectures at the College of Physicians and Surgeons of the Western District of New York at Fairfield, N. Y., and was licensed to practise in 1833. In 1835 he received the degree of M.D. from the University of Pennsylvania. For some time he gave private instruction in anatomy and surgery at Auburn, but in 1839, at the age of twenty-six, he was made professor of surgery at the Fairfield school. The next year he took the same chair in the Geneva Medical School, where he remained until 1844. Having decided to settle in Buffalo he first spent two years in study abroad and then (1846), with Austin Flint and others, founded the medical department of the University of Buffalo and became its first professor of surgery. After holding this chair for twelve years, he settled in Brooklyn as professor of surgery in the Long Island College Hospital.

In 1860 Hamilton published his *Practical Treatise on Fractures and Dislocations,* a work which went through eight editions and was translated into French and German, and in 1861 he was made professor of clinical and military surgery and fractures at the newly organized Bellevue Hospital Medical College. Having volunteered his services at the outbreak of the Civil War he was placed in charge of the field hospital at the first battle of Bull Run and was promoted rapidly from brigade surgeon to medical inspector of the Federal army. He resigned, however, in September 1863, and settled in New York. He had already published the first edition of his *Treatise on Military Surgery and Hygiene*

(1862). On the death of James R. Wood, Hamilton was made full professor of surgery and surgical pathology at Bellevue (1868) and remained there until 1875. Meanwhile he edited the *Surgical Memoirs of the War of the Rebellion* (2 vols., 1870–71) and published a treatise on *The Principles and Practice of Surgery* (1872). He was consulting physician to President Garfield when the latter was assassinated and was in constant attendance until the end came. In the last few years of his life he was largely incapacitated by fibroid phthisis which led to his death in 1886.

Hamilton was a tireless student throughout his life and made many technical contributions to surgery, one of the most notable being the healing of old ulcers by skin grafting. Although his report, *Elkoplasty or Anaplasty Applied to the Treatment of Old Ulcers,* did not appear until 1854, he had worked on this subject for some years. In addition to his larger textbooks he published a *Treatise on Strabismus, with Cases,* in 1844, and *Fractures of the Patella,* in 1880. As a young man he had a *flair* for painting in oils, and many of his anatomical plates were done by himself. He also had a discriminating literary taste and assembled a library and private museum which were purchased by the government after his death. Hamilton's first wife, whom he married Oct. 15, 1834, was Mary Virginia (van Arsdale) McMurran. She died in 1838 and on Sept. 1, 1840, he was married to Mary Gertrude Hart.

[C. A. Leale, *Eulogy Delivered before the N. Y. State Medic. Asso. on Prof. Frank Hastings Hamilton, M.D.* (1887); *In Memoriam. Prof. Frank Hastings Hamilton* (n.d.), published by the Society of Medical Jurisprudence and State Medicine; *Medic. and Surgic. Reporter,* Feb. 11, 1865; *Medic. Record,* Aug. 14, 1886; *Gaillard's Medic. Jour.,* Nov. 1886; *Brooklyn Medic. Jour.,* Sept. 1901; *N. Y. Times,* Aug. 12, 1886.]

E. P.

HAMILTON, GAIL [See DODGE, MARY ABIGAIL, 1833–1896].

HAMILTON, JAMES (*c.* 1710–Aug. 14, 1783), lawyer, lieutenant-governor, acting governor of Pennsylvania, son of Andrew [*q.v.*] and Anne (Brown) Preeson Hamilton, was born probably in Accomac County, Va. His father, a native of Scotland and an eminent Philadelphia lawyer, was famous as the defender of John Peter Zenger, the New York printer. His mother came of a wealthy and prominent Maryland family. James was educated in Philadelphia and England. He became a practising lawyer and in 1733 succeeded his father in the lucrative office of prothonotary of the supreme court of Pennsylvania. From 1734 to 1739 he was a member of the Pennsylvania Assembly. On his father's death in 1741 he inherited a considerable fortune, including the "Bush Hill" estate, then a rendezvous for distinguished visitors. In 1745 he was elected mayor of Philadelphia. On retiring from office he discontinued the customary banquet on such occasions, donating instead £150 toward the erection of a public building. He was also a member of the provincial council from 1745 to 1746. Toward the close of 1746 he visited England, returning to Pennsylvania on Nov. 23, 1748, with a commission as lieutenant-governor. His appointment elicited general satisfaction, Benjamin Franklin declaring, "we esteem him a benevolent and upright, as well as a sensible man" (A. H. Smyth, *The Writings of Benjamin Franklin,* 1905, II, 361).

Hamilton's term began auspiciously. He endeavored to settle the grievances of the Indians caused by encroachments on their lands and urged appropriations to build forts, arm men, and provide other protection for the trade, lives, and property of the frontier settlements. When the Assembly, however, proposed a tax on the proprietors for this purpose, Hamilton with great attachment to proprietary interests firmly opposed them. The quarrel thus precipitated soon extended to other questions. The Governor's contention in 1750 that the Assembly could not sit legally out of its appointed time without executive sanction provoked a bitter dispute. Frequent vetoes, especially of paper-money bills, caused further friction. Finally finding his position almost intolerable in the face of the complaints of the back-country, the Quaker Assembly's refusal to provide defense, and the interests of the Crown and proprietaries, Hamilton resigned, Oct. 3, 1754, retaining his seat in council. During his second term as lieutenant-governor (Nov. 17, 1759–Oct. 31, 1763), his relations with the Assembly were equally unpleasant. As president of council he served twice as acting governor in the absence of John Penn (May 6–Oct. 16, 1771, and July 19–Aug. 30, 1773). Since he had been devoted to the Crown and proprietors for so many years, it is not surprising that he did not espouse the American Revolution. Although prudently submitting to the new order of things, he was arrested in 1777 but in the following year was given his freedom. Under the new régime his claim to office and influence vanished. Disappointed at heart and broken in health from cancer, he survived the war but two years. Energetic, determined, self-confident, he possessed great ability and a high sense of civic duty and responsibility. He was an active promoter of public improvements, a patron of Benjamin West, warmly supported the College of Philadelphia, and contributed liberally to religious, educational, scientific, and philanthropic projects. He never married.

[Manuscript letters in the Pa. Hist. Soc.; *Pa. Archives,* 1 ser., vols. II–VIII (1853), 2 ser., vol. VI (1877), 3 ser., vol. VIII (1896); *Minutes of the Provincial Council of Pa.,* vols. V and VI (1851), VIII–X (1852); Benjamin Franklin, *An Hist. Rev. of Pa.* (1812); C. P. Keith, *The Provincial Councillors of Pa.* (1883); J. F. Watson, *Annals of Phila.* (3 vols., 1877–79), ed. by W. P. Hazard; J. H. Martin, *Bench and Bar of Phila.* (1883); *Pa. Mag. of Hist. and Biog.,* vol. XX (1896), p. 406, and Apr., July, Oct. 1892, Apr. 1901, Jan. 1902.] J. H. P—g.

HAMILTON, JAMES (May 8, 1786–Nov. 15, 1857), governor of South Carolina, the son of Maj. James and Elizabeth Hamilton, was born in Charleston. His father was a native of Pennsylvania; his mother, of South Carolina, a daughter of Thomas Lynch and, at the time of her marriage to Hamilton, the widow of John Harleston. Young Hamilton received his early education at Newport, R. I., and later completed his formal schooling in Dedham, Mass. He studied law in Charleston, was admitted to the bar in 1810, and served as secretary to Gov. Henry Middleton until the War of 1812, when both he and his father volunteered. He rose to the rank of major, and as one of General Izard's staff saw service on the Canadian border. On Nov. 15, 1813, he married Elizabeth Heyward, the daughter of Daniel and Ann Sarah Trezevant Heyward, who survived him. At the close of the war, after a brief experience as a cotton planter, he formed a law partnership with the brilliant James Louis Petigru [*q.v.*], which, while highly successful, lasted only long enough to cement a mutual affection which endured even the bitterness of the nullification controversy. In 1820 Hamilton began his political career with election to the lower house of the legislature, to which he was reëlected in 1821 and 1822. In the latter year he was also elected intendant of Charleston and as such crushed the conspiracy of Denmark Vesey [*q.v.*] for a slave insurrection. In the same year he was elected to Congress to succeed his close friend, William L. Lowndes, who had resigned. He took his seat Dec. 13, 1822, and served until Mar. 3, 1829, when he voluntarily retired. A vigorous, ready, and fluent debater, he quickly assumed a prominent part in the work of the House. Within a year he was chairman of the military-affairs committee, and from 1825 to 1829 he was the recognized leader of the Jacksonian opposition to the Adams administration. He was equally prominent in the anti-tariff group. He went to Washington an intense nationalist, but he quickly became a convinced and fervent advocate of state rights. Attacking the protective tariff incessantly, he became almost fanatical on the subject, and joined with William Smith and Dr. Thomas Cooper [*q.v.*] in an agitation of the question in South Carolina which at last brought Calhoun to their extreme position. Introduced by John Randolph to the Virginia and Kentucky Resolutions, Hamilton became thoroughly indoctrinated with their principles and found in them the remedy for the woes of his state. In a speech at Walterboro, S. C., on Oct. 21, 1828, he outlined the doctrine of nullification and opened the campaign for state action. In 1830 he was elected governor and began organizing the state. Speaking in every district, he established nullification clubs which became the organization of the state-rights and free-trade party. He was reëlected in 1831, and the passage of the tariff act of 1832 gave him a legislature favorable to his policy, which at once called a convention of the people. Calhoun had by now elaborated the theory of nullification for the intellectuals. Hamilton, intensely practical, had interpreted the doctrine to the people, had organized them, and now won a convention that was, in the words of Petigru, "in his palm." On him must rest the major responsibility for nullification in practice. He himself was elected to the convention and was chosen president. The ordinance of nullification was passed, and, upon his retirement from the governorship, he was placed in command of the state's troops with the rank of brigadier-general. He quickly organized and armed a force of 27,000 men. Up to the passage of the ordinance he had been very radical, but, having no desire for war or a dissolution of the Union, he now favored the compromise which secured tariff reduction, and joined with Petigru, the leader of the Union party, in averting violence between the opposing parties. To his mind the fight was won, even though nullification had died in the effort.

In the nullification controversy, as in his whole career, Hamilton was sincere and honest in purpose, sacrificing his national career to the cause. He was always frank and courageous, but entirely too sanguine and impetuous. Announcing that "he who dallies is a dastard; he who doubts is damned," he was primarily a man of action rather than of council, but he was no unreflecting hothead. His speeches, fluent and clever rather than profound, show thought and power of logical analysis. In action he was prompt and vigorous, with a genius for organization and manipulation. His tastes were simple, and, with none of the austerity of Calhoun, he was almost as restrained. Wine, women, and song had no appeal for him; life was always a serious matter, and he felt keenly its obligations. He had a fiery temper, but he had also a sweetness of disposition which won him many friends, even among his political opponents. He was a noted duelist and is said to have fought fourteen duels, always wounding his opponent. He was second to Randolph in the famous duel with Clay, and served as second to Oliver Perry, Stephen Decatur, and George McDuffie, among others.

He lost political strength after nullification. The radical state-rights group resented his conservatism and the Unionists never forgave him. He himself lost interest in politics and turned to business with brilliant, though temporary, success. He operated profitably five large rice plantations, two cotton plantations, a brick yard, and a rice mill. He organized the Bank of Charleston, then the largest in the United States, and became its president. He was an active director of the South Carolina and the Louisville, Cincinnati & Charleston railroads. He formed with his eldest son an exporting firm which carried on a large business. He engaged in tremendous land speculations in Alabama and Mississippi. For a time everything he touched succeeded, but presently a crash came and he lost the major part of his property and carried down with him many of his associates.

In the meantime, he had become enthusiastic over the struggle of Texas for independence, and, eager to aid, had advanced considerable sums of money to the cause. In 1835 he was made a perpetual citizen of the republic and a little later, by unanimous vote of the Texas congress, he was offered chief command of the army. In 1836, as state senator, he led the South Carolina legislature to express active sympathy with the revolution, but believing that it was to the interest of the South for Texas to remain a separate republic, he opposed annexation. In 1838 President M. B. Lamar [*q.v.*] made him commissioner of loans to raise money, which he did with considerable success, and in 1839 he went to Europe as diplomatic agent to France, Great Britain, Belgium, and the Netherlands. He quickly secured recognition of Texas by France and the Netherlands and favorable commercial treaties. In Belgium he secured recognition and began negotiations for a commercial treaty. In Great Britain he was equally successful, concluding with Lord Palmerston a treaty of recognition, a treaty for the suppression of the African slave trade, and a convention providing for a British offer of mediation to Mexico. He then sailed for the United States and, under authority of a commission from Texas, was seeking to secure a final settlement with Mexico in which he was assured of the good offices of Calhoun and Webster, when the news reached him that Sam Houston [*q.v.*], again president, had recalled him and repudiated the work in which he was then engaged. The indebtedness of Texas to Hamilton now amounted to $210,000 in gold, and the state's failure to pay any part of it embarrassed him deeply. Nothing that he attempted succeeded. He finally came to advocate annexation, supported Polk in 1844, and was reconciled to Jackson, who had so eagerly desired to hang him in 1833 and whom he had called "the Old Dotard and Despot." He favored the compromise measures of 1850, and, when Calhoun died, was appointed to the Senate to succeed him, but when the accusation was made that he was not a resident of South Carolina he immediately returned the commission, declining to accept an office to which any one would question his title.

In 1855 he moved to Texas where he had an enormous grant of land. Things began to brighten. There was hope that the United States would pay a part of his loan to Texas and, while he was in Washington temporarily, news reached him that Texas was ready to pay $35,000 more. Hastening to Texas, he took passage at New Orleans for Galveston. In the Gulf of Mexico the vessel collided with its sister ship and sank. Hamilton gave his life preserver to a woman for her child. His right arm was injured and he clung for a little while to a hatch cover with his left hand, then slipped off into the water and disappeared from view.

[Lewis Crueger, *A Brief Notice of the Death and Character of Gov. Hamilton* (1857); *Obit. Addresses on the Occasion of the Death of Gen. James Hamilton of S. C.* (1857); "Correspondence of John C. Calhoun," ed. by J. F. Jameson, *Ann. Report Am. Hist. Asso.*, 1899, vol. II; G. P. Garrison, "Diplomatic Correspondence of the Republic of Texas" (3 vols.), *Ibid.*, 1907, 1908; J. P. Carson, *Life, Letters and Speeches of James Louis Petigru* (1920); *S. C. Hist. and Geneal. Mag.*, Jan. 1902; *Charleston Daily Courier*, Nov. 19, 1857.]

J. G. deR. H.

HAMILTON, JAMES ALEXANDER (Apr. 14, 1788–Sept. 24, 1878), lawyer, politician, a New Yorker by birth, was the third son of Alexander [*q.v.*] and Elizabeth (Schuyler) Hamilton. In 1805 he was graduated from Columbia College and four years later, after studying in the law office of Judge Pendleton, was admitted to the bar. He began practice in Waterford, Saratoga County, N. Y., but in 1810 moved to Hudson, N. Y., and in October of that year married Mary, daughter of Robert Morris and a grand-daughter of Richard Morris [*q.v.*], once chief justice of New York. During the War of 1812 he served as brigade-major and inspector in the New York militia, but returned to the practice of law with the conclusion of peace. Unlike his distinguished father, he was a Clintonian Democrat and a member of Tammany, and in this connection he was for some time associated with Charles King and Johnston Ver Planck in the publishing of the *New York American*. Facile, smooth-tongued, and ambitious, he gradually worked his way into the inner circle of the foremost Democratic leaders of his day, being on especially intimate terms with Martin Van Buren and William H. Crawford [*qq.v.*]. In 1827–28, when the political star of Andrew Jackson was in the ascendancy, Hamilton was sent as one of the delegates of the Tammany Society to attend the anniversary celebration of the battle of New Orleans. He met the Jackson party at Nashville and journeyed with it down the Mississippi. His suavity and political standing soon won Jackson's friendship and confidence, and on his return from this trip he purposed to visit Crawford in Georgia in order to heal a political breach between the latter and Jackson. He did not see Crawford, but wrote to him, and the correspondence which ensued was instrumental in setting in motion the chain of events which ultimately led to political discord between Jackson and Calhoun. (See Van Buren, *post*, pp. 368 ff.).

The winter of 1829 found Hamilton in Washington acting as the trusted henchman for Van Buren when the latter was obliged to be absent. As a member of President Jackson's so-called Appointing Council he is said to have been influential in securing the secretaryship of state for Van Buren (Bassett, *Jackson, post*). Upon the suggestion of Van Buren, Hamilton himself was appointed by the President, on Mar. 4, 1829, to take charge of the department, which he surrendered to the regular appointee on Mar. 27. Of Jackson's cabinet as a whole, despite his part in selecting it, he was a caustic critic, later characterizing it as "the most unintellectual and uneducated cabinet we ever had" (*Reminiscences*, p. 314). Subsequently Jackson, wholly unknown to Van Buren and against his wishes, made Hamilton United States district attorney for the Southern District of New York, but the duties of the new office proved onerous, and he relinquished them in 1833. At Jackson's request he prepared a plan for a bank subordinate to the Treasury Department, but it was not used.

Always a stanch defender of his father's fiscal policies, in his later years he became a thorough Hamiltonian in his political philosophy. In 1840 he supported Harrison, and thereafter was identified with the Whigs and the Republicans. At every threat of war between 1833 and 1861 he offered his services to the army, but after 1833 he took part in politics only through the copious advice which he offered to statesmen of all parties. Abroad during the revolutions of 1848, he contributed plans of constitutional and financial reform to his French and Italian friends. He was an ardent nationalist, refusing to favor abolition because he believed that slavery was protected by the Constitution. With the outbreak of the Civil War, however, he urged emancipation as a military measure, and in 1862 drafted an emancipation proclamation. He published a number of pamphlets, among them *State Sovereignty: Rebellion against the United States by the People of a State is Its Political Suicide* (1862), and two in defense of his father: *The Public Debt and the Public Credit of the United States* (1864), and *Martin Van Buren's Calumnies Repudiated: Hamilton's Conduct as Secretary of the Treasury Vindicated* (1870). In his seventy-ninth year he began the preparation of his autobiography, *Reminiscences of James A. Hamilton; or Men and Events, at Home and Abroad, during Three Quarters of a Century*, which was published in 1869. He spent his declining years in and about New York City, where he died at the age of ninety.

[Hamilton's *Reminiscences*; "The Autobiography of Martin Van Buren," ed. by J. C. Fitzpatrick, in *Ann. Report Am. Hist. Asso., 1918* (1920), vol. II; J. S. Bassett, *The Life of Andrew Jackson* (1911), vol. II; David McAdam and others, *Hist. of the Bench and Bar of N. Y.*, vol. I (1897); J. S. Bassett, "Martin Van Buren," in S. F. Bemis, *The Am. Secretaries of State and Their Diplomacy*, vol. IV (1928); *N. Y. Tribune*, Sept. 26, 1878.]

H. J. C.

HAMILTON, PAUL (Oct. 16, 1762–June 30, 1816), governor of South Carolina and secretary of the navy, was the son of Archibald and Rebecca (Branford) Hamilton. His father's early death was soon followed by that of two brothers, leaving Paul Hamilton the sole surviving child. At sixteen, financial considerations compelled his withdrawal from school. When General Prevost invaded South Carolina, Hamilton joined a militia company. He participated in the unsuccessful siege of Savannah, and was with Gates's army when that officer was routed at Camden (Aug. 16, 1779). In the latter part of the Revolution, he served under various guerrilla chiefs, including Marion and Harden, and was a member of the latter's band when he captured Fort Balfour. On Oct. 10, 1782, Hamilton married Mary Wilkinson. His wife secured twenty-three negroes as her share of her father's estate and with these Hamilton began to plant indigo on

Edisto Island. Being unsuccessful, the next year he purchased a plantation in St. Paul's Parish and engaged in rice culture. He began his public career as collector of taxes for St. Paul's Parish, 1785–86, and justice of the peace, 1786. He was a member of the lower house of the state legislature, 1787–89, and of the convention of 1789 which ratified the Federal Constitution. He served successively as state senator, 1794, 1798–99, comptroller of finance, 1800–04, and governor, 1804–06. As governor, he advocated reforms in the penal code, believing that under the then-existing system punishments were not apportioned to offenses. He was an apostle of military preparedness, urging the repair of seacoast fortifications and the purchase of arms for state arsenals. He was a friend of the state college which opened in 1805. Though a slave owner, he protested against legalizing the African slave trade and urged the legislature to prohibit the traffic.

Three days after President Madison took office, he sent to the Senate Hamilton's appointment as secretary of the navy (Mar. 7, 1809). Why Madison should have chosen Hamilton is unknown, unless he was impressed by his zeal for fortification. A rice planter could not be expected to have any special knowledge of naval affairs. Until war with Great Britain became imminent, Hamilton's administration was uneventful. The navy was unpopular with the Republican Congress, which hindered the secretary by refusing to vote necessary appropriations. Arms and munitions at the disposal of the Navy Department were insufficient; the navy yards were neglected; the President was indifferent to the problem of preparedness. Hamilton secured the passage of an act establishing naval hospitals (Feb. 26, 1811), but no other important legislation was enacted. On the brink of war with a sea power of the first class, the navy consisted of eighteen vessels. Late in 1811, Hamilton made some preparation, but he could do little without funds. It was not until the war had virtually come that Congress awoke to the necessity of a less niggardly policy. On the approach of hostilities, economy and honesty ceased to be the only requirements for the successful administration of the navy. Hamilton was attacked as incompetent and resigned, Dec. 31, 1812 (*National Intelligencer,* Jan. 11, 1813). His death occurred some three and a half years later.

[Manuscript volume in Hamilton's handwriting, carrying his career down to his election as governor, in the possession of Mrs. Richard Smythe and her sister Mrs. Dewar Gordon, 57 Church St., Charleston; Hamilton letters in the MSS. Div., Lib. of Cong.; *S. C. Hist. and Geneal. Mag.,* Jan. 1922; Hamilton's messages to the legislature, in *Charleston Courier,* Nov. 29, 1805, and Dec. 1, 1806; *Am. State Papers: Naval Affairs,* I (1834), 193–282; C. O. Paullin, "Naval Administration under Secretaries of the Navy Smith, Hamilton and Jones, 1801–14," *Proc. U. S. Naval Inst.,* vol. XXXII (1906), reprinted in pamphlet form.]

J. G. V–D.

HAMILTON, PETER (Nov. 7, 1817–Nov. 22, 1888), lawyer, was born in Harrisburg, Pa., the son of William Thomas and Charlotte (Cartledge) Hamilton. The family was of Scotch origin, although the father had been born in Yorkshire, England. The son of a Presbyterian clergyman, Peter was educated in the schools maintained by that church. He attended academies at Newark, N. J., and at South Hadley, Mass., and after some private training entered the sophomore class at Princeton. Here he showed special ability in mathematics and graduated in 1835, ranking seventh in a class of fifty-four. After graduation, he went to Mobile, Ala., where his father was pastor of a Presbyterian church. He taught in Barton Academy for three years, at the same time studied law, and was admitted to the bar in 1838. He soon became a leader in his profession and with his brother formed the law firm popularly known as "Hamiltons," for many years one of the most important in the state. Hamilton specialized in chancery cases and cases in the United States courts and in the state supreme court. He was never fond of criminal cases. He always held himself apart from people and was reflective and reserved rather than aggressive and talkative. These qualities made him a much better pleader before judges than before juries.

He began his political career in 1847 as a member of the state legislature. He was elected to this body as a Whig and held the position through the difficult decade which preceded the Civil War. He was opposed to secession, but after Alabama seceded he loyally supported the state. After the war he identified himself with the Democratic party, although he never sought a position of leadership. Early in 1860 he became counsel for the Mobile & Ohio Railroad. For sixteen years he served the road in various positions, being at different times director, counsel, and vice-president. At the end of the war all bridges, trestles, stations, and cross ties had been destroyed for 124 miles. Only eighteen engines and two hundred freight cars were fit for use. The road had lost more than five million dollars in Confederate currency. Hamilton restored this road to usefulness and in so doing he rendered no small service to the state of Alabama.

Throughout the reconstruction period he was a leader of the Conservative party. His legal ability proved useful to the conservatives in many ways. He fought the legal battle to prevent the radical state board of education from destroying the independent school system of Mobile. He drew up the brief for the respondent in the case of *Stein* vs. *Bienville Company* (32 *Fed.*, 876) which overturned the monopoly controlling the Mobile water supply, and argued successfully in the case of *Waring* vs. *Lewis* (53 *Ala.*, 615) that his client, Waring, was not liable for trust funds invested by a trustee in Confederate bonds, although he was bondsman for him.

In 1872 Hamilton was elected to the state Senate and served until 1876. He was the representative of the conservative faction of this legislature sent to Washington to negotiate a union of the radical and conservative groups which met as two separate bodies after the election of 1872. He also served as a member of the committee of finance and taxation and was the author of the act funding the state debt, "the most complicated and difficult piece of legislation in all the history of the state" (*Memorial Record*, p. 543). He steered the act through the Senate and the restoration of the state's credit was in large part due to him. He repeatedly refused a position on the supreme bench of Alabama but in 1886 he assisted in preparing the state code. Two years later he died. Hamilton was married twice: on Dec. 27, 1842, to Anna Martha Beers of Mobile, and, after her death, on May 23, 1863, to Caroline (Cunningham) Goodman.

[T. M. Owen, *Hist. of Ala. and Dict. of Ala. Biog.* (1921), vol. III; *Memorial Record of Ala.* (1893), vol. II; W. L. Fleming, *Civil War and Reconstruction in Ala.* (1905); memoir in 86 *Ala. Reports*, ix–xi; *Daily Register* (Mobile), Nov. 23, 1888.] H. F.

HAMILTON, SCHUYLER (July 25, 1822–Mar. 18, 1903), soldier, engineer, was born in New York City, the son of John Church Hamilton and Maria Eliza Van den Heuval. At the age of fifteen he elected the career of soldier, in emulation of his grandfather, Alexander Hamilton, and of his great-grandfather, Philip Schuyler, and entered the United States Military Academy. He graduated in 1841, twenty-fourth in a class of fifty-two members, and was promoted second lieutenant of the 1st Infantry. After three years of duty in Iowa and Wisconsin, he spent a year as instructor in tactics at West Point, but he returned to the Middle West and was stationed there at the outbreak of the Mexican War. He was brevetted first lieutenant for gallantry at Monterey and captain for his conduct at the skirmish of Mil Flores. In both of these engagements he was severely wounded: in the first by a ball in the abdomen and in the second by a lance thrust through the lung, from the effect of which he suffered until his death. On Apr. 30, 1847, he was made aide-de-camp to General Scott, a position which he held for more than seven years. Shortly after leaving General Scott he resigned from the military service and went to the new state of California. Here, for a couple of years, he was *administrador* of a quicksilver mine, but the new occupation seems to have held him lightly, for in 1858 he moved to Connecticut and lived on a farm near Branford.

On the outbreak of the Civil War Hamilton marched to the relief of Washington as a private in the 7th New York. His previous service made him of immediate value, and within a few days he was made an acting aide to General Butler. Within the month his old commander, Scott, had learned of his presence in the army and had named him military secretary to the general-in-chief, with the rank of lieutenant-colonel. This position or the similar one of aide he held until General Scott's retirement. Thereupon he became assistant chief of staff to General Halleck, his brother-in-law, whom he accompanied to St. Louis. Almost immediately he received an appointment as brigadier-general of volunteers and took part in Grant's operations in western Kentucky and Tennessee. At Island Number 10 he is said to have suggested to Pope the cutting of a canal to turn the enemy's position. Here and at New Madrid he commanded a division with such skill as to win for himself his promotion to major-general of volunteers. Before he could accept his commission, however, he fell ill of malaria. His resignation followed, under the rule that no officer unfit for service should be named to Congress for confirmation. Hamilton felt that he had been victimized and for years after the war endeavored without success to have his name placed on the retired list. For two years he served as engineer in the department of docks in New York, but his health made regular occupation difficult. He lived quietly at his home in New York and died after a year and a half of severe suffering.

[G. W. Cullum, *Biog. Reg. U. S. Mil. Acad.* (ed. 1891), vol. II; F. B. Heitman, *Hist. Reg. and Dict. of the U. S. Army* (1903), vol. I; *Reg. of the Asso. of Grads. of the U. S. Mil. Acad.*, 1903; C. E. Fitch, *Encyc. of Biog. of N. Y.* (1916); M. A. Hamm, *Famous Families of N. Y.*, vol. I (1901); *N. Y. Tribune*, Mar. 19, 1903.] A. W. C.

HAMILTON, WILLIAM THOMAS (Sept. 8, 1820–Oct. 26, 1888), congressman, senator, governor of Maryland, the son of Henry and Anna Mary (Hess) Hamilton, was born at Hagerstown, Md., but spent his childhood in Boonsboro. After attending Jefferson College,

Canonsburg, Pa., and reading law under John Thomson Mason, he was admitted to the bar at Hagerstown in 1845. The following year he was elected to the Maryland House of Delegates as a Democrat. Here he upheld the payment of interest on the state debt and stanchly supported the general financial policy of the Whig governor, Thomas George Pratt. Owing largely to this lack of machine regularity, he failed of reelection in 1847, but he regained his seat in 1848, although western Maryland was temporarily swept into the Whig line, and in 1849 he began a service as representative of Maryland in Congress which continued until Mar. 3, 1855. As a member of the House he supported orthodox Democratic measures, for he viewed the South as the victim of tyrannical Northern sectionalism. He conducted his campaigns for reëlection by means of joint debates in which opposition to protective tariff was his principal argument and in 1852 won the election despite the fact that he was opposed by the veteran politician and debater, Francis Thomas. It was not until the Know-Nothing wave rose menacingly in 1854 that he was defeated.

Upon returning to private life in Hagerstown, Hamilton devoted himself to his law practice, and to municipal interests, personal affairs, and farming. He was especially active in encouraging all improved methods in agriculture. At the outbreak of the Civil War, like most influential Democrats in the border states, he found himself in a difficult position. He upheld the right of the South to secede although he deplored secession. His Southern sympathies were somewhat less pronounced than those of his law partner, Richard H. Alvey, but the two men were leaders in the so-called "Peace" party which was stigmatized by one of the local Unionist sympathizers as "Jeff Davis' masked battery." By 1867 the Democratic party had rallied in western Maryland, and in 1868 Hamilton was elected to the Senate, serving from 1869 until 1875. His activity was restricted during the radical Republican ascendancy. He favored rapid resumption of specie payments and upheld the bills for the admission of the Southern states and the resumption of home rule within them. Naturally, he voted against the Fifteenth Amendment. He strongly opposed the "salary grab," and refused to profit by it. In his last term he was chairman of the committee for the District of Columbia and was instrumental in securing improvements in the water system of Washington.

A split in the Maryland Democratic machine developed by 1871 and soon grew acute. Hamilton, as the recognized leader of one faction, deplored the dominance of the Chesapeake Canal interests in Maryland politics and on the expiration of his term in the Senate devoted his energies to advocating honesty and economy in the state administration, and reform in political methods. He particularly favored civil-service regulation of state appointments. In 1875 he failed to secure the nomination for governor although the convention was closely divided. In 1879, however, he carried the convention and was elected by an easy majority. His views regarding strict economy and political reform foredoomed him to an administration of trouble and friction. The state Senate was largely in the hands of the canal supporters and the treasury department was definitely controlled by his enemies. His message of 1882 was a masterly presentation of the measures necessary for a clean, efficient administration, but his appointments were blocked by the legislature and his measures were frequently rejected. From 1884 until his death he occupied himself with private matters and with the welfare of Hagerstown. He had married, in 1859, Clara Holmes Jenness, who with six children survived him.

[Brief biographies of Hamilton appear in H. E. Buchholz, *Governors of Md.* (1908); C. W. Sams and E. S. Riley, *The Bench and Bar of Md.* (1901); T. J. C. Williams, *A Hist. of Washington County, Md.* (1906); and the *Sun* (Baltimore), Oct. 27, 1888.]

K. J. G.

HAMILTON, WILLIAM THOMAS (Dec. 6, 1822–May 24, 1908), trapper, trader, scout, often called Wildcat Bill, was of mixed Scotch and English ancestry. He was born in the north of England, and his parents brought him to the United States when he was two years old. He grew up in St. Louis and went to school there. His health was delicate and in 1842 with hopes of improving it his father sent him to the Northwest with a band of "free" trappers. Bill Williams, a shrewd and clever trader and a man of courage and prestige on the frontier, headed the party. They traded first with the Cheyennes on the North Platte and later crossed into the Green River country. As "free" traders they were continually opposed by agents of the large fur companies, but by superior skill they obtained all the fur for which they could pay.

The years from 1842 to 1845 determined Hamilton's career. He grew to know the Indians and how to trade with them or to fight them as enemies. He learned the sign language so well, according to his own account, that he could use it better than any other white man and as well as any Indian. In later years he interpreted the pictures on the cliffs near Flathead Lake and no one disputed his explanations. In 1849 he went to California, but found no gold. He soon joined in attacking various Indian tribes that had been killing and robbing the miners and his party wiped out all the neighboring hostiles. He fought in the Rogue River War of 1855 and the Modoc War of 1856 and then traveled northeast to Walla Walla, where Col. George Wright [*q.v.*] was fighting the Yakima, Spokane, and other tribes. Wright wished to learn the disposition of the eastern Indians and Hamilton volunteered to ascertain it. He visited the Nez Percés, the Piegans, the Blackfeet, the Crows, and the Kootenai, traded with them, and secured the information desired. On his return in company with some Kootenai his party was attacked by Blackfeet, but after several desperate engagements the enemy was badly defeated. Hamilton then returned safely to Walla Walla with a fine collection of furs and presented his report to Colonel Wright. Having noted the confluence of Indian trails between the mouth of the Bitterroot and Hellgate Canyon, he moved there to trade. His post on the Rattlesnake, where Missoula now stands, was built in 1858 and was doubtless the first building within the present city limits. He remained here six years and in 1861 was elected sheriff of Missoula County. In 1864 he removed to Fort Benton and in 1869 went to the Yellowstone. In 1873 he was appointed marshal for the Crow Indians and at the outbreak of the Sioux War became a scout for Gen. George Crook [*q.v.*]. His services received praise, but accounts of them are vague. After the war he went to Columbus, Mont., where he lived the remainder of his life. He had married in 1850, while in California, but his wife died the next year. Thereafter he lived alone. During his later life he engaged in trapping and in guiding tourists and entertaining them with stories of his exploits. He was versed in the mysteries of nature and knew when fish would bite and where to look for game. To the end his body was active, his eyes keen, and his mind alert. He kept diaries and was fond of recounting his experiences. He wrote: "A Trading Expedition among the Indians in 1848 from Fort Walla Walla to the Blackfoot Country and Return," which was published in *Contributions to the Historical Society of Montana* (vol. III, 1900); *My Sixty Years on the Plains,* which was edited by E. T. Sieber and appeared in 1905; and "Trapping Expeditions 1848–9," which was printed in the *Contributions to the Historical Society of Montana* (vol. VII, 1910), after his death. In the Montana Historical Library are two unpublished manuscripts by him, "An Incident when Scouting with General Crook" and "My Experiences in Montana." His writings are highly colored and sometimes contradictory.

[Hamilton's writings are the chief source of information. *Contributions to the Hist. Soc. of Mont.,* vol. III (1900) contains a biographical sketch. See also Dan E. Conway, "Uncle Billy Hamilton" (Montana News Syndicate, 1927) in *Roundup Tribune,* May 27, 1927, and obituaries in *Anaconda Standard* and *Butte Miner,* May 26, 1908.]

P. C. P.

HAMLIN, ALFRED DWIGHT FOSTER (Sept. 5, 1855–Mar. 21, 1926), architect and teacher, the son of Cyrus Hamlin [*q.v.*] of Waterford, Me., and of his second wife, Harriet Martha Lovell, came of Puritan stock. His father founded Robert College in Turkey, and he was educated in the preparatory school of Robert College at Bebek, near Constantinople. At the age of fifteen he came to America to enter Amherst College. He was graduated in 1875 and the following year taught history in a high school at Worcester, Mass. In 1876–77 he studied architecture at the School of Architecture, Massachusetts Institute of Technology, then taught drawing for a year at Miss Porter's School, Farmington, Conn. In 1878 he went to France to study architecture in the École des Beaux-Arts, Paris, where he remained until 1881. Upon his return to America, he entered the office of McKim, Mead & White, architects, but after the founding of the department of architecture at Columbia, he went there to become special assistant to William R. Ware, his former preceptor at Massachusetts Institute of Technology. He remained with the school for the rest of his life, filling many positions. In 1887 he was made instructor in architecture; in 1889, assistant professor of architecture; in 1891, adjunct professor of architecture; in 1904, professor of the history of architecture, and in 1911–12, he was given the directorship of the department.

Hamlin was an accomplished linguist in both classical and modern languages. As commissioner for Greek relief of the Near East Relief, he made an extended and difficult inspection trip throughout the Near East in the summer of 1919, for which he was given the Cross of the Order of George I of Greece. As an authority on the history of architecture and ornament, he devised methods of analyzing and teaching these subjects which have widely influenced instruction in the rapidly growing number of architectural schools in America where his textbooks are standard. He was author of *A Text-Book of the History of Architecture* (1896 and later editions); "The Italian Formal Garden" in *European and Japanese Gardens* (1902); *In Memoriam: Rev. Cyrus Hamlin* (1903); *A History of Ornament, Ancient and Medieval* (1916); and *A History of Ornament, Renaissance and Modern* (1923). He was assistant editor for architectural terms for the *Standard Dictionary,* and a frequent contributor to architectural periodicals, especially noteworthy being the series on architecture and its critics published in the *Architectural Record* (May 1915 to December 1927). He was consulting architect and expert adviser on many public buildings, notably the public library of Brooklyn, New York; the City Hall, Cleveland; and the Carnegie libraries and the Brooklyn Institute for the Borough of Brooklyn, N. Y. From time to time he practised architecture. With William R. Ware he was architect of the American School of Classical Studies at Athens, and with C. P. Warren he designed several buildings at Robert College, and the Soldiers Monument at Whitinsville, Mass. On the evening of Mar. 21, 1926, he was struck by a passing automobile, and died shortly afterward. He was survived by his wife, Minnie Florence Marston of Hartford, Conn., whom he married in 1885, and by whom he had four children.

[*Who's Who in America,* 1924–25; H. F. Andrews, *The Hamlin Family* (1902); *Amherst Coll. Biog. Record of Grads. and Non-Grads., 1821–1921* (1927); *Jour. of the Am. Inst. of Architects,* May 1926; *N. Y. Times, Sun* (N. Y.), Mar. 22, 1926; autobiographical notes and family records in the possession of Hamlin's son, Talbot Faulkner Hamlin, New York City.]

W. A. B—g.

HAMLIN, CHARLES (Sept. 13, 1837–May 15, 1911), Union soldier, lawyer, business man, was born at Hampden, Me., the third son of Hannibal Hamlin [*q.v.*] and Sarah Jane (Emery) Hamlin. He attended Hampden, Bridgton, and Bethel academies, and graduated from Bowdoin College with the degree of A.B. in 1857. After reading law in his father's office he practised (1858–61) at Orland. He became the political lieutenant of his father, and witnessed his inauguration as vice-president in March of 1861. He recorded intimate, accurate accounts of the political background during the Civil War—notes later used by his son, Charles Eugene Hamlin, in *The Life and Times of Hannibal Hamlin* (1899). At the outbreak of war he recruited for the Union forces; on Aug. 21, 1862, he was commissioned major in the 18th Maine Infantry (afterwards the 1st Maine Heavy Artillery) and was soon engaged in constructing the defenses of Washington. Entering active service in May 1863 as assistant adjutant-general of the 2nd Division, III Corps, Army of the Potomac, he took part in the severe fighting of July 2, 1863, for the possession of Round Top at Gettysburg, and was officially commended by Gen. A. A. Humphreys "for valuable services rendered me on the field" (*War of the Rebellion, Official Records, Army,* 1 ser., XXVII, pt. 1, p. 535). He served through the actions at Kelly's Ford, Locust Grove, and Mine Run before his appointment as assistant to Gen. A. P. Howe, inspector of artillery, United States Army, stationed at Harper's Ferry and Washington, D. C. He was brevetted brigadier-general of volunteers on Mar. 13, 1865. Present at Ford's Theatre when President Lincoln was assassinated, Apr. 14, 1865, he immediately called out all the artillery at Camp Barry to face a rumored general uprising, and commanded the streets of the capital. Years afterward he wrote an account of this period, which was published by the Maine Commandery of the Military Order of the Loyal Legion in its *War Papers* (vol. I, 1898). Resigning from the army Sept. 14, 1865, he resumed the practice of law at Bangor, Me., where with his wife, Sarah Purinton Thompson of Topsham, whom he had married on Nov. 28, 1860, he resided until his death. His law practice was largely confined to the many enterprises he initiated or promoted. A pioneer in building and loan associations, he prepared and secured the passage of the Maine law of 1887 regulating such institutions and organized the Bangor Building & Loan Association (1885) and similar associations. He became interested in woolen-mills at Pittsfield and Old Town, in Bangor banks and in insurance companies. He lectured, 1899–1911, on bankruptcy law and federal procedure at the law school of the University of Maine. He held many minor offices: city solicitor, 1867–68; register of bankruptcy, 1867–78; United States commissioner, 1867–1911; reporter for the Maine supreme court 1888–1905 (81–99 *Maine Reports*); and member of the Maine legislature, 1883–87, being speaker of the House in 1885. Active in Civil War societies, he was a founder and later commander of the Maine chapter, Military Order of the Loyal Legion. He obtained the erection at Gettysburg of memorials to Maine soldiers, and edited and contributed to *Maine at Gettysburg* (1898). As president (annually elected, 1892–1911) he successfully developed the Eastern Maine General Hospital. With leisure and means at his command, less aggressive, more scholarly and painstaking, than his distinguished father, he collected rare books and prints, studied Maine genealogies, made after-dinner speeches, and published articles on the Civil War and on the jurists of Maine. He was the author of *Insolvent Law of Maine with Notes on Decisions* (1878); "The Supreme Court of Maine," six articles in the *Green Bag* (October 1895–March 1896); and "John Appleton," in *Great American Lawyers* (vol. V, 1908). He died in Bangor in his seventy-fourth year.

[H. F. Andrews, *The Hamlin Family* (1902); H. H. Shaw and C. J. House, *The First Maine Heavy Artillery* (1903); H. S. Burrage, *Mil. Order of the Loyal Legion . . . Hist. Address at the Fiftieth Anniversary of the Maine Commandery, Dec. 7, 1916* (1917); *Bangor Daily News*, May 16, 18, 19, 1911.] B. M—o.

HAMLIN, CYRUS (Jan. 5, 1811–Aug. 8, 1900), missionary and educator, was born near Waterford, Me., the son of Hannibal and Susan (Faulkner) Hamlin. His father and the father of Vice-President Hannibal Hamlin [*q.v.*] were twin brothers; his mother was a daughter of Francis Faulkner of Acton, Mass. Leading the rigorous life of poor and religious farmers, he attended public schools until apprenticed at the age of sixteen to his brother-in-law, a Portland silversmith. Having shown ambition and ability in night school, he was enabled to study for the ministry. Two terms at an academy in North Bridgton, Me., with study at home, prepared him for Bowdoin College. Able student, skilful constructor of scientific models, and leader in college life, he graduated in 1834 and spent the next three years at Bangor (Maine) Theological Seminary preparing for missionary work. Appointed by the American Board of Commissioners for Foreign Missions to establish a school in Turkey, he sailed in December 1838 and reached Constantinople the following February. After studying local languages, he opened in 1840 at Bebek on the Bosphorus a school and theological seminary which he directed for twenty years. Despite the disapproval of other missionaries, he established a workshop where his needy Armenian students manufactured iron stoves, stove pipes, and rat traps. A bakery and steam flour mill, begun to provide employment for boycotted Armenian Protestants, were expanded during the Crimean War to furnish bread for British hospitals, and washing machines were improvised for an establishment which cleaned the soldiers' vermin-infested clothing. The $25,000 thus earned paid for thirteen native Protestant churches. Differences with the American Board, which was replacing English with Armenian in its schools, caused Hamlin to resign in May 1860 and visit in New York Christopher Rhinelander Robert [*q.v.*], a wealthy merchant who wished to found a college at Constantinople. Plans were concerted and an endowment campaign begun when the Civil War interfered. In 1861 Hamlin returned to Constantinople and bought a magnificent site at Roumeli Hissar with money furnished by Robert. Since foreign opposition prevented immediate building, he opened Robert College in 1863 at Bebek. During the next eight years the institution grew rapidly, while its president persistently negotiated for a building permit which was only granted by the Sultan after Admiral Farragut's visit had been mistaken for an armed threat. Having moved the college in 1871 to its new building, constructed under his own minute supervision, Hamlin visited America on a brief but discouraging campaign for money. Leaving Constantinople again in October 1873, he continued his effort to obtain endowment, but was so seriously handicapped by his own dangerous illness and the outbreak of the Russo-Turkish War that the results were meager. Convinced that he would be better employed in directing the college, he decided in 1877 to return, but Robert, who had always been his intimate friend and loyal collaborator, was persuaded by the failure to obtain money and by an unfortunate misunderstanding to dismiss him without warning from the presidency. Deprived of his life-work at the age of sixty-six and deeply wounded, Hamlin never complained publicly. That summer he wrote the interesting story of his thirty-five years in Turkey, *Among the Turks* (1878), and in the autumn became professor at the Bangor Theological Seminary. Three years later, learning that his theological views were considered antiquated and his support of prohibition too ardent, he resigned to take the presidency of Middlebury College in Vermont. During five strenuous years he thoroughly reorganized the college and rescued it from imminent disaster. Retiring in 1885 to Lexington, Mass., he spent the last fifteen years of his life in preaching, lecturing, and writing in behalf of missions and especially of the persecuted Armenians. His autobiography, *My Life and Times,* was published in 1893. He married, Sept. 3, 1838, Henrietta Loraine Jackson, who died in 1850. On May 18, 1852, he married Harriet Martha Lovell, who died five years later. Mary Eliza Tenney, whom he married on Nov. 5, 1859, survived him. Alfred Dwight Foster Hamlin [*q.v.*], architect, was a son of his second marriage. Hamlin was uncompromising, quick-tempered, and dominating, but generous; with the resourcefulness of the pioneer. His monument stands on the shores of the Bosphorus—Robert College, which has sent out many political and intellectual leaders to the varied peoples of the Near East.

[H. F. Andrews, *The Hamlin Family* (1902); H. B. Genung, *The Story of Cyrus Hamlin* (1907); C. C. Crugan, "Cyrus Hamlin," in *Effective Workers in Needy Fields* (1902); C. Hamlin, *My Life and Times* (6th ed., 1924); A. D. F. Hamlin, *In Memoriam—Rev.*

Cyrus Hamlin (privately printed, 1903); *Missionary Herald,* 1838–60, *passim*; *Congregationalist,* Aug. 2, 16, 23, 1900; *Boston Transcript,* Aug. 9, 1900; letters and papers in the possession of Prof. Charles E. Estes of Robert College.] W. L. W—t., Jr.

HAMLIN, EMMONS (Nov. 16, 1821–Apr. 8, 1885), inventor, manufacturer of organs and pianos, was a descendant in the fifth generation from James Hamlin who came from England to settle in Barnstable County, Mass., about 1639. He was born in Rome, N. Y., the son of Henry and Laura (Munson) Hamlin. On Feb. 12, 1843, he married Elvira J. Patrick. His mechanical bent led him in his early twenties to seek employment in the melodeon factory of George A. Prince & Company in Buffalo. This firm was a pioneer in the industry and, during the early part of the nineteenth century, probably the largest maker of melodeons (free reed wind instruments with keyboard) in the United States. Hamlin was associated with it for about eight years. In 1850, as the result of numerous experiments, he made certain discoveries which revolutionized and perfected the "voicing" (tone-coloring) of the reeds, thus doing away with the thin, reedy, nasal tone with which the melodeon hitherto had justly been reproached. This radical discovery permitted an increase in the variety of the stops, making it possible for individual reeds to approximate the timbre respectively of violin, horn, clarinet, oboe, or other instrument.

Leaving the Prince Company in 1852, Hamlin went to Boston, where in 1854 he entered into a partnership with Henry Mason [*q.v.*], the firm being known as the Mason & Hamlin Organ Company. In 1855 this new house made its first Organ-Harmonium, with double bellows, which secured an unbroken continuance of tone. This instrument soon became popular, and in 1861, with further improvements, was renamed the American Cabinet Organ. Hamlin's inventive gift continued to be exercised in connection with the instruments his firm manufactured, which won recognition as superior to the product of foreign competitors (French harmoniums, Alexandre organs, etc.) and acquired an international reputation. In the heyday of the Second Empire, at the Paris Exposition of 1876, the Mason & Hamlin organs were awarded first prize. In the latter part of his life Hamlin took up the making of violins as an avocation. Through the influence of Ole Bull he obtained from Norway wood that was five hundred years old, and, studying the work of the great violin makers of Cremona, produced some instruments which were said to compare favorably with theirs. He was also a lover of art, and gathered a notable collection of paintings. He is said to have aided a number of musical students in their efforts to obtain education abroad. He died in Boston in his sixty-fourth year.

[See Alfred Dolge, *Pianos and Their Makers* (2 vols., 1911–13), I, 315; and H. L. Mason, *The Hist. and Development of the Am. Cabinet Organ* (n.d.); H. F. Andrews, *The Hamlin Family* (1902); *Boston Transcript,* Apr. 8, 1885.] F. H. M.

HAMLIN, HANNIBAL (Aug. 27, 1809–July 4, 1891), vice-president, United States senator, the son of Cyrus and Anna (Livermore) Hamlin, was born at Paris Hill, Me. He was a descendant in the fifth generation from James Hamlin who settled in Barnstable County, Mass., about 1639. His father, a twin brother of Hannibal Hamlin, the father of Cyrus [*q.v.*], had studied medicine at Harvard, but after taking up land in Maine, combined farming with the practice of his profession and the holding of sundry local offices. Hannibal grew up in the wholesome environment of a good New England home and attended the village school and Hebron Academy in preparation for college. The latter project had to be abandoned, owing to family misfortunes, and after trying his hand at surveying, printing, and school teaching for a brief period, he decided to study law. He was fortunate in being able to enter the office of Fessenden & Deblois of Portland, the senior partner of which firm, Samuel Fessenden [*q.v.*], was at once the leading lawyer and the outstanding anti-slavery advocate of the state. Hamlin was admitted to the bar in 1833 and in the same year settled at Hampden, not far from Bangor. He acquired a considerable practice, but his pronounced talent for party work soon diverted his attention to a political career. As a Jacksonian Democrat, he represented Hampden in the legislature from 1836 to 1841 and again in 1847. He served as speaker for three terms, 1837, 1839–40. The legislature, during his first five years of service, was an especially valuable training school, containing many members afterwards distinguished in state and national affairs and dealing with such important matters as the financial demoralization of 1837 and succeeding years, the Aroostook boundary embroglio, the abolitionist agitation, and the internal-improvement craze. Hamlin's attitude was usually cautious and conservative.

In 1842 he was elected to Congress and served without special distinction from Mar. 4, 1843, to Mar. 3, 1847. He had decided anti-slavery leanings but, like many of his contemporaries, regarded slavery as an institution beyond the legislative authority of the national government. It is to his credit, however, that he opposed the attempts of its supporters to suppress free discussion. The growing importance of this question eventually produced a serious schism in the Maine Democracy, and in 1848 Hamlin was elected to the United States Senate to serve the balance of the term of John Fairfield, deceased, by the anti-slavery wing of the party. He was reëlected in 1851 for a full term. Although a popular campaign orator, he preferred, as he afterwards stated, to be "a working rather than a talking member" of the Senate. As chairman of the committee on commerce he was the author of important legislation dealing with steamboat licensing and inspection and ship-owners' liability. Though a supporter of Pierce in 1852, he became increasingly dissatisfied with the Democratic policy toward slavery, and in 1856 went over to the Republicans. His speech of June 12, 1856, in which he renounced his Democratic allegiance, was widely quoted for campaign purposes and was one of his most effective utterances (*Congressional Globe,* 34 Cong., 1 Sess., pp. 1396–97). In the same year he was elected governor of Maine in an exciting contest which marked the beginning of a long period of Republican predominance. He served only a few weeks as governor, resigning from the Senate Jan. 7, 1857, only to resign the governorship in the following month in order to begin a new term in the Senate. He became increasingly prominent in the anti-slavery contest, and the political needs of 1860 made him a logical running-mate for Lincoln. He again resigned from the Senate on Jan. 17, 1861.

As vice-president during the Civil War, he presided over the Senate with dignity and ability, was on cordial terms with President Lincoln, and performed a great variety of wartime services for his former constituents in Maine. He was a strong advocate of emancipation and became identified with the "Radicals" of Congress. If his nomination in 1860 had been due largely to party exigencies, his failure to receive a renomination in 1864 may be attributed to the same causes. After retirement from the vice-presidency, he served for about a year as collector of the port of Boston, resigning because of his disapproval of President Johnson's policy. After two years as president of a railroad company constructing a line from Bangor to Dover, he was reëlected to the Senate, serving from Mar. 4, 1869, to Mar. 3, 1881. He was associated with the Radical group in reconstruction matters, supported Republican principles in economic issues, and steadily maintained his hold on the party organization of his native state. He was an influential opponent of the third-term movement for Grant in the convention of 1880. After retirement from the Senate he served as minister to Spain for a brief period (1881–82), an appointment of obviously complimentary character, without diplomatic significance. He spent his last years in Bangor, enjoying a wide reputation as a political Nestor and one of the last surviving intimates of President Lincoln.

Hamlin is usually grouped with the members of that remarkable dynasty of Maine statesmen beginning with George Evans and ending with Eugene Hale, all of whom he knew and some of whose fortunes he undoubtedly influenced. As a party manager and leader he did not display the unflinching courage and determination of William Pitt Fessenden or Thomas B. Reed, nor that mastery of a wide field of legislation possessed by George Evans or Nelson Dingley. He had, however, a great fund of shrewd common sense and a gift of stating things in clear and understandable phrase. When as chairman of the committee on foreign relations he urged the acceptance of the Halifax fisheries award in the interest of international arbitration and when, on the floor of the Senate, he opposed the Chinese exclusion law as a violation of treaty obligations (*Congressional Record,* 45 Cong., 3 Sess., pp. 1383–87), he displayed genuine statesmanship. It is also worth mention that if he quarreled with President Hayes over patronage and expressed his contempt for civil-service reform, he at least opposed the infamous "salary grab" and refused to take his share of the loot.

Personally Hamlin had many attractive qualities and retained the loyalty and affection of a host of supporters. Senator Henry L. Dawes, who knew him well, described him as "a born democrat," an interesting conversationalist, and an inveterate smoker and card player. He also mentioned as characteristic of the man that he wore "a black swallow-tailed coat, and . . . clung to the old fashioned stock long after it had been discarded by the rest of mankind" (*Century Magazine,* July 1895). Hamlin had a stocky, powerful frame and great muscular strength. His complexion was so swarthy that in 1860 the story was successfully circulated among credulous Southerners that he had negro blood. He was a skillful fly fisherman and an expert rifle shot. He was twice married: on Dec. 10, 1833, to Sarah Jane Emery, daughter of Judge Stephen A. Emery of Paris Hill, who died Apr. 17, 1855, and on Sept. 25, 1856, to Ellen Vesta Emery, a half-sister of his first wife. Charles Hamlin [*q.v.*] was his son.

[C. E. Hamlin, *The Life and Times of Hannibal Hamlin* (1899), a biography by his grandson, exaggerates Hamlin's importance in national affairs, but is useful in its presentation of Maine party history and occasional documents of personal interest. See also H. F. Andrews, *The Hamlin Family* (1902), and Howard Carroll, *Twelve Americans* (1883). The biographical literature of the period contains many references and the newspapers, probably because of Hamlin's association with Lincoln, published an unusually large amount of obituary material. See especially *N. Y. Tribune*, July 5, 9, 10, 1891.] W. A. R.

HAMLIN, WILLIAM (Oct. 15, 1772–Nov. 22, 1869), engraver, died in his ninety-eighth year and was active to the end, yet his disposition was so retiring that there are few outstanding events to record of his long life. A descendant of Giles Hamlin, who settled in Hartford, Conn., before 1651, he was a son of Capt. Samuel and Thankful (Ely) Hamlin. He was born in Providence, R. I., and spent his life there, marrying, on Apr. 2, 1810, Eliza Bowen, daughter of Isaac and Sarah (Whittaker) Bowen. His educational advantages were few and he picked up by himself much of his technical knowledge. He set up in business "At the Sign of the Quadrant" as a maker and repairer of nautical instruments, optical and mathematical. In this work he became interested in engraving processes and began to experiment on copper. He advertised that he would engrave business cards but later grew more ambitious. According to Weitenkampf (*post*, p. 111), he worked practically without instruction and with only fair success; his plates show "a somewhat weak mixture of mezzotint and stipple, frequently worked over with the roulette" (Stauffer, *post*. p. 117). He made at least three plates of the head of Washington, one of them being copied from the Savage portrait and another, engraved in his ninety-first year, from Houdon's bust. His print of "The Burning of the Frigate *Philadelphia* in Tripoli Harbor, February 1804" ("U. S. Ship *Philadelphia* at Tripoli," Stauffer, p. 210) is probably his best-known work. His interest to the collector of American prints is chiefly historical.

[H. F. Andrews, *The Hamlin Family* (1902); Frank Weitenkampf, *Am. Graphic Art* (1912); D. M. Stauffer, *Am. Engravers upon Copper and Steel* (1907); Wm. Dunlap, *A Hist. of the Rise and Progress of the Arts of Design in the U. S.* (rev. ed., 1918), vol. III.] K. H. A.

HAMLINE, LEONIDAS LENT (May 10, 1797–Mar. 23, 1865), clergyman, bishop of the Methodist Episcopal Church, born in Burlington, Conn., was of old New England stock, the son of Mark and Roxanna (Moses) Hamlin and a descendant of James Hamlin, born in England, who came to Barnstable, Mass., about 1639. For reasons unknown he added an *e* to the family name. (See H. F. Andrews, *The Hamlin Family*, 1902.) His father was a farmer and schoolmaster of limited means. A stanch Congregationalist, he hoped to see his son a minister of that persuasion, and so far as possible shaped his education to that end. Before he was eighteen Leonidas was teaching school winters and studying summers, and had become noted for his mental precocity, his speaking ability, and his religious activities. About 1815, because of a nervous breakdown, he went to South Carolina. After his return he became convinced that he had no religious fitness for the ministry, and turned to the law. The course of his career now becomes obscure for a time. He migrated to Ohio, and is quoted as stating that he was admitted to the bar in Lancaster in 1827 (Walter C. Palmer, *Life and Letters of Leonidas L. Hamline, D.D.*, 1866, p. 17). The records of Muskingum County, however, indicate that he was a member of the bar in Zanesville in 1825 (J. F. Everhart, *History of Muskingum County, Ohio*, 1882). At all events, he was married in that town, Mar. 6, 1824, to Eliza Price, daughter of a wealthy Irish business man. While on a sojourn in New York State in 1828 he came under Methodist influences, and after a long and painful struggle was converted. Returning to Ohio, he continued to practise law, but began to take an active part in camp-meetings and other religious assemblies. Soon the conviction that he must devote himself to proclaiming the gospel took possession of him, and in November 1829 he was licensed to preach, but with no expectation on his part, apparently, of entering the regular ministry. After traveling under the direction of presiding elders for several years, however, he was persuaded in 1832 to join the Ohio Conference on probation. He was ordained deacon in 1834, and elder in 1836. The first years of his service had been spent on long circuits in rough country, where he had gained the reputation of being a brainy and persuasive preacher. From 1834 to 1836 he was stationed as junior pastor at Wesley Chapel, Cincinnati, and in the summer of the latter year was sent to Columbus. His first wife died Mar. 27, 1835, and in 1836 he married Mrs. Melinda Truesdell.

In 1836 he was appointed assistant editor of the *Western Christian Advocate*, Cincinnati. He gave powerful support to the establishment of *Der christliche Apologete*, and to the extension of German missionary work in Cincinnati. A delegate to the General Conference of 1840, he was made chairman of the Committee on the Memorial to Establish a Periodical for Females. His report recommended that a periodical "blending the theology of the Bible as inculcated by Methodism with the attractions of a chastened literature should be placed within the reach of our female members." The General Conference authorized the publication of such a periodical under his supervision, and the *Ladies' Repository* was established, of which he was the able and popular editor until 1844. Elected to the General Conference of that year, he was warned by three medical advisers that, owing to a heart affection, attendance either as a debater or silent member "might increase the affection beyond the control of remedies." Indifferent through religious enthusiasm as to whether he lived or died, he was present at the Conference and took a leading part in the famous debate which resulted in the passing of a resolution advising Bishop James O. Andrew [*q.v.*] to desist from performing the offices of bishop, because of his connection with slave-holding. Hamline's speech on the constitutional authority of the General Conference remains one of the memorable addresses in the ecclesiastical history of his church. (See J. M. Buckley, *A History of Methodists in the United States,* 1896, ch. XVII.) The Conference elected him bishop, and despite his precarious health, he managed to perform the arduous duties of that office for eight years, being forced to relinquish active service in 1852. His resignation raised the question whether a Methodist bishop is an ecclesiastical officer, or a representative of a distinct priestly order—once a bishop, always a bishop. Its acceptance, after long discussion, committed the denomination to the former view.

The last period of his life was spent in steadily declining health at Mount Pleasant, Iowa, his last days being marked with great suffering and lofty endurance. Having inherited some wealth from his first wife, before his death he gave $25,000 to help establish what is now Hamline University, St. Paul, Minn., and $25,000 to Mount Vernon Institute, Iowa, besides smaller sums to various societies. He was impressive in appearance and an easy, graceful speaker with a melodious, bass voice, and good command of language. His sermons are analytical, argumentative, and somber, but were delivered, it is said, with deep feeling. Two volumes of his writings were published, *Works of Rev. Leonidas L. Hamline, D.D.* (vol. I, 1869; vol. II, 1871), both edited by **F. G. Hibbard**, who also prepared a *Biography of Rev. Leonidas L. Hamline, D.D.* (1880).

[For authorities, see references above.] H. E. S.

HAMMERSTEIN, OSCAR (*c.* 1847–Aug. 1, 1919), inventor, composer, theatrical manager, impresario, was born in Germany and came to New York a penniless run-away some time before the close of the Civil War. His first employment was in a Pearl Street cigar factory filling rush orders for the army. After he had been at work for a while, he devised and patented a machine for spreading and shaping the tobacco leaf by air suction. From this and from several later inventions he is said to have made over $1,000,000. Meanwhile he used his first royalties to start the *United States Tobacco Journal,* which he conducted successfully until 1885, began to speculate in Harlem real estate, and then, in accord with his strongest inclinations, ventured into the theatrical business. In 1868 he wrote three one-act comedies in German and got them produced in New York. Some years later, when he was well established as a manager, he made a wager with Gustave Kerker, the composer of *The Belles of New York,* that he could write an operetta, words and music, in forty-eight hours. He locked himself in a hotel room and set to work; a relay of organ-grinders, subsidized by Kerker, played in the street beneath his window; trays of cocktails and ham sandwiches were passed through his transom, and returned empty; and at the end of the stipulated period Hammerstein emerged smiling with the manuscript of *The Kohinoor.* Considerably revised, it was produced a few months later and made money. His first venture in management was the Stadt Theatre, in New York, which he leased in 1870. In 1880 he completed the Harlem Opera House, where, against the advice of his friends, he produced several operas in English. They were failures artistically and financially; but Hammerstein recouped his losses by erecting the Columbus Theatre. Among his other New York properties were the Olympia Music Hall (1895), the Victoria Music Hall (1899), which opened to the strains of his own "Victoria Festival March," and the Republic Theatre (1900). He was also part-owner of Koster and Bial's vaudeville house and of other theatres.

His lifelong ambition was to give grand opera in the English language at popular prices. The most gigantic of all his attempts to realize this ambition was the building of the Manhattan Opera House, on 34th Street. Before it was finished he decided to make it a rival of the Metropolitan and opened it Dec. 3, 1906, with a lavish production of Bellini's *I Puritani.* For some three years the two establishments engaged in furious and costly competition. Hammerstein forced his rivals to extend their repertoire and to improve their standards of production, but single-handed could not continue to maintain the struggle. In April 1910 he was compelled to sell his interests to the Metropolitan for $2,000,-000 and to agree not to produce grand opera in their territory until April 1920. He built the Philadelphia Opera House, opened Nov. 17, 1908, but sold it two seasons later. After his New York defeat he went to England and opened his London Opera House, Nov. 13, 1911, with a sumptuous performance of Nougués' panoramic *Quo Vadis,* but at the end of the season was forced to close for lack of patronage. Upon his return to New York he built the American Opera House (1912), but was enjoined from using it for opera. He renamed it the Lexington Theatre and devoted it to ordinary forms of entertainment. Probably no other theatrical manager of his day spent money more lavishly to realize his own artistic ideals.

Hammerstein was thrice married: first, to Rosa Blau; in 1879 to Malvina Jacobi of Selma, Ala.; and in 1914 to Mary Emma (Miller) Swift, who survived him. He died in New York City.

[Oscar Hammerstein: The Robinson Locke Collection of Dramatic Scrap Books, 3 vols., N. Y. Pub. Lib.; *Who's Who in America,* 1908–19; *N. Y. Times, Herald, World,* and *Eve. Post,* Aug. 2, 1919; *Musical Courier,* Aug. 7, 1919; *Musical America,* Aug. 9, 1919; *Theatre Mag.,* Oct. 1919; James Huneker, *Steeplejack* (1921).]

F. H. M.

HAMMETT, HENRY PINCKNEY (Dec. 31, 1822–May 8, 1891), cotton manufacturer, was born on his father's farm in Greenville County, S. C., the son of Jesse Hammett, whose father had come to Maryland from England, and Nancy Davis. After a country-school education, he went at the age of eighteen to Augusta, Ga., where he was a clerk in the cotton-firm of Matthews & Company. Returning to Greenville County, he taught school for a time, and then was employed in a country store near Batesville. Soon he began to keep the books at the Batesville Cotton Mill, married Deborah Jane, the daughter of William Bates, founder of the factory, and was taken into the firm with Bates and Thomas Cox. Bates had walked to South Carolina from Pawtucket, R. I., where he had been employed in Samuel Slater's celebrated cotton factory; after working in several small Southern mills, he built his own little plant on Rocky Creek about 1830, equipping it with second-hand English machinery. Hammett took charge of the purchase of cotton and sale of goods, the latter being hauled in heavy wagons and bartered over a wide area for grain, salted meat, and rags.

In 1863 the firm sold out to a Charleston company, and Hammett became tax assessor of Greenville County. He was elected to the legislature in 1865 and 1867, refusing reëlection in 1869. In 1866 he became president of the rundown Greenville & Columbia Railroad, which he improved before resigning office in 1870. When Batesville was sold, Hammett, probably with the assistance of Bates, bought the Garrison Shoals on the Saluda River, which was then entirely undeveloped except for a small dam which furnished power for a gristmill. On Apr. 30, 1873, Hammett organized and became president of the Piedmont Manufacturing Company, with subscribed capital of $75,000 (incorporated 1874 with $200,000 capital), to build a cotton factory at the Shoals, but construction had hardly begun when the panic of that year threatened to halt the enterprise. Subscribers refused to pay their instalments, and others sold out for what they could get. South Carolina was undergoing the rigors of Reconstruction. Hammett strained every resource to keep the work in progress, even arranging to pay wages with orders on a friendly grocery firm in Greenville. After a lapse of some months, operations were resumed in 1875, and the machinery was started in March 1876 with 5,000 spindles and 112 looms.

The mill was successful from the outset, and in 1877, with more capital from the North, 7,800 spindles and 112 looms were added. In 1878 a second mill was built, with 9,860 spindles and 320 looms; the next year 3,136 spindles were added to give this company more spindles and looms than any other in the state. A third mill was completed in 1890 with 22,848 spindles and 720 looms. The product was largely sheetings, of which half was exported to China. Hammett used the native poor-white labor, at first with superintendents from the North. He was deeply interested in his mill community, and the village which he built for the operatives became a pattern for others in the Southern Piedmont. Though not distinguished by personal temperance until the last years of his life, Hammett absolutely forbade liquor in his village and drove out the mountain wagons which came selling whiskey in tin cups at five cents a pint.

Hammett probably inspired more confidence in the practicability of manufacturing cotton in the South than any other one person. William Gregg [*q.v.*] was of greater ability, but the Civil War cut off much of his influence. The Piedmont Manufacturing Company refuted, with its excellent profits, the dire warnings of Edward Atkinson [*q.v.*] and others against Southern participation in what had been a Northern industry. Hammett selected his operatives with care and made promotions from his own ranks. His factory claims first place in number of men sent out to become superintendents and foremen of other mills. Hammett was a man of huge size, smooth-shaven, and with a bald head; he had a special buggy made to hold him. He wore a long coat and silk hat, and spoke with marked deliberation; but this ponderous manner was not a bar to extraordinarily cordial relations between him and his factory workers.

[See Greenville, S. C., *Daily News*, May 9, 1891; *Greenville Century Book* (Greenville, S. C., 1903); B. and G. S. Mitchell, *The Industrial Revolution in the South* (1930); *Cyc. of Eminent and Representative Men of the Carolinas*, vol. I (1892); J. M. Richardson, Hist. of Greenville County, S. C. (1930).] B. M—l.

HAMMETT, SAMUEL ADAMS (Feb. 4, 1816–Dec. 24, 1865), author, was born at Jewett City, New London County, Conn., the only child of Augustus and Mary (Wright) Hammett. He was taken by his parents to New York City, where his mother died Apr. 5, 1826. After receiving a good academic education, Hammett wandered to Texas as a young man and lived there some ten or twelve years. He served for a while as clerk of the district court of Montgomery County, engaged in merchandising, and was captain of a company of volunteers. It is evident from his writings that he enjoyed heartily the rough, outdoor life of the frontier and observed its inhabitants through clear, intelligent eyes. Returning to New York in 1848, he became a flour-merchant with a warehouse at 31 Water St. For the *Spirit of the Times*, the *Knickerbocker Magazine*, the *Literary World*, the *United States Magazine and Democratic Review* and the *American Whig Review* he wrote articles, which he later reworked for his books: *A Stray Yankee in Texas* (1853), *The Wonderful Adventures of Captain Priest* (1855), and *Piney Woods Tavern, or Sam Slick in Texas* (1858). His first volume appeared under the pseudonym of Philip Paxton, the others as "by the author of *A Stray Yankee in Texas*." Since Hammett had few or no literary associates, it is not surprising that he and his writings have been lost to sight, but his first book was a noteworthy contribution to the literature of the southwestern frontier and may still be read with enjoyment. Like other books of its genre, it is a narrative of personal adventure, seasoned with anecdote, dialect, and horseplay, but it is written with skill, its gusto is genuine, and it is uncommonly veracious. The author was particularly successful in reporting frontier and Yankee idiom. His second book, however, was a negligible collection of humorous tales and sketches; and in his third he returned, evidently with delight, to Texas. "Sam Slick," in the title of this third book, is used generically; Hammett was not, as has been sometimes supposed, an imitator of Thomas Chandler Haliburton. During his last years he lived in Brooklyn, where he died of pneumonia on Christmas Eve, 1865.

[*New-England Hist. and Geneal. Reg.*, Jan. 1881, p. 82; E. A. and G. L. Duyckinck, *Cyc. Am. Lit.* (rev. ed., 1875); *Trow's N. Y. City Directory*, 1858; J. Lain's *Brooklyn City Directory*, 1865; death notice in *N. Y. Daily Tribune*, Dec. 25, 1865.] G. H. G.

HAMMON, JUPITER (*c.* 1720–*c.* 1800), poet, was an African slave in the Lloyd family of Lloyd's Neck, Long Island. The first definite reference to him is found in a letter dated May 19, 1730, that shows him as being treated for a rheumatic disorder. He was first owned by Henry Lloyd, who died in 1763 and left him in the part of the inheritance that fell to Joseph Lloyd, one of his four sons. For some time during the Revolutionary War Jupiter lived in Hartford, Conn., since Joseph Lloyd had been compelled to leave Long Island when the British and Hessians overran it; and when this owner died in the course of the war, he fell into the possession of John Lloyd, Jr., Joseph's grandson. He was a dutiful and trusted servant, so highly esteemed by the members of the Lloyd family in his later years that they helped him to place his verses before the public. His first poem antedated by several years that of Phillis Wheatley [*q.v.*], who is commonly regarded as the first negro voice in American literature. This was *An Evening Thought. Salvation by Christ, with Penetential Cries: Composed by Jupiter Hammon, a Negro Belonging to Mr. Lloyd, of Queen's Village, on Long Island, the 25th of December, 1760*, printed as a broadside in New York, evidently in 1761. The poem consists of eighty-eight lines, and, like all of Hammon's work, emphasizes the religious motive, the word "salvation" appearing no less than twenty-three times. The second publication, a poetical address to Phillis Wheatley, dated Hartford, Aug. 4, 1778, was also in broadsheet form. Only one original copy, that of the Connecticut Historical Society, is now known to exist. This production, having more personal interest than the first, is somewhat stronger and more imaginative. Then followed *An Essay on the Ten Virgins* (1779); and *A Winter Piece* (Hartford, 1782), largely in prose but containing on the last two pages "A Poem for Children, with Thoughts on Death." *An Evening's Improvement*, written toward the close of the war, is of special biographical interest since it contains a poetical dialogue entitled "The Kind Master and Dutiful Servant." Of more intrinsic importance than any of the verse is *An Address to the Negroes of the State of New York,* originally presented to the members of the African Society in the City of New York on Sept. 24, 1786, and printed in New York early in 1787. It was immediately reprinted in Philadelphia by order of the Pennsylvania Society for promoting the Abolition of Slavery, and there was a third edition after Hammon's death. The strong style is the author's, but the spelling was corrected by the printers. The address shows Hammon as feeling it his duty to bear slavery with patience but as strongly disapproving of the system and urging that young slaves be manumitted. It is worthy of note that in his will, dated 1795, John Lloyd, Jr., directed that certain of his slaves be set free on arriving at the age of twenty-eight. The last definite reference to Hammon bears the date of Oct. 6, 1790, when he was sent by his master with money to pay a debt. Because of the difficulty in locating his poems, only within recent years has he begun to receive the attention he deserves.

[Oscar Wegelin, *Jupiter Hammon, American Negro Poet: Selections from his Writings, and a Bibliography* (1915), is the most accessible source and practically the sole authority.] B. B.

HAMMOND, CHARLES (Sept. 19, 1779–Apr. 3, 1840), lawyer, journalist, the son of George and Elizabeth (Wells) Hammond, was born near Baltimore, Md. His father was a farmer and a man of some culture, noted for his sound, practical judgment, uncompromising views, extensive reading, and retentive memory. In 1785 he moved with his family and slaves to the western part of Virginia and settled in Wellsburg, Brooke County (now part of West Virginia). Charles Hammond, under the direction of his parents and that of a tutor in mathematics and Latin, laid the foundation of the fund of information which he later acquired through his own efforts. He displayed an aptitude for writing, especially satirical verse, and it was his early ambition to become a printer. He made a trip to Washington with this object in mind but finding no encouragement decided, at the suggestion of his father, to study law. In 1800 he entered the law office of Philip Doddridge [*q.v.*]. The following year he was admitted to practice in the state courts and in 1803, in the federal courts. He began practising in Wellsburg, where he married Sarah Tillinghast in 1803, but he soon moved to Wheeling. In 1801 or 1802, his penchant for journalism and his strong Federalism led him to contribute a series of articles to the *Scioto Gazette* (Chillicothe), defending Governor St. Clair. These articles caused Hammond to become known throughout the region as a stanch Federalist. At twenty-four he won recognition as a lawyer when the argument he advanced in a case arising under the excise law was published in its entirety in the *United States Gazette* (Smith, *post,* p. 14).

In 1810 he removed to Belmont County, Ohio, where he settled on a farm near St. Clairsville. In his adopted state he was quickly recognized as leader of the Federalist party. In 1813 he was elected to the Ohio Senate and served 1813–15. From 1813 through 1817 he published the *Ohio Federalist.* In 1816 he was elected to the state House of Representatives and served in that body 1817–19 and 1820–21, declining renomination in 1821. Throughout his legislative career he was an ardent advocate of internal improvements and of a comprehensive system of education for the state. During his membership in the lower house, he revised the Ohio laws and drafted a number of important statutes, especially those regulating the course of descents, distribution of personal estates, and chancery proceedings. He was appointed the first reporter of the Ohio supreme court, holding the office from 1823 until his death and preparing the first nine volumes of the *Ohio Reports.*

In 1822 he moved to Cincinnati determined to devote himself to the law; but, in order to eke out his income, he also wrote for the *Cincinnati Gazette.* In 1823 he became an editorial writer on this paper and from 1825 until his death served as editor. From 1825 to 1830 he received no pay. He then demanded $1,000 a year and received this sum for a time, after which he was paid one-third of the profits. The *Gazette* was ably edited and became one of the most influential papers in the West. Through its columns Hammond vigorously attacked slavery and Andrew Jackson. For a time during the campaign of 1828 he edited a monthly known as *Truth's Advocate,* devoted to the interests of Henry Clay.

Hammond was the recognized leader of the Ohio bar in his generation. Chief Justice Marshall commented upon "his acuteness and accuracy of mind" (Randall and Ryan, *post,* III, 329), and Thomas Ewing declared that "Hammond spoke at the bar as good English as Addison wrote in the Spectator" (Smith, p. 13). His printed legal arguments won the admiration of the bar for their simplicity, conciseness, and originality of thought. His most celebrated argument was delivered in the case of *Osborn* vs. *Bank of the United States* (9 *Wheaton,* 738). Although a Federalist of the national school of Washington, he was a vigorous opponent of the Bank and led the attack upon it in the Ohio legislature. The case was argued in the United States Supreme Court in February 1824, by Hammond and John C. Wright for the plaintiff and Henry Clay for the Bank. Although Hammond lost, his review of Chief Justice Marshall's decision in *McCulloch* vs. *Maryland* was considered exceptionally able. President John Quincy Adams offered him a place on the United States Supreme Court bench (Greve, *post,* I, 806), but Hammond declined the honor. He died in his sixty-first year. His first wife had died some years before and he had been married a second time, to a sister of Thomas and Moses Moorehead of Zanesville.

[W. H. Smith, *Charles Hammond and His Relations to Henry Clay and John Quincy Adams* (1885); Jacob Burnet, *Notes on the Early Settlement of the North-Western Territory* (1847), p. 380; E. D. Mansfield, *Personal Memories* (1879); M. J. Roe, *Geneal. of Gen. James Wells* (1893); W. T. Coggeshall, *The Poets and Poetry of the West* (1860); E. O. Randall and D. J. Ryan, *Hist. of Ohio* (1912), vol. III, ch. IX; C. T. Greve, *Centennial Hist. of Cincinnati* (1904), vol. I; W. H. Venable, "Ohio Literary Men and Women," in *Ohio Centennial Anniversary Celebration* (1903), ed. by E. O. Randall; G. H. Payne, *Hist. of Journalism in the U. S.* (1920); *Bench and Bar of Ohio* (1897), vol. II; 9 *Ohio Reports,* 4.]
R. C. McG.

HAMMOND, EDWARD PAYSON (Sept. 1, 1831–Aug. 14, 1910), evangelist, was born at Ellington, Conn. His father, Elijah Hammond, a descendant of Thomas Hammond who settled in Hingham, Mass., in 1635, was a teacher. His mother, Esther Griswold, was a woman of deep Christian convictions whose devotion profoundly influenced Hammond's entire life. He studied at Phillips Academy, Andover, Mass., and graduated at Williams College in 1858. After two years at Union Seminary, New York, he completed his theological course in 1861 at Free Church College, Edinburgh. During his period of study there he held religious meetings in neglected places, with results so unusual as to arouse the attention and win the commendation of leading pastors in Edinburgh and other cities. As a consequence he was invited to conduct meetings in Edinburgh, Glasgow, and elsewhere in Scotland; later, in London and Liverpool. People came in crowds and intense interest was manifested. He introduced song services, which were then a novelty, using informal words and music; he gave attractiveness to evangelical themes by abundant illustrations from nature and everyday life; and made meetings for children a prominent feature of his work. In after years Rev. F. B. Meyer, widely known London clergyman, wrote of the deep impression made upon him, when a young clerk in London, by Hammond's meetings. Gen. William Booth, founder of the Salvation Army, attributed to the young evangelist important influence upon his own career.

Returning to America in 1861, Hammond conducted services in Massachusetts and Maine. On Jan. 2, 1862, he was ordained as an evangelist by the Presbytery of New York. He then held meetings in Brooklyn, Utica, Chicago (where D. L. Moody assisted him), Detroit, Philadelphia, and elsewhere. He was married, May 24, 1866, in Towanda, Pa., to Eliza Plemer Overton, and with his wife traveled in Europe, Egypt, and Palestine. Early in 1867 he held services for six weeks in London and through that year labored in Great Britain. He returned to the United States in 1868 and carried on work in various sections from the Atlantic to the Pacific, notably in a great revival at St. Louis in 1874. He made a missionary journey to Alaska in 1875. In 1881 he addressed great audiences in Canadian cities. At a later date he revisited Great Britain and conducted evangelistic services there and in Scandinavia. The Queen of Sweden invited him to her summer residence near Stockholm and expressed satisfaction at the results of his meetings. He continued active into the opening years of the twentieth century and after a considerable period of declining health died at his home in Hartford, Conn. Among his publications are *The Conversion of Children* (1878) and over a hundred small books and tracts. His children's hymns were translated into several languages of Europe and Asia.

[Some details of Hammond's life and many incidents of his work are give in P. C. Headley, *The Reaper and the Harvest* (1884). See also F. S. Hammond, *Hist. and Geneals. of the Hammond Families in America,* vol. II (1904); Alfred Nevin, *Encyc. of the Presby. Ch. in the U. S. of America* (1884); *Who's Who in America,* 1910–11; the *Presbyterian,* Aug. 24, 1910; *Hartford Courant* and *Hartford Times,* Aug. 15, 1910.]
E. D. E.

HAMMOND, EDWIN (May 20, 1801–Dec. 31, 1870), sheep-breeder, was descended from Benjamin Hammond who came with his mother to Boston in 1634, through a grandson, Elnathan, who moved to Newport, R. I., and was married there in 1728. Edwin's parents were another Elnathan Hammond and Deborah (Carr) Hammond, of Middlebury, Addison County, Vt., which was his birthplace. At an early age, Edwin and his brother William started farming together, devoting themselves chiefly to the raising of horses, sheep, and cattle. Sheep raising was then one of the most profitable branches of husbandry in northern New England, and one for which the rich pastures of Addison County were well adapted. The Hammond brothers at one time were keeping a flock of a thousand sheep, chiefly of the Saxony breed, but finding that changing conditions were making this breed less profitable, they turned their attention to the Merinos. This breed became permanently established in the United States in 1802 when David Humphreys [*q.v.*], United States minister to Spain, succeeded in importing seventy ewes and twenty-one rams, but they had been crossed with the Saxony sheep to such an extent that the Merinos as a pure-blooded stock were rapidly becoming extinct. The Hammond brothers visited the leading sheep-raising centers of New England in quest of the purest strain of Merinos obtainable. In January 1844, in company with R. P. Hall of Cornwall, they inspected the flock of Stephen Atwood at Woodbury, Conn., and after satisfying themselves that these sheep were full-blooded Merinos and obtaining documentary proof of descent from the original Humphrey importation, they purchased over a hundred ewes and rams. Using the Atwood sheep as a basis, they began through careful breeding and selection to build up a flock of pure-bred Merinos. Edwin devoted himself to the breeding side of the business and William attended to the management and practical care of the sheep, but after the death of the latter in 1858 Edwin carried on the work alone. He possessed keen judgment and an instinct which guided him in the determination of the qualities to be developed. Year after year the Merino breed improved under his management, blemishes and defects were eradicated, desirable traits strengthened, and the dominant characteristics intensified. Other sheep raisers of the county specialized in the Merinos and share the credit for the improvement of the breed, but Hammond was generally recognized as foremost in the field. For several decades following the Civil War Addison County was the chief Merino-breeding center of the country and its stock commanded fancy prices, five or six thousand dollars being paid for choice rams. In 1881 seventy-one carloads, containing 6,777 sheep, were shipped from Middlebury to various parts of the country as breeding stock.

Edwin Hammond was active also in other phases of agriculture. He was one of the founders of the Vermont State Agricultural Society (1851) and served as its president for several years. He gave aid and advice in the formation of the New England Agricultural Society and the National Woolgrowers Association and was a member of the executive committee of the latter. He was associated with the National Manufacturers' Association in framing the schedule on wool and woolens in connection with the tariff of 1867. He represented the town of Middlebury in the state legislature in 1858 and 1859 and was a delegate to the Republican National Convention in 1864. He was a member of the board of trustees of Middlebury College and contributed generously to its funds. On Dec. 29, 1828, he was married to Alpha Olmsted, of Middlebury, by whom he had three children.

[*Reg. of the Vt. Atwood Merino Sheep Club*, I (n.d., *c.* 1887), 808–13; *Reg. of the Vermont Merino Sheep Breeders' Asso.*, II (1883), 38–42; H. P. Smith, *Hist. of Addison County, Vt.* (1886), ch. xiv; Samuel Swift, *Hist. of the Town of Middlebury* (1859), ch. ix; files of the *New England Farmer*; Roland Hammond, *A Hist. and Geneal. of the Descendants of Wm. Hammond* (1894); H. K. Olmsted, *Geneal. of the Olmsted Family* (1912); certain information regarding family history from a grandson of Edwin Hammond.]

A. M. K.

HAMMOND, GEORGE HENRY (May 5, 1838–Dec. 29, 1886), packer, pioneer in the use of refrigerator cars, was born in Fitchburg, Mass., the third of the twelve children of John and Sarah (Huston) Hammond, and the eighth in descent from William Hammond, whose widow Elizabeth, a sister of Admiral Sir William Penn, emigrated from London to New England with her children in 1634. His father was a carpenter and joiner. As a boy Hammond did chores for a maker of leather pocket-books in Ashburnham, Mass., and took over the business, which employed a dozen girls, before he was twelve years old. His goods going out of fashion, he hired himself to a butcher and later worked in a mattress and palm-leaf hat shop. He soon bought the concern from his employer but sold it six months later in order to try his fortune in the West. Arriving in Detroit in 1854, he worked for two years and a half in a mattress and furniture factory and then started to make chairs on his own account. Several months later his plant burned, leaving him with thirteen dollars in cash and a fifty-dollar note. With this much capital he opened a meat market, attended a commercial school after hours, added a slaughter house to his retail business, and was soon thriving. In 1857 he married Ellen Barry of Detroit, by whom he had eleven children. Hammond was the first packer to see the possibilities of refrigerator cars, and his successful use of them, some years before they became general, brought him wealth and made him one of the most powerful influences in the centralizing of the meat industry. The car with which he began his experiments was built by William Davis, a fish dealer, who had been shipping fish in good condition from Lake Superior to Detroit in his patent ice-box. Just when Hammond dispatched his first carload of dressed beef to the Boston market is not known; the earliest dates given are October 1868 and May 1869. By 1870, however, the practice had proved remunerative and more cars were building; in 1885 Hammond had 800 in operation. The companies of which he was the head and directing genius established large slaughter houses at Omaha and at Hammond, Ind., which was founded and named for him by his business associate, Marcus M. Towle. As his fortune grew Hammond became heavily interested in Detroit real estate, banking, and insurance. He was a home-loving man and, having worked strenuously from his early years, had few recreations and no interest in religion, politics, literature, or society. He did take pleasure in travel, visiting Florida, California, and Europe; and in Detroit he was somewhat famous for his knack in telling tall stories. In manner he was quiet and placid, with little to indicate his shrewdness and enterprise. He died in Detroit in his forty-ninth year, of a heart ailment, after an illness of two weeks.

[*Detroit Free Press* and *Evening News,* Dec. 30, 1886; Silas Farmer, *Hist. of Detroit and Wayne County and Early Mich.,* vol. II (3rd ed., 1890), with portrait; Roland Hammond, *A Hist. and Geneal. of the Descendants of Wm. Hammond* (1894); *A Standard Hist. of Lake County, Ind., and the Calumet Region,* vol. I (1915), ed. by W. F. Howat.] R. A. C.

HAMMOND, JABEZ DELANO (Aug. 2, 1778–Aug. 18, 1855), historian and politician, was born in New Bedford, Mass., a descendant of Benjamin Hammond who came to Boston in 1634, and a son of Jabez and Priscilla (Delano) Hammond. Soon after his birth his parents removed to Woodstock, Vt. Educated in the common schools, he entered professional life as a school-teacher at the age of fifteen. After teaching several years and serving a short apprenticeship in a medical office, he qualified as a physician and began practice in Reading, Vt., in 1799. Since he found medicine uncongenial, however, he studied law, and after being admitted to the bar of New York, opened a law office in Cherry Valley, N. Y., in 1805. "Popular with the masses," wrote one who was his student and later his partner, "he . . . built up within a short time a reputable and profitable legal practice, and took a prominent stand as a politician . . . a man of sound practical good sense; not a fluent speaker or an eloquent debater" (Beardsley, *post,* p. 114). He began his public career with election in 1815 to the Fourteenth Congress. On concluding his congressional term he was elected to the state Senate for four years beginning in 1818. Previously uninstructed in the intricacies of Albany politics, he found himself in an atmosphere of plot and counterplot and soon, against his desire, a member of the widely responsible council of appointment. A sincere though discriminating admirer of Gov. DeWitt Clinton, he realized that he was selected by the governor's foes to help conceal the Anti-Clintonian character of the council. Here he observed the ideals and technique of party controversy which he was to set forth so clearly in his historical narrative (*History of Political Parties,* I, 447 ff.). This term completed his legislative career. He tried law practice for a few years in Albany, but returned to Cherry Valley where he spent the remainder of his life. During 1825 and 1826 he was a commissioner to settle the claims of New York against the federal government. Beginning in 1838, he served nine years as judge of Otsego County, acquiring a reputation not only for fairness and learning but for a benign and helpful attitude toward younger counsel (Roland Hammond, *post,* p. 175). While traveling through Europe in 1831 he took note of various systems of education. He was intensely interested in the schools of his state, made them the subject of addresses at Cherry Valley (1832) and Cooperstown (1838), served a term as county superintendent of schools, and in 1845 was appointed Regent of the University of the State of New York.

It is as the author of *The History of Political Parties in the State of New-York* that he has permanent fame. The two volumes published at Auburn in 1842 brought the narrative from 1789 through 1840. A few years later when he was considering the possibility of a third volume the death of Gov. Silas Wright [*q.v.*], whose biography he had desired to write, led him to combine the two projects. The result was a volume (Syracuse, 1848) cited both as Volume III of his history and as a Life of Wright, the latter occupying the first and last sections and being merged in the general history for the rest of the book. The entire work was enthusiastically received and passed through four editions and an extra printing. Covering more than a half century of New York politics familiar to the author, and distinguished for impartiality and candor, it has high value as an original source. It is far more than a work of reminiscence, however, for the author used all the material that energy and ingenuity could discover. He was too independent in mind to make a successful party man; though a Democrat, in 1828 he voted for Adams because he respected him and in 1844 withheld his vote from Polk because of his own detestation of slavery and his opposition to the annexation of Texas (see his *Letter to the Hon. John C. Calhoun on the Annexation of Texas,* 1844, p. 4).

He married, probably in 1810, Miranda Stoddard of Woodstock, Vt., who died in 1832, and in 1834 (or 1835) Laura Williams, also of Woodstock, who died in 1853. Two of his children by his first wife died young, but a son, Wells Stoddard Hammond, born in 1814, achieved respectable standing as a lawyer during his thirty-five years of life. A contemporary reports Mrs. Laura Hammond as being exceptionally solicitous as to her husband's health and comfort, accompanying him during court term so as to take care of special foods, but in his portrait (Roland Hammond, *post,* p. 176), with its broad forehead, deep-set eyes, and kindly mouth, there is no suggestion of a self-centered or exacting man. He was buried in the Cherry Valley cemetery.

[Hammond's character and opinions are revealed in his works cited above and in his *On the Evidence, Independent of Written Revelation, of the Immortality of the Soul* (1851). See also Roland Hammond, *A Hist. and Geneal. of the Descendants of Wm. Hammond* (1894); Levi Beardsley, *Reminiscences* (1852), 114–17; John Sawyer, *Hist. of Cherry Valley* (1898); *Biog. Dir. Am. Cong.* (1928); A. A. Werner, *Civil List . . . of N. Y.* (1886); *N. Y. Tribune,* Aug. 23, 1855.]

D. R. F.

HAMMOND, JAMES BARTLETT (Apr. 23, 1839–Jan. 27, 1913), inventor, manufacturer, was descended from Benjamin Hammond who came to Boston from London in 1634 with his widowed mother Elizabeth, sister of Admiral Sir William Penn, and from Richard Swan who joined the First Church at Rowley, Mass., in 1639. Born in Boston, Mass., the son of Thomas and Harriet W. (Trow) Hammond, James attended the public schools and by his unusual scholarship won the Franklin medal at the Mather School when he was twelve years old. During the following period, from 1851 to 1857, he entered successively the Boston High School and Latin School, and then Phillips Academy at Andover, Mass., where he prepared for college. He entered the University of Vermont in 1857 and was graduated in 1861. Here his scholarship won him Phi Beta Kappa honors. While in college he became interested in the art of shorthand writing and was soon an expert stenographer. In his senior year he made full reports of a series of lectures given in Boston by George P. Marsh on "The Origin and Growth of the English Language and Its Literature," which were printed in the New York *World.* Journalism presumably appealed to Hammond, since upon his graduation he began to report Henry Ward Beecher's sermons for the *Boston Daily Traveller.* Less than a year later, in 1861, he entered Union Theological Seminary, New York, but early in 1862 joined the *New York Tribune* and served as correspondent for that newspaper with the Army of the Potomac. As an avocation he continued to study philosophy and theology, and in 1863 reëntered Union Theological Seminary, from which he was graduated in 1865. He then found employment in religious editorial work in New York and assisted in the translation from the German of J. P. Lange's commentary on St. Luke. Upon the completion of this work he went to Germany to pursue his theological studies, chiefly at the University of Halle. Two years later, however, his health was completely undermined and he returned to the United States a physical and mental wreck. To regain his strength he busied himself with improving some property in Hyde Park, Mass., and then about 1871, at the request of former associates, began the independent translation of the Book of Psalms. This he did not complete on account of ill health, but instead turned to a business career. Writing manuscripts in longhand had always been irksome to Hammond, especially so since he was a master of shorthand, and from his college days he had from time to time considered the matter of designing some mechanical device to serve as a substitute for the pen. Once resolved to take up a business career, he focused his attention on the designing of a typewriter. For four years no material results attended his efforts. His basic idea was that of employing a typewheel carrying a full font of type instead of using, as in most present-day typewriters, a series of bars each carrying a single letter. When he started his work he knew of no other efforts being made in the field, but even when later he saw the typewriter invented by C. L. Sholes [*q.v.*] perfected by the Remington Company, he persevered with his own idea. In 1876, at the invitation of the Remington organization, Hammond went to Ilion, N. Y., and worked for a year there, assisted by the skilled mechanics of that organization, in an effort to perfect his machine. The mechanical problems remained unsolved, however, and he returned again to New York. For two years more he worked alone and in 1879 so far succeeded that he applied for a patent, which was granted Feb. 3, 1880 (No. 224,183). Four years more elapsed, however, before he succeeded in eliminating all of the mechanical difficulties and then, in 1884, the Hammond typewriter made its first official public appearance at the New Orleans Centennial Exposition, where it won the gold medal in competition with other typewriters. Subsequently Hammond received the Elliott Cresson gold medal bestowed by the Franklin Institute. With success practically assured, he organized a manufacturing company in New York City, of which he was president, and in the course of the succeeding twenty-five years he accumulated a large fortune. In the later years of his life he was extremely eccentric, and on two separate occasions a brother and a member of the Hammond Company tried unsuccessfully to have him legally declared insane. He died suddenly at St. Augustine, Fla., while on a yachting cruise, leaving his estate to the Metropolitan Museum of Art in New York. He never married.

[G. C. Mares, *The Hist. of the Typewriter* (1909); C. V. Oden, *Evolution of the Typewriter* (1917); *Who's Who in America*, 1906–07; *Gen. Cat. Union Theol. Sem.* (1919); Roland Hammond, *A Hist. and Geneal. of the Descendants of Wm. Hammond of London, England* (1894); *N. Y. Times*, Jan. 28, 1913; *N. Y. Financier*, Dec. 12, 1898; U. S. National Museum records.]

C. W. M—n.

HAMMOND, JAMES HENRY (Nov. 15, 1807–Nov. 13, 1864), governor of South Carolina, United States senator, was born at "Stoney Battery," Newberry District, S. C. His father, Elisha Hammond, a native of Massachusetts and a descendant of Benjamin Hammond who came to Boston with his mother in 1634 and later settled in Sandwich and Rochester, Mass., was a teacher, farmer, and merchant. His mother was Catherine Fox Spann of Edgefield District. Prepared by his father, he entered the junior class at South Carolina College and after two rather boisterous years was graduated in 1825. He wandered and taught for more than a year and then read law in Columbia and later in Augusta, Ga., where he also began newspaper writing. Admitted to the bar in 1828, he built up by his own exertions a lucrative practice at Columbia. Entering politics early as an opponent of protection and of submission to it, he established a newspaper, the *Southern Times* (first issue, Jan. 29, 1830), in support of nullification and, through his fiery advocacy of a convention, won the attention of the leaders of the state-rights party. On June 23, 1831, he married Catherine E. FitzSimons of Charleston, the daughter of Christopher FitzSimons, a wealthy merchant, and, abandoning his practice and his editorial work, moved to "Silver Bluff" on the Savannah River and began to operate a cotton plantation. He loved the soil, and for a time allowed agriculture to occupy his thoughts almost to the exclusion of politics.

He made a few speeches in 1832 and was an unsuccessful candidate for the nullification convention. When the state began military preparations, however, he threw himself with energy and success into the task of securing volunteers. He was elected colonel of the regiment from the Barnwell District, and was ready to turn over to the use of the state a large part of his crop of cotton and the services of all his negroes. He was opposed to allowing the intervention of the other states and to compromise, foreseeing in the suspension of the nullification ordinance to meet a lowered tariff the death of the doctrine of nullification. After the compromise he still urged military preparation. When the courts decided adversely to the test oath, he was a leader in advocating a constitutional amendment to authorize it. Without pretense of affection for the Union, he sought persistently for more than twenty years to secure the withdrawal from it of the Southern states. He was opposed to any consideration of secession by one state, desiring united action of at least five, and he may be regarded as one of the leading proponents of Southern nationalism. In 1834 he was elected to Congress. By now he was an advocate of the death penalty for abolitionists. Slavery he thought "the cornerstone of our Republican edifice." Emancipation he regarded as both impossible and undesirable and to be resisted by the Southern people even at the cost of their lives. In Congress he delivered his first speech on the subject of anti-slavery petitions and made it clear that secession held no terrors for him. To him it now seemed inevitable.

In 1836 his health failed rapidly and, resigning, he spent more than a year in European travel. Upon his return he was more than ever absorbed in farming and for a time resisted all pressure to return to public life. By 1839, however, he desired to be governor and was an unsuccessful candidate in 1840. He was still interested in the militia and was made general in 1841. He was elected to the governorship in 1842 and served two terms, during which he secured the transformation of the arsenal at Columbia and the Citadel at Charleston into military academies. He advocated public education, brought about a state agricultural survey, and directed an attack on the Bank of the State of South Carolina which resulted in the imposition of requirements beneficial to the state. This he regarded as his greatest achievement. There was much excitement in South Carolina over the tariff of 1842, and Hammond reached the conclusion that the time for secession had come and considered inquiring of the other Southern states whether they would unite in support of resistance by South Carolina. His message invited the legislature to take any action it saw fit to protect the state. Meanwhile he was taking steps to secure a plan of the defenses of Fort Moultrie.

At the close of his term he returned to "Silver Bluff" and remained aloof from politics without losing any of his keen interest in public affairs. He was anxious to avoid war with Mexico, but if it came wished to see it conducted on a grand scale, crushing English power in Canada and "grasping the whole continent from Panama to the North Pole." He was prevented from election to the United States Senate in 1846 by the threat of disclosure of a grave indiscretion in his past life. In 1850 his hope of succeeding Calhoun in the Senate was destroyed by the governor's appointment in succession of three other men, and when the legislature met he lost the election to R. B. Rhett and was greatly embittered by the defeat. He vigorously advocated the Southern Convention which met at Nashville in 1850 and attended as a delegate. He was "on all the committees and worked hard," but had no high opinion of the convention and declared that its results did not amount to much. In the crisis of 1850–52 in South Carolina he proposed "simply to cut every tie" between South Carolina and the federal government "which can be cut without affording a pretext for collision, & to remain thus with one foot out of the Union until a sufficient number of States take the same ground" (Merritt, *post,* p. 105). He refused to have anything to do with the convention of 1852.

In 1855 Hammond moved to "Redcliffe" on Beach Island in the Savannah River, where he built a beautiful house which was his home for the remainder of his life. He owned thousands of acres of land and more than three hundred negroes. He was a successful farmer, at once scientific and highly practical, and his plantations were superbly managed. He was one of the founders of the South Carolina Agricultural Society.

Elected to the Senate in 1857, he served until he resigned upon Lincoln's election in 1860. He was contemptuous of the Senate, a "vulgar set of sharp-shooters—county court lawyers & newspaper politicians" (Merritt, p. 116), but while a member of that body he began to doubt the wisdom of secession, believing that a majority of people in the South, if assured of their rights, would prefer to remain in the Union, and forming the opinion that the South could control the Union. He was outraged by Southern disregard of Northern sentiment, which, he saw, clearly furnished the abolitionists with much of their campaign material. The chief event of his senatorial career was his speech of Mar. 4, 1858, in reply to Seward's boast that henceforth the North would rule the South as a conquered province. In this speech he advanced the theory that the slaves in the South, the wage-earners in the North, constituted "the very mudsills of society," and declared, "You dare not make war on cotton —No power on earth dares make war upon it. Cotton is king" (*Congressional Globe,* 35 Cong., 1 Sess., p. 961). He did not attend the Charleston convention but hoped for the nomination of R. M. T. Hunter for the presidency. In the campaign he supported Breckinridge. He took no further part in politics, but gave his whole interest to economic questions. In June 1861 he went to Richmond to urge that cotton be held as a basis of credit. He abandoned free trade and became an advocate of protection. He was bitterly critical of Jefferson Davis and of the Confederate Congress, but he supported the Confederacy with all his power and when the end was in sight he collapsed.

Hammond published a large number of speeches and addresses, the more important of which are included in *Selections from the Letters and Speeches of the Hon. James H. Hammond of South Carolina* (1866), published two years after his death.

[Hammond Papers in Lib. of Cong.; Elizabeth Merritt, "James Henry Hammond, 1807–1864," in *Johns Hopkins Univ. Studies in Hist. and Pol. Sci.,* vol. XLI (1923); B. F. Perry, *Reminiscences of Public Men* (1883); Roland Hammond, *A Hist. and Geneal. of the Descendants of William Hammond* (1894); *Boston Daily Traveller,* Apr. 9, 1858; *Charleston Mercury,* Nov. 28, 1864.]

J. G. deR. H.

HAMMOND, NATHANIEL JOB (Dec. 26, 1833–Apr. 20, 1899), lawyer, was born in Elbert County, northeast Georgia, the son of Amos W. Hammond. During his boyhood the family removed to Monroe County in middle Georgia, whence, after preparatory schooling, Nathaniel was sent to the University of Georgia. He was graduated with honors in 1852, read law, was admitted to the bar, and began to practise at Atlanta in partnership with his father. Throughout the Civil War he served as solicitor general of the Atlanta circuit, and in 1865 he was a member of the convention in which was drafted the constitution embodying the changes made necessary by the war. In the same year he became reporter of the supreme court of Georgia, serving until 1872 when he resigned to accept the attorney-generalship of the state under Gov. J. M. Smith. He was a member of the constitutional convention of 1877. In 1879 he entered Congress as a Democrat and served for four terms, 1879–87.

Regarded as one of the leaders of the Georgia bar, Hammond was counsel in many important cases. In 1896, in association with ex-Senator Edmunds, of Vermont, he represented the government in the Long and Short Haul Case before the United States Supreme Court (*Cincinnati, New Orleans & Texas Pacific Railway Company* vs. *Interstate Commerce Commission,*

162 *U. S.*, 184). On the death of Justice William B. Woods, of the Supreme Court, the bar of Georgia recommended Hammond to succeed him. Higher education was one of his prime interests. For many years he was a member of the board of education of Atlanta and for twenty-five years a member of the board of trustees of the University of Georgia, being chairman much of the time, and championing the cause of the university before the people at a period when the institution was unpopular. He was also president of the board of trustees of the Atlanta College of Physicians and Surgeons.

A contemporary has described him as cold and reserved and with few of the traits that make for popularity. His intellect was of a high order. As a lawyer he was a student and scholar. He was a stanch believer in religion. Presiding Justice Lumpkin, of the supreme court of Georgia, in response to a memorial presented on the occasion of Hammond's death, stressed his great practical usefulness. In his every relation of life that trait seems to have been outstanding. In 1858 he was married to Laura Lewis, daughter of Custis Lewis of Griffin, Ga. His son was for seventeen years his law partner and survived him.

[Bernard Suttler in W. J. Northen, *Men of Mark in Ga.*, vol. III (1911); L. L. Knight, *A Standard Hist. of Ga. and Georgians* (1917), IV, 1865; *Report of . . . the Ga. Bar Asso.*, 1899 and 1902; *Atlanta Constitution*, Apr. 20, 21, 1899.]

R. P. B—s.

HAMMOND, SAMUEL (Sept. 21, 1757–Sept. 11, 1842), Revolutionary soldier, territorial governor of Missouri, banker, was born in Farnham's Parish, Richmond County, Va., the son of Charles and Elizabeth Hammond (Steele) Hammond. His parents were second cousins. He was still a youth when the struggle for American independence began, and immediately threw himself into the fray. Having had some military experience in Dunmore's War and Col. Andrew Williamson's expedition against the Cherokees, he raised a company of minute-men and commanded it at the battle of Long Bridge, near Norfolk, in December 1776. In 1779 he joined General Lincoln's army with the rank of captain and throughout the war served in the Southern colonies. He took part in the unsuccessful siege of Savannah (1779); and was present at the fall of Charleston. After that event he gathered round him a small band of patriots, headed for North Carolina, and there was joined by a detachment from Pickens' regiment. He participated in the important engagements in that area, Musgrove's Mills, King's Mountain, Blackstock, Cowpens; took part in the successful siege of Augusta; and was with Gen. Nathanael Greene in the battle of Eutaw Springs. At the end of the war he had been promoted to lieutenant-colonel in the South Carolina forces.

When peace was restored Hammond settled at Savannah, Ga., and engaged in mercantile pursuits which carried him to South America and France. In this way he acquired a knowledge of Spanish and French which was of much use to him later. He served several years in the legislature as the representative of Chatham County and was also appointed to the office of surveyor general. The year 1793 found him again in uniform commanding a battalion of Chatham County militia against the Creek Indians. In 1802 he was elected to the Eighth Congress. When Louisiana was purchased from France, and the territory divided, Jefferson appointed Hammond colonel commandant (military and civil commander) of the northern part, the District of Louisiana. He served in this capacity for two years, 1804–06, and in 1811 was appointed judge of the court of common pleas. After the territorial government of Missouri was set up, he was appointed to the territorial council, and at its first meeting, July 5, 1813, was elected president. In 1820 he was a member of the Missouri constitutional convention. For twenty years he made his home in the little French village of St. Louis on the extreme western frontier, and "the Hammond Mansion" became the center of the social and political life of the section. In 1824, acquiescing in his wife's desire, Hammond returned to the South. He had owned a place known as "Varello Farm" on the South Carolina side of the Savannah River, near Augusta, Ga. This place had been neglected and had been sold for taxes, but at the time of Hammond's return was in the possession of an old friend of his who relinquished it without protest. Though now nearly seventy years of age, Hammond continued in the public service. He was elected surveyor general of South Carolina in 1827 and secretary of state in 1831.

Apart from his official duties, Hammond organized and was the first president of the first bank in St. Louis. He acquired a considerable amount of property in that town which he apparently managed none too well. On the failure of certain local banks he became involved in a large debt to the United States government in connection with notes of the bank which had been accepted by the government in payment of public dues. He was arrested and prosecuted after his return to South Carolina, but was released on bail, sold his property in St. Louis, and liquidated the debt. Hammond was married in 1783 to Rebecca (Elbert) Rae, sister of Samuel Elbert [*q.v.*] and widow of Col. John Rae; she died in 1798, and on May 25, 1802, he married Eliza Amelia O'Keefe. There were children by both marriages. His second wife was said to be a woman of unusual charm. Hammond himself was described as polished in manner, a brilliant conversationalist and of exceptionally attractive personality.

[Memoir of Hammond by his son, A. S. Hammond, in Jos. Johnson, *Traditions and Reminiscences Chiefly of the Am. Revolution in the South* (1851), which also contains many of Hammond's notes on the battles and expeditions in which he participated; Geo. White, *Hist. Colls. of Ga.* (1855); Stella M. Drumm, memoir of Hammond, in *Mo. Hist. Soc. Colls.*, vol. IV, no. 4 (1923); *Am. State Papers, Misc.*, vol. I (1834); F. L. Billon, *Annals of St. Louis in Its Territorial Days from 1804 to 1821* (1888); obituary in the *Constitutionalist* (Augusta, Ga.), reprinted in the *Charleston Courier*, Sept. 27, 1842, and in the *Southern Recorder* (Milledgeville, Ga.), Oct. 4, 1842.] R. P. B—s.

HAMMOND, WILLIAM ALEXANDER (Aug. 28, 1828–Jan. 5, 1900), neurologist and surgeon-general of the United States Army, was born in Annapolis, Md. He was the son of Dr. John W. and Sarah (Pinkney) Hammond, members of two old Maryland families of Anne Arundel County. He received his academic education at Harrisburg, Pa., and his medical degree from the University of the City of New York in 1848. After a year spent in the Pennsylvania Hospital in Philadelphia, he settled in Saco, Me., for the practice of his profession. He was there but a few months when he took the examination for the army medical service and was appointed an assistant surgeon in 1849. For the following ten years he served at various frontier stations in New Mexico, Kansas, and Florida, with a tour of duty at the Military Academy at West Point. Between campaigns against hostile Indians, he occupied his time upon physiological and botanical investigations. In 1857 he published an exhaustive essay, *Experimental Researches Relative to the Nutritive Value and Physiological Effects of Albumen, Starch, and Gum, when Singly and Exclusively Used as a Food,* which was awarded the American Medical Association prize.

In the fall of 1859 he resigned from the army to accept the professorship of anatomy and physiology in the University of Maryland at Baltimore. Here he taught and practised his profession until the outbreak of the Civil War. As surgeon to the Baltimore infirmary he attended the wounded men of the 6th Massachusetts Infantry, who while on their way to the defense of Washington were fired upon by a Baltimore mob. He resigned his professorship and reëntered the army as an assistant surgeon, at the foot of a list upon which he had formerly held high place. His first Civil War service was as medical purveyor at Frederick, Md. Later he organized the Camden Street Hospital in Baltimore and was then transferred to the command of General Rosecrans in West Virginia, where he was made inspector of camps and hospitals. His work in this field attracted the attention of the Sanitary Commission, which, dissatisfied with the administration of the medical service of the army, successfully urged his appointment as surgeon-general. He assumed this office in the spring of 1862 with the grade of brigadier-general. His administration was one of marked efficiency. It was inevitable, however, that the masterful personality of Hammond should clash with the autocratic spirit of Edwin M. Stanton, secretary of war. Their official and personal relations early became strained, and after a period of friction Hammond was relieved from office; later charges were preferred against him alleging irregularities in the award of contracts for hospital supplies. He was brought before a court martial in 1864 and was dismissed from the army. In 1878 a bill was approved by Congress authorizing the President to review the proceedings of the court martial and to reinstate Hammond to the army rolls, if justice so indicated. As a result of this review he was restored to service and his name placed upon the retired list with the grade of brigadier-general.

Upon leaving the army in 1864 Hammond found himself in straitened circumstances from the expense of his trial. With help of friends he was able to establish himself in practice in New York and within a short time he became a leader in the practice and teaching of neurology, a specialty then in its infancy. Soon after his arrival in New York he was appointed lecturer on nervous and mental diseases in the College of Physicians and Surgeons. He resigned this position in 1867 to accept the professorship of the same subjects which was created for him in the faculty of Bellevue Hospital Medical College. In 1874 he transferred to a like professorship in the medical department of the University of the City of New York. At other times he was on the faculty of the University of Vermont at Burlington, and of the Post-Graduate Medical School of New York, of which he was one of the founders. In 1888, having acquired a comfortable fortune and being restored to the army retired list, he moved to Washington, where he practised until the time of his death from cardiac disease. During the later period he became much interested in the therapeutic employment of animal extracts and did much to instruct the medical profession in their use.

Throughout his career Hammond was a facile writer. While carrying the responsibilities of surgeon-general he found time to write a *Treatise on Hygiene with Special Reference to the Military Service* (1863). The more noteworthy of his other medical works were: *On Wakefulness: With an Introductory Chapter on the Physiology of Sleep* (1866), *Insanity in its Medico-Legal Relations* (1866), *Sleep and Its Derangements* (1869), *Physics and Physiology of Spiritualism* (1871), and *Insanity in its Medical Relations* (1883). In 1871 he published his *Treatise on Diseases of the Nervous System.* This was announced as "the first text-book on nervous diseases in the English language" (Dana, *post,* p. 1421). It was based largely on the lectures of Charcot, and was well and dramatically written. He was also a play-writer and novelist. His fiction includes *Robert Severne* (1867), *Dr. Grattan* (1884), *Mr. Oldmixon* (1885), *A Strong-Minded Woman* (1885), and *The Son of Perdition* (1898), the latter considered by some to be the best novel of the Christ ever written. Hammond was editor for a time of the *Maryland and Virginia Medical Journal,* published in Richmond and Baltimore. In 1867 he established the *Quarterly Journal of Psychological Medicine and Medical Jurisprudence,* of which he was editor until 1875. He also cooperated, 1867–69, in the founding and editing of the *New York Medical Journal* and the *Journal of Nervous and Mental Diseases,* 1867–83.

Hammond was undoubtedly a man of vision. During his two years as surgeon-general he accomplished many reforms in medical administration. He advocated others which have since become operative but which his feud with Secretary Stanton indefinitely postponed. He founded the Army Medical Museum and laid the foundation for the later production of the *Medical and Surgical History of the War of the Rebellion.* He proposed the establishment of an army medical school, the formation of a permanent medical-department enlisted force, and the location of a permanent general hospital in Washington, all of which have since been realized. Professionally he was a pioneer in the field of nervous and mental diseases in the United States: American neurology began in the Civil War, from the experience there gained by Hammond, Weir Mitchell, and W. W. Keen. In New York his forceful character brought him a ready following, together with many enemies. Of him C. L. Dana, himself a noted neurologist, wrote: "Dr. William A. Hammond was the dominant personality of the time. He was a big man and had a big mind. There was a shadow on his career and painful tales were told about his methods. The story went about that he once filled his hypodermic syringe with cream, plunged the needle into a patient's liver, showed him the withdrawn pus, and cured him of an abscess. The story was not true, but its recital was popular and gave comfort to the malevolent. Hammond put neurology in New York on its feet economically by his amazing audacity of charging $10 as his fee, and showing the bills on his table" (*post,* p. 1422). Hammond was married twice: in July 1849 to Helen Nisbet, daughter of Michael Nisbet of Philadelphia; and in 1886 to Esther D. Chapin.

[J. E. Pilcher, *Surgeons-General of the U. S. Army* (1905); C. L. Dana, "Early Neurology in the United States," *Jour. Am. Medic. Asso.,* May 5, 1928; symposium by various authors with complete bibliography and portrait, in the *Post-Graduate* (N. Y.), May 1900; H. A. Kelly and W. L. Burrage, *Am. Medic. Biogs.* (1920); *Who's Who in America,* 1899–1900; *Medic. News,* Jan. 13, 1900; *Evening Star* (Washington), Jan. 6, 1900.]

J. M. P

HAMMOND, WILLIAM GARDINER (May 3, 1829–Apr. 12, 1894), lawyer and legal educator, the son of William Gardiner Hammond and Sarah Tillinghast Bull, was born at Newport, R. I. He traced his ancestry to Joseph Hammond, born at Swansea, Mass., in 1690, who married Rachel Gardiner and settled in North Kingston, R. I., and was probably descended from William Hammond who was admitted a freeman of Lynn, Mass., in 1636. William Gardiner Hammond, Senior, was a lawyer, a scholar with a special enthusiasm and talent for languages, a leader in the Democratic party, and a surveyor of customs in Newport under four successive presidents. The younger William received most of his early education at home under the direction of his father and a Congregational minister, and for a while attended school at Wickford. He early gave evidence of aptness for languages and of literary taste. Disappointed in his hope to enter the Military Academy at West Point, he registered in Amherst College in the autumn of 1846 and graduated in 1849 with an excellent scholastic record, especially in the classics. After his graduation he began the study of law in the office of Samuel E. Johnson in Brooklyn. He was admitted to the bar in 1851 and practised law in Brooklyn until 1856. In that year, partly on account of his health, he went to Europe where he spent the greater part of the next three years. For a year he studied comparative and historical law at the University of Heidelberg. On his return from Europe in 1860 he went to Iowa to join his brother, a civil engineer, in order that his health might profit from the outdoor life of a surveyor. After a few months, he began the practice of law in Anamosa, Iowa, but soon transferred his practice to Des Moines in order that he might prepare for publication a digest of the reports of the supreme court of Iowa—the continuation of a work earlier undertaken by John F. Dillon. He established the *Western Jurist* on Jan. 1, 1867, and served as its chief editor until 1870. As a member of the commission appointed in that year to recodify the laws of Iowa, he was partly responsible for the Code of 1873. In cooperation with two judges of the supreme court, he opened a private school of law which in 1869 became the Law Department of the University of Iowa with himself as its chancellor. He served at the head of that department until 1881, when he was appointed dean of the school of law in Washington University, St. Louis, a position which he held at the time of his death. He was married twice: on May 26, 1852, to Lydia Bradford Torrey, daughter of Judge Joseph W. Torrey, and on May 3, 1865, to Juliet Martha Roberts, daughter of Rev. William Roberts, a Presbyterian minister.

In his day Hammond was probably the most eminent authority in America on the history of the common law. His erudite series of lectures in this field was given regularly in St. Louis, Boston, Ann Arbor, and Iowa City. In 1890 he published an edition of *Blackstone's Commentaries* based upon an excellent collection of materials. Other scholarly works which he published include his introduction to an edition in 1876 of Thomas Collett Sandar's *Institutes of Justinian,* and his edition in 1880 of Francis Lieber's *Legal and Political Hermeneutics.* It was in the improvement of the standards and methods of legal education that he made his greatest contributions, however. On this work he concentrated his efforts throughout the last quarter of his life. As a teacher he was characterized by magnetism, spontaneity of expression, profound and amazingly inclusive learning, a happy sense of humor, and sympathetic understanding of his students. He was a pioneer in the scientific teaching of the law and did much to discredit the formal lecture and the formal textbook as the chief staples in the professor's methodology. His method approached the case system of instruction later introduced at Harvard. As chairman of the committee on legal education of the American Bar Association, 1889–94, he labored incessantly and effectively for the improvement of the whole system of training for the profession of law. (See the reports of the committee, especially that of 1891.) The permanent agencies of the Bar Association dealing with legal education are due in no small measure to his persistent and constructive efforts.

[Hammond's letters, papers, publications, and collections are in the College of Law of the Univ. of Iowa; a good catalogue of them, together with a portrait, is available in the *Centenary Exhibit in Honor of William G. Hammond* (1928), being Univ. of Iowa Extension Bull., no. 201. See also Emlin M'Clain, in W. D. Lewis, *Great Am. Lawyers,* VIII (1909), 189–237; F. S. Hammond, *Hist. and Geneals. of the Hammond Families in America,* vol. I (1902); Wm. Hyde and H. L. Conard, *Encyc. of the Hist. of St. Louis* (1899), II, 978; *Am. Bar Asso. Reports,* XIII (1890), XIV (1891), XV (1892), XVII (1894); *Green Bag,* July 1889, May 1894; *Biog. Record of the Alumni of Amherst Coll.* (1883); *St. Louis Globe-Democrat,* Apr. 13, 1894; *St. Louis Evening Star-Sayings,* Apr. 12, 1894.]

A. J. L.

HAMPTON, WADE (1751 or 1752–Feb. 4, 1835), planter, congressman, soldier, was probably descended from Thomas Hampton, a clergyman, who was resident at Jamestown, Va., in 1630. The descendants of Thomas lived in Virginia through three generations, multiplying their homesteads as the colony expanded. Anthony, of the fourth generation, second son of John (1690–*c.* 1748) and Margaret (Wade) Hampton, followed the frontier southward by stages and when the Revolution began was settled on the Middle Fork of Tyger River (now Spartanburg County, S. C.) pursuing, according to tradition, the trade of "flax-breaker." Here in July 1776 he and his wife, whose maiden name is not known, a son, and a grandson were killed by Cherokee Indians (Draper, *post,* p. 83). Five sons escaped the massacre, however, and all served as officers in the American forces during the ensuing war.

Of these, Wade, probably the third son, subsequently rose to the greatest distinction. He was born in Halifax County, Va., and like the average frontier boy was "brought up to labor in the field; and was almost entirely without the advantages of even a common school education" (Hooker, *post,* p. 846). On Sept. 21, 1780, he declared himself to be a loyal subject of the Crown (*Royal South-Carolina Gazette,* Sept. 21, 1780), but at some time before Apr. 2, 1781, for reasons which he considered adequate, he renounced allegiance and joined the command of the patriot Gen. Thomas Sumter (Gibbes, *post,* pp. 47–48). At this time or shortly afterward he was commissioned colonel, and he continued to serve throughout the remainder of the war as one of Sumter's most daring and effective officers, performing especially meritorious service at the battle of Eutaw Springs. At various times between 1782 and 1794 he was a member of the state legislature, justice of the peace in Richland County, member of the convention which ratified the Federal Constitution (an act which he stoutly opposed), and sheriff of Camden District. From 1795 to 1797 and from 1803 to 1805 he represented South Carolina constituencies in the federal House of Representatives. Although normally a Republican, he followed an independent course in politics, supporting at times measures which were "characteristic of federalism" (Hooker, p. 847).

At the threat of war in 1808, Hampton offered for service in the army and in October 1808 was commissioned colonel and in February 1809, brigadier-general. First assigned to duty at New Orleans, where in the fall of 1809 he succeeded Gen. James Wilkinson [*q.v.*], the commanding officer, he was next, 1812–13, in charge of the fortifications of Norfolk, Va.; and in July 1813, having been advanced to the rank of major-general, was placed in command of the army on Lake Champlain in Military District Number Nine. Unhappily, circumstances shortly afterwards brought Wilkinson, for whom Hampton had the heartiest contempt, to the same district as senior officer. Bad feeling was renewed when Wilkinson assumed authority which he did not possess. Wilkinson blamed Hampton for the failure of the campaign which was undertaken against Montreal in the fall of 1813; and the latter resigned his commission. Hampton had carried out his part as well as his resources permitted, and he was in effect exonerated by the act of the War Department accepting his resignation (Adams, *post,* index, and "Defense of General Hampton," *Daily National Intelligencer,* June 6, 1814).

His many political and military responsibilities had not kept him from advancing his private interests. He had the qualities which made for success in the eighteenth-century South Carolina up-country: energy, foresight, and the frontiersman's attitude toward land; that is, the will to possess without an overscrupulous regard for the means of acquiring possession. (For his part in the Yazoo land speculations see Haskins, *post,* 411, 417.) Shortly after the Revolution he began the cultivation of a large plantation in Richland County. He was among the first of his section to plant cotton, and in 1799 raised a crop of six hundred bales with a value of about ninety thousand dollars. After 1811, in addition to these South Carolina lands he held sugar plantations on the lower Mississippi River, and such was his success in the management of all that when he died in 1835 he was reputed to be the wealthiest planter in America (Phillips, *post,* 98–99, and citations). He was three times married: in 1783 to Mrs. Martha Epps Howell, in 1786 to Harriet Flud, and in 1801 to Mary Cantey. He was survived by one son, Wade, and at least one daughter, who was the wife of John S. Preston. These were children of the second and third marriages respectively.

[J. S. Ames, "The Cantey Family," *S. C. Hist. and Geneal. Mag.,* Oct. 1910; J. B. O. Landrum, *Hist. of Spartanburg County* (1900), pp. 240 ff.; and *Colonial and Revolutionary Hist. of Upper S. C.* (1897), pp. 87–89; L. C. Draper, *King's Mountain and Its Heroes* (1881); "The Famous Hampton Family," *The State* (Columbia, S. C.), Dec. 24, 1911; E. L. Green, "Some Early Columbians," *Ibid.,* July 10, 1930; Edward McCrady, *Hist. of S. C. in the Revolution, 1780–83* (1902); R. W. Gibbes, *Doc. Hist. of the Am. Rev. in S. C., 1781–82* (1853); Wm. Johnson, *Sketches of the Life and Correspondence of Nathanael Greene* (1822), II, 167–68; James Wilkinson, *Memoirs of My Own Times* (1816), vol. III; J. Armstrong, *Notices of the War of 1812* (1840), vol. II; *Jour. of the Convention of S. C. Which Ratified the Constitution of the U. S.* (1928); J. Brannan, *Official Letters of the Mil. and Naval Officers during the War with Gt. Britain* (1823); C. H. Haskins, "The Yazoo Land Companies," *Papers Am. Hist. Asso.,* vol. V, pt. 4 (1891); *Am. State Papers, Mil. Affairs,* vol. I (1832); Henry Adams, *Hist. of the U. S. A.,* vols. V–VII (1889–91); U. B. Phillips, *Life and Labor in the Old South* (1929); "Diary of Edward Hooker," in *Ann. Report Am. Hist. Asso., 1896* (1897), vol. I; *Memoirs of Lieut.-Gen. Scott* (1864).]
J. H. E.

HAMPTON, WADE (Mar. 28, 1818–Apr. 11, 1902), Confederate soldier, governor of South Carolina, United States senator, was the grandson of Wade Hampton [*q.v.*]. His father (1791–1858), who likewise bore the Christian name of Wade, like other eldest sons of the men who had become great landlords of the South Carolina up-country in the years which followed the Revolution, took his place naturally among the planter aristocracy. After a brief experience in the army during the War of 1812, for which he left the junior class of South Carolina College, he assumed the management of "Millwood," a plantation near Columbia, where in addition to his normal occupations, he bred blooded horses which made his name famous on the Southern turf. "Millwood" also became in his hands a social center which drew into its circle such men as Dr. Samuel Gridley Howe, Henry Clay, and George Bancroft. Its proprietor seldom sought public office, but such was his influence in the politics of the state that he was called by a contemporary "the great Warwick of South Carolina" (Perry, *post,* p. 110). He married Ann, the daughter of Christopher FitzSimons, a well-to-do merchant who had come to America from Dundalk, Ireland, in 1783.

The eldest child of this marriage, Wade the third, was born in Charleston at the home of his mother's parents. His early years were spent chiefly at "Millwood" and at "Cashier's Valley," his father's summer home in the mountains of

North Carolina. Here he learned to ride and to hunt in the best Hampton tradition. He went to school first near "Millwood," then to the Columbia Academy, and in 1836 was graduated from the South Carolina College. At twenty he married Margaret, a sister of William C. Preston [*q.v.*], and after her death (1851) married again, his second wife being Mary Singleton McDuffie, the only child of George McDuffie [*q.v.*]. He had studied law, but, having no intention of following it as a profession, he took up the life of a planter. He devoted himself principally, particularly after the death of his father, to the Mississippi plantations, which he developed and expanded. From these lands alone his crop of cotton in 1861 was five thousand bales. From a sense of duty to the state, he became a candidate for the South Carolina legislature in 1852 and was elected to the House of Representatives from Richland County. He was returned twice subsequently and in 1856 was raised to the Senate where he sat until his resignation in 1861. On the questions of Southern policy his position was conservative. Having come to doubt the economic soundness of slavery, he vigorously opposed the movement in 1857 to remove the restrictions upon the importation of Africans. He supported the view that secession from the Union was correct constitutionally, but held that action in this direction in 1860 was inexpedient and without sufficient provocation.

Though he had not favored secession, Hampton gave himself and his resources unstintedly to the support of the Confederacy from the outset. He offered his cotton to be exchanged in Europe for arms and secured permission to raise, partly at his own expense, a legion to consist of infantry, cavalry, and artillery. At this time he was forty-three years of age—a powerful man in the physical sense—"six feet in height, broad-shouldered, deep-chested, . . . with legs which, if he chose to close them in a grip, could make a horse groan with pain" (Wells, *Hampton and Reconstruction,* pp. 16–17). His lack of military experience was in large measure offset by his skill as a horseman and the knowledge of woodcraft which he had gained through long devotion to the chase. These qualities marked him for the cavalry arm of the service, but he first served as an officer mainly of infantry. His command arrived in Virginia in time for the infantry portion to participate in the heaviest fighting of the first battle of Manassas, where he was wounded. During the greater part of the Peninsular campaign he commanded a brigade, and, having been favorably mentioned in the reports of his superior officers, he was advanced to the rank of brigadier-general, May 23, 1862. A week later at Seven Pines he was again wounded. His service as a cavalry officer began on July 28 following, when he was assigned to the 1st Brigade of Cavalry of the Army of Northern Virginia. After Sept. 2, as second in command, he had a part in practically all the major movements of Gen. J. E. B. Stuart: the Maryland campaign, the Chambersburg raid, the march around the flank of the Federal army before Gettysburg, the battle of Gettysburg itself where he was a third time wounded, and the defensive maneuvers of the Wilderness. During the winter of 1862–63 he led on his own account a series of successful raids from Martinsburg in the upper Shenandoah Valley. These, together with other successes, brought him on Aug. 3, 1863, a commission as major-general and after Stuart's death (May 12, 1864), the command of the cavalry corps.

The operations of the cavalry under Hampton were controlled by two factors. After he assumed command, the Confederate army in Virginia was never again on the offensive, and the supply of horses at his disposal was near the point of exhaustion. Accordingly, his tactics, with the exception of the Coggin's Point raid (Sept. 14, 1864) when he captured some 2,400 beef cattle from the Federal quartermaster's department, were those of defense. At Hawes' Shop (May 28) and Burgess Mill (Oct. 27) he endeavored, in the main successfully, to stay the Federal advance. Trevilian Station (June 11 and 12), Sappony Church (June 27), Reams' Station (Aug. 25), and many unnamed skirmishes were fought with even greater success to keep open the lines of communication from Richmond to the west and south. To offset the lack of sufficient remounts, Hampton resorted more and more to the practice of fighting his men dismounted, but in January 1865 it was necessary for him to take a part of his command out of Virginia in search of fresh horses. He did not return to this field, but instead was ordered to cover the retreat of Johnston's army then moving through South Carolina. He was promoted lieutenant-general on Feb. 14, 1865. Three days later the city of Columbia was burned. An effort was made by General Sherman to place the blame upon Hampton (*War of the Rebellion: Official Records,* 1 ser., XLVII, pt. 1, pp. 21–22; pt. 2, pp. 596–97), but on this score he has been exonerated (Hill, *post*).

When Johnston surrendered, Hampton regarded his command, on technical grounds, as exempt from the terms. He proposed to join President Davis, cross the Mississippi, and continue resistance in Texas. Davis agreed to accept his escort, but Johnston insisted that the troops were not free to go; so Hampton, feeling that he was in honor bound to do so, hastened alone to overtake the fleeing President though he realized that he was probably going under the "ban of outlawry." He was not able, however, to overtake Davis, and, abandoning a resolve to leave the country rather than submit, he returned to South Carolina. As in the cases of the majority of his class, the war had taken the greater part of his fortune.

Hampton gave his support to the plan of reconstruction prescribed by President Johnson, but, believing that his name would jeopardize its success, he was careful to withhold himself from the leading part which he might have had in putting it into effect in South Carolina. Such, however, was the esteem in which he was held that in spite of precautions to prevent his election he was almost chosen governor in 1865 (J. D. Pope in the *News and Courier,* Charleston, Apr. 12, 1902). When Congress substituted its more drastic reconstruction policy for that of the President, Hampton joined in the general protest and entered vigorously into both the presidential and state campaigns of 1868 with the object of defeating the party which was responsible for this program. Both campaigns, however, were unsuccessful, and for the next eight years, while the Republicans controlled the government of South Carolina, he devoted his attention to private affairs, spending much of his time on his Mississippi plantations.

In 1876 Hampton was nominated for governor by the "straight-out" Democrats. His acceptance did much to win the support of those Democrats who had opposed the "straight-out" movement believing that it would be better policy to work for the reëlection of D. H. Chamberlain, a Republican governor who had undertaken to reform the administration. Hampton's energetic county-to-county canvass, his appeals to the freedmen for their votes, and his immense popularity were important factors in the campaign which followed, but his election was probably secured in the end by the success of his followers in preventing large numbers of the Republican negroes from voting (Simkins, "The Election of 1876," *post*). Unquestionably, Hampton's greatest contribution toward the restoration of white supremacy in South Carolina was his influence in avoiding a general armed conflict, particularly between the election and the withdrawal of the United States troops (Apr. 10, 1877), when the Democrats were finally permitted to take possession of the government. In 1878 he was reelected governor, and not long afterward, while he lay desperately ill from a wound which he had received on a hunting expedition, he was made United States senator. He served in this office until 1891, taking an active but not a conspicuous part. His greatest effort was made on Jan. 16, 1891, in opposition to the Force Bill (*Congressional Record,* 51 Cong., 2 Sess., pp. 1418–21).

From 1876 to 1890 the name of Wade Hampton was the symbol of the political régime in South Carolina. Its traditions and practices were conservative—of the old rather than of the new South. There arose a party of opposition representing principally the farmer and artisan classes, led by Benjamin R. Tillman [*q.v.*], which demanded a more active legislative program on the part of the government. In 1890 this party was victorious at the polls and Hampton was defeated for reëlection to the Senate. Shortly afterward (1893) he was appointed commissioner of Pacific Railways, a position which he held until within three years of his death, which occurred in Columbia in a house which had been presented to him by the people of South Carolina when his own had burned a few years before.

[Hampton's career in the Civil War has been described by two of his companions in arms: D. B. Rea, *Sketches from Hampton's Cavalry, Embracing the Principal Exploits of the Cavalry in the Campaigns of 1862 and 1863* (1864), and E. L. Wells, *Hampton and His Cavalry in '64* (1899), the latter written largely from notes prepared by Hampton. The correspondence between Wells and Hampton relative to the preparation and publication of this book is in the possession of the Charleston Lib. Soc. See also *War of the Rebellion: Official Records (Army)*; *Battles and Leaders of the Civil War* (4 vols., 1887–88); E. A. Pollard, *Lee and His Lieutenants* (1867); *Confed. Mil. Hist.,* I (1899), 697; Dunbar Rowland, *Jefferson Davis, Constitutionalist* (10 vols., 1923); R. M. Hughes, *General Johnston* (1893); *Memoirs of Gen. Wm. T. Sherman* (1875). For certain phases of his career see: C. W. Ramsdell, "General Robert E. Lee's Horse Supply, 1862–65," *Am. Hist. Rev.,* July 1930; J. D. Hill, "The Burning of Columbia Reconsidered," *South Atlantic Quart.,* July 1926; F. B. Simkins, "The Election of 1876 in S. C.," *South Atlantic Quart.,* July, Oct. 1922, and *The Tillman Movement in S. C.* (1926); E. L. Wells, *Hampton and Reconstruction* (1907). Eulogies delivered by M. C. Butler in 1903 and 1906, *Address . . . on the Life, Character and Services of Gen. Wade Hampton before the Gen. Assem. of S. C.* (1903), and *Final Report of the Commission to Provide for a Monument to the Memory of Wade Hampton* (1907), and by D. C. Heyward in 1929 (*Sen. Doc. No. 18,* 71 Cong., 1 Sess.) have been published. For Hampton's father and family background see: B. F. Perry, *Reminiscences of Public Men* (1889); *Charleston Daily Courier,* Feb. 12 and 15, 1858; J. B. Irving, *The S. C. Jockey Club* (1857); article on "Millwood" by R. L. Allen, in *Am. Agriculturist,* Jan. 1847; W. H. FitzSimons, "Memoranda of the FitzSimons Family" (MS. in possession of Ellen M. FitzSimons, Charleston, S. C.).]

J. H. E.

HAMTRAMCK, JOHN FRANCIS (Apr. 19, 1798–Apr. 21, 1858), soldier, Indian agent, judge, was born in Fort Wayne, Ind. His father, Col. John Francis Hamtramck, although of Canadian birth, had served as captain of a New York company in the American Revolution and later, as a lieutenant-colonel commanding the left wing of Wayne's army, he had taken a conspicuous part in the battle of Fallen Timbers (1794); his mother was Rebecca Mackenzie, a sister of Sir Alexander Mackenzie. Upon the death of his father at Detroit in 1803, young John Francis was left under the guardianship of William Henry Harrison, at that time governor of Indiana Territory. From such an ancestry and environment it was inevitable that a military career should result. Youthful as he was, he took part in the War of 1812, serving as sergeant in the 1st Infantry on the expedition led by Zachary Taylor up the Mississippi River. At the close of the war, he was appointed to West Point, through the influence of Harrison and of his step-father, J. B. Thomas, later senator from Illinois. Graduated from West Point in 1819, he received his commission as second lieutenant of artillery and was stationed at Fort McHenry. He resigned his commission in 1822, apparently as a result of being transferred to a different artillery corps. In 1826 President John Quincy Adams appointed him agent for the Osage Indians. Removing to St. Louis, he continued in his duties as Indian agent until 1831, when he resigned and settled down as a planter near Shepherdstown, Va. (now W. Va.), the home of his wife. For the next fifteen years he pursued the career of a planter, the quietness of his life being accentuated rather than interrupted by the captaincy of the county militia. The even tenor of this existence was brought to an end by the war with Mexico. In recognition both of Hamtramck's past military record and his present civilian importance, on the last day of 1846 Governor Smith appointed him colonel of the 1st Virginia Regiment of Volunteers. He joined Taylor's army in Mexico, and was for a short time military governor of Saltillo. In June 1848 he was mustered out of service and returned to his home in Shepherdstown. He was mayor of the town from 1850 to 1854 and for the last four years previous to his death, was a justice of the Jefferson County Court.

Hamtramck was married three times. His first wife was a Miss Williamson of Maryland. After her death he married Ellen Selby of Shepherdstown, and upon her death married her sister Sarah. There were children by each of these marriages. Selby Mackenzie Hamtramck, a son of the third marriage, served in the Confederate army and died in prison at Fort Delaware.

[Most of the information for the above sketch has been furnished by Hamtramck's great-grand-daughter, Elise Selby Billmyer of Shepherdstown, from private and unprinted family records. There is a short account of Hamtramck in the *Shepherdstown Register*, published at the time of his death. See also *Jour. of the Exec. Proc. of the Senate of the U. S. A.*, vol. III (1828); F. B. Heitman, *Hist. Reg. and Dict. U. S. Army* (1903), and G. W. Cullum, *Biog. Reg. Officers and Grads. U. S. Mil. Acad.* (3rd ed., 1891).]

R. S. C.

HANAFORD, PHOEBE ANN COFFIN (May 6, 1829–June 2, 1921), Universalist minister and author, born on Nantucket Island, was the daughter of George W. and Phoebe Ann (Barnard) Coffin; she was descended from the Folger and Coffin families, both of which, as she often observed, possessed the honor and influence due "first families." Her early education was obtained in the public and private schools of Nantucket; Latin and mathematics she studied with an Episcopalian clergyman. At the age of eight she took the temperance pledge; at thirteen she began writing for the newspapers; at sixteen she taught school, and on Dec. 2, 1849, she married Joseph H. Hanaford, a teacher. She early devoted herself to bringing about that time "when right shall triumph over might, and every soul shall be saved from sin," laboring to this end in prose and verse, and with hymns and tracts, not hesitating to "go to the haunts of vice" with her gospel. She became chaplain and treasurer of the Daughters of Temperance in the dedication of halls and at the burial of members. *My Brother*, a negligible volume of verse and prose, she published in 1852, and the following year, *Lucretia, the Quakeress,* designed to illustrate the triumph of anti-slavery principles. In 1860 appeared *The Best of Books and Its History,* a series of lectures on the Bible which she had previously delivered to the Baptists of Nantucket. She had been reared in the doctrines and principles of the Quakers but she became a Baptist and later a Universalist. Having preached a year at the Universalist Church in Hingham, Mass., she was installed as pastor in 1868, the first woman regularly ordained in New England. Resigning in 1870, she was called to New Haven, Conn., where she remained until 1874, when she became pastor of the First, and later of the Second Universalist Church in Jersey City. She was the first woman to officiate as chaplain of the Connecticut legislature, which position she occupied several times in 1870 and 1872, and she was probably the first woman to act as chaplain to a legislative body of men. In 1865 she published three books: *The Young Captain,* a memorial of Capt. Richard C. Derby, killed at Antietam; *Frank Nelson, or the Runaway Boy,* a piece of juvenile fiction; and *Abraham Lincoln: His Life and Public Services,* of which a

German translation was published in New York the same year. Her *Life of George Peabody,* the philanthropist, was issued in 1870. The popularity of her books on Lincoln and Peabody was an indication of the condition of contemporary literary standards rather than of any merits in the biographies. *From Shore to Shore, and Other Poems* appeared in 1871. A chronicle of the achievements of American women, *Daughters of America; or, Women of the Century* (1882), was the last of her literary productions. Her active ministry ceased in 1891, and her death, at the age of ninety-two, occurred in Rochester, N. Y., at the house of a grand-daughter.

[Autobiographical material in *Daughters of America,* mentioned above; *Who's Who in America,* 1912–13; *Woman of the Century* (1893), ed. by F. E. Willard and M. A. Livermore; *Universalist Leader,* June 18, 1921.]
F. M.

HANBY, BENJAMIN RUSSEL (July 22, 1833–Mar. 16, 1867), song-writer, was born in Rushville, Fairfield County, Ohio, the eldest son of William Hanby, bishop of the United Brethren of Christ, and Ann (Miller) Hanby. He graduated from Otterbein University in 1858 and afterward traveled extensively as agent for the college. In June of the year of his graduation he married Mary Kate Winter. From 1859 to 1860 he was principal of the academy at Sevenmile, Butler County, Ohio, and in 1861 became pastor of the United Brethren Church, Lewisburg, Ohio. At this time he had already achieved a reputation as a popular song-writer. His first production, and the one which gives him distinction, "Darling Nelly Gray," was written while he was still in college. It is worthy of comparison with the Foster songs of like character in the sincerity of its expression and its genuine appeal. It had a phenomenal sale and was sung everywhere, not alone in America, but on the other side of the Atlantic as well. The author's sole compensation is said to have been ten complimentary copies. "Little Tillie's Grave" appeared in 1860. It was a rather weak imitation of the earlier song, but was also popular and enjoyed a large sale. Much better is "Ole Shady, the Song of the Contraband," published in 1861, and much sung and enjoyed by the men of the Northern armies. Here Hanby leaves the sentimental side of the negro character and attempts to express its exuberance and jollity. General Sherman in the *North American Review* for October 1888, under title of "Old Shady, with a Moral" pays high tribute to its genuineness and its vivid portrayal of the faithfulness and loyalty of the negro. The last of Hanby's songs of this type was "Now den, now den." It is quite probable that Bishop Hanby's firm stand as an anti-slavery man, and the fact that his home was used as a station of the "underground railroad" in those troublous and exciting times may have given this bent to his son's songs.

Feeling that he had become too liberal in his theological views to be in full sympathy with the United Brethren, in 1863 Hanby resigned his pastorate and withdrew from the Conference to which he belonged, though he never severed his connection with the Church. In 1864 he entered the employ of the John Church Music Company of Cincinnati, from which the following year he transferred to the music house of Root & Cady, Chicago. Here he took up the congenial task of writing Sunday-school and day-school songs and together with George F. Root issued a juvenile musical periodical, *Our Song Birds* (2 vols., 1866–67), to which Hanby contributed some sixty tunes and the words for about half that number. He was still engaged in this work at the time of his death.

[The chief source of information is an article by C. B. Galbreath on "Song Writers of Ohio," *Ohio Archaeol. and Hist. Soc. Quart.,* Apr. 1905, reprinted separately. See also *Twelfth Quadrennial Reg. of the Grads. of Otterbein Univ., 1857–1905* (1905).]
W. T. U—n.

HANCHETT, HENRY GRANGER (Aug. 29, 1853–Aug. 19, 1918), pianist, teacher of music, and author, was the great-great-grandson of John Hanchett, a lieutenant in the Colonial wars, and a great-grandson of Oliver Hanchett, a captain in the Revolution. Born in Syracuse, N. Y., the son of Milton Waldo and Martha Anna (Huntington) Hanchett, he was educated in the public schools of that city. At the age of seven he played the piano with some skill and at sixteen was a church organist. Recurrent attacks of blindness are said to have caused him to study medicine in order that he might understand and treat his own case. He received the degree of M.D. from the New York Homeopathic College in 1884 and practised for a time but soon made music his chief preoccupation. His interest in pathology continued, however, and he published several popular medical works, among them, *The Elements of Modern Domestic Medicine: A Plain and Practical Hand-book* (1887), and *Sexual Health* (1887; 4th ed., 1897).

His activities in the field of music were far flung and long continued. He gave courses in piano, musical history, pedagogy, appreciation of music, musical theory, or music pedagogy in Martha Washington College, Va. (1876–78);

Beethoven Conservatory, St. Louis, Mo. (1880–81); Adelphi College, Brooklyn, N. Y. (1899–1903); National Park Seminary, Forest Glen, Md. (1907–10); Brenau College, Gainesville, Ga. (1913–15). In addition he served as organist at the Church of the Ascension (1884–87) and Marble Collegiate Church (1889–93), New York; and at the Central Congregational Church, Brooklyn (1893–98); as a choral and orchestral conductor in various places; and as musical director at Chautauqua assemblies. Beginning in 1891, he toured the United States and Canada from Nova Scotia to the Pacific Coast, as a recital pianist and lecturer, appearing before universities, colleges, and women's clubs. He also lectured on music at the Brooklyn Institute (1894–1903) and in the public schools of New York (1896–1909). He made a specialty of "Beethoven Readings," and up to 1911 he had given some three hundred lecture recitals in New York alone. He was an active member of various scientific, historical, and musical societies, a founder of the American Guild of Organists, the inventor of the "sostenuto" or third tone-sustaining pedal now used on all grand pianos. He composed an Easter anthem, a *Te Deum* and a *Benedictus* for chorus, contributed many articles to the musical press, and published the following books: *Teaching as a Science* (1882); *The Art of the Musician* (1905); and *An Introduction to the Theory of Music* (1916).

He was twice married: first, on June 22, 1886, to Ophelia Murphey of Dover, Del., and second, on Feb. 22, 1896, to Grace Mather of New York. His death occurred at Siasconset, Mass.

[Albert Payne, *Celebrated Pianists of the Past and Present* (1894); *Musical America,* Aug. 31, 1918; *International Who's Who in Music* (1918); *Who's Who in America,* 1918–19.]

F. H. M.

HANCOCK, JOHN (Jan. 12, 1736/7–Oct. 8, 1793), merchant, politician, was born at Braintree, Mass., and baptized there four days later, on Jan. 16, 1736/7. His father, Rev. John Hancock, was pastor of the church at Braintree; his mother, Mary Hawke, was at the time of her marriage to John Hancock the widow of Samuel Thaxter. Since his father died while young John was a boy, he was adopted by his childless uncle, Thomas Hancock [*q.v.*], the richest merchant in Boston. Thus his future was made before he knew there was any difficulty in such making. He went, of course, to the Boston Latin School and Harvard, graduating in 1754. He then at once entered his uncle's mercantile office and there was trained in the lore of a general shipping merchant of the day. In 1760, under the tutelage of the former governor, Thomas Pownall [*q.v.*], he was sent to London to learn the English end of the business. There, as the heir of one of the richest of American merchants, with good manners, an expensive taste in dress, and a liberal purse, his way was undoubtedly easy. By October 1761 he was once more in Boston and on Jan. 1, 1763, he became a partner of Thomas Hancock & Company. When his uncle Thomas died of apoplexy in 1764, John, the poor minister's orphan, found himself at twenty-seven the head of Boston's leading mercantile house and the chief heir to £70,000. He was never much of a merchant but he continued the firm and in 1765 protested to his English correspondents about the Stamp Act. In 1767 he carried out his uncle's promise to Harvard to give them £500 worth of books, to which he added some of his own; but with characteristic vanity he informed the bookseller that the entire donation was a present from himself.

In 1768, he imported a large cargo of Madeira wine in his sloop *Liberty* and while the tidesman was forcibly confined between decks (according to his sworn statement) some of the cargo was smuggled ashore. Other merchants, less reputable than Hancock, had been smuggling wine; and accordingly, the government, strong in the presence of the ship *Romney,* decided on drastic action. The *Liberty,* then reloading for the outward voyage, was seized and towed out to the *Romney* and a riot on shore ensued (June 10, 1768). Suit was entered against Hancock, who was defended by John Adams, but the prosecution was dropped after a few months. The *Liberty* was condemned, however, and, converted into a coast guard, was ultimately burned by a mob at Newport, R. I. The whole episode, both because of the popular feeling aroused and because of the legal questions involved, was one of the most important in the prelude to revolution. (See *Proceedings of the Massachusetts Historical Society,* Vol. LV, 1923, pp. 239–84.)

The *Liberty* affair added much to Hancock's local prestige. In 1769 he was elected to the General Court, and in 1770, after the "Massacre," he was made head of the town committee. Samuel Adams, who recognized the importance of the rich young man, soon became a determining influence in his life. From now on Hancock became the idol of the populace and sided with the patriot party. In 1773 he took a leading part in the publication of the "Hutchinson Letters." The next year, he was chosen to deliver the oration on the anniversary of the "Massacre." He continued to be elected to the General Court and to minor offices. In 1774, when the Court transformed itself into a Provincial Congress, he was chosen president, and also chairman of a committee of safety with power to call out the militia. He was one of those especially excluded from the offer of amnesty made by the British. The following year he was again elected president of the Provincial Congress and a delegate to the second Continental Congress. On Aug. 28, 1775, at Fairfield, Conn., he was married to Dorothy Quincy.

Hancock was the richest New Englander on the patriot side and, quite apart from any personal ability, his value to the cause was obvious; though his ostentatious display on the way to Philadelphia and later at the Congress greatly exasperated the forthright and short-tempered John Adams. His wealth, judiciously expended among the people, and his espousal of the American side of the controversy, had made him immensely popular with those who did not work with him so closely as to perceive that his mind was of mediocre quality. He was elected president of the Congress, reëlected the following year, and signed the Declaration of Independence. Not realizing his own limitations, he desired to be made commander-in-chief of the army, but Congress promptly thwarted his ambitions by the appointment of Washington to that office. Hancock never forgave what he considered this slight to his ability and pretensions. He also never forgave Samuel Adams, whom he believed responsible for blocking a congressional vote of thanks for his services in 1777. He resigned the presidency of the Congress, Oct. 29, 1777, and although he continued a member of that body, he soon came to spend much of his time in Boston. In 1778 he commanded the Massachusetts contingent of 5,000 men who were to take part in a complicated movement against the British on Rhode Island. His performance of his minor rôle was neither able nor very creditable, although it was the union of many circumstances which made the expedition a failure.

During the latter part of the war his interest was much greater in Massachusetts politics than in Congress, and he did much to increase his local popularity. Although he had lost a part of his fortune, he was still wealthy and lavished money in various public ways. In one peculiar instance, however, he appeared to care nothing for his reputation. Being socially and financially prominent, he had been made treasurer of Harvard College in 1773, and for several years gave that institution infinite trouble. He refused to make accountings or to heed pointed suggestions that he resign. Finally, while he was away from Boston as president of the Continental Congress, one of the Harvard tutors was sent to him by the Corporation to receive the papers and securities in his hands, and succeeded in getting from him £16,000 of the college securities. The rest of the property he held was not returned until after his death. In June 1777, upon the recommendation of the Overseers, the Corporation elected a new treasurer.

In 1780 he was a member of the Massachusetts constitutional convention and in September of that year was elected first governor of the state by an overwhelming majority. He served until early in 1785 when in the face of serious conditions—which later culminated in Shays's Rebellion—he had an attack of gout and resigned. James Bowdoin [*q.v.*] carried the state through the rebellion and then Hancock again became a candidate for the governorship and was elected. In 1788 he presided at the convention to ratify the Federal Constitution. The convention, like the people, was much divided. Hancock had the gout and did not take the chair. A solution for the conflict was found in a series of amendments to be proposed, drawn up by some of the Federalists. It was suggested Hancock present them as his own. The gout fortunately disappeared, Hancock presented the amendments, became the popular peace-maker, and added much to his prestige (Harding, *post,* pp. 84 ff.; Morse, *post,* pp. 50 ff., 212 ff.; Parsons, *post,* pp. 65 ff.). He was again elected governor, for a ninth term, and was serving when he died at the age of fifty-six.

[A. E. Brown, *John Hancock, His Book* (1898), contains many letters and is useful; Lorenzo Sears, *John Hancock, the Picturesque Patriot* (1912), is popular and rather diffuse. Certain details are found in *Records of the Town of Braintree* (1886), p. 774, and L. R. Paige, *Hist. of Cambridge, Mass.* (1930), with a Supplement to the Index, by M. I. Gozzaldi, see esp. p. 336. See also J. T. Adams, "Portrait of an Empty Barrel," *Harper's Mag.*, Sept. 1930; Josiah Quincy, *The Hist. of Harvard Univ.* (2 vols., 1840); S. B. Harding, *The Contest over the Ratification of the Federal Constitution in the State of Mass.* (1896); A. E. Morse, *The Federalist Party in Mass. to the Year 1800* (1909); Theophilus Parsons, *Memoir of Theophilus Parsons* (1859); *The Works of John Adams* (10 vols., 1850–56), ed. by C. F. Adams; *The Writings of Samuel Adams* (4 vols., 1904–08), ed. by H. A. Cushing; *Warren-Adams Letters,* being *Mass. Hist. Soc. Colls.*, vols. LXXII and LXXIII (1917, 1925); *The Life and Correspondence of Rufus King* (6 vols., 1894–1900), ed. by C. R. King; *Letters of Members of the Continental Cong.* (vols. I–IV, 1921–28), ed. by E. C. Burnett; Hancock letters in *Proc. Mass. Hist. Soc.*, vols. XLIII (1910), XLVIII (1915), LX (1927), *Proc. Am. Antiq. Soc.*, n.s. XV (1904). Comparatively few of Hancock's papers have been preserved, but there are some in the possession of the Mass. Hist. Soc. A newspaper in 1884 stated that materials were collected for a biography but were purchased for $1,000 and suppressed (Sears, p. viii).]

J. T. A.

HANCOCK, JOHN (Oct. 24, 1824–July 19, 1893), Texas congressman and lawyer, was born in Jackson County, Ala., youngest of three sons of John Allen Hancock and Sarah (Ryan) Hancock, who had come from Virginia in 1819. He attended East Tennessee University and in 1840 made a visit to Texas where his older brother, George Hancock, was already established. In 1846, having completed his studies and being admitted to the bar, he returned to Texas where he soon commenced the practice of law in Austin as the partner of Andrew Jackson Hamilton [*q.v.*]. In 1851, Hancock was elected district judge. In 1855 he resigned to return to his practice, and in the same year was married to Susan E. Richardson of Brazoria, Texas. They had one son. Hancock soon became thoroughly familiar with the land laws of Texas, and for many years was engaged in almost every important case which involved a question as to the complex tenures by which the lands in the state were held. His practice in these cases was attended with remarkable success. He is described as a gentleman of great dignity of manner, wearing the conventional frock coat and tall hat which marked the lawyer. He was in his office or in court every hour of the business day. His one diversion was to drive behind his fine team of bays.

In 1860 Hancock was elected to the legislature as an avowed Unionist, but was soon expelled for refusing to take the oath of allegiance to the Confederacy. In company with other loyalists he seems to have meditated armed resistance, and even drilled in a company known as the "home guards," but when resistance proved vain, he continued to practise law. In 1864 he came into the limelight as the defender of four men arrested as Unionists, whose release he secured by making an able appeal to the fundamental rights of citizens. His own position was decidedly uncomfortable, however, and he fled through Mexico to the North where he awaited the end of the war. In 1865, he returned to Texas in the train of his former partner, A. J. Hamilton. In the constitutional convention of 1866, called in furtherance of President Johnson's plan of reconstruction, Hancock took a moderate position and sought with some success to mediate between the radicals and the conservatives. He was opposed to negro suffrage, and was the author of the resolution by which the personal rights of negroes were recognized while their testimony in courts was limited to cases in which members of their own race were involved.

Hancock had hoped to win election to the Senate and he was disappointed when the new legislature turned to two former Confederates. In 1870, however, he was elected as a Democrat to Congress, where he served for three terms. In 1876, as a part of the general movement to send only former Confederates to Washington, he was defeated, but in 1882 he again won a seat for a single term by a campaign in which much was said about free trade and little about the Civil War. Never an orator, he continued until his death to win a more brilliant reputation in the court room than on the political platform. He died at Austin.

[J. D. Lynch, *Bench and Bar of Texas* (1885); *Texas State Hist. Asso. Quart.*, Apr. 1908, Oct. 1910, and its successor, *S. W. Hist. Quart.*, Oct. 1912; *War of the Rebellion: Official Records (Army)*, 1 ser. XLVIII (pt. 2), 1026; C. W. Ramsdell, "Reconstruction in Texas," *Columbia Univ. Studies in Hist., Econ., and Pub. Law*, vol. XXXVI (1910); *Galveston Daily News*, July 20, 1893; files of the *Houston Telegraph* and *Galveston Daily News*; correspondence with Mrs. E. B. Hancock, Austin, Texas.]

R. G. C.

HANCOCK, THOMAS (July 13, 1703–Aug. 1, 1764), merchant, was among the foremost of eighteenth-century American business men. Descended from Nathaniel Hancock, who was in Cambridge, Mass., as early as 1634, he was the son of a poor parish minister, the Rev. John Hancock, and of Elizabeth Clark. He grew up in the new, sparsely populated settlement of Cambridge Farms, later Lexington, Mass., unschooled, except perhaps by his father, and was apprenticed to a bookseller and bookbinder in Boston when but thirteen years of age. Seven years later he was established in his own bookshop; and in the succeeding period his rise was rapid. With the aid of partners he engaged in paper manufacturing, exported codfish, whale oil, logwood, and potash, supplied rum, molasses, and other provisions to the Newfoundland fishing fleet, and controlled a group of freighting vessels. His marriage, on Nov. 5, 1730, to Lydia Henchman, daughter of Boston's most prominent book-dealer, marked the turning point in his career. From that date his business was operated on a larger scale. Determined and untiring, keen and diplomatic, proud, yet a close buyer who carefully priced a wanted commodity in many of the world's markets, farsighted, and an excellent manager of a much-ramified business, Hancock carefully built up a considerable fortune and a prosperous trade. He was soon mentioned as one of the wealthiest Bostonians of his era; and his wealth enabled him to secure influential friends among the most important officers of the Crown in England and the colonies. He made use of these friends skilfully to effect his ends. With their aid, he and his partner, Charles Apthorp, became government agents, and between 1746 and 1758 furnished supplies to all the British forces in Nova Scotia. It was Hancock who, in 1749, sent building material and foodstuff to Chebucto Bay to enable Col. Edward Cornwallis to found the city of Halifax. In 1755, Apthorp and Hancock, acting as agents for the Province of Nova Scotia, engaged the seventeen sloops used to transport the unfortunate Acadians to the colonies farther south. After Apthorp's death, in 1758, Hancock was able to secure even more of the supply business of Nova Scotia for himself. His wealth was further increased by his smuggling ventures. Tea, paper, Holland duck, and other goods were surreptitiously shipped from Amsterdam to St. Eustatius in the West Indies, from which port, together with contraband consignments of French molasses concealed in English hogsheads, they were run into Boston harbor as opportunity offered.

In his later years, gout and a "Nervous Disorder" almost forced him to withdraw from business, and in 1763 his nephew John Hancock [*q.v.*], the patriot leader, was made an equal partner in the concern so that he might continue it at the death of his uncle. Thomas Hancock died of apoplexy, Aug. 1, 1764, after being stricken in the Massachusetts State House, while he was serving as a member of the Governor's Council. He had inherited the Henchman fortune in 1761, and left an estate which has been moderately appraised at about seventy thousand pounds.

[The Hancock MSS., deposited in the Baker Library of the Harvard Graduate School of Business Administration, and the Hancock Letterheads and Hancock Account Books, at the New-England Historic Genealogical Society; C. A. Staples, "Sketch of the Life of Hon. Thomas Hancock, A Native of Lexington," in *Proc. Lexington Hist. Soc.*, vol. III (1905), incomplete and inaccurate; A. E. Brown, *John Hancock, His Book* (1898); Lorenzo Sears, *John Hancock* (1912); "Indenture of Thomas Hancock," *Bostonian Soc. Pubs.*, XII (1915), 99–101; T. B. Akins, *Selections from the Public Documents of Nova Scotia* (1869), esp. pp. 285–93, and p. 630; Justin Winsor, *Memorial Hist. of Boston,* II (1881), 519–20; *Boston Gazette,* Aug. 13, 1764; *Mass. Gazette and Boston News-Letter,* Aug. 2 and 16, 1764.]

E. Ed—n.

HANCOCK, WINFIELD SCOTT (Feb. 14, 1824–Feb. 9, 1886), soldier, presidential candidate, was named for Winfield Scott, already an outstanding figure in the War of 1812. His father was Benjamin Franklin Hancock (1800–1879), the son of Richard Hancock, a Philadelphia seaman, and his second wife, Anna Maria Nash, of Edinburgh, Scotland. Benjamin Hancock was reared by John Roberts, a Quaker; he was at first a teacher, but was admitted to the bar in 1828, and practised law in Norristown, Pa., for over forty years, where he had the reputation of being a well-read lawyer. His wife was Elizabeth Hoxworth, of English descent. Their son, Winfield Scott Hancock, was born at the village of Montgomery Square, and at the age of four years moved with his parents to Norristown, the county-seat. Here in due time he attended the Norristown Academy until it was merged into a high school, and showed a fondness for drill by organizing a military company among his schoolmates. He entered West Point on July 1, 1840, at the age of sixteen years and, though admittedly immature and not well grounded in his studies, graduated from the Military Academy on June 30, 1844, eighteenth in a class which had been reduced by elimination from one hundred to twenty-five members. Among his contemporaries at West Point, who later became distinguished generals, were Grant, McClellan, Franklin, W. F. Smith, Reynolds, Rosecrans, Longstreet, Pickett, and "Stonewall" Jackson. As a cadet he has been described by a fellow student as "of tall, slender, and handsome person, which he bore without haughtiness or condescension" (O. B. Willcox, in *Letters and Addresses, post*). In later years General Grant said of Hancock, "Tall, well-formed . . . young and fresh-looking,—he presented an appearance that would attract the attention of an army as he passed" (*Memoirs,* II, 540). Upon graduation, he was assigned to the 6th Infantry, and after two years' service in Texas, joined General Scott's army in Mexico in time to win brevets for gallantry at the battles of Contreras and Churubusco and to take part in the assaults upon Molino del Rey and Chapultepec. There followed some fourteen years of instructive, valuable experience for Hancock—the Seminole War in Florida, the Border War in Kansas, Harney's Utah Expedition, and quartermaster duty on the Pacific Coast. During this period he was married, Jan. 24, 1850, to Almira Russell, daughter of a St. Louis merchant. They had a son and a daughter, both of whom died before their father.

The outbreak of the Civil War found Hancock, then in his thirty-eighth year, active intellectually and physically, ripe in the experience of handling troops, and enjoying the confidence of his military superiors. Accordingly, on General McClellan's recommendation, he was promptly made a brigadier-general of volunteers, Sept. 23, 1861, and put to work organizing and training the newly assembled Army of the Potomac. His brigade—the 49th Pennsylvania, 43rd New York, 5th Wisconsin, and 9th Maine regiments—was early prepared for field duty, and took a prominent part in all the battles of Mc-

Clellan's Peninsular campaign, and at Crampton's Pass, South Mountain, and Antietam. In the latter decisive battle, Hancock succeeded to the command of the 1st Division, II Army Corps, and was promoted to major-general of volunteers, Nov. 29, 1862. He commanded his new division with distinction at the battle of Fredericksburg, Dec. 13, 1862. In the desperately contested battle of Chancellorsville, May 1–4, 1863, the steadiness of Hancock's division largely prevented overwhelming defeat, and he was promoted to command of the II Army Corps.

It was at Gettysburg, however, that he achieved lasting fame as one of the great soldiers of the Civil War. On the first day of the battle, it was Hancock, acting under broad discretionary powers from Meade, who virtually selected the field of Gettysburg upon which to fight and who by simulating a strongly held position on a broad front, dissuaded General Lee from attacking at once. On the second day, it was Hancock, commanding the left wing, who thwarted Lee's all-but-successful attempt to turn the Federal army's flank. On July 3, it was Hancock's corps which successfully repulsed the Confederate army's desperate thrust at the Federal center. During the battle, Hancock received a wound from which he never fully recovered. In the battles of the Wilderness and Spotsylvania, his corps again engaged in severe fighting which continued on to Appomattox; but on Nov. 26, 1864, he was recalled to Washington and entered upon a period of recruiting.

For gallant and distinguished services in all the operations of Grant's army in Virginia, Hancock was made a brigadier-general in the Regular Army (Aug. 12, 1864); and for his conspicuous share in the victory at Gettysburg he received the Thanks of Congress (Apr. 21, 1866). He was appointed a major-general in the Regular Army, July 26, 1866. During the ensuing years he personally led an expedition against hostile Indians while in command of the Central Military Department, 1867; commanded the Department of Louisiana and Texas, 1867, where his proclamation giving to civil tribunals jurisdiction over all crimes and offenses not involving forcible resistance to Federal authority failed to meet with the approval of Congress and led to his being relieved; commanded the Department of Dakota, 1870–72, the Division of the Atlantic, 1872–86, and finally, the Department of the East also, with headquarters at Governor's Island, N. Y.

Although he "had had absolutely no experience in politics and possessed but little knowledge of the problems of government" (Thomas, *post*, p. 54), in the National Democratic Convention of 1868 he received, as a military hero, a large number of votes for the presidential nomination, and in 1880, at Cincinnati, he was nominated for the presidency by the Democratic party. The campaign was notable for the lack of major issues and is chiefly remembered for Hancock's undeservedly ridiculed remark, "The tariff question is a local question" (interview in *Paterson Daily Guardian,* Oct. 8, 1880; widely quoted). He lost the election to James A. Garfield by a small popular plurality and fifty-nine votes in the electoral college.

Among those who knew him personally Hancock was characterized as possessing great industry, courage, ambition, lofty ideals, unfaltering loyalty to friends, and the quality of patient labor which has been called genius. In his *Memoirs* (II, 539–40), General Grant said of him: "Hancock stands the most conspicuous figure of all the general officers who did not exercise a separate command. He commanded a corps longer than any other one, and his name was never mentioned as having committed in battle a blunder for which he was responsible. . . . His personal courage and his presence with his command in the thickest of the fight, won for him the confidence of troops serving under him." He died, after a very brief illness, at Governors Island and was buried with military honors at Norristown, Pa.

[H. M. Jenkins, "Genealogical Sketch of Gen. W. S. Hancock," in *Pa. Mag. of Hist. and Biog.*, Apr. 1886; *Reminiscences of Winfield Scott Hancock* (1887), by his wife, Almira Russell Hancock; J. W. Dixon, "Across the Plains with General Hancock," *Jour. of the Mil. Service Inst.*, June 1886; F. A. Walker, *General Hancock* (1895); G. W. Cullum, *Biog. Reg.* (3rd ed., 1891); *War of the Rebellion: Official Records (Army)*; Abner Doubleday, *Chancellorsville and Gettysburg* (1882); *Personal Memoirs of U. S. Grant* (2 vols., 1886); *Letters and Addresses Contributed . . . in Memory of Winfield Scott Hancock* (1886); D. X. Junkin, and F. H. Norton, *Life of Winfield Scott Hancock* (1880), A. T. Freed, *Hancock* (1880), and other campaign biographies; H. C. Thomas, *The Return of the Democratic Party to Power in 1884* (1919), ch. III; *N. Y. Times*, Feb. 10, 1886.]

C. D. R.

HAND, DANIEL (July 16, 1801–Dec. 17, 1891), merchant, philanthropist, was born at East Guilford, now Madison, Conn. He was a descendant of John Hand who came to Lynn, Mass., from Maidstone, Kent, England, about 1635, and in 1649 became one of the patentees of East Hampton, L. I. Daniel's grandfather, Capt. Daniel Hand, with his company of East Guilforders joined Washington's army in the first Long Island campaign. The Captain's only son, Daniel, was a farmer of some literary tastes and a life-long magistrate. His son, Daniel, brought up on the farm and educated in the district school, went in his eighteenth year to Augusta, Ga., under the care of his maternal uncle, Daniel Meigs, long a merchant in the South, and ultimately succeeded to his uncle's business. He united with the First Presbyterian Church of Augusta, serving as superintendent of its Sunday school for thirty years. While frankly voicing his convictions as to the moral wrong of slavery, he admired the Southern people and had warm friends among them.

A branch business established in Charleston, S. C., outgrew that in Augusta, and Hand's large capital was transferred to the former city. When war between North and South appeared imminent, he was in New York on business, but at the urgent request of his Charleston partner, George W. Williams, a Southerner, he decided to return. On his way back, obliged to take a roundabout route, he was arrested at New Orleans, but was paroled on his promise to report to the Confederate authorities at Richmond. Proceeding thither, he stopped over night at Augusta. There a mob gathered about the hotel threatening him as a "Lincoln spy." To save him from violence, the mayor and other old friends escorted him to the city jail for temporary safe-keeping. When he reached Richmond he was sent to Libby Prison; but, after examination, was released on parole within the Confederacy. He made his home at Asheville, N. C., until peace was declared, when he returned to Connecticut. During the war it was proposed to confiscate his fortune; but after prolonged legal struggle the Confederate courts at Charleston confirmed his right to his property. This he left in charge of his partner, allowing him almost unlimited time for making settlement. Final accounting and full payment were made some twenty years later.

In his youth he married his cousin Elizabeth Ward. She and their children died early and he remained a widower, living in his later years in the home of a niece in Guilford. In 1888 he executed a deed of trust to the American Missionary Association of New York, conveying securities aggregating over a million dollars, thereby establishing the Daniel Hand Educational Fund for Colored People, the income to be used for the education of the colored people of the Southern states. He believed that by this means he would also render important service to the white population of those states. Up to that time this fund was the largest single gift made to a benevolent society in the United States by a donor during his lifetime. Hand was a vigorous personality, erect, alert, of wide reading, possessed of strong convictions which he unhesitatingly expressed. Wealth seemed valued by him chiefly as an instrumentality for beneficence. Among his gifts was one of an academy building for his native town.

[G. A. Wilcox, *A Christian Philanthropist: A Sketch of the Life of Mr. Daniel Hand* (1889); E. T. Nash, *Fifty Puritan Ancestors* (1902); B. C. Steiner, *A Hist. of the Plantation of Menunkatuck and of the Original Town of Guilford, Conn.* (1897); *News and Courier* (Charleston, S. C.), Oct. 26, 27, 1888; *New Haven Evening Register*, Dec. 17, 19, 1891.] E. D. E.

HAND, EDWARD (Dec. 31, 1744–Sept. 3, 1802), physician, Revolutionary soldier, son of John and Dorothy Hand, was born in King's County, province of Leinster, Ireland. He studied medicine and attended lectures at Trinity College, Dublin, and emigrated to Philadelphia in 1767 as surgeon's mate in the 18th Royal Irish Regiment. In 1772 he was commissioned ensign, accompanied his regiment to Fort Pitt, and returned to Philadelphia in 1774. He then resigned his commission and moved to Lancaster, Pa., to practise medicine. He was conspicuous throughout the Revolution as a soldier. In 1775 he was lieutenant-colonel in Colonel Thompson's battalion of riflemen at the siege of Boston. Later he was active in organizing and drilling the Lancaster County Associators, and on Mar. 7, 1776, he was elected colonel of riflemen. He performed gallantly against Cornwallis and Howe at Long Island and in the engagements at White Plains, Trenton, and Princeton. Promoted brigadier-general on Apr. 1, 1777, he was dispatched shortly thereafter to western Pennsylvania to mobilize the militia against the Indians and Tories. Late in 1778 he assumed command at Albany and in 1779 rendered valuable aid in Sullivan's expedition against the Indians and Tories in central New York. In 1780 he was assigned to a newly organized brigade of light infantry; on Jan. 8, 1781, he was elected adjutant-general; and in 1783 he became a major-general by brevet. His energy and daring as a soldier and his excellent horsemanship and skill in military science won the affection of his troops, albeit he was a strict disciplinarian. He was regarded highly by Washington for his zeal and ability.

After the war Hand resumed his practice of medicine, devoting considerable time to political and civic affairs. He was a member of Congress, 1784–85; in the Pennsylvania Assembly, 1785–86; a presidential elector, 1789; and a member of the Pennsylvania constitutional convention, 1789–90. As burgess of Lancaster (1789) he wrote to Congress urging the selection of that town for the permanent seat of government, assuring them that its advantages were unrivaled. In politics he was a stanch Federalist. An intimate friend of Washington during and after the Revolution, in 1798 he was recommended for adjutant-general and appointed major-general in the provisional army. He strenuously opposed Jefferson's election in 1800 and was active in holding the Federalists in the Pennsylvania Senate firm in the contest for that state's electors. His zeal was undoubtedly stimulated by the fact that from 1791 to 1801 he was inspector of revenue. Early in the Republican administration he encountered difficulty in settling his accounts, and in 1802 a petition was brought into court to sell his lands. In the midst of this trouble he died suddenly from an apoplectic stroke at "Rockford," his country home, near Lancaster. Hand actively promoted public improvements, held many local offices, and by his willingness to give medical aid gratuitously to the poor distinguished himself as a public benefactor. He married Catharine, daughter of John and Sarah (Yeates) Ewing, on Mar. 13, 1775.

[*Pa. Mag. of Hist. and Biog.*, Apr. 1883; "Orderly Book of Gen. Edward Hand," *Ibid.*, Apr., July, Oct. 1917; C. I. Landis, "Jasper Yeates and his Times," *Ibid.*, July 1922; *Papers Read before the Lancaster County Hist. Soc.*, vol. XVI, no. 8 (1912); "Papers of the Continental Cong.," no. 159, Division of MSS., Lib. of Cong.; *Minutes of the Supreme Executive Council of Pa.*, vols. XI–XIV (1852–53); *Pa. Archives*, 1 ser., vols. V–XII (1853–56); J. I. Mombert, *An Authentic Hist. of Lancaster County* (1869); *The Burd Papers* (1899), ed. by L. B. Walker; *The Unpublished Revolutionary Papers of Maj.-Gen. Edward Hand of Pa.* (1907), catalogued by A. J. Bowden.] J. H. P—g.

HANDERSON, HENRY EBENEZER (Mar. 21, 1837–Apr. 23, 1918), medical historian, born in Orange, Cuyahoga County, Ohio, was the son of Thomas and Catharine (Potts) Handerson. When he was two years old, his father died and he and his sister were adopted by an uncle, Lewis Handerson, a druggist of Cleveland. His childhood was that of an invalid, so that his schooling in Cleveland was much interrupted. In 1851 he was sent to Sanger Hall, a boarding school at New Hartford, N. Y., but was compelled to leave because of his health. Shortly after, his foster father moved, with his family, to Beersheba Springs, Tenn. Upon the latter's return to Cleveland in 1854, Henry entered Hobart College (Geneva, N. Y.), where he received the degree of A.B. in 1858. After graduation he went again to Tennessee, where he spent the next year in land-surveying and later became a private tutor in the family of a Louisiana cotton planter. In 1861 he entered the medical department of the University of Louisiana (later Tulane University), but his studies were interrupted by the Civil War. Following the bombardment of Fort Sumter (Apr. 12, 1861), he again took up tutoring in a Southern family, joined a company of plantation "homeguards," and on June 17, 1861, enlisted in the Stafford Guards, later Company B of the 9th Regiment of Louisiana Volunteers, commanded by Col. Richard Taylor, son of the former president, Zachary Taylor. Handerson served the Confederacy continuously during the war, and despite a gunshot wound and an attack of typhoid fever, he rose steadily in rank to the grade of major and adjutant-general of the 2nd Louisiana Brigade. In this capacity, he was captured by Northern troops on May 4, 1865, and remained a prisoner until June 17, 1865. At the age of twenty-eight he resumed his medical studies in the College of Physicians and Surgeons, New York City, where he was graduated M.D. in 1867. He engaged in the practice of medicine in New York until 1885, when he returned to Cleveland, to remain there to the end of his life.

During his Manhattan period, Handerson made his mark as a contributor to medical history by a scholarly paper, read to the Medical Society of the County of New York on Feb. 25, 1878, and published in 1883 as *The School of Salernum: An Historical Sketch of Mediæval Medicine*. This was followed in 1889 by his well-known *Outlines of the History of Medicine and the Medical Professor* (1876), translated from the German of Johann Hermann Baas, to which he added much interesting matter of his own, relating to English and American medicine. Through its fidelity to the original, its unfailing accuracy as a source of reference, and the piquant additions made by Handerson to a text already remarkable for droll humor and glancing wit, this translation became widely known and remained the authoritative textbook on the subject in this country for a whole generation. It gave him a high and justly deserved reputation in a subject little cultivated at the time, although he never sought publicity on that account but, true to type, remained a quiet recluse. Handerson's other contributions to medical literature include a number of effective sketches in Howard A. Kelly's *Cyclopædia of American Medical Biography* (1912), his *Gilbertus Anglicus: Medicine of the Thirteenth Century* (1918), and a series of articles on the sanitation, vital statistics, diseases, and medical history of Cleveland. All these evince the careful, accurate quality of his work.

From 1894 to 1896 Handerson was professor of hygiene and sanitation in the University of Wooster. When in the latter year the medical department at Wooster became the medical department at Ohio Wesleyan University, renamed the Cleveland College of Physicians and Surgeons, he transferred with it and remained ten years. He became president of the Cuyahoga County Medical Society in 1895, was a member of the Cleveland Academy of Medicine, the Ohio State Medical Society, and the American Medical Association, and was a founder of the Cleveland Medical Library Association and its president from 1896 to 1902. He was highly esteemed as a physician of acute mind and reliable character and had many affiliations and friendships both North and South. He eventually retired from practice, became totally blind about 1916, and died on Apr. 23, 1918, from the effects of cerebral hemorrhage. He was twice married: on Oct. 16, 1872, to Juliet Alice Root, and following her death, to Clara Corlett of Cleveland, June 12, 1888. In person he was tall and dignified, with the quiet, unassuming, genial manner of the gentleman and the scholar.

[S. W. Kelley, memoir of Handerson, with a bibliography of his writings, in Handerson's *Gilbertus Anglicus*; sketch of Handerson by the same author in H. A. Kelly and W. L. Burrage, *Am. Medic. Biogs.* (1920); F. H. Garrison, article in *Medic. Pickwick*, Mar. 1915; S. P. Orth, *A Hist. of Cleveland, Ohio* (1910), vol. II; *Who's Who in America*, 1917–18; Handerson's *Contribution to the Geneal. of the Handerson Family* (1885); *Cleveland Plain Dealer*, Apr. 24, 1918.] F. H. G.

HANDY, ALEXANDER HAMILTON (Dec. 25, 1809–Sept. 12, 1883), Mississippi jurist, belongs to that branch of the family, whose ancestor, Samuel, settled in Somerset County, Md., as early as 1665. Col. George Handy, of the third generation, father of Alexander, was an officer in Lee's Legion of Revolutionary fame. He married Betsy Wilson, daughter of James Wilson, and Alexander, his fifth son, was born in Princess Anne, Somerset County, Md. At the age of thirteen he was enrolled in Washington Academy, where he remained six years, being thoroughly grounded in the classics. He then became deputy clerk to his brother, George, who at that time was clerk of the county court. This aided greatly in his legal studies which he undertook during spare hours, and in 1834 he was admitted to the bar. The next year he married Susan Wilson Stuart, and several years later the couple decided to seek their fortune in Mississippi, then the far Southwest, settling in the town of Canton after living several years in Madisonville. Handy built up an extensive practice before the high court of errors and appeals, and in chancery and federal courts as well (*Mississippi State Gazette,* May 27, 1853). His prominence brought him before the public and in November 1853 he contested successfully the reëlection of William Yerger, a Whig, to a judgeship on the high court of errors and appeals. Handy was a Democrat and his known views on the constitutionality of the Union Bank bonds probably brought him the popular vote, though he maintained a strictly judicial reserve during the campaign. Yerger had rendered his noted decision in the case of *The State of Mississippi* vs. *Heyron Johnson* (25 *Miss.,* 625–882), which decreed that the Union Bank bonds, now worthless because of the failure of the bank, in which the state had a large interest, were therefore a valid obligation of Mississippi (*Mississippi State Gazette,* Dec. 2–9, 1853).

Shortly after the secession of Mississippi, Handy was appointed by the governor as commissioner to the authorities and people of Maryland to arouse secession sentiment in that state. After interviewing Governor Hicks, who refused to convene the legislature for the purpose of coöperating with the South, he delivered several speeches in the state. On Dec. 20, 1860, in Baltimore, he urged secession as a natural right, giving to his plea for the rights of the states great dignity and eloquence (Baltimore *Sun,* Dec. 19 and 20, 1860). During the war he continued to serve Mississippi as associate justice, and on Apr. 18, 1864, he was made chief justice of the high court of errors and appeals. On Oct. 1, 1867, he resigned in consequence of the court's being placed under military control and moved to Baltimore, where he resumed the practice of law and taught during the session 1870–71 in the University of Maryland Law School. In the fall of 1871 he returned to his old home at Canton, Miss., where he practised law and lived out the last uneventful and peaceful years of a well-rounded life, declining appointments to a professorship in the state university, and to his old position of chief justice, offered him by the governor. At the time of his death he was one of the leaders at the bar in Mississippi. His numerous opinions may be found through volumes 26 to 41 of the Mississippi *Reports.* They have contributed much to the law of that state and show independence of thought, clearness of reasoning, wide learning, and painstaking research.

[James D. Lynch, *The Bench and Bar of Miss.* (1881), pp. 328–31, 508–10; the *Sun* (Baltimore), Sept. 17, 1883; information as to certain facts from Handy's son, A. S. Handy, Canton, Miss.] C. W. G.

HANNA, MARCUS ALONZO (Sept. 24, 1837–Feb. 15, 1904), capitalist, politician, senator, was born at New Lisbon, Ohio. His father, Leonard Hanna, came of Scotch-Irish Quaker stock with a Welsh and an English or Dutch admixture, being descended from Thomas and Elizabeth Hanna who emigrated to America from the north of Ireland in 1763; his mother, Samantha (Converse) Hanna, a school-teacher from Vermont, was of mixed Huguenot, Irish, and English ancestry. Leonard Hanna practised medicine for a time, but shortly before his marriage became associated with his father and two brothers in a grocery business. Reverses in the late forties, occasioned by the decline of New Lisbon as a trading center, led to his removal with his family to Cleveland in 1852. There Marcus finished his public-school education and entered Western Reserve College. After a few months, however, disciplined for a student prank, he turned from school to employment in the grocery and commission firm of Hanna, Garretson & Company, in which his father was senior partner. A gay figure in a lively social set in Cleveland, he was none the less energetic in business and, when his father's health began rapidly to fail, he assumed new responsibilities that prepared him to become in 1862 a partner in the firm in his father's place. He had been reared in the old Quaker tradition of hostility to slavery; his father had been something of a reformer and a prominent "conscience" Whig, and young Hanna was identified with the Republican party almost from the start. Partly because of his filial obligations, however, his war record was limited to 110 days of service, in a volunteer regiment mustered in on May 5, 1864, and detailed to take part in the defense of Washington. On Sept. 27, 1864, he married Charlotte Augusta Rhodes, daughter of Daniel P. Rhodes, a strong-willed Cleveland coal and iron merchant of the Democratic persuasion, although at first differences in politics had threatened to prevent the union. In 1867, after flood and flame had wrecked a private venture in lake transportation and a petroleum refinery, Hanna transferred all his business interests to the new firm of Rhodes & Company, which undertook to continue the traditions that Daniel P. Rhodes had built up in the Cleveland coal and iron trade. The energetic qualities of the junior partner led to rapid expansion and brought about the reorganization of the firm in 1885, with the elimination of the Rhodes interest, under the name of M. A. Hanna & Company. Meantime, he helped to organize the Union National Bank, became proprietor of the *Cleveland Herald* and owner of the Cleveland Opera House, and established himself as the dominant figure in the street railway system of the city.

With the development of his business interests came a new interest in politics. He was quick to see that with the rise of the new industrialism business and politics were becoming more closely interrelated than ever before. His self-interest was seldom as simple and direct as when he supported candidates for the Cleveland city council whom he knew to be favorable toward his street railway, but it was real enough to make him first challenge the control of politics by "bosses" and later accept their cooperation as allies. In the Garfield campaign of 1880 he not only made liberal personal contributions but organized the business men of his city in support of the Republican candidate, a service which was rewarded by membership in the Republican state committee, where he ever remained a strong influence. He soon aspired to play a more active rôle in president making and took up the claims of Senator John Sherman, who became the "favorite son" of Ohio Republicans. Associated with him in this cause was the able young Joseph B. Foraker [*q.v.*], but in the convention of 1888, where Hanna directed the Sherman forces, Foraker seemed to waver in his loyalty to Sherman with the result that an estrangement took place between Hanna and Foraker that continued to be reflected in Ohio Republican politics until Hanna's death.

This breach led Hanna to take up another Ohioan, Congressman William McKinley [*q.v.*] of Canton, who had loyally supported Sherman's claims. His enthusiasm for McKinley grew when the latter was made chairman of the ways and means committee and as such became official sponsor for the tariff measure of 1890 that bore his name. This highly protectionist measure, antagonizing many voters as much as it pleased ardent protectionists like Hanna, led to a serious Republican setback and McKinley's defeat for reëlection to the House. Hanna, however, promptly brought out McKinley for governor and solicited contributions in his behalf even from Chicago and Pittsburgh manufacturers who were urged to save the cause of protection from another disaster. In 1891, a year of general Republican defeat, Hanna saw his candidate win an easy victory; he also had the satisfaction of contributing in a large way to the reëlection of Senator Sherman. He was now ready to press McKinley's claims to the presidency, but, since the year 1892 was unfavorable, did not at once bring out his candidate, although the Republican National Convention took generous notice of the Ohio governor. During the panic of 1893 Hanna first rescued McKinley from a financial embarrassment in which he found himself as a result of having signed a friend's paper and later helped the Governor to win a brilliant reëlection victory. At once the McKinley boom was launched, Hanna's protégé being heralded as the "advance agent of prosperity." In the winter of

1894–95, the president maker withdrew from active direction of his Cleveland firm, in order to devote his energies largely to politics. As the campaign for the nomination of McKinley was approaching its climax, Hanna took a house in Thomasville, Ga., where he later entertained Governor McKinley and brought him into touch with prominent Southern Republicans. Having assured himself of the support of a considerable majority of the Southern delegates to the national convention, he returned to Cleveland, where, again in the rôle of a gracious host, he promoted additional contacts for the Governor. As a result, complete success was assured before the meeting of the Republican convention at St. Louis, on June 15, 1896. On June 18, McKinley was nominated upon the first ballot. Whether or not Hanna was directly responsible for the adoption by the convention of the gold-standard principle which the Eastern business interests demanded, he unquestionably approved it, although his candidate was known to be a bimetallist and to wish to subordinate the currency issue to that of protection.

Almost the entire expense of the preconvention canvass, something over $100,000, was paid by Mark Hanna. So well had he demonstrated his ability as a political organizer that he was promptly selected as chairman of the national committee. Assuming a good deal of the work usually undertaken by the state committees, he gave that body a new importance. It brought together a group of 1,400 paid campaigners and distributed millions of pamphlets and broadsides. The unprecedented expenses of the national organization, which mounted to three and a half millions, were met not only by the gifts of generous individual donors and of corporations, but also by the returns from regular assessments upon banks, corporations, and other business institutions, which Hanna thought should be made to do their part in guaranteeing continued prosperity. The victory on election day exceeded all of Hanna's hopes and expectations.

He was offered the place of postmaster-general in McKinley's cabinet, but his one ambition in public life was to reach the United States Senate. This ambition was realized when John Sherman was made secretary of state under the new president and Hanna was appointed senator in his stead. In the fall of 1897 after an extensive stump-speaking campaign to insure his continuance in office by choice of the state legislature, he achieved a scanty victory despite a hostile combination of Democrats and Republican malcontents. As the contest reached its climax there were charges of bribery, which led to a legislative investigation, but the Senate committee on privileges and elections later refused to credit the reported findings of attempted bribery by Hanna's agents.

In the three years that followed, the most pressing national problems were those of foreign affairs, for which the new senator had little taste or talent. He was known to his friends as a sturdy opponent of intervention in Cuba and later as a critic of the new drift toward imperialism but, like McKinley, he was soon drawn into active support of both. In 1898, however, he was back in his element when he took an active part in raising the money for the Republican congressional campaign and generously contributed his rapidly developing talents for stump-speaking to the contest in Ohio. He now revealed himself as an outspoken champion of the prevailing tendency toward railroad and industrial combinations, which he presented as a natural business development and an essential factor for national prosperity and Republican success. As the most intimate adviser of the president, he aided in organizing the federal patronage to consolidate the strength of the party and of the administration; a frank critic of civil-service reform, he became a master hand in the effective distribution of the fruits of victory. Preparations were soon under way for the election of 1900. Early provision was made for McKinley's unanimous renomination but Hanna was only an eleventh-hour convert to the nomination of Theodore Roosevelt as vice-president. He took greater interest in sponsoring the "trust" plank which was incorporated in the Republican platform of that year. Again, as chairman of the national committee, Hanna was field-marshal of the Republican hosts; with the confidence placed in him by the big business men of the country, the war chest was soon filled to overflowing. Because of the importance of the Democratic-Populist forces in the West, the campaign was largely directed from Chicago; Hanna personally undertook a tour of the states of the upper Mississippi Valley which proved distinctly helpful to the party.

He was now ready to assume a more active rôle in the Senate. He soon became a leading champion of a ship-subsidy scheme designed to restore the American flag to its former place on the high seas. This he successfully pushed through the Senate, only to see it defeated in the House. Somewhat later he became an outstanding advocate of the Panama route for the isthmian canal. Gradually the man who had entered political life as a successful political manager and the representative in politics of business interests began to reveal qualities of statesmanship. When, therefore, in September 1901, upon the death of President McKinley, Theodore Roosevelt was elevated to the presidency, Hanna was continued in the rôle of a respected presidential adviser. Meantime he had made contributions toward the settlement of certain labor disputes in the anthracite coal industry. This led to his finally agreeing to serve upon the conciliation committee of the industrial department of the National Civic Federation; he was promptly made chairman of the executive committee. Before and during the great anthracite coal strike of 1902 he exerted himself to induce the operators to come to reasonable terms and made substantial contributions to the final settlement that was effected under the pressure of Roosevelt.

Hanna was known as a stout believer in the right of labor to organize, partly because of his own human qualities and partly as a corollary to his advocacy of big business and organized capital. Large corporations seemed unlikely to survive if their labor policy was oppressive, and it was simpler and more convenient to deal with the responsible spokesmen of labor than with the mass of unorganized employees. As an employer Hanna could always rely upon the loyalty of his own workers, in whose welfare he took a definite personal interest. His mining properties were somehow free from strikes and his street-railway employees refused to join the Cleveland railway strike of 1899.

Early in 1901 Hanna was being mentioned by certain newspapers as the "logical" nominee of the Republican party in 1904. His disclaimers of presidential aspirations together with the obvious ambition of Roosevelt caused a proposed Hanna boom to subside. It remained evident, however, that many large Eastern business interests looked with hope to Hanna's candidacy, if only as a means of getting rid of the "unsafe" Roosevelt. Following an overwhelming Republican victory in Ohio in 1903, in which Hanna's return to the Senate was assured, an organized campaign was launched in New York, although it was generally understood in political circles that he was not a candidate. Many were pondering the mystery of his failure publicly to concede the field to Roosevelt when news came of the illness that terminated in his death in February 1904.

Mark Hanna was a man of unbounded energies and of broad sympathies. He had a reputation for earnestness and honesty. In business he was one of the industrial pioneers who were ushering in a new era of American life. In the new scheme of things business and politics were natural allies and men like Hanna, assuming that individual and social profits are indistinguishable, generally did not scruple to use the government to advance their own personal and economic interests. The game of politics he played according to the rules; like his friend and associate, "Boss" Cox of Cincinnati, he had none of the instincts of the reformer. In 1902 he declared himself the champion of that "Stand-pattism," which, however much in his colloquial verbiage it may have appealed to his fellow Republicans of that day, soon carried all the connotations of reactionary politics. It may or may not be significant that his home city, Cleveland, which was usually strongly Republican, was seldom carried by the Hanna forces against the crusading followers of the sturdy democrat, Tom L. Johnson.

[A somewhat over-sympathetic account is H. D. Croly, *Marcus Alonzo Hanna* (1912). See also Thomas Beer, *Hanna* (1929); H. C. McCook, *The Senator: A Threnody* (1905); J. B. Foraker, *Notes of a Busy Life* (1916); H. H. Kohlsaat, *From McKinley to Harding* (1923); Carl Lorenz, *Tom L. Johnson* (1911); H. J. O'Higgins, *The Am. Mind in Action* (1924); C. S. Olcott, *The Life of Wm. McKinley* (1916); *The Autobiog. of Thomas Collier Platt* (1910); J. F. Rhodes, *The McKinley and Roosevelt Administrations* (1922); *Theodore Roosevelt, an Autobiog.* (1913); W. A. White, *Masks in a Pageant* (1928); C. W. Thompson, *Presidents I've Known and Two Near Presidents* (1929); Murat Halstead, in *Rev. of Revs.* (N. Y.), Oct. 1896; W. A. White, in *McClure's Mag.*, Nov. 1900; L. A. Coolidge, in *Rev. of Revs.* (N. Y.), Mar. 1904; R. M. Easley, "Senator Hanna and the Labor Problem," *Independent*, Mar. 3, 1904; memorial addresses in *Senate Doc. No. 321*, 58 Cong., 2 Sess.; *Cleveland Plain Dealer*, *N. Y. Times*, *Washington Post*, Feb. 16, 1904.]

A. C. C.

HANNEGAN, EDWARD ALLEN (June 25, 1807–Feb. 25, 1859), senator from Indiana, was born in Hamilton County, Ohio. During his infancy his parents moved to Lexington, Ky., where he received a good education and began to read law. In 1825 he journeyed to Vincennes, Ind., but finding too many lawyers there pushed on to the frontier town of Covington. While trying to make a start in the practice of his profession, he taught school and worked as a farm hand. In December 1829 he was chosen enrolling clerk by the lower house of the state legislature and on Jan. 23, 1830, was elected by the legislature on joint ballot to serve for two years as prosecuting attorney for the first judicial district of the state. In August 1831 he was elected a member of the lower house, and the following year, a member of the national House of Representatives, to which he was reëlected in 1834. As a member of the House (1833–37), he was a stanch supporter of the Jackson administration and won considerable repute as an orator. Failing to secure a third term in Congress, he offered himself as a candidate for the state House of Representatives in 1841 and was elected. Two years later he was elected—without a vote to spare and with one supporter a Whig—to the United States Senate, where he became an eloquent and aggressive champion of the policy of expansion, voicing the demand of the Old Northwest for the whole of the Oregon country, and leading his party before the nation with the cry "54° 40′ or fight." When Polk agreed to divide the Oregon country with Great Britain, Hannegan delivered philippics before the Senate against the President, but, thanks in part to Polk's tactfulness, the breach between them was afterward healed. In 1849, the Democrats in the General Assembly of Indiana deserted Hannegan and chose Gov. James Whitcomb to the Senate in his stead. On learning of Hannegan's defeat, his friends—both Whigs and Democrats—urged the President to find a place for him, and on Mar. 3, 1849, Polk appointed him to the new post of minister at Berlin. Hannegan's stay abroad was very brief. He was bold and outspoken, and also unable to control his appetite for drink. One or both of these failings would be sufficient to explain the request for his recall, which terminated his diplomatic service early in 1850.

He continued to have political aspirations, but his public career was ended. For a few years he again practised law at Covington, then moved to St. Louis, where he spent the last few years of his life, attaining a fair degree of success. This was after the death of his wife, Margaret Chambers Duncan, a sister of Capt. John R. Duncan of Newark, Ohio. At Covington, in 1852, Hannegan, under the influence of liquor, quarreled with this brother-in-law, whom he loved, and stabbed him. Captain Duncan, who seems to have been drinking also, had pressed the quarrel, and before he died absolved Hannegan from all blame. Hannegan, who lost his seat in the House in 1836 because of his intemperance, had then become a total abstainer. Aided by his wife, who stood by him through thick and thin, he struggled so successfully that he thought he had mastered himself. It was in this period of abstinence that he was elected to the Senate, but in Washington he again frequently fell into his old habits. He was a man of brilliant talents and was popularly believed to depend more on his natural gifts than on work, but he sometimes wrote out beforehand the eloquent speeches which were supposed to be spontaneous and he had an extensive library (*Lew Wallace: An Autobiography,* 1906, vol. I, ch. 23). He was a member of the Presbyterian Church. He was thoroughly sincere and hated dishonesty in private or public affairs.

[Two sketches of Hannegan's career, both inaccurate in details, are: W. W. Woollen, *Biog. and Hist. Sketches of Early Ind.* (1883), pp. 211–22; J. W. Whicker, "Edward A. Hannegan," in *Ind. Mag. of Hist.*, Dec. 1918. See also *The Diary of James K. Polk* (4 vols., 1910), ed. by M. M. Quaife; files of the *Indiana State Journal*, 1842, 1849, 1850, 1852, 1859, and of the *Indiana State Sentinel*, 1842, 1849, 1859; *Biog. Dir. Am. Cong.* (1928); *Sunday Morning Republican* (St. Louis), Feb. 27, 1859.]

W. O. L.

HANSEN, GEORGE (Apr. 15, 1863–Mar. 31, 1908), horticulturist, landscape architect, was born in the old town of Hildesheim in Hanover, Germany, the son of Adolph and Auguste Hansen. His mother was the daughter of J. G. K. Oberdieck, sometimes called the "father of German pomology," who on account of his services to the Prussian State had received the privilege of a free college education to such of his grandsons as desired to specialize in horticulture. Young Hansen, accordingly, after completing the Gymnasium course in his native town, was sent to Potsdam to become a student in the Royal College of Horticulture. After his graduation, in 1885, he went to England, entering the employ of F. Sander & Company. At first he worked with hybrids in the orchid house and later used his skill with a pencil in making illustrations for the orchid journal, *Reichenbachia.* His ability was soon recognized in London by election as fellow of the Royal Horticultural Society. It was at this time that he began the preparation of *The Orchid Hybrids,* a work requiring special knowledge and indefatigable industry and perseverance. An enumeration and classification of all the orchid hybrids made known up to that time, it was published in parts between 1895 and 1897.

After some two years in England, he determined to move far west, and accordingly, in 1887, settled in San Francisco, where he engaged in nursery propagation. His talents were soon in demand elsewhere, however. The central Sierra foothills, fertile and beautiful as found by the American pioneers in gold days, had been cruelly scarred and wastefully exploited by miner, logger, stockman, and hunter. To restore and improve the early-day agriculture, the University of California College of Agriculture established an experiment station in the Amador County foothills and, in 1889, appointed George Hansen as foreman of it. Here for seven years he used his science in behalf of the foothill farmer: introducing modern methods and new varieties; urging fencing and resting periods to restore the native grasses and clovers; and pleading always for protection of the native vegetative cover to save the land from erosion. No other botanist before him had been a resident of the foothills in the region of the Calaveras Big Trees. From the thin fringe of Digger Pine near the great plain of the Sacramento to the snowy summits of the Sierra he explored the plant formations at all altitudes and distributed herbarium sets of the native vegetation to the important botanical centers of the world, adding thereby a definite number of new species to the state's flora. In connection with this work he made the drawings for the second part (1890) of *West American Oaks* by Edward Lee Greene [*q.v.*]. This illustration work developed Hansen's field interest in the genus Quercus and enabled him to call the attention of botanists to remarkable variants of the native species of oak which he discovered in the region of the foothill station.

In 1896 he began work as landscape architect in Berkeley, especially in an advisory capacity to cities and towns confronted with park problems. Here he did a service in urging natural treatment. He was handicapped by an injury to his spine—the prime cause of his giving up the foothill station—but the Sierran experience had fortified his natural idealism and deepened his altruistic spirit; he continued his activities, buoyant, cheerful and eager, under a condition that to most men would have seemed crushing. With an especial love for children, he advanced the campaign for kindergartens as well as for city parks and playgrounds (see his *What is a Kindergarten?* 1901). He died in Berkeley, in his forty-fifth year, survived by his wife, Linda Frances (Rinehart) Hansen, whom he had married on Dec. 24, 1889.

[Chas. Murdock, in *Pacific Unitarian*, XVI, 180 (1908); W. L. Jepson, in *Madroño* (Berkeley, Cal.), Sept. 1928; *Who's Who in America*, 1908–09; Jepson Correspondence, vols. I, II (1894–97), MS.]

W. L. J.

HANSON, ALEXANDER CONTEE (Oct. 22, 1749–Jan. 16, 1806), jurist, was born in Annapolis, Md., the son of John [*q.v.*] and Jane (Contee) Hanson. His father was president of the Congress of the United States under the Articles of Confederation during the years 1781–82. Young Hanson obtained his education at the College of Philadelphia. After his graduation he studied law at Annapolis and was admitted to the Maryland bar about 1772. In August 1776, following the outbreak of the Revolution, he was appointed assistant private secretary to Gen. George Washington, but because of ill health, was forced to resign toward the close of the year. On Mar. 9, 1778, he became an associate judge of the general court of Maryland and held office until 1781. He was married on June 4, 1778, to Rebeca [*sic*] Howard at Annapolis. Their second son was Alexander C. Hanson [*q.v.*], the noted Federalist editor.

During the early months of 1780 a plan was formulated by certain Loyalists to release British prisoners of war held in Frederick County. On July 25, 1780, seven leaders of the movement were arrested and confined in Frederick Town. They were tried before a special court presided over by Hanson. The trial began June 27, 1781, and lasted ten days, all seven defendants being found guilty of high treason. In pronouncing sentence, Judge Hanson declared that "in view of the attitude of mockery of the accused and their apparent belief that America dared not punish Tories conspiring against her, and in view of the dreadful consequences if they had succeeded, they ought to suffer to the full the penalty for high treason" (Andrews, *post,* I, 654). He sentenced all seven to be hanged, drawn, and quartered. Such severity brought a quick reaction, and in 1782 a law was passed ordering that any one assisting or advising prisoners of war to escape should, if able-bodied, be sentenced to war vessels for three years; and if not able-bodied, should suffer fine or imprisonment, or both.

In 1786 in order to defeat the attempt of the City of Baltimore to remove the state capital from Annapolis, Hanson wrote *Considerations on the Proposed Removal of the Seat of Government; Addressed to the Citizens of Maryland by Aristides.* Under the same signature, in the following year, he published *Remarks on the Proposed Plan of a Federal Government,* designed to make clear the real object and purpose of government under the Federal Constitution, and on Apr. 28, 1788, in the convention at Annapolis, he gave his voice for the ratification of the Constitution. In both elections of Washington, he was a Maryland presidential elector. In 1787 he completed the compilation of the *Laws of Maryland Made Since M,DCC,LXIII* (1787), authorized by the legislature in 1784 and issued by the state printer at Annapolis. He was appointed chancellor of Maryland on Oct. 30, 1789, and served in that capacity until his death seventeen years later. Shortly after this appointment he was designated by the governor to prepare a digest of the testamentary laws of Maryland. In 1803, he issued under the signature "A Civil Officer of Maryland," *Publications Relative to the Difference of Opinion between the Governor and Council of Maryland on Their Respective Powers,* which consisted principally of reprints of political articles. He died of apoplexy, in Annapolis.

[G. A. Hanson, *Old Kent* (1876); *Md. Hist. Mag.*, June, Sept. 1911, Mar. 1926; *Tercentenary Hist. of Md.* (1925), vol. I, by M. P. Andrews, vol. IV, by H. F. Powell; G. M. Brumbaugh, *Maryland Records* (1928); E. S. Riley, *The Ancient City—A Hist. of Annapolis in Md.* (1887); *Federal Gazette & Baltimore Daily Advertiser,* Jan. 18, 1806.] W. G. E.

HANSON, ALEXANDER CONTEE (Feb. 27, 1786–Apr. 23, 1819), editor, representative and senator from Maryland, was born at Annapolis, the second son of Alexander Contee Hanson [*q.v.*] and Rebeca (Howard) Hanson. He was graduated from St. John's College in 1802, and practised law in his native city. He came from a line of fighting patriots and was nourished in Federalism as in a religion. In 1808 he founded a newspaper, the *Federal Republican,* in Baltimore, to represent extreme Federalist opinion. As editor-in-chief he secured Jacob Wagner, who had served in the State Department under Pickering and entertained an absolute aversion toward Jefferson and Madison. Hanson shared the conviction of most Federalists that the Republican statesmen were "bound over" to French interests, and Wagner's "inside information" concerning diplomacy was freely used to spread this view. For statements conceived to be "mutinous and highly reproachful to the President" made in an article on the Embargo, published Nov. 7, 1808, Hanson, who was a lieutenant in the 39th Regiment of Maryland militia, was court-martialed, but he defended himself with ability and success. As the country drifted toward war with England the *Federal Republican* became more bitter. Numerous threats were issued against it. On June 20, 1812, two days after the declaration of war, an editorial appeared, beginning "Thou hast done a deed whereat Valour will weep." The policy of the paper was defined as opposition to the war and hostility to Madison, who was stigmatized as the tool of Bonaparte. On June 22, a mob of infuriated Republicans demolished the newspaper plant, even tearing down the walls. Thereupon, following the advice of influential Federalists, Hanson decided to take a stand for freedom of opinion and of the press. A building was secured at 45 Charles St., and transformed into a veritable arsenal. On July 27, the paper was reissued from Georgetown, D. C., but circulated from Baltimore. This issue of the journal contained an attack upon the city government for favoritism toward the leaders of the Baltimore mob. The following day the house on Charles Street was surrounded and doors and windows were smashed. The Federalists responded with gun shots. One man was killed in the crowd. The militia deported itself irresolutely. Finally, when a cannon was dragged before the newspaper office, the defenders consented to compromise with the mayor of Baltimore and the commander of the militia. In return for promises of safety for life and property, they consented to a temporary surrender. Neither of these promises was fulfilled, however. The place of safety proved to be the jail, which, since the militia was immediately disbanded, was easily forced during the night. A butcher and a French tailor led the mob. The offending Federalists were clubbed into insensibility and hurled out upon the jail steps where the attack was continued with penknives, matches, and candle-grease poured upon the eyelids. Gen. James M. Lingan was killed and Gen. Henry (Light-Horse Harry) Lee received injuries from which he never fully recovered. Hanson was beaten into unconsciousness, but later was assisted to escape to his country estate. By Aug. 3, he was reissuing his paper from Georgetown.

Baltimore exonerated the rioters, and although the committee of grievances and courts of justice of the Maryland House of Delegates later upheld the Federalists, a wave of apprehension was felt lest this violent outbreak should prove the precursor of Republican terrorism. This Federalist reaction brought about Hanson's election to Congress. He took his seat in March 1813, continuing his anti-administration charges in the House. In 1816, he resigned in the hope of saving the local Federalist cause by entering state politics, but he failed in the elections for the House of Delegates. He was then appointed United States senator to complete the term of Senator Harper (resigned), and he served in this capacity from Jan. 2, 1817, until his death. Ill health prevented him from continuous activity in the Senate. Hanson married Priscilla Dorsey, June 24, 1805. He died at his estate, "Belmont," near Elkridge.

[The Md. Hist. Soc. possesses manuscript letters of Hanson to George C. Washington, 1817–18, and a collection called "Hanson Pamphlets," being the writings of Hanson's father, which contains a manuscript introduction, written (1851–52) by C. W. Hanson, treating of the family history. Accounts of the Baltimore riots are found in J. B. McMaster, *A Hist. of the People of the U. S.,* vol. III (1892); Henry Adams, *Hist. of the U. S. A.,* vol. VI (1891); J. T. Scharf, *Hist. of Md.* (1879), vol. III; and D. T. Lynch, *An Epoch and a Man: Martin Van Buren* (1929). See also *Trial of Alexander Contee Hanson, Esq., A Lieutenant in a Company of Militia,* etc. (1809); *Interesting Papers Relative to the Recent Riots at Baltimore* (1812); *Baltimore Patriot and Mercantile Advertiser,* Apr. 24, 1819; files of the *Federal Republican.*] K. J. G.

HANSON, JOHN (Apr. 13, 1721–Nov. 22, 1783), Revolutionary leader, member of the Continental Congress, son of Samuel and Elizabeth

(Story) Hanson, was descended from Roger de Rastrick, who was living in Yorkshire, England, in the middle of the thirteenth century. (The name was changed from De Rastrick to Hanson, Henry's son, in 1330.) A descendant married a connection of the Swedish royal family; and his son became an officer in the army of Gustavus Adolphus. In 1642 four sons of this soldier were sent by Queen Christina to the New World in the care of John Printz, governor of New Sweden. They removed from Tinicum Island, in the Delaware River, to Kent Island, Md., in 1653, and about three years later the youngest of the four, John Hanson, established the family in Charles County. His son, Samuel, was elected a member of the General Assembly of Maryland in 1716 and 1728, and served his county as sheriff, commissary, clerk, and member of the board of visitors of the county school. John, Samuel's son, was born at "Mulberry Grove," Charles County, in 1721. He entered public life in 1757 as a representative of Charles County in the Assembly, and served nearly every year from 1757 to 1773, when he removed to Frederick County. Under the influence of that progressive frontier section of the province he continued to serve in the Assembly until his election, in 1779, as a delegate to the Continental Congress.

Hanson was a member of the committee of the legislature which drafted instructions to the Maryland delegates to the Stamp-Act Congress in New York (1765). He signed the non-importation agreement of Maryland, which was adopted June 22, 1769, at a meeting of county committees as a protest against the Townshend Acts. He was chairman of the meeting in Frederick County which in June 1774 passed resolutions to stop all trade with Great Britain and the West Indies until the Acts of Parliament blockading the Port of Boston were repealed. As a member of the Maryland Convention, he signed July 26, 1775, the Association of the Freemen of Maryland which approved the use of arms to repel British troops. As chairman of the Committee of Observation, first for all Frederick County and subsequently for the Middle District, Hanson was active in raising troops and providing arms and ammunition. He was one of a committee of three chosen by the Maryland Convention to establish a gun-lock factory in Frederick. In July 1775 he wrote to the president of the Continental Congress warning him of an expedition by Loyalists and Indians against the Maryland frontier, a danger which was removed only by the arrest of the leaders, Nov. 19, 1775, near Hagerstown. Under Hanson's leadership the delegates from Frederick County to the Maryland Convention advocated independence several months before such sentiment was dominant in the other counties, and he held that every resolution of the Convention tending to separate Maryland from a majority of the colonies without the consent of the people was destructive of its internal safety. The Maryland Assembly elected him a delegate to the Continental Congress on Dec. 22, 1779. He took his seat in that body June 14, 1780. At this time the Maryland delegates were alone in refusing to ratify the Articles of Confederation. They had instructions not to ratify until Virginia and other states had relinquished their claims to the unsettled territory extending westward to the Mississippi River. John Hanson and his colleague Daniel Carroll [*q.v.*] labored successfully for this relinquishment. The ratification of the Articles of Confederation was completed Mar. 1, 1781, and on Nov. 5 of that year Hanson was elected president of the Congress of the Confederacy. He retired from public life at the close of his term of one year and died at Oxon Hill, Prince Georges County. Hanson's wife was Jane Contee of Prince Georges County. They had nine children, one of whom, Alexander Contee Hanson [*q.v.*], became chancellor of Maryland.

[Geo. A. Hanson, *Old Kent* (1876); J. T. Scharf, *Hist. of Western Md.* (1882); T. J. C. Williams, *Hist. of Frederick County, Md.* (1910); J. M. Hammond, *Colonial Mansions of Md. and Del.* (1914); *Tercentenary Hist. of Md.* (1925), vol. IV, by H. F. Powell; "Proceedings in the Senate and House of Representatives upon the Reception and Acceptance from the State of Maryland of the Statues of Charles Carroll of Carrollton, and of John Hanson, Erected in Statuary Hall of the Capitol," *Cong. Record*, 57 Cong., 2 Sess., pp. 1506 ff., 1541 ff., and *Sen. Doc. No. 13*, 58 Cong., Special Sess.; *Maryland Gazette* (Annapolis), Nov. 27, 1783.]

N. D. M.

HANSON, ROGER WEIGHTMAN (Aug. 27, 1827–Jan. 4, 1863), Confederate general, was born in Winchester, Ky., the second son of Samuel Hanson, lawyer and member of the legislature, and of Matilda (Calloway) Hanson. His father, who came of the Maryland Hanson family and was a native of Alexandria, Va., had moved to Kentucky in 1807. By nature impetuous and daring, Roger Weightman Hanson served as first lieutenant in the Mexican War under Capt. J. S. ("Cerro Gordo") Williams. In a duel after his return he received a wound which shortened one leg and gave him thereafter a peculiar gait. During convalescence he read law. He began to practise at home, then went to California with the gold rush, but returned with nothing added to his fortune. In 1851, opposing his old commander for a seat in the legislature, he lost by six votes; but two years later he was successful and became a representative from Clark County. In 1855 he removed to Lexington and won the election from Fayette County. He was an elector on the Fillmore ticket in 1856 and the following year ran unsuccessfully for Congress as a Know-Nothing. In 1860, on the eve of the great crisis, he stood forth as a conservative leader, favoring Bell and Everett in the presidential campaign; but, as events unfolded, resenting the domination of the Union by the North, he joined that neutrality movement peculiar to Kentucky, and was enrolled as colonel of the State Guards. When the crisis became acute, he joined the forces of the Confederacy, leading his regiment across the border to Camp Boone, Clarksville, Tenn., where his men formed the nucleus of the 2nd, 3rd, 4th, and 5th Kentucky regiments (Collins, *post,* I, 342). Here and elsewhere, known familiarly as "Old Flintlock," he excelled as a drillmaster, and at the same time won the loyalty of his men. On Feb. 13, 1862, he held the Confederate right at Fort Donelson, where he repulsed two attacks (*War of the Rebellion: Official Records, Army,* 1 ser., VII, 330). Two days later his regiment made a successful charge, "without firing a gun," against a superior force which broke and fled (*Ibid.*). On the same day he was captured. He was later exchanged, and in October 1862 was restored to his old command, the 2nd Kentucky Infantry. By order of General Breckinridge he received command of the 1st Brigade, consisting of the 2nd, 4th, 6th, and 9th Kentucky Infantry regiments, together with Graves's and Cobb's batteries. At Nashville he effectively aided Forrest, Nov. 5, and a month later, Dec. 7, 1862, while attached to Gen. J. H. Morgan's expedition against Hartsville, he captured and destroyed a Union force of some 2,000 men with a loss of only sixty-eight (*Official Records, supra,* 1 ser., XX, pt. 1, p. 68). For his conspicuous services he was promoted to be brigadier-general on Dec. 13. Less than three weeks later, at the battle of Stone's River or Murfreesboro, where his brigade held the left of the line, he was mortally wounded (Jan. 2, 1863). He died after two days of suffering, and was buried at Nashville. In 1866, with permission of the War Department, his body was removed by his widow, Virginia (Peters) Hanson, to Lexington, Ky., and reinterred with public honors. In many respects his career was typical of the gradual alienation of sympathy in his state from the strong Union views of the fifties to the anti-administration attitude in the late sixties, when honors readily bestowed upon Confederate heroes were rarely extended to former Union officers.

[Besides the *Official Records* cited above, see the *Lexington Observer and Reporter,* 1857–59; *Biog. Encyc. of Ky.* (1878); E. P. Thompson, *Hist. of the First Kentucky Brigade* (1868); *Reminiscences of Gen. Basil W. Duke* (1911), ch. VII; *Confed. Mil. Hist.* (1899), IX, 239; Lewis and R. H. Collins, *Hist. of Ky.* (1874), I, 342.] E. T.

HAPGOOD, ISABEL FLORENCE (Nov. 21, 1850–June 26, 1928), translator, journalist, author, opened to the English reading world the work of great Russian authors at a period when they were known in the West chiefly by distortions coming through the French. Nothing in her colonial English-Scotch ancestry appears to explain her extraordinary gift for languages. She was the daughter of Asa and Lydia (Crossley) Hapgood. Born in Boston, she grew up in Worcester, Mass., the family home between 1855 and 1881. She left school at eighteen, after three years at Miss Porter's seminary, Farmington, Conn. During the next decade or two she made her own practically all the languages of Continental Europe, including various Russian dialects and Old Church Slavonic. With Latin and French to her credit, she explored the Romance languages; after German lessons, she explored the Germanic tongues. She had labored for two years at Russian with dictionary and grammar before she chanced to meet a Russian lady who taught her the pronunciation. When, however, she made her first journey to Russia in 1887, she spoke freely enough to make friends in every walk of life. She says the very police dogs wagged their tails at her. For two years she traveled widely, meeting many literary lights, and making an extended visit to Count Tolstoy at his summer estate. Her experiences she embodied in a volume, *Russian Rambles* (1895), which, lighted by humor and shrewd observation, swept away many travelers' myths about country and people. She began to publish her translations from the Russian while dense ignorance of Russia still prevailed in the West. The year 1886 was marked by the appearance of Tolstoy's *Childhood, Boyhood, Youth,* several volumes of Gogol's tales and his great historical novel, *Tarás Búlba,* and *Epic Songs of Russia* with critical notes. Two years later appeared her authorized version of Tolstoy's *Life.* Her rendering of Tolstoy, Turgenev, Gorky, and Gogol set, according to the *Nation,* a new standard for fidelity in translation, and distinctly enriched our literature. They achieved immense popularity, the translator becoming as widely known as the author of a modern best-seller. She translated also from minor Russian authors, from the Dutch and Polish, the French of Victor Hugo, Renan, and De Coubertin, the Italian of De Amicis, and the Spanish of Palacio-Valdés.

In 1902 she published *A Survey of Russian Literature*; in 1906, a *Service Book of the Holy Orthodox Catholic Apostolic (Greco-Russian) Church,* designed for the use of the Russian Church in America, in which Old Church Slavonic ritual was collated with that of the Greek Church. She contributed to magazines articles on Russian subjects. For more than a score of years she served as foreign correspondent and reviewer for the *Nation* and the New York *Evening Post,* interpreting the literature of Europe to America. On her second visit to Russia in 1917 she had a long conference with the Czarina shortly before the Revolution. She was in Moscow at its outbreak, but her personal acquaintance with Russian officials enabled her to escape to Vladivostok. Her letters on phases of Soviet Russia appeared in the *New York Times.* A book on Russian church music, material for which she collected during her last trip, remains unpublished. Her home was in Boston from 1881 to 1889, after that in New York, where she died.

[Warren Hapgood, *The Hapgood Family* (1898); *Who's Who in America,* 1928–29; *Nation,* July 11, 1928; *N. Y. Times,* June 27, 1928, editorial, June 28.]
M. B. H.

HAPPER, ANDREW PATTON (Oct. 20, 1818–Oct. 27, 1894), Presbyterian missionary to Canton, China, was born in Washington County, Pa., near Monongahela City, the son of Baptist and Ann (Arrell) Happer. His mother early dedicated him to the ministry, and at the age of eleven he was sent to the preparatory department of Jefferson College. When he was fourteen years of age he resolved to become a missionary, and, to prepare for that profession, after graduating from Jefferson (1835) and teaching five years, he studied theology in the Western Theological Seminary, 1840–43. Having begun the study of medicine while still in theological school, in 1843 he went to Philadelphia to complete his medical course and in 1844 graduated from the University of Pennsylvania with the degree of M.D.

After first preferring India as a field for his life work, he finally chose China, then being partially opened to Protestant missionary efforts by the treaties of 1842 and 1844. He was ordained to the Presbyterian ministry Apr. 23, 1844, and in June of that year sailed for China, arriving late in October. For the first three years he spent most of his time in Macao, but in 1847 he was able to effect a residence in the suburbs of Canton, and that city henceforth became the center of his labors. For several years he engaged in preaching and in school and medical work. With the arrival of John G. Kerr [*q.v.*] in 1854, he largely discontinued the practice of medicine, but he maintained his pastoral and educational activities. In 1854, after ten years in China, he baptized his first convert. He was long in charge of the First Presbyterian Church of Canton, preaching there Sundays and weekdays, and ministered to offshoots of that body. For many years he conducted a school for the training of Chinese preachers and for a time was the head of a Chinese government school in Canton. He wrote voluminously, both in Chinese and English; from 1880 through 1884 he was editor of the *Chinese Recorder*; and he assisted in the revision of Bridgman and Culbertson's translation of the Bible, and in the translation of the New Testament into the Canton colloquial.

In 1884 Happer returned to the United States, ill, his life's work apparently at an end; but, partially recovering, he raised over $100,000 for the fulfilment of one of his dreams, the establishment of a Christian college in China. In 1888 he returned to Canton to found the institution—which was later to grow into Canton Christian College and then into Lingnan University—and was in charge of it until, in 1891, ill health again compelled his retirement to America, this time permanently. His last years were spent in Wooster, Ohio. He was married three times: Nov. 11, 1847, to Elizabeth S. Ball (died Dec. 29, 1864), the daughter of a missionary in Canton; Oct. 6, 1869, to Miss A. L. Elliott (died 1873); and Mar. 18, 1875, to Hannah J. Shaw. Three of his daughters served for longer or shorter periods as missionaries in Canton.

[*Ann. Reports of the Board of Foreign Missions of the Presbyt. Ch. in the U. S. A.*; *New York Observer,* Nov. 8, 1894; H. C. Trumbull, *Old Time Student Volunteers* (1902); S. P. Scovel, in *Missionary Review of the World,* Apr. 1895, based in part on a manuscript autobiography; *The Chinese Recorder and Missionary Jour.,* Jan. 1895; *China Mission Hand-Book* (Shanghai, 1896); *Commemorative Biog. Record of Washington County, Pa.* (1893).]
K. S. L.

HARADEN, JONATHAN (Nov. 11, 1744–Nov. 23, 1803), naval officer and privateersman of the Revolution, was born in Gloucester, Mass. His parents were Joseph and Joanna (Emerson) Haraden. As a boy he was taken to Salem by Joseph Cabot. His sea service in the Revolution began in July 1776, as lieutenant on the sloop *Tyrannicide,* of the Massachusetts state navy, commanded by Capt. John Fisk. Two successful cruises were made during the year. In 1777 Haraden was given command of the *Tyrannicide,* now changed to a brigantine. He cruised about the British Isles and France in company with Captain Fisk who had been transferred to the brigantine *Massachusetts.* They took several prizes, including a transport with Hessian troops. They were chased by a British squadron and the *Tyrannicide* had a narrow escape. She returned to Boston in August, sailed again in the fall, and during the winter cruised in the West Indies. In the summer of 1778 Haraden left the state service to begin his career as a privateersman in command of the 16-gun ship *General Pickering* of Salem. At first he sailed with cargoes to France and Spain and return, but later, as a privateer, devoted his ship wholly to commerce destroying. He was in many actions, sometimes with vessels of superior force, and took many prizes. In October 1779, off Sandy Hook, the *Pickering* engaged simultaneously three letters of marque, of 14, 10, and 8 guns. After an action of an hour and a half she captured all three and took them into port. In June 1780, in the Bay of Biscay, she took a 22-gun schooner and a few days later fell in with the British privateer *Achilles,* a much larger ship than the *Pickering* and of more than three times her force. They fought nearly three hours at close range and the *Achilles* then sheered off and sailed away. The *Pickering* was unable to follow, but recaptured her prize, which had been taken by the *Achilles.* This battle was fought close to the Spanish coast and was watched by a multitude of people. Early in 1781 the *Pickering* was captured by Admiral Rodney at St. Eustatius, and Haraden was made a prisoner of war. After regaining his liberty, he commanded the 14-gun ship *Julius Cæsar,* another Salem privateer, in which he sailed in 1782. In June he fought a British ship and brig, of 18 and 16 guns, for two and a half hours and then escaped from them. Haraden, besides being a thorough seaman, was a man of courage and resourcefulness. Cool and collected when the odds were against him, he never refused to fight a stronger foe, if brought to bay, and never knew when he was whipped. Although several times engaged with superior force, he was never captured until he fell into the trap set by Rodney for the unwary. His men were devoted to him, he inspired them with confidence, and they learned to expect victory. He was married three times: on June 8, 1767, to Hannah, daughter of William Deadman; on Mar. 11, 1782, to Mrs. Eunice (Diman) Mason, daughter of Rev. James Diman, of Salem; and on Oct. 12, 1797, to Mrs. Mary Scallon. He had two daughters. After the Revolution his health failed and he became reduced to narrow circumstances. At the end of a lingering illness he died in Salem at the age of fifty-nine.

[*Vital Records of Gloucester, Mass.* (1917), I, 318; *Vital Records of Salem, Mass.,* III (1924), 468, V (1925), 309; Sidney Perley, *Hist. of Salem* (1928); Freeman Hunt, *Lives of Am. Merchants* (1858), II, 34–42; *Diary of William Bentley,* III (1911), 62; *Salem Register,* Nov. 24, 1803; R. D. Paine, *The Ships and Sailors of Old Salem* (1909), ch. V; full references to the manuscript sources in the Mass. State Archives and to other material, in G. W. Allen, *Naval Hist. of the Am. Revolution* (2 vols., 1913), and *Mass. Privateers of the Revolution* (1927).]

G. W. A.

HARAHAN, JAMES THEODORE (Jan. 12, 1841–Jan. 22, 1912), railroad official, was born in Lowell, Mass., the son of Patrick and Rose (McCurn) Harahan. He attended the public schools of Lowell until he was seventeen, when he began his railroad career as clerk for the Boston & Providence Railroad Company at Boston. His work was interrupted by his enlistment in Company G of the 1st Massachusetts Infantry. He was in the army for three years, was wounded at the battle of Gettysburg, and was mustered out on May 25, 1864. He then returned to railroad service and began at the very bottom of the ladder as a switchman on the Orange & Alexandria Railroad in Virginia. During the years 1865 to 1870 he worked in various capacities, for a time in the employ of the Nashville & Decatur Railroad at Nashville, Tenn., and for a time in that of the Louisville & Nashville Railroad. Rising from clerk to section boss and finally railway executive, he went through every grade of railroad service, and his demonstrated capacity led to frequent calls from one company to another. From 1870 to 1872 he was in charge of the Shelby Railroad (eighteen miles long) in Kentucky, for seven years he was roadmaster of the Nashville & Decatur, for two years superintendent of the Memphis line of the Louisville & Nashville, and for the next two years superintendent of the New Orleans division of the same road. In 1883 he was made general superintendent of the road south of Decatur, and the following year general manager of the entire road. In 1885 he was off to the Baltimore & Ohio as general manager of the Pittsburgh division, but after three months he returned to the Louisville & Nashville, serving as assistant general manager and general manager. The period between Oct. 1, 1888, and Nov. 1, 1890, was again one of trial and promotion: he was successively assistant general manager of the Lake Shore & Michigan Southern, general manager of the Chesapeake & Ohio, and general manager of the Louisville, New Orleans, & Texas railroads. On the last date he became second vice-president of the Illinois Central Railroad, in charge of operation and traffic. One of his signal services in this position was his handling of the suburban traffic during the World's Columbian Exposition in 1893, when millions of passengers between the city and the fair grounds were adequately cared for by his road.

In 1906, Harahan was elected president of the Illinois Central in place of Stuyvesant Fish [*q.v.*], who had been deposed from the presidency. He retired from active service in 1911, at the age of seventy, and started work of a consulting character. He was killed in a railroad wreck in January 1912 while still in vigorous possession of his faculties and well qualified to carry on important work for a number of years.

Harahan was a successful railroad executive and seemed to have a peculiar faculty which fitted him to handle the railroad problems as they were constituted during the time he was engaged in railroad work. He believed in contact with the public so that they might appreciate the problems and difficulties of the railroads, and was a pioneer in developing that sort of railroad management. He was extremely industrious and very conscientious in the performance of his work. He was solicitous for the welfare of the employees, and was esteemed by them for his interest and justice in dealing with them. He took an active part in the life of the several communities in which he lived during his career. In 1866 he was married to Mary Kehoe, who died in March 1897, and on Apr. 19, 1899, he was married to Mary N. Mallory, daughter of Capt. W. B. Mallory of Memphis, Tenn. He had four children by his first marriage.

[*Who's Who in America*, 1910–11; *The Book of Chicagoans*, 1911; George Kennan, *E. H. Harriman: A Biog.* (1922), vol. II, ch. XX; *Railway World*, Jan. 26, 1912; *Railway and Engineering Rev.*, Jan. 27, 1912; *Nashville Banner*, Jan. 22, 1912; *Commercial Appeal* (Memphis), Jan. 22, 26, 1912; *N. Y. Times*, *Chicago Daily Tribune*, Jan. 23, 1912; names of parents and date of birth from Harahan's son, W. J. Harahan, Richmond, Va.]

E. L. B.

HARASZTHY DE MOKCSA, AGOSTON (*c.* 1812–July 6, 1869), pioneer, was born at Futtak, in the country of Bács-Bodrog, Hungary, the son of Charles Haraszthy, a landed proprietor. He entered the Royal Hungarian Body Guard, and was later private secretary to the viceroy of Hungary. He came to the United States in 1840 and eventually went to Wisconsin, where on the Wisconsin River he founded what is the present village of Sauk City, first named by him "Széptáj" (*i.e.*, Belleview), then "Haraszthy," and later called Westfield. Going into partnership with an Englishman, Robert Bryant, he began erecting a house, brick store (which still stands), school, and sawmill, and immediately attracted German, English, and Swiss emigrants. In 1842 he went to Hungary, sold his estate, and returned to America with his wife, Eleanora Dödinsky, and his three sons. He published an account of his adventures, in Hungarian, *Utazás Éjszak-Amerikabán* (2 vols., Pest, 1844). On his return to Sauk City, he opened a brick yard and began the manufacture of brick, Oct. 25, 1842. He planted the first hop yard in Wisconsin; operated the first ferryboat across the Wisconsin River at Sauk City (Oct. 14, 1844); and as the head of an emigrant association, brought colonists to the place. He also erected the first frame structure in the Baraboo Valley, at Baraboo, in 1845, and conducted a store there.

Afflicted with asthma and advised by physicians to seek a milder climate, in April 1849 he set out with his family for California, arriving in San Diego after an adventurous trip of nine months. Here he fought the Indians successfully and was elected county sheriff in 1850 and a member of the state legislature in 1852. In March of that year he imported the first vines which were planted in the vicinity of San Francisco. They were Tokay and Zinfandel, sent to him by friends in Hungary, and the celebrated Shiras vine from Persia. In 1857 he was appointed assayer and then smelter and refiner at the San Francisco Mint but resigned after a few months under a charge of embezzlement, of which he was later acquitted. Together with three Hungarians, Urnay, Wass, and Molitor, with whom he had been associated at the Mint, he bought a choice piece of land in the Sonoma Valley, a short distance from Buena Vista, and there in 1858 the first large vineyard in California was planted. He continued importing, and about the end of 1862 he and his associates had 300 acres of vineland under cultivation. In 1861 he was appointed by the legislature a commissioner "to report upon ways and means best adapted to promote the improvement and culture of the grape-vine in California," and in this capacity he made a tour of the wine-producing countries of Europe, bringing with him upon his return about three hundred distinct varieties of vines, and other fruit in addition. His report was published under the title, *Grape Culture, Wines, and Wine-Making; with Notes upon Agriculture and Horticulture* (1862). In 1863 he formed his Sonoma properties into a corporation, called "The Buena Vista Viticultural Society," with 300 acres of vineland and 5,000 acres of farm land. Having lost all his holdings in 1866, he moved with his oldest son, his wife, and his father to Nicaragua, where he acquired 100,000 acres of some of the best land in Central America and obtained a license to plant sugarcane and to manufacture sugar. Upon this plantation, the Hacienda San Antonio, near the port of Corinto, he met an accidental death by drowning. In addition to his report mentioned above, Haraszthy published a report on his farm, grapes, and wine, and on the early history of viticulture in California, in *Transactions of the California State Agricultural Society During the Year 1858* (1859). His catalogue of the trees and vines which he brought from Europe was published posthumously as *Addenda* to the second edition, revised (1881), of the *First Annual Report* of the Board of State Viticultural Commissioners, of which his son Arpad was president.

[Haraszthy's papers, letters, and documents are in the custody of the State Hist. Soc. of Wis., Madison. Published material includes: H. E. Cole, *A Standard Hist. of Sauk County, Wis.* (2 vols., 1892); W. H. Canfield, *Outline Sketches of Sauk County* (1861); A. J. Turner, "The Hist. of Fort Winnebago" in *Wis. Hist. Colls.*, vol. XIV (1898); V. S. Pease, "Agoston Haraszthy," in *Proc. State Hist. Soc. of Wis., 1906* (1907); *Trans. of the Old Settlers' Asso. of Sauk County, Wis.* (1872); H. H. Bancroft, *California inter Pocula* (1888), and *Hist. of Calif.*, vol. VII (1890); C. A. Menefee, *Hist. and Descriptive Sketch Book of Napa, Sonoma, etc.* (1873); W. G. Smith, *The Story of San Diego* (1892); W. E. Smythe, *Hist. of San Diego* (1907); Tom Gregory, *Hist. of Sonoma County, Calif.* (1911); Arpad Haraszthy, "Wine Making in California," *Overland Monthly*, Dec. 1871.] C. F.

HARBAUGH, HENRY (Oct. 28, 1817–Dec. 28, 1867), German Reformed clergyman, author, was born in Washington Township, Franklin County, Pa., almost on the Maryland line, the tenth of the twelve children of George and Anna (Snyder) Harbaugh. He was a great-grandson of Yost Harbaugh, a Swiss, who came to Pennsylvania about 1736 and settled eventually on Kreutz Creek in York County. Yost's descendants were devout, industrious, thrifty folk with little book-learning or concern for affairs beyond the confines of their parish. Henry, gnawed by vague ambitions, labored on his father's farm, attended a school in winter, conned an English grammar while the plowhorse rested in the furrow, and grew more restless each year. With his parents' reluctant consent he left home early in August 1836 and spent the next few years in Stark, Tuscarawas, and Carroll counties, Ohio, where he worked as a carpenter, organized singing classes, attended the New Hagerstown Academy, taught school, indited poems and elaborate letters to his friends, and gained his first experience as a public speaker. From 1840 to 1843 he was a student in Marshall College and the Seminary at Mercersburg in his native county; and under John Williamson Nevin [*q.v.*], his lifelong friend and master, he found himself. Licensed to preach Oct. 17, 1843, at Winchester, Va., he was pastor of the Lewisburg, Pa., charge, 1843–50, the First Church, Lancaster, 1850–60, and St. John's, Lebanon, 1860–63. He was married twice: on Dec. 14, 1843, to Louisa Goodrich of New Hagerstown, Ohio, who died Sept. 26, 1847, while visiting her parents; and on Nov. 14, 1848, to Maria Louisa Linn of Lewisburg, Pa., who survived him. One child by his first marriage and six by the second also outlived him.

He wrote constantly and well. In 1850 he launched a monthly magazine, the *Guardian*, and conducted it until December 1866, when he turned it over to Benjamin Bausman [*q.v.*] and revived the *Mercersburg Review*. Besides numerous minor publications and contributions to periodicals he was the author of *The Sainted Dead* (1848); *Heavenly Recognition* (1851); *The Heavenly Home* (1853); *Union with the Church* (1853); *The Birds of the Bible* (1854); *Life of Michael Schlatter* (1857); *Fathers of the German Reformed Church* (2 vols., 1857–58); *The True Glory of Woman* (1858); *Poems* (1860); *The Golden Censer* (1860); and *Christological Theology* (1864). A third volume of the *Fathers of the German Reformed Church* (1872) was edited for him after his death by David Y. Heisler, who added two more volumes to the series. He compiled a history of his family and was indefatigable in his search for papers, documents and traditions pertinent to the Reformed Church in Pennsylvania. At the suggestion of Philip Schaff [*q.v.*], who showed him Emanuel Rondthaler's "Morgeds un Oweds" (written about 1835), he produced a number of poems in the Pennsylvania-German dialect. Though he owed something to Burns and to Johann Peter Hebel, about whom he wrote an enthusiastic essay, Harbaugh was himself a genuine folk poet. The dialect was his mother tongue; he spoke it with a hearty appreciation of its earthy flavors and communicated through it, as he could have through no other medium, the reminiscences, whether tender or humorous, of his childhood and early youth. Fifteen of these poems were collected and published by Bausman as *Harbaugh's Harfe* (1870), which has been kept in print for over sixty years. Among Pennsylvania Germans "Das alt Schulhaus an der Krick," "Die Schlofschtub," "Der Pihwie," and "Heemweh" are esteemed as classics. Harbaugh also wrote several excellent hymns, including "Jesus, to Thy Cross I hasten," "Jesus, my Shepherd, let me share," and "Thou, by heav'nly hosts adored"; even better than these is his "Jesus, I live to Thee," the perfect expression of his own religious life.

He did more than any one else to popularize the "Mercersburg theology" and to make it a living force. A pulpit orator of extraordinary power, he filled the great churches of eastern Pennsylvania to overflowing wherever he preached. He was an active member of the committees that framed the *Liturgy, or Order of Christian Worship* (1857) and the *Order of Worship for the Reformed Church* (1866) and bore the brunt of the attack which they provoked from the conservative anti-liturgical wing of the denomination. In his own church at Lancaster Harbaugh was unable to preserve anything approaching unanimity of feeling, and in consequence he withdrew to the charge at Lebanon. In 1863 he was called to Mercersburg as professor in the Theological Seminary, and there during the few years still allowed him he did his best work. His theological lectures (preserved in manuscript in the Seminary archives at Lancaster) are still considered the best formulation of the Christological theology of his school. He died, at the height of his powers, after an illness of several months and was buried at Mercersburg.

[The fullest account, the *Life of the Rev. Henry Harbaugh, D.D.* (1900), by his son Linn Harbaugh, provides a complete bibliography and sufficient guidance to the sources. See also Henry Harbaugh, *Annals of the Harbaugh Family in America* (1856); J. I. Good, *Hist. of the Reformed Church in the U. S. in the Nineteenth Century* (1911), pp. 366–67; D. S. Schaff, *Life of Philip Schaff* (1897), pp. 242–43; H. H. Reichard, "Pennsylvania-German Dialect Writings and Their Writers," *Proc. Pa.-Ger. Soc.*, vol. XXVI (1918); U. H. Heilman, "The Genesis of 'Der Pihwie' with Reminiscences of its Author," *Lebanon County Hist. Soc. Papers*, vol. VII (Lebanon, Pa., 1919).]

G. H. G.

HARBEN, WILLIAM NATHANIEL (July 5, 1858–Aug. 7, 1919), novelist, son of Nathaniel Parks and Myra (Richardson) Harben, was born in Dalton, Ga., and died in New York City. His first Harben ancestor in America came to Virginia from Somersetshire in 1625; another ancestor was a brother of Daniel Boone; and on his mother's side he was related to the Bowman family of Virginia and Kentucky. As a child in Dalton he was an indifferent student, more engrossed in writing fiction after the manner of Cooper than in learning to cast accounts. Yet once out of school he was a merchant until he was thirty, sometimes in Georgia, sometimes in Tennessee, and always in arrears. In 1888 he determined to try his fortune as a writer, and shortly afterward he moved to New York. The next year he published *White Marie,* a book which dealt tragically with some of the complexities of life that grew out of the institution of negro slavery. Its reception in the North was mildly gratifying, but for all his claim that the book was not a hostile commentary, people in the South did not take to it or remember him for a while cordially. In seven slight books he published between 1890 and 1901 he kept safely apart from inter-racial subjects; after writing of the discrepancy that sometimes exists between religious profession and performance, he confined himself to stories of detectives, of far-wandering balloons, and of literary life in New York. During 1891–93 he was assistant editor of the *Youth's Companion.* In 1896 he was married to Maybelle Chandler of Williamsburg County, S. C. His *Northern Georgia Sketches* (1900), "dedicated to Joel Chandler Harris whose kindly encouragement made this book possible," is made up of ten stories that had already appeared in *The Century, Lippincott's,* and other magazines. Here he definitely struck the popular taste. The Harpers now solicited the manuscript "Westerfelt," which they had rejected, and, publishing it in 1901, inaugurated the series of novels which he was to write at a rate of slightly more than one a year for the rest of his life, dealing primarily with the land and people —chiefly the white people—of northern Georgia. He knew that region—man and woman, villager and countryman and mountaineer—and he set it forth with sound if not powerful realism, with some humor if without large philosophy, in an extended saga, with *Abner Daniel* (1902) and *Ann Boyd* (1906) as its most notable elements. Except for *Mam' Linda* (1907), which deprecates lynching, and *The Divine Event* (1920), which is laid in New York, all of his novels after 1901 occupy themselves mainly with very much the same setting and the same types of character; indeed, one character may appear in several different books. Many critics consistently applauded this long record, and William Dean Howells, perhaps the most distinguished of them, praised extravagantly (see Introduction to Harben's *The Triumph,* 1917) its portrayal of women. Harben once wrote of himself that he was afraid none of his books fairly represented him personally—he had "lived so very, very much and felt so much, and suffered, and enjoyed, and gloated and despaired" (*Library of Southern Literature,* V, 2075); but the photographs of him and the exemplary roster of his dedications to most of his family and to many friends seem to indicate that the turbulence of his spirit was sufficiently well disciplined not to set him beyond the ordinary reach of people's affection.

[*Library of Southern Lit.,* vol. V (1909); *Who's Who in America,* 1918–21; *N. Y. Times,* Aug. 8, 1919; M. L. Rutherford, *The South in Hist. and Lit.* (1907).]

J. D. W.

HARBY, ISAAC (Nov. 9, 1788–Dec. 14, 1828), journalist, playwright, was born and spent most of his life in Charleston, S. C. He was the son of Solomon Harby, whose father, lapidary to the Emperor of Morocco, fled to England for reasons unknown and there in 1787 married Rebecca, daughter of Meyer Moses. Solomon emigrated to Jamaica in his twenty-first year and thence to Charleston. His son Isaac attended Dr. Best's academy, evinced considerable precocity, and aspired to a literary career. After some experience at teaching he began the study of law in 1805 with the help of Langdon Cheves [*q.v.*] but dropped it shortly. He opened a school on Edisto Island in 1808, when the death of his father had left the family without support; and in 1809 he started an academy in Charleston. About this time he married Rachel Mordecai of Savannah. His next venture was a literary weekly, the *Quiver,* which soon failed. In 1814 he and a friend bought the *Investigator,* renamed it the *Southern Patriot and Commercial Advertiser,* and threw their political support to President Madison. Selling out in 1822, Harby joined the *City Gazette and Commercial Daily Advertiser,* for which, signing himself Junius, he wrote articles urging the nomination of Andrew Jackson for the presidency. His celebrity, such as it was, he owed to his theatrical criticism. Like his other writing, it is inflated and bedizened in a manner half provincial and half exotic, but it gained unmistakably by his practical acquaintance with the theatre. His first play, *Alexander Severus,* was written when he was seventeen and was rejected by Alexander Placide of the Charleston Theatre, but two later tragi-comedies, *The Gordian Knot, or Causes and Effects* (1810) and *Alberti* (1819), were played and published in Charleston. President Monroe, while sojourning in the city, saw a performance of the latter. Harby's blank verse is pliant and melodious, and the *Gordian Knot* has pleasant love scenes, but the two plays, though promising, belong to a tradition even then antiquated and are literary in the derogatory sense. Harby was one of the founders of the Reformed Society of Israelites, who seceded from the Sephardic Beth Elohim congregation in Charleston in order to adopt a simpler ritual. The society used English as well as Hebrew prayers and introduced an English sermon into the service. As the earliest movement of the sort in the United States, it had more than local significance. Harby's "Anniversary Address," *A Discourse Delivered in Charleston, S. C., on The Twenty-first of November, 1825* (1825), received sympathetic notice in the *North American Review* for July 1826 and elicited friendly comment from Thomas Jefferson and Edward Livingston. In June 1828, after the death of his wife, Harby removed to New York, hoping to benefit by the change of scene and wider opportunities. He opened a school on Howard Street and made a favorable impression with his theatrical criticism in the *Evening Post,* but in December he died unexpectedly, leaving his sister and his children destitute. Benefit performances were announced for them at the Park and Bowery theatres.

[Abraham Moise, memoir prefixed to *A Selection from the Miscellaneous Writings of the late Isaac Harby, Esq.* (Charleston, 1829); B. A. Elzas, *The Jews of S. C.* (1905); *N. Y. Mirror,* Dec. 20, 27, 1828, Jan. 10, 1829; obituary copied from the *Southern Patriot* in the Charleston *City Gazette,* Dec. 27, 1828; *Pubs. Am. Jewish Hist. Soc.,* no. 32 (1931); for other members of his family see the article "Harby" in the *Jewish Encyc.,* vol. VI (latest ed., 1925).] G. H. G.

HARDEE, WILLIAM JOSEPH (Oct. 12, 1815–Nov. 6, 1873), Confederate soldier, was born at "Rural Felicity," the Hardee estate, Camden County, Ga., a son of John and Sarah (Ellis) Hardee. He was descended from Anthony Hardy of Pembroke, Wales, who came to America in 1695 and settled in North Carolina. His grandfather, John, had been a Revolutionary soldier and later captain of a Continental galley on the Georgia coast. He moved to Georgia after the war, the state having made him a grant of 1,360 acres of land. William's father had also seen military service, having been a major of cavalry in the War of 1812. In 1838 William graduated from the United States Military Academy and was assigned as a second lieutenant to the 2nd Dragoons. He was promoted to a first lieutenancy in 1839 and to a captaincy in 1844. In 1840 Hardee was sent on a military commission to Europe to study cavalry operations. Returning, he was assigned to duty as tactical officer at Fort Jesup, La. In the war with Mexico he participated in the siege of Vera Cruz, the battles of Contreras and Molino del Rey, and the capture of the city of Mexico. Twice promoted for meritorious service, he emerged from this war as a lieutenant-colonel. In 1855 he published *Rifle and Light Infantry Tactics,* known as "Hardee's Tactics," which was adopted as a textbook for the army. In the same year he was attached as senior major to the 2nd Cavalry, of which Albert Sidney Johnston was colonel, Robert E. Lee, lieutenant-colonel, and George H. Thomas, Jr., junior major. In the following year Hardee became lieutenant-colonel and was assigned as commandant of cadets at West Point.

Hardee was on leave in Georgia when on Jan. 19, 1861, the state seceded from the Union. Two days later he resigned his commission in the United States army and was commissioned colonel, and in June, Brigadier-general, in the Confederate army. Assigned to a command in Arkansas, he organized the original Arkansas Brigade, afterwards known as "Hardee's Brigade." In the fall of 1861, now a major-general, he was transferred, with most of his command, to Kentucky. Hardee had no service in the Virginia campaigns where fame was most surely to be won. He was identified throughout the war with the western army, later known as the Army of Tennessee. He participated in the battles of Shiloh and Perryville, commanded the left wing at Murfreesboro, fought at Missionary Ridge, and played a leading rôle in the long contest against Sherman between Dalton and Atlanta. Meanwhile, in October 1862, he had been made a lieutenant-general. After the fall of Atlanta (September 1864), he was placed in command of the military department of South Carolina, Georgia, and Florida. Without adequate forces he made an ineffectual attempt to stem the tide of Sherman's advance through Georgia to Savannah. On the 18th of December Hardee evacuated Savannah, withdrawing across the river into South Carolina, and Sherman occupied the city. After a month in Savannah, Sherman also moved over the river, heading towards Charleston. Hardee, receiving no reinforcements, evacuated Charleston and led his small force into North Carolina, where a junction was made with the Army of Tennessee, again under the command of Joseph E. Johnston. Shortly after Hardee rejoined Johnston, the surrender at Appomattox occurred. High tribute was paid Hardee's military ability by his superior officers and by the Federal commanders. In his *Narrative of Military Operations* (1874), Joseph E. Johnston spoke of the "skill and vigor that Hardee never failed to exhibit in battle" (pp. 156–57), and referred to his personal gallantry in leading a certain notable charge at Bentonville. E. A. Pollard, in his *Lee and his Lieutenants* (1867), said of him: "His courage was of that order which inspires courage in others. An accomplished horseman, of commanding stature, and striking martial mien, his bearing in action was impressive and inspiring. To this was added, coolness that never failed; presence of mind never disturbed; and an intellect that rose, like his heart, in the tumult and dangers of battle" (p. 829). General Thomas of the Federal army is quoted by Sherman in his *Memoirs* (1875) as greatly admiring Hardee's handling of his four divisions in the battle of Cassville, May 1864 (II, 40). Sherman himself referred to him as a "competent soldier" (II, 195).

In January 1863, Hardee married Mary T. Lewis, of Greensboro, Ala. To this union one daughter was born. At the conclusion of the war Hardee settled down on a farm in Alabama which came to him through his wife (Snow, *post,* p. 492). He died in Wytheville, Va., and is buried in Selma, Ala.

[Sketch by Hardee's chief of staff, later his son-in-law, T. B. Roy, in W. J. Northen, *Men of Mark in Ga.*, vol. VIII (1911); T. B. Roy, "Gen. Hardee and the Military Operations around Atlanta," *Southern Hist. Soc. Papers,* vol. VIII (1880); *War of the Rebellion: Official Records (Army)*; G. W. Cullum, *Biog. Reg. of the Officers and Grads. of the U. S. Mil. Acad.* (3rd ed., 1891); *Confed. Mil. Hist.*, vol. I (1899); W. P. Snow, *Lee and his Generals* (1867); *Am. Ancestry,* vol. V (1890); *Selma Times,* Nov. 7, 1873; date of birth from A. D. Candler and C. A. Evans, *Georgia* (1906).]

R. P. B—s.

HARDENBERGH, HENRY JANEWAY (Feb. 6, 1847–Mar. 13, 1918), architect, son of John Pool and Frances Eliza (Eddy) Hardenbergh, was born in New Brunswick, N. J. He came of a Dutch family which had emigrated to New York about the middle of the seventeenth century, later had settled in Albany, and then in New Brunswick, where his great-great-grandfather, the Rev. Jacob Rutsen Hardenbergh [*q.v.*], was one of the founders and the first president of Queen's (Rutgers) College. After attending the Hasbrouck Institute at Jersey City, N. J., in 1865 Henry entered the office of Detlef Lienau in New York and there received his architectural education. Lienau had been educated at the École des Beaux-Arts in Paris under the famous Neo-Grec architect Labrouste, and the classical training of his master undoubtedly preserved Hardenbergh from the worst faults of the then fashionable Victorian Gothic. In 1870 he began to practise on his own account. His first work, the grammar-school at Rutgers, 1871, was a modified Victorian Gothic; but the Rutgers Library, 1873, although still Gothic, shows complete freedom from Victorian mannerisms. In the eighties he began to design large city buildings, which thereafter furnished the bulk of his practice. The earlier office buildings were frankly experimental attempts to produce purely new forms with slight classic inspiration, much as the Neo-Grec designers had worked in Paris, but with some additions from the Victorian Gothic. Though not beautiful to the modern eye they were nevertheless full of vitality and imagination and were interesting as early expressions of the desire to produce new forms for changing conditions.

In the Dakota Apartments, New York, 1884,

Hardenbergh's particular talents for practical planning, picturesque and compelling composition, and the free use of a historical style first achieved a complete synthesis. Despite its size, this structure is intimate and homelike; and despite its intimacy, it is monumental and, as a whole, impressive. The same qualities appeared in the Waldorf Hotel, 1891, which at once placed Hardenbergh as the foremost hotel designer of the time. The Dutch Renaissance style, chosen obviously because of the traditions of the name, lent itself well to restrained picturesqueness of outline combined with urbane dignity. The Waldorf was followed in 1896 by the Astoria, thus filling out the block. The Hotel Manhattan, 1896, is in a different style, an adaptation of the design of the house of Francis I in Paris. The Plaza, 1907, displays great elegance and dignity, although still retaining the broken outline. The Copley Plaza, Boston, 1910, is quieter, more classic, more monumental, its quiet restraint befitting its locality. Other important hotels designed by him were the New Willard and the Raleigh in Washington, the Martinique in New York, and the French Renaissance additions to the Windsor in Montreal. In the eighties and nineties he also designed many New York houses, the most successful of which were those on West Seventy-third Street, back of the Dakota, where twenty-seven houses, in a block, were brilliantly combined into one quiet composition. The Fine Arts building, New York, 1896, reveals completely the characteristics of his best work. The handling of precedent, the combination of richness of detail, the informal picturesqueness combined with the dignity necessary in city street design, and the simple and monumental plan, are the culmination of the qualities discernible in his earlier work.

Joining the American Institute of Architects in 1867, he was elected a Fellow in 1877. He became an Associate of the National Academy of Design, 1910, and was a founder of the American Fine Arts Society and the Municipal Art Society. He was a member of the New York Architectural League and its president, 1901–02. He was married in 1893 to Emily Irene (Leeds) Keene, who died Mar. 31, 1899. For most of the years of his life he lived with various members of his family in New York and at his own home in Bernardsville, N. J.

[Montgomery Schuyler, in *Architectural Record,* Jan.–Mar. 1897; Sadakichi Hartman, "Conversation with Hardenbergh," *Ibid.,* May 1906; M. Van V. Gillmore, "Hardenbergh Foundations in American History," *Jour. of Am. Hist.,* Jan.–Mar. 1913; obituaries in *N. Y. Times,* Mar. 14, 1918, and *Jour. Am. Inst. of Architects,* Apr. 1918; *Who's Who in America,* 1916–17; certain information received from Hardenbergh's brother, W. P. Hardenbergh.] T. F. H.

HARDENBERGH, JACOB RUTSEN (1736–Nov. 2, 1790), Dutch Reformed clergyman, first president of Rutgers College, was a descendant of Gerrit Janse Hardenbergh, who was in Albany in 1667, a grandson of Maj. Johannes Hardenbergh, recipient of the Hardenbergh patent, and the son of Col. Johannes and Maria (DuBois) Hardenbergh. He was born at Rosendale, N. Y. The date of his birth is not known, but he was baptized Feb. 22, 1736 (R. R. Hoes, *Baptismal and Marriage Registers of the Old Dutch Church of Kingston,* 1891, p. 215). At the age of eighteen, after attending the academy at Kingston for several years, he entered the household of John Frelinghuysen, pastor at Raritan (now Somerville), N. J., to study theology. In 1756, not long after his preceptor's early death, he married Mrs. Frelinghuysen (Dinah Van Bergh), a native of Holland, distinguished by unusual piety and strength of character. He was ordained in 1758, one of the first ministers of his faith to receive ordination in America, and at once took charge of a wide circuit embracing Raritan and four other towns. In a short time he became a leader of the Coetus, the faction that was advocating independence from the church in Holland and the establishment of a college at which young men might be trained in America for the Dutch Reformed ministry. When Hardenbergh went to Holland in 1763 to bring back his mother-in-law, he was authorized by the Coetus to petition the Classis (or local synod) at Amsterdam, which had direct control of the church in the colonies, for an independent American classis. He was told in no uncertain terms that such a proposal would not be considered and was warned against any attempt to establish an educational institution. Upon his return to America, however, with the cooperation of a few like-minded men, he brought about the issuance in 1766 of a royal charter for the founding of Queen's (now Rutgers) College. He was a member of the first board of trustees, and when the college actually began to function in 1771 at New Brunswick, N. J., he was one of three trustees appointed to govern the institution until a president could be secured.

When the Revolution interrupted his normal activities, Hardenbergh entered into affairs of state with characteristic energy and courage. So ardently did he preach resistance against England that a reward of £100 was offered for his apprehension, and he was obliged to sleep with a musket at his bedside, and several times to flee from his home. In 1776 he was a delegate to the Provincial Congress of New Jersey which ratified the Declaration of Independence and framed the constitution of the state. Subsequently, he served for several sessions as a member of the General Assembly of New Jersey. Between Hardenbergh and Washington a warm friendship was formed in 1779 when the General's headquarters were situated next door to the Dominie's house at Raritan.

In 1781 Hardenbergh returned to New York to take charge of several churches near Kingston. Having been elected to the still vacant presidency of Queen's College, of which he had served as president *pro tempore* on various occasions, in 1786 he left his pastorate and took over the full duties of the academic office. This post carried with it the responsibility of giving instruction in most of the subjects then taught, and also of serving as pastor of the New Brunswick church. Despite many hindrances, Queen's gained strength during Hardenbergh's administration, but the immense labor his triple position involved proved too great for his always frail health, and he died of tuberculosis after only four years in office. He left several children, two of whom, John and Jacob Rutsen, became prominent in the affairs of the college.

[W. H. S. Demarest, *A Hist. of Rutgers Coll.* (1924); T. W. Welles, *Ancestral Tablets From Colonial Days to the Present Era* (1893); E. T. Corwin, *A Manual of the Reformed Ch. in America* (1902), pp. 511–514; W. B. Sprague, *Annals Am. Pulpit*, vol. IX (1869); *Ecclesiastical Records, State of N. Y.*, 6 vols. (1901–05); Ralph LeFèvre, *Hist. of New Palz* (1903); R. H. Steele, *Hist. Discourse, Delivered at . . . First Reformed Dutch Ch. New Brunswick, N. J.* (1867). The tombstone in New Brunswick gives Oct. 30, 1790, as the date of Hardenbergh's death, but Nov. 2 is attested by Peter Studdiford, *A Funeral Sermon on the Death of the Rev. Jacob R. Hardenbergh* (1791); by the *N. Y. Journal and Patriotic Register*, Nov. 11, 1790; and by a letter from the widow to her brother-in-law written Nov. 9, 1790, and printed in the *Christian Intelligencer*, Aug. 26, 1869.] O. S. C.

HARDEY, Mother MARY ALOYSIA (Dec. 8, 1809–June 17, 1886), of the Society of the Sacred Heart, was a descendant of Nicholas Hardey who came to Maryland with Leonard Calvert in 1634, and the daughter of Frederick and Sarah (Spalding) Hardey. She was born in Piscataway, Md., but until she was six years old was brought up by her grandmother Spalding in Baltimore. When she was still a child her family removed to a plantation in Grand Coteau, La. Here in 1821 the Society of the Sacred Heart of Jesus, an institution of religious women devoted to the work of education, founded in France and introduced into America by Mother Philippine Duchesne [*q.v.*], established a convent. Mary Hardey was one of the first girls to receive instruction there, finishing her studies in 1824 with the highest honor attainable. In September of the following year she entered the convent desirous of joining the Order, and on Oct. 22, received the religious habit. The next day she accompanied Mother Audé and others to St. Michael's, where they took possession of a new convent. Although but sixteen at the time, she was tall, handsome, dignified in bearing, and mature beyond her years. She soon showed herself capable of self-abnegating obedience, sound judgment, great prudence, and marked organizing and administrative ability. In 1835 she became assistant superior and the next year, superior, of St. Michael's. The number of pupils increased to two hundred or more, an estate some two miles from the original location was secured, and the building of a new convent was begun. In 1841, however, before it was completed, she was transferred to New York, where with Mother Galitzin she established the first convent of the Order to be opened in the East. Going abroad the following year, she received the Pope's benediction, and in France conferred with Mother Barat, the foundress of the Order. Upon her return she was appointed superior of the convent in New York, which under her direction became a popular educational institution and the center of a far-spread influence. In 1844 she was made provincial of the houses of the Eastern states and Canada. For years she traveled extensively in the interest of the Society, establishing houses in the states of New York, New Jersey, Pennsylvania, Massachusetts, Rhode Island, Ohio, and Michigan, and in Canada and Cuba. In 1871 she was appointed assistant general and deputed to visit the convents in North America. When this mission was completed she took up her residence in the mother house, Paris. She still continued to supervise the foundations in America, making three visitations to this country between 1874 and 1882. Her duties also took her to Spain, Belgium, England, and Ireland. Worn out by her labors she died at Paris in her seventy-seventh year. Her body was placed in the crypt at Conflans, but in 1905 it was brought to America and buried at Kenwood, Albany.

[Mary Garvey, *Mary Aloysia Hardey* (1910); *Catholic World*, Sept. 1886, p. 844; Mary B. McCormack in *The Catholic Encyc.*, vol. VII (1910).] H. E. S.

HARDIE, JAMES ALLEN (May 5, 1823–Dec. 14, 1876), soldier, was born in New York City, the eldest child of Allen Wardwell Hardie, of Scotch and Dutch descent, and Caroline Cox, a descendant of James Cox, a Quaker, who settled on Long Island about 1650. His father was a real-estate broker. James received his early education at Western Collegiate Institute, Pittsburgh, and at the Poughkeepsie Collegiate School. At the age of sixteen he entered the United States Military Academy, the appointee of President Van Buren. He graduated in 1843, number eleven in a class of thirty-nine. For a year as brevet second lieutenant he served with his regiment, the 1st Artillery, at Hancock Barracks, Me., and then returned to West Point as assistant professor of geography, history, and ethics. While he was there the Mexican War began. He received a commission as major with a New York regiment raised for service in California and sailed with his command. While on the Pacific Coast he became a Roman Catholic and helped raise money to build the first cathedral church in San Francisco. After service in California, Oregon, and Lower California, he returned to the East and joined the 3rd Artillery, to which he had been assigned, with the grade of first lieutenant. During a tour of duty with his company at Jefferson Barracks, Mo., he married, 1851, Margaret Hunter, the niece of Colonel Mason, his commander in California. Five children of this marriage survived their father. Duty with his regiment both in the East and on the Pacific slope, where he saw service against the Indians near Spokane, occupied the years until the outbreak of the Civil War. His principal appointment during this period was as adjutant-general of the Department of Oregon, which position he left to return to the East. After a few weeks of recruiting in New England, he received an appointment as lieutenant-colonel on the staff of General McClellan. Here, under the immediate command of Gen. Seth Williams, he acted as assistant adjutant-general of the Army of the Potomac. Through the Peninsular campaign and the Maryland campaign of 1862, he followed the fortunes of McClellan, and later those of Burnside at Fredericksburg. His services had won him promotion to a brigadier-general of volunteers in November 1862. The faithfulness and accuracy of his work was such that in the controversy which arose between William Buel Franklin and Burnside [*qq.v.*] over the responsibility for the dismal failure on the Rappahannock, both contestants agreed to accept Hardie's field dispatches as the correct record of the orders given and of the resulting operations. Subsequently he filled in rapid succession several important positions. McClellan used him in preparing for the War Department the memorial which was to restore the fallen leader. Hooker made him judge advocate-general of the Army of the Potomac. He relinquished this office and his volunteer rank, however, to become a major on the regular staff with duty in Washington. His ability attracted the attention of the Secretary of War, and he was chosen to carry that secret, personal message which transferred command from Hooker to Meade in the tense days before Gettysburg. From the Secretary's office, he passed to the Inspector-General's office, of which he became chief. His career was rounded out by the receipt, Mar. 3, 1865, of brevet rank of brigadier-general for "distinguished and faithful services during the Rebellion," and of major-general, Mar. 13, 1865, for "faithful, meritorious and distinguished services in the Inspector-General's Department." All his subsequent service was as inspector either in Washington or elsewhere. He died in Washington from illness contracted on an arduous inspection tour.

[G. W. Cullum, *Biog. Reg. Officers and Grads. U. S. Mil. Acad.*, vol. II (3rd ed., 1891); old files, Adj. Gen. Office, War Dept., Washington; F. B. Heitman, *Hist. Reg. and Dict. U. S. Army*, vol. I (1903); C. F. Benjamin, *Memoir of James Allen Hardie* (1877); *Natl. Republican* (Washington), Dec. 16, 1876.] A. W. C.

HARDIN, BEN (Feb. 29, 1784–Sept. 24, 1852), lawyer, congressman, was a conspicuous member of a well-known family of Virginia origin, transplanted into Kentucky. His father, Benjamin, married his cousin, Sarah Hardin, a sister of John Hardin [*q.v.*], before they left Virginia. Their son Ben was born in Westmoreland County, Pa., and in 1787 the family moved to Nelson, later Washington County, Ky., settling near Springfield in March 1788. Ben's schooling began early, being conducted first by members of his family, then by Ichabod Radley, and lastly by Daniel Barry, an Irish linguist of some note, at Bardstown and at Hartford in Ohio County. He began the study of law at Richmond, Ky., in 1804, under the direction of his cousin, Martin D. Hardin [*q.v.*], and the next year he continued his work under Felix Grundy [*q.v.*] at Bardstown. The following year he was given license to practise and immediately set himself up as a lawyer at Elizabethtown, in Hardin County. Here he remained for two years, conducting his business for a year in partnership with Joseph Holt [*q.v.*], judge advocate-general of the army under President Lincoln. In 1808 Hardin moved to Bardstown, where he maintained his residence until his death. As a lawyer he developed a widespread prestige and a competent fortune. He practised in all the courts of his own county and the surrounding region, going at times even into Indiana. He also appeared frequently before the Kentucky court of appeals and occasionally before the United States Supreme Court, taking part in most of the prominent lawsuits of his day and state. He was a very effective speaker before a jury, never engaging in ornate and florid language but driving his argument home with an abundance of solid facts. His memory was remarkable; he never kept a note, yet he could with great accuracy marshal the testimony brought out in the court proceedings.

He first entered politics in 1810, when he became a member of the Kentucky House of Representatives. He was returned the next year and also in 1824 and 1825, and served four years in the Kentucky Senate, 1828–32. His greatest political renown was due, however, to his service in the United States House of Representatives, where he represented his district for five terms, in the Fourteenth (1815–17), Sixteenth (1819–21), Seventeenth (1821–23), Twenty-third (1833–35), and Twenty-fourth (1835–37) Congresses. Here he became a positive figure, well-known and respected by his colleagues. He took an active part in the debates, and by a direct and trenchant style of speaking attracted much attention, winning from John Randolph of Roanoke the comment, "Hardin is like a kitchen knife whetted on a brick, he cuts roughly but cuts deep" (Little, *post,* p. 63). Directly after the end of the War of 1812 he opposed what he called the "national glory" policy, urging the reduction of the army and navy and of taxes wherever possible (*Annals of Congress,* 14 Cong., 1 Sess., p. 756). He opposed the recharter of the second United States Bank and spoke for the admission of Missouri as a slave state. From 1844 to 1847 he was secretary of state under Governor Owsley, but in the latter year he resigned after a heated dispute with the governor. His last public service was in the state constitutional convention in 1849–50. He was in politics a Whig, and in 1833 and 1845 he served as a presidential elector, casting his votes in both instances for Clay.

Hardin married, on Mar. 31, 1807, Elizabeth Pendleton Barbour, a daughter of Ambrose Barbour of Washington County, Ky. She died in August 1852. In the summer of the same year Hardin fell from his horse and received an injury which brought about his death in the early fall. During his last illness he joined the Methodist Church.

[L. P. Little, *Ben. Hardin: His Times and Contemporaries* (1887); Lewis and R. H. Collins, *Hist. of Ky.* (2 vols., 1874); *The Biog. Encyc. of Ky.* (1878); H. Levin, *The Lawyers and Lawmakers of Ky.* (1897); T. M. Green, *Hist. Families of Ky.* (1889); *Louisville Daily Courier,* Sept. 25, 1852.] E. M. C.

HARDIN, CHARLES HENRY (July 15, 1820–July 29, 1892), governor of Missouri, philanthropist, was born in Trimble County, Ky., the son of Charles and Hannah (Jewell) Hardin, both of Virginia descent. His mother was a sister of Dr. William Jewell, founder of William Jewell College. Shortly after Charles Henry's birth, the family removed to Missouri, settling in 1821 in Columbia, where the boy was educated at the local academy. He attended Indiana University and Miami University, graduating from the latter in 1841. He studied law in Columbia, and in 1843 commenced practice in Fulton, Mo. On May 16 of the following year he married Mary Barr Jenkins. By heredity and by temperament a Whig, he was in a congenial political and social atmosphere. In 1848 he was elected circuit attorney for the second judicial district and in 1852 he commenced a legislative career in the lower house of the General Assembly, where he served continuously, except during 1856–57, until 1860. His chief interest was in railroad and banking legislation. In 1855 he was appointed a member of the committee to prepare *The Revised Statutes of the State of Missouri* (2 vols., 1856). He was a leader of the Whigs through several sessions when party and factional warfare was extremely bitter and the issue of slavery in the territories a continuous threat to the integrity and existence of the Whig party in Missouri. Upon the collapse of his party, he became an organizer of the American party, and a leader in 1860 of the Bell-Everett forces. He entered the state Senate in that year as a Conservative-Unionist opposed to secession and as a spokesman for the neutrality of Missouri. In 1861, however, he followed the disloyal state government in its peregrinations and became a member of the fugitive "rebel legislature," although he was the only senator who voted against the abortive secession ordinance (*Journal of the Senate, Extra Session of the Rebel Legislature . . . Begun and Held . . . on the Twenty-first Day of October, Eighteeen Hundred and Sixty-one,* 1865). Following the military defeat and political elimination of the disloyalists, Hardin was disfranchised, placed under bond by the test-oath law of 1862, and retired from politics. Remaining in comparative obscurity until the Liberal-Republican movement swept the Radicals from power in 1870, he reëntered politics as a stanch Democrat. He represented his district in the state Senate in 1872–74, and was nominated in the latter year for governor as a compromise candidate acceptable to the various factions of his party, although he was "the dryest campaign speaker that ever took the stump in Missouri" (Stevens, *post,* II, 490). He was easily elected over the Granger or People's-party candidate, becoming the first Democratic governor since the war. His administration, directed by a man of "inflexible methods and unrelaxing solemnity," was characterized by conservatism, retrenchment, and rigid economy. The extravagance of the Civil War period was abruptly terminated; the railroads and warehouses were brought under state control as to rates and services; the institutions of the state were conducted efficiently. Dull and uninteresting, the administration was one of "law and order" and of scrupulous honesty, a welcome reaction from the conditions of the previous decade. One of the Governor's proclamations which attracted comment was that setting a day of prayer for relief from a plague of grasshoppers. At the end of his term, Hardin was urged again to become a candidate but refused, retiring from public life in 1877. He was a leading layman of the Baptist church, and in 1873 the founder of Hardin College for Women at Mexico, Mo., his home after 1861.

[M. B. Hardin, *Life and Writings of Gov. Charles Henry Hardin* (1896), poorly arranged and uncritical; files of the *Missouri Statesman*, the *Missouri Republican*, and the *St. Louis Republican*, 1850–76; *Messages and Proclamations of the Govs. of the State of Mo.*, vol. V (1924); H. L. Conard, *Encyc. of the Hist. of Mo.*, vol. III (1901); *Hist. of Audrain County, Mo.* (1884); *The Bench and Bar of St. Louis, Kansas City, Jefferson City, and Other Mo. Cities* (1884); W. B. Stevens, *Centennial Hist. of Mo.* (1921), vol. II; *St. Louis Republic*, July 30, 1892.] T. S. B.

HARDIN, JOHN (Oct. 1, 1753–May 1792), soldier and Indian fighter, in whose honor were named counties in Kentucky and Ohio, was born in Fauquier County, Va., where his grandfather, Mark Hardin, had received grants of land in 1716. According to tradition the Hardins were of Huguenot stock. Martin Hardin, father of John, was the proprietor of an ordinary near Elk Run, and was apparently a man of solidity and strength. About 1765 the family left Fauquier, ultimately settling at George's Creek, in the southwestern Pennsylvania wilderness. Here young Hardin learned woodcraft and Indian ways and developed the skill as marksman and hunter that was to make his name anathema to the savages along the frontier. In 1774 he served as ensign in Dunmore's campaign and was wounded on McDonald's expedition but while still on crutches rejoined Dunmore's column. At the outbreak of the Revolution he changed his plans for moving to Kentucky, turned to recruiting, and entered the Continental Army as a second lieutenant. He soon joined Daniel Morgan's Riflemen and rendered conspicuous service with that noted regiment, winning the esteem and confidence of Morgan, who frequently assigned him to enterprises demanding intrepidity and discretion. At Saratoga his conduct elicited the thanks of General Gates, while James Wilkinson is said to have won his brigadier's brevet by appropriating credit for Hardin's discovery of the British position there (Walworth, *post*). Before he resigned from the army, in December 1779, he refused a major's commission on the ground that his services were more useful in a subordinate rank.

In 1786 he removed with his family—he had married Jane Davies in Pennsylvania—to Nelson (afterwards Washington) County, Ky. A few months later he volunteered under George Rogers Clark for the Wabash expedition, and was appointed quartermaster. Thenceforward, until his death, he participated in every excursion into Indian territory, with the exception of St. Clair's. In 1788 and again in 1789, when he was named county lieutenant with the rank of colonel, he conducted successful punitive forays against the Shawnees. He was one of the leaders in the ill-starred campaign of Josiah Harmar [*q.v.*] which resulted in the court-martialing of Hardin and his general. Both were honorably acquitted, while a second court-martial approved Hardin's conduct as "that of a brave and skillful officer" (*Kentucky Gazette*, Dec. 11, 1790). Despite his experience, eminent military talents, and unquestioned courage, Hardin was better qualified to command a company than a regiment, yet much of the blame for his double defeat upon the Maumee should be laid upon the cowardice of the Pennsylvania militia and the faulty generalship of Harmar. The following June, while with Charles Scott's expedition, Hardin redeemed his reputation by several brilliant successes. In May 1792 General Wilkinson sent him under a flag of truce to negotiate a peace with the Miami tribes, but at what is now the city of Hardin, Ohio, he was treacherously murdered by pretendedly friendly Indians—as was alleged, for his horse and equipment, although Marshall (*post*, II, 42) implies that Wilkinson's duplicity underlay the murder. A few days before his death he had been commissioned brigadier-general. Hardin's son Martin D. Hardin, his nephew Ben Hardin, and his grandson John J. Hardin [*qq.v.*], all attained distinction in Ohio Valley politics.

[Lewis and R. H. Collins, *Hist. of Ky.* (1874), vol. II; Humphrey Marshall, *Hist. of Ky.* (1824), II, 41 ff.; *Fauquier Hist. Soc. Bull.*, July 1924; R. M. McElroy, *Ky. in the Nation's Hist.* (1909); *Am. State Papers: Indian Affairs*, vol. I (1832), pp. 132, 337; *Am. State Papers: Mil. Affairs*, vol. I (1832), pp. 20–36; James Wilkinson, *Memoirs of My Own Times*, I (1816), 233; M. T. Walworth, "Colonel John Hardin." in *Hist. Mag.*, Apr. 1869.] A. C. G., Jr.

HARDIN, JOHN J. (Jan. 6, 1810–Feb. 23, 1847), soldier, congressman, was the son of Martin D. Hardin [*q.v.*], United States senator and secretary of state of Kentucky, and of Elizabeth (Logan) Hardin, daughter of Gen. Benjamin Logan. He was born at Frankfort, Ky., graduated from Transylvania University, and studied law under Chief Justice John Boyle [*q.v.*]. On Jan. 13, 1831, he married Sarah Ellen Smith of Locust Grove, Mercer County, Ky., and with her settled in Jacksonville, Ill. A major-general in the state militia, he saw service in the Black Hawk War. He espoused the Whig cause in Illinois politics; and was elected to the General Assembly for Morgan County in 1836, 1838, and 1840. In the General Assembly of 1837 he opposed the ill-starred internal-improvement scheme. He was the rival of Lincoln for the leadership of the Whig minority in the Illinois House. When Congressional reapportionment gave Illinois the right to choose seven congressmen in 1843, the Democratic majority districted the state in such fashion that there was but one Whig district, that containing Sangamon and Morgan counties. The seat found eager aspirants in Stephen T. Logan, E. D. Baker, Abraham Lincoln, and Hardin. In the election of 1843 Baker wrested the Sangamon County delegation from Lincoln only to suffer defeat at Hardin's hands in the district convention. Hardin was elected Aug. 7, 1843, polling 6,230 votes to 5,357 for his Democratic opponent. In Congress he voted against the gag resolutions, worked for river and harbor improvements, and as a Whig endeavored to make political capital for his party on the tariff and against Van Buren. He declined to stand for reëlection in 1844, and E. D. Baker succeeded him. In 1845–46, however, he came forward once more as a candidate for the Whig nomination against Lincoln, whose comment was, "Turn about is fair play." Hardin proposed to leave their candidacy to the decision of the Whig voters of the district, and when his offer was not accepted, withdrew from the race, leaving Lincoln an easy path to the honor. At the outbreak of the Mexican War, Hardin, who the year before had been in command of troops sent against the Mormons, was elected colonel of the 1st Regiment of Illinois Volunteers (June 30, 1846). His regiment, dispatched to Texas, was first put under the command of General Wool, with whom Hardin had one or two stormy scenes, then Wool's command was united to that of Gen. Zachary Taylor, and on Feb. 22–23, 1847, plunged into the battle of Buena Vista. On the second day Hardin, fighting at the head of his regiment, was killed. "We lost our best Whig man," said Lincoln a year later in speaking of Hardin's death (Beveridge, *post,* I, 461). Hardin was a handsome man of charming personality. His artless manner atoned for a trick of stammering which otherwise might have been a handicap. One of his four children, Martin D. Hardin, became a brigadier-general in the Union army during the Civil War.

[Martin D. Hardin, *"To the Members of the Hardin Family"* (1880); T. C. Pease, *The Frontier State* (1918), being vol. II of *The Centennial Hist. of Ill.*; T. C. Pease, *Illinois Election Returns, 1818–48* (1923), being *Colls. Ill. State Hist. Lib.*, vol. XVIII; A. J. Beveridge, *Abraham Lincoln, 1809–58* (1928), vol. I; C. M. Eames, *Historic Morgan and Classic Jacksonville* (1885); T. M. Green, *Hist. Families of Ky.* (1889); E. H. Walworth, "The Battle of Buena Vista," *Mag. of Am. Hist.*, Dec. 1879, an account by Hardin's daughter; *Illinois State Register* (Springfield), Apr. 2, 9, 1847.]

T. C. P.

HARDIN, MARTIN D. (June 21, 1780–Oct. 8, 1823), lawyer, soldier, United States senator, was born in the Monongahela River region of southwestern Pennsylvania. He was the son of John Hardin [*q.v.*], a soldier and Indian fighter, and Jane (Davies) Hardin, and a first cousin of Ben Hardin [*q.v.*]. Named for his grandfather, he is said to have adopted the initial "D." to distinguish himself from other Martins in the family (Green, *post,* p. 178). In 1786 his father moved his family to the district of Kentucky and settled in Nelson, later Washington, County, near Springfield. Martin received a classical education at Transylvania Seminary at Lexington, after which he took up the study of law under George Nicholas, one of the ablest men in Kentucky at that time. He began the practice of his profession at Richmond in Madison County, but soon thereafter he removed to Frankfort, the capital of the state. Here he established a reputation as a man of great legal talent, which assured him a position of leadership at the bar. In 1810 he published *Reports of Cases Argued and Adjudged in the Court of Appeals of Kentucky,* covering the years 1805–08. Although he was not politically ambitious, it is for his activities in statecraft that he is remembered. In 1805 while living at Richmond he made his first entry into politics, representing Madison County in the state House of Representatives for a term. In 1812, having moved his residence, he was elected to the same position to represent Franklin County, but in August of that year, Isaac Shelby [*q.v.*], who had just been elected governor, rewarded him for his support by appointing him secretary of state. During the war with England, Hardin, like most other Kentuckians of prominence, took an active part, serving as major in a regiment of riflemen led by Col. John Allen, under the general command of William Henry

Harrison. In 1816 he was appointed United States senator by Gov. Gabriel Slaughter to fill out the term of William T. Barry [*q.v.*], who had resigned. This appointment lasted only until the legislature met, but on the meeting of that body Hardin was elected. His term expired the following March. He took his seat on Dec. 4, and with only three months of official life allotted to him, took a rather prominent part in the deliberations. Distinctly a nationalist, he favored internal improvements at federal expense and advocated throughout a liberal construction of the Constitution. He was later accused by some of his fellow Kentuckians of being a Federalist. In point of fact he was a national Democrat who would undoubtedly have become a Whig had he lived long enough. He was a Monroe elector in 1821. Having no desire to continue in the Senate, he returned to Kentucky after Mar. 4, 1817, to continue his law practice. For the next two years he represented Franklin County in the Kentucky House of Representatives, and in 1819–20 served as speaker. Less than four years later he died, comparatively a young man. Hardin married Elizabeth Logan, a daughter of Gen. Benjamin Logan. Their son, Col. John J. Hardin [*q.v.*], served in Congress from Illinois from 1843 to 1845, and was later killed at the battle of Buena Vista.

[See Lewis and R. H. Collins, *Hist. of Ky.* (2 vols., 1874); T. M. Green, *Hist. Families of Ky.* (1889); *The Biog. Encyc. of Ky.* (1878); *Ky. Gazette* (Lexington), Nov. 18, 1816; *Argus of Western America* (Frankfort), Oct. 15, 1823; *Western Monitor* (Lexington), Oct. 14, 1823; the *Argus* and the *Biog. Dir. Am. Cong.* (1928) give Hardin the middle name "Davis."]

E. M. C.

HARDING, ABNER CLARK (Feb. 10, 1807–July 19, 1874), financier, Union soldier, congressman, was born in East Hampton, Conn., the son of Nathan and Philena Sears (Clark) Harding. The family was of Puritan origin, being descended from Joseph Harding who came to America in 1623 with Robert Gorges and ultimately settled at Chatham on Cape Cod. About 1750, descendants moved to Connecticut, and later to Plainfield, Herkimer County, N. Y., where Abner Harding spent the greater part of his boyhood. At the age of fourteen he attempted to enlist in the navy, but was rejected on account of his small stature. For the next four years he taught school and engaged in business. In 1826–27 he read law at Bridgewater, Oneida County, N. Y., but the following year moved to Pennsylvania where he was admitted to the bar at Lewisburg. Here he practised law for several years, rising rapidly in his profession. On Jan. 30, 1829, he had married Mrs. Rebecca L. Byers (*née* Leybricks), who died in 1833 leaving two children; on June 30, 1835, he was married a second time, to Susan A. Ickes. In 1838 he removed to Illinois and established a home in Monmouth, Warren County, which he maintained the rest of his life. He soon became interested in politics and took a prominent place in the Whig party, being elected to various offices. In 1847 he was a member of the convention which framed the constitution of 1848, under which the state was governed until 1870. In 1847–49 he was a county school commissioner; and in 1848–50 he was a member of the lower house of the General Assembly. Originally a Jackson Democrat, Harding next became a Whig, then an antislavery man, a Free-Soiler, and finally a Republican of the Sumner and Stevens school.

Failing eyesight compelled him to give up the practice of the law about 1851, and he turned to business. He organized the Second National Bank at Monmouth, and in company with Chancy Harding and Judge Ivory Quincy, under the firm name of C. Harding & Company, he engaged in the construction of the Peoria & Oquawka Railroad, building the line from Burlington to Knoxville. Harding also bought the contract for building the section of the road beyond Knoxville, which the original contractors were unable to carry out, and completed it in 1856. For a short time the Harding Company operated the road, but subsequently sold it to the Chicago, Burlington & Quincy system, of which it became a part. In 1853 Harding was a member of the first board of trustees of Monmouth College and later endowed a professorship there. During the Civil War, he was instrumental in organizing in Monmouth, in August 1862, the 83rd Illinois Volunteer Infantry, in which he enlisted as a private but of which he was soon elected and commissioned colonel. He saw service skirmishing in the region around Forts Henry and Donelson. On Feb. 3, 1863, he was in command of Fort Donelson when it was attacked by a Confederate force under Generals Wheeler, Forrest, and Wharton (*War of the Rebellion: Official Records, Army,* 1 ser., XXIII, pt. 1, pp. 34 ff.), and for gallantry in repelling the attack he was promoted to brigadier-general Mar. 13, 1863. For a time he was in command of Murfreesboro, Tenn. On June 3, 1863, because of the condition of his eyes, he resigned from the service. He was elected as a Republican to the House of Representatives of the Thirty-ninth Congress in 1864, and reëlected in 1866. He died in Monmouth in his sixty-eighth year, leaving a fortune of about $2,000,000, a large part of which was in farming lands in Warren and adjoining counties.

["In Memoriam—Gen. A. C. Harding," *Soc. of the Army of the Cumberland, Tenth Reunion* (1876); Newton Bateman and Paul Selby, *Hist. Encyc. of Ill. and Hist. of Warren County* (2 vols., 1903); *The Constitutional Debates of 1847* (Ill. State Hist. Lib., 1919), ed. by A. C. Cole; *Biog. Dir. Am. Cong.* (1928); G. A. Harding and F. H. Willard, *Hist. of Herkimer County, N.Y.* (1893); *Portr. and Biog. Album of Warren County* (n.d.); *The Past and Present of Warren County, Ill.* (1877); D. W. Lusk, *Eighty Years of Illinois: Politics and Politicians, 1809–89* (1889).] E. L. B.

HARDING, CHESTER (Sept. 1, 1792–Apr. 1, 1866), portrait painter, was born at Conway, Mass., a son of Abiel and Olive (Smith) Harding. The father was agreeable, moral, but shiftless, working at perpetual-motion machines while the mother struggled to keep the children decent. Chester, with almost no schooling, began work at the age of twelve. In 1806 the family moved to Madison County, N. Y., then unbroken wilderness, where the boys helped the father with a clearing and learned to make chairs. The War of 1812 arousing patriotic fervor, Chester enlisted as a drummer and almost died of dysentery at Sacketts Harbor. Discharged from the service, he made his way, thinly clad and suffering frightfully, to his parents' home. He obtained a contract to manufacture drums for the army and, after the war, undertook general cabinet making at Caledonia, N. Y. He married Caroline Woodruff and was arrested for debt on his wedding day. Opening a tavern, he "paid off some old debts by making new ones." Threatened with imprisonment, he fled the town, leaving his wife and new-born baby, and worked his passage on a raft down the Allegheny to Pittsburgh. He obtained work as a house-painter, saved a few dollars, tramped back to Caledonia, brought his family away secretly, and rafted them to Pittsburgh, where they arrived penniless. On the verge of starvation, Harding was advised by a barber to open a sign-painter's shop. He borrowed twenty dollars, bought paints and gold leaf, and began to solicit orders. He soon was working in his own busy shop. An itinerant portrait painter named Nelson made Harding's and his wife's likenesses at ten dollars each. Fascinated by the possibilities of this art, the young sign-painter set a palette with the pigments of his trade and did a head of Mrs. Harding which so nearly resembled her that he became "frantic with delight." A journeyman baker soon after offered him five dollars for a portrait and started him on his career. Chester's brother Horace, a chair-maker, had meanwhile established himself at Paris, Ky., and on his urgence the artist moved his family down the Ohio, again on a raft, and opened a studio adjacent to Horace's shop. He made many portraits at twenty-five dollars, then considered a large price, and began to have aspirations, not having previously thought of portraiture as "more honorable or profitable than sign painting." Having saved some money, he went to Philadelphia where he drew for two months at the Academy. Returning to Kentucky, he found a panic in progress. As sitters were unobtainable, he went to St. Louis with a letter of introduction to Governor Clark, whom he painted. Fifteen months of success followed. Harding at this time made a long trip to paint Daniel Boone in his cabin.

An ambition to visit Europe now possessed him. He had $1,000, a carriage and horses. With his wife and four children he drove to western New York, intending to leave his family there; but his mother, sensibly concerned by the lack of proper provision for them, persuaded him to postpone his foreign tour. He canceled passage on the *Albion,* which was wrecked with total loss of passengers, and spent a winter in Washington, adding to his savings. A friendship formed with Senator E. H. Mills of Massachusetts led the now prospering artist to summer at Pittsfield, where he increased his acquaintance and bank account. In the following autumn he visited Boston, "chiefly on a pilgrimage to [Gilbert] Stuart." He then painted at Northampton, was urged by several Bostonians to settle in their city, and presently yielded. Thus began in Boston the "Harding fever"—a term coined by Stuart, whose popularity was temporarily eclipsed. In six months Harding painted eighty portraits and acquired funds sufficient for two years abroad. He left his family at Northampton and sailed for Liverpool Aug. 1, 1823.

The journal which Harding kept in England and France is the naïve record of a backwoodsman who became a social lion. Through the American minister he was introduced to the Duke of Sussex, who sat for him, entertained him, and recommended him to the Duke of Hamilton, at whose Scottish palace he spent much time. Another friendly sitter was Robert Owen. Harding was so charmed by British life that he determined to stay and sent for his family. This move was unfortunate because of depressed financial conditions in Great Britain and a social difficulty thus recorded: "My profession entitled me to move in the highest circles, in which, at the same time, my wife and children would not be recognized" (*A Sketch, post,* p. 128). The Hardings sailed for Boston in 1826 and took a house which four years later was exchanged for one at Springfield, their permanent home during the rest of the artist's life.

Harding painted between 1826 and 1866 many celebrities whose portraits are now in important public or private collections: Timothy Pickering, Washington Allston, John Marshall, John Randolph of Roanoke, William Wirt, John C. Calhoun, Daniel Webster, William T. Sherman, and others. Of agreeable personality, striking appearance, and cultivated speech, he was everywhere socially popular. He was industrious and painstaking; his work deserves perhaps a better rating than that given in Kenyon Cox's depreciatory remark: "Harding appears to have attained to respectability but nothing more" (*Nation*, Jan. 21, 1921).

The Civil War found Harding in a tragic predicament. Two of his sons fought for the Union, two for the Confederacy. In his last year he sat, wearing his patriarchal white beard, for a head of St. Peter. His death came through his leaving Springfield in March 1866 to fish for trout at Sandwich, near Daniel Webster's old home. He caught a severe cold and died at the Tremont House, Boston.

[Harding contributed an account of himself to Wm. Dunlap, *A Hist. of the Rise and Progress of the Arts of Design in the U. S.* (1834; Bayley and Goodspeed ed., 1918, III, 65–72). His daughter, Margaret E. White, edited some of his papers as *My Egotistography* (privately printed, 1866; pub. 1890 as *A Sketch of Chester Harding, Artist*; new ed. with annotations by his grandson, W. P. G. Harding, 1929). See also: Osmond Tiffany, "Chester Harding, the Self-Made Artist," *Lippincott's Mag.*, Jan. 1874; Robt. Shackleton, "A Benvenuto of the Backwoods," *Harper's Mag.*, July 1916.]

F. W. C.

HARDING, GEORGE (Oct. 26, 1827–Nov. 17, 1902), lawyer, was born in Philadelphia, the son of Jesper Harding [*q.v.*], publisher of the *Pennsylvania Inquirer*, and of Maria (Wilson) Harding, and the brother of William White Harding [*q.v.*]. He was educated in the public schools and at the University of Pennsylvania, from which he was graduated in 1846. Accepted as an office student in that year by John Cadwalader [*q.v.*], later noted as United States district judge, he was admitted to the bar in 1849. The same year he was made secretary of the Law Academy of Philadelphia. His extraordinary abilities were recognized from the first. Within two years he assisted Edwin M. Stanton, representing the state of Pennsylvania, in a case of great importance before the Supreme Court of the United States (*Pennsylvania* vs. *Wheeling & Belmont Bridge Company*, 13 *Howard*, 518); and two years later he began his connection under circumstances extraordinarily flattering to him, with the early litigation over the Morse telegraph patent, which lasted for many years. Within a decade his reputation was established as one of the leading patent lawyers of the country. He was prominent in the litigation involving the McCormick reaper and other farm machinery, and also in a series of cases during three decades, remarkable for complexity and for his unvarying success, involving the manufacture of fat acids and glycerin. In more than a hundred cases before the federal circuit courts of appeal and the Supreme Court of the United States he was of counsel. His work was primarily in the fields of mechanics and chemistry; lacking both the requisite technical knowledge and the strength to acquire it, he took little part in the abundant litigation over electric problems which arose after he was fifty. He was at least partly responsible for the establishment of some of the fundamental doctrines of United States patent law; competent judges have pronounced him the greatest of American patent lawyers. It is a branch of practice which few, even of the legal profession, can either understand or appreciate. It was Harding's custom, in arguing cases in court, to perform chemical experiments and operate miniature models of machines and appliances (the telephone system between New York and Washington, a miniature grainfield and reaper, a felting machine, a furnace) to make clear the technical problems involved in the litigation. His strength seems to have lain as much in remarkable gifts of exposition as in intellectual power; and those gifts, coupled with his ardor and resourcefulness in argument and graces of manner, would probably have won him far greater fame, if otherwise no greater success, in other and less technical fields of practice. He was capable of joining humor and entertainment with scientific accuracy and curious learning in the dryest patent dispute. At the age of twenty-two he was elected a member of the Franklin Institute, and at twenty-seven, of the American Philosophical Society. He retired from practice in 1897.

In 1853 he delivered before the Franklin Institute an "Address" on the progress of the mechanic arts (*Journal of the Franklin Institute*, 1853); aside from stray reprints of his arguments in court he left no other writings. His wife was Charlotte Kenner of New Orleans, who bore him four children, of whom a son and a daughter survived him.

[A. H. Walker, in W. D. Lewis, *Great Am. Lawyers*, vol. VIII (1909); *Address Delivered Mar. 13, 1902, and Papers Prepared or Republished to Commemorate the Centennial Celebration of the Law Asso. of Phila.* (1906); W. J. Harding, *The Hardings in America* (1925); J. H. Martin, *Martin's Bench and Bar of*

Phila. (1883); *Public Ledger* (Phila.), Nov. 19, 21, 1902.] F. S. P.

HARDING, JESPER (Nov. 5, 1799–Aug. 21, 1865), publisher, was born in Philadelphia, Pa., the son of George and Mary (Hudd) Harding. At an early age he was apprenticed to Enos Bronson, the publisher of the *United States Gazette,* and was so apt a learner that at the age of sixteen he was able "to buy his time" and to engage in the printing business on his own account. An early imprint of his may be found on a pamphlet history of the organization of St. Paul's Protestant Episcopal Church in Philadelphia, dated 1818, when he was but eighteen years old. By 1820 his business was very successful and he added book binding to his activities. In 1829 he purchased the *Pennsylvania Inquirer* which had been established but a short time, soon thereafter acquired the *Democratic Press,* and in the next ten years absorbed several other contemporary journals. He also began the printing of Bibles, of which he subsequently became the largest publisher in the United States. As the first editor of the *Inquirer* he supported the administration of President Andrew Jackson and took a prominent part in the heated controversy between the President and the directors of the Bank of the United States. For a time the paper attempted the difficult task of supporting both the President and the bank, but when the government withdrew its funds from the bank, the *Inquirer* allied itself with the anti-Jackson wing of the Democratic party, supporting Harrison in 1836, and supporting the "Harrison Democrats" in the presidential campaign of 1840. Later, however, the editorial policy favored the Whigs and continued to do so until the party went out of existence. On Jan. 1, 1842, Harding acquired another important contemporary journal, the *National Gazette,* and the *Inquirer* was enlarged to nine columns, expanding again in 1851 to ten columns. In connection with his printing and publishing business he became interested in the manufacture of paper, and in 1835 erected a mill in Philadelphia. This plant was equipped with the best machinery then available, and it is said that it was not unusual to have rags enter the mill and be converted into paper which was printed and circulated in the shape of newspapers within six hours. In 1840, in order to take advantage of the greater water power of the Delaware, the mill was moved to Trenton, N. J., and was operated by him in that place until his retirement in 1859. Upon the passage of the Internal Revenue Act (1862), President Lincoln appointed Harding collector of the First District of Pennsylvania, which position he held until shortly before his death.

He was one of the most prominent figures in the early days of newspaper publishing, a man of unusual enterprise, a characteristic which was exemplified by the fact that during his administration of the *Inquirer* he obtained the advance sheets of several of Charles Dickens' novels for publication, thus presenting some of the work of this author to American readers for the first time. Early in life he had married Maria Wilson. He died in Philadelphia. One of his sons, William White Harding [*q.v.*] succeeded him as proprietor of the publishing business; another, George [*q.v.*], attained distinction as a patent lawyer.

[E. T. Freedley, *Phila. and Its Manufacturers* (1859); W. J. Harding, *The Hardings in America* (1925); E. P. Oberholtzer, *Phila.—A Hist. of the City and Its People* (n.d.), vol. IV; J. T. Scharf and T. Westcott, *Hist. of Phila.* (1884), vol. III; "The Phila. Inquirer 1829–1929" (MS.), in the possession of W. G. Harding, Esq., New York City; *Phila. Inquirer* and *Phila. Daily News,* Aug. 22, 1865.] J. H. F.

HARDING, ROBERT (Oct. 6, 1701–Sept. 1, 1772), Jesuit missionary in Maryland and pastor in Philadelphia, was born in Nottinghamshire, England. He entered the Society of Jesus, Sept. 7, 1722; and presumably pursued his ecclesiastical studies on the Continent. His missionary zeal not less than the demand for priests in the colonies led to his coming to America (1732) before he had completed the post-ordination *cursus* of his order, for he made on Apr. 2, 1735, a solemn profession of the Tertianship vows which he had taken two years earlier without submitting the customary fourth vow. For seventeen years he labored in Maryland with such devotion and success that in 1749, when Father Joseph Greaton, S. J. [*q.v.*] retired from the pastorate of St. Joseph's, Philadelphia, because of failing health, Father Harding received the position and later (1759) the headship of the Jesuits in Pennsylvania. In Philadelphia his interest in the affairs of the community developed a spirit of cooperation between the Catholics and Protestants which was rare in those days. Thus, when in 1755 Franklin promoted the founding of the Pennsylvania Hospital, Father Harding's name was on his subscription list. The same year he was prominently identified with the movement to aid the exiled Acadians in the city. Nevertheless, Catholics in 1755 were the target of a series of letters questioning their loyalty to the English cause in the war which had begun. The letters attracted attention in London and an investigation set on foot in the colonies revealed the presence of an "ingenious Jesuit in Philadelphia," upon whom the suspicions of disloyalty were centered. Father Harding promptly cleared himself of these suspicions, however, declaring that he was English by birth and sentiment; and assuaged the anxiety of the Protestant population by stating that there were not above 2,000 Catholics in the whole province of Pennsylvania. So convinced were Philadelphians of his integrity that when in 1763 he built St. Mary's Church on land he had bought for cemetery purposes in 1759, the generosity of the Protestants matched that of the Catholics. The English authorities, too, manifested confidence in him and in 1760 solicited him for a priest to work among the Indians of Illinois. He was active in the colonial cause and an intimate friend of George Meade, the Revolutionary patriot. Intellectually he was held in high repute: Ezra Stiles, president of Yale College, attended his chapel to hear him preach (Sept. 29, 1754). He may have written the articles on the attitude of the Fathers of the primitive Church toward the theatre, printed in the *Pennsylvania Gazette* (Feb. 5, 1767). On May 18, 1768, he became a member of the American Philosophical Association. The *Pennsylvania Gazette* of Sept. 2, 1772, in announcing his death "Early of the First Instant," referred to him as "a Gentleman, who for the Integrity of his Life, and exemplary Conversation, is greatly lamented."

[Extracts in the Woodstock College Library from the Catalogues of the Society (of Jesus) kept at Rome; *Pennsylvania Gazette,* Sept. 2, 1772; *Am. Cath. Hist. Soc. Researches,* and *Am. Cath. Hist. Soc. Records, passim*; T. A. Hughes, *Hist. of the Society of Jesus in North America* (3 vols., London, 1917); J. L. Kirlin, *Catholicity in Phila.* (1909); J. G. Shea, *The Catholic Ch. in the U. S.,* vol. I (1886).] F. J. T.

HARDING, SETH (Apr. 17, 1734–Nov. 20, 1814), naval officer, the son of Theodore and Sarah (Hamilton) Harding, was born at Eastham, Mass., of old Plymouth stock, a great-great-grandson of Joseph Harding who died at Plymouth in 1633. His youth was spent among seafaring folk and his education was nautical rather than academic. At nineteen, Apr. 27, 1753, he was married at Easthampton to Abigail Doane, who died after a few years. In his early twenties he moved to Norwich, Conn., and engaged in trade with the West Indies, commanding several merchant vessels during the hazardous periods of the French and Indian Wars. He was married a second time, at Norwich, Nov. 24, 1760, to Ruth Reed. In 1771 he removed to Liverpool, Nova Scotia, and acquired moderate wealth and political preferment, but the outbreak of the American Revolution caused his prestige and reputation to suffer in a community whose views were radically opposed to his own, and he therefore returned to Connecticut, where he offered his services to the governor. Commissioned to command the Connecticut brig *Defence,* Captain Harding consummated in June 1776 the most brilliant exploit of the American navy up to that time. During the night of June 16, he pursued two armed transports up Massachusetts Bay, ran his ship in between them, and called upon them to strike their colors. "Yes, I'll strike!" was the reply, as the British ships delivered broadsides at the *Defence.* Harding replied with port and starboard broadsides and after a hot engagement of an hour and a half compelled both ships to surrender. The following day by adroit maneuvering he captured a third transport. The capture included 466 officers and men of the 71st Highlanders and an invaluable stock of small arms and military stores, of which the army under Washington was in sore need.

Harding commanded successively the *Defence* (a new ship of the same name) and the *Oliver Cromwell* of the Connecticut state navy, making many valuable captures of British warships and armed merchantmen. In September 1778 Congress appointed him to command the Continental frigate *Confederacy,* yet to be constructed at Norwich, Conn. Gov. Jonathan Trumbull of Connecticut commented, "There is no one who can man a ship more expeditiously than him, from the opinion which the seamen in general entertain of him" (Howard, *post,* p. 61). President Laurens, in confirming the action of Congress, wrote, "Capt. Harding is a man of more dispatch than vanity" (*Ibid.,* p. 67). In October 1779 he was ordered to carry to Europe John Jay, newly appointed minister to Spain, and M. Gerard, the returning French envoy. Ten days out, the *Confederacy* was completely dismasted in a gale off the Newfoundland Banks, and only by the most skillful seamanship and good fortune were passengers and crew brought safely into Martinique, whence the former were transhipped to Spain. After a tedious period of refitting, the *Confederacy* engaged in raiding merchant vessels and in convoy service between United States and West Indian ports until it was captured by a superior British naval force on Apr. 14, 1781.

Exchanged in the following year, Harding assumed command of the letter of marque *Diana* but was soon captured and taken to Jamaica by a British warship. After his release he was picked up by Capt. John Barry at Cape François and voluntarily accepted the position of second in command on the *Alliance.* On Mar. 10,

1783, the *Alliance* encountered three British ships off the Florida coast. The engagement was indecisive. Harding was wounded but stuck to his post and participated with Barry in firing the last gun of the Revolution. After the close of the war, he resumed his activities in the merchant marine, trading largely with the Danish West Indies, where he acquired Danish citizenship for conveniences of trade without sacrificing his allegiance to the United States. Ill health, the effect of his wounds, forced him to retire from the sea, however, and left him with the barest means of livelihood. Congress was periodically petitioned for relief, but none was granted until 1807 when he was awarded half pay of a captain in the navy. His declining years were spent in Schoharie, N. Y., where he died.

[J. L. Howard, *Seth Harding, Mariner: A Naval Picture of the Revolution* (1930), containing full bibliography of printed and manuscript materials; L. F. Middlebrook, *History of Maritime Connecticut during the American Revolution* (2 vols., 1925).] J. L. H.

HARDING, WARREN GAMALIEL (Nov. 2, 1865–Aug. 2, 1923), twenty-ninth president of the United States, was born on a farm at Caledonia (now Blooming Grove), Morrow County, Ohio, the first of eight children of George Tryon and Phoebe (Dickerson) Harding. The father, then a farmer and later a physician, was of English and Scottish stock, the mother of English and Dutch (Clara Gardner Miller, *The Ancestry of President Harding,* 1928). After preparation in the local schools, Harding was sent to Ohio Central College, an institution of academy grade in Iberia, Ohio, where he attended for the three years 1879–82. Vacations and spare hours were spent in work on the farm, in a sawmill, in making brooms, and even as a laborer in helping to build the Toledo & Ohio Central Railroad. When his father removed in 1882 to the county seat, Marion, then a town of not quite 4,000 people, to practise medicine, Harding gave a brief trial to the study of law, which he disliked, and to the work of an insurance canvasser. He had gained some newspaper experience as printer's devil on the Caledonia *Argus* and as manager of a college paper, and in 1884 was employed on the Marion *Democratic Mirror,* a weekly journal, until in his enthusiasm for Blaine he found its strong Democratic views becoming irksome. He liked the calling, however, and immediately after the election joined a comrade named Jack Warwick in purchasing for $300 a struggling four-page sheet, the Marion *Star,* which was about to be sold at auction by the sheriff. For some years its circulation was less than 500 and its fate doubtful. Harding, who soon bought out his partner, collected news and advertising, set type, and oversaw the job-printing office until the growth of the town lifted the newspaper to prosperity.

Until near the close of the century, Harding devoted himself wholly to his newspaper and the activities of the town. He was a tall, handsome, likable young man, of some dissipated habits despite his industry, who played a variety of instruments in the Marion cornet band and led the neighborhood blades in their amusements. On July 8, 1891, he married Florence Kling De Wolfe, a widow with one child, the daughter of Amos Kling, a Marion banker. Her parents opposed the match, but she persisted, and, the union proving childless, assisted Harding greatly in transforming the *Star* from a weekly into a daily. As the journal enlarged its circulation, he grew in importance. He became a director of the Marion County Bank, the Marion Lumber Company, the Marion County Telephone Company, and other corporations, a trustee of the Trinity Baptist Church, and prominent in the Masonic and Elk organizations. In every respect he fitted the small-town environment. He was genial, interested in most sides of community life, a systematic promoter of civic enterprises, easygoing, and frank in admitting his lack of unusual abilities or intellectual tastes. His editorship and his talent for public speaking gradually won him political influence, and in political campaigns his resonant voice became known in much of central Ohio. Aligning himself with Joseph B. Foraker [*q.v.*] in state politics, he was nominated in 1898 for the state Senate in the district comprising Hardin, Logan, Union, and Marion counties, and was elected, promptly becoming floor leader for the Foraker group. In this campaign he made the acquaintance of Harry M. Daugherty, a former state representative, who at the end of his second term in the Senate (1902) helped him secure nomination and election as lieutenant-governor on the ticket headed by Myron T. Herrick. At the end of his undistinguished service he declined to stand for reelection. The Republican party in Ohio was passing under partial eclipse, and Harding found it convenient to give his entire attention to his newspaper until 1910, when he was nominated for governor but defeated by Judson Harmon by a plurality of approximately 100,000.

In these years he showed a conciliatory temper, keeping aloof from the numerous Republican factional quarrels; but he was distinctly friendly to machine elements, including the notorious Cincinnati boss, George B. Cox, whom at a state convention in 1904 he called "a peerless leader." His reputation as an orator increased, and in 1912 he was selected by President Taft to present his name at the Republican National Convention. Always a party regular, in the ensuing campaign he attacked Roosevelt vigorously. Under the guidance of Daugherty, now a highly experienced politician and lobbyist, he successfully ran against his old friend Foraker in 1914 for the Republican nomination to the United States Senate, and that fall was elected for the term 1915–21 by a plurality of 102,000. The size of the vote attracted attention, and when in 1916 he was chosen temporary chairman of the Republican National Convention in Chicago, making the "keynote speech," he was mentioned as a possible "dark-horse" candidate for president.

During his six years in the Senate, Harding became known as a safe and conservative member, attached to the standard Republican policies and especially sensitive to attacks upon big business. Personally attractive, he was of convivial habits, drinking a good deal and playing poker (White, *post*). He achieved no distinction whatever as a debater or an originator of legislation, and during the struggle over the Versailles Treaty made but one long speech, which went unnoticed. He found the Senate, as he said, "a very pleasant place." In 1916 he voted against the confirmation of Louis D. Brandeis as associate justice of the Supreme Court. In the same year he vigorously attacked Wilson's Mexican policy as indifferent to American investments and lives. He was a strong protectionist, and repeatedly avowed his belief in a ship subsidy. He favored the remission of tolls for American coastal shipping using the Panama Canal. In 1917 he voted for the bill to arm merchant ships, and shortly afterward for the declaration of war against Germany. He supported the Espionage Bill, the Selective Draft Bill, and the war revenue bills, but opposed high taxes on war profits in the belief that they would injure business and act to the final detriment of the nation. Throughout his career he had been on close terms with the Anti-Saloon League (Peter H. Odegard, *Pressure Politics. The Story of the Anti-Saloon League,* 1928, p. 172), and he not only supported the Eighteenth Amendment and Volstead Act but made suggestions for smoothing their way; while he voted for the equal suffrage amendment. As a member of the foreign relations committee he faithfully followed its chairman, Senator Lodge, in the issues raised by the peace. He signed the Lodge-Brandegee round-robin for the separation of the treaty and the League Covenant, and attacked the League as being either "a surrender of national sovereignty" or "an empty thing, big in name," that would "ultimately disappoint all of humanity that hinges its hope upon it." His subsequent view was that it was "a super-government of the world" (Schortemeier, *post,* p. 256). He declared that ratification was impossible without ample reservations, and voted against all alternatives to the Lodge resolution of conditional ratification. Later he supported the Knox resolution for a separate peace with Germany, asserting that "we are . . . giving notice to the world that the Chief Executive alone does not run the Republic" (*Congressional Record,* 66 Cong., 2 Sess., p. 7099).

The reaction from the tension and hardships of the war made Harding, with his conservatism, his cautious nationalism, his limited range of ideas, and his amiable temperament, a potential candidate for the presidency. In 1919 Harry M. Daugherty, at the head of the Ohio machine or "gang," began an astute campaign in his behalf. Harding's own faith wavered and he was more than once on the verge of withdrawal to assure his reëlection to the Senate. Though he showed no strength in the primaries and had even to divide the delegates of Ohio with Leonard Wood, Daugherty confidently predicted that after a long deadlock Harding would be chosen by a little two-o'clock-in-the-morning group. When the convention met in Chicago on June 8, 1920, he was in the minds of Lodge, Penrose, and others of the senatorial oligarchy which dominated the gathering. On the initial ballot he received only 65½ votes, and at first lost ground. But when Hiram Johnson grew weaker and Senator Borah announced that the progressives would bolt either Lowden or Wood, an early-morning meeting of leaders in George Harvey's room at the Blackstone Hotel, which included Senators Lodge, Smoot, Brandegee, McCormick, and Wadsworth, and was in close touch with Penrose by telephone, decided upon Harding. Distrust of his personal character appeared in the fact that this group called Harding before it and required him to make solemn affirmation that there was no reason in his past why he should not be nominated (Willis F. Johnson, *George Harvey, "A Passionate Patriot,"* 1929, p. 282). He was nominated that same day, June 12, on the tenth ballot, leading Wood by 692–1/5 to 156. The choice produced a feeling of national disappointment that was strongly voiced by even stanch Republican organs (*Literary Digest,* June 26, 1920; *Saturday Evening Post,* July 24, 1920).

A "front porch" campaign followed. Harding

receiving many delegations at his Marion home and making a series of speeches which were effective politically though they added nothing to his intellectual stature. He declared for a high tariff, a ship subsidy, the restriction of immigration, the rehabilitation of the railroads under private ownership, the creation of a department of public welfare, the encouragement of agricultural cooperation, and a policy of general deflation. On international issues he asserted that "our party means to hold the heritage of American nationality unimpaired and unsurrendered" (acceptance speech, July 22, 1920), and repeated in various forms an earlier exhortation: "Stabilize America first, prosper America first, think of America first, exalt America first!" (Schortemeier, *post*, p. 229). His opponent, Gov. James M. Cox, attempted under Wilson's inspiration to make the League of Nations the central issue. Harding refused an explicit statement of his position, straddling the question by condemning the Covenant in harsh terms while promising to labor for an "association of nations." The result was that while irreconcilables like Borah and Johnson supported him as an enemy of the League, a group of thirty-one Republican believers in the League idea, including Hughes and Hoover, signed an appeal for his election as the surest way of securing American entry into a satisfactory world organization (*New York Times*, Oct. 15, 1920). In a confused campaign, in which a heterogeneous mass of discontented elements vented their irritation upon President Wilson and the Democratic party, Harding neither offended nor impressed any one. A nation which accepted Senator Brandegee's view that the time did not require "first raters" gave him a staggering majority, the electoral vote being 404 for Harding and 127 for Cox, and the popular vote 16,152,000 for Harding and 9,147,000 for Cox (Edward Stanwood, *A History of the Presidency*, 1928, II, 423).

President Harding created a favorable impression by entering office without ostentation; he vetoed an inaugural display, and Mrs. Harding announced that they were "just folks." His cabinet appointments encountered considerable immediate criticism, and later it became evident that the body was a strange mixture of distinguished men, mediocrities, and politicians dangerously unfit for their offices. He was saved from the blunder of giving George Harvey the leading place only by that leader's generous refusal (Johnson, *George Harvey*, p. 282). The selection of Hughes as secretary of state, Hoover as secretary of commerce, and Mellon as secretary of the treasury commanded general approval and seemed to redeem the party's promise to use the "best minds." Paying political debts by other appointments, Harding fared less fortunately. Such intimate friends as Harvey promptly condemned Albert B. Fall, who was named secretary of the interior, as a man totally unfit by character and antecedents for the place, while the nomination of Harry M. Daugherty as attorney-general was, in view of his dubious record as a lobbyist, his entire lack of standing at the bar, and the fact that he had held no office higher than that of state representative, very widely attacked. Will H. Hays of Indiana, the new postmaster-general, was distrusted as an excessively adroit politician. A number of minor appointments, notably those of Charles R. Forbes as head of the Veterans' Bureau, Thomas W. Miller as alien property custodian, D. R. Crissinger, a Marion friend, as comptroller of the currency, E. Mont Reily as governor of Porto Rico, and Elmer Dover as assistant secretary of the treasury, were accepted without comment by the public, but filled experts on administration with consternation (Bruce Bliven, "The Ohio Gang," *New Republic*, May 7–June 4, 1924; New York *World* correspondence, 1921–22). As president, Harding quickly revealed to close observers an average common sense and conscientiousness, more than an average political skill and industry, and an undisciplined mind. There was "a certain softness about him mentally" (C. W. Gilbert, *The Mirrors of Washington*, 1921, p. 13). His intimate associates in the White House were selected from among the least intellectual of the senators and more irresponsible members of Washington society, with a sprinkling of Ohioans. Both the official and social atmosphere of the capital became obviously relaxed, careless, and open-handed. Harding worked hard and showed a wise reliance upon his ablest cabinet members, but the liquor and cards in the executive mansion, the gaiety of his pleasure trips, and the predatory aims of some of his associates quickly aroused critical comment (E. G. Lowry, *Washington Close-Ups*, 1921).

Harding called Congress to meet in special session on Apr. 11, 1921, and undertook to carry through a broad program. In his first message he recommended the creation of a federal budget system, an emergency tariff act, the restriction of immigration, assistance to the farmers, the readjustment of war taxes, and every possible effort at economy and retrenchment. His first step in international affairs was to sign the Knox resolution of peace with Germany, which Wilson had vetoed, and to appoint Alanson B. Houghton, a happy choice, as ambassador to

Berlin. But his presidential policies were all less his own than those of the Senate leaders and the three strongest members of the cabinet; it was quickly discovered that he had "a mind that bows to authority" (Gilbert, p. 14). Nor were his domestic achievements impressive. A competent observer declared at the close of his second year: "There has not been produced, during these two sessions, a single constructive piece of legislation that compares with the Congressional landmarks of the Wilson period" (W. B. Munro, "Two Years of President Harding," *Atlantic Monthly,* March 1923). Tariff revision had already commenced, and Harding signed without hesitation both the emergency tariff bill which Wilson had vetoed and the more permanent Fordney-McCumber Act (May 27, 1921; Sept. 21, 1922), though both were assailed by even protectionist Republicans as injuriously extreme measures. By the flexible tariff clause of the latter bill he was given power, following an investigation by the tariff commission, to raise or lower any duty by not more than 50 per cent., but he made practically no use of it. The adoption of a national budget, a reform which had been brought to the very point of completion under Wilson, took place early in the administration, Harding approving the bill on June 10, 1921, and appointing Charles G. Dawes first director of the budget.

In dealing with war taxes the President was guided by Secretary Mellon, who defined the administration program as one of steady reduction and of antagonism to high surtaxes. The first steps in the revision were to repeal the excess-profits tax and transportation tax, substituting for the former a small tax on corporate incomes, and to reduce the surtaxes. The President interposed to iron out differences between Secretary Mellon and those congressmen who thought him too tender of great aggregations of wealth, and at a White House conference on Aug. 9, 1921, secured a generally satisfactory agreement. In dealing with the economic depression of 1921–22, and the bitter strikes of the latter year in the hard and soft coal fields and the railway shops, Harding was guided chiefly by Secretary Hoover. He recommended a measure establishing a fact-finding coal commission, and a coal-distribution bill, both of which passed (August, September 1922); and he appointed Hoover chairman of a committee to control, through priority arrangements, the transportation and in part the price of all the available coal east of the Mississippi. But his personal efforts failed to contribute anything to the final agreement between operators and miners. In the shopmen's strike, moreover, he showed vacillation; "the President edged to one side and then to the other, ultimately emerging with a compromise after the psychological moment for it had gone by" (Munro, *ante*). The administration gave its approval to the Capper-Volstead Act legalizing cooperative-marketing associations for farmers (Feb. 18, 1922), and to enactments extending the privileges of government credit open to farmers, but a growing divergence appeared between it and the Western farm bloc.

Harding's failure to display a vigorous leadership sprang partly from weakness, and partly from his belief in cooperation with Congress and in a preservation of the traditional system of checks and balances. He was capable also of some persistence, as he proved in his futile advocacy of the ship subsidy bill which passed the House in November 1922, but failed in the Senate. But differences with Congress or any considerable portion of his party always disturbed him and frequently made him draw back. He tacitly dropped his plan for a department of public welfare. His proposal that the United States should adhere to the World Court had the support of a powerful body of non-partisan opinion, but was vehemently attacked by the irreconcilable Republicans, and in one of his last speeches (June 1923) he crippled it by approving drastic reservations, the purpose of which was the total divorce of the Court from the League (David Hunter Miller, *The World Court and Mr. Harding,* 1923). He gave much attention to the question of the payment of the European debts to the United States. In the form originally proposed by the administration the debt-funding bill allowed the president, acting through the secretary of the treasury, a wide discretion in settling upon terms with the debtor nations; but Congress, in passing the act signed on Feb. 9, 1922, would not permit this, and Harding yielded. As he lacked firm leadership, he also lacked vigilance and foresight. His worst single error was his failure to guard the public domain in the West from the marauders who wished to use it and who acted through Secretary Fall. In May 1921, this corrupt cabinet member induced the President to sign an executive order transferring the naval oil reserves from the Navy to the Interior Department. This unconstitutional act, for the courts later held that Congress alone had the right to make such a transfer, received little attention from the press. That autumn and winter Secretary Fall was involved in a series of sinister financial transactions with E. L. Doheny and Harry F. Sinclair, oil promoters, who in April 1922 secured the grant of leases of enormous value from the Department of the Interior. Within a fortnight after the signing of these Teapot Dome and Elk Hills leases Senator La Follette moved for an investigation of them; and though Fall induced Harding to inform the Senate that he entirely approved the acts of the Interior Department, the motion was carried. A storm was plainly brewing (M. E. Ravage, *The Story of Teapot Dome,* 1924).

In foreign affairs Harding accepted the guidance of Secretary Hughes, though both were fettered by their readiness to interpret the events of 1919–20 as a stern national mandate to avoid all foreign commitments. Harding announced in his first message that the United States would have nothing to do with the League of Nations; in one of his last speeches, that at St. Louis in June 1923, he proclaimed the League issue "as dead as slavery"; and while he early asserted that "we make no surrender of our hope and aim for an association to promote peace, in which we would most heartily join," he took no practical steps to achieve this object. In this attitude he was influenced by such associates as Senator Brandegee and Richard Washburn Child. For a time Hughes declined even to answer communications from the League, and the administration drew back sharply from most forms of cooperation with the outside world. It refused to follow Germany and Great Britain in resuming relations with Russia; it declined to recognize the Japanese claim to a mandate over the island of Yap; it drew up separate treaties of peace with Germany, Austria, and Hungary, including most of the advantages of the Versailles and St. Germain treaties, but rejecting all clauses which implied action with the League. Meanwhile, Borah and other senators had been urging the administration to grapple with the problem of the international limitation of navies. Under pressure of Borah's amendment to the naval bill passed on May 21, 1921, which authorized and urged the President to call an international conference, Harding on July 10 sent out preliminary invitations to Great Britain, France, Italy, and Japan, and final invitations a month later. The situation in the Far East, in view of the possible renewal of the Anglo-Japanese alliance, appeared dangerous, and as a consequence invitations were ultimately sent also to China, Holland, Belgium, and Portugal. In these steps Harding responded to rather than led Congress. He indicated that he regarded the conference as not merely a means of dealing with naval limitation and Far Eastern questions, but as the first of a series of international gatherings; but this intention remained wholly vague. The Washington Conference, which assembled on Nov. 12, 1921, was under the direct management of Secretary Hughes, and it is still uncertain what part Harding played in formulating the bold proposals with which the American delegates opened the first session. It represented the climax of the Harding administration, and its one really memorable achievement.

By the spring of 1923 difficulties were thickening fast around the President. In the elections of the previous autumn the Republican majorities in Congress had been reduced to a precarious level, dropping to eight in the Senate and five in the House. The farm bloc of radical Republicans obtained a clear balance of power. As a result the administration was crippled in all its proposals for further legislative action, and entered upon a period of political confusion. In Washington a series of scandals, still secret from the general public, were threatening to break. It was common rumor that the Department of Justice was corrupt, that some members of the "Ohio gang" were extorting money from violators of the prohibition law and other laws, and that one Jesse Smith, an associate of Daugherty, acted as collector until his sudden suicide or murder (May 30, 1923). Stories of wholesale looting by the Alien Property Custodian and the Director of the Veterans' Bureau were afloat. It was declared that Harding had cursed the latter as a traitor and thief and violently ejected him from his office (White, *post,* p. 430). Senator Thomas J. Walsh of Montana, as head of the Senate investigating committee, was collecting the material which was to result in exposure of the oil-lease scandal. There is evidence that Harding was deeply embarrassed by the existence of an illegitimate daughter born to Nan Britton, formerly of Marion, in October 1919 (Nan Britton, *post,* pp. 110 ff.). In the midst of these troubles, on June 20, 1923, President and Mrs. Harding, accompanied by a party of sixty-five, set off on a transcontinental tour. He was obviously harassed and worried as he made his initial speeches, and his anxiety is said to have been increased by a secret interview of an hour with the wife of Secretary Fall in the Hotel Muehlebach in Kansas City (Senator Capper, quoted by White, *post,* p. 432; partially denied by Mrs. Fall). He pushed on to Alaska, and after making a brief tour of part of that territory, was so disturbed by the receipt of a long Washington message in cipher that "for a day or so he was near collapse" (*Ibid.*). Returning to Vancouver, he spoke there, and on July 27 left Seattle for San Francisco. His worry continued, and he repeatedly asked Secretary

Hoover and certain trusted newspaper correspondents what a president whose friends had betrayed him should do. On July 28 he was reported suffering from ptomaine poisoning, and on reaching San Francisco went at once to the Palace Hotel for rest, his physicians declaring him in a state of utter exhaustion. His condition became grave on the night of the 28th with the development of bronchopneumonia, and at 7:30 P.M. on Aug. 2, after an apparent improvement, he suddenly died. The cause of his death was stated to be embolism (R. L. Wilbur, "The Last Illness of a Calm Man," *Saturday Evening Post,* Oct. 13, 1923). The body was brought to Washington for a state funeral on Aug. 8, and amid widespread expressions of sorrow, for he had retained his popularity, was buried two days later in Marion.

At the time, his sudden end was regarded as tragic, but before the lapse of many months it became evident that it was fortunate for him and his party. A series of public investigations, of which the chief was the inquiry of the Senate committee under Mr. Walsh into the naval oil leases, revealed the extent to which Harding had been victimized by treachery and corruption in many parts of his administration. These exposures, continued for several years, showed a looseness and dishonesty which paralleled those of the era just after the Civil War. They resulted in the revocation by the Supreme Court of the oil leases signed by Secretary Fall, and his sentence to a term in federal prison; the resignation of Attorney-General Daugherty and his narrow escape from the penitentiary on charges of corruption; the resignation under fire of Secretary Denby of the Navy; penitentiary sentences for Charles R. Forbes of the Veterans' Bureau and Alien Property Custodian Miller; proof that part of the enormous slush fund connected with the oil-lease transactions ($260,000 produced by the Continental Trading Company deal) had gone into the Republican party treasury to help liquidate the expenditures of 1920; and the punishment of various minor wrong-doers. In the trial of Daugherty in October 1926 the defense attempted to explain Daugherty's failure to take the stand and his destruction of bank records on the ground that any other course would have left a deep stain on Harding's memory. The extent to which he was aware of the evils boiling beneath the surface of his administration, and was either willing to palter with them or be blackmailed into overlooking them, cannot now be determined. The assessable evidence indicates that till near the end he was ignorant of a large part of the corruption surrounding him, and was stunned and completely perplexed when he discovered its proportions. Even if this is true, his responsibility for his appointments, for the general tone which he gave to his administration, and for such errors as his approval of the transfer of the oil reserves, cannot be palliated. In the first years after his death his name was so clouded that few would honor or defend it. Yet it must be recognized that a heavy responsibility for his record falls upon the party and nation which elected a man of moderate abilities, weak judgment of character, excessive amiability, and total lack of vigilance to so exacting an office. In minor station he was a useful and likable man, and it was his cruel misfortune that he was lifted to a post beyond his powers.

[There is no biography of Harding worthy of the name. Among the compilations treating of his life may be mentioned: Joe M. Chapple, *Warren G. Harding—the Man* (1920, 1924); T. H. Russell, *The Illustrious Life and Work of Warren G. Harding* (1923); Willis F. Johnson, *The Life of Warren G. Harding* (1923); and Sherman A. Cuneo, *From Printer to President* (1922). Light is thrown upon his character by Charles Willis Thompson, *Presidents I've Known and Two Near Presidents* (1929), and William Allen White, *Masks in a Pageant* (1928). The question of his illegitimate daughter is treated in Nan Britton, *The President's Daughter* (1927), and Joseph De Barthe, *The Answer* (1928). The "revelations" contained in Gaston B. Means, *The Strange Death of President Harding* (1920), have not been substantiated. The various collections of Harding's speeches, such as F. E. Schortemeier, *Rededicating America: Life and Recent Speeches of Warren G. Harding* (1920), are all defective, and his public utterances can as yet be fully studied only through the *Congressional Record* and the newspapers. The magazine literature upon his life is voluminous. Among articles of special value may be mentioned George T. Harding, "Warren Was a Good Son," *Collier's,* Mar. 6, 1926; Samuel G. Blythe, "Calm Review of a Calm Man," *Saturday Evening Post,* July 28, 1923; W. B. Munro, "Two Years of President Harding," *Atlantic Monthly,* March 1923; and Mark Sullivan, "Two Years of President Harding," *World's Work,* November 1922. Better than any American obituary article is that in the London *Times,* Aug. 4, 1923.]

A. N.

HARDING, WILLIAM PROCTER GOULD (May 5, 1864–Apr. 7, 1930), banker, governor of the Federal Reserve Board, was born in Greene County, Ala., the son of Horace and Eliza Procter (Gould) Harding and a grandson of Chester Harding [*q.v.*]. Graduating from the University of Alabama in 1880, he entered business as bookkeeper in a private bank, subsequently becoming cashier of the Berney National Bank of Birmingham, Ala., then vice-president and afterward president of the National Bank of Birmingham. On Oct. 22, 1895, he married Amanda Perrine Moore of that city. His knowledge of banking and his judgment of trade conditions brought him to the presidency of the Alabama State Bankers' Association in 1908 and of the Birmingham Chamber of Commerce in 1913, and appointment as Southern member of the newly organized Federal Reserve Board in 1914. In 1916 he was made governor of the Board. At that time it was believed that American intervention in the European war could not be long postponed. The first step taken under Harding's administration was the "mobilizing" with the Federal Reserve of all the gold previously held by private member banks as part of their own lawful reserve. After the declaration of war in April 1917, permission to export gold from the United States was made contingent on the assent of the Reserve Board. That proviso placed heavy responsibilities on Harding and his colleagues—responsibilities which were greatly increased when, in 1918, he became managing director of the government's War Finance Corporation, formed to lend public funds to industries whose products should be judged "necessary or contributory to the prosecution of the war." In these activities he won recognition as an efficient organizer, a tireless worker, and a sound though perhaps not brilliant, war-time executive. Genial and companionable, he displayed judgment and tact in maintaining harmony in the Reserve Board itself, and between the Board and the twelve Reserve banks on the one hand and the national government on the other.

On the return of peace, the immense requisitions on the Reserve banks' credit facilities were presently diverted into speculation of great magnitude which caused a rise in staple prices to an average of 20 per cent. above the highest of wartime and 147 per cent. above the pre-war level. As early as April 1919, Harding expressed his own belief that this misuse of credit should be checked by advancing the Reserve banks' discount rate, but such action was opposed at the time by the Treasury, in view of pending operations to reduce the government's floating debt, and no change in rate was made until November. Credit inflation was by that time wholly out of hand and, despite the moderate advance in the official discount rate, the ratio of the system's gold reserve to its note and deposit liabilities fell virtually to the legal minimum; in the New York Reserve bank, below it. To control the market's inroads on the system's credit fund, the Reserve bank rate was raised to 6 per cent.; then, in June 1920, to 7, though caution was observed by Harding, to avoid curtailing credit actually needed by industry when the inevitable "deflation" of the markets occurred. Even after the raising of the rate to 7 per cent., the Reserve banks increased by $485,000,000 in the subsequent five months their rediscount of purely commercial obligations.

With the collapse of speculation in commodities, the crash in staple prices, and the reaction in general trade, a great part of the industrial community angrily laid the responsibility on the Federal Reserve. Harding had publicly described the high prices of 1920 as artificial, and had boldly declared to agricultural associations that the Reserve system did not recognize maintenance of existing prices as its duty. These utterances were widely misinterpreted and misquoted; the governor and his colleagues on the board were charged in agricultural conferences with having promoted a policy of forcing down prices to "the pre-war basis" and with engaging deliberately in "a drive to force wheat from $2.55 to $1.60." Harding himself was assailed with special malignity, even to the extent of allegation, on the floor of the United States Senate, that he had personally been speculating in cotton and had pursued the "deflation policy" with his own interests in view. It was partly with the purpose of answering the charges of misjudgment made against his official policies that he wrote his book, *The Formative Period of the Federal Reserve System* (1925), which is primarily a careful historical sketch of the evolution of the system's policies in its earlier years but also a vigorous though good-tempered defense of the controverted policies of the author's own administration. When his official term expired in August 1922 the banking and conservative business community urged, unsuccessfully, that he be reappointed. After his retirement from the Board, he served for a time as special financial adviser to the Cuban government (1922) and declined an invitation (1924) from the League of Nations to become the financial administrator for Hungary, although he visited and gave unofficial aid to that country. In 1923 he was elected governor of the Federal Reserve Bank of Boston, and continued in that office until his death.

In addition to his book already mentioned there are in print a number of speeches made by Harding while in office: *The Present Position and Future Development of the Federal Reserve System* (1916), *Functions and Policies of the Federal Reserve Board* (1920), *The Federal Reserve System as Related to American Business* (1921), *The Federal Reserve System, What It Is, and What It Is Not* (1921), *Credit, Currency and Business* (1922).

[Harding's writings; H. P. Willis, *The Federal Reserve System* (1923); P. M. Warburg, *The Federal Reserve System: its Origin and Growth* (2 vols., 1930); *Who's Who in America*, 1928–29; *Commercial and Fi-*

nancial Chronicle, Apr. 12, 1930; *Journal of Commerce* (N. Y.); *N. Y. Times*, Apr. 8, 1930.] A. D. N.

HARDING, WILLIAM WHITE (Nov. 1, 1830–May 15, 1889), publisher, was born in Philadelphia, Pa., a son of Jesper Harding [*q.v.*] and Maria Wilson Harding and brother of George Harding [*q.v.*]. He attended the Northwest School, Philadelphia, and in 1846 became a clerk in the bookstore of George S. Appleton, where he remained three years. He then became associated with his father's business and in 1856 was made a partner, under the firm name of Jesper Harding & Son. Upon the retirement of his father, in 1859, he became the sole proprietor of *The Pennsylvania Inquirer* and the extensive Bible-publishing business which the elder Harding had built up. One of his first acts was to change the name of the paper to *The Philadelphia Inquirer.* Soon its size was increased from two to four pages and then to eight; the system of credit subscriptions was abolished; in connection with it stereotyping was introduced for the first time in Philadelphia; and in later years other innovations and mechanical improvements were made. The editorial and news items were also improved, no expense being spared to bring the paper up to the highest standard of journalism. During the Civil War—at which time Harding served as a colonel on the staff of Gov. James Pollock of Pennsylvania—the paper heartily supported the cause of the Union and showed great enterprise in obtaining news from the armies and from the government offices at Washington. Very efficient methods were maintained for circulating the paper in the armies and so highly was it regarded by officials that when any steps were taken in the prosecution of the war which it was thought advisable to communicate to the soldiers, a special edition was ordered by the authorities for free distribution in the field.

Early in his career as a publisher Harding adopted a plan for encouraging youthful talent. So many young men received their newspaper training at his hands that he became known as a judge of "raw material" and his paper as a school of journalism of the first rank. In addition to the development of the *Inquirer* he continued, with improvements, the publication of the "Harding Bible." In 1864 he established a paper-mill at Manayunk, near Philadelphia, and was prominently identified with the first attempts to make paper out of wood, having secured the rights to the process from its inventor. As a result of his initiative in this field of industry he was awarded a medal at the Philadelphia Centennial Exposition in 1876 as the only exhibitor at whose establishment paper was made, printed, and bound in book form. He also took a leading part in the development of the street-railway system of Philadelphia and gave much of his time and money to assist in the perfection of inventions of various kinds, especially those affecting the newspaper industry. In 1889 failing health caused him to relinquish the active management of the *Inquirer,* its ownership being transferred to a corporation—The Philadelphia Inquirer Company. He is described as a man of attractive personal appearance, simple in his habits and unostentatious in his manner. He did much to place newspaper publishing on a high plane and under his direction the *Inquirer* became a model for other papers in this country. Three months after his retirement he died of pneumonia at his home in Philadelphia. He had been married to Catharine Hart and there were six children.

[E. P. Oberholtzer, *Phila.—A Hist. of the City and Its People* (n.d.), vol. IV; J. T. Scharf and T. Westcott, *Hist. of Phila.* (1884), vol. III; Moses King, *Philadelphia and Notable Philadelphians* (1902); *Philadelphia's Industries* (n.d.); "The Phila. Inquirer 1829–1929" (MS.) in the possession of W. G. Harding, Esq., New York City; *Press* (Phila.), May 16, 1889.] J. H. F.

HARDY, ARTHUR SHERBURNE (Aug. 13, 1847–Mar. 13, 1930), mathematician, novelist, diplomat, was born in Andover, Mass., the son of Alpheus and Susan W. (Holmes) Hardy. His father was a wealthy and cultured merchant, a trustee of Amherst College and Andover Seminary, and chairman of the prudential committee of the American Board of Commissioners for Foreign Missions. As a boy of twelve Hardy was put in a school at Neuchâtel, Switzerland, where he acquired his excellent command of the French language. A few years later he made a voyage to Spain in the *Young Turk,* one of his father's ships. After attending the Boston Latin School, Phillips Andover Academy, and Amherst College (1864–65), he was appointed to the United States Military Academy and graduated in June 1869. A year on the Dry Tortugas as a second lieutenant of the 3rd Artillery gave him his fill of army life, and he resigned his commission as soon as he could. He was professor of civil engineering in Iowa (now Grinnell) College, 1871–73; an *élève externe* of the École des Ponts et Chaussées and the Conservatoire des Arts et Métiers in Paris, 1873–74; and professor of civil engineering, 1874–78, and of mathematics, 1878–93, in Dartmouth College. He was a good teacher, and his textbooks *Elements of Quarternions* (1881); *Imaginary Quantities* (1881), a translation of Argand's French treatise; *New Methods in Topographical Sur-*

veying (1883); *Elements of Analytic Geometry* (1889); and *Elements of Calculus* (1890)—were well received. Meanwhile his literary career had begun with the publication of a long poem, *Francesca of Rimini* (1878); with the appearance in 1883 of his first novel, *But Yet a Woman,* he leaped into prominence. The remarkable though transient vogue of this production was almost entirely a triumph of style; somewhat vague and unsatisfactory as a story, it won readers by its warm descriptive passages, spilth of aphorisms, and lustrous surface qualities. His next novel, *The Wind of Destiny* (1886), was a better literary performance, but its tragic tone was not so well liked by the public. In his third, *Passe Rose* (1889), an historical romance of the reign of Charlemagne, he displayed a growing power of character portrayal and a nice regard for historical accuracy. In 1891 he published the *Life and Letters of Joseph Hardy Neesima,* and from June 1893 to June 1895 he was editor of the *Cosmopolitan Magazine* in succession to William Dean Howells. After a few years of travel he entered the diplomatic service under President McKinley and served as minister resident to Persia, 1897–99, and as envoy extraordinary and minister plenipotentiary to Greece, Roumania, and Servia, 1899–1901, to Switzerland, 1901–03, and to Spain, 1903–05. Hardy could perform the social functions of a diplomat with perfect propriety and grace, and as he held only minor posts nothing more was required of him. He took his work seriously and appeared to be rising in the diplomatic service when President Roosevelt suddenly replaced him at Madrid. On Mar. 9, 1898, at Athens, he married Grace Aspinwall Bowen, daughter of Henry Chandler Bowen [*q.v.*]. By a previous marriage he had had one son, who was with him in Persia. After his retirement Hardy lived until his death at Woodstock, Conn., the home of his wife's family. Although he wrote fairly assiduously none of his later work attracted much attention. The separate publications consisted of *Dualty* (1893), a poem; *Songs of Two* (1900); *His Daughter First* (1903), a novel; *Aurélie* (1912), a children's story; *Diane and Her Friends* (1914), a volume of short stories; *Helen* (1916), a novel; *No. 13 Rue du Bon Diable* (1917), a novelette; and *Things Remembered* (1923), a volume of reminiscences, all of them thin in substance, mellifluous in style. Amid the changes in literary taste that came about in America during and immediately after the World War he was lost to sight, and by the time of his death his once great reputation had melted away. He died at Woodstock and was buried there.

[*Book Buyer*, Sept. 1890; *N. Y. Daily Tribune*, Mar. 11, 1898; *Who's Who in America*, 1928–29; *N. Y. Times*, Mar. 14, 1930.]

G. H. G.

HARDY, SAMUEL (*c.* 1758–Oct. 17, 1785), statesman, was born in Isle of Wight County, Va., the scion of a family settled in that county since 1636 or earlier. His father, Richard Hardy, was a vestryman of the church and a member of the House of Burgesses, 1772–74. Samuel was educated at the College of William and Mary, where, on July 30, 1778, he was initiated into the Phi Beta Kappa Society. He was admitted to the bar Oct. 1, 1778, and two days later, at a by-election, was chosen to the House of Delegates. Appointed escheator, Aug. 5, 1779, he resigned that office in April 1780, having meanwhile been again elected to the House of Delegates, in which body he continued to serve until June 12, 1781, when he was appointed to the Privy Council. He was lieutenant-governor of Virginia from May 29 to Oct. 11, 1782. On June 6, 1783, he was chosen as one of the delegates to the Continental Congress and was continued in the delegation until his death. His career in Congress, though brief, was notable. Monroe at first feared that Hardy might ally himself with the "intemperate" party, but he learned better. Jefferson said that Hardy had but one foible, that of being too good-humored. Yet this good humor must have been oil for the troubled waters through which he had to struggle. The period of his service in Congress was one of the stormiest in that body's history, a time when hot words and even challenges to duels were hurled across the narrow spaces of the assembly hall; yet Hardy, one of the most active members and a hard fighter despite his amiability, kept his serenity and his friendships through it all. When in the early summer of 1784 Congress adjourned, leaving a committee of the states to function in its stead, Hardy was chosen by his colleagues as Virginia's representative on the committee and by the committee itself to be its chairman. Thus he had for a time essentially the same powers and duties as a president of Congress. The committee soon went to pieces, but Hardy did his utmost to hold it together. During 1785 in the battle over the requisition and the state debts, he gave his last services to his country. Riding out to Kingsbridge afterward he broke a blood vessel, and death soon followed. The next day his remains were interred in a vault of St. Paul's Church, New York City (where Congress was then sitting), with funeral ceremonies more than usually elaborate. One friend, "Amyntor" (possibly Alexander Hamilton), wrote an elegy on his death. According to Hugh Blair Grigsby,

"Hardy was one of the most popular and beloved of our early statesmen." He was never married, the lady to whom he was engaged having preceded him in death.

[Biographical sketches of Hardy are found in: H. B. Grigsby, "The History of the Virginia Federal Convention of 1788," *Va. Hist. Soc. Colls.*, n.s. IX–X (1890–91), X, 139; R. S. Thomas, "The Old Brick Church near Smithfield, Va.," *Ibid.*, n.s. XI (1892), including an elegy by Hardy on the death of a friend; Stella P. Hardy, *Colonial Families of the Southern States* (1911), pp. 261 ff. Some of Hardy's letters are printed in *Calendar of Va. State Papers*, vols. III, IV (1883, 1884), and others will appear in a forthcoming volume of *Letters of Members of the Continental Congress*. The *Journals of the Continental Congress* (including the "Journal of the Committee of the States") are essential for following Hardy's career in that body. Accounts of his death and funeral are in the *Daily Advertiser* (N. Y.), Oct. 18, 19, 20, 1785.] E. C. B.

HARDY, WILLIAM HARRIS (Feb. 12, 1837–Feb. 18, 1917), lawyer, journalist, railroad promoter, judge, the son of Robert Williams Hardy and Temperance L. (Toney) Hardy, was born at Collirene, Lowndes County, Ala. At the age of seventeen he entered Cumberland University at Lebanon, Tenn., and was a student at that institution for two years, until a severe attack of pneumonia caused his withdrawal. In 1856 he visited some relatives near Montrose, Jasper County, Miss., and accepted a position as teacher of the Montrose school. He removed to Smith County and established the Sylvarena school. While teaching he studied law, and in 1858 located at Raleigh, Miss., for the practice of his profession. On Oct. 10, 1860, he married Sallie, daughter of Thomas H. Johnson of Raleigh, formerly of Gallatin, Tenn. On Apr. 27, 1861, he was elected captain of the Defenders of Smith County, a company which afterward became part of the 16th Mississippi Infantry in the Army of Northern Virginia. During the latter years of the Civil War he was aide-de-camp to Gen. James A. Smith.

In 1865 he removed to Paulding, Jasper County, Miss. In 1872 his wife died, leaving six children, and on Dec. 1, 1873, he married Hattie Lott of Mobile. In April 1873 he moved to Meridian, Miss., for the practice of law and for the promotion of the New Orleans & Northeastern Railroad, from Meridian to New Orleans, a project which he had been advocating since 1868 and in which he interested a London syndicate. He located the city of Hattiesburg and named it in honor of his second wife. In 1886 he reorganized the Gulf and Ship Island Railroad and was made president of the company. He had a new survey made from Jackson to the Gulf of Mexico and founded the city of Gulfport, the southern terminus of the road. He was elected state senator from Lauderdale County in 1895 and served from 1896 to 1900. He introduced a bill, which was passed by the Senate, for the building of a new capitol on the penitentiary site. In 1896 he was a candidate for Congress, but was defeated by John Sharp Williams.

In 1895 Hardy lost his second wife. He removed to Hattiesburg in 1899, and on May 14, 1900, married Ida V. May. He was appointed circuit judge of the second district by Gov. Vardaman in 1906 and was one of the commission which drafted the Mississippi code of 1906. He was a frequent contributor to the press of articles of a political, economic, and historical nature. In 1875 he edited the *Tri-Weekly Homestead*, published at Meridian, and was one of the first editors of the state to advocate the overthrow of Republican rule by the impeachment of Gov. Adelbert Ames. He was the author of "Recollections of Reconstruction in East and Southeast Mississippi," which appeared in the *Publications of the Mississippi Historical Society* (vol. IV, 1901). He was one of the first to foresee the industrial possibilities of the pine belt of south Mississippi and of the Gulf Coast region. The building of the Northeastern and the Gulf and Ship Island railroads was the principal factor in the opening up and development of those sections of the state, hitherto handicapped by the lack of transportation facilities. He died in Gulfport and is buried there.

[*Biog. and Hist. Memoirs of Miss.* (1891), I, 861–66; Dunbar Rowland, *Mississippi* (1907), vols. I, III; *Pubs. Miss. Hist. Soc.*, vol. IV (1901); records of the circuit court, second Miss. district, 1906–08; Gulfport and Biloxi newspapers, 1917.] D. R.

HARE, GEORGE EMLEN (Sept. 4, 1808–Feb. 15, 1892), Episcopal clergyman, educator, was born in Philadelphia and there spent the greater part of his long life. His father, Charles Willing Hare, brother of Robert Hare [*q.v.*] and son of Robert Hare who came to America from England in 1773, later marrying Margaret Willing, was a lawyer of high standing in Philadelphia; his mother was Ann Emlen, whose great-grandfather, George, came from England with William Penn. At an early age he entered Dickinson College, but transferred to Union College, Schenectady, N. Y., where he was under the influence of Eliphalet Nott [*q.v.*], and formed a lasting intimacy with Alonzo Potter [*q.v.*], afterward bishop of Pennsylvania. Graduating in 1826, he studied for a time at the General Theological Seminary, New York, and on Dec. 20, 1829, was ordained deacon by Bishop White in Christ Church, Philadelphia. He at once took charge of St. John's Church, Carlisle, Pa., and was ordained priest by Bishop Onderdonk. On June 4, 1830, he married Elizabeth C. Hobart, daughter of Bishop John Henry Hobart [*q.v.*]. In 1834 he became the first pastor of Trinity Church, Princeton, N. J., where he remained until 1843.

He then returned to Philadelphia where he was in temporary charge of St. James's Church, and from 1844 to 1845, assistant professor of Latin and Greek at the University of Pennsylvania. Essentially a scholar, he spent much of the remainder of his life in educational work. In 1846 Bishop Potter reëstablished the Academy of the Protestant Episcopal Church in Philadelphia, first opened in 1785, and put Hare in charge. During his headmastership, which continued until 1857, the school steadily expanded, until at one time it had 180 pupils and ten teachers. He was a dignified, remote, somewhat severe person. "There was a solidity and solemnity about the ministry of Dr. Hare in dealing with the boys," one of them wrote, "which had in it a feeling that it was a slice out of the day of judgment. . . . He was a clergyman, to be sure, but there was no loitering with him, and the janitor locked up the boys on Friday who failed in their catechism with the same perfunctory ease with which he locked up those who failed in Cæsar or algebra" (William Wilberforce Newton, *Yesterday with the Fathers,* 1910, pp. 46–47). As early as 1846, in compliance with Bishop Potter's desire for a diocesan training school, Hare began giving instruction to young men preparing for the ministry. In 1857 he resigned as master of the Academy, and Bishop Potter established a training school of which for several years Hare was dean and faculty. The Civil War necessitated the return of Northern students from seminaries in the South, and the institution expanded into the Divinity School of the Protestant Episcopal Church, Philadelphia, Hare taking the chair of Biblical learning. During all these years (1844–62), he also had charge of St. Matthew's Church, Francisville. He remained associated with the school until his death, becoming professor emeritus in 1889. An able Hebrew scholar, he was made a member of the Old Testament Company of the American Revision Committee. His published writings include: *Christians and Their Offspring, a Holy People* (1849), a sermon; "The Current Version of the Scriptures, as Compared with Our Present Needs," in *Anglo-American Bible Revision* (1879), by members of the American Revision Committee; and *Visions and Narratives of the Old Testament* (1889), a series of interpretative studies. Bishop William Hobart Hare [*q.v.*] was his son.

[J. T. Sharf and Thompson Wescott, *Hist. of Phila.* (3 vols., 1884); J. W. Jordan, *Colonial and Revolutionary Families of Pa.* (3 vols., 1911); the *Churchman,* Feb. 27, 1892; *Press* and *Public Ledger* (Phila.), Feb. 16, 1892; F. S. Edmonds, *Hist. of St. Matthew's Church, Francisville, Phila.* (1925); *Am. Ch. Almanac,* 1893; Bishop M. A. DeWolfe Howe, *Memoirs of the Life and Services of the Rt. Rev. Alonzo Potter, D.D., LL.D.* (1871); M. A. DeWolfe Howe, *The Life and Labors of Bishop Hare* (1911).] H. E. S.

HARE, JOHN INNES CLARK (Oct. 17, 1816–Dec. 29, 1905), jurist, was the son of Robert Hare [*q.v.*] of Philadelphia, a noted chemist, and Harriett (Clark) Hare of Providence, R. I. After graduation with honors from the University of Pennsylvania in 1834 he studied chemistry for nearly four years, two of them in Europe, before studying law. In 1841 he was admitted to the bar; on Nov. 16, 1842, he married Esther Coxe Binney, daughter of Horace Binney [*q.v.*]. His family connections, his unusual personality and culture, his evidently exceptional abilities, promised him an outstanding record in practice, but he inherited sufficient wealth to permit his acceptance of the less remunerative but more attractive honors of judicial office. In 1851 he was elected as a Whig to the district court of Philadelphia, wherein he served for twenty-four years, first as an associate and after 1867 as presiding judge. In 1875 he became president judge of the city court of common pleas, from which he resigned in 1896 because of ill health. He also served as a trustee of the University of Pennsylvania, 1858–68, and as a professor of law there from 1868 to 1888. His election to the offices of vice-provost, 1862–83, and provost, 1883, of the Philadelphia Law Academy expressed the honor in which he was held by the bar. Possessing a knowledge of technical law that was remarkable for depth, breadth, and exactness, he was also widely read in political history and in the European literature of jurisprudence and natural law. He served for forty-five years without reproach, with great industry and unvarying conscientiousness, lending to every lawyer before him a steady and even indulgent attention. His judicial conduct and his judgments were rigidly aloof and impersonal. He held, naturally, the admiration and affection of the bar, upon which he exerted a profound influence. Though political conditions kept him in a subordinate court, he was one of the half-dozen greatest judges that Pennsylvania has produced. He ascended the bench just after equity was introduced, as a general system, into Pennsylvania, and his contribution to its establishment was of great importance. On and off the bench he was characterized by gentle manners, sympathy, modesty, a perfect and equal courtesy toward all persons whatsoever, and an impressive dignity—though he was too kindly to be austere. His mind was astute and subtle, patient and precise, broad in outlook, retentive. Eminent as he was in ability and in scholarship, he showed no dogmatism or intellectual pride, nor any ostentation of learning. All his life he was keenly interested in politics and public problems, and read general literature omnivorously. He was elected in 1842 to the American Philosophical Society, from which he resigned in 1876.

He edited, in collaboration with Horace B. Wallace and successors, a number of collections of cases—all with additional notes and American citations—that enjoyed high repute and went through many editions; these included: J. W. Smith's *Selection of Leading Cases on Various Branches of the Law* (2 vols., 1847); F. T. White and O. D. Tudor's *Selection of Leading Cases in Equity* (2 vols., in 3, 1849–51); and *Reports of Cases . . . in the Courts of Exchequer and Chancery* (1853 ff.). He edited also *Select Decisions of American Courts in the Several Departments of the Law* (2 vols., 1847–48), later editions of which were published as *American Leading Cases.* Perhaps his most notable opinion was that in *Borie* vs. *Trott* (5 *Phila. Reports,* 366), reprinted as *Opinion . . . upon the Constitutionality of the Acts of Congress of February 5, 1862, Declaring the United States Notes "Lawful Money" and a "Legal Tender"* (1864). He also published "The Legal Tender Decisions" (*American Law Register,* February 1871); "The Ethical Basis of Jurisprudence" (*Legal Intelligencer,* Oct. 5, 1877); "Certain Points of Distinction between the English and American Constitutions" (*Ibid.,* Apr. 2, 1880); *Notes of a Course of Lectures on Contracts* (1882); *Notes of a Course of Lectures on Promisory Notes and Bills of Exchange* (1882); *The Law of Contracts* (1887); *American Constitutional Law* (2 vols., 1889); "Trial by Jury and the Right of Challenge" (*Albany Law Journal,* Mar. 18, 1899). Many of his judicial opinions may be found in the *Legal Intelligencer* of Philadelphia, and in the other repositories of Pennsylvania local reports.

[See *In Memoriam: Hon. John Innes Clark Hare* (1906), also printed in *Legal Intelligencer,* Jan. 12, 1906; Philadelphia *Public Ledger,* Dec. 30, 1905; J. H. Martin, *Martin's Bench and Bar of Phila.* (1883); D. P. Brown, *The Forum* (2 vols., 1856); Charles Morris, *Makers of Phila.* (1894); W. D. Lewis, in *Am. Law Register,* Dec. 1906; *Legal Intelligencer,* Jan. 5, 1906.]

F. S. P.

HARE, ROBERT (Jan. 17, 1781–May 15, 1858), chemist, was born in Philadelphia, the son of Robert and Margaret (Willing) Hare His father, an English immigrant of 1773, was a prominent business man and served in the Pennsylvania legislature and as a trustee of the University of Pennsylvania. Robert was educated at home and studied chemistry under James Woodhouse [*q.v.*]. For some years he managed his father's brewery, devoting his spare time to chemical research. In 1801 he discovered the oxy-hydrogen blow-pipe, source of the highest degree of heat then known, which enabled him to fuse the most refractory substances and led to the founding of the platinum industry and the development of the limelight and allied illuminators (see *Memoir of the Supply and Application of the Blow-Pipe,* 1802). At this time he formed with Benjamin Silliman [*q.v.*], who was spending the winter in Philadelphia, a friendship that became almost a partnership in research. Hare continued in business until 1816. After a few months' teaching at the College of William and Mary, he was elected professor of chemistry at the University of Pennsylvania. Though not a brilliant lecturer, he excelled in demonstration, utilizing much apparatus of his own invention. His greatest interest was in electricity. He invented the calorimotor, an ingenious piece of galvanic apparatus which became the model for Planté's secondary battery (1819), and the deflagrator (1821) for generating a high electric current. The use of the mercury cathode in the electrolysis of aqueous solutions of metallic salts was his discovery. In 1839 he built an electric furnace, in which he prepared phosphorus, calcium metal and calcium carbide, and artificial graphite from crude charcoal. His work on the constitution of salts anticipated the discoveries of Ira Remsen [*q.v.*]. He devised a means of using tar for lighting, new forms of eudiometers for the analysis and synthesis of gases, and demonstrated the use of platinized asbestos in the synthesis of ammonia.

Hare was a vigorous and prolific contributor to the *American Journal of Science,* invaribly displaying a tendency to turn a discussion into a controversy. He prepared papers which he read before the American Philosophical Society and edited William Henry's *Elements of Experimental Chemistry* (2 vols., 1819), and Andrew Ure's *Dictionary of Chemistry* (2 vols., 1821). His lectures, published in 1822 as *Minutes of the Course of Chemical Instruction in the Medical Department of the University of Pennsylvania,* appeared in 1827 as *A Compendium of the Course of Chemical Instruction,* and revised and enlarged, went through three subsequent editions. He received the Rumford Medal from the American Academy of Arts and Sciences in 1839. On his retirement from teaching in 1847, he gave his collection of apparatus to the Smithsonian Institution, and the next year was elected an honorary member of that body. Besides his scientific works, he published several pamphlets on banking and currency reform, and under the pen-name of "Eldred Grayson," a novel, *Standish the Puritan* (1850). In his old age he became convinced he had established communication with the dead by means of the "spiritoscope," and set forth his proofs, to the grief of his old friend Silliman, in *Experimental Investigation of the Spirit Manifestations, Demonstrating the Existence of Spirits and Their Communion with Mortals* (1855). Perhaps the most characteristic touch in the book was the alleged approval by Benjamin Franklin's spirit of Hare's electrical theories. When he sought to address the Association for the Advancement of Science on this subject, he obtained only the privilege of using the hall after the Association had adjourned. He married, Sept. 11, 1811, Harriett Clark of Providence, R. I. One of his sons, John Innes Clark Hare [*q.v.*], was a distinguished lawyer of Philadelphia.

[E. F. Smith, *The Life of Robert Hare* (1917) and *Chemistry in America* (1910); Benjamin Silliman, in *Am. Jour. Sci.*, July 1858, pp. 100–05, and *Am. Chemist*, Aug.–Sept. 1874, pp. 77–80; G. P. Fisher, *Life of Benjamin Silliman* (1866), I, 98 ff.; *Autobiog. of Samuel D. Gross* (1887), II, 297–98; Henry Simpson, *The Lives of Eminent Philadelphians* (1859); J. W. Jordan, *Colonial and Revolutionary Families of Phila.* (1911), I, 129–31; *Public Ledger* (Phila.), May 17, 1858.]

E. F. S.
H. C. B.

HARE, WILLIAM HOBART (May 17, 1838–Oct. 23, 1909), bishop of the Protestant Episcopal Church, "Apostle to the Sioux," was born in Princeton, N. J., son of Rev. George Emlen Hare [*q.v.*] and Elizabeth Catharine Hobart, daughter of Bishop John Henry Hobart [*q.v.*]. He received his schooling in the Academy of the Protestant Episcopal Church, Philadelphia, of which from 1846 to 1857 his father was headmaster, and in 1855 entered the sophomore class of the University of Pennsylvania. Eye trouble and the desire to save his father expense caused him to withdraw in his junior year. While studying for the ministry he taught at St. Mark's Academy, Philadelphia. On June 19, 1859, he was admitted to the diaconate and became assistant at St. Luke's Church under Dr. M. A. DeWolfe Howe [*q.v.*], whose daughter, Mary Amory Howe, he married on Oct. 30, 1861. In May of this year he had taken charge of St. Paul's Church in the Chestnut Hill suburb of Philadelphia, and on May 25, 1862, was ordained to the priesthood. In 1863 he went with his wife to Michigan and Minnesota in the hope of benefiting the latter's health, and there his interest in the needs of the Indians was awakened. Upon his return, having in the meantime resigned his rectorship, he conducted the affairs of St. Luke's parish during his father-in-law's absence, and in 1864 assumed care of one of its missions, the Church of the Ascension, which in 1867 became independent and chose him for its rector. On Jan. 7 of the previous year his wife had died.

His missionary career began in 1871 when he was appointed secretary and general agent of the Foreign Committee of the Board of Missions. The zeal and abilities which he displayed led the House of Bishops before the close of that year to elect him to the missionary episcopate of Cape Palmas and parts adjacent in Africa, but since the House of Deputies felt that he was more needed in his present position, the Bishops rescinded their action. On Nov. 1, 1872, however, he was notified that he had been elected missionary bishop of Niobrara, the ecclesiastical term for the country north of the Niobrara River, inhabited by the Sioux Indians. On Jan. 9, 1873, at St. Luke's Church, Philadelphia, he was consecrated. In this difficult field for nearly thirty-seven years, always under threat of a physical breakdown, he was a potent factor in the advancement of every civilizing influence. He won the trust and affection of the Indians, and his judgment and advice were held in high regard by government officials. He soon established boarding schools for Indian children which did efficient work, and in time the region became dotted with chapels and small missionary residences. In 1880 he was made defendant in a suit for libel instituted by one of his clergy whom he had brought to trial before a court of presbyters. The case was decided against him, but later the decision was reversed with the recommendation that the "case be left to the wise and judicious arbitrament of mutual friends." The affair brought him much painful notoriety, but did not reflect upon his character or impair his influence. By 1883 immigration into Dakota had brought many white people there, and the House of Bishops changed the limits of his jurisdiction and substituted the name South Dakota in its title for that of Niobrara. At Sioux Falls he established All Saints School for girls, opened in September 1885, that the daughters of his missionaries and other white girls might have suitable educational advantages. Sioux Falls became his Episcopal residence, and the school, his home. In February 1891 the House of Bishops requested him to proceed to Japan and administer the affairs of the jurisdiction for six months or a year, unless in the meantime a bishop should be elected. He was absent from March to August, and again in Japan and China, from January to April 1892. In 1893 he became leader in the long fight to reform the lax divorce laws in South Dakota. From as early as 1875 when his physician had sent him to Europe for rest he had labored under the knowledge that he was handicapped by mitral stenosis. In 1895 his condition became serious, and in 1896 he again went abroad. Upon his return, however, he bravely resumed his work. On Apr. 17, 1907, he underwent an operation at St. Luke's Hospital, New York, for a malignant growth on his face, which included the removal of his right eyeball; but later returned to his duties in South Dakota, now lightened by an assistant bishop chosen in 1905. Death came to him in Atlantic City in October 1909, and he was buried beside Calvary Cathedral in Sioux Falls.

[Much information about Bishop Hare's work may be found in his reports and communications in the *Spirit of Missions,* published by the Board of Missions, and after 1877 by the Domestic and Foreign Missionary Society of the P. E. Church. An address by him, *Reminiscences* was published in 1888. M. A. DeWolfe Howe, *The Life and Labors of Bishop Hare* (1911) gives a detailed account of his career. See also, *A Hand-Book of the Church's Mission to the Indians* (1914); J. B. Harrison, *The Latest Studies on Indian Reservations* (1887), p. 137, the *Churchman,* Oct. 30, 1909, and *Daily Argus-Leader* (Sioux Falls), Oct. 25, 1909, and Apr. 21, 25, 1910.] H. E. S.

HARGROVE, ROBERT KENNON (Sept. 17, 1829–Aug. 3, 1905), bishop of the Methodist Episcopal Church, South, son of Daniel Jones and Laodicea (Brantley) Hargrove, was born in Pickens County, Ala., and died in Nashville, Tenn. Through both his parents he was descended from families resident in Georgia and the Carolinas for several generations. His upbringing was intensely pious. One of his grandfathers, a kinsman of Bishop William McKendree, was a local preacher as well as a planter; his father was for fifty years a class leader; he was himself converted at the age of eleven. Promptly after his graduation from the University of Alabama in 1852, he married Harriet Cornelia Scott, daughter of a cotton manufacturer who lived in Tuscaloosa, and entered upon a professorship of mathematics which held him at his alma mater till 1858. Then he became a Methodist minister, and, except for a time when he was a chaplain in the Confederate army, he held pastorates at various towns in the mid-South till 1865. From 1865 to 1873 he was president successively of two small schools. Reëntering the itinerancy, he served different churches till 1882 when he was made a bishop. In 1876 he had acted as a delegate to a conference held between the Northern and Southern branches of his church with the aim of reconciling their differences, and after his elevation to the bishopric he attended another such conference in 1898. Other responsible posts fell to him. He was secretary of the college of bishops 1884–1900, president of the board of management of the Epworth League 1894–98, and president of the board of trust of Vanderbilt University from 1889 till the June preceding his death. He worked diligently to increase the activities of the Southern Methodist Church in the northwestern states and on the Pacific Coast, and, through a notable translator whom he brought to Nashville, he furthered Protestantism in Mexico. His second wife, whom he married in 1895, was Ruth Eliza Scarritt of Kansas City, Mo. He is said to have been distinguished by a pervading sweetness of character. His integrity and determination made him a capable executive, and it was only his increasing deafness which in 1902 brought about his superannuation. He continued to preach till within a few months of his death.

[T. M. Owen, *Hist. of Ala. and Dict. of Ala. Biog.* (1921), vol. III, p. 748; *Christian Advocate* (Nashville), Aug. 10, 24, 1905; *Nashville Banner,* Aug. 3, 1905; *Who's Who in America,* 1903–05; *A Reg. of the Officers and Students of the Univ. of Ala.* (1901).] J. D. W.

HARKNESS, ALBERT (Oct. 6, 1822–May 27, 1907), classical scholar, was born in Mendon, Mass., the son of Southwick and Phebe (Thayer) Harkness, and was of Scotch-Irish descent. His great-grandfather, Adam Harkness, son of John Harkness, came to Boston from Belfast about 1730 and settled in Smithfield, R. I. Albert graduated from Brown University in 1842, as valedictorian of his class, and after a novitiate as high-school teacher in Providence, 1843–53, studied from 1853 to 1855 at Berlin, Bonn, and Göttingen, receiving the degree of Ph.D. at the University of Bonn in 1854. He was professor of the Greek language and literature in Brown University from 1855 to 1892, when he became emeritus. He was elected a member of the Board of Fellows in 1904 and continued to serve the university in this capacity until his death. He was an enthusiastic devotee of Greek and Latin; and "his focussed teaching of Greek," to quote a former student, "made the teaching of English unnecessary!" He shared in moulding the utterance of men distinguished afterwards in academic life, in the professions, and in high position in the national government. Although he was professor of Greek, eighteen of his nineteen publications were textbooks in Latin. Five of these were editions of *Caesar, Cicero,* and *Sallust.* His *Latin Grammar* (1865; completely revised, 1898), justly famous for its clearness of presentation, carried his name and influence far beyond his immediate environment. In addition he contributed to the *American Journal of Philology,* the *Bibliotheca Sacra,* and other learned periodicals. On May 28, 1849, he married Maria Aldrich Smith of Providence. Their two children continued their father's classical interests. Their daughter married William Carey Poland, professor of art in Brown University; their son, Albert Granger Harkness, was professor of Latin at Brown from 1893 until his death and an annual director at the American School of Classical Studies in Rome.

Harkness was courteous, vigorous, dignified. Even after his retirement the genial hospitality dispensed by Mrs. Harkness and himself made their home the rendezvous for hundreds of returning graduates and other friends. His portrait, by William Merritt Chase, at the university, is an admirable presentation of his alert personality. He was president of the Rhode Island Historical Society, and was one of the founders of the American Philological Association and, in 1875–76, its annual president; he was also a founder of the American School of Classical Studies in Athens, and long a member of its managing committee. The "Albert Harkness Fund" (1902) secured to Brown University graduates free access to the Athenian School. He was also a member of the Archaeological Institute of America. In 1905 the University of Bonn confirmed *honoris causa* the doctorate conferred upon examination fifty years before. This honor was happily observed at the Brown Commencement by a Latin salutation from the faculty, to which Harkness responded in Latin unimpaired by his three and eighty years. He died two years later.

[*The Biog. Cyc. of Rep. Men of R. I.* (1881); *Who's Who in America,* 1906–07; *Providence Daily Jour.,* May 27, 1907; the *Nation,* May 30, 1907; *Memorial Exercises in Honor of Prof. Albert Harkness* (1907); *Proc. R. I. Hist. Soc. 1907–08* (1910); *Hist. Cat. Brown Univ.* (1924); personal acquaintance.]

F. G. A.

HARKNESS, WILLIAM (Dec. 17, 1837–Feb. 28, 1903), astronomer, was born at Ecclefechan, Scotland, the son of James and Jane (Weild) Harkness. His father was a Presbyterian clergyman and also a physician. The family came to New York in May 1839. William attended the Chelsea Collegiate Institute and private schools in Fishkill Landing and Newburgh, N. Y.; entered Lafayette College in 1854, and transferred to Rochester University in 1856, where he graduated with the degree of A.B. in 1858. He was a newspaper reporter in the New York legislature in 1858 and in the Pennsylvania Senate in 1860; then studied medicine in the New York Homeopathic Medical College, graduating in 1862; and during the Civil War served for brief intervals as volunteer surgeon. He was appointed aide in the United States Naval Observatory in 1862 and professor in 1863. During the cruise of the monitor *Monadnock* from Philadelphia to San Francisco, 1865–66, he made a careful investigation of the deviations of the compasses and observations of terrestrial magnetism (published in 1871, in *Smithsonian Contributions to Knowledge,* vol. XVIII). After a brief service in the Hydrographic Office he returned to the Naval Observatory in 1867. During the total solar eclipse of Aug. 7, 1869, he made his independent discovery of the coronal line K 1474 (λ 5303) announced in *Washington Observations . . . 1867,* Appendix II (1870). In 1870 he observed the eclipse in Sicily (*Ibid. . . . 1869,* Appendix I, 1872).

In 1871 he was appointed one of the original members of the Transit of Venus Commission and for many years thereafter was largely occupied with preparation for the observation of the transits of 1874 and 1882 and with the discussion of the results. He was in charge of the expedition sent to Hobart, Tasmania, to observe the transit of 1874, and he observed that of 1882 at Washington. These transits offered an opportunity to determine the distance of Venus, and hence of the sun. To determine the relative positions of the sun and Venus with accuracy from the photographs, Harkness devised a measuring machine, the spherometer caliper. Among his many publications, "The Solar Parallax and its Related Constants" (*Washington Observations . . . 1885,* Appendix III, 1891), and "On the Color Correction of Achromatic Telescopes" (*American Journal of Science,* September 1879 and February 1880) should be especially mentioned. He accepted, in 1894, appointment as astronomical director at the Naval Observatory, an office created at that time on the insistence of astronomers outside Washington. This office, continued for a few years only, provided its incumbent with a maximum of responsibility and a minimum of power. In 1897 Harkness was appointed director of the *American Ephemeris and Nautical Almanac* also. The labor entailed by these two positions was apparently too heavy for him, his health broke down completely, and after his retirement in 1899, with the rank of rear admiral, he found, to his great sorrow, that he was unable to take up some of the pieces of work that he had been obliged to postpone.

His tastes inclined him to the practical side

of astronomy. At the time of his death there was hardly a piece of apparatus in the Observatory which was not the work of his mind or which did not embody essential features which he had suggested. He was one of the founders of the Philosophical Society of Washington. He was never married, and lived at the Cosmos Club, of which also he was a founder. The American Association for the Advancement of Science chose him vice-president in 1881 and 1885, and president in 1893. He died at Jersey City, N. J.

[*Pop. Astron.*, June–July 1903; *Pubs. Astron. Soc. of the Pacific*, vol. XV (1903); *Science*, Mar. 13, Apr. 17, 1903; *Pop. Sci. Mo.*, May 1903; *Nature*, Mar. 12, 1903; *English Mechanic and World of Science*, Mar. 6, 20, 1903; *Memorie della Società degli Spettoroscopisti Italiani*, XXXII (1903), 212; *N. Y. Times*, Mar. 1, 1903.]

R. S. D.

HARLAN, JAMES (June 22, 1800–Feb. 18, 1863), Kentucky lawyer and legislator, congressman, was a son of James and Sarah (Caldwell) Harlan. His earliest American ancestor was George Harland, a Quaker from Durham, England, who in early manhood had removed to County Down, Ireland, from which place he emigrated to New Castle, Del., in 1687, settling finally in Chester County, Pa. In 1695 he was governor of Delaware. His grandson, George Harlan, emigrated to Frederick County, Va., where he became a member of the Presbyterian Church. Thence his son James, at the age of nineteen, crossed the mountains into Kentucky, being a companion of James Harrod [*q.v.*] in his abortive settlement at Harrodsburg in 1774. A quarter of a century later, at Harlan Station in what is now Boyle County, his son James Harlan was born. After an elementary education and a five-year interval of employment in a mercantile house, young Harlan studied law and in 1823, upon his admission to the bar, began the practice of his profession at Harrodsburg. In 1829 he began his public career in the office of commonwealth attorney. After holding this position for six years, he was elected in 1835 on the Whig ticket a member of the national House of Representatives, and was reëlected two years later for a second term. His short congressional career was without special incident except that in 1839 the House chose him chairman of the select committee to investigate the notorious Swartout defalcations (*Congressional Globe*, 25 Cong., 3 Sess., p. 132). At the conclusion of his two terms in the House, Harlan was one of the leaders of the Whig party in Kentucky, a predominantly Whig state. In 1840, immediately upon his return from Congress, he was selected secretary of state in the administration of Governor Letcher (Collins, *post*, I, 350), and in the same year was a delegate to the national convention which nominated Harrison for president. Upon the expiration of his term as secretary of state he was elected (1845) a member of the lower house of the Kentucky legislature, and in the August election of 1851, after refusing the Whig nomination for Congress from the Ashland district, he was chosen attorney-general of the state. This was the last elective office that Harlan held. With the approach of the Civil War, like most of the prominent Whigs of his state, he became a stanch Union man and opposed secession. In March 1861 he took an active part in preventing the passage by the legislature of a resolution which was avowedly the initial step toward secession. In May of the same year, in combination with John J. Crittenden, James Speed, and a few others, he formulated the plans for distributing the "Lincoln Guns" to Unionists in Kentucky (Daniel Stevenson, "General Nelson, Kentucky, and the Lincoln Guns," *Magazine of American History*, August 1883). It was no doubt in recognition of his services in opposing secession as well as in recognition of his legal abilities that Lincoln appointed him district attorney of Kentucky. This office he held until the time of his death.

Harlan's achievements in the various positions which he held were never of an extraordinary character, but there is tangible evidence that, as a lawyer, he had considerable ability and he certainly acquired a statewide reputation. In 1850 he was appointed by Governor Crittenden a member of a committee to simplify the rules of practice in the state courts, and the results of his labors may be seen in his book, *The Code of Practice in Civil and Criminal Cases*, published in 1854. The previous year he had published, with Benjamin Monroe, *Digest of Cases at Common Law and in Equity, Decided by the Court of Appeals of Kentucky from Its Organization in 1792 to the Close of the Winter Term of 1852–3* (2 vols., 1853). On Dec. 23, 1822, Harlan married Eliza Shannon Davenport, who bore him six sons and three daughters. Two of the sons attained distinction in their father's profession, James becoming vice-chancellor of the chancery court at Louisville and John Marshall [*q.v.*] associate justice of the Supreme Court of the United States.

[A. H. Harlan, *Hist. and Geneal. of the Harlan Family* (1914); *Biog. Encyc. of Ky.* (1878); Lewis and R. H. Collins, *Hist. of Ky.* (2 vols., 1874); *Louisville Daily Democrat, Louisville Daily Journal*, Feb. 20, 1863; *Daily Commonwealth* (Frankfort, Ky.), Feb. 20, 21, 1863; information from Richard D. Harlan, Esq.]

R. S. C.

HARLAN, JAMES (Aug. 26, 1820–Oct. 5, 1899), United States senator, secretary of the interior, was a product of the frontier, of its opportunity and of its limitations. He was descended from George Harland, a Quaker, who emigrated from the vicinity of Durham, England, to County Down, Ireland, and thence in 1687 to America, settling finally in Chester County, Pa. His parents, Silas and Mary (Conley) Harlan, natives of Pennsylvania and Maryland respectively, were married in Ohio and then joined the stream of western migration, locating in Clark County, Ill., where he was born. Four years later the family removed to the "New Discovery" in Parke County, Ind., a typical clearing settlement. Monotonous toil was relieved chiefly by visits of Methodist circuit riders who made the Harlan home their "preaching place." The frontier youth supplemented his log-school instruction by books secured from a county library. After teaching district school he attended a local "seminary" and entered Indiana Asbury (later DePauw) University in 1841. College life was interspersed by a trip to Iowa and a term of school teaching in Missouri. As a student his interest in politics was already marked; he was an ardent Whig. In 1845, the year that he took his degree, he was married to Ann Eliza Peck.

The young couple, true to type, sought the pioneer life in Iowa where Harlan became principal of the Iowa City College. Almost immediately his long and stormy political career began. In the first state election, in 1847, he was chosen superintendent of public instruction on the Whig ticket, but the election was declared illegal and in the contest to fill the vacancy he was defeated by methods that he regarded as highly irregular. Following this unfortunate experience, he studied law and was admitted to the bar in 1850 and in the same year declined the Whig nomination for governor. Before full establishment in his new profession, he was called to head the Iowa Conference University (now Iowa Wesleyan), which he served as president from 1853 to 1855. Under most discouraging conditions, both financial and academic, he was laying the foundations of one of the earliest trans-Mississippi colleges when the Free-Soil agitation put an end to his educational activities and career.

From the beginnings of the Free-Soil movement Harlan had been an active promoter. Put forward by friends as the new party's candidate for the United States Senate he was elected, in 1855, by a rump legislature after one house had formally adjourned. This irregularity led to the vacating of his seat in January 1857. He was promptly returned by a sympathetic legislature and in 1860 was the unanimous Republican choice for a second term. During his first senatorial contest he built up a personal organization throughout the state which he utilized effectively in later contests. As senator he concentrated on Western measures, homesteads, college land grants, and especially the Pacific railroad act, which he personally directed. He gave loyal support to the war measures of the administration and was intimate with President Lincoln; his daughter later married Robert Todd Lincoln [*q.v.*]. At the beginning of Lincoln's second term Harlan became secretary of the interior. This position was the disastrous turning-point of his career. Departmental policies created bitter enmities and led to charges of improper appointments and of corruption in the disposal of Indian and railroad lands. These charges persisted, although, according to one of Harlan's biographers, "each of the accusations was fairly and squarely met by facts which were a matter of record, and proven to be without foundation" (Brigham, *post,* p. 250). The most notable of his many dismissals in pursuance of his policy of economy was that of Walt Whitman [*q.v.*] from a clerkship in the Indian Office (*Ibid.,* p. 208). The reconstruction contest caused a break between Harlan and Johnson, and Harlan resigned his portfolio in July 1866.

Before leaving the cabinet he had been making plans for a return to the Senate, and he had so influential a following that he was elected in 1866, but at the cost of the friendship of Samuel J. Kirkwood and James W. Grimes [*qq.v.*]. Upon returning to the Senate he was definitely aligned with the radical administration group and his most notable acts were his support of Johnson's impeachment and his spirited defense of Grant's Santo Dominican policy. The growing cleavage in the party, which was to culminate in the Liberal Republican movement, was reflected in the Iowa senatorial contest in January 1872 in which Harlan's opponents combined so effectively that he was defeated by William B. Allison [*q.v.*]. This defeat ended his official career at a comparatively early age. Though candidate for senator and governor at various times, he was never again successful in an election. His only remaining official service was as a member of the second court of *Alabama* claims, 1882–86. He was an active member of the Methodist Church, and the support that he received from Iowa Methodists occasionally figured in political controversies. He was president of Iowa Wesleyan again for a short time in 1869–70. Tall, dignified, impressive looking, Harlan was strong of body and of will. He was a zealous partisan and a persistent fighter, tenacious of conviction whether based upon reason or prejudice.

[The Harlan papers, including autobiographical sketch of early years and a large correspondence, are in the possession of Harlan's daughter, Mrs. Robert Todd Lincoln, and were used and quoted extensively in Johnson Brigham, *James Harlan* (1913). See also *Cong. Globe,* 34–42 Cong.; *Report of the Sec. of the Interior,* 1865; *Diary of Gideon Welles* (3 vols., 1911); D. E. Clark, *Hist. of Senatorial Elections in Iowa* (1912); A. H. Harlan, *Hist. and Geneal. of the Harlan Family* (1914); *Hist. Sketch and Alumni Record of Iowa Wesleyan Coll.* (1917); E. H. Stiles, *Recollections and Sketches of Notable Lawyers and Public Men of Iowa* (1916); *Christian Advocate,* Oct. 19, 1899; *Iowa State Register* (Des Moines), Oct. 6, 1899.]

E. D. R.

HARLAN, JOHN MARSHALL (June 1, 1833–Oct. 14, 1911), jurist, was born in Boyle County, Ky. His mother was Eliza Shannon (Davenport) Harlan. His father, James Harlan [*q.v.*], a leading member of the Kentucky bar, served in Congress, as attorney-general of the state, and as federal district attorney. Young Harlan graduated in 1850 from Centre College at Danville, and studied law at Transylvania University at Lexington. Returning to Frankfort, he continued his legal studies in his father's office and under other prominent lawyers and was admitted to the bar in 1853. In 1858 he was elected judge of the county court of Franklin County for one year, his only judicial position prior to his appointment to the Supreme Court. In 1861 he moved to Louisville where he practised with W. F. Bullock.

Harlan participated actively in the bitter political struggles which racked Kentucky from the eve of the Civil War until reconstruction had been effected. In 1859 he ran for Congress against the Democrats in the Ashland district but was defeated by a small margin. A Southern gentleman and a slave-holder, and at heart a conservative, he was at first unable to follow the mass of Whigs into the Republican party. The critical campaign of 1860 found him, therefore, not supporting Lincoln, but serving as presidential elector on the ticket of the Constitutional Union party, headed by Bell and Everett, which sought the peaceful preservation of the *status quo.* At the outbreak of the war, he recruited the 10th Kentucky Volunteer Infantry, a regiment forming part of the original division of Gen. George H. Thomas. He served as colonel, participating in many engagements, until at the death of his father in 1863 he resigned his command. At this time his name was actually before the Senate for promotion to a brigadier-generalship. His letter of resignation (*Case and Comment,* July 1916, p. 120) expressed his continued devotion to the Union but urged the pressure of private affairs. Upon retiring from the army he ran successfully for the attorney generalship of Kentucky upon the Union ticket. He continued to hold this office until 1867, when he resumed the practice of law in Louisville. Although a firm defender of the Union, Harlan became a bitter critic of the Lincoln administration. In 1864 he took the stump in support of the presidential candidacy of Gen. George B. McClellan. He threw his influence against the Thirteenth Amendment, declaring that he would oppose it on principle "if there were not a dozen slaves in Kentucky" (*Cincinnati Gazette,* Aug. 2, 1865). To him the abolition of slavery by federal action seemed "a flagrant invasion of the right of self government" and a violation of the promises which had been made to Kentucky slave-holders (E. M. Coulter, *The Civil War and Readjustment in Kentucky,* 1926). The campaign of 1868, however, in which he supported Grant and Colfax, found him defending the war amendments as necessary to the reconstruction of the Union.

At the close of the war, Harlan occupied a position of leadership amongst the conservative Republicans, who bitterly assailed both the Democrats and their own more radical fellow partisans. A crushing Republican defeat in 1866 threw most of Harlan's conservative associates back into the Democratic fold; but Harlan himself, with two or three friends, cast in his lot with the radical Republicans. This realignment of forces put the Republican party in Kentucky on its feet, and in 1871 Harlan was reluctantly persuaded to accept the unanimous nomination for the governorship. His campaign was vigorous and effective, and while he was badly beaten he mustered Republican strength of ultimate significance. In 1872 his name was prominently mentioned as a vice-presidential possibility on the Grant ticket. In 1875 he ran again for the governorship and was again defeated. In 1876 Harlan headed the delegation from Kentucky to the Republican National Convention, pledged to B. H. Bristow, Blaine's strongest competitor at the outset for the nomination. When the Bristow cause became hopeless Harlan threw the Kentucky support to Rutherford B. Hayes, who was shortly thereafter nominated. Hayes's gratitude to Harlan for this service was keen. The cross-currents of party politics made Harlan's appointment to the attorney generalship in Hayes's cabinet politically inexpedient, although Hayes at first intended to offer Harlan this post and he would have been glad to accept it. He declined the tender of a diplomatic post on the ground that it would take him away from his profession. In April 1877, shortly after Hayes was inaugurated, Harlan was made a member of a commission appointed by the President to go to Louisiana to bring about the consolidation of the two rival legislatures so that the settlement of the rival claims to the governorship and other offices could be effected by the civil authority of the state, and to advise the President as to the expediency of the immediate withdrawal of the federal troops (President Hayes's "Letter of Instructions," *New York Tribune,* Apr. 4, 1877). The mission of the Louisiana Commission as outlined by the President was completely successful. On Oct. 17, 1877, Harlan was nominated to an associate justiceship on the Supreme Court of the United States. The appointment was criticized by the Southern conservatives on the ground that Harlan did not have proper regard for state rights, and by the Northern Republicans on the grounds of his opposition to Lincoln in 1864 and his attacks upon the war amendments. It was also urged that he had had no previous judicial experience. On Nov. 29, 1877, the Senate confirmed his appointment, and on Dec. 11, 1877, he took the oath of office and assumed his seat.

Harlan's long tenure on the bench made him a participant in the constitutional controversies of a third of a century. Coming to the Court as the country was just embarking upon economic and industrial revolution which was to influence so profoundly American politics and law, he was to share in the task of adjusting American constitutional principles and practice to the needs of the new industrial and capitalistic régime. During this time he wrote the opinion of the Court in 703 cases. His legal philosophy was built upon the foundation of an almost religious reverence for the Constitution. The simplicity and directness with which he viewed it approaches that of the layman. He believed that it should be construed in accordance with the views of the framers and the dictates of common sense. He had only impatience for refinements and subtleties of construction. He bore an even course between strong nationalism and state rights, as is well shown in a public address in which he declared that "the best friends of states rights . . . are those who recognize the Union as possessing all the powers granted to it in the Constitution, either expressly or by necessary implication." (See his toast, "Kentucky: United We Stand," at the dinner of the Kentucky Society of New York, 1907, *Chicago Legal News,* Dec. 28, 1907.) At the same time, he was quick to attack any infringement by the federal government upon what he deemed the legitimate powers of the states.

This balance of conflicting pressures is evident in his opinions on specific constitutional problems. His famous dissent (1895) in the income-tax cases (*Pollock* vs. *Farmers' Loan and Trust Co.,* 158 *U. S.,* 601) was largely a protest against what he regarded as impairment of the vital power of national taxation. It also shows his devotion to the doctrine of *stare decisis.* In the same vein he upheld the power of Congress to exclude lottery tickets from interstate commerce (*Champion* vs. *Ames,* 188 *U. S.,* 321). He also dissented strongly in the sugar-trust case (*United States* vs. *E. C. Knight Co.,* 156 *U. S.,* 1) urging that the commerce power may forbid a monopoly of manufacturing which must inevitably affect that commerce; and in 1904 he spoke for the Court in the Northern Securities case (193 *U. S.,* 197), when that holding company was declared to have violated the Sherman Act.

Justice Harlan was a stern defender of civil liberty and believed that the constitutional guarantees in its behalf should be strictly construed. This is apparent in his numerous opinions interpreting the clause forbidding the impairment of contracts by states or municipalities. In his defense of the rights of private property he even went so far as to hold that the right to hold public office was a form of property (*Taylor and Marshall* vs. *Beckham,* 178 *U. S.,* 548). He vigorously attacked the decision of the Court that a grand-jury indictment for crime is not essential to due process of law (*Hurtado* vs. *People of California,* 110 *U. S.,* 516). He had a profound reverence for the jury system and all its attributes. He dissented from the Court's ruling that the Thirteenth Amendment does not extend to seamen's contracts for labor which in effect subjected them to involuntary servitude (*Robertson* vs. *Baldwin,* 165 *U. S.,* 275). He protested strenuously in the Insular Cases against the doctrine that parts of the federal bill of rights do not apply of their own force in the unincorporated territories (*Hawaii* vs. *Mankichi,* 190 *U. S.,* 197; *Dorr* vs. *United States,* 195 U. S., 138). For him the Constitution "followed the flag," and he could not conceive of American territory deprived of the protection of the fundamental law. An important premise in his judicial philosophy was that the intentions of lawmakers should wherever possible be given effect without quibble or perversion. This attitude was made strikingly clear in his steady disagreement with his colleagues over the interpretation of the war amendments and the laws passed to give them effect. Thus he dissented strongly in the Civil-Rights Cases (109 *U. S.*, 3), which held that Congress had no power under the Fourteenth Amendment to protect the negro against discrimination practised by individuals, for he believed that such protection was intended by the framers of the amendment. He regarded this dissent as perhaps his most notable opinion. He objected vigorously to the Court's decisions that the guarantees of the federal bill of rights are not amongst the privileges and immunities of citizens of the United States which the states are forbidden by the Fourteenth Amendment to abridge or deny (*Maxwell* vs. *Dow,* 176 *U. S.*, 581; *Twining* vs. *State of New Jersey,* 211 *U. S.*, 78). Nor could he agree that the so-called "Jim Crow" laws effecting the segregation of negroes and whites in public places did not deny the negro the equal protection of the laws (*Plessy* vs. *Ferguson,* 163 *U. S.*, 537; *Berea College* vs. *Commonwealth of Kentucky,* 211 *U. S.*, 45).

Harlan believed that firm protection should be given to the police power of the states. Thus he dissented in the series of cases, including the famous "original package case," in which the states' power to keep intoxicating liquor from being shipped in through the channels of interstate commerce was cut down or denied (*Leisy* vs. *Hardin,* 135 *U. S.*, 100), in which he concurred in a dissent by Justice Gray (*Bowman* vs. *Chicago and Northwestern Railway Co.,* 125 *U. S.*, 465; *Rhodes* vs. *Iowa,* 170 *U. S.*, 412). He believed that in the exercise of the police power the legislative judgment and discretion should be accorded deep respect. He spoke for the Court in upholding state prohibition laws (*Mugler* vs. *Kansas,* 123 *U. S.*, 623), and a compulsory vaccination statute (*Jacobson* vs. *Massachusetts,* 197 *U. S.*, 11). He dissented in *Lochner* vs. *New York* (198 *U. S.*, 45), when the Court invalidated the New York ten-hour law for bakers, but he spoke for the Court in the case of *Adair* vs. *United States* (208 *U. S.*, 161), holding that a statute penalizing a common carrier for discharging an employee because of membership in a labor union was an arbitrary invasion of freedom of contract amounting to a denial of due process of law, as well as an unwarranted extension of the commerce power.

While Harlan firmly believed that the courts are the proper guardians of the Constitution and must invalidate laws which violate it, he had nothing but abhorrence for the doctrine of implied constitutional limitations which would permit the voiding of laws because they are deemed to violate "natural law" or "fundamental rights," and he rendered valiant service in helping to discredit this "natural rights" philosophy which Justice Field particularly had struggled to engraft upon American constitutional law. Furthermore, he resented with all his vigor what seemed to him to be judicial legislation. The first dissent which he ever uttered (*United States* vs. *Clark,* 96 *U. S.*, 37) and his last dissenting opinions written only a few months before his death, in the Standard Oil Company and American Tobacco Company cases, were alike strong denunciations of judicial legislation. In fact these last two opinions are probably his most famous, for they attracted wide attention and seemed to coincide with the views of the man in the street. In them he bitterly denounced the Court for reading into the prohibitions of the Sherman Act the word "unreasonable," so that instead of forbidding all restraints of trade, as the words read, it was held to forbid only unreasonable restraints (*Standard Oil Company of New Jersey, et al.* vs. *United States,* 221 *U. S.*, 1; *United States* vs. *American Tobacco Company,* 221 *U. S.*, 106).

In fact it is as the "great dissenter" that Harlan will be most widely remembered. By temperament he was a fighter, a controversialist, an advocate. He was endowed with a strong will, an indomitable confidence in the soundness of his own views, and a stern sense of his duty to adhere to them. The spirit of compromise was not in him. As Chief Justice White said of him, "he could lead but he could not follow." When he disagreed with his colleagues on the Court, as he frequently did, he was always constrained to voice his protest. Nor was his manner of doing so such as to smooth the edge of disagreement. His dissents were always vigorous, frequently impatient, sometimes almost bitter in their denunciation of the doctrines which he was seeking to refute. Sometimes they were delivered orally from the bench and the manuscripts prepared later: contemporary press accounts afford a striking picture of him as he uttered his famous dissent in the income-tax cases, pounding the desk in front of him, shaking his finger in the faces of the Chief Justice and Justice Field, and declaiming his protest with all the fervor of the stump orator. Altogether he dissented in 316 cases. In the ratio of dissents to agreements with his brethren he was exceeded only by Justice Daniel.

Harlan's judicial labors absorbed virtually his whole time. In 1892, however, he was appointed by President Harrison to serve as an American representative in the arbitration of the Bering Sea controversy with Great Britain (*Opinions of Mr. Justice Harlan at the Conference in Paris of the Behring Sea Tribunal of Arbitration,* 1893). From 1889 until 1910 he lectured on constitutional law at the Columbian (now George Washington) University. Harlan was a man of large and powerful physique. He had a powerful voice and was a most effective orator. (See his toast at the centennial celebration of the organization of the federal judiciary in New York in 1890, 134 *U. S. Reports,* 751, for an excellent example.) He built a fine house on the outskirts of Washington some three miles from the Capitol and for many years used to walk back and forth daily. In later life he took up golf, a game which he at first viewed with disdain only to follow with devotion. He was a man of great good humor and kindly interest in others, endowed with the gracious qualities and courtesy of the Southern gentleman, and was vastly popular. In spite of his many intellectual disagreements with them he was much beloved by his colleagues on the bench. He was a devoted Presbyterian, and for many years taught a Bible class each week. His intimate friend, Justice Brewer, once said of him: "He retires at eight with one hand on the Constitution and the other on the Bible, safe and happy in a perfect faith in justice and righteousness." His physical vigor remained with him to the end, his death occurring after an illness of less than a week. He had an ambition to set a new record for tenure on the Supreme Court and came near doing so. His service of thirty-three years, ten months, and twenty-five days was exceeded only by that of Justice Field and Chief Justice Marshall.

On Dec. 23, 1856, Harlan had married Malvina F. Shanklin of Evansville, Ind., who outlived him, and of this marriage six children were born.

[The opinions of Harlan are found in 95–221 *U. S. Reports.* See also: F. B. Clark, *Constitutional Doctrines of Justice Harlan* (1915); sketch by I. C. Willis, *Proc. Ky. State Bar Asso.* (1912), p. 36; sketch by R. T. W. Duke, Jr., *Va. Law Reg.,* Nov. 1911; "Militant Justice Harlan," *Current Literature,* July 1911; H. B. Brown, "Dissenting Opinions of Mr. Justice Harlan," *Am. Law Rev.,* May–June 1912, July–Aug. 1917; H. L. Carson, *The Supreme Court of the U. S.* (1891); Charles Warren, *The Supreme Court in U. S. Hist.* (1922); *Who's Who in America,* 1910–11; "Proceedings on the Death of Mr. Justice Harlan," 222 *U. S. Reports,* v; obituary in *N. Y. Times,* Oct. 15, 1911; A. H. Harlan, *Hist. and Geneal. of the Harlan Family* (1914).]

R. E. C.

HARLAN, JOSIAH (June 12, 1799–October 1871), soldier, adventurer, was born in Newlin Township, Chester County, Pa., the ninth child of Joshua Harlan, Philadelphia "merchant broker," and his wife, Sarah (Hinchman) Harlan, and a brother of Richard Harlan [*q.v.*]. Both parents were Friends. His father was the great-grandson of Michael Harlan (or Harland), who emigrated from his home near Durham, England, to County Down, Ireland, and in 1687 to Pennsylvania, where he settled in Chester County. In 1823 Josiah journeyed to the Far East, entered the employ of the East India Company as an officiating assistant surgeon, and was medical officer of Col. George Pollock's Bengal Artillery during the first Burmese war. Resigning in 1826, he proceeded to north India, where he attached himself to the fortunes of Shah Shooja-ool-Moolk, ex-king of Cabul, then living on a British pension at Loodiana. In 1828 Shah Shooja appointed his "Companion of the Imperial Stirrup" a secret agent, with a commission to revolutionize Afghanistan. In this capacity Harlan journeyed to the Afghan capital disguised as a dervish. Finding Dost Mohammed Khan, Amir of Cabul, firmly seated on his throne, Harlan returned to India and entered the service of Maharajah Ranjit Singh, sovereign of the Punjab. Here he remained for seven years, and was for a time governor of the province of Goozerath. The Sikh occupation of the town and citadel of Peshawar (May 1834) precipitated war between the Maharajah and the Amir, and in the spring of 1835 the latter brought an army through the Khyber Pass. Unprepared to meet the threatened invasion, the wily Ranjit Singh instructed Harlan to bribe Sultan Mohammed Khan, the Amir's disgruntled brother. This venture proving successful, Ranjit sent Harlan and Fakir Aziz-ud-din to the Amir's camp. Seduced by Sikh gold, the Afghan army slowly melted away, while the two Sikh envoys were ostensibly negotiating with the Amir (George B. Malleson, *History of Afghanistan,* London, 1879, p. 358). Informed that the Sikhs were surrounding his camp, Dost Mohammed Khan ordered a hasty retreat, after arresting the envoys and placing them in the custody of Sultan Mohammed Khan. The latter escorted them to safety. Becoming dissatisfied at the Court of Lahore, Harlan went to Cabul and urged the Amir to further hostilities. As aide-de-camp to Dost Mohammed Khan and general of regular troops, Harlan trained the Afghan infantry in European military tactics, and the Afghan army, commanded by the Amir's son, Mohammed Akbar Khan, defeated the Sikhs in the battle of Jamrud (April 1837). In the winter of 1838–39 Harlan commanded a division of the army sent to chastise Mir Murad Bey, prince of Koondooz. The expedition, accompanied by a train of artillery, proceeded through the mountains to Balkh, in ancient Bactria, along the route of Alexander the Great. This experience convinced Harlan that in modern times, as in Alexander's day, Balkh should properly be made the base of action for every military threat to India. The restoration of Shah Shooja to the throne of Cabul (August 1839) following the successful British invasion left Harlan without employment and he returned to Philadelphia in 1841. He then published *A Memoir of India and Avghanistaun* (Philadelphia, 1842) and wrote an article, "On the Fruits of Cabul and Vicinity" (*Senate Executive Document No. 39,* 37 Cong., 2 Sess.). He also prepared a "Personal Narrative of General Harlan's Eighteen Years' Residence in Asia," but it was never published. On May 1, 1849, he married Elizabeth Baker, by whom he had one daughter. During the summer of 1861 he raised the regiment known as Harlan's Light Cavalry, of which he was commissioned colonel (Oct. 5, 1861), and served in the Army of the Potomac until ill health forced his retirement (Aug. 20, 1862). A few years after the Civil War he moved to California and apparently practised medicine in San Francisco (H. G. Langley, *San Francisco Directory,* 1871). He died there in the autumn of 1871.

[See Harlan, *A Memoir of India and Avghanistaun* (1842); news articles based on information obtained from Harlan, in *Nat. Gazette* (Phila.), Aug. 25, 1841, and in *U. S. Gazette* (Phila.), Jan. 20, 1842. Not all the facts of Harlan's career in Asia can be checked by other sources but these show Harlan to be reasonably trustworthy: *Asiatic Jour.* (London), Apr. 1841, p. 194; Chas. Masson, *Narrative of Various Journeys in Balochistan, Afghanistan, and the Panjab* (London, 1842), III, 335–45; Mohan Lal, *Life of the Amir Dost Mohammed Khan, of Kabul* (London, 1846), I, 173–82, 240; Syad Muhammad Latif, *Hist. of the Panjab* (Calcutta, 1891), pp. 470–71; A. H. Harlan, *Hist. and Geneal. of the Harlan Family* (1914), pp. 139, 335; *Hist. of the Eleventh Pa. Vol. Cavalry* (1902); *Senate Ex. Doc. No. 27,* 33 Cong., 1 Sess., p. 61; J. S. Futhey and G. Cope, *Hist. of Chester County, Pa.* (1881), p. 316; Phila. *Press,* Nov. 4, 1871; *Sunday Dispatch* (Phila.), Nov. 12, 1871.] F. E. R.

HARLAN, RICHARD (Sept. 19, 1796–Sept. 30, 1843), naturalist, physician, was born in Philadelphia, the eighth child of Joshua and Sarah (Hinchman) Harlan and an elder brother of Josiah Harlan [*q.v.*]. He studied medicine at the University of Pennsylvania and while he was still a student made a voyage to India as ship's surgeon. Taking his degree in 1818 at the age of twenty-two, he began to practise in Philadelphia. For a time he was in charge of the private dissecting-room opened by his preceptor, Dr. Joseph Parrish. Three years after his graduation he was elected, in 1821, professor of comparative anatomy in the Philadelphia Museum and also surgeon to that institution. In 1832 he was a member of a commission sent to Canada and New York by the Sanitary Board of Philadelphia to study the epidemic of Asiatic cholera prevalent at that time. He was married on Jan. 30, 1833, to Margaret Hart (Simmons) Howell, a widow. Between 1832 and 1836 he was the corresponding secretary of the Geological Society of Pennsylvania and one of its three curators. In 1838 he visited Europe and after his return removed to New Orleans, where in 1843, the year of his death, he was elected vice-president of the Louisiana State Medical Society. His most important publications in the field of medicine and human anatomy were *Anatomical Investigations* (1824) and certain papers in his *Medical and Physical Researches* (1835).

Harlan's major interest was the study of zoölogy and vertebrate paleontology. His first publication in the latter field, "Observations on Fossil Elephant Teeth of North America," appeared in the *Journal of the Academy of Natural Sciences of Philadelphia* in June 1823, and was followed soon after, January 1824, by an article on the new genus Saurocephalus, a fossil reptile brought back by Lewis and Clark. In 1824 also he published his *Observations on the Genus Salamandra* and, as a result of an investigation of the West Jersey region in that year with Thomas Say and Titian Peale, he wrote a paper on an American Plesiosaur, a form hitherto supposed to be limited to Europe (*Journal,* February 1825). His most notable work *Fauna Americana,* the first systematic treatise on American mammals, appeared in 1825. A compilation based in large part on A. G. Desmarest's *Mammalogie* (1820–22), it dealt with both living and extinct forms, grouping the fossil forms with what the author presumed to be their nearest living representative. The work was received with hostile criticism (see Harlan's *Refutation of Certain Misrepresentations Issued against the Author of the Fauna Americana,* 1826), and the second part, which was to have dealt with the reptiles, was never published. Harlan was undiscouraged, however; in 1826 he wrote a brief monograph on the "Genera of North American Reptilia" (*Journal,* February 1826, February and June 1827), and in 1827 published as a pamphlet his *American Herpetology.* He was one of the first to support Featherstonhaugh's new *Monthly American Journal of Geology,* to which he contributed (August 1831) an interesting paper on the Jeffersonian genus Megalonyx. In a paper read in 1832 on the discovery of an Ichthyosaurus in Missouri, he forecast the beginning of the discovery of the great fossil treasures of the West (*Transactions of the American Philosophical Society,* n.s. IV, 1834). Although the modern science of odontography, or odontology, was then virtually unknown, he contributed to the Geological Society of Pennsylvania in 1834 a paper "On the Structure and Teeth of the Edentata Fossil" (*Transactions,* August 1834). During this same year he made his most extensive contribution to the science of vertebrate paleontology in his "Critical Notices of Various Organic Remains hitherto Discovered in North America" (*Ibid.*). This study was in large part a response to the desire of European naturalists for concrete information as to what had been accomplished in America. Harlan was a prolific writer for his day. He contributed papers to the Société Géologique de France, the Geological Society of London, and the British Association for the Advancement of Science. His chief service to American natural history was not his own research, however, so much as the collection and codification of the work of earlier writers in the field. After his removal to New Orleans he published little. He died there of apoplexy at the age of forty-seven.

[A. H. Harlan, *Hist. and Geneal. of the Harlan Family* (1914); Henry Simpson, *Lives of Eminent Philadelphians Now Deceased* (1859); H. A. Kelly, *Cyc. of Am. Medic. Biog.* (1912); J. T. Scharf and Thompson Westcott, *Hist. of Phila.* (1884); G. B. Goode, in *Report of the U. S. Nat. Museum, 1897,* pt. 2 (1901), pp. 450–51; bibliography of Harlan's writings in Max Meisel, *A Bibliog. of Am. Natural Hist.* (3 vols., 1924–29).] D. M. F.

HARLAND, HENRY (Mar. 1, 1861–Dec. 20, 1905), author, was born in New York City, the son of Thomas Harland, a lawyer. He was the last to bear the name of his family, which was established at Norwich, Conn., in 1773 by Thomas Harland [*q.v.*], clock-maker. Harland attended Adelphi Academy, Brooklyn, 1871–72, Public School No. 35, New York, 1872–77, and the College of the City of New York, 1877–80. During his college years he became interested in the Ethical Culture movement, then beginning under Felix Adler. After a year of private tutoring and writing he entered the Harvard Divinity School but did not remain long. Leaving Cambridge, his ministerial aspirations dispelled, he spent a year (1882–83) in Rome and Paris. After his return to New York in November 1883 he accepted a position in the office of his father's friend, Surrogate Daniel G. Rollins. On May 5, 1884, he married Aline Herminé Merriam, a talented musician and his constant, devoted companion. He resigned his clerkship in February 1886 to devote his time entirely to writing. His system of sleeping from supper time until two in the morning and then writing until breakfast had enabled him the year before to complete his first novel, *As It Was Written: A Jewish Musician's Story* (1885), which was published under the pseudonym of Sidney Luska. In rapid succession he then produced *Mrs. Peixada* (1886), *The Yoke of Thorah* (1887), and *My Uncle Florimond* (1888). These novels have for their background the life of those German Jews who were Harland's most intimate associates. The last of them is negligible but the others reveal a sense for melodramatic plot, moderate skill in verisimilitude, and a consistent if not brilliant power of characterization. The style, florid in spots, is in general commonplace and reveals no trace of his later manner.

In 1889 he went to Paris and thence to London, which was thereafter his headquarters. His next publications, *Grandison Mather* (1889), *A Latin-Quarter Courtship* (1889), *Two Voices* (1890), *Two Women or One* (1890), and *Mea Culpa* (1891) showed a continued inclination toward the autobiographical, melodramatic style of his early work. With the disappearance of the Jewish themes and background, however, Harland seemed to be groping for material. His next book, *Mademoiselle Miss* (1893), showed a distinct change. These short stories were half-romantic, half-realistic episodes laid in many parts of Europe. Their grace, felicity of language and characterization, and Zendaesque scenes mark the beginning of his new style. Richard Le Gallienne described him, in this period, as "one of those Americans in love with Paris who seem more French than the French themselves, a slim, gesticulating, goateed, snub-nosed, lovable figure, smoking innumerable cigarettes as he galvanically pranced about the room excitedly propounding the *dernier mot* on the build of the short story or the art of prose. . . . The polishing of his prose was for him his being's end and aim, and I have often seen him at that sacred task of a forenoon, in his study-bedroom, still in pajamas and dressing-gown, . . . bending over an exquisite piece of handwriting, like a goldsmith at his bench" (*The Romantic '90's,* 1925, pp. 233 ff.).

Meanwhile he had become associated with John Lane as a member of the editorial staff at the Bodley Head. Soon, with Aubrey Beardsley, they planned and established (April 1894) the *Yellow Book,* designed as a publication of high literary and artistic quality, uncontrolled by Mrs. Grundy. Harland proved an excellent editor. Precise and exacting in the mechanical parts of the work, he was enthusiastic in seeking important contributors and successful in retaining them. His apartment in Cromwell Road was the rendezvous of the *Yellow Book* set, and his spirit was the unifying force behind them. His own contributions consisted of a short story in each issue, and critical essays signed "The Yellow Dwarf" in Volumes VII, IX, and X. The stories appeared later, with others, in *Gray Roses* (1895) and *Comedies and Errors* (1898). The *Yellow Book* came to an end in April 1897. Harland had won fame within a limited circle; he had perfected a charming literary style and established himself as master of a form which blends the qualities of Maupassant and Henry James; but he was still to gain popular applause. This came soon with the publication of *The Cardinal's Snuff Box* (1900), his best-known work. Despite its slender plot it became one of the most widely read novels of its time. Its gracious characterization and vivacious, allusive style were everywhere admired. He followed this success with two others, *The Lady Paramount* (1902), and *My Friend Prospero* (1904), which resembled their predecessor too closely in substance and manner. *The Royal End* (1909) was completed by Mrs. Harland. During the last fifteen years of his life he endured the terrors of pulmonary tuberculosis. For relief he sought often the mild climate of San Remo, Italy, where he died in 1905, after weeks of suffering.

[G. Glastonbury (Mrs. Harland), "The Life and Writings of Henry Harland," *Irish Monthly*, Apr. 1911; Henry James, "The Story-Teller at Large," *Fortnightly Rev.*, Apr. 1, 1898; *Athenæum*, Dec. 30, 1905; *Bookman*, Aug. 1909; E. Lenore Casford, "The Magazines of the 1890's," *Univ. of Ore. Pubs.*, vol. I, no. 1 (Sept. 1929); C. H. Pope, *Merriam Geneal.* (1906); Laura Stedman and G. M. Gould, *Life and Letters of E. C. Stedman* (2 vols., 1910); S. L. Gwynn, *Experiences of a Literary Man* (1926); C. L. Hind, *Naphtali* (1926); *N. Y. Times*, Dec. 22, 1905; Holbrook Jackson, *The Eighteen Nineties* (1914).] D. A. R—s.

HARLAND, MARION [See TERHUNE, MARY VIRGINIA, 1830–1922].

HARLAND, THOMAS (1735–Mar. 31, 1807), watch- and clock-maker, silversmith, is said to have arrived in Boston from London on one of the famous tea ships. After a brief survey of that troubled town he decided that Norwich, Conn., offered greater opportunities for building up a business. The *Norwich Packet* on Dec. 9, 1773, carried his advertisement stating that he made "in the neatest manner and on the most improved principles, horizontal, repeating and plain watches in gold, silver, metal or covered cases, spring, musical and plain clocks; church clocks, regulators, etc." He also cleaned and repaired clocks and watches, engraved clock faces and made watch wheels for the trade, "neat as London and at the same price." It is illustrative of his versatility that when Norwich Town needed a fire-engine in 1778 it was Thomas Harland who superintended its construction. His business judgment was sound, as is shown by the fact that, in spite of the troubled times, his enterprise grew and prospered until, in 1790, his name was known all over the states as a master craftsman and apprentices were coming long distances to learn from him. Among these apprentices were Thomas Cleveland, grandfather of President Grover Cleveland, and Eli Terry [*q.v.*]. By this time twelve people were working in the Harland shop and it has been estimated that two hundred watches and forty clocks were being produced each year. One of his grandfather clocks is possessed by the Metropolitan Museum of Art. In addition Harland was fashioning jewelry and making silver table-ware marked with the name "HARLAND" in a rectangle or scroll, between profile and eagle displayed.

Not much is known of the life of Thomas Harland before his thirty-eighth year. He always advertised himself as a "London craftsman" but family tradition has it that he roamed over most of Europe, even reaching Warsaw. If this is so it is probable that contacts with foreign artisans improved his technique and knowledge. That he was a man of culture somewhat above the average for his station in life is shown by the inventory of his library, made at the time of his death. He possessed a number of serious volumes on philosophy and history, many of them in French. In his forty-fourth year, six years after he arrived in Norwich, he married Hannah Leffingwell Clark. He died at the age of seventy-two.

[Henry Terry, *Am. Clock Making* (t.p. date 1870; copyright 1871); M. E. Perkins, *Old Houses of the Ancient Town of Norwich* (1895); W. R. Cutter and others, *Geneal. and Family Hist. of the State of Conn.* (1911), vol. I; G. M. Curtis, *Early Silver of Conn. and Its Makers* (1913); *A List of Early Am. Silversmiths and Their Marks* (Walpole Soc., 1917); P. R. Hoopes, *Conn. Clockmakers of the Eighteenth Century* (1930); *Conn. Centinel* (Norwich), Apr. 7, 1807.] K. H. A.

HARMAR, JOSIAH (Nov. 10, 1753–Aug. 20, 1813), soldier, was born in Philadelphia. He was educated at the Quaker school of Robert Proud. In the Revolution he was made major of the 3rd Pennsylvania Regiment, Oct. 1, 1776, lieutenant-colonel of the 6th Pennsylvania, June 6, 1777, and was later transferred successively to the 7th, 3rd, and 1st Pennsylvania. He became colonel Sept. 30, 1783, and commander of the army (a very small force), Aug. 12, 1784. He had served under Washington, and at the end of the war under Henry Lee in the South. When the treaty of peace had been ratified by Congress, Harmar carried the ratification to France. Soon after his return he was married, on Oct. 19, 1784, to Sarah Jenkins. As commander of the army stationed on the Ohio frontier, he was present during the negotiation of the treaty of Fort McIntosh. In 1785, in accordance with the policy defined by the Indian treaties, he was ordered by the Indian Commissioners and by Congress to expel intruding settlers from the Indian country north of the Ohio River, a task in which he was only partly successful. He was engaged in Indian warfare in 1785 and 1786, was brevetted brigadier-general in 1787, and occupied in that year Vincennes and the Illinois towns. Vigorous measures became necessary against the Indians within the present Ohio and Indiana. In 1790 Harmar pursued the Shawnees along the Scioto River, and at the end of September he started from Fort Washington (Cincinnati) against the Indians in the valley of the Maumee, where he destroyed villages and considerable quantities of corn and other supplies, and to that extent harassed the enemy. A small detachment of his force was defeated. On the return march he unwisely sent back a body of 400 men to strike a blow, but in its encounter with the Indians, Oct. 22, it gained only a partial success. He was brave, but not suited for a commander against Indians, and was not in sympathetic touch with the frontiersmen. His army, composed of Kentucky and Pennsylvania troops, 1,400 to 1,500 in number, was of poor material, and imperfectly equipped; all but 320 were militia. Bad discipline prevailed, and although the expedition returned to its base, it was in its general results a failure. Indians followed upon Harmar's retreat, the struggling settlements in Ohio suffered, and the St. Clair expedition of the following year ensued. A court of inquiry was held in 1791, and its findings were "honorable" to Harmar. He continued to be commander of the army until Mar. 4, 1791, and resigned from the service Jan. 1, 1792. From 1793 to 1799 he served as adjutant-general of Pennsylvania.

[Harmar letters, 1784–96, and 1784–85, printed in *Mil. Jour. of Maj. Ebenezer Denny* (1859) and in the *Jour. of Capt. Jonathan Heart* (1885); *Am. State Papers: Indian Affairs,* vol. I, and *Mil. Affairs,* vol. I (both 1832); W. A. Brice, *Hist. of Fort Wayne* (1868); *Western Reserve Hist. Soc. Hist. and Archeol. Tract No. 6* (1871); Wm. H. Smith, *The St. Clair Papers* (2 vols., 1882); *Ohio Archeol. and Hist. Quart.,* Oct. 1910 and Jan. 1911; F. B. Heitman, *Hist. Reg. and Dict. U. S. Army* (1903); *Pa. Mag. of Hist. and Biog.,* Oct. 1922; *Poulson's Am. Daily Advertiser* (Phila.), Aug. 21, 1813.] E. K. A.

HARMON, DANIEL WILLIAMS (Feb. 19, 1778–Mar. 26, 1845), fur-trader, explorer, the son of Daniel and Lucrecia (Dewey) Harmon, was born at Bennington, Vt. Information regarding his life, except for the period covered by his journal, is meager, and nothing is known of his youth, nor of his education except that it was "not classical." At Montreal, in April 1800, he was engaged as a clerk by the North-West Company, and was assigned to the Far West. Leaving Montreal on the 28th, his party proceeded by the usual route of the trappers and arrived at Little Lake Winnipeg on Aug. 24. For ten years he served the company at various posts in the present Manitoba, Saskatchewan, and Alberta, and in the fall of 1810 crossed the mountains to British Columbia, where he remained nearly nine years. As clerk, regional superintendent, and ultimately a partner of the company, he made journeys through the wilderness that aggregated many thousands of miles. During the whole period he kept a record (though not a continuous one) of his travels and dealings with the Indians, to which he added many observations on the country and the character and customs of the savages, as well as occasional moral reflections. He jotted down, also, the various scraps of news that reached him—the arrival of Lewis and Clark at the Mandan villages in the fall of 1804; that of David Thompson and his party of Northwesterners at the mouth of the Columbia in 1811 only to find the Americans already in possession, and the sale of Astoria in 1813. For five years he resisted the custom of his fellow whites of taking a native woman for a companion, but on Oct. 10, 1805, he chose a fourteen-year-old half-breed girl, Elizabeth, who was to bear him eleven children and to accompany him back to civilization, where he formally married her. The return journey was made in 1819, and he seems to have arrived in Vermont early in 1820. On his marriage he probably settled his family in Burlington, and after intrusting his journal to the Rev. Daniel Haskell, of that town, he seems again to have started for the Northwest. Of his subsequent movements nothing is definitely known except that he returned to Montreal, where he died. His *Journal of Voyages and Travels in the Interiour of North America,* rewritten by Haskell, was published in Andover, N. H., in the fall of 1820, and in 1903 was reprinted, with a brief introduction by Robert Waite, in New York City. In spite of the labors of Haskell to make the work not only "literary" but somewhat pious, much remains of what must have been its original character—a descriptive narrative marked by a naïve simplicity and matter-of-fact straightforwardness.

[In addition to Harmon's *Journal,* see Geo. Bryce, *Notes and Comments on Harmon's Jour., 1800–20* (1883); M. D. Gilman, *The Bibliog. of Vt.* (1897); and J. W. Harman, *Harman-Harmon Geneal. and Biog.* (1928).] W. J. G.

HARMON, JUDSON (Feb. 3, 1846–Feb. 22, 1927), jurist, attorney-general, governor of Ohio, was born at the little village of Newtown, Hamilton County, Ohio, the eldest of the eight children of Benjamin Franklin and Julia (Bronson) Harmon. His father, a teacher and later a Baptist preacher, was descended from John Harmon who settled in Springfield, Mass., *c.* 1640. Educated partly at home and partly in the public schools, Judson Harmon at the age of sixteen entered Denison University, where he graduated four years later despite the need of contributing by his labors to his own support. A summer vacation of these Civil War college days was interrupted when he rode out with the home guards to help repel the incursion of the Southern cavalry raider, General Morgan. The young college graduate taught school for one year as principal at Columbia, Ohio, and then moved to Cincinnati to read law in the office of George Hoadly [*q.v.*], who afterward became governor of the state. In 1869 he received his law degree at the Cincinnati Law School and was duly admitted to the bar. After seven years of practice he was elected judge of the common-pleas court in Cincinnati but was ousted by a contest in the Ohio Senate. Two years later he was elected by a large majority to the local superior court, upon which he served until 1887 when he retired to take the place of Governor Hoadly in the eminent Cincinnati law firm of Hoadly, Johnson & Colston. In June 1870 he had married Olivia Scobey of Hamilton.

Originally inclined to support the Republican party on war issues, Harmon revolted against its drastic program of reconstruction and participated in the national Liberal Republican convention at Cincinnati in June 1872. Somewhat later he associated himself with the Democratic party of his state. In June 1895 President Cleveland recognized his talents and his claims upon the party when he appointed Harmon to succeed Richard Olney as attorney-general; in this office he rendered distinguished services and acquired national fame as a lawyer. He directed the prosecution, under the Sherman Act, of the Trans-Missouri Freight Association (166 *U. S.*, 290) and the beginning of suit against the Addystone Pipe & Steel Company (78 *Fed.*, 712). In 1897 Harmon returned to his lucrative legal practice in Cincinnati. In 1905 he was made a special commissioner to investigate charges of rebating by the Atchison, Topeka & Santa Fé Railroad; he helped to trace rebates of over a million dollars to the door of Paul Morton, the former traffic manager, who was now secretary of the navy (*Boston Transcript*, June 22, 1905; *Arena*, August 1905; *Nation*, June 22, 1905). President Roosevelt, however, interceded when Harmon urged proceedings against the responsible officials on the ground that "guilt is always personal," a slogan that later became the watchword of Harmon's efforts in politics, and Harmon accordingly withdrew from the case on June 5. From 1905 to 1909 he successfully labored as receiver to restore the financial stability of the Cincinnati, Hamilton & Dayton and the Pere Marquette Railroads. He was later criticized by Ex-President Roosevelt for continuing these services after his inauguration as governor, but was able to show that the court had refused to accept the resignation which he had tendered (*Cleveland Plain Dealer*, Nov. 6, 1910).

By 1908 the likable, hard-working, square-shouldered six-footer had established his reputation as the most intelligent and competent conservative in the ranks of the Ohio Democracy. He was generally known as a Tilden-Cleveland Democrat, standing somewhere between the old-time bosses of his party and the militant following of Tom L. Johnson [*q.v.*], an exponent of Bryan progressivism. Harmon now seemed the logical person to lead his party in challenging the long-standing and demoralizing Republican control of state politics. Accordingly, in spite of the open opposition of Johnson, the Ohio state Democratic convention of May 1908 chose Harmon as the nominee of the party for the gubernatorial office. In the election that followed, Harmon triumphed over the Republican incumbent with a plurality of 19,372, although the Republican candidate for the presidency, William H. Taft, an Ohioan, carried the state by over fifty thousand. The new governor soon won laurels for himself and his party. He waged war upon graft and corruption; he gave his state a business administration. When a hostile Republican legislature refused to cooperate in enacting the reform legislation that he repeatedly urged, he won renomination for a second term without opposition and made his pleas directly to the voters. In the spirited campaign of 1910, in which Ex-President Roosevelt enlisted his talents against Harmon, the latter led his party to victory over Warren G. Harding by a plurality of 100,377. His oft-renewed but good-natured recommendations now bore fruit in a number of measures that reflected Ohio's part in the progressive wave that was sweeping the nation. These included the ratification of the federal income-tax amendment, a law for the creation of a single board for the state's penal, benevolent, and reformatory institutions, and a new corrupt-practices act to insure against such traffic in votes as had prevailed in Adams and Scioto counties. Harmon's signature was also attached to a model workmen's-compensation act, a measure for the direct popular election of United States senators, and a statute creating a public-utility commission.

Harmon now became the favorite son of the Ohio Democracy for the presidency. When, however, he frankly declared his opposition to the statewide application of the then popular initiative and referendum, the Bryan progressive leaders of Ohio promptly declared that Harmon was not the prophet appointed to lead the party out of the wilderness of national politics. Indeed, the "Great Commoner" from Nebraska, "having learned . . . that Wall Street had picked out Governor Harmon as its Democratic candidate" (*The Memoirs of William Jennings Bryan*, p. 159), promptly entered the arena with denunciations of the Ohio "reactionary." None the less, as a result of the Ohio primaries of May 1912 and the control of the state Democratic convention by his followers, Harmon was assured the entire vote of the Ohio delegation at the Baltimore convention, as he was also the ninety votes of the New York delegation. At Baltimore, Bryan boldly attacked the favorites of "the privilege-hunting and favor-seeking class," a stand which was ominous for Harmon's candidacy. So, although the Ohioan started out auspiciously on the first vote as a fairly strong third in the race, he failed to build up his strength adequately in the prolonged balloting that finally led to the nomination of Woodrow Wilson. The victory of the latter in the November election, with the choice in Ohio of James M. Cox to the governorship, heralded Harmon's retirement from active politics. When, however he left office in 1913, he could take satisfaction in a well-established reputation for conservative contribution to the welfare of his commonwealth. Harmon now returned to Cincinnati and to the practice of law. He was widely known as an eminent corporation attorney and was for many years a professor in the law school which gave him his legal training. Efforts to induce him to reënter the field of active politics proved unavailing. He died at Cincinnati on Feb. 22, 1927.

[In the absence of a biography and even a satisfactory biographical sketch, materials may be found in the following: E. O. Randall and D. J. Ryan, *Hist. of Ohio: the Rise and Progress of an Am. State*, vol. IV (1912); J. K. Mercer, *Ohio Legislative Hist., 1909–13* (1913); T. E. Powell, *The Democratic Party of the State of Ohio*, vol. I (1913); J. B. Foraker, *Notes of a Busy Life* (2 vols., 1916); W. J. and M. B. Bryan, *The Memoirs of William Jennings Bryan* (1925). Among numerous articles in periodicals may be cited: E. B. Whitney, "Judson Harmon," *North Am. Rev.*, June 1908; S. Gordon, "Judson Harmon of Ohio," *Rev. of Revs.*, Sept. 1910; W. B. Hale, "Judson Harmon and the Presidency," *World's Work*, June 1911. See also obituary in *Cincinnati Enquirer*, Feb. 23, 1927, and A. C. Harmon, *The Harmon Genealogy, Comprising All Branches in New England* (1920).] A. C. C.

HARNDEN, WILLIAM FREDERICK (Aug. 23, 1812–Jan. 14, 1845), pioneer expressman and importer of labor, son of Ameriah and Sally Richardson Harnden, was born in Reading, Mass., where he obtained a public-school education. His father's occupation was that of house-painter, but the son was considered too delicate in health to earn his living thus, and in 1834 he began work for the Boston & Worcester railroad, acting as conductor on the first train which ran over this road, and later becoming a ticket agent for the road. With this assurance of employment, he married Sarah Wright Fuller of Newton, Mass., in December 1835. After he had been with the railroad five years it became obvious that he must find some less confining labor. James W. Hale, who ran the Tontine Coffee House at the corner of Wall and Pearl streets, New York, asserted many years later that he suggested to Harnden the notion of a messenger service between New York and Boston and likewise proposed using the name "express." Acting on this suggestion or on a plan of his own conception, Harnden established a regular carriage service for small and valuable packages which theretofore had been transported by stage-coach drivers, steam-boat captains, or the casual traveler. After the purchase of a half-bushel carpet-bag and the insertion of an advertisement in the Boston papers, he made his first trip, on Mar. 4, 1839. Without capital, health, or influence, his chances of success seemed small. His first two months were unprofitable, brokers and business men finding it difficult to accept the notion of paying a fee for what had often been performed gratuitously in the past. Gradually, however, the advantage of a messenger who was regular, prompt, and trustworthy won increasing favor with the press and with business men generally. Before the year had ended Harnden had added several employees. One was Adolphus Harnden, a younger brother, who lost his life the next year in the burning of the steamship *Lexington*. Another was Dexter Brigham, Jr., who soon became a partner in Harnden & Company and continued the business after Harnden's death.

For a time in 1840 it looked as if the precarious undertaking, made more difficult than usual by extremely inclement weather, must be abandoned, but the establishment of the Liverpool-to-Boston Cunard steamship line, with the resulting delivery in Boston of many packages for New York and Philadelphia, so increased business that more employees were added and the carpet-bag became a trunk. In 1841 branches of the company were created in Philadelphia and as far west as Albany, where the services of Henry Wells, as manager, were enlisted. Beyond Albany Harnden refused to go, having little faith in western profits. His own interest was in European expansion, and in the summer of 1841 Dexter Brigham and J. L. Stone were sent abroad to establish branches in Liverpool, London, and Paris.

About this time Harnden conceived of another possibility. Realizing the need for an increased labor supply, if the West were to be developed, and knowing that his influence in Europe would be enhanced if he interested himself in immigration, he added to his existing foreign offices others in Scotland, Germany, and Ireland and advertised the possibility of an easy transfer of money by the sale of bills of exchange on these foreign offices. Then he secured cheap passage for immigrants on a line of Boston packet boats and on Hudson River and Erie Canal boats as well. In this way he is said to have facilitated the movement of 100,000 laborers to the United States. But neither this business nor the express business was financially successful, and Harnden, broken by his unremitting labor, died a poor man. His energy, industry, and perseverance had far outrun his scant equipment of physical strength. His company, which after 1840 had had a rival in Burke & Adams, continued for some years after his death but was eventually absorbed in the Adams Express Company.

[A. L. Stimson, *Hist. of the Express Companies* (1858, rev. ed., 1881), contains the most complete account of Harnden's struggling business. See also W. H. Rideing, "An Am. Enterprise," *Harper's Monthly Mag.*, Aug. 1875; T. W. Tucker, *Waifs from the Way-Bills of an Old Expressman* (1872); Henry Wells. *Sketch of the Rise, Progress, and Present Condition of the Express System* (1864); E. R. Johnson, *Hist. of the Domestic and Foreign Commerce of the U. S.* (1915), vol. II; and the *Boston Transcript*, Jan. 14, 1845.]

E. D.

HARNETT, CORNELIUS (Apr. 20, 1723?–Apr. 28, 1781), statesman, son of Cornelius Harnett who was "bred a merchant in Dublin," and Mary (Holt) Harnett, was born probably in Chowan County, N. C. He inherited a good estate and seems to have had some educational advantages, for he is reported to have had "a fine taste for letters and a genius for music." From 1754 to 1775 he represented the borough of Wilmington in the General Assembly and rose rapidly to a place of leadership in the popular party. He was conspicuous in the revolutionary movement. As chairman of the Cape Fear Sons of Liberty in 1765–66, he led the successful resistance to the Stamp Act in North Carolina. Later he was a leader in the Assembly which, upon dissolution by the governor, met Nov. 7, 1769, as a convention and adopted a "Non-Importation Association," and was chairman of a committee of thirty appointed at Wilmington to enforce it. Hailed in 1773 as "the Samuel Adams of North Carolina" (Josiah Quincy, *Memoir of the Life of Josiah Quincy, Jr., of Massachusetts*, 1825, p. 120), he led the movement in the Assembly to create a committee of correspondence and was himself appointed one of its nine members. Though his absence from the colony prevented his election to the First Provincial Congress, Aug. 25, 1774, he served in each of the other four provincial congresses and succeeded Richard Caswell as president of the Congress of November 1776. As chairman of the committees of safety of Wilmington and New Hanover County, 1774–75, he made them the most effective revolutionary agencies in the colony, and from Oct. 18, 1775, to Aug. 21, 1776, he was president of the Provincial Council which put the colony on a war basis. Sir Henry Clinton, during his invasion of North Carolina, offered amnesty to all rebels who would return to their allegiance, "excepting only from the benefits of such pardon Cornelius Harnett and Robert Howes" [*sic*].

The Provincial Congress which met at Halifax, Apr. 4, 1776, appointed Harnett chairman of a committee to consider the question of independence, and on Apr. 12 he submitted a report recommending "That the delegates for this colony in the Continental Congress be empowered to concur with the delegates of the other Colonies in declaring Independency and forming foreign alliances." Unanimously adopted by the Provincial Congress, this resolution was forwarded to the Continental Congress where it was hailed with joy by the advocates of independence in that body. In the Fifth Provincial Congress, which met at Halifax Nov. 12, 1776, Harnett was a member of the committee which drafted the first state constitution. To him a well-founded tradition ascribes the authorship of the clause forbidding an established church and guaranteeing religious freedom. The new government went into operation Jan. 16, 1777, with Harnett as president of the Council of State, but on May 1 he was elected a delegate to the Continental Congress and took his seat in that body on July 22.

Harnett served three terms in the Continental Congress and there displayed a clear grasp of the country's situation and needs. Accordingly he urged his state to keep its military establishment up to full strength, to fortify the seacoast, and to levy taxes for maintaining the state and continental currency. He took particular interest in the Articles of Confederation, to which his name is signed, and urged their ratification upon the General Assembly. He found service in Congress extremely disagreeable. His health was poor, his expenses great. He missed the comforts of home, suffered from gout, and wearied of the quarrels and sectional jealousies of his colleagues. To a friend he wrote that his expenses had exceeded his salary by £6,000, but added: "Do not mention this complaint to anybody. I am content to sit down with this loss and much *more* if my country requires it." He accepted reëlection as a patriotic duty and retired from Congress only when he was no longer eligible, returning to his home near Wilmington, on Feb. 20, 1780. Upon the occupation of Wilmington by a British force, in January 1781, Harnett, who still rested under Clinton's proscription, attempted to escape but was overtaken about thirty miles from home, "thrown across a horse like a sack of meal," according to an eyewitness, and brought back to Wilmington "in an unconscious state" (Catherine DeR. Meares, *Annals of the DeRosset Family,* 1906, p. 50). There, on Apr. 28, 1781, he died a prisoner on parole. A visitor in 1775 described "Hilton," Harnett's home, as a very handsome house, fronting on "one of the finest pieces of water in the world." His wife, Mary, enjoyed a reputation as a pattern of industry and an agreeable woman of good sense. Harnett himself held high rank as a Mason, and though a deist in religion, he served for many years as vestryman of St. James Parish in Wilmington.

[R. D. W. Connor, *Cornelius Harnett: An Essay in N. C. Hist.* (1909); D. L. Swain, "Life and Letters of Cornelius Harnett," *N. C. Univ. Mag.*, Feb. 1861; C. A. Smith, "Our Debt to Cornelius Harnett," *Ibid.*, May 1907; *Colonial Records of N. C.*, vols. IV–X (1886–90); *State Records of N. C.*, vols. XI–XXX (1895–1914). For references to Harnett's wife, see *Jour. of a Lady of Quality* (1921), ed. by Evangeline W. Andrews.]

R. D. W. C.

HARNEY, WILLIAM SELBY (Aug. 22, 1800–May 9, 1889), soldier, was born in Haysboro, near Nashville, Tenn., the eighth and last child of Thomas Harney, a merchant and land surveyor, and Margaret (Hudson) Harney. He attended the academy conducted by Thomas Craighead in Haysboro, then received private instruction in navigation, since his mother had intended that he should enter the navy. Instead, on Feb. 13, 1818, he entered the army as second lieutenant in the 1st Infantry. He quickly showed his fitness as a soldier in the numerous expeditions into Florida against the Indians and rose rapidly in rank, until on Aug. 15, 1836, he was made lieutenant-colonel of the 2nd Dragoons. He was given the honorary rank of brevet colonel Dec. 7, 1840, for gallant and meritorious conduct in the Florida Everglades against the Indians, and on June 30, 1846, he was promoted colonel of the 2nd Dragoons. This promotion, which came about the time of the Mexican War, made Harney the ranking cavalry officer under General Scott. Harney and Scott were not on good terms, and Scott, who had never been able to manage Harney, and who thoroughly distrusted his judgment and impetuosity, attempted to detach Harney from his command and turn the cavalry over to a subordinate, Major Sumner. Harney at first relinquished command, only to resume it immediately in defiance of Scott's orders. Scott had Harney arrested and court-martialed. The court found Harney guilty of disobedience of orders and required him to apologize to Scott, which he did gracefully, saying he would not permit personal considerations to stand between him and his duty to his country. But Harney was not as guileless as his impetuous and forthright character might seem to have indicated. He appealed to his superiors in Washington with the result that Secretary of War Marcy, with President Polk's approval, upheld his position against Scott and administered a mild reprimand to Scott for depriving Harney of his command in such an arbitrary fashion.

Scott had in the meantime dealt generously with Harney by accepting his apology and by restoring his command over the cavalry. In the engagements which followed Harney justified the act by displaying heroic and brilliant leadership. In the battle of Cerro Gordo his charge up the heights of El Telegrafo in the face of a murderous fire at the head of General Smith's brigade won the victory. For this brilliant performance he was brevetted brigadier-general (Apr. 8, 1847). After the war he was stationed in the Platte country where he defeated the restless Sioux Indians in the battle of Sand Hill, adding greatly to his reputation. He was presently rewarded with the command of the Department of Oregon and the rank of brigadier (1858). But his Anti-British and expansionist proclivities, especially his seizure of the island of San Juan, claimed by the British, soon caused his recall. After this, until May 1861, he was in command of the Department of the West, stationed at St. Louis. Because of his agreement with General Price not to molest the state troops so long as they made no hostile move against the federal government, he was suspected of Southern sympathy and deprived of the command. Perhaps he was never trusted during the war, for no active command was given him, and he was finally retired in 1863. When the war was practically over, the government, recalling his long and brilliant services, brevetted him major-general. After his retirement he lived at his estate at Pass Christian, Miss., and at St. Louis. He had married, in 1833, Mary Mullanphy of St. Louis. They had three children but subsequently separated. Late in life he was married to his nurse, Mrs. St. Cyr. He died at Orlando, Fla., the scene of his youthful triumphs over the Indians.

[L. U. Reavis, *The Life and Mil. Services of Gen. Wm. Selby Harney* (1878); *The Mexican War and its Heroes* (1850), vol. II; F. B. Heitman, *Hist. Reg. and Dict. of the U. S. Army* (1903), vol. I; Justin H. Smith, *The War with Mexico* (2 vols., 1919); *House Ex. Docs.* no. 1, 30 Cong., 1 Sess., pp. 2–3, no. 56, *Ibid.*, pp. 57–61, 64–65, 67, 75–79, no. 59, *Ibid.*, pp. 5, 17, no. 60, *Ibid.*, pp. 1220, 1231–32; *War of the Rebellion: Official Records (Army)*, see Index; *Army and Navy Jour.*, May 11, 1889; *St. Louis Globe Democrat*, May 10, 1889.] F. L. O.

HARPER, FLETCHER (Jan. 31, 1806–May 29, 1877), printer and publisher, born at Newtown, Long Island, was the youngest son of Joseph and Elizabeth (Kolyer) Harper and the brother of James [*q.v.*], John, and Joseph Wesley Harper. When he was about ten, the family moved to New York City where he attended a school on Roosevelt Street taught by Alexander T. Stewart [*q.v.*]. After an apprenticeship with his brothers he joined the firm in 1825, completing the quartet later to be known as the house of Harper & Brothers. The same year the young man of nineteen took as his bride the seventeen-year-old Jane Freelove Lyon, by whom he had two sons.

Fletcher Harper was, perhaps, the ablest of the four brothers. In him "was concentrated more of the vigor, dash, enterprise and speculative spirit of the house than in any of the others, or perhaps all combined" (*New York Tribune*, May 30, 1877). Unusual administrative abilities are accredited to him, an immense energy, quick and true judgment, and efficient mastery of men. When in 1839 books were to be selected for the school district libraries of New York State, Fletcher, glimpsing an opportunity for a good stroke of business, went in person to get the order and secured it. John C. Spencer [*q.v.*], who had the matter in charge, later said that Fletcher Harper was the finest young man he ever met. His brother James originated *Harper's New Monthly Magazine* (1850), but Fletcher managed it as he did also his own creations, *Harper's Weekly* (1857) and *Harper's Bazar* (1867). He inspected everything that went into those periodicals. In this material "there might be questions of taste, but there must be none of morals" (*Harper's Weekly*, June 16, 1877). Although shunning political office, he exerted through the *Weekly* a strong political influence. When Nast with his cartoons was castigating unmercifully the "Tweed ring" and the Harper school-book business was in peril (see cartoon in *Harper's Weekly*, May 13, 1871), it took a great deal of courage for Fletcher to permit Nast to continue with a free hand. Arrangements for serial stories were made by him in person and, as these at the time were mostly available in England, he made many trips abroad. He most creditably represented the house in its personal relations and gained a wide acquaintance with the principal literary men at home and in Europe. Side by side in death, as they were in life, he now lies with James, John, and Joseph Wesley, in the tomb erected by their descendants at Greenwood Cemetery, Brooklyn.

[*The House of Harper*; A. B. Paine, *Thomas Nast, His Period and His Pictures* (1904); Chas. Nordhoff, *Reminiscences of Some Editors I Have Known* (1906); Algernon Tassin, *The Magazine in America* (1916); *Publisher's Weekly*, June 2, 1877; *Harper's Weekly*, June 16 and 23, 1877; *N. Y. Herald, Tribune*, and other N. Y. papers for May 30, and June 1, 1877; information from descendants.] A. E. P.

HARPER, IDA HUSTED (Feb. 18, 1851–Mar. 14, 1931), journalist and author, prominent in the woman's suffrage movement, was of New England ancestry, born in Fairfield, Franklin County, Ind., the daughter of John Arthur and Cassandra (Stoddard) Husted. When she was about ten years old her parents moved to Muncie, Ind., where she graduated from the high school. She then entered Indiana University but spent only a year there, becoming at the age of eighteen principal of the high school in Peru, Ind. On Dec. 28, 1871, she was married to Thomas W. Harper, a young lawyer, and as long as they lived together their home was in Terre Haute. Harper died in 1908, having married again in 1890 (*Indianapolis News*, Mar. 5, 1908).

During her residence in Terre Haute, Mrs. Harper began her career as a journalist, contributing to the papers of that city and of Indianapolis. For twelve years she conducted a department known as "A Woman's Opinion" in the Terre Haute *Saturday Evening Mail*, and for a short time was managing editor of the Terre Haute *Daily News*. She also wrote political articles for the *Indianapolis News.* In 1883 she became a contributor to the *Fireman's Magazine,* later called the *Locomotive Fireman's Magazine,* under the editorship of Eugene V. Debs [*q.v.*], and in May 1884 was put in charge of its woman's department. She was enrolled as a student at Leland Stanford University in 1893, at which time her daughter was pursuing the course there. For a considerable period her home was in New York, where she was for some time a department editor of the *Sunday Sun* and of *Harper's Bazar,* as well as a contributor to New York, Boston, Philadelphia, Washington, and Chicago papers.

She was a sturdy champion of the woman's suffrage movement and closely associated with its leaders. In 1899 she went to London as a delegate to the International Council of Women, and thereafter attended practically all the European meetings of the Council and of the International Suffrage Alliance. Her ability as a writer and her journalistic experience enabled her to give much aid to the suffrage campaign through the press, and in the years immediately preceding the adoption of the Nineteenth Amendment to the Federal Constitution she had charge of publicity for the National American Woman Suffrage Association. She wrote *The Life and Work of Susan B. Anthony* at Miss Anthony's request, the first two volumes, published in 1899, being written in the reformer's home at Rochester, N. Y. The third volume appeared in 1908. She also assisted Miss Anthony in preparing the fourth volume (1902) of *The History of Woman Suffrage.* In 1922 she published two more volumes, bringing the history down to 1920. Her last days were spent in Washington, where she died from a cerebral hemorrhage at the Homeopathic Hospital. Her body was cremated and the ashes were sent to Muncie, Ind., for interment.

[T. A. Wylie, *Ind. Univ., Its Hist. from 1830* (1890); E. F. Young, *The Biog. Cyc. of Am. Women,* vol. II (1925); *N. Y. Times,* Mar. 17, 1931; *Who's Who in America,* 1930–31.] H. E. S.

HARPER, JAMES (Apr. 13, 1795–Mar. 27, 1869), printer and publisher, was one of a family of six children, two of whom died in infancy. Of the four surviving sons he was the eldest. His father was Joseph Harper, a son of James Harper born in Ipswich, Suffolk, who came to America before the Revolution and settled at Newtown, Long Island. His mother was Elizabeth Kolyer, the daughter of a Dutch burgher. By these strict, but wise and loving, parents James and his brothers were trained in habits of industry, in integrity, and in sobriety; and a remarkable and enduring family loyalty was established. It was in their simple, frugal, religious farm home in Newtown, L. I., rather than in the small country school where James spent a few months each year, that the foundations were laid for his life of honor, usefulness, and success. Methodist preachers, as they rode their circuits, often stayed at the Harper home; and these men made their influence felt upon the youths of the household. James was a great reader. His interest in Franklin's *Autobiography* led him to choose printing for his own initial venture, and at sixteen he was apprenticed to a Methodist friend of the family, Abraham Paul, of the printing firm of Paul & Thomas, New York City, where according to custom he lived with his employer. His vigorous physique, industrious habits, and good-humored personality soon won him a place in the regard of his associates, who at first were rather inclined to scoff at the country youth in his homespun garb.

In 1817, after a younger brother, John (Jan. 22, 1797–Apr. 22, 1875), had completed a printer's apprenticeship with Jonathan Seymour, the two young men set up a business for themselves in a "dingy little room" in Dover Street under the name of J. & J. Harper. Their first big printing job was an edition of 2,000 copies of *Seneca's Morals.* "It soon became an understood thing that the young Harpers could do work better and quicker than anybody else" (*New York Times,* Mar. 29, 1869). The year 1818 was a dull one in the printing business and the new firm decided to venture upon a bit of publishing, choosing Locke's *Essay on the Human Understanding* for their first production. This was the earliest of about two hundred books issued by the two brothers. Soon the firm was enlarged by the admission of the remaining brothers, Joseph Wesley (Dec. 25, 1801–Feb. 14, 1870), commonly known as Wesley, and Fletcher [*q.v.*]. Wesley "bought into" the firm in 1823 and two years later Fletcher joined the organization, but it was not until 1833 that the still existing name of Harper & Brothers was assumed. As time went on, the growth of the business was such that a contemporary newspaper estimated that for several years prior to 1853 the Harpers had printed an average of twenty-five volumes a minute, averaging ten hours a day. This development was due in part to the loyalty that existed among the brothers. "Either one is the Harper, the rest are the Brothers," James once remarked (*The House of Harper, post,* p. 22). Until about 1859 each drew at will upon the common funds of the firm for his personal expenses. Furthermore, the capabilities of each supplemented those of the others. John, from the days of his apprenticeship, was known as an especially skilful compositor; he became a keen proof reader, and for years no important work went to press until specimen pages had passed his critical scrutiny. He was also the business manager of the concern. Joseph Wesley was noted for his literary judgment; he often made the final decision when the value of a book for publication was being considered. Many of the prefaces of the firm's publications are attributed to him. Courteous and tactful, he shone especially as letter writer for the house. He was also the almoner for the family. "You will have to see Wesley," said James to a Methodist solicitor, "he attends to God's business" (*New York Tribune,* May 30, 1877).

James Harper, from the beginning of his business career, was known as an accomplished pressman. When the work of the brothers became more or less specialized he assumed charge of the mechanical equipment of the house, which was among the first to use steam-run presses and the first to introduce electrotyping on a large scale. His personal relations with the employees were most intimate and friendly. Every day "for an hour or two he was looking through the working part of the establishment, joking or laughing with the workmen or workwomen but seeing everything that was done or left undone" (*New York Times,* Mar. 29, 1869). With him originated the idea of *Harper's New Monthly Magazine,* the first of the four periodicals issued by the firm. He was elected mayor of New York City as a reform candidate in 1844, at a time when the city was known as the "most prosperous and worst governed city in the world." He at once initiated numerous business-like improvements in city government. He was later proposed for governor of the state but refused to run. Driving a good horse was his chief recreation, and an accident while driving caused his death. He was twice married: first, to Maria Arcularius, by whom he had one son; second, to Julia Thorne, by whom he had one son and two daughters.

[See J. H. Harper, *The House of Harper* (1912); J. C. Derby, *Fifty Years Among Authors, Books and Publishers* (1886); G. H. Putnam, *George Palmer Putnam: A Memoir* (1912); *Harper's Weekly,* Apr. 10 and 17, 1869; obituaries in New York newspapers, Mar. 29 to Apr. 1, 1869, particularly *N. Y. Times,* Mar. 29, 1869; information from descendants. For John Harper see also *Publishers' Weekly,* May 1, 1875, and *Harper's Weekly,* May 8, 1875; for Joseph Wesley Harper see *Trade Circular Annual,* 1871, and *Harper's Weekly,* Mar. 5, 1870.]

A. E. P.

HARPER, JOHN (1797–1875). [See HARPER, JAMES, 1795–1869.]

HARPER, JOHN LYELL (Sept. 21, 1873–Nov. 28, 1924), mechanical and electrical engineer, was born at Harpersfield, Delaware County, N. Y., a town founded by his forefathers before the Revolution. His emigrant ancestor was James Harper of County Derry, Ireland, who settled in Maine about 1720. The son of Joseph and Quintilla Keturah (Hendry) Harper, John Lyell Harper spent his boyhood on his father's farm, attending the district school and the Stamford Seminary (Delaware County), from which he was graduated at the age of twenty after having won the New York state scholarship to Cornell University. He completed four years at Cornell, graduating in 1897 with the degree of M.E. and mention on his diploma that he had made a special study of electrical engineering. His first position after graduation was at Seattle, Wash., with the Oregon Improvement Company. At the end of four months he became electrician for the Union Electric Company of the same city. In June 1898 he was made operating and constructing engineer of the Twin City Rapid Transit Company (Minneapolis) in which position he was in charge of all their testing of 1200-volt and other underground systems, the designing and erecting of switchboards, and general operation. In the fall of the following year he was in charge, for Floy & Carpenter, a New York firm of consulting engineers, of the construction of the St. Croix Power Company's Apple River hydroelectric plant. The experience which he thus gained in hydroelectric work obtained for him in 1902 a position as assistant to Wallace C. Johnson, chief engineer of the Niagara Falls Hydraulic Power & Manufacturing Company. From this time until his death, Harper was actively interested in Niagara power. After two years as assistant he became chief engineer having responsible charge of all of the constructing and operating work of the company. In 1918, when the various power interests on the American side of Niagara Falls formed the Niagara Falls Power Company, a corporation under government direction, Harper was appointed its chief engineer. His most important achievement was the design and construction of the wartime hydroelectric power plant of the company in the gorge below the Falls. Under his leadership the plant had grown from one of 14,000 horsepower to one containing nearly 500,000 horsepower under one roof, the largest installed capacity in any power plant in the world at that time, a remarkable engineering feat from the standpoint of both power and size. After this accomplishment he became vice-president of the Company. He served also in the capacity of chief engineer of the Canadian Niagara Power Company, of the Niagara Junction Railway Company, and of the Cliff Electric Distributing Company, and was chief engineer and vice-president of the Harper-Taylor Company, consulting engineers. In addition to these interests, he developed and patented several electric furnaces, one of which is known as the Harper Electric Furnace for commercial firing of porcelain and other ceramic materials. His study of the Niagara River led him to publish a pamphlet, *The Suicide of the Horseshoe Fall* (1916), in which he set forth a plan for preserving the beauty of the famous Horseshoe Falls by the construction of remedial works to distribute the flow of water and thus prevent uneven erosion. He was considered one of the greatest hydroelectric engineers of his time. He was a member of several of the leading national and local engineering societies, and in recognition of his work of high standards was made a Fellow of the American Institute of Electrical Engineers. He married Linda E. Wheeler of Ithaca, N. Y., on Sept. 12, 1898. He died at Niagara Falls.

[*Who's Who in America*, 1924–25; *International Who's Who*, 1912; *Jour. Am. Inst. Electrical Engineers*, Jan. 1925; *Trans. Am. Soc. Mech. Engineers*, vol. XLVI (1925); E. D. Adams, *Niagara Power: Hist. of the Niagara Falls Power Co.* (2 vols., 1927); *Cornell Alumni News*, Dec. 11, 1924; *Buffalo Morning Express*, Nov. 29, 1924; for genealogy, H. R. Stiles, *Hist. and Geneals. of Ancient Windsor*, II (1892), 365–66, and Jay Gould, *Hist. of Delaware County* (1856).] F. A. T.

HARPER, JOSEPH WESLEY (1801–1870). [See HARPER, JAMES, 1795–1869.]

HARPER, ROBERT FRANCIS (Oct. 18, 1864–Aug. 5, 1914), Assyriologist, was the son of Samuel and Ellen Elizabeth (Rainey) Harper, and was born at New Concord, Ohio. He attended Muskingum College, 1879–80, and was graduated from the old University of Chicago in 1883. After studying three years in Germany under Professors Schrader and Friedrich Delitzsch, he received the degree of Ph.D. from the University of Leipzig in 1886. He became in the autumn of that year an instructor in Assyriology at Yale, a position which he filled until 1891, with the exception of the year 1888–89, when he went to Nippur as one of the Assyriologists of the first Babylonian expedition of the University of Pennsylvania. The year 1891–92 he spent at the British Museum inaugurating the researches which continued through later years formed the chief scientific work of his life, and the publication of which constitutes his chief literary monument—the editing of the *Assyrian and Babylonian Letters Belonging to the Kouyunjik Collections of the British Museum* (14 vols., 1892–1914). In 1892 he became associate professor of Semitic languages in the new University of Chicago, of which his brother, William Rainey Harper [*q.v.*], had become president. In 1900 he was advanced to a full professorship, a position which he held until his death. For the rest of his life he devoted himself mainly to the teaching of Assyriology, when in Chicago, and to the copying and editing of the Babylonian and Assyrian letters in London during his vacations. This program was interrupted in 1908–09, when he spent a year in Jerusalem as director of the American School of Oriental Research—a position which he filled with distinguished success. In addition to his major activities, he was curator, from 1900, of the Babylonian section of the Haskell Oriental Museum and director, from 1902 to 1906, of the Babylonian Expedition of the Oriental Exploration Fund of the University of Chicago, which under Dr. Edgar J. Banks as field director excavated Bismya. He was managing editor for some time of the *American Journal of Semitic Languages and Literatures*, and in February 1906 succeeded his brother in the editorship. He was also an associate editor of the *Biblical World* and the *American Journal of Theology*. In addition to the publication of the *Assyrian and Babylonian Letters*, he edited in 1901, *Assyrian and Babylonian Literature*, to which different scholars made contributions; published in 1904 *The Code of Hammurabi*, a volume containing the original text with transliteration, translation, sign list, and vocabulary—a volume that is still one of the best instruments for the study of that great body of legislation; and in 1908, as joint editor with Francis Brown and George F. Moore, published two volumes of *Old Testament and Semitic Studies in Memory of William Rainey Harper*, a worthy monument to the memory of his distinguished brother.

Robert Harper never married. Far from being simply a dry scholar, he was one of the most genial and social of men. He had a genius for friendship and companionship. This manifested itself at Chicago in the organization of the Quadrangle Club, where members of the faculty could enjoy social fellowship. He will be remembered by those who knew him, whether in America, London, or Germany as the possessor of a happy combination of the qualities of a devoted and accurate scholar and a genial and companionable man. He died in London.

[*Who's Who in America*, 1914–15; T. W. Goodspeed, *William Rainey Harper* (1928); J. D. Prince,

"Robert Francis Harper, 1864–1914," *Am. Jour. of Semitic Languages and Literatures,* Jan. 1915; F. F. Abbott, in the *Nation* (N. Y.), Oct. 1, 1914; *Univ. of Chicago Mag.,* July 1914; *Times* (London), Aug. 10, 1914; *Chicago Tribune,* Aug. 7, 1914.] G. A. B.

HARPER, ROBERT GOODLOE (January 1765–Jan. 14, 1825), politician, was born on a farm near Fredericksburg, Va. His father, Jesse Harper, was a member of a family which had lived in Spotsylvania County for many years; his mother was Diana Goodloe. When he was four years old the family moved to Granville County, N. C. There the boy was taught for a time and then sent away to school. When Cornwallis invaded the state after the battle of Camden, Harper joined a cavalry troop which served under General Greene until Cornwallis left the state. He then returned to his studies for a time, but he was eager for a military life and his father promised to educate him with that in view. He spent the year 1783 on a surveying tour of Kentucky and Tennessee, where he acquired a taste for land speculation in which he often thereafter dabbled. Upon his return he was dissatisfied and for a short time was idle, spending his time in gambling and dissipation. His father, hoping to save him, induced him to go to Princeton in 1784. He earned part of his expenses by teaching in the preparatory school and early in 1785 Richard Dobbs Spaight of North Carolina, then in New York, made him a loan which enabled him to go on to his graduation in September 1785. Soon afterward he went to Charleston, S. C., reaching there penniless and alone. By the help of a former pupil he secured a place as a teacher and an opportunity to study law, and through Benjamin Hawkins, of North Carolina, he was introduced to many men of prominence in Charleston whose acquaintance aided him. In 1786 he was admitted to the bar and began to practise at Ninety-Six. He indulged at the same time his interest in politics by writing for the press and upon his return to Charleston in 1789 he was elected to the lower house of the legislature. In 1791 he was made manager of a company interested in the Georgia western lands and went to Philadelphia to sell stock. The company failed, but Harper's stay in Philadelphia turned his mind toward a national career. He returned to South Carolina in 1794, bought a plantation in Ninety-Six District, and offering himself as a Republican candidate for the Fourth Congress in that district, was elected. He was still a member of the legislature when the death of Alexander Gillon made a vacancy in the Third Congress. Harper became a successful candidate for election and took his seat Feb. 9, 1795, serving until Mar. 4, 1801. During this period he frequently wrote long letters to his constituents in which he explained his course in Congress and urged upon them an approval of his policies. These letters were published and brought him something which he never overlooked—considerable public notice.

Up to the time of his election Harper had been an enthusiastic Republican. Madison, writing to Jefferson of his pleasure at his election, described him as "sound, able, and eloquent" (*Letters and Other Writings of James Madison,* 1865, II, 20). He had been radical in his pro-French sympathies, was vice-president of the Jacobin Club of Charleston, and in 1793 had almost haunted the French consulate and "dined there every day." But in Philadelphia the great and powerful were on the other side and almost immediately he began to shift his position, supporting the Jay Treaty in 1795, favoring Adams or Pinckney in 1796 instead of Jefferson for president, and displaying anti-French and pro-British feelings. He became at the same time a social lion, was a dandy in dress, acquired pomposity of appearance and manners, and, self-confident to the point of bumptiousness, he was presently the most insolent man in the House. Recognized finally as a leader of the Federalists, he was chairman of the committee of ways and means and was the most frequent and voluble debater in his party.

In 1797 Harper published his *Observations on the Dispute Between the United States and France* which attracted great attention at home and in Europe and ran through many editions. Praise of it so went to Harper's head that Fisher Ames remarked that it had "half spoiled him" (Seth Ames, *The Works of Fisher Ames,* 1854, I, 236). In 1798 he was an enthusiastic advocate of the alien and sedition laws and urged the limitation of citizenship to the native born. He was eager, too, for war with France. He saw in it boundless party advantage and implored Hamilton in April 1798 to become secretary of war (J. C. Hamilton, *The Works of Alexander Hamilton,* VI, 1851, 282). He personally had visions of military glory and although Hamilton recommended him for appointment as aide to Washington, as "a man of very considerable talents" (*Ibid.,* p. 334), Washington replied that he preferred men of experience. In 1799 Harper urged that the Sedition Act be retained in force, though he was most anxious that the debate on the question should not be allowed to reach the people. In 1800 he opposed reduction of the army and a little later he opposed reducing the navy. In the campaign he was bitter in his opposition to Jefferson and the Republicans, and when the election was thrown into the House, he voted for Burr until the final ballot when with the other South Carolina Federalists he refrained from voting. Throughout the final session he remained a stanch defender of Federalist legislation.

By 1801 the handwriting was on the wall for the Federalist party in South Carolina, and Harper himself was particularly unpopular, but he had already determined not to seek reëlection. He had become engaged to Catherine Carroll, the daughter of Charles Carroll of Carrollton, who violently opposed the match, and in May 1801 he married her and moved to Baltimore. Ultimately they established a handsome estate, "Oakland," four miles out in the country. In his profession Harper soon built up a productive practice and a considerable reputation. Justice Story, describing him as "diffuse but methodical and clear," added that he was "to be considered in some degree artificial" (W. W. Story, *Life and Letters of Joseph Story,* 1851, I, 162), but in view of the cases in which he was retained, he must have had genuine ability. He was one of the managers of the William Blount impeachment in 1798; he represented Judge John Pickering and Justice Chase in their impeachment trials; he was associated with John Quincy Adams in the case of *Fletcher* vs. *Peck,* and he appeared as counsel in many important cases in the appellate courts of Maryland and Pennsylvania. He was also prominent in Baltimore in civic and business affairs as well as in his profession and was active in the organization of a company which established the first water system, and in the organization of the Baltimore Exchange. Socially he was friendly, genial, and entertaining.

When the British attacked Baltimore in 1814, Harper took part in the battle of North Point and later in the year was appointed major-general of the Maryland troops. On Jan. 16, 1816, he was elected to the United States Senate. He was as of old a frequent and extended speaker, but he resigned in December on the ground that his business engagements would not allow him to serve. He was the Federalist candidate for vice-president in 1816, and in that year and in 1820 the Delaware electors voted for him. In his later years his greatest interest was the negro problem. In 1800 he had opposed the emancipation of slaves, though he favored the abolition of the slave trade. By 1817 he had become actively interested in the matter of colonizing the negroes outside the United States, hoping that it might lead to the establishment of a system of free white labor in the South. He was one of the original members of the American Colonization Society and defended it against pro-slavery and abolitionist critics. He was influential in the selection of Africa as the place for the colony and it was he who suggested Liberia and Monrovia as suitable names for the colony and its capital (*A Letter from Gen. Harper . . . to Elias B. Caldwell,* 1818). Early in 1825 Harper decided to give up his practice and all business connections, and to return to public life, but a few days after he had announced that he would be a candidate for Congress in the autumn of 1826, he died.

[C. W. Sommerville, *Robt. Goodloe Harper* (1899); *Select Works of Robt. Goodloe Harper* (1814); *Papers of James A. Bayard* (1915), ed. by Elizabeth Donnan and published as vol. II of the annual reports of the Am. Hist. Asso. for the year 1913; U. B. Phillips, "The S. C. Federalists, II," *Am. Hist. Rev.,* July 1909; *American and Daily Advertiser* (Baltimore), Jan. 15, 1825.]

J. G. deR. H.

HARPER, WILLIAM (Jan. 17, 1790–Oct. 10, 1847), nullification leader and judge, was born on the island of Antigua. His father, John Harper, a Scotch-Irish minister, was a Wesleyan missionary, but in 1795 he entered the South Carolina Conference and in 1799 he was a "stationed preacher" in Charleston. William was educated at the Mount Bethel Academy, in the Newberry District, and at the Jefferson Monticello Seminary. He entered South Carolina College in 1805, the first student to matriculate. A year later he left, but after earning enough money to provide for his brother's education, he returned and was graduated in 1808. In college he seemed a careless student, living apart in a world of his own, but he took a high stand in all his work. Leaving college, he began the study of medicine, but after a year he turned to law and was admitted to the bar, probably in 1813. When he heard of the capture of Washington by the British he entered the army as a private and served until his discharge in 1815 as a sergeant. On July 4, 1816, he married Catherine, the daughter of David Coalter of Columbia. He practised law in Columbia until 1818 as a partner of William C. Preston, who later married his wife's sister. In that year he was induced by Edward Bates, later attorney-general under Lincoln, Hamilton R. Gamble, war governor of Missouri, and David Harper Means, all three of whom also married sisters of Mrs. Harper, to move to Missouri. In 1819 he was appointed chancellor of the Missouri territory and was elected to that office after statehood was secured.

In 1823 Harper returned to South Carolina and was at once made reporter of the supreme court, holding the place for two years. Then following a short term as United States senator

(Mar. 28–Dec. 7, 1826), he moved to Charleston to practise law, but in 1828 he became a member and the speaker of the lower house of the legislature. In the same year he was elected chancellor of the state and held the position until 1830, when he was elected a judge of the court of appeals. Resigning in 1835, he again became chancellor and remained in that office until his death. In 1833, after the loss of two of his children from yellow fever, he moved to Fairfield where with little success he undertook to manage a plantation.

In 1826 Harper was a nationalist, but in 1828 he was the leader of the radical anti-tariff group in the legislature. Like most of his contemporaries in South Carolina, he had become convinced that protection was unconstitutional and too great a burden to be borne. By 1830 he was a convert to nullification. At the state-rights meeting at Columbia, in September 1830, he delivered a speech which was later published and circulated as *The Remedy by State Interposition* (1832). Criticized for political activity while on the bench, he defended and continued it, attending the anti-tariff convention at Philadelphia in 1831, and bearing its memorial, with one of his own, to Congress. He was a delegate to the convention of 1832 and wrote the nullification ordinance. At the adjourned session in 1833, he warned the convention that the compromise was only the beginning of the contest and expressed the belief that war would soon come. When the case involving the test oath (*State ex Relatione Ed. McCready* vs. *B. F. Hunt*) came before the court of appeals, it was held unconstitutional. Harper dissented, delivering an opinion which has been generally regarded as one of the most powerful statements of the state-rights case (II Hill's *Reports,* 1, 209–82). His political activity ended with nullification. In 1837 he wrote a *Memoir on Slavery,* an elaborate defense of the institution, which is regarded as one of the most important pro-slavery arguments in the history of the controversy. In it he took the position that slavery could not be proved a moral, political, or a social evil, or to be incompatible with a well-regulated and happy civil polity. In 1841 he published a memoir of Chancellor Henry W. De Saussure. Though Harper was given to excessive drinking in his younger days, he was a man of utter frankness and simplicity of character, a gentle spirit whose temper has been described as "soft and poetic." His mind was one of breadth and force and he had a genuine appreciation of learning.

[W. H. Brawley, article in *Great Am. Lawyers,* vol. III (1907), ed. by W. D. Lewis; J. B. O'Neall, *Biog. Sketches of the Bench and Bar of S. C.* (1859), vol. I; B. F. Perry, *Reminiscences of Public Men* (1883), pp. 85–89; *Jour. of the Convention of the People of S. C.* (1833); *South Carolinian* (Columbia), Oct. 19, 29, 1847; *Charleston Courier,* Oct. 15, 1847.]

J. G. deR. H.

HARPER, WILLIAM RAINEY (July 24, 1856–Jan. 10, 1906), Hebraist, educator, brother of Robert Francis Harper [*q.v.*], was born in New Concord, Muskingum County, Ohio. His ancestors on both sides were Scotch-Irish. His great-grandfather, Robert Harper, emigrated with wife and son from Ireland to western Pennsylvania in 1795. His father, Samuel Harper, was a drygoods merchant, Presbyterian churchman, and supporter of Muskingum College in New Concord. His mother was Ellen Elizabeth Rainey. In boyhood William was docile, intellectually precocious, and in spite of his energy, his ambition, and his gifts of leadership, extremely susceptible to the influence of strong personalities among his teachers and friends. He entered the preparatory school of Muskingum College at the age of eight and the College at ten. He received the degree of Bachelor of Arts at fourteen with a graduating class of seven and delivered the salutatory oration in Hebrew. For some two or three years after graduation he worked in his father's store, studied languages, especially Hebrew, by himself, played the piano with President Paul's daughter Ella, whom he afterward married, and was prominent in the conduct of a village band, in which he played the cornet. Though he took little interest in sports, he was then as in later life generally liked.

In the year 1872–73 he taught a class of three students in Hebrew in Muskingum College with the success and largely by the methods that later made him famous. In September 1873 he entered Yale College as a graduate student, and received the degree of Ph.D. at the age of eighteen, with a dissertation on "A Comparative Study of the Prepositions in Latin, Greek, Sanskrit, and Gothic." In the summer of 1875 he accepted the principalship of Masonic College at Macon, Tenn. He was married to Ella Paul, Nov. 18, and lived at Macon one year. Thence he was called to Denison University, Granville, Ohio, where he began work in September 1876 under the presidency of E. Benjamin Andrews [*q.v.*]. Friends made at Denison remained with him all his life, and some, including Ernest Burton, Clarence Castle, and Charles Chandler, later joined him at Chicago. He made his mark as an inspiring teacher, formally professed Christianity, and continued his private studies in the Semitic languages. He displayed little interest in writing, speaking, theological controversy, general literature, or philosophy.

The opportunity to teach Semitic languages came with a call to the Baptist Union Theological Seminary at Morgan Park (Chicago), where he began his work Jan. 1, 1879. Morgan Park added to the store of his permanent friendships, a number of those associated with him there later becoming his colleagues at the University of Chicago. After a year, partly spent in earning the degree of B.D., his abounding energy and initiative found vent in the development of correspondence courses in Hebrew, in a series of textbooks and vocabularies for the study of Hebrew, in the publication of two journals—the *Hebrew Student,* which in 1883 was renamed the *Old and New Testament Student* and later became the *Biblical World,* and the more technical *Hebraica,* afterwards continued as the *American Journal of Semitic Languages and Literatures*—and in the organization of a summer course in Semitic languages and Biblical studies, which between 1881 and 1890 became the parent of thirty such courses throughout the country. In 1886 he accepted a call to Yale, despite the endeavors of the Morgan Park trustees to retain him by the offer of the presidency of a proposed revival of the old University of Chicago. From 1885 on he took a prominent part in the work at Chautauqua, where he gave one of his summer courses and where after two years he was made president of the college of liberal arts, a position which he held for several years. This work supplemented the intensive teaching and study of his specialty by bringing him into touch with prominent men throughout the country, who accepted his invitations to lecture or teach at Chautauqua. During his five years at Yale, he multiplied his activities and won a national reputation as teacher, lecturer, organizer and editor. Here, as earlier at Morgan Park, he took no vacations and little sleep, passing smoothly from one occupation to another, teaching, editing, dictating his correspondence, directing secretaries and assistants, sitting on committees, presiding over societies and institutes, lecturing in many cities and at other colleges. His mail is said to have been larger sometimes than the entire mail of Yale University.

He received several calls to college presidencies and it was inevitable that when, with encouragement from John D. Rockefeller, the project of establishing a new University of Chicago was revived, he should be thought of by all interested as its predestined leader. Before accepting the call, however, Harper made plain to the trustees the nature of his conception of the new university, his own position in the conflict between the old orthodoxy of the letter and the modernism of Biblical criticism, and stipulated that there should be entire freedom of teaching and investigation both for himself and for the university. He also indicated what he afterwards urged more explicitly, that the new institution should not be, as was at first proposed, another ordinary American college, but a great university, a leader in education and research. At their fourth meeting, December 1890, the trustees adopted bulletins in which he outlined his plans. They included features more novel then than they seem today—university extension, a university press, university affiliations, the division of the year into four quarters, the summer school as an integral part of the academic year under the name of the summer quarter, the formal distinction of the two upper years of the undergraduate course as the senior college, faculty control of athletics, the concentration of the student's attention on a few studies at a time, the emphasis on graduate study and research.

The degree of Harper's originality and the possible sources of his ideas matter little in comparison with his power to promulgate and apply them. He did not, for example, invent the inductive method for studying language, and probably never considered critically its limitations, but he made it work in the teaching of elementary Hebrew. He did not invent university extension, but he called to Chicago its chief exponent, Professor Richard Moulton [*q.v.*], and made it a constituent part of the university. In his Decennial Report he enumerated ten experiments which were being tested in the experience of the University. These and his other ideas on education he expounded in numerous addresses which he delivered in response to invitations from many universities and civic and educational organizations. The most significant of these addresses were published in a volume entitled *The Trend in Higher Education* (1905). He wrote as he spoke, in an orderly, plain, forceful style, devoid of rhetoric, of wit, of the play of fancy and imagination, and of the charm of allusiveness, but the direct sincerity and lucid explicitness of these printed speeches still hold the attention of readers who are interested in such topics as "The University and Democracy," "Waste in Higher Education," "Are Schoolteachers Underpaid?," "Shall the Theological Curriculum be Modified and How?," "The Situation of the Small College," "Alleged Luxury Among College Students." The book that tells us most of Harper's inner self is the little volume of talks to students entitled *Religion and the*

Higher Life (1904). Nothing could be simpler or more sincere than these brief discourses. They contain no trace of cant and hardly any theology, only an earnest appeal to the hearers to give essential Christianity a trial in their lives and in the life of the University. Noteworthy is the statement in the modest preface, "With each recurring year it has required greater effort on my part to undertake this kind of service." Still more surprising and generally overlooked is the frank admission, "For several years I studied the Bible . . . for the purpose of discovering that which would enable me to convince others that it was only an ordinary book, and very ordinary at that." One would like to know more of this Voltairian or Ingersollian period in Harper's life. His two works on *The Priestly Element in the Old Testament* (1902) and *The Prophetic Element in the Old Testament* (1905), illustrate both the enormous industry of Harper and his secretary assistant, and the curious Benthamite minuteness of subdivision and classification which he carried into every field of activity.

Of his Semitic scholarship it can be said that he was recognized by his colleagues as a sound if not greatly creative scholar, and a very great teacher whose services in the revival of Hebrew scholarship rank him, in the words of Emil G. Hirsch, with Jerome, Reuchlin, the Buxdorfs, Gesenius, and Ewald (*Biblical World,* March 1906). His *Critical and Exegetical Commentary on Amos and Hosea* (1905), when it finally appeared shortly before his death, relieved the anxiety of those friends who feared that he had given too much of his strength to other occupations to complete it satisfactorily. It was favorably reviewed by experts. The *Old Testament and Semitic Studies in Memory of William Rainey Harper,* published on the second anniversary of his death, was such a tribute as few scholars of any age have received.

From 1892 to the year of his death Harper's life was inseparable from that of the University of Chicago. The attempt to create at once that product of secular growth, a great university, was the theme of many witticisms and well-invented anecdotes at the expense of the founders of Leland Stanford and Chicago universities. Harper, however, was not a man to be awed by epigrams. "It seems a great pity to wait for growth when we might be born full-fledged," he characteristically wrote to Mr. Rockefeller in 1890 (Goodspeed, *Harper,* p. 91). Within two or three years he assembled a brilliant faculty, attracted partly by higher salaries, partly by his personality and large designs; bought in Berlin a second-hand collection of more than 200,000 volumes and pamphlets, which, whatever its deficiencies and doublets, actually enabled many departments to start with a working library; established cooperation with his trustees and faculty; and had an entirely adequate, if not yet a great, university functioning and conferring earned degrees from A.B. to Ph.D. The demands upon his vitality were terrific, for though he never stinted his service to the university, he could not bring himself to renounce his other activities. He did what few if any university presidents have ever done, taught full time as chairman of his department. He retained for a period his presidency of Chautauqua and the editorship of various journals established before or after the foundation of the university. In 1893 he was chairman of the advisory committee of the World's Congress Auxiliary Department of Higher Education. From 1897 to 1905 he was superintendent of the Hyde Park Baptist Church Sunday school. From 1896 to 1898 he was an active member of the board of education of the city of Chicago. He attended educational conferences and gave lectures throughout the country. He planned, supervised, and lent his name to many textbooks. With all these other interests on his mind he not only administered the university, foresaw its successive developments, and kept in close touch with the faculty to whom he was always accessible, but he labored under the constant strain of the sense that everything thus far accomplished was precarious and could be secured only by pressing forward. Everything depended, he felt, on his own unrelaxing vigilance, and on his continuing power to interest, persuade, lead, guide, and, it might be, cajole. He did not complain, but there is a hint of the weight he was carrying in one of his addresses to students in *Religion and the Higher Life:* "To the unthinking mind the man who occupies a high position . . . is an object of . . . envy. If the real facts were known, in almost every case it would be found that such a man is being crushed—literally crushed—by the weight of the burdens which he is compelled to carry" (p. 46). He had to mediate and compromise between a divinity school and a faculty to whose members he had promised entire academic freedom, and the spokesman of an alarmed sectarian orthodoxy; between the requirements of an ideal for the university that constantly outran its budget, and the practical business sense of trustees and founders for whom living within an income was the first test of sound administration; between a public for whom a college was a school, and a band of scholars whose hearts were set upon research; between the promoters of immediate expansion into professional schools of every kind, with whom his own impatience sympathized, and the cautious advocates of consolidation within departments already established.

The story of his life for the next ten years is the history of his dealings with these problems, of "campaigns" for endowment, of the continuous growth of the university and the swift uprising of buildings, each falling into its appointed place in an architectural scheme which remains a symbol of Harper's forecasting and systematizing mind, though it owes its beauty doubtless to the architects and to the taste, the knowledge, and the devoted industry of Martin A. Ryerson, for thirty years president of the Board of Trustees. Among the marking events of this decade were the establishment of the Ogden Graduate School of Science; the transfer to Chicago of almost the entire faculty of science of Clark University, including such men as Michelson, Donaldson, and Loeb; the construction of the Hull Biological Quadrangle and the Haskell Museum; the securing of the Yerkes telescope, for which an observatory was constructed at Williams Bay, Lake Geneva; the Quinquennial Celebration, marked by a visit of the founder; the peace celebration and the conferring on President McKinley of the first honorary degree bestowed by the University, in 1898; the establishment of the College of Commerce and Politics in 1897, of the School of Education in 1901, and of the Law School in 1902; the Decennial Celebration (1901), which Harper felt to be in some respects the crowning of the edifice.

This Decennial Celebration was made notable by the laying of the corner-stones of five new buildings. In the lack of a suitable auditorium a huge tent was erected and there were bands and banquets, receptions, academic processions, and corner-stone addresses. To a superficial observer it might have seemed a great show, staged by a consummate manager and advertiser; but its deeper significance and the evidence of the true nature of Harper's ideals and the ripeness of the university to realize them, were to be found in the twenty-eight volumes of Decennial Publications. With pardonable exaggeration the president declared that "no series of scientific publications so comprehensive in its scope and of so great a magnitude has ever been issued at any one time by any learned society or institution" (*The University Record,* March 1904, p. 360). The Decennial Celebration marked an epoch in the life of the university and its president. The university was established and had taken its place among its peers. Harper was still under fifty, and might reasonably look forward to twenty years in which to guide and watch its growth and enjoy that "development of the æsthetic side of life and thought" which in his Decennial Report he predicted for the second decade.

Though not free from sickness in childhood, Harper had developed into a sturdy boy and a man whose iron constitution seemed to defy the ordinary laws of prudential hygiene. No constitution, however, could endure a regimen of incessant work, not unaccompanied by anxiety, no vacations, shortened hours of sleep, frequent irregular railway journeys, lunches of sandwiches consumed at the working desk, and a perpetual round of dinners and speeches. He had a slight warning that he was overdoing as far back as the summer of 1889, when he sought rest by a voyage to Europe to attend the Oriental Congress at Stockholm. In 1897 he had two illnesses and visited Europe again. On the advice of his physicians he gave up some of his multifarious activities. He had resigned his position on the Board of Education of the city of Chicago, partly for other reasons, in the year 1898. He had given up the principalship of Chautauqua in the year 1894. In 1902 he declined an invitation to preside over the organization of the Congress of Arts and Sciences at the Louisiana Purchase Exposition, St. Louis, though his part in it still remained so large that some Eastern wit styled it "Harper's Bazaar." On Feb. 29, 1904, he underwent an operation for appendicitis, from which he recovered sufficiently to return to work in a few weeks, in spite of the protests of physicians and friends. He attended banquets in honor of a group of German savants whom he had invited to visit the University in recognition of the debt of American to German scholarship, and presided at the March convocation when honorary degrees were conferred upon them. He delivered numerous Commencement addresses in June, spent the summer at Williams Bay, Lake Geneva, working with secretaries on his books, and returned to the president's office and the classroom in the fall; but his old vigor did not return. The operation had revealed to his physicians what they judged to be a cancerous infection, and when their diagnosis had been confirmed by further observation, they told him the truth, in January 1905. He called two of his closest friends to his home and informed them, as he once phrased it, that he had been notified of his impending execution. An attempted operation in February proved impossible to carry out, and nothing remained but the alternating hope and despair of X-ray treatment. Whatever his mental struggles, he calmly resumed his work and turned a cheerful face to the world. He taught large classes through the summer of 1905, and made his last public appearance, though very weak, at the September convocation. Tributes of love and admiration and letters of sympathy poured in upon him from every quarter. The end came Jan. 10, 1906. He was survived by his wife, a daughter, and three sons.

Like many of the world's most effective men, Harper found no time to achieve the type of culture that is defined as knowing the best that has been thought and said. He had a strong memory and astonishing ability to acquire the forms and vocabulary of a new language, and in youth he concentrated fiercely on his own special studies. In later life his many occupations left him little leisure for desultory reading. He acquired ideas largely by personal contacts and experience, and so preserved to the end a certain openness of mind toward new, or what were to him new, ideas. His belief in the value of concentrated study, for example, was largely derived from his experience as a teacher of language, but his formulation of it in the earlier programs for the University of Chicago was probably determined by the opinions of Professor George Herbert Palmer. He returned from his trip to Russia in the summer of 1900 with an entirely new conception of the necessity and value of a speaking knowledge of modern languages, and with a divination of the significance of Russia. In his Biblical studies he acknowledged his indebtedness to Moulton's literary study of the Bible. These illustrations could be indefinitely enlarged by one capable of tracing the converging influences of friends, conversations, and an ever-growing experience on Harper's mind.

He rarely answered personal criticism, whether of his orthodoxy, his methods, or his policies. The jests on his success in raising money he used to meet by the statement that he never asked for money but only presented opportunities. Favorite aphorisms of his in this connection were that a definite plan is more attractive than a vague suggestion, that it is as easy to do big things as little, and that men give money more readily for a beautiful and adequate building than for a cheap and meanly utilitarian structure. To the criticism that his own mind was materialized and that his quarterly statements materialized the atmosphere of the University it may be said that his sacrifice of the scholarly leisure for which one side of his diverse nature sincerely yearned, secured for his fastidious critics the still air of delightful studies which he envied but did not grudge them. He indeed bore no grudges. When a brilliant member of his faculty lost his head and his sense of proportion in assailing a presidential policy in faculty meeting, the president's only comment was, "Does Mr. —— take his facts from the newspapers?" Within a year he promoted that instructor and always worked in friendly cooperation with him. He liked to enlist other men in service and cooperation with him in the writing of textbooks which he planned; but those who stood aloof were left absolutely free from all pressure direct or indirect. He was wont to say in explanation of his policy that every member of the staff was expected to do something more than the routine teaching of his classes, but the choice of that something was left to the individual. He might devote himself to research, to the popularization (it was not then called humanization) of knowledge, or to administrative and committee work. It was enough for him to do something and be somebody. More than one type of man was needed to make a university.

Though he neither heeded nor seemed to remember personal attacks, he was extremely sensitive to any criticism that might impair the efficiency of the University. The charge that thought and speech were not entirely free there stung him to the quick, and he never lost an opportunity to repel it, whether it appeared in the crude expression of realistic American novelists, or in the innuendo of those dainty spokesmen of European culture who sneered at universities "growing ignobly rich on their hush money." In his Decennial Report he dealt with such calumnies in words which should be given a prominent place in every account of his life: "In the University of Chicago neither the Trustees nor the President . . . has at any time called an instructor to account for any public utterances. . . . In no single case has a donor to the University called the attention of the Trustees to the teaching of any officer of the University as being distasteful or objectionable. Still further it is my opinion that no donor of money to a university . . . has any right, before God or man, to interfere with the teaching. . . . Neither an individual, nor the state, nor the church has the right to interfere with the search for truth, or with its promulgation when found" (pp. xxi–xxii).

Like all strong executives, he wished to have his own way, mainly because it seemed to him the way of progress and efficiency. He was always willing, however, to listen to the other side, was ready to accept other methods of reaching his results, and was very flexible in adapting himself to modifications of his plans. He could the more readily be so because many of the plans, as he openly avowed, were put forward in conformity to his belief that a tentative and modifiable concreteness is more persuasive than abstract propositions so cautiously generalized as to commit nobody to anything. He won his way by the contagion of his energy and enthusiasm and his confidence in himself and his coworkers rather than by arbitrary self-assertion. It was not strange that a man who could set the whole country to studying Hebrew could secure a majority following in a board of trustees and a faculty. His was a dominating but not a domineering personality. He was urgent, but not in the last resort insistent. He could not bear to drive anybody to the wall and always contrived to save his opponent's face by the appearance, at least, of a compromise. The policy which he first proposed for the University of Chicago, of intense and concentrated study, with two recitations a day in the same subject, was well adapted to the earlier stages of learning a language, and was perhaps suggested to him by his success in teaching Hebrew by that method. With characteristic flexibility and good humor, however, he practically abandoned the plan when he found that his new faculty would not teach the same class and subject two hours a day and that subjects other than the elements of language required gradual growth and intervals of meditative assimilation. With similar adaptability he virtually gave up his plan for the partial segregation of men and women students in the Junior College when it was misinterpreted as a design to abolish coeducation altogether. He allowed himself to be convinced of the unwisdom of granting a distinct degree at the close of the Junior College, and he accepted a modification of four continuous quarters with only one intervening week in each case, by saving enough time out of the spring and summer quarters to leave the month of September free for reparations, whether of faculty or buildings. Though himself a devout and professing Christian, he remained, in the face of misunderstanding and calumny, the champion of the rights of higher criticism, and did more than Matthew Arnold to educate the general public to a recognition of the principle that scholars must be free to study the Bible like any other book. Though he had won his first fame by success in teaching Hebrew, he supported the abolition of the absolute requirement of Hebrew in the curriculum of the divinity school.

The University of Chicago is his monument, far more truly than the noble library building which was erected to commemorate his name. A quarter century after his death the University still in large measure embodies his spirit, and may not too fancifully be thought to exhibit both his qualities and what his censors regard as his defects. It has the self-confidence, the energy, the breadth, the tolerance, the hope, the enthusiasm for creative work, the determination to be a pace-maker, and the desire to prove all things, if not infallible success in holding fast that which is best.

[The chief authorities are T. W. Goodspeed, *William Rainey Harper* (1928), with a bibliography compiled by Edgar Goodspeed, and T. W. Goodspeed, *A Hist. of the University of Chicago* (1916). Goodspeed's sources were, in addition to his personal memories, the Harper files in the archives of the University of Chicago, and numerous letters from friends, colleagues, and pupils of Harper. The Decennial Report was published as *The President's Report—July 1892–July 1902* (1903), and also as Vol. I of the Decennial Publications (1904). The *Biblical World,* Mar. 1906, contains an excellent biography by Francis W. Shepardson, and tributes and appreciations from eminent men throughout the country. Estimates and characterizations of Harper were published in the *Am. Jour. of Theology,* Apr. 1906; *Harper's Weekly,* Jan. 27, 1906; *Outlook,* Jan. 20, 1906; *Independent,* Jan. 18, 1906; *Dial,* Jan. 16, 1906; and the *World Today,* Apr. 1905. Especially valuable are the discriminating estimates of Harper's scholarship by Prof. Francis Brown in the *Am. Jour. of Semitic Languages,* Apr. 1906, and in the introduction to *The Old Testament and Semitic Studies in Memory of William Rainey Harper* (2 vols., 1908).] P. S.

HARPSTER, JOHN HENRY (Apr. 27, 1844–Feb. 1, 1911), Lutheran missionary, was born at Centerhall, Pa., the youngest of the twelve children of George and Frances Harpster. On Apr. 22, 1861, a week after President Lincoln's first call for troops, he was mustered into the 7th Pennsylvania Volunteers for three months' service. In August 1862 he enlisted in the 148th Pennsylvania Volunteers. He was wounded in the head at Gettysburg, July 3, 1863, and on rejoining his regiment in September at Culpeper, Va., was assigned to ambulance duty. He was promoted successively to the grades of second lieutenant, first lieutenant, and captain, and was mustered out in June 1865. That autumn he entered the academic department of the Missionary Institute at Selinsgrove, Pa., where he soon displayed an aptitude for languages. In accordance with the wishes of his dying mother he abandoned his intention of studying law and turned to the ministry. While at Gettysburg Theological Seminary, 1869–71, he was persuaded by the Rev. Erias Unangst to offer himself for missionary work in India. Immediately after his ordination in Baltimore, Dec. 20, 1871, he set out for his post, visiting Europe, Palestine, and Egypt on the way. He began work in the General Synod's mission at Guntur,

Apr. 1, 1872. His eminent success in India was due to several factors. Army life had given him a knowledge of men and of practical affairs; he regarded Christianity more as a way of life than as a body of complicated and, to the Hindu mind, incomprehensible doctrine; he mastered the Telugu language with unusual thoroughness; and from the beginning he showed his confidence in the ability and integrity of the natives. Ill health, however, compelled him in 1876 to relinquish the work. For a short time he was a reader in an Episcopal congregation in San Francisco. He served as pastor of Lutheran churches in Ellsworth, Kan., 1879; Hays, Kan., 1879–82; Trenton, N. J., 1882–84; and Canton, Ohio, 1884–93. On Aug. 1, 1882, he married Julia, daughter of Prof. Michael Jacobs of Gettysburg, who outlived him. In 1893, accompanied by his wife, he returned to the work at Guntur, celebrating the day of his arrival, after an absence of seventeen years, by delivering a short address in Telugu. He labored with his customary success among the Guntur and Sattenappalli Taluks and in 1901 returned on furlough to the United States. The next year, at the urgent entreaty of his brother-in-law, Henry Eyster Jacobs, who was president of the General Council's Board of Foreign Missions, he entered the service of the General Council as "temporary director" of the mission at Rajahmundry. The work that he there undertook was of extreme difficulty, for dissensions among the resident missionaries and the impolitic conduct of the Board had rendered the situation all but hopeless. Harpster's achievement in restoring the prosperity of the Rajahmundry mission ranks him with J. C. F. Heyer [*q.v.*] as one of the great missionaries of the Lutheran Church in India. In 1909 he returned to the United States, and although much in need of rest he devoted himself whole-heartedly to lecturing and writing in behalf of the Rajahmundry mission. Contracting a cold which developed into pneumonia, he died at Mt. Airy, Philadelphia, in his brother-in-law's home, Feb. 1, 1911. He was buried at Gettysburg.

[A. R. Wentz, *Hist. of the Gettysburg Theol. Sem.* (1926); S. P. Bates, *Hist. of Pa. Volunteers 1861–65*, vol. IV (1870); J. W. Muffly, *The Story of Our Regiment: Hist. of the 148th Pa. Volunteers* (1904) with portrait and chapter by Harpster; T. F. Dornblaser, "A Reminiscence of Comrade Harpster," *Luth. Observer*, Feb. 24, 1911; L. B. Wolf, *Missionary Heroes of the Luth. Ch.* (1911); Geo. Drach and C. F. Kuder, *The Telugu Mission* (1914); *Public Ledger* (Phila.), Feb. 2, 1911.]
G. H. G.

HARPUR, ROBERT (Jan. 25, 1731?–Apr. 15, 1825), educator, statesman, was born at Ballybay, County Monaghan, Ireland, the only child of Andrew and Elizabeth Creighton Harpur, recent immigrants from Scotland. He was brought up under the severe discipline of puritanical Presbyterianism and was sent to Glasgow University to complete his education. Fearing that he lacked the necessary gift of oratory, he abandoned the idea of entering the Christian ministry, taught for a few years in Ireland, then set out for America, arriving in New York Sept. 1, 1761. Within three days after his arrival he was engaged as professor of mathematics and natural philosophy at King's College in New York City at a salary, fixed later, of eighty pounds sterling per annum. The following year he was appointed the first librarian of the college. Though he resigned as professor in February 1767, he must have retained an official connection with the college, apparently as a tutor, for the disciplinary records of the institution show that during the next few years he was the object of frequent student outbreaks, inspired apparently by his severe discipline. He seems to have remained at the college until it was closed at the outbreak of the Revolution. When it was reopened as Columbia College in 1784, Harpur was secretary of the Regents of the University of the State of New York, which governed the institution. This position he filled until 1787 when he became trustee and clerk of the board of trustees of the college. He resigned in 1795.

In the meantime he had taken an active part in the politics of New York state. Unlike others on the King's College faculty Harpur joined wholeheartedly in the rebellion. In 1776–77 he was a member of the Third and Fourth provincial congresses. In the latter body, which made the first state constitution, he was more conspicuous as a member of various important executive committees concerned with revolutionary business than as an author of the fundamental law. Indeed his extremely democratic ideas, shown in his demand for a broad franchise and a radical jury system, then as later may have excluded him from posts of importance to which his abilities would have entitled him. After the completion of the constitution and the dissolution of the Provincial Congress he served on the Council of Safety which directed the affairs of the state before the organization of the new government and thereafter when the legislature was not in session. Appointed to a seat in the Assembly in 1777, he continued in that body until 1784. During most of the war he served as a commissioner for detecting and defeating conspiracies in Dutchess County. In the spring of 1781 he appears as clerk of the council of appointments. From 1778 to 1795 he was deputy secretary of state and in this capacity he served as secretary of the Land Board. Here he may have been responsible for the classical names given to the towns of central New York.

In 1795 at the age of sixty-four Harpur abandoned his political and educational activities and established himself in the backwoods of Broome County, N. Y. He had long been interested in the possibilities of the back country. Indeed two years after his arrival in America he had tried to establish a colony of Scotch-Irish farmers, trained in the linen and hemp industries, on a tract to the eastward of Lake George. Now he purchased from the state over thirty thousand acres on the Susquehanna River, founded the village of Harpursville, and devoted the last years of a long life to the sale and development of his lands. He was twice married: first, on Sept. 29, 1773, to Elizabeth Crygier, and in April 1789 to Myra Lackey. He left two sons and three daughters.

[The sketch is based upon an unpublished memoir of Harpur, written by his grand-daughter, Julia C. Andrews. For printed sources see Herbert and Carol Schneider, *Samuel Johnson, President of King's College* (1929), vols. I and IV; *Cat. of Officers and Grads. of Columbia Univ.* (1912); *Calendar of N. Y. Colonial MSS. Indorsed Land Papers* (1864); H. P. Smith, *Hist. of Broome County* (1885); Asa Fitch, *A Hist. . . . Survey of the County of Washington* (1849); Chas. Maar, article in *Quart. Jour. N. Y. State Hist. Asso.*, July 1926; *Harpursville Budget*, June 27, 1920.]

P. D. E.

HARRAH, CHARLES JEFFERSON (Jan. 1, 1817–Feb. 18, 1890), promoter, capitalist, was born at Philadelphia, Pa., the son of John and Mary Harrah. While he was still an infant he was left to the care of his widowed mother and owing to their poor circumstances his attendance at school was limited to three days. As a boy he worked on farms near Philadelphia, but in 1832 he was apprenticed to Jacob Teese, a Philadelphia ship-builder. After the termination of his apprenticeship in 1836 he was employed in shipyards in Philadelphia, New York, and Erie, Pa., and in 1843 he contracted with Charles Deal of Rio Grande do Sul, in the southern part of Brazil, to build a steamship at that port. He sailed for Brazil on Apr. 10, 1843, established the shipyard, and remained at the port until 1852, when he moved to Rio de Janeiro and established another yard which he maintained until 1857. At this time the Brazilian government was beginning to realize the need for railroads in the development of the country and Harrah was among the first to grasp the opportunities thus presented. He returned to the United States to make a study of railroad construction and operation and formed a partnership with W. M. Roberts of Philadelphia, Jacob Humbird of Cumberland, Md., and Robert Harvey of Richmond, Va. Upon his return to Brazil in March 1858 he undertook to build the mountainous portion of the Dom Pedro II railroad, and although the contract was fulfilled in six years, it involved his complete financial ruin. To regain his fortunes he then engaged in a mercantile business with F. M. Brandon, under the firm name of Brandon & Harrah, and shortly afterward they established a branch house in London, England, a connection which was maintained until 1871.

Still interested in transportation, Harrah in 1868 cooperated with a few other Americans in organizing the Botanical Garden Railroad Company, which constructed and operated the first street railroad in Brazil, and in 1872 he organized the company which constructed the Leopoldina Railroad of Minas Geraes, Brazil. He established the first telegraph company in the country and served as its president until the enterprise was taken over by the government. He also aided materially in the formation of the Brazilian Navigation Company and was the official representative of that corporation in the United States when it was involved in litigation with the Garrisons of New York. Having won the confidence of the Emperor and the Imperial Government, in 1865 he was sent to the United States to attempt the purchase of gunboats and armament of which Brazil then stood in need, but he could not prevail upon the government to supply them. Two years later he was sent to the Rio de La Plata on a confidential mission to investigate irregularities and abuses in the commissariat department of the Brazilian army, and subsequently he filled other confidential positions. In 1870, with a few other merchants, he established at Rio de Janeiro the first public school in the empire. Returning to the United States in 1873, he became prominently identified with business enterprises in Philadelphia. For a number of years he held the office of president of the People's Passenger Railway of Philadelphia and served also as president of the Midvale Steel Works. He took an active part in organizations designed for the betterment of community conditions and was a member of various hospital and charity boards. He died in Philadelphia after a long illness. He had married, on Apr. 14, 1839, Anna Margaret Riehl of Philadelphia.

[J. T. Scharf and T. Westcott, *Hist. of Phila.* (1884), vol. III; G. Morgan, *The City of Firsts* (1926); Moses King, *Phila. and Notable Philadelphians* (1902); *Phila. Inquirer, Public Ledger* (Phila.), and the *Press* (Phila.) Feb. 19, 1890.]

J. H. F.

HARRELL, JOHN (Oct. 21, 1806–Dec. 8, 1876), clergyman, educator, "Apostle of early

Methodism in western Arkansas and eastern Oklahoma," was born in Perquimans County, N. C. At the age of seventeen he was licensed to preach, at twenty-one he was admitted on trial to the Tennessee Conference, and two years later he was admitted to full connection. In 1831, when Bishop Roberts called for volunteers to go to the Arkansas District of the Missouri Conference, John Harrell responded and was appointed to work along the border between Arkansas and the Indian Territory. A considerable proportion of his constituents were members of the newly transported Indian tribes from Georgia, and during the year 1832 he organized the first preaching "circuit" among the Cherokees. Though his principal labors were for and among the Indians, he built churches in Van Buren, Fort Smith, and Little Rock, served as the first delegate from Arkansas to the General Conference, and was sent to represent his brethren in the convention at Louisville, Ky., which set up the Methodist Episcopal Church, South (1845).

In 1850 Harrell transferred from the Arkansas Conference to the Indian Mission Conference, in which body for twenty-six years he worked with fatherly interest among these "first Americans." At one time or another he was presiding elder of every district in the Indian Mission Conference, giving fifteen years to that task, and for five years he directed the affairs of New Hope Seminary and the Asbury Manual Labor School, for Indian girls and boys respectively. During the war he served for three years as chaplain in the Confederate army. For three years also he was superintendent of the Indian Mission Conference, and on occasion, when it was impossible for the bishop to reach the seat of the annual conference, he was elected president. Five times he was sent as delegate to the General Conference. Harrell was married in 1832 to Eliza Williams, in Washington County, Ark. He survived his wife but a few weeks and was buried beside her at the Old Asbury Mission, Eufaula, Okla. Ministering to a people who were resentful toward the government and the "whites," he labored in a most difficult position, but he succeeded in winning the respect and the esteem of the Indians whom he served.

[Geo. McGlumphy, article in *Meth. Quart. Rev.*, July 1929; John B. McFerrin, *Hist. of Methodism in Tenn.*, vol. III (1873); Horace Jewell, *Hist. of Methodism in Ark.* (1892); *Christian Advocate* (Nashville), Dec. 16, 1876, Jan. 27, 1877.] R. W. G.

HARRIGAN, EDWARD (Oct. 26, 1845–June 6, 1911), playwright, actor, producer, was born on Scammel Street, New York. His ancestors had emigrated to Canada in the eighteenth century, one of them giving his name to Cape Harrigan on the northern coast of Labrador. William Harrigan, his father, was born in Carbonear, Newfoundland, and was a sea-captain and ship-builder, and in several of his plays Edward Harrigan revealed a knowledge of shipping. In Norfolk, Va., he met and married Helen Rogers, daughter of Matthias Rogers of Charlestown, Mass., who was killed in the War of 1812. Mrs. Harrigan had learned in Norfolk a great many negro songs, stories, and dances which she taught her son when he was a child. Leaving home on account of disagreements arising from his father's second marriage, Edward Harrigan went to San Francisco by way of Panama and in 1861 was singing duets with Lotta Crabtree [*q.v.*] at the Bella Union Theatre and elsewhere. He received a valuable training in the active theatrical life of California and became expert in impersonations, one of his most successful being that of Horace Greeley. Forming a partnership with another comedian, Sam Rickey, he returned to the East, playing first in New York at the Globe Theatre, Nov. 21, 1870, in *A Little Fraud.* It was, however, after his union in 1872 with Anthony Cannon, or "Tony Hart," as he was known on the stage, that the firm of Harrigan and Hart became widely known. In December of that year they appeared at the Theatre Comique, 514 Broadway, New York, in *The Day He Went West* and *The Big and Little of It.* In August 1876 they became managers of this house and made it a center of attraction until 1881, when it was torn down. Between 1870 and 1879 Harrigan wrote and produced nearly eighty vaudeville sketches, dealing with politics, life insurance, baseball, the army, the militia, and other themes, and exploiting Irish, German, Italian, and negro types. The programs of the Theatre Comique show that these sketches grew from a mere song to a duet, from a duet to a dialogue, and then to a one-act play, which later developed into several scenes and finally into a well-articulated play. Harrigan's work was soon known abroad, for the program of St. James's Hall in London, Nov. 7, 1877, announces as a feature "an entirely new musical sketch, . . . by Edward Harrigan, Esq., entitled *'Walking for dat Cake.'*" The most famous of Harrigan's productions began in 1873 when he presented a sketch, *The Mulligan Guard,* in Chicago and later in New York. It was a burlesque upon the excursions of military organizations which sprang up in New York City as "tributes" to a local politician, and which led sometimes to riots. Harrigan stated in 1874 that he composed the sketch as a protest against "this nuisance." In *The Mulligan Guards and the Skidmores* (1875) he dramatized the conflict between the Irish and the negroes, and in *The Mulligan Guard Ball* (1879), the racial pride and rivalry of the Irish and the Germans were celebrated. Dan Mulligan, an Irish immigrant who had fought in the Civil War with "the Sixty-Ninth," and, from his corner grocery ruled his political clan, is the hero of the Mulligan cycle of plays, which had its best expression in *Cordelia's Aspirations* (1883) and *Dan's Tribulations* (1884). Harrigan acted Dan and made that warm-hearted, courageous, quarrelsome character a real person to the audiences that thronged the Theatre Comique. When his mate Cordelia has social ambitions which lead him against his better judgment to move to Madison Avenue, to his consequent financial ruin, he returns to Avenue A with a quiet stoicism that is very appealing. Harrigan of course treated other phases of New York life. In *Squatter Sovereignty* (1882) he pictured the conflict between the owners of the rocky land near the East River about Eighty-second Street and the squatters who had taken possession of property which seemed then of little value. In *The Major* he played the central figure of the adventurer, Major Gilfeather. With this play Harrigan and Hart opened the New Theatre Comique, at 728 Broadway, Aug. 29, 1881. It was destroyed by fire Dec. 23, 1884. Undaunted by the heavy loss, Harrigan leased the Park Theatre at Thirty-fifth Street and Broadway, which he conducted as Harrigan's Park Theatre, with slight interruptions, until Apr. 13, 1891. In 1890 he built a theatre on Thirty-fifth Street near Sixth Avenue, which is now known as the Garrick Theatre. Of his later plays, *Pete* (1887), a drama of Southern life, in which he acted a negro servant, and *Reilly and the Four Hundred* (1890) were the best, although his last full-length play, *Under Cover* (1903), was enthusiastically received. He continued to act, especially in his own creations, one of his favorites being Old Lavender in a romantic play by that name, which had been one of his earliest successes. His last appearance in the legitimate drama was in *His Wife's Family,* at Wallack's Theatre, Oct. 6, 1908.

Disregarding variety sketches, Harrigan wrote thirty-nine plays, in all of which he acted the leading part. Only two of these are in print, *The Porter's Troubles* (1875) and *The Editor's Troubles* (1875), both one-act sketches. A novel, *The Mulligans,* was published in 1901. His ambition was to write of real people, and he studied his audiences carefully. In his own description of his methods (*Harper's Weekly,* Feb. 2, 1889, Supplement), he said he had treated the common people because their hopes and fears, their joys and sorrows, were more numerous and varied than those in other strata of society. He created "types" because he found them popular. The reason he dealt so often with the Irish immigrant and the negro was that these two races care most for the song and dance. As an actor his art was based on a long study of the masters of comedy, especially of Molière. When Brander Matthews took Coquelin to talk to Harrigan in his dressing room, Harrigan conducted the conversation in French. His songs, interspersed through the plays, were set to the music of Dave Braham, and reveal a lyric gift of no mean order, a phase of his imaginative power which lifts his work above that of nearly all the other writers of farce-comedy of his time. In 1870 he married Annie T. Braham, the daughter of the composer. She attended to his financial affairs, selected the costumes, and was his constant critic. He died in New York City.

[Unpublished MSS. are in the possession of Harrigan's son, Dr. A. H. Harrigan, of New York City, to whom the present writer owes much biographical information, differing frequently from printed accounts. For Harrigan's theatrical activity see T. A. Brown, *A Hist. of the N. Y. Stage* (3 vols., 1903); Arthur Hornblow, *A Hist. of the Theatre in America from its Beginning to the Present Time* (2 vols., 1909); *N. Y. Times,* June 7, 1911. For more detailed criticism of the plays and complete list with dates of first performance, see A. H. Quinn, *A Hist. of the Am. Drama from the Civil War to the Present Day* (2 vols., 1927).]

A. H. Q.

HARRIMAN, EDWARD HENRY (Feb. 20, 1848–Sept. 9, 1909), railroad executive, was born in Hempstead, Long Island, the son of Orlando and Cornelia (Neilson) Harriman. His great-grandfather, William Harriman, emigrated from England in 1795 and engaged successfully in trading and commercial pursuits. The descendants of William continued to follow commercial careers, Orlando Harriman, an Episcopal clergyman, being the one exception of his generation in a family of several brothers. Edward's mother, who belonged to a distinguished New Jersey family, was a woman of strong character who made a deep impression upon him. His boyhood was lived mostly in Jersey City, where he attended the public schools, later going to Trinity School in New York City.

At fourteen Harriman left school and entered Wall Street as an office boy. By the age of twenty-one he had acquired sufficient experience to warrant him in borrowing $3,000 from his uncle, with which he bought a seat on the stock exchange. But his ambition soon carried him beyond the mere making of money for its own sake and turned his attention to more constructive activities. Toward the end of the seventies he purchased a small boat running on the Hudson between New York and Newburgh. It was his first venture in the field of transportation to which he was to give his life. In 1879 he married Mary Williamson Averell, the daughter of William J. Averell, a banker of Ogdensburg, N. Y., who was president of the Ogdensburg & Lake Champlain Railroad Company. This relationship aroused his interest in up-state transportation and two years later his career as a rebuilder of bankrupt railroads began with a small broken-down railroad called the Lake Ontario Southern which he renamed the Sodus Bay & Southern, reorganized, and sold with considerable profit to the Pennsylvania, with which it connected.

In 1883 Harriman entered the Illinois Central directorate. He had been studying the road for some time and had acquired confidence in its future. He and Vice-President Stuyvesant Fish [*q.v.*], whom he had known for several years, worked together closely to secure improvement and expansion. In 1887 Fish became president and Harriman succeeded him as vice-president. He became a dominant influence in the financial policy of the Illinois Central. His skill was shown in the high credit which the road enjoyed and which carried it through the panic years of the nineties without loss of standing. Harriman was nearly fifty years old when in 1897 he became a director of the Union Pacific. Of the few people who knew anything about him many thought of him simply as a successful Wall Street operator. The unexpected knowledge he displayed of the intimate details of railroading was partly the result of natural aptitude. But it was in considerable measure the outcome of a rigorous training which began in Wall Street and continued through his years with the Illinois Central. In this period he developed judgment in the handling of financial problems and acumen in estimating the capital market, and acquired detailed knowledge of the various phases of railroad construction and operation that, by reason of his marvellous memory, became a permanent reservoir of pertinent information.

The Union Pacific, which had been built with the aid of a federal land grant and a government loan, had, after a checkered career, gone into the hands of receivers in 1893. In 1895 Kuhn, Loeb & Company undertook its reorganization. Harriman, who saw the traffic possibilities in the post-panic period if the road could be put into satisfactory physical condition, took a participation in the syndicate and became a member of the board of directors in the reorganized company in December 1897. By May 1898 he was chairman of the executive committee, and from that time until his death his word was law on the Union Pacific system, not only because of his dominant personality but also because of the respect of his colleagues for his judgment and vision. Characteristically, he spent the winter of 1897–98 in making himself familiar with the needs of the road, and it was during this period that he backed up his judgment as to its future by buying into its common stock and laying the foundation of his later fortune.

The condition of the property seemed almost hopeless. Track was poor, rails were light, rolling-stock was old and inadequate. Maintenance had been neglected on much of the line during the period of receivership, grades were heavy and curves short. Moreover, the business communities established along the line had suffered in the panic of 1893 and the prospects of traffic were discouraging. While still on his first inspection trip, Harriman telegraphed for authority from the board to purchase locomotives, cars, and rails and to start improvements to an amount aggregating twenty-five million dollars. The directors laid the project over until his return to New York. His confidence in the soundness of his proposals led him to conclude several contracts on his own responsibility before returning, and when he arrived in New York he promptly won the board to his point of view by a convincing presentation of the road's requirements. Less than a year after he became chairman, the Union Pacific had repossessed itself of the Oregon Short Line and gained control of the Oregon Railroad & Navigation Company giving it the necessary outlet to the Pacific at Portland. When expansion of the West began with the turn of the century, the Union Pacific was in position to handle the business economically. By 1901 the company was in an enviable financial situation, with abundant credit and the best of banking connections, a fact of significance in relation to the policy of expansion which followed. In 1903 Harriman assumed the office of president in addition to his other duties.

What was needed for a thoroughly efficient system to the coast was the ownership and rebuilding of the Central Pacific, which extended from Ogden to San Francisco and was owned by the Southern Pacific. In 1900 Collis P. Huntington died and his extensive holdings of Southern Pacific were for sale. In 1901 the Union Pacific board authorized the issue of $100,000,000 of convertible bonds, giving to the chairman of the executive committee the discretionary power to use the money "as in his judgment may be practicable and desirable." No clearer evidence could be adduced to show the absolute dominance that Harriman exercised over his directorate. With part of the proceeds of these bonds Harriman bought the Huntington holdings of the Southern Pacific. This purchase was added to until the Union Pacific owned forty-six per cent. of Southern Pacific stock which carried control of that corporation and ownership of the Central Pacific. The same policy of betterment was then inaugurated on the line from Ogden to San Francisco that had been pursued on the eastern division, the most spectacular improvement being the Lucin cut-off across Great Salt Lake, in the building of which difficulties of construction were overcome which many experts considered insurmountable. Harriman not only strengthened the physical condition of both the Union and Southern Pacific but he evolved an administrative organization for the combined system that attracted wide attention among railway men for the boldness of his conception and the perfection of its detail.

Having carried his roads to a high state of physical efficiency, Harriman had no intention of allowing other carriers to take traffic which belonged to him. Furthermore, he needed an entrance into Chicago. This was at the bottom of his struggle for control of the Chicago, Burlington & Quincy. With his dominating nature, he must have had in mind also the advantages of combination. As time went on, his ambition grew and he sought to satisfy it by acquiring a commanding position in the railway field as a whole, but at the beginning of this contest his strategy was actuated mainly by a desire to guard his territory. James J. Hill [*q.v.*], who dominated the northwestern situation, also wanted an entrance to Chicago and an opening into the traffic territory which the Burlington commanded. He succeeded in outgeneraling the Harriman interests and obtaining control of the road. Harriman then began buying stock of the Northern Pacific, which had been given a half-interest in the Burlington. The struggle between Hill and Harriman, now transferred to the Northern Pacific, resulted in the famous panic of May 9, 1901. This, however, did not affect the results of the strategy which preceded it. Harriman possessed a clear majority of the stock, preferred and common. Hill had a majority of the common. Whether the board of directors of the Northern Pacific could have postponed the annual meeting of the stockholders and retired the preferred stock on Jan. 1, 1902, and thus have ensured control to the Hill interests was a matter of dispute among lawyers, but there is no doubt that such a policy would have created animosities that would have affected adversely the railroad situation of the entire Northwest. This probability undoubtedly dictated the settlement under which the Northern Securities Company was organized to take over the stocks of the Great Northern and Northern Pacific. The Harriman interests were given representation on the board of the holding company. Three years later, in 1904, the Northern Securities Company was condemned by the Supreme Court (193 *U. S.*, 197) for having effected a combination in restraint of trade and was obliged to surrender its holdings of Great Northern and Northern Pacific stock. Harriman sought to get back the stock which he had turned in when the combination was formed and carried his contention to the Supreme Court, but the Court approved the pro rata distribution of Great Northern and Northern Pacific stock to the Northern Securities stockholders which had been arranged and which left the Hill interests in control of both roads. Harriman, being now unable to make his influence felt in the northwestern railroad situation, sold his holdings in the northern roads and aided by a rising market emerged from his experience with a profit of over fifty million dollars. These free assets, combined with the enormous net earnings of the Union Pacific, enabled him to pursue the policy of purchasing stocks in other railway companies in different sections of the country, apparently with the purpose of creating a community of interest for the Union Pacific and of influencing traffic relations between them. In some instances, however, this relationship was so remote that the only explanation for the purchase seemed to be a desire on the part of Harriman to make his influence felt in other portions of the railway field.

Harriman's policy of extended purchase of stocks of other railways led to an investigation of the Harriman lines in 1906–07 by the Interstate Commerce Commission. It has been charged that this investigation was a personal attack by Roosevelt because of a difference between him and Harriman that arose out of the campaign of 1904 in New York state in which Harriman raised a large fund for the election of the Republican candidates. But it can be explained more reasonably on broader grounds. Curbing of combinations and monopoly had been a Roosevelt policy from the beginning and he had secured amendments to the Interstate Commerce Act and had strengthened the personnel of the Commission to secure more effective railroad regulation. The investigation was started soon after the new law became effective. The public had become thoroughly alarmed over the situation disclosed by the Northern Securities case and demanded more knowledge of what the combination movement meant and whether the law was sufficient to cope with it. Among other financial transactions of Harriman, the Commission described the reorganization of the Chicago & Alton in 1899 and the juggling of its capitalization and surplus for the benefit of the syndicate that purchased its stock, characterizing the transaction as "indefensible financing." Although there was nothing in it that could be made the basis of prosecution, the transaction was an illuminating example of the manner in which a road may be drained of its resources for the benefit of insiders and at the expense of shippers, investors, and the public at large. The Commission's report also brought forth in striking fashion the range of Harriman's railroad holdings and the extent to which the Union Pacific system was being used as a holding company for the securities of other transportation corporations. Harriman's testimony before the Commission revealed the man's overpowering ambition and his expressed determination to push his conquests further if not stopped by governmental authority. From the standpoint of public welfare his offense was that he used the credit and resources of the Union Pacific system speculatively in the purchase of securities instead of devoting them to the interests of the road as an agency of transportation. He made the Union Pacific an investment company as well as a railroad company, a policy which the Commission held not to be in the public interest. That the public attitude has changed since 1907, and that combinations are now being permitted after approval by the Interstate Commerce Commission, does not justify Harriman's defiance of a law which had already been interpreted by the Supreme Court adversely to his view and which was being overwhelmingly supported by public opinion.

His ambitious plans for transportation development were not confined to the United States. He already had a line of steamships to the Orient and was planning a round-the-world transportation system in the interest of which he went to the Far East in 1905. But political conditions prevented the consummation of this project. His influence extended beyond the railroad field into banks and insurance companies. He was a director of the Equitable Life Assurance Society at the time of the ousting of James Hazen Hyde from the vice-presidency in 1905 and was a member of the committee which was responsible for the change in ownership and control. The insurance investigation which followed revealed nothing discreditable to Harriman, but his prominence in the insurance world, his break with Roosevelt, and the investigation by the Interstate Commerce Commission caused popular opinion to find in him the personification of all the evils of the existing business situation —monopoly, improper intercorporate relationships, political bribery, and Wall Street speculation for personal profit—and subjected him to an extraordinary storm of abuse. His characteristic silence only added to the denunciation. He was frank and direct on the witness stand but beyond that said nothing, which was a strategic mistake from the standpoint of his own interest and hardly justifiable from that of a public-service official. He has been variously characterized as the last great individualist and the last figure of an epoch. It is more correct to say that he belonged to an earlier period and that during his lifetime the methods he pursued were already becoming obsolete. It was for this reason that he became the subject of so much public disapproval.

Harriman's genius as a railroad administrator is generally admitted. His remarkable grasp of detail, his power to develop new traffic resources, and his unerring judgment as to the extent to which earnings should be reinvested in the property are all acknowledged. He was one of the great railway builders of all time. What deeply impressed his associates was his ability to grasp a multitude of facts and bring them to bear in an orderly fashion upon the problem in hand. Having formulated his case and declared his purpose, he drove ahead to its accomplishment, indifferent to all obstacles. What one close observer calls his "sheer persistency" was a marked characteristic. It derived its strength from a self-confidence based upon long study of a particular situation. With it went an extraordinary power over the wills of others which enlisted their support for his projects.

In 1899, as a relaxation from the responsibilities of business, Harriman organized and personally conducted a scientific expedition to Alaska, chartering a steamer for the purpose and taking with him twenty-five prominent scientists. The results, which were published (*Harriman Alaska Series,* 14 vols., 1902–14), are of great scientific value. In 1876, during his earlier years in New York, with a number of friends he organized the Tompkins Square Boys' Club on the East Side for boys of foreign parentage. It is said to have been the first organization of its kind in the United States and is still in existence. In 1885 he began his purchase of lands near Tuxedo, in Orange County, N. Y., for the purpose of preserving the wild forest area from the invasion of lumber interests. Eventually the estate, which he called "Arden," and which became his permanent residence, contained about twenty thousand acres. Interested in good roads because of his love of horses, he was the moving spirit in this work in Orange County.

In his business relations Harriman was cold and ruthless, sparing neither friend nor foe if they blocked his plans. Yet that he had another side was shown by his boys' club project, in which he retained his interest to the end, and by incidents in his business career such as his aid during the San Francisco earthquake and his work in saving the Imperial Valley from Colorado floods (George Kennan, *The Salton Sea: An Account of Harriman's Fight with the Colorado River,* 1917). Worn out by his responsibilities, he died on Sept. 9, 1909, in his sixty-second year. He left a widow, three daughters, and three sons.

[George Kennan, *E. H. Harriman: A Biography* (2 vols., 1922); Otto H. Kahn, *Edward Henry Harriman* (1911), reprinted as "The Last Figure of an Epoch: Edward Henry Harriman," in *Our Economic and Other Problems* (1920); John Muir, *Edward Henry Harriman* (1911); B. H. Meyer, *A Hist. of the Northern Securities Case* (1906); "In the Matter of Consolidations and Combinations of Carriers," *Interstate Commerce Commission Reports,* XII (1908); Wm. Z. Ripley, *Railroads: Finance and Organization* (1915); George Kennan, *E. H. Harriman's Far Eastern Plans* (1917); articles and estimates of his life and work in *Cosmopolitan,* Mar. 1903, July 1909; *Moody's Mag.,* Oct. 1906, Oct. 1909; *Am. Rev. of Revs.,* Jan. 1907, Oct. 1909; *McClure's Mag.,* Oct. 1909, Jan. 1911; *N. Y. Times* and N. Y. *Sun,* Sept. 10, 1909; *Railway World,* Sept. 17, 1909.]

F. H. D.

HARRIMAN, WALTER (Apr. 8, 1817–July 25, 1884), soldier, governor of New Hampshire, was the son of Benjamin Evans and Hannah (Flanders) Harriman and was descended from Leonard Harriman who emigrated to America from Yorkshire, England, in 1638, and settled at Rowley, Mass. He was born at Warner, N. H. After attending the public schools and Hopkinton Academy he began at seventeen to teach school in Warner and continued in this occupation for about seven years, holding positions in Massachusetts and New Jersey, as well as in New Hampshire. He spent ten years in the ministry of the Universalist Church, first at Harvard, Mass., after which he returned to Warner, N. H., in 1845. Becoming interested in business, he left the ministry in 1851 and conducted a general store at Warner in partnership with John S. Pillsbury, afterward governor of Minnesota. In politics he was a Democrat with anti-slavery leanings, and beginning in 1848, he became an active political worker. In the following ten years he served two terms in the New Hampshire House and one in the Senate (1849, 1858, 1859); two terms as state treasurer (1853–55); and in 1856 was appointed by President Pierce member of a commission for the classification of Indian lands in Kansas.

In the spring of 1861 Harriman became editor and part owner of the Manchester, N. H., *Union Democrat,* which he renamed the *Weekly Union,* and gave vigorous and effective support to the war policy of the Lincoln administration, a service of great importance in view of the numerical strength of the Democratic party in the state. In August of the following year he was commissioned colonel of the 11th Regiment of New Hampshire Volunteers and shortly afterward left for Virginia with his command. He took part in the battle of Fredericksburg in December. In 1863 his regiment was moved west and with the exception of a few weeks when he temporarily resigned, he spent the year in various operations in Kentucky, Tennessee, and Mississippi, including the siege of Vicksburg. In the spring of 1864 the regiment was again attached to the Army of the Potomac and at the battle of the Wilderness, Harriman was captured while leading an attack on the Confederate lines. He was exchanged a few months later, eventually resumed command of his regiment befor Petersburg, and participated with credit in the closing operations. He took part in the grand review, was honored with a brevet brigadier-generalship, and was mustered out June 11, 1865.

While still in the field Harriman had maintained an interest in politics and in 1863 accepted a nomination for the governorship from the War Democrats, diverting sufficient votes to force the election into the legislature, where the Republicans, actually a popular minority, were able to elect the governor. This maneuver gained the lasting gratitude of the Republicans and practically ended his former party affiliations. While on furlough after his release in 1864 he was an active campaigner for the Lincoln ticket in the presidential election. On leaving the army he was immediately elected secretary of state for New Hampshire and served two years, and in 1867 and 1868 he was elected governor after closely contested campaigns. After the inauguration of Grant, he was appointed and for the next eight years served as naval officer for the port of Boston. Having established a residence in Concord in 1872, he retired to it in 1877 and spent the rest of his life there, serving a single term (1881) as representative in the legislature, but devoting more attention to writing than to active party work. He contributed frequently to various New England newspapers and journals and in 1879 published a *History of Warner, N. H.*, containing in the appendix another historical study: "The Boundaries of New Hampshire." His last work was a volume entitled *Travels and Observations in the Orient, and a Hasty Flight in the Countries of Europe* (1883). He was twice married. His first wife was Apphia K. Hoyt, to whom he was married in September 1841. After her death he was married, in October 1844, to Almira R. Andrews.

[Amos Hadley, *Life of Walter Harriman with Selections from his Speeches and Writings* (1888); "Gen. Walter Harriman," *Granite Monthly*, Oct. 1879; Leander W. Cogswell, *A Hist. of the Eleventh N. H. Regiment, Volunteer Infantry* (1891); Otis F. R. Waite, *N. H. in the Great Rebellion* (1870); *War of the Rebellion: Official Records (Army)*; *Concord Evening Monitor*, July 25, 1884.] W. A. R.

HARRINGTON, CHARLES (July 29, 1856–Sept. 11, 1908), Boston sanitarian and educator, the son of George and Delphine Rose Eugénie (Saudray) Harrington, was born at Salem, Mass., where he received his preliminary education. He attended Bowdoin College in 1873–74 but graduated (A.B.) from Harvard College in 1878 and proceeded to the Harvard Medical School where he obtained the degree of M.D. in 1881. At the Medical School he came under the influence of Edward S. Wood [*q.v.*], professor of chemistry, who stimulated his interest in toxicology. While still an undergraduate he served as house pupil at the Massachusetts General Hospital and in 1881 won the Boylston Prize for an essay on accidental arsenic poisoning. After graduation he continued his studies in Germany (1881–83), during which time he became interested in hygiene and sanitation. In Strassburg he studied under Schmiedeberg and at Munich under von Pettenkofer, the veteran sanitarian, who more than any one moulded Harrington's career. On returning from Germany he was made an assistant in chemistry (June 25, 1883) and subsequently instructor in hygiene (June 8, 1885) at the Harvard Medical School. Three years later he was appointed instructor in materia medica and hygiene, in 1898 he became assistant professor of hygiene, and from 1906 to 1908 he served as professor of hygiene.

Harrington devoted his attention to the investigation of the sanitary conditions of the community and for many years rendered important services to the city of Boston as inspector of milk and vinegar. In 1892 he became secretary to the Massachusetts state board of health in succession to S. W. Abbot. In his day the science of preventive medicine was in its infancy, and through his numerous writings he did as much as any one of his time to arouse public interest in this branch of medical science. At the Chicago session of the American Medical Association in 1908 he delivered a memorable oration on state medicine, in which he described the history of the agitation for the national control for public health, discussed the constitutional difficulties, quarantine legislation, and the doctrine of state's rights, and suggested a constitutional amendment empowering the national government to act in health matters. He contributed more than fifty papers to various medical journals and in 1901 published *A Manual of Practical Hygiene for Students, Physicians and Medical Officers*, which before his death had passed through three editions. Two revised editions were subsequently brought out by M. Wyman Richardson, the last appearing in 1914. In its time it was referred to as one of the most satisfactory manuals in any language. He wrote extensively also on the methods of surgical disinfection in the *Boston Medical and Surgical Journal*, of which he was for many years a member of the staff, and in the *American Journal for Medical Sciences*. He was a genial and friendly man with a wide circle of friends. He died suddenly at Lynton in Devonshire, England. He had married, on Feb. 25, 1884, Martha Josephine Jones, daughter of John Coffin Jones, a Boston merchant.

[T. F. Harrington, *The Harvard Medic. School* (1905), III, 1437–38, 1563; *Harvard Univ. Quinquennial Cat.* (1925); *Harvard Grads.' Mag.*, Dec. 1908; *Boston Medic. and Surgic. Jour.*, Sept. 17, 1908; *Jour. Am. Medic. Asso.*, Sept. 26, 1908; the *Lancet* (London), Oct. 17, 1908; *N. Y. Medic. Jour.*, Sept. 19, 1908; *Boston Transcript*, Sept. 15, 1908.] J. F. F.

HARRINGTON, MARK WALROD (Aug. 18, 1848–Oct. 9, 1926), astronomer, meteorologist, son of James Harrington, a practising physician, and Charlotte (Walrod) Harrington, was born at Sycamore, Ill. He was educated at the Northwestern University and the University of Michigan, receiving from the latter the degrees A.B., 1868, and A.M., 1871. He was officially connected with the University of Michigan from 1868 to 1876, serving as assistant curator of the Museum, and ultimately teaching a range of subjects including mathematics, geology, zoölogy, and botany. The summer of 1871 he spent in Alaska as astronomical aid to the United States Coast and Geodetic Survey. In 1876–77 he was a student in Leipzig, and in 1877 he went to China as professor of astronomy in the cadet school of the Foreign Office in Peking. In 1878 he returned, owing to ill health, and for one year he was on the faculty of the University of Louisiana. In 1879 he became professor of astronomy and director of the observatory at the University of Michigan. He left this position to become chief of the United States Weather Bureau, on July 1, 1891, but on June 2, 1895, he was removed, and for the next two years he was president of the University of Washington. On Sept. 16, 1898, he reëntered the Weather Bureau and was sent to San Juan, Porto Rico, as section director. Unequal to the duties of the place, in the following March he was transferred to New York City, where on June 2, 1899, he retired from public service owing to failing mental and physical health. Shortly afterward, in 1899, he left home to attend a dinner and until 1908 was lost save for one or two strangely worded letters and an occasional news item indicating that a learned and cheerful philosopher was working in a lumber camp, on a sugar plantation, or in a shipyard. He had wandered far and wide, even to China, but at last, in June 1907, he applied for shelter at a police station in Newark, N. J. Being unable to identify himself, he was committed to an asylum where his reputation for great learning led to his identification the following year by his wife, Rose (Smith) Harrington, and his son. For a time he showed marked improvement, but never became well enough to be discharged.

In 1884 Harrington established the *American Meteorological Journal* and was its acting editor until 1892. During this time, and later, while chief of the Weather Bureau, he stimulated investigations in meteorology by requests for contributions on that subject. He was also influential in starting the Bureau's collection and publication of rainfall data of the United States and wrote the first of the Bureau's bulletins, an account of the climate and meteorology of Death Valley, California. This he followed with other bulletins, as well as occasional scattered articles, finally publishing his outstanding work, *About the Weather* (1899), based on material he had gathered at the Bureau. But however useful he was in government service, his tenure of office was not happy. He was the first civilian chief of the Weather Bureau and, coming from an academic institution, did not exercise the army discipline which had prevailed when it was a portion of the Signal Service. With his authority thus undermined, his usefulness as an executive was seriously impaired.

[*Who's Who in America*, 1901–02; *Portrait and Biog. Album of DeKalb County, Ill.* (1883), p. 285; *Alumni Cat. of the Univ. of Mich., 1837–1921* (1923); C. R. Bagley, *Hist. of Seattle* (1916), I, 155; E. W. Harrington, *The Harrington Family in America* (1907); official records, U. S. Weather Bureau.]

W. J. H.

HARRINGTON, SAMUEL MAXWELL (Feb. 5, 1803–Nov. 28, 1865), jurist, chancellor, railroad president, was born in Dover, Del., of English and German ancestry. During his boyhood he was employed in the office of the clerk of the supreme court at Dover. This inclined him to legal studies and after a course in Washington College, Md., from which he graduated in 1823 with first honors, he studied law in the office of Henry M. Ridgely and then with Martin W. Bates, being admitted to the bar in October 1826. With poor health, embarrassed circumstances, and the responsibility of the family after his father's death, he nevertheless rose rapidly in his profession and in 1828 was appointed secretary of state by Governor Polk. Two years later, on Oct. 16, 1830, he was appointed chief justice of the supreme court. During the following year, however, the constitutional convention changed the judicial system by setting up a superior court in lieu of the supreme court and the court of common pleas. On this superior court Harrington was appointed associate justice, Jan. 18, 1832, which position he held for twenty-three years, when, upon the death of James Booth, Jr., he was made chief justice, Apr. 3, 1855. On May 4, 1857, he was made chancellor. Coincident with his term as associate judge he held the position of law reporter, the first to be appointed in Delaware, and compiled five volumes of reports. He served also as chairman of the commission which revised the statute law of Delaware and prepared the code adopted by the legislature in special session in 1852.

Harrington's judicial attainments were of unusual calibre. His mind was keen and logical; his learning extensive. According to John M. Clayton, a contemporary, "his cases were announced with clearness of reasoning, aptness of illustration, and depth of research. Though based on the principles of the common law, they were qualified by a cautious and judicious recognition of doctrines of more recent origin" (see bibliography). A later estimate of his services came when the Delaware Bar Association, in 1924, selected him as the one who had been preëminent in judicial service to the state (Wilson L. Bevan, *History of Delaware, Past and Present,* 1929, III, 142).

Harrington was one of the prime movers, it

not the leading spirit, in the development of the Delaware Railroad, the beginning of a plan for a peninsular or Eastern Shore railroad, which would provide transportation direct from Norfolk to Philadelphia. Clayton conceived the plan (Harrington to Clayton, Mar. 1, 1852), but Harrington was made president when the company was organized in May 1852. The railroad became associated in the minds of many with monopoly and the cause of the Whig party in Delaware, and Harrington, who belonged to that party, labored to save his railroad from the shoals of party prejudice and the rivalry of other companies. The road was leased to the Philadelphia, Wilmington & Baltimore for construction, in 1855, completed in 1860, and finally taken over by that company. Harrington died at the close of the Civil War, while on business in Philadelphia. During the war he was an ardent Unionist. For two years before his death he had been almost prostrated by a stroke of paralysis but would not succumb to it. His wife, Mary (Lofland) Harrington, whom he had married in 1836, survived him.

[The best source on the life of Harrington is the sketch of him in *Portraits of Eminent Americans Now Living* (1853), vol. I, ed. by John Livingston. A letter from Harrington to Clayton, Dec. 29, 1851, in the "Clayton Papers," MSS. Division, Lib. of Cong., states that he was preparing a memoir of himself for Livingston to use in the above work. Clayton was asked to supply the estimate of his judicial services. This estimate is partly given in the text above. The "Clayton Papers" contain a series of ten letters from Harrington, dating from 1841 to 1855, most of which are important. Further sources include N. B. Smithers, sketch in 1 *Del. Chancery Reports,* 495; H. C. Conrad, *Hist. of the State of Del.* (1908), III, 929; and an obituary notice in the *Delaware State Jour. and Statesman,* Dec. 1, 1865.] C. W. G.

HARRINGTON, THOMAS FRANCIS (June 10, 1866–Jan. 19, 1919), physician, hygienist, was born in Lowell, Mass., the son of Mary Callaghan and Thomas Harrington. After a preliminary education in Lowell, he entered the Harvard Medical School, graduating in 1888. He took his interneship in the Rotunda, Dublin, and at the Children's Hospital, London, England, later returning to his native city to practise. Early in his career he became interested in public health and for three years was chairman of the Lowell board of health and visiting physician to St. John's hospital. From 1894 to 1907 he was secretary of the United States Pension Board. During this period he wrote an essay, *Dr. Samuel Fuller of the Mayflower (1620), the Pioneer Physician* (1903), and in 1905 he published a three-volume history, *The Harvard Medical School,* which became the standard work of reference on the subject. A year after Boston inaugurated its law of 1906 providing for medical inspection of its school children, Harrington was made director of physical training and athletics, a position which he held until 1915. At the same time he became president of the Boston Playground Association. He had continued to write and by 1910 had published *The Child and the Public School Curriculum* (1906); *Medical Supervision versus Medical Inspection* (1907); *Boston Public Schools: Report on Department of School Hygiene* (1908); *The Observance of Health Day in Schools* (1910); and *Boston Open-Air School Rooms* (1910). He was a pioneer advocate of yearly "health days" and recommended as early as 1898 open-air schoolrooms and hygienic physical culture. The employment of these and similar measures in Boston led to their adoption elsewhere in this country and in Europe. In 1910 Harrington attended the international school hygiene congress in Paris and in 1913 was chosen as a United States delegate to the seventeenth international congress of medicine in London. From 1915 until his death in 1919 he was deputy commissioner of the Massachusetts state board of labor and industry. During the World War he served as a lieutenant-colonel in the Massachusetts National Guards, being particularly active during the influenza epidemic in Boston in 1918. Harrington married, June 2, 1891, Mary Isabelle Dempsey of Lowell, who with three sons survived him.

[*Jour. Am. Medic. Asso.,* Feb. 1, 1919; *Boston Medic. and Surgic. Jour.,* Feb. 13, 1919; *Boston Transcript,* Jan. 20, 22, 1919; *Boston Herald,* Jan. 20, 1919; information as to certain facts from members of Harrington's family.] H. R. V.

HARRIS, BENJAMIN (fl. 1673–1716), bookseller, publisher, author, was the first American journalist. He began his publishing career by issuing a religious book, *War with the Devil,* from his shop in Bell Alley in Coleman Street, London, in 1673. Business prospered and during the next six years he published numerous religious books, including attacks against the Catholics and Quakers. Himself an Anabaptist, he became associated with Shaftesbury and the Whigs and in 1679 joined Titus Oates in exposing the Popish Plot. On July 7 of that year he published the first number of *Domestick Intelligence: or News both from City and Country,* later *The Protestant (Domestick) Intelligence,* and continued its publication, with several interruptions, until Apr. 15, 1681, when it was finally suppressed. Harris was both its publisher and editor. As Shaftesbury's campaign progressed Harris became more audacious and in the latter part of 1679 published the *Appeal from the Country to the City,* a seditious pamphlet written anonymously by Charles Blount. The following February Harris was tried, found guilty, and sentenced by Chief Justice Scroggs to stand in the pillory and pay a fine of £500, in default of which he was sent to King's Bench Prison. The House of Commons, under Whig influence, petitioned the King for his release, without effect, but in December he was illegally discharged. He celebrated his release by publishing his *Triumphs of Justice over Unjust Judges,* dedicating it to Scroggs, and resumed his propaganda against the papists. He opened a coffee-house near the Royal Exchange in Cornhill where he sold books, playing cards illustrating all the popish plots, and patent medicines. With the failure of Monmouth's Rebellion and the accession of James II, he acted with his old audacity and published *English Liberties,* of which five thousand copies were seized by the authorities. With that he agreed with his Whig friend John Dunton, then in Boston, that Old England was an "uneasie . . . Place for honest men," and he determined to seek refuge in New England.

He arrived in Boston, with his son Vavasour and a stock of books, in the fall of 1686 and opened a shop on the south corner of State and Washington streets. He was surrounded by seven booksellers, but the success of his first publication, John Tulley's *Almanach* for 1687, established his position, and on July 12, 1687, he returned to London to see his wife and to secure more books. Returning Jan. 25, 1688, he found that the business had further prospered under Vavasour and that the second issue of Tulley's *Almanach* had been published. Meanwhile, in 1687, his estate had been appraised for taxation purposes and was estimated at £16, as great as the estate of any Boston bookseller. In November 1688 he again sailed for London, with Judge Sewall as a fellow passenger. He soon returned and published a profitable edition of the new charter. His shop became known as the London Coffee House and in August 1690 he secured a license to sell "Coffee, Tee and Chucaletto." It became a social center, where women could come, though inns were denied them, and among its patrons were the Mathers, who published some of their books with Harris.

On Thursday, Sept. 25, 1690, Harris published *Publick Occurrences Both Forreign and Domestick,* the first newspaper printed in America. It contained three pages of news, with no advertisements, and was remarkable because the news was chiefly American. Harris had a marked sense of news value and a vigorous style in writing. He had planned to publish the paper monthly, "or if any Glut of Occurrences happen, oftener," but the first issue was promptly suppressed by the governor and the council. According to Sewall, it gave "much distaste because not Licensed; and because of the passage referring to the French King and the Maquas [Mohawk Indians]." Four days after the paper's appearance a broadside proclaimed the "high resentment and Disallowance" of the authorities and forbade any printing without license. Sometime before 1690 Harris had published *The New England Primer,* one of the most popular and influential books ever printed in America. He had brought out in London in 1679 *The Protestant Tutor,* a book designed to teach children spelling, the true Protestant religion, and the iniquities and dangers of the papists. Several similar books had been unsuccessfully published in Boston, perhaps in imitation of the *Tutor,* but Harris saw the necessity of a radical change, and though he borrowed parts of his *Tutor,* the *New England Primer* was a school book for children and not a savage political tract.

During 1690 Harris published at least ten books. The following year he formed a partnership with John Allen, and in 1692 he became the official printer to the governor, a position of influence, though one of difficulty and little profit. In 1693 Green superseded him as official printer and in 1694 he moved from his shop "over-against the old-Meeting-House" to new quarters "at the Sign of the Bible, over-against the Blew Anchor." Having determined to return to London, he went early in 1695, leaving Vavasour, assisted by Allen, to close up his business. His last publication was Tulley's *Almanach* for 1695. During his eight years in Boston he had established himself as the leading publisher and bookseller of seventeenth-century America.

In London he turned again to journalism and in May 1695 published the first number of *Intelligence Domestick and Foreign.* This was followed within three months by three newspapers which failed, but on June 6, 1699, he brought out *The London Slip of News, both Foreign and Domestick,* which, with its second issue, became the *London Post* and survived exactly six years. He sold it from his shop at the "Golden Boar's Head, against the Cross Keys in Gracechurch Street," along with sermons, books, almanacs, and patent medicines. His frequent quarrels with Dr. John Partridge, whose almanacs he plagiarized, probably attracted the attention of Jonathan Swift and brought about the famous Bickerstaff papers. In the *Post* he fought bitterly with his old friend Dunton, who replied in his *Living Elegy: or, Dunton's Letter (being a word of Comfort) to his Few Creditors* (London, 1706). It is to these quarrels that we owe most of our later knowledge of Harris. The *London Post* ceased publication in 1706 and his last edition of *The Protestant Tutor* was printed in 1716. The date of his death, like that of his birth, is unknown.

[Worthington C. Ford, *Boston Book Market, 1679–1700* (1917); Joseph G. Muddiman, *The King's Journalist, 1659–89* (1923), discursive and inaccurate; George E. Littlefield, *Early Boston Booksellers, 1642–1711* (1900), and *Early Mass. Press, 1638–1711* (2 vols., 1907); Paul L. Ford, *The New-England Primer* (1897); John Dunton, *Life and Errors of John Dunton* (2 vols., ed. 1818); W. G. Bleyer, *Main Currents in the Hist. of Am. Journalism* (1927); *Bibliog. Essays: A Tribute to Wilberforce Eames* (1924); S. A. Green, *Ten Fac-simile Reproductions Relating to Old Boston* (1901).]
F. M.

HARRIS, CALEB FISKE (Mar. 9, 1818–Oct. 2, 1881), merchant, bibliophile, was born in Warwick, R. I., the youngest of the five children of Dr. Stephen and Eliza (Greene) Harris. Through his father he was descended from Thomas Harris, a brother of the earnest but turbulent William Harris, who was associated with Roger Williams. Through his mother he was descended from John Greene, an English surgeon, who also was associated with Williams. The boy attended school at the Academy in Kingston, R. I., then entered Brown University in 1834. Eager to get into active employment, he left college before graduation to engage in the commission business in New York City. He remained in New York for twenty years, amassed an ample fortune, and returning to Providence, retired to enjoy it. Sometime in his career he developed a passion for collecting rarities in books and pictures. He bought books until they overflowed all shelf room in his house and piled up in the hidden recesses of closets, trunks, and boxes. Ranging from old missals and manuscripts on vellum, through the various types of early printing, and including a large number of first editions of English poets and dramatists, his collection covered a wide field of interests. It was already rich in American poetry and drama when it was augmented by the purchase of the library of Judge Albert Gorton Greene, of Providence, himself a book-lover and something of a poet. In 1874 Harris printed for private circulation a catalogue of his American items in poetry and drama. They numbered then over four thousand volumes, many of which were extremely rare. Had he lived to carry out all his intentions for increasing his collection it would have assumed even more impressive proportions, but his plans were tragically cut short by his sudden death by drowning while sailing on Moosehead Lake, in Maine. His wife, Emily Stevenson Davis of Philadelphia, whom he had married on Jan. 17, 1866, lost her life at the same time. As Harris left no heirs, his books were thrown on the market, but fortunately a cousin, Senator Henry B. Anthony, purchased the American poetry collection intact and at his death in 1884 he bequeathed it to Brown University. It bears Harris' name and, with extensive additions, has become the largest of its kind in the world.

[John C. Stockbridge, *The Anthony Memorial* (1886); Horatio Rogers, *Private Libs. of Providence* (1878); *New-Eng. Hist. and Geneal. Reg.*, July 1882; G. S. Greene and Louise B. Clarke, *The Greenes of R. I.* (1903); *Providence Jour.*, Oct. 4, 1881.]
E. R. B.

HARRIS, CHAPIN AARON (May 6, 1806–Sept. 29, 1860), dentist, editor, one of the founders of dentistry as an organized profession, was a son of John and Elizabeth (Brundage) Harris. He was born at Pompey, Onondaga County, N. Y., where he received his early education in the public school. In 1824–26 he studied medicine with his brother John at Madison, Ohio. On Jan. 11, 1826, he married Lucinda Heath Hawley of Loudoun County, Va., who became the mother of his nine children. He practised medicine at Greenfield, Ohio, in 1827–28, and in the latter year began the practice of dentistry in the same town, his interest in that profession having been aroused by his brother, who had become a dentist shortly before. He had the degrees of A.M. and M.D., but when and where he received them is uncertain. From 1831 to 1839 he practised dentistry in several cities of the South, with his headquarters in Baltimore, where he was licensed as a dentist in 1833 by the Medical and Chirurgical Faculty of Maryland. About 1833 he was in partnership with his uncle, James H. Harris, in Baltimore, and during the summer months of 1833 and 1834, with F. B. Chewning in Richmond, Va. From 1839 until his death he practised independently in Baltimore. In 1839 he published *The Dental Art, a Practical Treatise on Dental Surgery,* perhaps the most popular dental textbook ever written. Progressively revised and enlarged under the title of *Principles and Practice of Dental Surgery,* it went through twelve editions between 1845 and 1896, was translated into French, and had an extensive sale for half a century. Despite the opposition of Horace H. Hayden [*q.v.*], Harris interested several New York dentists in the establishment of the world's first dental periodical, the *American Journal of Dental Science,* the first number of which appeared in June 1839 with Harris as one of its editors. In the same year he obtained the cooperation of Hayden in the organization of the world's first dental college, the Baltimore College of Dental Surgery, which was chartered and began to function in 1840. Hayden was its first president and Harris its first dean and first professor of operative dentistry and dental prosthesis. In 1840 he was associated with Hayden and others in the organization of the first national dental association, the American Society of Dental Surgeons, of which he was the first corresponding secretary, and from which, as a member, he received one of the original titles of D.D.S. Upon Hayden's death in 1844, Harris succeeded him in the presidency of this society and in the presidency of the college. Harris was one of the organizers of the American Dental Convention in 1855, and president of that organization in 1856–57.

He contributed valuable articles and editorials to the pages of the *American Journal of Dental Science.* In its Library Supplement he published his own translations of two popular French dental works, *A Treatise on Second Dentition* (1845), by C. F. Delabarre, and *Complete Elements of the Science and Art of the Dentist* (1847), by A. M. Desirabode. In 1846 he issued an edition of the *Natural History and Diseases of the Human Teeth* by Joseph Fox, remodeled, with an introduction and additions. He also compiled *A Dictionary of Dental Science, Biography, Bibliography and Medical Terminology* (1849; and five later editions, 1854–98, without the original biographical and bibliographical notices). It was the only work of the kind in English for nearly three-quarters of a century.

Always a close student, Harris read extensively and accumulated a large private library. He died in his fifty-fifth year, a victim of overwork, and was interred in Mount Olivet Cemetery, Baltimore. His only son to reach maturity, Chapin B. Harris, practised dentistry with him for a time, but was an invalid and died in early manhood. Generous to a fault, Chapin A. Harris left practically no estate. A testimonial fund was raised among dentists for the benefit of his widow and unmarried daughters. There is a portrait bust of Harris at the intersection of Linden and North Avenues, Baltimore, and a Harris and Hayden memorial tablet has been placed in the Baltimore College of Dental Surgery.

[Family records; *Pa. Jour. Dental Sci.,* Jan. 1874; W. Simon, *Hist. of the Baltimore Coll. of Dental Surgery* (1904); J. R. Quinan, *Medic. Annals of Baltimore* (1884); E. F. Cordell, *Medic. Annals of Md.* (1903); B. L. Thorpe, in C. R. E. Koch, *Hist. of Dental Surgery,* vol. III (1910); L. P. Brown, "New Light on Dental History," *Dental Cosmos,* Aug. 1920; B. W. Weinberger, sketch of John Harris, *Ibid.,* Nov. 1929; obituaries in *Am. Jour. Dental Sci.,* Oct. 1860; *Dental Cosmos,* Dec. 1860, and the *Sun* (Baltimore), Oct. 1, 1860.]

L. P. B.

HARRIS, CHARLES KASSELL (May 1, 1865–Dec. 22, 1930), song-writer, music publisher, was the son of Jacob and Rachel Harris of Poughkeepsie, N. Y., where he was born. When he was about a year old his parents moved to Saginaw, Mich. The boy attended school in East Saginaw, and after school hours, perched on a fence between his father's tailor shop and the town hotel, he would watch variety entertainers rehearse their acts. One of the actors whom he admired gave him an old banjo, and soon he learned a few tunes by ear. When he was fourteen his family moved to Milwaukee. Two years later a disappointment in love inspired his first song, "Can Hearts So Soon Forget," which remained in manuscript until he himself published it, years later. During the following years he wrote a number of songs of the ballad type. He was not a trained musician, but he was apt at inventing melodies, and while he picked out his tunes by ear at the piano, a friend transcribed them and provided an accompaniment. In 1892 he wrote his biggest hit, "After the Ball," which netted him over $100,000 and was still selling at the rate of 5,000 copies annually more than thirty years later. It was a ballad with a story, founded on an actual incident witnessed by Harris at a ball he had attended in Chicago. He had difficulty in inducing a singer to perform it in public, but when James Aldrich Libby introduced it in Hoyt's *Trip to Chinatown,* at the Chicago Bijou Theatre, it swept the country. Sousa's band played it constantly at the Chicago World's Fair and carried its popularity far beyond that year.

Another outstanding song written by Harris was "Break the News to Mother" (1897), supposed to have been suggested by a line in the play, *Secret Service.* It languished for a time and then the Spanish-American War gave it a sudden vogue. Two schoolboy songs, "Always in the Way" (1903), and "Kiss and Let's Make Up" (1891), were also widely sung; and his "Hello, Central, Give me Heaven" (1901), sung in vaudeville by Charles Horwitz, was the first of a long line of telephone songs. Among the others which won more than momentary popularity were " 'Mid the Green Fields of Virginia," "I've a Longing in my Heart, Louise," "The Old Homestead," and "Only a Tangle of Golden Curls." Harris remained a firm believer in the sentimental popular ballad and claimed that the jazz song was merely a passing fad. In his later years, however, he himself wrote no songs that caught the popular fancy as had his earlier works.

Harris established publishing houses in Chicago and New York. In 1903 he moved to the latter city and spent the rest of his life there. As a publisher, aside from putting out his own songs, he will claim remembrance for having brought out Edgar Smith's and A. Baldwin Sloane's "Heaven Will Protect the Working Girl" (1909), sung by Marie Dressler in *Tillie's Nightmare.* He wrote several scenarios, one of which was based on "After the Ball." His autobiography, *After the Ball—Forty Years of Melody* (1926), vividly reflects his sincere, naïve pride in the achievements which permanently identified his name with American popular song writing. Harris died at his home in New York after a brief illness. He was survived by his wife, Cora (Lehrberg) Harris, of Owensboro, Ky., whom he had married Nov. 15, 1893.

[In addition to Harris' autobiography, see *Who's Who in America,* 1920–21; Mark Sullivan, *Our Times,* I (1926), 259–61; Sigmund G. Spaeth, *Read 'Em and Weep* (1926); and obituaries in the *N. Y. Herald-Tribune* and *Milwaukee Jour.,* Dec. 23, 1930.]

F. H. M.

HARRIS, DANIEL LESTER (Feb. 6, 1818–July 11, 1879), engineer, the son of Allen and Hart (Lester) Harris and a descendant of Thomas Harris who settled in Rhode Island with Roger Williams, was born at Providence, R. I. When he was two years old, his father took the family to Plainfield, Conn., where he operated a cotton-mill. Daniel attended the district school and the Plainfield Academy, spending his vacations in his father's mill. He is said to have worked from five in the morning to seven at night, returning to the mill as watchman through the night at the rate of four cents an hour. He entered Wesleyan University at Middletown when he was seventeen and spent three years in the technical school there. Upon graduation in 1838 he chose civil engineering as his field and went to work with the Norwich & Worcester Railroad. In 1839 he was employed on a survey for the Erie Railroad, and from 1840 to 1843 was an assistant engineer with the Troy & Schenectady. This work took him to Springfield, Mass., where he shortly accepted a position with a contractor building the road between Springfield and Hartford. In 1845 he became a member of the firm of Boody, Stone & Harris, and from this time to his death was active in railroad and bridge construction. He was one of the owners of the Howe Truss patent and as such was interested in bridge building throughout the country. Among the important contracts with which he was closely associated was that for the construction of twenty-seven bridges for the Hartford, Providence & Fishkill Railroad, including the bridge over the Connecticut River. From railroad constructing he naturally became interested in railroad management. In 1855 he was made a director of the Connecticut River Railroad and very soon afterward, president, in which position he served until 1879. Under his direction the road flourished and Harris was known as a leading railroad executive. In 1859, for the Russian Government, he made an examination and reported upon the condition and safety of the bridges of the St. Petersburg & Moscow Railroad. He was appointed a government director of the Union Pacific in 1869. An important part of his railroad work was the twelve years (1866–78) which he devoted to the Eastern Railroad Association as secretary and virtual manager during an early and crucial period of its life. He went to London for the Association in 1874, to assist in introducing the vacuum brake into England. In addition to his active business life, he devoted a great amount of time to public service. He was chosen a member of the Massachusetts House of Representatives five times between 1857 and 1873 and was mayor of Springfield, Mass., in 1860. He married Harriet Octavia Corson of Canastota, N. Y., May 25, 1843, and had eleven children. He died at Springfield, Mass.

[H. M. Burt, *Memorial Tributes to Daniel Lester Harris* (1880); *Alumni Record of Wesleyan Univ.* (1883); *Springfield Republican,* July 12, 1879.]

F. A. T.

HARRIS, ELISHA (Mar. 5, 1824–Jan. 31, 1884), pioneer sanitarian, was born at Westminster, Vt., the son of James and Eunice (Foster) Harris. As a child he was frail, but in adult life he was described as of good physique, temperate habits, and capable of a prodigious amount of work. He attended a country school near his father's farm, taught school before studying medicine under Dr. S. B. Woolworth, and in 1849 graduated from the College of Physicians and Surgeons in New York City. Soon afterward he married Eliza Andrews, daughter of Josiah B. Andrews. Mrs. Harris died in 1867. They had no children, and Harris did not remarry. He began the practice of medicine in New York City, and in 1855 became superintendent of the quarantine hospital on Staten Island. Four years later he was given charge of the construction of the floating hospital to be anchored below the Narrows. He was a member of the National Quarantine and Sanitary Association and a member of the committee which prepared the "code of marine hygiene" adopted at its Boston convention of 1860. This code comprehended all the essential details of the port quarantine practice in force in New York City for many years thereafter.

Upon the outbreak of the Civil War, he cooperated with Rev. Henry Whitney Bellows [*q.v.*] and others in bringing about the organization of the United States Sanitary Commission, of which he became a member on June 12, 1861. The only experienced sanitarian in that body, he urged the importance of the prevention as well as the relief of sickness and suffering in the army, and contributed *Hints for the Control and Prevention of Infectious Diseases in Camps, Transports, and Hospitals* (1863) to the series of monographs published by the Commission. The sufferings of the wounded during the journey to base hospitals from the battlefields of the Peninsular campaign impelled him to design a hospital car, which was immediately approved and put into use. This invention won two awards in France, and was used by the Prussian army during the Franco-Prussian War. Harris also originated an effective system of national records of the death and burial of soldiers and was one of the editors of the *Sanitary Memoirs of the War of the Rebellion* (2 vols., 1867–69).

As secretary of the Council of Hygiene of the Citizens' Association of New York, he summarized and published (1865) the report of the sanitary survey of the city conducted in 1864 under the direction of Dr. Stephen Smith [*q.v.*]. This report, by calling forceful attention to the existence of appalling conditions, led to the passage of the Metropolitan Health Act (1866) which established New York's first effective board of health. Harris, who had early recognized the importance of vital statistics, was made registrar of records under this board and later sanitary superintendent of the city. In the latter capacity he vigorously enforced the law of 1867 which provided for the regulation and inspection of tenement houses. In 1869 he organized the first free public vaccination service, by means of which in that year alone some fifty or sixty thousand persons were vaccinated. A change in administration in 1870 caused his retirement until 1873, when he was appointed registrar of vital statistics. He left that office in 1876, having reorganized the service and devised a system which was still in use at the time of his death.

In 1872 he was one of the organizers of the American Public Health Association, of which he was the first secretary, and in 1877, president. When the National Board of Health was organized by Act of Congress in 1879, he was one of eight appointed to inspect the sea-port quarantine stations. In 1880 he became one of the three original commissioners and the secretary of the newly organized New York State Board of Health; and also state superintendent of vital statistics, which offices he held until his death. He was active in a number of philanthropic organizations and wrote prolifically on public health and social welfare, most of his papers being published in official reports or in the transactions of the various organizations with which he was affiliated.

[In addition to official reports, see *Jour. Am. Medic. Asso.*, Feb. 16, 1884; *N. Y. Times*, *N. Y. Tribune*, Feb. 1, 1884; *Public Health, Papers and Reports of the Am. Pub. Health Asso.*, esp. vol. X (1885); *Albany Medic. Annals*, Feb. 1884; C. J. Stillé, *Hist. of the U. S. Sanitary Commission* (1866); Alfred Andrews, *Geneal. Hist. of John and Mary Andrews* (1872); S. W. Abbott, *The Past and Present Condition of Public Hygiene and State Medicine in the U. S.* (1900); *A Half Century of Public Health* (1921), ed. by M. P. Ravenel.]

E. W. K.

HARRIS, GEORGE (Apr. 1, 1844–Mar. 1, 1922), Congregational minister, educator, nephew of Samuel Harris [*q.v.*], was born in East Machias, Me., the son of George and Mary A. (Palmer) Harris. He graduated from Amherst College in 1866, and from Andover Theological Seminary in 1869. He was minister of the High Street Congregational Church, Auburn, Me., until 1872, and of the Central Congregational Church, Providence, R. I., until 1883. He married Jane A. Viall of Providence in 1873. In 1883 he became professor of Christian theology in Andover Seminary, succeeding Dr. Edwards Amasa Park. In 1899 he was called to the presidency of Amherst College. Resigning this post in 1912, he resided thereafter for some years in New York.

As minister of the Central Congregational Church in Providence, Harris maintained its high standard of preaching and exerted large influence upon the community and denomination. The movement in the direction of modern thought which he represented was making itself felt in Andover Seminary, and about the time of his arrival, the faculty was largely reconstituted. There was resistance by a part of the denomination, by one of the governing boards of the Seminary, the Visitors, and, incidentally, on the part of the American Board of Commissioners for Foreign Missions. The professors established in 1884 a monthly periodical, the *Andover Review*. Several careful articles, notably those on "Christianity and its Modern Competitors" (November 1886–May 1887), with many unsigned editorials, were written by Harris. In two small volumes, *Progressive Orthodoxy* (1886) and *The Divinity of Jesus Christ* (1893) published by the professors, Harris probably had part. In 1886, charges of heresy were preferred by certain individuals before the Board of Visitors against five professors, of whom Harris was one, but the complaint against Harris and three others was dismissed. In 1896 Harris published *Moral Evolution,* displaying the bent of his mind as somewhat more ethical and practical than strictly theological. This work was followed by *Inequality and Progress* (1897), inspired by his interest in social theory and endeavor. With characteristic common sense and humor, he spoke against the leveling tendency which social enthusiasts sometimes represented.

The opportunity opened before the Seminary was not followed up. Students were choosing seminaries with university connection and urban advantages. Prof. William Jewett Tucker resigned in 1893 to become president of Dartmouth College. Harris accepted, in 1899, the presidency of Amherst College. His years there were marked by no spectacular events. The number of students increased; large additions to endowment were made; he displayed administrative ability and a gift for dealing with men; and he chose teachers with insight. He made courageous modifications of the curriculum and to the end had the united support of students, faculty and alumni. After his retirement he published *A Century's Change in Religion* (1914), in which, with charming deference and humor, he described the surroundings of his own youth. With equal tolerance and sometimes with a sense of wonder he surveyed the theological hostilities which beset his maturer years. He trusted the future of religion in the midst of changes which no one was more quick to recognize than he.

[Geo. Harris and Geo. Harris, Jr., *Jane A. Harris* (n.d.); *Who's Who in America,* 1920–21; *Gen. Cat. of the Theol. Sem., Andover, Mass.* (1909); *Dates and Data* (1926), pub. by the Andover trustees; *Amherst Coll. Biog. Record of the Grads. and Non-Grads.* (1927); *N. Y. Tribune,* Oct. 29, 1891; *Boston Transcript,* Mar. 2, 1922.] E. C. M.

HARRIS, GEORGE WASHINGTON (Mar. 20, 1814–Dec. 11, 1869), humorist, was born in Allegheny City, Pa. At an early age, three or four, he was taken to Knoxville, and after only slight schooling was apprenticed to his half-brother, Samuel Bell, a jeweler. As a youth his craftsmanship and ingenuity, his fondness for steam and engineering, marked him for promotion. When of age he became captain of the *Knoxville,* the first steamboat regularly plying out of that city, and later he engaged in transporting the Cherokees westward. By 1843 he had become pretty well established, advertising in the *Knoxville Register* his new workshop, which was equipped to execute orders "in the metals generally" for "jewelry and silver-ware, copper-plate and wood-engraving, die-sinking, making models of new inventions, every variety of turning in steel, iron and brass, also racing cups." After the Civil War he turned to railroad engineering, becoming superintendent of the Wills Valley Railroad. Always mechanically minded, he completed a number of inventions and contributed to the *Scientific American.* As a writer Harris first contributed political articles in the vigorous Whig campaign of 1839 to the Knoxville *Argus,* then edited by his friend Elbridge G. Eastman. In 1843 he began writing humorous sporting letters to William Trotter Porter [*q.v.*], editor of the New York *Spirit of the Times*; and in 1845 (Aug. 2) contributed his first full-length humorous sketch, "The Knob Dance—A Tennessee Frolic," over the pseudonym Sugartail. From 1843 to 1857 Harris was one of the most popular contributors to the *Spirit,* taking rank with William T. Thompson, T. B. Thorpe, Johnson J. Hooper, and Joseph G. Baldwin. In 1854 the *Spirit* published his first story featuring that egregious Tennesseean Sut Lovingood. Subsequently Sut Lovingood yarns appeared in Knoxville, Chattanooga, and Nashville newspapers, and a collection of them was published in New York by Dick & Fitzgerald in 1867. No other published works are recorded, although it is known he contemplated issuing two other collections of stories, "Smoky Mountain Panther" (about 1843) and "High Times and Hard Times" at the time of his sudden death in 1869; but no trace of either survives. The *Sut Lovingood Yarns* (1867) and his other uncollected humorous sketches are unique in American literature, and except for their dialect and local setting would be nationally known for their rollicking humor. Sut Lovingood is a rough, lanky, uncouth mountaineer of the Great Smokies, whose particular delight in life is perpetrating hilarious pranks. In Harris' hands he immediately becomes a vivid character—in a sense an early prototype of Huck Finn—with a robust and hearty humor, sometimes rough but always funny. The *Yarns* are full of comic situation, plot, and phrase; and his other sketches as well are fresh and racy. Along with their rugged humor these sketches are colored with a sound, homely philosophy; and they delineate in a characteristic manner the localisms, dialect, thoughts, and superstitions of the mountain people of East Tennessee. In Knoxville Harris was a prominent and respected citizen, a Mason, a member of the First Presbyterian Church, a member of the Mechanics Association, treasurer of the Young Men's Literary Society, and postmaster, 1857–58. He was twice married: on Sept. 3, 1835, to Mary Emeline Nance of Knoxville, by whom he had six children; and six weeks before his death to Mrs. Jane E. Pride of Decatur, Ala.

[G. F. Mellen, articles in the Knoxville, Tenn., *Sentinel,* 1909–11; J. T. Brown, in *Library of Southern Lit.,* V (1909), 2099; *Tall Tales of the Southwest* (1930), ed. by F. J. Meine; private information.]

F. J. M.

HARRIS, IRA (May 31, 1802–Dec. 2, 1875), jurist, was born in Charleston, Montgomery County, N. Y., the son of Frederic Waterman and Lucy (Hamilton) Harris. His father's ancestors came from England to Rhode Island; his mother was of Scotch descent. The family moved to Cortland County in 1808 and the boy worked on the farm until he was seventeen. He attended Homer Academy, then entered the junior class of Union College in 1822, graduating with honors two years later. He began the study of law at home but later he was received into the office of Ambrose Spencer [*q.v.*] in Albany and in 1827 he was admitted to the bar. He began his career in Albany, where his success at the bar was immediate. In time he was drawn into politics. He was elected to the Assembly, as a Whig, with Anti-Rent support, for the sessions of 1845 and 1846, was a member of the state constitutional convention in 1846, and in 1847 was a member of the state Senate. Later in 1847 he was elected to the state supreme court for the short term of four years. In 1851 he was reëlected for a full term of eight years and in the same year became a member of the first faculty of the Albany Law School. In 1861, after a year in Europe, he was elected to the United States Senate as a Republican. He succeeded William H. Seward, defeating Horace Greeley and William M. Evarts. In the Senate he was a member of important committees and exercised considerable influence. Though he generally supported the administration and was a close friend of Charles Sumner, he was never an intense partisan and vigorously opposed the expulsion of Senator Jesse D. Bright, of Indiana, who had given a friend a letter of introduction to Jefferson Davis. While in Washington he lectured in the law school of Columbian College (later George Washington University). At the end of his term he was defeated in the Republican caucus by Roscoe Conkling but was chosen a delegate at large to the state constitutional convention the same year.

During Harris' stay in Washington his connection with the Albany Law School had not been entirely broken. On returning to Albany he resumed his place on the faculty and continued to lecture almost up to the time of his death. His interest in education was intense. He was one of the founders of the Albany Medical College (1838), for many years a trustee of Vassar College and Union College, and trustee and chancellor of the University of Rochester (1850–75). Prominent also in Baptist affairs, he was for many years a deacon in Emmanuel Baptist Church in Albany and served as chairman of the American Baptist Missionary Union. He was an eloquent advocate, a graceful orator, and an excellent judge. For almost fifty years he was a prominent figure in Albany and gave lavishly of his time and energy to any movement to advance the intellectual and moral interests of the community. He was twice married: first, to Louisa Tubbs, who died May 17, 1845, and second, to Mrs. Pauline Penny Rathbone, who with two sons and four daughters survived him. His brother, Hamilton Harris (1820–1900), was a prominent lawyer and Republican politician in Albany.

[A. I. Parker, *Landmarks of Albany County* (1897); G. R. Howell and Jonathan Tenney, *Hist. of the County of Albany, N. Y.* (1886); *Memorial of Ira Harris* (Albany, 1876); Irving Browne, "The Albany Law School," *Green Bag,* Apr. 1890; D. S. Alexander, *A Pol. Hist. of the State of N. Y.,* vol. II (1906); J. C. Cooley, *Rathbone Geneal.* (1898); *Albany Argus, N. Y. Tribune,* Dec. 3, 1875; *Albany Law Jour.,* Dec. 11, 1875.]

H. T.

HARRIS, ISHAM GREEN (Feb. 10, 1818–July 8, 1897), politician, the youngest of the nine children of Isham Green and Lucy (Davidson) Harris, of North Carolinian stock, was born near Tullahoma, Franklin County, Tenn. As a boy he displayed characteristics of seriousness and a sense of responsibility. At the age of fourteen, following a brief education in the common schools and at Winchester Academy, he left home and entered a store as clerk in Paris, Tenn. After a few years of successful merchandising in Paris and in Mississippi, he took up the law and was admitted to the bar in 1841. In 1843 he married Martha Travis; there were eight children from this marriage. As a lawyer he won a wide reputation for honesty, forcefulness, and remarkable clearness of mind, and soon he was drawn into a public career extending over fifty years, in the course of which he never suffered a defeat. He was elected to the state Senate in 1847, was a Cass elector in 1848, and was elected to Congress in 1849 and 1851. In 1853 he declined reëlection in order to take up the practice of law in Memphis, but in 1856, as a Southern Rights Democrat, he reëntered the political arena as a candidate for elector at large on the Buchanan ticket. He stumped the state in debate with his chief opponent Neill S. Brown, the former Whig governor, and for the first time since Andrew Jackson's election in 1832, Tennessee voted for a Democratic president. The next year Harris was elected governor against

Robert Hatton. In 1859 he carried the state against John Netherland, nominee of the Opposition state convention. On the local issue of bank restriction, he advocated specie payment. The national and more important issue was slavery. Harris insisted upon the complete support of the Dred Scott decision, which embodied extreme Southern demands, while Hatton and Netherland insisted upon ignoring the slavery issue.

When Lincoln was elected Harris urged secession. He assembled the state legislature on Jan. 7, 1861, and under his advice this body called an election for Feb. 9, to vote for or against a secession convention. Both the convention and secession were defeated by a large majority, but Harris realized that Tennessee would presently have to choose sides, as war was inevitable, and he determined that it should choose the Southern side. When Fort Sumter was fired upon and Lincoln called for volunteers, Harris spurned the call and assembled the legislature (Apr. 25), and pushed through two ordinances, one declaring Tennessee independent, the other providing for union with the Confederacy. This was a *coup d'état,* for the legislature had no authority to pass ordinances. Harris, however, submitted these ordinances to a plebiscite which supported them by a large majority (June 8, 1861). In the meantime he executed another revolutionary coup. He had the legislature pass an act May 7, 1861, allying Tennessee with the Confederacy and placing the state troops at the disposal of that government. This committed Tennessee to the Confederate cause regardless of the outcome of the plebiscite of the following June. However, the fact that Harris raised 100,000 troops for the Confederacy would indicate that he had followed the desires of the majority. He was elected in the autumn of 1861, and, though Robert L. Caruthers was elected in 1863, he was nominally governor of Tennessee until the war ended, owing to the fact that Caruthers did not qualify. After 1862, with the Federals in occupation of Tennessee, Harris was forced to leave the state. He became a voluntary member of the staffs of Albert Sidney Johnston, Braxton Bragg, and Joseph E. Johnston and fought in every important battle of the West except Perryville, Ky.

When the war ended Harris fled to Mexico with a price upon his head. From Mexico he went to England. In 1867 he returned to Memphis where he resumed the practice of law. In 1877 he was elected to the United States Senate where, until his death in 1897, he took an active part and held membership on such important committees as rules, finance, and claims. He fought to rid the South of the evils of radical rule and championed the agrarian demands for paper money and free silver, bank reforms and tariff reduction. Possessing great force of will, honesty, and courage, he was one of the strongest men of his times.

[*Memorial Addresses on the Life and Character of Isham G. Harris* (1898), delivered in the Senate and House of Representatives; J. W. Caldwell, *Sketches of the Bench and Bar of Tenn.* (1898); Jas. Phelan, *Hist. of Tenn.* (1888); J. T. Moore and A. P. Foster, *Tenn., the Volunteer State,* vol. I (1923); Will T. Hale and Dixon H. Merritt, *A Hist. of Tenn. and Tennesseans* (1913), vols. I–III; J. W. Fertig, *The Secession and Reconstruction of Tenn.* (1898); *Commercial Appeal* (Memphis), *Nashville American, Evening Star* (Washington), July 9, 1897.]

F. L. O.

HARRIS, JAMES ARTHUR (Sept. 29, 1880–Apr. 24, 1930), botanist, biometrician, the son of Jordan Thomas and Ida Ellen (Lambert) Harris, was born on a farm near Plantsville, Athens County, Ohio, and died at St. Paul, Minn. He was of old American stock of English origin, his great-grandfather, Watson Harris, having emigrated to Athens County from Maine about 1790. On his mother's side he was descended on the one hand from John Lambert, the noted English general under Oliver Cromwell, and on the other from Quaker ancestry, the Embrees. His fifth birthday was spent in a covered wagon, since his parents had begun the long trek of the pioneer migration across the plains. They went first to western Nebraska, then to western Kansas, and a little later to eastern Kansas where they settled on a farm. During this series of migrations the resources of the family became seriously depleted, and accordingly, when the boy was thirteen years old, he undertook to support himself completely. From that age on he received no further financial aid from his parents. His schooling was provided for wholly through his own efforts, and he likewise made provision for the education of his sister. In 1901 he received the degree of A.B. from the University of Kansas, followed by that of M.A. in 1902, and in 1903 the Ph.D. from Washington University, St. Louis. From 1901 to 1903 he was botanical assistant at the Missouri Botanical Gardens, from 1904 to 1907 he was librarian at the same institution, and over the same period of time, 1903–07, he was an instructor in the department of botany of Washington University. In 1907 he joined the staff of the Station for Experimental Evolution of the Carnegie Institution of Washington, with the title of botanical investigator, and held that position until 1924 when he was called to be head of the department of botany of the University of Minnesota, which place he filled with signal honor until his untimely death in his fiftieth year.

Harris was one of the few scientists who have made major contributions in many fields. There was no branch of science which he felt too trivial for exact investigation and accurate measurement. The experiences of his early youth left a profound influence upon his later life, for he was primarily a scientific pioneer. His philosophy of the life of such a pathfinder is expressed in "Frontiers," his presidential address before the Minnesota Chapter of Sigma Xi, June 1929 (*Scientific Monthly,* January 1930). As a man he abhorred artificiality and imitation; as a botanist he believed in studying plants in their own environment. Recognizing that with the advance of agriculture and population the natural environment becomes greatly altered, he was attracted to the wilder natural areas and spent many seasons in studying the vegetation of the Dismal Swamp, the coastal swamps of the Atlantic border of the United States, the Everglades, the deserts and rain-forests of Jamaica and Hawaii, and the deserts of Utah and Arizona. For ten successive seasons he studied the plant associations characteristic of the area lying in the basin of the prehistoric tertiary Lake Bonneville of Utah. His precise methods of thought and work caused him to adapt the more exact technique of physics and chemistry to his studies of plant geography, so that the data which he recorded might be without a personal bias. The United States Department of Agriculture early recognized the importance of his method of attack for agricultural problems, and from 1918 until his death he was a collaborator of the Bureau of Plant Industry, working largely upon problems of cotton and cereal growing in the arid or semi-arid regions of the West.

Early in his career he became interested in the applications of mathematics to biology. In 1908 and 1909 he studied with Karl Pearson in London, and in later years he became America's leading exponent of and contributor to biometrical theory and practice. In 1921 the University of Oxford conferred upon him the Weldon Medal and Weldon Memorial Prize, the highest award possible in the field of biometry. He was a member of many scientific societies, served on many important commissions, during 1926 was president of the American Society of Naturalists, and at the time of his death was a member-at-large of the Division of Biology and Agriculture of the National Research Council. His papers, contributed to scientific journals, number more than three hundred titles and include topics pertaining to almost every field of the biological sciences.

His avocation reflected his love of the frontier: he collected old Navajo rugs, old Pima and Papago Indian baskets, and the tales and traditions of the early West. The Indian wares manufactured for the tourist trade did not attract him, but those things which were a part of the native Indian life and the early days of the white man in the West he sought after and greatly prized. His collection of blankets and baskets rivaled in importance those to be found in the larger American museums. In his home life he was singularly happy. On Apr. 20, 1910, he married Emma Lay of New York City, who with four sons survived him.

[*Who's Who in America,* 1928–29; *Am. Men of Sci.* (1927); *James Arthur Harris: A Memorial Volume,* to be issued by the Univ. of Minn. Press; obituaries in *Minneapolis Tribune,* Apr. 25, 1930; *N. Y. Times,* Apr. 27, 1930; *Science,* May 9 and 23, 1930; *Gamma Alpha Record,* May 1930; *Jour. Am. Statistical Asso.,* Sept. 1930; *Industrial and Engineering Chemistry* (News Ed.), June 20, 1930; personal acquaintance and family records.]

R. A. G.

HARRIS, JOEL CHANDLER (Dec. 9, 1848–July 3, 1908), journalist, author, was born somewhere near Eatonton, Putnam County, Ga., the son of Mary Harris, of Newton County, who had eloped with a young Irish laborer only to be deserted by him before their child was born. His first fourteen years were lived with his mother at Eatonton, where she supported herself by dressmaking and received much kindly help from her neighbors. Listening to her reading of *The Vicar of Wakefield,* he early acquired his devotion to that classic and along with it a desire to write. He attended the local academy and in March 1862 became the printer's devil on the *Countryman,* a weekly newspaper just started by Joseph Addison Turner [*q.v.*] on his plantation, "Turnwold," some nine miles from the village. There he learned to set type and, having the freedom of the estate, an active mind, and unbounded curiosity, became thoroughly at home with all its resident population, animal and human. When he began to smuggle paragraphs of his own into the columns of the paper, Turner took him in hand, lent him books from his library, and schooled him rigorously and wisely in the art of writing. His command of a clear, pure English and his conviction that a writer must look to the life around him for his material Harris owed largely to Turner. This education ended abruptly in November 1864, when the left wing of Sherman's army swept across Putnam County, leaving confusion and desolation in its track. Emerging from the havoc, young Harris found work for a short time as type-setter on the *Macon Telegraph* and then sojourned in New Orleans for six months of 1866–67 as secretary to William Evelyn, publisher of the *Crescent Monthly.* He returned to Eatonton with a bad case of homesickness and never again left his native state for more than a brief outing. A friend, James P. Harrison of Forsyth, gave him employment on the *Monroe Advertiser.* By 1870 his reputation as a newspaper humorist was sufficient to secure him a generous offer from the *Savannah Morning News,* of which William Tappan Thompson [*q.v.*] was editor. In Savannah he met Esther LaRose, daughter of a French-Canadian landowner and steamboat captain, and on Apr. 21, 1873, they were married. When yellow fever visited the city in 1876, Harris, apprehensive for his wife and two children, resigned his position and took his family to Atlanta, where he soon joined the staff of the *Atlanta Constitution,* of which Evan P. Howell had just bought control. For twenty-four years Harris remained on the *Constitution,* writing political editorials, feature articles, fiction, book-reviews, and special items. Except for the first fourteen and the last eight years of his life he was thus an active journalist. Although he lacked the pyrotechnic qualities that won national attention for his colleague, Henry Woodfin Grady [*q.v.*], he was within his own state an influential liberal.

His literary career grew directly out of his newspaper work. One of his first duties on the *Constitution* was to write humorous sketches of negro character, sometimes with a political bearing, to take the place of similar matter that had been contributed by Sam W. Small. During his boyhood and apprenticeship at "Turnwold" he had been absorbing the negro speech and folk-tales as unconsciously as a melon draws its nutriment from soil and atmosphere; not until he read William Owens' "Folklore of the Southern Plantation" in *Lippincott's Magazine* for December 1877 did he realize what literary wealth he had in storage. He wrote the first of the animal tales with painstaking care, withholding them from the press until he could represent the middle Georgia negro speech of Uncle Remus with the utmost attainable fidelity. With Daddy Jack's Gullah dialect he appears to have been less successful. The tales were immediately popular, the *Springfield Republican* and the New York *Evening Post* giving them a hearty welcome in the North; Harris was deluged with letters of inquiry; and Joseph Cephas Derby, the energetic manuscript scout of D. Appleton & Company, induced him to publish *Uncle Remus: His Songs and His Sayings* (1880). This volume and its continuation, *Nights with Uncle Remus* (1883), seem secure of their place among the unforgettable books of American literature. Later additions to the Uncle Remus cycle were: *Daddy Jake the Runaway and Short Stories Told after Dark* (1889); *Uncle Remus and his Friends* (1892); *On the Plantation* (1892); *The Tar Baby and Other Rhymes of Uncle Remus* (1904); *Told by Uncle Remus* (1905); *Uncle Remus and Brer Rabbit* (1906); *Uncle Remus and the Little Boy* (1910); and *Uncle Remus Returns* (1918). These later volumes are addressed more exclusively to children and have some of the handicaps adherent to all sequels. Interest has often centered on the proportions of nature and of art in the stories. Harris insisted that he was a mere compiler and that the tales were "uncooked." That he was always faithful to the pattern of his original is hardly to be questioned, but many of them were worked up from bare outlines (for one example see Julia Collier Harris, *post,* pp. 197–98), and much of their piquancy results from the fact that Uncle Remus, or his amanuensis, was a close student of the masters of English prose. The subtlety and completeness of the characterization of the old negro have always been remarked; the suggestion of a whole animal community, the elaborate dialogue of the animals, and the rich background of the plantation are inseparable from the stories as Harris tells them and are almost certainly his creation (E. C. Parsons, "Joel Chandler Harris and Negro Folklore," *Dial,* May 17, 1919).

Harris also produced several volumes of children's stories, a few poems, various articles and editorials for the *Saturday Evening Post,* a quantity of miscellaneous matter, two inchoate novels, *Sister Jane, Her Friends and Acquaintance* (1896) and *Gabriel Tolliver, a Story of Reconstruction* (1902), and a number of short stories in which he depicted certain Georgia types and conditions with a tactful realism but honestly and out of ample knowledge. These stories were republished in *Mingo and Other Sketches in Black and White* (1884), *Free Joe and Other Georgian Sketches* (1887), *Balaam and his Master* (1891), *Tales of the Home Folks in Peace and War* (1898), *Chronicles of Aunt Minerva Ann* (1899), *On the Wing of Occasions* (1900), and *The Making of a Statesman* (1902). His strongest work in this kind is in the first two volumes. Like so many American writers, he never advanced beyond his initial successes. From June 1907 until his death he was editor of *Uncle Remus's Magazine,* a Southern monthly that failed to secure the support expected for it.

Twenty-eight years of literary fame could not alter his habits, which were those of a sedate, home-loving country journalist, or change his appearance, which corresponded to his habits. When not in his office he was at his home, the "Wren's Nest" in West End, or at work in his spacious garden. The hardships of his childhood had made him inveterately shy; among strangers his voice failed him; at a New Orleans hotel he could not muster enough courage to read aloud to a group of admiring children (Mark Twain, *Life on the Mississippi,* Chapter xlvii). Only after much persuasion did he spend a night with President Roosevelt at the White House, but among old friends, associates, and neighbors—among "folks"—he was sociable and brimming with good humor and he enjoyed a notable friendship with James Whitcomb Riley. Two weeks before his death, which was caused by cirrhosis of the liver, he was baptized into the Roman Catholic Church. His wife and five of his eight children survived him. He was buried in Westview Cemetery, Atlanta; his home is preserved as a memorial; and his birth is celebrated annually in the public schools of Georgia.

[*The Life and Letters of Joel Chandler Harris* (1918) by his daughter-in-law, Julia Collier Harris, is the only full biography. R. L. Wiggins' *The Life of Joel Chandler Harris from Obscurity in Boyhood to Fame in Early Manhood* (Nashville, Tenn., 1918), a study of his literary development up to the publication of *Uncle Remus: His Songs and His Sayings,* reproduces all his significant early writing. Both volumes include bibliographies, as does C. A. Smith's chapter, "Dialect Writers," *Cambridge Hist. Am. Lit.,* vol. II (1918). Later references may be traced most conveniently through G. G. Griffin's *Writings on Am. Hist.* (*Ann. Report Am. Hist. Asso., Supplement*). See also: F. P. Gaines, *The Southern Plantation: A Study in the Development and the Accuracy of a Tradition* (1924); J. H. Nelson, *The Negro Character in Am. Lit.* (Lawrence, Kan., 1926); H. W. Odum, *An Am. Epoch* (1930).]

G. H. G.

HARRIS, JOHN (1726–July 29, 1791), Indian trader, founder of Harrisburg, Pa., son of John and Esther (Say) Harris, was born at Harris Ferry. His parents came from Yorkshire, England, his father being of Welsh descent and a brewer by occupation. Coming to Pennsylvania at an early date, John Harris worked his way to the back-country by easy stages, established a trading-post at Paxtang on the Susquehanna, purchased 900 acres of land, opened a ferry there, and became a prosperous trader and farmer. Esther Harris, a typical pioneer's wife, was cool, alert, and quick-witted. On his father's death in 1748 the management of the farm, trading-post, and ferry devolved on John Harris, the younger. He proved to be as capable and energetic as his father had been. For thirty years, as trader, frontiersman, or officer in the provincial service, he wrote repeatedly to provincial or state officials urging defense against Indian raids, almost invariably giving warning that failure to take drastic action in protecting the frontier would lead to the abandonment or annihilation of the white settlements. Personally determined to hold his post to the last extremity, during the French and Indian War he recruited men, fortified his house, and in 1756 erected a stockade. Frequent conferences with the Indians were held at his place, one of which, on Apr. 1, 1757, a large delegation of warriors from the Six Nations attended. Although Harris was drastic and firm in his relations with the Indians, he nevertheless enjoyed their confidence. One of their chiefs, in requesting the removal of dishonest traders (Aug. 23, 1762), spoke of him as "the most suitable Man to keep Store" because "he is very well known by us all in our Nation, as his Father was before him (*Pennsylvania Colonial Records,* VIII, 1852, 754). Confident of the future development of Harris Ferry, he built a fine residence there in 1766 and in 1775 planned to lay out a town, but war intervened. To the Revolution he gave liberally of his money and influence. After the war he renewed his plans for a town. In 1785 Dauphin County was created with Harrisburg the county seat. Harris conveyed land for a court house, jail, and square to trustees, as well as his right and title to the ferry, and in return he was given authority to lay out a town and to sell lots. He lived to see the town prosper and died at the scene of his life's work. A lover of his gun, rod, and dog, he was very much a part of the back-country in which he lived. His wife was Elizabeth, daughter of David and Margaret McClure.

[W. H. Egle, *Centenary Memorial of the Erection of the County of Dauphin* (1886), *Hist. of the Counties of Dauphin and Lebanon* (1883), and *Notes and Queries, Biog. and Geneal.,* 3 ser., vol. II (1896), and annual vol., 1897 (1898); *Hist. Colls. of the State of Pa.* (1843), ed. by Sherman Day; *Minutes of the Provincial Council of Pa.,* vol. III (1852), vols. IV–VII (1851); *Pa. Archives,* 1 ser., vols. III–VI (1853).]

J. H. P—g.

HARRIS, JOHN WOODS (1810–Apr. 1, 1887), lawyer, was born in Nelson County, Va. His early education, which was obtained at the rural school near his home, was very meager, but as he approached manhood he became fired with an ambition to secure an education and become a lawyer. Accordingly he spent a year in Washington College, now Washington and Lee University, and five more at the University of Virginia, where he graduated in 1837, having "attained distinguished proficiency" in the law. In 1837, soon after leaving the university, he emigrated to the newly established republic of Texas and began the practice of law in Brazoria County. A little later he became affiliated with John A. Wharton and Elisha Marshall Pease, the former an outstanding man of the Texas Revolution, and the latter destined to serve the state as governor at two separate periods of its history. In 1839 Harris was elected a member of the Congress of the Republic. In this capacity he had a profound influence on the laws of the new state. As chairman of the judiciary committee, he introduced the bill, and secured its enactment into law, by which the existing Mexican laws were repealed and the common law of England was adopted in all civil matters. (The common law as to criminal matters had been established by the constitution of the republic adopted in 1836.) The act adopting the common law also established, or kept in force, the "community property" system substantially as it existed in Spanish law. This was an innovation in Anglo-Saxon countries which was later adopted in several states of the Union. At the same session of Congress he secured the enactment of a number of other important laws, based largely on the statutes of Virginia.

When Texas became a state of the Union in 1846, Harris was appointed its first attorney-general and was reappointed by the next governor. In this capacity he rendered signal service in defending the new constitution and statutes against hostile attacks in the courts. In 1854 Governor Pease named him as one of the commissioners, along with James Willie and O. C. Hartley, to revise the laws of the state. The penal code and code of criminal procedure drafted mainly by Willie and based on the codes drafted by Edward Livingston for the state of Louisiana were adopted by the legislature, but the code of civil procedure drafted by Hartley and the revised statutes prepared by Harris were not adopted. Harris' last public service was as a member of the Fourteenth Legislature, which met in 1874–75 and passed the bill calling for the constitutional convention of 1875. He was an able lawyer and acquired a competence from the practice of his profession. In politics he was an ardent Democrat, and though he had opposed secession, he supported the Confederacy. He died in Galveston, where he had settled after the war. His wife, Annie Pleasants (Fisher) Dallam, the daughter of S. Rhodes Fisher, whom he had married in 1852, survived him.

[Available sources of information regarding Harris include J. D. Lynch, *The Bench and Bar of Tex.* (1885); P. D. Barringer, J. M. Garnett, and Rosewell Page, *Univ. of Va.* (1904), vol. II; *Dallas News* and *Galveston News*, Apr. 2, 1887. Information as to certain facts has been supplied for this sketch by Harris' daughter, Mrs. Cora L. Davenport, San Antonio, Tex., and by the University of Virginia. The exact date of Harris' birth was unknown even to his wife.]

C. S. P.

HARRIS, JOSEPH (June 29, 1828–Nov. 18, 1892), farmer, writer, editor, was born at Shrewsbury, England, near the famous battlefield of Hastings. His parents were Henry and Anne (Webb) Harris. At an early age he developed an unusual talent for investigation, which was greatly increased by his being associated as a student with Sir John Bennet Lawes and Sir Joseph Henry Gilbert, experimenters and research workers in agriculture on the experiment farm at Rothamsted, England. He came to America as a young man, in 1849, and soon after establishing himself became a regular writer and contributor to farm magazines. In 1855 he was associate editor of the *Country Gentleman* and for a number of years he was owner and editor of the *Genesee Farmer*. In 1866, when he transferred the latter to the *American Agriculturist*, he became partner to Orange Judd [*q.v.*] and contributed to the journal until his death. He was an able writer and was particularly well known for his department on "Walks and Talks on the Farm," which was eagerly read by thousands of farmers. In 1879 he started a seed business, carrying it on until his death in 1892, after which it was operated under his name at Coldwater, N. Y.

Harris was the author of several farm books, among which were *Harris on the Pig* (1870), *Talks on Manures* (1878), and *Gardening for Young and Old* (1883). These books were written in the spirit of an investigator and research worker and were the answers to questions which he himself had put to the soils and animals instead of to men for the answers. He was one of the first to see the need of a good garden on every farm and developed this idea both in his magazine writings and in his book on gardening. His work on swine was used quite generally as a textbook by the earlier agricultural schools and colleges. Harris died at "Moreton Farm," near Rochester, N. Y., where he had maintained a home since 1862. He had married, in 1861, Sarah A. Mathews. As an agriculturist he will be remembered for his scientific approach to farm problems and for his ability to disseminate his information among farmers in a form which was understandable and usable.

[F. M. Hexamer, article in L. H. Bailey, *Cyc. of Am. Horticulture*, vol. II (1900); "Western N. Y. Horticultural Soc. Proc., 1893," in *Docs. of the Assembly of the State of N. Y., No. 67*, 1893; *Am. Agriculturist*

Jan. 1893; information as to certain facts from Harris' son, S. M. Harris.] E. R. E.

HARRIS, MAURICE HENRY (Nov. 9, 1859–June 23, 1930), rabbi, was born in London, England, the son of the Rev. Henry L. and Rachel (Levy) Harris. He was the brother of Isidore Harris, who became the scholarly minister of the Berkeley Street Synagogue in London. At nineteen he emigrated to the United States. After spending a short time in secretarial work in one of the early telegraph companies in New York, he followed his family tradition and natural bent towards the ministry and entered the Emanu-El Theological Seminary. In 1883 he became student preacher of an obscure synagogue, the Hand in Hand, which met over a store on East 116th Street, and with this congregation, the only one he ever served during his forty-seven years of ministry, Harris was associated until his death. In 1884 he was ordained by Rabbi Gustav Gottheil, and concurrently with his ministerial activities he studied at Columbia College, receiving the degrees of A.B., 1887; A.M., 1888; and Ph.D., 1889. On Aug. 14, 1888, he married Kitty Green of London, who bore him one son and two daughters.

Harris progressively led his congregation away from the orthodox traditions of the Hand in Hand Synagogue until it became one of the leading reform synagogues of the metropolis, Temple Israel. Through all the factional struggle which that transition involved, he retained the respect and the love of all his congregation. Greatly interested in social work, he was the founder (1905) and president of the Federation Settlement on East 106th Street, in a poor and congested neighborhood, and engaged in active work for the Jewish Protectory and Aid Society, which later became the Jewish Board of Guardians. In the rabbinical field he served as president of the New York Board of Jewish Ministers, and of the Association of Reform Rabbis of New York. He was one of the founders of the Jewish Institute of Religion, and one of its trustees from its foundation. His extensive library was given by his widow for the most part to that institute and to the Hebrew University in Jerusalem. Though he was at first opposed to Zionism, his visit to the Holy Land in the summer of 1921 gave him an understanding insight into the nature of Jewish aspiration and achievement in Palestine, and one of the results of that journey was his organization in America of an annual campaign among the children in American Jewish religious schools for the provision of school lunches for poor Jewish children in Palestine. This work, sponsored by the (American) Women's Zionist Organization, Hadassah, grew steadily in scope under Harris' direction, and after his death a model experimental station in school dietetics was established in Palestine in his memory.

Harris was a clear and painstaking writer. His principal publications were religious textbooks, among which may be mentioned *Judaism and the Jew* (1925) and his popular series of volumes of Biblical and post-Biblical Jewish history: *The People of the Book* (3 vols., 1886–90); *A Thousand Years of Jewish History* (1904); the *History of the Mediæval Jews* (1907); and *Modern Jewish History* (1910). His sermons, always carefully prepared and delivered with engaging simplicity and modesty, reflected extensive reading, sincerity, innate kindliness of judgment, and interest in human problems. He was essentially a lover of mankind. His relations with his congregation were beautifully intimate and fatherly, and his benign, pacific, and gentle nature drew to him the affection and good will of all of his people.

[*Central Conference of Am. Rabbis: Forty-first Ann. Convention*, 1930, pp. 220–22; *Who's Who in America*, 1930–31; the *Am. Hebrew*, June 27, 1930; *N. Y. Times*, June 24, 1930.] D. deS. P.

HARRIS, MERRIMAN COLBERT (July 9, 1846–May 8, 1921), missionary bishop of the Methodist Episcopal Church, was born at Beallsville, Ohio. His father was Colbert Harris, a landowner, farmer, and school-teacher in southeastern Ohio; his mother was Elizabeth Crupper of Virginia. Early in life he was influenced by a teacher, Robert L. Morris, who was interested in foreign missions, and by James M. Thoburn [*q.v.*], who took up his life work in India, and he decided to become a missionary. The course of his training was interrupted by the Civil War. He enlisted in the 12th Ohio Volunteer Cavalry in 1863 and remained until his regiment was mustered out in 1865, serving with Sheridan's Cavalry, and with Sherman's troops on the march through Georgia. After the war, with his scant savings of pay and bounties, he attended theological schools at Harlem Springs, Wash., and at Scio, Ohio, then he taught school for two years at Fairview, Ohio. In 1869 he joined the Pittsburgh Conference and was assigned to the pastorate at Urichsville, Ohio, but in 1871 he left the active ministry and entered Allegheny College at Meadville, Pa., where he graduated in 1873 with the degree of A.B. On Oct. 23, 1873, he married Flora Lydia Best, daughter of Dr. David Best of Meadville, Pa.

Appointed missionaries to Japan, Harris and

his wife at once set out for their chosen field, which proved to be the newly opened port of Hakodate, in the far north. In the short space of five years, and in spite of much anti-foreign sentiment, Harris had established a church, and his wife had opened the Caroline Wright School for girls. He had served also as consular representative of the United States, having been appointed vice-consul at Hakodate on Oct. 29, 1875, and consular agent, Jan. 3, 1877. In 1879 he was transferred to Tokio, as presiding elder. This work was interrupted by the illness of Mrs. Harris and they were transferred to San Francisco, where, from 1886 to 1904, Harris was superintendent of the Japanese mission of the Methodist Church. He established missions on the Pacific Coast and in Hawaii and organized them into a Pacific Japanese Mission. In 1904 he left this work to become bishop of Japan and Korea, an office which he filled with credit until 1916, when he asked to be relieved. Thereafter he was retained as bishop emeritus. On the eve of his departure for America in 1916 one hundred of the leading men of Japan gave him a banquet. In making a farewell address on that occasion, Viscount Kaneko, the foreign minister, said in part, "If all Americans dealt with us as openheartedly as Dr. Harris does, and if we revered Americans as we revere Dr. Harris, friendship between Japan and America would remain unchanged forever" (*Outlook*, June 28, 1916, p. 455). The Emperor honored the occasion by conferring on Harris the highest of his three decorations, giving him second-class rank in the order of the Sacred Treasure. On returning to Japan later in the same year he was presented with "a beautiful house fully furnished," situated on the Methodist grounds at Aoyama. Here he died, May 8, 1921, and was buried. The Emperor expressed his grief by the gift of 500 yen; floral offerings came from the highest officials of the government; and the Japanese press united in eulogizing his life and work.

In addition to his other activities Harris found time for writing. His published works include *One Hundred Years of Missions, Christianity in Japan* (1908), and *Japanese Proverbs.* Such was his enthusiasm for the Japanese and their institutions that he sometimes contended that they were occidental rather than oriental. The latter term seemed to connote "heathen" in his mind. Much of the success of his work was ascribed to the help and sympathy of his first wife. She was an accomplished writer and translator and was spoken of as his "poet-wife." She died in September 1909 and on Nov. 1, 1919, he married her cousin, Elizabeth Best, who survived him.

[*The Meth. Year Book,* 1922; *Who's Who in America,* 1920–21; *Christian Advocate,* May 12, June 30, Aug. 11, 1921; *Jour. of the Twenty-ninth Delegated Gen. Conference of the Meth. Episc. Ch.* (1924), pp. 852–53; *N. Y. Times,* May 9, 12, 1921; *Japan Times and Mail* (Tokio), May 11, 12, 1921; *Japan Advertiser* (Tokio), May 10, 11, 12, 1921.] H. N. A.

HARRIS, MIRIAM COLES (July 7, 1834–Jan. 23, 1925), novelist, daughter of Butler and Julia Anne (Weeks) Coles, was born at Dosoris, near Glen Cove, Long Island, N. Y. The Coles family in America was descended from Robert Coles, who came to Boston from Suffolk, England, in 1630, in the same fleet with Governor Winthrop. The widow and children of Robert Coles removed to Long Island, where the family acquired property and remained through succeeding generations. The grandfather of Miriam Coles was Nathaniel Coles, who was a direct descendant of Rev. Francis Doughty, the first patroon of the Newtown and Flushing section, and, it is said, the first preacher in English on Manhattan. Miriam Coles was educated at St. Mary's Hall, Burlington, N. J., and at Madame Canda's exclusive school in New York City. On Apr. 20, 1864, she married Sidney S. Harris, a New York lawyer. She had two children, a son and a daughter, and except for her writing, her early life was domestic and uneventful. Her first literary work was for periodicals. Her first novel, *Rutledge,* was published anonymously in 1860, after which others followed: *Louie's Last Term at St. Mary's* (1860), an autobiographical story; *The Sutherlands* (1862); *Frank Warrington* (1863); *Roundhearts and Other Stories* (1867); *St. Philip's* (1871); *Richard Vandermarck* (1871); *A Perfect Adonis* (1875); *Missy* (1880); *Happy-Go-Lucky* (1881); *Phoebe* (1884); *An Utter Failure* (1891); *A Chit of Sixteen, and Other Stories* (1892); and *The Tents of Wickedness* (1907). *A Corner of Spain* (1898) records some of her travels, and *A Rosary for Lent* (1867) and *Dear Feast of Lent* (1874) are devotional books. Her novels, which were considerably read during the late nineteenth century, are all of the same type. They are weak and melodramatic in plot, stilted and artificial in characterization, full of pious sentiments and moral maxims, and tedious and cumbersome in style. *Rutledge,* a sentimental story of the love of a middle-aged man and a young girl, is the book upon which her reputation rests and is representative of a type of romance popular in its period. In 1892 Mr. Harris died and thereafter Mrs. Harris spent much time abroad. She died at her home on the Boulevard des Pyrénées, at Pau, France.

[*Who's Who in America*, 1920–21; F. T. Cole, *The Early Geneals. of the Cole Families in America* (1887); obituary in the *N. Y. Times*, Jan. 25, 1925.] S. G. B.

HARRIS, NATHANIEL HARRISON (Aug. 22, 1834–Aug. 23, 1900), lawyer, and Confederate soldier, was born at Natchez, Miss., the son of William Mercer and Caroline (Harrison) Harris. He was given a collegiate education, took up the study of law, and was graduated from the University of Louisiana. He had an elder brother who was a lawyer at Vicksburg, and he himself settled there for the practice of his profession. On the outbreak of the Civil War he organized a company of infantry, the Warren Rifles, which was mustered into the state service May 8, 1861. On June 1 the company was enlisted in the service of the Confederate states as Company C, 19th Mississippi Infantry. The regiment left Richmond July 4, joined the forces of Gen. J. E. Johnston confronting Patterson's army in the upper Shenandoah Valley, and reached Manassas the day after the battle. Harris was praised by Col. L. Q. C. Lamar for gallantry at the battle of Williamsburg and was promoted major Mar. 5, 1862. After the Maryland campaign he was promoted lieutenant-colonel, and on Apr. 2, 1863, he was made colonel of his regiment. At the battle of Chancellorsville he was with Stonewall Jackson in his famous flank attack. At Gettysburg the 19th Mississippi, under command of Harris as a part of Posey's brigade, forced Meade's line from Cemetery Ridge. He was appointed brigadier-general Jan. 20, 1864. At Spotsylvania his brigade was ordered by Lee to meet the attack of Hancock's corps which had carried the salient held by Johnston's division and known to history as the "Bloody Angle," and was afterward engaged in all the sanguinary conflicts preceding the siege of Petersburg. The brigade occupied the Rives salient on the Petersburg line. In November 1864 it was relieved from duty in the trenches and put in reserve. In December and January it marched to thwart Grant's persistent efforts to cut the Weldon railroad. In March Harris was placed in command of the inner line of defenses of Richmond to meet Sheridan's raid. When at last the Confederate line was broken Harris was ordered to throw two regiments of his brigade into Battery Gregg and two into Battery Whitworth. These earthworks between the front line and the Appomattox River were held against terrific assaults for two hours until the arrival of Longstreet who formed an inner line of defense. At Appomattox Harris was in command of Mahone's division.

After the surrender of Lee's army Harris returned to Vicksburg and resumed the practice of law. When the Mississippi Valley & Ship Island Railroad was reorganized he was made its president. In 1885 he was appointed register of the United States land office at Aberdeen, S. Dak. In 1890 he visited California and later made San Francisco his home, engaging in business with John Hays Hammond. He died at Malvern, England, Aug. 23, 1900. In accordance with his wish his body was cremated. He was unmarried.

[N. H. Harris, "Defence of Battery Gregg," in *Southern Hist. Soc. Papers*, vol. VIII (1880); *Confed. Mil. Hist.* (1899), vol. VII; *War of the Rebellion: Official Records (Army)*; *Official and Statistical Reg. of the State of Miss.* (1908); *Movements of the Confederate Army in Va. and the Part Taken Therein by the 19th Miss. Reg. From the Diary of Gen. Nat. H. Harris* (1901), by Capt. W. M. Harris (his brother); Dunbar Rowland, *Mississippi* (1907), vol. I; *San Francisco Call*, Aug. 24, 1900; *Vicksburg Herald*, Aug. 24, 29, 1900.] D. R.

HARRIS, ROLLIN ARTHUR (Apr. 18, 1863–Jan. 20, 1918), oceanographer, mathematician, third of the six children of Francis Eugene and Lydia Helen (Crandall) Harris, was a great-grandson of John Harris, a Vermont farmer and surveyor who fought in the Revolutionary War. He was born on a small farm in Randolph, N. Y., but the family later moved to a farm near Jamestown, N. Y., and here he received his education in the local schools, graduating from Jamestown High School in 1881. That fall he entered Cornell University, where he was graduated four years later with the degree of Ph.B. Remaining at Cornell for postgraduate work, he specialized in mathematics and physics and received the degree of Ph.D. in 1888. He was then offered a fellowship at Clark University, where for a year he pursued special studies in mathematics. On June 13, 1890, he married Emily J. Doty of Falconer, N. Y., and in the following month entered the Coast and Geodetic Survey as computer. Here, in the mathematical development of the abstruse subject of the tides he found scope for his exceptional training and native ability. His "Manual of Tides" is the most exhaustive treatise on the subject to the present time (1931). It appeared in parts as appendices to the *Report of the Superintendent of the U. S. Coast and Geodetic Survey* for 1894, 1897, 1900, 1904, and 1907. In this "Manual" he forwarded the subject in many directions, on the technical side as well as on the hydrodynamic side; in it he developed his stationary-wave theory of the tide, published his cotidal maps, and suggested an improved form of tide predictor which is now used by the Coast and Geodetic Survey. In connection with the study of the tides of the Arctic Ocean (see his *Arctic Tides,* 1911), Harris directed attention to the possibility that the characteristics of the tide on the Arctic shores might throw light on the geography of the unexplored area lying northward of the known land masses. From a study of the very meager tidal data of that region he concluded that a large tract of land lay to the north of Alaska. Later observations and research have shown that the features of the Arctic tides on which he based his inference of land are due to other causes, but his hypothesis was fruitful in directing the attention of explorers to the importance of the geographical study of tides and in stimulating interest in Arctic exploration by suggesting the possibility of the discovery of a large land mass. He was an indefatigable worker and published a number of articles on mathematical and tidal subjects in various scientific journals, but owing to his modest bearing and somewhat retiring disposition, and to the restricted nature of his highly specialized and abstruse field, he did not command the position in American science to which his scientific contributions and his unquestioned ability entitled him. Among the students of tides and hydrodynamics, however, he has been accorded a secure place as one of the outstanding figures in that domain of science.

[*Who's Who in America,* 1918–19; *Science,* Feb. 15, 1918; *Cornell Alumni News,* Feb. 7, 1918; *Evening Star* (Washington), Jan. 21, 1918; J. P. Downs and F. W. Hedley, *Hist. of Chautauqua County, N. Y.* (1921), III, 466; official records Coast and Geodetic Survey; personal knowledge.] H. A. M.

HARRIS, SAMUEL (June 14, 1814–June 25, 1899), theologian, educator, was descended from Thomas Harris who settled in Charlestown, Mass., about 1630, through his son John, who moved to North Yarmouth, Me., before 1688. He was born in East Machias, Me., the son of Josiah and Lucy (Talbot) Harris. He entered Bowdoin College in 1829, the year in which Longfellow there assumed his duties as professor of modern languages and literature. To him Harris confessed indebtedness for a taste for literature, for solid foundations in the knowledge of German and French—languages in which later he became proficient—and for acquaintance with Italian and Spanish. Graduating in 1833, he served as principal of Limerick (Me.) Academy in 1833–34, was trained for the ministry at Andover Theological Seminary from 1835 to 1838, and for two years, 1838–41, was principal of Washington Academy in his native town. Ordained to the Congregational ministry on Dec. 22, 1841, he was pastor of the Congregational Church of Conway, Mass., from 1841 to 1851, and of the South Congregational Church of Pittsfield, Mass., from 1851 to 1855, when he was called to be professor of systematic theology in Bangor (Me.) Seminary. This position he held until 1867 when he was chosen president of Bowdoin College and professor of mental and moral philosophy. Finding executive duties uncongenial, he resigned his office in 1871 and accepted the Dwight professorship of systematic theology in Yale Divinity School. This chair he occupied with distinction for twenty-five years, resigning in 1895, and holding the title of professor emeritus until his death. He was twice married: on Apr. 30, 1839, to Deborah Robbins Dickinson, who died July 25, 1876; and on Oct. 11, 1877, to Mrs. Mary Sherman (Skinner) Fitch. He died in Litchfield, Conn., at the beginning of his eighty-sixth year.

Except for two pamphlets, *Zaccheus: or, the Scriptural Plan of Benevolence* (1844) and *Christ's Prayer for the Death of his Redeemed* (1863), a small volume of lectures entitled *The Kingdom of Christ on Earth* (1874), and an occasional sermon, Harris published nothing until he was sixty-nine years of age. Then appeared *The Philosophical Basis of Theism* (1883), which presented the grounds of theistic belief in a manner so profound and comprehensive, yet with such lucidity of statement, wealth of illustration, and emotional intensity that it made a deep impression on the ministers of that generation. Four years later appeared a supplementary volume entitled *The Self-Revelation of God* (1887), which carried his philosophical argument into the domain of doctrinal theology. In 1896, when he was eighty-two years old, he published two volumes bearing the title, *God: The Creator and Lord of All,* which comprised about half of his theological system.

As a theologian he belonged to no school, but occupied a transitional position between the old dialectical theology of New England and the more modern methods of thinking. Naturally conservative, he was open-minded to the scientific and critical information of his time and he embodied much of it in his thought. He taught that God, the Absolute Reason, is progressively revealing himself in the universe for the perfection of the individual and the establishment of the kingdom of Christ; and that man, because under the influence of rational motives he can determine the ends to which he will direct his energies, is a free moral agent, and makes a supreme choice either of God and all rational creatures or of himself only as the object of trust and service. The choice of self is sin. The love that is required in the law of God is the free choice of the will to trust and serve God and one's neighbor. Thus sin is selfish choice and love is primarily an act of the will. More than any of his predecessors Harris was a convincing interpreter of the intuitive powers of the mind, which, he claimed, apprehends five ultimate realities: the true, the right, the perfect, the good, and the absolute. These intuitions give man a real knowledge of the universe in which he lives and ample light for the direction of his choices.

While inheriting and accepting the great traditions of New England theology, Harris carried the doctrine of the freedom of the will to a higher point than had been attained by any of the able men who had preceded him, and he also relieved theology of its aridity by enriching the discussion of its themes with felicitous literary illustrations. Before him in America no mind more richly equipped had applied itself to theological problems. His wide knowledge of letters, however, served to ornament his style rather than to give his sentences the structural beauty which characterized the best writing of Edwards. He was not a subtle metaphysician chiefly interested in constructing and defending a closely articulated system of thought; rather, he was a thinker eager to comprehend and communicate truth which would influence the lives of men. His purpose was evangelical and his thought was the product of the pulpit as well as of the study. Consequently his books and his classroom lectures were quickened by a glowing spiritual ardor which enkindled the minds of readers and students. To them the truth he unfolded so luminously to the reason became at once a command to the will. Bold, independent, illuminating as a thinker, it was as an inspiring teacher that he most influenced the religious life of America. He was by nature a brooding, introspective man, but through long meditation on vast and lofty themes finally achieved a singular intellectual tranquillity and spiritual serenity. To commemorate their "lasting gratitude and affection" a bronze tablet in his honor was placed in Marquand chapel by his pupils.

[*Who's Who in America*, 1899–1900; *Andover Theol. Sem. Necrology* (1900); *Obit. Record Grads. Bowdoin Coll. . . . for the Decade Ending 1 June 1909* (1911); "Samuel Harris, Theologian, Author, Preacher, Teacher," by his nephew George Harris [*q.v.*,] president of Amherst College, in the *Congregationalist*, July 13, 1899; L. O. Brastow, *A Memorial Address Commemorative of the Life and Services of Samuel Harris* (1899); F. H. Foster, *A Genetic Hist. of the New England Theology* (1907); Herbert Harris, *Josiah Harris, 1770–1845, East Machias, Me.* (1903); *New Haven Evening Register*, June 26, 1899.] C. A. D.

HARRIS, THADDEUS MASON (July 7, 1768–Apr. 3, 1842), Unitarian clergyman, was born in Charlestown, Mass., a descendant of Thomas Harris who came to Boston from Devonshire about 1675 and the son of William and Rebekah (Mason) Harris. His father was a schoolmaster; after the battle of Lexington he fled with his family to Sterling, became a captain in the colonial army, and died in 1778 of a fever. Harris worked on farms at Sterling, Westminster, and Templeton, and then entered the household of Dr. Morse of Boylston, who prepared him for college, Harris meanwhile earning his keep by carpentry. In 1782 he visited his mother at Malden; she persuaded him to abandon the idea of going to Harvard and become a maker of saddle-trees; an injury to his wrist put an end to this occupation, however, and he entered the office of his maternal grandfather, who was clerk of the courts for Middlesex County. In his spare time he attended Samuel Kendal's school in Cambridge; and by putting out subscription papers Kendal enabled him in July 1783 to enter Harvard. He worked his way through college, being for two years a waiter in the commons hall; but was often miserably poor. On one occasion, when in need of money, he found a ring, for which a goldsmith gave him six dollars; this indication that Providence watched over him caused Harris in 1786 to become a church member. He graduated in 1787 and taught school at Worcester for a year; he was then invited to become Washington's secretary, but an attack of smallpox caused him to miss the opportunity. He returned to Harvard to study theology, was licensed to preach in 1789, took his A.M. and delivered the valedictory oration in 1790, and was librarian of the university from 1791 to 1793. He was then ordained pastor of the first church in Dorchester. On Jan. 28, 1795, he married Mary, daughter of Elijah and Dorothy (Lynde) Dix of Worcester. Their son Thaddeus William Harris [*q.v.*] also served as librarian of Harvard and was one of the first American economic entomologists. In 1795 and 1796 he edited the *Massachusetts Magazine*. In 1802 he caught yellow fever, and to renew his strength made a four-month western tour with Seth Adams and John Dix; in 1803 he published a four-volume *Minor Encyclopedia*; in 1805 he published a *Journal of a Tour into the Territory Northwest of the Alleghany Mountains* (reprinted in R. G. Thwaites' *Early Western Travels*, vol. III, 1904). From August 1810 to May

1811 he was in England on business connected with his father-in-law's estate. In 1820 appeared his *Natural History of the Bible,* a much shorter edition of which had been published by him in 1793; this was pirated in England, where it sold widely. In December 1833, after a long illness, he spent five months in Georgia; and gathered materials for his *Biographical Memorials of James Oglethorpe* (1841). He resigned his pastorate in 1836.

From 1837 until his death he was librarian of the Massachusetts Historical Society. He was an overseer of Harvard, a superintendent of public schools, and a member of numerous learned and humanitarian societies. He was for many years chaplain to the grand lodge of Freemasons in Massachusetts; in 1792 he published *Constitutions of the Ancient and Honorable Fraternity of Free and Accepted Masons,* he often spoke and wrote in defense of Masonry, and was subjected to much abuse during the anti-Masonic movement in the late eighteen-twenties. In addition to the works already mentioned, Harris published forty-eight sermons and addresses and twelve other works, including several in verse; he also assisted Jared Sparks in his edition of the writings of Washington. He was a man of wide learning; but his style was precious and pedantic. The journal of his western tour shows, however, a great delight in scenery.

Dorchester church called itself Unitarian, but Harris refused to accept the title and disliked all denominational distinctions. Though he considered the orthodox doctrine of the Trinity to be contradictory, he nevertheless believed in the atonement and in supernatural grace. He was of medium height, and in later life was "indescribably bent." He described himself as "naturally feeble and timid." He was tender, affectionate, and sensitive, and during his sermons would frequently burst into tears. Leonard Withington, writing under the name of John Oldbug, satirized him in *The Puritan* as Doctor Snivelwell.

[N. L. Frothingham, memoir in *Mass. Hist. Soc. Colls.,* 4 ser. II (1854), 130–55; W. B. Sprague, *Annals Am. Unitarian Pulpit* (1865); *Proc. Most Worshipful Grand Lodge Ancient Free and Accepted Masons Commonwealth Mass. 1826–44* (n.d.); T. B. Wyman, *The Geneals. and Estates of Charlestown* (1879).]

H. B. P.

HARRIS, THADDEUS WILLIAM (Nov. 12, 1795–Jan. 16, 1856), entomologist, librarian, was born in Dorchester, Mass., the son of Thaddeus Mason Harris [*q.v.*] and Mary (Dix) Harris. His father, librarian of Harvard College, 1791–93, and afterward pastor of the First Congregational Church in Dorchester, was an antiquarian and a naturalist, and the author of *The Natural History of the Bible* (1793; revised and enlarged, 1820). Young Harris entered Harvard in 1811 and graduated in 1815. His interest in entomology was inspired by the lectures of Prof. W. D. Peck [*q.v.*]. After graduation, he studied medicine and took his medical degree in 1820. He began to practise at Milton with Dr. Amos Holbrook, whose daughter Catherine he married in 1824. Later he returned to Dorchester. During these years he collected insects and studied them with the greatest interest and began a correspondence with other naturalists, notably Prof. N. M. Hentz. In 1831, on the death of Benjamin Peirce [*q.v.*] he was appointed librarian of Harvard College. He held this position for the rest of his life. From 1837 to 1842 he also gave instruction in natural history. Work in that field was not required, and attendance at the classes and lectures was voluntary. The subject proved so interesting, however, that Harris formed a private class in entomology which met one evening in every week. He apparently expected and hoped to be made full professor of natural history in the college, but to this chair Asa Gray [*q.v.*] was chosen in 1842. Meantime Harris had been contributing articles upon entomology and horticulture to scientific and agricultural journals. In 1831 he prepared Section VIII, "Insects," of the *Catalogue of the Animals and Plants of Massachusetts* (1833), which was also published as Part IV of Edward Hitchcock's *Report on the Geology, Mineralogy, Botany, and Zoology of Massachusetts* (1833). In 1837 Harris was appointed a member of the scientific commission to make a more extended geological and botanical survey, and as a member of this commission he wrote his *Report on the Insects of Massachusetts Injurious to Vegetation* (1841). Reprinted by the author in 1842 as *A Treatise on Some of the Insects of New England Which are Injurious to Vegetation,* it was again published in a revised form in 1852. After Harris' death an admirable new edition was ordered by the Massachusetts legislature and was published in 1862 under the editorship of Charles L. Flint. It was well illustrated, and the drawings by Antoine Sonrel and the wood engravings by Henry Marsh have hardly been excelled. The influence of this book was very great from the start. Harris' style was simple, lucid, and straightforward, without the slightest literary coloring such as one finds in the writings of J. H. Fabre; but it is probable that no work on any branch of natural history published in the United States during the nineteenth century was better done. It is probable also that no other work during the period had more loving or ardent students. It is a classic in entomology and is on the shelves of working entomologists today.

In the United States it is generally accepted that Harris' *Treatise* more than any other one thing started the trend of American entomology toward the practical. Down to that time insects had been studied largely as strange and interesting creatures. There had been occasional writers in the agricultural journals who recorded damage to crops and who proposed theoretical remedies, but here was a large book displaying life histories of many species that harmed crops and were detrimental to human interests in other ways, which indicated plainly the necessity for careful biological study of the different species before the exact character of their damage and the exact things to be done to circumvent them could be understood. Entomology in the United States from that date took on less of the dilettante aspect. While it is true that Harris received only $175 from the State of Massachusetts for the preparation of this report, it was the first instance of the employment of an entomologist for practical reasons.

While the treatise mentioned above represents Harris' principal work, his bibliography covers 120 titles on entomological subjects, and eight other titles. Much has been written of the admirable character of the man and in praise of his work, and he is generally considered as the father of American economic entomology. In his later years he was increasingly absorbed in the administration of the Harvard Library and was able to give correspondingly less time to his scientific research. "He seemed born with the librarian's instinct for alcoves and pamphlets and endless genealogies," and "described his methods to other librarians as lovingly as if he were describing a chrysalis" (Scudder-Higginson, *post,* p. xxxiii). He was often consulted in regard to genealogical problems and contributed several articles to the *New-England Historical and Genealogical Register.*

[Thomas Wentworth Higginson, "Memoir of Thaddeus William Harris," with bibliography of Harris' writings, published as the introduction to *Entomological Correspondence of Thaddeus William Harris, M.D.* (1869), ed. by S. H. Scudder; abridgement of Higginson's memoir in his *Contemporaries* (1899); A. R. Grote, "The Rise of Practical Entomology in America," in *Twentieth Ann. Report of the Entomological Soc. of Ontario, 1889* (1890); E. D. Harris, "Memoir of Thaddeus William Harris," in *Proc. Mass. Hist. Soc.,* vol. XIX (1882); *Boston Transcript,* Jan. 17, 1856.]

L. O. H.

HARRIS, THOMAS LAKE (May 15, 1823–Mar. 23, 1906), Christian mystic, poet, was born in Fenny Stratford, England. When he was about five years old his parents, Thomas and Annie (Lake) Harris, emigrated to America and settled in Utica, N. Y., where his father set up as grocer and auctioneer. Four years later Thomas' mother died. His stepmother apparently treated him harshly and thus caused the boy to dwell much on the memory of his mother and to cherish her love imaginatively. Befriended by the Universalist minister of the town, though his parents were "strict Calvinistic Baptists," he went frequently to the minister's house for instruction and finally lived there entirely. He wrote poetry and made several contributions to Universalist journals. He began to study for the Baptist ministry but was converted in 1843 to Universalism (*Universalist Union,* Oct. 28, 1843) and was soon given a small charge. While serving this charge he fell deeply in love with Mary Van Arnum, whom he married in 1845. In December of that year he accepted a call to the pastorate of the Fourth Universalist Society in New York City (*Ibid.,* Dec. 6, 1845). After two more years of preaching he became seriously interested in the evidences for spiritual survival contained in the phenomena of spiritualism. He became acquainted with Andrew Jackson Davis [*q.v.*] in 1847, who initiated him into the mysteries of mediumship and into the Harmonic philosophy, which Davis had constructed on a Swedenborgian basis. Under Davis' influence, he organized in 1848 an Independent Christian Congregation in New York, of which Horace Greeley was a member. It was as a direct result of one of his sermons here that the New York Juvenile Asylum was founded. In 1850, however, after the death of his wife, who left him with two sons—his only children—he abandoned his congregation and severed his connections with Davis. He was then associated for a time with James D. Scott and Ira S. Hitchcock who led a group of over a hundred followers to Mountain Cove, Fayette County, Va. (now W. Va.), where they expected to await the second coming of Christ (*New York Quarterly,* January 1853). The part Harris played in this little spiritualist community was apparently small, though he probably made some contributions to its publication, the *Mountain Cove Journal.* After it broke up, he wandered about for a while lecturing on spiritualism. About 1850 he had begun to go into trances and while in communication with the celestial world to compose long mystic poems on the theme of celestial love. In this manner he dictated *The Epic of the Starry Heaven* (1854), *A Lyric of the Morning Land* (1855), and *A Lyric of the Golden Age* (1856). These poems were the first of a long series and laid the basis for his own distinctive teachings.

He was attracted for a time by Swedenborgianism, but had begun to diverge from its beliefs when in May 1857 he founded a monthly journal, *The Herald of Light* (published until August 1861). In 1859–60 he went on a lecture tour to England, where he won the interest of Laurence Oliphant and his mother, Lady Oliphant, who later became his disciples. Upon his return to the United States, with a group of his followers who were seeking fitness for "the Brotherhood of the New Life," he settled on a farm at Wassaic, N. Y. Two years later the community was moved to Amenia, N. Y., where it prospered and about 1865 was joined by Lady Oliphant and later by her son. At the instigation of Lady Oliphant a larger tract of land (1,600 acres) was purchased at Brocton, near Dunkirk, N. Y., and the community was moved to this new location, called Salem-on-Erie. Harris, the Oliphants, and the other members (about forty in all), invested heavily in this colony, which was at first organized on a semi-communistic plan and carried on farming and vine growing. The communistic plan soon gave way to a "family partnership" and this in turn to a "patriarchal" society, in which Harris, as "Father," held and administered all the property.

This community was known as "The Use." All its members denied Self completely and surrendered themselves to the Divine Use or purpose. Their distinctive practices were "open breathing," a kind of respiration by which the Divine Breath (or Holy Spirit) entered directly into the body; and a system of celibate marriage whereby each person was left free to live in spiritual union with his or her heavenly "counterpart." The basis for Harris' teaching was the (Swedenborgian) doctrine that God "is not male merely, nor female merely, but the two-in-one"; and that in Heaven, or the "New Life," man attains union with God and the "conjugal spirits" are joined into a perfect unity. The "Brotherhood of the New Life" consisted of those who from the beginning of time had attained that felicity; its representatives on earth were the earthly focus for the spiritual regeneration of humanity.

In 1875, owing to a divergence between Harris and Oliphant, the community split; several of Harris' followers sold out to Oliphant and moved with Harris to Santa Rosa, Cal., where they purchased a 1,200-acre vineyard, which they called Fountain Grove. After 1881, when Oliphant broke away completely and recovered his share of the investment, Harris' California estate became the official home of the group. Meanwhile Harris himself was struggling "interiorly" to break through the natural forces of evil by rallying the "vortical atoms," and attain to his spiritual "two-in-oneness," or union with his heavenly counterpart (the Lily Queen). This he finally achieved in 1894 when he became technically immortal or "Theos." The "crisis" or end of the natural world was now eagerly expected and Harris predicted its imminence repeatedly. In *The New Republic* (1891), he praised the efforts of Bellamy and the Utopian Socialists, and his Theosocialism, as there set forth, attempted to give a theological justification and religious motivation for a new social system. In 1855 he had married his second wife, Emily Isabella Waters, with whom he lived in "The Use" until her death in 1883. In 1891 he married his secretary, Jane Lee Waring, the most prominent member of the community. After a visit to England, he moved with her to New York City, where he lived and wrote in retirement until his death. The most important of his numerous works, in addition to those mentioned above, are: *Hymns of Spiritual Devotion* (2 vols., 1861); *The Arcana of Christianity* (3 vols., 1858–78); *The Lord, the Two-in-One, Declared, Manifested and Glorified* (1876); *The Wisdom of the Adepts* (1884); *Star-Flowers* (1887); *The Brotherhood of the New Life: Its Fact, Law, Method and Purpose* (1891); *God's Breath in Man and in Humane Society* (1891); *The Song of Theos* (1903).

Most of those who knew Harris seem to have been impressed by the prophetic force of his personality, as well as by his remarkable eloquence and poetic gifts. He was opposed to creeds and to ecclesiastical organization, and insisted that he had not founded a new cult. His followers at one time were estimated to number about 2,000, including many adherents in England and Scotland.

[Sources include: A. A. Cuthbert, *The Life and World-Work of Thomas Lake Harris* (1908); Richard McCully, *The Brotherhood of the New Life and Thomas Lake Harris* (1893); *The Brotherhood of the New Life: An Epitome of the Work and Teaching of Thomas Lake Harris* (3rd ed., 1914); *Tribute to Sir Thomas Lake Harris* (Santa Rosa Commandery, Knights Templars, 1906); Laurence Oliphant, *Masollam* (2 vols., 1886); Margaret O. W. Oliphant, *Memoir of the Life of Laurence Oliphant* (2 vols., 1891); W. D. Howells, in "The Editor's Study," *Harper's Mag.*, Feb. 1892; *Rev. of Revs.* (London), Sept. 1906; Ray Strachey, *Religious Fanaticism* (1928). These works are mostly controversial; many of the accusations made against Harris have been either rescinded or refuted. The best collection of materials on the subject is in the hands of Mr. V. Valta Parma, Library of Congress. On Harris as a poet see Alfred Austin, *The Poetry of the Period* (1870). Certain details are found in R. N. Waring, *A Short Hist. of the Warings* (1898); W. A. Hinds, *Am. Communities* (2nd ed., 1908); H. C. Taylor, *Hist. Sketches of the Town of Portland* (1873).]

H. W. S.

HARRIS, TOWNSEND (Oct. 3, 1804–Feb. 25, 1878), merchant, politician, diplomat, the son of Jonathan Harris, was born of New England stock at Sandy Hill, Washington County, New York. The youngest boy in a family of six children, he had meager educational opportunities and at the age of thirteen was employed in a dry-goods store in New York, where he made his home for the following thirty years. With his father and brother John he joined in a partnership for the importation of china and earthen ware. Living with his mother, he remained a bachelor and supplemented his formal education with wide reading, acquiring a knowledge of French, Spanish, and Italian. In 1846, he was elected as a Democrat to the Board of Education, of which he served as president for two years. He plunged immediately into a campaign for the creation, under the Board, of a "Free College or Academy." The project excited the opposition not only of the friends of Columbia and the University of the City of New York, private institutions charging tuition, but also of those who were disposed to view with disfavor the higher education of the masses. Almost single-handed, according to the New York *World* (Mar. 1, 1878), Harris carried through the necessary legislation, and he was regarded as "almost the creator" of what is now the College of the City of New York.

After the death in 1847 of his mother, to whom he was much devoted, he fell into convivial habits, which, together with his public duties, led his brother to feel that he was neglecting his business. The partnership was dissolved. Townsend, having pledged himself to a reform of his personal habits, purchased an interest in a trading vessel and set out for California by way of Cape Horn. There he acquired full ownership of the vessel and embarked upon trading voyages in the Pacific and Indian Oceans, which ended a few years later in financial disaster.

When Commodore Perry was passing through China on his way to Japan, Harris was in Shanghai and vainly sought to accompany the expedition. In the spring of 1853 he applied for a consular post at either Hong Kong or Canton. Instead, he was appointed, Aug. 2, 1854, to Ningpo, an unimportant consulate. Hastening to the United States, he enlisted the support of his friends, including William L. Marcy, then secretary of state, and William H. Seward, then senator, and was appointed, Aug. 4, 1855, consul general to Japan, a post made possible by the ratification of the Perry Treaty. On Jan. 19, 1859, the position was raised to that of minister resident and consul general. Stopping at Bankok en route to Japan, he negotiated a new commercial treaty with Siam, many of the articles of which reappeared in the commercial agreement of June 17, 1857 and the treaty of July 29, 1858 with Japan.

Harris was put ashore at Shimoda, a lonely village some distance from Yokohama, and left by his government to shift for himself. Aided, however, by the success of the British and French war with China in 1858, he was able to convince the Japanese that they would do best to make their first comprehensive commercial treaty with the United States, which Harris represented as lacking the avarice of the Powers. In youth he had been taught by his mother "to tell the truth, fear God, and hate the British"; now at his lonely post, having become both a total abstainer and a devout churchman, he sought to carry out the precepts of his childhood. By plain-speaking and by persistence he won the confidence of the Japanese.

The outstanding characteristic of Harris' policy, incorporated in the treaty of 1858, was moderation, in contrast to the somewhat extravagant demands of the British, French, and Russian envoys who followed him. At the insistence of Marcy, Harris included a provision for extraterritoriality, but he drafted the treaty in such a way that, but for subsequent action by the Powers, it could have been revised in 1872 at the request of Japan. In other respects, both in the treaty and subsequently as resident in Yeddo (Tokio), Harris was forebearing with the Japanese and even advised and encouraged them in their conflicts with representatives of other Western nations. By the opening of its doors to the Western world Japan had been plunged into a domestic conflict which Harris understood and did not seek to turn to the advantage of the United States. No foreigner in the East ever so quickly attained such influence over the government of an Oriental people. Longford, the British historian, states that Harris' services were not "exceeded by any in the entire history of the international relations of the world" (Longford, *post,* p. 302). After the election of Lincoln, Harris resigned, returned to New York, became a War Democrat, joined the Union League Club, and spent his remaining years in New York, urbane, conservative, greatly interested in temperance, Christian missions, the Church, and foreign affairs. Though possessed of very moderate financial resources, he had the respect of his friends, and at his death his very substantial achievements were greatly honored.

[Harris Papers (College of the City of N. Y.); a small collection of personal letters (MSS. Div. N. Y.

Pub. Lib.); Dept. of State correspondence relative to his missions to Siam and Japan; *The Establishment of the College of the City of N. Y.* (1925) and *The Complete Journal of Townsend Harris* (1930) ed. by M. E. Cosenza; W. E. Griffis, *Townsend Harris* (1895), only partly trustworthy; J. H. Longford, *The Story of Old Japan* (1910); P. J. Treat, *The Early Diplomatic Relations between the U. S. and Japan 1853–65* (1917); R. S. Morris, *Townsend Harris: A Chapter in Am. Diplomacy* (n.d.); Tyler Dennett, *Americans in Eastern Asia* (1922).] T. D.

HARRIS, WILEY POPE (Nov. 9, 1818–Dec. 3, 1891), lawyer, judge, congressman, was born in Pike County, Miss., the son of Early and Mary Vivian (Harrison) Harris. His mother was the daughter of James Harrison of South Carolina, whose wife, Elizabeth, was the sister of the first Gen. Wade Hampton. His father, a lineal descendant of Lawrence, grandfather of George Washington, was a man of wealth in Georgia, but lost his property after moving to Mississippi Territory and died in 1821. Wiley Pope was adopted by his uncle, Gen. Wiley Pope Harris, for whom he was named. Gen. Harris moved from Pike to Copiah County, and took up land in the forest at Georgetown on Pearl River. The adopted son attended school at Columbus and Brandon. His uncle, Judge Buckner Harris, sent him to the University of Virginia where he began the study of law. He then studied at Lexington, Ky., under Chief Justice George Robinson, Justice Marshall and Judge A. K. Woolley. He began to practise in 1840 at Gallatin, then the county seat of Copiah County, as a partner of Philip Catchings. He soon moved to Monticello, where a district chancery court had been established. He was appointed circuit judge in 1847, and on the expiration of that term was elected judge. Though the youngest circuit judge when he went on the bench, he gained the reputation of being the ablest in the state. In 1851 he was married to Frances, daughter of Judge Daniel Mayes, a distinguished member of the Jackson bar.

He was a delegate from Lawrence County in the constitutional convention of 1851, known as the Union Convention, and a member of the committee of thirteen which reported resolutions. In 1853 he was elected a member of Congress where he served from December of that year to March 1855. After the expiration of his term he moved to Jackson. In January 1861 he was a member of the constitutional convention which adopted the ordinance of secession. He was a delegate to the Provisional Congress of the Confederate States, being the first man chosen by the convention, by unanimous vote. In keeping with a fixed policy about public office, he declined further service in the Confederate Congress, and retired to private life. From 1875 to his death Harris was the acknowledged leader and mentor of the Mississippi bar. In addition to his profound legal learning he had a sparkling and pungent wit which became proverbial throughout the state. His last public service was as a member of the constitutional convention of 1890, where he was chairman of the committee which framed the franchise clause of the constitution. He died at Jackson Dec. 3, 1891, and is buried in Greenwood Cemetery.

[Manuscript autobiography of Wiley Pope Harris in the possession of his grandson, Wiley Pope Harris, of Jackson, Miss.; Dunbar Rowland, *Mississippi*, vol. I (1907); H. S. Foote, *Bench and Bar of the South and Southwest* (1876); Reuben Davis, *Recollections of Miss. and Mississippians* (1889); *Jour. of the State Convention* (1861); *Jour. of the Proc. of the Constitutional Convention of the State of Miss.* (1890); Edward Mayes, *L. Q. C. Lamar, His Life, Times and Speeches, 1825–1893* (1896); *Memorials of the Life and Character of Wiley P. Harris of Miss.* (1892); *Clarion* (Jackson, Miss.), Dec. 10, 17, 1891.] D. R.

HARRIS, WILLIAM (Apr. 29, 1765–Oct. 18, 1829), Protestant Episcopal clergyman, college president, was born at Springfield, Mass., the son of Daniel and Sarah (Pynchon) Harris. He was descended on his father's side from Robert Harris who was a resident of Roxbury, Mass., as early as 1642, and on his mother's side from William Pynchon, the founder of Springfield. Fitted for college under the guidance of the Rev. Aaron Church, a Congregational minister of Hartland, Conn., he entered Harvard at the age of seventeen and was graduated in 1786. For two years he acted as "college butler" and studied theology. He was licensed to preach as a Congregationalist and at the same time became principal of an academy at Marblehead. Temporary ill health led him to take up medical studies, but the suggestions of a friend, the Rev. Thomas F. Oliver, an Episcopalian rector, impelled him to examine that faith and polity, with the result that he accepted it and with returning health was ordained a deacon and one week later a priest, in New York City (October 1791). In later years he affirmed that it was the reading of Richard Hooker's *Ecclesiastical Polity* which caused him to leave the Congregationalism of his fathers for Episcopal orders. On Nov. 3 following his ordination he was married to Martha Clark, daughter of Rev. Jonas Clark [*q.v.*], pastor of the church at Lexington.

Harris continued in charge of the academy at Marblehead and of St. Michael's Church there for a decade, but in 1802 became rector of St. Mark's in the Bowery, New York City, and established a classical school in the vicinity of the church. Ten years' residence in New York brought preferment of various kinds and especially social relationships that advanced his fortunes. In 1811 a peculiar situation in the affairs of Columbia College led to his election as president. Rev. John Mitchell Mason [*q.v.*] was the first choice of the trustees for that office, but a gift of real estate from Trinity Church had been conditioned on Columbia's president being a communicant of the Episcopal Church, and Dr. Mason was a Presbyterian. The powers of the office were divided, therefore, all the most important being transferred to the new office of provost, to which Dr. Mason was elected, while the presidency, conferred on Harris, retained a few rather inconsequential functions. Since the new president gave only a part of his time to college duties, he was able to continue in the rectorship of St. Mark's. The first college commencement in which he took part was the "riotous commencement of 1811" in Trinity Church, at which a senior was refused a degree because parts of his graduation oration were deemed offensive. After five years Mason retired and the trustees conferred on Harris the original powers of the presidency, at the same time doing away with the office of provost. Harris then resigned his rectorship and for the remaining thirteen years of his life devoted his whole time and strength to the college. He was especially successful in winning and holding the confidence of the faculty and in improving the college discipline. A contemporary declared him "a remarkable man, not so much for any one feature of his character as for a happy combination of the several qualities of mind and heart which go to make the effective guide, teacher and friend of young men" (Rev. Benjamin I. Haight, quoted in *Columbia University Quarterly,* June 1901, p. 224). During the greater part of his administration the students numbered from 125 to 140 and the faculty about twenty. The planning and opening of the Columbia Grammar School were due directly to his initiative. He died in office after a prolonged illness.

[L. M. Harris, *Robert Harris and His Descendants* (1861); J. B. Pine, "William Harris, S.T.D., Fourth President of Columbia College," *Columbia Univ. Quart.,* June 1901; H. T. Wade, "The Riotous Commencement of 1811," *Ibid.,* June, Sept. 1901; W. B. Sprague, *Annals Am. Pulpit,* vol. V (1859); funeral address by Rev. John McVicar in *Christian Jour.* (N. Y.), Nov. 1829.] W. B. S.

HARRIS, WILLIAM ALEXANDER (Oct. 29, 1841–Dec. 20, 1909), Kansas stockman, senator, was born in Loudoun County, Va., the son of William Alexander and Frances (Murray) Harris. His father, a lawyer, was a member of Congress, minister to the Argentine Confederation under Polk, editor for a time of the *Washington Union,* and printer to the Senate, 1857–59, under President Buchanan. The son received a primary education in Luray County, graduated from Columbian College (now George Washington University), and then worked six months on a preliminary inter-oceanic canal survey. He subsequently became a student at Virginia Military Institute, Lexington, was graduated with his class to enter the service of the state in 1861, and served throughout the war. He was promoted to be assistant adjutant general under Gen. C. M. Wilcox and later was ordnance officer under D. H. Hill and Robert E. Rodes in the Army of Northern Virginia. In 1865, he went to Kansas, where his training secured for him employment as resident engineer for the Union Pacific; he built one branch of the road. He had charge of the sale of some railroad lands, and in 1868 accepted the agency for the sale of the Delaware reservation and some other lands. After 1876, he devoted himself to his large farm at Linwood, near Lawrence, Kan. Recognizing the necessity of improving Kansas cattle, he made investigations which ultimately led him to specialize on a breed of Scotch Shorthorns which he imported. He built up a herd at Linwood which became famous among Shorthorn breeders, and his sales were widely attended. He was one of the founders of the American Shorthorn Breeders Association in 1893.

Harris filled various city offices of Lawrence, but as a Democrat and former Confederate he seemed barred from any political career in his state. When the Peoples Party was created to unite the agricultural sections, however, they jeered the "bloody shirt" as an evasion of the "real issues," and while Harris was in Europe in 1892, nominated him at the Wichita convention for congressman-at-large, as a concrete demonstration that the bloody chasm was closed. Democrats indorsed the Populist ticket, and Harris was elected with the others. In 1894, he was defeated when the fusion agreement failed. Following his defeat, he was elected state senator, but after the fusion victory in 1896, was chosen to the seat of United States Senator W. A. Peffer, Populist. In Congress, his training and experience qualified him to speak with some authority on railroad problems and on the Isthmian Canal; his work was solidly constructive rather than spectacular. Contemporaries credited him with saving fifteen million dollars in the settlement of the Pacific Railroad debt. After the expiration of his term, he was considered by President Roosevelt as a member of the Canal Commission. Harris left the Senate with his fortune seriously reduced, and accepted employment in Chicago with the National Livestock Association. He refused to consider the Democratic nomination for the governorship of Kansas in 1904, but in 1906, over his protests and in spite of eighteen months' actual residence in Chicago, he was named as the most available man in the party. He was narrowly defeated after an energetic canvass. Three years later he died in Chicago.

In person, Harris was tall and muscular, a farmer rather than a student. Though he was the last senator to drop the term Populist, he was in fact and in policy an agrarian Democrat, more conservative than his Populist contemporaries, and frequently acted independently. In 1863 he married Mary A. Lionberger, who died in 1894; soon thereafter he married Cora M. Mackey. He was a member of the Episcopal Church. A memorial bust was erected to his memory as a stockman and statesman at the Kansas State Agricultural College, of which he was long a regent.

[*Confederate Veteran,* Feb. 1910; W. E. Connelley, *A Standard Hist. of Kan. and Kansans* (1918), vol. III; sketch in Hill P. Wilson, *A Biog. Hist. of Eminent Men of the State of Kan.* (1901), probably authorized by Harris; *Who's Who in America,* 1908–09; *Cong. Dir.,* 53, 55–57 Cong.; *Biog. Dir. Am. Cong.* (1928); newspaper clippings of Harris' Eastern speeches and activities and files of Kansas newspapers in Kan. Hist. Lib.; obituary in *Topeka State Jour.,* Dec. 21, 1909.]
R. C. M—r.

HARRIS, WILLIAM LITTLETON (July 6, 1807–Nov. 26, 1868), jurist, was born in Elbert County, Ga., the son of Gen. Jeptha V. Harris, the descendant of a Virginia family which settled in Georgia before the Revolution. His mother, Sarah, was a daughter of Richardson Hunt. His early educational opportunities were good, and he entered the University of Georgia at the age of fifteen and was graduated in 1825. Immediately thereafter he began the study of law and in 1826 was admitted to the bar by a special act of the legislature which, on account of his minority, was necessary. He began the practice of his profession at Washington, Wilkes County, Ga., where he came into contact with noted lawyers, and on May 13, 1830, he married Frances Semmes. In 1837 he settled in Columbus, Miss. He was elected judge of the circuit court in 1853, and in 1856 served on the commission of three which drew up the excellent code of laws adopted as the code of 1857 at a special session of the legislature. He was reëlected circuit judge in 1857 and in 1858 was elected to the high court of errors and appeals. President James Buchanan is said to have offered him the appointment of justice of the Supreme Court of the United States to succeed Justice Peter V. Daniel of Virginia.

In pursuance of the resolutions adopted on Nov. 30, 1860, by the legislature of Mississippi, which authorized the appointment of commissioners to the other Southern states, to inform them that Mississippi had called a state convention, Gov. John Jones Pettus appointed Harris to visit Georgia. The latter appeared before the legislature and urged close cooperation between Georgia and Mississippi. He was again elected a justice of the high court of errors and appeals in 1865. During the Civil War he fulfilled the duties of his position, and stanchly supported the administration of Jefferson Davis. After the war, he continued, in the face of military interference with the civil authority, to fill the office to which he had been elected, but after the passage of the reconstruction act of Mar. 2, 1867, he resigned along with his two colleagues. He resumed the practice of law in Memphis, Tenn., where, on Nov. 26, 1868, he died of pneumonia.

[J. D. Lynch, *The Bench and Bar of Miss.* (1881); *Biog. and Hist. Memoirs of Miss.* (1891); D. Rowland, *Mississippi* (1907); 35–41 *Miss. Reports*; R. T. Semmes, *The Semmes and Allied Families* (1918); obituaries in *Daily Memphis Avalanche,* Nov. 28, 1868, *Clarion* (Jackson, Miss.), Nov. 30, 1868.]
D. R.

HARRIS, WILLIAM LOGAN (Nov. 14, 1817–Sept. 2, 1887), bishop of the Methodist Episcopal Church, a descendant of James Harris who emigrated in 1725 from Somersetshire, England, to Essex County, N. J., was born on his father's farm near Mansfield, Ohio. His parents, James and Mary (Logan) Harris, were Presbyterians, but William, converted at a camp-meeting when he was seventeen, became an earnest Methodist, and was moved to prepare for the ministry. He was encouraged in this ambition by his mother, but his father had died, and an uncle, who was virtually his guardian, wished to make a farmer out of him, and would give him no financial assistance. Supporting himself, however, he studied for two years in Norwalk Seminary, Norwalk, Ohio. With this meager education, in 1837 he was admitted on trial to the Michigan Conference, which then included northern Ohio, and embarked on his ministerial career. In 1839 he was ordained deacon, and in 1841, elder. On Aug. 9, 1840, he married Anna Atwell. As a young preacher on circuits and at various stations he proved himself an effective evangelical speaker, and revivals invariably attended his ministry.

He was pastor of the church in Delaware, Ohio, when Ohio Wesleyan University was opened in that town, and for a year, 1845–46, was tutor there. In 1848 he was elected principal of Baldwin Institute, at Berea, in which position he showed so much ability that in 1851 he was called to the principalship of the academic department of Ohio Wesleyan, and the following year was appointed professor of chemistry and natural science. In spite of his own meager schooling, he had so educated himself as to fill academic positions acceptably. He was a man of large stature, immense endurance, seemingly inexhaustible capacity for work, acquisitive mind, and unusual memory. During his tutorship at Ohio Wesleyan he had regularly met with Prof. William G. Williams at four o'clock each morning for instruction in Hebrew, and when he became professor he was proficient enough to give special courses in that subject. His taste, however, was for mathematics and science, and in the former field he was something of a genius. Circumstances later made him a close student of Methodist history, especially on its constitutional side. In spite of professional dignity and scholarly tastes, he gave the impression of being a "generous liver," and a "jolly old soul" (S. W. Williams, *Pictures of Early Methodism in Ohio,* 1909, p. 315).

His administrative ability and sound judgment, together with the fact that he was a person of method, thoroughness, and accuracy, brought him official positions in his denomination. From 1860 to 1872 he was assistant corresponding secretary of the Missionary Society. He was a member of all the General Conferences from 1856 to 1872 inclusive, and served as secretary of each. His work in this position was such that it came to be said that before Harris' time the Methodist Church never had a secretary. During the period when the question of the General Conference's powers with respect to excluding slave-holders from church membership was being hotly debated, Harris, in a series of articles in the *Western Christian Advocate* (later published under the title *The Constitutional Powers of the General Conference, with Special Application to the Subject of Slave-Holding,* 1860), ably opposed the arguments of those who maintained that slave-holders had a constitutional right to membership. He took an important part in determining the action of the General Conference on the admission of missionary conferences, and in preparing the plan by which lay representation was introduced. In 1872 he was elected to the board of bishops, and immediately became its secretary. Soon afterwards he made an eighteen months' trip around the world, during which he inspected missions in the East and presided at all the European conferences. In 1880 and in 1884–85 he made extensive tours in Mexico, and in 1881 visited South America, and again held the European conferences. Under the high pressure of his activity, his strong physique finally began to give way, and in 1887 he died at his home in Brooklyn, having almost completed fifty years in the ministry. He collaborated with William J. Henry in preparing *Ecclesiastical Law and Rules of Evidence, with Special Reference to the Jurisprudence of the Methodist Episcopal Church* (1879), and was the author of *The Relation of the Episcopacy to the General Conference* (1888), lectures at Drew Theological Seminary, published after his death.

[T. L. Flood and J. W. Hamilton, *Lives of Methodist Bishops* (1882); S. J. H. Keifer, *Geneal. and Biog. Sketches of the N. J. Branch of the Harris Family* (1888); *Meth. Rev.* (N. Y.), Jan. 1888; E. T. Nelson, *Fifty Years of History of the Ohio Wesleyan Univ.* (1895); *Christian Advocate* (N. Y.), Sept. 8, 1887; J. M. Buckley, *A Hist. of Methodists in the U. S.* (1896), Am. Ch. Hist. Series; *N. Y. Tribune* and other New York papers, Sept. 3, 1887.] H. E. S.

HARRIS, WILLIAM TORREY (Sept. 10, 1835–Nov. 5, 1909), philosopher, educator, son of William and Zilpah (Torrey) Harris, was born on a farm near the village of North Killingly, Conn. He attended the district school of the neighborhood, spent several terms in the city schools of Providence, R. I., where the country boy was thoroughly unhappy, and attended for one year each the academies at Woodstock, Conn., Worcester, Mass., and Andover, Mass., as well as two others of lesser note. This highly peripatetic training unfitted him to settle down at Yale, which he entered in 1854 but which he left in the middle of his junior year, dissatisfied with both the college and its curriculum. During this period, he had a youthful sympathy with every kind of revolt against authority and dabbled eagerly in spiritualism, mesmerism, and phrenology. In 1857 he began to teach in the public schools of St. Louis, where his immediate success and growing responsibility had a sobering effect upon his thinking. In the following year he was married to Sarah T. Bugbee. His rise in the educational system was rapid; he was soon made principal of the Clay School, became assistant city superintendent in 1866, and superintendent in 1868. Equally rapid was his philosophical development. Converted from phrenology by a lecture of Bronson Alcott, and led to a study of German literature and philosophy through his reading of Theodore Parker, he was already deep in Goethe and Kant when acquaintance with Henry C. Brokmeyer [*q.v.*], whom he met shortly after his own arrival in St. Louis, had a decisive effect upon all his later work. Under Brokmeyer's guidance he took up what was to prove a lifelong study of Hegel; in 1908 he was able to say that he had read Hegel's *Philosophy of History* sixteen times, while even more important to him was Hegel's *Logic,* which became his philosophical Bible. In the exposition of Hegel's thought and in the application of his principles to every department of knowledge but especially to education, Harris found his lifework. Hegel's doctrines of the solidarity of the individual with society and of the importance of the state temporarily met the needs of the new American feeling for national unity. In the Hegelian Absolutism Harris found an adequate defense against the agnosticism of Spencer, while he was able to interpret it without too much difficulty as a thoroughgoing theism. The infinite regression in natural causation, he was never tired of repeating, implies a self-active, directing causation in the whole; and self-activity, he held, implies consciousness and will. Harris' logic was far from impeccable, he was often guilty of verbalism, but his enthusiasm and devotion enabled him to become in time the foremost Hegelian scholar in America, though always a Hegelian of the extreme right wing. In 1867 he founded the *Journal of Speculative Philosophy,* continued until the close of 1893, which carried as its motto "Philosophy can bake no bread but it can give us God, Freedom, and Immortality." In its pages appeared the first English translations of important works of Hegel, Fichte, Schelling, and others; its critical articles offered the first systematic study of German philosophy to appear in this country; while in it such later writers as Howison, Peirce, Royce, Dewey, and James made their début. Meanwhile Harris' educational work was almost equally significant. His thirteen annual reports as superintendent (1868–80) were quoted nationally and even internationally as models of their kind. In 1880, somewhat weakened in health as a result of his tremendous exertions, he resigned his St. Louis position and moved to Concord, Mass., to assist in the establishment of the Concord School of Philosophy. To this rather fruitless enterprise he devoted much of his energy for the next nine years. It was his ambition to succeed Emerson as the leader of a great idealistic movement, but in this he signally failed. While his philosophy was in many ways more mature than that of the Transcendentalists, he utterly lacked their fire and originality. His system was derivative at best and really represented in America not the beginning but the end of a movement, the formalization of an idealism which had already lost its inspiration and become traditional. He himself was unable to develop his thinking beyond the point which he had already reached. The Concord School, held only in the summers, enjoyed merely a *succès d'estime,* its sessions attended mainly by women. In 1889, realizing that his philosophical career was virtually closed, Harris accepted the position of United States commissioner of education, which he held from Sept. 12, 1889, to June 30, 1906, when he voluntarily resigned. During these years, through his reports, lectures, and multitudinous articles in the magazines, his educational influence was very great. None of his contemporaries approached him in range of educational interest. He labored especially to place education upon a psychological basis, to bring about a rational correlation of studies, and to relate the school to other departments of institutional life. These were no new endeavors and Harris was no educational pioneer, but he was a great expositor of the best that was already known and thought in his field.

Sharp-featured, spare, and muscular, with something of the New England cleric in his mien, Harris created an impression of spiritual energy rather than of spiritual profundity. His bibliography contains 479 titles, nearly all in philosophy or education but otherwise of the most miscellaneous character. He spent himself largely in work which though important was for him a side-issue, such as the assistant editorship of *Johnson's New Universal Cyclopaedia* and the editorship of Appletons' International Education Series and of a new edition of *Webster's New International Dictionary of the English Language.* Excellent organizer though he was in the practical world, the task of organizing his thoughts on a large scale proved insuperable, and after many vain attempts he abandoned it. The nearest approach to a complete presentation of his philosophical views, his *Introduction to the Study of Philosophy* (1889), consists of a skilful compilation of selections arranged by Marietta Kies. His three volumes, *The Spiritual Sense of Dante's Divina Commedia* (1889), a somewhat too-Hegelian but otherwise good interpretation of Dante, whom Harris esteemed so highly that his friends needlessly feared his conversion to Catholicism, *Hegel's Logic, a Book on the Genesis of the Categories of the Mind* (1890), and *The Psychologic Foundations of Education* (1898), have all enjoyed up to date a precarious immortality rendered more precarious by their mechanical and unpregnant style. Harris' permanent influence upon American thought has proved to be far less than his contemporary reputation prophesied. Hardly any American philosopher was more widely acclaimed in his own time; hardly any is so little read today. Nevertheless he holds an assured position in the history of American philosophy and education as one who labored not unsuccessfully to emancipate these disciplines from provincialism and to accustom them to more spacious ways of thought. He died at Providence, R. I.

[*Who's Who in America*, 1908–09; *Providence Jour.*, Nov. 6, 1909; *Education*, June 1888; *Report of the Commissioner of Education 1907*, I, 37–66, containing bibliography; J. S. Roberts, *Wm. T. Harris: A Critical Study of his Educational and Related Philosophical Views* (1924); autobiographical material in the *Forum*, Apr. 1887; discussions of Harris' philosophy by Morris R. Cohen, *Cambridge Hist. of Am. Lit.*, III (1921), 236–39, and by Woodbridge Riley, *Am. Thought* (1915), 240–53.] E. S. B.

HARRISON, ALEXANDER [See HARRISON, THOMAS ALEXANDER, 1853–1930]

HARRISON, BENJAMIN (1726?–Apr. 24, 1791), Revolutionary statesman, governor of Virginia, was born at the family seat, "Berkeley," Charles City County, Va., the son of Benjamin Harrison and Anne Carter, daughter of Robert Carter [*q.v.*] of Corotoman ("King Carter"). Descended from Benjamin Harrison, who came to the colony before Mar. 15, 1633/34, he was the fifth of the name in the direct line of descent and, to distinguish him from others, all of whom sat in the House of Burgesses or held other high office in the province, he is usually referred to as "the Signer." This distinguished family later contributed two presidents of the United States, William Henry Harrison, the Signer's son, and Benjamin Harrison, his great-grandson.

At the time of his father's death in 1745, the fifth Benjamin Harrison was a student at the College of William and Mary, but he left without graduation and shortly afterward married Elizabeth Bassett. Already in charge of his father's estate, in 1749 he was elected to the House of Burgesses. He was reëlected successively until 1775, and was frequently chosen speaker. He was a member of the committee of that body which, in 1764, drew up a vigorous protest against the proposed Stamp Act, yet in the following year he was one of the conservative group who opposed Patrick Henry's resolutions as impolitic. When, however, the storm again broke in 1773 Harrison took a decided stand and as a member of Virginia's committee of correspondence helped to map out the program of resistance. Upon the dissolution of the House of Burgesses by Dunmore in May 1774, he joined with his fellow members in sending out a call for a general congress of the colonies, to which he was duly elected a delegate by the convention which assembled in August. "These gentlemen of Virginia," wrote John Adams, "appear to be the most spirited and consistent of any. Harrison said he would have come on foot rather than not come" (*Works of John Adams*, II, 1850, p. 362). That he should be returned to the Congress of 1775 was a matter of course, and, with a brief exception due to one of the frequent shifts in Virginia politics, he was retained in the delegation until 1778, although he withdrew in October 1777. In the meantime, he represented his county in the Virginia conventions of 1775 and 1776 and, upon the organization of the state government in the latter year, was elected to the new House of Delegates, to which he was successively returned until 1781.

In Congress, Harrison's career was one of importance and distinction. Perhaps none will agree with John Adams' querulous verdict in his latter years: "This was an indolent, luxurious, heavy gentleman, of no use in Congress or committee, but a great embarrassment to both" (*Works of John Adams*, III, 1851, p. 31). Harrison seldom took part in the debates, yet such of his remarks as have been recorded are usually pointed and apt. Certainly Washington leaned confidently upon him for the guidance of legislative measures pertaining to the army. Of the committee of secret correspondence created in November 1775 (later styled the committee for foreign affairs), Harrison was the first member named. In March 1776, he was placed on the marine committee, and in June he was chosen to the newly established board of war and ordnance. Thus in this formative period of national life Harrison had an important share in the establishment of three of the great departments of the American government, those of state, war, and the navy. He was not at any time a member of the treasury committee (or board of treasury), but he served on numerous committees concerned with financial problems. From March 1776 to August 1777, he was almost uniformly chairman of the committee of the whole and in that capacity he presided over the momentous debates which culminated in the Declaration of Independence (to which in due course he appended his signature), as he did also over the early debates upon the Articles of Confederation. The same fairness and decision for which he was distinguished as speaker in the Virginia assemblies likewise characterized his conduct as chairman of the committee of the whole in Congress.

Upon Harrison's retirement from Congress in October 1777, he took his seat in the House of

Delegates, of which in May 1778 he was chosen speaker, holding that office until 1781. In November of that year, when Governor Nelson resigned, Harrison was elected to the chief magistracy and was twice reëlected, three years being the constitutional limit of service. The most notable event of this trying period was the cession by Virginia of her claims to lands north and west of the Ohio. Harrison's administration was marked by characteristic vigor, firmness, and devotion to the interests of his state, but by an equal devotion to the Union which he had done so much to establish. Upon the termination of his service as governor (1784), Harrison was again elected to the House of Delegates and remained a member of that body until his death. In the Virginia convention of 1788, called to pass upon the federal Constitution, he was chairman of the committee on privileges and elections, but he did not engage extensively in the debates. In his principal speech, while reiterating his devotion to the Union, he declared his opposition to the Constitution as it stood, insisting that the inclusion of a bill of rights should precede, not follow, adoption. When, however, he was overruled, he refused to join the malcontents in further opposition but gave the Constitution and the new government his hearty support.

[The principal biography is that in John Sanderson, *Biog. of the Signers to the Declaration of Independence,* vol. VIII (1827). The latest and most extensive genealogical account of the Harrison family is W. G. Stanard, "Harrison of James River," in *Va. Mag. of Hist. and Biog.,* Oct. 1922–Oct. 1925. This includes a sketch of Harrison and reprints the principal part of Sanderson's biography. Much valuable material respecting Harrison's career is to be found in L. G. Tyler, *Letters and Times of the Tylers,* vol. I (1884). For the record of his service in Congress the *Jours. of Cong.* are a first requisite. Letters may be seen in E. C. Burnett, *Letters of Members of the Continental Cong.,* vols. I, II (1921, 1923); *Va. State Papers,* vol. I (1875); and in *Official Letters of the Govs. of the State of Va.,* vols. III (1929), IV (forthcoming). H. B. Grigsby, "Hist. of the Va. Federal Convention of 1788," *Va. Hist. Soc. Colls.,* n.s., vols. IX, X (1890–91) contains some account of his earlier career as well as of his part in that convention.] E. C. B.

HARRISON, BENJAMIN (Aug. 20, 1833–Mar. 13, 1901), twenty-third president of the United States, was descended from Benjamin Harrison, who came to Virginia from England and was elected to the House of Burgesses in 1642. The Harrisons belonged to the wealthy planter class and held the highest political positions in Virginia. The most prominent of the earlier members of the family was Benjamin Harrison [*q.v.*], signer of the Declaration of Independence and governor of Virginia. His son, William Henry Harrison [*q.v.*], established his home in Ohio on an extensive estate on the Ohio River just below Cincinnati; here he was residing in 1840 when elected president. On an adjoining farm lived his eldest son, John Scott Harrison, congressman for two terms. His second wife, Elizabeth Irwin, was the mother of Benjamin.

Private tutors and typical country schoolteachers prepared Benjamin Harrison for Farmer's College. He finished his college course with distinction in 1852 at Miami University. On Oct. 20, 1853, he married a college friend, Caroline Lavinia Scott, daughter of Dr. John Scott, president of the Oxford Female Institute; to them two children, Russell and Mary, were born. From 1852 to 1854 he read law in the offices of Storer and Gwynne, prominent attorneys in Cincinnati. In 1854, he settled in Indianapolis, then a growing Western town, and by indefatigable industry forged gradually to the front of his profession. His active interest in politics began during the first year of his law practice, when the struggle over slavery was at white heat. Harrison at once gave the Republican party unswerving allegiance; to him, moral principles were at stake. He soon established an enviable reputation as a campaign speaker. In 1858 he served as secretary to the Republican state central committee of Indiana; he was elected city attorney in 1857, and in 1860 and 1864 reporter of the supreme court of Indiana. He found the compilation of ten volumes of *Indiana Reports* equivalent to a postgraduate law course, while the salary and royalties placed him on his feet financially.

He was paying for a modest home at the outbreak of the Civil War. In 1862, he helped raise the 70th Indiana Infantry and was appointed its colonel by Gov. Oliver P. Morton. The regiment was hurried to Bowling Green, Ky., to assist in stopping Bragg, even though its colonel knew practically nothing of war and its rank and file knew less. Fortunately, it was given the prosaic duty of guarding the Louisville & Nashville Railroad. Two years of devotion to duty and study changed the untrained colonel into a seasoned brigade commander. Harrison soon became unpopular, however, because he insisted on turning raw recruits into disciplined soldiers. In 1864, his command was attached to Sherman's army and participated in the bloody battles of the Atlanta campaign, during much of which Harrison was in command of his brigade. His conduct won the praise of General Butterfield and a recommendation for promotion from General Hooker. After the capture of Atlanta, Harrison returned to Indiana at Governor Morton's request to help combat Copperhead influence in the political campaign of 1864. This service prevented his participation in the march through Georgia, but he rejoined his command in the Carolinas and led it in the grand review in Washington. On Mar. 22, 1865, he was brevetted brigadier-general "for ability and manifest energy and gallantry." Three years of war had fully matured him.

Returning to the practice of his profession, Harrison was immediately recognized as one of the ablest lawyers in his state. Like nearly all the lawyers of his time, he engaged in general practice; his work took him into the local, state, and federal courts in Indianapolis and some distance into the region roundabout. In 1881 he was admitted to practice before the United States Supreme Court. Among the leading cases in which he appeared were the Nancy Clem murder case, tried in a local court in 1869; *Milligan* vs. *Hovey, et al.*, in 1871 (3 Bissell, *U. S. Circuit Court Reports,* 13), in which he was appointed special assistant United States attorney by President Grant; and *R. S. Robertson* vs. *Indiana,* in 1887 (109 *Indiana,* 79). Harrison had an alert and ready mind, an extraordinarily retentive memory, unusual power of analysis, and great facility of expression. When a mass of confused and complicated facts was in the crucible of his mind, he would sometimes pass his friends on the street without seeing them, or if he gave them a "Good-morning," his earnest face with its absorbed and distant expression chilled their advances. Professional interest with him always stood before financial prosperity, yet his annual income soon rose from about $5,000 to over $10,000, a large income for an Indiana lawyer of this period. It enabled him to build a spacious house in Indianapolis and his family to acquire a prominent social position.

His active interest in public affairs and local philanthropy continued after the war. For forty years he was an elder in the Presbyterian Church; he taught a men's Bible class, was superintendent of a Sunday school, and several times a member of the General Assembly. During every state and national political campaign he spoke in various cities of the state. He was an ardent "radical" Republican during Johnson's presidency; during the 1870's, however, he was one of a few conservative leaders who fought for sound money and kept the Republican party in Indiana from supporting the Greenback doctrines. In 1872, Morton, who had developed an antipathy for Harrison, prevented his receiving the Republican nomination for governor. In 1876, however, Orth, the Republican candidate, was forced off the ticket in the middle of the campaign by an effective Democratic attack on his previous financial transactions. In this predicament, the Republican state committee persuaded Harrison, with his unsullied reputation, that it was his duty to his party to accept the nomination which he had previously declined. A bitterly fought campaign followed. Harrison appealed strongly to the old soldiers and to the cities. The Democratic candidate, James Douglas Williams, called "Blue Jeans," was a well-to-do farmer who had some of Lincoln's rugged honesty, simplicity of manner, and homely appearance. The Democrats capitalized these points further by speaking of Harrison as "Kid-glove" Harrison; and portraying him as being "as cold as an iceberg." From this charge he was to suffer as long as he was a candidate for or an occupant of public office. The Democrats carried the state by 5,139 majority. Harrison regretted the defeat of his party, but personally preferred to give his time to law. His fight had not been in vain. He had led his ticket by about three thousand votes, had made many friends over the state, and was considered by President Hayes for a cabinet position. In 1879, Hayes appointed him a member of the newly created Mississippi River Commission. This office he held until 1881. During the national railroad strike in 1877, Governor Williams appointed him a member of the citizens' committee to settle the strike in Indianapolis and also placed him in command of the state troops there. In 1878 he presided over the Republican state convention, and in 1880 he was chairman of the Indiana delegation to the Republican National Convention, where he and his delegation played a leading rôle in nominating Garfield. Harrison himself was suggested as a compromise presidential candidate. Conkling sought an interview to offer him second place on the Grant ticket, but Harrison refused to allow his name to be mentioned in connection with the vice-presidency. In the campaign that followed, he took a prominent part. Garfield would have been glad to give him a cabinet post, but Harrison declined to be considered because he had just been elected to the United States Senate.

While senator (1881–87), as chairman of the important committee on territories, Harrison successfully guided through the Senate a bill to grant civil government to Alaska and a bill to admit Dakota as a state, though the latter did not pass the House. The kindly, humane aspect of his nature was shown by his espousal of the interests of the Indians and homesteaders when they were threatened by the demands of powerful railroads seeking legislation; the cold, legal aspect was manifested in the debate on the Interstate Commerce Act, during which he supported fair, effective railroad regulation. He championed the Mississippi River Commission and its work, and supported labor legislation. He voted against the notorious river and harbor bill of 1882, though later he secured similar appropriations for his state. He favored passing a reasonable protective tariff bill in 1883. He advocated carrying out treaty obligations in good faith, opposing his Republican colleagues from the Pacific Coast when the Chinese Exclusion Bill was being debated and thus deliberately incurring a heavy future political liability. As was natural for an ex-soldier, he gave sympathetic, liberal support to general pension legislation and to the numerous individual Civil War pension petitions which came to him, and thus obtained the goodwill of many veterans, which constituted a valuable political asset. He made an important speech on civil-service reform on Mar. 26, 1886 (*Congressional Record,* 49 Cong., 1 Sess., pp. 2790–97). His speeches, though not oratorical, were with but few exceptions logical, short, and to the point. He generally aligned himself with the moderate, progressive group of his party. Meantime, the Democrats had carried Indiana in 1884, gerrymandered the state, and defeated him for reëlection in 1886 by a margin of one vote, after a dramatic campaign. His second major political defeat, however, like his first one in 1876, did not injure him politically.

As early as 1883, Wharton Barker, a wealthy Quaker banker of Philadelphia, had surmised that the bitter hostility between Blaine and Arthur would cause the defeat of either if nominated for the presidency and had suggested to independent Republican leaders in the East that Harrison would unite all elements of his party and carry the doubtful state of Indiana. Harrison attended the Republican National Convention at Chicago in 1884 and was seriously considered as a possible "dark horse" candidate. That his name was not presented was due to his own unwillingness to launch a personal campaign, to the failure of his civil-service record to satisfy Eastern independents, and, above all, to his inability to command the united support of his own state delegation. His lifelong rival and jealous opponent, Walter Q. Gresham [*q.v.*], was also hoping for the nomination and Indiana had not yet decided which was to be her favorite son. Beginning in 1887, Harrison's friends carried on a quiet but well-organized campaign to secure his nomination in 1888. Though he was fourth on the first ballot at Chicago, he was nominated on the eighth. A spectacular, spirited campaign followed with the tariff as the chief issue (see Cleveland, Stephen Grover). Harrison set a precedent by conducting an effective "front porch" campaign, making a large number of short speeches to visiting delegations. The archaic electoral college gave him 233 votes and Cleveland 169, in spite of the fact that the American people indorsed Cleveland's administration by a popular plurality of 100,000.

After long consideration Harrison appointed James G. Blaine [*q.v.*] secretary of state. Most of the other men selected for the cabinet were little known in national politics. The choice of some was criticized by party leaders, of others by reformers, but practically all made excellent department heads. The designation of John Wanamaker [*q.v.*], a wealthy Philadelphia merchant, as postmaster general was particularly obnoxious to the reform element because he had raised large campaign funds to elect Harrison and was recommended by Quay. Under him, however, the postal service was greatly increased in efficiency. Harrison gave him a free hand, even when the first assistant postmaster general, J. S. Clarkson, was removing Democratic incumbents with such rapidity that civil-service reformers were alienated.

Harrison appreciated the new forces which were sweeping the United States onward into imperialism. He took great pride in the new navy of steel ships being built under Secretary Benjamin F. Tracy and saw his policy of developing a merchant marine auspiciously begun. The Pan-American Congress was brilliantly conducted by Blaine. The frequent illness of the Secretary compelled Harrison, throughout the administration, to assume much of his work. Blaine pushed the American claims in Samoa with new vigor and received the credit for the result, but his hand was carefully guided by the President. The Samoan notes were revised and one was entirely rewritten, in accordance with Harrison's suggestions. Every effort was made to secure the Mole St. Nicholas in Haiti, but here even Machiavellian methods failed. In the bitter controversy with Chile, Harrison could not disregard an attack upon men wearing the uniform of the United States. During the closing days of his administration, Harrison sent to the Senate a treaty annexing Hawaii. To his great personal regret and mortification, his successor, Cleveland, promptly withdrew the treaty before the Senate had voted on it because in his opinion it had not been justly negotiated.

Civil-service reform proved a troublesome question to Harrison. He had been elected with the support of many of its friends and on a platform strongly favoring it. He was the first

Republican president since Lincoln to succeed a Democrat, however, and the hunger of his party for office was great. Harrison himself belonged to the moderates and soon aroused the antipathy of both the extreme reformers and the powerful politicians. In spite of a few unfortunate, though usually unimportant, acts which proved very helpful to his political enemies, his civil-service record was statesmanlike. He enlisted and kept the services of Theodore Roosevelt as civil-service commissioner; he respected the classified list, and he extended it from approximately 27,000 positions to 38,000. Nevertheless, during the campaign of 1892 he suffered severely because offended Republican leaders sulked, while extreme civil-service reformers left the party. Harrison gave much attention to administrative problems associated with the opening of Oklahoma Territory to settlement in 1889. When the Mormon church gave up polygamy in order to obtain statehood for Utah, Republican leaders, headed by Clarkson, persuaded Harrison to grant amnesty to accused Mormons (Jan. 4, 1893), but only after it had been proved that the renunciation was sincere and, the election of 1892 being over, he himself could not benefit from the action. Harrison's facility and felicity as a public speaker were never better displayed than in the many, gracious, and effective short speeches which he made on his 10,000-mile tour through the South and West in 1891.

Harrison's senatorial experience, together with his natural repugnance to wielding the "big stick," caused him to touch elbows with Congress, but to avoid important policies distinct from those which his party advocated there. He did not seek popularity, nor was he skilful in arousing and focusing public opinion in support of legislation which he desired. His searching, steel-gray eyes made the politician who came hoping for personal benefit feel ill at ease. His manner, even toward most senators and representatives of his own party, was reserved; this characteristic limited his influence with them, even though they had great respect for his intelligence in administration and his integrity of purpose and character. From 1888 to 1891, the Republican party was in the hands of leaders whom the president could not control. During the latter half of his term, his influence on legislation was severely curtailed by Democratic gains in the lower House. Before the Republicans lost their ascendancy in Congress, however, they passed many important laws. Long travail produced the McKinley Tariff Act. To make its high rates more palatable, Harrison was instrumental in obtaining the insertion of a reciprocity provision; in fact, he wrote the draft for this, the only popular section of the notorious bill. The Sherman Silver Act he signed because he was assured by Sherman, Aldrich, and Windom that he could safely do so and because he wanted to help the silver industry. The Sherman Anti-Trust Act he favored. In spite of all his efforts and to his great chagrin, the federal elections bill failed. He signed a river and harbors act which carried a large appropriation, and a dependent pension act which increased pension expenditures from $98,000,000 in 1889 to $157,000,000 in 1893. To him the increasing age and infirmity of Union veterans gave "the minor tones of sadness and pathos to the mighty appeal of service and suffering" (*Public Papers and Addresses of Benjamin Harrison,* 1893, p. 23). His attitude, however, was entirely different from that of "Corporal" Tanner, the commissioner of pensions, who followed an extravagant, materialistic policy. Tanner had been in office only a few months when Harrison stated privately that in giving him the place he had made one of the two great blunders in appointments. Tanner soon resigned, but the odium of his policy remained to harass Harrison. As a result of Republican legislation and general economic conditions, the surplus in the federal treasury soon disappeared and the advance shadows of the panic of 1893 became evident. As early as September 1890, Harrison exerted himself to increase circulation and avoid financial disaster.

By the second year of Harrison's term, Quay, Platt, Alger, "Czar" Reed, and others had begun to form an anti-Harrison wing in the Republican party to prevent his renomination. Had this situation not arisen, he, like Hayes, would probably have retired at the end of one term. He carried responsibility heavily, and to him the White House had no personal allurements. "Why should a man seek that which to him would be a calamity?" he wrote to his friend, Tracy, on May 5, 1896, when the latter, along with others, was urging him to become a candidate for the third time. The implacable hostility of the "bosses" increased as 1892 approached until its virulence is hard to overestimate. Harrison's friends rallied under the leadership of L. T. Michener and renominated him over Blaine and McKinley, but in the election he was overwhelmingly defeated by Cleveland. The defeat of the Republican party was caused principally by the following factors: the alienation of many labor votes because of the Homestead strike and Whitelaw Reid's candidacy for vice-president; the lethargy of leading organization men; Catholic opposition to Harrison's Indian school policy; his failure to make a strong popular appeal and his inability to exert his power as a campaigner because of the long illness and death of his wife; continued popular resentment against the over-reaching greed behind the McKinley Act; the business rumblings of the oncoming panic of 1893; and the deep-seated, nation-wide unrest which was soon to break out in the Populist and free-silver "whirlwind."

Harrison returned to his home in Indianapolis to engage in writing and in the practice of law. He accepted a considerable number of invitations to speak. Among his outstanding addresses were "The Obligations of Wealth," delivered in Chicago in 1898, and "The Status of Annexed Territory and of its Free Civilized Inhabitants," delivered in Ann Arbor in 1900. In these he espoused the cause of justice for the common citizen of the United States and personal liberty and civil rights for the people of Porto Rico and the Philippines. Many of his speeches were published, first in magazines and later in a book, *Views of an Ex-President* (1901). Edward Bok, editor of the *Ladies' Home Journal,* persuaded Harrison to write (1895–97) a notable series of articles on the nature of the federal government and the personal life of a president. These articles were later revised and published as a book, *This Country of Ours* (1897), which had a wide sale and for a generation was a standard reference work in high schools and colleges. It was republished in England under the title *The Constitution and Administration of the United States of America* (1897). The Carnegie Endowment for International Peace had it translated into Spanish under the title, *Biblioteca Interamericana: Vida constitucional de los Estados Unidos* (1919), and distributed it among influential persons in Latin America as one of five books which would best interpret to them the history and culture of the United States. During the campaign of 1894, Harrison spoke for his party; in 1896, he again took a leading part in the campaign, though he had little admiration for Mark Hanna and McKinley. The speech he made in Carnegie Hall in New York had wide influence; Richard Olney called it the "leading and best speech on the Republican side during the campaign" (Henry James, *Richard Olney and his Public Service,* 1923, p. 309). No other ex-president resumed the bona-fide practice of law on such a large scale and so successfully as did Harrison. He accepted retainers in outstanding civil cases in the highest state and federal courts, and he was selected by Venezuela as its senior counsel to present before the arbitration tribunal in Paris in 1899 its side of the boundary dispute with England. On this case he labored assiduously for almost two years. After his masterful, twenty-five hour, closing argument had proceeded for a day and a half, the English counsel dispatched a messenger to Lord Salisbury to prepare him for the loss of control over the mouth of the Orinoco River.

On Apr. 6, 1896, Harrison married Mrs. Mary Scott (Lord) Dimmick, a niece of his first wife; to them a daughter, Elizabeth, was born. During the mellowing years as ex-president, when he had no longer to labor constantly, nor put up a protecting barrier against office seekers, the kindly, considerate side of his character and his natural humor were given freer scope; his life broadened in outlook and he gave his influence to the liberal side of national and international problems, supporting what would now be termed "modernist" policies in the Presbyterian General Assembly, condemning extremes of imperialism, and emphasizing the obligations of wealth. He died of pneumonia on Mar. 13, 1901, and was buried in Crown Hill Cemetery, Indianapolis.

[Lew Wallace, *Life of Gen. Ben Harrison* (1888) is the best of seven campaign biographies. A biography by A. T. Volwiler, utilizing the numerous Benjamin Harrison manuscripts in the Lib. of Cong., hitherto unexploited by historians, is in preparation. E. W. Halford, private secretary to Harrison while president, published articles in *Century Mag.,* June 1912; N. Y. *Christian Advocate,* June 11, 18, and July 9, 1914; and *Leslie's Illustrated Weekly Newspaper,* Mar. 8–Oct. 11, 1919. The *Indianapolis Jour.* and *Indianapolis Sentinel* are invaluable for Harrison's life after 1854. See also Edward Stanwood, *A Hist. of the Presidency* (1898); Wm. A. White, *Masks in a Pageant* (1928); articles in *North Am. Rev.,* June, Oct. 1888, June 1892; N. Y. *Nation,* July 19, 1888, Mar. 21, 1901; *Forum,* July 1892; obituaries in *Indianapolis Sentinel, Indianapolis Jour.,* and *N. Y. Times,* Mar. 14, 1901.]

A. T. V.

HARRISON, BIRGE [See HARRISON, LOVELL BIRGE, 1854–1929].

HARRISON, CARTER HENRY (Feb. 15, 1825–Oct. 28, 1893), mayor of Chicago, was descended from Benjamin Harrison, clerk of the Royal Council of Virginia in 1634; his great-grandfather and Benjamin Harrison [*q.v.*], a signer of the Declaration of Independence and father of William Henry Harrison [*q.v.*], were brothers. Born near Lexington, Ky., the son of Carter Henry and Caroline (Russell) Harrison, he was prepared for college by Dr. Louis Marshall [*q.v.*], brother of the Chief Justice. He received the degree of A.B. from Yale in 1845. A most important part of his education for his future career in Chicago was his two years of travel and study in Europe (1851–53). He was a Kentucky planter for a few years, but having taken his law degree (LL.B.) at Transylvania University in 1855, he married Sophonisba Preston, sold his plantation, and settled in Chicago where he grew wealthy as a result of his real-estate ventures. Mrs. Harrison died in 1876 and six years later Harrison married Marguerite Stearns, who died in 1887. His engagement to Annie Howard of New Orleans was announced just before his death.

The Chicago fire of 1871 produced a non-partisan or "fire-proof" ticket on which Harrison, who was a regular Democrat to the day of his death but who up to that time had been interested only in business, was elected county commissioner. In this campaign he discovered a latent talent as a speaker which he had not dreamed he possessed. He was defeated for Congress in 1872 but elected on the Democratic ticket in 1874 and in 1876. Legislative business not being to his liking, he laid careful plans for his elevation to the mayoralty of Chicago, and was elected in 1879. In this office he was most happy and conspicuously successful. He was easily reëlected in 1881 and in 1883. His defeat for governor of Illinois in 1884 by a plurality of 14,599 was due to the fact that the Republicans normally carried the state by some 40,000 votes. He was again reëlected mayor in 1885, by a very narrow majority—375. He interrupted his political career in 1887–88 by a voyage around the world, which was the basis for his book, *A Race with the Sun* (1889), published originally as a series of letters to the *Chicago Tribune*. Two years later he published another book, *A Summer Outing and the Old Man's Story* (1891). the first part being the description of another trip, the second part an imaginative tale, originally planned as a novel. In 1891 he ran again for the office of mayor and was defeated by a small plurality, but was triumphantly elected as the party's regular candidate for "World's Fair Mayor" in 1893. The bullets of one Prendergast, a deluded young man who had vainly implored Harrison to make him corporation counsel, dramatically ended the Mayor's career the following October.

Harrison's success in Chicago was due to many factors. He won the support of business men of both parties because he was a successful business man himself and carried business principles to his office. He was both boss and mayor of Chicago—a very definite case of responsible government. Because of his sympathy with and appreciation of the moderate socialists he won their support. His liberal views on social and moral questions gave him the support of the saloon interests and the harpy classes, though these classes were never allowed to forget that Harrison was boss. He was a great champion of the naturalized citizens who enthusiastically gave him a big majority of their forty-nine per cent. of the Chicago vote. He was a superb campaigner of the "rough and tumble," stump-speaking variety. His physical courage was often demonstrated; his personal integrity was unquestioned; he was witty, quick, resourceful and always good-natured with his audience. His memory of men never failed him and he took good care that all should recognize him by his familiar black felt hat, which he wore with studied carelessness, and his fine Kentucky mare, which he rode like a "marshall of the empire." Despite the opposition of the pulpit and the partisan press, which alleged that he wallowed with the "unclean beast of his party" and had sold himself completely and irretrievably to Mike McDonald (the boss gambler) and the devil, he was greeted at nominating conventions with a "gutteral copper-distilled howl of joy," nominated "amid a perfect hurricane of applause and cheers" (*Chicago Daily News*, Mar. 29, 1883), and five times elected to the office of mayor. His name was the chief factor in electing his son mayor of Chicago in 1897.

[W. J. Abbot, *Carter Henry Harrison: A Memoir* (1895) and "The Harrison Dynasty in Chicago," *Munsey's Mag.*, Sept. 1903; F. O. Bennett, *Politics and Politicians of Chicago, Cook County, and Ill. . . . 1787–1887* (1886); Alexander Brown, *The Cabells and Their Kin* (1895); C. O. Johnson, *Carter Henry Harrison I, Political Leader* (1928); Adolf Kraus, *Reminiscences and Comments* (1925); J. T. McKenna, *The Four Assassins of Ellsworth, Lincoln, Garfield, Harrison* (1894).]

C. O. J.

HARRISON, CHARLES CUSTIS (May 3, 1844–Feb. 12, 1929), financier, and educator, was born, lived all of his life, and died in Philadelphia. He was a grandson of John Harrison [*q.v.*], a pioneer manufacturing chemist, and the son of George Leib and Sarah Ann (Waples) Harrison. Prepared for college at the Episcopal Academy in Philadelphia, he graduated from the College of the University of Pennsylvania in 1862, first in his class. Leaving college in the midst of war, he went almost immediately to the front, intending to enlist; but his youth, the state of his health, and his father's persuasions prevented his entering the military service. He contemplated the study of the law, but his father, who had purchased an interest in a sugar refinery, induced him to engage in business life, in which he might be joined later by his three younger brothers. He therefore became the head of the firm of Harrison, Newhall & Welsh, and continued for nearly three decades to direct the concern, under changing names, as its trade expanded in answer to his management. On Feb. 23, 1870, he married Ellen Nixon Waln, a great-grand-daughter of Robert Morris, the financier of the Revolution. He retired in 1892 when he and his brothers and a brother-in-law who were the sole proprietors of what had grown to be one of the most important enterprises of the country, sold it to the American Sugar Refining Company, known as the "Trust."

Harrison had a public outlook and he came to be regarded as one of Philadelphia's most useful and benevolent inhabitants. His aid and support were constantly sought and judiciously bestowed for the advantage of charitable and civic causes. He was elected a trustee of the University of Pennsylvania in 1876 when he was but thirty-two years old. Upon the resignation of Provost William Pepper [*q.v.*], in 1894, Harrison consented to act in his place *ad interim,* but at the end of a few months, in 1895, he became the provost in name as well as in fact, a place which he continued to occupy for fifteen years. His predecessor, Provost Pepper, had distinguished himself along with Eliot, Gilman, and Andrew D. White, in the work of modernizing and vitalizing higher education in America, and although Harrison did not possess Pepper's brilliant touch, he gave financial acumen and the energy of the business man to the execution of Pepper's program. In a few years he had fulfilled Pepper's plans and added new projects to the University's scheme of material development. When he resigned on Oct. 4, 1910, the number of acres in the University tract had nearly trebled, the value of its property had been quadrupled. The number of teachers had increased from 273 to 494, the student body from twenty-four hundred to more than five thousand. He had in that time collected more than ten million dollars for the needs of the institution, contributing liberally all the while from his own purse. Among his gifts was a half million for the George Leib Harrison Foundation in memory of his father, principally for the support of a number of scholarships and fellowships in the University. His retirement gave him more freedom for other benevolences, the principal object of his interest in later years being the University Museum, of which he was the president. His indomitable exertions made possible important archeological expeditions which brought to Philadelphia the fruits of scholarly research in ancient Babylonia, Egypt, and South America.

Harrison's advancement into a position of public service was at the cost of personal inclination and convenience. He was at ground a man of the simplest habits. His unremitting forays upon the wealthy in Philadelphia were made from a rather shabby office in the downtown business section of the city. Whether as provost or as citizen he was always friendly and accessible. His hours were long. His hurried daily luncheon at a "counter" with clerks and stenographers fitted his tastes better than the entertainment which he knew so well how to lavish upon his guests at his beautiful city and country homes. Between him and Mrs. Harrison, who died in 1922, there were the closest ties. He would say that a day never passed when he did not, at its end, unfold to her the results of its activities in the University's behalf.

[*Old Penn,* Oct. 8–Dec. 24, 1910; Phila. newspapers of Feb. 12 and 13, 1929, especially the *Evening Bulletin* of Feb. 12; W. W. Harrison, *Harrison, Waples and Allied Families* (1910); E. P. Oberholtzer, *Phila.: A Hist. of the City and Its People* (1912), vol. III; *Univ. of Pa.,* vol. I (1901) in Universities and Their Sons, ed. by J. L. Chamberlain; F. N. Thorpe, *William Pepper, M.D., LL.D.* (1904).]

E. P. O.

HARRISON, CONSTANCE CARY (Apr. 25, 1843–Nov. 21, 1920), author, novelist, daughter of Archibald and Monimia (Fairfax) Cary, was born in Fairfax County, Va. Her father was the son of William Jefferson Cary, nephew of Thomas Jefferson, and her mother was a daughter of Thomas, ninth Lord Fairfax, who never assumed his title. Archibald Cary was editor of the *Cumberland Civilian,* at Cumberland, Md., and died there before he was forty. His widow went with her three children to live with her mother on the Fairfax estate, "Vaucluse," near Alexandria, Va. There the family remained until "Vaucluse" was destroyed during the Civil War. The education of Constance Cary was often interrupted. At Cumberland she went to Miss Jane Kenah's day school and studied Latin with the rector of the parish. At "Vaucluse" she had a French governess; later she went to Richmond to the boarding-school of M. Hubert Lefebvre. During the Civil War, her mother became a volunteer nurse and she herself matured rapidly. She spent the war years in Richmond or its neighborhood and there met her future husband, Burton Norvell Harrison, the young secretary of Jefferson Davis. Her war experiences included nursing, making a Confederate flag, and writing magazine articles under the name "Refugitta." There were some pleasures: she saw the inauguration of Jefferson Davis, attended the receptions of Mrs. Davis, received a call from General Lee, and rode with Burton Harrison. After the fall of Richmond and the assassination of Lincoln, Harrison was imprisoned and Constance Cary, who had gone to stay with relatives in New Jersey, had no news of him for months. Finally, after continued efforts of the Carys, now in Washington, he was released and visited them there. In October 1866, Constance and her mother went to Europe, where the former studied music and French. On Nov. 26, 1867, she married Burton Harrison, in Saint Ann's Church, at Morrisania, N. Y., her aunt's home. Her husband was practising law in New York City and they went to live near Irving Place. Her social circle included many persons interested in music and literature. At the suggestion of Rev. Francis Vinton of Trinity Church, she began to write short stories. "A Little Centennial Lady," which appeared in *Scribner's Monthly,* July 1876, established her popularity. Thereafter she wrote continuously —tales, novels, plays, essays. She is best known by her novels and tales, the chief of which are: *Flower de Hundred; the Story of a Virginia Plantation* (1890); *Belhaven Tales* (1892); *A Daughter of the South and Shorter Stories* (1892); *Sweet Bells out of Tune* (1893); *A Bachelor Maid* (1894); *An Errant Wooing* (1895); *A Virginia Cousin and Bar Harbor Tales* (1895); *The Anglomaniacs* (1899); *A Princess of the Hills; an Italian Romance* (1901); *Sylvia's Husband* (1904); *The Carlyles; a Story of the Fall of the Confederacy* (1905); *Latter-Day Sweethearts* (1906). These tales, which had great popularity for years, have for subject matter rather superficial social life. The characters carry the story along pleasantly, if they make no lasting impression. Many of her backgrounds, which are well drawn, are European, and accordingly her novels are partly books of travel. Her style is vivacious and clever. After the death of her husband in 1904, she spent much time abroad, but finally settled in Washington. In 1911 she published an autobiographical volume, *Recollections Grave and Gay.* She died in Washington, survived by two sons.

[*Recollections Grave and Gay* (1911); *Who's Who in America,* 1918–19; C. W. Martin, "A Favored Daughter of the South," *Southern Mag.* (Louisville, Ky.), Aug. 1894; Fairfax Harrison, *Aris Sonis Focisque. . . . The Harrisons of Skinimo* (1910) and *The Va. Carys* (1919); *Evening Star* (Washington) and *N. Y. Times,* Nov. 22, 1920; information as to specific facts from Mr. Fairfax Harrison, of Belvoir, Va., son of Mrs. Harrison.] S. G. B.

HARRISON, ELIZABETH (Sept. 1, 1849–Oct. 31, 1927), kindergartner, came of a family of English origin, which was established in Virginia in 1699. She was born in Athens, Ky., the daughter of Isaac Webb Harrison and Elizabeth Thompson Bullock. A few months after her birth her parents moved to Midway, Ky., and when she was about seven, to Davenport, Iowa, where she received her elementary and high-school education. After the marriage of her sisters and the death of her mother, the home in Davenport was broken up, and in 1879, at the suggestion of a friend in Chicago, she went to that city to "look into a new system of education which . . . was destined to revolutionize the world" (*Kindergarten Magazine,* June 1893, p. 739). Becoming enthusiastic over the possibilities of this innovation—the kindergarten—she enrolled in the training class conducted by Mrs. Alice H. Putnam, graduated in 1880, and spent a year as assistant in Mrs. Putnam's kindergarten. The introduction to educational philosophy and practice which she here received led her to pursue further study under the direction successively of two of the pioneers of the kindergarten in America—Susan Elizabeth Blow [*q.v.*], in St. Louis, and Marie Kraus-Boelte [*q.v.*] in New York. During the year following her return to Chicago in 1883, she and Mrs. Putnam organized the Chicago Kindergarten Club for teachers and in 1884 she founded a free training class in a mission kindergarten. Two years later, with the cooperation of Mrs. John N. Crouse, she established a school dedicated to the training of mothers and teachers of young children. Of this institution, which in 1891 was incorporated as the Chicago Kindergarten College and in 1916 became the National Kindergarten and Elementary College, she was president for thirty-three years.

In 1890, accompanied by Mrs. Crouse, she went to Germany where she studied for some months under two pupils of Froebel, Frau Schrader and the Baroness von Marenholz-Bulow. In the same year she published her first series of lectures in book form, under the title *A Study of Child Nature* (1890). This publication has passed into fifty editions and has been translated into eight foreign languages. She was one of the first women to appear on the program of the National Education Association, was a speaker of note, and in demand as a lecturer. In 1894 she helped to organize a "convention of mothers" which ultimately grew into the National Congress of Parents and Teachers. She was one of the promoters of the Chicago "Literary Schools" in which Denton J. Snider and William Torrey Harris [*qq.v.*] took prominent part; in fact, these schools, which were held annually for eight years under the auspices of the Chicago Kindergarten College, may be said to have had their origin in a class of mothers organized for Dr. Snider by Miss Harrison in 1886. In 1912 the National Kindergarten Association sent her to Rome to investigate the work of Mme. Montessori. Her report, *Montessori and the Kindergarten* (1913), was published by the United States Bureau of Education. She was also the author of several volumes of stories for children and suggestions regarding kindergarten methods and child psychology, which served, at the time, to interpret and popularize the Child Study movement in its effort to create a better understanding of the child and his needs.

In 1920 she retired from active teaching, becoming president emeritus of the National Kindergarten and Elementary College. This institution is a memorial to her steadfast purpose and above all to her capacity to lend herself to progressive measures in education. While her work represents the best of her period, it bespeaks the emotional and ethical approach. Her claim to distinction lies in the growth and elasticity of mind which she showed during the last ten years of her active connection with the College. She approved of drastic changes in equipment, material, and technique when she might in her strategic position have offered disintegrating opposition. The closing years of her life were spent quietly in San Antonio, Tex., whither she had gone because of her frail health, and where she died.

[Elizabeth Harrison's autobiography, *Sketches Along Life's Road,* edited by Carolyn Sherwin Bailey, was published in 1930. See also: *Who's Who in America,* 1926–27; Ilse Forest, *Preschool Education* (1927); *Kindergarten Mag.,* June 1893; *In Memoriam* (1928), an appreciation by Edward Herbert Lewis, published by the College under the auspices of the International Kindergarten Union; *Experimental Studies in Kindergarten and Practice* (Teachers College, Columbia Univ., 1914); *Chicago Daily Tribune* and *N. Y. Times,* Nov. 1, 1927.]

B. C. G.

HARRISON, GABRIEL (Mar. 25, 1818–Dec. 15, 1902), theatrical manager, actor, author, painter, was cheated by a dangerous versatility out of the material rewards which should have come to any one of his varied gifts. He was of English descent. John Harrison, his great-grandfather, received an award from the British government for the invention of an important chronometer. His maternal grandfather wove the coronation robes of George III. William Harrison, his father's father, engraver to the Bank of England and map-engraver to the East India Company, came to America in 1794 to engrave notes for the State Bank of Pennsylvania. Gabriel was born in Philadelphia, the son of Charles P. Harrison, also an artist and engraver, and Elizabeth (Foster) Harrison, but he grew up in New York, whither his father removed in 1824. At his home in Reade Street the elder Harrison kept open house for men of letters and the arts. Gabriel remembered playing under the piano when the great Malibran was practising, and—a precocious, impressionable child—listening to the talk of Fitz-Greene Halleck, Nathaniel Parker Willis, and John Howard Payne. At eleven he scraped acquaintance with the aged Aaron Burr, who taught him to read aloud. At fourteen he saw Forrest act and was "wild for the stage." At seventeen he won amateur success with the American Histrionic Society, and at eighteen wrote a play. His professional début was made in 1838 at the National Theatre, Washington, as Othello to the elder Wallack's Iago and the Desdemona of Emma Wheatley. In 1845 he was supporting Charles Kean at the old Park Theatre, New York. Meanwhile, he had temporarily abandoned the stage for gainful occupations. He experimented successfully with Daguerre's newly perfected process, making portraits on silver which later won medals at the Crystal Palace, 1851, and the New York World's Fair of 1853. In 1843 he opened a general store at the corner of Broadway and Prince Street. Here the impecunious Poe discovered him. Harrison later pictured himself and Halleck drying Poe's coat over a flour-barrel while they plied the hungry poet with crackers and cheese, port and pleasant talk, in a sung nook among the tea chests ("Reminiscences of Poe," cited by Woodberry, *post*). Harrison became one of Poe's few intimates. While he was president of the White Eagle Club which aided Polk's election, Poe wrote for him a rousing campaign song. From 1848 Harrison was identified with Brooklyn (save for two seasons as actor-manager of the Adelphi Theatre, Troy), becoming a force in the dramatic, musical, and art life of the city. In 1853 he founded the Brooklyn Dramatic Academy, forming companies which played in towns about New York. In 1863 he opened the first established playhouse in Brooklyn, the Park Theatre, where he introduced his original device of concealed footlights. Here, in wartime, he launched the first American opera company with Theodore Thomas [*q.v.*] as conductor, scoring an artistic but scarcely a financial success. Thereafter he was often lessee of the Brooklyn Academy of Music, appearing with William Florence, Matilda Heron, and James W. Wallack. As secretary of the Brooklyn Academy of Design (1867), he promoted its free art schools. He helped to organize the Faust Club of actors, musicians, and authors (1872), and developed a dramatic department in the Long Island Historical Society, to which he gave his library of plays and manuscripts. By his publication of *The Life and Writings of John Howard Payne* (1875), he aroused interest in the poet which resulted in the bringing of his body from Tunis to the United States. From boyhood devoted to painting, in landscape and portraiture, Harrison often sold his work to further some civic cause. He prepared a biography, *Edwin Forrest, the Actor and the Man,* which was privately printed in 1889, and painted a portrait of Forrest, his lifelong friend, as Coriolanus. He contributed the chapter on drama, music, and the fine arts to Stiles's history of Kings County, and was the author of several plays, including *Melanthia,* a tragedy written in 1866 for Matilda Heron. In 1878 he appeared as Roger Chillingworth in his own dramatization of *The Scarlet Letter.* His acting was characterized by perfect enunciation and magnetic power of voice and manner. After a nervous illness persisting seven years, he gave his later life to the teaching of elocution and acting. He died of old age in Brooklyn.

[H. R. Stiles, *The Civil, Political, Professional and Ecclesiastical Hist. . . . of the County of Kings, and the City of Brooklyn, N. Y.* (1884); G. E. Woodberry, *The Life of Edgar Allan Poe* (2 vols., 1909); *Who's Who in America,* 1899, 1901–02; *N. Y. Times,* Dec. 16, 1902; *Brooklyn Daily Eagle,* Dec. 15, 1902.] M. B. H.

HARRISON, GEORGE PAUL (Mar. 19, 1841–July 17, 1922), soldier, politician, was born at "Monteith Plantation," near Savannah, Ga., the son of George Paul and Thurza Adelaide (Gwin) Harrison. His grandfather, Col. William Harrison, a veteran of the War of 1812 and of the Indian wars, seems to have been the first of the family in Georgia, though the date of his settling there is not known. The elder George Paul Harrison became a prominent rice planter. Prior to the Civil War he had risen to the rank of major-general of Georgia militia and during the war he commanded a brigade of state troops in and about Savannah. George Paul, Jr., was graduated in 1861 from the Georgia Military Institute, at Marietta, receiving the degrees of A.B. and C.E., and at once entered the Confederate army as a second lieutenant. During the first year of the war he saw service in Virginia. In 1862, however, he returned to Georgia to become colonel of the 5th, and six months later of the 32nd Georgia Infantry. His regiment was sent to form part of the garrison at Charleston and from that time on his service was in South Carolina, Florida, and Alabama. He commanded a brigade in the battle of Olustee, Fla., early in 1864, and on Feb. 7, 1865, was promoted to brigadier-general. Later in the year he protected Hardee in his retreat from Savannah, after Sherman had invested that city, and enabled Hardee to withdraw into South Carolina without serious loss. Shortly after the close of hostilities, Harrison, who had studied law during the war, began to practise in Alabama, first at Auburn and then at Opelika, and for the greater part of his life he was identified with that state. He was a delegate to the Alabama constitutional conventions of 1875 and 1901; a member of the state Senate, 1878–84, and again, 1900–04, and president of the Senate for two years; a delegate to the National Democratic Convention of 1892. He was elected to Congress in 1894 to fill a vacancy, and was reëlected for the following term, serving from 1894 to 1897. He was a prominent Mason, and twice Grand Master of the Grand Lodge of Alabama; he took great interest in the Association of Confederate Veterans and was four times head of the Alabama Division. He was always a regular Democrat and was a lifelong member of the Methodist Church. He was married four times: in 1863 to Mary Drake of Georgia; in 1886, to Mattie, daughter of Governor Ligon of Alabama; in 1896, to Frances Louise Witherspoon; and on Nov. 20, 1900, to Sarah Katharine Nunnally, of La Grange, Ga. One child, a daughter, was born to his first wife; and a son, to his third wife.

[*Who's Who in America,* 1914–15; W. J. Northen, *Men of Mark in Ga.,* vol. III (1911); B. F. Riley, *Makers and Romance of Ala. Hist.* (1915); T. M. Owen, *Hist. of Ala. and Dict. of Ala. Biog.* (1921), vol. III; *Confed. Mil. Hist.* (1899), VI, 421; *Biog. Dir. Am. Cong.* (1928); *Southern Hist. Soc. Papers,* vols. IX (1881) and XXXV (1907); *Confed. Veteran,* Aug. 1922; *Montgomery Advertiser,* July 18, 1922.]
R. P. B—s.

HARRISON, GESSNER (June 26, 1807–Apr. 7, 1862), teacher, classicist, was born in Harrisonburg, Va., the second son of Peachy and Mary (Stuart) Harrison. His father, a physician in large practice, universally esteemed for his learning and skill, named him for the Swiss poet of liberty, Salomon Gessner. The boy was quiet and sedate, diffident and retiring, and from an early age devoted to reading. He began his formal schooling at the age of four, and at eight was inducted into the Latin grammar. Instructed by a succession of Presbyterian ministers who demanded nothing short of absolute accuracy, he made uniform progress in mathematics, Greek, and Latin. Among his favorite books was Horne Tooke's *Diversions of Purley,* which undoubtedly awoke in him his lifelong interest in philology. In March 1825 he matriculated with his elder brother at the newly opened University of Virginia, where he continued as a student for three years. He and his brother did not sympathize with the riotous attitude of their fellow students, and they won a sort of student immortality by declining, on the grounds of religious scruples, the great Mr. Jefferson's rotatory invitation to Sunday dinner. In July 1828 Gessner graduated in the school of Greek and at the same time received the degree of Doctor of Medicine, expecting to return to his native town to practise with his father. He was appointed, however, at the suggestion of his preceptor, Prof. George Long, to succeed the latter in the chair of ancient languages, and, in spite of vigorous opposition occasioned by his youth and total lack of experience, entered the faculty of the University of Virginia at the age of twenty-one.

He was by nature timid and he was entirely at variance with the dominant sentiments of the student body. His first ten years of service at the University were the most tempestuous in its history. As the youngest member of the faculty and perhaps the most out-spoken in his denunciations of disorder, he was subjected to personal insults and violence, but he bore himself with extraordinary fortitude and self-control and was five times chosen as chairman of the faculty, serving twelve years in all. He deserves no small part of the credit for the adjustment of the relations between teachers and students, the growing helpfulness of mutual cooperation, and the birth of the honor system. Early in his career he reorganized the content and methods of the school of ancient languages. He was the first college teacher in America to recognize the new science of comparative grammar, threw himself into it with enthusiasm, and incorporated it organically in all his teaching. His *Exposition of Some of the Laws of the Latin Grammar* (1852) and his later *Treatise on the Greek Prepositions and the Cases of the Nouns with Which These are Used* (1858) show immense toil, and, antedating as they did the formulation of exact canons, some points of striking originality. His pamphlet, *The Geography of Ancient Italy and Southern Greece* (1834), became a standard textbook in many colleges and universities. In December 1830 he married Eliza Lewis Carter Tucker, daughter of his colleague, George Tucker, professor of moral philosophy. Of this union were born six sons and three daughters.

In person, Harrison was a small, slight man, alert in manner and movement. His face, though quite engaging, was rather homely, but "his dark eyes were singularly beautiful," and the tones of his voice exceedingly sweet (Broadus, *post*, p. 308). His mind was slow in its processes, but accurate and logical, and characterized by a rugged honesty which endeared him to colleagues and pupils alike. He was a man of deep religious convictions and of sincere piety in every relation of life. After thirty-one years of unbroken service, he resigned from his chair to establish a boarding-school for boys upon a plantation in Nelson County, Va. The life was suited to his tastes, and the revenues he was justified in expecting were needed for the expenses of his large family. His plans and hopes were frustrated by the Civil War, however, and his anxieties augmented by the desperate illness of his eldest son, invalided home, whom he nursed with unremitting care. He died in the spring of 1862, in his fifty-fifth year.

[Article by Gessner Harrison on the Univ. of Va. in E. A. and G. L. Duyckinck, *Cyc. of Am. Lit.* (1856), vol. II; J. A. Broadus, "Memorial of Gessner Harrison," printed in *Southern Rev.* (St. Louis), Oct. 1873, and in Broadus' *Sermons and Addresses* (1887); D. M. R. Culbreth, *The Univ. of Va.* (1908); L. G. Tyler, *Encyc. of Va. Biog.* (1915), vol. II; P. A. Bruce, *Hist. of the Univ. of Va.* (1920), vol. II.]

W. A. M.

HARRISON, HENRY BALDWIN (Sept. 11, 1821–Oct. 29, 1901), governor of Connecticut, the son of Ammi and Polly (Barney) Harrison, was born in New Haven. He prepared for college at the Lancasterian School there under John E. Lovell, its founder, and by private study with George A. Thacher, at that time a student in the Yale Divinity School. While he was a student Harrison taught for a time in the Lancasterian School. He entered Yale in 1842 and graduated as valedictorian of his class in 1846. After leaving college he studied law in the Yale Law School and in a New Haven law office. He was admitted to the bar in 1848 and began to practise in New Haven with Lucius G. Peck. Although he later was known especially as a corporation lawyer, he attracted attention in 1855 by his successful defense of a client charged with murder, on the then unusual plea of insanity. Active in politics, he was successively a Whig, a Free-Soiler, and a Republican. In 1854 he was elected to the state Senate on the Whig ticket. In the Senate he was chairman of the committee on corporations and a member of committees appointed to consider a revision of the statutes and to compile laws regarding education. He introduced the personal-liberty bill which was passed by this session of the General Assembly of Connecticut to nullify in the state the Fugitive-Slave Law passed by Congress. He was the Republican candidate for lieutenant-governor in 1856, but was defeated. In 1865 he was elected to the lower house of the Connecticut legislature as a representative of New Haven, and in this session was chairman of the committees on railroads and on federal relations. He advocated an amendment to the state constitution which would give the negro the ballot. He was again elected to represent New Haven in the legislature of 1873, and served as chairman of the committee on a constitutional convention—the bill for which was defeated—and as a member of the judiciary committee. In 1874 he was an unsuccessful candidate for the governorship. Representing New Haven in the lower house of the state legislature for the third time in 1884, he was chosen speaker of the House. In that year he was again a candidate for governor. No candidate received a majority of the popular vote, though the Democrats had a plurality. In the joint convention of the legislature made necessary by this situation Harrison was elected, 164 to 91. He served for two years, beginning Jan. 7, 1885. He was a member of Trinity Church (Episcopal), New Haven, and a member of the Yale Corporation, 1872–85, and, *ex officio,* 1885–87. He was married in 1856 to Mary Elizabeth Osborne, daughter of Thomas Burr Osborne. From this marriage there were no children. Harrison survived his wife. His death occurred in his eighty-first year at his home in New Haven.

[*Jour. of the Senate of the State of Conn.,* May Sess., 1854; *Jour. of the House of Representatives of the State of Conn.,* May Sess., 1865, May Sess., 1873, Jan. Sess., 1884; *New Haven Morning Jour. and Courier,* esp. Oct. 30, 1901; *New Haven Evening Register,* Oct. 29, 1901; *Yale College Class of 1846* (1871); *Obit. Record Grads. Yale Univ.,* 1902; E. E. Atwater, *Hist. of the City of New Haven* (1887); F. C. Norton, *The Governors of Conn.* (1905).]

DeF. V–S.

HARRISON, HENRY SYDNOR (Feb. 12, 1880–July 14, 1930), newspaper-man and novelist, was born in Sewanee, Tenn., where his father, Dr. Caskie Harrison, was professor of Greek and Latin in the University of the South. On the paternal side he came of a Virginia family established in America in 1634 by Richard Harrison, a native of Colchester, England. His mother was Margaret Coleman (Sydnor) Harrison of Halifax County, Va. In 1882 his parents moved to Mrs. Harrison's family home, and the next year Dr. Harrison established a private school known as the Brooklyn Latin School in Brooklyn, N. Y., where he was joined by his family in 1885. Having prepared for college in his father's school, Henry entered Columbia where he was graduated with the bachelor's degree in 1900. In college his literary bent was evidenced by his active participation in amateur theatricals and his service as editor of both *Morningside* and the *Spectator.* After his father's death in 1902, the family moved to Richmond, Va., where at the close of a brief experience with business, Henry joined the editorial staff of the *Richmond Times-Dispatch.* He was successful as the author of witty paragraphs and of a popular feature known as "Rhymes for the Day." By 1908 he had been made chief editorial writer. Early in 1910, encouraged by the reception of a first novel, *Captivating Mary Carstairs,* which he had published that year under the pseudonym Henry Second, he gave up newspaper work in order to devote all of his time to fiction, and moved to Charleston, W. Va. His second novel, *Queed,* was published in 1911. It won immediate success, justifying Harrison's decision to rely for a living wholly upon authorship, and was followed in 1913 by another success, *V. V.'s Eyes,* and in 1915 by *Angela's Business.* Harrison also republished *Captivating Mary Carstairs* in 1914 under his own name.

In 1915 he joined the American Ambulance Service and spent several months (March–July) on active duty in France. In 1917 he was commissioned lieutenant in the United States Naval Reserves, and, being over age for service at sea, was ordered to Washington, where he remained on duty until February 1919. From that time until his death his home was in New York City, whence he made occasional visits to Virginia and to Europe. His first literary work after the war was a tribute to his brother, who had fallen in action in the Argonne, and was entitled *When I Come Back* (1919). He returned to fiction in 1922 with his *Saint Teresa,* but with the publication of *Andrew Bride of Paris* (1925), he gave up novel writing. In 1929 he contributed a series of articles to the Richmond *News Leader.* His death occurred at a hospital in Atlantic City, N. J., four days after an operation for appendicitis and gall-stones. He was buried in Schockoe Cemetery, Richmond. He had never married.

Harrison was described by a literary acquaintance as "of medium height, slender, with light hair, and merry blue eyes that crinkle all up at the corners whenever he smiles" (Rood, *post*). The success of *Queed,* his best and most popular novel, was due in part to its timeliness. To choose for his hero a whimsical eccentric and for his background the local color of a provincial Southern city stirred by contemporary social problems was to fall in with the current of the hour. In *V. V.'s Eyes* he employed a similar setting and wrote a romance of purpose, with reforms in the tobacco factories as its motive. These works, in which the critics found evidences of the influence of Meredith and De Morgan, won him in the years just before the war a place among the most popular of American novelists.

[J. S. Wilson, in *Lib. of Southern Lit., Supp. No. 1* (vol. XVII, 1923); Henry Rood, "Flippant Portraits," *Bookman,* June 1914; J. A. Caskie, *The Caskie Family of Va.* (1928); Fairfax Harrison, *Aris Sonis Focisque . . . The Harrisons of Skinimo* (1910); E. M. Turner, *Stories and Verse of W. Va.* (1923); *Who's Who in America,* 1928–29; obituaries in *Richmond Times-Dispatch,* July 15, 1930; *Publisher's Weekly,* July 19, 1930; some autobiographical material in "Adventure with the Editors," *Atlantic Monthly*, Apr. 1914, in *Bookman*, Sept. 1913, and in *Everybody's Mag.*, Dec. 1920.] J. C. F.

HARRISON, JAMES (Oct. 10, 1803–Aug. 3, 1870), merchant, trader, and pioneer iron manufacturer of Missouri, was a native of Bourbon County, Ky., the second son of John and Betsy (McLanahan) Harrison. His ancestors were emigrants from the north of Ireland. His boyhood days were spent on his father's farm, and he received such school advantages as his section afforded. When he was nineteen he moved to Fayette, Howard County, Mo., where he soon showed a genius for business. He engaged in many successful enterprises, among these activities being shipment of livestock and grain to St. Louis and thence to New Orleans on flatboats. During 1831–32 he traded with Mexico, largely purchasing and transporting silver bullion, and personally conducted expeditions to Chihuahua. He experienced many of the perils incident to such expeditions, and was one of three survivors of a party of thirteen attacked by Indians between the "Jesus Marie" mine and Chihuahua. In 1832 he furnished Indian supplies under contract with the United States government. He also maintained profitable trading establishments in Arkansas from 1834 to 1840. In the latter year he removed to St. Louis and became a member of the firm of Glasgow, Harrison & Company. Three years later he initiated the development of the mineral resources of the state, stimulating enterprises of great value to the city of St. Louis, and to the individuals who speculated therein. Long before, the attention of scientists and capitalists had been attracted to the great deposits of iron ore in the vicinity of Pilot Knob. As early as 1836 Van Doren, Pease & Company purchased Pilot Knob and Iron Mountain and laid out plans for a large city. These plans failed, and it remained for James Harrison to accomplish results. His achievement was not without many costly experiments and bitter disappointments, but his unfaltering energy and confidence overcame the many obstacles. In 1843 he marshaled forces of men having wealth and business capacity, the most important of his organizations being the American Iron Mountain Company, which soon became known as one of the largest producers of iron in the world. In this company Harrison was associated with Pierre Chouteau, Jr., of St. Louis; Felix Vallé, C. C. Zeigler, and John Scott, of Ste. Genevieve; August Belmont, Samuel Ward, and Charles F. Mersch, of New York, and F. Pratte of Fredericktown, Mo. In 1850, Harrison organized the firm of Chouteau, Harrison & Vallé, which built an extensive rolling-mill, and took high rank in the business of the West. He promoted the organization of the Iron Mountain Railroad Company, and negotiated the seven-million-dollar loan when the Pacific Railroad Company was bought from the State of Missouri. He was a man of strong will, good judgment, public spirit, and generous impulses, who inspired confidence and stimulated charitable and other undertakings for the public good. The welfare of his employees was ever in his mind. For their benefit he built a handsome church and established schools at Iron Mountain.

At the time of the Civil War he maintained his usual conservatism, but his sympathies were with the South, and it was known among the stanch Southerners of the community that there was a horse saddled in his stable ready for any young man who wished to ride into the Southern lines and join the Confederate forces. His home was opposite Dr. McDowell's Medical College, which, used by the government during the war, was famous as Gratiot Street Prison. Harrison and the ladies of his family ministered to the Confederate prisoners, when permitted to do so, and many tales have since been told by former prisoners, of the warm clothing and much-needed food received. Harrison had a commanding personality: he was tall, stately, grave, and dignified; courteous without familiarity; serene in misfortune, conservative in prosperity. He was married in 1832 to Maria Louisa Prewitt, daughter of Joel Prewitt of Howard County. Mrs. Harrison died in 1847, leaving four children.

[L. U. Reavis, *St. Louis: Future Great City of the World* (1875); J. T. Scharf, *Hist. of Saint Louis City and County* (1883), II, 1264–65; *Missouri Republican*, Aug. 4, 1870; information as to certain facts from Harrison's grandson, George Fox Steedman.] S. M. D.

HARRISON, JAMES ALBERT (Aug. 21, 1848–Jan. 31, 1911), philologist, was born at Pass Christian, Miss. His father, James P. Harrison, a prosperous and influential lawyer, was of that Virginia family which gave a signer to the Declaration of Independence and two presidents to the Union; his mother, Mary Thurston, came of a family almost equally distinguished in the colonial history of Virginia. Young Harrison received his preparatory education in private schools in New Orleans and in 1866 entered the University of Virginia, where he pursued for two years advanced courses in Latin, Greek, and the modern languages. An invincible distaste for mathematics prevented his applying for any academic degree. The next two years, 1868–70, he gave to study in Europe, mainly in Germany, at

Bonn and Munich. Almost immediately after his return in 1871, he was elected professor of modern languages in Randolph-Macon College. Five years later, 1876, he was called to Washington and Lee University as professor of English and modern languages. In 1887 he married Elizabeth Letcher, daughter of John Letcher, governor of Virginia during the Civil War. Accepting a call from his alma mater in 1895, Harrison became professor of Romanic and Germanic languages in the University of Virginia, and in 1897 was made head of the newly created School of Teutonic Languages.

Despite a frail physique, he was a scholar of unremitting industry. His lectures, carefully written out in full, were frequently enlivened by a quaint humor, and though often over-ornate in style, drew their content from a linguistic scholarship as broad as it was profound and accurate. A pioneer in Old-English scholarship in America, he published in 1883 a volume containing *Beowulf* and *The Fight at Finnsburgh,* edited in collaboration with Professor Robert Sharp on the basis of Heyne's German edition. For many years this remained the only American edition. In 1884 appeared in *Anglia* his study of American-negro English. In collaboration with W. M. Baskerville he published an *Anglo-Saxon Prose Reader, for Beginners* (1898) and a *Dictionary of Anglo-Saxon Poetry* (1900). He was also for many years one of the etymological editors for the *Century* and *Standard* dictionaries, a frequent contributor of reviews to the press, and an editor of French and German classics for classroom use. During his vacation he was an indefatigable traveler, and he came to be completely at home in any country of Europe save Russia. With a sensitive and retentive mind, an extensive knowledge of languages and literature, and a fluent style, he found the literary reproduction of travel impressions a congenial occupation for his leisure hours. He thus published several books of a popular character, including: *A Group of Poets and Their Haunts* (1874); *Greek Vignettes* (1877); *Spain in Profile* (1879); *A History of Spain* (1883); *The Story of Greece* (1885). Of similar popular nature, though not originating in European travel, are *Autrefois, a Collection of Creole Tales* (1885) and *George Washington: Patriot, Soldier, Statesman* (1906).

The climax of Harrison's long career of scholarship was his work as editor in chief of the Virginia Edition of Poe (17 vols., 1902). This edition presented a scientifically corrected text of Poe's previously collected works and added nearly four volumes of hitherto uncollected critical articles, thus offering new material for the study of Poe's critical faculty. Volume I of the edition, the biography, was written by Harrison and brought much new material from sources first available to him. His last publication was *The Last Letters of Edgar Allan Poe to Sarah Helen Whitman,* issued in 1909. In that year failing health necessitated his retirement on the Carnegie Foundation. The remaining two years of his life were spent in Charlottesville, Va., in feeble health and almost total blindness. He died Jan. 31, 1911, and was buried in Lexington, Va.

[*Who's Who in America,* 1909–11; *Lib. of Southern Lit.,* vol. V (1909); *The Univ. of Va.* (2 vols., 1897–98); *Alumni Bull.,* Apr. 1911; *Times-Dispatch* (Richmond), and Baltimore *Sun,* Feb. 1, 1911.] W. H. F.

HARRISON, JOHN (Dec. 17, 1773–July 19, 1833), manufacturing chemist, was born in Philadelphia, the son of Thomas and Sarah (Richards) Harrison. His father, born in Thurstonfield, Cumberland, England, had come to America about 1764 and established himself as a merchant; his mother was a prominent minister of the Society of Friends. John Harrison was educated in Philadelphia and at an early age was apprenticed to a druggist, Townsend Speakman. Later he went to Europe to study the business of manufacturing chemicals, and during his two years abroad found opportunity to study the science of chemistry itself under the eminent Dr. Joseph Priestley. In 1793 he entered into partnership with Samuel Betton in Philadelphia, with whom he established a wholesale and retail trade in chemicals and drugs. In 1793–94 he began a series of experiments in the manufacture of sulphuric, nitric, and muriatic acids on a practical scale, and in 1801, having dissolved the partnership of Betton & Harrison, he became the first manufacturing chemist in the United States, devoting his entire time henceforth to that business. He added white lead to his manufactures in 1806, and then successively various other chemicals and colors. In 1807 he had built what was for his day a very large leaden chamber, eighteen feet high, eighteen feet wide, and fifty feet long, in which he was able to produce nearly a half million pounds of sulphuric acid annually. The acid prepared in this chamber was concentrated by boiling in glass retorts, and its cost was greatly increased by the constant breaking of the glass. In an effort to reduce costs, Harrison, with Dr. Eric Bollman, devised a method of concentration in a platinum still. The still they put into use weighed seven hundred ounces, and had a capacity of twenty-five gallons. It was in continuous service for fifteen years. This was perhaps the first instance of the use of platinum for such a purpose. Harrison's business grew to large proportions. In 1831 he admitted his sons Thomas and Michael into partnership, the firm being known as John Harrison & Sons. He found time for other than commercial activities, and displayed other interests: he was a captain of Philadelphia militia in 1792; on Mar. 23, 1796, he was elected a member of the famous Schuylkill Fishing Company; from 1821 to 1824 he served as recorder of the City and County of Philadelphia, and on Feb. 16, 1824, he was elected a member of the first board of managers of the Franklin Institute. He was married on Nov. 27, 1802, to Lydia Leib of Philadelphia. They had eight children, one of whom, George Leib Harrison, was the father of Charles Custis Harrison [*q.v.*], provost of the University of Pennsylvania. Harrison died in Philadelphia after a long illness. His portrait hangs in the John Harrison Laboratory of Chemistry, at the University of Pennsylvania, a memorial to him erected in 1892 by his grandsons.

[W. W. Harrison, *Harrison, Waples and Allied Families* (1910); J. T. Scharf and Thompson Westcott, *Hist. of Phila.* (1884), III, 2273; E. F. Smith, *Chemistry in Old Phila.* (1919); J. H. Martin, *Martin's Bench and Bar of Phila.* (1883); E. T. Freedley, *Phila. and Its Manufactures* (1858); *Poulson's Am. Daily Advertiser* (Phila.), July 25, 1833.] J. H. F.

HARRISON, JOSEPH (Sept. 20, 1810–Mar. 27, 1874), mechanical engineer, was born in Philadelphia, the son of Joseph and Mary (Crawford) Harrison. At the time of his birth the family fortunes were at low ebb, and he was able to obtain but little schooling. He early manifested an inclination for mechanical pursuits, and accordingly, in 1825, was apprenticed to Frederick D. Sanno, a builder of steam-engines. Sanno failed, and Harrison was then apprenticed to James Flint, of the firm of Hyde & Flint. In this shop he soon became proficient and at the age of twenty, before he was free from his indenture, was made foreman of part of the establishment. When he was twenty-two years old he was employed by Philip Garrett, who manufactured small lathes and presses. In 1833 he went to Port Clinton, Pa., for a short time, to establish a foundry for Arundus Tiers. The following year he was employed by William Norris, then engaged with Col. Stephen H. Long in building locomotives according to the latter's designs, and in 1835 he became foreman for Garrett & Eastwick, who had just begun the manufacture of locomotives. He was entrusted with designing the locomotive *Samuel D. Ingham,* the success of which led to the construction of others on the same plan. In 1837 Harrison became a partner in the firm of Garrett, Eastwick & Company, although his skill and energy were the only capital that he was able to contribute to the enterprise. Two years later, upon the retirement of Garrett, the firm took the name of Eastwick & Harrison.

These partners originated several important improvements in the locomotive. They were the first to design a practical eight-wheel engine, with four driving and four truck wheels. A method for equalizing the weight on the driving wheels was patented by Harrison in 1839, and he also devised an improvement in the forward truck, making it flexible so that it would accommodate itself to irregular undulations on the rails. Locomotives designed and built by this firm were among the first to burn anthracite coal successfully, and they surmounted higher grades than had previously been overcome in America or in Europe. In 1841 the firm built a locomotive called the *Gowan & Marx,* weighing but little over eleven tons, for the Philadelphia & Reading Railroad. Its performance in drawing 101 loaded coal-cars over that road caused much comment at the time as being without parallel in the history of railroad transportation. The achievement attracted the attention of two Russian engineers who had been commissioned by the Emperor Nicholas to examine and report upon railroads and railroad equipment then in operation in America and in Europe. When they reported on the construction of a railroad from St. Petersburg to Moscow, they recommended the adoption of an engine upon the plan of the *Gowan & Marx.* Accordingly Harrison went to St. Petersburg in the spring of 1843, where, in connection with Thomas Winans of Baltimore, he concluded a contract with the Russian government for building 162 locomotives and iron trucks for 2,500 freight cars. Eastwick & Harrison closed their plant in Philadelphia in 1844 and removed a portion of their equipment to St. Petersburg, where the firm of Harrison, Winans & Eastwick completed in 1851 the work for which they had contracted. Eastwick and Winans remained in Russia to undertake additional contracts, but Harrison returned to Philadelphia in 1852 after being decorated by the Emperor for his engineering accomplishments. He built an imposing residence in his native city and collected in it many paintings and works of art.

Years earlier, his attention had been directed to the means of improving steam-generation with a view to making steam-boilers less liable to explosion, and he now devoted himself for a time to this problem. In 1859 he patented the sectional Harrison Steam Boiler, which marked a distinct era in boiler construction, and after three years of European travel, he erected a factory in Philadelphia for its manufacture. On July 15, 1864, he was elected a member of the American Philosophical Society, and on May 30, 1871, he was awarded the gold and silver Rumford Medals of the American Academy of Arts and Sciences for his contributions toward insuring the safety of steam-boilers. He was a member of other learned societies, but, with the exception of reading a few papers, took no active part in the business of any of them. Toward the close of his life he turned his attention to recording some of his thoughts and experiences, and in 1869 published a folio volume entitled *The Iron Worker and King Solomon,* containing a poem of that name, some fugitive pieces, an autobiography, and many observations of life in Russia. He also published *An Essay on the Steam Boiler* (1867) and *The Locomotive Engine and Philadelphia's Share in its Early Improvements* (1872). He was married on Dec. 15, 1836, to Sarah Poulterer of New York and had seven children. He died in Philadelphia after a long illness.

[Harrison's writings mentioned above; sketch by Coleman Sellers in *Proc. Am. Phil. Soc.,* vol. XIV (1876); E. P. Oberholtzer, *Phila.: A Hist. of the City and Its People* (1912), vol. II; J. T. Scharf and Thompson Westcott, *Hist. of Phila.* (1884), III, 2258; J. L. Bishop, *Hist. of Am. Manufactures* (1864), vol. III; Phila. *Press,* Mar. 28, 1874.] J. H. F.

HARRISON, LOVELL BIRGE (Oct. 28, 1854–May 11, 1929), landscape painter, better known as Birge Harrison, was a son of Apollos W. and Margaret (Belden) Harrison, and a brother of Thomas Alexander Harrison [*q.v.*] and Butler Harrison. He was born in Philadelphia and obtained his elementary training as an artist in the school of the Pennsylvania Academy of the Fine Arts. In 1875, acting upon the advice of John S. Sargent, he went to Paris, where he continued his studies at the École des Beaux-Arts under Carolus-Duran and Alexandre Cabanel. His early works were figure pieces, and his first success in this line was a picture painted in 1880 called "November," which was bought by the French government in 1882 for the Marseilles Museum. Soon after this period his health became impaired and he left France, making extensive journeys in far countries—India, Australia, Ceylon, South Africa, Egypt, and most of the rest of the lands bordering on the Mediterranean; a little later he spent several seasons in California and the Southwest, and some months in Quebec. After the early nineties, so soon as his improved health permitted him to resume work, he made his home successively in Plymouth, Mass., New Hope, Pa., Bearsville, N. Y., and Woodstock, N. Y. At the latter place he directed with much success the summer school in landscape painting established by the Art Students' League of New York. He was the founder of the Woodstock art colony. He had married, in 1882, Eleanor Ritchie, who died on May 1, 1895. His second wife, whom he married Nov. 28, 1896, was Jennie Seaton Harrison.

His landscape work met with an uncommon degree of favor. He specialized in winter scenes and urban subjects. Most of his pictures are in the minor key, and are marked by a rare simplicity of design and a rather melancholy vein of sentiment. The best of them combine sturdy realism with the beauty of well-related values. His palette was restricted, and he was at his best when dealing with gray subjects without abrupt oppositions of light and dark. His nocturnal motives, winter twilights, rainy-day pictures, and snow effects, are the most characteristic and harmonious of his works. A good idea of his personal style is to be derived from the reproductions of his landscapes published in *Scribner's, Art and Progress,* and *Academy Notes.* His pictures have been widely exhibited, and excellent examples may be seen in almost all the important American art museums, including those of Philadelphia, Washington, Chicago, St. Louis, Detroit, Toledo, Indianapolis, St. Paul, and a dozen other cities. A long list of medals, together with membership in many artistic societies, the coveted *hors concours* of the Paris Salon, and other academic honors, such as the title of National Academician which came to him in 1910, testify to the full appreciation accorded his achievements.

In 1909 he published a book on *Landscape Painting,* which was in part the outgrowth of his counsels to his students at Woodstock. Naturally, there is much technical matter in it, but there is also much that should interest the general reader. It is never obscure, and contains a deal of sound esthetic doctrine. "As painters," he wrote, "our business is to transmit to picture-lovers . . . the emotions and the impressions of strength and power or of poetic beauty which have come to us direct from nature." Again, "This is the test of the highest form of art—that it should stimulate the imagination and suggest more than it expresses." Harrison was the writer of a number of magazine articles. One of his best friends was Robert Louis Stevenson.

[John E. D. Trask, in *Scribner's Mag.,* Nov. 1907; Leila Mechlin, in *Art and Progress,* Nov. 1911; Arthur Hoeber, in *Internat. Studio,* July 1911; C. L. Borgmeyer, "Birge Harrison—Poet Painter," in *Fine Arts Jour.,* Oct. 1913; Lorinda M. Bryant, in *What Pictures to See in America* (1915); *Am. Art Annual,* 1929; *Who's Who in America,* 1928–29; Henri Girardet, in *Les Tendances Nouvelles,* Dec. 1912; *Acad. Notes*

(Buffalo), Jan. 1909 and Oct. 1913; *Cat. of an Exhibition of Paintings by Alexander Harrison and Birge Harrison: The Art Inst. of Chicago* (1913), with preface by Arthur Hoeber; *N. Y. Times*, May 12, 1929.]

W. H. D.

HARRISON, PETER (June 14, 1716–Apr. 30, 1775), architect, was born in England, at York, the son of Thomas Harrison, Jr., and Elizabeth Denison. He went to Rhode Island in 1740 (not in 1729 with Dean Berkeley, as has been stated) and settled in Newport. There he engaged in agriculture and trade with his brother Joseph, dealing in wines, rum, molasses, and mahogany. On June 6, 1746, he married Elizabeth Pelham, a descendant of Benedict Arnold, the first governor of Rhode Island. In 1761 the Harrison brothers removed to New Haven, where Peter was made collector of the customs in 1768. He died in that town seven years later, leaving four children.

Peter Harrison's claim to remembrance rests on his work in architecture. By nineteenth-century writers (*e.g.*, David King, *Historical Sketch of the Redwood Library*, 1860) he was reputed to have been assistant architect of Blenheim House, and thus was supposed to have had professional training and experience under Sir John Vanbrugh, but his name does not appear in any of the English accounts of Blenheim. Furthermore, the nature of his work in America does not suggest a professional training and practice, but rather that cultivated amateurism which in the eighteenth century made architecture one of the accomplishments of the gentleman. In 1745, during the French war, he made maps of Cape Breton and of Newport (another of Newport dated 1755 is in the Public Record Office in London). In 1746 he assisted in the fortification of Newport. By designing the Redwood Library in that city (1748–50), King's Chapel, Boston (1749–54—the colonnade is a later addition of Bulfinch), the Brick Market, Newport (1761), Christ Church, Cambridge (1761), and the Synagogue, Newport (1762–63), Harrison became the most notable architect of colonial America. Except in the case of Christ Church, which was a little outside his orbit, all these services were entirely gratuitous. He took his pay in votes of thanks and pieces of plate. In the derivation of these designs Harrison depended, like other amateurs of his time, on the admirable engraved works which codified the academic forms: Hoppus' edition of Palladio, the *Vitruvius Britannicus*. Gibbs's *Book of Architecture* and *Rules for Drawing*, and Langley's *Treasury of Designs*; but he used them with exceptional ability, under the guidance of the strict Palladian tradition of Lord Burlington. His buildings were exceptional in the America of that time for their purity of detail and their monumental qualities. Within the Palladian tradition there was still room for personal individuality, welding derivative elements into a vital unity. Such unity and value are felt in Harrison's work. Despite its scholarly character, it does not smell of the lamp. Repose and suavity of proportion, a musical harmony, make it live, and give it distinction unique in the colonial period.

[The facts of Harrison's life are established by C. H. Hart in *Proc. Mass. Hist. Soc.*, vol. XLIX (1916), and S. F. Batchelder in *Bull. of the Soc. for the Preservation of New England Antiquities*, Jan. 1916; in the latter publication the Brick Market in Newport is completely studied by N. M. Isham. F. Kimball in "The Colonial Amateurs: Peter Harrison," *Architecture*, June–July 1926, studies his prototypes and relationships. The documents on the Redwood Library are given by G. C. Mason in his *Annals of the Redwood Library* (1891); measured drawings of some of Harrison's buildings appear in *The Georgian Period* (1900), and in R. C. Kingman, *New England Georgian Architecture* (1913). An obituary was published in the *Connecticut Journal* (New Haven), May 3, 1775.]

F. K.

HARRISON, THOMAS ALEXANDER (Jan. 17, 1853–Oct. 13, 1930), marine and figure painter, better known as Alexander Harrison, was born in Philadelphia, the eldest son of Apollos W. and Margaret (Belden) Harrison. He was the most eminent of a fraternal trio of painters which also included Lovell Birge Harrison [*q.v.*] and Butler Harrison. As a youth he worked for five years as a topographical draftsman in Florida for the United States Coast Survey, then he decided to become a painter, and after a brief course of study at an art school in San Francisco, Cal., he returned to Philadelphia and entered the Pennsylvania Academy of the Fine Arts. In 1879 he went to Paris and continued his training in painting under J. L. Gerôme at the École des Beaux-Arts. He was also for a time a pupil of Bastien-Lepage. In the summer he was usually to be found at Pont-Aven, Concarneau, or Begmiel, on the coast of Brittany, and there he became interested in marine painting. He remained unmarried, and continued to live in France for something like half a century, or until the time of his death.

His first *envoi* to the Salon was hung in 1880; it was a scene on the Breton coast. Two years later he sent to the Salon "Castles in Spain," an idle lad basking in the sun on the seashore. This canvas made a decided hit, and was acquired by the Metropolitan Museum, New York. The artist now turned his attention to marine pieces, and during the ensuing decade produced in rapid succession the series of surf motives that made him famous. Included in this series are the fine examples in the museums of St. Louis, Philadelphia, and Washington. These paintings, respectively known as *"Le Crépuscule,"* "Twilight," and "The Wave," were acclaimed as masterpieces; the last-named picture, in the Corcoran Gallery, Washington, was formerly in the Seney collection and was sold for $3,650 in 1891. It shows a moonlight effect at twilight, with the crests of the waves silvered by the moonbeams, and the long swells breaking on the beach with fringes of creamy foam. Similar is *"Le Crépuscule"* in the City Art Museum of St. Louis, which in 1885 received a prize of $2,500 at a New York exhibition and was the talk of the town. The Philadelphia picture is 40 x 109 inches in dimensions, and is warmly praised by the critics and much admired by the public. In 1886 Harrison made a new departure when he painted his "Arcady," now in the Luxembourg Museum, Paris. In this subtle and luminous vision of nude figures in a strong outdoor light the painter manifested his power of suggesting the actual effect of sunlight upon flesh tones with exceptional brilliancy and delicacy. "The effect was not alone of accuracy but of beauty," wrote Samuel Isham (*post*, p. 411); "the canvas shone with the joy of light and air." The recognition attained by Harrison may be inferred from the long list of honors bestowed upon him, from the impressive array of museums that have acquired his works—besides the galleries already named, those of Chicago, St. Paul, Dresden, Quimper (France), and, last but not least, the Wilstach Collection in Memorial Hall, Philadelphia, which contains five of his pictures—and from his membership in numerous societies and academies. His death occurred in Paris, in his seventy-eighth year.

[*Fine Arts Jour.*, Sept. 1913; Samuel Isham, *The Hist. of Am. Painting* (1905); *N. Y. Times*, Oct. 14, 1930; C. H. Caffin, *The Story of Am. Painting* (1907); Anna Seaton-Schmidt, "Some American Marine Painters," in *Art and Progress*, Nov. 1910; C. F. Browne, in *Brush and Pencil*, June 1899; *Cat. of Mr. George I. Seney's Important Coll. of Modern Paintings to be Sold at Auction* (Am. Art Asso., 1891); *The Pa. Acad. of the Fine Arts, Cat. of the T. B. Clarke Coll. of Am. Pictures* (1891); L. M. Bryant, *Am. Pictures and Their Painters* (1917); Wynford Dewhurst, *Impressionist Painting* (1904); *Acad. Notes* (Buffalo), Oct. 1913; *Gazette des Beaux-Arts*, June 1, 1886; *Am Art Annual*, 1930.]

W. H. D.

HARRISON, WILLIAM HENRY (Feb. 9, 1773–Apr. 4, 1841), ninth president of the United States, born at the plantation of "Berkeley," in Charles City County, Va., was the third son of Benjamin Harrison [*q.v.*]. His mother, Elizabeth Bassett, daughter of Col. William Bassett of "Eltham," was of a distinguished Virginia family. William Henry Harrison was apparently educated at home as a child, and in 1787 he entered Hampden-Sidney College. In 1790 he went to Richmond to take up the study of medicine, and after several months proceeded to Philadelphia to work under Dr. Benjamin Rush. In August 1791, following his father's death, he decided to enter the army and received the commission of ensign in the 1st United States Infantry.

Serving in the Northwest Territory against the Indians, Harrison acquitted himself well in the army, rising to the rank of lieutenant and acting as aide-de-camp to Anthony Wayne [*q.v.*]. After the battle of Fallen Timbers and the conclusion of the Treaty of Greenville in 1795, he remained on garrison duty at North Bend, and later at Fort Washington (now Cincinnati). In 1795 he married Anna Symmes, daughter of Judge John Cleves Symmes [*q.v.*]. Resigning from the army in 1798, he was appointed secretary of the Northwest Territory in July. When the territory advanced to the second grade of government in the following year, he was elected its first delegate to Congress. In this body, as chairman of the committee on public lands, he reported the bill which became the land act of 1800 and which to a considerable degree reflected the demands of the frontier. He was also instrumental in obtaining the passage of the act for the division of the Northwest Territory into the two territories of Ohio and Indiana. On May 12, 1800, he received the appointment as governor of Indiana, and for the next twelve years his career was interwoven with the history of that region.

Though criticized because he favored the continuation of a modified form of slavery and because he maintained to the full the prerogatives of his office, Harrison as governor did his work ably and conscientiously. The charges of fraud and corruption leveled at him were merely political ammunition, for in no case was proof adduced. He was instructed to exercise a general supervision over the Indians, standing for them *in loco parentis,* to win their confidence, and to secure for them justice at the hands of the settlers, as well as to exact fair dealings from them. He was also urged by President Jefferson, whose policy Madison later followed, to obtain for the government the cession of as much land as possible. On June 18, 1802, he was granted formal authority to make treaties. Harrison did his best to carry out both phases of his duty, and deplored the lack of justice accorded the Indians, but the two aims of the government were irreconcilable, and the interests of the settlers triumphed. During his terms of office Harrison obtained from the Indians the grant of millions of acres of land in what are now the states of Indiana and Illinois. As a result, the Indians' resentment of the invading tide of settlers was greatly augmented, and outbursts against remote settlements were constantly dreaded. In common with most Westerners of that time, Harrison attributed this hostility to the unfriendly intervention of British agents, but the land cessions exacted from the tribes constituted the basic cause for the Indians' attitude.

Beginning in 1805, there gradually developed a confederacy of the Indians under the Shawnee warrior Tecumseh [*q.v.*] and his brother Elskwatawa, the Prophet. Tecumseh's aim was to bind all the Indian tribes into an agreement to refuse to sell any more land. Indeed, he denied the power of any chief or any tribe to cede the land which belonged, he claimed, to all the tribes in common. When Harrison by the treaty of Fort Wayne in 1809 secured a grant of some two million and a half acres of land on the Wabash River, Tecumseh frankly warned him that he would oppose the occupation of that land by the whites. Undeterred by Harrison's counter-declaration to the effect that he would occupy the land, the Shawnee and their followers encamped in large numbers near the point at which Tippecanoe Creek empties into the Wabash.

Early in October 1811, Harrison led against the settlement at Tippecanoe his force of about a thousand men, composed of militia from the territory, volunteers from Kentucky and Indiana, and the 4th Regiment of regulars. At this date, Tecumseh was absent and the Indians were under the leadership of the Prophet. After toilsomely ascending the Wabash on Nov. 6, Harrison's army encamped near the Indian village and was attacked early the following morning by the Shawnee. Although Harrison succeeded in repulsing the Indians and was able to take possession of their settlement, 188 of his men were killed or wounded. Furthermore, the Indians returned to their encampment a few months later. Despite the acclaim with which Harrison was received upon his return to Vincennes, public opinion was not wholly satisfied with the results of the engagement. By spring the Indians became bold again and the necessity of a stronger punitive expedition became apparent.

Harrison himself was convinced of the expediency of a general war against the tribes of the Northwest, and throughout the opening months of 1812 repeatedly urged his plans upon President Madison. As early as April, however, feeling for war against Great Britain was running high at Washington. To Harrison's importunities, therefore, Madison turned a deaf ear. When war was finally declared against Great Britain, Harrison was fired with enthusiasm and used every line of influence to secure a command in the army. For some months he waited in vain, although his friends, one of whom was Henry Clay, exerted themselves in his behalf. In order to raise volunteers for the defense of Vincennes against the Indians, many of whom had allied themselves with the British under Tecumseh's lead, Harrison had gone to Frankfort, Ky., and was in that town when news was brought on Aug. 24, 1812, that Gen. William Hull [*q.v.*] was besieged in Detroit. Measures for his relief were imperative. By agreement of a conclave of the leading men of the state, Harrison was created, by brevet, major-general of the Kentucky militia for the purpose of going to Hull's aid. He at once proceeded to Cincinnati, where Gen. James Winchester with several regiments was encamped. Harrison took command of the army Winchester had enlisted, and on Aug. 28 received news of Hull's surrender. The following day, he set forth with his newly acquired army and, in the face of orders from the secretary of war, received on the march, establishing Winchester's preëminence in command, Harrison proceeded to the relief of Fort Wayne. After this had been accomplished, he reluctantly surrendered the army to Winchester on Sept. 19. Less than a week later, however, he received notice of his appointment, as of Sept. 17, to the supreme command of the Army of the Northwest. On Aug. 22, he had been appointed a brigadier-general in the regular army.

The task before Harrison presented great difficulties. Mackinac, Chicago, and Detroit were in the hands of the British. Before the winter set in, if possible, he was to transport a considerable army across Ohio and secure for it military stores, clothing, and food, as well as to train it in the rudiments of military art. Harrison's initial mistake may have been that he yielded to the popular clamor for a victory, and undertook with new troops a campaign that would have taxed hardy veterans. His plan of campaign was not free from objections, for he attempted to move his forces in three sections on the three different routes north across Ohio, with the intent of concentrating his army finally in one body at the Miami Rapids. To this plan the mischances of impassable roads and faulty communications proved fatal. General Winchester, in command of the left wing of the army, reached the Rapids on Jan. 10, 1813, considerably in advance of the other sections. Their delay proved disastrous, for on Jan. 22, following his rash and unsupported advance to the settlement of

Frenchtown, Winchester's force was surprised and overcome by Colonel (later Major-General) Procter. As a result, after some indecision, Harrison finally settled his army in winter quarters in the newly erected Fort Meigs, at the Miami Rapids.

For six months after the defeat of Winchester, Harrison pursued a generally defensive policy. Much of his time was spent in efforts to replace the troops whose enlistments expired and in trying to build up a large force for another offensive. Furthermore, the experiences of the winter's campaign had convinced him that control of Lake Erie must precede any offensive movement against Detroit. Twice General Procter invaded the Northwest. In May 1813 he besieged Fort Meigs for a week while Harrison was in command of the stockade, but at the end of that time was forced to withdraw. Again in July, the British commander invested Fort Meigs and after his failure to reduce that stronghold moved against Fort Stephenson on the Sandusky River. Harrison ordered George Croghan [*q.v.*], commander of that post, to abandon it; but Croghan gallantly withstood Procter's attack. This episode later involved Harrison in unpleasant arguments.

By the end of August 1813, Harrison had decided to take the offensive. Perry's victory over the British fleet on Sept. 10 gave the Americans the control of the lake, a factor of immense strategic importance. Harrison now hastened his offensive movements, and on Sept. 27 occupied Malden, a small British settlement opposite Detroit. The reoccupation of Detroit was made on Sept. 29; on Oct. 2, the Americans took up the pursuit of Procter, who had commenced a retreat after Perry's victory had rendered his position untenable. On Oct. 5, Harrison's forces overtook the British commander in the vicinity of a little settlement known as the Moravian town, on the Thames River. The battle lasted but a short time before the American victory was assured. Procter fled and Tecumseh was killed; the defeat of the British was complete. Never again did they recover the ground Procter lost nor attempt offensive operations in that quarter. Furthermore, the death of Tecumseh and the surrender of the Indian allies of the British brought about the pacification of the greater part of the Indians of the Northwest. Thus, the results of the battle of the Thames were most important. After his victory, Harrison remained in the army for six months. On Mar. 2, 1813, he had been raised to the rank of major-general and on the same date Thomas Posey had been appointed to succeed him as governor of Indiana. During the months immediately preceding his resignation from the army, he did not inaugurate any operations of importance. In May 1814, a controversy with Secretary of War Armstrong, together with the necessity of settling the estate of his father-in-law, induced Harrison to resign his commission. He was not a great general, but he served to the best of his ability in the face of great difficulties; and the controversies over his valor and ability raised later by Winchester, Desha, and Croghan were regrettable rather than conclusive.

In July 1814 at Greenville, and in August 1815 at Spring Wells, Harrison presided over councils with the Indians for the establishment of definitive peace with the tribes of the Northwest. After his resignation from the army, he took up his residence again at North Bend, near Cincinnati, where he cultivated his farm and engaged in several unfortunate commercial enterprises. From 1816 to 1819, he served as a representative from Ohio in Congress. He was in no sense an outstanding figure in the House. In general, he was a follower of Henry Clay, supporting his South American policy and his stand on the tariff and internal improvements, but his chief interest in these years centered in his work as chairman of the committee on militia. In 1819 he was elected a senator in the Ohio legislature. Here he was an important figure, but his attitude on the slavery question was not sufficiently positive to suit his constituents and he failed to obtain a reëlection. In 1824 he tried to secure the appointment as minister to Mexico in the hope of improving his finances, but he was passed over in favor first of Ninian Edwards, and then of Joel R. Poinsett. In 1825, however, he was elected to the United States Senate, where he was chiefly distinguished by his work as chairman of the committee on military affairs. He remained in the Senate three years. At the end of that period, through the influence of Henry Clay, he was appointed minister to Colombia, his appointment being confirmed on May 24, 1828.

When Harrison arrived at Bogotá, on Feb. 5, 1829, the government of Colombia was in a perilous condition. An insurrection against President Bolivar had been suppressed but six months before, another revolt was in progress, and in January 1829 the neighboring state of Peru had declared war on the republic. Accordingly, the utmost circumspection was required on the part of every foreign representative, a quality which Harrison proved to lack. Scarcely a month after his arrival, he became convinced that Bolivar was planning to make himself emperor of a greater Colombia, a plan which was repugnant to Harrison's republican principles. He was soon deeply in the confidence of a group of Colombians who, under the leadership of General Cordova, were plotting a new revolt against Bolivar. Harrison always maintained that he never gave any aid to the revolutionists, but his sympathies were clearly with them and aroused the resentment of the Colombian officials. In the summer of 1829, he received notice of his recall and of the appointment of T. P. Moore as his successor. This recall was in no way due to Harrison's behavior in Colombia, but was merely the result of President Jackson's desire to provide a place for one of his supporters. On Sept. 21, Moore arrived at Bogotá; four days later news reached the capital that Cordova had raised the standard of revolt. On Sept. 27, Harrison sent to Bolivar a letter of extraordinary temerity, urging him to adhere to the tenets of republicanism. When the contents of this letter became known some two weeks later, such was the animosity aroused that the Colombian government threatened to arrest him and did force him on Oct. 19 to set out on his return journey to the United States. While Harrison's devotion to republicanism may merit admiration, it must be admitted that he acted in a manner unbecoming to his office. (See *Remarks of General Harrison, Late Envoy . . . to the Republic of Colombia, on Certain Charges Made against Him by that Government,* 1830.)

For some years after his return from Colombia, Harrison encountered a series of financial reverses and family misfortunes. Except for the salary derived from the office of county recorder, to which he was appointed in 1834, he was dependent on the income derived from his North Bend farm for the support of a large family of children and grand-children. Apparently, however, he did not relinquish his interest in politics, and in 1835 a movement was started to nominate him for the presidency on an Anti-Van Buren ticket. In Kentucky, Ohio, and New York the movement gained considerable strength. In Pennsylvania the radical Anti-Masons supported Webster, but the moderates of that group indorsed the ticket of Harrison for president and Francis Granger for vice-president. In the electoral college, Harrison received only seventy-three votes, but his popular vote in the states north of the Ohio River ran close to that polled by Van Buren. Immediately after the election, Harrison and his friends began to lay plans to insure his success in the election of 1840. Webster, Clay, and Harrison were the three outstanding figures in the Whig party. When the Whig convention assembled at Harrisburg in December 1839, Webster had already withdrawn his name, so that Clay and Harrison were the outstanding rivals. Against Clay could be raised the objection that his political tenets were too clearly established and widely known to be pleasing to all the Anti-Van Buren groups. Furthermore, Clay was feared as a strong leader. The coalition of the Webster men with Thurlow Weed of New York, together with the strength of pledged Harrison delegates, secured for him the nomination. The second place on the ticket was given to John Tyler to placate the Southern Whigs. Clay felt bitterly his party's ingratitude and was never again on cordial terms with Harrison.

The election of 1840 has become famous because of the emphasis laid on emotional and demagogic appeal. The Whigs drew up no political platform; instead they emphasized Harrison as the candidate of the people and the military hero. "Tippecanoe and Tyler too" vied in popularity with transparencies showing the General seated before a log cabin with a barrel of cider at his side. The panic of 1837 and the hard times that followed contributed to the defeat of the Democrats; Van Buren received only 60 electoral votes while Harrison with 234 was triumphantly elected. His inauguration took place amid tremendous enthusiasm. His inaugural speech, in part the work of Webster, was an excellent disquisition on the rights and duties of the executive branch of the government, but was in no sense striking or remarkable. His cabinet, headed by Webster, was well-chosen. On Mar. 17, Harrison issued a call for an extra session of Congress to meet on May 31, in order to take action on the financial distress of the country. Scarcely a week later he contracted a chill that developed into pneumonia. Worn out by the strain of the election and by the ceaseless importunities of office seekers, he was unable to resist the disease and died on Apr. 4, 1841.

[Except for "A Discourse on the Aborigines of the Valley of the Ohio," *Trans. of the Hist. and Philos. Soc. of Ohio,* vol. I, pt. 2 (1839), Harrison's writings consist largely of letters and political speeches. The largest collection of his letters is in the MSS. Div., Lib. of Cong. The most complete published collection is that edited by Logan Esarey, "Governors Messages and Letters. Messages and Letters of Wm. H. Harrison," *Ind. Hist. Colls.* (2 vols., 1922). Primary materials are also contained in Moses Dawson, *A Hist. Narrative of the Civil and Mil. Services of Maj.-Gen. Wm. H. Harrison* (1824); and *Letters of Decius, to the Members of the Legis. of the Ind. Territory, to B. Park, . . . and to Wm. H. Harrison* (1805). Secondary accounts are: D. B. Goebel, *Wm. H. Harrison, a Pol. Biog.* (1926); Homer Webster, "Wm. H. Harrison's Administration of Indiana Territory," *Ind. Hist. Soc. Pubs.,* vol. IV, no. 3 (1907); E. A. Cruikshank, "Harrison and Procter. The River Raisin," *Royal. Soc. of Canada, Proc and Trans.*, 3 ser. IV, sect. 2 (1911); Ellmore Barce, "Gov. Harrison and the Treaty of Fort Wayne, 1809," *Ind. Mag. of Hist.*, vol. XI (1915). See also R. B. McAfee, *Hist. of the Late War in the Western Country* (1816); *Am. State Papers: Indian Affairs* (2 vols., 1832–34); Washington *Globe*, Apr. 6, 8, 1841; Washington *Daily Nat. Intelligencer*, Apr. 5, 6, 9, 1841; and "Autobiography," *Cincinnati Daily Enquirer*, Nov. 5, 1870.] D. B. G.

HARRISON, WILLIAM POPE (Sept. 3, 1830–Feb. 7, 1895), clergyman of the Methodist Episcopal Church, South, was born in Savannah but spent his boyhood in Oxford, Ga. Whatever early education he acquired was gained in his father's printing shop and under the instruction of Rev. Patrick H. Mell [*q.v.*]. A brief stay at Emory College taught him how to study and whetted an already keen desire for knowledge. He had no further schooling, but was a student all his life, and came to be recognized as the foremost bookman and one of the most versatile scholars in the ranks of Southern Methodism. He was admitted to the Georgia Conference on trial Jan. 15, 1850, and appointed junior preacher on the Watkinsville Circuit, but at the end of the year he withdrew because of ill health. In the meantime he had married Mary Hodges. Two years later he joined the Alabama Conference and until 1863 held various charges within its bounds, serving also from 1860 to 1862 as principal of Auburn Female College. Transferred to the Georgia Conference in 1863, he was appointed pastor of St. Luke's Church, Columbus, and in 1865, of Wesley Chapel, Atlanta, known after 1871 as the First Methodist Episcopal Church, South. By this time, although he appealed chiefly to the mind and conscience and but little to the emotions, he had become a preacher who attracted large congregations. "He did more to popularize church going in Atlanta than any other preacher ever did" (*Methodist Review*, July–August 1899, p. 299). He had acquired a large and varied fund of information upon which to draw, and "his voice was as soft as a lute and as clear as a silver trumpet; his diction classic; his imagination tropical in its opulence" (*Ibid.*, p. 297). The General Conference of 1870 established the *New Monthly Magazine* and made Harrison editor. A few numbers were issued early in 1871, after which the publication was suspended. With the exception of two or three short intermissions he was connected with the First Church, Atlanta, for some twelve years. In December 1877 he was chosen chaplain of the House of Representatives, being the third Southern Methodist to hold that position. Transferred to the Baltimore Conference the following year, he was appointed to the Mount Vernon Place Church, Washington. Here he remained until 1882, when he was sent to Winchester, Va. That year the General Conference elected him Book Editor to succeed Dr. Thomas O. Summers [*q.v.*], and he removed to Nashville, Tenn.

The position was one for which by temperament and knowledge he was well fitted. Shy and reticent, he had no liking for general society and found the pastoral duties of the ministry distasteful. He was happiest among books, and before his death had surrounded himself with a library of more than 10,000 volumes. Self-guided, he had become proficient in half a dozen languages and had considerable acquaintance with as many more. Besides being thoroughly versed in theology, he was a well-informed student of the political history of the United States, and had accumulated a valuable stock of scientific information. He was continued as Book Editor until 1894, when failing health caused his retirement. After 1886 he also edited the *Quarterly Review* (later the *Methodist Review*, Nashville), and some of his best theological and historical writings appeared in the "Editor's Table" of that periodical. His first published work was a theological novel, *Theophilus Walton, or the Majesty of Truth* (*c.* 1859), a contribution to the Baptist controversy then going on. It was a reply to *Theodosia Ernest; or the Heroine of Faith*, which had been issued in 1857 by Amos Cooper Dayton, a Baptist. Both books had a large circulation. In 1883 he published *The Living Christ; the Life and the Light of Men*; and in 1886, *The High-Churchman Disarmed; A Defense of Our Methodist Fathers*. In 1892 appeared *Methodist Union*, in which he discussed the division of the church, 1844–48, and suggested for the future, instead of reunion, a further division of American Methodism into Eastern, Southern, Western, and Colored General Conferences, all bound together by an advisory council. He also edited *The Gospel Among the Slaves: A Short Account of Missionary Operations Among the African Slaves of the Southern States* (1893); *Lights and Shadows of Forty Years* (1883), by Henry Heartwell; *The Wesleyan Standards, Sermons by Rev. John Wesley, A.M.* (2 vols., 1887). His death occurred in Columbus, Ga.

[*Methodist Review* (Nashville), Mar.–Apr. and July–Aug. 1895; *Minutes of the Annual Conferences of the M. E. Church, South* (1895); *Christian Advocate* (Nashville), Feb. 14, 1895; Nancy Telfair, *A Hist. of Columbus, Ga.* (1929), p. 352; W. J. Scott, *Biog. Etchings of Ministers and Laymen of the Georgia Conferences* (1895); Geo. G. Smith, *The Hist. of Georgia Methodism from 1786 to 1886* (1913); H. M. DuBose, *A Hist. of Methodism, . . . to the Year 1916* (1916); *Morning News* (Savannah), Feb. 8, 1895.] H. E. S.

HARROD, BENJAMIN MORGAN (Feb. 19, 1837–Sept. 7, 1912), civil engineer, was born in New Orleans, La., the son of Charles and Mary (Morgan) Harrod. His father, a native of New England, was a well-to-do business man; his mother was a daughter of Benjamin Morgan, a Pennsylvanian who settled in New Orleans before 1800 and about 1823 was regarded as a visionary in that city because he advocated the paving of the streets. Young Harrod was prepared for college in New Orleans and at Flushing, L. I. He entered Harvard, and received the degree of B.A. in 1856. After his graduation he studied engineering and architecture in New Orleans. In 1858 he began his career in the office of the United States Engineers, being assigned to the department in charge of construction of lighthouses and forts along the Gulf of Mexico from the Mississippi to the Rio Grande. He rapidly advanced from draftsman to assistant engineer and when the Civil War began had had two years' engineering experience. He enlisted in the Confederate army as a private, but his engineering skill won him a commission as lieutenant of artillery. He saw service under Gen. M. L. Smith as a brigade and division engineer, taking part in the fortification and subsequent defense of New Orleans and Vicksburg. After the surrender of Vicksburg he was commissioned captain of engineers in Virginia and helped in the construction of the defenses around Richmond and Petersburg, remaining there until the surrender at Appomattox. After the war, he resumed his profession in New Orleans, but was deeply interested, as were all the Southern white men of his time, in the reconstruction of the commonwealth and in establishing white supremacy. He was one of the prominent men connected with the White League.

In 1877, with his appointment as chief of the state board of engineers of Louisiana, he became prominent in the branch of engineering with which he was thereafter identified. The most important duty of the board was to protect the alluvial lands of the state from the flood waters of the Mississippi by the construction of levees. Harrod's work in this connection led President Hayes to appoint him in 1879 as a member of the Mississippi River Commission, formed in that year to undertake the improvement of navigation on the Mississippi River and its tributaries. This task involved the building of levees and ultimately resulted in the reclamation of 30,000 square miles of fertile land for agricultural purposes. In 1888 Harrod was appointed city engineer of New Orleans; later he served in an advisory capacity; and between 1897 and 1902 he was in charge of the design and construction of the drainage system of the city, which, because much of the town is below the level of the river, presented a unique problem. Recognized as one of the leading hydraulic engineers of the country, he was appointed by President Roosevelt to membership on the Panama Canal Commission and served (1904–07) until the plan of the canal had been determined.

He was president of the American Society of Civil Engineers in 1897, and in 1903 was a delegate to the International Congress of Navigation held that year at Düsseldorf, Germany. His last active work was in connection with the building of the Delgado Museum of Art in New Orleans, which now houses a large part of his valuable art collection. It has been said that while the Museum was in course of construction the committee would not hold a meeting without Major Harrod. In 1865 he married Harriet Shattuck Uhlhorn of New Orleans, and after her death he married, Sept. 11, 1883, her sister Eugenia Uhlhorn, who survived him. He died in New Orleans in his seventy-sixth year.

[*Who's Who in America*, 1912–13; *Memorial of Harvard College Class of 1856, Prepared for the Fiftieth Anniv.* (1906); *Trans. Am. Soc. Civil Engineers*, vol. LXXVI (1913); *Engineering News*, Sept. 19, 1912; *New Orleans Times-Democrat* and *Daily Picayune*, Sept. 8, 1912.]
W. B. G.

HARROD, JAMES (1742–July 1793), pioneer, soldier, was born at Big Cove in what is now Bedford County, Pa. His father came from England about 1734 and first settled in the Shenandoah Valley but soon moved on to Pennsylvania. James was a typical product of the unsettled frontier, skilful as a marksman, reveling in the great solitudes of the forest, and almost uncanny in his knowledge of woodcraft. He first saw military service in the French and Indian War as a private in General Forbes's forces. In 1773 he accompanied a party down the Ohio River in large canoes as far as the Falls, where Louisville now stands, and the next year he returned to the Kentucky region with thirty men. He went up the Kentucky River and began making surveys and building cabins at a place which came to be called Harrodsburg. In the midst of this work he and his men were warned out by Boone on account of an Indian uprising which developed into Lord Dunmore's War. Harrod hurried away, going through the Holston River country, and arrived at Point Pleasant in time to take part in the battle there. He soon afterward returned to Harrodsburg, completed the cabins, and thereby founded the first settlement in Kentucky—all before Richard Henderson and his Transylvania Company had arrived. Though

Harrod represented his stockaded settlement in Henderson's assembly, soon he and his followers were arrayed in opposition to the grandiloquent Transylvania scheme and he was among the signers of the petition sent late in 1775 to the Virginia legislature praying for the suppression of Henderson.

Harrod took an active part in the war in the West against the Indians. In 1777 he led a party to the Ohio River to carry back a consignment of powder sent out by Virginia; in 1779 he commanded a company in Bowman's expedition against Chillicothe; and in 1782 he took part in George Rogers Clark's invasion of the Shawnee country up the Miami River. He had no political ambitions, yet he was elected to the Virginia legislature in 1779 and in 1784 was sent as a militia representative to the Danville convention. A few years later he disappeared from his home under mysterious circumstances and never returned. The most probable explanation is that he was lured away by an enemy in search of the fabled Swift's silver mine and was murdered. He left a wife, Ann, and a daughter, and a considerable estate.

[H. Marshall, *Hist. of Ky.* (1824), vol. I; L. and R. H. Collins, *Hist. of Ky.* (1874); W. E. Connelley and E. M. Coulter, *Hist. of Ky.* (1922), vol. I; Archibald Henderson, *The Conquest of the Old Southwest* (1920); *Biog. Cyc. of Ky.* (1878).] E. M. C.

HARSHBERGER, JOHN WILLIAM (Jan. 1, 1869–Apr. 27, 1929), botanist, naturalist, teacher, was born and resided all his life in Philadelphia, Pa. His father, Dr. Abram Harshberger, was the great-grandson of an emigrant who came from near Coblenz, Rhineland, Germany, about 1735. His mother, Jane Harris Walk, was of Scotch-Irish, English, and Slavic ancestry; her family moved to Philadelphia after the burning of Chambersburg, Pa., during the Civil War. While still a boy, John Harshberger became interested in plants and made a small herbarium at the age of seven. His first paper, "A Few Pennsylvania Forestry Statistics," appeared in *Forest Leaves,* March–April 1889. After primary and secondary training in the Philadelphia public schools, he graduated, in 1892, with the degree of B.S. from the University of Pennsylvania. The following year he obtained his doctorate in philosophy, with the thesis *Maize; A Botanical and Economic Study* (1893), and was appointed instructor in biology at the same institution. He remained with this university until his death, becoming assistant professor of botany in 1907 and full professor in 1911. In addition, from 1892 to 1895, he taught general science in Rittenhouse Academy, was lecturer in the American Society for Extension of University Teaching (1896), and instructed for three seasons in farmers' institutes in Pennsylvania. He also was in charge of nature study at the Pocono Pines Assembly for five years (1903–08), was head professor in ecology at the marine biological laboratory, Cold Spring Harbor, Long Island (1913–22), and directed the study of botany at the Nantucket Maria Mitchell Association (1914, 1915).

Harshberger's early contributions were mainly observations in nature study. In 1896 he visited Mexico and afterward published several notes on the domestic and native plants of that country. In 1899 he brought out *The Botanists of Philadelphia and their Work,* followed in 1901 by a textbook: *Student's Herbarium for Descriptive and Geographic Purposes.* On June 28, 1907, he was married to Helen B. Cole, who died in 1923. His best-known work, the *Phytogeographic Survey of North America,* came out in 1911 as Volume XIII of *Die Vegetation der Erde* (published by A. Engler and O. Drude). Among his many other contributions to the study of plant distribution were *The Vegetation of South Florida* (1914) and *The Vegetation of the New Jersey Pine-Barrens* (1916). Although, throughout life, his viewpoint was evidently that of a naturalist and his dominant interest lay in the geographic panorama of floras, he also wrote *A Text-Book of Mycology and Plant Pathology* (1917) and a *Text-Book of Pastoral and Agricultural Botany, for the Study of the Injurious and Useful Plants of Country and Farm* (1920). He also published several papers on the botanical aspects of ethnology. Altogether, about three hundred of his dissertations on a wide variety of subjects connected with his special field appeared in print. Always affable and willing to help (despite a certain diffident dignity), Harshberger was very popular with his students and developed in many of them a creative interest in botany. A prominent advocate of the conservation of natural resources in Pennsylvania, he served during many years on the council of the Pennsylvania Forestry Association and was among the earliest to recognize the danger from the chestnut-blight fungus. He was the first president of the Pennsylvania Wild Flower Preservation Society and later became vice-president of the national organization. In summer trips, he visited most parts of the United States and also botanized in Mexico, the West Indies (1901), Europe (1907, 1923), Alaska (1926), and Brazil, the Argentine, Chile, Peru, and Panama (1927). The material which he obtained was deposited in the herbarium of the University of Pennsylvania. He was an indefatigable maker and collector of photographs, especially of those which showed characteristic plant formations. These he carefully labeled and arranged in bound volumes for the assistance of his students and colleagues. Practically all of his correspondence was methodically collated in a similar way. He was a member of many learned societies.

[*The Life and Work of John W. Harshberger, Ph.D.* (1928), an autobiography with bibliography; *Who's Who in America,* 1928–29; J. M. Cattell and D. L. Brimhall, *Am. Men of Science* (3rd ed., 1921); *Phila. Enquirer,* Apr. 28, 1929.] H. B. B.

HART, ABRAHAM (Dec. 15, 1810–July 23, 1885), publisher, philanthropist, was born in Philadelphia, Pa., the son of Abraham Hart, a shop-keeper, who came from Hanover, Germany, in 1804. His mother was Sarah Stork, a native of Holland. When the elder Hart died in 1823, the boy was put to work. Attracting the attention of Moses Thomas, auctioneer and former publisher, he was introduced to Henry C. Carey, of the publishing house of Carey & Lea, who gave him a position. When the business of the firm was divided in 1829 young Hart became associated with Edward L. Carey in the bookselling and publishing business under the style of E. L. Carey & A. Hart. Two years earlier Thomas had sent young Hart, then a boy of sixteen, to a Boston trade sale, giving him a letter of credit for $5,000 and depending upon his judgment to make purchases. Enterprising to a remarkable degree, the new firm, both of whose members were very young, made rapid progress. Several instances of their alertness have been recorded. One of these anecdotes refers to the first publication in America of Bulwer-Lytton's *Rienzi,* in 1836. Carey & Hart had purchased an advance copy from the English publishers, but the packet ship which brought it also brought an advance copy for Harper & Brothers in New York. On the day the copy was received by Carey & Hart, they divided it among twelve printing houses in Philadelphia, and the printers, by working continuously, had the sheets in the binder's hands at nine o'clock the following morning. On the afternoon of the same day five hundred complete copies of the book were placed in the mail stage for New York, which had been entirely reserved. With Hart accompanying them they were carried to New York, where they were on sale a full day ahead of the Harpers' edition.

For years Carey & Hart published an annual, the *Gift,* edited by Eliza Leslie [*q.v.*], to which Poe contributed some of his best-known tales. They had Longfellow prepare his *Poets and Poetry of Europe,* which they published in 1845, and also had Rufus W. Griswold compile *The Poets and Poetry of America* (1842), *The Prose Writers of America* (1847), *The Female Poets of America* (1849), and others of a similar character. Macaulay's *Critical and Miscellaneous Essays* (1842–44) they brought out in a five-volume edition. They also published many of Captain Marryat's romances and paid him on his last book, *Snarleyyow; or, the Dog Fiend* (2 vols., 1837), about the first copyright money ever given a foreign author by an American publisher. After the death of Edward L. Carey, in 1845, Hart conducted the business with Henry Carey Baird as partner until 1849, when the firm was dissolved. Hart then continued alone until his retirement in 1854. He then entered upon various enterprises as a capitalist, being at one time president of the Centennial Button-hole Machine Company, and vice-president of the American Button-hole Machine Company. For some time he was president of the Jewish Congregation Mickvéh Israel, the oldest in Philadelphia, and was prominent in Jewish educational and charitable organizations in the city, many of which he assisted in founding. In many more he was an honored officer. He died at Long Branch, N. J., having survived his wife, Rebecca Cohen Isaacks, whom he had married on Nov. 23, 1831.

[J. C. Derby, *Fifty Years Among Authors, Books and Publishers* (1884); H. S. Morais, *The Jews of Phila.* (1894); E. P. Oberholtzer, *The Lit. Hist. of Phila.* (1906), pp. 339–40; *Phila. Inquirer,* July 24, 1885.] J. J.

HART, CHARLES HENRY (Feb. 4, 1847–July 29, 1918), lawyer, art expert, author, was born in Philadelphia, Pa., the son of Samuel and Julia (Leavey) Hart, of Jewish stock. He was educated in private schools and under the direction of special tutors, later proceeding to the University of Pennsylvania to study law. He graduated in 1869, having been admitted to the bar the year before. For twenty-five years he practised law in Philadelphia, displaying throughout his legal career a remarkable keenness of perception in cases involving obscure questions, the most notable example, perhaps, being the North American Land Company's, which he brought to a settlement after eighty years of litigation. As a result of severe injuries received in 1894 in a railroad accident, he was incapacitated for fourteen months; when he became convalescent he determined to give up the practice of law and devote his time to literature and art, of which he had always been an ardent student. He was soon recognized, both in America and Europe, as an authority on historical portraiture. He made a special study of the work of Gilbert

Stuart. He waged bitter warfare constantly against dealers who attempted to dispose of spurious works and on many occasions saved intending purchasers from being victimized. His was an iconoclastic nature and delighted in the discovery and exposure of falsely labeled canvases. He always contended that the portraits of Don Josef de Jaudenes y Nebet, first Spanish minister to the United States, and of Don Matilde Stoughton de Jaudenes, both in the Metropolitan Museum of Art and believed to be the work of Gilbert Stuart, were spurious. His essay on "Frauds in Historical Portraiture" (*Annual Report of the American Historical Association,* 1913), destroyed many long-cherished artistic idols. He was a prolific writer of memoirs, monographs, and briefer articles on subjects of interest to him. In acknowledgment of an article in *Harper's Magazine* for March 1898, in which he proved that Gustavus Hesselius [*q.v.*] was the earliest known artist of repute in this country, he received the thanks of King Oscar of Sweden. Hart was the corresponding secretary of the Numismatic and Antiquarian Society of Philadelphia in 1865, and its historiographer in 1868; he was a director of the Pennsylvania Academy of the Fine Arts from 1882 to 1902, and in 1887, while chairman of the exhibition committee, was instrumental in the organization of the first exhibition of American historical paintings. His catalogue of this collection of paintings was a valuable work of reference. He was the only non-resident member of the committee of fifty in control of the arrangements for the celebration at New York, in 1889, of the one hundredth anniversary of the inauguration of George Washington. He married, first, in 1869, Armine, daughter of John Nixon; second, in 1905, Marianne Livingston Phillips, daughter of William Lacy Phillips, by whom he had one son; and third, in 1912, Anita Beatriz, daughter of Don Alfonso Gonzales y Arabe of Seville, Spain. He died in New York July 29, 1918.

[British *Who's Who,* 1903; *Who's Who in America,* 1918–19, with a full list of his numerous publications; *N. Y. Times,* July 31, 1918; H. S. Morais, *The Jews of Phila.* (1894); *New Eng. Hist. and Geneal. Reg.,* Apr. 1921 Supp.; *Am. Art News,* Aug. 17, 1918.]

G. C. H.

HART, EDMUND HALL (Dec. 26, 1839–Apr. 22, 1898), pioneer Florida horticulturist, was born at "Heartsease," Manchester Bridge, near Poughkeepsie, N. Y., the son of Benjamin Hall and Elizabeth (Nichols) Hart. He received a thorough training in horticulture from his father, and with his brothers, Walter and Ambrose, he settled in 1867 at Federal Point, Fla., and engaged in the culture of oranges and other citrus fruits. At this time American horticulturists were chiefly concerned with the adaptation of plant and fruit varieties to various parts of the United States. Hart developed an extensive stock and at one time had more than one hundred and fifty varieties of citrus alone under observation, as well as varieties of other fruits which could be grown in Florida. He introduced into the state under the name of Hart's Late or Hart's Tardiff (Tardive), the famous Valencia orange, which was later widely cultivated both in Florida and California. Of his other fruits his Choice banana, originally from the Bahamas, was an important product of his breeding. He was interested also in palms and other ornamental plants and was considered the best authority on palms in Florida, importing seeds and growing the plants of rare palms listed in the catalogues of the United States and Europe. It is said that he had probably the largest and finest specimens of several rare species of palms to be found in the United States, as well as many more common varieties.

Hart was a member of the old Florida Fruit Growers' Association, a charter member of the Florida State Horticultural Society, and an extensive exhibitor at Florida fairs and exhibitions. He was a member of the American Pomological Society, serving on the society's committee on tropical and sub-tropical fruits, and was also chairman for some time of the State Fruit Committee of Florida. His writings include the subtropical fruit section in J. J. Thomas' *American Fruit Culturist,* which appeared first in the twentieth edition of that work in 1897, and the various reports of his committees published in the *Proceedings* of the American Pomological Society from 1883 to 1889. In person he was modest and retiring in manner. He married Isabella Martense Howland on Dec. 1, 1870, and was survived at his death by his wife and three daughters.

[L. H. Bailey, *Cyc. Am. Agric.,* vol. IV (1909); Harold H. Hume, *The Cultivation of Citrus Fruits* (1926); Alfred Andrews, *Geneal. Hist. of Deacon Stephen Hart and his Descendants* (1875); *Proc. Am. Pomological Soc.,* 1895–99.]

R. H. S.

HART, JAMES MacDOUGAL (May 10, 1828–Oct. 24, 1901), painter, younger brother of William Hart [*q.v.*], was born at Kilmarnock, Scotland, the son of James and Marion (Robertson) Hart. His parents brought him to the United States in 1831 and apprenticed him when he was fifteen years old to a sign and banner painter at Albany, N. Y. Like his brother he advanced from signboards to portraits, and in 1850 went to Düsseldorf, then a frequented center, for three years of study under Schirmer and other teachers. The art of Düsseldorf was thin and sentimental, and students who attained distinction did so in spite of their instruction. On his return he opened a studio at Albany and taught and painted until his removal to New York in 1857. He was made an associate of the National Academy of Design in 1858 and a member in 1859; he served on the academic council for many years and was for three years a vice-president. In the period immediately after the Civil War New York swarmed with people newly rich and feverishly eager to acquire at once the trappings and paraphernalia of culture, oil paintings included. With such clients Hart and his brother found abundant employment, for they painted in a language intelligible to the artistically illiterate. James garnished his landscapes with barnyard animals, chiefly cows, and painted them with such fidelity that his delighted customers thought they could distinguish the Alderneys from the Guernseys; but his brother William, with a broad Scotch accent and a tinge perhaps of jealousy, dissented: "Jeames, he's a fair mon but he connot paint a coo." James was, in reality, deeply moved by the placid beauty of southeastern New York and did much, in spite of his immature technique, to stimulate a general appreciation of it. Among his better known works are: "The Drove at the Ford" (Corcoran Art Gallery, Washington), "At the Brookside" (Metropolitan Museum, New York), and "In the Autumn Woods" (Sayles Memorial Hall, Brown University). In 1866 he married Marie Theresa Gorsuch, by whom he had several children. He died at his home in Brooklyn.

[*Who's Who in America*, 1901–02; sketch, somewhat inaccurate, *Art Jour.*, n.s. I (1875), 180; *N. Y. Herald*, Oct. 26, 1901; information from his daughter, Letitia B. Hart.] K. H. A.

HART, JAMES MORGAN (Nov. 2, 1839–Apr. 18, 1916), philologist, was born at Princeton, N. J., the son of John Seely [*q.v.*] and Amelia Caroline (Morford) Hart. He spent his boyhood in Philadelphia. After graduating from the College of New Jersey in 1860, Hart studied at Geneva, Göttingen, and Berlin, becoming proficient in French, German, and Italian. He concentrated upon civil and canon law at the University of Göttingen and in 1864 won the degree of J.U.D. *vera cum laude*. After practising law in New York City for several years, he served, 1868–72, as an assistant professor of modern languages in Cornell University. Linguistic science fascinated him and in order to penetrate his chosen field more deeply he spent two years in Leipzig, Marburg, and Berlin, entering intensively into the study of English and German philology under noted philologists, among them Braune and Grein. He also wrote for American newspapers, as in the spring of 1873, when he was special correspondent of the New York *World* at the Vienna Exposition. In 1874 he was back in New York engaged in literary work, translating Auguste Laugel's *Angleterre, Politique et Sociale* (1874), editing German classics for college use, and writing his *German Universities: A Narrative of Personal Experience* (1874), which he dedicated to his college-mate and lifelong friend, George Haven Putnam. For more than a generation it was the standard work on the subject in America, a signpost directing young Americans toward the paths of graduate study. Its appearance was timely, its influence inestimable.

From 1876 till 1890 Hart occupied the chair of modern languages and English literature at the University of Cincinnati, where he found his first group of disciples, who carried his enthusiasm for advanced studies and scholarly research to other American colleges. He published a large number of reviews, *A Syllabus of Anglo-Saxon Literature* (1881), and made extensive collections for an Anglo-Saxon lexicon which unfortunately he never completed. In 1890 he was called back to Cornell University as professor of rhetoric and English philology. His reputation attracted numerous graduate students in English and Germanic philology who later filled important college and secondary-school positions. In harmony with this work he found a wider field for his activities. He was appalled by the poor English spoken and written by college students. He started a campaign for the improvement of the teaching of English in the schools of New York and threw his energy into this movement, attending teachers' meetings, organizing teachers' training courses, keeping the fires hot in educational magazines, writing textbooks on composition and rhetoric. He carried his crusade into the meetings of the Modern Language Association, of which he was president in 1895, appealing to all language departments to insist on the use of good English, and aiming to place English at the center of college education. In New York he may be said to have revolutionized the methods and practices of teaching and studying the English language. Among his scholarly writings book reviews preponderate. Most of them appeared in the *Nation,* not pleasing, faint notices, but virile, trenchant, and hard-hitting, never personal attacks, but straightforward, clear, precise investigations of the subject in hand. Severely critical as a teacher, he cultivated independence in his students.

Hart was twice married: first to Miss Wadsworth, a resident of New York, who died shortly after their marriage; second, in 1883 to Clara Doherty of Cincinnati, who survived him. At the age of sixty-eight (1907) he retired. He continued to live in Ithaca until 1914, when a southern climate was recommended to him by his physician. He died in Washington, D. C.

[*Cornell Univ.: A History* (1905) ed. by W. T. Hewett; *Who's Who in America*, 1899–1915; *Addresses at the Presentation of the Memorial Tablet to J. M. Hart in Sage Chapel, June 3, 1917* (*Cornell Univ. Official Pubs.*, vol. VIII, no. D, July 1917), ed. by C. S. Northrup.]

A. B. F.

HART, JOEL TANNER (Feb. 10, 1810–Mar. 2, 1877), sculptor, son of Josiah and Judith (Tanner) Hart, was born near Winchester, Ky. His parents had character, position, and education, but owing to family reverses, young Joel received only three months' schooling. Studious by nature and helped by his brothers, he learned what he could from books read by the evening firelight. Lacking work near his home, he went to Bourbon County, where he built stone walls and chimneys; on one of the latter he carved his name. At twenty-one, while working in a marble-yard at Lexington, he met the sculptor Shobal Vail Clevenger [*q.v.*], who was modeling a bust of Henry Clay. This meeting inspired Hart to attempt a bust of Cassius Marcellus Clay. The result being happy, he sought Andrew Jackson at the Hermitage, obtained from him sittings for a marble bust, and produced a good likeness. Returning to Lexington, he made busts of John J. Crittenden, Robert Wickliffe, and the Rev. Alexander Campbell; thereafter, his local fame was secure. He then visited Philadelphia, Washington, Baltimore, Richmond, and New York, studying the statuary in these cities, and getting, as he wrote to his brother, "attention enough for a lifetime." In Richmond, in 1846, he received from the "Ladies' Clay Association" an order for a life-size marble statue of Henry Clay, at $5,000. He had his subject daguerreotyped from many views, made casts of the face and other parts of the body, took measurements, and had sittings. His procedure was characteristic: a reliance on mechanical means, a leisurely, groping study from life. The work still exists—a poor thing enough, except for the fine head. After three years, the plaster model was ready for shipment to Italy, there to be copied in marble. Hart went abroad, visiting Rome and Florence and choosing Florence as his headquarters (1849), and while awaiting his plaster model, spent fourteen months in London, giving much time to the study of anatomy. He visited Paris, and viewed the old masters at the Louvre. When at last he returned to Florence, he learned that his long-expected model had been lost by shipwreck in the Bay of Biscay. He therefore sent for a duplicate, which arrived a year later. While convalescing from cholera and typhoid, he invented a measuring-machine to facilitate portrait work. His fellow sculptors would have none of it. "Powers, and the rest of them," he wrote to his brother in 1857, "hate it like the devil." The invention was patented in France and in England. Advertised in London, it brought Hart orders for ten marble busts of Londoners at 100 guineas each. These orders, with others, including that for the bust of Ex-President Fillmore, supported him while he waited final payment for his statue of Clay. Although it is signed "J. T. Hart, 1847," it was not until 1859 that the Clay statue was complete and in place. In that year Hart came to the United States for its unveiling and stayed eight months, lauded and fêted. He had planned to open a studio in New York, but on receiving from Louisville a commission for a duplicate of his statue, at $10,000, followed by another from New Orleans, he went instead to Florence to execute these works. The three statues set him on his feet, financially. He had time to reveal in marble his long-cherished vision of "Woman Triumphant," originally called "The Triumph of Chastity," a life-size nude female figure holding an arrow high above the reach of an imploring Cupid. For thirty leisurely years he kept this group by him in Florence, seeking its perfection by a study of more than a hundred and fifty models. It received extraordinary plaudits; at one time he refused $20,000 for it, and after his death, ladies of Lexington, Ky., bought a marble replica which was set up in the courthouse, but was later destroyed in a fire. Other ideal works by Hart were "Angelina," "Il Penseroso," and a "Child with Flowers." His best achievements were his portrait busts; he had a genuine talent for seizing likenesses. The Corcoran Art Gallery at Washington owns his excellent bust of Henry Clay as well as his bust of Crittenden.

Hart was tall, vigorous, bearded; in appearance, a pioneer; in reality, a dreamer. He wrote verses and played the flute. Gentle and blameless, he had a host of admiring friends of both sexes, but he remained a bachelor. He died and was buried in Florence. In January 1885, by special enactment, his body was brought home and reinterred with imposing ceremonies at Frankfort, Ky.

[S. W. Price, *The Old Masters of the Bluegrass* (1902), Filson Club Pubs. no. 17; Issa D. Breckinridge and Mary Desha, *"The Work Shall Praise the Master": A Memorial to Joel T. Hart* (1884); *The Biog. Encyc. of Ky.* (1878); G. W. Ranck, *Hist. of Lexington, Ky* (1872); H. T. Tuckerman, *Book of the Artists* (1867); J. J. Jarves, *The Art Idea* (ed. of 1877); Lorado Taft, *The Hist. of Am. Sculpture* (1903); E. D. Warfield, in *Mag. of Western Hist.*, May–Oct., 1885; *Louisville Commercial*, Mar. 3, 1877.]

A. A.

HART, JOHN (1711?–May 11, 1779), farmer, legislator, signer of the Declaration of Independence, was born in Stonington, Conn., the son of Edward Hart, who removed with his wife Martha and their children to Hopewell, N. J., about 1712. John had little or no schooling, but was a good farmer and in time acquired considerable property, including an interest in fulling mills at Glen Moore and grist and fulling mills at Rocky Hill. He was married, in 1740, to Deborah Scudder, the daughter of Richard and Hannah (Reeder) Scudder of Ewing, N. J. They had a large family. Having become "the most considerable man in his community," Hart was chosen justice of the peace of Hunterdon County in 1755 and in 1761 was elected to the Twentieth Assembly. He was reëlected to the Twenty-first Assembly and continued with the body until its dissolution late in 1771. A stanch supporter of popular rights, he opposed the Stamp Act of 1765, in 1768 he favored an address to the King which declared that rights to tax the colonies were vested in the colonies only, and led the opposition against further provision for royal troops in New Jersey. In 1775 he was serving as judge of the court of common pleas of New Jersey when he was elected, July 8, 1774, to the First Provincial Congress of New Jersey. He was successively reëlected and served until he was sent to the Continental Congress in June 1776. In January 1775 he was made chairman of the township committees of Hunterdon County, later he was appointed to the Committee of Correspondence and on Aug. 17, 1775, he was placed on the Committee of Safety. In the business of the New Jersey Congress he aided in the preparation of the estimates for defense, in formulating a method of issuing bills of credit, and was chairman of the committee which erected a Court of Admiralty. In the sessions of 1776 he was firm in his opposition to Gov. William Franklin [*q.v.*]. On June 15, 1776, he was elected vice-president of the Congress, and a week later, on June 22, with Richard Stockton, John Witherspoon, Francis Hopkinson, and Abraham Clark, he was elected a delegate to the Continental Congress. On August 2, he signed the Declaration of Independence. The same month he was elected to the first Assembly under the new state constitution of New Jersey and was unanimously chosen speaker. His main tasks were those which devolved upon him as a member of the Council of Safety, Mar. 18, 1777–Oct. 8, 1778. During the war his farm and mills, in the path of both armies, were laid waste and he himself was hunted through the hills around Sourland Mountains. After the victories at Princeton and Trenton he was able to return to his home. He was forced on account of his health to retire from public life in the fall of 1778 and died the following year. In 1865, the New Jersey legislature, wishing to honor his services to the state, provided for the erection of a monument in his memory at Hopewell, N. J.

[Sources include E. F. and W. S. Cooley, *Geneal. of Early Settlers in Trenton and Ewing, "Old Hunterdon County," N. J.* (1883); L. H. Patterson, sketch of Hart in *Proc. N. J. Hist. Soc.*, 4 ser., vol. X (1925); S. G. Arnold, *Biog. Sketches of Distinguished Jerseymen* (1845); *Docs. Relating to the Revolutionary Hist. of the State of N. J.*, vol. I (1901); *Minutes of the Provincial Cong. . . . of the State of N. J.* (1879); *Minutes of the Council of Safety of the State of N. J.* (1872); Theodore Sedgwick, Jr., *A Memoir of the Life of Wm. Livingston* (1833); Joel Parker, *Oration Delivered . . . at the Dedication of a Monument to the Memory of John Hart* (1896); *N. J. Archives*, 1 ser., vols. X (1886), and XVI (1891), 2 ser., vols. I (1901), and III (1906); *N. J. Gazette*, May 19, 1779. Nearly every date on the monument at Hopewell is incorrect.]

W. L. W—y.

HART, JOHN SEELY (Jan. 28, 1810–Mar. 26, 1877), educator, editor, the father of James Morgan Hart [*q.v.*], was born at Stockbridge, Berkshire County, Mass. He was the son of Isaac and Abigail (Stone) Hart and a descendant in the eighth generation of Deacon Stephen Hart who emigrated from England to Massachusetts Bay about 1632. When he was two years old the family moved to Pennsylvania and settled in Providence Township on the Lackawanna. From the deeply religious atmosphere of his home he went, after a period of preparation under Dr. Orton at Wilkes-Barre, to the College of New Jersey (later Princeton University). In 1830 he graduated with high honors and after a year of teaching in an academy at Natchez, Miss., he entered Princeton Theological Seminary, from which he graduated in 1834. During his last two years there he was tutor in the College of New Jersey and in 1834 was made adjunct professor of ancient languages. On Apr. 21, 1836, he married Amelia C. Morford. Having resigned his professorship, he purchased Edge Hill School, where he remained until December 1841. The following year he became principal of the Central High School of Philadelphia. For a time in 1844 he edited the Pennsylvania *Common School Journal* and from 1849 to 1851 he was co-editor of *Sartain's Union Magazine of Literature and Art*. In 1845 he published his

Elementary Grammar of the English Language and two years later his *Essay on the Life and Writings of Edmund Spenser, with a Special Exposition of the Fairy Queen.*

Hart had already achieved distinction by his success in the reorganization of the Philadelphia high school and by his editorial labors, when, in 1859, he became editor of the publications of the American Sunday-school Union. As the founder and first editor (1859–71) of the *Sunday School Times* he was the most influential writer in the Sunday-school movement then experiencing a successful revival. He attempted, with some success, to introduce into the Sunday schools the best methods of secular teaching. In 1862 he went to Trenton as head of the model department of the State Normal School of New Jersey and the next year was elected principal. While there he published *In the School-room* (1868), a conventional and fragmentary treatment of educational methods, which achieved a wide popularity. He was called to the College of New Jersey in 1872 as professor of rhetoric and English literature. Two years later he retired from active teaching to devote himself to private literary pursuits. The labors of these later years were anthologies and textbooks. In January of 1877 he fell on an icy pavement and sustained the injuries from which he died. He was distinguished as a teacher and as an editor, and throughout a tranquil though active life successfully upheld the family tradition of piety and public works.

[Alfred Andrews, *Geneal. Hist. of Deacon Stephen Hart and his Descendants* (1875); *Phila. Inquirer,* Mar. 27, 1877; *Sunday School Times,* Apr. 7, 1877; H. A. Boardman, *A Discourse Commemorative . . . of John Seely Hart* (1878); *Necrol. Report, Princeton Theol. Sem.,* 1877, p. 29.] F. M.

HART, SAMUEL (June 4, 1845–Feb. 25, 1917), theologian, the son of Henry and Mary Ann (Witter) Hart, was born at Saybrook, Conn. His father was descended from Stephen Hart, one of the Hartford proprietors and a deacon of Thomas Hooker's church in Newtown and Hartford. Another ancestor was the Rev. John Hart, one of the first students to receive a degree from the Collegiate School of Connecticut, later Yale College. Samuel was prepared in the Episcopal Academy at Cheshire, Conn., and graduated from Trinity College, Hartford, in the class of 1866. He was the first Trinity graduate to receive the title *optimus,* and at the time of his funeral President Luther stated that none had ever received such high marks during his college course. He graduated from the Berkeley Divinity School, then situated in Middletown, Conn., in the class of 1869. Even before his graduation from the Divinity School he was elected tutor in Trinity College, where he taught in turn almost all the subjects in the college curriculum. He was ordained to the diaconate of the Episcopal Church in 1869 and to the priesthood in 1870. In the same year he became adjunct professor of mathematics in Trinity College. Later made a full professor of mathematics and astronomy, he was in 1883 transferred to the professorship of Latin. In 1899 he became vice-dean of the Berkeley Divinity School and at the same time professor of doctrinal theology and the prayer book. He was elected dean of the school in 1908 and remained in that position during the remainder of his life.

In the diocese of Connecticut Hart became a member of the standing committee, chairman of many other committees, and a delegate to the General Convention. In 1886 he was elected custodian of the Standard Book of Common Prayer, in 1892 secretary of the House of Bishops, and in 1898 historiographer and registrar of the General Convention. He was a member of many learned societies and a trustee of a large number of institutions. From 1900 until the time of his death he was president of the Connecticut Beta of the Phi Beta Kappa, the longest record of service as secretary in the annals of the fraternity. His published writings include a *History of the American Book of Common Prayer* (1910), editions of several Latin texts for college use, a large number of sermons and historical addresses, and numerous articles contributed to periodicals and encyclopedias. His gracious personality, fine culture, and genial humor made him widely beloved. It was characteristic of his life of benevolent activity that for over thirty years he ministered every Sunday afternoon to the patients in the Hartford Hospital. A line of a Trinity College student song well expresses the impression he made upon others as well as upon students: "He lives pro bono publico." He was a thoughtful though not a brilliant preacher. His theological views might be described as of the liberal High-church order. In 1893 he was elected Bishop of Vermont but declined. It was reported at the time that he did this at the suggestion of Bishop Williams who desired to have him chosen bishop-coadjutor of Connecticut. He was, however, never again elected to the episcopate though his name figured prominently in several diocesan elections. The fact that he had had no parish experience and a certain temperamental moderation in practical affairs kept him perhaps from that high position in his Church for which he seemed otherwise so well qualified. He was never married.

[Trinity College, *Necrology, 1916–18* (1918); Berkeley Divinity School *Bulletin*, no. 28, Apr. 1917; *Who's Who in America*, 1916–17; Alfred Andrews, *Geneal. Hist. of Deacon Stephen Hart and his Descendants* (1875); *Hartford Daily Times*, Feb. 26, 1917.]

W. P. L.

HART, VIRGIL CHITTENDEN (Jan. 2, 1840–Feb. 24, 1904), Methodist missionary, who was to spend most of his life in China, was born in Lorraine, N. Y., the son of Augustus and Joanna (Horr) Hart. Reared on a farm under almost pioneer conditions, he received there a training which was probably both a preparation for and an incentive to the type of work to which his mature years were devoted. Although his father opposed his entering the ministry, his home appears to have been one of strong moral and religious conviction. When about fourteen years of age he passed through the experience of conversion in one of the "protracted meetings" which were then common. Before many years he determined to become a minister, and later, partially through reading an account of the work of David Livingstone—whose explorations were then thrilling the Anglo-Saxon world—he decided to be a missionary. His formal preparation was obtained in Gouverneur Wesleyan Academy, Northwestern University, and Garrett Biblical Seminary (B.D., 1865). True to his convictions, upon graduation from the seminary he accepted appointment under the foreign-mission board of the Methodist Episcopal Church. That same year he was ordained, and, shortly afterward, on Aug. 31, 1865, he was married to Adeline Gilliland.

Hart and his wife arrived at their station, Fuchow, China, in May 1866. The following year, 1867, Hart was chosen to inaugurate the work of his board in Central China, and the major part of the next two decades he spent in fulfilling that commission. He first established his residence in Kiu-kiang. From here he made long journeys and succeeded in opening stations in a number of different cities, among them Nanking. In pursuance of his task, he had often to face anti-foreign mobs and the indifference or actual opposition of Chinese officials. It was a day when, under the ægis of the toleration clauses of the treaties of 1858, foreign missionaries were penetrating the interior of China, often to the intense indignation of the Chinese. In the performance of what he believed to be his duty, Hart did not hesitate to insist upon his treaty rights or to appeal to American officials to support him in them. Whatever a later generation may believe to have been the ethics of this position, Hart maintained it with fine heroism and with no small cost to himself. In 1887, when about to start for America on a well-earned furlough, he was ordered by his bishop to West China, there to adjust the difficulties brought upon the Methodist mission in Chung-king by the severe riots of 1886. He fulfilled this commission and was greatly impressed by what he saw of the vast province of Sze-chuen. That same year, however, illness forced him to return to America, and in 1889 he resigned the superintendency of his mission and retired to a farm in Burlington, Ontario, to regain his health. While there, he was asked by the foreign-mission board of the Canadian Methodists to suggest a location for a new enterprise which it was about to begin in China. He advised Sze-chuen, and not only was his counsel taken, but he was asked to lead in the undertaking. This he did, sailing for China in 1891 with a large party. The following year he reached Cheng-tu, the capital of the province. He continued as head of the enterprise until 1900, when he was forced to the coast by the Boxer outbreak. His health finally gave way and he returned to America, worn out. After a few years of invalidism, he died in Burlington, Ontario.

[E. I. Hart, *Virgil C. Hart: Missionary Statesman* (1917); E. W. Wallace, *The Heart of Szchuan* (1903); O. L. Kilborn, *Our West China Missions* (1920); *Missionary Soc. of the Meth. Episc. Ch., Ann. Reports*, 1876–79; Geo. H. Cornish, *Cyc. of Methodism in Canada*, vol. II (1903); *Chinese Recorder and Missionary Jour.*, Apr. 1904.]

K. S. L.

HART, WILLIAM (Mar. 31, 1823–June 17, 1894), painter, elder brother of James MacDougal Hart [*q.v.*], was born at Paisley, Scotland, and came to America in 1831 with his parents, James and Marion (Robertson) Hart. The family settled at Albany, N. Y., and bound William to a carriage-maker who set him to painting carriages and eventually to doing the elaborate panel-decorating so much admired at the time. Fascinated by the possibilities of oil paints he attempted portraits and at eighteen was charging five dollars apiece for likenesses made in his father's woodshed. He also tried landscapes. Exhausting the local market, he set out for new territory and spent three years in Michigan, chiefly on portrait work. He was now charging twenty-five dollars for a portrait, but cash was so scarce that he frequently took his payment in board or barter. Malaria eventually drove him back to his father's home. A friend assisted him to make a trip to Scotland, where he studied briefly with rather obscure teachers and roamed about painting. Returning to America, he opened a studio in New York City. He had already exhibited at the National Academy, of which he was made an associate in

1855 and a full member in 1858. In 1865 he became the first president of the Brooklyn Academy of Design. He was also one of the organizers of the American Society of Water-Colorists and its president for three years. Like many other artists of the period he was charmed by the beauty of eastern New York and belonged to what is called "the Hudson River School." Because of his lack of formal instruction Hart's work had some of the freedom and freshness of the primitive. Though often thin and crude, it is never sentimental. His difficulty was that he had too little understanding of artistic problems and tried to convey his impressions by the reproduction of minute detail. His sincere efforts to encourage and organize artists were valuable to his generation. His home during his latter years was at Mt. Vernon, N. Y. His wife, Janet Wallace, a native of Scotland, predeceased him by only two months. They both were buried in Greenwood Cemetery, Brooklyn.

[H. T. Tuckerman, *Book of the Artists* (1867); G. W. Sheldon, *Am. Painters* (1881); C. H. Caffin, *The Story of Am. Painting* (1907); *N. Y. Tribune*, N. Y. *Evening Post*, June 18, 1894.] K. H. A.

HARTE, FRANCIS BRETT (Aug. 25, 1836–May 5, 1902), author, was born at Albany, N. Y. As a writer he used his middle name, spelling it with a single *t*, and is now known as Bret Harte; by his family and friends he was commonly called Frank. He was of English, Dutch, and Hebrew descent. His grandfather, Bernard Hart, was in the early part of the nineteenth century a prominent Jewish merchant of New York City. His son and Bret Harte's father, Henry Harte, was a man of scholarly tastes who supported, or failed to support, his family by teaching, lecturing, and translating. Henry Harte married Elizabeth Rebecca Ostrander in 1830. At the time of Bret Harte's birth his father was conducting a private school in Albany; he abandoned the venture, however, and left the city when his son was less than a year old. This was the prelude to later removals; during the next eight years the family resided in at least six different cities of the north Atlantic states. As might be expected, these frequent changes bespoke straitened circumstances. After Henry Harte's death in 1845 his widow with the four children lived in New York and Brooklyn until 1853, supported by the Ostranders and Bernard Hart. Harte's childhood was thus varied, and lacking in many of the advantages of life. He left school and went to work at thirteen, and at sixteen was supporting himself. At a very early age he began to show a literary interest which was encouraged by his family. As a boy he read vigorously in his father's more than usually large library, and gained a good knowledge of English literature. Of all books the novels of Dickens were his favorites, and their influence can be traced throughout his life. In addition to his reading, Harte also began to write while still a child. In spite of his admiration for Dickens, his first interest, which remained dominant until he had passed the age of thirty, was in writing verse. At the age of eleven he had a poem published in the *New York Sunday Morning Atlas*.

In 1853 Harte's mother went to California and married Col. Andrew Williams of Oakland. Harte followed her by the Nicaragua route early in 1854. From then until 1857 his life is at times obscure. At different periods he lived in his step-father's house, supporting himself by working in an apothecary's shop and perhaps by teaching. In 1856 he tutored for a while in a family living near Alamo in Contra Costa County. Early in 1857 he acted for a brief time as some kind of expressman, in what locality is not known. In the summer of 1857 he followed a married sister to Union (now Arcata) on Humboldt Bay. There he worked at odd jobs, tutored, taught school, worked again for an apothecary, and served on the town newspaper, the *Northern Californian*. Altogether he failed to advance in a material way and was frequently on the edge of poverty. He continued, however, to write assiduously in both prose and verse, and in a significant passage in his diary at the end of 1857 he dedicated himself definitely to a literary career. Much of this early writing was published in the San Francisco *Golden Era*, and a few poems were also accepted by some less important Eastern magazines. His work, on the whole, gave little promise of future eminence. On Feb. 26, 1860, the famous Gunther's Island massacre occurred near Arcata, in which about sixty peaceful Indians were murdered by white ruffians. Harte warmly espoused the cause of the Indians in the *Northern Californian*, the chief editor happening to be absent at the time. A month later Harte left Arcata and in view of the circumstances there is no reason to doubt that he was "run out." His conduct in the whole affair seems to have been extremely creditable.

This, in brief, is all that is certainly known of Harte's life between 1854 and 1860. There is, however, a considerable amount of legend, some of which may have a basis of fact. That Harte served in an Indian campaign or was a tax-gatherer rests upon no real evidence and is extremely improbable. That in his work as expressman he fought bandits is again unlikely. It is improbable that Harte, gentle, literary, and fresh from the East, ever engaged in such desperate activities. There is also no evidence that he ever mined, although he may well have tried his luck in a desultory way. In spite, moreover, of many statements and assumptions to the contrary, he had comparatively little first-hand knowledge of the mining country. There seems no reason to doubt, however, that he was in the so-called Southern Mines for some months, most likely in 1854–55. To this experience should be added his years in Arcata, a supply-base for mining country, where Harte could have become acquainted with the miners on their way to and from the Trinity River district. Finally, in accounting for the acquaintance with the mines which is displayed in his stories, we must add the facts which he must have accumulated through exchanges while working on the *Northern Californian,* and those coming to him through friends. His knowledge—by no means complete or always accurate—can easily have been attained in this way. His first six years in California form an extremely important period in his life. At this time he acquired in one way or another most of the information upon which his literary work was based and prepared himself by constant and conscientious application to the practice of writing.

Upon removing to San Francisco from Arcata in 1860 he first worked as a type-setter for the *Golden Era.* He soon began again to contribute, and in the next three years more than a hundred of his poems and sketches appeared in the *Era.* With a few exceptions, notably *M'liss,* these had no connection with life in the mines. In 1861, through the friendship of Mrs. Jessie Benton Frémont [*q.v.*] he received an appointment as clerk in the surveyor-general's office in San Francisco. On Aug. 11, 1862, he married Anna Griswold of New York. In 1863 he changed to a more lucrative post in the Branch Mint, which he held for six years; its duties, however, were not arduous, and did not greatly interfere with his writing. He was by this time a man of some note. He was a leader in literary circles in the city; his patriotic poems had done much to inspire Union sentiment throughout the state. After the establishment of the *Californian* in 1864, most of his work for two years was contributed to its pages and he occasionally acted as its editor. In 1865 (dated 1866) appeared what he liked to call his first book—*Outcroppings,* a volume of California verse that he selected. What was properly his first book, *The Lost Galleon and Other Tales,* a collection of poems, was published in San Francisco in 1867. In the same year his *Condensed Novels and Other Papers,* reprinted from magazines, appeared as his first volume of prose.

Harte's real burst of literary genius came after his establishment in 1868 as first editor of the *Overland Monthly.* In the first number (July) he was represented only by a poem, but to the second he contributed "The Luck of Roaring Camp." By a coincidence his first story in the new magazine was also the first product of his new style. It met with mediocre success in California—for the West has never particularly enjoyed being pictured as the West—but its enthusiastic reception in the East convinced the author that his true field was to be the short story of early California life. "The Luck" marks his literary maturity. He had at last managed to shake himself loose from the imitation of romantic models. His originality was displayed, however, not in the actual method, for that was essentially the tried and true formula of his beloved Dickens—the mingling of humor, sentiment, pathos, and whimsical character—but rather in his adaptation of the old method to new material, the California mining country. In this he became the teacher of the local-color writers who soon were ransacking the world for new scenes for the display of old characters and motifs. This constitutes his significance, though his work as a humorist and writer of dialect verse is also noteworthy.

Harte's second story in his new vein, "The Outcasts of Poker Flat" (January 1869), did not appear until six months after the first; in the meantime he was performing his duties as editor of the *Overland.* The success of "The Outcasts" showed that "The Luck" had not been mere accident; Harte continued to develop his California material, and in the course of a few years produced everything upon which his fame seems likely to rest. Most popular of all at the time was his poem, "The Heathen Chinee" (1870), which made him immediately famous as a humorist throughout the English-speaking world. In 1870, also, his first important book, *The Luck of Roaring Camp and Other Sketches,* was published in Boston. Not unnaturally, however, as his powers increased, he felt the urge to achieve in wider fields, and on Feb. 2, 1871, he started for the East.

He was received with enthusiasm. At this time we see Harte at his best, confident from recent success, enthusiastic and hopeful for the future. He presented to his readers in the East a strange contrast to the red-shirted miner whom they had expected. They saw a slender gentleman of middle height, but with a bearing that often made people think of him as tall. His beard was trimmed in the best fashion; he dressed stylishly, almost foppishly; he conversed without profanity and with all proprieties of grammar and diction. Far from being a frontiersman, Harte had in fact little liking for, or sympathy with, the kind of life which he depicted. Among the tangible fruits of his journey was a contract of $10,000 with the publishers of the *Atlantic Monthly* for his literary output—at least twelve contributions —during the ensuing year. He fulfilled his contract, but the quality of the work disappointed the publishers. The days of his prosperity were over.

The latter part of Harte's life may be passed over more rapidly. On the whole it lacks significance, since in spite of numerous later volumes his reputation rests upon the work completed in the few years preceding the end of 1871. His writing after that time shows ups and downs, but no real progress. From 1871 to 1878 he lived most of the time in or near New York City, although summering at various places. He wrote steadily, his work appearing first in magazines and later in book form. *Mrs. Skaggs's Husbands* (1873) and *Tales of the Argonauts* (1875) are his most important collections of short stories for this period; in addition he attempted a novel, *Gabriel Conroy* (1876), and two dramas, *Two Men of Sandy Bar* (1876), and *Ah Sin* (1877), the last in collaboration with Mark Twain. None of these was really successful. The decline of his popularity was the more disconcerting because of Mrs. Harte's expensive tastes and his own carelessness in money matters. Throughout much of his life he was embarrassed by debt, never more so than during his stay in the East, when a transient prosperity had accustomed him and his four children to more luxury than he could afford. During this period, although he must have been earning a good income, he lived generally from hand to mouth. He managed to supplement his revenue from literary work by several extensive lecture tours which took him from Canada to Georgia and as far west as Kansas. As a lecturer he was fairly well received, but the work was tiring and distasteful, and the financial returns disappointing. In 1877 he had high hopes in the establishment of the *Capitol Magazine* with himself as editor, but its collapse left him in desperate straits, for he had lost confidence in himself and his market had fallen off. Ready to snatch at any straw that offered, he eagerly accepted the consulate at Crefeld in Rhenish Prussia with a remuneration of about $2,500 yearly.

Harte sailed for Europe in June 1878 without his wife and family, and never returned. He remained about two years in Crefeld—discouraged, lonely, often ill. He wrote a little, but produced nothing to enhance his reputation. His performance of official duties was satisfactory; the routine, however, could not really interest him, and he transferred most of it to a deputy. The only bright spots of this period were visits to Switzerland and England. His reputation had not declined in England as it had in the United States; he was still fêted, invited to lecture, and sought as a friend.

In July 1880, he received the more important post of the consulate at Glasgow. There his situation was hardly more congenial, but England and his friends were more accessible. He wrote continually, supporting himself by his pen so that his official income could go to his family. His success with the English public helped him gradually to regain the confidence in his literary powers which had been so badly shattered by the experiences of his last few years in the United States. His term as consul was finally ended by a change of administration and his displacement in 1885.

For a living Harte was now cast entirely upon literature. In spite of many longings for America, he chose London as his place of residence because British editors still accepted his stories readily at good rates whereas in the United States he was receiving little or nothing. For the rest of his life he was little better than a hack-writer with neither leisure nor energy to escape from the rut. "I grind out the old tunes on the old organ and gather up the coppers" (*Letters*, p. 154). Story after story he turned out in which the old California characters, or their ghosts under the same names, were put through slightly new paces. For most of this time he wrote a thousand words daily, seven days a week, an appalling task to a man of his painstaking care in composition. He several times attempted drama, coveting its greater returns, but although *Sue* held the stage for a while in 1896, his plays were never really successful. Society palled upon him, and he no longer cared to play the Bohemian or the social lion. The letters of this period betray a great weariness. Mrs. Harte came to England in 1898, and thereafter the two saw each other frequently and Harte continued to give her the greater part of his earnings, but they lived apart. In his later years his health failed progressively. In 1901 he suffered badly from an "ulcerated sore throat," and on May 5, 1902, he died, the sore throat proving to be cancer. He worked almost to the end, but his entire estate amounted to only a few hundred pounds.

With his best writing done before he was thirty-five, Harte failed notably to fulfil the promise of his early years. This failure to develop cannot be attributed to lack of care, energy, or literary conscience; it seems rather to result from the shallowness of his intellectual resources. From the very beginning of his career, moreover, he was forced to think constantly of his family's support, and during most of his life he suffered from ill health. His great stroke was the application of simple, well-tested formulas to novel literary material. But the formulas were repeated too often, and his knowledge of the material was limited; all too soon he was left with an inflated reputation and with nothing to sustain it. In the brief years of his prime, however, he produced a body of work that still compels admiration by its vigor, color, and wit.

[T. E. Pemberton, *Life of Bret Harte* (1903); H. C. Merwin, *Life of Bret Harte* (1911); G. R. Stewart, Jr., *Bret Harte* (1931); *Letters of Bret Harte* (1926), edited by Geoffrey Bret Harte; *Overland Monthly*, Sept. 1902 (memorial number with reminiscences by several friends); Noah Brooks, "Bret Harte in California," *Century Mag.*, July 1899; *London Times*, May 7, 1902; bibliographies in *Cambridge Hist. of Am. Lit.*, vol. II (1918), *Book Lover*, July–Aug. 1902, and in Pemberton and Stewart.] G. R. S., Jr.

HARTLEY, FRANK (June 10, 1856–June 19, 1913), surgeon, was born in Washington, D. C., the son of John Fairfield Hartley, for many years assistant secretary of the treasury, and Mary (King) Hartley. His parents were originally from Saco, Me. He was educated in the public schools of Washington and at the same time was tutored in several languages. After preparing for college at Emerson Institute he attended the College of New Jersey (later Princeton), graduating in 1877. He received the degree of M.D. at Columbia in 1880. After serving as surgical interne at Bellevue Hospital, he spent two years, 1882–84, in further study in Germany and Austria. On his return to the United States he became office associate with Henry B. Sands. Without this obvious advantage he would probably have distinguished himself, for even as a very young surgeon his skill was recognized. He held hospital appointments as visiting surgeon at several institutions including the Bellevue, Roosevelt, and New York hospitals. In 1886 he entered the Columbia faculty as assistant demonstrator of anatomy. In 1889 he was made clinical lecturer on surgery and instructor in operative surgery, and in 1900 he became clinical professor of surgery.

Hartley is best remembered in medical annals for having devised the intracranial method for curing trigeminal neuralgia by bisecting the ganglion of the trigeminal nerve. Since Dr. F. Krause of Altona, Germany, performed a similar operation at about the same time the method bears the names of both surgeons. Hartley published two papers bearing upon the operation: "Intracranial Neurectomy of the Fifth Nerve," in the *New York Medical Journal*, Mar. 19, 1892, and "Intracranial Neurectomy of the Second and Third Divisions of the Fifth Nerve," in the *Annals of Surgery*, May 1893. Most of his other published works appeared in the latter journal. Hartley was reticent and taciturn to an extreme degree, which militated somewhat against his success as a lecturer. He was singularly indifferent to his surroundings and it has been said that when his duties kept him late in the anatomical room he would pass the night there. He was equally indifferent to public opinion and had no desire for publicity. He was married, on Aug. 1, 1897, to Mrs. Emma Allyce Parker, the daughter of George and Mary (Granville) Burton of Norfolk, England. She survived him.

[C. H. Peck, article in *Surgery, Gynecol. and Obstetrics*, July 1925; H. A. Kelly and W. L. Burrage, *Dict. of Am. Medic. Biog.* (1928); *Boston Medic. and Surgic. Jour.*, July 3, 1913; *Jour. Am. Medic. Asso.*, July 5, 1913; *N. Y. Medic. Jour.*, June 28, 1913; personal acquaintance.] E. P.

HARTLEY, JONATHAN SCOTT (Sept. 23, 1845–Dec. 6, 1912), sculptor, the son of Joseph and Margaret (Scott) Hartley, both of English origin, was born in Albany, N. Y. After attending Albany Academy in 1857–58, he found work in a monument yard. There the sculptor Calverley discovered him, a shy lad of sixteen, and encouraged him. A year or two later he became assistant to Erastus D. Palmer, whose successful career inspired young Hartley with the will "to follow the chisel no longer, but to lead it." In 1866 he went to London for three years' study at the Royal Academy, supporting himself meanwhile by part-time work as a stone carver. Having won a silver medal in 1869, he sought a broader field for his development, and chose Berlin, where for a year he worked conscientiously. This move he afterward considered a mistake. Returning home, he lived for a time in New York, where, in 1871, the sketch class which grew into the famous Salmagundi Club met for the first time in his studio, 596 Broadway. There he and his brothers John and Joseph modestly kept a Bohemian bachelors' hall, much enjoyed by the embryo Salmagundians. A drawing by Will Low depicts "An Evening with the Salmagundians in 1871." The foreground shows Hartley, lean in his sculptor's blouse, with his shock of curly hair and his pointed beard. His right hand stirs the evening sausages in the frying-pan, while his left wards off a pair of boxers.

From 1873 to 1875 Hartley studied in Rome, then for a time in Paris, after which he again returned, well-equipped, and established himself in New York City.

In the imaginative sculpture of his early period, Hartley revealed a Victorian quality in his rendering of such subjects as "King René's Daughter" (1872), and "The Young Samaritan," shown at the Centennial Exhibition in 1876. Other studies of the same period include "Priscilla," "Psyche," "Dawn," and "A Young Mother," the last a seated figure somewhat in the vein of the Tanagra idyls. His fame came suddenly in 1878, blown abroad by his spirited and original "Whirlwind," a female figure which roused fiery discussion because of its cyclonic drapery. More lasting is the fame he owes to his admirable portraits of men. From the passing of Palmer and his generation until the coming of Grafly, few American sculptors attained the eminence of Hartley in the field of virile portraiture. His analysis of character was keen; his findings were revealed with sympathy and technical excellence. Among his sitters were many stage celebrities. His "John Gilbert as Sir Peter Teazle," "Felix Morris as the Marquis," "John Drew as Sir Lucius O'Trigger," "Edwin Booth as Brutus," "Lawrence Barrett as Cassius," and his "Otis Skinner as Col. Bridau" were penetrating interpretations. Other valuable likenesses were those of Noah Davis, Susan B. Anthony, Henry George, the poet Bryant, Waldstein the archeologist, and the painters Thomas Wood, Daniel Huntington, J. H. Dolph, and George Inness. Hartley's bronze bust of W. T. Evans was the only sculpture in the Evans collection as originally presented to the National Gallery of Art. His busts of Hawthorne, Emerson, and Irving are on the façade of the Library of Congress. His monumental works include the Daguerre monument, Washington, D. C., and statues of Miles Morgan, an early settler, Springfield, Mass. (1882), John Ericsson, Battery Park, New York (1893), Alfred the Great, New Appellate Court, New York (1899), Rev. Thomas K. Beecher, Elmira, N. Y. (1901), and Pierre Laclède. The final decade of his life was given largely to ideal pieces, such as the "Water Baby," the "Boy with Frog," and "Nature's Sun Dial"; to family groups in bas-relief, and to portraits.

Hartley was greatly respected by his colleagues and received many honors. He was a member of the Players Club, the National Academy of Design, to which he was elected academician in 1891, the Architectural League of New York, and the National Sculpture Society, which he served as secretary for many years. A notable service to sculpture is his illustrated textbook, *Anatomy in Art,* published in 1891, after his long-continued work as instructor in anatomy at the Art Students' League had shown him the need of such a treatise. In 1888 he married Helen, daughter of George Inness [*q.v.*], and made his home in Montclair, N. J. A happy family life gave him many suggestions for the genre subjects in which he was skilled.

[Rupert Hughes, article in *Munsey's Mag.,* Aug. 1894, with eight illustrations; the *Am. Architect,* Feb. 22, 1911; the *Art Amateur,* Sept. 1898; Lorado Taft, *Hist. of Am. Sculpture* (1903); *Who's Who in America,* 1912–13; N. Y. *Evening Post,* Dec. 7, 1912.]

A. A.

HARTLEY, THOMAS (Sept. 7, 1748–Dec. 21, 1800), lawyer, Revolutionary soldier, congressman, son of George Hartley, early settler and well-to-do farmer, was born of an English family in Colebrookdale Township, Berks County, Pa. Receiving a liberal education at Reading, at eighteen he went to York, Pa., to study law with Samuel Johnston, a relative. He was admitted to the bar in 1769 and soon acquired a lucrative practice. In the Revolution Hartley enthusiastically embraced the colonial cause. He was vice-president of the York County Committee of Observation in 1774 and 1775; a deputy to the provincial conferences at Philadelphia in July 1774 and January 1775; and a lieutenant (later lieutenant-colonel) of Associators. On Jan. 10, 1776, Congress elected him lieutenant-colonel of the 6th Battalion of the Pennsylvania Line, with which unit he served in the Canadian campaign. In 1777 he commanded the 1st Pennsylvania Brigade at Brandywine, Germantown, and Paoli, playing a conspicuous part in the defense of Philadelphia. Hartley's major military achievement was his expedition in Pennsylvania in 1778 to avenge the Wyoming massacre. Marching into the enemy's country he killed many Indians, burned numerous villages, and carried away much plunder, thereby eliciting the commendations of Congress and paving the way for Sullivan's success a year later. On Feb. 13, 1779, he resigned his commission to accept a seat in the Pennsylvania Assembly.

Hartley spent the remainder of his life as a lawyer and politician. In the Council of Censors (1783–84), he advocated revision of the radical state constitution. In the state ratifying convention (1787) he was an outspoken champion of the Federal Constitution. From 1789 to 1800 he was in Congress. An avowed Federalist, he vigorously supported Hamilton's financial program, excepting his assumption plan, advocated protection for manufactures and an adequate military establishment, averring in 1793 that "the nation which is prepared for war can most easily obtain peace" (*Annals of Congress,* 2 Cong., 1 Sess., p. 779). He favored Wright's Ferry on the Susquehanna for the permanent seat of government. Although irritated by England's commercial policy, he considered war imprudent and opposed higher duties on British manufactures because they would cut off the revenue which was paying the national debt. Pleading ill health and derangement of his private affairs, he resigned on Sept. 8, 1800. Before the end of that year he died. He was a fluent speaker, energetic, determined, and independent in judgment, although somewhat vain, pretentious, and high-spirited. William Maclay characterized him as a "strange piece of pomposity" (*Journal, post,* p. 252). He was the first Pennsylvania lawyer admitted as counselor before the United States Supreme Court (Feb. 5, 1791). His wife, Catherine, daughter of Bernhart Holtzinger, and two children survived him.

[Manuscript letters in the Pa. Hist. Soc.; J. C. Jordan, "York, Pa., in the Revolution," *Pa. Mag. of Hist. and Biog.,* Oct. 1908; David Craft, "The Expedition of Col. Thos. Hartley Against the Indians in 1778," *Proc. and Colls. Wyo. Hist. and Geol. Soc.,* vol. IX (1905); *The Jour. of Wm. Maclay* (ed. 1927); J. B. McMaster and F. D. Stone, *Pa. and the Federal Constitution* (1888); *Minutes of the Provincial Council of Pa.,* vols. V–VII (1851), vol. XI (1852); *Pa. Archives,* 1 ser., vols. V–XI (1853–55); G. R. Powell, *Continental Cong. and York, Pa., and York County in the Revolution* (1914); S. T. Wiley, *Biog. Cyc. of Nineteenth Pa. Cong. District* (1897); W. C. Carter and A. J. Glossbrenner, *Hist. of York County, Pa.* (1834).]

J. H. P—g.

HARTRANFT, CHESTER DAVID (Oct. 15, 1839–Dec. 30, 1914), clergyman of the Reformed Dutch Church, educator, was born in Frederick, Montgomery County, Pa., the son of Samuel and Salome (Stetler) Hartranft and a descendant of Tobias Herterranft who settled in Pennsylvania about 1734. Both his parents were of German descent, his father's progenitors having been Schwenckfelders from Silesia. Samuel Hartranft was engaged in the manufacture of flour, and had the means to afford his son the best educational advantages. Chester graduated in 1856 from Central High School, Philadelphia, to which city the family moved when he was about seven years old, and later studied at Rambo's School, Trappe, and at the Hill School, Pottstown. He was nominated for West Point but was rejected because he was under age. Subsequently he entered the University of Pennsylvania, from which he graduated in 1861. For a time during the Civil War he was captain in the 18th Pennsylvania Volunteers, but saw no active service. His physical and intellectual energy, voracious mind, and capacity for leadership early manifested themselves. He first leaned toward the law as a profession, then turned to history, which was always one of his chief interests, but finally entered the Reformed Dutch Seminary, New Brunswick, N. J., graduating in 1864. The same year he married Anna Frances Berg, daughter of Rev. John F. Berg. After a two years' pastorate at South Bushwick, now a part of Brooklyn, in 1866 he became pastor of the First Reformed Dutch Church, New Brunswick, which he served until 1878. While here he gained a high reputation, not only as a preacher and organizer, but also as a patron of music. He was an organist, violinist, and capable director, his gifts having been recognized as early as 1861 when Rutgers College conferred upon him the degree of Doctor of Music. At New Brunswick in 1870 he founded a conservatory of music in which Leopold Damrosch and Samuel P. Warren [*qq.v.*] were instructors.

In 1878 he was called to the Hartford Theological Seminary and early in 1879 began his duties there as professor of ecclesiastical history. When in 1892 a chair of Biblical theology was created he was appointed to fill it, and in 1898 he was transferred to the chair of ecclesiastical dogmatics. For eight years he also served as librarian. In 1888 the office of president was reëstablished, and he was titular head of the institution until 1903. Having what at the time were radically advanced views on the subject of theological education, and being a man of powerful personality, he brought about great changes in the plan and scope of the school. He made the curriculum an inclusive, unified scheme of instruction, sought to put it on an undenominational basis, opened the regular courses to women, added a school of church music and one of sociology, and increased the Seminary's material resources. He was also active in promoting the musical, educational, and social interests of Hartford. His first wife died in January 1904, and on Nov. 22, 1911, he married her sister, Ida Thomas Berg.

Several of his addresses were published, including *The Aims of a Theological Seminary* (1878), and *Some Thoughts on the Scope of Theology and Theological Education* (1888). He also made contributions to *A Select Library of Nicene and Post-Nicene Fathers of the Christian Church,* edited by Philip Schaff and Henry Wace (see vol. IV, 1887, and 2 ser., vol. II, 1890). About 1882 he suggested to the Schwenckfelder Church of Pennsylvania, the collection and publication of the works of Kaspar von Schwenckfelder and all data concerning him. During trips to Europe he discovered a prodigious amount of material, and in 1903 he resigned the presidency of the Seminary in order to give his full time to editing it, the Seminary contributing to the project by making him honorary president and research professor. He took up his residence in Germany, where at Wolfenbüttel some eleven years later he died and was buried. At the time of his death four volumes of the material under the title, *Corpus Schwenckfeldianorum,* had been published. The work was continued by his collaborator, E. E. S. Johnson, and the tenth volume appeared in 1929.

[M. W. Jacobus and W. S. Pratt, *Memorial Addresses upon the Late Chester David Hartranft* (1915); *Corpus Schwenckfeldianorum,* vol. VI (1922); *The Geneal. Record of the Schwenkfelder Families* (1923), ed. by S. K. Brecht; *The Schwenckfeldian,* Mar. 1915; *Biog. Record Theolog. Sem., New Brunswick, 1784–1911* (1912), compiled by J. H. Raven; *Hartford Daily Courant* and *Hartford Times,* Jan. 21, 1915.] H. E. S.

HARTRANFT, JOHN FREDERICK (Dec. 16, 1830–Oct. 17, 1889), soldier, politician, was born near Fagleysville, six miles from Pottstown, in Montgomery County, Pa., the son of Samuel Engle and Lydia (Bucher) Hartranft, both of German descent. He attended Marshall and Union Colleges. At the latter institution he prepared for the profession of civil engineering, graduating in 1853. On Jan. 26, 1854, he was married to Sallie D. Sebring and in the same year became deputy sheriff of Montgomery County, deciding about the same time to shift from engineering to law and politics. He was admitted to the bar in October 1860. At the outbreak of the Civil War he was colonel of the 1st Regiment, Montgomery County Militia, which became the 4th Pennsylvania Regiment in a ninety-day enlistment. On Nov. 16, 1861, he was commissioned colonel of the 51st Regiment of Pennsylvania Infantry, which he had organized, and saw active service in numerous important battles throughout the war. On May 12, 1864, he was promoted brigadier-general of volunteers for gallantry at Spotsylvania Court House, and on Mar. 25, 1865, he was brevetted major-general of volunteers for conspicuous gallantry in driving back the enemy at Fort Stedman.

In 1865 Hartranft was elected on the Republican ticket as auditor-general of the state and was reëlected in 1868. In 1872 he was elected governor and served two terms in this office. During the era of great prosperity and rapid expansion following the war, large numbers of foreign workers had come into Pennsylvania. In the succeeding era of severe industrial depression beginning in 1873, unemployment and the menace of starvation kindled the flames of discontent. By 1877, disturbances bordering on civil war existed in various parts of the state, especially in Pittsburgh and Reading. The governor made frequent use of the state militia and in 1877 called on the federal government for soldiers, taking personal charge of the troops. Later, in looking back on the armed suppression of strikes, the governor doubted the expediency of "hedging property with bayonets" for maintaining industrial peace. His after-the-event proposals included the recognition by employers of workers' organizations and the adjustment of conflicting claims by arbitration. He also became convinced that an essential part of the remedy must be a much more extensive and thorough system of compulsory education, with provision for technical training. But as governor, he was chiefly noted for his attempt to solve industrial problems by force. Other events and policies of his administration included the completion in 1873 of the work of revising the state constitution; the centennial exposition of 1876; the inauguration of a series of geological surveys; a more effective public regulation of banking; and the reorganization of the state militia as a part of the National Guard. After the expiration of his second term as governor he was given command of the Pennsylvania National Guard. He was appointed postmaster at Philadelphia in 1879 and from 1881 to 1885 was collector of the port of Philadelphia.

[There is an extensive biography, not entirely uncritical, in Moses M. Auge, *Lives of the Eminent Dead and Biog. Notices of Prominent Living Citizens of Montgomery County, Pa.* (1879). See also F. B. Heitman, *Hist. Reg. and Dict. of the U. S. Army* (1903), vol. I; A. K. McClure, *Old Time Notes of Pa.* (1905), vol. II, a gossipy but important account of Hartranft's political connections; *Pa. Archives,* 4 ser., vol. IX (1902), for the governor's official papers; *The Geneal. Record of the Schwenkfelder Families* (1923), ed. by S. K. Brecht; and the *Phila. Enquirer,* Oct. 18, 1889. A small collection of letters is in the library of the Pa. Hist. Soc.] W. B.

HARTSHORNE, HENRY (Mar. 16, 1823–Feb. 10, 1897), physician, was born in Philadelphia, Pa., the son of Dr. Joseph Hartshorne and Anna Bonsall. He was educated at Haverford College, where he graduated in 1839. Subsequently he took his medical course at the University of Pennsylvania (M.D. 1845), and from 1846 to 1848 he was a resident physician at the Pennsylvania Hospital. On Jan. 8, 1849, he married Mary E. Brown of Philadelphia. He seems not to have been eager to study medicine and was not enthusiastic about practice. He had sufficient means without it, and it is likely that his interest in other things diverted him from medicine. He was active, however, during an epidemic of cholera in Philadelphia in 1849 and in Columbia, Pa., in 1854, and during the Civil War he was a surgeon in the Philadelphia hospitals. After the battle of Gettysburg he attended the sick and wounded on the battlefield. He held an extraordinary number of positions, medical and otherwise. He was professor of the institutes of medicine at the Philadelphia College of Medicine in 1853–54 and lecturer on natural history at the Franklin Institute in 1857–58. From 1859 to 1861 he was professor of the theory and practice of medicine in Pennsylvania College (later Gettysburg College), succeeding Dr. Alfred Stillé who had been elected to the chair of medicine in the University of Pennsylvania. He was a physician to the Protestant Episcopal Hospital, 1860–62, professor of hygiene at the University of Pennsylvania, 1865, and professor of diseases of children and later of physiology and hygiene at the Woman's Medical College, 1867–76. He also held appointments at the Philadelphia Central High School, the Pennsylvania College of Dental Surgery, Haverford College, and Girard College. He was active in the Academy of Natural Sciences, one of the founders of the American Public Health Association, and an active member of the American Philosophical Society, contributing papers especially in the field of physics. He was a prolific writer. His fondness for literature prompted him to publish a few volumes of his poetry as well as a novel, *Woman's Witchcraft* (1854), published under the pseudonym Corinne L'Estrange. In medicine his most important works were his *Essentials of the Principles and Practice of Medicine* (1867) and *A Conspectus of the Medical Sciences* (1869), both of which were translated into Japanese. For a time he was editor of a religious journal, *The Friends' Review.* The education of women interested him greatly and in 1876 he left Philadelphia to become president of Howland Collegiate School, Union Springs, N. Y. It proved an unsuccessful venture, however, and closed in 1878. Hartshorne returned to Philadelphia and opened a school for girls. He was a strong advocate of the right of women to study medicine. He was also interested in religion and religious work and in 1893 went to Japan to engage in missionary and philanthropic work, especially in connection with Quaker societies. He was particularly concerned with the prevention of the opium traffic. He died at Tokio and was buried there. It has been said that he would have accomplished more by concentrating on one branch of learning. His desire to achieve results was perhaps not accompanied with sufficient stability to carry any activity to an eminently successful conclusion.

[J. C. Morris, memoir, with bibliography, in *Proc. Am. Phil. Soc.*, vol. XXXIX (1900); James Darrach, "A Biog. Sketch of Henry Hartshorne, M.D., LL.D.," *Trans. of the Coll. of Physicians of Phila.*, 3 ser., vol. XIX (1897), Henry Simpson, *The Lives of Eminent Philadelphians* (1859), containing sketch of Hartshorne's father; *Biog. Cat. of the Matriculates of Haverford Coll.* (1900); *Public Ledger* (Phila.), Feb. 13, 1897; *Friends' Intelligencer*, Feb. 20, 1897.]

T. M.

HARTSUFF, GEORGE LUCAS (May 28, 1830–May 16, 1874), soldier, was born at Tyre, N. Y. At the age of twelve he moved with his parents to Michigan from which state he received his appointment to the United States Military Academy. In 1852 he graduated nineteenth in a class of forty-three members and received an assignment to duty at Fort Columbus, N. Y., as brevet second lieutenant of the 4th Artillery. Within a few months he went to the Texas frontier, whence after receiving his first promotion, he went to duty in the hostilities against the Seminole Indians. A surveying party which he was conducting was set upon by the Indians under Billy Bowlegs, and Hartsuff, severely wounded, saved his life by hiding under water in a pond. When the Indians left, he dragged himself fifteen miles before he was discovered three days later by a rescue party. Upon his recovery, he served as assistant instructor of tactics at West Point for three years (1856–59) and then returned to duty at Fort Mackinac, Mich. On Dec. 11, 1858, during his tour of duty at West Point, he married Sarah J. Maine, at Malden, Mass.

At the outbreak of the Civil War Hartsuff had just received his appointment as assistant to the adjutant-general. His first war service was at the defense of Fort Pickens, Fla., from which he passed to duty as chief of staff for General Rosecrans. In the spring of 1862 he was on duty at the War Department for a few weeks, but having meanwhile received a commission as brigadier-general of volunteers, he went into active service along the Rappahannock from May to July and in the campaign of Northern Virginia in July and August. He fought at Cedar Mountain and Manassas, and in the Maryland campaign, at South Mountain and Antietam, where he was severely wounded. For his conduct here he was brevetted colonel and in November 1862 was promoted to major-general of volunteers. From April to November of the following year he commanded the XXIII Army Corps in the operations in Kentucky and Tennessee. He still suffered so severely from the wound received at Antietam that until July 1864 he was inactive, and until March 1865, he performed no field duty. In the operations around Richmond, he commanded the Bermuda front of the works for the siege of Petersburg and later commanded at City Point and at Petersburg itself. During the war he had been regularly promoted to the grade of captain in 1861, to major in 1862, and to lieutenant-colonel in 1864. In the closing days of the war he was brevetted brigadier-general and major-general for his services. After being mustered out of the volunteer service in 1865 he took up his duties in the adjutant-general's department and continued them for another five years. Then the hardships of an unusually adventurous life began to tell upon him and he applied for retirement. Already Congress had begun to reward the leaders in the great war, and Hartsuff received his retirement as a major-general of the regular army. He lived uneventfully at his home in New York City until his death three years later.

[G. W. Cullum, *Biog. Reg. . . . U. S. Mil. Acad.* (ed. 1891), vol. II; F. B. Heitman, *Biog. Reg. and Dict. of the U. S. Army* (1903), vol. I; *Fifth Ann. Reunion, Asso. Grads. U. S. Mil. Acad.* (1874); *N. Y. Times,* May 17, 1874; *N. Y. Tribune,* May 18, 1874.]

A. W. C.

HARTWIG, JOHANN CHRISTOPH (Jan. 6, 1714–July 17, 1796), Lutheran clergyman, was born in Thüringen in the duchy of Saxe-Gotha and was educated for the ministry. Through Philip D. Kräuter, pastor of the German Trinity church in London, and Friedrich Wagner, pastor of St. Michael's in Hamburg, he was called to the congregations at Camp and Rhinebeck in the Hudson Valley. He was ordained in London Nov. 24, 1745, and reached his charges the next spring. Though a good, conscientious man, he was restless, desultory, eccentric, and uncouth. He preached in his blanket coat, changed his linen infrequently, and was so fanatical a misogynist that he would cross the road or leap a fence to avoid meeting a woman. His virtues, however, gained him the friendship of the Livingstons, the Van Rensselaers, and the Mohawk Indians, and he figures conspicuously in the annals of his denomination. Detesting Hartwig's Pietism and bad manners, Wilhelm Christoph Berkenmeyer [*q.v.*], then at Loonenburg, published four pamphlets attacking him as, among other things, a "crypto-Herrnhuter," stirred up trouble among his parishioners, and drove him temporarily from the province. Meanwhile, in Henry Melchior Mühlenberg [*q.v.*], whom he first visited at New Providence, Pa., in July 1747, he found a friend and counselor who was patient and helpful even when Hartwig himself was obtuse and ungrateful. Servants in the Mühlenberg household dreaded Hartwig's visits because of his inordinately long prayers at family worship. From 1748 until the end of the Revolution his life was congenially nomadic. Traces of him have been found in almost twenty congregations from Waldoboro, Me., to Winchester, Va., including Goshenhoppen, Pa. (1750–51), Reading (1757–58), New York (1761, 1782), Frederick, Md. (1762, 1768–69), Winchester, Va. (1762, 1769, 1781), and Boston (1784); but his journeyings cannot be charted completely. He aided Mühlenberg at various times and returned occasionally to the Hudson Valley, where he spent his old age. Out of his private means he bought from the Mohawks a tract of 21,500 acres in Otsego County, but legal troubles and the prestidigitations of his agent, William Cooper [*q.v.*], reduced his holdings to a third of their original extent. He died somewhat unexpectedly in the Livingston mansion at Clermont, while on his way to Albany from New York. He was buried ultimately in Ebenezer church in Albany. His will, to which he added codicils until an hour before his death, provided for the establishment of an institution for Indians and theological students, but the plans embodied in the will were quite impracticable. Finally, however, the institution was established as Hartwick Seminary (later Hartwick College) on the estate in Otsego County and began operations Dec. 15, 1815, with Ernst Lewis Hazelius [*q.v.*] as its director and John Anthony Quitman [*q.v.*] as his assistant. Among his English-speaking friends Hartwig was known as Hardwick or Hartwick.

[See W. J. Mann, B. M. Schmucker, and W. Germann, *Nachrichten von den vereinigten Deutschen Evangelisch-Lutherischen Gemeinen in Nord-America,* Erster Band (Allentown, Pa., 1886); W. J. Mann, *Life and Times of H. M. Mühlenberg* (1887); *Memorial Vol. of the Semi-Centennial Anniversary of Hartwick Sem.* (1867); M. L. Stoever, memoir in *Evangelical Rev.,* Oct. 1855; W. B. Sprague, *Annals Am. Pulpit,* IX (1869), 29–33; A. L. Gräbner, *Geschichte der Lutherischen Kirche in America* (1892). There are also other minor sources of information. The Luth. Hist. Soc. at Gettysburg, Pa., has the catalogue of his library and documents relating to his estate.]

G. H. G.

HARTZELL, JOSEPH CRANE (June 1, 1842–Sept. 6, 1928), missionary bishop of the Methodist Episcopal Church, was born in Moline, Ill., the fourth of the thirteen children of Michael Bash and Nancy Worman (Stauffer) Hartzell, both natives of Pennsylvania. He was descended from German ancestors who emigrated to Pennsylvania in the early part of the eighteenth century. Michael Hartzell was a farmer and cabinet maker, of rugged character. Both he and his wife were ardent Methodists, and their log cabin served as a preaching place for circuit riders. Under the religious influences by which he was surrounded, Joseph early resolved to enter the ministry, and though he had thought that he could prepare himself in two years he gave seven years to his training, working his way through Illinois Wesleyan University (B.A. 1868) and Garrett Biblical Institute (B.D. 1868). During this period he gave evidence of courage and physical stamina by rescuing the crew of a vessel wrecked in Lake Michigan.

Admitted to the Methodist ministry in 1868, he was stationed at Pekin, Ill. During the Civil War he had sought to enlist, and, rejected, had "felt impelled to stay in school and prepare for the battle of ideals which must follow the clash of arms." Interested in the problem of race-adjustment in the South, in 1870 he succeeded John Philip Newman [*q.v.*] as pastor of the Ames Church, New Orleans, where he began a period of notable service in the face of many difficulties. He loyally supported the federal government but did not condone the false representation of the Carpet-baggers and among those who differed with him on social and political matters he made many warm friends. For his tact then and later he earned for himself the title of "diplomat of the Church." In 1873 he was made presiding elder of the New Orleans district. In 1881 he was transferred to La Teche district. From 1883 to 1896 he was with the Freedmen's Aid and Southern Education Society at Cincinnati; as assistant corresponding secretary, 1883–88, and as corresponding secretary, 1889–96. In New Orleans he founded schools and a hospital for negroes, and in 1873 he founded the *Southwestern Christian Advocate,* an organ published weekly for the promotion of Methodist work among the negroes. From 1876 to 1896 he was delegate to the General Conference of the Methodist Episcopal Church, where he was influential in securing consideration for the Southern work, which developed into an extensive system of schools and churches for both races. In 1896 he was consecrated missionary bishop for Africa and gave himself to this continental field with amazing energy and substantial success. Fixing his official residence at Funchal, Madeira, in twenty years he made thirteen tours of Africa, traveling 1,300,000 miles by ship, train, cart, oxback, donkey-back, and hammock. In 1898 he acted as special representative for Liberia to ask Great Britain and the United States to establish a joint protectorate over Liberia. In recognition of this service he was made a Knight Commander of the Order for the Redemption of Africa (*Christian Advocate,* Sept. 13, 1928). Cecil Rhodes granted 13,000 acres equipped with buildings for his Rhodesia agricultural mission, supplemented by an annual grant for the maintenance of a school for children of white residents. Premier Clemenceau personally approved his project for a mission under the French flag in North Africa (1907), and the King of Portugal received him and granted liberties to Protestant missions in Angola and Inhambane. Meanwhile the bishop's personality kept the African field constantly before the church at home, which in 1909 responded to his leadership by pledging $330,000 in an Africa Diamond Jubilee Campaign. In 1916 he retired but continued to speak and work for Africa. On his eighty-sixth birthday he was assaulted by robbers in his home at Blue Ash, Ohio, and died some three months later from the effects of his injuries. He had married, on Nov. 14, 1869, Jennie Culver, who died in 1916.

[*Minutes of the Ann. Conferences of the Meth. Episc. Ch.,* 1870–96; *Jours. of the Gen. Conferences of the Meth. Episc. Ch.,* 1896–1916; *Southwestern Christian Advocate,* July 7, 1898, Mar. 18, 1920, June 28, 1923, Sept. 13, 1928; *Ann. Reports, Freedmen's Aid and Southern Educ. Soc.,* 1870–96; *Who's Who in America,* 1928–29; the *Christian Advocate* (N. Y.), Apr. 28, 1898, Sept. 13, 1928; *Meth. Rev.* (N. Y.), Jan.–Feb. 1930.]

J. R. J.

HARVARD, JOHN (November 1607–Sept. 14, 1638), for whom Harvard College was named, was the son of Robert Harvard, a butcher in the borough of Southwark, and Katherine Rogers, whose father (Thomas) was a cattle dealer and alderman of Stratford-on-Avon. John was baptized on Nov. 29, 1607, at St. Saviour's Church (now Southwark Cathedral, London). In 1625 his father and most of his brothers and sisters died of the plague, and his mother married again. On Dec. 19, 1627, he was entered pensioner at Emmanuel College, Cambridge (manuscript college records—not on Apr. 17, 1628, as often stated). He graduated bachelor of arts in Lent, 1631/32, and received his master's degree at Commencement, 1635. On Apr. 19, 1636, at South Malling, he married Anne Sadler (*Harvard Graduates' Magazine,* June 1907, p. 557), sister of one of his college mates, John Sadler (1615–1674). His mother's will (proved July 27, 1635) refers to him as "John Harvard Clarke," but no record is known of John's having preached or taken holy orders in England. Although he had inherited considerable property in London real estate, and was principal legatee and executor of his only surviving brother Thomas, a clothworker (will proved May 5, 1637), we find Harvard at this time making preparations to sail for New England, which he did not earlier than May 29, 1637 (*Publications of the Colonial Society of Massachusetts,* XXVI, 1927, 232). He was admitted an inhabitant at Charlestown, Mass., Aug. 1, 1637 (*City of Boston: Third Report of the Record Commissioners,* 1878, p. iv), made a freeman of the colony on Nov. 2 (*Records of the Governor and Council of Massachusetts Bay,* I, 1853, 373), and with his wife was admitted to the church on Nov. 6 (James F. Hunnewell, *Records of First Church in Charlestown, Mass.,* 1880, p. 9). He built a house, received considerable land in the divisions, served on an important town committee to help compile the Body of Liberties, and became teaching elder or colleague minister of the Charlestown church.

The college already founded by the colony in the fall of 1636, was opened under Nathaniel Eaton in a small house at Cambridge, at a date not long before Sept. 7, 1638. John Harvard died "at Charlstown, of a Consumption" (Mather, *Magnalia,* ed. 1702, Book IV, 126) on Sept. 14, 1638 (Samuel Danforth's *Almanack* for 1649, p. 14). According to the *Autobiography* of Thomas Shepard (p. 77 of the manuscript), written about ten years later, "The Lord put it into the hart of on Mr. Haruard who dyed worth 1600^{l} to giue halfe his estate to the erecting of the Schoole. The man was a scholler & pious in his life & enlarged toward the cuntry & the good of it in life & death." In addition he left the college his library, amounting to about four hundred volumes of classics, theology, and general literature. Various contemporaries estimated the value of the Harvard legacy, exclusive of the books, between £400 and £800; the treasurer of the college, about twenty years later, stated it to be £779 17*s.* 2*d.* (Josiah Quincy, *The History of Harvard University,* 1840, I, 460–62). This bequest so far exceeded all gifts to the college, public or private, that the General Court named it Harvard College on Mar. 13, 1638/39.

[Nothing certain was known of John Harvard's birth and parentage until 1885, when Henry F. Waters discovered the clue. The story of his search is in *Harvard Grads'. Mag.,* June 1907, pp. 544–60. The documentary results were published in the *New-England Hist. and Geneal. Reg.,* July 1885, pp. 265–84, Oct. 1886, pp. 362–80, and reprinted with additions in his *Geneal. Gleanings in England* (2 vols., 1901). Nothing material has come to light since. No contemporary portrait of John Harvard, and no letters of his are known to exist, although Henry C. Shelley has worked up Waters' facts, with much background and conjecture about Harvard's friendship with Shakespeare, Milton, etc., in *John Harvard and his Times* (1907). A. McF. Davis, "John Harvard's Life in America," *Pubs. Colonial Soc. of Mass.,* XII (1911), 4–45, is more accurate for that part of his career. The books that he left to Harvard College are described *Ibid.,* XXI (1920), 190–230. The monument erected in 1828 on the old burial hill at Charlestown, gives the date of his death incorrectly as Sept. 26, and Dr. George E. Ellis, in a note to Sewall's *Diary,* I (1878), 447, says that the spot was chosen because it then commanded a view of the college. The only contemporary record of Harvard's having become a minister at Charlestown is in John Wilson's elegy on "Johannem Harvardum, è suggesto Sacro Carolocnsi ad Coelos Evectum" (C. Mather, *Magnalia,* 1702 ed., Book IV, 139). Harvard's will was probably nuncupative, as no record of it has been discovered.]

S. E. M.

HARVEY, GEORGE BRINTON McCLELLAN (Feb. 16, 1864–Aug. 20, 1928), political journalist, editor, diplomat, son of Duncan and Margaret (Varnum) Harvey, was born in Peacham, Vt. He attended the Peacham Academy and busied himself in his father's country store until 1879, when he began his journalistic career on the *St. Johnsbury Index.* In the next few years, 1882–86, he reported successively for the *Springfield Republican,* the *Chicago News* and the New York *World.* For a time he edited the New Jersey edition of the *World* and in 1891 Joseph Pulitzer made him managing editor of the New York edition. While in New Jersey Harvey became a colonel on the governor's staff, thereby acquiring the title that clung to him throughout the rest of his life. On Oct. 13, 1887, he was married to Alma Arabella Parker of Peacham.

Harvey's political influence began in 1892 when he vigorously supported Cleveland and received from him in 1893 a tender of the consul-generalship at Berlin which he declined. In that year he temporarily forsook journalism. Valuable connections with William C. Whitney and others and his tireless efforts in the construction and operation of public utilities soon brought him a substantial fortune and a position of influence in Wall Street. In 1899 he purchased the *North American Review* and became its editor. His immediate success in this venture attracted the attention of Harper & Brothers, who had become financially embarrassed. With the consent of J. P. Morgan, the principal creditor, Harvey was made president of the company and was retained in the position after it went into receivership. He retained the editorship of the *Review* and in 1901 took on the editorship of *Harper's Weekly* as well. Harvey had a *flair* for president making, and at a dinner in honor of Professor Woodrow Wilson, given by the Lotos Club of New York, Feb. 3, 1906, he "nominated" the gifted Princetonian for the presidency. The suggestion was warmly received, and for the next five years Harvey carried on a skilful campaign through *Harper's Weekly* in Wilson's behalf. In 1910 he was influential in obtaining for his protégé the Democratic nomination for governor of New Jersey. Late in 1911, however, the Governor's friends became apprehensive of the effect in the progressive West of the support of an editor closely affiliated with Wall Street. At the same time Wilson's alleged radical tendencies incurred a distrust of him in financial circles. Strong pressure was brought on Harvey, particularly from Morgan, to desert his candidate, and he agreed to do so if he became convinced that Wilson was a dangerous man (*The Intimate Papers of Colonel House,* vol. I, 1926, p. 51). Soon afterward, the famous "break" between the two men occurred. In response to a frank inquiry from Harvey on Dec. 7, 1911, as to whether the support of *Harper's Weekly* was proving embarrassing, Wilson with equal frankness, though perhaps a little too bluntly, admitted that he thought it was. Harvey took offense, and immediately discontinued his advocacy. After Wilson was nominated, however, he publicly avowed that Democracy had chosen its best man and that Wilson was preferable to either Taft or Roosevelt. He thus joined the Governor's forces again and lampooned the opposition in his best style.

In May 1913 Harvey retired from the editorship of the *Weekly* and in 1915 from the presidency of the publishing house. Wilson's early domestic legislation and leadership received his commendation, but as the war in Europe progressed he became an outspoken critic of the President's policies and in the campaign of 1916 opposed him with as much vigor as he had ever employed in his behalf. He never supported the Democratic party again. In January 1918 he began the publication of *Harvey's Weekly* as a convenient vehicle for his satire, ridicule, and barbed shafts against Wilsonian officialdom and the President's "fourteen commandments." After the war and until its suspension in 1921, the magazine concentrated on Wilson's peace negotiations, the League of Nations, and other public questions upon which Harvey held pronounced views. In 1920 the Colonel turned to president-making again, choosing Warren G. Harding as his candidate. It was in his reception room in the Blackstone Hotel, Chicago, that the Lowden-Wood deadlock was broken and Harding chosen as the Republican nominee (*New York Times,* Aug. 21, 26, 1928). After the selection had been ratified by the convention delegates, Harvey went to Harding's home, aided in the preparation of the candidate's speeches, and in 1921 received as his reward the ambassadorship to Great Britain. He resigned in 1923, soon after President Harding's death. In June 1924 he assumed the editorship of the *Washington Post,* which he retained only until May 1925. In October 1926 he sold the *North American Review* and announced that he would henceforth give his undivided attention to historical and biographical writing. His *Henry Clay Frick, the Man,* a biography of an old friend, was published in 1928, a few months before the author's death at Dublin, N. H.

[A volume of Harvey's addresses, *The Power of Tolerance and Other Speeches,* was published in 1911; a biography by W. F. Johnson, *George Harvey 'A Passionate Patriot,'* appeared in 1929. See also R. E. Annin, *Woodrow Wilson, A Character Study* (1924), chap. X; Ray Stannard Baker, *Woodrow Wilson, Life and Letters,* vols. II, III (1927–31); *Mirrors of Washington* (1921); Wm. Inglis, "Helping to Make a President," *Collier's Weekly,* Oct. 7, 14, 21, 1916; J. H. Harper, *The House of Harper* (1912); *N. Y. Times,* Aug. 21, 26, 1928; *Washington Post,* Aug. 21, 1928.]

A. H. M.

HARVEY, HAYWARD AUGUSTUS (Jan. 17, 1824–Aug. 28, 1893), inventor, manufacturer, a descendant of William Harvey who settled in Dorchester, Mass., about 1636, was born at Jamestown, N. Y., the son of Thomas William and Melinda (Hayward) Harvey. Both his parents were natives of Vermont; his father, a blacksmith by trade and a skilled mechanic, went to western New York under contract to put up the machinery in a cotton-mill erected at Jamestown. He settled there as the village blacksmith and remained until his son was nine years old, when he moved to Ramapo, N. Y., to supervise the building of his newly invented screw-making machinery. In 1836 he took his family to Poughkeepsie, where he built up a flourishing screw-making industry and devised many inventions. Here young Harvey completed his schooling at the Poughkeepsie Academy and at the academy at New Paltz, N. Y., and then entered his father's factory to learn drafting. When the New York Screw Company was organized in New York City, about 1840, with the elder Harvey as president, H. A. Harvey became a draftsman in its service. During the next decade he patented a corrugated blind staple and invented a hay-cutter for which he received a silver medal at the American Institute Fair in New York in 1847; in 1849 he resigned from the New York Screw Company to take charge of a wire mill at Somerville, N. J., but within a year he was back in New York, where he established a wire mill of his own. Before this business was fairly under way, however, the factory was completely burned out, whereupon he joined the Harvey Steel & Iron Company at Mott Haven, N. Y., organized by his father in 1852. After the death of the latter in 1854, Harvey won several lawsuits which he brought against a number of screw companies for infringement of his father's patents awarded May 30, 1846, on the automatic screw machinery. He made a number of inventions, including a railway chair patented Dec. 25, 1859. About 1865 he organized a new screw company, the Continental, which was entirely successful. After selling this company to the American Screw Company of Providence in 1870, he devoted his attention for the next six years to wire nails and bolts, and in 1874 patented a "peripheral grip bolt" with a varying pitch of thread. He organized a company for its manufacture in 1876, but after a few years' operation sold it to a Western manufacturer. About 1880 he designed a machine for rolling instead of cutting the thread upon the screw blank. The company organized in 1881 to manufacture screws by this process was absorbed six years later by the American Screw Company. The cold-forged screw is now standard and Harvey is recognized as the original inventor. In 1885–86 he had a shop in Brooklyn where he conducted experiments with bolts and nuts, including the hardening of threads on bolts made of soft steel. Applying his peculiar process to other problems, he made, from a cheap grade of Bessemer steel, razor blades which were in all respects equal to those of the best refined steel. With friends, he organized the Harvey Steel Company in 1886 and the following year erected a plant in Jersey City where, by his method, file and tool steels were made from cheap grades of steel. A large variety of commercial articles, too, were treated, such as bicycle parts, punches and dies, railroad frogs, and plates for safes and vaults. In this connection Harvey started experimenting with thick blocks of steel in an endeavor to secure the greater resistance to blows and strains which armor plate must possess. As a result of these experiments he received patents Nos. 376,194 (Jan. 10, 1888) and 460,262 (Sept. 29, 1891) for treating armor plate. His treatment was brought to the attention of the Navy Department in May 1889, and after a large number of tests the Harvey Process was formally adopted by the United States government and by most European governments as well. While Harvey devoted the major part of his life to the perfection of automatic machinery and secured some hundred and twenty-five patents, it was the Harvey Process for treating armor plate that brought him world-wide reputation.

Harvey was extremely fond of music and could play almost any musical instrument, although he preferred the piano and the organ. He was twice married: on Dec. 29, 1849, to Mary Matilda Winant of New York, who died June 26, 1857, leaving one son; and on June 21, 1865, to Emily Alice Halsey of Bridgehampton, N. Y., who with one son and her stepson survived him at the time of his death in Orange, N. J.

[E. W. Byrn, *The Progress of Invention in the 19th Century* (1900); *Memoir of Hayward Augustus Harvey* (1900), by his sons; O. J. Harvey, *The Harvey Book* (1899); obituaries in *N. Y. Tribune* and *N. Y. Times,* Aug. 29, 1893; Patent Office records.]

C. W. M—n.

HARVEY, LOUIS POWELL (July 22, 1820–Apr. 19, 1862), secretary of state and governor of Wisconsin, was born in East Haddam, Conn., the son of David and Almira (Powell) Harvey and a descendant of Thomas Harvey who with his brother William emigrated from England to Massachusetts in 1636, settling at Dorchester. When he was a lad of ten, the family moved to Strongsville, Cuyahoga County, Ohio. He prepared himself for college while earning the money to that end and entered Western Reserve at Hudson at the age of seventeen. Ill health and lack of money interrupted his college course, and in his junior year he was forced to leave. He taught school for a time and in 1841 went to Wisconsin, where at Southport (now Kenosha) he started an academy. About two years later, in addition to his teaching, he took editorial charge of the *Southport American,* a Whig paper established in 1841. After his marriage in 1847 to Cordelia Adelaide Perrine of Barre, Orleans County, N. Y., he moved to Clinton, Wis., where he opened a store. He made his first appearance in a public capacity in 1847 as a member of the convention that framed the constitution of the state of Wisconsin. Three years later he settled in Waterloo (now called Shopiere), a small village in Rock County, which was his home thereafter. Here, in accord with his temperance principles, he purchased a distillery, tore it down, and in its place built a flour mill and retail store. Largely through his efforts a small stone Congregational church was erected, his uncle, Rev. O. S. Powell, being the first pastor. Elected state senator in 1853, he became an able speaker in the legislature, winning the favor of all classes by his earnest, genial, and courteous manner. He was reëlected for a second term in 1855, during which time he was chosen president *pro tempore.* After serving as secretary of state in 1860–61 he was nominated for governor by both the Union and Republican conventions and elected by a large majority. In April 1862 he went South himself to visit the hospitals in order to see that everything possible was done for the Wisconsin soldiers wounded in the battle of Shiloh. At Savannah, Tenn., about to embark on his steamer homeward bound, he made a misstep and fell between two boats into the river. In spite of every effort made to save him, the swift current drew him away and he was drowned. His body, found later some sixty-five miles below, was taken to Madison and with fitting ceremony buried in Forest Hill Cemetery.

[R. G. Thwaites, *Civil War Messages and Proclamations of Wisconsin War Governors* (Wis. Hist. Com. Reprints, no. 2, 1912); F. H. Lyman, *The City of Kenosha and Kenosha County, Wis.* (1916), vol. I; C. S. Matteson, *The Hist. of Wis.* (1893); *Portr. and Biog. Record of Waukesha County, Wis.* (1894); *The Biog. Dict. and Portr. Gallery of Representative Men of Chicago, Wisconsin, and the World's Columbian Exposition* (1895); David Atwood, in *Wis. Hist. Soc. Colls.*, vol. V (1868); C. R. Tuttle, *An Illus. Hist. of the State of Wis.* (1875); H. A. Tenney and David Atwood, *Memorial Record of the Fathers of Wis.* (1880); R. B. Way, *The Rock River Valley* (1926); O. J. Harvey, *The Harvey Book* (1899).] R. B. W.

HARVIE, JOHN (1742–Feb. 6, 1807), Revolutionary patriot, statesman, financier, was born in Albemarle County, Va., the son of Col. John Harvie (1706–1767) and Martha Gaines. John Harvie the elder (with whom his son is sometimes confused) was born in Gargunnock, Scotland, but settled about forty years before the Revolution in Albemarle County, where among other distinctions that came to him was the guardianship of young Thomas Jefferson. Of the education of John Harvie the younger little is known. He engaged in the practice of law in his native county, attaining, we are told, a high degree of success, and married Margaret, daughter of Gabriel Jones. At the outbreak of the Revolution he took an active part in raising troops and in 1776 was made colonel of Virginia militia. Meanwhile he was a delegate for Augusta and West Augusta counties, respectively, in the Virginia conventions of 1775 and 1776, and in the latter convention was one of the committee designated to prepare a declaration of rights and form of government. In these conventions also he had an important share in the proceedings relative to Indian affairs, and it may have been this fact which led to his appointment by the Continental Congress, May 11, 1776, as one of the commissioners for Indian affairs in the middle department. In conjunction with his fellow commissioners, Dr. Thomas Walker, John Montgomery, and Jasper Yeates, he conducted delicate negotiations with the Indians at Fort Pitt during the summer and autumn of that year. On Oct. 15, 1777, he took his seat in the Continental Congress in time to take part in the final debates and sign the Articles of Confederation. He became a member of the board of war, the committee on appeals, the marine committee, and the committee of commerce and was on most of the committees having to do with provisioning the army. One of his most important services was as a member of the committee sent to headquarters in January 1778 to concert with the commander-in-chief a reorganization of the army and a reform of abuses in the departments of supply. That committee presently ran amuck, but Harvie had already parted from it, apparently in disagreement. In Congress he was very apt to be found with the minority (he was one of two to vote against the notorious resolution suspending the embarkation of Burgoyne). Though again elected to Congress in May 1778, he withdrew in October, "for good," he hoped. Congressional politics evidently did not appeal to him. Besides, business, for which he had eminent qualities, was already beckoning to him (*Virginia Magazine of History and Biography*, January 1898, p. 293). He became purchasing agent for Virginia; then, in 1780, register of the land office for many years, and in the interval, 1785–86, mayor of Richmond; but it was chiefly as an enterprising builder and public-spirited citizen that Richmond knew him in his later years. His death, which took place at his home, "Belvidere," near Richmond, was in consequence of injuries received from a fall while inspecting the construction of what was afterward known as the Gamble House.

[Sketches are found in: *Va. Hist. Soc. Colls.*, n.s. VI (1887), 83; *The Harvie Family* (privately printed pamphlet); Edgar Woods, *Albemarle County in Va.* (1901). Some letters of Harvie are found in: *Calendar of Va. State Papers*, vols. IV and V (1884–85); E. C. Burnett, *Letters of Members of the Continental Cong.*, vols. II and III (1923–26); Jefferson Papers, Lib. of Cong. The *Journals of the Continental Congress* and the *Proceedings* of the Virginia conventions are essential. An obituary appeared in the *Richmond Enquirer*, Feb. 13, 1807.] E. C. B.

HASBROUCK, ABRAHAM BRUYN (Nov. 29, 1791–Feb. 23, 1879), lawyer, congressman, college president, was an outstanding representative, in his generation, of that group of Huguenot families which settled in Ulster County, N. Y., in the seventeenth century. He was a son of Judge Jonathan Hasbrouck of Kingston, N. Y., and Catharine (Wynkoop) Hasbrouck. Born at Kingston, he studied at Kingston Academy, entered Yale College in 1806, and was graduated in 1810. He then attended the famous law school at Litchfield, Conn., over which Judge Tapping Reeve presided. After spending some time there, he returned to his native town and in 1814 began to practise. On Sept. 12, 1819, he married Julia Frances Ludlum, who died in 1869. A man of scholarly bent, endowed with gifts of expression beyond the ordinary, he was successful in his profession. From 1817 to 1831 he was in partnership with Charles H. Ruggles and from 1833 to 1840 with his former student, Marius Schoonmaker. From its establishment in 1831 he was president of the Ulster County Bank. Meanwhile he was elected to Congress in the year 1824, but served only one term. He supported Clay's policy of internal improvements. Always more interested in church than in secular politics, he became increasingly prominent in the affairs of the Reformed Dutch Church and by 1840 was regarded as one of the foremost laymen in that body. In that year he was chosen president of Rutgers College at New Brunswick, N. J., then as always the leading literary institution supported by the denomination. The choice was logical and was well received in church circles, although Hasbrouck was the first layman to hold that office. His administration marked an increasing independence of the college from ecclesiastical control. The graduating classes at that period numbered between twenty and twenty-five members each year; the admission requirements consisted of the classics and arithmetic. Under Hasbrouck's administration modern languages were brought into the curriculum. He himself was an excellent classical scholar, and at various times while he was president gave instruction in the subjects of constitutional law, international law, political economy, moral philosophy, rhetoric, and belles-lettres. In his time student activities began to take a wider range; college publications and Greek letter fraternities were introduced. The president and his wife did much to enrich the college social life. Additions were made to the institution's property, and greater attractions were provided for students. Hasbrouck felt compelled by ill health to resign the presidency in 1849, but after a brief interregnum was reëlected by the trustees and continued to serve until April 1850, when a new president was chosen and he was permitted to retire. He spent a few years in New York City, but finally returned to the family home in Kingston, where he lived in "dignified retirement" until his death. He was the first president (1859) of the Ulster Historical Society. His *Inaugural Address* at Rutgers was published in 1840 and his address as president of the Ulster Historical Society in Vol. I (1860) of the Society's *Collections*.

[A. L. Snyder, "Lineage of the Abraham Hasbrouck Family," *Olde Ulster*, vols. IV and V (June 1908–Feb. 1909); F. B. Dexter, *Biog. Sketches Grads. Yale Coll.*, vol. VI (1912); N. B. Sylvester, *Hist. of Ulster County, N. Y.* (1880); W. H. S. Demarest, *Hist. of Rutgers Coll.* (1924); *Christian Intelligencer* (N. Y.), Aug. 1, 1850; *Rutgers Targum*, Mar. 1879; *N. Y. Tribune*, Feb. 25, 1879.]

W. B. S.

HASBROUCK, LYDIA SAYER (Dec. 20, 1827–Aug. 24, 1910), editor, and advocate of dress reform, was born in the town of Warwick, Orange County, N. Y., a descendant in the seventh generation of Thomas Sayer, one of the founders of Southampton, L. I. She was the daughter of Benjamin Sayer, a well-to-do farmer and distiller, and Rebecca Forshee, his wife, both prominent in the social life of the community. She grew up in an atmosphere of comfort, in a hospitable home—a fearless and self-reliant girl, notable for her skill in the domestic arts, her able horsemanship, and her keen interest in books. She received her formal education in the Warwick district school, Miss Galatian's Select School, the Elmira (N. Y.) High School, and Central College. About 1849 she became deeply interested in the dress-reform movement and in the doctrines of hygienic living proclaimed by the disciples of the water-cure. With characteristic independence she promptly adopted the "Bloomer" costume, and continued to wear it throughout her life, probably the only one of its early advocates who did so. Because of her unconventional dress she was refused admission to a seminary in Florida, N. Y., where she had hoped to continue her education. This action outraged her sense of justice and sent her into the ranks of the reformers. She began to speak and write on temperance, woman's suffrage, and dress reform, and in 1853 went as a delegate to the Whole World's Temperance Convention. A short time later she entered the Hygeia-Therapeutic College in New York City and graduated from it as doctor of medicine. She began her professional career in Washington, D. C., practising there for a year and lecturing frequently in the neighboring cities on the tyranny of fashion. Although she met constant criticism for her "immodest" costume and short hair, she was repeatedly described by reporters as "a pretty Bloomer doctress," graceful and self-possessed, with an intellectual face and a fascinating smile. In June 1856 she removed to Middletown, N. Y., and joined forces there with John W. Hasbrouck, proprietor of the *Whig Press*, in establishing a fortnightly reform paper called the *Sibyl*, "a Review of the Tastes, Errors, and Fashions of Society." She edited this lively periodical for eight years, vigorously denouncing all health-destroying fashions, advocating wider opportunities for women, and printing detailed accounts of dress-reform conventions. During the years 1864 and 1865 she acted as president of the National Dress Reform Association. On July 27, 1856, wearing a white bloomer costume, she married her business partner by a common-law marriage. Fifty years of companionship followed, during which time both husband and wife continued their reforming zeal. One daughter and two sons were born of this marriage. After giving up the *Sibyl,* Mrs. Hasbrouck assisted in editing her husband's paper, the *Press,* until 1868, and continued to work actively for woman's suffrage. In the first New York election that permitted women to vote for and hold school offices (1880), she was chosen a member of the Middletown schoolboard. The following year she and her husband started an independent weekly paper, the *Liberal Sentinel,* to defend the program of equal rights for women and men. She led an active intellectual life until the year before her death, never needing medical attention and always vigorous in mind. She died at her home, "Sibyl Ridge," in her eighty-third year, after arranging the details of her own funeral—an individualist unsubdued by convention, who had labored steadfastly for the causes in which she believed.

[E. M. Ruttenber and L. H. Clark, *Hist. of Orange County, N. Y.* (1881); obituaries in Orange County newspapers for Aug. 25, 1910; *N. Y. Herald,* Aug. 26, 1910; files of the *Sibyl*; family records.] B. M. S.

HASCALL, MILO SMITH (Aug. 5, 1829–Aug. 30, 1904), soldier, lawyer, and banker, was the son of Amasa and Phoebe Ann (Smith) Hascall. He was born at Le Roy, N. Y., and until he went to join three of his brothers at Goshen, Ind., spent his boyhood on his father's farm. At Goshen he worked for a time in one brother's store and for a time taught school. He received an appointment to the United States Military Academy in 1848, from which in 1852 he graduated, fourteenth in a class of forty-three members. His promotion as brevet second lieutenant took him to Fort Adams, R. I., where he received his commission as second lieutenant in the following year. The apparent stagnation of the pre-war years turned his thoughts to civil life and in September 1853 he resigned his commission. In 1854 he took a contract for building a section of the Michigan Southern & Northern Indiana Railroad. Until the outbreak of the Civil War he led a busy life in Indiana. He practised law in Goshen, served as prosecuting attorney for Elkhart and Lagrange counties and also as clerk of court. His first war service was as a private in a three months' volunteer regiment from Indiana. His previous training made him a marked man, and the governor of Indiana appointed him captain and aide-de-camp to General Morris. His services in training the Indiana volunteer regiments won him an appointment, June 12, 1861, as colonel of the 17th Indiana, with which he saw several minor engagements in the opening weeks of the war. In December 1861, he was ordered to Louisville, Ky., where he assumed command of a brigade of Ohio and Indiana troops, in the division of Gen. Thomas Wood. With this he served at the capture of Nashville in February 1862, and in the advance on Shiloh. On Apr. 25, 1862, he was commissioned brigadier-general of volunteers. From October of the same year to March 1863, he commanded a brigade in the Tennessee campaign, his principal action during this campaign being the battle of Stone River, in which he played a conspicuous part. At the close of the campaign, he spent several weeks on the unpleasant duty of collecting stragglers from Ohio, Indiana, and Illinois. At the request of General Burnside, he was transferred to the Army of the Ohio, and placed in command of the District of Indiana. In August 1863, in command of a division in the Army of the Ohio, he again saw field service in the operations in East Tennessee, especially at Chickamauga, Missionary Ridge, and in the engagements in defense of Knoxville. When Sherman began his march on Atlanta, Hascall was in command of the 2nd Division, XXIII Corps. In the brilliant campaign which followed, he took an active part, both in the many engagements north of Atlanta, and in the siege of the city itself. Before the conclusion of the campaign, however, he had decided to return to civil life. He resigned late in October 1864. In the years that followed, he engaged in banking at Goshen and at Galena. In 1890, he moved to Chicago where he became a dealer in real estate on a large scale, and where he continued to be active in business until his death.

Hascall was twice married. His first wife, whom he married in 1855, was Julia, daughter of Dean and Emeline Swift of Elkhart, Ind. Three years after her death in 1883, he married Mrs. Rose Miller, daughter of Jacob and Catherine Schwartz of Canton, Ohio. He left no children.

[G. W. Cullum, *Biog. Reg. Officers and Grads. U. S. Mil. Acad.* (3rd ed., 1891), vol. II; old files, Adj. Gen. Office, War Dept., Washington; *Who's Who in America,* 1903–05; F. B. Heitman, *Hist. Reg. and Dict. U. S. Army* (1903), vol. I; *Thirty-Sixth Ann. Reunion, Asso. Grads. U. S. Mil. Acad.* (1905); *Chicago Tribune,* Aug. 31, 1904.] A. W. C.

HASELTINE, JAMES HENRY (Nov. 2, 1833–Nov. 9, 1907), sculptor, the third of the eleven children of John and Elizabeth Stanley (Shinn) Haseltine, was born in Philadelphia, Pa., his parents being of American birth and English ancestry. His father was a prosperous merchant; his mother, as revealed in a portrait by Sully, was notably beautiful. A brother, William Stanley, was a painter and became a member of the National Academy of Design. A still younger brother, Charles Field, dealt in pictures and founded the Haseltine Art Galleries in Philadelphia. Clearly the family had artistic affiliations. James Henry studied sculpture under the French sculptor Joseph A. Bailly at the Pennsylvania Academy of the Fine Arts, where in 1859 he exhibited a copy of Rude's "Fisher Boy." He went to Paris and to Rome to pursue his art but in 1861 returned to enlist in the Union army, being mustered into service in September of that year. On Mar. 1, 1863, he was promoted from captain to major, Company E, 6th Pennsylvania Cavalry, 70th Regiment. He was discharged Nov. 12, 1863, and returned to his studies. Like his brother the painter, he spent most of his life abroad, chiefly in Rome, but also in Florence and in Paris. On July 5, 1881, in Paris, he was married to Marie N. F. Trombetti.

During his self-imposed exile, he sent home many works, pseudo-classic in type, and commented upon by critics of the day. H. T. Tuckerman regarded his several allegorical groups as showing "inventive expression and poetical significance" (*Book of the Artists,* 1867, p. 598). Among these were "Superstition," a heathen mother sacrificing her child to Moloch, and "Religion," a Christian mother presenting her child for baptism. His marble "Excelsior" Tuckerman considered an effective representation of aspiring youth, while his "New Wine," "America Victorious," and "Grateful and Ungrateful Love" he praised as having been "conceived with vividness and executed with skill" (*Ibid.*). Somewhat less flattering were the comments of Samuel Osgood ("American Artists in Italy," *Harper's New Monthly Magazine,* August 1870), who thought the sculptor "perhaps too eager to express his fancies in marble embodiment" and that his "America Victorious," though spirited, had "perhaps overmuch of symbolism in its details."

Haseltine also worked in portraiture, making studies of a number of well-known contemporaries. Among these were busts of the poets Longfellow and T. B. Read, and the generals Forsyth, Hartsuff, Merritt, and Sheridan. At the Centennial Exposition of 1876 he exhibited three figures, "Spring Flowers," "Captivity," and "Lucretia." For the Union League of Philadelphia he executed a commission for a monument, "America Honoring her Fallen Brave," the pedestal of which was adorned with bas-reliefs. During the last years of Haseltine's life little was heard of him. He died in Rome.

[In addition to sources mentioned see Josiah H. Shinn, *Hist. of the Shinn Family in Europe and America* (1903); Samuel P. Bates, *Hist. of Pa. Volunteers,* vol. II (1869), and catalogues of the Pennsylvania Academy of the Fine Arts. The date of Haseltine's death was supplied by the U. S. Bureau of Pensions.]

A. A.

HASELTON, SENECA (Feb. 26, 1848–July 21, 1921), jurist, son of Rev. Amos Haselton, a Methodist minister, and Amelia (Frink) Haselton, was born in the town of Westford, Vt. It is related that his father was fond of classical literature and wished to name his son Epictetus, but the mother objected and the parents compromised on Seneca. The lad attended the public schools of the period in the towns of Jericho and Underhill, and academies in Underhill and Barre. He entered the University of Vermont when James B. Angell was president of that institution. During his college career he eked out his income by teaching schools in several Vermont towns in the long winter vacation. After his graduation, in 1871, he became associate principal of Barre (Vt.) Academy, holding the position for one year. In 1873, he began the study of law in Burlington, Vt., in the office of Wales & Taft. A little later he secured a position as instructor of mathematics in the University of Michigan to which James B. Angell had gone in 1871 as president. This position enabled Haselton to continue his legal studies in the law department of the University, where he received the degree of LL.B. in 1875. He thereupon returned to Vermont, was admitted to the Chittenden County bar, and began the practice of law in Burlington. He was elected judge of the Burlington city court in 1878, holding office until 1886 when he was chosen a representative in the Vermont legislature. He was mayor of Burlington and welcomed President Benjamin Harrison to the city when the latter made a tour of Vermont in the centennial year of the Green Mountain State. In 1894, he was appointed United States minister to Venezuela by President Cleveland but resigned in 1895 because of the failure of his health, shortly before the culmination of the dispute between the United States and Great Britain over Venezuelan boundary affairs. When he had recovered his health he resumed the practice of law. In 1900 he was the Democratic candidate for United States senator to complete the unexpired term of Justin S. Morrill, but was defeated by William P. Dillingham.

Haselton held the office of reporter of the supreme court of Vermont from 1900 to 1902 (72–73 *Vermont Reports*), and when Chief Judge Russell S. Taft died in the last-named year, he was appointed to fill the vacancy caused by the promotion of the other judges. He served as a member of the supreme court until 1906, when the courts were reorganized, only a part of the original court being retained on the supreme bench. Haselton became chief judge of the new superior court, established that year, but in 1908 was again promoted to the supreme court bench, where he served with distinction until his resignation May 1, 1919, on account of failing health. He was the only Democrat on the bench during his period of service. He practised law a little after his retirement, but died July 21, 1921. Haselton was a trustee of the Vermont State Library, a member of the Vermont Historical Society, the American Society of International Law, and the Selden Society of England. He never married. He was a member of the Congregational Church. He had a remarkable memory, and it is related that in the trial of a will case in which he was counsel, he propounded orally to an expert witness a hypothetical question which took more than two hours in the asking, a question which included every circumstance in the case that bore upon the answer desired. He was noted for his profound learning and for the elegance of his diction, and although a modest, retiring man, was generally recognized as one of Vermont's great lawyers and jurists.

[*Proc. Vt. Bar Asso.*, vol. XV (1922); W. H. Crockett, *Vermont, the Green Mountain State* (1921), vols. IV and V; Hiram Carleton, *Geneal. and Family Hist. of the State of Vt.* (1903); J. G. Ullery, *Men of Vt.* (1894); *Burlington Free Press*, July 22, 1921.]

W. H. C.

HASENCLEVER, PETER (Nov. 24, 1716–June 13, 1793), iron manufacturer, was born at Remscheid, Prussia, the son of Luther and Klara (Moll) Hasenclever. His father was a merchant and owned iron and steel furnaces. Peter was placed early in the home of his maternal grandfather, the burgomaster of Lennep, where he attended the public school for three years, geography being his favorite study. For instruction in other branches he was later sent to Solingen. His next school was a steel mill in that city, where at the age of fourteen, a boy of slender constitution, he was set to work by the side of men whose laboring hours were from five in the morning until nine at night with slight interruption. At the end of two years he was sent to Liège, Belgium, to improve his French, and a short season there terminated his formal education. Before he was nineteen, the youth was making trips to France for the enlargement of his father's business, extending his travels to Bayonne and the Pyrenees; but, since that business was declining from various causes, he obtained permission to seek his fortune in enterprises of his own. In the employ of a cousin, a manufacturer of cloth and needles in Burtscheid, he began the series of journeys in Continental Europe as well as England that made him one of the best-equipped commercial men of his day. Deceived in the hope held out to him that he should become a partner in his kinsman's house, he found new friends, formed a profitable association in Lisbon, and extended his business to Cadiz. At Potsdam he attracted the attention of Frederick the Great, who consulted him on methods of improving the linen exports of Silesia.

Lured by stories of opportunities in America, he formed a company with an initial capital of £21,000 for the mining and manufacture of iron, the raising of flax and hemp, and the production of potash in the colonies; and, having become a British subject, he embarked for New York, arriving in June 1764. In Morris County, N. J., and Orange County, N. Y., and elsewhere, he established works for mining and smelting, also for producing potash, and engaged in raising flax and hemp. Altogether these industries covered 50,000 acres. He invested in draft animals, buildings, implements; built bridges, constructed dams for impounding waters, and tested mineral deposits. Eminent persons in England joined his company; and his iron was pronounced the best ever brought to England from America. Warned that an associate in England was handling the funds and credit recklessly, Hasenclever hastened to London to find this partner a bankrupt and the concern badly involved. After restoring his credit and reëstablishing the business, he returned to New York only to find his American interests involved in like misfortune. Trouble with English directors ensued, and they set out to draw his American enterprises wholly into their own hands, and leave him only the obligations. A commission appointed by Gov. William Franklin of New Jersey investigated Hasenclever's transactions and returned a report in 1768 commending his commercial character. He thereupon set out to pay the debts by which he was connivingly loaded, and to secure his rights in the English courts. His suit dragged on in chancery and only in 1787, at the end of twenty years, was he released from all claims and free to engage in trade in England. He had removed to Silesia in 1773 and spent his last days trying to improve the industries of that province. Six months after his death two of his persecutors were compelled to pay a large sum to a house to which Hasenclever had transferred his claim.

Hasenclever married in 1745 Katharine Wilds,

daughter of an English sea-captain, and was survived by a daughter, Maria Elisabeth Ruck.

[*Peter Hasenclever aus Remscheid-Ehringhausen: ein Deutscher Kaufman des 18. Jahrhunderts* (1922); ed. by Adolf Hasenclever, including biography, letters and memoirs; R. E. Day, *Calendar of the Sir Wm. Johnson MSS. in the N. Y. State Lib.* (1909); *The Papers of Sir Wm. Johnson*, vols. V (1927), VI (1928); H. A. Homes, *Notice of Peter Hasenclever* (1875, repr. in *Trans. Albany Inst.*, vol. VIII, 1876); Edmund Halsey and others, *Hist. of Morris County, N. J.* (1882); J. F. Tuttle, "Annals of Morris County," *Proc. N. J. Hist. Soc.*, 2 ser. II (1872); *Hist. of Morris County, N. J.* (1914), vol. I; *Docs. Relative to the Colonial Hist. of the State of N. Y.*, VII (1856), 888–90, VIII (1857), 35.]

R. E. D.

HASKELL, DUDLEY CHASE (Mar. 23, 1842–Dec. 16, 1883), politician, was born in Springfield, Vt., the son of Franklin Haskell and Almira Chase, both of whom were of New England ancestry. His father migrated from Massachusetts to Kansas Territory in 1854, reaching Lawrence with the second company of the Emigrant Aid Association. The following year he was joined by his wife and children. Dudley Haskell served with the Free-Soil militia while still a mere lad. Poverty, the bloody turmoil of early days in Kansas, the lure of the Pike's Peak country, the Civil War, a desire for learning, and possibly a restless vigor inherited from his father, all conspired to keep young Haskell on the move from 1855 to 1866. He went from Lawrence to school in New England, back again to Lawrence, out into the Pike's Peak region, back to Kansas, then into the Quartermaster's Corps of the Union army for more than a year's service, then into Yale College in 1864 for a course of special study, then to a business college in New Haven, and finally in December 1865 to Lawrence, Kan., with his bride, Harriet M. Kelsey of Stockbridge, Mass. For the next ten years he was a merchant in Lawrence but was only indifferently successful in business.

In 1871 Haskell definitely entered politics with his election on the Republican ticket to the lower house of the Kansas state legislature. He was reëlected in 1873 and 1875, and in 1876 was chosen speaker of the lower house. In 1874 he had been nominated for governor by the Temperance party of his state, but he declined the nomination. In 1876 he was nominated by the Republicans of the second congressional district of Kansas for the lower house of Congress. Elected by a safe margin, he was reëlected in 1878, 1880, and 1882. On entering Congress, he quickly gained the attention of party leaders by his power in debate, his indefatigable energy, and the range of his information. In most matters he was a conservative Republican and a consistent party man. He sought to liberalize the public land policy of the United States in the interests of his section, the West. He was the uncompromising foe of Mormonism, or rather of polygamy as practised by the Mormons. The Indian problem he thought should be solved through education and accordingly worked for the establishment of Indian schools. But his chief interest was the tariff. He was an out-and-out protectionist, probably the most prominent of his day from the purely agricultural West, and bore a leading part in the enactment of tariff legislation in 1882. He served on several important committees, notably on the committee of ways and means, and was one of the conferees on the Internal Revenue Bill of 1883, serving with Kelley and Randall of Pennsylvania, Carlisle of Kentucky, and William McKinley of Ohio. He died in Washington, survived by his wife and two daughters, and was buried in Lawrence, Kan.

[D. W. Wilder, *The Annals of Kan.* (1875); W. E. Connelley, *A Standard Hist. of Kan. and Kansans* (1918), vol. I; *Memorial Addresses on the Life and Character of Dudley C. Haskell* (1884); the *Nat. Republican* (Washington, D. C.), Dec. 17, 1883.]

W. W. D.

HASKELL, ELLA LOUISE KNOWLES (July 31, 1860–Jan. 27, 1911), lawyer, politician, club-woman, was throughout her life a militant crusader for equal rights for women. Her parents, David and Louisa (Bigelow) Knowles, were of English stock and were living at Northwood Ridge, N. H., when Ella was born. She grew up a studious girl and graduated from a local seminary in 1880. She then entered Bates College and in spite of some prejudice there against women won honors in oratory, debate, and journalism. After her graduation in 1884 she entered the law office of Henry E. Burnham, in Manchester, N. H., but owing to her frail health she decided to go West. In 1888 she was employed as a teacher in the schools of Helena, Mont., and the next year was made principal, but she resigned to resume her law studies. At that time no provision existed in Montana for the admission of women to the practice of law. She appealed to the territorial legislature to give them the right; her plea was granted, and in December 1889 she was admitted to the Montana bar. At first she handled many charity cases for she was a vigorous opponent of anything which she regarded as an injustice. She showed real ability as a lawyer, however, and gradually built up a lucrative practice.

Having established a reputation as a reformer, Miss Knowles was nominated in 1892 by the Populists for the attorney-generalship of the state. At first she regarded the nomination as a joke but later she decided to fight for the office. In the campaign she made more than one hundred speeches. She was defeated in the election, but her opponent, Henri J. Haskell, made her his deputy and on May 23, 1895, in San Francisco, she was married to him. In the attorney-general's office she was given charge of the legal work relating to public lands and made good the state's claim to school lands valued at $200,000. In 1896 she was sent by the Populists as delegate to their national convention, and for the next four years she served as national committeeman for Montana. She campaigned vigorously for Bryan and Watson in 1896, and for Bryan in 1900. On the platform she was persuasive and convincing.

A few years after her marriage Mrs. Haskell divorced her husband and in time went to Butte, Mont., where she opened a law office. She began buying mining property and was notably successful in her investments. She gained a reputation as a mining expert and became a member of the executive committee of the International Mining Congress. Her life continued to be varied. Law and mining took only a part of her time. She adored pretty dresses, fine pictures, and good music. She read, and traveled, and lectured, mostly in the interest of woman's rights. She was an active member of many clubs, and an ardent Theosophist. She had many friends, but few intimates; her vigorous assertion of her beliefs and her restless activities repelled those who came too close.

[Ella Knowles Haskell's activities can best be followed through the files of Montana newspapers. For brief notices and accounts of her life see *Progressive Men of the State of Montana* (n.d.); *Gen. Cat. of Bates Coll.* (1915); the *Helena Herald*, May 23, 1895; and the *Anaconda Standard*, Jan. 28, 1911.] P. C. P.

HASKELL, ERNEST (July 30, 1876–Nov. 2, 1925), painter, etcher, lithographer, was born in Woodstock, Conn., the son of Besture Haskell and Caledonia Raines Haskell, a member of a family of Norman-French nobility. Haskell's artistic career began very early when the editor of the New York *Mail and Express* recognized talent in some of his idle "scratchings" and published them. The delighted boy decided at once to become an artist and later obtained a position in the art department of the *New York American*. In 1897 he went to Paris, studied in the galleries, took a studio, and produced a series of clever monotypes, one of them being hung in the Salon de Mars. These monotypes, some of them in pastel, were skilfully executed and evinced a sound knowledge of the technique involved in this form of reproduction. Haskell returned to New York in 1898, making some successful caricatures and theatrical posters at a time when newspapers, magazines, and books were using them extensively for advertising. Among his posters were several of Minnie Maddern Fiske, which Weitenkampf says "attracted attention by their very reticence, by the simplicity of means used, crayoned with an almost pertly incisive characterization" (*post*, p. 283). He was unusually versatile. He worked delicately with crayon, making some notable drawings from nature; his silver-points were of Whistler-like lightness, and he was also a successful painter. One of his best-known portraits is that of Joan and "Jock" Whitney, daughter and son of Mr. and Mrs. Payne Whitney. Among his lithographs is one of Maude Adams as Juliet. In 1899 he had an exhibition at the Pratt Institute, Brooklyn.

In 1900 Haskell returned to Paris. He worked alone for two years studying the work of Rembrandt, Dürer, and Leonardo—an intensive study which he carried on during his entire life. Despite the variety of his work, he is perhaps best known as an etcher, and his prints are highly prized by collectors. An exhibition of his drawings, prints, silver-points, and monotypes was held in New York in 1911 and at the Art Institute of Chicago in 1916. A series of etchings and dry-points of trees and landscape subjects, inspired by a trip to California and Florida, were also exhibited in New York. He made a set of fifty water-colors in California, and in Maine a lovely series showing picturesque woods and country towns. Although he was an eager experimenter, he was an artist of rare taste, delicacy of feeling, and fine appreciation. After his marriage he made his home in Phippsburg, Me. His first wife was Elizabeth Louise Foley, who died Jan. 18, 1918. His second wife, whom he married June 5, 1920, was Emma Loveland Laumeister, who with four children survived him. He was killed in an automobile accident near Bath, Me., as he was on his way to his summer home from New York, where he had gone to arrange for a winter exhibition of his paintings. A memorial exhibition selected from his works was held in 1926 at the Macbeth Gallery, New York, when notable tributes were paid to him as a man and an artist by Childe Hassam, John Marin, Royal Cortissoz and many others.

[Frank Weitenkampf, *Am. Graphic Art* (ed. 1924); "Etchings by Ernest Haskell," *Century Mag.*, July 1919; *Bull. of the Art Inst. of Chicago*, Feb. 1916; A. E. Gallatin, *Whistler's Pastels and Other Modern Profiles* (1912), and article in the *Internat. Studio*, Aug. 1911; *Art News*, Nov. 7, 1925; *N. Y. Times*, Nov. 3, 1925.] H. W.

HASKET, ELIAS (Apr. 25, 1670–Mar. 9, 1739?), governor of the Bahamas, was born at Salem, Mass., the son of Stephen and Elizabeth (Hill) Hasket. Martha Hasket, sister of Elias, became the mother of Richard Derby, Jr. [*q.v.*]. Stephen Hasket, a soap-boiler and merchant of Salem, was a native of Henstridge, Somersetshire, where his ancestors, a race of prosperous yeomen and clothiers, were settled in the time of Queen Elizabeth. He came to Salem from Exeter, Devonshire, about 1666. The younger Hasket went in early life to Barbados, where he married Elizabeth Rich. He was a sea-captain, making frequent voyages to England, and in 1696 he was commanding the ship *New London.* In 1698 he became involved in a lengthy litigation with his relatives in England over the estate of his uncle, Elias Hasket, a prosperous Henstridge yeoman. Through his relations with London merchants engaged in the West India trade he procured an appointment as governor of New Providence, the largest of the Bahama Islands. After some delay the King approved his appointment, June 27, 1700, and Hasket took oath of office on the same day. Somewhat less than a year later he arrived in New Providence, where his career was brief and stormy. Early in October 1701 the people, under the leadership of John Graves, the collector of customs, with whom Hasket had quarreled, and instigated by Read Elding, one of the principal inhabitants of the island, whom the governor had imprisoned, rose in revolt against him. They imprisoned Hasket together with his brother-in-law, Benjamin Pickman of Salem, and seized the latter's ship. After keeping the governor in prison for six weeks they put him on board a small vessel bound for New York. On his arrival there he went to his relatives in Salem and thence to England. His wife escaped from the island during that winter, to Charleston, S. C., and thence went to her husband. On Oct. 5, 1701, before he had left New Providence, an assembly of the people addressed a memorial to the Lords Proprietors and the Commissioners of Trade setting forth their complaints against the governor, accusing him of extortion and tyranny in the performance of his duties, of illicit trading with the French at Cape François, and of harboring pirates, especially one of the crew of the notorious Captain Avery. To this remonstrance were appended depositions of several captains, among them the commander of a London ship, which set forth specific instances of his extortion and high-handed conduct toward them in the summer of 1701. Hasket replied with a long memorial, accusing the inhabitants of the island of disorderly and evil living, of illicit trade, robbery, and of giving assistance to the pirates of those parts. On Mar. 19, 1701/02 he styled himself "Governor of the Colony of New Providence" in a power of attorney to Samuel Browne, Esq., of Salem; but in a chancery suit which he commenced on Apr. 3, 1702, against one of his cousins in Henstridge, he calls himself "of Henstridge Marsh Esquire." On Sept. 27, 1702, the Queen in Council granted his petition for relief on account of his losses in the Bahamas and on Dec. 31, of the same year, the Privy Council referred to the Lord Admiral "the petition of Captain Elias Haskett for . . . the Command of a Fifth Rate Ship or some other Employment" (*Acts of the Privy Council, post,* p. 426). It is likely, therefore, that he returned to the sea and that he was the "Capt. Hasket, formerly a Sea Commander," whose death was recorded in the *Gentleman's Magazine* for March 1739.

[*New Eng. Hist. and Geneal. Reg.*, Jan., Apr. 1923, Jan. 1924, Apr., July, Oct. 1930; *Essex Inst. Hist. Colls.*, vols. XVI (1879), XLI (1905), XLII (1906), and LI (1915); *Calendar of State Papers, Colonial Ser., America and West Indies,* 1700–03; *Acts of the Privy Council of England, Colonial Ser., 1680–1720* (1910); *Articles, Depositions, &c. of the People of New Providence, in an Assembly held at Nassau, Oct. 5, 1701, Against Elias Haskett, Gov.* (1702); J. A. Emmerton and H. F. Waters, *Gleanings from English Records about New Eng. Families* (1880).]

G. A. M., Jr.

HASSARD, JOHN ROSE GREENE (Sept. 4, 1836–Apr. 18, 1888), journalist and litterateur, was born in Houston Street in New York City, the son of Thomas Hassard, a civil engineer, and Augusta (Greene) Hassard. His parents were Episcopalians and he was reared accordingly, but in 1851 he became a Catholic, and completed his education under Jesuit auspices. Graduated at the head of his class from St. John's College, Fordham, N. Y., in 1855, he acquired the master's degree two years later. He entered the diocesan seminary to prepare for the priesthood, but because of ill health abandoned his plan for a religious life. For a time he was secretary to Archbishop Hughes [*q.v.*], and during the same period he compiled articles for the *New American Cyclopaedia* and assisted its editor, George Ripley [*q.v.*], under whom he served an inspiring literary apprenticeship. He also gained some journalistic experience as a reporter on the *New York Tribune.* In 1865 he published *Reflections and Meditations Selected from the Writings of Fénelon,* and within two years of the death of Archbishop Hughes he undertook the preparation of a *Life of the Most Reverend John Hughes, D.D., First Archbishop of New York* (1866), making full use of the prelate's correspondence. Written with reasonable courage and a shrewd understanding of the redoubtable bishop, his problems, conflicts, and services, it remains an authoritative biography. In 1865 Hassard became editor of the newly established *Catholic World,* from which he was enticed by Charles A. Dana who was undertaking the editorship of the ill-starred *Chicago Republican.* On the failure of this journal (1866), Hassard returned to the *New York Tribune,* with which paper his life was thereafter identified. After Greeley's death, he acted temporarily as managing editor; but it was as an essayist and as music critic that he made his most distinctive contribution. Special representative of the *Tribune* at Bayreuth, he did much to make Wagner known in America through his criticisms, published first as letters in the *Tribune* and later as *Richard Wagner at Bayreuth: The Ring of the Niebelungs; a Description of its First Performance in August 1876* (1877). In 1875 he had illustrated his versatility by the publication of a pamphlet entitled *The Wonders of the Press,* and a short, popular *Life of Pope Pius IX.*

An ardent supporter of honest government, he lent a ready pen to political reform, relentlessly attacking municipal and national corruption. He was largely responsible for the solution of the mystery of the Tilden cipher dispatches. He defended local Catholic charitable institutions from attack by assigning accountants to make full investigations and publishing their reports. Believing in the necessity of civic education, he compiled *A History of the United States of America* (1878) which in abridged form was long used as a textbook in Catholic schools. At all times he could be depended upon by the editors of the *Catholic World* and the *American Catholic Quarterly Review* for reviews or clever essays on subjects of current interest. As New York correspondent of the London *Daily News,* he sympathetically interpreted America to English audiences until impaired health forced him to restrict his activities.

Never complaining and constantly occupied, Hassard spent several years in quest of health, always writing letters to the *Tribune,* whether from the shores of the Mediterranean or from Saranac Lake, from Southern California, France, or the Bahamas. Well-read in English, French, and German literature, he enjoyed his winter excursions especially when he could follow the trails of Thackeray and Pickwick and write of the various phases and extremes of English life (*A Pickwickian Pilgrimage,* 1881). In his fifty-second year he succumbed to tuberculosis, leaving a childless wife, Isabella Hargous Hassard, whom he had married in 1872. His funeral from St. Ann's Church, New York, was attended by churchmen, coreligionists with whom he was associated in charitable societies and in the Xavier Union, and coworkers with whom he was intimate at the editorial desk or at the Author's and Century clubs.

[*Cath. Encyc.*; *Illustrated Family Annual,* 1889; *Cath. World,* June 1888, June 1913; *N. Y. Times,* Apr. 19, 22, 1888; *N. Y. Tribune,* Apr. 19–22, 1888, including abstracts of editorial comments in other newspapers; J. B. Bishop, *Notes and Anecdotes of Many Years* (1925); Wm. Winter, *Old Shrines and Ivy* (1892); G. S. Greene and Louise B. Clarke, *The Greenes of R. I.* (1903).]

R. J. P.

HASSAUREK, FRIEDRICH (Oct. 8, 1831–Oct. 3, 1885), journalist, diplomat, and politician, was born in Vienna, Austria. Franz Hassaurek, his father, was a wealthy merchant and litterateur who speculated disastrously and died impoverished in 1836. His mother, Johanna Abele, a sister of Baron Vincenz von Abele, then married Leopold Markbreit, who sent Friedrich to the Piaristen Gymnasium. The boy proved a quick student and was editing a school paper at the outbreak of the revolution of 1848. Imbued with radical ideas, he joined the Student Legion and was slightly wounded fighting the imperial troops. After the failure of the revolution, he fled to Cincinnati, Ohio. Arriving in April 1849, he wrote articles for the German-American press and soon was appointed assistant editor of the *Ohio Staatszeitung* with an intermittently paid salary of $3.50 a week. Within a year he was able to establish with $100 borrowed capital the weekly *Hochwaechter,* through which the adolescent editor proclaimed vehemently the socialistic views of the most radical and anticlerical German revolutionists. In it he published serially his novel: *"Hierarchie und Aristokratie"* and waged a successful campaign against the fraudulent practices of agencies which were swindling German immigrants. Having become known as an impetuous and able public speaker in both German and English, he debated religious questions with Methodist ministers in 1852 and three years later successfully ran for the City Council as an Independent. Meanwhile, he had been studying law, and after his admission to the bar sold his newspaper. Almost at once he attracted attention as a lawyer by preventing the conviction for murder of Loeffler, an insane German criminal. Espousing ardently the anti-slavery cause, he organized the Republican party in Cincinnati, a Democratic stronghold, and by his brilliant oratory did much to attract to the new party the large German vote. A delegate to the Chicago convention which nominated Lincoln in 1860, he was rewarded by appointment in March 1861 as minister to Ecuador. At Quito he arranged the establishment of a mixed commission to settle the claims of both countries and served with distinction as American member. In 1864 he came home to campaign for Lincoln's reëlection and obtain the exchange of his half-brother, who was in Libby Prison. Returning to Ecuador in March 1865, he resigned after a year to become editor and part-owner of the *Tägliches Cincinnatier Volksblatt.* He had now lost his earlier socialistic beliefs and with great ardor opposed every policy which savored of paternalism, holding that the one essential function of government was the protection of private rights. Such views led him to criticize the Republican method of reconstructing the South, and in 1872 he joined the liberal movement which supported Greeley for the presidency. His backing of Tilden in 1876 caused a disagreement with the Republicans in control of the *Volksblatt,* and he retired from active editorship to spend a year traveling in Europe and writing delightful letters which the paper published. On his return he again became editor, and in disgust at both major parties conducted the paper on strictly non-partisan lines. In the hope of improving his broken health, he again went to Europe in 1882, accompanied by Eunice Marshall, his third wife. Though he still wrote steadily, his strength gradually failed until he died in Paris. A political orator and journalist of brilliant attainments, he was equally persuasive in English and German and possessed a sense of humor which made him especially popular as an after-dinner speaker. Out of his experience in Ecuador he wrote *Four Years among Spanish Americans* (1867; German translation, Dresden, 1887), a book full of accurate observation but lacking literary distinction. The same region provided local color for *The Secret of the Andes* (English edition 1879, German 1880), a fantastically sentimental and romantic novel. He also published an unimportant volume of *Gedichte* (1877).

[Armin Tenner, *Cincinnati Sonst und Jetzt* (1878); Max Burgheim, *Cincinnati in Wort und Bild* (1888); *Memoirs of Gustave Koerner* (2 vols., 1909), ed. by T. J. McCormack; *Das Ausland,* Dec. 14, 1885, p. 999; *Foreign Relations of the U. S.,* 1862–66; *Cincinnati Enquirer,* Sept. 20, Oct. 4, Oct. 20, 1885 and *Tägliches Cincinnatier Volksblatt,* Oct. 4, 21–23, 1885.]

W. L. W—t, Jr.

HASSELQUIST, TUVE NILSSON (Mar. 2, 1816–Feb. 4, 1891), Lutheran clergyman, editor, educator, was born at Hasslaröd, Ousby parish, Skane, Sweden, the son of a prosperous farmer, Nils Tufvasson, by his wife, Lissa Svensdotter. He was educated in the school at Kristianstad and at Lund University and was ordained into the ministry of the Church of Sweden in 1839. The large powerful man who served successively as curate in several parishes in the diocese of Lund gained the reputation of preaching sermons that soothed his hearers like a fresh breeze and of chanting like an angel. He was closely associated with, and influenced by, two pastors who were known for their Pietism and free-church tendencies, and throughout his life Hasselquist was an uncompromising critic of the state-church system, because "church and state are so interwoven that it is often difficult to distinguish between them" (*Det Rätta Hemlandet och Augustana,* October 1870). Through a letter from L. P. Esbjörn [*q.v.*], the only Swedish Lutheran pastor in the United States at the time, Hasselquist accepted the call to the Swedish Lutheran congregation at Galesburg, Ill., having been granted a leave of absence for three years from the State Church. He arrived at Galesburg, Oct. 28, 1852, and with the exception of a visit in the summer of 1870, partly for the purpose of recruiting men for the ministry, he never returned to his native land. He quickly adapted himself to the ways of his adopted country and became a leader in the Synod of Northern Illinois and in the Augustana Synod, serving as president of the latter body from 1860, when it was founded, to 1870, and as president of Augustana College and Theological Seminary from 1863 to 1891. He was undoubtedly the ablest leader and most versatile personality produced by the Swedish Lutheran Church in the United States, and his influence extended to other synods. Through the papers *Hemlandet,* which he founded at Galesburg, Jan. 3, 1855, and *Det Rätta Hemlandet,* in July 1856, he placed an enduring stamp on Swedish-American Lutheranism. He directed the editorial policies of the latter paper and of its successor, *Augustana,* the official synodical organ, until 1889. Although essentially a man of peace, he became more controversial with the passing years and with the increasing opposition to the Augustana Synod. He was a strong believer in centralization, advocating one synod, one college, one paper, and one central government, and his influence was probably decisive in checking the trend toward sectional and conference particularism. He favored the affiliation of the Augustana Synod with the General Council in 1870 and the transition from the use of Swedish to English as speedily as consistent with the obligations to the Swedish immigrants.

As a college president Hasselquist was loved by the students, who consulted with him as with a father and spoke of him as the patriarch of the synod. In spite of serious deficiencies as a parliamentarian, his winning personality claimed the respect and admiration of all although some thought he was too "free." In the earlier years of his ministry at the Sunday morning service he would appear dressed in a white linen coat, and as he walked to the front of the church he would sing a song in which the congregation joined. In the pulpit he was equally informal, often interrupting his sermon by singing a hymn. He saw no danger to Lutheran doctrine if the liturgy and certain forms were laid aside, although he was more conservative in his declining years. On May 24, 1852, he married Eva Helena Cervin of Kristianstad, a cultured woman of remarkable gifts and fine character, who adapted herself to pioneering as readily as her refined and scholarly husband.

[There is ample material for a comprehensive biography of Hasselquist in the manuscript collection of the Augustana Book Concern, Rock Island, Ill. In addition there are many important letters from him in the Wieselgren papers in the Gothenburg City library. G. M. Stephenson, *The Founding of the Augustana Synod 1850–60* (1927) gives citations to volumes containing selections from his correspondence. A collection of sermons has been published by the Augustana Book Concern. Erik Norelius, *T. N. Hasselquist. Lefnadsteckning* (n.d.), and Nils Forsander, *Lifsbilder ur Augustana-Synodens Historia* (vol. I, 1915), are tentative biographies.] G. M. S.

HASSLER, FERDINAND RUDOLPH (Oct. 7, 1770–Nov. 20, 1843), geodesist, mathematician, first superintendent of the United States Coast Survey, was born in Aarau, Switzerland, the only son of Jakob Hassler, a well-to-do watch manufacturer. Becoming interested in mathematics and geodesy while studying under Johann Georg Tralles of Hamburg at the University of Bern, he engaged in geodetic field work in Switzerland until troubled political conditions led him to join a land company which planned to form a Swiss colony in the southern United States, and in 1805 he emigrated to America with his wife and children. Although intending to take up farming, he brought with him a library of several thousand volumes and a number of scientific instruments. On his arrival in Philadelphia, he found the company financially embarrassed, leaving the would-be colonists stranded.

Hassler's interest in science soon brought him into contact with the members of the American Philosophical Society, who were responsible for recommending to President Jefferson a survey of the coasts of the United States. Upon executive recommendation Congress, on Feb. 10, 1807, passed a law authorizing such a survey. Plans were then invited for carrying it into effect; a commission, after considering the plans proposed, accepted Hassler's; and he was nominated to undertake the work. Because of troubled political conditions both at home and abroad, however, the active prosecution of the survey was held in abeyance.

Meanwhile, on Feb. 14, 1807, Hassler was appointed acting professor of mathematics at West Point. When, in 1809, the secretary of war decided that the law did not authorize the employment of civilians at the Military Academy, he became professor of natural philosophy and mathematics at Union College, but resigned in July 1811, upon being asked by the secretary of the treasury to proceed to London to procure the necessary instruments needed for starting the United States Coast Survey. The War of 1812 began soon after his arrival in London and it was not till 1815 that he returned to the United States with the instruments.

In 1816 he was formally appointed superintendent of the Coast Survey and immediately began field operations. These were continued until April 1818, when the law authorizing the survey of the coast was so modified that only naval and military officers could be employed in the work. This legislation excluded Hassler and led to a practical suspension of the Survey. During the following year he was engaged as one of the United States astronomers in settling the Northeastern boundary, but he spent the next decade farming, not very successfully, in New York state, teaching, writing mathematical textbooks, and, for a time, performing the duties of gager in the New York Custom House. In 1830 he returned to scientific work for the government as superintendent of Weights and Measures, to which position he was appointed by President Jackson. Two years later the Coast Survey was reëstablished and Hassler was again appointed superintendent. Although he was now sixty-two, he threw himself into the work with enthusiasm, again assembling the necessary instruments and training assistants, and himself carrying on observations in the field. While engaged in field work in the late fall of 1843 he became ill and died shortly afterward in Philadelphia, where he was buried.

As organizer and superintendent of the first scientific bureau under the government, Hassler had to contend with many difficulties. Although the survey of the coast was generally regarded as a problem to be attacked by ordinary surveying methods, Hassler's scientific temperament and familiarity with the best practice of geodetic surveying in Europe made him realize that the survey would possess permanent value only if it were carried out in accordance with the highest scientific standards. Time has justified the soundness of his ideas: the extension of the survey of the coast, to the present day, follows his plan, and the field work he carried out more than a century ago is of such high precision that it still forms part of the basic network.

Confident of his own ability, which was abundantly exhibited in coping with various technical problems arising in the conduct of the Coast Survey and in the design and improvement of various geodetic surveying instruments, he was impatient of what he considered as hampering and unnecessarily restrictive measures on the part of the administrative authorities in connection with the supervision and auditing of the accounts of the Survey. Consequently much of his energy during the last years of his life was expended in controversies over details regarding financial procedure. Conscious of his own integrity and wholly unfamiliar with the art of lobbying, he was not always politic in dealing with his administrative superiors or with Congressional committees. His sincerity, his devotion to the work, and his unquestioned scientific ability, however, won him the esteem and support of the scientific and political leaders of the time.

In 1798 Hassler married Marianne Gaillard. As the mother of nine children and the wife of a man whose greatest enthusiasm was for science and who at different times was in straitened financial circumstances, Mrs. Hassler's life was not easy. The want of society while they lived on the farm in New York state was an especial hardship to her, and accordingly, about 1823, when the two older girls were able to manage the household, she left home never to return. She spent the rest of her life first with friends and then with one or another of her children. Hassler saw her but once again, a few years after she had left.

[Letters written or received by Hassler, in the Ford Coll., N. Y. Pub. Lib.; *Principal Docs. Relating to the Survey of the Coast of the U. S. and the Construction of Uniform Standards and Weights* (3 vols., 1834–36); *North Am. Rev.*, Jan. 1836, Apr. 1842; *Translation from the German of the Memoirs of Ferdinand Rudolph Hassler, by Emil Zchokke, pub. in Aarau, Switzerland, 1877, with Supplementary Docs.* (1882); *Centennial Celebration of the U. S. Coast and Geodetic Survey* (1916); Florian Cajori, *The Chequered Career of Ferdinand Rudolph Hassler* (1929); *Niles' National Register*, Nov. 25, 1843.] H. A. M.

HASTINGS, SAMUEL DEXTER (July 24, 1816–Mar. 26, 1903), reformer, born at Leicester, Worcester County, Mass., was the son of Simon and Elizabeth (McIntosh) Hastings and a lineal descendant of Thomas Hastings who emigrated from England in 1634 and settled in Watertown, Mass. His early youth was spent in Boston; at the age of fourteen he moved to Philadelphia and there humbly began his mercantile career. Aided by a friend from Leicester, he was established in his own business at the age of twenty-one. During his sixteen years in Philadelphia he maintained a deep interest in social and religious questions. In 1835 he began his long connection with the anti-slavery movement that brought him into intimate association with William Lloyd Garrison, Wendell Phillips, and John G. Whittier. He was one of the active founders of the Liberty party in Pennsylvania and at the age of twenty-four was chairman of the state central committee. On Aug. 1, 1837, he married Margaretta Shubert and in 1846 moved to Walworth County in Wisconsin Territory. Two years later he was elected to the first state legislature by a large majority. In the first session he delivered a memorable speech against slavery and was the author of the resolutions which committed the new state to its opposition to the extension of the slave trade. He moved from Walworth County to La Crosse in 1852 and later to Trempealeau on the Mississippi. In 1856 he was returned to the legislature and the following year was elected treasurer of the state. He held this office for eight years, ably managing the state finances during the difficult period of the Civil War.

During his long career Hastings was a zealous foe of liquor and tobacco. He had spoken frequently, had encouraged legislation, and was an active member of many organizations to suppress these alleged evils. In the Sons of Temperance he became Grand Worthy Patriarch of Wisconsin and was six times elected Right Worthy Grand Templar, the highest office in the international order of Good Templars. In his youth he had been an ardent Presbyterian but withdrew from the church because of his anti-slavery views. He became prominent in the Congregational Church, was influential in establishing a free Congregational church in Philadelphia and, although remaining a layman, became moderator of the Wisconsin state convention. To this convention he made the remarkable address based on the text, "whatsoever ye do, do all to the glory of God," in which he effectively demonstrated that tobacco could not be used to the glory of God. He spoke for prohibition in nearly every state of the Union, in Canada, in Australia and New Zealand, and six times crossed the Atlantic to further the cause. For many years he contributed to prohibition and anti-slavery papers and in 1883 edited the speeches of John B. Finch under the title, *The People versus the Liquor Traffic*. He was for many years a member of the executive committee and treasurer of the national Prohibition party. Honest men sometimes quarreled with his methods, but he was never troubled by doubts of the value of his ends or his means to them. Throughout a long and active life he labored indefatigably for two great purposes: the emancipation of the negroes of the South and the imposition of prohibition upon the English-speaking peoples of the world. He died at Evanston, Ill.

[*Trans. Wis. Acad. Sci., Arts, and Letters,* 1903, pp. 686–90; *Internat. Good Templar,* Oct. 1889, *Columbian Biog. Dict.,* Wis. vol. (1895); *Proc. Wis. Hist. Soc.,* vol. XIV, pt. 2 (1904); L. N. H. Buckminster, *The Hastings Memorial* (1866); *Wis. State Jour.* (Madison), Mar. 26, 27, 1903.] F. M.

HASTINGS, SERRANUS CLINTON (Nov. 22, 1814–Feb. 18, 1893), jurist, was born in Jefferson County, N. Y. His ancestors emigrated from England and settled in Rhode Island early in the seventeenth century. His father, Robert Collins Hastings, commanded an army of soldiers at Sacketts Harbor in the War of 1812. His mother was Patience Brayton. He studied for six years at Gouverneur Academy, New York, and at the age of twenty became the principal of the Norwich Academy, Chenango County, N. Y. He commenced the study of law with Charles Thorpe of Norwich, but in a few months he moved to Lawrenceburg, Ind., where in 1834 he entered the law office of Daniel S. Major, under whom he completed his legal studies. In December 1836 he was admitted to the bar and in the following January moved to the Black Hawk Purchase (now the State of Iowa). In 1837 Governor Dodge of Wisconsin appointed him justice of the peace of the territory between Burlington and Davenport. When Iowa was erected into a separate territory, Hastings was elected on the Democratic ticket to the first territorial legislature. He became president of the Territorial Council and in 1846 became Iowa's first representative in Congress. At the expiration of his term in Congress he was appointed chief justice of the supreme court of Iowa, which position he resigned to go to California during the gold rush of 1849.

Within six months of his arrival in California Hastings was appointed by the legislature as first chief justice of the newly formed state supreme court. He was peculiarly well qualified by nature and experience to establish such a court since much of California's constitution had been modeled after the constitutions of New York and Iowa. He performed efficiently the difficult task of administering the law in a jurisdiction which was undergoing a transition from the Spanish to the American legal system. In 1851 he was elected attorney-general and while still holding this office he assumed private practice. He soon acquired a large fortune by successful investments in real estate and by his law practice. In 1878 he provided an endowment of $100,000 for the establishment of the Hastings' College of Law which was to be situated in San Francisco and affiliated with the state university at Berkeley. The charter provisions were very liberal. Instruction was not to be confined to those students who intended to become lawyers, but was to be extended to any one who wished it. The college proved to be one of the most important educational institutions in the state of California. Hastings married Azalea Brodt, at Muscatine, Iowa, in 1845. She died in Pau, France, in 1876. In 1885 he married Lillian Knust, from whom he was divorced five years later but subsequently remarried. At the time of his death he had given the greater portion of his wealth to his children and to educational endowments.

[Oscar T. Shuck's *Bench and Bar in Cal.* (1889) contains perhaps the fullest account of Hastings' career. There is a brief sketch of his life written by William W. Morrow in *Cal. Jurisprudence,* vol. I (1921), p. xl, and two short accounts in the *Hist. and Contemporary Rev. of Bench and Bar in Cal.* (1926). There is also a short sketch of his life by Thos. P. Madden in *Representative and Leading Men of the Pacific* (1870), ed. by Oscar T. Shuck. For an obituary notice see the *San Francisco Chronicle,* Feb. 19, 1893.] J. V. L.

HASTINGS, THOMAS (Oct. 15, 1784–May 15, 1872), hymn-writer and composer, was born at Washington, Litchfield County, Conn., the third of the eleven children of Dr. Seth Hastings, a farmer and physician, and Eunice Parmele. He was descended from Thomas Hastings of Ipswich, England, who emigrated to Massachusetts Bay Colony in 1634 and settled at Watertown. Thomas removed with his father to Clinton, Oneida County, N. Y. He developed an early interest in music, but he had little or no opportunity for cultivating it. Nevertheless, at the age of eighteen he was leading the village choir and in 1806 he began teaching music. In 1816, with Solomon Warriner, he published *Musica Sacra; or Springfield and Utica Collections United,* consisting of Psalms, hymn tunes, anthems, and chants. This book passed through several editions and was reissued as late as 1836. The original *Springfield Collection,* a hundred and fifty pages of sacred music from the works of European authors, had been issued by Warriner in 1813; the exact date of the publication by Hastings of the *Utica Collection,* a much smaller collection, but of original tunes, is not known. That it was compiled for the Handel and Burney Society, under whose patronage it was published, is stated in the introduction to the third edition (1822) of *Musica Sacra.* In 1817 Hastings published a *Musical Reader,* reissued in 1819. In 1817, also, he removed to Troy. He went later to Albany, and in 1823 he settled in Utica, where he conducted a religious journal, the *Western Recorder,* through the columns of which he was able to make known his special views on church music. During these years at Utica he published *The Union Minstrel, for the Use of Sabbath Schools* (1830), and with Lowell Mason, *Spiritual Songs for Social Worship* (1831).

In 1832 Hastings was called to New York by a committee from twelve churches, who urged him to come and put into practice in that city the theories for better church music which he had been promulgating. This he did, and for forty years gave himself unreservedly to his important task. During several years of this period he served as choirmaster in the Bleecker Street Presbyterian Church. In 1836 he published *The Musical Miscellany* (2 vols.), and, in collaboration with William Patton, *The Christian Psalmist, or Watts Psalms and Hymns* (2 vols.), with copious selections from other sources. Under his own editorship he later published *The Manhattan Collection* (1837); *The Sacred Lyre* (1840); and *Selah* (1856). With W. B. Bradbury he compiled *The Psalmodist* (1844), *New York Choralist* (1847), *Mendelssohn Collection* (1849), and *Psalmista* (1851); and with his son, Thomas S. Hastings, *Church Melodies* (1858). Aside from these musical works he also published. *Dissertation on Musical Taste* (1822, 1853), *Devotional Hymns and Religious Poems* (1850), *History of Forty Choirs* (1854), and *Sacred Praise* (1856). In 1858 he received the degree of doctor of music from the University of the City of New York, being one of the first in America to receive this degree.

It can readily be seen from the list of his published works how faithfully Hastings toiled through the years to carry out the purpose so near his heart. His work in New York seems to have quite paralleled that of Lowell Mason in New England. The numerous hymn books published by Hastings were of high rank for their time and successfully carried out the ambition of their author and compiler. Of Hastings' own tunes, of which he is supposed to have written about a thousand, it can be said that next to those of Lowell Mason they were the best of his time in America. They included "Ortonville," "Rock of Ages" (Toplady), "Retreat," "Zion," and many others. It is not always possible to identify his hymns for he often published them under assumed names, thinking that the public would have greater respect for the music if the composers' names bore a foreign aspect. In addition to writing tunes to words, he often wrote words to tunes, thus making possible the use of certain melodies for which there were then no hymns of appropriate meter. From this beginning he continued until he became one of the acknowledged hymn-writers of the country. Two of his best-known hymns are "Hail to the Brightness of Zion's Glad Morning," and "He that Goeth Forth with Weeping." Showing the spirit of the true musical educator and pioneer, he devoted many pages in all of his earlier works to the rudiments of vocal music, comprising the most elementary instruction in notation, scales, and rhythms.

Hastings was of unusual appearance as he was an albino and always gave the impression of being old. He lived long and worked diligently until within a few days of his death. He was married, Sept. 15, 1822, to Mary Seymour, in Buffalo. He died in New York City. His grandson, Thomas Hastings [*q.v.*], attained distinction as an architect.

[F. H. Hastings, *Family Record of Dr. Seth Hastings, Sr.* (1899); sketch in F. J. Metcalf, *Am. Writers and Compilers of Sacred Music* (1925), reprinted in the *Choir Leader* and the *Choir Herald* for Feb. 1916; Josiah Miller, *Our Hymns: Their Authors and Origins* (1866); J. T. Howard, *Our Am. Music* (1931); L. F. Benson, *The English Hymn* (1915); the *N. Y. Musical Gazette,* Apr. 1873.]

W. T. U—n.

HASTINGS, THOMAS (Mar. 11, 1860–Oct. 22, 1929), architect, was born in New York City, where his father, Thomas Samuel Hastings, was pastor of the West Presbyterian Church. A noted clergyman, he was later a professor, and from 1887 until his retirement in 1897, president of the Union Theological Seminary. Thomas Hastings' mother, Fanny de Groot, came from Dutch and English stock long in America. Hastings' immigrant ancestor, Thomas Hastings, came from Ipswich, England, in 1634 and settled in Watertown, Mass., where he served as town clerk, selectman, representative, and deacon, dying in 1685. From him Thomas Hastings was seventh in a line of distinguished clergymen and doctors. His grandfather, Thomas Hastings [*q.v.*], was a well-known composer of sacred music. To this background may be due the grandson's scholarly and even academic approach to his profession.

After spending a short time at Columbia Hastings left for Paris, where he entered the École des Beaux-Arts, studying in the atelier of Jules André. While in Paris he made the acquaintance of John M. Carrère [*q.v.*], his future partner. Upon his graduation and receipt of the French government *diplôme,* 1884, he returned to New York and entered the office of McKim, Mead & White, where he found Carrère at work. In 1886 they formed a partnership, and received as their first important commission (1887) the Ponce de Leon Hotel in Florida, for Henry M. Flagler. (For the further works of the firm, consult the article on John Merven Carrère.) In a partnership based on as close cooperation as that between Carrère and Hastings it is impossible to analyze all of the qualities contributed by each member individually. It has sometimes been said that Carrère was the chief originating mind. Such a claim is not strictly true. It would be more just to say that if Carrère's mind was more daring and more original in dealing with large elements, the sureness of taste, the careful execution and the delicacy of detail which characterized the greater part of the firm's work after Carrère's death would seem to indicate that at least some of these same qualities in the work of the earlier period came from the influence of Hastings.

After the death of Carrère the firm continued, under the same name, to preserve the tradition which it had built. In general, changing fashions and economic conditions produced a growing departure from the strict French inspiration of the earlier work and fostered the development of a more eclectic classicism. The Tower of Jewels at the Panama Pacific Exposition at San Francisco, 1914, was characteristic of this trend in its use of the classic orders to give the right character of gaiety for an exposition building. The Richmond County Court House, Staten Island, N. Y., with a dignified Corinthian colonnade, and the Frick house in New York City, with its Louis Sixteenth spirit, much modified in the picture gallery wing, are typical of this change. Other characteristic work of this time includes the building erected for the Knoedler Galleries, on Fifth Avenue, New York, with a façade inspired by Ely House in London; the Alexander building, in the same block, with exquisite graffito decoration, and the jewel-like chapel of St. Ambrose in the Cathedral of St. John the Divine.

The Memorial Amphitheatre in the national cemetery at Arlington, Va., is in a style almost Palladian classic, with its sweeping, elliptical colonnade. It is one of the many monuments designed by Hastings. Noteworthy among the others are: the Princeton Battle Monument, at Princeton, N. J., the base of the Lafayette monument in the court of the Louvre in Paris, and in Madison Square, New York, the Altar of Liberty and Victory Arch, built out of temporary materials to celebrate the victorious return of soldiers from the Great War in 1919. Hastings was also the architect of the permanent memorial flag pole later set up on the site of the Altar of Liberty, and of an ambitious design for a war memorial in Central Park, New York, never erected. He was consulting architect for the Cunard Company offices, 1919 (B. W. Morris, architect), and later (1923) the designer of the great office building for the Standard Oil Company, at the foot of Broadway, New York. The latter was a simple building on an irregular plot, capped by a pyramidal-topped tower, rich with classic detail.

Hastings was interested in city planning and with his partner was responsible for the city plan of Hartford, Conn., 1911, as well as a layout for Mt. Vernon Square and the civic center of Baltimore, Md. In the period after Carrère's death he was the designer of the industrial town for the United States Steel Company at Duluth, Minn. His interest in city beautification is exemplified in the Pulitzer fountain and the architectural treatment of the Plaza in New York City, the commission for which was won in competition. In the last few months of his life he completed the work on Devonshire House, London, a palatial apartment house done in association with C. H. Reilly, who gave Hastings credit for all of the details and the ornament. Hastings' last completed work was the reconstruction of the Senate chamber in the national Capitol at Washington. At the time of his death he was at work upon the architectural treatment of the Tri-Borough Bridge, New York City.

Hastings was of medium height, thick set, with an almost military bearing enlivened by a constant expression of energy. An enthusiastic worker, he made it a point, however busy he might be with executive matters, to draw or design every day. Genial and courteous to every one, he was widely liked both in and out of his profession. He was married, Apr. 30, 1900, to Helen R. Benedict, daughter of Commodore E. C. Benedict of Greenwich, Conn. He died after an operation for appendicitis at the Nassau Hospital, Mineola, L. I. His homes were in New York City and at Old Westbury, L. I. He was a member of many societies and one of the founders of the Federal Art Commission. On June 26, 1922, he was awarded the Royal Gold Medal of the Royal Institute of British Architects, an honor only twice before awarded to an American. He was also a chevalier of the Legion of Honor. He was the author of several magazine articles and a paper on modern architecture read before the Royal Institute of British Architects in 1913. With Ralph Adams Cram and Claude Bragdon he published *Six Lectures on Architecture* (1917), in which the section written by Hastings is a clear presentation of his own belief in the importance of an urbane, scholarly, and respectful attitude toward the tradition of the past, and specifically, his belief in the importance to modern American architecture of the classic tradition.

[L. N. H. Buckminster, *The Hastings Memorial* (1866); F. H. Hastings, *Family Record of Dr. Seth Hastings, Sr.* (1899); *Architectural Record,* Jan. 1910, Dec. 1929; the *Builder* (London), June 30, 1922; *Architecture,* Dec. 1929; the *Architect,* Nov. 1929; the *Am. Architect,* Dec. 1929; *N. Y. Times,* Oct. 23, 1929; and obituaries by C. H. Reilly in the following English periodicals: *Jour. of the Royal Inst. of British Architects,* Nov. 9, 1929; the *Builder,* Nov. 1, 1929; *Architect and Building News,* Nov. 1, 1929; *Architect's Jour.,* Oct. 30, 1929; *Carpenter and Builder,* Nov. 1, 1929.]

T. F. H.

HASWELL, ANTHONY (Apr. 6, 1756–May 22, 1816), printer, editor, ballad writer, was born at Portsmouth, England, son of William and Elizabeth Haswell. With his father and an elder brother he arrived at Boston at the end of 1769 or the beginning of 1770, and was apprenticed to a potter. He witnessed the "Boston Massacre," Mar. 5, 1770, and soon joined the Sons of Liberty, writing some crude songs which were sung at their meetings. He probably participated in the "Tea Party," Dec. 16, 1773. One of his songs led to his release by the potter to whom he was bound in order to become apprenticed to Isaiah Thomas [*q.v.*], the printer. When Thomas moved to Worcester, in April 1775, Haswell went with him. He served in the Revolutionary army during 1776–77. In June 1777 he became the publisher of the paper which Thomas had founded, the *Massachusetts Spy,* which on Aug. 14, 1777, appeared with a new title, *Haswell's Massachusetts Spy or American Oracle of Liberty.* In June 1778 he relinquished the paper and its publication was resumed by Thomas, Haswell remaining in his employ. Two years later *The New-England Almanack for 1781* appeared with the imprint, "Worcester: Printed by Anthony Haswell," but it was actually printed by the press of Hudson & Goodwin, Hartford, Conn., though Haswell was living at Worcester at the time. He moved to Hartford early in 1781 and was employed as a printer by George Goodwin. A year later, 1782, he moved to Springfield, Mass., where he and Elisha Babcock, a paper-maker, established a press. On May 14, 1782, they issued the first number of a weekly newspaper, the *Massachusetts Gazette or the Springfield and Northampton Weekly Advertiser*; and in addition they published many small books and pamphlets. After a year the partnership was dissolved and Haswell went to Bennington, Vt., where he spent the rest of his life. Vermont had not yet been admitted to the Union. In all its territory there was only one small press, from which was issued the only newspaper. On the western side, from the Massachusetts line to Canada, there was no printer. A committee from the Vermont legislature urged Haswell to establish a newspaper at Bennington, offering him as an inducement control of the post-offices of the commonwealth. He became the first postmaster general of Vermont, holding the office probably until the admission of the state into the Union. The first issue of the *Vermont Gazette, or Freemen's Depository* appeared June 5, 1783. Haswell kept the paper going with brief suspensions until his death in 1816, and it was continued for many years thereafter by his sons. He was less successful with another paper, the *Herald of Vermont, or Rutland Courier,* which he started at Rutland, June 25, 1792. Its career was ended in September by a fire which destroyed the press. In addition to these two journals, he edited and published, at various times, the *Monthly Miscellany, or Vermont Magazine* (April–September 1794), *The Congressional Register,* a monthly royal octavo of sixty-four pages (January–June, 1805), and *The Mental Repast, or Rays of Light from the Sun of Science* (January–June 1808). Books and pamphlets published by him exceed two hundred in number. Some of the books were compilations of prose and verse, original and selected, arranged for the benefit of his children. He compiled the *Memoirs of Captain Matthew Phelps* which he published in 1802.

Haswell was an early victim of the Sedition Act of July 14, 1798. His trial, which took place in the federal circuit court, at Windsor, Vt., in May 1800, was really a political persecution. He was sentenced to two months' imprisonment and a fine of $200. In 1844 Congress returned the fine to his heirs. Haswell was a prolific writer of doggerel ballads, through which he wielded extraordinary influence. He was twice married; his first wife, whom he married Apr. 23, 1778, was Lydia Baldwin of Worcester, who died Apr. 30, 1799. By her he had ten children. On Sept. 30, 1799, he married Betsey Rice, by whom he had seven children. She died Apr. 26, 1815. Haswell died the following year, in Bennington, at the age of sixty.

[Haswell Papers in the State Library of Vermont; files of the *Vermont Gazette* and Haswell's other periodicals; John Spargo, *Anthony Haswell, Printer, Patriot, Ballader . . . with a Selection of His Ballads and an Annotated Bibliog. of His Imprints* (1925); Francis Wharton, *State Trials of the U. S.* (1849); A. M.

Hemenway, *Vermont Quart. Gazetteer*, Oct. 1861; Isaac Jennings, *Memorials of a Century* (1869).]

J. S—o.

HASWELL, CHARLES HAYNES (May 22, 1809–May 12, 1907), engineer, was born in North Moore Street, New York City. His father, Charles Haswell, was a native of Dublin, at one time in the British diplomatic service; his mother, Dorothea Haynes, came of a prominent colonial family in Barbados. Reared in a cultured home, the boy received a classical education, graduating from Joseph Nelson's Collegiate Institute; then entered the shops of James P. Allaire [*q.v.*], the foremost steam-engine builder of the day. Here he became in time chief draftsman and designer. In 1829 he was married to Ann Elizabeth Burns, who bore him three sons and three daughters.

On Feb. 19, 1836, in pursuance of the purpose of Secretary Mahlon Dickerson, to introduce steam power into the navy, Haswell was commissioned to submit designs for engines for the frigate *Fulton*, then being built, and on July 12 he was appointed chief engineer to superintend their construction. He thus became the first engineer in the United States navy. The engines, installed during the summer of 1837, were double engines 50 x 108 inches, with cast-iron cranks and shafts, driving a side wheel 22 feet 9 inches in diameter, and with 11 feet face. The boilers, designed by Charles W. Copeland [*q.v.*], were of copper—standard practice at that time. In 1839–42, with Copeland, Haswell designed and supervised the building of the machinery for the naval vessels *Mississippi, Missouri,* and *Michigan,* in one instance going personally to the mould loft and laying out the shape and dimensions of each plate entering into the construction of the boilers he had designed. He took a leading part in the agitation by the naval engineers which resulted in the passage by Congress, in 1842, of an act providing for a force of engineers to be headed by a "skillful and scientific engineer in chief." The man first selected for this important post, Gilbert L. Thompson, was a lawyer and a business man, with no engineering experience. He indorsed a scheme to dispose of and thereby conceal the smoke from the boilers of a ship by discharging it into the water raised by the paddle wheels, and in the spring of 1843 ordered that the plan be put into operation on the *Missouri,* of which Haswell was then chief engineer. Haswell protested vigorously and pointed out the utter impracticability of the project, but he was over-ruled, and on the failure of the attempt, suspended from duty. The injustice of the suspension was soon recognized, and reinstatement offered him on condition that he apologize, whereupon he replied: "I would rather suffer injustice from another than to be unjust to myself." Taken from sea duty for a time, he was assigned to designing the machinery for four revenue cutters. The following year, however, he was fully reinstated, and succeeded Thompson as engineer in chief of the navy. In this capacity he drew up the general order of Feb. 26, 1845, defining the duties and responsibilities of the engineer afloat, which was for more than fifty years the basis for the navy's "steam instructions," and was instrumental in obtaining the passage of the Act of 1845 which fixed the relative rank of engineers and naval officers. In 1846 he placed slabs of zinc in the boilers of the *Princeton* to direct oxidation from the boiler plates, anticipating by nearly thirty years the introduction of this idea as a new invention in England. In 1852, as a result of overwork, controversy, and chronic dyspepsia, he returned to civil life.

For fifty-five years he was a consulting engineer in New York City. He designed commercial vessels, foundations for high buildings, harbor cribs and fills; was surveyor of steamers for Lloyd's and the New York underwriters, and a trustee of the New York and Brooklyn Bridge. From 1855 to 1858 he was a member of the Common Council of the city, and for a year its president; he served as consulting engineer for various departments of the city government. During the Civil War he saw active service under General Burnside.

Distinguished as he was in the history of the steam navy, Haswell was best known, probably, for his *Mechanic's and Engineer's Pocket Book,* first issued in 1842. This work, which gained the sobriquet, "The Engineer's Bible," carried through its seventy-fourth edition in 1913, with a total sale of more than 146,000 copies. Haswell's other professional publications included *Mechanics Tables* (1854) and *Mensuration and Practical Geometry* (1856). He also issued a work on *Bookkeeping* (1860), and in 1896 he was persuaded to publish *Reminiscences of an Octogenarian of the City of New York, 1816 to 1860,* which he had written down some years before. In 1898 and 1899 he contributed "Reminiscences of Early Marine Steam Engine Construction and Steam Navigation in the United States of America from 1807 to 1850" to the *Transactions of the Institute of Naval Architects* (London). He was internationally known and esteemed. Actively engaged in engineering until the end of his life, he died as the result of a fall, ten days before his ninety-eighth birthday.

[*Who's Who in America,* 1906–07; *Trans. Am. Soc. Civil Engineers,* vol. LXI (1908); *Trans. Am. Soc. Mechanical Engineers,* vol. XXIX (1907); *Jour. Am. Soc. Naval Engineers,* May 1907; F. M. Bennett, *The Steam Navy of the U. S.* (1896); *Minutes of Proc. of the Inst. of Civil Engineers* (London), vol. CLXX (1907); *Cosmopolitan,* May 1905; *Scientific American,* May 25, 1907; W. T. Bonner, *New York, The World's Metropolis* (1924); *N. Y. Times,* May 13, 1907.]

F. V. L.

HATCH, EDWARD (Dec. 23, 1832–Apr. 11, 1889), soldier, was born in Bangor, Me., the son of Nathaniel and Mary Elizabeth (Scott) Hatch. He married Evelyn Barrington of Philadelphia, Pa. After attending the schools of his native city he entered Norwich University, Vermont, in 1846, remaining two years. Determined to become a sailor, he made one voyage, but then, deciding to become a lumberman, he moved to Iowa. In the first summer of the Civil War, on Aug. 12, 1861, he was elected captain of a troop of the 2nd Iowa Cavalry, and after passing through all intermediate grades was commissioned colonel on June 13, 1862. The efficiency, excellent organization, and careful training of this distinguished regiment was largely the work of Hatch. He saw his first important service with the Western army, commanding his regiment at New Madrid, Island No. 10, and Booneville. At Iuka, Corinth, and Coffeeville he commanded a cavalry brigade. In the spring of 1863, Grant began his successful advance against Vicksburg, and as a means of diverting attention and to cut the hostile communications from the east, he sent a cavalry raiding force into central Mississippi under the command of Colonel Grierson. This force started from La Grange, Apr. 17, with three regiments, and on Apr. 21, Hatch was detached with one regiment to destroy the railroad between Columbus and Macon and then return to La Grange. He had a sharp action at Columbus, but completed successfully his task of destruction and returned to La Grange on Apr. 26. His conduct on this occasion attracted the favorable notice of his superiors (*Personal Memoirs of U. S. Grant,* vol. I, 1885, p. 488) and was partly responsible for the recommendation the following year that he be made a brigadier-general. During the fall of 1863 he was engaged in commanding a cavalry raiding force operating in Alabama.

After the fall of Atlanta he was given command of a part of Sherman's cavalry organized into a division and ordered to march to Tennessee and join the army of Thomas which was expecting an invasion of that state by the Confederate general Hood. Hatch's division was placed along the Tennessee River to observe Hood and delay his movements; it came into contact with Hood's cavalry as Hood advanced. Hatch commanded his division at the battles of Franklin and Nashville, distinguishing himself by his courage and ability. He was made brigadier-general of volunteers, Apr. 27, 1864; and brevet major-general of volunteers, Dec. 15, 1864, for gallant and meritorious services in the battles before Nashville.

Mustered out of the volunteer service, Jan. 15, 1866, he was commissioned colonel of the 9th United States Cavalry on July 28 of that year and brevetted brigadier-general and major-general United States Army, Mar. 2, 1867. As colonel of the 9th Cavalry he was in command, for a time, of the Department of Arizona and New Mexico. He was chairman of a commission which in 1878 concluded a treaty with the Ute Indians whereby they relinquished part of their reservation in Colorado. In 1880 he took the field against the Apache chief Victorio, who had escaped from the Mescalero Indian Reservation, but did not succeed in capturing him. During his career Hatch took part in forty battles and engagements. He was an able soldier, a man of decision, firm of character and with a well-balanced judgment. He died in his fifty-seventh year, at Fort Robinson, Nebr., from the effects of an accident.

[W. A. Ellis, *Norwich Univ., 1819–1911* (1911), II, 470; L. D. Ingersoll, *Iowa and the Rebellion* (1867); *Battles and Leaders of the Civil War,* vols. II and IV (1888); F. V. Greene, *The Mississippi* (1882), in Campaigns of the Civil War; F. B. Heitman, *Hist. Reg. and Dict. U. S. Army* (1903), vol. I; C. C. Rister, *The Southwestern Frontier 1865–81* (1928); *Appletons' Ann. Cyc.,* 1889; *Ann. Report Commissioner of Indian Affairs,* 1879, 1880; *Iowa State Register,* Apr. 12, 1889; *Army and Navy Jour.,* Apr. 13, 20, 1889; *Army and Navy Reg.,* Apr. 20, 1889.]

J. W. W.

HATCH, JOHN PORTER (Jan. 9, 1822–Apr. 12, 1901), soldier, was born at Oswego, N. Y., the descendant of a Kentish family which came to the American colonies early in the seventeenth century. His parents were Moses Porter Hatch and Hannah Reed. At eighteen he entered the United States Military Academy, from which in 1845 he graduated seventeenth in a class of forty-one. His graduation took him as a brevet second lieutenant to service with the 3rd Infantry in the military occupation of Texas. In the opening weeks of the Mexican War, he fought in the principal encounters of Taylor's campaign in the north of Mexico. After the battle of Resaca de la Palma, he transferred to the Mounted Rifles and with them he fought in the brilliant battles of Scott's campaign to capture Mexico City. He was brevetted first lieutenant for his conduct at Contreras and Churubusco, and captain for gallant and meritorious conduct at Chapultepec.

After the war he returned with his organization to Jefferson Barracks, Mo., but the new territories made many demands on the little United States Army, and the years which intervened before the Civil War brought Hatch varied duty in many remote corners of the country. He marched overland to Oregon, served there and in Washington, in Texas, and New Mexico. Again he saw active fighting in the campaigns against the Mogolon Indians and against the Navajos and took part in a number of scouting expeditions. He was serving as chief of commissariat in New Mexico when the crisis of 1861 called him to the East. He had received his captaincy in the regular service; now he took command, as brigadier-general of volunteers, of a brigade of cavalry at Annapolis. After a series of daring reconnaissances along the Rapidan and the Rappahannock, he commanded the cavalry of the V Army Corps under General Banks in the operations in the Shenandoah Valley from March to August of 1862. He fought at Winchester and took part in the retreat down the valley to the Potomac. In the campaign in Northern Virginia which immediately followed, he commanded a brigade of infantry, and again at Manassas, where he was lightly wounded. For a brief but eventful week, he commanded the 1st Division, I Army Corps, until a severe wound received at South Mountain disabled him for many weeks. Thereafter, until June 1864, although he was on active duty, his health kept him from combat service. Meanwhile he performed valuable service behind the lines, on court-martial duty, in command of draft rendezvous, and of a cavalry depot. After Sherman's march to Savannah, Hatch held command of various districts in the new Department of the South, and several times saw active fighting. The end of the war found him in command of the district of Charleston, whence he went to New York to be mustered out of the volunteer service. He now reverted to the rank of major of cavalry, United States Army, to which he had been promoted in 1863. During the twenty years following, until his retirement in 1886, he pursued the thankless and obscure tasks of the soldier on the frontiers, in Texas, the Indian Territory, Montana, and Washington. His promotion to lieutenant-colonel came in 1873 and to colonel in 1881. At the time of his retirement, he was in command of the 2nd Cavalry, at Fort Walla Walla. For his services in the Civil War he was brevetted in all grades to include brigadier-general in the Regular Army: major after Manassas, lieutenant-colonel after South Mountain, colonel and brigadier-general just before the close of the war. His other rewards were the brevet of major-general of volunteers for meritorious services in the war, and the Medal of Honor for his conduct at South Mountain. Following his retirement, he lived an uneventful life at his home in New York City, until his death at the age of seventy-nine. In 1851, he married Adelaide Goldsmith Burckle, daughter of Christian J. Burckle of Oswego. His widow, a son, and a daughter survived him.

[G. W. Cullum, *Biog. Reg. Officers and Grads. U. S. Mil. Acad.* (3rd ed., 1891), vol. II; old files, A. G. O., War Dept., Washington; F. B. Heitman, *Hist. Reg. and Dict. U. S. Army* (1903), vol. I; *Thirty-second Ann. Reunion, Asso. Grads. U. S. Mil. Acad.* (1901); J. S. Lawrence, *The Descendants of Moses and Sarah Kilham Porter* (1910); John P. Hatch Papers, 1843–68, MSS. Div., Lib. of Cong.; *N. Y. Times*, Apr. 14, 1901; *Army and Navy Reg.*, Apr. 20, 1901.] A. W. C.

HATCH, RUFUS (June 24, 1832–Feb. 23, 1893), financier and promoter, was born at Wells, York County, Me. His parents were Rufus and Huldah (Littlefield) Hatch. At nineteen he went to Rockford, Ill., where he was employed for a time in a grocery and later had an interest in a drygoods store. He became interested in railroad building and had some part in the laying of the first rails in Wisconsin (later a division of the Chicago & Northwestern). After about four years at Rockford, during which he seems to have prospered, he went to Chicago as a commission merchant, joining the firm of Armstrong & Company. When the business went to the wall in the panic of 1857, he assumed the debts and after a long struggle paid them all. For six years he was a member of the original Chicago Board of Trade, but in 1864 he went to New York, borrowing $2,000 with which to start a commission business. After the close of the Civil War he was unsuccessful in an attempt to get control of the Chicago & Northwestern Railroad, but later managed for Henry Keep [*q.v.*] the famous Northwestern pool, buying 10,000 shares of the stock and distributing profits of $225,000 to each of the participants. In a series of *Rufus Hatch's Circulars* he had attacked the Vanderbilt interests in 1869–70, exposing the stock-watering plans of the New York Central combination. His bear campaign at that time was unsuccessful and he failed for a considerable sum, but for a second time paid off his indebtedness. In the meantime he organized the Open Board of Brokers, which made itself so dangerous a competitor of the Stock Exchange that a merger soon became a matter of mutual interest and benefit. Upon its consummation, Hatch was offered the presidency of the Stock Exchange, but declined it. Throughout the Wall Street campaigns of the Erie and New York

Central and the failure of Jay Cooke, Hatch was an active operator and by 1874 he had become perhaps the best-known of the New York brokers. In that year he became president of the Pacific Mail Steamship Company, which was then making, through its new ships, the *Pekin* and the *Tokyo,* its first important bid for transpacific trade. The Iron Steamboat Company in New York Harbor was another of his interests. During this period Hatch was popular with brokers and with newspaper men. Unlike most operators, he wrote interesting and pointed articles for the press, and in his own person was regarded as good "copy." He shared with Daniel Drew the sobriquet of "uncle." The semi-clerical garb that he sometimes affected was considered a harmless foible. He is said to have coined the phrase, "lambs of Wall Street," and the label, "chromos," for securities which sold for more than he thought they were worth. In the Northern Pacific crash of 1883 he met his Waterloo. He sold his Stock-Exchange seat and went over to the Petroleum Exchange. For a time he was associated with James R. Keene [*q.v*]. in grain speculation. In 1884 he virtually retired from "the Street."

Hatch was twice married: to Charlotte T. Hatch, a distant relative, in 1853, and after her death some twenty years later, to Mary Gray, who survived him. He left two sons and a daughter by the first wife and three daughters and a son by the second. He was interested in music, gave elaborate musical entertainments at his home, and presented a pipe-organ to the pastor of the church at Rockford which he had served as organist in his youth. A sufferer from Bright's disease, he died suddenly after a coughing fit.

[C. A. Church, *Hist. of Rockford and Winnebago County, Ill.* (1900); Matthew Hale Smith, *Twenty Years among the Bulls and Bears of Wall Street* (1870); *Sketches of Men of Progress* (1870–71); Stephen Fiske, *Off-hand Portraits of Prominent New Yorkers* (1884); obituaries in *N. Y. Tribune, N. Y. Times, N. Y. Herald,* and *Sun* (N. Y.), Feb. 24, 1893; names of parents from the Town Clerk, Wells, Me.]

W. B. S.

HATCH, WILLIAM HENRY (Sept. 11, 1833–Dec. 23, 1896), congressman, was born near Georgetown, Ky., the son of Rev. William Hatch, a Campbellite minister, and Mary (Adams) Hatch, both members of pioneer Kentucky families. His education in the public schools of Lexington was supplemented by a year of legal training in a law office at Richmond. After his admission to the bar in 1854, Hatch, like many other Kentuckians, removed to Missouri. He settled at Hannibal where he began the practice of law, with politics as a major interest. Despite bitter internal warfare, the Democratic party in the state was uniformly successful, and Hatch shortly became favorably known as one of its leaders in northeastern Missouri. In 1858 he was elected circuit attorney for the sixteenth judicial district and was reëlected in 1860. In the national election of that year he supported Bell and Everett although his sympathies were obviously with the South. Despite these, and the extreme demoralization incident to civil war, he remained in office until 1862. Eliminated in that year because of his inability to subscribe to the necessary oath of loyalty to the Union, he entered the Confederate army and advanced in rank from captain to lieutenant-colonel. After the war he returned to Hannibal but, owing to the proscriptions of the Radical Republican régime, was barred from voting and from office-holding until 1871, when a combination of Democrats and bolting Liberals defeated the Radicals and regained political power. Immediately reëntering the political field, Hatch lost the nomination for governor in 1872 but, in 1878, when the Confederate tradition controlled the Missouri Democracy, he was elected from the old first district to the Forty-sixth Congress. He served from this strongly Democratic, agricultural region through eight successive terms. By his mastery of the intricacies of procedure, by his close friendship with J. G. Carlisle and C. F. Crisp [*qq.v.*], and by his aggressive leadership, he achieved great influence in the House of Representatives. From the first chiefly interested in agricultural legislation, he served for several sessions as chairman of the Committee on Agriculture. He proposed and successfully sponsored the act creating the Bureau of Animal Industry (1884), the first oleomargarine act (1886), and a meat inspection act (1890). He also wrote several anti-option laws to prevent speculation in grain. His most important service, however, was in connection with the establishment of the agricultural experiment stations. The proposal to appropriate federal funds to the colleges of agriculture to be spent for scientific research had long been before Congress, and by 1887 there were in existence fifteen state stations, so the way was prepared for national aid and a national agency (Conover, *post,* p. 34). By Hatch's persistent efforts, the bill, known as the Hatch Act, was passed by Congress and signed by President Cleveland on Mar. 2, 1887. The principle embodied in the legislation, that of direct aid for the study of scientific agriculture, was subsequently greatly enlarged and extended. Despite administrative weaknesses the operation of the law has had a remarkable influence upon experimental agricultural practice. Hatch was a leader in the agitation among the agricultural associations and in Congress for the elevation of the Department of Agriculture to the status of an executive department in the cabinet. This was finally accomplished in 1889, but Hatch did not achieve his ambition to become secretary. During the early nineties, he became a follower after the strange gods of Populism, although remaining in the Democratic party. After his defeat by Crisp for the speakership of the House in 1891 and his break with Carlisle over the silver issue, he lost much of his influence both in Congress and in his district. In non-partisan agricultural legislation, however, he remained an influential figure, while his close friendship with Speaker Reed, whom he greatly resembled in temperament and in method, partially compensated for his loss of support in his own party. He was defeated for reëlection in the Republican landslide of 1894 and retired to his farm, although he maintained his active leadership in agricultural legislation until his death. Hatch was twice married: to Jennie L. Smith, who died in 1858, and in 1861 to Thetis C. Hawkins, who survived him.

[F. B. Mumford, "William H. Hatch," in *Mo. Hist. Rev.*, July 1924; H. L. Conard, *Encyc. of the Hist. of Mo.* (1901), vol. III; Walter Williams, *A Hist. of Northeast Mo.* (1913), vol. III; L. H. Bailey, *Cyc. of Am. Agric.*, vol. IV (1909); Milton Conover, *The Office of Experiment Stations* (1924); *St. Louis Republic*, Dec. 24 and 25, 1896; names of parents through friends of the family.] T. S. B.

HATCHER, WILLIAM ELDRIDGE (July 25, 1834–Aug. 24, 1912), clergyman, author, the son of Henry and Mary (Latham) Hatcher, was born in Bedford County, Va., near the Peaks of Otter, and died at his country home, "Careby Hall," Fork Union, Va. The first of the family to set foot on American soil was William Hatcher, who served as a member of the Virginia House of Burgesses and took part in Bacon's Rebellion in 1676. After attending the schools of his native county, William Eldridge studied at Richmond College (later the University of Richmond), where he received the A.B. degree in 1858. Immediately upon graduation he was called to be pastor of the Baptist church in Manchester, now a part of the city of Richmond. There he witnessed some of the scenes of the Civil War. In 1867 he became pastor of the Franklin Square Baptist Church in Baltimore, remaining only one year. While successful here, his heart was really in his native state, where he was destined to spend the rest of his life. He returned to Virginia to take charge of the First Baptist Church in Petersburg; then for twenty-six years, from May 1875 to May 1901, he was pastor of the Grace Street Baptist Church in Richmond. Meanwhile, from 1882 to 1885, he was editor of the *Religious Herald*, to which he remained throughout life a frequent contributor. Always alert and active, he spoke frequently at religious gatherings in Washington, Philadelphia, and other cities. In 1888 he went to Europe and visited Spurgeon in London and his friend George B. Taylor in Italy. In 1899 he championed the cause of William H. Whitsitt, president of the Southern Baptist Theological Seminary in Louisville, Ky., who had been attacked on account of his views as to the history of immersion among English Baptists. When Whitsitt was forced to resign, Hatcher was instrumental in his being called to Richmond College as professor of philosophy.

Hatcher was a gifted preacher, masterly in the pulpit, and of commanding presence. His sympathies were with the masses, and especially after the Civil War he felt it his mission to reach out to them. His vivid personality made deep impress on his denomination, and throughout the South his leadership in Baptist circles was notable. He was president of the board of trustees of Richmond College, 1896–1908, and was the founder of Fork Union Academy (later Fork Union Military Academy) in 1898. His published works include: *Sketch of the Life and Writings of A. B. Brown* (1886), written in collaboration with his wife; *Life of J. B. Jeter, D.D.* (1887); *The Pastor and the Sunday School* (1902); and *John Jasper* (1908), the life of a noted and picturesque negro preacher of Richmond. *Along the Trail of the Friendly Years* (1910), is a charming autobiography. Hatcher was married, in 1864, to Oranie Virginia Snead. They had nine children, four of whom died in infancy.

[In addition to the autobiography, see E. B. Hatcher, *Wm. E. Hatcher* (1915); M. D. Ackerly and L. E. J. Parker, *"Our Kin": The Geneals. of Some of the Early Families who made History in the Founding and Development of Bedford County, Va.* (1930); files of the *Religious Herald*, 1858–1912; O. V. S. Hatcher, *The Sneads of Fluvanna* (1910).] S. C. M.

HATFIELD, EDWIN FRANCIS (Jan. 9, 1807–Sept. 22, 1883), distinguished in Presbyterian ecclesiastical administration and in hymnology, was born at Elizabeth, N. J. His father, Oliver S. Hatfield, was descended from Matthias Hatfield, who went from New Haven to Elizabeth in 1665. His mother, Jane Mann, numbered founders of Elizabeth and Newark among her ancestors. Edwin Francis graduated in 1829 from Middlebury College and studied theology for two years at Andover. He was ordained

May 14, 1832. After three years in the Second Presbyterian Church in St. Louis, in 1835 he began a pastorate of twenty-one years in the Seventh Presbyterian Church of New York, which flourished greatly under his care, receiving over twenty-one hundred members. When a portion of his congregation formed the North Presbyterian Church, Hatfield took the new pastorate, holding it till 1863, when illness compelled a year's retirement. After this he devoted much time to the interests of Union Theological Seminary, of which he had been a director since 1846. In 1864–65 he served as financial agent for the institution, increasing its funds by nearly half a million dollars, and for ten years, beginning in 1864, he was recorder of the board of directors.

In 1846 Hatfield was made stated clerk of the General Assembly of the New School Presbyterian Church. He held office throughout the church's history, by his vigorous administration contributing largely to its prosperity. He was secretary of the Joint Committee on Reunion of the two schools, formed in 1866. At the reunion of 1870, his preëminent qualifications and broad generous spirit led to his election as stated clerk in the reunited church. He served till his death, playing a great part in the church's life by his knowledge of its affairs and by his wisdom and counsel. In recognition of this service he was elected in 1883 moderator of the General Assembly.

In hymnology, a lifelong interest, Hatfield acquired large knowledge and collected an important library. A few of his own hymns were in congregational use for a time. He published a *Church Hymn Book* (1872, 1874), which was especially notable in that he had attempted to restore to their original forms the texts of the hymns and had made an effort to determine accurately their authorship and dates. An ardent anti-slavery man, he edited *Freedom's Lyre* (1840), a collection of hymns "for the slave and his friends," containing some of his own compositions. After his death there appeared his *Poets of the Church* (1884), a volume of biographies of hymn-writers. His other works include *Universalism as It Is* (1841), *Memoir of Elihu W. Baldwin* (1843), a valuable *History of Elizabeth, N. J.* (1868), and *Early Annals of Union Theological Seminary* (pamphlet, 1876), besides sermons and periodical articles, and biographical and statistical material for church history. His notable library of over six thousand volumes, partly collected in Europe, was bequeathed to Union Seminary. Hatfield was married on Apr. 27, 1837, to Mary E. Taylor, and had two sons and three daughters. In his later years he lived in Summit, N. J., where he died in the year of his moderatorship.

[*Minutes Gen. Assembly Presbyt. Ch., U. S. A.*, 1839–69; *Presbyt. Reunion Memorial Vol.* (1870); G. L. Prentiss, *The Union Theol. Sem.: . . . Hist. and Biog. Sketches of its First Fifty Years* (1889); John Julian, *A Dict. of Hymnology* (1891); S. A. W. Duffield, *English Hymns* (1886); general catalogues of Andover and Union seminaries; *N. Y. Times*, Sept. 23, 1883.]

R. H. N.

HATHORNE, WILLIAM (*c.* 1607–1681), Massachusetts colonial official, was born in Binfield, England, the oldest son of William and Sara Hathorne. In 1630, with his wife Anne, he emigrated to America in John Winthrop's company, and settled in Dorchester. Six years later he removed to Salem, which was his home for the rest of his life. From 1634, when he first secured admission to the highly select circle of freemen of the Massachusetts Bay Company, to 1679, when he withdrew from active participation in public affairs, Hathorne held a prominent place in the colony. One writer ranked him, next to Endicott, the most important personage in the early history of Salem (Waters, *post*, p. 203). Although a merchant, Hathorne had a liking for office holding, and for the influence and prestige which accompany a political career. In 1634 he was chosen to the board of ten selectmen of Dorchester, and in 1635 he became a deputy in the General Court. The next year he was one of the assessors in Dorchester. After his removal to Salem, he again became, 1637, a member of the General Court. In 1644, when for the first time the deputies met separately, Hathorne became speaker, a place which he held for six years. In spite of his active political life, he found time to acquire a military record. In May 1646 he became the captain of a militia company in Salem, and ten years later a major; he saw active service in King Philip's War. From 1662 to 1679 he was a member of the Board of Assistants, or Council. For four years, 1650–53, he was one of the eight commissioners of the Confederacy of New England.

On various occasions he was selected to serve on important commissions with other equally conspicuous political leaders of the colony. In 1646, he went with Gov. Thomas Dudley and Daniel Denison to treat with D'Aulnay at St. Croix. In 1657 the General Court sent Denison, Bradstreet, and Hathorne to the eastern settlements—Kittery, York, and other places—for the purpose of bringing these communities under the jurisdiction of Massachusetts. In 1666 Hathorne was one of the five principal citizens of Massachusetts ordered to England by Charles

II for refusing to submit to the authority of the royal commissioners.

Like some of his associates, he seems to have been a severe moralist. In 1641, he, with some other members of the General Court, "were very earnest to have some certain penalty set upon lying, swearing, etc." (Winthrop, *post,* II, 49), and he sometimes made himself objectionable to his associates by his determined insistence upon his own interpretation of the colony's charter. Winthrop records a dispute in 1644, over the powers of the Board of Assistants when the General Court was not in session. Hathorne, so Winthrop declared, was "the principal man in all these agitations" (*Ibid.,* II, 175). Even so, in spite of a tendency to bigotry and arbitrariness, he was a man of superior ability. Johnson, in his *Wonder-Working Providence* (p. 109), described him as "the godly Captaine William Hathorne, whom the Lord hath indued with a quick apprehension, strong memory, and rhetorick, volubillity of speech, which hath caused the people to make use of him often in publick service, especially when they have had to do with any foreign Government." Hathorne was the progenitor of a notable family, which in the sixth generation produced Nathaniel Hawthorne [*q.v.*].

[Sketches by H. F. Waters and G. M. Bodge in *New-Eng. Hist. and Geneal. Reg.,* Apr. 1884 and Oct. 1888, respectively; references in the same journal, July 1847, pp. 218, 219, July 1867, p. 275, July 1869, pp. 315, 320; *Winthrop's Journal* (2 vols., 1908), ed. by J. K. Hosmer; Edward Johnson, *Wonder-Working Providence* (1867, from the London ed. of 1654); J. A. Emmerton and H. F. Waters, *Hathorne Family of Salem, Mass.* (1880); J. B. Felt, *Annals of Salem* (1827).]

R. V. H.

HATTON, FRANK (Apr. 28, 1846–Apr. 30, 1894), journalist, postmaster general, was born in Cambridge, Ohio. His father was Richard Hatton of Fairfax County, Va.; his mother, Sarah Green, daughter of a Methodist minister, of Tyler County, Va. (now W. Va.). His grandparents had participated in the rush of settlers to the old Northwest and his father had become a frontier newspaper man, ultimately settling down as owner and editor of the *Republican* at Cadiz, Ohio. Young Hatton received little formal school instruction but was educated by his mother at home, and in his father's printery. He began to work in the printing office at eleven and served in every capacity from devil to local editor, learning the trade thoroughly. Early in the Civil War, he ran away and joined an Ohio infantry company as drummer boy. In 1864 he was commissioned first lieutenant in the 184th Ohio Volunteers and served in the Army of the Cumberland until mustered out. In 1866 the family moved to Mount Pleasant, Iowa, where the elder Hatton purchased the *Journal,* publishing it with the assistance of his son until his death in 1869. Frank Hatton and his brother-in-law then operated the plant for five years. In 1867 Hatton married Lizzie Snyder of Iowa, who bore him one son.

In 1874, Hatton acquired the *Burlington Daily Hawk-Eye,* a hardy pioneer journal, and moved to Burlington, where Robert J. Burdette [*q.v.*], the humorist, was his editorial associate. The *Hawk-Eye,* under Hatton's vigorous direction, developed into one of the most influential Republican organs in the Mississippi Valley and brought its owner into national prominence. Although a strong party man, he launched savage attacks against civil-service reform and his editorials were reprinted the country over. He became local postmaster in 1879. His most spectacular stroke as a journalist was persuading General Grant to spend three days in Burlington upon returning from his world tour, the visit advertising both city and aggressive editor widely. In the stormy campaign of 1880, Hatton gave Garfield ardent support, which brought political reward. On the recommendation of Grant, Conkling, and the Republican organization of Iowa, he was named assistant postmaster-general by President Arthur in October 1881. He capably performed the duties of that office for three years, greatly extending carrier service, speeding up the transmission of mail west of the Mississippi, and creating the special-delivery system. He was appointed postmaster general in October 1884, on Walter Gresham's resignation, and held this stop-gap appointment until Cleveland's inauguration, thus becoming the youngest cabinet member since Alexander Hamilton's day. His wife and he moved freely in Washington society during his official life; and, radiating geniality, his portly figure was a familiar one at the innumerable functions of the season, which he heartily enjoyed.

Craving the smell of printer's ink, he had written extensively for the *National Republican* of Washington even while holding office. He moved to Chicago in July 1885 and there assisted in reorganizing the *Mail,* which he edited until 1888. He then joined Robert Porter in founding the *New York Press* and, in 1889, in partnership with former Congressman Beriah Wilkins (Democrat), he purchased the *Washington Post,* which he edited as an independent paper. An inveterate foe of the civil-service régime, he at this time bitterly fought the reforming Roosevelt. He was an exacting employer, but was always keenly appreciative of work well done and himself set a high standard. On two occasions he brought out extras with the sole aid of the janitor. He developed a large personal following in these last years, and this, combined with an active club life, brought him marked social prominence. He suffered a stroke of paralysis at his desk on Apr. 24, 1894, and died six days later.

[A. M. Antrobus, *Hist. of Des Moines County Iowa and its People* (1915), I, 439; *Biog. Rev. of Des Moines County, Iowa* (1905); *Portr. and Biog. Album of Des Moines County, Iowa* (1888); *Iowa Hist. Record,* vol. X (1896); William Henry Smith, *Hist. of the Cabinet of the U. S. A.* (1925); files of the *Burlington Hawk-Eye,* 1874–81; *Baltimore American,* May 1, 1894; *Evening Star* (Washington), Apr. 30 and May 1, 1894; the *Sun* (Baltimore), May 1, 1894; *Washington Post,* 1889–94 (obituary, May 1, 1894); *Report of the Postmaster-General,* 1881–84; private information.]

L. J. R.

HAUGHERY, MARGARET GAFFNEY (*c.* 1814–Feb. 9, 1882), philanthropist, was born in Cavan, Ireland, the daughter of Charles and Margaret (O'Rourke) Gaffney. When she was about eight years old, her parents brought her with them to America. Almost immediately after their arrival both parents died in Baltimore, and Margaret's rearing was taken over by a Welsh family that had crossed in the vessel with her, people of great kindliness but of such poverty that they were unable to send her to school. In 1835 she married Charles Haughery. Within a year his health failed and the two moved from Baltimore to New Orleans. Later, seeking the benefits of a sea voyage, her husband went to Ireland, and while there died, leaving her with a young child and practically without money. His death and within a brief time the death of her child turned her toward religion. She worked for a while as laundress in a hotel, and later, having saved enough funds, bought two cows and started a dairy. Her business prospered, and she soon put both it and herself at the disposal of a practically defunct Catholic orphan asylum. In behalf of her new interest, she peddled her butter and milk through the city, devoting the proceeds and as much discarded food as she could beg to the support of the orphan protégés who were constantly becoming dearer to her. After a while, she took over for debt a small baker's shop. This business prospered also, becoming at length one of the largest bakeries in the South, and is said to have been the first there to employ steam. Thrifty, shrewd, and kindly, before long, she was known everywhere merely as "Margaret," one of the institutions of the city. Money somehow flooded in to her, and she was in haste to release it, particularly for the well-being of orphans, for whom she was instrumental in establishing and sustaining three homes capable altogether of looking after 600 children. She was as robust physically as she was sagacious. She personally nursed masses of the victims of yellow-fever epidemics, paddled her own relief boat when the overflowing Mississippi made people destitute, and once, it is alleged, set aside from her path a Civil-War sentry who attempted to halt her in a charitable expedition to a prison camp. She died in New Orleans, and two years after her death a statue, representing her as the city remembered her—shawled and seated on a chair at her bakery door, with her arm about a symbolic orphan—was erected in a small park, known since as Margaret Place.

[*Cath. Encyc.* (1910); Grace King, *New Orleans, the Place and the People* (1895); Alcée Fortier, *Louisiana* (1914); New Orleans *Times-Democrat,* Feb. 10, 11, 1882.]

J. D. W.

HAUGHTON, PERCY DUNCAN (July 11, 1876–Oct. 27, 1924), football coach, the son of Malcolm Graeme and Mary Nesbit (Lawrence) Haughton, was born on Staten Island, N. Y. His early school days were spent at the Staten Island Academy where his youthful skill as a football player, cross-country runner, baseball and tennis player, swimmer, and boxer indicated a future eminence in various sports. Entering Groton School in Massachusetts in 1891, he soon became known not only for his athletic skill but also for his sturdy championship of the ethics of sport, fair play, honest preparation, and adherence to the rules of the game. He left Groton with honors, having captained the eleven and having served as one of the mainstays of the baseball nine. Entering Harvard in 1895 as a member of the class of 1899, he immediately won a place as tackle on the freshman team and in 1896 he was substitute tackle on the varsity. Two years before (1894), Harvard and Yale had played a game at Hampden Park, Springfield, Mass., characterized by a bitterness resulting immediately in a number of serious injuries to players of both teams and ultimately in a break in athletic relationships between these ancient rivals which endured until 1897. Haughton never forgot the lessons of this distressing period, and in 1910 when he was a member of the Football Rules Committee he preached the cause of a game of football which should be safe for the player, enjoyable for the spectator, and amenable in all its phases to sportsmanlike construction, with eloquence so effective that many necessary reforms were then and there established. Winning a position of tackle on the 1897 varsity and used as fullback when kicks—drop, place, or punt—were called for, he gained for himself a reputation as a sound lineman and one of the outstanding kickers of all time. He played baseball with equal ability, captained the nine in his senior year, and had the satisfaction that year of defeating Yale both on the gridiron and on the diamond. Soon after his graduation he had an important decision to make: whether he should enter business or take up football coaching, the impelling issue being an invitation from Cornell to lift football at Ithaca out of the mire. He decided to go to Ithaca, and almost immediately the fallen fortunes of the gridiron sport at Cornell revived. In his two years there (1899–1900) sequential victories were won over Princeton, and other strong elevens were defeated. After leaving Cornell he was employed by E. H. Rollins & Sons, a Boston banking firm; subsequently was assistant secretary of the City Trust Company, Boston; and in 1910 became associated with Hamlin Nickerson & Company, stockbrokers. Meanwhile, in 1908, he was called to Harvard to reorganize the football system. In his first year he broke Yale's string of six successive victories. In 1909 his team lost to Yale and in 1910 a tie game was played, but thereafter until 1916 his elevens won regularly over both Yale and Princeton. Haughton did more than win, however. He wrought changes in methods of play which revolutionized the game and produced elevens that were perfectly coordinated machines. In the course of his career at Harvard he was a member of a syndicate which purchased the Boston Braves of the National Baseball League. He retired from coaching in 1916 and reëntered business. During the World War he was commissioned major in the Chemical Warfare Service, July 25, 1918, and saw active service in the Tryon Sector and the Meuse-Argonne offensive. After returning from France he again entered business, in association with White, Weld & Company, dealers in investment securities. Called in 1923 to coach Columbia, he had just completed a winning football system when in the middle of the season of 1924 he was taken suddenly ill and died in St. Luke's Hospital, New York City. Haughton wrote occasionally for newspapers and other periodicals and in 1923 published *Football and How to Watch It.* He was married, May 15, 1911, to Gwendolen (Whistler) Howell, widow of Rev. Richard L. Howell of Baltimore and grand-niece of James McNeill Whistler, and at his death was survived by his wife, a daughter, and two stepdaughters.

[*Harvard College Class of 1899* (1914, 1924); *Harvard Grads. Mag.*, Dec. 1924; *Lit. Digest*, Nov. 15, 1924; *Outlook*, Nov. 5, 1924; *N. Y. Times*, Oct. 28, 29, 31, 1924; *N. Y. Herald, Boston Transcript*, and *Boston Post*, all of Oct. 28, 1924; newspaper clippings, and the writer's personal recollections.] L. P.

HAUK, MINNIE (Nov. 16, 1852?–Feb. 6, 1929), dramatic soprano, was born in New York, the daughter of a German carpenter (her autobiography supplies no particulars regarding her mother's name or her parents' antecedents) who, when she was yet a child, moved first to Providence, R. I., and then to Sumner City, Kan., in a day when Indians still attacked the emigrant trains. At Fort Leavenworth, where her father worked at his trade while her mother kept a boarding-house, she went to school until, after another brief stay in Sumner, the family floated down the Missouri and the Mississippi in a houseboat to New Orleans. There the child studied with Curto, a well-known French singing teacher, and made her first appearance in concert singing the "Casta Diva" from *Norma* and a florid air from Auber's *Crown Diamonds.* During the same year the family removed to New York where, after studying with A. Errani and for a short time with Albites, she made her début in the Brooklyn Academy of Music, Oct. 13, 1866, as Amina in *Sonnambula* with pronounced success. Her appearance excited much interest, "from the fact that she [was] native-born . . . exceedingly pretty . . . and gave undoubted promise of future eminence" (*New York Tribune,* Oct. 15, 1866). Her New York début as Prascovia in *L'Étoile du Nord* occurred the same year. Now definitely launched on her career, she took further lessons from Moritz Strakosch and in 1867 sang the part of Juliette in the first American production of Gounod's *Roméo et Juliette.* She also took part in the American premières of other important operas, among them *Carmen* and *Manon.* In 1868 she made her London début at the Haymarket as Amina; she sang in Paris, Moscow, and St. Petersburg; and in Vienna she was the *prima donna assoluta* of the Komische Oper (later Ring Theater), where she created the rôles of Javotte, in Delibes' *Le Roi l'a dit,* and of Carlo Broschi in *La Part du Diable.* Later, at the Berlin Opera, she was a great favorite, notably as Katherine in Goetz's *Taming of the Shrew.* She was acclaimed as Carmen in Brussels and as Violetta in London (1878) and sang every season in the last-named city until 1881. That year she married the well-known traveler, author, and correspondent of the Vienna *Neue Freie Presse,* Baron Ernst von Hesse-Wartegg, with whom she made a three-year tour of the world, singing everywhere and everywhere well received. During her concert tour of the United States and

Canada, 1883–84, she sang at the White House for President Arthur. She retired in 1895.

The first and perhaps the most famous of American Carmens, Minnie Hauk had a rich, powerful soprano voice with a notable mezzo quality. Though she sang in few Wagnerian operas, her extensive repertory included more than one hundred rôles. She was acquainted with a host of petty German princes and was the recipient of numerous decorations, Prussian, French, and Italian. When she was left destitute by her husband's death in 1918, Geraldine Farrar and the Music Lovers Foundation raised funds to make her last years comfortable. She died at her home, Villa Tribschen, on Lake Lucerne.

[Her own *Memories of a Singer* (1925) is the chief source of information. See also: Moritz Strakosch, *Souvenirs d'un Impresario* (1887); H. S. Edwards, *The Prima Donna* (1888); Lucien Cleves, "Minna Hauk," *N. Y. Herald*, Feb. 29, 1920; *Musical America*, May 20, 1922; W. J. Henderson, obituary and article, N. Y. *Sun*, Feb. 6, 1929; *Musical Courier*, Feb. 14, 1929.]
F. H. M.

HAUPT, HERMAN (Mar. 26, 1817–Dec. 14, 1905), civil engineer, author, and inventor, was born in Philadelphia, Pa., the son of Jacob and Anna (Wiall) Haupt. He was educated in private schools in Philadelphia and at the United States Military Academy, where he graduated July 1, 1835, at the age of eighteen, and was appointed brevet second lieutenant in the 3rd Infantry. Three months later he resigned his commission to become assistant engineer in the survey of a railroad from Norristown to Allentown, Pa., and subsequently in the location of the Norristown & Valley Railroad. The following year he was appointed principal assistant engineer in the Pennsylvania state service, in which capacity he located a railroad from Gettysburg to the Potomac. Engaged in 1840 to aid in the construction of the York & Wrightsville Railroad, he began the study of bridge construction and a year or two later published the results of his experiments, anonymously, in a pamphlet entitled *Hints on Bridge Construction*, which attracted much attention and led to some controversy. Meanwhile he had given instruction in civil engineering and architecture at Pennsylvania College, Gettysburg, and from 1845 to 1847 he was professor of mathematics there. During this time he wrote his important book, *General Theory of Bridge Construction*, published in 1851, which has since been regarded as a leading authority on the subject. In 1847 he was appointed principal assistant to the chief engineer in charge of construction of the Pennsylvania Railroad, and on Sept. 1, 1849, became superintendent of transportation. In this capacity he examined the systems of bookkeeping and modes of operation of the more important railroads of New York and New England and arranged a plan of organization for the Pennsylvania Railroad Company which was adopted without change by the board of directors. From Dec. 31, 1850 to Nov. 1, 1852, he was general superintendent of the road, and after six months as chief engineer of the Southern Railroad of Mississippi, he was recalled to the Pennsylvania to take the post of chief engineer, which he retained until the completion and opening of the whole line to Pittsburgh, including the Alleghany Mountain tunnel. From Mar. 3 to Dec. 24, 1856, he served on the board of directors, elected by the city council of Philadelphia to represent the stock held by that city.

In 1855 he was requested to make an examination of the proposed Hoosac tunnel, on the line of the Troy & Greenfield Railroad in Massachusetts, and to give his opinion as to its practicability. Reporting favorably, he was prevailed upon to take an interest in the contract for its construction and to assist in raising the necessary capital. Accordingly, in 1856 he resigned from the Pennsylvania Railroad and began a vigorous prosecution of this new work. Despite the hostility of press and legislature, instigated by the rival Boston & Albany Railroad, and financial embarrassment resulting therefrom and from the failure of three of his partners, Haupt carried on the work, by advancing his personal funds and borrowing from friends, until it was so far completed as to permit his collecting the first payment due from the State of Massachusetts. After this the tunnel progressed without trouble until 1862 when the State of Massachusetts took over the work. Haupt was unable to secure a refund of his advances until 1884, when the State, in order to clear its title, made a settlement with him at the rate of about eight cents on the dollar. Throughout the controversy he never lost a point before bodies in which fairness and facts were permitted to control decisions, although he was not assisted by counsel until the matter was taken to the Supreme Court.

Meanwhile the Civil War had begun, and in April 1862 Haupt was called to Washington to become chief of construction and transportation on the United States military railroads, being appointed, Apr. 27, 1862, aide-de-camp on the staff of Gen. Irwin McDowell, with the rank of colonel. Accepting this post at great personal sacrifice, since at this time the tunnel controversy in Massachusetts was at its height, he directed the repairs and construction of railroads for facilitating the movements of the United States armies in Virginia. On Sept. 5, 1862, he was promoted to brigadier-general of volunteers, for meritorious services, which appointment he later declined to accept. Although he expressed his willingness to serve without official rank and without pay so long as no restriction was placed upon his freedom to attend to his business affairs, when this freedom was curtailed by the demand that he accept a military commission, he retired from the army, Sept. 14, 1863.

During his work on the Hoosac tunnel (1858) he had developed a pneumatic drill which was far superior to any in use up to that time, and in 1867, at the invitation of the Royal Polytechnic Society of Cornwall, he visited Europe to explain his system of mining and tunneling by power machinery. In 1870 he was chief engineer in charge of the location of the Shenandoah Valley Railroad; from 1872 to 1876 he was general manager of the Richmond & Danville Railroad, and during that time he prepared the plan for organizing the Southern Railway & Steamship Association which was adopted. In 1876 he was employed by the Pennsylvania Transportation Company to investigate and report upon the practicability of constructing a pipeline for the transportation of crude petroleum from the wells in the Allegheny Valley to tidewater. He decided that such a project was feasible, undertook its construction, and completed it despite the strong opposition of the trunk-line railroads and the Standard Oil Company.

As general manager of the Northern Pacific Railroad from the spring of 1881 to the fall of 1884, during which period the road was completed to the Pacific, he had charge of organizing the various divisions and departments necessary for its operation. For the next two years he was president of the Dakota & Great Southern Railroad. He was also president of the General Compressed Air & Power Company (1892–1905), as such being responsible for the practical introduction of compressed air for motors and mining machinery, and president of the National Nutrient Company (1899–1905) which was engaged in the evolution of foods from the waste products of the dairy. Throughout his career he was a voluminous writer, especially upon technical subjects. His most important publications, besides those already mentioned, were: *Military Bridges* (1864), *Tunneling by Machinery* (1876), *Street Railway Motors* (1893), and his account of his Civil War experiences, *Reminiscences of General Herman Haupt* (1901), prepared in collaboration with F. A. Flower. He was a member of the American Philosophical Society, the Pennsylvania Historical Society, and the Franklin Institute. In 1838 he married Ann Cecilia Keller of Gettysburg, Pa. They had eleven children. He died of heart failure on a railroad train at Jersey City, N. J., en route to his home in Washington, D. C.

[Haupt's Letter Book, 1862–63, in MSS. Div., Lib. of Cong.; sketch by F. A. Flower in Haupt's *Reminiscences* (1901); *Who's Who in America*, 1903–05; G. W. Cullum, *Biog. Reg. Officers and Grads. U. S. Mil. Acad.* (3rd ed., 1891), vol. I; *Thirty-seventh Ann. Reunion Asso. Grads. U. S. Mil. Acad.* (1906); W. H. Haupt, *The Haupt Family in America* (1924); W. B. Wilson, *Hist. of the Pa. R. R. Co.* (2 vols., 1895), and *General Supts. of the Pa. R. R. Co.* (1890); H. W. Schotter, *Growth and Development of the Pa. R. R. Co.* (1927); *War of the Rebellion: Official Records* (*Army*); "Use of Railroads in War an American Development," *Ry. Age Gazette*, June 22, 1917; obituaries in *Railroad Gazette*, Dec. 22, 1905, and N. Y. and Phila. newspapers, Dec. 15, 1905.] J. H. F.

HAUPT, PAUL (Nov. 25, 1858–Dec. 15, 1926), philologist, Assyriologist, was born in Görlitz, Germany, the son of Karl Gottlieb and Elise (Hülse) Haupt. He was graduated from the Gymnasium at Görlitz in 1876 and received the degree of Ph.D. from the University of Leipzig in 1878. He was the most distinguished pupil of Friedrich Delitzsch, the Assyriologist, and soon became associated with his teacher as an editor of two series of Assyriological researches, *Beiträge zur Assyriologie* and an *Assyriologische Bibliothek*. After taking his degree he spent two years in study at the Universities of Leipzig and Berlin and in the British Museum. He was privat-docent in Assyriology, 1880–83, at the University of Göttingen, and then promoted to a professorship. In the same year he became Spence Professor of Semitic Languages and director of the Oriental Seminary at the Johns Hopkins University in Baltimore, a position which he held until his death. Until 1889 he also maintained his connection with the University of Göttingen, but after that date devoted himself wholly to his American work. At various times he held honorary curatorships in the United States National Museum in Washington. He was a prolific author, the list of his publications including 522 titles. His third publication, *Die Sumerischen Familiengesetze* (1879), attracted wide attention, and his various studies of the Gilgamesh Epic, which he called the Babylonian *Nimrodepos*, made him for years the chief interpreter of that oldest of epics. Haupt was, however, much more than an Assyriologist. Few men have had a wider or more accurate knowledge of the various Semitic languages and dialects, or a keener philological sense. Had he chosen to write a comparative Semitic grammar, it would have been a masterly production. His articles on this subject invariably reveal the breadth and accuracy of his knowledge and the keenness of his insight. Many of his publications were in the field of Old Testament criticism. The best known of these is *The Sacred Books of the Old Testament* (1893–1904), commonly known as the "Polychrome Bible" because the various documents which critics find in the books were printed on a background of different colors. Of this work only six volumes—*Leviticus, Joshua, Judges, The Psalms, Isaiah, Ezekiel*—appeared in English, for the publishers found the undertaking unprofitable. Sixteen volumes of the subsidized Hebrew edition made their appearance. The volumes were prepared by various scholars, but Haupt as editor furnished numerous notes for each book. He also published *Biblical Love-Ditties* (1902); *The Book of Canticles* (1902); *Koheleth* (1905); *The Book of Ecclesiastes* (1905); *Purím* (1906); *The Book of Nahum* (1907); *Biblische Liebeslieder* (1907); *Jonah's Whale* (1907); *The Book of Esther* (1908); *The Aryan Ancestry of Jesus* (1909); *The Burning Bush and the Origin of Judaism* (1910); *The Book of Micah* (1910); and numerous articles of a similar character in various journals. His contributions to Biblical criticism are, however, inferior to his work in Assyriology and Semitic philology. In the nature of the case, the "Polychrome Bible" could only record the opinions of a scholar and editor at a given moment of time. In many instances, too, the notes inserted by the editor are somewhat irrelevant. In such works as *Canticles, Ecclesiastes, Nahum, Micah,* and in his articles on the Psalms, Haupt's limitations as a Biblical critic are most apparent. He could not discriminate between what his fertile imagination suggested as possible and what sound critical principles allow one to accept as probable. He was of the opinion, too, that Hebrew poets always wrote in rigid metrical forms, which later editors spoiled by insertions, but which he was able to restore; hence, instead of interpreting an Old Testament text he usually rewrote it. This habit, together with the notion that much Old Testament literature originated in the Maccabaean period, vitiated all his critical work. If his literary and historical judgment had been as good as his philological judgment, he would have been a great Biblical scholar. As it was, however, his works are not safe guides in this field. On June 9, 1884, he married Margaret Giede, who died on Aug. 19 of that year. On Mar. 8, 1886, he married Minna Giede, who with two sons and a daughter survived him. Haupt's positive personality, his skill and eminence as a teacher, his wide learning, his sound judgment in Assyriological and philological matters, his assiduous attendance at the meetings of learned societies, and his productivity as a writer combined to make him one of the greatest influences in advancing Oriental studies in the United States.

[*Who's Who in America,* 1924–25; the *Sun* (Baltimore), Dec. 16, 1926; W. F. Albright, "Prof. Haupt as Scholar and Teacher," *Oriental Studies . . . in Commemoration of the Fortieth Anniv. of Paul Haupt as Director of the Oriental Seminary of the Johns Hopkins Univ.* (1926); Aaron Ember, bibliography, *Ibid.*]

G. A. B.

HAUSER, SAMUEL THOMAS (Jan. 10, 1833–Nov. 10, 1914), pioneer miner, capitalist, territorial governor of Montana, was descended from Martin Hauser, a Moravian, who came from eastern France to America before 1700 and settled in North Carolina; his grandfather, George Hauser, served in the American Revolution; and his father, Samuel Thomas Hauser, graduated in law from the University of North Carolina and moved to Falmouth, Ky., where he became prominent as a lawyer and judge. Here he married Mary Ann Kennett of a Maryland family, and here their son, Samuel Thomas Hauser, was born and reared. He attended the Chittenden school for a time, but his more advanced studies were carried on under the direction of his father and of a cousin, Henry Hill, a graduate of Yale and a railway engineer. When young Hauser was nineteen he became an assistant to Hill, who was in charge of construction work for the Kentucky Central. In 1854 he went to Missouri and had charge of surveying a right of way for a railroad that later became part of the Missouri Pacific.

The secession movement attracted Hauser, but because his father was strongly Unionist the young man decided to remain neutral. Railroad work was stopped, and in 1862 he started up the Missouri River to the Salmon River mines in Idaho. In June he was at Gold Creek, where he met Granville and James Stuart, with the latter of whom he formed a lasting friendship. After mining at Bannack for a while with considerable success, he joined James Stuart in 1863 to search for gold in the Yellowstone country. No gold was found by this party, but a small group endeavoring to join it stumbled upon the fabulous riches of Alder Gulch. There is no record to show it, but it seems probable that Hauser was given one of the richer claims reserved for the discoverers. Within two years he had accumulated several thousand dollars. Perceiving the advantage of more capital to develop mining, he went to St. Louis to get it. There apparently he interested two wealthy cousins, a friend of theirs, George C. Swallow who was state geologist of Missouri, and others. On his return he and Stuart bought six silver mines and at Argenta built the first furnace in Montana for reducing silver ore. In 1866 Hauser built a silver mill at Philipsburg, and near Helena some time later he built smelters that treated ore from his own mines and from all the silver-mining regions of the Northwest. He also opened many coal mines which became profitable as the territory developed. Obtaining a franchise from the first legislature of Montana, Hauser and others built a toll road and telegraph line from Virginia City to the mouth of the Yellowstone, and a telegraph line to Salt Lake City. In 1865 he organized a bank at Virginia City; in 1866, the First National Bank of Helena; and he took part in organizing other national banks, one at Missoula in 1873, and one at Butte in 1878.

Seeing the need of railroads, he first urged a line from Ogden to Butte and then built the Helena & Jefferson County Railway to connect Helena with this road. He was interested in the Northern Pacific and built many short railroads to connect with the main line. He was probably the first to see the possibilities of water power to develop electricity in the Northwest and constructed a high-tension line to Butte that furnished the city with light and power to run its mining machinery. He planned the first large reclamation project in Montana to irrigate extensive tracts of land along the Missouri. He was one of the first to engage in large-scale stock raising in the territory and owned large interests in the Pioneer Cattle Company which ran great herds of cattle on the open ranges of eastern Montana. With his many interests, it was inevitable that he should be drawn into Montana politics. In 1885 he was appointed territorial governor by President Cleveland, and in his *Report of the Governor of Montana to the Secretary of the Interior* (Washington, 1885) he presented the silver miners' classic arguments for free silver. His predecessors had been from outside the territory and were generally called "carpetbaggers." His appointment therefore was popular, but the office took too much time from business, and in less than two years he resigned. He continued an active Democrat and sided with W. A. Clark [*q.v.*] in his contest with Marcus Daly [*q.v.*].

Hauser was a man of adventurous spirit. In 1863 he carried $14,000 through a country infested with road-agents and later as a *Vigilante* helped rid the mining camp of bandits. In spite of business he went on the Washburne expedition of 1870 to explore the country that later became Yellowstone Park. He was a benefactor to pioneer ministers and an enthusiastic student of Montana history. In his last years he gave much encouragement and help to business enterprises which he no longer had the strength to guide. In 1871 he married Ellen Farrar of St. Louis, grandniece of George Rogers Clark, and to them two children were born.

[*Montana Hist. Soc. Contributions*, vols. I, II, V, VII (1876–1910); Granville Stuart, *Forty Years on the Frontier* (2 vols., 1925); N. P. Langford, *Vigilante Days and Ways* (2 vols., 1890); Helen F. Sanders, *Hist. of Mont.*, vol. I (1913); Tom Stout, *Montana* (1921); W. H. Maguire, "Samuel T. Hauser, An Early Governor of Montana," in *Mag. of Western Hist.*, vol. XIII (1890); *Northwest Mag.*, Aug. 1885 and Aug. 1886; files of the *Helena Independent* and *Helena Herald*; *Who's Who in America*, 1912–13; obituaries in *Helena Independent* and *Montana Daily Record* (Helena), Nov. 11, 1914; letters and papers in the possession of Hauser's son, Thomas Hauser, Helena, Mont.]
P. C. P.

HAVELL, ROBERT (Nov. 25, 1793–Nov. 11, 1878), engraver, painter, the son of Robert and Lydia (Phillips) Havell, was born at Reading, Berkshire, into a famous family of English engravers. (See sketches of Robert and William Havell in *Dictionary of National Biography.*) He early mastered aquatint engraving in the Havell establishment and evinced marked artistic ability in water color. His father, however, seeking to force him into one of the learned professions, succeeded, in 1825, in driving him from home. Two years later, while in search of a paragon among engravers to execute the plates for Audubon's *Birds of America,* the elder Havell discovered his son, a finished artist in aquatint, in the employ of Colnahgi & Company, publishers. Reconciliation followed and a partnership was formed; Robert, Junior, undertook the engraving and his father the coloring and printing of the huge "elephant folio" plates. In 1828 the partnership was dissolved. The fact that after his father's death in 1832, Robert Havell dropped the "Junior" from his signature has led some writers to ascribe the Audubon plates to the elder man, whereas except for the first ten plates, executed by William Lizars of Edinburgh, Robert Havell, Jr., was the sole engraver of this series—"the most sumptuous work to which aquatint was ever applied in illustration" (Stauffer, *post*). After the first, he was responsible for the coloring as well. Assistants applied the first crude washes, but Havell's brush laid the more salient tones, the delicate touches. Williams (*post*) notes that Havell largely overcame the limitations of his medium, securing not only the softness suited to bird plumage, but, by judicious use of etched and engraved lines, a crisp definition giving to bird and plant forms both delicacy and force. By deft use of feathering he secured soft gradations and telling accents and achieved "a chiaroscuro seldom, if ever, equalled in aquatint." To his genius, which reproduced both the scientific truth and the artistic charm of Audubon's drawings, was due much of the extraordinary success of the work. Havell, his courage as indomitable as Audubon's, his temperament more equable, also did much to sustain the naturalist through the long struggle of publication, offering, too, considerable financial support. In appreciation Audubon in 1834 presented his engraver with a silver loving-cup. In 1838 the vast work, 435 plates, was completed. The following year Havell, with his wife and a daughter, followed Audubon [*q.v.*] to America and after staying with him for a time, and then in Brooklyn, settled at Sing Sing, now Ossining, on the Hudson. Here and at Tarrytown, where in 1857 he built a house and studio, he passed the remainder of his life, chiefly in painting and sketching for his own pleasure the scenery of the Washington Irving country, although he also engraved and published important views of the Hudson and of several American cities. Shortly before his death he exhibited some seventy-five canvases in oils, for which medium he had forsaken water color. He died within sight of his beloved Hudson and was buried in Sleepy Hollow. Havell married Amelia Jane Eddington, and they were the parents of two sons and two daughters.

[G. A. Williams, "Robert Havell, Jr.," *Print Collector's Quart.*, Oct. 1916; D. M. Stauffer, *Am. Engravers upon Copper and Steel* (1907); S. T. Prideaux, *Aquatint Engraving* (1909); Ruthven Deane, "The Copper Plates of the Folio Edition of Audubon's 'Birds of America,'" *Auk*, Oct. 1908; Harry Harris, "Uncolored Prints from Havell's Engravings of Audubon's 'Birds of America,'" *Auk*, Jan. 1918; F. H. Herrick, *Audubon the Naturalist* (2 vols., 1917).]

M. B. H.

HAVEMEYER, HENRY OSBORNE (Oct. 18, 1847–Dec. 4, 1907), sugar refiner and capitalist, a member of a family long identified with the sugar industry in America, was born in New York City, a son of Frederick Christian and Sarah Osborne (Townsend) Havemeyer. The family had already amassed wealth from the sugar trade. When Henry was fourteen years old his grandfather, Frederick Christian, died leaving an estate of $3,000,000. His father had been a partner of a cousin, William Frederick [*q.v.*], who was three times mayor of New York. Notwithstanding the affluence into which he was born, the boy received barely the equivalent of a high-school education and was then apprenticed in the sugar-refining business. At the time of his entrance into the organization the processes had undergone great changes since the Havemeyer brothers from Germany had set up their little refinery in lower Manhattan some sixty years before. Large plants had been erected on the Brooklyn waterfront and important economies had been effected in the handling of imported raw sugar. In course of time Henry and his older brother Theodore came into a controlling interest in the Brooklyn refineries during a period of rapid expansion in the industry. Both brothers knew the technology of the business, and Henry, in addition, was experienced in buying and selling. In 1887 they succeeded in forming a merger of all the important refining interests in New York and Brooklyn (controlling fifteen plants in all), to be known as the Sugar Refineries Company. Henry Havemeyer was made president. Soon the combine, which came to be known as the sugar trust, was attacked in the courts. A lengthy litigation followed, and finally, in June 1890, the court of appeals decided unanimously against its legality and the necessary steps for its dissolution were at once taken (*People of the State of New York, Respondent* vs. *North River Sugar Refining Company, Appellant,* 121, *N. Y.*, 582–626).

The corporation was reorganized in 1891 under a New Jersey charter as the American Sugar Refining Company and was not thereafter impeded by legal proceedings. In the reorganization Henry Havemeyer took charge of the financial side of the operation. He now had a considerable acquaintance in Wall Street and could command support among capitalists because he was a dividend producer. He was a persistent advocate of the lowering of tariff barriers to the importation of raw sugar, but joined other manufacturers in demanding protection for the finished product. It was in his administration that the long and bitter contest took place with John Arbuckle [*q.v.*], the coffee merchant. At Havemeyer's death, in 1907, the American Sugar Refining Company, still under his direction, owned more than twenty-five plants and manufactured approximately half of the sugar consumed in the United States.

With wealth and leisure, Havemeyer was able to indulge his taste for country life. On the shore of Great South Bay, Long Island, he had an estate valued in his lifetime at $250,000. He was twice married: first to Mary L. Elder, and then to her niece, Louisine W. Elder. With the latter, who outlived him twenty-one years, he became a discriminating collector of European art objects. By his widow's will, probated in January 1929, the Metropolitan Museum of Art received nearly one hundred paintings, including works by Rembrandt, Corot, Degas, and others as well known.

[Robert N. Burnett, "Captains of Industry: Henry Osborne Havemeyer," *Cosmopolitan*, Apr. 1903; Franklin Clarkin, "The Great Business Combinations of To-day: The So-called Sugar Trust," *Century Mag.*, Jan. 1903; *House Report 3112*, 50 Cong., 1 Sess.; the *Sun* (N. Y.), Dec. 5, 1907.] W. B. S.

HAVEMEYER, WILLIAM FREDERICK (Feb. 12, 1804–Nov. 30, 1874), sugar refiner, capitalist, mayor of New York City, was descended from a family which had figured in the bakers' guild of Bückeburg, capital of the German principality of Schaumburg-Lippe, since the middle of the seventeenth century. He was born in New York City five years after his father, William Havemeyer, had emigrated from England, where he had learned the trade of sugar refining. The elder Havemeyer followed that calling in America and early in the century founded a business of his own. His refinery was in Vandam Street and in that neighborhood the boy grew up. He attended private schools and Columbia College, from which he was graduated in 1823, a student of fair ability, showing some aptitude for mathematics. After graduation he studied law for a short time but soon left it for a clerkship in his father's sugar business. In 1828 he formed a partnership with his cousin, Frederick Christian Havemeyer, in owning and operating a refinery, which was successful, but for reasons not disclosed he disposed of his interest to his brother Albert and retired from the business in 1842, at the early age of thirty-eight. He was already well-to-do.

For a time Havemeyer took an interest in local politics. In 1844 he was a delegate to the Democratic General Committee of the city (then controlled by Tammany Hall) and was one of the Polk presidential electors that year. Soon Tammany made him chairman of its finance committee. In 1845 he was nominated and elected mayor over James Harper. On the whole he satisfied all factions during his incumbency, but he declined reëlection in 1846. In 1848 he was again elected, but after serving his term, he withdrew as before. In the decade of the fifties he turned his attention to banking activities, becoming president of the Bank of North America and of the New York Savings Bank. He resigned both offices in 1861. In the meantime he had acquired interests in the Pennsylvania Coal Company and the Long Island Railroad. With the exception of interference in a contest between state and city authorities for the control of the local police in 1857 and an unsuccessful candidacy for mayor in 1859, he was out of the political limelight during that period. At the outbreak of the Civil War he presided at one of the great meetings in Union Square to uphold the cause of the Union. As a War Democrat he supported the Lincoln administration.

For another ten years New York's citizens lost sight of Havemeyer. Then came the "Tweed ring" disclosures and the demand of an outraged city for the punishment of the bandits. At this juncture Havemeyer came forward, after almost a quarter of a century in retirement, and in company with Samuel J. Tilden set up a standard to which all decent citizens might rally. Heading the New York city council of reform, he won support, on the single issue of clean government, from men of all parties. On Apr. 6, 1871, and again on Sept. 4 he presided over mass-meetings in Cooper Union from which emerged the Committee of Seventy, pledged to hunt down the thieves and banish them from office. With Tilden he obtained from the Broadway Bank, in which the "Tweed ring" kept its accounts, legal proof of the stealings from the city and enabled suits to be brought for the recovery of the loot. When the mayoralty election of 1872 drew near, Tammany put up a highly respectable candidate to reassure the honest voter. The Republican organization, seeing a chance of victory, named Havemeyer, who was elected.

Within six months after assuming his duties in the City Hall for the third time, Havemeyer had apparently forfeited the good opinion of all who had counted on the success of his administration. Not a newspaper in the city continued its support. Not one influential leader of public opinion commended his acts or policies. His seventieth birthday found him as nearly friendless as a man in public life can be. His reappointment of two police commissioners (one of whom was an intimate personal friend), after their conviction for offenses involving the violation of their oaths of office, astounded the city. The greater part of the two-year term for which he was inaugurated was taken up with wranglings over appointments with the Board of Aldermen. At length a petition was sent to Gov. John A. Dix for the mayor's removal. The Governor's comment on the charges—a stern arraignment of Havemeyer's official conduct—did not go so far as to order removal because there was no imputation of corrupt motives and no assertion that the mayor had been unfaithful to his constituents. On Nov. 30, 1874, after his successor had been chosen, and while a suit for libel brought against him by John Kelly, former sheriff, was being tried, Havemeyer died suddenly of apoplexy in his office. With the shock that followed this tragic end of a career recently marked by startling vicissitudes there was a demonstration of popular grief, for it was remembered that no charge of dishonesty or cowardice had been brought against the man in the thirty years since his first election, and of few New York politicians in those days could as much be said. Havemeyer had married Sarah Agnes Craig in 1828. She, with several children, survived him.

[For the family history, see *Life, Letters and Addresses of John Craig Havemeyer* (1914); also *In Memoriam: Wm. Frederick Havemeyer, Mayor of the City of N. Y.* (1881). Obituaries appeared in the New York newspapers of Dec. 1, 1874. Havemeyer's part in the citizens' movement of 1870–72 is described in the reports of the New York City Council of Political Reform and of the Committee of Seventy. "Our Wonderfully Reformed City Government," by Edward I. Sears, in the *Nat. Quart. Rev.*, June 1873, is a survey of the same activities from a hostile viewpoint.]

W. B. S.

HAVEN, ALICE B. [See HAVEN, EMILY BRADLEY NEAL, 1827–1863].

HAVEN, EMILY BRADLEY NEAL (Sept. 13, 1827–Aug. 23, 1863), author, editor, was the daughter of George and Sarah (Brown) Bradley of Hudson, N. Y. When she was three years old her father died, and several years later she was adopted by her mother's brother, the Rev. J. Newton Brown, a scholarly clergyman, who directed her education. She attended schools in Boston and in Exeter, N. H., while her uncle resided in those cities, and received further training in an academy at New Hampton, N. H. There her youthful poems and sketches received high praise, and, encouraged by the admiration of her companions, she sent several of her compositions, signed Alice G. Lee, to a popular Philadelphia weekly, *Neal's Saturday Gazette and Lady's Literary Museum.* Acquaintance with Joseph C. Neal [*q.v.*], the editor of this paper, followed, and in December 1846 she became his wife, retaining thereafter, at his request, her pen name of Alice, instead of her baptismal name of Emily. For a few months following her marriage she acted as assistant editor of the paper, contributing to it a lively column of social and literary chat over the signature of Clara Cushman. In July 1847 her husband died, and the young widow, not yet twenty, assumed his responsibilities on the periodical and carried it on for the next six years in partnership with Charles J. Peterson. She was greatly admired in Philadelphia literary circles, where her beauty, charm, and talent made her a somewhat romantic figure among editors. While writing regularly for her own weekly, she also contributed to *Sartain's, Graham's,* and *Godey's* and as Cousin Alice, a name by which she became widely known, produced several popular books for children. For older readers she published *Helen Morton's Trial* (1849) and *The Gossips of Rivertown* (1850). On Jan. 1, 1853, she married Samuel L. Haven, a New York broker, and removed to Mamaroneck, occupying there during her later years James Fenimore Cooper's "Closet Hall," which she renamed "The Willows." Two sons and three daughters were born of this marriage. She continued her literary work as Alice B. Haven, contributing regularly to the *Lady's Book* for the rest of her life and frequently to *Harper's.* She wrote for the Appletons between 1851 and 1859 a series of seven Home Books, designed "to show the bravery of a self-reliant and humble spirit," with such titles as *Contentment Better Than Wealth* (1853), *All's Not Gold That Glitters* (1853), *Out of Debt, Out of Danger* (1855). Her work was well paid, and, having learned that "water-colors sell best," she produced pleasant, easily understood tales intended to inculcate a moral or correct a fault. Regarding her talent as a sacred trust, she employed a large part of her earnings in relieving the needs of others. Her last long work, *The Good Report* (1867), was published after her death. Always delicate and fragile in body but strong and determined in spirit, she devoted herself so actively to her household, her charities, her friends, and her writings that a prominent contemporary editor declared, "Her life unites all that is most worthy of imitation in female excellence." In a vain attempt to arrest the development of tuberculosis, she spent her last winters in Florida and Bermuda. She died in Mamaroneck shortly before her thirty-sixth birthday and was buried in the cemetery at Rye.

[C. B. Richards, *Cousin Alice: A Memoir of Alice B. Haven* (1865), with extracts from Mrs. Haven's journal; S. J. Hale, *Woman's Record* (1874 ed.); *N. Y. Tribune,* Aug. 24, 1863; "Alice B. Haven," *Godey's Lady's Book,* Jan. 1864; files of *Neal's Saturday Gazette,* Am. Antiq. Soc. Lib.; information from the family.]

B. M. S.

HAVEN, ERASTUS OTIS (Nov. 1, 1820–Aug. 2, 1881), educator, bishop of the Methodist Episcopal Church, a first cousin of Gilbert Haven [*q.v.*], was born in Boston, Mass. His father was Jotham Haven, a Methodist local preacher and a descendant of Richard Haven who emigrated from England to Lynn, Mass., in 1644; his mother was Betsy Spear. At Wesleyan University, where he was graduated with honors in 1842, he joined the Methodist Episcopal Church. In 1843, while teaching at Sudbury, Mass., where he had started a private academy, he began to preach, though he did not join the New York Methodist Conference until 1848.

Meanwhile he taught for a time in Amenia (N. Y.) Seminary, of which he was principal in 1846–48. For five years thereafter he was pastor of Methodist churches in and near New York City, until in 1853 he was called to the chair of Latin in the University of Michigan. The following year he became professor of history and English literature, serving for two years. At this time he advocated the opening of the institution to women. From 1856 to 1863 he was editor of *Zion's Herald,* the Boston Methodist weekly, which he piloted with steady hand through the anti-slavery storms that preceded the Civil War. Though not an abolitionist, he demanded the exclusion of slave-holders from church-membership. Temperance reform he warmly supported. He served on the state Board of Education and was twice a member of the Senate, in which capacity he framed the law which established the Massachusetts Agricultural College and greatly strengthened the Massachusetts Institute of Technology. He also represented the state on the Board of Overseers of Harvard College. In 1863, he was recalled to Ann Arbor as professor of rhetoric and English literature and president of the University of Michigan. He found the school greatly agitated over the removal of President Henry Philip Tappan [*q.v.*], but his moderation, self-control, and understanding restored peace and order. It was he who conceived the plan of annual legislative appropriations for the support of the University, and he had the satisfaction of seeing it provided for by law in 1867, ensuring the permanent support of the institution, hitherto precarious. All state universities have profited by this act. In 1869 he accepted the presidency of Northwestern University, a struggling young Methodist institution near Chicago. Here his constructive plans for the development of professional schools were interrupted by the Chicago fire (1871), and in 1872 he resigned to become corresponding secretary of the newly organized Board of Education of the Methodist Episcopal Church, an administrative and advisory position for which his wide educational experience had given him extraordinary qualifications. He was at the same time chancellor of Syracuse University (1874–80), then in its formative stages. Here again, his prestige, his wisdom, his conciliatory spirit, and his courage, saved an imperiled institution. In 1878 he bore greetings to the Methodists of Great Britain, where he secured Wesleyan cooperation in the plan for an Ecumenical Methodist Conference. Elected bishop in May 1880, he went to reside in San Francisco, Cal. Sedentary life had unfitted him for the long journeys and arduous labors of a Methodist general superintendent, and he succumbed in less than a year, dying at Salem, Ore., whither he had gone to preside at a conference. He was survived by his wife, Mary Frances, daughter of the Rev. George Coles of New York City, and by three sons and two daughters.

Haven was a polished writer and speaker; he had marked intellectual and organizing gifts. In the Methodist Episcopal General Conference of 1860 he exerted himself to secure the exclusion of slave-owners from the church, and in 1868 he was chairman of the committee which framed the provision admitting laymen to membership in the General Conference. His books and pamphlets include: *The Young Man Advised* (1855); *Universities in America* (1863); *Lincoln, Memorial Address* (1865); *The Legal Profession in America* (1866); *The Pillars of Truth* (1866); *The Medical Profession* (1869); *Rhetoric* (1869); *The National Handbook of American Progress* (1876). He also prepared an autobiography which was published after his death.

[*Autobiog. of Erastus O. Haven* (1883), ed. by C. C. Stratton; H. H. Moore, in *Lives of the Methodist Bishops* (1883), ed. by T. L. Flood and J. W. Hamilton; memorial discourse by Alexander Winchell, delivered in 1881, in *Report of the Pioneer Soc. of the State of Mich.,* vol. VI (1884); Josiah Adams, *The Geneal. of the Descendants of Richard Haven of Lynn, Mass.* (1843); and *Continuation of the Geneal.* (1849); the *Christian Advocate* (N. Y.), Aug. 11, 1881.] J. R. J.

HAVEN, GILBERT (Sept. 19, 1821–Jan. 3, 1880), abolitionist, bishop of the Methodist Episcopal Church, was born in Malden, Mass., being the fifth of the ten children of Gilbert and Hannah (Burrill) Haven, of old New England stock. He was a cousin of Erastus Otis Haven [*q.v.*]. He attended Wesleyan Academy, Wilbraham, Mass., where he experienced a Methodist conversion; and Wesleyan University (B.A. 1846), where he was noted for his scholarship, his genial personality, his anti-slavery opinions, and his gift for leadership. After five years in Amenia (N. Y.) Seminary, where he taught Greek and German and was for three years principal, he entered the Methodist Episcopal ministry in the New England Conference in 1851. During his early pastorate in Massachusetts he distinguished himself by his interest in public affairs, especially the moral questions that were involved in the political issues of the time. His sermons, and notably his articles in the religious and secular press, were vigorous expressions of fiery convictions on slavery, temperance, *et cetera.* At Lincoln's first call for troops he volunteered and was commissioned chaplain of the 8th Massachusetts on Apr. 30, 1861.

After a year in Europe (1862) he returned to the ministry in Boston. He was now bent on securing for the freedmen the full fruits of emancipation. He advocated civil rights and absolute social equality, even to racial amalgamation. He resisted the wish of the bishops to send him South as a missionary because they limited his field to the blacks. From 1867 to 1872 as editor of *Zion's Herald,* the Boston Methodist weekly, he was a powerful ally of Charles Sumner and the radical Republicans, as well as a strong advocate of prohibition, woman's suffrage, and lay representation. He compelled the nation to take notice of him, while his own church echoed with his sayings—"Havenisms." In 1868 he was a member of the General Conference and mentioned for the episcopacy. In 1872 he was elected, to the dismay of conservatives and the rapturous delight of the negroes and radicals. His residence was fixed in Atlanta, Ga. Socially ostracized and threatened with violence because he practised the racial equality which he preached, he energetically pressed the freedmen's claims, gave his own money and solicited gifts to found schools and colleges for them, and enlisted Northern college graduates to come South and teach the former slaves and their children. By his articles, sermons, and lectures he kept the North informed with regard to the Southern policy of repression, and fearlessly denounced the secret organizations which "murdered people for their opinions." He visited Mexico in 1873 with the Rev. William Butler, and cooperated with him in planting Methodism in the capital. In 1876 he visited the Methodist missions in Liberia, where he contracted the African malaria which tormented him ever after. He finally succumbed on Jan. 3, 1880, in Malden, Mass., leaving a son and a daughter, both of whom became noted in religious work. His wife, Mary Ingraham, whom he married at Amenia, N. Y., in 1851, died in 1860.

Bishop Haven was of medium height, compactly built, with ruddy face and red hair. His voice was unattractive and his delivery forced, but he carried his hearers and his readers with him by the strength and warmth of his own convictions. As a writer he was journalistic rather than literary. His publications were: *The Pilgrim's Wallet* (1866); *National Sermons* (1869); *Father Taylor, the Sailor Preacher* (1872), with Thomas Russell; *Our Next Door Neighbor: A Winter in Mexico* (1875); *Christus Consolator* (1893), with a preface and notes by his son; and pamphlets including: *Parkerism* (1860), *Lay Representation in the Methodist Episcopal Church* (1864), *Te Deum Laudamus: the Cause and the Consequence of the Election of Abraham Lincoln* (1860), *The Uniter and Liberator of America* (1865)—a memorial discourse on Lincoln, *An Appeal to Our People for Our People* (1875). Some years after his death there was published *Heavenly Messenger* (1890), which, it was alleged, was a communication from Haven through a spiritualist medium.

[Erastus Wentworth, *Gilbert Haven: A Monograph* (1880); George Prentice, *The Life of Gilbert Haven* (1883); *Memorials of Gilbert Haven* (1880), ed. by Wm. H. Daniels; T. L. Flood, "Gilbert Haven," in *Lives of Methodist Bishops* (1882), by T. L. Flood and J. W. Hamilton; Josiah Adams, *The Geneal. of the Descendants of Richard Haven of Lynn, Mass.* (1843) and *Continuation of the Geneal.* (1849); the *Christian Advocate* (N. Y.), Jan. 8, 1880.] J. R. J.

HAVEN, HENRY PHILEMON (Feb. 11, 1815–Apr. 30, 1876), whaling merchant, Sunday-school superintendent, descended from Richard Haven, a resident of Lynn, Mass., in 1645, was born in Norwich, Conn., the son of Philemon and Fanny (Manwaring) Caulkins Haven. When he was four years old his father died, leaving his family of five in ragged poverty. Henry learned to sew, to cook, and to do the work on the little farm. He obtained a meager education in the public schools. He attended Sunday-school assiduously and founded a juvenile society against swearing. These influences of his youth, a grim theology and grim poverty, moulded his entire life. In 1830 the family moved to New London where he was indentured to Thomas W. Williams, a wealthy ship-owner. Six years later he became a confidential clerk and at the age of twenty-three a partner in the firm of Haven & Smith, a company already successfully engaged in whaling and sealing. Haven possessed indomitable energy, shrewdness and efficiency, the ability and the desire to drive hard bargains. At this time the American whale fishery was enjoying its greatest prominence and extent. He prospered and scattered his ships over the Atlantic, the Pacific, and distant seas in search of profits. Sea-elephants from the Indian Ocean and guano from islands in the Western Pacific were among the sources of his wealth. In 1867, while negotiations were in progress for the purchase of Alaska, he corresponded with Seward about the opening of the seal fisheries to Americans. When Alaska was ceded his vessels were sealing there before Californians had begun to realize the new opportunities. He was active in forming a company of Eastern and Western ship-owners which in August 1870 obtained a monopoly of the seal fisheries at St. Paul's and St. George's Islands. He reorganized and became president of the New London & Northern Railroad Company and was prominent in three Connecticut banks. In 1852 he was elected mayor of New London and in the same year was elected to the state Assembly. He was the Republican candidate for governor in 1873. When he, with the entire ticket, was defeated he recollected that man's judgment was but a little thing: and looked forward to his weighing in the Lord's balances.

Haven's success as a merchant was considerable, yet his success as a Sunday-school superintendent was greater. He became a Sunday-school teacher at the age of fifteen; six years later he went to combat the evils of rum, prostitution, and unbelief in the seaport town of Waterford. This struggle he continued until his death. In 1858 he became superintendent of the Sunday school of the Second Congregational Church in New London. To this task he brought a restless energy and a militant piety. With thoroughness and efficiency he reorganized it as he had reorganized banks and railroads. He was one of the first and principal contributors to the International Sunday-school Lessons. Many of his innovations are still employed in Sunday schools. In 1869 he prepared for the *New-England Historical and Genealogical Register* (October 1869) a memoir of his half-sister, Frances Manwaring Caulkins (1795–1869), historian of Norwich and New London. The death in 1874 of his wife, Elizabeth Lucas Douglas, whom he had married, Feb. 23, 1840, induced him to go to Europe the following year. He attended various meetings of religious groups abroad and had returned and resumed his usual duties when he died of heart failure.

[H. C. Trumbull, *A Model Superintendent: Sketch of the Life, Character, and Methods . . . of Henry P. Haven* (1880); *New-Eng. Hist. and Geneal. Reg.*, Jan. 1879; Alexander Starbuck, *Hist. of the Am. Whale Fishery . . . to 1876* (1878); D. H. Hurd, *Hist. of New London County, Conn.* (1882); Josiah Adams, *The Geneal. of the Descendants of Richard Haven of Lynn, Mass.* (1843).] F. M.

HAVEN, JOSEPH (Jan. 4, 1816–May 23, 1874), clergyman, teacher, scholar, was born in Dennis, Mass., the son of Rev. Joseph and Elizabeth (Sparrow) Haven and a descendant of Richard Haven who was a resident of Lynn, Mass., in 1645. While he was still a child, his parents removed to Amherst, and here, in the quiet, cultural atmosphere of a clergyman's home and amid the outdoor delights of one of the most charming of Massachusetts towns, he passed his boyhood. Prepared at the local academy, he entered Amherst College in 1831. His studies were largely confined to the classical languages and history, with scattered courses in mathematics, science, and philosophy. At his graduation in 1835, he delivered the class oration on "Sources of Superstition." For two years he taught in an institution for deaf mutes in New York City, and at the same time began his theological studies at the Union Theological Seminary. In 1837 he went to the Andover Theological Seminary. Here he won his professional degree (1839) and a wife—Mary, daughter of Prof. Ralph Emerson, whom he married on Sept. 23, 1840. He had ten children, four of whom, with Mrs. Haven, survived him.

In the November following his graduation, Haven was ordained and installed pastor of the Congregational church in Ashland, Mass. From this pastorate he was called in 1846 to the Harvard Congregational Church in Brookline, Mass., where he remained four years. In addition to his pastoral duties in this large and important parish, he did editorial work on the *Congregationalist,* of which with Edward Beecher and Dr. Increase N. Tarbox, he was one of the original editors. A crisis came in his career in 1850, when he was called to the chair of mental and moral philosophy in Amherst College. Assuming the duties of this professorship in January of the next year, he definitely abandoned the ministry, and gave himself henceforth to a life of teaching and study. After seven years at Amherst, he resigned, in August 1858, to accept a call to the chair of systematic theology in the Chicago Theological Seminary, which had been chartered in 1855 without faculty or sufficient funds. Haven opened the school with Franklin W. Fisk and Samuel C. Bartlett [*q.v.*] as his associates. "These three men," writes President Ozora Stearns Davis, "are known in our tradition and history as the great trinity of the early days." Haven remained at Chicago until 1870, when he resigned on account of failing health. After a period of travel in Europe and the Near East, including Palestine, and of preaching and lecturing after his return home, he became in 1873 acting professor of mental and moral philosophy in the University of Chicago, and was engaged in the duties of this office until his death, from typhoid fever complicated with inflammatory rheumatism, in the fifty-eighth year of his age.

Joseph Haven had real genius as a teacher. It was said of him in his early years at Amherst that "he taught the Scotch philosophy with a logical clearness and force worthy of the system, and with a felicity of illustration and a vein of humor that were all his own." In his maturer days he had the reputation of "making even the driest subject interesting." Not an imparter of facts merely, he was a living force of eloquence and passion (*Obituary Record of the Graduates of Amherst College,* 1874). As a scholar and author he exercised authority and influence in his time. His books, *Mental Philosophy* (1857), *Mental Science as a Branch of Education* (1857),

Moral Philosophy (1859), *Studies in Philosophy and Theology* (1869), and a posthumous *History of Philosophy* (1876), were widely read in this country and abroad. When traveling in the Near East he found classes in Syria and Turkey conducted with his textbooks as guides. His greatest work was undoubtedly done at the Chicago Theological Seminary which he served during the first decade of its history while in the full maturity of his powers and ripeness of his scholarship. In religion he was evangelical, but "one of the most liberal and progressive theologians of the time." His preaching had simplicity and elegance, and was welcomed in churches of many denominations.

[Official records at Amherst College, Union Theological Seminary, Andover Theological Seminary, and the University of Chicago; C. D. Helmer, *A Sermon in Memory of Joseph Haven* (1874); *Chicago Theol. Sem. Quarter Centennial Hist. Sketch* (1879); Josiah Adams, *The Geneal. of the Descendants of Richard Haven, of Lynn, Mass.* (1843); *Chicago Daily Tribune* and *Daily Inter Ocean*, May 27, 1874; letter from the late President O. S. Davis, Chicago Theol. Sem.]

J. H. H.

HAVENS, JAMES SMITH (May 28, 1859–Feb. 27, 1927), congressman, lawyer, was born in Weedsport, Cayuga County, N. Y., the son of Dexter Eber and Lucy Bell (Smith) Havens. After preparing for college in the public schools of Weedsport and in Monroe Collegiate Institute, Elbridge, N. Y., he entered Yale with the class of 1882, but his college course was interrupted by illness, and he was not graduated until 1884. He studied law in the office of William F. Cogswell of Rochester, was admitted to the bar in 1886, and practised in Rochester for more than forty years. He was soon recognized as a wise counselor and a powerful advocate with a high standard of personal and professional ethics. His cases were always well prepared, and his presentation was marked by unusual simplicity and clarity. For many years he was ranked as one of the leaders of the bar in Western New York. An enthusiastic Democrat by inheritance and conviction, he was at all times willing to work for the party, and was an effective campaigner, but was never a candidate for public office until 1910. In that year, after a campaign which attracted nation-wide attention, he overcame a large adverse majority and was elected (Apr. 19) to the United States House of Representatives for the unexpired term (1910–11) of his deceased law-partner, James Breck Perkins [*q.v.*], defeating George W. Aldridge, the Republican leader of Monroe County (see *Review of Reviews*, New York, May 1910). Havens refused to consider a nomination for the succeeding term and returned to his profession at the end of his few months of service. In 1918, he became assistant treasurer of the Eastman Kodak Company, though his duties were more legal than financial. The next year he was made secretary and vice-president in charge of the legal department. In this latter capacity he was instrumental in settling many complicated questions which had arisen between the company and the United States government as a result of the World War. He also retained a limited private practice for a few old clients, and continued to serve as director in various financial, industrial, and civic organizations. His death occurred in Rochester after several months of failing health.

During his long residence in Rochester, Havens was much respected for his legal and financial ability and his sense of civic responsibility, while his high character, friendly nature, and unfailing courtesy made him many warm friends. His attitude toward the younger members of the bar was especially considerate. He married, Jan. 16, 1894, Caroline Prindle Sammons of Rochester, who with a daughter and two sons survived him.

[*Who's Who in America*, 1926–27; *Cong. Record*, 61 Cong., 2 Sess.; *A Hist. cf the Class of Eighty-Four, Yale College* (1914); *Biog. Dir. Am. Cong.* (1928); sketch in *Democrat and Chronicle* (Rochester), Feb. 28, 1927, prepared by Havens' secretary in anticipation of his death; obituary in *N. Y. Times*, Feb. 28, 1927; information as to certain facts from Havens' nephew and former law-partner, Samuel M. Havens.] H. T.

HAVERLY, CHRISTOPHER (June 30, 1837–Sept. 28, 1901), "Col. Jack H. Haverly," theatrical manager, the son of Christopher and Eliza (Steel) Haverly, was born at Boiling Springs (now Axemann) near Bellefonte, Pa. He began his career in 1864 by the purchase of a variety theatre in Toledo, Ohio, where he remained for two years. His first minstrel show opened at Adrian, Mich., on Aug. 1, 1864, and played about four weeks. Burgess and Haverly's Minstrels were inaugurated on Oct. 8, 1864, at Toronto, Canada, but by the end of the month Burgess had withdrawn and the troupe was again Haverly's Minstrels. In 1866 his troupe toured with that of Dick Sands; the following years he took over the management of Billy Arlington's Minstrels. He became manager of Cal Wagner's Minstrels in 1870. During the next several years Haverly purchased interests in other minstrel troupes and acquired theatres. He secured from Tom Maguire an interest in Emerson's Minstrels in 1875 and became part owner of the New Orleans Minstrels in 1876 and of Callender's Colored Minstrels two years later. He bought the old Adelphi Theatre in Chicago in 1876 and quickly came to own or control more than a dozen theatres in Chicago, New York, Philadelphia, and San Francisco. His most famous show was Haverly's Mastodon Minstrels, sometimes known from its advertisements as the "Forty, Count 'Em! Forty!" troupe, which he organized in 1878.

At the height of his career Haverly took his Mastodon Minstrels to England and, after a sensational advertising campaign, opened at Her Majesty's Theatre in the Haymarket, London, on July 31, 1880. For seventeen weeks he played to crowded houses. Following a tour of the provinces and another engagement in London he took his troupe to Germany, where for a time he was in danger of arrest for fraud, because he presented his company of white entertainers as a troupe of negro minstrels. He returned to New York in the early summer of 1881. The following July he again opened at Her Majesty's Theatre, but with a large troupe composed entirely of negroes. After an unsuccessful season of several months he returned to America early in 1882. In May 1884 Haverly opened in London at the Drury Lane Theatre with his Mastodon Minstrels, the most brilliant company he had ever assembled, but a prolonged heat wave and the competition of Callender's All-Colored Minstrels made this venture a financial failure. When he returned to New York in August, his fortune was gone, for during his absence abroad his affairs had become involved. Haverly, whose income had once been between ten and twenty thousand dollars a day, was reduced to running a small and unsuccessful museum in Brooklyn. He was a constant poker player and a daring speculator in mining stocks. During his career he is said to have won and lost five fortunes. Under the guidance of John Cudahy [*q.v.*] he speculated in pork and in an attempt to gain control of the New York stock exchange one of his fortunes crashed. During the last three years of his life he was engaged in mining in the West. Although he is considered to have been the greatest minstrel manager in America his name was unknown when he died of typhoid fever in Salt Lake City in 1901. He was twice married—to the Duval (Hechinger) Sisters, vocalists. Sara, whom he married first, died at Toledo, Ohio, in March 1867, but Eliza, his second wife, survived him. He published in 1879 *Haverly's Genuine Georgia Colored Minstrels' Songster,* a collection of negro jubilee and camp-meeting songs and hymns. *Negro Minstrels* (1902), a collection of recitations and stories attributed to him, was chiefly the work of an enterprising publisher.

[Edward Le Roy Rice, *Monarchs of Minstrelsy* (1911); Dailey Paskman and Sigmund Spaeth, *"Gentlemen, Be Seated!"* (1928); Harry Reynolds, *Minstrel Memories . . . Minstrelsy in Great Britain from 1836 to 1927* (London, 1928); Ike Simond, *Old Slack's Reminiscences* (Chicago, 1891); *Deseret Evening News* (Salt Lake City), Sept. 30, 1901; information from Byron Haverly Blackford of Bellefonte, Pa.] F. M.

HAVERLY, JACK H. [See HAVERLY, CHRISTOPHER, 1837–1901].

HAVILAND, CLARENCE FLOYD (Aug. 15, 1875–Jan. 1, 1930), physician and psychiatrist, was born in Spencertown, N. Y., the son of Dr. Norman H. Haviland, a physician, and Henrietta (Newman) Haviland. While he was a boy the family moved to Fulton, N. Y., where he attended the public schools and graduated from the local high school in 1893. He at once entered the medical school of Syracuse University from which he received the degree of M.D. in 1896. In the following year he became an interne at the Manhattan State Hospital, New York City, and was promoted in succession to junior physician and second assistant physician, under Dr. William Mabon. After thirteen years of service here he was promoted in 1910 to first assistant physician at King's Park State Hospital. In 1914 he prepared at the request of the National Committee for Mental Hygiene a survey of the care of the insane in Pennsylvania, which was published in book form the following year (*Treatment and Care of the Insane in Pennsylvania,* 1915). In 1915 he left the King's Park hospital to take charge of the Connecticut State Hospital at Middletown, Conn. During his connection with this institution, from 1916 to 1921, he was chairman of the executive committee of the Connecticut Society for Mental Hygiene. In 1921 he was made president of the Connecticut Conference for Social Work, but in the same year returned to New York to serve until 1926 as medical member and chairman of the New York State Hospital Commission. On July 1, 1926, he became superintendent of the Manhattan State Hospital and during this year was chosen president of the American Psychiatric Association. In 1927 he was appointed professor of clinical psychiatry at the College of Physicians and Surgeons, New York. On Dec. 3, 1929, accompanied by Mrs. Haviland, he sailed from New York for a Mediterranean cruise; in Cairo he was attacked by influenza-pneumonia, and although he was treated by American medical men at the Anglo-American Hospital there, he succumbed to the infection. He was survived by his wife, Amy Amelia Miller, whom he married June 26, 1908, by his father, and by a brother, also a psychiatrist.

Although Haviland lacked the academic training received by many of his contemporaries in modern psychiatry, he was, nevertheless, an able representative of that school. Enthusiastic and with a tremendous capacity for work, he devoted his entire professional life to improving the care of the insane and to efforts toward the prevention of insanity. Influential only after he became a member of the New York State Hospital Board, he is given the major share of credit for various advances made during his few years' incumbency. In the belief that mass insanity could be benefited by occupational therapy, he succeeded in having such treatment standardized throughout all the state hospitals. He caused the quality of service rendered in the state hospitals by doctors, nurses, and attendants to be investigated, and instituted courses of instruction for attendants and nurses, and a series of mental diagnostic clinics for the enlightenment of the staff physicians. The mental clinics were extended to include problem children. He also formulated a building program designed to prevent overcrowding and give the best fire protection, in accordance with which plan two new state hospitals were constructed and additions were made to others. Among his favorite projects were state psychiatric clinics at the Medical Center, New York, and at Syracuse University. He was greatly interested in mental hygiene and all forms of social prophylaxis, including eugenics. He was one of the editors (1923–30) of the *Modern Hospital,* and the author of a number of professional papers.

[*Who's Who in America,* 1928–29; *Am. Jour. of Psychiatry,* Jan. 1930; *Jour. Am. Medic. Asso.,* Jan. 25, 1930; *Psychiatric Quart.,* Jan., Apr. 1930; *Modern Hospital,* Feb. 1930; *Mental Hygiene,* Jan. 1930; *Archives of Neurology and Psychiatry,* Mar. 1930; *Alumni Record and Gen. Cat. of Syracuse Univ., 1872–1910,* vol. III. pt. 1 (1911); *N. Y. Times,* Jan. 2, 1930.]

E. P.

HAVILAND, JOHN (Dec. 15, 1792–Mar. 28, 1852), architect, was born at Gundenham Manor, Somerset, England, the son of James Haviland, a small squire, and Ann, daughter of Benjamin Cobley, a rector of the Church of England. On his mother's side he was connected with Benjamin Robert Haydon, the artist. After an academic education he studied architecture in London with James Elmes and superintended several buildings in London. His mother's sister had married Admiral Count Morduinoff, whom he visited in St. Petersburg before removing to America in 1816. He landed at Philadelphia in September of that year. Among his letters of introduction was one from General von Sonntag, whose sister he subsequently married.

In Philadelphia Haviland, with Hugh Bridport, conducted an architectural drawing school (advertisements of 1818 reproduced in the *Journal of the American Institute of Architecture,* October 1916, pp. 420, 421) and in 1818–19 they published *The Builders Assistant for the Use of Carpenters and Others,* in two volumes (2nd edition, 3 vols., 1825). Haviland designed many buildings in Philadelphia, including the First Presbyterian Church, St. Andrew's Episcopal Church, and the Pennsylvania Institute for the Deaf and Dumb (now the School of Industrial Art), with its fine, sober Greek-Doric front. Other buildings from his designs were the United States Naval Asylum at Norfolk, the State Insane Asylum at Harrisburg, the County Halls of Pittsburgh, Newark, York and other towns, and numerous churches and private houses. He is said to have received the first premium for a design for the New York Exchange, but this building, as well as the Philadelphia City Hall (see his printed *Communications to the County Commissioners, City Councils, and County Board on the Subject of the New Public Buildings for Philadelphia,* 1849), was entrusted to other architects.

The most notable work of Haviland, however, was in the creation of the architectural type of the modern prison, on the "radiating plan." The Philadelphia Society for Alleviating the Miseries of Public Prisons, pioneering in prison reform along lines related to the work of the English reformer Howard, secured in 1818 an act providing a prison at Pittsburgh which it was hoped might give opportunity for improvements in management and design. For this institution Haviland unsuccessfully submitted a competitive plan, not preserved, in which he is believed to have adopted the radial type. In 1821 an act was passed providing for the Eastern State Penitentiary at Cherry Hill, Philadelphia. Haviland competed, won, and supervised the building—still in use—until its completion. In this structure, according to the *Pennsylvania Journal of Prison Discipline* at the time of Haviland's death (*post,* p. 101), "the chief objects of prison architecture . . . were for the first time attained." The improvements were instantly recognized, and Haviland was entrusted in following years with the Western Penitentiary at Pittsburgh (succeeding within a few years the building which had been preferred to his first design), the New Jersey, Missouri, and Rhode Island state penitentiaries, the Allegheny, Dauphin, Lancaster, Berks, and many other jails, including the Halls of Justice and City Prison ("The Tombs," replaced 1888) in New York.

The success of his work was so striking that the British, French, and Russian governments sent commissioners to the United States to study and report (William Crawford, *Report on the Penitentiaries of the United States,* London, 1834; F. A. Demetz and G. A. Blouet, *Péniten-*

ciers des États-Unis, Paris, 1837). Blouet, one of the leading architects of France, wrote to Haviland: "As you may see by our report, the establishments constructed by yourself have been the chief source from which we have drawn; they are also the models which we propose as the best" (*Journal of Prison Discipline,* p. 102). Personally very modest, though recognizing his achievement, Haviland was frank, amiable, and liberal in helping others in his profession. He was one of the founders, in 1836, of the short-lived American Institution of Architects, forerunner of the present Institute, and a corresponding member of the Royal Institute of British Architects. He died suddenly, in Philadelphia, in his sixtieth year.

[An obituary in the *Pa. Jour. of Prison Discipline,* July 1852, is a chief source for Haviland's life and contributions to prison design. It gives a portrait in mezzotint, showing a strong, determined face. The *Builder* (London), May 29, 1852, contains a list of Haviland's works, quoted from the *Daily National Intelligencer* (Washington, D. C.), Apr. 16, 1852. His status in his profession is discussed by G. C. Mason in the *Jour. Am. Inst. of Architects,* Sept. 1913. A manuscript by Haviland, "Description of the Halls of Justice or House of Detention, New York," with drawings, is preserved by the Royal Institute of Architects. A drawing for an unidentified building, dated Oct. 25, 1831, exists in the office of the Supt. of the U. S. Capitol at Washington, among papers presented by the Misses Walter.]

F. K.

HAWES, CHARLES BOARDMAN (Jan. 24, 1889–July 15, 1923), writer of tales of adventure, was a descendant of English ancestors who came to Massachusetts in the first half of the seventeenth century, and the son of Charles Taylor and Martha (Boardman) Hawes. He was born in Clifton Springs, N. Y., where his parents were temporarily staying, but was brought up in Bangor, Me., in the schools of which city he prepared for college. He entered Bowdoin in 1907, graduating four years later. Here his interest centered in literature and composition. In his junior and senior years he was class poet, and later in his career occasional bits of verse by him were published; but prose was to be his chosen medium of expression. Three prizes were awarded him during his senior year: one for being "the best scholar in English literature and original English composition"; another as the author of the best short story—even in childhood his gift for story-telling had attracted attention; and the third as the author of the best Commencement part. He was also awarded the Henry W. Longfellow Graduate Scholarship, devised to afford students exhibiting marked ability in English opportunity for graduate work in some other institution. A year at Harvard followed. Both the forest and the sea appealed to him, and he spent his summers with surveying parties in the Maine wilderness where he acquired a knowledge of woodcraft and found inspiration for some of his earlier stories. Fencing and chess were his favorite diversions. After leaving Harvard he taught at Harrisburg Academy, Pa., for a brief period, and then joined the staff of the *Youth's Companion,* Boston. Short stories of distinction from his pen now began to appear in various periodicals and he commenced to gather material for the "swinging yarns of high adventure and the sea" which gave him rank as a writer. He frequented the wharves, talked with seafaring men, perused old chronicles, and collected charts, maps, and logs.

His earliest book, *The Mutineers* (1920), a tale of old days at sea and of adventures in the Far East, first appeared as a serial in the *Open Road,* 1919, a magazine for boys, of which Hawes became associate editor in 1920. For the same periodical were written *The Great Quest,* a romance of 1826, and *The Dark Frigate,* published in book form in 1921 and 1923 respectively. They are vigorous, vivid stories of reckless exploits on sea and land, of pressgang, piracy, slave ships, and bloody fights, in which striking personalities are skilfully depicted and imagination and accuracy of historical background are joined, written in rhythmic prose that lays a spell upon the reader, young or old. A few days after Hawes's sudden death in his thirty-fifth year, his *Gloucester, by Land and Sea* (1923) was published. In 1924 *The Dark Frigate* was awarded the Newbery Medal as the most distinguished contribution of 1923 to American literature for children. The same year appeared *Whaling* (1924), in which is set forth in a wealth of detail the history of that industry from the first whalemen of whom we have record down to the days of its decline. It was completed by his wife, Dorothea, daughter of George W. Cable [*q.v.*], whom he married in June 1916. In 1926 a tablet to his memory was placed in the Bowdoin Library.

[Clayton H. Ernst, *Chas. Boardman Hawes, An Appreciation* (pamphlet, n.d., Little, Brown & Company); *Boston Evening Transcript,* July 17, 1923; *Publishers' Weekly,* Aug. 18 and 25, 1923, July 5, 1924; *Jour. Nat. Educ. Asso.,* Sept. 1924; information furnished by Chas. T. Hawes.]

H. E. S.

HAWKINS, BENJAMIN (Aug. 15, 1754–June 6, 1818), United States senator, Indian agent, the third son of Philemon and Delia (Martin) Hawkins, was born in Warren County, N. C. His father, of English descent, was born in Virginia in 1717 and as a young man removed to North Carolina, where he became a man of substance and importance. On the outbreak of the American Revolution Benjamin was a member of the senior class at the College of New Jersey. At the time General Washington had need of an interpreter to facilitate intercourse with his many French officers and, in some way learning of Hawkins' unusual proficiency in the French language, attached him to his staff. Hawkins returned to North Carolina in 1779 and was immediately pressed into the service of the state in various capacities. In 1781 he was elected to the Congress of the Confederation and served until 1784; and again he was a member in 1786–87. On the adoption of the new constitution of the United States he was one of the two senators first elected to represent North Carolina and by lot drew the six-year term. He was described as a stanch Federalist, "aristocratic, conservative, proud and wealthy." On the turning of the political tide in 1795 he was defeated for reëlection by Timothy Bloodworth [*q.v.*], a Jeffersonian.

For some years before this time Hawkins had become interested in Indian affairs. In 1785 he had been appointed commissioner to treat with the Cherokees and other Southern Indians. The treaty of Hopewell resulted, defining the boundaries of the Cherokees. Later, treaties were negotiated with the Choctaws and Chickasaws (1786). In 1795 President Washington appointed Hawkins and two others to treat with the Creek Confederacy. Hawkins negotiated with them the important treaty of Coleraine (1796) and thus made contacts with the Indians which so furthered his interest in them that when the President tendered him the post of agent to the Creeks and general superintendent of all Indian tribes south of the Ohio, he accepted the appointment. This decision, which was made against the strong opposition of his family and friends and which changed the whole course of his career, reveals the caliber of the man. Highly educated, wealthy, held in the highest esteem by the people of his native state, surrounded by all the comforts of his plantation home, he abandoned all of his old connections and spent the rest of his life among untutored savages with no reward in prospect except the satisfaction of rendering important public service. His domain as Creek agent covered an immense territory in middle and lower Georgia, Alabama, and Mississippi, extending 400 miles east and west and 200 miles from north to south. His headquarters were originally at Fort Hawkins near Macon, but later he removed to the "Old Agency" on the Flint River. His kindly and sympathetic attitude toward the Indians won for him the title "Beloved Man of the Four Nations." So great was his influence that for sixteen years the Creeks were at peace. He taught them pasturage and agriculture. In order to lead them in their painful transition from savage to semicivilized life, he brought his slaves down from his Roanoke plantation and created a large model farm, where he produced quantities of grain and raised herds of cattle and made farm tools and implements. His plantation was an embryonic agricultural college for the Indians.

This peaceful development was interrupted by the War of 1812. British emissaries and Tecumseh fomented the always latent war spirit of the Indians and those Creeks farthest removed from Hawkins' influence rose and began to harry the frontier settlements. Hawkins raised a regiment of friendly Creeks, supported it with his own funds, and became its titular head, though the half-breed chief, William McIntosh, actually commanded the force. The Creeks were completely crushed by Andrew Jackson and peace was restored in 1814. The national government penalized the Confederacy by compelling them to cede a large portion of their land, including important areas occupied by those Creeks who had remained friendly. The spirit of the Creeks was forever broken. Hawkins was bitterly grieved by this untoward war and its consequences, and his death, which followed shortly thereafter, has been attributed in part to his disappointment at the unfortunate interruption of his work of development. He lies in the Old Agency in Crawford County where his later life work had been done. Hawkins was not only conspicuously successful as an administrator of Indian affairs; he was a man of letters and a keen observer as well. His "Sketch of the Creek Country" (*Georgia Historical Society Collections,* vol. III, pt. 1, 1848) is an interesting, authentic account of the native customs and characteristics of the Creeks. Though many of his manuscripts remain unpublished, the Georgia Historical Society brought out in 1916 a volume of his letters (*Collections,* vol. IX) covering the period from 1796 to 1798.

[An excellent sketch of Hawkins by Stephen B. Weeks was published in the *Biog. Hist. of N. C.,* vol. V (1906), and was reprinted in the *Ga. Hist. Soc. Colls.,* vol. IX (1916). Other accounts may be found in A. H. Chappell, *Miscellanies of Ga.* (1874); L. L. Knight, *A Standard Hist. of Ga. and Georgians* (1917), vol. I; and W. J. Northen, *Men of Mark of Ga.,* vol. II (1910).]

R. P. B—s.

HAWKINS, DEXTER ARNOLD (June 24, 1825–July 24, 1886), lawyer, educator, political reformer, was born in Canton, Me., the son of the Reverend Henry and Abigail (Fuller) Hawkins. He was a descendant of Sir John Hawkins. One grandfather had served in the Continental Army, the other had been under John Paul Jones. His father had been sent as a missionary from Providence, R. I., to the province of Maine. The boy's education in the ordinary district school was supplemented by the teaching of his father, who was an active evangelist in the causes of education, temperance, and abolition. Before entering Bowdoin College in 1844, Hawkins had already gained practical experience as a teacher of mathematics in the academies at Bethel and later at Bridgton, and had completed his own secondary education in the latter. In the year of his graduation from college, 1848, he was appointed by the state board of education as lecturer on public instruction before teachers' institutes—in which capacity during the next three years he gave a course of forty-five lectures attended by three thousand teachers. At the end of that time he was offered the secretaryship of the state board of education; but in spite of his great interest in educational problems the attraction of the law proved greater. Accordingly he entered an office in Portland, Me., and later attended lectures at the Harvard Law School. After two years in Europe, which he divided between courses at L'École des Droits in Paris and a first-hand study of the judicial and educational systems of the various countries, he opened his law office in New York City, Jan. 2, 1854. By the time of the outbreak of the Civil War, he had built up an influential practice. An accident, received in childhood, prevented his active participation in the army, but otherwise he exerted his influence to the utmost in the cause which he so fervidly approved. In 1867 he devoted his energies once more to the cause of education and was instrumental in the establishment of the Department of Education. Three years later—much to the disappointment of Hawkins, who wished the national head of education to be a powerful administrator—this department was relegated to the rank of a bureau in the Department of the Interior. During the remainder of his life Hawkins was an ardent champion, by speeches, pamphlets, and newspaper articles, of a system of free, independently controlled public schools. To him education presented the truest panacea for social evils since it was the surest preventive of pauperism. In 1874 he drew up provisions which were passed into law by New York State under the title, "Act to Secure to Children the Benefits of Elementary Education." Many states followed the New York precedent. In the case of the Southern states, whose educational backwardness he deplored, he advocated corrective interference by the national government. His attacks on parochial schools were bitter, "A child trained in the parochial school . . . is more than three and a quarter times as likely to get into jail as the child trained in the free public school" (*Archbishop Purcell Outdone,* 1880, p. 13). He was equally outspoken in his denunciation of political corruption and extravagance in New York City. The statistics contained in his various pamphlets were instrumental in the overthrow of the Tammany ring and in the correction of other less glaring irregularities. In contrast to the corrupted leaders of municipal politics and parochial schools, the Anglo-Saxon American was praised by Hawkins as being and bidding "fair to be for centuries to come, the best composite, harmonious development, the highest perfection of humanity" (*The Anglo-Saxon Race,* 1875, p. 26). Hawkins died suddenly at Groton, Conn. He had married, Apr. 12, 1859, Sophia T. Meeks.

[*Am. Jour. Educ.,* Mar. 1881; W. B. Lapham, *Centennial Hist. of Norway, Oxford County, Me.* (1886); Nehemiah Cleaveland, *Hist. of Bowdoin Coll. with Biog. Sketches of its Grads.* (1882); *N. Y. Times, N. Y. Tribune,* July 25, 1886.] E. M—s., Jr.

HAWKINS, RUSH CHRISTOPHER (Sept. 14, 1831–Oct. 25, 1920), soldier, collector of incunabula, was born in Pomfret, Vt., the son of Lorenzo Dow and Maria Louisa (Hutchinson) Hawkins. He received no formal education but was trained by members of his family. While under age he served in the Mexican War. In 1851 he took up the study of law in New York City. Success in his profession and fortunate investments in real estate gave him leisure in later life. In June 1860 he married Annmary Brown, the daughter of the Hon. Nicholas Brown of Providence, and the grand-daughter of Nicholas Brown [*q.v.*] after whom Brown University was named. He served in the Civil War from May 1861 until May 1863, heading the "Hawkins Zouaves," the 9th New York Volunteers which he organized and commanded. He saw active service at Hatteras Inlet, Roanoke Island, Winton, South Mills, South Mountain, Antietam, Fredericksburg, and Suffolk, and in 1865 was raised by brevet to the rank of brigadier-general. Equally patriotic and courageous in civil life, he was constantly attacking evils in public morals and was active in promoting remedial legislation. In 1872 he served in the New York legislature, and in 1889 he was United States commissioner of the fine arts at the Universal Exposition, Paris.

Aside from his services rendered during the Civil War, Hawkins' most notable achievement was his assembling of a superb collection of incunabula, now deposited in the Annmary Brown Memorial, the mausoleum which he erected in Providence, R. I. He began early to collect and in 1855 purchased his first fifteenth-century book.

In 1878 he met Henry Bradshaw, librarian of Cambridge University, when the latter was formulating his epoch-making method of studying incunabula. From that moment until his death, Hawkins zealously collected specimens of early printing. In 1884 his list of *Titles of the First Books from the Earliest Presses* introduced into America the system originated by Bradshaw and subsequently developed by Robert Proctor, which was destined to become the basis for modern research in this field. Using this work as a checklist, Hawkins sought to acquire if possible a copy of the first book from each press, thus illustrating the diffusion of the art of printing between 1462 and 1500. His activities as a collector were highly specialized, but in a representative sense he acquired a remarkably complete collection. Of the 238 towns into which printing was introduced during the fifteenth century, the British Museum in 1909 had specimens from 166 of them and Hawkins, 141. Of the 111 towns in which printing was known between 1450 and 1480, 94 were represented at the Museum and 84 in the Hawkins collection. Although a born fighter, and usually involved in some controversy, the General was a very earnest student of his cherished books. That his scholarly traditions might endure, he created the curatorship of the Annmary Brown Memorial as a chair for bibliographical study. He and his wife had intended to erect a memorial to Gutenberg, in which to house the more than five hundred specimens of incunabula and the paintings which they had collected. Mrs. Hawkins died before this had been accomplished. In her name, and in recognition of the benefactions of the Brown family, the Memorial with its treasures was placed in Providence in 1907. Hawkins' death, thirteen years later, came as the result of his having been knocked down by an automobile in New York.

[J. H. E. Whitney, *The Hawkins Zouaves, . . . Their Battles and Marches* (1866); A. W. Pollard, *Cat. of Books Mostly from the Presses of the First Printers . . . Collected by Rush C. Hawkins* (1910), and "Gen. Rush C. Hawkins," the *Library*, Dec. 1920; Frank Dilnot, *The New America* (1919); Margaret B. Stillwell, "Gen. Hawkins as He Revealed Himself to His Librarian," *Papers of the Bibliog. Soc. of America*, vol. XVI, pt. 2 (1923), and *The Annmary Brown Memorial* (1925); Henry H. Vail, *Pomfret, Vt.* (2 vols., 1930); *Providence Jour.*, Oct. 26, 1920.] M. B. S.

HAWKS, FRANCIS LISTER (June 10, 1798–Sept. 27, 1866), Protestant Episcopal clergyman, historian, second son of Francis and Julia (Stephens) Hawks, and grandson of John Hawks [*q.v.*], was born at New Bern, N. C. Graduating with first honors at the University of North Carolina in 1815, he began the study of law under William Gaston and later went to the famous law school of Tapping Reeve and James Gould at Litchfield, Conn. He was immediately successful at the bar and in 1820 was made reporter of the supreme court of North Carolina, filling the place until 1826, when he gave up the practice of law. In 1821 he represented the borough of New Bern in the House of Commons. A devoted member of the Episcopal Church, he finally decided to enter its ministry. After studying theology under Rev. William M. Green, later bishop of Mississippi, in 1827 he was successively ordained deacon and priest. After serving (in 1829) as assistant in Trinity Church, New Haven, and then assistant in the parish of St. James in Philadelphia, he was elected (1830) professor in the divinity school of Washington (now Trinity) College, Hartford, Conn. In 1831 he became rector of St. Stephen's, and later of St. Thomas' Church, in New York City, holding the latter place until 1843. During this period he was assistant secretary of the General Convention of 1832, and secretary of the New York diocesan convention in 1834, was elected (1835) missionary bishop of the Southwest but declined that office, and was professor of ecclesiastical history at the General Theological Seminary, 1833–35. In 1837 he was editor, for a few months, of the *New York Review*, for which he wrote frequently, contributing to its early numbers severely critical articles on Jefferson and Burr. In 1839 he established a church school, St. Thomas' Hall, at Flushing, L. I. The venture resulted in the loss of a great deal of money and drew such criticism that Hawks resigned as rector of St. Thomas' Church and moved to Mississippi, where he was soon elected bishop, but declined the office. He was an original trustee of the University of Mississippi. In 1844 he became rector of Christ Church, New Orleans, and was elected the first president of the University of Louisiana, which began operations under his guidance.

In 1846 he volunteered to become professor of history at the University of North Carolina, but the chair was not established. Three years later he resigned his charge in New Orleans and his presidency of the University and returned to New York as rector of the Church of the Mediator. Subsequently he went to Calvary Church, but in 1862, on account of his sympathy with the South, he resigned and went to Christ Church, Baltimore. During this period in New York he was instrumental in establishing (1853) the *Church Journal*. He returned to New York in 1865 and formed the parish of Our Savior, and also that of Iglesia de Santiago where he preached and conducted services in Spanish. He died the following year. In 1852 he had declined election as bishop of Rhode Island and in 1859 as professor of history in the University of North Carolina. In 1823 he married Emily Kirby of New Haven, Conn., who died in 1827. Later he married Mrs. Olivia (Trowbridge) Hunt of Danbury, Conn., who survived him. He had two children by his first marriage and six by his second.

Hawks was a man of great ability and unusual charm. Interested in many subjects, an omnivorous reader, possessed of quick wit, and remarkable gifts as a conversationalist, he was widely popular. As a lawyer he proved himself learned, logical, and powerful before a jury or appellate court, and as a preacher he was noted for the force, felicity, and sincerity of his sermons. He had a quick temper and was inclined to unrestrained and angry speech, but he was quick to repent and atone for any unkindness. In 1835 the General Convention of the Episcopal Church appointed him to collect material on the colonial history of the church, and he went to England and brought back a great mass of manuscript material, some of which he utilized in *Contributions to the Ecclesiastical History of the United States: Virginia* (1836) and *Maryland* (1839). Thereafter he devoted much time to writing. His work was of high literary quality, scholarly, original, and, in view of the material then available, remarkably accurate and sound. In the field of church history, besides the *Contributions,* his most important publications were: *Journals of the General Convention of the Protestant Episcopal Church in the United States,* volume I (1861), covering the period 1785–1808, and *Documentary History of the Protestant Episcopal Church in the United States of America* (2 vols., 1863–64), both prepared in collaboration with W. S. Perry. He wrote a number of books, historical and otherwise, for children, and to secular American history contributed *Early History of the Southern States* (1832); *The Mecklenburg Declaration of Independence* (1836); *Narrative of the Expedition of an American Squadron to the China Seas and Japan . . . under the Command of Commodore M. C. Perry* (1856); *History of North Carolnia* (2 vols., 1857–58), and other works. He also edited *The Official and Other Papers of the Late Major-General Alexander Hamilton* (1842). Suggestive of the scope of his interests are: *The Monuments of Egypt* (1850); *Peruvian Antiquities* (1853); *Romance of Biography* (1855); *The English Language* (1867). For a time he was editor of *Appletons' Cyclopaedia of Biography*. A posthumous volume, *Poems Hitherto Uncollected,* was published in 1873. Hawks was a leader in the reorganization of the New York Historical Society and one of its most active members. He was one of the founders of the American Ethnological Society and its vice-president from 1855 to 1859, and also a founder of the American Geographical and Statistical Society, which he served as president for several years.

[E. A. Duyckinck, *A Memorial of Francis Lister Hawks, D.D., LL.D.* (1871); *A Tribute to the Memory of Rev. Francis L. Hawks, D.D., LL.D.* (1867); Henry Fowler, *The Am. Pulpit* (1856), pp. 381–88; "Francis Lister Hawks," in *Putnam's Mag.*, Jan. 1868.]

J. G. deR. H.

HAWKS, JOHN (1731–Feb. 16, 1790), architect and builder, was born at Dragby, Lincolnshire. Nothing definite is known of his early career; that he was a man of consequence and probably held some position at Court seems apparent from the fact that he was selected to design and superintend the construction of the mansion of the colonial governor of North Carolina at New Bern, "the most magnificent in America." In this project both King George III and Queen Charlotte were interested (Haywood, *post,* p. 63). The Queen, who had built "Stratford" in Virginia for Thomas Lee out of her private purse, seemed eager to develop a domestic architecture in the American dominions.

John Hawks arrived in North Carolina in company with Governor Tryon in 1764. They were immediately confronted by the difficulty of raising funds for the architectural project, and for a time it seemed doubtful whether work on it could begin for some years. In 1767 Tryon recommended Hawks for the post of comptroller of the port of Beaufort (*Colonial Records,* VII, 548), but he did not have occasion to accept that office, for in the same year the General Assembly appropriated £5,000 for building the palace. The corner-stone was laid Aug. 26, 1767, and the building was completed late in 1770. During January and February of the next year the government records were moved into it. The edifice was a three-storied structure, built in the best traditions of the early Georgian style; with quarter-circle colonnades connecting it with two small square Georgian buildings placed at either side. The central portion bore unmistakable signs of having been fashioned after the favorite residence of the King and Queen, Kew Palace at Kew Gardens, Surrey, in the rebuilding of which, not many years before, Hawks may well have had a hand. The interior of the North Carolina mansion was elaborately designed and furnished. The entire cost amounted to nearly fifteen thousand pounds. This sum, after much difficulty and trouble which paved the way for much of the subsequent civil commotion in the colony, was finally appropriated by the General Assembly (*Colonial Records,* vol. VII, Preface). For his services in making the designs of the palace and overseeing its erection, John Hawks received £300 "proclamation money" yearly. He built other structures in New Bern, including the Craven County prison of which he was one of the trustees. From 1770 to 1773 he was a kind of commissioner of finance for Governor Tryon. In the latter year he was chosen clerk of the upper house of the General Assembly upon the recommendation of Governor Martin (*Colonial Records,* IX, 370), which office he retained until it became extinct in 1784. During this time he was also a justice of the peace for Craven County and district auditor for New Bern. In 1784 he became the first auditor of the state of North Carolina, continuing in that position until the time of his death. In December 1788 he was appointed judge of the court mercantile and maritime for New Bern by Gov. Samuel Johnston, but resigned the office, for which he had not applied, because he thought himself unqualified "for the undertaking." He died at New Bern, Feb. 16, 1790. Eight years later, on the night of Feb. 27, 1798, the beautiful and costly Governor's Palace was destroyed by fire.

About the year 1770 Hawks married Mary Fisher, only daughter of George Fisher of Craven County. They had one son, Francis, who was the father of Francis Lister Hawks [*q.v.*] and Cicero Stephens Hawks.

[*The Colonial Records of N. C.*, ed. by Wm. L. Saunders, vols. VII, IX (1890), XX (1902), XXII (1901), XXIV (1905); manuscript records of the N. C. Hist. Commission, at Raleigh; M. De L. Haywood, *Gov. Wm. Tryon* (1903), which also contains a view of the palace, made from the original design by Hawks now in the N. C. State Archives; information as to certain facts from a descendant of Hawks.] E. L. W. H.

HAWLEY, GIDEON (Nov. 5, 1727–Oct. 3, 1807), missionary to the Indians, a descendant of Joseph Hawley, who emigrated to America in 1629, was born at Stratfield (Bridgeport), Conn., the son of Gideon and Hannah (Bennett) Hawley. His mother died at his birth; his father three years later. Little is known of his youth before he entered Yale, where he graduated in 1749. He was licensed to preach by the Fairfield East Association, May 23, 1750. Hawley seems to have been a man with a single purpose in life, to be a missionary to the Indians. In many ways he was temperamentally unfitted for such a career, for his letters give the impression of uncompromising Puritan virtue and a lack of sympathy with Indian character. Yet just because he believed the Indians inferior to the white men, he felt a more insistent call to serve them. His career began in 1752 when he accepted a position at Stockbridge in the pay of the Society for Propagating the Gospel among the Indians, under the supervision of Jonathan Edwards [*q.v.*]. He described his duties as those of a school-master for the Iroquois, many of whom came from great distances to his school. On the Lord's Day he preached to them. Edwards visited his school occasionally and gave him advice about his work. Hawley was not happy in this place, however, because of the existence of opposing cliques among the controlling authorities, who hampered each other's efforts and hindered the work of the missionaries. Consequently, he was glad to accept an offer from the Society to establish a mission among the Six Nations on the Susquehanna. He was ordained for this task in July 1754 at Boston, and left for his frontier post, near the present Windsor, N. Y. Apparently his services at this place were much more extensive than they had been at Stockbridge. Besides trying to convert and civilize the Indians he seems to have acted as interpreter, and, of greater importance on the eve of war, to have been highly respected in their diplomatic councils. Outbreak of war did not at first interfere with his labors, but in May 1756 he was forced to leave. He went to Boston and accepted a commission as chaplain to Col. Richard Gridley's regiment, about to depart for Crown Point, but unfortunately illness compelled him to return in October. After an unsuccessful attempt to resume his mission labors, he was sent by the Commissioners of the Society on a temporary mission to the Indians at Marshpee, Mass., who had been long without an English minister. He succeeded so well at Marshpee that the Indians requested his appointment as their permanent preacher. Their petition was granted, and on Apr. 8, 1758, he took up the work which he carried for half a century. Hawley married for his first wife Lucy Fessenden, on June 14, 1759, by whom he had three sons and two daughters. After her death in 1777, he married, Oct. 7, 1778, Mrs. Elizabeth Burchard. He died at Marshpee in his eightieth year.

[Hawley's manuscript journal and letters covering the period from 1753 to 1805, in the library of the Am. Congreg. Asso., Boston; letters printed in *Mass. Hist. Soc. Colls.*, 1 ser. IV (1795), 50–67 and 6 ser. IV (1891), 617–19, 627–30; W. B. Sprague, *Annals Am. Pulpit,* vol. I (1857); F. B. Dexter, *Biog. Sketches Grads. Yale Coll.*, vol. II (1896); Samuel Orcutt, *A Hist. of the Old Town of Stratford and the City of Bridgeport, Conn.*, pt. 2 (1886); E. H. Everett, *Hawley and Nason Ancestry* (1929); *Columbian Centinel* (Boston), Oct. 7, 1807.] V. F. B.

HAWLEY, GIDEON (Sept. 26, 1785–July 17, 1870), lawyer, educational administrator, the son of Gideon Hawley and Sarah (Curtiss) Hawley and a descendant of Joseph Hawley who came to America in 1629 and later settled in Stratford, Conn., was born in Huntington, Conn., but moved with his parents to Ballston, N. Y., in 1794 and in 1798 to Charlton, N. Y. He graduated from Ballston Academy, entered Union College, was graduated (B.A.) in 1809, and was appointed tutor in the college for the following year. After studying law with Henry Yates in Schenectady and in the office of Bleecker & Sedgwick, Albany, he was admitted to the Albany bar in May 1812. On Oct. 19, 1814, he married Margarita Lansing, member of an Albany family of social, political, and financial distinction. Two children were born to them. He was master in chancery from 1812 to 1830. As director of the Mohawk & Hudson Railroad and treasurer of the Utica & Schenectady Railroad, he shared in the pioneer work of railroad development in New York State. From 1819 to 1853 he was secretary of the Albany Insurance Company.

His most notable service to the state, however, was in the field of education. In 1812, the year of his admission to the bar, he was chosen the first superintendent of public instruction for the state of New York, and between 1812 and 1821, when the office was abolished, he laid the foundations for the public elementary schools of the state. The Board of Regents, who were guiding the development of the private academies, appointed him secretary in 1814, an office which he held until 1841. In his dual capacity as secretary of the Board of Regents and superintendent of public instruction he became the dominant figure in state education. He created the executive functions of the official variously known as superintendent and commissioner of education and gave especial significance to the judicial functions of the educational executive (see J. S. Brubacher, *Judicial Powers of the Commissioner of Education in New York State,* Teachers College Publications, 1927). In 1842 he became a member of the Board of Regents of the University of the State of New York and continued in that office until his death twenty-eight years later. He was largely responsible for the establishment of the first normal school in New York State, that in Albany. His total service to public education extended from 1812 to 1870, while his connection with the Board of Regents, as secretary and as member, covered a period of fifty-six years. From 1846 to 1861 he was a member of the Board of Regents of the Smithsonian Institution. Aside from official reports, his only publication of any consequence seems to have been *Essays on Truth and Knowledge* (1856), containing an essay previously issued under the title, *Definitions of Knowledge and Truth.* The Gideon Hawley Library at the State College for Teachers, Albany, commemorates his service.

[Cuyler Reynolds, *Hudson-Mohawk Valley Geneal. and Family Memoirs* (1911), vol. III; *Bibliotheca Munselliana, a Catalogue of Books and Pamphlets by Joel Munsell* (1872), an annotated copy of which is owned by the American Antiquarian Society, Worcester, Mass.; E. S. Hawley, *The Hawley Record* (1890); S. V. Talcott, *Geneal. Notes of N. Y. and New England Families* (1883); *Eighty-Fourth Ann. Report of the Regents of the Univ. of the State of N. Y.* (1871); *Am. Jour. Educ.,* Mar. 1862; Minutes of the Board of Regents (MS.).]
A. R. B—r.

HAWLEY, JAMES HENRY (Jan. 17, 1847–Aug. 3, 1929), lawyer and governor, the son of Thomas and Annie (Carr) Hawley, was born in Dubuque, Iowa. His mother died during his infancy and his father remarried. At the age of fourteen young Hawley tried to enlist in a company of Iowa volunteers recruited in Dubuque for Civil-War service but was rejected because of his youth. Accompanying an uncle to California in 1862, he arrived in San Francisco in time to join the stampede to the Salmon River and Boise Basin placer mines of Idaho. In 1864 when still only seventeen years old he returned to California and entered the San Francisco City College to study law. At the end of a year he had finished the limited curriculum of that day and was graduated. After a year at sea in which he visited the Orient, he returned to Idaho where he temporarily resumed his mining activity while establishing himself in his profession. From his admission in 1871 to the bar of the supreme court of the Territory, with the exception of such periods as he held public office, he was continuously engaged in practice until his death. From 1878 to 1886 his residence was Idaho City; then he moved to Boise, of which city he was mayor 1903–05. He participated in practically all the early mining and irrigation litigation in Idaho and practised criminal law extensively. He served several terms in the territorial assembly, first in the House, 1870–71, and then in the Senate, 1874–75. From 1878 to 1882 he was district attorney and from 1886 to 1890, United States attorney. He failed of election to the federal House in 1888 and to the Senate in 1914.

It was as chief prosecutor in the Haywood, Pettibone, and Moyer case, 1907, that he gained, for a time, national prominence. Labor unrest in the Cœur d'Alène mining area of northern Idaho culminated in 1898 and 1899 in a series of riots, burnings, and murders, alleged to have been incited by the Western Federation of Miners, with which the local authorities were incapable of coping. Governor Steunenberg (Populist) appealed for federal troops. The presence of soldiers and the drastic measures taken by them resulted in breaking the influence of the Federation. On Dec. 30, 1905, however, Governor Steunenberg was assassinated. When one Harry Orchard confessed the crime, implicating the president of the Western Federation of Miners, Charles Moyer, the secretary, William D. Haywood, and a former member of the executive committee, George Pettibone, Hawley and W. E. Borah were selected to prosecute them. Hawley undertook to prove that the Western Federation of Miners was a criminal organization, the officers of which were guilty of the murder of Steunenberg at the hands of Harry Orchard. The defense, conducted by Clarence Darrow of Chicago and E. F. Richardson of Denver, relied largely on what were alleged to be Orchard's personal motives. To the general surprise, the jury found Haywood not guilty, a verdict which was said to have been returned because in his charge Judge Wood, who presided at the trial, cited with emphasis the well-known rule of evidence that a person cannot be convicted of crime upon the testimony of an accomplice unless it be corroborated by other evidence, which of itself and without the aid of the testimony of the accomplices tends to convict the defendant.

Backed by a wide reputation and personal following, Hawley was elected governor (1911–13) but was defeated for reëlection. He married Mary Elizabeth Bullock, July 4, 1875, at Quartzburg. He had eight children, six boys and two girls. All but two children, who died in infancy, survived him. During his later years he gave his attention chiefly to matters of civic and fraternal interest. On the title-page of a two-volume *History of Idaho, the Gem of the Mountains* (1920) his name appears as editor.

[*Hist. of Idaho, the Gem of the Mountains* (1920); *Who's Who in America*, 1928–29; *Outlook*, Apr. 6, 1907, and issues during June 1907; *N. Y. Times*, Aug. 4, 1929; *Idaho Statesman*, Aug. 4 and 18, 1929.]

H. C. D.

HAWLEY, JOSEPH (Oct. 8, 1723–Mar. 10, 1788), lawyer, public servant, "Son of Liberty," was born in Northampton, Mass., the son of Joseph and Rebekah Hawley. Through his father he was descended from Thomas Hawley who with his brother Joseph came to America in 1629; his maternal grandfather was the Rev. Solomon Stoddard [*q.v.*], for nearly sixty years pastor of the Northampton church and a religious leader in western Massachusetts. On the maternal side also he was a cousin of Col. Israel Williams of Hatfield, Mass., and of Jonathan Edwards [*qq.v.*]. After attending the schools of Northampton he entered Yale College in 1739 and was graduated in 1742. He planned to enter the ministry and may have studied for a time with Jonathan Edwards. He served as chaplain of one of the Massachusetts regiments against Louisbourg in 1745, but his experiences on the expedition and his conversion to Arminianism turned him from theology to law. Soon after his return from Louisbourg he began his law studies and in 1749 was admitted to the bar. Eventually he became one of its leaders in western Massachusetts and did a great deal to raise the standing of the profession. During the dispute between the Northampton church and its pastor, Jonathan Edwards, in 1749–50, Hawley led the group opposed to Edwards and was largely influential in his dismissal from the church. Hawley's headstrong and impetuous conduct in the affair was long a reason for self-reproach. Thereafter he was a leader in Northampton and throughout western Massachusetts. He served on the Northampton board of selectmen with but few interruptions from 1747 until his death, and during most of the time as chairman. In 1754 he was commissioned a major of Hampshire County and, without actually participating in the fighting, he was active throughout the French and Indian War in matters of organization and supply. Meanwhile, on Nov. 30, 1752, he had married Mercy Lyman of Northampton.

He was elected to the Massachusetts General Court in 1751, 1754, and 1755 but played an unimportant part. His election in 1766, however, was the beginning of a decade of activity that made him one of the Revolutionary leaders of the province. He became associated on equal terms with Otis and the Adamses in their constant opposition to the royal power. Gov. Thomas Hutchinson attributed many of the difficulties of the time to Hawley's influence, but recognized that unlike some of the other leaders he was not the complete partisan. Hawley worked sincerely for political freedom. In 1773 he was instrumental in settling a boundary dispute between Massachusetts and New York, one of his few constructive achievements during these years. The next year he was elected to the Continental Congress but declined to serve, presumably because of ill health, and John Adams was elected in his place. At Philadelphia Adams soon received from Hawley a searching analysis of the colonial situation with an exhortation for resistance to the limit unless Great Britain yielded to the American demands (*Works of John Adams,* vol. IX, 1854, App.; Hezekiah Niles, *Principles and Acts of the Revolution,* 1822, p. 324). Hawley wrote: "Fight we must finally, unless Britain retreats." Between 1774 and 1776 Hawley served on all the important committees of the province and was besides the guiding spirit of the Revolution in the Connecticut Valley. For many months before July 4, 1776, his constant letters to the Adamses, Thomas Cushing, and Elbridge Gerry at the Continental Congress urged a declaration of independence and the setting up of a unified colonial government. Unfortunately his exertions in the cause of the Revolution undermined his health, and in 1776 he fell a victim to the family's curse of insanity. While the remainder of his life was spent in retirement, he was able in 1780 to write from a liberal standpoint a vigorous criticism of the Massachusetts constitution. Although pious and for many years a deacon of the church at Northampton, Hawley long favored the disestablishment of Congregationalism. In 1780 he refused to take his seat in the state Senate because of the religious test for office-holding. During the riots in western Massachusetts in 1782 he was active in upholding law and order, although at the same time urging a policy that would secure justice for the discontented (letter to Ephraim Wright, printed in *American Historical Review,* July 1931). At his death in 1788 his estate was left to Northampton for the support of education.

[Hawley Papers and Samuel Adams Papers in the N. Y. Pub. Lib.; Mass. Archives; Judd MSS. in the Forbes Lib., Northampton, Mass.; E. F. Brown, *Joseph Hawley, Colonial Radical* (1931); E. S. Hawley, *Hist. Sketch of Maj. Joseph Hawley* (1890) and *The Hawley Record* (1890); *Joseph Hawley's Criticism of the Constitution of Mass.* (1917), ed. by M. C. Clune; F. B. Dexter, *Biog. Sketches Grads. Yale Coll.,* vol. I (1885); Thomas Hutchinson, *The Hist. of the Province of Mass. Bay,* vol. III (1828); J. R. Trumbull, *Hist. of Northampton, Mass.,* vol. II (1902); *The Boston Gazette and the Country Journal,* Mar. 17, 1788.] E. F. B.

HAWLEY, JOSEPH ROSWELL (Oct. 31, 1826–Mar. 18, 1905), editor, soldier, senator, was descended in the eighth generation from Joseph Hawley who came from England to Boston in 1629 and later settled in Stratford, Conn. Hawley's father, the Rev. Francis Hawley, a native of Farmington, Conn., married Mary McLeod of North Carolina and at Stewartville in the latter state Joseph was born. In 1837 the family returned to Connecticut and the boy received his early schooling at Hartford and at Cazenovia, N. Y. After graduating with honor from Hamilton College in the class of 1847, winning distinction as a speaker and debater, he taught school and read law. In 1850 he was admitted to the bar in Connecticut and secured enough clients to make a living. Drawn into the ranks of the anti-slavery crusaders, he was a delegate to the national convention of the Free-Soil party in 1852. Four years later he called the meeting of a hundred Connecticut citizens—among whom was his friend, Gideon Welles [*q.v.*]—which organized the Republican party in the state. He took an active part in the Frémont campaign, developing a vigorous and epigrammatic style on the stump. In 1857 he abandoned his law practice for the editor's chair when he took charge of the Hartford *Evening Press,* the organ of the new party. Associated with him on the *Press* was a college chum and life-long friend, Charles Dudley Warner [*q.v.*].

While the telegraph was still bringing the reports of the bombardment of Fort Sumter to his newspaper office, Hawley drew up the paper for enlisting the first company of volunteers from his state. He followed this action with a rousing speech on the evening of Apr. 17 before a memorable Hartford mass-meeting. On the following day he was mustered into the service with the rank of captain. On Jan. 15, 1866, he returned to civil life, having been brevetted major-general of volunteers to date from Sept. 28, 1865, "for gallant and meritorious services during the war." He saw service in thirteen "battles and actions," most of them along the eastern coast of the Confederacy. In the operations in Virginia in 1864, he served under Benjamin Butler [*q.v.*] and later under Terry. He was cited for meritorious conduct at the first battle of Bull Run and at the battle of Olustee, Fla., Feb. 20, 1864. Twice during the war his ability as a speaker was capitalized when he was sent North on recruiting duty.

In the year of his discharge he was elected governor of Connecticut by a people anxious to honor war veterans. In 1867 he became editor of the *Hartford Courant* with which the *Evening Press* was merged. He liked speaking better than writing, however, and politics remained to the end of his life his primary interest. He was as much at home in the conservative Republican party after the war as he had been in the crusading group in the years preceding it. In 1868, when the proposal to pay government bonds in depreciated currency was gaining favor west of the Appalachians, he uttered, as President of the Republican National Convention, his most-quoted political epigram, "Every bond, in letter and in spirit, must be as sacred as a soldier's grave" (*Official Proceedings, post,* p. 24). Two years later he opposed openly the political aspirations of his former chief, the then discredited Butler who was seeking office in Massachusetts. Butler retaliated with a speech in Springfield on Aug. 24, 1871, in which he accused Hawley, while under his command, of incompetency and hinted at cowardice. Hawley, always impulsive and at times irascible, lost no time in calling his former commanding officer a "liar and blackguard." The resulting controversy, in which Butler hedged, was widely discussed throughout the North with public opinion running strongly in Hawley's favor.

Between 1868 and 1881 Hawley was twice defeated for and thrice elected to the House of Representatives, where he served on committees on claims, banking and currency, military affairs, and appropriations. At the Republican National Convention of 1872 he was secretary of the committee on resolutions and in 1876 chairman of that committee, playing no small part in shaping the issues on which his party went before the electorate. He was president of the United States Centennial Commission and disclosed his Puritan heritage by causing the exposition to be closed on Sundays. From 1881 to within two weeks of his death he was United States senator from Connecticut. He was able but not conspicuous. He was a consistent protectionist and advocate of sound money. He did his most useful work as chairman of the Senate committee on civil service and on military affairs. In the latter capacity he had charge in the upper house of bills for increasing the coast defenses, providing for a volunteer army, and reorganizing the regular army which were made necessary by the Spanish-American emergency in 1898. Hawley was married twice: in 1855 to Harriet Ward Foote, who died in 1886, and subsequently to Edith Anne Horner, a native of England. He died in Washington, D. C.

[E. P. Parker, "Memorial Address," in *Joint Report of the Commission on Memorials to Senators Orville Hitchcock Platt and Joseph Roswell Hawley to the Gen. Assem. of the State of Conn.* (1915); letters by Hawley as president of the Centennial Commission and scrapbooks kept by him in Conn. State Lib.; *Sen. Report 6947*, 59 Cong., 2 Sess.; files of the *Hartford Courant*; *War of the Rebellion: Official Records (Army)*, 1 ser. esp. II, 355, and XXXV (pt. 1), 289; *Official Proc., Nat. Republ. Conventions, 1868–80* (1903); *Springfield Republican*, Aug. 25, 1871; *The Brilliant Military Record of Maj. Gen. Hawley* (pamphlet, n.d.), reprinted from the *Hartford Courant* at the time of the Butler controversy; E. S. Hawley, *The Hawley Record* (1890); *Biog. Dir. Am. Cong.* (1928); *Evening Star* (Washington), and *Hartford Courant*, Mar. 18. 1905.]

R. H. G.

HAWORTH, JOSEPH (Apr. 7, 1855?–Aug. 28, 1903), actor, was born in Providence, R. I. He was the son of an English artist and engineer, Benjamin Haworth, who came to this country before the Civil War, and Martha (O'Leary) Haworth, of Irish ancestry and English birth. During the war his father died in a southern prison camp, whereupon Martha Haworth took her family to Cleveland. Joseph went to work in a newspaper office and in leisure hours devoted himself to elocution. When he was eighteen Charlotte Crampton, John Ellsler's leading lady, heard him read. Struck by his personality, his musical voice, his immense earnestness, she tendered him the part of the Duke of Buckingham to her Richard III at her benefit. This led to his engagement as general utility man in Ellsler's stock company, an excellent school for a young actor. For several seasons he trod the boards with stars, working his way to leading parts. Before he was twenty he had supported Barrett, who commended his reading of his lines, and Booth, whose appreciation of his Laertes in *Hamlet* led to his offering Haworth, in 1878, a place in his company. The young actor accepted instead an engagement with the Boston Museum stock company, then in the zenith of its reputation. At his farewell to the Ellsler company he played Hamlet for the first time to the Ophelia of Effie Ellsler, for whom he had an unrequited attachment. During the next three years he played everything, from Gilbert and Sullivan opera (he had a magnificent voice) to old English comedies and Shakespeare. In November 1878 his singing of "He remained an Englishman" at the first performance in America of *Pinafore* brought down the house. In 1881, having played an effective Romeo with Mary Anderson, he was offered the post of leading man at the Boston theatre. He chose rather to join McCullough on a starring tour, and for two seasons, until McCullough's tragic collapse, he played such parts as Iago, Ingomar, Cassius, and Icilius. Thereafter until 1895 he was starring, first in *Hoodman Blind*, then in *Paul Kauvar*, which he made famous by four years of success, and later in an arduous repertory in which he alternated such plays as *The Leavenworth Case*, *The Bells*, *Ruy Blas*, and *Rosedale*, with Shakespearian revivals. In 1895 he played a long engagement at the Castle Square Theater, Boston. For the next two seasons he played opposite Modjeska in her varied repertory. The more important of his later successes were made as the original John Storm in Hall Caine's play, *The Christian*, Rafael in *The Ghetto*, Vinicius in *Quo Vadis*, Cassius in Richard Mansfield's production of *Julius Caesar*, and, his last rôle, Prince Dimitri in *Resurrection*. He died, unmarried, at the peak of his achievement.

Haworth was one of the most intellectual and conscientious performers of serious parts on the American stage. If his ambition to become great in the full meaning of the word was scarcely realized, he was much more than talented. He had real feeling, and in temperament he was an artist. A good (popularly reputed a "great") Hamlet, he was a fine Malvolio, an impressive Richelieu. Modjeska called his Macbeth "well-characterized," effective in the banquet and fight scenes. Winter, however, thought him unequal to the exacting demands of the part. An erratic genius, "half dashing man-about-town, half recluse," morbidly sensitive, generous even to his enemies, Haworth was a prey to fits of tragic depression which he tried to drown in drink. In appearance he was "not tall, but so slender he appeared so," dark of skin, with dark hair, fine dark eyes, and a mouth, "firm-set for one so vacillating." It has been said of him that he lost no opportunity to appear in classic drama and failed in no classic rôle he undertook.

[*Memories and Impressions of Helena Modjeska* (1910); J. B. Clapp and E. F. Edgett, *Players of the Present*, 3 pts. (1899–1901), I, 144; L. C. Strang, *Famous Actors of the Day in America* (1900); "A Conversation with Jos. Haworth," *Arena*, Jan. 1901; *Who's Who in America*, 1901–02, 1903–05; *N. Y. Dramatic Mirror*, Sept. 5, 1903; Wm. Winter, *Shakespeare on the Stage* (1911), p. 493; *N. Y. Times*, Aug. 29, 1903; information as to certain facts from Haworth's niece, Martha Haworth Ford.] M. B. H.

HAWTHORNE, CHARLES WEBSTER (Jan. 8, 1872–Nov. 29, 1930), painter, was born at Lodi, Ill., where his parents, Joseph Jackson and Cornelia J. (Smith) Hawthorne, from the state of Maine, were temporarily resident. He passed his boyhood at Richmond, Me., then at eighteen he went to New York to study art. He was obliged to earn his way, and, supposing himself employed as a designer, he took work in a stained-glass factory. His job at first was to sweep the floors and run errands, but he persisted, and presently he was allowed to take part in designing and making windows. The simple and elemental qualities of his later painting undoubtedly reflected in considerable degree this training in the glass shop. While thus employed, Hawthorne studied in the classes of the Art Students' League of New York under Frank Vincent DuMond and George DeForest Brush. Facile painting he learned in William M. Chase's class, and when the latter quit the League Hawthorne was one of the secessionists, taking a prominent part in founding the Chase School, later the New York School of Art. At this school Hawthorne taught and for several years served as its manager. He also assisted Chase at the summer school, Shinnecock Hills, Long Island. His canvases of this period were direct, vigorous, brisk of facture, exemplifying Chase's familiar advice to his students: "Take plenty of time for your pictures—take two hours if you need it."

During a painting tour of Holland, as he studied old masters, Hawthorne began to add something of his own—serious and subjective—to his acquired cleverness in quickly recognizing and developing artistic motives. He was already outgrowing the limitations of the sketch class when chance led him to settle at Provincetown, Mass. In 1903 he was married to Marion Campbell, also an artist. Their summer home in the dunes and their adjacent Cape Cod School of Art became a Mecca of American art students. Hawthorne's criticisms, delivered to his students at their easels in the streets and on the wharves, were thorough and searching, with insistence on a sound technique as a basis for subsequent self-expression. Among the Portuguese people of Provincetown Hawthorne found models for paintings in which he sought to recreate the spirit of the early Italian artists. He depicted dark-eyed fisher folk at work and play. His canvases became inevitable prize winners. He won the first Hallgarten prize, National Academy of Design, 1904; a silver medal at the Argentine International Exposition, 1910; the Altman prize and Isidor gold medal, National Academy of Design, 1914; a silver medal at the Panama Pacific Exposition, 1915; and the Norman Wait Harris prize and bronze medal, Art Institute of Chicago, 1917. He became a fellow of the National Academy in 1908.

Although Hawthorne, unlike most of his artistic contemporaries, had never studied in Paris, his work was fully appreciated in Europe. He was elected an associate member and, in 1913, a full member of the Société Nationale des Beaux-Arts. Reviewing Hawthorne's works in the Champ de Mars exhibition, Emile Henriot (quoted by Alvan F. Sanborn in the *Boston Transcript*, June 6, 1914) wrote: "Hawthorne . . . is an admirable painter, charming, vigorous, warm, personal. . . . I am constrained to praise . . . the prodigious technique of the artist who utilizes, with incomparable mastery, all the resources of his art." Hawthorne was never of robust physique and suffered from heart disease in his last years. He died while he was undergoing treatment at the Johns Hopkins Hospital, Baltimore. He was buried from the Hawthorne winter home, 280 West Fourth Street, New York. Several of his paintings were acquired by American art museums during his life, among them "The Trousseau," Metropolitan Museum of Art, New York; "The Mother," Boston Museum of Fine Arts; "Refining Oil," Detroit Institute of Arts; "Fisherman's Daughter," Corcoran Art Gallery, Washington; and "Venetian Girl," Worcester (Mass.) Art Museum.

[Sadakichi Hartmann, article in *Internat. Studio*, Sept. 1905; Arthur Hoeber, article in *Ibid.*, May 1909; Anna Seaton-Smith, article in *Art and Progress*, Jan. 1913; editorial in the *Outlook*, Mar. 14, 1917; review by F. W. Coburn in the *Boston Herald*, Mar. 26, 1916; obituary in *N. Y. Times*, Nov. 30, 1930; *Who's Who in America*, 1928–29; information as to certain facts, including Hawthorne's place of birth, from Marion Campbell Hawthorne.] F. W. C.

HAWTHORNE, NATHANIEL (July 4, 1804–May 18 or 19, 1864), novelist, was born in Salem, Mass., the son of Nathaniel Hawthorne and Elizabeth Clarke Manning, his wife. The earliest Hawthorne (or Hathorne, as the name was spelled until the novelist changed it) in America was Maj. William Hathorne [*q.v.*], who came to Massachusetts in 1630 and settled first at Dorchester and then at Salem. His son, John Hathorne, served as judge in the Salem witchcraft trials; the curse pronounced upon him by one of his victims was remembered by his descendants and was blamed for any evil fortune which befell the house. The third Hathorne of the line was a farmer; the fourth, the "bold Hathorne" of the Revolutionary sea ballad; the fifth, likewise a ship captain, who died four years after the birth of his son, the future novelist. Elizabeth Clarke Manning was descended from ancestors who settled in Salem in 1679. The younger Nathaniel was the first Hawthorne to choose a sedentary calling, a choice which he made the more easily because the will to action had by this time faded out of the stock, to be succeeded by a mild pride of blood and a quiet loyalty to the concerns of the mind.

The death of his father in 1808 plunged his mother into a perpetual widowhood, which she observed by keeping her own room so far as possible and never taking her meals at the common table of the household. Naturally the son grew up in what he later called the "cursed habits" of solitude. These seem not, however, to have made themselves felt during his pre-adolescent years, even during the years between nine and twelve when a slight lameness shut him off from sports and turned him to a course of reading in books as romantic as *The Faerie Queene* and as realistic as *The Newgate Calendar* and made him by fourteen acquainted with Shakespeare, Milton, Bunyan, Clarendon, Froissart, Rousseau, and novels and romances of all sorts. At fourteen, however, about the age when, if the father had lived, the boy would presumably have gone to sea and have begun to study the world, he went instead to Raymond, Me., where his maternal uncles owned a tract of land on Sebago Lake in the midst of the wilderness. There the youth had his imagination touched by the forest, which was for him a school in which the principal instruction was in contented loneliness. It is true that after a year in Maine he went back to his studies in or near Salem, and that from 1821 to 1825 he was at Bowdoin College, where he gambled a little, drank rather more, and skylarked a good deal in a robust, athletic, innocent way, but after taking his degree he felt no impulse to enter a profession or to venture abroad into the expanding America of his age, and so settled down in Salem to a dozen years devoted to making himself a man of letters. After some early exercises in deliberate gloom he arrived at a levelness of temper which marked both his life and his work. In the end he did not regret his long retreat. "If I had sooner made my escape into the world, I should have grown hard and rough, and been covered with earthly dust, and my heart might have become callous by rude encounters with the multitude.... But living in solitude till the fullness of time was come, I still kept the dew of my youth with the freshness of my heart" (*Passages from the American Note-Books,* p. 219). In spite of what may be suspected from this argument, Hawthorne was neither particularly priggish nor excessively shy. He was only trusting to his imagination. "I used to think I could imagine all passions, all feelings, and states of heart and mind" (*Ibid.*). Indeed, until he reached his maturity at about thirty-three, Hawthorne's imagination does seem to have been competent to sustain and interest him.

At the same time, he did not confine his imagination to an exclusive diet of itself. At least once a year, ordinarily in the summer, he was likely to shake off his solitude, leave Salem and his mother's house behind, and strike out on a kind of wary vagabondage through other districts of New England. His *American Note-Books* show him to have used his eyes and ears on his travels, as do several of his tales and sketches. The White Mountains furnished the scene for "The Ambitious Guest," "The Great Carbuncle," and "The Great Stone Face"; some crossroads north of Boston, for "The Seven Vagabonds"; Martha's Vineyard, for "Chippings with a Chisel"; the Shaker community at Canterbury, N. H., which he visited in 1831, for "The Canterbury Pilgrims" and, with changes, "The Shaker Bridal"; Greylock in the Berkshires, for "Ethan Brand." If the "Sketches from Memory," "Old Ticonderoga," and "My Visit to Niagara" are as autobiographical as they look, Hawthorne visited Lake Champlain, followed the Erie Canal between Utica and Syracuse, stopped at Rochester, saw Niagara Falls, and may even have gone as far as to Detroit. Everywhere he was attentive to the manners and customs that he found. Merely as historian he has genuine value. In especial he had a decided taste for low life, for toll-gatherers, pedlars, cattle-drovers, hawkers of amusement, stage-agents, tavern-haunters. He must himself have experienced the longing of the narrator in "The Seven Vagabonds" to join a crew of chance-met nomads and live by telling stories to random audiences along the road.

Such longings, however sincere for this or that brief moment, did not move Hawthorne to become the picaresque romancer which New England has never had. In a community of scholars, he read more than he tramped, ruffling the history of his native section in search of color and variety. "The knowledge communicated by the historian and biographer," he wrote in one of the earliest pieces of prose known to be his, "is analogous to that which we acquire of a country by the map—minute, perhaps, and accurate, . . . but cold and naked" (*Tales, Sketches, and Other Papers,* 1883 edition, p. 227). He aimed to enliven and warm the record by reconstructing typical "moments of drama, little episodes of controversy, clashes between the parties and ideas which divided the old New England." In "The Gentle Boy," the first of his stories to attract attention, he went back to the Quaker persecutions; in "Young Goodman Brown," to the witchcraft mania; in "The Gray Champion," to the last days of Governor Andros; in "The Maypole of Merry Mount" and "Endicott and the Red Cross," to the early days of the settlement; in the "Legends of the Province House," to the Revolution. In these, and in others of slighter value, Hawthorne tended always to look for the conflict rather of ideas than of parties. "The future complexion of New England," he wrote concerning the struggle between the Puritans and the jolly rioters of Merry Mount, "was involved in this important quarrel. Should the grizzly saints establish their jurisdiction over the gay sinners, then would their spirits darken all the clime and make it a land of clouded visages, of hard toil, of sermon and psalm forever. But should the banner of Merry Mount be fortunate, sunshine would break upon the hills, and flowers would beautify the forest, and late posterity do homage to the Maypole." Himself a descendant of the Puritans, Hawthorne nevertheless sympathized, lightly ironical as his language might now and then be, with the other side, with the humane and expansive rebels against the order of austerity and orthodoxy.

That this was less an historical than a moral position on his part is indicated by the theme which occupied him most in the short stories. He was solitary by habit, but he deeply feared the solitude which comes from egotism, the proud, hard isolation which shuts the essential egotist away from society. In "Wakefield," telling the story of a man who had left his family to live twenty years in secret in the next street, Hawthorne closely studied the motives which might have accounted for such an experiment of selfishness and vanity. "The Minister's Black Veil" represented what might follow if even a virtuous egotist should hide his face in fact as others do in effect. "Rappaccini's Daughter" took up the ancient legend of a girl so long fed on poisons that no poison could hurt her, and found behind it the tragedy of an involuntary egotist so far removed from nature as to have become herself a poison. "Ethan Brand" revived a later legendary idea, that of the unpardonable sin, and showed a Calvinist who believed he had committed it, and who grew, as he brooded, into a conviction that he was a sinner without equal, and finally reached a state of pride, of egotistic desperation, which as Hawthorne saw it was less pardonable than any other sin the man might have committed. Solitude, these early stories sought to illustrate, leads to egotism; egotism leads to pride; and pride, by different roads, leads always away from nature. "The Birthmark" showed a husband so crazed by a lust for perfection that he employed dark sciences to remove a birthmark from the cheek of his otherwise flawless wife and thereby caused her death. "The Christmas Banquet" showed the punishment of pride to be an incurable inner sense of coldness and emptiness, "a feeling," the victim says, "as if what should be my heart were a thing of vapor—a haunting perception of unreality. . . . All things, all persons . . . have been like shadows flickering on the wall." There can be no question that Hawthorne was, as it is traditional to say, concerned from the first with sin, but neither can there be any question that he was concerned with the sin least likely to be involved with meanness and brutality, the sin which of all the deadly sins is perhaps closest to a virtue.

Aside from the stories which he wrote there are virtually no events to mark the progress of his life from 1825 to 1837. Early in that period, though the exact date is not known, he tried to find a publisher for a book which he meant to call "Seven Tales of My Native Land." Exasperated by his failure with established publishers, and by the delays of the Salem printer who said he would take the chance, the author destroyed the manuscript. In 1828 he issued, at his own expense and anonymously, the undistinguished *Fanshawe,* of which the scene was more or less Bowdoin and the hero more or less Hawthorne. The novel, though it got him no readers, got him a publisher, the energetic Samuel Griswold Goodrich [*q.v.*] of Boston, who was just then founding an annual, the *Token.* During the fourteen years of its persistence the

Token, with the *New England Magazine,* to the editors of which Goodrich introduced him, was to be Hawthorne's chief outlet. Not till 1832, however, did anything from the lonely venturer at Salem rise much above the elegant melancholy which characterized this and similar annuals, and even "The Gentle Boy," in that year, did not rise too far above it. This tale was quickly followed, however, by enough short masterpieces to justify the publication in 1837 of the first series of *Twice-Told Tales,* with which, though the book was calmly received, the dozen years of solitary experiment came to an end, as did also the earlier plans for a book to be called "Provincial Tales" and another to be called "The Story-Teller." For another dozen years or so, which saw a second series of *Twice-Told Tales* (1842), *Mosses from an Old Manse* (1846), and *The Snow-Image and Other Twice-Told Tales* (1851), Hawthorne continued to write short stories, but he had an increasing reputation, and he lived approximately in the visible world.

During 1836 he had already acted as editor for seven months of the *American Magazine of Useful and Entertaining Knowledge,* published by Goodrich in Boston, where Hawthorne not only edited but also wrote or compiled the whole of every issue. After this he compiled *Peter Parley's Universal History* (1837), a piece of hackwork which is said to have sold over a million copies before it went out of print. As Oliver Goldsmith had done before him, Hawthorne put his smooth, clear prose into routine service for young readers, whom later he served by writing *Grandfather's Chair* (1841), *Famous Old People* (1841), *Liberty Tree* (1841), *Biographical Stories for Children* (1842), and, finally, the books in which his serviceable pen became silver, *A Wonder-Book for Girls and Boys* (1852) and *Tanglewood Tales for Girls and Boys* (1853), two of the lasting triumphs of their mode. All these undertakings were, of course, for the sake of money, the want of which did as much as anything else to break up Hawthorne's career of solitude. With the help of his friend Franklin Pierce [*q.v.*], the emerging recluse tried in 1837 for the post of historian to an expedition to the Antarctic then being planned, and, failing that, became weigher and gager in the Boston Custom House from 1839 to 1841. Having resigned his place, which he knew he would probably lose when the Whigs came again into office, he went to live at West Roxbury, with the Transcendental enthusiasts who had founded Brook Farm. Hawthorne invested his savings in the little Utopia, but he was otherwise not an enthusiast, and he left after an intermittent year of residence had proved to him that the association did not suit his temper or solve his problem.

Neither the Custom House nor Brook Farm had enabled him to enter the world enough to get his living from it and yet to keep his imagination free in the security thus obtained. In both he had been disappointed by the realities to which he had looked forward with the hope that they might give the needed stir and substance to his life. Temporarily abandoning any such hope, he was married July 9, 1842, to Sophia Amelia Peabody of Salem, his love for whom during the past four years had steadily increased his dissatisfaction with solitude. "Indeed," he had written to her, "we are but shadows; we are not endowed with real life, and all that seems most real about us is but the thinnest substance of a dream,—till the heart be touched. That touch creates us,—then we begin to be,—thereby we are beings of reality and inheritors of eternity" (*Passages from the American Note-Books,* p. 219). In the Old Manse at Concord, where Hawthorne made his home for the next three years, he discovered in love, of which he seems to have had no previous experience, a reality which he had not discovered in "encounters with the multitude." Profoundly happy with his wife, he was not, for some time, too much disturbed by his serious lack of money or by his unproductiveness as a writer. Nor was he distracted by the presence near him of the most distinguished group of men who have ever come together in a single American village. He was merely bored by Bronson Alcott, and was chiefly tolerant towards Ellery Channing. He listened to Emerson with interest but without the customary reverence and without catching the infection of abstract thought. Only with Thoreau did Hawthorne arrive at anything like intimacy, and that was based upon the habits of silence which they had in about an equal degree, and upon a taste for things, as distinguished from opinions, in which Thoreau had gone further than Hawthorne but in which Hawthorne was eager to follow him. Though the effects of so much happiness were not immediately visible, these three years were in the long run the most fruitful, or at least the most stabilizing, of all that Hawthorne ever lived through.

The Concord idyll, however, was broken up by the pressure of necessity. Hawthorne removed his wife and child to Salem in 1845, tried to become post-master, and instead was appointed surveyor of the port. Before taking up the duties of his office he brought together what he believed was to be his final collection of short stories, *Mosses from an Old Manse* (1846), and wrote for it an introductory paper exquisitely describing the circumstances of his pastoral interlude. By comparison his next three years, about which he was later to write in his introduction to *The Scarlet Letter,* were an interlude of comedy. The custom house at Salem depressed and troubled him as much as that at Boston had done, but he now stood on surer ground and could smile at what would once have made him fret. Nevertheless, he resented his dismissal when the Democrats went out of power in 1849, and he thereafter held a grudge against his native town. He had written little during the period, though to it belong "The Great Stone Face" and "Ethan Brand," and had finally lost interest in short stories, but when, once more forced into private life, he resumed his proper occupation, he found, or at least showed, how much he had stored up during his two interludes. *The Scarlet Letter* (1850), *The House of the Seven Gables* (1851), and *The Blithedale Romance* (1852), which brought his art to its somewhat tardy peak, poured from him in a serene flood.

The novels marked no decided break with the tales. In style, tone, tempo, themes, Hawthorne proceeded much as he had always done. Only his dimensions were different. *The Scarlet Letter,* for which a hint had already appeared in "Endicott and the Red Cross," is really a succession of moments of drama from the lives of the principal characters, almost without the links of narrative which ordinarily distinguish a novel from a play. What binds the parts together is the continuity of the mood, the large firmness of the central idea. Both mood and idea lift the story to a region more spacious than seventeenth-century Salem might have been expected to furnish. This novel again portrays a clash between elements opposed in old New England, but, at the same time, the universal clash between egotism and nature. Dimmesdale is destroyed by the egotism which leads him to keep the secret of his offense, even though another must bear the whole punishment. Chillingworth is destroyed by the egotism which leads him to assume the divine responsibility of vengeance. Hester, whose nature no less than her fate makes it impossible for her to be a stealthy egotist, is the only one of the three who survives the tragedy and grows with her experience. If *The Scarlet Letter* was an extended study of such egotism as Hawthorne had dealt with in many of his tales, *The House of the Seven Gables* was an extended description of such houses and households as he had dealt with in many of his sketches. This house was described from an actual house in Salem, and this household was in some respects like the household of Hawthorne's own youth—withdrawn, solitary, declining, haunted by an ancestral curse. Into the story he distilled all the representative qualities, all the typical memories of decadent New England, without, however, bringing in that New England complacency which made a virtue out of decay and refused to admit the existence of any evil in adversity. The Pyncheons inevitably dwindle to ashes, and the life of their proud line has to be carried on, collaterally, by nature, by the infusion of less genteel blood. With *The House of the Seven Gables* Hawthorne said farewell to the Salem in which he had grown up. In *The Blithedale Romance* he turned to the contemporary world. His setting was more or less what he remembered from Brook Farm, which he used in order "to establish a theatre, a little removed from the highway of ordinary travel, where the creatures of his brain may play their phantasmagorical antics, without exposing them to too close a comparison with the actual events of real lives." This was as near as he cared to come to "certainly the most romantic episode of his own life—essentially a day-dream, and yet a fact," as Hawthorne characterized Brook Farm in his preface. By a kind of softness in the tone, by a kind of charming formalism in the characterization and dialogue, he dimmed the lights and suffused the colors of his drama. Yet he no less firmly indicated his guiding thesis, which was that philanthropy, of the sort displayed by Hollingsworth, is at bottom only another egotism and may bring the philanthropist into tragic conflict with nature.

The Scarlet Letter was written and published, with great success, while Hawthorne was still living in Salem, after he had lost his place in the custom house. The second novel he wrote at Lenox in the Berkshires, to which he had gone with his family in 1850 and where he lived in a farm house during a cold winter and two agreeable summers. Though again in retirement, he saw a good many friends, and in particular made the acquaintance of Herman Melville [*q.v.*], who was then writing *Moby Dick* at Pittsfield. How relatively contented Hawthorne was in his solitude, how steady in his skepticism, is made clear by the contrast between him and this bitter, violent man of genius. In 1851 the household was again moved, to West Newton, where the third novel was completed the next spring. The novels brought Hawthorne money as well as an increase of reputation. He bought a house in Concord and returned to the scene of his greatest happiness. Once more, however, there were interruptions, even less congenial to the novelist than those which, at Lenox, had seen him taking advantage of his new fame by collecting *The Snow Image and Other Twice-Told Tales* and writing *A Wonder-Book*. Pierce, nominated for president by the Democrats, asked his old friend to prepare a campaign biography. Hawthorne was totally uninterested in politics, but he had hitherto benefited by political appointments, and he had a strong sense of obligation to the man who had most aided him. He consequently wrote, with great labor, *The Life of Franklin Pierce* (1852), and, after some hesitation on his part, was rewarded by another appointment, this time that of United States consul at Liverpool. In 1853, at the age of nearly fifty, Hawthorne for the first time left the New World for the Old, where he was to remain for seven years.

The seven years came too late to work any important changes in either his art or his thought. In his native province he had inclined toward the universal; in a larger universe he inclined toward the provincial. During the whole of his stay in England, from 1853 to 1858, he made friends with no men or women of first-rate quality, very few of whom he even saw. Instead he faithfully, if now and then complainingly, discharged his consular duties, visited historical scenes in the spirit of the conscious tourist, and waited two years before he went for the first time to London. London, however, delighted him. In Italy, where Hawthorne lived during 1858 and the first months of 1859, he felt most at home among the American and British residents and travelers. Though he believed he was not homesick, he felt overpowered by Europe, by the rush of countless new impressions. With the eagerness of a very young American he tasted the pleasures of antiquity in the expected places. With the patience of a man long withheld from the masterpieces of architecture, music, painting, sculpture, he gorged cathedrals and galleries. Often he was bored. At the end of his journey he could still seriously condemn the representation of the nude in works of art. But his provincialism, because it remained honest, did not become disagreeable. What small men may learn earlier Hawthorne was learning late, and he gave himself to the task with a temper which was observant, sensitive, and resolute. When, after another year in England, he came back to Concord in 1860, he remained a provincial, but he also regretted the world he had left behind.

Hawthorne's stay abroad had not stimulated his pen. After *Tanglewood Tales,* written before he left Concord, he did not publish another book before *The Marble Faun* (1860), begun in Italy and completed in England. It, with *Our Old Home* (1863), a beautiful, shrewd, slily satirical commentary upon England, summed up what he had acquired in Europe. He was enough a son of New England to feel an obligation to describe Rome in his romance with something of the thoroughness of a guidebook, though of a guidebook remarkably suave and melodious. He was also enough of a son of his province to show, in his central idea, that he had been frightened by paganism and driven back to Calvinism. Miriam and Donatello are both creatures of nature, of a sort to which Hawthorne had given his sympathy in the earlier tales and novels; but these two, surprised into the crime of murder, see it as a sin even more than as a crime, and are driven by conscience along a path which a Puritan might have traveled. Their sense of sin is their teacher, and from it they receive their moral education. Indeed, Donatello, who is pure nature, becomes truly human only after sin has touched him. The conclusion seems a long way from the position which Hawthorne had taken in his drama of Merry Mount.

The four years after his return saw, except for *Our Old Home,* nothing further by him. He was constantly tempted by another theme for a romance, or rather, by two: the idea of an elixir of life and that of the return to England of an American heir to some hereditary estate. Yet though Hawthorne experimented with them in four fragments, *The Ancestral Footstep, Septimius Felton, Dr. Grimshaw's Secret,* and *The Dolliver Romance,* all published posthumously, he could not fuse or complete them. The Civil War fatally interrupted his reflections. Moreover, his imagination was dissolving, his vitality was breaking up, along with the New England era of which he had been, among its poets and romancers, the consummate flower. He could not survive his age. He could not even endure the tumult of its passing. In 1862 he visited Washington, called upon Lincoln with a delegation from Massachusetts, and wrote a magazine article called "Chiefly About War Matters" which vexed many readers of the *Atlantic* (July 1862) who could not understand the novelist's unconcern with the specific issues of the conflict. The death of Thoreau in 1862 weighed upon Hawthorne, as did the illness of his daughter Una. He wrote *Our Old Home* with difficulty and could not bring himself to undertake a serial for the *Atlantic.* In May 1864 he set out from Concord somewhat as he had been accustomed to do in his years at Salem, except that now, too feeble to go alone, he was accompanied by his friend Pierce, and went by carriage. In Plymouth, N. H., Hawthorne died quietly in his sleep. He was mourned as a classic figure and has ever since been so regarded.

[Hawthorne himself furnishes a good deal of valuable biographical material in the *Passages from the Am. Notebooks* (1868), *Passages from the English Notebooks* (1870), and *Passages from the French and Italian Notebooks* (1871), edited from his journal by his wife. The published notebooks do not always represent the original manuscripts in the Pierpont Morgan Library with complete fidelity. His wife in *Notes in England and Italy* (1869), his son Julian Hawthorne in *Nathaniel Hawthorne and His Wife* (1884) and in *Hawthorne and His Circle* (1903), his daughter Rose Hawthorne Lathrop in *Memories of Hawthorne* (1897), and his son-in-law George Parsons Lathrop in *A Study of Hawthorne* (1876) all have the special authority which comes from their relationship. In addition there have been numerous biographical and critical studies by other writers, among whom may be mentioned: Newton Arvin, *Hawthorne* (1929); Horatio Bridge, *Personal Recollections of Nathaniel Hawthorne* (1893), Moncure Daniel Conway, *Life of Nathaniel Hawthorne* (1890), L. Dhaleine, *Nathaniel Hawthorne: sa vie et son œuvre* (1905), Herbert Gorman, *Hawthorne: a Study in Solitude* (1927), Henry James, *Hawthorne* (1879), Lloyd Morris, *The Rebellious Puritan: Portrait of Mr. Hawthorne* (1927), F. P. Stearns, *The Life and Genius of Nathaniel Hawthorne* (1906), Caroline Ticknor, *Hawthorne and His Publisher* (1913), George Edward Woodberry, *Nathaniel Hawthorne* (1902). There is a careful bibliography of the writings by and about Hawthorne in *The Cambridge Hist. of Am. Lit.*, II (1918), 415–24.] C. V–D.

HAWTHORNE, ROSE [See ALPHONSA, MOTHER, 1851–1926].

HAY, CHARLES AUGUSTUS (Feb. 11, 1821–June 26, 1893), Lutheran clergyman, spent his life in the service of the General Synod and was for thirty-two years a professor in its theological seminary at Gettysburg. Born at York, Pa., the son of John and Eliza (Ebert) Hay, he attended the York County Academy and the German Reformed High School and received private instruction from his uncle, John Gottlieb Morris [*q.v.*]. After graduating from Pennsylvania (now Gettysburg) College in 1839 and from Gettysburg Theological Seminary in 1841, he went to Germany for two years of study at the universities of Berlin and Halle. At Halle, like many another American student, he won the fatherly interest of Friedrich Tholuck. Returning in 1843, he was licensed to preach and, after nine months' labor at Middletown, Md., was made professor of Biblical literature and German, at a salary of $500 a year, in Gettysburg Seminary. On May 5, 1845, he married Sarah Rebecca Barnitz of York, who with five of their eight children survived him. Himself a lover of peace and moderate views, he was dismayed to see the General Synod split into two hostile camps, the "American Lutherans" and the advocates of "Old Lutheranism," and realized that the Seminary was to be the scene of a pitched battle between the contending forces. He also felt keenly his lack of pastoral experience and was in need of additional income. Accordingly, on the advice of his uncle and of his former teacher, Charles Philip Krauth [*q.v.*], he resigned in 1848 and, after a brief pastorate at Hanover, Pa., accepted a call in 1849 to Zion Church, Harrisburg, Pa., to which he ministered with notable success for sixteen years. During the Civil War he was a good friend of the soldier and an ardent, in fact a too ardent, Unionist. For some unwise criticism of Gen. John Ellis Wool's lenience to Southern sympathizers he was once arrested and arraigned before the military authorities in Baltimore, but he was quickly released. Hay remained loyal to the General Synod when it was disrupted in 1864. Conservative though he was in theology, he had previously shown his repugnance to strict confessionalism by withdrawing with his congregation in 1857 from the Ministerium of Pennsylvania and joining the Synod of East Pennsylvania. In 1865 he was recalled to Gettysburg as professor of Hebrew and Old Testament theology, pastoral theology, and German. There he taught, preached, and studied until his death twenty-eight years later. He had been president of the board of directors of the Seminary from 1861 to 1863 and of the East Pennsylvania Synod in 1860; he was president of that synod again in 1874 and of the General Synod in 1881. For forty years he was a trustee of Pennsylvania College. As librarian of the Seminary and curator of the Lutheran Historical Society he showed foresight and energy in collecting manuscripts, books, and documents; he has an honorable place among historians of the Lutheran Church in America. He wrote articles on historical and biographical subjects, published short lives of Jacob Goering, George Lochman, and Benjamin Kurtz (in one volume, 1887), translated Luther's *Commentary on the Sermon on the Mount* (1892), and was cotranslator with Henry Eyster Jacobs of Heinrich Schmid's influential *Doctrinal Theology of the Evangelical Lutheran Church* (1876; 1889). In a generation fierce with doctrinal strife, he bore himself with unvarying modesty, courtesy, and dignity. He died at Gettysburg after an illness of only a few days and was buried at Harrisburg.

[*Hist. of the Evangelical Luth. Synod of East Pa., 1842–92* (Phila., n.d.); *Patriot* (Harrisburg), June 27, 29, 1893; A. R. Wentz, *Hist. of the Gettysburg Theol. Sem.* (1926).] G. H. G.

HAY, GEORGE (Dec. 15, 1765–Sept. 21, 1830), jurist, was born in Williamsburg, Va., the son of Anthony Hay and Elizabeth Davenport. His father, traditionally reputed to be a son of one of the earls of Errol, established himself in Williamsburg as a cabinet maker sometime between the years 1740 and 1750 but soon changed to an industry for which the colonial appreciation was more pronounced, purchasing the Raleigh Tavern in 1767 and becoming the keeper of an ordinary of more than local reputation. Elizabeth Davenport, second wife of Anthony Hay, was the daughter of Joseph Davenport, first town clerk of Williamsburg. George studied law and became a lawyer classified either as "eminent" or "ordinary" according to the political prejudice of the classifier. He began his political career with his election to the Virginia House of Delegates where his service was of such a nature that he has been described as a prominent legislator (L. G. Tyler, *Encyclopedia of Virginia Biography,* II, 1915, 196). When Jefferson became president of the United States he appointed Hay United States attorney for the District of Virginia, and this position he held for many years. It fell to him as his most conspicuous task in this capacity to conduct the prosecution of Aaron Burr for treason. Although it is the consensus of opinion among historians that he showed himself unequal to the occasion, it is probably true that no one could have handled the case better than Hay did, and at any rate he seems to have had the approval of Jefferson. In 1811, with William Wirt and Littleton W. Tazewell he appeared for Jefferson in the "Batture Case" and in 1814 he appeared for the defendant in *Hunter* vs. *Martin.* Upon the entrance of John Quincy Adams to the presidency, Hay was appointed judge of the United States district court for eastern Virginia.

There may be some doubt in regard to Hay's ability as a lawyer and as a judge; there can be none as to his courage and probity. During much of his life he was a fierce controversialist. He was a confirmed Jeffersonian Republican and kept the pen of a ready writer always loaded with diatribes against the Federalists. It has been said that his two pamphlets on the liberty of the press, issued in 1799 and 1803, had "profound effect" (Charles Warren, *A History of the American Bar,* 1913, p. 238). Much of his controversial writing appeared in the *Richmond Enquirer* and was signed "Hortensius"—a name which may have been suggested to him by the name of his daughter Hortense. In addition to his polemics Hay wrote several legal treatises and a eulogistic memoir of James Thompson, one of the early Republican pamphleteers of Virginia. He was twice married, his second wife being Elizabeth Gouverneur Monroe, elder daughter of President James Monroe. By his first marriage he had two children, one of whom, Charles, was chief clerk of the Navy Department during the administration of the younger Adams. By his second marriage he had one child, Hortense. During Monroe's presidency Hay lived in the White House and there is evidence that Monroe had great confidence in him and relied upon his counsel.

[Hay family data is to be found in *Tyler's Quart. Hist. and Geneal. Mag.,* Apr. 1927, and in the *Wm. and Mary Coll. Quart.,* Apr. 1897. Hay's conduct of the Burr prosecution is presented in A. J. Beveridge, *The Life of John Marshall* (4 vols., 1916–19), vol. III. There are allusions to his private life in Meade Minnegerode, *Some Am. Ladies* (1926).] R. S. C.

HAY, JOHN MILTON (Oct. 8, 1838–July 1, 1905), poet, journalist, historian, and diplomat, was born at Salem, Ind., the fourth child of Dr. Charles and Helen (Leonard) Hay. On his father's side he was of Scotch and German ancestry; his great-great-grandfather, a soldier of adventure, took part in the wars of the first half of the eighteenth century in Germany. The latter's son, Adam, emigrated to America about 1750 and settled in Virginia. Thence a son, John, crossed the mountains in 1793 to Kentucky and later moved northward to Illinois. His son, Dr. Charles Hay, married Helen Leonard, who was born in Assonet, Mass., and came of direct New England lineage. Moving from Salem, Ind., this family settled finally at Warsaw, Ill., on the banks of the Mississippi. The original name of the town had been Spunky Point, which was abandoned by the genteel readers of Jane Porter's *Thaddeus of Warsaw* (1803). Later John Hay was to write, "I hope every man who was engaged in the outrage is called Smith in Heaven."

At Warsaw, Hay grew to youth; his education was at first in local schools, and at a private academy at Pittsfield, Pike County, Ill.; in 1852 he progressed to a college, which was little more than a high school, at Springfield. Three years later, at the age of seventeen, he entered Brown University as a sophomore. The records of his boyhood are meager but they seem to suggest a good-looking lad, "chock full of fun and devilment," who had a most retentive memory, a happy imagination, and a capacity for easy study which marked him as the scholar of the family. His father's family helped financially in John's education, for the conditions of life in a country doctor's household almost on the frontier were arduous. As Hay wrote, "the life was a hard one, with few rational pleasures, few wholesome appliances." Yet, whatever the limitations of Western surroundings, Hay, at a state capital such as Springfield, had in those years opportunity to watch the wheels of political life go round, to see on the sidewalks of the town such men as Douglas, Trumbull, Davis, and Lincoln, and to listen to vigorous debates, most of which naturally turned on the great national issues of the time. Hay, though a lover of books, was by no means a drudge; his natural brightness and gay spirits brought him now and later in his life to an enjoyment of social festivity and an appreciation of feminine beauty. At Brown he seems to have lived a quiet life. His class rank was high; in novel surroundings he did not lose his passion for reading or his early habit of rhyming; and at his graduation he was chosen class poet. He was already saturated with the idea of a career of letters, but no opening presented itself. In 1858 he went back, reluctantly, to the bleak life of Warsaw, thankful that he had had at least a glimpse into a life of culture before he returned to what he then called "this barbarous West."

There followed a period of youthful melancholy. Such times of depression were to afflict him in after life as well. Now there was in particular the uncertainty of his future career. Letters as a source of sustenance he reluctantly abandoned, for, however flourishing might be the economic prospects of the West at this period, a poet and a man of letters could find no appreciation or haven of refuge there, and least of all his daily bread. The Church he also avoided. As he wrote to his uncle: "I would not do for a Methodist preacher, for I am a poor horseman. I would not suit the Baptists, for I dislike water. I would fail as an Episcopalian for I am no ladies' man" (Thayer, *post,* I, 59). Thus he was gradually forced to the law, not as a real profession but as a choice among evils. In 1859 he entered the law office of his uncle, Milton Hay, at Springfield. In that office he found a "nursery for cradling public men." The law and politics were two sides of the same coin. Next door was the office of Abraham Lincoln, and the contacts resulting from this circumstance, together with the influence of a young friend, John G. Nicolay [*q.v.*], whom Hay had first known in Pittsfield, soon brought about the opportunity of Hay's lifetime. Nicolay persuaded Lincoln that Hay would be useful as an assistant private secretary to the President-Elect. "Well, let Hay come," said Lincoln; and forthwith there came to Hay the chance to play a small rôle in national politics which was to affect profoundly his future life. The young ladies of Springfield missed the polite and amusing verses of the youthful lawyer as he plunged into a new environment and undertook a novel and exciting task at Washington.

Daily and even nightly relations with the President during more than four years of national peril gave the young man (for even in 1865 he was only twenty-seven years old) an abiding sense of the greatness of Lincoln. The wonder was that in all the atmosphere of political intrigue Hay was able to keep his head and to emerge at the end unspoiled. His reputation for honesty and sincerity remained unblemished; he sharpened his wits against many of the ablest men of his day; he faced social glamour with amusement; and he acquired that directness of thought and familiarity with great issues which were to stand him in good stead in years to come. The work at first was somewhat varied. To receive callers, many of them cranks; to act as the tactful messenger for impatient or frightened politicians, demanding to see the President at once; to write a constantly increasing number of letters; to do his duty by Mrs. Lincoln, whom he found difficult; and to be a sort of general yet genial factotum: these were among the ordinary labors of the day. Often at night, before he and Nicolay moved to Willard's, Hay would be wakened by the President, tall and gaunt in his nightshirt, to laugh with him at some joke in the book he was reading while vainly seeking sleep. The "Ancient" and the "Tycoon" were affectionate nicknames bestowed by Hay on his beloved chief. Early in 1864 Hay became assistant adjutant-general in the army with rank of major (later lieutenant-colonel, then colonel) and was detailed to the White House. The equivalent of military aide, he became in some sort the President's eyes. That he was quick to grasp a situation, discreet, and modest soon became evident. Hay, of course, was no military expert, but his vision of the complexities of the Civil War may be well seen in a quotation from Nicolay and Hay: "War and politics, campaign and statecraft, are Siamese twins, inseparable and interdependent; to talk of military operations without the direction and interference of an Administration is as absurd as to plan a campaign without recruits, pay, or rations" (*Abraham Lincoln, A History,* IV, 360). Hay himself was, at times, astounded by the magnanimity of Lincoln toward members of his political household who were intriguing against him. Yet the "backwoods Jupiter," as Hay termed him, could on occasion talk "pretty d—d plainly" to men engaged in intrigue. Thus Hay saw the firmness as well as the kindness of the President, and by both qualities was profoundly impressed.

Such intimate companionship with one of the most sincere men in all history was in itself a graduate course in the art of living. Yet Hay's experience at Washington did not provide him with a career. He was only an amateur. This was to become more evident in the years immediately to follow. His appointment, in March 1865, as secretary to the American legation in Paris was evidence both of the friendship of Secretary Seward and of Hay's capacity. He had wearied of the work at Washington; now he was to experience the delights of life abroad. The social experiences of diplomatic life in Paris at the period when the court of Napoleon III was most brilliant occupied Hay to the full. His chief, the American minister, was John Bigelow, who had an important influence in turning the young man again toward writing. He now found time to indulge himself in composing verse and in describing in prose some of the gay scenes which he witnessed. His ardent belief in democracy gave to his writings for the next few years a tone and a color which may offend the judicious historian. This dream, this vision, of a republican millennium in Europe founded on liberty and peace was common at the time, especially among young men. Such views, however, took small stock of the facts in the case. Hay enjoyed his brief stay in Paris (1865–67) and profited by its social joys, but apparently did not exert any influence on the diplomatic negotiation of the time. He had learned much but was to learn more before he acquired that real knowledge of European affairs which could entitle him to be called a "cosmopolite" (see, however, Thayer, *post,* I, 244).

After six months in America, Hay once more took diplomatic office, this time as chargé d'affaires at Vienna, thanks again to Secretary Seward. En route, he stopped in London. There he showed again how faulty was his judgment of British politics, for he wrote in July 1867: "If the Republicans are not distracted by false issues they will conquer at last, by the force of numbers" (Thayer, I, 281). His year and a half in Paris had scarcely given him a notion of the forces at work in the European world. At Vienna, where diplomatic duties sat lightly, he greatly enjoyed the music and the picture galleries. His chief interest, however, was in society and in the observation of the life of the people afforded him by frequent excursions and occasional night rambles. The spectacle of an entire nation so largely influenced by clerical forces, the degradation of the Ghetto in Vienna, and the menacing danger of militarism seem particularly to have attracted his attention. His mistaken notion of the immediate future of Europe is shown in a passage in a letter of Feb. 5, 1868, to Seward: "No honest statesman can say that he sees in the present attitude of politics the necessity of war. No great Power is threatened. . . . Why then is this awful waste of youth and treasure continued? I believe from no other motive than to sustain the waning prestige of Kings" (Thayer, edition of 1915, I, 303). Journeys to Poland and to Turkey filled out the year that Hay was stationed at Vienna; he resigned in August 1868. Long office holding had now converted him into a persistent office seeker. As a result of his reiterated requests he was offered, in June 1869, the post of secretary of legation at Madrid. In Spain, Hay collected impressions which later were included in that admirable book of travel, *Castilian Days* (1871). Of Spain, however, he soon wearied; he was pressed financially; and he was eager to return to lively America. Accordingly he went back, landing in New York in September 1870. He had decided, under the influence of Bigelow, to become a journalist.

Hay had expected to take a position, under Nicolay, on the *Chicago Republican,* which was the enterprise of Springfield capitalists, but the paper failed even before he reached Chicago. He then turned to his literary friends in the East and at length accepted a position as editorial writer and night editor on the *New York Tribune,* under Whitelaw Reid, whom he had known as a press correspondent in Washington. An event of prime importance to his future career was his marriage, on Jan. 8, 1874, to Clara L. Stone, the daughter of wealthy parents living in Cleveland, Ohio. Within a year, in 1875, Hay gave up journalism, both because of the desire of his father-in-law and because of his own poor health, and removed to Cleveland, in order occasionally to assist Amasa Stone [*q.v.*] in financial matters and, more important still, to continue his own literary efforts. The change of residence, of interest, and of friends was of major importance in Hay's development. He never liked Cleveland and maintained his reserve of manner. "No matter how intimate you were," his best friend in that city told Thayer, "or how merry the occasion, nobody ever slapped John Hay on the back" (Thayer, I, 330). As soon as convenient after the death of his father-in-law, he transferred his residence to Washington.

As a journalist, Hay had been partly anonymous, but when he began a literary career his name soon became familiar to thousands. His notable literary successes came in his first year on the *Tribune.* "Little Breeches" and "Jim Bludso," after appearing in that paper, were included in his *Pike County Ballads and Other Pieces* (1871), which were followed a few weeks later by *Castilian Days.* At once Hay became one of the leading literary figures of the United States. His *Poems* were published in 1890. The *Ballads,* which introduced to poetry a new character in his homeland and constituted Hay's most important contribution to American literary development, exposed him to scorching criticism. This disclosed the important fact that the author, however facile and gifted, lacked both conviction and courage. Distrustful of his true literary gift, he later sought to minimize his *Ballads,* but they survive, while most of his conventional poems have been forgotten. (See Benét, *post,* p. 151; Ward, *post,* p. 55; Kreymborg, *post,* p. 177). In 1884 he published anonymously a novel, *The Bread-Winners.* A satirical attack on labor unions and a defense of economic individualism, it had a wide sale and well expressed the spirit of upper-class America in the eighties, but it now seems partisan, if not "smeared with unctuous morality" (Parrington, *post,* III, 173–79). The Paris Commune, his own experience of wealth, and the danger of great industrial strikes had all combined with middle age to curb Hay's youthful enthusiasms.

More important than any of these occasional forms of self-expression was his publication, with John Nicolay, of *Abraham Lincoln: A History* (10 vols., 1890). Back in White House days, the two secretaries had discussed the question of writing the story of the momentous times in which they lived. Nothing was decided until with the passing years the figure of Lincoln grew in popular imagination and Hay's marriage and his retirement from the *Tribune* gave him the necessary wealth and leisure. Then a plan of cooperation was agreed on. Even so, because of his ill health and a variety of other activities, including both travel and the acceptance of a temporary diplomatic post at Washington, this plan did not bring ripened results for fifteen years. Nicolay had returned from Paris, where he had been consul, and was now established in Washington as marshal of the Supreme Court. His library became the chief clearinghouse for material, which included a mass of documents loaned by Robert T. Lincoln, the President's son. The schedule for the work was laid down by Nicolay; then he and Hay arranged for the division of the task. On completing his chapter, each would send his manuscript to the other for revision. Thus the book was in every sense a cooperative work, possible only because of the friendship and common experience of the two authors. After ten years of labor, they signed in 1885 a contract for the serial publication of the work in the *Century*; for this they received fifty thousand dollars, an unprecedented sum at the time. It is of course impossible to declare, chapter by chapter, that this particular section was written by Hay or that by Nicolay; but from Hay's letters it is possible definitely to assign to him the chief responsibility for the chapters dealing with the first forty years of Lincoln's life. Hay on the whole was in favor of a more compact treatment, while Nicolay was at times obsessed by his desire for thoroughness. As was natural, fatigue told heavily on Hay; he was driven to dictation, which, as Thayer wisely remarks, is "the foe of durable writing." The authors, however, maintained a fairly good average. Both of them were so influenced by their memory of the martyred President that at times they portray an idealized character. None the less, the work remains an indispensable record, based on original sources, which will continue both as a monument to Abraham Lincoln and as an invaluable narrative of the history of his presidency.

In November 1878 Hay became assistant secretary of state and moved to Washington. There he found his most important friendship, that with Henry Adams [*q.v.*]. A few years later they built adjoining houses, designed by H. H. Richardson; there at 800 Sixteenth St., N. W., across the square from the White House, Hay renewed, under most favorable circumstances, the memories of his earlier days. Thither came Adams, Clarence King, Mrs. Cameron, the Lodges, and Cecil Spring-Rice. A few distinguished artists and literary men, birds of passage, were welcome guests. In Cleveland, Hay had occasionally spoken to political audiences and there was talk of his running for Congress. Garfield urged him in 1880 to become his private secretary, but Hay wisely declined. At the Department of State he learned about the mechanism of diplomacy and the various ways in which policies were determined. For six months in 1881 he was again in journalism, taking Whitelaw Reid's place as editor of the *Tribune* during the latter's absence from the country. It was during the years 1881–96 that Hay also made frequent trips to Europe, there to absorb the information and to acquire the point of view which were to be invaluable in the nation's service. He decided in 1881 to give up politics but never for long was able to resist the temptation to return to them. He had the misfortune often to back men who were unsuccessful aspirants for the presidency and no actual opportunity to hold office was again provided him until the McKinley administration was inaugurated. During the campaign of 1896 Hay, who had long been a friend of the Republican candidate, was brought within the circle of McKinley's intimate advisers. His appointment as ambassador to Great Britain in 1897 was received with some surprise by many Americans, although it was in accord with the tradition which had sent Motley and Lowell to London; Hay's work on the Lincoln history had made him a literary figure in Republican eyes.

He went to London at a time of great significance for the United States. The controversy with Great Britain regarding the proper method of settling the Venezuelan boundary dispute was barely ended. American difficulties with Spain as to the conduct of affairs in Cuba were soon to flare into actual war. In England his charm and dignity soon won for him a distinguished place in society and he was welcomed on all sides. Bimetallism and seal-fisheries were at first the subjects for diplomatic correspondence; but with the outbreak of the Spanish-American War in April 1898, all of Hay's resources were used to secure the goodwill of Great Britain. In this endeavor he was successful, for the Court, the politicians, and the financial interests in London all rallied to the support of the United States; and Balfour for the Government stated privately to Hay that "neither here nor in Washington did the British Government propose to take any steps which would not be acceptable to the Government of the United States" (State Department Archives). By June and July 1898, Washington was asking Hay's advice in regard to possible terms of peace with Spain. At this time Hay agreed with President McKinley that only a port in the Philippines should be retained by the United States but that American approval should be deemed necessary for the lease or alienation to a third power of any portion of the islands. Later in the year Hay changed his mind and was completely in favor of the cession of the entire group to the United States. In the meantime (August 1898) he was urged by the President to accept the place of secretary of state. With great reluctance, chiefly on grounds of uncertain health, he consented and at the end of September took office at Washington. His term as ambassador had been brief but pregnant; but his very success in London was to label him to political opponents in America as an Anglophile. This charge was again and again to interfere with Hay's plans in America. The story that a secret alliance with Great Britain had been made was often current; this of course was arrant nonsense. Hay wrote privately, however: "As long as I stay here [in Washington] no action shall be taken contrary to my conviction that the one indispensable feature of our foreign policy should be a friendly understanding with England" (to Henry White, Sept. 24, 1899; quoted in Thayer, II, 221).

Hay showed himself an imperialist in the settlement with Spain, and steadfastly supported the President in his final determination that Spanish misrule should cease in the West Indies and that the Philippines should become American. He likewise favored the attack on Aguinaldo; and in general was determined that the new interests of the United States should be maintained. He was aware of the rivalry of European powers in the Far East and was ambassador when the Department of State rejected the suggestion of Great Britain in 1898 that a joint declaration by the two powers might be made in favor of freedom of commerce in China and voicing their opposition to the cession of Chinese coastal territory to foreign states. In 1899, the war with Spain having been liquidated, the time seemed ripe for a proposal to the great powers, including Japan, that a declaration should be made in favor of the "Open Door" in China. The final draft of the notes on the subject which Hay dispatched abroad followed almost word for word the language used in a memorandum written in August 1899 by William W. Rockhill [*q.v.*], formerly of the diplomatic service and an expert in Far-Eastern affairs. The doctrine of the "Open Door," or of equal opportunity, was based on earlier American policy and was at this time largely formulated by Rockhill; but it came to the world as a policy particularly associated with Hay's name. He chose to sponsor it and his diplomatic skill and courage were responsible for its general acceptance. The next year, in 1900, there came the Chinese outbreak against the policy of spoliation which various European countries had been following at the expense of China. The Boxer movement, as this revolt was called, was accompanied by brutal outrage on the part of the Chinese and violation of international law and courtesy. Hay's policy at this crisis was to use force when necessary and to punish when practicable but to assume that the revolution was purely local and to persist in dealing with the Peking government, with a view to preventing the partition of China. In later times the indemnity forced from China by the United States was remitted. Through the succeeding years of Hay's life, he was continually faced by the unscrupulous and deceitful policy of Russia which sought to extend influence and territory at the expense of China. In voicing American opposition to this policy of Russian expansion, Hay was handicapped by the lack of firmness shown by China and by his knowledge that the United States would not go to war to maintain American policies in the Far East. With the signature of the Anglo-Japanese alliance in 1902, there followed naturally the Russo-Japanese War (1904–05), which involved among other questions that of the neutrality of China. Here Hay was again perplexed by the lack of courage and consistency shown by China. American policy toward Far-Eastern matters, notwithstanding the accession of Roosevelt in September 1901, displayed lack of vigor and decision. After the presidential election of 1904, Hay's hand relaxed because of his ill health, and Roosevelt became the director of Far-Eastern policy. Hay's most notable accomplishment in China was the prevention of the dissolution of the empire in 1900.

Hay had followed the historical policy of approaching Far-Eastern problems through European paths and in his negotiations with regard to American questions he was continually and necessarily in contact with Europe. Thus the partition of the Samoan island group involved delicate negotiation with both Germany and Great Britain. The long-drawn-out disputes with Canada naturally required the intervention of British diplomacy. The settlement finally arrived at with respect to the Alaskan boundary question (1903) resulted in a victory for the United States, chiefly because Hay first refused to submit the matter to arbitration along the lines of the Venezuela reference, and, by devising a *modus vivendi* in 1899, postponed the decision until passions had cooled and the Canadians were willing to accept a tribunal composed of equal numbers for the United States and for Great Britain. With these negotiations with Canada he also refused to permit any entanglement of the question of the abrogation of the Clayton-Bulwer Treaty and the development of a new settlement regarding an interoceanic canal. Thus, although continually charged with being an Anglophile, Hay stood firm and secured from Great Britain greater concessions than had been obtained by any other secretary of state in fifty years.

In the treaties relating to the Panama Canal, Hay was to suffer a severe disappointment, for his first agreement with Great Britain was so amended by the Senate that it failed in England. The second canal treaty (1901), which did away with the Clayton-Bulwer Treaty and under guise of the exercise of police power ultimately provided for the fortification of the canal zone by the United States, was successful. Hay's language in private letters during the months of conflict with the Senate, while angry and contemptuous, did not greatly differ from his earlier and later views regarding the power of the Senate as to treaties. He was strongly opposed to the constitutional requirement of a two-thirds majority in the Senate for approval, and he was critical of the right of amendment. Negotiations with Colombia, however, regarding the construction of a canal across the Isthmus of Panama, proved even more arduous. Hay once said to a friend: "Talking with those fellows from down there ... is like holding a squirrel in your lap and trying to keep up the conversation" (J. B. Bishop, *Theodore Roosevelt and His Time,* 1920, I, 279). After much labor, a treaty was actually signed in January 1903, but it was never ratified by Colombia. This result intensely disgusted the Administration in Washington. Hay wrote Roosevelt in September: "It is altogether likely that there will be an insurrection on the Isthmus against that government of folly and graft that now rules at Bogotá. It is for you to decide whether you will (1) await the results of that movement, or (2) take a hand in rescuing the Isthmus from anarchy, or (3) treat with Nicaragua" (*American Secretaries of State,* IX, 163–64). Hay was opposed to haste, but Roosevelt took the matter out of his hands. In November a successful revolution at Panama took place. The President's prompt recognition of the new republic of Panama and the threat of the use of force to prevent Colombian intervention were sufficient. Whatever of blame attaches to the precipitate recognition of Panama should be assigned to Roosevelt, although it must be admitted that Hay acquiesced in this *coup* and even attempted subsequently to defend the policy.

The pressure brought to bear on Germany in 1902–03, to warn her not to endanger the Monroe Doctrine by hasty naval action against Venezuela, was due primarily to Roosevelt. Yet it is hard at times to distinguish Hay's part and Roosevelt's. As regards the protection of American interests in Turkey, it was Hay who acted; in regard to the rescue of Perdicaris from the hands of the Moroccan chieftain Raisuli, it was Roosevelt, though Hay coined the telegraphic phrase of instruction, "Perdicaris alive or Raisuli dead." In 1905 Hay's health failed completely and he went abroad for medical treatment. He returned in June somewhat better, but collapsed almost at once on attempting to work at Washington. He had been ill for at least five years. On July 1 he died at his country home in New Hampshire, survived by his wife and three of his four children, a son of great promise having met with an accidental death four years before.

Theodore Roosevelt, notwithstanding many contrary assertions during Hay's lifetime, subsequently declared that the latter was "not a great Secretary of State" (to Henry Cabot Lodge, Jan. 25, 1909). There were, in fact, after Seward, no great secretaries of state in the nineteenth century if Hay is not to be included. His best work was done under McKinley; the least creditable achievements of his term of service belong actually to Roosevelt. The famed Open-Door Policy was largely an illusion, but the China policy in 1900 was masterful and stood the most exacting test: China escaped dissolution. To Hay must be given very great credit that the government of the United States did not in 1900 abruptly abrogate the Clayton-Bulwer Treaty in a manner which would have left a stain on the national honor. To him belongs the credit for having settled the Alaskan boundary question, although Roosevelt subsequently disputed it. Under his secretaryship began an era of good relations with Great Britain such as did not ensue from the work of Adams or of Webster, Clayton, Seward, or Fish. It seems probable that with the passing of years Hay's reputation and place in American history will be raised—not to the rank which popular enthusiasm assigned it at the time of his death, but to a more estimable place than Roosevelt was willing to concede.

[Hay unfortunately destroyed most of his letters home, but the papers in the possession of his daughter, Mrs. J. W. Wadsworth, Jr., are essential, as are the Archives of the Dept. of State, and the Roosevelt Papers in Lib. of Cong. The more important printed sources are: *Addresses of John Hay* (1907); *Letters of John Hay and Extracts from Diary* (3 vols., 1908); *A Poet in Exile. Early Letters of John Hay* (1910), ed. by Caroline Ticknor; *The Complete Poetical Works of John Hay* (1916), with introduction by his son, Clarence L. Hay. The chief biography is W. R. Thayer, *Life and Letters of John Hay* (2nd ed., 2 vols., 1916), containing original source material. See also sketch by A. L. P. Dennis in S. F. Bemis, ed., *Am. Secretaries of State and Their Diplomacy,* vol. IX (1929); Dennis, *Adventures in Am. Diplomacy, 1896–1906* (1928); Tyler Dennett, *Americans in Eastern Asia* (1922), and *Roosevelt and the Russo-Japanese War* (1925); Lorenzo Sears, *John Hay, Author and Statesman* (1914); *Theodore Roosevelt: An Autobiography* (1913); *The Education of Henry Adams* (1918); W. R. Benét, *Poems for Youth: An Am. Anthology* (1925); Alfred Kreymborg, *Our Singing Strength: An Outline of Am. Poetry, 1620–1930* (1929); Sister Saint Ignatius Ward, *The Poetry of John Hay* (1930); V. L. Parrington, *Main Currents in Am. Thought,* vol. III (1930); J. B. Moore, "Mr. Hay's Work in Diplomacy," *Rev. of Revs.* (N. Y.), Aug. 1905; W. D. Howells, "John Hay in Literature," *North Am. Rev.,* Sept. 1905; J. B. Bishop, "A Friendship with John Hay," *Century Mag.,* March 1906; A. S. Chapman, "The Boyhood of John Hay," *Century Mag.,* July 1909. The editor has received from Dr. Tyler Dennett, who is preparing a biography of Hay, suggestions which were invaluable, especially because the untimely death of Prof. Dennis prevented his making a final revision of his article.] A. L. P. D.

HAY, MARY GARRETT (Aug. 29, 1857–Aug. 29, 1928), civic worker, the daughter of Andrew Jennings and Rebecca (Garrett) Hay, was born in Charlestown, Clark County, Ind. Her father, a physician, was a man of wide interests, who took an active part in the politics of his state. Mary Hay attended Western College for Women at Oxford, Ohio, in 1873–74, but did not graduate. At an early age she began attending political meetings with her father and developed an interest in public affairs which she retained throughout her life. The first organization to absorb her interest was the Women's Christian Temperance Union, of which she became a state officer. Through the contacts made in this work she became interested in the woman's suffrage movement. First a local and then a state officer, she soon became affiliated with the national suffrage association which she served as an organizer, campaigning in many states. She assisted in organizing the New York City Woman's Suffrage party and it was under her leadership that suffrage was won in New York state in 1917 through the city's vote. New York was the first large city to adopt woman's suffrage and the victory was largely due to Miss Hay's courage, energy, and executive ability. She was appointed chairman of the Republican Women's National Executive Committee and held that office during the two years of the committee's existence. When the vote was won she saw the need of training women to exercise the franchise and took an active part in the work of the New York City League of Women Voters. A born leader, she held a long list of offices in a variety of organizations, over twenty of which were represented at memorial services held for her in New York City after her death. She assisted in organizing the first Conference on the Cause and Cure of War, held in Washington, D. C., in 1926, and took an active part in the succeeding conferences in 1927 and 1928, but the last three years of her life were devoted chiefly to the subject of her first interest, prohibition. At the time of her death she was engaged on plans for a dry ticket for the New York Women's Committee for Law Enforcement of which she was chairman. To her, right and wrong were clearly defined and she worked indefatigably for the cause she felt to be right, accepting no compromises. Her death came suddenly on her seventy-first birthday, in New Rochelle, N. Y., where she had long made her home.

[*Biog. Hist. of Eminent and Self-Made Men of the State of Ind.* (1880), vol. I; *Who's Who in America,* 1928–29; the *Nation,* Sept. 19, 1928; *Woman's Jour.,* Oct. 1928; *Gen. Federation News,* Sept. 1928; *Western Coll. Alumnæ News,* Nov. 1928; *N. Y. Times,* Aug. 31, Sept. 1, Oct. 11, 1928; *World* (N. Y.), Aug. 31, Sept. 1, 1928.] B. R.

HAY, OLIVER PERRY (May 22, 1846–Nov. 2, 1930), paleontologist, was born near Hanover,

Ind., the eldest son of Robert L. and Margaret Crawford Hay. His formal education began in a little country schoolhouse in central Illinois, whither the family had moved when he was about four years of age. With a view to becoming a minister, he entered Eureka College, Ill., and in spite of many interruptions due to financial difficulties, graduated in 1870. After attempting his first sermon, he decided that preaching was not his vocation. His interest in natural science, developed while in college, now stood him in good stead: he was appointed professor of natural sciences at Eureka College where he remained until 1874, when he went in a like capacity to Oskaloosa College, Iowa. He spent the academic year 1876–77 as a graduate student at Yale, the next two years as professor of natural sciences at Abingdon College, Ill., and was then appointed professor of biology and geology at Butler College, Indianapolis, where he remained from 1879 to 1892, assisting meanwhile in the state geological survey of Arkansas, 1884–88, and of Indiana, 1891–94. During this time he helped to organize the Indiana Academy of Science and was its president in 1890–91. He received the degree of Ph.D. from Indiana University in 1884. In 1895 he joined the staff of the Field Museum of Natural History, Chicago, where he was assistant curator of zoölogy until 1897. In 1900 he went to New York to become assistant and later associate curator of vertebrate paleontology, in the American Museum of Natural History, a position which he held until 1907. After five years of private research in vertebrate paleontology, he was appointed research associate in the Carnegie Institution of Washington, where he remained until his retirement in 1926, at the age of eighty.

From his first paleontological expedition into western Kansas about 1889 or 1890, Hay's whole scientific interest was devoted to paleontology, although his first publication on the subject did not appear until 1895. Two of his outstanding contributions to the science were *The Fossil Turtles of North America* (1908), a complete discussion of classification, distribution, and osteology, together with a detailed description of the orders, families, genera, and species, and *The Pleistocene Geology of North America and its Vertebrated Animals* (1923–27), three volumes dealing with the animals of the eastern, middle, and western portions of North America. In the latter work the divisions of the Pleistocene with their stratigraphical and time limits, the extinction of species, and the distribution by states of such groups as the horses, the elephants, the tapirs, bison, deer, beaver, and whales, were all carefully investigated and recorded. Hay's most notable service to science, however, was probably his *Bibliography and Catalogue of the Fossil Vertebrata of North America* (1902), supplemented by his *Second Bibliography and Catalogue* ... (2 vols., 1929–30). The first of these covered the literature of the eighteenth and nineteenth centuries and the last two volumes that of the first twenty-eight years of the twentieth century. They constitute a monumental work, revealing years of painstaking effort and patient recording. Their careful investigation of synonyms, their logical classification of the entire vertebrate phylum—often involving fresh grouping and nomenclature—their accuracy and reliability, make them immeasurably valuable to the research worker.

Hay possessed an extraordinary capacity for concentration upon special questions, but at the same time maintained a view of the whole field. In every undertaking he showed the utmost care, very close attention to detail, and a tireless pursuit in running down obscure points. The study of languages was his only hobby. While in college he studied Latin and Greek; at Yale he began to study French and later German; only three years before his death he undertook to learn Italian and made considerable progress in that language. He was a man of kindly disposition, absolute integrity, and possessed of a rare sense of humor. Though slow and cautious in drawing conclusions, when once convinced of their truthfulness, he held tenaciously to his decisions. He was an active member of many organizations of scientific character. From 1902 to 1905 he was associate editor of the *American Geologist,* and in 1904 he was a delegate to the International Congress of Zoölogy in Berne. In 1870 he was married to Mary Emily Howsmon, of Eureka, Ill., who with two sons and two daughters survived him.

[*Who's Who in America,* 1928–29; *Am. Men of Sci.,* 1927; R. S. Lull, "Memorial of Oliver Perry Hay" in *Bull. Geol. Soc. of America,* Mar. 1931, with bibliography; *Evening Star* (Washington), Nov. 3, 1930; personal letters.]

R. S. L.
N. E. W.

HAYDEN, AMOS SUTTON (Sept. 17, 1813–Sept. 10, 1880), minister of the Disciples of Christ, educator, was born in Youngstown, Ohio, the eighth and youngest child of Samuel and Sophia Hayden who had emigrated to that place from Pennsylvania in 1804. He spent his early days on a farm, and although his opportunity for schooling was limited he succeeded in getting a fair classical education. His parents were devoted Baptists and he was an eager reader of religious books. In March 1828, under the preaching of Walter Scott [*q.v.*], one of the leaders in the Disciples movement, he was converted. When about nineteen years old he became an independent evangelist. On May 31, 1837, he married Sarah M. Ely of Deerfield, Portage County, Ohio, and in 1840 became pastor of a church in Collamer, then Euclid, Cuyahoga County, Ohio. He was one of those instrumental in the founding, in 1850, of the Western Reserve Eclectic Institute at Hiram, Ohio, which developed into Hiram College, and was chosen its first principal. He did good pioneer work there, but by 1857 the institution had outgrown his abilities and he resigned to be succeeded by James A. Garfield [*q.v.*], who had fitted for college there. In 1858 he was chosen principal of McNeely Normal School, Hopedale, Ohio, and also acted as pastor of the church in that town, but the following year he returned to Collamer, where the most of his remaining life was spent. He had a natural gift for music and was one of the earliest compilers of hymns for use in the churches of the Disciples. The *Christian Hymn and Tune Book* (1870) lists three previous works by him, *Sacred Music*, the *Sacred Melodeon*, and *The Hymnist*. The second of these is reviewed in the *Millennial Harbinger* of April 1849, which states that it contains approved pieces of old standard authors and many original compositions. He was also the author of the *Early History of the Disciples in the Western Reserve* (1875), prepared at the request of the Western Reserve Preachers Association. His older brother, William [*q.v.*], was a prominent leader of the early Ohio Disciples.

[F. M. Green, "The Life and Character of A. S. Hayden," *The Disciple*, Apr. 1886; W. T. Moore, *The Living Pulpit of the Christian Church* (1869), containing biographical sketch and a sermon on "Conscience and Christianity"; F. M. Green, *Hiram Coll. and Western Reserve Eclectic Inst.—Fifty Years of Hist.* (1901); *Annals of the Early Settlers Asso. of Cuyahoga County*, no. II (1881); *Cleveland Leader*, Sept. 12, 1880.]

H. E. S.

HAYDEN, CHARLES HENRY (Aug. 4, 1856–Aug. 4, 1901), landscape painter, born at Plymouth, Mass., was the son of Edward Boyd and Ann Flower (Goodspeed) Hayden. His father was a cotton manufacturer, with mills at Chiltonville, Plymouth. He began the study of drawing and painting at the age of twenty under John B. Johnston, the cattle painter, in Boston, but remained with him only two or three months. When, in 1877, the school of drawing and painting of the Museum of Fine Arts, Boston, was opened, he followed the advice of his teacher and entered that institution, where he worked for two years. The ensuing four years he devoted to out-of-door work and to attendance on evening life classes, Johnston still acting as adviser and critic. In 1882 he secured a situation as designer in the stained-glass establishment of Cook, Redding & Company, Boston, remaining there until December 1886, when he went to Paris and entered the atelier of Raphael Collin. In the spring of 1887 he passed a few months in Italy for the purpose of study, with a view to specializing in decorative work.

In 1888 Hayden settled in St. Léger, a picturesque village in the forest of Rambouillet, where he gave all his time to landscape work, continuing there until the opening of the Paris Exposition of 1889. He sent to the Salon of that year a landscape entitled "Near the Village" and also exhibited in the international exposition, where he received a mention. Returning to America in July 1889, he settled in Belmont, Mass., a suburb of Boston, where he built a studio, making that place his home for the rest of his life. In 1895 he received the Jordan prize of $1,500 for his picture of "The Turkey Pasture," exhibited at the Jordan Gallery, Boston, and subsequently presented to the Museum of Fine Arts, Boston, by Eben D. Jordan. The same year, 1895, the artist received a medal at the Atlanta Exposition for one of his best landscapes, "A Connecticut Hillside," which was later acquired by the Cincinnati Art Museum. "The Poplars, Chatham, Massachusetts," belongs to the Corcoran Gallery, Washington. An exhibition of his pictures was opened at the St. Botolph Club, Boston, in 1897.

Hayden died, unmarried, at Belmont, on the forty-fifth anniversary of his birth. He left $50,000 to the Boston Art Museum. A memorial exhibition of his paintings which was held at the St. Botolph Club from Dec. 30, 1901, to Jan. 18, 1902, contained fifty-three works painted at Belmont, on Cape Cod, in the Berkshires, and at Mystic, Conn. His landscapes are serene and sober in an unusual degree, so much so that a casual observer is likely to wonder what there is in them that artists should esteem them so highly. Most of his pictures deal with nature's undemonstrative moods. Their excellence is best realized by close observers of nature. The merits of his pictures correspond to the unassuming and sensitive character of the man.

[Catalogue of a memorial exhibition at the St. Botolph Club, 1901, with biographical sketch and appreciation by Philip L. Hale; W. A. Goodspeed, *Hist. of the Goodspeed Family* (1907); *Brush and Pencil*, May 1899; *Am. Art Ann.*, 1903–04; the *Bostonian*, Feb. 1895; *Boston Transcript*, Aug. 5, Dec. 31, 1901; information as to certain facts from Hayden's sister.]

W. H. D.

HAYDEN, FERDINAND VANDIVEER (Sept. 7, 1829–Dec. 22, 1887), geologist, son of

Asa and Melinda (Hawley) Hayden, was born in Westfield, Mass. Of his earlier ancestry little is known beyond the fact that his grandfathers on both sides lived to an age of approximately a hundred years and served in the Continental Army during the Revolution. When the boy was about ten years old his father died and, as his mother married again soon afterward, he went to live with an uncle on a small farm near Rochester, N. Y. Here he remained until he was eighteen, teaching after he was sixteen in the local country schools during the winter.

Refusing an offer of adoption from his uncle, and quite without funds, he then walked to Oberlin College determined either to gain an education or to learn a trade. From President Finney he received advice, encouragement, and assistance which enabled him to enter the college in 1847 and graduate with the class of 1850. His life during that time was hard. A poor, apparently timid, and absent-minded boy, the youngest in his class, little understood by his classmates who regarded him as a dreamer and predicted for him small success in after life, he nevertheless "made good" as a student and was always well prepared. He presented on graduation a thesis indicative of his tendency to dream, "The Benefit of a Refined Taste." Soon afterward he entered upon the study of medicine in the Albany Medical College, graduating in 1853 with the degree of M.D. In Albany he formed an acquaintance with the New York state paleontologist, James Hall [*q.v.*], which changed the course of his career. Instead of entering at once upon the practice of his profession, in the spring of 1853, under Hall's patronage, he joined a fellow enthusiast, F. B. Meek [*q.v.*], on a collecting trip into the Bad Lands of South Dakota. In the description of the large collections of fossils which they brought back Hayden had little part, though he submitted a brief vertical geological section showing the order of superposition of the strata. This is worthy of mention as being his first contribution to geology, though it was not published under his name. In the spring of 1854 he again ascended the Missouri River, this time under the auspices, in part, of the American Fur Company. During the next two years he made his way up the valley of the Missouri as far as Fort Benton in Montana, traveling on foot or by whatever form of conveyance was available and dependent for subsistence on such friends as he made as he went along. During 1856 and 1857 he served as geologist under Lieut. G. K. Warren in his explorations of the Yellowstone and Missouri rivers and the Black Hills of Dakota. In 1858 he was associated with F. B. Meek in explorations of the Territory of Kansas and in 1859 with Capt. W. F. Raynolds in explorations of the headwaters of the Yellowstone, Gallatin, and Madison rivers in Montana. With the outbreak of the Civil War he entered the Union army in the capacity of surgeon and served until his retirement in June 1865 with the rank of lieutenant colonel. In the fall of the last-named year he was elected professor of geology in the University of Pennsylvania, holding the position until 1872 when he resigned to give all his time to the duties of the United States Geological Survey. In the spring of 1866, under the auspices of the Academy of Natural Sciences of Philadelphia, he made a second expedition to the Bad Lands and in 1867, under direction of the General Land Office, he entered upon a survey of the Territory of Nebraska, in so doing laying the foundation for the United States Geological Survey as it exists today. From this date on, with governmental appropriations varying from year to year and a like variation in the personnel of his field parties, Hayden continued his geological and natural-history surveys in the West, mainly in Colorado, Idaho, Montana, Wyoming, and Utah, until the consolidation of all the individual surveys under the general management of Clarence King [*q.v.*] in 1879. Under the new organization Hayden was appointed to the position of geologist and authorized to continue the work already under way in Montana. Unfortunately his health failed, and his disease—locomotor ataxia—made such rapid progress that he was forced to resign in 1886, thus closing a record of nearly thirty years as naturalist, surgeon, and geologist in the service of the government. He died the following year.

In considering the character and value of Hayden's work, the conditions under which he labored must be taken into consideration. There were no good maps, topographic or otherwise, of the country traversed; such maps had to be made as the work progressed. Railways west of the Mississippi were few and of little avail for transportation. Yet he covered a vast area of the Rocky-Mountain region which prior to his investigations was mostly unknown territory. His work was necessarily largely in the nature of reconnaissance—indeed so rapidly did he move from point to point that according to Cope the Indians applied to him a name the meaning of which was "the man who picks up stones running." The work which gave him immediate reputation was that which resulted in the setting aside as a public reservation of an area in southern Wyoming and adjacent portions of Montana and Idaho now known as Yellowstone National

Park. "There can be no doubt that among the names of those who have pioneered in the marvellous geology of western North America that of F. V. Hayden will always hold a high and honored place," wrote Sir Archibald Geikie (White, *post,* p. 406). Hayden was a member, active, corresponding, honorary, or otherwise of a large number of societies including the Academy of Natural Sciences of Philadelphia, the National Academy of Sciences, the Geological Societies of London and Edinburgh, the Geologische Reichsanstalt of Vienna, the Société Impériale of Moscow. In accordance with the custom of naming genera and species of various organisms, living or extinct, after individuals—of creating a progeny for the childless as some one has expressed it—Hayden has been complimented with a progeny of forty-four, ranging in character from a living moth to a fossil dinosaur.

Hayden was excitable in temperament and frequently impulsive in action, yet generous and always ready to give full credit to whomever it was due. The apparent diffidence which had impressed his fellow students while in college and caused them to doubt his future success remained characteristic of his later years; the secret of his achievement lay in his enthusiastic frankness and determination to carry through whatever he undertook. On Nov. 9, 1871, he was married to Emma C. Woodruff, daughter of a Philadelphia merchant. They had no children.

[Sources of information include: personal acquaintance; correspondence; an unpublished biography by Hayden's assistant, A. C. Peale; memoir by C. A. White in *Nat. Acad. Sci. Biog. Memoirs,* vol. III (1895), which contains full bibliography of Hayden's publications. See additional references in Max Meisel, *A Bibliog. of Am. Natural Hist.,* I (1924), 193; and obituary in *Phila. Press,* Dec. 23, 1887.] G. P. M.

HAYDEN, HIRAM WASHINGTON (Feb. 10, 1820–July 18, 1904), brass-manufacturer, inventor, the son of Joseph Shepard [*q.v.*] and Ruhamah (Guilford) Hayden, was born at Haydenville, Mass. His father was a skilful mechanic. Hiram grew up in Waterbury, Conn., attending the academy and working as his father's helper. In time he was known as a capable mechanic and when the firm of J. M. L. & W. H. Scovill began the manufacture of chased gilt buttons, he was asked to assist in this new work. In 1838 he went to Wolcottville in the employment of Wadhams & Company, manufacturers of buttons, but returned to Scovills & Company as a die maker in 1841. At Wolcottville the Wolcottville Brass Company was making kettles by the battery process, which was not entirely satisfactory. Hayden became interested in this work and spent much time on the development of a better method. On Dec. 16, 1851, he patented "machinery for making kettles and articles of like character from disks of metal," patent No. 8,589. In this process a disk of thin sheet metal is fastened to a die which is the exact shape of the article to be formed. The die with the disk of metal is then rotated at high speed while a tool is brought to bear against the disk, rolling the metal over until it has conformed very closely to the shape of the die. This invention was the first important American improvement in brass manufacturing methods. Because of it the business of the Wolcottville Brass Company was undermined, and the Waterbury Brass Company to whom Hayden sold the process in 1853 became one of the most important firms in the industry.

In 1853 Hayden with Israel Holmes, John C. Booth, and H. H. Hayden organized Holmes, Booth & Haydens, to cast, roll, draw, and manufacture brass. In this firm Hiram Hayden had charge of the manufacture of sheet brass into finished articles. At this time the introduction of petroleum as a cheap and satisfactory illuminant increased the demand for brass lamp burners and fittings. In order that the company might command as much of this new business as possible, Hayden with L. J. Atwood, an employee, made a study of the requirements for efficient lamp burners and designed some that could be made cheaply from sheet brass. This was the first extensive use of sheet brass for this class of articles and Hayden and Atwood took out many patents for improvements in the field, becoming known as authorities on oil-lighting. Hayden continued with this firm until his death, developing many improvements in brass-manufacturing methods, including a machine for making solid metal tubing. He also patented several improvements in firearms and is credited with having made one of the first successful attempts at making a positive photograph without the use of a negative. Hayden married Pauline Migeon, daughter of Henri and Marie (Bandelot) Migeon at Litchfield, Conn., July 31, 1844. They had three children. Hayden died at Waterbury.

[C. E. Leonard, *The Fulton-Hayden-Warner Ancestry in America* (1923); Jos. Anderson, *The Town and City of Waterbury, Conn.* (1896), vol. II; Wm. G. Lathrop, *The Brass Industry in the U. S.* (1926); W. J. Pape, *Hist. of Waterbury and the Naugatuck Valley* (1918), vol. III.] F. A. T.

HAYDEN, HORACE H. (Oct. 13, 1769–Jan. 26, 1844), dentist, geologist, was a son of Thomas and Abigail (Parsons) Hayden. Born in Windsor, Conn., where his ancestor William Hayden had settled in 1642, he received his early education in his native town and at the age of fourteen made two voyages to the West Indies as cabin boy on a brig. At sixteen, after a further term at school, he began the study and practice of architecture with his father, with whom he was associated for some five years. He returned twice to the West Indies, but was driven home both times by the yellow fever. In 1792 he removed to New York City, where he studied dentistry with the help of John Greenwood [*q.v.*]. About 1800 he began the practice of his new profession in Baltimore, and was licensed as a dentist by the Medical and Chirurgical Faculty of Maryland (in 1810, according to J. R. Quinan, *Medical Annals of Baltimore,* 1884). Hayden practised also in other cities and villages of Maryland, and quickly attained success. On Feb. 23, 1805, he married Marie Antoinette Robinson. Having studied medicine and surgery in connection with dentistry, he was able to act as assistant surgeon as well as sergeant of militia when the British attacked North Point at the mouth of the Patapsco in 1814. During the next few years he published in medical journals several articles on subjects relating to dental physiology and pathology. He was first secretary of the Baltimore Physical Association in 1818, and vice-president of the Maryland Academy of Sciences and Literature in 1826. Two of his brothers, Anson B. Hayden and Chester Hayden, became his student assistants and proved successful dentists.

At an early date Hayden taught small classes in dentistry in his own office at night, and delivered one course of lectures on dental physiology and pathology to medical students in the University of Maryland ("about the year 1825," according to Chapin A. Harris in his *Dictionary of Dental Science,* 1849, p. 360). In 1839 he joined Chapin A. Harris [*q.v.*] and others in a petition to the Maryland legislature for the establishment of the first dental college in the world, the Baltimore College of Dental Surgery, which was chartered Feb. 1, 1840. He was the first president of the college, and the first professor of the principles of dental science; but he shortly took the chair of dental physiology and pathology, which he occupied until his death. He was one of the prime movers in the organization of the first national association of dentists, the American Society of Dental Surgeons (New York, 1840), a project which had been a favorite with him since 1817. He received the degree of D.D.S. as a member of that society, and in the same year (1840) an honorary M.D. was conferred upon him by the Medical School of the University of Maryland. In spite of his long-continued labors for the elevation of the profession, he was opposed to the first dental periodical, the *American Journal of Dental Science,* which was established by Harris and others in 1839. He held that he had labored too hard and too long in the acquisition of professional knowledge to sow it broadcast through the land by means of a magazine (see Solyman Brown, "Early History of Dental Surgery," *Dental Science and Art Journal,* February 1875, p. 5). In the first volume of the *American Journal* three of his dental articles were reprinted from medical publications, and his portrait by Rembrandt Peale appeared as the frontispiece to the second volume, but his only voluntary contribution was a long series of "Comments" in Vol. III on an essay by Harris ("Diseases of the Maxillary Sinus") which had been published in the *Journal.* Hayden had read an essay on the same subject before the American Society, which did not appear in the *Journal,* and he included some caustic criticisms of that periodical in his sarcastic "Comments" on the Harris essay. Harris replied in a similar tone (June 1843) thus sustaining a controversy which marked the culmination rather than the beginning of a regrettable estrangement.

Hayden was a deeply religious and studious man, and at the same time an ardent sportsman with gun and rod. He was interested in botany and wrote on silkworm culture, but geology was his chief hobby. In 1820 he published *Geological Essays; or, An Inquiry into Some of the Geological Phenomena to be Found in the Various Parts of America, and Elsewhere,* which was favorably reviewed in Silliman's *American Journal of Science and Arts* (vol. III, 1821), but adversely criticized in the *North American Review* (January 1821) by a reviewer who opposed Hayden's theory that the alluvial or glacial deposits of North America were formed at the time of the Biblical deluge. In Parker Cleaveland's *Elementary Treatise on Mineralogy and Geology* (1816) Hayden is one of the authorities followed, and in the Appendix to the second edition (1822), Cleaveland stated that he applied the name "Haydenite" to a mineral "recently discovered" by Hayden near Baltimore. This name is still the recognized designation of that form of chabazite. When he died in his seventy-fourth year Hayden was recognized as one of the foremost dentists of his time, and he had lived to see the realization of his most cherished project, the establishment of dentistry as an organized profession. He was buried in Greenwood Cemetery, Baltimore. His native town, Windsor, Conn., has erected a monument to his memory, and there is a Harris and Hayden memorial tablet in the Baltimore College of

Dental Surgery. Of his six children, two died in infancy. One of his sons, Handel M. Hayden, became a dentist as did Gillette Hayden (1880–1929), a great-grand-daughter through another son.

[Sources include: B. L. Thorpe, in C. R. E. Koch, *Hist. of Dental Surgery*, vol. III (1910); L. P. Brown, "New Light on Dental History" in *Dental Cosmos*, Aug. 1920; H. R. Stiles, *Hist. and Geneals. of Ancient Windsor*, vol. II (1892); J. H. Hayden, *Records of the Conn. Line of the Hayden Family* (1888); Wm. Simon, *Hist. of the Baltimore Coll. of Dental Surgery* (1904); obituary in the *Sun* (Baltimore), Jan. 27, 1844. It is said that Hayden had no middle name, but adopted the "H." in order to distinguish himself from another Horace Hayden (Second Official Cat., Lib. of Cong.).]
L. P. B.

HAYDEN, JOSEPH SHEPARD (July 31, 1802–Feb. 17, 1877), inventor, manufacturer, the son of Daniel and Abigail (Shepard) Hayden, was born in Foxborough, Mass. He was descended from John Haiden who emigrated from England to America about 1632 and settled ultimately in Braintree, Mass. His father was an ingenious mechanic and after obtaining such an education as the local schools afforded, Joseph took up mechanical work, first with his father and later, after his marriage in 1819 to Ruhamah Guilford, with relatives in Haydenville, Mass. He shortly moved with his family to Waterbury, Conn., which offered greater opportunity. The brass industry, then in its infancy, centered more or less in the vicinity of Waterbury. Among the many brass products being made were brass and gilt buttons as well as cloth-covered buttons—the latter made by hand. Joseph and his father, who had preceded him to Waterbury, became interested in the possibility of designing a machine to make cloth-covered buttons and about 1828 succeeded in building some crude machinery for this purpose. They thereupon started a small button factory in Waterbury and prospered, for, with their crude machine, they were able to make as many as forty gross of cloth-covered buttons a day. This was a phenomenal increase in output over that possible by the old hand methods. No record exists that the Haydens, father and son, applied for or received a patent for their invention. The result was that around 1830 Josiah Hayden, a cousin of Joseph, who was a button manufacturer in Haydenville, Mass., incorporated the essential features of Joseph's machine in one of his own design and with it established an extensive cloth-covered button industry in Haydenville. Joseph presumably did not continue to improve his machine but turned his attention to other things. Thus on Oct. 1, 1830, a patent (granted to his cousin Festus Hayden) was awarded to his invention of wire-eyed buttons and the machinery for making them. Then with his father, he began the manufacture of this commodity and enjoyed considerable success. By 1838 they were employing over 200 operatives and the following year they added the manufacture of steel pens to their line. Very little information concerning Hayden's activities is available after this time. He seems to have been a mechanical genius, more interested in invention and machine design than in managing a button factory. He is said to have constructed the first engine lathe ever seen in Waterbury. He imparted, too, to his son, Hiram Washington Hayden [*q.v.*], his mechanical and inventive skill. At the time of his death in Waterbury he was survived by his widow and his son.

[Jos. Anderson, *The Town and City of Waterbury, Conn.* (1896), vol. II; *Waterbury American*, Feb. 18, 1877; *Americana*, Apr. 1928; Patent Office records; J. L. Bishop, *A Hist. of Am. Manufactures*, II (1864), 348, 411, 766.]
C. W. M—n.

HAYDEN, WILLIAM (June 30, 1799–Apr. 7, 1863), a pioneer evangelist of the Disciples of Christ, was born in Rosstrevor Township, Westmoreland County, Pa. He was the oldest of the eight children of Samuel and Sophia Hayden, the youngest being Amos Sutton [*q.v.*], also prominent among the early Disciples. In 1804 the father migrated westward, and settled in Youngstown, Ohio, where amid frontier surroundings William grew up. Of questioning mind and having access to few books, he studied the Bible assiduously. Although at one period on the verge of atheism, for he was an independent thinker, he was finally converted and joined the Baptist Church. On Dec. 20, 1818, he married Mary McCollum and took up land in Austintown. While he carried on the work of developing his farm with diligence, he was actively interested in everything pertaining to religion. A sermon which he heard Alexander Campbell [*q.v.*] preach at Warren in October 1821 awakened in him a struggle over the doctrines of Calvinism, and in time he adopted the views of the gospel being promulgated by the Disciples. The preaching of Walter Scott [*q.v.*] resulted in the reconstituting on a Campbellite basis of numerous practically defunct Baptist churches in northeastern Ohio. Among these was the church in Austintown, reëstablished in June 1828, and of this Hayden, having been licensed to preach in May by the Canfield church, of which he was then a member, was put in charge. When the Mahoning Association met that year, however, and it was proposed to confine Scott's activities within the Association's borders, the evangelist said: "Brethren, give me my Bible, my head, and Brother William Hayden, and we will go out and convert the world." The Association acquiesced, and Hayden was ordained at Austintown. Scott said later that he chose Hayden not because he could preach better than anybody else, but because there was not a man in the Association who could sing like him. He was the Sankey of his day. When Scott's appeal failed, he would retire, saying: "I'll send Willie, and he'll sing you out." Nevertheless, he was also a most effective preacher and was especially successful in personal conferences. His connection with Scott was the beginning of thirty-five years of remarkable evangelistic work, during which he is said to have traveled 90,000 miles, two-thirds of them on horseback. His journeys extended from Syracuse, N. Y., to the Mississippi, and from Canada to Virginia, although his chief field was in the Western Reserve. He broke new ground, starting churches, turning them over to someone else, and moving on. He was interested in education and was associated with his brother Amos in establishing the Western Reserve Eclectic Institute, later Hiram College, serving as agent to secure funds for its building. He was also an early advocate of system and organization in the activities of the Disciples. After suffering for two years from paralysis, he died in his sixty-fourth year at his home in Chagrin Falls, Ohio.

[A. S. Hayden, *Early Hist. of the Disciples in the Western Reserve* (1875); *Millennial Harbinger*, May 1863; Robt. Richardson, *Memoirs of Alex. Campbell*, vol. II (1870); Wm. Baxter, *Life of Elder Walter Scott* (1874); F. D. Power, *Sketches of Our Pioneers* (1898); W. T. Moore, *A Comprehensive Hist. of the Disciples of Christ* (1909); Alanson Wilcox, *A Hist. of the Disciples of Christ in Ohio* (1918).] H. E. S.

HAYES, AUGUSTUS ALLEN (Feb. 28, 1806–June 21, 1882), chemist, was born at Windsor, Vt., the son of Thomas Allen and Sophia (West) Hayes. He attended the military academy at Norwich, Vt., where he graduated in 1823. Immediately afterward he began to study chemistry in the medical school at Dartmouth College under James Freeman Dana [*q.v.*]. Here he started a laborious investigation of the proximate constituents of American medicinal plants, and in 1825 published, among other results, an account of the isolation of an alkaloidal compound which he called sanguinaria. It attracted attention more from the brilliant colors of its derivatives than from its medicinal properties. For the next two years, 1826–28, he investigated certain compounds of chromium, and the paper containing his results was commended by the eminent Swedish chemist Berzelius. In 1828 he moved to Boston, Mass., and devoted the rest of his life to chemical research in that city or its vicinity. He became successively the director of a large plant in Roxbury, Mass., which manufactured colors and other chemicals, the consulting chemist of several of the most important dyeing, bleaching, gas-making, and smelting establishments in New England, and the assayer of the state of Massachusetts. He discovered a process for making chloroform by alcohol and chlorin, but this process was not utilized to any extent. On the other hand, the methods he devised for shortening the time needed in smelting iron and refining copper were widely used. The oxids of iron were added to the mixture in the puddling furnace and a better quality of malleable iron was obtained. Scales of copper oxid, added at the proper point, made the operation of refining more certain. He investigated the formation of guano and studied the composition and specific differences of numerous varieties of this fertilizer. In 1837 he started an intensive investigation of methods of economizing fuel in generating steam, and his results soon led to fundamental improvements in the construction of furnaces and the arrangement of steam boilers. While acting under a commission from the United States Navy Department, his investigations on the use of copper and copper sheathing in the construction of national vessels led to an extended study of the composition of sea water and its action below the surface and at the mouths of rivers. In 1859–60 Hayes conducted an investigation of the water supply of Charlestown, Mass., and devised and used a simple electrical method of detecting the limits of slight impurities in drinking water. He proved that a copper strip or wire if placed vertically into two layers of water, slightly different in composition, would exhibit electrolytic action. By applying this method, he showed that a sulfur compound, when decomposed, could be detected by the formation of black copper sulfid, and the limits of the compound could be read on the strip. At the beginning of the Civil War he pointed out the uncertainty of the foreign, as well as domestic, supply of saltpeter needed for gunpowder, and the urgent necessity for increasing domestic production. Through his researches an excellent quality of potassium nitrate was manufactured for the Navy Department from sodium nitrate and potassium hydroxid. He received the honorary degree of M.D. from Dartmouth College in 1846. He was a member of the American Academy of Arts and Sciences and other learned societies. His scientific papers, which numbered about sixty, covered a wide range, and were published for the most part in the *Proceedings* of the Academy and the *American Journal of Science*. His opinions as a consulting chemist were highly valued. The last thirteen years of his life were hampered by invalidism, which was borne with the same cheerfulness and fortitude that characterized his active life. His wife was Henrietta Bridge Dana, the daughter of the Rev. Samuel Dana of Marblehead, whom he married July 13, 1836.

[*Proc. Am. Acad. Arts and Sci.*, n.s. X (1883); G. M. Dodge and W. A. Ellis, *Norwich Univ., 1819–1911* (1911), II, 133–34; J. J. Dana, *Memoranda of Some of the Descendants of Richard Dana* (1865); *Gen. Cat. Dartmouth Coll., 1769–1925* (1925); J. C. Poggendorff, *Handwörterbuch*, vol. III (1898); *Boston Transcript*, June 23, 1882.] L. C. N.

HAYES, CHARLES WILLARD (Oct. 8, 1858–Feb. 8, 1916), geologist, oldest son and fifth child of Charles Coleman and Ruth Rebecca (Wolcott) Hayes, was born at Granville, Ohio. His forebears had migrated to Ohio in the early part of the nineteenth century. His ancestors were from the North of England, whence they emigrated to Maryland in the latter part of the seventeenth century. Hayes's father was a tanner by trade—or profession—who moved to Hanover, Ohio, in 1868. The boy is described as a "sturdy youngster, full of enterprise and without fear," but with a pronounced scholarly tendency which he apparently inherited from his mother, who was a seminary graduate and before her marriage a teacher. His early training was that of the common schools of the region, where however he showed no geological inclinations, although he was fond of natural history subjects. From the elementary schools he passed to the Denison University preparatory school and at the age of nineteen entered the sub-freshman school of Oberlin College whence he was graduated from the classical and scientific department in 1883, with inclinations toward teaching. He is stated to have been a good student, having a certain mental poise uncommon among students of his own age. After a year spent in teaching at the Brecksville High School, Hayes entered in 1884 the graduate school of Johns Hopkins University as a student in chemistry. Here he came in contact with George H. Williams—young, of pleasing personality, fresh from Heidelberg, and filled with enthusiasm over the recently developed science of micropetrology. Dull and unimpressible indeed must have been the man who would not have succumbed, and it was not long before Hayes was found taking part in all the geological excursions and was one of the "inner circle" of geological students. Nevertheless he received his doctorate in 1887 with chemistry as his major and mineralogy and geology his minor subjects.

Still dreaming of a professorship in chemistry, Hayes went to Washington in the spring of 1887 and while there agreed to become assistant to I. C. Russell of the United States Geological Survey for work in the Southern Appalachians at a monthly salary of fifty dollars. He is said never to have regretted this move. He remained with the Appalachian division of the Survey until the spring of 1897, interrupting his service only by a trip of exploration in company with Lieutenant Schwatka into Alaska and down the Yukon basin in the summer of 1891. His executive ability was soon recognized by his superiors. In 1899 he was given charge of the section of non-metalliferous resources in the division and three years later he was placed in administrative charge of all the geological work of the Survey. At the time the Nicaragua Canal Commission was organized he was appointed geologist and later (1910) he was assigned to similar duties in the Panama Canal Zone. In 1911 he succumbed to the financial inducements of the Aguila Oil Company of Mexico and his services as a geologist came to an end.

Hayes was a vigorous and careful worker and spared no pains to insure accuracy in his results. He was an original thinker and brought new life into the organizations with which he became associated. From the beginning his tastes ran strongly along the lines of physiography. He was nevertheless interested in economic problems and while he was in charge of the section of the Survey devoted to the non-metallic minerals, he became particularly interested in the southern deposits of rock phosphate and of bauxite. As an administrator both with the Survey and in Mexico he was successful to a marked degree, largely because he had "a genius for applying what is generally called common sense to any problem that arose" (Brooks, *post*, p. 112). He remained with the Mexican oil companies until the Americans were driven out by revolution. He then returned to Washington. Later he took a trip to London to prepare for future explorations for oil. Failing rapidly from an internal cancer, however, he returned to his home in Washington, where, after a painful illness, he died in 1916. Though given somewhat to crowding his workers, he was not unreasonable, but endeavored to be uniformly fair in his treatment of his subordinates. He was a member of the geological societies of America and of Washington, of the American Institute of Mining Engineers, and of the Mining and Metallurgical Society of America. In 1897 he received the Walker grand prize from the Boston Society of Natural History. He was married on Mar. 22, 1894, to Rosa E. Paige of Washington. His widow and eight children, three daughters and five sons, survived him.

[A. H. Brooks, memorial in the *Bull. of the Geol. Soc. of America*, Mar. 31, 1917, with full bibliography of Hayes's publications; C. W. Hayes, *Geo. Hayes of Windsor* (1884); *Engineering and Mining Jour.*, Feb. 19, 1916; *Mining and Sci. Press*, Mar. 4, 1916; *Mining and Metallurgical Soc. of America, Bull.*, Feb. 29, 1916; *Science*, July 28, 1916; *N. Y. Times*, Feb. 10, 1916; personal recollection.] G. P. M.

HAYES, ISAAC ISRAEL (Mar. 5, 1832–Dec. 17, 1881), physician and explorer, was born in Chester County, Pa., the son of Benjamin and Ann (Borton) Hayes, and a descendant of Henry Hayes of Fulwell, Oxfordshire, who settled in Chester County in 1705. He was educated at Westtown Academy and the University of Pennsylvania, where he received the degree of M.D. in 1853. In the same year he sailed in the *Advance* as surgeon to the second Arctic expedition of Elisha Kent Kane [*q.v.*]. From the winter quarters at Van Rensselaer Harbor, 78° 37′ N., 71° 14′ W., Hayes explored the unknown coast of Ellesmere Land northwest of Cape Sabine. Leaving on May 20, 1854, he crossed Smith Sound to Dobbin Bay and traced the coast to Cape Frazer, 79° 43′ N., whence he was turned back by a broken sled and snow blindness—a notable journey, conditions considered. The *Advance* frozen in and a second winter before him, Kane granted permission for the dividing of his command. On Aug. 28, 1854, Hayes with eight men started in a boat for the Danish outposts in Greenland, as related in his book, *An Arctic Boat Journey* (1860). The attempt was disastrous, and the party would have perished but for the food and transportation furnished by the Eskimo, which enabled the party to reach the *Advance* on Dec. 12.

Returning home in 1855 with a mutilated foot, Hayes found that his extreme sufferings instead of abating increased his enthusiasm for arctic explorations. Through lectures and personal appeals to societies and individuals, he succeeded in organizing a new expedition, financed largely by the American Geographical Society and Henry Grinnell [*q.v.*]. With a crew of fourteen he sailed from Boston on July 9, 1860, in the schooner *United States,* planning to reach, via Smith Sound, the ice free Arctic Ocean reported by Morton. At the Greenland ports he obtained furs, sleds, dogs, and Eskimo natives to serve as hunters and dog-drivers. Profiting by the experience of his predecessor, he made his winter quarters south of Kane Sea, and established his base in Foulke Fiord, near Littleton Island. Abundant game and friendly relations with the Etahs made his prospects unusually favorable. The autumn began well, with a journey to the inland ice, to an elevation of 5,000 feet. Later an epidemic killed all but nine dogs, and an Eskimo hunter strayed or deserted and died of starvation. More distressing was the death of the astronomer, August Sonntag, who perished in a journey with Hans Hendrik to obtain dogs from the natives near Cape York. Hayes was not deterred from his explorations by these misfortunes. He turned to the Etahs with excellent results as to comradeship and assistance in the way of dogs. On Apr. 3, 1861, he started to navigate and determine the extent of the Arctic Ocean. Besides two dog-sledges, he carried on a man-drawn sled a metallic ice-boat for navigation. Ice conditions were so bad that after twenty-six days of most exhausting labor he recognized the failure of his main journey, and sent the main party back with the boat.

Remaining, with three men and fourteen dogs, he decided to explore Grinnell Land. On May 11 he reached Cape Hawks, having made only eighty miles in thirty-one days. Accidents occurred, but Hayes struggled northward and reached his farthest on May 19. A single inaccurate observation placed him in 81° 35′ N., but reliable researches, agreeing with his sledge journal, make it evident that his farthest was Cape Joseph Goode, in 80° 14′ N. Ascending the high cape he recorded: "There was no land visible except the coast upon which I stood. . . . The sea beneath me was a mottled sheet of white and dark patches . . . [which] receded until the belt of the water-sky blended them all together. . . . All the evidences showed that I stood upon the shores of the Polar Basin, and that the broad ocean lay at my feet" (*Open Polar Sea*, p. 349). In fact he was gazing on Kennedy Channel, where high spring tides and strong currents clear for days large spaces from its winter ice-covering. His book, *The Open Polar Sea* (1867) was widely criticized, but, errors aside, his main story stands. With Kane and Charles Francis Hall [*q.v.*] he opened the way to the North Pole.

Returning to Boston in October 1861 he learned of the outbreak of the Civil War, immediately offered his schooner to the government, and enlisted in the Union army as a surgeon. He was put in charge of the Satterlee Hospital at West Philadelphia and was successively promoted major and brevet colonel. At the close of the war he settled in New York City where he engaged in business and gave considerable time to lecturing and writing. His "Physical Observations in the Arctic Seas" appeared in Vol. XV (1865) of the Smithsonian Institution *Contributions to Knowledge* and his account of his adventures written for children was published under the title *Cast Away in the Cold* in 1868. His third voyage to the Arctic, in 1869, with William Bradford in the *Panther,* resulted in an accurate and lively sketch of Greenland, *The Land of Desolation* (London, 1871; New York, 1872). He attended the Iceland millennial celebration as correspondent for the *New York Herald* in 1874. The following year he was elected as a Republican to the New York Assembly, where he served until 1881, the year of his death, being active in canal affairs and in the promotion of the Hudson River Tunnel. He was unmarried.

[In addition to Hayes's own publications see: E. K. Kane, *Arctic Explorations: The Second Grinnell Expedition* (2 vols., 1856); biographical sketch by G. W. Cullum in *Jour. Am. Geog. Soc.,* XIII (1881), 110–24; J. S. Futhey and Gilbert Cope, *Hist. of Chester County, Pa.* (1881); S. C. Harry, T. H. Windle, and J. C. Hayes, *Proc. of the Bi-Centennial Gathering of the Descendants of Henry Hayes* (1906); *N. Y. Tribune,* Dec. 18, 1881.] A. W. G.

HAYES, JOHN LORD (Apr. 13, 1812–Apr. 18, 1887), lawyer, author, scientist, was born in South Berwick, Me., the son of William Allen Hayes, for many years judge of the probate court of York County, Me., and Susan (Lord) Hayes, daughter of John Lord of South Berwick. He received his early education at the South Berwick Academy and entered Dartmouth College in 1827 at the age of fifteen. During his college years he became interested in science, studying principally natural history and geology. Immediately upon his graduation in 1831, he entered the law office of his father, from which he entered Harvard Law School, remaining there for one year (1833–34). Admitted to the New Hampshire bar in 1835, he removed to Portsmouth to practise his profession. On May 29, 1839, he married Caroline S. Ladd, daughter of Alexander Ladd of Portsmouth. The following year he was appointed clerk of the United States circuit court for New Hampshire. Hayes never lost his interest in geology. On May 4, 1843, he presented a paper on "The Probable Influence of Icebergs upon Drift" before the American Association of Geologists and Naturalists at Boston. It was published in 1844. In 1845, in recognition of his scientific researches, he was elected a member of the Boston Society of Natural History.

Hayes became interested in tariff protection for native New England industries and in 1850 was appointed representative of the Iron Masters of New England to petition Congress to alter the tariff act of 1846. In 1851 he removed to Washington, D. C. He practised law and appeared in many important cases, one of which was the *Creole* case, tried before the Mixed Commission under the Convention of Feb. 8, 1853, between the United States and Great Britain (J. B. Moore, *A Digest of International Law,* 1906, vol. II, pp. 351–55, 358–61). In May 1861 President Lincoln appointed him chief clerk of the United States Patent Office, a position which he held until the close of the Civil War. In 1865 when the National Association of Wool Manufacturers was formed, he was elected its secretary. Largely through his efforts, in this office, in bringing together wool-growing and wool-manufacturing interests, the West was induced to support the East in urging protection for the industry, thus fostering the passage of the tariff act of 1867 which provided a high tariff on wool and woolens. The Association was an early example of a successfully organized business lobby and was the first great business interest so to organize. In 1869 Hayes became editor of the *Bulletin of the National Association of Wool Manufacturers* published quarterly in Boston, to which he contributed over fifty essays and reviews. Some years later he headed the tariff commission appointed by the President in 1882 and wrote the introductory address and report which was subsequently incorporated into the tariff act of 1883. From 1883 until his death practically all of his time was devoted to writing and study. He died in Cambridge, Mass., in his seventy-sixth year. Several of his studies, representing his varied interests, were published in pamphlet form.

[W. T. Davis, *Bench and Bar of the Commonwealth of Mass.* (1895), vol. II; H. K. Beale, "The Tariff and Reconstruction," *Am. Hist. Rev.,* Jan. 1930; *House Misc. Doc. 6,* pt. 1, 47 Cong., 2 Sess.; G. T. Little, *Geneal. and Family Hist. of the State of Me.* (1909), vol. III; *Boston Daily Advertiser,* Apr. 19, 1887.] W. G. E.

HAYES, RUTHERFORD BIRCHARD (Oct. 4, 1822–Jan. 17, 1893), president of the United States, was born at Delaware, Ohio, the posthumous son of Rutherford Hayes, a farmer, who had married Sophia Birchard in 1813. Both parents sprang from old New England families and through the paternal line he was descended from George Hayes who emigrated from Scotland as early as 1680 and settled in Windsor, Conn. The place of a father was taken for him by his uncle Sardis Birchard, a Vermonter by birth, who helped furnish means for his education. From the academy at Norwalk, Ohio, the boy was sent to the private school of Isaac Webb at Middletown, Conn. He dreamed of Yale, but the expense and lack of full preparation decided the family to send him to Kenyon College at Gambier, Ohio. Here he displayed great earnestness. "I am determined," he wrote at eighteen, "from henceforth to use what means I have to acquire a character distinguished for energy, firmness, and perseverance" (*Diary and Letters,* I, 57). When graduated in 1842 he had obtained a fair literary training, good moral discipline, and a Middle-Western point of view that he would have missed at Yale. He had early made up his mind to the law, and some dull months in reading Blackstone and studying German in the office of Sparrow and Matthews in Columbus, Ohio, were followed by a year and a half in the Harvard Law School. Here he studied under Joseph Story and Simon Greenleaf, attended lectures by Jared Sparks, and was fired by glimpses of J. Q. Adams and Daniel Webster. In addition, he found time to attend theatres, dabble in Latin and French, and read philosophy. The experience also had social value. He discovered that his chief defect was "boyish conduct" and that he needed "greater mildness and affability." Returning to Ohio, he was admitted to the bar on Mar. 10, 1845, and began practice in Lower Sandusky (later Fremont), Sardis Birchard's home.

Lower Sandusky held Hayes for five leisurely years, spent over small cases, the English and French classics, and natural science, for he always had a roving intellectual taste. He considered volunteering for the Mexican War in order to benefit a bronchial affection, but gave up the plan on the advice of physicians (*Ibid.,* I, 203–09). In the winter of 1848, however, he journeyed to Texas to visit a college classmate, Guy M. Bryan, studying plantations at close range, seeing the rough, lawless side of the frontier, and finding slavery a kindly rather than cruel system. Not returning till spring, he witnessed impassively the feverish gold rush to California. "There is neither romance nor glory in digging for gold," he concluded. The value of this trip in enlarging his horizon was increased by steady later correspondence with Bryan. At the beginning of 1850 he opened his own law office in Cincinnati, still so poor that his first hotel bill worried him and he slept in his office to keep expenses at thirty dollars a month. But his business grew steadily and he sorely regretted "the waste of those five precious years at Sandusky." He also made friends rapidly and was keenly alive to the world about him. He joined the Literary Club of Cincinnati, helped it to entertain Emerson, saw Charlotte Cushman play "Meg Merrilies," heard Beecher and Edward Everett lecture and Jenny Lind sing, attended the Episcopal church, though his own views tended toward agnosticism, and joined the Sons of Temperance and Odd Fellows. In several criminal trials, notably that of one Nancy Farrer accused of murder, he distinguished himself by clever defenses (Eckenrode, *post,* p. 33). By the end of 1852 he had saved enough money to marry, on Dec. 30, a boyhood sweetheart, Lucy Webb, whose attractiveness, shrewdness, and poise contributed much to his later success. By September 1854, largely through the generosity of his uncle (*Diary and Letters,* I, 469), he was able to move into his own $5,500 house, where two of his eight children were born.

In 1851 Hayes entered the local politics of Cincinnati, attending ward and county meetings, and making stump speeches. His Ohio associations had made him a Whig of the Thomas Corwin school, and he spoke for Winfield Scott in 1852. The struggle over the Kansas-Nebraska Bill intensified his interest in public affairs; in 1855 he was a delegate to the state Republican convention; and in 1856 he supported Frémont, as he wrote, "hopefully, ardently, joyously," though he predicted defeat. Naturally cool of temperament, he refused to condemn slavery in the extreme terms used by other Free-Soilers, but strongly opposed its extension. In 1857 he was mentioned for Congress and in 1858 was elected city solicitor at a salary of $3,500 a year. In the campaign of 1860 he characteristically refused to grow excited, making only a few speeches for Lincoln and writing his uncle that "a wholesome contempt for Douglas, on account of his recent demagoguery, is the chief feeling I have" (*Diary and Letters,* I, 564). He hoped to see war averted, advocating conciliation, negotiation, and even compromise; but when the conflict began he could not be restrained. "I would prefer to go into it if I knew that I was to die or be killed in the course of it than to live through and after it without taking any part in it," he said (*Ibid.,* II, 16). He made patriotic speeches, helped recruit men, and accepted the post of major (June 27, 1861) in the 23rd Ohio under Col. William S. Rosecrans [*q.v.*]. Serving first in western Virginia, he enjoyed the guerrilla fighting "as if it were a pleasure tour"; by the end of the year, now a lieutenant-colonel, he was in command of the regiment.

Hayes's military service was varied and capable but not distinguished. He acted for a time as judge-advocate, trying court-martial cases under Gen. Jacob Cox and General Rosecrans; he fought under Frémont at the time of "Stonewall" Jackson's Valley Campaign, was ordered east as a part of General Cox's division in August 1862, was wounded in the arm at the battle of South Mountain the following month, and later was sent back to West Virginia for the winter. In July 1863 he was sent with the troops who administered to Morgan's raiders a sharp check near Gallipolis, Ohio. Later placed in command of Gen. George Crook's first infantry brigade, he was with Sheridan in the Shenandoah Valley during the campaign of 1864, fought well at Winchester, where his flags were the first to enter the town, and was at Cedar Creek when Sheridan defeated Early. From that time until the end of the war he was chiefly on garrison duty. Somewhat tardily, on Oct. 19, 1864, he was commissioned brigadier-general, and on Mar. 13, 1865, he was brevetted a major-general of volunteers.

Meanwhile, in July 1864, Hayes had been nominated for the House of Representatives from the 2nd Ohio (Cincinnati) district, but had wisely refused to take the stump, writing that "an officer fit for duty who at this crisis would abandon his post to electioneer for a seat in Congress ought to be scalped" (*Diary and Letters,* II, 497). In October he was elected by a heavy majority. Resigning his commission in June 1865, he took his seat in December. In Congress he obeyed the Republican caucus on important questions and was hostile to the "rebel influences . . . ruling the White House," but disapproved of the extreme radicalism of Thaddeus Stevens. When General Schenck proposed an amendment by which Southern representation would be based on suffrage, he suggested an educational test for the ballot. His best work was as chairman of the library commission, for he sponsored a bill shifting the Smithsonian Institution's collection of books to the Library of Congress, carried an appropriation of $100,000 to purchase Peter Force's collection of Americana, and developed the botanical gardens. He served his constituents well and gained the name of the soldier's friend. He was reëlected in 1866, but his congressional career was brief. The Ohio Republicans needed him as candidate for governor, for Jacob Cox was unpopular in that office, and when nominated in June 1867 he resigned from Congress. An arduous campaign, in which Hayes made more than seventy speeches, ended in his election over Allen G. Thurman by the narrow majority of 2,983, though the proposed amendment to the state constitution for universal manhood suffrage, which he favored, was defeated by about 50,000 votes. A Democratic legislature sent Thurman to the Senate and thwarted the chief recommendations of Hayes. He was able, however, to carry through important prison reforms and a measure for the better supervision of charities. In 1869 a campaign for reëlection against weakened opposition gave him a majority of about 7,500 and some measure of national prestige; and this time the Republicans gained control of the legislature. Hayes made a determined stand against extravagance and higher taxes, obtained reforms in the care of the insane, urged the establishment of a state agricultural college, and denounced current abuses in railway management. He recognized the merit principle in his appointments, placing able Democrats in office; he combated election frauds; he helped create the geological survey of Ohio, and chose an accomplished scientist as its head; and he encouraged the preservation of historical records. As his reputation as a courageous administrator grew, some of his public addresses were widely reported and read. Urged in 1871 to stand for a third term, he refused to violate the unbroken precedent of the state.

An astute governor, Hayes was also an astute politician. In 1872 he shrewdly rejected the suggestion that he seek election to the Senate as an opponent of the cold, unpopular, but able John Sherman. In that year, though sympathizing with many aims of the Liberal Republicans, of whom his friend Stanley Matthews was a leader, he refused to leave his party and campaigned vigorously for Grant. He was himself beaten for Congress because of the party split. Retiring to the "Spiegel Grove" estate near Fremont which his uncle Sardis Birchard had bequeathed him, he devoted himself to law, the real-estate business, and the promotion of public libraries. His successor as governor, Gen. E. F. Noyes, was badly beaten by William Allen in 1873, while in 1874 the Democrats carried Ohio by 17,000 plurality and elected thirteen out of twenty congressmen. As Republican leaders sought his aid, Hayes's ambition awoke. In his diary, on Apr. 14, 1875, he wrote: "Several suggest that if elected governor now, I will stand well for the Presidency next year. How wild! What a queer lot we are becoming!" None the less, he dreamed of the presidency. Nominated for governor by an overwhelming vote in the state convention of 1875, he opposed William Allen in a campaign which drew national attention and which brought in Carl Schurz and Oliver P. Morton to stump the state. His election by a majority of 5,544 was a triumph which made him a national figure. By virtue of his liberalism, taste for reform, war record, and loyalty to his party he was one of the distinctly "available" figures for the next presidential nomination, and he added to his reputation by another wise state administration.

Hayes was brought forward for the presidency by John Sherman and Garfield, with Ohio Republicans united behind him. In May 1876, he ingratiated himself with the Eastern reformers by a letter of sympathy for Richard H. Dana of Massachusetts, just rejected by the Senate for the mission to England (*Diary and Letters,* III, 318). His Ohio managers won a preliminary victory when they succeeded in having Cincinnati made the convention city, for the friendliness of the crowds and press counted heavily. The leading rival candidates were Blaine, Conkling, Bristow, and O. P. Morton. For a time it seemed that Blaine might be named, but the refusal of the convention to ballot immediately after Robert G. Ingersoll's brilliant nominating speech destroyed his chances. Repeated conferences were held by the managers of the Hayes, Morton, and Bristow candidacies, with Stanley Matthews, who was ostensibly for Bristow but really for Hayes, in a key position. The result was that when Blaine made dangerous gains on the sixth ballot the opposing delegates united on Hayes, and on the next ballot nominated him with 384 votes against 351 for Blaine. Hayes had awaited the result calmly. Just before it came he wrote in his diary: "I have kept cool and unconcerned to a degree that surprises me. The same may be said of Lucy. I feel that defeat will be a great relief—a setting free from bondage. The great responsibility overpowers me" (*Diary and Letters,* III, 326). His nomination pleased the reformers under Schurz, Bristow, and G. W. Curtis, satisfied the practical politicians, was applauded by Civil War veterans, and did much to hold the recently chaotic Republican party together. In the vigorous campaign which followed Hayes benefited by the activities of an unexampled group of stump speakers—Blaine, Evarts, Sherman, Schurz, Bristow, Curtis, Ingersoll, Logan, Garfield, Harrison, and even Mark Twain (Eckenrode, *post,* p. 145). He himself played an inactive part, though late in October he visited the Centennial Exhibition for Ohio Day and inspired extraordinary interest. In October Hayes stated that the chances of his opponent, Tilden, appeared better than his. The first returns on Nov. 7 seemed to show that the election was lost and he went to bed apparently in that belief.

His hopes revived when on Nov. 8 Zachariah Chandler sent out his telegram "Hayes has 185 votes and is elected." That day, according to the *Ohio State Journal* of Nov. 9, he "received those who called in his usual cordial manner, and was very unconcerned, while the greatest office on the American continent was trembling in the balance." When it became clear that the result hinged on contested returns from South Carolina, Florida, Louisiana, and Oregon, he was resolutely opposed to any attempt at a "compromise." At the outset he was dubious regarding Louisiana, but his misgivings were soon stilled by friends and party managers, and on Dec. 6 he telegraphed Schurz: "I have no doubt that we are justly and legally entitled to the Presidency" (*Diary and Letters,* III, 386). His original demand was that the electoral votes be counted by the president of the Senate, but chiefly as a result of Schurz's arguments he consented to the creation of the Electoral Commission. When the composition of this body was decided he awaited the issue with confidence. There is evidence that as the work of the Electoral Commission approached its close, especially after Louisiana's votes were counted for Hayes, Republican agents were in close touch with Southern Democrats who cared less about the presidency than the restoration of white rule in Louisiana, South Carolina, and Florida. The speech of Charles Foster, representative from Hayes's former Cincinnati district, who on Feb. 23, 1877, declared that it would be Hayes's policy to wipe out sectional lines and conciliate the South, was regarded as an olive branch from Hayes himself. In the conferences with Southerners in Washington, Foster, Stanley Matthews, Ex-Gov. Wm. Dennison, and John Sherman were the chief representatives of Hayes. These meetings bore fruit in "the bargain," an agreement in the interests of party peace and sectional amity, dictated by powerful public considerations (P. L. Haworth, *The Hayes-Tilden Disputed Presidential Election of 1876,* 1906, pp. 271 ff.). Hayes even gave verbal assurances in his Ohio home. L. Q. C. Lamar wrote him on Mar. 22, 1877: "It was understood that you meant to withdraw the troops from South Carolina and Louisiana. . . . Upon that subject we thought that you had made up your mind, and indeed you so declared to me" (Hayes Papers). Once the alliance between the Hayes forces and the Southern Democrats was cemented the end came quickly. On Mar. 2 Hayes was awarded the presidency with 185 electors to Tilden's 184. Hayes had left for Washington the previous day, was entertained at dinner by President Grant on Saturday evening, Mar. 3, and took the oath of office that night privately and on Mar. 5 in public.

Hayes made his administration notable by his policy of Southern pacification, his attention to reform, and his insistence on a conservative treatment of financial questions. The choice of his cabinet indicated a partial break with the elder statesmen. Before leaving Ohio he had selected William M. Evarts for secretary of state, John Sherman for the treasury, and Carl Schurz for the interior. He had also considered nominating Gen. Joseph E. Johnston, the Confederate leader, as secretary of war, but encountered an opposition too fierce; he compromised by selecting Senator David M. Key, a former Confederate of Tennessee, to be postmaster-general. Though the "Stalwart" Republicans in the Senate showed their indignation by referring all the cabinet nominations to committees, public pressure forced a prompt confirmation. Hayes's first important measure was to carry out "the bargain" by withdrawing the Federal troops from the South. He called Wade Hampton and D. H. Chamberlain, rival claimants for the governorship of South Carolina, to Washington, discussed the situation with them, and on Apr. 3 ordered the Secretary of War to end the military occupation of the South Carolina state house. An investigating commission was sent to Louisiana, it advised Hayes to remove the Federal soldiery, and orders to that effect were issued on Apr. 20. For these steps he was fiercely attacked by Ben Wade, Garrison, Blaine, Wendell Phillips, and Ben Butler, and lost so many Republican machine workers "that it could be said that within six weeks after his inauguration Hayes was without a party" (J. F. Rhodes, *History of the United States from Hayes to McKinley,* 1919, p. 12; see also *Letters of Mr. William E. Chandler Relative to the So-Called Southern Policy of President Hayes,* 1878). But the wisdom of his course was shown by the immediate end of violence and the establishment of relative prosperity and contentment at the South. The restoration of full autonomy to the states was his greatest achievement, and one which Tilden could not have effected without arousing a far greater storm. Hayes continued to excite the hostility of the "Stalwarts," and particularly the New York faction under Conkling, by his measures of civil-service reform. He had declared in his inaugural that there must be such reform, that it must be "thorough, radical, and complete," and that it must comprehend appointment on the ground of ability alone, security of tenure, and exemption from the demands of partisan service. With Hayes's encouragement, Secretary Schurz at once reformed the interior department. Other department heads took similar action. Hayes had Secretary Sherman appoint an investigating committee under John Jay to examine the New York custom house, and he made the recommendations of this body the basis for a vigorous letter (May 26, 1877) forbidding partisan control of the revenue service, political assessments upon revenue officers, and any participation by such officers in the management of conventions, caucuses, or election campaigns. This order, which caused consternation, was reinforced by another letter on June 22, 1877. When Chester A. Arthur, collector at New York, and Alonzo B. Cornell, naval officer, defied these orders, Hayes asked for their resignations; and when they ignored his request, he appointed two men to take their places. The Senate, with Roscoe Conkling as leader, at first refused to confirm these nominations. But Hayes bided his time, presented two new names when the Senate reassembled in December 1878, and, by the skilful use of a letter from Secretary Sherman which thoroughly exposed the custom-house scandals, secured the needed confirmation.

Facing an unsatisfactory monetary situation, Hayes declared in his inaugural against "an irredeemable paper currency" and for "an early resumption of specie payments." His courage and skill were tested by a dangerous demand in both parties for repeal of the act for resumption of specie payments on Jan. 1, 1879, and for the free and unlimited coinage of silver as a full legal tender. Bills for both purposes were carried in the House in the fall of 1877. Hayes met the threat by a vigorous discussion of the monetary question in his December message, insisting on resumption and on payment of the public debt in gold or its equivalent. His determined stand helped prevent the Senate from passing the bill to postpone resumption, but did not defeat the Bland-Allison Bill. He vetoed it on Feb. 28, 1878, and, after it passed over his veto, urged in his message of December 1879 that Congress suspend the silver coinage. In 1880, pointing out that the market value of the silver dollar had declined to eighty-eight and a half cents, he vainly urged that the treasury be authorized to coin "silver dollars of equivalent value, as bullion, with gold dollars," instead of silver dollars of 412½ grains. With his support, Secretary Sherman successfully effected resumption at the date fixed. The early part of the administration was marked by business distress and labor troubles. Hayes did not fully understand the social and economic problems of the time and did nothing to strike at the root of unrest, but he showed firmness in calling out federal troops to suppress the railroad riots of 1877. The latter years of his term saw a revival of business prosperity. He showed firmness also in vetoing a popular Chinese exclusion bill as a violation of the Burlingame treaty, and in combating congressional usurpation. He waged a successful struggle with Congress in 1879 over its action in tacking "riders" to two essential appropriation bills, maintaining that this process was an effort to force the president into submission to Congress in a fashion not contemplated by the Constitution. Congress gave way and removed the riders. But Hayes remained unsuccessful in his attempts to persuade Congress to pass a permanent civil-service act. Little by little his hard-working habits, conscientiousness, system, and responsiveness to moral forces impressed the nation; the original Democratic bitterness decreased; and he became genuinely esteemed. Lucy Hayes, though ridiculed for her temperance rules, was even more generally liked.

Hayes firmly believed that a president could most effectively discharge his duties if he refused to entertain the idea of a second term; and in his letter accepting the nomination in 1876 he expressed an inflexible determination to serve but one term. He returned from Washington in March 1881 to "Spiegel Grove," where his modest house was enlarged into a mansion. Here he spent his remaining years, devoting much time to his extensive library, filling many engagements as a speaker, and enlisting in a variety of humanitarian causes. He was president of the National Prison Association from 1883 to the end of his life, was a member of the board of trustees of both the Peabody Education Fund and Slater Fund, and was interested in the Lake Mohonk conferences. The death of his wife in June 1889 was a heavy blow, but he remained active to the last. Exposure while attending a meeting of trustees of the state university hastened his end. His funeral was the occasion for a national tribute to his strong though not brilliant abilities, patriotic devotion, and zeal for common-sense reforms.

[An exceedingly full biographical record is presented in Chas. R. Williams, *Life of Rutherford Birchard Hayes* (2 vols., 1914); while there is a shorter, more incisive, and genuinely critical biography by H. J. Eckenrode, *Rutherford B. Hayes, Statesman of Reunion* (1930). A campaign life worthy of notice is William Dean Howells, *Sketch of the Life and Character of Rutherford B. Hayes* (1876). Special interest attaches to the conscientious *Diary and Letters of Rutherford Birchard Hayes,* edited by C. R. Williams (5 vols., 1922–26). J. W. Burgess, *The Administration of President Hayes* (1916), is a eulogistic set of lectures; there is a better-balanced estimate by James Ford Rhodes in his *Hist. Essays* (1909). Special aspects of Hayes's life are treated in Paul L. Haworth, *The Hayes-Tilden Disputed Presidential Election of 1876* (1906), and V. L. Shores, "The Hayes-Conkling Controversy, 1877–79," *Smith Coll. Studies in Hist.,* vol. IV (1919). Illuminating first-hand impressions of the administration are contained in both volumes of John Sherman's *Recollections of Forty Years* (1895), and James G. Blaine's *Twenty Years of Congress,* vol. II (1886). The Hayes Papers, with other material on his life, are housed in a memorial library at Fremont, Ohio.] A. N.

HAYES, WILLIAM HENRY (1829–March 1877), trader, adventurer, generally known as Bully Hayes, is said to have been born in Cleveland, Ohio, and to have sailed from New York on Mar. 4, 1853, in the American bark *Canton,* Elisha Gibbs master, which arrived at Singapore from Sydney, N. S. W., July 11, 1854 (Saunders, *post,* p. 1). Disposing of the *Canton,* he made voyages to San Francisco and Shanghai, then bought back his old ship, renamed it the *C. W. Bradley*—in honor of Charles William Bradley [*q.v.*]—mortgaged it for $3,000, secured goods and supplies on credit, and scurried out of Singapore Nov. 20, 1856, without obtaining clearance papers. With modifications to suit circumstances he continued to use this technique for twenty years. Most of his transactions were as legitimate probably as those of the ordinary trader; many of the stories that grew with tropical luxuriance around his name are merely fabulous, some having been started by himself; but his malodorous, far-reaching reputation is grounded on a substantial, however indeterminable, stratum of swindling and miscellaneous rascality. His success was due in large part to his fine appearance and ingratiating address, to his skill in evading the English, American, and Spanish authorities, and to the difficulty of running him down and getting tangible evidence against him. He was arrested at various times but usually managed to escape or to obtain his discharge. Into certain of his exploits, too, he injected a breezy waggery that won him in some quarters toleration and even admiration. His operations extended from San Francisco to the Hawaiian Islands, the Fijis, the Samoas, New Zealand, Australia, and many remote islands of the South Seas. Edward Reeves, who met him in New Zealand about 1864, describes him as a "stout, bald, pleasant-looking man, of good manners; chivalrous, with a certain, or rather uncertain, code of honour of his own; loyal to anyone who did him a good turn; gentle to animals, fond of all kinds of pets, especially of birds. Of these he had a number, and he treated them with tender care" (*Brown Men and Women,* 1898, p. 5). In 1867 he made himself useful and agreeable to James Chalmers, the English missionary (Richard Lovett, *James Chalmers: His Autobiography and Letters,* 1902, pp. 66–68, 70). Later he engaged in blackbirding—that is, in kidnapping Polynesians and selling them as slaves in the Fiji Islands. For this he was arrested by the British authorities but as usual came off scot free. In 1870 he raided and demolished the German consulate at Apia (Samoan Islands). In 1875 he was arrested by Spanish officials while attempting to rescue prisoners from Guam, and was imprisoned for some months at Manila. He was notorious for his brutal treatment of native women on various islands. On Aug. 25, 1857, at Penwortham, Western Australia, he married a Mrs. Amelia Littleton, who with two sons and a daughter survived him. He was killed at sea by a mutinous sailor.

[Notices of Hayes are scattered, fragmentary, and unauthentic, but A. T. Saunders, in *Bully Hayes: Barrator, Bigamist, Buccaneer, Blackbirder, and Pirate* (Sunday Times Pub. Co., Ltd., Perth, Western Australia, 1915), attempted a full, discriminating account and gave a list of references. Sydney Wm. Dutton, 103 Newgate St., London, E. C. 1, has a collection of materials relating to him. For a characteristic sketch of Hayes see W. B. Churchward, *My Consulate in Samoa* (1887), pp. 245–55.] E. L. W. H.

HAYFORD, JOHN FILLMORE (May 19, 1868–Mar. 10, 1925), geodesist, civil engineer, was born on a farm at Rouse Point, N. Y., the son of Hiram Hayford and Mildred Alevia (Fillmore) Hayford. He received his early education in the local public schools and in 1885 entered Cornell University, graduating with the degree of C.E. in 1889. Upon graduation he entered the United States Coast and Geodetic Survey, Washington, D. C., serving in various capacities both in the office and in the field until 1895, when he resigned to become instructor in civil engineering at Cornell. The year before he had married Lucy Stone of Charlotte, N. Y. After three years at Cornell, Hayford returned to the Coast and Geodetic Survey as expert computer and geodesist, and in 1900 he was placed in charge of the geodetic work. Here his engineering abilities found wide scope in the improvement of geodetic instruments and in the standardization of geodetic field practice. He was responsible for the adoption of the United States Standard Datum for the triangulation of this country. Later this datum was also adopted by Canada and Mexico, and it then became known as the North American Datum.

In connection with his geodetic studies it occurred to Hayford that the theory of isostasy could be applied to the problems of geodesy with advantage. In pursuance of this idea he carried out extensive investigations summarized in his *Figure of the Earth and Isostasy from Measurements in the United States* (1909) and in *Supplementary Investigation in 1909 of the Figure of the Earth and Isostasy* (1910). These investigations brought forth two notable results: the existence of isostasy was proved conclusively; and by the application of isostasy to the determination of the figure of the earth, values were derived which were adopted in 1924 by the International Geodetic and Geophysical Union as best serving both practical and scientific purposes.

In 1909 Hayford assumed the directorship of the College of Engineering of Northwestern University, at Evanston, Ill., a position which he held until the time of his death. He was also a research associate of the Carnegie Institution of Washington. For the latter institution he carried out an investigation of the laws of evaporation and stream flow, the results of which were published in *Effects of Winds and of Barometric Pressures on the Great Lakes* (1922). In addition to various monographs and reports dealing with geodesy and isostasy, he published also numerous articles in technical and scientific journals dealing with engineering and geodetic matters. He was active in many scientific organizations, his outstanding abilities being recognized by such signal honors as election to the National Academy of Sciences and by membership in the National Advisory Committee for Aeronautics. It is, however, in connection with the establishment on a sound basis of the theory of isostasy that Hayford is best known, and it was in recognition of his work in that field that the Royal Geographical Society of Great Britain conferred upon him its Victoria Medal in 1924.

[Otis Hayford, *Hist. of the Hayford Family* (1901), pp. 247–48; *Who's Who in America*, 1924–25; *Science*, Mar. 27, June 5, 1925; *Evanston News-Index*, Mar. 10, 1925; *Chicago Tribune*, Mar. 10, 11, 1925; official records, Coast and Geodetic Survey.] H. A. M.

HAYGOOD, ATTICUS GREEN (Nov. 19, 1839–Jan. 19, 1896), bishop of the Methodist Episcopal Church, South, educator, was born in Watkinsville, Ga. He had in him strains of English and Welsh blood. His father, Green B. Haygood, a lawyer, was a native of Clarke County, Ga. His mother, Martha Ann Askew, a teacher, was born in North Carolina. A sister of young Haygood, Laura Askew [*q.v.*], became a noted missionary in China. He was reared in an atmosphere of piety and of loyalty to the church. When fifteen years old he subscribed twenty-five dollars to the building of Trinity Methodist Church in Atlanta, whither the family had moved in 1852, and paid it by working for the contractor in carrying brick and mortar. His mother prepared him for the sophomore class of Emory College, from which he graduated in 1859. In the same year he married Mary F. Yarbrough and was admitted on trial into the Georgia Conference of the Methodist Episcopal Church, South. He was a chaplain in the Confederate army during the Civil War. Afterward he served as pastor and presiding elder until 1870 when he was elected Sunday-school secretary of his Church. In this capacity he made marked improvement in the lesson helps for pupils and teachers and edited a number of books for Sunday-school libraries.

Elected president of Emory College in 1875 he continued in that office until 1884. He found the college with a debt larger than its endowment. During his presidency new buildings were erected, the endowment grew to $100,000, and the number of students was almost doubled. He attracted young men to him and inspired many a youth to seek a college education. During his presidency he also edited (1878–82) the *Wesleyan Christian Advocate*, a weekly paper which was the organ of Methodism in Georgia and Florida. As an outgrowth of editorials in this paper he wrote *Our Brother in Black, His Freedom and His Future* (1881). It was a sympathetic and hopeful account of the accomplishments of the negroes during the first fifteen years of their freedom. Though moderate in tone, it gave offense to many Southern people. In 1882 he was elected to the office of bishop but declined ordination, being the first in his Church to reject this honor. There were a number of students, thirty of whom were preparing for the ministry, whom he was helping to carry on their college studies. He felt that if he accepted the bishopric most of these students would have to leave college (Bishop Duncan's funeral address, *Wesleyan Christian Advocate,* Jan. 22, 1896). In 1883 he became the agent of the John F. Slater Fund, established by a citizen of Connecticut for aiding the education of the negro. He gave up the college presidency in 1884 in order to devote his full time to his new work. *Pleas for Progress* (1889) consisted in good part of addresses on negro education.

In 1890 he was elected bishop at a General Conference of which he was not a member, and this time he accepted ordination. Taking with him several Georgia preachers, he moved to California and made his home there until 1893. He was low in stature and stocky in build. In manner he was cordial, quietly self-confident, and gave the impression of having unusual stores of reserve power. He strove after simplicity and clearness in public speech and in his writings. He despised show and pretense. When ordained bishop he insisted on wearing his usual business suit. He made no attempt at oratory, but he was a man of strong feeling and affection and some of his sermons had great and evident effect. He believed in federal aid for negro education and opposed the leasing of convicts. While a loyal Southerner he strove to restore good will between North and South and was popular on platforms in both sections. It was an occasional practice of his, especially when he had on hand a task which he wished to finish, to spend an entire night in reading and writing. In addition to the works already mentioned he published: *Go or Send* (1874); *Our Children* (1876); *Sermons* (1883); *Man of Galilee* (1889); *Jack Knife and Brambles* (1893); *The Monk and the Prince* (1895). He assisted his friend and neighbor, Prof. R. M. McIntosh in editing three songbooks for Sunday-school and other church services.

[*Jour. of the Thirteenth Gen. Conference of the M. E. Ch., South* (1898), pp. 131–35; G. B. Winton, *Sketch of Bishop Atticus G. Haygood* (1915); Hiram P. Bell, *Men and Things* (1907), ch. xxix; *Christian Advocate* (Nashville), Jan. 23, 1896; the *Morning News* (Savannah), Jan. 20, 1896. A sketch of Haygood's ancestors may be found in O. E. and A. M. Brown's *Life and Letters of Laura Askew Haygood* (1904).] E. H. J.

HAYGOOD, LAURA ASKEW (Oct. 14, 1845–Apr. 29, 1900), missionary, was born in Watkinsville, Ga., but spent the most of her youth in Atlanta, to which place her family moved when she was six years old. The influences under which she grew up were such as to incline her both to religious activity and to study and teaching. Her father, Green B. Haygood, a Georgian of English and Welsh ancestry, and a lawyer by profession, was a stanch Methodist, prominent in church work; her mother, Martha Ann Askew, born in Burke County, N. C., was the daughter of a Methodist preacher, Josiah Askew. She was a teacher in the high school at Salem, Ga., when she met Green Haygood, and after her marriage to him she continued to teach for some years. She fitted her two sons for Emory College, one of whom, Atticus Green Haygood [*q.v.*], afterward became its president and a bishop of the Methodist Episcopal Church, South; and her two daughters for Wesleyan Female College, Macon, Ga. Entering this institution when she was about seventeen, Laura was able by hard work to finish the required course in two years.

Meantime her father had died and the Haygoods, driven from their Atlanta home by the coming of Sherman's army, were living in Oxford. Here at the Palmer Institute she began a teaching career which had its completion in China many years later. She soon returned to Atlanta and opened a private school for girls, which she conducted until 1872. She then became an instructor in the newly established Girls' High School, and in 1877 its principal. Along with her teaching, which was carried on with a deep sense of responsibility for the moral and spiritual concerns of her pupils, she took a prominent part in church, Sunday-school, and home-missionary activities. So dominant in her life was the religious motive that when in 1884 there was a call for a person of experience and administrative ability to help direct the work for women being carried on in Shanghai by the

Woman's Board of Missions of the Methodist Episcopal Church, South, she offered her services. They were at once accepted, and on Nov. 17, she was at her station in China. Of massive frame, abounding energy, and optimistic spirit, able to meet difficult situations with serenity and confidence, accustomed to direct others, and zealously devoted to furthering human welfare, she was well fitted by temperament, training, and character for her duties. Although almost forty years old, she set about acquiring the language. "The Chinese," she said in a letter home, "pay great deference to my age and *size* and spectacles." The Clopton School, which was a boarding school for girls, and one or two day schools were at once put under her charge. The former she developed into a normal school to train Chinese girls for teaching. From a small nucleus she also built up a thorough and comprehensive organization of day schools. Her most memorable achievement, however, was the establishment of the McTyeire Home and School. The home afforded a place where new missionaries could spend a year or two, acquire the language, and receive training for their work; the school, originally the idea of Dr. Young J. Allen [*q.v.*], was designed to give Chinese girls a broad education, first in the classics of their own land, and then in Western learning. In the face of many difficulties, largely through Miss Haygood's planning and energy, funds were secured and the school finally opened on Mar. 16, 1892. In May 1889, upon the resignation of Dr. Allen as superintendent of the work of the Woman's Board in China, she was appointed agent for the Shanghai District, "to communicate the purposes and orders of the Board, and to provide for the execution of its plans." The condition of her health caused her to spend two years in the United States (1894–96), during which time, however, she did much traveling and speaking. Upon her return she became agent for the entire work of the Woman's Board in China. Illness brought her activities practically to a close in the summer of 1899. Refusing to go home until it was too late, she died and was buried in Shanghai. The Laura Haygood Home and School in Soochow was established as a memorial to her.

[Oswald E. and Anna M. Brown, *Life and Letters of Laura Askew Haygood* (1904); James Cannon, *Hist. of Southern Methodist Missions* (1926), pp. 108–09; *Christian Advocate* (Nashville), May 3, 10, 1900; *Review of Missions,* July 1900; *Atlanta Constitution,* Apr. 30, 1900.]

H. E. S.

HAYNE, ISAAC (Sept. 23, 1745–Aug. 4, 1781), Revolutionary soldier, became celebrated in the annals of the Revolution as a victim of British action. He was the son of Isaac and Sarah (Williamson) Hayne and the grandson of John Hayne who emigrated from England to Colleton District, S. C., about 1700. He was married, July 18, 1765, to Elizabeth Hutson, daughter of Rev. William Hutson. Prior to the Revolution he was a planter and breeder of fine horses. With William Hill he bought the iron works in York District, S. C., and made a contract with Governor Rutledge of South Carolina for the manufacture of ammunition for the use of the Continental forces. Later the works were destroyed by British and Loyalists under Captain Huck. In the Revolution he served first as a captain in the Colleton militia, then, when a junior officer was placed over him, he resigned his commission and reënlisted as a private. He was serving in the outposts at the time of the siege of Charleston. After the surrender of the city he retired to his farm on parole. In 1781 the crisis of affairs was approaching in the South, and the British authorities were increasingly severe. Hayne was summoned either to come to Charleston as a prisoner, or to swear allegiance to the Crown. His wife and two children were desperately ill with smallpox, and Hayne was assured that military service would never be required of him. Armed with this assurance, and unwilling to leave his family, he took the required oath of allegiance. Nevertheless he was soon ordered to join the British army, and he considered this action as a release from his parole. For a short time he was colonel of South Carolina militia, and in July he captured the renegade general, Andrew Williamson, near Charleston. This exploit was soon punished by his surprise and capture at a place called Horse Shoe by a British force under Col. Nisbet Balfour. Hayne was taken to Charleston and brought before a court of inquiry; there was no trial in the ordinary sense, and there were no witnesses. Lord Rawdon, commander in Charleston, charged that Hayne was a spy and guilty of treason and his condemnation followed. When he was informed that he had received the death sentence Hayne wrote to Rawdon and Balfour, July 29, 1781, demonstrating with legal argument that either as a prisoner of war or as a prisoner of state he was entitled to a legal trial. He was told in reply that his execution had been ordered "by virtue of the authority with which the commander-in-chief of South-Carolina and the commanding officer in Charleston are invested" (Ramsey, *post,* II, 516). Hayne was hanged at Charleston. The intense indignation among Americans was but the beginning of a prolonged controversy. Bancroft says: "Feeling the act as a stain upon his name, he (Rawdon) attempted, but not until after the death of Balfour, to throw on that officer the blame that belonged to himself" (*History of the United States*, 1892, vol. V, p. 503). Of Balfour it has been said that he "incurred much odium for carrying out the execution . . . which Lord Rawdon had ordered." Rawdon has been described as "a stern martinet, . . . guilty of several acts of impolitic severity during the American war."

[Sources include: David Ramsey, *Hist. of the Revolution of S.-C. from a British Province to an Independent State* (1785); Isaac W. Hayne, memoir in *Hist. Mag.*, Aug. 1867; Henry Lee, *Memoirs of the War in the Southern Dept. of the U. S.* (2 vols., 1812); Edward McCrady, *The Hist. of S. C. in the Revolution, 1780–83* (1902); R. Y. Hayne, article in the *Southern Rev.*, Feb. 1828, reviewing H. Lee, *Campaign of 1781 in the Carolinas* (1824), and *Letter of the Earl of Moira* [Rawdon] *to Henry Lee* (1824). The comments on Balfour and Rawdon have been taken from their respective biographies in the *Dict. of Nat. Biog.*]

E. K. A.

HAYNE, PAUL HAMILTON (Jan. 1, 1830–July 6, 1886), poet, was born in Charleston, S. C., where his ancestors had been prominent for a century, the only child of Lieut. Paul Hamilton Hayne, U. S. N., and Emily (McElhenny) Hayne. His father dying early, the boy grew up under the joint care of his mother, from whom he inherited poetic ability, and his distinguished uncle, Robert Young Hayne [*q.v.*], whose home became his own. After preparing at Mr. Coates's school, where began his lifelong intimacy with Henry Timrod, at twenty he graduated from Charleston College and turned to the law, with its prospect of political preferment. He had already felt "the thirst for beauty's balmy fount," however, and soon abandoned his practice in favor of a literary career. In 1852 he married Mary Middleton Michel, of Charleston, daughter of a French surgeon who had won distinction under Bonaparte.

During a decade of apprenticeship he alternated between journalism and poetry, contributing to the *Southern Literary Messenger* and the *Charleston Evening News*, holding editorial positions with the short-lived *Southern Literary Gazette* and Washington *Spectator*, and publishing three volumes: *Poems* (1855), *Sonnets and Other Poems* (1857), and *Avolio, a Legend of the Island of Cos* (1860). His verses, though occasionally imitative, showed an idyllic delicacy and deep-rooted love of nature which won them immediate appreciation, Holmes, Bryant, Longfellow, and other poets extending generous hands of fellowship. Meanwhile he drifted naturally into that company of brilliant young men who, in the fifties, under Simms's leadership, were to make Charleston the literary center of the South. The most important outcome of their gatherings at John Russell's bookstore was the launching, Apr. 1, 1857, of *Russell's Magazine*, with Hayne and W. B. Carlisle as editors. Despite the magazine's merit it lasted only three years, its Southern policy arresting circulation in the North without increasing it at home. Hayne subsequently referred to his editorship—he did all of the editorial work—as "one of the most difficult, exacting, and thankless positions imaginable," yet from it he gained invaluable practice and added reputation. Then, just when success seemed assured, came the Civil War.

Unfit for field service, Hayne became an aide on Governor Pickens' staff. His physical frailty soon compelled his retirement, and he thenceforth sought outlet in patriotic verses which, if not equal to Timrod's in fire and artistry, were popular and often meritorious. Conspicuous in his martial pieces is his affectionate pride in his state and city, foreshadowing the tender reminiscences of "Ante-Bellum Charleston" which he later contributed to the *Southern Bivouac*: he was as truly the poet of Charleston as Holmes was of Boston. Yet when, after the war, his home and library having been burned in the bombardment, his family silver stolen by Sherman's men, and his competency gone, he determined to start afresh, it was not unnatural that he should turn from the wreckage of his beloved "Queen City of the Sea" to an exile hardly less tragic.

With his wife and son he moved to Groveton, near Augusta, Ga., where he owned a few acres of poor pine land, and himself built Copse Hill, "a little apology for a dwelling," which he furnished with "three mattresses and a cot" and stocked with "a box of hardtack, two sides of bacon, and four-score . . . smoked herring." In time chairs, tables, and shelves, made of packing-boxes, were added, Mrs. Hayne supplying the decoration by papering walls and furniture with pictures cut from magazines. The closing years of the war had inured him to hardship, however, and in this rough "shanty of uncouth ugliness" the poet lived out his days, cultivating his flowers and vegetables, poring over a few favorite books, grinding out quantities of prose hack-work, and writing his best verse, with more which was not his best, while standing at the carpenter's workbench which served him for desk. If ever poet lived on sixpence a day and earned it, it was Hayne in the lean years after the Confederacy fell, but his courage never faltered, his ideals never dimmed. To Mrs. Preston he wrote, "By . . . my literary craft I will win my bread and water; by my poems I will live or I will starve," and more than any American author of his time he depended upon poetry alone for his income. When the other Southern war poets fell silent, Hayne, despite poor health, worked serenely, confidently, copiously on, and developed as an artist. His wife helped him inestimably. English friends—including Tennyson, Swinburne, Jean Ingelow, Blackmore, Marston—wrote encouraging letters and praised his work. Longfellow, Bryant, Whittier, Holmes, Bayard Taylor, Boker, and other Northern literary men, conscious of his fairness of nature, his devotion to art, and his brave fight with poverty and illness, added their appreciation. Nor was he without honor at home, although the South was too impoverished to buy his books: he inherited Simms's mantle as literary high priest, wrote numberless sage advices to young Southern authors, and gave guidance or encouragement to Lanier, Timrod, Clinton Scollard, and others who sought him out. He had even less money for travel than for book-buying, but, although denied his wish to visit England and the home of his ancestors in Shropshire, he made one memorable post-war journey to New England to see his fellow poets there.

In 1872 appeared *Legends and Lyrics,* perhaps his best single volume, containing, as he wrote his friend Charles Warren Stoddard, "the only two *narrative* poems I really value." The next year he edited the poems of his friend Timrod, prefacing them with a memoir as penetrating as it was sympathetic and sincere; then followed *The Mountain of the Lovers* (1875), *Lives of Robert Young Hayne and Hugh Swinton Legaré* (1878), and an unpublished life of Simms. In 1882 Lothrop issued an illustrated edition of his collected *Poems,* his last volume except the little Confederate memorial, *The Broken Battalions* (1885); but despite his now rapidly failing health he wrote on, contributing prose articles to the magazines, making occasional addresses, and leaving, besides an unfinished novel, enough verses—some of them among his finest—to fill a fair-sized book.

Time has so edited his works that few of his poems remain widely known, which is, within limits, fitting: under the spur of necessity he wrote too much and blue-penciled too seldom. Sometimes his verse echoed the English poets, especially Tennyson, Keats, William Morris; sometimes it was marred by mid-century sentimentalism and romantic prettiness; but at its best, when he sang from his heart of the trees, the birds, the skies which he knew, it was at once individual and Southern. Lacking in depth of philosophy and thought, in compression, in imaginative reach, it was nevertheless strong in its dignity, calmness, spiritual sweetness, color, and weighing of words; he was ever the gentle lover of what he held beautiful and true, the almost commonplace subjects through which he sought "to come near and to rouse the great heart of humanity." His somewhat feminine fancy and delicacy of feeling made him sensuously responsive to the picturesqueness of Southern forest and landscape; above all he was the poet of the pines, which he celebrated as enthusiastically as Lanier did the marshes. His craftsmanship improved steadily in grace and melody, although the spirit of his work remained essentially the same: he became the threnodist of the ante-bellum régime, whose ideals he interpreted in his poetry and illustrated in his character. Yet, if sectional, he was not partisan, never bitter, paying sincere tribute after the Civil War to numerous Northern men of letters and laboring effectively to foster a national spirit. His place is definitely among the minor singers, but his worth has oftener been underestimated in the North than overestimated in the South: Tennyson praised his sonnets (which he wrote more profusely than any of his countrymen) as the best by an American; his simpler nature lyrics ring finely true; some of his personal pieces, not least those to Timrod, Longfellow, and Lanier, are eloquent and final. He deserves to be better known, not simply for his poetry, but as a delightful letter-writer and raconteur, an outspoken critic, and a high-hearted, naïve, wholly charming gentleman—"the last literary Cavalier," as Maurice Thompson aptly called him (*Critic,* April 1901) in an essay which, pointing out his strong facial resemblance to Robert Louis Stevenson, contains the best description of his physical appearance.

[There is no adequate biography of Hayne, no volume of his letters, no properly edited collection of his poems. See however: *Lib. of Southern Lit.* (1909); *Cambridge Hist. Am. Lit.,* vol. II (1918); S. A. Link, *Pioneers of Southern Lit.* (1903); C. W. Hubner, *Representative Southern Poets* (1906); W. P. Trent, *Wm. Gilmore Simms* (1892); Sidney Lanier, *Music and Poetry* (1881); W. H. Hayne, "Paul H. Hayne's Methods of Composition," *Lippincott's Mag.,* Dec. 1892; M. J. Preston, article in *Southern Bivouac,* Sept. 1886; *S. C. Hist. and Geneal. Mag.,* July 1904.]

A. C. G., Jr.

HAYNE, ROBERT YOUNG (Nov. 10, 1791–Sept. 24, 1839), lawyer, United States senator, governor of South Carolina, railroad president, was in all his capacities an eloquent advocate of the interests of Charleston and South Carolina. He was descended from John Hayne who emigrated from England to Colleton District, S. C., about 1700. Born on a rice plantation, of a well-established family, he would presumably have been sent to college had there not been thirteen other sons and daughters of William Hayne and his wife Elizabeth Peronneau. Instead, after schooling in Charleston he studied in the office of Langdon Cheves, was admitted to the bar shortly before attaining the age of twenty-one, and at once acquired a substantial clientage. His marriage to Frances Henrietta Pinckney and after her death to Rebecca Motte Alston allied him to families of lowland influence, and the second wife brought him wealth. The Democratic-Republicans of Charleston elected Hayne to the state legislature in 1814, and four years afterward he was made speaker of the House. A year in this office was followed by two as attorney-general of the state. With the aid of Calhoun he was elected to the United States Senate in December 1822, defeating William Smith; and in 1828 he was chosen for a second term without opposition. His intelligence and industry together with fluency and personal charm brought him esteem and affection from a widening circle (T. H. Benton, *Thirty Years' View,* 1856, II, 186).

In the Senate Hayne's chief endeavor was to check the heightening of protective tariff rates. Opposing a bill in 1824, he said: "In attempting to gratify the wishes of interested individuals, we are legislating in the dark, distributing the national funds by a species of State lottery—scattering abroad bounties and premiums of unknown amount" (*Annals of Congress,* 18 Cong., 1 Sess., col. 623). Again (*Ibid.,* col. 649): "This system is in its very nature progressive. Grant what you may now, the manufacturers will never be satisfied. . . . If we go on in our course, the time is at hand when these seats will be filled by the owners of manufacturing establishments; and do you believe that, when a numerous party here, . . . shall call upon you with one voice 'for a monopoly of the raw material at their own prices,' and shall quote British authority for their demands, you will dare to refuse?" The Senate, in short, would become its own insatiate lobby. Except as to munitions of war he held protective legislation to be both improper and unconstitutional. Resuming this theme upon renewed occasion in 1828, he said that the continuance and increase of exploitation by means of the tariff was producing between the sections of the country a jealousy "founded on a settled conviction, on the one part, that they are the victims of injustice, and on the other, that our complaints, if not groundless, may be safely disregarded" (*Register of Debates in Congress,* 20 Cong., 2 Sess., p. 56).

Thus far the supporters of protection had shown more voting strength than eloquence. But in 1830, Daniel Webster having shifted with New England from low to high tariff and from strict to broad construction of the Constitution, the stage was set for an oratorical tournament. Foot's resolution, presented on Dec. 29, 1829, looking to the restraint of surveys and sales of public lands, gave occasion. Benton as champion of the West opposed the resolution of the senator from Connecticut as a piece of Eastern enmity. Hayne, alert to the Southern need of Western alliance against the manufacturers, went to Benton's aid. Alluding to a recent official suggestion that a restriction of land sales would benefit manufacturers by reducing wage rates, Hayne denounced any program to deprive citizens of the fullest opportunity for prosperous livelihood; and he expressed a dread that if the public lands were administered as a source of great revenue the treasury would be swollen, corruption would be fostered, and the federal government would be "consolidated" in a manner "fatal to the sovereignty and independence of the states" (*Register of Debates in Congress,* 21 Cong., 1 Sess., p. 34). Webster followed, Jan. 20, taking Hayne to task: "Consolidation!—that perpetual cry, both of terror and delusion—consolidation! . . . The East! the obnoxious, the rebuked, the always reproached East! . . . I deny that the East has, at any time, shown an illiberal policy towards the West" (*Ibid.,* pp. 38, 39).

These were but preliminaries. Thrust and parry, point and counter, the forensic duel occupied most of a fortnight and ranged over the tariff, negro slavery, the merits of Massachusetts and South Carolina in the Revolution, the due fame of Nathan Dane, the character of the Constitution, the meaning of phrases from Jefferson and Madison in its interpretation, the purposes of the Hartford convention, and the virtues and vices of nullification. In peroration Webster was unequaled, but in sustained argument Hayne was his match. Day after day the chamber was thronged with listeners to the cadenced flow. The newspapers crowded their columns, and manuals of oratory still print extracts among their choicest examples. A few sentences from Hayne must here suffice: "Who, then, are the friends of the Union? Those who would confine the Federal Government strictly within the limits prescribed by the constitution; who would preserve to the States and the People all powers not expressly delegated, who would make this a Federal and not a National Union, and who, administering the Government in a spirit of equal justice, would make it a blessing, and not a curse. And who are its enemies? Those who are in favor of consolidation; who are constantly stealing power from the States, and adding strength to the Federal Government. Who, assuming an unwarrantable jurisdiction over the States and the People, undertake to regulate the whole industry and capital of the country. But, sir, of all descriptions of men I consider those as the worst enemies of the Union, who sacrifice the equal rights which belong to every member of the Confederacy to combinations of interested majorities, for personal or political objects" (*Ibid.*, p. 56). Again: "It is in vain to tell us that all the States are represented here. Representation may, or may not, afford security to the people. The only practical security against oppression, in representative Governments, is to be found in this, that those who impose the burthens are compelled to share them. Where there are conflicting interests, however, and a majority are enabled to impose burthens on the minority, for their own advantage, it is obvious that representation, on the part of the minority, can have no other effect than to 'furnish an apology for the injustice.' . . . Of what value is our representation here, on questions connected with the 'American system,' where . . . the 'imposition is laid, not by the Representatives of those who pay the tax, but by the Representatives of those who are to receive the bounty?'" (*Ibid.*, p. 89).

Contending that checks and balances of sundry sorts were essential to freedom and equity, Hayne indorsed the doctrine, now grown popular among his constituents, that upon drastic occasion a state might lawfully estop within its own area the enforcement of an act of Congress if its enactment had involved an exercise of unauthorized power. To buttress this contention he argued that the Constitution had been established as a compact between the several states and the federal government. Webster in reply was able to show that the federal government was not a party to such a compact. Calhoun, presiding over the Senate in his capacity as vice-president of the United States, must have winced when this joint in Hayne's armor was pierced. He was forging at the time his own coat of mail with no gaps between its links of syllogisms. When the crisis came in 1832 Calhoun resigned his high seat of silence, and to give him place upon the floor Hayne withdrew from the Senate to become governor of South Carolina. Meanwhile he had tilted with Clay on the tariff bill of 1832, creditably as concerns argument but without avail in preventing enactment.

His appeal for moderation having failed in the Senate, Hayne played a leading rôle in the South Carolina convention which adopted the nullification ordinance, and then as governor defended the policy of the state with vigor and yet with temperance. To Jackson's proclamation he replied in similar form defiantly, and as commander-in-chief he summoned the commonwealth to furnish ten thousand citizen soldiers ready to repel invasion. But when Clay proposed in the Senate a compromise of the tariff question Hayne readily concurred first in an informal suspension of the ordinance and then in its rescindment. His own concern, as had been made clear in the debate with Clay, was with an equable basis for a harmonious future: "Restore that harmony which has been disturbed—that mutual affection and confidence which has been impaired. . . . And be assured that he to whom the country shall be indebted for this blessing, will be considered as the second founder of the republic" (*Register of Debates in Congress,* 22 Cong., 1 Sess., col. 104). In local affairs his counsels of moderation did much to mitigate factional strife and to prevent any lingering resentment among those who had opposed nullification.

After the end of his term as governor Hayne was mayor of Charleston for a year, but his main interest was now turned to the project of a railroad which by tapping the traffic of the Ohio Valley at Cincinnati was in his fancy to make Charleston the rival of New York in the commerce of the continent and at the same time was to bind the West to the South in friendly sentiment. The South Carolina Canal & Railroad Company, chartered in December 1827, had already built within five years what was then the longest line in the world, 136 miles, from Charleston to the bank of the Savannah River opposite Augusta. This road might become part of a continental system either by connections across Georgia to Chattanooga or Memphis, or by a branch to Columbia and extension through Asheville and Knoxville. The Georgia line would avoid mountain grades, but it would serve Savannah no less than Charleston, and in sentiment it would tend to consolidate the South more than to cultivate alliance with the West. This was Calhoun's preference, but Hayne committed himself with ardor to conquering the Blue Ridge, threading the valley of the French Broad, penetrating Cumberland Gap, and reaching Cincinnati. After mass-meetings, and conventions at Knoxville and elsewhere to frame plans and arouse enthusiasm, charters were procured from the legislatures of South and North Carolina, Tennessee and Kentucky, and the Louisville, Cincinnati & Charleston Railroad Company was organized in 1836 with Hayne as president. Appeals which he made in print and in speeches along the projected line were eloquent enough, but only in South Carolina did subscriptions to stock meet expectations. The twelve million dollars needed for construction were never in prospect, although the shares were to be paid for in instalments of five per cent. at intervals of not less than two months. Ohioans displayed no interest, and Kentuckians little more. A purchase of the South Carolina Railroad's property was undertaken, which might have proved advantageous had credit continued easy, but which actually brought great embarrassment. The panic of 1837 caused many defaults of the third instalment from subscribers and a lopping of the Kentucky lines from the company's plan of construction. As the general depression of industry and finance persisted, only a loan by the South Carolina legislature enabled the corporation to survive long enough to build a few miles of track (U. B. Phillips, *A History of Transportation in the Eastern Cotton Belt to 1860,* 1908, pp. 168–220). For Hayne the end came at a stockholders' meeting at Asheville in September 1839. High debate over the disordered finances and the future program of the company led only to an adjournment to another time and place, for Hayne, prostrated by fever after the first day's session, died within the week. Later the trains of the Southern Railway followed the course projected by Hayne; but in his generation enthusiasm, good will, and eloquence could not summon enough money to level the roadbed and lay the rails.

[T. D. Jervey, *Robt. Y. Hayne and His Times* (1909), and "The Hayne Family," *S. C. Hist. and Geneal. Mag.,* July 1904; Paul H. Hayne, *Lives of Robt. Young Hayne and Hugh Swinton Legaré* (1878); *Niles' Nat. Reg.,* Oct. 12, 1839; *Charleston Courier,* Sept. 30, 1839.]

U. B. P.

HAYNES, JOHN (1594?–Jan. 1653/54), governor of Massachusetts, first governor of Connecticut, was the son of John Haynes of Old Holt, Essex, England, and Mary Mitchell. He was the owner of the manor of Copford Hall, Essex, in 1624. He emigrated to America in 1633, sailing in July in the *Griffin,* the vessel that carried John Cotton and Thomas Hooker to the New World, and arriving in Massachusetts Bay Sept. 4. He is described at this time as "a gentleman of great estate." He took up his residence at Newtown (Cambridge), was admitted a freeman of Massachusetts Bay on May 14, 1634, and was immediately made an assistant of the colony. He was chosen to oversee the construction of an ammunition house at Newtown in the following September and was appointed townsman for Newtown in February 1634/35. On May 6, 1635, he was chosen governor of Massachusetts Bay and agreed to serve without salary "partly in respect of their love showed towards him, and partly for that he observed how much the people had been pressed lately with public charges, which the poorer sort did much groan under" (*Winthrop's Journal, post,* vol. I, p. 150). It was during this period that he accused Winthrop of administering justice too leniently (*Ibid.,* I, 171), and he himself pronounced sentence of banishment upon Roger Williams, later expressing regret for his action (*Massachusetts Historical Society Collections,* 1 ser., vol. I, 1806, p. 280). Upon the expiration of his term as governor, Haynes was again chosen assistant. He was appointed colonel of a Massachusetts regiment in December 1636.

Haynes removed to Connecticut in May 1637 and settled at Hartford. Upon the outbreak of the Pequot War, the General Court at Hartford sent Haynes and Roger Ludlow "to the mouth of the River to treate & Conclude with our frendes of the Bay either to joine with their forces in prosecutinge our designe against our enemies or if they see cause by aduise to interprise any Accon accordinge to the force we haue" (*The Public Records of the Colony of Connecticut, post,* p. 10). Haynes opposed the killing of Pequot women and children (*Massachusetts Historical Society Collections,* 4 ser., vol. VI, 1863, p. 196). In 1638 he was one of the signers of a treaty made between Connecticut and the Narragansetts and Mohicans (Samuel G. Drake, *Biography and History of the Indians of North America,* ed. 1837, vol. II, p. 61). The Fundamental Orders of Connecticut were adopted Jan. 14, 1638/39, and Haynes was chosen the first governor of the colony under those orders Apr. 11, 1639. Under the early laws of Connecticut the governor could not be reëlected for a consecutive term but Haynes was chosen governor of Connecticut every alternate year, and usually served as deputy governor in the intervening years, until his death. He was appointed a member of a committee to secure an enlargement of the liberties of the Warwick patent for Connecticut in 1645. From 1637 to 1643 he worked to establish a union of the New England colonies and after the formation of the New England Confederation in 1643, he represented Connecticut at meetings of the commissioners of the united colonies in 1646 and 1650.

Haynes was twice married: in England, to Mary, the daughter of Robert Thornton of Nottingham, by whom he had two sons, Robert and Hezekiah, and a daughter Mary; and in Newtown, to Mabel, the sister of Roger Harlakenden of Newtown, by whom he had three sons, John,

Roger, and Joseph, and two daughters, Ruth and Mabel. He died at Hartford in January 1653/54 (not Mar. 1, as is usually stated; see letter of William Goodwin to John Winthrop, Jr., Jan. 10, 1653/54, *Massachusetts Historical Society Collections,* 4 ser., Vol. VII, 1865, pp. 49–50). His English property passed to the sons of his first wife; his Newtown property had been sold before his death to Mrs. Glover; his Connecticut property passed to his second wife and to her sons.

[Thos. Wright, *The Hist. and Topography of the County of Essex* (1836), vol. I; *Records of the Gov. and Company of the Mass. Bay in New Eng.,* vol. I (1853); *Winthrop's Jour.* (2 vols., 1908), ed. by J. K. Hosmer; *The Records of the Town of Cambridge (formerly Newtowne), Mass., 1630–1703* (1901); *The Reg. Book of the Lands and Houses in the "New Towne" and the Town of Cambridge* (1896); *The Public Records of the Colony of Conn.,* vol. I (1850); "Acts of the Commissioners of the United Colonies of New Eng.," *Records of the Colony of New Plymouth in New Eng.,* vols. IX and X (1859); "Original Distribution of the Lands in Hartford among the Settlers, 1639," *Conn. Hist. Soc. Colls.,* vol. XIV (1912); "The Wyllys Papers," *Ibid.,* vol. XXI (1924); "Records of the Particular Court of Conn., 1639–63," *Ibid.,* vol. XXII (1928); "Will of Gov. Haynes," *New-Eng. Hist. and Geneal. Reg.,* Apr. 1862, pp. 167–69; *Dict. of Nat. Biog.*] I. M. C.

HAYNES, JOHN HENRY (June 27, 1849–June 29, 1910), archaeologist, the son of John W. and Emily (Taylor) Haynes, was born at Rowe, Mass. He attended the public schools of North Adams and Drury High School, from which he went to Williams College, graduating in 1876. For the next four years he was principal of the Williamstown High School. In the fall of 1880 he took a similar position at the South Hadley High School but resigned after a few weeks to go with W. J. F. Stillman on his expedition to Crete. In 1881–82 he was a member of the expedition of the Archaeological Institute of America which excavated at Assos. Leaving Assos, he tutored until 1884 in Robert College, Constantinople, then went as business manager and photographer of the Wolfe Expedition to Mesopotamia led by William Hayes Ward in 1884–85, to reconnoiter for the most promising site to excavate. For the following three years he taught at Aintab, Turkey. In 1888 the first expedition of the University of Pennsylvania was organized by John P. Peters [*q.v.*] for the excavation of Nippur, and Haynes became its business manager and photographer. In the same year an American Consulate was established at Bagdad and he became the first American consul at that place. He was continuously in Mesopotamia from 1888 to 1890, assisting Peters in his two seasons of excavation at Nippur and performing his work as American consul at Bagdad. Later two additional expeditions were entrusted to him as field director and he excavated almost continuously at Nippur from early in 1893 to 1895, and again from 1896 to 1900. He married in March 1897. Without undervaluing in any way the work of Peters, it must be said that it was owing to the long, continuous, and systematic work of Haynes that the more important discoveries, which gave the expedition its scientific importance, were made. It was he who laid bare the lower strata of the mounds and who discovered by far the larger portion of the tablets. While Haynes was field director, Herman V. Hilprecht [*q.v.*] in 1895 became scientific director of the expedition. When, in the early months of 1900, Haynes reported that he had discovered an archive of some hundreds of tablets, Hilprecht at once set out for Babylonia, and afterward, as Haynes's superior officer, took the credit of the discovery of the tablets, which he designated the "Temple Library." Afterward in his book, *Explorations in Bible Lands During the Nineteenth Century* (1903), Hilprecht was at pains systematically to belittle the work of Haynes, to represent it as unscientific, and to magnify his mistakes. Haynes had returned from Nippur in broken health—a martyr to science—and this treatment from his chief broke his heart. Hilprecht's criticisms were regarded by all who knew the facts as ungenerous and unjust, and, although the University of Pennsylvania in 1895 conferred upon Haynes the honorary degree of B.Sc., the injustice of the treatment and the loss of credit for what he had done cast a deep shadow over his last years. Williams College conferred on him the honorary degree of D.Sc. in 1896 and Robert College, Constantinople, the Ph.D. degree in the same year. He died in North Adams, Mass. Of the many scientists of the United States who have in the spirit of high endeavor carried American ingenuity and initiative into many fields of activity in all parts of the world where it has borne rich fruit, the name of John Henry Haynes is by no means the least, and among the Babylonian treasures stored in the University Museum in Philadelphia are many mute but eloquent witnesses to the fruitfulness of his scientific labors.

[J. P. Peters, *Nippur* (2 vols., 1897), and "The Nippur Library," *Jour. Am. Oriental Soc.,* XXVI (1905), 145–64; *Obit. Record of the Soc. of Alumni of Williams Coll., 1910–11* (1911); *Boston Transcript,* June 29, 1910.] G. A. B.

HAYS, ALEXANDER (July 8, 1819–May 5, 1864), soldier, was born of Scotch-Irish ancestry at Franklin in Venango County, Pa. His father was Samuel Hays, a general in the Pennsylvania militia and a member of Congress; his mother was Agnes (Broadfoot) Hays. He attended Venango Academy, Mercer Academy, and Allegheny College, but having developed an interest in military affairs, he left Allegheny College in his senior year in order to take advantage of an opportunity to enter West Point. At the Military Academy he graduated in 1844, in the class following that of General Grant. Two years later, on Feb. 19, 1846, he was married in Pittsburgh to Annie Adams McFadden. After leaving West Point, Hays served on frontier duty at Natchitoches, La., in the military occupation of Texas, and in the war with Mexico. For gallant conduct in the battles of Palo Alto and Resaca-de-la-Palma, he was brevetted first lieutenant on May 9, 1846. Following a period of recruiting duty, he returned to the Mexican conflict in 1847, serving until the end of the war. He resigned from the army Apr. 12, 1848. Returning to civil life, he engaged in the iron industry at the Victory Forge near Franklin, Pa., but with little success. When news came of the discovery of gold in California he forsook the irksome routine of business and joined a party of "Forty-niners" in quest of gold. From Pittsburgh the party went by steamboat by way of St. Louis to Independence on the Missouri River. From this point, a popular rendezvous for emigrants to the West, the party, regularly organized and officered, set out across the plains. The route lay by way of Fort Kearney, Fort Laramie, Salt Lake, and Sacramento. The journey from Independence to Sacramento required four months and six days. After typical experiences, described vividly in his surviving correspondence, Hays returned in 1851 to Pennsylvania. He then engaged in engineering and construction work, particularly bridge-building, for railroads and municipalities in western Pennsylvania.

At the outbreak of the Civil War, Hays returned to the army with the rank of captain in the 16th Infantry. As colonel of the 63rd Pennsylvania, he served in the defense of Washington, D. C., until March 1862, and later, in the Army of the Potomac, receiving a brevet of major for gallant and meritorious service in the battles of Fair Oaks, the Peach Orchard, and Glendale, Va. For his conduct in the battle of Malvern Hill he was brevetted lieutenant-colonel, July 1, 1862. He was severely wounded in the battle of Manassas, but after a month's leave of absence he returned to the forces in defense of Washington. In June 1863 he was given command of a division in the Army of the Potomac, was brevetted colonel for his conduct in the battle of Gettysburg, and served successively in the pursuit to Warrenton, in the Rapidan campaign, and in the Richmond campaign. He was killed in action on the second day of the battle of the Wilderness. His character is revealed by his rigorous orders to his men to refrain from violence against civilians in enemy territory. "God help the violator," he wrote, "so long as I command."

[G. T. Fleming, *Life and Letters of Alexander Hays* (1919), is a full but uncritical biography. See also G. W. Cullum, *Biog. Reg. . . . U. S. Mil. Acad.* (3rd ed., 1891), vol. II; C. A. Babcock, *Venango County, Pa.* (1919), vol. I; *Hist. of Venango County, Pa.* (1890); *Personal Memoirs of U. S. Grant*, vol. II (1886).]

W. B.

HAYS, HARRY THOMPSON (Apr. 14, 1820–Aug. 21, 1876), lawyer, Confederate soldier, brother of John Coffee Hays [*q.v.*], was the son of Harmon and Elizabeth (Cage) Hays. He was born in Wilson County, Tenn., near "The Hermitage," which General Jackson purchased from Hays's grandfather, John Hays, an officer under Jackson in the Creek war. Both parents died within a month of each other when the boy was very young, and he was brought up by his uncle, Harry Cage, of Wilkinson County, Miss. He graduated from St. Mary's College in Baltimore and later studied law in the office of S. T. Wallis, a leading lawyer in the same city. In 1844 he began the practice of his profession in New Orleans in the office of Baillie Peyton, a relative of his mother's. At the outbreak of the Mexican War he joined a Mississippi cavalry regiment and served with distinction until the end of the struggle, returning to New Orleans to form a successful legal partnership with W. C. Hamner, under the firm name of Hamner & Hays. During the early fifties Hays was also active in politics as a member of the Whig party. He was a delegate from Louisiana to the national nominating convention of that party in the summer of 1852, and in the fall a presidential elector on the Scott ticket. A year or two prior to 1860 he married his first cousin, Elizabeth Cage, the daughter of Robert Cage of Yazoo County, Miss.

At the commencement of the Civil War Hays left his law practice and entered the Confederate service as colonel in the 7th Louisiana Regiment of the Army of Northern Virginia. His initial action was in the first Bull Run. In 1862 he took part in Stonewall Jackson's Shenandoah Valley campaign, where his unit was attached to the brigade of Gen. Richard Taylor of Ewell's division. At Port Republic he received a wound which prevented his participation in the Seven Days' battles and at the second Bull Run. During his absence from active duty on account of his wound, he was commissioned brigadier-general, July 25, 1862, and assigned the brigade formerly commanded by General Taylor, who had been ordered to Louisiana to take charge of operations there. Again in action, Hays served at Sharpsburg, where his brigade was in the thickest of the fighting, and also at Fredericksburg, Chancellorsville, and Gettysburg. On May 9, 1864, he was severely wounded at Spotsylvania Court House, but by the fall of the year he had recovered sufficiently to attend to duties in Louisiana, where he had been assigned. On May 10, 1865, he was commissioned major-general, but the Confederacy had ceased to exist except in the Trans-Mississippi Department, where he then was, and this section soon gave up the struggle. Returning to New Orleans after the war, Hays formed a law partnership with Gen. Daniel Adams and Judge E. Waller Moise but retired from the office when he was made sheriff of Orleans Parish in 1866. After about a year he was removed—by General Sheridan, it is said—and went back to the law. His old firm having dissolved, he associated himself with Major John H. New and practised until he was disabled by Bright's disease. He died at his New Orleans home and was buried in the Washington Street Cemetery.

[There are short sketches of Hays's life in Alcée Fortier, *Louisiana* (1909), vol. I, and in the *New Orleans Times* and *New Orleans Republican* for Aug. 22, 1876. For his Civil War record see C. A. Evans, *Confed. Mil. Hist.* (1899), vol. X. Information as to certain facts was supplied by members of the Hays family.]

M. J. W.

HAYS, ISAAC (July 5, 1796–Apr. 13, 1879), physician, ophthalmologist, medical editor, the eldest son of Samuel and Richea Gratz Hays, was born in Philadelphia, Pa. He entered the University of Pennsylvania in 1812 and received the degree of B.A. in 1816. His father, a merchant engaged in the East India trade, was eager that his son should enter his business but a short trial proved that the younger Hays was not interested in a mercantile life, and in 1817 he began the study of medicine. He was an office pupil of Dr. Nathaniel Chapman and graduated in medicine at the University of Pennsylvania in 1820. Having developed a special interest in ophthalmology, in 1822 he was given a position on the staff of the Pennsylvania Infirmary for Diseases of the Eye and Ear. From the strictly professional point of view his work in ophthalmology may be regarded as his chief contribution to medicine, as he was an extensive contributor to ophthalmologic literature and was one of the first to detect astigmatism and to study color blindness. He also invented a special knife for cataract operations. In 1834 he was appointed one of the surgeons to the Wills Eye Hospital on its organization, a position which he held until 1854. Meanwhile, in 1843, he edited and enlarged the work of Sir William Lawrence, *Treatise on the Diseases of the Eye,* which went through three editions and aided greatly in advancing a sound knowledge of ophthalmology in the United States. He was elected the first president of the Ophthalmological Society of Philadelphia.

Hays's work as an editor extended over many years. In 1827 he was appointed to the staff of the *Philadelphia Journal of the Medical and Physical Sciences* which had been founded in 1820 by Nathaniel Chapman. Within a few months he assumed the editorship of the periodical, changed its title to the *American Journal of the Medical Sciences,* and secured the coöperation of many representative medical men in all parts of the country. In 1869 his son, Isaac Minis Hays, was appointed assistant editor and succeeded his father as editor after his death. Dr. John Billings once said that if all other medical literature of this period were destroyed, it would be possible to reproduce most of the real contributions of medical science from this journal. Hays remained its editor until his death. His other editorial ventures were no less ambitious. In 1834 he projected the *American Cyclopedia of Practical Medicine and Surgery,* with many contributors, but the time was not ripe for such an extensive work and only two volumes (1834–36) were issued. In 1843 he brought out a new monthly journal, the *Medical News,* which later became a weekly journal and was published until 1906. In 1874 he began the publication of the *Monthly Abstract of Medical Science,* the fore-runner of subsequent abstracting journals, but in 1880 it was merged with the *Medical News.*

Hays's other works indicated his interest in science and natural history as well as in medicine. He edited Alexander Wilson's *American Ornithology* (3 vols., 1828), which prompted an interesting correspondence with Charles Lucien Bonaparte, and in collaboration with Dr. R. E. Griffith he published *Chronic Phlegmasiae* (1831) and *Principles of Physiological Medicine* (1832), translated from the French of Broussais. In 1848 he brought out *Elements of Physics,* a revision of the work of Neil Arnott, and in 1855 a new edition of R. D. Hoblyn's dictionary of medical terms. He was a member of the Academy of Natural Sciences of Philadelphia, serving as its president from 1865 to 1869, and was one of the founders of the Franklin Institute and of the American Medical Association.

He was also an active member of the American Philosophical Society. In 1834 he was married to Sarah, daughter of Isaac Minis of Savannah, Ga., who with four children survived him. He is described as of striking appearance, with gentle manners and a reputation for remarkable punctuality. He can be regarded as an outstanding American medical editor and as one whose influence on American medical literature was of value and importance. He died in Philadelphia.

[Alfred Stillé, memoir in *Trans. Coll. of Physicians of Phila.*, 3 ser., vol. V (1881); *Standard Hist. of the Medic. Profession of Phila.* (1897), ed. by F. P. Henry; H. S. Morais, *The Jews of Phila.* (1894); S. D. Gross, obituary notice in *Am. Jour. of the Medic. Sci.*, July 1879; *Public Ledger* (Phila.), Apr. 14, 1879.] T. M.

HAYS, JOHN COFFEE (Jan. 28, 1817–Apr. 28, 1883), soldier, surveyor, brother of Harry Thompson Hays [*q.v.*], was born at Little Cedar Lick, Wilson County, Tenn., the son of Elizabeth Cage, of Virginian origin, and Harmon Hays, a Tennessee volunteer under Jackson. He began surveying at the age of fifteen. He worked in Mississippi four years, later surveyed many of the Texas headrights, and finally served one term as surveyor-general of California. His chief claim to distinction, however, rests upon his military service under the Republic of Texas and in the Mexican War. One of the volunteers who went to Texas to help in the Revolution, he arrived shortly after the battle of San Jacinto, Apr. 21, 1836. He enlisted in the army and served about four years on the frontier against hostile Mexicans and Indians under two scouts, Henry W. Karnes and Erastus ("Deaf") Smith. In 1840, the Ranger forces, light-armed cavalry first used in 1836, were enlarged, and despite his youth Hays was made captain of one of the new companies. He served on the frontier in the region between the Rio Grande and the Nueces and for gallantry in action was promoted to major. Although he was not commanding in physique, he held the respect and allegiance of his Rangers through his natural superiority and his genuine interest in them. Young, daring, good horsemen, good marksmen, good fighters, fast-moving as Indians and better armed, the Rangers coped for the most part successfully with superior numbers of hostile Indians and Mexicans and contributed largely in pushing back the frontier and making possible the permanent settlement of Texas.

Hays served practically throughout the Mexican War, most of the time as colonel of a regiment of Texas volunteer cavalry, and won especial distinction at the battle of Monterey. After his discharge in 1848, he led an important though partly unsuccessful expedition in search of a new San Antonio-Chihuahua trade route. In 1849 he emigrated to California, and early in 1850 he was elected sheriff of San Francisco County because of his military reputation. Reelected in 1851, he served until 1853, when he resigned to accept President Pierce's appointment as surveyor-general of California. After this, his last public office, he went into real-estate business, acquiring valuable property in the "Eastbay" region. He also had large banking, public service, and industrial interests in Oakland. An invalid in his later years, he died at "Fernwood," his home, near Piedmont, Alameda County. He was married in Texas, in 1847, to Susan Calvert, a native of Alabama. Of their six children only two lived to maturity.

[The chief official sources are the few remaining Ranger service records, Hays's reports in the Texas State Library, and the Mexican War records in the U. S. War Dept. His own narrative, in manuscript, is in the Bancroft Library, San Francisco. Printed sources include A. J. Sowell, *Early Settlers and Indian Fighters in Southwest Tex.* (1900); *Hist. of Alameda County, Cal.* (1883); Z. T. Fulmore, *The Hist. and Geog. of Tex. as Told in County Names* (1915); *The Papers of Mirabeau Buonaparte Lamar*, vols. IV (1924), V (1927), ed. by C. A. Gulick, Jr.] E. H. W.

HAYS, WILLIAM JACOB (Aug. 8, 1830–Mar. 13, 1875), painter of animals, was born in New York City, the only son of Aaron Burr Hays and the grandson of Jacob Hays, who for nearly half a century was high constable of New York and a noted terror to criminals. His mother was Sarah Pool Forman. The artist studied drawing under John Rubens Smith, but in the subsequent development of his work as a painter he relied upon his own efforts and attained a notable degree of success in his specialty. In 1850 he exhibited his first picture, "Dogs in a Field," at the National Academy of Design, and in 1852 he sent to the same institution his "Head of a Bull-dog," which was highly commended for its accuracy and spirit. He was made an associate of the Academy in 1852 but resigned five years later. In 1865 he was married to Helen Dummer.

In 1860, when Colorado, Wyoming, and the Rocky Mountains were but little known and offered an inviting new field for the painter, Hays visited that region and made a studious survey of its fauna and landscape. The results of the journey were not only interesting as delineations of novel subjects but presented a record of historic value. The picture of "The Wounded Buffalo" was pronounced one of the most successful paintings of animal life ever executed by an American painter. "The Stampede," a spirited picture of a vast herd of frightened bison about to be precipitated over the brink of a canyon,

"The Herd on the Move," depicting a horde of bison crossing an arroyo in search of food or water, and the "Prairie-dog Village" were all well known in their day.

Though Hays owed his reputation chiefly to these western scenes, he painted a great number of pictures of dogs, deer, squirrels, partridges, quail, and other game birds, and fish, fruit, and flower pieces. In search of his subjects he traveled to Nova Scotia, the Adirondacks, and other northern regions. His paintings of flowers were especially popular. In the later years of his life he did not send his works to the exhibitions, and for this reason his name was not well known to the public. Nevertheless, when he died in New York in 1875, after a long and painful illness, the *Art Journal* spoke of him as one of the ablest painters in the country; the *New York Tribune* ranked him among the first of animal painters; and the eight pall-bearers at his funeral were the leading painters in New York.

[H. T. Tuckerman, *Book of the Artists* (1867); the *Art Jour.*, Apr. 1875; *New Am. Cyc.* (1860); C. E. Clement and Laurence Hutton, *Artists of the Nineteenth Century* (1879); J. D. Champlin, Jr., and C. C. Perkins, *Cyc. of Painters and Paintings* (1886); genealogical notes in *Pubs. of the Am. Jewish Soc.*, no. 2 (1884); *N. Y. Tribune*, Mar. 16, 1875; information as to certain facts from Hays's son, William J. Hays, Millbrook, N. Y.]

W. H. D.

HAYS, WILLIAM SHAKESPEARE (July 19, 1837–July 23, 1907), ballad writer, composer, was born in Louisville, Ky., where he also died. His father, Hugh Hays, was born in Pennsylvania, but he went to Louisville in 1832, married Martha Richardson, and became a prosperous manufacturer of farm implements. William early developed a faculty for music, but he took lessons in the art for only a few weeks, since, says an admirer, "instructors in music, as in literature, seemed superfluities to him." He none the less, after attending primary school, went successively to three small colleges, one in Hanover, Ind., one in Clarksville, Tenn., and one in Georgetown, Ky., at the last of which he was listed as a freshman in 1856–57. His first published ballad, *Little Ones at Home,* appeared in 1856. It proved popular, and it was not long before Hays found work as a reporter on the *Louisville Democrat* and as amanuensis for George D. Prentice. At about this time, he composed for the delight of a house party the song "Evangeline," first writing it, words and music, impromptu, with a charred stick upon a white board fence. During the Civil War, he was in command of a river transport named the *Gray Eagle,* but he so incensed the Federal general in command at New Orleans that he was thrown into prison. Always he was working at some song or other, or at some poem which might as well have been a song. They were mostly reminiscent and sentimental, descriptive of joys that could never be again, but they were bought, one after another, by thousands, through the entire repertory of over 300, until at last Hays had sold millions of them. At sixty he wrote as he wrote at twenty, with just the proper dash of dialect to make his work poignant. He always maintained that it was he who wrote the original words and music for "Dixie," but as this authorship has been disputed, a more certain claim to remembrance rests with "Mollie Darling," the most popular of all of his ballads. In 1865 he was married to Belle McCullough of Louisville. During the late sixties and early seventies he was a riverman, plying regularly from Pittsburgh to New Orleans. Later he resumed his work with the Louisville *Courier-Journal,* serving as its marine editor and conducting a daily marine column. He sought not merely to amuse and instruct his readers, but to create public opinion, for it seemed to him most urgently important that the rivers be made more easily navigable. He exerted himself powerfully, and with some effectiveness, to that end. All his life he dabbled in black-face comedy, and in the late eighties a company in Louisville which bore his name advertised as "the Creme de la Creme of Negro minstrelsy." He published three booklets, all in Louisville: *The Modern Meetin' House and Other Poems* (1874), *Will S. Hays' Songs and Poems* (1886), and *Songs and Poems* (1895). On the page following the title-page of his last book, he printed this note: "To my Friends: If I have done wrong in publishing this book, forgive me. Yours truly, Will S. Hays."

[*Hist. of Ky., the Blue Grass State* (Chicago, Louisville, 1928), vol. IV; *Who's Who in America,* 1906–07; *Cat. of the Officers and Grads. of Georgetown Coll., Ky.,* 1856–57; "A Southern Singer," the *Musician,* Oct. 1906; Louisville *Courier-Journal,* July 24, 1907.]

J. D. W.

HAYWARD, GEORGE (Mar. 9, 1791–Oct. 7, 1863), Boston surgeon, the first to employ ether anesthesia during a major operation, was the son of Lemuel Hayward (1749–1821), surgeon of the Revolution, and was brought up in his father's house at Jamaica Plain, Mass., in an atmosphere of strong medical tradition. After graduating from Harvard College in 1809, he studied medicine at Philadelphia where he came under the influence of Benjamin Rush, Benjamin S. Barton, and Caspar Wistar [*qq.v.*]. He received the degree of M.D. from the University of Pennsylvania in 1812 and then went abroad for several years, where he had contact with Sir Astley Cooper and John Abernethy. On his return to Boston he found his father's practice awaiting him, which he entered upon conscientiously and with success. He was appointed physician to the Almshouse and in 1818 was made a fellow of the American Academy of Arts and Sciences. With John Collins Warren and Enoch Hale [*qq.v.*] he founded in 1830 a medical school supported by private subscription, which existed for a period of eight years. In 1834 he became a lecturer at the Harvard Medical School and in 1835, when a new professorship was established in the principles of surgery and clinical surgery, Hayward was made the first incumbent. He had become an assistant surgeon to the Massachusetts General Hospital in 1826 and in 1838 he was made one of the surgeons-in-chief. After 1835 he began to give regular clinics at the hospital, and through his association with this institution he linked his name with the introduction of anesthesia. On Oct. 16, 1846, Warren removed a fatty tumor from the neck of a patient who had been anesthetized by W. T. G. Morton [*q.v.*]. Hayward, on the following day, removed a similar tumor from the upper arm of another patient and on Nov. 7 performed the first major operation under ether, involving the amputation of a thigh. The procedure lasted one minute and three-quarters exclusive of ligation of the vessels. Hodges, in describing the operation, says (*post,* p. 47) that this painless amputation "is justly regarded as the first decisive operation performed" under ether. Hayward published an account of his early experiences with ether in the *Boston Medical and Surgical Journal,* Apr. 21, 1847.

On Nov. 4, 1846, Hayward read the introductory lecture at the opening of the new building of the Harvard Medical School on North Grove Street. He was secretary of the Massachusetts Medical Society, 1832–35, and president, 1852–55. He retired from the chair of surgery, Mar. 31, 1849. In 1852 he was made a fellow of Harvard College—an unusual honor for a physician—and served until his death. His medical writings are of considerable importance. With the translation of Bichat's *Anatomie Générale* which appeared in Boston in a three-volume edition in 1822, he introduced into America the spirit of the French school of pathological anatomists. In 1834 he wrote the first American textbook of physiology: *Outlines of Human Physiology,* in which the breadth of his reading was creditably reflected, but which offered little that was new in the way of physiological experiment. His various surgical papers were reprinted in 1855 under the title: *Surgical Reports and Miscellaneous Papers on Medical Subjects.* All his writings are precise and clear, but not brilliant, his reputation coming rather from his unusual skill as a surgeon. He was beloved as a teacher and gave much time to preparation for lectures and to the affairs of the medical school. Personally he was retiring and abhorred publicity. Shortly before his death he destroyed all of his papers which might have been of use to biographers.

[*Proc. Am. Acad. Arts and Sci.,* vol. VI (1866); *Medic. Communications of the Mass. Medic. Soc.,* vol. X, no. 3 (1863); T. F. Harrington, *The Harvard Medic. School* (1905), vol. II; R. M. Hodges, *A Narrative of Events Connected with the Introduction of Sulphuric Ether into Surgical Use* (1891); J. C. Warren, *Etherization, with Surgical Remarks* (1848); W. L. Burrage, *A Hist. of the Mass. Medic. Soc.* (1923); *Boston Transcript,* Oct. 7, 1863.]

J. F. F.

HAYWARD, NATHANIEL MANLEY (Jan. 19, 1808–July 18, 1865), inventor, manufacturer, was born in Easton, Mass., the son of Jerahmeel Hayward. He was descended from Thomas and Susannah Hayward who came from England in 1635, resided for a time in Duxbury, Mass., and finally settled in Bridgewater. As a very young man he went to Boston and operated a livery stable. He had received practically no education, but he was of an inventive turn of mind, and when, in the early thirties, there was much public interest in Boston in India-rubber products he attempted to manufacture a waterproof shoe-blacking with India rubber. He was on the point of making a satisfactory material when his attention was turned to the preparation of India-rubber fabric. This occurred in the summer of 1834. After continuing experiments quietly through the winter Hayward sold out his livery business in the spring of 1835 and went to his home at Easton where he continued experimenting secretly for a number of months. Having no knowledge of chemistry or of the action of any of the chemicals which he used, he worked in a purely blind fashion. His aim was, of course, to produce a fabric which would not become soft and sticky in the summer time. For some reason not known to himself, he succeeded in making one satisfactory piece of cloth and on the strength of this was given employment with the Eagle India Rubber Company in Easton. He worked for this company for several years both at Easton and at Woburn, Mass., where the company moved late in 1835, serving in the capacity of general superintendent.

Some time in 1836, in an attempt to make white rubber aprons, Hayward subjected rubber-coated cloth to sulfur fumes to bleach it and found, to his surprise, that in addition to being whitened it did not soften and become sticky as before. This was his first intimation of the value of sulfur in rubber compounding. For several months thereafter he experimented more or less secretly with sulfur and in the fall of 1836, in partnership with a friend, bought out the Eagle India Rubber Company. In the spring of 1838 he himself took over the business. He continued to make rubber cloth with various degrees of success, utilizing sulfur in the compound and subjecting it to the heat of the sun's rays. He thus brought about a partial, superficial vulcanization. Although he planned to secure a patent on his process he met Charles Goodyear [*q.v.*] about that time and in September 1838 sold his factory to him. The two drew up an agreement, too, that Hayward should secure his patent and in consideration of $1,000 assign all rights in it to Goodyear. The agreement, furthermore, gave Hayward the privilege of making three hundred yards of rubber cloth a day until Goodyear had paid him an additional sum of $2,000. On Feb. 24, 1839, Hayward, "Assignor to Charles Goodyear," was granted United States Patent No. 1090.

After working a year for Goodyear in the plant at Woburn, Hayward carried on a business of his own until 1841, during which time he manufactured rubberized articles amounting in value to about $1,000. He then returned to work for Goodyear and assisted the latter in his experiments on rubber vulcanization. In 1842 he went into business for himself again but after struggling along for another year he sold out to Leverett Candee and went to work in the latter's manufactory at Hamden, Conn., making rubber shoes. After a year here he went to Lisbon, Conn., and under the firm name of N. Hayward & Company, engaged in the manufacture of shoes on his own account. Shortly after this venture began Hayward discovered a method of giving rubber shoes a luster. He kept the secret for two years and in this time the company prospered. In the spring of 1847 the business was sold to a stock company called the Hayward Rubber Company, organized in the town of Colchester, Conn. Hayward was active manager of this firm until 1854 and president from 1855 until his death. He was also largely interested in the Boston Rubber Shoe Company at Malden, Mass., and started a factory at Wyoming, Mass., called the Red Mills. During the Civil War he had large government contracts for blankets, haversacks, and canteens, and also constructed rubber pontoons. When the first renewal of the Goodyear patent was sought, Hayward was its strong advocate and spent a large sum of money to secure its success. He opposed, however, the second application. Hayward was married when very young to Louisa Buke of Boston. At the time of his death in Colchester he was survived by his widow and seven children.

[*Some Account of Nathaniel Hayward's Experiments with India Rubber* (Norwich, Conn., 1865); *India Rubber World*, Oct. 1890; G. W. Hayward, *Centennial Gathering of the Hayward Family* (1879); Chas. Goodyear, *Gum-Elastic and Its Varieties* (2 vols., 1853).]

C. W. M—n.

HAYWOOD, JOHN (Mar. 16, 1762–Dec. 22, 1826), jurist, historian, was born in Halifax County, N. C., the son of Egbert and Sarah (Ware) Haywood and the grandson of Col. John Haywood, founder of the family in North Carolina. The Haywoods were of English derivation and settled in Virginia a generation before the removal of the grandfather to North Carolina. Egbert Haywood was a member of the Halifax Committee of Safety and of the first Provincial Congress of his state, in 1776. Later he was a member of the General Assembly and of the constitutional convention of 1788 which refused to ratify the Federal Constitution. John Haywood received a limited education at an academy in an adjoining county. Near the close of the Revolutionary War he served a short time as aide on an officer's staff. He began, unaided and untutored, the study of law and was soon admitted to the Halifax bar. Brought into contest at the bar with the able general, William R. Davie, of the same county, and James Iredell, young Haywood displayed such ability that the General Assembly elected him (Dec. 28, 1785) judge of a superior court it had just established for Davidson County at Nashville in the faraway Cumberland country, but he declined the commission for fear of loss of life "through hostile savages" in that region. About this time he was married to Martha Edwards.

Possessed of an unusually powerful and logical mind, he developed it by an intensive reading of the English reports and texts. He was elected solicitor-general of the state, Dec. 11, 1790; raised to the post of attorney-general the next year, and to the bench of the superior court, then the court of last resort, June 24, 1793—at first by temporary appointment. His election followed in 1794. He reported the decisions of that court in two volumes which are the earliest in the series of law reports of North Carolina. Although he was rapidly gaining a reputation as a judge, he resigned from the bench in 1800 under circumstances which brought upon him severe criticism and near-odium: his friend, James Glasgow, secretary of state, was indicted with other leading men of the state for fraudulently issuing land-warrants, and Haywood is said to have accepted a retainer of one thousand dollars for the defense before the court from which he had resigned. The letter of resignation indicated that he had taken the step owing to the inadequacy of his salary as judge. At the time Haywood resided in Franklin County. For vindication he stood for election as presidential elector, in 1800, but lost even his own county by a humiliating majority. He threw himself into the practice of law, summoning all of his powers, and was eminently successful. His vigorous mind found outlet, also, in the production of *A Manual of the Laws of North-Carolina* (2 vols., 1808) and *The Duty and Authority of Justices of the Peace* (1810).

About 1807 Haywood removed to Tennessee. There he was assured of steady employment and large professional returns through the landed interests of his connections and friends. At the bar he at once took rank with Felix Grundy and Jenkin Whiteside, the acknowledged leaders, and soon demonstrated his superiority over them and all others in points of profound legal learning and forceful argumentation. On Sept. 14, 1816, he was elected to the supreme court of Tennessee and continued in service until his death, his fame increasing all the while. The one flaw in his make-up, according to his contemporaries, was his inclination to avarice. As in North Carolina, he edited and reported the opinions of his court, and in association with Robert L. Cobbs, he compiled *The Statute Laws of the State of Tennessee* (2 vols., 1831). His estate, "Tusculum," was seven miles south of Nashville. His law office he built of logs. In it were written many of the great judgment-opinions that laid the foundations of Tennessee jurisprudence. Another office of logs was added when Haywood established a law school, the first in the Southwest, in order that aspirants to the bar might have systematic training which he himself had been denied.

As Haywood grew older his active mind sought outlet in extra-professional activities. Seeing the need of preserving the history of his state while many of the earlier pioneers were yet alive, he turned to the writing of history. As an aid, he organized in 1820 and became the first president of the Tennessee Antiquarian Society, which existed about two years. He published in 1819 *The Christian Advocate,* a curious book in which much learning was displayed, somewhat in medley, to prove the truth of prophecy and Christianity. In it he advocated fixing a time-limit for slavery's existence. His next works, *The Natural and Aboriginal History of Tennessee* (Nashville, 1823) and *The Civil and Political History of Tennessee* (Knoxville, 1823), are in a sense companion works, giving accounts of the Tennessee country down to 1796. For their preparation he interviewed many early settlers and conducted a wide correspondence. He had almost no archival aid or guidance. Notwithstanding, the two volumes have always been deemed high authority. Haywood was the pioneer in this field in the Southwest. His style as historian is quaint, compressed, and entertaining. All three of these works in the first edition are exceedingly rare and fetch very high prices. Haywood County, Tenn., was named in his honor.

Haywood was stockily built, and in middle age he became exceedingly corpulent, weighing three hundred and fifty pounds, so that, sitting, "his abdomen came down on his lap and nearly covered it to his knees." His physiognomy was most unusual: head conical in shape, and high above the ears; lips protruding, with pointed tips, and under-jaws massive. About this remarkable personality there grew up a rich anecdotage. At his death, in 1826, he was possessed of a large estate. He was buried at Tusculum.

[W. C. Allen, *Hist. of Halifax County* (copyright 1918); W. J. Peele, *Lives of Distinguished North Carolinians* (1898); M. DeL. Haywood, sketch in S. A. Ashe, *Biog. Hist. of N. C.,* vol. VI (1907); J. C. Guild, *Old Times in Tenn.* (1878), pp. 78–79; *The Papers of Archibald D. Murphey* (2 vols., 1914), ed. by W. H. Hoyt; W. W. Clayton, *Hist. of Davidson County, Tenn.* (1880); biographical sketch by A. S. Colyar in the 1891 edition of Haywood's *Civil and Pol. Hist. of the State of Tenn.*; H. S. Foote, *The Bench and Bar of the South and Southwest* (1876); S. A. Ashe, *Hist. of N. C.,* vol. II (1925); *The State Records of N. C.,* vols. XVIII (1900), and XXI (1903); the *Am. Hist. Mag.,* Oct. 1901; J. W. Caldwell, *Sketches of the Bench and Bar of Tenn.* (1898); *Univ. of N. C. Mag.,* Nov. 1860; the *Green Bag,* Mar. 1893; *Raleigh Reg. and N.-C. Gazette,* Jan. 19, 1827.]
S. C. W.

HAYWOOD, WILLIAM DUDLEY (Feb. 4, 1869–May 18, 1928), labor agitator, was born in Salt Lake City, Utah. His father, also named William Dudley, was born near Columbus, Ohio, of colonial stock, and at an early age went west. His mother was born in South Africa of Scotch-Irish parents who came to America during the later days of the gold rush. The boy had but passed his third birthday when his father died, and four years later his mother remarried. At the age of nine he suffered the loss of an eye. In the same year he worked with his step-father for a few months in a mine, and with several intervals of schooling was employed during the next six years at various odd jobs. His given name of William Richard he insisted on altering to that of his father; and his mother, consenting, had the change confirmed at an Episcopalian service—the last religious service, according to the son, that he ever attended.

At fifteen he became a miner with his stepfather at Eagle Canyon, sixty miles north of Winnemucca, Nev. About 1889, in the same state, he married Nevada Jane Minor. He was for a time a cowboy; later he took up a homestead, which he lost through its cancellation by the government, and then he returned to mining in Silver City, Idaho. He had first become interested in the labor question in 1886 when reading about the Haymarket episode in Chicago. In 1896 he joined the Western Federation of Miners as a charter member of the Silver City local. Two years later he was elected a delegate to the national convention; in 1899 he was made a member of the national executive board, and in 1900 secretary-treasurer, with headquarters in Denver. He soon became dominant in the leadership of the Federation, and his aggressive policy was warmly approved by the membership. Determined resistance to the organization on the part of the mine and smelter owners brought on a clash, and the Telluride strike of May 1, 1901, marked the opening of an industrial war in Colorado in which, during a period of four or five years, acts of savage violence were perpetrated on both sides. As an advocate of industrial unionism, Haywood strongly opposed the craft unionism of the American Federation of Labor and was active in the effort to reorganize the American labor movement. He presided at the convention that met in Chicago on June 27, 1905, and founded the Industrial Workers of the World, of which the Western Federation of Miners became at once a subordinate body.

The assassination, on Dec. 30, 1905, of Frank R. Steunenberg, former governor of Idaho, led to the arrest of Harry Orchard, a member of the Federation. In a long statement Orchard asserted that he had committed many crimes, including this one, at the instigation of Haywood and other officials of the organization. On the night of Feb. 17, 1906, Haywood, Charles H. Moyer, the president of the Federation, and George A. Pettibone, a local merchant, were arrested in Denver and on the following day were taken on a special train to Boisé and lodged in the Idaho penitentiary, whence later they were transferred to the Ada County jail. A period of intense excitement followed. Largely attended meetings were held throughout the country; resolutions denouncing the "kidnapping" were passed, and thousands of dollars were contributed for the prisoners' defense. The Socialist party of Colorado nominated Haywood for governor, and in the November election he polled some 16,000 votes. His trial, which attracted nation-wide attention, ended on July 28, 1907, with an acquittal. Pettibone was later tried, with the same result, and Moyer was then released.

Haywood returned to Denver and began a speaking campaign in behalf of the Western Federation of Miners and such of its members as were in prison. Difficulties between him and the other leaders of the organization, which in the meantime had withdrawn from the I.W.W., soon came to a head, and on Apr. 8, 1908, he was formally repudiated as one of its representatives. Henceforth, for several years, he was actively engaged as a campaigner for both the Socialist party, which he had joined in 1901, and for the I.W.W. In 1908 a considerable minority of the former organization favored his nomination for the presidency, and he was later elected to its national executive board, but in 1912, because of his advocacy of violence, he was dismissed from this office. He became national secretary-treasurer of the I.W.W., and in September 1917, with many fellow members, was arrested for sedition. After a trial extending over four months, he and ninety-four others were convicted, Aug. 17, 1918, and he was sentenced to be imprisoned for twenty years and to pay a fine of $10,000. Released on bail, pending a decision on the application for a new trial, he left the country in disguise on Mar. 31, 1921, and next appeared in Soviet Russia. He was at first ostentatiously welcomed by the Soviet government but later was relegated to an inconspicuous place and was never admitted to the councils of the leaders. Toward the end he made several speaking tours through the country in behalf of revolutionary agitators in foreign lands, and spent considerable time on the preparation of his autobiography. On Mar. 16, 1928, he was prostrated by a paralytic stroke. Two months later he died in the Kremlin Hospital, of hemiplegia. He had taken a Russian wife in 1927. Haywood was more than six feet tall and of powerful build. Though assertive and rough-mannered, he was a genial companion. He was a forceful though by no means an eloquent speaker, and an industrious writer, contributing many articles to the radical press. In 1911, in collaboration with Frank Bohn, he published *Industrial Socialism.* His autobiography, published after his death, is a disappointing work, abusive of his opponents, careless as to details, and evasive as to many of the outstanding episodes of his career.

[See W. D. Haywood, *Bill Haywood's Book* (1929); *Official Proceedings* of the annual conventions of the Western Federation of Miners, 1901–08; P. F. Brissenden, *The I.W.W.: A Study of Am. Syndicalism* (1919); files of the *Miners Mag.* (Denver), 1904–09; W. M. Feigenbaum, "'Big Bill' Haywood Was Long a Storm Centre," *N. Y. Times,* May 27, 1928. Haywood was the subject of many articles in periodicals and of innumerable news items in the daily press.] W. J. G.

HAZARD, AUGUSTUS GEORGE (Apr. 28, 1802–May 7, 1868), merchant and manufacturer, was born in South Kingstown, R. I., the son of Thomas S. and Silence (Knowles) Hazard. He was descended from Thomas Hazard who emigrated to Massachusetts Bay early in the seventeenth century and settled in Rhode Island. When Augustus was six, his father, a retired sea-captain and farmer, moved his family to a farm near Columbia, Conn. Here the boy remained until he was fifteen, leaving then to learn the trade of painter, at which he continued until he was eighteen. In 1818 he felt the urge to travel and with his savings purchased passage on a packet to Savannah, Ga., where he spent a profitable two years at his trade. In 1822 he revisited New England to marry Salome Goodwin Merrill of West Hartford, Conn. He then returned to Savannah, purchased a store dealing in paints, oils, and similar merchandise, and was remarkably successful. When only twenty-five he returned to New York to expand his activities to include a commission house for handling southern produce, the resident purchasing agency for his own and other commercial establishments in the South, and the shipping agency of a line of New York-to-Savannah packets of which he became part owner. He later added foreign importing to his activities and had a connection with the London house of George Wildes & Company. Every phase of the varied business prospered and although he suffered a serious loss in the panic of 1837, Hazard maintained his credit and financial standing.

Having acted as the general agent for Loomis & Denslow, manufacturers of black powder, for many years, Hazard in 1837 acquired a fourth interest and joined the firm which reorganized as Loomises, Hazard & Company. In 1843 he and Denslow bought out the other owners and organized a joint-stock company under the name of the Hazard Powder Company. Hazard was the principal owner and president from 1843 to 1868. The Mexican and Civil wars, together with the large amount of internal improvement carried on in that period, were responsible for a steadily growing market for explosives. The company flourished, and in time a plant covering some five hundred acres grew up at Hazardville, near Enfield, Conn., with smaller mills at Canton and East Hartford. But as the business grew, departments were established in practically every state and territory in the Union, and Hazard as the owner was reputed to possess real estate in more states than any other citizen of the country. The company became one of the important manufacturers of powder and in 1872, four years after Hazard's death, it was one of the three largest members of the Gunpowder Trade Association. In 1876 a majority of the stock was purchased by the Du Pont Company. Hazard combined the social manner of the Southern trader with the business ability of the New England manufacturer. He is described as generous, forceful, and conservative. He was an active Whig, chairman of the Connecticut state committee, and a friend and companion of Daniel Webster. Hazardville, Conn., is named for him. He died at Enfield, survived by three of his eight children.

[A. P. Van Gelder and Hugo Schlatter, *Hist. of the Explosives Industry in America* (1927); J. L. Bishop, *A Hist. of Am. Manufactures,* vol. II (1864); James Parton and others, *Sketches of Men of Progress* (1870–71); Caroline E. Robinson, *The Hazard Family of R. I.* (1895).] F. A. T.

HAZARD, EBENEZER (Jan. 15, 1744–June 13, 1817), editor of historical records, postmaster-general, was the son of Samuel Hazard, a merchant of Philadelphia, and his wife, Catherine Clarkson of New York. He was born in Philadelphia, Pa., and was educated at the academy of Samuel Finley [*q.v.*] at Nottingham, Pa., and at the College of New Jersey (later Princeton University), where he graduated in 1762. From 1769 to 1775 he was a partner in the publishing firm of Noel & Hazard of New York, and later a member of the firm of Benedict & Hazard. On May 1, 1775, he was authorized by the Committee of Safety of New York to reorganize the local postal service and on Oct. 5 he was commissioned by the Continental Congress postmaster of the city of New York. Appointed surveyor-general of the Post-Office of the United States late in 1776, he was made postmaster-general, succeeding Richard Bache [*q.v.*], on Jan. 28, 1782. Hazard managed his office with economy and efficiency and was one of the few postmasters-general who have made the post-office pay its way. Nevertheless, on the reorganization of the government after the adoption of the Federal Constitution, he was replaced in September 1789 by Samuel Osgood [*q.v.*] of Massachusetts. He had resided in Philadelphia from 1782 to 1785 and in New York from 1785 to 1789.

Finding it difficult to make a living in New York after the loss of his position under the government, Hazard returned to Philadelphia in 1791 and lived there during the remainder of his life. He was the first secretary of the Insurance Company of North America and for many years was manager of the Schuylkill Bridge Company and of the Delaware & Schuylkill Canal Company. He was moderately successful in these enterprises, but his real interests were primarily intellectual. His duties as surveyor-general of the post (1777–82) made it necessary for him to travel extensively and he took advantage of the opportunity to collect the source-materials of early American history. In response to a petition which he presented to the Continental Congress, July 11, 1778, he received permission to copy documents in the Continental archives and also a grant of one thousand dollars for expenses. Most of his local material was collected before 1782, because when he became postmaster-general he had to give up his wandering existence and live at the seat of government. His two volumes of *Historical Collections* (1792–94) were published in Philadelphia. The first volume contains an assortment of documents relating to the discovery of America and to the early period of colonization; the whole of the second is devoted to the records of the New England Confederation. Several other volumes were planned, but the two which were published sold so badly that the scheme was abandoned. Although most of this material has been superseded by later collections, Hazard is entitled to great credit. He was a careful and conscientious editor and a pioneer in the collection and publication of original historical records. An excellent Greek scholar, he assisted Charles Thomson [*q.v.*], secretary of the Continental Congress, in making his translation of the New Testament. He carried on a correspondence for many years with Jedidiah Morse [*q.v.*], the geographer, and Jeremy Belknap [*q.v.*], the historian. It was owing to his advice that the first volume of Belknap's famous *History of New Hampshire* (1784) was published in Philadelphia. He was keenly concerned about the welfare of the Indians and published a paper entitled "Remarks on Mr. Schermerhorn's Report Concerning the Western Indians" (*Massachusetts Historical Society Collections,* 2 ser., vol. IV, 1816). On Sept. 11, 1783, he was married to Abigail Arthur of Shrewsbury, N. J. Their son, Samuel Hazard [*q.v.*], apparently inherited his father's interest in the preservation of historical sources.

[The best sketch of Hazard's life is that by his grandson, A. G. Vermilye, in the *Mag. of Am. Hist.,* Feb. 1885. For an appraisal of his work as an editor see J. S. Bassett, *The Middle Group of Am. Historians* (1917), and for the Hazard-Belknap correspondence see the *Mass. Hist. Soc. Colls.,* 5 ser., vols. II and III (1877), and 6 ser., vol. IV (1891). Other sources include W. E. Rich, *The Hist. of the U. S. Post Office to the Year 1829* (1924), and the inaccurate though informative chapter by Willis P. Hazard on the Hazards of the Middle states in T. R. Hazard, *Recollections of Olden Times* (1879). There are several unpublished letters from Hazard to Jedidiah Morse in the Pa. Hist. Soc.]

W. R. S.

HAZARD, JONATHAN J. (b. 1744?), political leader, called "Beau Jonathan" because of his scrupulous regard for dress and courtliness of manner, was of the Narragansett Hazards, the son of Jonathan and Abigail (MacCoon) Hazard and a descendant of Thomas Hazard, one of the founders of Newport. He was born about 1744, and died after 1824. His native ability, ready oratory, and political skill put him in the forefront of Rhode Island affairs. For a long time, says Wilkins Updike, he was "the idol of the country interest, manager of the State, leader of the Legislature, in fact, the political dictator in Rhode Island" (*History of the Episcopal Church in Narragansett, R. I.,* 1847, p. 329). He took an early stand for liberty and in 1776, as a delegate to the Rhode Island House of Representatives from Charlestown, was a member of the General Assembly which, on May 4, enacted the law containing Rhode Island's Declaration of Independence. In the same year he had the difficult and dangerous task of apprehending disaffected persons on Block Island. In 1777 he was paymaster of the Continental Battalion and in 1778 he became a member of the Council of War. In the latter year also he was again elected to the lower house of the General Assembly and, repeatedly chosen, served with intermissions during most of the period of the Revolution and after. In 1787 he was elected a delegate from Rhode Island to the Congress of the Confederation but did not take his seat until the next year, when he was again selected. In May 1789 he was once more elected a delegate although Rhode Island was not in the Union.

Beau Jonathan stood at the height of his power perhaps in 1786. At the May session of the Assembly in that year he was the victorious champion of the agricultural element of the state in its struggle with the mercantile element. Using all the qualities of his leadership, he aided in forcing through the Paper Money Act which was set at naught, however, by the decision of the court in the famous case of *Trevett* vs. *Weeden.* The year 1790 saw him again on the losing side and saw too the end of his active power in state affairs. He had fought in the General Assembly against the adoption of the Federal Constitution; he continued the fight as a delegate to the state convention held at South Kingstown in March 1790, and at the adjourned convention held in Newport in May. On May 29, ratification was agreed to by a vote of 34 to 32. Beau Jonathan said in a letter written in an after year that he was sold out by his friends. In his later life he removed to

Verona in Oneida County, N. Y. There, too, he continued his interest in public affairs. Elegant and courtly to the last, after he was eighty years old he was married for the third time. His first wife was his second cousin Patience, daughter of "Stout Jeffrey" Hazard, "who had the strength of six common men"; his second wife was Hannah Brown; his third, Marian, daughter of Moses Gage.

[See Caroline E. Robinson, *The Hazard Family of R. I.* (1895); *Records of the State of R. I. and Providence Plantations in New Eng.*, vols. VIII (1863), IX (1864), and X (1865); W. B. Weeden, *Econ. and Social Hist. of New Eng., 1620–1789* (1890), and *Early R. I.* (1910); and F. B. Bates, *R. I. and the Formation of the Union* (1898). The "J." in Hazard's name was not originally used; it was probably adopted to distinguish the subject of this sketch from other Jonathan Hazards.] W. A. S.

HAZARD, ROWLAND GIBSON (Oct. 9, 1801–June 24, 1888), manufacturer, writer on philosophical subjects, the son of Rowland and Mary (Peace) Hazard, and a younger brother of Thomas Robinson Hazard [*q.v.*], was born in South Kingstown, R. I. Rowland Hazard, his father, born also in South Kingstown, became engaged in foreign commerce as a member of the Charleston, S. C., firm of Hazard & Robinson (afterward Hazard & Ayrault), and married Mary Peace of that city. About the turn of the century he went back to South Kingstown and took up his residence at Peacedale, a name chosen by him to commemorate the family in which he had found his wife, and which celebrated too the charm of the Kingstown countryside. In 1802 he began at Peacedale the woolen industry which successive generations of the Hazard family carried on in the same place. Rowland Gibson, his third son, studied at the schools at Burlington, N. J., and Bristol, Pa., and at the Friends' School at Westtown, Chester County, Pa. When about eighteen he returned to South Kingstown, became associated with his elder brother Isaac Peace Hazard in the business at Peacedale, from which their father had now retired, and continued in it for nearly fifty years. He was a Free-Soiler and later a Republican, a member of the Pittsburgh convention of 1856, of the convention in the same year that nominated Frémont, of the convention in 1860 that nominated Lincoln, and of the convention of 1868 that nominated Grant. He aided the free-school movement and was an advocate of temperance reform. In 1851, 1854, and 1880, he was a member of the Rhode Island House of Representatives, and in 1866 a member of the state Senate. While in the General Assembly he worked for the suppression of lotteries and for the prevention of bribery in elections. His financial articles, written during the Civil War, gained for him a wide reputation. Some of them were collected and published as *Our Resources* (1864), which was republished in London, and several were translated into Dutch and published in Amsterdam. He performed notable service in Europe in the effort to sustain the national credit.

In 1866 Hazard retired from the business at Peacedale. Still possessed of the habit, or with the instinct born with him, of looking for general principles, and of applying the results of abstract thinking to practical ends, he engaged himself with problems of Reconstruction and other questions of the day. He helped to put the first railroad across the continent. As other demands lessened, he found time for study and writing, for travel, and for his philanthropies. With his son Rowland Hazard he established the Hazard Professorship of Physics in Brown University. He was a trustee of Brown from 1869 to 1875, and a fellow from 1875 until his death in 1888. He married Caroline Newbold, daughter of John Newbold of Bucks County, Pa., Sept. 25, 1828. Their two sons, Rowland and John Newbold Hazard, were the third consecutive generation of Hazards to carry on the manufacture of woolen goods at Peacedale.

As a youth, Rowland Gibson Hazard had a certain precocity in mathematics. Before leaving school he discovered, it is said, an original and simple method of describing the hyperbola. In his maturer years his underlying interests were philosophical. When on his business trips, while traveling on packets and stage-coaches, on boats and trains, he made notes for later books. His first considerable publication, *Language: Its Connexion with the Present Condition and Future Prospects of Man* (1836), possibly had its inception in discussions with his friend—and Poe's friend—Mrs. Sarah Helen Whitman, on the nature of poetry. The book attracted the attention of William Ellery Channing, who became intimate with him. Following the latter's death in 1842, Hazard wrote an *Essay on the Philosophical Character of Channing,* published in 1845. At some time prior to 1840, Channing suggested that Hazard should undertake a refutation of Jonathan Edwards on the Will. Hazard began to make notes and by 1843 had elaborated his main points only to lose all the material he had collected through a mishap to a Mississippi steamer on which he had taken passage to New Orleans. Fourteen years later he returned to the work and published it in 1864 under the title: *Freedom of Mind in Willing; or Every Being That Wills a Creative First Cause.* The book gained for Hazard the friendship of John

Stuart Mill, who wrote to him: "I wish you had nothing to do but philosophize, for though I often do not agree with you, I see in everything you write a well-marked natural capacity for philosophy" (*Freedom of Mind in Willing,* ed. 1889, p. v). In 1864, while in Europe, he sought out Mill. His *Two Letters on Causation and Freedom in Willing, Addressed to John Stuart Mill* (1869) were the result of his conversations and correspondence with the British philosopher.

[Hazard's numerous writings, including several for the first time printed, were brought together by his grand-daughter, Caroline Hazard, and published under her editorship in four volumes in 1889. Each volume bears a separate title. Of these, the *Essay on Language, and other Essays and Addresses* contains a biographical preface by Miss Hazard, and *Freedom of Mind in Willing* contains an introductory essay by George P. Fisher on Hazard's philosophical writings. William Gammell's *Life and Services of the Hon. Rowland Gibson Hazard, LL.D.* (1888), contains a paper by President E. G. Robinson of Brown University on Hazard's philosophical writings and a bibliography of his works. Other sources include J. R. Cole, *Hist. of Washington and Kent Counties, R. I.* (1889); *The Biog. Cyc. of Representative Men of R. I.* (1881); Wm. R. Bagnall, *The Textile Industries of the U. S.* (1893); and the *Providence Jour.*, June 25, 1888.] W. A. S.

HAZARD, SAMUEL (May 26, 1784–May 22, 1870), editor, antiquarian, was the son of Ebenezer Hazard [*q.v.*] and his wife Abigail Arthur. He was born in Philadelphia, Pa., and received his early education at an academy at Woodbury, N. J. During the early years of his adult life he was a merchant in Philadelphia and made several voyages to the West Indies and the Mediterranean. In 1818 he moved to Huntsville, Alabama Territory, where he conducted a cotton brokerage and general mercantile business until 1827. On Mar. 18, 1819, he was married, in Alabama, to Abigail Clark Hetfield of Elizabeth, N. J. In January 1828 he founded a weekly periodical in Philadelphia entitled the *Register of Pennsylvania,* but the enterprise was not financially successful and was abandoned in 1836. The sixteen volumes of the series contain state papers and public documents, legal decisions, documents relating to the early history of the state, Indian history, treaties, anecdotes and antiquities, biographical memoirs, meteorological tables, mineralogical notes, and other interesting information. They are especially rich in historical material. Some of the manuscripts in the American Philosophical Society relating to the early settlements on the Delaware were published for the first time in volumes IV and V of this series. Hazard also edited the *United States Commercial and Statistical Register* (July 1839–June 1842), which is still useful for its financial and economic data.

The title of Hazard's third work, *The Annals of Pennsylvania, from the Discovery of the Delaware, 1609–82* (Philadelphia, 1850), is somewhat misleading. The book is really a prologue or introduction to the *Annals,* being devoted primarily to the Swedish and Dutch settlements on the Delaware. It is based on original material, collected from a variety of sources, most of which had not been published before. Considering the state of historical knowledge in 1850, it is a very creditable piece of work. Shortly after the *Annals* appeared, Hazard received a commission from the governor of Pennsylvania to edit the *Pennsylvania Archives: Selected and Arranged from Original Documents in the Office of the Secretary of the Commonwealth.* Of these there were twelve volumes (Philadelphia, 1852–56), covering the period from the English conquest of New Netherland in 1664 to the adoption of the second state constitution in 1790. Although Hazard had nothing to do with the editing of the *Colonial Records,* he supervised the preparation of a general index to both the *Records* and the *Archives,* published in Philadelphia in one volume in 1860. In the index he left much to be desired, but as editor of what has come to be known as the first series of the *Pennsylvania Archives,* he set a high standard for his successors, and in the *Register of Pennsylvania* and the *United States Commercial and Statistical Register* he left mines of information for the student of American economic history. Hazard died at Germantown, Pa., just a few days before his eighty-sixth birthday.

[The records of Hazard's life are very scanty. There is a sketch of his life in *Appletons' Ann. Cyc.* for 1870 and there are a few references to his early career in the manuscript letters of Ebenezer Hazard to Jedidiah Morse in the library of the Pa. Hist. Soc. The Hazards of the Middle states are treated by Willis P. Hazard in T. R. Hazard, *Recollections of Olden Times* (1879).] W. R. S.

HAZARD, THOMAS (Sept. 15, 1720–Aug. 26, 1798), Abolitionist, was called by the distinguishing name of "College Tom," since there were of this clan, according to one computation, thirty-two other Thomas Hazards contemporary with him. He was of the fifth generation from Thomas Hazard, progenitor of the Hazard family of Rhode Island and one of the nine founders of Newport in 1639. Robert Hazard, of the second generation, removed to that region of Rhode Island known as the Narragansett Country, with which the Rhode Island Hazards have been continuously identified. Life in the Narragansett Country was highly individualistic. The Hazards were wholly typical of it, "handing down and retaining certain peculiarities from generation to generation," such as "a peculiar decision of character, a certain amount of pride, and a pronounced independence, coupled with a slight amount of reserve" (W. P. Hazard, in T. R. Hazard's *Recollections of Olden Times,* 1879, p. 227). Physically they were strongly marked, being generally speaking of good stature and vigorous frame, and with a firmly set jaw. "College Tom," son of Robert and Sarah (Borden) Hazard, had the Hazard characteristics of mind and body. He studied at Yale College for several terms (whence his appellation) but did not graduate, it is said, because he could not reconcile his Quaker principles and collegiate honors (Wilkins Updike, *History of the Episcopal Church in Narragansett, R. I.,* 1847, p. 322). In 1742 he was admitted a freeman of the colony from South Kingstown and in the same year was married to his third cousin Elizabeth, daughter of Gov. William and Martha (Potter) Robinson. Perhaps also in 1742, certainly before 1745—the year of his father's death—he had his memorable conversation with the Connecticut church deacon who told him that Quakers were not Christians because they held their fellow men in slavery. The idea was a novel one to the young man. In the region about him there was one negro slave to every two or three white men; his father, their friends and neighbors were all slave-owners; and at least two of his connections imported negroes to be sold into slavery. Nevertheless, the words of the church deacon did their work; he took the view that slave-holding was an evil, and despite the arguments, even the threat of disinheritance by his father, he began cultivating his farm with free labor and to work against slavery—one of the first members of the Society of Friends to take the stand. At first he seems to have had but a single convert, his friend Jeremiah Austin, who had liberated the one slave he possessed, his sole inheritance from his father.

The movement in Rhode Island slowly grew till, in 1774, College Tom found himself a member of a committee of the Yearly Meeting which went to the General Assembly with a bill, passed by it, affirming personal freedom as the greatest of the rights which the inhabitants of America were then engaged in preserving, and prohibiting the importation of negroes into the colony. During the Revolution he was a member of the Meeting for Sufferings. In 1783 he was a member of the committee of the Yearly Meeting which brought to the General Assembly a petition for the abolition of slavery which was answered by an act to that end, adopted by the Assembly in February 1784. Shortly afterward, he was enrolled as one of the founders of the Providence Society for Abolishing the Slave Trade, which saw the fruit of its endeavors in the act for its prevention, adopted by the Assembly in 1787. He was one of the incorporators in 1764 of Rhode Island College, later Brown University, and afterward assisted in the establishment of the Friends' School, later the Moses Brown School, in Providence. "In his latter days, to illustrate the deceitfulness of the human heart, he used to say . . . he at last discovered that he himself had 'ruled South Kingstown monthly meeting forty years, in his own will, before he found it out'" (*Recollections of Olden Times,* p. 108).

[In addition to the books named in the text see Caroline Hazard, *Thos. Hazard, son of Robt., Call'd College Tom* (1893); Caroline E. Robinson, *The Hazard Family of R. I.* (1895); Rufus M. Jones, *The Quakers in the Am. Colonies* (1911); W. Dawson Johnston, "Slavery in R. I.," *R. I. Hist. Soc. Pubs.,* n.s. II, no. 2 (1894); J. R. Brackett, "The Status of the Slave, 1775–89," in *Essays in the Constitutional Hist. of the U. S., 1775–89* (1889), ed. by J. F. Jameson; I. B. Richman, *Rhode Island* (1905).] W. A. S.

HAZARD, THOMAS ROBINSON (Jan. 3, 1797–Mar. 26, 1886), agriculturist, manufacturer, social reformer, author, the second son of Rowland and Mary (Peace) Hazard, the grandson of Thomas Hazard [*q.v.*], called "College Tom," and the brother of Rowland Gibson Hazard [*q.v.*], was born in South Kingstown, R. I. After a few years of schooling at the institution maintained by the Society of Friends at Westtown, near Philadelphia, Pa., he returned to Rhode Island and became interested in sheep-raising in Narragansett, whence he came to be called "Shepherd Tom," a name which greatly pleased him. In 1821 he began the manufacture of textiles and combined sheep-raising with it. By the time he was forty-three he had put aside a fortune sufficient to permit him to retire from active business. The remainder of his life was spent at "Vaucluse," the estate he had purchased on the island of Rhode Island, near Newport. He was married to Frances, daughter of Jonas Minturn of New York, Oct. 12, 1838. After her death, some sixteen years later, he became "an earnest worker in the cause of what is called 'Modern Spiritualism,'" and left it on record that he had "no higher ambition than that his name should be handed down to the coming generations associated with this fact alone" (*Recollections of Olden Times,* 1879, p. 192).

He was interested in African colonization and for a time was vice-president of the American Colonization Society. In 1851 he made to the General Assembly of Rhode Island a detailed report on the care of the poor and insane of the state from which important reforms resulted. He opposed capital punishment, and in 1852, a bill originating with him, providing for its abolition and forbidding the pardon of long-term convicts excepting by vote of the General Assembly, was passed. He shared in the establishment of common schools in Rhode Island and was a promoter of relief work in the United States during the Irish famine of 1846–47. He wrote in opposition to slavery, to war, and to the exclusion of woman from the suffrage; his writings discuss among other subjects taxation, the law for the collection of debts, and Rhode Island turkeys. "In his later writings denunciation takes full possession, and supplants religion in his mind; in fact, it *became* a religion, negative yet positive" (R. G. Hazard, *The Jonny Cake Papers of "Shepherd Tom,"* ed. 1915, p. xvii). His *Recollections of Olden Times,* written when he was in his eighty-first and eighty-second years, casts a rich after-glow on life in the Narragansett Country and contains genealogies of the Hazard family. In 1882 a collection of discourses called the *Jonny-Cake Letters,* first printed in the *Providence Journal,* was published by Sidney S. Rider. In 1915 a new edition in the typography of Merrymount Press was brought out under the title: *The Jonny Cake Papers of "Shepherd Tom,"* containing also "Reminiscences of Narragansett Schools of Former Days." "The Jonny Cake Papers" cut across the Narragansett Country into regions more delightfully whimsical than soberly geographical.

[A short biographical sketch of Thomas Robinson Hazard is printed in *The Biog. Cyc. of Representative Men of R. I.* (1881). The biographical sketch by Rowland G. Hazard, of the ninth generation in Peacedale, is an affectionate, yet frank, appreciation of his kinsman of two generations before. See also Caroline E. Robinson, *The Hazard Family of R. I.* (1895), and the *Providence Jour.,* Mar. 27, 1886.] W. A. S.

HAZELIUS, ERNEST LEWIS (Sept. 6, 1777–Feb. 20, 1853), Lutheran clergyman, was descended from a line of Swedish clergymen that began with a court preacher to Gustavus Vasa. Eric Hazelius, his father, had also been intended for the ministry and had studied theology at the University of Upsala, but after a shipwreck, of which he was the sole survivor, he became a Moravian, married a Moravian girl, Christiana Brahtz of Stettin, and settled as a watchmaker at Neusalz, Silesian Prussia, where his son was born. The boy's earliest memory was of being in the arms of an old man, Bishop Polycarp Müller at Herrnhut, who blessed him and devoted him to the ministry. He narrowly escaped another destiny: Catherine II of Russia had been a schoolmate of his mother's, was interested in the boy, and with difficulty was prevented from adopting him. Left an orphan by the time he was sixteen, Hazelius lived in poverty while securing his education in the Moravian institutions at Barby and Niesky. He learned Latin, he said afterward, by doing exercises for his fellow students in return for gifts of potatoes. In 1800 he was licensed to preach and sent to Pennsylvania to teach Latin and Greek in the Moravian school at Nazareth. His ability was quickly recognized, and in 1807 he was made the first professor of theology in the school. His first three pupils—William H. Van Vleck, Samuel Reinke, Peter Wolle—became bishops of the Moravian Church. In 1809 he resigned his position and became a Lutheran. This change seems to have been due to some dissatisfaction with his position at Nazareth; it involved no change in his theological convictions, and his relations with the Moravians remained friendly. On his birthday in 1809 he was ordained by the Lutheran Ministerium of New York as pastor of three scattered congregations—New Germantown, German Valley, Spruce Run—in Hunterdon and Morris counties, N. J. He also conducted a school in Hunterdon County, and in 1810 married Hulda Cummings Bray of Lebanon, N. J., who survived him for a few years. In 1815 he became professor of theology in Hartwick Seminary, Otsego County, N. Y., and devoted the rest of his life to training ministers. While at Hartwick he acquired a reputation as a scholar, received the degree of D.D. from Union and Columbia Colleges in 1824, and declined professorships at Lafayette and Princeton. He was busy, then and later, as a writer, his published works being a biography of Luther (1813); *Materials for Catechisation on Passages of Scripture* (Cooperstown, N. Y., 1823); *The Augsburgh Confession . . . with Notes and Observations* (Schoharie, N. Y., 1828); *The Life of John Henry Stilling* (Gettysburg, Pa., 1831); Volume I (Baltimore, 1842) of a projected *History of the Christian Church from the Earliest Ages to the Present Time*; and a *History of the American Lutheran Church* (Zanesville, Ohio, 1846). Published for the most part in remote towns, his books never enjoyed an extensive circulation and are now rare. Hazelius was the second professor in the Gettysburg Theological Seminary, 1830–33, but was unhappy there and on Jan. 1, 1834, became the professor of theology in the Classical and Theological Institute of the Synod of South Carolina at Lexington, S. C. There he remained, isolated but apparently content, until his death, taking his leave of his pupils only four days before the end. In 1842 he visited Germany, was urged to stay, but returned. His thirty-seven years as a professor of theology exerted a strong, though quiet, influence on the Lutheran Church. Himself childless, he lavished his affection on his pupils, who venerated him in turn. By temperament he was irenic and evangelical. Denominational distinctions did not hedge him in. Church historians, writing from the confessionalist point of view, have underestimated his services as a teacher and have overlooked the essential conservatism of his theological position.

[M. L. Stoever, memoir in *Evangelical Rev.*, Jan. 1856; W. B. Sprague, *Annals Am. Pulpit*, IX (1869), 132–41; J. G. Morris, *Fifty Years in the Luth. Ministry* (Baltimore, 1878); G. D. Bernheim, *Hist. of the German Settlements and of the Luth. Church in North and South Carolina* (1872); A. L. Gräbner, *Geschichte der Luth. Kirche in America* (St. Louis, 1892); W. A. Schwarze, "Hist. of the Moravian Coll. and Theol. Sem.," *Trans. Moravian Hist. Soc.*, vol. VIII (1909); A. R. Wentz, *Hist. of the Gettysburg Theol. Sem.* (1926).]
G. H. G.

HAZELTINE, MAYO WILLIAMSON (Apr. 24, 1841–Sept. 14, 1909), literary critic, journalist, born at Boston, Mass., was the son of Mayo and Frances A. (Williamson) Hazeltine. After graduating at Harvard in 1862 he studied at Oxford and traveled widely in Europe. Returning to America he studied law and was admitted to the bar in New York City, where he practised in partnership with a former classmate, William Tucker Washburn. Hazeltine was the original of the Sybaritic Harvard junior of *Fair Harvard: A Story of American College Life,* published anonymously by Washburn in 1869. His interest and his success in the law were small. Lawyers said of him that he could draw a will conforming to every principle of Roman jurisprudence, of the common law, of the Code Napoléon, and of the laws of inheritance in every state of the union—and then would forget to have it properly witnessed.

In 1878 he submitted to Charles A. Dana, the editor of the New York *Sun,* specimens of essays and book criticisms and was at once offered the literary editorship, a position which he held until his death more than thirty years later. He brought to his task an erudition and industry akin to genius. His legal training was reflected in his reviewing: his writing was clear, impersonal, and judicial. He was convinced that the reader was interested in the book and its author and not in the personality of the reviewer. In criticising Henry James's *Life of Hawthorne* he said that American criticism to be appropriate or helpful must borrow "the manner of the pedagogue, and not that of the courtier; we need plain speech, not pretty speech." Skilful in paraphrasing, Hazeltine usually brought out the best qualities of the book under notice and with these he quietly merged his own scholarship and knowledge. His reviews became a feature of the Sunday edition of the *Sun* and often occupied an entire page. In 1883 a collection of his reviews was published under the title of *Chats About Books: Poets and Novelists.* His trenchant notice of Henry James's *Life of Hawthorne,* his critical estimate of Longfellow, and his appreciation of Zola are noteworthy among articles marked by their subtlety and penetration. Hazeltine wrote slowly but with a tireless energy. He worked year after year with no vacations except those infrequently necessitated by illness. Though he was always on space compensation his prolific pen brought him moderate wealth. While writing book reviews, special articles, and editorials for the *Sun* he contributed to the *North American Review, Harper's Weekly,* and *Collier's.* His articles were frequently reprinted, the *American Woman in Europe* (1879) and *British and American Education* (1880) achieving a considerable popularity. Few things disturbed the even tenor of his life. He once aspired to a career in statesmanship and unsuccessfully spent thousands of dollars in Staten Island and New Jersey attempting to win nominations that would have opened a career in Congress to him. He married Sophie B. Dallas. In January 1901 while crossing Broadway he was run down by a cab and permanently injured. He died some eight years later in Atlantic City, N. J.

[*Class Report . . . Fiftieth Anniversary . . . Class of 'Sixty-Two Harvard Univ.* (1912); Frank M. O'Brien, *The Story of the Sun, 1833–1928* (1928); Edward Page Mitchell, *Memoirs of an Editor* (1924); *Harper's Weekly,* Sept. 25, 1909; *Sun* (N. Y.), Sept. 15, 16, 1909.]
F. M.

HAZELTON, GEORGE COCHRANE (Jan. 20, 1868–June 24, 1921), actor, lawyer, playwright, novelist, son of George and Ellen (Van Antwerp) Hazelton, was born at Boscobel, Wis. His father was of Scotch-Irish and his mother of Dutch descent. The earlier years of his life were spent in the vicinity of his birthplace where, according to his own statement, he lived mostly out-of-doors, fishing, hunting, and riding. After his father was elected to Congress, he spent his winters in Washington. In 1884 he entered Greylock Institute at South Williamstown, Mass., specializing in the study of Latin and Greek, history and mathematics. After two years at Greylock he matriculated at Columbian (later George Washington) University in Washington. A few years later he decided to become an actor in order to acquaint himself with the technique of the drama, for he had ambitions to become a dramatist. He acted various rôles in Edwin Booth's company and was with Booth in Brooklyn on the occasion of his last appearance in 1891. He subsequently played in Helena Modjeska's company for two seasons, returning after that to Columbian University to study law. He received the degree of LL.B. in 1895 and LL.M. in 1896. In 1897 he published *The National Capitol: Its Architecture, Art, and History.* For some years after he was admitted to the bar he built up a considerable legal practice in Philadelphia and New York, but the persistence of his early desire to write plays at last forced him to give up his practice.

The first of Hazelton's plays to be produced was *The Raven* (1895), a biographical play about Poe which served as the basis for a novel, published in 1909. In October 1901, *Mistress Nell,* one of his most popular dramas, opened with Henrietta Crosman in the title rôle. This he also converted into a novel. Neither *Captain Molly* (1902) nor *The Cracksman* (1908) was very successful in the theatre. But in 1912 came *The Yellow Jacket,* a "play in the Chinese manner," written in collaboration with J. Harry Benrimo. Although it attracted some attention on the occasion of its original production in New York and aroused the enthusiasm of practically all the critics, it was so delicately acted and charmingly unemphatic that it could not attract large paying audiences. Somewhat later it was revived, the acting was made more obvious and "pointed," and the production became financially successful. Besides being translated into a dozen languages and acted in as many foreign countries, it is one of the few plays of American authorship prior to 1920 that deserves to be remembered. Among his last dramatic works was an adaptation of Pierre Louÿs' *Aphrodite,* produced in New York in 1919.

Hazelton can scarcely be classed as a professional playwright. He worked slowly, exercising considerable care over the purely literary side of his work. A romantic by temperament, he was attracted by the more colorful personalities and epochs of history. Neither an original thinker nor a great dramatist, he was none the less a fastidious writer and a picturesque personality. He married Byrd C. Quin in 1899.

[Hazelton left manuscript notes for an autobiography, "My Book," which was neither finished nor published. For printed sources see *Who's Who in America,* 1918–19; W. B. Lapham, *Geneal. Sketches of Robt. and John Hazelton and Some of their Descendants* (1892); *Bookman,* Jan. 1904; *N. Y. Dramatic Mirror,* Nov. 13, 1912; *N. Y. Clipper,* June 29, 1921; *N. Y. Times,* June 25, 1921. Information as to certain facts was supplied for this sketch by Hazelton's widow, Byrd C. Hazelton.]

B. H. C.

HAZELWOOD, JOHN (*c.* 1726–Mar. 1, 1800), Revolutionary naval officer, was born in England, became a mariner early in life, and later emigrated to Pennsylvania. As early as 1753 he was in command of various merchant ships plying between Philadelphia and foreign ports, the *Rebecca,* in 1774, being one of the largest sailing at the time. At the outbreak of the Revolution Pennsylvania sought his services as a naval leader. In July 1775 he assisted the Committee of Safety in the construction of warships, floating batteries, and fire rafts, and also in sinking *chevaux-de-frise* in the Delaware River. On Dec. 28, 1775, he was named captain of ten fire rafts and temporarily superintendent over a fleet of rafts, an appointment made permanent the following June. During 1776 he surveyed the Delaware at Philadelphia and in July went to Poughkeepsie, N. Y., to devise plans for obstructing the North River by fire vessels. For the latter services he received a three-hundred-dollar gift from the convention of New York and the praises of the Secret Committee of Congress. Early in 1777 he was promoted commodore in the Pennsylvania navy, and on Sept. 6, 1777, as Howe was approaching the city, the Pennsylvania Council placed him in full command of the naval forces of the state.

Shortly after entering Philadelphia Howe demanded the surrender of the Pennsylvania fleet. Hazelwood's curt reply that he would defend it to the last extremity so gratified Congress that on Oct. 17 they commended him for his bravery. When the British fleet attempted to pass up the river on Oct. 22, Hazelwood drove them back, destroying two men-of-war and compelling four others to retire. For this conduct Congress presented him with a sword. Later, when Fort Mifflin fell, and the fleet was ordered up the river beyond Philadelphia, he succeeded in conveying thirteen galleys, twelve armed boats, the brig *Convention,* and some minor craft to a refuge above Burlington without having a shot fired at them. Throughout the campaign for the defense of Philadelphia Hazelwood gave ample evidence that he was a daring and brilliant naval officer, skilled in seamanship and naval affairs.

In the summer of 1778, with the British out of Philadelphia, the Assembly decided that a large navy was unnecessary and the fleet was disbanded. Hazelwood, however, retained his rank. Late in 1778, while on furlough, he visited the West Indies on private business. In 1779 he helped to raise money for the army by house-to-house canvass. On June 23, 1780, he was appointed commissioner of purchases for the Continental Army in Philadelphia and in December 1780 receiver of provisions for the Pennsylvania militia. Little is known of his life after the war except that in 1785 he was a port warden in Philadelphia, and that he was owner or part owner of vessels engaged in the foreign trade. He was twice married: on Aug. 10, 1753, to Mary, daughter of Charles Edgar, Philadelphia merchant, and after her death, to Esther, widow of Samuel Leacock and daughter of Plunket Fleeson. Hazelwood's portrait, painted by Peale, was purchased by the city and hung in Independence Hall.

[J. G. Leach, "Commodore John Hazelwood, Commander of the Pa. Navy in the Revolution," *Pa. Mag. of Hist. and Biog.*, Apr. 1902; *Ibid.*, vols. XVIII (1894), and XIX (1895); *Minutes of the Provincial Council of Pa.*, vols. X–XII (1851–52); *Pa. Archives*, 1 ser., vols. V–IX (1853); J. T. Scharf and Thompson Westcott, *Hist. of Phila.* (1884), vol. I; manuscript letters in the Pa. Hist. Soc.]

J. H. P—g.

HAZEN, HENRY ALLEN (Jan. 12, 1849–Jan. 23, 1900), meteorologist, was the son of Reverend Allen Hazen, a missionary of the Congregational Church, and Martha (Chapin) Hazen, and was descended from Edward Hazen who had settled in Rowley, Mass., in 1649. He was born in Sirur, India, about 100 miles east of Bombay, and at ten came to the United States, where he remained the rest of his life. His primary schooling was obtained at St. Johnsbury, Vt., and his academic training at Dartmouth College, where he graduated in 1871. After his graduation he spent one year at the Thayer School of Civil Engineering. During the next four years he was an instructor in drawing in the Sheffield Scientific School, then until 1881 he was assistant at the same institution to Prof. Elias Loomis in physics and meteorology and also aided the latter in the preparation of several of his meteorological papers. In the spring of 1881, Prof. Cleveland Abbe recommended that Hazen be appointed a computer in the "Study Room," a division of the meteorological section of the United States Signal Service, in Washington, established for the purpose of developing the scientific aspects of its work. This appointment was made on May 1, 1881. Later he was promoted, and often took his turn, beginning with October 1887, in making the official forecasts of the weather, and also, beginning with December 1888, in editing the *Monthly Weather Review.* At the same time he assisted in the work of the records division. In July 1891, on the transfer of the meteorological service from the Army to the Department of Agriculture, he was made professor of meteorology in the Weather Bureau, a position of major rank, and was assigned to the forecast division. While hurrying on a bicycle to his duties as forecaster, on the night of Jan. 22, 1900, he was so injured by a collision with a pedestrian, that he became unconscious and passed away the following evening.

During his entire connection with the meteorological service Hazen was exceedingly active in assembling statistics, conducting experiments, and developing theories. One of his publications, *Reduction of Air Pressure to Sea Level* (1882), concerned the difficult problem of finding from the actual readings of barometers what their readings would be under like weather conditions at sea level, a matter essential to the construction of weather maps. Another monograph dealt with the climate of Chicago. He also published a great number of smaller papers, covering a wide range of subjects. His experimental work involved studies on the measurements of humidity, the determination of the dew point, the proper exposure of thermometers to secure accurate values of the temperature of the air, and other instrumental problems. The thermometer shelter he devised was adopted by the Weather Bureau for general use in 1885 because it was both simple and efficient. His theoretical work, also, was voluminous, but in this he was not so successful. Some of his ideas appeared to his less emotional colleagues as no less than wild, but their weaknesses he never would admit. He was an enthusiast in regard to the value of a knowledge of the condition of the free air and made several balloon ascents for the purpose of studying the vertical distribution of temperature and humidity. He was also greatly interested in family history and genealogy and compiled *The Hazen Family: Four American Generations* (1879), which appeared first in the *New-England Historical and Genealogical Register.* He never married.

[Cleveland Abbe, biographical sketch in the *Monthly Weather Rev.*, Jan. 1900; *Who's Who in America*, 1899–1900; *Service in Memory of Henry Allen Hazen* (1900); *U. S. Signal Service Notes*, nos. 6, 7, 15, 20 (1882–85); the *Evening Star* (Washington, D. C.), Jan. 23, 1900; official records of the Weather Bureau.]

W. J. H.

HAZEN, MOSES (June 1, 1733–Feb. 3, 1803), Revolutionary soldier, was born at Haverhill, Mass., the son of Moses and Abigail (White) Hazen, and a descendant of Edward Hazen, who had settled in Rowley in 1649. He served in the French and Indian War, in McCurdie's company of rangers, fighting at Crown Point, Louisburg, and Quebec. When McCurdie died, Hazen became captain of the company and won General Wolfe's commendation. In 1761 he was commissioned lieutenant in the 44th Regiment. Two years later he retired on half pay and settled at St. John's, Quebec, where he became a prosperous farmer and maintained sawmills, a forge, and a potash house. He also had a share in the land grants which his brother William, a trader of Newburyport, had acquired in New Brunswick. In December 1770 he married Charlotte de La Saussaye at Montreal.

When the Revolutionary War began, Hazen fell under suspicion from both sides. In May 1775 he brought to Governor Carleton the news of Arnold's seizure of St. John's; his brother took refuge in New Brunswick in June. Both Montgomery's forces and the Canadian authorities imprisoned him and seized his property, although later Congress indemnified him for his losses. He joined Montgomery and took part in the attack on Quebec and in the siege of Montreal. On the retreat he fell out with Arnold, who found him too independent a subordinate and brought him before a court-martial, but Hazen was honorably acquitted. He spent the winter at Albany, recruiting for the 2nd Canadian Regiment, of which he was made colonel Jan. 22, 1776. The regiment, known as "Congress" or "Hazen's Own," he had raised partly in Canada and among Canadian refugees. It took part in the Staten Island campaign, in the battles of Germantown and Brandywine, and in the siege of Yorktown. Having urged another Canadian campaign, Hazen in 1778 served with General Gates on a board selected to prepare a plan for a second expedition and also gathered stores for that proposed under Lafayette. Though this project was abandoned, he pressed the Vermonters to support the plan and got himself sent north, in the summer of 1779, to begin the construction of a military road to the Canadian border. Later he was recalled to New Jersey, where in addition to his military duties, he was busy securing an acquittal from another court-martial, this time for an infraction of Steuben's discipline, and trying to get funds from Congress to pay the expenses of his soldiers. A week after the Board of Treasury reported that it had no funds, Congress made him a brigadier-general, June 29, 1781. At the close of the war he resigned and settled in Vermont, where he had bought land during the war. He died in Troy, N. Y.

[H. A. Hazen, *The Hazen Family: Four Am. Generations* (1879), reprinted from the *New-Eng. Hist. and Geneal. Reg.*, Apr. 1879; J. H. Smith, *Our Struggle for the Fourteenth Colony* (2 vols., 1907); E. B. O'Callaghan, "Le Brig.-Gen. Moses Hazen," *Bulletin des Recherches Historiques*, May 1901, p. 159; I. W. Hammond, *N. H. State Papers*, vol. XVII (1889); Peter Force, *Am. Archives*, 4 ser., vols. IV–VI (1843–44), 5 ser., vol. I (1848); F. W. Baldwin, "The Hazen Military Road," the *Vermonter*, Nov. 1906.]

E. K. A.
H. C. B.

HAZEN, WILLIAM BABCOCK (Sept. 27, 1830–Jan. 16, 1887), soldier, was in the military service from his entrance to West Point as a cadet in 1851 until his death as brigadier-general and chief signal officer in 1887. He was born in Vermont, a descendant of Edward Hazen who emigrated to the Massachusetts Bay Colony in the seventeenth century and settled at Rowley. He spent his boyhood in Hiram, Ohio, whither his parents Stillman and Sophrona (Fenno) Hazen took him. Here he was brought into a profitable friendship with James A. Garfield. His four years at West Point, 1851–55, were followed by tours of duty in the Far West, where he served creditably in Oregon and Texas. A lucky wound received while on the latter station sent him home on sick leave and thereby enabled him to avoid capture by Confederate forces in the Civil War. He was a captain of infantry in 1861, but before the year was out he, like Garfield, had received his regiment. Hazen became colonel of the 41st Ohio Volunteers and led the regiment into action in the spring of 1862. In command of an infantry brigade he took part on the second day of Shiloh, and he continued active thereafter through the Mississippi movement, Chickamauga, Missionary Ridge, the march through Atlanta to the sea, and the northern march through Columbia. He became a major-general of volunteers after Savannah, but too late to please him for he objected to the prevailing methods of promotion. After the grand review, May 24, 1865, in which he marched at the head of the XV Corps in the Army of the Tennessee, he saw long years of service on the border with the 38th and then with the 6th Infantry. He reverted to the rank of colonel in the regular army, faced Custer, and restrained him from destroying the friendly Kiowa camp near Fort Cobb in 1868 (W. B. Hazen, *Some Corrections of "Life on the Plains,"* 1875), visited Europe as military observer with the German armies in the war of 1870, commanded at Fort Buford, Dakota Territory, in the years thereafter, and wrote pointedly and truthfully of the railroad promoters who were exaggerating the rainfall and fertility of the western plains. (See his report on the plains between Fort Kearney and the Rocky Mountains, *House Executive Document 45*, 39 Cong., 2 Sess., and his letters in the *New York Tribune*, Feb. 7, 1874, Jan. 22, 1876.) He also revealed to Garfield and others, including a committee of the House of Representatives, a belief that the administration of the post-trader system in the War Department was extravagant and corrupt.

The publication of Hazen's comments on War Department corruption (*New York Tribune*, Feb. 16, 1872) had no immediate results, although the *Tribune* declared that an army officer had seen the John S. Evans-Caleb P. Marsh contract respecting the Fort Sill post. But four years later, when a Democratic majority in the House of Representatives was worrying the members of the Grant administration, the story came again to life (*Proceedings of the Senate Sitting for the Trial of William W. Belknap, post,* pp. 718–19). Marsh testified before the House committee on expenditures in the War Department with the result that on Mar. 2, 1876, the impeachment of the secretary of war, William W. Belknap, was demanded by that committee. Grant accepted Belknap's resignation the same day. The impeachment was fatally embarrassed; but Hazen was called upon to testify before the trial was over.

In December 1880 President Hayes appointed Hazen to the post of chief signal officer in the War Department, with the rank of brigadier-general. Here were two inconsistent duties. The business of military signaling had no real connection with that of managing the Weather Bureau, but the two had become attached because of the necessary reliance of the Weather Bureau upon the military telegraphs for data from the Far West. Out of the Weather Bureau came a great controversy and a humiliation. One of the earliest duties of the Signal Corps under Hazen's command was the organization of the scientific expedition under Lieut. A. W. Greely which was sent to Lady Franklin Bay in 1881. Hazen had much upon his conscience the relief expeditions that were to follow it (*Annual Report of the Chief Signal Officer of the Army,* 1882, p. 67, 1883, p. 8, 1884, p. 14). The first relief by the *Neptune* failed in 1882. The second, by the *Proteus,* in 1883, was broken up by ice; and when in September 1883 the party came back to St. John's, Newfoundland, their outfitting place, the Secretary of War decided that it was too late in the year to attempt another relief, and Greely was left with his party for a third winter in the Arctic. When relief under Commander W. S. Schley at last reached Greely, June 22, 1884, only seven of the twenty-five members of his party were alive. Hazen never forgave Secretary Lincoln for inaction in 1883. In his annual report for 1884 Lincoln censured Hazen for his criticism. Hazen replied in a letter to the Secretary which was returned to him with the warning to keep it private. Instead Hazen published a statement that he had written such a letter in the Washington *Evening Star,* Mar. 2, 1885. He was ordered before a general court-martial which convened Mar. 11, 1885, under the presidency of Maj.-Gen. W. S. Hancock, and by sentence of this court he was reprimanded by the President for "unwarranted and captious criticism" of his superior (*New York Herald,* Apr. 18, 1885). Despite the findings of the court-martial, however, the feeling was general among experts, including Greely, that Hazen was clearly in the right. His service in the signal office was only temporarily interrupted by the controversy. He died in 1887, leaving a widow, Mildred McLean, the daughter of Washington McLean of Cincinnati, and one son. He wrote rather freely on controversial matters and published *The School and the Army in Germany and France, with a Diary of Siege Life at Versailles* (1872); *Our Barren Lands: The Interior of the United States West of the 100th Meridian and East of the Sierra Nevadas* (1875); and *A Narrative of Military Service* (1885). He was a conscientious professional officer, strongly opposed to rum in the army, and was convinced that "the iron hand which is just but always firm can alone make soldiers that can be relied upon" (*Narrative of Military Service,* p. 125).

[There are fairly good obituaries in the *N. Y. Times* and *N. Y. Tribune,* Jan. 17, 1887. See also Henry Allen Hazen, *The Hazen Family: Four Am. Generations* (1879); W. H. Tucker, *Hist. of Hartford, Vt.* (1889); *Proc. of the Senate Sitting for the Trial of Wm. W. Belknap, Late Secretary of War* (1876); Frederick Whittaker, *A Complete Life of Gen. Geo. A. Custer* (1876); and T. J. Mackey, *The Hazen Court-Martial* (1885).]

F. L. P.

HEADLEY, JOEL TYLER (Dec. 30, 1813–Jan. 16, 1897), author, was born at Walton, Delaware County, N. Y., the son of Isaac and Irene (Benedict) Headley, and by family tradition a descendant of Leonard Headley, who emigrated from England to New Jersey in 1665. Phineas Camp Headley [*q.v.*] was his younger brother. Graduating from Union College in 1839, he studied at Auburn Theological Seminary, was licensed to preach in New York, and was called to a New York church. Because of poor health his physician dissuaded him from accepting, but, reluctant to abandon the profession of his father, he accepted a small charge at Stockbridge, Mass. After several years he suffered a complete breakdown and in the summer of 1842 went to Italy. To New York newspapers he contributed travel letters that achieved considerable popularity and were republished as *Italy and the Italians* (1844). In Europe his health had grown worse and, returning to America, he definitely gave up the ministry. The success of his book had made him an author, and a second volume, *Letters from Italy,* appeared in 1845. Having succeeded Henry J. Raymond, in 1846, as associate editor of the *New York Tribune,* he devoted himself assiduously to journalism and to popular historical writing. *Napoleon and his Marshals* (2 vols., 1846) and *Washington and his Generals* (2 vols., 1847) were quickly and widely successful. An attack on the brain induced him to spend the summer of 1847 in the Adirondacks, then a wild and little-known region. He returned the following summer; his many letters describing the beauty and predicting the popularity of the region were collected under the title *The Adirondack* (1849). Despite his poor health Headley for almost half a century applied amazing and unwearied industry to the production of printed matter. In May 1850 he married Anna Allston Russel and settled at Newburgh, N. Y. In 1854 he served a term as a member of the New York Assembly and, elected the following year on the Know-Nothing ticket, served as secretary of state from 1855 to 1858. His later life, spent in editing and writing, passed quietly at his home in Newburgh, where he died in 1897.

Prolific and popular, he produced during his long career more than thirty biographies, histories, and books of travel. Their patriotic, moral tone and sweet vivacity appealed to many thousands. In 1853 his books had reached a total sale of 200,000 volumes; eight years later *Napoleon and his Marshals* had gone into a fiftieth edition. In 1866 the New York *Nation* remarked that *Washington and his Generals* was one of the five secular books to be found on the typical American bookshelf. While a large public regarded him as a scholar and a historian, many of his books were mere compilations without taste, judgment, or insight. His vivid, nervous style often sank to bombast and prolixity, as in his *Sacred Mountains* (1847) which Edgar Allan Poe declared was "written in that kind of phraseology in which John Philpot Curran, when drunk, would have made a speech at a public dinner." Headley's industry and enthusiasm were but little compensation for his lack of training; Poe dubbed him "The Autocrat of all the Quacks."

[A. J. Fretz, *A Geneal. Record of the Descendants of Leonard Headley* (1905); H. M. Benedict, *The Geneal. of the Benedicts in America* (1870); *N. Y. Tribune,* Jan. 17, 1897; *Critic,* Jan. 23, Feb. 13, 1897; *U. S. Mag. and Democratic Rev.,* Sept. 1845, Oct. 1848; E. A. Poe, *Southern Lit. Messenger,* Oct. 1850; private information.]

F. M.

HEADLEY, PHINEAS CAMP (June 24, 1819–Jan. 5, 1903), clergyman, writer of popular biographies, was the son of Rev. Isaac and Irene (Benedict) Headley. The former was pastor of the Congregational church of Walton, N. Y., from 1813 to 1829, and in this town Phineas was born. His older brother, Joel Tyler Headley [*q.v.*], also became widely known as a writer. Phineas had rather limited educational opportunities, but when he was twenty-eight years old, having studied for a time in the law office of Hon. Walter Hubbell of Auburn, N. Y., he was admitted to the bar. Yielding to his mother's wishes, and to certain religious proclivities of his own, he soon turned to the ministry and entered Auburn Theological Seminary, from which he graduated in 1850. Amherst College conferred the degree of A.M. upon him in 1859. The year of his graduation from Auburn he took charge of the Presbyterian church in Adams, N. Y., where in 1851 he was ordained by the Watertown Presbytery. On May 13 of this year he married Dora C. Bartlett of New Bedford, Mass. He left Adams in 1854, and his subsequent pastorates were in West Sandwich, Mass., 1854–57; Greenfield, Mass., 1857–61; and Plymouth, Mass., 1861.

From the beginning of his ministry he gave much time to writing. After 1861 he devoted himself for many years almost wholly to this work, residing in Boston until 1894, and thereafter in Lexington, Mass. His confessed purpose was to portray persons of historical significance in a way adapted to the popular mind. A moral and patriotic motive was also present, though never in an offensive degree. A number of his books were written for boys, both to give them information and to inspire them to noble deeds. He was a wide reader but in no sense a critical scholar. Using easily available material, he wrote in a clear, facile, and sometimes picturesque style. His first published work was *Historical and Descriptive Sketches of the Women of the Bible* (1850). Following this in rapid succession came, *The Life of the Empress Josephine* (1850), *The Life of General Lafayette* (1851), *The Life of Louis Kossuth* (1852), *The Life of Mary Queen of Scots* (1857), *The Life of Napoleon Bonaparte* (1859). His Young Folks' Heroes of the Rebellion series includes lives of Generals Grant, Sherman, Sheridan, and Mitchel, and of Admiral Farragut and John Ericsson. Among his other publications were *Massachusetts in the Rebellion* (1866), *The Island of Fire; or a Thousand Years of the Old Northmen's Home* (1875), and *Public Men of Today* (1882).

[See *Gen. Biog. Cat. Auburn Theol. Sem., 1818–1918* (1918); *Who's Who in America,* 1901–02; A. J. Fretz, *A Geneal. Record of the Descendants of Leonard Headley* (1905); *Boston Transcript,* Jan. 5, 1903. *Who's Who in America* gives the date of Headley's birth as June 29; all other sources as June 24.]

H. E. S.

HEALY, GEORGE PETER ALEXANDER (July 15, 1813–June 24, 1894), portrait painter, was born in Boston, Mass., the eldest son of William Healy, a sea-captain of Irish descent, and Mary Hicks. While George was still young his father died, and he was obliged to support his mother and his younger brothers and sister until after his marriage. His artistic talent appeared in marked degree early in life. Encouraged by Sully, at eighteen he opened a Boston studio and the next year he was exhibiting his paintings. He is said to have got his start as a portrait painter through the kindness of Mrs. Harrison Gray Otis, who permitted Healy to paint her and brought him other patronage. In 1834 he set out for Paris to continue his studies. Though he possessed no knowledge of French, he was admitted to the studio of Baron Gros, shortly before the latter's death, and while working under him met Thomas Couture with whom he later formed a close friendship. In England he met Louisa Phipps, whom he married.

Healy remained in Paris, where he developed a large patronage and painted portraits with astonishing ease. His reputation brought him distinguished subjects, including the king, Louis-Philippe, Lewis Cass, the American minister, Marshal Soult, François Guizot, and Léon Gambetta. In 1855 he received a medal at the Universal Exposition for his tremendous composition, "Franklin Urging the Claims of the American Colonies before Louis XVI," which he exhibited along with a number of portraits. In the same year, 1855, he returned to the United States and established himself in Chicago. His family followed him in 1856 and the next year, with them, he moved into the country. During his stay he was made a member of the National Academy of Design. When he returned to Europe, some ten years after his coming to Chicago, he had painted more than five hundred portraits as well as historical and genre subjects.

After a year in Paris, Healy went to Rome in 1867. While he was there he was invited to contribute a portrait of himself to the collection of self-portraits in the Uffizi Gallery in Florence—the first American to receive the honor. In 1873 he returned to Paris, remaining there until 1892. By that time he had become aware of the changed outlook on art, and feeling out of sympathy with the new men, he returned to Chicago. There he died two years later. His pictures hang in representative American and European galleries. Several portraits, including one of Daniel Webster and one of Longfellow, were acquired by the Boston Museum of Fine Arts. His series of the presidents hangs in the Corcoran Gallery, Washington, and a portrait of Chief Justice Taney is in the Capitol. Others of his works were acquired by the Art Institute of Chicago and by the Metropolitan Museum, New York. His best-known historical composition, "Webster Replying to Hayne," hangs in Faneuil Hall, Boston. In the year of his death he published *Reminiscences of a Portrait Painter.* Healy was a facile rather than a subtle artist. His knack of catching a likeness made him acceptable to a generation of Americans who asked of a portraitist little more than a gift for getting a resemblance and a certain polish of workmanship.

[In addition to Healy's *Reminiscences* see Mary Bigot (Healy's daughter), *Life of Geo. P. A. Healy* (n.d.); H. T. Tuckerman, *Book of the Artists* (1867); *Biog. Sketches of the Leading Men of Chicago* (1868); *Chicago Tribune,* June 25, 1894.]

W. P.

HEAP, SAMUEL DAVIES (Oct. 8, 1781–Oct. 2, 1853), naval surgeon, consul, was born at Carlisle, Pa., the son of Judge John Heap and Margaret (Kerr) Heap. His grandfather, George, was sent by the British government to Pennsylvania as an assistant surveyor-general, and made one of the earliest known maps of Philadelphia. Graduating from the Jefferson College of Medicine, Philadelphia, in 1803, Samuel received a commission in the United States navy as surgeon's mate on Apr. 5, 1804, and on June 17, 1808, was promoted to surgeon. During the following years he was stationed at various times at New Orleans, Norfolk, Boston, and Philadelphia. In 1817 he was ordered to the Mediterranean to take charge of the hospital of the American fleet in those waters. He conceived a desire to enter the consular service at one of the Mediterranean ports, and when Major Stith, American consul at Tunis, retired unexpectedly in 1823, Heap was appointed chargé d'affaires.

Arriving at Tunis in December, his first act was to settle with dispatch a troublesome misunderstanding with the local government. At his second audience with the Bey, on Jan. 24, 1824, he took advantage of a favorable opening in the conversation to propose an amendment to the treaty of 1797 between the United States and Tunis, which contained some objectionable clauses. Negotiations went swiftly forward, and exactly a month later the new treaty was signed. This brought him criticism from various quarters. It was asserted that he had had no diplomatic experience; that he was too simple to match his wits against the wily Barbary traders; that a treaty so speedily and informally concluded must be open to suspicion; that he had no authority to negotiate a treaty at all. The administration at Washington officially indorsed his action, however; the Senate ratified the treaty;

and it stood without further amendment for eighty years, being superseded in 1904 by a treaty with France, after Tunis had become one of its colonies. It appears clear that Heap had won the confidence and friendship of the Tunisians by an attitude which they had too rarely experienced from Western representatives. He was frank, sincere, and scrupulously fair. "He walked in a straight line," they said. Although firm when occasion demanded, his manner was warmed by a tolerant sympathy and genuine friendliness, without a trace of the suspicious or patronizing. "I have not only avoided collision with this government," he truthfully wrote the Secretary of State later in his career, "but have preserved our relations with it upon the most friendly footing."

Heap's first appointment at Tunis was of brief duration. A consul was sent out from Washington and took over the office in December 1824. The following November, however, he received a permanent appointment to the Tunis consulate, which continued to the end of his life except for two intervals when new consuls were appointed in his place. Each of the four times he came to Tunis he was obliged to smooth out a ruffled situation left by his immediate predecessor. When, in 1852, the consul who had displaced him died in office, the Bey of Tunis paid Heap the honor of petitioning the President for his return. He was appointed on Mar. 16, 1853, and proceeded to his post; but late in the summer he was stricken with paralysis, and after a month's illness he died. He was buried in the Protestant cemetery at Tunis. In 1810 he married Margaret Porter, a sister of Commodore Porter. Five children were born to them.

[*Am. State Papers, Foreign Relations,* vol. V (1858); T. H. S. Hamersly, *Gen. Reg. of the U. S. Navy and Marine Corps* (1882); *Memoirs of John Quincy Adams,* vol. XI (1876); official correspondence in Office of Library and Records and the Navigation Bureau of U. S. Navy Dept., and in the archives of the U. S. Dept. of State; information from Mrs. Evelina Heap Gleaves of Philadelphia, Pa.] I. L. T.

HEARD, AUGUSTINE (Mar. 30, 1785–Sept. 14, 1868), sea-captain and merchant, was the fifth of the eight children of John Heard and Sally Staniford, his father's second wife. He was born at Ipswich, Mass., where his father was a leading ship-owner and merchant dealing in the West Indies and China. The elder Heard was also prominent in state politics and served as a state senator and as chief justice. Augustine entered Phillips Exeter Academy in 1799, but it does not appear that he was graduated from that institution. In 1803 he was in the employ of Ebenezer Francis, one of the principal merchants of Boston, and in his twentieth year, 1805, he sailed to Calcutta as supercargo of a vessel belonging to his employer. He was absent two years on this voyage. He continued to go to sea, and on Feb. 18, 1812, in the brig *Caravan,* he sailed for the first time as master, being both captain and supercargo. On this voyage eighty thousand dollars in cargo and treasure were entrusted to his care. His skill as a navigator and success as a merchant were of such a high order that he soon became one of the foremost captains in the East-India trade, and he had the choice of some of the best ships trading with the Orient.

He had been able to build up a comfortable fortune through his numerous ventures, and in 1829 he completed his active sea career. On June 7, 1830, while in his forty-sixth year, he sailed for Canton to become a partner in the famous firm of Samuel Russell & Company, in which he had a three-sixteenths' interest. His work was marked with success, but being in bad health he returned to America in 1834 at the end of his term. He then settled in Boston, from which city he directed his business and investments. Owing to internal friction, Russell & Company was reorganized in 1840, and the new firm of Augustine Heard & Company was established with Joseph Coolidge, formerly of Russell & Company, as the active partner in Canton. In 1841, Heard returned to China to assume charge of the business there, taking with him his nephew, John Heard, who later became the managing partner in Canton. The Opium War was in progress when Heard arrived, and during the period of hostilities his place of business was attacked by a mob which caused him serious loss, although his coolness and fearlessness enabled him to save a large share of his goods and specie. Later he was compensated for his loss by the Chinese government. Carrying on the general merchant and commission business common to the China merchants of his day, he had the confidence and respect of the Chinese, as well as of his competitors and employees. In contrast to the sharp practices of the small firms, he maintained high standards of business in conjunction with the few large houses at Canton. With those of Samuel Russell, D. W. C. Olyphant [*q.v.*], and W. S. Wetmore, his firm was one of the four American houses to survive the competition of decades at Canton. In that highly individualistic period of American foreign policy, it had an important influence in shaping the Far Eastern policy of his government.

Heard returned to America in 1844 and never again went to China, although he made several trips to Europe. Each of his four nephews, however, served his turn as manager of the firm in China, and the second of them, Augustine Heard, was American minister to Korea from 1890 to 1893. As long as Heard lived, the business was very profitable, but after the Civil War it suffered from the same deleterious conditions that affected all American firms in the Orient. In 1828 with his brother, G. W. Heard, and Joseph Farley he incorporated the Ipswich Manufacturing Company and in 1852 became sole owner. He founded and endowed the Ipswich Public Library. Never marrying, he devoted his affections to his friends and relatives, whom he assisted in numerous quiet ways. He died at Ipswich in the same house in which he was born.

[The chief published source, which is based on a collection of letters in the possession of the Heard family, is Thos. Franklin Waters, "Augustine Heard and His Friends," *Ipswich Hist. Soc. Pubs.*, XXI (1916); *Boston Transcript*, Sept. 14, 1868; R. B. Forbes, *Personal Reminiscences* (3rd ed., 1892); T. F. Waters, *Ipswich in the Mass. Colony*, vol. II (1917).]

H. J. N.

HEARD, DWIGHT BANCROFT (May 1, 1869–Mar. 14, 1929), investment banker, farmer, publisher, nephew of Franklin Fiske Heard [*q.v.*], was born in Boston, Mass., the son of Leander Bradford and Lucy (Bancroft) Heard. He was a descendant of Zachariah Heard, born in 1675, who lived in Cambridge and later in Sudbury, now Wayland, Mass. Leander Heard was engaged in the wholesale grocery business and was especially interested in building up trade with the West. Dwight received a public-school education which terminated in the Brookline, Mass., high school, and at the age of seventeen he went to work for the wholesale hardware firm of Hibbard, Spencer & Bartlett, Chicago. On Aug. 10, 1893, he married Maie Pitkin Bartlett, daughter of A. C. Bartlett, president of the firm. One child, a son, was born to them.

Because of impaired health Heard went to the Southwest in 1894, and, after spending some time in Texas, in 1895 he settled in Phoenix, Ariz. Here he engaged in the investment and loan business and in farming. His principal interests were the Dwight B. Heard Investment Company, and the Bartlett-Heard Land & Cattle Company, the holdings of which included 7,000 acres of land near Phoenix. This land was intensively cultivated with a view to turning it into small homesteads, a purpose which Heard lived to see well on the way toward realization. Upon the affairs of the growing territory he exerted a dominating influence. He was one of the Western leaders in the movement resulting in the United States Reclamation Act of 1902, the first undertaking under which was the Roosevelt project in the Salt River Valley, Ariz. He took an energetic part in opposing a bill for the admission of Arizona and New Mexico into the Union as one state; attended and read a paper at the conference of governors called by President Roosevelt in 1908 to consider measures for the conservation of natural resources; and was active in various phases of war work during the World War. In 1912 he was a delegate to the Republican National Convention, and one of the signers of the call for the Progressive Convention, to which also he was a delegate. This same year his interest in the Progressive movement led him to secure control of the *Arizona Republican*. He was interested in politics only as a part of good citizenship. In 1924 he accepted the Republican nomination for governor of Arizona and was defeated by a majority of 800, although the normal opposition majority was 15,000. He was one of the foremost advocates of the development of the Colorado River with full protection of Arizona's rights. From 1914 to 1917 he was president of the American National Live Stock Association, and was long a member of the United States Chamber of Commerce, serving as a director and as chairman of the agricultural division. Among his manifold activities was that of promoting the cultivation of long staple cotton in Arizona. In the interest of this enterprise he visited Egypt, and published "Cotton and the Sudan" in the *American Review of Reviews*, July 1926, a periodical to which he was an occasional contributor. Interested in American antiquities, he had in his private museum a considerable collection of New England antiquities and specimens of the crafts of primitive peoples.

[J. H. Edwards, *A Hist. of the Heard Family of Wayland, Mass.* (1880); J. H. McClintock, *Arizona*, vol. III (1916), pp. 434–36; *Hist. of Ariz.* (1930), III, IV; *Who's Who in America*, 1928–29; *Ariz. Republican*, Mar. 15, 1929.]

J. W. S.

HEARD, FRANKLIN FISKE (Jan. 17, 1825–Sept. 29, 1889), legal author, was born in East Sudbury, now Wayland, Mass., a descendant of Zachariah Heard (b. 1675) of Cambridge and Sudbury, and an uncle of Dwight Bancroft Heard [*q.v.*]. His father was Jonathan Fiske Heard, a wheelwright, and his mother, Harriet Stratton, formerly of Weston. He graduated from Harvard College in 1848, studied law at Wayland under Judge Edward Mellen, and was admitted to the bar at Concord in 1850. After five years' practice in Framingham, he removed to Boston where he spent most of his active life. From about 1884 he practised law at his residence in Saxonville, Mass. In his practice Heard was prominent in the argument of questions of law in appellate cases and particularly excelled in the preparation of civil and criminal cases for trial and argument, for which he was much used by other lawyers. He was accurate in his methods and was said to have a more intimate knowledge of books and cases than any other lawyer in Boston, and to possess an exhaustive familiarity with the criminal law. He held no office except for a brief service as assistant district attorney of Middlesex County.

He began the authorship of legal works soon after his admission to the bar by editing Daniel Davis' *Practical Treatise upon the Authority and Duty of Justices of the Peace in Criminal Prosecutions* (3rd ed., 1853), and later published over twenty books, besides acting as associate editor of the *Monthly Law Reporter* from 1861 until its expiration in 1866. His publications include: *A Treatise on the Law of Libel and Slander* (1860), the first American work on this subject; *Criminal Abortion* (1868), with Dr. Horatio R. Storer; *The Principles of Criminal Pleading* (1879); *A Practical Treatise on the Authority and Duties of Trial Justices, District, Police, and Municipal Courts* (1879), a second edition under the title, *Heard on the Criminal Law*, appearing in 1882; *Pleading in Civil Actions* (1880); *A Concise Treatise on the Principles of Equity Pleading* (1882); *Precedents of Equity Pleadings* (1884); besides editions of others' writings and collaborative books. He varied his technical labors by editing *Bacon's Essays, with Annotations by Richard Whately* (1868); by collecting amusing cases in his *Curiosities of the Law Reporters* (1871) and *Oddities of the Law* (1881); and by writing *The Legal Acquirements of William Shakespeare* (1865) which was enlarged and published under the title, *Shakespeare as a Lawyer* (1883), in which legal passages in the plays are brought together with interesting but not profound comments. His more serious books must be valued largely for the useful service which they performed to the legal profession of his own time. Like most legal treatises they have been almost entirely superseded by statutory changes and by the accumulation of subsequent judicial decisions. Heard's chosen field of procedure has been nearly made over since he wrote. His books were not saved from this general oblivion by any novelty of approach or comprehensive reasoning, and they have had little influence on the writings of later men. Probably his only treatise still to be consulted is *Equity Pleading*, a clear and concise statement of the principles of a branch of procedure which has met with little alteration in states where suits in equity have not been abolished.

Like his father, who had been violinist in the Wayland Unitarian Church, Heard was proficient in music and was an excellent organist. He was twice married: first, Apr. 24, 1855, to Harriet Hildreth of Lowell, Mass., a sister of Mrs. Benjamin F. Butler, who died in 1866, leaving a daughter; and second, Apr. 5, 1868, to Martha B. Stone of Saxonville, Mass., by whom he had a son. Heard died in a hospital at Boston.

[J. H. Edwards, *Hist. of the Heard Family of Wayland, Mass.* (1880); *Wayland, Mass., Vital Records to 1850* (1910); obituary notices in *Boston Advertiser* and *Boston Post*, Oct. 1, and *Boston Transcript*, Oct. 5, 1889; manuscript records of Harvard Class of 1848 (Widener Library).]

Z. C., Jr.

HEARN, LAFCADIO (June 27, 1850–Sept. 26, 1904), author, was the son of Charles Bush Hearn, surgeon-major in the British army. There was English, Irish and a touch of Gypsy in the Dorsetshire family of his father, who, ordered to duty on the Grecian island of Santa Maura, there met and married a lovely Greek girl, Rosa Tessima, whose family probably had a strain of Arab and Moorish blood. Patricio Lafcadio Tessima Carlos Hearn was born of this union. When he was two years old his father, ordered to the West Indies, deposited his wife and child with relatives in Dublin. Mrs. Hearn, impetuous and extremely high-tempered, found the environment impossible and eventually fled—it is hinted with a former lover—leaving Lafcadio, now aged seven, to the none too tender mercy of his father's aunt, Mrs. Brenane, a bigoted convert to Catholicism. The boy spent a lonely childhood in her big house until, in 1863, she decided to educate him, presumably for the priesthood, and sent him to St. Cuthbert's College, England. Here an accident occurred that embittered his whole life. While he was playing "Giant's Stride," the handle on the end of a rope flew back, struck him in the face, and destroyed the sight of his left eye, leaving the iris covered with a milky film. Always an omnivorous reader, he so abused the other eye that it became permanently swollen to twice its normal size and its vision was impaired. A nervous breakdown ensued, and as a result he developed the morbid obsession of being physically repulsive to every one, especially women—an inferiority complex he never overcame.

Hearn's father remarried and Mrs. Brenane lost her fortune; so, when Lafcadio was expelled from St. Cuthbert's for some trifling insubordination and had later run away from a Jesuit school in France, Mrs. Brenane determined to free herself from her burden by paying his passage to New York. He arrived there in 1869, friendless, half-blind, shy—grotesquely unfitted to cope with a strange environment. For a while he earned a bare living by menial jobs such as waiting in a cheap restaurant, and finally went to Cincinnati. Again he suffered hardships, sleeping half-starved in haylofts or in rusty boilers junked in vacant lots. He was a messenger boy for a day, and a job of peddling mirrors for a Syrian was equally transient. Always improvident and impractical, he was discharged from a position in the Public Library because he read so much that he neglected his work. By good fortune he made a real friend—Henry Watkin, a kindly old English printer, who let him sleep in his shop, taught him to set type and finally got him his first position on a paper, the *Trade List.* Hearn soon gave this up to do feature articles for the Sunday *Cincinnati Enquirer* (1873). They were written not in journalese but in pure literary English and gave evidence of indefatigable reading. By 1874 he was a full-fledged reporter and had made a reputation by the gruesomely vivid way in which he had covered a particularly revolting murder. His three intimate friends were Henry Edward Krehbiel [*q.v.*], a reporter on a rival newspaper, from whom he learned much about music, and two artists, Frank Duveneck [*q.v.*] and H. F. Farney. With the latter he embarked in the publication, as a side issue, of a short-lived weekly—*Ye Giglampz,* for which he supplied well-written but *macabre* articles.

From his Greek mother Hearn had inherited a love of the beautiful and, possibly, his marked lubricity. It was natural, therefore, that the French Romanticists—especially Flaubert, Gautier, and Baudelaire with their elaborate sensuality and the thrice-polished beauty of their craftsmanship—should enthrall him. At odd times he made a painstaking translation of Gautier's *Avatar,* but destroyed it, knowing it could never be published in that period of virtuous surfaces and fatuous blindness to facts. It was not time wasted, however, for this practice immeasurably refined and enriched his style. Possibly through Baudelaire's example, or because the outlets for his own sexuality were circumscribed by poverty and the obsession that he was repulsive to women, he lived openly with a mulattress and was only prevented from marrying her by the law against miscegenation. The resulting scandal caused his dismissal from the *Enquirer,* but the *Cincinnati Commercial* immediately employed him. During his years in Cincinnati he had worked twelve to sixteen hours a day as a reporter and in addition translated from the French. Under this terrific strain his health broke, and in 1877, sick and semi-ostracized on account of his liaison, he decided to go to New Orleans, the *Commercial* commissioning him to write of political conditions in Louisiana.

As he scoured that semi-tropical city, on fire with curiosity and enthusiasm, he must have been a strange figure. He was only five feet three inches tall; the peajacket he affected was much too large and his very low collar with its black string tie much too big, giving him the appearance of a miniature but serious-minded scarecrow. His hands were delicate and well-bred, and his coarse boots could not quite hide the fact that his feet were small. A species of railroad conductor's cap concealed his intellectual forehead, the visor casting into friendly shadow his abnormal eyes. The nose was hawk-like, with nostrils finely chiseled, and a long brown mustache hid a sensuously sensitive mouth. He suggested a small, shy, studious, shipwrecked sailor.

His descriptions of the city, signed "Ozias Midwinter," were charming but made no mention of politics—an omission which caused his dismissal and stranded him a penniless stranger in New Orleans. An appalling yellow-fever epidemic broke out; people fled the city; he could find no employment. He almost died of dengue and starvation, and it was seven months before he got work on the *Item.* His unhappy experiences, coupled with an inherent love of children and animals, intensified his sympathy for the oppressed, and he wrote editorials against child labor, police extortion, vivisection, and lynching. He contributed book reviews, a column, in all seriousness, of advice to young people, delightful bits of translation from contemporary French literature, and a series of eerie short stories which he called "Fantastics." He worked so painstakingly that every article helped, as an exercise, to develop the faultless literary style of his maturity.

Never happy long in one place, he hankered for the West Indies and to finance the voyage started a five-cent restaurant called the "Hard Times." When his partner disappeared with the cash and the cook, Hearn lost all his savings. Two leading papers were merged into the *Times-Democrat* in 1881 and offered him a larger salary. Realizing his value, they gave him only congenial work, editorials and a Sunday feature called the "Foreign Press." Under this heading he published splendid translations of the most imaginative and curious specimens of French and Spanish literature encountered in his reading. His initial book, *One of Cleopatra's Nights* (1882), an almost perfect rendering of six of Gautier's stories, was an outgrowth of this work. His leisure and money having increased, he combed the world for books on all sorts of strange and exotic subjects, especially folklore. These studies were reflected in a series of articles, the best of which were afterwards published as *Stray Leaves from Strange Literatures* (1884). *Gombo Zhèbes* (1885), a collection of proverbs in the French patois of the negroes of Louisiana and the West Indies, followed and at the same time appeared anonymously *La Cuisine Créole* (1885), for which he had supplied the recipes and an introduction. Already the *Century Magazine* and *Harper's Weekly* had accepted work, and he was becoming known in New York. In 1887 *Some Chinese Ghosts,* a group of beautifully polished Oriental legends, was published, and *Harper's Magazine* accepted his first novel "Chita," a tale of the terrible tidal wave that swept Last Island. He imagined he could earn his salt in the North, his reborn Wanderlust persuading him that he had sucked New Orleans dry of inspiration.

That spring he arrived in New York and stayed at the apartment of his friend Krehbiel, now music critic of the *Tribune.* Such a confined, well-ordered life could not hold Hearn long, and he yearned again for the tropics. Krehbiel introduced him to Henry Mills Alden, editor of *Harper's,* who commissioned him to do articles on the West Indies. He made the trip, returning in the autumn fascinated with the country, and the sketches were a great success. New York, however, appalled him as usual with its noise and immensity. His friends were out of town, and his near blindness made it almost impossible for him to get about. Hating it all and yearning for the peace and brilliant sunshine of Martinique, he decided to return on the same steamer that brought him. Memories of the "waspcolored" bodies of the sensuous but childlike women of the islands may have had a secret pull, for his inferiority complex made social intercourse with his equals, except in the case of a few old friends, much too painful. It is probable that he found in these golden women of an inferior race a *milieu* he could frequent without pain, and that this was a major part of the lure that kept him a romantic wanderer. Having no contract for his literary output, he led a precarious existence in Martinique for two and a half years, dependent for weeks at a time upon the charity of colored persons. Nevertheless, the country and its people enchanted him and the articles which *Harper's* accepted, later published as *Two Years in the French West Indies* (1890), reflect this fascination in every line. They still remain the most perfect picture of the islands that has yet been painted. He also wrote *Youma* (1890), a novel of the slave insurrection.

In the spring of 1889 he returned to New York, going almost immediately to Philadelphia to visit George Milbry Gould [*q.v.*], an oculist with whom he had been in correspondence, although they had never met. His host, educated for the ministry, undertook to reform this Latin-minded man of forty and force him to write of moral conflicts in which virtue was invariably the victor. *Karma* was the only *opus* produced under this influence, and was Hearn's worst. Realizing this, and having developed a grievance against the doctor, he returned to New York, as usual almost penniless. After a few months he decided to go to Japan and made certain arrangements with the Harpers. C. D. Weldon was to accompany him. To gather funds he sold several magazine articles and translated Anatole France's *Le Crime de Sylvestre Bonnard* in the short space of two weeks, for which he received one hundred dollars. Weldon and Hearn started in March 1890, and they had no sooner arrived than Hearn developed one of the delusions of persecution to which he was subject. Imagining that Alden and the Harpers were plotting to hold him a literary slave at starvation wages, he wrote a most insulting communication severing his connection with the firm. Prof. Basil Hall Chamberlain of Tokio University, to whom he had brought a letter, obtained for him a position as teacher in a school at Matsue, a small town in which many feudal customs survived. This experience provided him with material for *Glimpses of Unfamiliar Japan* (1894). Becoming ill again as a result of his past overwork, privations, and excesses, he realized that, were he to continue writing, he must have care. When a fellow teacher suggested that he take to wife Setsuko Koizumi, the twenty-two-year-old daughter of an excellent though impoverished Samurai family, he married her in 1891. He adopted Japanese dress in his home and became a model of connubial faithfulness.

As the winters in Matsue had been very cold, seriously affecting his constitution accustomed to tropical heat, he had applied for a transfer and, before the birth of his first son, Kazuo, in 1893, had moved to the Government College at Kumamoto. His entire energies were now devoted to providing for the future of his family, greatly increased by the addition of Mrs. Hearn's relatives. He discovered that if he formally registered her as his wife, she would be considered a foreigner, forced, in the event of his death, to live in the open ports cut off from her kin, and that his son also would suffer from certain legal drawbacks. To solve this tangle he became a Japanese citizen and took the name of Koizumi Yakumo. Since native teachers received a much smaller salary than foreigners, Hearn's stipend was reduced when he became naturalized. This preyed upon his mind and seemed to turn his admiration and affection for the Japanese into dislike and suspicion. After teaching at Kumamoto for three years he resigned and joined the staff of the *Kobe Chronicle* in 1894. The work proving too arduous, Chamberlain secured him the chair of English Literature at the Imperial University of Tokio, which he occupied until 1903. His lectures were published posthumously from verbatim transcripts by his students and make four volumes of splendid informative criticism.

He had become homesick and dissatisfied and for over a year had been trying to obtain work in the United States. Cornell University offered him $2,500 for a series of lectures. He prepared them, but before they were finished the invitation was withdrawn. The rejected lectures were later published as *Japan: An Attempt at Interpretation* (1904). This was the summation of all his sympathetic and acute observation of Japan. His previous books, he had been averaging one a year, had presented the minutiae of life and custom, and details concerning birds, insects, cats, and flowers. His last book was the essence of all Japan, a real interpretation of the mind and soul of the people of his adoption. He did not live to see it in final form, dying on Sept. 26, 1904, of a heart attack, leaving a widow, three sons, and a daughter.

Hearn's achievement of writing twelve distinguished books about a country whose language he had never learned was possible only because he supplemented his own talent for microscopic observation by employing his wife and his students to gather the raw material which he so carefully refined—even to the point of once working eight months to perfect seventy-three lines. He had a genius for choosing harmonious words with which to convey imponderable niceties of meaning, and, of all modern writers in English, his prose was possibly the most polished, beautiful, lyrical. This should have classed him with the immortals had it not been that his judgments were too often the children of his prejudices, and that he lacked too much in breadth of view, ordinary common sense, and knowledge of human nature for his message to be of first importance to mankind. Even though Hearn possibly overromanticized his picture of Japan—he has been accused of being a chameleon who reflected stronger colors than were found in the actual pigments of his background—he nevertheless rendered a signal service to international amity, interpreting the East to the West, and the West to the East.

[Elizabeth Bisland, *The Life and Letters of Lafcadio Hearn* (1906) and *The Japanese Letters of Lafcadio Hearn* (1910); Henry Watkin, *Letters from the Raven* (1907); G. M. Gould, *Concerning Lafcadio Hearn* (1908), with bibliog. by Laura Stedman; Yone Noguchi, *Lafcadio Hearn in Japan* (1911); N. H. Kennard, *Lafcadio Hearn* (1911); E. L. Tinker, *Lafcadio Hearn's Am. Days* (1924); Oscar Lewis, *Hearn and his Biographers: The Record of a Lit. Controversy* (1930).]

E. L. T.

HEARST, GEORGE (Sept. 3, 1820–Feb. 28, 1891), mining prospector, mine-owner, senator from California, was identified with the growth of that state from the time of his arrival there in October 1850. His father, William G. Hearst, had married Elizabeth Collins of Georgia and had gone to Missouri from South Carolina in 1808. George Hearst, born near Sullivan, Franklin County, Mo., attended the public schools and the Franklin County Mining School, and, upon the death of his father in 1846, inherited the latter's farm property. Leaving Missouri, however, four years later, he crossed the plains on foot beside an ox-wagon, and, arriving in California, turned first to quartz-mining, and later to placer mining. His success was not marked until 1859, when, speculating on the rich finds in western Nevada, he laid the foundations of a great fortune. Gradually his many interests spread to other states, as well as into Mexico, where the principal mine was San Luis at San Dimas, in the state of Durango. Among his famous holdings were the Ophir in Nevada, the Ontario in Utah, the Homestake in South Dakota, and the Anaconda in Montana. His chief business associates were James Ben Ali Haggin, Lloyd Tevis, and in later years, Marcus Daly [*qq.v.*]. In 1866 and again in 1874 his financial condition became precarious, but in each case he recovered. He came to know from personal observation most of the country west of the great plains. This firsthand knowledge, of which he was proud, gave him influence with his allies in business and later with his colleagues in the Senate. It was generally agreed that he was a born prospector, and that he came to be, for practical mining purposes, one of the best geologists that the country had produced. As a multimillionaire he lived on a lavish scale and contributed to manifold charities, personifying to many in the West the open-handed generosity of the early days. This generosity came to be related in the popular mind with the more careful philanthropies of his wife, Phoebe Apperson Hearst [*q.v.*], whom he married on June 15, 1862, upon a return to Missouri.

Except for a brief service in the California Assembly in 1865–66, Hearst did not have an active part in politics until 1882, when he appeared as a candidate for governor before the Democratic state convention. Two years before this he had acquired the San Francisco *Daily Examiner* (later the *Examiner*). In his candidacy he had the backing of the San Francisco delegates and he was said by his managers to be opposed to railway domination of politics. The nomination was won by George Stoneman, who was elected. Hearst entered into political alliance with Christopher Buckley, Democratic boss of San Francisco, contributed heavily to campaign funds in 1884, and after receiving the nomination of the Democratic caucus for the Senate was defeated by Leland Stanford in January 1885. On Mar. 23, 1886, upon the death of John T. Miller, Governor Stoneman appointed Hearst to the United States Senate. Two years later he was elected for the full term. In the Senate, as in business life, his interest was in matters touching upon mining, railways, agriculture, and land grants. He spoke seldom and claimed on one occasion to be "the silent man of the Senate." He impressed his colleagues as an unusual man whose life had been a romance in westward expansion and who brought to the work of the Senate the fruits of a rich experience. His abounding humor and emphatic honesty were long remembered. Tall, gainly, with large nose and deep-set eyes, he had the long bushy beard which in earlier years marked the Western miner, and miner he remained to the last. Within a week of the close of the Fifty-first Congress, he died in Washington, survived by his wife and one son, William Randolph Hearst, then a young man of twenty-eight, who in March of 1887 had taken over the management of his father's newspaper, the San Francisco *Examiner.*

[*Jour. of the Assembly* (California), 17 Sess., 1865–66; *Biog. Dir. Am. Cong.* (1928); memorial addresses of Mar. 25, 1892, and Feb. 24, 1894, 52 Cong., 2 Sess., *Senate Miscellaneous Doc. No. 65*, published separately as *Memorial Addresses on the Life and Character of George Hearst* (1894); Edith Dobie, *The Pol. Career of Stephen Mallory White* (1927); J. K. Winkler, *W. R. Hearst, An Am. Phenomenon* (1928); Winifred B. Bonfils, *The Life and Personality of Phoebe Apperson Hearst* (p.p., 1928); San Francisco *Examiner*, Mar. 1, 1891.]

E. E. R.

HEARST, PHOEBE APPERSON (Dec. 3, 1842–Apr. 13, 1919), philanthropist, was born in Missouri, where she spent the first twenty years of her life. Her parents, Randolph Walker Apperson, and Drucilla (Whitmire) Apperson, were farmers of substantial means. A brief period of teaching in the public schools preceded her marriage on June 15, 1862, to George Hearst [*q.v.*], who had returned to Missouri after twelve years in California. By way of Panama they traveled to San Francisco, where they made their home. Her only son, William Randolph Hearst, was born in 1863. Soon afterward her parents moved to California, and in 1866, accompanied by her younger brother, Elbert, she visited the Sandwich Islands. A long-cherished wish was realized in 1873, when she went to Europe. Previous study of art and literature brought rich returns upon this trip, as her diary and her letters to her husband reveal (Bonfils, *post*). It was four years before she again went to Europe, for in 1874–75 her husband suffered heavy financial losses and for a time she gave up her house in San Francisco.

After her return from her second trip to Europe in the spring of 1880, welfare activities became the marked feature of her life. She gave freely to hospitals and orphan asylums, served upon committees to carry forward their work, and devoted much attention to the establishment of kindergartens. Though particularly interested in San Francisco charities, she provided in her later years libraries and kindergartens in the Utah, Dakota, and Montana mining communities which had grown up around the Hearst properties. The center of her philanthropic work was transferred to Washington, D. C., in 1886, when she and her husband took up residence at 1400 New Hampshire Avenue. She continued to aid kindergarten work and hospital service, but her greatest interest appeared to be in the education of girls, finding expression in the foundation and support of the National Cathedral School for girls. Upon the death of her husband in 1891, she turned much of her attention to her vast properties, yet she continued her former interests, serving as president of the Columbia Free Kindergarten in 1893. In 1899 she was present at the laying of the corner-stone of the St. Albans School, which her generosity had made possible.

The later years of her life were identified with California and particularly with the state university at Berkeley. She became a regent of the institution in 1897 and lived for a time in Berkeley, where she took great interest in the women of the university. In 1901 she gave Hearst Hall for their use. As early as 1894 she had provided funds for the establishment of an ethnological museum, which was built around her own collection. In subsequent years she gave large sums to make possible scientific expeditions and the service of experts in the field of anthropology. In 1896 she furnished the means for an international architectural competition which was to provide a plan for the university grounds and buildings. On Nov. 18, 1902, the corner-stone of the Hearst Memorial Mining Building was laid. Constructed at a cost of $645,000, it was formally presented to the university in 1908. Her benefactions in lectureships, fellowships, scholarships, and book funds were innumerable. Mrs. Hearst was a woman of unusual energy, great tenacity of purpose, and remarkable aptitude for philanthropy. She was small of stature, erect and graceful, with much tact and wit. She had a gift for the discovery of talent, encouraged ambition wherever she found it, and made her houses in California centers for the entertainment of interesting figures in the worlds of literature, music, scholarship, and politics.

["Regent Phoebe Apperson Hearst." *Univ. of Cal. Chronicle,* July 1919; J. K. Winkler, *W. R. Hearst, An Am. Phenomenon* (1928); Winifred B. Bonfils, *The Life and Personality of Phoebe Apperson Hearst* (p.p., 1928); *Who's Who in America,* 1918–19; San Francisco *Examiner,* Apr. 14, 15, 16, 1919.] E. E. R.

HEATH, JAMES EWELL (July 8, 1792–June 28, 1862), author and state official, often designated inexactly the first editor of the *Southern Literary Messenger,* was born in Virginia, probably in Northumberland County. He was the son of John Heath, first president of the Phi Beta Kappa society and a member of the Third and Fourth congresses, and his wife Sarah Ewell. Elected to the legislature from Prince William County in 1814, during his third term he became a member of the Privy Council and in 1819 was made state auditor, continuing in this office for thirty years and finding recreation in occasional excursions into literature. As late as 1841 Poe referred to him as "almost the only person of any literary distinction" residing in Richmond (*Works, post,* vol. XV, p. 241). He was known further as one of the first officers of the Virginia Historical and Philosophical Society, a friend of religious and educational institutions, and a progressive, public-spirited citizen. He married, first, his cousin, Fannie, daughter of "Parson" Weems, and second, in 1820, Elizabeth Ann, daughter of Col. William Hartwell Macon of New Kent County.

In 1828 Heath published anonymously *Edge-Hill, or The Family of the Fitzroyals,* a two-volume romance of plantation life in Virginia during the closing years of the Revolution, with an aristocratic and patriotic hero and an equally conventional love plot. The story is afflicted with most of the ills that then beset American fiction, but it holds interest for the student of the American novel in its early employment of native material, its avowed modeling after Scott, and in the relative prominence accorded the negro body servant. Although Poe praised it and George Tucker ranked it with the novels of Cooper, Bird, and Kennedy, its circulation was disappointingly small. Six years later, when its publisher, Thomas W. White, determined to establish a monthly magazine in Richmond, he obtained, gratuitously, Heath's advice and assistance through the better part of the *Messenger's* birth year by representing the venture in a patriotic light. After eight numbers White announced that he had engaged "an Editor . . . who would devote his whole attention to the work," but at various later times he had occasion to invoke Heath's counsel. It is reasonable to assume that the *Messenger* would hardly have lasted out the year without some such supervision as Heath supplied, for White, who lacked education, was seldom sure of his own literary judgment unless the contributor chanced to be a friend. Heath's only other volume was a three-act comedy, *Whigs and Democrats, or Love of No Politics,* published anonymously in Richmond in 1839 and played in Philadelphia five years later. Written to demonstrate that "our own country furnishes ample materials for the drama" as well as to ridicule "the despicable arts of demogoguism," it showed advance over *Edge-Hill* in dialogue and characterization, and contained such forceful satire on rural election practices that the Democrats were said to have ousted him from the auditorship in 1849 in revenge for his attack. His last important public office was that of commissioner of pensions, 1850–53, under President Fillmore.

[B. B. Minor, *The Southern Lit. Messenger* (1905); Horace E. Hayden, *Va. Geneals.* (1891); *Works of Edgar Allan Poe,* Harrison edition (1902), vols. I, XV, XVII; *Southern Lit. Messenger, passim*; E. G. Swem and J. W. Williams, *A Reg. of the Gen. Assembly of Va.* (1918).] A. C. G., Jr.

HEATH, PERRY SANFORD (Aug. 31, 1857–Mar. 30, 1927), newspaper man and politician, was one of the six sons of Jacob W. and Rhoda A. (Perdieu) Heath, of Muncie, Ind. The father was a lay preacher of the Methodist Church. Perry shifted for himself from an early age. At twenty-one he was editor and proprietor of Muncie's first daily newspaper, and three years later he was publishing the *Pioneer* at Aberdeen, Dakota Territory. For the next twelve years he worked as a newspaper correspondent at Washington. There he became engrossed in national politics, managed the details of Harrison's prenomination campaigns in 1888 and 1892, and extended his acquaintance widely among Republican politicians. From 1894 to 1896 he was editor of the *Cincinnati Commercial-Gazette* and took part in the McKinley nomination campaign in 1896. In the election contest of that year between McKinley and Bryan, fought on the issue of free-silver, Heath had a significant part in directing the publishing and printing for the Republican National Committee. This had not in former campaigns been a function that commanded much attention, but in the unusual efforts put forth in 1896 to educate the public on the money question it became important. Under Heath's supervision 135 carloads of printed matter were distributed and 350 writers were employed, supplying copy for 12,000 publications of all kinds. This was quite unprecedented in American political contests.

When the McKinley administration took office Heath was made first assistant postmaster-general, the head of the department being Charles Emory Smith of the Philadelphia *Press.* Heath installed the rural free-delivery system although some experimenting had been done during the Cleveland administration, and within three years the number of routes provided in this service was increased from 44 to 1,214. It fell to him to organize the system under comparatively small appropriations from Congress and this he did so successfully as to induce a large increase in the amounts appropriated for the purpose. When he resigned from the service in July 1900, serious irregularities had come to light in the Cuban postal service, then administered by the United States. Officials whose appointments he had recommended were found guilty and received prison sentences for embezzlement and extensive frauds in printing contracts. In 1903 came disclosures involving men in the department at Washington, several of whom owed their places to him. In a memorandum with the report of Fourth Assistant Postmaster-General Bristow, President Roosevelt named Heath, who had been serving as secretary of the Republican National Committee since he left the department. Bristow believed that Heath's appointments would have justified his removal from office, but when charges were made against him after his resignation, the District Attorney did not find sufficient evidence to indict him. In the meantime he had returned to newspaper work, having bought the *Salt Lake Tribune* in 1901, and established the *Telegram,* an evening paper, in the following year. He had married Ella Conway, of Louisville, Ky., in 1890.

[There are brief sketches of Heath's life in *Who's Who in America,* 1926–27; the *Evening Star* (Washington, D. C.), Mar. 30, 1927, and the *Indianapolis Star,* Mar. 31, 1927. See also *House Doc. 383* and *Senate Doc. 151,* 58 Cong., 2 Sess., and *A Portrait and Biog. Record of Delaware and Randolph Counties, Ind.* (1894).] W. B. S.

HEATH, WILLIAM (Mar. 2, 1737–Jan. 24, 1814), Revolutionary soldier, was born in Roxbury, Mass., the son of Samuel and Elizabeth (Payson) Heath. He was primarily a farmer by occupation. On Apr. 19, 1759, he was married to Sarah Lockwood of Cambridge. Although he did not serve in the Seven Years' War, he was enrolled in a militia company, and in 1765 he joined the Ancient and Honorable Artillery Company of Boston, subsequently becoming a captain, and supplementing his training by a careful study of works on military science and tactics. In the growing dispute with Great Britain, he exerted an influence in arousing a spirit of resistance. Over the pseudonym of "A Militia Man" he published in the *Boston Gazette* in 1770 two articles advocating military preparedness. In 1761 he had represented Roxbury in the General Court. In 1771 he was again elected to that body and remained a member until its dissolution by Governor Gage in 1774. When the crisis became imminent he was a member of the Provincial Congress of Massachusetts and served on the committees of safety and supplies. In February 1775 the Provincial Congress commissioned him a brigadier-general, and at the battle of Bunker Hill he won promotion to the rank of major-general. When the Continental Congress took charge of the army before Boston, Heath became a brigadier-general under Washington. A year later he was commissioned major-general in the Continental service. In January 1777, while attempting to carry out Washington's orders in connection with an attack on Fort Independence, Heath handled the affair so badly that he brought upon himself a reprimand from the commander-in-chief. Thenceforth he was used for staff work rather than for active fighting.

During 1777 and 1778, after the Fort Independence episode, Heath was placed in command of the Eastern district, with headquarters in Boston. It fell to him in this position to act as guardian of Burgoyne's surrendered army, until it was removed to Virginia. Then, in the summer of 1778, when Gen. John Sullivan and the Boston populace were threatening the French admiral, D'Estaing, with vengeance, because of disappointment over the proposed attack upon the British in Rhode Island, Washington wrote to Heath to try to prevent the Bostonians from casting unwarranted aspersions upon the French. In June 1779 he was transferred once more to the lower Hudson and remained in command there until the end of the war, with the exception of a period in 1780 when he was sent to Rhode Island to prepare for the arrival of Rochambeau's French army. On July 1, 1783,

Heath returned to his farm in Roxbury, where he spent the remaining thirty years of his life. He served as a member of the state convention which in 1788 ratified the Federal Constitution, in 1791 and 1792 was a member of the state Senate, and in 1792 was judge of probate. In 1806 he was elected to the lieutenant-governorship, but he declined to serve. He seems to have been a man of solid rather than brilliant parts, and probably a better farmer than a strategist or tactician.

[For Heath's letters and papers see the *Mass. Hist. Soc. Colls.*, 5 ser., vol. IV (1878), 6 ser., vols. IV (1904) and V (1905). For his own record of his military career see the *Memoirs of Maj.-Gen. Heath* (1798), reprinted by Wm. Abbott in 1901 and by R. R. Wilson in 1904. Other sources include J. M. Bugbee, *Memorials of the Mass. Soc. of the Cincinnati* (1890), and the *Boston Daily Advertiser*, Jan. 28, 1814.] R. V. H.

HEATHCOTE, CALEB (Mar. 6, 1665/66–Mar. 1, 1720/21), merchant, statesman, churchman, was the son of Gilbert Heathcote, one-time mayor of Chesterfield, in the hundred of Scarsdale, Derbyshire, England, and Anne Dickens, his wife. Disappointed in love, he removed in 1692 to New York, where he was almost immediately appointed to the governor's council. This position he held, except for the years 1698–1702, until his death. He prospered as a merchant, a contractor, and a farmer of Westchester County taxes, but was conspicuously free from the scandals then prevalent in public life. Beginning in 1692, he served for life as colonel of militia, presiding judge of the court of sessions, judge of the prerogative court, and (after 1693) first judge of the court of common pleas, all for Westchester County. In 1696 he took up residence in Westchester borough town, then chartered at his instance, and was its mayor throughout life. Near here he erected gristmills, a leather-mill, a fulling-mill, a linseed-oil mill, and a sawmill.

Living in an atmosphere of land speculation, he associated eight others with him and in 1697 patented the "Great Nine Partners" tract in Dutchess County; similarly he patented three Westchester tracts running from near Croton Point to Connecticut. Partnerships he found necessary from political, not financial, considerations. He owned land also in Ulster and Richmond counties and in New York City. Purchasing from Ann Richbell about twenty square miles running back from Mamaroneck, he had it and two small adjoining tracts erected into the Manor of Scarsdale (1701) with customary rights, the last manor granted in the British Empire. He forewent his manorial courts, being county judge himself.

In 1695 and again during 1702–03 he was a commissioner to conduct the offices of collector and receiver general. Strongly urged in 1708 for the governorship, he had to content himself with the mayoralty of New York, 1711–13. He unfolded schemes to the British government for the production of naval stores with the aid of garrison soldiers, calling attention to his own success with flax and hemp. The ministry passed over his apparently practicable proposals, however, preferring to experiment—futilely, it proved—with New Englanders and, later, German immigrants. He made an early suggestion (1715) of a general conference of colonial administrators to discuss defense and Indian relations, without success. Rejecting his plans but respecting his capacity, the ministry in 1715 made him surveyor-general of the customs for the northern department, that is, to the Delaware River. To free imperial administration of obstructive assemblies, he proposed in 1716 that Parliament provide increased customs revenue and pay governors and other officials out of it. Finding Connecticut smoothly insolent to customs officers and Rhode Island uproariously defiant, he urged in 1719 that these charter governments be strictly reformed. The High Admiralty Court of England made him judge of vice-admiralty of New York, Connecticut, and the Jerseys (1715), but it was Lewis Morris, an appointee of the governor, who actually served, this duplication confusing admiralty jurisdiction in colonial New York.

Heathcote was a devoted and energetic churchman. Sustaining Governor Fletcher in the partial establishment of Anglicanism in New York, he led in founding Trinity Parish and building the edifice. Meanwhile in Westchester he had threatened his militia with hard Sunday drill unless they maintained regular worship, and had begun the establishment of his church. Cleverly circumventing the local New England majority, he set up Episcopal worship in Westchester, Rye, New Rochelle, Eastchester, and Yonkers. He steadily supported the Society for the Propagation of the Gospel in Foreign Parts, of which he became a member, established a day school and a Sunday school in Rye, and more than any other colonial mayor encouraged schools in New York City. After careful plans, he made in 1706 the first of five missionary journeys into Connecticut and was chiefly responsible for planting Episcopacy in that colony at Stratford.

Caleb Heathcote was an important force for civilization in New York. His death from apoplexy in 1721 came, appropriately enough, when he was collecting funds for a charity. Two sons and two daughters died as minors and after the death in 1736 of his widow (Martha, daughter of

"Tangier" Smith, whom he had married on Sept. 7, 1699), the manor was jointly held by his daughters, Anne, wife of Chief Justice James De Lancey [*q.v.*], and Martha, wife of Dr. Lewis Johnston, until it was dissolved in 1774.

[The only extensive account is, D. R. Fox, *Caleb Heathcote, Gentleman Colonist* (1926), where all authorities are given.] D. R. F.

HÉBERT, LOUIS (Mar. 13, 1820–Jan. 7, 1901), engineer, soldier in the Confederate army, was the son of Valéry and Clarisse (Bush) Hébert, both of Iberville Parish, La. He was a descendant of Louis Hébert who settled in Canada in 1604. In 1755, Paul Gaston Hébert, his great-grandson, left Port Royal (Annapolis), Nova Scotia, and in 1767 settled in Louisiana. His son, Armand Valéry, was Louis's grandfather and also grandfather of Paul Octave Hébert [*q.v.*], Louis's cousin. Young Hébert's early education was directed by private teachers on his father's plantation, and later he was sent to Jefferson College in St. James Parish, from which he graduated in 1840. Receiving an appointment to West Point, he was graduated there in 1845, third in his class, and was made brevet second lieutenant of engineers. For two years he served as assistant engineer in the construction of Fort Livingston, Barataria Island, La. In 1847, he resigned from the army to take charge of his father's sugar estate in Iberville Parish, and the following year he married Malvina Lambremont. Three sons were born of this union. From 1847 to 1850 he was major in the Louisiana militia and colonel from 1858 to 1861; from 1853 to 1855, a member of the state Senate; and from 1855 to 1859, chief engineer of Louisiana. In the latter year this office was abolished and he became a member of the board of public works.

At the opening of the Civil War, he entered the service of the Confederate states as colonel of the 3rd Louisiana Infantry, a well drilled and equipped organization chiefly made up of men from northern Louisiana, which was placed in the brigade of General McCulloch. At the battle of Wilson's Creek his division did gallant work. At Pea Ridge, where both his senior officers, McCulloch and McIntosh, were killed, Hébert and numbers of his officers and men were captured. On May 26, 1862, he was commissioned brigadier-general, and, after being exchanged, led the 2nd Brigade, Little's division, Price's army, in northern Mississippi. He took a gallant part in the battle of Iuka, bearing the brunt of Rosecrans' attack. He was afterward for a time in command of Little's division, distinguished himself in the battle of Corinth, and served in the siege of Vicksburg. After the fall of that city, Hébert was in charge of the heavy artillery in the Cape Fear department under Major-General Whitney and acted as chief engineer of the war department of North Carolina. When peace was declared he went back to his native parish and became editor of the *Iberville South*, a weekly paper published in the town of Plaquemine. Later he taught in private schools both in Iberville and St. Martin parishes, taking no part in politics. He was still teaching at the age of eighty-one when his death occurred in St. Martin Parish.

[Alcée Fortier, *Louisiana* (1914), vol. I; C. A. Evans, *Confed. Mil. Hist.*, vol. X (1899); W. H. Tunnard, *A Southern Record: The Hist. of the Third Regt., La. Cavalry* (1866); *Thirty-Second Ann. Reunion Asso. Grads. U. S. Mil. Acad.* (1901); Lucinda Boyd, *The Irvines and Their Kin* (1898); family records supplied by Ellis L. Hébert of St. Martinville, La.] W. B. G.

HÉBERT, PAUL OCTAVE (Dec. 12, 1818–Aug. 29, 1880), soldier, Louisiana governor, the son of Paul Gaston and Mary Eugenia (Hamilton) Hébert, was born on a plantation on the banks of the Mississippi twelve miles above Bayou Goula, Iberville Parish, La. His grandfather, Armand Valéry Hébert, was also the grandfather of Louis Hébert [*q.v.*]. After attending elementary schools near his home, Paul was sent to Jefferson College, St. James Parish, La., where he graduated in 1836 at the head of his class. Four years later he was first in the class of 1840 at the United States Military Academy at West Point, where William T. Sherman and George H. Thomas [*qq.v.*] were his classmates. He was commissioned second lieutenant in the Engineer Corps but was shortly appointed assistant professor of engineering at West Point, a position he held until July 21, 1842, when he was ordered to Barataria, La., to superintend the construction of some Mississippi River defenses. On Aug. 2, 1842, he was married to Cora Wills Vaughan, daughter of a sugar planter living near Bayou Goula. In 1845 he left the army to accept an appointment from Gov. Alexander Mouton as chief engineer of Louisiana but resigned early in 1847. The Mexican War being then in progress, he was commissioned lieutenant-colonel in the 14th Infantry, in the brigade commanded by Gen. Franklin Pierce. He took part in all important battles of the Mexico City campaign and at Molino del Rey so distinguished himself that he was personally complimented by General Scott and brevetted colonel for gallantry.

At the close of the war Hébert retired to his sugar plantation, but soon afterward, in an attempt to improve his health, he made a tour of

Europe. After his return to the United States he was a member of the Louisiana constitutional convention in 1852 and in the same year was elected governor of the state on the Democratic ticket. He is said to have been the youngest man elected to the office up to that time. Commissioned a brigadier-general in the Confederate army at the outbreak of the Civil War, he was in command in Louisiana during 1861. After being transferred to the Trans-Mississippi Department he was given command of the Department of Texas, then put in charge of the defenses of Galveston, and finally given command of the sub-district of North Louisiana, where he took part in the battle of Milliken's Bend, the only engagement of consequence in which he participated during the war. After General Lee surrendered, General Kirby-Smith turned his command over to General Magruder, who immediately transferred it to Hébert, and by him it was surrendered to Gen. Granger of the Union army. The war over, Hébert resumed business in his native state. His political disabilities were soon removed by President Johnson. In 1873 he was appointed state engineer by Gov. W. P. Kellogg, and commissioner and civil engineer of the Mississippi levees by President Grant. In 1872, with the slogan "All Roads from Greeley Lead to Grant," he had led the wing of the Louisiana Democrats which supported Horace Greeley for the presidency. In 1879 he began to suffer from cancer, and a year later he died at the New Orleans home of his father-in-law, John Andrews, a prominent sugar planter of Iberville Parish. Hébert's first wife died in 1859, and on Aug. 3, 1861, he had married Penelope Lynch Andrews. He was buried at Bayou Goula.

[See Lucinda Boyd, *The Irvines and Their Kin* (1898); Arthur Meynier, *Meynier's La. Biogs.* pt. I (1882); H. and A. Cohen, *Cohen's New Orleans Directory,* 1854; C. A. Evans, *Confed. Mil. Hist.,* vol. X (1899); Chas. Gayarré, *Hist. of La.,* vol. IV (1866); *New Orleans Times,* Aug. 30, 1880. Information as to certain facts was supplied by Hébert's grand-daughter, Mrs. G. W. Pigman, New Orleans, La.] M. J. W.

HECK, BARBARA (1734–Aug. 17, 1804), "Mother of Methodism in America," was born in Ballingrane, County Limerick, Ireland, where German refugees from the Palatinate had been permitted to settle in 1709. Her father was Sebastian Ruckle. With her husband, Paul Heck, she came to New York in 1760 on the ship *Perry,* which also brought Philip Embury [*q.v.*] and his wife, and other Ballingrane people. The most of the company had been converted to Methodism in Ireland, but, divorced from former associations, their fervor seems to have waned. Barbara Heck was greatly distressed by their backsliding, and one day in 1766 a card game which she found going on set her on fire with indignation, and she became a flaming angel of rebuke and exhortation. Sweeping the cards from the table, she denounced the players in no uncertain terms, and then went across the street to the home of Embury, who had been a local preacher in Ireland, and startled that individual from his spiritual lethargy by declaring: "Philip, you must preach to us, or we shall all go to Hell, and God will require our blood at your hands!" When he objected on the ground that he had no place in which to preach, she retorted, "Preach in your own house! And at once! The Lord will protect you!"

From this incident most Methodists date the beginning of the Wesleyan movement in America (Jesse Lee, *A Short History of the Methodists,* 1810, ch. II). Embury preached, Barbara Heck was there to encourage him and was a vitalizing agency in subsequent activities which, in 1768, resulted in the erection of the first Wesleyan chapel in this country. She decided the plan of it, divinely inspired, as she believed, and is said to have helped raise the necessary funds. The Hecks moved to Salem, in what is now Washington County, N. Y., in 1770, where again they helped Embury found a Wesleyan Society. Being Loyalists, just before the Revolution they removed to Montreal and Paul Heck served in the English army. Later they made their home in Augusta, Canada. Barbara died there on a summer day, sitting outdoors by the St. Lawrence River, her Bible in her lap.

[For discussion of the erroneous statement that her name was "Hick," and that she was buried in New York, see John Atkinson, *Hist. of the Origin of the Wesleyan Movement in America* (1896), ch. V; Wm. Crook, *Ireland and the Centenary of Am. Methodism* (1868). See also: J. B. Wakeley, *Lost Chapters Recovered from the Early Hist. of Am. Methodism* (1858); *Methodist Rev.* (N. Y.), Jan.–Feb. and May–June 1928; *Christian Advocate* (N. Y.), Jan. 1, 8, 1885; S. A. Seaman, *Annals of N. Y. Methodism* (1892); J. M. Buckley, *A Hist. of Methodism in the U. S.* (2 vols., 1897); and other denominational histories.] H. E. S.

HECKER, FRIEDRICH KARL FRANZ (Sept. 28, 1811–Mar. 24, 1881), German revolutionist, Union soldier, farmer, was born in Eichtersheim, Baden. His father was well-to-do, a court counsellor under Fürst-Primas von Dalberg; his mother, née Von Lueders, was of noble family. After an early training in the Lyceum at Mannheim, he studied law and history at the universities of Heidelberg and Munich, receiving at the latter his doctor's degree in law. After a visit to Paris in 1835, he settled down in Mannheim and rapidly gained distinction as an advocate. Drawn into politics by his election in 1842 to the Second Chamber of Baden, he led, with Itzstein and Sander, the liberal movement for parliamentary government. His speech in the Chamber of Baden opposing the incorporation of Schleswig-Holstein with Denmark won him fame throughout Germany, and his popularity increased when on a visit to Berlin in 1845 he was expelled from Prussia. Not willing to compromise on halfway measures, as were his colleagues Bassermann and Welker, he resigned in 1847 and made a trip to Southern France and Algiers, but he was soon recalled by his constituents. Regarded as the champion of popular rights, he drew up, with Gustav Struve, the program of the Claims of the People of Baden at the Offenburg popular convention, Sept. 12, 1847. Idealist that he was, he thought the German people were ready to throw over their monarchistic and particularistic traditions at once and declare themselves for a united republic. Such a resolution he brought forward in the Preliminary Parliament (*Vorparlament*) at Frankfurt, Mar. 31, 1848. The moderates won, however, and when the government of Baden resorted to energetic measures, Hecker proclaimed the German Republic from Constance, and summoned the people of the Lake District (*Seekreis*) and the peasants of the Black Forest to armed resistance. He hoped for a spontaneous uprising in vast numbers of such as had been carried away by his fiery eloquence and magnetic personality, but the poorly armed force of a few thousand that gathered about him was no match for the combined troops of Baden and Hessen under General von Gagern. In the engagement near Kandern, Apr. 20, 1848, Hecker's little army was badly routed and the leader fled across the Swiss border. Hecker was honored with reëlection to the Chamber, but the Baden government would not respect his immunity, and the new Frankfurt Parliament refused to admit him to a seat as a member. He decided to emigrate, with the hope of collecting funds for the support of the revolution. The defeated Hecker was received like a conquering hero in New York City, and the ovations were repeated in Philadelphia, Cincinnati, and St. Louis. With the aid of friends he selected a farm near Belleville, Ill., and planned to join the colony of "Latin farmers," but when in May 1849 the Baden government was overthrown, the revolutionary Provisional Government called him home. He got as far as Strasbourg, where he learned that the Prussian armies had already vanquished the revolutionary forces in the Palatinate and Baden, and that the cause upon which he had staked all was lost. Emigration was now compulsory. With his wife (née Josephine Eisenhardt of Mannheim) and two children he set sail from France and returned to his Belleville farm, situated near what later became the village of Summerfield, St. Clair County, Ill.

Hecker became a successful farmer, cattle raiser, and viticulturist. A born leader, he could not keep out of politics when great questions agitated his adopted country. Though never accepting political office, he was one of the early Republicans, was on the Frémont electoral ticket, stumped the East and West against slavery, especially where Germans had settled, and was an ardent supporter of Lincoln. At the age of fifty when the Civil War began he served as a private soldier under General Sigel, until he was made colonel of the 24th Illinois. Difficulties with superior officers caused him to resign hotheadedly, but soon another regiment was recruited for him in Chicago, the 82nd Illinois, which he led for the greater part of the war. He was wounded severely at Chancellorsville, but recovered quickly and did his part in the battles of Chattanooga, Missionary Ridge, and elsewhere. He returned to his farm after the war, but remained a chosen leader of the German element on public occasions and in public affairs. His speech at St. Louis in 1871 (*Festrede zur St. Louiser Friedensfeier*) was noteworthy, showing his adherence to republican principles. Another address, delivered July 4 of the same year at Trenton, Ill., is included in D. J. Brewer's *World's Best Orations* (1899, vol. VII). He was active in the Liberal Republican movement of 1872 and, although he opposed Greeley's nomination and spoke against him in the campaign, gave hearty support to the state Liberal Republican ticket. In 1873 he visited Germany. He died of pneumonia at his Summerfield farm on Mar. 24, 1881, after a very brief illness. His wife and five children survived him. Hecker's winning personality and inspiring oratory, his integrity, wholeheartedness, and readiness to sacrifice all for the cause in which he believed, made him almost a legendary hero, in spite of his impetuosity, tactlessness, and vanity.

[*Allegemeine Deutsche Biographie, Bd.* 50 (1905); F. K. F. Hecker, *Die Erhebung des Volkes in Baden für die Deutsche Republik im Frühjahr 1848* (1848); Friedrich von Weech, *Badische Biographieen, Bd.* 4 (1891); Karl Mathy, *Aus dem Nachlass: Briefe aus den Jahren 1846–1848* (1898), ed. by Ludwig Mathy; *Friedrich Hecker und sein Anteil an der Geschichte Deutschlands und Amerikas* (1881); *Erinnerung an Friedrich Hecker* (1882); *Reden und Vorlesungen von Friedrich Hecker* (1872); *Memoirs of Gustave Koerner 1809–1896* (1909), ed. by T. J. McCormack; *Reminiscences of Carl Schurz* (1907); *1848: Der Vorkampf deutscher Einheit und Freiheit* (1914); F. I. Herriott, "The Conference in the Deutsches Haus, Chicago, May

14–15, 1860," *Trans. Ill. State Hist. Soc. . . . 1928* (1928); *St. Louis Globe-Democrat*, Mar. 25, 1881.]
A. B. F.

HECKER, ISAAC THOMAS (Dec. 18, 1819–Dec. 22, 1888), Roman Catholic priest, founder of the Paulists, youngest son of John and Caroline (Freund) Hecker, natives of Prussia, was born in New York, where at the age of eleven he was forced to leave school to aid his brothers in their bakery. Stimulated by an early acquaintance with Orestes Brownson [*q.v.*], Hecker attempted to educate himself by propping a copy of Kant's *Critique of Pure Reason* in front of the doughboard that he might read as he worked. Led by Brownson, he joined the Workingmen's Party and while in his teens made numerous political speeches. From philosophy and political science he turned his thoughts to religion and theology, subjects more compatible with his mystic nature. In January 1843, advised by Brownson, he went as a visitor to Brook Farm, where for six months he studied philosophy and theology. Learning of Bronson Alcott's colony, Fruitlands, near Harvard, Mass., he went there on July 11. Exactly two weeks later he returned to his brothers' bakeshop in New York. Less than a year after his return, his ascetic nature again asserted itself, and he went to study in Concord, Mass., where he lived with the Thoreau family. The individualism of the Transcendentalists repelled him and turned his thoughts toward the ritualistic religions. Rejecting the Episcopal Church after long consideration, he decided in June 1844 to become a Roman Catholic. After attempting unsuccessfully to convert Henry Thoreau and George William Curtis to Catholicism, he went to New York, where on Aug. 1 he was baptized by Bishop McCloskey. Attracted by the idea of life in a religious community, he applied for admission into the Redemptorist order, a society of priests in charge of the German congregations in New York. He was admitted, was confirmed in 1845, added Thomas to his name in honor of St. Thomas Aquinas, and in July 1845 sailed for Belgium, where he began his novitiate at St. Trond. Obtuse superiors and the unwonted regimen of the order made him miserable, but he kept doggedly at his study, and after becoming a member of the Redemptorist congregation on Oct. 15, 1846, he left on the following day for further training at Witten, Holland. In September 1848 he was sent to Clapham, England, and on Oct. 23, 1849, he was ordained in London by Bishop Wiseman.

Father Hecker returned from England to the United States in March 1851 as a Redemptorist missionary to the increasingly numerous German immigrants. For five years he worked with Fathers Baker, Deshon, Hewit, and Walworth. During these years he wrote two books, *Questions of the Soul* (1852) and *Aspirations of Nature* (1857), expositions of Catholic doctrine. His own conversion and his contacts with Protestants convinced him of the need of an English-speaking Redemptorist house. His four colleagues also felt the need and in August 1857 sent Hecker to Rome to lay the matter before the general of the order. Having come without first obtaining permission, he was promptly expelled from the order. Pope Pius IX dispensed the five American priests from their Redemptorist vows, and Hecker returned to New York in May 1858, ready to found a new order with St. Paul as patron. When the new order, The Missionary Priests of St. Paul the Apostle, was founded in New York in July 1858, Hecker became superior and retained the office until his death.

He worked with tremendous energy, continued his doctrinal lectures, and espoused the cause of the Catholic press. In 1865 he founded the *Catholic World*; in 1866 he organized the Catholic Publication Society; in 1870 he began the *Young Catholic,* a paper for children; and in 1871 he had raised more than half the fund needed to establish a Catholic daily when his health failed and he abandoned the project. He went south in 1872, and to Europe in 1873, where he recovered some of his strength and engaged again in writing. He died in New York.

Hecker conceived of the Catholic Church as essentially democratic; and in his lectures, books, and periodicals he sought to commend this conception to democratic America. After his death he was attacked in France as one who had endeavored to establish an independent American Catholicism. The charge seems to have been without foundation, for Hecker himself yielded to the will of the Holy See and never countenanced the least deviation from the strictest Catholic doctrine.

[The definitive biography is Walter Elliott, *The Life of Father Hecker* (1891). The controversy about his alleged advocacy of an American church is presented in Charles Maignen's *Études sur l'Américanisme—Le Père Hecker, Est-il un Saint?* (Paris and Rome, 1898) and in the English version of the same book, *Father Hecker, Is He a Saint?* (Rome, Paris, and London, 1898).]
R. W. A.

HECKEWELDER, JOHN GOTTLIEB ERNESTUS (Mar. 12, 1743–Jan. 31, 1823), missionary of the renewed Unitas Fratrum, or Moravian Church, to the Indians of Ohio, was born in Bedford, England, and died in Bethlehem, Pa. His father was the Rev. David Heckewelder, a native of Moravia, who had been sent to England in the service of the Brethren's Church. John's early education was acquired at Moravian schools in that country. After coming to America with his parents in 1754, he attended the boys' school in Bethlehem for three years and was then sent to assist in the operation of the Economy Farm at Christian's Spring, near Nazareth. In 1759 he was indentured to a cedar cooper at Bethlehem, though at that time he had offered his services as an evangelist and had expressed a strong desire to be allowed to assist in the work of David Zeisberger and Christian Frederick Post [*qq.v.*], who were planning a mission on the Muskingum River in the Ohio territory. In 1762 he received a call to assist Post in the transfer of several parties of Christian Delaware Indians from the Susquehanna region. A preliminary journey to Ohio was made, but, just as arrangements for the transfer were ready, Pontiac's War blazed out in the Western area and the proposed migration was temporarily abandoned. When the Pontiac affair collapsed, Post and Zeisberger carried out the plan and Heckewelder was compelled to remain in the cooper shop, chafing under the restraints imposed upon his dreams.

From 1763 to 1771, however, he was occasionally dispatched as a messenger to the Indian settlement at Wyalusing, Pa., and even to the Indian towns on the west branch of the Susquehanna. In this work he showed, to an unusual degree, the ability to understand both the customs and the language of the Indians, and he occupied many hours of those years in acquiring their language, traditions, and legendary history. His regular mission service was begun in 1771 and lasted fifteen years, during which, as assistant to David Zeisberger, he lived with the Moravian Christian Indians, guiding and accompanying them from the Susquehanna to the Big Beaver River and thence to Schoenbrunn and Gnadenhütten on the Muskingum. During these years he was constantly on horseback between Bethlehem and Detroit, usually as the leader of Indian groups and always as their passport on the way; for the idea of Indians as peaceful and God-fearing people was not conceivable to many frontiersmen in those troublous days. In 1781 he and all his companions were made prisoners by a wandering company of English and Indians and taken to Upper Sandusky where they were held as prisoners of war on the charge of being American spies. Heckewelder was twice summoned to Detroit and arraigned before the commandant of the post, but all were finally allowed to return to the Ohio work. It was during this absence from Ohio that ninety-six Christian Indians of Gnadenhütten were massacred by the whites.

In 1780 Heckewelder married Sarah Ohneberg of Nazareth, Pa., their wedding, the first of a white couple in Ohio, taking place in the chapel of the station at Salem. Six years later he retired to Bethlehem and withdrew from the active mission service, though not from the service of his church. Additional duties were imposed upon him by the new government of the United States, which availed itself of his special knowledge of Indian language and life. In 1792 General Knox, secretary of war, appointed him to accompany General Putnam [*q.v.*] and a commission to arrange the peace treaty at Vincennes, Ind. The next year he acted as adviser for a similar group consisting of General Lincoln, Colonel Pickering, and Gov. Beverly Randolph, going by way of the Iroquois country to Detroit. In 1801 he returned to Gnadenhütten, and for nine years administered the Indian "estate" on the Muskingum, held in trust by the Society for Propagating the Gospel, for the benefit of the descendants of the Indians of the former mission. By this time most of these had been transferred, largely through his efforts and energy, to Fairfield, Canada.

He returned with his family to Bethlehem in 1810 where new labors awaited him. At the solicitation of Caspar Wistar of the American Philosophical Society he gave the last years of his life to the work of recording some of the knowledge of Indian life that he had acquired. As a result his "Account of the History, Manners, and Customs of the Indian Nations, Who Once Inhabited Pennsylvania and the Neighboring States" was published in *The Transactions of the Historical & Literary Committee of the American Philosophical Society*, vol. I (1819). A German edition appeared in Göttingen, 1821, and a French, in Paris, in 1822. This work was denounced in the *North American Review*, January 1826 for its alleged naïve acceptance of Indian traditions as facts, but was vindicated with some success by William Rawle, in *Memoirs of the Historical Society of Pennsylvania*, vol. I (1826). Among his other published works are *Johann Heckewälders Reise von Bethlehem in Pensilvanien bis zum Wabashfluss* (Halle, 1797; English translation in *Pennsylvania Magazine of History and Biography*, January, April, and July 1888), an account of the journey made in 1792 with Putnam; *A Narrative of the Mission of the United Brethren among the Delaware and the Mohegan Indians from its Commencement in the Year 1740 to the Close of the Year*

1808 (1820; new edition, edited by William E. Connelley, 1907); *Names which the Lenni Lennape or Delaware Indians Gave to the Rivers, Streams, and Localities within the States of Pennsylvania, New Jersey, Maryland, and Virginia, with their Significations* (1872); "Map and Description of Northeastern Ohio . . . in 1796" (*Magazine of Western History,* December 1884). An interesting meteorological journal kept by Heckewelder at Gnadenhütten in 1800 is printed in the *Philadelphia Medical and Physical Journal,* vol. I, pt. 2 (1805), and his journal of a tour made with Putnam in 1797 for the survey of the Indian "estate" is printed in the *Pennsylvania Magazine of History and Biography,* April 1886. Heckewelder's work is, of course, supplementary to that of David Zeisberger, by whom the original investigations into Indian languages were made. It was Heckewelder's eminent common sense and adaptability, however, that carried the mission work through to success; it was his simple straightforwardness that won against prejudice at Detroit; and in the end it was through Heckewelder that the story of Indian life and of colonial Indian affairs in the Ohio country was given a proper perspective in history.

[Heckewelder's Autobiography, MS., Bethlehem Archives; E. Rondthaler, *Life of John Heckewelder* (1847); G. H. Loskiel, *Geschichte der mission der evangelischen brüder unter den Indianern in Nordamerika* (1789); Wm. C. Reichel, in Heckewelder's *Names which the Lenni Lennape or Delaware Indians gave to the Rivers, Streams, and Localities,* . . . (1872), in *Trans. of the Moravian Hist. Soc.,* vol. I (1876), and in *Memoirs of the Hist. Soc. of Pa.,* vol. XII (1876); J. M. Levering, *A Hist. of Bethlehem, Pa., 1741–1892* (1903); E. A. De Schweinitz, *Life and Times of David Zeisberger* (1870); C. W. Butterfield, *Hist. of the Girtys* (1870); *Memoirs of Rufus Putnam* (1903); *Ohio Arch. and Hist. Pubs.,* vol. VII (1899).]

A. G. R.

HECTOR, FRANCISCO LUIS [See CARONDELET, FRANCISCO LUIS HECTOR, BARON DE, *c.* 1748–1807].

HEDDING, ELIJAH (June 7, 1780–Apr. 9, 1852), elected bishop of the Methodist Episcopal Church after twenty-four years' pioneer work as circuit rider, stationed preacher, and presiding elder, was born in what is now Pine Plains, Dutchess County, N. Y. He was of English descent, the son of James Hedding. When he was about eleven years old his parents moved to Starksborough, Vt., in which frontier settlement he became hardy in spirit and rugged in physique. Both educational and religious opportunities were all but wanting there, but Methodism finally made conquest of the region, and, after much mental perturbation, Hedding was soundly converted. Prior to this event he had been accustomed to read Wesley's sermons at services held in the home of a pious family, for he was a good reader and had a resounding voice. In the early days of his preaching, it is said, he could be heard a mile away. He now became an exhorter. In 1799 when Lorenzo Dow [*q.v.*] left the neighboring Essex Circuit in order to preach to the Catholics in Ireland, Hedding, not yet twenty, took his place, and on June 16, 1801, was admitted to the New York Conference on probation. In 1803 he was ordained deacon by Bishop Whatcoat, and in 1805, elder, by Bishop Asbury. He traveled long and difficult circuits, enduring hardships and exposure which brought on bodily infirmities from which he never fully recovered. Like other itinerants he carried books in his saddle bags, and by studying grammar, the English language, and theology, he became a clear, correct speaker and better informed than the average of his confreres. Changes in the boundaries of the New York and New England conferences in 1805 made him a member of the latter. From this time until he was elected bishop, he was one of the foremost agents in the extension of Methodism in New England. His work carried him into all its states, he was presiding elder of several different districts, and was stationed at Boston, Lynn, Nantucket, Portland, and New London. While in Boston in 1822, he was instrumental in the establishment of *Zion's Herald* (first issue, Jan. 9, 1823), the earliest exclusively Methodist periodical.

In the General Conferences, all of which he attended either as delegate or bishop from 1808 until his death, he was a conspicuous figure. At the first of these, when a resolution establishing "delegated" General Conferences had been defeated, which action was later rescinded, he helped to prevent the breaking up of the Conference by persuading the disgruntled New England representatives not to return home. In the long-continued but unsuccessful effort to make presiding elders elective by the annual conferences he was a leader, though in his later years his views on the matter changed. As a bishop, to which office he was elected in 1824, his exposition of the spirit and intent of the disciplinary statutes of the church came to be held in high regard, and his decisions, and especially his *Discourse on the Administration of Discipline* (1842) did much to put the economy of the church on a uniform and fair basis. He strongly opposed the extreme abolitionist agitation in the northern conferences and thereby brought upon himself much abuse and persecution. Conscious perhaps of his own early limitations, he was a strong advocate of education. Hedding College, Abingdon, Ill., founded in 1856, is named for him. As a presiding officer he was unexcelled. His physical presence suggested power and authority, for he was six feet tall, large-framed, and corpulent. He was preëminently a simple, practical man, keen-minded, shrewd in his estimate of others, quick-witted, and of sound judgment. His piety, however, was deep and sincere. During his later life his home was in Poughkeepsie, N. Y., where he died in his seventy-second year. His wife, whom he married Jan. 10, 1810, was Lucy Blish of Gilsum, Cheshire County, N. H.

[Autobiographical letter dated July 31, 1846, repr. from *Northern Christian Advocate* in A. M. Hemenway, *The Vt. Hist. Gazetteer,* I (1868), p. 104; D. W. Clark, *Life and Times of Rev. Elijah Hedding, D.D.* (1855); Wm. B. Sprague, *Annals Am. Pulpit,* vol. VII (1859); Nathan Bangs, *A Hist. of the Meth. Episc. Church* (4 vols., 1838–41); Abel Stevens, *Memorials of the Introduction of Methodism into the Eastern States* (1848); *Meth. Quart. Rev.,* Jan. 1853; Theo. L. Flood and John W. Hamilton, *Lives of Meth. Bishops* (1882); John J. Tigert, *A Constitutional Hist. of Am. Episcopal Methodism* (rev. ed., 1904); J. M. Buckley, *Constitutional and Parliamentary Hist. of the M. E. Church* (1912); Jas. Mudge, *Hist. of the New Eng. Conference of the M. E. Ch. 1796–1910* (1910); *Zion's Herald,* Apr. 14, 28, 1852; *Christian Advocate* (N. Y.), Apr. 8, 15, 1852.]

H. E. S.

HEDGE, FREDERIC HENRY (Dec. 12, 1805–Aug. 21, 1890), Unitarian clergyman, Transcendentalist, translator of German literature, was born at Cambridge, Mass., the second child of Levi [*q.v.*] and Mary (Kneeland) Hedge. Showing an early talent for language, he memorized the *Eclogues* of Virgil before he was seven years of age and much of Homer before he was ten. His father, professor of logic at Harvard, sent Frederic to Germany with George Bancroft in 1818, a boy of thirteen in the care of a youth of eighteen. He returned in 1822 and entered Harvard with advanced standing, graduating in 1825. After studying at the Divinity School, 1825–29, he was ordained at West Cambridge (now Arlington), Mass., May 20, 1829, and served as minister of Unitarian churches at West Cambridge, 1829–35; Bangor, Me., 1835–50; Providence, R. I., 1850–56; and Brookline, Mass., 1857–72. In 1830, at West Cambridge, he married Lucy L. Pierce, daughter of Rev. John Pierce. He was editor of the *Christian Examiner,* 1857–61; professor of ecclesiastical history in the Harvard Divinity School, 1857–76, and an especially appointed instructor in ecclesiastical history for the year 1877–78; and professor of German literature in Harvard College from 1872 until his retirement in 1884. He continued to live in Cambridge until his death.

Although his adolescent years in Germany had allowed Hedge more freedom than was good for him, they had given him, as he said, " a thorough knowledge of the language, some acquaintance with its literature, and an early initiation in the realm of German idealism, then to our people an unknown world" (quoted by Chadwick, *post*). He came back to America well grounded in German literature and philosophy and continued to read Kant, Fichte, and Schelling. In 1836, when he joined Emerson and George Ripley in organizing a group of Transcendentalists, he was the only one of them who knew the German philosophical background of Transcendentalism at first hand. Recognizing Hedge's leadership, the group made his visits from Bangor to Boston the occasion for calling meetings and referred to themselves as "The Hedge Club," although in literary history they are known as "The Transcendental Club." Hedge's enthusiasm for German philosophy passed first to Margaret Fuller, then to Ripley, and to James Freeman Clarke. As a philosopher Hedge was neither Kantian nor Hegelian and avoided identifying himself with any one school of thought, but he was always with the idealists and intuitionalists against the realists and experimentalists. By 1836 many other American scholars could have given the Transcendental group an understanding of German philosophy; Hedge's unique service lay in bringing to it something of the very atmosphere of German thought.

He was president of the American Unitarian Association, 1859–62, and all his life a powerful leader in the Unitarian movement. No party in the church claimed him; in theology, as in philosophy, he belonged to no school. He was cautious about accepting the theory of evolution; yet he was bold, daring, even rash in his own speculation. As editor of the *Christian Examiner* he espoused no cause, though he was frankly intolerant of attempts to organize the Unitarian societies into large associations; he frowned on any move to make a denomination out of the free churches. As professor at the Harvard Divinity School he objected to the audacities of the western Unitarians when he himself was complacently doubting personal immortality and relegating the whole realm of nature to the devil. He formulated neither his theology nor his philosophy, and because he did not conform to any one party he exerted an influence on all factions.

His ability as a creative writer was displayed in his hymns and lyrics and in his orations of the decade after 1872, particularly the Luther oration (published 1888) and those published in *Ways of the Spirit and Other Essays* (1877);

but his chief service to literature was as a translator. His most noted single translation is the familiar English version of Luther's *"Ein feste Burg."* His *Prose Writers of Germany* was published in 1848. This collection of translations, with critical introductions, exhibited not only breadth of reading but discerning appreciation and literary skill in the translations from his own hand. Together with his indefatigable effort in periodicals and in conversation, it introduced German literature into America. His appointment to the German professorship at Harvard was a somewhat tardy recognition of his scholarship and zeal.

In addition to the scores of articles which he contributed to periodicals and the books previously mentioned, he published several volumes, including: *Conservatism and Reform* (1843); *Christian Liturgy; For the Use of the Church* (1853); *Hymns for the Church of Christ* (1853); *Recent Inquiries in Theology* (1860); *Reason in Religion* (1865); *The Primeval World of Hebrew Tradition* (1870); an edition of Goethe's *Faust* (1882); *Atheism in Philosophy* (1884); *Hours with German Classics* (1886); *Personality and Theism* (1887); *Martin Luther and Other Essays* (1888); *Metrical Translations and Poems* (1888), with Annis Lee Wister; and *Sermons* (1891).

[J. H. Allen, "A Memory of Dr. Hedge" and "Frederic Henry Hedge," *Unitarian Rev.*, Sept., Oct. 1890, the latter issue containing an autobiographical chapter on his youth in Germany; J. W. Chadwick, *Frederic Henry Hedge; A Sermon* (n.d.); *Nation* (N. Y.), Aug. 28, 1890; G. W. Cooke, *Unitarianism in America* (1902); H. C. Goddard, *Studies in New England Transcendentalism* (1908); S. A. Eliot, *Heralds of a Liberal Faith*, vol. III (1910); S. F. Kneeland, *Seven Centuries in the Kneeland Family* (1897).] R. W. A.

HEDGE, LEVI (Apr. 19, 1766–Jan. 3, 1844), philosopher, was born in Warwick, Mass. He was the second of the six sons of the Rev. Lemuel Hedge, a Harvard graduate and Congregational clergyman at Warwick, and of Sarah, daughter of the Rev. David White. Owing to the slender income of his father, and in accordance with the democratic customs of the day and place, Levi was early apprenticed to a mason and made his own way through college, graduating from Harvard in 1792. He was married to Mary Kneeland, daughter of Dr. William Kneeland and grand-daughter of President Holyoke of Harvard, on Jan. 15, 1801, at Cambridge, Mass. (S. P. Sharples, *Records of the Church of Christ at Cambridge in New England, 1632–1830*, 1906). From 1795 to 1800 he was annually appointed tutor in philosophy at Harvard, and in the latter year became the first "permanent tutor" there. In 1810 he was appointed professor of logic and metaphysics, and in 1827 Alford Professor of Natural Religion, Moral Philosophy, and Civil Polity, which position he held until 1832. In 1808 he received the honorary degree of A.M. from Brown and in 1823 that of LL.D. from Yale. For over forty years he was a familiar and respected figure in Cambridge, often seen under one of the "three eminent umbrellas" in the town, "vast and heavy structures, equally hard to spread or furl" (T. W. Higginson, *Old Cambridge*, 1899, p. 23).

In 1816 Hedge published his *Elements of Logick, or a Summary of the General Principles and Different Modes of Reasoning*, which ran through numerous editions and was translated into German (reviewed in the *North American Review*, November 1816). In this remarkably clear and simple work, the author, far in advance of his times, took a broad view of his subject, which, he asserted, should "teach the principles of every species of reasoning, which we have occasion to make use of, both in the pursuits of science, and in the ordinary transactions of life" (Preface). Accordingly he devoted much attention to the grounds of probable reasoning, included a chapter on the calculation of chances, and, all in all, produced a more practical textbook than many of a later date. In addressing his classes in regard to this book, Hedge, if tradition be correct, was accustomed to say, "It took me fourteen years, with the assistance of the adult members of my family, to write this book, and I am sure that you cannot do better than to employ the precise words of the learned author" (S. A. Eliot, *A History of Cambridge, Mass.*, 1913, p. 113). Besides being a philosopher, Hedge was also something of an orator and in 1818 delivered an edifying *Eulogy on the Rev. Joseph McKean.* His last work was to edit in two volumes the hitherto unpublished *Treatise on the Philosophy of the Human Mind* (1827) by Thomas Brown of Edinburgh. Frederic Henry Hedge [*q.v.*] was his son.

[Records of Harvard Univ.; Josiah Quincy, *Hist. of Harvard Univ.* (1840); S. A. Eliot, ed., *Heralds of a Liberal Faith* (1910), III, 159–60; Benj. Rand, "Philosophical Instruction in Harvard Univ. from 1636 to 1906," *Harvard Grads. Mag.*, Sept. 1928.] E. S. B.

HEENAN, JOHN CARMEL (May 2, 1835–Oct. 25, 1873), pugilist, son of Timothy and Mary (Morrissey) Heenan, was born in West Troy, N. Y., where his father was a foreman in the federal arsenal. As soon as the boy finished elementary school he was apprenticed as a machinist, but in 1852 the lure of gold and adventure drew him to California. Here he prospected, fought all comers, and labored in the Benicia shops of the Pacific Mail Steamship Company, where he threw a thirty-two-pound sledge for twelve hours per day. As the Vigilantes became active and fighters scarce, in 1857 Heenan with his manager, Jim Cusick, left for New York where strong-arm work in an election won him a sinecure in the customs service. With no desire to reënter the ring, he was forced by clamor and gibes to fight champion John Morrissey at Long Point, Canada, for $2,500 a side (Oct. 20, 1858). Heenan lost the technical decision, but in sportdom he was considered the better man. Modest and laughingly good-natured, the "Benicia Boy" was a popular figure; and his popularity was not lessened by his marriage, Apr. 3, 1859, to the fascinating actress, Adah Isaacs Menken [*q.v.*]. Unable to get a return match with Morrissey until he should have fought Tom Sayers, the holder of the English belt, Heenan accepted the latter's general challenge and went to England, where he established training quarters at Salisbury Plain.

Interest was keen in America and in the British Isles, and the newspapers pandered to this interest by emphasizing the international character of the conflict in lengthy articles. Finally, Sayers, a middle-sized, lithe man of superb training, faced Heenan in an enclosure near Farnborough (Apr. 17, 1860). Despite secrecy to avoid police interference, there were 12,000 spectators of every degree from costermongers to peers. Even Queen Victoria is said to have requested that news of the result be conveyed to her. In a suppressed note of approval, the crowd marveled at Heenan's powerful physique, for he was more than six feet tall, and when in condition weighed 196 pounds. In the thirty-seventh round, the ring was broken by the "bobbies," but the enraged "Benicia Boy" fought on, while some sixty Yankees held off the constables. Although he had knocked down Sayers repeatedly and the time was poorly kept, the referees declared a draw, a decision which the American press denounced as due to British partisanship.

On Heenan's return, he was greeted by enormous crowds in Eastern cities and given a considerable purse. The following year, he went back to England and challenged any Englishman for a side bet of $10,000. He and Sayers gave exhibition matches under the auspices of Joe Cushing, an American showman, and later he toured the kingdom with Howe's circus. Again, he fought a championship battle (Dec. 10, 1863), this time with Sailor Tom King at Wadhurst, England, losing the decision in the twenty-fifth round. Heenan was drugged, and the contest aroused hostility against the prize ring. He continued in England as a book-maker and, his first wife having divorced him in 1862, he married Sarah Stevens, an American actress. Returning to New York after the Civil War, he was charged with corruption in connection with the "Tweed ring," established a gambling parlor, and fought as a sparring partner of Jem Mace. On his way to California, he expired in Cusick's arms at Green River Station, Wyo.

[Frederick Locker-Lampson, *My Confidences* (1896); Joseph Irving, *Annals of Our Time* (1875); *Ann. Reg.; or a View of the Hist. and Politics of the Year 1860*, Apr. 1860; F. L. Dowling, *Fistiana* (1861); W. E. Harding, *John C. Heenan, His Life and Battles* (1881); Ed James, *The Life and Battles of J. C. Heenan* (1879); S. Sowden, *The Heenan and Sayers fight* (1860); *Career of the Champions; a Reliable Hist. of Tom Sayers and John C. Heenan* (1860); Jeffery Farnol, *Famous Prize Fights; or Epics of "The Fancy"* (1928); *N. Y. Times* and *N. Y. Herald*, Oct. 27, 1873; R. J. Purcell, "Fists Across the Sea," *Columbia*, Apr. 1926, based upon contemporary material in newspapers and magazines.]

R. J. P.

HEGEMAN, JOHN ROGERS (Apr. 18, 1844–Apr. 6, 1919), third president of the Metropolitan Life Insurance Company, was the son of John G. and Charlotte Owen Rogers Hegeman. His early education in public schools near his birthplace, Flatlands, now a part of Flatbush, Brooklyn, N. Y., was followed by study at a private school at Poughquag, Dutchess County, and a year at Brooklyn Polytechnic Institute. His progress in the business world was rapid, for within four years, 1866–70, he rose from book-keeper in the Bank of the Republic of New York City, to accountant and later secretary to the board of directors of the Manhattan Life Insurance Company. In June 1870 he became secretary of the Metropolitan Life Insurance Company, and on Oct. 25 of the same year he was elected vice-president, an office which he held for twenty years, succeeding Joseph F. Knapp to the presidency in 1891. During the years of Hegeman's connection with the Metropolitan, the business grew from a struggling company, carrying on a precarious existence in rented offices, to a nation-wide concern. From 1870 to 1918 it increased its insurance policies from less than ten thousand to almost twenty million; and from the time Hegeman became president until his death, the company's income rose from $11,423,496.68 to $200,218,763.48.

In its early days the Metropolitan carried on its life insurance business through the *Hildise Bund*, an organization made up of lodges with members who paid weekly premiums. Financial troubles in 1873 slowed down the ordinary insurance business, but when industrial insurance was introduced in 1875, Knapp and Hegeman worked out a system of industrial policies which the Metropolitan began writing in 1879 and concentrated upon until 1891. In that year Hegeman became president and Haley Fiske [*q.v.*] vice-president. Together these men revived the ordinary department, instructing the agents to write both ordinary and industrial policies. This enterprise met with immediate success, as did the practice, begun in 1896, of writing five-hundred-dollar policies for persons between those paying weekly premiums and those holding policies of a thousand dollars or more. Hegeman was particularly interested in the liberalization of policy provisions, and in health and welfare work. The Armstrong investigation of life insurance companies by the New York State legislature in 1905 brought about a limitation of the amount of ordinary business the company could write, but no restrictions were made regarding industrial insurance. As a result of the Armstrong investigation Hegeman himself was indicted in May 1907 on ten counts—seven of forgery and three of perjury. He was charged with having altered items in the annual reports of the Metropolitan Life Insurance Company submitted to the state life insurance commissioner. Although the fact that the alterations had been made was admitted, Judge Dowling of the New York supreme court dismissed the forgery indictments in 1907 on the ground that no intent to defraud was proved. The perjury indictments were allowed to stand but were dismissed in June 1910 by Judge Davis for the same reasons given by Judge Dowling.

Aside from his interest in insurance, Hegeman was a trustee of the Hamilton Trust Company and of the Union Dime Savings Bank, and a director of the Metropolitan Bank & National Surety Company. He and his wife were active Baptists, having a special interest in the Salem Baptist Church of New Rochelle, N. Y., which they helped to build. His wife was Evelyn Lyon of Brooklyn, whom he had married on Oct. 26, 1870. Ill health during his last years prevented Hegeman from actively carrying on his duties as president of the insurance company. After his wife's death in 1914 he traveled, especially in the Orient. He died in Mamaroneck, N. Y., in 1919. He bequeathed funds for a tuberculosis research laboratory which was completed at Mount McGregor, N. Y., in 1923 and is known as the John Rogers Hegeman Memorial.

[Sources include: a manuscript biography of Hegeman lent by the Metropolitan Life Insurance Company, New York; *The Metropolitan Life Insurance Company Hist.* (1908); *An Epoch in Life Insurance* (1924); *Docs. of the Assembly of the State of N. Y., No. 41*, 1906; *N. Y. Law Jour.*, Dec. 3, 1907, June 24, 1910; *Insurance Monitor*, Jan., Apr. 1909, Apr. 1919; *Insurance Press*, Apr. 9, 1919; the *Intelligencer*, pub. by the Metropolitan Life Insurance Company, July 1919; *N. Y. Times*, Aug. 3, Oct. 25, Nov. 10, 11, 14, 1905, May 23, 1907, Apr. 7, 8, 10, 22, 1919.] E. M. G.

HEILPRIN, ANGELO (Mar. 31, 1853–July 17, 1907), geologist, paleontologist, and explorer, son of Michael Heilprin [*q.v.*] and Henrietta (Silver) Heilprin, was born in Sátoralja-Ujhely, Hungary, whither his father had gone from Russian Poland, and was brought to the United States by his parents in 1856. He received his first education in the schools of Brooklyn and Yonkers, N. Y. While still a youth, scarcely out of school, he assisted his father, who was associate editor of the *New American Cyclopaedia*, by contributing several important articles. Since he displayed a fondness for science, he was encouraged to go to Europe in 1876, and at the Royal School of Mines (now the Normal School of Science), London, he studied biology under Huxley, geology under Judd, and paleontology under Etheridge. The next year he received the Forbes medal for proficiency in biology and paleontology. Subsequently he studied in Paris; in the University of Geneva, where he took up mineralogy; in Florence, and in Vienna. In the later city he attended lectures at the Imperial Geological Institute.

Returning to the United States in 1879, he was selected as a correspondent of the Academy of Natural Sciences, Philadelphia, the following year, and soon after was made professor of invertebrate paleontology in that institution. In 1883 he was elected curator in charge of the Academy, but resigned that position in 1892. He was selected as professor of geology in the Wagner Free Institute of Science, Philadelphia, in 1885, and three years later curator of the Institute's museum. In 1891 he was one of the founders and the leading spirit of the Geographical Club of Philadelphia, becoming its first president. It was subsequently known as the Geographical Society of Philadelphia. About ten years later he founded the Alpine Club, membership in which was limited to actual mountain climbers. In 1904 he was elected lecturer at the Sheffield Scientific School, Yale University, and he was the chief editor of *Lippincott's Pronouncing Gazetteer*, in 1905.

It was as a traveler and explorer, however, that he was best known. In 1886 he explored the Florida peninsula and the Everglades. In 1888 he made his first visit to Mexico, and his investigations led to the conclusion that the Peak of Orizaba (18,200 ft.), by which name Citlaltepetl is popularly known, was the highest summit of the North American continent, with the possible exception of Mount Logan. Prior to his explorations in Mexico, the volcanic peak of

Popocatepetl was generally believed to be the summit of North America, but all these beliefs were dispelled by the scaling of Mount McKinley, Alaska, which reaches to the height of 20,300 feet. In 1889 Heilprin made investigations of the physical history and zoölogy of the Bermuda Islands. When Lieut. Robert Peary [*q.v.*] made his first exploration of the Arctic in 1891, Heilprin headed the scientists accompanying him, representing the Academy of Natural Sciences, and the following year he led the expedition sent to relieve that explorer. He visited Morocco, Algeria, and Tunis in 1896, and Alaska and the Klondike in 1898, when the gold rush was beginning.

On May 8, 1902, Mont Pelée, which had shown signs of activity for three days, suddenly burst forth "with a violence that surpasses description," and overwhelmed 40,000 persons in the city of St. Pierre. A few days later Heilprin started on a steamer for Martinique. The eruption had not ceased when he arrived, and on May 20 the mountain was in violent convulsion again; but the Philadelphia scientist braved the danger and ascended its slopes. He made numerous photographs at ranges so close to the fiery crater as to place his life in constant jeopardy, but he continued his observations as coolly and calmly as if he had been examining a fossil in a museum. He remained in Martinique for several months, and made subsequent visits to the island. On his return from his first visit he made a report which added materially to the knowledge of vulcanology. His last expedition was a journey up the Orinoco River, British Guiana, in 1906. He contracted a fever and the disease so undermined his health that he never recovered, although his death, which was due to heart disease, was unexpected. It occurred at the home of a sister in New York City. He was gifted as a painter and pictures by him were exhibited at several exhibitions; he also drew the illustrations for some of his publications. He was granted a patent, January 1882, for a contrivance to turn the leaves of music on a piano, and one in April 1896 for a ventilating railroad-car window. For the latter he was awarded the Edward Longstreth Medal of the Franklin Institute in 1897.

Among his printed contributions to science are the following: *Contributions to the Tertiary Geology and Paleontology of the United States* (1884); *Town Geology: the Lesson of the Philadelphia Rocks* (1885); *Explorations on the West Coast of Florida, and in the Okeechobee Wilderness* (1887); *The Geological Evidences of Evolution* (1888); *The Bermuda Islands; a Contribution to the Physical History and Zoology of the Somers Archipelago* (1889); *Principles of Geology* (1890); *The Arctic Problem and Narrative of the Peary Relief Expedition* (1893); *The Earth and its Story* (1896); *Alaska and the Klondike* (1899); *Mont Pelée and the Tragedy of Martinique* (1903); *The Tower of Pelée* (1904). He contributed the article on Mexico to *The International Geography* (1900).

[*Bull. Geog. Soc. of Phila.*, vol. VI (1908); Gustav Pollak, *Michael Heilprin and his Sons* (1912); H. S. Morais, *The Jews of Phila.* (1894); *Who's Who in America*, 1906–07; *Who's Who in Pa.*, 1904; *Public Ledger* (Phila.), July 18, 1907; *N. Y. Times*, July 18, 1907.]

J. J.

HEILPRIN, MICHAEL (1823–May 10, 1888), scholar, writer, encyclopaedia expert, and worker in patriotic and philanthropic causes, was born at Piotrkow, Poland, of Hebrew ancestry, the son of Phineas Mendel and Hannah (Lipschitz) Heilprin. His father, though a merchant, was a scholar of high rank and an earnest student of philosophy, and among his ancestors there had been noted scholars during many generations. Michael never was sent to school nor had any teacher except his father; but from his earliest childhood he evinced the love of learning which he maintained throughout life. The family were ardent Polish patriots, and, finding Russian oppression intolerable in the years that followed the failure of the Polish insurrection of 1830, emigrated to Hungary in 1842. For two years after his arrival Michael devoted himself to the study of the language, literature, and history of his adopted country; and he entered, heart and soul, into the great national liberal movement which culminated in the Hungarian Revolution of 1848. Although he was a recent immigrant, such was his command of the Magyar language that his revolutionary poems had become widely popular before the outbreak of the Revolution; and in the revolutionary government he was offered and accepted the post of secretary to its literary bureau.

Upon the collapse of the Revolution, Heilprin escaped imprisonment only by fleeing the country. After a sojourn in France he returned to Hungary, but in 1856 emigrated to the United States. Here, though he was making but a precarious living by teaching, he at once became deeply interested in politics, and especially in the anti-slavery cause. In preparation for his coming, he had set about mastering the English language, and almost from his first arrival his facility in it was so great as to enable him to undertake any literary labor that might present itself. When, in 1858, he met George Ripley and Charles A. Dana [*qq.v.*], editors of the *New American Cyclopaedia,* then in its third volume, these gentlemen, impressed with the extent and accuracy of his scholarship, at once intrusted him with the revision of all the geographical, historical, and biographical articles. This was the first of a series of important connections with encyclopaedic works, some of which, especially the comprehensive revision of the *American Cyclopaedia* (1872–76), involved years of arduous labor, and drew upon his extraordinary store of accurate knowledge.

Apart from the periods covered by his encyclopaedia engagements, he made his living by teaching and writing. After the *Nation* was founded, Heilprin contributed articles on historical and linguistic subjects and on European politics. At the time of his death the editors declared his loss to the journal almost irreparable, "so largely has he contributed during the past twenty years to whatever reputation the *Nation* may have acquired for literary accuracy or breadth of information" (*Nation,* May 17, 1888). His life was brought to a premature close by his self-sacrificing labors in behalf of the Russian Jews driven from their native land by the barbarous fury of the persecution which broke out in 1881. His exertions were chiefly directed to the establishment of farm colonies for the refugees; but in many other ways he stood in the breach during several critical years.

Since nearly all of his writing was anonymous, and since he never formed any academic connection, it was only to a few that his quality, either as a scholar or as a writer, became known. His only published book, *The Historical Poetry of the Ancient Hebrews* (2 vols., 1879–80), a critical study, with original translations, of the poetical books of the Old Testament, was received with appreciation by eminent scholars, American and European. He was an enthusiastic talker and an appreciative listener; conversation with him was a delight, yet could not fail to impress the hearer with a sense of the amazing range and thoroughness of his knowledge. His beauty of soul and nobility of character were felt by all who knew him. In his twentieth year he married Henrietta Silver, who survived him. During the most strenuous years of his encyclopaedia labors he had the assistance of his three daughters and two sons. Of the latter, Louis became an encyclopaedia expert and Angelo [*q.v.*] a noted geologist and explorer.

[Gustav Pollak, *Michael Heilprin and his Sons* (1912); H. L. Morais, *The Jews of Phila.* (1894); John W. Chadwick, in the *Unitarian Rev.*, Sept. 1888; *Nation,* May 17, 1888; *N. Y. Times,* May 11, 1888.]

F. F.

HEINEMANN, ERNST (Feb. 19, 1848–May 11, 1912), wood-engraver, was a German, born in Brunswick, the son of J. August and Marie (Fricke) Heinemann. He studied under Adolf Closs and Richard Brend'amour of Düsseldorf. On May 4, 1872, he married Bertha Manzel of Stuttgart and the same year came to the United States. It was the dawn of the golden age of American reproductive engraving and he was drawn hither by the growing demand for artistic work for magazine and book illustration. On his arrival in New York he at first executed work for *Harper's Weekly* and other periodicals, and then allied himself for a time with the so-called "shop" of Frederick Juengling, at that date still an old-school engraver. Soon starting out on an independent career, he showed a command of the possibilities of the block which won him plenty of commissions. He was a contributor to the *de luxe* edition of Longfellow's poems issued by Houghton, Osgood & Company in 1879. Later he did work for *St. Nicholas* and the *Century.* As the new movement in wood-engraving gained headway, he was influenced by its spirit, but did not, according to Koehler, fall into its heresies. He displayed a quiet elegance and delicacy and a sensitive feeling for the original, which enabled him to render the manner, tone, and texture of a painter's work. He reproduced such strongly contrasted effects as the silvery tone and "airy, translucent manner," of F. S. Church in "Nymphe des Eaux," Frans Hals's jovial "Guitar Player," and the "rich, unctuous" chiaroscuro of Ribot's "Studio," which won a medal at the Pan American Exposition of 1901. Weitenkampf cites as his best work, Christopher Plantin's "Proofreaders."

When the perfecting of cheap photo-mechanical processes put a period to the brilliant success of American wood-engravers, Heinemann, like many another good craftsman, was forced to adapt himself to the new order. Thereafter he devoted his skill and his artistic feeling chiefly to the retouching of half-tone plates for school-book illustration, and to this impersonal work, in connection with the art department of the American Book Company, he was doomed from 1902 to the close of his life. An eager attendant at the sketch class of the Art Student's League during his prosperity in the eighties, he now enlivened his years of eclipse and financial struggle by pursuing for his own pleasure the study of painting and produced some delightful sketches in oils and watercolor of the landscape of Staten Island, his home for more than thirty years. He was a typical German of the old school, tall, athletic, soldierly, as befitted a veteran of the Franco-Prussian War, genial, bluff and kind-hearted, a favorite with the artists of the Salmagundi Club, of which he was long a member. He died at his home at Fort Wadsworth. A memorial exhibition of his work was held at the New York Public Library.

[Frank Weitenkampf, *American Graphic Art* (1912); *Abendblatt der New Yorker Staats Zeitung*, May 13, 1912; G. H. Whittle, "Monographs on American Wood Engravers," VIII, in *Printing Art*, Jan. 1918; S. R. Koehler in *Die Vervielfältigende Kunst der Gegenwart*, vol. I (1887); *Who's Who in America*, 1912–13; *N. Y. Times*, May 19, 1912; N. Y. *Evening Post*, May 18, 1912.]

M. B. H.

HEINRICH, ANTONY PHILIP (Mar. 11, 1781–May 3, 1861), composer, born at Schönbüchel, Bohemia, was adopted by a rich manufacturer and died in extreme poverty in New York after a strange, erratic, and partly uncharted career. He emigrated to America in 1805, as he claimed in 1850, "actuated by curiosity," although it is more than likely that he came for financial reasons. About 1810 he was director of music at the Southwark Theatre in Philadelphia. Before 1814 he revisited Europe by way of London, returning to America in 1816. After acting in Philadelphia and Baltimore as agent for a Trieste merchant, Heinrich retired in 1818 to Bardstown, Ky., where his career as a composer seems to have begun. A few years later he reappeared at Boston after having published at Philadelphia in 1820 *The Dawning of Music in Kentucky, or, The Pleasures of Harmony in the Solitudes of Nature. Opera Prima.* This collection of compositions for piano, voice or voices, violin, and other instruments, the most ambitious American publication of its kind and time, was reviewed at length in 1822 in the *Euterpiad* of Boston where Heinrich in 1823 is known to have been organist at the Old South Church. As late as 1910 a reviewer in the *Musical Times* of London pronounced the music almost equal to that of Sir Henry Bishop.

Some time after 1826 Heinrich made a second visit to England where in 1831 he was a violinist at the Drury Lane Theatre. In 1832 he reappeared in Boston. From 1834 to 1837 he revisited Europe, giving a concert of his works at Gratz in Styria on June 9, 1836. Soon afterward he settled in New York where he presided in 1842 at the meeting for the foundation of the Philharmonic Society. He left America in 1856 or 1857 for a last professional trip to Europe where, at Prague, on May 3, 1857, a concert of his works took place as "Vater Heinrich's Concert." He had become familiarly known in America as "Father Heinrich." This sobriquet certainly answered the fitness of things better than that of "the Beethoven of America," bestowed upon him by enthusiasts on such occasions as the "grand festivals" of his music at the Broadway Tabernacle, New York, June 16, 1842, or Tremont Temple, Boston, June 13, 1846.

After his Kentuckian "opera prima" Heinrich produced an amazing quantity of works, small and large, but only a few of his "fugitive pieces" and "occasional compositions," of which he presented two volumes on Sept. 23, 1857, to the National Museum in Prague, were published. Among the unpublished apparently was the very bulky "Sylviad or Minstrelsy of Nature. . . . An old Work, Vocal and for the Pianoforte" which he listed as "lost by fire in Boston" and as "No. 72" in the "Nomenclature" of his works. This list, compiled about 1857, forms a part of his voluminous book of "Memoranda" which is now a principal source of information about his career. It was acquired by the Library of Congress with many of his major works, the majority in his own hand. (See *Report of the Librarian of Congress . . . 1917.*) Most of them employ an unusually large orchestra. If only the orchestral technique and musical substance had measured up to Heinrich's ambitious demands! Nevertheless, while these works, even in their own day of somewhat obsolete style, have lost their musical interest, historically they retain their significance because Heinrich, an odd mixture of simple-minded sincerity and freakish eccentricity, presumably was the first composer deliberately to essay "Americanism" in music, and to build many of his works on American subjects. Occasionally he employed Indian themes for the purpose. A few characteristically bombastic titles of these pioneer works suffice as proof: *The Columbiad. Grand American National Chivalrous Symphony* (1837?); *The Indian War Council: Gran Concerto Bellico for Forty-one Instrumental Parts* (1834?); *The Treaty of William Penn with the Indians, Concerto Grosso* (1834?); *Wild-wood Spirit's Chant or Scintillations of Yankee Doodle, Forming a Grand National Heroic Fantasia Scored for a Powerful Orchestra in Forty-four Parts.* Heinrich was twice married. His second wife, an American, died in Boston in 1817.

[See Gustav Schilling, *Encyc. der gesammten musikalischen Wissenschaften*, vol. III (1836); F. J. Fétis, *Biog. Universelle des Musiciens et Bibliog. Générale de la Musique*, vol. V (1839); *Allgemeine Musikalische Zeitung*, Feb. 1836; *Dwight's Jour. of Music*, Apr. 20, May 11, 1861; F. A. Mussik, *Skizzen aus dem Leben des sich in Amerika befindenden deutschen Tondichters Anton Philipp Heinrich* (1843); *Anthony Philip Heinrich ("Vater Heinrich"), zur Lebensgeschichte des Veteran Kompositeurs* (1857); H. T. Drowne. "Memories of the Grand Musical Festival . . . by Anthony Philip Heinrich in the Broadway Tabernacle,

N. Y., June 16, 1842," MS. in the Lib. of Cong.; J. H. Hewitt, *Shadows on the Wall or Glimpses of the Past* (1877); *The New Encyc. of Music and Musicians* (1929), ed. by W. S. Pratt; *N. Y. Times,* May 4, 1861. Heinrich's name is variously spelled; he himself wrote it as it is given here.] O. G. T. S.

HEINRICH, MAX (June 14, 1853–Aug. 9, 1916), concert baritone, was born in Chemnitz, Saxony. After studying music at the Zwickau Gymnasium under Karl Emanuel Klitzsch from 1865 to 1869, and later at the Dresden Conservatory, he emigrated to the United States in 1873, at a time when concert life was well developed, especially in the East. He taught music in Philadelphia until 1876, when he accepted a position in the Judson Institute, Marion, Ala. In 1882 he left the South, went to New York, and began his career as a concert artist with his appearance in the rôle of Elijah in Mendelssohn's oratorio, with the New York Choral Society. His success was immediate. He frequently sang at orchestral concerts conducted by Seidl, Thomas, Gericke, Paur, Nikisch, and Walter Damrosch, and for a short time appeared in opera, but it was in his individual song recitals, at which he played his own accompaniments, that he made his chief contribution to the furtherance of good music in America as a pioneer in the cultivation of a taste for the German *Lied.* In these recitals he presented the songs of Schubert, Franz, Schumann, Brahms, and other German composers. He frequently changed his scene of activity. In 1884 he visited California on a tour with Theodore Thomas' orchestra, and he lived and sang successively in Chicago, 1894–1903, in Boston, 1903–10, and in New York, 1910–16. For only five years, from 1888 to 1893, when he was in London as professor of singing at the Royal Academy of Music, did he live outside of the United States after his first arrival. He translated into English the texts of many of the classics in his repertory; composed songs, and arranged musical settings to accompany the recitation of Poe's "The Raven" and Waller's "Magdalena," anticipating later works of this kind by Max von Schillings, Richard Strauss, and Rossiter G. Cole. He was the author of a technical treatise, *Correct Principles of Classical Singing* (1910). These creative activities, however, were less important than his activity as an exponent of German *Lieder.* Heinrich was twice married. His first wife was Anna Schubert who died in 1900. About 1904 he was married to Anna Held, from whom he later separated.

[*Internat. Who's Who in Music and Musical Gazetteer* (1918); *Music,* Oct. 1900; *Who's Who in Music* (2nd ed., 1915); *Musical Observer,* Oct. 1911; *Musical Advance,* Sept. 1916; *Musical America,* Dec. 11, 1909, Aug. 19, 1916.] F. H. M.

HEINTZELMAN, SAMUEL PETER (Sept. 30, 1805–May 1, 1880), soldier, was born at Manheim, Lancaster County, Pa., the son of Peter and Ann Elizabeth (Grubb) Heintzelman. He received a fair elementary education and was appointed a cadet at West Point in 1822. Graduating four years later, he became a lieutenant in the 2nd Infantry and was promoted to captain in 1838. On Dec. 5, 1844, he married Margaret Stewart of Albany, N. Y. In 1847 he joined General Scott's expedition against the City of Mexico and was brevetted major for gallant and meritorious conduct at the battle of Huamantla. He was promoted to major in 1855 and served with the 1st Infantry in California, being again brevetted, this time for gallantry in action against Indians. He founded Fort Yuma, Ariz., afterwards operating along the Rio Grande border, then infested with marauders.

Early in 1861 he was called to Washington as inspector of the forces there collecting. In May he was appointed colonel of the 17th Infantry, and a few days later brigadier-general of volunteers. On May 24 he captured Alexandria, Va., initiating the military operations near Washington. Soon after he was assigned to the 3rd Division of McDowell's army, which he commanded in the ensuing Bull Run campaign. In the battle of Bull Run he led his division to the support of Hunter's troops, already engaged. Heintzelman's troops were slow to arrive, and no united attack was made; yet they captured the Henry house, the key point of the battle-field. The enemy, through an unfortunate error being mistaken for friends, was able to seize the Union artillery, which had advanced to a line near the Henry house. Heintzelman personally directed numerous efforts to recapture the lost guns, and fought desperately but unsuccessfully. His division was driven from the field, and he himself was severely wounded. In the spring of 1862, he commanded the III Corps, in General McClellan's army during the Peninsula campaign. He led the advance on Yorktown, again initiating operations. His report to McClellan that an assault was impracticable was one of the causes of the protracted siege, which ended on May 4 when the Confederates quietly marched away. Heintzelman started in pursuit, and late the same day his corps gained contact with the enemy near Williamsburg. On May 5 a severe battle was fought, the main attack being largely under Heintzelman's direction. The result was indecisive, owing to lack of coördination between the Union commanders. Three years later Heintzelman was brevetted for his gallant conduct in this battle. At the battle of Seven Pines, May 31, he was the senior officer south of the Chickahominy. When the news of the Confederate attack upon the front line reached him, he at once sent his own corps to the front to resist the advancing enemy. He himself went forward and attempted to restore order among the retiring troops; but personal bravery did not compensate for absence of leadership, and unorganized efforts only prolonged the fighting into the next day without securing victory. Heintzelman was selected to lead what was intended to be the final attack on Richmond, commencing June 25. This started the Seven Days' battles. A slight initial gain was counterbalanced on June 26 by the Confederate attack elsewhere on the battle-field. McClellan decided to withdraw his army. Heintzelman fell back, on June 29, rather precipitately, due to a misunderstanding of the situation. On June 30, his corps fought well. On July 1, at Malvern Hill, it was engaged, but not as seriously as other troops. On July 4, Heintzelman was promoted to major-general of volunteers. His next service was in August 1862, when his corps, withdrawn from the Peninsula, was sent to reenforce Pope's army in the Manassas campaign. Two days, Aug. 27–28, were spent in exhausting marches. On Aug. 29 Heintzelman attacked what he supposed to be a retreating enemy, but instead found the redoubtable Jackson awaiting him. His attack was repulsed. Its renewal the next day met with no greater success, and the Union army withdrew.

Heintzelman was now assigned to the defenses of Washington, on which duty he remained until October 1863. Early in 1864, he was sent to command the Northern (Central States) Department, from which he was relieved in October of the same year. He was employed on courts-martial duty for the remainder of the war. Mustered out of the volunteer service in August 1865, he assumed command of the 17th Infantry, and served with it, mostly in Texas, until retired in February 1869. A few months later, he was made a major-general retired, by special act of Congress. He resided in Washington until his death. He had a stern, rather unkempt appearance, with full beard and long, thin hair. Although he was gifted with personal bravery, his gallant conduct failed to make him a successful leader; he lacked initiative, and magnified difficulties.

[The principal source for Heintzelman's war record is *War of the Rebellion: Official Records (Army)*; the *Report of the Joint Committee on the Conduct of the War at the Second Session, Thirty-eighth Congress* (1865) contains interesting matter; G. B. McClellan in *McClellan's Own Story* (1887) gives an account of his relations with Heintzelman, in the main correct. See also G. W. Cullum, *Biog. Reg. of the Officers and Grads. U. S. Mil. Acad.*, vol. I (3rd ed., 1891); F. B. Heitman, *Hist. Reg. and Dict. U. S. Army*, vol. I (1903); Third Army Corps Union, *Obit. Notice of Maj.-Gen. Samuel P. Heintzelman, First Commander of the Third Army Corps* (1881); *Eleventh Ann. Reunion Asso. Grads. U. S. Mil. Acad.* (1880); *Evening Star* (Washington), May 1, 1880; A. K. Hostetter, in *Hist. Papers and Addresses of the Lancaster County Hist. Soc.*, vol. XVII (1913).] C. H. L.

HEINZ, HENRY JOHN (Oct. 11, 1844–May 14, 1919), manufacturer of prepared food, was born in the Birmingham section of Pittsburgh, of German parents, the eldest of the eight children of Henry and Margaretha (Schmidt) Heinz, and spent his boyhood and youth in Sharpsburg, Pa. After completing the course in Duff's Business College he became the bookkeeper and factotum of his father's brickyard and was taken into partnership when he came of age. He put the business on a year-round basis by installing heating flues and drying apparatus in the plant, and to the end of his life he was a connoisseur of bricks and brick-laying. He always attended personally to the buying and laying of brick for the buildings of his company, and his office desk, which he seldom used for anything else, was frequently piled with samples collected on his travels. The paternal brickyard was only an interlude, however, in his real career, which began, when he was eight years old, by his peddling the surplus produce from the family garden. Using hotbeds and intensive cultivation, he obtained two or three crops a year and steadily enlarged his acreage and market until in 1860 he employed several women and made three wagon deliveries a week to Pittsburgh grocers. In 1869 he and L. C. Noble formed a partnership to make and sell grated horseradish and later admitted E. J. Noble to the firm and moved their business to Pittsburgh. They went bankrupt in 1875, Heinz later paying his share of their debts in full. The next year, with his brother John and his cousin Frederick as partners and himself as manager, he started the partnership of F. & J. Heinz to manufacture pickles, condiments, and other prepared food. In 1888 this partnership was reorganized as the H. J. Heinz Company, and in 1905 it was incorporated with Heinz as president. In 1919 it had 6,523 employees, twenty-five branch factories, eighty-five pickle-salting stations, its own bottle, box, and can-factories, and its own seed farms, and was putting the annual harvests from 100,000 acres into bottles, cans, and barrels. In 1896 Heinz invented the advertising slogan of "fifty-seven varieties," which became an American proverbial expression; he knew at the time that his factories were making more than that many kinds of goods, but "fifty-seven" sounded to him like a magic number and proved to be one. The H. J. Heinz Company was a pioneer in the pure-food movement in the United States and in welfare work among employees. During its whole history under its founder, it never suffered from labor troubles.

Heinz was married on Sept. 23, 1869, to Sarah Sloan Young, of Irish descent, by whom he had five children. After her death in 1894 he built and endowed a settlement house, the Sarah Heinz House, in her memory. Through accident rather than through any changes of doctrinal opinion, he became a member successively of the Lutheran, the Methodist Episcopal, the Methodist Protestant, and the Presbyterian churches. He was a Sunday-school superintendent for twenty-five years and prominent in state, national, and international Sunday-school associations. He supported various educational enterprises, became in his later years an enthusiastic traveler, and collected watches and ivories that are now in the Carnegie Museum of Pittsburgh. He died of pneumonia at his home in Pittsburgh on the day when he had expected to attend a Sunday-school convention in New York.

[*Who's Who in America,* 1906–19; *Henry J. Heinz* (H. J. Heinz Co., 1919); *The Story of the Sunday School Life of Henry J. Heinz* (privately printed, 1920); E. D. McCafferty, *Henry J. Heinz* (1923); *Pittsburgh Post,* May 15, 1919.]

A.I.

HEINZE, FREDERICK AUGUSTUS (Dec. 5, 1869–Nov. 4, 1914), Montana copper king, was born in Brooklyn, N. Y. His father, Otto Heinze, was a German; his mother, Lida March Lacey, was a Connecticut Yankee with a strain of Irish blood. His father named him Fritz, but while still a schoolboy he dropped the name as too German and thereafter generally signed himself F. Augustus; he gave his first name as Frederick when applying for a marriage license. He was educated at the Brooklyn Polytechnic Institute, the Columbia School of Mines, and in Germany. After graduating from Columbia in 1889 he went to Butte, Mont., where he found employment as an engineer with the Boston & Montana Mining Company. Although William A. Clark and Marcus Daly [*qq.v.*] were then developing their organizations and beginning to control the copper market, Heinze, keen, alert, and resourceful, saw opportunities that they had missed. After spending the year 1891 in New York on the editorial staff of the *Engineering and Mining Journal,* he returned to Montana and leased the rich Estella mine from James Murray, "the shrewdest operator in Butte," and manipulated the deal so that he got all the profits. In 1893 he organized the Montana Ore Purchasing Company and built a smelter for the small independent producers. He leased the abandoned Glengarry mine and found a rich vein of copper. In 1895 he bought the Rarus mine for $400,000, and made it pay him millions. From Miles Finlen, Marcus Daly's partner, he bought the unproductive Minnie Healy mine, and within a month uncovered the richest copper vein in Butte. When this business was prospering, Heinze decided to invade the Kootenay region in Canada. There he built a smelter and obtained a land grant to build a railroad to the coast, but the Canadian Pacific, alarmed, soon bought him out at a high price.

Heinze was doubtless willing to sell because he saw impending a fight with the large copper companies at Butte. The chief weapon on both sides was the "apex law," under the terms of which the owner of the apex of a vein of ore could follow the vein downward even under the land of another. Heinze's intimate knowledge of the ore deposits around Butte and his clever imagination enabled him to turn the "apex law" to his advantage. The Boston & Montana Company began the fight by suing Heinze. When the newly created Amalgamated Copper Company absorbed the former company it inherited this suit along with a number of others. Since these were equity cases, to be decided by judges elected by the people, there ensued a bitter political struggle. Heinze was popular, while the "trust" was dreaded. The Amalgamated cut miners' wages and Heinze maintained them. He bought newspapers, hired bands and speakers, and succeeded in electing his men as judges. Then he claimed much Amalgamated property under the "apex law," and since the apex could not be determined except by excavating, it was difficult to disprove his contentions. He secured many injunctions against the Amalgamated and exploited its property until the trust gave up and closed its mines. Finally in 1903 the legislature, in special session, passed the "fair trial" bill which enabled the Amalgamated to carry its suits to other judges, and Heinze's control of the Butte mines was weakened. In 1906 he sold most of his holdings there for $10,500,000. He then organized the United Copper Company and gained control of a number of banks, including the Mercantile National Bank of New York City. The Standard Oil Company, which controlled the Amalgamated, continued the fight. One of the first breaks in the panic of 1907 was the fall of United Copper stocks, which was followed by a run on the Heinze banks. The Heinze group was notified by the New York Banks

Clearing House Committee that they must relinquish their offices before aid would be given their banks, and it then appeared that the panic was precipitated by the struggle to get rid of Heinze. Thereafter he never wielded his former power, although he continued to be interested in several mining and railway projects. He was married, Aug. 31, 1910, to Berenice (Golden) Henderson, an actress, the divorced wife of Charles A. Henderson. Heinze and his wife were divorced in 1912, shortly after the birth of their only child, but became reconciled in 1913, just before the death of Mrs. Heinze. Heinze died suddenly at Saratoga Springs, N. Y.

A handsome man of powerful build, Heinze had the faculty of winning and holding the loyalty of all sorts of people. He was equally at ease in a group of miners, in cultured society, and in the gambling dens of Butte. He was a convincing speaker and in political campaigns won votes by his eloquence as well as by bribery and trickery. Five of his speeches were published in 1902 in a volume entitled *The Political Situation in Montana, 1900–1902.* He made bitter enemies and was himself a fearless and unrelenting enemy. In Butte the Heinze days were among the most vivid of its colorful history.

[C. P. Connolly, "The Fight of the Copper Kings" and "The Fight for the Minnie Healy," in *McClure's Mag.*, May, June, July 1907; W. R. Stewart, "F. Augustus Heinze," in *Cosmopolitan*, Jan. 1904; "The Story of Heinze, a Tale of Copper and Brass," in *Current Lit.*, Jan. 1908; Helen Sanders, *A Hist. of Mont.* (1913), vol. I; Tom Stout, *Montana* (1921) vol. I; files of the *Anaconda Standard*, the *Butte Miner*, and Heinze's *Daily Evening News*; C. A. Conant, *A Hist. of Modern Banks of Issue* (1909); obituaries in *Anaconda Standard*, *N. Y. Times*, Nov. 5, 1914, and *Engineering and Mining Jour.*, Nov. 14, 1914.] P. C. P.

HEINZEN, KARL PETER (Feb. 22, 1809–Nov. 12, 1880), German revolutionist, journalist, and author, was born in Grevenbroich, in the Düsseldorf district of Rhenish Prussia, son of Joseph and Marie Elisabeth (Schmitz) Heinzen. His father during the French Revolution was one of the most ardent of Rhenish republicans, but turned conservative when he accepted the post of Prussian forest inspector in 1815. The early death of his mother deprived the boy of her sympathy and love, and the restraint put upon him at home and at school served to foster a ruling passion for opposing all arbitrary authority. After completing his studies in the Gymnasium of Cleve, he began the study of medicine at Bonn in 1827, but on account of a revolutionary speech was dismissed from the university. Wishing to see the world, he entered the Dutch military service, which brought him the rank of a subaltern officer and a trip to the East Indies in 1829. Some years after he published a graphic picture of his eighteen months' sojourn there, in a work entitled *Reise nach Batavia* (1841). After he had returned home in 1833, though he had suffered mental tortures under the monotony of a soldier's life, he performed the required year of Prussian military service. His deep attachment for the accomplished and beautiful Luise Schiller during this period was a turning point in his early life. She was the daughter of the lawyer Moras in Cleve, and widow of the cavalry captain, Richard Schiller. She inspired the most beautiful of Heinzen's poems, those lamenting her early death. The care and education of her four children Heinzen, then twenty-six years of age, took upon himself, sacrificing eight years of his life in most distasteful and ill-paid clerical service under a bureaucratic government, a life especially galling to a man of his independent spirit. In 1840 the oldest daughter, Henriette Schiller, became his wife, to whom and their son, Karl Frederick, born in 1844, Heinzen dedicated his autobiography, *Erlebtes,* in remembrance of their having borne bravely and cheerfully the persecutions and miseries of which the book gives account. His positions in the Prussian civil service were first, that of a tax-collector, later clerk in the Rhenish railway system at Köln. He then accepted a better paid position with the Aachen Fire Insurance Company, the duties of which also left him some leisure for writing. A volume of poems, *Gedichte* (1841), was favorably reviewed by the leading critics Menzel and Kurz, who saw in his work virility, genuine emotion, and unconventionality. It was in satire, however, that Heinzen early found his proper sphere. *Die Ehre* (1842), and *Die geheime Konduitenliste* (1842) sharply criticized Prussian civil government, and he became even bolder in his contributions to the radical journals *Leipzige Allgemeine Zeitung* and *Rheinische Zeitung,* which were both forbidden in Prussia. This interdict angered Heinzen into writing his severe arraignment of Prussian bureaucracy, *Die preussische Büreaukratie* (1844), which was widely circulated in spite of the order of confiscation. Criminal proceedings were instituted against the author, who, however, escaped to Belgium and in 1846 went to Switzerland, whence he sent his broadsides of revolutionary propaganda into German territory, aided secretly and skilfully by liberal friends. Noteworthy among his bitter satires were *Ein Steckbrief* (1845), *Mehr als zwanzig Bogen* (1845), *Politische und unpolitische Fahrten und Abenteuer* (1846), *Macht euch bereit* (1846). The pens of Heine and of Börne in the preceding decade were not more caustic and effective. The radical of radicals was banished successively from Zürich, Basel-Land, Bern, and Geneva, and in January 1848 he came to the United States. In New York, in conjunction with Ivan Tyssowski, the Krakau revolutionist, he edited *Die deutsche Schnellpost,* founded by Eichthal. When the Paris revolution broke out in February 1848, Heinzen hastened back and took active part in the second Baden revolution, but antagonized most of the other leaders. After the collapse he was not tolerated in France or Switzerland, but was transported with his family to London. When all hope of a third revolution had to be abandoned, he set sail for America, arriving in New York in 1850. There he founded the radical paper *Der Völkerbund,* only one number of which appeared. After its financial failure he again edited *Die deutsche Schnellpost,* subsequently the *New Yorker Deutsche Zeitung,* and finally the *Janus,* all of which failed in quick succession. Finding a new great cause in the abolition of slavery, which he wished to agitate in a slave state, he removed to Louisville, Ky., in 1853 to become editor of the *Herold des Westens.* His establishment was burned, but German friends gave him a new start with a paper called the *Pionier,* founded in 1854, removed to Cincinnati, then to New York, and finally in 1859 to Boston. Into this weekly journal he poured his intellectual powers and his soul for more than twenty years. Extremely radical, always advocating unpopular causes, it yielded at best a hand-to-mouth existence, but the editor never considered his material welfare, and his able wife for long periods reduced publication expenses to a minimum by serving as type-setter and business manager. The *Pionier* appeared until December 1879, a year before Heinzen's death.

A born satirist, he spared neither friend nor foe; opposition he could not tolerate; the value of tact and cooperation he never learned. A courageous seeker after truth, he could not compromise with truth as others saw it. The most intellectual of all the German revolutionists, he never mastered the English language and his works with very few exceptions became known to only a limited few. His masterful German style with its clear flow, caustic wit, and brilliant sallies could not easily be transferred into another language. He thought a truly democratic republic must not be based alone on equal political but also on equal social rights. He did not believe in communism, for that could be maintained only through an unendurable despotism. The sacredness of property based on individual work he considered a necessity for personal independence. Heinzen's philosophy was materialistic, his religion ethical, non-Christian, anti-institutional. He was opposed to all strongly centralized government, but had nothing constructive to offer in its place.

An edition of his collected works was to comprise twelve volumes, but only five appeared. There is a four-volume collection of his essays and addresses under the title: *Teutscher Radikalismus in Amerika: Ausgewahlte Vortrage* (1867–79). Among his essays, editions of which appeared in English are: *Mankind the Criminal* (1864); *Six Letters to a Pious Man* (1869); *The True Character of Humboldt* (1869), an oration; *What is Real Democracy?* (1871); *Lessons of a Century* (1876), a Fourth of July oration; *What is Humanity?* (1877); *Separation of State and Church* (1882); *The Rights of Women and the Sexual Relation* (1891).

[*Erlebtes,* autobiog., erster Theil (1864), zweiter Theil (1874); *Allgemeine Deutsche Biographie, Bd.* 50 (1905); Heinrich Kurz, *Geschichte der deutschen Literatur, Bd.* 4 (5th ed. 1894); *Deutsch-amerikanisches Conversations-Lexicon, Bd.* 5 (1877), ed. by A. J. Schem; H. A. Rattermann, *Der Deutsche Pionier,* Apr.–Sept. 1881; P. O. Schinnerer, in *Jahrbuch der Deutsch-Amerikanischen Historischen Gesellschaft von Illinois . . . 1915* (1916); *Boston Transcript,* Nov. 13, 1880; manuscript sources in the possession of Henriette M. Heinzen, Cambridge, Mass.]

A. B. F.

HEISS, MICHAEL (Apr. 12, 1818–Mar. 26, 1890), Roman Catholic missionary, educator, and bishop, was born in Pfahldorf, of Bavarian peasant stock, the son of Joseph and Gertrude (Frei) Heiss. After completing his grammar-school course in Pfahldorf without showing much promise, his parents risked sending him to high school in Eichstätt. He was finally told to make good in Latin or go home. He managed to escape this penalty, and thereafter his school record was invariably satisfactory. In 1831 he went to the Gymnasium of Neuburg on the Danube; from 1835 to 1839 he was at the University of Munich; and from 1839 to 1840, in the diocesan seminary of Eichstätt. The university in his day was celebrated by such names as Görres, Döllinger, and Moehler. Heiss stated that the last of these influenced the turn of his life, and that Moehler's work, *Symbolik,* and Friedrich von Hurter's *Geschichte Papst Innocenz des Dritten,* formed the basis for his future career. After ordination at Nymphenburg, Oct. 18, 1840, he resided as curate in Raitenbuch, but his work lay in four nearby missions.

A visit of Bishop John Purcell [*q.v.*] of Cincinnati, Heiss's interest in news-letters in the French, Austrian, and Bavarian missionary pamphlets and the stimulus of an American friend, Rev. Charles Boeswald, influenced him to come to the United States. He arrived late in 1842 and was assigned to Covington, Ky., where he remained about a year, and in 1844, as secretary, accompanied Bishop John Henni [*q.v.*] to Milwaukee. For a number of years he acted as pastor for the Germans of St. Mary's, Milwaukee, and visited missions within a radius of fifty miles. He was the first rector of St. Francis Seminary, St. Francis, Wis. (1856–68), an institution which he helped to found and in which he did heroic teaching in the branches of theology, canon law, and scripture. As the first bishop of La Crosse, Wis. (1868–80), he carried heavy burdens. One of his letters tells of eleven addresses given in one day and naïvely goes on about the next day and its tasks. Contemporaries considered him apostolic in humility and zeal, a characteristic which he unwittingly betrayed in his pen name *Caecus Videns,* "Blind (himself) Seeing (for others)." His letters, published as "Reminiscences" (*post*), are as edifying and piquant as the *Confessions* of St. Augustine. He became archbishop of Milwaukee in 1880, and in the ten years of his incumbency paid off the diocesan debt and effected the definitive organization of the diocese, by planning and directing the first Provincial Council of Milwaukee (1886). Probably his influence did more than that of any other one person to secure the repeal of the Bennett Law, a public school act which created much commotion in Wisconsin in 1889 and 1890. He was considered one of the leading theologians and canonists in the United States, and enjoyed special consideration for his work at the second and third Plenary councils of Baltimore (1866, 1884) and the Vatican Council (1870). He was called to Rome in 1883 to advise the Pope on American church affairs. He was one of five bishops who planned a curriculum for Catholic seminaries and colleges and helped to establish the Catholic University at Washington.

The activities associated with his career as missionary, rector, bishop and archbishop, would seem to preclude much else; nevertheless, he found time to write two scholarly books, one on marriage for the American clergy, *De Matrimonio* (Munich, 1861), the other, *The Four Gospels* (Milwaukee, 1863), and to make a remarkable contribution to the history of the eleventh century, centering around St. Peter Damian, which he left in manuscript. He also furnished articles to the *Pastoral-Blatt,* and contributed to newspapers, especially the *Wahrheitsfreund.*

[The best source of information is Heiss's letters published as "Reminiscences" in *Salesianum,* Feb. 1908–July 1919. See also D. J. O'Hearn, *Fifty Years at St. John's Cathedral* (n.d.); *Milwaukee Sentinel,* Mar. 27, 1890; and bibliography under sketch of John Martin Henni.] P. L. J.

HELBRON, PETER (1739–Apr. 24, 1816), Catholic missionary, son of Joannes Matthias and Maria Magdalene (Gottlieb) Helbron, was born in Hilbringen im Kreise Merzig, Rhenish Province, and was baptized on July 9, 1739. Little is known of his career in Germany save that he served in the Prussian cavalry and later was ordained a priest in the Capuchin order, which was conversant with American conditions since several of its members were chaplains in the French service during the American Revolution. Influenced by the knowledge they had disseminated and by the letter of Rev. James Pettentz (one of the few German priests in America) in the *Mainzer Monatschrift von Geistlichen Sachen* (1785) urging German priests for their brethren in America, Helbron decided to enter the American mission field despite the lack of an official invitation. Sailing from Rotterdam with his brother, John Charles Baptist Helbron (1746–Nov. 25, 1793), he arrived at Philadelphia on Oct. 14, 1787, and the following month was assigned to the important German center of Goshenhoppen, Berks County, Pa., from which he attended distant missions. A man of refinement, he was precise in his attire and in attention to duties and a good preacher in his native tongue. Hence he so won the favor of his people that the trustees of the Church of the Holy Trinity, Philadelphia, invited him to succeed his brother who went to Spain in 1791 on a collection tour for the new church, and later, although a constitutional priest, was guillotined at Bayonne, France, for his refusal to close his church. In Philadelphia Helbron, whose military training made him an invaluable nurse in the cholera epidemic of 1793, succeeded despite troublesome trustees and the fears of Bishop John Carroll [*q.v.*] that the presence of a Capuchin in a German parish would tend to incite racial schism. At length, however, Father John Nepomucene Goetz intrigued with the trustees until they expelled Helbron and established himself as pastor. Followed by the less contentious portion of the flock, Helbron went to St. Joseph's Church as a curate (Nov. 16, 1796). Three years later, he was assigned to Sportsman's Hall, where Rev. Theodore Brouwers, a Hollander (d. 1790), had organized a considerable German and Irish congregation. Here he built a chapel and log house, tilled his own farm for a livelihood, settled racial difficulties which confronted his friend, Demetrius Gallitzin [*q.v.*], made astonishing missionary excursions on horseback over all western Pennsylvania and as far as Buffalo, built a chapel at Greensburg, and gathered together the first congregation in Pittsburgh aided by his temporary assistant, Thomas O'Flynn, and Col. James O'Hara [*q.v.*], the glass-manufacturer. His activities drew the attention of the reformed trustees of Holy Trinity and in 1804 they urged his return to their pulpit, but he had become too much attached to the Pennsylvania frontier, whither he was drawing numerous German immigrants and where he was laying the foundations for two prospective dioceses, to be lured away. With advancing age, he was troubled with an incurable tumor. Returning from Philadelphia where he had consulted a specialist, he was forced to halt at Carlisle and there he died, leaving his pittance of an estate to the local church, in which his remains were buried.

[N. H. Miller, "Pioneer Capuchin Missionaries in the U. S. 1784–1816" (manuscript essay, 1930, in Cath. Univ. Lib.); *Katholische Volks-Zeitung*, June 1869; A. A. Lambing, *A Hist. of the Cath. Ch. in the Dioceses of Pittsburg and Allegheny* (1880); H. G. Ganss, "Hist. of St. Patrick's Church, Carlisle, Pa.," *Records Am. Cath. Hist. Soc.*, Dec. 1895, and M. I. J. Griffin, "The Rev. Peter Helbron," *Ibid.*, Mar. 1912; *Poulson's Am. Daily Advertiser* (Phila.), May 8, 1816; information from Dr. Felix Fellner, O. S. B.] R. J. P.

HELFFENSTEIN, JOHN ALBERT CONRAD (Feb. 16, 1748–May 17, 1790), German Reformed clergyman, was born at Mosbach in the Palatinate, the son of Peter Helffenstein, Reformed pastor at Mosbach and Obrigheim and later at Heidelsheim and Sinsheim, by his wife, Anna Margaretha Dietz, widow of Johann Peter Helffrich. He matriculated May 7, 1764, at the University of Heidelberg and, after passing his theological examinations, was vicar to his father and other clergymen for several years. In 1771 he and his half-brother, John Henry Helffrich, were ordained by the synods of Holland for the Coetus of Pennsylvania and embarked Sept. 6 from Amsterdam. With them sailed John Gabriel Gebhard, who was the Reformed pastor from 1776 to 1826 at Claverack, N. Y. The voyage was a succession of head winds and violent storms, but on Jan. 14, 1772, with their provisions and water exhausted, the three missionaries landed safely at New York and were hospitably received by John Henry Livingston [*q.v.*]. On their proceeding to Philadelphia, Helffrich was assigned to the Maxatawny charge in Berks and Lehigh counties, which he served until his death in 1810, and Helffenstein to Germantown and Frankford. His father, who would gladly have gone with him, wrote from time to time, sending him books, underwear, and matrimonial advice. On Feb. 11, 1773, Helffenstein married Catharine Kircher, who with four children survived him. Despite the strenuous opposition of his parishioners, he left Germantown late in 1775 and accepted a call to the Reformed congregation at Lancaster. The best remembered events of his two and one-half years in that town were the mordant sermons that he preached to the interned Hessian prisoners on such texts as Isaiah lii, 3, and John viii, 36. He returned as pastor to Germantown in the summer of 1779 and remained there until his death from consumption eleven years later. He was a zealous member of the Coetus, of which he was clerk in 1779 and 1787 and president in 1781 and 1788. He was famous throughout German Pennsylvania for the eloquence and pungency of his sermons. His methods of preparation and manner of delivery were carefully observed by his contemporaries, and so lasting was his reputation that twenty years after his death nineteen of his sermons were published as *Eine Sammlung Auserlesener Predigten* (Carlisle, 1810, and later editions). This was translated by Israel Daniel Rupp [*q.v.*] as *A Collection of Choice Sermons* (1832), and in 1835 another *Sammlung Auserlesener Predigten* was issued at Chambersburg. Helffenstein's eldest son, Samuel, was pastor for thirty years of the Reformed Church in Philadelphia.

[Henry Harbaugh, *The Fathers of the German Reformed Church in Europe and America*, vol. II (Lancaster, 1858); J. H. Dubbs, "Some Helffenstein Letters," *Lancaster County Hist. Soc. Papers*, I (1896–97), 218–25; J. I. Good, *Hist. of the Reformed Church in the U. S., 1725–92* (Reading, 1899); *Minutes and Letters of the Coetus of the German Reformed Congregations in Pa., 1747–92* (1903); Gustav Toepke, *Die Matrikel der Universität Heidelberg*, vol. IV (1903); Wm. J. Hinke, "Diary of the Rev. J. H. Helffrich Sept. 6, 1771–Jan. 14, 1772," *Pa. Mag. of Hist. and Biog.*, Jan. 1914; additional notes by Prof. Hinke.] G. H. G.

HELLER, MAXIMILIAN (Jan. 31, 1860–Mar. 30, 1929), rabbi, born in the Bohemian city of Prague, was the only son and the third of five children born to Simon and Mathilde (Kassowitz) Heller. On both sides of the family, which was of the German or Ashkenasic strain of Jews, he was descended from a long and distinguished line of European rabbis and scholars. His childhood and early youth were spent in the ghetto of Prague, where his father was a well-to-do wool-merchant. In 1877, while he was a student at the Prague Gymnasium, his father suffered such severe financial reverses that the family decided to emigrate to the United States. In order not to interrupt his preparation for a career in medicine, the son was left behind. The family settled in Chicago, Ill., where the father eked out a precarious living by preparing young boys for confirmation and by serving as a lodge secretary. In 1879, Maximilian, hearing that the mother, who was afflicted with tuberculosis, had but a short time to live, followed the family to the United States. Upon his arrival in Chicago, he saw before him the necessity of having to help support the family and decided that his best course was to prepare himself for the rabbinate. He therefore entered the Hebrew Union College, at Cincinnati, Ohio, at the same time enrolling for courses at the University of Cincinnati. This period of his life was a very strenuous one, since he was compelled to support himself by extensive tutoring, the strain and privation of his college years being such as to result in the permanent impairment of his health. His efforts, however, brought him the degrees of B.L. (1882) and M.L. (1884) from the University of Cincinnati and the degree of Rabbi (1884) from Hebrew Union College.

Upon graduation, he was appointed associate to Rabbi Bernard Felsenthal of Chicago, in which capacity he served for a year and a half. For a period of five months, he was next in charge of the Reform Jewish Congregation of Houston, Tex. In 1887, he was elected rabbi of the Temple Sinai Congregation of New Orleans, La. He was in charge of this congregation until 1927, when he was made rabbi emeritus. On Mar. 6, 1889, he was married to Ida Annie Marks, daughter of an old Portuguese Jewish family of New Orleans, by whom he had four children. In New Orleans, he soon revealed himself as a man who was diffident and timid in matters about which he did not feel himself sufficiently informed to have a conviction, but who did not hesitate to take a determined and courageous stand when he thought a moral principle was involved. Together with Dr. Benjamin Morgan Palmer [*q.v.*], a Presbyterian divine, and Senator (later Chief Justice) Edward Douglas White [*q.v.*], he led the bitter and historic fight which resulted in the abolition of the Louisiana Lottery, although his friends advised him against such a course and some of the officers of his own congregation opposed it. Equally characteristic was his early espousal of the cause of Zionism, a position he assumed when support of this cause meant vilification and loss of merited recognition. He was also actively engaged in promoting the cause of public education. From 1892 to 1896 he was a member of the State Board of Education. The Tulane University of Louisiana recognized his scholarship by appointing him, in 1912, professor of Hebrew language and literature. He was made professor emeritus in 1928. His co-religionists recognized his leadership in Jewish education and culture by electing him vice-president of the Central Conference of American Rabbis in 1907 and 1908, and president in 1909 and 1910.

His literary work was extensive, though largely composed of published articles, sermons, and addresses. He was editor of the *Jewish Ledger* from 1896 to 1897, leader writer on the *American Israelite* from 1902 to 1914, and contributor of a column of Jewish current events to the *B'nai Brith News* until shortly before his death. His more extended works comprise *Jubilee Souvenir of Temple Sinai 1872–1922* (1922), a history of his New Orleans congregation; "The Place of the Jew in a Racial Interpretation of the History of Civilization" which appeared in the *Year Book of the Central Conference of American Rabbis* (1913), and *My Month in Palestine* (1929), published after his death by his children. He was one of the most respected and best loved religious leaders of New Orleans and the South. His associates in every field recognized him as a man of firm moral convictions and yet of great intellectual tolerance; as a writer and speaker, gifted with a fine sensitiveness to delicacy of thought and expression; and as a personality, of rare gentleness, simplicity, and charm.

[*American Jewish Year Book*, 1903–04; *Who's Who in America*, 1928–29; *Who's Who in Am. Jewry* (1926); *Times-Picayune* (New Orleans), *New Orleans States*, and *New Orleans Item-Tribune*, Mar. 31, 1929; information from a son, Isaac Heller, and from other relatives; biographical material in the *Jubilee Souvenir*.]

M. ten H.

HELLER, ROBERT [See PALMER, WILLIAM HENRY, 1828–1878].

HELM, CHARLES JOHN (June 21, 1817–February 1868), United States consul general and later Confederate agent at Havana, was born at Hornellsville, N. Y., the son of Francis T. and and Sallie (McKinney) Helm. His father, who was of an old Virginia family, moved to Newport, Ky., in 1817, where his descendants still live. Charles Helm was educated locally, read law in the office of John W. Tibbatts, and was admitted to the bar in 1842. He was associated in practice with his preceptor, and in the Mexican War was for a time a first lieutenant in the 16th Kentucky Regiment under Col. Tibbatts. He subsequently served as aide to General Wool. At the close of the war he resumed the practice of law at Newport. In 1851 he was elected to the Kentucky legislature, but his political career closed after one term, and in 1853 he was appointed United States commercial agent at the island of St. Thomas. There he became friendly with the governor and was instrumental in securing the abolition of certain duties. Helm was the representative of the United States at St. Thomas at the time of the events which originated the Butterfield claims against Denmark. Two ships from New York, one of them laden with ammunition, were detained at St. Thomas at the end of 1854 partly because of the need of repairs and partly because of a suspicion that they were intended to give aid to a rebellion in Venezuela. The ships were eventually sold to the Mexican government, but the events of their detention at St. Thomas led to claims for damages against the Danish government. Helm, as the arbitrator's award of 1890 finally showed, evinced a quite proper willingness to cooperate with the governor in the exaction of guarantees against violation of Danish neutrality; but his action was posthumously reprimanded by the Department of State when used by Denmark as an argument against the claim (S. J. M. P. Fogdall, *Danish-American Diplomacy, 1776–1920* (1922), pp. 87 ff.; *House Executive Document 33,* 45 Cong., 2 Sess., pp. 21, 59, 85; *Foreign Relations of the United States,* 1889, p. 159).

In 1858 Helm became consul general at Havana, where he enjoyed friendly relations with the captain-general, Serrano. On the opening of the Civil War in 1861, he resigned his post, and it is said that Seward, in urging him to remain loyal to the Union, gave him a silk American flag. In July 1861 he was appointed special agent of the Confederacy in the West Indies, to reside in Havana, and he arrived in Cuba, by way of Canada and London, in October. His services to the Confederacy were considerable but not spectacular. He found Havana sympathetic with the Southern cause and his friend the captain-general not less so. In fact Helm promised General Serrano informally that he would not encourage or allow any breach of Spanish neutrality by his compatriots, with the understanding that the Cuban government would behave as benevolently toward the Confederacy as neutrality permitted. This agreement, continued with Serrano's successor, was eminently satisfactory. Helm several times commented to his home government that in Cuba "our people" were treated with all the kindness and consideration possible, and on two occasions the ship *Florida* received something more than neutral hospitality at Havana. In general Helm's work consisted in the purchase and shipment of arms, in supervision of matters connected with blockade-running, and in arranging for the transmission of dispatches and the conveyance of passengers between the Confederate States and Europe. In 1854 he had married Louise A. Whistler, by whom he had five children. After the war he lived with other former Confederates in Toronto, where he died.

[*Biog. Encyc. of Ky.* (1878), p. 705; *War of the Rebellion: Official Records (Army),* 2 ser. II, 93, 99; and *(Navy)* 2 ser. III, *passim*; *House Ex. Doc. 7,* 36 Cong., 2 Sess.; Dunbar Rowland, *Jefferson Davis, Constitutionalist* (1923), VII, 117 ff.; J. D. Bulloch, *The Secret Service of the Confed. States in Europe* (1884), II, 232; certain information from Webster Helm, Esq.]

H. D. J.

HELM, JOHN LARUE (July 4, 1802–Sept. 8, 1867), governor of Kentucky, was the son of George and Rebecca (Larue) Helm. He was born near Elizabethtown, Ky., on the old Helm place, formerly Helm Station, founded on the Kentucky frontier in 1781 by his grandfather, Thomas Helm, an emigrant from Prince William County, Va. This estate was Helm's home throughout his life. In 1830 he married Lucinda Barbour Hardin, daughter of Ben Hardin [*q.v.*], the noted frontier lawyer. They upheld the family tradition by rearing twelve children.

Early disclosing a mind above the average, John Helm attracted the attention of Duff Green [*q.v.*], at that time a partner of one of his uncles, who took a great interest in the boy's career and education. In his teens he went to work in the office of the clerk of the circuit court and began the reading of law. His first tutor was the venerable Samuel Haycraft. In 1821 he entered the law office of Ben Tobin of Elizabethtown, and after two years was admitted to the bar. He soon acquired a large practice, owing in part to his ability, in part to his many well-connected relatives, but especially to the hopelessly tangled condition of Kentucky land lines which gave rise to almost as many civil suits as there were acres of land and to a large number of trials for homicide. At the age of twenty-two, he was made county attorney, and two years later, in 1826, his friends and relatives sent him to the state legislature. Here he served with one or two interruptions for eleven years, rising to a position of leadership in state politics and being chosen speaker of the House several times in succession. In 1844 he was elected to the state Senate, where he served until 1848. Throughout his legislative career he stood boldly for the Clay program on tariff, internal improvements, and the national bank. In the exciting presidential year of 1848, when the country was about to divide upon the Wilmot Proviso, Helm was elected lieutenant-governor on the Whig ticket, with J. J. Crittenden [*q.v.*]. After Crittenden resigned in 1850 to enter Fillmore's cabinet, Helm served out his term, extending through 1851, and proved himself a strong governor. In 1853 he was a presidential elector on the Scott ticket. This ended his political career for twelve years. From 1854 to 1860 he was president of the Louisville & Nashville Railroad, one of the most important lines in the South.

In 1860 Helm openly denounced the election of Lincoln and in the critical time that followed strove at first to preserve Kentucky's neutrality, hoping eventually to have her join the South. During the war he was subjected to much inconvenience as a Confederate sympathizer, and one of his sons, Ben Hardin Helm, a general in the Confederate army, was killed at Chickamauga. When the war had ended Helm reëntered politics as a Democrat. He was elected to the state Senate in 1865 and as chairman of the committee on federal relations led a successful fight for the removal of all restrictive and punitive laws against ex-Confederates. As soon as he had accomplished this task he became a candidate for the governorship, and in the memorable election of 1867, when nearly every mayor and alderman, almost all the state legislature, the nine congressmen, and two federal senators went Democratic, he was elected by a clear majority of 43,000 over his combined radical and conservative opponents. He did not long survive his victory, however. He took the oath of office at his home on Sept. 3 and died five days later, before assuming his official duties.

[Lewis and R. H. Collins, *Hist. of Ky.* (1874); W. E. Connelley and E. M. Coulter, *Hist. of Ky.* (1922); E. M. Coulter, *Civil War and Readjustment in Ky.* (1926); letters from Helm in *War of the Rebellion: Official Records (Army)*, see Index; W. H. Perrin and others, *Ky., a Hist. of the State* (1886); H. Levin, *Lawyers and Lawmakers of Ky.* (1897); *Biog. Sketch of the Hon. John L. Helm* (1868), pub. by direction of the Ky. Gen. Assem.; *Biog. Encyc. of Ky.* (1878); *Frankfort Commonwealth*, Sept. 6, 13, 1867.]

F. L. O.

HELMER, BESSIE BRADWELL (Oct. 20, 1858–Jan. 10, 1927), lawyer, editor, and publisher, was born in Chicago, Ill., and died in Battle Creek, Mich. Her father, James B. Bradwell, was a man of learning, a warm advocate of women's advancement, and the first judge to hold that a marriage made during slavery was valid after emancipation. Her mother, Myra Colby Bradwell, was the first woman in the United States to apply for admission to the bar. She was refused on the ground that she was a woman, but the supreme court of Illinois granted her a license as attorney and counselor at law, whereupon she devoted her knowledge and ability to securing the recognition of the equal rights of women before the law. Bessie Bradwell graduated from the Chicago High School as valedictorian in 1876. She received the degree of A.B. in 1880 and that of A.M. in 1882 from Northwestern University. In the latter year, valedictorian of her class in the Union College of Law, Chicago, she received her LL.B. and was admitted to the Illinois bar. On Dec. 23, 1885, she married in Chicago Frank Ambrose Helmer, also a lawyer. In 1894 she became assistant editor of the *Chicago Legal News,* the first legal journal in the West, which had been founded, edited, and managed by her mother; in 1907 she became the editor-in-chief, and president of the company which owned it. From 1905 to 1923 she was editor of Hurd's *Revised Statutes of the State of Illinois* and also edited nine volumes of *Reports of Cases Determined in the Appellate Court of Illinois.* She was an honorary member of the Illinois State Bar Association and a member of the American Bar Association.

Among the many activities which appealed to her interest there was none to which she gave of her strength and thought more generously than to the Association of Collegiate Alumnae, now the American Association of University Women. Her character and personality early brought her leadership in this organization and in 1890 she became for a year its president. She was president of the Chicago branch in 1894–95. Her outstanding contribution to the Association was made in connection with the fellowships which it awarded. In 1890 all the fellowship work was put in charge of a committee under the chairmanship of Alice Freeman Palmer [*q.v.*]. Of this committee Mrs. Helmer was a member, and in 1891 she became chairman, which onerous position she held for fifteen years. In the files of the Association for 1892–93 appears her report of the Committee on Fellowships—"the first of a remarkable series which when presented to the Association always called forth both official and informal appreciation and make a notable contribution to the early history of graduate study by American women." To the effort involved in raising the needed funds and in spreading interest in fellowships and to the difficult task of selecting from the many candidates those best qualified and most promising, she gave all her strength and her fine qualities of judgment and discrimination. It was to her labors that the Association owes in large part the firm foundation upon which its fellowship work has for forty years been continuously carried on.

[*Pubs. of the Asso. of Collegiate Alumnae, passim*; *Annual Report of the Ill. State Bar Asso.*, 1927; *Who's Who in Jurisprudence* (1st ed., 1925); *Who's Who in America*, 1926–27; Marion Talbot and L. K. M. Rosenberry, *Hist. of the Am. Asso. of Univ. Women, 1881–1931* (1931); *N. Y. Times*, Jan. 12, 1927.]

L. K. M. R.

HELMPRAECHT, JOSEPH (Jan. 14, 1820–Dec. 15, 1884), superior of the Redemptorist Fathers, was born at Niederwinkling in Bavaria. From a religious home, he was sent to a Benedictine school at Metten where Boniface Wimmer [*q.v.*], later founder of the Benedictines in America, was his tutor. Thereafter, he followed courses in philosophy and theology at the University of Munich and at Louvain. In 1843 he entered the novitiate of the Congregation of the Most Holy Redeemer at Altotting. In this year he was sent to Baltimore, Md., with a group of volunteer priests. On Dec. 8, 1844, he pronounced his final vows and on Dec. 21 of the following year was ordained by Archbishop Eccleston. For three years he served as a priest of St. James's Church and gave missions to neighboring German congregations. With this valuable apprenticeship, he was fitted for his next assignment, superior of St. Mary's Church and the Redemptorist House in Buffalo (1848–54), where he won the gratitude of Bishop John Timon [*q.v.*] for his zealous care of the Germans of the city and provincial towns, the erection of a new church and parochial school, and the foundation of an orphanage. In 1854, as rector of the important Church of the Most Holy Redeemer in New York with jurisdiction over the Church of St. Alphonsus, he built another German orphanage and gained a reputation as an understanding confessor whom so severe a critic as James McMaster [*q.v.*] could depict as "a man simple in his ways and pretentions; singularly sincere in all his works and acts; singularly seeking in all things for God's glory and the good of men." At the end of his term, he served a few months in Philadelphia, was an assistant at St. Philomena's in Pittsburgh (1861), and prefect of the Second Novitiate at Annapolis, Md. (1863). In 1865 he was called to Rome as a counselor on business concerning his society in the United States.

On Helmpraecht's return from Europe, he was named provincial of the American Redemptorists by the Superior General in the place of the recently deceased John de Dycker. For four terms (1865–77), he held this office, during which he established mission-houses for English as well as German-speaking people in New York, Baltimore, Boston, and St. Louis; founded Redemptorist churches in Quebec and Philadelphia; erected houses of studies at Ilchester, Md., and at Chatawa, Miss.; and assisted materially in the development of the society and its labors. After being relieved he served as pastor of St. Michael's Church in Baltimore, and of the Church of the Most Holy Redeemer in New York, in which relationship he continued until his painful death from cancer. A saintly man, he humbly thanked God for the excruciating pains which he endured in the agonies of his last months on earth.

[M. A. Corrigan, in the U. S. Cath. Hist. Soc. *Records and Studies,* Nov. 1907; *Annalen der Verbreitung des Glaubens, Bd.* xxxiv, Munich, 1866; James McMaster in *N. Y. Freeman's Journal,* Dec. 27, 1884; *Katholische Volks-Zeitung,* Baltimore, Dec. 27, 1884; *N. Y. Times,* Dec. 17, 1884; the *Sun,* Baltimore, Dec. 18, 1884. A history of the Redemptorists by J. F. Byrne, C.SS.R., is now in press.] R. J. P.

HELMUTH, JUSTUS HENRY CHRISTIAN (May 16, 1745–Feb. 5, 1825), Lutheran clergyman, was born at Helmstedt, Duchy of Brunswick, Germany, the son of Johann Christoph and Justina Helmuth. He was educated in the Halle Orphanage and at the University of that city, in both institutions coming under the influence of Gotthilf August Francke. Karl Heinrich von Bogatzky heard his first sermon and gave it his approval; to the end of his long life Helmuth always began the day with a half-hour's reading in Bogatzky's *Güldenes Schatzkästlein.* In his twenty-fourth year, while acting as preceptor in the Orphanage, he accepted a call to Pennsylvania, was ordained at Wernigerode, said goodby to his mother, and landed at Philadelphia, Apr. 2, 1769, accompanied by his friend, John Frederick Schmidt. Succeeding John Siegfried Gerock, he was pastor at Lancaster from 1769 to 1779. On July 5, 1770, he married Maria Barbara Keppele, who bore him five children and predeceased him by about a year. In March 1779 he became co-pastor of St. Michael's and Zion's in Philadelphia and held office until his retirement in September 1820. His colleagues during these forty-one years were John Christopher Kunze, John Frederick Schmidt, and Frederick David Schaeffer. Helmuth was noted for the mildness and serenity of his temper and for the moving eloquence of his preaching. During the yellow-fever epidemic of 1793 his mettle was put to a severe test. In the course of a few months 625 members or adherents of his congregation died. Helmuth spent the greater part of each day in the churchyard, committing bodies to the ground as fast as the graves were made ready. Each morning he held a brief service in his church, speaking to his hearers as one dying man to another. "Never, during the entire period of our ministry," he wrote, "was preaching to us such a heartfelt work as we found it during these weeks of suffering; and never, we confidently believe, were we more serviceable to the Lord than at that time." He trained many men for the ministry, among them Jacob Goering (at Lancaster), John George Butler, John Michael Streck, Christian Endress, John George Lochman, John George Schmucker, and Samuel Simon Schmucker. Some of his great service to the Lutheran church was offset, however, by his persistent and damaging opposition to the use of English in the services. He was a member of the American Philosophical Society and for eighteen years professor of German in the University of Pennsylvania. Characteristic of him was his devoted friendship for several of the Moravian clergymen and for J. W. Hendel and J. A. C. Helffenstein [*qq.v.*] among the Reformed. His publications include: *Empfindungen des Herzens in einigen Liedern* (1781); *Denkmal der Liebe und Achtung, Welches seiner Hochwürden dem Herrn D. Heinrich Melchior Mühlenberg . . . ist Gesetzet Worden* (1788); *Betrachtung der Evangelischen Lehre von der Heiligen Schrift und Taufe* (1793); *Kurze Nachricht von der Sogenannten Gelben Fieber in Philadelphia* (1793; English translation by Charles Erdmann, 1794); *Kurze Andachten einer Gottsuchenden Seele* (1786; several later editions); *Plan einer Anstalt zur Erziehung der Jungen Prediger* (1805); *Etliche Kirchenlieder* (1809). Enough of his devotional and occasional poems, printed as leaflets, have been preserved to fill a large volume. C. F. Gellert was his principal model. In 1812 he founded the *Evangelisches Magazin,* the first Lutheran church paper in the United States. He lived his last years in retirement.

[Helmuth's journals, papers, and correspondence are preserved in the archives of the Ministerium of Pa. at Mt. Airy, Phila. See also: *Nachrichten von den Vereinigten Deutschen Evangelischen-Lutherischen Gemeinen in Nord-America* (2 vols., Halle, 1787); *Documentary Hist. of the Ev. Luth. Ministerium of Pa.* (1898); C. R. Demme, *Die Letzte Ehre des Christlichen Predigers: Zur Gedächtniss-Feier des Pastors J. H. C. Helmuth* (1825); M. L. Stoever, memoir in *Evangelical Rev.,* July 1854; W. B. Sprague, *Annals Am. Pulpit,* vol. IX (1869); W. J. Mann, *Life and Times of Henry Melchior Mühlenberg* (1887).]

G. H. G.

HELMUTH, WILLIAM TOD (Oct. 30, 1833–May 15, 1902), surgeon, author, was born in Philadelphia, Pa., the son of John Henry and Jeanette (Tod) Helmuth, and the great-grandson of Rev. Justus Henry Christian Helmuth [*q.v.*], who came to Pennsylvania from Germany in 1769. William received his early education under James Pastor and later went to St. Timothy's College near Baltimore, remaining there through his junior year. He studied medicine with his uncle, Dr. William S. Helmuth, then professor of medicine in the Homeopathic Medical College of Pennsylvania, and graduated from that institution in 1853. From 1854 to 1855 he was one of the dispensary physicians there and prosector of surgery to Dr. James Beakley. On July 17, 1856, when not yet twenty-three years old, he was made professor of anatomy. He early began to write and in 1855 published his first book, *Surgery and Its Adaptation to Homœopathic Practice.* He removed to St. Louis in 1858 and was one of the founders of the Homeopathic Medical College of Missouri, in which he became the first professor of anatomy. He was also made surgeon to the Good Samaritan Hospital. In 1867 he was president of the American Institute of Homeopathy and the following year studied surgery in Europe. He organized the St. Louis College of Homeopathic Physicians and Surgeons in 1869. During these years he continued to make contributions to the literature of medicine and surgery.

When the New York Homeopathic Medical College was undergoing reorganization in 1870, Dr. Helmuth had gained such a reputation that he was called to the professorship of surgery in that college and to the position of surgeon to Hahnemann Hospital. His success as a surgeon and teacher was outstanding and in 1893 he became dean of the college, which position he held until his death. He was married, Feb. 10, 1859, to Fannie Ida Pritchard of St. Louis, by whom he had two children. She became prominent as a leader in philanthropic and hospital work in St. Louis and New York. Among Helmuth's extensive writings are: *A Treatise on Diphtheria; Its Nature, Pathology and Homœopathic Treatment* (1862); *An Essay on Cleft Palate* (1867); *A System of Surgery* (1873), which went through five editions; *A Record of Surgical Clinics* (1875); *Nerve Sketching; with a Short History of the Operation and Illustrative Cases* (1879); *Epi-cystotomy; Hypogastric Lithotomy; Supra-pubic Lithotomy; the High Operation for Stone* (1880); *The Present Status of Antiseptic Surgery* (1883); *Fourteen Consecutive Cases of Ovariotomy* (1885); *A Contribution to the Study of Renal Surgery. Nephrectomy for Pyo-nephrosis, and Nephrectomy for Renal Calculi* (1892); *A Glance at Japanese Medicine, Ancient and Modern* (1893); and *A Plea for the Increased Study of Anatomy in our Colleges* (1898). His non-technical writings include, *Medical Pomposity, or the Doctor's Dream* (1866), a satire; *"Scratches" of a Surgeon* (1879), anecdotes; *With the "Pousse Café," being a Collection of Post Prandial Verses* (1892); *Various Verses* (1901). He also edited the *Western Homœopathic Observer* (1863–

71); and was co-editor of the *North American Journal of Homœopathy* (1862–69), *New England Medical Gazette* (1871–72), *New York Journal of Homœopathy* (1873–74), and the *New York Homœopathic Times* (1875–77).

[T. L. Bradford, *Hist. of the Homœopathic Medic. Coll. of Pa.; The Hahnemann Medic. Coll. and Hospital of Phila.* (1898); W. H. Bishop, "William Tod Helmuth," in Appendix to *Trans. of the Homœopathic Medic. Soc. of the State of N. Y.*, for the year 1902, vol. XXXVII; *Biog. Index of the Homœopathic Medic. Coll. of Pa. and the Hahnemann Med. Coll. and Hospital of Phila.* (n.d.); *N. Y. Times*, May 16, 1902; H. A. Kelly and W. L. Burrage, *Dict. of Am. Med. Biog.* (1928).] C. A. B.

HELPER, HINTON ROWAN (Dec. 27, 1829–Mar. 8, 1909), author, was born in Rowan (now Davie) County, N. C. He was the youngest child of Daniel and Sarah (Brown) Helper. His father, whose parents (spelling their name Helfer) emigrated to North Carolina from the vicinity of Heidelberg, Germany, in 1752, had acquired a small farm and several slaves but died the year after Helper was born so the boy grew up in straitened circumstances. He managed to graduate from Mocksville Academy in 1848 and for a time worked in a store in the neighboring town of Salisbury. In 1850 he went to New York and from there, by way of Cape Horn, to California. He returned three years later with his mind greatly stimulated and wrote *The Land of Gold* (1855). He afterward claimed his publisher forced him to eliminate from this certain criticisms of slavery based upon his observation of free labor in California and thus intensified his dislike of the institution, but the book itself (pp. 221–22, 275–79), hardly supports that explanation of his opinions during the following year when he wrote *The Impending Crisis.* He moved to New York as a safer place to live after the appearance of this work, which was a brief in behalf of the non-slaveholding whites of the South. Contrasting the economic condition of the free and slave states, he attributed the backwardness of the South to the impoverishment of free labor by slavery. There was no trace of interest in the negro and his real or fancied wrongs. He attacked the slave-holders violently and threatened a slave uprising if necessary to overthrow the system. The book had a significance not then realized as an expression of the growing feeling against slavery among non-slave-holders and small slave-holders in North Carolina. Published in 1857, it caused a sensation, one far greater than *Uncle Tom's Cabin* produced. It was furiously attacked in the South but few dared to read it and it thus remained without an adequate answer. Instead of pointing out the real weakness of the book, those who read it cast doubts on Helper's integrity. Samuel M. Wolfe in *Helper's Impending Crisis Dissected* (1860, p. 75) accused him of stealing money from his employer. This charge continued to be repeated and believed in spite of Helper's denial (Bassett, *post,* p. 16) and his attempts to prove its falsity by a certificate from the employer (*New Englander,* Nov. 1857, p. 647). In the North the book was read and in 1859 a fund was raised to print one hundred thousand copies of it for Republican campaign use in 1860. John Sherman's indorsement of it caused his defeat for speaker of the House in 1859 and the heat which it aroused was a powerful contributing cause of the Civil War.

In 1861 Lincoln appointed Helper consul at Buenos Aires, where he tried to establish closer relations with South America, in 1863 married Maria Luisa Rodriguez, and served satisfactorily though uneventfully until he resigned in 1866. He returned to the United States and wrote in quick succession three books on the negro question. *Nojoque* (1867), often described as an inconsistency, was to Helper logically the next step. It is a furious denunciation of the negro as a menace to the South and to white labor, and the purpose avowed in its preface was "to write the negro out of America . . . and out of existence." Helper was naturally opposed to congressional reconstruction, foreseeing its results and detesting its theory of negro equality. *Negroes in Negroland* (1868) was an even more elaborate continuation of the theme, while *Noonday Exigencies* (1871) was a plea for a new political party. His detestation of the negro continued to the end of his life and, as long as his circumstances allowed him any choice, he would not stay where negroes were employed.

After resigning from the consulship Helper acted as attorney to citizens of the United States in the collection of their claims against South American governments and interested himself in the various phases of political and commercial relations with South America, such as the establishment of regular steamship communication, the building of a canal at one of the three feasible sites, the subsidy of a commercial marine, and the character and efficiency of the navy, which he felt failed in its duty to represent a friendly United States in South American waters. His *Oddments of Andean Diplomacy* (1879) is a collection of papers and letters pertaining to these activities. More and more, however, his time and thought were absorbed in plans to promote a railroad from Hudson Bay to the Strait of Magellan. He offered prizes to the amount of $5,000 for the best essays and poem on the subject and published five of the papers as *The Three Americas Railway* (1881). He wrote thousands of letters, memorialized Congress, interviewed hundreds of influential men, and paid several visits to South America in the interests of the plan. Becoming a monomaniac on the subject, he called himself "the new Christopher Columbus." He was a man of keen intellect, with a touch of genius akin to madness.

Helper's last years were spent in poverty. Having sacrificed comfort, fortune, and family to his dream, when hope waned he grew despondent and bitter, finally committed suicide in Washington, and was buried by strangers.

[J. S. Bassett, "Anti-Slavery Leaders of N. C.," *Johns Hopkins Univ. Studies in Hist. and Pol. Sci.*, 16 ser., no. 6 (1898); S. A. Ashe, *Biog. Hist. of N. C.*, vol. VIII (1917); *Charlotte Observer*, Apr. 18, 1909; W. S. Pelletreau, "Hinton Rowan Helper and His Book," *Americana*, Aug. 1911; *The South in the Building of the Nation*, vol. XI (1909); *Nation*, Mar. 11, 18, 1909; *Washington Post*, Mar. 10, 1909.]

J. G. de R. H.

HEMENWAY, MARY PORTER TILESTON (Dec. 20, 1820–Mar. 6, 1894), philanthropist, was born in New York of old New England ancestry, the daughter of a shipping merchant, Thomas Tileston, and of Mary (Porter) Tileston. She went to a private school in New York, and at home "was reared," as she said, "principally on household duties, the Bible, and Shakespeare" (*Memorial Services*, p. 21). On June 25, 1840, she married Augustus Hemenway, a successful merchant, and thereafter she was identified with Boston, Mass. Her husband died in 1876, but she survived him eighteen years, devoting her wealth and her energies to the development of numerous educational and philanthropic projects. She read carefully, loved pictures, and knew well leading writers and citizens. She was a member of James Freeman Clarke's Church of the Disciples. A queenly woman without affectation or condescension, she combined in her philanthropic work enthusiasm with effectiveness. She sought able helpers and her benefactions were generally the result of careful thought.

After the Civil War she helped the establishment of schools on the southern seaboard for both whites and blacks. Later, she made gifts to Armstrong at Hampton and Booker Washington at Tuskegee for the further education of the freedmen. In the course of her welfare work for soldiers' families during the war she had discovered that many of the soldiers' wives did not know how to sew; accordingly, in 1865 she provided a teacher and materials for systematic instruction in sewing in a Boston public school. The experiment brought good results, and the instruction was taken over by the city. In 1883, she started an industrial-vocation school in Boston and two years later, in 1885, she opened a kitchen in a public school, the first venture of its kind in the United States. After three years the city assumed the cost of the kitchen, and cooking as well as sewing became part of the program of public education. Meantime, in 1887, Mrs. Hemenway had started the Boston Normal School of Cooking, which after her death became the Mary Hemenway Department of Household Arts in the State Normal School at Framingham. Next, for a year, she furnished a hundred Boston teachers free instruction in gymnastics, using the Swedish system as best adapted to schoolrooms. In order to interest the public, she promoted in 1889 a conference on physical training, held in Boston, which led to the introduction of gymnastics into the city's public schools, by action of the School Committee, and was influential in stimulating nationwide interest in the cause of physical education (F. E. Leonard, *A Guide to the History of Physical Education*, 1923). In 1889, also, she established the Boston Normal School of Gymnastics, which twenty years later became the Department of Hygiene and Physical Education of Wellesley College. She promoted, at much personal effort, the Boston Teachers' Mutual Benefit Association.

In 1876, in order to save from destruction the Old South Meeting-house, famous for meetings of Revolutionary days, she gave $100,000—a quarter of the total sum required—her hope being to make the old church a center for the cultivation of patriotic idealism through education in history. Prizes were offered for essays by high-school pupils, historical lectures were given, the Old South Leaflets, a series of reprints of historical "sources" edited by Edwin D. Mead, were issued, and the young persons who had competed for prizes were organized into a historical society. At a time when the history of the United States had no place in the school curriculum, the "Old South work" was almost unique. Such scholars as John Fiske and James K. Hosmer [*qq.v.*] furthered Mrs. Hemenway's plans and were helped by her to publish lectures and biographies. Her interest in American history was further evidenced by her promotion of the Hemenway Southwestern Archaeological Expedition begun in 1886 under Frank H. Cushing [*q.v.*] of the United States Bureau of Ethnology and continued after 1900 under J. W. Fewkes [*q.v.*] of the Bureau. The collections made by the expedition are kept in the Hemenway Room at the Peabody Museum at Harvard; the results of its investigations are set forth in five volumes, *A Journal of American Ethnology and Archaeology* (1891–1908), edited by Fewkes and published at Mrs. Hemenway's expense. Her will provided for the support of her various enterprises for fifteen years, during which time her trustees were able to put them on a permanent basis.

[*A Memorial of the Life and Benefactions of Mary Hemenway, 1820–1894* (privately printed, 1927), preface signed by Mary Wilder Tileston; *Memorial Services in Honor of Mrs. Mary Hemenway by the Boston Public School Teachers* (1894), ed. by Larkin Dunton; Katherine H. Stone, "Mrs. Mary Hemenway and Household Arts in the Boston Public Schools," in *Jour. of Home Economics*, Jan. 1929; E. D. Mead, *The Old South Work* (1899); L. V. Briggs, *Hist. and Geneal. of the Cabot Family* (1927), vol. II; M. D. R. Young, *An Ideal Patriot of Peace* (1894); E. E. Hale in *Lend a Hand*, Apr. 1894; C. G. Ames, *Ibid.*, July 1894; Agnes Crane in *Leisure Hour*, Sept. 1894; *Boston Evening Transcript*, Mar. 6, 15, 1894; *Boston Post*, Mar. 7, 1894.] J. R. B.

HEMMETER, JOHN CONRAD (Apr. 26, 1863–Feb. 25, 1931), physiologist, composer, was born in Baltimore, Md., of German parents. His father, John, came from Baiersdorf near Erlangen and his mother, Mathilde Ziegler, from Hanau. His father was chief emigration agent of the Baltimore & Ohio Railroad. Hemmeter attended the Baltimore public schools; at ten years of age he spent some time in school in Hanau, Germany, and later attended the Realgymnasium in Wiesbaden. On his return to Baltimore in 1877 he entered the Baltimore City College. He graduated M.D. at the University of Maryland in 1884, was appointed one of the physicians to Bay View Asylum, and two years later was made resident physician. He continued his studies and received the degree of Ph.D. in 1890 from the Johns Hopkins University; his thesis was "On the Comparative Physiological Effects of Certain Members of the Ethylic Alcohol Series" (*Johns Hopkins University: Studies from the Biological Laboratory*, vol. IV, no. 5, 1889). Subsequently he made frequent trips to Germany and pursued special courses in physiology under Emil Du Bois-Reymond in Berlin and in diseases of the digestive system under Hermann Nothnagel in Vienna. In 1902 he was made professor of physiology in the University of Maryland Medical School and at the same time gave instruction in diseases of the digestive system. He retired from this position in 1915.

His chief researches were in physiology and gastroenterology. In summer he would spend much time at the Marine Biological Laboratory, Woods Hole, Mass. He was probably the first to use Röntgen rays for studying the size and location of the stomach (*Boston Medical and Surgical Journal*, June 18, 1896, p. 609), and he invented a method of intubating the duodenum and obtaining specimens of the contents of the upper part of the intestines (*Johns Hopkins Hospital Bulletin*, April 1896). He published some 170 articles, chiefly medical, and was the author of *Diseases of the Stomach* (1897, and later editions), *Diseases of the Intestines* (2 vols., 1901–02), and *Manual of Practical Physiology* (1912).

Hemmeter was a pianist of unusual ability, and while living in Wiesbaden had been a pupil of Wilhelm Jahn. He wrote some thirty compositions for piano and voice, as well as for orchestra, male chorus, and mixed chorus, and composed a musical setting for the Twenty-third Psalm. At a meeting of the American Medical Association in Baltimore, his *Hymn to Hygeia*, a cantata for orchestra and male chorus, was rendered for the first time. It is in praise of the science and art of medicine, and he composed both music and words. He contributed numerous articles on music to American and German musical journals. His interest in the history of medicine increased as he grew older and led to a number of contributions to various journals and to his *Master Minds in Medicine* (1927). The first eight articles in this volume deal with the sources, aims, and methodology of medical history; the remainder are studies of such men as Rudolph Virchow, Albrecht von Haller, Henry Rose Carter [*q.v.*], Michael Servetus, Leonardo Da Vinci, and Goethe.

Hemmeter was a tall man, of commanding presence, precise in dress and speech, with the manners and bearing of a German professor of two generations ago. He had a lively appreciation of the importance of his position and work. His personality, habits of thought, and opinions are admirably revealed in his autobiography in L. R. Grote's *Die Medizin der Gegenwart in Selbstdarstellungen* (vol. III, 1924). On Jan. 18, 1893, he married Helene Emilie Hilgenberg, of Baltimore. He was a member of American, German, and Austrian medical societies. He died in Baltimore.

[Autobiography in *Die Medizin der Gegenwart in Selbstdarstellungen* (vol. III, 1924), ed. by L. R. Grote; E. F. Cordell, *Univ. of Md.*, I (1907), 329–32, and *The Medic. Annals of Md.* (1903); *Men of Mark in Md.*, I (1907), 179–82; *Who's Who in America*, 1930–31; *Sun* (Baltimore), Feb. 26, 1931. In the Johns Hopkins University *Register*, 1889–90, and in subsequent sources, including *Who's Who in America* down to 1919, Hemmeter's middle name is given as Cohn. Later it appears as Conrad.] J. R.

HEMPEL, CHARLES JULIUS (Sept. 5, 1811–Sept. 24, 1879), homeopathic physician, author, translator, was born in Solingen, Germany. When he had completed his college education, he took the military examination which excused him from army service until the end of his twenty-third year. He then went to the Collège de France in Paris and there came to know Jules Michelet whom he assisted for a time in the preparation of the latter's *Histoire de France*. He lived with Michelet's family for six months. While in Paris, especially when associated with Michelet, young Hempel became acquainted with many Americans and it was through them that he decided to emigrate to America. In 1835, on his twenty-fourth birthday, he arrived in New York City. Immediately he began the study of the English language in which he soon became proficient. After his first six or seven years of residence in America when his activities were largely literary, he began the study of medicine, and on Mar. 1, 1845, he received his M.D. degree from the medical department of the University of the City of New York. Even before his graduation he had shown an inclination toward homeopathy and in practice he came to be known as a leading homeopathic physician. In 1855 he was married to Mary (Coggeshall) Calder, the daughter of George Coggeshall of Grand Rapids, Mich., and the following year he accepted the professorship in materia medica at the Hahnemann Medical College of Philadelphia. This position he was obliged to resign in 1861 because of the death of his father-in-law, necessitating his removal to Grand Rapids. During the last ten years of his life he was an invalid. As the result of an injury to his spinal cord, he suffered a progressive paralysis, and during his last years he was blind. Despite these handicaps, however, his mind remained active.

Hempel's interest in literary activity manifested itself throughout his life. In medicine he translated the outstanding German and French works on homeopathy and wrote numerous articles on homeopathic subjects. In 1859 he published his most important work, *A New and Comprehensive System of Materia Medica and Therapeutics,* which was enlarged and republished in later editions. Outside of the field of medicine his interests were varied. As early as 1842 he published a two-volume *Grammar of the German Language,* and in 1870, as the result of a long study, he published *Schiller's Complete Works* (2 vols.), with new translations of his own. Hempel was a strongly religious man and a member of the Swedenborgian Church.

[*Trans. of the Thirty-third Session of the Am. Inst. of Homœopathy* (1880); the *U. S. Medic. and Surgic. Jour.*, Jan. 1873; T. L. Bradford, *Hist. of the Homœopathic Medic. Coll. of Phila.* (1898); *British Jour. of Homœopathy*, Jan. 1880; Egbert Cleave, *Biog. Cyc. of Homœopathic Physicians and Surgeons* (1873); Albert Baxter, *Hist. of the City of Grand Rapids, Mich.* (1891); *Detroit Post and Tribune,* Sept. 26, 1879.]

C. B.

HEMPHILL, JOHN (Dec. 18, 1803–Jan. 4, 1862), jurist, was born near the present village of Blackstock, S. C. His father, Rev. John Hemphill, was a native of Ireland and a minister in the Associate Reformed Church, who came to America at the close of the Revolutionary War. His mother, Jane Lind, a native of Pennsylvania, was the daughter of a minister of the same church, and was related to Robert Fulton. John's early education was obtained in the common schools. He taught school for one year and then entered Jefferson College, Pennsylvania, from which, after an attendance of only two years, he was graduated, in 1825, as the second ranking man of his class. After his return to South Carolina he again engaged in teaching. In 1829 he began the study of law in the office of D. J. McCord, an eminent lawyer of Columbia, S. C., in November of that year was admitted to practice in the court of common pleas, and two years later was admitted to practice in the court of Chancery. The next seven years he spent in the practice of his profession. In 1838 he removed to the newly founded Republic of Texas and began the practice of law at "Old Washington on the Brazos." Here he found in use the Spanish law written in the Spanish language. With characteristic thoroughness he went into retirement until he could master the language and familiarize himself with the law. Early in 1840, after a residence of only two years, he was elected district judge, and, in December of the same year, chief justice of the supreme court, a position he held continuously under republic and state for a period of eighteen years.

Hemphill's duties as judge were interrupted by two military episodes and a brief excursion into constitution-making as a member of the convention of 1845. In the first military episode he participated (though it is not known how he happened to be present) in the famous council-house fight with the Comanche chiefs in San Antonio, and, being attacked and slightly wounded, he was "reluctantly compelled . . . to disembowel his assailant with his bowie knife." In the second he served as adjutant-general to General Somervell in his fruitless expedition to the Rio Grande in 1842. When the question of annexation arose he became an earnest advocate of that policy and as a member of the constitutional convention of 1845 supported and signed the ordinance agreeing to the resolution of the Congress of the United States providing for annexation. He was appointed the first chief justice of the new state and was elected by popular vote in 1851 and again in 1856. In 1858 he resigned to accept election to the United States Senate but withdrew from that body when Texas seceded from the Union and served for the remainder of his life as a representative of Texas in the Congress of the Confederate States of America.

Hemphill has been called the John Marshall of Texas. It was his task to preside over the court that interpreted the constitutions of the republic and of the state, and to make smooth the transition from the civil law to the common law. It was his decisions largely that gave form and content to the two new institutions, the community property system and the homestead exemption law. He did much to bring about a complete blending of law and equity in the courts of Texas and preserved for the future something of the liberal spirit of the civil law, which he regretted to see supplanted by the common law. He was a man of dignity and of seeming austerity, but of a very kindly nature. "He spent a solitary life, without wife or relatives in the state of his adoption, whose prosperity and greatness he loved and worked to achieve."

[The best biography of Hemphill is that by former Chief Justice R. R. Gaines in *Great Am. Lawyers* (1908), vol. IV, ed. by W. D. Lewis. See also J. D. Lynch, *Bench and Bar of Tex.* (1885), 69–73; H. S. Thrall, *A Pictorial Hist. of Tex.* (1879); *Biog. Encyc. of Tex.* (1880); 59 *Tex. Reports*, vii–xi; *Jours. of the Convention Assembled . . . for the Purpose of Framing a Constitution for the State of Tex.* (1845); *Richmond Enquirer*, Jan. 6, 1862.] C. S. P.

HEMPHILL, JOSEPH (Jan. 7, 1770–May 29, 1842), lawyer, congressman, judge, son of Joseph and Ann (Wills) Hemphill, was born in Thornbury Township, Chester (later Delaware) County, Pa. His father, a native of Londonderry, Ireland, was a well-to-do farmer. Joseph attended grammar school at West Chester and received the bachelor's degree from the University of Pennsylvania in 1791. He then studied law and in 1793 was admitted to the bar. From 1797 to 1800 he was a member of the state Assembly, where he was active in securing the final adjustment of the Wyoming controversy. In 1800 he was elected to Congress as a Federalist. His first speech, in opposition to the repeal of the judiciary act (Feb. 16, 1802), earned for him the title, "Single-Speech Hemphill." Charging that the Republicans aimed at destroying the Constitution, he predicted that if the act were repealed, "it will become as much a matter of course to remove the judges as the heads of departments, and in bad times the judges would be no better than a sword in the hands of a party, to put out of the way great and obnoxious characters for pretended treasons" (*Annals of Congress,* 7 Cong., 1 Sess., col. 544). In 1804 he moved to Philadelphia to continue his growing law practice. Although he was a Federalist, many of his best friends and clients were Republicans. In the Constitutionalist victory (1805) he was sent to the state legislature, where he assisted in revising the judiciary. In 1811 Governor Snyder, arch-Jacobin, appointed him first president-judge of the district court for Philadelphia City and County, an unusual tribute for those partisan times. He was recommissioned in 1817 but resigned in 1819 owing to his delicate health and weak eyes.

From 1819 to 1831, except for two years, 1827–29, Hemphill was again in Congress. As chairman of the committee on the slave trade he attacked as unconstitutional (Dec. 11, 1820) Missouri's discrimination against free negroes and mulattoes, contending that the provision in the federal Constitution regarding privileges and immunities was a condition precedent and, until complied with, no state was or could be created. A report on the enormities of the slave trade (*House Report 59,* 16 Cong., 2 Sess.), which he and Charles Fenton Mercer prepared, evoked favorable comment in England. An administration man throughout this period, a member of the committee on the judiciary and of that on the Cumberland Road (1822), he advocated internal improvements, the encouragement of domestic manufactures, and relief for war veterans. His political career ended with a term in the state Assembly, 1831–32. Having become interested in porcelain manufacturing, after visiting European factories in 1827 he engaged in that business in Philadelphia. The enterprise failed and was soon abandoned. Hemphill married Margaret, daughter of Robert Coleman of Lancaster, on Sept. 11, 1806.

[Sources include: Gilbert Cope and H. G. Ashmead, *Hist. Homes and Institutions and Geneal. and Personal Memoirs of Chester and Delaware Counties, Pa.* (1904), I, 112–13; J. S. Futhey and G. Cope, *Hist. of Chester County, Pa.* (1881); and *North Am. and Daily Advertiser* (Phila.), May 30, 1842. For reception of slave trade report in Great Britain see the *Edinburgh Rev.*, Oct. 1821, p. 50, and T. C. Hansard, *Parliamentary Debates,* 2 ser., vol. VII (1823), cols. 1400–02.]
J. H. P—g.

HEMPL, GEORGE (June 6, 1859–Aug. 14, 1921), philologist, was born at Whitewater, Wis., the son of Henry Theodore and Anna (Häntzsche) Hempel, from Dresden, of German and Slavic descent. When he was six years old the family moved to Chicago, and two years later to Battle Creek, Mich. In 1879 he graduated from the classical course in the University of Michigan. He was teacher and principal in the high schools of Saginaw, Mich., and La Porte, Ind., for five years, and instructor in German in the Johns Hopkins University, 1884–86. During the next three years he studied in the universities of Berlin, Göttingen, Jena, Strassburg and Tübingen, and in 1889 took the degree of Ph.D. at Jena. Among the scholars who most influenced him were Eduard Sievers and Ernst Haeckel. He had always a thoroughly scientific habit of mind, and felt at least as much at home among natural scientists as among humanistic scholars. Besides linguistic studies, archeology became one of his chief interests. In 1889 he returned to the University of Michigan, where he served as assistant professor of English, 1889–93, junior professor, 1893–97, and professor of English philology and general linguistics from 1897 to 1906. From January 1907 till his death he was professor of Germanic philology in the Leland Stanford Junior University. In 1890 he married Anna Belle Purmort of Saginaw.

His main interest throughout his life was in adding to knowledge, and with this he was unwilling to allow even his teaching to interfere. His productions, numbering nearly a hundred and fifty titles, are chiefly articles and notes in learned periodicals. The larger number are on the etymology, meaning, usage and pronunciation of single words, especially in modern and early English. Many are on the development of English sounds and other phonological matters. For this work he had the special qualifications of a strongly auditory memory, imagination, and analytical ability. He became one of the pioneers in the movement for the scientific reformation of English spelling, and a member of the Simplified Spelling Board. With characteristic root-and-branch consistency he habitually used simplified spelling in his correspondence and extirpated an unphonetic *e* from his own surname. He was a pioneer also in the scientific study of American dialects, and collected a vast amount of material on local vocabulary, usage and pronunciation, which has since been made available for projected dictionaries of American English. His knowledge of this subject was immense and minute. No subject interested him more, and his mind was continuously alert to it. In companies of people he would hang on the words of a fluent talker, whose gratification was sometimes dashed by discovering that the attraction had been some unsuspected local peculiarity of his own speech. Among Hempl's most important publications are a dozen papers on the origin of the Germanic runes and interpretations of runic inscriptions. This interest in early writing drew him to studies on some of the obscurer languages of Mediterranean countries, and on their methods of representing sounds, studies which filled his later years. These might have been his most important contribution had his health not failed about 1914, and also had he not been prone to be off after some new problem before he had finished with the old. He became particularly interested in the non-Latin languages of ancient Italy, Venetic and especially Etruscan, which he believed to be Italic. Later he turned to the pictographic writing of the near East. He studied some of the "Minoan-Greek" inscriptions in Crete, and, beginning about 1912, some of the Hittite inscriptions in Asia Minor, which he believed to be in an early form of Attic Greek. While at times he guessed wildly, and often failed to see difficulties, he had a rare grasp of the principles involved and extraordinary resourcefulness.

[*Who's Who in America*, 1920–21; *Univ. of Mich. Cat. of Grads., Non-Grads., Officers and Members of the Faculty* (1923); memoir and list of publications in Hempl's posthumous *Mediterranean Studies* (3 vols., 1931), published by Stanford University; private information; personal knowledge.] J. S. P. T.

HENCK, JOHN BENJAMIN (Oct. 20, 1815–Jan. 3, 1903), engineer and educator, was born at Philadelphia, Pa., the son of George Daniel and Caroline (Spiess) Henck, both German born. The father died in 1831 leaving a family of eight children, the eldest seventeen, with the result that John Henck had little opportunity for formal education. He taught himself so well, however, that he was able to enter Harvard when some of the other children of the family became old enough to earn their own support. He graduated as valedictorian of his class in 1840 in spite of the fact that he had to tutor throughout his entire course in order to meet expenses. The next year he was principal of the Hopkins Classical School in Cambridge, Mass., and in 1841 he went to the University of Maryland as professor of Latin and German. In 1843 he left this position for a similar one at the Germantown Academy and the same year married Mary Ann Kirby of Philadelphia.

The requirements of a growing family caused him to leave the academy in 1848 for a more lucrative position in the office of Felton & Parker, civil engineers at Charlestown, Mass. After a year in the office and a year of field work on the Fitchburg Railroad, he left the firm to form a partnership with William S. Whitwell, who had served as engineer in connection with the construction of the Cochituate water-works. Under the name of Whitwell & Henck they opened offices in Boston for general engineering work and made a profitable connection with the first street railways there. Whitwell retired in 1859 and Henck continued the business alone. In 1855 they had been employed by the commission in charge of the Charles River basin and Back Bay development as engineers for this work. Henck continued in this capacity after the retirement of Whitwell, and up until 1881 was in charge of the filling in, laying out, and paving of the Back Bay district. This development was one of the most important achievements of the period and the position Henck held was probably the most responsible in the engineering field.

From the first proposals to establish the Massachusetts Institute of Technology, Henck was closely associated with President William B. Rogers [*q.v.*] and in 1865 he took charge of the department of civil engineering, at the head of which he remained until he retired in 1881. By requiring from the students a high standard of scholarship and a thorough and accurate knowledge of the courses in his department, he is said to have done more than any other one man to establish for the institution the reputation which it maintains. He was the author of *Field-book for Railroad Engineers* (1854), a standard textbook in wide use for many years. After his retirement from active work he spent four years in Europe and then settled at Montecito, Cal. There he died in his eighty-eighth year, survived by his wife, two sons, and a daughter.

[*Engineering News,* Feb. 12, 1903; *Harvard Grads. Mag.,* Mar. 1903; *Technology Rev.,* Apr. 1903; *Popular Sci. Monthly,* Sept. 1903; *Quinquennial Cat. of the Officers and Grads. of Harvard Univ. 1636–1910* (1910); information as to certain facts from a son, John B. Henck, Esq.] F. A. T.

HENDEL, JOHN WILLIAM (Nov. 20, 1740–Sept. 29, 1798), German Reformed clergyman, was born at Dürkheim in the Palatinate, the eldest of the three sons of Johann Jacob Hendel, a master baker, by his wife, Anna Sybilla Otten. He matriculated, May 10, 1759, at the University of Heidelberg and was still there Feb. 10, 1762, when, for their part in some obscure disorder, he and ten other students were sentenced to three days in the Carcer on bread and water (Gustav Toepke, *Die Matrikel der Universität Heidelberg,* IV, 1903, p. 185). He was examined at The Hague June 27, 1764, by the deputies of the Synods of Holland and was sent to Pennsylvania with a warm letter of recommendation. John Daniel Gros [*q.v.*] accompanied him and, on Hendel's testimony to his character and education, was ordained by the Coetus. This incident was of more than passing moment, since it forshadowed the complete separation of the Coetus of Pennsylvania from the Dutch synods. Hendel was pastor at Lancaster, 1765–69, Tulpehocken, 1769–82, Lancaster again, 1782–94, and Philadelphia, 1794–98. In 1766 he married Elizabeth Le Roy, a sister-in-law of Philip William Otterbein [*q.v.*]. His only son, William Hendel, Jr., also became a prominent Reformed clergyman. While at Lancaster, Hendel made several missionary journeys to isolated groups of German settlers in Maryland and Virginia, especially in the Shenandoah Valley. In 1773, when John Christian Stahlschmidt visited him at Tulpehocken, he was ministering to nine congregations. During the Revolution he frequently preached in Lykens Valley, a guard escorting him to the church and standing in the doorways during the service to forestall attacks by Indians. He was president of the Coetus in 1768, 1779, 1789, and 1791, was vice-president of Franklin College, 1787–94, and was the leading spirit in the movement that resulted in the organization of the Synod of the United States in 1793. He trained a number of candidates for the ministry and was noted for the eloquence of his sermons and for his integrity of character. He died in Philadelphia of yellow fever, one of the last victims of the epidemic of 1798, and was buried in what is now Franklin Square.

[J. C. Stahlschmidt, *Pilgerreise zu Wasser und zu Land* (Nürnberg, 1799); Henry Harbaugh, *The Fathers of the German Reformed Church in Europe and America,* vol. II (Lancaster, 1858); J. I. Good, *Hist. of the Reformed Church in the U. S., 1725–92* (Reading, 1899); *Minutes and Letters of the Coetus of the German Reformed Congregations in Pa. 1747–92* (1903); information as to certain facts from Prof. Wm. J. Hinke.] G. H. G.

HENDERSON, ARCHIBALD (Aug. 7, 1768–Oct. 21, 1822), congressman, lawyer, was the son of Richard [*q.v.*] and Elizabeth (Keeling) Henderson of Granville County, N. C., and the brother of Leonard Henderson [*q.v.*]. He was educated in a Warren County academy and studied law under Judge John Williams. About 1790 he began the practice of law in the western village of Salisbury but returned to Granville County, where he was clerk of the county court from 1795 until he removed permanently to Salisbury in 1798. In 1801 he married Sarah Alexander. He believed whole-heartedly in the principles of Federalism and viewed with genuine alarm the rising tide of Jeffersonianism. In the congressional election of 1798 he overwhelmingly defeated Matthew Locke, Republican representative of the Salisbury district for three terms, whose extreme opposition to the popular administration measures for national defense in the French crisis of 1798 was keenly resented. He defeated Locke again in 1800.

While he was in Congress, 1799–1803, Henderson favored the Judiciary Act of 1801; voted steadily for Burr in the presidential election of 1801 in the House; and supported the bill to continue the Sedition Law, believing that it should be made perpetual as a necessary bulwark of the government. In public letters to his rural constituents he frankly explained his positions. Against the recommendation of the state legislature, he opposed the repeal of the Judiciary Act of 1801 in an able, Federalistic address, attacking the Republican measure as unconstitutional and destructive of the independence of federal judges. Triumphant Republicanism in North Carolina made it impossible for Federalists to aspire hopefully to high public office, and Henderson, always a Federalist of the old school, did not offer himself as a candidate for reëlection in 1803 nor did he ever afterward hold public office except as representative of the borough of Salisbury in the House of Commons, 1807–09, 1814, and 1819–20. His chief distinction was gained in a long and extensive practice of law in the federal circuit and state courts. His vigor of intellect, knowledge of the law, and power of analysis and argument gave character to the state bar and won for him the estimate by John Marshall that he was unquestionably among the ablest lawyers of his time. For several years he was president of the Salisbury branch of the State Bank of North Carolina and in 1819 was elected vice-president of the Raleigh chapter of the American Colonization Society. After his death his associates at the bar erected a monument over his grave in Salisbury.

[See sketch of Henderson in the *N. C. Booklet*, July, Oct. 1917; A. D. Murphey, "Sketch of the Character of Archibald Henderson as a Lawyer," Raleigh *Star*, Jan. 10, 1823, reprinted in *The Papers of Archibald D. Murphey* (1914), ed. by W. H. Hoyt, vol. II, pp. 312–19; *The Papers of John Steele* (2 vols., 1924), ed. by H. M. Wagstaff; *Raleigh Reg. and N. C. Gazette*, Nov. 1, 1822.]
A. R. N.

HENDERSON, CHARLES RICHMOND (Dec. 17, 1848–Mar. 29, 1915), Baptist clergyman, sociologist, was born in Covington, Ind., the son of Albert and Loranna (Richmond) Henderson. His education was received at the old University of Chicago (A.B., 1870) and at the Baptist Union Theological Seminary (B.D., 1873). In 1901 he received the degree of Ph.D. from the University of Leipzig. He was ordained to the Baptist ministry and became pastor of the First Baptist Church of Terre Haute, Ind., in 1873, and was married the same year to Ella Levering of Lafayette, Ind. In 1882 he accepted a call to the pastorate of the Woodward Avenue Baptist Church, Detroit, where he remained until 1892 when he was invited to join the faculty of the new University of Chicago as university chaplain, assistant professor of sociology, and university recorder. From 1894 to 1897 he was associate professor of sociology, and from the latter date to his death, professor of sociology, becoming head of the department of practical sociology in 1904. Throughout these years he remained the chaplain of the University.

As a student he served a small church back of the stockyards in Chicago, and from this experience dates his interest in social problems. At Terre Haute he was the first president of the local charity organization, and on going to Detroit he at once allied himself with the charitable organizations of that city. While still a pastor he made a study of prisons and prison management and became a recognized authority in that field. He took an active interest in labor problems, and when a strike on the Detroit street car lines was imminent he was largely responsible for settling the differences between the contending parties. At the University of Chicago he found opportunity to give himself more freely to social studies and during his service there he published sixteen books and more than one hundred articles. Many of these publications are of pioneer importance in the field of penology, industrial insurance, and industrial legislation. Among his most important books are, *Introduction to the Study of the Dependent, Defective and Delinquent Classes,* which first appeared in 1893, and was revised and improved in 1901; *The Social Spirit in America* (1896); "Modern Prison Systems" (*House Document 452,* 57 Cong., 2 Sess.); *Modern Methods of Charity* (1904); *Industrial Insurance in the United States* (1907). Besides contributing frequently to sociological and religious journals, he served for many years as associate editor of the *American Journal of Theology*; the *American Journal of Sociology,* and the *Journal of the American Institute of Criminal Law and Criminology.* He was president of the National Conference of Charities, 1898–99, and president of the United Charities of Chicago, 1913. Among his chief interests was that of prison reform, and he was a member of national and international organizations to advance that cause, serving as president of the National Prison Association, 1901–02.

As a teacher and investigator he was a pioneer in a new field. His chief traits as a scholar were open-mindedness and loyalty to truth, and although dealing in his study with the lowest conditions among men, he never lost faith in mankind. He was deeply religious, but broad-minded, and was loved and respected by all religious groups, a fact exemplified in the great memorial meeting held, in his honor, on Apr. 11, 1915, shortly after his death. He was characterized, by those who knew him and his work, as both academic and practical, respected both by scientists and men of practical affairs. Overwork was responsible for his sudden death, which occurred at Charleston, S. C., to which place he had gone with Mrs. Henderson in March 1915, expecting to recover his health.

[*Community Memorial Meeting in Honor of Charles Richmond Henderson* (1915); *Univ. Record* (Chicago), Jan. 1915; *Chicago Daily Tribune*, Mar. 30, 1915; *Who's Who in America*, 1915–16; *Proc. Ann. Cong. Am. Prison Asso.* (1915); *Jour. Am. Inst. Criminal Law and Criminology*, May, Nov. 1915; *Outlook*, June 9, 1915; *Survey*, Apr. 10, 1915; *Univ. of Chicago Mag.*, Apr. 1915.] W. W. S.

HENDERSON, DANIEL McINTYRE (July 10, 1851–Sept. 8, 1906), bookseller, poet, was born in Glasgow, Scotland, the son of Thomas and Margaret Henderson. An easy distance from the city lay Blackhill Locks, and thither the family removed ten years later. The new neighborhood possessed no educational facilities, and the boy was obliged to attend the parish school of Saint Enoch in Glasgow, walking there each morning, and returning home each afternoon. After leaving school he took a situation in a wholesale draper's shop with the intention of learning the business. He presently relinquished it, however, and, after filling two or three other positions, accepted that of bookkeeper to the Scottish Permissive Bill and Temperance Association.

In 1873, he emigrated to the United States, and established a permanent home in Baltimore, returning in 1876, to marry Alice M. Ashcroft. Of this union six sons and four daughters were born. In Baltimore, after acting for some years as bookkeeper to a firm of furniture manufacturers, he became a bookseller, and for the rest of his life was the proprietor of the University Book Store, on the corner of Howard and Madison Streets. He was a bookish man, and his knowledge of literature, particularly of that directly connected with poetry, was broad and deep, and served him well in his agreeable calling. The little shop became a stopping-place for the professors connected with the Johns Hopkins University, which was close at hand. Students strolled in to buy, and to ask the modest, mild-eyed man for his quaint and wise opinions upon their purchases.

Every Scotchman is at heart a poet, and in 1888 Henderson published a collection of poetry, under the title of *Poems, Scottish and American*, and in 1905, a second volume, called *A Bit Bookie of Verse*. These ventures brought him new friends, in all parts of the country. James Whitcomb Riley, coming into the shop one day, went out of it his enthusiastic brother-in-verse. Stevenson, Stedman, Whittier, and Lowell, wrote him warm and appreciative letters.

His walks back and forth to Saint Enoch school had given his sensitive spirit opportunity for mature thought, for recalling scraps of Burns's and other poets' verse, and for stringing together musical words of his own. All these went into the developing and nourishing of his poetic gift. His poetry reveals him as a gentle-natured and devout man, with an intense affection for both the Old World and the New, and for humble and lovely things. His songs are simple, direct, spontaneous. Perhaps this very spontaneity at times produces an over-facility of expression. As a whole they are delicate in feeling, and full of touching lines. A gift of the old west-country flowers, imperially purple, impelled him to write "The Heather"; the sight of pink-petaled blossoms coming up in a Baltimore public square resulted in "Daisies in Baltimore." The latter poem, together with many of the others, is written in Scottish dialect. These, along with much else in the two small books, hold the essence and flavor of real poetry.

Henderson was not only a poet and a scholar, but an alert citizen interested in public matters, a member of the Saint Andrew's Society, and, at his death, its president, and also a deacon in the Associate Congregational Church. He died in the Maryland General Hospital, Baltimore, after a two-weeks' illness of typhoid fever.

[J. D. Ross, *Scottish Poets in America* (1889); *The Scottish American*, 1906; the *Sun*, Baltimore, Sept. 10, 1906; information from the family.] L. W. R.

HENDERSON, DAVID BREMNER (Mar. 14, 1840–Feb. 25, 1906), pioneer, soldier, speaker of the House of Representatives, the son of Thomas and Barbara (Bremner) Henderson, was born in Old Deer, Scotland, and emigrated with his parents to America in 1846. The family first settled in Illinois, moving three years later to Fayette County in northeastern Iowa where David worked on the farm in the summer and went to the district school in the winter. He attended Upper Iowa University for a time but left in 1861 to enlist as a volunteer private in the Union army. When Company C of the 12th Iowa Infantry was organized he was elected first lieutenant. He was wounded in the neck at Donelson, and at Corinth he was so severely wounded in the left leg that part of it had to be amputated. It never healed satisfactorily and further amputation in later life undermined his strength and terminated prematurely his career. Retiring for a time from military service, he was appointed commissioner of the board of enrolment of the 3rd congressional district of Iowa, serving from May 1863 to June 1864. He then reëntered the army and was appointed colonel of the newly organized 46th Iowa Volunteers of which he assumed command for the "hundred days' service." At the close of the war he began the practice of law in Dubuque and on Mar. 4, 1866, he was married to Augusta A. Fox of West Union, Iowa. He held several minor federal offices, and in 1882 he was nominated for Congress in the 3rd district and was elected. He was a member of Congress for ten consecutive terms. In 1899 and again in 1901 he was the unanimous choice of his party for the speakership of the House and he would have been chosen again in 1903 had he not declined a renomination for Congress. After his retirement he practised law in New York City; but he returned home soon thereafter and remained, except for a brief sojourn in California, until his death.

Henderson never attained distinction as a lawyer, nor was his congressional career marked by any constructive statesmanship. As an ardent "stand-pat" Republican he participated in a number of debates in which he distinguished himself as an orator rather than as a statesman; as an able advocate before the House of Representatives rather than as a profound student of legislation. His most distinguished services were in behalf of the veterans of the Civil War. He fought for pensions. This was his life-long hobby, and it may be doubted whether there was another man in Congress who did more than he for the soldiers, widows, and orphans. The war spirit dominated his career. He treated foreign relations from the standpoint of the soldier and with a view to the possibility of war. He was also an earnest advocate of high protection. Although he was personally opposed to prohibition, in his political speeches he supported the crusade against intemperance.

[*Who's Who in America*, 1906–07; *Annals of Iowa*, Apr. 1906; B. F. Gue, *Hist. of Iowa* (1903), IV, 126–27; Johnson Brigham, *Iowa: Its Hist. and Its Foremost Citizens* (1915), I, 553–60; Wm. H. Smith, *Speakers of the House of Representatives of the U. S.* (1928); *Dubuque Daily Times*, Feb. 27, 1906; information as to certain facts from E. E. Wilson, Waterloo, Iowa, and E. R. Harlan, curator of the State Historical Department, Des Moines, Iowa.] L. B. S.

HENDERSON, JAMES PINCKNEY (Mar. 31, 1808–June 4, 1858), first governor of Texas, was born in Lincoln County, N. C., the son of Lawson Henderson and Elizabeth Carruth. He was prepared for college at the Lincoln Academy and spent several years at the University of North Carolina, leaving before graduation to begin reading law. He was admitted to the bar in 1829. He practised for a time in North Carolina and was deeply interested in the militia in which he became a colonel. In 1835 he moved to Canton, Miss., and was establishing a good practice and an excellent reputation there when early in 1836 he became enthusiastic over the struggle of Texas for independence. Raising a company he went ahead of it with Memucan Hunt, another North Carolinian living in Mississippi, and arrived just after the battle of San Jacinto had been fought. He was at once commissioned brigadier-general and returned to the United States to raise troops, sending one company from North Carolina to Texas at his own expense. He returned to Texas in the fall and was immediately appointed attorney-general of the republic. In November he became secretary of state and served until June 1837, when President Houston made him diplomatic agent of Texas to England and France. In England he made many friends but was unable to secure the recognition of Texas, although he did negotiate an informal commercial arrangement by which trade could be carried on. In 1838 he went to France and for a time was unsuccessful, but there also he was able to make a commercial arrangement similar to the one made with England. After long delays and the untangling of a number of diplomatic complications by Henderson and James Hamilton, who joined him in 1839, a treaty of recognition was signed Sept. 25, 1839. In Paris Henderson met Frances E. Cox, the daughter of John Cox of Philadelphia, who had just completed her education abroad, and in October 1839, before he returned home, he was married to her in London.

Henderson returned to Texas in 1840. President Lamar had planned to make him secretary of state again but circumstances prevented him from awaiting Henderson's return. Consequently Henderson settled at San Antonio, and, resuming practice, established in four years a deserved reputation as a trial lawyer. In 1844 he was appointed special envoy to the United States to assist Isaac Van Zandt in negotiating a treaty of annexation which was presently signed. The treaty failed of ratification, but when Texas was annexed by resolution Henderson was a delegate from San Augustine County to the convention which framed the state constitution and, upon its ratification, was elected governor. When the Mexican War began, in response to the invitation of the legislature, Henderson took command of four regiments furnished by Texas and became a brigadier-general of volunteers. For his gallantry at Monterey Congress voted him a sword. There Taylor appointed him one of the commission which arranged with Ampudia the terms of capitulation. Declining to be a candidate for reëlection to the governorship Henderson once more returned to his profession and declined to consider public office until 1857 when he was unanimously elected United States senator. He was in delicate health when he took his seat on Mar. 1, 1858, and very soon thereafter he had to go for treatment to Philadelphia. He died the following June in Washington.

[F. B. Sexton, memorial address delivered Aug. 21, 1858, printed in *Quart. of the Tex. State Hist. Asso.*, Jan. 1898; *Biog. Dir. Am. Cong.* (1928); *The Papers of Mirabeau Buonaparte Lamar* (6 vols., 1921–28); G. P. Garrison, "Diplomatic Correspondence of the Republic of Tex.," *Ann. Report of the Am. Hist. Asso.*, 1907, vol. II, 1908, vol. II; "Secret Jours. of the Senate, Republic of Tex., 1836–45," in *First Biennial Report of Tex. Lib. and Hist. Commission* (1911); *Jour. of the Convention Assembled . . . for the Purpose of Framing a Constitution for the State of Tex.* (1845); J. H. Smith, *The Annexation of Texas* (1911); *Cong. Globe*, 35 Cong., 1 Sess., pp. 2717–18, 2720–21; *Washington Union*, June 5, 1858.]

J. G. de R. H.

HENDERSON, JOHN (Feb. 28, 1795–Sept. 16, 1857), lawyer, United States senator, was born in Bridgeton, N. J. His father was a native of Scotland. As a youth he engaged in flatboating on the Mississippi River, read Blackstone in leisure moments, and later studied law in Cincinnati, Ohio. While still a young man he emigrated to Mississippi and practised law at Woodville and Pass Christian. In 1835 and 1836 he represented Wilkinson County in the state Senate where as chairman of a committee to which his own resolutions had been referred he drafted a report which declared that the House of Representatives assembled was not a legal House and that the legislature was not the legislature authorized by the constitution and the laws, because of the admission of representatives from new counties not recognized in the act of apportionment. The resolutions were adopted by the Senate. The House refused unanimously to concur. The governor broke the deadlock by proclaiming on Jan. 31, 1835, the adjournment of both houses. Henderson was a Whig in politics, but he supported the doctrine of the sovereignty of the states in all governmental functions not delegated to the federal government. He was elected to the United States Senate in 1839 as a Whig and served for six years, though in 1840 the Mississippi House of Representatives demanded his resignation for opposing the independent treasury bill. A warm supporter of the annexation of Texas and of the conquest of Cuba and Mexico, he was closely connected with John A. Quitman in enterprises looking to the continental expansion of the United States and was active in the support of Lopez in his filibustering expeditions against the Spanish authorities in Cuba. After the defeat of the Cadenas expedition Lopez went to New Orleans to prepare for another invasion of Cuba and there he had the support and sympathy of Henderson, who at the time was a practising lawyer at the New Orleans bar. In 1851 Henderson was tried in the United States district court in New Orleans for violation of the neutrality law of 1818 for complicity in the Lopez expedition. After three attempts at conviction in which neither acquittal nor conviction was procured, the government dropped the case. Henderson's name is carved on the memorial erected by the Cuban government in Havana to American citizens who took part in the long struggle of its people for independence. He continued to practise law in New Orleans and died at Pass Christian in 1857. He was twice married. His second wife was Louisa (Fourniquet) Post, whom he married in 1830.

[*Biog. and Hist. Memoirs of Miss.* (1891), I, 907–08; Dunbar Rowland, *Mississippi* (1907), vol. I; J. D. Lynch, *Bench and Bar of Miss.* (1881); J. F. H. Claiborne, *Life and Correspondence of John A. Quitman* (2 vols., 1860); *The Writings and Speeches of Daniel Webster* (1903), XV, 432–33; J. B. McMaster, *A Hist. of the People of the U. S.*, vol. VIII (1913); *Daily Picayune* (New Orleans), supp. to issue of Mar. 8, 1851, and death notice in issue of Sept. 18, 1857.]

D. R.

HENDERSON, JOHN BROOKS (Nov. 16, 1826–Apr. 12, 1913), United States senator, was born in Danville, Va., the son of James and Jane (Dawson) Henderson. In 1832 the family moved to Lincoln County, Mo., where a few years later his father was accidentally killed. His mother died soon afterward and he went to live for some years on the farm of a minister where he worked to the advantage of both brain and brawn, acquiring rugged health and obtaining a firm grounding in his studies. From then until the end of his life he was an omnivorous reader and a prodigious worker. At fifteen he began teaching in Pike County and also read law. Admitted to the bar in 1844, he began practice at Louisiana, the county-seat, rapidly built up a large practice, and, fortunate always in investments, accumulated a considerable property which developed ultimately into a large fortune. In politics he was an ardent Democrat and was elected to the legislature in 1848 and again in 1856. In both sessions he was prominent in railroad and banking legislation. During this period he was president of one of the branches of the state bank. He was defeated for Congress in 1850, 1858, and 1860, but he was judge of the court of common pleas for a short time and was offered a seat in the supreme court. In 1856 and in 1860 he was a presidential elector. Independent then as always, he opposed President Buchanan's Kansas policy; and in 1860, supporting Douglas, he was a delegate to the Charleston and Baltimore conventions. He was a state-rights Democrat, or at least so considered himself, but when the issue was drawn in 1861, he strongly opposed the secession of Missouri and was a Union delegate to the convention and one of the most influential forces in preserving the state to the Union. But he was opposed to the coercion of the seceded states. "Has it ever been supposed, by any member of this convention, that any man could be elected President of the United States who could so far disregard his duties under the Constitution and forget the obligation of his oath as to undertake the subjugation of the Southern States by military force? . . . If so . . . this Government is at an end" (*Journal and Proceedings of the Missouri State Convention, post,* pt. 2, pp. 91–92). Declaring secession "a damnable heresy," he was bitter against the North and the Abolitionist element of the Republican party which he thought had provoked the trouble and declared that revolution would be the better course for Missouri if Abolitionist doctrines were to prevail. He served on the federal relations committee and its report expressed his views. In the report of the commission appointed to receive the commissioner from Georgia he made a powerful argument for the Union, and his speech, made by request of the convention on Mar. 5, was fiery and eloquent. The fall of Sumter and the call for troops changed his opinion as to coercion, and he raised a brigade of militia of which he became brigadier-general. He saw no active service and on Jan. 17, 1862, was appointed United States senator to replace Trusten Polk. The following year he was elected for a full term.

In the Senate, where he was next to the youngest member, Henderson quickly became prominent. He served on a number of important committees, including finance, foreign relations, and Indian affairs, and was responsible for much of the financial legislation of the war. He was greatly interested in the purchase of Alaska and aided Seward in arranging the terms. As chairman of the committee on Indian affairs he urged better treatment of the Indians, and in 1867, as chairman of the Indian peace commission, he concluded advantageous treaties, bringing peace with several tribes. He was friendly to Lincoln's plan for compensated emancipation and voted for the resolution indorsing it. At Lincoln's request he went to Missouri to urge the policy, later introducing a bill to carry it into effect there. Lincoln informed him in the summer of 1862 of the proposed emancipation proclamation, but while approving, he, like Seward, urged its delay. In 1864, believing that an amendment abolishing slavery would pass only if proposed by a border-state member, he introduced the Thirteenth Amendment despite his belief that it meant his political death. He voted for the Wade-Davis bill, but he supported Lincoln's plan of reconstruction. In the session of 1865–66, however, he acted with the radicals, voting for the Freedmen's Bureau and Civil Rights Bills, and in February 1866, while opposing the Fourteenth Amendment as inadequate, he advocated negro suffrage and offered an amendment to the resolution which was almost identical to the wording used later in the Fifteenth Amendment. In the end he voted for the Fourteenth Amendment, but in 1869, when the Fifteenth Amendment was under discussion, he did not speak in its behalf and was absent when it was passed. He doubted the wisdom of the provision for military government in the Reconstruction acts but yielded the point. He was a severe critic of Johnson and voted for the Tenure of Office Act, but, alone of the regular Republican senators, voted against the bill forbidding the president to issue military orders except through the general in command of the army. From a sense of decency he would not vote for the resolution declaring Stanton's removal illegal and during the progress of the trial of Johnson he was liberal with respect to the admission of evidence. He found it hard to reach a decision, harder still to vote against his party, and visibly wavered, even offering to resign that his successor might vote guilty. When an insolent telegram of instructions came from Missouri his poise was restored, and he replied: "Say to my friends that I am sworn to do impartial justice according to law and conscience, and I will try to do it like an honest man" (Henderson, *post,* p. 208). He voted "not guilty," defied the attempt of the managers to fasten corruption upon him, assuring the Senate that he had no appropriate epithets for B. F. Butler's report, and, if he had, could not, in justice to himself or to the Senate, use them, and filed an unanswerable defense on legal grounds for his votes. He was denounced, threatened, and burned in effigy by Missouri radicals, but more than any other of the recalcitrant Republicans he was forgiven by his party. He was, of course, not a candidate for reëlection. Returning to the law, he began to practise in St. Louis. In 1870 he supported the Liberals, but in 1872 he was back in the fold and the party candidate for governor and in 1873, candidate for senator. In 1875 he was appointed special federal district attorney to investigate and prosecute the whiskey ring, but he was soon removed for a speech attacking General Babcock, which Grant thought reflected upon him as well. Henderson knew Grant well and had sought in 1867 and 1868 to guide him away from some of his undesirable political associates. He did not approve of Grant's administration and supported him reluctantly in 1872. In 1876 and 1880 he was a determined opponent of the third-term movement. In 1884 he was president of the Republican national convention and was eager for the nomination of his friend and neighbor, Gen. W. T. Sherman.

In 1889 Henderson retired from practice and moved to Washington, D. C., where he spent the rest of his life. He was an interested delegate to the Pan-American Congress of 1889 and for many years, 1892–1911, a regent of the Smithsonian Institution. He wrote constantly for magazines and the press, preserved a lively interest in public affairs, entered into the social life of the capital with zest, entertaining a great deal, and grew gracefully to old age. He died after a brief illness and was buried at Arlington. Although Henderson was a man of warm and affectionate nature, he had a gusty temper not infrequently aroused. In politics he was courageous and never hesitated to differ with his party. A touch of intellectual uncertainty in him is indicated by his frequently voting for measures he opposed in speech. He married, in 1868, Mary Newton Foote, the daughter of Elisha Foote of New York, who survived him.

[J. B. Henderson, "Emancipation and Impeachment," *Century Mag.*, Dec. 1912; *Jour. and Proc. of the Mo. State Convention Held . . . Mar. 1861* (1861); D. P. Dyer, *Autobiog. and Reminiscences* (1922); Wm. Hyde and H. L. Conard, *Encyc. of the Hist. of St. Louis* (1899), vol. II; *Evening Star* (Washington, D. C.), and *St. Louis Republic*, Apr. 13, 1913.]

J. G. deR. H.

HENDERSON, LEONARD (Oct. 6, 1772–Aug. 13, 1833), jurist, brother of Archibald Henderson [*q.v.*], was the third son of Richard [*q.v.*] and Elizabeth (Keeling) Henderson and was born at his father's plantation home on Nutbush Creek in Granville County, N. C. His father died when Leonard was twelve years old and his mother five years later. He was educated, like his father, by private tutors, reading Greek and Latin with a Presbyterian minister of the community. Inevitably inclined to the profession in which so many of his relatives were engaged and in which his father had attained eminence, he studied law in the office of his kinsman, Judge John Williams, at Hillsboro, and was admitted to the bar in 1794 (J. H. Wheeler, *Reminiscences and Memoirs of North Carolina and Eminent Carolinians*, 1884, p. 182). It was not until 1800, however, that he began the practice of law, the intervening years being spent as clerk of the district court at Hillsboro. His native ability, powerfully reinforced by his family connections, soon brought him into prominence, with the result that in 1808 he was elected a judge of the superior court of North Carolina, a position held by his father in pre-Revolutionary days. This position he held until 1816, when he resigned (J. H. Wheeler, *Historical Sketches of North Carolina*, 1851, vol. II, p. 163). Subsequently the judicial system of North Carolina was revised involving the erection of a supreme court of three members. To the bench of this court Henderson was elected in 1818 and eleven years later, upon the death of John Louis Taylor [*q.v.*], he was appointed to succeed him as chief justice. In this, the highest judicial position in the state, he continued until his death.

It was probably in the rôle of teacher that Henderson exerted the greatest influence on the history of his state. For thirty years he conducted a law school in connection with his law office and the most eminent of the North Carolina lawyers of the next generation received their legal training from him. As a judge he was esteemed by his contemporaries more for his acumen and sound judgment than for his knowledge of or respect for precedents. His impatience with precedents, however, was probably due rather to his self-confidence than to defective legal training. In religious matters he was a free-thinker and seems to have made no profession of religion until at a very advanced age. Upon his death he was survived by his wife, Frances Starr Henderson, and by four children.

[In addition to the references cited see W. H. Battle, "A Memoir of Leonard Henderson," *N. C. Univ. Mag.*, Nov. 1859; T. B. Kingsbury, "Chief Justice Leonard Henderson," *Wake Forest Student*, Nov. 1898; *N. C. Law Jour.*, Nov. 1901; J. L. Seawell, *Law Tales for Laymen* (1925), ch. xii; and the *Green Bag*, Oct. 1892.]

R. S. C.

HENDERSON, PETER (June 9, 1822–Jan. 17, 1890), horticulturist, seed-merchant, writer, was born at Pathhead, near Edinburgh, Scotland. He was the youngest of the three children of James Henderson, a land-steward, and his wife, Agnes Gilchrist. He was sent at an early age to the parish school, where he showed a dislike for anything not of a strictly utilitarian nature. At the age of fifteen he went to Edinburgh and found employment in a liquor store, but he remained only a few months. He was then indentured as an apprentice in the gardens of Melville Castle, near Dalkeith, which under the direction of the head-gardener, George Stirling, was considered the best garden training-school in Scotland. While still an apprentice, he won the medal offered by the Royal Botanical Society of Edinburgh for the best herbarium of native and exotic plants in a competition open to entrants from the whole of Great Britain. Emigrating to America in the spring of 1843, he arrived in New York with but three sovereigns in his pocket. He obtained a position with George Thorburn at Astoria, Long Island, and remained with him one year. From there he went to Philadelphia to work for Robert Buist, Sr., at that time the leading nurseryman and florist in the United States. After some months with Buist he became private gardener for Charles F. Spang, at Pittsburgh.

Henderson remained in Pittsburgh until he had saved $500, then he went into partnership in 1847 with his brother James, who possessed an equal amount of money, in the market-gardening business in Jersey City, N. J. After a few years the partnership was dissolved. James Henderson established a new business and concentrated on vegetable growing. Peter continued at the same place, adding to his stock an increasing proportion of ornamental plants until his garden stock was superseded. About 1853 he opened an office in New York City, where during the spring and early summer months he sold greenhouse and vegetable plants. In 1864 he left the Jersey City establishment and moved into what was then known as South Bergen. Here he erected model greenhouses. He retained the original New York office until 1862, when he moved into a seed store on Nassau Street with two young Scotchmen. In 1871, after buying out the two partners, he established the seed and garden supply house of Peter Henderson & Company.

Henderson was a prolific writer, his first horticultural writings appearing in the *Magazine of Horticulture.* Later he began to write for the *Horticulturist,* the *Gardener's Monthly,* Moore's *Rural New-Yorker,* the *Country Gentleman,* and similar publications. For some time he wrote on vegetable culture almost exclusively but as he drifted into ornamental horticulture, his articles began to cover that field also. His first book, *Gardening for Profit,* was written in the summer of 1866 when he was working at least sixteen hours a day, largely at manual labor. It was twice revised, in 1874 and 1886, and went through many editions. *Practical Floriculture* (1869 and later editions), and *Gardening for Pleasure* (1875, 1888), followed the first book, then in 1881 he published his most pretentious work, *Henderson's Hand Book of Plants.* This volume of more than four hundred pages was devoted to the botanical classification, propagation, and culture of economic plants. His revision of the work was finished only one week before he contracted his fatal illness. In 1884 he published two books: *Garden and Farm Topics,* which was a collection of essays containing special agricultural information in condensed form, and *How the Farm Pays,* which he produced in collaboration with William Crozier. The latter was in the form of a stenographical report of a series of questions put by Crozier and answered by Henderson. Besides these books and magazine articles he is said to have written many anonymous articles on various controversial matters in horticulture. One of his outstanding papers was that read before the New York Horticultural Society in 1881 entitled "Popular Errors and Scientific Dogmas in Horticulture," in which he attacked the graft-hybrid theory of the origin of certain species as proposed by Darwin.

Scarcely second to the personal influence exerted by his published writings was Henderson's enormous following as a result of his personal correspondence. In the last thirty-five years of his life he was said to have written or dictated at least 175,000 letters. More than two-thirds of these were written by his own hand. He lived nearly all his life in Jersey City, where he established his home in 1851 at the time of his marriage to Emily Gibbons, of Bath, England. She died in 1868 and three years later Henderson married Jean H. Reid, the daughter of his friend Andrew Reid.

[Alfred Henderson, *Peter Henderson, Gardener—Author—Merchant* (1890); L. H. Bailey, *Cyc. of Am. Horticulture,* vol. IV (1900); C. R. Woodward, *The Development of Agric. in N. J., 1640–1880* (1926); *N. Y. Tribune,* Jan. 18, 1890.]

R. H. S.

HENDERSON, RICHARD (Apr. 20, 1735–Jan. 30, 1785), the promoter of the Transylvania colony in Kentucky, was a descendant of Thomas Henderson who emigrated to Virginia early in the seventeenth century and settled ultimately in Hanover County. His father, Samuel Henderson, who married Elizabeth Williams, moved with his family to Bute (later Granville) County, N. C., in 1742. Here in the backwoods of North Carolina on the turbulent frontier their son Richard grew to manhood, relying on private tutors for his education in a region barren of schools and making a beginning of his career as constable and deputy sheriff to his father who had become high sheriff of the county. He studied law in the office of his neighbor and kinsman, John Williams, and upon his admission to the bar became a junior member of the firm of Williams & Henderson. On Mar. 1, 1768, he was appointed an associate justice of the superior court. Both in his capacity of sheriff and of counsel, Henderson came into frequent contact with Daniel Boone, already a noted hunter and explorer and a decidedly indigent farmer, and as early as 1764 Richard Henderson & Company, a land company, had been organized and Boone was acting as Henderson's agent. In 1769 Henderson sent Boone on his well-known second trip into Kentucky in order to secure a trustworthy account of the land in which it would seem he was already meditating a settlement. The latter years of Henderson's term on the bench were stormy owing to the Regulator troubles in western North Carolina and at one time he was compelled by rioters to close his court. In 1773 he retired to private life and from this time on gave his entire attention to the promotion of those Western projects with which his name is connected in history.

With the intention of establishing a proprietary colony in the West and of securing recognition of it by England, he organized in 1774 the Louisa Company, soon renamed the Transylvania Company, for the purpose of promoting the enterprise. The members of the company were his neighbors and kinsmen and he himself was its president. Fortified with an opinion from Lord Mansfield that his course was legal, Henderson made his arrangements to purchase from the Indians the land which he designed for his colony, despite the fact that the governor of North Carolina had issued a proclamation forbidding the company to proceed. In a treaty at Sycamore Shoals on the Watauga River he bought from the Cherokee Indians in March 1775 the land lying between the Kentucky and the Cumberland rivers, thus (if the treaty was legal) clearing this region of Indian title, since the northern Indians had given up their title to the land south of the Ohio by the treaty of Fort Stanwix in 1768. Preceded by Boone who blazed the famous Warrior's Trace and cut the equally famous Boone's Trace, Henderson made his way into Kentucky through Cumberland Gap and the mountains of Kentucky and established his first settlement, Boonesborough, on the bank of the Kentucky River in the extreme eastern limit of his colony. It is interesting to speculate on what the future of Transylvania colony would have been if there had been no Revolution. But the Revolution made it impossible for Henderson to secure recognition from England or to make headway against the opposition of Virginia and North Carolina within whose chartered limits he had made his settlement. Both these states denounced his project, and although Henderson appealed to the state legislature of Virginia and to the Continental Congress as well, Virginia and North Carolina asserted jurisdiction and the Transylvania colony collapsed, although ultimately Henderson was reimbursed with large land grants.

On two other occasions Henderson appeared in Western enterprises and each time with dramatic effect. In the winter of 1779–80 he served as one of the North Carolina commissioners working with Virginia commissioners to survey the boundary between the two states and in the same winter promoted and carried through the colonization of what is now western Tennessee, establishing a settlement at French Lick, later Nashville. His appointment on the boundary commission shows that his Transylvania project had not hurt his standing with the government of North Carolina. As a matter of fact he was elected to the North Carolina legislature in 1781 and to the council of state in 1782. He died rich in honors and respect at his plantation home on Nutbush Creek. Henderson had married on Dec. 28, 1763, Elizabeth Keeling. Archibald and Leonard Henderson [*qq.v.*] were their sons.

[The best secondary accounts of Henderson are by Archibald Henderson. Chief of these are: *The Conquest of the Old Southwest* (1920); "Richard Henderson and the Occupation of Ky.," *Miss. Valley Hist. Rev.*, Dec. 1914; "The Creative Forces in Westward Expansion: Henderson and Boone," *Am. Hist. Rev.*, Oct. 1914; "Richard Henderson: The Authorship of the Cumberland Compact and the Founding of Nashville," *Tenn. Hist. Mag.*, Sept. 1916; and *The Star of Empire* (1919). Lyman C. Draper's unfinished manuscript life of Boone has an exhaustive account of Henderson. It is in the library of the State Historical Society at Madison, Wis., where there is also much source material on Henderson and his associates. Other sources include: W. P. Palmer, *Calendar of Va. State Papers*, vol. I (1875); G. W. Ranck, *Boonesborough* (1901), No. 16 of the Filson Club Publications, which contains Henderson's journal as well as other documents; Walter Clark, "The Colony of Transylvania," *N. C. Booklet*, Jan. 1904, which also prints Henderson's journal; *The Colonial Records of N. C.*, vols. VII–X (1890); *The State Records of N. C.*, vols. XII (1895) and XIX (1901).] R. S. C.

HENDERSON, THOMAS (Aug. 15, 1743–Dec. 15, 1824), physician, soldier, public servant, was born in Freehold, N. J., the fourth son and seventh child of John Henderson, a devout Presbyterian and a prosperous farmer, and Ann Stevens. He was descended from Scotch Covenanters who emigrated from Fifeshire in 1685 and settled in Monmouth County, N. J. Graduating from the College of New Jersey in 1761, he studied medicine with Nathaniel Scudder [*q.v.*] and in 1764 began practice, first in Freneau and then in Freehold, where he remained for the rest of his life. In 1766 he became a member of the New Jersey Medical Society, the first society of its kind in the country. As the breach with England approached Henderson actively sided with the Revolutionists. He was made a member of the Freehold Committee of Observation and Inspection, Dec. 10, 1774, and lieutenant of local militia in 1775. On Feb. 15, 1776, he was commissioned major of Stewart's minute men, and two months later, major of militia. From June 14 he held the rank of major in Heard's battalion, later he was commissioned lieutenant-colonel in Heard's brigade, and on Jan. 12, 1777, he was made lieutenant-colonel of Forman's Additional Continental Regiment. At Monmouth, in June 1778, he served as brigade-major and took word to Washington of Gen. Charles Lee's retreat. Elected to the Continental Congress Nov. 17, 1779, he declined the office, but served from 1780 to 1784 in the New Jersey Assembly, and from July 1, 1780, on the local committee of retaliation. He also held judicial office, serving as surrogate of Monmouth County, 1776, judge of common pleas, 1783 and 1799, and master of Chancery in 1790. Elected to the New Jersey Council for the term 1793–94, he was vice-president of that body and consequently acting-governor while Richard Howell [*q.v.*] led the New Jersey troops sent to aid in putting down the Whiskey Rebellion. He was also a member of the commission appointed to settle the New Jersey-Pennsylvania boundary dispute. Chosen representative to the Fourth Congress at Philadelphia, he served from 1795 to 1797. He was an independent Federalist, not strict in attendance. In the work of the Congress he urged the protection of the frontier and the strengthening of the army and navy. He also favored sound finance, land sales, and a tariff for revenue. His only speech of any length, Apr. 22, 1796, urged the granting of the appropriation necessary for the execution of Jay's treaty, and is in great contrast to the flood of excited partisan discussion which that matter evoked (*Annals of Congress*, 4 Cong., 1 Sess., pp. 1158 ff.). He was not reëlected and, save in 1812–13, when he served on the New Jersey Council, he held no further political office. Henderson was married on Sept. 23, 1767, to Mary Hendricks, the daughter of John Hendricks, who died a few months after their wedding. On Jan. 2, 1778, he was married to his second wife, Rachel Burrowes. They had seven daughters. Henderson was a devoutly religious man and was both a trustee and elder of the Tennent Church. As candidate for public office "he never sought a vote, and would not even be seen at the polls on election day."

[Stephen Wickes, *Hist. of Medicine in N. J.* (1879); F. R. Symmes, *Hist. of the Old Tennent Church* (ed. 1904); *Minutes of the Provincial Cong. and the Council of Safety . . . of N. J.* (1879); W. S. Stryker, *Official Reg. of the Officers and Men of N. J. in the Revolutionary War* (1872); *N. J. Archives*, 2 ser., vol. II (1903) and IV (1904); *Trenton Federalist*, Dec. 20, 1824.]

W. L. W—y.

HENDRICK (*c.* 1680–Sept. 8, 1755), Mohawk sachem, sometimes referred to by the Indian name Tiyanoga, was born about 1680, possibly even earlier. It is probable that he was a Mohican by birth, but he was adopted by the Mohawks and elected a sachem of the tribe as a young man. He became a Christian, in name at least, and throughout his life was in close contact with those who were responsible for English policy along the New York frontier. He usually resided in the Mohawk Valley, near the Upper or Canajoharie Castle. In 1710, with a party taken over by Col. Peter Schuyler, he visited England and was presented to Queen Anne. For many years he acted as official spokesman for the Mohawks, who occupied a position of great strategic importance. His friendship was assiduously cultivated by William Johnson [*q.v.*] and various colonial governors, by whom he was held in high esteem. Between the outbreak of King George's war and his death he was active in his efforts to hold the Six Nations to the English interest. He supplied the English with information of French activities and occasionally participated in raiding expeditions against the common enemy. At the same time he was loyal to his own people and endeavored to protect them from loss of their lands and the promiscuous sale of liquor. In 1751 he was invited to Stockbridge, Mass., where he was consulted by Jonathan Edwards in regard to a project for educating members of the Mohawk tribe. During the years immediately preceding the French and Indian War, Hendrick frequently represented the tribe at councils between the Six Nations and the English leaders. These meetings culminated in the famous Albany Congress of 1754, at which Hendrick delivered the greatest speech of his career. With stinging sarcasm he took the English to task for neglecting the defense of their frontiers and leaving his own people, their allies, exposed to the French menace. The address made a profound impression and was even published in England (*Gentleman's Magazine,* June 1755). In the late summer of 1755 he helped to enlist the aid of the Indians for Johnson's expedition against Crown Point, and himself accompanied Johnson, at the head of a force of fifty Mohawks. Hendrick was killed at the battle of Lake George on Sept. 8, as he was leading the Indians in an attack against the French under Dieskau. His death called forth sincere expressions of grief and respect from his English associates. He was perhaps the outstanding Indian of this period in North America. During his later years he was often referred to as "King Hendrick." According to Timothy Dwight (*Travels in New England and New York,* 1823, III, 164), one who saw him declared that "his figure and countenance were singularly impressive and commanding; that his eloquence was of the same superior order; that he appeared as if born to control other men, and possessed an air of majesty unrivaled within his knowledge."

[E. B. O'Callaghan, *Docs. Relative to the Colonial Hist. of the State of N. Y.,* vols. IV–VII (1854–56); *The Papers of Sir William Johnson,* vol. I (1921), vol. II (1928); letter of Jonathan Edwards in the *Mass. Hist. Soc. Colls.,* 1 ser., X (1809); N. S. Benton, *A Hist. of Herkimer County* (1856); W. L. Stone, *The Life and Times of Sir William Johnson* (2 vols., 1865), especially vol. I, app. IV.] W. E. S.

HENDRICK, ELLWOOD (Dec. 19, 1861–Oct. 29, 1930), chemist, broker, author, was born at Albany, N. Y., the second of the six children of James and Judith Anne (Wands) Hendrick. He was of English, Scotch, Dutch, and Irish ancestry. His father (1825–99), born at Walsall, England, was brought to the United States in childhood, was admitted to the New York bar, built up a large insurance business at Albany, was a colonel of militia, and maintained a dairy farm and nurseries at "Font Grove," Slingerlands, Albany County. Ellwood completed his formal education at the University of Zürich, 1878–81, where he became a member of the Corps Tigurinia. Though chemistry was his specialty—he never forgot that he had been a pupil of Victor Meyer, Victor Merz, and Wilhelm Weith—he was during his active life as much a business man as a chemist, and his interests extended to other branches of science, to literature, art, music, philosophy, sociology, even to theology. After four years, 1881–84, as manager of the Albany Aniline and Chemical Works, he entered the insurance business and was connected for sixteen years, first as surveyor and later as special agent, with the Commercial Union Assurance Company of London. Meanwhile, on Nov. 15, 1897, he married Josephine Pomeroy, daughter of Daniel Pomeroy of New York, who with one son and one daughter survived him. From 1900 to 1915 he was connected with Pomeroy Brothers (later Denny, Pomeroy & Company), members of the New York Stock Exchange, a firm controlled by his brothers-in-law, Henry Keney Pomeroy and Horace Arthur Pomeroy. He was with Arthur D. Little, Inc., of Cambridge, Mass., 1917–22; consulting editor of *Chemical and Metallurgical Engineering,* 1918–23; and curator of the Chandler Chemical Museum of Columbia University from 1924 until the end of his life. He was the master of a style remarkable alike for its lucidity and ease. His *Everyman's Chemistry* (1917) and *Opportunities in Chemistry* (1919) were unusually succesful attempts to make chemistry intelligible to the layman, but the range of his ideas and the charm of his language are best revealed in a collection of his magazine essays, *Percolator Papers* (1919). He also published *Lewis Miller: A Biographical Essay* (1925) and he was a contributor to the *Dictionary of American Biography.*

His dignified, impressive, and picturesque figure, florid countenance, generous features, and iron gray hair were well known in American scientific, artistic, musical, and literary circles. In London he was often pointed out as a typical Englishman and in Berlin as a German. He had a genius for winning friends, one of whom was Lafcadio Hearn who was his frequent correspondent. During the later period of his life he exerted a wide influence. His appreciation of the pleasant things of life and his fresh, sparkling, whimsical accounts of his experiences made his spoken word even more effective than his writings. By his conspicuously successful lectures at Columbia and elsewhere, by his friendly and inspiring contacts with professors and students, and by his breadth of understanding, he became a conspicuous man among his university associates, and his pattern has been woven into the fabric of many lives. He died at his home, 139 East Fortieth St., New York, after a brief illness.

[*Who's Who in America,* 1930–31; *Who's Who in N. Y.,* 1924; *The Chemist* (Bull. of the Am. Inst. of Chemists), vol. VIII, no. 1, Oct. 1930; *N. Y. Times,* obituary Oct. 30 and editorial Oct. 31, 1930; *Industrial and Engineering Chemistry,* news edition, Nov. 10, 1930; *Percolator,* Nov. 1930; *Chemical and Metallurgical Engineering,* Nov. 1930; *Jour. of the Soc. of Chemical Industry,* Nov. 14, 1930; *Science,* Jan. 30,

1931; F. A. Virkus, *Abridged Compendium of Am. Geneal.*, I (1925), 335, which gives his name as Alfred Ellwood; A. A. Pomeroy, *Hist. and Geneal. of the Pomeroy Family* (1912); *Albany Evening Jour.*, July 25, 1899 (obituary of James Hendrick).] D. D. J.

HENDRICKS, THOMAS ANDREWS (Sept. 7, 1819–Nov. 25, 1885), representative, senator, governor of Indiana, vice-president of the United States, was born near Zanesville, Ohio. Before the Revolution Abraham Hendricks, who was of Huguenot stock, was living in western Pennsylvania, where John, brother of William Hendricks [*q.v.*] and father of Thomas Andrews, was born. Jane Thomson, mother of the latter, was of Scotch descent. The family were Presbyterian in faith, though in later life the son became an Episcopalian. In 1820 they moved to Madison, Ind., but two years later established themselves in Shelby County. Young Hendricks spent his boyhood on his father's farm, and received his early education in the Shelby County Seminary and the Greenburg (Ind.) Academy. After a year in preparatory studies at Hanover College, a Presbyterian institution near Madison, he entered in 1837 the freshman class, graduating in 1841. He achieved some distinction as a college debater. He began to read law in 1842 under Judge Major, in Shelbyville, and in 1843 went to a law school in Chambersburg, Pa., to be under the tutelage of an uncle, Judge Thomson. Admitted to the bar in Shelbyville, he became a highly successful lawyer. On Sept. 26, 1845, he married Eliza C. Morgan, of Northbend, Ohio. Their only child, a son, died at the age of three.

In 1848 Hendricks was elected on the Democratic ticket to the lower house of the Indiana Assembly, in which he became chairman of the committee on banking. Two years later he was elected without opposition to the convention called to revise the constitution of the state. He became an influential member of that body, taking a prominent part in the debates, and by this service added to his friends and influence. In the convention he opposed allowing negroes to come into Indiana, and he supported the provision of the new constitution to that effect, though he disclaimed any sympathy with the institution of slavery. He was elected to Congress from the Indianapolis district in 1851, the only time he had to contend vigorously for a party nomination. He was reëlected in 1852 (the new constitution having transferred the election to the even years), but was defeated in 1854 by the candidate on the "Fusion" ticket, representing a combination of Know-Nothings, members of the People's party, old Whigs, "Maine law" men, and inchoate Republicans. Hendricks had supported the Kansas-Nebraska bill and was an ardent Douglas Democrat. Appointed in 1855 commissioner of the general land office by President Pierce, he held this office till 1859, when, being out of harmony with President Buchanan, he resigned.

In 1860 Hendricks was the Democratic candidate for governor of Indiana but was defeated by Henry S. Lane, Republican. In that year he moved from Shelbyville to Indianapolis. In January 1863 he was elected to the United States Senate by a Democratic legislature, which had come into power in Indiana because of the reaction following military reverses and because of various unpopular measures of the Lincoln administration. During his single term in the Senate (1863–69) he won prominence as one of the leaders of the Democratic opposition. He voted for supplies to carry on the war but was a constant critic of the administration. He opposed the draft, emancipation, the heavy tax bills, and the issue of greenbacks, though later he became a Democratic "Greenbacker" and opposed the retirement of that currency by the resumption of specie payments. He opposed the Thirteenth Amendment on factional and partisan grounds, claiming that the times were not propitious, that the negro was inferior and no good would come from his freedom, that emancipation was a matter for the states and the Southern states were not in a condition to consider it; and he put forward the extremely conservative plea that he "would not disturb the foundations of the fathers." After the war he supported Johnson's plan of reconstruction, holding that since the states in "rebellion" had at no time been out of the Union they were entitled to full representation in Congress; and that the white people of the South should have full control of their state governments with the same body of voters as before the war. He opposed the Freedmen's Bureau Bill and the Civil Rights Bill and any new apportionment of representation. He objected to the Fourteenth Amendment because the Southern states were not represented when Congress offered it for ratification. He would "not amend the constitution amid hate and passion," he said, but only when "the public should be in a cool, deliberative frame of mind." He also opposed the Fifteenth Amendment and the impeachment of Johnson. In the National Democratic Convention of 1868 he was one of the prominent contestants for the presidential nomination. In the same year his party in Indiana nominated him a second time for the governorship, but he lost the election to

Conrad Baker by the narrow margin of 961 votes.

After retiring from the Senate, Hendricks returned to his law practice in Indianapolis, but in 1872 he was nominated a third time for the governorship. Supported by the temperance forces and aided by his own personal popularity, he was elected by a majority of 1,148 votes, though only one other Democrat on the state ticket was successful. As one of the first Democrats chosen to a governorship in a Northern state after the Civil War, he occupied a position of considerable political prominence. When Horace Greeley, candidate of the Democrats and Liberal Republicans for president in 1872, died between the election and the meeting of the electoral college, Hendricks received by compliment forty-two electoral votes of the sixty-two won by his party. In 1876 he was the vice-presidential candidate on the ticket with Samuel J. Tilden and helped to carry Indiana for the Democrats. Four years later his party in the state urged his candidacy for the presidency. His nomination as Cleveland's running-mate in 1884 served to balance that successful ticket, for Hendricks was from the Middle West, had been identified with "soft money," and was acceptable to the machine faction, though not to the reform element that favored Cleveland (Thomas, *post,* p. 194). As in 1876, his strength in his own state helped to carry it in the election. On Nov. 25, 1885, less than nine months after his inauguration as vice-president, he died suddenly at his home in Indianapolis.

[J. W. Holcombe and H. M. Skinner, *Life and Pub. Services of Thos. A. Hendricks* (1886); "Memorial Addresses on the Life and Character of Thos. A. Hendricks," *Sen. Miscellaneous Doc. No. 120,* 49 Cong., 1 Sess.; address by David Turpie, printed in *Souvenir: Unveiling the Hendricks Monument July 1, 1890* (1891); Mrs. Hope Graham, "Hendricks in Reconstruction," master's thesis, Univ. of Ind. (1912); H. C. Thomas, *The Return of the Democratic Party to Power in 1884* (1919); Jas. G. Blaine, *Twenty Years in Cong.* (2 vols., 1884–86); David Turpie, *Sketches of My Own Times* (1903); *Lew Wallace; An Autobiography* (2 vols., 1906); *A Biog. Hist. of Eminent and Self-made Men of the State of Ind.* (2 vols., 1880); *Indianapolis Jour.,* and *Indianapolis Sentinel,* Nov. 26, 1885.]
J. A. W.

HENDRICKS, WILLIAM (Nov. 12, 1782–May 16, 1850), congressman, governor of Indiana, was born at Ligonier, Westmoreland County, Pa., the son of Abraham and Ann (Jamison) Hendricks. He received an elementary education in the common schools at Cannonsburg, Pa., and graduated from Jefferson (later Washington and Jefferson) College in 1810. In early manhood he moved to Cincinnati where he taught school and studied law, and in 1813 he removed to Madison, Ind., while that state was still a territory. Madison remained his home until his death. In the year of his arrival he joined with a partner in publishing the *Western Eagle* and in the same year he was elected to the territorial legislature. Reëlected in 1814, he was chosen speaker of the Assembly. He was also made territorial printer. In 1816, when the territorial convention met at Corydon to draw a constitution for the new state, Hendricks became secretary of the convention although he was not a delegate. In the first election under the constitution in August 1816 he was elected to Congress and was reëlected in 1818 and 1820. In the latter year he favored placing an anti-slavery restriction on Missouri in the controversy over the admission of that state. He denounced slavery as "morally wrong," and "an epidemic in the body politic." Contending that Congress had power to impose conditions on a territory, he held that the people of a territory "are not possessed of sovereign State powers when making a constitution, nor when it is made, until Congress shall admit them to the Union" (*Annals of Congress,* 16 Cong., 1 Sess., p. 1345).

In 1822 Hendricks was elected governor of Indiana without opposition, receiving nearly all the votes that were cast. He resigned from Congress to accept the governorship, but in 1825 he was elected to the United States Senate and resigned the governorship to take his seat there. In December 1830, he was elected to a second term in the Senate. During his twelve years of senatorial service he was a member of the committee on roads and canals, acting as chairman from 1830 to 1837. Although he was a Jackson Democrat he was a firm believer in internal improvements and favored the building of roads and canals in all parts of the country. He sought to have the public lands ceded to the states in which they lay, since otherwise he saw no escape from federal appropriations. There was, he contended, no equality between the old states and the new so long as the old states owned their lands while the new states did not. He particularly insisted that the Western states should have title to the public lands within their borders. In financial matters he stood for a central national bank, with its seat in Washington, empowered to establish branches in the states, but only by the consent of the states themselves.

In 1837 Hendricks retired from public life as the result of Whig triumphs in his state. During his nearly twenty years of service in Congress he had followed the habit of sending an annual letter, or report, to his constituents giving an account of his stewardship and setting forth the leading topics and features of the session just closed. He gave faithful and competent service, and his long public life was above reproach. He helped to lay the foundations of his state and made the first revision of the laws of Indiana which he had printed on his own press. He was married, on May 19, 1816, to Ann P. Paul. Vice-President Thomas A. Hendricks [*q.v.*] was his nephew.

[Logan Esarey, ed., *Governors Messages and Letters*, vol. III, which is vol. XII (1924) of the *Ind. Hist. Colls.*; *A Biog. Hist. of Eminent and Self-made Men of the State of Ind.* (2 vols., 1880); *Biog. and Hist. Cat. of Washington and Jefferson Coll., 1802–89* (1889); *Biog. Dir. Am. Cong.* (1928).] J. A. W.

HENDRIX, EUGENE RUSSELL (May 17, 1847–Nov. 11, 1927), bishop of the Methodist Episcopal Church, South, was of Huguenot extraction on his father's side, and of Scotch and Welsh, on his mother's. He was a descendant of Hendrick Hendricks, who came to America with three brothers sometime before 1700 and settled in Pennsylvania. Hendrick's son, Adam, changed the spelling of the family name to Hendrix. The latter's grandson, Adam, left his home in New Freedom, Pa., in 1840 and went to Fayette, Mo., where he established a bank. Four years later he returned East to marry and take back to Missouri Isabella Jane Murray of Baltimore County, Md. Eugene Russell was the second of their five children, the third being Joseph Clifford [*q.v.*]. Both parents were devoted adherents of the Methodist Church. At the age of sixteen Eugene entered Wesleyan University, Middletown, Conn., from which he received the degree of A.B. in 1867. Having graduated from Union Theological Seminary, New York, two years later, he joined the Missouri Conference of the Methodist Episcopal Church, South, and in 1870 was ordained. On June 20, 1872, he married Ann Eliza Scarritt, daughter of Dr. Nathan Scarritt of Kansas City, Mo.

Circumstances decreed that during the greater part of his career Hendrix should be engaged in administrative work, for which, indeed, he was well fitted. Only eight years was he in charge of churches. He was pastor at Leavenworth, Kan., 1869–70; Macon, Mo., 1870–72; and St. Joseph, Mo., 1872–76. In 1876 he made a trip around the world in company with Bishop Enoch M. Marvin [*q.v.*], who was sent to visit the missions in China. This experience broadened Hendrix's outlook and quickened his interest in missionary activities. He published an account of the journey in 1878 under the title *Around the World.* From 1877 to 1878 he was pastor at Glasgow, Mo., and in the latter year became president of Central College, an institution established by Missouri Methodists some two decades before in his home town, Fayette. This office he filled until he was elected bishop in 1886, strengthening it in every way and having notable success in enlisting the interest of those who could give it financial support.

During his more than forty years in the episcopal office he became one of the most widely known and influential leaders of his Church. His duties took him to all its Conferences, to South America, and to the Far East. In 1900 he was fraternal messenger to the British Wesleyan Conference. Tall and impressive physically, his emotions always in control, urbane, and formal in manner, he maintained an invariable dignity. His keenness of perception, tact, and knowledge of parliamentary procedure made him an exceptional presiding officer. Good judgment, especially in financial matters, won him the confidence of men of affairs. Comparatively free from local and sectarian narrowness, he was a pronounced advocate of interdenominational fellowship and cooperation. In recognition of his activities in this field, he was elected the first president of the Federal Council of the Churches of Christ in America in 1908, and served until 1912. He read widely and his writings are copiously adorned from the contents of his well-stocked mind. Besides contributing frequently to the *Methodist Quarterly Review,* he published: *Skilled Labor for the Master* (1901), a collection of short discourses addressed chiefly to ministers, designed to promote greater efficiency in Christian service; *The Religion of the Incarnation* (1903), Cole Lectures at Vanderbilt University, and *The Personality of the Holy Spirit* (1903), Quillian Lectures at Emory College, works which present the subjects from a conventional orthodox viewpoint; *Christ's Table Talk: A Study in the Method of Our Lord* (1908); and *If I Had Not Come: Things Taught by Christ Alone* (1916). After some five years of invalidism, he died at Kansas City, Mo., in his eighty-first year.

[*Alumni Record of Wesleyan Univ.* (1911); *Alumni Cat., Union Theol. Sem. 1836–1926* (1926); *Who's Who in America,* 1926–27; *Meth. Quart. Rev.,* Apr. 1928; *Christian Advocate* (Nashville), Nov. 18, 25, 1927; *Kansas City Jour.,* Nov. 12, 13, 1927.] H. E. S.

HENDRIX, JOSEPH CLIFFORD (May 25, 1853–Nov. 9, 1904), banker and congressman, was born at Fayette, Howard County, Mo., the third son of Adam and Isabella Jane (Murray) Hendrix. He was a descendant of Hendrick Hendricks who settled in Pennsylvania sometime before 1700, and a brother of Eugene

R. Hendrix [*q.v.*]. Joseph received his academic education at Central College, Fayette, and later studied for three years at Cornell University, Ithaca, N. Y. While a student at Cornell he became interested in journalism and for a short time was editor of the *Ithaca Daily Leader*. He removed to New York in 1873 and became the Brooklyn reporter of the New York *Sun*. He was soon promoted to night city editor, but retained his residence in Brooklyn. There he early took an active part in local politics. In 1882 he was appointed a member of the board of education. In 1887 he was elected president of the board and held this position until 1892. In 1883 he received the Democratic nomination for mayor of Brooklyn, but was defeated in the election by Seth Low [*q.v.*], who later became mayor of Greater New York. In 1884 he was appointed a trustee of the New York and Brooklyn Bridge, and the next year was made secretary of the trustees. In 1886 he was appointed postmaster of Brooklyn by President Cleveland and served in this position for two years. He was elected to the Fifty-third Congress (1893–95) as a Democrat, and strong defender of the gold standard, receiving a large majority of votes over his Republican opponent Michael J. Dady.

His banking career began in 1889 when he organized the Kings County Trust Company in Brooklyn. He was serving as president of this institution at the time of his election to Congress. While in Congress he was offered and accepted the presidency of the newly created National Union Bank of Commerce in New York. This institution, organized by leading New York financiers with a capital of $1,200,000, was merged into the National Bank of Commerce on Jan. 9, 1900, but Hendrix retained his position as president, serving in this capacity until 1903, when the National Bank of Commerce and the Western National Bank consolidated. He retired to private life on Oct. 5, 1903, and hardly more than a year thereafter he was stricken with typhoid fever and died at Brooklyn, in his fifty-second year.

He took a very active part in banking affairs. In 1899 he was appointed a member of a committee on admissions to the New York Clearing House and in 1901 was made chairman of its committee on arbitration. In 1896 he was elected vice-president of the American Bankers' Association and the following year was made president. He filled both positions with efficiency. In addition to his office as president of the National Bank of Commerce he was a trustee of the Kings County Trust Company of Brooklyn, the Fifth Avenue Trust Company, and the Morton Trust Company of New York. His interest in educational affairs continued throughout his career and at the time of his death he was one of the life trustees of Cornell University. On Oct. 28, 1875, he married Mary Alice Rathbone, daughter of Abel Rathbone, of Norwich, Conn.

[*Who's Who in America*, 1903–05; *Congressional Directory* (1893); *Biog. Dir. Am. Cong.*, (1928); *Commercial and Financial Chronicle*, Nov. 12, 1904; *Bankers' Mag.*, Oct. 1897; *Am. Banker*, Nov. 12, 1904; *Brooklyn Daily Eagle*, Nov. 9, 1904; *Cornell Alumni News*, Nov. 16, 1904.]

A. M. S.

HENING, WILLIAM WALLER (1767/8–Apr. 1, 1828), legal writer, was born in Virginia, probably in Spotsylvania County, and at an early age began the practice of law at the Fredericksburg bar, his patience, learning, and vigor of mind soon raising him to a position of local prominence. About 1791/2 he removed to Albemarle County, where he built up a successful practice, dealt less happily in real estate, and acquired a distillery with which his name was long associated. In 1804 and 1805 he represented Albemarle in the legislature, and while in this capacity was elected to the Privy Council. Several years later he was appointed clerk of the chancery court for the Richmond district, and retained this office until his death.

Hening did little creative writing, but, despite professional duties that were exacting as well as heavy, worked tirelessly at legal compilations which were contemporaneously important and have proved often invaluable historically. His first book was *The New Virginia Justice* (1795), a handbook of procedure for magistrates, which was both serviceable and popular, was indorsed and distributed by the state, and went through four—perhaps five—editions. In 1808 he drew up a pamphlet of the militia laws of Virginia, and the same year, with William Munford, issued the first of four volumes of Virginia court of appeals reports (1808–11). He published *The American Pleader and Lawyer's Guide* (1811); edited a collection of the legal maxims of Noy, Branch, and Francis, *Maxims of Law and Equity* (1824); and assisted Benjamin Watkins Leigh in preparing his *Revised Code of the Laws of Virginia* (2 vols., 1819).

Soon after his removal to Richmond he began to engage actively upon the work which has made his name revered by Virginia lawyers and antiquarians and which led the historian Bancroft to observe that "no other State in the Union possesses so excellent a work on its legislative history." His thirteen volumes of *The Statutes at Large; Being a Collection of all the Laws of Virginia* (1809–23), published under enactment of the legislature, comprise the laws of Virginia from the first session of the colonial Assembly in 1619 down to 1792, together with the mass of official papers necessary to a complete understanding of the legislation and the political history of the state. Undoubtedly the example, if not the direct precept, of Thomas Jefferson induced him to undertake this task. Jefferson had already expended much money and effort in gathering together the manuscript and printed laws of the commonwealth, alone among the states at that time in owning no complete collection of her statutes, and, confident of his former neighbor's scholarly exactness, willingly turned over his materials to Hening. After laborious research and considerable drudgery, Hening, practically unaided, filled the lacunae in Jefferson's accumulation of documents and, although hampered by various vicissitudes, finally saw his work in the permanence of print. He died in Richmond, after a lingering illness, his wife Agatha, daughter of Gerard Banks of Stafford County, surviving him only ten days.

[Edgar Woods, *Albemarle County in Va.* (1901); P. L. Ford, *Writings of Thos. Jefferson,* vol. IX (1898); *Richmond Enquirer,* Apr. 4, 1828; *Constitutional Whig,* Apr. 12, 1828; 11 and 12 *Va. Reports* (1 and 2 Hening and Munford *Reports*), *passim; Jour. of the House of Delegates of the Commonwealth of Va.,* 1801–25, *passim*; G. B. Goode, *Va. Cousins* (1887).]

A. C. G., Jr.

HENKEL, PAUL (Dec. 15, 1754–Nov. 27, 1825), Lutheran clergyman, was born in Rowan (now Davidson) County, N. C., in the Dutchman's Creek neighborhood thirteen miles from Salisbury, the eldest of the ten children of Jacob Henkel by his wife, Mary Barbara Teter (Dieter). His great-grandfather Anthony Jacob Henckel (1668–1728) of Mehrenberg, Nassau, Germany, matriculated at the University of Giessen in 1688, was ordained in 1692, emigrated with his family to Pennsylvania in 1717, and until his death ministered to the Lutherans at Tulpehocken, New Hanover, Germantown, and Philadelphia. About one hundred of Anthony Jacob's descendants have been Lutheran ministers. Weary of Indian depredations, Paul's father left Rowan County in 1760 and finally settled at Upper Tract, West Augusta County, Va. (now Pendleton County, W. Va.), some distance from his brothers and brothers-in-law at Hinkle's Fort in Germany Valley. Even there the family was in danger; during an Indian attack Paul's sister Hannah was burned to death. Paul grew up speaking both German and English, attending school when opportunity offered, and strengthening his Lutheran orthodoxy on daily drafts from the *Nürnberger Bibel,* Arndt's *Wahres Christenthum,* and Starck's *Tägliches Handbuch.* He learned the cooper's trade, married Elizabeth Negeley Nov. 20, 1776, and in 1781 preached what he considered his first sermon. Encouraged by the Rev. John Andrew Krug of Frederick, Md., he resolved to devote himself to the ministry, studied Latin, Greek, and theology with the Rev. Christian Streit at Winchester, Va., was licensed by the Ministerium of Pennsylvania at York, Pa., June 16, 1783, and was ordained by the same body at Lancaster June 6, 1792. A born frontiersman, Henkel became the great Lutheran home missionary of his generation. His devotion was indefatigable. Traveling each year through a good part of Virginia, North Carolina, Tennessee, Kentucky, Ohio, or Indiana, he preached the gospel, administered the sacraments, formed permanent congregations, and sought out pastors to take charge of them. His wife, who bore him six sons and three daughters and outlived him by some seventeen years, accompanied him at times and shared in the work. For a few years he received support from the Ministerium of Pennsylvania, to which he sent detailed reports, but most of his journeys were made at his own cost. He was one of the founders of the North Carolina Synod in 1803, of the Joint Synod of Ohio in 1818, and of the Tennessee Synod in 1820. From 1790 until his death his headquarters, with several intermissions, was at New Market, Va. His house he turned into a family theological seminary in which he trained four of his brothers and five of his sons for the ministry. From 1800 to 1805 he lived in Rowan County, N. C.; during the War of 1812 and at other times he established himself at Point Pleasant, Va., on the Ohio River. He was always a copious diarist, and when his sons set up their press at New Market he helped to supply them with copy, preparing *Das Neu Eingerichtete Gesang-Buch* (1810); *Der Christliche Catechismus* (1811); *The Christian Catechism* (1811); *Kurzer Zeitvertreib* (1810)—a volume of satiric and didactic verse; and the *Church Hymn Book* (1816), as well as some lesser works. All of them were widely circulated, Henkel himself acting as colporteur. Though he produced a large quantity of verse, both English and German, he was no poet. In his latter years his position was that of a patriarch. A paralytic stroke compelled him to retire in 1823, but he continued to preach and write until six weeks before his death in 1825. He was buried in Emmanuel Cemetery, New Market.

Henkel's sons continued his work. Solomon (1777–1847) became a distinguished physician at New Market; the other five were Lutheran ministers. Philip (1779–1833) and David (1795–

1831) were leaders of the Tennessee Synod, Andrew (1790–1870) and Charles (1798–1841) of the Joint Synod of Ohio. Ambrose (1786–1870) combined preaching with printing, which he learned under John Gruber, the German printer of Hagerstown, Md. In 1806 he and Solomon established at New Market the first Lutheran publishing house in the United States. It continued in existence for over a century, supplying the Lutherans of the South with many books and several periodicals. The greatest undertaking of the firm was the first English translation of the *Christian Book of Concord, or Symbolical Books of the Evangelical Lutheran Church* (1851; rev. ed., 1854). Philip's sons, Eusebius and Irenæus, and David's sons, Polycarp Cyprian and Socrates, became prominent clergymen and authors in the Tennessee Synod. All the Henkels were noted for their orthodoxy and for their bitter opposition to the General Synod. With them began the confessional movement which ultimately spread through almost the whole Lutheran Church in America.

[See A. Stapleton, "Rev. Gerhardt Henkel and his Descendants," *Pa.-German*, Apr. 1903; "An Important Historical Error Corrected," *Ibid.*, Dec. 1906; *The Henkel Memorial*, 1 ser., nos. 1–4 (1910–12); Elon O. Henkel, *The Henckel Family Records*, nos. 1–7 (1926–31); Andrew Henkel, memoir in W. B. Sprague, *Annals Am. Pulpit*, vol. IX (1869); M. L. Stoever, memoir in *Evangelical Review*, July 1869; J. G. Morris, *Fifty Years in the Luth. Ministry* (1878); *Doc. Hist. Ev. Luth. Ministerium of Pa. . . . 1748–1821* (1898); Socrates Henkel, *Hist. Ev. Luth. Tenn. Synod* (1890); G. D. Bernheim and G. H. Cox, *Hist. Ev. Luth. Synod and Ministerium of N. C.* (1902); C. V. Sheatsley, *Hist. of the Joint Synod of Ohio* (1919); C. W. Cassell and others, *Hist. Luth. Ch. in Va. and East Tenn.* (1930); W. J. Finck, "Paul Henkel, the Lutheran Pioneer," *Luth. Quart.*, July 1926; A. L. Gräbner, *Geschichte der Lutherischen Kirche in America* (1892); C. L. Martzolff and F. E. Cooper, "Rev. Paul Henkel's Journal: His Missionary Journey to the State of Ohio in 1806," *Ohio Archaeol. and Hist. Quart.*, Apr. 1914. Henkel family papers are in the possession of Elon O. Henkel and Dr. Casper O. Miller of New Market, Va., and of other members of the family. Some of Henkel's missionary journals are in the archives of the Ev. Luth. Ministerium of Pa. at Mt. Airy, Phila.] G. H. G.

HENLEY, ROBERT (Jan. 5, 1783–Oct. 6, 1828), naval officer, was born at Williamsburg, James City County, Va., a descendant of Reynold or Reginald Henley who settled in James City County as early as 1661. He was the second son of Leonard Henley and his wife, Elizabeth Dandridge, sister of Martha Dandridge Custis Washington, and was a younger brother of Capt. John Dandridge Henley, U. S. N., and of Frances Dandridge, the wife of Tobias Lear [*q.v.*]. Originally intended for the law, he entered the College of William and Mary, at Williamsburg; but his interest in the navy was such that his family allowed him to apply for a midshipman's warrant, which he obtained on Apr. 8, 1799. He served throughout the war with France, and was on the *Constellation* with Commodore Truxtun during the engagement with the French frigate *La Vengeance,* Feb. 1–2, 1800. His bravery and gallant behavior in that battle drew from his commander the compliment, "That stripling is destined to be a brave officer" (Peterson, *post,* p. 479). After the war he obtained a leave of absence and returned to Williamsburg for a course of lectures in navigation and naval science. He was commissioned lieutenant, Jan. 29, 1807, and placed in command of a gunboat at Norfolk. He was in command of one of two divisions of fifteen gunboats, arranged in crescent formation, which drove three English frigates from Hampton Roads, June 20, 1813.

It was, however, at the battle of Lake Champlain, Sept. 11, 1814, that Henley won his chief fame. He commanded the brig *Eagle,* which headed the American line, and was second in command to Commodore Macdonough. The *Eagle* was the first to open fire and bore an important and aggressive part in the entire engagement. Family tradition has it that Henley planned the battle; and certainly his report to the Secretary of the Navy (Bowen, *post,* pp.153–54) indicates his belief that he had not received sufficient acknowledgment from his superior, although Commodore Macdonough wrote officially, "To Captain Robert Henley, of the brig *Eagle,* much is to be ascribed; his courage was conspicuous, and I most earnestly recommend him as worthy of the highest trust and confidence" (Peterson, p. 480). Henley received from Congress a vote of thanks and a gold medal; Governor Nicholas, of Virginia, presented to him the thanks of the legislature of that state; and he was promoted to the rank of master-commandant. Ordered to the Naval Station at Norfolk, he was subsequently made post-captain. Serving next on the *Hornet,* he captured the piratical schooner *Moscow* off Santo Domingo, Oct. 29, 1821. He was promoted to the rank of captain, Mar. 3, 1825. After a tour of duty in North Carolina, he was ordered to the Naval Station at Charleston, S. C., and died there, at Sullivan's Island, where he was buried with military honors. Henley married in early life, but left no children.

[Thos. Wyatt, *Memoirs of the Generals, Commodores, and Other Commanders* (1848); C. J. Peterson, *The Am. Navy* (1858); T. H. S. Hamersley, *Gen. Navy Reg.* (1882); H. B. Dawson, *Battles of the U. S. by Sea and Land* (1858), vol. II; *Niles' Weekly Reg.*, Oct. 5, 1816; Dec. 8, 1821; Oct. 25, 1828; Abel Bowen, *The Naval Monument* (1816); Barber Badger, *The Naval Temple* (1816); E. S. Maclay, *A Hist. of the U. S. Navy, 1775–1901* (3 vols., 1901); *Wm. and Mary Coll.*

Quart. Hist. Mag., July 1896; *Charleston Courier,* Oct. 7, 1828; *Southern Patriot* (Charleston), Oct. 8, 1828.]
W. K. D.

HENNEPIN, LOUIS (Apr. 7, 1640–1701 or later), Recollect friar, author of books on North America, was a native of Ath in the Flemish province of Hainaut. His father, Gaspard, and his mother, Robertine (Leleup) Hennepin, were the parents of six children. The future friar was baptized under the name of Johannes; he is thought to have changed his name upon entering the Recollect order. His novitiate was passed at Bethune in Artois, under Father Gabriel de la Ribourde who years later was with his former novice in Canada. Hennepin says of himself that he was especially fond of traveling, that he visited Italy and Germany, preached in Artois and Hainaut, and carried his beggar's bowl to Calais, where he eagerly listened to the tales of overseas sailors. Once he had an opportunity to go as a missionary to the East Indies; his preference, however, was for Canada, and to journey thither he set forth in July 1675. The previous year he had succored the wounded at the battle of Seneffe.

On the vessel in which Hennepin embarked was Robert Cavelier de la Salle [*q.v.*], who was returning to Canada equipped for western exploration. La Salle preferred Recollect to Jesuit missionaries, and in 1678 obtained the services of Hennepin as chaplain at his Fort Frontenac seigniory on Lake Ontario. Fort Frontenac was the base from which La Salle set forth to explore and colonize the Mississippi Valley. He prepared to build a vessel to carry him around the Great Lakes and in 1678 established his shipyard on the Niagara River above the falls. Thither he sent Father Hennepin to be chaplain for his shipbuilders; on the way, the friar saw the cataract of Niagara, of which he later gave in one of his books the first printed account, greatly exaggerating its height. Hennepin claimed that while in this region he visited the Iroquois country, where he met several Jesuit missionaries, and accompanied the tribesmen to Orange, now Albany, N. Y. That he took so long a journey seems doubtful, for in 1679 he accompanied La Salle in his newly built ship, the *Griffon,* on his expedition through the Great Lakes to the Illinois country. In passing from Lake Erie to Lake Huron Hennepin suggested the name for Lake St. Claire. From Green Bay the *Griffon* was sent back laden with furs, while La Salle and his men in Indian canoes navigated Lake Michigan and reached central Illinois before the close of the year. From Fort Crèvecœur, which he built on the banks of Lake Peoria, La Salle dispatched a party led by Michel Aco [*q.v.*], in February 1680, to explore the upper Mississippi. The other members of the party were Antoine Auguel, called Picard du Gay, and Louis Hennepin.

In Hennepin's first book, *Description de la Louisiane* (Paris, 1683), the author gave an account of his adventures, describing himself as the head of the expedition and claiming credit for considerable exploration. From other sources, we learn that Aco and his party were captured on Apr. 11 by Sioux Indians, were nearly put to death, and suffered many indignities. They were rescued by Duluth [*q.v.*], who had formerly made a treaty with the Sioux and who gave up his plans of western exploration to release Hennepin and carry him to safety. During his captivity Hennepin had traveled over much of Minnesota and had discovered and named St. Anthony's Falls, at the site of the present city of Minneapolis. Duluth took Hennepin to Canada, whence in 1682 he returned to France, where he published the next year his *Description de la Louisiane,* called the "most prominent, most interesting, and most minute of all the narratives of early American exploration." Its success was immediate and the author's fame assured. About 1690, for some reason not understood, Hennepin was expelled from France and returned to his native land. There he published at Antwerp in 1696 *Nouveau Voyage* and the next year at Utrecht, *Nouvelle Decouverte,* both dealing with his travels in North America. The second book appeared in English dress in 1698 as *A New Discovery,* dedicated in fulsome terms to William III of England. In these latter books Hennepin claimed to have discovered the Mississippi River and to have sailed down it to its mouth, appropriating without credit the account of his fellow missionary, Membré [*q.v.*], who acted as La Salle's chaplain on his voyage of 1682.

Even while soliciting the patronage of the English king the friar was begging from William's rival in France the privilege of returning to Canada. Louis XIV replied with an edict ordering Hennepin's arrest if he should attempt to sail from a French port. The French envoy in Holland wrote of the missionary, "He is a very restless man, now he wants to go to Italy." He is known to have been in Rome in March 1701; after that no trace of him has been found. Hennepin was a charming writer of travels, observing minutely and describing graphically all he saw, but his works are marred by his garrulity, his inordinate vanity, his inability to tell the truth, and his habit of appropriating without credit what others had written. The maps accompanying his books were the best issued up to that time.

[*Hennepin's New Discovery* (1903), ed. by R. G. Thwaites, contains a good biography and a complete bibliography of Hennepin's works, by V. H. Paltsits; W. W. Folwell, *Hist. of Minn.* (1921), vol. I, maintains that the question of Hennepin's veracity is still open; J. E. LeRoy in *Pubs. of the Canadian Archives*, VI (1911), 59, gives some recently found documents on his later life. See also *Bull. des Recherches Historiques* (Lévis), June 1907, p. 184; J. G. Shea's translation, with notes, of Hennepin's *Description of Louisiana* (1880); P. Jerome Goyens, in *Archivum Franciscanum Historicum*, July 1925; H. A. Scott, in *Trans. Royal Soc. of Canada*, 1927, p. 113; address by Prince Albert de Ligne, Belgian ambassador, at the celebration of the 250th anniversary of the discovery of the Falls of St. Anthony, in *Minn. Hist.*, Dec. 1930.]

L. P. K.

HENNESSY, JOHN (Aug. 20, 1825–Mar. 4, 1900), Roman Catholic prelate, was a native of Bulgaden, a village in the county of Limerick, Ireland. He was the oldest of eight children born to William Hennessy, a farmer, and Catherine (Meaney) Hennessy. After receiving his primary education in the Bulgaden schools, he began, at the age of twelve, a course of studies in private schools, where he developed a strong predilection for the humanities, a partiality which displayed itself markedly even in the later years of his life. He studied a short while at All Hallows College, Dublin, and at the age of twenty-two left Ireland, and emigrating to the United States, entered the theological seminary at Carondelet near St. Louis, Mo. Three years later, Nov. 1, 1850, he was ordained to the priesthood by Archbishop Peter Kenrick [*q.v.*].

After spending a few years in pastoral and missionary work, he was installed in 1854 as a professor in Carondelet Seminary and made vice-president of that institution, becoming president in 1857. He spent the year 1858–59 in Rome as personal representative of the Archbishop of St. Louis, and here attended the Vatican Council. The year following his return to America saw him appointed to the important parish of St. Joseph in the city of St. Joseph, Mo. It was while laboring here that he was elected bishop of Dubuque and on Sept. 30, 1866, he was consecrated by Archbishop Kenrick, the same prelate who had ordained him. The zeal he displayed in his many constructive works and the successes he achieved won for him further recognition from his Church, in that Dubuque was created an archdiocese in 1893 and he was appointed its first archbishop.

The outstanding work of his episcopal life was the spread of Christian education. A Catholic school in every parish for the religious training of the children was his objective. In the Third Plenary Council of the American bishops held in Baltimore in 1884, he was the stanchest advocate of the parochial school system, even, it is alleged, in the face of strong opposition from certain Eastern prelates; and there is a sound tradition that he was the deciding influence that committed the Church to the policy that was adopted. In the West his methods met with continued criticism because they were considered by some to be an attack on the public-school system. That he succeeded in his program can be seen from the figures: when he went to Iowa in 1866 there were twenty-nine schools under Catholic auspices in the state; at his death, there were 187 primary schools and academies. His example influenced other Western dioceses. To assist him in the schools and to raise their standards, he welcomed into his diocese several teaching sisterhoods, among them, the Sisters of the Third Order of St. Francis of the Holy Family, an order exiled from Germany by Prince Bismarck during the "Kulturkampf." In 1873 he founded in Dubuque a school for the higher education of young men, Columbia College. He was a gifted orator on the rostrum as well as in the pulpit.

[*Souvenir-Volume, Silver Jubilee Rt. Rev. John Hennessy, D.D., Bishop of Dubuque* (1891), gives a detailed account of his episcopal activities. The *Cath. Encyc.*, vol. V (1909), treats of him in the article on the Dubuque archdiocese; some of his sermons and orations have appeared in print in general collections; and original data are found in his letters and documents in the Dubuque archdiocesan archives. See also J. G. Shea, *The Hierarchy of the Cath. Ch. in the U. S.* (1886); J. F. Kempker, *Hist. of the Cath. Ch. in Iowa* (1887); *Hist. of Dubuque County, Iowa* (1911), ed. by F. T. Oldt; *Dubuque Daily Telegraph* and *Dubuque Daily Times*, Mar. 5, 1900.]

M. M. H.

HENNESSY, WILLIAM JOHN (July 11, 1839–Dec. 26, 1917), painter and illustrator, was born at Thomastown, County Kilkenny, Ireland, the son of John and Catherine (Laffin) Hennessy. His father escaped from Ireland after the unsuccessful rising of the Young Ireland party in 1848, and made his way to Canada, whence he proceeded to New York City and became a citizen of the United States. His wife and family joined him there in 1849. William's education was for the most part derived from private tutors; he began to make drawings from life at the age of fifteen; and two years later, in 1856, he entered the school of the National Academy of Design. For the ensuing fourteen years he had a studio in New York and produced in rapid succession a large number of paintings and illustrations which were so well received that his reputation was fairly established. His subjects were landscapes and genre pieces. In the latter he made a strong appeal to the taste and sentiment of that large constituency which likes above all things a well-told story with abundant human interest. Many of his themes were trite—the baby learning to walk, the old woman reading her Bible, and the like—but their sincerity of feeling and clever workmanship made them acceptable and interesting. As a landscapist he was equally able and prolific. His outdoor work was luminous and his skies were especially fine.

It was more particularly in his work as illustrator, however, that he made his mark during the New York period. He illustrated the works of Tennyson, Longfellow, Whittier, Stedman, Mrs. Browning, J. G. Holland, and W. C. Bryant. In a certain vein of sentimentality he was so thoroughly in sympathy with these poets that it might be said he was the predestined graphic laureate of the period that produced "Maud," "Evangeline," "Enoch Arden," and "Maud Muller." The series of eleven drawings for the last-named ballad was typical of the rest in its unrestrained appeal to the susceptibilities of the Victorians. These drawings, published in Boston in 1867, were engraved by Anthony, Davis, and Marsh; but the set of twelve drawings of Edwin Booth in as many dramatic characters (Boston, 1872), engraved by Linton, is doubtless the most widely known of his works in black-and-white.

In the course of his professional life in New York, Hennessy, having been elected an associate of the National Academy in 1862 and an Academician in 1863, sent his pictures to the Academy exhibitions with considerable regularity. He was one of the founders of the Artists' Fund Society, and honorary member of the American Society of Painters in Water Colors. In June 1870 he married Amelia Charlotte Mather and went abroad, remaining in England five years, where he exhibited many paintings at the Royal Academy and became a member of several artistic societies, including the Institute of Oil Painters. He was wont to spend his summers in Normandy and he became so fond of that province that in 1875 he moved to France and leased a manor on the coast near Honfleur. Later, in 1886, he removed to Saint-Germain-en-Laye. In 1891 he made a tour in Italy, after which he moved to Brighton, England (1893), and later to Rudgwick, Sussex. After 1887 he ceased to send his works to the large exhibitions. His "Wreck of the Old Chain Pier, Brighton," belongs to the Corporation Art Gallery in Brighton.

[H. T. Tuckerman, *Book of the Artists* (1867); *L'Art*, Paris, Oct. 6, 1878; Ulrich Thieme and Felix Becker, *Allgemeines Lexikon der Bildenden Künstler*, vol. XVII (1923); J. D. Champlin and C. C. Perkins, *Cyc. of Painters and Paintings*, vol. II (1886); Henry Blackburn, *Acad. Notes*, 1875–82; *Am. Art Annual*, vol. XVI (1919); *Who's Who in America*, 1918–19.]

W. H. D.

HENNI, JOHN MARTIN (June 15, 1805–Sept. 7, 1881), Roman Catholic prelate, was born at the hamlet of Misanenga in the canton of Grisons, Switzerland, eldest of the seven children of Johann Georg Henni, a prosperous farmer, and his wife Maria Ursula (Henni) Henni. After attending a parish school in Misanenga he went to a private school conducted at Meyerdorf by Johann Peter Mirer, later Bishop of St. Gall, then followed his teacher to the Gymnasium at St. Gall, and subsequently studied in the Lyceum and Gymnasium at Lucerne. His residence with an uncle, chaplain of a Swiss regiment in the service of Holland, to whom he was indebted in part for his education; his study under Mirer; and a course at the Urban College of the Propaganda at Rome determined his vocation and eventual missionary career. Visiting Rome in 1828, the Rev. Frederic Rese, vicar general of Cincinnati, won Henni for the American mission. The young man arrived in New York on May 28, 1828, and proceeded to the seminary at Bardstown, Ky., where he completed his studies. After ordination on Feb. 2, 1829, he taught philosophy at the Athenaeum, Cincinnati (today St. Xavier University), and in his spare time took a census of German Catholics in Ohio. In 1834 he was appointed vicar general of Cincinnati and pastor of Germans there. Two years later he published *Ein Blick in's Thal des Ohios* (Munich, 1836). He was the founder, in 1837, and the editor for six years of the *Wahrheitsfreund,* Cincinnati, the first German Catholic newspaper in the United States. Under his editorship this journal achieved a reputation as a medium of correct news and clear thinking, in matters political, moral, social, and religious. The first issue carried the Declaration of Independence, the story of Columbus, an appreciation of American unity, and a civilian creed, the keynote of which was obedience to law. Henni hated slavery, but was against war as the means of abolishing it. Prohibition found no favor with him. He steadily expressed his opposition to autocratic governments, such as that of Prussia, which "make the foot fit the shoe." Though courageous in politics, he was tactful and never coercive. One of his guiding lines was, "Germans may be political enemies of nativist Whigs but not enemies of Whigs as natives" (*Wahrheitsfreund,* Oct. 4, 1838). His separate writings, which include a German *Catechism* (1835), and a pamphlet, *Facts against Asser-*

tions (1844), belonged to passing literature, but his periodic Pastorals contained some excellent observations in history and religion.

When Wisconsin became a diocese in November 1843 with Milwaukee as headquarters, Henni was selected as bishop. He was consecrated on Mar. 19, 1844, in Cincinnati. Less than a month after his arrival in his new field he set out for a four-months' trip of discovery throughout the state, guided by his deep study of the Jesuit Relations and his untiring questioning of aged Indians. Everywhere in Wisconsin are found the fruits of his wise foresight and constructive administration. He established St. Francis Seminary, which has been the cradle for Catholicity in the Northwest; he introduced into the diocese the Sisters of Notre Dame, the Sisters of Charity, the Sisters of St. Francis, the Capuchins, and the Jesuits. The cathedral is filled with trophies he garnered in Belgium, Bavaria, Italy, Mexico, and Cuba. During the Civil War, he aided recruiting by his addresses and his provision for chaplains. In 1875 he became archbishop, amid demonstrations of regard by citizens of all creeds. Six years later he died, in his seventy-seventh year.

[Martin Marty, *Dr. Johann Martin Henni, Erster Bischof und Erzbischof von Milwaukee* (1888); *The Cath. Ch. in Wis.* (1895–98), ed. by H. H. Heming; Joseph Rainer, *A Noble Priest: Joseph Salzmann, D.D.* (1893), tr. by Joseph Berg; P. M. Abbelen, *Venerable Mother M. Caroline Friess* (1893); *Salesianum* (St. Francis, Wis.), *passim,* and esp. July 1927, Apr.–July 1928; *Wis. Mag. of Hist.,* Sept. 1926–Sept. 1928; files of *Berichte der Leopoldinen-Stiftung* (Vienna), 1831 ff., *Annalen der Verbreitung des Glaubens herausg. d. den Ludwig-Missions Verein* (Munich), 1838 ff.; *Wahrheitsfreund* (Cincinnati), 1837 ff., *Seebote* (Milwaukee), 1852 ff., and *Columbia* (Milwaukee); *U. S. Cath. Hist. Soc. Hist. Records and Studies,* IX, 203 (June 1916); *Der Deutsche Pionier,* Jan. 1881–May 1882; *Milwaukee Sentinel,* Feb. 7, 1879.] P. L. J.

HENNINGSEN, CHARLES FREDERICK (Feb. 21, 1815–June 14, 1877), soldier and author, was of Scandinavian ancestry. His tombstone asserts that he was a "Briton by birth," but other evidence points to Belgium as his birthplace. He early became a British citizen, however, and in 1830 his parents established their residence in England. At nineteen he entered the service of the Carlists in Spain, where he was knighted in 1835 and made a captain of lancers. He served in this capacity until the death of his general, Zumalacarregui, in 1836, returned after a peace convention to England, but at a fresh outbreak of hostilities reëntered the struggle and won new laurels. At some time before 1845 he campaigned with the revolutionist prophet of the Caucasus, Schamyl, fighting in the snows against Russian mountaineers. Later, a fugitive in Asia Minor, he rushed back to Europe to help the Hungarians in their uprising against Austria and distinguished himself as commander at Comorn. At the close of this revolution he followed its leader, Kossuth, first to Turkey, then, in 1851, to the United States, serving as his confidential secretary.

Remaining in the United States, he married a widow, Williamina (Belt) Connelly, a niece of Senator John McPherson Berrien [*q.v.*] of Georgia, and learned to know the Southern people and their problems. In October 1856, he joined the expedition to Nicaragua under the filibuster William Walker [*q.v.*], taking with him $30,000 worth of stores, arms, and ammunition given by himself, his wife, and others. He had previously supervised the conversion into Minié rifles of several thousand old army muskets purchased for the expedition by George Law [*q.v.*]. Appointed brigadier-general and given charge of the artillery, he served until the end of the war. Returning to the United States in 1857 he took up his residence in Georgia. In 1861 he offered his services to the Confederate States and on Oct. 14 of that year was appointed colonel of the 59th Regiment, Virginia Infantry (originally known as the Wise Legion), to date from Aug. 1. As senior colonel he commanded the post at Dogwood Gap. He resigned on Nov. 5, 1862. Although he was recommended for promotion to brigadier-general, there is no evidence that he received the appointment. Despite his military experience he never attained distinction in the Confederate service. Later he became interested in Cuban independence.

He was a man of striking appearance and sturdy, patient character; a scholar and linguist of unusual ability; and "an accomplished man of the world." He had some ability as a poet and translator of verse, but his chief medium of expression was prose, which was notable for its forceful style, its wide range of vocabulary, and its facile use of English idiom. His writings deal accurately and fearlessly with the social, cultural, military, and political aspects of peoples and countries. They are the records of his own observations and are in the main descriptive, historical, and didactic in character. Written in a direct, lucid, serious, and convincing vein, where fact excludes fancy, they are both valuable and entertaining. Especially noteworthy are his accounts of Polish, Russian, and Finnish literature. Several of his works appeared in two or three volumes; many in several editions; not a few were translated into foreign languages; and some were published simultaneously in the United States and in England. His descriptions of Russia opened the eyes of Europe to conditions in that country. The list of his works includes: *The Siege of Missalonghi,* a poem written before 1830; *The Last of the Sophis* (1831), a poem; *Scenes from the Belgian Revolution* (1832); *The Most Striking Events of a Twelvemonth's Campaign with Zumalacarregui* (2 vols., 1836); *Revelations of Russia* (2 vols., 1844); *The White Slave* (1845); *Eastern Europe and the Emperor Nicholas* (3 vols., 1846); an edition of *Revelations of Austria* (2 vols., 1846), by Michael Kubrakiewicz; *Sixty Years Hence* (1847); *Analogies and Contrasts* (2 vols., 1848); *The National Defences* (1848); *Kossuth and The Times* (1851); *The Past and Future of Hungary* (1852); *Letter from General C. F. Henningsen in reply to the letter of Victor Hugo on the Harper's Ferry Invasion* (1860). The last years of his life he resided under needy circumstances in Washington, D. C., where he died and was buried in the Congressional Cemetery.

[Henningsen's own works; private correspondence; Confederate records and letters in the War Dept.; *War of the Rebellion: Official Records (Army)*; *Jour. of the Cong. of the Confed. States of America,* I (1904), 507, V (1905), 469; *Cat. of the Printed Books in the Lib. of the Faculty of Advocates* (Edinburgh), III (1874), 725; B. H. Wise, *The Life of Henry A. Wise of Va.* (1899); William Walker, *The War in Nicaragua* (1860); D. M. Hall, *Six Centuries of Moores of Fawley* (1904), pp. 83, 90; J. J. Roche, *The Story of the Filibusters* (1891), with portrait; W. O. Scroggs, *Filibusters and Financiers* (1916); *N. Y. Herald,* June 2, 1856; *Harper's Weekly,* May 23, 1857; *Evening Star* (Washington), June 14, 1877; *National Republican* (Washington), June 15, 1877.] A. B. B.

HENRI, ROBERT (June 25, 1865–July 12, 1929), painter and teacher, was a native of Cincinnati, Ohio. He was the son of John and Theresa Henri; the family, in which French, English, and Irish blood was mingled, had lived for several generations in Virginia, Kentucky, and Ohio. Educated in Cincinnati, Denver, and New York schools, Henri began the study of art at the age of twenty, and in 1886 entered the school of the Pennsylvania Academy of the Fine Arts. After two years of training there in drawing and modeling under Thomas P. Anschutz [*q.v.*], he went to Paris in 1888 with Charles Grafly [*q.v.*] and other students, to enroll himself at the Julian Academy under Bouguereau and Fleury. He also studied for a time in the École des Beaux Arts but chafing under the academic rigidity and dryness of the schools, he sought to develop his artistic personality in independent work outside of them, and traveled in Brittany, Italy, and Spain. In 1891 he returned to the United States and settled in Philadelphia, where he became instructor in the Women's School of Design, and was a conspicuous member of a lively little coterie of realists comprising such men as John Sloan, W. J. Glackens, George Luks, Everett Shinn, E. W. Redfield, and Elmer Schofield. In 1894 he and Glackens were sharing a studio. Henri then went back to Paris and taught a class there for about two years. In 1898 he married Linda Craige of Philadelphia. The year following he exhibited at the Paris Salon a street scene, "Snow," which was bought by the government for the Luxembourg Museum. With his wife he passed the summer of 1899 at Concarneau, then returned to America, where he made his home in New York, having his studio in an old house in East Fifty-eighth street, overlooking the East River. He taught successively and successfully at the Veltin school, the Chase school, the Henri school, the Ferrar school, and the Art Students' League, establishing a great reputation by his zeal, his personal methods, and his faculty for encouraging and inspiring his pupils. He laid emphasis on visual honesty, the avoidance of aping other artists' styles, and the supreme importance of being true to one's self. His wife died in 1905, and between 1906 and 1914 he traveled extensively, painting portraits and character studies in many parts of the world—Irish and Gipsy types, Down-East Yankees, the Indians of California and New Mexico. In 1908 he married Marjorie Organ of New York, herself an artist. The same year the group known as The Eight was organized for the purpose of holding exhibitions; it was composed of Henri, John Sloan, Arthur B. Davies, George Luks, Maurice Prendergast, Everett Shinn, W. J. Glackens, Ernest Lawson.

A book entitled *The Art Spirit,* published in 1923, was compiled from Henri's scattered essays and class-room notes. It contains much that is stimulating and spontaneous in the way of generalizations. Like his painting, his writing is sketchy; but it has the vitality of direct and candid impressions. He was a radical by nature, but not by any means an unreasonable insurgent. He "had learned to respect plain vitality in art, whether in Hals and Rembrandt or in Hogarth," says Morton D. Zabel, who quotes Henri's concise characterization of Hogarth's superb head of a fish girl in the National Gallery: "It is like the wind that blows" (*New Republic, post,* p. 289). This quality of naturalness and spontaneity is likewise the chief merit of Henri's brisk and dashing character studies. It is true that they are sketchy, but they preserve the freedom and freshness that are so likely to be impaired by over-elaboration. Above all they have vitality, a quality so momentous that its presence atones for many defects. That they are widely appreciated is shown by the fact that Henri's work is represented in more than thirty public art museums. In 1929, when the Arts Council of New York sought the opinion of American artists, collectors, dealers and museum officials as to the "hundred most important living artists," Henri was one of the three whose names were given first place.

During the last part of his life he had a summer home, "Boycott House," in County Mayo, Ireland, where he enjoyed the trout fishing and was wont to spend a part of each day at the sport. In the autumn of 1928, while on the way to New York from Ireland, he became ill; on landing he was taken to St. Luke's Hospital, where he died after a sickness of more than seven months. He was survived by his wife and a brother.

[*Robert Henri, His Life and Works* (1921), 40 illus., ed. by William Yarrow and Louis Bouche; *Robert Henri* (1922), 64 illus., compiled by Nathaniel Pousette-Dart; M. D. Zabel, in *New Republic*, July 31, 1929; O. S. Tonks, in *Am. Mag. of Art*, Oct. 1916; C. W. Barrell in *Independent*, June 25, 1908; G. P. du Bois, in *Arts and Decoration*, Apr. 1912; *Current Literature*, Apr. 1912; F. B. Ruthrauff, in *Fine Arts Jour.*, July 1912; *N. Y. Times*, July 13, 1929; *Who's Who in America*, 1928–29.]
W. H. D.

HENROTIN, CHARLES (Apr. 15, 1843–July 25, 1914), Chicago banker, brother of Fernand Henrotin [*q.v.*] and son of Joseph F. Henrotin and Adèle (Kinson) Henrotin, was born in Belgium but was brought to America in 1848 by his parents, who settled in Chicago. After receiving his preliminary schooling, he was sent back to Belgium to the Polytechnic School at Tournai. At the age of eighteen he returned to Chicago where he entered the employ of the Merchants' Savings, Loan & Trust Company. After a period of seven years he was made cashier, succeeding Lyman J. Gage [*q.v.*]. He remained in this position until 1878 when he became an independent banker and broker. He acted as the American representative of important financial interests in London and on the Continent. On the death of his father in 1876, he was appointed to fill the position of Belgian consul which his father had occupied. In 1877 he was made consul for the Ottoman Empire, later becoming consul-general. He continued in these services until his death.

During the administration of the elder Carter Harrison [*q.v.*], Henrotin did notable service for the city and county by purchasing the depreciated scrip of the local governments after it had been declared illegal, thus protecting the incomes of city and county employees. The scrip was subsequently redeemed at par. During the period 1878–83 he introduced railroad bonds into the Chicago financial market. It was at this time that he took a leading part in organizing the Chicago Stock Exchange, of which he was the first president (1882–84). In 1887 he became involved in serious financial failure as a result of an attempted corner in wheat in which customers of his bank had participated, but he recovered, and in 1889–91 served again as president of the Chicago Stock Exchange. He was also a member of the Chicago Board of Trade and helped to promote the building of the Chicago Opera House. He was an active Democrat and took great interest in the Free Silver issue of the Bryan campaigns, writing numerous articles and pamphlets.

On Sept. 2, 1869, he married Ellen M. Martin of Portland, Me., who in 1887 was joint author with K. B. Martin of *The Social Status of European and American Women* and in 1894 became president of the General Federation of Women's Clubs. Henrotin continued to be identified with banking interests in Chicago until his death, which occurred in his seventy-second year.

[A. N. Marquis, *The Book of Chicagoans*, 1911; *Who's Who in America*, 1914–15; *The Biog. Dict. and Portr. Gallery of Representative Men of Chicago* (1892); Wallace Rice, *The Chicago Stock Exchange* (1923); *Chicago Tribune, Chicago Herald*, July 26, 1914.]
E. A. D.

HENROTIN, FERNAND (Sept. 28, 1847–Dec. 9, 1906), surgeon, brother of Charles Henrotin [*q.v.*], was born in Brussels, Belgium, to Dr. Joseph F. and Adèle (Kinson) Henrotin. His father was a graduate of the University of Liège, and served as surgeon in the Belgian army. In 1848 he emigrated to the United States and settled in Chicago. He became Belgian consul in 1857 and held that position until his death in 1876. Having received his preliminary education in the public schools of Chicago, Fernand graduated from Rush Medical School in the class of 1868 and joined his father in a well-established practice to which he later succeeded. He began his teaching career as prosector at Rush Medical College. He was one of the founders of the Chicago Polyclinic and from its beginning until his death served as professor of gynecology there. During the greater part of his medical career he was surgeon to the municipal police and fire departments, and he wrote a manual of first aid for their use. He served for many years on the surgical staff of the Cook County Hospital, was senior surgeon of the Alexian Brothers Hospital, and consulting gynecologist at St. Joseph's and at the German Hospital. Though he never entirely gave up general practice, his leaning was toward operative gynecology and in this field he achieved an international reputation, contributing to the literature of his specialty many valuable and practical monographs. He wrote the chapter on ectopic gestation in *The Practice of Obstetrics, by American Authors* (1899), edited by Charles Jewett; that on gynecology in *The International Text-book of Surgery* (2 vols., 1900), by J. C. Warren and A. P. Gould; and that on vaginal hysterectomy in *Gynecology and Abdominal Surgery* (2 vols., 1907–08), by H. A. Kelly and C. P. Noble. He also wrote *Democracy of Education in Medicine* (1903), a plea for higher standards in medical education and for post-graduate study. A textbook on pelvic surgery was left uncompleted at the time of his death. He was a member and one-time president of the Chicago Medical Society, and a member of the Chicago Gynecological Society and of the American Gynecological Society. Inheriting from his father an interest in military medicine, he was for a time surgeon of the 1st Brigade, Illinois National Guard, and one of the founders of the Association of Military Surgeons of Illinois. Tied down by these varied interests and a large and exacting practice, he was looking forward to retirement to the quiet of his country home and to the writing of a novel on social life when he died quite unexpectedly of myocarditis.

His chief personal attractions were his good-nature and his unfailing kindness and courtesy. His portrait shows a full, round, good-humored countenance of distinctly Gallic type. On Apr. 24, 1873, he married Emilie B. Prussing of a prominent German family of Chicago. When in 1907 the Chicago Polyclinic built its new hospital it was given the name Henrotin Hospital.

[Nicholas Senn, "Dr. Fernand Henrotin," in *Surgery, Gynecology and Obstetrics*, Jan. 1907; *Hist. of Medicine and Surgery and Physicians and Surgeons of Chicago* (1922); H. A. Kelly and W. L. Burrage, *Am. Medic. Biogs.* (1920); *Jour. Am. Medic. Asso.*, Dec. 15, 1906; *Military Surgeon*, Mar. 1908; *Chicago Tribune*, Dec. 10, 1906.] J. M. P.

HENRY, ANDREW (*c.* 1775–June 10, 1833), fur trapper, lead miner, was the son of George and Margaret (Young) Henry and was born in York County, Pa. For a time he lived in Nashville, Tenn., and from there, in April 1800, he went to Ste. Genevieve, in the present Missouri. He was again in Nashville two years later, but in 1803 returned to Ste. Genevieve, soon afterward settling in the present Washington County and engaging in lead mining. He was married, Dec. 16, 1805, to Marie Villars, but separated from her early in the following January and obtained a divorce from her on Oct. 15, 1807. On Mar. 7, 1809, he joined with Manuel Lisa, Pierre Chouteau [*qq.v.*], and others in the organization of the St. Louis Missouri Fur Company, and three months later left with its first and most noted expedition for the upper Missouri. As second in command of Pierre Ménard's detachment, he took part (April 1810) in the first organized invasion of the region about the Three Forks of the Missouri; and though Ménard [*q.v.*] and a majority of the men, discouraged by the attacks of the Blackfeet, returned to St. Louis, Henry and some fifteen or twenty of the more venturesome spirits for a time stayed on. Abandoning the fort in June or July, he led his men south, and traversing a region never before seen by white men, ascended the Madison, crossed the continental divide, descended Henry's Fork of the Snake, and near its mouth erected another fort. Here the party wintered, the first American trappers to operate west of the Rockies. The venture was a complete failure, and in the spring of 1811 the party broke up. Henry reached St. Louis in the fall and returned to his mines. In 1814 he was major of the local regiment of which W. H. Ashley [*q.v.*] was lieutenant-colonel commanding.

Early in 1822 he joined Ashley in the latter's project of trapping the mountain regions, and on Apr. 15 set out with him up the river on the first expedition. At the mouth of the Yellowstone, whence Ashley returned to bring up a second expedition, Henry built a fort, and directed the winter's trapping. In the spring of 1823, undismayed by his former experience with the Blackfeet, he set out with a party for the upper waters of the Missouri, but in May, near the Great Falls, was attacked and compelled to retreat. Reaching his fort, he learned of Ashley's defeat by the Arikaras and hurried to his commander's relief, arriving in time for the battle of Aug. 9. A week later he started again for the Yellowstone, and in the fall abandoned the fort and led his men to the mouth of the Bighorn, where they wintered. In the spring of 1824 he followed the Smith-Fitzpatrick party through South Pass to Green Valley, dispatching his trappers in various directions. Collecting the furs of all the Ashley parties, he started for St. Louis, arriving late in the summer. Evidently discouraged by his experiences in the mountains, he returned to the mines, where he remained. He died at his home in Harmony Township.

Henry was married a second time, in 1819, to Mary Fleming, of Ste. Genevieve. He was tall and slender, and of commanding presence. He played the violin well and he was fond of reading. He was highly respected for his intelligence, enterprise, daring, and honesty. At one time he had considerable wealth, but lost it by becoming surety for others. Because of his adventurous exploits he figures largely in the early annals of the frontier, and no trapper of his time, with the possible exception of John Colter [*q.v.*], had wider renown as a hero.

[Thos. James, *Three Years Among the Indians and Mexicans* (1916), ed. by W. B. Douglas; H. M. Chittenden, *The Am. Fur Trade of the Far West* (1902).]
W. J. G.

HENRY, CALEB SPRAGUE (Aug. 2, 1804–Mar. 9, 1884), clergyman, educator, and author, was born in Rutland, Mass., the son of Silas and Phebe (Pierce) Henry. He was a descendant of Robert Henry who was a native of Scotland and came to America from Ireland in 1718. Caleb graduated from Dartmouth College with the degree of A.B. in 1825, studied theology at Andover, Mass., and at New Haven, and was ordained to the Congregational ministry on Jan. 1, 1829. He was pastor of Congregational churches in Greenfield, Mass., 1829–31, and West Hartford, Conn., 1833–35. Transferring his allegiance to the Protestant Episcopal Church, he was ordained deacon in that communion in 1835 and priest in 1836. The remainder of his active life was largely devoted to literary and educational pursuits.

He was professor of intellectual and moral philosophy at Bristol College, Pennsylvania, from 1835 to 1838. In the latter year he was appointed professor of the same subjects at the University of the City of New York, now New York University, holding that chair until 1852. Soon instruction in belles-lettres and history were added to his duties, so that from 1840 to 1852 he bore the formidable title of "Professor of Intellectual and Moral Philosophy, Belles-Lettres and History." That he was able to bear up under this heavy load is evidenced by the fact that he occupied, in addition, the position of rector of St. Clement's Church in New York City from 1847 to 1850. After 1852, except from 1870 to 1873, when he was rector of St. Michael's Church, Litchfield, Conn., he held no official position, but devoted himself to literary work.

He was an inspiring teacher of great personal magnetism, awakening in his students interest in life in its manifold phases. A member of the class of 1850 at the University of the City of New York reveals an engaging, dynamic personality in the following description: "He was an intellectual force, charged to the full with animal vitality, sparkling vivacity, mental activity, and literary enthusiasm. . . . And into his talk he threw, or rather tumbled, his entire *personnel*—body, mind, heart and spirit" (F. N. Zabriskie, quoted in *New York University, post.*)

It was as editor and author, however, that he left his greatest imprint upon his day and generation. In 1834 he published a pamphlet entitled *Principles and Prospects of the Friends of Peace,* and in the same year founded the *American Advocate of Peace,* which shortly became the organ of the American Peace Society. He was one of the founders of the *New York Review* in 1837, holding the position of editor until 1840. A stanch churchman, he was a constant contributor on theological subjects to religious and secular periodicals. In 1847 he was appointed editor of the *Churchman* and conducted that organ of the Protestant Episcopal Church until 1850. He also served for several years as political editor of the *New York Times.* His wide range of intellectual interests is further evidenced by voluminous publications in book, pamphlet, and periodical form. He published Victor Cousin's *Elements of Psychology* translated from the French, with introduction and notes, in 1834, a book which ran through four editions. He also edited W. Hazlitt's translation of Guizot's *General History of Civilization in Europe* (1842) and translated Bautain's *Epitome of the History of Philosophy* (2 vols., 1841) which he brought down to date. *Dr. Oldham at Greystones and His Talk There* (1860) was followed by the more substantial work *Considerations on Some of the Elements and Conditions of Social Welfare and Human Progress* (1861), and that by *Satan as a Moral Philosopher* (1877). He also wrote *About Men and Things* (1873), and "History of the United States of America," in W. C. Taylor's *Manual of Ancient and Modern History* (1845). In March 1838 he married Cornelia M. Heard, daughter of James Heard of New York. During the Civil War he was an ardent supporter of the Union cause and raised several companies.

[W. H. Eldridge, *Henry Geneal.* (1915); *Vital Records of Rutland, Mass., to the End of the Year 1849* (1905); *Gen. Cat. of the Theolog. Sem., Andover, Mass., 1808–1908* (1909); *Gen. Alumni Cat. of N. Y. Univ. 1833–1905* (1906); E. A. and G. L. Duyckinck, *Cyc. of Am. Literature* (2nd ed. 1875); *N. Y. Univ.* (1901) in "Universities and Their Sons," ed. by F. L. Chamberlain; *North Am. Rev.*, Apr. 1862; *Churchman*, Mar. 29, 1884; *N. Y. Tribune,* Mar. 4, 1884; *Lit. World,* Apr. 5, 1884, with a list of Henry's works; *Outlook,* Mar. 28, 1914; *N. Y. Univ. Alumnus,* Jan. 9, 1929.]
M. S. B.

HENRY, EDWARD LAMSON (Jan. 12, 1841–May 9, 1919), historical painter, the son of Frederick and Elizabeth (Fairbanks) Henry, was born in Charleston, S. C. When he was seven years old he was taken to New York City, where he received his academic education. He began his art education at the Pennsylvania Academy of the Fine Arts in Philadelphia and continued it in Paris under Suisse, Gleyre, and

Courbet, returning to America in 1864. Henry's major interest was in the past life and customs of the United States, especially during the first half of the nineteenth century. He began soon after his return to paint pictures which were accurate to the last chair and the most minute button. Owing in part to his attention to detail, his work was of greater historic than artistic merit. In his desire to include as many personages as possible in his representation of notable occasions he frequently crowded his canvases. Primarily an illustrator in oils, he found an appreciative public in that vast majority which demands of a picture first of all that it tell a story. "The Reception to Lafayette," "Off for the Races," "Leaving at Early Morning in a Northeaster," were titles of some of his best-known paintings; his "Railway Station—New England" was sold in 1876 for $530. In 1867 he was made an associate of the National Academy of Design and in 1869, became a member. He exhibited his pictures at all the large national fairs, receiving a medal or honorable mention at each; at the Paris Exposition of 1889 he received honorable mention. He was married in June 1875 to Frances Livingston Wells and lived with her in New York City and in the Hudson Valley until his death in 1919, at "Cragsmoor," Ellenville, N. Y.

[*American Art News,* May 17, 1919, which quotes a letter by Will Low from the N. Y. *Evening Post* of May 12, 1919; Sadakichi Hartmann, *A Hist. of Am. Art* (1902), vol. I; Samuel Isham, *The Hist. of Am. Painting* (new ed., 1927); *Who's Who in America* (1919); *Am. Art Annual,* vol. XVI (1919); C. E. Clement and Laurence Hutton, *Artists of the Nineteenth Century* (1885); W. E. Hunt, *Concerning a Painting by Edward L. Henry, Entitled The Uplands at Bow* (1914), with biographical sketch; Eugen Neuhaus, *The Hist. and Ideals of Am. Art* (1931); L. F. Fuller, in *Scribner's Mag.,* Aug. 1920.] K. H. A.

HENRY, JOHN (1746–October 1794), actor, theatrical manager, was born in Dublin, Ireland. After receiving a liberal education, he made his début in 1762, according to J. N. Ireland (*Records of the New York Stage,* vol. I, 1866, p. 43), at Drury Lane, London. It has been stated that he came out under the patronage of Thomas Sheridan, the father of Richard Brinsley Sheridan, but that he did not succeed. Leaving England, he played for a time in Jamaica, West Indies, and then made his American début at the Southwark Theatre, Philadelphia, Oct. 6, 1767. He was quickly recognized as one of the handsomest actors ever seen in the Colonies and one of the most capable—admirable as Othello and inimitable in Irish parts. When war with England impended and colonial theatres were closed by recommendation of Congress, the American Company of Comedians early in 1775 departed for Jamaica, where it remained until peace was restored. For the season of 1779–80 Henry was engaged at Drury Lane, acting Othello among other rôles (John Genest, *Some Account of the English Stage,* vol. VI, 1832, pp. 125 ff.). In 1782 he was again in America looking after the property of the company and giving lectures and readings in New York. About this time he adapted *The School for Soldiers; or, The Deserter,* a version of a French play, for the Old American Company, as it was now called. Leading his actors back to these shores in 1785, he almost immediately united forces with Lewis Hallam [*q.v.*], a prominent member of the pre-Revolutionary company, who for some months had been managing a feeble troupe in this country.

During their partnership Hallam and Henry were often at violent odds, being rival actors and quarrelsome by nature, but for the next seven years they had a monopoly of the American theatre from New York to Annapolis. In 1791, however, the comedian Thomas Wignell, after disagreements with Henry, resigned from the organization and set about forming a company of his own. Thus threatened, Henry sailed for England in 1792 to obtain reënforcements and brought back some able actors, chief among them being John Hodgkinson [*q.v.*]. This amazing person, as unscrupulous as he was gifted and ambitious, at once set about robbing Henry of the rôles he had long played, and in this procedure the newcomer had the connivance of the crafty Hallam, who was glad to see his partner undone. Henry resisted for a time, but his spirit was soon broken, and in 1794 he sold his half of the property for $10,000 to Hallam, who promptly resold it to Hodgkinson. Henry's death from rapid consumption, perhaps aggravated by distress of mind, followed shortly upon this transaction. His wife, a popular actress, who was formerly Maria Storer, the third of the Storer sisters to bear his name with or without legal sanction, was driven insane by the shock of his death and died six months later. An intelligent director, an accomplished actor both in tragedy and comedy, a pantomimist, an acrobat, and a good musician, John Henry was one of the most useful men on the early American stage.

[In addition to the sources cited above see: Wm. Dunlap, *A Hist. of the Am. Theatre* (1832); G. O. Seilhamer, *Hist. of the Am. Theatre* (3 vols., 1888–91); W. B. Wood, *Personal Recollections of the Stage* (1855); John Hodgkinson, *A Narrative of His Connection with the Old Am. Company* (1797); G. C. D. Odell, *Annals of the N. Y. Stage,* vol. I (1927). Henry's tombstone at Bristol, Pa., records that he died "in the 48th year of his age." It gives as the date of his death Oct. 16, 1794, while the *N. Y. Daily Advertiser* and the *Herald* (N. Y.), for Oct. 27, 1794, give Oct. 23, which is probably correct.] O. S. C.

HENRY, JOHN (November 1750–Dec. 16, 1798), lawyer, delegate from Maryland to the Continental Congress, senator, and governor, was the grandson of Rev. John Henry, a Scotch Presbyterian minister who emigrated to America early in the eighteenth century, and of his wife Mary (King), daughter of an Irish baronet. His father, Col. John Henry, married Dorothy Rider, a descendant of one of the early settlers of Dorchester County, Md., and of this union the third John Henry was born, at "Weston," the Henry homestead in that county. He attended West Nottingham Academy, in Cecil County, until prepared to enter the College of New Jersey (now Princeton University), from which institution he was graduated in 1769. During the next six years he was engaged in the study of law, and while completing his legal training at Middle Temple, London, he was a member of the Robin Hood Club, in the discussions of which he frequently had occasion to defend the rights of the colonies. He sailed from England in 1775, enjoyed much popularity on his return to Maryland, was soon elected to the General Assembly, was chosen a delegate to the Continental Congress on Dec. 22, 1777, took his seat in that body Jan. 20, 1778, and with the exception of an interval of three years (1781–84) when he served in the Maryland Senate, held it until 1787. He had been in Congress less than one week when he wrote the governor of his state that the army for want of pay, clothes, and provisions was "decreasing every hour, not by one or two at a time, but from seven to twelve"; that "The avarice of our people and the extravagant prices of all commodities, joined with the imperfect management of our affairs, would expend the mines of Chili and Peru" (*Letters and Papers,* p. 4). Against these conditions he directed his efforts. He procured funds for the Maryland recruiting service, appealed to the governor for clothing and other supplies, and advocated the concentration of the army for "strengthening the hands of General Washington." He served on many committees, such as that to procure flour for the army, to procure aids and supplies from France, on ways and means, on taxes, on a motion for erecting new states out of the western territory. When Virginia and other states had yielded with regard to their claims to the western lands, Henry voted in the Maryland Senate to authorize the Maryland delegates to ratify the Articles of Confederation. When in December 1788, after the adoption of the federal Constitution, the two houses of the General Assembly of Maryland met in joint session for the first election of United States senators, Henry received the required majority on the second ballot and Charles Carroll of Carrollton was elected his colleague on the third ballot. Henry took his seat in the Senate Apr. 20, 1789, and when lots were cast to determine who should serve for two years, who for four years, and who for six years, he drew the six-year term. Disregarding instructions by the Assembly, he voted, in March 1792, against a resolution for open sessions of the Senate. The House of Delegates censured him, but he was reëlected for the term commencing Mar. 4, 1795. Two years later, Nov. 13, 1797, the Maryland Assembly elected him governor of the state. He resigned his seat in the Senate to accept that office, served a full term of one year, refused to be considered for reëlection, retired in ill health from public life, and died within a month on his estate along the Nanticoke River in Dorchester County.

Henry was recognized by his associates as a man of integrity and was highly respected for his knowledge of law. On Mar. 6, 1787, he married Margaret Campbell, daughter of John and Elizabeth (Goldsborough) Campbell. They had two sons.

[Many of Henry's papers were lost in a fire soon after his death and only a few letters and a meager sketch of his life are published in J. W. Henry, *Letters and Papers of Gov. John Henry of Md.* (1904). See also H. E. Buchholz, *Govs. of Md. from the Revolution to the Year 1908* (1908); Elias Jones, *Revised Hist. of Dorchester County, Md.* (1925).] N. D. M.

HENRY, JOHN (fl. 1807–1820), adventurer, was born in Ireland about 1776 and was sent to America at about sixteen and placed under the care of an uncle, a New York merchant. He is said to have married a French *émigrée,* who died early, leaving him with two daughters; and, during the administration of John Adams, to have obtained a commission in the United States army as an artillery officer, which about 1802 he resigned. For five years he seems then to have lived on an "estate" in Vermont near the Canadian border. In 1807 he was a student-at-law in Montreal, Lower Canada. Here he succeeded in ingratiating himself with the "fur-barons" of the North West Company by defending them against attacks in the newspapers. In 1808 his friends attempted to secure for him an appointment as a puisne judge in Upper Canada; but Francis Gore, the lieutenant-governor of Upper Canada, who had met him, opposed the appointment, on the ground that Henry was "an Irish adventurer, not even called to the Bar, and . . .

a citizen of the United States" (Gore to Cooke, Sept. 16, 1808, Canadian Archives, Q, 311). Meanwhile, an opening for his talents occurred in another direction. He had made the acquaintance of Herman W. Ryland, the civil secretary of the province and the confidential adviser of the governor-general, Sir James Craig, and when on a visit to Vermont and Boston in the spring of 1808 he wrote a number of letters to Ryland on the political situation in the United States. These letters were shown by Ryland to Craig (as was no doubt intended), and were in turn forwarded to Castlereagh, the secretary of state in London. The result was that early in 1809 Henry was commissioned by Craig to proceed to the United States on a secret and confidential mission with the object of reporting on "the state of the public opinion both in regard to their internal politics and to the probability of war with England" (*Report on Canadian Archives,* 1896, p. 47). He was also authorized, if the Federalists should wish to enter into any communication with the Canadian government, to transmit any such communication to the governor-general.

Henry went to Vermont and to Boston; and in the latter place he placed himself in touch with some of the leaders of the Federalist party. He wrote a number of letters to Craig and he was recalled after a stay in the United States lasting only four months. On his return to Canada he devoted himself to trying to obtain preferment as a reward of his services. Two years later he went to London to prosecute his claims, but his applications to the government resulted only in the reference of the matter back to Quebec; and finally, with his resources at a low ebb, he was compelled to return to America in the autumn of 1811. On board ship, he met another adventurer, the *soi-disant* Count de Crillon, whose true name was Soubiran, and who was really the son of a French goldsmith. Soubiran, to whom he confided his troubles, immediately urged him to sell his papers to the government of the United States and offered to act as intermediary. On their arrival at Boston, the two proceeded to Washington, and there Soubiran succeeded in selling Henry's letters to President Madison for the very large sum of $50,000. The letters, somewhat garbled and abbreviated, were communicated to Congress; and the uproar which they caused against the "infamous intrigues" of the British had an important influence in bringing about the declaration of war in 1812. Before the letters were published, however, Henry was smuggled out of the country on the United States dispatch boat, the *Wasp*; and in due course he landed in France. He was in Paris on July 2, 1814; for Soubiran saw him there on that date, and apparently in the interval Henry had lost an eye. Six years later, in 1820, he was a paid informer sent to Italy to discover evidence against Queen Caroline of England, but after this episode he disappears from view.

[The "Henry Letters," in *Report on Canadian Archives, 1896* (1897), note B, and in *Niles's Weekly Register,* Mar. 14, 1812. See also *Niles's Weekly Register,* Mar. 21, 28, 1812; Henry Adams, "Count Edward de Crillon," in *Am. Hist. Rev.,* Oct. 1895; Robert Christie, *Interesting Pub. Docs. . . . Supplementary to the Hist. of Lower Canada,* vol. VI (1855); *The Jour. of Duncan M'Gillivray of the North West Company* (1929), ed. by A. S. Morton; and occasional references in the Canadian Archives (Q 311–12)—see *Report . . . 1893* (1894)—the *Quebec Gazette,* and the manuscript journal of Joseph Frobisher in the McGill Univ. Lib., Montreal.] W. S. W.

HENRY, JOSEPH (Dec. 17, 1797–May 13, 1878), investigator in physics, first secretary and director of the Smithsonian Institution, was born in Albany, N. Y., the son of William and Ann (Alexander) Henry. His grandparents on both sides were immigrants from Scotland. His father was a day-laborer, and the family was poor. Early in life Henry went to live with his maternal grandmother at Galway, N. Y., where he attended the district school and from his tenth year worked in his spare time as a clerk in the village store. When he was thirteen or fourteen he returned to Albany to live with his mother, who by that time was a widow. For a year or two he was apprenticed to a watchmaker and jeweler, but his master failed in business, and he was left for a time without employment. At Galway he had read all the novels and plays that the village library afforded and had become fascinated with the stage. When he went to Albany he joined a group of young people who were interested in amateur theatricals, became their president, wrote two plays for them in which he acted himself, and gave much of his time to acting and stage management. An accidental encounter with a popular book on natural science interested him so much, however, that he determined to give up his lighter pursuits and to devote himself to the acquisition of knowledge. He resigned the presidency of the dramatic society, and by study under tutors qualified himself for admission to the advanced classes of the Albany Academy. While a student at the Academy he supported himself by teaching school and subsequently by serving as an assistant in the Academy itself. After completing his course he was for two years tutor in the family of Stephen Van Rensselaer, and continued his studies with the intention of fitting himself for the practice of medicine. He was diverted from this purpose by receiving an appointment to a surveying party which was engaged for the State of New York in laying out a road through the southern counties from West Point to Lake Erie. After finishing this work with credit and while he was considering another engineering engagement in Ohio, he was elected in the spring of 1826 to the professorship of mathematics and natural philosophy in the Albany Academy.

On entering upon this position he took up research in the comparatively new field of the relation of electric currents to magnetism. His first notable success was the improvement of William Sturgeon's electromagnet, which was made by covering an iron core with an insulating coat of wax and winding a wire in a single loose spiral around it. Such a magnet would sustain at most a weight of a few ounces. Henry insulated the wire and coiled it in many turns and in several layers around the iron core. The magnetic condition of the core was increased by this arrangement, when the current was sent through the coils, to an unparalleled degree. This plan of making magnets was at once adopted everywhere, and the electromagnets of the present day are precisely like those which Henry designed. Using an experimental magnet, with the wire wound on in sections with projecting ends so that the coils could be joined in different combinations, he discovered that when the coils were each joined similarly or in parallel to the battery, the magnet was strongly excited even by a small battery, so long as the external circuit was short, but that the same arrangement gave almost no effect when a long wire was introduced into the circuit. On the other hand, when the coils were joined successively or in a series to each other, the arrangement, which was not so effective in the short circuit, was much more satisfactory than the first arrangement in the long circuit, particularly when the battery consisted of a number of elements in series. Henry called these two types quantity and intensity magnets respectively, and pointed out in the *American Journal of Science* as early as January 1831 that the intensity magnet was the type to be used in the electromagnetic telegraph. In fact, before that date, he had set up a circuit of over a mile of wire strung around a large room in the Academy and transmitted signals through it. Later, at Princeton, a similar telegraphic circuit joined his laboratory with his house, and was used by him for sending messages.

In the course of his experiments Henry discovered that when a long circuit or one containing a spiral conductor is broken, a bright spark appears at the gap. He published an account of this discovery in the *American Journal of Science* in July 1832, but did not continue his investigations of it at that time, in consequence of the duties imposed upon him by his removal to Princeton. In 1835, stimulated thereto by the announcement that Faraday had made a similar discovery, he presented an account of his researches to the American Philosophical Society, and gave an explanation of his results by ascribing them to the inductive action of the current on the conductor in which it is flowing. It is because of these researches on self-induction that the modern practical unit of induction has been called the Henry.

Meanwhile, in a paper presented to the Royal Society, Nov. 24, 1831, Faraday had announced the discovery of the induced current. The first account of this discovery was received by Henry in June 1832 in a copy of the *Annals of Philosophy* for the previous April. He immediately resumed a research on which he had been engaged and which had been interrupted by the opening of the school year of the Academy, and published in the *American Journal of Science* in July 1832 an account of a method for obtaining these induced currents which, he said, had been used by him before having any knowledge of Faraday's methods. Henry always recognized Faraday's priority in this most important discovery and made no claims for himself, but the evidence points to Henry's having been the first to detect the induced current, possibly as early as the summer of 1830. That he was an independent discoverer his own statement leaves no doubt. That his discovery antedated Faraday's is less certain, but that it did do so is rendered probable by the fact that it was Henry's custom to do his scientific work in the summer vacation, when he could set up his apparatus in the auditorium of the Academy, and to lay it aside for other duties when the school term opened. The experiment which he was able to describe in such detail as soon as he heard of Faraday's success was most probably performed in the previous summer, or perhaps even a year earlier. His daughter, Mary A. Henry, relates (*post*) that her father often expressed his regret that he had neglected to publish his first results. These, she says, were obtained in 1830, but he refrained from announcing them because he wished to amplify them before publishing. He was so hampered by lack of time and means that he did not take up the subject again until roused to it by Faraday's success.

During this period of activity at Albany Henry also invented an electromagnetic motor, a little machine, called by him "a philosophical toy," so arranged that a horizontally poised bar electromagnet would rock to and fro as the current through it was automatically reversed.

In May 1830 he was married to Harriet L. Alexander, of Schenectady, N. Y., his first cousin. Two of his children died in infancy; a son, William Alexander Henry, died in 1862; his widow and three daughters survived him.

In 1832 Henry was elected to the professorship of natural philosophy in the College of New Jersey at Princeton. The labors incident to the development of his courses interrupted for a few years his scientific activity. His first communication from Princeton was the paper on the current of self-induction already referred to. He then undertook an investigation of the induction of a current by another current. His researches in this field during the period from 1838 to 1842 brought out some important facts and curiously anticipated some of the modern developments in the science of electricity. They are too extensive to be easily summarized, but it may be stated that he showed that an induced current could be made to induce another current in a neighboring circuit, and this to currents of the fourth and fifth order; that a quantity current which would make a strong magnet, decompose water, and deflect the needle of a low-resistance galvanometer could induce in a neighboring conductor an intensity current which would give perceptible shocks when taken through the body though it would hardly actuate a magnet or deflect an ordinary galvanometer; and that an intensity current properly employed could induce a quantity current. These actions are analogous to those now exhibited by the step-up and the step-down transformers. He invented low and high resistance galvanometers to use with these types of current. He showed also that similar inductive effects were produced when the discharge of a Leyden battery was used in the primary circuit, and that the inductive effect could be transmitted from primary to secondary through considerable distances. In one instance he obtained it in a secondary wire which was set up parallel to a long straight primary wire two hundred and twenty feet away from it. As he showed that he could obtain the inductive effect from the Leyden-jar discharge when the secondary was interrupted by a non-conducting gap, he came in these experiments very near to the fundamentals of wireless telegraphy. By studying the way in which the electric discharge through a spiral will magnetize needles placed in the axis of the spiral, sometimes in one direction and sometimes in the other, he convinced himself that the discharge consisted in a series of oscillations of gradually diminishing intensity, as had been suggested by Savary, and he gave so clear and satisfactory an explanation of the facts observed that he is usually credited with the discovery of the oscillatory nature of the discharge. While at Princeton, Henry collaborated with his brother-in-law, Stephen Alexander [*q.v.*], in the investigation of solar radiation and the heat of sun spots. He was also greatly interested in capillarity and the cohesion of liquids.

His connection with the College of New Jersey was broken on Dec. 14, 1846, when he left Princeton for Washington to become the first secretary and director of the Smithsonian Institution, though his formal resignation of his professorship was delayed until 1848. A few years before, the United States of America had received a bequest from James Smithson, a British subject, to found at Washington "an establishment for the increase and diffusion of knowledge among men." After much discussion Congress at last determined in August 1846 to vest the control of the Institution in a Board of Regents. The Regents, desiring a man for the position of secretary who was distinguished as an investigator and who besides possessed good judgment, catholic sympathies, and weight of character, offered the post to Henry. He was very reluctant to leave his congenial labors as a professor at Princeton and the opportunities he there had for research to take a position in a new enterprise which had been the subject of lively discussion in Congress, and as to the proper development of which great diversity of opinion prevailed; but he yielded to what he thought was a call of duty.

The development of the Smithsonian Institution followed the course marked out for it in Henry's first report to the Board of Regents. In that report he analyzed the intent of Smithson in making his bequest: "Increase of knowledge" was to be furthered, not by furnishing lectures or providing libraries at Washington, but by stimulating and supporting original research. "Diffusion of knowledge" could be best effected by the wide distribution of papers containing original researches or accounts of the most recent results obtained in the various fields of natural science. He deprecated the use of a large portion of the income of the Institution for the support of the museum, art gallery, laboratory and library settled upon it by the action of Congress, and pointed out that in process of time the care of these establishments would require the whole income of the fund. While he loyally carried out the terms of the act, he let no opportunity pass to urge upon the Regents and upon Congress the importance of relieving the Institution of these irrelevant burdens. As time went on and the success of Henry's plan for the development of the Institution became increasingly evident, his wisdom in regard to these matters was recognized, and one by one they were provided for either by transfer to other agencies or by direct appropriations.

The labors of his office were so onerous that Henry found it impossible to continue his researches in pure science. As director of the Smithsonian Institution he initiated various enterprises, among them the system of receiving weather reports by telegraph and basing on them predictions of weather conditions and storm warnings. This work was started by Henry about 1850 and was carried on by the Smithsonian Institution until the outbreak of the Civil War. Henry was appointed a member of the Light House Board when it was established in 1852, and was its president from 1871 on. He served continuously on its committee on experiments, and in this connection carried out important experiments on the relative value of different illuminating oils and on the curious regions of inaudibility sometimes observed when fog horns are sounding.

He was elected a member of the American Philosophical Society in 1835. He helped to organize the American Association for the Advancement of Science and was its president at its second meeting, held at Cambridge in 1849. He assisted in founding the Philosophical Society of Washington (1871), and served continuously thereafter as its president. He was an original member of the National Academy of Sciences, its vice-president in 1866, and its president from 1868 until his death. He was the recipient of many honorary degrees and countless honorary elections to scientific and literary societies. Twice he visited Europe, first in 1837, when the college at Princeton gave him a year's leave of absence on full salary, and again in 1870, on leave granted by the regents of the Smithsonian Institution.

Henry was a man of vigorous frame, with a benignant countenance marked with strong Scottish features. In character he was eminently just and fair, mild, considerate, and sympathetic, and yet firm in adherence to his own views of what was right. He united with the Presbyterian Church after going to Princeton and maintained throughout his life a firm belief in the Christian faith which he then professed. He was adored by his family circle and revered by all who knew him. His death, which occurred at his home in Washington, May 13, 1878, from nephritis, was felt as a public calamity. By concurrent resolution a memorial service in his honor was held on the evening of Jan. 16, 1879, in the Hall of the House of Representatives, attended by the president and his cabinet, by both houses of Congress, by the justices of the Supreme Court, by the regents of the Smithsonian Institution, and by many other distinguished men. At this service eulogistic addresses were delivered by members of Congress and of the Board of Regents. By act of Congress a bronze statue of Henry by W. W. Story was erected at Washington in his memory.

[The date of Henry's birth, often assigned to 1799, is settled by the record in the Baptismal Register of the First Presbyterian Church of Albany, where it was discovered by Dr. John H. Finley. *The Scientific Writings of Joseph Henry* (2 vols., 1886) were published by the Smithsonian Inst. *A Memorial of Joseph Henry,* published by order of Congress in 1880 and included also in *Smithsonian Misc. Colls.,* vol. XXI (1881), contains the proceedings of the memorial service at the Capitol, the memorial proceedings of the most important scientific societies, a list of Henry's publications, and several important biographical sketches. Among these last are memoirs by Asa Gray, also pub. in *Ann. Report . . . Smithsonian Inst., 1878* (1879); by Simon Newcomb, also pub., with bibliography, in *Nat. Acad. Sci. Biog. Memoirs,* vol. V (1905); and by W. B. Taylor—the last an extended account of his scientific work, with bibliography, also pub. in *Bull. Phil. Soc. of Washington,* vol. II (1875–80). See, in addition, Benjamin Silliman, Jr., in *Am. Jour. Sci.,* June 1878; G. B. Goode, "The Three Secretaries," in *The Smithsonian Inst., 1846–96* (1897); W. B. Taylor, "Henry and the Telegraph," in *Ann. Report . . . Smithsonian Inst., 1878* (1879); M. R. Waite, *Address at the Unveiling of the Joseph Henry Statue at Washington* (1884); E. W. Stone, "Joseph Henry," in *Scientific Monthly,* Sept. 1931; *Evening Star* (Washington), May 13, 1878; Mary A. Henry, "America's Part in the Discovery of Magneto-Electricity—A Study of the Work of Faraday and Henry," in *Electrical Engineer* (N. Y.), Jan. 13–Mar. 9, 1892, and "The Invention of the Electromagnetic Telegraph," in *Electrical World,* Nov. 23–Dec. 21, 1895.]

W. F. M.

HENRY, MORRIS HENRY (July 26, 1835–May 19, 1895), physician, was born in London, England, the son of Henry A. and Esther Henry. The father is said to have been a distinguished Orientalist and educator, and was presumably a friend of Sir Moses Montefiore, who acted as godfather to the son. Morris studied in the polytechnic school at Brussels and also took art courses at the Government School, Somerset House, London. In 1852 he came to New York and devoted his first two years in the United States to art and literature. The study of art anatomy turned his attention to medicine and in 1857, although not yet a graduate, he was prosector and assistant to the chair of surgery in the New York Medical College. In 1860 he received the degree of M.D. from the University of Vermont. He studied in Europe during 1860–61 and in the latter year entered the United

States navy as assistant surgeon. He was first stationed in Virginia and later went through the entire Mississippi campaign with Farragut. After three summers of service in the South he resigned in July 1863 because of ill health. Settling in New York the following year, he engaged in general practice and was appointed surgeon to the Northern Dispensary. In 1869 he received the appointment of surgeon to the New York Dispensary, and in 1873, that of surgeon-in-chief to the state Emigrant Hospital, which position he held until 1880. From 1872 to 1884 he was chief police surgeon of New York, and in that period organized the ambulance service.

He founded in 1870 and edited for five years the *American Journal of Syphilography and Dermatology.* This journal represented a pioneer effort to awaken American physicians to the importance of a knowledge of skin and venereal diseases and syphilis. In 1871 Henry published an American edition of W. T. Fox's monograph, *Skin Diseases: Their Description, Pathology, Diagnosis, and Treatment,* which was adopted as the textbook of the medical departments of the United States army and navy. As a result Henry was recognized both in the United States and England as a leading authority on the subjects involved. Opposed, however, to anything suggestive of narrowness in specialism, he achieved equal repute as a surgeon. He invented numerous instruments, notably forceps and scissors for various purposes; and became especially identified with an operation for varicocele which consisted essentially of removing a redundant portion of the scrotum. His first paper on this subject appeared in the *American Journal of Syphilography and Dermatology,* July 1871, and was followed by others in 1881 and 1888. His operation became widely known and was so much esteemed in Greece and Turkey that he received decorations from the sovereigns of both countries. In 1878 he reported a successful reduction of a dislocation upward and forward upon the pubes of the hip twenty-six days after the accident, thus establishing a record.

As early as 1879 Henry discovered that he was suffering from chronic nephritis. He did not abandon his practice, although he spent much time in traveling for his health. For the last four or five years of his life, however, he was a confirmed invalid. In 1893 he published a forty-nine-page catalogue of his private medical library. Although a facile and prolific writer he produced no major work. He was known as a crusader for the higher medical education and a foe of quackery under any disguise. His first wife whom he married in 1872 was Elizabeth Rutherford Hastings, a daughter of Hugh Hastings. She died in 1876, and in 1880 he married the widow of Harrison Everett Maynard. A son by his first wife survived him.

[*Medic. Record,* May 25, 1895; *New Eng. Medic. Mo.,* Mar. 1884; H. A. Kelly and W. L. Burrage, *Am. Medic. Biogs.* (1920); *Jour. Am. Medic. Asso.,* Nov. 3, 10, 1888; *N. Y. Tribune,* May 20, 1895.] E. P.

HENRY, O. [See PORTER, WILLIAM SYDNEY, 1862–1910.]

HENRY, PATRICK (May 29, 1736–June 6, 1799), Revolutionary statesman, orator, was born in Hanover County, Va., among frontier farmers and of a parentage typical of the region. His father, John Henry, who had come to the province from Aberdeen, Scotland, before 1730, was a man of moderate means, sturdy character, good education, and stanch loyalty to the reigning house of Hanover; he was a vestryman of the local branch of the established church, a justice of the peace, colonel of the militia, and the master of a small estate on the South Anna River which bore the pretentious name of "Mount Brilliant." The mother, Sarah, daughter of Isaac Winston, a Presbyterian immigrant from Yorkshire and likewise a planter of moderate means, was a woman of marked abilities and social charm. She was the widow of Col. John Syme before her marriage to John Henry. The Rev. Patrick Henry, a brother of John, was rector of St. Paul's parish, Hanover. From his father young Henry learned enough Latin to read with ease the great Roman classics the rest of his life; and there was an atmosphere of eighteenth-century culture both at "Mount Brilliant" and at the rector's home. Another and an important influence came into the neighborhood in 1747 when Samuel Davies [*q.v.*] settled there as the stated pastor of the scattered New Light congregations of Hanover and neighboring counties. Although young Henry was early baptized and made a member of his uncle's parish church, he often went with his mother to hear the stirring, tearful sermons of the greatest of all the Southern preachers of that time.

Averse, it seems, to the daily toil of setting and worming tobacco, Patrick became a clerk in a cross-roads store at fifteen; at sixteen he opened a store in partnership with his older brother, William. Within a year the brothers had lost whatever capital they had ventured or borrowed. He was hardly eighteen when he married Sarah Shelton, daughter of John Shelton, who brought him a small dowry. The young couple began with six slaves and three hundred acres of sandy, half-exhausted land, eight or ten miles from river transportation. At the age of twenty-one Henry lost his house and furniture by fire and he and his wife now turned once more to the unfortunate store-keeping. In two years they were hopelessly in debt but known to everybody in the county and particularly to Capt. Nathaniel West Dandridge, one of the elect in Virginia. With ruin staring him in the face and with three or four children about him, Henry now turned his thoughts to law. In the spring of 1760, with a little knowledge of "Coke upon Littleton" and a speaking acquaintance with a digest of Virginia acts, he appeared before Sir John Randolph and three other members of the bar and obtained license to practise law. He returned home, studied diligently the customary book of forms, closed out his store, took quarters with his father-in-law, who kept a tavern at Hanover Courthouse, and opened his door to clients.

He won immediate success. In three years he had managed 1185 suits, had won most of his cases, and was known throughout that poor region which stretches from Hanover Courthouse to Fredericksburg—the New Light Presbyterian, Baptist, and Quaker country. During these years there was a quarrel brewing between the tobacco planters and the clergy of the established church, who were paid in that fluctuating commodity. The vestrymen tended to leave the clergy to care for themselves when the price of tobacco was low; when it was high they set twopence a pound as the proper rate for settlement. In 1755 and again in 1758, when tobacco was scarce, the Assembly decreed that, during a limited period, creditors might be paid at the rate of twopence a pound. The clergy made loud complaint and sent agents to London to argue against the constitutionality of these laws, which at length were disallowed. This action was tantamount to a plain announcement that the Virginia practices of a hundred years were henceforth not to be permitted. The question of self-government was involved and there was much popular excitement. None the less, the clergy began suits for the unpaid portions of their salaries. In April 1762, James Maury, rector of a parish in Louisa County, where there was no chance to win, brought suit in the Hanover County court, John Henry being the presiding justice. In November 1763 the court declared the law unconstitutional. A jury was empanelled to determine the amount of the award due Maury. There was intense interest. Patrick Henry was engaged to argue the defense. Maury declared that three members of the jury, who were known dissenters, were not gentlemen and that the jury, accordingly, was not legal (Ann Maury, *Memoirs of a Huguenot Family,* 1853, pp. 418–24). Henry insisted, with precedent on his side, that plain farmers made an honest jury. He made a speech which turned less upon the law in question than upon the policy of the clergy in demanding salaries for preaching the gospel and in declining to observe the law of their "country," and above all upon the dangerous encroachment of the Crown upon the rights of Virginia freemen. He stirred the jealousies and hatreds of a community, fast losing its loyalty to the established church, to such depths that the parsons who had come to the court to enjoy their own triumph fled from the scene before the verdict was announced. The jury awarded one penny to Maury, and the fame of the man who in effect had won the case quickly spread to every parish in the colony.

The next year Henry, though still living in Hanover, became a freeholder in Louisa County and was chosen to the House of Burgesses from that frontier region. He took his seat on May 20, 1765. He was now almost twenty-nine years old, well-to-do, widely known, ill-dressed. He faced John Robinson [*q.v.*], speaker of the House, treasurer of the colony, and leader of the elder statesmen of the low country; around him sat Randolphs, Pendletons, Harrisons, Carys, and Braxtons, widely known for their acres and their high pretensions. The colony had issued large sums of paper money to meet the expense of the long war but recently closed. The paper was receivable for taxes and was to have been burned by Treasurer Robinson, but he loaned the money to political friends on meager security and was so involved in 1765 that he sought to set up a public loan office to which, it was charged, he planned to shift his loans and thus escape exposure. Henry opposed the plan and caused a strong alignment of the western and northern counties against the old tidewater region. The leaders of the latter managed to effect a compromise by which a committee was appointed to maneuver them out of their dilemma. The next year it became plain that Robinson had caused the colony a loss of more than a hundred thousand pounds in Virginia currency.

Meanwhile, the expected copy of the Stamp Act circulated among the burgesses, and Patrick Henry, after consultation with at least two up-country members, offered (May 29, 1765) seven radical resolutions to the committee of the whole house. The last of these claimed for Virginia the complete legislative independence which had been enjoyed under the Commonwealth. The older leaders, Robinson, Peyton Randolph, Edmund Pendleton, and the rest, foresaw a future régime of frontier leadership. Henry pressed his resolutions in a speech which closed with the famous comparison: "Caesar had his Brutus —Charles the first, his Cromwell—and George the third—may profit by their example" (Wirt, *post,* p. 65; see also *American Historical Review,* July 1921, pp. 726–29, 745). The resolutions passed the committee amidst an uproar unprecedented in that staid Assembly. On the next day the leaders of the old order endeavored to defeat the propositions in the full house. Henry fought for his program and secured the adoption of five of his resolutions on May 30, though one of these was reconsidered the next day, after his nonchalant departure, and lost. The work of the committee was reported to the people outside the hall and immediately the seven unrevised resolutions were hurried off to the other colonies and became the basis of violent agitation from Boston to Charleston. Thus at twenty-nine years of age Henry was the leader of a new party. When the Assembly met in the fall Henry was again a member and more influential than Governor Fauquier himself. Between 1765 and 1770 he was as complete a master of the public life of Virginia as Samuel Adams was of that of Massachusetts. The Townshend Acts and the concerted efforts at resistance which followed them enabled Henry to consolidate the opposition to Great Britain to such an extent that in 1769 when a new and sympathetic governor, Lord Botetourt, reached Virginia there was no other possible solution of the colonial problem except upon the basis of complete autonomy. Meanwhile, the conflicts between the popular party of Massachusetts and the British troops stationed in Boston and the growing discontent in Virginia about the British land policy, as revealed in the proclamation of 1763, prepared the way for the next outbreak. On May 24, 1774, a message from the Massachusetts Committee of Correspondence informed the Virginians of the closing of the port of Boston. There was already a similar committee in Virginia with Henry for a guiding spirit. The burgesses appointed June 1 a day of fast and prayer in order "to give us one heart and one mind firmly to oppose . . . every injury to American rights." The governor, Lord Dunmore, dissolved the Assembly; but the same men assembled on May 27 in the Raleigh Tavern, under the leadership of Henry, to ask all the colonies to meet in a continental congress and to call a Virginia convention for Aug. 1, 1774 (Peter Force, *American Archives,* 4 ser., I, 1837, cols. 350–51).

The first Virginia convention met and appointed Henry with six other leaders as a delegation to the first Continental Congress. He arrived in Philadelphia on Sept. 4, 1774, and took active part in the proceedings of the Congress, always leaning toward radical measures and showing strong nationalist tendencies. The declaration of grievances and the Association of the colonies for the purpose of boycotting British goods in American markets received his hearty support. He was less interested in the petition to the king imploring a change of policy. In Virginia, Lord Dunmore called the Assembly to meet late in November, but, finding all the colonies organized to enforce the recommendations of the continental Association against British commerce, and the Assembly composed of the leaders of the party of revolution, prorogued the body. The same members met in Richmond on Mar. 20, 1775, to decide upon the course which Virginia should follow. Unwilling to wait for the British reply to the petition of the Continental Congress, Henry offered three resolutions, one of which provided that "this Colony be immediately put into a posture of defence"; and that a committee be appointed "to prepare a plan for the embodying, arming, and disciplining such a number of men as may be sufficient for that purpose" (Force, 4 ser., II, 168). Randolph and others now of the party of resistance were alarmed and sought to delay matters; but Henry pressed his resolutions with the third great speech of his life, in which occurred his most famous saying: "Give me liberty, or give me death" (W. W. Henry, *post,* I, 266).

Under the spell of his burning words, the convention authorized the arming and training of companies of infantry, cavalry, and artillery but took inadequate measures to collect the taxes to meet the expense. Another delegation, including Henry, was selected to attend the second Continental Congress, but as he was about to set out for Philadelphia, messengers brought news of the battle of Lexington. Meanwhile, he had learned that Lord Dunmore had seized the ammunition in the colonial arsenal at Williamsburg and lodged it in a war vessel on the James River. Henry collected the militia of Hanover County and marched toward the little capital, sending a messenger demanding restoration of the gunpowder to representatives of the colony. There was great excitement in Williamsburg. After a moment of delay the Governor complied with the demand; and Henry made ready to depart for Philadelphia. Dunmore issued a proclamation on May 6, outlawing "a certain Patrick Henry" for disturbing the peace of the colony.

Henry took his seat in the second Continental Congress on May 18 and had a share in the legislation under which a continental army was organized and George Washington was made general-in-chief.

From the anxious deliberations of Philadelphia Henry hurried during the early days of August to Richmond, where the second Virginia convention considered the ways and means of putting three regiments of soldiers in the field and of dealing with Dunmore, who had taken flight to the British war ships in Chesapeake Bay and was then preparing an attack upon the lower counties. Henry's party promised immunity from taxes for a year and a half and put out large issues of paper money to meet the expenses of the war. He himself was made colonel of the first regiment, this appointment making him commander-in-chief of all the forces of the colony. Washington opposed the appointment, though he did not protest. The opponents of Henry in the convention chose a committee of public safety and put it under the control of Edmund Pendleton, Henry's most resolute opponent. The new colonel went home for a short vacation, during which he witnessed the death of his wife, and then went to take charge of the recruits who waited on the grounds of the College of William and Mary. Henry wished to lead his army to the defense of Norfolk, now threatened by Dunmore, but Pendleton, acting for the convention, ordered Henry's subordinate, William Woodford, to take command of the proposed expedition and a little later authorized Robert Howe of North Carolina to share the general command in the Norfolk region. Smarting under this affront and resenting the attitude of the military committee of the Continental Congress, Henry resigned his commission on Feb. 28, 1776, and returned to his home in Hanover County. He was promptly elected a member of the third revolutionary convention which was to assemble on May 6 in Williamsburg. There he took a decisive part in the drafting of the new constitution of Virginia and in urging the passage of a resolution which authorized Congress to declare independence and appeal to France for help. The resolution passed on May 15, the constitution was soon completed and accepted, and on June 29 Henry was elected governor. He at once took control of the state and somewhat later set up housekeeping with his second wife, Dorothea Dandridge, the daughter of his friend, Nathaniel West Dandridge. He was twice reëlected.

If he had failed as a military commander, he was certainly not an inactive governor. With the support of George Mason and Thomas Jefferson, he sent George Rogers Clark in 1778 on a secret military mission to the Illinois country, which resulted in the expulsion of the British from the Northwest; and in 1778–79, when there was a widespread intrigue to remove Washington from the command of the continental armies, he was the first to send the latter evidence which led to the defeat of the movement (W. W. Henry, *post,* I, 544–52). But Sir George Collier took him by surprise when he landed a British force at Hampton Roads in May 1779, captured Portsmouth without difficulty, and then seized the great collection of military supplies at Suffolk. After urging the French admiral at Newport, R. I., to station a part of the fleet inside the entrance to Chesapeake Bay, Henry retired from the governorship in the summer of 1779 to a great tract of wild land in Henry County, two hundred miles southwest of Richmond, on the eastern slopes of the Blue Ridge Mountains. His close friend and political lieutenant, Thomas Jefferson [*q.v.*], succeeded to the governorship; but Henry came down from his mountain fastness to attend the sessions of the Assembly in 1781 when the military situation was critical. Following the expiration of Jefferson's term in June 1781, the legislature chose Thomas Nelson, an opponent of both Henry and Jefferson, and passed a resolution which asked for an investigation of the latter's conduct as governor. Henry joined in the hue and cry against Jefferson and thus laid the foundation for a feud which lasted as long as either of them lived (W. W. Henry, II, 137–68).

In 1783, when the acceptance of the treaty of peace by Virginia raised the question as to the status of the vanquished Loyalists, Patrick Henry in the legislature urged an act of oblivion and restoration, in so far as the latter might be possible. In so doing he surprised and even angered many of his followers. He declared that the country needed people and that the former opponents of the revolution would make good citizens. At the same time he urged a great enlargement of the powers of the Confederation in the hope of lending vigor to the inchoate national authority, and of paying the burdensome war debts. The chaotic finances of Virginia he endeavored to remedy by the laying of tariff duties on imports far more onerous than any Stamp or regulation duties which the British had endeavored to lay in 1765 or 1774. When James Madison, the leader in the Assembly next in influence to Henry himself, proposed measures for the disestablishment of the ancient church and for entire freedom of conscience,

Henry turned conservative and offered a bill for the incorporation of all churches in Virginia and for the regular assessment of a moderate tax for religious purposes upon all citizens. Madison was known as Jefferson's close friend and was able to divide the followers of Henry. The economic outlook in Virginia was hardly better in 1784, when Henry again became governor, than it had been in 1774. He sought to collect large quantities of tobacco due on the continental debt; and he endeavored to pay the Virginia war debt by grants of land to returned soldiers. At the moment a committee of Congress labored over the sketch of a treaty between the thirteen states and Spain, the news of the death of Henry's brother-in-law, Col. William Christian [*q.v.*], at the hands of Indian warriors in Kentucky, came to him. Henry indited a vigorous letter to Congress urging that it was the duty of the Confederation to protect the frontier. On Aug. 12, 1786, James Monroe, a friend of Henry and a member of Congress, wrote that seven of the eastern states were committed to a treaty with Spain in which the navigation of the Mississippi was to be abandoned for a period of twenty-five years in return for most desirable commercial arrangements in the markets of that country and her American possessions (W. W. Henry, II, 291–98). Henry saw at once, as he thought, a conspiracy of the trading states to sacrifice the interests of the South and the settlements in the Mississippi Valley. From this time he showed an increasing dread of a closer union of the southern with the eastern states. But when, upon the urgent advice of Washington and others, the legislature of Virginia agreed to appoint delegates to the proposed Federal Convention, Henry made no public objection. His fifth term as governor expired on Nov. 30, 1786, and he made ready to settle his family in Prince Edward County, near Hampden-Sidney College.

Fifty years old, his health broken, his fortune depleted, and with a score of children and grandchildren around him, he turned now to the practice of his profession. But he had hardly reached his new home before he received official notice of his election as a member of the Virginia delegation to the Federal Convention. He declined at his leisure and in tones which gave evidence of unmistakable opposition to the objectives of the convention; and when the assembly met the following October, he was in his accustomed seat. When the Virginia convention met in Richmond on Oct. 20, 1788, he occupied a seat for Prince Edward County and at once took the leadership of those who opposed adoption. His opinion of the proposed Federal constitution is fairly indicated in the following statement: "This is a consolidated government . . . and the danger of such a government is, to my mind, very striking . . . our rights and privileges are endangered, and the sovereignty of the States will be relinquished . . . and . . . they may, if we be engaged in war, . . . liberate every one of your slaves" (W. W. Henry, II, 379, 400–01). For twenty-three days Henry resisted adoption with every resource at his command. He spoke every day but five, and on some days five times. When the conflict was over and the Constitution was accepted, he announced that he would abide the result; but he had so advertised the faults of the new system that when the Virginia Assembly met the following October four-fifths of the members were ready to do his bidding. He wrote the Virginia appeal to the first Congress and the other states for amendments to the Constitution (*Journal of the House of Delegates, . . . 1788,* 1828, pp. 42–43). He caused the counties of the state to be districted in such a way that nearly all the Virginia members in the first House of Representatives were likely to be antifederal in character; and later it proved very difficult for the friends of Washington and Marshall to procure the election of Madison in his own district. Similarly, Henry dictated the election of Richard Henry Lee and William Grayson, known opponents of the new Constitution, to the United States Senate. Henry was probably more responsible than any or all others for the adoption of the first ten amendments to the federal Constitution.

After these stormy events he turned again at the end of the year 1788 to the practice of law and the recouping of his personal fortunes. It was a time of important lawsuits in Virginia. After the Constitution of 1787 made the treaty of 1783 part of the law of the land, British creditors, who had sought in vain to collect from Virginia debtors during the period of the Confederation, appeared in federal courts to present their claims. In the first test case in the state under the Constitution, that of *Jones* vs. *Walker,* Henry and John Marshall served for the defense (B. R. Curtis, *Reports of Decisions in the Supreme Court of the United States,* I, 1855, p. 164, referring to the case as *Ware, Administrative of Jones, Plaintiff in Error* vs. *Hylton et al.*). The trial began on Nov. 23, 1791, in the United States district court at Richmond, Judges Griffin of the district and Johnson and Blair of the Supreme Court being present. Henry spoke for three days and showed himself an unsuspected master of the law and the complications of the case; in his appeals based upon the history of the Revolution and upon the passions of men he was then, as in 1763, as complete an artist as the times afforded. If he did not win the case, he made it almost certain that the plaintiffs would never be able to collect their debts in Virginia. Every one who heard him on that occasion pronounced him as much a master in the realm of international law as he had been in that of politics, although as a matter of fact his semi-victory was the result as much of emotional appeal as of reason (W. W. Henry, III, 601–48, gives the only known report of this speech). The decision of the judges was reserved and the case was reargued at the same place in May 1793, Henry again appearing on the side of the Virginia debtors. He was not less successful than he had been two years before. The judges found for the plaintiff and left it to a jury to determine the amount to be paid; but the jury disagreed, and the case was substantially lost.

Henry was now an old and a broken man, though less than sixty years of age. He retired to his last home, the "Red Hill" plantation on the Staunton River, and gave up his law practice. He was to be drawn, however, into embarrassments which his biographers have never quite clearly described. Before the last great speech in the federal court, Jefferson, unforgetful of the events of 1781, and Madison had begun to organize the remnants of the party which Henry had commanded throughout the revolution. Henry had never been willing to serve a day under the newly constituted federal government; but when Jefferson and Madison became the chief opponents of the administration, Washington's friends paid assiduous court to the master of "Red Hill," and he was not averse to the attentions. On Oct. 9, 1795, Washington offered to Henry the position of secretary of state, which Jefferson had relinquished two years before. The offer was declined, but within three months the President, then smarting under the extravagant strictures of the opposition press, asked Henry to become chief justice (W. W. Henry, II, 563; Tyler, p. 359). Henry declined this offer also, but made the public aware of his reviving admiration for the President. It was a sensation of the first magnitude. Henry's own children condemned the new turn in the orator's career and the old man wrote an explanation to Mrs. Patrick Henry Aylett, one of his married daughters. Spencer Roane, who had married Anne Henry, was never reconciled. The fiercest party warfare spread over the state; and Jefferson rapidly drew to himself nearly all the prominent followers of Henry and the great mass of the voters. Henry was now ready to burn all his bridges. When John Marshall became a candidate for a seat in the House of Representatives in 1798, Henry made it known that he was heartily in favor of the declining Federalist party. This led in January 1799 to an earnest request on the part of Washington that Henry offer as a candidate for the Virginia House of Delegates in order to resist there the theories of Madison and nearly all the former associates of Henry, expressed in the Kentucky and Virginia resolutions (W. W. Henry, II, 600–03). Henry consented, although his health forbade him to stand long upon his feet. He made his last speech on a cold March day at Charlotte Courthouse, young John Randolph offering as a candidate and an opponent in debate. Henry was elected but death intervened to prevent his appearance as a Federalist member of the Assembly the next autumn. He died on June 6, 1799, and was buried in the garden near his last residence.

[Wm. Wirt, *Sketches of the Life and Character of Patrick Henry* (1817), is a combination of authentic facts, traditions, and old men's recollections. M. C. Tyler, *Patrick Henry* (1887), is careful and faithful, though marred by forced interpretation of the events and attitudes of the last decade of Henry's career. W. W. Henry, *Patrick Henry: Life, Correspondence and Speeches* (3 vols., 1891), contains extensive documentary materials, but gives none of the speeches in full and only comparatively few letters. See also: H. B. Grigsby, *The Va. Convention of 1776* (1855); Jonathan Elliott, *The Debates, Resolutions, and Other Proc., in Convention, on the Adoption of the Fed. Constitution,* vol. II (1828); E. C. Burnett, *Letters of Members of the Continental Cong.*, vol. III (1926); John Burk, *The Hist. of Va.*, vols. III (1805), IV (1816); Chas. Campbell, *Intro. to the Hist. of the Colony and Ancient Dominion of Va.* (1847); W. E. Dodd, "Va. Takes the Road to Revolution," in *The Spirit of '76* (1927), by C. Becker, J. M. Clark, and W. E. Dodd; writings and biographies of contemporary statesmen.]

W. E. D.

HENRY, ROBERT (Dec. 6, 1792–Feb. 6, 1856), clergyman, educator, was born in Charleston, S. C. He was the son of Peter Henry, a native of Banffshire, Scotland, who went to the West Indies and became a successful merchant. In Jamaica he met Anne Adelaide (Schwiers) Angel, a widow with one child, whom he married. In May 1792 they came to Charleston, S. C. Peter Henry went back to the West Indies to settle up his business affairs, and as he was returning to Charleston, the ship on which he traveled was captured by a French privateer and he was so harshly treated that he died in Savannah in September 1794. His wife opened a dry-goods store for the support of herself and her children. In 1803 she took Robert to England that he might have the best educational advantages. Here he attended a school conducted by the Rev. James Lindsay near London. In 1811, with a view to entering the ministry, he enrolled at the University of Edinburgh, from which he received the degree of M.A. in 1814. After traveling on the Continent, he returned to Charleston. He had been licensed to preach according to the rites of the Scottish Church, and was soon invited to supply the Calvinistic Church of French Protestants in that city. He ministered to it for about two years, preaching alternately in French and English. On May 25, 1817, he was ordained by the Presbytery of Charleston, and the following year he married Elizabeth Henrietta Connors, a daughter of Charles Connors of Clarendon, S. C., by whom he had six children.

Henry had command of several modern languages, was well versed in the classics, and was especially proficient in philosophy. On Nov. 26, 1818, he was elected professor of logic and moral philosophy in South Carolina College, now the University of South Carolina, with which, either as teacher or executive, the rest of his life, except for a brief interval, was spent. For a time after the death of President Jonathan Maxcy [*q.v.*] in 1820, he also gave instruction in metaphysics. Maxcy was succeeded by the stormy petrel, Thomas Cooper [*q.v.*]. So turbulent was Cooper's administration (1820–34), that Henry, who acted as president *pro tempore* after Cooper's resignation, reported to the board of trustees that only twenty students remained. Henry held the college together for a year, when he was succeeded by Robert W. Barnwell [*q.v.*], who restored the fortunes of the institution. Henry failed of election himself because he was suspected of sharing Cooper's heretical religious views, a suspicion which seems to have been unfounded. Keenly disappointed, he withdrew from the college, although the administrative board desired him to remain as professor, and went to live on a farm near Columbia. Later he was discount clerk in the Branch Bank of the State, Columbia. In 1839, however, he accepted an invitation to return to the college as professor of metaphysics, logic, and belles-lettres. Always inclined to regard the apostolic succession a mark of the true church, on Mar. 10, 1841, he was ordained deacon in the Episcopal Church, and on Sept. 25, 1842, priest. Upon the resignation of President Barnwell, in 1841 Henry was made chairman of the faculty and on Dec. 2, 1842, was elected president. He also taught metaphysics and moral philosophy and gave instruction in Greek. He performed his duties as president most conscientiously, but his administration was a troubled one and he was so sensitive that every untoward incident worried him almost to the point of illness. On Nov. 28, 1845, a committee on the state of the college recommended that the presidency be declared vacant and that Henry be offered the professorship of Greek literature. He accepted and served the college in that capacity for the remainder of his life. A man of much learning and piety, genial and benevolent, he exerted no little influence on the institution during his more than thirty years' connection with it. He was buried in the Episcopal churchyard, Columbia, where the students erected a monument to his memory. He contributed articles to the *Southern Review* and published a number of sermons and addresses, among them, *Eulogy on Jonathan Maxcy, Late President of the South Carolina College* (1822); *Mysteries of Religion Worthy the Assent of the Human Understanding* (1834); *The Cultivation of the Fine Arts, Favorable to the Perfection of Private Character and the Development of Public Prosperity* (1840); *Eulogy on the Late Honorable John Caldwell Calhoun* (1850).

[Maximilian LaBorde, *Hist. of the S. C. College* (2nd ed., 1874); E. L. Green, *A Hist. of the Univ. of S. C.* (1916); *Sou. Quart. Rev.*, Apr. 1856; E. A. and G. L. Duyckinck, *Cyc. of Am. Literature* (2nd ed., 1875); *Charleston Daily Courier*, Feb. 7, 1856.]

S. C. M.

HENRY, WILLIAM (May 19, 1729–Dec. 15, 1786), gunsmith, patriot, was born in West Caln Township, Chester County, Pa. He was the son of John and Elizabeth (De Vinne) Henry, the former having come to America with his parents from Ireland in 1722, the latter being of Huguenot descent. Henry's early youth was spent on the farm and in the acquisition of an elementary education. When he was fifteen years old he went to Lancaster, then the largest inland town in Pennsylvania, and was apprenticed to a gunsmith, Matthew Roesser. He continued with this master for six years and because of his mechanical aptitude became an expert in this difficult craft. In 1750, at Lancaster, he formed a partnership with a wealthy Jew, Joseph Simon, for the making of firearms. The unusually accurate performance of his rifles soon made his name known throughout the colonies and his business prospered to such a degree that in the course of his life it yielded him a considerable fortune. During the Indian wars which desolated the frontier from 1755 to 1760, Henry served as principal armorer of the troops then called into service. After his return to Lancaster he bought out his partner and thereafter conducted his business alone. He was an enthusiastic student of natural philosophy and maintained a well-equipped laboratory at his gun works, where he engaged continuously in research. He had made some experiments with steam, when, in 1761 on a business trip to England, he met

James Watt who explained his own steam-engine inventions to him. Upon his return he concentrated his experimental work on the application of steam to the propelling of boats and by 1763 had completed a stern-wheel steamboat. Although its trial on the Conestoga Creek at Lancaster was unsuccessful, Henry should be credited with being the first person in the United States to make such an experiment. After 1761 and until the beginning of the Revolution he was busy in his gunshop and laboratory and enjoying a delightful home life. He was the first to recognize the genius of Benjamin West [*q.v.*] and to extend to him both moral and material help. Fulton, too, in his youth received much knowledge and inspiration from Henry and was a welcome visitor to his home and factory. Henry joined the American Philosophical Society in 1768, taking his seat at the same time as his lifelong friend David Rittenhouse. He contributed an article to the first volume of the society's *Transactions* (1769–71), describing his invention of a so-called "sentinel register," an apparatus utilizing the expansive force of air when heated to open and close the flue-damper in a furnace. He also devised many labor-saving machines for his gun works. He is credited with the invention of a screw auger; he perfected a steam-heating system; and he was at work on the construction of a "steam wheel" when he died.

Having no little aptitude for public affairs, he held important civil and military offices. He was made a justice of the peace when twenty-nine, and at thirty-six began a ten-year service as assistant burgess of Lancaster. He served three terms as an assistant justice of the county courts and was a member of the state canal commission in 1771. He was a delegate to the state Assembly in 1776 and later, in 1777, became a member of the Council of Safety. As treasurer of Lancaster County from 1777 to his death he rendered noteworthy service in a critical financial period. Finally, he was elected by the Assembly to the Continental Congress in 1784 and died while in office. Throughout the Revolution he was assistant commissary general and disbursing officer of the government for the district of Lancaster. In addition, he served as superintendent of arms and accoutrements and in this capacity established workshops in various parts of the state and directed the making of boots, shoes, hats, and ordnance. He married Ann Wood, daughter of Abraham Wood of Darby, Pa., in January 1755, and was survived by his wife, a daughter, and six sons.

[Francis Jordan, Jr., *The Life of William Henry* (1910); Alexander Harris, *Biog. Hist. of Lancaster County, Pa.* (1872); *Trans. Am. Phil. Soc.* . . ., vol. I (1769–71); R. H. Thurston, *Robert Fulton: His Life and its Results* (1891); Franklin Ellis and Samuel Evans, *Hist. of Lancaster County, Pa.* (1883); *Early Proc. Am. Phil. Soc. . . . 1744–1838* (1884); H. M. J. Klein and E. M. Williams, *Lancaster County, Pa. A Hist.* (1924), vol. I.]

C. W. M—n.

HENRY, WILLIAM WIRT (Feb. 14, 1831–Dec. 5, 1900), lawyer, historian, was born at "Red Hill," in Charlotte County, Va., where his grandfather, Patrick Henry, had lived during his last years and was buried, and was named for that statesman's biographer, whom he was destined to emulate. His father, John Henry, was the youngest son of the Revolutionary orator and his second wife, Dorothea Spotswood Dandridge. His mother, Elvira Henry McClelland, was the daughter of Thomas S. McClelland and the grand-daughter of Col. William Cabell of "Union Hill." After taking the M.A. degree at the University of Virginia in 1850, young Henry read law with Judge Hunter H. Marshall, began practice in his native county in 1853, and served for some years as commonwealth's attorney. Like his father a Whig in politics in ante-bellum days, he opposed secession. He enlisted, however, in a local artillery company and did relatively brief and inconspicuous military service. Emerging from the Civil War without bitterness, he removed in 1873 to Richmond, where he was speedily recognized as a leader of the bar. His political career, which was confined to a term of two years in the House of Delegates, 1877–79, and a year in the state Senate, 1879–80, was not notable except for his brave opposition to the readjustment of the state debt. Aloof from politics during the remainder of his life, he was none the less a prominent public figure, both in the state and in the nation, and received countless tokens of the esteem of his contemporaries.

His prominence was in no small degree due to his historical writings, which give him his chief title to fame. These consist chiefly of addresses and papers, delivered before various patriotic and historical gatherings, and his *Patrick Henry: Life, Correspondence and Speeches* (3 vols., 1891), which is still indispensable to students of the period covered by it. The grandson of the "forest Demosthenes" was a self-trained historian, and was never fully emancipated from localism and hero worship. Practically all his historical work was confined to the Virginia field, and was primarily motivated by a desire to quicken interest in, and gain proper recognition for, the contributions made to American life and institutions by his state, the Scotch-Irish settlers, and his distinguished ancestor. Upon many occasions, he championed Capt. John Smith and upheld that doughty warrior's title to historical veracity. His *magnum opus,* which is distinctly a family biography, is valued today chiefly for its rich personal documentary material and its wealth of information about local conditions.

Though he did not belong to the small group of American scholars who had gained technical training abroad or in one of the few graduate schools of history, he cooperated in a modest way in the production of Justin Winsor's *Narrative and Critical History of America* (III, 1885, ch. IV, "Sir Walter Ralegh"). Though his interest was primarily local, he was prominently associated not only with the Virginia Historical Society, which delighted to do him honor, but also with the Massachusetts Historical Society, the Long Island Historical Society, the American Antiquarian Society, and the American Historical Association. He was president of the latter organization, 1890–91. (His presidential address was published in the *Annual Report of the American Historical Association for the Year 1891,* pp. 15–29.) If always to a considerable extent a patriotic, rather than a critical, historian, he was not unaffected by the new emphasis on thoroughness and fairmindedness which characterized the last two decades of his life, and occupies a place of dignity in American historiography.

He was married in 1854 to Lucy Gray, daughter of Col. James P. Marshall of Charlotte County, Va. His widow and four children survived him.

[For a brief sketch of Henry's life, entirely uncritical as regards his historical scholarship, see *Va. Mag. of Hist. and Biog.,* Jan. 1901, pp. xiii–xvi. For a practically complete list of his writings, see E. G. Swem, *A Bibliography of Va.,* I (1916), 259–60. See also *Eminent and Representative Men of Va. and the D. C.* (1893), p. 461; and obituary in the *Richmond Dispatch,* Dec. 5, 6, 1900.] D. M.

HENSHALL, JAMES ALEXANDER (Feb. 29, 1836–Apr. 4, 1925), physician, naturalist, and writer on angling, was born in Baltimore, Md., the son of the Rev. James Gershom Henshall and Clarissa (Holt) Henshall. He received his early education in the schools of Baltimore, New York, and Cincinnati, graduated from the Eclectic Medical Institute of Cincinnati in 1860, and pursued post-graduate studies in the Eclectic Medical College of the City of New York in 1867. His career as a practising physician extended over thirty years, although the latter part of the period was marked by an increasing attention to angling and the publication of several books upon the subject. In 1864 he was married to Hester S. Ferguson of Cincinnati, where he established his home. In 1896 the call of the waters and woods became irresistible, and he entered the service of the United States Bureau of Fisheries as superintendent of its hatchery at Bozeman, Mont. His successful work at this point was terminated in 1909 when he was transferred to the hatchery at Tupelo, Miss., to carry on the propagation of black bass. He was president of the American Fisheries Society in 1891 and held a life-long membership in that organization. He was various times secretary of the Cincinnati Society of Natural History, president of the Montana Society of Natural Sciences, and honorary president of the Izaak Walton League of America. He was chief of the fisheries department at the Chicago exposition of 1893 and for his contributions to fish culture and conservation was awarded medals at the Paris and St. Louis expositions.

The numerous books on game fish and fishing coming from his pen were based upon an extensive experience as an angler in various parts of the United States and foreign countries. One of his fishing companions was Judge Longworth of the prominent Cincinnati family, who accompanied him on an angling tour around the world. The fruit of his services as a professional fish culturist appeared in the development of several improved methods and devices for the propagation of game fishes, particularly the grayling and the black bass. Several technical articles based on the results of his studies are found in the *Transactions* of the American Fisheries Society. More than thirty-five titles are credited to Henshall, the majority being technical articles or contributions to sportsmen's publications. His longer writings, some of which achieved considerable popularity, were: *The Book of the Black Bass* (1881); *Camping and Cruising in Florida* (1884); *More about the Black Bass* (1889); *Ye Gods and Little Fishes* (1900); *Bass, Pike, Perch and Others* (1903); *Favorite Fish and Fishing* (1908). His writings reflect the gentle kindly soul of the author and express charmingly his knowledge and appreciation of the denizens of woods and waters. Failing eyesight necessitated his resignation from the government service in 1917, and he retired to his Cincinnati home to busy himself with further writing and revision of his earlier works. He died in Cincinnati.

[*Who's Who in America,* 1924–25; H. A. Kelly and W. L. Burrage, *Dict. of Am. Medic. Biog.* (1928); *Trans. Am. Fisheries Soc.,* 1925; *Jour. Am. Medic. Asso.,* May 16, 1925; *Cincinnati Enquirer, N. Y. Times, N. Y. Herald Tribune,* Apr. 5, 1925; records of the U. S. Bureau of Fisheries.] M. C. J.

HENSHAW, DAVID (Apr. 2, 1791–Nov. 11, 1852), politician, secretary of the navy, was a descendant of Joshua Henshaw of Lancashire, England, who settled in Dorchester, Mass., about 1653. Born in Leicester, Mass., the fifth son of David and Mary (Sargent) Henshaw, David attended the free schools and the academy of his native town. At the age of sixteen he became a druggist's apprentice and at twenty-one went into business for himself. Before he was thirty-three he had acquired means to become a banker and to establish an insurance company, and by 1828 he had entered actively into the project for a railroad through the Berkshires to Albany, N. Y. Later he became an incorporator of the Western Railroad which, with the Boston & Worcester of which also he was a director, completed the interstate line.

In 1821, Henshaw and his associates established the *Boston Statesman,* under the editorship of Nathaniel Greene [*q.v.*], and about it gathered a faction opposed to the Federalists who were then in power in Massachusetts. The *Statesman's* editorials preferred Crawford of Georgia to John Quincy Adams in the campaign of 1824; but Henshaw later made terms with the party of President Adams and, on its ticket, gained election to the state Senate in 1826. This political alliance was short-lived however; for Henshaw, interested in the real estate of South Boston, advocated free bridges. Bostonians who had property rights in the toll bridge to Charlestown were thoroughly aroused (see *The Proprietors of the Charles River Bridge* vs. *The Proprietors of the Warren Bridge and Others,* 11 *Peters,* 420); old Federalists and Republicans sank their enmities and rallied around Governor Lincoln, Senator Webster, and President Adams to form a new conservative party which overwhelmed Henshaw and his free-bridge party at the polls in April 1827. Henshaw lost no time in finding another political alliance. Standing for "Republican friends of Jackson," he sought election to Congress in July, appealing to the ship-owners and importers who opposed the protective tariffs which Adams and Webster were beginning to favor in behalf of New England's rising textile industry. He was again defeated, but he was given the collectorship of the port of Boston and the patronage of that office, which made him the Democratic boss of Massachusetts. When he attempted, however, to hand over the collectorship to an intimate friend and to seek the place of postmaster-general, he learned that Marcus Morton [*q.v.*], his perennial candidate for the governorship, had been given the disposal of the office. Close upon this disappointment came the panic of 1837, which forced Henshaw's Commonwealth Bank into bankruptcy and himself into political repudiation. He withdrew to his home in Leicester to bide his time, meanwhile making a tour of the West and representing the town of Leicester in the state legislature of 1839.

The return of Calhoun to influence, after the break between Tyler and Clay, gave Henshaw his opportunity. In the spring of 1843 he gathered his old associates to form a Tyler-Calhoun faction and challenged the authority of the Van Buren organization by seeking the nomination for Congress from Worcester County. Although unable to regain control of the Democratic party at this time, he was so nearly reëstablished that he obtained the President's nomination to be secretary of the navy. He administered the Department satisfactorily from July 23, 1843, to Feb. 19, 1844, when, the Senate having rejected his appointment in deference to Webster and other Whigs, he was succeeded by Thomas W. Gilmer [*q.v.*]. In spite of this occurrence, Henshaw was now so prominent in his party, owing to the support of Southern Democrats, that he continued to dominate Democratic affairs in Massachusetts until the slavery issue began to disrupt parties. He died in 1852.

Henshaw's democracy was conservative. He himself was a capitalist, a Mason, an opponent of prohibition, a friend of slaveholders. A political rival characterized him as "a shrewd, selfish, strong-minded (but I believe corrupt-hearted) man" who directed the party "with a rod of iron" and would "see it damned ere others should" (J. G. Harris to George Bancroft, February 1838, Bancroft MSS.). Henshaw's will to rule was unmistakable; but there is little reason for questioning the sincerity of his convictions. He read much and possessed a keen knowledge of men. Although he never married, he dispensed a generous hospitality at his country home in Leicester.

Among his separately published writings are: *Remarks on the Bank of the United States* (1831); *Remarks upon the Rights and Powers of Corporations* (1837); *Letters on the Internal Improvements and Commerce of the West* (1839); *The Exchequer and the Currency* (1842).

[Henshaw letters in the Chamberlain collection, Boston Pub. Lib., and in the Ebenezer Baldwin papers, Yale Univ. Lib.; *A Refutation by His Friends of the Calumnies against David Henshaw* (1844); A. H. Ward, in *Memorial Biogs. of the New Eng. Hist.-Geneal. Soc.,* vol. I (1880); *New Eng. Hist. and Geneal. Reg.,* Apr. 1868; J. S. Loring, *The Hundred Boston Orators* (1852); J. B. Derby, *Political Reminiscences* (1835); *Memoirs of John Quincy Adams,* VIII (1876), 181, 392–93; L. G. Tyler, *Letters and Times of the Tylers,* II (1885), 389; A. B. Darling, *Political Changes in Mass. 1824–48* (1925); *Boston Daily Advertiser,* Nov. 12, 1852.]

A. B. D.

HENSHAW, HENRY WETHERBEE (Mar. 3, 1850–Aug. 1, 1930), naturalist, ornithologist, ethnologist, was born at Cambridge, Mass., the youngest of the seven children of William and Sarah Holden (Wetherbee) Henshaw. He was educated in the Cambridge public schools and planned to go to Harvard, but in 1869, shortly before he was to take the entrance examination, his health gave way, and, although it was restored by a winter in Louisiana, his plans for a college course were abandoned. His subsequent training as a naturalist comprised chiefly outdoor study. As a boy he had been interested in the varied wild life of the woods and marshes about his home but he soon developed a preference for birds, and the enthusiastic study of ornithology, largely in the field, occupied much of his time for many years. In 1872 he was attached as a naturalist to the Wheeler Survey, which was engaged in general explorations west of the one-hundredth meridian. Annual field trips in this connection to various parts of the West, and the preparation of reports in Washington, kept him busy until the Survey was terminated in 1879. He made notable collections of birds, and his interest extended also to several other branches of natural history—mammals, fishes, reptiles, insects, and even plants. In 1885 his collection of birds and eggs was acquired by the British Museum.

After the conclusion of the Wheeler Survey, since no opening in ornithological work was then available, he joined the staff of the Bureau of Ethnology. Because of administrative duties his ornithological studies were largely discontinued for some years. He was editor of the *American Anthropologist* from 1889 to 1893. In the latter year, owing to ill health, he was compelled to ask for an indefinite leave of absence. He went in December 1894 to the Hawaiian Islands, where he remained about ten years, studying the birds and natural history in general and devoting much time to outdoor photography with notable success. Finding himself once more in condition for serious work, he returned in 1904 to the United States, and in 1905 was appointed administrative assistant in the Bureau of Biological Survey of the Department of Agriculture, becoming assistant chief in December of the same year. As his administrative duties were heavy, he again found little time for collecting and observing bird life in the field. While in Hawaii he had taken up the use of the microscope in the examination of land shells, and after returning to Washington derived much pleasure in noting under a high-power lens the surpassing beauty and infinite variety of form presented by diatoms. In 1910 he became chief of the Biological Survey. The work of the Bureau developed rapidly along diversified lines, with direct bearing upon wild-life administration, and with the increasing responsibilities of his position his health again began to suffer and he resigned on Dec. 1, 1916. He never entirely recovered his full powers, and thereafter did comparatively little active work. He died at Washington, unmarried.

Henshaw was the author of a *Report on the Ornithology of Nevada, Utah, California, Colorado, New Mexico, and Arizona* (1875); *Birds of the Hawaiian Islands* (1902); "Birds of Town and Country" (*National Geographic Magazine,* May 1914); "American Game Birds" (*Ibid.,* August 1915); "Friends of our Forests, the Warblers" (*Ibid.,* April 1917); and also of a number of important papers contributed to scientific journals, on ornithology and ethnology. In the latter field, he contributed many articles to the "Handbook of American Indians" (*Bulletin 30, Bureau of American Ethnology,* 2 vols., 1907, 1910). He was a fellow of the American Ornithologists' Union, and was vice-president of that organization from 1891 to 1894 and from 1911 to 1918. The most notable contribution of his later years was his autobiography, which was published in several numbers of the *Condor,* an ornithological journal, during 1919 and 1920.

[The chief sources are Henshaw's autobiography, in the *Condor,* May 1919–June 1920, and personal acquaintance. A full bibliography of Henshaw's writings, now in the possession of the Bureau of Biological Survey, U. S. Dept. of Agric., Washington, D. C., will be published together with a memoir, in the *Auk* in the near future. See also *Who's Who in America,* 1916–17; *New England Hist. and Geneal. Reg.,* Oct. 1862; *Evening Star* (Washington), Aug. 2, 1930; *N. Y. Times,* Aug. 3, 1930.] E. A. G.

HENSON, JOSIAH (June 15, 1789–May 5, 1883), an escaped slave, active in the service of his race, and the reputed original of Uncle Tom in Harriet Beecher Stowe's *Uncle Tom's Cabin,* was born in Charles County, Md., on a farm belonging to Francis Newman, about a mile from Port Tobacco. In his early years, under the system of slavery, he saw his mother brutally assaulted and his father mutilated. The master, Riley, into whose hands he fell while still a young boy, was harsh and incompetent. Josiah, however, became a strong and vigorous youth. Before he was grown his ability made him superintendent of the farm, and the crop doubled under his management. At the age of eighteen, never before having heard a sermon, he was deeply moved by the discourse of a godly baker, John McKenny, who was opposed to slavery. One evening, in rescuing his master at a convivial gathering, he offended the overseer of a neighboring plantation, who later attacked him with the assistance of three slaves, broke one of his arms, and otherwise abused him. At the age of twenty-two he married a slave girl, who became the mother of twelve children. In 1825, Riley, about to be ruined by his improvidence, exacted from Josiah a promise that he would conduct the slaves of the plantation, about twenty in number, to a brother living in Kentucky. In passing through Ohio they were urged to assert their freedom, but Josiah remained true to his word. In Kentucky he worked under more favorable conditions and in 1828 was admitted as a preacher of the Methodist Episcopal Church. After trying in vain to purchase his freedom, he was sent to New Orleans to be sold.

Deciding to make a bid for freedom he set forth one night with his wife and four young children. It took him two weeks to reach Cincinnati. Later a Scotchman named Burnham, captain of a boat, assisted him in getting to Buffalo, and, Oct. 28, 1830, he crossed over to Canada. He worked hard, learned his letters from his oldest boy, who now went to school, became a preacher in Dresden, Bothwell County, Ont., and rapidly advanced in influence and esteem. He was interested not only in helping other slaves to escape from bondage but also in cultivating in the negroes the spirit of thrift and in encouraging them to acquire land. He tried to develop a community and to found an industrial school at Dawn, in the territory between Lake St. Clair and the Detroit River, to which place he took his family in 1842. Committees in both England and America were interested, but through the incompetence of an agent the project dragged on for years, little being done. Henson's own integrity was called in question both in England and by the negroes in the settlement; but he cleared himself to the satisfaction of all concerned. In 1851, on the second of three trips to England, he was awarded a bronze medal for some black walnut boards that he exhibited at the World's Fair, was honored before a distinguished company at the home of Lord John Russell, prime minister, and invited by Lord Grey to go to India to supervise cotton raising. Late in life, his first wife having died, he married a widow in Boston, who accompanied him on his third visit to England in 1876. A farewell meeting in Spurgeon's Tabernacle was attended by thousands, and Queen Victoria at Windsor Castle presented him with a photograph of herself framed in gold.

A quarter of a century before, on passing through Andover, Mass., Henson had told his story to Harriet Beecher Stowe. In *A Key to Uncle Tom's Cabin* (1853) she had referred to his career; henceforth he was famous as Uncle Tom, though his claim was not without dispute. In 1849 he published *The Life of Josiah Henson, Formerly a Slave, Now an Inhabitant of Canada, as Narrated by Himself.* It appeared enlarged and with an introduction by Harriet B. Stowe in 1858, under the title *Truth Stranger than Fiction: Father Henson's Story of His Own Life,* and further enlarged was published in 1879 under the title, *"Truth Is Stranger than Fiction": An Autobiography of the Rev. Josiah Henson,* with a preface by Harriet B. Stowe and introductory notes by Wendell Phillips. He died in Dresden, Ont.

[In addition to works already mentioned, see *N. Y. Tribune,* May 6, 1883.] B. B.

HENTZ, CAROLINE LEE WHITING (June 1, 1800–Feb. 11, 1856), author, was born in Lancaster, Mass., the youngest of the eight children of John and Orpah Whiting, and the sixth in descent from the Rev. Samuel Whiting [*q.v.*] who emigrated to Massachusetts in 1636. Her father, who had fought in the Revolution, and three of her brothers became officers in the United States army. On Sept. 30, 1824, she married Nicholas Marcellus Hentz, a native of Metz, who had left France for political reasons. He was a man of various accomplishments, a miniature painter, an entomologist, and the author of at least one novel, *Tadeuskund, the Last King of the Lenape: An Historical Tale* (1825). His monograph on the spiders of the United States (*Boston Journal of Natural History,* January 1842–December 1847) was once famous and is still consulted. At the time of their marriage he was employed under George Bancroft [*q.v.*] in the Round Hill School in Northampton. He was a professor in the University of North Carolina, 1826–30, and conducted a girls' school in Covington, Ky., 1830–32; in Cincinnati, 1832–34; in Florence, Ala., 1834–43; in Tuscaloosa, 1843–45; in Tuskegee, 1845–48; and in Columbus, Ga., 1848–49. Besides bearing and rearing four children and supervising her household, Mrs. Hentz assisted him in his school work. Meanwhile, she engaged in authorship. Composition cost her no effort; she could write in spare half-hours, in a room filled with children, or with friends looking on and reading over her shoulder. Thus at intervals she contributed poems and tales to several magazines. In 1831 a prize of $500 offered by William Pelby, the Boston actor, for a play based on the Moorish conquest of Spain was awarded to her *De Lara or The Moorish Bride* (Tuscaloosa, 1843), which was performed at the Arch Street Theatre, Philadelphia, and at the Tremont Theatre, Boston. Pelby, in financial straits and unable to pay the full amount of the award, returned the copyright to her. Touched apparently by his honesty, she favored him with another play, *Constance of Werdenberg* (said to have been published in the Columbus, Ga., *Times and Sentinel*), which was performed at the Park Theatre, New York, in 1832. A third play, *Lamorah or the Western Wild,* was performed in Cincinnati in 1832 and in Caldwell's Theatre, New Orleans, Jan. 1, 1833. *Aunt Patty's Scrap Bag,* one of her best-known tales, appeared in 1846. In 1849 her husband became an invalid, and she herself was ill for many months. They had to close their school, and thereafter Mrs. Hentz supported the family. Working assiduously, she produced a series of novels amazingly popular in their generation and republished as late as 1889: *Linda or The Young Pilot of the Belle Creole* (1850); *Rena or The Snow Bird* (1851); *Marcus Warland or The Long Moss Spring* (1852); *Helen and Arthur or Miss Thusa's Spinning Wheel* (1853); *The Planter's Northern Bride* (2 vols., 1854), her most ambitious effort; *Robert Graham: A Sequel to Linda* (1855); *Ernest Linwood* (1856); and a number of others. Her shorter tales were collected and published in several volumes, including *The Victim of Excitement and Other Stories* (1853); *Wild Jack* (1853); *Courtship and Marriage or The Joys and Sorrows of American Life* (1856); and *The Banished Son, and Other Stories of the Heart* (1856). Mrs. Hentz was pained by the widening breach between North and South and strove in her novels to represent negro slavery as a beneficent social arrangement. Two years before her death she visited her old home in Massachusetts. She and her husband spent their last years with their grown children in Marianna and St. Andrews, Fla. She died in Marianna of pneumonia, her strength weakened by long attendance on her sick husband, and was buried in the Episcopal cemetery.

[Wm. C. Langdon, memoir prefixed to *Linda* (1889); H. S. Nourse, *The Birth, Marriage, and Death Reg. . . . of Lancaster, Mass., 1643–1850* (1890); Wm. Whiting, *Memoir of Rev. Samuel Whiting, D. D.* (privately printed, 1873); G. M. West, *St. Andrews, Fla.* (1922); J. S. Hart, *Female Prose Writers of America* (1852), with portrait; A. H. Quinn, *A Hist. of the Am. Drama from the Beginning to the Civil War* (1923); R. L. Rusk, *The Lit. of the Middle Western Frontier* (1925); *Times and Sentinel* (Columbus, Ga.), Feb. 20, 1856; J. G. Johnson, *Southern Fiction prior to 1860: An Attempt at a First-Hand Bibliog.* (Charlottesville, Va., 1909).]

G. H. G.

HEPBURN, ALONZO BARTON (July 24, 1846–Jan. 25, 1922), banker, philanthropist, born in Colton, St. Lawrence County, N. Y., was the son of Zina Earl Hepburn and Beulah (Gray) Hepburn. His father was descended from Peter or Patrick Hepburn, a Scotchman who settled at Stratford, Conn., about 1700. His mother came from similar stock: the Grays, Scotch-Irish, who came to Worcester, Mass., in 1718. Hepburn's American ancestors were pioneers throughout, moving across Vermont to the wild country of northern New York. The conditions of life in his early years were hard, and every child in the family of eight was called upon to be an "asset in the family economy"; hunting and fishing were economic activities as well as sports; but the family also gathered about the fireplace reading good books aloud by turn. Hard work in local academies and finally, for a year, in Middlebury College gave young Hepburn his education. In 1902 he was awarded the degree of A.B. as of the class of 1871. For a few years he taught school and read law, beginning his legal practice in Colton, N. Y., where he served as school commissioner, instituting reforms against strong opposition. In 1875, over the opposition of the local Republican bosses, he was elected as a Republican to the New York legislature, where he continued for five successive terms. He early became known as a master of legislation.

Hepburn's first great public service was performed during his legislative career. He was chairman of the legislative committee appointed to inquire into railway-rate discrimination, and the "Hepburn Report" of 1879 is a landmark in railroad history (*Proceedings of the Special Committee on Railroads Appointed under a Resolution of the Assembly to Investigate Alleged Abuses in the Management of Railroads Chartered by the State of New York,* 8 vols., 1879). This report was followed by corrective legislation, the "Hepburn Laws," and influenced the Federal Interstate Commerce Act adopted eight years later. In 1880 Hepburn became superintendent of the state banking department of New York, in which capacity he introduced drastic reforms, including regular bank examinations. Declining reappointment in 1883, he lived in St. Lawrence County from 1883 to 1889, laying, in successful land and lumber operations, the foundation for his large fortune of later years. This was the only period of his life given primarily to his personal financial affairs. From 1889 to 1892 he was United States bank examiner in New York City. In 1892 he became comptroller of the currency in Washington, resigning in 1893.

He was president of the Third National Bank of New York from 1893 to 1897, when that institution was absorbed by the National City

Bank, of which, from 1897 to 1899, he was vice-president. In 1899 he became vice-president of the Chase National Bank, with which institution he remained until his death, being president from 1904 to 1911, chairman of the board of directors from 1911 to 1918, and chairman of the advisory board from 1918 to 1922. It was as head of this bank that Hepburn became an international figure, playing a significant rôle in international finance and diplomacy through his friendships with statesmen and bankers in both Europe and Japan. This service was of greatest importance between 1914 and 1918, but he was constantly called upon for advice by high officials of many countries to the very end of his life.

A life-long student of the theory and history of money, Hepburn was a leader in defending the gold standard against free silver. In 1903 he published *History of Coinage and Currency in the United States and the Perennial Contest for Sound Money*. The enlarged revision of this work, *A History of Currency in the United States: with a Brief Description of the Currency Systems of All Commercial Nations* (1915), is a classic. As chairman of the currency commission of the American Bankers Association, he was largely responsible for the organization of the National Monetary Commission under Senator Nelson W. Aldrich [*q.v.*]. An advocate of the Aldrich Plan, which involved a central bank with branches, he opposed the Federal Reserve Act, with its plan for regional reserve banks, until he succeeded in having incorporated in it the provision requiring one Federal Reserve bank to rediscount for another, thus pooling all of the gold in the system. He then supported the measure (see Mrs. Hepburn's preface to the 1924 edition of Hepburn's *History of Currency in the United States*). In addition to a long list of published articles, addresses, reports, and interviews, many of them of very great importance, covering the period from 1875 to 1922, Hepburn published *Artificial Waterways and Commercial Development* (1909), revised as *Artificial Waterways of the World* (1914), and *The Story of an Outing* (1913).

His philanthropies were widespread. He dotted the North Country from which he came with public libraries and built a hospital at Ogdensburg. The School of Business of Columbia University, St. Lawrence University, Middlebury College, Princeton, Williams College, New York University, Wellesley College, the Commercial Education Fund of the Chamber of Commerce of the State of New York, and the University Club of New York City, all received benefactions. He endowed a chair in the University of Tokyo on "The Constitution, History and Diplomacy of the United States." From his youthful environment Hepburn derived a life-long interest in big-game hunting. He was a man of great personal charm, who made and kept loyal friends. He was married in 1873 to Hattie A. Fisher who died in 1881. In 1887 he was married to Emily Lovisia Eaton, who, with her two daughters and a son of the first marriage, survived him.

[*Ann. Report of the Supt. of the Bank Dept. of the State of N. Y.*, 1880–82; *Ann. Report of the Comptroller of the Currency*, 1892; B. C. Forbes, *Men Who Are Making America* (1917); J. B. Bishop, *A. Barton Hepburn, His Life and Service to His Time* (1923); *Bankers' Mag.*, Feb. 1922 and Feb. 1924; *Monthly Bull., Chamber of Commerce of the State of N. Y.*, Feb. 1922; *The Chase* (a monthly pub. of the Chase National Bank), 1918–22, *passim*, esp. Feb. 1922, Feb., Mar. 1924, Mar. 1929; *Who's Who in America*, 1920–21; *N. Y. Times*, Jan. 26, 1922.] B. M. A., Jr.

HEPBURN, JAMES CURTIS (Mar. 13, 1815–Sept. 21, 1911), medical missionary, came of Scotch-Irish stock on the side of his father, Samuel Hepburn, and of English stock on that of his mother, Ann Clay. His great-grandfather, Samuel Hepburn, had emigrated from Belfast to Pennsylvania in 1773, and James Curtis Hepburn was born at Milton, in that state, where his father was practising law. Graduating (B.A.) from the College of New Jersey at Princeton in 1832, he received the degree of M.D. from the University of Pennsylvania in 1836. While practising in Norristown he met Clarissa Leete, whom he married in 1840. Four of the five children born to them died in infancy. In 1834 he had joined the Presbyterian church, and the March following his marriage he sailed with his wife for Singapore to become a medical missionary under the American Board of Commissioners for Foreign Missions. After serving at Singapore and in Amoy (1843–45), they returned to the United States, where Hepburn practised his profession in New York City for thirteen years.

Immediately after the opening of Japan to American residents in 1859, Hepburn and his wife sailed, under commission of the Presbyterian Board, for Kanagawa, at which port they arrived Oct. 18, 1859. They were among the earliest of American missionaries in Japan. Hepburn opened a dispensary, where by 1869 he was ministering to thirty to fifty patients daily. Here he carried on a medical training class for young men. He was one of the founders and the first president of the Meiji Gakuin, a boys' school in Tokyo; held the chair of physiology and hygiene there for some years; and raised the money to build a dormitory, which was named Hepburn Hall. He served often as mediator between the mercantile and the missionary elements in the foreign population of Yokohama. He had a share in the organization of the Union Church (for foreign residents) and the Shiloh Church (for Japanese). The latter was built chiefly through the gifts of his personal friends in America. Mrs. Hepburn began in 1863 a class for girls which was one of the first steps ever taken toward the education of Japanese women. In 1867 Hepburn's English-Japanese dictionary, a pioneer work in its field, was issued from the press of the American Presbyterian Mission at Shanghai, and in 1891 he published a Bible dictionary. The profits from his books were used for the Shiloh Church in Yokohama and the Meiji Gakuin in Tokyo. He also took an active part in the translation of the Bible into Japanese, being responsible for about three-fourths of the work. The New Testament was completed in 1880 and the Old Testament in 1887.

In 1892, after a generation of service, during which their home had been a center of hospitality for both Japanese and foreigners, the Hepburns returned to the United States, where, surviving his wife by several years, Hepburn lived quietly in East Orange, N. J., until his death at the age of ninety-six.

[W. E. Griffis, *Hepburn of Japan* (1913), and article in *Missionary Review of the World,* Dec. 1911; E. B. Greene, *A New-Englander in Japan: Daniel Crosby Greene* (1927); *The Christian Movement in Japan: Tenth Annual Issue* (1912); *N. Y. Times,* Sept. 22, 1911; other material in Foreign Mission Library of the Presbyterian Board, New York City.] E. W. C.

HEPBURN, WILLIAM PETERS (Nov. 4, 1833–Feb. 7, 1916), congressman, author of the Hepburn Law and of the Pure Food and Drug Law, was born in Wellsville, Columbiana County, Ohio. He was the son of James S. and Ann Fairfax (Catlett) Hepburn and the grandson of James Hepburn, an emigrant from Scotland to New York. His father was a graduate of West Point, an artillery officer, and a physician, who died of cholera in New Orleans before William was born. His mother was the daughter of Hanson Catlett, an army surgeon, who sailed against the Barbary pirates and fought in a number of Indian wars. The widowed mother married George S. Hampton, a prosperous commission merchant in Wellsville, who, emigrating to Iowa after the panic of 1837, moved the family in 1841 to a farm near Iowa City. Here William lived for three years until he was taken to Iowa City where his step-father became clerk of the supreme court and his mother a teacher in the "female department" of Mechanics' Academy. He attended several private schools and served an apprenticeship in the printing office of the *Iowa Republican.*

Hepburn read law with William Penn Clarke and was admitted to the bar in 1854. On Oct. 7, 1855, he married Melvina A. Morsman of Iowa City. The same year he settled in Marshalltown, Iowa, where his professional and political career began. He attended the first Republican state convention held in Iowa in 1856 and in the same year was elected prosecuting attorney for Marshall County. In 1858 he became chief clerk of the House of Representatives and also won the district attorneyship of the 11th judicial district, which he continued to hold until he entered the army in 1861. He raised and became the captain of a company of cavalry which was mustered into the service of the Union as Company B, 2nd Iowa Cavalry, rose to the rank of major commanding the first battalion, and finally was lieutenant-colonel, serving on the staffs of Sheridan and of Rosecrans. He was also detailed as judge-advocate of general courts martial. At the close of the war he engaged in the practice of law and in business in Memphis, Tenn., until 1867 when he returned to Iowa, opened a law office at Clarinda, and bought a half interest in the *Page County Herald.* He soon became eminently successful in the practice of law and abandoned his newspaper work. In 1872 he joined the Liberal Republican movement, supporting Horace Greeley for the presidency, but returned to the party shortly afterward and remained a stanch defender of its principles.

In 1880 Hepburn was nominated for Congress in the 8th district and was elected for three terms during which he distinguished himself as a vigorous opponent of "pork-barrel" legislation and an earnest champion of military and pension legislation. When he was defeated for reëlection in 1886 by A. R. Anderson, after a spirited campaign in which railroad regulation constituted the main issue, he resumed his law practice until President Harrison appointed him in 1889 to the office of solicitor of the treasury, which he held for four years. In 1892 Hepburn again became a candidate for Congress and was elected eight consecutive times. For fourteen years chairman of the committee on interstate and foreign commerce and for ten years a member of the committee on Pacific railroads, he worked on the transportation problem. His work, in this connection, culminating in the Hepburn rate law of 1906, constitutes his principal achievement. Hepburn was also the joint author and leading advocate of the Pure Food and Drug Act of 1906, champion of the bill of 1904 providing for the construction of the Panama Canal—in spite of his own preference for the Nicaragua route, a consistent opponent of civil service reform, and one of the leaders in the movement to limit the powers of the speaker.

In 1908 his party renominated him, but the rise of the radical Republicans, his opposition to trade unions, and the small enmities he had made in his career caused his defeat by a narrow margin. He opened an office in Washington and began again the practice of law. On Feb. 7, 1916, he died at Clarinda, Iowa.

[Sources include J. E. Briggs, *Wm. Peters Hepburn* (1919); *Annals of Iowa*, Oct. 1923; J. F. Meginness, *Geneal. and Hist. of the Hepburn Family of the Susquehanna Valley* (1894); *Des Moines Register and Leader*, Feb. 8, 1916; information from Mrs. Wm. P. Hepburn and Margaret Hepburn Chamberlain on his ancestry and boyhood. It was Hepburn's own estimate that the *Cong. Record* contained everything worth while he ever did.] L. B. S.

HEPWORTH, GEORGE HUGHES (Feb. 4, 1833–June 7, 1902), clergyman, editor, was born in Boston, Mass., the son of George Hepworth, machinist, a native of Dewsbury, England, by his second wife, Mrs. Charlotte (Salter) Smith. The latter, a sister of William Salter, the English painter, was born in London but was of French and Spanish descent on her mother's side. When George Hughes was six years old, the family moved to a farm in Newton where he acquired a love of outdoor life which he never lost. After a trip to Europe in 1844, the Hepworths lived in Boston again, and in 1846 George enrolled in the Latin School. His gift for writing early manifested itself in stories and verses contributed to the *South Boston Gazette*. His parents were Unitarians, and from boyhood he had anticipated becoming a minister. Accordingly, in 1852 he entered the Harvard Divinity School, from which he graduated in 1855.

His first parish was on the island of Nantucket, where, Sept. 12, 1855, at the Second Congregational Church, Unitarian, he was ordained. After two years' stay he returned to Cambridge for graduate work at the Divinity School; and on Oct. 6, 1858, he was installed pastor of the recently organized Church of the Unity, Boston, which he served until Oct. 6, 1869. On Apr. 25, 1860, he married Adaline A. Drury, daughter of Gardner P. Drury of Boston. Granted nine months' leave of absence in 1862, he accompanied the 47th Regiment to Louisiana as chaplain. General Banks secured him a commission as first lieutenant of the 4th Louisiana Native Guards, a negro regiment; detailed him as aide-de-camp; and made him supervisor of the negro labor system. After his return he published *The Whip, Hoe, and Sword* (1864), a highly partisan account of Southern life. The following year one of his sermons, *The Criminal; the Crime; the Penalty*, an intemperate arraignment of Jefferson Davis concluding with a demand for his execution, was issued. *Two Sermons* (1865) inspired by Lincoln's death, and a Fourth of July oration, 1867, voice the implacable post-war spirit of the North. His preaching—practical, fervid, colorful—attracted many. He was especially interested in bringing religion to the masses and in 1867 instituted theatre preaching in Boston. He also established the short-lived Boston School for Ministers, designed to train earnest young men for mission work.

In 1869 he became pastor of the Church of the Messiah, New York, and the following year published *Rocks and Shoals: Lectures to Young Men*. Evangelical in temperament, and having attempted without success to persuade the Unitarians to issue a positive statement of their beliefs, in 1872 he affiliated with the Congregationalists. The Church of the Disciples, institutional in its design, was organized, and he was its pastor until the spring of 1879. During this period he revealed his nautical knowledge and love for the sea in *Starboard and Port* (1876). At the time of the Irish famine in 1880 he was abroad, and James Gordon Bennett [*q.v.*] made him the American representative on the committee for the distribution of the *New York Herald's* relief fund. After his return he was pastor of the Belleville Avenue Congregational Church, Newark, until 1885, but became increasingly occupied with writing and editorial work. Besides contributing essays and stories to periodicals, he had for some time written "Chat by the Way" for the *Herald*, and in 1882 Bennett made him one of its editorial writers, appointing him superintending editor in 1885, and in 1893 putting the *Telegram* in his charge. Beginning in 1892 he published weekly sermons in the *Herald*, which attracted wide attention. Four volumes of these were printed, *Herald Sermons* (1894); *Herald Sermons* (1897); *We Shall Live Again* (1903); *Making the Most of Life* (1904). Among his other publications are *! ! !* (1881), a story suggested by the doctrine of reincarnation; *Hiram Golf's Religion* (1893), more than thirty-five thousand copies of which were sold; *Brown Studies, or Camp-Fires and Morals* (1895); *The Farmer and the Lord* (1896); *The Queerest Man Alive and Other Stories* (1897). In 1897 Bennett sent Hepworth to Anatolia to make a survey of the Armenian situation. His observations were published in *Through Armenia on Horseback* (1898), highly commended for its sound judgment and impartial spirit.

[Susan H. Ward, *George H. Hepworth* (1903); *Who's Who in America,* 1901–02; *Gen. Cat. of the Divinity School of Harvard Univ.* (1905); *N. Y. Herald,* June 9, 1902; *Independent* (N. Y.), June 12, 1902.]

H. E. S.

HERBERMANN, CHARLES GEORGE (Dec. 8, 1840–Aug. 24, 1916), editor, writer, teacher, was born at Saerbeck, Westphalia, Germany. He was the first of the seven children of George Herbermann, a native of Glandorf, Hanover, and his wife, Elizabeth Stipp of Osnabrück. At the age of nine he had completed the course at the village school and had begun the study of Latin. The family emigrated to New York where they landed on Jan. 21, 1851, after a tempestuous voyage of eighty-two days in the course of which two of the children, one of whom had been born on shipboard, died. Charles attended the parochial school attached to the Church of Saint Alphonsus for two years and then entered the College of Saint Francis Xavier. At his graduation in 1858 the degree of bachelor of arts was conferred on him by Saint John's College, the predecessor of Fordham University, since Saint Francis Xavier's College had not yet obtained its charter. For the next eleven years he taught at the college, continuing his studies and receiving the degrees of A.M. (Saint John's, 1860) and Ph.D. (Saint Francis Xavier's, 1865). On Nov. 1, 1869, he began his duties as professor of the Latin language and literature at the College of the City of New York. This institution he served for forty-five years, with broad and sound scholarship and patient and skilful pedagogy in the classroom, and with prudence and foresight in the faculty chamber. He published editions of Sallust's *Jugurthine War* (1886) and *Bellum Catilinæ* (1900).

In 1888 the *United States Catholic Historical Magazine* published Herbermann's translation from the Latin of Torfason's "History of Ancient Vinland." The United States Catholic Historical Society made him its president in 1898 and continued him in office until his death. Under his editorship of its publications, the Society enriched the field of Americana with such contributions as *Unpublished Letters of Charles Carroll of Carrollton* (1902) and *The Cosmographiæ Introductio of Martin Waldseemüller* (1907). The latter volume was a facsimile reprint of the original work published in 1507, with a translation into English and a facsimile of the first map on which appeared the name "America." In January 1905, he was appointed editor-in-chief of *The Catholic Encyclopedia,* an epochal product of Catholic scholarship, with fifteen hundred contributors from forty-three countries (vols. I–XV, 1913, vol. XVI, Index, 1914). During the progress of the work, Pope Pius X honored Herbermann with knighthood in the Order of Saint Gregory (1909), and again, at its completion (1913), with the medal *Pro Ecclesia et Pontifice.* In 1916, the year of his death, he published *The Sulpicians in the United States.*

Herbermann was twice married, first, in 1873, to Mary Theresa Dieter of Baltimore, who died in 1876, and second, in 1880, to Elizabeth Schoeb of New York City, a native of Marburg in Hesse, who died in 1893. He was the father of nine children, seven of whom survived him. A sufferer from glaucoma, he spent the last years of his life in total blindness, performing his scholarly tasks with the help of his children who read to him, wrote at his dictation, and accompanied him at all times. He died in his seventy-sixth year.

[*U. S. Cath. Hist. Soc., Hist. Records and Studies,* vol. X (1917); *City College Quart.* (N. Y.), Dec. 1916; *Who's Who in America,* 1916–17; *Cath. Hist. Rev.,* Jan. 1917; *America* (N. Y.), Sept. 2, 1916; *N. Y. Times,* Aug. 25, 1916.]

P. H. L.

HERBERT, HENRY WILLIAM (Apr. 7, 1807–May 17, 1858), writer, better known as Frank Forester, under which pseudonym he published the works on field sports for which he is chiefly remembered, was born in London, a descendant of English peers, educated at Eton and Cambridge, and after a colorful career in America died by his own hand in a New York hotel at the age of fifty-one. His father, Rev. William Herbert, son of Henry Herbert, first Earl of Carnarvon, was dean of Manchester, and a noted classicist, linguist, and naturalist; his mother was Hon. Letitia Emily Dorothea, daughter of Joshua, fifth Viscount Allen. The dean was an ardent sportsman and Henry, early taught to ride and shoot, acquired a passionate fondness for outdoor life. At the University he was prominent among the convivially inclined and a member of the Cambridge Yeomanry Cavalry, but graduated B.A. from Caius College in 1830 with a high reputation for scholarship, especially in the classics. Financial difficulties soon prompted him to leave England for the Continent and in 1831 he came to the United States.

Settling in New York, he was for some eight years Latin and Greek preceptor in a school conducted after the Eton plan by Rev. R. Townsend Huddart. Hunting and fishing expeditions, in which he took rare and intelligent delight, consumed much of his spare time. As a classical scholar he had few equals in this country, his *Prometheus and Agamemnon of Aeschylus, Translated into English Verse* (1849) receiving high praise from Prof. C. C. Felton (*North*

American Review, October 1849); his knowledge of English history and literature was extensive; he was a pen-and-ink artist of marked ability; as a sportsman he was unsurpassed; his pupils idolized him. He soon became acquainted with many of the leading writers of the day and began a literary career to which, after giving up teaching, he devoted himself almost exclusively. In a short time he was a well-known character, not only because of his brilliant gifts, but also because of his eccentricities. Always a *poseur,* he attracted attention on the street, "usually attired in sporting costume, and bearing a luxuriant moustache—an appendage rather unusual in those days—cavalier boots upon his feet, and massive King Charles' spurs setting off the whole" (*Frank Forester's Sporting Scenes and Characters,* 1881, pp. 15, 16). Later in life he frequently appeared in a checked suit with a Scotch plaid shawl thrown over his shoulder. In 1839 he married Sarah, daughter of John Barker of Bangor, Me., whom he met while he was on a hunting trip. She died in 1844, leaving him a son, William George, who was later sent to England and remained there. In 1845 Herbert built a cottage in a wooded retreat on the Passaic River near Newark which he called "The Cedars." Here, surrounded by his books and sporting accoutrements, he did much of his writing.

Happy and companionable as a sportsman, he had unfortunate characteristics which made his social life in general hectic and regrettable, and alienated his friends. He gloried in his English lineage and maintained aristocratic pretensions, was ambitious for literary recognition, sensitive, quarrelsome, and of violent temper; nevertheless, he held tenaciously to certain high standards and in his writing was extremely conscientious. In a letter penned just before his death, he declared: "I have put forth nothing that I did believe to be false or evil, or anything which I did not believe to be good and true."

His literary output was prodigious and varied. In 1833, with A. D. Patterson, a colleague of his at Huddart's school, he started the *American Monthly Magazine,* a rival of the *Knickerbocker.* He continued as editor until the end of 1835, when a quarrel with Charles Fenno Hoffman [*q.v.*], who had become associated with him, caused him to retire. In the meantime, 1835, he had published anonymously his first historical romance, *The Brothers, a Tale of the Fronde,* which was well received. This was followed by a number of others, several of which went through more than one edition and were republished abroad. In general, however, they were prolix, lacking in imagination and humor, and in their studied fidelity to fact, more historical than romantic. In his later years he turned to purely historical writings, such as *The Knights of England, France and Scotland* (1852); and *The Captains of the Roman Republic* (1854). All the while he was contributing to periodicals and turning out miscellaneous work of various kinds including translations of some of the novels of Eugène Sue and Alexandre Dumas. His poems were numerous and of considerable merit. Selections from them, *Poems of "Frank Forester,"* with a memoir of the author by Morgan Herbert (Margaret Morgan Herbert Mather) were published in 1888.

He consented in 1839 to write a series of articles for the *American Turf Register,* lately acquired by William T. Porter [*q.v.*]. In order that they might not interfere with his ambition to be known as a writer of great romances, he concealed their authorship under the pseudonym, Frank Forester. Although of secondary importance in his own estimation, his contributions to the literature of field sports, of which these sketches were the beginning, are the portion of his work which has greatest interest and permanent value. They were published in 1845 under the title, *The Warwick Woodlands, or Things as They Were There Ten Years Ago*; a second edition, *The Warwick Woodlands,* illustrated by the author, appeared in 1851. The background is that of Orange County, N. Y., country of which Herbert was especially fond. He wrote with enthusiasm and spirit; his characters are skilfully portrayed; humor is not lacking; the descriptions are accurate and vivid; and through all a thread of poetic imagination runs. In 1846 *My Shooting Box* and in 1849 *The Deerstalkers* were issued, both of which had appeared in part in *Graham's Magazine.* A work of some scope, *Frank Forester's Field Sports of the United States, and British Provinces, of North America,* was issued in 1849, in two volumes, having appeared in London the previous year under a slightly different title. It has since gone through many editions and is still considered an authority. *Frank Forester's Fish and Fishing of the United States and British Provinces of North America* was issued in London in 1849 and in New York in 1850. In 1852 he published *The Quorndon Hounds; or A Virginian at Melton Mowbray,* and in 1857, *Frank Forester's Horse and Horsemanship of the United States and British Provinces of North America,* two volumes, a work to which all writers on sport of early times must turn. Many of his writings are illustrated by his own drawings. With respect to *Fish and Fishing* he states: "All the cuts were drawn by myself, on wood, either from the dead fishes themselves, or from original drawings in the possession of Professor Agassiz." In 1856 he brought out *The Complete Manual for Young Sportsmen.* As a pioneer in this field he made a distinct contribution both to American literature and to sportsmanship.

In February 1858, Herbert married Adela R. Budlong of Providence, R. I. Not many weeks afterward she left him. Her desertion threw him into one of his frequent moods of melancholy and on May 17, in the Stevens House, New York, he shot himself. His remains were buried in Mount Pleasant Cemetery, Newark, and eighteen years later the Newark Herbert Association erected a simple stone at his grave. In 1881 *Frank Forester's Sporting Scenes and Characters,* two volumes, edited by Will Wildwood (Fred E. Pond), was published, and in 1882, the *Life and Writings of Frank Forester,* two volumes, edited by D. W. Judd with memoir by Thomas Picton. On Oct. 23, 1920, a memorial to him by the sportsmen of America was unveiled at Warwick, Orange County, N. Y. In 1930 the Hitchcock edition of his sporting novels was issued.

[John Venn, *Biog. Hist. of Gonville and Caius College 1349–1897,* vol. II (1898); memoirs by "Will Wildwood" (Fred E. Pond) in *Frank Forester's Fugitive Sporting Sketches* (1879) and *Frank Forester's Sporting Scenes and Characters* (1881), vol. I; *The Newark Herbert Association to "Frank Forester": In Memoriam* (1876); *Dict. of Nat. Biog.,* in which date of birth is incorrectly given; *International Mag.,* June 1, 1851; *Porter's Spirit of the Times,* May 22, Aug. 21, 1858; F. L. Mott, *A Hist. of Am. Magazines* (1930); E. B. Hornby, *Under Old Rooftrees* (1908); *N. Y. Herald, N. Y. Times,* and *N. Y. Tribune,* May 18, 1858; *N. Y. Herald,* Nov. 26, 1893; *Warwick Valley Dispatch,* Oct. 27, 1920; *The Spur,* June 15, 1922; *N. Y. Herald Tribune,* Nov. 9, 1924; *Saturday Rev. of Lit.,* Jan. 10, 1925; *N. Y. Herald Tribune,* Nov. 30, 1930; *N. Y. Evening Post,* Aug. 29, 1931. The best collection of Forester material is in the possession of Harry Worcester Smith, No. Grafton, Mass., who has made some of it available for use in this sketch; see also his introductions to *The Warwick Woodlands* (1921, 1924), and his memoir of Forester in the Hitchcock Edition of Frank Forester, vol. IV (1930).] H. E. S.

HERBERT, HILARY ABNER (Mar. 12, 1834–Mar. 6, 1919), Confederate soldier, congressman, secretary of the navy, was born at Laurensville, now Laurens, S. C. He was descended from English ancestors who settled in Virginia in 1630. His father, Thomas Edward Herbert, was a planter; his mother, Dorothy Teague Young, had been educated in a Moravian school for young women at Salem, N. C., and was the founder of a successful school for girls which was continued after her marriage in Laurens and, after 1847, in Greenville, Ala. Thomas Herbert had many advanced theories of education which he applied in the rearing of his son. Hilary was ready for college at sixteen, but his father regarded him as too young to begin a college course, and kept him on the plantation two years longer. He entered the sophomore class at the University of Alabama in 1853 and quickly became a leader of the group. This was the year of "Doty's Rebellion," when the sophomore class withdrew from school in indignation at the treatment of one of their number by the faculty. Hilary left with his class and never returned. In 1855 he entered the University of Virginia, but was forced to withdraw after one year because of ill health. He began reading law in 1856 and after four months passed the required examinations and was admitted to the bar. He practised in Greenville until the outbreak of the Civil War.

Entering the Confederate army as a second lieutenant of the Greenville Guards, he went with his company when it was ordered to Mobile to take charge of the fort. When the Guards were incorporated in the 8th Alabama Infantry in May 1861 he was made captain of the company. He was given the rank of major during the Peninsula campaign and later was promoted to that of lieutenant-colonel. At Fair Oaks he was wounded and captured, but was exchanged after two months. He fought at Manassas, Fredericksburg, Antietam, and Gettysburg. He was permanently disabled in the Wilderness and retired from active service in 1864. Although he was only a lieutenant-colonel, he had commanded his regiment and was retired with the rank of colonel because of the protest of his fellow officers, who urged that his gallantry in action had earned the reward of promotion.

Herbert resumed the practice of law in 1864 at Greenville, and on Apr. 23, 1867, married Ella B. Smith of Selma, Ala. In 1872 he opened an office in Montgomery. Five years later he was elected to Congress from the Montgomery district, which he represented for sixteen years. He attracted attention in his first session when he opposed a forty-million-dollar appropriation for the building of the Texas & Pacific Railroad, in spite of a memorial from the Alabama legislature demanding his vote for the project. When the supporters of the measure carried the fight to his district in the next election, the district supported Herbert. He was a member of the committee on ways and means and three times chairman of the committee on naval affairs. In the latter capacity he was largely responsible for the increased appropriations which led to the revival of the American navy. In 1893 he was appointed secretary of the navy in President Cleveland's cabinet. He had a definite program in view which centered construction work upon battle-ships and torpedo boats and, constantly urging increased construction upon a reluctant Congress, he was able in spite of the financial depression to get support for an enlarged navy. He was one of the authors of *Why the Solid South? or, Reconstruction and Its Results* (1890), a book of propaganda designed to arouse public opinion in the North against the Force Bill which was before Congress at that time. Dedicated to the Northern business man, it attracted no little attention, winning favor as a fair presentation of the Southern white man's view of the problem of negro suffrage. In 1912 Herbert published *The Abolition Crusade and its Consequences.* From 1897 to the end of his life he practised law in Washington. He died in Tampa, Fla., shortly before his eighty-fifth birthday.

[T. M. Owen, *Hist. of Ala. and Dict. of Ala. Biog.* (1921), vol. III; *Memorial Record of Ala.* (1893), vol. II; B. F. Riley, *Makers and Romance of Ala. Hist.* (n.d., 1915); *Who's Who in America,* 1918–19; *Confed. Veteran,* June, July 1919; *Evening Star* (Washington, D. C.), Mar. 6, 1919; *Montgomery Advertiser,* Mar. 7, 1919; manuscript material in the Ala. Dept. of Archives and Hist., Montgomery.] H. F.

HERBERT, VICTOR (Feb. 1, 1859–May 26, 1924), musician, the son of Edward Herbert and Fanny Lover, the daughter of the Irish novelist Samuel Lover, was born in Dublin, Ireland. He was sent to Germany at seven to study music and specialized in the 'cello under Cossman at Baden. After appearing as a solo 'cellist in Germany, France, and Italy, he became first 'cellist of Strauss's orchestra in Vienna in 1882, and from 1883 to 1886 he was with the Stuttgart court orchestra. In Stuttgart he studied composition with Max Seifritz and wrote his "Suite in F" for 'cello and orchestra. In 1886 he met and married Therese Förster, prima donna at the Vienna *Hofoper,* and came to America as first 'cellist at the Metropolitan Opera House. Later he held the same place in Thomas' orchestra, and then in the New York Philharmonic Society, conducted by Seidl, in which he was also assistant conductor. From 1888 to 1891 he was an associate conductor at the festivals in Worcester, Mass., where in 1891 his oratorio, *The Captive,* was performed. In 1893 he succeeded Gilmore as bandmaster of the 22nd Regiment, New York National Guard. From 1898 until 1904 he was the conductor of the Pittsburgh Symphony Orchestra, then after 1904 he conducted his own—Victor Herbert's New York Orchestra—appearing at times as guest conductor with other orchestras.

In 1893 Herbert launched upon his career as a composer of comic opera when William MacDonald, manager of the Bostonians, induced him to write a light opera for his company. The result, *Prince Ananias,* produced in New York Nov. 20, 1894, determined Herbert's musical future. From that time on his main energies were devoted to dramatic music. *Prince Ananias* was but the first of a series of comic operas which in quantity of output exceeded and in imaginative quality often excelled, the operas of Sullivan. *The Wizard of the Nile* (1895); *The Serenade* and *The Idol's Eye* (1897); *The Fortune Teller* (1898), Alice Nielsen's greatest hit; *Babes in Toyland* (1903); *Mlle. Modiste* (1905), containing the waltz-song "Kiss Me Again"; and *The Red Mill* (1906), were immediately successful and some of them have been many times revived. Later works included *Little Nemo* (1908); *Naughty Marietta* (1910); *The Madcap Duchess* and *Sweethearts* (1913); *Princess Pat* (1915); and *Her Regiment* (1917). Herbert also wrote the musical scores of the Ziegfeld Follies of 1919, 1921, and 1924. In his later years his spontaneity flagged, and unlike Sullivan, he did not always have a Gilbert for a librettist. That his remarkable gift of musical invention would have found an even richer development in grand opera seems certain. His *Natoma* (Philadelphia, 1911), set to an inadequate book, remains, musically, one of the best among American grand operas; his shorter score in the same form, *Madeleine* (New York Metropolitan, 1914) shows his mastery of humorous descriptive music. His comic opera triumphs did not console him for his unrealized dream of grand opera composition. He made a successful departure as a dramatic composer in 1916, however, in the elaborate dramatic score for the photoplay *The Birth of a Nation* and later wrote the music for *Little Old New York, The Great White Way,* and *Yolanda.* His non-dramatic compositions include piano pieces, songs, male choruses, a symphonic poem, "Hero and Leander," and three suites for orchestra. His "Second 'Cello Concerto" he himself played with the New York Philharmonic Society, Mar. 10, 1894.

Herbert was generous and impulsive by nature and was devoted to his friends. Retaining a love for his native country he was active in many Irish societies and at the time of his death was president of the Friendly Sons of St. Patrick and the Sons of Irish Freedom. He was one of the founders of the American Society of Composers, Authors, and Publishers, which endeavored to prevent radio corporations from broadcasting copyrighted music without payment, and shortly before his death he headed a delegation which presented the Society's case in Washington. As a musician, largely through the radio dissemination of his works, he attained a popularity which no other American composer had won. In 1913, when he was at the height of his career, it was said of him that "his characteristic utterance is in its way as distinctive, as individual, as free as that of every great foreign composer of comic opera from Strauss to Arthur Sullivan" (H. F. Peyser, in *Musical America,* Oct. 11, 1913), and Deems Taylor, writing at the time of his death (*New York World,* June 1, 1924), said of him that he had "raised light opera music to a degree of harmonic sophistication that it had never before reached."

[Rupert Hughes and Arthur Elson, *Am. Composers* (1914); *Jour. of the Am. Soc. of Composers, Authors, and Publishers,* Dec. 1927; *Musical America,* May 31, 1924, giving a full bibliography of Herbert's compositions; *Musical Observer,* Aug. 1923; *Musical Courier,* Mar. 3, 1927; *N. Y. Times,* May 27, 29, 1924; *N. Y. Herald Tribune,* May 27, 1924.] F. H. M.

HERDIC, PETER (Dec. 14, 1824–Mar. 2, 1888), lumberman, inventor, was the son of Henry Herdic and was born on a farm at Fort Plains, N. Y. His father died when Peter was still an infant and his mother with her seven children moved to Ithaca, N. Y., in 1826. Four years later upon her second marriage she settled with her family on a farm near Ithaca. Here the boy lived until he was thirteen years old and secured a bit of schooling. In 1837 his stepfather died and the family settled on a virgin tract of land on Pipe Creek, N. Y. Herdic and his brothers cleared and cultivated the land, built a home, and in every way aided in the support of the family. In 1844 when he was twenty years old Herdic began to work for a lumberman and through earnest application and hard work learned the business and added to his capital as well. Two years later he went to Lycoming County, Pa., and near Williamsport began the operation of a shingle mill. His earnings in three years enabled him to purchase a farm of 150 acres in the neighborhood and to build a modest home to which he took his bride, Amanda Taylor, whom he married on Christmas Day, 1849. For the succeeding four years he operated his farm and a steam sawmill as well. Then in 1853 he moved to Williamsport, and from that time on until his death his seemingly inexhaustible energy was directed toward the development and growth of that city. He purchased hundreds of acres of land on which he erected mills and factories, and he induced manufacturers to establish themselves there. Residences, stores, bank buildings, and hotels rose as if by magic, and municipal projects such as water-works, gas-manufacturing plants, and street-paving jobs became actualities under his guiding hand, especially during his term as mayor following his election in 1869.

In 1878 Herdic failed with large liabilities and all of his undertakings in Williamsport had to be abandoned. Shortly afterward he became interested in city and interurban transportation and turned his attention first to the design of a suitable vehicle. On Apr. 20, 1880, he obtained his first patent for an improved vehicle running-gear and a few months later, on June 8, he patented a fare-collecting box to be used on his proposed coach and cab. He then removed to Philadelphia, Pa., where he organized the Herdic Coach Company and began the construction of coaches and the operation of transport lines. The "Herdic" soon became popular; its inventor continued to improve it, and in a measure his fortune was restored. Unfortunately, however, he met with an accident while on a business trip to New York which caused his death there within a month. Herdic's first wife died in 1856 and on Jan. 12, 1860, he married Encie E. Maynard who with two sons survived him. He was buried in Williamsport.

[E. Collins and J. W. Jordan, *Geneal. and Personal Hist. of Lycoming County, Pa.* (1906), vol. I; *N. Y. Times,* Mar. 3, 1888; *Ann. Report of the Commissioner of Patents for the Year 1880* (1881).] C. W. M—n.

HERING, CARL (Mar. 29, 1860–May 10, 1926), electrical engineer, was born at Philadelphia, Pa., the son of Constantine [*q.v.*] and Theresa (Buckheim) Hering, and a younger brother of Rudolph Hering [*q.v.*]. He was educated at Lauterbach's Academy in Philadelphia and at the University of Pennsylvania, from which he received the degree of B.S. in 1880. He remained at the university as an instructor and in 1882 became interested in electrical engineering, then a new course of study. Upon the completion of the courses offered at Pennsylvania, Hering continued his study at the Polytechnikum at Darmstadt, Germany, 1883–84, and in 1885 obtained a position as an electrical engineer with Henry Moehring & Company, manufacturers of electrical machines at Frankfurt-am-Main. In 1886 he returned to the United States, received the degree of M.E. from the University of Pennsylvania, and began the practice of consulting engineer at Philadelphia. He continued his studies and extended them to include researches in the new fields of electrochemistry and electrophysics. He investigated the regeneration of battery solutions and patented several improvements in battery construction. In 1900 he began the study of electric furnaces when making tests for the reduction of arsenic ores. Six years later his experiments resulted in the design of an electric furnace in which the electromagnetic force known as the "pinch effect" was employed. This force, which tends to contract any conductor through which a current is flowing, was used to impart a desirable circulating motion to the molten mass within the furnace. The furnace which he developed required close adjustment of many elements and was too delicate of operation to enjoy more than a limited commercial use. In 1892 Hering became technical editor of *Electrical World* and in 1893 established the *Digest of Current Electrical Literature* in connection with this publication. In 1902 he was instrumental in founding *Electrochemical Industry,* which later became *Chemical and Metallurgical Engineering.* Before 1890 he was well known in the profession and was sent as a delegate to many of the important expositions and congresses, including the Electrical Exhibition in Vienna, 1883, the Paris Exposition, 1889, and the International Electrical Congress in Paris, 1900. In 1889 the French government appointed him an Officer of Public Instruction and in 1891 made him a Knight of the Legion of Honor. He was president of the American Institute of Electrical Engineers 1900–01, and a founder and president of the American Electrochemical Society, 1906–07. His published works include: *Principles of Dynamo-Electric Machines* (1888); *Table of Equivalents of Units of Measurements* (1888); *Universal Wiring Computer* (1891); *Ready Reference Tables* (1904); and a *Standard Table of Electrochemical Equivalents and Their Derivatives* (1917). He also published a *Road Book of Pennsylvania* (1900) and compiled a summary of *Recent Progress in Electric Railways* (1892). Hering married Harriet Truesdell, by whom he had one child. He died at Philadelphia.

[*Jour. of the Am. Inst. of Electrical Engineers,* June 1926; *Electrical World,* May 15, 22, 1926; *Chem. and Metallurgical Engineering,* May 1926; F. J. Moffett, *The Electric Furnace* (1921); *Studies in Applied Electricity* (1901); *Phila. Record,* May 11, 1926; *Pa. Gazette,* May 21, 1926.]

F. A. T.

HERING, CONSTANTINE (Jan. 1, 1800–July 23, 1880), physician, homeopathist, was born in Oschatz, Saxony, the son of Christian Gottlieb Karl Hering, an accomplished musician and educator, and of Christiane Friedericke (Kreutzberg) Hering. At the age of eleven he was placed in the classical school at Zittau, where he displayed strong interest in natural history and made a valuable collection of minerals, herbs, and bones. He began his medical studies at the Surgical Academy of Dresden in 1820 and subsequently attended the University of Leipzig, taking seven courses in medicine. While there he became a special pupil and assistant of J. Henry Robbi, a celebrated French surgeon who had served under Napoleon. When a publishing house requested Robbi to prepare a pamphlet inveighing against homeopathy, designed to deal a deathblow to that rising system of therapeutics, Robbi declined the assignment but made the suggestion that it be given to young Hering. The latter accepted the task with enthusiasm and proceeded, with the industry that characterized him throughout life, to make his work one of superexcellence. Studying, to this end, the teachings of Hahnemann, he became converted to Hahnemann's theories. His convictions were soon strengthened by a personal experience: he contracted a severely infected dissecting wound which seemed to demand amputation, but homeopathic prescribing—the remedy being arsenicum—effected a cure without the aid of surgery. Attracted by the reputation of Schönlein, he pursued further studies in the University of Würzburg, from which institution he received his diploma in medicine, surgery, and obstetrics on Mar. 23, 1826. Following graduation, he was appointed teacher in mathematics and the natural sciences at the Blochmann Institute in Dresden, a school for the education of young noblemen. After several months of work here, upon the recommendation of the president of the school to the King of Saxony, Hering was delegated to go to Surinam in South America to make researches in zoology. His ability and industry while in Surinam enabled him in addition to his zoological researches to engage in some medical practice, study drug action, and contribute articles to Stapf's *Archiv.* These outside activities were disapproved by the physician to the King; the Minister of the Interior wrote Hering a letter of criticism, and the young scientist promptly resigned, although no fault had been found with the character of his research work. He then practised medicine in Paramaribo, and there began his studies of the venomous Lachesis and made provings of numerous remedies. One of his enthusiastic pupils, Dr. George H. Bute, a Moravian missionary, left South America in 1831 for the United States and began practice at Nazareth, Pa. At his solicitation, in 1833, Hering took up his residence in Philadelphia, where he practised medicine until his death.

He was instrumental in organizing, at Allentown, Pa., in 1835, the first school of homeopathic therapeutics in the world—the North American Academy of the Homeopathic Healing Art, chartered June 17, 1836. He was president and principal instructor until 1842, when the institution was obliged to close its doors for want of funds. Two years later Hering presided at the first session of the American Institute of Homeopathy (1844). In 1848, with Jacob Jeanes and Walter Williamson, he founded the Homeopathic Medical College of Pennsylvania. He was elected professor of materia medica in the first faculty, but resigned before the beginning of the session. In 1864 he accepted the chair of institutes of homeopathy and practice of medicine, which he held for three years. In 1867, when the controlling stockholder decided to abolish the chair of pathology, Hering resigned, being followed by several members of the faculty. Securing a charter, he immediately formed a new college, the Hahnemann Medical College of Philadelphia, with which, two years later, the Homeopathic Medical College united. Of the new institution Hering was dean, 1867–71. He also served as professor of institutes and materia medica, 1867–69, 1870–71, and of institutes and practice, 1869–70. From 1876 until his death he was professor emeritus of institutes and materia medica.

Throughout his long career Hering was an indefatigable worker. Bradford's *Homœopathic Bibliography* credits him with 325 articles, mostly on remedies and their indications, and eighty-nine books and pamphlets. His first important work was *The Homœopathist or Domestic Physician* (pt. 1, 1835; pt. 2, 1838), which passed through fourteen editions in German; seven editions in the United States, and two in England; it was also translated into French, Spanish, Italian, Danish, Swedish, and Russian. From 1851 to 1853 he was one of the editors of the *North American Homœopathic Journal*; from 1854 to 1856, of the *Homœopathic News,* and from 1867 to 1871, of the *American Homœopathic Materia Medica.* He was the author of *Materia Medica* (1873), *Analytical Therapeutics* (1875), and *Condensed Materia Medica* (1877). He translated from the German R. H. Gross's *Comparative Materia Medica* (1867). His *opus magnum* was *Guiding Symptoms* (10 vols., 1878–91). He died while arranging the third volume; the remaining seven were published under the supervision of his literary executors. Hering was an indefatigable "prover," over eighty remedies standing to his credit. His most notable work in this line was that which he began in 1828 on Lachesis. He was an ardent admirer of Paracelsus, of whose writings he had a notable collection, which after his death was deposited in the library of the Hahnemann Medical College of Philadelphia.

Hering's medical teachings were liberal; his examinations of patients were complete, including the investigation of all data, organic, functional, and mental. He contended that anatomy, physiology, chemistry, pathology, surgery, and diagnosis were essential to the homeopathic practitioner, herein bringing upon himself the criticism of less liberal colleagues. He was married three times, first, in 1829, to Charlotte Kemper, who died in 1831; second, to Marianne Hussmann, who died in 1840; and third, in 1845, while on a visit to Germany, to Theresa Buckheim, who survived him. Carl and Rudolph Hering [*qq.v.*] were his sons. Hering died in his eighty-first year. In religious faith he was a Swedenborgian.

[*A Memorial of Constantine Hering, . . . 1800–1880* (Phila., n.d.); "Dr. Constantine Hering," by his daughter, in *Mittheilungen des Deutschen Pionier-Vereins von Philadelphia,* 1907; A. M. Eastman, "Life and Reminiscences of Dr. Constantine Hering," in *Hahnemannian Monthly,* Aug. 1917; Herman Faber, in *Jour. Am. Inst. of Homeopathy,* June, July, Aug. 1915; T. L. Bradford's "Biographies of Homeopathic Physicians," vol. XVI, in library of Hahnemann Medic. Coll., Phila.; T. L. Bradford, *Homœopathic Bibliography of the U. S., 1825–91* (1892), *The Pioneers of Homœopathy* (1897), and *Hist. of Hahnemann Medic. Coll. and Hospital of Phila.* (1898); Egbert Cleave, *Biog. Cyc. of Homœopathic Physicians and Surgeons* (1873); W. H. King, *Hist. of Homœopathy and its Institutions in America* (1905), vol. I; *Trans. of the World's Homœopathic Convention Held at Phila., 1876,* II (1880), 773–98; H. A. Kelly and W. L. Burrage, *Am. Medic. Biogs.* (1920); *Phila. Press,* July 26, 1880; appreciation by Rudolph Hering, in *Jour. Am. Inst. of Homeopathy,* Feb. 1919.]
C. B.

HERING, RUDOLPH (Feb. 26, 1847–May 30, 1923), pioneer sanitary engineer, brother of Carl Hering [*q.v.*], was born at Philadelphia, Pa., the son of Dr. Constantine Hering [*q.v.*], one of the founders of homeopathy in America, and of his third wife, Theresa (Buckheim) Hering. At the age of thirteen, Rudolph was sent to Germany where he attended the Dresden public high school and later the Royal Polytechnical School, from which he was graduated in 1867 as a civil engineer. He then returned to the United States and worked on the surveys for Prospect Park in Brooklyn, N. Y., and the extension of Fairmount Park in Philadelphia. In 1872 he went to the Yellowstone as an astronomical observer with the government party sent to explore this newly established national park. Returning to Philadelphia, he entered the office of the city engineer, and from 1876 to 1880 served as assistant city engineer in charge of bridges and sewers. Though his first work in this office was in connection with the construction of the Girard Street Bridge, his later work had more to do with sewage disposal and definitely established his interest in that field, in which very little real engineering had been done. In 1880 serious yellow-fever epidemics in many cities of the United States caused the National Board of Health to consider more fully the problems of city sewage disposal. To further this investigation Hering was sent abroad to study European practice. His *Report on European Sewerage Systems,* published in 1881, was the first comprehensive American writing in the field, and remained for many years the most important work on the principles of sanitary engineering. Upon his return from this survey, Hering opened an office in Philadelphia and began his practice as a consulting sanitary engineer, probably the first in the country. From 1882 to 1885 he supervised an exhaustive study of new sources of water supply for Philadelphia, and from 1885 to 1887 acted as chief engineer for the Drainage and Water Supply Commission of Chicago, the report of which was the basis for the establishment of the Chicago Drainage Canal. He then moved to New York, where he practised for more than thirty years. It is estimated that in the course of his career he made reports for more than 250 cities and towns in North and South America. He made water-supply investigations for the cities of Philadelphia, Washington, New Orleans, Columbus, Montreal, Quebec, and Toronto, and was a member of the Burr-Hering-Freeman Commission that made the report (1903) on an additional water supply for New York City, which was the basis for the Catskill Aqueduct project. In the field of sewage disposal he was associated with most of the larger undertakings in America and was called the dean of sanitary engineers. President Harrison appointed him (1889) chairman of a commission to prepare a program for sewerage improvements for Washington, D. C., and he was engineer for the sewerage systems of Mexico City and of Santos, Brazil. He wrote extensively on the subject of hydraulics for technical journals. In collaboration with John C. Trautwine, Jr., he translated *A General Formula for the Uniform Flow of Water in Rivers and Other Channels* (1889), by E. Ganguillet and W. R. Kutter. This translation introduced American and English engineers to the important Kutter's Formula for determining the mean velocity of flow of water in open channels. Hering had previously (January 1879) expanded this formula in a paper in the *Transactions* of the American Society of Civil Engineers (vol. VIII, 1879). After 1917 he confined most of his time to writing *Collection and Disposal of Municipal Refuse* (1921), of which he was joint author with Samuel A. Greeley. Hering was a member of many engineering and scientific societies in both America and Europe. In recognition of his work the American Society of Civil Engineers established the Rudolph Hering Medal, to be awarded for the best contributions to its *Transactions* on the fundamentals of sanitary engineering. He was married twice: in 1872 to Fanny Field Gregory, by whom he had two children, and in 1894, to Hermine Buckheim, by whom he had three children. He died in New York City.

[*Trans. Am. Soc. Civil Engineers,* vol. LXXXVII (1924); *Proc. Am. Soc. for Testing Materials,* vol. XXIII (1923); *Who's Who in America,* 1908–09; *Fire and Water Engineering,* June 6, 1923; *Am. Jour. Pub. Health,* July 1923; *N. Y. Times,* May 31, 1923.]

F. A. T.

HERKIMER, NICHOLAS (1728–Aug. 16, 1777), a Revolutionary officer, was born near the present town of Herkimer, N. Y., the son of Johan Jost and Katharine Herkimer. The family, whose German name was written Herchheimer or Erghemer, emigrated from the Rhine Palatinate, and various members received grants of land in the Mohawk Valley in 1725. Nicholas became acquainted with woodcraft and was a lieutenant of militia in the French and Indian War, defending Fort Herkimer against an attack by Indians. He acquired moderate wealth, and as the Revolution drew on, he became chairman of the Committee of Safety of Tryon County (Mohawk Valley). Already a colonel, he was made brigadier-general of militia, charged with the local defense against Indian and Tory attacks. The Valley was badly divided in sentiment, and nowhere in the state was the feeling between Whigs and Loyalists so bitter. It was a civil war, separating neighbors and even members of families. In 1776 Herkimer led a force against Sir John Johnson. The crisis came in the following year, with Burgoyne's invasion by way of Lake Champlain, and, a more immediate danger to the Valley, St. Leger's band of Tories and Indians advancing on Fort Schuyler (Fort Stanwix) by way of Oswego. Herkimer issued a proclamation July 17, calling out the militia, and later appointed a rendezvous at Fort Dayton (Herkimer). Starting from his home near Little Falls, he collected his men, about eight hundred in number, and marched to the relief of Fort Schuyler.

As he neared the fort, Herkimer attempted to arrange with its commandant for a combined attack on St. Leger and a sortie from the fort. The march had been conducted incautiously, and the General, overruled by his officers and taunted unjustly with cowardice, gave the order to proceed. Near the modern village of Oriskany his army was ambushed in a heavily wooded country whose chief feature was a ravine. The hostile detachment, mainly of Tories and Indians, was commanded by Butler and the famous chief Brant. The battle in the woods was long and desperate, and especially bitter because it bore the character of civil warfare, though the exaggerated accounts of extreme and gruesome ferocity are unfounded. During the fight, which was temporarily suspended by a sharp thunderstorm, Herkimer was severely wounded in the leg. The familiar story tells how he was placed at the foot of a tree and thence directed the struggle. The Americans fell back and retreated down the valley, taking Herkimer with them to his home. He died less than a fortnight after the battle as the result of an unskilful amputation of his leg. The loss of the enemy is estimated as between seventy and a hundred. The Americans had probably more than two hundred killed, and almost as many wounded or taken as prisoners. It was therefore one of the bloodiest fights in the war. It has been variously described as a drawn battle; a British victory, because the Americans retreated; an American victory, on account of its effect on the larger issues, St. Leger's repulse and Burgoyne's failure. A monument was erected on the battle-field in 1884. The campaign, to an unusual degree, has been the subject of illustrative literature, the best example of which is Harold Frederic's *In the Valley* (1890). Herkimer was twice married. His first wife was Lany Dygert (Tygert) and the second was Myra Dygert (Tygert), a niece of the first. He had no children by either marriage.

[Sources include: Phoebe Strong Cowen, *The Herkimers and Schuylers* (1903); *Eighteenth Ann. Report, 1913, of the Am. Scenic and Hist. Preservation Soc.* (1913); W. W. Campbell, *Annals of Tryon County* (ed. 1924); Daniel Häberle, *Aus Wanderung und Koloniegründungen der Pfälzer in 18. Jahrhundert* (1909); Henry R. Schoolcraft, "Hist. Considerations on the Siege and Defence of Fort Stanwix in 1776," in App. to *Proc. N. Y. Hist. Soc. . . . 1845* (1846); Ellis H. Roberts, *The Battle of Oriskany: Its Place in Hist.* (1877); C. W. Schlegel, *Schlegel's German-Am. Families in the U. S.*, vol. I (1916); W. L. Stone, *Life of Jos. Brant* (1838), vol. I; and W. M. Willett, *A Narrative of the Mil. Actions of Col. Marinus Willett, Taken Chiefly from His Own Manuscript* (1831). Date of death is taken from F. B. Heitman, *Hist. Reg. of Officers of the Continental Army* (1914).] E. K. A.

HERMAN, LEBRECHT FREDERICK (Oct. 2, 1761–Jan. 30, 1848), German Reformed clergyman, was born at Güsten in the principality of Anhalt-Cöthen, the son of Johann Friedrich Gottlieb Herrmann, an organist and school teacher, by his wife, Dorothea Wartman. He was an inmate for six years of the Halle Orphanage, matriculated May 10, 1781, at the University of Halle, became a teacher and vicar in Bremen, and was ordained at The Hague in February 1786 for the Coetus of Pennsylvania. He was pastor at Easton, Plainfield, Dryland, and Greenwich, Pa., 1786–90, and at Germantown and Frankford, succeeding J. A. C. Helffenstein [*q.v.*], 1790–1800. In 1787 he married Maria Johanna Feidt. For the ten days Nov. 1–10, 1793, he had Washington for a boarder at the Germantown parsonage, the President paying him $37.94 for three rooms, breakfasts, suppers, and candles for himself and Bartholomew Dandridge. Herman, it is recorded, declined to provide the dinners also. Although he used English as much as possible in conversation, he found it so burdensome to preach in that language on alternate Sundays that he resigned in 1800 and accepted the Falkner Swamp, Pottstown, and Vincent charge, where he remained for the rest of his long life. Like the other ministers of his generation he preached at a number of places as opportunity offered and was instrumental in organizing several congregations. As a theological preceptor he wielded a far-reaching influence over his denomination, his house at Pottstown becoming famous as the "Swamp College." He gave his pupils a systematic three-years course of instruction in the classical languages, exegesis, and dogmatics, and made them speak Latin at the table. Five of his six sons became ministers. His *Catechismus* (Reading, 1813), a simplification of the *Heidelberg Catechism*, went through four editions. By maintaining a respectable educational standard during the long, critical period from the founding of the Synod of the United States to the growth of an efficient seminary under its control, Herman performed a useful service with his "Swamp College," but trouble eventually arose. In 1820, in order to kill competition with its projected seminary at Frederick, Md., the Synod passed a resolution forbidding its ministers to direct the theological studies of candidates. The next year Herman's gifted but wayward son Frederick was deposed from the ministry and his father notified of the action in a manner definitely though perhaps unintentionally offensive. Insult having thus been added to injury, Herman and his friends left the Synod and organized at Maxatawny, Apr. 24, 1822, the Synod of the Free German Reformed Congregations of Pennsylvania. This synod grew to include fifty-seven ministers and more than one hundred congregations and received support, not entirely desired, from anti-clericals like the erratic Carl Gock of Lancaster. In 1837 it returned in a body to the mother synod. Herman survived all his friends and contemporaries and, though blind and greatly distressed by the death of his wife, remained in good health and spirits until the end. He died at Pottstown in his eighty-seventh year.

[Sketch by Ruben T. Herman, a son, appended to *Gebet-Liebling, enthaltend Morgen und Abend-Segen für jeden Tag der Woche nebst mehreren andern Gebeten* (1850); Henry Harbaugh, *The Fathers of the German Reformed Church*, vol. II (1858); *Minutes and Letters of the Coetus of the German Reformed Congregations in Pa. 1747–92* (1903); D. N. Schaeffer, "Rev. Lebrecht Frederick Herman, D.D.," *Pa.-German*, Mar. 1909; J. I. Good, *Hist. of the Reformed Church in the U. S. in the Nineteenth Century* (1911); C. F. Jenkins, *Washington in Germantown* (1905); information from Prof. Wm. J. Hinke.] G. H. G.

HERNDON, WILLIAM HENRY (Dec. 25, 1818–Mar. 18, 1891), law partner of Abraham Lincoln, was born in Greensburg, Ky. His mother, Rebecca (Day) Johnson, in 1816 had taken as her second husband Archer G. Herndon, who moved to Illinois in 1820, settling in Sangamon County in 1821 and in Springfield in 1825. Here he engaged in politics and business. William Herndon entered the preparatory department of Illinois College, only to imbibe its anti-slavery atmosphere. An emphatic public utterance on the death of Lovejoy caused his father to recall him, and a breach developed between father and son. Herndon was a great admirer of Lincoln and probably in 1844 he joyfully accepted an invitation to become his junior law partner. Thereafter he worked loyally to further Lincoln's political ambitions. His influence on Lincoln's opinions on slavery can probably be overestimated; but Herndon, who was in close correspondence with Theodore Parker and in touch with anti-slavery literature, undoubtedly called to his partner's attention on this, as on other subjects, many papers and books which would have otherwise escaped him. Herndon's own political ambitions were easily satisfied. He was mayor of Springfield for a term, state bank examiner, and candidate for presidential elector in 1856. But he sedulously nursed Lincoln's fortunes through the setback in 1848, and through the trials and vicissitudes of the years from 1854 to 1860. Lincoln's last request of him on leaving their office was to keep the old sign, Lincoln & Herndon, till his return. After his partner's death, Herndon had successively as partners Charles Zane and Alfred Orendorff. Business reverses, due as he frankly admitted to his long habits of intemperance, overtook him about 1871. For the latter part of his life he turned his attention not very successfully to a small fruit farm. On Mar. 26, 1840, he had married Mary J. Maxey by whom he had six children; after her death he married, July 31, 1861, Anna Miles, who bore him two children.

Herndon's chief claim to fame is as the biographer of his great friend. Immediately after Lincoln's death he traveled in Kentucky and Indiana collecting reminiscences of Lincoln's childhood and boyhood, from men still living who could speak of them at first hand. He laboriously exhausted the recollections of John Hanks and Dennis Hanks. Although he himself planned to write an elaborate biography based on his researches, he generously gave of his stores to biographers like Holland, Barrett, and Arnold, who made scanty acknowledgment of their debt. About 1870 his financial straits induced him to sell copies of his notes to the persons engaged on the Lamon *Life of Abraham Lincoln* (1872); that he had any further share in that work he strenuously denied. As an old man he published in association with Jesse W. Weik *Herndon's Lincoln: The True Story of a Great Life* (3 vols., 1889). The original publishers, Belford, Clarke & Company, went bankrupt, and in 1892 D. Appleton & Company republished it in two volumes with important alterations. At the time of its publication the work met savage criticism for its statements as to the birth of Lincoln's mother, Lincoln's religious beliefs, and other details. The best recent opinion acquits Herndon of any very serious blunders on these heads and endorses his attempt to keep Lincoln a human personality and to save him from too uncritical an apotheosis; it finds more vulnerable his attempts to dramatize his materials and to find the motifs of Lincoln's career in an unhappy marriage and the blighted romance with Ann Rutledge. For introducing the Rutledge interpretation of Lincoln's career, so popular with the romantic, Herndon's lecture of Nov. 16, 1866, has justly to do penance (*Abraham Lincoln, Miss Ann Rutledge, New Salem, Pioneering and the Poem*, 1910). But the debt of all serious Lincoln students to his researches is very great.

[Sources include: J. C. Power, *Hist. of the Early Settlers of Sangamon County, Ill.* (1876); Jesse W. Weik, *The Real Lincoln* (1922); Joseph Fort Newton, *Lincoln and Herndon* (1910); A. J. Beveridge, *Abraham Lincoln* (2 vols., 1928); Paul M. Angle, *Where Lincoln Practiced Law—Lincoln Centennial Asso. Papers* (1927); *Ceremonies at the Unveiling of Monument to Wm. H. Herndon* (n.d.); *Chicago Tribune*, Mar. 19, 1891. Date of birth is taken from the inscription on Herndon's tombstone.] T. C. P.

HERNDON, WILLIAM LEWIS (Oct. 25, 1813–Sept. 12, 1857), naval officer, was born in Fredericksburg, Va., the son of Dabney and Elizabeth (Hull) Herndon, and a descendant of William Herndon who came to America some time before 1674. One of seven children and left an orphan at an early age, William Lewis developed self-reliance and steadfastness in his younger years. At the age of fifteen, Nov. 1, 1828, he entered the United States navy as a midshipman. He went through the usual preparatory years of duty and on Feb. 25, 1841, was commissioned lieutenant. A few years later he was actively engaged in the Mexican War and from 1847 to 1848 commanded the *Iris*, a steamer in the home squadron, operating in the Gulf of Mexico. Shortly afterwards he was attached to the Naval Observatory in Washington. This scientific duty led to his being detached in 1851 in order that he might make a thorough exploration of the Amazon River. The expedition started from Peru and Herndon made a very complete survey of the main branch of the Amazon system. His report was submitted to Congress on Jan. 26, 1853, and the government published it under the title *Exploration of the Valley of the Amazon* (2 vols., 1853–54). Owing to its use in published articles and otherwise by Lieutenant (afterwards Commodore) Matthew F. Maury [*q.v.*], a brother-in-law of Herndon, it was instrumental in helping to open up the Amazon River to merchant ships of all nations.

On Sept. 14, 1855, Herndon was promoted to the grade of commander and in this same year he was given leave of absence by the Navy Department to take command of the Pacific Mail steamer, *George Law*, afterwards renamed *Central America*, the steamers of this line then being commanded by United States naval officers. The *Central America* ran regularly between New York and Aspinwall, now called Colon, and carried passengers as well as freight. Herndon successfully commanded the vessel for two years without encountering any mishap, but on Sept. 11, 1857, he ran into a heavy gale off Cape Hatteras. Besides a cargo of mail and gold from California, there were approximately 575 persons on board, including the crew of about one hundred. The storm increased in violence and although everything possible was done to weather the gale, parts of the ship's rigging were carried away and finally a leak developed which let in so much water that the fires were extinguished. Passengers and crew worked to save their lives but exhaustion gradually overcame many of them. Herndon, seeing that in spite of hard work, professional skill, and excellent seamanship, the ship would in all probability founder, bent his energies to attract assistance and save as many lives as possible. On Sept. 12, the brig *Marine* came near and all the women and children were transferred safely to her decks. Night soon set in, however, and the raging seas doomed many who were unable to be conveyed to the brig. Herndon went down with his ship. He was survived by his widow, Frances Elizabeth Hansbrough, whom he married Mar. 9, 1836, and by a daughter, Ellen Lewis, who later became the wife of Chester A. Arthur [*q.v.*], president of the United States. In 1919 Herndon was honored by having a naval destroyer named for him. He also has the distinction of having a monument to his memory on the grounds of the Naval Academy at Annapolis.

[See *U. S. Navy Department, Ships' Data* (1922); R. W. Neeser, *Ship Names of the U. S. Navy* (1921); F. A. Virkus, *The Abridged Compendium of Am. Genealogy*, vol. II (1926); C. L. Lewis, *Matthew Fontaine Maury* (1927); Nathan Crosby, *Ann. Obit. Notices of Eminent Persons Who Died in the U. S., for 1857* (1858); *Va. Mag. of Hist. and Biog.*, Apr. 1904; *Evening Star* (Washington), Sept. 18, 19, 21, 1857, and *N. Y. Times*, Sept. 18, 19, 1857. The *U. S. Naval Inst. Proc.*, Jan. 1928, contains a copy of an excellent report on Herndon and the loss of his ship, written to the Secretary of the Navy by Lieut. M. F. Maury.]

A. R. B—g.

HERNE, JAMES A. (Feb. 1, 1839–June 2, 1901), actor and playwright, was born in Cohoes, N. Y., the son of Patrick and Ann Temple Ahern. Patrick Ahern was an emigrant from the south of Ireland, converted from Catholicism to the Dutch Reformed faith. He was honest and hardworking, but narrow-minded and strict in the discipline of his numerous children, in whom he inspired little affection. When young James was thirteen, his father took him from school and put him to work. His employer, recognizing the boy's alertness, offered to pay for his further schooling, but the father would not permit it. Accordingly, all James's subsequent education was self-achieved. At about this time, an elder brother took him to the old Albany Museum to see his first play, and he decided then and there to become an actor. He secretly saved what money he could, till at twenty he had $165, which he sank in a barnstorming company that permitted him to act a small part in return. In April 1859 he secured a real engagement at the Adelphi Theatre, Troy, at six dollars a week, playing George Shelby in *Uncle Tom's Cabin*, and felt he was launched on his life career. He changed his name from James Ahern to James A. Herne, and was soon acting Horatio, Bassanio, and numerous other rôles in the familiar stock repertoire. Soon he transferred to the Gayety Theatre, Albany, where his disgusted father saw him perform, and remarked: "The fools aren't all dead yet."

Herne was evidently a "born actor," for at the outbreak of the Civil War he was engaged by John T. Ford [*q.v.*] of Baltimore and Washington and for several years was a favorite player in the companies of that famous manager. He acted in support of Junius Brutus Booth, and his son, Edwin [qq.v.], Forrest, Davenport and other stars, greatly admired Forrest's acting (though not his plays), and early excelled in character parts, such as Cap'n Cuttle; but he lacked ambition, and evidently lived gaily from day to day. Presently he was engaged as leading man for Lucille Western [q.v.], a favorite actress of the period, and toured the country with her. In 1866 he married her sister Helen, but the union was not happy, and they were soon divorced. For a time Herne managed the Grand Opera House in New York for Jim Fiske, but in the middle seventies went to San Francisco as stage director of the Baldwin Theatre. In that city, then at the heyday of its boiling life, his real talents were finally wakened. Two facts were chiefly responsible: first, in April 1878 he married Katherine Corcoran, who had recently made her stage début under his guidance and was thereafter the dominant influence in his life; and second, he worked with a young stage manager of driving energy and ambition, named David Belasco. His new wife urged him to collaborate with Belasco on an original play (they had tinkered one or two manuscripts previously), and together they wrote *Chums,* which later was called *Hearts of Oak.* This was produced at the Baldwin Theatre Sept. 9, 1879, with Herne as Terry and Mrs. Herne as Chrystal. It was taken thence to Chicago, where its success was repeated. Herne bought out Belasco's interest, and continued to act the play for seven years. It made him a small fortune, and he bought a home in Dorchester, Mass., where his children, Julie, Chrystal, and Dorothy, were reared.

Hearts of Oak was, in its day, unusual because of its simplicity, its lack of a stage villain, its simple, kindly, genuine sentiment. Both Herne and his wife acted their rôles with simplicity and without the over-emphasis then common. They were pioneering in realism. On Apr. 5, 1886, at the Chestnut Street Theatre, Philadelphia, Herne produced his next play, *The Minute Men,* a melodrama of the Revolution. It was not a success. It was followed by *Drifting Apart* (People's Theatre, New York, May 7, 1888), a play dealing with the havoc of drink among Gloucester fishermen. Here, again, there was pioneering in realism, which frightened off the conventional managers. For his next play, *Margaret Fleming,* Herne could find no sponsor. It was a somber story of marital infidelity, written in the spirit of the new Continental naturalists whom Herne had been reading, urged on by his friends Hamlin Garland and William Dean Howells, both then in Boston. Herne had to produce the play himself. It opened in Lynn, Mass., July 4, 1890 (probably the only time that city ever cradled a revolution in the arts!), but not until May 4, 1891, in Chickering Hall, Boston, did it get a metropolitan hearing. Its "frankness" (pale enough today), its lack of artifice and "situation," which at that time were looked for and relished, its advocacy of a single sex standard, and above all its disturbing reality, shocked most Bostonians who saw it; but a group of young liberals rallied to it, and its production had much to do with the special performances of Ibsen, the formation of "Stage Societies," and other pioneer movements which followed in the nineties. It cost Herne his fortune, however, and in 1891 he had to move to New York and become stage manager for Klaw and Erlanger—producing *The Country Circus. Margaret Fleming,* presented by Palmer's stock company with Mrs. Herne in the cast, had a hearing in December of that year, but New York also was unsympathetic.

Herne, however, hewed to his line. He now had a manuscript, *Shore Acres,* with a part for himself, embodying his realism but also full of homely sentiment. For a time it went begging, but was finally produced at McVicker's Theatre, Chicago, May 23, 1892, with Herne as Nat Berry and Mrs. Herne as Helen. It was played without the silent ending, however, which McVicker feared, and did not disclose its full effect. In February 1893, supported by the famous stock company of the Boston Museum, Herne at last acted *Shore Acres* with the beautiful benediction of the silent kitchen to close the play, and in the land of the Yankees this Yankee play came into its own. With a new company Herne continued it for five years, making a fortune thereby. On the proceeds, he built a home at Southampton, L. I., where he wrote two more plays. The first, *Griffith Davenport,* was a drama of the Civil War, but showed no battles. It was the tragedy of a family divided against itself, based on the novel, *An Unofficial Patriot,* by Helen H. Gardener [q.v.], and it was first produced in Washington, D. C., Jan. 16, 1899, and two weeks later, in New York. As in the case of *Margaret Fleming,* the play and the performance were hailed by the few and neglected by the crowd. Israel Zangwill, however, who witnessed the production, insisted that only Herne in America be permitted to stage his new play, *Children of the Ghetto*—another drama which proved too much of a pioneer for financial success but which blazed a path into the future. Herne's last play, *Sag Harbor,* returned to the homely-folk field of *Shore Acres* and was filled with the quaint sayings, racy atmosphere, and wholesome sentiment of an old seafaring village. It was produced at the Park Theatre, Boston, Oct. 23, 1899, with Herne as Cap'n Dan Marble, and doubtless would have served the actor-author as a vehicle for many years—for its success everywhere, except in New York, was tremendous—had his health not failed. This failure was due in part, perhaps, to his ardent campaigning for Bryan in 1900 and his disappointment over the Commoner's defeat. In the spring of 1901 he broke down completely and died in New York the following June.

It is unfortunate that a fire which destroyed the Herne home on Long Island a few years later also destroyed the only existing copies of *Margaret Fleming* and *Griffith Davenport,* his two most advanced plays. Mrs. Herne rewrote the former from memory, but the latter is gone. There is ample testimony, however, to the effect they produced on many sensitive beholders, and no question as to the honorable place they hold in the development of American drama toward simplicity and truth, and away from the tricks and postures of the older stage. In *Shore Acres* and *Sag Harbor,* both available in print, can be studied the realism of homely detail and the warm, genial sentiment, which so endeared these plays, and Herne's acting in them, to the country; and in the silent ending of the former, especially, when the old kitchen becomes the hero of the drama, can be felt the thrilling forward step Herne took away from the pumped-up emotionalism of the old-style "climax," into the quieter and deeper places of the heart.

In the days of his fame Herne was a sturdy man with a large head, a face which bore the actor's wrinkles and in repose was rather sad but could and did light up with the most beneficent of smiles, and Celtic eyes that twinkled and flashed. At his best as a character comedian in parts of mellow geniality, in which he radiated charm, he was a thoroughly competent actor in any line. Since he was his own stage director and meticulously careful in all details, his companies were excellent schools for many younger players. Unquestionably the influence of the American and European realists strengthened and gave direction to his work, but it is evident even in *Hearts of Oak* that Herne was by his own instinct feeling toward a new style of drama, and that as early as the eighties both he and his wife were consciously working toward simplicity and naturalness in acting. Most Americans had never been so close to reality on the stage as *Shore Acres* brought them. All subsequent actors and dramatists who felt the new urge found their way made easier by the work which Herne had done.

[*Shore Acres and Other Plays* (1928), with biog. introduction by Julie A. Herne; recreated text of *Margaret Fleming* in A. H. Quinn, *Representative Am. Plays* (5th ed., 1930); Herne Scrap-book, Locke Coll., N. Y. Pub. Lib.; Hamlin Garland, *A Son of the Middle Border* (1917); Norman Hapgood, *The Stage in America, 1897–1900* (1901); J. A. Herne, "Old Stock Days in the Theatre," *Arena,* Sept. 1892; M. J. Moses, *The Am. Dramatist* (3rd ed., 1925); A. H. Quinn, *A Hist. of the Am. Drama from the Civil War to the Present Day* (1927); *N. Y. Tribune,* June 3, 1901.] W. P. E.

HEROLD, DAVID E. [See BOOTH, JOHN WILKES, 1838–1865].

HERON, MATILDA AGNES (Dec. 1, 1830–Mar. 7, 1877), actress, was born in County Londonderry, Ireland, the daughter of John and Mary Laughlin Heron. At an early age she was brought to Philadelphia, Pa., where she was reared by her brother Alexander. After attending a French academy in that city, she became a pupil of the actor Peter Richings and despite her brother's opposition made her début at the Walnut Street Theatre, Philadelphia, Feb. 17, 1851. Her success was followed by an engagement for leading rôles at the Bowery Theatre, New York, beginning Aug. 23, 1852. The next year she made a trip to California. Arriving unknown and almost penniless, she yet contrived a début at San Francisco, Dec. 26, 1853, and at once became an immense favorite. On June 10, 1854, she was clandestinely married to Henry Byrne, a San Francisco lawyer, but a permanent separation followed within a few months. Shortly thereafter she went abroad and at Paris saw Mme. Doche in Dumas' *La Dame aux Camélias.* She quickly translated the play into English and acted the leading part in America in October 1855. Her Camille was not the first this country had seen, but the drama did not create a furore here until she presented it in New York, Jan. 22. 1857. Her intense and impulsive nature had found a peculiarly congenial medium, and, although her naturalistic method was sometimes condemned, her sincerity and power were irresistible. Critics and audiences alike hailed the advent of a brilliant genius. After a long run in Camille, she brought out in New York her translation of Legouvé's *Medea,* another drama well suited to her tempestuous spirit. An event of this year was her marriage to Robert Stoepel, a New York musician, whom she later divorced. In 1860 she took *Camille* to London, but the censor so mangled the play that it almost failed. On her return to America she repeated her former triumphs in it, playing time after time in most of the large theatres of the country, and in 1865 making a second visit to California, where she was received with high honor. This period was also marked by her appearance, though without great success, in several of her own original plays. During her later years her popularity waned. The fortune she had made from *Camille* had been dissipated by extravagance and lavish generosity, and she was reduced to poverty. On Jan. 17, 1872, a benefit for her relief was held in New York, in which Edwin Booth and other noted players participated, and which yielded over $4,000. Except for this aid her support was derived from the training of aspirants for the theatre. Among her most gifted pupils was her own daughter, Hélène Stoepel, later known to the stage as Bijou Heron. Early in 1877 her ill-health necessitated an operation, from which she did not recover. Matilda Heron's range of characters was not wide, but in such parts as Camille, Medea, and Nancy in the dramatization of *Oliver Twist,* she displayed a strange, wild beauty, or an elemental passion that overwhelmed her spectators and exerted a distinct influence on the acting of her time.

[Wm. Winter, *Vagrant Memories* (1915); Laurence Hutton, *Plays and Players* (1875), and *Curiosities of the Am. Stage* (1891); T. A. Brown, *A Hist. of the N. Y. Stage* (1903); obituary notices in the *N. Y. Times,* the *N. Y. Herald,* and the *Sun* (N. Y.), Mar. 8, 1877; information as to certain facts from Mrs. Henry Miller, formerly Hélène Stoepel.] O. S. C.

HERON, WILLIAM (1742–Jan. 8, 1819), Revolutionary spy, was born at Cork, Ireland. Little is known of him until he settled on Redding Ridge, Conn., a few years before the Revolution. He is said to have graduated from Trinity College, Dublin, but his name is not to be found in the register of graduates. His first years in America he spent as a school teacher and surveyor. During the Revolution he openly sided with the colonies. Besides holding a succession of important town appointments, he represented Redding for four sessions, between 1778 and 1782, in the Connecticut Assembly and was friendly with officers of the Continental Army. According to his next-door neighbor, Maj.-Gen. Samuel Holden Parsons [*q.v.*], he was also a volunteer who "in every trial proved himself a man of bravery." From September 1780 to March 1782, however, this "consistent national whig" was engaged, as "Hiram the Spy," in a secret correspondence with Maj. Oliver De Lancey, head of the British secret service. His communications, usually in cipher and in a skilfully disguised hand, contained such items as the strength and location of the French and American troops, minutes of the Connecticut Assembly, and plans of campaign. At the same time he was endeavoring, if his word is to be accepted, to "improve" the "soul" of General Parsons to the advantage of the Royal cause. Such was his success that he was able by July 1781 to inclose a letter of intelligence in Parsons' own writing. The letter was addressed to Heron, but this, he announced, was in accordance with the plan concerted between them. It is doubtful, however, whether the general ever knew the destination of his letter or received the hundred guineas paid for it. Meanwhile, Heron's chief concern was yet another scheme for the benefit of the mother country and, incidentally, of himself. In the first conversation with De Lancey he had suggested that with a British passport for one of his vessels he might ship goods to Ireland. He aroused suspicion among his neighbors by frequent trips to New York to expedite this business, which nevertheless met with one delay after another. When nearest success in July 1781, Heron, as a "rebel," was captured with his boat by a band of Loyalists, and to save appearances at home, was, at his own request, locked up for a while in the British provost.

In all this, Heron seems to have served the British more from self-interest than from zeal for his King. This is further evidenced by the fact that Parsons recommended him to Washington (Apr. 6, 1782) as a spy who had given him most accurate accounts of the numbers of the enemy and best descriptions of their posts. He described Heron as "a man of very large knowledge, and a great share of natural sagacity, united with a sound judgment, but of as unmeaning a countenance as any person in my acquaintance" (*Magazine of American History,* XX, 293). These together with shrewdness, fluency, and a gift of flattery equipped him perfectly for the rôles he played. That he was not suspected of his treasonable correspondence is indicated by the fact that he was again elected to the Connecticut Assembly after the war, serving several terms between 1784 and 1796. His wife, Mary, died July 16, 1819, having borne him eight children.

[The original Heron-De Lancey correspondence is included in the Sir Henry Clinton Papers at the W. L. Clements Library, University of Michigan. Copies of a few of the documents have been printed in "Sir Henry Clinton's Original Secret Record of Private Daily Intelligence," *Mag. of Am. Hist.,* Nov. 1883–Aug. 1884, Oct. 1888. Heron's "Information," Sept. 4, 1780, is given in B. F. Stevens, *Facsimiles,* vol. VII (1891); another copy is in *Docs. Relative to the Colonial Hist. of the State of N. Y.,* vol. VIII (1857). Perhaps the best biographical sketch is in W. E. Grumman, *The Revolutionary Soldiers of Redding, Conn.* (1904); inadequate sketches are given in C. B. Todd, *The Hist. of Redding* (1880), and Lorenzo Sabine, *Loyalists of the Am. Revolution* (1864). Other references include Mrs. L. L. Armstrong, "Eight Cemeteries in the Town of Redding, Conn.," in the Connecticut State Library; C. S. Hall, *Life and Letters of Samuel Holden Parsons* (1905); and G. B. Loring, "Vindication of Gen. Samuel Holden Parsons," *Mag. of Am. Hist.*, Oct. 1888. Compare Winthrop Sargent, *The Life and Career of Maj. John André* (1861), pp. 254, 258, with Hall, *op. cit.*, p. 307 ff.] J. C.

HERR, JOHN (Sept. 18, 1781–May 3, 1850), founder of the sect of Reformed Mennonites, was born on his father's farm in West Lampeter, Lancaster County, Pa., the fifth of the eight children of Francis and Fanny (Barr) Herr. He was descended from Hans Herr, a Mennonite bishop, born in or near Zürich, Switzerland, in 1639, who in spite of his years led a band of his persecuted brethren from Switzerland and the Palatinate to Pennsylvania in 1709 and settled on Pequea Creek in what later became Lancaster County. His daughter and six of his sons followed him to the new home in 1710 and became the ancestors of one of the most numerous of Mennonite families. In the fourth generation Francis Herr developed separatist tendencies. His opponents declared that he had been excommunicated for unfair dealing in a horse trade; according to his own story, he was distressed by the growing worldliness of the sect and came out from among them on his own initiative. He held public meetings in his house and was sometimes called upon by sympathizers to preach or to exhort at funerals. After his death in 1810 his son John, although unbaptized, carried on the work and rapidly increased in influence. Deciding that the Mennonites had departed from the ways of Menno Simons and had therefore ceased to be the Visible Church, he and his followers met in his farmhouse in Strasburg on May 30, 1812, and constituted themselves the Reformed Mennonites. Abraham Landis baptized Herr, who in turn rebaptized Landis and Abraham Groff. Herr was elected pastor and bishop; then, or soon after, Groff was made a deacon and Landis a minister. Professing to uphold the teachings of Menno Simons in their ancient integrity, the new sect drew to itself many of the ultraconservative, but it provoked the quiet, stubborn opposition of many more, who resented its condemnation of the Old Mennonites. A note of apology runs through all of Herr's writings, which include *Der Wahre und Selige Weg* (1815), *Eine Kurze und Apostolische Antwort . . . auf den Brief von Abraham Reinke* (1819), and *Erläuterungs Spiegel, oder Eine Gründliche Erklärung von der Bergpredigt* (1827, 1854), an *Anhang* to which presents a short account of his early religious experiences. The first and third of these writings were translated as *The True and Blessed Way* (1816) and *The Illustrating Mirror* (1834). Herr also wrote an introduction for Israel Daniel Rupp's translation of Menno Simons' *Foundation and Plain Instruction* (1835, 1863). He died in Humberstone, Welland County, Ontario, while on a visit to the churches of his sect in western New York and Canada. His wife, whom he married Apr. 7, 1807, was Betsey Groff.

[T. W. Herr, *Geneal. Record of Rev. Hans Herr and his Direct Lineal Descendants* (1908); I. D. Rupp, *Hist. of Lancaster County, Pa.* (1844); Daniel Musser, *The Reformed Mennonite Church* (1873; 2nd ed., 1878); J. F. Funk, *The Mennonite Church and her Accusers* (1878); C. H. Smith, *The Mennonites of America* (1909); H. S. Bender, *Two Centuries of Am. Mennonite Literature* (1929); *John Herr's Complete Works* (1890), with an appendix on Herr's life.] G. H. G.

HERRESHOFF, JAMES BROWN (Mar. 18, 1834–Dec. 5, 1930), inventor, was born at Papposquaw, near Bristol, R. I., the eldest of the nine children of Charles Frederick and Julia Ann (Lewis) Herreshoff, and a grandson of Karl Friedrich Herreschoff, son of one of Frederick the Great's guardsmen, who emigated from Prussia to Rhode Island in 1783 and married Sarah, daughter of John Brown [1736–1803, *q.v.*], a wealthy merchant and politician. From 1853 to 1856 James studied at Brown University, taking courses in general science but specializing in chemistry. Upon finishing his work there he found employment as a chemist at the Rumford Chemical Works, Rumford, R. I., and in 1858 became superintendent, serving in this capacity until 1863, during which period he improved Horsford's substitute for cream of tartar. In 1863, in partnership with his father, he began the manufacture of fish oil and fertilizer on Prudence Island, R. I., utilizing a novel oil press of his own invention. This partnership continued until 1869, when Herreshoff went to Europe as the representative of his younger brothers, John Brown [*q.v.*] and Nathaniel, the famous yacht-designers and builders of Bristol, R. I. For the next fourteen years he spent most of his time abroad, traveling extensively in the interests of his brothers and devoting what time he could spare to inventing various needed devices. As early as 1858, for example, he had perfected a cross plank design of boat; in 1860 he invented a sliding seat for rowboats, which subsequently came into general use in all racing shells; in 1864 he developed an improved process and apparatus for making nitric and hydrochloric acids; and in 1866 he patented a thread-tension regulator for sewing machines. During his sojourn in Europe in 1872, he devised a bicycle driven by a gasoline engine, and also patented an apparatus for measuring the specific heat of gases. In 1874 he and his brothers devised a tubular marine steam-boiler constructed in the form of a beehive and having coils of iron pipe. It was tried out in a specially constructed 48-foot launch which made a speed of fifteen miles an hour. Subsequently the coil-boiler was adopted for the first torpedo-boat built for the United States navy, and on a trial trip made a speed of twenty-one miles an hour. Five years later, in 1879, he devised a steam-engine to utilize superheated steam, the cylinder of which was made of hardened slab steel. Around 1875 Herreshoff began experimenting with and subsequently perfected the fin keel for racing yachts, which was incorporated to great advantage in later years in *America's* Cup defender yachts designed and constructed by his brothers. In fact, between 1877 and 1889 Herreshoff was engaged in extensive experiments with his fin keel, first in Switzerland, and then in Bristol Harbor, R. I., having taken up his residence in Bristol in 1883 for the express purpose of conducting this work. During this period he did some successful work with a yacht equipped with metal plates and lead bulb, and also perfected a mercurial anti-fouling paint for boats. He invented, too, what he called a "rowcycle," a three-wheeled vehicle with handlebars designed to propel the vehicle as one rows a boat. From 1893 until 1904 he resided in Coronado, Calif., but in the latter year he removed with his family to New York, where he lived for the rest of his life. He married Jane Brown of Dromore, Ireland, in 1875, and at his death in his ninety-seventh year he was survived by five children. He was buried in Bristol, R. I.

[*Who's Who in America,* 1928–29; *Hist. Cat. Brown Univ.* (1914); *The Biog. Cyc. of Representative Men of R. I.* (1881); *N. Y. Times,* Dec. 7, 1930; *Providence Jour.,* Dec. 8, 1930; Patent Office records.]

C. W. M—n.

HERRESHOFF, JOHN BROWN (Apr. 24, 1841–July 20, 1915), ship-builder, yacht-designer, younger brother of James Brown Herreshoff [*q.v.*], was born at "Point Pleasant," near Bristol, R. I., the son of Charles Frederick and Julia Ann (Lewis) Herreshoff. His maternal grandfather was a sea-captain; his father was a farmer and ship-builder. At the age of twelve John constructed a rope walk and a machine shop with a foot lathe; but in 1855, while engaged in building his first boat, he became totally blind. After a few months of despondency, he took a fresh hold on life, built a longer rope walk, a machine shop, and, with the help of his father and brother Nathaniel, finished his boat, the *Meteor.* He built other boats and in 1863, with his brother James, doubled Cape Cod on his twenty-six-foot *Kelpie.* On the return voyage the *Kelpie* so far outsailed another yacht, the *Qui Vive,* that her owner, Thomas Clapham, followed the Herreshoff boys to Bristol and gave John his first commission. More orders followed, among them one for a schooner yacht *Faustine,* which made the transatlantic passage in seventeen days. About this time Herreshoff built a number of small boats on the same model or in duplicate, being one of the first to discern the business possibilities of mass production. After a brief partnership with Dexter S. Stone, he resumed boat building by himself and in 1868 constructed his first steam yacht, the *Annie Morse,* for Samuel Shove of Providence, followed by a steam fisherman for Church Brothers of Tiverton, R. I. In 1874 he and his brothers contrived a tubular or coil-boiler, which proved such a success that an order for a small torpedo-boat was received from the United States navy. This was followed by a commission, apparently legitimate, for a fast steamer, but the vessel was seized as a prospective Cuban filibuster.

In 1878 John and Nathaniel formed the Herreshoff Manufacturing Company, John having charge of the finances and construction, Nathaniel of the drafting, engineering, and experimentation. The first fifteen years were devoted chiefly to the building of steam yachts and torpedo-boats. They did not neglect the sailing-yacht, however, for in 1881 their sloop *Shadow* was the only American boat able to beat the Scotch cutter *Madge.* The Herreshoffs were original in their designs and building methods. They were among the first to construct yachts over molds, keel upward, with double skins and iron floors and knees. Turning once again to sail, the brothers produced in 1891 the forty-six-foot sloop *Gloriana* built on radical lines, with a shortened bow, scarcely any forefoot, and a decreased but rounder and fuller waterline that enabled her to carry an unusual amount of sail. The success of the *Gloriana* and of her successor, the *Wasp,* was so marked that when in the fall of 1892 a challenge was received from England for the *America's* Cup, the leading international yachting trophy, the Herreshoffs received orders for two prospective defenders. Their bronze sloop *Vigilant* was chosen and vanquished the *Valkyrie II* in three straight races. In the four matches for the *America's* Cup which followed in the next ten years, all the defenders were Herreshoff boats, the *Defender* in 1895, the *Columbia* in 1899 and 1901, and the *Reliance* in 1903. John Herreshoff conducted the negotiations for these yachts as well as for the *Constitution,* which failed to qualify in 1901, and supervised much of their construction. The designs and details were worked out by Nathaniel, through whose engineering skill the *Reliance* was able to carry as mainsail the largest piece of canvas ever fashioned for a sailing craft. For the proposed match of 1914, the sailing of which was postponed by the war, they built the seventy-five-foot sloop *Resolute,* which in 1920 defeated the *Shamrock IV* in three out of five races, making a record for the Herreshoffs of eighteen races in twenty starts in twenty-seven years against the fastest of English yachts. Scores of other yachts nearly as notable were also built, including the large schooners *Queen, Westward, Elena, Katoura,* and two *Vagrants,* as well as a quartette of one design seventy-foot sloops, a pair of sixty-five-footers, a trio of fifty-seven-footers and many smaller one-design classes such as the Newport thirties of 1896, the Bar Harbor thirty-ones of 1903, the New York thirties of 1905, and the New York fifties of 1912.

In 1870 Herreshoff married Sarah Lucas Kilton of Boston, by whom he had a daughter Katherine. The marriage ended unhappily, and in 1892 he married Eugenia Thames Tucker of Providence, who survived him.

[*Representative Men and Old Families of R. I.*, (1908), I, 615; W. P. Stephens, *Am. Yachting* (1904); J. S. Hughes, *Famous Yachts* (1928); articles in *Providence Jour.*, July 21, 1915; *N. Y. Times*, Aug. 31, 1924; *Yachting,* Dec. 1924; *Who's Who in America,* 1903–15.] W. U. S.

HERRICK, EDWARD CLAUDIUS (Feb. 24, 1811–June 11, 1862), librarian, scientist, was a native and lifelong resident of New Haven, Conn. From his earliest years the influence of Yale College enveloped him. His father, Rev. Claudius Herrick, born in Southampton, Long Island, where his ancestor, James, had settled in 1640, was a graduate of Yale, and at the time of his son's birth was conducting a school for young ladies on the present site of Battell Chapel. Edward's mother was Hannah Pierpont, a descendant of Rev. James Pierpont [*q.v.*], one of the founders of Yale. He received a good classical training, but an affection of the eyes prevented him from taking the college course. At the age of sixteen he became clerk in the bookstore of Gen. Hezekiah Howe, a library of books of all descriptions, publishing house for the college, and the resort of professors and men of literary tastes. In 1835 he became one of its proprietors, but retired, financially embarrassed, three years later. Such were his scholarly attainments by this time, however, that Yale conferred upon him the honorary degree of master of arts. During the next three years his occupations included service as clerk of the City of New Haven and in the office of the *American Journal of Science.* The erection of a library building at Yale and Herrick's appointment as librarian in 1843 began a new era in the library's development and usefulness. He remained its head until 1858, when he resigned to give full time to the duties of treasurer of the college, to which office he had been elected in 1852. After the death of Professor James L. Kingsley [*q.v.*], along with his other duties he edited the triennial catalogue, prepared the records of deceased graduates, and delved into the early history of the institution.

Necessity in the form of financial obligations compelled him to do clerical and administrative work when he would gladly have occupied himself with other pursuits. A tireless worker, never taking a vacation, he performed every duty with extreme conscientiousness and marked business ability. His habitual manner, according to a contemporary, was that of one who had no time to lose. When going anywhere "he . . . took the most direct way from point to point, regardless of the paths which others used." He never married and had few social responsibilities to distract him from his labors. By taste and mental characteristics he was preëminently a scholar. He had an encyclopedic knowledge in a variety of fields, which others drew upon freely; but his major interest was in the natural sciences, and his entomological and astronomical investigations, though carried on in his spare hours, won him an international reputation. In 1837 in collaboration with Professor James D. Dana [*q.v.*] he published in the *American Journal of Science* (vol. XXXI) "Description of the Argulus Catostomi, a New Parasitic Crustaceous Animal." Thereafter until his death there was scarcely an issue of the *Journal* which did not have some contribution from him. In 1832 he began a study of the Hessian fly, which he carried on for years. A portion of a long correspondence with Dr. T. W. Harris [*q.v.*] on this and other subjects appears in S. H. Scudder's *Entomological Correspondence of Thaddeus William Harris* (1869); and in the *American Journal of Science* (April–June 1841) he published "A Brief, Preliminary Account of the Hessian Fly and its Parasites." He was also the first to find and to describe the parasites of the eggs of the spring canker-worm moth. His work marks him as "one of the best of the early economic entomologists" (Dr. Leland O. Howard). The remarkable shower of meteors which occurred Nov. 13, 1833, awoke his interest, and in the October and November numbers of the *American Journal of Science* for the year 1837 he propounded the theory of the periodic occurrence of a large number of meteors about the 9th of August. News of the announcement of a similar theory by M. Quetelet, director of the Observatory at Brussels, antedating Herrick's, did not reach America until a few days after Herrick's second article. A correspondence between the two, lasting for more than twenty years, ensued, and Quetelet in a letter written Nov. 9, 1861, acknowledged great indebtedness to Herrick for observations made in this country. The aurora borealis also attracted his interest, and he corresponded and wrote on this phenomenon.

Herrick died at the early age of fifty-one. Regarding him Professor James D. Dana wrote: "There is no person living whose example and advice have had more influence on my scientific character than Herrick's. From him I learnt how to investigate; his thorough method of research, and his accuracy were the models I studied" (quotation from private letter: *New Englander,* October 1862, p. 836). Modest and frugal in his life, he left instructions that his funeral service be simple; biographical notices, as brief as possible; and the cost of his monument be limited to thirty dollars. A memorial window in Battell Chapel bears his name.

[*Obit. Records Grads. Yale Coll.,* 1862; *Am. Jour. Sci.,* July 1862; *New Englander,* Oct. 1862; Wm. L. Kingsley, *Yale Coll., A Sketch of its Hist.,* vol. I (1879); Jedediah and L. C. Herrick, *Herrick Geneal.* (1885); letter from Dr. Leland O. Howard; *Hartford Courant,* June 13, 1862.] H. E. S.

HERRICK, MYRON TIMOTHY (Oct. 9, 1854–Mar. 31, 1929), lawyer, banker, diplomat, was descended from ancestors who migrated from New England and New York state to Ohio. The progenitor of the family in America was Henerie Hericke, who emigrated from England and was one of the founders of the first church in Salem in 1629. Myron Herrick was born at Huntington, Lorain County, Ohio, in a log cabin built by his grandfather. His father, Timothy R. Herrick, was a farmer who won for himself political recognition in his community and was reputed to be a forceful speaker. His mother was Mary, daughter of Orrin Hulbert. Both his grandfathers fought in the War of 1812. At Huntington, and later at Wellington, Herrick attended the local schools, and when about sixteen he was appointed teacher of a district school at Brighton. The effort to fit himself for college by study at night, added to the strain of his duties as a schoolmaster, impaired his health and led him to embark upon a business venture which carried him to St. Louis. Stranded there by the financial failure of his enterprise, but enriched by his experience, he undertook writing for a newspaper, in which his vivid powers of description won him success. By this means, and later by selling to the farmers dinner bells and parlor organs, he was enabled to pass a year and a half at Oberlin Academy and later to enter Ohio Wesleyan University, Delaware, Ohio, where he remained about two years.

In 1875 he moved to Cleveland and entered the law offices of G. E. and J. F. Herrick as a student, subsisting on his slight compensation as an office boy. He was admitted to the bar in 1878 and opened an office in his own name. Soon after he went to Cleveland the young lawyer joined the military organization known as the Cleveland Grays, with which he served as a trooper for twelve years. On June 30, 1880, after a courtship of two years, he was married to Carolyn M. Parmely, daughter of M. B. Parmely of Dayton, Ohio. He regarded her as his wisest counselor. Collaterally with his law practice he undertook several profitable business ventures which led to his becoming in 1886 secretary and treasurer of the Society for Savings, a highly successful banking institution. In 1894 he was chosen as the president, and later as the chairman of the board. Having become a director in several railroads and trust companies in various parts of the country, in 1901 he was elected president of the American Bankers Association.

A man of such vigor and enterprise could not be long kept out of politics. Elected to the city council of Cleveland in 1885, after serving two terms he refused to be again a candidate. In 1888, in opposition to Marcus A. Hanna [*q.v.*], he succeeded in securing control of the district convention of the Republican party to select delegates to the national convention of that year. He insisted however that Hanna himself should be the first delegate, thus beginning a lifelong friendship. His association with Hanna and his close friendship with William McKinley [*q.v.*], both before and during the time the latter was governor of Ohio, when Herrick was appointed a colonel on his staff, drew him into active political relations and he became a leading member of the Republican state and national committee. As a prospective candidate for the presidency, Governor McKinley found himself deeply embarrassed by pecuniary debts incurred by his generosity in indorsing the notes of a friend. By Herrick's aid and advice, with the assistance of James H. Hoyt, H. H. Kohlsaat, Hanna, and other friends, a sum was raised sufficient to take over these debts. In 1896 Herrick played an influential part in the nomination and election of McKinley to the presidency, and strenuously advocated the gold standard. After McKinley's election Herrick was offered the position of secretary of the treasury, but declined this offer because, as he said, he was a comparatively unknown man, and also because he was at the time deeply engaged in business enterprises to which he was already committed.

In June 1903, he received the nomination for governor of Ohio, an honor which his friend Hanna persuaded him to accept. After a speaking tour of the state, in which the tax theories of Henry George and Tom L. Johnson [*q.v.*] were advocated by his opponent, he was elected by a majority of 113,812 votes. His administration as governor was characterized by a conservative conduct of public affairs, with close attention to sound fiscal policy, and the veto of several measures which he thought inimical to the best interests of the state. Conflicts arising from some of his decisions awakened a bitter opposition which in his second gubernatorial campaign, in 1905, caused his defeat. This result, however, did not prevent his presiding in September 1906 as temporary chairman of the Ohio Republican convention. From this time until 1912, while manifesting a continuous interest in political affairs, he was chiefly engaged in large financial transactions and in the reorganization of several railroads.

The crown of his career still awaited him, and it was found where he least expected to find it, in the diplomatic service. When President McKinley entered upon his second term in 1901, he had offered Herrick an appointment as ambassador to Italy, to be followed by one as secretary of the treasury; but, in view of his preoccupations, these offers had been declined. In 1912 conditions had greatly changed, and on Feb. 15, 1912, Herrick accepted an appointment from President Taft as ambassador to France. He hoped that he might be able to take advantage of his short stay by studying in Europe the operation of rural credits, upon which subject he was later to publish a book (*Rural Credits,* 1914). Though he was without what in Europe would be accounted the necessary technical preparation for a diplomatic post, circumstances were to give this handsome, kindly American an exceptional opportunity to display his native qualities of mind and heart, and these were to win for him, not only the respect, but also the deep affection of the French people.

When Wilson entered upon the presidency in 1913, Herrick, following the custom, sent in his resignation, which he expected would be accepted. Owing to some difficulties, however, Wilson did not name his successor, William G. Sharp, until June 1914, and the latter arranged to delay his arrival in France until the following August. The coming of war rendered Herrick's position unique and his services indispensable. Remaining until December at the request of Wilson, he performed by authority, but under conditions of embarrassment, the functions and manifold duties of office, while his chagrined successor, who arrived in September, was hunting a house in which to live. Only the barest mention can be made of the varied activities of Herrick during the four remaining months of his mission. The expansion of the American Hospital into an American ambulance hospital was made possible by his cooperation. He aided in the repatriation of American citizens stranded in Europe. He took over the interests of Germany and Austria, of Servia, Japan, and Turkey, and, after the diplomatic corps had followed the government to Bordeaux in September, even those of Great Britain. He himself remained in Paris in order to protect not only his fellow citizens but also the churches, museums, and monuments of the city. Finally, he established the American Relief Clearing House for the care of the disabled, the widows, the orphans, and other victims of the war. This American man of business was an admirable organizer, and by his simple and brave fidelity in a time of great peril he became a dramatic figure, a symbol of American good will. While at sea on his return home in December, he was informed by a wireless message that the French government had conferred on him the Grand Cross of the Legion of Honor.

Defeated as a candidate for the Senate in 1916, Herrick held no public office in the United States after his return, but when his friend Harding became president in 1921, he was named a second time ambassador to France. Arriving at his post, dramatically on July 14, the French national holiday, he was welcomed with enthusiasm. It seemed to him almost as if he were returning home. His wife, however, was no longer with him, for she had died on Sept. 15, 1918. His son Parmely remained, and his daughter-in-law helped make a home for him. Soon he was comfortably settled in the De Broglie house where he narrowly escaped the bomb of a communist. Later, with his own money he paid 5,400,000 francs (then about $200,000) for the Grévy house, which afterward became the permanent home of the American embassy.

This time, there was a long term of service before him. The problems of financial settlement presented many difficulties, with which, however, because of his experience as a banker and his friendship for the French people, he was particularly fitted to deal. Criticism of the

United States in France caused him much unhappiness, but he served to remind the French of past American kindness, and personally did much to ease the situation. In May 1927, when the atmosphere was tense, came Lindbergh's famous flight across the Atlantic. Herrick comprehended its immense import, gave the young hero his undivided attention, and shared the sunshine temporarily restored to Franco-American relations by this redoubtable exploit.

The years were now weighing upon him. In the summer of 1927 he made a visit to his birthplace and the scenes of his early life in Ohio. Another visit home in the autumn of 1928 appeared to be of benefit to him and he returned refreshed to Paris. The death of Marshal Foch affected him deeply. For five hours he was exposed, marching or standing, at the funeral of his friend. Five days later, on the morning of Easter Sunday, Mar. 31, 1929, he himself died in the embassy he had acquired for his government. A French warship, the *Tourville,* which was met by two American cruisers off Nantucket, bore his body to New York, where it was received by a civil and military escort on its way to his home in Cleveland.

[*Myron T. Herrick, Friend of France* (1929), by T. Bentley Mott, containing many passages dictated by Herrick and extracts from letters, is appropriately described as "An Autobiographical Biography." See also Jas. K. Mercer, *Representative Men of Ohio* (1908); Jedediah and L. C. Herrick, *Herrick Geneal.* (1885); *Who's Who in America,* 1928–29; *N. Y. Times,* Apr. 1, 21, 1929; *Le Monde Illustré,* Apr. 6, 1929.] D. J. H.

HERRICK, SOPHIA McILVAINE BLEDSOE (Mar. 26, 1837–Oct. 9, 1919), editor, author, was born in Gambier, Ohio, the eldest child of Albert Taylor Bledsoe [*q.v.*], Southern educator and writer, and Harriet (Coxe) Bledsoe, descendant of a well-known New Jersey family. She received her early education in a boarding school conducted by her aunt, Margaret Coxe, first in Cincinnati, afterward in Dayton, Ohio; later, she was largely self-taught. From her eleventh year until her marriage she lived in a university community, her father being professor of mathematics, first at the University of Mississippi, and after 1854, at the University of Virginia. In this environment her strong natural interest in drawing, mathematics, and such scientific knowledge as she encountered found helpful encouragement. In June 1860 she married James Burton Herrick, a young clergyman from the Episcopal Theological Seminary, Alexandria, and went with him to his mission parish in New York City. A son and two daughters were born to them. During this period of her life, in the midst of war-time anxieties, she turned for relief to a systematic reading of the newly published works of Darwin, Huxley, and Tyndall, bringing to them an extraordinary memory and a remarkably alert intelligence.

In 1868, finding herself unable to accept the social views that were leading her husband into the Oneida Community, she assumed the responsibility of supporting her children and joined forces with her father in Baltimore, where he was conducting a school for girls and editing the *Southern Review.* She took charge of the school for a time, but soon devoted herself almost entirely to writing. For ten years she contributed regularly to the *Southern Review,* furnishing a substantial part of its contents. From 1875 to 1878 she acted as its associate editor, carrying it on alone for a year after her father's death in 1877. Her constant study and tireless industry enabled her to supply the paper not only with comprehensive articles and reviews dealing with many aspects of science, but also with historical, critical, and biographical sketches. After a course in biology at the Johns Hopkins University in 1876, where she had her first opportunity of working in a scientific laboratory, she wrote for *Scribner's Monthly* (November 1876–December 1877) a series of articles, illustrated with her own delicately precise drawings, entitled "Hours with a Microscope." In 1879 she accepted a position on the staff of *Scribner's* and was soon highly valued by its editor as an expert on everything relating to popular science. When *Scribner's* became the *Century* she continued to act as editorial assistant and reader of manuscripts, serving the magazine for twenty-five years with her wide range of knowledge. In the early issues she frequently wrote for the department known as "Home and Society." Painting was her favorite recreation, and some of her flower and still-life canvases were exhibited in New York. She retired in 1906 and devoted the leisure of her late years to books, art, and travel. Her published works are: *The Wonders of Plant Life Under the Microscope* (1883); *Chapters on Plant Life* (1885); *The Earth in Past Ages* (1888); *A Century of Sonnets* (1902). Her "Personal Recollections" appeared in the *Methodist Review* (Nashville), October 1915.

["Personal Recollections"; R. U. Johnson, *Remembered Yesterdays* (1923); L. F. Tooker, *The Joys and Tribulations of an Editor* (1924); *Letters of James Russell Lowell* (1894), ed. by C. E. Norton; *Southern Review,* Oct. 1870, Apr. 1875; Jedediah and L. C. Herrick, *Herrick Geneal.* (1885); *N. Y. Tribune,* Oct. 10, 1919; information from representatives of the family.]

B. M. S.

HERRING, AUGUSTUS MOORE (Aug. 3, 1867–July 17, 1926), pioneer in aviation, the son of William Francis and Chloe Perry (Conyers) Herring, was born at Covington, Ga., and died at Brooklyn, N. Y. He was married to Lillian Mellen of Freeport, Long Island. Educated in mechanical engineering at Stevens Institute of Technology, he offered in 1888 a thesis on "The Flying Machine as a Mechanical Engineering Problem" but, disappointed by the Institute's refusal to accept his thesis because of its supposed chimerical character, he left shortly before graduation. Almost immediately entering his chosen field, he experimented with gliders, at first copying those of Lilienthal. His work on light engine construction brought him into the notice of Samuel Pierpont Langley [*q.v.*], whom he assisted at the Smithsonian Institution from June to November 1895. In 1896, Herring assisted Octave Chanute [*q.v.*] in making and flying gliders near Chicago. Of the four types experimented upon by Chanute, the Herring biplane with flexible-rudder stabilizer proved best. Herring and others made many glides with it ranging from 250 to 1,000 feet.

On Dec. 11, 1896, Herring applied for a patent (Serial No. 615,353) on a heavier-than-air powered flying machine. He showed superposed wings, a wheeled chassis, a horizontal and vertical rudder with flexible controls, two screw-propellors of opposite pitches driven oppositely on a common central shaft, and wing sections of special curvatures both above and below. Since the Patent Office required a working model, he submitted an affidavit reciting his gliding experiences and his work on light engines, and accompanied it by three photographs: one, of a two-foot elastic-band propelled model in flight, another, of himself gliding with a full-sized machine, and the third, of a light two-cylinder gasoline engine. The Patent Office found nearly twenty claims not anticipated by the prior art. Among these are highly important ones covering curved wing sections of unequal curvatures above and below. Although these and other claims would have been allowable in an application for a glider, the Office totally rejected the application in 1898, saying: "So far as the examiner is aware no power driven aeroplane has yet been raised into the air with the aeronaut or kept its course wholly detached from the earth for such considerable time as to constitute proof of practical usefulness." Conceiving the Office to demand as proof of operability an actual power-driven flight with pilot, Herring worked on gasoline and on steam engines for several years but only succeeded so far that in 1898, powered with compressed air, he made a hop of seventy-five feet with his full-sized machine. A fire in 1901 destroyed his shop and partly-completed engines. Almost without funds, he nevertheless made, about 1902, a 2½ H.P. gasoline engine of four pounds to the horsepower, which was exhibited in Germany.

About 1909, the Herring-Curtiss Company was formed. Herring and his friends contributed his patent applications besides funds, and held a majority of the stock. Successful machines were turned out, and Herring petitioned for a revival of the patent application of December 1896 after he had actually flown a machine constructed on that plan by Starling Burgess. The Patent Office found, however, "that the delay in prosecuting this case has not been shown to have been unavoidable within the meaning of Section 4894 R.S.," and the petition was denied. In 1910, the Herring-Curtiss Company was made a defendant in the famous suit by the Wrights, in which the lower court held against the defendants. Appeals still pending were settled out of court in 1917 by the celebrated "cross-licensing agreement," whereby to meet the war exigency all patents were made available to all builders on certain terms. Disagreements had arisen between Curtiss and Herring, however. Their company became bankrupt about 1910, and its assets were purchased at auction by Curtiss, who also secured an injunction against Herring. At its expiration, Herring brought suit for damages against Curtiss for $5,000,000. Appeals are still pending (1931) therein. Several further attempts to revive the patent application of December 1896 were made by Herring and his assignee after 1920, and even carried to the court of appeals, but the Patent Office was finally sustained in its action disallowing the petitions on the ground of fatal delay.

With much ingenuity, devotion and enthusiasm, Herring tried hard for many years to promote heavier-than-air gliding and power flying. He wrote many articles, both technical and popular, he gave generous praise to the Wrights in their success, but he, himself, seemed almost continuously pursued by misfortune.

[*Libertarian* (Greenville, S. C.), Oct. 1924; *Aeronautical Annual* (Boston, Mass.), no. 2, 1896, no. 3, 1897; *The Wright Company* vs. *The Herring-Curtiss Company et al.*, transcript of record, appeal from the Circuit Court for the Western District of New York; *N. Y. Times*, July 19, 1926; records of the Smithsonian Institution; family records.]

C. G. A.

HERRING, JAMES (Jan. 12, 1794–Oct. 8, 1867), portrait painter, was born in London, England. His father, James Herring, moved his family to New York City when the lad was about ten years old and was first a teacher, then a brewer. James completed his schooling at an academy in Flatbush, L. I., and then started in business as a distiller with a location in the Bowery near his father. War with England played havoc with his business, and in order to keep the wolf from the door—for he had ventured into matrimony at eighteen—he began to color prints and maps. One of his employers was John Wesley Jarvis [*q.v.*], but in time his best patron was Mathew Carey [*q.v.*], publisher in Philadelphia, whither he moved. Meantime he tried his hand at drawing profiles and coloring them. Then he attempted to delineate the full face, experimenting with water colors and then with oil. Having been successful in these ventures he gained a reputation as a portrait painter and was employed throughout northern New Jersey. His initiation into Solomon's Lodge of Masons in Somerset County served to bring him further employment and gave him a lifelong interest in Masonry. When his skill attracted New York patronage and led him in 1822 to establish a studio not far from his former distillery, he became actively engaged as an officer in the several bodies comprising the various branches of the fraternity. For a long period beginning in 1829, he was grand secretary of the grand lodge of New York state. He was orator on the occasion of the "first sorrow lodge" of St. John's Lodge, No. 1, Feb. 25, 1847 (Transactions of St. John's Lodge), and was much in demand for public addresses. In order to provide for the financial welfare of his family he established on Broadway, about 1830, a circulating library of 10,000 volumes, called the Enterprise Library. It proved highly successful. An undertaking of another sort was *The National Portrait Gallery* (4 vols., 1834–39), which he published in collaboration with J. B. Longacre. Some portraits of his own found in this work are those of Noah Webster, Oliver Ellsworth, Dr. John W. Francis, and Gov. Morgan Lewis. Herring also projected the Apollo Gallery at 410 Broadway and prepared the *Catalogue of the First Fall Exhibition of the Works of Modern Artists at the Apollo Gallery* (1838). This led to the organization of the Apollo Association for the Promotion of the Fine Arts in the United States (later the American Art Union), of which he was the corresponding secretary. His final years were passed in Paris, where he died, but he was interred in Greenwood Cemetery, Brooklyn. A son, Frederick W. Herring, also a portrait painter, survived him.

[Wm. Dunlap, *Hist. of the Rise and Progress of the Arts of Design in the U. S.* (ed. 1918), vols. II and III; C. T. McClenachan, *Hist. of the . . . Masons in N. Y.*, vol. II (1892); *Somerset County Hist. Quart.*, July 1919; T. S. Cummings, *Hist. Annals of the Nat. Acad. of Design* (1865); *N. Y. Tribune*, Oct. 23, 1867; manuscript letters in the N. Y. Pub. Lib.] A. E. P.

HERRING, SILAS CLARK (1803–June 23, 1881), safe-manufacturer, was born in Salisbury, Vt., the son of Otis and Mary (Olds) Herring who were married at Brookfield, Mass. At sixteen he went to work in an uncle's grocery store at Albany, N. Y., and continued there for six years. Later he engaged in the business of selling lottery tickets, with his uncle. Becoming interested in military matters he was appointed paymaster and colonel of the 5th Regiment of New York Artillery. He removed to New York City in 1834 and had just embarked in a wholesale grocery business when his goods and prospects were wiped out by the great fire of 1835. After he had made a new start the financial crisis of 1837 dealt him another severe blow, from which he recovered with difficulty. At that low stage of his fortunes he met, by the merest chance it would seem, one Enos Wilder, who held a patent on an invention of a plaster-of-Paris lining for metallic safes. At that time (1840) no steel safe had been built which had stood the fire test with its contents unimpaired. Wood was the material commonly used for lining, and safe-manufacturers were still looking for a satisfactory non-conductor of heat to take its place. Herring was convinced that in plaster-of-Paris Wilder had that substance. He bought the manufacturing rights, paying Wilder a royalty of one cent a pound, and began to build the "Salamander" safe on a small scale. One factor in the rapid expansion of his business was advertising. In this Herring was aided by providence. New York in those days was the scene of many destructive fires. Whenever a Salamander safe emerged from one of these tests with its contents untouched by flame Herring lost no time in apprising the public of the fact, and he was continually challenging rival safe-manufacturers to a test of their products. His safe survived the *Tribune* building fire of 1845 triumphantly, the only one which did. The Wilder patent expired in 1852, having made both the patentee and Herring rich men for that day, but in the meantime Herring had added improvements with a view to making his product burglar-proof as well as fireproof. Although his safes have long since been superseded, for years they enabled the manufacturer to hold his own in competition. Herring married Mary A. Draper, of Brookfield, in 1831. She died six years later, and on May 9, 1843, he was married to Caroline S. Tarbell of Brimfield, Mass. One of his sons, Francis Otis, in after years succeeded to his father's business.

[*Vital Records of Brookfield, Mass.* (1909); *Vital Records of Brimfield, Mass.* (1931); T. W. Draper, *The Drapers in America* (1892); *Fighting Fire for Twenty-Six Years: Being the Actual Experience of Herring's Celebrated Safes* (n.d.); obituary in the *N. Y. Tribune*, June 25, 1881; certificate of death.]

W. B. S.

HERRMAN, AUGUSTINE (*c.* 1605–1686), colonial cartographer, merchant, land-holder, was born in Prague, Bohemia. His father, Augustin Ephraim Herrman, was a merchant and a councilor of Prague; his mother Beatrix, daughter of Kaspar Redel, was a member of a patrician Protestant family. Spending his early years in Bohemia, Herrman acquired a knowledge of English, French, and German, and at an early age took a decided interest in geography and map-making. In 1618 his father was outlawed for his political activity and the family escaped to Amsterdam. Young Herrman is said to have served for a time in the army of Gustavus Adolphus, but, forsaking a soldier's career, he soon entered the employ of the Dutch West India Company. Later he claimed to have been the founder (1629) of its Virginia tobacco trade (Rattermann, *post*; O'Callaghan, *Calendar*, p. 204). In 1633 he was a witness to a transaction whereby the Dutch bought from the Indians all the land now occupied by Philadelphia (Samuel Hazard, *Annals of Pennsylvania*, 1850, p. 35). During the following decade he was engaged, apparently, in trade with Brazil or Surinam; in 1643 he went from Curaçoa to New Netherland, where, the next year, he became an agent for Peter Gabry & Sons, a great mercantile firm of Amsterdam. After the death of the elder Gabry in 1651, quarrels arose between Herrman and the sons which led to the severing of the connection. Meanwhile, Herrman had built up a large business in beaver skins under his own name in New Amsterdam; had introduced and grown indigo successfully on Manhattan Island (Van der Donck, *post*, p. 156); had bought large tracts of land on Manhattan Island and in the present state of New Jersey, not only for himself, but also for Govert Loockermans, another prominent merchant of New Amsterdam; and with his partner, George Hack [*q.v.*], had become the largest exporter of tobacco in America.

Upon the reorganization of the government of New Netherland in 1647, Herrman was appointed one of Governor Stuyvesant's "Nine Men," but on July 28, 1649, he was one of the signers of the *Vertoogh* or "Remonstrance" to the States-General of the Netherlands, by which act he gained Stuyvesant's enmity. The vindictive old governor ruined him financially, together with his two powerful associates, Van der Donck and Loockermans, but in 1653 he was released from his creditors and for a while enjoyed the favor of Stuyvesant, who sent him on several diplomatic missions. Going to Maryland in 1659 to discuss with Lord Baltimore the Dutch-Maryland boundary dispute, he remained in that province for the rest of the year, sketching a map of the territory. Early in 1660 he presented a rough sketch of this map to Lord Baltimore, who was so pleased that he ordered papers of denization to be prepared for Herrman. In 1663, the latter petitioned for naturalization, and three years later he and his family became citizens of Maryland.

The map, *Virginia and Maryland as it is Planted and Inhabited This Present Year 1670 Surveyed and Exactly Drawne by the Only Labour & Endeavour of Augustin Herrman Bohemiensis*, is Herrman's outstanding achievement. Ten years were spent in making the necessary surveys. It was engraved in London in 1673 by William Faithorne and published the same year. One copy is in the British Museum and another in the John Carter Brown Library, Providence, R. I., where there is also a manuscript copy, formerly the property of William Blathwayt, secretary to the Lords Commissioners of Trade and Plantations. Lord Baltimore characterized it as "the best mapp that was ever Drawn of any Country whatsoever" (Phillips, *post*), and liberally rewarded Herrman for his services by granting him more than thirteen thousand acres of rich land in the extreme northeast corner of Maryland, now Cecil County. This land Herrman erected into a manor of which he became the first lord. Until the American Revolution, Bohemia Manor was an hereditary manor. On Dec. 10, 1651, Herrman had married Jannetje Verlett (or Varleth) of New Amsterdam, who bore him two sons and three daughters. His second wife was Catherine Ward of Cecil County, Maryland, by whom he had no children. Until his death Herrman lived in considerable magnificence in the great house which he built on the north bank of the Bohemia River. He was buried in his vineyard, beside his wife. His will was proved Nov. 11, 1686, the title "Lord of the Manor" descending to his eldest son, Ephraim.

[*Docs. Relative to the Colonial Hist. of the State of N. Y.*, vols. I, II (1856–58), XII (1877), XIV (1883); E. B. O'Callaghan, *Calendar of Hist. MSS. in the Office of the Secretary of State* (Albany, N. Y., 1865); Benthold Fernow, *The Records of New Amsterdam* (7 vols., 1897), esp. vols. I–III; W. H. Brown, *Archives of Md.: Judicial and Testamentary Proc. of the Provincial Court, 1649/50–1657* (1891), *Proc. and Acts of the Gen. Assem., 1637/8–1664* (1883) and *1666–1676* (1884), *Proc. of the Council of Md., 1667–1687/8* (1887) and *1687/8–1693* (1890); H. A. Rattermann, "Augustin Herrman" in *Deutsch-Amerikanisches Maga-*

zin, Jan.–July 1887; P. L. Phillips, *The Rare Map of Va. and Md. by Augustine Herrman* (1911); C. P. Mallery, "Ancient Families of Bohemia Manor," *Papers Hist. Soc. of Del.,* no. VII (1888); J. G. Wilson, "Augustine Herrman, Bohemian," *Proc. N. J. Hist. Soc.,* 2 ser. XI (1892); N. Y. *Sun,* Oct. 23, 1892; Adriaen Van der Donck, "A Description of New Netherlands," *N. Y. Hist. Soc. Colls.,* 2 ser. I (1841); *L. I. Hist. Soc. Memoirs,* vol. I (1867); *N. Y. Hist. and Geneal. Record,* Apr. 1878; L. C. Wroth, *John Carter Brown Library . . . Report,* 1930; *Pa. Mag. of Hist. and Biog.,* Oct. 1891; C. F. Hall, *Narratives of Early Md.* (1910); memoranda, a journal, and documents of Augustine Herrman in Md. Hist. Soc.] E. L. W. H.

HERRMANN, ALEXANDER (Feb. 10, 1844–Dec. 17, 1896), magician, was the son of parents whose names, according to himself, were Anna Meyer and Samuel Herrmann. The mother was from Hamburg; the father was a Berlin Jew, a physician, and magician of much ability. They had sixteen children, the younger of whom were born in Paris. The oldest son, Carl or Compars, was twenty-nine years old and a magician of established reputation when Alexander, the youngest child, was born. He was greatly attached to the child and aided him in running away when he was ten years old, taking him as his assistant to St. Petersburg. Two years later the mother insisted on placing the boy in school in Vienna. He was already spoiled for the quieter life and in 1859, much against their father's wish, Compars took him again as his assistant. They appeared in Spain that year and in the following year emigrated to America. Their American début at the New York Academy of Music, Sept. 16, 1861, was very successful. In 1862 Alexander left his brother to set up his own show and did not see him again until 1867, when they met in Vienna. They formed a temporary partnership and in 1869 Compars announced his brother as his successor. Alexander, traveling alone, covered much of the civilized world, including South America. He was so popular in London that an engagement at Egyptian Hall ran for a thousand nights. In 1875 he married Adelaide Scarsez, a dancer, who became his assistant. In the following year he took out papers of citizenship in the United States. He and his brother had made a friendly agreement to keep out of one another's way, for each had great drawing power. In his later years Herrmann published a number of books on the art of magic including *Herrmann's Hand-Book of Parlor Magic* (n.d.), *Herrmann's Black Art* (copyright 1898), *Herrmann's Conjuring for Amateurs* (1901), and *Herrmann's Book of Magic* (copyright 1902).

"Chevalier Alexander Herrmann," or "Herrmann the Great," with his Mephistophelian beard and mustache, his personal charm, his exceedingly clever sleight-of-hand, has been rated as one of the three leading American magicians. His repertoire changed little from year to year but his showmanship was good and his manner of presentation so skilful that his audiences came again and again to see him perform. In his time magicians ran their own shows, booked themselves, carried all of their theatrical equipment, including curtains, and usually did their own advertising. It was Herrmann's custom to play practical jokes in public places and, when a crowd had assembled, to announce himself and his performances.

[See H. J. Burlingame, *Herrmann the Magician* (1897); H. R. Evans, *Adventures in Magic* (1927); T. T. Timayenis, *A Hist. of the Art of Magic* (1887); the *Sphinx,* May 1903; *N. Y. Tribune,* Dec. 18, 1896; *N. Y. Dramatic Mirror,* Dec. 26, 1896. That the name Herrmann may have been assumed for the stage is indicated by the statements of Herrmann's niece, Mrs. Corelli, given in H. J. Burlingame, "Two Great Magicians," *Mahatma,* July, Aug. 1900.] K. H. A.

HERRON, FRANCIS JAY (Feb. 17, 1837–Jan. 8, 1902), the youngest major-general in the Civil War, was born at Pittsburgh, Pa., of an old and prominent family, his parents being John and Clarissa (Anderson) Herron. He entered the Western University of Pennsylvania (later the University of Pittsburgh) but left at sixteen to work in a bank. Two years later, in 1855, seeking the business opportunity of the West, he went to Dubuque, Iowa, where he and three brothers established a bank. His military interest developed early, and in 1859 he helped to organize an independent company known as the "Governor's Grays." This company, with himself in command, Herron offered to Lincoln as early as January 1861 and in the following April it became a unit of the 1st Iowa Regiment. After hard service with Lyon in Missouri through the disastrous reverse at Wilson's Creek, it was mustered out in August 1861. Herron acquitted himself so well that, in the following month, he was named lieutenant-colonel in the 9th Iowa. This regiment was in the thick of the Arkansas campaign, and at Pea Ridge Herron in a hand-to-hand encounter was wounded and taken prisoner. For his conduct on this occasion he was promoted, July 1862, to brigadier-general and in 1893 won a congressional medal. In his first command the young general achieved his outstanding personal success in December 1862 at Prairie Grove, Ark., where after a spectacular march he saved Blunt's command and turned apparent defeat into decisive victory. It was a choice, he wrote to a friend, of risking an immediate attack against great odds or retreating and losing his supplies. The battle was of such consequence in the conquest of Arkansas that it won for the commander the highest reward, and

Herron, after barely eighteen months in active service, was accorded a major-generalship, dating from Nov. 29, 1862.

With Grant at Vicksburg in 1863 Herron commanded the left division and was one of the three generals selected to take possession of the city. Transferred to the Department of the Gulf he took part in an international crisis by timely aid to President Juarez of Mexico. In February 1865 he assumed command of the northern district of Louisiana; he resigned the following June. After the war, like many other Union officers, Herron remained in the South to practise law and engage in politics. He was not successful in any connection. His investments resulted disastrously and his participation in Louisiana Reconstruction politics did not add to his fame. He was United States marshal, 1867–69, and for about a year, 1871–72, by designation of the notorious Governor Warmoth, he was *de facto* secretary of state. In 1877 he removed to New York City where he was connected with a manufacturing establishment until his death. He survived his second wife, Adelaide Wibray Flash, by only a few weeks.

[*War of the Rebellion: Official Records (Army)*; A. A. Stewart, *Iowa Colonels and Regiments, Being a Hist. of Iowa Regiments in the War of the Rebellion* (1865); *Battles and Leaders of the Civil War* (1888); Gretchen Carlson, article in the *Palimpsest*, Apr. 1930; *Annals of Iowa*, Jan. 1867; S. H. M. Byers, *Iowa in War Times* (1888); Ella Lonn, *Reconstruction in La. After 1868* (1918); *Telegraph-Herald* (Dubuque), and the *Sun* (N. Y.), Jan. 9, 1902; *N. Y. Tribune*, Oct. 8, 1893, Jan. 9, 1902.] E. D. R.

HERRON, GEORGE DAVIS (Jan. 21, 1862–Oct. 9, 1925), clergyman, lecturer, and writer, was born at Montezuma, Ind., of devoutly religious parents of Scotch origin, William and Isabella (Davis) Herron. His childhood he describes as obsessed with premonitions of a religious world mission, out of which, perhaps, grew the vivid and passionate conviction of messiahship and of an imminent kingdom of heaven on earth which in changing forms dominated his mature life. He attended the preparatory department of Ripon College, Ripon, Wis., from 1879 to 1882, working at the printer's trade to secure funds. In 1883 he married Mary Everhard and entered the ministry. His further education consisted of reading and independent reflection.

Herron first attracted public notice in 1891 when as pastor of the First Congregational Church of Lake City, Minn., he addressed the state Association of Congregational Ministers, meeting at Minneapolis, upon the theme: "The Message of Jesus to Men of Wealth." This address, published that same year, was an earnest and moving appeal for the application of Christian ethics to business, and resulted in Herron's being called to the pastorate of the First Congregational Church of Burlington, Iowa. Seventeen months later a professorship of applied Christianity was founded for his occupancy in Iowa College (later Grinnell) by Mrs. E. D. Rand of Burlington. During the six years of his service Iowa College became the center of nation-wide interest because of his attempt to translate Christianity into social, political, and economic terms. He brought to this work a fervor and eloquence which attracted students and impressed many men and women of insight and influence. His scathing criticism of existing institutions aroused bitter antagonism, however, and ultimately alienated many of his most loyal supporters.

As a consequence, he resigned his professorship in 1899. Joining the Socialist party, he tried to organize within it a "social crusade," which should give religious character to the movement. Mrs. E. D. Rand and her daughter, Carrie Rand, cooperated with him in various undertakings to this end in Chicago and in New York. Partly through his influence the Rand School of Social Sciences was founded in New York City in 1906 by Mrs. Rand. In March 1901 his wife divorced him for "cruelty culminating in desertion," and was given for the support of herself and the five children the personal fortune of Carrie Rand, amounting to sixty thousand dollars. On May 25, 1901, he and Carrie Rand were married in New York City by a ceremony, wherein "each chose the other as companion," thus dramatizing his avowed opposition to "all coercive institutions." He was at once deposed from the ministry and shortly afterward took up permanent residence with his wife and her mother upon an estate near Fiesole, Italy. He continued to exercise a large influence with the Socialist party, especially in its international activities, but devoted the major portion of his energy to literary work, aiming to give wider and more universal form to his ideas. As early as 1901 he had asserted that Jesus' view of life was "inadequate to the Social Revolution" and by 1910 he avowedly dropped the Christian phraseology, though his temper and teaching remained dominantly religious to the end of his life.

Like many Socialists, he viewed the World War at its outbreak as the capitalist catastrophe prophesied by Karl Marx. Later, however, he became violently anti-German, abandoned his pre-war pacifism, and broke with the Socialist party for its tolerance of Germany and of Bolshevism, trying even to divert from the Rand School the funds of the Rand estate. America's entrance into the war he envisioned as a "sacred crusade" wherein "for the first time in the earth's annals, a great and powerful people has gone to war for humanity" (*Germanism and the American Crusade,* 1918, p. 23). Of Woodrow Wilson he wrote an extravagant eulogy, *Woodrow Wilson and the World's Peace* (1917). During the negotiations for peace he appears to have had a large place in the confidence of the German emissaries and of President Wilson. He influenced the German representatives to trust Wilson's power to enforce upon the Allies conditions favorable to Germany and as Wilson's personal emissary persuaded Kurt Eisner to advocate the acknowledgment by Germany of her war guilt. He sided with the Bavarian Revolution against the German Republic of which he sent bitter denunciations to the American press. Early in the Russian Revolution he seems to have been favorable to the Bolshevists but he soon became alienated from their program. President Wilson's appointment of Herron and William Allen White as America's representatives to the abortive Prinkipo Conference aroused a storm of protest in the American press, based chiefly upon Herron's views regarding marriage. When the terms of peace became known he was inevitably discredited with both radicals and conservatives and was bitterly hated in Prussia. He turned to Italy as a final Utopian hope and in 1920 published in periodicals of Europe and America his "ecstatic confidence" that Italy would become a "more Christly society than the world has yet known." On the death of his second wife in 1914, he married Friede B. Schoeberle. His books are for the most part collections of sermons and lectures, or reprints of articles in American and European periodicals. Besides those already mentioned, the more important are: *The Larger Christ* (1891), *The Call of the Cross,* and *A Plea for the Gospel* (1892), *The Christian State* (1895), *Social Meanings of Religious Experiences* (1896), *Between Cæsar and Jesus* (1899), *Why I am a Socialist* (1900), *The Day of Judgment* (1904), *From Revolution to Revolution* (1907); *The Menace of Peace* (1917), *The Defeat in the Victory* (1921). His war papers, two volumes of which were sealed for twenty-five years, were deposited in the Hoover Library of Stanford University. He died at Munich, Bavaria, in his sixty-fourth year.

[*Arena,* Apr. 1896; *Who's Who in America,* 1918–19; *Our Day,* June 1895; *Rev. of Revs.* (N. Y.), Dec. 1899; *Independent,* June 13, 1901; *Current Opinion,* Aug. 1913; *Outlook,* Feb. 19, 1919; *N. Y. Times,* Feb. 8, 1919, and Oct. 11, 1925; *Das Literarische Echo,* Dec. 1, 1922; information from relatives and associates.]

C. M. S.

HERSCHEL, CLEMENS (Mar. 23, 1842–Mar. 1, 1930), hydraulic engineer, was born in Boston, Mass., and spent his boyhood in Davenport, Iowa. Prepared by a tutor, he entered the Lawrence Scientific School of Harvard University at sixteen, graduating with distinction in 1860. He wished then to attend the École des Ponts et Chaussées in Paris, but since the quota of foreign students there was filled, he went instead to the Carlsruhe Technical School, where he completed the course in 1863. Returning to the United States, he established his headquarters in Boston, and engaged in diverse works of engineering, including roads, drainage, roofs, and bridges. He was engineer of the Quinnipiac drawbridge in New Haven, 1874–78, and in 1875 he published *Continuous Revolving Drawbridges: Principles of Construction and Calculation of Strains.* He abandoned bridge engineering in 1879, however, because he saw in its future the survival only of the large bridge companies in which the individual engineer was obscured. Not wishing to become a mere "cog in a wheel," as he expressed it, he turned his attention to hydraulics where he could be more independent, and accepted employment with the Holyoke Water Power Company at Holyoke, Mass.

In this field, under James B. Francis [*q.v.*], to whom he later referred as "my former master," Herschel found his proper *milieu.* He soon became chief engineer at Holyoke. In this capacity he rebuilt the early-type wooden dam of the Holyoke Company across the Connecticut River, constructed the Holyoke testing flume which marked the beginning of scientific study of water turbines, and invented the Venturi meter, a device without moving parts for the measurement of the flow of water in pipes. The last of these is the achievement for which he will be best and longest remembered. The Venturi meter is in ever-increasing use the world over in substantially the same form in which Herschel produced it originally. For a paper describing it (1888), he received the Rowland prize of the American Society of Civil Engineers, and in 1899 the Franklin Institute of Philadelphia awarded him its Elliott Cresson medal for his invention.

He left Holyoke in 1899 to become chief engineer of the East Jersey Water Company. His service there continued until 1900, during which time he built works providing a large additional water supply for Newark, N. J., and nearby places. He was the author of *115 Experiments on the Carrying Capacity of Large, Riveted*

Metal Conduits (1897). After 1900 he engaged in consulting engineering practice. Among his engagements, some of which antedated this year, were those with the power companies at Niagara Falls and with the City of New York in relation to the water tunnel and aqueduct for the Catskill supply. In 1899 he published a translation of *The Two Books on the Water Supply of the City of Rome* by Sextus Julius Frontinus, water commissioner of the Imperial City in 97 A.D., who recorded in these books a history and description of the water supply and the famous aqueducts and a statement of his interpretation of hydraulic principles. The translation was made with the help of French and German versions from the Latin manuscript copy which Herschel located in the Benedictine monastery of Monte Cassino, Italy, and of which he had photographic reproductions made.

Herschel's most notable achievements reflect his abhorrence of sham, dishonesty, and misrepresentation. The measurement of water appealed to him as a bulwark against these and against waste. He championed the Venturi meter as a weapon for conservation. His Holyoke testing flume was a device to test the claims of the many water turbines then being foisted on the market under a screen of inaccurate and often deceitful representation. In his study of the work of Frontinus he scored earlier French and German translators for their "unfounded but grandiloquent" estimates of the carrying capacities of the Roman aqueducts. He advocated the association of purchasers of hydraulic equipment for the purpose of testing the many articles offered under various names, in order to promote scientific buying. His name was ever prominent in the discussions of papers before the American Society of Civil Engineers on the side of thorough search for truth. With halfway studies, with promises loosely assumed, he had no sympathy, and he was outspoken in his attack upon them.

In 1922, he was made an honorary member of the American Society of Civil Engineers, being at the time of his death one of eighteen to enjoy that distinction. He had been president of the Society in 1916. He was an early member of the Boston Society of Civil Engineers, its president in 1890–91, and later an honorary member. In 1890 he became a member of the Institution of Civil Engineers (London). Herschel married Grace D. Hobart of Boston in 1869. She died in 1898, and in 1910 he married Jeannette B. Hunter of Thompsonville, Conn. Two sons and a daughter were born of his first marriage and one son of his second. As if to plead his age and seek release from exacting professional duties, he caused the word "retired" to be inserted below his name on his letterhead in the last few years of his life. To the end, however, he maintained a vigorous interest in public affairs, particularly in those that affected engineering. He died shortly before the close of his eighty-eighth year at his home in Glen Ridge, N. J.

[W. G. Kent, *An Appreciation of Two Great Workers in Hydraulics* (London, 1912); memoir of Clemens Herschel prepared for Am. Soc. Civil Engrs., by J. W. Smith and W. H. Burr; *Proc. Am. Soc. Civil Engineers,* vol. LVI, pt. 2 (1930); *Who's Who in America,* 1928–29; *Engineering News Record,* Mar. 6, 1930; *N. Y. Times,* Mar. 3, 1930; "Frontinus, etc.," *Trans. Asso. Civil Engrs. Cornell Univ.,* vol. II (1894); *Trans. Am. Soc. Civil Engrs.,* 1869–1930.] M. K.

HERTER, CHRISTIAN (Jan. 8, 1840–Nov. 2, 1883), designer, head of the firm of Herter Brothers, interior decorators on a grand scale, was an influential figure in American art during the period after the Civil War when the "palaces" of the pioneer millionaires were rising. He was the son of another Christian Herter, a German woodcarver and cabinetmaker of repute, who had a furniture establishment in Stuttgart. His mother was Christiana, *née* Schaeffer, who when she married Herter was a widow with one son, Gustave, to whom her husband gave the Herter name. Both Christian and his half-brother were well educated, and both early displayed artistic gifts. Gustave was the first to emigrate to America. After two years in the atelier of the German architect Leins, where he designed the interior woodwork for the Royal Villa at Berg, he appeared in New York about 1848 as a silver designer at Tiffany's. By 1854 he had established a business, under the caption, "Gustave Herter, Decorations."

Meanwhile, Christian was a student at the Stuttgart Polytechnic. He seems to have been but fifteen when he entered the École des Beaux Arts in Paris. Some five years later he joined Gustave in New York, where, in 1864, he married Mary Miles, daughter of Dr. Archibald Miles of Cleveland. As a designer apparently first at Tiffany's and later in Gustave's atelier, he showed such brilliant endowment that about 1868 his brother sent him to Paris for further study. There he worked under Pierre Victor Galland, whose success as a decorative artist was broadly based on knowledge of architecture, sculpture, and painting. Young Herter's lifelong desire to become a painter was intensified by his contacts in Galland's studio with most of the distinguished brushmen of France. This ambition he sacrificed, however, out of a sense of responsibility toward his family, for the surer returns of business. Returning to New York in 1870, he bought Gustave out, and during the ensuing decade, by his originality, independence, business acumen, and many-sided artistic skill, he advanced the reputation of Herter Brothers to the front rank. Among great houses unconditionally intrusted to him for their interior decorations and fittings were those of Governor Latham and Mark Hopkins in San Francisco, D. O. Mills in Menlo Park, Heber R. Bishop, David Dows, Pierpont Morgan, and William H. Vanderbilt in New York. For the Vanderbilt houses (Fifth Avenue at Fifty-first Street) Herter was responsible for both exterior and interior plans, designing also most of the furniture, textiles, mosaics, and carvings. It was his last contract. Retiring with a fortune, about 1880, he returned to Paris to study under Jean Paul Laurens, hoping at last to realize his old dream of success as a painter, but after about a year he contracted tuberculosis and came home to die.

Christian Herter drew on the resources of all periods, all countries, to feed his invention. After the Centennial, he was the first to bring to the United States Chinese porcelains, Persian pottery and embroideries, Japanese art objects, and to employ Oriental *motifs* in his interiors, thus changing the taste in America and revolutionizing textile design. A man of great physical beauty, magnetism, and charm, musical, well-read in the literature of four languages, socially gifted, he was as popular among his workmen as with his fellow designers or his millionaire patrons. Upon the talented young men who were associated with him in his work—among them being Charles B. Atwood [*q.v.*] and Alexander Sandier—he left the stamp of his high idealism and his artistry.

[W. G. N., *In Memory of Christian Herter* (n.d.); Wm. Baumgarten, "Christian Herter's Verdienste," in *N. Y. Staats-Zeitung*, Feb. 20, 1898; *Am. Architect and Builder*, May 2, 1881; *Artistic Houses*, vol. I (1883); *N. Y. Times*, *N. Y. Tribune*, Nov. 3, 1883; information as to certain facts from members of the family.]

M. B. H.

HERTER, CHRISTIAN ARCHIBALD (Sept. 3, 1865–Dec. 5, 1910), physician, biochemist, was the son of Christian Herter [*q.v.*] and Mary (Miles) Herter. His father, who was of German parentage, was well known as an artist and interior decorator. Young Herter, who chanced to be born in Glenville, Conn., was brought up mainly in New York City. Although he was a graduate of the Columbia Grammar School, most of his preliminary education was private, under the direction of his father, and comprised music and the fine arts. Selecting for himself the career of a physician, he received his medical degree from the College of Physicians and Surgeons (Columbia) in 1885. In December 1886 he was married to Susan Dows. The years following his graduation were passed at Johns Hopkins, where he came under the influence of Professor William Welch, and in Europe. In 1888 he settled in New York and on the uppermost floor of his sumptuous residence, 819 Madison Ave., he established a laboratory where for many years he experimented in bacteriology, chemistry, pharmacology, and pathology. At the same time he led the life of a practising physician, and even after his laboratory and teaching efforts came to encroach more and more heavily on his work in clinical medicine, he retained his connection with hospitals. From 1894 to 1904, for example, he was visiting physician to the New York City Hospital. In 1898 he was given the chair of pathological chemistry at Bellevue Hospital Medical College, but in 1903 he joined the faculty of his alma mater, Columbia, as professor of pharmacology and therapeutics, retaining this chair until his death. Beginning with 1901 he became closely identified with the new Rockefeller Institute for Medical Research; he was its treasurer for several years, a director, and for a time, one of the visiting physicians to its hospital.

Very early in his career Herter developed strong leanings toward clinical neurology, and in 1892 he published his first book, *The Diagnosis of Diseases of the Nervous System.* He also contributed "Diseases of the Cranial Nerves" to F. X. Dercum's *Textbook of Nervous Diseases by American Authors,* which appeared in 1895. Eventually he seems to have lost his interest in neurology, however, for when a second edition of his textbook on diagnosis was issued in 1907 (*The Diagnosis of Organic Nervous Diseases*) he turned the revision over to Dr. L. Pierce Clark and took no part in the work himself. In 1902 appeared his second book, *Lectures on Chemical Pathology in Its Relation to Practical Medicine,* regarded as somewhat of an epoch-making work. This was followed by *The Common Bacterial Infections of the Digestive Tract and the Intoxication Arising from Them* (1907); *On Infantilism from Chronic Intestinal Infection* (1908), which work, regarded as a classic, was at once translated into German and served to make the condition now known as "Herter's infantilism" generally familiar; and the posthumous work, *Biological Aspects of Human Problems* (1911), in which the author entered into the rare domain of medical philosophy. In addition he contributed to periodical literature more than seventy scientific articles, largely the results of his own research. In 1905, with Professor J. J. Abel of Johns Hopkins he founded and edited the *Journal of Biological Chemistry,* of which in 1909–10 he was sole editor; and he was a charter member of the American Society of Biological Chemists, which was established in 1908. For several years before his death he was in failing health and endured considerable suffering, but he was active to the last. He died in his forty-sixth year, survived by his wife and three daughters.

Herter's most notable contribution to medicine was the foundation, with Mrs. Herter, of two lectureships, at Johns Hopkins and Bellevue respectively. Even during his lifetime some of the foremost scientists in the world—Ehrlich, Schaefer, Starling, and others equally eminent—gave Herter Lecture courses. The Herter Lectures attract many distinguished Europeans who otherwise might never choose to make the voyage across the Atlantic, and remain today one of the most advanced media for the dissemination of European medical culture in the United States.

[*Bio-Chemical Jour.* (Liverpool), V (1911), xxi; *Jour. of Biological Chem.*, Dec. 1910; *Bull. Johns Hopkins Hospital,* May 1911; *Who's Who in America,* 1910–11; H. A. Kelly and W. L. Burrage, *Am. Medic. Biogs.* (1920); *N. Y. Times, N. Y. Tribune,* Dec. 6, 1910.] E. P.

HESSELIUS, GUSTAVUS (1682–May 25, 1755), portrait painter and organ builder, was born at Folkarna, Dalarne, Sweden, and went to Philadelphia in 1711. He belonged to a family conspicuous for learning and piety. His father and four brothers were clergymen, and his maternal uncle was the father of Emanuel Svedberg, or Swedenborg, founder of the Swedenborgian Church. A nephew attained distinction as an artist. Gustavus Hesselius arrived May 1, 1711, at Christina (now Wilmington), Del., with his brother Andreas, who had been commissioned by Charles XII to take charge of the church there. A few weeks later he went to Philadelphia "on account of his business" but remained there only a few years. Somewhat later he may have lived for a short time in Wilmington, as one of his children was baptized there in 1716. Between 1716 and 1720 he removed to Prince George's County, Md., where he remained until the early thirties, when he returned to Philadelphia to live there until his death in 1755. He married, probably in Philadelphia or Delaware, his wife Lydia, whose family name is unknown. He was survived by one son, John Hesselius [*q.v.*], and three daughters. Contemporary records indicate that Hesselius began his American career as a painter. Although nearly forty portraits in public and private collections are attributed to him, the attribution in many instances is decidedly questionable. Very few signed portraits by him are known. The painting that has given Hesselius a distinctive position in the history of the fine arts in America is the large and elaborate altar-piece, "The Last Supper," which in 1721 he was commissioned by the vestry to paint for St. Barnabas' Church, Prince Georges County, Md. This was the first public art commission in the colonies of which we have a record. This painting, for which he received £17, was removed when the church was demolished in 1773 and is now in a private collection. He also painted a "Crucifixion." Of his first Philadelphia period almost nothing is known, nor have any portraits definitely attributable to him then been traced. Of his Maryland period, covering some fifteen years from about 1718 to 1733, little is known except what is gleaned from the church records and from the dozen or more Maryland portraits by him still extant. After his return to Philadelphia about 1735 and his purchase in that year of a house on High Street, he becomes less nebulous. A number of portraits painted by him in this second Philadelphia period are known. Two very characteristic portraits are those of himself and his wife Lydia in the Pennsylvania Historical Society. The portraits of the Rev. John Eversfield and his wife, his neighbors in southern Maryland, and those of Thomas Bordley, attorney-general of Maryland, and of the Rev. William Brogden, are equally typical, all showing the peculiar modeling and the sombre colors which he so much used. In "The Last Supper," which seems to be an original composition, the same coloring is employed. Brought up as a Swedish Lutheran, in Maryland Hesselius affiliated with the Church of England. Afterward in Philadelphia he joined the Moravian Brethren, and in 1746 was paid £25, 9s., for building an organ for the Moravian church in Bethlehem. A few years before his death, however, he reverted to his original Lutheran faith. In his latter years he seems to have devoted more time to organ-building and after about 1750 to have diverted as much portrait work as possible to his son John.

["Gustavus Hesselius, the Earliest Painter and Organ-Builder in America," *Pa. Mag. of Hist. and Biog.*, Apr. 1905; C. H. Hart, "The Earliest Painter in America," *Harper's Mag.*, Mar. 1898; Charles Henry Hart MSS., Frick Art Reference Library; manuscript records of Queen Anne's Parish, Prince Georges County, Md., of Old Swedes' Church, Phila., of the Moravian churches, Phila. and Bethlehem; Wertmüller's Jour., Pa. Hist. Soc.; will of Gustavus Hesselius, Phila.] J. H. P—s.

HESSELIUS, JOHN (1728–Apr. 9, 1778), portrait painter, son of Gustavus Hesselius [*q.v.*] and his wife, Lydia, was probably born in Prince

Georges County, Md. His youth was spent in Philadelphia where his father had returned in the early thirties, and there is no question that it was under his father's tutelage that he first learned to paint. It was doubtless on one of his frequent painting expeditions to Maryland that he met and married, on Jan. 30, 1763, a wealthy young woman, Mary Woodward. She was the widow of Henry Woodward of "Primrose Hill," an Anne Arundel County planter, and the daughter of Col. Richard Young who lived near Annapolis. This marriage into the prominent Young family insured Hesselius the patronage of the wealthy landholding aristocracy of the province. While his early portraits show the effect of his father's teaching, during the fifties he came under the influence of John Wollaston [*q.v.*], the English artist who "in the grand style" painted very extensively in Maryland and Virginia at this time. Not only the "almond eyes" but a certain similarity in the pose of the figure characterized the work of both artists. In the later sixties and down to the time of his death in 1778 Hesselius' work deteriorated, portraits painted during the last ten years of his life being rather wooden and stereotyped in their execution. At this period nearly all the women he painted looked middle-aged and strangely similar, and were dressed in costumes almost identical. In only a slightly lesser degree is the same similarity to be found in his portraits of men and of children.

Hesselius was probably the most prolific painter of the pre-Revolutionary period, his known portraits numbering nearly a hundred. Writing to William Dunlap about 1824, Robert Gilmor of Baltimore, perhaps the first American art collector of importance, refers to him as "Hesselius by whom the greater part of the family portraits in the old mansions of Maryland was painted, and that in a respectable manner" (William Dunlap, *History of the Rise and Progress of the Arts of Design in the United States,* 1834, I, 131). The old mansions of Virginia and Philadelphia might well have been included in the statement. To say that he was the equal of any American-born artist whose career was confined to the pre-Revolutionary period is perhaps fainter praise than he really deserves. The portraits of Samuel Chew and his wife, and the three charming portraits of the children of Benedict Calvert, show strongly the Wollaston influence. The later portrait of Governor Johnson in the Maryland Historical Society and that of his wife, and those of Mrs. John Moale and of Col. Edward Fell and his wife, are typical of the more conventionalized style which usually characterized his later work. Many of Hesselius' portraits are found signed. Occasionally they are dated and signed on the front, but the great majority of his portraits show in his large, clear, round handwriting on the back of the canvas the name and age of the subject, as well as the signature of the artist and the date.

Hesselius lived until his death at "Bellefield," a fine plantation of about a thousand acres on the Severn River near Annapolis, which he acquired through his wife. He had the affection and respect of the community in which he lived and was for several years a vestryman and warden of St. Anne's Church, Annapolis. Although of independent means he continued to work actively at his profession until within a short time of his death. He died in his fiftieth year, leaving a widow, one son, and three daughters, and is buried on his plantation.

["Gustavus Hesselius, the Earliest Painter and Organ-Builder in America," *Pa. Mag. of Hist. and Biog.,* Apr. 1905; "Young-Woodward-Hesselius Family Record, 1737–1820," *Md. Hist. Mag.,* Sept. 1926; Charles Henry Hart MSS., Frick Art Reference Library; register of St. Anne's Parish, Anne Arundel County, Md.; will of John Hesselius.]
J. H. P—s.

HESSOUN, JOSEPH (Aug. 8, 1830–July 4, 1906), Roman Catholic priest, was born in Vrcovice near Pisek in Bohemia, the son of Albert and Marie (Strabochova) Hessoun. His father, an overseer of a large tract of land, died when Joseph, the youngest of seven children, was a child, and whatever virtue he possessed, as he later touchingly admitted, was due only to his good mother. On the advice of teachers and pastor, he was sent to Pisek for his preparatory studies; for his philosophical studies he went to Budweis; and thence to the seminary, where he took high rank. On July 31, 1853, he was ordained by Bishop Jirsik. After twelve years' service as priest in his native land, he answered the call of Msgr. Joseph Melcher, who had complained that there were five thousand Czechs in St. Louis without a priest able to speak their tongue. Upon his arrival in that city, Oct. 4, 1865, he took charge of St. John of Nepomuk, the first American Bohemian church, where, as a result of the Civil War, he found finances involved and religious zeal flagging. He soon organized a model parish, built a large Gothic church in 1870 which he was forced to reconstruct after the cyclone of 1896, established two thriving parochial schools which assisted in perpetuating the language as well as the faith, and aided in developing the second Bohemian parish of St. Wenceslas. As a means of counteracting the Hussite, rationalistic, and radical propaganda among American Bohemians, he joined with Fathers Joseph Maly and Joseph Molitor in establishing at Chicago in 1868 the weekly *Katolicke Noviny.* Since this journal soon failed, in 1871 he founded the ephemeral *Hlas* of St. Louis. Two years later, he revived it and with the aid of a lay editor managed the paper until 1899 during which time it became the outstanding Bohemian Catholic publication. In 1877, he was instrumental in organizing the first Czech Central Roman Catholic Union under which all the local and sectional Bohemian beneficial societies were federated. He assisted the Bohemian Benedictines in the foundation of an abbey in Chicago (1885), supported St. Procopius Abbey and College in Lisle, Ill., and promoted the Bohemian Benedictine Press in Chicago, which city had superseded St. Louis as the Bohemian center.

Hessoun was a national leader, known as the "Little Father" to a half million of his countrymen. A speaker of force and learning, he lectured and preached in all Bohemian centers and in fraternal conventions, so that a rationalist writer could describe him as "the greatest prelate the American Čech Catholics have had" (Thomas Căpek, *The Cechs in America,* 1920, p. 248). In 1896, Pope Leo XIII raised him to the rank of domestic prelate in lieu of episcopal honors for which he was racially unavailable. In 1899, he was partially incapacitated by an apoplectic stroke but lived on several years. In 1903 his golden jubilee was celebrated by all his people; the bishop of Budweis in Bohemia named him an honorary canon; the Bohemian Societies built as a memorial the Hessoun Bohemian Orphanage at Fenton, Mo. In 1929 a memorial tablet in his honor was erected in the town of his birth by American Bohemians.

[A. P. Houst, *Krátkě Dějiny a Seznam Čezko-Katolických Osad ve Spoz-Statech Amerických* (1890); Jan Habenicht, *Dějiny Čechůi Amerických* (1904); *The First Čech Cath. Convention . . . held in St. Louis, Sept. 24–26, 1907;* J. E. Rothensteiner, *Hist. of the Archdiocese of St. Louis,* vol. II (1928); *Nat. Cath. Welfare Council Rev.,* Sept. 1930; *Hlas Almanac* (1907); *Katolik Almanac* (1907); *Narod* (Chicago), July 5, 1906; *St. Louis Globe-Democrat,* July 6, 11, 1906.]

A. V. T.

HETH, HENRY (Dec. 16, 1825–Sept. 27, 1899), soldier, was born at Black Heath Estate, Chesterfield County, Va., the son of John and Margaret (Pickett) Heth, and a cousin of Gen. George E. Pickett [*q.v.*]. His paternal grandfather, Henry Heth, and three brothers were officers in the Revolution, and his father was an officer in the navy in the War of 1812 and later served as a colonel of Virginia volunteers. Henry Heth was educated in private schools of Virginia until he was twelve, when he entered Georgetown College where he remained for one year. He afterwards attended schools in New York. Refusing an appointment to the Naval Academy in 1842, he accepted from President Tyler, the following year, an appointment as cadet in the United States Military Academy. Upon his graduation in 1847 he was appointed brevet second lieutenant. He served through the war with Mexico and later married his first cousin, Harriet Selden, daughter of Miles and Harriet (Heth) Selden, by whom he had three children. Until the outbreak of the Civil War Heth served in various Western posts, becoming a first lieutenant in 1853 and captain in 1855. During the Sioux expedition of 1855 he saw action, Sept. 3, at Blue Water, Nebr. He was on a board for testing breech-loading rifles in 1857 and in 1858 wrote *A System of Target Practice,* which was published by the War Department as a textbook. It was largely a translation from the French and curiously foreshadowed the present methods.

Heth resigned from the army Apr. 25, 1861, and joined the Confederacy, serving in various staff capacities from captain to colonel during that year. In the fall he organized Floyd's command for the West Virginia campaign, taking part in the battle of Carnifax Ferry and conducting Floyd's retreat. On Jan. 6, 1862, he became a brigadier-general and assumed command of a military district in the vicinity of Lewisburg, Va. In engagements during May 1862, against Frémont and Crook, he came off second best, but in June President Davis recommended him highly to Kirby-Smith and assigned him to that officer for duty. He served as a post and division commander in Bragg's army during the expedition into Kentucky, in Kirby-Smith's corps and later he commanded the Department of East Tennessee. General Lee, on Nov. 25, 1862, asked for Heth's transfer to the Army of Northern Virginia, and in January 1863, he was so transferred. At first commanding a brigade in A. P. Hill's division, he took command of the division when Hill was wounded at Chancellorsville, and was commended by both Lee and Stuart. Following a personal recommendation of Lee to President Davis, he became a major-general on May 24, and was given four brigades with which to form a division for Lee's northward thrust which ended at Gettysburg. His most conspicuous action was at the battle of Gettysburg, when, as part of Hill's III Corps his outposts unexpectedly engaged a superior force of the enemy and precipitated the general battle on July 1. In twenty-five minutes his division lost more than a third of its strength, and Heth was wounded. Two days later, under Pettigrew, his division, the smallest in the army, advanced on the left of Pickett in the charge and suffered severely.

He was not a particularly successful general, being defeated more times than he won and never winning a decisive victory, but he was held in high esteem for his personal qualities and retained command of his division until the surrender at Appomattox. After the war he engaged in the insurance business in Richmond. From 1880 to 1884 he was in the government service as a civil engineer on river and harbor work. For some years thereafter he was special agent for the office of Indian affairs. Prior to his becoming ill in December 1898, he had been serving as commissioner for marking the graves of the Confederate dead at Antietam battlefield. His death occurred in Washington, D. C.

[Data regarding Heth's family and schooling given in an unpublished autobiography, extracts from which are used by consent of surviving relatives; L. G. Tyler, *Encyc. of Va. Biog.*, vol. III (1915); *Proc. Va. Hist. Soc. . . . 1891* (1892); G. W. Cullum, *Biog. Reg. of the Officers and Grads. of the U. S. Military Acad.* (3rd ed., 1891), vol. II; *Battles and Leaders of the Civil War*, 4 vols. (1884–88); *War of the Rebellion: Official Records (Army)*; C. B. Evans, *Confed. Mil. Hist.*, vol. III (1899); *Richmond Times*, and *Evening Star* (Washington), Sept. 27, 1899; *Confed. Veteran*, Dec. 1899.] D. Y.

HEWAT, ALEXANDER (*c.* 1745–*c.* 1829), Presbyterian clergyman, Loyalist, historian, was born in Scotland and educated at Kelso Grammar School and the University of Edinburgh. He emigrated to Charleston, S. C., in 1763, arriving in November of that year, and became pastor of the First Presbyterian, or Scots Church in Charleston, which he served for about twelve years. Soon after his arrival he was admitted to membership in the Saint Andrew's Society. According to tradition, he became intimate with the family of Gov. William Bull [*q.v.*]. He was a royalist and, therefore, not in sympathy with the spirit of revolt in the colonies. As the Revolution approached and the conflict between the colonies and the mother country seemed inevitable he left South Carolina, probably in 1775, and went to England. There, in 1779, he published *An Historical Account of the Rise and Progress of the Colonies of South Carolina and Georgia,* in two volumes. It covers the period from the discovery of America to the repeal of the Stamp Act in 1766. In the preface Hewat stated: "The Southern provinces in particular have been hitherto neglected, insomuch that no writer has favored the world with any tolerable account of them. Therefore it is hoped, that a performance which brings those important, though obscure, colonies into public view, and tends to throw some light upon their situation, will meet with a favorable reception." Despite the assistance he is supposed to have obtained from his friend William Bull, Hewat was hampered by lack of historical material. The sources of colonial history were not published and the manuscripts were difficult to use even when they were available. The records in South Carolina were not accessible. He expressed his regret that he was sometimes obliged to have recourse to very confused materials, and he was sometimes mistaken in his statements; nevertheless his work is noteworthy as the first history of South Carolina. He also published *Sermons* (2 vols., 1803–05), which have been characterized as "chiefly on duties rather than doctrines" (Howe, *post,* I, 404). In 1780 he was awarded the degree of D.D. by the University of Edinburgh. He appeared as a witness before the Royal Commission on the losses and services of American Loyalists in 1785. His interest in South Carolina continued until the end of his life. In 1792 he was one of those requested to help select a pastor for his old charge, the Scots Church. He married a Mrs. Barksdale, a widow from Carolina, who was visiting England for the sake of her children's health. She was probably the "Eliza, wife of Rev. Dr. Hewat" whose death is recorded in the *Gentleman's Magazine* for May 1814. Hewat corresponded with his old friends in America, and by his will left to the church in Charleston the sum of fifty pounds, which was received by its treasurer on Oct. 4, 1829. Apparently his last years were spent in London and there, it is supposed, he died.

[Although Hewat's name has been spelled differently by different writers, there seems to be no doubt as to the spelling he himself used. The matter is discussed in W. B. Sprague, *Annals Am. Pulpit*, vol. III (1858). For the facts of his career see also: *A Catalogue of the Graduates . . . of the University of Edinburgh* (1858); George Howe, *Hist. of the Presbyt. Ch. in S. C.*, vol. I (1870); Edward McCrady, *S. C. under Proprietary Govt.* (1897), p. 17, and *S. C. under the Royal Govt., 1719–76* (1901), I, 443; G. A. Wauchope, *The Writers of S. C.* (1910); *The Royal Commission on the Losses and Services of Am. Loyalists, 1783–85, Being the Notes of Mr. Daniel Parker Coke, M.P.* (1915), ed. by H. E. Egerton; Hew Scott, *Fasti Ecclesiae Scoticanae*, new ed., VII (1928), 663.] P. S. F.

HEWES, JOSEPH (Jan. 23, 1730–Nov. 10, 1779), signer of the Declaration of Independence, was born in Kingston, N. J. His parents, Aaron and Providence (Worth) Hewes, were Quakers, and the son grew up in their faith, but he gradually drifted away from it in North Carolina and definitely abandoned it at the outbreak of the Revolution. After finishing school he was apprenticed to a Philadelphia merchant and later, going into business for himself, acquired a comfortable fortune. Sometime between 1756 and 1763, he moved to Edenton, N. C., where he established a thriving mercantile and shipping business. He became engaged to Isabella Johnston, but she died within a few days of the time set for their wedding, and he never married. In Edenton he was "a particular favorite with everybody," being generally regarded as "one of the best and most agreeable men in the world," "the patron and the greatest honor of the town." In 1766 he began a service as borough member of the colonial assembly, in which he continued until the end of the royal government in 1775. In 1773 he was a member of the committee of correspondence and as a matter of course he was a delegate to all five provincial congresses. In 1774 he was elected to the Continental Congress and served until 1777, when he failed of election. A few days later he declined, partly on account of ill health, to allow the use of his name in another election. He was borough member of the House of Commons in 1778 and in 1779 was again elected to Congress and died in Philadelphia during the session.

In Congress Hewes rendered distinguished service. At the first session he aided in preparing the statement of the rights of the colonies and in spite of his knowledge of the effect it would have upon his personal fortunes strongly supported the policy of non-importation. In 1776, when he spent the entire year in Philadelphia, he was a member of the secret committee, the committee on claims, and the committee to prepare a plan of confederation. He was the active member and real head of the committee to fit out armed vessels, and as chairman of the committee of marine, was in actual fact the first executive head of the navy of the United States. His business training and ability and his experience as a ship-owner made his selection for that position a fortunate one. He had known John Paul Jones in North Carolina, and it was he who appointed Jones an officer of the navy and found him a ship. He is said to have aided Washington in planning the campaign of 1776. In the beginning, however, Hewes had not desired a permanent break with Great Britain. He wrote an English correspondent: "We do not want to be independent; we want no revolution. But every American to a man is determined to die or be free" (Ashe, *post,* 176). He gloried in rebellion while he shrank from independence, hanging back in his support of the resolution in spite of the peremptory instructions of the North Carolina provincial congress, until John Adams convinced him of the popular strength of the independence movement in his province. Then, as Adams described it, he "started suddenly upright, and lifting up both his hands to Heaven, as if he had been in a trance, cried out, 'It is done! and I will abide by it'" (C. F. Adams, *The Works of John Adams,* vol. X, 1856, p. 35). His labors were tremendous. Regularly he worked twelve hours a day without interruption and without food or drink, and in consequence his health failed utterly. His death, which occurred after a brief collapse, came as a direct result of overwork. He was buried in Christ Church, Philadelphia.

[S. A. Ashe, *Biog. Hist. of N. C.,* vol. III (1905); Eben Putnam, *Lieut. Joshua Hewes . . . and a Sketch of Joseph Hewes the Signer* (1913); E. C. Burnett, *Letters of Members of the Continental Congress,* vols. I–IV (1921–28); John Sanderson, *Biog. of the Signers to the Declaration of Independence,* vol. VII (1827); G. J. McRee, *Life and Corresp. of James Iredell* (2 vols., 1857–58); *N. C. Booklet,* Sept. 1904.]

J. G. de R. H.

HEWES, ROBERT (1751–July 1830), glass-maker, instructor in fencing, bone-setter, was born in Boston, Mass., shortly after his parents' arrival from London, England. His mother was Ann Rose Frye. Upon settling in America his father took up the trade of tallow-chandler; the business prospered, and upon the death of the elder Hewes Robert inherited $50,000, a large sum of money for those days. The boy was well-educated, versatile, ambitious, and had no desire to continue solely with his father's business. Looking through an encyclopedia, he noticed an account of the history and manufacture of glass, and it appealed to his imagination. Contrary to friendly advice he determined to erect glass-works and spent much time experimenting in the manufacture of glass. The stringent embargo on manufactures before the Revolution prevented him from carrying out his desires until after the war, but by that time the conditions were favorable, and glass was becoming exceedingly scarce.

Accompanied by Hesse-Waldeckian impressed deserters from the British forces—glass blowers in their native country—Hewes arrived at Temple, N. H., in May 1780. He had selected this location because of cheap land and living conditions, an abundance of wood for fuel, ashes for potash, and near-by sand beds. The factory was built and the furnace fired but a few times when the plant was destroyed by fire. Hewes immediately erected a new factory, but upon its completion a severe frost cracked the furnace, causing the structure to give way at the initial firing. Having exhausted his ready money, Hewes tried to interest the inhabitants of Temple in financing a third venture, appealing to various bodies for aid, but the former catastrophes made the citizens unwilling to assume the risk. He was finally offered a loan, but because of the rigid stipulations involved, he declined it. He next planned a lottery, but the tickets would not sell. The Hewes family then determined to return to Boston, but before they could migrate, smallpox ravaged the Hessians, and thus the precarious experiment was ended. Hewes was still determined to make glass, however, and in 1787 he helped organize the Essex Glass Works of Boston, the General Court of Massachusetts granting the company exclusive manufacturing privileges in the commonwealth for a period of fifteen years. The buildings stood on Essex Street. Expert artisans were brought from the Duchy of Brunswick and from Glassboro, N. J., and for many years the firm was successful, becoming the leading cylinder or window-glass manufacturing establishment in the country. In 1809 the company reorganized and adopted the trade-name of the Boston Crown Glass Company. Hewes probably withdrew from the concern in 1824. It failed in 1827.

Hewes's other interests were varied. He was part owner of a glue factory, a soapworks, and a slaughter-house. He compounded liniments and "embrocations for fractures," and, having a familiarity with surgery, gained a reputation for skilful bone-setting. He was also a teacher of the art of fencing to the élite of Boston. He published the standard *Rules and Regulations for Sword Exercise of Cavalry* (1802) and *On the Formation and Movements of Cavalry* (1804), and for many years he was an instructor in military tactics. At the age of seventy-five, it was said, he could wield a sword as well as any young Bostonian. He had a charming house and garden, where he spent many hours among his flowers and peacocks. His grave is in the old burying-ground on the Boston Common.

[H. A. Blood, *The Hist. of Temple, N. H.* (1860); C. B. Heald, "First Glass Making in America," *Granite State Mag.*, Jan. 1907; W. G. Harding, "Glass Manufacture in the Berkshires," *Berkshire Hist. and Sci. Soc. Colls.*, II (1894), 29–44; L. H. Burbank, "Glass-making in N. H.," *Antiques*, Oct. 1923; Rhea Mansfield Knittle, *Early Am. Glass* (1927); *Boston Weekly Messenger*, July 22, 1830; *Am. Traveller* (Boston), July 23, 1830.] R. M. K.

HEWETT, WATERMAN THOMAS (Jan. 10, 1846–Sept. 13, 1921), educator, editor, was born at Miami, Saline County, Mo., the son of Waterman Thomas and Sarah Woodman (Parsons) Hewett, and a descendant of English ancestors who arrived in New England about 1635. The elder Hewett began his career as a lawyer in Maine but followed the course of settlement to the Southwest as a planter in Mississippi and Missouri, where he died. The family returned to Maine, where the son received his preparation for college at the Maine State Seminary in Lewiston. He graduated at Amherst College, receiving the degree of A.B. in 1869. Especially interested in the classics, he went to Athens and then to Heidelberg to study. After a period of teaching at Cornell University in the department of "North European Languages," 1870–77, he resumed his studies abroad at the universities of Leipzig, Berlin, and Leyden, 1877–78, specializing in Germanic philology. On his return he was awarded the Ph.D. degree at Cornell University in 1879. He remained at the university, as assistant professor of German until 1883, then as full professor of the German language and literature, a position which he held until his retirement in 1910.

Hewett was one of the American pioneers of modern-language study who went abroad to imbibe the spirit of scientific philological investigation prevailing mainly in German universities. Philology in the broad sense included linguistic and literary science treated from the historical and comparative points of view. These philological ideals he upheld during a long life and career as a teacher against the opposition of an old tradition which held German and other modern languages to be handmaids to other departments of study. As a teacher and scholar, Hewett was more stimulating in personal intercourse than in the lecture-room, a greater editor than original writer. As an editor of textbooks he was at his best. His edition of *Hermann und Dorothea* (1891) led him into textual criticism which was recognized at its true value in the publications of the Goethe-Gesellschaft of Weimar (*Goethe-Jahrbuch*, XIII, 1892, 304). His *Poems of Uhland* (1896) is a notable work, while his *Cornell University: A History* (4 vols., 1905), for skilful compilation, is deserving of special mention. In addition to these, he published articles and addresses on literary, educational, philological, and bibliographical subjects which give evidence of his scholarly activity.

Hewett was twice married, on June 22, 1880, to Emma McChain, who died in 1883, and on Dec. 18, 1889, to Katherine Mary Locke, who died in 1910. He was not in good health at the time of his retirement in 1910, but after some years he recovered remarkably and for almost a decade was able to enjoy the leisure of a professor emeritus, passing the winters in Egypt, Italy, and Southern France, and at other seasons residing in Oxford, England. With indefatigable zeal he collected materials and wrote on favorite themes. At the time of his death he had completed but not published a "Bibliography of the Works of Goldwin Smith." He had also collected materials from Southern archives on Sherman's march to the sea. He was a member of the American Philosophical Society, the Goethe-Gesellschaft of Weimar, and, through his *Frisian Language and Literature* (1879), a foreign member of the Frisian societies of language and literature, and history, antiquities, and philology. He died in London.

[*Hist. of the Class of 1869, Amherst Coll.* (1889, 1894, 1899); *Amherst Coll. Biog. Record of the Grads. and Non-Grads.* (1927); *Cornell Alumni News,* Sept. 29, 1921; *Cornell Univ.: A Hist.* (1905), vol. II; *Who's Who in America,* 1920–21; *N. Y. Times,* Sept. 14, 1921; *Times* (London), Sept. 15, 17, 1921; information as to certain facts from H. W. Hewett-Thayer, Princeton, N. J.] A. B. F.

HEWIT, AUGUSTINE FRANCIS (Nov. 27, 1820–July 3, 1897), Catholic priest, was the son of Rev. Nathaniel and Rebecca (Hillhouse) Hewit, and was christened Nathaniel Augustus. He was born at Fairfield, Conn., where his father, a founder of Hartford Theological Seminary, was minister of the Congregational Church. He prepared for college at Phillips (Andover) Academy and graduated from Amherst College in 1839. In 1840 he entered the Theological Institute of Connecticut at East Windsor, and in 1842 he was licensed to preach in the Congregational Church. Calvinistic Protestantism was not attractive to him, however, and in recording his religious feeling he wrote in 1887, "I was attracted to the Episcopalian form of Protestantism from childhood, and to no other" (*Catholic World,* October 1887, p. 33). It is not surprising, then, that he entered the Episcopal Church almost as soon as he was licensed as a preacher in his father's denomination. He was ordained a deacon in October 1843 and served in the Episcopal Church until early in 1846. Having developed symptoms of consumption in the summer of 1845, he spent the following winter on a plantation near Edenton, N. C., serving as chaplain for the slaves.

The conversion of Newman in 1845 caused Hewit to examine critically the validity of the Anglican episcopacy and to conclude that apostolic succession resided only in the Roman Catholic Church. On Easter Sunday, 1846, he took his first communion in a Catholic church. The following winter, while he was still in North Carolina, he began studying theology under the direction of Dr. Patrick N. Lynch, afterward bishop of Charleston. He was ordained a priest of the Catholic Church on Mar. 25, 1847, the first anniversary of his communion, and took the name Augustine Francis. He at once became vice-principal of Charleston Collegiate Institute, and at the same time aided Bishop Reynolds in preparing the writings of Bishop England for publication. This work took him to Philadelphia and Baltimore. There the Redemptorist congregation attracted him, and in 1849 he joined the Congregation of the Most Holy Redeemer in Baltimore and became associated with Fathers Hecker, Baker, Deshon, and Walworth, all of whom had been Protestants like himself. He made his religious profession Nov. 28, 1850, and engaged in the missionary work of the order until 1858. In the latter year he was released from his vows, along with Father Hecker and others of his associates, and together they formed the Missionary Society of St. Paul the Apostle in New York. Hewit wrote the constitution of the new order and was active in establishing and managing the *Catholic World,* serving from 1869 to 1874 as editor of the periodical. He taught theology and philosophy to the novitiates in the Paulist seminary in New York and in 1888 succeeded Father Hecker as superior of the order. He immediately pledged the Paulist community to support the Catholic University of America, in Washington, D. C., and in 1889 secured the establishment of the College of St. Thomas Aquinas at that university.

Father Hewit was a prolific writer, the author of numerous articles in the *Catholic World* and the *American Catholic Quarterly Review,* some of which were gathered into a volume entitled *Problems of the Age, With Studies in St. Augustine on Kindred Subjects* (1868). His books were chiefly tracts seeking to explain Catholicism to American Protestants, the only notable exception being *The Life of Reverend Francis A. Baker* (1865). When Hewit died in New York, he had been for twenty years one of the foremost Catholic apologists in the United States.

[For autobiographical sketches see *Statistical Cat. of the Amherst Coll. Class of 1839* (1854), and "How I Became a Catholic," *Catholic World,* Oct. 1887. Other sources include: *The Cath. Encyc.*; H. E. O'Keefe, "Very Rev. Augustine F. Hewit," *Am. Cath. Quart. Rev.,* July 1903; the *Cath. Univ. Chronicle,* July–Oct. 1897; Walter Elliott, *Life of Father Hecker* (1891); C. A. Walworth, *The Oxford Movement in America* (1895); Hewit's *Life of Rev. Francis A. Baker* (1865); and the *N. Y. Times,* July 4, 1897.] R. W. A.

HEWIT, NATHANIEL AUGUSTUS [See HEWIT, AUGUSTINE FRANCIS, 1820–1897.].

HEWITT, ABRAM STEVENS (July 31, 1822–Jan. 18, 1903), iron manufacturer, statesman, philanthropist, son of John and Ann (Gurnee) Hewitt, was born at Haverstraw, N. Y. His father, a native of Staffordshire, came to the United States in 1790 and in 1793 assisted in the construction of the first steam-engine ever built in America; his mother's family, the Garniers (Anglicized Gurnee), of old Huguenot stock, settled in Rockland County, on the farm where Abram was born. There he grew up, spending his summers working on the farm and his winters attending the public schools in New York, where his father was engaged in business. Having won a scholarship in a competitive examination, he entered Columbia College, graduating in 1842 with high rank. He continued there for a time as instructor in mathematics, studied law, and in 1845 was admitted to the bar; although, owing to defective eyesight, he never practised.

Meantime, in 1843–44, accompanied by his college associate, Edward Cooper, son of Peter Cooper [*qq.v.*], he visited Europe. The ship on which they returned was wrecked and they drifted about in an open boat for twelve hours before they were picked up. The adventure cemented their friendship and, with the aid of Peter Cooper, who gave over to them his Trenton Iron Works, they formed a partnership under the firm name of Cooper & Hewitt and engaged in the manufacture of iron. Though the firm was a pioneer in the making of iron girders and beams, its success from the beginning was marked. It maintained excellent relations with its employees; at one time it had on its payroll more than three thousand men; during the depression of 1873–78, to keep as many as possible of them employed, the plant was kept running at a great loss.

In 1862, Hewitt visited England to study the making of gun-barrel iron and on his return he erected at Weston the first American open-hearth furnace. Here, during the latter part of the Civil War, he produced for the United States government all the gun-barrel material it needed at bare production cost, and in 1870 produced the first steel of commercial value manufactured in the United States. As the iron and steel industry grew, Cooper, Hewitt & Company expanded with it until the firm operated the Trenton, Ringwood, Pequest, and Durham Iron Works. Hewitt thus found himself a force in financial and industrial affairs. He was at one time or another, president of the United States Smelting Company and of the New York & Greenwood Lake Railroad Company; vice-president of the New Jersey Steel & Iron Company, and a director of the Erie Railroad, the Lehigh Coal & Navigation Company, and the Alabama Coal & Iron Company.

In 1855, he married Sarah Amelia Cooper, only daughter of Peter Cooper. When Peter Cooper established Cooper Union, Hewitt took a leading part in the undertaking. He was the chairman of the board of trustees that drew up the charter and plan for the institution and afterwards became secretary of the board. In this capacity he directed all its educational and financial details for more than forty years—a task not less difficult than that of being president of a college. His interest in the institution was unflagging and in 1902, together with his wife and Edward Cooper, he contributed $600,000 to its endowment.

Hewitt's public career began in 1867 when he was appointed by President Johnson commissioner to the Paris Exposition and produced a report on the steel industry which was widely read and translated into several foreign languages. His entrance into political life was due largely to his association with Samuel J. Tilden [*q.v.*]. With Tilden and Edward Cooper, in 1871, he joined in a campaign against the "Tweed Ring," and when reform was brought about he had a prominent part in the reorganization of Tammany Hall. In 1874, he was elected to Congress as the regular Democratic candidate, and continued in office with the exception of one term, until 1886, winning a position of authority on questions of labor, finance, and the national resources. In 1876 he served as chairman of the Democratic National Committee in the Hayes-Tilden presidential campaign. In the crisis that followed he took a leading part, writing the proclamation which set forth the claims of his party and urging the boldest action. Tilden, however, counselled compromise and Hewitt, respecting his wishes, became a member of the committee which drew up the Electoral Count Act, under which the Electoral Commission was constituted and Hayes elected to the presidency.

In 1886, Hewitt was chosen mayor of New York in one of the most exciting elections in the history of the city. The other candidates were Henry George, on the United Labor ticket, and Theodore Roosevelt on the Republican. Hewitt's plurality of 22,500 votes over George and 30,000 over Roosevelt marked a personal triumph. It opened a vigorous administration made notable by reforms and improvements, among which was the plan for the municipal construction of the Rapid Transit Railroad. For this service he was later awarded a gold medal by the Chamber of Commerce. His thoroughgoing reforms, his fearlessness of speech, and his intolerance of partisanship made enemies within his own party, produced an open break with Tammany Hall, and led to his retirement from politics.

The last ten years of his life were devoted to

the public interest, especially in education and charity. He was a trustee of Columbia University, chairman of the board of trustees of Barnard College, one of the original trustees of the Carnegie Institution, the first chairman of its board, and a member of its executive committee. Twice (1876 and 1890) he served as president of the American Institute of Mining Engineers. He died, at the age of eighty-one in Ringwood, N. J., which had been his home for nearly fifty years. Peter Cooper Hewitt [*q.v.*] was his son.

[E. M. Shepard, "Abram S. Hewitt, a Great Citizen," *Rev. of Revs.* (N. Y.), Feb. 1903; R. W. Raymond, memoir, in *Trans. Am. Inst. of Mining Engineers*, vol. XXXIV (1904); *Unveiling of the Statue of Abram S. Hewitt in the Chamber of Commerce of the State of N. Y., May 11, 1905* (1905); *N. Y. Times*, *N. Y. Tribune*, Jan. 19, 1903.] W. B. P.

HEWITT, JAMES (June 4, 1770–1827), violinist, composer, the father of John Hill Hewitt [*q.v.*], was born in Dartmoor, England, the son of Capt. John Hewitt of the British navy. James entered the navy but later resigned and turned to music, becoming in time the leader of the court orchestra of George III. In 1790 he married a Miss Lamb, who died in 1791. The next year he appeared in New York City, and on Jan. 25, 1793, at Corre's Hotel, he gave his first concert. In December 1795 he was married to Eliza King, the daughter of Sir John King of the British navy. He was a good performer and his compositions, though not intrinsically valuable, were well liked. Thus he established himself as a violinist and concert manager, became the orchestra leader of the Old American Company and other orchestras, and until shortly before his death was an active figure in American musical life. In 1797 he bought the New York branch of Carr's Musical Repository in order to facilitate carrying on the business of publishing music, into which he had already ventured. He did not, however, give up his activity as a conductor. In 1800 he was leading his "grand band" in Corre's Columbia Gardens, facing the Battery, and also regularly conducting "grand concerts" in the Mount Vernon Gardens in Leonard Street. In 1812 he moved to Boston, where he took charge of the music at the Federal Street Theatre. About 1818 he returned to New York.

Hewitt's musical productivity kept pace with his activities as a conductor and publisher. The compositions attributed to him include a "Battle Overture" (1792), in nine movements; a "Storm Overture" (1795); and a setting of Collins' "Ode on the Passions," recited by John Hodgkinson at a concert of the Columbian Anacreontic Society, June 11, 1795. He was highly rated in his time, and his "Grand Sinfonie Characteristic of the Peace of the French Republic," played by his orchestra at Lovett's hotel in 1802, received as much consideration from contemporary critics as the works of distinguished composers have received in a later day. Of all his compositions, however, perhaps the most interesting, because of its political associations, is the score of *Tammany or the Indian Chief* (1794), the libretto of which was written by Mrs. Anne Julia Hatton, poetess of the Tammany Society. This quasi-opera became a symbol of Republican protest against the Federalist party and was dubbed "wretched" or "one of the finest things of its kind" depending upon the political prejudices of its critics (O. G. T. Sonneck, *Early Opera in America*, 1915, p. 97). Its performances were marked by stormy scenes created by "the poorer classes of mechanics and clerks who would be much better employed on any other occasion than disturbing a theatre" (New York *Daily Advertiser*, Mar. 7, 1794). Hewitt also wrote incidental music for plays and dramas, including *The Patriot* (1794); *Columbus* (1797); Harriet Lee's *The Mysterious Marriage* (1799); and *Pizarro* (1800), and as late as Nov. 29, 1824, he supplied the "orchestra accompaniments" for Micah Hawkins' operatic piece, *The Saw-Mill*, produced at Chatham Gardens. He died in Boston, about the first of August, 1827. For a time he had been estranged from his wife and had lived in New York while she maintained a home in Boston.

[O. G. T. Sonneck, *Early Concert Life in America* (1906); J. T. Howard, *Our Am. Music* (1930), and "The Hewitt Family in Am. Music," *Musical Quart.*, Jan. 1931; G. C. D. Odell, *Annals of the N. Y. Stage*, vols. I and II (1927); *Boston Patriot & Mercantile Advertiser*, Aug. 3, 1827.] F. H. M.

HEWITT, JOHN HILL (July 11, 1801–Oct. 7, 1890), journalist, musician, poet, was born in New York City, the eldest son of James [*q.v.*] and Eliza (King) Hewitt. The family moved to Boston while John was a child, and there he received a common-school education and was apprenticed to a sign-painter. Finding this trade uncongenial he ran away and after varied experiences and adventures returned to New York in 1816. Two years later he received an appointment to the military academy at West Point. While he was a cadet he studied music under the leader of the academy band and at the end of his course resigned to take up his father's profession. As a member of a theatrical company organized by his father, he found himself in Augusta, Ga., when the venture failed, and remained in that city as a teacher of music. In 1823 he moved to Columbia, S. C., and from there to

Greenville, in the same state, where he read law in the office of Judge Thompson, and where he established a paper known first as the *Republican* and later as the *Mountaineer*. Tiring of this he returned to Augusta, whence he was called to Boston in 1827 by the death of his father.

In 1828 Hewitt went to Baltimore, where for some years journalism distracted him from his interest in music. In 1829 he was associated with Rufus Dawes in the editorship of the *Baltimore Minerva and Emerald*, which in July 1830, became the *Minerva and Saturday Post* and was edited by Hewitt alone. In February 1832 Charles F. Cloud established a literary weekly, the *Baltimore Saturday Visitor,* under the editorship of Lambert Wilmer, who was succeeded in a few months by Hewitt. In the summer of 1833 the proprietor offered prizes of one hundred dollars for the best story and fifty dollars for the best poem contributed to its columns. Edgar Allan Poe won the hundred-dollar prize with his "MS. Found in a Bottle" and with it the friendship and literary guidance of John P. Kennedy, one of the judges. The poetry prize, for which the choice lay between Poe's "The Coliseum" and Hewitt's "The Song of the Wind," entered under the pseudonym Henry Wilton, was awarded to Hewitt, partly, it would seem, because the judges did not wish to award both prizes to one person. This decision displeased Poe and was a source of controversy between himself and Hewitt. In 1835 the *Visitor* changed hands, and in 1839 Hewitt became editor and part owner of a daily newspaper, the *Baltimore Clipper*. The next year he sold his interest and moved to Washington.

In the capital Hewitt resumed the teaching of music and enjoyed the favor of Henry Clay, whose political views he supported with his pen. He soon returned to Baltimore and remained in that city until the beginning of the Civil War, when he went South. Living in Richmond for a time, he made use of his military training by serving as a drill-master, and then he moved to Savannah, where he edited the *Evening Mirror*. At the close of the war he taught music in various southern cities and returned early in the seventies to Baltimore, which was his home until his death. He was twice married. Not long after leaving West Point he married Estella Mangin, the daughter of Major Mangin, of the French army. She died in 1863, leaving seven children. His second wife was Alethia Smith, of Savannah, Ga., who was eighteen at the time of her marriage. She bore him four children.

Hewitt's publications include a small book of verse entitled *Miscellaneous Poems,* issued in Baltimore in 1838, and a volume of rambling reminiscences, *Shadows on the Wall, or Glimpses of the Past,* published in 1877. The latter volume includes a few poems. He wrote the words and music of many popular ballads, among the most successful of which were "The Minstrel's Return from the War," "Rock Me to Sleep, Mother," and "Carry Me Back to the Sweet Sunny South." He composed also some thirty operas and oratorios, of which the oratorio *Jephtha* was regarded as the best, and wrote a number of ephemeral plays and stories, using the pseudonyms Eugene Ramon, Col. Marcus Kennedy, and Jenks.

[G. C. Perine, *The Poets and Verse-Writers of Md.* (1898); J. T. Howard, *Our Am. Music* (1930), and "The Hewitt Family in Am. Music," *Musical Quart.,* Jan. 1931; J. T. Scharf, *Hist. of Baltimore City and County* (1881); *Baltimore American,* Oct. 8, 1890.]

J. C. F.

HEWITT, PETER COOPER (May 5, 1861–Aug. 25, 1921), scientist, inventor, the son of Abram S. Hewitt [*q.v.*] and Sarah Amelia Cooper, and grandson of Peter Cooper [*q.v.*], was born in New York City. There he was educated by private tutors, at Stevens Institute of Technology, and at Columbia College. There also he married on Apr. 27, 1887, his first wife, Lucy Work, and there he lived for the greater part of his life. He inherited a genius for mechanism and a marked gift for invention from his grandfather, Peter Cooper, who perceived his talent at an early age and gave it full encouragement, placing at his disposal an old greenhouse for workshop and experiment station. There he began those researches and experiments in mechanics, physics, and especially in electricity which later led to a number of discoveries and inventions, including the mercury vapor lamp (1903), a static converter or rectifier, an electrical interrupter, and a wireless receiver. His friend Michael Pupin speaks of Hewitt's imaginative power and his artistic gift, and comments upon his grace of body, and especially the extraordinary deftness of his hands. "Those who knew him . . . watching him at work, felt that a part, at least, of Hewitt's thinking apparatus was in his hands." His methods were unacademic, often incomprehensible to the orthodox investigator; he designed and constructed his own instruments and apparatus, which, though sometimes apparently crude, proved by use to be peculiarly adapted to the problem in hand. He is best known by the mercury vapor lamp bearing his name, which because of its high efficiency has been widely adopted for industrial illumination. This invention marked progress in a department of electrical science at that time little developed—the motion of electricity through rarefied gases and vapors. Hewitt was the first to establish the fact that the reacting force at the negative electrode is the principal determining factor in these motions and the first to find a means of overcoming this reaction. He was the first also to recognize the importance of the rectifying characteristic of electrodes in a rarefied gas, to employ it in the wireless art, and to discover "the third or pilot electrode, usually called the 'grid,' which inserted in the path of moving electricity in a vacuum tube and suitably electrified can influence that motion to any extent" (Pupin, *post*). This last discovery is the fundamental principle of the vacuum-tube amplifier, which is so important in radio telephony. Hewitt was a pioneer in the development of hydro-airplanes and of high-speed motor boats. He was early interested in the problem of the helicopter, and in 1918 succeeded in building a machine that would rise into the air without a horizontal take-off. In 1915 he was made a member of the Naval Consulting Board, and in that capacity designed an aërial torpedo. In recognition of his achievements he was given the honorary degree of doctor of science by Columbia University in 1903 and by Rutgers College in 1916. On Dec. 21, 1918, he married his second wife, Maryon J. (Andrews) Bruguiere, daughter of Tunstall T. Andrews of Virginia.

Hewitt had large business interests and was director in a number of corporations, including Cooper, Hewitt & Company, the New York & Greenwood Lake Railway, and the Midvale Water Company. He was also a trustee of Cooper Union and of the Hospital and House of Rest for Consumptives, and was a member of many learned and scientific societies. He died at the American Hospital in Paris.

[Michael Pupin, *In Memoriam of Peter Cooper Hewitt* (1921); George Iles, *Inventors at Work* (1906); *Who's Who in America*, 1920–21; *Jour. Am. Inst. Electrical Engineers*, Oct. 1921; *Trans. Soc. Naval Architects and Marine Engineers*, vol. XXIX (1922); *N. Y. Times, N. Y. Evening Post*, Aug. 26, 1921.]

W. B. P.

HEYDT, HANS JÖST [See HITE, JOST, d. 1760].

HEYER, JOHN CHRISTIAN FREDERICK (July 10, 1793–Nov. 7, 1873), missionary, the son of Johann Gottlieb and Frederike Sophie Johanne (Wagener) Heyer, was born in Helmstedt, in the duchy of Brunswick, Germany. From his third until his fourteenth year he attended the local school. In 1807 he was confirmed in the village church of St. Stephen's, and shortly thereafter sailed from Friedrichstadt, Denmark, to join the family of an uncle in Philadelphia. Here he attended Pastor Passey's private school, and learned from his uncle the furrier's trade. He attended Zion's German Lutheran Church and took part in many of its activities. Having decided to devote his life to the Christian ministry, he studied theology from 1809 until 1814 with Dr. Justus H. C. Helmuth and Dr. Frederick D. Schaeffer [*qq.v.*]. From Sept. 15, 1813, he taught the parochial school conducted by Zion's Church in Southwark, Philadelphia, and preached occasionally. In the spring of 1815 he returned to Germany to visit his parents and to engage in university study. Finding Halle University closed on account of war, he entered Göttingen. After a year's study there he returned to the United States and in 1817 was licensed to preach by the Pennsylvania Ministerium. He was assigned to itineration among the Lutheran churches of Crawford and Erie counties, making Meadville his headquarters. After a year, he was assigned to the Cumberland parish, Maryland, where he labored for the next six years. In 1819 he married Mary (Webb) Gash, a widow, who bore him six children. He was ordained at Lancaster, Pa., in 1820 by the Ministerium and appointed to make a short tour through parts of Indiana and Kentucky. In 1824 he was called to be pastor at Somerset, Pa., and in 1827 accepted the pastorate at Carlisle. In 1828 he was elected secretary, and in 1831, president of the West Pennsylvania Synod. Becoming the agent of the Sunday School Union of the Evangelical Lutheran Church in the United States in 1830, he served in that capacity until January 1832, when he resumed the pastorate at Somerset. Five years later he removed to Pittsburgh and took a leading part in the organization of Lutheran work in that area.

In May 1840, the German Foreign Missionary Society asked him to consider foreign missionary service. He accepted the call and spent the fall and winter of 1840–41 at Baltimore in the study of medicine and Sanskrit, his purpose being to work in India. He went to India as agent of the Pennsylvania Ministerium. On July 31, 1842, at Guntur, he began the founding of the first foreign mission of his Church. His service in India falls into three periods, with furloughs in 1846–47, and 1857–69. His second furlough, except for a year which was spent in Germany, was given to home-missionary work in Minnesota, where he was president of the Synod for ten years. Guntur and Gurjal were the centers of his work in India until 1855, when he entered the Rajahmundry field. He conducted services both in English and in Telugu, made many converts, especially from among the weavers, organized several congregations, translated Luther's small catechism into Telugu, and established schools of various grades, including training schools for mission workers. For a time the greater part of the expense of his work was borne by friends in Guntur. In 1846 the Guntur mission, and in 1851, the Rajahmundry mission passed into the control of the Foreign Missionary Society of the General Synod of the Lutheran Church. The latter mission, however, reverted in 1869 to the control of the Pennsylvania Ministerium, and Heyer hastened to India to make the transfer effective. In 1872 he returned to America and became chaplain of the Lutheran Theological Seminary in Philadelphia, where he died in his eighty-first year. He was buried at Friedensburg, Pa., beside the remains of his wife.

[W. A. Lambert, *Life of Rev. J. F. C. Heyer, M.D.* (1903); G. H. Trabert, *Eng. Lutheranism in the Northwest* (1914); L. D. Reed, *The Hist. of the First English Evangelical Lutheran Ch. in Pittsburgh* (1909); C. H. Gerberding, *Life and Letters of W. A. Passavant, D.D.* (1906); George Drach and C. F. Kuder, *The Telugu Mission of the Gen. Council of the Evangelical Lutheran Ch. in North America* (1914); E. B. Burgess, *Memorial Hist. of the Pittsburgh Synod of the Evangelical Lutheran Ch.* (1925).] J. C. A.

HEYWARD, THOMAS (July 28, 1746–Mar. 6, 1809), signer of the Declaration of Independence, Revolutionary soldier, jurist, was generally known as Thomas Heyward, Junior, because there were others of the same name in his family. He was the eldest son of Col. Daniel Heyward, one of the wealthiest planters of colonial South Carolina, and of Mary (Miles) Heyward, daughter of William Miles, and was born on his father's plantation in that part of St. Helena's Parish which later became St. Luke's Parish. After receiving his early education in South Carolina, he was admitted to the Middle Temple, London, on Jan. 10, 1765, and to the bar in South Carolina on Jan. 22, 1771. The following year he was elected to the Commons House of Assembly from St. Helena's Parish. He was a delegate to the provincial convention which met July 6, 1774, at Charleston, when the news of the blockading of the port of Boston was received, and to a provincial congress which met there, Jan. 11, 1775. Heyward was one of the thirteen members of the council of safety, chosen by this congress a few months later, which practically took over the functions of government. He was elected to the second provincial congress which met Nov. 1, 1775, and in its second session, beginning Feb. 1, 1776, he served on a committee of eleven to prepare a constitution for the state, which was adopted on Mar. 26, 1776. He was chosen by the provincial congress as one of the five delegates from South Carolina to the Second Continental Congress, he signed the Declaration of Independence, and served in the Continental Congress until the end of 1778, when he returned to his native state and became a circuit judge.

He was a member of the militia of the state and captain of a battalion of artillery in Charleston. He participated, with his battalion, in Moultrie's defeat of the British, Feb. 4, 1779, on Port Royal Island, and was wounded. He took part in the defense of Charleston and upon the fall of that city, May 12, 1780, was paroled as a prisoner of war. Soon afterward, however, his parole was recalled and he was sent to St. Augustine, Fla., where he was held until exchanged July 1781. On his return, he represented Charleston in the legislature for two years (1782–84), and, resuming his duties as circuit judge, served until 1789, when he resigned and devoted his attention to agriculture. He was one of the founders of the Agricultural Society of South Carolina in 1785 and its first president. His plantation, "White Hall," was situated in St. Luke's Parish; his house in Charleston was rented by the city and placed at the disposal of President Washington on the occasion of his visit to South Carolina in May 1791.

Heyward was twice married: first, Apr. 20, 1773, to Elizabeth Mathewes, daughter of John Mathewes and sister of Governor John Mathews, and after her death, to Susanna Savage, daughter of Thomas Savage, May 4, 1786. He died in his sixty-third year and was buried in the family cemetery on his father's plantation in St. Luke's Parish. In 1920 the General Assembly of South Carolina appropriated $2,500 for a monument which was erected over his grave, in recognition of his services as "patriot, statesman, soldier, jurist."

[A. S. Salley, Jr., *Delegates to the Continental Congress from S. C.* (1927), and *Marriage Notices in the S. C. Gazette . . . 1732–1801* (1902); E. C. Burnett, *Letters of Members of the Continental Cong.*, vols. I–IV (1921–28); Edward McCrady, *S. C. under the Royal Govt. 1719–1776* (1899), *S. C. in the Revolution, 1775–1780*, and *1780–1783*; John Sanderson, *Biog. of the Signers to the Declaration of Independence*, vol. IV (1823); J. B. Heyward, *The Colonial Hist. of the Heyward Family of S. C.* (1907).] P. S. F.

HEYWOOD, EZRA HERVEY (Sept. 29, 1829–May 22, 1893), radical pamphleteer, was the son of Ezra Hoar, an enterprising farmer related to Senator George F. Hoar [*q.v.*], and Dorcas (Roper) Hoar, a collateral descendant of John Locke. After the father's death in 1845 the children took the name Heywood in 1848 by legislative sanction. Heywood was born in

Princeton, Mass., a country village, where he spent the greater part of his life. From Westminster Academy he went to Brown University, graduating in 1856, but remaining for two years' further study, with the Congregationalist ministry in view. He was already an advocate of women's rights, and his commencement address was on "Milton—The Advocate of Intellectual Freedom." An encounter with William Lloyd Garrison at an abolitionist meeting in Framingham influenced Heywood to become an active agent of the Massachusetts Anti-slavery Society. Thus he became a frequent and popular platform speaker. After the Civil War, which he opposed as a pacifist, he carried over the abolitionist spirit and methods into social and economic radicalism.

He married, June 6, 1865, a woman who shared his every interest, Angela Fiducia Tilton of Worcester. Heywood removed to that city where he lived until 1871, when he returned to Princeton. The Heywoods (under the name of The Co-operative Publishing Company), set up a press from which, aided only by their children, they poured out an astonishing volume of propaganda. Abbreviated titles of his chief pamphlets are: *Cupid's Yokes,* on marriage reform, which ran to fifty thousand copies and for mailing which Heywood and De Robigne M. Bennett [*q.v.*] were prosecuted; *Uncivil Liberty,* advocating women's rights, which ran to eighty thousand copies; *Social Ethics . . . Free Rum . . . Assures Temperance*; *The Labor Movement*; *Hard Cash*; *Free Trade*; *The Great Strike . . . of 1877.* In May 1872, appeared the first number of *The Word,* a monthly journal of reform, which continued until April 1893, interrupted only by Heywood's imprisonment. Mrs. Heywood supplied some of the most daring contributions, which her husband never revised, even when he disapproved of them, so strong was his belief in women's rights. Heywood's writings were courageous, plainspoken, earnest, but without humor and very lengthy. Their importance lies less in their substance than in the fact that they were so much in advance of contemporary thought and so widely read. These two fiery spirits soon attracted others. The Heywoods established in Princeton The Mountain Home, a kind of summer hotel for agitators and spiritualists. They organized a radical society, the Union Reform League, which held conventions in Princeton. They joined in forming the New England Free Love League in 1873, which Heywood thenceforth regarded as the beginning of a new chronology, dating his letters and journal Y. L. (Year of Love), instead of the outworn A. D. The federal statute of 1873 against mailing obscene matter, obtained by Anthony Comstock [*q.v.*], was bitterly opposed by Heywood, whose publications were equally objectionable to Comstock. In November 1877, Comstock arrested Heywood in Boston at a meeting of the Free Love Society. Heywood was convicted, June 1878, in the United States court, for mailing obscene publications to Comstock, who had applied for them under an assumed name. He was sentenced to $100 fine and two years' imprisonment at hard labor in Dedham jail. An indignation meeting in Faneuil Hall, attended by six thousand persons, resulted in a pardon from President Hayes after Heywood had served six months' imprisonment. A second arrest in 1882 by Comstock, at Princeton, for similarly induced mailing was followed by acquittal, Heywood appearing in his own defense. Upon a third arrest, under the Massachusetts obscenity law, in 1883, Heywood's neighbors, despite their strong disagreement with his views, formed a defense committee and petitioned against the prosecution, which was not pressed. In 1890 he was convicted in the United States court for obscene passages in *The Word,* written by Mrs. Heywood, and sentenced to two years' imprisonment, which he served.

Those who knew him well attest his kindliness of spirit, sincerity of motive, and the integrity of his private life. He and his wife, despite their advocacy of free love, were a faithful, devoted, and happy couple, who gave excellent training to their four children, Hermes, Angelo, Vesta, and Psyche Ceres. The family were somewhat ostracized in a small village, but were nevertheless respected. The neighbors used occasionally to buy *The Word* to see what shocking statements it contained; yet a Princeton farmer once concealed a whole issue in his barn to avoid its seizure by the authorities. A few months after his last release Heywood died in Boston, while on a visit for medical treatment. His funeral was typical of his life, without minister, prayers, or Scripture, but the friends who were present spoke as they were impelled to do. He was buried in the family lot at Princeton, in a plain unpainted pine box.

[See *Proc. of the Indignation Meeting Held in Faneuil Hall . . .* (1878); *Free Speech: Report of Ezra H. Heywood's Defense* (1883); *Boston Herald,* May 23, 25, 1893; Heywood Broun and Margaret Leech, *Anthony Comstock, Roundsman of the Lord* (1927); *Providence Jour.,* June 28, 1893. The petition of the neighbors on his third arrest is in the Harvard University library. Much use has been made of numerous letters about Heywood in the Brown University library, which also possesses a death mask, a photograph, and a file of *The Word.*]

Z. C., Jr.

HEYWOOD, LEVI (Dec. 10, 1800–July 21, 1882), manufacturer, inventor, was born at Gardner, Worcester County, Mass., the son of Benjamin and Mary (Whitney) Heywood, and a descendant of John Heywood who came from England and settled in Concord, Mass., about the middle of the seventeenth century. His early life was that of the normal farmer's boy of the time and included the usual short terms in the village school. When he was twenty years old he had, in addition, two terms at the academy in New Salem, Mass., and for the succeeding two winters he taught school in his native town and in the adjoining village of Winchendon. For a year he engaged in general contracting in Rochester, N. Y., and then returned to Gardner and in partnership with a brother operated a country store for six years. In the meantime, 1826, he began in Gardner the manufacture of wood-seated chairs. Five years later Heywood closed his factory and went to Boston where he opened a store for the sale of chairs. In partnership with a second brother and a friend, he also started a sawmill in Charlestown, Mass., for sawing veneers from mahogany and other woods. This mill was destroyed by fire in 1835, and the following year, after giving up his retail store in Boston, Heywood returned to Gardner and, with a third brother, again engaged in the manufacture of chairs. For the first few years Heywood Brothers & Company, as the firm was called, made chairs mainly by hand, the only machinery being turning-lathes and circular saws operated by water power. About 1841 Levi turned his attention to the invention of machinery especially adapted to the various processes of chair manufacture. His brother, however, not being at all enthusiastic in this direction, sold out his interests in the business to Levi. Thereafter the latter gave his every thought to the devising and constructing of special machinery for chair construction, and to the adapting of existing wood-working machinery to that purpose. He introduced constantly new and valuable features into the methods of manufacture which, in turn, resulted in the enlargement and variety of the style of product. The inventions which contributed most to his success were one for a wood chair seat; another for a tilting chair; a third for a combination of three machines for splitting, shaving, and otherwise manipulating rattan; and a fourth for machinery for bending wood. One of his inventions not connected directly with chair manufacture was a substitute for whalebone which he made by injecting India rubber into rattan. Probably the most original and valuable of his inventions was that for bending wood. Through the introduction of Heywood's machinery, his business grew steadily during the first twenty years until in 1861 it yielded over $300,000 a year; a decade later it brought in more than a million dollars annually. The factory employed between twelve and fourteen hundred workmen, and in addition, nine wholesale warehouses employing over five hundred people were maintained in various parts of the United States. Besides his own interests at Gardner, Heywood was a partner with W. B. Washburn in the manufacture of chairs and wooden ware at Erving, Mass. These partners, too, engaged in the manufacture of lumber, owning large acreages of timber land in various sections of New England. After he had secured his patents for machinery to utilize rattan, Heywood's company about 1876 began the manufacture of rattan furniture and a second company, known as the American Rattan Company, in which he was a large stockholder, was organized. Heywood erected, too, in 1876, as part of his establishment, a foundry to make the various iron parts used in chair manufacture.

In 1853 he represented the town of Gardner in the convention for revising the constitution of the State of Massachusetts, and in 1871 he served a term in the lower house of the state legislature. He was married, Dec. 29, 1825, to Martha Wright of Gardner, who with five children survived him.

[W. D. Herrick, *Hist. of the Town of Gardner, Worcester County, Mass.* (1878); J. D. Van Slyck, *New England Manufacturers and Manufactories* (1879); G. F. Bacon, *Leading Business Men of Fitchburg and Vicinity* (1890); Patent Office records; *Worcester Daily Spy,* July 22, 1882.] C. W. M—n.

HIACOOMES (*c.* 1610–1690), Indian preacher, of Great Harbor, now Edgartown, Martha's Vineyard, was a member of the Pokanauket Tribe, a subdivision of the Narragansetts. A grave, thoughtful native, apparently about thirty years of age, he was the first convert of the younger Thomas Mayhew [*q.v.*], who in 1643, three years before John Eliot commenced his labors on the mainland, began missionary work among the Indians of Martha's Vineyard. Hiacoomes placed himself under Mayhew's instruction, learned to read English, and became a student of the Bible. He first acted as interpreter to his pastor and taught him how to approach the Indians, but by 1644 was himself doing personal work among them. The immunity of Hiacoomes and his family during the great sickness of 1645 made an impression on the natives, led to their desire for Christian instruction, and resulted in his beginning to preach. The medical skill of Mayhew, the boldness of

Hiacoomes, and the miraculous deliverance of one of their own number from assassination, broke down the determined opposition of the chiefs and medicine men. By 1651 there were 199 converts and two Indian congregations ministered to by Mayhew and Hiacoomes, the latter, who now preached twice a Sunday, coming to Mayhew each Saturday for advice about his sermons. Schools were established and in 1659 an Indian church was founded. By 1666 the last tribes toward Gay Head were converted. Hiacoomes was ordained, Aug. 22, 1670, by John Eliot and John Cotton of Plymouth. Just before his death in 1690 he ordained his successor, and he left a son who became a preacher.

[Cotton Mather, *Magnalia Christi Americana* (1702); C. E. Banks, *Hist. of Martha's Vineyard,* vol. I (1911); Experience Mayhew, *Indian Converts* (London, 1727), reprinted in abridged form as *Indian Narratives* (Boston, 1829); *Strength out of Weakness* (1652), and Henry Whitfield, *The Light Appearing More and More Towards the Perfect Day* (1651), both reprinted in *Mass. Hist. Soc. Colls.,* 3 ser., IV (1834); Daniel Neal, *The Hist. of New England,* vol. I (1720).] F. T. P.

HIBBARD, FREEBORN GARRETTSON (Feb. 22, 1811–Jan. 27, 1895), Methodist Episcopal clergyman, a descendant of Robert Hibbard who settled in Salem, Mass., sometime between 1635 and 1639, was born in New Rochelle, N. Y., the son of Rev. Billy and Sybil (Russ) Hibbard. His father, a native of Norwich, Conn., son of Nathan, tanner and shoemaker, was a pioneer Methodist preacher, "abounding in labors, grace, and eccentricities." At the request of his friend, Bishop Asbury, he kept a journal, which he published in 1843 under the title, *Memoirs of the Life and Travels of B. Hibbard.* After another of his friends, Freeborn Garrettson, he named the eighth of his sons. Since his father was absent from home on long circuits much of the time, Freeborn was brought up chiefly by his mother, a frail little woman, without whose frugality and good management the family would often have been in want. He began to preach when he was seventeen years old, taking some of his father's appointments when the latter was ill. "About this time," his father records, "he was very desirous to get to Wilbraham School, for the purpose of perfecting his studies, and particularly in Greek and Hebrew. This could not be done, as I was unable to bear the expense." Accordingly he read through three times the works of Fletcher, Wesley, and one or two others, and in 1830 he was admitted to the New York Conference on trial. In 1832 he was received into full connection, and ordained deacon. This same year that body was divided and he was assigned to the Troy Conference, where, in 1834, he was ordained elder. He transferred to the Genesee Conference (called Central New York Conference 1872–82) in 1837, of which, except for the lifetime of the East Genesee Conference, when he belonged to its jurisdiction, he was a member till his death.

Although never rising to conspicuous leadership, he became one of the prominent figures in New York Methodism, and achieved more than local eminence through membership in six General Conferences—that of 1844 and those from 1856 to 1872 inclusive—and as an editor and writer. He was a person of great dignity, suavity, refinement, and conscientiousness, holding strongly to the Wesleyan doctrine of Christian perfection. He had scholarly tastes, and was a thorough investigator, although inclined to idealize a subject in which he was deeply interested. For the first fifteen months of its history he was sole editor of the *Northern Christian Advocate*; then, for about a year, Rev. William Hosmer was his associate (*Northern Christian Advocate,* Jan. 30, 1895). In 1848 the General Conference elected Hosmer editor, and in 1856 he was succeeded by Hibbard, who continued in that office until 1860. This paper was one of those which strongly opposed all slave-holding by members of the Methodist Church. During his ministry Hibbard published a number of books, several of which had wide use. They include *Christian Baptism: Its Mode, Obligation, Import, and Relative Order* (1841); *A Treatise on Infant Baptism* (1843); *The Psalms Chronologically Arranged with Historical Introductions* (1856); *The Religion of Childhood* (1864); *Palestine: Its Geography and Bible History* (1851); *Biography of Rev. Leonidas L. Hamline, D.D.* (1880); commentary on the Psalms in D. D. Whedon's *Commentary on the Old Testament,* vol. V (1882); *History of the Late East Genesee Conference* (1887); *Eschatology, or the Doctrine of the Last Things According to the Chronology and Symbolism of the Apocalypse* (1890). He was also the editor of *Works of Rev. Leonidas L. Hamline, D.D.,* vol. I (1869), vol. II (1871). His first wife, Mary Whipple, died a comparatively short time after their marriage, leaving him one son, and in 1846 he married Maria Hyde, who survived him.

[A. G. Hibbard, *Geneal. of the Hibbard Family* (1901); *Minutes Ann. Conferences M. E. Church,* 1830, 1832, 1834, 1895; minutes of the Genesee Conference, 1895, 1913; *Christian Advocate* (N. Y.), Feb. 7, 1895; *Northern Christian Advocate,* Mar. 13, 1895.]
H. E. S.